W9-ACG-928

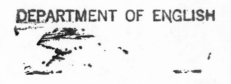

The Reader's Encyclopedia of SHAKESPEARE

The Reader's Encyclopedia of SHAKESPEARE

Edited by
OSCAR JAMES CAMPBELL
Associate Editor
EDWARD G. QUINN

THOMAS Y. CROWELL COMPANY
New York / Established 1834

The editors wish to express their thanks to Levi Fox of The Shakespeare Birthplace Trust and to Lewis M. Stark of the Rare Book Division of The New York Public Library who, with their associates, were most helpful in obtaining many of the illustrations.

Throughout the encyclopedia, line numbers cited for extracts from the plays are those of The Globe Edition of Shakespeare.

Published in Canada by Fitzhenry & Whiteside Limited, Toronto.
Designed by Laurel Wagner
Illustrations editor, Robert H. Snyder, Jr.
Manufactured in the United States of America
Library of Congress Catalog Card No. 66-11946
ISBN 0-690-67412-0
5 6 7 8 9 10

Permission of publishers to reprint the following copyright materials is gratefully acknowledged.

Extracts from Elizabethan and Jacobean documents, from *William Shakespeare* (1930) by E. K. Chambers, reprinted with the permission of The Clarendon Press, Oxford.

Drawings by C. Walter Hodges, accompanying the articles "playhouse structure," "Fortune Theatre," and "Hope Theatre," from *The Globe Playhouse Restored* by C. Walter Hodges, reprinted with the permission of Coward-McCann, Inc., and Oxford University Press. Copyright © 1954 by C. Walter Hodges.

Illustration of Leslie Hotson's reconstruction of the Globe Theatre accompanying the article "playhouse structure," from *Shakespeare's Wooden 'O'* (1959), reprinted with the permission of The Macmillan Company and Rupert Hart-Davis, Ltd. Copyright © by Leslie Hotson, 1959.

Quotations and paraphrases from *The Living Shakespeare* (1949) by Oscar James Campbell, reprinted with the permission of The Macmillan Company.

Quotations and paraphrases from *Shakespeare and the Artist* (1959) by W. Moelwyn Merchant, reprinted with the permission of Oxford University Press.

The editors are also indebted to many other publishers and authors for permission to reprint critical comments on the works of Shakespeare from copyright materials. Acknowledgment for these excerpts is made in Authors Quoted in Selected Criticisms, p. xi.

Preface

The Reader's Encyclopedia of Shakespeare has been compiled in the hope of offering in a single volume all the essential information available about every feature of Shakespeare's life and works. Its compact form permits convenient reference to persons, places, literary works, and other subjects relevant to Shakespeare. It thus becomes a compendium of the results of studies made by scholars and biographers, by historians, literary, political, and social, and by editors and critics from the poet's own time to the present day.

Almost every statement in the volume is based on some exhaustive study made by an expert through the years. In presenting this mass of material, however, the editors and their staff have kept in mind that they are addressing not only the specialist, but also everyone with an interest in Shakespeare and delight in his works that has been awakened in the classroom, the library, or the theatre. They hope that the volume will at once arouse and satisfy the reader's curiosity about the greatest of all English playwrights and poets.

Nothing that casts even a feeble ray of light on Shakespeare's life, his career, or his reputation has been rejected as too trivial to deserve a place in the encyclopedia. The volume contains an entry for nearly every individual with whom Shakespeare is known or suspected to have established a relationship, for the playwrights thought to have influenced him or been influenced by him, for every significant character in the plays, for important actors remembered for performances in principal roles of the plays, for celebrated critics or editors of his works.

The encyclopedia contains many essays written for the volume by outstanding scholars on the subjects of their particular competence. Taken together these articles form a spectrum of views of the poet and of methods adopted for discovering the essential character of each drama. They also become a composite picture of current methods of criticism as applied to Shakespeare.

Generally accepted biographical details of the dramatist's life are summarized in the first entry under his name and treated more fully in separate entries. A less conventional feature of the encyclopedia is a brief survey of Shakespeare's intellectual and theatric growth and development—doubtless a piece of presumption. Although they realize that the mainsprings of this development lie hidden in the secret places of the poet's personality, the editors have hoped to discern some of its outlines. For example we can see how the elements of many of the early comedies and tragedies were reworked with telling effect in the works of Shakespeare's maturity. Obviously, such transformations as these are evidence of profound changes in Shakespeare's conceptions of tragedy and in his ideas of mortality.

The editors have given a full examination to each play in the accepted canon, including a summary of its plot, an investigation of its sources, the probable date of its composition, and finally a critical opinion of the work. Although this comment is usually an expression of the editors' ideas, dissident opinions are given full spread elsewhere in the book, which thus becomes a variorum of the interpretations of Shakespeare's work for three hundred years.

No other author of the Western world has stimulated so much thought among the best minds of each generation, so much research by its most gifted scholars, such keen insight by professional philosophers, so much eloquence by masters of rhetoric, and, alas!, so much tortured ingenuity expended by enthusiasts in support of rival claimants to the authorship of dramas they believe to be falsely attributed to a "village ignoramus." One could say, without being accused of idolatry, that the mental vigor and aesthetic sensibility of each English-speaking generation can be partly measured by its acceptance of Shakespeare's genius and the fervor of its response to his vision of life and his scrutiny of death.

This is a fortunate moment for the appearance of a Shakespeare encyclopedia. Critical attention to him has reached a new high. Never before has some acquaintance with the playwright and his work been so widespread. His plays are taught and minutely examined in secondary schools, colleges, and graduate schools. Many candidates for the Ph.D. degree in English departments present dissertations dealing with Shakespeare or with subjects related to him and his career. Literally millions of paper-backed editions of his plays crowd the bookstalls. Volumes of essays on his life, his plays, and his poems stream from the presses in many lands. Scores of festivals by groups organized for staging his dramas take place each year in England, Canada, and the United States. To these festivals pilgrims of adjoining regions go as to shrines. Some educators impatient with what they believe unhealthy overemphasis on this study refer to it as the Shakespeare Industry.

The Reader's Encyclopedia of Shakespeare, by giving its readers an all-embracing view of Shakespeare criticism up to the present, can serve as a warning to future scholars against fastidious judgments, against bold, ill-supported generalities, and above all, against unsuccessfully disguised repetition of stale opinions. In this way the body of future study of the poet can be based on a secure historical and aesthetic foundation.

OSCAR JAMES CAMPBELL

Contents

Contributors

(The titles of major articles are here cited with their authors' names.)

R. H. B. — Robert Hamilton Ball
Queens College of the City University of New York
"George Chapman"

P. B. — Patrick Barrett

J-A. B. — Jean-Albert Bédé
Columbia University
"France"

A. B. — Adam Berkley
Paterson State College

G. M. B. — Gerald M. Berkowitz
Indiana University

F. B. — Fredson Bowers
University of Virginia
"Textual Criticism"

M. C. B. — Muriel Clara Bradbrook
Girton College, Cambridge University
"Folk Festivals"

E. B. — Ernest Brennecke
Columbia University
"Germany"
"Music Based on the Plays"
"Music in the Plays"

D. B. — Douglas Bush
Harvard University
"Classical Myth in Shakespeare"

M. St. C. B. — Muriel St. Clare Byrne
"Elizabethan Life in the Plays"

O. J. C. — Oscar James Campbell
Columbia University

J. C. — Joan Cenedella

J. L. C. — James L. Clifford
Columbia University
"Samuel Johnson"

L. C. — Lois Cohen

H. D. — Helen Delpar

E. V. K. D. — Elliott V. K. Dobbie
Columbia University
"Pronunciation"

D. P. D. — Donald P. Duclos
Paterson State College

W. F. — Willard Farnham
University of California, Berkeley
"Medievalism in Shakespeare"

R. C. F. — Robert C. Fox
St. Francis College

E. G. — Ernest Gallo
University of Massachusetts

G. G. — George Gibian
Cornell University
"Russia"

M. H. G. — Martha Hester Golden
University of California, Riverside
"Stage Imagery"

P. G. — Peni Golden

E. V. G. — Edward V. Grice

M. G. — Maureen Grice

A. G. — Alice Griffin
Hunter College of the City University of New York
"American Shakespeare Festival"
"Stratford Shakespearean Festival, Canada"

T. S. H. — Talât Sait Halman
"Turkey"

A. H. — Alfred Harbage
Harvard University
"Style"

R. H. — Richard Harrier
New York University
"Imagery"

G. B. H. — G. B. Harrison
University of Michigan
"Topical References"

M. H. — Murray Hartman
Long Island University

T. H. — Terence Hawkes
University of Wales, Cardiff
"Samuel Taylor Coleridge"

C. W. H. — C. Walter Hodges
"Playhouse Structure"

J. H. — John Holloway
Queens College, Cambridge University
"Criticism—20th Century"

L. H. — Lucyle Hook
Barnard College
"Elizabeth Barry"
"Anne Bracegirdle"

M. H. H. Michael H. Horowitz

R. D. H. Robert D. Horn
University of Oregon
"Oregon Shakespearean Festival"

S. F. J. S. F. Johnson
Columbia University
"Enemies of the Stage"

S. M. J. Sister Miriam Joseph, C. S. C.
Saint Mary's College
"Rhetoric"

S. K. Seymour Kleinberg
Long Island University

G. W. K. G. Wilson Knight
University of Leeds
"Symbolism"

J. F. L. James F. Lacey
St. Francis College

N. L. Nino Langiulli
St. Francis College

C. L. Clifford Leech
University of Toronto
"John Fletcher"

O. LeW. Oswald LeWinter
"Poland"

R. E. L. Robert E. Lynch
Brooklyn College of the City University of New York

J. G. M. James G. McManaway
The Folger Shakespeare Library
"Folger Shakespeare Library"

L. M. Louis Marder
University of Illinois at Chicago Circle
"Scholarship—20th Century"

S. G. M. Sister Grace Maria
Saint Joseph's College for Women

G. W. M. George Wilbur Meyer
Newcomb College, Tulane University
"Christopher Marlowe"

M. M. Masao Miyoshi
University of California, Berkeley
"Japan"

N. M. Nils Molin
"Scandinavia"

K. M. Kenneth Muir
University of Liverpool
"Sources"

A. N. Allardyce Nicoll
University of Birmingham
"Language and Characterization"

M. P. Mario Praz
Rome University
"Italy in the Plays"

E. Q. Edward Quinn
City College of the City University of New York

J. R. John Reilly
Queens College of the City University of New York

I. R. Irving Ribner
University of Delaware
"Ben Jonson"

M. R. Martha Robinson

I. A. S. Isaac Avi Shapiro
Shakespeare Institute, University of Birmingham
"Shakespeare Institute of the University of Birmingham"

P. N. S. Paul N. Siegel
Long Island University
"Psychology"

C. J. S. Charles Jasper Sisson
University of London
"The Jig"

G. W. S., Jr. George Winchester Stone, Jr.
New York University
"David Garrick"

J. C. T. J. C. Trewin
Drama Critic, *The Illustrated London News* and *The Birmingham Post*
"Royal Shakespeare Theatre"

D. T. Dorothy Tuck

D. M. Z. David M. Zesmer
Illinois Institute of Technology
"John Dryden"

Oscar James Campbell, Ph.D., Litt.D., is Professor Emeritus at Columbia University, where he was formerly chairman of the Department of English. He has written *Comicall Satyre and Shakespeare's "Troilus and Cressida"* (1938), *Shakespeare's Satire* (1943), and is the editor of *The Living Shakespeare* (1940), *Sonnets, Songs, and Poems of Shakespeare* (1965), and, with others, of the Bantam Shakespeare series. Edward G. Quinn, Ph.D., is a professor of English at the City College of the City University of New York.

Authors Quoted in Selected Criticisms

The entry for each of Shakespeare's major works closes with a section entitled "Selected Criticism," which contains a collection of brief comments excerpted from the writings of past and present-day critics. These writers are named here in alphabetical order, with references to the Shakespearean works on which they have been quoted. The editors are grateful to many authors and publishers for their kind permission to reprint from copyright materials. Specific acknowledgments are made in the list which follows.

JOHN QUINCY ADAMS. Comments on *Othello* and *Romeo and Juliet*, reprinted from James Henry Hackett's *Notes, Criticisms, and Correspondence upon Shakespeares Plays and Actors* (1863).

WILLIAM ARCHER. Comment on *Twelfth Night*, reprinted from *Macmillan's Magazine* (August, 1884).

W. H. AUDEN. Comment on *Othello*, reprinted from "The Joker in the Pack," *The Dyer's Hand and Other Essays* (1962), by permission of Random House, Inc. and Faber and Faber, Ltd. Copyright © 1960 by W. H. Auden.

GEORGE P. BAKER. Comments on *King John* and *Two Gentlemen of Verona*, reprinted from *The Development of Shakespeare as a Dramatist* (1907).

C. L. BARBER. Comments on *As You Like It*, *Henry IV*, *Love's Labour's Lost*, *A Midsummer Night's Dream*, and *Twelfth Night*, reprinted from *Shakespeare's Festive Comedy* (1959), by permission of Princeton University Press. Copyright © 1959 by Princeton University Press.

S. L. BETHELL. Comments on *Antony and Cleopatra* and *Troilus and Cressida*, reprinted from *Shakespeare and the Popular Dramatic Tradition* (1944), by permission of The Staples Press.

ADRIEN BONJOUR. Comment on *King John*, reprinted from "The Road to Swinstead Abbey," *English Literary History*, XVIII (1951), by permission of The Johns Hopkins Press.

MURIEL C. BRADBROOK. Comment on *Measure for Measure*, reprinted from "Authority, Truth, and Justice in *Measure for Measure*," *Review of English Studies*, XVII (October, 1941), by permission of Oxford University Press. Comment on *Much Ado About Nothing*, reprinted from *Shakespeare and Elizabethan Poetry* (1951), by permission of Chatto & Windus Ltd. and Oxford University Press.

A. C. BRADLEY. Comments on *Antony and Cleopatra*, *Henry IV*, reprinted from *The Oxford Lectures on Poetry* (1909), by permission of Macmillan & Co Ltd, The Macmillan Company of Canada, and St. Martin's Press. Comment on *Coriolanus*, reprinted from *A Miscellany* (1929), by permission of Macmillan & Co Ltd, The Macmillan Company of Canada, and St. Martin's Press. Comments on *Hamlet*, *Macbeth*, and *Othello*, reprinted from *Shakespearean Tragedy* (1904), by permission of Macmillan & Co Ltd, The Macmillan Company of Canada, and St. Martin's Press.

GEORG M. BRANDES. Comments on *The Merchant of Venice* and *A Midsummer Night's Dream*, reprinted from *William Shakespeare: A Critical Study* (1896), by permission of William Heinemann Ltd., Publishers.

J. P. BROCKBANK. Comment on *Henry VI*, reprinted from "The Frame of Disorder—'Henry VI,'" *Early Shakespeare*, Stratford-Upon-Avon Studies 3 (1961), by permission of Edward Arnold, Ltd. and St. Martin's Press.

HAROLD BROOKS. Comment on *The Comedy of Errors*, reprinted from "Themes and Structure in 'The Comedy of Errors,'" *Early Shakespeare*, Stratford-Upon-Avon Studies 3 (1961), by permission of Edward Arnold, Ltd. and St. Martin's Press.

JOHN RUSSELL BROWN. Comments on *As You Like It*, *A Midsummer Night's Dream*, and *The Taming of the Shrew*, reprinted from *Shakespeare and His Comedies* (1957), by permission of Methuen & Co., Ltd.

JAMES L. CALDERWOOD. Comment on *King John*, reprinted from "Commodity and Honour in *King John*," *University of Toronto Quarterly*, XXIX (1960), by permission of the University of Toronto Press and the author.

THOMAS CAMPBELL. Comments on *Much Ado About Nothing* and *The Winter's Tale*, reprinted from *The Dramatic Works of Shakespeare* (1838).

GEORGE CHALMERS. Comment on *The Sonnets*, reprinted from *A Supplemental Apology for the Believers in the Shakspeare-papers* (1799).

E. K. CHAMBERS. Comments on *The Comedy of Errors*, *The Merry Wives of Windsor*, and *A Midsummer Night's Dream*, reprinted from *Shakespeare: A Survey* (1925), by permission of Sidgwick & Jackson, Ltd.

R. W. CHAMBERS. Comment on *Measure for Measure*, reprinted from *Man's Unconquerable Mind* (1939), by permission of Jonathan Cape, Ltd.

H. B. CHARLTON. Comments on *The Comedy of Errors* and *The Two Gentlemen of Verona*, reprinted from *Shakespearian Comedy* (1938), by permission of Methuen & Co., Ltd.

WOLFGANG CLEMEN. Comment on *A Midsummer Night's Dream,* reprinted from the Introduction to *A Midsummer Night's Dream* (Signet Edition, 1963), by permission of The New American Library. Comments on *Richard III* and *Romeo and Juliet,* reprinted from *The Development of Shakespeare's Imagery* (1951), by permission of Harvard University Press and Methuen & Co., Ltd.

NEVILL COGHILL. Comments on *The Comedy of Errors* and *The Merchant of Venice,* reprinted from "The Basis of Shakespearian Comedy: A Study of Medieval Affinities," *Essays and Studies,* n.s. III (1950), by permission of the author.

SAMUEL TAYLOR COLERIDGE. Comments on *All's Well That Ends Well, Antony and Cleopatra, The Comedy of Errors, Hamlet, King Lear, Love's Labour's Lost, Measure for Measure, Richard II, Romeo and Juliet, The Sonnets,* and *The Tempest,* reprinted from *Shakespearean Criticism* by S. T. Coleridge, T. M. Raysor, ed., Everyman Library Edition (1960), by permission of E. P. Dutton & Co., Inc. and J. M. Dent & Sons Ltd.

R. S. CRANE. Comment on *Macbeth,* reprinted from *The Languages of Criticism and the Structure of Poetry* (1953), by permission of The University of Toronto Press and the author.

BENEDETTO CROCE. Comments on *Antony and Cleopatra,* and *The Sonnets,* reprinted from *Ariosto, Shakespeare and Corneille* (1920), by permission of George Allen & Unwin, Ltd.

PATRICK CRUTTWELL. Comment on *The Sonnets,* reprinted from *The Shakespearean Moment* (1955), by permission of Columbia University Press and Chatto & Windus, Ltd.

JOHN DENNIS. Comment on *Coriolanus,* reprinted from *An Essay on the Genius and Writings of Shakespear* (1712).

THOMAS DE QUINCEY. Comment on *Macbeth,* reprinted from "On the Knocking at the Gate in Macbeth," *Miscellaneous Essays* (1851).

MADELEINE DORAN. Comment on *Henry IV,* reprinted from "Imagery in *Richard II* and in *Henry IV,*" *The Modern Language Review,* XXXVII (April, 1942), by permission of The Modern Humanities Research Association and the author.

EDWARD DOWDEN. Comments on *All's Well That Ends Well, As You Like It, Henry VI, Macbeth,* and *The Tempest,* reprinted from *Shakspere: A Critical Study of His Mind and Art* (1875).

JOHN DRYDEN. Comment on *The Tempest,* reprinted from "The Prologue," *The Tempest* (Davenant-Dryden adaptation, published 1670).

T. S. ELIOT. Comment on *Hamlet* reprinted from "Hamlet and His Problems" and comment on *Othello* reprinted from "Shakespeare and the Stoicism of Seneca" in *Selected Essays of T. S. Eliot,* New Edition, copyright, 1932, 1936, 1950, by Harcourt, Brace & World, Inc.; copyright, 1960, 1964, by T. S. Eliot. Reprinted by permission of Harcourt, Brace & World, Inc. and Faber and Faber, Ltd.

UNA ELLIS-FERMOR. Comment on *Troilus and Cressida,* reprinted from *The Frontiers of Drama* (1945), by permission of Methuen & Co., Ltd.

WILLIAM EMPSON. Comment on *Henry IV,* reprinted from "Falstaff and Mr. Dover Wilson," *Kenyon Review,* XV (Spring, 1953), by permission of *The Kenyon Review* and the author. Comment on *Measure for Measure,* reprinted from "Sense in *Measure for Measure,*" *The Structure of Complex Words* (1951), by permission of Chatto and Windus, Ltd. Comment on *Pericles,* reprinted from "Hunt the Symbol," *The Times Literary Supplement* (April 23, 1964), by permission of The Times Publishing Company, Limited.

WILLARD FARNHAM. Comment on *Coriolanus,* reprinted from *Shakespeare's Tragic Frontier* (1950), by permission of the University of California Press and the author.

FRANCIS FERGUSSON. Comments on *The Comedy of Errors, Measure for Measure,* and *Much Ado About Nothing,* reprinted from *The Human Image in Dramatic Literature* (1957), by permission of the author. Comment on *Macbeth,* reprinted from "*Macbeth* as the Imitation of an Action," *English Institute Essays 1951* (1952), by permission of Columbia University Press.

F. J. FURNIVALL. Comment on *The Winter's Tale,* reprinted from *The Leopold Shakespeare* (1877).

G. G. GERVINIUS. Comments on *Henry VI, Henry VIII, Love's Labour's Lost, The Merry Wives of Windsor, Pericles,* and *The Two Gentlemen of Verona,* reprinted from *Shakespeare* (1849–1850), translated as *Shakespeare Commentaries* (1863).

GOETHE. Comment on *Hamlet,* reprinted from *Wilhelm Meister's Apprenticeship* (1795–1796; translated by Thomas Carlyle, 1824).

HARLEY GRANVILLE-BARKER. Comments on *Cymbeline* and *King Lear,* reprinted from *Prefaces to Shakespeare* (Vol. I, 1946), by permission of Princeton University Press. Copyright 1946 by Princeton University Press. Comments on *Coriolanus* and *Othello,* reprinted from *Prefaces to Shakespeare* (Vol. II, 1947), by permission of Princeton University Press. Copyright 1947 by Princeton University Press.

FRANK HARRIS. Comments on *All's Well That Ends Well, Coriolanus, Henry VI,* and *The Taming of the Shrew,* reprinted from *The Women of Shakespeare* (1911) by permission of Methuen & Co., Ltd. Comment on *The Merry Wives of Windsor* and *Timon of Athens,* reprinted from *The Man Shakespeare* (1909).

WILLIAM HAZLITT. Comments on *As You Like It, The Comedy of Errors, Coriolanus, Cymbeline, Hamlet, Henry IV, Henry V, Henry VI, Love's Labour's Lost, The Merchant of Venice, The Merry Wives of Windsor, Othello, The Tempest, Twelfth Night,* and *The Two Gentlemen of Verona,* reprinted from *The Characters of Shakespear's Plays* (1817).

ROBERT B. HEILMAN. Comment on *Othello,* reprinted from *Magic in the Web,* by permission of The University of Kentucky Press. Copyright © 1956 by The University of Kentucky Press.

HEINRICH HEINE. Comment on *The Merchant of Venice,* from *Shakespeares Mädchen und Frauen* (1839; tr. in *Complete Works,* 1892–1895, by C. G. Leland *et al.*).

JOHN HOLLANDER. Comment on *Twelfth Night,* reprinted from "Twelfth Night and the Morality of Indulgence," *The Sewanee Review,* No. 67 (1959), by permission of *The Sewanee Review* and the author.

JOHN HOLLOWAY. Comments on *King Lear* and *Othello*, reprinted from *The Story of the Night* (1961), by permission of Routledge & Kegan Paul, Ltd.

EDWARD HUBLER. Comment on *The Sonnets*, reprinted from *The Sense of Shakespeare's Sonnets*, by permission of Princeton University Press. Copyright 1952 by Princeton University Press.

VICTOR HUGO. Comments on *Love's Labour's Lost*, *The Tempest*, and *The Winter's Tale*, from *Œuvres Complètes de Shakespeare* (1859–1866); translations from New Variorum editions of *Love's Labour's Lost* (1904), *The Tempest* (1892), and *The Winter's Tale* (1898). Comment on *Othello*, from *William Shakespeare* (1864); reprinted from a translation by M. B. Anderson (1898).

LEIGH HUNT. Comments on *Julius Caesar* and *King John*, reprinted from *Leigh Hunt's Dramatic Criticism, 1808–1831* (1949), edited by L. H. and C. W. Houtchens, by permission of Columbia University Press.

HENRY JAMES. Comment on *Cymbeline*, reprinted from "Mr. Henry Irving's Production of 'Cymbeline,'" *Harper's Weekly*, Nov. 21, 1896.

ANNA BROWNELL JAMESON. Comments on *Antony and Cleopatra* and *Much Ado About Nothing*, reprinted from *Shakespeare's Heroines;* originally published in *Characteristics of Women* (1832).

HAROLD JENKINS. Comment on *As You Like It*, reprinted from "As You Like It," *Shakespeare Survey 8* (1955), by permission of Cambridge University Press.

SAMUEL JOHNSON. Comments on *All's Well That Ends Well*, *Antony and Cleopatra*, *Coriolanus*, *Cymbeline*, *Hamlet*, *Henry IV*, *Henry VI*, *Henry VIII*, *King Lear*, *Macbeth*, *Othello*, *Richard III*, *Romeo and Juliet*, *Timon of Athens*, *Titus Andronicus*, and *The Two Gentlemen of Verona*, reprinted from *The Plays of William Shakespeare* (1765).

ERNEST JONES. Comment on *Hamlet*, reprinted from *Hamlet and Oedipus* (1949), by permission of Victor Gollancz, Ltd. and W. W. Norton & Company, Inc. Copyright 1949 by Ernest Jones.

THOMAS KENNY. Comments on *All's Well That Ends Well*, *Cymbeline*, *Henry V*, *Henry VI*, and *A Midsummer Night's Dream*, reprinted from *The Life and Genius of Shakespeare* (1864).

FRANK KERMODE. Comment on *Henry VIII*, reprinted by permission from "What is Shakespeare's *Henry VIII* About?" *Durham University Journal*, n.s. IX (1948). Comment on *The Merchant of Venice*, reprinted from "The Mature Comedies," *Early Shakespeare*, Stratford-Upon-Avon Studies 3 (1961), by permission of Edward Arnold (Publishers) Ltd. and St. Martin's Press. Comment on *Pericles*, reprinted from *Shakespeare: The Final Plays* (1963), No. 155 in the Writers and Their Work series, by permission of the British Council and the author. Comment on *The Tempest*, reprinted from the Introduction to *The Tempest* (The Arden Shakespeare, 1958), by permission of Harvard University Press and Methuen & Co., Ltd. Comment on *The Winter's Tale*, reprinted from the Introduction to *The Winter's Tale* (Signet Edition, 1963), by permission of The New American Library, Inc.

ALVIN KERNAN. Comment on *Othello*, reprinted from the Introduction to *Othello* (Signet Edition, 1963), by permission of The New American Library, Inc.

CHARLES KNIGHT. Comments on *The Comedy of Errors*, *Henry V*, *King John*, *A Midsummer Night's Dream*, and *Titus Andronicus*, reprinted from *Studies of Shakspere*, 1849.

G. WILSON KNIGHT. Comments on *Cymbeline*, *Henry VIII*, *Pericles*, and *The Winter's Tale*, reprinted from *The Crown of Life* (1947), by permission of Methuen & Co., Ltd. Comment on *Julius Caesar*, reprinted from *The Imperial Theme* (1954), by permission of Methuen & Co., Ltd. Comments on *King Lear* and *Troilus and Cressida*, reprinted from *The Wheel of Fire* (1930), by permission of Methuen & Co., Ltd.

CHARLES LAMB. Comments on *King Lear*, *Richard III*, and *Twelfth Night*, reprinted from *Lamb's Criticism* (1923), E. M. W. Tillyard, ed., by permission of Cambridge University Press.

W. W. LAWRENCE. Comment on *All's Well That Ends Well*, reprinted from *Shakespeare's Problem Comedies* (1931).

CLIFFORD LEECH. Comment on *Henry IV*, reprinted from "The Unity of 2 Henry IV," *Shakespeare Survey 6* (1953), by permission of Cambridge University Press.

CHARLOTTE LENNOX. Comment on *The Winter's Tale*, reprinted from *Shakespear Illustrated* (1753).

HARRY LEVIN. Comment on *Hamlet*, reprinted from *The Question of Hamlet* (1959), by permission of Oxford University Press. Copyright © 1959 by Harry Levin.

ABRAHAM LINCOLN. Comment on *Hamlet*, from a letter to James K. Hackett, reprinted in *American Shakespearean Criticism*, A. V. Westfall, ed. (1939).

THE LONDON CHRONICLE. Comment on *Richard III*, from an anonymous review of Spranger Barry as Richard III in a production at Covent Garden, *The London Chronicle*, Jan. 29–Feb. 1, 1757; reprinted in *The English Dramatic Critics*, James Agate, ed. (1932).

JAMES RUSSELL LOWELL. Comment on *Richard III*, reprinted from *The Complete Writings of James Russell Lowell* (1904). Comment on *The Tempest*, reprinted from *Among My Books* (1870).

MARY MC CARTHY. Comments on *Julius Caesar*, and *Macbeth*, reprinted from *Mary McCarthy's Theatre Chronicles, 1937–1962* (Farrar, Straus & Giroux, Inc., 1962).

MAYNARD MACK. Comment on *Antony and Cleopatra*, reprinted from the Introduction to *Antony and Cleopatra* (The Pelican Shakespeare ed., 1960), by permission of Penguin Books, Inc. Comment on *Hamlet*, reprinted from "The World of Hamlet," *The Yale Review*, XLI (1952), by permission of *The Yale Review*. Copyright 1952 by Yale University Press. Comment on *The Taming of the Shrew*, reprinted from "Engagement and Detachment in Shakespeare's Plays," *Essays on Shakespeare and Elizabethan Drama*, Richard Hosley, ed. (1962), by permission of University of Missouri Press.

JOHN MASEFIELD. Comment on *King John*, reprinted from *William Shakespeare* (1911), by permission of Oxford University Press.

J. C. MAXWELL. Comment on *Titus Andronicus*, reprinted from the Introduction to *Titus Andronicus* (The Arden Shakespeare, 1953), by permission of Harvard University Press and Methuen & Co., Ltd.

ARTHUR MIZENER. Comment on *The Sonnets*, reprinted from "The Structure of Figurative Language in Shakespeare's Sonnets," *The Southern Review*, V (1940), by permission of Louisiana State University Press.

MAURICE MORGANN. Comment on *Henry IV*, reprinted from "An Essay on the Dramatic Character of Sir John Falstaff" (1777).

R. G. MOULTON. Comment on *Julius Caesar*, reprinted from *Shakespeare as a Dramatic Artist* (1885).

KENNETH MUIR. Comments on *Pericles* and *Two Noble Kinsmen*, reprinted from *Shakespeare as Collaborator* (1960), by permission of Methuen & Co., Ltd.

GILBERT MURRAY. Comment on *Hamlet*, reprinted from *The Classical Tradition in Poetry* (1927), by permission of Harvard University Press.

J. MIDDLETON MURRY. Comment on *King John*, reprinted from *Shakespeare* (1936), by permission of Jonathan Cape, Limited.

GEORGE ORWELL. Comment on *King Lear*, reprinted from "Lear, Tolstoy, and the Fool" in *Shooting an Elephant and Other Essays*, by permission of Harcourt, Brace & World, Inc., and Martin Secker & Warburg, Ltd. Copyright 1945, 1946, 1949, 1950 by Sonia Brownell Orwell.

THOMAS MARC PARROTT. Comments on *All's Well That Ends Well*, *Much Ado About Nothing*, and *The Taming of the Shrew*, reprinted from *Shakespearean Comedy*, by permission of Oxford University Press, Inc. Copyright 1949 by Thomas Marc Parrott.

WALTER PATER. Comment on *Love's Labour's Lost*, reprinted from *Macmillan's Magazine* (December, 1885). Comment on *Richard II*, reprinted from *Appreciations* (1889).

H. T. PRICE. Comment on *Titus Andronicus*, reprinted from "The Authorship of Titus Andronicus" in the *Journal of English and German Philology*, XLVII (1943), by permission of University of Illinois Press.

IRVING RIBNER. Comments on *Henry VI* and *Henry VIII*, reprinted from *The English History Play in the Age of Shakespeare* (1957), by permission of Princeton University Press. Copyright © 1957 by Princeton University Press.

WILLIAM AND BARBARA ROSEN. Comment on *Julius Caesar*, reprinted from the Introduction to *Julius Caesar* (Signet Edition, 1963), by permission of The New American Library, Inc.

A. P. ROSSITER. Comment on *Richard III*, reprinted from *Angel with Horns* (1961), by permission of Longmans, Green & Co., Ltd., and Theatre Arts Books, New York, N.Y. Copyright © 1961 by Longmans, Green & Co., Ltd.

THOMAS RYMER. Comment on *Othello*, reprinted from *A Short View of Tragedy* (1693).

HANNS SACHS. Comment on *Measure for Measure*, reprinted from "The Measure in 'Measure for Measure,'" from *The Creative Unconscious* (2nd ed., 1951), by permission of Sci-Art Publishers and Miriam Lazrus.

GEORGE SANTAYANA. Comment on *Hamlet*, reprinted from the Introduction to *Hamlet* (The University Press Shakespeare, Renaissance Edition, 1908).

A. W. SCHLEGEL. Comments on *As You Like It*, *Measure for Measure*, *Twelfth Night*, and *The Winter's Tale*, from *A Course of Lectures on Dramatic Literature* (1809–1811; trans. John Black, 1846).

ARTHUR SEWELL. Comment on *King Lear*, reprinted from *Character and Society in Shakespeare* (1951), by permission of Oxford University Press.

GEORGE BERNARD SHAW. Comment on *Cymbeline*, reprinted from *The Saturday Review* (Sept. 26, 1896), and on *The Taming of the Shrew*, from *The Saturday Review* (Nov. 6, 1897), by permission of The Public Trustee and The Society of Authors.

WILLIAM SPALDING. Comment on *Two Noble Kinsmen*, from *A Letter on Shakespeare's Authorship of The Two Noble Kinsmen* (1833).

THEODORE SPENCER. Comment on *Two Noble Kinsmen*, reprinted from "The Two Noble Kinsmen," *Modern Philology*, 36 (1938), by permission of The University of Chicago Press.

BERNARD SPIVACK. Comment on *Othello*, reprinted from *Shakespeare and the Allegory of Evil* (1958), by permission of Columbia University Press.

CAROLINE SPURGEON. Comments on *Antony and Cleopatra*, *Hamlet*, and *Pericles*, reprinted from *Shakespeare's Imagery* (1935), by permission of Cambridge University Press.

DONALD A. STAUFFER. Comment on *Romeo and Juliet*, reprinted from *Shakespeare's World of Images* (1949), by permission of W. W. Norton & Company, Inc. Copyright © 1949 by W. W. Norton & Company, Inc.

GEORGE STEEVENS. Comment on *The Sonnets*, from *The Plays of William Shakespeare* (1793).

GEORGE STEINER. Comment on *Much Ado About Nothing*, reprinted from *The Death of Tragedy* (1961), by permission of Alfred A. Knopf, Inc.

J. I. M. STEWART. Comment on *Henry IV*, reprinted from *Character and Motive in Shakespeare* (1949), by permission of Longmans, Green & Co., Limited.

BRENTS STIRLING. Comment on *Julius Caesar*, reprinted from *Unity in Shakespearian Tragedy* (1956), by permission of Columbia University Press. Comment on *The Merchant of Venice*, reprinted from the Introduction to *The Merchant of Venice* (The Pelican Shakespeare ed., 1959), by permission of Penguin Books, Inc.

E. E. STOLL. Comment on *The Merchant of Venice*, from "Shylock, The Complete Villain," *Shakespeare Studies* (1927).

JOSEPH H. SUMMERS. Comment on *Twelfth Night*, reprinted from "The Masks of *Twelfth Night*," *The University of Kansas City Review*, Vol. 22 (Autumn, 1955), by permission of *The University Review* and the author.

ALGERNON CHARLES SWINBURNE. Comments on *Antony and Cleopatra* and *Love's Labour's Lost*, reprinted from *A Study of Shakespeare* (1880).

WYLIE SYPHER. Comment on *Hamlet*, reprinted from

the Appendix to *Comedy* (Doubleday-Anchor, 1956), by permission of the author. Comment on *Much Ado About Nothing*, reprinted from "Nietzsche and Socrates in Messina," *Partisan Review* (1949), pp. 710–711. By permission of *Partisan Review* and the author. Copyright © 1949 by *Partisan Review*.

BERNHARD TEN BRINK. Comments on *Julius Caesar* and *The Merchant of Venice*, reprinted from *Five Lectures on Shakespeare* (1895).

JOHANN LUDWIG TIECK. Comment on *Romeo and Juliet*, from *Dramaturgische Blätter* (Vol. 1, 1826). Translation reprinted from *Romeo and Juliet*, New Variorum Edition (1871).

E. M. W. TILLYARD. Comments on *Henry IV* and *Henry VI*, reprinted from *Shakespeare's History Plays* (1944), by permission of Chatto and Windus, Ltd.

LEO TOLSTOY. Comment on *King Lear*, reprinted from *Tolstoy on Shakespeare* (1907); translation by V. Tchertkoff.

DEREK TRAVERSI. Comments on *The Taming of the Shrew* and *The Two Gentlemen of Verona*, reprinted from *Shakespeare: The Early Comedies* (rev. ed., 1964), No. 129 in the Writers and Their Work series, by permission of the British Council and the author.

IVAN SERGEYEVICH TURGENEV. Comment on *Hamlet*, reprinted from "Hamlet and Don Quixote," *Current Literature* (January, 1907).

PETER URE. Comment on *Richard II*, reprinted from the Introduction to *Richard II* (The Arden Shakespeare, 1956), by permission of Harvard University Press and Methuen & Co., Ltd.

MARK VAN DOREN. Comments on *As You Like It*, *Henry VI*, and *Timon of Athens*, reprinted from *Shakespeare* (1939), by permission of Holt, Rinehart and Winston, Inc. Copyright 1939 by Mark Van Doren.

EUGENE WAITH. Comment on *Titus Andronicus*, reprinted from "The Metamorphosis of Violence in *Titus Andronicus*," *Shakespeare Survey 10* (1957), by permission of Cambridge University Press.

BARRETT WENDELL. Comments on *Henry V*, *King John*, *The Taming of the Shrew*, *Timon of Athens*, and *The Sonnets*, reprinted from *William Shakspere: A Study in Elizabethan Literature* (1894).

WALTER WHITER. Comment on *Romeo and Juliet*, reprinted from *A Specimen of a Commentary on Shakespeare* (1794).

CHARLES WILLIAMS. Comment on *Henry V*, reprinted from *Shakespeare Criticism, 1919–1935*, A. Bradby, ed. (World Classics 436, 1936), by permission of Oxford University Press.

J. DOVER WILSON. Comment on *Henry IV*, reprinted from *The Fortunes of Falstaff* (1943), by permission of Cambridge University Press. Comments on *The Merchant of Venice* and *The Merry Wives of Windsor*, reprinted from *Shakespeare's Happy Comedies* (1962), by permission of Faber and Faber, Ltd. and Northwestern University Press.

W. K. WIMSATT. Comment on *Antony and Cleopatra*, reprinted by permission from "Poetry and Morals: A Relation Reargued," *Thought*, 23 (1948).

WILLIAM BUTLER YEATS. Comments on *Henry V* and *Richard II*, reprinted from *Essays and Introductions* (1961), by permission of A. P. Watt & Son, Macmillan Co. of Canada, Ltd., Macmillan & Co., Ltd., The Macmillan Company, and Mr. M. B. Yeats. Copyright © Mrs. W. B. Yeats, 1961.

STARK YOUNG. Comment on *Twelfth Night*, reprinted from *Immortal Shadows* (1948), pp. 220–221, by permission of Charles Scribner's Sons.

ROSE A. ZIMBARDO. Comment on *Henry V*, reprinted from *Shakespeare Encomium*, Anne Paolucci, ed., The City College Papers I (1964).

The Reader's Encyclopedia of SHAKESPEARE

A

Aaron. In *Titus Andronicus,* the malevolent Moorish lover of Tamora, queen of the Goths. He devises the plan whereby Tamora's sons murder Bassianus, after which Titus' sons Quintus and Martius are executed for the crime. Aaron arranges, moreover, that Titus shall cut off his own hand in a vain attempt to ransom the lives of his sons. As punishment, Lucius orders him buried breast-deep in earth and starved to death.

Abbott, Edwin Abbott (1838–1926). Educator and scholar. From 1865 to 1889 Abbott was headmaster of the City of London School, in which capacity he achieved renown for his educational reforms. Some of his innovations were the introduction of the study of science and English literature, with Shakespeare forming an integral part of the sixth-form curriculum. Among the students whom he inspired were A. H. Bullen and Sir Sidney Lee. Abbott's writings include textbooks, literary scholarship, and theological studies. His *Shakespearian Grammar* (1869), while designed primarily for the student, was a pioneer study of Shakespeare's language which for generations proved to be an indispensable guide. His *Bacon and Essex* (1877) brought to light much hitherto neglected material and presented conclusions different from those of James Spedding, the outstanding 19th-century authority on Bacon. In later life Abbott devoted much of his time to theological studies, one of his important works being *The Anglican Career of Cardinal Newman* (2 vols., 1892).

Abergavenny, George Neville, Lord (c. 1471–1535). Eldest son of George, 2nd Baron Abergavenny. Though he had been a trusted retainer of Henry VII, his marriage to Mary Stafford, daughter of the duke of Buckingham, led to his being suspected by Henry VIII of involvement in the duke's royal ambitions. He was pardoned after a year in prison, but never fully regained the king's favor. In *Henry VIII,* Abergavenny shares Buckingham's detestation of Cardinal Wolsey and is arrested with the Duke (I, i), at Wolsey's instigation, on charges of treason.

Abhorson. In *Measure for Measure,* an executioner. His name suits his occupation. Abhorson objects to the Provost's hiring Pompey, a prostitute's tapster, as an assistant executioner, claiming that he "will discredit our mystery." Reprimanded by his superior, Abhorson accepts his new helper and teaches him the trade (IV, ii).

above. See UPPER STAGE.

Abraham. In *Romeo and Juliet,* a servant to Montague.

abridged texts. Texts of Elizabethan plays that have evidently been shortened for a particular type of performance. It is not clear, however, which theatrical conditions called for abridged versions. Some have suggested that court performances were abbreviated, others that winter performances in the public theatres were shortened for lack of light. The most generally held opinion, however, is that plays were abridged for tours in the provinces when a reduced number of players required the elimination of superfluous small parts.

Abridgment is apparent in all of the "bad quartos" of Shakespeare's plays, some of which, notably the *Romeo and Juliet* and the *Henry VI* bad quartos, were probably cut for a provincial tour. The practice is also evident in authoritative texts, such as *The Two Gentlemen of Verona, The Comedy of Errors,* and *Macbeth,* first published in the 1623 Folio. J. Dover Wilson has also suggested that the Folio text of *The Tempest* is an abridged one. [W. W. Greg, *The Shakespeare First Folio,* 1955.]

academic plays. See UNIVERSITY DRAMA.

Achilles. In Greek mythology, the king of the Myrmidons, a Thessalian tribe, and the most illustrious Greek warrior in the Trojan War, in which he killed Hector. As the hero of Homer's *Iliad,* Achilles became the prototype of the Greeks' conception of manly beauty and valor. In *Troilus and Cressida,* he appears as one of the Greek generals and is presented as a man frustrated by two conflicting motives. Achilles is pledged, on the one hand, to cease warring on the Trojans because of his love for Polyxena, Hector's sister. His public duty as a Greek soldier, on the other hand, is to continue fighting, and he is continually reminded of this duty by the skillful Ulysses. Ultimately, however, Achilles' decision to rejoin the fight is based on an unrelated motive—the death of Patroclus. His triumph over Hector in the play is not as Homer gives it, but is the dishonorable murder of an unarmed man. In all of these scenes Shakespeare consistently undercuts the heroic picture of Achilles, as he does with most of the other characters in this sharply cynical play.

Achilles has been thought by some to be Shakespeare's portrait of the earl of Essex. See TOPICAL REFERENCES. [Robert Kimbrough, *Shakespeare's Troilus & Cressida and Its Setting,* 1964.]

Acolastus, his After Witte (1600). A poem by Samuel Nicholson (fl. 1600), poet and divine. The poem is notable for its numerous and apparently unashamed plagiarisms of lines from *Venus and Adonis* and *The Rape of Lucrece.* Nicholson also borrowed the line from *3 Henry VI* ("O tigers heart wrapt in a woman's hide"), which Robert Greene parodied in his

ACOLASTVS
HIS AFTER-
WITTE.

By S. N.

Semel insaniuimus omnes.

AT LONDON
Imprinted for Iohn Baylie, and are to be
sold at his shop, neere the little North-
doore of Paules Church.
1600.

TITLE PAGE OF NICHOLSON'S *Acolastus* (1600).

attack on Shakespeare. The greatest indebtedness of *Acolastus* is, however, to *Venus and Adonis.* While *Acolastus* might be considered a competent poem in its own right, it never achieves the distinction of the work it imitates. [J. M. Bemrose, "A Critical Examination of the Borrowings from *Venus and Adonis* and *Lucrece* in . . . *Acolastus,*" *Shakespeare Quarterly,* XV, 1964.]

acting. There are two current theories concerning acting style in the Elizabethan theatre. One theory asserts that Elizabethan actors employed a highly formalized, rigidly restricted style derived from textbooks on oratory and rhetoric used in 16th-century schools and universities. This formal system relied on conventional gestures used by the actors to represent and convey various emotional states. Thus the Elizabethan actor was less concerned with the modern idea of "interpreting" a part than he was with representing it. His own personality had little or no impact on his presentation of the role and an actor was judged by his oratorical ability. Proponents of this theory usually cite Hamlet's advice to the players ("Suit the action to the word, the word to the action," III, ii, 20) as evidence of the use of the formal style. This was almost certainly the case in academic productions (see UNIVERSITY DRAMA), but it was not necessarily employed by the professionals in the public theatres.

The opposing theory argues that a flexible, comparatively naturalistic style was employed by companies such as the King's Men, who were saluted by a dramatist in 1630 as "the true brood of actors, that alone keep naturall unstray'nd Action in her throne." It is argued that Elizabethan actors attempted "to hold . . . the mirror up to nature" and were therefore concerned with imitating life as they knew it.

A middle ground between these two views is held by those who suggest an acting style which operated within a conventional and formal framework but which left room within this framework for the expression of distinctive, individual characteristics. [Bertram L. Joseph, *Elizabethan Acting,* 1951; Bertram L. Joseph, *The Tragic Actor,* 1959; Bernard Beckerman, *Shakespeare at the Globe,* 1962.]

acting companies. The origin of Elizabethan acting companies is to be found in the early trade guilds' presentations of dramatized episodes from the Old and New Testaments and the lives of saints and heroes. An especially popular play was apt to be shown in neighboring villages at first and then farther afield in larger towns, giving rise in effect to traveling companies. On their journeys about England, players were likely to come into contact with groups of itinerant entertainers of all sorts: jugglers, tumblers, tightrope adepts, sleight-of-hand artists, and animal trainers, as well as ordinary beggars and vagabonds. The groups often came into conflict with each other and with local populaces: players, entertainers, and vagabonds enjoyed equally unsavory reputations. They were accused of horse-thievery, purse-snatching, and general pilfering from farmers.

With the passage of time the nature of the dramatic offerings of the strolling players changed. Into their repertories they began gradually to insert plays, usually farces, full of slapstick and often obscene. Later they added morality plays; into these dramas of supposedly moral instruction, they also inserted obscenities and the like. Such fare, while it delighted some audiences, offended many others, and efforts were made to control and suppress the content of the companies' offerings, and the companies themselves. See CENSORSHIP.

Vagabondage itself was offensive in the medieval and Elizabethan order of things. More practically, by the end of the 14th century a labor shortage was beginning to make itself felt, and an attempt was made to compel able-bodied vagabonds to return to their original homes and seek work. The Tudors continued and developed this policy. In 1531 Henry VIII issued an act requiring able-bodied vagabonds and beggars without master, land, merchandise, craft, or mystery to be brought before the local justice of the peace (or the mayor in incorporated towns) and whipped. In 1550 the act was revived and kept in force through frequent renewals, the last occurring in 1563.

Players and minstrels were not named as such in the statutes. Playing was not considered a craft, but the Tudor players were not legally vagabonds because they were not "masterless." They were the "servants" of a noble lord or wealthy gentleman, and this status was affirmed by a "certificate," or letter, which a law of 1554 required them to carry as proof of identity. The players were not paid by their patron, but lived on earnings from public performances. Frequently, especially on festival days, they would give a performance before their patron and his guests.

During the early years of the Elizabethan drama the stage was dominated by boy acting companies. The boys came from the trained musical establishments of the royal chapels and the major cathedrals and colleges (see CHILDREN'S COMPANIES; CHILDREN OF THE CHAPEL; CHILDREN OF PAUL'S). There were several reasons for the prominence of the boys. At court, for example, the Gentlemen of the Chapel had ceased giving performances under Henry VIII, and the customary royal INTERLUDES were allowed to disappear. The adult companies had no permanent economic base in London, and their playwriting proficiency was not up to courtly standards. The performances of the boys, on the other hand, were polished and professional and under the guidance of clever, talented, and energetic masters.

With the erection of the first permanent public theatres in 1576, the adult acting companies began to gain in popularity. After this date it became fashionable for men in high office, the lord chamberlain or the lord high admiral, or the queen's favorites, to sponsor London companies. By 1578 there were eight public theatres (six inns used as theatres, the Theatre, and the Curtain) occupied by players, but an order of the privy council that year limited performances in the court revels to six companies: Leicester's, Warwick's, Sussex's, Essex's, Children of the Chapel, and Children of Paul's. Other companies existing at the time—Lord Vaux's, Arundel's, Berkeley's, and Abergavenny's—were never summoned to court and disappeared into the provinces.

From 1583 to 1590, the boy companies went into a decline, despite the plays written for them by John Lyly. The adult companies gained the services of the so-called UNIVERSITY WITS—Marlowe, Peele, Greene, Lodge, and Nashe—to write plays for court presentation, with lesser literary lights composing chronicle histories and other popular material for public consumption.

The most popular group during this time was the QUEEN'S MEN, making 21 appearances at court. They wore the royal livery, transferred to them from the Interluders, and included the best actors. Led by Richard Tarlton, there were Robert Wilson and John Laneham (from Leicester's), Robert Adams (Sussex's), and John Dutton (Oxford's). After 1587 Leicester's and Oxford's men ceased to play at court. Only by coalition with other companies were the ADMIRAL'S MEN able to perform (see AMALGAMATION). The last coalition, of Admiral's and Strange's Men, from 1589, was able to gain dominance at court and seriously rival the Queen's Men after Tarlton's death in 1588.

The years from 1592 to 1594 were marked by virulent epidemics of plague, and the consequent shutting down of the theatres resulted in truncated theatrical seasons in London. The acting companies toured the provinces, occasionally in combination (see PROVINCIAL TOURS). The Queen's Men continued as a provincial group, capitalizing on the royal name, never returning to London. Edward Alleyn's group (a coalition of Strange's and Admiral's) split into Chamberlain's and Admiral's. The last two companies maintained a fierce competition with each other, evidenced by rival plays with similar themes, such as Chamberlain's *1 Henry IV* against Admiral's *Sir John Oldcastle* or Admiral's two Robin Hood plays vs Chamberlain's *As You Like It*. Measured by frequency of court performances between 1594 and 1603, Chamberlain's were the more popular with 32 to Admiral's 20. In 1597 both companies were granted a virtual monopoly of the London stage by the PRIVY COUNCIL; other companies, in defiance of the privy council's order, however, continued to play. The latter included Pembroke's, Derby's, Worcester's, and Hertford's, which were also seen at court. A third permanent company was created by an amalgamation of Oxford's and WORCESTER'S MEN in 1602. During this period, too, there was a revival of interest in the boy companies, Paul's in 1599, and Chapel, 1600, appealing to a new generation of playgoers.

At the death of Elizabeth and accession of James in 1603, there was a change in the names and the patrons of the leading companies, but no significant internal change. Chamberlain's came under the direct patronage of James and was called the King's Men; Admiral's Men became Prince Henry's; and Worcester's became Queen Anne's. At the death of Henry in 1612, his company came under the patronage of the Elector Palatine. Anne also became patroness of the Children of the Chapel, which took the name Children of the Queen's Revels.

The royal family's liberal patronage of the theatre brought about the formation of new companies desiring to make profit from this fact. The Duke of York's Men were patented in 1610, and Lady Elizabeth's Men in 1611. In 1613 Lady Elizabeth's and the Children of the Queen's Revels combined, and in 1615 they were joined by Prince Charles' Men (the company formerly known as the Duke of York's). By March 1615 there were four major companies in London: King's at the Globe and Blackfriars; the Palsgrave's at the Fortune; the Queen's at the Red Bull (moving to the Cockpit in 1617); and Prince's at the Hope. The King's Men maintained their supremacy from 1603 to 1616, giving 127 of the 299 court performances recorded for that period. Next were the Prince's (47), Queen's (28), York's (20), Queen's Revels (15), Elizabeth's (9), and Paul's (3). For acting companies originating in the Restoration theatre, see DUKE'S COMPANY; KING'S COMPANY. [E. K. Chambers, *The Elizabethan Stage*, 1923; Muriel C. Bradbrook, *The Rise of the Common Player*, 1962; G. E. Bentley, *The Jacobean and Caroline Stage*, 5 vols., 1941–1956.]

Act of Supremacy. (1) An act marking the end of Roman leadership of the Church in England. The Act of Supremacy of 1534, in which "the King's Majesty [was] justly and rightfully [held] to be the Supreme Head of the Church of England," had been occasioned by Henry VIII's desire to legitimize his divorce from Katharine of Aragon.

(2) An act issued in 1559 restoring royal supremacy over the English Church. Queen Mary's espousal of the Roman Church during her reign (1553–1558) had created serious religious divisions in England. Attempting to re-establish religious and national

unity in the embittered country, the second Act of Supremacy declared the queen, i.e., Elizabeth, to be "Supreme Governor of this realm . . . as well in all spiritual or ecclesiastical things or causes as temporal," and required an oath recognizing her supremacy from all officials of church and state. Characterizing Elizabeth as "Governor" rather than "Head" of the church, the act was indicative of her generally aloof and uncommitted attitude to the religious controversy. See ENEMIES OF THE STAGE; RECUSANCY.

actors. The Elizabethan theatre owed its glory in large measure to the invention of its playwrights, but the freedom granted players to play is an equally important factor in its development. The early strolling players' status was that of ROGUES AND VAGABONDS; players normally found it quite difficult to rise above the stigma of the disreputable (see RATSEIS GHOST). They were considered "masterless" and "without craft" (see ACTING COMPANIES). Actors, however, managed to acquire masters by becoming members of the households of some lord or other noble personage. Although the lord did not pay their wages, he was in a position to secure for them the right to play where they wished; he might also petition the authorities for special privileges. The actors, in turn, wore their master's badges or liveries, and would perform for him both spectacular and more subdued entertainments.

The most important legal development which favored the actor was the transfer of control over his activities from local authorities to the court and privy council. This development occurred in a relatively short period of time, from the initial patent granted LEICESTER'S MEN in 1574, and the more reasonable London regulations of that year, until 1597, when the crown assumed complete administrative control of all actors in the London area, through the agencies of the PRIVY COUNCIL, the LORD CHAMBERLAIN, and the MASTER OF THE REVELS.

Between 1584 and 1597 actors increasingly received assurance that the government recognized their occupations as legitimate and respectable. In the patent granted Leicester's Men, playing was referred to as an "arte and facultye"; in 1581 the privy council called acting a "trade"; in 1582, a "profession"; and in 1593, a "qualitie." The London actor may have amused his audience as well as the medieval minstrel before him, but the actor was a householder and property owner, with the concomitant privileges and obligations. The minstrel had been not only masterless, but homeless; the London actor became involved in the affairs of his home and parish (see John HEMINGES).

Permitted by law to follow his "qualitie," the actor had to observe the laws regulating his conduct as a citizen and a player. A license was required for him to establish a theatre and perform plays or to take to the roads when the London theatres were closed (see PROVINCIAL TOURS). Playing was permitted in certain areas, on specific days of the week, seasons, and hours of the day. Despite the large measure of protection from the central government, actors continued to encounter local opposition. Citizens objected to theatres in their neighborhoods because of the traffic congestion, crowds, noise, pickpockets, bawds, and various other undesirable adjuncts to the entertainment business. The Puritans attacked actors as immoral and held their blasphemy and "indecency" responsible for the frequent deadly visitations of plague, which were held to be direct punishment for society's sins. Municipal authorities, whether influenced by considerations of their citizens' comfort, citations of the players' ungodliness by the Puritans, or the desire to avoid the large crowds congenial to the spread of the plague, were also frequently averse to the players.

The ultimate status of actors as household servants was reached when they came under the royal patronage. The members of the royal companies—the QUEEN'S MEN, the King's Men (see CHAMBERLAIN'S MEN), and Queen Anne's Men (see WORCESTER'S MEN)—were integral parts of the royal household; they belonged to the department supervised by the lord chamberlain, and were sworn grooms of the chamber. Although their exact duties are obscure, the office of groom was not entirely honorary. In at least one instance, the visit of the constable of Castile to the English court in 1604, the King's and Queen's Men performed the services of grooms. The difficulty in establishing their duties is owing to the fact that grooms were sworn (orally) rather than patented (written) and records which might outline their duties do not exist. The actors who served the king received the royal livery every two or three years. This might consist of three or four yards of bastard scarlet (see COSTUMES) for a cloak and one quarter yard of crimson velvet for a cap (according to court records, the velvet cost 26s. 8d. the yard). The actors in the service of the king also received "watching" liveries of less expensive (5s. the yard) medley cloth. New players entering the royally patronized companies were sworn in as "grooms in ordinary without fee."

The economics of the Elizabethan and Jacobean players were complicated and varied from company to company. The actor who was best off is epitomized in the career of one such as John Heminges and other of his fellows: Shakespeare, Henry Condell, Richard Burbage. The worst off were apparently the members of LADY ELIZABETH'S MEN, who appear to have been almost bonded servants of Philip Henslowe. The members of Shakespeare's company owned their own company, and they shared in the ownership of their two principal theatres, the Globe and the Blackfriars, as HOUSEKEEPERS. The members of Lady Elizabeth's Men presented an outraged petition to the lord chamberlain concerning their relations with Henslowe, and their quarrel with him was not resolved until after his death. On the other hand, the members of Lady Elizabeth's Men were lucky to have had a chance at London under any circumstances; very few acting companies managed to escape the stigma of being provincial, poor, and obscure. With the dissolution of their company, the Lady Elizabeth's Men were able to find places in other companies.

A contract concluded by Henslowe and a Lady Elizabeth's actor, Robert Dawes, reveals the nature of Henslowe's demands on the players. The contract, for three years, fined the player for being late to a rehearsal (1s.), not donning his costume by three o'clock in the afternoon (10s.), drunkenness (10s.), and absence from a performance for a reason other than sickness (20s.).

The Elizabethan actor had to memorize and retain the lines of a very large number of roles. Henslowe's record in his diary of the plays produced by the Admiral's Men reveals the enormous repertory. In one season (August 1595 to February 1596) the company gave 150 performances of 30 different plays. Of these, 14 were new plays. During the three-year period from June 1594 to June 1597, Edward ALLEYN, the leading actor of the Admiral's Men, was forced to learn and retain in his memory 70 different roles. That he was completely successful is evident from even the briefest glance at his career. Although no similar record exists for the Chamberlain's Men, there is no reason to assume that they produced fewer plays or that the demands on the actors were less severe; in fact, they were even more popular than the Admiral's Men, if the great number of performances they gave at court is any gauge of popularity.

Although each actor had a general "line," it is hazardous to assign definite parts to any of them (other than those known from record, of course). Except for the clown, the actors were required to play many varied roles (see CAST). When a very large number of players was required, the hired men were called into service, or the cast resorted to the practice of doubling. New actors entered the companies very frequently, though not as sharers at first (see SHARERS' PAPERS). They came from other adult companies or from the attrition of the children's companies. [E. K. Chambers, *The Elizabethan Stage*, 1923; T. W. Baldwin, *The Organization and Personnel of the Shakespearean Company*, 1927; G. E. Bentley, *The Jacobean and Caroline Stage*, 5 vols., 1941–1956; Bernard Beckerman, *Shakespeare at the Globe*, 1962; Muriel C. Bradbrook, *The Rise of the Common Player*, 1962.]

Acts and Monuments. See THE BOOK OF MARTYRS.

act-scene division. Conventional interruption of the action in a play. Modern editions of Elizabethan plays are generally misleading in their indications of act and scene divisions and in their identification of locations, such as "a room in the palace" and "another room in the palace."

Early printed plays rarely show scene divisions and seldom act divisions. Texts of Tudor interludes and Elizabethan popular plays show no interruption in the continuity of performance. Plays which indicate precise separation are usually the product of the university dramatists, derived from academic analysis of Latin comedies. Such markings may be found in the academic comedies of Nicholas Udall, some of the court tragedies, in translated plays, and in Lyly's comedies. Plays that were written for and produced in the public theatres were usually printed without specific divisions. See PROMPT-BOOK.

Plays produced in private theatres were ordinarily divided into acts, but not into scenes; the usual explanation for this distinction is that the private theatre performances were generally given by boy actors and the act intervals were provided to allow time to rest. The intervals were probably filled with music, the forte of the children's companies, which in turn ultimately influenced the increased use of music in the public theatres.

The supposition that major changes of locality coincided with act divisions is negated by plays in which such changes may occur within an act. In *All's Well That Ends Well*, the second and third acts are at Paris, the fourth at Florence, and the fifth at Marseille, but the shift from Roussillon to Paris occurs in the middle of Act I. Similar abrupt changes may be found in *The Winter's Tale* where the scene shifts from Sicily to Bohemia in the middle of Act III, while in *Henry V* the Agincourt scenes begin in the middle of Act III.

Though not always indicated in early texts, some intervals or shifts in time and place seem clear: in *A Midsummer Night's Dream* the lovers sleep through the interval between Acts III and IV; the introduction of a dumb-show often coincides with what might have been an act interval; the use of choruses (as in *Romeo and Juliet* and *Pericles*) also indicates such divisions. In many plays, act intervals could not have been too long, if the plays were to occupy the "two hours' traffic of the stage." Music may have been used, especially in the private theatres, to give the spectators an opportunity to stretch.

Clearly, a "scene" in Elizabethan drama is not to be confused with the "French scene" of a later period, in which the entrance or exit of a significant character constitutes the beginning or termination of a scene by providing a new motivational unit. Nor can the clearing of the stage always be a determinant for the end of a scene.

Lapses of time and change of location are usually to be imagined by the audience or reader. Characters who exit at the close of a scene rarely return to the stage early in the next scene; a long speech or another scene may intervene before their reentry. Playwrights schooled in the university and trying to adhere to the classical unities frequently employed fewer scenes than other playwrights.

One theory advanced for determining scene divisions and the functional use of the Elizabethan stage has been called "the alternation theory," which maintains that a fluidity and flexibility of performance and change of scene was probably achieved by alternating scenes enacted on the forestage, within the inner stage, and upon the upper stage or within the gallery. Modern scholarship has demonstrated enough inconsistency in and contradiction of such practice to make the alternation theory untenable.

The most conclusive proof of intentional division into acts and scenes may be found in some prompt-books and in a few printed copies (for example, the First Quarto of *Romeo and Juliet*) in which dotted lines or some similar devices are sometimes drawn across the page to separate segments of the play; other proof of division may be found in the practice (unfortunately not always consistent or regular) of some playwrights who allow their characters to identify time and place in dialogue (e.g., Hamlet's " 'Tis now the very witching hour," or Rosalind's "This is the forest of Arden"). [A. H. Thorndike, *Shakespeare's Theater*, 1916; E. K. Chambers, *The Elizabethan Stage*, 1923.]—D.P.D.

Adam. In *As You Like It*, a faithful old servant of the De Boys family. Adam warns Orlando of Oliver's plots to kill him and urges him to flee. He generously offers his own savings for the journey and accompanies Orlando into exile (II, iii). After the second act of the play there is no further allusion to this character. It is thought that Shakespeare played this part himself. See LAMENESS; William OLDYS.

Adams, John Cranford (1903–). American scholar and educator, president emeritus of Hofstra

University. Adams' *The Globe Playhouse: Its Design and Equipment* (1942) contains his theories concerning the construction of Shakespeare's theatre (see PLAYHOUSE STRUCTURE). While president of Hofstra (1944–1964), Adams built a replica of the Globe for the performance of Elizabethan plays. A similar replica based on Adams' conjectures is at the University of Illinois. In collaboration with Irwin Smith, Adams constructed a one-twelfth scale model which is on display at the Folger Shakespeare Library. An account of this project, together with scale drawings suitable as an aid for building similar models, is found in Smith's *Shakespeare's Globe Playhouse: A Modern Reconstruction* (1956). For a while Adams' theories were widely accepted, but there has been a tendency to take a more critical view; Adams has been accused of misapplying evidence and of taking conjectures for proof. [A discussion of his and other recent theories can be found in James Stinson, "Reconstruction of Elizabethan Public Playhouses," in *Studies in the Elizabethan Theatre,* Charles T. Prouty, ed., 1961.]

Adams, Joseph Quincy (1881–1946). American scholar. Director of the FOLGER SHAKESPEARE LIBRARY from 1931 to his death, Adams helped develop the Folger into the greatest Shakespearean library in the world. Prior to this time he had established his scholarly reputation with a number of important publications, including *Shakespearean Playhouses* (1917) and his authoritative *Life of William Shakespeare* (1923). He edited *The Dramatic Records of Sir Henry Herbert, Master of the Revels* (1917), *The First Quarto of Titus Andronicus* (1936), and *The Passionate Pilgrim* (1939). Adams also served as general editor of the New Variorum Shakespeare. See VARIORUM EDITIONS.

adaptations. The official CLOSING OF THE THEATRES between 1642 and 1660 not only created a gap in the history of English drama, but changed the course of its development as well. After the Restoration it became apparent that taste and ideals had changed. The rich disorder of Elizabethan drama seemed rude and shapeless to the new generation of writers. They admired French theory and practice and strove for consistency and reasonableness in their characters and form; they aimed at clarity in every aspect of their art. Shakespeare's greatness was acknowledged, but he seemed rough and undisciplined to them, and in need of editing and rationalizing before he could meet the requirements of their more civilized age. See CRITICISM—17TH CENTURY.

The most persistent adapters of Shakespeare's plays in this period were William DAVENANT, John DRYDEN, and Nahum TATE. Each thought that he was "improving" Shakespeare by cutting away unnecessary verbal flourishes and remodeling the plays along classical lines. In a few cases, such as Dryden's *Troilus and Cressida* (1679) or Thomas Shadwell's *Timon of Athens* (1678), the "improvements" were dramatically effective, but most of the adaptations ranged from the barbarous to the ludicrous. The 17th-century adapters were trying to bring order into what they considered chaos; they failed to realize that Shakespeare's genius had created an order of a new and different kind.

The following list includes all plays written from the Restoration to 1820 which directly use Shakespeare's plays as their source. They are listed for each play of Shakespeare; more complete information is to be found for the most important adaptations in the stage history section of the play discussion, and under the entries for the authors of the adaptations as well. The dates in parentheses refer to first performances, unless otherwise indicated.

All's Well That Ends Well. Frederick Pilon, *All's Well That Ends Well; a Comedy* (1785); and John Philip Kemble, *All's Well That Ends Well* (1793).

Antony and Cleopatra. John Dryden, *All for Love: or, The World Well Lost. A Tragedy, As It is Acted at the Theatre-Royal; and Written in Imitation of Shakespeare's Stile* (1678); Edward Capell (also attributed to David Garrick), *Antony and Cleopatra; an Historical Play Written by William Shakespeare: Fitted for the Stage by Abridging Only* (1758); and Henry Brooke, *Antony and Cleopatra* (pub. 1778).

As You Like It. Charles Johnson, *Love in a Forest. A Comedy* (1723); James Carrington(?), *The Modern Receipt: or A Cure for Love. A Comedy. Altered from Shakespeare* (1739); and John Philip Kemble, *As You Like It* (1805).

The Comedy of Errors. William Taverner and Dr. Brown, *Every Body Mistaken. A Farce.* (1716); William Shirley, *All Mistaken. A Comedy* (neither printed nor performed, written between 1739 and 1777); anon., *See If You Like It* (1734); Thomas Hull, *The Comedy of Errors. With Alterations from Shakespeare. Adapted for Theatrical Representation* (1762); also known as *The Twins; or, The Comedy of Errors* (pub. 1770); William Woods, *The Twins; or, Which Is Which? In Three Acts. Altered from Shakespeare's Comedy of Errors* (1780); John Philip Kemble, *Oh! It's Impossible!* (1780); and John Philip Kemble, *Comedy of Errors* (1808, based on Hull's version).

Coriolanus. Nahum Tate, *The Ingratitude of a Common-wealth: Or, the Fall of Caius Martius Coriolanus* (c. 1681, pub. 1682); John Dennis, *The Invader of his Country: or, The Fatal Resentment. A Tragedy* (1720); Thomas Sheridan, *Coriolanus: or, The Roman Matron. A tragedy. Taken from Shakespeare and Thomson* (1754); and John Philip Kemble, *Coriolanus, or the Roman Matron, (A Tragedy) Altered from Shakespeare and Thompson, by Mr. J. P. Kemble; and Printed Conformably to the Representation* (pub. 1789).

Cymbeline. Thomas D'Urfey, *The Injured Princess, or the Fatal Wager* (1682); Charles Marsh, *Cymbeline: King of Britain. A Tragedy, Written by Shakespear. With Some Alterations by Charles Marsh. As It Was Agreed to be Acted at the Theatre-Royal in Covent Garden. The Part of Posthumus to Have Been Performed by Mr. Barry, and the Character of Imogen, by Mrs. Cibber* (not acted, pub. n.d., c. 1755); William Hawkins, *Cymbeline. A Tragedy, Altered from Shakespeare.* (1759); David Garrick, *Cymbeline. A Tragedy. By Shakespear. With Alterations* (1761); Henry Brooke, *Cymbeline* (not acted, pub. 1778); and John Philip Kemble, *Cymbeline* (1801).

Hamlet. William Davenant, *The Tragedy of Hamlet Prince of Denmark* (1676); David Garrick, *Hamlet* (1772); Tate Wilkinson, *Hamlet* (1773); Joseph George Holman, *Hamlet* (1793); and John Philip Kemble, *Hamlet, Prince of Denmark* (1796).

1 Henry IV. Thomas Betterton, *K. Henry IV. With the Humours of Sir John Falstaff. A Tragi-comedy* (1700); and John Philip Kemble, *Henry IV, Part I* (1803).

2 Henry IV. Thomas Betterton, *The Sequel of Henry the Fourth: With the Humours of Sir John Falstaffe, and Justice Shallow* (1707); anon., *The Humours of Sir John Falstaff, Justice Shallow, and Ancient Pistol* (1734); Theophilus Cibber, *The Humourists* (1754); Richard Valpy, *The Second Part of King Henry The Fourth, Altered from Shakespeare* (1801); and John Philip Kemble, *King Henry the Fourth, (The Second Part)* (1804).

Henry V. Charles Molloy, *The Half-Pay Officers; a Comedy* (1720); Aaron Hill, *King Henry the Fifth. Or The Conquest of France By the English. A Tragedy.* (1723); anon., *The Conspiracy Discovered* (1746); and John Philip Kemble, *King Henry V., or the Conquest of France, A Tragedy* (1789).

1, 2, and 3 Henry VI. Anon., *Richard, Duke of York; or the Contention of York and Lancaster. As Altered from Shakespeare's 3 parts Henry VI* (1817).

2 Henry VI. John Crowne, *Henry the Sixth, The First Part. With the Murder of Humphrey Duke of Gloucester* (1681); and Ambrose Philips, *Humfrey, Duke of Glocester, a Tragedy* (1723).

3 Henry VI. John Crowne, *The Misery of Civil-War. A Tragedy* (1680); Theophilus Cibber, *An Historical Tragedy of the Civil Wars Between the Houses of York and Lancaster in the Reign of King Henry VI. (Being a Sequel to the Tragedy of Humfrey Duke of Gloucester: And an Introduction to the Tragical History of King Richard III)* (1723); and Richard Valpy, *The Roses; or King Henry the Sixth; an Historical Tragedy* (1795).

Henry VIII. John Dryden, *K. Henry VIII. A Tragedy. Written by W. Shakespear, with Alterations by Dryden, as It Is Now Acted in the Theatres-Royal of London and Dublin* (1752); anon., *King Henry the Eighth. With the Coronation of Ann Bullen. Written by Shakespear. With Alterations* (1762); and John Philip Kemble, *King Henry the Eighth, a Historical Play* (1804).

Julius Caesar. William Davenant and John Dryden, *The Tragedy of Julius Caesar: With the Death of Brutus and Cassius; Written Originally by Shakespear, and Since Alter'd by Sir William Davenant and John Dryden Late Poets Laureat* (1719); John Sheffield, duke of Buckingham, *The Tragedy of Julius Caesar, Altered* (pub. 1723); and John Sheffield, duke of Buckingham, *The Tragedy of Marcus Brutus* (pub. 1723).

King John. Colley Cibber, *Papal Tyranny in the Reign of King John. A Tragedy* (1745); John Philip Kemble, *King John* (1800); and Richard Valpy, *King John, an Historical Tragedy* (1803).

King Lear. Nahum Tate, *The History of King Lear* (1681); David Garrick, *King Lear, a Tragedy* (1756, pub. 1773); George Colman the Elder, *The History of King Lear* (1768); and John Philip Kemble, *King Lear* (n.d., 1795).

Love's Labour's Lost. Anon., *The Students. A Comedy. Altered from Shakespeare's Love's Labours Lost, and Adapted to the Stage* (pub. 1762).

Macbeth. William Davenant, *Macbeth a Tragedy. With All the Alterations, Amendments, Additions, and New Songs* (1674); David Garrick, *Macbeth* (1744); John Lee, *The Historical Tragedy of Macbeth* (1754, pub. 1761); and John Philip Kemble, *Macbeth. A Tragedy.* (1794).

Measure for Measure. William Davenant, *The Law Against Lovers* (1662); Charles Gildon, *Measure for Measure, or Beauty the Best Advocate* (1699/1700); and John Philip Kemble, *Measure for Measure* (n.d., 1795).

Merchant of Venice. George Granville, Lord Lansdowne, *The Jew of Venice. A Comedy* (1701); John Philip Kemble, *The Merchant of Venice* (1795); and Richard Valpy, *The Merchant of Venice, a Comedy* (1802).

Merry Wives of Windsor. John Dennis, *The Comical Gallant: or the Amours of Sir John Falstaffe. A Comedy* (1702); and John Philip Kemble, *The Merry Wives of Windsor* (1797).

A Midsummer Night's Dream. Robert Cox, *The Merry Conceited Humors of Bottom The Weaver. . . .* (1661); Elkanah Settle, *The Fairy-Queen: an Opera* (1692); Richard Leveridge, *Pyramus and Thisbe. A Comic Masque* (1716); John Frederick Lampe, *Pyramus and Thisbe. Mock Opera, set to music by Mr. Lampe* (1745); David Garrick, *The Fairies. An Opera. Taken from A Midsummer Night's Dream, Written by Shakespear. . . . The Songs from Shakespear, Milton, Waller, Dryden, Lansdown, Hammond, &c. The Music Composed by Mr. Smith* (1755); David Garrick, *A Midsummer Night's Dream. Written by Shakespeare: With Alterations and Additions, and Several New Songs.* (1763); George Colman the Elder, *A Fairy Tale. In Two Acts. Taken from Shakespeare* (1763); George Colman the Elder, *The Fairy Prince. A Masque* (1771); and Frederick Reynolds, *A Midsummer Night's Dream, Written by Shakespeare: With Alterations, Additions, and New Songs* (1816).

Much Ado About Nothing. William Davenant, *The Law Against Lovers* (1662); James Miller, *The Universal Passion. A Comedy* (1737); Robert Jephson, *The Law of Lombardy* (1779); and John Philip Kemble, *Much Ado About Nothing* (1797).

Othello. David Garrick, *Othello* (1745); John Philip Kemble, *Othello* (1804).

Pericles. George Lillo, *Marina* (1738).

Richard II. Nahum Tate, *The History of King Richard the Second Acted at the Theatre Royal, Under the Name of the Sicilian Usurper* (1681); Lewis Theobald, *The Tragedy of King Richard the II; Alter'd from Shakespear* (1719, pub. 1720); Francis Gentleman, *King Richard II. A Tragedy altered from Shakespeare* (1754); James Goodhall, *King Richard II. A Tragedy. Alter'd from Shakespear, and the Stile Imitated* (pub. 1772); and Richard Wroughton, *King Richard the Second; an Historical Play. Adapted to the Stage, with Alterations and Additions* (1815).

Richard III. Colley Cibber, *The Tragical History of King Richard III* (pub. 1700); and John Philip Kemble, *King Richard III* (1810).

Romeo and Juliet. James Howard, *Romeo and Juliet. A Tragi-Comedy* (1661); Thomas Otway, *The History and Fall of Caius Marius. A Tragedy* (1679); Thomas Sheridan, *Romeo and Juliet* (1746); Theophilus Cibber, *Romeo and Juliet, a Tragedy, Revis'd, and Alter'd from Shakespear* (1744); David Garrick, *Romeo and Juliet. A Tragedy. With Alter-*

ations and an Additional Scene (1748); Charles Marsh, *Romeo and Juliet* (written before 1762); and John Lee, *Romeo and Juliet* (1777).

The Taming of the Shrew. John Lacy, *Sauny the Scott: or the Taming of the Shrew: a Comedy* (1667); Christopher Bullock, *The Cobler of Preston. A Farce* (1716); Charles Johnson, *The Cobler of Preston* (1716); James Worsdale, *A Cure for a Scold. A Ballad Farce of Two Acts* (1735); David Garrick, *Catherine and Petruchio. A Comedy in Three Acts* (1756); and John Philip Kemble, *Katharine and Petruchio. A Comedy* (1801).

The Tempest. John Dryden and William Davenant, *The Tempest, or the Enchanted Island. A Comedy* (1667); Thomas Shadwell, *The Tempest, or the Enchanted Island. A Comedy* (1674); David Garrick, *The Tempest. An Opera. Taken from Shakespear . . . The Songs from Shakespear, Dryden, &c. The Music Composed by Mr. Smith* (1756); Richard B. Sheridan, *Songs and Chorusses in the Tempest* (1777); *The Shipwreck, Altered from Shakespeare and Dryden, with the Original Music by Smith, as Performed at the Patagonian Theatre, Exeter-'Change* (1780); John Philip Kemble, *The Tempest, or The Enchanted Island* (1789); and John Philip Kemble, *The Tempest, or The Enchanted Island* (1806).

Timon of Athens. Thomas Shadwell, *The History of Timon of Athens, the Man-Hater . . . Made into a Play* (1678); James Love (pseud. of James Dance), *Timon of Athens . . . Altered from Shakespeare and Shadwell* (1768); Richard Cumberland, *Timon of Athens. Altered from Shakespear. A Tragedy* (1771); Thomas Hull, *Timon of Athens* (1786); and George Lamb, *Timon of Athens, . . . Altered and Adapted for Representation* (1816).

Titus Andronicus. Edward Ravenscroft, *Titus Andronicus, or the Rape of Lavinia* (1686).

Troilus and Cressida. John Dryden, *Troilus and Cressida, or, Truth Found Too Late* (1679).

Twelfth Night. William Burnaby, *Love Betray'd; or, The Agreeable Disappointment. A Comedy* (1703); and Charles Molloy, *The Half-Pay Officers* (1720).

Two Gentlemen of Verona. Benjamin Victor, *The Two Gentlemen of Verona. A Comedy, Written by Shakespeare. With Alterations and Additions* (1762; pub. 1763); and John Philip Kemble, *The Two Gentlemen of Verona* (1808).

The Winter's Tale. McNamara Morgan, *The Sheep-Shearing: Or, Florizel and Perdita. A Pastoral Comedy* (1754); Charles Marsh, *The Winter's Tale, a Play. Alter'd from Shakespear* (printed 1756); David Garrick, *Florizel and Perdita. A Dramatic Pastoral, in Three Acts* (1756); Thomas Hull, *The Winter's Tale* (1773); and George Colman the Elder, *The Sheep-Shearing: A Dramatic Pastoral* (1771).

[George C. Branam, *Eighteenth-Century Adaptations of Shakespearean Tragedy*, 1956; Charles Beecher Hogan, *Shakespeare in the Theatre, 1701–1800*, 2 vols., 1952–1957.]

Addenbrooke, John (fl. 1607–1610). A resident of Warwickshire against whom Shakespeare brought a suit in the Stratford court of record in 1608 to recover a debt of £6. Addenbrooke was brought into custody but released when Thomas Hornbey, a local blacksmith, agreed to act as his surety. In 1609 a jury awarded Shakespeare the debt and 24 shillings to cover costs and damages. Addenbrooke, however, had absconded in the interim, and Shakespeare then had to seek recovery of the money from Hornbey. [Mark Eccles, *Shakespeare in Warwickshire*, 1961.]

Addison, Joseph (1672–1719). Essayist and critic. Born at Milston, Wiltshire, and educated at the Charterhouse School in London and Queen's College, Oxford, Addison secured a fellowship at Magdalen College and attracted the notice of influential Whigs who granted him a pension for his literary services. After four years of travel and study on the continent, Addison wrote *The Campaign* (1705), a poem celebrating Marlborough's victory at Blenheim. This poem launched his political and literary career. He entered parliament in 1708, held a number of political offices, including that of lord commissioner for trade and the colonies, and was appointed secretary of state in 1717. He wrote three plays, the most noteworthy of which is *Cato* (1713), a classical tragedy.

Addison is remembered primarily for his essays, published in issues of *The Tatler* (1709–1711) and *The Spectator* (1711–1712). These essays, among the finest examples of periodical prose in English, aimed at the improvement of English taste and manners. Neoclassical in tone, they reveal the influence of Longinus, as in the judgment that "productions of a great genius, with many lapses and inadvertences, are infinitely preferable to the works of an inferior kind of author which are scrupulously exact, and conformable to all the rules of correct writing." Addison considered Shakespeare to be such a wild and natural genius, and he was one of the first critics of the period who refused to judge Shakespeare by classical standards. Shakespeare is reproved for excessive punning and for a tendency toward obscurity and over-elaborateness in his poetry, but Addison's criticism is never categorically strict. Although he preferred French classical tragedy to the Elizabethan drama, Addison believed that the ability to stimulate the imagination was more important than perfection of form or style. [Herbert Spencer Robinson, *English Shakespearian Criticism in the Eighteenth Century*, 1932.]

Adlington, William. See Lucius APULEIUS.

Admiral's Men (1585–1596) **[Lord Howard's Men** (1576/7–1585), **Earl of Nottingham's Men** (1596–1603), **Prince Henry's Men** (1603–1612), **Elector Palatine** or **Palsgrave's Men** (1612–1625)]. Acting company, originally under the patronage of Charles Lord Howard, 1st earl of Nottingham and lord high admiral. The Admiral's Men were the principal rivals of Shakespeare's company (Chamberlain's and King's Men) throughout their career. When Howard was appointed lord admiral in 1585, his players, active since 1576, became known as the Admiral's Men. By 1589 Edward ALLEYN, one of the greatest actors of the Elizabethan age, had joined the company.

In 1590 they allied themselves with Strange's Men, the troupe which was to form the nucleus of Shakespeare's company, at James Burbage's Theatre. After a quarrel with Burbage in 1591, the amalgamated company left the Theatre for Philip Henslowe's Rose playhouse, on the Bankside. In 1594 the amalgamation was dissolved, with Strange's Men becoming, for the most part, Chamberlain's Men and returning to the Theatre. The Admiral's company, under the leadership of Alleyn, remained at the ROSE THEATRE.

The Admiral's Men toured the provinces on several occasions. In some places they appeared with Strange's Men, or other companies. In 1588/9 they appeared in Cambridge. In 1589/90, they visited Ipswich (two performances), Maidstone, Winchester, Marlborough (July 25), Gloucester, Coventry, and Oxford. In 1590/1 they were at Southampton and again at Winchester; they appeared at Bath, where they received 16s. 3d., while Strange's got 17s.; they toured Gloucester and Oxford again. In 1591/2 they were at Aldeburgh, Ipswich (with "Darby's" or Strange's, on August 7, 1592), and Leicester (in December). In 1592/3, Admiral's and Lord Norris' players appeared jointly for two performances; they were at Shrewsbury, Coventry, and Norwich singly, and at Shrewsbury (also with Strange's), Ipswich (jointly with Lord Stafford's), York (with Lord Morden's), and Newcastle (with Lord "Morleis").

From 1594 we have a full account of the company's activities as recorded in *Henslowe's Diary* (W. W. Greg, ed., 1904–1908). From 1594 to 1597 the diary notes 728 performances of 55 plays by the company. In addition to Alleyn, their chief actors were John Singer (fl. 1583–1609), Richard Jones (fl. 1583–1625), Thomas Towne (n.d.), Martin Slater (fl. 1594–1625), and Edward Juby (fl. 1594–1618). In 1596 Lord Howard was elevated to the rank of earl of Nottingham, and the company is sometimes mentioned in records as Nottingham's Men. In 1597 Alleyn retired from the stage but returned in 1600 when the company moved to Henslowe's new FORTUNE THEATRE (in which Alleyn evidently also had an interest). The plays given by the company during this period were written by a group of free-lance playwrights whom Henslowe paid with money he loaned to the company. The more productive dramatists included Henry Chettle, Thomas Dekker, Anthony Munday, George Chapman, and Thomas Heywood.

At the accession of James I the company came under the patronage of his eldest son, Henry, the prince of Wales, and became known as Prince Henry's Men. In 1606 they received a royal patent, from which Alleyn's name is omitted, indicating that he had again retired from the stage. Alleyn did, however, retain a share in the company, as well as co-ownership with Henslowe of the Fortune.

In 1612 Prince Henry died and the Elector Palatine of the Rhine (or the Palsgrave), Frederic V, who married Princess Elizabeth, James' daughter, in 1613 became the company's patron. In 1616 Henslowe died and Alleyn became the sole owner of the Fortune. Two years later he leased it to the company for a period of 31 years at an annual rental of £200. In 1621, however, the theatre was burned to the ground. The fire and its effect on the company was described in a letter by John Chamberlain:

> On Sonday night here was a great fire at the Fortune in Golden-Lane, the fayrest play-house in this towne. It was quite burnt downe in two howres, & all their apparell & play-bookes lost, wherby those poore companions are quite undone.

The loss not only of their playhouse but of their costumes and prompt-books as well was a virtual death blow to the company. The Fortune was rebuilt during the following year but the company never managed to regain their former position, and they apparently did not resume playing after the closing of the theatres because of the plague in 1625. [E. K. Chambers, *The Elizabethan Stage*, 1923; G. E. Bentley, *The Jacobean and Caroline Stage*, 5 vols., 1941–1956.]

Adrian. In *The Tempest*, one of the lords attending the King of Naples. To Adrian's innocent senses, the island's "air breathes upon us here most sweetly." When Sebastian and Antonio wager whether Gonzalo or Adrian will first begin "to crow," Adrian causes Sebastian to lose, and the wager, "a laughter," is paid (II, i).

Adriana. In *The Comedy of Errors*, jealous wife of Antipholus of Ephesus. Adriana pursues Antipholus of Syracuse to an abbey, imagining that he is her husband. She is scolded by the abbess as being responsible for her husband's "madness," but is finally reconciled with her husband when the errors are resolved.

Aegeon. In *The Comedy of Errors*, an aged merchant from Syracuse, condemned to death for landing in Ephesus while searching for one of his twin sons. In the final act, Aegeon, reunited with both his sons and his long-lost wife, Aemelia, is pardoned by the Duke of Ephesus.

Aemelia. In *The Comedy of Errors*, the wife of Aegeon. Believing her sons, the Antipholus twins, and her husband lost to her, Aemelia becomes the abbess of Ephesus. She unknowingly gives sanctuary to Antipholus of Syracuse, then recognizes Aegeon on his way to his execution. Ultimately, a reunion takes place.

Aemilius. In *Titus Andronicus*, a noble Roman. He informs the Emperor, Saturninus, that a Gothic army led by Lucius is advancing toward Rome (IV, iv), and conveys to Lucius the Emperor's request for a parley (V, i).

Aeneas. In Greek legend and in Homer's *Iliad*, a Trojan general. As the hero of Vergil's *Aeneid* and the legendary progenitor of the English people, Aeneas was for Shakespeare's audience among the greatest of Homeric heroes. In *Troilus and Cressida*, however, he has a relatively minor role as a Trojan general and as a friend and advisor to Troilus.

Aeneid, The. See VERGIL.

Agamemnon. In Greek legend, Homer's *Iliad*, and Shakespeare's *Troilus and Cressida*, the high King of Mycenae (Argos), brother of Menelaus, and leader of the Greeks at the siege of Troy.

Agas, Ralph or **Radulph** (c. 1540–1621). A land-surveyor who is remembered for his unusual and valuable maps of 16th-century Oxford, Cambridge, and London. The London engraving measures 6½ feet in length by 2 feet 4½ inches in width and was printed from wooden blocks. It was based on a map of London printed in 1572 (see HOEFNAGEL MAP). Agas' map was probably drawn before 1590, although it was not printed until 1633. The Agas map shows no theatres in Southwark, but does indicate a bullbaiting and a bearbaiting ring—both of which are depicted as circular structures. See ENGRAVINGS OF LONDON. [Irwin Smith, *Shakespeare's Globe Playhouse*, 1957.]

Agrippa, Marcus Vipsanius (63–12 B.C.). Commander of Octavius' fleet at Actium and subsequently his son-in-law; in *Antony and Cleopatra*, a friend of Octavius who proposes that Antony marry Octavius' sister Octavia (II, ii).

Aguecheek, Sir Andrew. In *Twelfth Night*, a foolish knight. As a joke, Sir Toby Belch persuades Sir Andrew Aguecheek to compose a swaggering challenge to Cesario, but at Sir Toby's invented report of that youth's ferocity, Sir Andrew shrinks back from the encounter. Despite having been the butt of Sir Toby's humor, this absurd nobleman has decidedly enjoyed that rogue's company and has shared happily in the Illyrian delirium.

Ajax. In classical legend, the king of Salamis and, as treated by Homer in the *Iliad*, the most daring Greek hero of the Trojan War except Achilles; in *Troilus and Cressida*, Ajax appears as a Greek warrior and provides the most striking example in the play of Shakespeare's showing up of classical heroes. From the towering figure of the *Iliad* he is transformed into a surly, envious, slow-witted muscleman. It has been argued that Ajax is Shakespeare's portrait of Ben Jonson and that this portrait is the "purge" referred to in *2 Return from Parnassus* (see PARNASSUS PLAYS). What is more probable, however, is that Ajax is Jonson as pictured by Thomas Dekker, Jonson's enemy during the War of the Theatres—just as Thersites is Dekker as portrayed by Jonson. In other words, Shakespeare was not so much directly satirizing Dekker and Jonson as he was the "war" which had erupted between them. See WAR OF THE THEATRES.

Still another view of *Troilus and Cressida*, one which sees Achilles as a portrait of Essex, argues that Ajax's position as the envious hero eclipsed by Achilles corresponds to that of Sir Walter Raleigh, who had long since been replaced by Essex as England's foremost courtier and nobleman. [*Troilus and Cressida*, New Variorum Edition, Harold Hillebrand and T. W. Baldwin, eds., 1953.]

Alarbus. In *Titus Andronicus*, the eldest son of Tamora, queen of the Goths. The four surviving sons of Titus sacrifice Alarbus to the spirit of their brother, killed in the wars against the Goths.

Albany, Duke of. In *King Lear*, the husband of Goneril. Though Albany comes to hate his wife for her ingratitude and treachery toward her father, duty compels him to repulse the French army which Cordelia has brought to help Lear.

Alcester. A town 10 miles west of Stratford and the home of Thomas Shakespere (d. 1539), father of a William Shakspere, and thought by some to be a grand-uncle of the dramatist. Alcester was also the home of the poet Fulke GREVILLE who, according to one 17th-century story, was "Shakespear's and Ben Johnson's Master." [Mark Eccles, *Shakespeare in Warwickshire*, 1961.]

Alchemist, The (1610). A satiric comedy by Ben JONSON. First acted by Shakespeare's company, the King's Men, in 1610, the roles of the arch-cozeners Face and Subtle in *The Alchemist* were probably played by Richard Burbage and John Heminges. John Lowin played the part of Sir Epicure Mammon. Shakespeare had apparently long since abandoned acting to devote his full time to writing plays and thus had no part in the play.

An anecdote in John Aubrey's *Brief Lives* says that one John Dee "used to distill egge-shells and 'twas from hence that Ben Johnson had his hint of the alkimist . . . ." (See ALCHEMY.) Regarded by many as Jonson's finest comedy, *The Alchemist* was admitted to illustrious company by Coleridge in his famous remark, "I think the *Oedipus Tyrannus*, *The Alchemist*, and *Tom Jones*, the three most perfect plots ever planned." [*Ben Jonson*, C. H. Herford and Percy Simpson, eds., 11 vols., 1925–1952.]

alchemy. The medieval and 16th-century chemical science and speculative philosophy the aims of which were the transmutation of base metals into gold and the discovery of a panacea. Alchemy was based upon the assumption of the essential unity of all matter. Basic matter was said to fill space and to be capable of assuming various forms, identifiable by the impressions that they created. All matter was thus either hot, cold, dry, or moist. The four elements, derived from combinations of these properties, were fire (hot and dry), air (hot and moist), earth (cold and dry), and water (cold and moist). All substances were thought to be composed of compounds of the four basic elements, and only when the action of these elements was properly balanced was the substance thought to be perfect. Imperfect substances were those in which one element predominated. Perfect substances manifested themselves in form without any elemental character, so harmonious and balanced were their natures. See PSYCHOLOGY.

The notions of perfection and balance were the themes of this quasi-scientific atmosphere. Society

TITLE PAGE OF GEORGE BAKER'S *The Newe Iewell of Health* (1576).

¶ The newe Iewell of Health, wherein is contayned the most excellent Secretes of Phisicke and Philosophie, deuided into fower Bookes. In the which are the best approued remedies for the diseases as well inwarde as outwarde, of all the partes of mans bodie: treating very amplye of all Dystillations of Waters, of Oyles, Balmes, Quintessences, with the extraction of artificiall Saltes, the vse and preparation of Antimonie, and potable Gold. Gathered out of the best and most approued Authors, by that excellent Doctor *Gesnerus*. Also the Pictures, and maner to make the Vessels, Furnaces, and other Instrumentes therevnto belonging. Faithfully corrected and published in Englishe, by George Baker, Chirurgian.

338

Printed at London, by Henrie Denham.
1576.

regarded gold as the perfect metal and good health as the optimum human state. Thus it was assumed that "medicine" was either an agent for transmuting baser metals to gold or a means of guaranteeing longevity and assuring excellent health (since anything less than perfect was thought to be diseased). Alchemists sought a "philosopher's stone" as the means by which base metals would be turned to gold and an "elixir" to prolong human life. In *2 Henry IV*, Prince Hal, thinking his father dead, removes the King's crown and places it on his own head. The alchemist's relationship between health and gold is implicit in Hal's explanation of his actions; the gold crown

> Hath fed upon the body of my father;
> Therefore, thou best of gold art worst of gold:
> Other, less fine in carat, is more precious,
> Preserving life in medicine potable.
> (IV, v, 160–163)

Shakespeare's allusions to alchemy are few. Unlike Ben Jonson in The Alchemist, he makes no use of the jargon of the profession. In *King John*, King Philip blesses a marriage-day:

> To solemnize this day the glorious sun
> Stays in his course and plays the alchemist,
> Turning with splendour of his precious eye
> The meagre cloddy earth to glittering gold.
> (III, i, 77–80)

The deeper concern of alchemy—the transmutation of the imperfect to the perfect—is expressed in a reference to Brutus in *Julius Caesar:*

> And that which would appear offence in us,
> His countenance, like richest alchemy,
> Will change to virtue and to worthiness.
> (I, iii, 158–160)

Similarly, in Sonnet 114, love teaches an alchemy

> To make of monsters and things indigest
> Such cherubins as your sweet self resemble,
> Creating every bad a perfect best.

The alchemists' claim that gold might be multiplied inspired much naïve popular interest and occasioned a great deal of chicanery. Though some honest investigators were drawn to the study of alchemy, most practitioners were thoroughly dishonest. Ben Jonson's *Alchemist* is an excellent characterization of the pseudoscientific charlatan of the period and his naïve, gullible victims.

The official attitude toward alchemy was one of encouragement. Elizabeth patronized certain alchemists who were brought to her attention; the most notable of these was John Dee (1527–1608), a mathematician and astrologist. His favored position was not, however, of long duration, and he was left to pursue his alchemical studies in ultimate obscurity. His career followed the pattern of that of most alchemists. At some point in their careers they often enjoyed brilliant reputations, then followed a period of eclipse—into obscurity, poverty, and even jail. [Robert Steele, "Alchemy," *Shakespeare's England*, 1916.]

Alcibiades (c. 450–404 B.C.). An anti-democratic Athenian general and politician; in *Timon of Athens*, an Athenian captain. Spurred on by Alcibiades' speech favoring an expedition against Sicily, in 415 B.C. the Athenians sent him at the head of a huge fleet. He was recalled to be tried for sacrilege in the destruction of the sacred herms, but he escaped. Sentenced to death in absentia and his property confiscated, he joined the Spartan side against Athens, but was later forced to flee the jealousy of Spartan leaders. He was welcomed back to Athens for a time but was soon distrusted again. He fled to the Persians, but was killed in Bithynia at Spartan instigation.

In *Timon of Athens*, Alcibiades is the Athenian captain whose request for a friend's pardon is refused by the Senate and whose angry reply results in his banishment. With Timon's gold to help finance his attack on the city, he takes Athens and wreaks revenge on both his and Timon's enemies.

Aldridge, Ira Frederick (c. 1805–1867). American actor. Aldridge is considered to be one of the ablest and most faithful interpreters of Shakespeare of his era, but his origin and many details of his life are obscure. He was probably born in New York City. Edmund Kean took him to England with him as a personal attendant and aided him in studying for the stage. A Negro, Aldridge made his debut as Othello in 1826 at the Royalty Theatre, London, and was soon being hailed as the "African Roscius." He made numerous tours, including one to Ireland where he played Othello to the Iago of Charles Kean. He made many appearances in London—notably in 1833, 1858, and 1865 as Othello, Lear, Macbeth, and Aaron. In 1853 he embarked on a three-year tour of Europe, playing in Germany with a group of German supporting actors. Crowds were attracted and intrigued by the novelty of the Negro tragedian and he was much praised and honored by the crowned heads of Europe. He had amassed a considerable fortune by the time of his death in 1867 in Łódź, Poland. It was generally thought that Aldridge never acted in the United States, but recent researchers have discovered evidence which points to an unsuccessful attempt in Baltimore in the 1830's. He became a naturalized British subject in 1863. [*Dictionary of American Biography*, 1927; *Oxford Companion to the Theatre*, Phyllis Hartnoll, ed., 1951.]

Alençon, John, 2nd duke of (d. 1476). Son of the 1st duke of Alençon, who died at Agincourt and is mentioned in *Henry V*. The younger Alençon was captured at Verneuil by Fastolfe in 1424 but was subsequently released on parole. In 1429 he led the French army at Jargeau. Although Alençon attended the coronation of Charles VII, he plotted against the crown and was imprisoned on a charge of treason. Later, after rebelling against Louis XI, Alençon was executed. In *1 Henry VI*, after the French are checked in a skirmish with the English before Orléans, Alençon speaks admiringly of the courage and audacity of the "lean raw-boned rascals" (I, ii). [W. H. Thomson, *Shakespeare's Characters: A Historical Dictionary*, 1951.]

Alexander. In *Troilus and Cressida*, Cressida's servant. Alexander's description of Ajax is regarded by some as a satirical portrait of Ben Jonson. See Parnassus Plays.

Alexander, Peter (1894–). Scholar. In his *Shakespeare's Henry VI and Richard III* (1929), Alexander continued the work inaugurated by A. W.

Pollard in identifying "bad quartos." He adduced convincing evidence that the CONTENTION PLAYS are bad quartos of *2* and *3 Henry VI* and not, as hitherto believed, earlier plays which Shakespeare had revised. The same position had been taken by Thomas Kenny in his *Life and Genius of Shakespeare* (1864), but Alexander was unaware of this forgotten work while pursuing his own investigation. He has also written *Shakespeare's Life and Art* (1939), an analysis of the individual plays indicating Shakespeare's development; *Hamlet, Father and Son* (1955), provoked by Sir Laurence Olivier's motion-picture version; and *Shakespeare* (1964), a popular introduction in the Home University Library series. His text of the complete works (1951) has appeared under various imprints, including the four-volume Collins Classics edition. Introductions to the latter have been published separately as *Introductions to Shakespeare* (1964). *Studies in Shakespeare* (1964) is his selection of 10 of the Annual Shakespeare Lectures presented to the British Academy.

Alexas. In *Antony and Cleopatra*, an attendant to Cleopatra. In IV, vi, Enobarbus reveals that when Alexas went to the Jews to transact Antony's affairs, he tried to turn King Herod against Antony. Upon learning of Alexas' treachery, Octavius Caesar hanged him. The same episode is told by Plutarch.

Alfieri, Vittorio. See ITALY.

Alice. In *Henry V*, one of the ladies in attendance on Princess Katharine of France. In III, iv, Alice gives her mistress a lesson in speaking English.

Aliena. In *As You Like It*, the name assumed by Celia when she accompanies Rosalind into exile disguised as a country maid.

Allde, Edward (fl. 1584–1628). London printer of several Shakespeare quartos. The son of a printer, Allde was admitted to the Stationers' Company in 1584. He printed the work of Samuel Daniel, Thomas Dekker, Christopher Marlowe, and other noted authors, as well as some Catholic polemical literature, an act for which his press was seized in 1597. He was reinstated as a stationer and continued the business until his death sometime around 1628. His Shakespearean publications include the printing of the 1611 Quarto (Q3) of *Titus Andronicus*. In the same year he printed *The Anuals of Great Brittaine* (1611) as a second edition, with a new title, of Robert Chester's *Love's Martyr*, the collection of verse which includes Shakespeare's *The Phoenix and the Turtle*. Allde may also be the printer of the First Quarto of *A Midsummer Night's Dream*, although Richard Bradock and James Roberts are other possibilities. [R. B. McKerrow, ed., *A Dictionary of Printers and Booksellers . . . 1557–1640*, 1910.]

Alleyn, Edward (1566–1626). Actor. Probably the most distinguished of the Elizabethan-Jacobean actors, Alleyn was born in London, the son of an innholder and porter to the queen. He began his acting career about 1583 with Worcester's Men, and joined the ADMIRAL'S MEN some time later in the 1580's, becoming the "fellow" of his brother John. In 1592 he married Joan Woodward, stepdaughter of manager Philip Henslowe, and became involved in Henslowe's various enterprises.

Alleyn had already achieved an enviable reputation as an actor by the time the amalgamated Admiral's-Strange's company was playing at Henslowe's Rose

EDWARD ALLEYN, THE FOUNDER OF DULWICH COLLEGE, WHERE HIS PORTRAIT IS PRESERVED. (BY PERMISSION OF THE GOVERNORS)

theatre during the early 1590's. Witness to this are several contemporary allusions, the earliest of which is a defense of English actors in Thomas Nashe's *Pierce Penilesse his supplication to the divell* (1592).

> Our Players are not as the players beyond Sea, . . . our Sceane is more statelye furnisht than euer it was in the time of *Roscius* . . . . Not *Roscius* nor *Æsope*, those admyred tragedians that haue liued euer since before Christ was borne, could euer performe more in action than famous *Ned Allen* . . . .

Nashe's *Strange newes* (1592) refers to Edmund Spenser, the poet: "his very name (as that of Ned Allen on the common stage) was able to make an ill matter good." E. K. Chambers suggests that Alleyn's success with the Admiral's Men (1590–1597) was due to the superior dramatic works he chose for his repertory as much as to his acting ability. His company purchased all of Christopher Marlowe's plays (with the exception of *Dido* and *Edward III*), as well as works by Peele, Lodge, Greene, and Porter. Alleyn acted the title roles in *Faustus* and *Tamburlaine*, and the role of Barabas in *The Jew of Malta*. His part as

Orlando in Greene's *Orlando Furioso* (1591) is the only extant Elizabethan actor's PART.

In 1597 Alleyn announced that he was retiring from the stage. A quaint, but apocryphal, story attributed his retirement to a strange happening during a performance of Marlowe's *Dr. Faustus* (which the Admiral's gave a total of 24 times between October 1594 and October 1597) in which Alleyn took the title role. This legend had particular appeal for the Puritans, who disliked actors and the stage, for it confirmed the notion that plays and actors were willy-nilly in league with the devil. The story derives from several sources. *The Blacke Booke* (1604) by "T. M." (probably Thomas Middleton) describes an apparition of the devil suddenly visible on the stage while the company was performing *Dr. Faustus:*

> Hee had a head of hayre like one of my Diuells in Dr. Faustus when the old Theatre crackt and frighted the audience.

The legend has it that not only was the audience "frighted" but Alleyn himself was so scared that he retired to private life. In 1633 the story was revived in William Prynne's *Histriomastix:*

> The visible apparition of the Devill on the stage at the Belsavage Play-house, in Queen Elizabeths dayes (to the great amazement both of the actors and spectators) while they were there prophanely playing the History of Faustus (the truth of which I have heard from many now alive, who well remember it) there being some distracted with that feareful sight.

Whatever may have been the influence of the supernatural, Alleyn did retire in 1597. In 1600, however, he returned to the stage. Extant documents indicate that his return was due to several factors. In 1600 Alleyn was involved in constructing a new theatre, the Fortune, which was opposed by many of the local citizenry. A letter from the privy council in April that year interceded in his behalf with the Middlesex justices of the peace; the communication was signed by the earl of Nottingham, Lord Hunsdon, and Robert Cecil, two of whom were patrons of acting companies themselves. In the letter they cite the queen's wish to see her favorite actor once again perform before her.

Alleyn's venture at the Fortune turned out to be quite successful, and by this time he was a very rich man. (See RATSEIS GHOST.) An anonymous play given by the Children of Paul's in 1600, *Jack Drum's Entertainment,* had in it a character, Sir Edward Fortune, whose name probably alludes to Alleyn, his new theatre, and his wealth. Alleyn's success derived from his association with Henslowe as well as his own name as a great actor. In addition, his share, upon his return to the Admiral's Men, was a privileged one; he was free of the liability of contributions normally assumed by actors for maintenance and other expenses.

By 1605 Alleyn had again retired from acting, but he continued in the theatre as manager and theatre-owner. He had bought for £10,000 a manor originally belonging to the Cluniac monks of Bermondsey in West Dulwich, Surrey. There he established the College of God's Gift, which was inaugurated (1619) in the presence of several dignitaries, including the lord chancellor. The school, now known as Dulwich College, flourishes today; its library contains Alleyn's and Henslowe's papers, which are a valuable resource for scholars studying the Elizabethan-Jacobean stage, and its private art gallery is one of the best in Great Britain. In 1623 Alleyn's wife Joan died and he married Constance Donne, daughter of the poet and dean of St. Paul's, John Donne. Alleyn himself died in 1626 and is buried in Dulwich.

In the years following Henslowe's death in 1616, Alleyn had become involved in a long, complicated series of legal disputes over Henslowe's will. Recently available evidence seems to indicate that Alleyn resorted to chicanery and fraud to secure greater control of the estate. Whatever the verdict of history on Alleyn's personal character or the nature of his business dealings, however, there can be no gainsaying his great stature as an actor. [E. K. Chambers, *The Elizabethan Stage,* 1923; John Briley, "Edward Alleyn and Henslowe's Will," *Shakespeare Quarterly,* IX, 1958.]

Alleyn, Giles (fl. 1600). The owner of the land on which the THEATRE stood. When Shakespeare's fellows razed the Theatre and transported the lumber across the Thames to the Bankside in order to build the Globe, Alleyn brought an unsuccessful suit against them. See GLOBE THEATRE.

Alleyn, John (c. 1557–1596). Actor and elder brother of Edward Alleyn. John was listed in 1589 as a member of the Admiral's Men and as part owner, with his brother Edward, of "playinge apparelles, playe-Bookes, Instrumentes and other commodities." In the Brayne-Burbage dispute (see the THEATRE), he testified as a witness when the case was brought to court in 1592. At his death, he was survived by his son John, who was later also involved in the theatrical enterprises of Edward Alleyn. [Edwin Nungezer, *A Dictionary of Actors,* 1929.]

All's well that ends well.

All's Well That Ends Well. A comedy by Shakespeare.

Text. For the text, the only authority is that of the First Folio. And, as Arthur Quiller-Couch once wrote, "a vile one" it is. There are many omissions, much carelessness in the distribution of speeches, and, in several instances, the first sentence of a speech, or sometimes only the first words, have become detached and assigned to the wrong speaker. Much of the prose and many rhymed passages are either examples of Shakespeare's first, rough draft or, as J. Dover Wilson believes, the work of a reviser, a lesser dramatist with a passion for sententious couplets and bawdry, who, for some reason, was engaged to expand the text. Quiller-Couch's characterization of the text as "largely a palimpsest, overwritten upon juvenile work, after a considerable amount of time," expresses the opinion of modern editors who postulate a reviser. Others argue that the corruption of the text is best explained by assuming that the printer's copy was Shakespeare's uncorrected FOUL PAPERS.

Date. To fix a probable date for the composition of the comedy it is necessary to assume that the Folio text was all written at one time. If we further assume that Shakespeare designed the part of the clown Lavache for Robert Armin, who replaced Will Kempe as the low-comedy actor in the latter part of 1599, *All's Well That Ends Well* must have been written after that date.

Many scholars have considered this play to be identical with the *Love's Labour's Won* referred to by Meres in his PALLADIS TAMIA (1598). This theory is particularly favored by those who believe that the Folio text is an incomplete revision of Shakespeare's earlier work (see above under *Text*). Most scholars, however, accept E. K. Chambers' assignment of the play to the years 1602–1603. It is so much like *Measure for Measure* in theme, language, characterization, and construction that the two "dark comedies" must have been composed at about the same time, *Measure for Measure* (1604) being the later play.

Sources. The ultimate source of *All's Well That Ends Well* is the ninth Novella of the third day in Boccaccio's *Decameron.* It is the story of Beltramo de Rossiglione and Giglietta de Narbone, which Shakespeare probably read in the English translation appearing in William PAINTER's *Palace of Pleasure* (2 vols., 1566–1567). Professor H. G. Wright has raised the possibility that a French translation of Boccaccio's story by Antoine le Maçon may have been the version that Shakespeare read. However, it is unlikely that the poet would have used a French version when Painter's was at hand in a volume that was among his favorite books.

For the character of Parolles, Shakespeare may have drawn upon the life and adventures of his fellow poet Barnabe BARNES.—O. J. C.

Plot Synopsis. Act I. Helena, the orphaned daughter of the celebrated physician Gerard de Narbon, has been reared in the household of the Countess of Rousillon. She is in love with the Countess' son, Bertram, but despairs of ever winning his affection because of the difference in their rank. Upon the death of the Countess' second husband, Bertram, who is now the ward of the ailing King of France, leaves Rousillon for Paris in the company of the cowardly Parolles and Lafeu, an honest old lord. Helena, who is in possession of some of her father's medical secrets, decides to go to Paris herself in the hope of curing the King of the ulcerous sores that afflict him and thus elevate herself in the eyes of the world.

Act II. Bertram reaches Paris as several noblemen are departing to serve in the army of the Duke of Florence, but the King insists on his staying behind because of his youth. When Helena arrives at the court, the King is at first doubtful that she can succeed where so many learned doctors have failed, but she is willing to stake her life on the effectiveness of her remedies. As payment for her services, she asks to be permitted to choose a husband from the bachelors of the court. When the King is restored to health through her ministrations, she claims her fee and selects Bertram, who strongly objects to what he considers a degrading alliance. Fearful of the King's displeasure, he finally agrees to marry Helena, but with the encouragement of Parolles he decides to go secretly to Florence immediately after the wedding.

Act III. Helena has returned to Rousillon at Bertram's request and there receives a letter from him in which he states that he will not be her husband until she can obtain the ring he always wears on his finger and beget a child by him. The Countess, who has always loved Helena like a daughter, is incensed at his conduct.

Grieved by the knowledge that she has been the cause of Bertram's flight from France, Helena disguises herself as a pilgrim and sets out for the shrine of Saint Jaques le Grand. Arriving in Florence, she learns from an old widow that Bertram has attempted to seduce her daughter, Diana, who blames Parolles, "that jack-an-apes with scarfs," for leading the young Count astray. After convincing the widow that she is Bertram's wife, Helena promises to provide Diana with a generous dowry if she will pretend to yield to his importunity; she is to demand the ring that he wears and then fix a time for an assignation, when Helena will take her place.

Act IV. Parolles' posturing has earned the contempt of his fellow officers in Florence, and they are determined to enlighten Bertram as to his true character. When he leaves his camp after boasting that he would recapture a drum taken by the enemy, he is seized and blindfolded by his comrades, who pretend to speak a strange foreign tongue. Questioned by an "interpreter" in Bertram's presence, he readily reveals much information about the French forces, describes the Count as "a dangerous and lascivious boy," and abjectly pleads for his life. Upon learning of the deception, however, Parolles betrays little shame; resolving to make the best of his situation, he concludes that "there's place and means for every man alive."

Meanwhile, Diana has persuaded Bertram to part, albeit reluctantly, with his ring, a treasured family heirloom, and has arranged a midnight tryst. Unknown to Bertram, it is Helena who occupies Diana's bed and gives him a ring which she had received from the King. In the belief that his wife is dead, he decides to return to France.

Act V. The report of Helena's death has reached the King as well as the Countess and Lafeu, who offers Bertram his own daughter as a second wife. Bertram agrees to the match and, as a favor for his bride-to-be, gives Lafeu the ring he had received from the woman he took to be Diana. The King immediately recognizes it as Helena's and, suspecting Bertram of responsibility for her death, orders his arrest. Diana now arrives with her mother and accuses Bertram of seducing her and reneging on his promise to marry her after his wife's death. Bertram's reply is to blacken her reputation. She now proceeds to talk in riddles, claiming that Bertram is both guilty and innocent and that he got his wife with child though she is dead. Exasperated, the King is about to send Diana to jail when she asks her mother to bring her "bail." The widow reappears with Helena, who declares that she has fulfilled Bertram's conditions and asks whether he will be hers, now that he has been "doubly won." He replies that he is prepared to "love her dearly, ever, ever dearly."—H. D.

Comment. *All's Well That Ends Well* is generally designated, along with *Troilus and Cressida* and *Measure for Measure,* as one of Shakespeare's dark comedies or problem plays (see COMICAL SATIRE). These plays all share an ambivalent, ironic, occasionally cynical view of human behavior. Accordingly they mark a significant departure from the poet's earlier romantic comedies.

Various attempts have been made to explain these curiously complex achievements written during a period (1601–1604) when Shakespeare was at the height of his mastery of tragic drama. Until the 20th century these plays were regarded as anomalies, best explained as Shakespeare's hasty revisions of other men's work. Critics of this century, however, sympathetically drawn to the disenchantment and negative picture of human nature presented in the plays, have come to regard them as significant artistic accomplishments. As a result there has been a greater effort in recent years to come to an understanding of these plays on their own terms in an attempt to determine their place in the total pattern of the Shakespeare canon.

One explanation of the apparent cynicism at the heart of *All's Well* is that it is the result of the poet's realistic treatment of two typically medieval stories. One is a "virtue" tale, exalting a woman's devotion to a husband or a lover who treats her with contempt. In the play this takes the form of a tale of a "clever wench," a girl who is able to fulfill designedly impossible conditions imposed on her by an alienated husband before he will consummate their marriage. That her wits proved to be more than a match for his awakens his admiration and makes him more than willing to have so clever a girl for his wife. A second popular narrative device in medieval tales, which W. W. Lawrence has named the "bed-trick," forms an important part of Helena's achievement. This stratagem is the heroine's substitution of herself in the bed of a wanton with whom the husband has made an assignation. The success of this "trick" enables her to present him with a child that he has unknowingly begotten.

Helena is a sympathetically designed representative of this girl of folklore. In spite of the bold part she must play, she is a modest, reserved creature. It is Bertram's mother who discovers her foster daughter's love; and it is to her, never to Bertram, that Helena betrays her hopeless love for one so much higher in the social scale. She confesses:

> I know I love in vain, strive against hope;
> Yet in this captious and intenible sieve
> I still pour in the waters of my love.
> . . . . .
> Religious in mine error, I adore
> The sun, that looks upon his worshipper,
> But knows of him no more.
> (I, iii, 207–209, 211–213)

This is the secret idolatry of a girl who does not remotely aspire to possession. She does not plan to go to the court where Bertram resides; it is the Countess who urges her to go there in order to cure the King of a fatal malady with a sovereign remedy that her doctor-father has bequeathed her. If she harbors the hope that by restoring the King to health she may win Bertram's affection, she never betrays it. Yet we may suspect that the idea has occurred to her from her earlier expression of her philosophy of action in the famous lines, "Our remedies oft in ourselves do lie, / Which we ascribe to heaven" (I, i, 231–232). Throughout the play her concealment of her thoughts and intentions forms an important part of her clever-wench role. The reward that she demands of the King for healing his fistula, the betrothal of a husband of "the royal blood of France," is presumptuous, but he grants it. Of the lords lined up by royal command for inspection she naturally chooses Bertram. The proud, boyish aristocrat is outraged that his sovereign should force him to marry a "poor physician's daughter," exclaiming, "I cannot love her, nor will strive to do't" (II, iii, 152). As the King begins to put pressure on the recalcitrant youth, she interrupts him with, "That you are well restored, my lord, I'm glad: / Let the rest go" (II, iii, 154–155). She is too gentle and too well-mannered to accept a husband forced to take her by a king's command. The King, however, refusing to accept her renunciation, compels Bertram to take her hand in token of official troth-plight. This forces his agreement to wed her, though clearly not to bed her. He at once sends her home to his mother's estate and, threatening never to return, hurries to Florence, from where he sends word of the seemingly impossible conditions under which he will make her truly his wife.

At this point, Helena appears undecided which of two courses of action to take: either to give up all claim to her nominal husband, or to do as Giletta does in Painter's version of the tale—make directly for her errant husband in Florence on the pretext that she is going on a pilgrimage. Her first impulse is to take the former course. She will leave the Countess' estate for good, so that Bertram can go home whenever he wishes. Yet if she is eager to avoid him, why does she go to the one place where she knows Bertram now resides? Is this a sign of her duplicity or a sign that Shakespeare could not decide which course to have Helena take? The latter was the solution of many 19th-century critics, who could not accept the idea that the poet would permit one of his sympathetically drawn women to pursue a man in so unladylike a fashion as the tale dictated. The only sensible and simple solution of this critic-created puzzle is to admit that the poet expected his audience to regard Helena's quiet duplicity as one of the clearest examples of the ingenuity of a "clever wench." It was proof of a wife's cleverness that she was capable of bringing a husband back into her arms.

Coincidence plays a large part in the success of her venture. Having arrived in Florence, she seems concerned only to find the road to St. Jaques, where the pilgrims usually lodge. It is by chance that she learns that Bertram is wooing a certain Diana, and this news gives her the idea of substituting herself for the girl in her assignation with Bertram. In this way Helena is able to present her husband with a child of his begetting without his knowledge of the means.

The atmosphere of *All's Well* is as "dark" as the story itself. Parolles is no adulterous braggart-soldier, no cousin to Falstaff. He is, rather, a shrewdly drawn portrait of a type of degraded gentleman who haunted London as an aftermath of the wars on the continent. He is contemptible in many ways besides his cowardice. That he should be Bertram's boon companion increases our initial contempt for the man whom Helena so irrationally desires. Having been given no reason for her infatuation, we find no satisfaction in the final reconciliation and completed marriage of the ill-suited pair.

The play contains satire in the savage spirit of Juvenal. Even the clown is far from gay. His exchanges with both Helena and the Countess are crude and foul. The Countess is so disgusted with his dirty impertinence that she once orders him off, as the editors of The New Cambridge edition suggest, "with a stamp of her foot." He has at least one of the characteristics of the buffoonish commentator whose progenitor is Carlo Buffone of Jonson's *Every Man Out of his Humour*. He is given to figures of speech that are preposterously irrelevant. His description of Parolles, as he introduces him to Lafeu, is a good example of his "similes of comfort."

> Here is a purr of fortune's, sir, or of fortune's cat, —but not a musk-cat,—that has fallen into the unclean fishpond of her displeasure, and, as he says, is muddied withal. (V, ii, 20–23)

This is ridicule of Elizabethan dramatists' indiscriminate and tedious employment of similitude.

The final scene is a good example of Shakespeare's newly adopted tendency to prolong his last acts artificially with spun-out crises of suspense and surprise—surprise to the dramatis personae, certainly not to the audience. This exhibition of a playwright's ingenuity diverts attention from that part of the denouement important for the fortunes of the principal characters. It is a naked exhibition, a professional tour de force that only gives the author further chances to blacken Bertram and to make the immature, spoiled fellow seem progressively more unworthy of Helena's inexplicable devotion.—O. J. C.

Stage History. *All's Well That Ends Well* has been one of the least often staged of any of Shakespeare's plays. There is no record of a performance before the closing of the theatres. The first production after 1660 did not occur until March 7, 1741, at the unfashionable Goodman's Fields Theatre, where David Garrick first appeared in that year. The next year, Theophilus Cibber gave the play a brief spurt of popularity by excelling in the part of Parolles at Drury Lane; Peg Woffington acted Helena in this production, which was played for 10 performances. Cibber was succeeded in his role by Henry Woodward, who from 1746 acted Parolles for 30 years, becoming so obviously the star that the romantic roles were cut down. The attention of audiences was focused on Woodward and the various actors who played the clown Lavache. At Drury Lane on December 12, 1794 John Philip Kemble restored the proper balance between the romantic and low-comedy features with a version in which he himself played Bertram with Mrs. Jordan (Dorothy Bland) as Helena. The production was not a success, nor was that of Charles Kemble, who produced the same version at Covent Garden in 1811. On October 12, 1832 *All's Well*—transformed into an opera, with songs inserted from other of Shakespeare's plays, and a masque of *Oberon and Goodfellow*, based on material culled from *A Midsummer Night's Dream*—was presented at Covent Garden. On September 1, 1852 Samuel Phelps put on the play during his ninth season at Sadler's Wells; he played Parolles, but the production enjoyed little success.

Frank Benson may have regretted reviving the play in 1916 at the Memorial Theatre in Stratford-upon-Avon, for he never toured with it. He took the part of Parolles opposite Florence Glossop-Harris' unilluminating portrayal of Helena as a calculating opportunist. On May 20, 1920, when William Poel staged a "vocal recital" of *All's Well* at the Ethical Church in Bayswater, his treatment of the play was somewhat eccentric. Edith Evans and Winifred Oughton assumed the roles of the brothers Dumain. When Clare Greet, a happy, maternal actress, abandoned the part of Parolles after a disturbing first rehearsal, Poel took over the role himself. Helena wooing Bertram was represented as signifying the new emancipated woman and, so the audience would make no mistake about the seriousness of his condition, a uniformed nurse wheeled the King on in a Bath chair. The playbill failed to identify the production's stage manager, Robert Atkins.

Sir Barry Jackson, with the Birmingham Repertory Theatre, produced a modern-dress version in 1927.

Laurence Olivier's portrayal of Parolles as a pleasant sophisticate especially pleased George Bernard Shaw.

During the late summer of 1940, the comedy was staged for its first public run in London since 1811. Robert Atkins played Lafeu in his production at the Vaudeville, with Catherine Lacey as Helena and Ernest Milton as the King of France. The eloquence of their performances completely engrossed the premiere audience, who seemed unaware that one of the worst daylight bombings of the war was taking place. It was 13 years before London saw another *All's Well*, Michael Benthall's disappointing revival at the Old Vic in 1953. The one saving feature of this production was the Parolles of Michael Hordern. Lines were rushed and garbled, the King of France reduced to a ridiculous senile invalid, his fantasticated court overrun by flatterers. Claire Bloom played Helena and Fay Compton was the Countess.

At Stratford in 1955 *All's Well* was staged in Louis XIII costume and, in 1959, in combined Edwardian and modern dress, under Tyrone Guthrie's direction. Guthrie had originally designed the latter production for the 1953 season of the Shakespearean Festival Theatre at Stratford, Ontario. For this version, the director completely eliminated the role of Lavache and, by means of inconsequential comic panoply, expanded III, iii, from its original 10 lines into his own idea of the military establishment. This lively rendition was memorable for the benevolent Countess of Edith Evans, the sympathetic Helena of Zoe Caldwell, and for Cyril Luckham's swaggering Parolles.—M. G.

Bibliography. TEXT: *All's Well That Ends Well*, New Cambridge Edition, A. Quiller-Couch and J. Dover Wilson, eds., 1929; *All's Well That Ends Well*, New Arden Edition, G. K. Hunter, ed., 1959. DATE: New Arden Edition. SOURCES: H. G. Wright, "How Did Shakespeare Come to Know the Decameron?" *Modern Language Review*, L, 1955; Goeffrey Bullough, *Narrative and Dramatic Sources of Shakespeare*, Vol. II, 1958. COMMENT: New Arden Edition; W. W. Lawrence, *Shakespeare's Problem Comedies*, 1931; E. M. W. Tillyard, *Shakespeare's Problem Plays*, 1949; M. C. Bradbrook, *Shakespeare and Elizabethan Poetry*, 1951. STAGE HISTORY: New Cambridge Edition; G. C. D. Odell, *Shakespeare from Betterton to Irving*, 1920; J. C. Trewin, *Shakespeare on the English Stage, 1900-1964*, 1964.

Selected Criticism

SAMUEL JOHNSON. This play has many delightful scenes, though not sufficiently probable, and some happy characters, though not new, nor produced by any deep knowledge of human nature. Parolles is a boaster and a coward, such as has always been the sport of the stage, but perhaps never raised more laughter or contempt than in the hands of *Shakespeare*.

I cannot reconcile my heart to *Bertram;* a man noble without generosity, and young without truth; who marries *Helen* as a coward, and leaves her as a profligate: when she is dead by his unkindness, sneaks home to a second marriage, is accused by a woman whom he has wronged, defends himself by falsehood, and is dismissed to happiness.

The story of *Bertram* and *Diana* had been told before of *Mariana* and *Angelo*, and, to confess the truth, scarcely merited to be heard a second time.

The story is copied from a novel of *Boccace*, which may be read in *Shakespear Illustrated*, with remarks not more favourable *to Bertram* than my own. [*The Plays of William Shakespeare*, 1765.]

SAMUEL TAYLOR COLERIDGE. I cannot agree with the solemn abuse which the critics have poured out upon Bertram in "All's Well that Ends Well." He was a young nobleman in feudal times, just bursting into manhood, with all the feelings of pride of birth and appetite for pleasure and liberty natural to such a character so circumstanced. Of course he had never regarded Helena otherwise than as a dependent in the family; and of all that which she possessed of goodness and fidelity and courage, which might atone for her inferiority in other respects, Bertram was necessarily in a great measure ignorant. And after all, her *prima facie* merit was the having inherited a prescription from her old father the Doctor by which she cures the King—a merit, which supposes an extravagance of personal loyalty in Bertram to make conclusive to him in such a matter as that of taking a wife. Bertram had surely good reason to look upon the king's forcing him to marry Helena as a very tyrannical act. Indeed, it must be confessed that her character is not very delicate, and it required all Shakespeare's consummate skill to interest us for her; and he does this chiefly by the operation of the other characters—the Countess, Lafeu, &c. We get to like Helena from their praising and commending her so much. [*Table Talk*, 1835; reprinted in *Shakespearean Criticism* by S. T. Coleridge, T. M. Raysor, ed., Everyman Library Edition, 1960.]

THOMAS KENNY. The unamiable character of Bertram seems to constitute the great defect of this drama. He is young, brave, handsome, and high-born; but he is, at the same time, petulant, arrogant, cold, and selfish, and his very vices present no feature of impressive interest. The unwelcome part which he plays is, no doubt, in some measure, the result of the false position in which he has been unfairly placed by the understanding between the King and Helena; but his own character appears to have been made unnecessarily repulsive. We lose all trust in him when, immediately after his apparent repentance, we find him insolently untruthful in his account of his relations with Diana; and this unexpected aggravation of his demerits seems to be somewhat unaccountably introduced, as we have no such scene in the original tale of Boccaccio . . . . The disagreeable character of the young Count tends greatly to diminish the interest which we should, under other circumstances, be disposed to feel in the adventures of the beautiful and afflicted Helena. We can entertain no very intense desire that she should succeed in the pursuit of an object which seems hardly to deserve her devotion; and, besides, we cannot quite conceal from ourselves that she only attains it by the employment of an extravagant and a not very delicate stratagem. She is herself brought before us with some drawbacks from the general beauty and elevation of her character. She has clearly no very strong regard for rigid, unequivocating truthfulness. She does not really mean to go, as she announces, on a pilgrimage to the shrine of St. Jaques. It is not true, as she states to Diana, that she does not know Bertram's face. And, again, we find that she does not hesitate to cause false intelligence of the accomplishment of her pilgrimage and of her death to be conveyed to the camp at Florence. These departures from strict veracity harmonise, no doubt, readily enough with the rude spirit of old romance; but they contrast somewhat disagreeably with that general ideal perfection with which Shakespeare has invested many of his female characters, and Helena herself, in no small degree, among the number. [*The Life and Genius of Shakespeare*, 1864.]

EDWARD DOWDEN. In *All's Well that Ends Well*, a subject of extreme difficulty, when regarded on the ethical side, was treated by Shakspere with a full consciousness of its difficulty. A woman who seeks her husband, and gains him against his will; who afterwards by a fraud—a fraud however pious—defeats his intention of estranging her, and becomes the mother of his child; such a personage it would seem a sufficiently difficult task to render attractive or admirable. Yet Helena has been named by Coleridge "the loveliest of Shakspere's characters." Possibly Coleridge recognized in Helena the single quality which, if brought to bear upon himself by one to whom he yielded love and worship, would have given definiteness and energy to his somewhat vague and incoherent life. For sake of this one thing Shakspere was interested in the story, and so admirable did it seem to him that he could not choose but endeavor to make beautiful and noble the entire character and action of Helena. This one thing is the energy, the leap-up, the direct advance of the *will* of Helena, her prompt, unerroneous tendency towards the right and efficient *deed* . . . .

The mode by which Helena succeeds in accomplishing the conditions upon which Bertram has promised to acknowledge her as his wife seems indeed hardly to possess any moral force, any validity, for the heart or the conscience. It can only be said, in explanation, that to Helena an infinite virtue and significance resides in a *deed*. Out of a word or out of a feeling she does not hope for measureless good to come; but out of a deed, what may not come? That Bertram should actually have received her as his wife, actually, though unwittingly; that he should indeed be father of the child she bears him—these are facts, accomplished things, which must work out some real advantage. And now Bertram has learned his need of self-distrust, perhaps has learned true modesty. His friend (who was all vain words apart from deeds) has been unmasked and pitilessly exposed. May not Bertram now be capable of estimating the worth of things and of persons more justly? Helena, in taking the place of Diana, in beguiling her husband into at least material virtue, is still "doing him wrong, for his own sake." The man is "at woman's command," and there is "no hurt done."

Even at the last, Bertram's attainment is but small; he is still no more than a potential piece of worthy manhood. We cannot suppose that Shakspere has represented him thus without a purpose. Does not the poet wish us to feel that although much remains to be wrought in Bertram, his welfare is now assured? The courageous title of the play, *All's Well that Ends Well*, is like an utterance of the heart of Helena, who has strength and endurance to attain the end, and who will measure things, not by the pains and trials of the way, not by the dubious and difficult means, but by that end, by the accomplished issue. [*Shakspere: A Critical Study of His Mind and Art*, 1875.]

FRANK HARRIS. The truth is that, owing partly to the puerile affectations of the first sketch and partly to the later revision, the character of Helena is a mere jumble of contradictions, without coherence or charm; she is not realized clearly enough or deeply enough to live; she is an unconsidered attempt; an exasperating failure.

The whole story of the play is unsuited to the character of a young girl, and perhaps no care could have made a girl charming, or even credible, who would pursue a man to such lengths or win him by such a trick; at any rate no dramatist has yet succeeded with such a theme, though it might be within the larger compass of the novelist. [*The Women of Shakespeare*, 1911.]

W. W. LAWRENCE. *All's Well* is artificial in effect; almost entertainment provided according to a formula. The technique of transforming narrative into drama is in good order, but the imagination of the dramatist has seldom been kindled, or his sensibilities aroused. A curious hardness and indifference are often evident. There are flashes of tenderness and fineness, as in the portraiture of Helena and the Countess, but these are all too rare. Parolles and the Clown lack the genial human qualities which make us love such eccentric characters as Falstaff and Touchstone. One is driven to the conclusion that Shakespeare, needing a play for the company, took a well-tried theme, developed it according to principles which he had by this time fully mastered, but never put his whole heart and soul into it. He relied for effect, not on emotion or truth to life, but on the familiarity and popularity of the story, and upon the theatrical effectiveness of individual scenes. And this, I think, is why the modern reader, who has no feeling for the traditions of story, and who cannot judge from the stage effects, finds *All's Well* highly puzzling. [*Shakespeare's Problem Comedies*, 1931.]

THOMAS MARC PARROTT. Shakespeare may have modeled Parolles after Bobadil in Jonson's *Every Man in his Humour*, in which Shakespeare himself took part; but Parolles is both a more complex and a more realistic character than Jonson's Elizabethan Miles Gloriosus. . . . Even in a satiric portrait of an unlovely contemporary type Shakespeare recognizes the essential humanity of a liar and a coward. The exposure of Parolles is a scene of broad farce; the rogue is tricked and laughed at, but he is spared the shame and pain that Bobadil suffered under the cudgel of Downright. Parolles slinks off with something like repentance in his heart; he will let his idle sword rust and try to live by 'fooling': after all—and here we may catch Shakespeare's own voice—'There's place and means for every man alive.' And a place, as a matter of fact, is reserved for him at Lafeu's table; the honest lord, who was the first to see through him, is willing to entertain and make sport with him; 'though you are a fool and a knave you shall eat.' Shakespeare has none of Jonson's bitter indignation at fools and knaves. [*Shakespearean Comedy*, 1949.]

Alonso. In *The Tempest*, the King of Naples,

father of Ferdinand, and brother of Sebastian. Although Alonso helped Antonio to usurp Prospero's dukedom, this rather irresolute ruler is capable of honest remorse. Reminded by Ariel of his misdeeds, and sorrowing over the presumed loss of his son, the King contemplates suicide. Alonso is alone among the miscreants to entreat Prospero's pardon, and he subsequently restores Prospero's dukedom. The unhappiness of this true penitent fully dissolves when he discovers Ferdinand quite alive and betrothed to Miranda.

amalgamation. A practice, common among Elizabethan acting companies, whereby two or more companies combined to form a single company. The amalgamation could be either temporary or permanent; the usual motive was economic, but it is generally difficult to determine the exact nature of the arrangements.

Many examples of amalgamation are known. In 1591 Sussex' Men and the Queen's Men combined for a brief period, then recombined, apparently permanently, in 1594. In 1597 the Admiral's Men absorbed the leading members of Pembroke's Men. In 1602 the privy council, seeking to limit the number of acting companies permitted to play in London, ordered Oxford's Men and Worcester's Men to play together at the Boar's Head Inn. In 1615 Prince Charles' Men absorbed Lady Elizabeth's Men, which had previously been combined in 1612/3 with the Children of the Queen's Revels.

The most important amalgamation, however, was that which lasted from approximately 1588 to 1594 between STRANGE'S MEN, which later became Shakespeare's company the Chamberlain's Men, and the Admiral's Men. The exact nature of the alliance is unknown, but it is clear that although the companies played together, they did not abandon their separate identities. [E. K. Chambers, *The Elizabethan Stage*, 1923.]

Amazons. In *Timon of Athens*, characters in the masque held in Timon's banquet hall. The Amazons dance, play lutes, and mix with the lords in the audience (I, ii).

Ambassadors to the King of England. In *Henry V*, they present Henry with a gift considered by Lewis the Dauphin to suit his character: tennis balls (I, ii).

American Shakespeare Festival, The. An annual dramatic festival held at Stratford, Connecticut. On July 12, 1955 the American Shakespeare Festival Theatre and Academy opened in a handsome gray building, slightly resembling Shakespeare's Globe. It was the culmination of efforts by Lawrence Langner, codirector of the Theatre Guild, to "give Shakespeare a home in America to keep his plays alive, and to give an opportunity to younger actors to learn classical acting, which may otherwise become a lost art in America." Inspired in 1950 by the achievements of the Shakespeare Memorial Theatre at Stratford-upon-Avon, England, Mr. Langner at first planned a similar theatre for Westport, Connecticut, where he lived, but later decided upon Stratford on the Housatonic River, near Bridgeport.

Costing $1,000,000, the building, designed by Edwin L. Howard, housed a 1550-seat auditorium, paneled in wood contributed from all over the world. Its exterior design combined the hexagonal auditorium and a taller, rectangular stage house, high enough so that scenery could be raised, or "flown," for fast changes. Attributed to Edward C. Cole, the stage was of a conventional 19th-century type, fronted by a proscenium, or frame, like those on Broadway. A gesture toward the Elizabethan stage was reflected in a 14-foot forestage, actually an apron, in front of the proscenium, but it bore little resemblance to the large platform stage of Shakespeare's day. This Stratford stage (on which it was announced that opera, ballet, and concerts would be seen in the winter months) and cavernous auditorium, with its steeply graded balcony affording a pocket-sized view of the action, hardly promoted the feeling of intimacy between actor and audience as did the Elizabethan theatre.

Not only the stage and auditorium, but also the productions, looked back to 19th-century practices: the use of star "names" heading an indifferent cast, declaiming of lines for sound rather than sense, and scenery and costumes either so conventional as to be dull or so outlandish as to be distracting. However, even though its spirit is staid rather than exciting, the Festival has made some gains. Early attempts to camouflage the stage with gray venetian-blind-like slats failed, but more recently it has been converted by shrewd lighting and scenery into a highly effective playing area.

The theatre's most notable achievement has been to give good actors the opportunity to play the best roles ever written. Among the younger talents which have enriched the Stratford scene have been those of Christopher Plummer, Nancy Wickwire, John Colicos, Hal Holbrook, and Roddy McDowall. Two established American actors have given unforgettable performances at the Festival in roles they probably would never have played elsewhere—Morris Carnovsky as Shylock and as Lear and Alfred Drake as Iago. Other casting has often been less felicitous. Younger actors have been given major roles for which they were unprepared, and Hollywood stars have been brought to Stratford to play parts for which they were unsuited.

The opening season, July 12 to September 3, presented *Julius Caesar* and *The Tempest*, with Raymond Massey as Brutus and Prospero, Jack Palance as Cassius and Caliban, Christopher Plummer as Antony and Ferdinand, and Roddy McDowall as Octavius Caesar and Ariel. Directed by an Englishman, Denis Carey, the productions were listless and lacking in poetry. In *Julius Caesar* impressive performances were given by Roddy McDowall, portraying Octavius as a cold and bloodless young man, and by Christopher Plummer, whose voluptuary of an Antony was devoted as much to himself as to Caesar.

The following year, 1956, saw a "clean sweep" in the artistic direction of the Festival. The reins were taken over by John Houseman, whose considerable stage and motion picture experience in this country included the Mercury Theatre and the film of *Julius Caesar*. Under Mr. Houseman's direction for the next five years, the productions were all acceptable; a few were memorable. His assistant director, Jack Landau, often applied the practice of taking the plays out of their own periods and setting them in others, hoping to point up their timelessness. Too often this device proved only an annoying interference with the play itself.

Of *Measure for Measure* in Victorian dress that second season, directed by Messrs. Houseman and Landau with Kent Smith and Nina Foch as Angelo and Isabella, Walter Kerr wrote in the New York *Herald Tribune* that the colloquial, nonpoetic production "scuttles what is most arresting and most difficult in Shakespeare's troublesome play. What is left, though, is an extended lark among low-brows, an impudent parade of fetching folk from Vienna's rowdier cellars, and I think you'll find the brawl entertaining." Concentrating on the novelty and comedy at the expense of the serious aspects of the plays became a persistent tendency at Stratford. The second season also included *King John,* with John Emery in the title role, directed by Houseman, and *The Taming of the Shrew,* directed by Norman Lloyd. Rouben Ter-Arutunian's permanent setting of gray slats was inaugurated and kept on for succeeding seasons.

One of the Festival's best years, 1957, saw Morris Carnovsky playing Shylock and Katharine Hepburn, Portia in *The Merchant of Venice;* Miss Hepburn and Alfred Drake as Beatrice and Benedick in *Much Ado About Nothing;* and Earle Hyman and Mr. Drake as Othello and Iago. Although Miss Hepburn brought charm, Hollywood glamor, and her familiar type of tremulous, awkward heroine to the *Merchant,* the production still would have been as effectively sunlit and musical without her. Morris Carnovsky was an excellent Shylock, subtly executed, not as a self-pitying hero, but as a thoroughly human villain, filled with self-love and blind to human values. Young Earle Hyman lacked the heroic stature for Othello, but as Iago, Alfred Drake revealed exceptional talents for delivery and variety in quick changes of mood. *Much Ado About Nothing* was set in the American Spanish Southwest at the turn of the century, complete with whooping cowboys twirling lassoes and shooting off pistols.

Hamlet, A Midsummer Night's Dream, and *Romeo and Juliet* were offered in 1958. Of Fritz Weaver's Hamlet, Herbert Whittaker wrote in the *Herald Tribune:* "He is not notably princely, is not a romantic figure, nor especially musical . . . . his is a Hamlet happiest in the prose." Inga Swenson and Richard Easton were not ideally cast as Juliet and Romeo, and *A Midsummer Night's Dream* so overstressed the comedy that Brooks Atkinson commented in the *Times* that Jack Landau, the director, "might do better to concentrate on the lyricism rather than the comedy . . . ." After this uninspired season, the Festival in 1959 offered a happier bill, with members of its company taking the leading roles: Nancy Wickwire and Nancy Marchand as Mistresses Ford and Page and Larry Gates as Falstaff in an infectiously spirited *Merry Wives of Windsor,* John Colicos as the troubled Leontes and Miss Wickwire as the wronged Hermione in *The Winter's Tale* and as a shy Helena in *All's Well That Ends Well.*

For the next three years the Festival went back to its earlier policy of hiring star names for the leading roles. In 1960 Robert Ryan and Katharine Hepburn reminded one more of a midwestern businessman and a New England spinster than of Antony and Cleopatra, while *Twelfth Night,* another of the "novelty" productions, set at a fashionable seaside resort in the Regency period, was reminiscent of *H.M.S. Pinafore.* Walter Kerr, writing of *Twelfth Night,* contrasted "the carefree nonsense of Shakespeare's plot and the calculated nonsense of the present production." The season's greatest success, and one of the best productions in Stratford's history, was *The Tempest,* directed by William Ball as a spectacle in the tradition of the 17th-century masques.

Broadway stars played leading roles in 1961, with Pat Hingle as a one-dimensional, nonpoetic Macbeth opposite Jessica Tandy as an effective Lady Macbeth; and Kim Hunter as a prosaic, uninspired Rosalind in *As You Like It.* That year's novelty was a *Troilus and Cressida* set in the American Civil War, so striving to match the play to the period that any over-all meaning or effect was lost. Helen Hayes, Maurice Evans, and Richard Basehart were the stars in 1962, in which year Joseph Verner Reed took over the artistic direction of the Festival. Miss Hayes and Mr. Evans offered "Shakespeare Revisited," a program of recitations which was more successful in its lighter moments than in its serious ones. Richard Basehart was unique in portraying a colloquial interpretation of Richard II, Shakespeare's most lyric king. *1 Henry IV,* with no stars, came off best, with Eric Berry an impressive Falstaff and Hal Holbrook as a vigorous Hotspur. One of the most dramatic events of that season was offstage, with Miss Hayes attacking the "first-string" critics on the New York papers for not attending the Festival, and one of the critics replying that when the productions were worth it, they would make the trip.

By 1963 the nonstar policy was back in favor, and it produced one of the finest offerings of the Festival. Morris Carnovsky, who had played supporting and leading roles at Stratford since 1956, portrayed King Lear most impressively. Other productions were *2 Henry IV,* with relatively the same cast as the year before, and *The Comedy of Errors* set in the Cavalier period, with the same actors doubling as the twins Dromio and Antipholus.

Among the events held at Stratford in 1964 to celebrate the 400th anniversary of Shakespeare's birth was an exhibit of paintings presented to the Festival by Lincoln Kirstein and of memorabilia presented by Harvard University. Most of the cast that season had participated in an extensive training program, underwritten by the Ford Foundation. The productions were *Hamlet,* directed by Douglas Seale, with Lester Rawlins in the title role, Philip Bosco as Claudius, and Carmen Mathews as Gertrude; *Much Ado About Nothing,* with Jacqueline Brookes as Beatrice and Philip Bosco as Benedick; and *Richard III* with Douglas Watson in the title role.

The outstanding event of the 1965 season was a revival of *King Lear,* in which Morris Carnovsky achieved new heights in the title role and received standing ovations for his portrayal of a monarch of tragic stature, who was yet profoundly human. The inadequacy of most of the supporting cast was in part disguised by expert use of the stage and lighting. A production of *Coriolanus,* with Philip Bosco as the protagonist and Aline McMahon as Volumnia, caught some of the ironies of this difficult play. A hectic performance of *The Taming of the Shrew,* with Ruby Dee miscast as Kate, had little to recommend it. Terence Scammell and Maria Tucci played Romeo and Juliet to mixed notices.

In addition to its summer seasons, the Festival has consistently sent its productions on tour, these including the 1960 presentation of *A Midsummer Night's Dream,* with Bert Lahr as Bottom, which visited 18 cities, and the Helen Hayes–Maurice Evans bill, which toured successfully in the 1962/3 season. In addition, pre-season and post-season performances are always offered at reduced rates for students, with over 150,000 schoolchildren from 10 states seeing the plays each year in this way.

An evaluation of the Festival during its first decade finds most serious critics agreeing that the country is fortunate to have such an institution devoted solely to professional productions of the plays of Shakespeare, but wishing at the same time that the Festival might achieve a happy mean between the too pallid and respectful and the overcute, a point where it might be both vigorous and lyric, like the plays themselves, and from there evolve a distinctive style, character, and point of view.—A. G.

Amiens. In *As You Like It,* a follower of the banished Duke in Arden Forest. He sings "Under the greenwood tree" (II, v) and "Blow, blow, thou winter wind" (II, vii).

Amyot, Jacques (1513–1593). French writer. Amyot's version of Plutarch's *Lives* (*Vie des hommes illustres,* 1559), translated into English by Sir Thomas North in 1579, was the source of Shakespeare's Roman plays. Amyot was a classical scholar, but his translations are marked by a liveliness and freedom which do not generally accompany scholarship. His work thus served as a suitable model for North's memorable translation. Amyot was frequently honored during his life, serving first as a professor of classical languages at Bourges and later as the bishop of Auxerre until his death in 1593.

Anderson, Dame **Judith** (1898–). Actress. Born in Australia, Dame Judith made her debut in Sydney in 1915. In 1918 she began acting in New York, graduating from bit parts to leads within a year. She has since acted primarily in England and America. In 1936 she played Gertrude in Sir John Gielgud's *Hamlet* in New York, and the following year appeared as Lady Macbeth at the Old Vic. Her Lady Macbeth and Medea have established her as a powerful heroic tragedienne, and she has been called upon to repeat both roles many times. She has appeared in two television productions of *Macbeth.* [*Who's Who in the Theatre,* 1961.]

Anderson, Mary (1859–1940). American actress. At a very early age, Miss Anderson came under the influence of Charlotte Cushman and, at her urging, made her debut at 16 in Louisville, Kentucky, playing Juliet. She was an extraordinarily beautiful woman and was endowed with a remarkable voice. Within two years of her debut, she had formed her own company and had successfully toured the United States. She arrived in England in 1883 and won acclaim in a contemporary play. At the opening of the Shakespeare Memorial Theatre at Stratford-upon-Avon in 1885, she played Rosalind in *As You Like It.* Among her other Shakespearean successes were Juliet and Lady Macbeth, and she was the first actress to double the roles of Hermione and Perdita in *The Winter's Tale.* She unexpectedly retired at the age of 30, married, and settled in England. [*Oxford Companion to the Theatre,* Phyllis Hartnoll, ed., 1951.]

MARY ANDERSON AS JULIET.

Andrewes, Robert (d. 1616). London scrivener who drew up the documents for Shakespeare's purchase of Blackfriars Gate-House. Andrewes' business was located in the parish of St. Gregory. In 1603 he prepared the will of Marie James, mother of Elias JAMES, a brewer for whom Shakespeare is alleged to have written an epitaph. [Leslie Hotson, *Shakespeare's Sonnets Dated,* 1949.]

Andromache. In Greek legend and in Homer's *Iliad,* the wife of Hector; in *Troilus and Cressida,* she appears in the same role. Andromache makes a vain appeal to her husband not to engage Achilles in battle: "Unarm, unarm, and do not fight today" (V, iii, 3).

Andronicus, Titus. See TITUS ANDRONICUS.

Angeli, Diego. See ITALY.

Angelica. See NURSE.

Angelo. In *The Comedy of Errors,* a goldsmith. Angelo's attempts to force one Antipholus to pay for a gold chain he has made for the other precipitate much of the action.

Angelo. In *Measure for Measure,* the deputy appointed by the Duke to enforce laws against immorality during his supposed absence. Angelo condemns Claudio to death for seducing Juliet, but offers Claudio's sister, Isabella, her brother's life in exchange for her favors. When, at the disguised Duke's intervention, Angelo's jilted fiancée, Mariana, takes Isabella's place in the deputy's bed, he believes that he has possessed Isabella, but nonetheless orders Claudio's execution. His treachery is thwarted by the Duke, and at the end of the play Angelo is forced to marry Mariana.

Angus. In *Macbeth,* a Scottish nobleman. He fights with Malcolm's rebel army against Macbeth (V, iv).

Anne, Queen (1574–1619). Wife of James I of England, whom she married in 1589. Anne was a princess of Denmark, the sister of King Christian IV (1588–1648). After her removal from the chilling sobriety of Scotland to become queen of England in 1603, she manifested a strong penchant for lavish entertainments at court. Under her leadership the English court became a center of elaborate and costly dramatic spectacles, notably the brilliant masques written by Ben Jonson and Samuel Daniel and staged by Inigo Jones. She personally appeared in Jonson's *Masque of Blackness* (1604) and his *Masque of Queens* (1609). See MASQUE.

Anne was also a generous and enthusiastic supporter of the regular theatre, acting as patron for two companies, the Children of the Queen's Revels and Queen Anne's Men. Although essentially frivolous herself, she had an important impact on the more serious drama of her time. Her love of spectacle and costume, for example, stimulated the development of the aristocratic tastes which Shakespeare gratified with his romances.

Anne Hathaway's Cottage. Name given to the farmhouse at Hewlands Farm in Shottery, occupied by the Hathaway family in the 16th century. In 1610 it was purchased by Bartholomew Hathaway, nephew of Anne, and it remained in the Hathaway family until well into the 18th century. In 1892 it was purchased by the trustees of the Shakespeare "birthplace" and has since become one of the most popular tourist attractions in the Stratford area. See HATHAWAY FAMILY.

Anne Neville, Lady (1456–1485). Younger daughter of Warwick the Kingmaker. Although in 1470 Lady Anne was betrothed to Edward, son of Henry VI and Queen Margaret, it is not certain that a marriage took place. After the rise to power of Richard, duke of Gloucester, Anne was sent into concealment by her brother-in-law, the duke of Clarence. However, Richard discovered and married her in 1474. Their only child, Edward, was born in about 1476 but died eight years later.

In *Richard III,* Anne appears as the widow of Edward, Prince of Wales. In I, ii, she curses Richard for the deaths of her father and her husband but consents to marry him. After her coronation, Anne mysteriously dies. Her ghost, appearing to Richard on the eve of the battle of Bosworth Field, bids him "despair, and die!" (V, iii).

Annesley, Sir Brian (d. 1603). Gentleman pensioner of Queen Elizabeth. Annesley's relationship with his daughters parallels that of King Lear. In 1600 Annesley made a will which was apparently unfavorable to his two married daughters, Lady Wildgoose and Lady Sandys. Three years later, shortly before his death, the two women sought to have their father declared insane and his will invalidated. Their attempt was, however, frustrated by a third daughter, Cordell, who wrote the queen's minister, Robert Cecil, and asked that her father be spared such treatment. After the death of her father, Cordell "at her own proper cost and charges" erected a monument to her father and mother, "against the ungrateful nature of oblivious time." Subsequently Cordell married Sir William Harvey (a frequently proposed candidate for the role of Mr. W. H.), husband of the late countess of Southampton and stepfather of Shakespeare's patron, the earl of Southampton. Through his association with the family Shakespeare may have become aware of the Annesley incident and could have used it in *King Lear,* especially for the idea of Lear's madness, which does not appear in any of the recognized sources of the play. [G. M. Young, *Today and Yesterday,* 1948; *King Lear,* New Arden Edition, Kenneth Muir, ed., 1952.]

Antenor. In Homer's *Iliad,* a Trojan who advises Helen to return to Menelaus; in *Troilus and Cressida,* a Trojan warrior. In the play Antenor is captured by the Greeks during the battle and exchanged for Cressida at the request of Calchas, Cressida's father.

Antigonus. In *The Winter's Tale,* a lord of Sicilia and Paulina's husband. Antigonus is a worthy spouse of his honest, outspoken wife and speaks openly to Leontes his opinion that the jealous King is "abus'd, and by some putter-on that will be damn'd for't." Visited by an apparition of Hermione while loyally executing Leontes' command to abandon the innocent infant Perdita in some remote place "where chance may nurse or end it," the good Antigonus is warned that "for this ungentle business . . . , thou ne'er shalt see thy wife Paulina more." After leaving the baby on the deserts of Bohemia, he is attacked by a bear and killed.

antimasque. Term used to describe the contrasting interlude in a MASQUE, designed to act as a foil to the main masque. The earliest recorded use of the term "antimasque" is in the preface to Ben Jonson's *The Masque of Queens* (1609) in which he speaks of using an "anti-masque of boyes" in his previous masque, *The Hue and Cry After Cupid* (1608). Although originally intended as a contrasting interlude of grotesque comedy, the antimasque developed under Jonson's skillful hands into an organic part of the main masque. It is possible that Jonson drew his inspiration for his demonic antimasques from the witches' scenes in *Macbeth.* [*Ben Jonson,* C. H. Herford and Percy Simpson, eds., 11 vols., 1925–1952.]

Antioch Shakespeare Festival. See GREAT LAKES SHAKESPEARE FESTIVAL.

Antiochus. In *Pericles,* the evil king of Antioch. He has decreed that all aspirants for his daughter's hand must solve a riddle containing the hideous secret of his incestuous relationship with her. When Pericles interprets the rhyme correctly, Antiochus, fearing that the Prince will reveal his infamy, commissions an assassin to murder him. Gower reports the deaths of the King and his daughter in III, i.

Antipholus. In *The Comedy of Errors,* the name of identical twin brothers, sons of Aegeon and Aemilia. One is Antipholus of Ephesus, the other Antipholus of Syracuse. Separated as infants in a shipwreck, they are reunited after a series of entanglements, in which each is mistaken for his twin.

anti-Stratfordians. See CLAIMANTS.

Antonio. In *The Merchant of Venice,* the title character. In order to lend his friend Bassanio 3000 ducats, Antonio pledges his ships and merchandise to borrow the amount from Shylock. When the young man is unable to repay the money, Shylock demands a pound of his flesh as compensation. In the ensuing trial, Bassanio's wife Portia acts as Antonio's defense attorney and cleverly turns the tables on Shylock, who emerges as the criminal in the affair. Though the court decrees that Shylock must forfeit his fortune, Antonio generously requests that the old man be allowed to keep half of it. His request is granted.

Antonio. In *Much Ado About Nothing,* Leonato's brother. In V, i, Antonio advises Leonato, who is sorrowing over the dishonor and supposed death of his daughter, Hero, that instead of killing himself with grief he should "make those that do offend you suffer too." When Antonio himself undertakes to challenge the offending Claudio, he explodes in such violent insults that his brother has difficulty calming him. In the denouement, Antonio gives his "daughter," actually the masked Hero, to the repentant Claudio.

Antonio. In *The Tempest,* Prospero's brother and the usurping Duke of Milan. Evil ambition led the villainous Antonio to supplant his negligent brother and to set Prospero and his daughter, Miranda, adrift in a rotting boat. Twelve years later, shipwrecked and cast ashore on a strange island but with his villainy still intact, Antonio plans to murder the sleeping Alonso. The intended victim is awakened in time and the killing is averted.

Antonio. In *Twelfth Night,* a sea captain and Sebastian's friend. Exposing himself to the danger of arrest for an old offense, the dedicated and kind Antonio nevertheless accompanies Sebastian to Illyria and gives him his purse (III, iii). Later he mistakes the page Cesario for Sebastian, and is astonished and dismayed when Cesario refuses to return the purse.

Antonio. In *The Two Gentlemen of Verona,* father of Proteus. Antonio dispatches his son to the Emperor's court in Milan, believing that Proteus "cannot be a perfect man, not being tried and tutor'd in the world."

Antony, Mark. Anglicized name of **Marcus Antonius** (c. 83–30 B.C.). Roman triumvir and general; in *Julius Caesar,* one of the triumvirs; in *Antony and Cleopatra,* the hero. Historically, Antony, though somewhat a profligate, gained distinction as a soldier and joined with Julius Caesar, whose consul he became (44). After Caesar's murder, Antony determined to make himself sole ruler of Rome, but he was defeated by Octavius. He later came to terms with Octavius and formed with him and Lepidus the second triumvirate, defeating the republican army led by Brutus and Cassius. Later he met Cleopatra, queen of Egypt; they became lovers, Antony remaining with her until called back to Rome by the death of his wife, Fulvia (40). In Rome he made a diplomatic marriage with Octavia, the sister of Octavius Caesar, but divorced her a few years later to return to Cleopatra. Becoming despotic, Antony provoked a war with Octavius that culminated in his defeat at Actium (31); shortly afterward he killed himself.

In *Julius Caesar,* Antony turns the populace against Brutus and his fellow conspirators with his funeral oration upon Caesar's death. The spirit of Caesar living on in him, he triumphs with Octavius over the republican army led by Brutus and Cassius. As a character, Antony is morally inferior to Brutus but politically more effective; less noble, perhaps, but superior in terms of the larger values of proper order.

Antony and Cleopatra opens with Antony's delay in Egypt because of his love for Cleopatra. To his soldiers Antony is "the triple pillar of the world transform'd/ Into a strumpet's fool" (I, i), but his friends, notably Enobarbus and Dolabella, later confirm the fact of the Queen's vast charm and beauty. The lovers' relationship follows its fateful course in the death of Antony's wife, Fulvia, his return to Rome and marriage to Octavia, Cleopatra's jealousy, their defeat by Octavius at Actium, Antony's despair, his suicide and then Cleopatra's.

Antony is a tragic figure, caught between Cleopatra's timeless sensuality and his own ambition. Although he loses his political being by choosing Cleopatra's world, he is to an extent graced by partaking of that world. While the "proper" order of things triumphs with Octavius' victory at Actium, there is the suggestion, in the nobility of their deaths, that Antony and Cleopatra have themselves triumphed. [*Antony and Cleopatra,* New Variorum Edition, H. H. Furness, ed., 1907.]

THE TRAGEDY OF

ANTHONY and CLEOPATRA.

Antony and Cleopatra. A tragedy by Shakespeare.

Text. The only authority for the text is the FIRST FOLIO (1623). This text, over 3000 lines in length, is far too long to represent the acting version of the piece. This fact indicates that it was probably set up, not from the company's PROMPT-BOOK, but either from

Shakespeare's own manuscript or from a carefully prepared transcript of it. The Folio text is an unusually good one, except for many misprints, most of which were corrected in the Second Folio (1632).

Date. The play was entered in the Stationers' Register, along with *Pericles*, on May 20, 1608, as follows:

> Edward Blount. Entred for his copie under thandes of Sir George Buck knight and Master Warden Seton A booke called. The booke of Pericles prynce of Tyre. vj[d].
>
> Edward Blount. Entred also for his copie by the like Aucthoritie. A booke Called Anthony. and Cleopatra, vj[d].

In 1607 Samuel Daniel published a revised edition of his play *The Tragedie of Cleopatra*, first published in 1594. Daniel's revisions are so much like distinctive features of *Antony and Cleopatra* that some critics think that they prove that Daniel had seen Shakespeare's play on the stage before he embarked upon his altered version. If that is the case, *Antony and Cleopatra* must have been produced, at the latest, early in 1607. However, this relationship between the two works cannot be definitely established. The similarities may have resulted from Shakespeare's having copied Daniel. In this case, *Antony and Cleopatra* would probably have been written late in 1607 or early in 1608. Most scholars incline to the former view, seeing Daniel as the borrower and dating the play 1606–1607.

Sources. The main source is Thomas North's translation (1579) of Plutarch's life of Antony in his *Lives*. Many passages in this work suggested scenes in Shakespeare's play and often furnished the actual words, which were transmuted by the dramatist into poetry. The most famous example of this transformation is Enobarbus' description, to the entranced Agrippa, of Cleopatra sailing down the Cydnus river (II, ii, 196–223). Most of the details in the passage are found in Plutarch. The poet probably also saw a copy of Samuel Daniel's above-mentioned *Tragedie of Cleopatra*, which takes up the story after Antony's death. Daniel's narrative poem "Letter from Octavia," printed in his *Poeticall Essayes* (1599), may have provided an account of the Octavia-Antony relationship. Certain historical details were added to the play from Appian's *Civil Wars*, translated by "W. B." in 1578. Shakespeare may also have consulted Robert Garnier's French neoclassical tragedy *Marc-Antoine* (1578), translated (1590) into English by Mary Herbert, countess of PEMBROKE.—O.J.C.

Plot Synopsis. Act I. In Alexandria the triumvir Mark Antony has become enmeshed in the silken coils of Egypt's Queen, Cleopatra, and devotes himself to revelry and love. Urgent summonses from Rome go unheeded and his followers grumble to see "the triple pillar of the world transform'd / Into a strumpet's fool." He is forced to bestir himself, however, when he learns that his wife, Fulvia, who was in rebellion against Octavius Caesar, has died and that Sextus Pompeius, son of Pompey the Great, is challenging Caesar on the seas. In his absence, Cleopatra scolds her maid Charmian for comparing Julius Caesar to Antony, her "man of men," and sends him greetings every day.

Act II. At a meeting in Rome in the house of Lepidus, the third member of the triumvirate, Octavius Caesar accuses Antony of abusing his messengers and inciting Fulvia to make war on him. They are on the verge of a quarrel when, at the suggestion of the general Agrippa, Antony agrees to marry Octavia, Caesar's sister, in order to strengthen the bonds between them. After Antony and Caesar have gone to see Octavia, Agrippa and Mecaenas, another supporter of Caesar, question Enobarbus, an old friend of Antony, about the splendors of Egypt and its Queen. Enobarbus describes for them the occasion of Cleopatra's first meeting with Antony, when she appeared on the river Cydnus in a barge "like a burnish'd throne." Mecaenas believes that Antony will now leave Cleopatra, but Enobarbus disagrees.

After his marriage to Octavia, Antony asks an Egyptian soothsayer whether Caesar's fortunes shall rise higher than his. The soothsayer replies that Antony's guardian spirit advances only when he is far from Caesar, and Antony ruefully admits that the very dice seem to obey Caesar. He decides to return to Egypt, but first he accompanies Caesar and Lepidus to Misenum, Sicily, where they meet with Pompey. Pompey invites them aboard his galley for a night of feasting, during which Lepidus gets drunk and must be carried to bed. Menas, Pompey's lieutenant, whispers to Pompey that he can become master of the world merely by ordering him to murder his guests. Pompey rejects Menas' proposal but rebukes him for not having acted on his own initiative.

In Alexandria, meanwhile, Cleopatra's gay reminiscences about her life with Antony are rudely interrupted by the arrival of a messenger from Italy, whose countenance betrays the ill-tidings that he bears. When the poor fellow reveals that Antony has married Octavia, he comes close to losing his life at the hands of the enraged Cleopatra.

Act III. Having regained her composure, Cleopatra calls back the messenger and quizzes him about the appearance of her rival. She is relieved to hear that Octavia is a widow of 30, low-voiced, and short of stature—"dull of tongue, and dwarfish," as Cleopatra interprets it—with a round face and a narrow forehead.

Having proceeded to Athens with his bride, Antony is informed that Caesar has spoken slightingly of him and has violated their agreement by making war on Pompey. It is also revealed that Caesar has imprisoned Lepidus. Octavia returns to Rome in an attempt to heal the resulting breach between her husband and her brother, but Caesar, who has learned of Antony's return to Egypt and his division of the Eastern provinces among Cleopatra and her offspring, is in no mood to bargain with him. Declaring himself affronted by Octavia's meager train, Caesar convinces her of Antony's perfidy. He now moves against Antony openly and appears with lightning speed near Actium in Greece. Against the advice of Enobarbus and Canidius, his lieutenant-general, Antony decides to oppose Caesar in a naval engagement. At the height of the battle, before the sickened gaze of Enobarbus, Cleopatra's 60 ships turn tail and flee, and Antony, "like a doting mallard," meekly follows. At this, Canidius resolves to go over to Caesar with all his troops. Antony, overcome with shame for his cowardice, at first reproaches Cleopatra for her flight, but soon asserts that a kiss of hers repays him.

He sends his old schoolmaster, Euphronius, to parley with Caesar, who has arrived in Egypt, but the latter rebuffs him and dispatches one Thyreus to try to separate Cleopatra from Antony. Upon hearing the report of Euphronius, Antony challenges Caesar to personal combat. Enobarbus observes that Caesar has routed not only Antony's soldiers but his judgment as well. Cleopatra receives Thyreus cordially, but Antony orders him whipped and denounces Cleopatra, whom he says he found "as a morsel cold upon / Dead Caesar's trencher." They are soon reconciled, however, and Antony decides to stake everything on another battle. Meanwhile, Enobarbus looks on Antony's frenzied valor with dismay and seeks an opportunity to leave him.

Act IV. Caesar laughs at Antony's challenge and resolves to wage the final battle on the morrow. Enobarbus makes his way to Caesar's camp, but he is overwhelmed with remorse when Antony sends him the chests and treasure he had left behind, and during the battle he dies of a broken heart. Although the battle goes favorably for Antony at first, the desertion of the Egyptians costs him the victory on the second day of fighting. He bitterly accuses Cleopatra of betraying him, and his rage so frightens her that she hides in her monument and instructs her servant Mardian to inform Antony that she has killed herself. Antony resolves to follow her example and asks his friend Eros to kill him. Eros refuses and, while Antony's back is turned, takes his own life instead. Antony then falls on his sword. When Cleopatra, suspecting his intentions, sends word that she is still alive, he asks to be taken to her. He bids her remember that he was once "the greatest prince o' the world" and that he does not die basely but "a Roman by a Roman / Valiantly vanquish'd." After he dies, Cleopatra wonders why she should remain in this "dull" world which in Antony's absence is "no better than a sty."

Act V. Upon hearing of Antony's death, a mournful Caesar sends Proculeius to inform Cleopatra that she has nothing to fear from him. From Dolabella, however, she learns that he plans to lead her in triumph through Rome. Meanwhile, guards are placed outside her monument. Caesar himself comes to the monument and treats her affably, though he warns her not to attempt suicide. She gives him an inventory of her money, plate, and jewels, adding that she has omitted only a few items, and calls Seleucus, her treasurer, to verify her statement. He, however, declares that she has left out enough to purchase what she included. Cleopatra berates Seleucus, but Caesar makes light of the incident. After Caesar's departure, Dolabella tells her that Caesar plans to set out for Syria and to take her and her children with him. Repelled by the thought of becoming the object of the gibes of the Roman rabble, she declares that she is going to join Antony and dons her finest garments. In response to her summons, a clown brings a basket of figs in which some asps are hidden. She applies one asp to her breast and another to her arm and dies tranquilly, together with her maids, Charmian and Iras. Upon returning to the monument and seeing the bodies, Caesar orders that Cleopatra be buried in the same grave as Antony.—H. D.

Comment. *Antony and Cleopatra* displays many of the distinctive features of a chronicle history play: a critical political situation, battles by land and sea, and episodic diversity. Yet all these salient points merely serve to build a theatre in which the tragedy of this peerless pair can be presented. The restless movement of scene from Syria to Rome, to Alexandria, to Caesar's camp, and so on, fulfills the author's purpose: to stage all the martial exploits of his hero and to set the gorgeous panorama of the storied east as a background for his two protagonists. Yet even this great exotic world is too small for the scope that their love demands. Some part of the alien universe impinges on their love, threatens it, and finally destroys it along with the lovers. As *Romeo and Juliet* exalts first love, so *Antony and Cleopatra* presents, with a slight touch of satire, middle-aged love. For the idealism and headlong rashness of *Romeo and Juliet, Antony and Cleopatra* substitutes all the ways of civilized passion, in which both principals are adepts. Their glorifying of their own emotions becomes an obsession. Antony becomes a victim of *hybris,* for he is so obsessed by Cleopatra and her arts of seduction that he almost arrogantly ignores the threat they offer to his military operations and his public duties. He betrays his infatuation in his first colloquy with her:

> Let Rome in Tiber melt, and the wide arch
> Of the ranged empire fall! Here is my space.
> . . . . .
> the nobleness of life
> Is to do thus; when such a mutual pair [*embracing*]
> And such a twain can do't . . . .
> (I, i, 33–34, 36–38)

After his disgraceful flight from battle at Actium, he feels that the ground on which he stands should be ashamed to bear him. Yet, when Cleopatra, all in tears, begs him for pardon, he falls completely under her spell, exclaiming:

> Fall not a tear, I say; one of them rates
> All that is won and lost: give me a kiss;
> Even this repays me.
> (III, xi, 69–71)

Antony, like Shakespeare's other tragic protagonists, is a slave of one of the passions. The lovers' sacrifice of everything else in life to their mutual captivation never renders them despicable. Bernard Shaw's comment that in *Antony and Cleopatra* Shakespeare turns "hogs into heroes" since the modern equivalent of the pair "can be found in every public house" (tavern) is nonsense. Their passion is referred to in terms that lend it grandeur; as Eros, in attempting to obey Antony's command to kill him, says:

> Turn from me, then, that noble countenance,
> Wherein the worship of the whole world lies.
> (IV, xiv, 85–86)

Cleopatra remembers that when he first wooed her

> Eternity was in our lips and eyes,
> Bliss in our brows' bent; none our parts so poor,
> But was a race of heaven: they are so still.
> (I, iii, 35–37)

Throughout the drama this romantic mutual inflation of the lovers continues.

Another serious blemish on Antony's heroic image, his lack of honor in public life, partly results from the decadent political atmosphere in which he has to forge his career. It is a world in which no loyalties, save those of self-interest, prevail. Even the Roman generals on the frontiers of the empire plan their campaigns less to meet the thrusts of the enemy than to insure their political survival in the maze of conflicting selfish ambitions in which they must move. Ventidius, for example, refuses to press his victory over the Parthians to complete triumph for fear of awakening the envy of his superior officers.

This moral decay is most striking in Enobarbus' tragedy. He is a scoffing, realistic commentator, yet Shakespeare puts his qualities in the service of his extraordinary loyalty. His desertion to the enemy destroys him, for in deserting his master he demolishes the cornerstone of his nature, his devotion to Antony. Nothing is now left for him but a ditch wherein to die.

Antony, despite his attractive personal traits—generosity, affability, and magnanimity—is a deeply flawed dramatic protagonist. His suicide is a love-death as surely as that of Isolde in Wagner's opera. It is all for love that he falls upon his sword, for as soon as he receives the false news of Cleopatra's suicide, he finds the glory of his triumph has become meaningless. "Unarm Eros," he cries, "the long day's task is done, / And we must sleep" (IV, xiv, 35–36). All the kingdoms of the world have become clay to him. Cleopatra's supposed suicide to escape disgrace seems to him an act of supreme courage, a tribute paid to honor. His tardiness in taking his own life seems base. The only noble act left for him to perform is the conquest of himself. In death he will again stand up peerless with her. He will overtake her in Elysium, where she will again be his bride. So exulting, he can give his imagination free rein.

> I will be
> A bridegroom in my death, and run into 't
> As to a lover's bed.
>
> (IV, xiv, 99–101)

In his dying farewell to Cleopatra he bids her remember his former fortunes: "Wherein I lived, the greatest prince o' the world, / The noblest" (IV, xv, 54–55). The beauty of imagery in Antony's death scenes and the nobility of his attitude evoke such strong sympathy that recent critics are prone to place the play beside the four great tragedies.

In the early part of the play Cleopatra is little more than a royal courtesan, devising new ways to attract, hold, and influence Antony. Being an Egyptian, she was to Elizabethan audiences a cousin to the gypsies, and, like them, adept at conjuring. It is the infinite variety in her practice of the art of love that makes it like the work of a magician. Her swift and fascinating changes of mood are not so much calculated as instinctive, a coquette's compulsion to attract. "She is cunning past man's thought," exclaims Antony. As he falls deeper and deeper under her spell, he finds his personality disintegrating. To Eros he says in rueful surprise, "Here I am Antony; / Yet cannot hold this visible shape, my knave" (IV, xiv, 13–14). At this point in the story Cleopatra's influence on Antony has become in no way ennobling, but destructive of all the martial virtues that have made him a hero.

Although in the last two acts she continues to dally with Antony's infatuation, the false news of her death that she sends her lover is the supreme example of her juggling with his love. His death in her arms purges her love of its trickery, but not completely of its parade. In preparation for her suicide, she orders her women to array her in all her royal splendor, partly to do Antony honor when she meets him in Elysium, but partly that all those who may chance to see her dead body—Octavius in particular—will wonder at her queenly beauty. She does not take her life in the high Roman fashion, but "pursues conclusions infinite of easy ways to die," so that her suicide, like other events in her life, is a sensuous experience. She imagines the asp that stings her to death to be a baby "that sucks the nurse asleep." Her death is a coda to Antony's tragedy. It does not ennoble her; it merely offers her a transcendent opportunity of exhibiting the artful self-indulgent creature that she has always been. Her death is not, like Antony's, heroic. She is merely a lovely object that Antony's fall topples to ruin with him.

The theme of the action may be said to be the ancient one of the hero's choice of love over empire. The basic structure of the drama is that of a chronicle history, but it is one that serves as the setting of a hero's slavery to one of the passions. The brilliant colors in which the poet has decked his play relates it to Shakespeare's later romances. Like them it appeals to wonder and delight in a world of far away and long ago.—O. J. C.

Stage History: England. A document in the lord chamberlain's records, dated January 1669, lists *Antony and Cleopatra* as one of Shakespeare's 21 plays assigned to the King's Company. It describes the play as "formerly acted at the Blackfryers," indicating that the drama had been staged there sometime after the King's Men had taken possession of the building in 1608. There is no record of any other production before the closing of the theatres in 1642. After the Restoration it was driven from the stage for 100 years by Dryden's *All for Love*, first produced at Drury Lane in 1678. In 1759 David Garrick revived *Antony and Cleopatra*. The acting text of this production was prepared by the Shakespeare scholar and editor Edward Capell. Capell made generous cuts, reduced the number of characters, and transferred speeches to other characters than those Shakespeare had assigned them to. Garrick, playing Antony to the Cleopatra of George Anne Bellamy, spent large sums on lavish sets and costumes, but his production ran for only six nights. On November 15, 1813 John Philip Kemble revived the tragedy, making, however, many alterations and reinserting many passages from *All for Love*. The last act, a strange mixture of Dryden and Shakespeare, ended with a funeral procession accompanied by instrumental music and choral singing. In spite of Kemble's efforts to add glamor to the play, the production was presented only nine times. At Drury Lane, Charles Macready gave three performances, on November 21 and 22 and December 2, 1833, and expressed dissatisfaction with almost every feature of the production, including his own portrayal of Antony. The next revival was produced by Samuel Phelps at Sadler's Wells in 1849. But when, in 1867, Phelps' Cleopatra, Miss Glyn, repeated her role in Charles Calvert's mangled version of the play at the Princess' Theatre, the production failed. Another failure followed in 1873 at Drury Lane. Andrew Halliday had gone even further than Calvert in reducing the tragedy to a mere episodic review of the loves of Antony and Cleopatra for this spectacle. Lily Langtry's pretentious revival at Princess' Theatre featured herself as an inadequate Cleopatra opposite Charles Coghlan's Antony. This was in 1890, and once again the lovers failed despite their sumptuous surroundings.

Frank Benson first produced the play at Stratford-upon-Avon in 1898 in an ornate setting, and later in 1912. In between, he brought this production to the Lyceum Theatre in 1900. Benson's Antony and Oscar Asche's Pompey were singled out for praise by the critics.

Beerbohm Tree staged a scenic extravaganza which opened December 27, 1906. This production was notable for the naturally imperious Cleopatra of Constance Collier, the harsh Enobarbus of Lyn Harding, but even more for the splendor of the sets and the beauty of the costumes.

On December 4, 1922 a revolution in the style of producing *Antony and Cleopatra* occurred when Robert Atkins staged it at the Old Vic Theatre. Abandoning the traditional method of giving a realistic setting to each of the 42 scenes, Atkins used an almost bare stage and brought the curtain down only once during the entire performance. All subsequent producers have followed Atkins and adopted the idea of symbolic scenery and of few, if any, interruptions.

There were productions in 1925 at the Old Vic with the seasoned Baliol Holloway as Antony opposite Edith Evans; in 1927, at Stratford, Wilfrid Walter played Antony and Dorothy Green was Cleopatra. In 1930 Harcourt Williams directed *Antony and Cleopatra* at the Old Vic with Dorothy Green as Cleopatra and John Gielgud as Antony. W. Bridges-Adams staged the play at Stratford the next year, but his Antony and Cleopatra, Gyles Isham and Dorothy Massingham, did not equal the portrayals of Miss Green and Gielgud.

In 1934 the Old Vic presented the tragedy again, this time less successfully. Henry Cass, directing his first production for that company, calamitously miscast Wilfrid Lawson in the role of Antony, and the play failed, although Maurice Evans was a successful Octavius. For his first season at Stratford in 1935, B. Iden Payne also chose *Antony and Cleopatra*, staging a picturesque presentation with Catherine Lacey as Cleopatra and Randle Ayrton as Enobarbus.

A drastically cut version was offered by Theodore Komisarjevsky at the New Theatre in 1936. Disastrous in this elaborate production was Eugenie Leontovich, a Russian comedienne, who, cast as Cleopatra, made the verse unintelligible. Donald Wolfit played Antony, but his talents, combined with those of Leon Quartermaine, Ion Swinley, George Hayes, and Margaret Rawlings in supporting roles, could not save this injudicious experiment. Komisarjevsky's *Antony and Cleopatra* had only four performances.

Ten years later another much-discussed production was staged by Glen Byam Shaw. For his set Shaw used a permanent structure, the recess of which was contrived to denote specific localities, such as a barred door for the monument. Edith Evans, playing Cleopatra for the first time since 1925, and Godfrey Tearle as Antony were both disappointing. Shaw enjoyed success with the play when, in 1953 at Stratford, his cast included Peggy Ashcroft, temperamentally perfect as Cleopatra; Michael Redgrave, abandoned as Antony; and Harry Andrews as Enobarbus.

In 1951 Laurence Olivier and Vivien Leigh played *Antony and Cleopatra* at the St. James. Theirs were somewhat hushed yet effective portraits in Michael Benthall's swiftly moving production, set on a revolving stage devised by Roger Furse. Robert Helpmann directed a London production at the Old Vic in 1957.

Stage History: America. *Antony and Cleopatra* was first performed on the American stage in April 1846 at the Park Theatre in New York. It featured an excellent cast, including George Vandenhoff and Harriet Bland in the title roles, John Dyott as Octavius, and Humphrey Bland as Enobarbus. Although well acted and elaborately staged, the production ran for only six performances. In 1854 and 1855 the tragedy was presented at the Old Broadway Theatre and appeared again, with completely new scenery and historically accurate costumes, as that theatre's final production, opening on March 7, 1859. The last two performances of that revival, both given on April 2, 1859, were for the benefit of the Old Broadway's manager, Edward Eddy, who played Antony opposite Mme. Ponisi's alluring Cleopatra. The previous year James Collier and Maggie Mitchell had starred in the tragedy at the Bowery Theatre, and in April 1859 Julia Dean Hayne portrayed Cleopatra at Niblo's Garden. At that same theatre in April 1877 Joseph Wheelock, Sr., and Agnes Booth impersonated Antony and Cleopatra, while H. B. Phillips acted Enobarbus in a lavish production which sacrificed the essence of the tragedy to elaborate pageantry. That November another opulent presentation of *Antony and Cleopatra*, produced by Rose Eytinge, appeared at the Broadway Theatre. Miss Eytinge gave a highly commendable impersonation of a fiery and capricious Cleopatra, opposite Frederick B. Warde's Antony, and was the most significant interpreter of the Nile Queen seen in the United States throughout the 1800's. In 1889 the tragedy achieved its longest American run up to that time with 57 consecutive performances, beginning on January 8 at Palmer's Theatre. Kyrle Bellew, this production's Antony, arranged the play in 6 acts and 14 scenes, cut Octavia's part, and presented the tragedy solely as a drama of sensuality. Neither Bellew nor his co-star, Cora Urquhart Potter, supported by Ian Robertson's Octavius and Henry Edwards' Enobarbus, approached adequacy in the leading roles. In 1892 R. D. MacLean and Marie Prescott acted Antony and Cleopatra at the Union Square Theatre, and for the first production at the ill-fated New Theatre in November 1909, Edward H. Sothern and Julia Marlowe took the title roles under Louis Calvert's direction. Defective acoustics blighted the performances, which, though intelligent, generally lacked passion. After a short time, Sothern and Miss Marlowe dropped the characterizations from their repertory. Jane Cowl appeared opposite Rollo Peters in 1924. In 1937 Tallulah Bankhead appeared in a costly revival at the Mansfield Theatre which closed after only five performances. Miss Bankhead's courageous attempt to deviate from tradition with an historical portrait of Cleopatra as a designing woman devoid of queenly qualities lacked subtlety and received little support from the ponderous Antony of Conway Tearle. Despite a valiant effort by Thomas Chalmers in the drastically cut role of Enobarbus, the character became ineffectual and the production was labeled most discouraging. A highly successful *Antony and Cleopatra* followed 10 years later. Under Guthrie McClintic's direction, and starring Godfrey Tearle and Katharine Cornell in the title roles, with Kent Smith as Enobarbus, the production ran for 126 performances from November 26, 1947.

The American Shakespeare Festival's production at Stratford, Connecticut, in 1960 featured Robert Ryan as a rather foolish Antony and Katharine Hepburn as a peculiarly unseductive Cleopatra. Joseph Papp's concert reading of the tragedy in 1959, with the cast seated on chairs arranged in a straight row, proved most satisfactory to those who like Shakespeare readings. A more conventional offering by Papp at the New York Shakespeare Festival in 1963 was of little consequence; most of the verse was spoken indifferently and, although Michael Higgins performed competently as Antony, Colleen Dewhurst was miscast as Cleopatra.—M.G.

Bibliography. TEXT: *Antony and Cleopatra*, New Cambridge Edition, J. Dover Wilson, ed., 1950; *Antony and Cleopatra*, New Arden Edition, M. R. Ridley, ed., 1954. DATE: Arthur Norman, "Daniel's *The Tragedie of Cleopatra* and the Date of *Antony and Cleopatra*," *Modern Language Review*, LIV, 1959. SOURCES: Kenneth Muir, *Shakespeare's Sources*, Vol. I, 1957; Geoffrey Bullough, *Narrative and Dramatic Sources of Shakespeare*, Vol. V, 1964. COMMENT: M. W. MacCallum, *Shakespeare's Roman Plays and Their Background*, 1910; Levin L. Schücking, *Character Problems in Shakespeare's Plays*, 1922; Caroline Spurgeon, *Shakespeare's Imagery and What It Tells Us*, 1935. STAGE HISTORY: New Cambridge Edition; T. Alston Brown, *A History of the New York Stage . . . to 1901*, 1903; William Winter, *Shakespeare on the Stage*, 3 vols., 1911–1916; G. C. D. Odell, *Shakespeare from Betterton to Irving*, 1920; J. C. Trewin, *Shakespeare on the English Stage, 1900–1964*, 1964.

Selected Criticism

SAMUEL JOHNSON. This Play keeps curiosity always busy, and the passions always interested. The continual hurry of the action, the variety of incidents, and the quick succession of one personage to another, call the mind forward without intermission from the first Act to the last. But the power of delighting is derived principally from the frequent changes of the scene; for, except the feminine arts, some of which are too low, which distinguish *Cleopatra*, no character is very strongly discriminated. *Upton*, who did not easily miss what he desired to find, has discovered that the language of *Antony* is, with great skill and learning, made pompous and superb, according to his real practice. But I think his diction not distinguishable from that of others: the most tumid speech in the Play is that which *Caesar* makes to *Octavia*.

The events, of which the principal are described according to history, are produced without any art of connection or care of disposition. [*The Plays of William Shakespeare*, 1765.]

SAMUEL TAYLOR COLERIDGE. This play should be perused in mental contrast with Romeo and Juliet;—as the love of passion and appetite opposed to the love of affection and instinct. But the art displayed in the character of Cleopatra is profound in this, especially, that the sense of criminality in her passion is lessened by our insight into its depth and energy, at the very moment that we cannot but perceive that the passion itself springs out of the habitual craving of a licentious nature, and that it is supported and reinforced by voluntary stimulus and sought-for associations, instead of blossoming out of spontaneous emotion.

But of all perhaps of Shakespeare's plays the most wonderful is the *Antony and Cleopatra*. [There are] scarcely any in which he has followed history more minutely, and yet few even of his own in which he impresses the notion of giant strength so much, perhaps none in which he impresses it more strongly. This [is] owing to the manner in which it is sustained throughout—that he *lives* in and through the play—to the numerous momentary flashes of nature counteracting the historic abstraction, in which take as a specimen the [death of Cleopatra]. [Notes on the Tragedies, c. 1819; reprinted in *Shakespearean Criticism* by S. T. Coleridge, T. M. Raysor, ed., Everyman Library Edition, 1960.]

ANNA BROWNELL JAMESON. What is most astonishing in the character of Cleopatra is its antithetical construction—its *consistent inconsistency*, if I may use such an expression—which renders it quite impossible to reduce it to any elementary principles. It will, perhaps, be found, on the whole, that vanity and the love of power predominate; but I dare not say it *is* so, for these qualities and a hundred others mingle into each other, and shift, and change, and glance away, like the colors in a peacock's train.

. . . in Cleopatra it is the absence of unity and simplicity which strikes us; the impression is that of perpetual and irreconcilable contrast. The continual approximation of whatever is most opposite in character, in situation, in sentiment, would be fatiguing, were it not so perfectly natural: the woman herself would be distracting, if she were not so enchanting.

I have not the slightest doubt that Shakespeare's Cleopatra is the real historical Cleopatra—the "rare Egyptian"—individualized and placed before us. Her mental accomplishments, her unequalled grace, her woman's wit and woman's wiles, her irresistible allurements, her starts of irregular grandeur, her bursts of ungovernable temper, her vivacity of imagination, her petulant caprice, her fickleness and her falsehood, her tenderness and her truth, her childish susceptibility to flattery, her magnificent spirit, her royal pride, the gorgeous eastern coloring of the character—all these contradictory elements has Shakespeare seized, mingled them in their extremes, and fused them into one brilliant impersonation of classical elegance, Oriental voluptuousness, and gipsy sorcery. [*Shakespeare's Heroines;* originally published in *Characteristics of Women*, 1832.]

A. C. SWINBURNE. It would seem a sign or birth-mark of only the greatest among poets that they should be sure to rise instantly for awhile above the very highest of their native height at the touch of a thought of Cleopatra. So was it, as we all know, with William Shakespeare: so is it, as we all see, with Victor Hugo. As we feel in the marvellous and matchless verses of *Zim-Zizimi* all the splendour and fragrance and miracle of her mere bodily presence, so from her first imperial dawn on the stage of Shakespeare to the setting of that eastern star behind a pall of undissolving cloud we feel the charm and the terror and the mystery of her absolute and royal soul.

Never has he given such proof of his incomparable instinct for abstinence from the wrong thing as well as achievement of the right. He has utterly rejected and disdained all occasion of setting her off by means of any lesser foil than all the glory of the world with all its empires. And we need not Antony's example to show us that these are less than straws in the balance. . . . Even as that Roman grasp relaxed and let fall the world, so has Shakespeare's self let go for awhile his greater world of imagination, with all its all but infinite variety of life and thought and action, for love of that more infinite variety which custom could not stale. Himself a second and a yet more fortunate Antony, he has once more laid a world, and a world more wonderful than ever, at her feet. He has put aside for her sake all other forms and figures of womanhood; he, father or creator of Rosalind, of Cordelia, of Desdemona, and of Imogen, he too, like the sun-god and sender of all song, has anchored his eyes on her whom 'Phoebus' amorous pinches' could not leave 'black,' nor 'wrinkled deep in time'; on that incarnate and imperishable 'spirit of sense,' to whom at the very last 'The stroke of death is as a lover's pinch, That hurts, and is desired.' To him, as to the dying husband of Octavia, this creature of his own hand might have boasted herself that the loveliest and purest among all her sisters of his begetting, 'with her modest eyes, and still conclusion, shall acquire no honour, Demurring upon me.' To sum up, Shakespeare has elsewhere given us in ideal incarnation the perfect mother, the perfect wife, the perfect daughter, the perfect mistress, or the perfect maiden: here only once for all he has given us the perfect and the everlasting woman. [*A Study of Shakespeare*, 1880.]

A. C. BRADLEY. Why is it that, although we close the book in a triumph which is more than reconciliation, this is mingled, as we look back on the story, with a sadness so peculiar, almost the sadness of disenchantment? Is it that, when the glow has faded, Cleopatra's ecstasy comes to appear, I would not say factitious, but an effort strained and prodigious as well as glorious, not, like Othello's last speech, the final expression of character, of thoughts and emotions which have dominated a whole life? Perhaps this is so, but there is something more, something that sounds paradoxical: we are saddened by the very fact that the catastrophe saddens us so little; it pains us that we should feel so much triumph and pleasure. In *Romeo and Juliet, Hamlet, Othello*, though in a sense we accept the deaths of hero and heroine, we feel a keen sorrow. We look back, think how noble or beautiful they were, wish that fate had opposed to them a weaker enemy, dream possibly of the life they might then have led. Here we can hardly do this. With all our admiration and sympathy for the lovers we do not wish them to gain the world. It is better for the world's sake, and not less for their own, that they should fail and die. At the very first they came before us, unlike those others, unlike Coriolanus and even Macbeth, in a glory already tarnished, half-ruined by their past. Indeed one source of strange and most unusual effect in their story is that this marvellous passion comes to adepts in the experience and art of passion, who might be expected to have worn its charm away. Its splendour dazzles us; but when the splendour vanishes, we do not mourn, as we mourn for the love of Romeo or Othello, that a thing so bright and good should die. And the fact that we mourn so little saddens us.

A comparison of Shakespearean tragedies seems to prove that the tragic emotions are stirred in the fullest possible measure only when such beauty or nobility of character is displayed as commands unreserved admiration or love; or when, in default of this, the forces which move the agents, and the conflict which results from these forces, attain a terrifying and overwhelming power. The four most famous tragedies satisfy one or both of these conditions; *Antony and Cleopatra*, though a great tragedy, satisfies neither of them completely. But to say this is not to criticise it. It does not attempt to satisfy these conditions, and then fail in the attempt. It attempts something different, and succeeds as triumphantly as *Othello* itself. In doing so it gives us what no other tragedy can give, and it leaves us, no less than any other, lost in astonishment at the powers which created it. [*Oxford Lectures on Poetry*, 1909.]

BENEDETTO CROCE. The tragedy of the good and evil will is sometimes followed, sometimes preceded, by another tragedy, that of the will itself. Here the will, instead of holding the passions in control—making its footstool of them—allows itself to be dominated by them in their onrush; or it seeks the good, but remains uncertain, dissatisfied as to the path chosen; or finally, when it fails to find its own way, a way of some sort, and does not know what to think of itself or of the world, it preys upon itself in this empty tension.

A typical form of this first condition of the will is voluptuousness, which overspreads a soul and makes itself mistress there, inebriating, sending to sleep, destroying, and liquefying the will. When we think of that enchanting sweetness and perdition, the image of death arises at the same instant, because it truly is death, if not physical, yet always internal and moral death, death of the spirit, without which man is already a corpse in process of decomposition. The tragedy of *Antony and Cleopatra* is composed of the violent sense of pleasure, in its power to bind and to dominate, coupled with a shudder at its abject effects of dissolution and of death. [*Ariosto, Shakespeare and Corneille*, 1920.]

CAROLINE F. E. SPURGEON. The group of images in *Antony and Cleopatra* which, on analysis, immediately attracts attention as peculiar to this play, consists of images of the world, the firmament, the ocean and vastness generally. That is the dominating note in the play, magnificence and grandeur, expressed in many ways, and pictured by continually stimulating our imaginations to see the colossal figure of Antony, 'demi-Atlas of this earth', 'triple pillar of the world', built on so vast a scale that the whole habitable globe is but a toy to him, as it were a ball or apple which he quarters with his sword, playing with 'half the bulk of it' as he pleases, 'making and marring fortunes'.

Antony himself touches this note at once in his royal love-making, when he tells Cleopatra that if she would put a bourn to the measure of his love, she must 'needs find out new heaven, new earth'. . . .

This vastness of scale is kept constantly before us by the use of the word 'world,' which occurs forty-two times, nearly double, or more than double, as often as in most other plays, and it is continually employed in a way which increases the sense of grandeur, power and space, and which fills the imagination with the conception of beings so great that physical size is annihilated and the whole habitable globe shrinks in comparison with them. Caesar, lamenting his differences with Antony, cries,

> if I knew
> What hoop should hold us stanch, from edge to edge
> O' the world I would pursue it;
> (II, ii, 115)

and Octavia declares that wars between these two mighty ones, her husband and her brother, would be

> As if the world should cleave, and that slain men
> Should solder up the rift.
> (III, iv, 31)

The emotional effect of such a simile as this is incalculable, with its amazing picture of the gigantic gaping fissures in the round globe packed tight with the bodies of the dead. Were the feeling in it not so intense, it would verge on the grotesque, as do some others among these vast world images. Such, for instance, is the kind of huge gargoyle depicted by the saturnine Enobarbus when he hears that Caesar has deposed Lepidus, thus leaving only Antony and himself in power. He imagines them as the two mighty jaws in the world's face, grinding and destroying everything that comes between them, and exclaims,

> Then, world, thou hast a pair of chaps, no more;
> And throw between them all the food thou hast,
> They'll grind the one the other.
> (III, v, 14)

Antony's imagination moves on this same vast plane, and the pictures that he draws stimulate our vision and keep us ever conscious of the puny size of even the greatest of worldly princes, powers and spaces compared to his stupendous force. Especially is this so when power is slipping from him, when the old lion is dying, and the tragedy is thus increased by contrast. With what a sublime sweep of simple words he sums up his earlier activities:

> I, that with my sword
> Quarter'd the world, and o'er green Neptune's back
> With ships made cities;
> (IV, xiv, 57)

and how vivid is the picture of the kings of the earth starting forth at his call, like small boys in a scramble, crying out to know what is his will! When he is angry, the insolent magnificence of his images surpasses that of all others in Shakespeare. [*Shakespeare's Imagery*, 1935.]

S. L. BETHELL. Egypt and Rome are thus opposed throughout the play: they represent contradictory schemes of value, contradictory attitudes to, and interpretations of, the universe. It is difficult to isolate these opposed systems in a brief space without appearing to dogmatise, and the reader must understand that a great many supporting quotations have been omitted in order to reduce the argument into a reasonable compass. The whole play should be read with the opposition of Egyptian and Roman values in mind. First, then, Egypt and Rome stand respectively for love and duty, or for pleasure and duty, or even love-pleasure and duty. Supporting quotations are hardly necessary here: Cleopatra embodies the love-pleasure principle, of which the 'Roman thought' (I. ii. 87), the call to duty, is the negation. Closely related to this is the opposition of indulgence and restraint: in Egypt 'Epicurean cooks' (II. i. 24) provided breakfasts as horrifying to Mecaenas as to the modern mind. . . .

Antony chose Egypt, intuition, the life of the spontaneous affections, with its moral and aesthetic corollaries; of all which Cleopatra is the focus and symbol. Shakespeare does not satisfy the psychologists with his character of Cleopatra; but he does not attempt a character in the sense of Trollope, or George Eliot, or even Dickens. In Cleopatra he presents the mystery of woman, the mystery of sensuality, an exploration of the hidden energies of life, and a suggestion of its goal. Intuition or spontaneous feeling is opposed to practical wisdom, generosity to prudence, love to duty, the private affections to public service; and the former in each instance is preferred. Not that the Roman values are entirely repudiated: there is a case for Caesar, 'Fortune's knave' (V. ii. 3) though he be. But the Egyptian values are affirmative; the Roman, negative or restrictive: the good life may be built upon the Egyptian, but not upon the Roman. It is a way of saying that the strong sinner may enter heaven before the prudential legislator. In *Antony and Cleopatra* the strong sinners meet their purgatory here. They do not desire or seek it; it is forced upon them from without—grace which visits them in the guise of defeat. Changes of character inexplicable by psychological determinism are readily explained if we perceive that Shakespeare is applying theological categories. Earthly defeat is the providential instrument of eternal triumph: it comes undesired, but when it comes, is freely accepted, and so converted into a process of necessary cleansing. Antony's purgatory lies in military failure and a bungled suicide prompted by the false report of Cleopatra's death; Cleopatra's in surviving Antony, and in the thought of a Roman triumph. In the end the better Roman qualities are needed to transmute the Egyptian into eternal validity. [*Shakespeare and the Popular Dramatic Tradition*, 1944.]

W. K. WIMSATT. What is celebrated in *Antony and Cleopatra* is the passionate surrender of an illicit love, the victory of this love over practical, political and moral concerns, and the final superiority of the suicide lovers over circumstance. That is a crudely one-sided statement which makes the play as plainly immoral as it can be made. There is of course far more—the complex, wanton and subtle wiles of the voluptuary queen, her infinite variety which age cannot wither nor custom stale, the grizzled and generous manhood and the military bravery of Antony—the whole opulent and burnished panorama of empire and its corruptions. Such intricacies and depths surely at least add to the interest of immorality and—without making it any more moral—yet make it more understandable, more than a mere barren vileness, a filthy negation. It is to be noted that the reasons on the side of morality are so far as possible undercut, diminished or removed from the play. The politics from which Antony secedes are not a noble Roman republicanism, the ideals of a Brutus or a Cato, but the treacheries and back-stabbing of a drunken party on a pirate's barge. The victimized Octavia is a pallid and remote figure, never (as in Dryden's version) made to appear as a rival motive to the Egyptian seductions. The suicides which provide the catastrophe have at least the subjective palliation that they are within the Stoic code which is the standard of the whole scene.

> Give me my robe, put on my crown; I have
> Immortal longings in me; now no more
> The juice of Egypt's grape shall moist this lip.
> Yare, yare, good Iras; quick. Methinks I hear
> Antony call; I see him rouse himself
> To praise my noble act; I hear him mock
> The luck of Caesar, which the gods give men
> To excuse their after wrath: husband, I come:
> Now to that name my courage prove my title!
> I am fire and air; my other elements
> I give to baser life.

There is no escaping the fact that the poetic splendor of this play, and in particular of its concluding scenes, is something which exists in closest juncture with the acts of suicide and the whole glorified story of passion. The poetic values are strictly dependent—if not upon the immorality as such—yet upon the immoral acts. Even though, or rather because, the play pleads for certain evil choices, it presents these choices in all their mature interest and capacity to arouse human sympathy. The motives are wrong, but they are not base, silly, or degenerate. They are not lacking in the positive being of deep and complex human desire. It is not possible to despise Antony and Cleopatra. If one will employ the classic concept of "imitation," the play imitates or presents the reasons for sin, a mature and richly human state of sin. ["Poetry and Morals; a Relation Reargued," *Thought*, No. 23, 1948.]

MAYNARD MACK. Are we to take the high-sounding phrases which introduce us to this remarkable love affair in the play's first scene as amorous rant?

> *Cleopatra*. If it be love indeed, tell me how much.
> *Antony*. There's beggary in the love that can be reckoned.
> *Cleopatra*. I'll set a bourn how far to be beloved.
> *Antony*. Then must thou needs find out new heaven, new earth.

Or is there a prophetic resonance in that reference to "new heaven, new earth," which we are meant to remember when Cleopatra, dreaming of a transcendent Antony—

> His face was as the heav'ns, and therein stuck
> A sun and moon, which kept their course and lighted
> The little O, th' earth. . . .
> His legs bestrid the ocean: his reared arm
> Crested the world: his voice was propertied
> As all the tunèd spheres—

consigns her baser elements to "baser life"? Does the passion of these two remain a destructive element to the bitter end, doomed like all the feeling in the play "to rot itself with motion"? Or, as the world slips from them, have they a glimmering of something they could not have earlier understood, of another power besides death "Which shackles accidents and bolts up change"? Is it "paltry to be Caesar," as Cleopatra claims, since "Not being Fortune, he's but Fortune's knave"? Or is it more paltry to be Antony, and, as Caesar sees it, "give a kingdom for a mirth," as well as, eventually, the world?

To such questions, *Antony and Cleopatra*, like life itself, gives no clear-cut answers. Shakespeare holds the balance even, and does not decide for us who finally is the strumpet of the play, Antony's Cleopatra, or Caesar's Fortune, and who, therefore, is the "strumpet's fool." Those who would have it otherwise, who are "hot for certainties in this our life," as Meredith phrased it, should turn to other authors than Shakespeare, and should have been born into some other world than this. [Introduction to *Antony and Cleopatra*, The Pelican Shakespeare, 1960.]

Apemantus. In *Timon of Athens*, a cynical philosopher. Timon disregards Apemantus' warnings that his friends are false. On discovering the truth, however, the openhanded nobleman becomes an even greater misanthrope than the old philosopher.

apocrypha. Plays outside of the 37 (including *Pericles*) in the CANON that have been attributed to Shakespeare. Since the 17th century about 50 Elizabethan plays have been ascribed to Shakespeare with little or no evidence to support the ascriptions. Only three plays in the apocrypha have any serious claim to be considered Shakespearean: TWO NOBLE KINSMEN and SIR THOMAS MORE, which have received general acceptance as partly by Shakespeare, and EDWARD III, which has strong evidence in favor of its acceptance.

The remaining plays in the apocrypha have received little or no credence as Shakespeare's. They include six plays that were published in the Third Folio (1663): LOCRINE, SIR JOHN OLDCASTLE, THOMAS LORD CROMWELL, THE LONDON PRODICAL, THE PURITAN, and A YORKSHIRE TRAGEDY. Other plays ascribed to Shakespeare in the 17th century include THE BIRTH OF MERLIN, THE MERRY DEVIL OF EDMONTON, MUCEDORUS, THE SECOND MAIDEN'S TRAGEDY, and FAIR EM. In the 18th century the list was expanded to include the lost play CARDENIO, and ARDEN OF FEVERSHAM. More recent has been the attempt to ascribe the manuscript play EDMUND IRONSIDES to Shakespeare. In addition, three lost plays were entered in the Stationers' Register as Shakespeare's by the bookseller Humphrey Moseley; these are DUKE HUMPHREY, IPHIS AND IANTHA, and KING STEPHEN.

To this list might be added three Shakespearean

source plays, *The Troublesome Raigne of King John, The Taming of A Shrew,* and THE FAMOUS VICTORIES OF HENRY V. The first two, it has been suggested, are not sources, but "bad quartos" of Shakespeare's *King John* and *The Taming of the Shrew; The Famous Victories* has been seen as Shakespeare's early attempt at chronicle drama. [Baldwin Maxwell, "The Shakespeare Apocrypha," *Shakespeare Newsletter*, XIV, 1964.]

Apollonius of Tyre. See John GOWER.

Apologie for Actors. A pamphlet written by Thomas HEYWOOD around 1608 but not published until 1612. *Apologie* was written in response to the Puritan attacks on the stage (see ENEMIES OF THE STAGE). Heywood's defense of the theatre is distinguished by its comparative objectivity. He readily grants that in part the Puritan opposition to actors for their licentiousness and loose living is justified. He also deplores the growing satiric element in drama, specifically the comedy of humours popularized by Jonson. Nevertheless he asserts that the great majority of actors are men "of sober lives and temperate carriages," and he presents an elaborate case for the moral and practical virtues which acting can inculcate, at one point echoing Hamlet's advice to the players (III, ii, 19–20) by asserting that acting enables one "to fit his phrases to his action and his action to his phrase."

Heywood's *Apologie* is important for its apparent reference to Shakespeare in the Epistle. (See THE PASSIONATE PILGRIM.) It has also been useful to scholars attempting to date the careers of some Elizabethan and Jacobean actors, whom Heywood refers to as having been before his time and about whom information is otherwise unavailable.

Apothecary. In *Romeo and Juliet*, a minor character. In V, i, the Apothecary accepts Romeo's offer of 40 ducats and, breaking the law of Mantua, sells him a dram of deadly poison.

apparitions. See GHOSTS AND APPARITIONS.

Apuleius, Lucius (c. 125–?). Orator and rhetorician. Apuleius' *Metamorphoses*, better known as *The Golden Ass*, was excellently translated into English in 1566 by William Adlington. A picaresque narrative of the adventures of a young man who has been transformed into an ass, the *Metamorphoses* is probably the source of Bottom's transformation in *A Midsummer Night's Dream* (see MIDSUMMER NIGHT'S DREAM: *Sources*). It has also been suggested that Shakespeare is indebted to Apuleius for Valentine's adventures among the outlaws in *Two Gentlemen of Verona*, for the episode of the hunting of the boar in *Venus and Adonis*, for the witches' incantation scene in *Macbeth* (IV, i, 1–94), and for the plot of the Queen's attempt to poison Imogen in *Cymbeline*. [D. T. Starnes, "Shakespeare and Apuleius," *PMLA*, 60, 1945.]

Aquitaine, Eleanor or **Elinor of.** See ELEANOR OR ELINOR OF AQUITAINE.

Arber, Edward (1836–1912). Antiquary. For 24 years a clerk in the admiralty office in London, Arber became an English lecturer at University College, London, then professor of English at Mason College, Birmingham, and finally emeritus professor in London and fellow of King's College. An editor of old books and documents, he published three series of reprints of English authors to meet the need for reliable texts at reasonable prices; for years some of them remained the only readily available texts. These were: *English Reprints* (30 vols., 1868–1871), including Gosson's *School of Abuse* and *Tottel's Miscellany; An English Garner* (8 vols., 1877–1896); and *The English Scholar's Library* (16 vols., 1878–1884). Along with his *Term Catalogues, 1668–1709* (3 vols., 1903–1906), his most valuable contribution to English studies is his *Transcript of the Registers of the Company of Stationers of London, 1554–1640* (5 vols., 1875–1894). Arber himself privately printed these works, which he compiled from booksellers' lists and which contain certain material not accessible elsewhere.

Arcadia (1590). A long pastoral romance in prose and verse written by Sir Philip SIDNEY for the entertainment of his sister Mary Herbert, countess of PEMBROKE. The *Arcadia* is preserved in two different versions: a relatively straightforward account which existed only in manuscript until the 20th century, and a highly involved and ornate revision, unfortunately never completed because of Sidney's death in 1586. The latter was published in 1590 as *The Countess of Pembroke's Arcadia* and, in various formats, went through a number of editions. The earlier version of *Arcadia* represents a fusion of the traditions of PASTORALISM and GREEK ROMANCES; the revised version represents an attempt to recast this romance into something approaching a prose epic. The book exerted a considerable influence on subsequent literature, helping to bring about the popularity of the

TITLE PAGE OF THE FIRST EDITION OF SIDNEY'S *The Countesse of Pembrokes Arcadia* (1590).

THE
COVNTESSE
OF PEMBROKES
ARCADIA,
WRITTEN BY SIR PHILIPPE
SIDNEI.

LONDON
Printed for William Ponsonbie.
Anno Domini, 1590.

so-called romances in drama, such as *Cymbeline, Pericles,* and *A Winter's Tale.* It is certain that Shakespeare knew *Arcadia,* for he used one of the episodes—the tale of the blind king of Paphlagonia—for the Gloucester subplot in *King Lear.* See KING LEAR: *Sources.*

Archer, Edward (fl. 1656). London bookseller and publisher of plays. In 1656 Archer issued a catalogue titled *An Exact and perfect Catalogue of all the Plaies that were ever printed together with all the Authors names* in which he gratuitously ascribed to Shakespeare the authorship of George Peele's *Arraignment of Paris,* Henry Chettle's *Tragedy of Hoffman,* Beaumont and Fletcher's *Chances,* and Thomas Kyd's *Spanish Tragedy,* as well as the anonymous *London Prodigal* and *Mucedorus.*

archery. Since medieval times the longbow had been the Englishman's principal weapon of war. Shakespeare was born in an era when every male child was legally required to demonstrate his facility with the longbow, and he was therefore familiar with the terms normally associated with archery.

There were three principal types of shooting: prick or clout, butt, and roving. In the first, the canvas-covered target was located at a distance of 160 to 240 yards from the bowman. The target, or clout, which was about 18 inches across, had on it a white circle, in the center of which was a wooden peg; one "hit the white" or "cleft the pin." In the second type, butt shooting, the archer aimed at targets on earthen butts at a distance of 100 to 140 yards. In the third type, roving shooting, the archer shot at unknown distances over open ground.

There are numerous references to the various types of shooting in several plays. In *Romeo and Juliet,* for example, Mercutio mockingly describes Romeo, smitten by love, as

> . . . stabbed with a white wench's black eye; shot thorough the ear with a love-song; the very pin of his heart cleft with the blind bow-boy's butt-shaft . . .
>
> (II, iv, 13–16)

In *3 Henry VI,* when the army of Queen Margaret has won the field, Richard cries out "I am your butt, and I abide your shot" (I, iv, 29).

Arrows varied with the type of shooting. For prick and roving, light arrows were required. For butt shooting, arrows were heavier, as were the barbed war arrows. Two or three matched arrows, known to fly exactly alike, were called a flight. In *The Merchant of Venice,* Bassanio recalls his prowess:

> In my school-days, when I had lost one shaft,
> I shot his fellow of the self-same flight
> The self-same way with more advised watch,
> To find the other forth, and by adventuring both
> I oft found both.
>
> (I, i, 140–144)

[H. Walrond, "Archery," *Shakespeare's England,* 1916.]

Archidamus. In *The Winter's Tale,* a Bohemian lord. Archidamus and Camillo discuss Polixenes' visit to Sicilia (I, i).

Arcite. In *The Two Noble Kinsmen,* one of the kinsmen of the title and a nephew to Creon, King of Thebes. Though banished by Theseus from Athens, Arcite so loves Emilia that he disguises himself, returns to court, and wins a place in her service. After defeating his cousin Palamon in the contest decreed by Theseus for Emilia's hand, he is mortally wounded in a fall from his horse. With his dying breath Arcite gives Emilia to Palamon.

Arden Family. Shakespeare's maternal ancestors. His mother's family may have been related to the Ardens of Park Hall, Warwickshire, whose lineage could be traced back to the 11th century. There were Ardens living in Snitterfield, near Stratford, in the 15th century, but the earliest Arden known to be an ancestor of Shakespeare is the poet's great-grandfather ***Thomas Arden*** of Wilmcote (d. c. 1525), who in 1501 bought property in Snitterfield. His son ***Robert Arden*** (d. 1556) apparently prospered as a farmer. In addition to owning his house and farm in Wilmcote, Robert owned two freeholds in Snitterfield, on one of which his tenant was Richard Shakespeare, the poet's paternal grandfather. An 18th-century tradition identifies Robert's house as the one now called Mary Arden's House, purchased and restored by the Shakespeare Birthplace trustees in 1930.

Robert was married twice, first to a woman whose name is not known, and later to Agnes, widow of John Hill, a farmer. Robert had eight daughters by his first wife, six of whom married: Agnes (d. before 1576) to Thomas STRINGER, Joan (d. 1593) to Edmund Lambert, Katharine to Thomas EDKINS, Elizabeth to a John Scarlett, Margaret to Alexander Webbe (d. 1573, see WEBBE FAMILY) and Edward CORNWELL, and Mary to John SHAKESPEARE. Alice and Joyce did not marry. Robert Arden's will, dated November 24, 1556, left to his youngest daughter Mary "all my lande in Willmecote, cawlide Asbyes, and the crop apone the grounde sowne and tyllide as hitt is." It is possible, but not likely, that this Asbyes was the property which John and Mary Shakespeare subsequently mortgaged to their brother-in-law Edmund Lambert (see LAMBERT FAMILY).

Mary Arden (d. 1608) married John Shakespeare probably some time in 1557. After her husband's death in 1601, she continued living in the Shakespeare house on Henley Street. She was buried in Stratford on September 9, 1608.

Robert Arden's will is of interest for the light it sheds on his religious opinions. The reference in the will to "our bleside Laydye, Sent Marye" is viewed by some as an indication that Shakespeare's grandfather remained a Catholic (see RELIGION). The will, from the original in the Registry Court of Worcester, is reprinted below:

> In the name of God, Amen, the xxiiij.th daye of November, in the yeare of our Lorde God, 1556, in the thirde and the forthe yeare of the raygne of our soveragne lorde and ladye, Phylipe and Marye, kyng and quene, &c., I, Robart Arden, of Wyllmecote in the parryche of Aston Caunntlowe, secke in bodye and good and perfett of rememberence, make this my laste will and testement in maner and forme folowyng.—Fyrste, I bequethe my solle to Allmyghtye God and to our bleside Laydye, Sent Marye, and to all the holye compenye of heven, and my bodye to be beryde in the churchyarde of Seynt Jhon the Babtyste in Aston aforsayde. Allso

I give and bequethe to my youngst dowghter Marye all my lande in Willmecote, cawlide Asbyes, and the crop apone the grounde sowne and tyllide as hitt is; and vj.li.xiij.x. iiij.d. of monye to be payde orr ere my goodes be devydide. Allso I gyve and bequethe to my dowghter Ales the thyrde parte of all mye goodes, moveable and unmoveable, in fylde and towne, after my dettes and leggeses be performyde, besydes that goode she hathe of her owne att this tyme. Allso I gyve and bequethe to Annes my wife vj.li.xiiij.s. iiij.d. apone this condysione, that shall sofer my dowghter Ales quyetlye to ynyoye halfe my copyehoulde in Wyllmecote dwryng the tyme of her wyddowewhoode; and if she will nott soffer my dowghter Ales quyetlye to ocupye halfe with her, then I will that my wyfe shall have butt iij.li.vj.s. viij.d. and her gintur in Snyterfylde. Item, I will that the resedowe of all my goodes, moveable and unmoveable, my funeralles and my dettes dyschargyde, I gyve and bequethe to my other cheldren to be equaleye devidide amongeste them by the descreshyon of Adam Palmer, Hugh Porter of Snytterfylde, and Jhon Skerlett, whome I do ordene and make my overseres of this my last will and testament, and they to have for ther peynestakyng in this behalfe xx.s. apese. Allso I ordene and constytute and make my full exceqtores Ales and Marye, my dowghteres, of this my last will and testament, and they to have no more for ther paynes-takyng now as afore geven them. Allso I gyve and bequethe to every house that hathe no teme in the parryche of Aston, to every howse iiij.d.—Thes beyng wyttnesses,—Sir Wylliam Borton, curett; Adam Palmer; Jhon Skerlett; Thomas Jhenkes; Wylliam Pytt; with other mo.—Probatum fuit, &c., Wigorn., &c., xvj.° die mensis Decembris, anno Domini 1556.

[J. O. Halliwell-Phillipps, *Outlines of the Life of Shakespeare*, 1881; Mark Eccles, *Shakespeare in Warwickshire*, 1961.]

Arden of Feversham. Elizabethan play, published in 1592 and attributed to Shakespeare by Edward Jacob (d. 1788), who reprinted the play in 1770. Modern scholars are almost unanimous in rejecting any Shakespearean connection with the play, the majority of them tending to assign it to Thomas Kyd. The play is an interesting and very capably written example of the minor Elizabethan genre known as DOMESTIC TRAGEDY.

Arden Shakespeare, The (1899–1924). A 37-volume edition of the works of Shakespeare under the general editorship first of W. J. Craig from 1899 to 1906 and then of R. H. Case from 1909 to 1924. The Arden Shakespeare became a standard scholarly edition because of the extensive introductions, textual and critical notes, and variant readings. A revision, usually referred to as The New Arden Shakespeare, was inaugurated in 1951 under the general editorship of Una Ellis-Fermor who was succeeded, after her death in 1958, by Harold F. Brooks and Harold Jenkins. Originally conceived of as a revision, The New Arden is in practice a new edition; corrections and supplementary material have been added, and the original critical introductions have, for the most part, been replaced. See SCHOLARSHIP—19TH CENTURY.

Ariel. In *The Tempest*, an airy, mischievous spirit. Having been rescued by Prospero from imprisonment in a cloven pine, Ariel now obediently serves his liberator. At Prospero's bidding he has managed the storm that has caused the shipwreck. Afterward he lures Ferdinand to the meeting with Miranda, singing "Come unto these yellow sands," and later he awakens Gonzalo in time to frustrate the plot to murder the King. Anticipating his release from servitude, the dainty Ariel sings "Where the bee sucks, there suck I," concluding "Merrily, merrily shall I live now." After he has provided a calm sea and good wind for the voyage to Milan, the blithe spirit is at last freed.

Ariodante and Genovara (1583). A lost play given at court in 1583 by the boys of the Merchant Taylor's School. *Ariodante and Genovara* is presumably an adaptation of the episode of Ariodante and Genevora in Ariosto's *Orlando Furioso*. This episode is the source of the Hero-Claudio plot in *Much Ado*

WOODCUT FROM *Arden of Feversham*, FROM THE THIRD QUARTO (1633).

About Nothing. See MUCH ADO ABOUT NOTHING: *Sources*.

Ariosto, Lodovico (1474–1533). Italian poet and dramatist. One of the great figures of the Italian Renaissance, Ariosto began his career as a law student, later turning to the study of the classics. His earliest literary endeavors were prose comedies, among which *I Suppositi* (1509), a Plautine farce translated into English by George Gascoigne as *Supposes* (pub. 1573), became the source of the subplot of Bianca's suitors in *The Taming of the Shrew* (see THE TAMING OF THE SHREW: *Sources*). In 1503, Ariosto began work on his great epic poem *Orlando Furioso*, first published in 1516, and devoted the remainder of his life to revising and perfecting it. The completed version was published in 1532, the year before his death.

Orlando Furioso had a considerable influence on the literature of 16th-century England. Robert Greene dramatized a portion of the epic in his *Orlando Furioso* (1589), and Sir John HARINGTON translated the entire work in 1591. However, the poem achieves its finest expression in English in *The Faerie Queene* of Edmund Spenser, who used Ariosto's work as a main source. Spenser's work, together with Peter Beverly's *Ariodante and Genevra* (1566), a dramatized version of which was performed in 1583 and which is also derived from *Orlando Furioso*, provide the main sources of *Much Ado About Nothing*. It is possible that, in addition to these versions, Shakespeare knew and used *Orlando Furioso* itself, either in the original or in Harington's translation, and J. S. Smart has argued that the account of the handkerchief in *Othello* is based on a description in the last canto of Ariosto's poem. See MUCH ADO ABOUT NOTHING: *Sources*. [J. S. Smart, *Shakespeare: Truth and Tradition*, 1929.]

Aristotle (384–322 B.C.). Greek philosopher. Aristotle's pre-eminence as the "master of them who know," the greatest of the philosophers, remained unchallenged in the Renaissance as it had throughout the Middle Ages. The rediscovery of his *Poetics* at the beginning of the 16th century provided Renaissance humanists with an authoritative text on which to base their aesthetic theory. Unfortunately their codification of Aristotle's *ad hoc* judgments resulted in a stifling of creative expression on the continent, if not in England.

Aristotle's work was frequently translated into the vernacular languages during the 16th century, but there is no indication that Shakespeare was familiar with any of it. The celebrated error in *Troilus and Cressida* (II, ii, 166)—that Aristotle regarded young men as unfit to hear moral philosophy—is derived from a mistranslation of the philosopher which appears in Erasmus' *Colloquia*. The fact that the same error has been found in Bacon's *Advancement of Learning* (1605) has been used by Baconians as evidence of the identity of the two men. See NEOCLASSICISM.

Armada. Spanish fleet consisting of 130 ships which in 1588 attempted to control the English Channel in order to pave the way for a Spanish invasion of England. From July 21 to August 8 the lighter, more maneuverable English ships engaged them off the coast of Calais, where one-third of the Spanish fleet was destroyed. The value of the victory lay less in the comparatively slight losses suffered by the Spanish than in the psychological impact of the battle. The defeat completely demoralized Spain, whose decline as an imperial power can be dated from this time. The English, on the other hand, were sparked to an outburst of enthusiasm and energy which pervaded every area of life and gave to the next decade of the era those qualities of exuberance and vitality which we characterize as Elizabethan.

Shakespeare's allusions to the Armada are surprisingly few. Leslie Hotson believes that Sonnet 107 ("The mortal moon hath her eclipse endured") is a reference to the great victory. He argues that the battle formation of the Spanish fleet was crescent-shaped and cites contemporary documents which refer to the Armada as the moon. A reference in *King John* (III, iv, 2–3) to "A whole armado of convicted sail/ . . . scatter'd and disjoin'd from fellowship" refers to the abortive second Armada of 1596, which was "scatter'd and disjoin'd" by a storm in the Bay of Biscay, rather than to the 1588 Armada.

Armado, Don Adriano de. In *Love's Labour's Lost*, a verbose, pompous Spaniard who is made sport of by the King and his lords. Don Armado is Costard's rival for Jaquenetta's affections, and when a love letter that he has written to her is mistakenly delivered to Rosaline, its grandiose language causes much amusement. He portrays Hector in the interlude of the Nine Worthies. As a type, Don Armado is derived from the Italian Renaissance idea of an offensive soldier (see LOVE'S LABOUR'S LOST: *Sources*), and is thought to be a caricature of Sir Walter Raleigh, Gabriel Harvey, or Antonio PÉREZ.

Armin, Robert (c. 1568–1615). Actor and dramatist. A native of Norfolk, Armin served a goldsmith's apprenticeship after which he is said to have become the protégé of the famous clown Richard Tarlton. He began his acting career with Lord Chandos' Men, for whom he wrote his play *Foole upon Foole*. By the time this play was published (1600), Armin had become a member of Shakespeare's company, the Chamberlain's Men, for on the title page of the play he is described as "Clonnico de Curtaino Snuffe." This is a reference to the Curtain theatre where the Chamberlain's Men played until the opening of the Globe in 1599. Armin succeeded Will Kempe, chief clown of the Chamberlain's Men, and the significant change in the comic roles of Shakespeare's plays at this time is generally attributed to Armin's talent (see CAST).

Armin showed a lifelong interest in fools, the all-licensed court jesters, and it is likely that Shakespeare drew upon this interest in creating the distinctive fools which Armin very likely played, namely, Touchstone in *As You Like It*, Feste in *Twelfth Night*, Lavache in *All's Well*, and Lear's Fool. Leslie Hotson has suggested that Armin may also have played Polonius in *Hamlet*. An allusion in the dedication of Armin's *The Italian Taylor and his Boy* (1609) has been taken as evidence that Armin played Dogberry in *Much Ado*: "I pray you the boldnes of a beggar who hath been writ down an Asse in his time." This is an echo of Dogberry's famous line (V, i, 263–265).

Armin was the author of one other play, *Two Maids of More-clack* (pub. 1609). Its main character, Tutch, may be a recollection of Touchstone unless, as Charles Felver has suggested, Armin's play preceded Shakespeare's, in which case Shakespeare may have adapted the name from Armin. [Leslie Hotson, *Shakespeare's Motley*, 1952; Charles Felver, "Robert Armin," *Dissertation Abstracts*, 1956.]

Armstrong, John (1709–1779). Scottish physician and poet. Armstrong referred to Shakespeare in a few of his *Sketches*, published in 1758 under the pseudonym of Launcelot Temple. He cited Shakespeare as the notable exception to the formal rules and criticisms he made. He objected, for example, to the introduction of artificial masques or processions into the drama, but admitted that the masque in *Romeo and Juliet* had an important part in the action. Armstrong was strongly in favor of adherence to the dramatic unities, but acknowledged that they were hard to maintain and that Shakespeare's success in ignoring them was a good argument in defense of occasional violations by other writers. [Herbert Spencer Robinson, *English Shakesperian Criticism in the Eighteenth Century*, 1932.]

Arne, Thomas Augustine (1710–1778). Composer. Educated at Eton, Arne studied music privately. He gave up legal studies to write the music for Addison's *Rosamund* (1733); Fielding's *The Opera of Operas* (1733), altered from *Tom Thumb;* Milton's *Comus* (1738); Congreve's *Judgment of Paris* (1740); and Thomson and Mallet's *Alfred* (1740), which included the song "Rule Britannia." For the Drury Lane production of *As You Like It* in 1740 he set to music the songs "Under the greenwood tree" and "Blow, blow thou winter wind." In 1744 he was appointed composer to the Drury Lane theatre. He composed music for songs from *The Tempest* and *Twelfth Night* and for the *Ode* by Garrick for the Shakespeare Jubilee at Stratford-upon-Avon in 1769.

Arragon, Prince of. In *The Merchant of Venice*, one of Portia's suitors who fails the test of the caskets. The Prince of Arragon chooses the silver chest containing "the portrait of a blinking idiot" (II, ix).

Arraignment of Paris, The (c. 1584). A pastoral play by George PEELE. One of the earliest examples of PASTORALISM in English drama, *The Arraignment of Paris* was written for a court performance by the Children of the Chapel before Queen Elizabeth. The plot deals with the "golden apple" myth, and at the climax of the play an actor delivers the golden apple to the person of the queen herself.

In the *Catalogue of . . . Plaies* which was printed in 1656 by Edward Archer, the play is attributed to Shakespeare.

arras. See CURTAINS.

art. In Shakespeare's time the pictures that could be seen in England were few in number and limited in kind. There were no English paintings of flowers, still life, or animals; there were no scenes from ordinary life (genre painting); and landscape painting had not yet been developed. In fact, except for a few private collections of continental art, most of the paintings in England were portraits. Pictures in books were rare and consisted chiefly of crude woodcuts. English illustration was still in its infancy and grew as a separate tradition somewhat apart from other artistic production. The art of illustration developed as an elaboration of the illustrated title page, or frontispiece, which was engraved with ornamental type and sometimes included a portrait of the author.

The first illustrated edition of Shakespeare, edited by Nicholas ROWE (1709), drew on two major sources: European art, represented by the classical painting of the French Academy and the more modest Dutch and Flemish schools; and the stage conventions of the theater, masques, and opera, both contemporary and earlier. Since many of Shakespeare's plays were not performed during this period, any theatrical quality in the engraving must in those instances be due to the imagination of the engraver. These early illustrations have a puppet-like stiffness, and the costuming conventions themselves add a peculiar note. During most of the 18th century, theatrical wardrobes consisted of a curious grab bag of clothing—the fashion of the moment augmented by traditional costumes and a few exotic accessories. The illustrations do not suggest Shakespeare to modern eyes; the gentleman in the periwig is not recognizable as Macbeth. The convention, too, was to depict characters in the most typical poses, rather than in a single moment of action on the stage. Although these illustrations often provide valuable indications of the exact stage productions, their stiffness and staginess fail to express the dramatic quality of the plays.

A drawing by William HOGARTH of Falstaff reviewing his troops (c. 1728) is the first illustration of Shakespeare to strike an immediately vivid note. The very casualness of the picture, its sketchiness of line, and the informality of Falstaff's stance and gesture bring the scene to life. Lewis Theobald's 1733 edition of Shakespeare, however, reflects nothing of Hogarth's influence, but merely re-engraves, in a smaller size, the Rowe edition's illustrations. The Thomas HANMER edition of 1744, however, is of a more ambitious artistic quality; Francis HAYMAN, one of the original members of the Royal Academy, designed the plates. The engravings were executed by Hubert GRAVELOT, a highly accomplished French artist whose 20 years of work in England did much to raise the standards of English illustration. Theobald's 1740 edition had 36 plates designed by Gravelot, of which he himself engraved 8. Gravelot's fluent and delicate style is well suited to the romances and comedies, but the influence of French classicism visible in the tragic scenes makes the murder of Desdemona and the amputations in *Titus Andronicus*, for example, oddly unaffecting. Hayman and Gravelot combined to produce the illustrations for Hanmer's 1744 edition; 31 plates were drawn by Hayman, while Gravelot drew 5 and engraved all 36.

Around 1750 it became fashionable for contemporary leading actors to commission portraits of themselves in their favorite roles. The engravings of such portraits sold very well, and the theatrical tableau became popular. Equally chic were group portraits set in intimate surroundings and group portraits of actors with theatrical sets as backgrounds. John ZOFFANY was the most talented and important painter of these conversation pieces, as they are called, and his work reflects the changing theatrical taste of the time—the increasing preference for more natural and spontaneous gesture.

Despite a lively market in theatrical prints, the enterprise of the richest and most successful printseller of the time, John Boydell, was sparked by cultural ambition rather than the desire for profit (see BOY-

"ELIZABETH AND THE THREE GODDESSES" BY HANS EWORTH (1569). THE SUBJECT MATTER OF THIS PAINTING CLOSELY PARALLELS PEELE'S *The Arraignment of Paris.* IN THIS VERSION, HOWEVER, ELIZABETH AWARDS THE APPLE TO HERSELF. THIS IS THE FIRST PORTRAIT OF ELIZABETH AFTER SHE BECAME QUEEN. (HAMPTON COURT, BY GRACIOUS PERMISSION OF H. M. QUEEN ELIZABETH II.)

DELL SHAKESPEARE GALLERY). Boydell was eager to establish a British school of history painting which could meet the exalted standards of the French Academy. The idea of history painting as a separate genre was essentially a 17th-century conception; the French Academy had decreed that a picture was important only if its subject was glorious. The heroes of the past thus offered the artist the opportunity to transcend everyday life and present a lasting, universal image of human nobility.

By the middle of the 18th century, however, the growing forces of nationalism and democracy had vitiated to a great extent the classical ideals. Where the 17th century had viewed man's reason as responsible for his triumph over barbarism, the 18th century glorified the ideal of man himself who, by dint of his own creativity and skill, was building new societies and settling new worlds. History painting reflected this new vision and became more nationalistic and eclectic. Benjamin WEST, an American, was the acknowledged master of the new style of history painting, while Sir Joshua REYNOLDS, president of the Royal Academy, was the exponent of the older tradition. History painting, however interpreted, was still officially the most valued of all art forms, and Boydell's project was evidence of England's desire to claim a share of the form's glory and prestige.

Beginning with "King Lear in the Storm" (1767) by John RUNCIMAN, the romantic vision, imparting a new coherence to English painting, was slowly coming to the fore. Contemporary illustration contributed nothing to this movement; popular taste was being fed by the puerile work of men like C. R. Leslie, whose engravings of 45 pretty girls (allegedly Shakespearean heroines) were issued in 1836. In painting and the theatre, however, the taste for both the wilder aspects of nature and the more imaginative and emotional aspects of man reflected the new sensibility of the age. The attraction of the romantic temperament to Shakespeare is not difficult to comprehend, and the period produced some of the finest paintings on Shakespearean themes ever to be created. Only on one artist, however, was Shakespeare to exercise an overriding influence: this was Henry FUSELI, who did hundreds of drawings, engravings, and paintings on a wide variety of Shakespearean subjects.

William BLAKE did fewer drawings based on Shakespeare than did Fuseli, but his work exhibits a more highly personal approach. Blake measured the value of art by its ability to stimulate the imagination, and Shakespeare's artistry was well able to awaken Blake's mind. Blake's illustrations of characters and scenes from Shakespeare are less striking than the metaphorical drawings which were suggested by Shakespeare's imagery.

John Constable (1776–1837), William Turner (1775–1851), and Richard Bonington (1802–1828), among the most famous artists of their day, produced important paintings on Shakespearean subjects. In France, Eugène Delacroix (1799–1863) painted "Hamlet and the Gravedigger," while Jean-Baptiste Corot (1795–1875) created "Macbeth and the Witches," noteworthy for its expressive use of landscape. Between 1834 and 1843, Delacroix also published a set of 16 lithographs of scenes from *Hamlet* which are distinguished for their economy of line.

Dante Gabriel Rossetti (1828–1882), who led the pre-Raphaelite movement (the later phase of English Romanticism), began to produce in 1857 a series of elaborate drawings and watercolors illustrating Shakespearean scenes. In his pictures the tempestuous landscapes of earlier painters yield to careful detail, and the emotional energy of Shakespeare's characters fades into yearning and melancholy.

Serious modern artists of the period following the pre-Raphaelites—with the exception of some isolated work, notably by Walter Sickert (1860–1942) and Wyndham Lewis (1884–1957)—have paid little attention to Shakespeare. The modern artist is most likely to be directly interested in scenic design, if he manifests any interest in Shakespeare at all. See PORTRAITS OF SHAKESPEARE. [W. M. Merchant, *Shakespeare and the Artist*, 1959; *Encyclopedia of World Art*, 1959–1964.]

Artemidorus of Cnidos. In *Julius Caesar*, a teacher of rhetoric. Artemidorus presses on Caesar a document warning of the conspiracy and begs him to read it instantly, "for mine's a suit that touches Caesar nearer," but he is dismissed as a madman (II, iii and III, i). According to Plutarch, Artemidorus was, because of his profession as doctor of rhetoric, acquainted with several of the conspirators and learned of the plot against Caesar. Having recorded this information on a scroll, the Sophist managed to give it to Caesar who was, however, distracted from reading it by the crush of other petitioners.

Artesius. In *The Two Noble Kinsmen*, an Athenian captain. Theseus, Duke of Athens, orders Artesius to prepare the army for war against Thebes to avenge the killing of the three Queens' husbands (I, i).

Arthur Plantagenet, duke of **Brittany** (1187–1203). Posthumous son of Geoffrey Plantagenet (3rd son of Henry II) and Constance of Brittany. Since Geoffrey was older than his brother John, Arthur's claim to the throne of England was more valid than that of John. When, however, the latter became king, Arthur was nonetheless acknowledged by the nobles of the English possessions in France as their ruler. He consequently became a most dangerous threat to his uncle who, after capturing Arthur in battle, is thought to have killed him.

In *King John*, the King takes his nephew, Arthur, prisoner and entrusts him to Hubert de Burgh to be put to death. Hubert, unable to muster the cruelty to blind the boy as John's written instructions require, hides him and informs the King that he is dead. Arthur subsequently dies while attempting to escape Hubert's custody.

Arundel's Men. An early Elizabethan acting company. Arundel's Men seem to have played at the Curtain in the 1580's and to have dispersed after the imprisonment of their patron, Philip Howard, 13th earl of Arundel (1557–1595), in 1585. [E. K. Chambers, *The Elizabethan Stage*, 1923.]

Arviragus. In *Cymbeline*, the King's younger son. Arviragus is kidnapped with his brother, Guiderius, by Belarius and reared as Belarius' son under the name of Cadwal. Although more sensitive than Guiderius, Arviragus is his brother's equal in bravery. When the Romans invade Britain, Belarius' plan to find safety in the mountains is rejected by Arviragus with the protest, "What pleasure, sir, find we in life, to lock it from action and adventure?" Whereupon the young Prince joins his brother in fearless combat with the enemy.

Ascham, Roger (c. 1515–1568). Educator and scholar. Among the various posts occupied by Ascham were those of tutor to Elizabeth I and Latin secretary to Mary Tudor. He is the author of *The Scholemaster* (1570), a description of the ideal education for an Elizabethan gentleman, chiefly notable for its spirited defense of the "vulgar tongue" (English) and for its opposition to the standard educational practice of flogging students. *The Scholemaster* is also an early example of the sternly moralistic view of literature and, particularly, the theatre which was the source of Puritan opposition to the stage. See ENEMIES OF THE STAGE.

Asche, Oscar. Real name **John Stanger Heiss** (1871–1936). Actor and theatre manager. Born in Australia, Asche came to England as a young man. After many early struggles, he joined, in 1893, the Benson Repertory Company, where he had the opportunity to act a variety of roles from Biondello in *The Taming of the Shrew* to Claudius in *Hamlet*. In 1904, Asche became co-manager of the Adelphi Theatre with a fellow actor, Otto Stuart, and during the next several seasons produced and played in *A Midsummer Night's Dream, The Taming of the Shrew,* and *Measure for Measure*. His most notable success was his portrayal of Othello in his own production (1907) of the play at His Majesty's Theatre where he had become manager in the same year. He participated in the Shakespeare tercentenary (1916) at the Drury Lane, playing Casca in *Julius Caesar*. His final Shakespearean venture was an unsuccessful production of *The Merry Wives of Windsor* in modern dress in 1929. [*Dictionary of National Biography*, 1885– ; *Oxford Companion to the Theatre*, Phyllis Hartnoll, ed., 1951.]

Ashley, Sir **John.** See Sir John ASTLEY.

Aspinall, Alexander (d. 1624). Schoolmaster at the Stratford grammar school from 1582 until his death in 1624. Born in Lancashire, Aspinall was educated at Oxford where he received a B.A. in 1575 and an M.A. in 1578. Sir Francis Fane (1611–1680) records the following note in his commonplace book:

> The gift is small
> The will is all:
> A shey ander [Alexander] Asbenall.
>
> Shaxpaire upon a peaire of gloves that mas[t]er sent to his mistris.

E. I. Fripp suggests that the anecdote refers to a purchase of gloves from John Shakespeare by Aspinall for Anne Shaw, whom he married in 1594. Fripp also argues that Aspinall is the prototype of HOLOFERNES, the pedantic schoolmaster in *Love's Labour's Lost.* [E. I. Fripp, *Shakespeare, Man and Artist,* 2 vols., 1938; Mark Eccles, *Shakespeare in Warwickshire,* 1961.]

Aspley, William (c. 1574–1640). London bookseller. The son of William Aspley of Raiston, Aspley served as an apprentice printer from 1588 to 1597, being admitted to the Stationers' Company as a freeman on April 11, 1598. He was the joint publisher with Andrew Wise of the first editions of *Much Ado About Nothing* (1600) and *2 Henry IV* (1600). He was one of the publishers, along with William Jaggard, Edward Blount, and John Smethwicke, of the First Folio (1623) and one of the group who published the Second Folio (1632). His shops were located at the sign of the Tiger's Head and of the Parrot, both in St. Paul's Churchyard. In 1640, the year in which he died, he was made Master of the Company of Stationers. [R. B. McKerrow, ed., *A Dictionary of Printers and Booksellers . . . 1557–1640,* 1910.]

assembled texts. It has been suggested that the texts of some of the plays in the First Folio were reconstructed for the printer by "assembling" or integrating each actor's PART with the PLOT (the prompter's abstract of the play). The theory of assembled texts was first put forth by Edmund Malone and seeks to explain what COPY the printer of the First Folio used when the company's PROMPT-BOOK had been lost and when the play had not previously been published in quarto. Dover Wilson, who popularized the theory, argues that evidence of assembled texts can be seen in *The Two Gentlemen of Verona, The Merry Wives of Windsor,* and *The Winter's Tale.* His argument is based on a distinctive feature common to all these plays: all the characters appearing in a given scene are listed in the beginning of the scene regardless of whether they appear in the beginning or later on. This feature would be characteristic of a plot, but not of a prompt-book which lists entrances and exits of characters as they occur in any scene. The theory has been contested by W. W. Greg, who argues that the massing of entrances at the beginning of the scene is a phenomenon to be noted in plays outside the Folio, such as the 1623 edition of Webster's *The Duchess of Malfi,* the text of which was almost certainly derived from the author's foul papers (unrevised, original manuscript). Greg also suggests that the practice of massing entrances at the beginning of the scene was a common convention among continental dramatists which was imported to England by Ben Jonson. [W. W. Greg, *The Shakespeare First Folio,* 1955.]

Astley or **Ashley,** Sir **John** (d. 1641). Master of the Revels, 1622/3. Astley was the son of John Astley (d. 1595), who held a high position in Elizabeth's royal household. The younger Astley was himself a gentleman of the privy chamber under James I, and succeeded to the Revels post in 1622 when his predecessor, Sir George Buc, became mad. On July 20, 1623, however, he sold his post to Henry Herbert for £150 a year, although technically retaining the title of Master until 1629. Astley is generally thought to be the author of the entry in Herbert's office book which records a performance of *Twelfth Night* on February 2, 1623: "At Candlemas *Malvolio* was acted at court, by the kings servants." See MASTER OF THE REVELS. [G. E. Bentley, *The Jacobean and Caroline Stage,* 5 vols., 1941–1956.]

Aston Cantlow. A parish northwest of Stratford which included within its boundaries the hamlets of Aston Cantlow and WILMCOTE, the home of Shakespeare's mother, Mary Arden. Shakespeare's father and mother were probably married in the parish church of Aston Cantlow and in 1579 they forfeited some property within the parish to their brother-in-law Edmund Lambert when they failed to pay the mortgage.

astronomy and astrology. Most Elizabethans accepted the geocentric theory of astronomy which had come down from Ptolemy. Some scientists, however, were beginning to regard Ptolemy's theory as obsolete; in addition, the voyages of exploration began to demand more accurate astronomical observations and navigational methods. The disillusionment with Ptolemaic astronomy was hastened by Copernicus (1473–1543) in his *De Revolutionibus Orbium Coelestium* (1543). The Copernican hypothesis of the sun as the center of the solar system received confirmation from Johannes Kepler (1571–1630), whose *De Motibus Stellae Martis* (1609) set forth laws of planetary motion, and from Galileo (1564–1642), who published his observations in the *Sidereus Nuncius* (1610). English scientists, however, were excited by the Copernican theories even before they received corroboration from Kepler and Galileo. English and continental observers maintained close contact with each other: Thomas Harriot (1560–1621), tutor to Sir Walter Raleigh, was in communication with Kepler, for example. Robert Recorde (c. 1510–1558) in *The Castle of Knowledge* (1556) described both Copernican and Ptolemaic theory. Another student of astronomy, John Field (c. 1525–1587), also lent credence to the new Copernican theory in his *Ephemeris anni 1557 currentis juxta Copernici et Reinhaldi canones* (1556). Other Copernican supporters were Thomas Digges (d. 1595), the father of Leonard DIGGES, who objected to the confusion of the Ptolemaic system in his *A Geometricall Practise* (1571), and John Dee (1527–1608). Dee embodied within himself the transition between the old and new scientific methods. His popular reputation was based on his work as an alchemist, astrologer, and magician; yet he was also a serious mathematician and geographer, and advocated adoption of the Gregorian calendar. William Gilbert (1540–1603), famous for his work on magnetism (*De magnete,* 1600), was also an advocate of the Copernican astronomy.

The Copernican orientation was, however, confined to a very small group of scientists. The vast majority still adhered to a Ptolemaic conception, and one of the best minds of the period, Sir Francis Bacon, was not content with either hypothesis. He devised an improbable, eclectic system of his own.

Most stargazing in Elizabethan England was not done by scientists at all, but by astrologers and for purposes of divination, not observation. As they had been doing for centuries, astrologers continued to read astral portents and make predictions. For the superstitious populace, including the nobility and the queen, they interpreted astronomical phenomena such as eclipses, comets, and ordinary heavenly bodies. The ancient belief that man's fate was controlled by the stars still prevailed. Astrology was regarded by all the major religious authorities as a dangerously pagan practice. Calvin's attitude in the 16th century was as censorious as that of the Roman Catholic Church two centuries earlier. As the years passed, astrology was to become increasingly discredited. When Shakespeare wrote the following well-known lines in *Julius Caesar,* he was aware to some degree of the growing disrepute of astrological determinism among the learned:

> The fault, dear Brutus, is not in our stars,
> But in ourselves, that we are underlings.
>
> (I, ii, 140–141)

In the same play, however, he could communicate to a sympathetic, comprehending audience Calpurnia's fears about the significant omens in a violent thunderstorm:

> Fierce fiery warriors fought upon the clouds,
> In ranks and squadrons and right form of war,
> Which drizzled blood upon the Capitol;
> The noise of battle hurtled in the air,
> Horses did neigh, and dying men did groan,
> And ghosts did shriek and squeal about the streets.
> O Caesar! these things are beyond all use,
> And I do fear them.
> *Caesar.* What can be avoided
> Whose end is purposed by the mighty gods?
> Yet Caesar shall go forth; for these predictions
> Are to the world in general as to Caesar.
> *Calpurnia.* When beggars die, there are no comets seen;
> The heavens themselves blaze forth the death of princes.
>
> (II, ii, 19–31)

Similarly, in *King Lear* (I, ii, 112–113), Gloucester sees ill omens in "These late eclipses in the sun and moon" (see TOPICAL REFERENCES). Edmund, in a famous speech, comments:

> This is the excellent foppery of the world, that, when we are sick in fortune,—often the surfeit of our own behaviour,—we make guilty of our disasters the sun, the moon, and the stars: as if we were villains by necessity; fools by heavenly compulsion; knaves, thieves, and treachers, by spherical predominance; drunkards, liars, and adulterers, by an enforced obedience of planetary influence; and all that we are evil in, by a divine thrusting on: an admirable evasion of whoremaster man, to lay his goatish disposition to the charge of a star! My father compounded with my mother under the dragon's tail; and my nativity was under Ursa major; so that it follows, I am rough and lecherous. Tut, I should have been that I am, had the maidenliest star in the firmament twinkled on my bastardizing.
>
> (I, ii, 129–146)

Edmund ends his speech with a refutation of the astrological belief that the stars or planet under which one was born determined the fate of the individual.

The Elizabethan audience was very much aware of the significance of the language of astrology, and could grasp the symbolism in passages which are unintelligible to the modern playgoer. Each heavenly body was recognized as exercising its own special kind of influence on human affairs. The moon, for example, controlled the tides and precipitation, and it was referred to by Shakespeare as the "watery star" (*The Winter's Tale,* I, ii, 1) and the "moist star" (*Hamlet,* I, i, 118). It was held responsible for causing madness and provoking thievery, and certain men were "the moon's men" of whom Hal says:

> for the fortune of us that are the moon's men doth ebb and flow like the sea, being governed, as the sea is, by the moon.
>
> (*1 Henry IV,* I, ii, 35–37)

In addition, the signs of the zodiac were associated with various parts of the body.

While the recondite lore of astrology is no longer considered *de rigueur* for the common reader or playgoer, those interested in the subject might glean further insights by studying one of the astrological treatises which the Elizabethans took as their sources, namely, the *Liber Novem Iudicum in Iudiciis Astrorum* (1509), the writings of John Dee, or Richard Harvey's *An astrological discourse* (1583). [E. B. Knobel, "Astronomy and Astrology," *Shakespeare's England,* 1916.]

As you like it.

As You Like It. A comedy by Shakespeare.

Text. The sole authoritative text, in the First Folio, is a good one. The copy for it appears to have been the PROMPT-BOOK of the Chamberlain's Men, or a transcript of it. Stage directions are relatively meager, but those that are given appear to be the work of a BOOK-KEEPER.

Date. On August 4, 1600 an entry in the Stationers' Register directs four plays, all owned by the Chamberlain's Men, "to be staied," that is, kept from being printed in a pirated edition (see BLOCKING ENTRIES). The plays were *As You Like It, Much Ado About Nothing, Henry V*, and Ben Jonson's *Every Man In his Humour*. That the pirates were after *As You Like It* suggests that it was very popular in 1600. There is a disputed theory that Shakespeare wrote a much earlier version of the play, of which the present text is a revision. The evidence adduced for this hypothesis is the appearance of blank verse lines embedded in the prose. Those who make this assumption find particularly in the first 18 lines of V, ii, conclusive evidence that they had been originally written in verse, and later rewritten as prose. But G. L. Kittredge, among other scholars, points out that the best English prose runs easily into blank verse, as it does here. For this and other equally good reasons, the idea that the present text of *As You Like It* represents a revision of a text composed as early as 1593 has not been widely accepted. The play is not mentioned in Meres' PALLADIS TAMIA (1598). Rosalind's famous quotation (III, v, 82) from Marlowe's *Hero and Leander* ("Who ever loved that loved not at first sight?") is also taken as evidence of a post-1598 date, since Marlowe's poem was not published until that year. The date usually given for the comedy, therefore, is 1599–1600.

Sources. The direct and principal source of *As You Like It* is Thomas LODGE's novel *Rosalynde, Euphues' golden legacie*. Shakespeare's play follows Lodge's novel relatively closely. However, the poet did change the names of most of the characters and invented Jaques, Touchstone, Audrey, William, and Sir Oliver Martext. More importantly, he eliminated the slow-moving and cumbersome features of Lodge's plot in order to bring the theme of the play into sharper focus. Lodge had based his story on *The Tale of Gamelyn*, a 14th-century poem of 902 lines which was incorrectly ascribed to Chaucer and found in many manuscripts of *The Canterbury Tales*. The idyllic green world of the forest was being exploited at the end of the century in two popular plays about Robin Hood. They were being performed in 1598 by the chief rivals of Shakespeare's company, the Admiral's Men. These plays were Anthony Munday's *The Downfall of Robert Earl of Huntingdon* and *The Death of Robert Earl of Huntingdon*, by Munday and Henry Chettle. *As You Like It* is Shakespeare's contribution to (and comment on) the vogue of the pastoral. Sir Philip Sidney's *Arcadia*, written in 1580–1581, had awakened interest in the depiction of an idealized world of innocent shepherds set in an idealized landscape. But it was Bartholomew Yonge's translation (1598) of Jorge Montemayor's Spanish original, *Diana Enamorada* (1552), that most stimulated the movement in England, of which Lodge's novel was a part. In his comedy, Shakespeare frequently undercuts the extravagant romanticism of the pastoral world. Some of these realistic touches may derive from an anonymous play, *Sir Clyomon and Clamydes*, written between 1570 and 1590 and published in 1599.—O.J.C.

Plot Synopsis. Act I. Orlando, the youngest son of Rowland de Boys, has been kept "rustically at home" by his older brother, Oliver, who has withheld his inheritance and prevented him from acquiring any formal education. Now Orlando demands his birthright, and the two brothers come to blows. Upon learning that Orlando plans to challenge a wrestler called Charles, Oliver, who is envious of his brother's virtues, falsely warns Charles that Orlando is determined to defeat him, even if he must resort to treachery.

The match is to take place at the court of Duke Frederick, who has recently usurped the title of his older brother. The rightful Duke has been banished and, together with several lords who chose to follow him, has taken refuge in the Forest of Arden where they live like Robin Hood and his Merry Men. His daughter, Rosalind, has remained in the ducal palace at the insistence of her cousin Celia, Frederick's daughter. Having been informed of the contest by an affected courtier named Le Beau, the two girls watch as Orlando throws Charles to the ground. Duke Frederick is displeased to learn the identity of Orlando's father, for he had been a friend of the banished Duke, but Rosalind gives the victor a chain from her neck. He is struck dumb with love for her. Following the advice of Le Beau, who warns him against the Duke, Orlando decides to flee from the court.

Rosalind has fallen in love with Orlando, to the amusement of Celia, who is surprised that her cousin could be smitten so suddenly. When Duke Frederick, fearful that Rosalind's presence in the court may become a threat to him, orders her to leave, Celia insists on sharing her exile. They decide to travel in disguise, Rosalind as a youth called Ganymede, and Celia as his sister Aliena. Their sole companion will be the court fool, Touchstone.

Act II. Having ventured into Arden Forest, Rosalind, Celia, and Touchstone listen as young Silvius reveals to Corin, an old shepherd, the depth of his passion for the disdainful Phebe. Their conversation prompts Touchstone to recall the excesses to which his own youthful ardor for one Jane Smile had tempted him. When Corin informs the weary travelers that his master has a cottage and some sheep to sell, Rosalind asks him to purchase the property for her.

Meanwhile, Orlando has left his brother's palace accompanied by Adam, a faithful old servant of the family. After they reach the forest, Adam becomes faint with hunger, and Orlando sets out in search of food. He finds the banished Duke about to enjoy a sylvan feast with his followers, among whom is the melancholy Jaques, an erstwhile libertine who would now like to "cleanse the foul body of th'infected world." Orlando demands food at sword's point, but the Duke disarms him by graciously inviting him to the table. Before he will accept any food, however, he leaves to fetch Adam. Orlando's account of his sufferings leads the Duke to remark on the fact that "this wide and universal theatre" presents sadder histories than their own. Jaques observes that "all the world's a stage, / And all the men and women merely players."

Act III. Orlando is still so enamored of Rosalind that he takes to composing verses to her and hanging them on trees. Rosalind is inclined to be critical of their literary merit until she learns that the anonymous poet is Orlando, who soon arrives in person but fails to recognize her in her male attire. After indulging in some good-natured raillery at his expense, she promises to cure his love if he will woo her as if she were Rosalind. Touchstone's fancy, meanwhile, has lighted on Audrey, an ill-favored country wench whom he proposes to marry.

Silvius pays ardent court to Phebe, but the hard-hearted shepherdess spurns his advances. Rosalind, who has witnessed the scene, angrily chides Phebe for her pride, admonishing her to thank heaven for the love of a good man like Silvius. Unfortunately, Phebe responds by becoming infatuated with Rosalind.

Act IV. Jaques' melancholy, which he claims is the result of observations gleaned during his travels, arouses the scorn of Rosalind, who asserts, "I had rather have a fool to make me merry than experience to make me sad." Orlando arrives nearly an hour late for an appointment, leading Rosalind to observe that such tardiness does not betoken true love. At her bidding he describes how he would woo Rosalind, maintaining that he would die if she refused him, but she replies that "men have died from time to time and worms have eaten them, but not for love." When Orlando states that he must leave her for two hours, she declares that if he is even so much as a minute late, she will think him "a most pathetical break-promise," unworthy of his Rosalind. She later confides to Celia that her love for Orlando is so deep that it cannot be sounded.

Another recent arrival to the forest is Oliver, who has been ordered by Duke Frederick to find Orlando. He comes in search of Rosalind, to whom he gives a bloody handkerchief belonging to his brother. Oliver explains that his life has been saved by Orlando, who killed a hungry lioness that lay in wait for him as he slept. He identifies himself as Orlando's elder brother and declares that they are now reconciled. Orlando, who had been wounded in his struggle with the lioness, had asked Oliver to take the handkerchief to Rosalind in order to explain his failure to return at the appointed hour. At sight of the handkerchief she swoons.

Act V. Oliver informs Orlando that, despite their brief acquaintance, he and Celia are in love. When Orlando reveals to Rosalind that the wedding is to take place before the Duke the following day and contrasts his own "heart-heaviness" with his brother's happiness, she says that she knows a magician who will enable him to marry Rosalind. She also promises to satisfy both Silvius and Phebe, who is still sighing for Ganymede.

Rosalind makes good her pledge the next day when she reveals her identity to her father, the Duke, and to Orlando, while Hymen, the god of marriage, looks on. Thus, Orlando wins Rosalind as his bride, and Phebe must settle for Silvius. Touchstone and Audrey and Oliver and Celia bring to four the number of couples to be united.

Jaques de Boys, the brother of Orlando and Oliver, arrives unexpectedly with good news: Duke Frederick had invaded the forest to capture his brother, but, after conversing with an old hermit, has decided to forsake the world and restore his brother's title and estate to him. The only discordant note in the happy scene is struck by the ever-cynical Jaques, who announces his intention of joining the penitent Frederick and his followers in religious life.—H.D.

Comment. *As You Like It* is at once a distillation of the spirit of pastoral romance and a satire—sometimes a travesty—of the pastoral idea. Shakespeare's Forest of Arden is his equivalent of the scenes painted by Montemayor and other authors of pastoral romance. Yet Shakespeare has made it more real and familiar by his memories of the Warwickshire Forest of Arden which intrude upon the conventional landscape. So the play is not, like its predecessors, set in a never-never land, but in an English woodland, where one might catch faint echoes of Robin Hood's horn and the shouts of his Merry Men. Love is the absorbing interest of all the principal characters in *As You Like It.* It is awakened at first sight. For Rosalind, it is sheer exhilaration, lighting a fire in her wit. Orlando is the stricken sonneteering suitor of Renaissance poetry. Among other conventions of romance that Shakespeare adopted is that of an ideal friendship, dearer than love to Tudor gentlemen. But the poet applies it here for the first time to two women, Rosalind and Celia. Another old convention of romance is that of the dedicated devotion of a retainer to the head of a gentle household; thus Adam shows his master "the constant service of the antique world."

Jaques is entirely the poet's creation. He takes no part in the plot, but stands aloof to make misanthropic comment on every situation and every character that attracts his attention. Yet he should not be

hearted humor. British audiences who witnessed her initial efforts as Rosalind were kinder than her countrymen, who first saw her in the role at the Astor Place Opera House in 1850 and who preferred a more tender heroine. The following year Fanny Wallack starred in *As You Like It* at Burton's Chambers Street Theatre, and in 1852 Anna Cora Mowatt, an exceptionally charming Rosalind, acted in the comedy at the Old Broadway. For the opening of Laura Keene's Varieties on November 18, 1856, Miss Keene, previously the heroine of Wallack's production of the play in 1853, repeated the role with an exceptional cast. Earlier that spring Louise Howard played Rosalind for her American debut at the Lyceum Theatre. The next year Julia Bennett Barrow acted the role at Tripler Hall.

During the last half of the 19th century, the popularity of *As You Like It* in America soared, and the part of Rosalind continued to appeal to the most attractive and popular actresses. On November 14, 1868 Mrs. Scott-Siddons acted Rosalind for the first time in America at the Boston Museum and on the 30th of that month made her New York debut playing the same role. Her performance, ideally balancing tenderness, mischievousness, vitality, and ardor, was repeated at least three more times that year. The following October she alternated as Rosalind and Celia with Clara Jennings at the Fifth Avenue Theatre. They were supported by William Davidge, a clever performer of low comedy, as Touchstone, and George Clarke as a pleasantly romantic Orlando. Both revivals were produced by Augustin Daly, as was an *As You Like It* presented in 1876. In the last, Fanny Davenport was starred opposite Lawrence Barrett's Orlando. Her father, E. L. Davenport, combined dignity with pathos as a humorously eccentric Jaques, a role he had previously taken in 1871. This production was given in May at the Fifth Avenue Theatre. The following November Daly mounted an elaborate production of the comedy, again with Miss Davenport, who was, however, a disappointing, one-dimensional Rosalind. Fortunately the scenery was in excellent taste, the costumes handsome, and Davidge was on hand as Touchstone.

Before this, during the 1872 season, Adelaide Neilson had made her initial New York appearance as the heroine, giving a performance which benefited from repetition and won considerable recognition by the end of the decade. In 1879 Ada Cavendish made her first appearance as Rosalind at Wallack's Theatre, but proved inadequate to the more profound sentiments of the heroine. The same criticism was leveled at Rose Coghlan in Lester Wallack's revival on September 30, 1880.

Lily Langtry and Helena Modjeska made their first New York appearances in the role of Rosalind within a month of each other, Mrs. Langtry at Wallack's Theatre on November 13, 1882, Mme. Modjeska at Booth's Theatre on December 11. Of the two, the Polish actress gave the superior interpretation, but no doubt the perfect Rosalind would have synthesized Langtry's sparkle with Modjeska's innate refinement and delicate expression of tenderness. Although the critics preferred Mme. Modjeska's tragic impersonations, she professed Rosalind her own favorite.

During the 1885/6 season Mary Anderson, after brilliant success as Rosalind at Stratford-upon-Avon, essayed the role at the Star Theatre. Her sympathetic heroine embodied all the animation, intelligence, tenderness, and sensitivity of the character, deftly making the transitions from quiet reflection to coy merriment. Adelaide Moore appeared in 1885 at the Star; Marie Wainwright acted the part at the same theatre in 1889. Credit for the most brilliant production of *As You Like It* in the 19th century goes to Augustin Daly. With Ada Rehan playing Rosalind for the first time, he presented what has been judged the finest production of the play on the American stage. All solemn overtones were studiously avoided in a springtime setting. Miss Rehan invested her portrayal with steady animation, perfect innocence, charming impulsiveness, and unfailing femininity. In this staging John Drew, who had previously acted Silvius with Fanny Davenport, portrayed Orlando with competence but little passion; George Clarke was a good-natured, cynical, convincing Jaques. *As You Like It* ran for 60 performances that season, and throughout the decade Miss Rehan appeared regularly in the comedy, continuing after Daly's death in 1898. Clarke appeared regularly with her.

Although Julia Marlowe played Rosalind in productions spanning more than 20 years, her performance in the part was hardly inspired. She first appeared at Tompkins' Fifth Avenue Theatre during the 1889/90 season and at the Knickerbocker Theatre in 1898. Orlandos in the several productions of the 1890's included Otis Skinner, W. S. Hart, and Maude Banks, who enacted the hero in an all-female *As You Like It* at Palmer's Theatre in 1893. Early in 1902 Henrietta Crosman, who had played Celia with Ada Rehan in 1899, made her first appearance as Rosalind in New York at the Republic. Familiarity with Miss Rehan's impersonation apparently gave little advantage, since Miss Crosman's portrayal, though intelligent, was devoid of spontaneity.

Julia Marlowe resumed the role during a repertory season at the Academy of Music, New York, in 1910. Her husband, E. H. Sothern, portrayed Jaques in this and subsequent presentations of the comedy during the next three years, but his delivery added no new significance to the character. *As You Like It* was included in Robert Mantell's repertory productions, and he played Orlando at Daly's Theatre in 1911, with Marie Booth Russell as Rosalind. In 1914 Margaret Anglin portrayed the heroine for the first time in New York at the Hudson Theatre. William Winter characterized Miss Anglin's performances in Shakespearean roles as being worthy of nothing more than qualified praise at their best. That critic had even harsher words for her Orlando, Pedro de Cordoba ("neither poetic nor romantic"), and devastated the production's Touchstone, Sidney Greenstreet ("silly, vacuous, vulgar, and offensive, and beneath criticism"). On February 8 and 9, 1918, Edith Wynne Matthison played Rosalind at the Cort Theatre.

In 1923 the comedy was presented as the first endeavor of the newly formed American National Theatre at the 44th Street Theatre. This presentation, produced by Augustus Thomas and staged by Robert Milton, opened on April 23 and closed after six performances, frustrating the movement for a national stage. While Ian Keith's Orlando convinced with a truly fervent impersonation, Marjorie Rambeau indulged in mechanical coquetry which lacked spirit and was further hampered by overly precise diction. Alexander Woollcott summarized the general opinion of this *As You Like It* with "a mighty good looking bore." Later, several repertory groups adopted the play. Fritz Leiber's company, based at the Civic Theatre in Chicago, presented it there during 1929/30 and again during 1930/1, giving performances also at the Shubert and Ambassador theatres in New York. During 1932/3, the Shakespeare Theatre Company staged the comedy 16 times at the Shakespeare Theatre in New York.

On October 30, 1930 the Surrey Players opened at the Ritz with a visually interesting and unpretentious production, spoiled, however, by excessive romping. Katherine Emery's Rosalind, though attractive, was too self-consciously coy, but Shepperd Strudwick gave an outstanding performance of Orlando that was remarkable for its honesty. Most later productions of the comedy likewise suffered from inadequate Rosalinds. In 1941 Ben A. Boyar's revival, clumsily directed by Eugene S. Bryden, was performed eight times at the Mansfield Theatre. Although Alfred Drake presented a virile, poetic, and intelligible Orlando, his Rosalind, Helen Craig, succumbed to the temptation of general coyness that never matched Drake's spirit. Leonard Elliott was an unusually young Touchstone, and Philip Bourneuf, as a sardonic Jaques, gave fresh meaning to the Seven Ages speech, recited most casually and without buffoonery.

A group of students from the University of Washington attempted unsuccessfully to impress New York with a modern-dress, three-act adaptation by John Burgess at the President Theatre on July 4, 1945. Margaretta Ramsey made a convincingly boyish Rosalind and Burgess acted with competence as Orlando; only Norman Budd, a New York professional, genuinely impressed audiences as Touchstone. Donald Wolfit's repertory group played an engagement at the Century Theatre in 1947, giving four performances of *As You Like It.* In 1950 Katharine Hepburn starred in a scenically sumptuous production at the Cort Theatre which ran for 145 performances, thanks in part to a publicity campaign emphasizing Miss Hepburn's considerable physical charm. Michael Benthall directed this commercially successful presentation, with William Prince as Orlando, Ernest Thesiger as Jaques, and Bill Owen as Touchstone.

The New York Shakespeare Festival offered two productions of *As You Like It.* The first, in 1958, directed by Stuart Vaughan, introduced a remarkable Jaques, George C. Scott, who gave a fresh reading of the Seven Ages speech. Walter Kerr, praising Scott's communication of sophisticated despair, pronounced that "the figure that emerges is stunningly new." Nancy Wickwire gave a winning performance as Rosalind, combining innocence and impetuosity. The second of Joseph Papp's productions of the comedy during the 1963 season fared less well. Jaques, as played by Frank Schofield, was competent, but offered no new insights, and Rosalind was reduced to shrillness in the hands of Paula Prentiss.

In between these productions, the comedy appeared at both Stratford Festivals, in Ontario in 1959 and in Connecticut in 1961. The earlier *As You Like It,* staged by Peter Wood, was a handsome production, but only Douglas Campbell as Touchstone, a shrewd buffoon, contributed anything more than a just satisfactory performance. Irene Worth's Rosalind and William Sylvester's Orlando were quite dull. The American-based company, directed by Word Baker, placed the action in a modern period, dressing a barefoot Orlando in overalls and the banished Duke's men in dungarees, while the courtiers wore madras jackets, the ladies, stylish dresses, and Sir Oliver Martext traveled about by bicycle. Kim Hunter, in her Shakespeare debut, was pleasant as Rosalind, as was Donald Harron as Orlando.

One of the latest American efforts with the play was a musical adaptation by Dran and Tani Seitz, twin sisters operating from the Theatre de Lys in New York, who portrayed Celia and Rosalind, respectively. Much of Shakespeare was retained in the lyrics, and the company, directed by Val Foralund, provided pleasant diversion for an afternoon, but nothing more.—M.G.

Bibliography. TEXT: *As You Like It*, New Cambridge Edition, Arthur Quiller-Couch and J. Dover Wilson, eds., 1926; W. W. Greg, *The Shakespeare First Folio*, 1955. DATE: New Cambridge Edition; *As You Like It*, George Lyman Kittredge, ed., 1939. SOURCES: Geoffrey Bullough, *Narrative and Dramatic Sources of Shakespeare*, Vol. II, 1958; Marco Mincoff, "What Shakespeare Did to Rosalynd," *Shakespeare-Jahrbuch*, 96, 1960. COMMENT: W. W. Greg, *Pastoral Poetry and Pastoral Drama*, 1906; Oscar James Campbell, *Shakespeare's Satire*, 1943; Alfred Harbage, *As They Liked It*, 1947. STAGE HISTORY: New Cambridge Edition; T. Alston Brown, *A History of the New York Stage, . . . to 1901*, 1903; William Winter, *Shakespeare on the Stage*, 3 vols., 1911–1916; G. C. D. Odell, *Shakespeare from Betterton to Irving*, 1920; J. C. Trewin, *Shakespeare on the English Stage, 1900–1964*, 1964.

Selected Criticism

A. W. SCHLEGEL. It would be difficult to bring the contents of *As You Like It* within the compass of an ordinary relation; nothing takes place, or rather what does take place is not so essential as what is said; even what may be called the denouement is brought about in a pretty arbitrary manner. Whoever perceives nothing but what is capable of demonstration will hardly be disposed to allow that it has any plan at all. Banishment and flight have assembled together in the Forest of Arden a singular society: a Duke dethroned by his brother, and, with his faithful companions in misfortune, living in the wilds on the produce of the chase; two disguised princesses, who love each other with a sisterly affection; a witty court fool; lastly, the native inhabitants of the forest, ideal and natural shepherds and shepherdesses. These lightly-sketched figures pass along in the most diversified succession; we see always the shady dark-green landscape in the background, and breathe in imagination the fresh air of the forest. The hours are here measured by no clocks, no regulated recurrence of duty or toil; they flow on unnumbered in voluntary occupation or fanciful idleness, to which every one addicts himself according to his humour or disposition; and this unlimited freedom compensates all of them for the lost conveniences of life. One throws himself down solitarily under a tree, and indulges in melancholy reflections on the changes of fortune, the falsehood of the world, and the self-created torments of social life; others make the woods resound with social and festive songs to the accompaniment of their horns. Selfishness, envy, and ambition have been left in the city behind them; of all the human passions, love alone has found an entrance into this wilderness, where it dictates the same language to the simple shepherd and the chivalrous youth, who hangs his love-ditty to a tree. A prudish shepherdess falls instantaneously in love with Rosalind, disguised in man's apparel; the latter sharply reproaches her with her severity to her poor lover, and the pain of refusal, which she at length feels from her own experience, disposes her to compassion and requital. The fool carries his philosophical contempt of external show and his raillery of the illusion of love so far, that he purposely seeks out the ugliest and simplest country wench for a mistress. Throughout the whole picture it seems to have been the intention of the poet to show that nothing is wanted to call forth the poetry which has its dwelling in nature and the human mind, but to throw off all artificial constraint and restore both to their native liberty. In the progress of the piece itself the visionary carelessness of such an existence is expressed; it has even been alluded to by Shakespeare in the title. Whoever affects to be displeased that in this romantic forest the ceremonial of dramatic art is not duly observed, ought in justice to be delivered over to the wise fool, for the purpose of being kindly conducted out of it to some prosaical region. [*A Course of Lectures on Dramatic Literature*, 1809–1811; trans. John Black, 1846.]

WILLIAM HAZLITT. It is the most ideal of any of this author's plays. It is a pastoral drama in which the interest arises more out of the sentiments and characters than out of the actions or situations. It is not what is done, but what is said, that claims our attention. Nursed in solitude, 'under the shade of melancholy boughs,' the imagination grows soft and delicate, and the wit runs riot in idleness, like a spoiled child that is never sent to school. Caprice and fancy reign and revel here, and stern necessity is banished to the court. The mild sentiments of humanity are strengthened with thought and leisure; the echo of the cares and noise of the world strikes upon the ear of those 'who have felt them knowingly,' softened by time and distance. 'They hear the tumult, and are still.' The very air of the place seems to breathe a spirit of philosophical poetry; to stir the thoughts, to touch the heart with pity, as the drowsy forest rustles to the sighing gale. Never was there such beautiful moralising, equally free from pedantry or petulance. . . . Within the sequestered and romantic glades of the Forest of Arden, they find leisure to be good and wise or to play the fool and fall in love. Rosalind's character is made up of sportive gayety and natural tenderness; her tongue runs the faster to conceal the pressure at her heart. She talks herself out of breath, only to get deeper in love. The coquetry with which she plays with her lover in the double character which she has to support is managed with the nicest address. . . . The silent and retired character of Celia is a necessary relief to the provoking loquacity of Rosalind. . . . The unrequited love of Silvius for Phoebe shows the perversity of this passion in the commonest scenes of life, and the rubs and stops which Nature throws in its way where fortune has placed none. [*The Characters of Shakespear's Plays*, 1817.]

EDWARD DOWDEN. Upon the whole, *As You Like It* is the sweetest and happiest of all Shakspere's comedies. No one suffers; no one lives an eager intense life; there is no tragic interest in it as there is in *The Merchant of Venice*, as there is in *Much Ado About Nothing*. It is mirthful, but the mirth is sprightly, graceful, exquisite; there is none of the rollicking fun of a Sir Toby here; the songs are not "coziers' catches" shouted in the nighttime, "without any mitigation or remorse of voice," but the solos and duets of pages in the wildwood, or the noisier chorus of foresters. The wit of Touchstone is not mere clownage, nor has it any indirect serious significances; it is a dainty kind of absurdity worthy to hold comparison with the melancholy of Jacques. And Orlando in the beauty and strength of early manhood, and Rosalind,

> A gallant curtle-axe upon her thigh,
> A boar-spear in her hand,

and the bright, tender, loyal womanhood within—are figures which quicken and restore our spirits, as music does, which is neither noisy nor superficial, and yet which knows little of the deep passion and sorrow of the world.

Shakspere, when he wrote this idyllic play, was himself in his Forest of Arden. He had ended one great ambition—the historical plays—and not yet commenced his tragedies. It was a resting place. He sends his imagination into the woods to find repose. [*Shakspere: A Critical Study of His Mind and Art*, 1875.]

MARK VAN DOREN. "As You Like It" is a criticism of the pastoral sentiment, an examination of certain familiar ideas concerning the simple life and the golden age. It is not satire; its examination is conducted without prejudice. For once in the world a proposition is approached from all of its sides, and from top and bottom. The proposition is perhaps multiple: the country is more natural than the court, shepherds live lives of enviable innocence and simplicity, the vices that devour the heart of civilized man will drop from him as soon as he walks under a greenwood tree, perversion and malice cannot survive in the open air, the shade of beech trees is the only true Academy, one impulse from the vernal wood will teach us more than all the sages can. Yet it is single too, and pastoral literature has monotonously intoned it. Shakespeare relieves the monotony by statement which is also understanding, by criticism which is half laughter and half love—or, since his laughter is what it is, all love. The result is something very curious. When Rosalind has made her last curtsy and the comedy is done, the pastoral sentiment is without a leg to stand on, yet it stands; and not only stands but dances. The idea of the simple life has been smiled off the earth and yet here it still is, smiling back at us from every bough of Arden. The Forest of Arden has been demonstrated not to exist, yet none of its trees has fallen; rather the entire plantation waves forever, and the sun upon it will not cease. The doctrine of the golden age has been as much created as destroyed. We know there is nothing in it, and we know that everything is in it. We perceive how silly it is and why we shall never be able to do without it. We comprehend the long failure of cynicism to undo sentiment. Here there is neither sentiment nor cynicism; there is understanding. [*Shakespeare*, 1939.]

HAROLD JENKINS. In Corin Shakespeare provides us with a touchstone with which to test the pastoral. Corin's dialogue with the Touchstone of the court, dropped into the middle of the play, adds to the conventional antithesis between courtier and countryman a glimpse of the real thing. Our picture of the court as a place of tyranny, ambition and corruption is no doubt true enough. But its colours are modified somewhat when Touchstone gives us the court's plain routine. For him, as he lets us know on another occasion, the court is the place where he has trod a measure, flattered a lady, been smooth with his enemy and undone three tailors. Though Touchstone seeks to entangle Corin in the fantastications of his wit, his arguments to show that the court is better than the sheepfarm have a way of recoiling on himself. What emerges from the encounter of these two realists is that ewe and ram, like man and woman, are put together and that though the courtier perfumes his body it sweats like any other creature's. In city or country, *all* ways of life are at bottom the same, and we recognize a conclusion that Jaques, by a different route, has helped us to reach before.

The melancholy moralizings of Jaques and the Robin Hood raptures of the Duke, though in contrast, are equally the product of man's spirit. There has to be someone in Arden to remind us of the indispensable flesh. It was a shrewd irony of Shakespeare's to give this office to the jester. Whether he is wiser or more foolish than other men it is never possible to decide, but Touchstone is, as well as the most artificial wit, the most natural man of them all; and the most conscious of his corporal needs. After the journey to the forest Rosalind complains of a weariness of spirits, to which Touchstone retorts "I care not for my spirits, if my legs were not weary." And when he displays his wit at the expense of Orlando's bad verses, saying "I'll rhyme you so eight years together," he remembers to add "dinners and suppers and sleeping-hours excepted." A "material fool," as Jaques notes. This preoccupation with the physical makes Touchstone the obvious choice for the sensual lover who will burlesque the romantic dream. So Touchstone not only deprives the yokel William of his mistress, but steals his part in the play, making it in the process of infinitely greater significance. ["As You Like It," *Shakespeare Survey 8*, 1955.]

JOHN RUSSELL BROWN. To follow Jaques through the play is to become aware of Shakespeare's preoccupation with the ideal of order in society, in Arden, and in love, and of the subtlety and range of his consequent judgements. But Jaques alone cannot suggest the light-footed gaiety, the warmth, and the confidence with which this comedy is written. Some of these qualities derive from the apparently easy interplay between the varied and individually conceived characters; for example, the absurdly single-minded Silvius is first introduced talking to the simply and sensibly satisfied Corin, and overheard by Rosalind and Touchstone, and then, later, Touchstone and Corin meet and compare their individual 'simplicities'. But the play's generosity and confidence spring chiefly from the characterization of Rosalind. She ensures that Shakespeare's ideal of love's order is not presented as a cold theorem; in her person love's doubts and faith, love's obedience and freedom, coexist in delightful animation. . . .

In the two central scenes between Orlando and Rosalind, Shakespeare shows us the growing assurance of their mutual love, its generosity, truth, and order. And at the close of the play, he directs that they should take hands in the forefront of the other lovers and, after the final dance affirming the creation of mutual order, that they should go back with the duke to the court, away from purely subjective content—they go to play their part on the great stage of society and to affirm order and harmony there. [*Shakespeare and His Comedies*, 1957.]

C. L. BARBER. . . . the reality we feel about the experience of love in the play, reality which is not in the pleasant little prose romance, comes from presenting what was sentimental extremity as impulsive extravagance and so leaving judgment free to mock what the heart embraces. The Forest of Arden, like the Wood outside Athens, is a region defined by an attitude of liberty from ordinary limitations, a festive place where the folly of romance can have its day. The first half of *As You Like It*, beginning with tyrant brother and tyrant Duke and moving out into the forest, is chiefly concerned with establishing the sense of freedom; the traditional contrast of court and country is developed in a way that is shaped by the contrast between everyday and holiday, as that antithesis has become part of Shakespeare's art and sensibility. Once we are securely in the golden world where the good Duke and "a many merry men . . . fleet the time carelessly," the pastoral motif as such drops into the background; Rosalind finds Orlando's verses in the second scene of Act III, and the rest of the play deals with love. This second movement is like a musical theme with imitative variations. . . . The love affairs of Silvius and Phebe, Touchstone and Audrey, Orlando and Rosalind succeed one another in the easy-going sequence of scenes, while the dramatist deftly plays each off against the others. ["The Alliance of Seriousness and Levity in *As You Like It*," *Shakespeare's Festive Comedy*, 1959.]

Athenian. In *Timon of Athens*, a citizen whose daughter is being courted by Timon's servant Lucilius. The old Athenian asks Timon to forbid the courtship. Ascertaining that his servant and the girl love one another, Timon arranges the match and wins the old man's consent by matching the girl's dowry and inheritance (I, i).

Atkins, Robert (1886–). Actor and director. Atkins began his professional career with Herbert Beerbohm Tree's company in London, and later joined the companies of Forbes-Robertson and Frank Benson, gaining much experience in Shakespearean roles. He joined the youthful Shakespearean repertory company at the Old Vic in 1915, where he played Iago, Jaques, Prospero, and Cassius. From 1920 to 1925 he was a director of the company. During this time he mounted a number of Shakespearean productions, among which were the then rarely performed complete *Henry VI* and *Titus Andronicus*. From 1933 to 1939 he directed and performed in such plays as *Twelfth Night*, *A Midsummer Night's*

Dream, and *The Tempest*, and during the war years mounted Shakespearean plays at Regent's Park. He produced *Henry V* at Stratford-upon-Avon in 1934 and from 1944 to 1945 was director of the Stratford-upon-Avon Shakespeare Memorial Theatre, now the Royal Shakespeare Theatre. In 1953 he directed *Twelfth Night* again, appearing in one of his favorite roles, Sir Toby Belch, and in 1955 directed *A Midsummer Night's Dream*. [*Who's Who in the Theatre*, 1961.]

Atkinson, William (b. 1571). A witness to Shakespeare's purchase of the Blackfriars Gate-House in 1613. Atkinson was a resident of St. Mary Aldermanbury parish in London, the parish of John Heminges and Henry Condell, Shakespeare's fellow actors. He was also the clerk of the Brewers Company, in which capacity he probably knew two of Shakespeare's trustees in the purchase, John Jackson and William Johnson, the host of the Mermaid Tavern. The third trustee was Heminges. [Leslie Hotson, *Shakespeare's Sonnets Dated*, 1949.]

Aubrey, John (1626–1697). Gentleman antiquary. Aubrey lived a gay, irresponsible life, spending much of his time visiting friends in the country and pumping them for information about celebrities. The biographical information he collected was largely for inclusion in Anthony à Wood's *Athenae Oxonienses* (1692), a biographical register of distinguished graduates of Oxford. Aubrey's collection is generally known as *Aubrey's Brief Lives* (first published in 1813).

Aubrey's method of obtaining information was to visit one of his cronies at his country seat, there to spend an evening in gossip and conviviality. Early the next morning he would get up before his host had stirred and, his head not completely clear, would write down what he hazily remembered of the last night's talk. He made no attempt to produce a fair copy. He left blanks for dates and many other facts and inserted fresh material at random. Thus while Aubrey's biographical notes are always interesting and frequently hilarious, their authority is something less than unimpeachable.

In collecting information for his biography of Shakespeare, however, he chose at least one reliable source—William Beeston, whose father Christopher was a fellow actor in Shakespeare's company (see BEESTON FAMILY). Aubrey's account includes the information that in his younger days Shakespeare was a schoolmaster in the country, a theory that has been revived by a number of recent scholars. Aubrey's account of Shakespeare is as follows:

> Mr. William Shakespear. [*bay-wreath in margin*] was borne at Stratford vpon Avon, in the County of Warwick; his father was a Butcher, & I have been told heretofore by some of the neighbours, that when he was a boy he exercised his father's Trade, but when he kill'd a Calfe, he would doe it in a *high style*, & make a Speech. There was at that time another Butcher's son in this Towne, that was held not at all inferior to him for a naturall witt, his acquaintance & coetanean, but dyed young. This Wm. being inclined naturally to Poetry and acting, came to London I guesse about 18. and was an Actor at one of the Play-houses and did act exceedingly well: now B. Johnson was never a good Actor, but an excellent Instructor. He began early to make essayes at Dramatique Poetry, which at that time was very lowe; and his Playes tooke well: He was a handsome well shap't man: very good company, and of a very readie and pleasant smooth Witt. The Humour of . . . the Constable in a Midsomersnight's Dreame, he happened to take at Grendon [*in margin*, I thinke it was Midsomer night that he happened to lye there.] in Bucks which is the roade from London to Stratford, and there was living that Constable about 1642 when I first came to Oxon. Mr. Jos. Howe is of that parish and knew him. Ben Johnson and he did gather Humours of men dayly where ever they came. One time as he was at the Tavern at Stratford super Avon, one Combes an old rich Usurer was to be buryed, he makes there this extemporary Epitaph
>
> Ten in the Hundred the Devill allowes
> But *Combes* will have twelve, he sweares & vowes:
> If any one askes who lies in this Tombe:
> Hoh! quoth the Devill, 'Tis my John o' Combe.
>
> He was wont to goe to his native Country once a yeare. I thinke I have been told that he left 2 or 300li per annum there and therabout: to a sister. [*In margin*, V. his Epitaph in Dugdales Warwickshire.] I have heard Sr Wm. Davenant and Mr. Thomas Shadwell (who is counted the best Comoedian we have now) say, that he had a most prodigious Witt, and did admire his naturall parts beyond all other Dramaticall writers. He was wont to say, That he never blotted out a line in his life: sayd Ben: Johnson, I wish he had blotted out a thousand. [*In margin*, B. Johnsons Underwoods.] His Comoedies will remaine witt, as long as the English tongue is understood; for that he handles mores hominum; now our present writers reflect so much upon particular persons, and coxcombeities, that 20 yeares hence, they will not be understood. Though as Ben: Johnson sayes of him, that he had but little Latine and lesse Greek, He understood Latine pretty well: for he had been in his younger yeares a Schoolmaster in the Countrey. [*In margin:* from Mr ——— Beeston.]

Audeley, John. See John SHAKESPEARE.

Auden, W[ystan] H[ugh] (1907–). Poet and critic. Educated at Christ's Church, Oxford, Auden taught school at Malvern from 1930 to 1935. With his *Poems* (1930) and *The Orators* (1932), he was recognized as a dominant figure among the intellectual leftists of the 1930's. He moved to the United States in 1939 and in 1946 became an American citizen. Besides a large and varied literary output—poetry, criticism, translations, libretti—he has been active as an editor, teacher, and lecturer. He received the Pulitzer Prize in 1947 for *The Age of Anxiety* and served as professor of poetry at Oxford from 1956 to 1960. His *Collected Poetry* (1945) and *Selected Poetry* (1959) contain the bulk of his early poems; *Homage to Clio*, containing his later poems, was published in 1960. Both as poet and critic, Auden has been concerned with Shakespeare. *The Sea and the Mirror*, published in 1944 with *For the Time Being*, is a closet drama drawing upon *The Tempest* for both characters and structure. The subtitle, "A Commentary on Shakespeare's *The Tempest*," suggests an interpretation of the play, but that end is subordinate to Auden's own theme of the relationship of art to reality. The second part of *The Age of Anxiety* is "The Seven Ages," a psychological interpretation of Jaques' speech in *As You Like It* (II, vii, 139 ff.). *The Dyer's Hand* (1962), the title taken from Shakespeare's Sonnet 111, is a miscellany of criticism with a number of observations on Shakespeare. Section IV, "The Shakespearian City," consists of several essays which deal with the nature of tragedy, Falstaff, *The Merchant of Venice*, and *Othello;* the final essay is entitled "Music in Shakespeare." Auden has also written introductions to the Laurel Shakespeare *Romeo and Juliet* (1958) and the Signet Shakespeare *Sonnets* (1964). [Monroe K. Spears, *The Poetry of W. H. Auden*, 1963.]

audiences. The audiences that gathered at the Globe represented almost every element in London's immensely varied population. The prices were distinctly popular, designed to fit the purse of the great mass of the citizens. The bulk of a typical audience was made up of shopkeepers, craftsmen, and other persons in the lower income groups. Though these bourgeois folk were the "groundlings" (i.e., those who stood on the ground in the orchestra where there were no seats), a title which has come to be opprobrious, they were solid, well-behaved citizens, in no sense an undisciplined rabble. There were many apprentices in most audiences. Ranging in age from 17 to 24, they formed a class by themselves. Though they seem to have frequently created disturbances within the theatre and in its neighborhood, their demonstrations were little more than expressions of youthful exuberance, a spirit that inside the playhouse provided an enthusiasm for which both playwright and actor were grateful. As a group they were intelligent and well-bred, for they always came from well-to-do families and had usually enjoyed a grammar school education.

The gentry in the audience included professional men, attendants at the court or in noble households, and lesser gentlemen. These were the occupants of the two- and three-penny seats in the galleries. Earls and other great lords often appeared either in the conspicuous seats on the stage or in the 12-penny rooms. It is difficult to determine how large a part of an average audience at the Globe was composed of men at the lower end of the social scale. Professor Alfred Harbage, author of the excellent *Shakespeare's Audience* (1941), believes that members of the proletariat constituted never more than 10 per cent of an Elizabethan audience.

Women, not merely "light" women but the respectable wives and daughters of ordinary tradesmen, attended the London theatres as a matter of course. The evidence establishing this fact is overwhelming. Foreign visitors to London during the years in which Shakespeare wrote his plays remark with some surprise that "women-folk" and "many respectable women" attend the theatre without scruple.

This heterogeneous yet on the whole intelligent crowd was frequently large. A thousand spectators often gathered for a performance in the Globe or the Fortune, both of which probably had a capacity of somewhat over 2000. A typical audience of this size was probably not so badly behaved as diatribes by Puritan enemies of the stage have led many modern historians to believe. That purses were sometimes "cut," or stolen, was inevitable among members of a close-packed crowd whose attention was riveted to the stage. Some prostitutes certainly attended the theatres and occasionally solicited. But the insinuation of some Puritan writers that an Elizabethan theatre was a kind of anteroom to a house of assignation is mere slander.

Judged by modern standards, Elizabethan audiences were very demonstrative. There is much evidence to show that they wept unashamedly at pathetic or stirring scenes. Nashe reports that the "teares of ten thousand spectators" were called forth by the death of brave Talbot, the hero of *1 Henry VI*. Laughter and applause were also unrestrained. Shouts of approval or expressions of violent displeasure, such as catcalls and hisses, frequently interrupted the action and the speeches. For such audiences the Elizabethan dramatist was forced to endow even his gentler characters with animation and to keep the action of his play continuously stirring. The spectators thus played no small part in establishing the virile character of the Elizabethan plays. [Alfred Harbage, *Shakespeare's Audience*, 1941.]—O.J.C.

Audrey. In *As You Like It*, a stolid, illiterate country wench. Audrey jilts her former lover, William, for a more attractive match with Touchstone, who describes her as "a poor virgin, an ill-favoured thing, but mine own" (V, iv).

Aufidius, Tullus. In *Coriolanus*, the Volscian general. Aufidius accepts an alliance with the banished Coriolanus, who promises to lead an attack on Rome. When Coriolanus wavers in his resolve and instead offers an advantageous peace with Rome, Aufidius jealously gathers a band of conspirators and murders him.

Aumerle, Edward of Norwich, duke of (c. 1373–1415). Eldest son of Edmund of Langley, 1st duke of York. One of Richard II's most active supporters, Aumerle participated in the arrest of Gloucester, Arundel, and Warwick, who had formed an alliance against the king. In Henry IV's first parliament in 1399, Aumerle was charged with Gloucester's death but was pardoned. Although he was thought to have been involved in the conspiracy of January 1400 against the life of the new king, it is doubtful that Aumerle actually participated. On his father's death in 1402, he became 2nd duke of York. Subsequently accompanying Henry V to France, Aumerle, now York, was killed in the battle of Agincourt.

In *Richard II*, as in history, Aumerle supports his cousin Richard against his other cousin Bolingbroke. At Henry's parliament, Sir John Bagot and Lord Fitzwater accuse Aumerle of murdering Gloucester (IV, i), and later, Aumerle's father, the Duke of York, denounces his son for treason. On the latter's confession, Henry pardons him (V, iii). In *Henry V*, as Duke of York, he dies after fighting bravely (IV, vi). [W. H. Thomson, *Shakespeare's Characters: A Historical Dictionary*, 1951.]

Austen, Jane (1775–1817). Novelist, considered by many the greatest of women novelists. Jane Austen wrote six complete novels of which *Pride and Prejudice* (1813) and *Emma* (1816) are often considered her finest. Several critics have made brief comments about a similarity in humor and technique between the comedies of Shakespeare and Jane Austen's novels. The parallelism is most striking between *Much Ado About Nothing* and *Pride and Prejudice*. The main plot of each concerns the fortunes of two lovers—Claudio and Hero, Bingley and Jane—their estrangement, and eventual reunion. The subplot of each deals with a second pair of lovers—Benedick and Beatrice, Darcy and Elizabeth—who engage in a spirited battle between the sexes; it is this pair, rather than the somewhat colorless lovers of the main plot, who capture the interest of the reader or audience. In both works the male figure of the subplot must prove his worth by aiding the lovers of the main plot. Reconciliation, in both the novel and the play, is brought about accidentally through the blunders of minor characters (Dogberry and the watch, Lady de Bourgh). In many respects *Pride and Prejudice* captures the spirit of *Much Ado About Nothing* and places it in a middle-class, 19th-century setting.

Austria, duke of. See LYMOGES.

Autolycus. In *The Winter's Tale*, a peddler and pickpocket. Modeled on the rogues and knaves of the CONY-CATCHING PAMPHLETS, Autolycus escapes the audience's moral disapprobation as a result of his irrepressible gaiety and light heart. He confesses amorality in both song and verse with a disarming candor and spirited wit. His character serves a necessary function in the play, undercutting the potentially cloying idyllic atmosphere of Act IV. His lightly cynical portrait of the gulls whom he fleeces offers us an indirect critique of pastoral simplicity without entirely negating that view of life. His own properly qualified love of life is exhibited in his songs, five of which he sings during the play. His opening song ("When daffodils begin to peer," IV, iii, 1–12) is an indication of the new mood in which the atmosphere of the play is to be enveloped, a heralding that the winter of the first three acts has been succeeded by the joyous springtime which the remainder of the play celebrates.

Auvergne, Countess of. In *1 Henry VI*, the French noblewoman who tries unsuccessfully to capture Lord Talbot in her castle (II, iii). The Countess of Auvergne may have been modeled on Mary, wife of Bertrand III, count of Auvergne. [W. H. Thomson, *Shakespeare's Characters: A Historical Dictionary*, 1951.]

Ayrer, Jakob (c. 1543–1605). German dramatist. The author of over 60 plays, published in 1618 as *Opus Theatricum*, Ayrer was heavily influenced in his dramaturgy by the troupes of English actors who toured Germany in the 16th and 17th centuries (see GERMANY). He borrowed many of the techniques, as well as the character of the clown, from these companies. At least three of Ayrer's plays have strong similarities to Shakespeare's. His *Comedia von zweyen Brudern aus Syracusn* (written before 1605) parallels the *Comedy of Errors* and is probably derived from Plautus' *Menaechmi*. His *Die Schöne Phänicia*, written between 1593 and 1605, is analogous to *Much Ado About Nothing*, being based on the same story in Bandello's *Novelle* from which Shakespeare ultimately derived his plot. His *Die Schöne Sidea* (written before 1605) reveals many similarities to *The Tempest*, for which no source has been found. It is generally assumed, however, that here, as in the other two instances, both dramatists were working independently from common sources.

Ayscough, Samuel (1745–1804). Scholar and librarian. In 1785 Ayscough was appointed assistant librarian at the British Museum where he worked indefatigably compiling indexes and catalogues to the manuscripts and books there. In 1790 Ayscough published his *Index to Shakespeare* which was in fact the first concordance to the plays and which remained the standard one until superseded by the concordances of John Bartlett and Mary Cowden Clarke.

B

Bach, Carl Philip Emanuel. See MUSIC BASED ON SHAKESPEARE: *18th century*.

Backstead, William. See William BARKSTEAD.

Bacon, Delia (1811–1859). American author and teacher whose essays and books popularized the notion that Shakespeare is not the author of the plays ascribed to him (see BACONIAN THEORY). Delia Bacon's ideas were first expressed in an article in *Putnam's Monthly Magazine* (1856) and later expanded into a book titled *The Philosophy of the Plays of Shakespeare Unfolded* (1857). Her book, to which Nathaniel Hawthorne wrote a preface, sets forth the theory that a group of leading Elizabethan thinkers under the direction of Francis Bacon wrote the plays in order to advance, in allegorical form, the philosophical position identified with Bacon. Technically, therefore, she did not suggest that Bacon wrote the plays but that he was the presiding genius of the group who did, which she identifies as "Raleigh's school." Shortly before the publication of her book, Miss Bacon traveled to England in order to obtain the proof of her theory. She was convinced that the evidence was to be found under the gravestone of Shakespeare. Apparently, however, she was unable to bring herself to remove the stone. Shortly thereafter she became hopelessly insane and was confined to a sanatorium where she remained until her death in 1859. [Frank W. Wadsworth, *The Poacher from Stratford*, 1958.]

Bacon, Francis (1561–1626). Philosopher, essayist, and statesman. Bacon, whose name is inextricably linked with Shakespeare's as a result of the notion that he is the author of Shakespeare's works (see BACONIAN THEORY), was born in London and educated at Cambridge and Gray's Inn. In 1584 he became a member of parliament, some time thereafter securing the friendship of Robert Devereux, earl of Essex and favorite of the queen. The friendship, however, came to an abrupt end with the fiasco of Essex' attempt to seize the throne in 1601. Bacon, at this time a member of the queen's counsel, was an official at the Essex trial, and to him fell the unhappy task of justifying to the public the government's execution of Essex. The result was the *Declaration of the Practices and Treasons attempted and committed by Robert, late Earle of Essex* (1601), a document which makes reference to the fact that on the day before the Essex rebellion, a group of his fellow conspirators had deliberately arranged for Shakespeare's company to present "the play of deposing King Richard the second." The document makes no attempt, however, to implicate the players in the rebellion.

Bacon's subsequent career reads like an illustration of the medieval notion of the "wheel of fortune," wherein one is raised to the heights of success only to be cast down at the whim of Dame Fortune. In 1617 he was designated as lord keeper; in 1618 lord chancellor with the title Baron Verulam. In 1621 he was again honored, receiving the title of Viscount St. Albans, but in May of that year he was convicted of taking bribes and deprived of his official position. He devoted the rest of his life to writing and scientific experiment.

Of Bacon's literary works the best known are the *Essays* (1597, rev. 1625), but his most significant achievement is his overstated but important critique

FRANCIS BACON. PORTRAIT BY DANIEL MYTENS. (NATIONAL PORTRAIT GALLERY)

of the existing philosophical "establishment" in the *Novum Organum* (1620) and *The Advancement of Learning* (1605). As a constructive thinker he had serious limitations, but his influence on succeeding generations has been considerable.

Bacon, Matthew [Mathias] (fl. 1590–1615). The defendant in a friendly suit brought by Shakespeare and a number of other tenants of the Blackfriars district. The BLACKFRIARS GATE-HOUSE, which Shakespeare purchased from Henry Walker in 1613, had formerly belonged to Bacon, who had sold it to Walker in 1604. Bacon had inherited the gatehouse and adjacent properties from his mother, Ann Bacon, and had long since disposed of them. However, he required court authorization before surrendering the relevant deeds and documents. Thus the suit was a formality which enabled the *de facto* owners to become the legal owners. The suit was instituted by Shakespeare and his neighbors on April 26, 1615 by a petition in chancery court:

> Humblie complayninge sheweth vnto your Honorable Lordship your daylie oratoures Sir Thomas Bendishe Baronet, Edward Newport and Willyam Thoresbie Esquiours, Robert Dormer Esquiour and Marie his wife, Willyam Shakespere, gent., and Richard Bacon Citezen of London, That whearas your oratours be and are seuerallye lawfullie seised in there demesne as of fee of and in one capitall messuage or dwellinge howse with there appurtenaunces with two court yardes, and one void plot of grownd sometymes vsed for a garden on the east parte of the said dwellinge howse, and so much of one edifice as now or sometymes served for two stables and two haye loftes over the said stables and one litle colehowse adioyninge to the said stables, lyinge on the south side of the said dwellinge howse, and of another messuage or tenemente with thappurtenaunces now in the occupacion of Anthony Thompson and Thomas Perckes and of there assignes, & of a void peece of grownd whervppon a stable is builded to the said meassuage belonginge, and of seuerall othere howses devided into seuerall lodginges or dwellinge howses, toginther with all and singuler sellours, sollers, chambers, halls, parlours, yardes, backsides, easementes, profites and comodityes hervnto seuerallie belonginge, and of certaine void plotes of grownd adioyninge to the said messuages and premisses aforesaid or vnto some of them, and of a well howse, All which messuages, tenementes and premisses aforesaid be lyinge within the precinct of Black Friers in the Cittye of London or Countye of Middlesex, late the messuages, tenementes and enheritances of Willyam Blackwell thelder, Henrie Blackwell and Willyam Blackwell the younger, and of Ann Bacon, or some or one of them, Vnto which foresaid capitall messuages, tenementes and premisses aforesaid seuerall deedes, charteres, letters patentes, evidences, munimentes and wrightinges be and are belonginge and apperteyninge and do belonge vnto your oratours, and doe serve for the provinge of your oratours lawfull right, title, interest and estate in, to and vnto the foresaid messuages and premisses, All which foresaid letters patentes, deedes, evidences, charteres, munimentes and wrightinges aforesaid were left in trust with Ann Bacon deceassed for and vnto the vse and behooffe of your orators; Now so yt is, may yt please your Honorable Lordship, that the said Ann Bacon beinge latelie dead and Mathy Bacon being her sole executour the foresaid letters patentes, deedes, charteres, and evidences, muniments and wrightinges aforesaid be since her death come vnto and now be in the handes and possession of the foresaid Mathy Bacon, who doth not clayme any right, estate or interest at all in or vnto the foresaid messuages or tenementes Yet neuertheles the said Mathy Bacon, knowinge the messuages, tenementes, letters patentes, deedes, evidences, charteres, munimentes and wrightinges aforesaid to be belonging and onelie to belonge to your oratours, doth neuertheles withhould, keepe and deteyne awaye from your oratours the foresaid letters patentes and other deedes, evidences, charteres, munimentes and wrightinges aforesaid and will not deliuer the same vnto your oratours, wherby your oratours be in great danger for to loose and be disinherited of the messuages, tenements and premisses aforesaid;

Bacon's reply was delivered in court on May 5, 1615. He denied any claim to the title of the property, asking only to be relieved of responsibility regarding the papers:

> The answeare of Mathye Bacon gent. defendant to the bill of complaynte of Sir Thomas Bendishe Baronett, Edward Newport esquier, William Thoresbye esquier, Robert Dormer esquier and Mary his wife, William Shakespeare gent. and Richard Bacon citizen of London, complaynantes.
>
> The said defendant, savinge to himselfe nowe and all tymes hereafter all advantage and benefit of excepcion to all and every the incertenties & insufficiencies of the said bill of complaynte, saieth that hee thinketh it to be true that the said complaynantes are lawfullye severally seised in theire demesne as of fee of and in one capitall messuage or dwellinge house with thappurtenances and other the tenementes, stables, edefices and voide groundes mencioned in the said bill of complaynte, and likewise thinketh it to be true that the same were late the messuages, tenementes and inheritances of William Blackwell the elder deceased, Henry Blakwell and William Blakwell the yonger, and of Anne Bacon deceased mother of the said defendant, or of some of them. And this Defendant further saieth that hee doth not nowe clayme to haue any estate, right, title or interest of, in or to the said premisses or any parte or parcell thereof.

On May 22 the court decreed that the defendant be ordered to deliver the documents to court in order to have them distributed to the rightful owners:

> It is therevppon ordered that the said defendant shall bringe into this corte all the said letters patentes, deedes, evidences, writinges & mynumentes soe by him confessed to be in his custodye or possession vpon his oath, here to remayne to bee disposed of as shalbe meate, and for that purpose the plaintiffes maye take proces against the defendant if they will.

Bacon, a resident of Holborn, London, was admitted to Gray's Inn in 1597 and was employed as a scrivener. [C. W. Wallace, "The Newly Discovered Shakespeare Documents," *University of Nebraska Studies,* 5, 1905; E. K. Chambers, *William Shakespeare,* 1930.]

Baconian theory. A theory that ascribes the works of Shakespeare to Francis Bacon. The Baconian theory is the oldest and the best-known expression of a widely held, popular belief that Shakespeare was not the author of the plays that bear his name.

The theory was first advanced by Herbert Lawrence in 1769 in *The Life and Adventures of Common Sense,* but was apparently disregarded or overlooked until almost 80 years later when Joseph C. Hart in *The Romance of Yachting* (1848) reasserted the hypothesis. Hart's ideas were further expanded and elaborated upon by W. H. Smith in *Was Bacon the Author of Shakespeare's Plays?* (1856), but they achieved their highest emotional pitch in the writings of Delia BACON who, while not advocating Bacon's sole authorship, furiously discredited the "Stratford poacher" as a "vulgar, illiterate man" and described his company as a "dirty, doggish group of players." Miss Bacon thus sounded what has always been the basic premise of the Baconian position—that it is virtually impossible for the barely literate country bumpkin from Stratford to be the author of the immortal literature which has been attributed to him.

In 1885, The Bacon Society was founded and in 1892 its journal, *Baconiana,* began to appear regularly. At the same time, in the United States, Mrs. C. F. Ashmead Windle, acting on a reference in Delia Bacon's work to a hidden cipher, was working on a study of what she called the "VEILED ALLEGORY" of the plays. Her ideas were taken up with many ingenious modifications by Ignatius DONNELLY, whose giant book *The Great Cryptogram* (1888) claimed to have solved the cipher which Bacon had supposedly planted in the First Folio. The cipher proved that Bacon was the author not only of the known Shakespeare plays, but also of most of the plays classified under the Shakespearean APOCRYPHA, as well as the works of Christopher Marlowe, the essays of Montaigne, and Burton's *Anatomy of Melancholy* (1621).

By the time Donnelly's book appeared, the authorship question had already become an international *cause célèbre,* but his work opened the floodgates of inspiration and speculation which continued unabated into the 20th century. The most notable disciples of Donnelly were Mark Twain, who wrote *Is Shakespeare Dead?* (1909) under another pseudonym, and Sir Edwin Durning Lawrence, whose *Bacon Is Shakespeare* appeared in 1910. Sir Edwin verified his theory by reference to the long word, "Honorificabilitudinitatibus," that appears in *Love's Labour's Lost* (V, i, 44); a rearrangement of the word, he argued, revealed the Latin message "HI LUDI F. BACON NATI TUITI ORBI" ("these plays, offspring of F. Bacon, are preserved for the world"). See NORTHUMBERLAND MS.

At this time, however, a number of heretical movements began to spring up, claiming authorship of the plays for other prominent Elizabethans. (See CLAIMANTS.) The result of the division among "anti-Stratfordians" has been a lessening of the impact of the Baconians. Nevertheless, The Bacon Society continues to be active today, publishing its findings with undiminished zeal, continuing its demand that Shakespeare's tomb be opened, and defying all disbelievers—even schismatics like J. Freeman Clarke, who argues that Shakespeare wrote the works of Bacon. [W. and E. Friedman, *The Shakespearean Ciphers Examined,* 1957; Frank W. Wadsworth, *The Poacher from Stratford,* 1958; John Crow, "Heretics Observed," *Times Literary Supplement,* April 23, 1964.]

Badger, George (fl. 1565–1606). A woolen draper of Stratford to whom John Shakespeare in 1597 sold a "toft" of land on the west side of his property in Henley Street. A "toft" was the name usually given to a piece of land on which a building had formerly stood. However, since the "toft" sold by Shakespeare was only ½-yard wide and 28 yards long, it is unlikely that a building had once been there. Badger owned the property immediately west of John Shakespeare's, and he probably bought the strip of land in order to build a wall.

Badger, the father of 16 children, was a successful and well-known figure in Stratford. He served as an alderman from 1594 to 1598. [Mark Eccles, *Shakespeare in Warwickshire,* 1961.]

bad quartos. Name given to a group of corrupt early editions of Shakespeare's plays. The term "bad quarto" was first employed by the great bibliographical scholar A. W. Pollard in an attempt to distinguish those quarto editions referred to by Heminges and Condell in the Preface to the First Folio as "stolne, and surreptitious copies." The editions cited by Pollard were the First Quartos of *Romeo and Juliet, Henry V, Hamlet,* and *The Merry Wives of Windsor.* This canon of bad quartos was enlarged in 1929 by Peter Alexander when he conclusively demonstrated that the CONTENTION PLAYS were not, as had long been thought, sources of *2* and *3 Henry VI,* but were in fact bad quartos of Shakespeare's plays.

Another text sometimes regarded as a bad quarto is the so-called "pied bull" edition (1608) of *King Lear,* although the *Lear* play does not exhibit the radically corrupt features of the earlier bad quartos (see KING LEAR: *Text*). Similarly, the 1609 edition of *Pericles* bears some of the earmarks of a bad quarto. See PERICLES: *Text.*

Two other plays have been suggested as possible bad quartos. These are the two Shakespearean source plays *The Troublesome Raigne of King John,* conjectured to be a bad quarto of *King John,* and *The Taming of A Shrew,* which Peter Alexander has argued is a bad quarto of the Shakespeare Shrew play. Although the arguments in support of these hypotheses have been advanced with considerable ingenuity, they have not as yet gained general acceptance.

The major distinction of the bad quartos is the radical nature of the corruption which exists in the texts. Thus there are found in the quartos frequent omissions, garbled passages, or interpolations of speech when the texts are compared with later quartos of the same plays or to the folio version. In the bad quarto of *Hamlet,* for example, Hamlet's advice to the players (III, i) is followed by a series of jokes which were later printed in *Tarlton's Jests* (1638); the "To be or not to be" soliloquy appears in the following distorted and incoherent form:

Ham. **To be,or not to be, I there's the point,**
To Die, to ſleepe,is that all? I all:
No,to ſleepe,to dreame, I mary there it goes,
For in that dreame of death, when wee awake,
And borne before an euerlaſting Iudge,
From whence no paſſenger euer retur'nd,
The vndiſcouered country, at whoſe ſight
The happy ſmile,and the accurſed damn'd.
But for this,the ioyfull hope of this,
Whol'd beare the ſcornes and flattery of the world,
Scorned by the right rich,the rich curſſed of the poore?
The widow being oppreſſed,the orphan wrong'd,
The taſte of hunger, or a tirants raigne,
And thouſand more calamities beſides,
To grunt and ſweate vnder this weary life,
When that he may his full *Quietus* make,
With a bare bodkin, who would this indure,
But for a hope of ſomething after death?
Which puſles the braine, and doth confound the ſence,
Which makes vs rather beare thoſe euilles we haue,
Than flie to others that we know not of.
I that,O this conſcience makes cowardes of vs all,
Lady in thy orizons, be all my ſinnes remembred.

(REPRODUCED FROM THE *Hamlet* QI IN THE HUNTINGTON LIBRARY)

Various attempts have been made to explain the source of the bad quartos. Some scholars have suggested that an agent of the printers sat in the audience taking notes which were later transcribed and printed (see STENOGRAPHIC REPORT). The more commonly held explanation, however, is that the texts were reconstructed from memory by an actor or actors who had performed in the play (see MEMORIAL RECONSTRUCTION). The evidence for this view rests upon the fact that the lines of certain roles, such as those of Marcellus in *Hamlet* and the Host in *The Merry Wives of Windsor*, are reproduced with an accuracy unmatched in the rest of the play. Presumably the actor involved was betraying his fellows or former fellows, but this is only a presumption. There is no evidence of any traitorous activity by an actor, nor was the amount of money a printer was likely to pay for a play sufficient to induce betrayal. It appears almost certain, however, that these plays were printed without the knowledge or consent of the acting company. [A. W. Pollard, *Shakespeare Folios and Quartos*, 1909; E. K. Chambers, *William Shakespeare*, 1930; Leo Kirschbaum, *Shakespeare and the Stationers*, 1955.]

Bagley, Edward (fl. 1647–1675). Kinsman of Elizabeth Hall, Shakespeare's granddaughter. A resident of London, Bagley purchased the Blackfriars Gate-House, probably about 1647. He was named as one of the legatees of Elizabeth Hall's will, as a result of which he eventually acquired Shakespeare's house, New Place, in 1674. In 1675 he sold the property to Sir Edward Walker for £1060. [E. K. Chambers, *William Shakespeare*, 1930.]

Bagot, Sir William (fl. 1397). A minister of Richard II. When Henry Bolingbroke returned from exile, Bagot fled to Ireland where the king had gone to settle some affairs. Bagot returned to England with Richard, and after the latter's resignation of the crown, was charged by the duke of Aumerle with instigating Richard's misdeeds. He was committed to the Tower and, some historians say, was not seen again. Others, however, claim that Bagot was released and brought back to favor. In *Richard II*, it is Bagot who charges Aumerle with the murder of the Duke of Gloucester (IV, i). [W. H. Thomson, *Shakespeare's Characters: A Historical Dictionary*, 1951.]

Baker, George Pierce (1866–1935). American scholar. One of the most celebrated teachers of his day, Baker was a professor of English at Harvard (1905–1924) where he founded the "47 Workshop," a training ground for drama students that produced some of the most successful American dramatists and authors. In 1925 Baker became director of the drama department at Yale. His *The Development of Shakespeare as a Dramatist* (1907) did much to emphasize Shakespeare's role—too often disregarded by 19th-century critics—as a practical man of the theatre.

Balakirev, Mily Alexeivich. See MUSIC BASED ON SHAKESPEARE: *19th century, 1850–1900.*

Baldwin, Thomas Whitfield (1890–   ). American scholar, professor emeritus at the University of Illinois, and since 1958, visiting professor at the University of Southern Illinois. Baldwin's first book, *The Organization and Personnel of the Shakespearean Company* (1927), is an elaborate attempt to reconstruct the history of the Chamberlain's Men, Shakespeare's acting company, and assign specific roles to the individual members of the troupe. Because there is little evidence to support his theory, most scholars are reluctant to accept his inferences and conclusions without qualification. They do, however, recognize and admire his resourcefulness and perspicacity, and the enormous amount of factual detail which characterizes most of his work makes his books invaluable for reference. Baldwin's other works include *William Shakspere's Petty School* (1943) and *William Shakspere's Small Latine and Lesse Greek* (2 vols., 1944), which are exhaustive studies of the primary and secondary schools of Shakespeare's day. In *Shakspere's Five-Act Structure* (1947) Baldwin argues that Shakespeare wrote his plays in five acts because he was influenced by classical dramatic principles. Two later works are concerned with sources: *On the Literary Genetics of Shakspere's Poems and Sonnets* (1950) and *On the Literary Genetics of Shakspere's Plays, 1592–1594* (1959). [*Studies in Honor of T. W. Baldwin*, Don Cameron Allen, ed., 1958.]

Baldwin, William. See MIRROR FOR MAGISTRATES.

Bale, John. See ENEMIES OF THE STAGE; KYNGE JOHAN.

Balthasar. In *The Merchant of Venice*, one of Portia's servants. She orders Balthasar to take a letter to her cousin, Doctor Bellario, in Padua (III, iv). Portia adopts this name when she disguises herself as a lawyer.

Balthasar. In *Much Ado About Nothing*, an attendant on Don Pedro. Balthasar sings the song "Sigh no more, ladies" in II, iii. Stage directions in the First Folio indicate that the role was played by "Jacke Wilson." See John WILSON.

Balthasar. In *Romeo and Juliet*, Romeo's servant. When Romeo is banished to Mantua, Balthasar brings him word of Juliet's apparent death and accompanies him to the Capulet tomb but, hiding outside, is captured by the guard.

Balthazar. In *The Comedy of Errors*, a merchant. Invited to dinner by Antipholus of Ephesus, Balthazar advises restraint when his would-be host, ordered away from his own house, threatens to break in.

Bandello, Matteo (1480?–1562). Italian writer. Bandello was born at Castelnuovo Scrivia in Tortona, Lombardy. In the best Renaissance tradition his occupations included that of priest (later bishop of Agen in France), courtier, and soldier. His multivolume *Novelle* (1554–1573), containing 214 racy prose romances, was translated into French by François de BELLEFOREST and Pierre Boaistuau (d. 1566) as *Histoires Tragiques* (1559–1582), which in turn was Englished by Geoffrey Fenton under the title *Certaine Tragicall Discourses* (1567). Painter's *Palace of Pleasure* (1567), a collection of prose tales, also includes a number of Bandello's stories. It is doubtful that Shakespeare used Bandello directly as a source but he is indirectly indebted to him for a number of plots. Arthur BROOKE's *Romeus and Juliet* (1562), the main source of Shakespeare's play, is based on Boaistuau's translation of Bandello. Barnabe Riche's "Apolonius and Silla" (1581), a major source of *Twelfth Night*, is based on Belleforest's version of a tale in *Novelle*, while another tale recounts a version of the Hero-Claudio plot in *Much Ado About Nothing*.

Banister, John. See MUSIC BASED ON SHAKESPEARE: *17th century*.

Banks' Horse. A performing horse trained by John Banks (fl. 1591) which was extraordinarily popular in London during the 1590's. According to a pamphlet entitled *Maroccus extaticus Or Bankes Bay Horse in a Trance* (1595), "This horse would restore a glove to the due owner after the master had whispered the man's name in his ear; would tell the just number of pence in any piece of silver coin newly showed him by his master." He is alluded to by Shakespeare in *Love's Labour's Lost* (I, ii, 55–57) in Moth's comment: "how easy it is to put 'years' to the word 'three,' and study three years in two words, the dancing horse will tell you." According to Ben Jonson, Banks and his horse were eventually burned for witchcraft while traveling in Europe in the early years of the 17th century.

Bankside. A district within the borough of Southwark on the southern bank of the Thames and the site of most of the Elizabethan public theatres, including the Hope, the Rose, the Globe, and the Swan. Along the river in the Bankside were 20 houses which served as public brothels and were collectively known as the Bordello or the Stews. These were suppressed by law in 1546, but were apparently still operating in Shakespeare's time. Also within the Bankside was Winchester House, the palace of the bishop of Winchester, and the Church of St. Mary Overies now St. Saviour's. In 1596 Shakespeare was living in or near the Bankside, where he had moved from St. Helen's Parish in London. [Edward H. Sugden, *A Topographical Dictionary to . . . Shakespeare . . .*, 1925.]

Banquo. In *Macbeth*, a Scottish general and nobleman. With Macbeth, he vanquishes the rebel forces

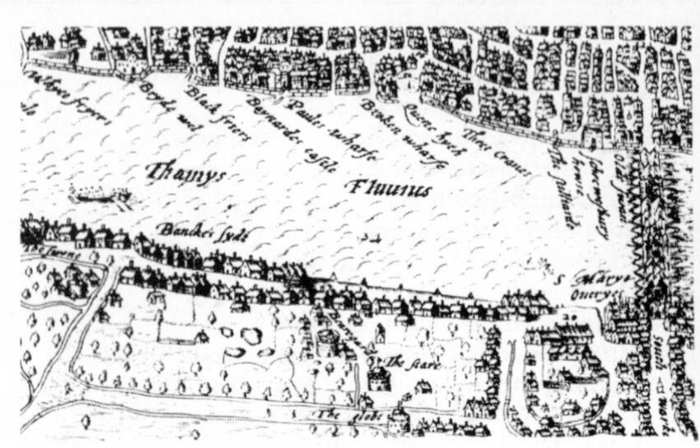

BANKSIDE IN 1600 FROM NORDEN'S *Civitas Londini*. THIS MAP ALSO SHOWS THE BANKSIDE THEATRES. (ROYAL LIBRARY, STOCKHOLM)

of Macdonwald and his Norwegian allies. On their return from battle, the two generals meet three Witches, who prophesy that Banquo is to be the ancestor of the kings of Scotland. Macbeth, who subsequently becomes king, arranges Banquo's murder in order to thwart the witches' prediction, but the dead man's son Fleance escapes the assassins, thus assuring the survival of the family line. Banquo's ghost returns to haunt Macbeth at a great banquet.

Baptista Minola. In *The Taming of the Shrew*, a wealthy merchant of Padua. Baptista refuses to acknowledge suitors for his much-courted younger daughter until the elder daughter, a notorious shrew, is wed.

Bardolfe, George. See RECUSANCY.

Bardolph. In *1* and *2 Henry IV*, one of Falstaff's cronies. In the first play Bardolph joins Falstaff in robbing the travelers; in the second play he assists in the selection of Feeble, Shadow, and Wart to serve in the army. In *The Merry Wives of Windsor*, Falstaff arranges for Bardolph to serve as tapster at the Garter Inn and predicts that he will thrive in this life that he has long desired. In *Henry V*, Bardolph is hanged for having looted French churches during the campaign.

Bardolph, Thomas, 5th Baron (1368–1408). Eldest son of William, 4th Baron Bardolph. He fought for Henry IV in the invasion of Scotland in 1400, subsequently playing a part in Hotspur's rebellion, without, however, losing the king's favor. In 1405 Bardolph joined the faction of the earl of Northumberland, becoming a traitor to the crown, and in 1408 he was killed fighting Rokesby's troops at Bramham Moor.

In *2 Henry IV*, Lord Bardolph is a supporter of the Earl of Northumberland, to whom he brings false word that Hotspur has won the battle at Shrewsbury. He subsequently seems to desert Northumberland's cause and to join Richard Scroop, Archbishop of York; however, the deaths of Northumberland and Bardolph are reported together in IV, iv.

Baretti, Giuseppe. See ITALY.

Barkstead or **Backsted, William** (fl. 1607–c. 1630). Actor and poet. Barkstead is the author of two books of poetry, *Mirrha the Mother of Adonis* (1607) and *Hiren* (1611). On the title page of *Hiren* he describes himself as "one of the servants of his Maiesties Revels," but it is difficult to determine which acting company he meant. As an actor he has been tentatively identified as having been with the Children of the Queen's (or King's) Revels (1607, 1609), Lady Elizabeth's Men (1611, 1613), and Prince Charles' Men (until 1615/6).

In *Mirrha*, a poem which owes much to *Venus and Adonis*, Barkstead makes a direct allusion to Shakespeare:

His Song was worthie merrit (*Shakspeare* hee)
sung the fair blossome, thou the withered tree
Laurell is due to him, his art and wit
hath purchast it, *Cypres* thy brow will fit.

In 1631, the third edition of the play *The Insatiate Countess* was published with two alternate title pages, one with "Written, By William Barksteed," and the other with "Written by Iohn Marston." It has been generally assumed that Barkstead completed writing Marston's play for production by the Children of the Queen's Revels, c. 1610. [E. K. Chambers, *William Shakespeare*, 1930; G. E. Bentley, *The Jacobean and Caroline Stage*, 5 vols., 1941–1956.]

Barnard, Sir John. See Sir John BERNARD.

Barnardine. In *Measure for Measure*, a dissolute prisoner, "careless, reckless, and fearless of what's past, present, or to come." A condemned murderer, Barnardine has enjoyed nine years' residence at the prison by virtue of regular reprieves and would not escape if he could, as he enjoys the liberty of continual drunkenness in the jail. The Duke persuades the Provost to execute Barnardine and substitute his head for that of Claudio, which Angelo has demanded, but Barnardine refuses execution on the ground that he is drunk and unfitted to die. Luckily another prisoner dies, and that prisoner's head is used instead. At the play's end, the Duke pardons Barnardine his earthly crimes and hands him over to Friar Peter for regeneration.

Barnes, Barnabe (1571–1609). Poet. Barnes, the son of the bishop of Nottingham, was born in York. He attended Brasenose College, Oxford, but left without taking a degree. After leaving college he joined the growing numbers of young men in the service of the earl of Essex. In 1593 he published his first volume of verse, *Parthenophil and Parthenophe*, with one of the dedicatory sonnets written to the earl of Southampton, Shakespeare's patron. This dedication and the fact that Barnes appears to have been a member of the Southampton circle have led some scholars to identify him as the RIVAL POET of Shakespeare's sonnets.

In 1598 Barnes was charged with attempted murder and brought before Star Chamber court. Confined in the Marshalsea prison awaiting trial, he escaped and fled to the north. Apparently no effort was made to recapture him, probably as a result of the intercession of one of the powerful nobles whom he numbered among his friends. Barnes turned to playwriting and in 1607 his tragedy *The Divils Charter* was presented at court by Shakespeare's company, the King's Men. Some commentators have seen parallels between a scene in Barnes' play and a scene (V, iv) in *Cymbeline*.

From all accounts Barnes appears to have been a braggart, a coward, and a Machiavellian intriguer, qualities which have prompted some to suggest that he was Shakespeare's model for Parolles in *All's Well That Ends Well*. [Mark Eccles, "Barnabe Barnes," *Thomas Lodge and Other Elizabethans*, C. J. Sisson, ed., 1933.]

Barnes, Joshua (1654–1712). Greek scholar and antiquary who allegedly purchased stanzas of Shakespeare's ballad about Sir Thomas LUCY. Barnes, a professor of Greek at Cambridge, was a man of wide-ranging interests. His many publications demonstrate his lively and active mind, but they are frequently marked by inaccuracies and, occasionally, distortions. Edmund Malone discovered the stanzas in a manuscript titled *History of the Stage*, which has since been lost. According to Malone the manuscript was "full of forgeries and falsehoods" which he suspected were the work of the forger William CHETWOOD. Malone dated the manuscript between 1727 and 1730:

Here we shall observe, that the learned Mr Joshua Barnes, late Greek Professor of the University of Cambridge, baiting about forty years ago at an inn in Stratford, and hearing an old woman singing part of the above-said song, such was his respect for Mr Shakespeare's genius, that he gave her a new gown for the two following stanzas in it; and, could she have said it all, he would (as he often said in company, when any discourse has casually arose about him) have given her ten guineas:

Sir Thomas was too covetous,
To covet so much deer,
When horns enough upon his head
Most plainly did appear.

Had not his worship one deer left?
What then? He had a wife
Took pains enough to find him horns
Should last him during life.

[E. K. Chambers, *William Shakespeare*, 1930.]

Barnfield, Richard (1574–1627). Poet. Barnfield's chief claim to fame rests on his early admiration for Shakespeare. His *Cynthia, with certain sonnets*, published in 1595, bears a resemblance to the technique and manner of Shakespeare's sonnets. *The Encomion of Lady Pecunia* (1598), including *Poems of Divers Humours*, contains a poem ("A Remembrance of some English Poets") which marks one of the earliest metrical allusions to Shakespeare:

And *Shakespeare* thou, whose hony-flowing Vaine,
(Pleasing the World) thy Praises doth obtaine,
Whose *Venus*, and whose *Lucrece* (sweete, and chaste)
Thy Name in fames immortall Booke have plac't.

Three of Barnfield's poems were included in *The Passionate Pilgrim*, a collection of verse printed as Shakespeare's in 1599. Barnfield may also be the "R. B." who wrote GREENE'S FUNERALLS. [*The Shakspere Allusion-Book*, J. Munro, ed., 1909.]

Barrault, Jean-Louis (1910–   ). French actor and director. Barrault began as a pupil of Charles Dullin at the Théâtre de l'Atelier in 1930 and later worked with the famous Comédie-Française. After World War II, with his wife, actress Madeleine Renaud, he established his own theatrical troupe, successfully combining presentations of classical and modern works. Although Barrault's achievements as an actor have been numerous, perhaps his most famous role has been that of Hamlet. He first approached the role in 1939 in a version written by the French poet Jules Laforgue. Laforgue's *Hamlet* emphasized humorous qualities and the character became a sort of tragic clown. Two years later, in 1941, Barrault appeared for the first time in Shakespeare's *Hamlet*, in an adaptation into French by Guy de Pourtalès. Having already made two attempts at the difficult role, which he called the "Annapurna" of the theatre, Barrault turned to it once again to open his repertory company in 1946 at the Théâtre Marigny, this time in an adaptation by André GIDE. Moreover, Barrault himself had been partly responsible for the adaptation, having encouraged Gide to complete the work back in 1942. The combination of the two talents created one of the great successes in France's postwar theatre. In 1952, Barrault continued his triumph in the part with a production of the play in New York at the Ziegfeld Theatre.

Barrault considers Hamlet a super-hero who is able to reach out to today's audiences, and he calls the work the best play of modern times. He views the character of Hamlet as a representation of man who hesitates before the many problems of existence, a sort of Everyman in whom consciously appear, simultaneously, the best and the worst.—J.R.

Barrett, Lawrence (1838–1891). American actor. Though he was one of the most distinguished American Shakespearean actors of the 19th century, Barrett's career was overshadowed by that of his friend and close associate, Edwin Booth. Barrett began his association with Booth in 1871 and in that year played Cassius to Booth's Brutus, roles that the two men were to repeat throughout their careers. Barrett also played with Booth in *The Merchant of Venice*, *King Lear*, *Hamlet*, *Macbeth*, and *Othello*, playing Bassanio to Booth's Shylock, Edgar to Booth's Lear, Laertes to Booth's Hamlet, and Macduff to Booth's Macbeth. In *Othello* he and Booth alternated in the roles of Othello and Iago.

When not in tandem with Booth, Barrett frequently played star roles, including those of Wolsey in *Henry VIII*, Benedick in *Much Ado About Nothing*, Romeo, Richard III, Hamlet, and Macbeth. In the testimonial performances of *Hamlet* given by an all-star cast at the Metropolitan Opera House in 1888, Barrett played the Ghost. Barrett's performances were distinguished by their dignity, grace, and intelligence.

Barry, Ann. Born **Ann Street** (1734–1801). Actress. Born in Bath, Mrs. Barry made her first recorded stage appearance in 1756 at Portsmouth, with her first husband, an actor named Dancer. In 1758 in Dublin, she played Cordelia to Spranger Barry's Lear, and spent nine years in his company. Later, in London, she married Barry and achieved a growing reputation as an actress. After Barry's death in 1777 she married Thomas Crawford. As a tragedienne, Mrs. Barry equaled Peg Woffington and Mrs. Cibber, and she was a better comedienne. She played a wide variety of roles in Shakespearean plays and adaptations: Beatrice, Cordelia, Constance, Imogen, Lady Macbeth, Lady Percy, Portia, Rosalind, Viola, Catharine (in *Catharine and Petruchio*, Garrick's adaptation of *The Taming of the Shrew*), Evanthe (a character added by Cumberland to his version of *Timon of Athens*), and Perdita (in *Florizel and Perdita*, MacNamara Morgan's alteration of *The Winter's Tale*). [*Dictionary of National Biography*, 1885– ; Charles Beecher Hogan, *Shakespeare in the Theatre, 1701–1800*, 2 vols., 1952–1957.]

Barry, Elizabeth (1658–1713). First great actress on the English stage. Born presumably in London, Elizabeth Barry was the daughter of Robert Barry, a barrister who lost his fortune fighting for Charles I. Various accounts are given of her training as an actress, the most credible being that in 1672 or 1673, Lady Davenant, the widow of Sir William Davenant, took her at the age of 15 with other newly recruited young women to be trained for the DUKE'S COMPANY, one of the two theatres that had been authorized by Charles II at the Restoration in 1660. The story of her mediocrity and even failure on the stage until she was tutored by John Wilmot, earl of Rochester, has been told repeatedly, perhaps as a contrast to the unprecedented success that she enjoyed from 1680 to 1710 as the leading actress, patentee, and joint arbiter with Thomas Betterton of the theatrical company that dominated English drama for more than 30 years. She created at least 125 new roles and appeared in innumerable revivals of Elizabethan, Jacobean, and Carolinian plays, in many of which she played feminine roles that had never before been acted by a woman.

Acknowledged to be one of the most fascinating, although not one of the most beautiful, women of the Restoration period, she became a powerful force in the dramatic circles of London, all of the playwrights drawing their female characters to fit her particular talents in both comedy and tragedy. She was the mistress of Rochester for at least two stormy years, bearing him an acknowledged daughter in December 1677. At the same time, Thomas Otway, in whose *Alcibiades* she created her first recorded minor role, had fallen desperately in love with her and wrote a succession of plays in which his hopeless love is recorded. In 1689, after the death of both Rochester and Otway, she was the mistress for a short time of Sir George Etherege, perhaps bearing him a daughter.

Elizabeth Barry's first essay in Shakespeare was probably Lavinia (Juliet) in Thomas Otway's *Caius Marius*, an adaptation of *Romeo and Juliet*. Her success in the convincing tragic role of Lavinia was undoubtedly due to the careful training of Rochester, who insisted that she know the meaning of each word and phrase before committing the lines to memory and that she enter into the emotion of each speech and scene. This naturalistic technique was startlingly new in the training of actresses, who, up to that time, had been instructed in the art of acting the part of a woman as a young boy would have been trained. She evidently carried the same technique to her role of Cordelia in Nahum Tate's drastically rewritten *King Lear*. After the success of *Caius Marius*, Otway wrote *The Orphan* (1680), in which Mrs. Barry played Monimia, and *Venice Preserv'd* (1682), in which her portrayal of Belvidera justified her designation thereafter as "The Great Mrs. Barry."

After the union of the Duke's and King's Companies in 1682, Elizabeth Barry, acknowledged by then to be the leading actress in London, could choose any part she wished from the repertory of both companies. The company's main fare was contemporary plays. One of the most famous roles of her subsequent career was that of Cleopatra in Dryden's *All for Love*. She also played *Hamlet*, possibly appearing first as Ophelia to Mrs. Betterton's Gertrude and later as Gertrude with Anne Bracegirdle as Ophelia. Although there is no definite record that Elizabeth Barry played Desdemona, the many presentations of *Othello* with Betterton in the title role should be sufficient proof that she did.

In 1695 the Betterton group, including Elizabeth Barry, Anne Bracegirdle, and nine other veteran players, broke away from the tyranny of Christopher Rich at the Theatre Royal and set up their own theatre in Lincoln's Inn Fields, where they turned to Shakespeare for plots to be refurbished and for plays to be revived. According to John Dennis, *Coriolanus* was played for 20 nights at Lincoln's Inn Fields during the season of 1698/9. No one but Mrs. Barry in the small company would have played Volumnia to Betterton's Coriolanus. At the beginning of the next season, in November 1700, she must have played Queen Katharine in *Henry VIII*, in which Betterton was the King and Cave Underhill, Cardinal Wolsey, for she is listed for the part for the next eight years. Mrs. Barry did not appear in another Shakespeare-inspired play until the production of Burnaby's *Love Betray'd, or, The Agreeable Disappointment* (*Twelfth Night*, 1703), in which she appeared as Villaretta (Olivia) to Mrs. Bracegirdle's Cesario (Viola). On April 24, 1704 *The Merry Wives of Windsor* was played at court as a command performance for Queen Anne with Betterton as Falstaff, Mrs. Barry as Mrs. Page, and Mrs. Bracegirdle as Mrs. Ford.

Since Elizabeth Barry was co-arbiter with Thomas Betterton of dramatic fare in England for three decades, she helped to establish many British acting traditions that persist today. Colley Cibber's admiration for her acting is significant:

> Mrs. Barry in Characters of Greatness, had a Presence of elevated Dignity, her Mien and Motion superb and gracefully majestick; her Voice full, clear, and strong, so that no Violence of Passion could be too much for her: And when Distress or Tenderness possess'd her, she subsided into the most affecting Melody and Softness. In the Art of exciting Pity she had a Power beyond all the Actresses I have yet seen, or what your Imagination can conceive.

Other evidence in the scanty dramatic comment of the time reveals that she brought to Shakespearean roles a complete understanding of their significance and was the first to convey reality to the female characters. Moreover, she shared with Betterton the first deep appreciation of Shakespeare and helped to establish the Bardolatry for which Sir William Davenant may be said to be the originator.

On April 24, four days before Betterton's death on April 28, 1710, Elizabeth Barry played Lady Macbeth, her last Shakespearean role, opposite John Mills, who had fallen heir to the part of Macbeth. On June 13, 1710 she played Lady Easy of Cibber's *The Careless Husband*, thus saluting, in her last appearance on the stage, the sentimental drama of the 18th century. [Edmund Curll, *Betterton's History of the English Stage*, 1741; Allardyce Nicoll, *A History of Early Eighteenth Century Drama, 1700–1750*, 3rd ed., 1952; Allardyce Nicoll, *A History of Restoration Drama, 1660–1700*, 4th ed., 1952; J. H. Wilson, *All the King's Ladies*, 1958; Lucyle Hook, "Portraits of Elizabeth Barry and Anne Bracegirdle," *Theatre Notebook*, XV, 1961.]—L.H.

Barry, Spranger (1719–1777). Irish actor. Barry was one of the greatest Shakespearean actors of his day, second only to David Garrick. He made his first stage appearance in Dublin as Othello, and brought his interpretation to the Drury Lane in 1746. Subsequently, David Garrick moved to the Drury Lane and his jealousy of Barry's success as Macbeth and Hamlet induced him to take on these roles himself. In 1750, Barry went into open competition with Garrick by playing Romeo, Lear, and Richard III. He was less successful in the last two roles, but his fine Romeo provoked the "Romeo and Juliet War"—the play being presented simultaneously at Drury Lane and Covent Garden. Barry's success continued until 1758 when his building of the Crow Street Theatre in Dublin ruined him financially. He returned to London, where he played for a time under Garrick, then moved to Covent Garden. During this time, his first wife died and he married Ann Dancer, who, as Ann Barry, became an outstanding actress. [*Dictionary of National Biography*, 1885– ; *Oxford Companion to the Theatre*, Phyllis Hartnoll, ed., 1951.]

Barrymore Family. American actors. ***Maurice Barrymore*** (real name Herbert Blythe; 1847–1905) was born in Fort Agra, India, where his father was a surveyor. Intended for a civil-service career or the law, he took up acting at Oxford. He began his career in London and in 1875 came to America, where he had a long career as a supporting actor to such stars as Modjeska, Lily Langtry, Olga Nethersole, and Mrs. Fiske. With Modjeska he played Romeo

SPRANGER BARRY.

and Orlando. In 1876 he married Georgiana Drew (1856–1893), sister of the prominent actor John Drew. She began her career at her parents' Arch Street Theatre, where on one occasion she appeared as Celia in *As You Like It*, with Fanny Davenport as Rosalind and Charles Coughlan as Orlando. Georgiana Barrymore played opposite Edwin Booth, Lawrence Barrett, and John McCullough. She and her husband had three children, Lionel, Ethel, and John.

Lionel Barrymore (1878–1954) made his first stage appearance in New York in 1893. He was successful in character roles, both on stage and in films. In 1921 he played Macbeth at the Apollo Theatre, New York.

Ethel Barrymore (1879–1959) was a prominent and distinguished actress and manager. She made her first New York appearance in 1894 as Julia in *The Rivals.* In 1922 she acted Juliet, and also in 1925 played opposite Walter Hampden as Ophelia, and as Portia in *The Merchant of Venice.* In 1928 she opened the Ethel Barrymore Theatre in New York. Her most memorable performances were in *The Constant Wife*, *School for Scandal*, and *The Corn Is Green*, and she made many films from 1914 until her death.

John Barrymore (1882–1942) made his first stage appearance in Chicago in 1903 and from there went on to establish himself as one of the most colorful leading men of the theatre and films. His Shakespearean roles included Richard III in New York in 1920 and Hamlet in New York and London in 1923–1925. His performance in the latter recalled the major 19th-century interpretations of the role (see HAMLET: *Stage History*). Barrymore's autobiography, *The Confessions of an Actor*, appeared in 1926. [*Dictionary of American Biography*, 1927– ; *Who's Who in the Theatre*, 1939, 1952, 1957.]

Bartholomew Fair (1614). A saturnalian comedy by Ben JONSON, published in the second folio edition of his *Workes* (1631). It was first acted at the HOPE THEATRE by Lady Elizabeth's Men (several of the latter are cited by name in the play, including Nathan Field and John Taylor and Will Ostler of the King's Men). The play is set in the fairgrounds at Smithfield, where every St. Bartholomew's Day (August 24) the citizens of London, along with a goodly number of pickpockets and thieves, flock in order to sample the variety of foods and entertainment available. The play has a fierce vitality and an exuberant pace unmatched by any comedy of its time.

Bartholomew Fair contains a number of topical allusions, including a probable reference to *Two Noble Kinsmen* and one to *Titus Andronicus.* In the Induction to his play, Jonson ridicules the old-fashioned taste of one who "will sweare, *Ieronimo* [Kyd's *Spanish Tragedy*], or *Andronicus* are the best playes yet." The Induction also censures plays which feature a "*Seruant-monster*," Jonson declaring that he is "loth to make Nature afraid in his *Playes*, like those that beget *Tales*, *Tempests*, and such like *Drolleries*." Here, he is clearly referring to the elements of fantasy and romance which had recently been exhibited in Shakespeare's *The Winter's Tale* and *The Tempest*, with the "*Seruant-monster*" undoubtedly an allusion to Caliban in *The Tempest.*

Bartlett, John (1820–1905). American editor and publisher. Best known for his compilation of *Familiar Quotations* (1855), Bartlett, a partner in the Boston publishing firm of Little, Brown and Company, was also the editor of *The Complete Concordance to Shakespeare's Dramatic Works and Poems* (1894). This massive compilation is still the standard Shakespeare concordance.

Barton-on-the-Heath. A hamlet 15 miles south of Stratford and the home of Edmund Lambert, a brother-in-law of Shakespeare's mother. Shakespeare alludes to the spot in *The Taming of the Shrew* in describing Christopher Sly, "Old Sly's son of Burton heath."

Bassanio. In *The Merchant of Venice*, a lighthearted gentleman who is forever in straitened circumstances. In order to court Portia in grand style, Bassanio borrows 3000 ducats from his friend Antonio, who in turn secures a loan from Shylock on the agreement that he will forfeit a pound of flesh should he fail to make repayment. Traveling to Portia's residence at Belmont, Bassanio passes the test of the three caskets, choosing the leaden one bearing the legend "Who chooseth me must give and hazard all he hath." The casket contains Portia's portrait, and Bassanio claims her as his bride. When Antonio is brought to trial for nonpayment of the loan, the wealthy Portia sends her new husband to Venice, where he offers Shylock twice the money owed. The offer refused, Portia, who has secretly come to the Venetian court disguised as a lawyer, cleverly turns the case against Shylock.

Basse, William (1583?–?1653). Poet. Basse is known chiefly for his epitaph "On Mr. Wm. Shakespeare." The poem exists in a number of versions and in 1633 was included among the poems of John Donne. In at least six different versions, however, Basse is listed as the author. The poem doubtless was written before 1623, for Ben Jonson's poem on Shakespeare in the First Folio (1623) makes a definite allusion to it.

On Mr. Wm. Shakespeare
he dyed in Aprill 1616.

Renowned Spencer, lye a thought more nye
To learned Chaucer, and rare Beaumont lye
A little neerer Spenser to make roome
For Shakespeare in your threefold fowerfold
  Tombe.
To lodge all fowre in one bed make a shift
Vntill Doomesdaye, for hardly will a fift
Betwixt this day and that by Fate be slayne
For whom your Curtaines may be drawn againe.
If your precedency in death doth barre
A fourth place in your sacred sepulcher,
Vnder this carued marble of thine owne
Sleepe rare Tragoedian Shakespeare, sleep alone,
Thy vnmolested peace, vnshared Caue,
Possesse as Lord not Tenant of thy Graue,
  That vnto us and others it may be
  Honor hereafter to be layde by thee.

[E. K. Chambers, *William Shakespeare*, 1930.]

Basset. In *1 Henry VI*, a member of the Lancastrian faction who quarrels with Vernon, one of the Yorkist group (IV, i). This character has been identified with Robert Basset or Philip Basset, both of whom fought at Agincourt and were members of a prominent Cornish family. [W. H. Thomson, *Shakespeare's Characters: A Historical Dictionary*, 1951.]

Bassianus. In *Titus Andronicus,* the younger son of the deceased emperor of Rome and brother of the newly elected emperor, Saturninus. When the Emperor announces his intention to marry Bassianus' beloved, Lavinia, Bassianus claims her as his own, carries her off, and marries her. He is subsequently murdered by Tamora's sons, Demetrius and Chiron, as part of a complicated plot against the family of Titus.

Bates, John. In *Henry V*, an English soldier. In a conversation with some fellow soldiers on the eve of the battle of Agincourt, Bates wishes aloud, in the disguised King's presence, that Henry were there alone, since he would surely be ransomed and "a many poor men's lives saved" (IV, i).

Battle of Alcazar, The (c. 1589). Historical play generally ascribed to George PEELE. The chief interest of *The Battle of Alcazar* lies in the fact that it is the only Elizabethan play for which there is extant both the full text and the "plot" used by the actors. Thus it provides important primary evidence of the techniques employed in adapting a play to the Elizabethan theatre. Unfortunately, the published text (printed in 1594) had been revised before publication to provide a reading, rather than an acting, text. The result is that many of the stage directions in the plot have no corresponding treatment in the text. It was given 14 times in 1592/3 by Strange's Men, and later revived by Edward Alleyn and the Admiral's Men. [*Two Elizabethan Stage Abridgments: The Battle of Alcazar and Orlando Furioso,* W. W. Greg, ed., 1922.]

Baty, Gaston. See FRANCE.

Baudelaire, Charles. See FRANCE.

Bawd. In *Pericles*, wife of the Pandar and keeper of a brothel at Mytilene. She instructs Marina in her duties, advising her to "seem to do that fearfully which you commit willingly" (IV, ii). When her recalcitrant pupil threatens to "undo a whole generation" by managing to preserve her virtue, the Bawd commissions Boult to "crack the glass of her virginity."

bawdy. The use of obscene and suggestive language in Shakespeare. "Bawdy" has been extensively studied by Eric Partridge in his *Shakespeare's Bawdy: A Literary and Psychological Essay and a Comprehensive Glossary* (1947, rev. ed. 1955). Partridge finds abundant evidence of sexual punning in the plays and poems. According to Partridge, *Richard II* is the "cleanest" of the plays and *Measure for Measure* and *Othello* "the most sexual, the most bawdy."

Baylis, Lilian (1874–1937). Theatre manager at the Old Vic, where she instituted the universally admired Shakespearean repertory associated with that playhouse. The daughter of professional musicians, Lilian Baylis began her career as a musician and music teacher. In 1912 she succeeded her aunt, Emma Cons, as the manager of the Royal Victoria Hall and Coffee Tavern, which later became known as the OLD VIC. Miss Baylis immediately began a series of innovations there, introducing opera and Shakespearean drama fashioned to appeal to a broad, popular audience. In its first decade the theatre won international fame as the home of Shakespeare in England. Having succeeded in establishing Shakespearean drama as an artistic and commercial success, Miss Baylis took over the Sadler's Wells Theatre in 1931 with the idea in mind that it might serve north London as the Old Vic served the south. In time, however, it proved to be more practicable to concentrate on ballet and opera at Sadler's Wells while emphasizing Shakespearean drama at the Old Vic. Miss Baylis acted as manager of both of these theatres with continued success until her death.

THE BULLBAITING AND BEARBAITING ARENAS IN BANKSIDE. FROM AGAS' MAP OF LONDON (BEFORE 1590).

bearbaiting, bullbaiting, and cockfighting. Three sports dating in England as early as the 12th century and considered legitimate and highly popular sports in the Elizabethan age. Bearbaiting and bullbaiting were given royal patronage in the 16th century when Henry VIII made the mastership of the bears, bulls, and mastiff dogs a court office and in 1526 sponsored the building of the Paris Garden on the Bankside in Southwark for bullbaiting and bearbaiting exhibitions. The Bankside was outside the jurisdiction of London and thus immune to Puritan opposition to the sports on the grounds of their cruelty and the scheduling of the most important matches on Sundays. By the end of the 16th century, however, several theatres which had been erected on the Bankside offered such competition to the Bear Garden that the theatres were ordered closed on Thursdays.

Bearbaiting and dramatic amusements were evidently regarded as having much in common. Philip Henslowe, a leading theatrical manager, and the actor Edward Alleyn devoted as much time to organizing baiting matches as they did to their theatrical enterprises. In 1613 Henslowe, who had acquired the Paris Garden, tore it down and erected the Hope theatre, which was to be used both for plays and for baiting matches.

So popular was the sport that it was almost inevitable that Shakespeare should draw metaphors from it. Macbeth likens himself to the bear chained to a stake in the center of the ring:

> They have tied me to a stake; I cannot fly,
> But, bear-like, I must fight the course.
> (V, vii, 1–2)

Similarly, Gloucester cries in *King Lear:*

> I am tied to the stake, and I must stand the course.
> (III, vii, 54)

The "course" was a bout or round in which the bear was set upon by four to six mastiff dogs. The bear often killed or disabled one or two at the first encounter, and the rest would hang back and bark at a safe distance. Thus in *3 Henry VI* Richard III describes his father in battle, comparing him to a

> . . . bear, encompass'd round with dogs,
> Who having pinch'd a few and made them cry,
> The rest stand all aloof, and bark at him.
> (II, i, 15–17)

The baiting match continued, with fresh dogs entered as necessary, until the bear was either beaten (few bears actually died) or proved himself more than a match for the dogs. The baiting of bulls, which occurred less frequently, followed the same pattern. Exhibitions sometimes ended with "pleasant sport with the horse and ape"—the spectacle of a horse, an ape on his back, pursued by the dogs. Bearbaiting was as popular among the common people as it was with the nobility, and the bawling and yelling of enthusiastic spectators made bear gardens synonymous with noisy disorder. In *Henry VIII* a porter reproves the noisy crowd in the palace yard awaiting the christening procession of the infant Elizabeth:

> You'll leave your noise anon, ye rascals: do you take the court for Paris-garden?
> (V, iv, 1–2)

Cockfighting was equally popular among the Elizabethans. In the reign of Henry VIII the sport was officially organized and the first cockpit was built. Like bearbaiting, cockfighting had existed in England since medieval times. Henry's original cockpit in St. James' Park was also used as a theatre after the reign of Elizabeth (see COCKPIT AT COURT). Another famous cockpit, St. Giles in the Fields, was converted into the Phoenix or Cockpit Theatre late in the reign of James I and was used both for dramatic presentations and for cockfighting. In *Henry V* Shakespeare describes the stage on which the play is to be performed as "this cockpit" (prologue, 11). [Sidney Lee, "Bearbaiting, Bullbaiting, and Cockfighting," *Shakespeare's England*, 1916.]—D.T.

Beatrice and **Benedick.** In *Much Ado About Nothing*, the witty pair of lovers who are engaged in a "merry war" of words. Ostensibly the protagonists of the subplot, Beatrice and Benedick come to dominate the proceedings very early in the play, sweeping all before them, even the melodramatic and stagy main plot of Claudio and Hero's romance. That this has always been the case in the history of the play is attested to by the 17th-century references to it as "Benedicte and Betteris." In his copy of the Second Folio King Charles I wrote the words "Benedick and Beatrice" on the title page of *Much Ado;* in his commemorative poem to the 1640 edition of the *Poems*, Leonard Digges attested to the popularity of the pair with the audience of his day. See MUCH ADO ABOUT NOTHING: *Stage History*.

The source of this popularity is the verbal brilliance which the two lovers display in their battle of wit, disguising their mutual attraction under a barrage of repartee. Benedick is, in Mark Van Doren's words, "a virtuoso in hyperbole," but he is more than matched by "my Lady Tongue," Beatrice, who is "born to speak all mirth and no matter." Their war of words provides the base not only for this play, but for the witty exchanges of the young couples of the later Restoration comedy. Shakespeare's characters, while matching the later figures in wit, have a greater warmth and humanity than the brilliant but brittle creations of the Restoration theatre. [Mark Van Doren, *Shakespeare*, 1939; John Palmer, *Comic Characters of Shakespeare*, 1946.]

Beattie, James (1735–1803). Scottish poet and educator. In his essay *Memory and Imagination* (1783) Beattie defends Shakespeare from his critics, arguing that the dramatic rules Shakespeare broke were merely mechanical and therefore not absolutely binding. He does not salute Shakespeare as a great untutored poet, but says that Shakespeare made up for his lack of formal education by a close study of nature, humanity, and the English language.

In letters to various friends, Beattie notes that Shakespeare's greatest genius lay in his psychological and emotional insights. He also defends Shakespeare's use of tragicomedy on the ground that an unrelieved tragic action of the proportion of *Hamlet* or *King Lear* would be an unbearable strain on the audience. [Herbert Spencer Robinson, *English Shakespearian Criticism in the Eighteenth Century*, 1932.]

Beaufort, Henry. See Henry Beaufort, bishop of WINCHESTER.

Beaufort, John. See John Beaufort, 3rd earl of SOMERSET.

Beaufort, Thomas. See Thomas Beaufort, duke of EXETER.

Beaumont, Francis (c. 1584–1616). Dramatist and poet. The son of Sir Francis Beaumont, a justice of common pleas in Leicestershire, Beaumont studied law at the Inner Temple. His first publication is probably the anonymous *Salmacis and Hermaphroditus*, an Ovidian narrative poem published in 1602. His dramatic career appears to have begun about 1606 with the performance of *The Woman Hater*, a play which shows the influence of Beaumont's friend Ben Jonson. Around 1608 he began the famous collaboration with John Fletcher which lasted for about five years. During that time the playwrights produced jointly at least six plays. However, the establishment of a Beaumont-Fletcher canon has been complicated by the fact that collected editions of the plays (published in 1647 and 1679) describe no fewer than 53 pieces as being "by Francis Beaumont and John Fletcher." Although Fletcher probably had a hand in all or most of these plays, Beaumont, who retired from the stage in 1613, could have had a share in only a small portion. E. K. Chambers estimates that the Beaumont-Fletcher combination produced the following plays: *Philaster* (c. 1610), *The Maid's Tragedy* (c. 1611), *A King and No King* (1611), *Four Plays in One* (c. 1608), *Cupid's Revenge* (1612), *The Coxcomb* (1608–10), and *The Scornful Lady* (c. 1613). Beaumont is probably also responsi-le for THE KNIGHT OF THE BURNING PESTLE (1607). For a discussion of the relationship of Shakespeare to the Beaumont-Fletcher plays, see John FLETCHER.

Bedford, John of Lancaster, duke of (1389–1435). Third son of Henry IV and Mary de Bohun. He was created duke of Bedford in 1414, after his brother became King Henry V. During Henry's campaigns in France, Bedford officiated as lieutenant of the kingdom, and on Henry's death, he became guardian of his brother's son Henry and protector of the realm. Bedford continued the conquest of France, where he was made regent, defeating the French and Scots at Verneuil and retaking many towns that had fallen to the French. He suffered reverses, however, after Joan of Arc raised the siege of Orléans in 1429. After Joan was captured, Bedford bought the Maid and allowed her to be tried and burned at the stake in Rouen (1431). The duke himself died in that city four years later.

In *1 Henry IV*, John of Lancaster appears only at the battle of Shrewsbury (V, i), where his brother Henry commends him for his valor and dispatches him to deal with the rebels in the north. In *2 Henry IV*, Lancaster, with Westmoreland's aid, captures the rebel leaders by trickery: after promising to redress their grievances and inducing them to dismiss their troops, he orders them arrested and executed (IV, ii). In *Henry V*, Lancaster appears as the Duke of Bedford at Agincourt—a historical impossibility. In *1 Henry VI*, Bedford is Regent of France. After taking Orléans and Rouen, he dies in the latter city.

Bedford, Lucy Harington, countess of (1580–1627). Patroness of poets. The friend and patroness of some of the greatest poets of the Elizabethan age, the countess of Bedford was celebrated in their poems as a paragon of virtue and beauty. Among those who showered praise upon her were Drayton, Donne, Chapman, Daniel, and Jonson. Jonson seems to have been particularly devoted, addressing two poems to her, in one of which he characterizes her as ". . . faire and free and wise / Of greatest bloud and yet more good than great."

An extant copy of the poem which Jonson contributed to *Love's Martyr* (1601), the collection of verse which first included Shakespeare's *The Phoenix and the Turtle,* contains the heading "To: L:C:of B:" Bernard Newdigate has concluded from this that the countess of Bedford is the anonymous recipient of the poems in *Love's Martyr* and thus the "phoenix" of Shakespeare's poem. In 1594 the countess had married Edward Russell, 3rd earl of Bedford. The marriage was childless until 1601 (the approximate year when Shakespeare's poem was written). The child born in that year died soon after his birth. These events correspond to those apparently alluded to in *The Phoenix and the Turtle*. The attribution, however, has not been generally accepted by scholars. [Bernard Newdigate, "The Phoenix and Turtle: Was Lady Bedford the Phoenix?" *Times Literary Supplement*, October 24, 1936; *The Poems*, New Variorum Edition, Hyder Rollins, ed., 1938.]

Beeston Family. Actors and theatre-owners. ***Christopher Beeston*** (d. 1638) probably began his career in Shakespeare's company as an apprentice to the actor Augustine Phillips, who left 30 shillings in his will to "my Seruante Xofer Besone." Beeston is listed in the cast of Ben Jonson's *Every Man In his Humour* (1598). In 1602 he left the Chamberlain's Men for Worcester's Men, which later became Queen Anne's company. He formed a close friendship with the playwright Thomas Heywood, contributing commendatory verse to the latter's *Apologie for Actors* (1612). In 1612 he became the manager of the Queen's Men, and in 1617 he moved them to his own theatre, the Phoenix, which he had built. In subsequent years a number of companies—Prince Charles', Lady Elizabeth's, Queen Henrietta's, and "Beeston's Boys"—occupied the Phoenix, and Beeston, although owner of the theatre, always acted with the companies. Beeston, apparently a skillful and shrewd manager, had a reputation for sharp practices in his relations with the players. The last company he managed was the King and Queen's Young Company, also known as "Beeston's Boys." The company was not an ordinary boys' company but seems to have included a large number of younger players. They enjoyed considerable prestige and patronage from their inception in 1637 until Beeston's death in 1638.

Christopher's son, ***William Beeston*** (c. 1606–1682), probably began as an actor in one of his father's companies. At his father's death in 1638, he inherited his land holdings and a one-twelfth interest in the company known as "Beeston's Boys" at the Phoenix theatre. Under his direction in 1640 the company performed an unauthorized play which gave direct offense to King Charles. As a result Beeston was removed from his position as their "governor" and imprisoned for a short period. After the closing of the theatres in 1642, Beeston remained active in theatrical affairs. By 1651 he had repaired the Phoenix (which had been razed in 1649), and was training a boys' company, and in 1652 he obtained the lease of the Salisbury Court theatre. Leslie Hotson argues that he was the "ill beest" who in 1653 betrayed a company of players at Gibbon's Tennis Court who were performing at a time when parliament had closed all theatres. With the Restoration, Beeston apparently lost control of the Phoenix and, as the owner of the Salisbury Court theatre, was engaged in litigation with the company playing there under the direction of George Jolly. The theatre was burned down in 1663, at which time Beeston's theatrical activities ceased.

Beeston is important as a transitional figure from the pre-1642 theatre to the Restoration stage. His training of young actors, for which he was frequently praised, helped establish a continuity of acting styles from Shakespeare's time to the latter half of the 17th century. His transitional status also enabled him to serve as the source of the information about Shakespeare recorded by John AUBREY. Beeston's recollections included the suggestion that Shakespeare "had been in his younger yeares a Schoolmaster in the Country." [Leslie Hotson, *The Commonwealth and Restoration Stage*, 1928.]

Beethoven, Ludwig van. See MUSIC BASED ON SHAKESPEARE: *19th century to 1850.*

Belarius. In *Cymbeline,* a banished lord disguised under the name of Morgan. Twenty years before, Belarius revenged his unjust banishment by kidnapping Cymbeline's two sons; he has reared Guiderius and Arviragus as their natural father in the wilds of Wales. In this idyllic setting, the good Belarius exhorts the young men to an appreciation of the simple virtues as opposed to courtly complexities. He is somewhat uneasy over their subtle alienation from his philosophy and the clear manifestations of their princely natures. Unable to restrain their noble instincts, Belarius joins Guiderius and Arviragus when they enlist in the battle against Rome and, together, the "old man and two boys" perform with such extraordinary valor that they miraculously turn defeat into a British victory.

To save Guiderius from a death sentence, Belarius reveals the identity of the two boys and Cymbeline restores him to royal favor.

Belch, Sir Toby. In *Twelfth Night,* Olivia's roistering uncle. An established fixture in Olivia's somewhat cluttered household, coarse Sir Toby represents himself to the gullible Sir Andrew Aguecheek as the ideal gentleman. He acts as the affluent knight's guide, steering him through drunken revels, directing his romantic visions toward Olivia, and encouraging his aspirations to swordsmanship. Sir Andrew is fair game and Sir Toby has benefited by "two thousand strong, or so."

Invulnerable as a master deluder, Sir Toby becomes ludicrous only when, as a swashbuckling swordsman, he joins the deceived company in mistaking Sebastian for Cesario. [Joseph H. Summers, "The Masks of *Twelfth Night,*" *University of Kansas City Review,* XXII, 1955.]

Belgium. See FLEMISH PRODUCTIONS.

Belgrade Theatre, The. A civic theatre in Coventry, England. The civic theatre is one of a line of such endeavors in Coventry, but has the distinction of being the first full-scale professional theatre ever to be built entirely at the expense of a municipal authority. Its name derives from a gift of timber extended by Belgrade, Yugoslavia, to the city for the purpose of reconstruction after the war. The theatre opened on March 27, 1958.

Although the theatre's repertory has been varied, it has to its credit numerous Shakespeare productions. Included in these productions have been *Julius Caesar, Much Ado About Nothing, Twelfth Night, Hamlet, Taming of the Shrew,* and *The Merchant of Venice.*

Belleforest, François de (1530–1583). French poet, translator, and historiographer. Belleforest began his career as a provincial poet, but lack of acceptance by the more sophisticated audiences of Paris, where he had gone in order to establish a reputation, forced him to turn to prose. He wrote a series of volumes on the history of France, for which he received (but later forfeited) the title "historiographe de France." His most significant work, however, was his continuation of *Histoires Tragiques,* the French translation by Pierre Boaistuau (d. 1566) of Matteo BANDELLO's *Novelle.* Boaistuau completed only six stories before abandoning the project. Belleforest's continuation ran to seven volumes, published from 1559 to 1582, ultimately including tales from sources other than Bandello. The most famous of Belleforest's tales is his rendering of an old legend translated from Saxo Grammaticus which eventually became the source of *Hamlet* (see HAMLET: *Sources*). Belleforest may also be the indirect source of *Much Ado About Nothing, Twelfth Night,* and *All's Well That Ends Well.* The *Histoires Tragiques* was translated into English by Geoffrey FENTON.

Bellenden, John (fl. 1533–1587). Scottish translator. A member of the court of James V of Scotland, Bellenden was commissioned by the king to translate into Scots the Latin history of Scotland, *Scotorum Historiae* (1526), of Hector BOECE. Bellenden's translation (1535) subsequently became the source of *Macbeth,* probably through the English version in Holinshed. Some scholars have suggested that Shakespeare used Bellenden directly, but the evidence in support of this view is slight.

Bell Inn. An Elizabethan inn which offered presentations of plays. In existence prior to 1560, the Bell Inn was located on "Gracyous-strett" (or Gracechurch Street). (This is known because extant records show that on June 12, 1560, the wife of the Bell's innkeeper was carted through the streets as punishment for being a bawd and whore.) It is known that by 1576/7 plays were being presented at the Bell; the Revels Accounts for that season show an expenditure of 10d.

> ffor the cariadge of the partes of ye well counterfeit from the Bell in Gracious strete to St. Iohns to be performed for the play of Cutwell.

A civic order of November 28, 1583 assigned it and the Bull to the Queen's Men for their first winter season. *Tarlton's Jests* (entered in the Stationers' Register 1609) confirms that Tarlton and the Queen's Men played "at the Bell by the Cross Keys," another inn in Gracious Street. When in 1596 the London authorities were prevailed upon by the Puritans to disallow plays in the area within the city's jurisdiction, the Bell was one of the theatres put down. See Richard RAWLIDGE. [E. K. Chambers, *The Elizabethan Stage,* 1923.]

Belott-Mountjoy suit. A legal dispute in which Shakespeare acted as a witness. The Mountjoys were a French Huguenot family whose home and business were located in the northwest section of London in Cripplegate. Christopher Mountjoy (d. 1620), the father, was a tire (tiara)-maker, a creator of elaborate headdresses for women; one of his customers was the queen of England. It is now known, as the result of the industrious research of C. W. Wallace, that in 1604 the Mountjoys had Shakespeare as a lodger in their home. Shakespeare's residence is established as a result of a suit brought against Christopher Mountjoy by his son-in-law Stephen Belott. According to Belott, a former apprentice of Mountjoy, he had married Mountjoy's daughter Mary on November 19, 1604 upon the promise that he would receive a dowry of £60 and a bequest of another £200 in Mountjoy's will. By 1612 neither of these promises had been fulfilled and Belott brought suit against his father-in-law, during which a number of witnesses were called to testify as to the original terms of the dowry. The testimony consisted of depositions signed by the witnesses, the principal one of whom was Shakespeare. In the following extracts, as given by E. K. Chambers, matter scratched out in the documents appears in broken brackets and editorial additions appear in square brackets.

The first witness was Joan Johnson, a former maid of the Mountjoys. She testified that the relationship between Stephen and Mary was abetted by Mary's parents, who had enlisted Shakespeare's aid:

> And as she remembereth the defendant did send and perswade one Mr Shakespeare that laye in the

> house to perswade the plaintiff to the same marriadge.

A second witness was Daniel Nicholas:

> he herd one Wm: Shakespeare saye that the defendant did beare a good opinion of the plaintiff and affected him well when he served him, and did move the plaintiff by him the said Shakespeare to haue [a] marriadge betweene his daughter Marye Mountioye [and] the plaintiff, and for that purpose sent him the said Sh[akespeare] to the plaintiff to perswade the plaintiff to the same, as Shakespere tould him this deponent, which was effected and solempnized vppon promise of a porcion with her . . . the plaintiff did requeste him this deponent to goe with his wyffe to Shakespe[are] to vnderstande the truthe howe muche and what the defendant did promise to bestowe on his daughter in marriadge with him the plaintiff, who did soe. And askinge Shakespeare thereof, he answered that he promissed yf the plaintiff would marrye with Marye his the defendantes onlye daughter, he the defendant would by his promise as he remembered geue the plaintiff with her in marriadge about the some of ffyftye poundes in money and certayne househould stuffe.

At a later deposition on June 19, 1612 there were two other witnesses, William Eaton and Nowell Mountjoy. Eaton testified that "he hath herd one Mr Shakspeare saye that he was sent by the defendant to the plaintiff to move the plaintiff to haue a marriadge betweene them . . . ." Nowell Mountjoy, brother of the defendant, deposed that he was not aware of the alleged encouragement of the marriage on Mountjoy's part, but he did confirm that "the plaintiff [Belott] tould this deponent that one Mr. Shakespeare was imployed by the defendant about that buysnes . . . ."

Shakespeare's deposition was given on May 11, 1612. It confirms the argument that he had assisted Mountjoy in bringing about the marriage. Shakespeare, however, had by this time forgotten the details of the dowry:

> William Shakespeare of Stratford vpon Aven in the Countye of Warwicke gentleman of the age of xlviij yeres or thereaboutes sworne and examined the daye and yere abouesaid deposethe & sayethe
>
> 1. To the first interrogatory this deponent sayethe he knowethe the partyes plaintiff and deffendant and hathe know[ne] them bothe as he now remembrethe for the space of tenne yeres or thereaboutes.
>
> 2. To the second interrogatory this deponent sayeth he did know the complainant when he was servant with the deffendant, and that duringe the tyme of his the complainantes service with the said deffendant he the said complainant to this deponentes knowledge did well and honestly behaue himselfe, but to this deponentes remembered he hath not heard the deffendant confesse that he had gott any great profitt and comodytye by the service of the said complainant, but this deponent saithe he verely thinkethe that the said complainant was a very good and industrious servant in the said service. And more he canott depose to the said interrogatory.
>
> 3. To the third interrogatory this deponent sayethe that it did evydentlye appeare that the said deffendant did all the tyme of the said complainantes service with him beare and shew great good will and affeccion towardes the said complainant, and that he hath hard the deffendant and his wyefe diuerse and sundry tymes saye and reporte that the said complainant was a very honest fellow: And this deponent sayethe that the said deffendant did make a mocion vnto the complainant of marriadge with the said Mary in the bill mencioned beinge the said deffendantes sole chyld and daughter, and willinglye offered to performe the same yf the said complainant shold seeme to be content and well like thereof: And further this deponent sayethe that the said deffendantes wyeffe did sollicitt and entreat this deponent to move and perswade the said complainant to effect the said marriadge, and accordingly this deponent did moue and perswade the complainant thervnto: And more to this interrogatorye he cannott depose.
>
> 4. To the ffourth interrogatory this deponent sayth that the defendant promissed to geue the said complainant a porcion ⟨of monie and goodes⟩ in marriadg[e] with Marye his daughter, but what certayne ⟨some⟩ porcion he rememberethe not, nor when to be payed ⟨yf any some weare promissed,⟩ nor knoweth that the defendant promissed the plaintiff twoe hundered poundes with his daughter Marye at the tyme of his decease. But sayth that the plaintiff was dwellinge with the defendant in his house, and they had amongeste them selues manye conferences about there marriadge which [afterwardes] was consumated and solempnized. And more he cann[ott depose.]
>
> 5. To the vth interrogatory this deponent sayth he can saye noth[inge] touchinge any parte or poynte of the same interrogatory, for he knoweth not what implementes and necessaries of houshould stuffe the defendant gaue the plaintiff in marriadge with his daughter Marye.
>
> Willm Shakp

The evidence of the testimony reveals that Shakespeare was residing with the Mountjoys probably as early as 1602, and that in 1612 he was a resident of Stratford, not of London. The document also gives one of the few undisputed examples of Shakespeare's signature.

The suit itself was referred from the Court of Requests to the elders of the French Huguenot church in London. The elders decided in favor of Belott, requiring Mountjoy to pay him 20 "nobles," which a year later still had not been paid. In 1614 Mountjoy was excommunicated from the French church for licentiousness. He died in 1620. His will, dated January 26, 1619, leaves no marriage portion to his daughter and son-in-law and, indeed, deprives them of their legal inheritance. Stephen Belott died sometime around 1646. [C. W. Wallace, "Shakespeare and his London Associates . . . ," *Nebraska University Studies*, 10, 1910; E. K. Chambers, *William Shakespeare, A Study of Facts and Problems*, 1930; B. Roland Lewis, *The Shakespeare Documents*, 1940.]

Bel Savage Inn. An inn used as a playhouse and located on Ludgate Hill. Bel Savage Inn is not to be confused with another inn of a similar name in Gracechurch Street of which the comedian Richard Tarlton was the keeper. The inn was apparently the winter quarters of the Queen's Men in the 1580's and of the Admiral's Men in the 1590's when, according to William Prynne's *Histrio-mastix* (1633), *Dr. Faustus* was performed there. It was apparently also used for boxing matches. The inn was probably one of those which were "put down" in 1596 when the city fathers succeeded in prohibiting public plays within the city limits. See Richard RAWLIDGE.

Benedick. See BEATRICE AND BENEDICK.

Benedicte and Betteris. See MUCH ADO ABOUT NOTHING: *Stage History*.

Benfield, Robert (d. 1649). Actor with the King's Men. Benfield probably began his acting career with the Children of the Queen's Revels and then joined Lady Elizabeth's Men; he appears in the acting lists of the latter's productions of Beaumont and Fletcher's *The Coxcomb* and *The Honest Man's Fortune*, both given in 1613. By 1619 he had joined the King's Men, for his name is among those in the new patent granted to that company that year. Very likely he was a replacement for Will Ostler, who had died in 1614, for his name is listed with Ostler's as having played Antonio in *The Duchess of Malfi* (pub. 1623). He is in many acting lists of the King's Men, and T. W. Baldwin has conjectured that his roles were mainly those requiring a dignified mien—kings, senators, and old men.

His name is in the First Folio list of principal actors who appeared in Shakespeare's plays, and he was one of three actors who sued for the right to purchase shares in the Globe and Blackfriars in 1635 (see SHARERS' PAPERS). He probably remained with the company until its end, for he signed the dedication to the Beaumont and Fletcher Folio in 1647. [T. W. Baldwin, *The Organization and Personnel of the Shakespearean Company*, 1927; G. E. Bentley, *The Jacobean and Caroline Stage*, 5 vols., 1941–1956.]

Benson, Sir Francis Robert (1858–1939). Actor and theatre manager. Although not a great actor, Benson contributed greatly, through his management and productions, to the Shakespearean theatre. He was born at Tunbridge Wells and educated at Oxford, where he was a leader in the movement which led to the founding of the Oxford University Dramatic Society. At this time, the actress Ellen Terry witnessed his amateur performance as Clytemnestra in *Agamemnon*, and encouraged him in a professional career. In 1882, he played Paris in Irving's *Romeo and Juliet* at the Lyceum; Ellen Terry played Juliet.

In 1883, with the aid of his family, he purchased the Bentley acting company, in which he had worked for a season. In a short time Benson's management created a provincial company which was the mainstay of the Shakespearean theatre in England for 33 years. With the exception of *Titus Andronicus* and *Troilus and Cressida*, Benson produced all of Shakespeare's works. His presentations were neither ostentatious nor tricky, and they proved a training ground for many young actors. Benson himself appeared in many of his productions. His most notable roles were Richard II, Richard III, Petruchio in *The Taming of the Shrew*, and Caliban in *The Tempest*.

Benson was the first actor to be knighted in a theatre; the ceremony took place at the Drury Lane in 1916 following his portrayal of Julius Caesar. Benson was a governor of the Shakespeare Memorial Theatre and a trustee of the Shakespeare Birthplace. [*Oxford Companion to the Theatre*, Phyllis Hartnol ed., 1951. J. C. Trewin, *Benson and the Bensonian* 1960.]

Benson, John (d. 1667). London publisher of bal lads and broadsides. In 1640 Benson published a edition of poems purportedly by Shakespeare. Thi edition has very little textual authority, althoug 18th-century scholars relied upon it heavily. Its titl page bore the following inscription: "Poems: Writ ten by Wil. Shake-speare. Gent. Printed at Londo by Tho. Cotes, and are to be sold by Iohn Benson dwelling in St. Dunstans Church-yard. 1640." Oppo site the title page is a cut of the Droeshout engraving signed "W. M. *sculpsit*." The engraver was appar ently William MARSHALL. Printed below the engrav ing is Ben Jonson's First Folio eulogy of Shakespeare Other preliminary matter includes two poems writ ten in praise of Shakespeare, one by Leonard DIGGES the other by John WARREN.

Benson's edition failed to include *Venus an Adonis* or *The Rape of Lucrece*, substituting fo those legitimate works of Shakespeare a host o poems known to be written by other men. It con tained all the poems in the 1612 edition of *The Pas sionate Pilgrim*, *The Phoenix and the Turtle*, *Th Lover's Complaint*, and all the Sonnets with the ex ception of numbers 18, 19, 43, 56, 75, 76, 96, and 126 The non-Shakespearean poems in Benson's collectio include Marlowe's "The Passionate Shepherd to hi Love" and Sir Walter Raleigh's "Nymph's Reply to the Shepherd," which also appear in *The Passionat Pilgrim*. Also included in Benson's collection ar John MILTON's "Epitaph," reprinted from the Secon Folio; an elegy "On the Death of William Shake speare" by William BASSE; and the anonymous "A Elegie on the death of that famous Writer and Actor M. William Shakespeare":

I dare not doe thy Memory that wrong,
Unto our larger griefes to give a tongue;
Ile onely sigh in earnest, and let fall
My solemne teares at thy great Funerall;
For every eye that raines a showre for thee,
Laments thy losse in a sad Elegie.
Nor is it fit each humble Muse should have,
Thy worth his subject, now th'art laid in grave;
No its a flight beyond the pitch of those,
Whose worthles Pamphlets are not sence in Prose.
Let learned *Johnson* sing a Dirge for thee,
And fill our Orbe with mournefull harmony:
But we neede no Remembrancer, thy Fame
Shall still accompany thy honoured Name,
To all posterity; and make us be,
Sensible of what we lost in losing thee:
Being the Ages wonder whose smooth Rhimes
Did more reforme than lash the looser Times.
Nature her selfe did her owne selfe admire,
As oft as thou wert pleased to attire
Her in her native lusture, and confesse,
Thy dressing was her chiefest comlinesse.
How can we then forget thee, when the age
Her chiefest Tutor, and the widdowed Stage
Her onely favorite in thee hath lost,
And Natures selfe what she did bragge of most.
Sleepe then rich soule of numbers, whilst poore we,
Enjoy the profits of thy Legacie;

And thinke it happinesse enough we have,
So much of thee redeemed from the grave,
As may suffice to enlighten future times,
With the bright lustre of thy matchlesse Rhimes.

The remainder of Benson's volume is entitled "An Addition of Some Excellent Poems, to those precedent, of Renowned *Shakespeare*, By other Gentlemen." This section includes poems by Jonson, Francis Beaumont, Robert Herrick, Thomas Carew, and some unidentified poets.

Benson's edition was probably unauthorized, since he entered in the Stationers' Register only the non-Shakespearean poems in the volume. His culpability is increased by the disingenuous Epistle with which he prefaced his edition:

To the Reader.

I Here presume (under favour) to present to your view, some excellent and sweetely composed Poems, of Master *William Shakespeare*, Which in themselves appeare of the same purity, the Authour himselfe then living avouched; they had not the fortune by reason of their Infancie in his death, to have the due accommodation of proportionable glory, with the rest of his everliving Workes, yet the lines of themselves will afford you a more authentick approbation than my assurance any way can, to invite your allowance, in your perusall you shall finde them *Seren*, cleere and eligantly plaine, such gentle straines as shall recreate and not perplexe your braine, no intricate or cloudy stuffe to puzzell intellect, but perfect eloquence; such as will raise your admiration to his praise: this assurance I know will not differ from your acknowledgement. And certaine I am, my opinion will be seconded by the sufficiency of these ensuing Lines; I have beene somewhat solicitus to bring this forth to the perfect view of all men; and in so doing, glad to be serviceable for the continuance of glory to the deserved Author in these his Poems.

—I.B.

[Hyder Rollins, ed., *Poems: Variorum Edition*, 1938.]

Benthall, Michael (1919–). Director. Benthall, educated at Eton and Oxford, was a member of the Oxford University Dramatic Society, with whom he acted the role of Claudio in *Much Ado About Nothing* in 1938. He made his professional debut in Newcastle-on-Tyne in 1938, and in 1939 he began to act small parts with the Old Vic company. In February 1944 he co-directed *Hamlet* with Tyrone Guthrie for the Old Vic at the New Theatre. In 1947 he directed *The Merchant of Venice* for the Shakespeare Memorial Theatre at Stratford-upon-Avon and in the two years following he directed *King John, Hamlet, The Taming of the Shrew, A Midsummer Night's Dream*, and *Cymbeline* at Stratford. He directed the 1950 production of *As You Like It* in New York, and in 1951 did *Antony and Cleopatra* in London and *The Tempest* at Stratford. In 1953 he became director of the Old Vic and has been responsible for productions of *Hamlet, All's Well That Ends Well, Coriolanus, Macbeth, Richard II, Julius Caesar, The Winter's Tale, Henry V, Measure for Measure, Timon of Athens*, and *Twelfth Night*. Most of these plays have been seen abroad on Old Vic tours, as well as at the Edinburgh Festival; the 1954 *Hamlet* was also given at Elsinore. Benthall directed the production of *Macbeth* at Covent Garden in 1960. [*Who's Who in the Theatre*, 1961.]

Bentley, Gerald Eades (1901–). American scholar. Bentley, a professor of English at Princeton University, is the author of *The Jacobean and Caroline Stage* (5 vols., 1941–1956), an exhaustively detailed history of the theatre from 1616 to 1642. His work is a continuation of E. K. Chambers' four-volume *The Elizabethan Stage* (1923), which ends with the year 1616. Bentley has also written *Shakespeare and Jonson* (2 vols., 1945) and *Shakespeare: A Biographical Handbook* (1961). The latter is a scrupulous presentation of the facts—as distinguished from inferences and fantasies—of Shakespeare's life as revealed in existing records. He is also the author of an important article, "Shakespeare and the Blackfriars" (*Shakespeare Survey, 1*, 1948), which argues that the acquisition in 1608 of the Blackfriars, a private playhouse catering to a select audience, by Shakespeare's company required "new and different plays for a new and different audience" with the result that Shakespeare produced the experimental romances *Cymbeline, The Winter's Tale*, and *The Tempest*.

Benvolio. In *Romeo and Juliet*, the friend and cousin of Romeo. Benvolio's steady self-control and geniality balance the extremes of Romeo's passionate romanticism and Mercutio's inspired cynicism.

Berkeley. See TRESSEL AND BERKELEY.

Berkeley, Thomas, 5th baron (d. 1417). Berkeley was dispatched by the duke of York to Henry Bolingbroke, in 1399, to demand an explanation for Bolingbroke's armed re-entry into England. In *Richard II*, Lord Berkeley is rebuked by Bolingbroke for addressing him as lord of Hereford instead of Lancaster, the title Bolingbroke has returned to England to claim (II, iii). [W. H. Thomson, *Shakespeare's Characters: A Historical Dictionary*, 1951.]

Berlioz, Hector (1803–1869). French composer. Two, at least, of Berlioz' greatest works were inspired by Shakespeare. His dramatic symphony *Roméo et Juliette* (1839) is scored for a large orchestra, chorus, and soloists; the composer's own text is versified by Emile Deschamps. His two-act comic opera *Béatrice et Bénédict* was produced successfully at Baden in 1862. Again Berlioz wrote his own libretto. *Hamlet* inspired two works for orchestra and chorus, "La mort d'Ophélie" and a "Marche Funèbre" for the final scene (1848). Berlioz also wrote an overture, "Roi Lear" (1831), and a cantata, *Cléopâtre* (1829), inspired by *Antony and Cleopatra*, but not directly based on it. His fantasia with choruses on *The Tempest* (1828) he incorporated three years later into his "monodrama" *Lélio, ou Le Retour à la Vie*. [Christopher Wilson, *Shakespeare and Music*, 1922.]

Bernard, Elizabeth. See Elizabeth HALL.

Bernard or **Barnard, Sir John** (1605–1674). The second husband of Shakespeare's granddaughter Elizabeth HALL. Barnard married Elizabeth in 1649, about 14 months after the death of her first husband, Thomas Nash (see NASH FAMILY). Bernard had eight children. The second marriage was without issue, however, and the direct descendants of Shakespeare ended with Elizabeth.

The couple lived at Bernard's ancestral home of

Abington Manor, in Northamptonshire, moving to New Place after the death of Elizabeth's mother, Susanna Hall, in 1649. They returned to Abington shortly before the Restoration and lived there for the remainder of their lives. Bernard was knighted by Charles II in 1661 in recognition of his support of the king during the Commonwealth period. Upon the death of his wife in 1670, Bernard inherited New Place. His heirs, in turn, sold it to Sir Edward Walker after Bernard's death in 1674. [Joseph Q. Adams, *A Life of William Shakespeare*, 1923.]

Bernardo. In *Hamlet*, the officer who, with Marcellus, first sees the Ghost. After the spectre has twice appeared on the battlements, Bernardo and Marcellus bring Horatio to the scene of the apparition, and together the three inform Hamlet of the strange event they have witnessed (I, ii).

Berners, John Bourchier, 2nd Baron (1467–1533). Statesman and translator. Berners served both Henry VII and Henry VIII in various diplomatic and administrative roles and was rewarded in 1520 with an appointment as deputy of Calais. While at Calais he completed his translation from the French of the *Chronicles* (2 vols., 1523, 1525) of Jean FROISSART which provided Shakespeare with some important details in *Richard II*. Berners also translated *Huon of Bordeaux* (c. 1534), an extremely popular book in the Elizabethan age, from which Shakespeare may have drawn the name Oberon for *A Midsummer Night's Dream*. Berners' translation (*The Golden Boke of Marcus Aurelius*, 1534) of a French version of Antonio de Guevara's *El Reloj de Príncipes* was an important landmark in the development of English prose style and one of the sources of the style known in Shakespeare's time as euphuism.

Berowne or **Biron.** In *Love's Labour's Lost*, the skeptical analyst of love who himself falls victim to the malady he so wittily describes. One of the four young noblemen who forswear the company of women in order to devote themselves to study, Berowne early emerges as the least deluded of the quartet. He frankly acknowledges the implausibility of the attempt to triumph over love, and in so doing serves as the spokesman of the audience. He himself is not exempt from satire and is frequently impaled by the witty thrusts of dark Rosaline. Their relationship, highlighted by exchanges of raillery, is a foreshadowing of the even more brilliant "merry war" of Beatrice and Benedick in *Much Ado*.

Bertram. In *All's Well That Ends Well*, the young Count of Rousillon and the unwilling husband of Helena. Easily the most maligned and generally disliked of Shakespeare's heroes, Bertram has emerged as one of the major obstacles to appreciation of the play. His churlish rejection of Helena, his subsequent unsuccessful philandering, and the stubbornness—often verging on stupidity—with which he refuses to acknowledge his wife's virtue and beauty, have elicited contempt from most modern readers. They are quick to point out the difficulty of responding to a comedy in which the hero is, in Mark Van Doren's words, "a commonplace cad."

Recent commentary, however, has tended to reverse this view. Critics such as M. C. Bradbrook have come to see the character of Bertram as a development of the central figure of a medieval morality play. In the morality plays the hero, representing mankind, was the object of a contention between the forces of good and evil (see PSYCHOMACHIA). Although frequently succumbing to temptation, the erring hero would eventually be captured by the forces of good, as in the Biblical story of the Prodigal Son. Bertram is thus presented as the object of the struggle between Helena and the low-lived intimate, Parolles. Bertram emerges from the struggle with an insight into the nature of "true nobility," as exemplified in the character of Helena. [Mark Van Doren, *Shakespeare*, 1939; M. C. Bradbrook, *Shakespeare and Elizabethan Poetry*, 1952.]

Bestrafte Bruder-mord, Der (Fratricide Punished). An early 18th-century German version of the Hamlet play. The *Tragoedia der bestrafte Bruder-mord oder: Prinz Hamlet aus Dännemark* appears to be either a revision of the older play, *Hamlet*, which was the source of Shakespeare's play (see UR-HAMLET), or a version of the pirated, corrupt First Quarto of Shakespeare's *Hamlet*, or both. The German version, first published in 1781 from a manuscript dated 1710, contains a number of elements which appear to predate Shakespeare's play, including an introductory prologue and the use of the name Corambis for the character Polonius. (Corambis is the name given Polonius in the First Quarto.) *Der Bestrafte Bruder-mord* thus provides some clue to what was contained in the *Ur-Hamlet*, but its provenance remains obscure and conjectural. G. I. Duthie believes that *Der Bestrafte Bruder-mord* is a memorial reconstruction based on the First Quarto, and that it was performed during a continental tour made in the early 17th century by a company of actors led by John Greene. This troupe's repertory included a *Tragoedia von Hamlet einen printzen in Dennemark*. Duthie suggests that this play was based on the First Quarto, with an occasional borrowing from the *Ur-Hamlet*. See GERMANY. [G. I. Duthie, *The "Bad" Quarto of Hamlet*, 1941.]

Bethell, Samuel Leslie (1908–1955). Critic. Author of *The Winter's Tale: a Study* (1947) and *Shakespeare and the Popular Dramatic Tradition* (1944), Bethell emphasizes the nonrealistic aspects of Shakespeare's plays in order to correct the tendency to view them in terms of "psychological naturalism." He argues that Shakespeare is "somewhere between two practical extremes," the naturalism of Ibsen's *A Doll's House* and the "conventionalism" of *Everyman*.

Betterton, Thomas (c. 1635–1710). Actor. Betterton is ranked as the outstanding actor of the Restoration. Although many of the facts concerning his early career are obscure, it is fairly certain that his first major Shakespearean role was that of Pericles in 1660. He joined William Davenant's Duke's Company at Lisle's Tennis Court in 1661 and during the next two years achieved acclaim for his portrayals of Hamlet, Macbeth, Mercutio, and Sir Toby Belch. With the death of Davenant, Betterton and Henry Harris assumed management of the company. In 1671, their company merged with a rival company at the Theatre Royal. Betterton discontinued this arrangement in 1695 and reopened the theatre at Lisle's Tennis Court. Finally, in 1705, he settled at a new theatre built for him at the Haymarket. Colley Cibber, Pope, Pepys, and the hard-to-please critic Aston agreed that Betterton had no peer as an actor; their praise was unqualified. His magnificent portrayal of

Hamlet could be traced to Richard Burbage's interpretation. Betterton also was admired as Lear, Henry VIII, and Othello.

Betterton married the accomplished actress Mary Saunderson in 1662. She has been called the first actress of the English stage, but this claim is doubtful. Cibber considered her Lady Macbeth the finest he had ever seen. [*Dictionary of National Biography*, 1885– ; R. W. Lowe, *Thomas Betterton*, 1891.]

Bevis, George. In *2 Henry VI*, one of the men who join the rebel band of Jack Cade and follow him on his plundering, murdering march to London.

Beyle, Marie Henri. See STENDHAL.

Bianca. In *Othello*, the mistress of Cassio. Bianca is an unwitting instrument in the schemes of Iago.

Bianca. In *The Taming of the Shrew*, the gentle, sweet younger daughter of Baptista Minola. Bianca is forbidden suitors by her father until her older sister, the shrewish Katharina, is wed. Bianca elopes with Lucentio and proves to be a less obedient wife than her sister.

Bible, 16th-century translations. At the beginning of the 16th century there were only two complete English versions of the Bible, both of which were made by the followers of John Wyclif (c. 1324–1384). The Wycliffite versions had been made from the Vulgate, and their language was somewhat archaic. An increasing demand for new translations, particularly from the original languages, was the result of several factors: the underground current of Lollardy, the inspiration from the continental reformers, and the availability of critical texts recently edited by such humanists as Erasmus. Further, the invention of the printing press made it possible to distribute new versions more widely. The first important Englishman in this new movement was William Tyndale (c. 1494–1536). Unable to carry out his project in England, he moved to Germany and at Worms in 1526 published his version of the New Testament based on the Greek text of Erasmus. A new edition issued in 1534 exerted a major influence because most of its text was later incorporated into the Authorized Version (1611). Tyndale did not live to complete his translation of the Old Testament but was apprehended in Flanders and executed by Charles V. Another exile, Miles Coverdale (1488–1569), was meanwhile preparing a version which he published in 1535. His New Testament was basically Tyndale's, revised in the light of German versions, while the Old Testament drew upon various Latin and German versions and the portions completed by Tyndale. The Coverdale Bible was published in London under a royal license in 1537. The same year a license was also granted for the "Matthew's Bible," so-called because the translation was attributed to one Thomas Matthew, a pseudonym of John Rogers, a former associate of Tyndale's. The Matthew's Bible was basically a compilation of Tyndale and Coverdale. Meanwhile, the church, under Henry VIII and Thomas Cromwell, wished to make an official version. Coverdale was given charge of its preparation and the result was the "Great Bible" (1539), sometimes called "Cranmer's Bible" from the long Preface which he contributed to the second edition (1540). Because of its official status and timely appearance, the Great Bible was used to supply the appropriate texts for the

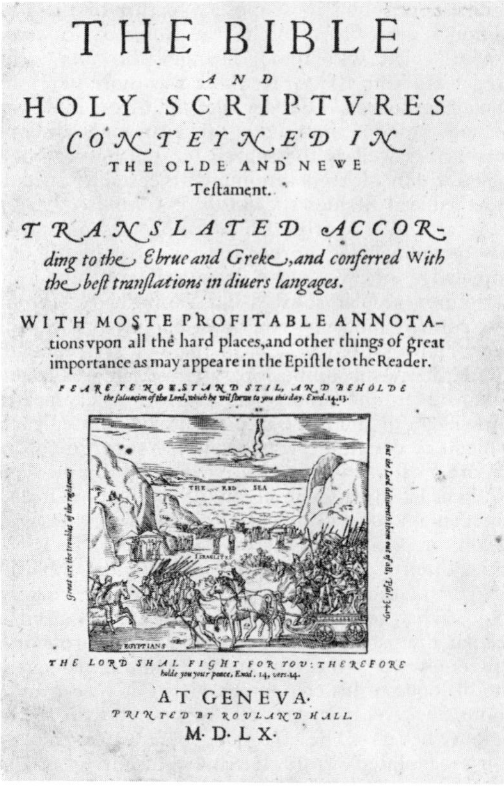
THE BIBLE
AND
HOLY SCRIPTVRES
CONTEYNED IN
THE OLDE AND NEWE
Teſtament.

TRANSLATED ACCOR-
ding to the Ebrue and Greke, and conferred With
the beſt tranſlations in diuers langages.

WITH MOSTE PROFITABLE ANNOTA-
tions vpon all the hard places, and other things of great
importance as may appeare in the Epiſtle to the Reader.

FEARE YE NOT, STAND STIL, AND BEHOLDE
the saluacion of the Lord, which he wil ſhewe to you this day. Exod. 14, 13.

THE LORD SHAL FIGHT FOR YOU: THEREFORE
holde you your peace. Exod. 14, vers. 14.

AT GENEVA.
PRINTED BY ROULAND HALL.
M. D. LX.

TITLE PAGE OF THE GENEVA BIBLE, SOMETIMES CALLED THE "BREECHES BIBLE" (1560).

Book of Common Prayer (1549). The persecutions under Queen Mary again found English Protestant exiles (including, perhaps, Coverdale) preparing fresh translations. The "Genevan (or "Breeches") Bible" (1560) became enormously successful—150 editions from 1560 to 1644—and by its extensive notes it exerted a formative influence on English religious thought. To counteract the strongly Calvinistic tenor of the glosses, Elizabethan prelates prepared a new official version, the "Bishops' Bible" (1568). The need for an official Roman Catholic version was supplied by the English College located alternately at Rheims and Douai. The New Testament was published at Rheims in 1582; the Old Testament, at Douai in 1609/10.

The nature and extent of Shakespeare's use of the Bible has been the subject of much speculation resulting in widely divergent opinions. The most balanced discussion is that of Richmond Noble in his *Shakespeare's Biblical Knowledge* (1935) in which the author gives careful consideration to earlier scholarship in addition to presenting his own conclusions. With regard to the version used, Noble offers a corrective to the once-prevalent view that Shakespeare relied almost exclusively on the Genevan version. It now appears that he used the Bishops' Bible for his earlier plays and that subsequently he tended to rely more heavily on the Genevan Bible. For the New Testament he apparently used Lawrence Thomson's revision (1576) rather than the original Genevan text. His quotations from the

Psalms correspond most closely to that of the 1540 edition of the Great Bible; the *Book of Common Prayer* which, with minor changes, drew its Scriptural texts from the Great Bible was more likely his immediate source. The fact that the Great Bible was the ancestor of both the Genevan and Bishops' versions, as well as the source for the prayer book, makes it difficult to determine with certainty specific indebtedness. Besides the *Book of Common Prayer*, there are other works that Shakespeare could have used as immediate sources for much of his Biblical knowledge: the HOMILIES drew primarily upon the Scriptures, secular sources like Holinshed's *Chronicles* contain Biblical quotations, and even the ordinary conversation of Elizabethans was frequently interlarded with Biblical paraphrases and allusions.

Whatever the immediate source, Shakespeare's knowledge of the Bible was extensive, although it is difficult to determine whether it was superior to that of other alert, intelligent, well-read Elizabethans. There is hardly a scene in any of the plays that does not contain some Biblical quotation, paraphrase, allusion, or parallel; furthermore, his use of such material often assumes a familiarity with the Bible on the part of the audience. The nature of the borrowings is what we would expect on the part of a skilled secular dramatist; Biblical material is not brought in for its own sake but appears as a natural element in the dialogue of his characters. Hence it reveals more about Shakespeare's dramatic technique than his religious beliefs. The frequent references to "the Lord's anointed" from II Samuel occur as natural allusions in the history plays. The three instances in which the Virgin Mary is alluded to are in the parts of historical characters—John of Gaunt, Joan of Arc, and Henry VIII—who Shakespeare felt would naturally make such allusions. When he came to depicting a Jew, Shakespeare had Shylock make frequent reference to Old Testament figures—Hagar, Jacob, Laban, Daniel. When Mistress Quickly refers to Falstaff as being "in Arthur's bosom" (*Henry V*, II, iii, 9–11), the point of the joke depends upon the audience knowing that she has misquoted the "Abraham's bosom" of Luke 16: 22–23. One of Shakespeare's most common uses of Biblical material is found in Portia's speech on "The quality of mercy" (*Merchant of Venice*, IV, i, 184 ff.). Noble notes that Shakespeare has interwoven quotations from Ecclesiasticus (35: 19) and Deuteronomy (32: 2); but the speech also has an analogue in Seneca's *De Clementia* (I, 19). Shakespeare merely drew upon whatever sources were most appropriate—Biblical, classical, or other—in order to achieve his aim. An example of Shakespeare's subtlety in this regard can be found in the fact that the two characters who most frequently quote the Bible are Henry VI and Richard III; with the former it is the natural result of his sincere piety, with the latter it is an example of the devil citing Scripture for his own purpose. [Richmond Noble, *Shakespeare's Biblical Knowledge*, 1935.]—R.C.F.

Bidford or **Biddeford.** A village 7½ miles west of Stratford where Shakespeare is alleged to have engaged in a disastrous drinking bout according to a popular legend anonymously recorded in 1762:

> . . . [Shakespeare] having heard much of the men of that village as deep drinkers and merry fellows, one day went over to Bidford, to take a cup with them. He enquired of a shepherd for the Bidford drinkers; who replied they were absent; but the Bidford sippers were at home; and, I suppose, continued the sheepkeeper, they will be sufficient for you: and so, indeed, they were. He was forced to take up his lodging under that tree for some hours.

[E. K. Chambers, *William Shakespeare*, 1930.]

Bigot, Lord. In *King John*, Bigot, together with the Earls of Pembroke and Salisbury, finds Arthur's body and concludes that he was murdered by Hubert de Burgh on King John's orders. All three men revolt from John and join Lewis the Dauphin. However, they return their allegiance to the English King when they learn that the Dauphin plans to execute them when his purpose is accomplished.

Historically this character was probably Roger Bigot or Bigod, 2nd earl of Norfolk (d. 1221). He joined the barons whose quarrels with King John resulted in the signing of the Magna Carta, and when Louis of France invaded England, Bigot became the foreign king's ally. On the accession of Henry III, the earl returned his allegiance to his own country. [W. H. Thomson, *Shakespeare's Characters: A Historical Dictionary*, 1951.]

Biondello. In *The Taming of the Shrew*, one of Lucentio's servants. Biondello aids in his master's exchange of identity with Tranio, a ruse designed to give Lucentio access to Bianca (I, i).

Bird or **Borne, William** (d. 1624). Actor. Bird was with Pembroke's Men early in 1597 and, after the collapse of that organization, with the Admiral's Men. He was one of the most important members of the latter company until his retirement from the stage about 1622. Occasionally, he did some "doctoring" of plays for the Admiral's Men. He and William Rowley, for example, added parts to Marlowe's *Dr. Faustus* in 1602.

Conjectures that Bird may have been a member of the Chamberlain's Men before joining Pembroke's in 1597 have led to the suggestion that he and Gabriel Spencer were the reporters of the "bad quarto" of *Romeo and Juliet*. See MEMORIAL RECONSTRUCTION. [Harry R. Hoppe, *The Bad Quarto of Romeo and Juliet*, 1948.]

Birmingham Repertory Company. Acting company in Birmingham, England, inaugurated in 1913 under the direction of Sir Barry JACKSON, with the stated purpose of serving "art instead of making that art serve a commercial purpose." The Birmingham Repertory Company has produced nearly all of Shakespeare's plays, as well as hundreds of non-Shakespearean plays. The company presented its first play on February 15, 1913; this was *Twelfth Night* with Felix Aylmer as Orsino, John Darnley Drinkwater as Malvolio, Cecily Byrne as Viola, E. Stuart Vinden as Feste, and W. Ribton Haines as Sir Toby.

Many well-known actors received their earliest experience at Birmingham. Among these are Dame Peggy Ashcroft, Dame Edith Evans, Albert Finney, Gwen Ffrangcon-Davies, Maud Gill, Stewart Granger, Sir Cedric Hardwicke, Margaret Leighton, John Neville, Robert Newton, Sir Laurence Olivier, Donald Pleasance, Eric Porter, Sir Ralph Richardson, and Paul Scofield. Its principal producers and directors have been John Drinkwater, A. E. Filmer, H. K. Ayliff, John Moody, William Armstrong, Bernard Hepton, Margaret Webster, and John Harrison.

Other directors, engaged for single productions during the season, have included Peter Brook for *Romeo and Juliet* (1947); Michael Benthall for *The Merchant of Venice* (1947 and 1948), *King John, Hamlet,* and *The Taming of the Shrew* (all 1948); Nugent Monck for *Pericles* (1947); Anthony Quayle for *The Winter's Tale* and *Troilus and Cressida* (both 1948); and Godfrey Tearle for *Othello* (1948).

The Birmingham Repertory Company has given many of its plays during the London season, as well as at the Malvern and Stratford-upon-Avon festivals. In a representative season, such as 1962, the works of such diverse playwrights as Robert Bolt, George Bernard Shaw, Jean Giraudoux, Eugene Ionesco, John Osborne, Arnold Wesker, Harold Pinter, Peter Ustinov, Oliver Goldsmith, Chekhov, and Richard Sheridan have been presented. [James C. Trewin, *The Birmingham Repertory Company 1913–1963*, 1963.]

Birmingham Shakespeare Memorial Library. Library established as an adjunct of the Birmingham Public Library in 1864. By 1877 there were 6739 volumes in the Birmingham Shakespeare Memorial Library. Two years later, on January 11, 1879, it was all but completely destroyed by fire. The library was rebuilt through the generosity of the townspeople of Birmingham and the donations of organizations such as the German Shakespeare Society. The Birmingham Memorial owns more than 37,000 volumes of Shakespeareana. These include copies of the four Folios and a large collection of 18th-century Shakespearean items. There are also more than 200 scrapbooks containing playbills, souvenirs, and illustrations of the plays. [F. J. Patrick, "The Birmingham Shakespeare Memorial Library," *Shakespeare Survey* 7, 1954.]

Biron. See BEROWNE.

birthday. The exact date of Shakespeare's birth is unknown; it is certain, however, that he was baptized on April 26, 1564, and therefore that he was born a few days earlier, since baptisms usually took place a few days after birth. The tradition that Shakespeare was born on April 23 is fancifully derived from the fact that he died on April 23; furthermore, April 23 appeals to national sentiment since it is the feast day of St. George, patron saint of England. The insubstantiality of these grounds for the birth date has led scholars, notably J. O. Halliwell-Phillipps, to suggest another date. Halliwell-Phillipps suggests April 22 on the grounds, equally insubstantial, that the poet's only grandchild, Elizabeth Hall, was married on April 22, 1626. He suggests that she chose the date to commemorate her grandfather's birthday. An argument in favor of either date is that they are both a few days before Shakespeare's baptism. [J. O. Halliwell-Phillipps, *Outlines of the Life of Shakespeare,* 1881.]

Birth of Merlin, The. A play, probably by William ROWLEY, attributed to Rowley and Shakespeare by Francis Kirkman in his *Catalogue* (1661) of plays. The following year Kirkman and Thomas Marsh published the play as "Written by William Shakespeare and William Rowley." There is nothing in the play to support the ascription to Shakespeare, and most scholars assign it to Rowley, with Thomas Middleton considered as a possible collaborator.

birthplace. One of two adjacent houses owned by the poet's father, John Shakespeare, in Henley Street in Stratford. The eastern-most house of the pair is usually called the WOOLSHOP; the western house is called the "birthplace" in accordance with the tradition that Shakespeare was born there. According to J. O. Halliwell-Phillipps, however, this belief "rests solely . . . on the unvarying tradition of the inhabitants of Stratford." Tradition and nomenclature notwithstanding, scholars are still uncommitted as to the place of Shakespeare's birth.

John Shakespeare was a resident in Henley Street in 1552. In 1556 he bought the eastern house or woolshop, but it is not known exactly when he acquired the birthplace. He may have bought it before Shakespeare's birth, or it may have been one of two houses in Henley Street that he bought in 1575, 11 years after Shakespeare's birth. Other possible sites of Shakespeare's birth include a house in Greenhill Street, Stratford, purchased by his father in 1556 or the Old Rectory at Clifford Chambers, a hamlet about a mile and a half south of Stratford where a John Shakespeare is recorded as living in 1560. Another possibility is that Shakespeare was born in the woolshop.

By 1597 at least, John Shakespeare was residing in the house now known as the birthplace. At his death he bequeathed it to William, who in turn left it to his daughter Susanna. Susanna's daughter Elizabeth Bernard bequeathed the house to the Hart family, the descendants of Shakespeare's sister, Joan Hart. In the meantime, the eastern house had become an inn during the 17th century, possibly as early as 1603. The inn was known as "The Maidenhead" and later as "The Swan and Maidenhead." The Hart family owned the house until 1806. In 1847, it was purchased by the Shakespeare Birthplace Committee of London and Stratford for £3000. [J. O. Halliwell-Phillipps, *Outlines of the Life of Shakespeare*, 1881; Levi Fox, "The Heritage of Shakespeare's Birthplace," *Shakespeare Survey 1*, 1948.]

Bishop, Sir **Henry Rowley** (1786–1855). Composer and opera conductor. Most widely known for his setting of Shakespeare's "Lo! here the gentle lark," from *Venus and Adonis* (1853), Bishop wrote a series of operatic pastiches of Shakespearean plays. These were patchworks of music by various composers drawn from songs out of several plays, the whole grouped together under a single Shakespearean title. The first of these was *A Midsummer Night's Dream* (1816); *As You Like It* appeared in 1819, *Twelfth Night* in 1820, and *Two Gentlemen of Verona* in 1826. Bishop sometimes contributed music of his own to these productions. For *The Comedy of Errors* he wrote an overture, songs, two duets, and glees. He also composed an "Epicedium," or funeral dirge, for *Antony and Cleopatra* when it was produced at Covent Garden in 1813.

Bishop, Sir **William** (1626–1700). A native of the Stratford district who is alleged to be the source of two apocryphal stories related to Shakespeare. One of these was recorded by John Roberts (fl. 1729) in his *An Answer to Mr. Pope's Preface to Shakespeare* (1729). Roberts attributes to Bishop the story that Shakespeare's personal papers were destroyed in a fire which occurred in the town of Warwick in 1694:

> How much is it to be lamented, that *Two* large *Chests* full of this GREAT MAN's *loose Papers* and *Manuscripts*, in the Hands of an ignorant *Baker* of WARWICK, (who married one of the Descendants from *Shakespear*) were carelesly scatter'd and

thrown about, as Garret Lumber and Litter, to the particuler Knowledge of the late *Sir William Bishop*, till they were all consum'd in the generall Fire and Destruction of that Town?

Bishop is also cited as the source of an anecdote recorded by Sir William Oldys which relates that the character of Falstaff was a satiric portrait of an unnamed resident of Stratford with whom Shakespeare had quarreled. [E. K. Chambers, *William Shakespeare*, 1930.]

bishops' bonfire. See John WHITGIFT.

Bishopton. A rural hamlet about a mile northwest of Stratford and the location of some parts of the STRATFORD TITHES purchased by Shakespeare in 1605 for £440.

Blackfriars Gate-House. A house purchased by Shakespeare from Henry WALKER in 1613, for £140. It was erected over and beside a large gate, which led to the main house of a former "Blackfriars," or Dominican friars, estate. The house was about 600 feet from the Blackfriars theatre, the winter home of Shakespeare's company. Despite its proximity to the theatre, the house was not intended as a residence for Shakespeare who, by 1613, had probably retired from the stage and was living in Stratford. Both Walker's and Shakespeare's copies of the deed are extant. The extract below is from Walker's copy:

> This Indenture made the tenthe day of Marche . . . Between Henry Walker citizein and Minstrell of London of th'one partie; And William Shakespeare of Stratford Vpon Avon in the countie of Warwick gentleman, William Johnson, citizein and Vintener of London, John Jackson and John Hemmyng of London gentlemen, of th'other partie; Witnesseth that the said Henry Walker (for and in consideracion of the somme of one hundred and fortie poundes of lawfull money of England to him in hande before th'ensealing hereof by the said William Shakespeare well & trulie paid, whereof and wherewith hee the said Henry Walker doth acknowledge himselfe fullie satisfied and contented, and thereof, and of every part and parcell thereof doth cleerlie acquite and discharge the saide William Shakespeare, his heires, executours, administratours and assignes, and every of them by theis presentes) hath bargayned and soulde and by theis presentes doth fullie, cleerlie, and absolutlie bargayne and sell vnto the said William Shakespeare, William Johnson, John Jackson, and John Hemming, their heires, and assignes forever; All that dwelling house or Tenement with th'appurtenaunces situate and being within the Precinct, circuit and compasse of the late black Fryers London, . . . abutting vpon a streete leading downe to Pudle wharffe on the east part, right against the Kinges Maiesties Wardrobe; part of which said Tenement is erected over a great gate leading to a capitall Mesuage which sometyme was in the tenure of William Blackwell Esquiour deceased, and since that in the tenure or occupacion of the right Honorable Henry now Earle of Northumberland; And also all that plott of ground on the west side of the same Tenement which was lately inclosed with boordes on two sides thereof by Anne Bacon widowe, soe farre and in such sorte as the same was inclosed by the said Anne Bacon, and not otherwise, and being on the third side inclosed with an olde Brick wall; Which sai plott of ground was sometyme parcell and take out of a great peece of voide ground lately vse for a garden; And also the soyle wherevppon th said Tenement standeth; And also the said Bric wall and boordes which do inclose the said plott c ground; . . .

Shakespeare apparently paid £80 cash for th property, with Walker holding a mortgage of £6 according to the terms drawn up the day after th sale:

> This Indenture made the eleaventh day of Marcl . . . Betweene William Shakespeare, of Stratfor vpon Avon in the countie of Warwick, gentlemar William Johnson, citizein and Vintener of Londor John Jackson and John Hemmyng, of Londor gentlemen, of th'one partie, and Henry Walke citizein and Minstrell of London, of th'other partie Witnesseth that the said William Shakespeare, Wil liam Johnson, John Jackson and John Hemmyng have dimised, graunted and to ferme letten, and b theis presentes doe dimise, graunt and to ferme let vnto the said Henry Walker, All that dwellin house or Tenement, with th'appurtenaunces, situ ate and being within the precinct, circuit and com passe of the late Black Fryers, London . . . .

The William JOHNSON, John Hemmyng (Hem inges), and John JACKSON mentioned in the dee with Shakespeare were acting as his trustees in th sale. The use of trustees had the effect of barrin Shakespeare's widow from any right to the property In his will he left the property to his daughter an son-in-law, Susanna and John Hall. See Matthev BACON. [E. K. Chambers, *William Shakespeare*, 1930.

Blackfriars theatre. Elizabethan theatre in the pre cinct of the Blackfriars. In 1576 a suite of room within the precincts of the dissolved Blackfriars (Dominican friars) monastery was leased to Richar Farrant, Master of the Children of Windsor an deputy to William Hunnis, Master of the Childre of the Chapel. Farrant wanted a room in which th Children could give public performances of play prior to their appearances at court. The site appeare to be well suited for a theatre: because of its erst while ecclesiastical status, Blackfriars was legally a enclave or "liberty" not under the jurisdiction of th city of London, and therefore not subject to th local citizens' protests against theatrical enterprises

After Farrant's death in 1580, legal difficulties were encountered by his widow, Anne, who attempted tc sublease the premises to other theatrical entrepre neurs such as John Lyly and Henry Evans wh were connected with the Children and probably alsc with Oxford's Men. The original landlord, Sir William More, recovered the premises and the Blackfriars returned to private usage until 1596. In tha year James Burbage bought one section of the buildings for the sum of £600 and attempted to conver his property into a theatre. In this purpose he was frustrated by his neighbors who petitioned the privy council to prevent the establishment of a theatre ir their select residential area. Among the petitioners were Sir George Carey, Lord Hunsdon, and Richard Field, the first printer of Shakespeare's poems. Burage died in 1597 and it was not until 1600 that his on Richard was able to bring players to the Black-riars. Richard circumvented (or precluded) the ob-ections of his neighbors by emulating the tactics em-loyed by Farrant's children's company, who had iven public performances "vnder the name of a pri-ate howse." The Children of the Chapel under Nathaniel Giles undertook a lease for 21 years at £40 per year rent. The business manager of the roup, Henry Evans, set up a company and the thea-re ran for five years with the Children of the Chapel iving constant performances in serious competition vith the adult companies. In 1605 the company was uspended for its performance of the satire *Eastward Io!* The Children were reconstituted shortly there-fter under the name of the Children of Blackfriars. Their chief manager at this time was Robert KEYSAR. n the spring of 1608 the Children performed Chap-nan's *Conspiracy and Tragedy of Charles Duke of Byron*, giving serious offense to the French. The rench ambassador complained to the king and ames immediately suppressed the company. The Children's performances thus ended abruptly.

In August 1608 Richard Burbage, faced with a risis requiring new tenants for his theatre, organized new syndicate composed of his brother Cuthbert nd several leading players of the King's Men. They rranged to have the Blackfriars used by the King's Men alternately with the Globe, an arrangement which lasted from the autumn of 1609 to 1642.

The new organization was composed of seven artners who were HOUSEKEEPERS (as opposed to harers who shared in the profits accruing to the ctors). Aside from Richard Burbage, the lessees vere Cuthbert Burbage, John Heminges, William hakespeare, Henry Condell, William Sly, and Thomas Evans. Each lease was for a 7th part of the layhouse, requiring 1/7 of the £40 annual rent to e paid for by each housekeeper for 21 years (begin-ing from the previous year, i.e., 1607). Sly died nly five days later and his share was first divided mong the others, and then transferred to Will Ost-er in 1611. (See Thomasina OSTLER.) Between 1608 nd 1624 John Underwood was admitted to a share. After the termination of the leases in 1629, it is likely hat new leases were assumed. In 1633 the rent was ncreased to £50 per year, and in 1635, according to xtant records, the lease had four years to run and vas divided into eight parts: one held by Cuthbert Burbage; two by the widows of Richard Burbage nd Henry Condell; two shares, bought from Hem-nges' son, by John Shank; one part in Underwood's ame, but a third of that was held by Eyllaerdt wanston; one by John Lowin; and one by Joseph Taylor. As a result of the SHARERS' PAPERS dispute, hank was ordered by the lord chamberlain to re-ign one of his shares; this was divided among Swan-ton, Thomas Pollard, and Robert Benfield.

The theatre was a great success with the "carriage rade," and the Blackfriars inhabitants were roused o petition the city authorities in 1619 to end the uisance of the theatre. The city corporation or-ered the Blackfriars suppressed on January 21, 1619, stensibly for the following reasons:

> There is such a resort of peoplle and such multitudes of coaches . . . that sometimes all our streets cannot contain them, but they clog up Ludgate also, in such sort that they both endanger the one the other, break down stalls, throw down men's goods from their shops, and the inhabitants there cannot come to their houses, nor bring in their necessary provisions of beer, wood, coal or hay, nor the tradesmen or shopkeepers utter their wares.

The corporation order was not applied, but, evidently to avert further trouble with the city, the King's Men appealed for a new patent in 1619, wherein the king made explicit their right to play at "their private house scituate in the precinctes of the Blackfriers" and at the Globe. In 1631 a move to buy them out was instituted by some of the local citizenry, who asked the influential Bishop Laud to intercede for them. In 1633 a group of Middlesex justices offered the players £2900, a sum considerably at variance with the players' own estimate of their worth at £21,900. The offer was evidently dropped. Later in 1633 the privy council forbade coaches to stand in Ludgate or St. Paul's churchyard while performances were going on, but this order was amended in council at a meeting the king himself chaired.

About the precise physical structure of the rooms used for the theatre there seems to be some doubt, according to Chambers. The dimensions of the hall were 66 feet from north to south and 46 feet east to west; it was paved, with a stage, galleries, and seats. The stage was at one end of the hall.

By the time of Charles I, the Blackfriars had become the principal, and more profitable, of the two houses used by the King's Men. It was closed with the rest of the theatres in 1642. In 1653 it was still standing, disused, and Richard Flecknoe's *Miscellania* glorified it with an "Epilogue":

> From thence passing on to the Black-fryers, and seeing never a Play-bil on the Gate, no Coaches on the place, nor Doorkeeper at the Play-house door, with his Boxe like a Churchwarden, desiring you to remember the poor Players, I cannot but say for Epilogue to all the Playes were ever acted there:
>
> Poor House that in dayes of our Grand-sires,
> Belongst unto the Mendiant Fryers:
> And where so oft in our fathers dayes
> We have seen so many of Shakspears Playes.

It was razed in August 1655, and the site was used for tenements. For a discussion of the impact of the aristocratic audiences at the Blackfriars on Shakespeare, see SHAKESPEARE, WILLIAM: HIS PLAYS AND POEMS—*The Romances*. [Joseph Quincy Adams, *Shakespearean Playhouses*, 1917; E. K. Chambers, *The Elizabethan Stage*, 1923.]

Blair, Hugh (1718–1800). Scottish clergyman, educator, and critic. Blair's Shakespearean criticism is contained in his *Lectures on Rhetoric and Belles-Lettres* (1783), a collection culled from 20 years of lectures delivered at the University of Edinburgh. In discussing the classical rules of drama, Blair sees them, not as absolute laws, but as helpful guides for the playwright, citing the existence of great plays—notably Shakespeare's—in which the rules are violated. Shakespeare's departure from the rules is excusable, according to Blair, because his merits are so great. Blair particularly praises Shakespeare for his characterizations and for his understanding and perfect expression of human passions. For Blair, Shakespeare is on a level with the Greek tragedians, and above the French, in his ability to move his audience profoundly: his tragic masterpieces are *Othello* and *Macbeth* and his most enduring comedy is *The Merry Wives of Windsor*. [Herbert Spencer Robinson, *English Shakesperian Criticism in the Eighteenth Century*, 1932.]

Blake, William (1757–1827). Poet, painter, and engraver. Most of Blake's pictorial work was done for the purpose of book illustration. As an artist he is best known for his great series of drawings from Milton, the Book of Job, and Dante. He also produced a considerable body of Shakespearean drawings. Unlike many of his contemporaries, Blake was not commissioned by John Boydell to paint or execute engravings for the Boydell Shakespeare Gallery. Even without such patronage, and lacking other material incentive, Blake produced over 20 treatments of Shakespearean themes. A complex and highly original artist, Blake did not limit himself to literal renderings of character and scene; often, he produced drawings that embody Shakespeare's figurative language. The connection between the illustration and Shakespeare in this type of drawing is often tenuous. It has been suggested, for example, that one of his earliest engravings, "Jocund Day," illustrates an image from *Romeo and Juliet* (III, v, 9–10):

Night's candles are burnt out, and jocund day
Stands tiptoe on the misty mountain tops.

However, the title of the drawing is not Blake's ar other sources for it have been suggested. Clear from Shakespeare is "Pity" (1795), a color pri which illustrates a metaphor from Macbeth (I, v 21–25):

And pity, like a naked new-born babe,
Striding the blast, or heaven's cherubim, horsed
Upon the sightless couriers of the air,
Shall blow the horrid deed in every eye,
That tears shall drown the wind.

A group of small, neatly drawn heads of vario Shakespearean characters (most of which are in t Boston Museum of Fine Arts) are not among the ar ist's best work. Far more vivid are two studies Glendower and Hotspur, now in private collection Of Blake's drawings of scenes from Shakespeare, t most notable are four interpretations (c. 1807–180 of Queen Katharine's dream from *Henry VIII*. S ART. [W. M. Merchant, *Shakespeare and the Artis* 1959.]

Blanche of Castile (1185–1252). Third daughter Alphonso VIII of Castile and Eleanor of Englan and wife of Louis the dauphin, who later becan Louis VIII of France. Blanche was betrothed to hi as a result of a treaty between King John of Englan

WILLIAM BLAKE'S *Pity*. (TATE GALLERY)

and Philip II of France. She was a steadfast supporter of her husband's invasion of England, and after his death when she became regent, she successfully repelled an attack by the English king.

In *King John*, "Blanch" appears as John's niece. She becomes the bride of Lewis the Dauphin, and the marriage leads to a temporary alliance between England and France.

Bloch, Ernest. See MUSIC BASED ON SHAKESPEARE: *20th century*.

blocking entry. A term coined by the scholar A. W. Pollard. Pollard conjectures that certain of the entries for Shakespeare's plays in the STATIONERS' REGISTER were inserted, not as indication of the intention to publish, but to prevent their publication until their runs were concluded. Presumably, this was an effort to maintain the popularity of the plays and to keep them out of the hands of rival companies. The conjecture has been challenged by a number of scholars. See James ROBERTS.

Blount, Edward (1564–1632). London bookseller and one of the publishers of the First Folio (1623). Blount was admitted to the Stationers' Company in 1588 and became one of the most successful of London publishers. He was a friend of Christopher Marlowe, some of whose plays and poems he published. He also published the first and second editions of John Florio's translation of Montaigne's *Essays* and the first edition of *Love's Martyr* (1601), the collection of poems which includes Shakespeare's *The Phoenix and the Turtle*. On May 20, 1608 he entered *Antony and Cleopatra* and *Pericles* in the Stationers' Register, but never published them. It has been suggested that Blount's entry was a BLOCKING ENTRY, an attempt by Shakespeare's company to prevent publication of popular plays. Another explanation of Blount's failure to publish may be that he moved his shop in that year. [R. B. McKerrow, ed., *A Dictionary of Printers and Booksellers . . . 1557–1640*, 1910.]

Blunt or **Blount, Sir James** (d. 1493). Grandson of Sir Walter Blunt, who appears in *1 Henry IV*. In *Richard III*, Sir James Blount is a captain in Richmond's army (V, iii).

Blunt or **Blount, Sir John** (d. 1418). Son of Walter Blunt (d. 1403). In *2 Henry IV*, Prince John of Lancaster orders Blunt to guard the prisoner Colevile (IV, iii).

Blunt or **Blount, Sir Walter** (d. 1403). A well-known adherent of John of Gaunt and, after John's death, of his son Henry. Blunt was standard-bearer for King Henry IV at the battle of Shrewsbury, where, mistaken for the king, he was killed. In *1 Henry IV*, Blunt is sent by Henry to ask the insurgents to state their grievances (IV, iii). In V, iii he is killed onstage by Douglas. [W. H. Thomson, *Shakespeare's Characters: A Historical Dictionary*, 1951.]

Boaistuau, Pierre. See Matteo BANDELLO; François de BELLEFOREST.

Boar's Head Inn. At least six inns in the city of London bore this name from the last half of the 16th century through the middle of the 17th century. A Boar's Head Inn in St. Michael's parish on the south side of Great Eastcheap was traditionally regarded in the 17th century as the locale of the *Henry IV* plays' tavern scenes.

A Boar's Head Inn in 1557, located outside Aldgate, was the scene of one of the earliest plays ever to be given in a London inn yard: *The Sackful of Newes*. In 1602 the privy council ordered the combined Worcester's and Oxford's Men to play only at "the house called the Bores head" which was "the place they haue especially vsed and doe best like of." The license Queen Anne granted Worcester's Men in 1603, in which she assumed patronage of the company, permitted them to play "within there now vsuall Howsen, called the Curtayne, and the Bores head, within our County of Middlesex." In another context the Boar's Head is considered the place in which the duke of York's company performed around 1608. This was said to be a theatre located in Whitechapel. [E. K. Chambers, *The Elizabethan Stage*, 1923.]

Boatswain. In *The Tempest*, a seasoned, energetic petty officer. Contemptuous of the royal passengers interfering with his duties during the violent storm, the Boatswain roars "Keep to your cabins! You do assist the storm" (I, i).

Boccaccio, Giovanni (1313–1375). Italian author, humanist, and poet. Boccaccio is known to the world chiefly as the author of the celebrated *Decameron* (1353). The *Decameron* is a collection of 100 fabliaux and folk tales told by 10 people who have taken refuge from the plague in Florence. The tales were justly popular on the continent and in England, providing Chaucer with the general framework and some of the stories of *The Canterbury Tales* (c. 1387–1400). William Painter's *Palace of Pleasure* (1567) included a number of the tales (in English versions), thus making them readily available to the Elizabethans. There is, however, an increasing belief in the theory that Shakespeare may have consulted his Italian sources in their original versions. In any event he derived the plot of *All's Well That Ends Well* from the story of "Giletta of Narbona," the ninth novel of the third day of the *Decameron*, a version of which is found in Painter (see ALL'S WELL THAT ENDS WELL: *Sources*). Shakespeare may also be indebted to the *Decameron* for the wager on the chastity of Imogen in *Cymbeline*, the motif of which is used by Boccaccio in the second novel of the ninth day.

Boccaccio's *Il Filostrato* (c. 1338) was one of the earliest romantic versions of *Troilus and Cressida* and the source of Chaucer's poem which in turn was one of the sources of Shakespeare's play. Among his Latin works is *De casibus virorum et feminarum illustrium* (1355–1360), translated into French by Laurent de Premierfait. The French version was the basis of John Lydgate's English translation, *Falle of Princis* (1494), which eventually became the basis of the most popular of Elizabethan verse narratives, *A Mirror for Magistrates* (1559).

Bodenham, John (c. 1558–1610). Literary patron. Bodenham, the son of a prosperous grocer, was able to act as a patron of literature by virtue of an ample inheritance. At one time he was thought to be the editor of a group of Elizabethan verse and prose anthologies, the best known of which is *England's Helicon* (1600). It is now evident, however, that Bodenham was not the editor, but the originator of the idea behind the miscellanies.

England's Helicon contains the Shakespearean lines from *Love's Labour's Lost* (IV, iii, 101–120) that had been reprinted in *The Passionate Pilgrim*, a collection of poems attributed to Shakespeare and published in 1599. Another Bodenham-sponsored anthology is *Belvedere or The Garden of the Muses* (1600); it is not, properly speaking, a miscellany, but a dictionary of verse quotations, edited by A. M., who is probably the ubiquitous Anthony MUNDAY. The prefatory epistle to the work cites the authors being quoted, among whom are:

Christopher Marlow.
Beniamin Iohnson.
VVilliam Shakspeare.

Shakespeare is the most frequently quoted author in the book. The compiler cites 213 quotations drawn from *Love's Labour's Lost, Romeo and Juliet, 1* and *2 Henry IV, Richard II, Richard III, Venus and Adonis, The Rape of Lucrece*, and *3 Henry VI.* [*The Shakspere Allusion-Book*, J. Munro, ed., 1909.]

Bodleian Library. The library at the University of Oxford founded by Sir Thomas Bodley (1545–1613). When the Bodleian Library first opened in 1602, it contained more than 2000 books. Since that time the holdings of the library have increased to more than 500,000 volumes and MSS., including many early editions of Shakespeare's plays and poems. The Bodleian's early Shakespeare holdings, acquired primarily from the private library of Edmund Malone, consist of 43 early quartos, 2 First Folios, 3 Second Folios, 1 Third Folio, and 2 Fourth Folios. The library also owns the original manuscripts of Simon Forman's *Book of Plaies*, John Aubrey's "Life" of Shakespeare, Edward Pudsey's commonplace book, and a number of Elizabethan plays in manuscript, including Middleton's *The Witch*, songs from which were interpolated into *Macbeth*. [L. W. Hanson, "The Shakespeare Collection in the Bodleian Library, Oxford," *Shakespeare Survey 4*, 1951.]

Bodmer, Martin (1899–). Swiss bibliophile and owner of the largest collection of early editions of Shakespeare outside England and America. The scion of a wealthy Swiss family, Bodmer began his collection in his native Zurich, moving to Geneva in 1951. His library, known as the *Bibliotheca Bodmeriana*, includes first editions of the *Sonnets* (1609), *Love's Labour's Lost* (1598), *2 Henry IV* (1600), *Much Ado About Nothing* (1600), *King Lear* (1608), *Troilus and Cressida* (1609), *Othello* (1622), and the 1640 edition of the *Poems*. It also contains copies of the first four Folios (1623; 1632; 1663 and 1664; 1685). [Georges Bonnard, "Shakespeare in the Bibliotheca Bodmeriana," *Shakespeare Survey 9*, 1956.]

Boece, Hector (c. 1465–1536). Scottish historian and biographer. Boece was a graduate of the University of Paris, where he had been a friend of Erasmus. For many years he served as principal of the University of Aberdeen, which he helped to found. Boece is known for his *Scotorum Historiae* (1526), a multivolume, highly inaccurate history of Scotland written in classical Latin in imitation of Livy. John BELLENDEN translated the work into Scots in 1535, and through Holinshed it became the historical source of *Macbeth*.

Boleyn, Anne. See Anne BULLEN.

Bolingbroke, Henry. See HENRY IV.

Bolingbroke, Roger. A sorcerer who encouraged the duchess of Gloucester to believe that her husband would be king. Bolingbroke was arrested in 1441 for treason and was later hanged, drawn, and quartered. In *2 Henry VI*, Bolingbroke invokes a spirit in the Duchess' presence and questions it as to the fate of the King and the Dukes of Suffolk and Somerset. [W. H. Thomson, *Shakespeare's Characters: A Historical Dictionary*, 1951.]

Bolton, Edmund (1575?–?1633). Minor critic, historian, and poet. Bolton is best known for his *Hypercritica* (written c. 1610–1618; pub. 1722), in which he cites as "among the cheife" of those books "out of which wee gather the most warrantable English . . . Shakespere, Mr Francis Beaumont, & innumerable other writers for the stage." [*The Shakspere Allusion-Book*, J. Munro, ed., 1909.]

Bona of Savoy (d. 1485). Third daughter of the 1st duke of Savoy and the younger sister of the queen of Louis XI of France. In *3 Henry VI*, Bona appears as the projected bride of Edward IV of England, a match arranged by Warwick in the play but for which there is little basis in history. On learning that Edward has married Lady Grey, Bona urges King Lewis to support Queen Margaret in her effort to depose Edward and reinstate Henry VI. [W. H. Thomson, *Shakespeare's Characters: A Historical Dictionary*, 1951.]

Bonduca. A tragedy by Francis BEAUMONT and John FLETCHER which was written for Shakespeare's company sometime between 1609 and 1614. A manuscript version of *Bonduca*, dating from about 1625, is extant. The manuscript, probably a transcript prepared by the book-keeper for a private collector, is missing one or two scenes, a fact the scribe accounts for by noting that the prompt-book, the acting version of the play, had been lost and that the transcript was made from the author's rough manuscript, or foul papers. In the Second Folio of Beaumont and Fletcher's *Works* (1679), a prefixed note indicates that the "Principal Actors" in the play had been "Richard Burbadge, Henry Condel, William Eglestone, Nich. Toolie, William Ostler, John Lowin, John Underwood, and Richard Robinson." [W. W. Greg, *Dramatic Documents from the Elizabethan Playhouses*, 1931.]

Bonian or **Bonion, Richard** (fl. 1598–1611). London bookseller who, in conjunction with Henry Walley, published the First Quarto of *Troilus and Cressida* (1609). The Quarto, printed by George Eld, had two printings, the title pages of which are significantly different. See TROILUS AND CRESSIDA: *Text*.

book. See PROMPT-BOOK.

book-keeper [book-holder or **prompter].** The official of an Elizabethan acting company who had custody of the PROMPT-BOOKS or texts of the plays. The book-keeper probably also served as book-holder or prompter during the performances of the plays. As W. W. Greg points out, "It does not perhaps necessarily follow that the book-keeper and the book-holder were always the same person, but since it must be difficult to distinguish their functions it is simpler to assume that they were." An important member of the company, the book-keeper obtained the license for each play, and it was his duty to purge the manuscript of anything offensive before it met the eyes of the official censor, the Master of the Revels.

The book-keeper's duties as prompter probably lso embraced those assigned in the modern theatre) the stage manager, such as arranging for the neces- ıry properties and cueing the music and off-stage ›unds. T. W. Baldwin even elevates him to the :atus of the modern-day director, claiming that he etermined the area in which each scene was to be ıounted. Baldwin also suggests this official is farci- ally presented in the figure of Peter Quince, car- enter of Athens and impresario in *A Midsummer Night's Dream.* At the rehearsal of the play the mechanicals" are going to present at the wedding estivities of Theseus and Hippolyta, Quince gives ıe actors a general idea of the drama, assigns the arts, discusses the problems of presentation, and olds Bottom, his temperamental star, in subjection) the demands of his substantial part of Pyramus.

Contemporary evidence, however, indicates that ıe playwright himself supervised and directed his wn plays. In 1613 the German dramatist Rhenanus vrote:

> As for the actors, they (as I have noted in England) are instructed daily as though at school; even the most prominent actors must permit themselves to be instructed in their parts by the poets, and this is what endows a well-written comedy with life and grace. Thus it is no wonder that the English comedians (I speak of the practiced ones) are more excellent than others.

Then too there is the tradition recorded by John Downes, the Restoration theatrical historian, that Shakespeare coached John Lowin in the role of Henry VIII and Joseph Taylor in the role of Hamlet, although the latter case is highly improbable.

Even without directorial responsibilities, however, the book-keeper's duties were extremely important. n addition to those already listed, they included as- embling copies of the players' individual "parts" rom the prompt-book and the drawing up of the plot," that is, the record of exits and entrances for ach play.

According to John Taylor (the "water-poet"), vriting in 1638, a Thomas Vincent "was a Book- eeper or prompter at the Globe play-house" proba- ly around 1600. T. W. Baldwin suggests that John Rhodes, who formed a company of actors at the Restoration, was the book-keeper for the King's Men in the 1620's. In 1633 Sir Henry Herbert, Master f the Revels, in connection with a King's Men's lay, sent a note to "Knight, their book-keeper." This was either Anthony or Edward Knight (proba- ly the latter), both of whom were listed as HIRED MEN with the company. Herbert's note indicates the ook-keeper's duties in connection with censoring lays and the possible unpleasant repercussions if he ailed in this duty.

> Mr. Knight,
> In many things you have saved mee labour; yet wher your judgment or penn fayld you, I have made boulde to use mine. Purge ther parts, as I have the booke. And I hope every hearer and player will thinke that I have done God good servise, and the quality no wronge; who hath no greater enemies than oaths, prophaness, and publique ribaldry, whch for the future, I doe absolutely forbid to bee presented unto mee in any playbooke; as you will answer it at your perill. [21 Octob. 1633.]

[T. W. Baldwin, *The Organization and Personnel of the Shakespearean Company*, 1927; W. W. Greg, *The Editorial Problem in Shakespeare*, 1942.]—E.Q.

Book of Martyrs, The (1563). Popular name for the book originally entitled *Actes and Monuments* by John Foxe (1516–1587). Having embraced Protestantism at an early age, Foxe was in exile during the reign of Mary (1553–1558). At Strasbourg in 1554 he published a Latin account of the precursors of Protestantism. As reports reached him of new persecutions under Mary, he incorporated accounts of the deaths of contemporary Protestant martyrs into an expanded version which appeared at Basel in 1559. That same year he returned to England, received orders, and became prebendary of Salisbury Cathedral. In 1563 he issued the first English version of *The Book of Martyrs,* a folio of 1741 pages, under the title *Actes and Monuments of These Latter Perilous Days.* Revised editions and abridgments, such as that made by Timothy Bright in 1589, followed. Copies were installed in the churches and the book became a familiar item in many English households, especially in shorter versions. The dramatic power of the biographical sketches, the forceful style, the edifying nature of the subject matter, and the impressive wood-cuts made it a powerful book, and it exerted an influence that is difficult to overestimate. Foxe's militant Protestantism is combined with a strong nationalism; England is seen as enjoying the special providence of God because of her fidelity to the Gospel even during the height of Rome's power. The religious and national prejudices are apparent, and even in his own day Foxe's probity was questioned. (For an objective view, see J. F. Mozley, *John Foxe and His Book,* 1940.) Shakespeare is indebted to *The Book of Martyrs* for his account of the conspiracy against Cranmer in *Henry VIII* and possibly for the feigned miracle of Simpcox in *2 Henry VI.*

Booth, Barton (1681–1733). Actor. Booth received his early training in Dublin and in the provinces. In 1700, he joined Thomas Betterton's company, playing a variety of roles. His career was not marked by any outstanding successes until his performance of Othello in 1711 at Drury Lane. Although his reputation never reached great heights, he was evidently an extremely competent actor. Among his successes were Coriolanus, Lear, and Henry VIII. In 1719, he married Hester Santlow, a fine actress who played in many Shakespearean productions. [*Dictionary of National Biography,* 1885– ; *Oxford Companion to the Theatre,* Phyllis Hartnoll, ed., 1951.]

Booth Family. American actors. ***Junius Brutus Booth*** (1796–1852) was the leading Shakespearean actor of his day in America. Born in London, he claimed Jewish ancestry and later played Shylock with a Jewish accent. When he appeared in 1817 as Richard III, the similarity of his performance to that of Edmund Kean resulted in a rivalry between Keanites and Boothites. For one performance in 1817 he played Iago to Kean's Othello. His first Shylock was played in 1818, followed by Lear in Nahum Tate's version of Shakespeare's play in 1820. In that year he again appeared with Kean, playing Iago and Edgar.

In a noteworthy *Julius Caesar* at Drury Lane, Booth was Cassius, James W. Wallack was Brutus, and John Cooper was Antony.

In 1821 Booth moved to America, scoring notable successes touring and managing theatres. In 1831, as manager of Baltimore's Adelphi Theatre, he introduced Charles Kean in his first American appearance and, in deference to Kean, played the Second Gravedigger to Kean's Hamlet. He also presented Edwin Forrest, to whom he gave leading roles, and did *Othello* with Forrest in 1831 in New York. His career was troubled by intermittent bouts with insanity and alcoholism, and his passions were reflected in the characters he played best—Shylock, Iago, and Richard III. Booth wrote *Ugolino*, a blank-verse tragedy, which his son John Wilkes Booth produced unsuccessfully at the Boston Museum in 1863.

The eldest of Booth's children, ***Junius Brutus Booth, Jr.*** (1821–1883), was an excellent manager and producer and acted with his father as Iago in 1835 and 1852. His two sons also had theatrical careers.

The second of the elder Booth's surviving children, ***Edwin Thomas Booth*** (1833–1893), became immersed in Shakespeare while acting as his father's quasi-business manager. His first role was that of Tressel in *Richard III* (1849), and he continued to play minor roles until, in 1851, he substituted unsuccessfully for his father as Richard III in New York. His popularity began after his return to San Francisco from a disastrous Pacific tour with Laura Keene in 1854. He played Lear in Tate's version of Shakespeare's play at San Francisco, and by the time of his return to New York in 1856 he had become an accomplished actor in the tradition of Kean and his father but, unlike either of them, capable of a sustained, rather than erratic, power. In 1860 he married a young actress, Mary Devlin; in 1861 he captivated London audiences as Richelieu in Bulwer Lytton's *Richelieu*, probably his greatest part. He played for a while with a Manchester stock company, which included young Henry Irving, before returning to New York. His grief over the death of his wife in 1863 resulted in his temporary retirement from the stage; when he returned he also assumed management of the Winter Garden Theatre, New York, and became co-owner of the Walnut Street Theatre, Philadelphia. In 1865 he played Hamlet for 100 nights, in a portrayal overcast with his own melancholia and characterized by his intellectual, aristocratic temperament. That same year his brother's assassination of Lincoln led to a second period of retirement. His loyalty was to the North, however, and by 1866 his audiences welcomed him back to the stage. In 1867 a relatively successful run of lavishly staged productions at the Winter Garden was interrupted by the burning of that theatre. Booth built a new theatre which he opened on February 3, 1869, with *Romeo and Juliet*. His leading lady was Mary McVicker, whom he was later to marry. He reached the high point of his career between 1869 and 1874, although he continued to suffer domestic and financial misfortune.

Edwin Booth's roles in Shakespeare included Romeo, Othello, Macbeth, Hamlet, Cassius, Brutus, Mark Antony, and Benedick. Under his management appeared many famous contemporary stars including Joseph Jefferson, John McCullough, Lawrence Barrett, and Charlotte Cushman. The Panic of 1873 resulted in Booth's financial ruin. His theatre con tinued until 1883, when it was closed and torn down Booth's later career was taken up with tours, an was characterized by a steady decline in his talen and his health. In 1884, however, the year in whic his second wife died after years of insanity, he ha a triumphant engagement with Henry Irving i *Othello*, the two great actors alternating as Iago an Othello. In 1878 *Edwin Booth's Prompt-Books*, ed ited by William Winter, were published; these con tained the acting texts of 15 plays, namely, *Richar II, Richard III, Henry VIII, Hamlet, Macbeth Othello, King Lear, The Merchant of Venice, Muc Ado About Nothing, Katherine and Petruchic Richelieu, The Fool's Revenge, Brutus, Ruy Blas* and *Don Caesar de Bazan*. He also contributed som perceptive notes to the Furness Variorum Edition of *Othello* and *The Merchant of Venice*.

John Wilkes Booth (1838–1865), Junius Brutu Booth's notorious son, was a talented actor, but i better known as the assassin of President Lincoln Although early in his career he seemed inadequatel prepared, he developed into one of the leadin Shakespearean actors of his time. His roles include Richard III, Romeo, Hamlet, Macbeth, Othello, an others. His passionate delivery compensated to large degree for his careless diction.

John Wilkes Booth was the only member of th family with Southern sympathies. In 1859 he ha been part of the Virginia militia company which ha arrested and hanged John Brown, and early in 186 he had become part of the conspiracy to murde Lincoln. Among his last stage appearances was on as Julius Caesar at the Winter Garden with Edwi as Brutus and Junius Brutus Booth, Jr., as Cassius [*Dictionary of American Biography*, 1927– Stanley Kimmel, *The Mad Booths of Marylana* 1940; *Oxford Companion to the Theatre*, Phylli Hartnoll, ed., 1951.]

Borachio. In *Much Ado About Nothing*, a fol lower of Don John. Having informed his villainou master of the intended marriage between Claudi and Hero, Borachio originates a scheme "to misus the Prince, to vex Claudio, to undo Hero and kil Leonato." His part in the conspiracy is to stage wooing of Hero; actually, he makes love to Hero' attendant Margaret, who is disguised as Hero. Th ruse is discovered and Borachio is arrested. In hi confession, Borachio clears Margaret of blame an avows that he would "rather seal with my deat than repeat over to my shame" this treachery.

Borne, William. See William BIRD.

Boswell, James (1778–1822). Scholar. Boswell i known as James Boswell, the younger, in order t distinguish him from his father, the famous biogra pher of Dr. Johnson. Through his father he becam acquainted at an early age with Edmund MALONE whose second edition of Shakespeare's works h completed after the famous scholar's death. It wa published in 1821 as the Third Variorum editio of Shakespeare in 21 volumes. The edition include Malone's biography of Shakespeare and his histor of the stage. Boswell died shortly after the publica tion of this valuable work. See VARIORUM EDITIONS.

Bottom, Nick. In *A Midsummer Night's Dream*, weaver and the star actor among the rude mechani cals who present the playlet of "Pyramus an Thisbe." A creature whose harmless self-conceit i matched only by his empty-headedness, Bottom veathers a series of adventures which, however niraculous, never manage to topple his marvelously omic complacency. His transformation into an ass nd the divine Titania's subsequent infatuation with im disturb not at all his superbly simpleminded quanimity. As an actor he is sublimely indifferent o the catcalls and criticism of his audience. He has een seen by some critics as Shakespeare's slyly sairic portrait of the professional actor, existing in a elf-contained world and feasting on the praise of his ans, the mechanicals who, because of his histrionic bility, regard him as "a very Paramour for a sweet oice."

Boult. In *Pericles,* a servant to the Pandar at the rothel in Mytilene. Boult arranges the purchase of Aarina and cries her beauty through the market. Vhen the innocent virgin threatens to ruin the rothel's business by converting its customers to hastity, the indelicate Boult determines to ravish Aarina. However, she bribes him to place her amongst honest women" where she can teach singng, dancing, and sewing.

Bourbon, John, duke of (d. 1433). Uncle of Charles /I of France. In *Henry V,* Bourbon is captured at Agincourt (IV, viii).

Bourchier, Cardinal. See Thomas Cardinal Bourhier, archbishop of CANTERBURY.

Bowdler, Thomas (1754–1825). Clergyman and edior. Bowdler is known chiefly for his expurgated dition called *The Family Shakespeare,* which gave urrency to the verb "bowdlerize." It first appeared n a 4-volume edition in 1807, and in 1818 in 10 olumes. His object was to offer a text "in which othing is added to the original; but those words nd expressions are omitted which cannot with ropriety be read in a family." Shakespeare had, fter all, "provided an almost inexhaustible fund of nstruction as well as pleasure which even the severst moralists would not wish to withhold from inocent minds." Therefore, his version (based on George Steevens' edition) offered a text which vomen and children could read "unmixed with anyhing that could raise a blush on the cheek of modsty," or that would be unfit "to be read aloud by a entleman to a company of ladies."

Bowdler excised substantial portions of the openng scenes of *Romeo and Juliet, Othello,* and *Lear,* mong many others. Nevertheless, some noxious expressions were too firmly embedded in the text to vield to the scalpel; though "bitch" was banished, 'whore," "harlot," and "strumpet" were spared long with many double entendres, the meanings of vhich seem to have escaped the editor.

In 1836 the word "bowdlerize" was coined by one Perronet Thompson, in the pejorative sense, meanng to exhibit prurient editorial squeamishness. Nevertheless, *The Family Shakespeare* persisted in ts popularity throughout the 19th century. It was ot only admired by conventional Victorians, but lso honestly praised by some radicals, including Swinburne, who declared in *Studies in Prose and Poetry* (1894) that "no man ever did better service o Shakespeare than the man who made it possible to out him into the hands of intelligent and imaginative children."

Bowers, Fredson [Thayer] (1905–). American scholar. Professor of English at the University of Virginia, Bowers has contributed significantly to TEXTUAL CRITICISM of the works of Shakespeare. Among his works are *On Editing Shakespeare* (1955) and *Textual and Literary Criticism* (1959).

Boy. In *Henry V,* a minor character who makes frequent appearances. In II, i, he summons Pistol and Nell Quickly to help put his sick master, Falstaff, to bed. Having subsequently accompanied Nym, Bardolph, and Pistol to Harfleur, the Boy, disapproving of their constant thievery, decides to abandon them for some better service (III, i). After Nym and Bardolph have been hanged for their crimes, the Boy appears on the battlefield with Pistol and acts as interpreter when Pistol captures a French soldier (IV, iv). When Pistol leaves, the Boy determines to stay at the camp with the lackeys and guard it against the French.

Boy. In *Macbeth,* one of Macduff's children. After Macduff's flight to England, Macbeth orders the murder of Lady Macduff and her children (IV, ii).

Boy. In *The Two Noble Kinsmen,* a figure in the wedding celebration of Theseus and Hippolyta. He sings the song "Roses, their sharp spines being gone" (I, i).

boy-bishop. The "bishop of the boys" (*episcopus puerorum,* or *innocentium*), who had been traditionally chosen since medieval times in connection with the festival of Holy Innocents (Feast of Fools). In England the boy-bishop reigned from December 6 (feast of St. Nicholas, patron saint of children) to December 28 (Holy Innocents' day). He wore a bishop's vestments and symbols and made a circuit of the town, blessing all the people. The custom originated in the large cathedrals and then spread to local parishes, where it became very popular. Many of the children's acting companies had their origin in the revels celebrating the boy-bishop. See CHILDREN'S COMPANIES. [F. A. Gasquet, *Parish Life in Mediaeval England,* 1906.]

boy companies. See CHILDREN'S COMPANIES.

Boydell's Shakespeare Gallery. An 18th-century project established by John Boydell (1719–1804), with the dual purposes of founding a school of English history painting and illustrating the works of Shakespeare. Boydell was an engraver, a phenomenally successful publisher of prints, and a patron of the arts; in 1790 he was elected lord mayor of London. In 1786 he proposed to commission two series of paintings by all the notable artists of England and build a gallery for their permanent exhibition. A set of small paintings was to be engraved for elegant, illustrated editions of the plays; large paintings were to be engraved for a folio collection without text.

The Shakespeare Gallery was opened in Pall Mall in June 1789 with 34 paintings; 33 were added during the following year. The illustrated volumes of the plays, with texts edited by George Steevens, were published between 1791 and 1805, and in the latter year the folio collection of prints appeared. Before that, however, heavy expenditures for the project, and reverses suffered as a result of his firm's loss of foreign trade during the French Revolution, brought Boydell close to bankruptcy. He had ceded the Shakespeare Gallery to the nation, but an act of Parliament in 1804 allowed him to dispose of all of his property by a lottery. There were 62 prize lots which, Boydell claimed, reflected an investment of more than £375,000; the lottery consisted of 22,000 three-guinea tickets. Boydell sold all of them and paid his creditors, but he died about nine weeks before the drawing, which was held on January 28, 1805. The winner of the 62nd prize—the Shakespeare Gallery and its paintings—sold them at auction a few months later. Boydell had paid his artists and engravers more than £150,000 in commissions; the paintings sold for a total of £6128 16s.

Altogether, 170 paintings had been completed, with almost half of them produced by four men: Robert SMIRKE, 26; William HAMILTON, 23; Richard WESTALL, 22; and Francis WHEATLEY, 13. The work produced varied widely in style, conception, and quality. This was due not only to differences in talent and training among the artists, but also to the complex state of English painting at the time. More sophisticated artists, such as George ROMNEY, Sir Joshua REYNOLDS, and Benjamin WEST, were well acquainted with French and Italian art and seriously attempted to synthesize the requirements of classic history painting and the illustration of Shakespeare (see ART). However, the native English tradition (whose exponents ranged from William HOGARTH through Francis HAYMAN) included many popular and prolific artists who were uncomfortable in a tragic or idealizing vein. Their artistic training was practical rather than theoretical; they were either theatrical scene painters who often showed a strong flair for landscape (as William HODGES and Francis Wheatley), or book illustrators who were particularly successful in comic or sentimental scenes (Robert Smirke and William Hamilton).

In addition to this divergence of tradition an entirely new artistic vision appeared, particularly in the work of Henry FUSELI, who contributed nine paintings to the collection. His emphasis on the expression of mood and character heralded the beginning of Romanticism and a new critical interpretation of the meaning of Shakespeare's work. Such great diversity resulted in confusion. An observer sympathetic to the Shakespeare illustrated by Reynolds was likely to find Smirke trivial and Fuseli absurd, and the collection was generally considered a hodgepodge.

Others among the 35 Gallery artists were James NORTHCOTE, Matthew PETERS, and Nathaniel DANCE-HOLLAND. [W. M. Merchant, *Shakespeare and the Artist*, 1959.]

Boyet. In *Love's Labour's Lost*, one of the lords attending the Princess of France. Boyet's function is chiefly that of messenger; he reveals to the Princess and her ladies that the supposed Muscovite visitors are in fact the King and his nobles (V, ii).

Boys from Syracuse, The. See MUSIC BASED ON SHAKESPEARE: *20th century*.

Brabantio. In *Othello*, a Venetian senator and the father of Desdemona. Appearing only in I, iii, the scene of the Senate meeting, Brabantio accuses Othello of stealing his daughter and warns that she may deceive the Moor as she has deceived her father. In V, ii, Gratiano reveals that Brabantio has died of grief over his daughter's marriage.

Bracciano, Don **Virginio Orsini,** duke of (b. 1573). Orsini, whose parents' sensational deaths provide the historic background for Webster's *The White Devil*, visited England in January 1601. Leslie Hotson has argued that *Twelfth Night* was first performed on the occasion of his visit and that the "Duke Orsino" is named as a compliment to the guest of honor. Hotson's thesis has met some opposition among scholars who admit the connection of the two dukes but who argue that the play was first performed in the following year, 1602. Hotson has discovered two long letters written by the duke to his wife from England, in which he describes in detail his reception and the festivities attendant upon his arrival. See TWELFTH NIGHT: *Date*. [Leslie Hotson, *The First Night of Twelfth Night*, 1954.]

Bracegirdle, Anne (c. 1673–1748). Actress. Born near Wolverhampton, Staffordshire, Anne Bracegirdle was adopted by Thomas and Mary Betterton, leading players of the Duke's Company in London at the age of three or four just after the death of her father. Edmund Curll states that at the age of six she played Cordelio, a page, in Otway's *The Orphan* (1680), thus starting her long professional association with Elizabeth Barry and Thomas Betterton. (The three players were known later as the Three B's and ruled English drama from the 1690's to 1707.) According to the customary personal epilogue given to her as a young actress making her debut in an adult role, she was "not yet Thirteen" when, billed in the dramatis personae as "Miss Nanny," she played the part of Clita in Thomas D'Urfey's *A Commonwealth of Women* (1685).

In contrast to Elizabeth Barry, Anne Bracegirdle led an exemplary life, refusing to be compromised by many would-be lovers, one of whom, Captain Richard Hill, tried to kidnap her in 1692; the attempt ended in the death of William Mountfort, one of her fellow players, and in the trial in the house of lords of the notorious Lord Mohun, accomplice of Hill in the attempted abduction. She was rewarded on one occasion with the sum of £800 sent to her, "with Encomiums on her Virtue," by Lord Halifax and the dukes of Dorset and Devonshire. For years her name was associated with that of William Congreve, who wooed her in vain on and off the stage.

Mrs. Bracegirdle created at least 85 new roles and took part in many revivals of Elizabethan, Jacobean, and Carolinian, as well as early Restoration plays during her adult career of 22 years. She began to play mature roles after 1685, without doubt playing Ophelia in *Hamlet* when Elizabeth Barry relinquished the part. By 1690 she had inherited many of the young comic parts of Mrs. Barry and Mrs. Betterton as well as most of the repertoire of Elizabeth Boutell, notably the role of Statira in Nathaniel Lee's *The Rival Queens*, which she played opposite Betterton's Alexander and Mrs. Barry's Roxana. With this play and Dryden's *All for Love*, the three players started the pattern that would be maintained until 1707: Elizabeth Barry as the strong, sometimes villainous and usually lustful heroine; Anne Bracegirdle as the virtuous, sometimes piteous, and usually successful rival for the love of Betterton; and Betterton as the all-conquering, always admired but somewhat flawed hero. In comedy the same pattern held, with Mrs. Bracegirdle as the brisk, witty, virtuous heroine, and Mrs. Barry as her socially soiled satiric rival for the love of the swaggering worldly hero, Betterton. Congreve's comedy *Love for Love* (1695) and his tragedy *The Mourning Bride* (1697) are excellent illustrations of the formula that was developed by the dramatists in writing for the Three B's.

After the Betterton group seceded from the Theatre Royal in 1695 and set up their own theatre in

Lincoln's Inn Fields, they relied extensively on Shakespeare revivals and rewritten plays. Mrs. Bracegirdle had already been given Mrs. Barry's youthful parts, including Ophelia in *Hamlet,* Lavinia (Juliet) in Otway's *Caius Marius* (*Romeo and Juliet*), and with these roles must have gone Desdemona, for she was still playing the part opposite Betterton as Othello in 1707, the year of her retirement. Charles Gildon's *Measure for Measure* (1699) furnished her with the bowdlerized part of Isabella opposite the Angelo of Betterton. Although there is no written record of her having played Anne Bullen with Betterton as the King and Mrs. Barry as Queen Katharine in a revival (1700) of *Henry VIII,* it is difficult to assign, in the small company, any other actress to the role. There was also Portia opposite Betterton's Bassanio in Lansdowne's *The Jew of Venice* (*The Merchant of Venice*) early in 1701, and possibly Imogen, for *Cymbeline* was played by the company at least twice in the early part of the season of 1702/3, and according to usual casting, Anne Bracegirdle would have played opposite Betterton or Verbruggen as Posthumus. In Burnaby's *Love Betray'd, Or, The Agreeable Disappointment* (*Twelfth Night,* 1703), she played the breeches role of Cesario (Viola) with Mrs. Barry as Villaretta (Olivia).

The Shakespearean revivals dating from 1703 to 1710 were generally at the request of the town to see the aging Betterton in his justly celebrated roles of Othello, Lear, Brutus, Timon of Athens, Falstaff, Antony, Henry VIII, Hamlet, and Macbeth. Opposite him, Anne Bracegirdle played Desdemona in *Othello,* Cordelia in *The True and Antient History of King Lear* (as differentiated from Tate's 1681 version), Portia in *Julius Caesar,* Mrs. Ford in *The Merry Wives of Windsor* with Mrs. Barry as Mrs. Page, Octavia opposite Mrs. Barry's Cleopatra and Betterton's Antony in Dryden's *All for Love,* and Ophelia opposite Betterton's Hamlet and Mrs. Barry's Gertrude. It should be noted that Mrs. Bracegirdle was more suited to the female characters in plays in which the male role was dominant, in contrast to Mrs. Barry's acknowledged superiority in such striking roles as Cleopatra, Gertrude, Volumnia, and Lady Macbeth. Her last recorded Shakespearean part was that of Lavinia (Juliet) on February 18 and 19, 1707 in *Caius Marius,* which Otway had written for Elizabeth Barry in 1678.

Anne Bracegirdle retired at the height of her career in February 1707, following a dispute with Christopher Rich over some of her accustomed roles which he insisted on giving to a younger actress, Anne Oldfield. With the exception of a benefit for Betterton on April 7, 1708, for which she returned to speak a special prologue and to play her part of Angelica in Congreve's *Love for Love,* she never appeared on the stage again. Her permanent retirement at the age of 34 was made financially possible by a legacy of £1000 from one of the admirers of her virtue, the earl of Scarsdale, who died in 1707. [Edmund Curll, *Betterton's History of the English Stage,* 1741; J. H. Wilson, *All the King's Ladies,* 1958; Emmett L. Avery, ed., *The London Stage,* Vol. I, 1955, Vol. II, 1960; Lucyle Hook, "Portraits of Elizabeth Barry and Anne Bracegirdle," *Theatre Notebook,* XV, 1961.]—L. H.

Brackenbury, Sir **Robert** (d. 1485). Constable of the Tower of London. Commanded by Richard III to kill the young princes, Brackenbury delegated the task to Sir James Tyrrel, to whom he gave his keys. In *Richard III,* Brackenbury appears as Lieutenant of the Tower. On Richard's order he surrenders the sleeping Duke of Clarence to the two murderers. It is presumed that he also gives up the Princes to Tyrrel.

Bradbrook, Muriel C. (1909–). Scholar. A fellow of Girton College, Cambridge, Miss Bradbrook has written *Themes and Conventions in Elizabethan Tragedy* (1935), *The Growth and Structure of Elizabethan Comedy* (1955), and *The Rise of the Common Player: a Study of Actor and Society in Shakespeare's England* (1962). Her *Elizabethan Stage Conditions: a Study of Their Place in the Interpretation of Shakespeare's Plays* (1932) examines Elizabethan dramatic conventions. In *Shakespeare and Elizabethan Poetry* (1952), a comprehensive work which relates Shakespeare's poetry to that of Sidney, Spenser, Marlowe, and Chapman, Miss Bradbrook emphasizes Elizabethan conceptions of love, honor, duty, and wit and describes the stylistic development of Shakespeare.

Bradley, A[ndrew] C[ecil] (1851–1935). Critic, scholar, and professor of poetry at Oxford. Bradley's most important book is *Shakespearean Tragedy* (1904), which contains a penetrating analysis of *Hamlet, Othello, Lear,* and *Macbeth.* Despite criticism of his tendency to treat Shakespeare's characters as if they were real people who have an off-stage existence (see CHARACTER CRITICISM), Bradley's interpretation of the plays is regarded as one of the greatest pieces of Shakespearean criticism ever written.

Less well known but equally brilliant are Bradley's essays on "The Rejection of Falstaff" and on *Antony and Cleopatra,* both of which were included in his *Oxford Lectures on Poetry* (1909). His lecture on *Coriolanus* published in 1912 is still regarded as one of the most significant studies of that play.

In *Shakespearean Tragedy* Bradley suggests that almost all of Shakespeare's tragic heroes display "a marked one-sidedness, a predisposition in some particular direction; a total incapacity, in certain circumstances, of resisting the force which draws in this direction; a fatal tendency to identify the whole being with one interest, object, passion, or habit of mind."

Central to his analysis of Shakespearean tragedy is Bradley's conviction that the moral force in Shakespeare's world, which compulsively and recklessly corrects a violation of order, destroys the best in man as well as the worst. This "mystery" brings about the tragic impression of waste, but it never leaves us feeling "crushed, rebellious or desperate." Shakespeare exhibits "greatness of soul . . . oppressed, conflicting and destroyed" yet "makes us realize so vividly the worth of that which is wasted that we cannot possibly seek comfort in the reflection that 'all is vanity.'" See CRITICISM—20TH CENTURY.

Bradock, Richard (fl. 1577–1615). London printer. Bradock was admitted to the Stationers' Company in 1577. He printed the sixth and seventh editions of *Venus and Adonis* (1599, 1602), and *A Yorkshire Tragedy* (1608) with the ascription "Written by W. Shakespeare" on the title page. Bradock may have been the anonymous printer of *A Midsummer Night's Dream.* This conjecture is based on an elaborate ornament in the 1600 Quarto, which is also found in an edition of Christopher Marlowe's *Edward II* (1594), which Bradock is known to have printed. Other possible candidates for the printing of the Quarto are James Roberts and Edward Allde. [R. B. McKerrow, ed., *A Dictionary of Printers and Booksellers . . . 1557–1640*, 1910.]

Brahms, Johannes. See MUSIC BASED ON SHAKESPEARE: *19th century, 1850–1900.*

Brander Matthews Dramatic Museum. The theatre collection of Columbia University, first opened in 1911 and named for its founder, Brander Matthews, who had been a professor of literature at Columbia from 1892.

Among its Shakespeareana is a special collection from Roger Wheeler, which, with material from Brander Matthews and scholar George C. D. Odell, make the museum particularly rich in Shakespearean material. Illustrations in all forms—engravings, etchings, mezzotints, lithographs, photographic prints, transparencies, and halftones and gravures from newspapers and periodicals—are to be found here; most are of actors in their roles, but there are also scenes from the plays based on specific productions or drawn from the imagination. There are also views of playhouses, both exteriors and interiors. Some of the best prints date from the 18th century, such as those of Garrick as Hamlet, as Lear, and as Richard III. Prints from the 19th century document the productions of actor-managers Henry Irving and Beerbohm-Tree; the collection also has the handsome Boydell series of book illustrations. The major Shakespearean productions of this century, up to the inauguration of the summer festivals, are recorded in photographs and prints made from photographs.

The museum's original model of the (first) Globe theatre was constructed under the supervision of Shakespeare scholar H. H. Furness, Jr. Built on a scale of 1:24, it incorporated all the basic features of the building which have appeared in models since. The Furness Globe was damaged in 1948 and a new model was commissioned. It was completed over a period of three years by stage designer Frances Malek and model-maker Steve Lansing. It is one of the most striking of the models on permanent display in the museum. The most remarkable feature of the model is its elaborate decoration, reflecting the Elizabethan taste for carvings, gilt, marble effects, and brilliant colors, and suggesting the strong influence of the Italian renaissance, which inspired English builders to make London the "new Rome."

The museum holds another architectural model of interest to students of Elizabethan drama: the Fortune theatre, Edward Alleyn and Philip Henslowe's theatre, built the same year as the Globe. The model is based on original specifications preserved at Dulwich College, supplemented by the views of William Archer.—T. K.

Brandes, Georg Morris. Original surname **Cohen** (1842–1927). Danish scholar and critic. A champion of the spirit of liberalism and rationalism, Brandes dedicated himself to the task of bringing Denmark out of cultural isolation. His lectures at the University of Copenhagen appeared in an English translation as *Main Currents in Nineteenth Century Literature* (6 vols., 1901–1905). Taking the period from the beginning of the century to the Revolution of 1848, he traced literary developments in France, Germany and England with emphasis on the struggle between revolution and reaction. In 1873 Brandes settled in Berlin for several years, but returned to the University of Copenhagen in 1877, where he was appointed professor of aesthetics in 1902. Despite his rationalism, he was one of the first to champion Kierkegaard, whose biography he wrote. He also wrote biographies of Disraeli, Goethe, Voltaire, Michelangelo and Julius Caesar. His three-volume life of Shakespeare was translated into English as *William Shakespeare, A Critical Study* (2 vols., 1898); it exerted a strong influence in both Germany and England, and was considered of sufficient importance to be reissued in 1963. Several of Brandes' topics were of particular interest to English readers: Shakespeare viewed in relationship to continental literature, with frequent parallels to Calderón, Goethe, and Corneille; a lengthy study of the "Hamlet problem" by a Dane; and the autobiographical interpretation of the sonnets and plays. Brandes read the sonnets as Shakespeare's personal history and identified the Fair Youth as the 3rd earl of Pembroke and the Dark Lady as Mary FITTON. He further related the Dark Lady to many of the female characters in the plays. Frank Harris has followed Brandes in this approach. [J. Moritzen, *Georg Brandes in Life and Letters*, 1922.]

Brandon. In *Henry VIII*, an officer who somewhat reluctantly arrests the Duke of Buckingham, on the King's orders. The actual arrest was made by Henry Marne or Marney. Brandon is not a historical character, unless Shakespeare intended him to be Charles Brandon, who is referred to elsewhere in the play as the Duke of SUFFOLK.

Brandon, Sir William. Standard-bearer for the earl of Richmond at the battle of Bosworth Field in 1485. Because of Sir William's function, Richard III made a point of killing him personally. In *Richard III*, Brandon, though he is not listed in the cast of characters, appears in V, iii, where he is asked to bear Richmond's standard. In V, v, he is reported dead. [W. H. Thomson, *Shakespeare's Characters: A Historical Dictionary*, 1951.]

Brayne, John (d. 1586). The brother-in-law and partner of James Burbage, the builder of the THEATRE. Brayne was apparently an unwilling partner in the transaction. According to one account he was duped by Burbage into putting up most of the money for the erection of the playhouse and was subsequently defrauded of his share of the receipts. Their partnership was marked by violent quarrels. When Brayne died in 1586, his widow Margaret's attempt to claim her share of the receipts of the Theatre resulted in a continuation of the quarrels with Burbage. The final result of the disputes was a violent pitched battle between the Burbage and Brayne factions on the site of the playhouse. It has been suggested that this imbroglio provided Shakespeare with hints for a similar scene in *King John* (II, i). See also RED LION INN. [E. K. Chambers, *The Elizabethan Stage*, 1923.]

Brend, Thomas (d. 1599). A citizen of London whose property, when surveyed after his death, was found to include a house occupied by Shakespeare:

> . . . vna domo de novo edificata . . . in parochia S[ci] Salvatoris praedicta in comitatu Surria prae-

dicta in occupacione Willielmi Shakespeare et aliorum [a house newly built in the parish of St. Saviour aforesaid in the county of Surrey aforesaid in the occupation of William Shakespeare and others].

Brend was the father of Nicholas Brend who owned the property on which the Globe was built. Shakespeare had apparently become a tenant of the Brends as a result of an acquaintanceship growing out of negotiations over the Globe. [G. E. Bentley, *Shakespeare: A Biographical Handbook*, 1961.]

Brent, Faukes de (d. 1225). Friend and faithful servant of King John of England. A brave but fierce native of the Welsh border lands, Faukes fought on the king's side during the many battles which marked that turbulent period. Described by the historian Holinshed as "a man of great stomach and more rashnesse," he may have been the model for Shakespeare's colorful Faulconbridge, the Bastard in *King John*. [W. Watkiss Lloyd, *Essays on Shakespeare*, 1875; Geoffrey Bullough, *Narrative and Dramatic Sources of Shakespeare*, Vol. IV, 1962.]

Bretagne, Arthur, duke of. See ARTHUR PLANTAGENET, duke of Brittany.

Bretchgirdle, John (d. 1565). Vicar of Stratford who probably baptized Shakespeare on April 26, 1564. Bretchgirdle was an M.A. from Christ Church, Oxford. In his will he left many books to residents of Stratford, including the Latin-English dictionary compiled by Sir Thomas Elyot, which was bequeathed to the Stratford grammar school.

Bridges-Adams, W[illiam] (1889–1965). Director. Born in Harrow, Bridges-Adams was educated at Oxford. He played Prospero and Leontes with the Oxford University Dramatic Society and, after graduation, accumulated some provincial acting experience before moving to London in 1910. He played Shakespearean repertory with various companies and also directed and managed for the Bristol and Liverpool repertory companies. In 1919 he directed the Stratford-upon-Avon Shakespeare Festival, and founded and organized the New Shakespeare Company, which later became the Stratford-upon-Avon Festival Company. From 1919 to 1934 he directed 29 of the 36 plays in the First Folio at Stratford, producing plays for the Oxford University Dramatic Society as well between 1920 and 1926.

From 1919 to 1924 he was also the scenic designer for revivals of Gilbert and Sullivan. He took the Stratford Company on several tours of Canada and the United States. He supervised the installation of the new Memorial Theatre at Stratford, and in 1934 was named governor of the Shakespeare Memorial (now Royal Shakespeare) Theatre. Bridges-Adams is the author of *The Shakespeare Country* (1932), *The British Theatre* (1944), *Looking at a Play* (1947), *The Lost Leader* (1954), and *The Irresistible Theatre* (1957). [*Who's Who in the Theatre*, 1961.]

Bright, Timothy (c. 1551–1615). Physician and clergyman. After leaving Cambridge, Bright studied medicine and eventually was licensed to practice. In 1584 he published in one volume his *Hygiena, id est Sanitate tuenda medicinae* (1582) and *Medicinae therapeuticae* (1583), works dealing with preventive and curative medicine. His *Treatise of Melancholy* (1586) presents both the physical and the psychological aspects of the subject; religious melancholy, which afflicts those tormented by remorse of sin and fear of divine retribution, is given special attention. It has been conjectured that Shakespeare was familiar with the treatise and drew upon it for his depictions of Hamlet, Jaques, and other melancholic figures. Robert Burton (1577–1640) in his *Anatomy of Melancholy* (1621) followed Bright's general outline of the subject and occasionally quoted him. Bright also devised a system of shorthand which he explained in his *Characterie* (1588; see STENOGRAPHIC REPORT). Eventually he abandoned the practice of medicine and took holy orders; his abridgment of *The Book of Martyrs* (1589) was popular.

Bristol Old Vic Company. A permanent repertory company at the Theatre Royal in Bristol. In 1946 the noted Old Vic Company accepted the invitation of the Arts Council of Great Britain to set up and administer a resident company at the Theatre Royal. In subsequent years, the Bristol Old Vic has established itself as Britain's leading provincial repertory company, having developed the talents of many of England's leading and, in some cases, internationally famous actors. With the advent of the National Theatre in 1963 and the consequent demise of the Old Vic Company, a new company, the Bristol Old Vic Trust Limited, was formed to continue and develop the work at Bristol.

Although the fare at the Theatre Royal is catholic and international, and Shakespeare is one of the many who are performed, the Shakespeare productions are generally acknowledged to be of the highest caliber. In the spring of 1964, to celebrate the 400th anniversary of Shakespeare's birth, and using all the available resources of the Theatre Royal, the Little Theatre, and the university, an ambitious program was devised to illustrate the sources which contributed to Shakespeare's work. The climax of the season was the production of a comedy, a tragedy, and a history by Shakespeare, with a specially augmented company, at the Theatre Royal. Two of these productions, *Henry V* and *Love's Labour's Lost*, formed the repertoire of the subsequent six-month tour of Europe, Israel, and the British provinces.

British Museum. The chief national museum and library of England. The British Museum is the home of one of the richest and most varied collections of material related to Shakespeare and the English drama. Among its many collections are David Garrick's library of 1000 plays, bequeathed to the museum in 1779, which included 37 Shakespeare quartos. Another significant Shakespeare collection is to be found in the books bequeathed by George III in 1823, among which are 23 early quartos. In 1858 the museum acquired from James Halliwell-Phillipps 18 more Shakespearean and pseudo-Shakespearean quartos. In addition to these the museum owns five copies of the First Folio, four of the Second, and three of the Third. In the Department of Manuscripts of the museum is the manuscript of *Sir Thomas More*, three pages of which are thought to be in Shakespeare's hand, as well as an undisputed Shakespeare signature in the deed to the Blackfriars' Gate-house. There are also extensive collections of Shakespearean sources and of allusions to him. [F. C. Francis, "The Shakespeare Collection in the British Museum," *Shakespeare Survey 3*, 1950.]

Britten, Benjamin. See MUSIC BASED ON SHAKESPEARE: *20th century*.

Brome, Richard (c. 1590–1652). Dramatist. Brome first appears on record as the servant and disciple of Ben Jonson, and he is cited in the Induction to Jonson's *Bartholomew Fair* (1614). In 1629 **Brome** achieved his first success as a playwright with *The Lovesick Maid,* written for the King's Men. The enthusiastic reception of this play followed hard on the heels of an unsuccessful play by Jonson, and Jonson was enraged at what he termed "Brome's sweepings." For the next 10 years Brome continued to supply the King's Men with plays, the most successful of which was *The Northern Lass* (1632). His last play, *A Jovial Crew* or *The Merry Beggars,* was acted in 1641.

Brome excelled in complicated comedies of intrigue such as *The Madd Couple well matcht* (1637) and *The Antipodes* (1638). In the latter there is an allusion to Shakespeare's writings:

> These lads can act the Emperors lives all over,
> And Shakespeares Chronicled histories, to boot,
> And were that *Caesar,* or that English Earle
> That lov'd a Play and Player so well now living,
> I would not be out-vyed in my delights.

Brontë, Emily (1818–1848). Novelist and poet. Emily Brontë spent most of her short life in her native Yorkshire. Trained as a teacher, her real education came from her creative sisters and brother. Her poems, with those of her sisters, appeared in 1846; her only novel, *Wuthering Heights* (1847), was published shortly before her death. Mr. Lockwood's allusions to *King Lear* and *Twelfth Night* lend support to recent suggestions that Shakespeare was an important influence on *Wuthering Heights.* Catherine Earnshaw's "mad scene" (Chapter 12) has been compared to Ophelia's and to the ravings of Lear. Heathcliff's motivations and actions are similar to those of Edmund and Richard III, and Lockwood himself, the narrator, to Christopher Sly of *The Taming of the Shrew.* [Lew Girdler, "*Wuthering Heights* and Shakespeare," *Huntington Library Quarterly,* XIX, 1956.]

Brook, Peter [Stephen Paul] (1925–). Producer and co-director, Shakespeare Memorial Theatre (now the Royal Shakespeare Theatre). Born in London, Brook was educated at Oxford. He directed his first play, *Dr. Faustus,* in 1943. In 1945 he directed *Love's Labour's Lost* at the Chanticleer and *King John* during a season with the Birmingham Repertory Theatre. His productions at Stratford-upon-Avon have included *Romeo and Juliet* (1947), *Love's Labour's Lost* (1947), *Measure for Measure* (1951), *The Winter's Tale* (1951), *Titus Andronicus* (1954), *The Tempest* (1956), and *King Lear* (1962). For *Titus Andronicus* and *The Tempest,* Brook also composed the music and designed the sets. In 1955 he directed *Hamlet* at the Moscow Art Theatre. He also has directed opera in London and New York, several films, including *The Beggar's Opera* (1953) and *Lord of the Flies* (1962), and a television production of *King Lear* (1953) in New York. [*Who's Who in the Theatre,* 1961.]

Brooke, Arthur (d. 1563). Poet and translator. Brooke's sole claim to fame is his long poem *The Tragicall Historye of Romeus and Juliet* (1562), a metrical version of a story in Boaistuau's *Histoires Tragiques* (1559) and the main source of Shakespeare's tragedy (see ROMEO AND JULIET: *Sources*). Brooke's poem is a pedestrian narrative of 3020 lines written in rhyming couplets. The preface to the poem is highly moralistic and heavily tinged with Protestant polemics; the tragedy is seen as the result of filial disobedience, "meddlesome friers," and the practice of confession. Brooke, however, adds a number of features not in the French version, which Shakespeare adopted, including the comic garrulity of the nurse and the notion of Fortune as the controller of the lovers' fates. Of Brooke's life little is known. He died, apparently a young man, the year after the publication of his poem.

Brooke, Henry. See ADAPTATIONS.

Brooke or **Brook, Master.** In *The Merry Wives of Windsor,* the name assumed by Master Ford in order to spy on Falstaff. Perhaps because it was regarded as an insult to William Brooke, 7th Lord COBHAM, the name was changed to "Broome" in the First Folio.

Brooke, [Charles Frederick] Tucker (1883–1946). American scholar. Sterling professor of English at Yale until 1946, Brooke was the general editor, with W. L. Cross, of The Yale Shakespeare (40 vols., 1918–1928) and the author of a biographical volume, *Shakespeare of Stratford* (1926), included with that edition. He also edited *The Shakespeare Apocrypha* (1908) and *The Works of Christopher Marlowe* (1910).

Brookes, Baldwin (fl. 1636–1641). A mercer of Stratford who in 1637 brought a suit for recovery of debt against Shakespeare's daughter Susanna and her son-in-law Thomas Nash. Brookes' suit claimed that he had won a judgment against the estate of John Hall (Susanna's husband, who had died in 1635) of £77. 13s. 4d., which had not been paid to him because Hall's will had never been probated. Brookes requested that the court order the defendants to make public the terms of Hall's will. The reply of Susanna and Nash, extracts of which are printed below, is particularly interesting, for it shows that in 1637 the Blackfriars Gate-house, purchased by Shakespeare in 1613, and the land purchased from William and John Combe in 1602 was still owned by his daughter. Even more interesting, however, is the accusation in the reply that Brookes had employed bailiffs to invade the study at New Place and carry off "Divers bookes boxes Deskes moneys bonds bills and other goods of greate value . . . ." This latter incident may be one of the principal reasons why none of Shakespeare's personal papers has survived.

> The Joynte and severall Answeres of Susan Hall widowe & Thomas Nashe gent Defendants to the Bill of Complaynte of Baldwyn Brooks Complaynaunte . . . .
>
> The said Defendantes . . . sayth
>
> That they take yt to bee true that John Hall gent in the Bill of Complaynte named was in his life tyme and at the tyme of his Deceass seised of the Messuages Landes tenementes and hereditamentes in the Bill of Complaynte menconed in manner and forme followinge That is to saye,
>
> That hee was seised of Two Messuages and of certayne Land meadowe & pasture contayninge by estimacion ffoure yard Land w[th] thappurtennces lyeinge w[th]in the parishes of Stratford vppon

Avon old Stratford Bishopton and welcombe in the Countye of Warwicke and of one Messuage lyeinge and beinge in Blackefriers London in the right of the Defendant Susan as given to her the said Susan by the last Will and testament of Willm. Shackspeare gent her late ffather . . .

And the Defendant Susan sayth that shee by force and vertue of the guifte & bequeste of her said late ffather as aforesaid hath ever since the Deceasse of the said John Hall her late husband Deceassed entred into and vppon the Messuages and ffoure yard land wth Thappurteunces lyeinge in Stratford vppon Avon old Stratford Bishopton & Welcombe And the messuage lyeinge in Blackfriers london And hath taken the Rentes ussyes and profittes thereof as she hopeth vnder the favo[r] of this most honorable Courte was & is lawfull for her to Doe . . . .

And theis Defendantes Susan Hall and Thomas Nash saye That the said John Hall did make a nuncupatyve will but nomynated noe executo[r] . . .

And saie that they doo Contynue their habitacion in the messuage in Stratford aforesaid wherein the said John Hall lyved and Died . . .

And saie that the said Complt. since the death of the said John Hall by force of some execucion as hee p[r]tended taken forth againste the said Susan eyther as Executrix or administratrix of the said John Hall procured the said vndersheriffe and sone of his Bayliffes w[ch] Bayliffes as theis Defendantes Conceave were men of meane estate or worth violently and forceablie to breake open the house in Stratford aforesaid where theis Defendants dwell & inhabite And that the said Bayliffes Did then and there breake open the Doores and studdy of the said howse and Rashlye seise vppon and take Divers bookes boxes Deskes moneyes bonds bills and other goods of greate value as well w[ch] were of the said John Halls as of the proper goods of this Defendant Thomas Nashe the perticulars or value whereof theis Defendantes saie they are not able to expresse for that they had not then taken a full viewe survey or note of the personall estate of the said John Hall deceassed . . . .

Subsequently Susanna Hall instituted a counter-complaint against Brookes, charging that the damages resulting from the bailiffs' invasion of her home had amounted to more than the original debt of £77. The ultimate resolution of the case is not known, nor is anything else known of Baldwin Brookes other than that he served as bailiff of Stratford in 1640/1. [Frank Marcham, *William Shakespeare and His Daughter Susannah*, 1931; B. Roland Lewis, *The Shakespeare Documents*, 1940.]

Brooks, Cleanth (1906–). American critic, Gray professor of rhetoric at Yale University. As one of the outstanding figures among the "new critics," Brooks has adopted as his methodology a close analysis and explication of texts, stressing such elements as metaphor, ambiguity, irony, and paradox. His technique of close reading is exemplified in *Modern Poetry and the Tradition* (1939) and *The Well Wrought Urn* (1947). The latter includes an essay entitled "The Naked Babe and the Cloak of Manliness" in which two images in *Macbeth* are analyzed to show how they enter into the larger symbols that dominate the play. Brooks wrote several widely used texts which have strongly influenced undergraduate teaching: *Understanding Poetry* (with R. P. Warren, 1938; rev., 1950, 1960) and *Understanding Drama* (with R. B. Heilman, 1945). *Understanding Drama* includes the texts of *1 Henry IV* and *King Lear* together with detailed critical analyses of these plays; briefer critical notes are given for *Othello*, *Macbeth*, and *Antony and Cleopatra*.

Brother to the Jailer. In *The Two Noble Kinsmen*, he brings back the Jailer's Daughter, who has gone insane with love for Palamon and, having followed her beloved into the forest, has not been able to find him. The Brother humors the Daughter in her madness and exhorts the others to do likewise (IV, i).

Browning, Robert (1812–1889). Poet. Modeled first upon Byron, then upon Shelley, Browning's early works were considered failures. The influence of the two poets waned, however, as he wrote six plays and a collection of verse under the title *Bells and Pomegranates* (1841–1846). He courted Elizabeth Barrett, whose fame as a poet was, at the time, greater than his own, and the two eloped to Italy in 1846. His finest dramatic monologues—a genre that he perfected—appeared in *Men and Women* (1855) and *The Ring and the Book* (1868). Though abundant, his later work did not reach the level of the poems of these middle years.

Whenever Browning refers to Shakespeare, whether in his letters, plays, or poems, it is with a reverence that approaches deification. In the poem "Christmas Eve" (1850) he compares Shakespeare to Christ, and in "The Names" (1884) he asks that the same respect be accorded the name of Shakespeare as that of Jehovah. A resulting influence is evident in Browning's thought and work. In the clearest statement of his poetic theory, the "Essay on Shelley" (1852), Browning stresses the need for an objective poetry, a dissociation of the poet from his work, and uses *Othello* as his model. Later, in "At the Mermaid" (1876), he has Shakespeare himself demand that dissociation, and in "House" (1876) Browning rejects the autobiographical reading of the *Sonnets*.

A line from *King Lear* (III, iv, 187) inspired "'Childe Roland to the Dark Tower Came'" (1855), and *The Tempest* was the source for "Caliban Upon Setebos" (1864). Shakespeare had more influence, however, on Browning's plays than on his poems. In *Paracelsus* (1835) Browning's poetic techniques, such as the distribution of metrical pauses, indicate a strong Shakespearean influence, while themes and allusions point especially to *Hamlet*. *A Blot in the 'Scutcheon* (1843) suggests *Romeo and Juliet* as a model, and *Luria* (1846) closely resembles *Othello*, with the city of Florence taking on a role analogous to that of Desdemona.

In his final years, Browning lamented his failure to achieve his highest ambition: to write a great tragic drama. The failure was rooted in Browning's attempt to create a kind of 19th-century Shakespearean drama and in the dramatic monologue "Bishop Blougram's Apology" (1855) he has the speaker assert the futility of a poet's attempt to emulate Shakespeare. [G. R. Elliott, "Shakespeare's Significance for Browning," *Anglia*, XXXII, 1909.]

Brutus, Decius Junius (c. 84–43 B.C.). One of Julius Caesar's generals who joined the conspiracy against the dictator; in *Julius Caesar*, one of the conspirators. Confident that he can flatter Caesar into proceeding to the Senate house, Decius, as "fresh and merrily" as Marcus Brutus has prescribed, gives a favorable interpretation of Calpurnia's ominous dream. This friendly fellow is prompted by his "dear dear love" for the ruler to mention that the Senate is prepared to give Caesar a crown, but might change its mind if he failed to appear that day. Decius' final caution—should anyone learn that Caesar was absent because of fear he might be subjected to mockery—succeeds, and Caesar yields to his lure (II, ii).

Brutus, Junius. See SICINIUS VELUTUS and JUNIUS BRUTUS.

Brutus, Marcus (85–42 B.C.). Roman general and leader in the conspiracy against Julius Caesar; in *Julius Caesar*, a tragic figure, if not the hero. Historically, Brutus joined Pompey in the civil war (49), was pardoned by Caesar after the battle of Pharsalus, but nonetheless joined the conspirators who assassinated Caesar (44) in hope of restoring republican government. In a subsequent battle at Philippi (42) he and Cassius were defeated by Antony and Octavius Caesar, whereupon Brutus took his own life. His wife was Portia, daughter of Cato and Utica.

Shakespeare's characterization of Brutus has puzzled many readers. Traditionally regarded as a speculative man of high motives and refined sensibility—an embryonic Hamlet—he has of late been seen in a new light. Many modern readers, disillusioned with idealism and perhaps overly sensitive to its limitations, have come to see Brutus as the object of ironic satire. For them he represents an embryonic Woodrow Wilson, the ineffectual, self-righteous reformer whose political and personal delusions invite disaster. As in most Shakespeare criticism, however, this rather extreme position is more revealing about the age which holds it than it is about the character himself. [John Palmer, *Political Characters of Shakespeare*, 1945; Ernest Schanzer, *The Problem Plays of Shakespeare*, 1963.]

Bryan, George (fl. 1586–1613). Actor. Bryan was a member of an English traveling company which visited Helsingör (Elsinore) in Denmark and Dresden in 1586/7. He is one of the three actors referred to as "Mr." in the "plot" of *The Seven Deadly Sins*, given by the combined Admiral's-Strange's Men in 1590/1. He traveled with Strange's in 1593, and is a payee for a court performance by the Chamberlain's Men in December 1596, after which there is no longer any mention of him as an actor. Probably he left the company to take up court duties as an ordinary groom of the chamber, in which post he is cited in records up to 1613. His name appears in the First Folio (1623) list of the "principall Actors" in Shakespeare's plays. [E. K. Chambers, *The Elizabethan Stage*, 1923.]

Buc or **Buck**, Sir **George** (c. 1562–1622). Master of the Revels (1610–1622). The nephew of Edmund Tilney, Master of the Revels from 1579 to 1609, Buc served as Tilney's deputy before succeeding to the mastership. He was educated at Middle Temple, fought against the Armada in 1588 and was a member of parliament in 1593 and 1597. In 1596 he took part in the expedition to Cádiz, after which he served the lord admiral as a diplomat and courier. After the death of Tilney in 1609 he succeeded as Master of the Revels, a post he held until 1622 when he became mad and was removed from office.

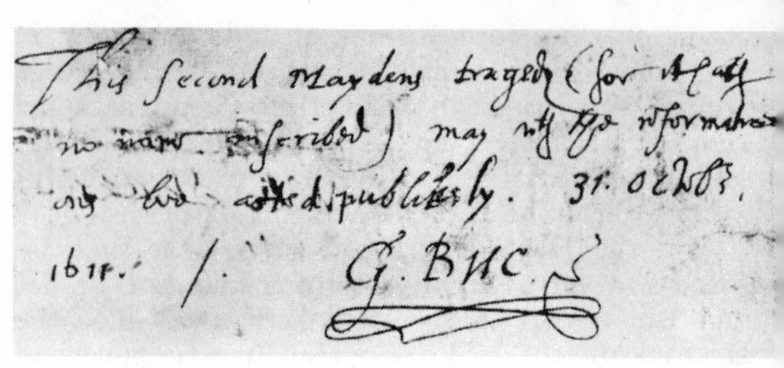

GEORGE BUC'S ALLOWANCE ON THE LAST SHEET OF THE MANUSCRIPT OF *The Second Maiden's Tragedy*. (BRITISH MUSEUM) FOR A TRANSCRIPT SEE APPENDIX.

Buc was also a poet and historian. He is the author of *The Third Universitie of England* (1615), in which he mentions another work of his entitled *The Art of Revels*, a treatise on the history and function of the Master of the Revels. Unfortunately, the latter work, which would doubtless be a valuable source of information on the drama of the period, is not extant. He is also the author of *The History of the Life and Reigne of Richard the Third*, published in 1646, which is an interesting early attempt to vindicate that ruler. The original manuscript of Buc's history, dated 1619, is extant and of considerable interest, since Buc occasionally used wastepaper from the Revels Office for his manuscript. On the back of some of these papers are play-lists, including the following plays:

The Winters Tale
The 2. Noble Kinesmen
The Tradgedy of Ham. . .
nd Part of Falstaff
laid theis 7. yeres.
Henrye the vna
Titus, and Vespatian

E. K. Chambers has suggested that the reference to "nd Part of Falstaff" is to *2 Henry IV*, and that the original comment on the play was probably "not plaid theis 7. yeres." The entry of "Titus, and Vespatian" has provoked considerable discussion as to whether or not this is Shakespeare's *Titus* (see TITUS ANDRONICUS: *Sources*). The list probably represents plays that were being considered for court performances. A direct connection between Buc and Shakespeare has been argued on the grounds of a note, said to be in Buc's handwriting, on the title page of a copy of the anonymous play *George a Greene* (1599). The note reads "Written by . . . a minister, who acted the pinners part in it himself. *Teste W. Shakespea*." The note apparently implies that the information about the authorship is based on the testimony of Shakespeare. See MASTER OF THE REVELS. [E. K. Chambers, *William Shakespeare*, 1930; Mark Eccles, "Sir George Buc, Master of the Revels" in *Thomas Lodge and Other Elizabethans*, C. J. Sisson, ed., 1933.]

Buckingham, Edward Stafford, 3rd duke of (1478–1521). Eldest son of the 2nd duke, Henry Stafford. Early in his reign Henry VIII held Buckingham in favor, making him lord constable. In 1521, however, the duke's ill-concealed ambition to succeed to the throne played into the hands of his influential enemy Cardinal Wolsey, and he was executed for high treason. In *Henry VIII*, Buckingham, together with his son-in-law Lord Abergavenny, is arrested on the evidence of his disgruntled Surveyor, at the instigation of Wolsey (I, i). Later he addresses the common people as he is led to his execution (II, i).

Buckingham, George Villiers, duke of (1592–1628). Courtier and favorite of James I. The son of a Leicestershire knight, Villiers rose rapidly in the Jacobean court, by virtue of his wit and good looks, until in 1623 he was created duke of Buckingham. His ascent to power was apparently facilitated by his performance in a court masque, Ben Jonson's *The Golden Age Restored* (1615).

An ambitious and controversial figure, Buckingham exercised a virtual dictatorship over English foreign policy from 1618 to 1628. His attempt to arrange a marriage between the infanta of Spain and Prince Charles (later Charles I) created a national scandal. In 1626 he was impeached by parliament, but his hold on the king was so strong that his power continued unabated. On October 23, 1628 he was assassinated by one of his followers. About a month prior to his assassination, Buckingham attended a Globe performance of *Henry VIII* which he had personally requested.

Buckingham, Henry Stafford, 2nd duke of (1454?–1483). Grandson of Humphrey Stafford, 1st duke. Although he was married to Catherine Woodville, sister of Edward IV's queen, Buckingham did not rise to political importance until after that king's death. Assisting Richard, duke of Gloucester, in the arrest of Rivers, Grey, and young Edward V, he then endeavored to persuade the people that the late king's heirs were illegitimate and urged them to support Gloucester's claim to the crown. A short time after the latter's accession as Richard III, Buckingham, for reasons that are not clear, defected to Richmond's party. He was betrayed by one of his own men and given over to Richard, who ordered him beheaded.

In *Richard III*, Buckingham is Gloucester's staunch supporter, called his "other self." After assisting Richard in the execution of Rivers, Grey, and Hastings, Buckingham maligns the dead King Edward to the people of London. He nevertheless fails to respond to Richard's hint that he murder the young Princes in the Tower, thereby incurring the new King's enmity. Knowing that the evil Richard now plans to be rid of him, too, Buckingham attempts to join Richmond but is intercepted, captured, and executed.

Buckingham, Humphrey Stafford, 1st duke of (1402–1460). Son of Edmund, 5th earl of Stafford, on whose death at Shrewsbury Humphrey became earl of Stafford at the age of one. Stafford campaigned under Henry V in France, joined the Council of Regency for young Henry VI, and went with the latter king to France, where he was made constable of that country. After his return to England, Stafford was made duke of Buckingham (1444). Loyal to the king, he participated in the arrest of the duke of Gloucester and subsequently aided Queen Margaret against the ambitious duke of York. Buckingham was killed on the eve of the battle of Northampton.

In *2 Henry VI*, Buckingham is chiefly responsible for the downfall of the Duke and Duchess of Gloucester. When, later, the Duke of York returns to England with a large number of Irish troops, he is persuaded to disband his men on Buckingham's assurance that York's enemy Somerset is imprisoned in the Tower. On Somerset's appearance with Queen Margaret, the infuriated York goes to battle with the royal forces. Buckingham's death is reported in *3 Henry VI*.

Buckingham, John Sheffield, duke of. See ADAPTATIONS.

Budbrooke. A small parish near the city of Warwick and only a short distance from Stratford. In 1523 it was the home of a "Richard Shakyspere" who may be Shakespeare's grandfather. In 1573 an Anthony Shaxpere was married at the Budbrooke church and his son Henry was christened there in 1575. There does not appear, however, to be any direct relation between Anthony and the Stratford Shakespeares. [Mark Eccles, *Shakespeare in Warwickshire*, 1961.]

bullbaiting. See BEARBAITING, BULLBAITING, AND COCKFIGHTING.

Bullcalf, Peter. In *2 Henry IV*, a recruit who asks to be excused from the King's service because he is "a diseased man." He buys his release for "four Harry ten shillings" (III, ii).

Bullen, Anne (1507–1536). Queen consort of Henry VIII, mother of Elizabeth I. Anne Bullen's father, Sir Thomas Bullen, was descended from prosperous merchants; her mother was the daughter of Thomas Howard, duke of Norfolk. Shortly after becoming maid of honor to Queen Katharine, she caught the eye of the king. He waited 11 years,

ANNE BULLEN. PORTRAIT BY AN UNKNOWN ARTIST. (NATIONAL PORTRAIT GALLERY)

then married her in 1533, before his divorce from Katharine was made formal. Three years later he had her beheaded for alleged infidelity. In *Henry VIII*, the masked King first meets and dances with Anne during a masque at the home of Wolsey (I, iv); shortly thereafter he makes her Marchioness of Pembroke (II, iii). Later she is seen in the procession after her coronation at Westminster Abbey (IV, i).

Bull Inn. An inn used as a playhouse and located at No. 91 Bishopsgate Street. The Bull Inn is mentioned as a prominent playhouse in John Florio's *Firste Fruites* (1578) and in Stephen Gosson's *Schoole of Abuse* (1579). From 1583 until 1588 it was used by the Queen's Men, and it was here that the company acted the anonymous play THE FAMOUS VICTORIES OF HENRY THE FIFTH. The inn was still being used as a playhouse in 1594 and it was probably among the theatre-inns which were "put down" by municipal order in 1596. See Richard RAWLIDGE.

Bullock, Christopher (c. 1690–1724). Actor and dramatist. The son of William Bullock (1657–1742), a well-known actor who excelled as Falstaff, Christopher Bullock played important secondary roles at Lincoln's Inn Fields. His Shakespearean parts included Slender in a 1704 production of *The Merry Wives of Windsor*, Poins in a 1719 production of *1 Henry IV*, and Osric in a 1721 *Hamlet*. In January 1716, Bullock's company at Lincoln's Inn Fields was engaged in a rivalry with the Drury Lane company who were planning a production of THE COBLER OF PRESTON, an adaptation of the Induction to *The Taming of the Shrew*. Bullock wrote an adaptation of the same section of the play, using the same title. Bullock's *The Cobler of Preston* was first produced on January 24, 1716 and easily eclipsed in popularity the rival play at Drury Lane.

Bullock's actress-wife, Jane Rogers (d. 1739), subsequently established a reputation in a number of Shakespearean roles, including Lady Macbeth in Davenant's adaptation of *Macbeth* and Cressida in Dryden's alteration of *Troilus and Cressida*. [C. B. Hogan, *Shakespeare in the Theatre, 1701–1750*, 1952.]

Bullough, Geoffrey (1901–). Scholar. Professor of English at Kings College, University of London, Bullough is the editor of *Narrative and Dramatic Sources of Shakespeare*, of which six volumes have been completed. The work is a collection of the major sources for each of the plays, prefaced by a detailed discussion of the use Shakespeare made of them.

Burbage, Cuthbert (1566–1636). Theatre owner. The son of James and the brother of Richard Burbage, Cuthbert Burbage was apparently never an actor himself but he appears to have always been involved in theatre activities. He is mentioned as assisting his father at the THEATRE in 1589. After the death of James Burbage in 1597, he inherited his father's interest in the Theatre, and later became a part owner of the Globe and Blackfriars theatre. Living in St. Leonard's, Shoreditch, in Southwark all his life, he maintained close association with the actors in Shakespeare's company. His reply to the petition of the King's Men in 1635 gives the history of the theatrical interests of the Burbage family. See SHARERS' PAPERS; BLACKFRIARS THEATRE. [G. E. Bentley, *The Jacobean and Caroline Stage*, 5 vols., 1941–1956.]

Burbage, James (1530 or 1531–1597). Actor and theatre owner. Burbage was a member of Leicester's Men in the early 1570's. In 1576 he and his brother-in-law, John Brayne, built the Theatre, the first regular public playhouse. His subsequent career as a theatre owner was prosperous but stormy, punctuated by frequent quarrels with both the Brayne family and the acting companies who occupied the playhouse (see the THEATRE). Burbage was a shrewd and occasionally unscrupulous businessman. In 1596 he acquired the Blackfriars priory with the intention of creating a private theatre there. He died before completing this task; the plan was realized by his sons Richard and Cuthbert.

Burbage, Richard (c. 1567–1619). Actor. The son of James Burbage, builder of the Theatre, Richard Burbage was the leading actor in Shakespeare's company until his death. He is first officially mentioned in extant records of the 1590 dispute over the Theatre (see John BRAYNE; the THEATRE). A direction in the "plot" of the anonymous DEAD MAN'S FORTUNE, given by the Admiral's Men about 1590/1, reads "Burbage a messenger." The plot of Richard Tarlton's *Seven Deadly Sins* (1590/1) casts "R Burbadg" in the two important roles of Gorbuduc and Terens, but E. K. Chambers assigns the plot to a revival of the play by Admiral's or Strange's Men about 1590.

Burbage began his long career with Shakespeare's company in 1594, when they were formed from the remnants of the recently divided Admiral's-Strange's company. He became leading actor of the Chamberlain's Men and, after 1603, of the King's Men. His relationship with his fellow actors seems to have been one of affection and mutual respect, a circumstance which is truly remarkable in view of the fact that he was also the company's landlord. He was one of the three fellow actors to whom Shakespeare willed 26s. 8d. each to buy memorial rings, and he is mentioned in the wills of two other players, Nicholas Tooley and Augustine Phillips.

RICHARD BURBAGE. POSSIBLY A SELF-PORTRAIT. (DULWICH COLLEGE, BY PERMISSION OF THE GOVERNORS)

He was lionized by the public. The charisma of his performance of the title role in Shakespeare's *Richard III* was enough to create an almost total identification of the two Richards in the eyes of the public. (This is well communicated in a famous anecdote told by John MANNINGHAM concerning Burbage, Shakespeare, and a lady citizen of London.) In addition to Richard III, Burbage's roles included Lear, Othello, Hamlet, Hieronimo in Thomas Kyd's *Spanish Tragedy*, and Ferdinand in Webster's *Duchess of Malfi*. It has been argued that Shakespeare also wrote the part of the Bastard in *King John* for Burbage (see Philip FAULCONBRIDGE).

In 1597 James Burbage died, leaving his interest in the Globe and Blackfriars theatres to his sons Cuthbert and Richard (see GLOBE THEATRE; BLACKFRIARS THEATRE). Both brothers lived in Halliwell Street, Shoreditch. In the registers of St. Leonard's are recorded the births and deaths of Richard's children and Richard's own death. Of his seven children, only his son William seems to have survived childhood. Burbage died on March 13, 1619; on the preceding day he had executed a nuncupative (oral, not written) will, creating his wife Winifred sole executrix of what was then a considerable estate. Both William and Winifred, who later married Richard Robinson, one of Burbage's fellow King's Men, were alive in 1635, according to the extant SHARERS' PAPERS.

The measure of Burbage as an actor would seem to be how well his reputation survived his death. But Burbage's reputation was already well established during his lifetime, according to the myriad allusions made to his acting ability by his contemporaries. We have already mentioned John Manningham on Burbage as Richard III. John Davies of Hereford in his *Microcosmus* (1603) cited Burbage as a player loved for his "painting, poesie." In one of the PARNASSUS PLAYS of 1602, Burbage is himself a character. Burbage is also one of the participants in a dialogue in the Induction to Marston's *The Malcontent* (1604). Jonson's *Bartholomew Fair* (1614) alludes to both Burbage and Nathan Field, when Cokes asks the master of the puppets: "Which is your *Burbage* now . . . your best *Actor*. Your *Field?*"

Burbage was reputed to be a painter as well as actor. Attributed to him have been a self-portrait, hanging in the gallery at Dulwich, the Chandos portrait of Shakespeare, and the original of the Droeshout engraving. In the gallery at Dulwich there is also a portrait, presented by William Cartwright, of a "womans head on a boord done by Mr. Burbidge ye actor." He is also said to have designed an *impresa* for the earl of Rutland in collaboration with a "Mr. Shakspeare" (see Francis Manners, 6th earl of RUTLAND).

Burbage's death in 1619 (old style, 1618) elicited both the shortest and the lengthiest of epitaphs: Camden's *Remaines* (1674 edition) has simply "Exit Burbage," while a longer poem, existing in versions of both 86 and 124 lines, is "An Elegie on the death of the famous actor Rich: Burbage, who died 13 Marij Ao. 1618" and is ascribed to "Jo ffletcher." The elegy refers to Burbage's famous roles:

Hee's gone & with him what a world are dead,
Which he reuiud, to be reuiued soe.
No more young Hamlett, ould Heironymoe.
Kind Leer, the greved Moore, and more beside,
That liued in him, haue now for ever dyde.
Oft haue I seene him leap into the graue,
Suiting the person which he seem'd to haue
Of a sadd louer with soe true an eye,
That theer I would haue sworne, he meant to dye.
Oft haue I seene him play this part in iest,
Soe liuely, that spectators, and the rest
Of his sad crew, whilst he but seem'd to bleed,
Amazed, thought euen then hee dyed in deed.

The *Burley MS*, containing a number of John Donne's poems, is also the source of Ben Jonson's epitaph on Burbage:

Epi: B: Jo:

Tell me who can when a player dies
In wch of his shapes againe hee shall rise?
What need hee stand at the iudgment throne
Who hath a heaven and a hell of his owne.
Then feare not Burbage heavens angry rodd,
When thy fellows are angells & old Hemmīgs
is God.

[C. C. Stopes, *Burbage and Shakespeare's Stage*, 1913; E. K. Chambers, *The Elizabethan Stage*, 1923.]

Burbage, William (fl. 1582–1589). Stratford resident who in 1582 had a judgment rendered for him against Shakespeare's father, John Shakespeare. Burbage was apparently Shakespeare's tenant who was seeking to recover a debt of £7. Burbage's claim was upheld in court in 1589 and a further record in 1592 indicates that the debt remained unpaid and that a judgment was executed against Shakespeare. It might be relevant to note that in that same year John Shakespeare was presented in a list of recusants (see RECUSANCY) who had failed to attend church "for feare of processe for Debtte." [Leslie Hotson, *Shakespeare's Sonnets Dated*, 1949.]

Burby, Cuthbert (d. 1607). London bookseller who published two plays of Shakespeare. Burby entered the Stationers' Company in 1592. In 1598 he published the first extant quarto of *Love's Labour's Lost* and in the following year the Second Quarto of *Romeo and Juliet* (1599), both of which were carelessly printed. In the year of his death his copyrights to these two plays were transferred to Nicholas Ling. [R. B. McKerrow, ed., *A Dictionary of Printers and Booksellers . . . 1557–1640*, 1910.]

Burgh, Nicholas (fl. 1650). A resident of Windsor who about 1650 collected a number of verses in a manuscript (Bodleian Ashmolean MS. 38) which includes two epitaphs allegedly written by Shakespeare, one on John Combe (see COMBE FAMILY) and the other on Ben Jonson:

On John Combe a Coveteous rich man Mr. Wm. Shakspear wright this att his request while hee was yett liveing for his Epitaphe

Who Lies In this Tombe
Hough; Quoth the Devill, Tis my Sonn
John A Combe.

finis

but being dead, and making the poore his heiers hee after wrightes this for his Epitaph

How ere he lived Judge not
John Combe shall never be forgott
While poor, hath Memmorye, for hee did gather
To make the poore his Issue; hee their father

As record of his tilth and seede
Did Crowne him In his Latter deede.
finis W: Shak.

m^r Ben: Johnson and m^r. W^m: Shake-speare Being Merrye att a Tavern, m^r Jonson haveing begune this for his Epitaph

Here lies Ben Johnson that was once one he gives ytt to m^r Shakspear to make upp who presently wrightes

Who while hee liv'de was a sloe thinge
and now being dead is Nothinge.
finis

The poem on Combe is interesting because it seems to correspond with known facts: in his will Combe actually did leave £1000 to the poor. The Ben Jonson verse may have had its source in Jonson's reputation as a slow writer, a circumstance for which he was frequently twitted by his contemporaries. [E. K. Chambers, *William Shakespeare*, 1930.]

Burghley, William Cecil, Lord (1520–1598). Lord Treasurer of England (1572–1598) and Elizabeth's chief adviser throughout most of her reign. A member of a middle-class family that had a long tradition of service to the state, Burghley served as secretary of state in 1553, the last year of the reign of Edward VI. He was out of favor during the rule of Queen Mary (1553–1558), but at the accession of Elizabeth (1558) he became a member of the privy council. From that time until his death, although occasionally eclipsed by more flamboyant rivals, such as Leicester and Essex, he was the most respected and trusted of Elizabeth's advisers. His advocacy of prudence and noncommitment became the hallmark of English foreign policy and resulted in the achievement of relative peace and prosperity in England for over 40 years.

WILLIAM CECIL, LORD BURGHLEY. PORTRAIT BY AN UNKNOWN ARTIST. (NATIONAL PORTRAIT GALLERY)

A master of craft himself, he had a striking capacity to ferret out the conspiratorial designs of others. In the 1590's his chief opponent at court was Essex, whose faction Shakespeare is said to have supported. As a result many scholars have argued that Burghley is being satirized as Polonius in *Hamlet*. Evidence of this view is believed to be found in Burghley's *Certaine Preceptes, or Directions* (1616), which he wrote for his son, Robert Cecil, and which Shakespeare may have seen in manuscript. Polonius' famous advice to Laertes (I, iii, 58–80) is strikingly similar to Burghley's precepts in this treatise. Hamlet's reference to Polonius as a "fishmonger" may also be an allusion to Burghley's attempt as treasurer to stimulate the fish trade.

Burgundy, Duke of. In *King Lear*, one of Cordelia's suitors. Though Burgundy professes great love for her, when Lear offers her with no dowry other than his curse, Burgundy backs down. He does not appear after the first scene of the play.

Burgundy, Philip, duke of. Called Philip the Good (1396–1467). Son of John the Fearless, duke of Burgundy. When his father was assassinated in 1419, Philip signed the treaty of Arras, which recognized Henry V of England as heir to the French throne, and in 1420 he signed the treaty of Troyes. Burgundy continued to be an ally of the English, and in 1423 his sister Anne married the duke of Bedford, leader of the English army in France. After Anne's death, however, he returned his allegiance to the French king, Charles VII. On Charles' death, Burgundy gave his support to Louis XI; however, the new king's arrogance so angered the duke's son Charles that Burgundy was persuaded to make war on France.

In *Henry V*, Burgundy appears as the peacemaker between Henry of England and Charles VI of France, and arranges the treaty of Troyes. In *1 Henry VI* he is at first an ally of the English, and with Talbot makes a daring night attack on the French at Orléans. After an appeal from Joan of Arc, however, Burgundy abandons the English in favor of his own countrymen.

Burnaby, William (c. 1673–1706). Dramatist whose *Love Betray'd* (1703) is an adaptation of *Twelfth Night*. Burnaby was educated at Oxford and Middle Temple. He is credited with the authorship of three other plays and with the first English translation (1694) of the *Satyricon* of Petronius Arbiter.

Love Betray'd leaves most of Shakespeare's characters and the basic *Twelfth Night* plot unchanged, but the verbal texture is considerably altered. Many of the names are new, most of the play is in prose, and a masque is added at the end. Malvolio and Sir Andrew Aguecheek are dropped, and their dramatic functions are combined in the character of a butler named Taquilet. Very few of Shakespeare's speeches are left intact. *Love Betray'd*, the last Restoration adaptation of Shakespeare to be produced, appeared on the stage in 1703, but it was not particularly successful. See TWELFTH NIGHT: *Stage History*. [Hazelton Spencer, *Shakespeare Improved*, 1927.]

Burney, Charles. See MUSIC BASED ON SHAKESPEARE: *18th century*.

Burt, Nicholas (fl. 1630–1660). Actor. Burt may

have been the "Nick" who played an attendant in Philip Massinger's *Believe As You List* performed in 1631 by the King's Men. In his *Historia Histrionica,* James Wright states that "Burt was a Boy first under Shank at the Blackfriers," evidence that he began his career as a member of Shakespeare's company. Subsequently, according to Wright, Burt joined Beeston's Boys at the Phoenix. During the civil war, Burt was a soldier in the Royalist army. At the Restoration, he joined Killigrew's King's Company.

Burton, Richard (1925–). Actor. Born in South Wales and educated at Oxford, Burton made his acting debut in Liverpool in 1943. In 1944 he played Angelo in the Oxford University Dramatic Society's *Measure for Measure.* In 1953 he played with the Old Vic in their Edinburgh Festival production of *Hamlet,* and continued in the title role for the Old Vic's longest run on record, 210 performances. He also played Sir Toby Belch, Coriolanus, the Bastard (*King John*), and Caliban. In 1956 he again appeared at the Old Vic, alternating with John Neville as Iago and Othello. Burton's appearance in John Gielgud's 1964 rehearsal-dress *Hamlet* in Canada and New York was an indifferent success. He has appeared in films since 1948, and played for a year in the Broadway musical *Camelot.* [*Who's Who in the Theatre,* 1961.]

Busby, John (fl. 1576–1619). London publisher of several unauthorized Shakespearean quartos. Busby was admitted as a freeman to the Stationers' Company in 1585. In 1600 he collaborated with Thomas Millington in issuing a "bad quarto" of *Henry V;* later in the year the copyright for *Henry V* was transferred to Thomas Pavier. In 1602 Busby registered *The Merry Wives of Windsor,* transferring it on the same day to Arthur Johnson, who published it. In 1607, in conjunction with Nathaniel Butter, he registered *King Lear,* which was published by Butter in the following year.

Bushy or **Bussy, Sir John** (d. 1399). A favorite of Richard II, Bushy attained his status by constant adulation. When Henry Bolingbroke returned from exile in 1399, Bushy fled to Bristol with Sir Henry Green and the earl of Wiltshire. There the three were seized and executed by Bolingbroke's followers. In *Richard II,* Bushy and his fellow courtier Green flee to Bristol, where Bolingbroke captures and executes them. In II, iii, Bolingbroke describes these followers of Richard as the "caterpillars of the commonwealth." [W. H. Thomson, *Shakespeare's Characters: A Historical Dictionary,* 1951.]

Bussy d'Ambois. See George CHAPMAN.

Butler, Samuel (1612–1680). Poet. Butler is best known as the author of *Hudibras* (1663–1678), the famous verse satire on Puritanism based on *Don Quixote.* The poem won the approval of Charles II, who awarded Butler a pension of £100 a year. Apparently one of Butler's court-appointed tasks was the vindication of Charles I from the charge of worldliness which the Puritans had lodged against him. One of the Puritan accusations had claimed that Charles would not have met the fate he did "Had he but studied Scripture half so much as *Ben: Johnson* or *Shakespear* . . . ." Butler's defense was published in *The Plagiary Exposed* (1691), an attack upon the affected language of the Puritan pamphlet:

> . . . therefore you do ill to accuse him of reading *Johnsons* and *Shakespears Plays,* which should seem you have been more in yourself to much worse purpose, else you had never hit so right upon the very Dialect of their railing Advocates . . . .

Another comment of Butler's illustrates the commonly held opinion of the late 17th century that Jonson was superior to Shakespeare because of his greater learning and discipline.

> Hence it is that Virgil who wanted much of that Natural easiness of wit that Ovid had, did nevertheless with hard Labour and long Study in the end, arrive at a higher perfection then the other with all his Dexterity of wit, but less Industry could attaine to: The same we may observe of Johnson, and Shakespeare. *For he that is able to thinke long and study well,* will be sure to finde out better things then another man can hit upon suddenly, though of more quick and ready Parts, *which is commonly but chance,* and the other Art and Judgment.

[*The Shakspere Allusion-Book,* J. Munro, ed., 1909.]

Butter, Nathaniel (d. 1664). Journalist and publisher who issued the PIED BULL QUARTO of *King Lear* (1608). Butter was admitted to the Stationers' Company in 1604 and four years later had established a shop at the sign of the Pide Bull, from which he published his quarto of *King Lear.* In 1605 Butter published *The London Prodigal,* ascribed on the title page to Shakespeare. In 1622 he turned to journalism, publishing a series of volumes of foreign news semiannually. In 1639 he transferred all the plays in his possession to Miles Fletcher (d. 1664). [H. R. Plomer, *A Dictionary of Booksellers and Printers . . . from 1641 to 1667,* 1907.]

Butts, Dr. **William** (d. 1545). Chief physician to Henry VIII. One of the outstanding medical men of his age, he helped to found the College of Physicians. In *Henry VIII,* Butts calls to the King's attention the shameful treatment of Cranmer (V, ii).

Byron, George Gordon, 6th Baron (1788–1824). Romantic poet. Educated at Cambridge, Byron's first book of poems, *Hours of Idleness* (1807), had such a hostile reception that he retorted with the scathing *English Bards and Scotch Reviewers* (1809). He espoused radical causes in the house of lords and fell under further public censure after his wife left him in 1816. That year he left England forever, first for Switzerland, then for Italy where he completed *Manfred* (1817) and *Childe Harold* (1819) and began *Don Juan.* He died in 1824 of a fever while fighting for Greek independence, leaving *Don Juan* incomplete.

It is apparent from innumerable allusions in his letters and journals that Byron often associated himself, his life and problems, with the plights of Shakespeare's heroes. At 19 he spoke of himself as Timon of Athens, the melancholy misanthrope. In the house of lords he saw himself as a Shylock in his alienation from his fellow nobles and as a Coriolanus in his scorn of them. But the character with whom he felt the closest affinity was Hamlet, and he constantly sought Hamlet's words to express his own discontent (although he thought Hamlet less of a man than Richard III). These identifications, however, were not always serious, for he noted in his journal in 1814: " 'Man delights not me,' and only one woman —at a time."

On the basis of direct references, oblique allusions, and, most of all, Byron's "rhetorical patterns," G. Wilson Knight concluded that "there is no more Shakespearean writing than the prose of Byron's Letters and Journals." There are references to Shakespeare (again most often to *Hamlet*) in the poems as well, and Byron sometimes directed the reader to the source in a footnote. In a note (iv, 75) to *Childe Harold*, Byron praises the "To be or not to be" soliloquy, which he refers to again in *Don Juan* (ix, 16). And he chose as epigraph to this great satire a line from *Twelfth Night:* "Dost thou think, because thou art virtuous, there shall be no more cakes and ale?" (II, iii, 123). Characteristically, Byron disliked *Othello* because he could not take the theme of jealousy seriously, and in *Beppo* (1818) he mocks the Moor's insistence on marital fidelity.

Byron is known to have enjoyed attacking Shakespeare before Shelley, but it would seem that his motive was to bait his friend, for Shelley would thereupon leap to Shakespeare's defense. And it is only in a context of praising Alexander Pope and boasting of the nonconformity of his own tastes that he made his famous remark that he did not think Shakespeare "without the grossest of faults." [R. G. Howarth, "Allusions in Byron's Letters," *Notes and Queries*, CLXXI, 1936; G. Wilson Knight, *Byron's Dramatic Prose*, 1953, and *Byron and Shakespeare*, 1966.]

C

C., I. (fl. 1603). The author of the poem *Saint Marie Magdalens Conversion* (1603), in which there is an apparent allusion to several of Shakespeare's works.

Of Helens rape and Troyes beseiged Towne,
Of Troylus faith, and Cressids falsitie,
Of Rychards stratagems for the English crowne,
Of Tarquins lust, and Lucrece chastitie,
Of these, of none of these my muse nowe treates,
Of greater conquests, warres, and loves she speakes.

If the allusion to "Troylus" and "Cressids" refers to characters in Shakespeare's *Troilus and Cressida,* an important clue for dating the play is provided. No identification of "I. C." has been made, but one possibility is the John Cooke (fl. 1604–1614) who made another, indirect allusion in 1604 (see A MOURNEFUL DITTIE). [*The Shakspere Allusion-Book,* J. Munro, ed., 1909.]

Cade, John. Called **Jack** (d. 1450). English rebel. In 1450 Cade became leader of the Kentish rebellion against corrupt officers of the king. He claimed to be John Mortimer and the rightful heir of Richard II. After a victory over the royal army at Sevenoaks, Cade proceeded to London and proclaimed himself lord of the city. The citizens of London, who had at first been sympathetic, became alarmed at the eruption of violence. Led by Matthew Gough, they marched on the rebels at London Bridge. Thereafter Cade's men deserted him. He continued to foment discord, however, and a proclamation setting a price of £1000 on his head was issued. Cade was finally captured in a wooded area of Sussex by Alexander Iden, the new sheriff of Kent. The rebel died of a wound while being taken to London.

In *2 Henry VI,* as in history, Cade claims to be John Mortimer. Launching his rebellion in Blackheath, he promises that when he is king seven halfpenny loaves shall be sold for a penny.

Cadiz. An important seaport on the west coast of Spain. In 1587 Sir Francis Drake (c. 1546–1596) conducted a series of daring raids on Cadiz, capturing a richly laden Spanish carrack and causing enough damage to delay the sailing of the Armada for a full year. In 1596 under the joint command of Charles Howard, lord high admiral, and the young earl of Essex, an expedition to Cadiz destroyed 40 Spanish vessels and captured the town. The victory marked the high point of Essex' career. Two large Spanish ships, the *St. Matthew* and the *St. Andrew,* were captured. Shakespeare refers to the *St. Andrew* in *The Merchant of Venice* where Salanio speaks of "my wealthy Andrew" (I, i, 27). (See THE MERCHANT OF VENICE: *Date.*) Some scholars have also seen references to the expedition in *King John* (V, vii, 115–118).

Cadwal. In *Cymbeline,* the name which Belarius gives Arviragus upon kidnapping the infant and raising him as his own son (III, iii).

Caesar, Julius (100–44 B.C.). Roman general, statesman, and writer; in *Julius Caesar,* the plot revolves around his assassination which occurs early in the play. Historically, Caesar was elected consul in 59 B.C. and joined with Pompey and Crassus that same year in the first triumvirate. As governor of Gaul, he spent the following nine years (58–49) conquering Central Europe. In 49 Pompey, fearing Caesar's great prestige, led a Senate rebellion against him, but was overcome at Pharsalus (48). After defeating Pharnaces, son of Mithridates, at Zela (47), Caesar crushed the remaining Pompeian senators at Thapsus in North Africa (46).

On his return to Rome in 46, Caesar was made dictator for 10 years, and in 44, the dictatorship was extended to his lifetime. While in power, Caesar introduced many reforms, and members of the old conservative aristocratic families, fearing that their rights and powers were being usurped, joined the conspiracy against his life.

In Shakespeare's play, Caesar is presented in an ambivalent fashion, quite in keeping with the modern conception of the drama as a "problem play" (see JULIUS CAESAR: *Comment*). Shakespeare's portrait is a complex and, to some, disturbing amalgam of the mythical hero, "the foremost man of all this world," and the all too fallible human being. The cleavage within the character is reflected in the commentaries on him. Critics have been divided between those who view Caesar as essentially noble and those who regard him as a pompous, insecure braggart. Some modern critics, notably Ernest Schanzer, have argued that these apparently irreconcilable aspects of Caesar's character are both part of Shakespeare's conscious design—that in this play Shakespeare is acutely aware of the disparity between the private and the public life, and that he presents this disparity objectively, without judgment. [Ernest Schanzer, *The Problem Plays of Shakespeare,* 1963.]

Caesar, Octavius (63 B.C–A.D. 14). First emperor of Rome and great-nephew of Julius Caesar; in *Julius Caesar* and *Antony and Cleopatra,* a member of the second triumvirate. Historically, Octavius pressed war against Julius Caesar's assassins, Brutus and Cassius, helping to crush the rebels at Philippi in 42 B.C. Octavius subsequently maneuvered Mark Antony into accepting as his share of the empire the eastern

Mediterranean provinces, and consolidated his own control over the West in the years 40–31 B.C. After defeating the combined naval forces of Antony and Cleopatra at Actium in 31 B.C., Octavius was greeted by Rome as her savior, and on January 17, 27 B.C., he became her first emperor, taking the name Augustus. The greatest achievement of his 41-year reign was the long periods of peace he was able to maintain through his mastery of the art of statesmanship.

Octavius Caesar appears only briefly in *Julius Caesar,* where, as in history, he forms with Mark Antony and Lepidus the second triumvirate after Caesar's assassination. He subsequently helps to defeat his great-uncle's assassins at Philippi. In *Antony and Cleopatra,* Octavius is presented as a cold and puritanical man of relentless purpose and ruthless ambition; he imprisons his co-triumvir Lepidus, defeats Antony at the battle of Actium, and after invading Egypt, is left master of the Roman Empire.

Caithness. In *Macbeth,* a Scottish nobleman. He fights with Malcolm's rebel army against Macbeth (V, iv).

Caius. In *Titus Andronicus,* a kinsman of Titus. At Titus' bidding, Caius shoots an arrow to which is attached a message to Saturn (IV, iii). He does not speak.

Caius, Doctor. In *The Merry Wives of Windsor,* a French physician and one of Anne Page's suitors. Somewhat peevish in temperament, Doctor Caius challenges Sir Hugh Evans when he learns that the parson favors Slender's suit to Anne. The Host of the Garter Inn directs each to a different place to await his opponent and then arranges for a confrontation at which he reveals his deception. These two murderers of the King's English realize that they have been made sport of and agree to "knog [their] prains together" to gain revenge.

Doctor Caius has received the support of Mistress Page in his courtship of her daughter, and she arranges to have him carry Anne off during the baiting of Falstaff at Windsor Park. However, Anne and Fenton sabotage this arrangement, and Doctor Caius, stealing away with a fairy in green, discovers he has married "oon garsoon, a boy!"

Caius Lucius. See Caius LUCIUS.

Calchas. In Homer's *Iliad,* a priest of Apollo serving with the Greek army; in *Troilus and Cressida,* Cressida's father. In the play Calchas has deserted the Trojans for the Greeks. After the capture of the Trojan commander Antenor, Calchas asks for "my Cressid in right great exchange" (III, iii). The exchange is made, thus precipitating Cressida's betrayal of Troilus.

Caliban. In *The Tempest,* the brutish, unwilling slave of Prospero. The name "Caliban" is probably an anagram of "cannibal," a term that had come into use, by Shakespeare's time, to describe the inhabitants of the American continent and used by Montaigne in his famous essay "Of Cannibals," one of the sources of *The Tempest.* Deformed in mind and body, Caliban is the product of an unnatural union between his mother, the witch Sycorax, and a diabolic spirit. He exists on a level slightly below man and above beasts. In such a position he represents the brutish instincts in human nature. Caliban is man stripped of his two ennobling gifts, reason and grace. His natural limitations, however, mitigate his vileness. Since improvement is beyond him, he is les culpable than those human creatures in the play, lik Antonio, who are committed to evil despite their ad vantages. Thus Caliban, despite his negative char acter, serves as an example of the principle that th naturally debased is superior to a perverted goo As Shakespeare says in Sonnet 94, "Lilies that feste smell far worse than weeds." [J. E. Hankins, "Cali ban the Bestial Man," *PMLA,* LXII, 1947.]

Calpurnia. Julius Caesar's third wife, married t him in 59 B.C.; in *Julius Caesar,* she is haunted b ominous dreams and begs her husband not to leav the house. At first Calpurnia's frightened pleas hav no effect but, in the face of her obsessive anxiety her loving husband begins to waver. Calpurnia's hin of victory collapses with the arrival of cheery Deciu Brutus, who interprets her latest dream favorabl and when Caesar invites his "Good friends, go in an taste some wine with me;/ And we, like friends, wil straightway go together," Calpurnia is a voiceles pathetic bystander (II, ii).

Cambridge, Richard, earl of (c. 1374–1415). Sec ond son of Edmund of Langley and Isabella o Castile. In 1414 Henry V made him earl of Cam bridge, as his father had been. After the revelatio that Cambridge, Lord Scrope, and Sir Thomas Gre had plotted to assassinate the king, the three wer arrested and condemned to death. Although Cam bridge confessed his guilt and begged for mercy, th sentence was carried out. In *Henry V,* as in history he is a traitor who, with Scroop and Grey, has con spired to murder Henry. Not suspecting that thei plot has been discovered, they enter the King' presence. After declaring that "Never was monarc better fear'd and loved / Than is your majesty, Cambridge advises Henry to punish a certain ma who has complained against the King. His counsel i turned on himself and his associates (II, ii).

Cambridge Shakespeare, The. A nine-volume edi tion of Shakespeare's works. The Cambridge Shake speare was the most important 19th-century critica edition. The first edition appeared between 1863 an 1866 under the editorship of W. G. Clark, J. Glove and W. A. Wright. A second edition (1891–1893 was revised by Wright. The text was reprinted a the convenient, one-volume Globe Shakespeare i 1864. See SCHOLARSHIP—19TH CENTURY.

Cambyses (c. 1569). A bombastic tragedy b Thomas Preston (fl. 1569–1589). Entered in the Sta tioners' Register as "An enterlude a lamentabl Tragedy full of pleasaunt myrth," *Cambyses* serve to illustrate the transitional nature of English dram written during the first half of Elizabeth's reign. I a primitive fashion, the play combines elements o both the native and classical traditions of drama. It plot is derived from the classical story of Cambyses king of Persia, but it is heavily larded with the comi scenes and other elements derived from Tudor inter ludes. Cambyses was apparently popular long enoug for Shakespeare to allude to it with amusement i *1 Henry IV,* where Falstaff requests

> . . . a cup of sack to make my eyes look red, tha it may be thought I have wept; for I must spea in passion, and I will do it in King Cambyses' vei
> (II, iv, 424–426)

Camden, William (1551–1623). Antiquarian an historian. Camden was the headmaster at Westmin er School when Ben Jonson was a student there, ıd they formed a lifelong friendship to which Jonon frequently alluded. Camden became famous for is *Britannia* (1586), a comprehensive topographicalistorical survey of Great Britain. The Latin text vent through seven editions before it was translated ıto English by Philemon Holland in 1610. Camden's *emaines of a Greater Worke Concerning Britain* 1605) contains what he called his "rubbish," that is, miscellany of antiquarian lore which he compiled rom his *Britannia* and translated into English. It inludes a list of contemporary poets, beginning with ir Philip Sidney and ending with Shakespeare:

> These may suffice for some Poeticall descriptions of our auncient Poets, if I would come to our time, what a world could I present to you out of Sir *Philipp Sidney, Ed. Spencer, Samuel Daniel, Hugh Holland, Ben: Johnson, Th. Campion, Mich. Drayton, George Chapman, Iohn Marston, William Shakespeare,* & other most pregnant witts of these our times, whom succeeding ages may iustly admire.

;amden also wrote a history of the Elizabethan age, *nnales rerum Anglicarum et Hibernicarum regante Elizabetha* (Vol. I, 1615; Vol. II, completed in 617 and published posthumously in 1625). Elizaeth's lord treasurer, Lord Burghley, supplied many fficial documents, thus making it an invaluable ource for all subsequent studies of the period.

In 1597 Camden was appointed Clarenceux kingf-arms. As such he is mentioned in the 1599 draft equesting permission for the Arden arms to be imaled on the Shakespeare arms (see COAT OF ARMS).

Camden's *Remaines* may have been the source of hakespeare's "fable of the belly," in the speech by Ienenius in *Coriolanus* (I, i, 99–150). [Marchette :hute, *Ben Jonson of Westminster*, 1953.]

Camden Society, The. A scholarly society founded n 1838 and named in honor of William Camden, the :lizabethan historian. The purpose of The Camden ociety has been to make accessible material for the ivil, ecclesiastical, and literary history of the United ingdom. The popularity of this society led to the ounding of several others similar in purpose, but estricted to more specialized fields. Reprinted maerial includes chronicles, rolls, personal memoirs, etters, genealogy, heraldry, and popular literature. The bulk of this material comes from the late medival and early modern periods. The first series of 05 volumes was completed in 1872. A second series 1871–1901) consists of 94 volumes. A third series vas begun in 1900 and by 1963 included 94 volumes. John G. Nichols, *A Descriptive Catalogue of the irst Series of the Works of the Camden Society*, nd ed., 1872.]

Camillo. In *The Winter's Tale*, a lord first in the ervice of Leontes, King of Sicilia, and later in that f Polixenes, King of Bohemia. Camillo serves an nportant unifying function in the action of the lay: he is the link between Bohemia and Sicilia and he benevolent assistant of the young lovers.

Campbell, Lily B[ess] (1883–). American cholar. Professor Emeritus at the University of Caliornia, Professor Campbell wrote *Scenes and Mahines on the English Stage during the Renaissance* 1923), a book reflecting the interest which recent hakespeare scholars have taken in the staging of the plays. In *Shakespeare's Tragic Heroes: Slaves of Passion* (1930) and *Shakespeare's Histories: Mirrors of Elizabethan Policy* (1947) she analyzes the character of Shakespeare's tragic heroes and argues that Elizabeth's attitude toward Mary, Queen of Scots, is suggested by King John's relation to Arthur in Shakespeare's play. See William DAVISON.

Campbell, Oscar James (1879–1970). American scholar, long-time professor of English at Columbia University. Campbell is the author of *Comicall Satyre and Shakespeare's Troilus and Cressida* (1938), which argues that in *Troilus and Cressida* Shakespeare is imitating a new genre invented by Jonson. His *Shakespeare's Satire* (1943) considers the satiric elements in the plays and arrives at some provocative analyses, such as the characterization of *Timon of Athens* as a tragic satire (see TIMON OF ATHENS: *Comment*). Campbell was editor of *The Living Shakespeare*, an edition of 21 of Shakespeare's most popular plays, and, with others, of the Bantam Shakespeare, a paperback series.

Campbell, Mrs. **Patrick.** Born **Beatrice Stella Tanner** (1867–1940). Actress. Mrs. Campbell made her first professional stage appearance in Liverpool in 1888. She then appeared with Ben Greet as Rosalind, Viola, Helena, and the Princess of France. Her first London appearance was in 1890, but it was not until she appeared as Paula Tanqueray in *The Second Mrs. Tanqueray* in 1893 that her reputation was established. She made frequent stage appearances until about 1933 and was in films after 1934. Her other Shakespearean roles included Juliet opposite Forbes-Robertson (1895) and Ophelia with him in 1897 and in 1898 at Berlin. She made her first New York appearance in 1902; in 1904 she played Melisande to Sarah Bernhardt's Pelleas; in 1920 she played Lady Macbeth to James Hackett's Macbeth. Other famous roles included the leads in *Pygmalion* and *Hedda Gabler*. [*Who's Who in the Theatre*, 1939.]

Campeggio, Lorenzo. See Cardinal Lorenzo CAMPEIUS.

Campeius (L. for **Campeggio**), Cardinal **Lorenzo** (1461–1539). Italian cardinal and papal legate. A distinguished lawyer, Campeggio entered the church in 1510 and rose rapidly. The pope made him protector of England (an office within the curia) and bishop of Bologna; Henry VIII added the bishopric of Salisbury to his honors. In 1528 he and Wolsey were made co-legates by Clement VII to try the case of Henry's divorce, but the pope, dominated by Catharine's nephew Charles V, instructed Campeggio to prolong the proceedings and later refused the divorce. Deprived of the see of Salisbury by the angry Henry, Campeggio left England.

In *Henry VIII*, Campeius upbraids Wolsey for having obtained the dismissal of Henry's distinguished secretary, Dr. Pace (II, ii). Later Campeius and Wolsey postpone the divorce trial (II, iv), and shortly thereafter counsel the distrustful Queen not to oppose the King (III, i).

Campion, Thomas (1567–1620). Poet and musician, by profession a physician. Five of Campion's earlier poems appeared in the unauthorized edition of Sir Philip Sidney's *Astrophel and Stella* (1591). In 1601 Campion published, in collaboration with Philip ROSSETER, *A Booke of Ayres*, followed by *Two Bookes of Ayres* (1610) and *The Third and Fourth Booke of Ayres* (1617?). In these collections the lyrics are accompanied by musical settings, the simple monophonic form of the air. Related to Campion's interest in the relationship of music and poetry were his views on English prosody set forth in his *Observations in the Arte of English Poesie* (1602). Campion's strong classical bias led him to argue in favor of quantitative meter over accentual and to denounce rhyme as "gross, vulgar, barbarous." Ironically, Campion's best-known poems are in rhyme and they observe accent as well as quantity. A prompt rejoinder to Campion was made by Samuel Daniel in *A Defense of Rime* (1603).

cancel. In textual criticism, the term used to describe a page (technically a leaf) which replaces one that has been removed by the printer. The leaf which has been removed is called a *cancelland*. See TROILUS AND CRESSIDA: *Text*.

Canidius. In *Antony and Cleopatra*, the lieutenant-general of Antony's land forces. Canidius vainly advises Antony against engaging Octavius Caesar in naval battle (III, vii). Later Canidius defects to the enemy.

canon. The 37 plays generally assigned to Shakespeare, all but one of which—*Pericles*—appeared in the First Folio (1623). The canon has been established on the strength of the title page of the First Folio ("Mr William Shakespeares Comedies Histories & Tragedies . . .") and the Preface of its editors, Shakespeare's fellow actors Heminges and Condell (see FIRST FOLIO). Doubt as to the authenticity of the canon has existed since the 18th century (see DISINTEGRATION); at that time, and ever since, examination of the plays has raised the question as to whether Shakespeare was the sole author of every play in the canon, or whether there was a little, or even a great deal, in the plays that was the work of other men. Other contemporary evidence supporting the authority of Heminges and Condell and the First Folio are the 19 plays entered as Shakespeare's in the Stationers' Register (3 of which were subsequently published as quartos, the other 16 being among 18 that were not printed until the publication of the First Folio); the attribution to Shakespeare of 15 of the 18 plays that were published in quarto (see QUARTO); the citation of Shakespeare as the author of 12 plays referred to in Francis Meres' PALLADIS TAMIA; and other scattered contemporary references to Shakespeare as the author of a particular play.

The Shakespearean canon has been enlarged as well as undermined. Spurious plays were attributed to Shakespeare in the early 17th century; in the Third Folio (1664) seven plays were added to the canon, and remained there until 18th-century editors removed them (see APOCRYPHA). More recently, however, as a result of the efforts of close textual criticism, there has been a tendency to enlarge the canon to include as partially Shakespeare's *Two Noble Kinsmen*, *Sir Thomas More*, and, with considerably less certainty, *Edward III*. [Kenneth Muir, *Shakespeare as Collaborator*, 1960.]

Canterbury, Henry Chichele or **Chicheley,** archbishop of (1362?–1443). A yeoman's son who, after being educated at Oxford, became a Carthusian monk. On the accession of Henry V to the throne, Chichele, who had risen rapidly in rank, was sent with the earl of Warwick as ambassador to France (1413). After his return, he was made archbishop of Canterbury. Although Chichele agreed to the war on France, Shakespeare's portrayal of the archbishop as urging it for purposes of the Church alone is not borne out by fact. In *Henry V*, he is the King's learned counselor. After promising Henry that the Church will assist him financially (I, i), he urges the King to assert his claim to the French crown (I, ii).

Canterbury, John Whitgift, archbishop of. See John WHITGIFT.

Canterbury, Thomas Cardinal **Bourchier,** archbishop of (c. 1404–1486). Third son of William Bourchier and Anne Plantagenet. Bourchier was a mediator between the disputing houses of Lancaster and York, and in 1458 assisted in formulating a temporary agreement between them. Bourchier crowned Edward IV in 1461 and, after Edward's death, presided over the coronation of Richard III. He was angered, however, over the murder of the young princes, whose protection he had undertaken, and was consequently overjoyed when the king was defeated at Bosworth. The cardinal crowned Henry VII and married him to Elizabeth of York, thereby joining the two factions he had sought so long to unite.

In *Richard III*, Bourchier is persuaded by the Duke of Buckingham, one of Richard's supporters, to remove the young Duke of York from sanctuary (III, i).

Canterbury, Thomas Cranmer, archbishop of. See Thomas CRANMER.

Capell, Edward (1713–1781). Scholar and editor. A graduate of Cambridge, Capell was appointed deputy inspector of plays in 1737, a post which left him considerable time to devote to the study of Shakespeare. His first publication was *Prolusions or Select Pieces of Antient Poetry* . . . , an anthology in which Capell included the anonymous play *Edward III*, tentatively attributing it to Shakespeare. In 1768 he published a 10-volume edition of Shakespeare based upon a careful collation of the early quartos and folios. In 1774 he published the first part of the notes and comments to his edition as *Notes and various Readings to Shakespeare, Part I*. Later he recalled this volume of annotations, which was later published by subscription along with two other volumes as *Notes and various Readings to Shakespeare* (1779–1783). Capell's notes include a number of apocryphal stories about Shakespeare, including one which is another version of the ballad which the young Shakespeare was alleged to have written about Sir Thomas Lucy and an account of Shakespeare's having played the role of Adam in *As You Like It*:

> A traditional story was current some years ago about Stratford,—that a very old man of that place,—of weak intellects, but yet related to Shakespeare,—being ask'd by some of his neighbours, what he remember'd about him; answer'd,—that he saw him once brought on the stage upon another man's back; which answer was apply'd by the hearers, to his having seen him perform in this scene the part of Adam: That he should have done so, is made not unlikely by another constant tradition,—that he was no extraordinary actor, and therefore took no parts upon him but such as this: for which he might also be peculiarly fitted by an accidental lameness, which,—as he himself tells us

twice in his "*Sonnets*", v.37, and 89,—befell him in some part of life; without saying how, or when, of what sort, or in what degree; but his expressions seems to indicate—latterly.

At his death Capell left to Trinity College his valuable collection of early editions of the plays. His chief distinction, however, lies in the fact that he was the first editor to apply the principle that the earliest text, i.e., the good quarto editions, should, where possible, be made the basis of the editions of Shakespeare's plays. In this approach Capell not only broke with the traditions of his own age, but anticipated one of the editorial principles of modern textual criticism. [Alice Walker, *Edward Capell and his Edition of Shakespeare*, Annual Shakespeare Lecture of the British Academy, 1960.]

Caphis. In *Timon of Athens*, the servant of a senator to whom Timon is in debt. Caphis' master orders him to collect the debt, but Timon cannot pay (II, i and ii).

Capilet, Diana. In *All's Well That Ends Well*, the Widow's daughter. Modestly resisting Bertram's seduction attempts, Diana arranges a tryst at which Helena, Bertram's wife, is to take her place. Later, when the faithless young man is about to be betrothed to his second wife, Diana exposes him in the presence of the King of France. At the play's end, the King rewards her with a dowry.

Captain. In *King Lear*, a minor character. In V, iii, after the capture of Lear and Cordelia, the Captain is given a piece of paper by Edmund instructing him to hang Cordelia and sets out to execute the order. Later in the same scene, Lear states that he has killed the Captain, and a second captain confirms the truth of his words.

Captain of a band of Welshmen. In *Richard II*, believing that the King is dead, the Captain refuses to remain with Richard's party (II, iv).

Capucius (L. for **Chapuys**), **Eustachius.** Ambassador to England from Charles V. In *Henry VIII*, Shakespeare follows Holinshed's account that Capucius attended Queen Katharine at her death and promised to deliver her last letter to the King (IV, ii).

Capulet. In *Romeo and Juliet*, the testy, short-tempered father of Juliet whose obstinate insistence on Juliet's marriage to Paris precipitates the tragedy. Although Capulet is a blustering, badly spoiled domestic tyrant, he is nevertheless a warmly human figure. The Italian setting of the play cannot disguise his origin as a typical English squire or well-to-do merchant.

Capulet, Lady. In *Romeo and Juliet*, the mother of Juliet and wife of Capulet. Like her husband, Lady Capulet desires Juliet's marriage to Paris.

Cardenio. A lost play attributed to Shakespeare and John Fletcher. A play of this title was acted by the King's Men in 1613. In 1653 the publisher Humphrey Moseley entered it in the Stationers' Register as "The History of Cardenio, by Mr Fletcher & Shakespeare." If the play was ever published, no extant copies have been discovered, but in 1727 Lewis Theobald, the famous Shakespearean editor, prepared for the stage a play entitled *Double Falsehood, or the Distressed Lovers*. Theobald claimed that the play had been written by Shakespeare and had been made available to him in manuscript form. The apparent source of the lost play and of *Double Falsehood* was the episode of Cardenio and Lucinda in the 1612 English translation of *Don Quixote*. *Double Falsehood* enjoyed considerable success when it was produced and in the following year (1728) it was published with an explanatory preface by Theobald:

> It has been alledg'd as incredible, that such a Curiosity should be stifled and lost to the World for above a Century. To This my Answer is short; that tho' it never till now made its Appearance on the Stage, yet one of the Manuscript Copies, which I have, is of above Sixty Years Standing, in the Handwriting of Mr. *Downes*, the famous Old Prompter; and, as I am credibly inform'd, was early in the Possession of the celebrated Mr. *Betterton*, and by Him design'd to have been usher'd into the World. What Accident prevented This Purpose of his, I do not pretend to know: Or thro' what hands it had successively pass'd before that Period of Time. There is a Tradition (which I have from the Noble Person, who supply'd me with One of my Copies) that it was given by our Author, as a Present of Value, to a Natural Daughter of his, for whose Sake he wrote it, in the Time of his Retirement from the Stage.

Theobald's explanation is far from satisfactory, and doubt as to the legitimacy of his claim is increased by the fact that he did not include the play in his edition of Shakespeare. Nevertheless, there are quite a few passages in *Double Falsehood* which are reminiscent of the style and technique of Fletcher and, less often, an occasional passage which would not be unworthy of Shakespeare. [Kenneth Muir, *Shakespeare as Collaborator*, 1960.]

Carew, Richard (1555–1620). Poet and antiquary. Carew's chief contribution is to topographical literature; his connection with Shakespeare is a result of his obscure "Epistle," appearing in the second edition (1614) of William Camden's *Remaines*. This little essay, titled "An Epistle concerning the excellencies of the English tongue," compares (in the course of demonstrating that English writers were the equal of the classical poets) Shakespeare and Marlowe with Catullus:

> Will you reade *Virgill?* take the Earle of Surrey.
> *Catullus? Shakespheare* and *Barlowes* fragment.

"Barlowes [a misprint for Marlowe's] fragment" apparently refers to Marlowe's *Hero and Leander*, left incomplete at his death. In citing Shakespeare, Carew apparently had in mind *Venus and Adonis* and *The Rape of Lucrece*. The comparison with Catullus was not in reference to that poet's better known lyrics, but probably to his *Lament of Attis*.

Carew, Thomas (c. 1594–1640). Poet. Educated at Oxford and the Middle Temple, Carew served abroad as a secretary at various embassies before becoming attached to the court of Charles I. During his lifetime he circulated in manuscript a number of his poems, largely courtly and amorous in nature, but including translations of the Psalms and other religious pieces. He also wrote a masque, *Coelum Britannicum*, which was produced at Whitehall in 1633. Carew is in the line of development from the school of Ben Jonson, but he also shows the influence of John Donne in his use of metaphysical conceits. His

"Elegy Upon the Death of Dr. Donne" is an important contemporary document for the student of metaphysical poetry. "A Pastoral Dialogue" depicts the parting of a shepherd and a nymph at dawn; in situation, characters, and language it recalls *Romeo and Juliet* (III, v, 1–36).

Carey, George. See 2nd Lord HUNSDON.

Carey, Henry. See 1st Lord HUNSDON.

Carlisle, Thomas Merke, bishop of (d. 1409). A Benedictine monk of Westminster who was much involved in secular affairs under Richard II. Carlisle protested Richard's deposition and was allegedly present at the meeting of the conspirators who were plotting to murder the new king, Henry IV. He was consequently imprisoned in the Tower, but was later pardoned by virtue of his excellent character. In *Richard II,* Carlisle, a loyal adherent of Richard, is with the King when he surrenders to the usurper, Henry Bolingbroke. He is implicated in the plot, devised by the Abbot of Westminster, to do away with Bolingbroke. Henry nevertheless pardons Carlisle, saying, "High sparks of honour in thee have I seen" (V, vi).

Carlyle, Thomas (1795–1881). Scottish essayist and historian. Carlyle was one of the writers of Victorian England who, through his social and moral criticism, received the epithets of "sage" and "prophet." His principal works are *Sartor Resartus* (1836), *Chartism* (1840), *On Heroes, Hero-Worship, and the Heroic in History* (1841), *Past and Present* (1843), *Oliver Cromwell's Letters and Speeches* (1845), *Latter-Day Pamphlets* (1850), and his massive biography of Frederick the Great (6 vols., 1858–1865).

Carlyle's observations on Shakespeare are to be found principally in *On Heroes and Hero-Worship,* where, in the third lecture, titled "The Hero as Poet," Shakespeare is coupled with Dante. Just as Dante embodied the inner life of the Middle Ages, so Shakespeare embodied its outer life, giving a concrete expression of that age at the time when it was about to dissolve. For Carlyle, Shakespeare possesses all human gifts and owes his power to his ability to see; he embodies English patriotism, but more than that, he is a prophet and priest of the universal church of the future and of all times.

Carlyle, then, was in the Romantic tradition of rhapsodic praise of Shakespeare. He had little to say about his art beyond some general remarks concerning his universal sympathy and his ability to depict living characters. Carlyle helped to perpetuate the image of Shakespeare as the "Stratford peasant," the untutored genius who, thanks to the relentlessness of Sir Thomas Lucy, was driven from his idyllic life in Warwickshire to seek a living in London. [F. W. Roe, *Thomas Carlyle as a Critic of Literature,* 1910.]

Carpenter, John Alden. See MUSIC BASED ON SHAKESPEARE: *20th century.*

Carrington, James. See ADAPTATIONS.

Cartwright, William (1606?–?1654). Actor. The son of William Cartwright, who was an actor with the Admiral's Men from 1598 to 1622, the younger Cartwright probably began as a child actor with his father's company. In the years prior to the closing of the theatres, he was a member of Queen Henrietta's Men and, after 1642, one of a group of actors who continued giving clandestine performances. See CLOSING OF THE THEATRES.

Cartwright, William (1611–1643). Dramatist an[d] divine. After receiving his M.A. from Oxford i[n] 1635, Cartwright entered holy orders and becam[e] "the most florid and seraphical preacher in the uni[-]versity." His reputation as a writer was extremel[y] high among his contemporaries, a fact attested to b[y] the 56 commendatory verses prefixed to the collecte[d] edition of his plays and poems (1651). He himself [is] the author of a commendatory poem, "Upon th[e] Dramatick Poems of Mr. John Fletcher," in whic[h] he makes two slighting references to Shakespeare:

> Twixt *Johnsons* grave, and *Shakespeare's* lighter sound
> His muse so steer'd that something still was found . . .
> *Shakespeare* to thee was dull, whose best jest lyes
> I' th Ladies questions, and th Fooles replyes,
> Old fashion'd wit, which walkt from town to town
> In turn'd Hose, which our fathers call'd the Clown;
> Whose wit our nice times would obsceanness call,
> And which made Bawdry pass for Comicall:
> Nature was all his Art, thy veine was free
> As his, but without his scurility.

[*The Shakspere Allusion-Book,* J. Munro, ed., 1909.]

Casca. In *Julius Caesar,* one of the conspirator[s.] The blunt Casca who delivers a cynically humorou[s] description of Caesar's triple rejection of a crown ([I,] ii) is unrecognizable in the next scene when, fearfu[l] and trembling, he describes the portentous "tempes[t] dropping fire." Casca is, however, easily enlisted int[o] the conspiracy against Caesar and, as planned, is th[e] first to stab him (III, i).

Cassandra. In Greek mythology, a daughter o[f] Priam and Hecuba. Apollo gave Cassandra the powe[r] of prophecy, but when she refused the god's ad[-]vances, he ordained that no one would believe he[r] predictions, although they were invariably correct[.] In *Troilus and Cressida,* Cassandra appears as th[e] sister of Hector. Although her prophetic powers en[-]able her to foresee the fall of Troy, she join[s] Andromache (V, iii) in a futile attempt to dissuad[e] Hector from doing battle with Achilles.

Cassio, Michael. In *Othello,* the newly appointe[d] lieutenant of Othello. An attractive and charmin[g] figure, Cassio is nevertheless guileless and easily de[-]ceived by Iago. His loyalty to Othello is matche[d] only by his reverence for Desdemona. At the end o[f] the play Cassio is designated as the ruler of Cypru[s] and to him, fittingly, falls the task of executing Iago[.]

It has been suggested that a parallel to Cassio's pro[-]motion is to be seen in the elevation of Lord Mount[-]joy as second in command to the earl of Essex. Se[e] TOPICAL REFERENCES.

Cassius. Full Latin name, **Caius Cassius Longinu[s]** (d. 45 B.C.). Roman general and politician; in *Juliu[s] Caesar,* originator of the conspiracy against Caesar[.] Passionate and jealous, but cynical and dangerous t[o] friends as well as to enemies, Cassius "loves no play[s] . . . , he hears no music; seldom he smiles" (I, ii)[.] Cassius' motives in planning the conspiracy agains[t] Caesar are not clearly spelled out in the play. He is[,] in Ernest Schanzer's words, a combination of "th[e] Machiavel and the loving friend." This dual role while a possible source of confusion for the audience, serves a coherent dramatic function. The opposition of personal and political morality in Cassius mirrors the thematic polarity of the play as a whole. [Ernest Schanzer, *The Problem Plays of Shakespeare*, 1963.]

Casson, Sir Lewis T. (1875–). Actor, producer, and director. Sir Lewis began acting in 1900 as an amateur with Charles Fry, for whom he played Sebastian, Dumain, and Hotspur. In 1903 he made his professional debut as Polixenes and Cassius, and from 1904 to 1907 acted with William Poel as Eglamour, Servilius, and Don Pedro. In 1905 at the Adelphi he acted Rosencrantz and Laertes with Henry Irving, Oscar Asche, and Lily Brayton. His career as an actor has been a long and productive one, and has included many Shakespearean roles, including Troilus, Brutus, Banquo, Petruchio, Shylock, Benedick, Henry V, Macbeth, Coriolanus, Kent, Edmund, and Gloucester. He has either directed or produced innumerable Shakespearean productions. He was knighted in 1951. [*Who's Who in the Theatre*, 1961.]

cast. The assignment of the parts in a play to the several actors; conversely, the set of actors to whom the parts in a particular play are assigned. In the Elizabethan theatre, acting companies were essentially of a repertory character. In creating plays for a particular company, a dramatist had to bear in mind the physical and personal characteristics of the actors, their ages, appearance, and special abilities, and the number of actors available to the company at any particular time. It was necessary to provide a part for nearly every permanent member of a company. Shakespeare, for example, never wrote a play for fewer than 15 actors. The complement of permanent actors in his company available for major roles (the sharers) ranged in number from about 9 in 1600 to 12 in 1619. In addition to the sharers, the cast was composed of HIRED MEN, who assumed minor speaking roles; boys, who played the roles of women; and occasional supernumeraries, who might be required to fill out a particularly demanding mob scene. Shakespeare's history plays, containing as many as 50 speaking parts, also required the actors to double in several roles in the same play (see DOUBLING); actors on provincial tours also found doubling a necessity.

Apart from the company's numerical composition, a playwright usually took into consideration the talents of individual actors. In Shakespeare's writing of comedy roles, for example, there is a marked change after 1598, when Robert Armin succeeded Will Kempe as the Chamberlain's Men's leading comedian; the change in roles is from the erstwhile obvious, bumbling clown to the clever, more subtle fool. Kempe's comic style had been that of an acrobat and dancer of jigs. His humor was broad; in the tradition of Richard Tarlton, Kempe would bounce and jingle across the stage, interpolating the playwright's lines with his own ad libs, a practice to which Shakespeare evidently took exception (cf. Hamlet's advice to the players, III, ii, 42–50). Armin, on the other hand, was an actor capable of greater subtlety, better able to communicate complexity and depth of characterization, and the roles of Touchstone in *As You Like It*, Feste in *Twelfth Night*, and the Fool in *King Lear* were probably created specifically to take advantage of his superior acting ability. Similarly, it is apparent that from about 1594 to 1601 the Chamberlain's Men were endowed with two extraordinarily talented boy actors, one tall, the other short. For them Shakespeare is thought to have written the contrasting roles of Portia and Nerissa in *The Merchant of Venice*, Beatrice and Hero in *Much Ado About Nothing*, Rosalind and Celia in *As You Like It*, and Viola and Olivia in *Twelfth Night*. [G. E. Bentley, *Shakespeare and His Theatre*, 1964.]

Castelnuovo-Tedesco, Mario. See MUSIC BASED ON SHAKESPEARE: *20th century*.

Castiglione, Baldassare (1478–1529). Italian writer and diplomat. Castiglione was a skilled and experienced diplomat, his missions including a trip to England in 1506. His best-known work is *Il Libro del Cortegiano* (*The Book of the Courtier*). Written between 1508 and 1518 and published in 1528, the work attempts to refashion the medieval ideal of the chivalrous knight and to fuse it with the Renaissance virtues of learning and grace. Castiglione's work was translated into English in 1561 by Sir Thomas Hoby (see THE COURTIER) and exerted a strong influence on the courtly ideals of Elizabeth's reign. The "merry war" of Beatrice and Benedick in *Much Ado About Nothing* may be derived from a similar exchange of wit in *The Courtier*.

casting-off copy. In textual criticism the name given to the procedure in an Elizabethan printing house by which a printer would estimate the amount of copy to be printed on a given number of pages. The term has recently come into use as a result of Charlton Hinman's discovery that the First Folio was set by "formes," i.e., that the first pages set in every gathering of the Folio were the sixth and seventh. This meant that the printer or compositor had to "cast-off" the number of lines needed to fill the first five pages of each gathering. If the printer made an error in "casting-off" there would be either too much or too little copy to accommodate the first five pages. This is what frequently happened in the printing of the Folio, a fact which accounts for a number of odd typographical features of that volume (see FIRST FOLIO). As a result of Hinman's discovery, work is now in progress to determine the extent to which "casting-off" was practiced in the printing of the early quartos. [Charlton Hinman, *The Printing and Proof-Reading of the First Folio of Shakespeare*, 1963.]

Castle, William (b. 1614). A parish clerk of Stratford in 1693, Castle recounted a story to a Mr. DOWDALL of Shakespeare's having been in his early years "apprentice to a butcher; but that he run from his master to London, and there was Received Into the playhouse . . . ."

Catesby, William (d. 1485). One of Richard III's chief advisors. In *Richard III*, Catesby is erroneously called Sir William. Sent by Gloucester to determine Hastings' loyalties, he finds Hastings loyal to the young Edward V (III, ii).

Catesby Family. A leading Catholic family of Warwickshire, one of whose members was the chief figure in the GUNPOWDER PLOT. Sir ***William Catesby*** (1547–1598) was appointed high sheriff of Warwickshire in 1577. His house, Lapworth Hall, although located 12 miles to the north of Stratford, was technically a part of the town. Catesby was a Catholic recusant, accused of harboring the Jesuit priest Edmund Campion in 1581 (see RECUSANCY). His son

Robert Catesby (1573–1606) was an adherent of the earl of Essex' faction and was imprisoned in 1601 for his role in the earl's attempted overthrow of Elizabeth. After his release he formed a circle of discontented Catholic recusants and conceived the disastrous Gunpowder Plot. Catesby was killed resisting capture after the discovery of the plot. Leslie Hotson has shown that Catesby was distantly related to Shakespeare through the marriage of Judith Shakespeare to Thomas Quiney and that Catesby had a number of intimate and important connections with Stratford. [Leslie Hotson, *I, William Shakespeare*, 1937.]

Catharine & Petruchio. See TAMING OF THE SHREW: *Stage History*.

Catholicism. See JESUITS; RECUSANCY; RELIGION.

Catiline. A tragedy by Ben JONSON. *Catiline*, based on the career of the Roman conspirator Catiline (d. 62 B.C.), was first acted in 1611 by Shakespeare's company, the King's Men. The actor list for the play, published with the 1616 Folio edition of Jonson's works, lists 10 actors from the company. The list does not include Shakespeare's name, an indication that he had presumably ceased acting before 1611.

Cato, Young. In *Julius Caesar*, a son of Marcus Cato of Utica. Cato is a supporter of Brutus and Cassius at Philippi, where he is slain. According to Plutarch, he fought bravely in the battle, calling out his own and his father's name. Shakespeare preserves the tradition (V, iv).

Cawdrey Family. Neighbors of Shakespeare in Stratford. ***Ralph Cawdrey*** (d. 1588), a butcher, was fined in 1559 for assaulting Alexander Webbe, John Shakespeare's brother-in-law. He served as alderman and high bailiff of Stratford in 1568. Leslie Hotson has discovered a document showing that in 1582 John Shakespeare petitioned for "sureties of the peace against Ralph Cawdrey, William Russell, Thomas Logginge, and Robert Young for fear of death and mutilation of limbs." Sureties of the peace were petitions requiring anyone named in the petitions to keep the peace for a specified time under penalty of forfeiture of a bond which the cited party was obliged to post. There is no indication of the nature of the dispute between Cawdrey and Shakespeare or of its eventual outcome.

Cawdrey had two sons approximately the same age as Shakespeare: ***Arthur*** (b. 1562) and ***George*** (b. 1565). In 1580 George left England to study in France and in 1583 he was at the English Catholic seminary in Rheims. The Stratford recusant list of 1592, in which John Shakespeare's name was listed (see RECUSANCY), recorded that George was suspected of being "a Seminarye Preeste or a Jhesuite . . ." and indicated that his mother and sister were suspected of "harboring seminaries." In a similar recusant list, published in 1606, there is recorded, in addition to Shakespeare's daughter Susanna, a Sybil Cawdrey, another member of the strong Catholic family. [Leslie Hotson, *Shakespeare's Sonnets Dated*, 1949.]

Caxton, William (1421–1491). Translator and the first English printer. Caxton spent the early years of his life as an apprentice in the silk trade. Subsequently he entered this business, residing in the low countries as an agent for the English merchants doing business there. In 1471–1472 he visited Cologne where he learned the new art of printing. In 1474 he set up his own press and printed the first book in English, *The Recuyell of the Histories of Troy* (1475), a translation by Caxton of Le Fevre's *Recueil des histoires de Troye*. Caxton's *Recuyell* is one of the sources of Shakespeare's *Troilus and Cressida*. Returning to England in 1476, Caxton printed over 70 books before his death in 1491, including such important works as Chaucer's *The Canterbury Tales* (1478?), and *Troilus and Creseide* (1483), John Gower's *Confessio Amantis* (1483), and Sir Thomas Malory's *Morte d'Arthur* (1485).

Cecil, Robert. See Robert Cecil, 1st earl of SALISBURY.

Cecil, William. See William Cecil, Lord BURGHLEY

Celia. In *As You Like It*, the daughter of the usurping Duke Frederick. A sympathetic and devoted friend to her lively, witty cousin Rosalind. Celia is not moved by her father's argument that she herself will seem brighter with Rosalind gone. Celia accompanies her cousin into exile disguised as a peasant girl, Aliena. It is she who suggests that they look for Rosalind's father in the Forest of Arden. There Celia meets Oliver, and in one of the happy events of the denouement, they are married.

censorship. In the context of the Elizabethan stage, government control and licensing of plays. Dramatic censorship had two functions, one moral, the other political. The former resulted from militant Calvinist opposition to drama, specifically because of the prohibition, in Deuteronomy (22:5): "A woman shall not be clothed with man's apparel; neither shall a man use woman's apparel." This passage, cited by Calvin himself, was the focus of Puritan opposition to the stage.

It was, however, political censorship which was the most commonly practiced under the Tudors (see ENEMIES OF THE STAGE). Elizabeth issued a proclamation in 1559 which imposed upon mayors and justices of the peace the task of examining plays in order to insure the absence of any material dealing with "matters of religion or of the governaunce of the estate of the common weale." In 1581, however, this rule was amended by an order of the privy council, bestowing on the MASTER OF THE REVELS the power to "order and reforme, auctorise and put down" all plays. Although ostensibly giving the Master of the Revels control over all the plays in the kingdom, it was in reality aimed at overcoming the opposition of the city fathers in London to the players within their jurisdiction. In 1607 this authority was extended to include the licensing of all plays being prepared for the press. Despite this close supervision, frequent violations by the players are recorded. By 1606 infringements were so severe that parliament passed "an Act to restrain the abuses of the players," in which censorship was exerted on the use of oaths or the name of God in plays.

The procedure for obtaining a license involved submitting the manuscript of a play to the Master of the Revels, who read it for a stipulated fee, deleting any objectionable material before issuing the license. Some of the manuscripts submitted to the Master of the Revels are extant, including one, *Sir Thomas More*, in which three pages are thought to be written in Shakespeare's hand.

Celebrated examples of censorship in Shakespeare's plays include the omission of the deposition scene in

Richard II (see Richard II: *Text*), and the alteration of "Oldcastle" to "Falstaff" in *Henry IV*, and of "Brooke" to "Broome" in *The Merry Wives of Windsor* (see 7th Lord Cobham). [E. K. Chambers, *The Elizabethan Stage*, 1923.]

Ceres. In *The Tempest*, a role assumed by one of the island's spirits in the masque arranged by Prospero to entertain Ferdinand and Miranda. A personification of the fruits of harvest, Ceres is summoned by Iris to bestow her gifts of prosperity and wealth on the newly betrothed couple. She sings her blessings to Ferdinand and Miranda (IV, i).

Cerimon. In *Pericles*, a prosperous lord of Ephesus and a skillful physician whose honor and charity are renowned throughout the city. When the apparently dead body of Thaisa is brought to Cerimon, he revives her and later offers her his assistance in realizing her desire to become a priestess. He confirms Thaisa's identity when Pericles visits the temple of Diana at Ephesus.

Cervantes [Saavedra], Miguel de (1547–1616). Spanish novelist, dramatist, and poet. Born in Alcalá de Henares, Cervantes left Spain as a young man, became a soldier, and fought in the battle of Lepanto (1571). Subsequently he returned to Spain where he obtained a position as a government agent. In 1605 he published the first part of *Don Quixote*, which became an immediate success. The work was translated into English in 1612 by Thomas Shelton and one of its incidents—the story of Cardenio and Lucinda—may have provided the source of *Cardenio*, a play no longer extant, which Lewis Theobald ascribed to Shakespeare and John Fletcher. Another Cervantes story, *La Señora Cornelia*, published in his *Novelas Ejemplares* (1613), provided the source of Fletcher's comedy The Chances (c. 1617).

Cesario. In *Twelfth Night*, the name adopted by Viola when she disguises herself as a page.

Chalmers, George. See William Henry Ireland.

Chamber Accounts. Records, kept by the treasurer of the chamber, of the disbursement of funds for various court entertainments, including masques and plays. The presentation of the plays themselves was the responsibility of the Revels Office, which compiled a summary account of expenditures (see Revels Accounts). This was submitted to the treasurer of the chamber who in turn submitted the account to the auditors of the chamber. Here an extract of the original account was made and recorded as the Chamber Accounts. The Chamber Accounts were essentially duplicates of the Revels Accounts except that the Chamber Accounts usually omitted the names of the plays performed. The exception to this omission appears in the records of 1612/3 when 6 Shakespearean plays are cited among two groups of 20 plays for which the King's Men were paid on May 20, 1613:

> Item paid to John Hemynges . . . fowerteene severall playes, viz: one playe called Filaster, One other called the Knott of Fooles, One other Much Adoe abowte Nothinge, The Mayeds Tragedy, The Merye Dyvell of Edmonton, The Tempest, A Kinge and no Kinge, The Twins Tragedie, The Winters Tale, Sir John Falstaffe, The Moore of Venice, The Nobleman, Caesars Tragedye, And one other called Love lyes a bleedinge . . .
>
> Item paid to the sayd John Heminges . . . for presentinge sixe severall playes, viz: one playe called A badd begininninge makes a good endinge, One other called the Capteyne, One other the Alcumist, One other Cardenno, One other the Hotspur, And one other called Benedicte and Betteris, . . .

The reference to "Sir John Falstaffe" is probably either to *2 Henry IV* or *The Merry Wives of Windsor;* "Caesars Tragedye" is undoubtedly *Julius Caesar;* "Hotspur" is probably *1 Henry IV* and "Benedicte and Betteris," *Much Ado About Nothing*. See John Stanhope. [E. K. Chambers, *The Elizabethan Stage*, 1923.]

Chamberlain, John (1553–1627). Scholar and letter writer whose correspondence is an important private source of information about events occurring in the Elizabethan and Jacobean periods. Chamberlain was educated at Cambridge, which he left without receiving a degree. He was a man of leisure who spent a good deal of his time traveling, studying, and corresponding with various friends, to whom he wrote an account of the burning of the Globe in 1613:

> The burning of the Globe or playhouse on the Bankside on St. Peters' Day cannot escape you; which fell out by a peal of chambers (that I know not upon what occasion were to be used in the play), the tampin or stopple of one of them lighting in the thatch that cover'd the house, burn'd it down to the ground in less than two hours . . . .

A letter of Chamberlain's a year later refers to the "New Globe . . . which is said to be the fairest that ever was in England." In a letter written in December 1621 Chamberlain described the burning of the Fortune theatre in that year and the destruction of the players' costumes and prompt-books. [Joseph Quincy Adams, *Shakespearean Playhouses*, 1917.]

Chamberlain's Men (1594–1603) [**Lord Hunsdon's Men** (1596–1597) **King's Men** (1603–1642)]. The greatness of Shakespeare and the significance of his achievement have resulted in a tendency to undervalue the organization within which he functioned as the creative nerve center and from which, it is fair to assume, he drew artistic as well as material sustenance. Without Shakespeare, of course, the Chamberlain's Men might have been relegated to an obscure footnote in the history of Elizabethan drama. What it is equally important to keep in mind, however, is that Shakespeare without the Chamberlain's Men would have been a lesser Shakespeare. At a time when most playwrights were living a hand-to-mouth existence as free-lance writers, Shakespeare enjoyed the advantages of a permanent and prominent position with a group of experienced and talented actors with whose limitations and capacities he could become intimately acquainted. Added to this is the evidence that the members were friends as well as colleagues, that they were, throughout most of their careers, free of the economic oppression of theatre owners like Philip Henslowe and, finally, that membership in the company was extraordinarily stable during most of Shakespeare's career. The very stability of these conditions has sometimes been looked upon as a confining influence which Shakespeare was forced to overcome. Closer acquaintance with the theatre suggests that they were aids, not hindrances to his genius, that

Shakespeare enjoyed the indisputable advantages of repertory theatre.

The Chamberlain's Men were formed early in the summer of 1594, with a nucleus of actors from the old STRANGE'S MEN. The patron of the company was Henry Carey, 1st Lord Hunsdon, who from 1585 had held the powerful post of lord chamberlain. Hunsdon had been the patron of a provincial company as early as 1564, and of another Chamberlain's Men for which performances are recorded between 1585 and 1590.

The company newly organized in 1594 included Will KEMPE, John HEMINGES, Augustine PHILLIPS, George BRYAN, Richard COWLEY, and Thomas POPE, all formerly of Strange's Men. (See CAST.) At the time of formation or very shortly thereafter, two other names were added to the roster. One of these was the brilliant young actor, Richard BURBAGE, who would subsequently emerge as the company's star. The other was William Shakespeare, who had already established a reputation as a "Johannes Factotum" (see GROATS-WORTH OF WIT) with either Strange's or Pembroke's Men.

The first recorded performances of the company were given early in June 1594 in collaboration with the Admiral's Men, at NEWINGTON BUTTS THEATRE. Among the plays performed during this period were *Titus Andronicus*, *Taming of A Shrew*, and the *Ur-Hamlet*. Shortly thereafter the company separated from the Admiral's Men and moved to the THEATRE, which was owned by Richard Burbage's father, James. The company's winter quarters during this period was apparently the CROSS KEYS INN within the city of London, and available to them only through the permission of the lord mayor. On December 26 and 27, 1594 the company made its initial appearance at court in two plays, the payment for which was received the following March; the joint payees of the company at this time were Burbage, Kempe, and Shakespeare. The appearance of Shakespeare's name with that of the two leading actors is an indication of the prominence which he had already achieved within the troupe.

In July 1596 Henry Carey died and his son George Carey succeeded him as Lord Hunsdon and as patron of the company. George Carey was not, however, immediately appointed lord chamberlain. That post fell to Lord Cobham, who held it until his death on March 5, 1597. At Cobham's death the office passed to George Carey. Thus for the period from July 1596 to March 1597 the company was known as Lord Hunsdon's Men and reverted to the name Chamberlain's Men only when Carey received his appointment.

From 1594 to 1596 the company appeared at the Theatre. By 1596, however, there is reason to believe they had moved to the Swan (see Francis LANGLEY). In the following year a performance of Thoma Nashe's scandalous *The Isle of Dogs* by Pembroke' Men resulted in the closing of the theatres, and th Chamberlain's Men were forced to tour the prov inces. When they returned to London they bega to play at the Curtain theatre. In 1598 the company produced Ben Jonson's *Every Man In his Humour* the edition of the play published in 1616 provides list of the principal actors and includes Shakespeare Christopher Beeston, William Sly, and John Duke

By the fall of 1599 the company had constructe its own theatre, the GLOBE, where for the nex decade it had the privilege of introducing the sur passing masterpieces of the world's greatest drama tist. During this period the company's position a the foremost theatrical company in London wa largely unchallenged, except for a brief threat fron the children's companies in the first years of th century. It is worthy of note that this most pro ductive period was marked by remarkably fev changes in personnel. Some time before 1599 Kemp had left the company and was replaced by Rober Armin. With that exception the sharers remaine unchanged except for the deaths of Pope an Phillips and the addition of Henry CONDELL, Alex ander COOKE, Will OSTLER, John UNDERWOOD, an William ECCLESTONE.

The fortunes of the company might have suf fered a setback in February 1601 when they per formed *Richard II* on the eve of the Essex rebellio (see Robert Devereux, earl of ESSEX). Evidently however, they were not held responsible for partici pating in the abortive revolt, for they appeared a court in a play two weeks later.

After the death of Elizabeth in 1603 the company' eminence was recognized by the new king, James I who on May 19 of that year issued a royal paten bringing it directly under his patronage:

> Knowe yee that Wee of our speciall grace, cer teine knowledge, & mere motion haue licenced an auchtorized and by theise presentes doe licenc and aucthorize theise our Servauntes Lawrenc Fletcher, William Shakespeare, Richard Burbage Augustyne Phillippes, Iohn Heninges, Henrie Con dell, William Sly, Robert Armyn, Richard Cowly and the rest of theire Assosiates freely to vse an exercise the Arte and faculty of playinge Come dies, Tragedies, histories, Enterludes, moralls, pas toralls, Stageplaies, and Suche others like as thei haue alreadie studied or hereafter shall vse o studie, aswell for the recreation of our loving Subjectes, as for our Solace and pleasure when we shall thincke good to see them, duringe our pleas ure. And the said Commedies, tragedies, historie Enterludes, Moralles, Pastoralls, Stageplayes, an suche like to shewe and exercise publiquely t

THE DECLARED ACCOUNTS OF 1594/1595 RECORDING A PAYMENT TO THE CHAMBERLAIN'S MEN FOR THEIR PERFORMANCES AT COURT. (PUBLIC RECORD OFFICE) FOR A TRANSCRIPT SEE APPENDIX.

theire best Commoditie, when the infection of the plague shall decrease, aswell within theire nowe vsual howse called the Globe within our County of Surrey, as alsoe within anie towne halls or Moute halls or other conveniente places within the liberties and freedome of anie other Cittie, vniversitie, towne, or Boroughe whatsoever within our said Realmes and domynions. Willinge and Commaundinge you and everie of you, as you tender our pleasure, not onelie to permitt and suffer them herein without anie your lettes hindrances or molestacions during our said pleasure, but alsoe to be aidinge and assistinge to them, yf anie wrong be to them offered, And to allowe them such former Curtesies as hath bene given to men of theire place and quallitie, and alsoe that further favour you shall shewe to theise our Servauntes for our sake wee shall take kindlie at your handes.

'he name of Lawrence FLETCHER was included mong those of the King's Men apparently because e was a personal favorite of the king's; there is no vidence that he ever took any active role in the ompany.

In 1608/09 the King's Men, as they were now alled, leased a private indoor theatre in the Blackriars district. (See BLACKFRIARS THEATRE.) This nove had a decisive impact both on the company nd the plays they performed. Attempting to appeal o a smaller, more select audience, the troupe ltered the style and content of the dramas they resented. The change is reflected in Shakespeare's ate plays, his so-called romances, and in the plays f Beaumont and Fletcher, who began writing for he company at this time. Although the company ontinued to play at the Globe in the summer, the 3lackfriars soon became the more important of the wo theatres.

By this time Shakespeare had evidently long since eased performing as an actor with the company see William SHAKESPEARE: *London*); his last reorded appearance was in a 1603 performance of onson's *Sejanus*, and by 1612 he was apparently iving in semiretirement at Stratford. The loss of heir chief playwright had no immediate impact on he fortunes of the King's Men, the gap being filled y the popular plays of Beaumont and Fletcher. Then too Shakespeare continued to supply the comany with an occasional play either alone or in ollaboration with Fletcher, who was apparently eing groomed as his successor.

After Shakespeare's death in 1616 the company ontinued to prosper. In 1619 a new royal patent was ssued to them, confirming their right to play at the Globe and Blackfriars. The players named in the locument were John Heminges, Richard Burbage, Henry Condell, John LOWIN, Nicholas Tooley, John Underwood, Nathan Field, Robert Benfield, Robert Gough, William Ecclestone, Richard Robinson, and ohn Shank. On March 13, 1619 the company's star, Richard Burbage, died; in 1620 they lost Nathan Field, but despite their losses the company continued o dominate the London theatrical scene, and at some ime about 1619 added Joseph TAYLOR as a replacement for Burbage.

The First Folio of Shakespeare's plays, containing he fullest extant list of actors in the plays, was pubished in 1623 by Heminges and Condell, doubtless with the approbation of the full company. In 1624 the company again offended the king, indirectly, with a performance of Middleton's sensational A GAME AT CHESSE, but when James died the following year and was succeeded by Charles I, the company's royal patent was nevertheless reissued. The company maintained their prosperity in the following years, a circumstance attested by the figures cited in the SHARERS' PAPERS dispute of 1635. In 1636/7, however, the theatres were closed for 17 months because of the plague and the company suffered. In 1641 the plague reappeared, forcing further curtailment of theatrical activity, and on September 21, 1642 a parliamentary order required that "publike Stage-Playes shall cease, and bee foreborne." (See CLOSING OF THE THEATRES.)

With that event the company's nearly half-century of continuous theatrical activity came to a close. Its organization, stability, and longevity were unique in the history of the English theatre. But its major achievement remains that of providing a productive and fruitful theatrical climate in which the genius of Shakespeare could flourish. [E. K. Chambers *William Shakespeare*, 1930; Bernard Beckerman, *Shakespeare at the Globe, 1962.*]—E.Q.

Chambers, Sir E[dmund] K[erchever] (1866–1953). Scholar. Educated at Marlborough and Corpus Christi colleges, Oxford, Chambers served with the educational department from 1892 to 1926 and was knighted in 1925. He established his scholarly reputation with the comprehensive study *The Medieval Stage* (2 vols., 1903) followed by *The Elizabethan Stage* (4 vols., 1923). In 1924, he delivered the British Academy Annual Shakespeare Lecture, "The Disintegration of Shakespeare," largely a discussion of J. M. Robertson's criticism; this lecture has been reprinted in *Shakespearean Gleanings* (1944), edited by J. W. Mackail. In *Shakespeare: A Survey* (1925) he published a collection of essays which had previously appeared as introductions to the plays for the general reader. Chambers issued another of his comprehensive studies with *William Shakespeare: A Study of Facts and Problems* (2 vols., 1930); the massive body of material, particularly the second volume which consists of reprints of the relevant documents, makes it a work for reference rather than for general reading. The latter purpose is better served by the abridgment made by Charles Williams entitled *A Short Life of Shakespeare* (1933). A useful tool is the comprehensive index to both *The Elizabethan Stage* and *William Shakespeare* made by Beatrice White in 1934. Other works by Chambers include *Shakespearean Gleanings* (1944) and *Sources for a Biography of Shakespeare* (1946).

In the area of medieval studies, Chambers wrote *Arthur of Britain* (1927), *The English Folk Play* (1933), and *English Literature at the Close of the Middle Ages* (1945), a volume in the Oxford History of English Literature. Among several collections of essays and articles is *Sir Thomas Wyatt and Some Collected Studies* (1933), which is concerned with medieval and Tudor literature. Chambers also wrote full-length studies of Samuel Taylor Coleridge and Matthew Arnold. His editions include the works of Landor, Milton, and Vaughan; collections of English pastorals and early English verse; and *The Oxford Book of Sixteenth Century Verse* (1932).

Chambers, Raymond Wilson (1874–1942). Scholar.

A professor of English at University College in London, Chambers was primarily a medievalist. In *The Jacobean Shakespeare and Measure for Measure* (1937) Chambers interprets *Measure for Measure* as a Christian comedy of redemption. He has also shown in an essay on "King Lear" (1940) that Shakespeare ends this play on a more optimistic note than do his sources. Chambers' essay on SIR THOMAS MORE, published in A. W. Pollard's symposium, *Shakespeare's Hand in The Play of Sir Thomas More* (1923), and reprinted in his own *Man's Unconquerable Mind* (1939), brilliantly establishes a close correspondence between the political philosophy of Shakespeare and that of the anonymous "Hand D" who was in part author of the play. The essay is regarded as one of the most important arguments in identifying Shakespeare with "Hand D."

Chambrun, Clara Longworth, comtesse **de** (1873–1954). American-born author and scholar. A member of a distinguished Cincinnati family, the comtesse de Chambrun married a French official and adopted the citizenship of his country. During her residence in Paris, Washington, and Morocco, she wrote various works in both English and French. Her first work on Shakespeare was *The Sonnets of William Shakespeare: New Light and Old Evidence* (1913). In a long introduction she identified the Young Man of the *Sonnets* as the earl of Southampton and drew upon much hitherto neglected 16th-century material. Departing from the traditional order of the *Sonnets,* she rearranged them to present a more coherent story. In 1921 she received a doctorate from the Sorbonne for her *Giovanni Florio*, which threw new light on Italian and French influences in Elizabethan England. Two scholarly works on Shakespeare are *Shakespeare Actor-Poet* (1927) and *Shakespeare Rediscovered by Means of Public Records* (1938). *My Shakespeare, Rise!* (1935) is a fictional account of Shakespeare purportedly told by John Lacy, a Restoration actor. The special contribution of the comtesse de Chambrun was to call attention to unknown or neglected documents relating to Shakespeare, such as those pertaining to the Catholicism of Shakespeare's family. However, her handling of these documents has not always satisfied professional scholars. She sometimes made fanciful interpretations of her discoveries, and she neglected contemporary scholarship and criticism. This neglect led her at times to oversimplification and overstatement.

Chances, The. A comedy by John FLETCHER based on one of the *Novelas Ejemplares* (1613) of CERVANTES. The date of *The Chances* has not been determined but it appears to have been written around 1617 and revised in 1627 after Fletcher's death. In his *Catalogue of . . . Plaies* (1656), Edward Archer ascribed the play to Shakespeare.

Chandos portrait. See PORTRAITS OF SHAKESPEARE.

Changeling, The. See Thomas MIDDLETON.

Chapel Lane. The location in Stratford where Shakespeare purchased a cottage in 1602. New Place, Shakespeare's home, was located at the corner of Chapel Street and Chapel Lane, and the cottage, which Shakespeare purchased from Walter Getley, stood across from the gardens of New Place. The record of the transaction was entered in the court rolls of the manor of Rowington, since the property was considered part of the manor:

> Ad hanc curiam venit Walterus Gentley . . . e sursum reddidit in manus domine manerii predic unum cotagium, cum pertinenciis, scituatum. jacer et existens in Stratford-super-Avon, in quodam vico ibidem vocato Walkers Streete alias Dea Lane, ad opus et usum Willielmi Shackespere e heredum suorum imperpetuum, secundum con suetudinem manerii predicti; et sic remanet i manibus domine manerii predicti, quousque pre dictus Willielmus Shakespere venerit ad capiendu premissa predicta.
>
> [Walter Getley . . . came to this court . . . an returned to the hand of the mistress of the afore said manor, a cottage with appurtenances, locate lying and existing in Stratford-upon-Avon in th street there known as Walker's Street alias Dea Lane, to the needs and use of William Shakespear and his heirs in perpetuity according to the custor of the aforesaid manor, and thus it remains in th hands of the mistress of the aforesaid manor, unt the aforesaid William Shakespeare will come to th aforesaid premises.]

Chapel Lane was also known as Walker's Street o Dead Lane, the names referred to in the documen The mistress of the manor alluded to was the count ess of Warwick, the widow of Ambrose Dudley earl of Warwick (1528–1590).

Surveys of the area taken in 1604 and 1606 show that "William Shakespeare lykewise holdeth ther one cottage and one garden, by estimation a quarte of one acre, and payeth rent yeerlye i j^{s}, v j^{d}." In hi will Shakespeare directed his daughter Judith to sur render her interest in the property to her siste Susanna. In 1617 it was mentioned as the property o "John Haule [Hall] and Susan his wief . . . afte the decease of Wm. Shakespeare, gen. late father o Susan." The Halls held their interest in the propert until at least 1638. [C. C. Stopes, *Shakespeare's In dustry*, 1916; Tucker Brooke, *Shakespeare of Strat ford*, 1926; G. E. Bentley, *Shakespeare: A Biographi cal Handbook*, 1961.]

Chapman, George (c. 1560–1634). Poet, play wright, and translator. Chapman forged a literar career which spanned approximately the same year as that of Shakespeare. He was born about 30 mile north of London at Hitchin, Hertfordshire, and i said to have attended Oxford and to have taugh school at Hitchin. In the service of Sir Ralph Sadler he arrived in London by about 1585 and went sol diering in the low countries. By 1596 Chapman wa writing plays for Philip Henslowe's Lord Admiral' company at the Rose. Some of his work of thi period has not survived. Chapman's first unmistak able dramatic success, in February 1596, was with *Th Blind Beggar of Alexandria*, later printed in a text based on stage copy, which cut down the romanti elements and emphasized the farcical incidents. An other comedy, *An Humourous Day's Mirth,* ap peared the next year and was well received; even more strikingly it anticipated Jonson's *Every Man In his Humour*, a year later. Chapman was well on hi way as a playwright; indeed, he was listed in 1598 by Francis Meres as among "our best for Tragedy" a well as "for Comedy." None of his early tragedie has survived.

Chapman's completion of Marlowe's amatory

›oem *Hero and Leander* was published in 1598 and ıcluded lines which stressed their friendship and ›ommon inspiration. In its full form it was imnensely popular and went through 9 additional ediions within the next 40 years. 1598 also marks the ırst printed portions of Chapman's translations from Iomer, a task which occupied him for many years nd for which he wished to be, and is, chiefly nown. A few years later he transferred his services s playwright to the newly organized Children of he Chapel, later called the Queen's Revels, at Blackriars, and thereafter most of his dramatic work was or child actors. His plays for the Children included *Ill Fools* (1604?), *May Day* (c. 1609), *The Gentlenan Usher* (1602?), *Monsieur d'Olive* (1604), and *The Widow's Tears* (between 1603 and 1609). One ›lay merits our special attention because of its conequences; this was a collaboration with Jonson and ohn Marston called *Eastward Ho!* (1605). The title vas evidently suggested by Dekker and Middleton's *Vestward Ho!*, written for the rival children's comany of Paul's. The new play, a realistic picture of ondon life, contained a minor action about the olonization of America. This scene was almost cerainly written by Chapman, who showed his interest n exploration in his poetry. This section, however, ncluded some incidental satire on the Scots, apparntly inserted by Marston, which proved offensive o King James. There was much to-do, and though Marston escaped, Chapman and Jonson found themelves in prison under threat of dire penalties. Forunately, their friends at court interceded, the two playwrights were released, and the play, slightly mended, enjoyed a rousing success.

Meanwhile, Chapman had been appointed sewer n ordinary to Prince Henry, who promised support o his translations of Homer. He published books I, II, VII–XI of the *Iliad* in 1598. Twelve books of the *Iliad* appeared in 1609, the complete translation in 1611, and the complete *Odyssey* in 1615. There were original poems too, frequently occasional; translations of Petrarch, Hesiod, and Juvenal; and, for a while, tragedies.

Chapman's tragedies, with one exception, are dramatic poems, serving more as vehicles for the expression of his philosophical and political ideas than for performance in the theatre. The exception was *Bussy D'Ambois* of 1604, acted by Paul's Boys and much more successful on the stage than any of the others. It dramatized the *virtu* of a well-known Frenchman and his defeat by worldly forces. Its sequel, *The Revenge of Bussy D'Ambois* (c. 1610), a further "excitation to heroical life," continued to demonstrate Chapman's independence of thought, but it could hardly have won applause for its dramaturgy. Between them came the two-part *Conspiracy and Tragedy of Charles Duke of Biron* (1608), which daringly depicted French policy and manners and brought the protest of the French ambassador. Performance was suspended and the author escaped arrest, but not some of the actors; on its publication in 1608, in much cut form, Chapman spoke of "these poor dismembered poems." After 1616 he wrote little except in revision. He died on May 12, 1634 and was buried in the cemetery of St. Giles-in-the-Fields.

In a period other than the Elizabethan, Chapman might not have been a dramatist at all. He was a man of letters and he considered himself a man of learning: Stoic, Platonic, and speculative. He was deeply concerned with seeking, following, and teaching ethical values and with political wisdom and its application to contemporary conditions. Since he was a proud, somewhat irritable, and exacerbated man, he frequently did not satisfy himself or others, and as a poet he was often self-consciously opaque or unconsciously strained.

There is no external evidence whatever that Chapman and Shakespeare actually met. Though Chapman addressed poems to a number of poets and playwrights, he wrote none to Shakespeare, and Shakespeare avoided the literary epistle. Moreover, considerably more than a word of caution is in order upon the specific literary relations between Chapman and Shakespeare: influences, borrowings, reminiscences, personal references, and suggested attributions. According to one view, they fenced with each other for years. According to another, Chapman was the primary author of *All's Well*, *Troilus and Cressida*, and *Measure for Measure*, and his hand was to be found in *Henry VI*, *The Taming of the Shrew*, *Henry V*, *Julius Caesar*, *The Merry Wives of Windsor*, *Timon of Athens*, *Pericles*, and the masque in *The Tempest*, not to mention the fragmentary *Sir Thomas More*, *A Lover's Complaint*, the interludes in *Hamlet*, and possibly about 50 of the *Sonnets.* And, of course, if Shakespeare was really Lord Oxford, then Shakespeare and Chapman represented the opposing Protestant and Catholic points of view, and both Bussy and Feste were Oxford. Competent Shakespeare scholars do not accept such nonsense; nor is there any support for the theory that *Timon of Athens*, left fragmentary by Shakespeare, was reworked by Chapman.

Skepticism should greet two persistently mentioned theories: first, that Chapman is the Rival Poet of Shakespeare's *Sonnets;* and second, that in *Love's Labour's Lost* Shakespeare is commenting on the group of kindred spirits with whom Chapman was early associated, the so-called SCHOOL OF NIGHT. The case for Chapman as the Rival Poet, a theory proposed almost a century ago, rests in part on Sonnets 80, 85, and 86, where the "familiar ghost" allegedly aims at Chapman's claim of supernatural inspiration and nightly visitation. "The proud sail of his great verse" refers, somewhat prematurely, to the Homeric translations, and "every hymn that able spirit affords" to the two "Hymns" of his poem *The Shadow of Night* (1594). In addition, Chapman wrote sonnets to Southampton and Pembroke, the most popular candidates for the role of the Fair Youth or Friend of Shakespeare's sonnets. This is conjecture, not evidence. It is possible that Chapman may have been the Rival Poet; but, without external documentation, no identification is possible.

Firmer ground is gained by attempting to establish the influences one dramatist had upon the other. It is quite clear that Chapman and Shakespeare made use of each other's work. In *Bussy d'Ambois*, Chapman's lines (III, i, 23–25) about "empty clouds,/ In which our faulty apprehensions forge/ The forms of dragons, lions, elephants . . ." recall Hamlet's words (III, ii, 392–399) to Polonius. Perhaps Shakespeare returned the compliment in "a cloud that's dragonish;/ a vapour sometime like a bear or lion" in *Antony and Cleopatra* (IV, xiv, 2–3). In *The Revenge of Bussy,* Chapman not only made use of Hamlet's delayed revenge after the charge of the familial ghost, but where the ghost of Bussy appears (V, i), imitated the closet scene between Hamlet and his mother. In *Chabot* (c. 1613) he picked up Hamlet's pun on Brutus, and a scene (III, ii) of *Eastward Ho!,* probably his, had a footman named Hamlet addressed, " 'S foot, Hamlet, are you mad?" He also echoes a line in *Hamlet* (I, ii, 180–181) "the cold meat left at your wedding [which] might serve to furnish their nuptial table" (*Eastward Ho!,* II, i, 257–258) and made comic play with one of Ophelia's songs (*Eastward Ho!,* III, ii, 77–79; *Hamlet,* IV, v, 190 ff.). Evidently Chapman knew *Hamlet* and *Romeo and Juliet* well. The words in *The Revenge of Bussy D'Ambois:* "See how he hangs upon the ear of Guise, / Like to his jewel" (I, i, 152–153) recall Romeo's "It seems she hangs upon the cheek of night / Like a rich jewel in an Ethiope's ear" (I, v, 47–48). In addition, Chapman's familiarity with *Twelfth Night* was shown in *May Day* (III, iii).

A complementary influence can be seen in Shakespeare's *Troilus and Cressida.* Let us remove from consideration the so-called War of the Theatres, Chapman's connection with a play called *Histriomastix* and its relation to Shakespeare's play, as well as the absurd identification of Chapman with Thersites. We may avoid, too, any application to contemporary affairs. What is important is the relation between Chapman's translation of Homer and Shakespeare's characters and incidents. Chapman's *Seven Books of the Iliads* (I, II, VII–XI) and *Achilles' Shield* (XVIII) were first published in 1598; the other books were issued after Shakespeare's play was written and are not germane. The stories of the heroes were well known in Shakespeare's time, through Chaucer and medieval romances; there were foreign translations of Homer, and there were English adaptations which Shakespeare undoubtedly used. Some of the latter explain his attitudes to characters, particularly Cressida. Shakespeare knew more of the background material than Chapman provided, and he referred in earlier plays to both title characters and to others present at the siege of Troy. Since Shakespeare read widely and Chapman was well known, it might be assumed that he had read Chapman's translation; it can be confidently affirmed that he did.

It is difficult to prove that Shakespeare consciously imitated Chapman's epic diction. However, his "When rank Thersites opes his mastic jaws, / We shall hear music, wit and oracle" (*Troilus and Cressida,* I, iii, 73–74) is incontrovertibly derived from Chapman. The application of the imagery is Chapman's and is not to be found in Homer, or anywhere else. Indeed, Shakespeare's conception of Thersites stemmed from Chapman:

> The filthiest Greek that came to Troy
> A man of tongue, whose raven like voice a tuneless jarring kept,
> Who in his rank mind copy had of unregarded words,
> That rashly and beyond all rule used to oppugn the Lords . . .
> To mighty Thetides
> And wise Ulysses he retain'd much anger and disease
> For still he chid them eagerly; and then against the state
> Of Agamemnon he would rail.
> (1598 ed., II, 205–216)

And Shakespeare's character does rail at Agamemnon at his first entrance.

It is significant, too, that Shakespeare drew material from Books I, II, VII, IX, XI and XVII of the *Iliad,* but ignored Books III through VI which Chapman had not yet translated. It is not maintained that Shakespeare knew no more of the *Iliad* than Chapman had given him, but that he apparently had read his contemporary with considerable interest, picking up a detail here, a hint for character there, and had generally refreshed his memory of the old tales. [The standard edition of Chapman's plays is by Thomas Marc Parrott, *The Tragedies* (1910), *The Comedies* (1914), now reprinted in four volumes, 1961; of the *Poems,* by Phyllis Brooks Bartlett, 1941, reprinted, 1962. See also *Chapman's Homer . . . ,* Allardyce Nicoll, ed. 1956. The only satisfactory full length and general book on Chapman is Jean Jacquot, *George Chapman . . . sa vie, sa poésie, son théâtre, sa pensée,* 1951 which contains a valuable bibliography.]—R.H.B.

character criticism. Term used to refer to the emphasis in some Shakespearean criticism placed on Shakespeare's capacity to create convincing and memorable characters. The development began in the late 18th century with the publication of Maurice Morgann's *An Essay on the Dramatic Character of John Falstaff* (1777). With the gradual triumph of Romanticism and its consequent emphasis on individuality, the preoccupation with the problems of character—notably that of Hamlet—came to be considered the most fruitful critical approach to the plays. This was particularly true in the criticism of Coleridge and Hazlitt. By the Victorian period this approach had reached, at its extreme, a tendency to view the characters in the plays as living people with biographies that might be reconstructed by an ingenious critic. Thus, in 1851–1852 Mary Cowden Clarke published in three volumes *The Girlhood of Shakespeare's Heroines,* an attempt to picture the life of the major female figures in the plays before the opening of the plays.

After Coleridge, character criticism achieved its finest expression with the publication of A. C. BRADLEY's *Shakespearean Tragedy* (1904), a book which dominated critical thought for many years. The reaction against Bradley was signaled by the HISTORICAL CRITICISM of E. E. Stoll but achieved its most celebrated expression in L. C. Knight's essay "How Many Children Had Lady Macbeth?" (1933), which came to be regarded as a manifesto of the "new critics'" approach to Shakespeare. Since the 1930's pure character criticism has been replaced by a more sophisticated concept of character as an inseparable aspect of the entire design of the play, as individual embodiments of ideas, values, and attitudes. Recently, however, there has been discernible a tendency to a view in which character is once again dominant as the instrument by means of which the author recreates a unique and intensely human, personalized xperience. See CRITICISM—20TH CENTURY. [L. C. Knights, "The Question of Character in Shakepeare," *More Talking of Shakespeare*, John Garrett, d., 1959.]

Charlecote. See Sir Thomas LUCY.

Charles. In *As You Like It*, Duke Frederick's wrestler. Charles challenges all comers, but, on learning of Orlando's intention to wrestle with him, he sks Oliver to dissuade his brother from the match ince Orlando is bound to be injured and disgraced. Oliver, in the hope that the wrestler will kill Orlando, naliciously incites Charles against him. At the conest, however, Orlando defeats the wrestler, who carried away half-dead.

Charles I (1600–1649). King of England (1625–649). The second son of James I and Queen Anne, Charles succeeded his father as king in 1625. In the ame year he married Henrietta Maria, the daughter of Henry IV of France. Very early in his reign he was drawn into conflict with parliament; in 1629 he dissolved the existing body, refusing to call another or the next 11 years. In 1640, the rebellion of the Scots forced him to convene parliament in order to aise revenues to put down the rebellion. The new parliament proved completely intractable, however; Charles' attempt to arrest five of its members was to provoke the civil war which erupted in 1642. In 646 Charles surrendered to the Scots, who then turned him over to the English parliament. Three years later, on January 30, 1649, he was executed.

CHARLES I. PORTRAIT BY VAN DYCK. (NATIONAL PORTRAIT GALLERY)

Charles and his queen were active and enthusiastic patrons of the drama. Charles himself collaborated on a play, *The Gamester* (1633), with James Shirley. After Charles' execution, one of the Puritan justifications for the regicide was based on his dissolute character, exemplified for them in his love of plays. As one Puritan pamphlet expressed it, he would have succeeded as king "Had he but studied Scripture half so much as Ben: Johnson or Shakespear . . . ." See Samuel BUTLER.

Charles VI (1368–1422). King of France, son of Charles V and Jeanne of Bourbon. Because Charles succeeded to the throne at the age of 12, his uncles struggled for the royal power. Eventually emerging victorious, Charles himself began to govern in 1388, conducting affairs ably until the first of his many attacks of insanity. At this juncture his uncles regained power.

In 1396 the king's daughter Isabella was married to Richard II of England, thus securing peace between the two countries until the Lancastrian revolution in 1399. Then there sprang up two factions, one led by the count of Armagnac, the other by John the Fearless, duke of Burgundy, who in 1411 made a treaty with Henry IV of England. The king appealed to the Armagnacs for help, but when in 1415 Henry V invaded the divided country, he won a decisive victory at Agincourt. Civil war continued in France until the treaty of Troyes was concluded (1420). By its terms Henry V became master of France.

In *Henry V*, Charles appears as the French King who yields to the demands of King Henry by granting him the hand of his daughter Katharine and acknowledging him heir to the French crown.

Charles VII (1403–1461). King of France, fifth son of Charles VI and Isabella of Bavaria. He became dauphin in 1417 and was crowned at Rheims in 1429, two months after Orléans was taken by Joan of Arc. There followed 15 years of anarchy, as French and English armed men roamed the country. At last, however, the French people drove the English from France. In *1 Henry VI*, Charles appears first as the Dauphin, later as King. He is in love with Joan la Pucelle, after whose capture he dispiritedly allows himself to be reduced to the position of viceroy, subject to Henry.

Charles' Men. See PRINCE CHARLES' MEN.

Charlton, Henry Buckley (1890–1961). Scholar. Educated at the universities of Leeds and Berlin, Charlton became professor of English literature at the University of Manchester and on occasion served in various administrative posts. His early works include *Castelvetro's Theory of Poetry* (1912) and *The Senecan Tradition in Renaissance Tragedy* (1921; reissued, 1946). In 1939 he delivered the British Academy Annual Shakespeare Lecture, "*Romeo and Juliet* as Experimental Tragedy." Charlton is best known for his two general works, *Shakespearian Comedy* (1938) and *Shakespearian Tragedy* (1948). The latter is a development and refinement of the psychological approach which A. C. Bradley used in his *Shakespearean Tragedy*. Noting that the assault on Bradley has been the most striking trend of the past generation in the interpretation of the tragedies, Charlton proclaimed himself "a devout Bradleyite" whose approach would be that of "the Bradley outlook." Like Bradley, he concentrates on the four major tragedies—*Hamlet, Othello, Macbeth,* and *King Lear*—but he also makes passing remarks on the others and includes the substance of his British Academy lecture on *Romeo and Juliet.* With R. D. Waller, Charlton edited the 1933 edition of Marlowe's *Edward II.*

Charmian. In *Antony and Cleopatra,* an attendant on Cleopatra. After setting her dead mistress' crown straight, Charmian applies an asp to herself and dies (V, ii).

Chastes, Le Sieur Aymar de (fl. 1596). Governor of Dieppe. De Chastes frequently served as the king of France's envoy to England. On one of these missions, which took place in September 1596, de Chastes was required to make a hurried return to Dieppe in order to prepare to receive an English embassage to the French court. He and his servants encountered difficulty in securing post horses to take them to their ship in Dover. De Chastes and his men finally resorted to force in order to secure the horses and the resultant scandal caused a stir in Elizabethan court circles. The incident may have provided Shakespeare with the source of the horse-stealing subplot in *The Merry Wives of Windsor* (IV, iii; IV, v). See Frederick, duke of WÜRTTEMBERG. [John Crofts, *Shakespeare and the Post Horses,* 1937; William Green, *Shakespeare's Merry Wives of Windsor,* 1962.]

Chatillon. In *King John,* an ambassador from Philip II of France to John of England. Chatillon threatens the latter with war if he does not surrender the throne to his nephew, Arthur. It is probable that this character was Hugh de Chatillon, a high-ranking nobleman who attended parliament in Paris in 1223. [W. H. Thomson, *Shakespeare's Characters: A Historical Dictionary,* 1951.]

Chaucer, Geoffrey (c. 1340–1400). Poet. Chaucer's reputation in the Elizabethan age was generally quite high. He was praised by some as a forerunner of the Reformation and, ironically enough, as a serious theologian and moralist. For others, as for Edmund Spenser, he was that "well of Englishe undefyled."

Shakespeare's debt to Chaucer is revealed in *Troilus and Cressida,* which is based primarily on Chaucer's great poem *Troilus and Criseyde* (c. 1385) (see TROILUS AND CRESSIDA: *Sources*). Shakespeare drew on Chaucer's *Legend of Good Women* (c. 1386) for the accounts of Ariadne and Dido in *The Merchant of Venice* (V, i) and possibly also for *The Rape of Lucrece.* Of Chaucer's famous collection of stories in verse, *The Canterbury Tales* (c. 1387–1400), Shakespeare appears to have made use of only "The Knight's Tale." This serves as the source of the legend of Theseus and Hippolyta in *A Midsummer Night's Dream,* as well as the romantic subplot of that play. "The Knight's Tale" also provided the primary inspiration for Shakespeare and John Fletcher's *Two Noble Kinsmen.*

Chester, Robert. See LOVE'S MARTYR.

Chettle, Henry (c. 1560–1607). Printer and playwright. Chettle began his career as a printer's apprentice and eventually became a partner of the printer John DANTER. Chettle was still associated with Danter in 1592 when he edited *Groats-worth of Wit,* the pamphlet by Robert Greene which includes a famous attack on Shakespeare. In the following year Chettle published a pamphlet of his own, *Kind Harts Dreame Conteigning fiue apparations wit Their Inuectiues against abuses raigning,* and in hi epistle "To the Gentlemen readers" apologized fo Greene's abuse and vindicated Shakespeare (se GROATS-WORTH OF WIT). A reference in the epistl to Shakespeare's "honesty" is often cited by scholar seeking to determine whether or not Greene had accused Shakespeare of plagiarism.

Sometime after the appearance of *Kind-Hart Dreame,* Chettle turned his hand to playwriting. H is mentioned in Francis Meres' *Palladis Tamia* (1598) as being among "the best for comedy." From 1598 t 1603 he turned out 48 plays for the Admiral's Men Of these, only five or six are extant, however. H collaborated with Anthony Munday on *The Deat of Robert Earl of Huntingdon* (1598), a play whose popularity may have prompted the "green world" setting of Shakespeare's *As You Like It;* and he wrote with Thomas Dekker a now lost play, "TROILUS AN CRESSIDA." In 1603, on the death of Queen Elizabeth Chettle penned a eulogy, *Englande's Mourning Garment,* in which he appealed to a number of contemporary writers (citing them by fanciful names) t write poems commemorating the death of the queen The reference to "Melicert" is usually regarded as a allusion to Shakespeare:

> Nor doth the siluer tonged *Melicert,*
> Drop from his honied muse one sable teare
> To mourne her death that graced his desert,
> And to his laies opend her Royall eare.
> Shepheard, remember our *Elizabeth,*
> And sing her Rape, done by that *Tarquin,* Death.

Chettle's handwriting has also been identified as one of those in the manuscript of SIR THOMAS MORE.

Chetwood, William Rufus (d. 1766). Dramatist, translator, bookseller and prompter at the Drury Lane and Smock Alley (Dublin) theatres. In 1749 Chetwood brought out his *A General History of the Stage,* where he makes the first specific reference to the story that Sir William DAVENANT was the natural son of Shakespeare. In 1750 he published in Dublin *The British Theatre, Containing the Lives of the English Dramatic Poets; with an Account of all their Plays* (published in London in 1752). The book was written while Chetwood was in prison, a fact which partially accounts for the gross inaccuracies of the work. The volume, described by W. W. Greg as "the source of nothing but error," contains a biography of Shakespeare taken largely from that of Nicholas Rowe. Appended to the biography is a list of Shakespeare's plays which includes many imaginary editions concocted by Chetwood. [W. W. Greg, "Notes on Dramatic Bibliographers," *Malone Society Collections,* I, 1911.]

Child, Harold Hannyngton (1869–1945). Author and critic. Child abandoned law for acting, and later became assistant editor of the *Academy* and the *Burlington Magazine,* dramatic critic for the *Observer* between 1912 and 1920, and, later, reviewer for The *Times.* His personal experience on the stage enabled him to appreciate all aspects of production, and he established himself as an authoritative historian of Shakespearean theatre. A contributor to The *Times Literary Supplement* for more than 40 years, he also wrote articles on stage history for The New Cam-ridge Shakespeare, a number of chapters for the *'ambridge History of English Literature*, and no-ices on theatrical figures for the *Dictionary of Vational Biography*. His other literary work in-ludes a novel, a book of poems, a book on Thomas Hardy, and the libretto for Vaughan Williams' *Iugh the Drover*.

Children of Blackfriars. See CHILDREN OF THE CHAPEL.

Children of Bristol. Company of boy actors on the acobean stage. In June 1615 Queen Anne signed a ignet bill authorizing a patent for the Children of Bristol to be granted to John Daniel. Although the roup was ostensibly under the queen's patronage, here are no records of any London performances. n 1616/7 Daniel brought the Children to Norwich. By April 1618 he had transferred his interest in the ompany to Martin Slater, John Edmonds, and Na-haniel Clay, who secured permission to play as "her Maiesties servants of her Royall Chamber of Bristoll." n the following year there is evidence (a letter of omplaint from the mayor of Exeter to Sir Thomas ake) that several adults had joined the company, lthough the group's patent had been issued for boy ctors only. [E. K. Chambers, *The Elizabethan Stage*, 923.]

Children of Paul's. An Elizabethan company of oy actors, originating primarily from the choir chool of London's St. Paul's Cathedral. The Chil-dren of Paul's' first recorded public performance in a lay took place at Christmas 1378 in a Biblical drama. Under the leadership of John Ritwise, master of the grammar school from 1522 to 1532, the Children pre-ented humanist-inspired interludes, such as an anti-utheran play given in French and Latin before Henry VIII and the French ambassadors in 1527.

The next court presentations were directed by Se-astian Westcott, master of the choir school from 557 to 1582. During Westcott's mastership the boys ecame extremely popular, performing at court 27 imes. In addition to these court productions, the Children also performed before the public in their wn quarters, either in the cathedral courtyard or in he choir school.

After Westcott's death in 1582 there is some evi-dence that the Paul's boys joined the Children of the Chapel for performances at the Blackfriars theatre. With a group of "boyes" under the patronage of the arl of Oxford, they presented two plays by John Lyly: *Campaspe* (1584) and *Sapho and Phao* (1584), oth of which Lyly brought to court in 1584. In 1584 the Blackfriars theatre was no longer available, and it is assumed that the combined performances of he boy companies ended.

Thomas Giles, almoner of the Paul's charity school, became master of the choir school on May 22, 1584. Under his direction the company gave nine court performances in four winter seasons of several plays by Lyly, including *Endymion* (1588), *Galathea* (1588), and *Midas* (1590). After Giles' mastership he boys are not listed in the court records for a period of about nine years.

In 1598 they opened their own private theatre, en-gaged John Marston and Thomas Dekker as their playwrights, and began their last period of theatrical activity. Edward Pearce (or Piers) was appointed master of the choir school in 1600, and the boys gave their first recorded court performance under his direction January 1, 1601. Several plays, however, were produced before their appearance at court, and by the end of 1600 their repertory probably included John Day's or Lyly's *The Maid's Metamorphosis* (1600), the anonymous *Wisdom of Dr. Dodipoll* (1599/1600), and Marston's *Jack Drum's Entertainment* (1600).

While they did not appear at court in 1601 or 1602, they probably produced several plays publicly, including the second part of Marston's *Antonio and Mellida* (1602), *What You Will* (1601), and *Satiromastix* (1601, co-authored with Dekker).

The Children's last performance before Elizabeth took place January 1, 1603, and their first performance for King James, on February 20, 1604. There were no court performances between 1604 and 1605, although *Westward Ho!* and *Northward Ho!* by John Webster and Dekker may have been added to the repertory during this time. Between 1605 and 1606 two plays were presented by the boy actors for Princes Henry and Charles.

The last recorded appearance of the Children of Paul's was on July 30, 1606 in the anonymous *The Abuses*, given before James and King Christian of Denmark. While a large number of the company's play-books reached the printers in 1607 and 1608, it is likely that the Children's performances had been discontinued before that time. [E. K. Chambers, *The Elizabethan Stage*, 1923.]

Children of the Chapel (1501–1603) **[Queen's Revels** (1603–1605), **Children of the Revels** (1605–1606), **Children of Blackfriars** (1606–1609), **Children of Whitefriars** (1609–1610), **Children of the Queen's Revels** (1610–1616)]. The Chapel had been an established part of the royal household since the 12th century, consisting mainly of chaplains and clerks up to the 14th century. Children of the Chapel appear during the reign of Henry IV who in 1401 appointed a chaplain to be their master of grammar. In the reign of Henry VI the Children became known for their high level of musical accomplishment. The Chapel establishment moved with the rest of the court at the will of the sovereign, except to houses which already had choirs and chapels of their own. Up to 1526 the number of Children varied from 8 to 10; it was then fixed by Henry VIII at 12. The chaplains were known as the Gentlemen of the Chapel and among them was included the master of the Children.

The boys received no wages, but were, according to extant records, well fed. When their voices matured they were placed at the university or otherwise provided for. Early in the 16th century they appeared in a series of one or two plays per year given by the Gentlemen of the Chapel (until 1506–1512). The Gentlemen are not recorded in any other plays until Christmas of 1553, when they performed a morality play. The performance of a regular series of plays had in 1517 been taken over by the Children alone under the directorship of William Cornish (fl. 1509–1523). It was Cornish who was responsible for organizing the Children into a definite dramatic company in the later years of his leadership, but from the beginning his energetic spirit made itself felt, especially in the elaborate disguisings which glorified the court of the young King Henry VIII from 1511 to 1522. Nearly everyone in the court took part in the disguisings, which were often designed as a setting for interludes requiring more skilled actors. Cornish was succeeded as master upon his death in 1523 by William Crane (fl. 1523–1545), and then by Richard Bower, who held the office continuously under Edward VI, Mary, and Elizabeth, until 1561. Under Crane and Bower the Children still offered court performances, but their popularity had diminished since the mastership of Cornish.

Richard EDWARDS, who had already established an enviable dramatic reputation, followed Bower as master. At Christmas 1564/5 the Children performed what might have been Edwards' own tragedy, *Damon and Pythias*. Under Edwards' successor, William Hunnis (fl. 1566–1597), and Hunnis' deputy, Richard FARRANT, the boys performed with reasonable regularity at court until 1584, pleasing Elizabeth with their well-trained, cultured performances. Under Farrant and Hunnis the Children began to give plays in some old priory buildings in the Blackfriars precinct which Farrant had rented in 1576. Hunnis took over the lease on the Blackfriars when Farrant died in 1580, and the Children continued to perform there and at court until 1583. The complicated court records do not contain sufficient evidence to indicate what financial arrangements had been made to pay for the boys' performances at court. Their public performances were probably arranged to offset the lack of profit to be derived from performing at court. This possibility would be consistent with the policies of the queen and her economical ministers. However, by November 1583 the Blackfriars venture had proved to be financially unsuccessful, and this, together with the competition from the Queen's Men, put an end to public performances. At this time Hunnis evidently made some sort of arrangement with the Children of Paul's and the earl of Oxford and his agents, John Lyly and Henry Evans, to enable the Children to appear at court in the winter of 1584/5. That season they gave five plays, including Lyly's *Campaspe* (1584) and *Sapho and Phao* (1584). From 1584 to 1589, the Children of the Chapel and the Children of Paul's acted in eight of Lyly's plays given before the queen. For the next 17 years, however, the Children cease to be part of the history of court performances. They are recorded as having traveled to Ipswich, Norwich (1586/7), and Leicester (Michaelmas, 1591).

Hunnis died on June 6, 1597 and on June 9 Nathaniel Giles was appointed master of the Children. Three years later the Children resumed their theatrical activity when Giles, in partnership with Henry EVANS, rented a building in the Blackfriars which Burbage had converted into a theatre. The boys again became serious rivals of the adult companies. They gained the support of Ben Jonson who in 1601 produced there his *Poetaster*, ridiculing John Marston and Thomas Dekker and provoking a reply by the latter in their *Satiromastix* (1601). The acting list of the 1616 Folio of *Poetaster* contained the names of "Nat. Field, Sal Pavy, Tho. Day, Ioh. Underwood, Wil. Ostler and Tho. Marton." Giles brought the boys to court twice in January and once in February 1602. At the same time he was summoned before the Star Chamber, charged with impressing boys (under the powers granted in the royal patent) for service in his own theatre in Blackfriars. The Chamber also censured Henry Evans, who subsequently transferred his lease on the theatre in Blackfriars to his son-in-law to avoid implication in the legal action.

By December 1603 Evans had made repairs at the theatre in Blackfriars and the theatrical enterprise continued under a new royal patent which James issued February 4, 1604, calling the company "Children of the Revells to the Queene" and authorizing them to play "within the Blackfryers in our Cytie of London, or in any other convenient place where they shall thinke fit for that purpose." The patent was issued in the names of Edward Kirkham, Alexander Hawkins, Thomas Kendall, and Robert Payne. The newly patented company enjoyed a renewed success and performed at court three times between February 1604 and February 1605. They gave Chapman's *All Fools* on January 1, 1605, and by that time had added three other plays to their repertory: Chapman's *Monsieur D'Olive* (1604), *Bussy D'Ambois* (1604), and Day's *Law Tricks* (1604). In 1604 they acquired the talents of John Marston, who had himself invested in the undertaking, and wrote for the group *The Malcontent* (1604) and *The Dutch Courtesan* (1603/4). With *The Dutch Courtesan* the company found itself commencing a series of conflicts with the authorities, climaxed by the publication in 1605 of *Eastward Ho!* by Marston, Chapman, and Jonson. The aspersions cast on the Scots in *Eastward Ho!* occasioned the imprisonment of Jonson and Chapman; Marston was reported to have fled abroad. The company did not appear at court during the winter of 1605/6, although they performed such plays as Marston's *Sophonisba* (1606) and Day's *Isle of Gulls* (1606) in the Blackfriars. The conflict over *Eastward Ho!*, however, had cost the Children direct royal patronage. Thereafter they were called Children of the Revels. Day's *Isle of Gulls* gave additional offense and some of those responsible were imprisoned in Bridewell. A new reorganization of the company was imperative, and by Christmas of 1606 their direction had been assumed by Robert KEYSAR, a London goldsmith. In November 1606 a new commission, issued to Giles, dissociated the acting company from the royal chapel's "Choristers or Children." Under Keysar they took the name Children of the Blackfriars. In 1608 they encountered further difficulty when the king threatened a permanent ban on theatrical presentations because of two particularly offensive plays. The first, Chapman's *The Conspiracie, and Tragedie of Charles Duke of Byron, Marshall of France* (1608), dealt with the French king's domestic affairs and interfered with James' diplomacy (when it was published in 1608, the offending scene had been deleted). The other, which is not extant, appears to have been a play by Marston which made uncomplimentary references to the king's silver mines in Scotland. Marston was summoned before the privy council and then committed to Newgate in June 1608. When, in August 1608, the Evans syndicate's lease on the Blackfriars terminated, Burbage transferred it to a new group which represented the King's Men. See BLACKFRIARS THEATRE.

The winter of 1608/9 the company under Keysar performed three plays at court, still under the name Children of the Blackfriars. In the autumn of 1609, however, Keysar found new quarters at the Whitefriars which had been vacated by the short-lived King's Revels group. Under a new name, Children of Whitefriars, they performed at court in no less than five plays in the winter of 1609/10. The autumn of 1611 found them traveling, and the summer of 1612 found them with a new director, Ralph Reeve. They visited Norwich, Bristol, and, sometime between 1612 and 1613, Coventry. (It has been suggested that Reeve's traveling company was a group distinct from the London Children of Whitefriars, however.) The London group continued under the direction of Philip ROSSETER, one of Keysar's partners during 1610 and a lutenist in the royal household. Under Rosseter they gave four court performances in 1612/3, presenting Beaumont and Fletcher's *Coxcomb* and *Cupid's Revenge*. They gave Chapman's *Revenge of Bussy D'Ambois* at Whitefriars before its publication in 1613; Chapman's *Chabot* (1613?) and Beaumont and Fletcher's *Monsieur Thomas* (between 1610 and 1616) and *The Nightwalkers* (pub. 1640) might also have been plays done by the children that season. During this time, as the Children of the Queen's Revels, they appear to have amalgamated with Lady Elizabeth's Men, and then added Prince Charles' Men to the combination in 1615. Theoretically, however, the Children of the Revels maintained their separate identity during this time. This is evident from a patent licensing Rosseter and Reeve, together with Robert Jones and Philip Kingman, to build a new theatre for the Children of Blackfriars. This theatre, PORTER'S HALL, was demolished after a short time, owing to public hostility. The one play which the Children of the Revels almost certainly gave in the new theatre was Beaumont and Fletcher's *Scornful Lady* (pub. 1616). After 1615 and the death of Philip Henslowe early in 1616, the amalgamation dissolved and the Children disappeared from the London stage. [E. K. Chambers, *The Elizabethan Stage*, 1923.]

Children of the King's Revels. Jacobean boys' acting company. The Children of the King's Revels were possibly in existence as early as the first half of 1607. Included in their repertory were Day's *Humour Out of Breath* (1608); Markham and Machin's *The Dumb Knight* (1608); and Armin's *Two Maids of More-clack* (1609).

The company was short-lived; it had tried to establish itself at a time when a performance of John Day's *The Isle of Gulls* by the Children of the (Queen's) Revels had caused a prohibition on all plays and when the plague was visiting London with particular virulence. (See CHILDREN OF THE CHAPEL.) Very little is known of the company after 1609. In 1615 a license for a company of the King's Revels was granted, but this company was primarily a provincial one. The following year, however, the company was condemned and had its warrant revoked by the lord chamberlain, and the year after that (about 1617) it was to be found touring the provinces with relics of the provincial Queen's Revels company. [E. K. Chambers, *The Elizabethan Stage*, 1923.]

Children of the Queen's Revels. See CHILDREN OF THE CHAPEL.

Children of the Revels. See CHILDREN OF THE CHAPEL.

Children of Whitefriars. See CHILDREN OF THE CHAPEL.

Children of Windsor. Company of boy actors in the Elizabethan theatre. The Children of Windsor developed from a group of six choristers of Windsor's Chapel Royal. During Elizabeth's reign their number was increased to 10. Under the mastership of Richard FARRANT, the Children gave seven plays at court between 1567 and 1576. E. K. Chambers has surmised that while Farrant was the deputy of William Hunnis, master of the Children of the Chapel, the Chapel and Windsor boys had been combined for the winter season of 1576/7. The CHILDREN OF THE CHAPEL continued to perform until about 1616, but there are no further dramatic performances recorded for the Children of Windsor. [E. K. Chambers, *The Elizabethan Stage*, 1923.]

children's companies. Name given to the troupes of boy actors in the Elizabethan private theatres. The children's companies dominated performance of the drama during the first half of Elizabeth's reign. They developed from the choir schools, some of which were established as early as the 12th century as adjuncts to a chapel or cathedral. The earliest record of boys training as performers dates back almost as far as the founding of the choir schools. For the two and a half centuries after their inception, the boys' training was concerned only with performances in old sacred dramas, the revels of the BOY-BISHOP, and Latin plays. Later in their history, the boys often performed in court pageants and ceremonies and, early in Elizabeth's reign, their main function, in addition to their religious duties, was to provide entertainment at court on holidays.

During the latter part of Elizabeth's reign, however, the children's companies were formed into regularly organized professional troupes and they began to perform outside the court. Each company had its own place in London for public performances, either at the choir school of the cathedral or chapel with which they were associated, or in a specially constructed theatre.

The number of actors varied from 8 to 12 boys in each company. They were well trained by the choirmasters of their respective schools. During the period of the boy companies' greatest popularity, choirmasters had to become theatrical managers as well. Their duties included designing pageants, writing plays, teaching the boys to act, keeping accounts, and arranging for court and public performances. The choirmasters often seriously abused their privilege of impressing boys for service in the companies.

Although the CHILDREN OF PAUL'S and the CHILDREN OF THE CHAPEL enjoyed the greatest success, other boy companies became popular as well. As a group, the boy companies seriously rivaled the adult acting companies from Elizabeth's time to the early years of the Jacobean period. The court preferred the well-trained, sophisticated, and graceful performances of the boy actors to the comparatively unpolished presentations of the adult companies. The latter, appealing to a primarily popular audience, had great difficulty establishing themselves on a permanent economic basis in London while competing with the royally-favored boys.

With the construction of the first permanent theatre in 1576, the adult companies began to gain in popularity, despite the boys' performance of John Lyly's well-received, specially-written plays for the child actors. For a short time at the turn of the century, the boy companies did enjoy a revival, once more offering the adults serious competition. Shakespeare noted the major role the boys played in the Elizabethan theatre, referring to them in *Hamlet* (II, ii, 354–357) as "an aery of children, little eyases, that cry out on the top of question and are most tyranically clapped for't." See WAR OF THE THEATRES.

By 1610 the popularity of the boy companies was in permanent decline. The adult companies had secured greater financial stability and a superior status, and the boys were no longer of any importance in the theatre. See also CHILDREN OF BRISTOL; CHILDREN OF THE KING'S REVELS; CHILDREN OF WINDSOR. [E. K. Chambers, *The Elizabethan Stage*, 1923.]—L. C.

Chiron. See DEMETRIUS AND CHIRON.

Cholmeley's Men. A provincial acting company under the patronage of Sir Richard Cholmeley who toured throughout Yorkshire in the first two decades of the 17th century. The Cholmeley's Men company was apparently made up exclusively of Catholics and their activities were watched closely by the authorities. In 1610 they were brought before a local justice to testify as to the plays they were performing. Among these indicated as being in their repertoire were "Perocles prince of Tire, And . . . Kinge Leere." According to the players' testimony they had performed these plays on two successive nights at Gowthwaite Hall, Nidderdale, in the western part of Yorkshire. The testimony is also interesting in that it indicates that this provincial company was in the habit of using recently printed versions of London plays (*King Lear* had been printed in 1608; *Pericles* in 1609) as their PROMPT-BOOKS. [C. J. Sisson, "Shakespeare Quartos as Prompt Copies: With Some Account of Cholmeley's Players and a new Shakespeare Allusion," *Review of English Studies*, XVIII, 1942.]

Chorus. In several of Shakespeare's plays, a figure who sets the background or fills in details of the plot in prologues or interludes. Before Acts I and II of *Romeo and Juliet* there are prologues spoken by the Chorus. Rumour, "painted full of tongues," recites the Induction to *2 Henry IV*, and a dancer speaks the Epilogue. In *Henry V*, each act is introduced with a speech by the Chorus. The poet Gower serves as Chorus in *Pericles*, reciting rhymed iambic tetrameter prologues to each act. In *The Winter's Tale*, the passage of 16 years between Acts III and IV is bridged by the speech of "Time, the Chorus," in IV, i. *Henry VIII* opens with a spoken prologue; and there is a spoken prologue and epilogue to *The Two Noble Kinsmen*.

Chronicles of England, Scotland and Ireland, The. See Raphael HOLINSHED.

chronology. The term referring to the problem of reconstructing the order in which Shakespeare's plays were written. Determining the chronology of the plays involves the attempt on the part of scholars to establish a date *before* which the play could not have been written (the *terminus a quo*) and the date *after* which the play could not have been written (the *terminus ad quem*). This is achieved by a study of external and internal evidence. External evidence derives from allusions to the plays in the books, records, and other writings of the period. Internal evidence derives from an examination of the style, structure, thematic patterns, and metrical characteristics of the plays themselves. Finally, there is a combination of internal and external evidence, probably the least reliable, derived from seeking in the plays allusions to contemporary events.

The two most important sources of external evidence are Frances Meres' list of plays in his PALLADIS TAMIA (1598) and the entries of the plays in the STATIONERS' REGISTER before publication. Internal evidence is considerably less exact since, despite pseudoscientific verse tests and other approaches, there is inevitably a large subjective element present. Nevertheless, there is a clear and undeniable stylistic development in Shakespeare's work which can be traced in its outline at least.

The first scholar to consider the problem of chronology was Nicholas Rowe who in 1709 speculated on "what was the first essay of a fancy imagination like Shakespeare's." Rowe, however, made no attempt to pursue his idle speculation. In 1778 Edmund Malone published his famous *An Attempt to Ascertain the Order in which the Plays of Shakespeare were written* (rev. ed. 1790), the first and most important single study of the chronology. Malone's work was extended in the 19th century by F. G. Fleay, F. J. Furnivall, and the members of the NEW SHAKSPERE SOCIETY, all attempting to establish the chronology and order of the plays by means of an intense analysis of the verse (see VERSE TESTS). Fleay's account was published in his *Shakespeare Manual* (1876, 1878) and Furnivall's in his Introduction to the *Leopold Shakespeare* (1877). The standard treatment of the chronology in the 20th century is E. K. Chambers' chapter on the problem in his *William Shakespeare: A Study of Facts and Problems* (2 vols., 1930). The dates of composition of the plays, according to Malone, Fleay, and Chambers are:

PLAY	MALONE	FLEAY	CHAMBERS
Titus	. .	. .	1593/4
1 H. VI	1589	1595, part	1591/2
2 H. VI	1591	. .	1590/1
3 H. VI	1591	. .	1590/1
M N D	1592	1592, rev. 1599	1595/6
C of E	1593	1592	1592/3
Shrew	1594	1589, 1602, parts	1593/4
L L L	1594	1591, rev. 1597	1594/5
Two G	1595	1595, completed	1594/5
R & J	1595	1596, 1st rev., 1597, finished	1594/5
Hamlet	1596	1601, 1st draft 1603, completed	1600/1
K. John	1596	1595	1596/7
R. II	1597	1593, rev. 1597	1595/6
R. III	1597	1595, Q version 1602, F version	1592/3
1 H. IV	1597	1597	1597/8
2 H. IV	1598	1598	1597/8
M of V	1598	1596	1596/7
All's Well	1598	1604, rewritten	1602/3
H. V	1599	1599	1598/9
Much Ado	1600	1599	1598/9
A Y L I	1600	1600	1599/1600
M W W	1601	1598, 1st draft 1605, complete	1600/1

H. VIII	1601	1611, part	1612/3
T & C	1602	1594, begun 1607, finished	1601/2
M F M	1603	1603	1604/5
W T	1604	1611	1610/1
Lear	1605	1605	1605/6
Cymb	1605	1608, begun 1610, finished	1609/10
Macb	1606	1606	1605/6
J C	1607	1600	1599/1600
A & C	1608	1608	1606/7
Timon	1609	1606, part	1607/8
Cor	1610	1609	1607/8
Oth	1611	1604	1604/5
Temp	1612	1610	1611/2
T N	1614	1594, begun 1601, finished	1599/1600
Per	..	1607, part	1608/9
T N K	..	1609, part	1612/3

Since the publication of Chambers' book, there has been a slowly developing tendency to date the plays somewhat earlier. Many scholars assert, with Peter Alexander, that the earliest plays were written in the 1580's and probably revised at a later date. Alexander's "approximate" chronology for the plays (given in *Introductions to Shakespeare*, 1964, and discussed in detail in *Shakespeare's Life and Art*, 1939, rev. ed., 1964) is:

PERIOD	COMEDIES	HISTORIES	TRAGEDIES
1584?	*Shakespeare arrives in London*		
	C of E	1 2 3 H. VI	Titus
	Shrew	R. III	
	Two G	K. John	
	Greene calls him "upstart crow" (1592)		
	L L L (and poems: Venus, Lucrece)		
1594	*Shakespeare joins Lord Chamberlain's Men*		
	M N D	R. II	R & J
	M of V	1 H. IV	
	M W W	2 H. IV	
	Much Ado	H. V	
	A Y L I		
1599	*The Globe theatre is opened*		
	T N		J C
	T & C		Ham
	M F M		Oth
	All's Well		T of A
			Lear
			Macb
			A & C
			Cor
1608	*King's Men take over the Blackfriars*		
	Per		
	Cymb		
	W T		
	Temp	H. VIII	
1613	*The Globe is destroyed by fire*		

Of these earlier dates the ones which have received the greatest measure of acceptance have been those given for *The Comedy of Errors*, *King John*, and *The Merry Wives of Windsor*. The arguments for earlier dating of *The Comedy of Errors* and *King John* are still being debated, but the early date for *Merry Wives* is now accepted by most scholars. For a discussion of the most recent evidence, see the *Date* sections of the entries for the above plays. [J. G. McManaway, "Recent Studies in Shakespeare's Chronology," *Shakespeare Survey 3*, 1950; Marco Mincoff, "The Chronology of Shakespeare's Early Works," *Zeitschrift fur Anglistik und Amerikanistik*, XII, 1964.]—E.Q.

Chute, Marchette (1909–). American biographer and literary historian. Miss Chute began to write professionally immediately after her graduation from the University of Minnesota in 1930. Among her early works were three books of verse for children. She is best known for three biographies: *Geoffrey Chaucer of England* (1946), *Shakespeare of London* (1949), and *Ben Jonson of Westminster* (1953). All three works are remarkable for their vivid re-creation of the times in which their subjects lived, and have won her recognition as an authority in English literary history.

Her *Shakespeare of London*, read widely by students of Shakespeare and laymen alike, presents Shakespeare from the point of view of his times, thus avoiding the prejudices and distortions of subsequent commentators. Her sources are entirely contemporary, and the result is not the mounting of a legend but the portrait of a great playwright and poet working in one of the richest periods of English dramatic history. Miss Chute has also written *An Introduction to Shakespeare* (1951) and *Stories from Shakespeare* (1956).

Cibber, Colley (1671–1757). Dramatist, actor, and poet laureate. The son of an emigrant Danish sculptor, in 1690 Cibber joined the Theatre Royal under the directorship of Thomas Betterton. He quickly developed a reputation as an actor and playwright after his *Love's Last Shift* was produced in 1696. For many years he acted as the chief playwright and manager of the Drury Lane Theatre, and in 1730 he was awarded the position of poet laureate. Cibber was so clearly undeserving of the post that he was subjected to severe ridicule by Pope, Fielding, Dr. Johnson, and others. His adaptations of Shakespeare include a famous version of *Richard III* (1700), in which he cut the play in half and inserted additional material from the other Shakespeare histories (see KING RICHARD III). Cibber's adaptation proved so popular that it was the most frequently performed version until well into the 20th century (see RICHARD III: *Stage History*). Cibber also adapted *King John* as *Papal Tyranny in the Reign of King John* (1745) in order to exploit anti-Catholic feeling in London. Despite his labors, which include the composition of over 30 plays, he is still best known as the satirical butt of Pope's second *Dunciad* (1742) and for the reminiscences of the Restoration theatre in his *Apology for the Life of Mr. Colley Cibber, Comedian* (1740). [*The Shakespeare Newsletter*, XI, December 1961.]

Cibber, Susannah Maria (1714–1766). Actress. Born in London, the daughter of an upholsterer in Covent Garden and the sister of the composer Thomas Arne, Mrs. Cibber began her career in opera. In 1736 she made her first appearance as actress, having married Theophilus Cibber two years before. She was a favorite of Handel, who wrote the part of Galatea in *Acis and Galatea*, Micah in *Sampson*, and the contralto portions of the *Messiah* for her. Mrs. Cibber developed a reputation as a great tragic actress, in spite of acting lessons from her father-in-law, Colley Cibber, known for his affected style. Garrick gave her the chance to play Constance in his revival of *King John* at Drury Lane in 1744, and she proved her great abilities beyond doubt. According to Tate Wilkinson, she was also the best Ophelia of the age. After a series of early triumphs at Covent Garden, she rejoined Garrick at Drury Lane and remained there from 1753 until her death. Contemporaries considered her the "opposite" or "sister" of Garrick, and the latter commented at her death, "Then tragedy is dead on one side." Among her Shakespearean roles were Lady Anne, Cordelia, Desdemona, Queen Elizabeth (in *Richard III*), Isabella, Juliet, Lady Macbeth, and Perdita. She was the author of a one-act comedy, *The Oracle*, which was produced in 1752.

Cibber, Theophilus (1703–1758). Actor and playwright. Son of Colley Cibber, Theophilus Cibber was educated at Winchester College and made his first stage appearance in 1721 at Drury Lane. Through the influence of his father and the patronage of literary men such as Steele, as well as his own ability, he rose in public favor. He was ugly and had a shrill voice, but these faults were balanced by technical proficiency and a certain charm. In 1731 and 1732 he was the patentee of Drury Lane, and then migrated to the Haymarket. Upon his return to Drury Lane in 1734 he married Susannah Maria Arne (see Susannah Maria CIBBER). His extravagance resulted in 1738 in his flight to France to escape his creditors.

Between 1741 and 1755, in London and Dublin, he played a great many character parts in Shakespearean plays and adaptations.

Cibber himself adapted two of Shakespeare's plays: *3 Henry VI* as *An Historical Tragedy of the Civil Wars Between the Houses of York and Lancaster in the Reign of King Henry the Sixth*, first given in 1723, and a version of *Romeo and Juliet*, first given in 1744. The published version of his *Romeo and Juliet* (1748) contains an appended "Serio-Comic Apology for part of the life of Mr. Theophilus Cibber, Comedian," an account of his difficulties in getting a license for the Haymarket.

Cicero, Marcus Tullius (106–43 B.C.). Roman statesman, orator, and writer; in *Julius Caesar*, a senator. Cicero encounters Casca in a thunderstorm and listens to Casca's narration of the portents he has witnessed (I, iii). In II, i, Cassius proposes that Cicero be asked to join the conspiracy against Caesar, but Brutus objects, saying that "he will never follow any thing/ That other men begin." After Caesar's assassination, Cicero is reported killed at the orders of the second triumvirate (IV, iii).

Cimber, Metellus. In *Julius Caesar*, one of the conspirators against Caesar. Adding his voice to those who wish to make an accomplice of Cicero, Metellus suggests that the age of the silver-haired orator would compensate for the youthfulness of the conspirators and win them the good opinion of the people. At the Senate house, he prostrates himself before Caesar to present a petition for the recall of his banished brother, Publius Cimber, thereby signaling the assassination.

Cinna, Gaius Helvius. A Roman poet. In *Julius Caesar*, Cinna is on his way to Caesar's obsequies when the frenzied mob mistakes him for Cinna the conspirator. On learning that he is the poet, the mob tears him limb from limb, just the same, "for his bad verses" (III, iii). The historical Cinna, a poet of some celebrity and a friend of Caesar's, was, in Plutarch's account, dispatched in a similar fashion.

Cinna, L. Cornelius. In *Julius Caesar*, one of the conspirators. It is Cinna's duty to throw into Brutus' window letters that are purportedly from Roman citizens who fear Caesar's ambition (I, iii).

Cinthio. Real name **Giovanni Battista Giraldi** (1504–1573). Italian dramatist and novelist. A native of Ferrara, Cinthio was a professor of rhetoric at the University of Pavia. His tragedies, the best known of which is *Orbecche* (1541), were imitations of Seneca which popularized the notion of "horror" as an element in tragedy. Cinthio is also the author of *Hecatommithi* (1565?), a collection of prose tales told on board a ship traveling from Rome to Marseilles. The most interesting stories are those of "Disdemona and the Moor," the main source of *Othello*, and of "I and Epitia." The latter story was later dramatized by Cinthio and became, by way of George Whetstone's English version, *Promos and Cassandra* (1578), the source of *Measure for Measure*. Cinthio is also the author of two *Discorsi* (1543, 1549), critical treatises on comedy and tragedy upholding the neoclassicist

TITLE PAGE OF CINTHIO'S *Hecatommithi* (1565).

DE GLI
HECATOMMITHI
DI M. GIOVANBATTISTA
GYRALDI CINTHIO
NOBILE FERRARESE.
PARTE PRIMA
PRINCIPIS AMOR, CIVIVM FELICITAS.
NEL MONTE REGALE
Appresso Lionardo Torrentino
M D LXV.

position while at the same time defending the literature written in modern languages.

ciphers. See BACONIAN THEORY.

Citizens' Theatre, The. Started against great odds by James Bridie in 1943, the ultimate aim of the Citizens' Theatre in Glasgow was to establish a genuine civic theatre. After more than two decades of private funding and innumerable crises the town council of Glasgow became actively interested and involved in the idea of a civic theatre. It was the original policy of the theatre, and continues to be, that under no circumstances must a leveling of artistic standards be permitted to take place, and the result has been a spirit of uncompromising excellence.

The Citizens' Theatre's Shakespeare productions have included *A Midsummer Night's Dream*, *Macbeth*, *Merchant of Venice*, *As You Like It*, *King Lear*, *Taming of the Shrew*, *Much Ado About Nothing*, *Julius Caesar*, *Richard II*, *Twelfth Night*, *Othello*, *Hamlet*, and *Romeo and Juliet*.

Civil Wars. An historical epic poem by Samuel DANIEL dealing with events in English history from the reign of Richard II (1377–1399) to the accession (1485) of Henry VII. The work was published in two parts; in 1595 as *The First Fowre Bookes of the civile warres* . . . and in 1609, enlarged and revised, as *The Civile Wares betweene the Howses of Lancaster and Yorke* . . . . The poem was an important source of Shakespeare's *Richard II*, and it was also used by the dramatist for his Henry IV plays and *Henry V*. Shakespeare was indebted to Daniel in *Richard II* for the details of John of Gaunt's apostrophe to England and for the opening scene in Act V in which Queen Isabella meets her now deposed husband, Richard. Daniel on the other hand seems to have drawn upon Shakespeare's plays when revising his poem for the 1609 edition. The most striking change which Daniel introduced in his revision was to modify considerably his portrait of Richard, bringing it closer to that presented in Shakespeare's play. [*Samuel Daniel's The Civil Wars*, Laurence Michel, ed., 1958.]

claimants. Persons other than Shakespeare to whom his works have been attributed. The earliest claimant was Francis Bacon, whose claim to authorship of the plays was advanced as early as 1769. The BACONIAN THEORY held the field among "anti-Stratfordians" for more than a century. Since the late 19th century, however, Bacon's claims have been overshadowed by those of a growing roster of other prominent Elizabethans. Among the hypotheses most diligently put forward have been the MARLOVIAN THEORY, the OXFORDIAN THEORY, the RUTLAND THEORY, and the DERBYITE THEORY.

Claims have also been put forward for the following as full or part authors:

William Alexander, earl of Stirling
Anthony Bacon (Francis Bacon's brother)
Barnabe Barnes
Richard Barnfield
Sir John Bernard
Sir Charles Blount, Lord Mountjoy, earl of Devonshire
Richard Burbage
Robert Burton
William Butts
Robert Cecil, earl of Salisbury
Henry Chettle
Samuel Daniel
Thomas Dekker
Robert Devereux, 2nd earl of Essex
Walter Devereux, 1st earl of Essex
John Donne
Michael Drayton
Sir Edward Dyer
Queen Elizabeth
Henry Ferrers
John Fletcher
John Florio
Robert Greene
Bartholomew Griffin
Thomas Heywood
The Jesuits
Ben Jonson
Thomas Kyd
Thomas Lodge
John Lyly
Mary, queen of Scots
Thomas Middleton
Anthony Munday
Thomas Nashe
Henry, Lord Paget
George Peele
Henry Porter
Sir Walter Raleigh
The Rosicrucians
Thomas Sackville, Lord Buckhurst, earl of Dorset
Sir Anthony Shirley
Elizabeth Sidney, countess of Rutland
Mary Sidney, countess of Pembroke
Sir Philip Sidney
Wentworth Smith
Edmund Spenser
William Warner
Thomas Watson
John Webster
Anne Whateley
Robert Wilson
Thomas, Cardinal Wolsey
Henry Wriothesley, earl of Southampton
See also Michelangelo FLORIO.

The proponents of these theories have expended enormous ingenuity in erecting elaborate edifices of theory on unfounded assumptions. The one premise shared by all of them seems to be that such profound and wide-ranging works could not possibly have been written by an ill-educated man from the country. [Frank W. Wadsworth, *The Poacher from Stratford*, 1958; George McMichael and Edgar M. Glenn, *Shakespeare and His Rivals*, 1962; H. N. Gibson, *The Shakespeare Claimants*, 1962.]

Clarence, daughter of. See Margaret PLANTAGENET.

Clarence, George Plantagenet, duke of (1449–1478). Third surviving son of Richard, duke of York, and brother to Edward IV and Richard III. Created duke of Clarence in 1461, after Edward's accession, he married the daughter of the earl of Warwick in 1469 and joined him in restoring Henry VI. But Clarence's own desire to be king compelled him to abandon Warwick and the Lancastrian party; in 1471 he rejoined Edward at Barnet and Tewkesbury and helped to re-establish the Yorkist dynasty. In 1478, on charges of plotting King Edward's murder by necromancy, Clarence was secretly executed in the tower.

In *3 Henry VI*, Clarence appears first as an ally of Edward IV. Disapproving of Edward's marriage to Lady Grey, he defects with Warwick to the Lancastrian forces; but before the battle of Barnet, Clarence turns again, deserting Warwick to support Edward. At Tewkesbury, he is a party to the murder of young Prince Edward, son of Henry VI.

In *Richard III*, Clarence appears as one of the short-lived obstacles to Richard's ambitions to the throne. After King Edward, whom Richard sets against his brother, has been warned that the letter G will be his downfall, Clarence is imprisoned in the tower because his name is George. There he is murdered at Richard's command.

Clarence, son of. See Edward Plantagenet, earl of WARWICK.

Clarence, Thomas, duke of (1388?–1421). Second son of Henry IV. Clarence was killed at Beaugé after rashly attacking a superior French force. In *2 Henry IV*, the King describes Prince Hal's affection for

Clarence and urges him to be of assistance to his older brother (IV, iv).

Clark, W[illiam] G[eorge] (1821–1878). Scholar. Educated at Trinity College, Cambridge, Clark was elected a fellow in 1844 and continued in residence until 1873. He helped to found, and served as editor of, the *Journal of Philology*. His principal work was The Cambridge Shakespeare (1863–1866), which he planned and co-edited. For the first volume, John Glover was his collaborator, but he was subsequently joined by William Aldis Wright. Clark and Wright were also joint editors of the one-volume Globe Shakespeare (1864), which was based on the Cambridge text.

Clarke, Charles Cowden (1787–1877). Scholar and lecturer. The husband of the scholar Mary Cowden Clarke, Clarke was the early and beloved schoolmaster of Keats. In 1834 he began his famous lectures on Shakespeare which proved to be one of the major factors of the tremendous popular interest in Shakespeare in mid-Victorian England. Some of his lectures were published, including *Shakespeare Characters, chiefly those Subordinate* (1863) and *Shakespeare's Contrasted Characters* (1864). In collaboration with his wife, he edited *The Shakespeare Key* (1879) and a multivolumed edition of the plays (1864–1868).

Clarke, Mary Cowden. Born **Mary Victoria Novello** (1809–1898). Scholar. The daughter of a famous musician, Mrs. Clarke numbered among her friends Keats, Shelley, Lamb, and Leigh Hunt. She married Charles Cowden Clarke, the Shakespearean scholar, and spent 16 years painstakingly compiling her *Complete Concordance to Shakespeare* (1845). Her most popular book, however, was *The Girlhood of Shakespeare's Heroines* (3 vols., 1851–1852), an extreme expression of the tendency in the 19th century to identify Shakespeare's characters as real human beings (see CHARACTER CRITICISM). She was also the editor, with her husband, of *The Shakespeare Key* (1879), a kind of topical concordance; in addition she and her husband edited a massive edition (1864–1868) of the plays.

classical drama. Strictly speaking, the plays of ancient Greece and Rome. By extension, classical drama also includes any plays of a later period which are modeled on the drama of Greece and Rome, although here the term neoclassical is perhaps more appropriate. See UNIVERSITY DRAMA.

Classical drama, in the strict sense of the term, never reached the popular Elizabethan theatres; there is no record of a classical play having been performed at a public theatre. In a broader sense, however, the influence of classical drama was pervasive and powerful, although not as powerful as the native tradition. Elizabethan playwrights had studied the classical comedies in school and from them had learned the value of a five-act structure for presenting coherent and developed plot action, something totally absent from the popular English tradition.

Classical tragedy for the Elizabethans was represented by one name, SENECA. In their plays the Elizabethans incorporated some of the standard fixtures of Senecan drama such as the moralizing chorus, the Ghost, the confidant to the hero or heroine, and the tendency to see the death of the hero as the distinguishing characteristic of tragedy. The classical influence, while it stifled the development of the drama in those countries such as France and Italy, where it completely dominated the vernacular, was beneficial in England because it was properly subordinated to the vital, productive, popular medieval theatrical tradition. (See MEDIEVALISM IN SHAKESPEARE.) The Senecan elements enumerated here can, of course, be found in Shakespeare as abundantly as in any other Elizabethan dramatist, but some scholars have suggested that Seneca's was not the sole classical influence operative on Shakespeare. J. A. K. Thomson asserts that through the biographies of Plutarch (in North's translation), Shakespeare became acquainted with the true spirit of Greek tragedy. This spirit, lacking in Seneca, is represented as a capacity to reveal, in the account of a given individual's life and death, the tragic condition of universal man. [J. A. K. Thomson, *Shakespeare and the Classics*, 1952.]

classical myth in Shakespeare. During the Renaissance there was hardly any sort of verse or prose in which a reader did not meet with classical mythology; it provided themes for sensuous poems and moral *exempla* for sober treatises. Before we come to our main concern, Shakespeare's use of myth in his plays, we must look briefly at his first formal contribution to "literature" (though it was not his first writing), that is, *Venus and Adonis*, dedicated in 1593 to the earl of Southampton. The elaborately decorative retelling of a single classical myth had already been practiced extensively on the continent, and the genre was established in England by Thomas Lodge's *Scylla's Metamorphosis* (1589) and especially by Marlowe's unfinished *Hero and Leander* (1593), which, though not printed until 1598, was widely known in manuscript. *Venus and Adonis* quickly attained second place in popularity.

Like most poems of its kind, *Venus and Adonis* was based on Ovid's *Metamorphoses:* the main story came from the 10th book; the conception of a warm Venus and cold Adonis being presumably indebted to the tale of Salmacis and Hermaphroditus in Ovid's 4th book; the boar came from the 8th book. But most of the substance is Shakespeare's own and has parallels with his sonnets and early plays; especially his own are such authentic rural vignettes as the account of "poor Wat," the dew-bedabbled hare. While the sweating Venus is passionate as well as voluble in amatory persuasion, Shakespeare seems more consistently detached than Marlowe, more coolly intellectual, and more preoccupied with the devices of rhetoric and wit (notably Ovidian antithesis). The treatment of myth in Renaissance poetry, painting, and sculpture could be learnedly and complexly allegorical and symbolical, as in Spenser, George Chapman (for example, his continuation of *Hero and Leander*), and Jonson's masques; and, our own age being steeped in myth and symbol, various recent critics have seen various symbolic themes in *Venus and Adonis,* from the ideal of Platonic love and beauty to the fall of man. Some of these themes may be there, although the recorded comments of the earliest readers show an awareness of nothing more than Ovidian eroticism. In the non-mythological *Lucrece* (1594), which appealed to "the wiser sort," Shakespeare reversed the situation and presented an innocent woman as the victim of male lust.

To come to mythological allusion in the plays, we may remember that, whether it was used by the greatest or the flattest writers, the dominant conceptions and intentions were the same all over Europe. Mythology was a language, a kind of shorthand, which embodied and illustrated the elements and forces of nature and, especially, human virtues and vices on a superhuman scale. The figures of myth might be called pagan counterparts of the angels; well-educated people knew indeed that the gods were the evil angels who fell with Satan, but that theological tradition of their origin did not restrict their literary functions. They might be evil or morally neutral or good, but in any case they symbolized power or beauty or passion beyond human limits; they freed the imagination—though seldom the moral sense—from the values and restraints of Christian belief and morality. On the other hand, they could be readily assimilated into the Christian tradition, since such pagan myths as those of the golden age and the flood seemed to be variant versions of Biblical truth; and, for such devout poets as Spenser and Milton, Pan, the god of shepherds, could stand for Christ the good shepherd. Whether or not *Venus and Adonis* develops philosophic themes, in the plays Shakespeare, like Chaucer, has small concern with the widespread allegorical uses of myth; the vision of both poets was focused primarily on individual man rather than abstract and learned concepts. Of course there may be a thin line between allegory and moral *exempla*, but Shakespeare, as we might expect, rarely goes beyond elementary and familiar ideas.

One external fact is that Shakespeare's abundant use of mythology in plays for the popular stage implies responsive knowledge in a large proportion of his audience. The grammar schools, including the one at Stratford, were wholly devoted to classical education (see EDUCATION). Shakespeare had read and could read with competence the more familiar Latin authors; he was at one with a sufficient number of playgoers to refer to classical myths as freely as a modern dramatist may refer to Freudian formulas. Besides, so many myths were common coin inside as well as outside the theatre that even the groundlings would, without books, acquire a tincture. The *dramatis personae* of the Trojan war were more familiar than the leaders in the Wars of the Roses.

Comparative statistics on allusions in Shakespeare yield little interest and enlightenment because of various factors, among them the differing material and character of the plays, the frequency of conventional items like the ubiquitous Cupid, and simplicity or complexity of reference. However, to give a brief catalogue, these are the plays with the highest number of allusions, according to R. K. Root's count in his *Classical Mythology in Shakespeare* (1903): *Troilus and Cressida*, 56; *Titus Andronicus*, 53; *Antony and Cleopatra*, 39; *Love's Labour's Lost*, 38; *A Midsummer Night's Dream*, 37; *Cymbeline*, 31; *Much Ado About Nothing*, 30; *The Merchant of Venice*, 28; *As You Like It*, 27; *Coriolanus*, 26; and *Romeo and Juliet*, *All's Well That Ends Well*, and *Pericles*, 25 each. Obviously such a list does not link high frequency of mythological allusions with either high or low quality or with comedy or tragedy; nor is it a mark of Shakespeare's novitiate, though several of the early plays are among those with the highest scores. Most of the great tragedies do not appear in the list; for them the figures are more or less low: *Julius Caesar*, 5; *Hamlet*, 19—exclusive of the player's speech; *Othello*, 11; *King Lear*, 7; *Macbeth*, 8. But what matters is the poetic and dramatic quality of allusions, and a short discussion can offer only some headings and representative examples; these last will be much more suggestive than an effort to cover more ground by way of summary description.

Shakespeare's mythology may be roughly classified either horizontally or vertically. The first way involves the simple division into comic and serious allusions, and both kinds may occur in plays of all three groups, histories, comedies, and tragedies. What was said earlier about Renaissance mythologizing implied chiefly serious uses, but comic uses were universal too, and that meant no real contradiction. It is only in an age of faith that the religious can make jokes about religion, and deep veneration for ancient moral wisdom or the ideal beauty of myth was, during the Renaissance, wholly compatible with robust irreverence. Examples on various levels might be the two kinds of fustian—both burlesques of older modes of writing—represented by Pistol (*2 Henry IV*, II, iv, 169) and the play of Pyramus and Thisbe in *A Midsummer Night's Dream;* the conscious playfulness of two very different speakers, Rosalind's disparagement of those renowned lovers, Troilus and Leander (*As You Like It*, IV, i, 97), and Doll Tearsheet's exaltation of Falstaff in comparison with Hector, Agamemnon, and the Nine Worthies (*2 Henry IV*, II, iv, 236–239); and the delicate, half-comic, half-romantic fancies of Berowne's speech on love (*Love's Labour's Lost*, IV, iii, 339). And the same myth may, in diverse contexts, run the whole gamut of emotions, comic and serious. The mocking Mercutio can say that Romeo's heart is "cleft with the blind bowboy's butt-shaft," and urge him to "Borrow Cupid's wings/ And soar with them above a common bound." The same image reappears, with others, in the giddy intensity of Troilus' sensual expectations:

> I stalk about her door,
> Like a strange soul upon the Stygian banks
> Staying for waftage. O, be thou my Charon,
> And give me swift transportance to those fields
> Where I may wallow in the lily-beds
> Propos'd for the deserver! O gentle Pandarus,
> From Cupid's shoulder pluck his painted wings,
> And fly with me to Cressid!
> (*Troilus and Cressida*, III, ii, 9–16)

To take a vertical or chronological view of Shakespeare's mythology, there is a general pattern of development, however numerous the exceptions. His serious handling of myth naturally partakes of his general literary, imaginative, and moral growth, and it carries us from the pedantry of Renaissance classicism up to a rich and individual power of re-creation. In the earliest plays—not all of undisputed authenticity throughout, though opinion nowadays is less skeptical than it used to be—the tyro's hand appears in Marlovian grandiloquence that often falls short of Marlowe's impassioned vision, in allusions that lack dramatic relevance or are worked out in undramatic detail. For one brief example out of many, while Talbot's heroic rodomontade was popular on the stage, he can, when about to be killed in battle by the French, address his staunchly loyal son with "Then follow thou thy desp'rate sire of Crete,/ Thou Icarus" (*1 Henry VI*, IV, vi, 54). A large number of allusions are merely one kind of poetic diction, the small change of Renaissance mythologizing, such as the use of the name Neptune for the sea. This sort of thing may turn up even in the most mature plays, as when Mark Antony recalls his past greatness:

I, that with my sword
Quarter'd the world, and o'er green Neptune's back
With ships made cities . . .
(*Antony and Cleopatra*, IV, xiv, 57–59)

On a higher level, many brief allusions, present in plays early and late, register the kind of human or superhuman ideal already noted as the main function of mythology. Thus Hamlet, showing his mother the portrait of his murdered father and contrasting it with that of Claudius, urges:

See, what a grace was seated on this brow;
Hyperion's curls; the front of Jove himself;
An eye like Mars, to threaten and command;
A station like the herald Mercury
New-lighted on a heaven-kissing hill . . .
(III, iv, 55–59)

Sometimes such brief references may be given an added dimension. As Professor Eugene Waith has shown, various elements of Hercules—a figure especially familiar through the Senecan plays as well as general knowledge—could be infused into some notable characters in Elizabethan and Jacobean drama. Shakespeare's many allusions are mostly inconsequential, but some acquire, or should acquire, a deeper significance when Hamlet thinks of the hero of action *par excellence*. Yet it is a question if a full effect comes through when he speaks of

My father's brother, but no more like my father
Than I to Hercules.
(I, ii, 152–153)

or when, after talking with the ghost, he declares that each muscle in his body is "As hardy as the Nemean lion's nerve" (I, iv, 83); or when, after the encounter with Laertes in Ophelia's grave, he says:

But it is no matter.
Let Hercules himself do what he may,
The cat will mew and dog will have his day.
(V, i, 313–315)

In *Antony and Cleopatra*—a play rich in both the quality and the number of its mythological allusions—more effective use is made of Hercules, whom, according to Plutarch, Antony, "this Herculean Roman" (I, iii, 84), looked back to as his ancestor. While we do not have what we might expect, a reference to Hercules' bondage to Omphale, there are two items that make a strong impact. When, as Antony's fortunes sink, his soldiers wonder at the meaning of "Music i' th' air," one explains

'Tis the god Hercules, whom Anthony loved
Now leaves him.
(IV, iii, 15–16)

In Plutarch, it is Bacchic music and song; Shakespeare's change to Hercules was a potent dramatic and poetic stroke. Later, when Cleopatra's betrayal has brought ruin, the tortured Antony cries:

The shirt of Nessus is upon me. Teach me,
Alcides, thou mine ancestor, thy rage.
Let me lodge Lichas on the horns o' th' moon;
And with those hands, that grasp'd the heaviest club,
Subdue my worthiest self. The witch shall die . . . .
(IV, xii, 43–47)

Here the Senecan Hercules becomes Shakespearean.

Three variations on one theme, in plays spanning a large part of Shakespeare's career, will suggest characteristic stages in his imaginative and artistic growth. In the early and bloody *Titus Andronicus*, the ruthless Tamora sees herself and her ruthless lover, Aaron, in these terms:

And, after conflict such as was suppos'd
The wand'ring prince and Dido once enjoy'd,
When with a happy storm they were surpris'd
And curtain'd with a counsel-keeping cave,
We may, each wreathed in the other's arms . . .
(II, iii, 21–25)

This is merely a literal, literary, undramatic reminiscence of Vergil. But, in the moonlight dialogue between Lorenzo and Jessica, scene and emotion are vivified in a lyrical strain befitting the young lovers, Dido being modeled apparently on Chaucer's deserted Ariadne:

In such a night
Stood Dido with a willow in her hand
Upon the wild sea banks and waft her love
To come again to Carthage.
(*The Merchant of Venice*, V, i, 9–12)

Finally, on Shakespeare's highest level of dramatic relevance and tragic poignancy, there is the later Aeneas who had not quitted his Dido to found the Roman state, but had lost the world and (as he thinks) Cleopatra, too, and is about to order his freedman to kill him:

Eros!—I come, my queen!—Eros!—Stay for me!
Where souls do couch on flowers, we'll hand in hand,
And with our sprightly port make the ghosts gaze.
Dido and her Æneas shall want troops,
And all the haunt be ours.
(*Antony and Cleopatra*, IV, xiv, 50–54)

Two more passages will further illustrate the difference between the young and imitative and the mature and completely individual poet. The seductive pictures offered Christopher Sly are, quite properly in their context, literal, graceful, Ovidian description:

Adonis painted by a running brook,
And Cytherea all in sedges hid,
Which seem to move and wanton with her breath,
Even as the waving sedges play with wind . . . .

Or Daphne roaming through a thorny wood,
Scratching her legs that one shall swear she bleeds,

And at that sight shall sad Apollo weep,
So workmanly the blood and tears are drawn.
(*The Taming of the Shrew*, Ind., ii, 52–55, 59–62)

But in the half-mythic pastoral setting of *The Winter's Tale*, on the lips of Perdita, the ancient divinities come to life with the budding of the English spring:

O Proserpina,
For the flowers now that, frighted, thou let'st fall
From Dis's waggon! daffodils,
That come before the swallow dares, and take
The winds of March with beauty; violets dim,
But sweeter than the lids of Juno's eyes
Or Cytherea's breath; pale primroses,
That die unmarried, ere they can behold
Bright Phoebus in his strength . . .
(IV, iv, 116–124)

There are other kinds of mythological poetry, in Spenser and Milton, that Shakespeare did not attempt, but the reverse is no less true. If, like many of his contemporaries, he is often merely bookish, his best writing in this vein is quite unbookish, a kind of imaginative and expressive inspiration that resists analysis. [Along with Robert K. Root's now old book, mentioned above, some writings of varying focus and scope are: Thomas W. Baldwin, *Shakspere's Small Latine & Lesse Greeke*, 2 vols., 1944; J. A. K. Thomson, *Shakespeare and the Classics*, 1952; DeWitt T. Starnes and E. W. Talbert, *Classical Myth and Legend in Renaissance Dictionaries*, 1955; J. Dover Wilson, "Shakespeare's 'Small Latin'—How Much?" *Shakespeare Survey, 10*, 1957; Eugene M. Waith, *The Herculean Hero in Marlowe, Chapman, Shakespeare & Dryden*, 1962; D. Bush, *Mythology and the Renaissance Tradition in English Poetry*, rev. ed., 1963.]—D.B.

Claudel, Paul [Louis Charles Marie] (1868–1955). French dramatist, poet, and diplomat. Claudel has been likened to Shakespeare more often than any other Frenchman by his compatriots—admirers and detractors alike. He was often suggested as the ideal translator of the plays, but although he did some translation (e.g., Aeschylus, and the English Catholic poets Francis Thompson and Coventry Patmore) he never turned to Shakespeare. He did, however, comment on Shakespeare, and interestingly. A fervent Catholic, Claudel expressed a repugnance for Shakespeare's world as one without God, measured solely in human terms. The loss of heaven in Shakespeare imparts to his plays an unrelieved horror, suffering, and darkness in the absence of the sense that there exists something more important than human affairs. Alive to the poetry and passion of Shakespeare, Claudel was nevertheless deterred by what he considered Shakespeare's secular humanism. For Claudel, Shakespeare's psychological profundity lacked a correspondingly profound metaphysic.

Like many French commentators, Claudel also compared Shakespeare unfavorably with Racine. Racine, he felt, was more ordered in composition and maintained a perfect equilibrium between passion and logic. [Henri Peyre, "Shakespeare and Modern French Criticism," *The Persistence of Shakespeare Idolatry*, Herbert Schueller, ed., 1964.]

Claudio. In *Measure for Measure*, a young Viennese gentleman, Isabella's brother. The first victim of the reform Deputy's stern rule, Claudio is condemned to death under an old blue law for having "upon a true contract got possession of Juliet's bed." His betrothed is pregnant and he is to be made an example to any whose morals would be as lax. When his sister reveals to Claudio that his life might be spared at the loss of her honor, he nobly agrees with Isabella that "O heavens! it cannot be!" But soon overwhelmed by visions of death, he suffers a moment of weakness and pitiably begs her to sacrifice her virtue for his life. The fierceness of his sister's attack on his cowardice causes Claudio to regret his moral lapse and he asks for Isabella's pardon "so out of love with life that [he] will sue to be rid of it."

Claudio. In *Much Ado About Nothing*, a young Florentine lord. Having accomplished "in the figure of a lamb the feats of a lion," Claudio turns from warring to look at Hero with a lover's eyes. He soon becomes, however, a victim of his own credulity, first suspecting Don Pedro of wooing Hero for himself. This suspicion dispelled and his betrothal announced, Claudio's vision is clouded by Don John's slander. Renouncing his intended bride before the wedding assembly, he accuses her of being "an approved wanton." When Borachio reveals the deception perpetrated by Don John, Claudio is filled with remorse. In reparation to Hero's father, Leonato, he agrees to publicize the presumably dead girl's innocence by hanging an epitaph on her tomb and, after this, to marry Leonato's niece, whom Leonato describes as "almost a copy of my child." When Claudio's masked bride is unveiled, he discovers "another Hero."

Claudius. In *Hamlet*, the King of Denmark, Hamlet's uncle, and the murderer of Hamlet's father. As a villain Claudius has none of the diabolism of Iago in *Othello* or the defiant rationalism of Edmund in *King Lear*. Claudius is on the other hand a much more believable figure. While capable of ruthlessly pursuing his goals, he is at the same time privately remorseful. He is both smooth and subtle, yet expresses sincere emotion, notably in his relationship with his wife. The strain of his guilt is revealed only obliquely, as in the various allusions to his excessive drinking. The result is a character who is less theatrically effective than Shakespeare's other villains but, to many critics, more interesting.

Claudius. In *Julius Caesar*, a servant (see VARRO AND CLAUDIUS).

Clayton, John (fl. 1593–1600). A yeoman of Willington, Bedfordshire, who, in 1600, was sued for recovery of a debt of £7 to "William Shackspeare." However, Leslie Hotson has discovered a "William Shakespeare" who lived in Compton, Bedfordshire, a short distance from Willington and it is undoubtedly this William Shakespeare and not the poet who was involved in the suit. [Leslie Hotson, *Shakespeare's Sonnets Dated*, 1949.]

Clemen, Wolfgang H. (1909–). German scholar. Educated at German universities and at Cambridge, Clemen has been a professor at the University of Munich since 1946. His *Development of Shakespeare's Imagery* (1951) is a revised and augmented translation of *Shakespeares Bilder* (1936). In the preface to the English translation, J. Dover Wilson notes that it is the first survey to consider Shakespeare's imagery as an integral part of the development of his dramatic art. Wilson describes Clemen's work as concentrating upon "the form and significance of particular images or groups of images in their context of the passages, speech or play in which they occur." Clemen's approach contrasts with Caroline Spurgeon's, hers being statistical in method and partly biographical in aim. Clemen's other works include *English Tragedy before Shakespeare* (1961); *Chaucer's Early Poetry* (1964), an augmented translation of his *Der junge Chaucer* (1938); and *Shakespeare's Soliloquies* (1964).

Cleomenes. In *The Winter's Tale,* a lord of Sicilia. With Dion, Cleomenes is dispatched to Apollo's temple at Delphi, and returns with the oracle's judgment that "Hermione is chaste." Sixteen years later, Leontes' penitence is considered sufficient by Cleomenes, who tells the King, "Do as the heavens have done: forget your evil; with them, forgive yourself."

Cleon. In *Pericles,* governor of Tarsus and husband to Dionyza. Gower forewarns that this benign lord "will prove awful both in deed and word." Grateful to Pericles, who has provided relief to his country during a famine, Cleon is entrusted with the care of Marina and dutifully fulfills his vow "to give her princely training." When he learns that his wife has plotted Marina's murder, Cleon decries the treachery but adds a cowardly approbation of the deed by participating in the display of mourning devised by Dionyza to deceive Pericles as to her real feelings.

Cleopatra (69–30 B.C.). Queen of Egypt (51–49; 48–30); in *Antony and Cleopatra,* the heroine. Historically, Cleopatra was the eldest daughter of Ptolemy Auletes, king of Egypt. Heir to the kingdom with her brother Ptolemy, she was driven from the throne by his guardians (49) but restored to it by Julius Caesar, whose mistress she was, and to whom she bore a son. After Caesar's death she met Antony (41) and became his mistress; she supported him against Octavius, but the defection of her fleet hastened his defeat at Actium (31). In despair at the reversal of his fortunes, Cleopatra caused a false rumor of her death to be spread, whereupon Antony took his life. To escape the humiliation of being taken captive by Octavius, Cleopatra killed herself.

Shakespeare characterizes her beauty, charm, candor, and immense fascination. She epitomizes, in the play, the sensuality and timelessness of Egypt as opposed to the immediacy of the political world of Rome. Antony's whole being responds to her influence. Constantly changing—the word "becoming" is often used in connection with her—Cleopatra represents at one time the capricious as well as the cyclical aspect of life. Her dual nature is clearly seen at the end of the play, where she practices a cheap courtesan's trick—the rumor of her death—which brings about Antony's death; but in preparing for her own death, Cleopatra attempts to shift her values away from herself, and in so doing achieves a certain nobility. She meets death sensuously—dying by holding an asp to her breast—but succeeds in making the triumphant Octavius look like a fool when he comes to fetch her. Thus she carries to the grave her enigmatic essence, confounding all attempts, whether of the romantic or the moralist, to reduce her "infinite variety" to an easily defined, limited category. [*Antony and Cleopatra,* New Variorum Edition, H. H. Furness, ed., 1907; D. G. Cunningham, "The Characterization of Shakespeare's Cleopatra," *Shakespeare Quarterly*, 1955.]

Clerk of Chatham. In *2 Henry VI,* he is hanged by Jack Cade for the crime of being able to "write and read and cast accompt" (IV, ii).

Clifford, John de, 9th Baron of Westmoreland (1435?–1461). Son of Thomas de Clifford. An avowed enemy of the house of York, Clifford is said to have murdered York's son, the earl of Rutland, after the battle of Wakefield, and to have beheaded the dead earl's father, presenting the head, bearing a paper crown, to the victorious Queen Margaret. Clifford was killed on the eve of the battle of Towton. In *2 Henry VI,* Clifford sees his father killed in battle and vows to avenge himself on the sons of York. Accordingly, in *3 Henry VI,* Clifford (now Lord) kills both the Duke of York and his son. He himself dies at Towton.

Clifford, Thomas de, 8th Baron of Westmoreland (1414–1455). Son of John, 7th lord, and Elizabeth Percy, Hotspur's daughter. Clifford campaigned under the duke of Bedford in France, staunchly supported King Henry VI on the eruption of the Wars of the Roses, and was killed in that cause at the first battle of St. Albans. In *2 Henry VI,* Lord Clifford supports the King. He persuades Cade's rebellious followers to abandon their leader in favor of Henry and fights in the royal army at St. Albans, where he is killed by the Duke of York.

Clifford Chambers. A village in the county of Gloucestershire, about a mile and a half south of Stratford. It was the home of Lord and Lady Henry Rainsford at whose home Michael Drayton was a frequent visitor. Drayton's sonnet sequence *Idea* was a tribute to Lady Rainsford (Anne Goodyere). That Drayton and Shakespeare knew each other has never been proven but is generally accepted. Shakespeare's son-in-law Dr. John Hall was Drayton's physician. A John Shakespeare (d. 1610), who may have been a relation of the poet's, lived in Clifford Chambers.

Clitus. In *Julius Caesar,* a servant of Brutus. After the defeat at Philippi, Brutus asks Clitus to kill him. He refuses, saying, "I'll rather kill myself." When the alarms signal the approach of Octavius and Antony, Clitus runs off with Volumnius and Dardanius, calling for Brutus to fly with them (V, v).

Clive, Kitty [Catherine] (1711–1785). Actress. Kitty Clive became one of the outstanding comic actresses of her time. She made her debut at Drury Lane at the age of 17, and became a favorite almost immediately. Her first Shakespearean role was Dorinda, in the Dryden-Davenant version of *The Tempest.* Except for one season, her entire career was spent at Drury Lane. She established her reputation under the direction of Colley Cibber. When Garrick formed his company at Drury Lane, Kitty Clive came under his management. Many stories recount the blustery relationship which developed between her and Garrick. Although they respected each other professionally, Garrick opposed her obsessive desire to be a tragedienne. On the occasions she did attempt tragic roles, the reasons for Garrick's opposition were apparent. Her forte lay in low, broad comedy and she brought a robustness to Shakespeare unmatched at the time. Among her greatest successes were Catherine in *Catherine and Petruchio*, Garrick's adaptation of *The Taming of the Shrew;* Olivia; and Portia in *The Merchant of Venice.* Although Portia was a popular success, Kitty Clive herself acknowledged that her burlesque of the role was somewhat less than in keeping with the spirit of the play. She retired in 1769. [*Dictionary of National Biography*, 1885– ; *Oxford Companion to the Theatre*, Phyllis Hartnoll, ed., 1951.]

Clopton Family. Residents of Stratford. The Clopton family was the most prominent in Stratford. Sir Hugh Clopton (d. c. 1496), who served as lord mayor of London in 1491, was the builder of New Place, later owned by Shakespeare. Sir Hugh also financed the rebuilding of the Gild hall in 1492 and of the Clopton Bridge over the Avon. Sir Hugh's descendant Sir William Clopton (1538–1592) owned property in the parish of Hampton Lucy in which John Shakespeare, the poet's father, was a tenant.

The Cloptons moved from New Place early in the 16th century to an estate just outside of Stratford known as Clopton Manor. The manor achieved great notorietv in 1605 when it became known that it had served, without the owner's knowledge, as a rendezvous for the conspirators in the Gunpowder Plot. [Edgar I. Fripp, *Shakespeare, Man and Artist*, 1938.]

closing of the theatres. The parliamentary suppression of plays in 1642. The civil war between the Royalists and the Puritans broke out on August 22, 1642 and London immediately came under control of parliament. On September 2, parliament seized the opportunity to pass a resolution prohibiting plays as

> . . . spectacles of pleasure, too commonly expressing lacivious Mirth and Levitie: It is therefore thought fit and Ordeined by the Lords and Commons in this Parliament Assembled, that while these sad Causes and set times of Humiliation doe continue, publick Stage-playes shall cease, and bee forebone.

In defiance of the ordinance, a small band of players continued to perform surreptitiously. In 1647 the actors began playing again in a more or less public manner at the Cockpit, Salisbury Court, and Fortune theatres—the Globe having been pulled down in 1644. Parliament again ordered the lord mayor and justices of the peace to "suppress all publick Plays and Playhouses." Nevertheless the players continued their performances, evidently with the support of a substantial portion of the population. Parliament then retaliated with an order, dated October 16, 1647, requiring the imprisonment of all actors caught during performance. As a result of this order, dramatic performances were seriously curtailed, although never entirely suppressed, until the Restoration. See Robert Cox. [Leslie Hotson, *The Commonwealth and Restoration Stage*, 1928.]

Cloten. In *Cymbeline*, the King's stepson. Cloten, a barbaric nobleman who is a crass fool and lecherous brute, is ridiculed by his courtiers, who recognize him for the bullying coward that he is. His love suit for Imogen, who is already married, is scorned by her as being "fearful as a siege," but at the direction of his mother, Cloten bombards her with "music a-mornings."

When at the reception of Augustus Caesar's envoy this knave dismisses out of hand the Roman General's demand for tribute, there is a glimmer of some mental capacity in his verbal thrusts. Moreover, Cloten incomprehensibly attains a kind of nobility in response to the departing Lucius' request for his hand: "Receive it friendly; but from this time forth I wear it as your enemy."

This regeneration is short-lived, and learning that Imogen has fled, Cloten manifests his baseness in his attempt to pursue and ravish her. [Harley Granville-Barker, "Cymbeline," in *Prefaces to Shakespeare*, 1946.]

Clown. In *Othello*, a servant of Othello who engages in a verbal exchange with a musician (III, i, 3–32). In *Shakespearean Tragedy* (1904), A. C. Bradley acutely pointed out that most readers of Shakespeare are unaware of the existence of a clown in Othello, so brief and insignificant is the clown's role. For Bradley, this aspect of the play highlights one of the important distinguishing features of *Othello*—its painful intensity, unrelieved by humor.

Clown. In *The Winter's Tale*, the Old Shepherd's son, foster brother to Perdita, and dupe of Autolycus. The Clown is the Good Samaritan who buries Antigonus and offers charitable assistance to that "robbed and beaten" rogue, Autolycus; he is the generous swain who buys ballads from Autolycus for both Mopsa and Dorcas; and he is the wise counselor who advises his father to reveal the manner of Perdita's discovery in Bohemia. When for four hours he has been "a gentleman born," the Clown is ready to assume the licenses of this newly acquired station: to swear and lie.

Clunes, Alec S. (1912–). Actor, manager, and director. Clunes, whose parents were also actors, was born in London, and amassed considerable amateur experience before taking up the stage professionally. He played Orlando in 1934, and later that year joined the Old Vic, with which he remained until 1941. His first role was as Proculeius in *Antony and Cleopatra;* later portrayals included Octavius, Clarence, Autolycus, Edmund, Berowne, and Lucentio. In 1939 he played Petruchio, Richmond, Iago, Benedick, and Coriolanus at the Shakespeare Memorial Theatre, Stratford-upon-Avon. In 1942 he founded the Arts Theatre Group of Actors, a repertory group for whom he produced and directed more than 100 plays. In 1950 he joined the re-opened Old Vic and subsequently appeared as Orsino, Ford, and Henry V. In 1952 he played Claudius with the troupe presenting *Hamlet* at the Moscow Art Theatre. In 1957 he played a season at the Shakespeare Memorial Theatre in such roles as the Bastard (*King John*), Brutus, and Caliban. Among his many films is *Richard III.* His *The British Theatre*, an illustrated history, was published in 1965. [*Who's Who in the Theatre*, 1961.]

coat of arms. In 1596 John Shakespeare applied to the College of Arms with a "patierne" (probably the motto "non sanz droict") of a coat of arms which had been received 20 years before, preparatory to a grant. His delay in applying for a grant is due to the apparent decline his fortunes suffered in the 1580's. It is usually inferred that the reapplication at the close of John's life was made with the assistance of his son William, who, by 1596, had already established himself as an extremely popular poet (*Venus and Adonis* and *The Rape of Lucrece*) and whose reputation, as the author of the popular histories *Richard III* and *Richard II*, was steadily rising.

The grant of arms, entitling him to be known as "gentleman," was received by John Shakespeare on

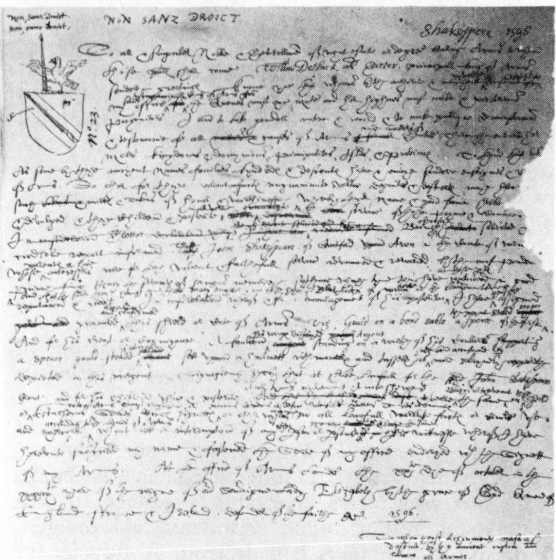

THE DRAFT IN THE COLLEGE OF ARMS OF JOHN SHAKESPEARE'S COAT OF ARMS (1596). (PHOTOGRAPH SUPPLIED BY SHAKESPEARE BIRTHPLACE TRUST)

October 20, 1596. The original manuscript on which the grant was written is decayed and a number of erasures and corrections have been made in it. In the transcript below, missing letters and phrases are placed in brackets:

> Wherefore being solicited and by credible report [info]rmed, That John Shakespeare of Stratford vppon Avon, [in] the count[e of] Warwike, [whose] parentes [& late] grandfather for his faithfull & va[leant service was advanced & re-war]ded [by the most prudent] prince King Henry the seventh of [famous memorie, sithence which tyme they have] continewed in those partes being of good reputacon [& credit, and that the s]aid John hath maryed the daughter [& one of the heyres of Robert Arden of Wilmcoote in the said] Counte esquire, and for the encouragement of his posterite to whom [these achivmentes by the a]uncyent custome of the Lawes of Arms maye descend. I the Said G[arter king] of Arms have assigned, graunted, and by these presentes confirmed: This shi[eld] or [cote of] Arms, viz. Gould, on a Bend Sables, a Speare of the first steeled argent. And for his creast or cognizaunce a falcon his winges displayed Argent standing on a wrethe of his coullers: suppo[rting] a Speare Gould steeled as aforesaid sett vppon a helmett with mantelles & tasselles as hath ben accustomed and doth more playnely appeare depicted on this margent: Signefieing hereby & by the authorite of my office aforesaid ratefieing that it shalbe lawfull for the said John Shakespeare gentilman and for his children yssue & posterite (at all tymes & places convenient) to beare and make demonstracon of the same Blazon or Atchevment vppon theyre Shieldes, Targetes, escucheons, Cotes of Arms, pennons, Guydons, Seales, Ringes, edefices, Buyldinges, vtensiles, Lyveries, Tombes, or monumentes or otherwise for all lawfull warlyke factes or ciuile vse or exercises, according to the Lawes of Arms, and customes that to gentillmen belongethe without let or interruption of any other person or persons for vse or bearing the same. In wittnesse & perpetuall remembrance hereof I have herevnto subscribed my name & fastened the Seale of my office endorzed with the signett of my Arms. At the office of Arms London the xx daye of October the xxxviiith yeare of the reigne of our Soueraigne Lady Elizabeth by the grace of God Quene of England, France and Ireland Defender of the Fayth etc. 1596.
>
> This John shoeth A patierne herof vnder Clarent Cookes hand.
> —paper. xx years past.
>
> A Justice of peace And was Baylyue The Q officer & cheff of the towne of Stratford vppon Avon xv or xvi years past.
>
> That he hath Landes & tenementes of good wealth, & substance 500^{li}.
>
> That he ma[rried a daughter and heyre of Arden, a gent. of worship].

Three years later in 1599 John Shakespeare requested the right to bear the arms of his wife's family impaled upon his own. The request was apparently granted, although William Shakespeare's monument bears only the Shakespeare arms.

Both grants were made by William Dethick, who was Garter king of arms. Dethick had many enemies, among whom was Ralph Brooke, herald of Yorkshire, who in 1602 claimed that Dethick, motivated by greed, had granted arms to 23 unworthy "base persons." Among the 23 persons listed was John Shakespeare. John, however, by virtue of having served as a bailiff of Stratford was fully entitled to the grant. The arms were later used by Shakespeare's daughter and son-in-law, Susanna and John Hall, impaled on those of Hall.

The motto of Shakespeare's coat of arms, "non sanz droict" ("not without right"), is thought to be parodied in Ben Jonson's *Every Man Out of his Humour* (1599) where Sogliardo's coat of arms is described by another character as "Let the word be, *not without mustard*." [E. K. Chambers, *William Shakespeare*, 1930.]

Cobham, Henry Brooke, 8th Lord (d. 1619). The son of William Brooke, 7th Lord Cobham and lord chamberlain. Cobham was a familiar figure in Elizabethan court circles. He was early allied to that faction opposed to the earl of Essex, who strove unsuccessfully to prevent Cobham's appointment to the office of warden of the Cinque Ports in 1596.

Cobham was a descendant of Sir John OLDCASTLE, the name originally given by Shakespeare to the character Falstaff. Despite the fact that the name "Oldcastle" was changed to "Falstaff," the association between Cobham and Falstaff, in the minds of his enemies at least, remained. Thus in 1598, a letter from the earl of Essex to Robert Cecil, 1st earl of Salisbury, then on a diplomatic mission in France, contains the postscript:

> I pray you commend me allso to Alex. Ratcliff and tell him for newes his sister is maryed to S^{r} Jo. Falstaff.

The reference to the sister of "Alex. Ratcliff" is to Margaret Ratcliffe, Elizabeth's maid of honor, who was courted in vain by Cobham, the reference obviously being intended as a joke.

On July 8, 1599, the wife of the earl of Southampton, Shakespeare's patron and a close friend of Essex, wrote to her husband, who was at that time in Ireland with Essex:

> Al the nues I can send you that I thinke will make you mery is that I reade in a letter from London that Sir John Falstaf is by his M[rs] Dame Pintpot made father of a go[o]dly milers thum, a boye thats all heade and veri litel body, but this is a secrit.

Leslie Hotson has pointed out that the reference to "milers thum" in the letter is a further allusion to Cobham, since "cob," a type of fish, was also known as a "miller's thumb." At this time Cobham was also negotiating a marriage with the daughter of Charles Howard, lord admiral. Hotson suggests that the attempt of the Admiral's Men to vindicate the original Oldcastle in their play SIR JOHN OLDCASTLE may have been as the result of a request by the lord admiral or his daughter. [Leslie Hotson, *Shakespeare's Sonnets Dated*, 1949.]

Cobham, William Brooke, 7th Lord (d. 1597). Courtier, diplomat, and lord chamberlain of Elizabeth's household from August 1596 until his death on March 5, 1597. Cobham was a direct descendant of Sir John OLDCASTLE, the 15th-century soldier whose name Shakespeare originally gave to Falstaff in *1 Henry IV*. It is generally agreed that the change of name from Oldcastle to Falstaff resulted from a protest by a member of the Cobham family, either William or his son Henry Brooke, who succeeded his father as 8th Lord Cobham in 1597. Coupled with this is the striking fact that the name which Master Ford assumes in *The Merry Wives of Windsor* was originally "Brooke," not "Broome," the name that appears in the First Folio. As in the Oldcastle case there had apparently been a name change in order to avoid offending the powerful Cobhams.

Leslie Hotson (*Shakespeare Versus Shallow*, 1931) argues that these two affronts to the Cobham family were intentionally directed at William Brooke as the result of an alleged antitheatrical bias which he displayed as lord chamberlain. Other scholars have suggested that the insults were directed at William's son Henry (see Henry Brooke, 8th Lord COBHAM), who was an archenemy of the earls of Essex and Southampton, Shakespeare's patron. William Green (*Shakespeare's Merry Wives of Windsor*, 1962), however, argues that the affronts were unintentional, that Shakespeare derived the name "Oldcastle" directly from the source play, *The Famous Victories of Henry the Fifth*, and that the name Brooke was hit upon as a punning parallel to "Ford," but that it was probably changed during rehearsals of the comedy when the similarity to Cobham's name was realized.

Cobler of Preston, The. The title of two plays, both adaptations of the Induction to *The Taming of the Shrew* (see TAMING OF THE SHREW: *Stage History*). The two plays, written in January of 1716, were produced by rival companies at the Drury Lane and Lincoln's Inn Fields theatres. The author of the play produced at Drury Lane was Charles JOHNSON, who was later to adapt *As You Like It* to the 18th-century stage as *Love in a Forest*. The play at Lincoln's Inn Fields was written by Christopher BULLOCK, who began work on his play when he heard that Johnson's work was in progress. Bullock's version proved to be more popular and held the stage for a number of years.

Cobweb. In *A Midsummer Night's Dream*, one of Queen Titania's fairies. Cobweb is commissioned by Bottom to kill a bee and bring him its honey-bag (IV, i).

cockfighting. See BEARBAITING, BULLBAITING, AND COCKFIGHTING.

cockpit at court. An octagonal cockpit located near St. James Park on the grounds of Whitehall Palace. The cockpit at court was apparently built in 1604 by King James I and used for both cockfights and occasionally for plays. In the early Jacobean era it was the scene of plays given for Princess Elizabeth and Prince Henry. The office-book of Sir Henry Herbert, Master of the Revels, records the performance there of three Shakespearean plays in 1639:

> . . . At the Cocpit the 29th of May the princes berthnyght —ould Castel [probably *1 Henry IV*] At the Cocpit the 13th of November —Caeser. At the Cocpit the 15th of November —The mery wifes of winsor.

[G. E. Bentley, *The Jacobean and Caroline Stage*, 5 vols., 1941–1956.]

Cockpit theatre. See PHOENIX THEATRE.

Coghill, Nevill (1899–). Scholar, since 1957 Merton professor of English literature at Oxford. Coghill's work on William Langland includes the introduction to H. W. Wells' modernized version of *The Visions of Piers Plowman* (1935); "The Pardon of Piers Plowman," Gollancz Memorial Lecture, British Academy (1945); and his own modernized version, *Visions from Piers Plowman* (1949). He also wrote a modernized version of *The Canterbury Tales* (1951) and two popular introductions to Chaucer, *The Poet Chaucer* (1949) and *Geoffrey Chaucer* (1956). Active in the Oxford University Drama Commission, Coghill has numerous Shakespearean productions to his credit. His practical experience is reflected in *Shakespeare's Professional Skills* (1964), in which he discusses production problems, the soliloquies, the juxtaposition of scenes, and similar matters; there is also an essay revaluating *Troilus and Cressida*.

Cokayne or **Cokain,** Sir **Aston** (1608–1684). Poet. A member of an ancient and wealthy family, Cokayne owned several large estates, his favorite being located in Shakespeare's native county of Warwickshire. In his poetry he frequently refers to the county and to Shakespeare.

Cokayne was also a devoted patron of the theatre. His other great passion was "a fine little glass" as is evidenced in this poem which alludes to the Induction of *The Taming of the Shrew:*

> *Shakspeare* your *Wincot*-Ale hath much renownd,
> That fo'xd a Beggar so (by chance was found
> Sleeping) that there needed not many a word
> To make him to believe, he was a Lord:
> But you affirm (and in it seem most eager)
> 'Twill make a Lord as drunk as any Beggar.

Bid *Norton* brew such Ale as *Shakspeare* fancies
Did put *Kit Sly* into such Lordly trances:
And let us meet there (for a fit of Gladness)
And drink our selves merry in sober sadness.

The poem is addressed to "*Mr.* Clement Fisher *of* Wincott," which is Wilnecote, a small village near Stratford. [E. K. Chambers, *William Shakespeare*, 1930.]

Coleman, Charles. See MUSIC BASED ON SHAKESPEARE: *17th century*.

Coleridge, Samuel Taylor (1772–1834). Poet and critic. Born at Ottery St. Mary in Devonshire, Coleridge was educated at Christ's Hospital in London. He attended Jesus College, Cambridge for about three years, but did not receive a degree. His friendship with William Wordsworth, whom he met in 1795, coincides with the period of Coleridge's greatest achievement as a poet. To this period belong *Kubla Khan* (1797?, pub. 1816), *The Rime of the Ancient Mariner* (1798), and *Christabel* (First Part, 1797; Second Part, 1800; pub., 1816). Wordsworth and Coleridge together published *Lyrical Ballads* in 1798. In the same year they traveled to Germany where Coleridge steeped himself in German criticism and philosophy; he studied philosophy at the Göttingen university and mastered the German language.

The most significant English literary critic of his time, Coleridge's critical works include *Biographia Literaria* (1817) and *Literary Remains* (1836–1839). His criticism of Shakespeare ranks, by most standards, as the finest of the romantic period and, as far as British criticism is concerned, may be said to mark the effective beginning of a new and truly sympathetic approach to the plays.

Characteristically, Coleridge never collected or collated his Shakespearean criticism in any cohesive form and only two essays on Shakespeare were ever actually put together and seen through the press by him: "The specific symptoms of poetic power elucidated in a critical analysis of Shakespeare's *Venus and Adonis* and *The Rape of Lucrece*" (published as Chapter XV of *Biographia Literaria*) and "On Method in Thought" (published as the General Introduction to *Encyclopaedia Metropolitana*, 1818, and in the same year revised and published in *The Friend*). The entire bulk of what remains exists in the form of lecture notes, coherent and otherwise, marginalia, passing mentions in letters, newspaper reports, shorthand notes taken by members of lecture audiences, records of dinner-table conversations, and the accounts of a diarist. The most reliable reports of the lectures were not in fact even generally available until 1883 when Thomas Ashe collected J. P. Collier's shorthand notes, together with those of an anonymous Bristol reporter, some records from London newspapers, and some details from the diary of Henry Crabb Robinson, in his edition of Coleridge's *Lectures and Notes on Shakespeare and other English Poets* published in that year. An inaccurate conflation of marginalia and fragments of lecture notes, which had earlier been made by the poet's nephew H. N. Coleridge, was published in *Literary Remains* and enjoyed acceptance as a "standard" text in many later editions. Not until 1930 was that garbled version replaced by T. M. Raysor's edition of *Coleridge's Shakespearean Criticism* which, by printing Coleridge's own words from the original manuscripts, became and has remained definitive (a second, slightly revised edition was published in 1960 by Everyman's Library).

Most of this material comprises the remains of at least seven or eight courses of lectures on literary and philosophical topics given between 1808 and 1819 in London and Bristol. Slightly less than half of the lectures seem to have been concerned directly with Shakespeare, in particular with seven plays, *Richard II*, *Romeo and Juliet*, *Hamlet*, *Othello*, *Macbeth*, *The Tempest*, *Love's Labour's Lost*, and with the narrative poems. *King Lear* was apparently somewhat skimped; the marginalia and notes on the play are relatively sketchy, and Coleridge pronounced it "not a good subject for a whole lecture, in *my* style." *Antony and Cleopatra* he hardly touched on, though a manuscript note refers to it as "of all perhaps of Shakespeare's plays the most wonderful." The *Sonnets* were neglected, *Measure for Measure* misunderstood ("It is a hateful work"), and a course of lectures on the comedies, though planned, seems never to have been given.

The lectures suffered by remaining unpublished in Coleridge's lifetime, for the digressions, which indicate a lively responsiveness to his audience, inevitably detract from their trenchancy and would, hopefully, have been cut from a printed version. But the audience, for better or worse, was a popular not an academic one. It wanted entertainment as well as instruction, and since Coleridge depended on the continued admission fees for a good deal of his livelihood in these years, his style took on the anecdotal and digressive quality which delighted his listeners and, he tells us, proved most comfortable for himself.

As a result, readers have sometimes found the cold print disappointingly repetitious and fragmentary. But the repetitions, caused by making the same point to different groups of people, nevertheless frequently become revisions and restatements, and an impressive critical edifice accumulates. More often than not, too, the fragmentary remarks have a peculiar pregnancy which hints at the profundity of the intended oral expatiation. Some of these, for example the well-known comment on *Othello*, ". . . The last speech, Iago's soliloquy, shows the motive-hunting of motiveless malignity—how awful!" have a vital quality not only delightful in themselves but perfectly in keeping with Coleridge's avowed purpose to "keep the audience awake and interested during the delivery, and to leave a *sting* behind—i.e., a disposition to study the subject anew, under the light of a new principle."

That principle seems to have been twofold. As early as 1804, in a letter to Sir George Beaumont, Coleridge had spoken of his intention to "exhibit the characteristics of the Plays—and of the mind—of Shakespeare" by means of a consideration of

> the Diction, the Cadences and Metre, the character, the passion, the moral or metaphysical Inherencies and fitness for theatric effect

of the plays, and a discussion of

> what proportion they bear to each other . . . so as to see and be able to prove what of Shakespeare belonged to his Age and was common to all the

first-rate men of that true Saeculum aureum of English Poetry, and what is his own and his only . . . .

This ambitious plan was never fulfilled. However, glimpses of it recur, together with hints of an even grander design. In 1807, Coleridge wrote to Sir Humphry Davy about a proposed course of lectures on "The Principles of Poetry as illustrated by Shakespeare, Spenser, Milton, Dryden, Pope, and modern poetry" of which five lectures would be devoted to "the genius and writings of Shakespeare." In them, he proposed to expound

> the whole result of many years' continued reflection on the subjects of taste, imagination, fancy, passion, the source of our pleasures in the fine arts, on the *antithetical* balance-loving nature of man, and the connexion of such pleasures with moral excellence.

In practice, the first part of Coleridge's aim, the "placing" of Shakespeare together with his contemporaries in their cultural "background," was never completed, or even fully attempted. His achievement lies rather in the second direction which the "continued reflection" on the subjects mentioned above indicates: the treatment of Shakespeare's plays as autonomous works of art, pleasing to the "*antithetical* balance-loving nature of man" because they are products of that most remarkable of all human possessions, the Imagination.

Coleridge's notion of the Imagination (set forth in Chapters XIII and XIV of his *Biographia Literaria*) is central to his criticism of Shakespeare. The principal role of that faculty is said to be one of synthesis, balance, and the creation of harmony and unity. Imagination

> reveals itself in the balance or reconcilement of opposite or discordant qualities: of sameness, with difference; of the general with the concrete; the idea with the image; the individual with the representative; the sense of novelty and freshness with old and familiar objects; a more than usual state of emotion with more than usual order . . .

This activity represents, to Coleridge, exactly the spirit embodied in Shakespeare's plays: they are themselves unified and harmonious, they illustrate the virtues of unity and harmony, and they inculcate these in the minds of their audience.

Such ideas gain additional interest by being placed in context. The orthodox neoclassical view of Shakespeare (which held sway from the middle of the 17th century pretty well to the time when Coleridge was writing) argued that his numerous triumphs came about in spite of his numerous faults; his "natural" genius imposed itself on an essential lack of real taste, which had resulted in an abandonment of the three unities, and a consequent absence of over-all unity from his plays. Before Coleridge, this view had come under considerable attack from such critics as Lord Kames (*Elements of Criticism*, 1762) and Dr. Johnson (*Preface* to Shakespeare, 1765), but as late as 1815, in the *Essay Supplementary to the Preface to the Lyrical Ballads*, Wordsworth could still refer scathingly to the current opinion of Shakespeare as "a wild irregular genius, in whom great faults are compensated by great beauties."

However, a rigid insistence on the kind of "unity" which the doctrine of three unities was supposed to inculcate had virtually crumbled under the arguments of Kames and Johnson, and the effect on Shakespearean criticism over the years had been to arouse a compensating and equally restrictive interest in the "characters" of the plays. But however much this may seem to coincide with the romantic movement's concern with the individual, it sprang effectively from the older neoclassic source, and both antedates and is distinct from Coleridge's sort of interest in Shakespeare. Perhaps its best exemplars are Maurice Morgann's *Essay on the Dramatic Character of Sir John Falstaff* (1777) and an account of *Hamlet* by the playwright Henry Mackenzie (1745–1831) published in *The Mirror* (1779–1780), which much impressed A. C. Bradley.

In fact, Coleridge's prime concern was to demonstrate the larger *organic* unity of Shakespeare's plays, an aim much more in keeping with the true spirit of Aristotle than the mechanical dogma of time, place, and action. One of the most sustained examples of this principle at work in his criticism may be found in his account of *The Tempest:*

> a drama, the interests of which are independent of all historical facts and associations, and arise from their fitness to that faculty of our nature, the imagination I mean, which owes no allegiance to time and place,—a species of drama, therefore, in which errors in chronology and geography, no mortal sins in any species, are venial, or count for nothing.

Later on, he explains his use of terms, specifically

> what is meant by mechanic and organic regularity. In the former the copy must appear as if it had come out of the same mould with the original; in the latter there is a law which all the parts obey, conforming themselves to the outward symbols and manifestations of the essential principle. If we look to the growth of trees, for instance, we shall observe that trees of the same kind vary considerably, according to the circumstances of soil, air or position; yet we are able to decide at once whether they are oaks, elms or poplars.
>
> So with Shakespeare's characters: he shows us the life and principle of each being with organic regularity.

The purpose here is much wider than a simple attack on classicism in the name of romantic drama. The ultimate intention is to show, as Wordsworth put it,

> that the judgement of Shakespeare in the selection of his materials and in the manner in which he has made them, heterogeneous as they often are, constitute a unity of their own, and contribute all to one great end. . . . [*Essay cit.*]

A considerable degree of success must be granted to this endeavor in the bulk of Coleridge's criticism, and the absence of a certain amount of originality does not detract from that. German romanticism had been attracted to Shakespeare in much the same spirit as Coleridge, and the great German critic A. W. von Schlegel (1767–1845) had reached conclusions in his *Vorlesungen über dramatische Kunst und Literatur* (lectures, delivered at Vienna in 1808, published 1809–1811) that are in some cases indistinguishable, word for word, from those of Coleridge. In spite of the evidence, Coleridge considered the charges of plagiarism unjust. He and Schlegel, he said, had both read Kant.

Coleridge has often been assumed to be the "father" of a school of Shakespearean criticism whose major interest lies in the "characters" of the plays, and whose work is most formidably exemplified in the writings of A. C. Bradley. Accordingly, in the modern reaction against Bradley's limitations, Coleridge's criticism has acquired a kind of associative guilt, and he has not been well regarded by numbers of contemporary "historical" critics.

However, as suggested above, it can be argued that Bradley inherits a neoclassic tradition much older than, and antipathetic to, the principles on which Coleridge's view of Shakespeare rests. In fact, a more recent tendency has been to resist any such simple dismissal of his work on the ground that throughout his analyses of the plays there runs the notion that the "characters" are in some way "universal," as well as particular, embodiments of a larger vision of mankind than that of mere psychological verisimilitude. As Coleridge says, "Shakespeare's characters are all *genera* intensely individualized." Moreover, like many post-Bradleyan critics who, aware that they write from the disabling standpoint of an age in which poetry and drama are quite separate realms of activity, recognize the danger of imposing this view on Shakespeare and of treating his plays as prosaic studies of human motives, Coleridge insists that their distinctive feature is that their author was both a poet *and* a dramatist. He recognizes too the resultant "depersonalized" quality of Shakespeare's greatness which modern critics admire. Coleridge's Shakespeare is no 19th-century literary "personality" with an individual "point of view," but a "Proteus" with an "oceanic mind": he is the "Spinozistic deity—an omnipresent creativeness"—a man who himself embodied the principle of unity in multitudinousness which his "characters," by being both universal and particular, exhibit on another level.

Finally, Coleridge never leaves any doubt of his wholehearted opposition to the sort of quasi-naturalism which most "character" criticism presupposes the plays' mode to be. His ideas about the nature of dramatic illusion clearly indicate so much, dependent as they are on a typical account of Imagination:

> the Shakespearean drama appealed to the Imagination rather than the senses . . . the Imagination has an arbitrary control over both [time and space]; and if only the poet have such power of exciting our internal emotions as to make us present to the scene in imagination chiefly, he acquires the right and privilege of using time and space as they exist in the imagination, obedient only to the laws which the imagination acts by.

Hence his account of the way in which ". . . that willing suspension of disbelief for the moment which constitutes poetic faith" actually works in the theatre, in the case of poetic drama,

> to produce a sort of temporary half-faith, which the spectator encourages in himself and supports by a voluntary contribution on his own part, be cause he knows that it is at all times in his powe to see the thing as it really is.

This contains in a nutshell most modern ideas o the way Shakespeare's plays communicated wit their contemporary audience.

Of course, in practice, Coleridge frequently in dulges in character-analysis to excess (as in his analy sis of Edmund in *King Lear*) and in conjecture which reach far beyond the bounds of the play. I would be presumptuous to "excuse" such events a "lapses," or as instances of obsessiveness about psy chological matters (although members of his audi ence quickly detected a similarity between Cole ridge's version of Hamlet's "character" and himsel Nor was he unaware of this, though his reported " have a smack of Hamlet myself, if I may say so" i surely playful). But in any event these do not, as i the case of lesser critics, constitute a principle o procedure, or mark the limit of an interest.

There is no Coleridge "school" of Shakespearea criticism: he was unique, and his influence remain oblique, unacknowledged, or unrecognized. But i ought to be remembered that he outlined the whol basis of modern historical criticism, even though h never built upon it himself: his concern to plac Shakespeare in an appropriate "world-picture" wa frequently expressed. His rigorous scrutinies of th text, his interest in ambiguity, and above all hi highly developed sense of each play's autonomou unity and innate organic form are fundamentally i harmony with present-day views. Although he wa not the originator of many of these notions, Cole ridge was perhaps their most forceful expositor. Hi heirs, if he has any, are the critics of the mid-20t century. See IMAGERY. [I. A. Richards, *Coleridge o Imagination*, 1950; Barbara Hardy, "'I have a smac of Hamlet': Coleridge and Shakespeare's characters," *Essays in Criticism*, VIII, 3, 1958; Alfred Harbage "Introduction" to *Coleridge's Writings on Shakespeare*, Terence Hawkes, ed., 1959; M. M. Badawi "Coleridge's Formal Criticism of Shakespeare' Plays," *Essays in Criticism*, X, 3, 1960; *Coleridge' Shakespearean Criticism*, T. M. Raysor, ed., rev. ed. 1960; Richard Harter Fogle, *The Idea of Coleridge' Criticism*, 1962.]—T.H.

Colevile, Sir John. In *2 Henry IV*, a rebel leade captured by Falstaff (IV, iii). He may have been Si John Coleville, governor of Wisbeach Castle. [W. H Thomson, *Shakespeare's Characters: A Historica Dictionary*, 1951.]

collaboration. In literature, a term referring t joint authorship. That collaboration was a commo practice among Elizabethan playwrights is easil established from records, especially from theatre-manager Philip Henslowe's accounts in his diary Although collaboration usually involved two play-wrights (Beaumont and Fletcher in the 17th centur being the most famous example of such a partnership), Henslowe's records indicate that the practice sometimes involved as many as five hands. The reasons for such an association were usually based o necessity resulting from the arbitrary condition under which a play was commissioned. Plays generally had short runs and those that did not draw audiences had to be replaced almost immediately, creating a constant demand for new plays.

Shakespeare's collaborative efforts are difficult to etermine. Of the plays included in the First Folio, any critics believe that *Henry VIII* was done in ollaboration, probably with Fletcher. Of the plays utside the Folio, *Pericles* is generally attributed nly in part to Shakespeare, and *The Two Noble Kinsmen* is regarded as a result of another joint effort vith Fletcher. There is strong evidence to support he view that Shakespeare was a minor collaborator n the play *Sir Thomas More* and that he penned vith Fletcher the lost play *Cardenio*. Kenneth Muir as recently marshaled a strong argument for Shakespeare's collaboration on the early chronicle play *Edward III*. [E. K. Chambers, *William Shakespeare,* 1930; Kenneth Muir, *Shakespeare as Collaborator,* 1960.]

Collier, Jeremy (1650–1726). Clergyman and enmy of the stage. Collier is best known as the author of *A Short View of the Immorality and Profaneness f the English Stage* (1698), an onslaught against the lleged blasphemy and profanity of the Restoration tage. While directed at the contemporary stage, his emarks allude to Shakespeare, particularly his depictions of the clergy. He does, however, applaud he treatment accorded to Falstaff at the end of *2 Henry IV:*

> Shakespear takes the Freedom to represent the clergy in several of his Plays: [*in margin:* Measure for Measure, Much ado about Nothing. Twelf-Night. Henry 4th, pt. 1st. Hen. 6. pt. 3rd. Romeo and Juliet. Merry Wives of Windsor.] But for the most part he holds up the Function, and makes them neither Act, nor Suffer any thing unhandsom. In one Play or two He is much bolder with the Order. Sr. Hugh Evans a Priest is too Comical and Secular in his Humour. However he understands his Post, and converses with the Freedom of a Gentleman. I grant in *Loves Labour lost* the Curate plays the Fool egregiously; And so does the Poet, too, for the whole Play is a very silly one. In the History of Sr. John Oldcastle, Sr. John, Parson of Wrotham Swears, Games, Wenches, Pads, Tilts, and Drinks; . . . Shakespears Sr. John has some Advantage in his Character. He appears Loyal, and Stout; He brings in Sr. John Acton, and other Rebels Prisoners. He is rewarded by the King, and the Judge uses him Civilly and with Respect. In short He is represented Lewd, but not Little; And the disgrace falls rather on the Person, then the Office. But the Relapsers [Collier's term for the Restoration dramatists] business, is to sink the Notion, and Murther the Character, and make the Function despicable: So that upon the whole, Shakespear is by much the gentiler Enemy.

See James DRAKE.

Collier, John Payne (1789–1883). Scholar and forger. The son of a newspaperman, in 1809 Collier succeeded his deceased father as a reporter for the London *Times* and for the London *Morning Chronicle*. His study of early English literature led to the publication of his three-volume *History of English Dramatic Poetry and Annals of the Stage* (1831), as a result of which he gained access to the great private collections in the libraries of the duke of Devonshire and the earl of Ellesmere. From this source he published the first of his many books relating to Shakespeare: *New Facts* (1835), *New Particulars* (1836), and *Further Particulars* (1839). These were the first of Collier's many curious studies in which genuine scholarly discoveries were placed alongside outright forgeries. At the time, however, Collier was not suspected of fraud and his reputation as a Shakespeare scholar continued to grow. He was one of the founders of the original SHAKESPEARE SOCIETY (1840), for whom he published *Memoirs of E. Alleyn* (1841), the *Alleyn Papers* (1843), and the *Diary of Philip Henslowe* (1845). These were all edited from the manuscript collection at Dulwich College and Collier's forged entries on the original papers have created enormous problems for later scholars.

Collier's downfall came as a result of his announcement in 1852 that he owned a copy of the Second Folio (1632) which had annotations and textual emendations written in 17th-century handwriting. He published these as *Notes and Emendations to the Text of Shakespeare's Plays* (1852), but he refused to allow the Folio to be examined by experts. In 1859, however, it was deposited with the British Museum where the annotations were exposed as modern forgeries. Collier died without confessing his fabrications, but evidence found among his papers after his death gives undeniable proof of his culpability. A detailed list of his known fabrications can be found in E. K. Chambers' *William Shakespeare* (Vol. II, 384–393). Collier also produced an edition (1842–1844) of Shakespeare in eight volumes.

Collins, Francis (d. 1617). Stratford attorney who drew up Shakespeare's will. Collins was deputy town clerk of Stratford from 1602 to 1608 and town clerk from April to September 1617. He not only drew up the will, but was one of the two overseers of it, the other being Thomas RUSSELL. He was apparently a close friend of Shakespeare, since he is designated in the will for a legacy of £13 6s. 8d. [E. I. Fripp, *Shakespeare, Man and Artist,* 2 vols., 1938.]

Collins, John Churton (1848–1908). Critic. Educated at Balliol College, Oxford, Collins devoted a number of years to journalism, teaching, and public lecturing. In 1904 he was appointed professor of English literature at the University of Birmingham. He is the author of *Studies in Shakespeare* (1904) and of miscellaneous essays which have been reprinted in several collections, namely, "Shakespeare's Sonnets" and "The Religion of Shakespeare" (*Ephemera Critica,* 1901); "The Predecessors of Shakespeare" and "The Porson of Shakespearian Criticism" (*Essays and Studies,* 1895); and "Shakespearian Theatres" (*Posthumous Essays,* 1912). Among his numerous editions are the poems and plays of Cyril Tourneur (2 vols., 1878) and Robert Greene (2 vols., 1905). [L. C. Collins, *The Life and Memoirs of John Churton Collins,* 1912.]

colloquialisms. Although the language of the Elizabethan stage was to a great extent the colloquial language of the times, it contained relatively little current slang. Among the most common instances of slang usage in Shakespeare are profane oaths or their euphemistic substitutes—"God's blood," "God's wounds," "God's body," and their weakened variations such as "'sdeath," "'slife," and "zounds." There are also a number of reduplicating words, a common slang formation: "helter-skelter," "hugger-mugger," and "hurly-burly," all used by Shakespeare; and "fiddle-faddle," "flim-flam," "higgledy-piggledy," and "riff-raff," found in other Elizabethan writers. The slang of the people in general was almost certainly much more extensive than that which appears in contemporary writings; for instance, there are only a few humorous terms for drunkenness in the literature of the period (e.g., "foxed," "columberd"), but there must have been then, as now, many words in general usage. A distinct form of 16th-century slang was the cryptic jargon used by thieves and vagabonds and known as thieves' cant. Though some of Shakespeare's contemporaries, notably Robert Greene and Thomas Dekker, were interested in it, thieves' cant does not appear in Shakespeare except for a few older words, such as filch, rogue, and foist, which had already made their way into general usage. [Henry Bradley, "Shakespeare's English," *Shakespeare's England*, 1916.]

Colman, George. Called **Colman the Elder** (1732–1794). English dramatist and producer. In *Literary Offerings in the Temple of Fame*, a dream-vision published in 1753, Colman imagined all the major literary figures destroying the worst parts of their writings. Generally, the standards he employed were strictly classical. Shakespeare, however, was only purged of some puns, bombast, and "incorrectness." The poet's variations on the classical rules were permissible because his genius was said to rise above his lapses, and he was ranked by Colman with Homer in his degree of supremacy over other poets.

Colman's dramatic output includes two adaptations of *A Midsummer Night's Dream—A Fairy Tale. In Two Acts. Taken from Shakespeare* (1763) and *The Fairy Prince. A Masque* (1771)—and *The Sheep-Shearing: A Dramatic Pastoral* (1771), a version of *The Winter's Tale*. Colman's version of *King Lear*, first produced in 1768, is based on the adaptation by Nahum TATE. Colman eliminated Tate's romance between Edgar and Cordelia, as well as Gloucester's imagined leap from Dover cliff. He followed Tate, however, in dropping the Fool, and retaining the happy ending. [Herbert Spencer Robinson, *English Shakesperian Criticism in the Eighteenth Century*, 1932.]

Colonne, Guido delle. See GUIDO DELLE COLONNE.

colophon. Information about a publisher or a printer appearing at the end of a book. When this information is included on the title page it is called an imprint. Early printed books generally had colophons or "finishing touches," but toward the end of the 16th century these began to be replaced by imprints. The colophon, if used at all, was retained only for the name of the printer.

Colorado University Shakespeare Festival. An annual dramatic festival held at Boulder, Colorado. In 1958 the University of Colorado inaugurated its annual two-week summer Shakespeare Festival with *Hamlet, Julius Caesar*, and *The Taming of the Shrew*. The second season offered *1 Henry IV, Macbeth*, and *A Midsummer Night's Dream*, the policy being to present a comedy, a tragedy, and a history play each year. Dr. J. H. Crouch is the executive director and founder of the festival, which includes films, fencing demonstrations, lectures, and discussions. Plays are staged in the beautiful new outdoor Mary Rippon Theatre on the campus at Boulder. Built of the pink stone native to the state, the 1000-seat amphitheatre rises in tiers from a semicircular grass apron. Surrounded by grass, trees, and shrubs, the stone-fronted stage rises three feet, and quarter-circles of stone form the wings. There are slopin entries of grass at stage right and left, with wic central steps at back, used for such scenes as Caesar assassination. At the back of the stage is the un versity museum building, the bronze doors of whic may be used in such scenes as that before Glouce ter's castle in *King Lear*, while the shrubber used for the hovel in *King Lear*, has also formed useful hiding place for Toby, Fabian, and S Andrew during Malvolio's letter-reading scene i *Twelfth Night*.

Using this unlocalized stage, the productions focu attention on the poetry and the actors, as the scen flow one into the other. Outstanding productions the festival have included *King Lear* in 1961, wit K. Lype O'Dell in the title role, and *Measure fo Measure* in 1963, with George Nicovich as Angel Presented for the quatercentenary were *As Yo Like It, Troilus and Cressida*, and *King John*.—A.C

Combe Family. Stratford neighbors of Shake speare. The origins of the family are obscure, bu their first connection with Stratford is recorded i 1534 when ***John Combe*** (d. 1550) married Katherin Quiney, the widow of Adrian Quiney (d. 1533 John's posthumous son, ***William Combe*** (1551–1610 was educated at Middle Temple. He served in parlia ment in 1588, 1593, and 1597 and as high sheriff i 1607. In 1593 he purchased land in the hamlet of OL STRATFORD, which he subsequently sold to Shake speare in 1602. William's elder brother, ***John Comb*** (d. 1588), lived in Stratford's only stone hous called the College, and was prosperous enough t secure a coat of arms in 1584. He had seven childrer one of whom was another ***John Combe*** (c. 1560 1614), a usurer, the wealthiest man in Stratford, an apparently the friend of Shakespeare, to whom h left £5 in his will: "Item, I give . . . to Mr William Shackspere five pounds."

This John Combe appears frequently in the Strat ford records, usually as the plaintiff in suits to re cover debts. In 1598 he acted as an agent of John an Mary Shakespeare in their suit against John Lamber (see LAMBERT FAMILY). In 1602 he acted in conjunc tion with his uncle William in the sale of the Ol Stratford property to Shakespeare. As he had n children, his property was left to his nephev Thomas.

Besides his bequest to Shakespeare, Combe lef £1000 to the poor and £60 for a tomb to be erecte in the Stratford church. In 1618 Richard Braithwait printed "An Epitaph vpon one Iohn Combe of Strat ford vpon Auen, a notable Vsurer, fastened vpon Tombe that he had caused to be built in his lif time":

Ten in the hundred must lie in his graue,
But a hundred to ten whether God will him
haue?
Who then must be interr'd in this Tombe?
Oh (quoth the Diuell) my *John a Combe*.

In 1634 the verse was attributed to Shakespeare by one Lieutenant HAMMOND of Norwich and in 165 by Nicholas BURGH. In 1672 Robert Dobyns reprinted the verse with slight variations and appended a convenient explanation of its disappearance:

Tenn in the hundred here lyeth engraved
A hundred to tenn his soule is now saved

If anny one aske who lyeth in this Tombe
Oh ho quoth the Divell tis my John a Combe.

Since my being at Stratford the heires of Mr Combe have caused these verses to be razed, so yt now they are not legible.

John AUBREY, as was his wont, elaborated on the tale little further, claiming that Shakespeare extempoized the lines while sitting in a tavern:

Ten in the Hundred the Devill allowes
But *Combes* will have twelve, he sweares & vowes:
If any one askes who lies in this Tombe:
Hoh! quoth the Devill, 'Tis my John o' Combe.

These many variations are indicative of the unreliability of attributing the epitaph verse to Shakespeare; furthermore, similar lines were printed as early as 1608 in reference to another usurer.

John's brother, ***Thomas Combe*** (d. 1609), held half the sublease of the Stratford tithes, of which the other half belonged to Shakespeare. An 18th-century tradition, traceable to Francis PECK, attributes still another epitaph, this one on Thomas Combe, to Shakespeare. Thomas Combe had two sons, ***William*** (1586–1667) and ***Thomas*** (1589–1657). William Combe, educated at Oxford and Middle Temple, was his father's heir. His failure to pay his portion of the rent due on the STRATFORD TITHES caused Shakespeare, Thomas Greene, and Richard Lane to enter a complaint against him in 1611. He was also a prominent figure in the dispute over the Welcombe ENCLOSURE. He was sheriff of Warwickshire in 1615/6. During the civil war he was an active supporter of the parliamentary faction, as a result of which his house was pillaged by royalist forces.

William's younger brother, Thomas Combe, is best known as the recipient in Shakespeare's will of his sword. He supported his brother in his efforts to bring about the enclosure of Welcombe in 1614. During the Commonwealth period he served as sheriff of Warwickshire (1648) and recorder of Stratford (1648–1657). [Mark Eccles, *Shakespeare in Warwickshire*, 1961.]

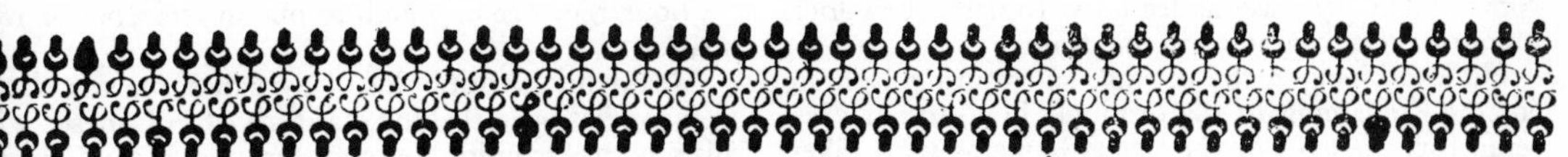

The Comedie of Errors.

Comedy of Errors, The. An early comedy, possibly the earliest, by Shakespeare.

Text. The play was first printed in the First Folio (1623), after being entered in the Stationers' Register, along with 15 other previously unpublished Shakespeare plays, on November 8, 1623. It is the shortest of Shakespeare's texts, consisting of only 1777 lines. The action requires no inner stage, only the typical setting of Latin comedy—three houses opening upon a square from which issue two streets. It is likely, therefore, that the play was written to be performed on some special occasion on a simple stage in one of the inns of court or perhaps on a platform erected at the end of the great hall in the queen's palace at Whitehall. This is the poet's only play for which there is no extant text designed for the public theatre.

Several mistakes and inconsistencies in the characters' names suggest that the copy for the Folio text was the author's FOUL PAPERS. J. Dover Wilson's theory that the source of the text was a scribe's transcription has not been generally accepted.

Date. The first recorded performance of the play was staged at Gray's Inn on December 28, 1594 (see INNS OF COURT). Until recently scholars argued for either 1592 or 1593 as the date of its composition, but recent Shakespearean scholars assign it a much earlier date, through what they believe is a correct interpretation of some lines in a punning, off-color conversation between Dromio and Antipholus about an amorous kitchen wench. Dromio of Syracuse declares that he finds in her unsavory body many countries of Europe. In her forehead, exposed by receding hair, he discerns France "armed and reverted [revolted] making war against her heir" (III, ii, 126). The play upon "hair" and "heir" is obvious. The events evidently referred to are the following: The death in 1584 of the duke of Anjou, brother of Henry III, made Henry king of France and the Protestant Henry of Navarre heir presumptive, but the new king's assassination in 1589 led to four years of civil war before Henry of Navarre was accepted as king. Two different interpretations of these facts have led to two different dates for the play. Peter Alexander and others argue that Henry of Navarre was recognized in Protestant England as the rightful king of France from 1589 on and that any reference to him as "heir" must precede this date. Many other scholars argue, however, that the "revolt" referred to was the civil war, and therefore date the play between 1589 and 1593. Within this period, 1591 would be a likely date, for in that year an expedition under the command of the earl of Essex was dispatched to France in order to aid Henry.

T. W. Baldwin, on the other hand, argues for 1589 on the basis of a parallel which he sees between the death penalty imposed on Aegeon and the execution of a seminary priest in October 1588 in Finnsbury Fields. Still other scholars argue that the play may have been written expressly for the 1594 Christmas revels at Gray's Inn. This comparatively late date would explain similarities between Shakespeare's play and William Warner's translation of the *Menaechmi*. Though not published until 1595, this translation was entered in the Stationers' Register in June 1594 and may have been available then to

Shakespeare. Nevertheless, the earlier dates are more frequently invoked for what is still generally regarded as Shakespeare's first comedy.

It is natural enough that he should begin his career as a playwright with an imitation of a comedy of Plautus, whose work he had been taught in the Stratford grammar school. And if, as seems likely, he was in his younger days a schoolmaster in the country, he may have taught the comedy to his pupils. With no play would he have been more familiar.

Sources. *The Comedy of Errors* is an adaptation of Plautus' *Menaechmi*, with some incidents added from his *Amphitruo*. An "error" in this play means a mistake in identity. From the rediscovery in 1429 by Nicholas of Treves of 12 of Plautus' plays lost during the Middle Ages, all schoolmasters and grammar-school-trained men considered Plautus and Terence to be the best models for English comedies. Seeking to enlarge the *Menaechmi* and to multiply its confusions, the dramatist made the two servants of the twin brothers in the Latin comedy also identical twins, of the same age as their masters. Through this invention Shakespeare was able to double the "errors" and to increase at least twofold the bewilderment of every character in the drama.

He also changed the setting, substituting Ephesus for the Epidamnus of the original. The servant Messenio lists the evils of the place. It teems with rakes, drunks, harlots, swindlers, and sharpers. Shakespeare has Antipholus of Syracuse transfer to Ephesus the deceit and sorcery that flourished by classical tradition in Epidamnum. "They say the town is full of cozenage," he soliloquizes (I, ii, 97–102). Ephesus had acquired a bad name in Tudor times. According to T. W. Baldwin, the Ephesus Shakespeare envisages is that of the 19th chapter of the Acts of the Apostles. His traveler follows St. Paul's route that brought him to Ephesus, where, among other miracles, Paul cast out evil spirits. Geoffrey Bullough believes that the playwright chose Ephesus for two reasons. First, the city was well known to Elizabethans as a great seaport and was famous also for its temple of Diana. Secondly, the play was to be concerned with family relationships, and he found that some of the lessons taught in Paul's Epistle to the Ephesians dealt impressively with this subject. For example: "Wives, submit yourselves unto your own husbands . . . . For the husband is the head of the wife, even as Christ is the head of the Church . . . . Husbands love your wives . . . let every one of you in particular so love his wife, even as himself and let the wife see that she feare [reverence] her husband" (Epistle to the Ephesians, V). This is the same advice that Luciana gives Adriana (II, i, 6–31).

Shakespeare's most elaborate addition to the plot of the *Menaechmi* is the story of Aegeon, taken from the prose romance *Apollonius of Tyre*, which he was to use again in *Pericles*.

A lost play, *The Historie of Error*, acted by Paul's Boys at Hampton Court on January 1, 1577 has been put forward as a direct source of *The Comedy of Errors*, but this is mere conjecture, with not a shred of supporting evidence.

The rhetorical features of the comedy betray the influence of John Lyly that was strong during the formative years of Shakespeare's art. The symmetrical arrangement of the characters is the most obvious sign of that influence. The nature of the verse i many of the passages shows almost as clearly the ir fluence of the rhetoric taught in grammar school which Lyly had developed in his own ingeniou fashion.—O. J. C.

Plot Synopsis. Act I. Aegeon, a Syracusan me chant who has been condemned to death for ente ing Ephesus in violation of a law banning all inte course between the two hostile cities, explains h presence there by narrating a sorrowful tale. Ove 20 years ago, Aegeon's wife had borne him twi sons, and at the same time the couple had adopte another set of identical twins as attendants to the sons. During a voyage from Epidamnum their shi had been wrecked in a storm. Aegeon, with th younger of his infant sons and one of the little slave had been rescued by a ship from Epidaurus, while h wife and the other boys had been taken up by som Corinthian fishermen. Eighteen years later, the so whom Aegeon had reared had left Syracuse with h slave to search for his brother, and now Aegeon i looking for his Syracusan son. Moved by Aegeon story, Duke Solinus of Ephesus gives the merchant 24-hour reprieve in which to obtain a ransom of 100 marks.

Meanwhile, Antipholus of Syracuse, the son who Aegeon has been seeking, has arrived in Ephesus wit his servant Dromio. He sends Dromio to the Centau the inn where they lodge, with 1000 marks for safe keeping, only to see him return a few moments late This Dromio is, however, actually the slave of An tipholus' lost twin brother and namesake, who, un known to the Syracusan, lives in Ephesus. Seeing man he takes to be his master, Dromio tells him t hurry home to dinner, for his wife is "hot becaus the meat is cold." Bewildered by Dromio's messag and by the fact that he denies knowledge of the 100 marks, Antipholus recalls that Ephesus is said to b full of sorcerers and charlatans.

Act II. Adriana, the wife of Antipholus of Ephesu is angry at the male sex in general and at her dilator husband in particular, but her sister Luciana argue that women are meant to be subservient to me When Dromio of Ephesus, still smarting from th blows he has received from the Syracusan Antipho lus, reports his supposed master's strange behavio Adriana becomes even more irate and expresse doubts of her husband's fidelity.

The Syracusan Dromio, returning from his erran at the Centaur, is also rewarded with a beating fro his master when he professes ignorance of any sum mons to dinner. Adriana now arrives and reproache Antipholus of Syracuse for neglecting her. Ignorin his demurrers, she takes him along to dinner.

Act III. Antipholus of Ephesus arrives before h home with his servant Dromio; Balthasar, a me chant; and Angelo, a goldsmith who is making a gol chain for Adriana. When Antipholus tries to ente his house, he is refused admittance by Dromio o Syracuse, who guards the door from within. The in dignant Antipholus is dissuaded from breaking i with a crowbar only by the expostulations of Bal thasar. He decides instead to dine at the Porpentin upon whose hostess he will bestow the necklace h had intended for his wife.

Inside, Luciana urges Antipholus of Syracuse t treat Adriana with greater consideration and affec on, even if he is insincere. To her distress, however, ntipholus responds with a declaration of love for uciana. His servant is having romantic problems of nother sort, for he reports that the kitchenmaid, a spherical," swarthy wench, "all grease," claims that e is promised to her. By now thoroughly perplexed, ntipholus decides to leave Ephesus, where "none ut witches do inhabit," and asks Dromio to find out hether any ships are sailing that night. At this oint, Angelo appears and presents Antipholus with ne gold chain.

Act IV. After dining at the Porpentine, Antipho-us of Ephesus orders Dromio to bring him a rope to se on his wife. Meeting Angelo, he inquires about he chain, but the goldsmith's reply is to ask him for ayment, since he is being pressed by a creditor. ntipholus insists that he will pay when he receives he chain, and Angelo insists that he already has iven it to him. Antipholus is finally arrested at the uit of Angelo's creditor. Dromio of Syracuse now eturns to state that a bark of Epidamnum awaits hem and asserts that he knows nothing of a rope. owing to punish Dromio later, Antipholus sends im to seek bail money from Adriana.

As Luciana describes her interview with Antiph-lus to Adriana, Dromio of Syracuse brings word of he arrest of his supposed master and is dispatched vith 500 ducats for the Ephesian's bail. Encounter-ng Antipholus of Syracuse on the street, Dromio is urprised to see him at liberty, but gives him the oo ducats. Antipholus, convinced that both he and Dromio are "distract" and "wander in illusions," be-omes even more confused when a courtesan de-nands the chain he had promised her at dinner in xchange for a ring, worth 40 ducats, that she had iven him.

Meanwhile, Antipholus of Ephesus, who is still in ustody, becomes enraged when Dromio of Ephesus rings him a rope instead of the money for his bail. Adriana, Luciana, and the courtesan arrive with Doc-or Pinch, a conjuror who is to restore the mad Antipholus to his senses, but the Ephesian responds o his ministrations by boxing him on the ears. Both e and Dromio are seized as lunatics and hauled way. When Antipholus and Dromio of Syracuse ap-ear, the women assume that they have eluded their uards, while the Syracusans take them to be witches.

Act V. On a street before a priory, Angelo sees Antipholus of Syracuse wearing the chain he had upposedly denied receiving. Adriana, Luciana, and he others burst in, causing Antipholus and Dromio o seek refuge in the priory, whose Abbess emerges o ask the reason for the uproar. Adriana explains hat her husband is distracted. When Adriana re-eals, as a result of the Abbess' skillful questioning, hat she had continuously carped at her husband hrough jealousy, the Abbess makes her realize that er railing has provoked Antipholus' "madness." The Abbess, however, refuses to surrender Antipholus.

Just then the Duke passes by with the doomed Aegeon, and Adriana pleads with him to intercede vith the Abbess. Suddenly Antipholus of Ephesus, vho has escaped his jailers, appears to seek justice rom the Duke. Berating his wife, Angelo, and Doc-or Pinch, Antipholus eloquently describes his mis-dventures to the baffled Duke, who can conclude only that they "all have drunk of Circe's cup."

Aegeon, who thinks that he recognizes Antipholus and Dromio of Ephesus and hopes that his ransom now will be paid, is heartbroken when they deny ever having seen him. The "errors" finally end when the Abbess reappears with Antipholus and Dromio of Syracuse. The Antipholuses, she explains, are twin sons of Aegeon and she is his wife, Aemilia, who had been separated from her son after the shipwreck. During the happy reunion that follows, Aegeon re-gains his freedom, Antipholus of Syracuse plans to pursue his courtship of Luciana, and Dromio of Syra-cuse realizes that he soon will have a fat kitchen wench for a sister-in-law.—H.D.

Comment. Although Shakespeare set his play in Ephesus, he transformed that city into a typical Eng-lish seaport, with a central market and inns pictur-esquely named "The Tiger" or "The Centaur." The houses, like those in London, are identified by the signs on the shops below the living quarters; Adri-ana's dwelling, for example, is called "The Phoenix." The ever-hungry Parasite remains a character of Roman comedy, and the slaves are still the clownish servants they were in Plautus, given to horseplay and indulgence in verbal quips, rhetorical distortions, and routines of forced logic. However, since a lout from the barnyard or a pantry boy—the British equivalents of the Dromios—could not realistically have become his master's confidant or fellow-plotter, Shakespeare allows neither Dromio to plan and ma-nipulate the intrigue. But in Dromio of Syracuse's efforts to resist the blandishments of Nell, the greasy kitchen wench, the spectators could recognize a sit-uation that often developed belowstairs in their own houses. Fat Nell herself was a caricature of the servants who mucked about in far-from-spotless Elizabethan kitchens. And when Dromio of Ephesus beat on his master's door, the audience must have laughed boisterously to hear him call the kitchen wenches by the names they commonly bore in Eng-land—Maud, Bridget, Marian, Cicely, Gilliam, Ginn.

In adapting Plautus to the English stage Shake-speare altered more than the plot elements and set-ting of the *Menaechmi* and *Amphitruo;* he seriously modified the tone of these two plays by injecting the feature of romantic love. In the *Menaechmi* there is sexual adventure but no love. The Romans saw nothing ennobling in sexual attraction. The frustra-tions met in the incessant pursuit of women, they thought ridiculous. Hence, in Plautus sex arouses no tenderness—only scornful laughter.

The Elizabethan attitude toward love was much more like ours. Centuries of the practice of courtly love and knightly devotion to a lady (never a wife) lay between Plautus and Shakespeare. His audiences expected to find romantic courtship in his comedies, and he fully satisfied this expectation in *The Comedy of Errors*. In the Latin comedy the citizen's wife, named merely "Mulier" (woman), is a conventional stage figure. Her "business" is incessant complaining and nagging. It is her fretting and nosing into what he thinks are his private affairs that drives the citizen Menaechmus into the arms of a courtesan. Adriana, too, is sometimes a scold. More often, her distress at her husband's long absences from home is sincere enough to seem pathetic. He is no shameless lecher, like his Roman prototype. The Elizabethans did not share the Roman tolerance of a husband's infidelity.

Antipholus of Ephesus would have completely lost the sympathy of the audience if he had posted off to a harlot every time he became tired of his wife's shrewishness. He seeks the extramarital companionship of another woman only after he has been locked out of his house, where he is certain that his wife is carrying on with another man. His "friend" is no whore but a ". . . wench of excellent discourse, / Pretty and witty, wild and yet, too, gentle." She is a lady. Her conversation, though entertaining, is decorous, good-mannered, and relaxing. We think no worse of the husband for forgetting his domestic problems at her table. Luciana has no prototype in the *Menaechmi;* she is Shakespeare's invention. It is she who introduces into the play sentiment completely foreign to the spirit of Roman comedy. In her conversation with Adriana, already referred to, she urges her sister almost in St. Paul's words to be subservient to her husband. She announces, "Ere I learn love, I'll practice to obey." She charges the man whom she supposes to be Adriana's husband to treat his wife with kindness; and, if he must seek the company of another woman, to do so stealthily. Her feminine sweetness awakens love in the serious-minded traveler, an upright man, who rejects the temptations of a harlot in order to court Luciana. He woos her in a long lyrical passage in highly figured language of which the following lines may serve as an example.

> Sing, siren, for thyself and I will dote:
> Spread o'er the silver waves thy golden hairs,
> And as a bed I'll take them and there lie,
> And in that glorious supposition think
> He gains by death that hath such means to die.
> (III, ii, 47–51)

This utterance represents Shakespeare's first awkward attempt to express sympathetically the emotions of a romantic lover.

Shakespeare opens his comedy on a note of grief and despair with the story of Aegeon. By coming to Ephesus, Aegeon has walked into a trap. A Tudor audience familiar with the dangers of the intense commercial rivalry of 16th-century Italian city-states could have seen Aegeon's predicament, not as part of a contrived romantic tale, but as a plausible incident in the life of many a trader sailing the Mediterranean. Aegeon's account of his unlucky-lucky shipwreck was calculated to excite amazement and then expectation. It introduced suspense into a plot where there had been none before. It therefore induced the audience to listen attentively to Aegeon's long and complicated narration, in which he piles wonder upon wonder. At his first appearance his advanced age, his hopeless hope of finding his lost wife and the infants, and his fear of being hanged, awaken instant sympathy and anticipation of relief. It comes in a happy ending that unties all the tangles of the plot and introduces the Abbess in the role of a moral counselor against jealousy and nagging. She offers her convent as a sanctuary in the shelter of which the uproar dies away and an atmosphere of joy is established.

However, to dwell on the drawing of real character and the endowing of trivial events with near-tragic importance is to throw a view of the comedy out of focus. The action moves from one scene of physical farce to another. A Dromio is beaten almos every time he appears. In one of the speeches o Dromio of Ephesus the dramatist seems to be apolo gizing for the incessant rain of blows and perhap appealing for a little sympathy for the rogue, wh ruefully describes his punishment:

> When I am cold, he heats me with beating; whe I am warm, he cools me with beating: I am wake with it when I sleep; raised with it when I sit driven out of doors with it when I go from home welcomed home with it when I return. . . .
> (IV, iv, 34–39)

The farcical spirit mounts to its apogee in the wil goings-on when Dr. Pinch,

> a hungry lean-faced villain,
> A mere anatomy, a mountebank,
> A threadbare juggler and a fortune-teller,
> A needy, hollow-eyed, sharp-looking wretch . . .
> (V, i, 237–240)

attempts to exorcize the devils who, he pronounces possess Antipholus of Ephesus and his Dromio.

When Shakespeare designed his comedy, his sol object was doubtless to provide his audience with a occasion for an hour or two of boisterous laughte but his developing interest in the actions and motive of his characters produces a conviction that the des tiny of all of them is a matter of human significance The invasion of *The Comedy of Errors* by seriou emotion slows down the traditional speed of a farc and diminishes its wild gaiety. For these reason Shakespeare's play is not as pure and satisfactory farce as its Plautine models. It does, however, offer richer and more complex experience than pure farc and thus, in however crude a fashion, it serves t foreshadow some of the later great achievements o Shakespearean comedy.—O.J.C.

Stage History. The first recorded performance o *The Comedy of Errors* took place at the Christma revels at Gray's Inn on the evening of December 28 1594. The guests of the Inn's law students were thei fellow barristers from the Inner Temple and many gentlewomen. The actors were, almost surely, mem bers of Shakespeare's company who had acted befor the queen on the afternoon of the same day, conceiv ably the same comedy. As part of other Christma festivities 10 years later to the day, *The Comedy o Errors* was presented to the court at Whitehall. Ther is no record of a subsequent performance until Octo ber 9, 1734, when the comedy, reduced to two act and called *See If You Like It or Tis All A Mistake* was staged at Covent Garden. During the season o 1741/2, it was acted five times at Drury Lane wit Charles Macklin playing Dromio of Syracuse, bu never at that theatre during David Garrick's long term as manager. Thomas HULL's alteration, re named *The Twins,* successfully held the stage fron 1762 until 1808 when John Philip Kemble made con siderable additions to this adaptation. He enlarge the role of Dromio of Syracuse, which he played and prolonged the sentimental exchanges betwee Adriana and Luciana. Indulging his predilection fo naming Shakespeare's nameless characters, Kembl caused the Second Merchant to be called Charles. In 1819 Frederick REYNOLDS' operatic version of th farce elicited the following criticism from John

Genest: "Reynolds may be assured that the only sentiments which the real friends of Shakespeare can feel towards him are—indignation at his attempt, and contempt for the bungling manner in which he has executed it." The play that Shakespeare wrote was restored by Samuel Phelps on November 8, 1855 at Sadler's Wells when it was tacked onto a play entitled *Hamilton of Bothwellhaugh*, written by an otherwise unknown A. R. Slous. However, in 1856 Phelps gave it the sole place on his bill. The brothers Charles and Henry Webb presented almost identical Dromios in their production at the Princess' Theatre in 1864. The play was acted in its entirety without interruption. At J. S. Clarke's Strand Theatre in 1883, Clarke, an accomplished comedian and brother-in-law of Edwin Booth, played Dromio of Syracuse. Frank Benson produced the comedy for the Adelphi during the scorching summer of 1905, but managed to attract only a small audience. When Ben Greet staged his production at the Old Vic he introduced a new actress to the company, Sybil Thorndike, who made her first appearance there on November 30, 1914 in the role of Adriana. With the text cut almost in half and the Dromios in blackface, Henry Baynton presented *The Comedy of Errors* at the Savoy on September 1, 1924 as part of a double bill with *The Bells*. Eric Portman, then 21, was Antipholus of Syracuse. The Open Air Theatre saw Ion Swinley play his last role, that of Duke Solinus in *The Comedy of Errors*, just before his sudden death in September 1937.

In an otherwise indifferent festival year of 1938, Theodore Komisarjevsky's colorful, lively production of *The Comedy of Errors* was a box-office success. His costumes were a mixture of many periods, with the males wearing plumed bowler hats and the women in hoop skirts, carrying modern handbags. Tedium was diverted with a song or balletic romp performed by the citizens of Ephesus to music by Handel and Anthony Bernard. Although widely acclaimed, Komisarjevsky's burlesque of Shakespeare was resented by some. Since then, the play has been staged as a Victorian musical comedy (Cambridge, 1951) and as an Edwardian spectacular with music by Sir Arthur Sullivan (London, 1952). An operatic version with music by Julian Slade was televised in 1954 and presented at the Arts Theatre in 1956.

Of the straightforward productions, the most notable were by the Birmingham Repertory Theatre under the direction of Douglas Seale in 1948, with Donald Pleasance's excellent portrayal of a Dromio; by Robert Atkins, who in 1949 included *The Comedy of Errors* in an ingenious double bill with *Two Gentlemen of Verona* at the Open Air; and by Walter Hudd, who in 1957 at the Old Vic cut the play to an hour and presented it on a double bill with *Titus Andronicus*. Clifford Williams' invigorating production of the play was staged alternately at Stratford-upon-Avon and at the Aldwych during 1962 and 1963 and was presented in the United States in 1964.

The first American actors to play in the drama were Henry and Thomas Placide. In those cities and towns of the United States that could then boast a theatre, they appeared together as the two Dromios every year up to 1877, when Thomas committed suicide. In the next year William Henry Crane and Stuart Robson continued the success of the Placide brothers as the Dromios. The farce was an important part of the repertory of Ben Greet's company, which played first in London in 1905 and the next year indoors and outdoors in many communities in the United States, often on college campuses. *The Boys From Syracuse*, an hilarious and impudent musical version of the comedy by Richard Rodgers and Lorenz Hart, delighted New York audiences during the 1938/9 season at the Alvin Theatre and was successfully revived in 1963/4 for a long run.—M.G.

Bibliography. TEXT: *The Comedy of Errors*, New Cambridge Edition, Arthur Quiller-Couch and J. Dover Wilson, eds., 1922; *The Comedy of Errors*, New Arden Edition, R. A. Foakes, ed., 1962. DATE: New Cambridge Edition; New Arden Edition; T. W. Baldwin, *William Shakspere Adapts a Hanging*, 1931; Sidney Thomas, "The Date of *The Comedy of Errors*," *Shakespeare Quarterly*, VII, 1956. SOURCES: T. W. Baldwin, *Shakspere's Five-Act Structure*, 1947; Geoffrey Bullough, *Narrative and Dramatic Sources of Shakespeare*, I, 1957. COMMENT: G. R. Elliott, "Weirdness in *The Comedy of Errors*," *University of Toronto Quarterly*, IX, 1939; T. W. Baldwin, *Shakspere's Five-Act Structure*, 1947; Northrop Frye, "The Argument of Comedy," *English Institute Essays*, 1948; Nevill Coghill, "The Basis of Shakespearian Comedy," *Essays and Studies*, n.s. III, 1950; M. C. Bradbrook, *The Growth and Structure of Elizabethan Comedy*, 1955; Bertrand Evans, *Shakespeare's Comedies*, 1960; Harold Brooks, "Themes and Structure in *The Comedy of Errors*," *Early Shakespeare*, 1961. STAGE HISTORY: New Arden Edition; G. C. D. Odell, *Shakespeare from Betterton to Irving*, 1920; J. C. Trewin, *Shakespeare on the English Stage, 1900–1964*, 1964.

Selected Criticism

WILLIAM HAZLITT. This comedy is taken very much from the Menæchmi of Plautus, and is not an improvement on it. Shakespear appears to have bestowed no great pains on it, and there are but a few passages which bear the decided stamp of his genius. He seems to have relied on his author, and on the interest arising out of the intricacy of the plot. The curiosity excited is certainly very considerable, though not of the most pleasing kind. We are teazed as with a riddle, which notwithstanding we try to solve. In reading the play, from the sameness of the names of the two Antipholises and the two Dromios, as well from their being constantly taken for each other by those who see them, it is difficult, without a painful effort of attention, to keep the characters distinct in the mind. And again, on the stage, either the complete similarity of their persons and dress must produce the same perplexity whenever they first enter, or the identity of appearance which the story supposes, will be destroyed. We still, however, having a clue to the difficulty, can tell which is which, merely from the practical contradictions which arise, as soon as the different parties begin to speak; and we are indemnified for the perplexity and blunders into which we are thrown by seeing others thrown into greater and almost inextricable ones.—This play (among other considerations) leads us not to feel much regret that Shakespear was not what is called a classical scholar. We do not think his *forte* would ever have lain in imitating or improving on what others invented, so much as in inventing for himself, and perfecting what he invented,—not perhaps by the omission of faults, but by the addition of the highest excellencies. [*Characters of Shakespear's Plays*, 1817.]

SAMUEL TAYLOR COLERIDGE. The myriad-minded man, our, and all men's, Shakspeare, has in this piece presented us with a legitimate farce in exactest consonance with the philosophical principles and character of farce, as distinguished from comedy and from entertainments. A proper farce is mainly distinguished from comedy by the license allowed, and even required, in the fable, in order to produce strange and laughable situations. The story need not be probable, it is enough that it is possible. A comedy would scarcely allow even the two Antipholuses; because, although there have been instances of almost indistinguishable likeness in two persons, yet these are mere individual accidents, *casus ludentis naturae*, and the *verum* will not excuse the *inverisimile*. But farce dares add the two Dromios, and is justified in so doing by the laws of its end and constitution. In a word, farces commence in a postulate, which must be granted. [Notes on the Comedies; reprinted in *Shakespearean Criticism* by S. T. Coleridge, T. M. Raysor, ed., Everyman Library Edition, 1960.]

CHARLES KNIGHT. Nothing can be more beautifully managed, or is altogether more Shaksperean, than the narrative of Ægeon: and that narrative is so clear and so impressive, that the reader never forgets it amidst all the errors and perplexities which follow. The Duke, who, like the reader or spectator, has heard the narrative, instantly sees the real state of things when the *dénouement* is approaching:—

"Why, here begins his morning story right."

The reader or spectator has seen it all along,—certainly by an effort of attention, for without the effort the characters would be confounded like the vain shadows of a half-waking dream;—and, having seen it, it is impossible, we think, that the constant readiness of the reader or spectator to solve the riddle should be other than pleasurable. It appears to us that every one of an *audience* of "The Comedy of Errors," who keeps his eyes open, will, after he has become a little familiar with the persons of the two Antipholuses and the two Dromios, find out some clue by which he can detect a difference between each . . . [*Studies of Shakspere*, 1849.]

E. K. CHAMBERS. From one point of view, then, *The Comedy of Errors* is to be classed as a comedy. But the label hardly applies to it as a whole, since, as I have already pointed out, the ethical element, no less than the element of romance, in the play has been imported into the original design under the promptings of the Elizabethan mood. Stripped of these ornaments, the interest declares itself as almost entirely one of plot, arising out of a succession of ingeniously interwoven situations brought about by the facial resemblances of the two pairs of twin brothers and the accident of their coming together, unknown to each other, in the same city. Too much praise cannot be given to the technical skill with which the idea is worked out; nor can it be denied that in this respect many improvements have been made in the original scheme of the *Menaechmi*. The supplementing of the Antipholuses by the Dromic quadruples the possibilities of misunderstanding, an the fun grows fast and furious, as error is piled upo error. If the rehandling of the Plautine structure is t be attributed to Shakespeare himself, he was alread a master of stage-craft. To this particular type c drama it is possible to give the name of farce rathe than of comedy, if certain distinctions are observec Farce, indeed, is a term which has been used b literary historians in two rather different shades c meaning. In one acceptation, derived from its use a applied to *Maître Pathelin* and other examples o fifteenth-century French dramatic humour, it doe not so much connote something other than comedy as a variety of comedy itself. It is a matter of tempe and *milieu*. Farce is comedy translated from th speech and manners of a cultivated society into th speech and manners of the *bourgeoisie;* or perhaps i would really be more historical to say that comed represents a development out of farce, due to th sharpening of the wits and the refinement of th moral issues which accompany or form part of th growth of a cultivated society as distinct from *bourgeoisie*. Such farce is a comedy of the rude vices and the more robust virtues, a comedy in whic fisticuffs, literal and verbal, take the place of rapier play. [*Shakespeare: A Survey*, 1925.]

H. B. CHARLTON. Adriana is doubtless shrew, virag and vixen to boot. She breaks the servants' pate across, though that hardly gives her characteristi distinction in a play in which fisticuffs are th regular means of intercourse. She rails at bed an board, and jealousy gives venom to her clamours adding to them a virulence of which Plautus coul scarcely avail himself, for it is only love in th modern sense "which is full of jealousy." An Eng lish shrew, moreover, much more than a Roma one, is hampered by memories of the affection sh once had for the man of her choice. Adriana eve fondles at times. But her single lapse into the broken hearted bride who will weep and die in tears is fall both from type and from character. A mor credibly humanising trait appears in her excited en largement of the tale of her husband's frenzied acts the duke is treated to a display of rumour's growth as facts swell with fancy when she recounts th incidents she thought she had seen (V. i. 136ff.) Yet at the end of the play, the shrew is not so muc out of countenance as she was meant to be. On cannot but remember that the person solemnly re proving Adriana for her shrewishness is not, as i Plautus, her own natural parent, but her mother-in law. Nor does her husband appear to suffer muc spiritual disquiet from her moods. A man who con ducts a domestic tiff by calling his wife a dissemblin harlot, and by threats to pluck out her eyes, is no too sensitive a fellow and has a sufficient protectio in the thickness of his skin. Indeed, the genera temper of the life depicted in *The Comedy of Error* is so crude, coarse, and brutal, that Adriana's faul appears to be not so much her shrewishness as he undiplomatic use of it. [*Shakespearian Comedy* 1938.]

NEVILL COGHILL. . . . anyone (caring for poetica form) who compares *The Comedy of Errors* with it source in the *Menaechmi*, will find significant differ ences in the shape and content of these two plays. I is not simply a matter of doubling the pairs of twins hakespeare's play has a new beginning, a new end nd an infusion of tenderness; there is love in it. In act he medievalized the story, starting it off in troule, ending it in joy. It begins (daringly for a comdy) with a man led seriously out to execution; it is *:geon,* the father of the Antipholus twins, a major haracter; this gambit is not in Plautus. Execution on *:geon* is deferred by the Duke, but he remains (albeit ff-stage) under sentence of death until the last cene. When, however, he is at last led out once nore to suffer, there emerges from an improbable bbey, a more improbable abbess, who, most imrobably of all, is discovered to be his long-lost wife, he mother of the Antipholi, and the means of his eliverance and their reunion. She is also Shakepeare's invention, and turns catastrophe into general oy. The scene gathers in the whole cast and conludes in rejoicing, a model to all subsequent comdy, with a stage crammed at the end with happy eople. The play-world has been led into delight, and vith it the world of the audience.

Although its main business is the fun of mistaken dentity, *The Comedy of Errors* is given a touch of lelicacy by the language of *amour courtois* (a thing nknown to Plautus) and the invention of a romanic sub-plot—the love-affair between Antipholus of Syracuse and Luciana:

> Teach me deere creature how to thinke and
> speake:
> Lay open to my earthie grosse conceit:
> Smothred in errors, feeble, shallow, weake,
> The foulded meaning of your words deceit:
> Against my soules pure truth, why labour you,
> To make it wander in an vnknowne field?
> Are you a god? would you create me new?
> Transforme me then, and to your power Ile
> yeeld. . . .

Thus could the fantasy of the Middle Ages transform the stolid fun of the world of Roman imagination. ["The Basis of Shakespearian Comedy: A Study in Medieval Affinities," *Essays and Studies*, n.s. III, 1950, 1–28.]

FRANCIS FERGUSSON. The play belongs in the stream of popular comedy, from Menander to Minsky; but it also shows an intelligence and control, on the part of the author, which is rare in any kind of play. It is much lighter and funnier than *The Two Menaechmuses*. This mastery is revealed, not so much in the language, though that is perfectly adequate to its modest purposes, as in the consistency with which its farcical limitations are accepted, and in the ingenuity of the plot. This plot really is built like the proverbial "Swiss watch": it is as absurdly neat as Leibnitz's pre-established harmony. Comedy of this type, or taste—rationalistic, built on a Latin base—was to be more fully explored in the succeeding age of the Enlightenment, in the innumerable comedies which lighted the theaters of Europe from Molière through Mozart. But Shakespeare was developing in a different direction, not toward the univocal perfection of the geometric diagram, but toward the harmonizing of complementary perspectives; not toward further ingenuity, but toward deeper insight.

The Comedy of Errors, like other comedies of that taste, is so clear that it *ought* to be reducible to a formula. Molière's comedies often strike us in the same way. Certainly one can find in them many standard and publicly available devices, whether of plotting, attitude, or conventional characterization. Without that heritage I do not suppose Shakespeare could, at so early an age, have written anything so easy and assured. Yet he uses it for his own purposes, like a good cook who first learns and then forgets the basic recipes, or a dress designer who assumes the clichés of fashion only to go beyond them to something not quite predictable. Only Shakespeare could derive *The Comedy of Errors* from Plautus, and only he could proceed from that simple fun to the enigmatic humor of his maturity. [*The Human Image in Dramatic Literature*, 1957.]

HAROLD BROOKS. The play begins and ends with relationship: a family torn asunder and reunited. Relationship is the motive that has brought Egeon, and the alien Antipholus and Dromio, to the hazards of Ephesus; relationship is threatened by the tensions in the marriage of Antipholus the denizen. The chief entanglements spring from mistaken identity and mistiming:

> I see we still did meet each other's man,
> And I was ta'en for him, and he for me,
> And thereupon these ERRORS are arose.

The twins appear the same, but in reality are different; those who meet them are led by appearance into illusion. Repeatedly one of the persons assumes that he shared an experience with another, when in reality he shared it with a different one. In consequence, the persons cease to be able to follow each other's assumptions, and become isolated in more or less private worlds. Mistakes of identity all but destroy relationship, and loss of relationship calls true identity yet more in question; the chief persons suspect themselves or are suspected of insanity, or of being possessed, surrounded, or assailed by supernatural powers—madness or demoniac possession would be the eclipse of the true self, and sorcery might overwhelm it. The alien Antipholus and Dromio fear Circean metamorphosis; Egeon, that he has been deformed out of recognition by time. Yet the hazard of metamorphosis and of the loss of present identity is also the way to fresh or restored relationship. Antipholus the bachelor desires that Luciana will transform him and create him new; and Adriana's belief that in marriage the former identities coalesce and emerge identified with each other, is true if rightly interpreted. How the possessive interpretation, not relinquished by Adriana till almost the end, is at odds with the free giving and hazarding in which the wealth and debts of love differ from those of commerce, is another central theme, well traced by J. R. Brown. Adriana's envy of a husband's status contravenes principles of order that for Shakespeare and orthodox Elizabethans extended through the whole cosmos. The status of husband, and of wife, Kate's lines in *The Shrew* imply, are related to their places in this hierarchical order:

> Such duty as the subject owes the prince
> Even such a woman oweth to her husband.

Adriana comes to style her husband lord, and they each lay their case, as each has come to see it, before the Duke, reminding themselves and him that the match was first made by his authority. By this point, disorder from the various disruptions of relationship has gone so far in the community, that only the appeals for justice addressed to the Abbess and to him, God's viceroys spiritual and temporal, are capable, the time now being ripe, of leading to a solution. ["Themes and Structure in 'The Comedy of Errors'" in *Early Shakespeare*, Stratford-Upon-Avon Studies 3, 1961.]

Comical Gallant, The, or The Amours of Sir John Falstaff. See John DENNIS.

comical satire. A term invented by Ben Jonson for a type of drama. In 1599 Jonson's *Every Man Out of his Humour* was produced by the Chamberlain's Men, perhaps at the new Globe theatre. He called it a "comicall satyre," meaning that it combined traditional features of comedy and satire. This was perhaps Jonson's answer to the restraining order, issued on June 1, 1599 by the archbishop of Canterbury and the bishop of London, which prohibited further publication of verse-satires, particularly those of Joseph Hall, John Marston, and Sir John Davies (see Archbishop WHITGIFT). Searching for a dramatic equivalent of these satires, Jonson adapted from classical comedy and commedia dell' arte a method of ridiculing the objects of his satire that became standard practice with him. He first drew a portrait of a fool or knave, then, through the action, forced him into an exaggerated display of his folly. Finally, he brought about either the character's reform, or his scornful ejection from the action as incorrigible.

In order to focus the derision of the audience upon the victim, Jonson employed two commentators in *Every Man Out of his Humour:* Asper-Macilente, who spoke for Jonson himself as an ideal castigator of follies and sins, and Carlo Buffone. The latter, as a typical buffoon, was, according to Renaissance critical theory, an improper agent of satire, for he observes fitness of neither time nor place in launching his ridicule. Moreover, he does not even pretend to want to improve the figure he derides. He seeks merely to show off his verbal virtuosity and to entertain with a display of detraction and scurrility. These forms of abuse find their most characteristic expression in what Jonson names "adulterate similes," grotesque and vulgar figures of speech. Although each in its context may possess a kind of preposterous pertinency, these extravagant sallies make the buffoon seem as absurd as his victim, and often distasteful. Thus, the satire is double-edged.

Shakespeare, in his "dark comedies" adopted methods of satire very similar to these of Jonson. Earlier, in such incidents as the exposure of Falstaff's cowardice (*1 Henry IV*, II, ii and iv) and of Malvolio's pretensions (*Twelfth Night*, II, v and III, iv), the poet had invented situations in which a fool is encouraged to betray his own folly, but the tone of these episodes was such as to elicit from the audience only good-natured laughter at human foibles. In *All's Well That Ends Well*, however, although the exposure of Parolles (IV, i and iii) is similar in many respects to that of Falstaff (another *miles gloriosus*), the laughter of the audience, guided by the reaction of the other characters in the play, must have been of a far harsher sort. In the end, Parolles, like some of the figures of scorn in Jonson's comical satires, is contemptuously expelled from the action.

In the same play Shakespeare presents a buffoon of the breed of Carlo Buffone. Although the clown Lavache functions as a typical court fool, his preposterous figures of speech are borrowed from the buffoon's unsavory store. Introducing Parolles after his disgrace, he says:

> Here is a purr of fortune's, sir, or of fortune's cat,—but not a musk-cat,—that has fallen into the unclean fishpond of her displeasure, and, as he says, is muddied withal.
>
> (V, ii, 20–23)

On a still lower level of vulgarity he characterizes Parolles as "a paper from Fortune's close-stool." Here the clown has clearly no other purpose than to exhibit his cleverness in inventing gross, even indecent, figures of speech.

In *Troilus and Cressida* Thersites, though based on a classical model, also shows the characteristics of the buffoon of comical satire. He is indefatigable in the invention of tortured figures of speech, all of them derogatory. He calls Patroclus, "thou idle immaterial skein of sleave-silk, thou green sarcenet flap for a sore eye, thou tassel of a prodigal's purse, thou" (V, i, 35–37). Of Agamemnon he says, "He has not so much brain as ear-wax . . . a thrifty shoeing-horn in a chain, hanging at his brother's leg" (V, i, 58–59, 62–63). Pandarus, too, is a figure from satire. It is his cynical attitude that sets the tone of the doomed love affair.

The strong infusion of satire in the "problem plays" accounts to a considerable degree for their dark and pessimistic tone. If these plays give the impression that their disparate elements are imperfectly fused, it may be that Shakespeare was forcing his art into channels uncongenial to his mind and spirit. [Oscar James Campbell, *Comicall Satyre and Shakespeare's Troilus and Cressida*, 1938.]

commedia dell' arte. Name given to a type of improvisational comedy which began in Italy in the Middle Ages. It reached the height of its fame during the 16th century at which time its influence was felt all over Europe. Its distinguishing character was the fixed types, performed by highly specialized actors, which recurred in virtually every skit. The basic pattern included two pairs of lovers (amorosos and amorosas), two comic servants (*zanni*, whose comic business was known as *lazzi*), a braggart captain (an adaptation of the classical *miles gloriosus*), and a serving maid. For a detailed account of Shakespeare's adaptation of commedia dell' arte features, see LOVE'S LABOUR'S LOST: *Comment* and THE TEMPEST: *Sources*.

Cominius. In *Coriolanus*, consul and commander-in-chief of the Roman army which conquers the Volscian town of Corioli. Cominius gives his own horse to Caius Marcius in recognition of his bravery in the battle, and bestows on him the name "Coriolanus." When the Roman people decide to banish Coriolanus, Cominius pleads on his behalf, citing his performance in the Volscian campaign. His plea unsuccessful, he subsequently attempts to persuade Coriolanus against leading a Volscian attack on Rome.

compositor. The typesetter in a printing shop. Modern TEXTUAL CRITICISM has begun to make an intensive study of the habits of the compositors of Shakespeare's plays in order to determine what disinctive features of the text may result from a given compositor's idiosyncrasies or abilities. An Elizabethan compositor set his type by hand, letter by letter, a practice which made it difficult to keep the sense of the text in mind and which therefore gave rise to a number of meaningless passages in Elizabethan printed books. Then, too, the lack of uniform spelling procedures left each compositor free to spell a given word according to his personal predilection. As a result scholars have been able to identify a compositor's share of a printed text by a close study of spelling habits and other idiosyncrasies.

Charlton Hinman's *The Printing and Proof-Reading of the First Folio of Shakespeare* (1963) is an exhaustive study of the typographical features of the First Folio, printed at the shop of Isaac and William Jaggard. Hinman sees the hands of five compositors at work on the Folio. He identifies these five by the letters *A*, *B*, *C*, *D*, and *E*. According to Hinman, the major part of the Folio, more than 450 pages, was set by *B*, who did most of the comedies and tragedies. Compositor *A* set most of the histories, while the work of *C* and *D*, relatively inexperienced men, is to be seen primarily in the comedies. Compositor *E*, probably an apprentice, worked exclusively on the tragedies, the last section of the book. He set almost all of *Romeo and Juliet* and *Titus Andronicus*, more than half of *King Lear*, and sections of *Troilus and Cressida*, *Hamlet*, and *Othello*. The names of the compositors at the Jaggards' shop are not known, although from 1610 to 1617 one of their apprentices, who might very well have remained in their employ and worked on the Folio, was a John Shakespeare of Warwickshire. [Alice Walker, *Textual Problems of the First Folio*, 1953; Charlton Hinman, *The Printing and Proof-Reading of the First Folio of Shakespeare*, 1963.]

computer scholarship. With the distinct possibility of over 100,000 books—articles, editions, reviews, etc. —on Shakespeare by the end of the 20th century, it is useful, if not absolutely necessary, to consider some electronic means of storing and making accessible Shakespearean scholarship and criticism. As far back as 1957 Kodak had almost completely developed its Minicard system, a system which made it possible to store 12 legal-size pages or 18 smaller-size pages on a film ⅝ inch high by 1¼ inches wide—along with the necessary coding information to make the material on those sheets available: these minicards could be scanned and withdrawn from the file at the rate of 1000 per minute for immediate reference. Kodak had to drop the system after fully developing it, however, because of the expensive complex of machines required. Their Recordak system is far less expensive and almost as effective, except that infiling on a completed roll of film is impossible unless splicing is used. However, IBM and other companies have developed other methods of electronic storage which are capable of doing almost anything that a scholar requires for research in an amazingly brief period of time. It is possible that the Shakespearean student and scholar will, within a hundred years, sit at his desk and merely dial for the information he needs, the information then appearing on a television screen before him in a matter of seconds. In a world where the contents of a 645-page book can be reproduced microscopically on a film one inch square and where such information can be optically researched in thousandths of a second, it is unthinkable that scholars will long continue to do the time-consuming Shakespearean research they did in the past.

Equally as exciting as the opportunities for investigative research in past scholarship are the opportunities for original research, especially of the kind that takes hundreds of hours of mechanical, repetitive operations, as in the making of a concordance, or which requires an almost infinite memory, as in the minute comparison of the work of two authors.

In England Trevor H. Howard-Hill has been investigating the influence of Ralph Crane on the folio texts of the plays that he transcribed for the King's Men. A report of his activities indicated that he was making a study of the 4000 known preferences in spelling used by Crane as a clue to further analysis.

At the time of this writing the whole of the First Folio has been taped for further investigation and there are plans to tape some of the plays in the still-unpublished old-spelling edition of Ronald B. McKerrow and Alice Walker. These tapes will be used by Howard-Hill of Oxford, by a group of scholars at the University of Edinburgh, and will be available to anyone who wishes to have them reproduced for studies elsewhere. We may also assume that electronically produced tapes of the quartos will eventually be available. As scholars for this kind of research increase we would expect to have taped copies of Shakespeare's sources, the plays, poetry, and prose works of his contemporaries, and similar materials. Once these have been taped, the number of studies that could be performed is limited only by the imaginative resources of the investigator. The electronic data-processing machines could also be used to perfect or corroborate the work of the scholars of the past.

While it is impossible to conceive that electronic data processing will solve all problems facing Shakespeareans, it is a distinct possibility that all problems which can be solved by the accumulation of massive statistical evidence will be solved by the end of the 20th century. [Trevor Howard-Hill, "Computer Analysis of Shakespearean Texts," *The Shakespeare Newsletter*, XIV, 6, 1964; Louis Marder, "The Computer in Shakespearean Scholarship," *The Shakespeare Newsletter*, 1965.]—L.M.

concordance. An alphabetical index of the words used by an author. The first Shakespeare concordance was the *Index to the Remarkable Passages and Words made use of by Shakspeare* (1790) compiled by Samuel Ayscough. In 1845 Mary Cowden Clarke painstakingly constructed her *Complete Concordance*, which was superseded by John Bartlett's *New and Complete Concordance* (1894). Bartlett's *Concordance* is the standard work in the field.

Condell, Henry (d. 1627). Actor and co-editor, with John Heminges, of the First Folio of Shakespeare (1623). By 1598, when he appeared in a production of *Every Man In his Humour*, he had become a member of the Chamberlain's Men, Shakespeare's company. He was not one of the original housekeepers of the Globe when it was built the following year, but he did subsequently acquire an interest in that playhouse and in the Blackfriars theatre. He acted in Ben Jonson's *Sejanus* (1603), *Volpone* (1605), *The Alchemist* (1610), and *Catiline*

(1611); however, the only known role attributable to Condell is the Cardinal in *The Duchess of Malfi* (pub. 1623).

Condell retired from the stage about 1623, and removed to his country estate at Fulham. Condell's will, dated December 13, 1627, named his wife Elizabeth executrix and John Heminges, Cuthbert Burbage, Herbert Finch (his son-in-law), and Peter Saunderson ("grocer") overseers. His widow was the chief legatee and received his shares in the Globe and Blackfriars. Condell had evidently maintained warm and cordial relationships with the other actors in the troupe. He is named in several of his fellows' wills, including that of Shakespeare, who bequeathed him 26s. 8d. to buy a memorial ring. Both Heminges and Condell were active in the parish affairs of St. Mary's Aldermanbury, where Condell was buried. In 1896 a monument outside the church was erected to the memories of Heminges and Condell in recognition of their work on the Folio.

Condell was never famous in his own right as an actor, but he was evidently a highly esteemed personage in the theatre. The work for which both Heminges and Condell are best known is their overseeing the publication of the First Folio in 1623, though scholars consider that the actual editing of the Folio was done by someone else (see FIRST FOLIO). The importance of their work on the Folio was recognized almost immediately, as the epigram in the SALISBURY MANUSCRIPT suggests. [E. K. Chambers, *The Elizabethan Stage*, 1923; G. E. Bentley, *The Jacobean and Caroline Stage*, 5 vols., 1941–1956.]

Conrad, Joseph. Original name **Teodor Jósef Konrad Korzeniowski** (1857–1924). Polish-born novelist. After miscellaneous youthful adventures, Conrad joined the British merchant service, becoming a ship's master in 1886; in 1894 he retired to devote himself to writing. Among his principal works are *The Nigger of the "Narcissus"* (1897), *Lord Jim* (1900), *Heart of Darkness* (1902), *Nostromo* (1904), *Chance* (1913), and *Victory* (1915).

Shakespeare made an early and lasting impression on Conrad; as a boy he had read Shakespeare in translations made by his father. With his first earnings he bought a copy of the complete works and kept the volume with him during his years at sea. He was familiar with A. C. Bradley's *Shakespearean Tragedy* (1904), which he read a few months before he finished *Victory* and which may have exerted an influence on that work. Several of his novels contain epigraphs from Shakespeare, and in some instances the direct influence of Shakespeare is discernible. *Chance* has suggestions of *Othello:* the Desdemona-Othello-Iago triangle has a parallel in the relationship of Flora, Anthony, and de Barral, and there are a number of verbal echoes throughout. There is also a parallel between *Victory* and *The Tempest*. The hero Heyst lives on an island where, like a Prospero without magic, he must protect the Miranda-like Lena; peace is restored only after an invasion by forces of violence and fraud. In addition, some resemblances of Heyst to Hamlet were noted by an early reviewer and repeated by James Huneker in an appreciative chapter on Conrad in *Ivory Apes and Peacocks* (1915). [Frederick R. Karl, *A Reader's Guide to Joseph Conrad*, 1960.]

Conrade. In *Much Ado About Nothing*, a follower of Don John, who has been worsted in battle b Don Pedro. Conrade advises Don John to suffer hi defeat patiently and to ingratiate himself with th victor, but promises that when the opportunity arise to cross Claudio, he will assist his lord "to the death. Although he is not involved in the actual plot, Con rade is arrested while listening to Borachio's repor of his part in it. In the ensuing interrogation, he call Dogberry an ass (IV, ii).

Conspirators with Aufidius. In *Coriolanus*, the con spirators aid Aufidius in murdering Coriolanus (V, vi)

Constable of France. In *Henry V*, a leader of th French army at Agincourt, where he is killed in bat tle. Historically, he was Charles de la Bret, an illegiti mate son of Charles le Mauvais, king of Navarre, an a half brother to Henry V of England by virtue o the marriage of his stepmother, Joan of Navarre, t Henry IV. [W. H. Thomson, *Shakespeare's Charac ters: A Historical Dictionary*, 1951.]

Constance of Brittany (d. 1201). Daughter o Conon le Petit, duke of Britanny; wife of Geoffre Plantagenet, and mother of Arthur. After Geoffrey' death, Constance was married twice more. In *Kin John*, she is determined that her son wear the Eng lish crown. When John defeats her allies and cap tures Arthur, Constance goes mad and dies.

Contention plays. Phrase used to designate tw plays now generally regarded as "bad quartos" o *2* and *3 Henry VI*. The Contention plays, firs

TITLE PAGE OF *The First Part of the Contention*, NOW CONSIDERED A BAD QUARTO OF *2 Henry VI* (1594).

THE
First part of the Con-
tention betwixt the two famous Houses of Yorke
and Lancaster, with the death of the good
Duke Humphrey:

And the banishment and death of the Duke of
Suffolke, and the Tragicall end of the proud Cardinall
of *VVinchester*, vvith the notable Rebellion
of *Iacke Cade*:

And the Duke of Yorkes first claime vnto the Crowne.

LONDON
Printed by Thomas Creed, for Thomas Millington,
and are to be sold at his shop vnder Saint Peters
Church in Cornwall.
1594.

The true Tragedie of Richard Duke of Yorke, and the death of good King Henrie the Sixt,

with the whole contention betweene the two Houses Lancaster and Yorke, as it was sundrie times acted by the Right Honourable the Earle of Pembrooke his seruants.

Printed at London by P. S. for Thomas Millington, and are to be sold at his shoppe vnder Saint Peters Church in Cornwal. 1595.

TITLE PAGE OF *The True Tragedie*, NOW CONSIDERED A BAD QUARTO OF *3 Henry VI* (1595).

rinted in 1594 and 1595, have the following title ages:

The First part of the Contention betwixt the two famous Houses of Yorke and Lancaster, with the death of the good Duke Humphrey: And the banishment and death of the Duke of Suffolke, and the Tragicall end of the proud Cardinall of Winchester, with the notable rebellion of Iacke Cade: And the Duke of Yorkes first claime vnto the Crowne. *Thomas Creede for Thomas Millington.*

The true Tragedie of Richard Duke of Yorke, and the death of good King Henrie the Sixt, with the whole contention betweene the two Houses Lancaster and Yorke, as it was sundrie times acted by the Right Honourable the Earle of Pembrooke his seruants. *P.S. for Thomas Millington.*

Both plays were reprinted in 1600 and in a combined form in 1619 as part of a collection of falsely lated Shakespearean and pseudo-Shakespearean plays. The title pages of the 1619 edition attributed the uthorship to Shakespeare:

The Whole Contention betweene the two Famous Houses, Lancaster and Yorke. With the Tragicall ends of the good Duke Humfrey, Richard Duke of Yorke, and King Henrie the sixt. Diuided into two Parts: And newly corrected and enlarged. Written by William Shakespeare, Gent. *For T.P.*

From the time of Edmund Malone until well into the 20th century, scholars generally believed that the Contention plays were written by one of the University Wits and later revised by Shakespeare into *2* and *3 Henry VI.* The leading candidates for the authorship were Christopher Marlowe, Robert Greene, and George Peele. Greene's attack on Shakespeare in GROATS-WORTH OF WIT has been seen as evidence for this belief. In 1929, however, Peter Alexander, echoing an argument first put forth by Thomas Kenny in 1864, argued that the Contention plays were BAD QUARTOS of Shakespeare's plays, based on MEMORIAL RECONSTRUCTION.

Alexander's arguments have generally been accepted, although doubt still exists among some scholars, notably J. Dover Wilson and Charles T. Prouty. [Peter Alexander, *Shakespeare's Henry VI and Richard III*, 1929; Charles T. Prouty, *The Contention and Shakespeare's 2 Henry VI*, 1954.]

continuous copy. In TEXTUAL CRITICISM, a term used to describe the theory advanced by J. Dover Wilson and A. W. Pollard that the original PROMPT-BOOK of a play, regardless of how much revision and alteration it might be subject to, would continue to be retained as the prompt copy. The basis of the continuous-copy theory is the belief that the acting companies would be extremely reluctant to reproduce any copies of a play which could fall into the hands of a printer or a rival troupe of actors. The promptbook usually cited in support of the theory is the manuscript of *Sir Thomas More*, a play which received extensive alteration and revision by a number of hands but which still retained its original sheets.

This theory has been rejected by W. W. Greg on the ground that it overemphasizes a reluctance to publish on the part of members of the acting companies, who, on the contrary, frequently sold plays to the publishers. Greg also argues that there is no evidence to support the idea that *Sir Thomas More* ever reached the stage or that the extant manuscript was ever used—or indeed could have been used in its chaotic condition—as a working prompt-book in an Elizabethan playhouse. [W. W. Greg, *The Editorial Problem in Shakespeare*, 1942.]

Conway, William Augustus. Real name **Rugg** (1789–1828). Born in London, Conway was educated in Barbados. At the age of 18, in weak health, he returned to England and became stagestruck. His success in Young's tragedy *The Revenge* at Chester led to an offer from Macready and to a provincial tour as Macbeth. In 1813 he was hired to replace the star in Dublin, and there developed a passion for Eliza O'Neill. An encounter with Charles Mathews resulted in his debut at Covent Garden the following year. His Shakespearean roles included Romeo, Othello, Henry V, Coriolanus, Antony (in *Julius Caesar*), Petruchio, Orlando, Richmond, the Prince of Wales, Macduff, and Faulconbridge. In 1816 Conway played Henry V in the Garrick Jubilee on the bicentenary of Shakespeare's death. In 1824 he appeared in America as Coriolanus and Petruchio, with great success, and also delivered some religious discourses in public. He died a suicide in the United States. He was noted for the effectiveness of his portrayals of agony and sorrow, and his brilliant declamation, but he was ill at ease and given to fantastic gesture designed to startle an audience into applause.

Hazlitt, in his *View of the English Stage* (1818), described Conway as Romeo (with Miss O'Neill as Juliet) as characterized by "unwieldy" motion, with a voice comparable to Gargantuan thunder in its effect on the ear ". . . but when he pleases to be soft he is 'the very beadle to an amorous sigh.'" [*Dictionary of National Biography*, 1885- .]

cony-catching pamphlets. A series of exposés of the activities of the Elizabethan underworld written by Robert GREENE. A cony-catcher was a confidence man or swindler whose tricks and schemes are detailed by Greene in vivid, racy prose. The first of these pamphlets, *A Notable Discovery of Cozenage,* appeared in 1591. Its success was such that it was followed by a *Second Part of Cony-Catching* (1592), a *Third Part of Cony-Catching* (1592), and *A Disputation between a He Cony-Catcher and a She Cony-Catcher* (1592). Shakespeare drew upon the cony-catching pamphlets for the tricks and the dialogue of that supreme cony-catcher AUTOLYCUS in *The Winter's Tale.* [Kenneth Muir, *Shakespeare's Sources,* Vol. I, 1957.]

Cooke, Alexander (d. 1614). Actor. Cooke probably became a full member (a SHARER) of the King's Men, Shakespeare's acting company, in 1603. Before that he was most likely a hired man (see HIRED MEN), perhaps apprenticed to John Heminges. W. W. Greg and F. G. Fleay have attempted to identify Cooke with the Saunder who is listed in the "plot" of Tarlton's *Seven Deadly Sins* (given as a revival by the amalgamated Admiral's-Strange's Men about 1591) in the roles of Videna in the Envy episode and of Progne in Lechery, both female roles. Both Edmund Malone and T. W. Baldwin have conjectured that Cooke took female roles exclusively, especially portraying so-called strong-minded women, such as Tamora in *Titus Andronicus* and Katharina in *The Taming of the Shrew,* but little evidence exists to support any of the above identifications. His name does, however, appear in several printed acting lists. His is among "the names of the principall Actors in all these playes" of the 1623 First Folio of Shakespeare's plays. He is also in the acting lists of the King's Men's productions of Ben Jonson's tragedies *Sejanus* (1603) and *Catiline* (1611), Jonson's comedies *Volpone* (1605) and *The Alchemist* (1610), as well as *The Captain* (1612/3), a play usually attributed to Beaumont and Fletcher.

In Augustine Phillips' will of 1605 Cooke was a legatee of the following bequest from Phillips: "To my fellowe Alexander Cook twenty shillings in gould." Cooke himself died in February 1614. In his own will, executed in January 1614, he named Henry Condell and John Heminges trustees, referring to Heminges as his "master." [E. K. Chambers, *The Elizabethan Stage,* 1923; T. W. Baldwin, *The Organization and Personnel of the Shakespearean Company,* 1927.]

Cooke, John. See C., I.; A MOURNEFUL DITTIE.

Cooper, James Fenimore (1789–1851). American novelist. America's earliest major novelist, Cooper is remembered primarily for his *Leatherstocking Tales* (1823–1841), five novels that portray the career of Natty Bumppo, a frontier hero. Other significant works include *The Spy* (1821), *The Pilot* (1823), and *Satanstoe* (1845), a novel that deals with the social history of New York State.

According to his daughter Susan, Cooper was "al ways ready" to read Shakespeare to the family, "en tering with unfeigned delight into the spirit of hi works." In *Jack Tier* (1848) Cooper describes Shake speare as "the great poet of our language, and th greatest that ever lived, perhaps, short of the inspire writers of the Old Testament, and old Homer an Dante." Cooper's familiarity with Shakespeare is at tested to by his quoted chapter headings, more tha 40 per cent of which are from the plays. Cooper ha left no significant criticism of Shakespeare.

In his "Cooper's Indebtedness to Shakespeare, W. B. Gates argues that the novelist borrowed nu merous incidents from the plays and that many o Cooper's characters have Shakespearean prototypes *The Spy,* for example, contains echoes of *Much Ad About Nothing* and *Measure for Measure.* A sugges tion of Claudio's situation in the latter play occur when Henry Wharton, under sentence of death awaits a reprieve, but when the messenger arrives h confirms the sentence. Cooper himself invited com parison by opening the chapter describing Wharton' predicament with a quotation from *Measure fo Measure:* "Have you no countermand for Claudi yet/ But he must die tomorrow?"

Gates suggests, too, that *The Pioneers,* the firs novel of the Leatherstocking series, is an adaptatio of *King Lear.* In both works a man, driven mad afte giving away his property, is cared for by a faithfu retainer. The storm scene in the play is paralleled b a forest fire and storm in the novel, and Natty Bumppo, like Kent, is "put into the stocks." Further more, when Edward Effingham learns of his grand father's poverty, he removes him to a hut. Since ther is no reason for this development in the novel, Gate suggests that Cooper, in including this incident, wa merely following Shakespeare.

Several other parallels have been noted by Gates *The Pilot* (1823) relies on characters and situation from *As You Like It* and *1 Henry VI; Lionel Lincol* (1825) is based on the Gloucester plot of *Lear; Th Last of the Mohicans* (1826) and *The Prairie* (1827 are reminiscent of *As You Like It* and *Romeo an Juliet* respectively; the plot of *The Wept of th Wish-ton-Wish* (1829) was derived from *Cymbeline* incidents in *Homeward Bound* and *Home as Foun* (1838) have parallels in *The Winter's Tale;* and *Th Crater* (1847), which involves a feud between th families of the hero and heroine, is based upo *Romeo and Juliet.* Captain Peter Polwarth in *Lione Lincoln,* Captain Burroughcliffe in *The Pilot,* an Hector Homespun in *The Red Rover* (1827) are al reminiscent of Falstaff. The chapter that introduce Polwarth, in fact, is headed by Falstaff's descriptio of himself: "A goodly portly man, i' faith, and corpulent." Similarly, E. P. Vandiver has argued con vincingly that Dr. Battius of *The Prairie* is based o Holofernes in *Love's Labour's Lost.*

Many of the "parallel" incidents which Gate points to may have been adopted from sources othe than Shakespeare. Many of them, as Gates is aware are stock situations in the historical romance and i the classics as well. Even granting a direct borrowin from the plays, as the frequency of quoted chapte headings from the plays may suggest, the influenc would appear to be related largely to plot, an area i which neither Shakespeare nor Cooper was especiall outstanding or original. Thomas Philbrick, however, has suggested recently that *The Water-Witch* (1830) resembles *The Tempest* because of its "dreamlike mood" and its interest in "rhetorical experimentation." Since Cooper was familiar with the plays, it might be of interest to consider whether Shakespeare's idea of order or his concept of nature had any effect on the American novelist. [Edward P. Vandiver, Jr., "James Fenimore Cooper and Shakespeare," *Shakespeare Association Bulletin*, XV, 1940; William B. Gates, "Cooper's Indebtedness to Shakespeare," *PMLA*, LXVII, 1952; Edward P. Vandiver, Jr., "Cooper's *The Prairie* and Shakespeare," *PMLA*, LXIX, 1954; Thomas Philbrick, *James Fenimore Cooper and the Development of American Sea Fiction*, 1961.]

Cooper, Thomas (c. 1517–1594). Bishop of Winchester (1584–1594) and lexicographer, whose *Thesaurus Linguae Romanae et Britannicae* (1565) was the standard reference work on classical mythology in the Elizabethan age. An active polemicist in defense of the Church of England, Cooper was the author of numerous religious works, including one of the treatises in the Marprelate controversy. Cooper's *Thesaurus* is a Latin-English lexicon and phrase book with a separate section for proper names. Shakespeare seems to have drawn from it the description of Tarquin in *The Rape of Lucrece* and the famous lines in *Antony and Cleopatra* spoken by Cleopatra at the moment of her death when she refers to the fatal asp applied to her breast as "my baby . . . / That sucks the nurse asleep." [De Witt T. Starnes and Ernest William Talbert, *Classical Myth and Legend in Renaissance Dictionaries*, 1956.]

Cooper, Thomas Abthorpe (1776–1849). English-born American actor. Cooper began his career in England playing minor parts in provincial acting companies before making his London debut as Hamlet at Covent Garden in 1796. He then came to the United States, where he remained for most of his career. With Hamlet in 1804, Cooper entered into a peak period in his career, becoming involved in management and direction and marrying into a socially prominent New York family. He maintained his position until 1827, but his popularity waned thereafter. Handsome and majestic, Cooper was in the first rank of contemporary Hamlets, Macbeths, and Othellos early in his career and he did Falstaff with some success. [*Dictionary of American Biography*, 1927– .]

Cope, Sir Walter (d. 1614). Courtier and antiquary. Knighted in 1603 and appointed a chamberlain of the exchequer shortly thereafter, Cope was a prominent and profligate member of the Jacobean court. During the Christmas season of 1604/5 he wrote the following note to Robert Cecil, 1st earl of Salisbury:

> Sir,
>
> I have sent and bene all thys morning huntyng for players Juglers & Such kinde of Creaturs, but fynde them harde to finde, wherfore Leavinge notes for them to seeke me, Burbage ys come, & Sayes ther ys no new playe that the quene hath not seene, but they have Revyved an olde one, Cawled *Loves Labore lost*, which for wytt & mirthe he sayes will please her excedingly. And Thys ys apointed to be playd to Morowe night at my Lord of Sowthamptons, unless yow send a wrytt to Remove the Corpus Cum Causa to your howse in Strande. Burbage ys my messenger Ready attendyng your pleasure.
>
> Yours most humbly,

Another letter referring to the same event indicates that the performance was held at Cecil's house in January 1605. [E. K. Chambers, *William Shakespeare*, 1930.]

Copeau, Jacques. See FRANCE.

Copland, Aaron. See MUSIC BASED ON SHAKESPEARE: *20th century*.

copy. The manuscript or printed text used by the printers of Shakespeare's plays. The question of the copy used for the printed editions of the plays has become one of the most important and vexing problems of modern TEXTUAL CRITICISM. Determining the nature of the copy that has been used by a printer of the plays helps to determine how close, or far removed, a printing may be from Shakespeare's original. The copy used by the printers was any one of a number of sources: the author's FOUL PAPERS, or rough first draft; his FAIR COPY, corrected and revised by the author or a professional scribe; the acting company's PROMPT-BOOK; earlier printed editions of the play, sometimes with corrections and additions inserted; a manuscript based on a MEMORIAL RECONSTRUCTION; a text based on a STENOGRAPHIC REPORT made by someone in the audience of the theatre where the play was acted; an ASSEMBLED TEXT, arrived at by putting together the actors' individual parts with the PLOT used by the acting company.

According to W. W. Greg, a pioneer in the study of the copy of the plays, examples of texts derived from foul papers include the First Quartos of *Love's Labour's Lost* and *Richard II* and the Second Quarto of *Romeo and Juliet*. Examples of fair copy sources for the text have been seen in the First Quarto of *Othello*, as well as in the Folio texts of *All's Well That Ends Well* and *Measure for Measure*. The King's Men prompt-books, or transcripts of them, appear to have been used for the Folio texts of *The Two Gentlemen of Verona*, *The Merry Wives of Windsor*, *Julius Caesar*, *As You Like It*, *Twelfth Night*, *Macbeth*, and *Cymbeline*. Earlier printed editions (quartos) with annotations from the prompt-book or an authorial manuscript probably provided the Folio texts of *A Midsummer Night's Dream*, *The Merchant of Venice*, *Richard II*, *Much Ado About Nothing*, *Troilus and Cressida*, *Othello*, and *King Lear*. Texts based on a memorial reconstruction or a stenographic report are those classified as BAD QUARTOS and include *The First part of the Contention betwixt the two famous Houses of Yorke and Lancaster* (*2 Henry VI*) and *The true Tragedy of Richard Duke of Yorke* (*3 Henry VI*), as well as the First Quartos of *Romeo and Juliet*, *Hamlet*, *Henry V*, *The Merry Wives of Windsor*, and possibly *King Lear*. *The Taming of A Shrew* is seen by some scholars as a "bad quarto" of Shakespeare's Shrew play. The theory of assembled texts as copy, advanced by Dover Wilson to explain certain distinctive characteristics in the Folio texts of *The Two Gentlemen of Verona*, *The Winter's Tale*, and other Folio plays, has not been generally accepted.

It should be added that the question of the copy for the texts of the plays is receiving intensive study at the present time and that the classifications listed above are largely tentative and subject to change under the light of further investigation. [Fredson Bowers, *On Editing Shakespeare and the Elizabethan Dramatists,* 1955; W. W. Greg, *The Shakespeare First Folio,* 1955.]

copyright. Authorial copyright in England was practically nonexistent before the first Copyright Act of 1710. Before this an author held a more or less implicit common-law right in his work, and in some cases a direct copyright from the crown insured the author's control over the publication of his material. Publisher's copyright on the other hand was secured through the Stationers' Company, but it is not entirely clear what the procedure for acquiring copyright involved. It was thought that copyright was conferred simply by entering the publication in the Stationers' Register. However, Leo Kirschbaum (*Shakespeare and the Stationers,* 1955) has argued with some effectiveness that copyright was secured by publication, not by registration. Thus Kirschbaum's thesis suggests that even in the case of unregistered, surreptitiously published plays, such as the Shakespearean "bad quartos," the publishers of these plays retained copyright. This thesis explains some otherwise inexplicable facts, such as the fact that Nicholas Ling, the publisher of the bad quarto of *Hamlet* (Q1) in 1603, was also the publisher of the good quarto (Q2) in 1604. It also accounts for the fact that an estimated one-third of the books published during the Elizabethan period were never entered in the Register.

Kirschbaum's theory has been rejected by C. J. Sisson who, as a result of a study of a dispute within the Stationers' Company, has concluded that copyright could only be ensured by registration, provided the book being registered had never before been printed. An unregistered book, according to Sisson, ran the risk of being subsequently printed by another stationer. In such a case, the only recourse the original printer would have would be to bring his case before the court of the Stationers' Company. [Leo Kirschbaum, "The Copyright of Elizabethan Plays," *The Library,* 3rd series, XIV, 1959; C. J. Sisson, "The Laws of Elizabethan Copyright: the Stationers' View," *The Library,* 3rd series, XV, 1960.]

JAGGARD AND BLOUNT'S ENTRY IN THE STATIONERS' REGISTER OF NOVEMBER 8, 1623 FOR THOSE OF SHAKESPEARE'S PLAYS THAT HAD NOT BEEN PUBLISHED IN QUARTO. FOR SIX SHILLINGS THEY REGISTERED 16 PLAYS AND SECURED THE RIGHT TO PUBLISH THE FIRST FOLIO. (STATIONERS' HALL, BY PERMISSION OF THE WORSHIPFUL COMPANY OF STATIONERS.)

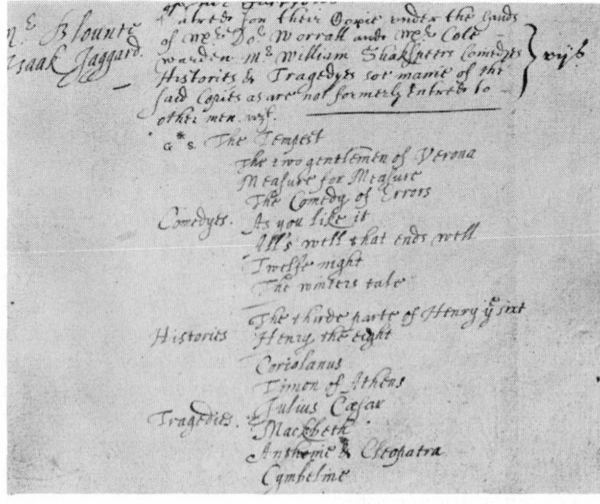

Corbet, Richard (1582–1635). Prelate and poet. Corbet served successively as bishop of Oxford and Norwich, but the dignity of those offices apparently never interfered with his establishing a reputation as a witty, satirical poet. His poems were first printed in 1647 under the title *Certain Elegant Poems written by Dr. Corbet, bishop of Norwich.* In one of these poems he recounts a visit to Bosworth Field:

Mine host was full of ale and history,
And, on the morrow, when he brought us nigh
Where the two Roses joyned, you would suppose
Chaucer nere writ the Romant of the Rose.
Heare him,—See yee yond' woods? there Richard lay
With his whole army. Looke the other way,
And loe where Richmond in a bed of grosse
Encamp'd himselfe o're night with all his force.
Upon this hill they met. Why, he could tell
The inch where Richmond stood, where Richard fell;
Besides what of his knowledge he could say,
Hee had authentique notice from the play,
Which I might guesse by's mustring up the ghosts,
And policies not incident to hosts;
But chiefly by that one perspicuous thing
Where he mistooke a player for a king,
For when he would have said, King Richard dy'd,
And call'd a horse, a horse, he Burbage cry'd.

The quotation is an amusing testimony to the acclaim accorded Richard Burbage for his portrayal of Richard III. [J. O. Halliwell-Phillipps, *Outlines of the Life of Shakespeare,* 1881.]

Cordelia. In *King Lear,* the youngest daughter of the King. Although Cordelia makes only a few relatively brief appearances in the play, she leaves a profound impact on the audience. Many critics, including Coleridge, have censured Cordelia for her pride and obstinacy in the opening scene in which she refuses to humor her father by professing her love. Others argue that her candor is a measure of the strength of her affection and the beauty of her character. None deny the attraction of her character in the last part of the play, although Freud provided the most startling explanation of it when he characterized her as the embodiment of the death-wish. In recent Christian interpretations of the play, Cordelia has come to assume increasing importance. John F. Danby, for example, asserts that "to understand Cordelia is to understand the whole play." In Danby's analysis, Cordelia represents Charity, which for him is the overriding principle of the play. [John F. Danby, *Shakespeare's Doctrine of Nature: A Study of King Lear,* 1949.]

Corin. In *As You Like It,* an old shepherd who arranges the purchase of his master's house, sheep, and pasture for Rosalind and Celia. Touchstone pronounces Corin a natural philosopher but humorously judges him damned for the sin of never having been at court. The old man defends himself against this condemnation, but rests his case acknowledging Touchstone to "have too courtly a wit for me" (III, ii).

Coriolanus. Real name **Caius Marcius** (1st half of 5th c. B.C.). Roman general and hero of *Coriolanus.* The known historical facts relating to Caius Marcius, surnamed Coriolanus, are few, for his story is based largely on legend, but these facts agree in general with those given in Shakespeare's play. He was a noble and distinguished warrior whose open contempt for the common people resulted in his being exiled from Rome in 491 B.C. His march against Rome and his subsequent yielding to his mother's request that he spare the city are all recorded in Plutarch, Shakespeare's source, through the splendid translation of Sir Thomas North.

Coriolanus, like the play he inhabits, usually commands a respectful but rather frigid admiration. His attitude toward the common people inevitably evokes a critical attitude in modern audiences. Thus many modern readers have come to regard the play as a form of "tragic satire" in which both the hero and his adversary, the mob, are presented as objects of derision. [O. J. Campbell, *Shakespeare's Satire,* 1943.]

The Tragedy of Coriolanus

Coriolanus. A tragedy by Shakespeare.

Text. The only authoritative text is that of the First Folio. It contains many errors, chiefly in mislineations and some printing of verse as prose, and prose as verse, the result of the printer's miscalculations as to the space required for the play (see CASTING OFF COPY).

Date. Verse tests and the style fix the date of *Coriolanus* between the dates of *Antony and Cleopatra* and *Pericles.* Shakespeare probably began to write this play soon after completing *Antony and Cleopatra.* Verbal echoes of *Coriolanus* have been detected in two nearly contemporary works, Ben Jonson's *Epicœne* (1609) and Robert Armin's *Phantasma the Italian Taylor and His Boy* (pub. 1609). The so-called "echoes" in Jonson's comedy are of words and phrases too common in Elizabethan literature to serve as evidence for dating a play, but the quotation of *Coriolanus* in Armin's work furnishes better evidence. In Shakespeare's tragedy Caius Marcius, in reporting the absurd delight of the plebeians at having their complaints listened to, says in scorn, "They threw their caps / As they would hang them on the horns o' the moon" (I, i, 216–217). In Armin's Preface to his work he writes:

> A strange time of taxation, wherein every Pen and inck-horn Boy will throw his Cap at the hornes of the Moone in censure although his wit hang there, not returning unless monthly on the wane.

Armin's borrowing of this striking figure lends support to the view that *Coriolanus* was written before 1609. His membership in Shakespeare's company from 1599 to 1610 made it possible for him to hear this easily remembered figure spoken during the rehearsal and production of *Coriolanus.* It is possible, but unlikely, that Shakespeare borrowed the phrase from Armin. G. B. Harrison points out that the theme of a class struggle would have had peculiar interest in the year 1608, for in early summer of the previous year just such a conflict had led to a number of outbreaks in the northern and midland counties of England. All available external evidence points to the year 1608 as the date of the first production of *Coriolanus* (see TOPICAL REFERENCES).

Sources. The principal source of the play is the account of the life of Caius Marcius Coriolanus in the translation (2nd ed., 1595) of Plutarch's *Lives* made by Sir Thomas NORTH by way of Jacques Amyot's French translation. Plutarch's account of the events dramatized in the play was designed to teach a lesson in political restraint and accommodation. Shakespeare took the central facts from Plutarch and, where it suited his dramatic purpose, enlarged and embellished them, as in the characters of Menenius and Volumnia.

Menenius' "fable of the belly"—the speech that he delivers to the plebeians (I, i, 99 ff.)—is found in Plutarch, but Shakespeare seems to have used other versions of the fable, particularly the account given by William Averell (fl. 1584) in his *Meruailous Combat of Contrarieties* and by William CAMDEN in his *Remaines of a Greater Worke Concerning Britaine* (1605). Shakespeare may also have known Livy's version in his *Annales* (Book XXXII), either in the original Latin or in Philemon Holland's English translation (1600). A. L. Rowse suggests that the discussion of the three servingmen in Aufidius' house on the advantages of war over peace (IV, v, 233–

250) derived some of its substance from *Foure Paradoxes, or Politique Discourses* (1604), by Thomas and Dudley Digges.—O.J.C.

Plot Synopsis. Act I. The citizens of Rome, on the verge of rebellion because of a scarcity of grain, are especially bitter toward the patrician Caius Marcius, known as the "chief enemy to the people." Though he has performed great services to the state, it is said that he was moved mainly by his pride and his desire to please his mother. Menenius Agrippa, a friend of Marcius and "one that hath always loved the people," tries to persuade the hungry plebeians that the patricians are genuinely interested in their welfare, recounting a fable in which the members of the body revolt against the belly but eventually realize that the belly sustains them all. Marcius, however, bluntly denounces the commoners for their inconstancy and presumption and reveals with disgust that, in response to their petition, the senators have appointed five tribunes to protect the commoners' interests. Shortly thereafter, Marcius, with the consul Cominius and Titus Lartius, is sent to quell an uprising of the Volscians led by Tullus Aufidius, whom Marcius describes as a lion that he is proud to hunt. Virgilia, Marcius' wife, is sorrowful over his departure and refuses to leave her home until he returns, but his mother, Volumnia, rejoices in his military exploits and recalls with pleasure the day he won his first oaken garland in battle against the Tarquins.

Near Corioli, the Volscian capital, Marcius curses his soldiers for their faintheartedness, and by his own bravery inspires them to capture the city. Although Marcius refuses his share of the booty and scorns the praise of his comrades, Cominius declares that henceforth Marcius shall be known as Coriolanus in memory of his victory. His deeds have also won him the implacable enmity of Tullus Aufidius, who vows to destroy him even if he must resort to trickery.

Act II. The tribunes Sicinius Velutus and Junius Brutus try to convince Menenius that Marcius is overly proud, but that "humorous patrician" replies by deriding the ambition and servility of the tribunes. Upon his triumphal return to Rome amid the applause of the multitude, Coriolanus becomes a candidate for the consulship and quickly wins the approbation of the senate. With great reluctance he bows to the custom that requires office seekers to don a gown of humility and to solicit the citizens' votes by displaying their wounds. Although they readily give him their votes, some of the plebeians later assert that there was mockery in his appeal and, encouraged by the tribunes, decide to withdraw their approval.

Act III. As Coriolanus discusses the news that Tullus Aufidius, who now makes his headquarters at Antium, is preparing to take up arms again, Sicinius and Brutus announce that the citizens no longer consent to his election. The tribunes charge that Coriolanus opposed the free distribution of grain to the citizens. He replies that, since they were unwilling to fight in their country's defense, the citizens did not deserve the grain. Summoned by the tribunes, the outraged citizens try to seize Coriolanus, but he and the senators manage to repel them. When the tribunes demand the death of Coriolanus, Menenius appeases them by promising to bring him to the Forum to answer to the citizens' complaints. Coriolanus, however, refuses Menenius' request, yielding only to the entreaties of his mother, who argues that policy combined with honor is as necessary in peace as in war. When Coriolanus appears in the Forum, the plebeians accuse him of harboring tyrannical ambitions, and, forgetting his promise to speak mildly, he launches into a tirade against the people and their tribunes. At this, Sicinius orders him to leave the city immediately. While the citizens shout their approval of his exile, Coriolanus utters a final denunciation of the Romans: he hopes that they will banish their defenders and quake before their enemies until they have delivered themselves into the power of their foes.

Act IV. As his mother weeps, losing for once her "ancient courage," Coriolanus leaves Rome and goes to Antium. Disguised by his mean attire, he forces his way into the house of Tullus Aufidius and, after revealing his identity, puts himself at the disposal of his old enemy, offering to become the victim or the ally of the Volscians. Tullus declares himself overjoyed to greet Coriolanus as a comrade and offers to share his command with him in a new war against Rome.

The satisfaction of the tribunes over their successful campaign against Coriolanus is rudely disturbed by rumors that he has joined Tullus and is devastating the countryside. Menenius ironically congratulates the tribunes for their "fair work" in banishing Coriolanus, and the citizens begin to regret his exile. One observes, "Though we willingly consented to his banishment, yet it was against our will."

Tullus, meanwhile, is displeased by the pride of Coriolanus and by his growing popularity among the Volscians. He is confident, nevertheless, that, though Coriolanus will undoubtedly regain the favor of the Romans, some flaw in his nature will cause him to lose it again.

Act V. Having gone to the Volscian camp to plead for Rome, Cominius tells the Romans that Coriolanus is determined to destroy the city. At the request of the tribunes, Menenius visits Coriolanus but, somewhat to his surprise, the general remains impervious to the pleas of his old friend, offering only the terms that the Romans had previously rejected. The next suppliants are Volumnia, Virgilia, and the small son of Coriolanus. Kneeling before her son, Volumnia asks him to take pity on her and Virgilia, for they are torn between their devotion to Rome and their love for him. She does not ask him to harm the Volscians, but merely to negotiate a peace honorable to both sides. Coriolanus seems unmoved and the women turn to go, but he takes Volumnia by the hand and declares that she has won "a happy victory to Rome," though it is one that bodes ill for him.

While the Romans welcome Coriolanus with flowers and music, Tullus returns to Antium, bitterly angry at Coriolanus for usurping his position among the Volscians and then deserting them on the eve of victory. Coriolanus arrives in Antium to explain his conduct to the Volscians. Reminding them of the spoils they had won under his leadership, he shows them the peace treaty with Rome. When Tullus accuses him of betraying the Volscians, Coriolanus retorts with an insulting reference to his triumph at Corioli. Incited by Tullus' henchmen and recalling kinsmen who had died at Roman hands, the citizens fall upon Coriolanus and murder him. His rage now spent, Tullus decrees that Coriolanus shall have "a noble memory" in Antium.—H.D.

Comment. Coriolanus is a political tragedy. Its subject is a class struggle set in the Rome of 490 B.C. It confronts the plebeians with the patricians, the poor with rich, the weak with the powerful. The subject was of very present interest to Shakespeare, as a landowner, and to his audiences, because it reflected a contemporary social situation. In May 1607 there erupted in England a popular revolt against the gentry because of their enclosure of great stretches of agricultural land for the pasturage of sheep. This brought about a scarcity of "corn" (that is, wheat) and sent its price skyrocketing. Shakespeare presents a similar economic crisis as the cause of the uprising of the plebeians. They ignorantly blame the patricians for their destitution, whereas the real cause of their suffering is a prolonged drought. In any case, the patricians, insensible to the plight of the common people, refuse to alleviate their distress by gifts of grain from their stores. A tragic protagonist given the principal part in this drama of an economic situation was of necessity different from those in the earlier great tragedies. One of his flaws is political: he is a bad ruler. He breaks one of the most important rules for the conduct of a successful prince formulated by Renaissance writers of treatises on government, namely that a governor should treat his subjects as though they were his own dear children. But Coriolanus, far from acting as their kind and sympathetic father, despises them. In his role of military captain he holds his common soldiers in contempt. When, in a battle with the Volsces, his men have been beaten back to their trenches, he vehemently berates them:

> All the contagion of the south light on you,
> You shames of Rome! you herd of—Boils and plagues
> Plaster you o'er, that you may be abhorr'd!
> (I, iv, 30–32)

Thus, his personal courage is sullied by his brutal treatment of his troops.

He attacks even more outrageously the mob of plebeians, who revolt against their natural governors, seeking to establish a democracy of wills in place of a leader's authority:

> What's the matter, you dissentious rogues,
> That, rubbing the poor itch of your opinion,
> Make yourselves scabs?
> . . . . . .
> He that will give good words to thee will flatter
> Beneath abhorring. What would you have, you curs,
> That like nor peace nor war? the one affrights you,
> The other makes you proud.
> (I, i, 167–169, 171–174)

He has also serious personal faults. Two members of a crowd of mutinous citizens discuss Coriolanus' services to his country and his motives for his patriotic actions. The first citizen insists that "what he hath done famously," he did to flatter his pride. And he concludes ". . . though soft-conscienced men can be content to say it was for his country, he did it to please his mother, and to be partly proud; which he is, even to the altitude of his virtue" (I, i, 37–41). His pride is class pride, not the self-conceit of an ordinary man, but a demand that his patrician position in the state and his achievements in war and peace be not only recognized but also admired. Above all, he cannot brook any opposition from the plebeians or their wretched tribunes. He responds to their baiting with bursts of temper that are obviously spasmodic efforts to make clear that he is his own master. This mixture of hot-headedness and self-assertion is evidence of his emotional immaturity. In battle his class pride becomes honor and his shows of temper, courage. But in the political arena his headlong emotions sweep away his plans to show the primary political virtues of patience and restraint.

This pride is his besetting sin. When it is injured, his temper explodes. Its volcanic nature Shakespeare picturesquely illustrated in Valeria's account of Coriolanus' son, young Marcius', pursuit of a butterfly. She says,

> I saw him run after a gilded butterfly; and when he caught it, he let it go again; and after it again; and over and over he comes, and up again; catched it again; or whether his fall enraged him, or how 'twas, he did so set his teeth and tear it; O, I warrant, how he mammocked it!
> (I, iii, 66–71)

Volumnia remarks with obvious approval, "One on's father's moods." In this early part of the play Shakespeare makes it clear that he is drawing a portrait of the choleric man (see PSYCHOLOGY). As we shall see, his foes learn how to arouse his anger automatically and manipulate it to his undoing.

The tribunes, the villains of the piece, realizing the inflammability of Coriolanus' temper, teach their followers how to provoke his paroxysms of rage. By following their leaders' instructions, the mob is able to produce at will his explosions of choler. The simple plan works. One of the plebeians calls him traitor, a charge that maddens him. He shouts insults at the tribunes and their creatures. When he calls them a "common cry of curs," they fall upon him and "whoop him" out of Rome into exile.

Plutarch describes Coriolanus as a born warrior driven into battle by an irresistible impulse of his deepest nature. Shakespeare explains that it is Volumnia, "poor hen, that clucked him to the wars and home again," a figure so homely that it greatly reduces the glory of his martial exploits. In both war and politics he is his mother's creature. He finds distasteful the time-honored Roman custom of a candidate for the highest office of the state flattering the people and winning their gratitude by displaying the wounds he has received in their defense. His first response to his mother's entreaty that he go through the nauseating business is a flat "I will not do it." This brusque refusal arouses his mother's ire and she roundly scolds her boy. Her chiding breaks his will and reduces the great soldier to the stature of a frightened child cowering before a parent's threats. And he almost whimpers, "Pray be content: Mother, I am going to the market-place; Chide me no more . . . . Look, I am going." His mother's power over him is shown at its most dangerous in the great scenes in which various ambassadors from Rome meet Coriolanus, now leader of an attacking Volscian army, at the city's gates. He brusquely rejects the humble suit for mercy of his fellow consul and an old companion in arms. Old Menenius, confident that he can influence his protégé, can extract from the stubborn turncoat only a second offer of the peace terms already rejected. Finally his mother, his wife, his little boy, and his wife's friend Valeria appear. This group visibly moves him. He kisses his wife, gives his son a warrior's greeting, and significantly kneels before his mother. Yet neither Virgilia's tears nor Volumnia's appeals weakens his stubborn determination to proceed with his attack on Rome. At last Volumnia loses her temper, saying,

> Come, let us go:
> This fellow had a Volscian to his mother;
> His wife is in Corioli and his child
> Like him by chance. Yet give us our dispatch:
> I am hush'd until our city be afire,
> And then I'll speak a little.
> (V, iii, 177–182)

Her fierce indignation, as always, cows her son. Yielding to her, he cries out like a helpless child:

> O my mother, mother! O!
> You have won a happy victory to Rome;
> But, for your son,—believe it, O, believe it,
> Most dangerously you have with him prevail'd,
> If not most mortal to him.
> (V, iii, 185–189)

It is the soldier's infantile attitude toward his mother that prompts him to spare Rome and precipitates his final catastrophe. But it is his slavery to anger that brings about his destruction.

Aufidius, now jealous of Coriolanus, sees a chance to wreak vengeance on him for his betrayal of the Volscians' victory. He incites the mob by using the same method of provoking his wrath that the tribunes had employed to force the plebeians to "whoop him out of Rome." There it was the word "traitor" that maddened him. Here it is the phrase "boy of tears" that stirs his nature into an uproar. Shouting taunts at the Volscian commoners, he infuriates them, until, crying "Kill, kill, kill, kill, kill him!" they fall upon him and tear him to pieces, an outrageously unheroic death.

Coriolanus is different from most of Shakespeare's other tragic protagonists. In none of the crises of his career is he master of his conduct. Instead, his enemies manipulate him into tantrums that serve not his purposes but theirs. Even his death is an automatic response to artfully contrived provocation. He is a puppet, whose strings are pulled by his enemies. The catastrophe of such a marionette is almost funny. It may arouse some melodramatic excitement, but more scorn than pity or terror. For this reason, *Coriolanus,* on the analogy of Jonson's "comical satire," might appropriately be called a "tragical satire."—O.J.C.

Stage History: England. The first recorded production of *Coriolanus,* in 1681, was an adaptation made by Nahum TATE entitled *The Ingratitude of a Common-Wealth: or, The Fall of Caius Martius Coriolanus.* In 1719 John Dennis also tried his hand at an adaptation called *The Invader of his Country or the Fatal Resentment,* a dull piece that met deserved failure. James Thomson's *Coriolanus,* first staged in 1749, was a new and original work. It is of importance only because it was later blended with Shakespeare's play to form a hybrid drama that long held the stage in both England and America. The first compilation, as altered by Thomas SHERIDAN who acted the title role, was staged at Covent Garden on December 10, 1754. In anticipation of this production, Drury Lane had revived the unalloyed Shakespeare on November 11 of that year with Henry Mossop as Coriolanus and Hannah Pritchard as Volumnia. Then, on February 7, 1789, at Drury Lane, John Philip Kemble mounted his alteration of Shakespeare and Thomson, the most noted of the hybrid productions, with Sarah Siddons in the role of Volumnia. By the time Kemble transferred his version to Covent Garden on November 3, 1806, both he as the hero and Mrs. Siddons as Volumnia had fully developed their interpretations. Coriolanus had become Kemble's favorite role and his best.

Edmund Kean acted Coriolanus in one of the first presentations of the tragedy as written by Shakespeare, "with omissions only." This laudable effort to restore the original opened on January 24, 1820 at Drury Lane and closed four nights later. Kean's small stature made him a poor representative of the hero and contributed to the production's failure. William Charles Macready, who had played the hero in 1819, staged a magnificent presentation of the tragedy at Covent Garden on March 12, 1838. Samuel Phelps produced the play on four separate occasions; the first, on September 27, 1848, was received with great enthusiasm at Sadler's Wells. Frank Benson staged *Coriolanus* at Stratford in 1893 and 1898 and in London at the Comedy Theatre on February 13, 1901 with Genevieve Ward winning laurels as Volumnia. He and Miss Ward repeated their triumph at the Stratford Memorial Theatre in six different years from 1907 to 1919 and acted it for Beerbohm Tree in the sixth annual Shakespeare Festival (1910) at His Majesty's. *Coriolanus* was Henry Irving's last Shakespearean revival and played at the Lyceum on April 15, 1901. Both he, as Coriolanus, and Ellen Terry, as Volumnia, were ill-suited to their roles and the costly production failed.

At the Old Vic, in April 1920, Genevieve Ward recreated her Volumnia opposite Charles Warburton's Coriolanus and, in March 1924, Robert Atkins produced the tragedy with a cast which included Ion Swinley as Coriolanus and George Hayes as Aufidius.

W. Bridges-Adams opened the 1926 spring season at Stratford-upon-Avon with his production of *Coriolanus* and, in 1933, restaged the play, using an inner proscenium and rolling sets. Anew McMaster, playing for one season at Stratford, triumphed in the role. In between, a production of *Coriolanus* was played at the Chelsea Palace in May 1931. Staged by William Poel, then 78 years old, the play ran for one and a half hours.

The most interesting modern production of *Coriolanus* was given in Paris at the Comédie Française in the spring of 1934. At that time the *Action Française* and other antirepublican groups began to agitate for a revolution which they hoped would overthrow what they believed was a weak and corrupt democracy. As part of their campaign they induced the Comédie to produce a version of *Coriolanus* by René Louis Pichaud, which he advertised as "freely translated from the English original" and "adapted to the conditions of the French stage." He should have written "adapted to the conditions of contemporary French politics." The producers cooperated with M. Pichaud in making the play seem to be a devastating criticism of all the processes of democracy. Though it did stimulate violent demonstrations in the theatre and near riots in the streets, it failed to usher in a revolution.

Meanwhile, an Old Vic *Coriolanus* (1938) featured Laurence Olivier, giving a magnificent performance in his portrayal of the contemptuous aristocrat, and Sybil Thorndike, rising from the somewhat complacent domesticity of the earlier scene to become the symbol of Rome in her supplication, as Volumnia. Lewis Casson produced this powerful dramatization. Olivier played Coriolanus again, 21 years later, in Peter Hall's production at Stratford. Now even more arrogant, his professional soldier revealed throughout the influence of his mother, climaxed by his collapse when he reaches toward her as he agrees to save Rome. Edith Evans as Volumnia delicately combined the sorrowful mother with a victorious matriarch.

In 1939 Ben Iden Payne at Stratford staged the tragedy with Alec Clunes as Coriolanus and Dorothy Green playing Volumnia. The next London production was in 1948. The Old Vic company, at the New Theatre, was sustained by Alec Guinness, whose portrayal of Menenius Agrippa, the "humorous patrician," was finely balanced, never reduced to gruff eccentricity. In 1952 Anthony Quayle was Stratford's Coriolanus in Glen Byam Shaw's production with Michael Hordern as Menenius. Richard Burton, at the Old Vic for a season, played the title role in Michael Benthall's *Coriolanus* which opened on February 23, 1954.

When Tyrone Guthrie staged *Coriolanus* in 1963 at the Nottingham Playhouse, a program note called attention to the development of a psychological interpretation of the characters and promised an examination of the "love-hate between Coriolanus and Aufidius."

Stage History: America. David Douglass acted the title role in the first American production of *Coriolanus* at the Southwark in Philadelphia on June 8, 1767. The arrangement used for this presentation was the Sheridan-Thomson-Kemble version. The second recorded *Coriolanus* seen in the United States, also at Philadelphia, purportedly gave the original text. This production at the New Theatre on June 3, 1796 starred John P. Moreton, an American actor of excellent reputation, supported by a prominent cast, including William Green as Aufidius. Thomas Abthorpe Cooper portrayed Coriolanus in the first New York revival of the tragedy, which opened at the Park on June 3, 1799. Since no description of his performance in the role is available, its quality can only be inferred from the documented success of his interpretation of other tragic Shakespearean heroes. With Cooper were Mrs. Barrett as Volumnia and Ellen Westry (Mrs. William B. Wood) as Virgilia. A specific description of James W. Wallack's Coriolanus seen at the Park in 1818 is also lacking, but general commendation of his performance conveys the impression that his interpretation contained all the elements of intrinsic nobility in the character.

The first prominent impersonator of the hero on the American stage was Edwin Forrest, who took up the role on May 9, 1831 and thereafter retained it in his repertory, winning greater commendation in the part than any other Coriolanus in this country. Forrest never went beneath the virility and insolence to communicate the intellectual aspects of the character, but admirers of his arrogant patrician were blind to this dimension in Coriolanus and therefore fully satisfied. He had not played the part for seven years when the most elaborate and well-cast production of the drama opened at Niblo's Garden on November 2, 1863. A tableau showing the incineration of the body of Coriolanus on a large funeral pyre closed this presentation. Forrest as Coriolanus has been immortalized in a marble statue executed by Thomas Ball. Other actors attempting Coriolanus during Forrest's supremacy in the part were less successful. In 1837 John Vandenhoff portrayed Coriolanus at the National Theatre and one commentator stated that "supercilious disdain was never more powerfully expressed." James R. Anderson gave a respectable performance as the warrior in 1844 at the Park, and Thomas Hamblin proved only competent when he essayed the role at the Bowery in 1849 and 1852. His Aufidius in the latter production, Edward Eddy, graduated to the title role in 1862 at the New Bowery with George Boniface appearing in Eddy's former role and Mrs. M. A. Farren as Volumnia. Although Eddy's performance was judged skilled, it never threatened Forrest's position.

A few years after Forrest's death, however, a significant contribution to the conception of the hero as the intellectual superior of the masses he despises was made by John E. McCullough at the Grand Opera House on December 16, 1878. Especially effective were his scornful reaction to banishment and his ability to evoke the pathos of the scene with Volumnia and Virgilia. After McCullough, only two other representatives of Coriolanus—both European—appeared on the American stage in the 19th century and both acted the part in their native tongues: Ludwig Barnay, in German, making his American debut in 1883, and Tommaso Salvini, in Italian with an English-speaking company, at the Metropolitan Opera House in 1886. Both performers succeeded in creating sympathetic portraits of the scornful nobleman torn between an affectionate nature and vengeful will.

In February 1938 Charles Hopkins brought his New York State Federal Theatre Project production of the rarely acted tragedy to Maxine Elliott's in New York. Erford Gage, in the title role, was effective in the more tender moments, but his characterization, full of scorn, generally lacked power and the *Post*'s critic described his performance as reminiscent of "an irrepressible Harvard Republican thumbing his nose at the Campus Communists." Leonore Sorsby presented a youngish, dignified Volumnia.

Sixteen years later *Coriolanus*, staged by John Houseman at the Phoenix, featured the Shakespearean debut of Robert Ryan as a virile, headstrong hero. His vocally disappointing performance, at times lapsing into ineffectual snarling, lacked the range required to sustain the role and some of the best speeches were rasped. Accomplished support, however, accounted for some excellent readings with special notice given to Alan Napier, a vital, distinguished Menenius, and John Emery's representation of Aufidius, a fascinating exhibition of treachery. Mildred Natwick, as Volumnia, while not affecting in the most stirring scenes, delivered the domestic passages most competently and Lori March enacted Virgilia with charm.

In 1965 *Coriolanus* was presented at both the New York Shakespeare Festival Theatre in Central Park, with Robert Burr as Coriolanus and Jane White as Volumnia, and at the American Shakespeare Festival at Stratford, Connecticut, with Philip Bosco and Aline McMahon.—M.G.

Bibliography. TEXT: *Coriolanus,* New Cambridge Edition, J. Dover Wilson, ed., 1960; W. W. Greg, *The Shakespeare First Folio,* 1955. DATE: New Cambridge Edition; G. B. Harrison, "A Note on *Coriolanus,*" *Joseph Quincy Adams Memorial Studies,* 1948. SOURCES: Kenneth Muir, *Shakespeare's Sources,* Vol. I, 1957; A. L. Rowse, *William Shakespeare,* 1963. COMMENT: A. C. Bradley, *Coriolanus,* 1912; Oscar James Campbell, *Shakespeare's Satire,* 1943; Willard Farnham, *Shakespeare's Tragic Frontier,* 1950. STAGE HISTORY: New Cambridge Edition; T. Alston Brown, *A History of the New York Stage . . . to 1901,* 1903; William Winter, *Shakespeare on the Stage,* 3 vols., 1911–1916; G. C. D. Odell, *Shakespeare from Betterton to Irving,* 1920; J. C. Trewin, *Shakespeare on the English Stage, 1900–1964,* 1964.

Selected Criticism

JOHN DENNIS. The Good must never fail to prosper, and the Bad must be always punish'd. Otherwise the Incidents, and particularly the Catastrophe which is the grand Incident, are liable to be imputed rather to Chance than to Almighty Conduct and to Sovereign Justice. The want of this impartial Distribution of Justice makes the *Coriolanus* of Shakespear to be without Moral. 'Tis true indeed Coriolanus is kill'd by those Foreign Enemies with whom he had openly sided against his Country, which seems to be an Event worthy of Providence, and would look as if it were contriv'd by infinite Wisdom, and executed by supreme Justice, to make Coriolanus a dreadful Example to all who lead on Foreign Enemies to the Invasion of their native Country; if there were not something in the Fate of the other Characters, which gives occasion to doubt of it, and which suggests to the Sceptical Reader that this might happen by accident. For Aufidius the principal Murderer of Coriolanus, who in cold blood gets him assassinated by Ruffians, instead of leaving him to the Law of the Country, and the Justice of the Volscian Senate, and who commits so black a Crime, not by an erroneous Zeal, or a mistaken publick Spirit, but thro' Jealousy, Envy, and inveterate Malice; this Assassinator not only survives, and survives unpunish'd but seems to be rewarded for so detestable an Action by engrossing all those Honours to himself which Coriolanus before had shar'd with him. . . . The Good and the Bad then perishing promiscuously in the best of Shakespeare's Tragedies, there can be either none or very weak Instruction in them: For such promiscuous Events call the Government of Providence into Question, and by Scepticks and Libertines are resolv'd into Chance. [*An Essay on the Genius and Writings of Shakespear,* 1712.]

SAMUEL JOHNSON. The Tragedy of *Coriolanus* is one of the most amusing of our author's performances. The old man's merriment in *Menenius;* the lofty lady's dignity in *Volumnia;* the bridal modesty in *Virgilia;* the patrician and military haughtiness in *Coriolanus;* the plebeian malignity and tribunition insolence in *Brutus* and *Sicinius,* make a very pleasing and interesting variety: and the various revolutions of the hero's fortune fill the mind with anxious curiosity. There is, perhaps too much bustle in the first act, and too little in the last. [*The Plays of William Shakespeare,* 1765.]

WILLIAM HAZLITT. Shakespear has in this play shewn himself well versed in history and state-affairs. *Coriolanus* is a store-house of political common-places. Any one who studies it may save himself the trouble of reading Burke's *Reflections,* or Paine's *Rights of Man,* or the Debates in both Houses of Parliament since the French Revolution or our own. The arguments for and against aristocracy or democracy, on the privileges of the few and the claims of the many, on liberty and slavery, power and the abuse of it, peace and war, are here very ably handled with the spirit of a poet and the acuteness of a philosopher. Shakespear himself seems to have had a leaning to the arbitrary side of the question, perhaps from some feeling of contempt for his own origin; and to have spared no occasion of baiting the rabble. What he says of them is very true: what he says of their betters is also very true, though he dwells less upon it. The cause of the people is indeed but little calculated as a subject for poetry: it admits of rhetoric, which goes into argument and explanation, but it presents no immediate or distinct images to the mind, 'no jutting frieze, buttress, or coigne of vantage' for poetry 'to make its pendant bed and procreant cradle in.' The language of poetry naturally falls in with the language of power. . . . The love of power in ourselves and the admiration of it in others are both natural to man: the one makes him a tyrant, the other a slave. Wrong dressed out in pride, pomp, and circumstance has more attraction than abstract right. Coriolanus complains of the fickleness of the people: yet the instant he cannot gratify his pride and obstinacy at their expense, he turns his arms against his country. If his country was not worth defending, why did he build his pride on its defence? He is a conqueror and a hero; he conquers other countries, and makes this a plea for enslaving his own; and when he is prevented from doing so, he leagues with its enemies to destroy his country. [*Characters of Shakespear's Plays,* 1817.]

FRANK HARRIS. The high interest of Coriolanus is that Shakespeare is intent on showing us in it how he loved his mother, the confidante of his dreams and ambitions in boyhood, and how deeply he regretted her: . . . "no man in the world," he declares, "owed more to his mother . . . the most noble mother of the world." . . .

He paints her for us too; Volumnia has quick temper but more insight and good sense; she is always able to control herself in deference to judgment. Shakespeare's mother, Mary Arden, who could not read or write, had in her probably the wisdom of the finest English natures; she saw her own faults and her son's, and usually counselled moderation. It was not his quick, adventurous and unfortunate father whom Shakespeare adored; but his wise, loving mother. Every mention of her in the play is steeped in tenderness; even the paltry prejudiced tribune

Sicinius has to admit that Coriolanus "loved his mother deeply."

The professor-mandarins will naturally pooh-pooh all this as if it were the very extravagance of conjecture; but after all it is for the reader to judge between us. I am not afraid of the ultimate verdict, though teaching professors to read is, I confess, ungrateful, hard labour. [*The Women in Shakespeare*, 1911.]

A. C. BRADLEY. *Coriolanus* is beyond doubt among the latest of Shakespeare's tragedies; there is some reason for thinking it the last. . . .

We cannot say that it shows any decline in Shakespeare's powers, though in parts it may show slackness in their use. It has defects, some of which are due to the historical material; but all the tragedies have defects, and the material of *Antony and Cleopatra* was even more troublesome. There is no love-story; but then there is none in *Macbeth*, and next to none in *King Lear*. Thanks in part to the badness of the Folio text, the reader is impeded by obscurities of language and irritated by the mangling of Shakespeare's metre; yet these annoyances would not much diminish the effect of *Othello*. It may seem a more serious obstacle that the hero's faults are repellent and chill our sympathy; but Macbeth, to say nothing of his murders, is a much less noble being than Coriolanus. All this doubtless goes for something; but there must be some further reason why this drama stands apart from the four great tragedies and *Antony and Cleopatra*. And one main reason seems to be this. Shakespeare could construe the story he found only by conceiving the hero's character in a certain way; and he had to set the whole drama in tune with that conception. In this he was, no doubt, perfectly right; but he closed the door on certain effects, in the absence of which his whole power in tragedy could not be displayed. He had to be content with something less, or rather with something else; and so have we.

Dr. Johnson observes that 'the tragedy of *Coriolanus* is one of the most amusing of our author's performances.' By 'amusing' he did not mean 'mirth-provoking'; he meant that in *Coriolanus* a lively interest is excited and sustained by the variety of the events and characters; and this is true. But we may add that the play contains a good deal that is amusing in the current sense of the word. When the people appear as individuals they are frequently more or less comical. Shakespeare always enjoyed the inconsequence of the uneducated mind, and its tendency to express a sound meaning in an absurd form. Again, the talk of the servants with one another and with the muffled hero, and the conversation of the sentinels with Menenius, are amusing. There is a touch of comedy in the contrast between Volumnia and Virgilia when we see them on occasions not too serious. And then, not only at the beginning, as in Plutarch, but throughout the story we meet with that pleasant and wise old gentleman Menenius, whose humour tells him how to keep the peace while he gains his point, and to say without offence what the hero cannot say without raising a storm. Perhaps no one else in the play is regarded from beginning to end with such unmingled approval, and this is not lessened when the failure of his embassy to Coriolanus makes him the subject as well as the author of mirth. If we regard the drama from this point of view, we find that it differs from almost all the tragedies, though it has a certain likeness to *Antony and Cleopatra*. What is amusing in it is, for the most part, simply amusing, and has no tragic tinge. It is not like the gibes of Hamlet at Polonius, or the jokes of the clown who, we remember, is digging Ophelia's grave, or that humour of Iago which for us is full of menace; and who could dream of comparing it with the jesting of Lear's fool? Even that Shakespearean audacity, the interruption of Volumnia's speech by the hero's little son, makes one laugh almost without reserve. And all this helps to produce the characteristic tone of this tragedy. ["Coriolanus," British Academy Lecture, 1912; reprinted in *A Miscellany*, 1929.]

HARLEY GRANVILLE-BARKER. Coriolanus cannot be ranked with the greatest of the tragedies. It lacks their transcendent vitality and metaphysical power. But while neither story nor characters evoke such qualities, those they do evoke are here in full measure. The play is notable for its craftsmanship. It is the work of a man who knows what the effect of each stroke will be, and wastes not one of them. And while ease and simplicity may sometimes be lacking, an uncertain or superfluous speech it would be hard to find. Was Shakespeare perhaps aware of some ebbing of his imaginative vitality—well there may have been after the creation in about as many years of *Othello*, *King Lear*, *Antony and Cleopatra* and *Macbeth*! and did he purposefully choose a subject and characters which he could make the most of by judgment and skill? . . .

Throughout the play action and words are expressively keyed together, the action of as great an import as the words. Marcius' share in the scene of the wearing of the gown of humility is as much picturing as speaking; and the mere sight of him later in his Roman dress, surrounded by the Volsces in theirs, sitting in council with them, marching into Corioles at their head—the graphic discord vivifies the play's ending. The sight of the silently approaching figures of Volumnia, Virgilia and Valeria makes double effect; directly upon us, and upon us again through the effect made upon Marcius. And little though Virgilia says (and Valeria not a word), Volumnia so insistently joins them to her plea that their simple presence has an all but articulate value; while the actual spectacle of Marcius fighting singlehanded "within Corioles gates" is better witness to his prowess than any of the "acclamations hyperbolical" which he somewhat selfconsciously decries. The memory of it, moreover, will not fade, only lie dormant until at the last it is rekindled by the magnificently trenchant

> "Boy"! false hound!
> If you have writ your annals true, 'tis there,
> That, like an eagle in a dove-cote, I
> Fluttered your Volscians in Corioles:
> Alone I did it.

Here, then, we have a play of action dealing with men of action; and in none that Shakespeare wrote do action and character better supplement and balance each other. [*Prefaces to Shakespeare*, 1927–1947.]

WILLARD FARNHAM. The tragedy made by Shakespeare out of Plutarch's story of Coriolanus is not that of a noble spirit ruined by lack of education, which is the tragedy that Plutarch outlines. It is the tragedy of a noble spirit ruined by something in itself which education cannot touch, or at least does not touch. We do not hear anything in Shakespeare's play about the hero's lacking instruction because of his father's death and thus acquiring a faulty character. On the contrary, we learn that Volumnia, the strong-willed mother of the hero, has been both father and mother to him, has devoted herself, according to her lights, to the education of his character, and has certainly not failed to teach him how to be manly. By her precepts and her praises she has stimulated his valor. We have her own word for it that she does not approve of his unbending pride, and presumably she has done what she could to check it when she saw it standing in the way of his advancement. She is not the best of teachers to show him how to overcome his pride, but at least she can condemn it as something not drawn from her:

> Thy valiantness was mine, thou suck'dst it
> from me,
> But owe thy pride thyself.
>
> (III, ii, 129–130)

The pride she condemns is what she says it is, a thing of his own, fixed in his nature. It is in the original substance of his character and is not an untutored churlishness acquired through the accident of his father's death.

But there is that about the pride of her son which Volumnia is quite incapable of understanding. Though she sees clearly that it can keep him from gaining the highest honors in Rome, she does not see that it can also keep him from base timeserving. It is more worthy of condemnation than she knows, but at the same time it is worthy of praise in a way that she does not even suspect. Her pupil shows reaches of nobility for which she is not responsible, and he shows them even in his valor, which is not a virtue of her creation, as she seems to think, but a virtue grounded in his natural pride. This valor has been developed but not called into being by her instruction.

The pride of Coriolanus has two very contradictory faculties. It is the tragic flaw in his character and therefore has the well-known power of pride the preëminent deadly sin to produce other faults and destroy good in the spirit of its possessor; but it is at the same time the basis of self-respect in his character and thus has power to produce good in his spirit. Whether destructive of good or productive of good, it is a fierce pride, accompanied by a wrath that makes it work at white heat. The wrath is like the pride it accompanies in not always having the qualities of a deadly sin; it can at times be righteous wrath, directed against human baseness. Hence both the pride and the wrath of Coriolanus can be admirable as well as detestable. [*Shakespeare's Tragic Frontier*, 1950.]

Cornelius. In *Cymbeline*, a physician. Correctly suspecting the Queen's designs against her stepdaughter, Imogen, the good Cornelius supplies her with a harmless drug that makes "a show of death," rather than the poisoning compounds she has ordered. When this "remedy" is taken by Imogen, she loses consciousness temporarily and is thus mistakenly presumed dead. Cornelius later relates to Cymbeline the wicked Queen's deathbed confession of her ruthless schemes to secure the throne for her son, Cloten.

Cornelius. In *Hamlet*, one of the two courtiers whom Claudius dispatches to Norway in a diplomatic attempt to prevent Fortinbras' invasion of Denmark (I, ii). The mission is successful.

Cornelius, Peter. See MUSIC BASED ON SHAKESPEARE: *19th century, 1850–1900*.

Cornwall, Duke of. In *King Lear*, Regan's husband. Cornwall orders Lear's messenger, Kent, put in the stocks, and later commands Gloucester to lock the doors on the raving Lear, leaving him to wander the heath exposed to the storm. Cornwall blinds Gloucester for having helped Lear, but is in turn killed by a servant.

Cornwell, Edward (d. 1624). The second husband of Shakespeare's aunt, Margaret Arden (d. 1614, see ARDEN FAMILY). Cornwell married Margaret, the widow of Alexander Webbe, before 1574. The Cornwells leased land in Snitterfield, the home of Richard Shakespeare, the poet's grandfather. In 1574, while serving as constable in Snitterfield, Cornwell was assaulted by Shakespeare's uncle, Henry Shakespeare. In 1576 he bought a share of the Arden estate from Thomas Stringer which he sold two years later to his stepson, Robert Webbe. [Mark Eccles, *Shakespeare in Warwickshire*, 1961.]

Coryat, Thomas (c. 1577–1617). Traveler. Coryat left Oxford without taking a degree and became a hanger-on and wit, first at the court of James I and later in the household of the king's eldest son, Prince Henry. In 1608 he began his travels, mainly on foot, through western Europe. In 1611 he published the journal of his trip, *Coryats Crudities*, an instructive account of the chief cities of Europe. It was the first and for some time the only, handbook for continental travelers. An appendix to the book contained commendatory verses and testimonials by many of the famous literary figures of the day, including Ben Jonson and John Donne. The appendix was later published separately as *The Odcombian Banquet* with a Preface that reflected satirically upon Coryat. Coryat wrote that in Venice he saw women act, "a thing I never saw before, though I have heard that it hath been sometimes used in London." In 1612 he set out for further travels in the Near East and India. Fragments of his writings were included in *Purchas his Pilgrimage* (1613).

Coryat was an habitué of the Mermaid Tavern where he made the acquaintance of a number of Shakespeare's friends and, probably, of Shakespeare himself. Leslie Hotson has shown that Coryat was an acquaintance of John JACKSON, one of Shakespeare's trustees in his purchase of the Blackfriars Gate-house and of William JOHNSON, the host of the Mermaid, who also acted as Shakespeare's trustee in the Gatehouse purchase. [Leslie Hotson, *Shakespeare's Sonnets Dated*, 1949.]

Costard. In *Love's Labour's Lost*, a clown who parodies voguish phrases. Costard is jailed when discovered consorting with Jaquenetta contrary to the King's proclamation. Don Armado, Costard's rival for Jaquenetta's love, releases him from custody to deliver an amatory message to her. Also entrusted with a message from Berowne to Rosaline, Costard confuses the two letters and the mix-up affords the ladies much amusement. He plays Pompey the Great in the interlude of the Nine Worthies.

costumes. Theatrical costuming in the Elizabethan and Jacobean theatre must be regarded as an extension of the ordinary dress of the period, which was characterized by its lavishness and sumptuousness. The actors' dress competed in magnificence with that of the audience, with the most fashionable of the audience for a time taking their seats on the stage. Actors of the period were also expected to continue a long tradition of rich costume on the stage, a heritage of the ecclesiastical vestments worn in liturgical drama, the lavish outfits of the participants in the miracle and morality plays, and the splendid liveries of the entertainers and other retainers in the households of royalty and nobility.

Spectacular dress on stage made up for the lack of visual splendor in surroundings. A scene was normally mounted with only the barest suggestion of location, a minimum of furniture, and only utilitarian hangings or curtains. Costumes were required to suggest the dignity, beauty, holiness, or cruelty of the wearer. The apparel worn by the players confirmed critics of the theatre in their opinion that the clothes actors wore were too good for them. Puritanical critics were not the only ones to scorn the vagaries of fashionable apparel; the bizarre fashions were often satirized in the plays themselves. One of Portia's suitors, for example, is mocked in the following fashion:

> How oddly he is suited! I think he bought his doublet in Italy, his round hose in France, his bonnet in Germany, and his behaviour everywhere.
> (*Merchant of Venice,* I, ii, 79–82)

Benedick is described as having a tendency to strange disguises:

> . . . a Dutchman to-day, a Frenchman to-morrow, or in the shape of two countries at once, as a German from the waist downward, all slops, and a Spaniard from the hip upward, no doublet.
> (*Much Ado About Nothing,* III, ii, 33–37)

The cost of clothing actors was a major expense of the Elizabethan acting company. The company's leading actors evidently furnished their own wardrobes, which were usually made to measure for them personally and which they might later sell to their company. The common stock of apparel for the company could be accumulated in various ways. The manager of the company might agree to provide the apparel, as Francis Langley did for Pembroke's Men at the Swan, at a cost he estimated at £300. In 1610 the Duke of York's Men bought some "olde clothes or apparell which formerly weare players clothes or apparrell" from John Heminges of the King's Men for £11. Typical of the many costume expenditures recorded in Henslowe's diary are the following:

	£	s	d
Bought damske casock garded with velvett		18	
....a payer of paned rownd hosse of cloth whiped with sylk, drawne out with tafitie			
....j payer of long black wollen stockens		8	
....j black satten dublett			
....j payer of rownd howsse paned of vellevett	4	15	
....a robe for to goo invisibell			

Occasionally actors bought used clothing from the nobility, or servants of nobles would receive their masters' clothes as bequests when their masters died, and, being unable to wear anything but livery, would sell the clothes to actors. Companies acting in Revels at court would often be rewarded with the costumes they had worn, supplied by the Revels Office. This Office also sold worn-out or unfashionable costumes used in the masques at court.

In historical dramas the costumes worn could be quite varied. The LONGLEAT MANUSCRIPT, which is the only extant picture of an Elizabethan stage production, may or may not be accurate in its depiction of the principals in a sort of historical dress and the lesser hirelings in Elizabethan dress. Much was left to the audience's imagination.

The costumes used color for more than visual enhancement and excitement. Color symbolism had been part of the visual spectacle of the drama from the earliest times and in Elizabethan drama, too, it conveyed the character's station in life and emotional qualities. The color watchet, for example, an aquamarine or pale turquoise, was worn by the queen and her courtiers, or even by a courtesan, and suggested deceptive love. Servants wore dark navy blue, or tawny liveries. The color tawny, a yellowish tan, meant sadness as well as servitude. Blood red clothed the bold and mighty, and purple, traditionally, was the color of royalty. Willow green, a somber gray-green, was the traditional color of the lovelorn. Green sleeves were part of the costume of a courtesan. The color russet, of the rough homespun woolen garments, was a dusky reddish brown and signified steadfastness; the color was also used to dye more expensive fabrics. A soft dove-gray called ash by Elizabethans was frequently used to dye velvet and made a fitting background for bright-hued embroidery and trimmings, while a dull, dark gray called rat's color was worn by the poor. [E. K. Chambers, *The Elizabethan Stage,* 1923; Cecile de Banke, *Shakespearean Stage Production: Then and Now,* 1953; *Henslowe's Diary,* R. A. Foakes and R. T. Rickert, eds., 1961.]

Cotes, Richard (d. 1652) and **Thomas** (d. 1641). Printers of the Second Folio (1632) of Shakespeare. In 1627 Thomas and Richard Cotes succeeded to the business and all the copyrights of the printers William and Isaac JAGGARD. The Jaggards had been the printers of the First Folio, and the printing of the second edition of the Folio naturally fell to the Coteses. They also printed the 1640 edition of Shakespeare's *Poems* for the publisher John Benson. [H. R. Plomer, *A Dictionary of Booksellers and Printers . . . from 1641 to 1667,* 1907.]

Country People. In *The Two Noble Kinsmen,* four unnamed characters. They resolve to go to the Maying (II, iii), where they perform the morris dance (III, v).

coursing. See HUNTING, COURSING, AND FOWLING.

Court, Alexander. In *Henry V,* an English soldier. On the eve of the battle of Agincourt, he converses with several fellow soldiers; they are joined by King Henry in disguise (IV, i).

Courtezan. In *The Comedy of Errors,* a minor

speaking role in IV, ii and V, i. Confusing Antipholus of Syracuse with his brother, the Courtezan asks him for the chain he promised her and for the ring he took and invites him to dinner. She later testifies to Solinus, Duke of Ephesus, that Antipholus took her ring, inadvertently incriminating the wrong brother.

Courthope, William John (1842–1917). Scholar. Educated at Corpus Christi and New College, Oxford, Courthope was professor of poetry at Oxford from 1895 to 1900. His lectures there were published under the title *Life in Poetry, Law in Taste* (1901). Courthope's first major scholarly undertaking was the Elwin-Courthope edition of Pope, which he brought to completion himself when Elwin abandoned the project.

Courthope's other major scholarly work was his *History of English Poetry* (6 vols., 1895–1910), a comprehensive survey tracing the continuity of English poetry and its correspondence with the great movements of English history. The fourth volume of the *History* contains a number of chapters on Shakespeare as well as an important appendix which considers the authenticity and chronology of the early plays. In determining the authenticity of a given play, Courthope departed from the then popular practice of VERSE TESTS and made a comparative study of structure and of characters. Among other conclusions was that the two CONTENTION PLAYS were early drafts of *2* and *3 Henry VI* and not, as then commonly believed, sources. While it is now generally maintained that these are "bad quartos," Courthope was closer to the truth than most of his contemporaries. Courthope also maintained that *The Troublesome Reign of King John* was by Shakespeare. Without the benefit of modern textual science, Courthope anticipated some recent judgments and has won high praise from Tillyard (*Shakespeare's History Plays,* 1944) for his opinions on authenticity and as "a most enlightened interpreter of the early Shakespeare." [W. J. Courthope, *The Country Town and Other Poems,* with a memoir by A. O. Prichard, 1920.]

Courtier, The (The Courtyer of Count Baldessar Castilio done into Englyshe by Thomas Hoby). Sir Thomas Hoby's translation (1561) of *Il Cortegiano* by Baldassare CASTIGLIONE. *Il Cortegiano* (pub. 1528) grew out of the author's experience at the court of Urbino from 1505 to 1508. The work is in dialogue form, ostensibly covering four evenings in which a number of courtiers meet to discuss the qualities of the ideal courtier and his obligations to his prince, to his lady, and to society. It culminates in a discourse on Platonic love, the substance of which appears in Edmund Spenser's *Fowre Hymnes* (1596) and in numerous other Renaissance works.

Sir Thomas Hoby (1530–1566) was educated at Cambridge where he came under the influence of the humanists Sir John Cheke and Roger Ascham; later he spent much time abroad as a traveler, as a diplomat under Edward VI, and as an exile during the reign of Mary. While in exile, probably at Padua, he completed his translation of Castiglione but did not publish it until 1561. The translation won acclaim as a masterpiece of prose, and by means of it Castiglione's book became one of the most influential of the Renaissance courtesy books in England as well as on the continent. Its accommodation of Christian ethics to the requirements of political self-preservation offered a semi-ironic model of moral as well as social behavior. Shakespeare may have derived the "merry war" of Beatrice and Benedick in *Much Ado About Nothing* from an account of a similar battle in *The Courtier.*

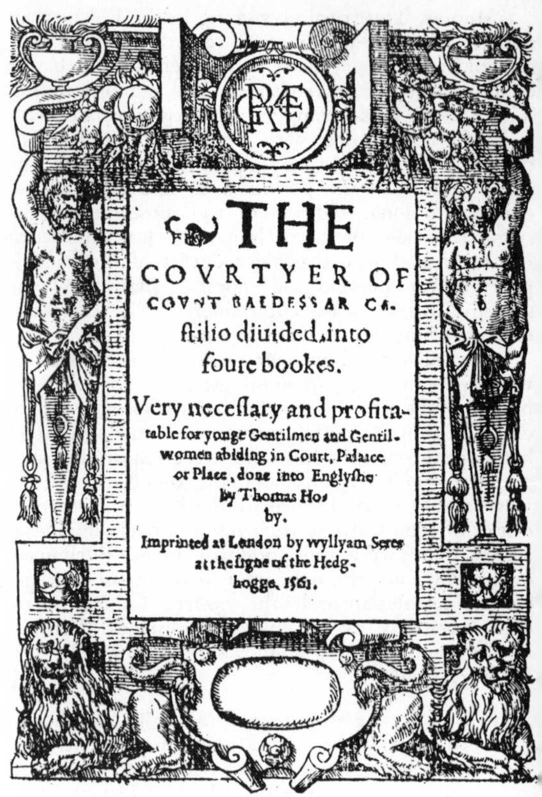
THE
COVRTYER OF
COVNT BALDESSAR CA-
stilio diuided into
foure bookes.
Very necessary and profita-
table for yonge Gentilmen and Gentil-
women abiding in Court, Palaice
or Place, done into Englyshe
by Thomas Ho-
by.
Imprinted at London by wyllyam Seres
at the signe of the Hedg-
hogge. 1561.

TITLE PAGE OF HOBY'S TRANSLATION OF *The Courtyer* (1561).

court performances. See REVELS OFFICE.

Covell, William (d. 1614). Poet. Covell is probably the "W. C." who made an early allusion to Shakespeare in a verse epistle appended to his *Polimanteia or the Meanes Lawful and Unlawfull to Judge of the Fall of a Commonwealth* (1595), a tract on astrology printed at Cambridge. The allusion occurs in two side-notes to a section of the epistle praising Samuel Daniel and Spenser. The notes are apparently designed as examples of the author's thesis and do not have any direct relevance to the text itself. The extract below shows the position they occupy in the original work:

	Let o-
	ther countries (sweet *Cambridge*) enuie,
All praise	(yet admire) my *Virgil,* thy petrarch, di-
worthy.	uine *Spenser.* And vnlesse I erre, (a thing
Lucrecia	easie in such simplicitie) deluded by
Sweet Shak-	dearlie beloued *Delia,* and fortunatelie
speare.	fortunate *Cleopatra; Oxford* thou maist
Eloquent	extoll thy courte-deare-verse happie
Gaueston.	*Daniell,* whose sweete refined muse, in
	contracted shape, were sufficient a-

mongst men, to gaine pardon of the	*Wanton*
sinne to *Rosemond,* pittie to distressed	*Adonis.*
Cleopatra, and euerliuing praise to her	*Watsons*
louing *Delia.*	*heyre.*

Covell, a native of Lancashire, was educated at Cambridge, where he received an M.A. in 1588 and a D.D. in 1601. He was employed by the Anglican church as a polemicist and wrote a number of treatises refuting the doctrines of Catholicism. [J. O. Halliwell-Phillipps, *Outlines of the Life of Shakespeare*, 1881.]

Covent Garden Theatre. Playhouse in Bow Street, Covent Garden, built by John Rich in 1731 as a replacement for Lincoln's Inn Fields Theatre. In the ensuing years Covent Garden established itself as the chief rival of Drury Lane, although the great 18th-century performers who played there, including James Quin, Spranger Barry, and Peg Woffington, were never a match for the Lane's David Garrick. In 1767, the theatre and company patent were sold to George Colman the Elder and his partners for £60,000. In 1773, Charles Macklin made his first appearance as Macbeth at the Covent Garden. In 1787, the theatre was rebuilt and enlarged.

John Philip Kemble took over the management in 1803 and brought to the Covent Garden stage his sister Sarah Siddons in a number of memorable Shakespearean performances. In 1808, the theatre was burnt down; when it was rebuilt several months later, new higher prices were instituted and the "Old Prices" riots were set off. In 1817 Kemble gave his farewell performance on its stage in the role of Coriolanus and his younger brother Charles assumed control in 1823; Charles' management is notable for the staging of *King John* with authentic costumes and scenery designed by James Robinson Planché, and for his enormously successful production of *Romeo and Juliet* in 1829 with his daughter Fanny Kemble as Juliet.

At Covent Garden in 1833 Edmund Kean collapsed into the arms of his son while giving his last performance as Othello. William Charles Macready assumed the management of the theatre in 1837 and there gave elaborately staged productions of *Coriolanus* (1838) and a *King Lear* (1838) which restored the original text of Shakespeare's play for the first time since the Restoration. Macready did not permit long enough runs of his more successful plays and he failed financially. He was succeeded by Charles Mathews and his wife, Elizabeth Vestris, who scored a great success with an opening production of *Love's Labour's Lost* in 1839. In 1848 Charles Kemble again took the management of Covent Garden, but it had passed its heyday and was used primarily as an opera house. In 1856 the theatre was again destroyed by fire and the building constructed in 1858 is the Covent Garden Theatre in use today.

Coverdale, Miles. See BIBLE, SIXTEENTH-CENTURY TRANSLATIONS OF.

Cowley, Abraham (1618–1667). Poet. Born in London and educated at Westminster and Cambridge, Cowley published his first book of poems, *Poetical Blossoms* (1633), at the age of 15. During the civil wars he served the royalist cause and was imprisoned as a spy by the Commonwealth forces. His *Poems* (1656) included *Davideis*, a Biblical epic that had a minor influence on *Paradise Lost;* the *Pindaric Odes*, on which his early reputation was based; and a number of fine lyric poems in the metaphysical strain of John Donne. His dramatic works include *The Guardian* (1641), an anti-Puritan comedy that accurately predicted the fate of the theatre in the event of a successful Puritan rebellion: "The first pious deed will be, to banish *Shakespear* and *Ben Johnson* out of parlour, and to bring in their rooms *Marprelate*, and *Pryn's* [William Prynne] works."

In the Preface to his *Poems*, Cowley included an attack on those printers who capitalize on a popular poet's name by including spurious and inferior work in their editions. Thus they "are content to diminish the value of the *Author*, so they may encrease the price of the *Book*." He goes on to say that "This has been the case with *Shakespear*, *Fletcher*, *Johnson*, and many others." Cowley's attack provides some contemporary support for the theory that holds suspect the authenticity of plays attributed to Shakespeare during the late 17th century. [*The Shakspere Allusion-Book*, J. Munro, ed., 1909.]

Cowley, Richard (d. 1619). Actor. Cowley was probably one of the original members of Shakespeare's company, the Chamberlain's Men. He is listed in the letters patent of May 19, 1603 granted to Chamberlain's in which they are named the king's "Servauntes" and become the King's Men. The earliest mention of him on the stage is in the list of actors in the "plot" of the revival of Tarlton's *Seven Deadly Sins* given by the amalgamated Admiral's-Strange's company in 1590/1. According to the correspondence of Edward Alleyn, Cowley was also with the contingent of Strange's Men touring the provinces in 1593.

He acted in the 1598 production of *Much Ado About Nothing*, according to the stage directions affixed to the Quarto of 1600. He was apparently very thin and gangling, with a pale face. E. K. Chambers speculates that his appearance led to his being cast as Verges, in contrast to Will Kempe as Dogberry. T. W. Baldwin conjectures that other roles played by Cowley might have included Silence in *2 Henry IV*, Slender in *Merry Wives of Windsor*, William in *As You Like It*, and Aguecheek in *Twelfth Night*.

In 1601 Cowley was listed as a payee for a Chamberlain's Men's performance at court along with Heminges, and this fact has led scholars to infer that he was a full sharer in the company. He was among the members of the King's Men who were provided with "iiij yardes" of "red clothe . . . by his Maiestie . . . against his Maiesties sayd royall proceeding through the Citie of London" March 15, 1604 for James I's delayed coronation procession. Cowley was one of the "fellows" to whom Augustine Phillips left 20s. in "gould" in the will the latter executed in 1605. He was also one of the actors in the First Folio (1623) list of "principall Actors" in Shakespeare's plays.

Cowley died in March 1619. His will, dated January 13, 1618, named his daughter Elizabeth Birch executrix, and was witnessed by John Heminges, Cuthbert Burbage, John Shank, and Thomas Ravenscroft. [E. K. Chambers, *The Elizabethan Stage*, 1923; T. W. Baldwin, *The Organization and Personnel of the Shakespearean Company*, 1927.]

Cox, Robert (1604–1655). Actor who won fame during the suppression of the theatres (1642–1660) for his "drolls." Short, comic scenes extracted from popular plays, Cox's drolls were a practicable form of entertainment at a time when actors were de-

FRONTISPIECE OF KIRKMAN'S *The Wits* (1662) SHOWING AN IMPROVISED STAGE.

prived of their right to act. One of the earliest of drolls was "The Merry Conceits of Bottom the Weaver" which Cox had contrived out of *A Midsummer Night's Dream.* It was published along with 26 other drolls in 1672 by Francis Kirkman, who mentions in the Preface that they enjoyed great popularity during the Commonwealth period because of the skill of the "incomparable Robert Cox." The title of the collection is *The Wits, or, Sport Upon Sport* (1672), and not the least important aspect of it is the frontispiece providing one of the few contemporary pictures of a pre-Restoration stage. Another droll in *The Wits,* titled "The Bouncing Knight, or, the Robbers Rob'd," was derived from *1 Henry IV,* chiefly from II, iv; III, iii; and V, iv. Cox was betrayed to the military by some of his fellow actors and arrested during a performance in 1653. He died two years later.

Crab. In *The Two Gentlemen of Verona,* the dog belonging to Launce and a silent participant in many of his comic scenes.

Craig, Hardin (1875–1968). American scholar. Upon his retirement from Stanford University in 1942, Craig taught at the universities of North Carolina (1942–1949) and Missouri (1949–1960). He became well known for his *The Enchanted Glass* (1936), a stimulating essay on the intellectual assumptions of the Elizabethan age (see HISTORICAL CRITICISM). *An Interpretation of Shakespeare* (1948) is a survey of the plays and poems, together with an introductory chapter which includes the substance of his earlier book. His editions of Shakespeare's complete works (1951) and of 21 plays (1958) are heavily annotated and contain extensive historical-critical introductions. Other works include *English Religious Drama of the Middle Ages* (1955), *New Lamps for Old: A Sequel to The Enchanted Glass* (1960), and *A New Look at Shakespeare's Quartos* (1961). Craig has also served as general editor of *A History of English Literature,* for which work he wrote the second section, *The Literature of the English Renaissance, 1485–1660* (1950; issued as a separate volume, 1962). [*Renaissance Studies in Honor of Hardin Craig,* Baldwin Maxwell and others, eds., 1941; *Essays on Shakespeare and Elizabethan Drama in Honor of Hardin Craig,* Richard Hosley, ed., 1962.]

Craik, George Lillie (1798–1866). Scottish author and educator. Educated at the University of St. Andrews, Craik moved to London where he became associated with Charles Knight and the Society for the Diffusion of Useful Knowledge. His numerous popularizations are largely in the field of English language and literature, and range from periodical articles to three-volume studies of Spenser and Bacon. In 1849 he was appointed professor of English literature at Queen's College, Belfast. His most important scholarly work is *The English of Shakespeare* (1856), a long essay on Shakespeare's language with a detailed linguistic analysis of *Julius Caesar.* His *English Prose* (5 vols., 1893–1896) is a useful collection with critical introductions, illustrating the development of English prose from the 14th to the 19th centuries. Craik was also one of the founders of the first Shakespeare Society in 1840.

Crane, Ralph (1550[60?]–c. 1632). Scrivener. Crane's work, done principally for lawyers, included occasional transcriptions of plays for the acting companies. The most important of Crane's extant transcripts are his manuscripts of Middleton's *A Game at Chesse* (1624) and *The Witch* (c. 1610–1616). The latter play contains songs which were interpolated into *Macbeth,* and Crane's transcript is the earliest authority for their text. Crane very probably played an important part in preparing the copy of the First Folio for the printers. It has been suggested that his scribal peculiarities are present in the Folio texts of *The Tempest, The Merry Wives of Windsor, The Two Gentlemen of Verona, Measure for Measure,* and *The Winter's Tale.* An analysis of Crane's spelling characteristics, based on the computations of an electronic computer, has been undertaken by T. H. Howard-Hill of Oxford University. Dover Wilson's theory of ASSEMBLED TEXTS—that in some cases the copy for the Folio was derived from the actor's "parts" together with the "plot"—implies that Crane's role was editorial as well as scribal. See COMPUTER SCHOLARSHIP. [W. W. Greg, *The Shakespeare First Folio,* 1955; T. H. Howard-Hill, "Computer Analysis of Shakespearean Texts," *The Shakespeare Newsletter,* December 1964.]

Cranmer, Thomas (1489–1556). Archbishop of Canterbury. Cranmer was a professor of divinity at Cambridge when, in 1529, his view that Henry VIII's marriage to Catherine might be declared invalid without reference to Rome brought him to the delighted notice of the king. Four years later he reluctantly accepted the post of archbishop of Canterbury, and very shortly thereafter nullified the royal marriage, approved Henry's four-month-old marriage to Anne Bullen, and crowned her queen. Cranmer became, to a large degree, the architect of the Church of England, being largely responsible for the circulation of the English Bible and the preparation of the Book of Common Prayer. He was an influential advisor to Henry and, later, to the boy-king Edward VI. Having against his own judgment opposed the accession of Mary Tudor at Edward's death, he was both condemned for treason and burned as a heretic.

In *Henry VIII,* Cranmer is present at a session of the divorce trial and (off-stage) crowns the new Queen, but his only active role, through much of Act V, is to defend himself meekly to the King against his many detractors, who seek his imprisonment. The King remains loyal to him. At the end of the play Cranmer apostrophizes the baby Elizabeth at her christening.

Creede, Thomas (fl. 1578–1617). London printer of several of Shakespeare's plays. Creede was made a freeman of the Stationers' Company in 1578 and opened his own shop at the Catherine Wheel in Thames Street in 1593. In 1594 he printed *The First part of the Contention betwixt the two famous Houses of Yorke and Lancaster,* a "bad quarto" of *2 Henry VI.* In 1595 he was the printer of *The Lamentable Tragedy of Locrine,* attributed to "W. S." on the title page. He printed the Second, Third, Fourth and Fifth Quartos of *Richard III* (1598–1612) and the Second Quarto of *Romeo and Juliet* (1599). In 1600 he printed *The Chronicle History of Henry the fifth,* a bad quarto reprinted in 1602. In the same year he printed the First Quarto of *The Merry Wives of Windsor,* another bad quarto. He is also the T. C. who printed the apocryphal *London Prodigal* in 1605, the title page of which ascribes the play to Shakespeare. [R. B. McKerrow, ed., *A Dictionary of Printers and Booksellers . . . 1557–1640,* 1910.]

Cressida. In medieval and subsequent literature, the beloved of Troilus, though she does not so appear in classic legend. As Criseida she is the heroine of Boccaccio's *Filostrato,* and as Criseyde, that of Chaucer's *Troilus and Criseyde.* From Chaucer's time to Shakespeare's, Cressida had suffered a severe debasement in English literature, so that she had come to be regarded as the archetypal prostitute, a conception expressed by Ancient Pistol in *Henry V* when he describes Doll Tearsheet as a "lazar kite of Cressid's kind" (II, i, 80).

In *Troilus and Cressida* Shakespeare did not alter this conception so much as he humanized it. Cressida is indeed the embodiment of female frailty, but she is neither deceitful nor corrupt. She is an incorrigible flirt, witty, and charming, but essentially a frivolous creature incapable of sustaining a sincere relationship. Thus she emerges from her mythic past a less significant but more recognizably human creature.

criticism—17th century. The earliest critical references to Shakespeare are in Francis Meres' *Palladis Tamia* (1598), which, while invaluable as a source of information, is from a critical standpoint little more than a repository of clichés. The only notable criticism of Shakespeare by his 17th-century contemporaries is to be found in Ben Jonson's justly famous remarks, which included the comment that "Shaksperr wanted Arte," a phrase which sounded the theme of Shakespearean criticism for the rest of the century (see William DRUMMOND). Taking their cue from Jonson, commentators almost invariably referred to Shakespeare as a natural genius, lacking the discipline and learning necessary to elevate his work to the highest level. (See NEOCLASSICISM.) There were some notable exceptions to this view, however. John HALES of Eton in 1633 defended Shakespeare from the charge of ignorance, and the remarkable poem prefixed to the Second Folio (1632) gives us a striking picture of Shakespeare as "a mind reflecting ages past." See THE FRIENDLY ADMIRER. Another stout defender of the dramatist was Leonard DIGGES who in the preface to the 1640 edition of the *Poems* refers to this "art unparaleld."

By mid-century, however, Jonson's criticism had taken firm hold, and while Shakespeare still shared membership with Jonson and Fletcher in the "triumvirate of wit," there were distinct indications of his being overshadowed by those more fashionable dramatists. The nadir of Shakespeare appreciation, however, was yet to be reached. This achievement belongs to Thomas RYMER, described by George Saintsbury as "the worst critic who has ever been." Rymer, a dogmatic adherent of the neoclassical principles of dramatic construction, ridiculed and derided *Othello* as a "bloody farce without salt or savour."

Rymer's views had some influence on the next generation of critics, but they were overshadowed by a far greater critical and creative mind, that of John DRYDEN. Dryden is the first great Shakespearean critic and one of the most influential. His praise of Shakespeare, tempered by his own neoclassical predilections, offset the fanaticism of Rymer and served as a pervasive influence in the first half of the 18th century. [Augustus Ralli, *A History of Shakespearian Criticism,* 1932.]

criticism—18th century. The tone of the dominant mode of Shakespearean criticism in the early years of the 18th century had been set by John Dryden. Critics of the 18th century did not fail to acknowledge Shakespeare's genius; they did, however, like Dryden, qualify their praise with certain strictures relating to the construction of the plays and to their occasional display of factual errors. Chief among these critics were the critical descendants of Thomas Rymer who censured the dramatist severely for his violation of the neoclassical rules of the drama. By the end of the first decade of the century, however, this group proved a dying breed. The new critical mode was expressed by Nicholas Rowe in the Preface to his edition (1709) of Shakespeare:

> If one undertook to examine the greatest part of these [the Tragedies] by those rules which are established by Aristotle, and taken from the model of the Grecian stage, it would be no very hard task to find a great many faults: but as Shakespeare lived under a kind of mere Light of Nature, and had never been made acquainted with the regularity of those written precepts, so it would be hard to judge him by a law he knew nothing of.

Rowe's position was extended by Joseph ADDISON in one of his *Spectator* essays, arguing that there is "more beauty in the work of a great genius who is ignorant of the rules of art than those of a little genius who knows and observes them." In their defense of Shakespeare both of these critics touched upon the topic which was to be of consuming interest to later critics of the century: the question of Shakespeare's learning. For the problem of Shakespeare's violation of classical precepts on the drama was seen to be related to his ignorance of these rules. Thus John DENNIS, writing in 1712, argued that Shakespeare could not have known the classical prescriptions for the dramatic art, else he could never have failed to have profited by the knowledge. The debate over Shakespeare's learning was eventually resolved by Richard FARMER's *Essay on the Learning of Shakespeare* (1767), which demonstrated that a good deal of the foreign sources of the plays had been read in translation.

As the question of Shakespeare's violation of the rules died in England, it was renewed in France by VOLTAIRE and others who rejected the English "barbarian" in favor of Corneille and Racine. (See FRANCE.) The opposition to this position was expressed, ineffectually, by Lady Elizabeth MONTAGU in her *Essays on the Writings and Genius of Shakespear* (1769). The soundest refutation of Voltaire's criticism, however, had already been given in Samuel JOHNSON's Preface to his edition (1765) of the plays. Johnson, while enumerating at great length the many flaws in Shakespeare, never lost sight of the poet's genius for creating "human sentiments or human actions." Johnson's Preface was far from being a definite manifesto of a break with neoclassicism; it did, however, usher in an era of Shakespearean criticism in which the application of "the rules" was no longer significant.

The last quarter of the century is notable for its growing interest in an aspect of Shakespeare which was to become increasingly important in the 19th century: his characters. This interest was exhibited at the Stratford Jubilee of 1769, where the parade of Shakespearean characters was one of the major events of the festival. The earliest examples of character criticism were to be seen in the essays of William RICHARDSON and Thomas WHATELY, but the most significant of these studies of Shakespearean character was Maurice MORGANN's *Essay on the Dramatic Character of Sir John Falstaff* (1777), the earliest example of that imaginative, often idolatrous elevation of Shakespeare as the supreme creator of character which came to be the hallmark of Romantic criticism. Unique among the critical commentaries of the age was the work of Walter Whiter, whose *A specimen of a Commentary on Shakespeare* (1794) anticipated the modern study of Shakespeare's image patterns. (See IMAGERY.) Other critics of note during the period include John ARMSTRONG; James BEATTIE; Hugh BLAIR; Richard CUMBERLAND; Charles GILDON; Georg Wilhelm HEGEL; Johann Gottfried HERDER; John HUGHES; Henry Home, Lord KAMES; Charlotte Ramsay LENNOX; Gotthold Ephraim LESSING; Henry MACKENZIE; Corbyn MORRIS; George SEWELL; Richard STEELE; Joseph WARTON; and Edward YOUNG. [D. Nichol Smith, *Eighteenth Century Essays on Shakespeare*, 1963.]

criticism—19th century. In the first two decades of the 19th century in England and on the continent, Shakespearean criticism flourished in rebellion against the reservations about Shakespeare of 18th-century neoclassicism. The romantics in England, France, and Germany succeeded in shifting the intellectual climate of opinion about Shakespeare from something that had ranged from erratic enthusiasm in England and Germany to contempt in France, to something closer to wild adulation. But from 1815 in Germany and 1820 in England, by which times Shakespeare had become universally accepted by critics, criticism ceased to be an active or important part of contemporary literary history; it became eulogium: adoring, uncurious, sonorous, and, above all, redundant of the earlier decades of Coleridge and Schlegel. Not until George Bernard Shaw's iconoclastic essays appeared at the end of the century was there any abatement of adoration. See FRANCE; GERMANY.

In England, while Wordsworth, Byron, and Keats invoked Shakespeare to justify their own practices as poets, the major romantic critics, Coleridge, Lamb, and Hazlitt, developed the trends of late 18th-century Shakespeare criticism.

Samuel Taylor COLERIDGE dominated Shakespearean criticism until the appearance of Bradley's *Shakespearean Tragedy* (1904). In two short essays, Coleridge changed the nature of Shakespearean criticism in England. In "Shakspeare's Judgment Equal to his Genius," he defined the concept of organic form as that which emerged to suit the individual nature of each play, in contrast to mechanical form imposed by outside standards, thus refuting the neoclassical reservations about Shakespeare's aesthetic judgment. In "Recapitulation and Summary of the Characteristics of Shakspeare's Dramas," he emphasized the unity of feeling rather than of time and place in the plays. In answer to Johnson's accusation of moral and verbal grossness, Coleridge took pains to point out that Shakespeare's language is poetic and integral, never merely decorative, and that his essential morality is beyond question. In his lectures and notes published in *Literary Remains* (1836–1839), it is clear that Coleridge considered Shakespeare the greatest artist who ever lived, more prophet than poet, certainly the ultimate philosopher of human nature and the absolutely universal artist.

Charles LAMB wrote of both Shakespeare and his contemporaries, pointing to a body of playwrights and a golden age of drama. Although he wrote only a small amount of criticism, his lively style and insight rescue his work from neglect. He was one of the first critics to feel that the tragedies, *King Lear*, for example, and even some of the comedies, such as *The Tempest*, are disappointing on stage compared to a reading of them; such plays, almost beyond human grasp, cannot be contained in a theatre.

William HAZLITT hailed Shakespeare as the greatest, most universal genius who ever lived in his *The Characters of Shakespear's Plays* (1817), in "Shakespear's Genius" (*Lectures on the English Poets*, 1818), and in *Lectures on the Dramatic Literature of the Age of Elizabeth* (1820). Indebted to Schlegel, Coleridge, and Lamb, Hazlitt nevertheless had his own trenchant and often remarkable insights into the plays. He was generally concerned with human motivation, and he constantly recognized the complexity of behavior as he considered the dramatic poetry of the plays. With a sure grasp of the nature of dramatic poetry, Hazlitt insisted on psychological realism as the standard for his criticism.

Thomas De Quincey's (1785–1859) "On the Knocking at the Gate in *Macbeth*," in *London Magazine* (October 1823), is a brilliant description of the writer's reaction to a piece of stage business; his other work on Shakespeare was written for the seventh edition of the *Encyclopaedia Britannica* (1838).

Victorian criticism of Shakespeare is noteworthy only for its quantity. Beginning with Anna Brownell Jameson's (1794–1860) *Characteristics of Women, Moral, Poetical, and Historical* (1832), some 70-odd writers ventured opinions about Shakespeare, now mostly forgotten, in both England and the United States. Thomas CARLYLE, in his discussion of the hero as poet in *On Heroes, Hero-Worship, and the Heroic in History* (1841), showed himself a disciple of romantic German professorial adulation. Matthew Arnold in his preface to his *Poems* (1853) was more judicious, if cursory.

In the United States, Edgar Allan POE's negative review of Hazlitt's *Characters of Shakespear's Plays* ushered in American Shakespearean criticism. Both Ralph Waldo EMERSON in *Representative Men* (1850) and James Russell Lowell in "Shakespeare Once More" in the *North American Review* (1868), though critical, were often concerned with eulogizing Shakespeare. See UNITED STATES.

The work of three important critics appeared in England in the latter part of the century. One of them, Edward Dowden, was influenced by Coleridge and in turn influenced A. C. Bradley. His *Shakspere, A Critical Study of his Mind and Art* (1875) is regarded as the best critical work of the second half of the century. Barrett Wendell (1855–1921) follows in the footsteps of Dowden in his *William Shakespeare, A Study in Elizabethan Literature* (1894), as does F. S. Boas in *Shakspere and his Predecessors* (1896).

Of major figures in the last decades, Algernon Charles SWINBURNE's *A Study of Shakespeare* (1880) was the first detailed criticism of the plays by a poet of rank since Coleridge, although that is its only distinction. Walter Pater's (1839–1894) essays on the history plays and some of the early comedies are generally more perceptive (see LOVE'S LABOUR'S LOST: *Selected Criticism*). While both Swinburne and Pater were unstinting in their admiration, the young George Bernard SHAW in his capacity as drama and music critic for *The Saturday Review* wrote a series of consistently negative reviews of the plays (1895, 1896, 1897), which can best be characterized by the following citation: "Shakespear is for an afternoon, but not for all time" (*The Saturday Review*, XXIV, May 2, 1896).—S.K.

criticism—20th century. In the first 60 years of the 20th century, Shakespeare criticism has become more intricate and difficult than ever before; and those who turn to it, not from an interest in criticism as such, but because of their first-hand enthusiasm for the dramatist himself and his incomparable works, may decide that the trend toward intricacy and difficulty has gone further than they would wish. After all, they will say, it is not right for criticism to exercise the reader's mind simply for its own sake. Its function is to equip him to turn from criticism back to literature. One of the main problems of this essay, therefore, is to make clear why this intricacy and difficulty have come into the criticism of Shakespeare.

Two things must be borne in mind. The first is something which nearly all of us, however little we like difficult criticism, are really prepared to admit or, more accurately, to insist on. It is that Shakespeare is universally regarded as a dramatist of extraordinary richness, variety and—one may add—profundity. We cannot be surprised if the work of critics who seek to reveal this wealth and complexity of material should itself become intricate and difficult; and it is important to bear in mind that even the criticism in which one finds really unnecessary difficulty was not written out of willfulness. It was written by some critic who—distant though his point of view may have been from one's own—wrote as he did because he sincerely felt that if he were to elucidate Shakespeare's wealth, he had to write in that way. Even the critics who seem to offer us least, offer us one thing of decisive importance: they remind us that Shakespeare is not just one more important writer, but one of the giants of the literature of the whole world, and that his variety and richness are so great that his work can offer to others excitement and meaning wholly different from our own.

The second thing to bear in mind is that the criticism of a great writer never develops in an intellectual vacuum. Critics bring to it—some perhaps one thing, and some another—the whole spectrum of intellectual and cultural interests of their time. Criticism belongs to its period. Rightly understood, it seems sometimes to be nothing short of an image of its period. Any study of 20th-century Shakespeare criticism must necessarily begin with A. C. BRADLEY's *Shakespearean Tragedy* (1904), and two passages from the opening pages of this book will immediately make the point clear in his particular case.

The first of these concerns Bradley's conception of the link between drama and poetry; and in reading it, one should remember that Shakespeare is of course our greatest poet as well as greatest dramatist:

> Even what, in a restricted sense, may be called the 'poetry' of [the tragedies]—the beauties of style, diction, versification—I shall pass by in silence. Our one object will be what, again in a restricted sense, may be called dramatic enjoyment . . . to learn to apprehend the action and some of the personages of each [play] with a somewhat greater truth and intensity.

In another passage toward the beginning of the book, Bradley shows more fully what he understands by "action" and "personages":

> We see a number of human beings placed in certain circumstances; and we see, arising from the co-operation of their characters in these circumstances, certain actions. These actions beget others, and these others beget others again, until this series of inter-connected deeds leads by apparently inevitable sequence to a catastrophe.

The first of these passages reflects clearly how its

author was writing under the influence of the revival of realist prose drama toward the end of the 19th century. That in a poetic drama the poetry is a delightful addition which can be abstracted not merely from this or that other aspect of the drama, but from the drama as a drama strikes us today as strange. But the second passage also shows the critic as a product of his time. For this picture of settled character and determinate environment, in systematic interaction, springs from the sense of universal and determined causality, in society as well as nature, which was one of the great intellectual inventions of the 19th century. The world of a play, Bradley believes, is a world of causal law and of determined "inevitable" consequence, just like the world of reality. Behind his criticism lies the thought of Mill and Herbert Spencer; just as, along with their thought, and constituting another movement of mind toward seeing human society as shaped everywhere by the rule of scientific, systematic law, there lies the fiction of George Eliot; or in another way, and coming much nearer to Bradley's own time, that of Thomas Hardy.

On the other hand, to see Bradley as mere creature of the *Zeitgeist* would be grotesque. When he speaks in his essay "Coriolanus" of the "profound sense of sadness and mystery" which comes from Shakespeare's work, of its "supreme imaginative appeal . . . terrible, heart-rending or glorious to witness"—and such testimony is common in his work—one cannot escape the impression of a man whose response to the magnitude of Shakespeare's achievement is first-hand and alive. Moreover, in giving one a sense—at least in intention—of wholly unwavering submission and allegiance to his author, of total exemption from the urge to substitute his own interests, views, or attitudes for those of Shakespeare, he seems to excel all his successors down to the present day. But, nevertheless, his implicit acceptance of that 19th-century idea of all-pervasive causality is perhaps what gives Bradley's criticism its most distinctive quality. In the first place, it explains why his chapter on "Construction" in the tragedies is by far the slightest in his book. As the passage quoted above made clear, for Bradley the organization of a play was in essence the same as the rational, causal order of experience. There remained to discuss only such matters as how Shakespeare's tragedies may be divided into phases of Exposition, Development up to Crisis, and Catastrophe; or how the succession of events in a play displays "a constant alternation of rises and falls of tension"; or how, in a number of the tragedies, one group of characters becomes more and more successful up to a maximum point, and then progressively declines in fortune.

Bradley's main insight lies elsewhere. It lies on the side not of action, but his other dramatic dimension: "personages." It was to the richness and profundity of Shakespeare's characters that Bradley above all responded: the elaborate springs of their conduct and the elaborate and brilliant play of their consciousness. Here he is at his best, often both penetrating and exhilarating; and this interest also helps to place Bradley in his own age—or rather, at the end of an age, in the period of the 19th-century novel with its elaborate and often magnificent development of the individual character. The connection shows especially clearly, perhaps, in the essay on *Antony and Cleopatra* included in his *Oxford Lectures on Poetry* (1909). Beginning with a reference to "the full analysis and illustration of the character" of Cleopatra, Bradley goes on to write:

> Cleopatra stands in a group with Hamlet and Falstaff . . . They are inexhaustible. You feel that, if they were alive and you spent your whole life with them, their infinite variety could never be staled by custom; they would continue every day to surprise, perplex and delight you. Shakespeare has bestowed on each of them . . . his own originality, his genius. He has given it most fully to Hamlet, to whom none of the chambers of experience is shut.

Reading this, it is impossible not to recall that Bradley's Shakespeare lectures were being delivered during the very years when Henry James was writing his later novels; variety and inexhaustible potentiality were exactly what James aimed at and offered in his major characters. In fact, the very idea (at the level of high consciousness) of opening all the doors of experience is exactly the idea which governs the development of several of James' major novels, and it would be easy, if space permitted, to show how it was one of the seminal literary ideas of the end of the 19th century.

Bradley's criticism has been discussed at length because the easiest way to understand later work is to see it as supplementing or qualifying his own, and standing in the perspective of his insights and emphases or over-emphases. Harley Granville-Barker's series of *Prefaces to Shakespeare* (1927–1947), for example, deals in great detail with the staging of the plays, acting of the parts, and speaking of the lines—all of them matters which Bradley, concentrating on what might be termed the dramatic as against the theatrical, legitimately disregarded. If Granville-Barker's discussions lack profundity (as they do), they have retained their considerable value partly because of the help they give to actors and directors, and partly because of their unfailing good sense and freedom from the false ingenuity and cleverness which have marred a good deal of more recent criticism.

Bradley's scanty attention to the theatrical side of the plays found more sophisticated compensation in the work of E. E. Stoll. What Stoll rejects is exactly Bradley's implicit assumption, that the world of a play and the characters in it may be explained by means of the same modes of explanation as are valid for the world of real life. This, Stoll cogently argued (*Art and Artifice in Shakespeare*, 1933), is to ignore the whole spectrum of dramatic convention as it existed for Shakespeare (see historical criticism). "What is structure is turned into psychology," he succinctly says, by this false method. Bradley had argued that Macbeth's first response to his meeting with the witches proved for us that Macbeth had already been plotting the murder of Duncan with his wife. Stoll argues that subtleties of this kind fail to allow for the fact that Shakespeare was writing within a convention whereby the protagonist's succumbing to a temptation could be accepted with a certain special readiness as creating part of the *données* of a play and was therefore not available for ingenious speculation as to what it showed about the depths of his nature or the recesses of his past. Similarly, if Othello readily believed Iago's slanders on his wife, or Hamlet accused himself of being slow to revenge, these were not facts which the dramatist offered us as a basis for character-analysis: that the slanderer should be believed, that the revenger should not "sweep to his revenge" but delay it long enough to make the length of the play, were conventions of the theatre.

Stoll's keen sense of dramatic stylization, of the essential difference between real world and play-world, was a valuable insight, and it is perhaps a pity that his work has not been more influential. That it has not probably results from the fact that in stressing how Shakespeare's plays relied on conventions, which may be traced widely in the drama of his time, Stoll dealt insufficiently with what it was that made those plays so much superior to those of Shakespeare's contemporaries, where the conventions also held. His references, left curt and vague, to Shakespeare's "manipulating" his characters "more deftly" or to "the all-reconciling power of poetry" left something unexplained; later critics justly saw it as perhaps the most important thing of all.

The truth is that most critics since Bradley would regard Stoll's virtual refusal to touch on the poetry of the plays as revealing not awareness, but a disabling *un*awareness of their drama, as neglect of a convention, a stylization, which is far more central to poetic drama than any convention relating to action or character because it is the convention which makes poetic drama what it is. Bradley's willingness to make a sharp distinction between poetic convention and theatrical convention was mentioned above. This, combined with his interest in character, led him into some obvious errors. It led him to claim that we must see Macbeth and Antony as men of poetic nature, because at times they speak fine poetry; and that Coriolanus is unimaginative because he does not. But again, that more recent Shakespeare criticism has seen Shakespeare's poetry not as a character-revealing aspect of the major roles, but as something which subordinates all the roles to a greater whole, a greater unity, and one which is in the first place a unity of language—this is no mere novel idea that has developed by chance. It, too, is of its time. To begin with, it is the reflection in Shakespeare studies of the general break in modern art (both literary and pictorial) with the realism which was dominant in the 19th century. Yeats' essay on "The Tragic Theatre" (1904) rejects the shallowness of contemporary theatrical realism, and rejects the very distinction that Bradley started from:

> In poetic drama there is, it is held, an antithesis between character and lyric poetry . . . yet when we go back a few centuries and enter the great periods of drama, character grows less and sometimes disappears, and there is much lyric feeling . . . suddenly it strikes us that character is continuously present in comedy alone . . .

Yeats clinches this contrast between realist (predominantly comic) drama and poetic (more characteristically tragic) drama by a contrast between 19th-century realist painting ("How perfectly that woman is realized as distinct from all other women that have lived or shall live") and Byzantine painting, which leaves out certain elements of reality so that it may be more expressive of emotion and more symbolic. It is clear that he was conscious of how his views were part of a general movement in art and criticism.

Yeats was the first in the modern period to recognize the distinctive nature and deeper potentiality of poetic drama; in fact, his conception was something like fully formed as early as the *Letters to the New Island*, which were published in two American newspapers during 1889–1891, though not collected in book form until more than 40 years later. But a much more influential figure in the field of criticism was T. S. Eliot. In his essay "Four Elizabethan Dramatists: a Preface to an Unwritten Book" (1924), Eliot completely alters the perspective. He saw the belief in a division between poetry and drama as bringing about the unstageable closet-drama of Tennyson, Browning, and Swinburne on the one hand, and the fallacious concept of an illusionist prose drama on the other. The fault of the Elizabethans was not what William Archer had argued—that they allowed dramatic convention to impede the illusion of reality—it was that they so much as compromised with the realist heresy, so much as let it enter their calculations. "Realistic drama," writes Eliot, ". . . is drama striving steadily to escape the conditions of art." In others of his early dramatic essays Eliot develops his conception, though it must be remembered that for the most part he does so (as indeed is his usual method of argument) more by hint and implication than anything blunt or direct. Thus in the "Dialogue on Dramatic Poetry" (1928), it is the character suggestively denominated by the initial "E" who claims that the illuminating analogy for drama is with the ceremony of the Mass—drama is not a "slice of life" so much as a liturgy—and implies that the decisive distinction between drama in prose and in verse is that in the latter the "form" is more profoundly operative.

Again, this emphasis might be related to its period: the concept of form and formal unity were central to the aesthetic movement of the end of the 19th century, which drew to itself the main opponents of realism at that time, and was a key to the philosophical work of F. H. Bradley (brother of the critic), who had more than one link with the aesthetic movement, and on whom the young Eliot produced his doctoral thesis. But Eliot gave a quite special emphasis to this idea of form, and thereby gave the criticism specifically of "poetic" drama an immense new strength and substance, because he linked it to the main general interest of both poets and critics of poetry at that time. In "Rhetoric and Poetic Drama" (1919), Eliot had already carefully made it clear that if drama of this kind called for rhetoric it was rhetoric in the sense not of bombast but of style: such style as was demanded by the nature of the whole work as a work of art. In fact, poetic drama at its highest made possible and was (more important) made possible by a use of language at the polar opposite from bombast:

> Examination of the development of Elizabethan drama shows . . . development from monotony to variety, a progressive refinement in the percep-

tions of the variations of feeling, and a progressive elaboration of the means of expressing these variations. This drama is admitted to have grown away from the rhetorical expression, the bombast speeches, of Kyd and Marlowe to the *subtle and dispersed* [italics mine] utterance of Shakespeare and Webster....

The next phase of Shakespeare criticism was therefore no mere adjustment from the standpoint we have noticed in Bradley's work, but in essence a diametric contrast. So far from setting "the poetry" on one side in pursuit of the drama, it started from the position that the one and only way to locate the dramatic significance of the work was to give primacy of consideration to the poetry; and that to do this meant to give primacy of attention to the "subtle" and intricately interwoven texture of the language of the play, through which its levels or layers of poetic meaning would be pervasively "dispersed." Shakespeare criticism therefore aligned itself with the major trend in modern criticism of poetry: to criticize was in the first place to analyze, and to analyze the texture of language in the work in such a way as to bring out all the richness and complexity created by verbal interaction and evocation. The emergence of analytic criticism in the work of Eliot, Pound, and also, one might add, T. E. Hulme; its inheritance from the thought of Mallarmé and others associated with the symbolist movement in France; and its development and dissemination during the 1920's in books by Herbert Read, Robert Graves, and (most influential of all, probably) I. A. Richards are well known and need not be discussed here. But on the other hand, it would be quite wrong to see the Shakespeare criticism of the time as merely reflecting a movement toward analysis which enjoyed a full and independent existence unconnected with Shakespeare. On the contrary, Eliot did not write at length on Shakespeare, but it was to the dramatic verse of the early 17th-century—a style of verse which was ultimately a Shakespearean creation through and through—that he turned for his main illustration and confirmation of the complexity of linguistic texture that interested him and that criticism ought, in his view, to study. In Read's *The Problem of Style* (first delivered as lectures in 1921) Shakespeare's own later verse was most insistently taken as the poetic achievement which demands, justifies, and shows the potential of detailed analytical criticism. It was Shakespeare who came to Richards' mind in illustration of the idea, so characteristic of the movement, that what distinguishes the poet from the plain man is the "range, delicacy, and freedom of the connections he is able to make between different elements of his experience" (*Principles of Literary Criticism*, 1925 ed.). Only a few years after Richards, F. R. Leavis was writing about the texture of language essential to poetry from the same point of view (though in a way which seems better to have stood the test of time), and, once more, it was repeatedly in the verse of Shakespeare's later plays that he found his obvious, his decisive examples and confirmation.

The earliest really explicit and detailed statement of how this critical approach should be applied to Shakespeare is probably L. C. Knights' *How Many Children had Lady Macbeth?* (1933): ". . . the total response to a Shakespeare play can only be obtained by an exact and sensitive study of the verse, of the rhythm and imagery of the controlled associations of the words [etc.] . . . we start with so many lines of verse on a printed page which we read as we should any other poem. We have to . . . unravel ambiguities . . . estimate the kind and quality of the imagery . . . As we read other factors come into play . . . 'plot,' aspects of 'character' and recurrent 'themes' . . . there is a constant reference backwards and forwards" (quoted from Knights' *Explorations*, 1946). Caroline Spurgeon's *Shakespeare's Imagery and What It Tells Us* (1935) was a detailed and influential study of its subject, but systematically analytical rather than critical. (See IMAGERY.) M. M. Mahood's *Shakespeare's Wordplay* (1957) is a full discussion of detailed associations and verbal ambiguity in the plays.

What might loosely be termed the "linguistic movement" in criticism was also integral to the whole intellectual spectrum of the period (linking notably with developments in philosophy—between which discipline and that of criticism, Richards himself stood as an intermediary figure). But here one must notice a distinction of absolutely first-rate importance. While linguistic analysis in philosophy went on the whole with a skeptical temper of mind, it was linked in criticism with an emphatic stress on the place of moral values; or at least a sense that complexity resulted from no mere self-contained skill with words, but rather from a richer development of the whole self of the poet, a fuller capacity on his part to receive experience in all its range, variety, and difficulty, and to order and master it without omission or crudification. Verbal complexity was thus an index of superiority of character, a superiority of not the aesthetic but the moral life. To put the point briefly and in the key terms of this school of criticism, the complex was the moral, and the moral was the mature.

The idea that ability to produce verse which used language the complex way was ultimately a quality of character, of general cultural adequacy, is of course clear in Eliot's criticism (the essays on "Andrew Marvell" and "The Metaphysical Poets" might be cited), as also is a sense that in the modern world both writer and critic have a special concern and responsibility for identifying and maintaining values (in this connection the essay on Pascal has much relevance). The intimate connection between soundness from a general ethical standpoint and the power of poets to emerge successfully from close verbal analysis had, in fact, already been stressed since 1908 by A. R. Orage. That a newer school of Shakespeare criticism should have made these its basic tenets was, given the conditions of the age, natural enough; and by now we have before us two of the three fundamental moments of that criticism. The third is something of rather a different order, and by no means follows from the other two. Eliot had, in fact, recurrently stressed the *im*personality of major and successful art. He saw it as not an expression of personality, but an escape from personality. But after all, Shakespeare had written his plays steadily and continuously, and over a period of many years. Moreover, he had not gone to and fro between plays of various types and with varying outlooks. There was undoubtedly something steadily sequacious in how he moved on from phase to phase in his work. Finally, it is more than easy to see in the sequence from "cynical" plays like *Troilus and Cressida* through the major tragedies to the last "romance" plays something like an access of doubt and uncertainty, then a greater effort to confront at their worst and most powerful the aspects of life that caused that doubt, and finally a resolving of the crisis that resulted from this effort. Shakespeare came to be seen rather in the image of some of his modern readers who felt that the modern world presented them also with a disjointed and frightening vision of life, and had struggled to reduce it to sense and order. "What *for*, what ultimately for?" "What do men live by?" "How to live?" F. R. Leavis, and Matthew Arnold before him, saw these as the questions that in general concerned both writer and critic if they were serious. Shakespeare criticism adopted Keats' viewpoint ("Shakespeare led a life of Allegory"), and saw the dramatist's achievement as the record and the product of a private struggle, intense and spiritual, over the years from the late 1590's until the close of his life as a writer.

Although Leavis' own Shakespearean criticism is small in bulk, its impact has been out of all proportion to its volume. More than this, it is Leavis' practice and advocacy of what may for brevity be termed moral-analytical criticism that have undoubtedly been most sustained, influential, and impressive. But although this strong affinity between the newer Shakespeare criticism and the general work of Leavis is one of the fundamentals of the situation, as a matter of chronology and in practice the real originator of the new approach was not Leavis but—insofar as any one name can be cited—G. Wilson KNIGHT. In the first essay Knight published, *Myth and Miracle: An Essay on the Symbolism of Shakespeare* (1929), the three "moments" mentioned above are all clearly stated. First, Shakespeare's final plays (the essay claims in its opening words) are "the culmination of a series which starts about the middle of Shakespeare's writing life." This series, of "remarkable coherence and significance," is the progressive revelation of Shakespeare's personal spiritual voyaging, his struggle with or arrival at "the questioning, the pain, the profundity and grandeur." Moreover, there is no question of our mere awareness of character, story, emotional absorption: "all these plays are to the reader, what they must have been to the author, revelations of profundity and grandeur: the mystery of human fate . . . is intuitively apprehended." Here is the second major point, that the plays constitute an ordering and profound comprehension of life and the values of life: "tragedy and our religion are inter-significant." The third may be seen in Wilson Knight's insistence that where "the language of conceptual thought fails," the plays succeed by offering to us a semi-mystical vision through "poetic atmosphere" and through "symbolism" which integrates the basic "themes" of each play into a kind of poetic orchestral score, from which as a whole the ultimate vision of the play emerges and "The artist expresses a direct vision of the significance of life." No mere conceptualized statements, but the symbolism of storm and music, for example, is what runs through play after play and gives expression to Shakespeare's sense of the cosmic battle between good and evil, life and death, order and chaos. See SYMBOLISM.

In his first full-length work, *The Wheel of Fire* (1930), Wilson Knight included an introductory essay, "On the Principles of Shakespeare Interpretation," in which he elucidated his approach to the plays more fully: contrasting "analysis," mere superficial discussion of the sequence of the plot or detail of character, and "interpretation," which sees each play as a "set of correspondences" (or equally well, perhaps, contrasts) between areas of ultimate meaning—themes of "death," "evil," "intuition against intelligence"—embodied in imagery, incident, or the *dramatis personae* themselves (Knight writes not of Othello, but of "the Othello conception"). "We should regard each play as a visionary whole, close-knit in personification, atmospheric suggestion, and direct poetic symbolism . . . we should not look for perfect verisimilitude to life, but rather see each play as an expanded metaphor."

J. Dover Wilson's *The Essential Shakespeare* (1932) advanced much the same view of Shakespeare as engaged, from about 1599 on, in a passionate spiritual struggle to reach balance of mind through insight into order; and gave this conception new strength in his vivid but scholarly biographical study. In *Approach to Shakespeare* (1938) by D. TRAVERSI there is much that is similar to Wilson Knight, but also, though it is not immediately obvious, much that is quite different. Traversi also opens his discussion with a firm though courteous rejection of Bradley's approach, and concentrates on the poetry of the plays, on their sense of value, and on how they constitute a record of their author's inquiring mind as it moved forward in a spiritual voyage. But Traversi's sense of the poetic dimension was not, like Knight's, one of the impact of imagery and event sensed as it were for their substance and *en bloc*, mapping out the play as a spatial entity ("spatial" was, in fact, Knight's word). It derived from Traversi's general adherence to Leavis as a critic, concentrated on the detailed local texture of Shakespeare's language, emphasized (in accordance with the more general views of critics of this kind) how its poetic strength could not be separated from its racy vernacular quality, and—perhaps the distinctive and crucial issue—saw the scheme of values embodied in a play, its structure as a moral entity, as thrown everywhere into relief by a local verbal texture of which the poetic merit lay exactly in this power to intimate a nuance of value at every point. "The compression of the syntax . . . is a sign of the moral pressure felt in the speech." That Cressida's "youth and freshness" were such that they "made *stale* the morning" brings to life, through the double sense of "stale," the whole value-scheme of the work. Indeed, in his enthusiastically keen sense of how analysis of the verse reveals the play's decisive moral life, Traversi seems even to exaggerate: "the juxtaposition of . . . 'freshness' and 'stale' is *vital to the whole play* [italics mine]."

The difference between the two critics is not merely their differing interests in language. Unobtrusively but fundamentally, their senses of the moral life of the plays are in contrast. Wilson Knight's writing is sometimes almost febrile, because his mind is so full of Shakespeare as marvelously and passionately in contact with the mystic ultimates of the cosmos—and he enthuses from below. Traversi very often sees Shakespeare's sense of value as concerned with what is life-enhancing or the reverse at a wholly everyday level, manifesting itself in such things as that Macbeth, once hardened in crime, is lacking in intensity and "played out," or that Isabella in *Measure for Measure* is defective in her chastity because it seems to take no account of the "natural roots of feeling" as manifested in Claudio's fornication. It is a morality of quotidian conduct, though one notably liberal, tolerant of sensuousness and "for life," that Traversi chiefly traces in Shakespeare.

Also, the tone of his work differs much from Knight's. He does not follow Shakespeare as disciple, so much as adjudge, from the position of the critic, how near the dramatist comes to full success. Shakespeare "has gained solidity and actuality" by the time of *Henry IV*. There is something in the so-called problem plays which is "not . . . adequate." The "mature tragedies" are "more adequate." *Othello* represents an "advance in Shakespeare's *experience*," but he "came *nearer*" to unifying his experience in *Antony and Cleopatra.*

If Knight's criticism leaves the reader dissatisfied in that he cannot accept the critic's often febrile, emotionalized quality as an accurate index to a writer so conspicuously free from these defects, what takes the place of this in Traversi's work is a not infrequent impression of arbitrariness. The reader feels this critic could give any interpretation to anything if he wished. As mere indication of what is meant by that comment, two examples must suffice. Here is the first. The "fact that makes *Othello* the first of the mature tragedies" is that by contrast with the "inextricable interdependence" of good and evil in *Measure for Measure,* the later play indeed links its positive and negative sides by related imagery, but "for the first time the links are subsidiary to and less important than the division." But *Antony and Cleopatra* is "the most . . . completely realized of the last plays." We might therefore expect the "division" between positive and negative to be yet more sharply and maturely made. On the contrary, its poetry turns no longer upon "cleavage" between good and evil, but "perfect continuity." In the end, the attentive reader doubts if he knows where he is.

Another example, of a different kind, may be found in Traversi's repeated treatment of a celebrated speech in *The Winter's Tale*. In the first edition of *Approach to Shakespeare,* we read that in Perdita's "great list of flowers" (IV, iv) "one can discern a certain pathetic weakness, a kind of wilting from life." The whole discussion, nearly 200 words long, was repeated virtually unchanged 18 years later in the work more modestly entitled *An Approach to Shakespeare* (1956), and closely paraphrased in *The Age of Shakespeare* (1955), a volume in the Pelican Guide to English Literature. Here we read that "the love" expressed by the flower speech "still lacks the necessary maturity. The emphasis laid in the imagery, upon Spring, that is upon birth, inexperience, virginity, is subtly balanced by an implicit sense of death . . ." In Traversi's fourth printing of his analysis of the speech—in *Shakespeare: the Last Phase* (1954)—we read once again of the "certain pathetic weakness, a kind of wilting from life" in the "great list of flowers." But here, and only here, there is also something quite different. "Meanwhile the vitality which, in spite of what we have said about her flower speech, underlies Perdita's love for Florizel is indicated by the reference to . . ." (the ox-lips and crown-imperials, in fact, which are part of the flower speech), and by "the intense feeling for life"—which comes at the end of the same speech. How, the reader is left wondering, does one and the same speech express pathetic weakness and also vitality, wilting before life and also intense feeling for life, in respect of the same person and apparently the same emotion? And if the contrast between wilting and vitality needed bringing out in 1954, why did the wilting alone suffice in 1955 and 1956?

The points are not points merely of detail, if they lead to a sense of the standing danger implicit in this type of criticism, as those in Bradley were noticed earlier. This standing danger in the work of Knight and Traversi seems to be a tendency to substitute self-expression for interpretation, to be always under the temptation to impose on Shakespeare (at least to some degree) the critic's own convictions about life and its values, rather than find the dramatist's. That these critics should find in Shakespeare very much the moral sensibility they find in other authors, of quite different periods, whom they greatly admire; and that they should make little or no use of the considerable body of recent scholarship which has clarified how the moral sensibility of Shakespeare's time differed profoundly from anything we can find in the spectrum of today, lends support to the suggestion that their findings belong to themselves, and today, rather than to Shakespeare and the 16th century.

It could be argued that even a scholarly and self-effacing critic like L. C. Knights somewhat illustrates the same trend. In *An Approach to Hamlet* (1960), for example, Knights endorses virtually *in toto* Leavis' discussion of the character of Othello in his essay "Diabolic Intellect and the Noble Hero," despite the fact that this took for granted expressed attitudes toward woman, sexual love, and public life characteristic of our own time as they would not have been of Shakespeare's. But if occasionally Knights' own views rather than Shakespeare's find expression in his criticism, they do so with modesty and delicacy. It is at a deeper level that his work raises problems about the validity of this kind of criticism.

For this purpose the works of A. Sewell (*Character and Society in Shakespeare,* 1951) and D. G. James (*The Dream of Learning,* 1951) are also relevant. The fact is that in all these critics there seems to be a deep and revealing uncertainty about the *mode* in which the author's moral sensibility is present in his work, or the status which it has in it. In part, as will transpire, this is not greatly open to objection. But the fact remains that Sewell, for example, says at one point that Shakespeare "created drama out of the *question* . . . simply, 'What shall we do to be saved?' " but elsewhere speaks of Shakespeare's "fundamental . . . *study* of the moral nature of man's address to his world" or of "social and moral *judgements* implicit" in a play; or again of "that *representation* of the human soul which is the business of the great tragedies." For Knights, Shakespeare comes to terms with "obstinate *questionings*," *King Lear* is a "great *exploratory* allegory," *Antony and Cleopatra* "makes it impossible for us not to *question* . . ." In *Some Shakespearean Themes* (1959), Knights speaks of "themes that shape themselves into a developing *pattern*," of "answers . . . to urgent questions," of the "complete endorsement of a certain quality of being . . . affirmation in spite of everything," and of the *moral theme* in *Timon* being "presented for examination." In *An Approach to Hamlet* he uses expressions like "question that [Shakespeare] *asks with some insistence*," "*defining* the weakness . . . of a particular attitude to life," "a play *about* death," and "*Hamlet* . . . is the *exploration and implicit criticism* of a particular state of mind." James also vacillates: *King Lear* "represents a great labor of *knowledge*" (in the sense of perception), our judgment on it is necessarily a judgment on its "veracity," but "we certainly cannot say that it brings us to a state of belief; instead it confronts us with mystery." Shakespeare "provided knowledge," but "he had . . . nothing to say about human nature and its destiny," he "showed it only"; and yet again "he will not resolve, but behold." (Italics in above quotations are mine.)

It is, of course, reasonable to claim that no significant work of art will have a moral vision such as can be abstracted and encapsulated. Could one do this, capsule might replace work. It is therefore to some extent unreasonable to demand any rigorous formula expressing how moral vision is present in a drama. But even so, these quotations suggest an indeterminateness or even confusion of mind which goes beyond that. These critics are fundamentally undecided as to what it is of value that they find in Shakespeare. Perhaps it is simply his raising and defining of certain questions which are urgent or elusive; perhaps, his exploring of such questions; or his holding before us a vision of life which may intimate something exactly (words like "define" and "clarify" are not infrequently used), or indeterminately and suggestively, or not at all. Perhaps it is his creating, from something cognitive, a "structure" or "developing pattern" which has value and interest in part for its formal qualities; or perhaps, his offering us an exact and detailed answer to some question and in this case either presenting a *possible* answer for our own ultimate judgment or endorsing and affirming an answer with all his power. Perhaps it is several or all of these things at once.

It seems as if these critics cannot say. But this lack of clarity has its own special interest, resulting, perhaps, from more than mere confusion of mind or failure to think out an approach (though it may well connect with these things). If we concede as much as is possible to this general kind of criticism (the discussion must at this stage concentrate upon what unites, rather than distinguishes, these authors), we shall surely see much of high value in their insistence on the unity of the work as a unity created in the first place by poetry, that is, by a texture of language. We shall surely concede also that Shakespeare's sense of human nature and of good and evil enter prominently into his works and deserve our highest respect, and that the plays can fill our minds with moral ideas and attitudes which (depending rather upon the existing state and development of our own moral education and convictions) we find of value or perhaps irreplaceable value. But it looks, at the same time, as if the lack of definition noted above occurs not because it is the essence of a great drama to advance a question or statement of some peculiarly elusive type—and the difficulty is simply that of exactly indicating so elusive a something—but rather that the lack of precision and constant shift of emphasis enable these critics to do much that really lies outside their chosen province, while supposing that it lies inside. It enables them to respond to pattern and formal organization, to sense the excitement, exhilaration and delight of the plays, to respond to their incomparable variety and intensity of emotional situation, while remaining all the time within a *schema* of quite another kind: one of question, answer, statement, solution and knowledge, matters whose connection with delight and exhilaration is normally, and perhaps of necessity, slight and subordinate.

It is not extravagant, I think, to see in these features of more recent Shakespeare criticism a reflection, once again, of certain conceptions or preconceptions which are prominent in our own time. In brief, it is a criticism which takes the image of knowledge, of the informative, as archetype of what is valuable, and which finds in Shakespeare such knowledge as addresses itself to a question like: What shall we do to be saved? Such preoccupations accord well with an age of universal information, education, and anxiety. What is taken for granted comes out well toward the close of *The Dream of Learning:* "Shakespeare indeed provided knowledge . . . we can find enough emotion, presumably, in a hundred and one ways . . . if we speak of these things in this way, I do not see that we can . . . justify the importance we attach to the *study and teaching* of Shakespeare." The dangers implicit in this passage are surely three: the assumption that the nature of great drama may well be studied from such a starting point as its importance to educators; the assumption of adequacy in the knowledge-emotion dichotomy; and above all, perhaps, the failure to see necessity for decisive distinctions within the field denoted by "emotion." Eliot's suggestion, mentioned earlier, that there is a significant analogy between drama and the Mass is enough, in fact, to challenge all of these assumptions; and it may be that Shakespeare criticism, developing this suggestion, could derive in the future even more from Eliot than it has derived already. [A. C. Bradley, "Coriolanus," *A Miscellany*, 1929; T. S. Eliot, *Selected Essays*, 1932; D. Traversi, *Approach to Shakespeare*, 1938; F. R. Leavis, "Diabolic Intellect and the Noble Hero," *The Common Pursuit*, 1952; W. B. Yeats, *Essays and Introductions*, 1961.]—J.H.

Croce, Benedetto (1866–1952). Italian philosopher, historian, and critic. A metaphysician in the idealistic tradition and a liberal historian, Croce wrote *Aesthetic as the Science of Expression* (1902), a significant contribution to the philosophy of art. His *Ariosto, Shakespeare, and Corneille* (1920) characterizes Shakespeare's manner and the development of his art and attacks historical and biographical approaches to the study of Shakespeare. Croce argues that any attempt to construe Shakespeare's philosophy from an insight into the "purpose" of individual plays is questionable. By distinguishing the artist's "poetical" personality from his "practical" one, Croce suggests that speculation about the poet's personal experience from data found in the plays is useless. As J. M. Robertson argues in his polemical *Croce as Shakespearean Critic* (1922), Croce's denunciation of all approaches but the aesthetic, as dealing with questions "not worth settling," ignores "relevant knowledge" in a rather doctrinaire fashion.

Cromwell, Thomas (c. 1485–1540). Son of a tradesman, and successively a merchant, a moneylender, and a lawyer, Cromwell rose through a series of honors to become earl of Essex. Though he was hated for his venality and harshness, his shrewdness made him useful first to Wolsey and later to the king. Partly as a result of his arranging Henry's marriage with an ugly woman, Anne of Cleves, he fell from favor and was executed for treason. In *Henry VIII*, however, he appears merely as Wolsey's loyal servant (III, ii), though his later preferments from the King are enviously catalogued by Sir Thomas Lovell and Gardiner, Bishop of Winchester (V, i).

Crosse, Samuel (d. ?1605). Actor. A member of the King's Men, Shakespeare's company, Crosse is listed with the "principall Actors" who appeared in Shakespeare's plays, in the First Folio (1623) list. No other facts are known about him. Scholars have speculated that he is the Crosse alluded to in Thomas Heywood's *Apologie for Actors* (c. 1607). E. K. Chambers conjectures that Crosse joined the King's Men about 1604, but was carried off by the plague almost immediately and was replaced by Nicholas Tooley. T. W. Baldwin speculates that Crosse was possibly Heminges' apprentice and played comic female roles. Baldwin attributes to Crosse the roles of Maria in *Twelfth Night*, Mistress Quickly in *The Merry Wives of Windsor*, Mistress Overdone in *Measure for Measure*, and Livia in Jonson's *Sejanus*. [E. K. Chambers, *The Elizabethan Stage*, 1923; T. W. Baldwin, *The Organization and Personnel of the Shakespearean Company*, 1927; E. K. Chambers, *William Shakespeare*, 1930.]

Cross Keys Inn. An inn used as a playhouse and located on Gracechurch Street within the city limits of London. The first reference to the Cross Keys Inn dates from 1579 when James Burbage, the builder of the Theatre, was arrested "as he came down Gracious Street towards the Cross Keys there to a play." An anecdote about the comedian Richard Tarlton asserts that he saw BANKS' HORSE there. In 1589 Strange's Men defied an admonition against playing within the city by performing at the inn. In 1594 when Strange's Men were reorganized as the core of the Chamberlain's Men, they obtained permission to perform at the Cross Keys during the winter months. It is not known how long Shakespeare's company (the Chamberlain's Men) used the Cross Keys, but it was apparently not in use after 1596. The inn was evidently one of the "Play-houses in Gracious Streete" which were "put down" after the prohibition against public plays within the city in 1596. See Richard RAWLIDGE. [E. K. Chambers, *The Elizabethan Stage*, 1923.]

Crowne, John (1640?–?1712). Dramatist. A successful Restoration playwright about whom little is known, Crowne was a favorite of Charles II. He is the author of two plays, *The Misery of Civil-War* (1680; reissued in 1681 as *Henry the Sixth, The Second Part; or, The Misery of Civil-War*) and *Henry the Sixth, The First Part. With the Murder of Humphrey Duke of Glocester* (1681), which are derived from Shakespeare's *Henry VI* trilogy.

Both are little more than political tracts, the first attacking the rebellion-threatening Whigs, and the other directed against the Catholics. Although Crowne claimed in each case to have invented almost all of the action himself, he actually lifted whole sections and plots from the *Henry VI* plays (see 3 HENRY VI: *Stage History*). He generally expands scenes and speeches to meet his requirements, but sometimes adds new material of his own. Shakespeare's poetry and characterizations are ruthlessly sacrificed to the cause of royalist propaganda.

Henry the Sixth, The First Part is the less artistically successful of the two plays. Based on the first three acts of Shakespeare's *2 Henry VI*, it makes few structural changes, achieving an anti-Catholic bias by additions to the original scenes. One such change is the murder of Gloucester, which Crowne presents onstage. The murderers are religious fanatics who affirm their beliefs at length, partly in conversation with the Cardinal, before actually killing the Duke. Characters are consistently simplified and broadened—particularly the Cardinal—in order to play a more effective role as tools or targets of propaganda. Despite all of its additions, Crowne's play has only four acts.

The Misery of Civil-War opens in the middle of *2 Henry VI* with a combination of several of Shakespeare's scenes of Cade and the mob. It follows the action of *2 Henry VI* and *3 Henry VI* with a few modifications, chiefly in rearrangements of the scenes. Edward's lechery is emphasized by having him pause in the midst of battle for amorous dalliance. The weaknesses of other characters, particularly of the rebels, are insistently developed, and the loose construction of the original is tightened by an emphasis on political motivation throughout.

Scenes of soldiers raping, pillaging, and slaughtering innocent peasants are added to dramatize the horror of civil war, and every patriotic speech and every reference to the Whigs or the folly of rebellion is expanded or rewritten.

The Misery of Civil-War is superior to its predecessor; Crowne is very careful here in presenting motivations of characters and even effects a unification of scenes that are disjointed in Shakespeare. On the other hand, his tampering with characterization and diction overshadows any structural improvements that can be credited to him. *The Misery of Civil-War* was first produced in 1680, while *Henry the Sixth, The First Part* did not appear until 1681, although it was probably written first. Both plays were presented at Dorset Garden. [Hazelton Spencer, *Shakespeare Improved*, 1927.]—G.B.

Cuffe, Henry (1563–1601). Author and personal secretary to the earl of Essex. Educated at Oxford, where he distinguished himself as a gifted scholar, Cuffe entered the service of the earl of Essex in 1594. He accompanied Essex on the expedition to Cadiz in 1596 and was with him in Ireland in the ill-fated campaign of 1599. In 1600, during the earl's estrangement from the queen, Cuffe was his constant dviser, and it was he who formulated the policy hich resulted in the Essex rebellion. Although uffe did not take part in the rebellion, he was xecuted for his complicity in it.

G. B. Harrison and Dover Wilson have argued nat *Troilus and Cressida* is an allegory of the forines of Essex during 1600 and that Cuffe is reprented by the figure of Thersites. See TOPICAL REFERNCES. [G. B. Harrison, "Shakespeare's Topical ignificances," *Times Literary Supplement*, Novemer 20, 1930; J. Dover Wilson, *The Essential Shakeeare*, 1932.]

Culman, Leonard (1498–1562). German clergyman nd anthologist whose collection of Latin maxims, *ententiae Pueriles* (1544), had a strong influence on hakespeare. Culman was born at Crailsheim, Geriany. He was first a schoolmaster and later the astor of an evangelical church. His *Sententiae ueriles* is an alphabetically arranged collection of roverbs from various Latin authors. In Tudor Engind it was a frequently used textbook for beginning udents of Latin. According to Charles G. Smith here are 209 proverbs in Shakespeare for which here are Latin parallels in Culman, including the amous proverb garbled by Dogberry in *Much Ado bout Nothing* (III, v, 18), "Comparisons are odorus." [Charles G. Smith, *Shakespeare's Proverb ore*, 1963.]

Cumberland, Richard (1732–1811). Dramatist and ovelist. Several essays in Cumberland's collection *he Observer* (1785) deal with Shakespeare, paricularly with a comparison of *Macbeth* and *Richard II* similar to that of Thomas Whately. Cumberland onsiders *Macbeth* the better play because its proagonist is basically honorable and therefore pitiable. *ichard III* is technically fascinating to him because hakespeare made a one-sided character interesting nd sympathetic. Cumberland considers Lady Maceth's role the natural counterpart of the witches' in nspiring her husband's ambition. He praises the anquet and sleepwalking scenes as unique devices or adding to the characterization of Macbeth and is wife. Similarly, Cumberland admires the battle cenes in *Richard III*, because they show that galantry and bravery were parts of Richard's personalty. Other essays deal with Falstaff and his comanions, approving particularly the comedy of hallow and Silence. [Herbert Spencer Robinson, *nglish Shakespearian Criticism in the Eighteenth entury*, 1932.]

Cunningham, Peter (1816–1869). Scholar. Cuningham was employed from 1834 to 1860 as a clerk n the audit office in London, where he had access to nany early official documents related to fiscal maters. He was also treasurer of the Shakespeare Soiety, for which he edited *Extracts from the Acounts of the Revels at Court in the reigns of Queen lizabeth and King James I* (1842). These are from he REVELS ACCOUNTS, the account books of the evels Office, which provided, among other informaion, evidence for the earliest performances of *thello* (1604) and *The Tempest* (1611). The records are extremely valuable, but their authenticity as been questioned by a number of scholars, chiefly amuel Tannenbaum, whose *Shakspere Forgeries in he Revels Accounts* (1928) branded the records as further forgeries of John Payne Collier. Collier was a friend and associate of Cunningham, and Tannenbaum established a strong case. However, modern scholars tend to accept the records as genuine.

Cupid. In *Timon of Athens*, a character who appears in the masque held in Timon's banquet hall. Cupid praises Timon's lavish generosity (I, ii).

Curan. In *King Lear*, a courtier. Curan informs Edmund of gossip concerning a breach between the Dukes of Albany and Cornwall (II, i).

Curio. In *Twelfth Night*, a gentleman attending on Duke Orsino.

Curry, Walter Clyde (1887–). American scholar. Professor of English at Vanderbilt University, Curry is known primarily for approaching literature from the viewpoint of science. He has written on Milton's cosmology and on Chaucer and the medieval sciences. Curry discusses Shakespeare's ideas in *Shakespeare's Philosophical Patterns* (1937).

curtains. Cloth hangings draped on the stage of a playhouse. In the Elizabethan and Jacobean theatre, curtains were primarily used as background and for concealment of alcoves on the main stage and upper stage. They were also commonly seen in the form of bed-curtains, as in Desdemona's death-chamber scene (*Othello*, V, ii). Veil, arras, and traverse were contemporary terms for curtains. An arras, the Elizabethan name for any tapestry hanging, was hung as a wall decoration projected on a frame, thus providing a space for concealment of actors between the wall and the hanging. Concealment behind an arras is a requisite for the murderers in *King John* (IV, i) and the eavesdropping Polonius in *Hamlet* (III, iv). Falstaff ensconces himself behind an arras in order to sleep (*1 Henry IV*, II, iv) and to hide (*Merry Wives of Windsor*, III, iii). It has also been suggested that curtains were suspended both from the base of the stage and from the "heavens" (see PLAYHOUSE STRUCTURE).

Contemporary writers on the theatre alluded to the use of curtains in one form or another. John Florio's dictionary, *A Worlde of Wordes, Italian and English* (1598), described the tiring-house façade as "being trimmed with hangings." In the induction to *Cynthia's Revels* (1600), Ben Jonson wrote:

> I am none of your fresh Pictures, that use to beautifie the decay'd dead Arras, in a publique Theatre.

Melpomene in Thomas Heywood's *An Apology for Actors* (1612) says:

> Then did I tread on arras; cloth of tissue
> Hung round the forefront of my stage.

Richard Flecknoe's *Short Treatise of the English Stage* (1664) alluded to the decoration of the earliest theatres:

> Theatres . . . of former times . . . were but plain and simple, with no other scenes, nor decorations of the stage, but onely old tapestry, and the stage strew'd with rushes.

Curtains in the public theatres were movable, although they did not rise and fall or conceal the proscenium as on the modern stage. Hung from a straight rod, the curtains could be slid along and drawn (either opened or closed). It is not known which member of the acting company was responsible for attending to the curtains. Scholars have proposed for this task some actor taking part in the play's action directly on stage, the speaker of a prologue, or a "servitor" (a stagehand employed by the theatre operators). Curtains for setting a tragedy were suitably black. The fabric used is not always indicated. Curtains for the court masques were made of sarcenet, a soft silk material which could be dyed in many colors.

Court masques made varied use of curtains. In staging *Tethys' Festival* in 1610, Inigo Jones ordered the proscenium curtained until the audience was seated. For a masque in 1565 the court Revels Office had supplied "a vayle of sarsnett drawen vpp and downe before . . . a rock or hill for the ix musses to singe vppone."

In Jacobean masques the curtains were painted to represent part of the setting, such as clouds, the night, a red cliff, the wall of a city, and the like. Early in the action of the masque, the curtain was removed to "discover" a more solidly set scene (see DISCOVERY SPACE). There is no evidence in masques of curtains being drawn up (by means of rollers) or drawn diagonally (by cords), although E. K. Chambers does not discount the possibility that either method might have been used. [Lily B. Campbell, *Scenes and Machines on the English Stage during the Renaissance*, 1923; E. K. Chambers, *The Elizabethan Stage*, 1923.]

Curtain theatre. An Elizabethan playhouse located just south of the Theatre in the parish of Shoreditch, a northern suburb of London. The Curtain was probably built in 1577, a year after the Theatre, and from 1585 to 1592 served as an "easer" to handle the overflow crowd of the Theatre. The origin of the Curtain's name is obscure, but it almost certainly had nothing to do with the theatrical connotation of the word; curtains, in the modern sense, were nonexistent in the Elizabethan theatre. It was owned in 1585 by Henry Lanman, but it is not clear whether he was the original owner.

It is not known what companies occupied the Curtain in the 1580's and early 1590's. Shakespeare's company was probably there from 1597 to 1599, the period between the permanent closing of the Theatre and the building of the Globe. In 1600, Robert Armin, the chief clown of Shakespeare's company, published his *Fool Upon Fool*, describing himself as "Clonnico del Curtaino Snuffe," while the 1605 edition of the same work uses the epithet "Clonnico del Mondo Snuffe." Many scholars agree with J. Dover Wilson that the allusion in *Henry V* to the playhouse as a "wooden O" refers to the Curtain and not to the Globe. The "wooden O" reference may also be an indication that the Curtain was circular in shape. A privy council order on May 10, 1601 referred to a serious offense by "the actors at the Curtain," and in 1603 it was cited as the home of Queen Anne's Men, formerly Worcester's Men. Queen Anne's Men remained at the Curtain until 1605 when they moved to their new theatre, the Red Bull, although they still retained control of the Curtain. In 1622 it was occupied by Prince Charles' Men. This is its last recorded use as a theatre, but the building was still standing in 1660. [J. Q. Adams, *Shak spearean Playhouses,* 1917; E. K. Chambers, *T Elizabethan Stage*, 1923.]

Curtis. In *The Taming of the Shrew,* servant Petruchio. Having made the domestic preparatio for his master's homecoming, Curtis presses Grumi another servant, for news of the newlyweds (IV, i

Cushman, Charlotte Saunders (1816–1876). Ame ican actress. Born in Boston, Miss Cushman studi for the opera and made her debut in *The Marria of Figaro* in 1835 as Countess Almaviva. On a visit New Orleans later that year she turned to dram acting Lady Macbeth with J. H. Batton, a visitin English actor. Her next success came at Alban where she played Romeo for the first time. Fro 1842 to 1844 she was the manager of Philadelphia Walnut Street Theatre, acting with George Vande hoff and Macready. Her performances became mo polished and she was ambitious to act in Londo where in 1845 she became the second America actress to appear. She played there successfully wit Edwin Forrest. She soon added Rosalind to h repertory and played Romeo convincingly with h sister, Susan, as Juliet. In London in 1849 she acte for the first time her greatest role, Queen Katharin in *Henry VIII.* From 1849 to 1852 she toured Ame ica as the leading actress of the stage, playing bot feminine roles and Hamlet and Wolsey. In 1852 sh was rich enough to retire and until 1857 lived i England. She made return appearances in New Yor as Wolsey, and after farewell performances in 185 she retired to Rome. Her last appearances were i 1874 in New York as Queen Katharine and as Me Merrilies in *Guy Mannering*, the latter one of he earliest successes. She died two years later in Bosto leaving behind her the memory of a strong, inte lectual, powerful actress, tall and deep-voiced, no quite feminine, but capable of great depth of feelin Her male impersonations were not entirely convinc ing, but her Queen Katharine was noted for it power, passion, poetry, and dramatic effectivenes She never married, but engaged in many philan thropic works; the Cushman School in Boston named after her. [*Dictionary of American Biograph* 1927– .]

Custom of the Country, The. See John FLETCHER.

Cymbeline or **Cunobelinus** (d. c. 43). King of th Britons and ally of Augustus; in Shakespeare's *Cym beline*, the King of Britain and an opponent o Roman domination. Little is known of the historica Cymbeline except that he made his capital at Col chester and in A.D. 40 exiled his son Adminius, wh surrendered to the authority of the Roman empero In the year 43, after Cymbeline's death, Claudius sen Aulus Plautius to conquer Britain, long deemed par of the Roman Empire, but Cymbeline's sons Togo dumnus and Caractacus fought the invasion.

Though Cymbeline is the title role in Shakespeare' play, the character has little relation to the historica figure and performs but a minor and chiefly self destructive part in the action. He takes as his Quee and second wife a hypocritical woman who loathe him and has designs on his throne. Offended that hi daughter by his first wife has married a poor thoug honorable man, he exiles her husband. He refuses t pay the annual tribute due the Romans and thereb provokes an invasion of Britain. He unjustly exile general Belarius, thus driving the general to kidp his two sons. When Belarius and the sons lead : victory over the Romans, Cymbeline knights :m all but fails to recognize them in their disises. Learning that one of the lads has killed his pson, Cloten, he orders the boy's arrest, even though the Queen has just died confessing a plot to murder the King and put Cloten on his throne. Fortunately Belarius reveals the sons' noble identity and his own. Amid the ensuing celebration, Cymbeline declares that in the interests of friendship he will continue paying tribute to the defeated Romans.

The Tragedy of CYMBELINE.

Cymbeline. A romance by Shakespeare.

Text. The only authoritative text is that of the rst Folio (1623), where it is titled *The Tragedie ' Cymbeline*. The Second Folio (1632) corrects a w misprints in the First. Many scholars believe that ıe vision in V, iv, is, at least in part, not of Shakeeare's authorship. The text of the Folios was set ther from a PROMPT-BOOK or, more likely, from scribe's transcript made from the author's FOUL PERS.

Date. In his *Book of Plaies*, Simon FORMAN records tending a performance of *Cimbalin, King of England*. The entry is undated, but Forman died Sepmber 8, 1611. Most scholars accept the hypothesis at *Cymbeline* was the first play that Shakespeare rote for audiences in the Blackfriars theatre, which e King's Men bought in 1608. The best guess for ıe date of composition is 1609–1610.

Sources. The plot of the play consists of three disnct narrative strands: the history of the reign of ıe pseudohistorical British ruler Cymbeline, who ecame king in 33 B.C.; the wager story; and the story f Belarius and the kidnapped princes. The material n the half-legendary, half-historical king was found HOLINSHED's *Chronicles*. Moreover, the Scottish ection of the *Chronicles*, to which Shakespeare had ecourse in writing *Macbeth*, was also a source for ıe heroism of Belarius, Guiderius, and Arviragus V, iii). There Shakespeare found an account of a cotsman and his two sons who defeated the Danes t the battle of Loncart (A.D. 976). The playwright vas also slightly indebted to two tragedies about Guiderius, to be found in the additions to A MIRROR OR MAGISTRATES. The first, called "The Complaint of Guiderius," appeared in Blenerhasset's *Second part of he Mirror for Magistrates* (1578); the second, called 'The Tragedy of Guiderius," by John Higgins, apeared in the 1587 edition of that popular collection.

The probable source of the wager plot is the ninth ıovel of the second day in Boccaccio's *Decameron*. However, Shakespeare could have read the story in ll its important details in a pamphlet entitled *Frederyke of Jennen* [Genoa], an English translation of Dutch version of Boccaccio's story. This translation was first printed in Antwerp in 1518, and reprinted in London in 1520 and 1560. Although the pamphlet story is in all essentials like Boccaccio's, it agrees with *Cymbeline* at some points at which the play differs from the *Decameron*.

The most likely principal source of the Belarius story is a romantic drama entitled *The Rare Triumphs of Love and Fortune*, presented at court on December 30, 1582 and first printed in 1589. In 1901 Ashley Thorndike advanced the theory that Beaumont and Fletcher invented the formula for the dramatic romance and first revealed it in their *Philaster*, which Shakespeare used as a model for *Cymbeline*. Thorndike's premise, accepted for a number of years, now has few supporters. The exact date for the composition of *Philaster* has never been definitely established, and most scholars believe it unlikely that a successful playwright would imitate the work of two novices.—O.J.C.

Plot Synopsis. Act I. Imogen, daughter of King Cymbeline of Britain, has stirred her father's wrath by marrying against his wishes "a poor but worthy gentleman," Posthumus Leonatus. He has lived in the court since childhood and is so named because his mother died as he was being born. Banished to Italy for his offense, Posthumus gives Imogen a bracelet as a parting gift and receives a diamond ring from her. Although the Queen, Cymbeline's second wife, feigns sympathy with the unhappy lovers, she really wishes to see her own son, the lumpish Cloten, on the throne. She tries to persuade Pisanio, a servant of Posthumus, to betray his master and gives him a drug which she says is a powerful restorative, but which she believes to be a deadly poison. In reality, Cornelius, the physician who supplied her with the potion, is suspicious of her designs and has substituted a harmless sleeping draught.

Having arrived in Rome, Posthumus goes to the house of Philario, an old friend of his dead father. There he meets an Italian called Iachimo, to whom he boasts of the virtue of his lady. Iachimo doubts that any woman is unassailable and wagers 10,000 ducats to Posthumus' ring that he can induce Imogen to betray her husband. Despite Philario's protests,

Posthumus accepts the challenge and gives Iachimo a letter of introduction to Imogen. When Iachimo meets Imogen at the British court, he immediately realizes that he will have to use deceit to gain his ends; he accuses Posthumus of infidelity and proposes that Imogen avenge herself by taking him as a lover. She spurns this suggestion at once, whereupon he explains that he was merely testing her devotion to her husband. After she accepts his apologies, he asks if he may leave some valuables with her overnight for safekeeping. She agrees and bids him send his trunk to her bedchamber.

Act II. After Imogen falls asleep that night, Iachimo emerges from the trunk. He carefully takes note of the furnishings in the chamber and, as he slips Imogen's bracelet off her arm, sees a mole on her left breast, a detail that will surely convince Posthumus of his success. When the clock strikes three, he returns to his hiding place. Later in the morning, Cloten tries to woo Imogen by ordering musicians to sing before her chamber. She finally appears, in response to his knocks, and bluntly declares that the meanest garment of Posthumus is dearer to her than Cloten. As she speaks, she notices with concern that her bracelet is missing. Iachimo, meanwhile, returns to Rome and, armed with his information about Imogen's room and person as well as her bracelet, persuades Posthumus that she has been unfaithful. Damning women as the source of all vice, Posthumus vows vengeance.

Act III. Cymbeline receives Caius Lucius, a Roman general who bears a message from Caesar Augustus. The Romans are indignant because Cymbeline has failed to pay the annual tribute levied on Britain since the time of Julius Caesar. Supported by the Queen, Cymbeline states that Britain is determined to shake off the Roman yoke and deprecates Lucius' threat of force. Even Cloten makes a strong, if brash, defense of British freedom.

Pisanio, meanwhile, has received instructions from Posthumus to kill Imogen, but he refuses to believe that she is an adulteress. In order to give Pisanio an opportunity to do the deed, Posthumus has sent her a letter asking her to join him in Milford Haven. She immediately leaves for Wales with Pisanio, who, upon their arrival, shows her Posthumus' letter to him. Now it is her turn to inveigh against the falseness of men. Pisanio suggests that she don male disguise and seek employment in the service of Lucius, so that she can go to Rome and find Posthumus. After offering to send some bloody token to Posthumus to convince him of her death, Pisanio gives her the potion he obtained from the Queen.

Having followed Pisanio's advice, Imogen wanders through the mountainous Welsh countryside for two days until, tired and hungry, she comes to a cave where she finds food. The cave is the abode of Belarius, a general who has been unjustly exiled by Cymbeline. In retaliation, he has abducted Cymbeline's infant sons, Guiderius and Arviragus, and has reared them as his own in the wilds of Wales, far from the vanities of cities and courts. Guiderius and Arviragus welcome Imogen, who calls herself Fidele, and soon feel strong affection for the unknown lad.

Act IV. While her hosts are hunting, Imogen, sick at heart, swallows the drug given to her by Pisanio and falls into a slumber resembling death. Meanwhile, Cloten has forced Pisanio to show him t letter summoning Imogen to Milford Haven; recal ing Imogen's remark about Posthumus' garments, l has dressed himself in clothes belonging to his riv and has set out for Wales with the intention of kil ing Posthumus and ravishing Imogen. Before Bela ius' cave, however, Cloten and Guiderius quarr and Guiderius beheads Cloten. When Guiderius an Arviragus find Imogen, they believe her to be dea and gently lay her in a rustic grave bedecked wit flowers. After their departure, she awakens and, se ing the decapitated body of Cloten clothed in Pos humus' garments, assumes that her husband has bee killed by Cloten and Pisanio. Lucius, commander the Roman forces preparing to attack Britain, no passes by and takes Fidele into his service. Upo learning that a battle between the British and R mans is imminent, Belarius wants to leave the are but his charges, betraying their noble stock, a weary of their secluded existence and are eager play a part in the great world beyond their cave.

Act V. Posthumus, who already regrets his desi for Imogen's death, has arrived in Wales with th Roman forces. Unwilling to do battle against h countrymen, he disguises himself as a peasant order to seek death fighting in the British ranks. A first the battle goes badly for the British, but the da is saved by the heroism of an old man and two strij lings, in reality Belarius and his charges. Posthumu who also distinguishes himself, is seized as a Roma While in prison, he sees a vision in which Jupite promises that both Britain and Posthumus will b happy when "a lion's whelp shall . . . be embrace by a piece of tender air; and when from a statel cedar shall be lopped branches, which, being dea many years, shall after revive, be jointed to the ol stock and freshly grow."

After knighting Belarius, Guiderius, and Arvira gus, Cymbeline learns that the Queen has died, cor fessing her misdeeds. Lucius and Iachimo, who ar among the Roman prisoners, are brought in togethe with Imogen and Posthumus. At Lucius' reques Cymbeline agrees to spare Fidele and offers to grar the lad a boon. Imogen speaks privately to the Kin who then asks Iachimo where he obtained the dia mond ring he wears. After Iachimo has admitted hi treachery, Posthumus bitterly curses his own foll and when Imogen tries to comfort him, throws he to the ground. Pisanio now reveals Imogen's identit and with the help of the physician Cornelius succeed in convincing her that he was ignorant of the power of the drug he gave her. When Guiderius disclose that he has slain Cloten, the King orders his arres but Belarius asserts that he and his brother are a nobly born as Cloten, and relates the story of thei origin. During the reunion that follows, Posthumu asks a soothsayer to interpret the message he receive in prison. The soothsayer replies that he, Leonatus, i the lion's whelp who is to be embraced by the tende air—"mollis aer" or "mulier"—that is, Imogen. Cym beline is the stately cedar, and the lopped branche are his sons. The King now caps the general rejoic ing by declaring that, despite his triumph on the bat tlefield, he will pay tribute to Caesar, so that th Roman and British ensigns may wave together i amity and peace.—H.D.

Comment. Although the editors of the First Foli

laced *Cymbeline* last among the tragedies, after *Anony and Cleopatra*, the play is best understood if it regarded as a romance.

Along with *Pericles, Cymbeline* represents the ramatist's first efforts to compose a play that would tisfy the taste of the audiences that the King's Men xpected to attract to their new Blackfriars theatre. hat audience was composed of courtiers and other embers of the gentry, who did not go to the theae expecting profound revelations of character or resentations of problems of conduct, but looked for xcitement, surprise, suspense, and wonder. Any draatist writing for such an audience would inevitably uckle to its expectations. The poet evidently ought that the components of traditional romances ould solve his problem. They were stories of love nd adventure, of faithful love triumphing over hosle circumstance and wicked enemies. These were e usual ingredients of GREEK ROMANCE, the product f decadent Alexandrian taste, and of early 16thentury crude romantic comedies.

The poet's attempt to satisfy all these new demands n his invention in *Cymbeline* was only partly sucessful. His old skill in uniting a number of narrative rands to form one master plot seems to have derted him, along with his expertise in exposition. He rites soliloquies that furnish information about the rogress of the story and the motives of the characers, but that do not reflect thoughts and feelings. inally, hostile critics find the rhymed verse in the ision of Sicilius Leonatus and his sons (V, iv, 30–22) unworthy of the poet. These serious blemishes ave led many scholars to accept Furness' explanaon in his New Variorum edition of the play (1913) hat they are the work of an inferior collaborator. his invention of a whipping boy for Shakespeare's nfelicities is an easy but unconvincing way of exonrating the dramatist. The best explanation of these hows of incompetence is that Shakespeare had no nodel for the type of play he was writing and that e was annoyed at having to perform a task imposed n him by what were, in the last analysis, business onsiderations.

Many commentators, particularly in the days of hakespeare idolatry, would have dissented from his unfavorable judgment. Furness called *Cymbeline*, nce the work of his assumed collaborator had been ubtracted, "the sweetest, tenderest, profoundest of lmost all the immortal galaxy." Joseph Quincy dams tells a moving story of the poet Tennyson's eep love of the play. Just before his death he called vith trembling voice for his copy of Shakespeare; fter his death his family discovered that almost his ast act had been to open the volume at his favorite lay, *Cymbeline*, a copy of which was buried with im. Others who are deeply moved by the drama ave clearly been entranced by Imogen, whom they udge not as a character in a play but as a captivating voman—an ideal Victorian lady, "as chaste as ununned snow" and exhibiting in her intimate relations vith her husband "rosy pudency." Her reaction to achimo's feigned report of her lord's pursuit of Roman harlots: "My lord, I fear, / Has forgot Britin" (I, vi, 112–113) is a model of Victorian restraint nd good taste. There are many scenes filled with ervous tension and lyrical speech, of which the most amous are Iachimo's intrusion into Imogen's bedchamber (II, ii, 11 ff.) and the noble sons' burial of the supposedly dead Imogen (IV, ii, 197 ff.). Two of the poet's most loved songs appear in this play: "Hark, hark, the lark" (II, iii, 21–30), widely known in Schubert's musical setting, and the pagan threnody sung by the exiled princes, "Fear no more the heat o' the sun" (IV, ii, 258–281).

The last scene is a tour de force, an excellent exhibition of the author's technical skill, as full of suspense and surprise as any Blackfriars audience could wish. The scene presents eight surprises and has evoked wonder that Shakespeare could cram into 480 lines two dozen situations, any one of which would have been enough to carry a whole act. Imogen's apparent rising from the dead, like Hermione's in *The Winter's Tale*, becomes a symbol of complete regeneration, an entrance into a brave new world.—O.J.C.

Stage History. Simon Forman wrote of seeing a performance of *Cymbeline* some time before September 1611 (see above under *Date*). On January 1, 1634 the play was presented before King Charles I and Queen Henrietta Maria. Thomas D'URFEY's adaptation, entitled *The Injured Princess or The Fatal Wager*, was written about 1673 and printed in 1682. It supplanted Shakespeare's play for many years and was revived in 1720 and 1738. The first production of the real *Cymbeline* since Caroline times occurred at Covent Garden in 1746. But in 1759 William HAWKINS' alteration was staged at that theatre. In this version, which was not revived, Iachimo was given the name Pisanio and Pisanio was called Philario. David Garrick mounted a slightly altered version at Drury Lane in 1761, and Posthumus became one of his favorite roles. His first Imogen was an incompetent actress, Elizabeth Bride, but more professional performers, such as Mary Ann Yates, Ann Street Barry and Dorothy Jordan, assumed that role in later Drury Lane productions during the 18th century. John Philip Kemble played Posthumus at Drury Lane in 1785 and in 1787, when his leading lady was Sarah Siddons, a most notable Imogen. By the time he revived the play in 1806 at Covent Garden, Kemble had christened the previously nameless lords "Madan" and "Locrine."

At Covent Garden, Barton Booth played Posthumus in 1817, William Charles Macready in 1818, and in 1820, Charles Kemble took the part, while Macready acted Iachimo. Second to Mrs. Siddons' Imogen was that of Helen Faucit, who played the role in 1837 at Covent Garden, again in 1838, opposite Samuel Phelps, and was still impersonating the heroine as late as 1865.

In 1827 Charles Kemble dressed the play in historically accurate costumes and scenery and included "Dr. Cooke's favorite Glee of 'Hark! the Lark.' " When Henry Irving produced *Cymbeline* in September 1896, the song was inserted into Act III. Ellen Terry was a perfect Imogen, but Irving's portrayal of Iachimo was not one of his best, and the production failed.

Cymbeline has been something of a collector's item in the 20th century. Stratford presented it in 1909, 1920, and the summer of 1922. At the Old Vic under Robert Atkins' direction from 1920 to 1925 *Cymbeline* was the only Folio play to be excluded from production. Sybil Thorndike played Imogen in 1918 for the Old Vic and again at the New Theatre in 1923, but the role was hardly suited to her talents as a major tragedienne. The latter production, a two-act version, was guided by Lewis Casson and described in the *Times* as "more or less futuristic." Five months earlier, Barry Jackson had staged a modern-dress version at the Birmingham Repertory Theatre. Cedric Hardwicke as Iachimo wore evening clothes when he initiated the wager at a dinner party; Imogen effected her disguise with knickers and a cap, and those noble savages, Guiderius and Arviragus, donned flannel shirts and shorts. It was this production that originated the critical phrase "Shakespeare in plus-fours."

The Old Vic's next effort, in 1932, this time under Harcourt Williams, was disappointing despite Peggy Ashcroft's Imogen, but, in 1937, B. Iden Payne succeeded at Stratford-upon-Avon with an effective Jacobean court masque treatment and a cast including Baliol Holloway as Cloten and Donald Wolfit as Iachimo. That same year, in November, André van Gyseghem staged the play at the Embassy using George Bernard Shaw's last act, *Cymbeline Refinished*. Shaw, who in his words "ruthlessly cut out the surprises that no longer surprise anybody," had originally offered it to both the Old Vic and Stratford, but neither had taken him seriously. After this production, *Cymbeline Refinished* was not repeated in any major theatre, but this act was used in 1952 at Sloan School and, in 1963, at Nottingham Playhouse.

In 1946 Donald Wolfit produced *Cymbeline* and played Iachimo at the Winter Garden, and Nugent Monck staged the play at Stratford, with Paul Scofield as Cloten. There was another Stratford production in 1949 by Michael Benthall; one at the Open Air in 1952; and, for the first time in over 20 years, one at the Old Vic in 1956. Peggy Ashcroft, a believable Imogen, played the role again at Stratford in 1957 in Peter Hall's fairy-tale treatment of the drama. *Cymbeline* was given again at the Memorial Theatre under William Gaskill, with Eric Porter playing Iachimo and Vanessa Redgrave as Imogen.—M.G.

Bibliography. TEXT: *Cymbeline*, New Arden Edition, J. M. Nosworthy, ed., 1955; *Cymbeline*, New Cambridge Edition, J. C. Maxwell, ed., 1960. DATE: New Arden Edition. SOURCES: New Arden Edition; New Cambridge Edition; Ashley H. Thorndike, *The Influence of Beaumont and Fletcher upon Shakespeare*, 1901. COMMENT: Sir Arthur T. Quiller-Couch, *Shakespeare's Workmanship*, 1918; Harley Granville-Barker, *Prefaces to Shakespeare*, 1927–1947; E. C. Pettet, *Shakespeare and the Romance Tradition*, 1949; E. M. W. Tillyard, *Shakespeare's Last Plays*, 1938. STAGE HISTORY: New Arden Edition; New Cambridge Edition; G. C. D. Odell, *Shakespeare from Betterton to Irving*, 1920; J. C. Trewin, *Shakespeare on the English Stage, 1900–1964*, 1964.

Selected Criticism

SAMUEL JOHNSON. This Play has many just sentiments, some natural dialogues, and some pleasing scenes, but they are obtained at the expence of much incongruity.

To remark the folly of the fiction, the absurdity of the conduct, the confusion of the names and manners of different times, and the impossibility of the events in any system of life, were to waste criticism upon unresisting imbecillity, upon faults too evident for detection, and too gross for aggravation. [*The Pla of William Shakespeare*, 1765.]

WILLIAM HAZLITT. The pathos in *Cymbeline* is n violent or tragical, but of the most pleasing and an able kind. A certain tender gloom overspreads t whole. Posthumus is the ostensible hero of the piec but its greatest charm is the character of Imoge Posthumus is only interesting from the interest s takes in him; and she is only interesting herself fro her tenderness and constancy to her husband . . Of all Shakespeare's women she is perhaps the mc tender and the most artless. Her incredulity in t opening scene with Iachimo, as to her husband's i fidelity, is much the same as Desdemona's backwar ness to believe Othello's jealousy. Her answer to t most distressing part of the picture is only, 'My lo I fear, has forgot Britain.' Her readiness to pard Iachimo's false imputations and his designs agair herself, is a good lesson to prudes; and may she that where there is a real attachment to virtue, it h no need to bolster itself up with an outrageous affected antipathy to vice. [*Characters of Shak spear's Plays*, 1817.]

THOMAS KENNY. But we must still regard th drama as one of Shakespeare's comparative failur In it he never rises to his finer and more imaginati presentment of life. All the higher purposes of dr matic composition are here more or less sacrificed the necessities of mere romantic narration. The mo rapid examination of "Cymbeline" will show, v think, that it is not largely distinguished by viv characterisation. The King is old and feeble, and h no striking part to perform. The two young princ are also comparatively unimportant figures; tr enough to the very exceptional circumstances which they are placed, but in no sense great dramat creations. The Queen is a sort of diminutive Lad Macbeth, but without any opportunity, througho these intricate and improbable episodes, of distinct developing her character. Cloten is a more origin portraiture; and although he is but slightly sketche and in spite of some apparent contradictions he and there, which make him sometimes better ar sometimes worse than we are prepared to expect, w seem to catch in his brutal but not wholly unman nature, glimpses of a real unmistakable human bei of a very unconventional type. The "yellow Iachim is one of the many villains in Shakespeare's dram who sin without any intelligible motive, and wh afterwards, at the desired moment, appear to r nounce their wickedness with an equally unaccoun able facility . . . .

Imogen is the redeeming figure in this work; it she alone that gives to it any deep vital interes Without any apparent effort, or any straining aft effect, the poet places her before us in the light the most natural and engaging loveliness. The char of her divine purity and tenderness is finely blende with the rapid but enchanting glimpses we obtain her personal grace and attractiveness. She is undoub edly one of the most exquisite of all Shakespeare female creations. But we still cannot class such a fig ure among the greatest achievements of his geni for it is evidently one that arose out of a refined se sibility rather than out of the highest creative ima ination. [*The Life and Genius of Shakespeare*, 1864

GEORGE BERNARD SHAW. . . . I do not defend Cyn

line. It is for the most part stagey trash of the west melodramatic order, in parts abominably writ- n, throughout intellectually vulgar, and judged in int of thought by modern intellectual standards, lgar, foolish, offensive, indecent, and exasperating yond all tolerance. There are moments when one ks despairingly why our stage should ever have en cursed with this "immortal" pilferer of other en's stories and ideas, with his monstrous rhetorical stian, his unbearable platitudes, his pretentious re- ction of the subtlest problems of life to common- aces against which a Polytechnic debating club ould revolt, his incredible unsuggestiveness, his ntentious combination of ready reflection with mplete intellectual sterility, and his consequent in- pacity for getting out of the depth of even the ost ignorant audience, except when he solemnly ys something so transcendently platitudinous that s more humble-minded hearers cannot bring them- lves to believe that so great a man really meant to lk like their grandmothers. With the single ex- eption of Homer, there is no eminent writer, not ven Sir Walter Scott, whom I can despise so en- rely as I despise Shakespear when I measure my ind against his. The intensity of my impatience ith him occasionally reaches such a pitch, that it ould positively be a relief to me to dig him up and row stones at him, knowing as I do how incapable e and his worshippers are of understanding any less bvious form of indignity. To read Cymbeline and think of Goethe, of Wagner, of Ibsen, is, for me, imperil the habit of studied moderation of state- ent which years of public responsibility as a jour- alist have made almost second nature in me. ["Blam- g the Bard," *The Saturday Review*, September 26, 896.]

HENRY JAMES. Those lovers of the theatre with hom it is a complaint that they are not more often eated to Shakespeare encounter in *Cymbeline* one f those stumbling-blocks with which the path of his particular regret is not unplentifully strewn: it rings them face to face with so many of the ques- ons that flutter up in the presence of all attempts to ut the plays to the proof of the contemporary stage. None of them practically takes so little account as *ymbeline* of the general effort of the theatre of our ay to hug closer and closer the scenic illusion. The hing is a florid fairy-tale, of a construction so loose nd unpropped that it can scarce be said to stand up- ight at all, and of a psychological sketchiness that ever touches firm ground, but plays, at its better imes, with an indifferent shake of golden locks, in he high, sunny air of delightful poetry. Here it dis- orts itself beyond the reach of all challenge. Mean- while the mere action swings, like a painted cloth in he wind, between England and Italy, flapping mer- ily back and forth and in and out, alternately crum- ling up the picture and waving it in the blue. ["Mr. Henry Irving's Production of 'Cymbeline,'" *Harper's Weekly*, Nov. 21, 1896.]

HARLEY GRANVILLE-BARKER. A fair amount of the lay—both of its design and execution—is pretty cer- ainly not Shakespeare's. Just how much, it is hard to ay (though the impossible negative seems always he easier to prove in these matters), for the suspect tuff is often so closely woven into the fabric. It may ave come to him planned as a whole and partly written. In which case he worked very thoroughly over what are now the Folio's first two acts. Thereafter he gave attention to what pleased him most, saw Imogen and her brothers and Cloten through to the end, took a fancy to Lucius and gave him reality, did what more he could do for Posthumus under the circumstances, generously threw in the First Gaoler, and rescued Iachimo from final futility. This relieves him of responsibility for the poor planning of the whole; he had been able to refashion the first part to his liking. But why, then, should he leave so many of the last part's ineptitudes in place? Or did the unknown cling affectionately to them, or even put them back again after Shakespeare had washed his hands of the business? We are dabbling now, of course, in pure "whipping-boy" doctrine, and flaws enough can be found in it. Of the moments of "unresisting imbecility" Shakespeare must be relieved; careless or conscienceless as he might sometimes be, critical common sense forbids us to saddle him with them. . . . No one will rank *Cymbeline* with the greater plays. It is not conceived greatly, it is full of imperfections. But it has merits all its own; and one turns to it from *Othello*, or *King Lear*, or *Antony and Cleopatra*, as one turns from a masterly painting to, say, a fine piece of tapestry, from commanding beauty to more recondite charm. [*Prefaces to Shakespeare*, 1927–1947.]

G. WILSON KNIGHT. *Cymbeline* is a vast parable, with affinities to Lyly's *Endimion*, though far more compacted and weighty and with no stiffness of allegory. A sense of destiny is pointed by two transcendental incidents: (i) the appearance of Jupiter and (ii) the Soothsayer's vision; the reference of the one being mainly personal; of the other national; though the two interests dovetail.

The action reaches a climax at Jupiter's appearance to Posthumus. This scene we shall study in detail presently. The extraordinary event cannot be properly received without full appreciation of the more-than-personal significance of Posthumus and the social and national implications of his marriage. Jupiter leaves an oracular tablet, reminiscent of the dream-book in *Endimion*, foretelling in cryptic phraseology the King's recovery of his lost sons and Posthumus' union with Imogen. The King is called a 'royal cedar', Posthumus Leonatus a 'lion's whelp', and Imogen 'a piece of tender air', the phrase being derived by the Soothsayer through *mollis aer* to *mulier*, to emphasize her typifying of womanhood, at its gentle best (V. v. 436–53). So Posthumus' representative function, whereby his successful marriage becomes at once the matrimonial peace of the individual, the social integrity of the nation and the union of British manhood with the essence—Imogen is just that, an 'essence'—of royalty, which is also the union of strength with gentleness, becomes peculiarly clear:

> . . . then shall Posthumus end his miseries, Britain be fortunate and flourish in peace and plenty.
> (V. v. 441)

Posthumus' happiness is one with Britain's welfare. His marriage-happiness is assured by Jupiter, in whose 'Temple' he was married (V. iv. 106); and indeed the will to preserve the marriage bond inviolate, so strong in Shakespeare's work, may well be derivative from Roman rather than Hebraic sources. So young Britain receives, through Posthumus, the blessing and protection of great Jupiter, the guardian deity of ancient Rome. [*The Crown of Life*, 1947.]

Czechoslovakia. The fact that the Czechs of Bohemia, Silesia, and Moravia and the Slovaks of Slovakia were under German and Austrian rule until 1918 had two major effects on the history of Shakespeare in their country. The first was that Shakespeare was introduced through Germany rather than Russia, as was the case with other Slavic peoples. The earliest attempts to translate Shakespeare into Czech were stimulated by the performances of Heufeld's German translation of *Hamlet* in Prague in 1776 and in Bratislava, the capital of Slovakia, in 1773. Furthermore, these early attempts were based on German translations. The second effect was the association of Shakespeare, and particularly Shakespearean stage productions, with the nationalistic aspirations of the Czechs. As a non-German writer of patriotic inclination whose genius was widely recognized, Shakespeare provided the Czechs with a task of translation that would expand and enrich the Czech language and gain recognition for it as a language into which important literary works had been rendered.

translation. The earliest translations were for the most part adaptations from German translations. The first of these was K. H. Thám's *Macbeth* (1786) which was shortly followed by J. J. Tandler's *Hamlet* (1791) and P. F. Sedivy's *King Lear* (1792). Of these three "translations," only Thám's was published. The first two Czech translators to break away from the German models and to turn directly to the English text were Michal Bosy, working under the pseudonym Bohuslav Křižák, and A. Marek. The former was working on a verse *Hamlet* as early as 1810; the latter's prose *Comedy of Errors* appeared in 1823. These two were followed by another early translator of note, Josef Kajetán Tyl, the father of the Czech theatre. Tyl's *King Lear* (1835) was the first verse translation of Shakespeare to appear on the stage.

It remained, however, for another prominent figure in the Czech theatre, Joseph Jirí Kolar, and his pupil and collaborator Jakub Malý to begin a systematic translation of the plays. The success in 1853 of Kolar's *Hamlet* led to plans for a standard edition of all the plays to be published under the auspices of the Bohemian Museum. Malý, co-editor of the first Czech encyclopedia, translated 11 of the plays and Kolar, 4. The other translators were Frantisek Doucha, a priest and children's poet (nine plays), Jan Josef Čejka, professor of medicine (nine plays), and Ladislav Čelakovský, botanist and son of the poet Frantisek Ladislav Čelakovský (four plays). Each play was submitted for approval to two experts before being included in the collection. The first two plays appeared in 1855, and the project was completed in 1872.

The last volume of the Bohemian Museum edition had been in print only a few years when its inadequacies became apparent and work was started on a new translation, this time under the imprint of the National Academy. The number of translators in the earlier edition and their varied preparations had resulted in unevenness. In addition, the language was going through a period of rapid change. Jaroslav Vrchlický, who had reshaped the diction and prosodic techniques of Czech poetry, was the movin[g] force behind the new translations. He translated 1[?] sonnets and *Venus and Adonis*, leaving the re[st] of the work to his friend Josef Václav Sládek. At th[e] time of his death in 1912, Sládek had translated [?] plays. The remainder of the plays, poems, and all th[e] sonnets were completed by his disciple Antoni[n] Klášterský by 1925.

The Academy edition has come to be regarded [as] the standard translation, but it has also drawn muc[h] criticism. Sládek's efforts to achieve accuracy led t[o] his adding lines, which resulted in a loss of the ters[e]ness of the original. Furthermore, he toned dow[n] Shakespeare's grosser expressions and bawdry. [?] Baudiš, Celtic scholar and medievalist, expressed th[e] opinion that the Bohemian Museum edition wa[s] closer to Shakespeare's intentions. However, th[e] main direction of recent translation derives fro[m] neither of these earlier editions, but rather from th[e] pleas for freer translation by Otakar Fischer, criti[c] and dramatist.

Following the lead of Fischer, Bohumil Stepáne[k] translated 20 plays, of which 18 have appeared i[n] print. However, Stepánek's translations have bee[n] criticized for departing from the author's intende[d] meaning. Another follower of Fischer, Erik Ado[r] Saudek, has been more warmly received. He ha[s] translated 10 plays, by 1955, into a conversationa[l], sometimes slangy, Czech. Although this approach ha[s] succeeded with the comedies, his translations of th[e] tragedies lack grandeur and nobility. O. F. Babler ha[s] contributed an additional three plays to the editio[n] being prepared by Saudek.

Slovak translations have been few. In 1806 Bo[-]huslav Tablic included a redaction of the "To b[e] or not to be" soliloquy in his *Poezie*. The 1830's sa[w] the production of three translations by the sam[e] Bohuslav Křižák who had translated *Hamlet* in[to] Czech. However, the high points of Slovak transla[-]tion are the *Hamlet* (1903) and *A Midsumme[r] Night's Dream* (1905) of Pavel Országh Hviezdo[-]slav. These latter two plays were rendered fro[m] Czech, Polish, Hungarian, and German translation[s] since Hviezdoslav's knowledge of English was lim[-]ited.

stage production. Shakespeare production in Bo[-]hemia goes back almost as far as the Czech theat[re] itself, but a distinct Shakespeare tradition begins onl[y] with the productions of J. J. Kolar, mentioned abov[e] in connection with the Bohemian Museum editio[n]. Kolar's interpretation of *Hamlet* was not surpasse[d] until Edward Vojan, generally acknowledged to b[e] Bohemia's greatest actor, appeared on the Czec[h] stage with his characterizations of Hamlet, Othell[o] and Shylock. Hana Kvapilová, who often played op[-]posite Vojan, was (until her death in 1907) the lea[d]ing interpreter of Shakespeare's heroines. In 1916, i[n] spite of the fact that Bohemia was still the provin[ce] of a Germany at war with England, a Shakespea[re] festival was staged at the National Theatre by Jaro[-]slav Kvapil, Bohemia's leading Shakespeare produce[r]. Vojan, who was still alive, appeared in many of th[e] productions. Thirty-three years later, Czech nationa[l]ism expressed itself again through the medium o[f] Shakespeare in a production of *Macbeth* in whic[h] the title role was played by Z. Stěpánek wearing [a] dark costume suggestive of the S.S. uniform. In 195[?]

when Prague audiences saw a production of *Othello* which stressed the racial elements and the "fascist" character of Iago, the political overtones of the interpretation were clearly within the tradition of Czech Shakespeare production.

The history of Shakespeare on the Slovak stage is less impressive. There has been a professional Slovak theatre only since 1921. Although there have been some Shakespeare productions in recent years, particularly of the comedies, which were believed to be more likely to arouse public interest, a Shakespeare tradition has yet to be established.

influence. Shakespeare's influence in Bohemia extends beyond the limits of literature. Czech composers have been particularly susceptible to this influence. Benda wrote a "Singspiel" based on *Romeo and Juliet* (1776); Smetana contributed a march to the Shakespeare Festival of 1864 and at the time of his death was working on an opera based on Krásnohorská's libretto of *Twelfth Night;* Vrchlický adapted the libretto of *The Tempest* (1895) for Fibich's opera; and Dvořák wrote an overture to *Othello.* Evidence that Shakespeare's appeal for Czech composers is still strong may be found in the composition and staging in 1956 of two ballets: *A Midsummer Night's Dream,* by D. C. Vackár, and *Othello,* by Jan Hanuš. In addition, 1959 saw the completion of a puppet film by Jiří Trnka, the famous Czech puppeteer, based on *A Midsummer Night's Dream.*

criticism. Czech Shakespeare criticism until World War II followed the line set down for it by its progenitor, J. Malý, who derived his point of view from Samuel Johnson. Both of the leading Shakespeare scholars of the pre-World War II period, F. Chudoba (*Book about Shakespeare,* 1941) and Jindřich Vodak (*Shakespeare, A Critic's Breviary,* pub. posthumously in 1950), died in Nazi concentration camps. Since World War II the important figures in Shakespeare criticism have been predominantly Marxist. Of special note are Jaroslav Pokorný (*Shakespeare's Theatre and Shakespeare's Age,* 1956) and the critics listed in the bibliography that follows. [O. F. Babler, "Shakespeare's *Macbeth* in Czech Literature," *Notes and Queries,* CXCIII, June, 1948; O. F. Babler, "Shakespeare's *King Lear* in Czech Translations," *Notes and Queries,* CXCVI, February, 1951; Ján Šimko, "Shakespeare in Slovakia," *Shakespeare Survey 4,* 1951; O. F. Babler, "Shakespeare's *Tempest* in Czech," *Notes and Queries,* CC, January, 1955; Otakar Vocadlo, "Shakespeare and Bohemia," *Shakespeare Survey 11,* 1956; O. F. Babler, "Shakespeare's *Midsummer Night's Dream* in Czech and Slovakian," *Notes and Queries,* CCII, April, 1957; reports on Shakespeare activities in Czechoslovakia by B. Hodek appear in the "International Notes" section of numbers 5, 10, 11, 12, and 13 of *Shakespeare Survey.*]—A.B.

D

Daborne, Robert (d. 1628). Dramatist. Daborne's career as a dramatist was brief and obscure. Habitually in debt, he wrote for the Queen's Revels and Lady Elizabeth's Men. He is less well known for his plays than for his extensive correspondence with Philip Henslowe, which provides much information about the hazards and financial problems of a free-lance 17th-century playwright. He has been suggested as a collaborator on some of the plays attributed to Beaumont and Fletcher. By 1618 Daborne had quit the stage and entered the ministry, and in 1621 he was named dean of Lismore.

Daly, [John] Augustin (1838–1899). American playwright and producer. Daly started out as a dramatic critic. In the 1860's he was successful as an adapter and producer of French and German plays on the American stage; he also dramatized novels, notably *Pickwick Papers.* His first original play, *Under the Gaslight* (1867), introduced melodrama to the American theatre; his best play, *Horizon,* a drama of Western American life, established him as the first realist among American playwrights. Beginning in 1870 he produced older English comedies along with European adaptations and took his company to London and Europe. His production of *Taming of the Shrew* (1888) was probably the first Shakespearean comedy done in Europe by an American cast. He opened his own theatre in London, where he produced *As You Like It* in 1891 and *Twelfth Night,* which ran for 100 performances. Tennyson chose Daly to stage his dramatic poem *The Foresters* in 1892. Returning to America, Daly continued to produce Shakespeare; his *Tempest* (1897) was particularly successful. Besides raising the standard of Shakespearean production, he was the author or adapter of some 90 plays.

Danby, John Francis (1911–). Scholar. Danby has written *Shakespeare's Doctrine of Nature: a Study of King Lear* (1949), an intellectual history which opposes the Hooker-Bacon and the Hobbesian conceptions of nature. His *Poets on Fortune's Hill: Studies in Sidney, Shakespeare, Beaumont and Fletcher* (1952) questions symbolic interpretations of the later plays.

Dance-Holland, Sir **Nathaniel** (1735–1811). History, portrait, and genre painter. A scion of the Dance family, Nathaniel Dance was one of the founding members of the Royal Academy. He studied under Francis Hayman in Italy and upon his return to England became a noted portrait painter. His work includes portraits of George III and his consort; Captain Cook; and David Garrick as Richard III. The latter painting, exhibited in the Royal Academy in 1771, is probably the most famous of the Garrick portraits. Dance contributed "The Death of Mark Antony" and the Garrick portrait to BOYDELL'S SHAKESPEARE GALLERY. In 1790 he became a member of parliament, representing East Grinstead, and was awarded a baronetcy in 1800. [W. M. Merchant, *Shakespeare and the Artist,* 1959.]

Dancer. In *2 Henry IV*, speaker of the EPILOGUE.

dancing. Despite Puritan opposition, dancing enjoyed great popularity in Elizabethan England. It was a favorite recreation of all people, the yeomanry participating in country dances and courtiers stepping to more stately measures.

Of the country dances, the most popular was the morris dance, or morisco, a mixture of dance and pantomime, which was performed by dancers dressed in traditional costumes, wearing bells on their legs. Shakespeare refers to dancers' bells in *2 Henry VI;* Jack Cade, wounded by many arrows in his thighs, is described as capering

> upright like a wild Morisco,
> Shaking the bloody darts as he his bells.
> (III, i, 365–366)

A Moor, a Hobby Horse, Robin Hood, Friar Tuck, and Maid Marian were at various times characters in the morris dances. The simplest country dance was the round or roundel; other dances, such as the hay and the jig, were based on the roundel form. See FOLK FESTIVALS.

One of the most stately and solemn of society dances was the measure. The King in *Love's Labour's Lost* plays on the name of the dance:

> Say to her, we have measured many miles
> To tread a measure with her on this grass.
> (V, ii, 184–185)

Shakespeare made many plays on the names of dances. In *Much Ado About Nothing* Beatrice advises Hero as follows:

> The fault will be in the music, cousin, if you be not wooed in good time: if the prince be too important, tell him there is measure in every thing and so dance out the answer. For, hear me, Hero: wooing, wedding, and repenting, is as a Scotch jig, a measure, and a cinque pace: the first suit is hot and hasty, like a Scotch jig, and full as fantastical; the wedding, mannerly-modest, as a measure, full of state and ancientry; and then comes repentance and, with his bad legs, falls into the cinque pace faster and faster, till he sink into his grave.
> (II, i, 72–83)

The cinquepace was a lively dance and a part of the galliard. (It is thought that cinquepace was the original name for the galliard because it had five steps; as the galliard developed new steps, the name cinquepace was reserved for the original dance form.) The galliard was also used as the last movement of a pavane, giving a sprightly ending to an otherwise stately processional dance.

Most of the court dances of the Elizabethans had their origin on the continent. The *bransle*, or *branle à mener* (from the French *branler*, to vibrate) was known in England as the brawl. Led by one or two dancers, whom all the rest followed, it was a precursor of the minuet. In *Love's Labour's Lost*, Moth asks Armado, "Master, will you win your love with a French brawl?" To which Armado replies, "How meanest thou? brawling in French?" (III, i, 8–10).

The volte, a form of the galliard, was characterized by a turn made with two steps and a high spring. Shakespeare refers to this dance as lavolta:

> They bid us to the English dancing-schools,
> And teach lavoltas high and swift corantos.
> (*Henry V*, III, v, 32–33)

The courante, or coranto, was somewhat like the volte but, as its name implies, had more of a running step. In *Twelfth Night* Sir Toby Belch cites the coranto in a speech made up of puns on dancing terms:

> Why dost thou not go to church in a galliard and come home in a coranto? My very walk should be a jig; I would not so much as make water but in a sink-a-pace.
> (I, iii, 136–139)

[A. Forbes Sieveking, "Dancing," *Shakespeare's England*, 1916.]

Daniel, Sir **George,** of Beswick (1616–1657). Minor Cavalier poet. Daniel was a loyal disciple of Ben Jonson, whom he described as "of English Dramatickes, the Prince." Probably as a consequence of his devotion, he tended to disparage Jonson's rival as "Comicke Shakespeare." In his *Trinarchodia* (1647), Daniel deplores the misrepresentation of Sir John Fastolfe as Falstaff.

> Here to Evince the Scandall, has bene throwne
> Vpon a Name of Honour, (Charactred
> From a wrong Person, Coward, and Buffoone;)
> Call in your easie faiths, from what y'ave read
> To laugh at Falstaffe, as an humor fram'd
> To grace the Stage, to please the Age, misnam'd.

[*The Shakspere Allusion-Book*, J. Munro, ed., 1909.]

Daniel, Samuel (1562–1619). Poet and dramatist. Daniel was born in Somerset, the son of John Daniel, a musician. Leaving Oxford without a degree, he traveled in Italy and on his return to England became associated with the circle of Mary Herbert, countess of Pembroke.

Twenty-eight of Daniel's sonnets were appended to the first, unauthorized edition of Philip Sidney's *Astrophel and Stella* (1591). In the following year Daniel issued his own collection under the title *Delia* (1592) with a dedication to the countess of Pembroke. Its popularity is attested to by the several editions, all with extensive revisions, which were published before the end of the century. The majority of the sonnets are in the English form, first used by the earl of Surrey and later by Shakespeare.

Included in the 1592 edition of *Delia* was "The Complaint of Rosamond," echoes of which have been found in *The Rape of Lucrece*, *Love's Labour's Lost*, and *Romeo and Juliet*. At this time Daniel also wrote *The Tragedie of Cleopatra* (1593), a closet drama. Daniel now turned his attention to history and in 1595 published the first four books of his *Civil Wars* (see CIVIL WARS). By 1609 he had completed eight books of the *Civil Wars*, bringing the narrative down to the marriage of Edward IV; he announced his intention to continue his account to the period of Henry VII, but instead turned to a prose *History of England*. He also wrote *Musophilus* (1599), a poetical dialogue in defense of learning, and *A Defence of Rhyme* (1602), a rejoinder to Thomas Campion's attack on rhyme and accentual verse. Among those who identify William Herbert, earl of Pembroke, as the Fair Youth of the *Sonnets*, Daniel is sometimes mentioned as the RIVAL POET.

Daniel's connection with the stage began in 1604 when he was appointed licenser of the Queen's Revels, probably as a result of the successful masque, *The Vision of the Twelve Goddesses* (1604), which he had written for Queen Anne. There are a number of verbal echoes of Daniel's *Cleopatra* in *Antony and Cleopatra*, and Shakespeare may be indebted to Daniel for the sympathetic portrait of the heroine, which is not in Plutarch. [Arthur Norman, "Daniel's *The Tragedie of Cleopatra* and *Antony and Cleopatra*," *Shakespeare Quarterly*, IX, 1958.]

Danter, John (fl. 1582–1598). London printer. Danter served as an apprentice from 1582 to 1588, during which time he was engaged in illegal printing activities. In 1589 he entered into partnership with Henry Chettle and William Hoskins (d. c. 1604). In 1591 he set up his own shop at Duck Lane, near Smithfield, and in the following year at Hosier Lane. In 1594 he printed the First Quarto of *Titus Andronicus*, of which there is only one copy extant, discovered in Sweden in 1905. (See TITUS ANDRONICUS: *Text*.) His edition of *Romeo and Juliet* (1597) is a "bad quarto," lacking about 800 lines found in the authoritative text. [R. B. McKerrow, ed., *A Dictionary of Printers and Booksellers . . . 1557–1640*, 1910.]

Dardanius. In *Julius Caesar*, a servant to Brutus. After his defeat at Philippi, Brutus asks Dardanius to kill him, but he refuses (V, v). According to Plutarch, Dardanius was Brutus' armor-bearer.

Dark Lady. A term used to describe the woman allegedly referred to in Sonnets 126–152.

Some critics believe that the Dark Lady is not the portrait of any real woman, but a creature of the poet's imagination, a sister of Rosaline in *Love's Labour's Lost* and a convincing illustration of the superiority of masculine friendship to physical passion. Other critics hold that the sonnets devoted to the Dark Lady were inspired by at least two sirens. The attempts to identify her by scholars who believe her to be one real woman have been many, some of them fantastic. George Chalmers, in *An Apology for the Believers in the Shakespeare Papers* (1797), originated the quaint theory that Shakespeare addressed all the sonnets to Queen Elizabeth. Other critics advance the notion that the sonnets were commissioned by the earl of SOUTHAMPTON to serve as gifts to Elizabeth Vernon, his mistress and later his wife (see Elizabeth Wriothesley, countess of SOUTHAMPTON). G. B. Harrison in his *Shakespeare Under Elizabeth* (1933) asserts that the Dark Lady was a courtesan of notoriety among the young gentlemen of the Inns of Court, a certain Lady Negro, abbess of Clerkenwell, certainly a dark woman! (See Luce MORGAN.) Edgar I. Fripp in his two-volume work, *Shakespeare, Man and Artist* (1938), accepts this identification and states without qualification that Lady Negro was Shakespeare's model for the Dark Lady.

Other attempts at identification have included the name of Mrs. Jane Davenant, the wife of an Oxford vintner, who with her husband John kept the tavern at Oxford where Shakespeare is supposed to have put up on his frequent trips between London and Stratford. This identification was accepted and developed by Arthur Acheson in his *Mrs. Davenant, The Dark Lady of Shakespeare's Sonnets* (1913). In other books Acheson "discovered" that the Avisa of WILLOBIE HIS AVISA (1594) was the Dark Lady and that she was Jane Davenant, the mother of an illegitimate son, Sir William DAVENANT, of whom Shakespeare was the father. According to John Aubrey, Sir William "seemed contented enough to be thought his [Shakespeare's] son." Indeed he took pains to spread the legend abroad. Acheson later made another discovery, that the distinction belonged not to Jane but to a suppositious Anne, John Davenant's first wife. But there is no proof that such a woman existed. She is apparently the figment of Acheson's imagination.

The identification of Mistress Mary FITTON with the Dark Lady has of late been accepted by many reliable historians. Her claims were first advanced by Thomas Tyler, in a paper read before the New Shakspere Society at its meeting on May 30, 1884, and defended in his *The Herbert-Fitton Theory of Shakespeare's Sonnets* (1898). Those who accept Pembroke as the young aristocrat (see MR. W. H.) to whom Shakespeare addressed his sonnets find that the known facts of Mary Fitton's career as a maid of honor at the queen's court correspond to what Shakespeare tells us in the sonnets about the Dark Lady. [*The Sonnets*, New Variorum Edition, Hyder Rollins, ed., 1944.]

Daughter of Antiochus. In *Pericles*, the Princess of Antioch. "So buxom, blithe and full of face" that, despite the King's edict decreeing that all suitors for her hand must, under penalty of death, solve a riddle, she nonetheless has many wooers. Pericles discovers the incest between Antiochus and his daughter. She later dies by fire with her father.

Davenant, Sir **William** (1606–1668). Poet and playwright. Born and educated at Oxford, where his father kept a tavern, Davenant came to London at an early age and served as a page in the establishments of the duchess of Richmond and Fulke Greville (Lord Brooke). His first play, *The Tragedy of Albovine, King of the Lombards* (pub. 1629) was followed by many plays and masques at court. He stood high in royal favor and in 1638, after the death of Ben Jonson, was awarded a pension and the quasi-official title of "poet laureate." During the Civil War, Davenant was a royalist; he executed many commissions for Henrietta Maria, the queen consort of Charles I, who was in exile in France, and in 1643 he was knighted by the king for his support at the siege of Gloucester. One product of this period is the epic poem *Gondibert* (1651). Davenant was in prison many times during the Commonwealth period; in 1650 he was apprehended by parliamentary forces while en route to America, and held in the Tower of London. His release in 1654, according to legend, was effected by the intervention of the poet John Milton, for whom Davenant in turn interceded at the Restoration.

At the time of the closing of the theatres in 1642 Davenant had been a theatre manager. Upon his release from prison he began to present various entertainments, among which were the *First Days Entertainment at Rutland House* (1656) and *The Siege of Rhodes Made a Representation by the Art of Prospective in Scenes, And the Story sung in Recitative Musick* (1656). The latter afterward became known as one of the first "operas." At the Restoration Davenant and Thomas KILLIGREW were the only two men who received patents enabling them to form acting companies and run theatres. Davenant's group, the DUKE'S COMPANY, played at LISLE'S TENNIS COURT and after Davenant's death, moved to Dorset Garden. The company presented many of Davenant's adaptations of Shakespeare's plays, as well as original plays and operas which he and others created. Davenant is buried in Westminster Abbey.

One of the myths surrounding the life of Shakespeare is the legend of his "relationship" with Sir William Davenant. According to the best-known account (that of John AUBREY), Davenant let it be known that he was Shakespeare's natural son. In the following transcription, the bracketed matter consists of Aubrey's asides to the reader:

> Sr William Davenant Knight Poet Laureate was born in ——— street in the city of Oxford, at the Crowne Taverne [*in margin*, V.A.W.Antiq: Oxon:]. His father was John Davenant a Vintner there, a very grave and discreet Citizen: his mother was a very beautifull woman, & of a very good witt and of conversation extremely agreable . . . . Mr William Shakespeare was wont to goe into Warwickshire once a yeare, and did commonly in his journey lye at this house in Oxon: where he was exceedingly respected. I have heard parson Robert D [avenant] say that Mr W. Shakespeare here gave him a hundred kisses. Now Sr. W^m would sometimes when he was pleasant over a glasse of wine with his most intimate friends e.g. Sam: Butler [author of Hudibras] &c. say, that it seemed to him that he writt with the very spirit that Shakespeare, and was seemed contented enough to be thought his Son: he would tell them the story as above. in which way his mother had a very light report, whereby she was called a whore.

Although there is very little of substance to the story, by 1709 Shakespeare was actually regarded as Davenant's godfather, and probably as his father, too. By this time, too, attached to the legend was a jest which, in its original form, derives from the early 17th century (see Thomas HEARNE). Davenant's mother is elsewhere referred to as a virtuous and loving wife although she is also described as high-spirited and witty. Some attempt has been made to identify her as the heroine, Avisa, of WILLOBIE HIS AVISA. Another tradition asserts that Davenant possessed a letter written to Shakespeare by King James (see JAMES I).

Davenant's adaptations of a number of Shakespearean plays were performed on the Restoration stage. Most famous is THE TEMPEST, OR THE ENCHANTED ISLAND, produced by Davenant and John Dryden in 1667, which held the stage well into the 18th century. *Macbeth, Hamlet,* and *Much Ado About Nothing* were other sources of Davenant's adaptations (see THE LAW AGAINST LOVERS). Davenant's *Macbeth. With all the Alterations, Amendments, Additions, and New Songs* (pub. 1674) was adapted for the stage in 1663. It was very popular, primarily because of its operatic spectacle, and held the stage until Garrick revived the original in 1744. It follows closely the story of Shakespeare's play, although there are instances of the combination of several characters into one and of the transference of one character's speeches to another. The few major changes in structure are almost all attempts to create the classical symmetry absent from the original. Other elements are introduced, such as the addition of speeches and scenes that establish Lady Macduff as the symbol of virtue (to counterbalance Lady Macbeth as evil). The sleepwalking scene is drastically cut, but Davenant makes up for this by giving Lady Macbeth a scene in which she sees Duncan's ghost, a counterpart to Macbeth's banquet scene. Macduff's role is also expanded; in Act II he meets the witches, who give him a triple prophecy to match those of Banquo and Macbeth.

The witches themselves are given a new emphasis —the most striking features of the play are the special "operatic" effects used in their scenes. Written into their parts are several songs and dances, with the interpolations from Thomas Middleton's *The Witch* ("Come away, come away . . . ," etc.) included in the First Folio. Mechanical devices were employed in the production that enabled the witches to fly around the stage and the ghosts to rise and disappear.

Davenant's greatest violence to his source is verbal —almost all the speeches in the play are rewritten with Davenant's characteristic concern for absolute purity and clarity. He evidently could not see, or chose not to see, the intended effect of Shakespeare's irregularities; even slightly ambiguous passages are rephrased in concrete terms.

Another adaptation, *Hamlet* (1661), is attributed to Davenant; although only circumstantial evidence justifies the attribution, it was first produced by his company, under his direction, and it incorporates the characteristic changes in diction which Davenant was known to favor. The play suffers from none of the violent structural changes that characterize his other adaptations. Although Davenant did not seriously cut the original, he thoroughly "corrected" Shakespeare's diction. The printed version (1676) contains scenes omitted in the original production, and sets them apart from the rest of the text. The deleted passages include most of the material about Fortinbras, Polonius' advice to Laertes, and Hamlet's lecture to the players. Other scenes appear in greatly reduced form: Hamlet's first meeting with the Ghost, his scene with the First Player, the play-within-a-play, and the soliloquies "O, that this too too solid flesh would melt" and "O, what a rogue and peasant slave am I!" Assuming that the adapter's aim was to facilitate the action and eliminate purely rhetorical and reflective passages, most of the cuts seem justified.

Verbal changes, however, affect the entire play, including the scenes cut in production. They follow Davenant's typical pattern: all coarse, blasphemous, or inelegant phrases are tidied up, and the slightest ambiguities and unnecessarily poetic or symbolic passages are rendered entirely clear and simple. Davenant was rather more ambitious than his wont in the elimination from *Hamlet* of indelicate words. Among the inadmissible phrases are "by heaven," "poor wench" (which becomes "gentle maid"), and "the devil take thy soul." Phrases that Davenant felt required clarification include "my operant powers" (which becomes "working powers"), "the general gender" (changed to "the people"), and "my inky cloak" ("mourning"). [Hazelton Spencer, *Shakespeare Improved,* 1929; E. K. Chambers, *William Shakespeare,* 1930; Alfred Harbage, *Sir William Davenant,* 1935.]

Davenport, Robert (fl. 1624–1640). Dramatist. Davenport first appears in the records of the Master of the Revels in 1624 as author of *The City-Night-Cap* and the *History of Henry I.* The latter play was written for the King's Men, and is apparently one of the two plays entered in the Stationers' Register by Humphrey MOSELEY in 1653 as "Henry ye first, & Henry ye 2^d^. By Shakespeare and Dauenport." John Warburton records these two plays among the manuscripts burned by his cook. In Davenport's comedy *A New Tricke to Cheat the Divell* (1639) there is an allusion to Falstaff followed by a parody of Falstaff's famous monologue on honor. In Davenport's best-known work, *The City-Night-Cap,* he is indebted to the language of *Measure for Measure, Antony and Cleopatra, Cymbeline, The Winter's Tale, Othello.* If 1624 is accepted as the date of *The City-Night-Cap,* it is apparent that Davenport's wide and varied use of Shakespeare is a result of his access to the then recently published First Folio (1623).

Davies, John, of Hereford (c. 1565–1618). Poet. Davies, a graduate of Oxford, earned his living as a writing-master, drawing his pupils from the leading noble families of England. His publications include *The Scourge of Folly* (c. 1610), a collection of epigrams. One of the epigrams is entitled "To our English Terence, Mr. Will. Shake-speare":

> Some say (good *Will*) which I, in sport, do sing,
> Had'st thou not plaid some Kingly parts in sport,
> Thou hadst bin a companion for a *King;*
> And, beene a King among the meaner sort.
> Some others raile; but, raile as they thinke fit,
> Thou hast no rayling, but, a raigning Wit:
> *And* honesty *thou sow'st, which they do reape,*
> *So, to increase their* Stocke *which they do keepe.*

The cryptic allusion to Shakespeare's having played "Kingly parts" has been interpreted by some as an indication that Shakespeare's specialty as an actor was playing the roles of kings. Others believe that it has a specific reference to the censure which the King's Men received for having performed, in December of 1604, *The Tragedy of Gowry*, a play in which James I was a character. Leslie Hotson argues that the passage refers to Shakespeare's relationship with Mr. W. H. (see William HATCLIFFE).

Two additional works by Davies, *Civile Warres of Death and Fortune* (1609) and *Microcosmos* (1603), while alluding to contemporary actors, include in the margins the initials "W. S. R. B.," probably referring to William Shakespeare and Richard Burbage. [*The Shakspere Allusion-Book*, J. Munro, ed., 1909; Leslie Hotson, *Mr. W. H.*, 1964.]

Davies, Sir John (1569–1626). By profession a lawyer, now remembered as the author of *Orchestra* (1596) and *Nosce Teipsum* (1599). *Orchestra*, subtitled "a poem of dancing," uses the dance to symbolize the order, degree, and correspondences which pervade the universe. E. M. W. Tillyard has drawn upon it to illustrate the commonplaces of the age discussed in his *The Elizabethan World Picture* (1943). *Nosce Teipsum* is a philosophical poem in defense of the immortality of the soul. In the process it touches upon virtually every aspect of psychology: reason, knowledge, the faculties, sense, memory, etc. Its value lies in the fact that it summarizes the psychological beliefs generally held in the Elizabethan age.

Davies, Richard (d. 1708). Clergyman. In 1695, Davies, educated at Oxford, became rector of Sapperton, a small village in Gloucestershire not too far from Stratford. Davies was apparently a friend of another Gloucestershire clergyman, William Fulman. Fulman died in 1688, and Davies came into possession of his personal manuscripts. Included among these were a few sentences relating to Shakespeare's life, to which Davies added additional information:

> William Shakespeare was born at Stratford upon Avon in Warwickshire about 1563·4. *much given to all unluckinesse in stealing venison & Rabbits particularly from Sr Lucy who had him oft whipt & sometimes Imprisoned & at last made Him fly his Native Country to his great Advancemt. But His reveng was so great that he is his Justice Clodpate and calls him a great man & yt in allusion to his name bore three lowses rampant for his Arms.*
>
> From an Actor of Playes he became a Composer. He dyed Apr. 23, 1616, AEtat. 53, probably at Stratford, for there he is buryed, and hath a Monument *on wc He lays a Heavy curse upon any one who shal remoove his bones. He dyed a papist.*

The information in italics is in Davies' handwriting; it contains the first allusion to Shakespeare's alleged participation in deer-stealing (see Sir Thomas LUCY). It is also the principal source of the belief that Shakespeare may have been a Catholic. [J. O. Halliwell-Phillipps, *Outlines of the Life of Shakespeare*, 1881.]

Davison, William (c. 1541–1608). Secretary to Queen Elizabeth. Davison served in a number of important diplomatic missions to Scotland and the Netherlands. In 1586 he was appointed assistant to Sir Francis Walsingham, Elizabeth's secretary of state. In his official capacity Davison was required to submit to Elizabeth the warrant for the execution of Mary, Queen of Scots, which Elizabeth was extremely reluctant to sign. She eventually signed the warrant while at the same time hinting to Davison that Mary not be formally executed but covertly assassinated. Through no fault of Davison's, however, the formal execution was carried out, much to Elizabeth's displeasure. Seizing on Davison as a scapegoat she denied any responsibility for the act, and had Davison imprisoned for disobedience. He was released from prison in 1589, but never allowed to reenter the Queen's service, despite the warm advocacy of his cause by Elizabeth's favorite, the earl of Essex.

Some scholars have seen in Elizabeth's handling of the execution of Mary and her subsequent repudiation of Davison a strong parallel to Shakespeare's *King John*. In the play, John commands the death of his rival claimant to the throne, young Arthur, and then furiously repudiates Hubert de Burgh, whom he believes to have carried out the command:

> *K. John.* Why seek'st thou to possess me with these fears?
> Why urgest thou so oft young Arthur's death?
> Thy hand hath murder'd him: I had a mighty cause
> To wish him dead, but thou hadst none to kill him.
> *Hub.* No had, my lord! why, did you not provoke me?
> *K. John.* It is the curse of kings to be attended
> By slaves that take their humours for a warrant . . . .
> *Hub.* Here is your hand and seal for what I did.
> (IV, ii, 203–209, 215)

The parallel may seem tenuous at best, but there is other evidence to support the view that Shakespeare had Elizabeth's reign in mind when writing *King John*. [Lily B. Campbell, *Shakespeare's Histories: Mirrors of Elizabethan Policy*, 1947.]

Davy. In *2 Henry IV*, Shallow's servant. He persuades his master to ignore a complaint against William Visor of Woncot, explaining that, although the latter is an arrant knave, "a knave should have some countenance at his friend's request," for "An honest man, sir, is able to speak for himself, when a knave is not" (V, i).

Day, John (c. 1574–1640). Dramatist. Day attended Cambridge but was expelled for stealing. In 1598 he sold a play to the Admiral's Men and soon became regularly employed by Philip Henslowe as part of his stable of playwrights. Leslie Hotson has uncovered evidence to show that he was the same John Day who killed the playwright Henry PORTER in a quarrel in 1599. Day continued with Henslowe until 1603, and from 1604 to 1608 did free-lance work. Nothing further is known of him until 1619 when he is mentioned disparagingly by Ben Jonson.

Most of Day's work was done in collaboration, usually with Thomas Dekker. The finest work of which he is the sole author is *The Parliament of Bees* (1634–1640), a series of dialogues in which bees represent various vices and virtues. Day has been suggested as the author of the PARNASSUS PLAYS, an attribution for which there is little evidence. He has also been cited as Shakespeare's collaborator in at least the first and third scenes of Act II of *Pericles*. The argument for this identification is based on a number of parallels between lines in Day's plays and in the second act of *Pericles*. The most striking of these is the parallel between lines from Day's *Law Tricks* (1608) and the dialogue of the fishermen (II, i, 30–46) in *Pericles*.

Dead Man's Fortune, The. A lost play of which the only extant element is the "PLOT," an outline of the play used as a backstage cue of entrances and exits. The plot of *The Dead Man's Fortune* indicates that there were at least 12 characters in the play, of whom only 4 actors are cited by their names, Richard Darlowe, Robert Lee, and a boy actor referred to simply as "Sam." The fourth actor, however, is Richard Burbage, whose appearance in the play has led to speculation as to which acting company might have owned it. A general consensus argues that the play probably dates back to about 1590 when the Admiral's Men were performing at James Burbage's Theatre and that Richard Burbage was then beginning his career as a member of that company. [W. W. Greg, *Dramatic Documents from the Elizabethan Playhouses*, 2 vols., 1931.]

Debussy, Claude. See MUSIC BASED ON SHAKESPEARE: *19th century, 1850–1900.*

Decameron. See Giovanni BOCCACCIO.

Dee, John. See ALCHEMY; ASTRONOMY AND ASTROLOGY.

deer-stealing episode. See Sir Thomas LUCY.

degree. The Elizabethans regarded degree as the agent of order at work both in the heavens and on earth; it most directly represents the unifying power of God binding creation together and preventing the variable universe from dissolving back into chaos. Degree creates hierarchy; things are ordered in terms of degrees of superiority. Thus, in all classes of existence, natural, human, and heavenly, all things that exist are assigned their rightful place; and in all categories of being can be found innate aristocracy and inherent inequality. Between the different categories exist correspondences which reinforce and elucidate each other and the propriety of relationships within each class (God, the sun, the king, gold are all correspondents; the angels are to God what subjects are to their king, or the planets to the sun, or other metals to gold).

QUEEN ELIZABETH PRESIDING OVER THE SPHERES OF STATE. WOODCUT FROM CASE'S *Sphaera civitatis* (1588).

The image of degree in action was known as the Great Chain of Being, the "ladder to all high designs" (*Troilus and Cressida,* I, iii, 102). The ordering and unity of the universe was expressed as an unfaltering chain stretching from the throne of God to the meanest speck of creation. The links of this chain include every category of being: from inanimate existence (matter); to existence and life (vegetable); to existence, life, and feeling (animal); to existence, life, feeling, and understanding (man); and finally, a purely spiritual class. Sir John Fortescue gave one of the best accounts of the chain in his 15th-century Latin work on the Law of Nature, as did Raymond de Sebonde in his *Natural Theology* in the 16th century. A detailed account of the chain was made by Arthur O. Lovejoy in his *The Great Chain of Being* (1936).

The chain is considered by Shakespeare explicitly in *The Tempest,* where exponents of all levels of the chain are represented by Ariel (the angelic or divine), Prospero (at the apex of humanity), Trinculo and Stephano (at the lowest point in the scale for humanity), and by Caliban (the bestial).

The necessity for degree was occasioned by Variety, the expression of God's abundant glory in the multiplicity of creation. Variety ordered by Degree yields Harmony. This sense of prolific life and fruitfulness is summed up by Ulysses in *Troilus and Cressida* in his famous speech on degree (I, iii, 82–129). Shakespeare is always concerned with the theme of order, and most of the plays refer to it. Degree is particularly noted in *Henry V* (I, ii, 183–204). In *Richard II* (III, iv), the noted "gardener's scene" in which the royal gardener and garden become emblems for the King and for England shows the proper ordering of variety contrasted with Richard's inept rule, which has permitted chaos to assert itself in England by his failure to maintain degree within his realm. The play which most concerns itself with the upsetting of order and degree and the chaotic consequences of such an event is *King Lear.*

For contemporary accounts of order, see Sir Thomas Elyot's *The Governor,* The Church Homily *Of Obedience,* the first book of Richard Hooker's *Laws of Ecclesiastical Polity,* and the preface to Sir Walter Raleigh's *History of the World.* The best modern discussion of order and degree is found in E. M. W. Tillyard's *The Elizabethan World Picture* (1943) and in Hardin Craig's *The Enchanted Glass* (1936).—S.K.

Deiphobus. In Greek legend, a son of Priam and Hecuba of Troy. He appears only very briefly in *Troilus and Cressida,* with a line in IV, i.

Dekker, Thomas (c. 1572–1632). Dramatist and pamphleteer. Dekker was apparently born in London and was of Dutch ancestry, but his early life is shrouded in obscurity. His career may be divided into three periods: the early years as a playwright for Henslowe and the Admiral's Men; a second phase as a busy and successful pamphleteer; and a final period in which he worked at both. Throughout his life, despite considerable success, Dekker never managed to avoid being in debt. From 1598, Henslowe's diary records the many advances on plays paid to Dekker, and from 1613 to 1619 the dramatist was imprisoned for debt.

During his early years with the Admiral's Men at the Rose and the Fortune theatres, Dekker was one of the busiest of the "hacks" who worked for Henslowe; he was responsible, either alone or in collaboration, for 44 plays, of which only 6 are extant. He also revised many older plays, and evidently was available to Henslowe's other theatrical companies and to the Chamberlain's Men and the Children of Paul's as well. During this period he wrote *The Shoemaker's Holiday* (1599), a delightful comedy imbued with the atmosphere of Elizabethan London. In 1601 (possibly in collaboration with John Marston) he was working on a tragicomedy, to which he hurriedly added a subplot attacking Ben Jonson. The play was called *Satiromastix or the Untrussing of the Humorous Poet* (1601), and was a reply to Jonson's caricature of Dekker as "Demetrius Fannius," a "dresser" of plays, in the *Poetaster* (1601). See WAR OF THE THEATRES.

Dekker's best romance, *Old Fortunatus*, was written in 1600. In 1604 he wrote *The Honest Whore*, his most interesting play, in which the hand of Thomas Middleton is also visible. About this time, too, he began to produce his prose pamphlets. *The Wonderful Year* (1603) was the beginning of a series of tracts on the plague in London. His *News From Hell* (1606) and *The Seven Deadly Sins of London* (1606) were in the tradition of social criticism and pungent satire established by Thomas Nashe. The *Belman of London* (1608) and *Lanthorn and Candlelight* (1608) were popular versions of Robert Greene's CONY-CATCHING PAMPHLETS. Dekker's versions tend to emphasize the charming, witty confidence man, a figure from which Shakespeare may have drawn Autolycus in *The Winter's Tale*. Dekker's most famous work, however, is probably THE GUL'S HORNE-BOOKE, a satiric view of London life during the early years of the 17th century.

In 1602 Dekker had been employed to revise the play of SIR JOHN OLDCASTLE, which has some references to Falstaff. *The Wonderful Year* includes passages distinctly reminiscent of *1 Henry IV*. Dekker's other dramatic works reveal to a certain extent the influence of *A Midsummer Night's Dream*, *Romeo and Juliet*, and *Hamlet*. Dekker is also cited as the author of a lost play, *The Jew of Venice*, about which nothing is known except that it was entered in the Stationers' Register in 1653. Thus, it is impossible to determine what relationship, if any, it bears to Shakespeare's *Merchant of Venice*. [Mary L. Hunt, *Thomas Dekker: A Study*, 1911.]

Delacroix, Eugène. See FRANCE.

Delaram, Francis. See ENGRAVINGS OF LONDON.

Delius, Frederick. See MUSIC BASED ON SHAKESPEARE: *20th century*.

Deloney or **Delone, Thomas** (1543?–?1607). Writer of tales. By trade a silk weaver, Deloney turned to writing street ballads and prose narratives, the latter proving to be very popular. *Jack of Newberry* (1597) is a series of 11 anecdotes about an apprentice and his rise to prosperity. *The Gentle Craft* (two parts, 1597 and c. 1598) is a collection of tales dealing with shoemakers; it apparently suggested to Thomas Dekker his play *Shoemaker's Holiday*. *Thomas of Reading* (c. 1599) consists of stories of a variety of people during the reign of Henry I; the vivid description of the death of Old Cole recalls the death scenes in *Macbeth*. The charming song "Crabbed age and youth" which is ascribed to Shakespeare in *The Passionate Pilgrim* is also included in a collection attributed to Deloney, *Garland of Good Will*, the earliest surviving edition of which is dated 1631.

Demetrius. In *Antony and Cleopatra*, a friend to Antony. Demetrius appears only in I, i, where he serves as Philo's audience.

Demetrius. In *A Midsummer Night's Dream*, an Athenian youth who is rejected by Hermia but favored over Lysander by her father. Informed by Helena, who loves him, that Hermia and Lysander have fled Athens, Demetrius pursues the couple to the wood where Puck's magic turns his love from Hermia to Helena.

Demetrius and Chiron. In *Titus Andronicus*, the two younger sons of Tamora, queen of the Goths. After raping Lavinia, they cut off her hands and tongue, and, having previously murdered Bassianus, they contrive to make Titus' sons Quintus and Martius seem guilty of the crime, causing their execution. In revenge, Titus cuts the throats of Demetrius and Chiron and serves their flesh in a pie to their mother.

Denham, Sir **John** (1615–1669). Poet. Born in Dublin, Denham served in the royalist army during the civil war. His best-known works are *The Sophy* (1642), a tragedy written for the Blackfriars theatre, and *Cooper's Hill* (1642), a topographical poem. Denham also wrote a commendatory poem to the 1647 edition of Beaumont and Fletcher's *Works*, in which he makes the familiar 17th-century reference to Shakespeare and Jonson as representing, respectively, nature and art.

When JOHNSON, SHAKESPEARE, and thy selfe did sit,
And sway'd in the Triumvirate of wit—
Yet what from JOHNSONS oyle and sweat did flow,
Or what more easie nature did bestow
On SHAKESPEARES gentler Muse, in thee full growne
Their Graces both appeare, yet so, that none
Can say here Nature ends, and Art begins
But mixt like th' Elements, and borne like twins,
So interweav'd, so like, so much the same,
None this meere Nature, that meere Art can name.

[*The Shakspere Allusion-Book*, J. Munro, ed., 1909.]

Denmark. See SCANDINAVIA.

Dennis. In *As You Like It*, a servant to Oliver (I, i).

Dennis, John (1657–1734). Dramatist, critic, and adapter of two of Shakespeare's plays. Dennis is now remembered chiefly for his critical works, most important of which are *The Grounds of Criticism in Poetry* (1704) and *An Essay on the Genius and Writings of Shakespear with some Letters of Criticism to the Spectator* (1712). A patronizing and insensitive critic, Dennis gives Shakespeare's faults and virtues equal weight. He considers poetic justice the most important feature of tragedy: "It is the duty of every tragic poet by an exact distribution of a Poetic Justice to imitate the Divine Dispensation." According to Dennis, Shakespeare's violations of poetic justice are to be blamed on the poet's failure to read Aristotle and Horace.

Dennis' adaptation *The Comical Gallant: or the Amours of Sir John Falstaffe* (1702) attempts to improve on *The Merry Wives of Windsor* by making the plot tighter and the comedy lower. Written entirely in prose, the play was produced and published in the same year. The romance of Fenton and Anne Page is made the unifying center of the play. Fenton arranges to have Falstaff told that Mrs. Page and Mrs. Ford are in love with him and also to have the two husbands informed of Falstaff's activities; all this is designed to draw attention away from the young lovers so they can elope. From this point on, however, the play progresses as in the original, and Anne and Fenton do not reappear until the final scene, when her parents give their consent to the match. Two scenes are added, which give Dennis an opportunity to exercise his penchant for bawdy dialogue (see MERRY WIVES OF WINDSOR: *Stage History*). Dennis' adaptation of *Coriolanus* titled *The Invader of His Country: or, The Fatal Resentment. A Tragedy*, appeared briefly on the Drury Lane stage in 1720. (See CORIOLANUS: *Stage History*.) Neither of Dennis' adaptations was successful, however. [Hazelton Spencer, *Shakespeare Improved*, 1927.]

Denny, Sir Anthony (1500–1549). Courtier and favorite of Henry VIII. In *Henry VIII*, Denny brings Cranmer to the King's presence (V, i).

De Quincey, Thomas (1785–1859). Essayist and critic. De Quincey made two significant contributions to Shakespeare criticism. His article on the poet in the seventh edition of the *Encyclopaedia Britannica* (1838) is an early and excellent example of the type of Romantic criticism which De Quincey had absorbed from his friend and associate, Coleridge.

Considerably more important, however, is his famous essay "On the Knocking at the Gate in *Macbeth*," first published in *The London Magazine* in October 1823. In highly charged prose De Quincey describes the imaginative effect of the murder of Duncan in *Macbeth* whereby the atmosphere of the play is temporarily transformed into a "world of devils." The subsequent knocking at the gate (see PORTER) becomes the signal that "the human has made its reflux upon the fiendish; the pulses of life are beginning to beat again." De Quincey concludes his essay with an impassioned apostrophe to Shakespeare, which, for all its flamboyant bardolatry, makes the sensible point that the reader should approach Shakespearean drama with a faith in its inherent order and design.

Derby, Thomas Stanley, 1st earl of. See Sir Thomas STANLEY.

Derbyite theory. Term used to describe the claim that William Stanley, 6th earl of Derby (1561–1642), is the author of the plays ascribed to Shakespeare. The Derbyite theory was first put forth by a British archivist, James Greenstreet, in a series of essays published in *The Genealogist* (1891–1892). It was revived in 1915 by Robert Frazer in *The Silent Shakespeare* and elaborately developed by a French scholar, Abel Lefranc, in his *Sous le Masque de "William Shakespeare": William Stanley, VIe comte de Derby* (1919). Lefranc's position, restated in two subsequent volumes in 1923 and 1945, was based on the belief that the plays betray an intimate knowledge of court life with which only a courtier like Derby would have been familiar. Lefranc's views were supported by Dr. A. W. Titherley, former dean of the faculty of science at the University of Liverpool, in *Shakespeare's Identity* (1952). Dr. Titherley set about the problem by reducing it to a series of scientific formulas—based, unfortunately, on a number of untenable hypotheses—which showed Derby to be the author. A. J. Evans asserts in *Shakespeare's Magic Circle* (1956) that Oxford, Bacon, Rutland, and Derby collaborated on the plays, the major share of the partnership being Derby's. Evans' theory has the advantage of including all the major CLAIMANTS, except Marlowe, and thereby providing the anti-Stratfordians an opportunity to close ranks and unite against the skeptical majority. [Frank W. Wadsworth, *The Poacher from Stratford*, 1958; G. Lambin, *Voyages de Shakespeare en France et en Italie*, 1962.]

Derby's Men. See STRANGE'S MEN.

Dercetas. In *Antony and Cleopatra*, a friend to Antony. After Antony falls on his sword, Dercetas brings the bloody weapon to Octavius Caesar and offers him his services (V, i). The name of this character is sometimes given as Decretas. North, following Plutarch, calls him Dercetaeus, and both Dercetas and Decretas appear in the First Folio.

Dering Henry IV. A manuscript version of *1* and *2 Henry IV*, written about 1613 and revised about 1623 by Sir Edward Dering (1598–1644) for a private performance at his house in Kent. The original version of the Dering *Henry IV* was copied from the 1613 Quarto (Q5) of *1 Henry IV* and the 1600 Quarto (Q1) of *2 Henry IV*. Three-quarters of it is taken from *1 Henry IV* and the rest from *2 Henry IV*. It may have originally been written for a performance at court and subsequently passed into the possession of the Dering family. Dering's alterations are interesting: he divided the play into acts and scenes and added nine original lines (at I, i, 25 in *1 Henry IV*). Aside from the fragment of the play of *Sir Thomas More*, thought to be by Shakespeare, the Dering *Henry IV* is the earliest known manuscript of a Shakespearean play. [*Henry IV, Part I*, New Variorum Edition, S. B. Hemingway, ed., 1936.]

Desdemona. In *Othello*, the wife of Othello and one of Shakespeare's greatest heroines. Desdemona's gentleness and innocence are underlined by a quiet strength which enables her in the early scenes to withstand the pressures of her father and in the later scenes to transcend and forgive Othello's brutality. Curiously enough, her character has not escaped censure by some of the sterner moralizing critics of the 18th and 19th centuries. She has been represented as a liar, a moral coward, and as a disobedient daughter whose tragic fate is justly deserved. This view, however, is that of a decided minority. In general, critics have recognized the beauty and delicacy of her character. She manages to evoke sympathy without sentimentality and to reflect larger values while remaining a recognizable and attractive human being. Diametrically opposite to Iago, who emerges from the allegorical figure of Vice in medieval drama, Desdemona may be said to embody the abstraction Virtue, particularly the virtue of love and charity. The opposition of these two figures and the idea of Desdemona's ultimate triumph in death are rooted in the medieval tradition which provides the structural framework of the play. See PSYCHOMACHIA. [Bernard Spivack, *Shakespeare and the Allegory of Evil*, 1958; Marvin Rosenberg, *The Masks of Othello*, 1961.]

Deutsche Shakespeare Gesellschaft. See GERMANY: *The 20th Century*.

devices of printers. Ornamental figures used as a distinguishing trade-mark by early printers and publishers. A study of these devices makes it possible to determine at what print shop a given book was published and in some instances helps to establish the date of the book. An account with reproductions of early devices is given in Ronald B. McKerrow's *Printers' and Publishers' Devices in England and Scotland 1485–1640* (1913).

De Witt, Johannes (fl. 1583–1596). Dutch student who visited London in the 1590's. De Witt wrote an account of his visit, including in the account a rough sketch of the interior of the Swan theatre. The sketch and the manuscript were lost, but not before De Witt's friend and fellow student Arend Van Bushell was able to make a copy of De Witt's drawing. The sketch is the most important source of our knowledge of the structure of Shakespeare's stage and the basis of all attempts to reconstruct it. See PLAYHOUSE STRUCTURE.

Diana. Roman name for Artemis, Greek goddess of the chase and the chaste. In *Pericles*, she visits the protagonist in his sleep and commands him to make a sacrifice at her temple in Ephesus (V, i). There he is reunited with his lost wife, Thaisa, who has become a votaress to the Goddess. Since Diana of Ephesus was a notoriously unchaste Asiatic goddess, Shakespeare probably had in mind her classical counterpart.

Diana. See CAPILET, DIANA.

Dick. In *2 Henry VI*, a butcher from Ashford and follower of Jack Cade. Dick is skeptical of Cade's claims to exalted ancestry (IV, ii), but earns the rebel leader's praise for dealing with enemies as if he had been in his own slaughterhouse (IV, iii).

Dickens, Charles (1812–1870). Novelist, considered by some the greatest of his country. Dickens' earliest pieces, *Sketches by Boz* (1836), were satires of London life and were originally serialized in *The Monthly Magazine*. With *Pickwick Papers* (1837) and *Oliver Twist* (1837–1839), Dickens began his career as England's most popular novelist, developing with *Bleak House* (1853) and *Hard Times* (1854) into a satirist with a view to social reform. In addition to his writings, Dickens became known as an editor and actor, his specialty being readings from his own work.

Much of Dickens' interest in Shakespeare can be traced to his interest in acting. His fine articles on *King Lear* and *Much Ado About Nothing* and on the characterizations of Iago and Hamlet were primarily criticisms of particular productions. Dickens himself acted in Shakespearean drama, playing Justice Shallow in *The Merry Wives of Windsor*—once before Queen Victoria. In *Nicholas Nickleby* (1838–1839), he has a rehearsal of *Romeo and Juliet* and

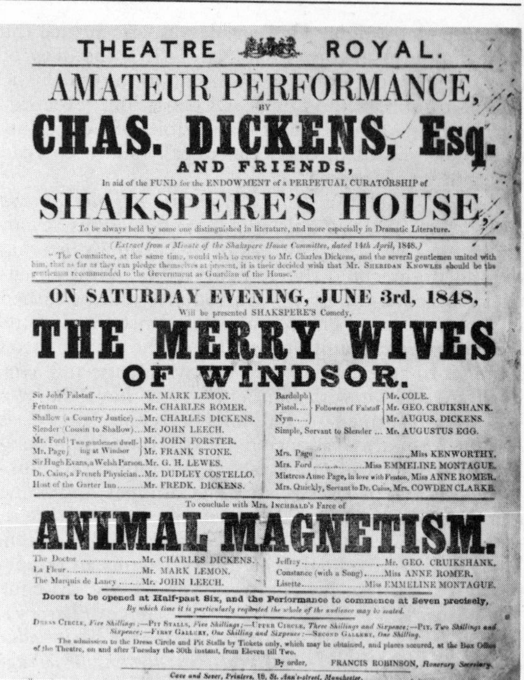

PLAYBILL FOR A PERFORMANCE OF *The Merry Wives* GIVEN BY DICKENS TO RAISE MONEY FOR THE "BIRTHPLACE." DICKENS PLAYED THE PART OF SHALLOW. (SHAKESPEARE BIRTHPLACE TRUST)

satirizes a pretentious scholar who praises "Bill" as a fine "adapter." In the same novel a character tells of her impressions upon visiting Shakespeare's home, undoubtedly reflecting Dickens' own feelings, for he had visited Stratford in 1838. The names of two of the magazines he edited were taken from Shakespeare. *Household Words* is drawn from Hal's speech to his soldiers (*Henry V*, IV, iii, 52); *All the Year Round* was inspired by a line from *Othello* (I, iii, 129–130) which, slightly corrupted, Dickens put at the head of each issue. Because so many of the references to Shakespeare in his letters, speeches, and novels were misquotations, the extent of Dickens' knowledge of Shakespeare has often been questioned, but there can be no doubt as to his love. During his disastrous first trip to America in 1842, described in *Martin Chuzzlewit* (1843–1844), Dickens carried a copy of Shakespeare and called it "an unspeakable source of delight." He lived his last years at a house at Gads Hill (the scene of Falstaff's "robbery") and he was proud of its Shakespearean associations. [Edward P. Vandiver, Jr., "Dickens' Knowledge of Shakspere," *Shakespeare Association Bulletin*, XXI, 1946.]

Dido. In the *Aeneid* of VERGIL, the name given to Elissa, founder and queen of Carthage, who, through the intervention of Venus and Cupid, is compelled to suffer an all-consuming love for Aeneas. In Book IV, at the command of the gods, Aeneas deserts her and she kills herself. In the Renaissance her plight caused her to become a frequent subject for tragedy, a figure of heroic stature and dignity who is destroyed by love. Christopher Marlowe's *Tragedie of Dido Queene of Carthage* (1593) gives us a sympathetic portrait of the great queen at the mercy of the gods. The legend of Dido also had a strong impact on Shakespeare (see CLASSICAL MYTH IN SHAKESPEARE). She is mentioned in six of his plays and Aeneas' unconscious wooing of her with his story of the fall of Troy may be paralleled in Othello's courtship of Desdemona. [*Shakespeare Quarterly*, X, 1959.]

Dido, Queen of Carthage (before 1593). A tragedy by Christopher MARLOWE. It was first published in 1595 as "The Tragedie of Dido Queene of Carthage: Played by the Children of her Maiesties Chappell. Written by Christopher Marlowe, and Thomas Nash. Gent."

Dido, probably Marlowe's maiden venture in the drama, is an imperfect but interesting effort designed to show what a Cambridge M.A. could do. Much of it is straight translation from the *Aeneid*, but there is also much true Marlowe. The play begins with "Jupiter dandling Ganymede upon his knee." Jupiter speaks the opening lines:

> Come, gentle Ganymede and play with me;
> I love thee well, say Juno what she will.

Ganymede, after minor dalliance, replies:

> I would have a jewel for mine ear,
> And a fine brooch to put in my hat,
> And then I'll hug with you an hundred times.

The drift of the passage is unmistakable; it serves also to introduce a plot device that controls the main issue of the play. The love affair between Dido and Aeneas—for Aeneas it is little more than a troglodytic stopover between the fall of Troy and the founding of Rome—is controlled by supernatural power. Whether Shakespeare had Dido in mind when he wrote *A Midsummer Night's Dream* and *The Tempest*, plays in which the central love affair is influenced by magic, one can only guess at. In any event, Marlowe forgets the gods, and his play ends naturalistically with the suicide by fire of the hapless Dido. Meanwhile, Aeneas, in his description of the death of Priam and the fall of Troy, has provided Shakespeare with matter he needed for the player's speech that provokes Hamlet's second soliloquy ("Oh what a rogue and peasant slave . . ."). Then in her pretty vacillation over what to do with Aeneas' tackling, oars, and sails (one of the many logistical problems with which Marlowe puzzles his audience), and knowing that he is torn between the conflicting worlds, Carthage and Rome, of the Terrene Sea, Dido gives us a striking preview of the ambivalence shown, some 20 years later, by Shakespeare's Cleopatra.—G.W.M.

Digges, Leonard (1588–1635). Poet and translator. Digges contributed a commendatory poem to the Shakespeare First Folio (1623). He was the son of Thomas Digges (d. 1595), an eminent mathematician, and the brother of Sir Dudley Digges (1583–1639), a prominent member of the East India Company. Digges was educated at University College, Oxford (M.A. 1606), where he developed his natural gift for languages. (One of his acquaintances there was William Combe of Stratford, the man with whom Shakespeare was to have some difficulty in the matter of the Stratford tithes in 1611.) In 1617 Digges translated from the Latin Claudian's *The Rape of Proserpine* and in 1622 published his translation of a Spanish novel, *Gerardo, the Unfortunate Spaniard*, by G. de Céspedes y Meneses.

After the death of his father, Digges' mother married Thomas Russell, a friend of Shakespeare's and overseer of his will. Digges' acquaintance with Shakespeare probably developed through Russell, since the Russells lived at Alderminster, not far from Stratford. Their relationship may account for the warmth and understanding which Digges displayed in his First Folio poem, "To the Memorie of the deceased Author, Maister W. Shakespeare":

> *Shake-speare*, at length thy pious fellowes giue
> The world thy Workes: thy Workes, by which, out-liue
> Thy Tombe, thy name must: when that stone is rent,
> And Time dissolues thy *Stratford* Moniment,
> Here we aliue shall view thee still. This Booke,
> When Brasse and Marble fade, shall make thee looke
> Fresh to all Ages: when Posteritie
> Shall loath what's new, thinke all is prodegie
> That is not *Shake-speares;* eu'ry Line, each Verse,
> Here shall reuiue, redeeme thee from thy Herse.
> Nor Fire, nor cankring Age, as *Naso* said,
> Of his, thy wit-fraught Booke shall once inuade.
> Nor shall I e're beleeue, or thinke thee dead
> (Though mist) untill our bankrout Stage be sped
> (Impossible) with some new strain t' out-do
> Passions of *Iuliet*, and her *Romeo;*
> Or till I heare a Scene more nobly take,
> Then when thy half-Sword parlying *Romans* spake,
> Till these, till any of thy Volumes rest
> Shall with more fire, more feeling be exprest,
> Be sure, our *Shake-speare*, thou canst neuer dye,
> But crown'd with Lawrell, liue eternally.

Digges' poem is also notable for its allusion to the Shakespeare MONUMENT, which helps to date that sculpture.

A second poem by Digges was prefixed to the 1640 edition of Shakespeare's *Poems* and is justly celebrated for its lively description of Shakespeare's comic characters.

> Poets are borne not made, when I would prove
> This truth, the glad rememberance I must love
> Of never dying *Shakespeare*, who alone,
> Is argument enough to make that one.
> First, that he was a Poet none would doubt,
> That heard th' applause of what he sees set out
> Imprinted; where thou hast (I will not say)
> Reader his Workes (for to contrive a Play
> To him twas none) the patterne of all wit,
> Art without Art unparaleld as yet.
> Next Nature onely helpt him, for looke thorow
> This whole Booke, thou shalt find he doth not borrow,
> One phrase from Greekes, nor Latines imitate,
> Nor once from vulgar Languages Translate,
> Nor Plagiari-like from others gleane,
> Nor begges he from each witty friend a Scene
> To peece his Acts with, all that he doth write,
> Is pure his owne, plot, language exquisite.
> But oh! what praise more powerfull can we give
> The dead, than that by him the Kings men live,

His Players, which should they but have shar'd
the Fate,
All else expir'd within the short Termes date;
How could the Globe have prospered, since
through want
Of change, the Plaies and Poems had growne
scant.
But happy Verse thou shalt be sung and heard,
When hungry quills shall be such honour bard.
Then vanish upstart Writers to each Stage,
You needy Poetasters of this Age,
Where *Shakespeare* liv'd or spake, Vermine
forbeare,
Least with your froth you spot them, come not
neere;
But if you needs must write, if poverty
So pinch, that otherwise you starve and die,
On Gods name may the Bull or Cockpit have
Your lame blancke Verse, to keepe you from the
grave:
Or let new Fortunes younger brethren see,
What they can picke from your leane industry.
I doe not wonder when you offer at
Blacke-Friers, that you suffer: tis the fate
Of richer veines, prime judgements that have
far'd
The worse, with this deceased man compar'd.
So have I seene, when Cesar would appeare,
And on the Stage at halfe-sword parley were,
Brutus and *Cassius:* oh how the Audience,
Were ravish'd, with what wonder they went
thence,
When some new day they would not brooke a
line,
Of tedious (though well laboured) *Catilines;*
Sejanus too was irkesome, they priz'de more
Honest *Iago,* or the jealous Moore.
And though the Fox and subtill Alchimist,
Long intermitted could not quite be mist,
Though these have sham'd all the Ancients, and
might raise,
Their Authours merit with a crowne of Bayes.
Yet these sometimes, even at a friend's desire
Acted, have scarce defraied the Seacoale fire
And doore-keepers: when let but *Falstaffe* come,
Hall, Poines, the rest you scarce shall have a
roome
All is so pester'd: let but *Beatrice*
And *Benedicke* be seene, loe in a trice
The Cockpit Galleries, Boxes, all are full
To heare *Maluoglio* that crosse garter'd Gull.
Briefe, there is nothing in his wit fraught Booke,
Whose sound we would not heare, on whose
worth looke
Like old coynd gold, whose lines in every page,
Shall passe true currant to succeeding age.
But why doe I dead *Sheakspeares* praise recite,
Some second *Shakespeare* must of *Shakespeare*
write;
For me tis needlesse, since an host of men,
Will pay to clap his praise, to free my Pen.

[E. K. Chambers, *William Shakespeare,* 1930; Leslie Hotson, *I, William Shakespeare,* 1938.]

D'Indy, Vincent. See MUSIC BASED ON SHAKESPEARE: *19th century, 1850–1900.*

Diomedes. In *Antony and Cleopatra,* an attendant on Cleopatra. Diomedes brings word to Antony, who has been falsely told that Cleopatra is dead, that she is still alive (IV, xiv).

Diomedes. In Greek mythology, a king of Argos, described in Homer's *Iliad* as one of the bravest Greek warriors in the Trojan War. In *Troilus and Cressida* he appears as a Greek general with whom Cressida makes an assignation before the disbelieving eyes of Troilus (V, ii).

Dion. In *The Winter's Tale,* a lord of Sicilia. Leontes sends Dion and Cleomenes to Apollo's priest at Delphi and they return with a sealed oracle containing the proclamation of Hermione's innocence. Sixteen years after the Queen's supposed death, Dion begs the King to forgo his mourning and rewed; he accuses Paulina of considering "little what dangers, by his Highness' fail of issue, may drop upon his kingdom and devour incertain lookers-on."

Dionyza. In *Pericles,* wife of Cleon, governor of Tarsus, and mother to Philoten. Though Dionyza has promised Pericles that his daughter Marina will be held no less dear than her own daughter Philoten, Dionyza plots "with envy rare" to murder her charge, whose beauty and accomplishments have eclipsed those of Philoten. Believing the treachery accomplished, Dionyza then poisons the hired assassin, Leonine. Gower reports her death at the hands of an outraged citizenry, who burn Cleon's palace when the story of this deed, "although not done, but meant," is spread.

discovery space. Name given to the curtained area of the Elizabethan stage used for the unveiling of certain interior scenes. All scholars agree that there must have been a curtained area on the stage and most of these agree that it was at the rear of the stage. Richard Hosley, who has made an extensive study of the use of "discoveries" in Shakespearean plays, suggests that the discovery space was located behind curtains running the entire width of the rear of the stage. He concludes that the entire canon only calls for 11 discoveries, 3 of which are in *The Merchant of Venice* and one each in eight other plays. His list of discoveries is as follows: *The Merchant of Venice* (II, vii; II, ix; III, ii), the scenes in which Portia's caskets are revealed; *Romeo and Juliet* (V, iii), the scene in which Romeo discovers Juliet in the tomb; *The Merry Wives of Windsor* (I, iv), the scene in which Simple is discovered hiding in Dr. Caius' room; *1 Henry IV* (II, iv), the scene in which Falstaff is discovered asleep behind the arras; *Troilus and Cressida* (III, iii), the scene in which Achilles and Patroclus are discovered at the entrance of Achilles' tent; *Pericles* (V, i), the scene in which Pericles is discovered reclining on a couch; *The Winter's Tale* (V, iii), the scene in which Hermione is discovered by the drawing of a curtain; *The Tempest* (V, i), the scene in which Ferdinand and Miranda are discovered playing chess in Prospero's cell; and *Henry VIII* (II, ii), the scene in which the King is discovered reading.

To this list might be added the discovery of Polonius' body behind the arras after he is stabbed by Hamlet (III, iv), although Hosley feels that Polonius probably fell forward onto the stage and thus was not, technically speaking, "discovered." The importance of Hosley's discovery-space theory is that it acts as a reasonable alternative to the two other major conjectures about these scenes, that they were enacted on an INNER STAGE or in a curtained "booth" or "pavilion" set up against the tiring-house wall. See PLAYHOUSE STRUCTURE. [Richard Hosley, "The Discovery Space in Shakespeare's Globe," *Shakespeare Survey 12*, 1959; Richard Hosley, "Shakespearian Stage Curtains," *College English*, 25, April 1964.]

disintegration. Term used to describe the tendency among certain scholars to deny Shakespeare's sole authorship of many of the plays within the CANON. The disintegration movement reached its peak during the latter half of the 19th century and the first two decades of the 20th. However, doubts as to the authenticity of the Shakespeare canon existed as early as 1687. In that year Edward Ravenscroft prefaced his adaptation of *Titus Andronicus* with the remark that the play had been written by someone else and that Shakespeare merely "gave some Master touches to one or two of the Principal Parts or Characters."

In the 18th century, Alexander Pope doubted Shakespeare's authorship of large portions of *The Comedy of Errors*, *Love's Labour's Lost*, and *The Winter's Tale*, and Samuel Johnson saw an alien hand at work in *Richard II*. The great scholar Edmund Malone brought some stability to these conjectures by establishing a tentative CHRONOLOGY of the plays which presented them in terms of a coherent development from apprenticeship to mastery. Within this framework, he suggested that only the Henry VI plays and *Titus Andronicus* were substantially not Shakespeare's.

Malone's conjectures remained largely unchallenged until the 1870's when the investigations of Shakespeare's verse conducted by the New Shakspere Society (see VERSE TESTS) led to new doubts about the authenticity of certain of the plays. Chief among the skeptics was F. G. Fleay whose hypotheses were based upon analyses of what he conceived to be inconsistencies in the metrical patterns of the plays. His conclusions resulted in the assignment of parts of *The Taming of the Shrew* to Thomas Lodge, of *Romeo and Juliet* to George Peele, of *Julius Caesar* to Ben Jonson as well as in the identification of a number of alleged collaborators on the early plays *Titus Andronicus*, *Henry VI*, and *Richard III*.

Fleay's conjectures were arrived at in an age when the prestige of science had reached a new high; his reliance on statistics and quantitative analysis gave his ascriptions an air of "scientific" authority which won him a number of enthusiastic disciples. The most forceful of these was J. M. Robertson, whose procedure differed somewhat in that it relied on a number of subjective judgments as to what portions of a given play would not have been written by Shakespeare. On the basis of his impressions he proceeds to attribute these inferior parts to other playwrights with a similar style or vocabulary. Thus he sees Marlowe as the major contributor to earlier versions of *Richard III*, *Richard II*, *Henry V*, and *Julius Caesar*. Robert Greene is seen as the major author of *Two Gentlemen of Verona*, again in an earlier form which evolved into the present version of the play as the result of a complicated series of drafts and redrafts. Similarly, Robertson argues that in *Hamlet*, *All's Well That Ends Well*, *The Merry Wives of Windsor*, *Troilus and Cressida*, *Timon of Athens*, and *Pericles*, Shakespeare was working from earlier drafts or versions of those plays written by George Chapman. Many of Robertson's arguments are not without force, but the vast majority of them rest on equivocal, subjective evidence which has been rejected by most scholars.

A more formidable theory of disintegration, and one which commands many adherents, is that set forth by Dover Wilson. Wilson's conjectures are based upon insights provided by modern TEXTUAL CRITICISM which examines the techniques and practices of Elizabethan printing houses, the nature of the copy that the printer used, and the possibilities of alteration that the copy might undergo. A more moderate disintegrationist than his predecessors, Wilson argues that in almost all of the early histories and comedies Shakespeare's versions were essentially revisions of earlier plays. Thus, for example, he argues that *The Merry Wives of Windsor* is Shakespeare's revision of *The Jealous Comedy*, an anonymous play, possibly also written by Shakespeare. See THE MERRY WIVES OF WINDSOR: *Text*.

Later studies of the texts of the plays, however, have moved generally in the direction of affirming the authenticity of the canon, acknowledging, at the same time, the presence of non-Shakespearean hands in *Pericles* and *Henry VIII*, and possibly in *Timon of Athens* and *Titus Andronicus*, and of interpolations in *Macbeth*. For example, *2* and *3 Henry VI*, long regarded as revisions of the anonymous CONTENTION PLAYS, are now generally accepted as original Shakespearean dramas of which the Contention plays are "bad quartos."

Revisions of old plays and the collaboration of playwrights were common practices in the Elizabethan theatre, and it is clear that Shakespeare engaged in both (see COLLABORATION; REVISION). Nevertheless, despite the tireless efforts of the distintegrationists, nothing as yet has been advanced that substantially alters the claim of Heminges and Condell, editors of the First Folio (1623), that the 36 plays in the Folio are the work of William Shakespeare. [E. K. Chambers, "The Disintegration of Shakespeare," *Shakespearean Gleanings*, 1944.]

Dittersdorf, Carl Ditters von. See MUSIC BASED ON SHAKESPEARE: *18th century*.

Doctor. In *King Lear*, a minor character. The Doctor appears in IV, iv and IV, vii as a member of Cordelia's retinue, and ministers to the demented Lear.

Doctor. In *The Two Noble Kinsmen*, a friend of the Jailer. He decides that, in order to cure the madness of the Jailer's Daughter, her wooer should impersonate Palamon (IV, iii; V, ii).

Doctors. In *Macbeth*, two minor characters. In V, i, the ***English Doctor***, referred to as "a Doctor of Physic," witnesses Lady Macbeth's sleepwalking. In V, iii, the ***Scotch Doctor*** informs Macbeth that Lady Macbeth is "troubled with thick-coming fancies."

Dogberry. In *Much Ado About Nothing*, the head constable of Messina, who is given to malapropisms and other absurdities of speech and logic. Charging the night watch to "comprehend all vagrom men," Dogberry further enjoins them: "If you meet a thief, you may suspect him, by virtue of your office, to be no true man." With his final exhortation to "be vigitant," Dogberry sets the watch which presently seizes Borachio and Conrade (III, iii). During the interrogation of the two criminals, Dogberry accuses them of the wrong crimes. Nevertheless, it is this "shallow fool" who brings to light what the wisdom of others could not discover. For his trouble he is called an ass (IV, ii).

Dogget, Thomas (c. 1670–1721). Actor. Born in Dublin, Dogget played several years in the English provinces before London audiences became aware of his remarkable abilities in low comedy. His reputation grew, however, and Congreve, in 1695, wrote the role of Ben in *Love for Love* for him. Dogget was remembered for his portrayal of Shylock in George Granville's *Jew of Venice* (a weak adaptation of *The Merchant of Venice*), a role which he performed twice, the first time to Betterton's Bassanio and Mrs. Bracegirdle's Portia in 1701. Dogget co-managed the Drury Lane for a time with Colley Cibber and Robert Wilks. He virtually retired from the stage in 1713. He was the author of a comedy, *The Country Wake*. [*Dictionary of National Biography*, 1885– .]

Dolabella. In *Antony and Cleopatra*, a friend to Octavius Caesar. Sent by Caesar to persuade Antony to surrender, Dolabella finds Antony dead. Dolabella notifies Cleopatra of Caesar's intention to lead her in triumph through Rome, thus precipitating her suicide (V, ii).

domestic tragedy. A type of tragedy based upon the lives of contemporary, middle-class people rather than on historical figures or persons of high rank. Domestic tragedy originated in the Elizabethan theatre with plays based upon contemporary murder stories, such as ARDEN OF FEVERSHAM (c. 1592), and *A Yorkshire Tragedy* (c. 1606). Both of these anonymous plays are among the best examples of domestic tragedy and both have been attributed to Shakespeare, although general critical opinion assigns *Arden of Feversham* to Thomas Kyd and *A Yorkshire Tragedy* to Thomas Heywood or George Wilkins. *Arden* is the dramatization of the murder of a husband by his wife and her lover which took place in 1551. *A Yorkshire Tragedy* is based on a father's murder of his children which occurred in 1605.

Probably the finest examples of domestic tragedy are Thomas Heywood's *A Woman Killed with Kindness* (c. 1603) and *A Warning for Fair Women* (c. 1599), the latter an anonymous play generally regarded as having been written by Heywood. Domestic tragedy must have enjoyed great popularity at the end of Elizabeth's reign for there are more than a score of dramas of this type extant and at least that many which have been lost.

Donalbain or **Donald Bain.** Second son of Duncan I of Scotland. On his father's death and Macbeth's accession to the throne, Donalbain fled to the Hebrides, where he seems to have remained throughout the reign of Macbeth. After the death of his older brother Malcolm, Donalbain claimed the crown, but in 1097 he was deposed by Malcolm's son Edgar. In *Macbeth*, Donalbain flees to Ireland after Duncan's murder, and his brother Malcolm flees to England. They are consequently suspected of being their father's assassins. [W. H. Thomson, *Shakespeare's Characters: A Historical Dictionary*, 1951.]

Donne, John (1572–1631). Poet and churchman. Of a staunchly Catholic family, Donne studied at Oxford and Cambridge before being admitted to Lincoln's Inn. Like others residing at the inns of law, he devoted himself to letters and became known as a fashionable wit and man about town. He then served under Essex in the expeditions to Cadiz in 1596 and to the Azores in 1597. On his return to London, he entered the service of Sir Thomas Egerton, keeper of the great seal. In 1601 he fell into disfavor by marrying without the queen's permission Anne More, a niece of Lady Egerton, and for a brief time was imprisoned. Ostracism, poverty, and religious skepticism brought Donne to a state of despair, and apparently he contemplated suicide. His religious difficulties seem to have been settled in favor of Anglicanism by 1607, the year in which he was urged by Thomas Morton, dean of Gloucester, to take orders. But Donne hoped for secular preferment. In 1615, after repeated urging by James I, he was ordained and six years later became dean of St. Paul's.

Donne is the leading exponent of the metaphysical school of poetry. In rebelling against the conventions of both Petrarch and Spenser, he developed techniques such as ingenious conceits, a highly intellectualized approach to subject matter, and a vast range of imagery, which make his style conversational, dramatic, and at times abrupt. These characteristics appear in the secular love lyrics, presumably the fruit of Donne's early years, and in the religious verse. Most of the poems circulated in manuscript and were not published until after his death. Among the few poems printed in Donne's own lifetime are the two verse meditations *An Anatomy of the World* (1611) and *The Progress of the Soul* (1612). Prose works include *Ignatius His Conclave* (1611), an attack upon the Jesuits with incidental references to Copernicus and Galileo; *Devotions Upon Emergent Occasions* (1624), a series of meditations on death; and numerous sermons delivered in his capacity of dean of St. Paul's. It has been suggested that Donne, who knew the earl of Southampton, is the Rival Poet of the *Sonnets*. See RIVAL POET.

Donnelly, Ignatius (1831–1901). American author, public official, and historian. Donnelly was the first to propound the theory that Bacon's authorship of the plays ascribed to Shakespeare could be proven by a careful study of the "cipher" embedded in the plays. (See BACONIAN THEORY.) A man of extraordinary energy and zeal, Donnelly was the founder of a utopian community, a member of Congress, a candidate for the vice presidency on the Populist Party ticket, and the author of a number of unusual books in a wide variety of fields. In 1888 he published a massive, 998-page study titled *The Great Cryptogram.* According to Donnelly, Bacon managed to conceal within the 1623 Folio a hidden message which establishes his authorship. On the basis of this cipher Donnelly asserts that Bacon was the author of a number of anonymous plays, as well as Burton's *Anatomy of Melancholy*, Montaigne's essays, and the complete works of Marlowe. He elaborated his theories in a later work, *The Cypher in the Plays and on the Tombstone* (1899). Donnelly's books created a *cause célèbre* and gave birth to a number of imitations. [Frank W. Wadsworth, *The Poacher from Stratford*, 1958.]

Dorcas. See MOPSA AND DORCAS.

Dorrell, Hadrian (fl. 1594). Author. Dorrell wrote

a prefatory epistle to WILLOBIE HIS AVISA (1594), a poem which may contain some allusions to Shakespeare's private life. In his epistle, Dorrell describes himself as a student at Oxford and a "very good friend and chamber fellow" of Henry Willobie, whom he describes as the author of the poem.

There is no record of a Hadrian Dorrell at Oxford during the 1590's although there is a "Thomas Darrell" who matriculated on the same day as Willobie in 1596. The name "Dorrell" might possibly be one invented by Willobie or a pseudonym of one of his classmates. "Dorrell" is also the author of an "Apology showing the true meaning of *Willobie his Avisa*," which was added to the second edition (1596) of the poem.

Dorset, Thomas Grey, 1st marquis of (1451–1501). Elder son of Sir John Grey and Lady Elizabeth Woodville, later queen of Edward IV. In *Richard III*, Dorset is sent by his mother to join the Earl of Richmond (IV, i).

Dorset Garden Theatre (Duke's House). Playhouse built in 1671 as the home of the Duke's Company. The Dorset Garden, built at a cost of £9000, was designed by Christopher Wren and was the largest and most sumptuous theatre of its day. It was located on the Thames near Salisbury Court. Its original manager and leading actor was Thomas Betterton, and the theatre in time became known for its operas, including Sir William Davenant's adaptation of *Macbeth* and the Thomas Shadwell version of *The Tempest*, known as *The Enchanted Island* (1673). One of the most successful plays given there was Shadwell's adaptation of *Timon of Athens* (1678).

In 1682 the Duke's Company amalgamated with the King's Company and the combined group performed at the Drury Lane. In 1689 the Dorset Garden was renamed the Queen's Theatre, in honor of Queen Mary (1662–1694), and while some operas and acrobatic and animal exhibitions continued to be given there for a short while, it is not mentioned after the first decade of the 18th century.

Dostoevsky, Fyodor. See RUSSIA.

Douai MS. A manuscript dated 1694/5 now in the Public Library at Douai, France, which contains transcripts of six Shakespearean plays. The plays are *Twelfth Night, As You Like It, Comedy of Errors, Romeo and Juliet, Julius Caesar*, and *Macbeth*. The texts of the plays were transcribed from a copy of the Second Folio (1632). The MS appears to have been used in early amateur presentations of the plays and provides some valuable clues as to late 17th-century acting versions of the plays. [G. Blakemore Evans, "The Douai Manuscript—Six Shakespearean Transcripts," *Philological Quarterly*, 41, 1962.]

Double Falsehood. See CARDENIO.

doubling. The common Elizabethan practice of an actor's assuming more than one part in a play. The earliest trace of doubling is in the 15th-century miracle play, the Croxton *Play of the Sacrament* (c. 1480). The procedure was continued by the strolling players of the early Tudor period. In the professional Elizabethan theatre, the practice required the playwright to take particular care in constructing his plays in those frequent cases where a large CAST was necessary. In *2 Henry VI*, for example, Shakespeare wrote 47 parts for a company of no more than 18 actors. This practical theatre problem required considerable concessions from the dramatist. It might account, for example, for the sudden disappearance of the Fool in *King Lear* in Act IV and the apparently wanton death of Antigonus in *The Winter's Tale*. It may have been that actors playing these roles were needed to double in other roles. The Fool, it might be noted, is never on the stage at the same time as Cordelia or the King of France. [W. J. Lawrence, *Pre-Restoration Stage Studies*, 1927.]

Douce, Francis (1757–1834). Scholar and antiquarian. A librarian and rare-book collector, Douce was keeper of the manuscripts in the British Museum. His *Illustrations of Shakespeare* (2 vols., 1807), a valuable collection of notes on the plays, includes one of the earliest critical accounts of Shakespeare's clowns.

Douglas, Archibald, 4th earl of (1369?–1424). Son-in-law of Robert III of Scotland. In 1402 he invaded England on behalf of the duke of Albany, but was taken prisoner at Homildon Hill by Hotspur and Sir Edmund de Mortimer (1402). When Hotspur revolted against Henry IV, Douglas was freed. He fought with Hotspur at Shrewsbury but was taken prisoner by the king's army. In *1 Henry IV*, Douglas is defeated at Holmedon and imprisoned by Hotspur. Joining his captor's rebellion against Henry, Douglas fights at Shrewsbury. He kills Sir Walter Blunt and engages the King in personal combat (V, iii). Eventually captured, he is freed without ransom by Prince Henry.

Dowdall, [John?] Mr. (fl. 1693). Antiquary. Dowdall composed the following account of his visit to Stratford in 1693, during a jaunt through Warwickshire.

> The 1st Remarkable place in this County y[t] I visitted was Stratford super avon, where I saw the Effigies of our English tragedian, M[r] Shakespeare . . . Neare the Wall where his monument is Erected Lyeth a plaine free stone, vnderneath w[ch] his bodie is Buried with this Epitaph, made by himselfe a little before his Death.
>
> Good friend, for Jesus sake forbeare
> To digg the dust inclosed here
> Bles't be the man that spares these stones
> And Curs't be he that moves my bones!
>
> The clarke that shew'd me this Church is aboue 80 y[rs] old; he says that this *Shakespear* was formerly in this Towne bound apprentice to a butcher; but that he Run from his master to London, and there was Rec[d] Into the playhouse as a serviture, and by this meanes had an opportunity to be w[t] he afterwards prov'd. he was the best of his family, but the male Line is extinguished; not one for feare of the Curse aboues[d] Dare Touch his Grave Stone, tho his wife and Daughters Did Earnestly Desire to be Layd in the same Graue wth him.

The most interesting piece of information in this report is that Shakespeare's first position in the theatre was that of a servitor or hired man. [E. K. Chambers, *William Shakespeare*, 1930.]

Dowden, Edward (1843–1913). Irish biographer and critic. Dowden was born in Cork and educated at Queens College, Cork, and Trinity College, Dublin. In 1867 he was elected professor of oratory and English at Dublin University. His first book, *Shake-*

speare: A Critical Study of his Mind and Art* (1875), made him widely known as an authority on Shakespeare and was translated into German and Russian. His later works in this field were editions of *Shakespeare's Sonnets* (1881) and *The Passionate Pilgrim* (1881), *Introduction to Shakespeare* (1893), and editions of *Hamlet* (1899), *Romeo and Juliet* (1900), and *Cymbeline* (1903). He was also Irish commissioner of education from 1896 to 1900 and trustee of the National Library of Ireland.

Dowden regarded the plays as accurate indices of Shakespeare's moods and personal attitudes. *Shakespeare: A Critical Study of his Mind and Art* uses F. J. Furnivall's division of Shakespeare's career into four periods which are characterized as "In the Workshop," "In the World," "In the Depths," and "On the Heights." The standard critical biography of Shakespeare of its time, it was the first book in English to present a comprehensive picture of Shakespeare's development. As a result of Dowden's biographical bias in interpreting the plays, however, subsequent critics have tended to underrate his achievement.

Dowland, John (1563–1626). Lutenist and composer. Dowland popularized once again the "air," the traditional English song form which had been eclipsed in the 16th century by the more complicated madrigal. He published four books of airs under the following titles: *The First Booke of Songes or Ayres . . .* (1597); *The Second Booke of Songs or Ayres . . .* (1600); *The Third and Last Book of Songs or Aires* (1603); and *A Pilgrimes Solace. Wherein is contained Musicall Harmonie of 3.4. and 5. parts* (1612).

TITLE PAGE OF DOWLAND'S *First booke of Songes or Ayres* (1597).

THE FIRST BOOKE of Songes or Ayres of fowre partes with Tableture for the Lute: So made that all the partes together, or either of them seuerally may be song to the Lute, Orpherian or Viol de gambo. Composed by *Iohn Dowland* Lutenist and Batcheler of musicke in both the Vniuersities. Also an inuention by the sayd Author for two to playe vpon one Lute.

Nec prosunt domino, quæ prosunt omnibus, artes.

¶ Printed by Peter Short, dwelling on Bredstreet hill at the sign of the Starre, 1597

Dowland served as lutenist for King Christian IV of Denmark, the brother-in-law of James I, for whom he also acted as personal lutenist. His contemporary reputation rested more upon his ability as a performer than as a composer. He was complimented on his playing by Richard Barnfield in a poem later published in *The Passionate Pilgrim* (1599), a collection of poems ascribed to Shakespeare. This fact probably accounts for the idea recorded by William OLDYS that Shakespeare had praised Dowland:

> Shakespeare was deeply delighted with the singing of Dowland the Lutanist, but Spencer's deep conceits he thought surpassed all others. See in his Sonnets *The friendly Concord*. That John Dowland and Thos. Morley are said to have set several of these Sonnets to musick, as well as others composed by Sir P. Sydney, Sr. Edwd. Dyer, Sr. Walter Raleigh, and Kit Marlow and Spencer. When the King of Denmark had heard that Dowland, he requested (as may be seen by his Letter in Harleian Library) King James to part with him, and he had him over to Denmark where he died.

It should be mentioned, however, that Dowland is thought to have died in London.

Downes, John (c. 1640–c. 1710). Actor and theatrical historian. Downes began as an actor in William Davenant's Duke's Company at Lisle's Tennis Court in 1662. His acting career, however, came to an end in that year as a result of severe stage fright suffered during a performance of Davenant's *Siege of Rhodes*. He remained with the company as book-keeper (prompter).

In 1708 he published his *Roscius Anglicanus, or an Historical Review of the Stage from 1660 to 1706*. *Roscius Anglicanus* is riddled with inaccuracies but is invaluable for its information concerning the casts of particular plays, such as the following list of actors in the Duke's Company's production of *Hamlet:*

> The Tragedy of *Hamlet; Hamlet* being Perform'd by Mr. *Betterton*, Sir *William* (having seen Mr. *Taylor* of the Black-Fryars Company Act it, who being Instructed by the Author Mr. Shaksepeur) taught Mr. Betterton in every Particle of it; which by his exact Performance of it, gain'd him Esteem and Reputation, Superlative to all other Plays Horatio by Mr. Harris; The King by Mr. Lilliston; The Ghost by Mr. Richards, (after by Mr. Medburn) Polonius by Mr. Lovel; Rosencrans by Mr. Dixon; Guilderstern by Mr. Price; 1st, Gravemaker, by Mr. Underhill: The 2d, by Mr. Dacres; The Queen, by Mrs. Davenport, Ophelia, by Mrs. Sanderson: No succeeding Tragedy for several Years got more Reputation, or Money to the Company than this.

The information that Shakespeare coached Joseph Taylor in the role of Hamlet is probably inaccurate, since Taylor apparently did not join the King's Men until the death of Richard Burbage in 1619, three years after Shakespeare's death.

Downes records a similar incident in connection with a Duke's Company production of *Henry VIII:*

> The part of the King was so right and justly done

by Mr. Betterton, he being Instructed in it by Sir William, who had it from Old Mr. Lowen, that had his Instructions from Mr. Shakespear himself . . . .

Downes also includes an account of Davenant's adaptation of *Macbeth*, and he notes that *Macbeth*, along with *King Lear* and *The Tempest*, was also acted during the Restoration "exactly as Mr. Shakespear Wrote it." [*Restoration Stage*, John L. McCollum, Jr., ed., 1961.]

Downton or **Dowton, Thomas** (d. c. 1625). Actor. Downton first appears in extant records in an entry in the St. Saviour's registry where he is called a musician. He is probably the "Mr Doutone" who toured the provinces with Edward Alleyn and Strange's Men in 1593, and he probably joined the Admiral's Men the following year. Later he became one of Pembroke's Men, but rejoined Admiral's upon the dissolution of Pembroke's in 1597. For the next 20 years he was a prominent member of the Admiral's Men, sometimes acting as their payee for performances at court. In 1617 or 1618 he married the widow of a vintner and himself became a vintner, leaving the stage. Edward Alleyn's diary mentions Downton as having been a dinner guest in 1622.

The registry of St. Saviour's records the baptisms of two sons, Christopher (b. 1592) and Thomas (b. 1600 or 1601), the "baseborne, . . . supposed son of Thomas Dowton, a player." The latter evidently also became an actor, but his career was apparently limited to provincial companies. His father's will of 1625 refers to him exasperatedly: "because my sonne hath bine a desperate sonne to me I giue a desperat Legacye." [Edwin Nungezer, *A Dictionary of Actors*, 1929; G. E. Bentley, *The Jacobean and Caroline Stage*, 5 vols., 1941–1956.]

Draghi, Giovanni Baptista. See MUSIC BASED ON SHAKESPEARE: *17th century*.

Drake, James (1667–1707). Writer. Drake is the author of the refutation of a famous attack by Jeremy COLLIER on the Restoration stage and, indirectly, on Shakespeare. Drake's answer to Collier appeared in his *The Antient and Modern Stages survey'd* (1699). His defense of Shakespeare involves an extended account of the highly moral qualities of *Hamlet* and its "admirable distribution of Poetick Justice." He concludes with a summary of the moral of the play and of the similarly exemplary aspects of Shakespeare's other plays:

> The Moral of all this is very obvious, it shews us, *That the Greatness of the Offender does not qualifie the Offence, and that no Humane Power, or Policy, are a sufficient Guard against the Impartial Hand, and Eye of Providence, which defeats their wicked purposes, and turns their dangerous Machinations upon their own heads.* This Moral *Hamlet* himself insinuates to us, when he tells *Horatio*, that he ow'd the Discovery of the Design against his Life in *England*, to a rash indiscreet curiosity, and thence makes this Inference.
>
> *Our Indiscretion sometimes serves as well,*
> *When our dear Plots do fail, and that shou'd teach us*
> *There's a Divinity, that shapes our ends,*
> *Rough hew 'em how we will.*
>
> The Tragedies of this Author in general are Moral and Instructive, and many of 'em such, as the best of Antiquity can't equal in that respect. His *King Lear*, *Timon of Athens*, *Macbeth* and some others are so remarkable upon that score, that 'twou'd be impertinent to trouble the Reader with a minute examination of Plays so generally known and approved.

[*The Shakspere Allusion-Book*, J. Munro, ed., 1909.]

Drake, Nathan (1766–1836). Scholar and physician. Drake received his M.D. from the University of Edinburgh in 1789 and served as a general practitioner in Suffolk. His leisure time was devoted to literary pursuits. In 1817 he produced a two-volume study, *Shakespeare and his Times*, one of the earliest attempts to synthesize the efforts of various 18th-century scholars. The work includes a suggested chronology and the earliest identification of Mr. W. H. with the earl of Southampton. In 1828 he edited *Memorials of Shakespeare*, probably the first anthology of Shakespeare criticism.

dramatic irony. Name given to the discrepancy between the expectations of a given character in a play and the eventual outcome of those expectations. Also known as "tragic irony," dramatic irony is a frequent feature of tragedy, its classic example being Oedipus' unwitting self-condemnation in Sophocles' *Oedipus Rex*. In Shakespeare, dramatic irony is most pronounced in *Macbeth*, to cite two examples, in Lady Macbeth's complacent assurance after the murder of Duncan that "A little water clears us of this deed" (II, ii, 67), and in Macbeth's conviction, imbibed from the witches (whose entire prophecy is presented in ironic terms), that he need fear no man born of woman. Both of these statements are ironically significant in the light of Lady Macbeth's subsequent remorseful delusion about her irrevocably bloodstained hands and Macbeth's defeat by Macduff, who was not "born" but "untimely ripped" from his mother's womb.

Dramatic irony is employed in several other Shakespearean tragedies, notably in *Othello* and *Hamlet*, but it nowhere else assumes the significance which it does in *Macbeth*. [John Holloway, "Dramatic Irony in Shakespeare," *Northern Miscellany*, I, 1953.]

Drayton, Michael (1563–1631). Poet. Born in Hartshill, Warwickshire, Drayton served as a page to Sir Henry Goodere and in 1591 went to London to begin his literary career. He eventually became one of the most popular and voluminous authors of the day, frequently trying his hand at whatever form was currently fashionable. In narrative poetry alone he ranged from the ballad to the lengthy historical narrative, and for material he drew upon Biblical, legendary, historical, and mythological sources. Other forms he attempted include the sonnet, ode, epistle, elegy, pastoral, and drama. Drayton's most ambitious work was the *Polyolbion* (1612, enlarged 1622), a guide to the individual counties of England and Wales which incorporates a vast body of descriptive, legendary, and historical material. The 13th book, covering Warwickshire, is a useful guide to Shakespeare's native county.

It is highly probable that Drayton and Shakespeare were acquainted; according to some legends, there was a close personal friendship between the two. One rumor current in Stratford was that Shakespeare's death had been hastened as a result of a drinking bout with Drayton. On more substantial evidence we

MICHAEL DRAYTON. PORTRAIT BY AN UNKNOWN ARTIST. (DULWICH COLLEGE, BY PERMISSION OF THE GOVERNORS)

know that Drayton had once been treated by Dr. John Hall, Shakespeare's son-in-law.

Some affinities have been noted between the works of the two poets. Drayton's *Legend of Matilda*, published in the same year as Shakespeare's *Rape of Lucrece* (1594), contains a reference to Lucrece. Shakespeare's *Venus and Adonis* (1593) may have exerted some influence on Drayton's *Endimion and Phoebe* (1595); both are examples of the Ovidian-mythological poem then in vogue. As one of Philip Henslowe's hacks, Drayton collaborated on *Sir John Oldcastle* (1599), an answer to the misrepresentation of Oldcastle as Falstaff in *1 Henry IV*. Drayton's *The Baron's War* (1603) contains a description which closely resembles that of Brutus in *Julius Caesar* (V, v, 68–75). Drayton made a direct allusion to Shakespeare in his elegy on Henry Reynolds (1627). Surveying the English poets from Chaucer to his own day, he observed that Shakespeare had as smooth a "comic vein," as "strong a conception," and as "clear a rage" as any who "trafficked with the stage." His "natural brain" contrasts with that of the "learned Jonson" who had "drunk deep of the Pierian spring." These and other affinities have led some to conclude that Drayton was the RIVAL POET of Shakespeare's *Sonnets*.

Drew, John (1853–1927). American actor. The son of Mr. and Mrs. John Drew, who managed the Arch Street Theatre in Philadelphia, Drew made his first stage appearance at his parents' theatre in 1873 and played there for two years. From 1875 to 1892, with the exception of a tour in 1878/9, Drew played at Augustin Daly's theatre in New York, where he took parts in productions of *Hamlet, Othello, Richard II, The Merchant of Venice, King Lear, The Taming of the Shrew, As You Like It, The Merry Wives of Windsor*, and *A Midsummer Night's Dream*. In 1892 he was hired as a "star" by Charles Frohman, with whom he remained until 1915, playing many parts including Benedick in *Much Ado About Nothing*. In 1916 he played the part of Shakespeare in Percy MacKaye's *Caliban by the Yellow Sands*, a production given at the stadium of what was then New York College in honor of the Shakespeare Tercentenary. [*Who's Who in the Theatre*, 5th ed., 1925.]

Drew, Louisa Lane (1820–1897). American actress and producer. She came to America in 1827 with her mother, who was also an actress. She appeared that year in Philadelphia as the Duke of York in Junius Brutus Booth's *Richard III*. As a child mimic, she toured with her mother until after her marriage in 1836 to Henry B. Hunt, when she began to play more mature parts. During this time she supported Edwin Forrest and Macready and in 1847 emulated Charlotte Cushman by doing Romeo and Antony in New York. In 1850 she married her third husband, John Drew, by whom she had three children, John, Giorgiana, and Louisa (see John DREW). Her son's memoirs, *My Years on the Stage* (1921), are a tribute to her. [*Dictionary of American Biography*, 1927– .]

drink. See FOOD AND DRINK.

Droeshout, Martin. See PORTRAITS.

drolls. See ROBERT COX.

Dromio. In *The Comedy of Errors*, the name of identical twin slaves, one serving Antipholus of Ephesus, the other Antipholus of Syracuse. On good terms with their masters, they are involved in the confusion of identities and enjoy a reunion in the final act.

Drummond, William, of Hawthornden (1585–1649). Scottish poet and friend of Ben JONSON, whose observations on Shakespeare he recorded. Drummond was educated at Edinburgh University, after which he studied and traveled abroad. On the death of his father in 1610, he became laird of Hawthornden where he devoted the rest of his life to literature. His poetry is fluent and graceful after the manner of Spenser, but even in its own day it was regarded by Drummond's contemporaries as somewhat mannered and old-fashioned.

In the winter of 1618/9 he was visited by Ben Jonson, and during the visit Drummond recorded their talks in a notebook which was ultimately published as *Conversations of Ben Jonson with William Drummond of Hawthornden* in 1842. Among the observations of Jonson recorded by Drummond is the remark "That Shaksperr wanted Arte," i.e., that he violated the neoclassical rules to which Jonson was devoted (see CRITICISM—17TH CENTURY). Drummond also recorded Jonson's remark criticizing Shakespeare for referring to a shipwreck in Bohemia (in *The Winter's Tale*) when there is no seacoast near that country. [E. K. Chambers, *William Shakespeare*, 1930.]

Drury Lane Theatre [King's House, Theatre Royal]. Playhouse, probably the most famous in English theatrical history, built in 1662 by Thomas Killigrew and Robert Howard in conjunction with eight actors from Killigrew's King's Company. The Drury Lane was located between Drury Lane and Bridges Street; it was first occupied on May 7, 1663 by the company which had previously been playing at Gibbon's Tennis Court. It was officially designated the Theatre Royal and constructed by right of a patent from Charles II; the patent still forms part of the theatre's lease. In 1672 a fire destroyed the building, but it was subsequently rebuilt under the aegis of the famed architect Christopher Wren.

For a short time the theatre prospered, but Killigrew had entrusted it to the hands of unskilled and incompetent managers and by 1681 it was forced to close. The Drury Lane reopened in 1682 with a resident troupe consisting of the amalgamated Duke's and King's companies under the leadership of Thomas Betterton. In 1690, however, an unscrupulous owner, Christopher Rich, gained control; Rich's mistreatment of the actors eventually resulted in their rebellion, led by Betterton, and the desertion by Betterton's faction in 1695 (they moved temporarily to the Lincoln's Inn Fields Theatre).

The Drury Lane remnants and the Betterton troupe engaged in a fierce rivalry, with the Drury Lane group faring rather poorly. In 1709 the Drury Lane was purchased by Colley Cibber, Thomas Doggett, and Robert Wilks. Under the leadership of the "Triumvirate," as they were called, the place prospered. The period of its greatest fame came, however, under the direction of David Garrick. In 1794 playwright Richard Brinsley Sheridan, Garrick's successor, assumed control and ordered the theatre enlarged and rebuilt. From 1809 to 1812 the theatre was closed because of the damage wrought by a disastrous fire. When it reopened, its stage witnessed the myriad triumphs of Edmund Kean, but despite his enormous successes the gross mismanagement of the theatre was evident in the net annual loss of income.

Success was again evident with the productions in the 1840's of William Charles Macready, but losses reappeared with his successors. One of the latter, Frederick Chatterton, delivered the famous dictum, "Shakespeare spelt ruin and Byron bankruptcy." Nevertheless, the Drury Lane has survived and continues to flourish.

Throughout the Drury Lane's long history, its name and that of Shakespeare have been inseparably linked. During the Restoration it was the scene of the King's Company revivals of *The Merry Wives of Windsor*, *Henry IV*, *Julius Caesar*, and *Othello*, and from 1682 to 1695 of Betterton's portrayals of Shakespearean heroes. Less memorable were the numerous "adaptations" of Shakespeare which were also staged at the Drury Lane; these included Nahum Tate's *Richard II* (1680) and Colley Cibber's version of *Richard III* (1700), which held the stage for many years. The Drury Lane witnessed Charles Macklin's great 1741 portrayal of Shylock, but the greatest era of Shakespearean production at the theatre came during the 30-year period of David Garrick's magnetic performances, from 1746 to 1776. The tradition established by Garrick was upheld by later successors, such as John Philip Kemble and Sarah Siddons toward the end of the century, and the financial difficulties in which its managers frequently found themselves in the course of the 19th century in no way diminished the Drury Lane's great productions starring Edmund Kean and William Charles Macready. In the 20th century the theatre's Shakespearean efforts have continued to capture audiences, largely through the notable presentations of Sir Henry Irving, Ellen Terry, and Sir Johnston Forbes-Robertson. [W. J. Macqueen-Pope, *Theatre Royal, Drury Lane*, 1946.]

Dryden, John (1631–1700). Poet, playwright, and critic. Born at Aldwinkle, Northamptonshire, Dryden was educated at the Westminster School in London and Trinity College, Cambridge. Although his family was Puritan, Dryden's religious sympathies turned to the Church of England and ultimately to Roman Catholicism. His political views, reflecting changes in the government of England, similarly became more conservative.

The most important English man of letters of his age, Dryden wrote a number of plays in addition to the lyric and satirical poetry for which he is chiefly remembered. Among his plays are *Marriage à la Mode* (1672), a salacious comedy of manners; *The Indian Emperor* (1665); *The Conquest of Granada* (in two parts, 1670; 1671) and *Aureng-Zebe* (1675), heroic tragedies done in rhymed couplets. Dryden's *Essay of Dramatic Poesy* (1668) is considered the most important English contribution to literary criticism in the 17th century. In it Dryden is concerned with the practical problem of deciding which models the contemporary playwright should follow: the ancients, the French, or the Elizabethan. The discussion leads to an evaluation of Shakespeare which defines, essentially, the course that was to be taken by Shakespeare criticism until the Romantic revolution of the following century.

It has been said of Dryden that "his virtues were his own, his faults those of his age." Nowhere is this attribute better illustrated than in his attitude toward Shakespeare. When he judges according to those critical canons which the Restoration derived from Italian and French Aristotelian formalists of the 16th and 17th centuries, Dryden deplores Shakespeare's irregularities and his lapses from good taste. But when Dryden liberates himself from neoclassic rules and speaks from the fullness of his intuitions as an artist, he reveres Shakespeare as "the man who of all modern, and perhaps ancient poets, had the largest and most comprehensive soul."

A child of his time, Dryden criticizes Shakespeare for not constructing unified plots. The histories "are rather so many chronicles of kings, or the business many times of 30 or 40 years, cramped into a representation of two hours and a half." By looking at nature "through the wrong end of a perspective," Shakespeare in these plays renders a distortedly small image of life. Other plays—*Pericles*, *The Winter's Tale*, *Love's Labour's Lost*, and *Measure for Measure*—are "either grounded on impossibilities" or else so badly written as to be unsatisfactory both in their comic and in their serious parts. Shakespeare and his contemporaries—with the solitary exception of Ben Jonson—ignore the neoclassic unities of time, place, and action. Although *Troilus and Cressida* begins promisingly, the end "is nothing but a confusion of drums and trumpets, excursions and alarms" (*Preface to Troilus and Cressida*, 1679). Moreover, it violates poetic justice: "Cressida is false, and is not punished." Shakespeare cannot be blamed entirely, however, for he wrote for a benighted age that doted upon ridiculous stories. Audiences demanded "magic supernatural things . . . And he then wrote, as people then believ'd" (*Prologue to The Tempest*, 1667).

Dryden's chief complaint against Shakespeare is that his language is improper, "his comic wit degenerating into clenches, his serious swelling into bombast." Every page yields "either some solecism of speech, or some notorious flaw in sense" (*Defence of the Epilogue*, 1672). So thoroughly has the English language been purified since Shakespeare's day, "that many of his words, and more of his phrases, are scarce intelligible. And of those which we understand, some are ungrammatical, others coarse; and his whole style is so pestered with figurative expressions, that it is as affected as it is obscure" (*Preface to Troilus*). Dryden selects for particular censure the player's speech in *Hamlet*, describing Hecuba's clamorous reaction to the death of Priam: "Wise men would be glad to find a little sense couched under all these pompous words; for bombast is commonly the delight of that audience which loves Poetry, but understands it not: and as commonly has been the practice of those writers, who, not being able to infuse a natural passion into the mind, have made it their business to ply the ears, and to stun their judges by the noise." Shakespeare could be carried away "beyond the bounds of judgment, either in coining of new words and phrases, or racking words which were in use, into the violence of a catachresis [misuse of words]."

The foregoing quotation belongs to a period in Dryden's life (c. 1679) when he seems especially to have felt the influence of Thomas Rymer, the neoclassic critic who attacked Shakespeare with single-minded vigor. Interestingly enough, he even assumes Rymer's manner, and, in fact, makes Rymer's customary mistake of not judging a speech in its appropriate dramatic context. (The Player's lament for Hecuba is *supposed* to be artificial and bombastic.) But it is characteristic of Dryden to accept Rymer's detailed strictures on Shakespeare without losing sight of the fact that Shakespeare was a genius.

Ultimately, then, Dryden rejects a narrow formalism. While acknowledging that Restoration poets are more polished and correct, he concedes that they cannot match their Elizabethan ancestors in strength. "Theirs was the giant race, before the flood" (*Epistle to Congreve*, 1694). Anyone can write regular plays and adhere to the unities. "But genius must be born, and never can be taught." Congreve is Shakespeare's spiritual descendant. "Heav'n, that but once was prodigal before, / To Shakespeare gave as much; she could not give him more." Although Dryden may be pleased with his own accomplishments, he confesses that "a secret shame/ Invades his breast at Shakespeare's sacred name" (*Prologue to Aureng-Zebe*, 1675). He draws inspiration from a portrait of Shakespeare that Sir Godfrey Kneller had painted and given to him. "With reverence [I] look on his majestic face; / Proud to be less, but of his godlike race" (*Epistle to Kneller*, 1694). It does not matter to Dryden that Shakespeare lacked formal learning. "He was naturally learn'd: he needed not the spectacles of books to read Nature; he looked inwards, and found her there." In this respect Shakespeare and Homer are alike, "in either of whom we find all arts and sciences, all moral and natural philosophy, without knowing that they ever studied them" (*Discourse Concerning Satire*, 1693).

By looking "inwards" Shakespeare created distinctive characters, among them Henry IV, Mercutio, Falstaff, and Caliban. In Caliban he brought forth "a person which was not in Nature," an extraordinary boldness yet one that Shakespeare carries off successfully. The quarrel between Brutus and Cassius is "incomparable," and there is nothing in any other language to match the passion and poignancy of the deposition scene in *Richard II*. Shakespeare is not consistent, but he is capable of sublimity. "He is always great, when some great occasion is presented to him; no man can say he ever had a fit subject for his wit, and did not then raise himself as high above the rest of the poets [as the tall cypresses generally tower above the lowly viburnum shrubs]."

Dryden's attitude toward Shakespeare is revealed not only in his poems and prefaces, but also in his actual writing for the stage. When the theatres were reopened in 1660 after having been closed during the Puritan interlude, the new companies, in the absence of a continuing performing tradition, depended initially upon revivals of Elizabethan plays, often "improved" to meet the allegedly superior tastes of Restoration playgoers. (See ADAPTATIONS.) The practice continued throughout the period. Apart from scattered verbal echoes and borrowings, Dryden derived three plays directly from Shakespeare: THE TEMPEST, OR THE ENCHANTED ISLAND (1667), a collaboration with Sir William Davenant; *All for Love* (1677), inspired by *Antony and Cleopatra;* and *Troilus and Cressida* (1679), an attempt to bring order out of Shakespeare's chaotic original.

Neither *The Tempest* nor *Troilus and Cressida* really resembles its Shakespearean source. Among the fanciful innovations in the Restoration *Tempest*—Davenant's ideas, one hopes!—are a male counterpart of Miranda, a man who has never seen a woman; a sweetheart for Ariel; and a sister for Caliban. Prospero is de-emphasized, and the low comedy scenes are expanded. In *Troilus and Cressida*, a better play, the heroine, who encourages Diomedes only that she might protect her father Calchas, kills herself to demonstrate her fidelity to Troilus. There is a strong scene between Troilus and Hector, and Dryden's Ulysses speaks somewhat in the vein of the speech on degree that is the ethical focus of Shakespeare's play. The Greek and Trojan warriors, however, are glorified rather than ridiculed. Shakespeare wrote a bitter satire against war and lechery; Dryden, a heroic tragedy—tidier, no doubt, but intellectually much less stimulating.

All for Love is a true adaptation rather than an "improvement." Where Shakespeare covers 11 years of history in 42 scenes that stretch throughout Egypt and the Roman empire, Dryden restricts the action to Alexandria during the lovers' last splendid day. Shakespeare's 34 characters are reduced to 12, with Octavius being omitted from the stage and with Ventidius absorbing many of the qualities of Enobarbus. Dryden introduces a confrontation between Cleopatra and Antony's wife Octavia—the two rivals do not meet in Shakespeare. What is indeed remarkable about Dryden's performance is that he has reshaped a massive romantic tragedy to meet the rigid requirements of neoclassic drama, attaining formal correctness and at the same time preserving the grandeur and intensity of tragic poetry. [John Dryden, *Works*, Sir Walter Scott, ed., 1808, revised by George Saintsbury, 18 vols., 1882–1893; Allardyce Nicoll, *Dryden as an Adapter of Shakespeare*, 1922;

ugustus Ralli, *A History of Shakespearean Criticism*, 2 vols., 1932; John O. Eidson, "Dryden's riticism of Shakespeare," *Studies in Philology*, XXIII, 1936; Ruth Wallerstein, "Dryden and the nalysis of Shakespeare's Techniques," *The Review f English Studies*, XIX, 1943; *The Critical Opinions f John Dryden: A Dictionary*, John M. Aden, ed., 963; George Watson, "Dryden's First Answer to ymer," *The Review of English Studies*, New Seies, XIV, 1963.]—D. M. Z.

Duchess of Malfi, The (1613–1614, pub. 1623). A ragedy by John WEBSTER, generally regarded as the reatest Jacobean drama outside of the works of hakespeare. *The Duchess of Malfi* was first acted y Shakespeare's company, the King's Men, at the lackfriars and the Globe. The play was published n 1623 with the names of the cast:

> The Actors Names. Bosola, *J. Lowin.* Ferdinand, *I, R. Burbidge, 2 J. Taylor.* Cardinall, *I H. Cundaile, 2 R. Robinson.* Antonio, *I. W. Ostler, 2 R. Benfeild.* Delio, *J. Underwood.* Forobosco, *N. Towley.* Pescara, *J. Rice.* Silvio, *T. Pollard.* Madmen, *N. Towley, J. Underwood, etc.* Cardinals Mis, *J. Tomson.* The Doctor, etc., *R. Pallant.* Duchess, *R. Sharpe.*

Vill Ostler, who played Antonio, died in 1614; thus he play must have been performed before that date. The indication that Joseph Taylor replaced Burbage n the role of Ferdinand makes it clear that the play ontinued to be performed after Burbage's death in 619. The play has a number of unimportant verbal choes of Shakespeare (Webster was a prolific colector of other men's lines), but its deepest affinity vith Shakespearean tragedy lies in its relentless, unentimental confrontation with the fact of death.

Ducis, Jean François (1733–1816). French dramaist. After several unsuccessful attempts at original laywriting, Ducis began a series of adaptations of Shakespeare's plays for the Comédie Française. His irst adaptation was a version of *Hamlet* presented in 1769. This was followed by adaptations of *Romeo nd Juliet* (1772), *King Lear* (1783), *Macbeth* (1784), and *Othello* (1792). Ducis' versions were ased not on the originals but on translations of Shakespeare, and he further diluted Shakespeare in n attempt to have the plays conform to the neolassical orientation of the French stage. See FRANCE.

dueling. See FENCING AND DUELING.

Dugdale, Sir William (1605–1686). Antiquary whose *Antiquities of Warwickshire* (1656) is an important early history of Shakespeare's native county. Dugdale was attached to the court of Charles I, holding a number of positions which gave him enough freedom to devote himself to antiquarian research. His publications included *Monasticon Anglicanum* (3 vols., 1655–1673), a massive historical account of English monasteries, and *The Baronage of England* (1676), a history of the English peerage.

Antiquities of Warwickshire concludes its account of the history and topography of Stratford with the following sentence:

> One thing more, in reference to this antient Town is observable, that it gave birth and sepulture to our late famous Poet *Will. Shakespere*, whose Monument I have inserted in my discourse of the Church.

An engraving of the monument mentioned in Dugdale's account was reproduced in his book; his diary, not published until the 19th century, mentions the sculptor of the monument as "Gerard Johnson." See Gerard JANSSEN.

Dukas, Paul. See MUSIC BASED ON SHAKESPEARE: *19th century, 1850–1900.*

Duke. In *As You Like It*, Rosalind's father. Deposed by his younger brother Frederick and living in exile in the Forest of Arden, the Duke accepts his banishment philosophically and, attended by a cheerful company of lords, can translate the "stubbornness of fortune" into a pleasantly peaceful existence. When Orlando arrives in Arden and violently demands food, the Duke gently invites him to his table. With the subsequent news of the restoration of his title and possessions, the Duke promises to share his good fortune with his faithful lords but, for the present, prefers to "forget this new-fall'n dignity" and exhorts the company to "rustic revelry" to celebrate the several weddings that have just taken place.

Duke, John (d. 1613). Actor. Duke is mentioned in the "plot" of the second part of THE SEVEN DEADLY SINS, which belongs to a revival of the play by Strange's Men about 1591. In that play Duke had the roles of the pursuivant in the Induction, a soldier in Envy, Will Fool in Sloth, and a lord in Lechery. In the 1590's he became a member of the Chamberlain's Men, and he appears in the actor list of *Every Man In his Humour* (1598). By 1602 he had become a member of Worcester's Men (which was renamed Queen Anne's Men the following year). He acted as payee for their court performances and was active in the company until 1612.

Duke Humphrey. An historical play, no longer extant, entered in the Stationers' Register as Shakespeare's in 1660 by Humphrey Moseley. The play undoubtedly dealt with the life of Humphrey, duke of Gloucester, who figures in *1* and *2 Henry VI.*

Duke of Venice. In *Othello*, a minor character who appears only in I, iii, the scene of the Senate meeting. The Duke appoints Othello commander of Cyprus and attempts to persuade Brabantio to accept the Moor as a son-in-law.

Duke of York's Men. See PRINCE CHARLES' MEN.

Duke's Company. A Restoration company of actors under the patronage of the duke of York, later James II. Originally formed by John Rhodes in 1660, the Duke's Company performed at the Phoenix theatre, later moving to the Salisbury Court. Shortly thereafter, William Davenant took charge of the company, and it was moved to LISLE'S TENNIS COURT in June 1661. Following Davenant's death in 1668, the company moved to a new theatre, the DORSET GARDEN. Here, under the leadership of Thomas Betterton, they continued to prosper until 1682 when they amalgamated with the King's Company and moved to the Drury Lane.

The original plays, as well as a number of adaptations of Shakespeare, were an important part of the repertory of the Duke's Company. On December 12, 1660 an edict of the lord chamberlain set aside certain plays as belonging to the company, including *The Tempest, Measure for Measure, Much Ado About Nothing, Romeo and Juliet, Twelfth Night, Henry VIII, King Lear, Macbeth,* and *Hamlet.* The company was also given sole rights for two months to produce *Pericles*. On August 20, 1668 the lord chamberlain added to the list of plays "allowed to be acted by his Royale Highnesse ye Duke of Yorkes Comoedians . . . *Timon of Athens, Troylus and Crisseida,* and *Three parts of H:ye 6*." The best remembered of the company's Shakespearean productions was that of *Hamlet* (1661) with Betterton in the title role, described by Pepys as "the best part, I believe, that ever man acted." See John DOWNES. [Hazelton Spencer, *Shakespeare Improved*, 1927.]

Dull, Anthony. In *Love's Labour's Lost*, an ignorant, unimaginative constable who arrests Costard on the complaint of Don Armado. In V, i, Dull is invited to perform in the presentation of the Nine Worthies; he agrees to dance or play on the tabor.

Dulwich College. See Edward ALLEYN.

Dumain. In *Love's Labour's Lost*, a handsome optimist and one of the three lords who are comrades in the vow, proposed by the King of Navarre, to lead the contemplative life and to reject women for three years. Dumain is, however, smitten with love for "the most divine Kate" and concocts an ode to her. Dumain's counterpart in history was the duc de Mayenne. See LOVE'S LABOUR'S LOST: *Sources*.

Dumas, Alexandre, *père*. See FRANCE.

Duncan I, King of Scotland (d. 1040). Grandson of Malcolm II, whose throne he inherited in 1034. It is probable that Duncan ruled the land south of Forth and Clyde, while his cousin Thorfinn ruled northern Scotland. Between the two domains lay Moray, ruled by Macbeth. Duncan granted the northern lands to his nephew Moddan, who was defeated by Thorfinn when he went to claim them; Duncan went to Moddan's assistance and was killed in battle by Macbeth, who had joined Thorfinn. In *Macbeth*, while a guest in Macbeth's castle, Duncan is murdered by his host, who has been prompted by ambition and by the urgings of Lady Macbeth. The regicide upon which Shakespeare based the incident in his play is historically that of King Duff, slain in 972 at the behest of Donwald, who had been urged to the deed by his ambitious wife. [W. H. Thomson, *Shakespeare's Characters: A Historical Dictionary*, 1951.]

Dunois, Jean. See ORLÉANS, BASTARD OF.

D'Urfey, Thomas (1653–1723). Dramatist and balladeer whose prolific literary productions include a Restoration adaptation of *Cymbeline*. Educated as a lawyer, D'Urfey turned to the more hazardous but exciting occupation of playwright and song-writer. His plays were distinguished by a boisterous vitality which won him as much favor at court as in the playhouses.

His adaptation of *Cymbeline* is called *The Injured Princess, or the Fatal Wager*. It follows Shakespeare's plot in the main, but introduces a subplot which requires some alteration of the ending. The Queen sentences Clarina (Shakespeare's Helen) to be raped by Jachima (a new character, not Shakespeare's Iachimo) for her supposed aid to Eugenia (Imogen). Pisanio kills Jachima as the sentence is about to be carried out under the direction of Cloten, and the old man is in turn blinded by Cloten. This whole affair is recounted in the final act as a rather effective demonstration of the extent of Cloten's villainy.

D'Urfey's alterations of Shakespeare's diction are minor except for some changes in the order of the scenes. The subplot, of course, required original writing. In addition to the changes in the names of the characters already mentioned, D'Urfey changes Posthumus to Ursaces and Iachimo to Shatillion, evidently not realizing the significance of "Little Iago." D'Urfey also attempts to tighten the construction of the final act by simplifying and condensing its many confrontations of characters and explanations of the preceding events, but he is not wholly successful. *The Injured Princess* was first produced at Dorset Garden in 1682 and was published the same year. [Hazelton Spencer, *Shakespeare Improved*, 1927.]

Dutton, John and **Lawrence.** See OXFORD'S MEN.

Dyce, Alexander (1798–1869). Scholar. A native of Scotland, he early became interested in literature and devoted his life principally to the publication of editions of earlier writers. He edited the work of Middleton, Greene, Webster, Beaumont and Fletcher and Marlowe. In 1857 he brought out his six-volume edition of Shakespeare, the textual accuracy of which made it highly regarded in its day. His later years were spent in revising and correcting his editions.

Dyer, Sir Edward (1543–1607). Courtier and poet. After studies at Oxford and travels abroad, Dyer entered the Elizabethan court and came under the patronage of Robert Dudley, earl of Leicester. He was knighted in 1596 after serving on diplomatic missions to the Netherlands and Denmark. Dyer had a high poetic reputation in his day, but little of his work has survived. He is most famous for the elegy on the death of his friend Sir Philip Sidney and for the lyric "My mind to me a kingdom is." Alden Brooks has constructed an elaborate thesis (*Will Shakspere and the Dyer's Hand*, 1943), "proving" that Dyer is the author of Shakespeare's plays.

E

Earl of Nottingham's Men. See ADMIRAL'S MEN.

Eastward Ho! (1605). A comedy written by George CHAPMAN, Ben JONSON, and John MARSTON. *Eastward Ho!* was first performed by the Children of the Queen's Revels in 1605 at the Blackfriars. Since it contained "something against the Scots," the play was regarded as personally insulting to King James. Consequently, the company lost the patronage of the Queen; Marston fled to the continent, and Chapman went to prison, where he was voluntarily joined by Jonson. Somehow, the play itself escaped censure. It was revived by Lady Elizabeth's Men in 1613, and given by them at court in January, 1614.

Eaton, William (fl. 1604–1612). An apprentice of Christopher Mountjoy who testified as to Shakespeare's involvement in the BELOTT-MOUNTJOY SUIT.

Eccles, John. See MUSIC BASED ON SHAKESPEARE: *17th century*.

Eccles, Mark (1905–). American scholar, professor of English at the University of Wisconsin. Eccles' *Christopher Marlowe in London* (1934) depicts the milieu of the poet. His *Shakespeare in Warwickshire* (1961) supplies information about Shakespeare's contemporaries in his native county.

Ecclestone or **Eglestone, William** (d. post 1625). Actor. Ecclestone was a member of the King's Men, Shakespeare's company, but little is known of his origins. He was with the King's Men in 1610 and 1611, when he appeared in Jonson's *Alchemist* and *Catiline*. For the next two years he acted and toured with Lady Elizabeth's Men (from 1611 to about 1613). He had already left that company when its members drew up a list of grievances in 1615 against their manager, Philip Henslowe. He is in the King's Men official lists of 1619 and 1621, and is one of the "principall Actors" cited in the 1623 First Folio of Shakespeare. He is in every King's Men acting list from *Bonduca* (1613 or 1614) to *The Spanish Curate* (1622). In the stage directions for the Folio of *All's Well That Ends Well*, the inscription of the initial "E." has led to a conclusion that Ecclestone may have played one of the minor roles.

He was a resident of St. Saviour's parish, in the registry of which is recorded his marriage in 1603 to Anne Jacob. It is not known, however, when he left the company, although his name does not appear in the patent the company received from Charles I in 1625. Traditionally, he is thought to have lived to a very old age, but it is not known when he died. [E. K. Chambers, *The Elizabethan Stage*, 1923; G. E. Bentley, *The Jacobean and Caroline Stage*, 5 vols., 1941–1956.]

Edgar. In *King Lear*, the legitimate son of the Earl of Gloucester. Forced into hiding by the machinations of his illegitimate half-brother Edmund, he assumes the disguise of a half-naked "Tom o'Bedlam," a term used to describe inmates of Bedlam Hospital, a London insane asylum, who were released periodically to beg for money to pay their keep. When Lear, the Fool, and Kent take refuge from the storm in a hovel (III, iv), they find the supposedly mad beggar there, and the sight of Edgar's wretchedness prompts Lear to observe that "unaccommodated man is no more but such a poor, bare, forked animal as thou art" and to tear off his own clothes. Later Edgar, still wearing his disguise, hears the blind Gloucester acknowledge his errors and becomes his guide. At the end of the play he is left to rule England and sustain "the gored state."

Edkins or **Etkyns, Thomas** (fl. 1550–1595). Shakespeare's uncle. Edkins married Katharine Arden (see ARDEN FAMILY), the sister of Shakespeare's mother, sometime before 1550. Edkins had at least two sons, Thomas and Adam. In 1576 he and his wife sold their share in the Arden estate to their brother-in-law Thomas Stringer. [Mark Eccles, *Shakespeare in Warwickshire*, 1961.]

Edmund. In *King Lear*, the illegitimate son of the Earl of Gloucester. Resentful of his inferior status and determined to obtain the property of his legitimate half-brother Edgar, he contrives the latter's banishment. Later, his perfidy results in Gloucester's blinding by Cornwall and Regan. After Edmund has ordered that the captive Cordelia be hanged, he is mortally wounded by Edgar in formal combat and, repenting of his misdeeds, vainly tries to countermand his execution order. Like two of Shakespeare's other great villains, Richard III and Iago, Edmund has affinities with the familiar figure of medieval morality plays, the Vice. His villainy is never modulated by self-deception or indecision; in fact, his extraordinary self-awareness and personal insight are his most striking qualities.

Edmund Ironside. A manuscript play attributed to Shakespeare. *Edmund Ironside* is found in a manuscript collection of 15 plays (*Egerton MS. 1994*) now in the British Museum. The play deals with the life of Edmund Ironside (d. 1016), a Saxon ruler in 11th-century Britain. A recent student of the play, E. B. Everitt, dates its writing between 1585 and 1590 and argues that in theme, style, and imagery it bears a strong resemblance to Shakespeare's works. Everitt argues further that the manuscript is in Shakespeare's hand. His theory, however, has not been accepted by most authorities. [E. B. Everitt, *Young Shakespeare; Studies in Documentary Evidence*, Anglistica, II 1954.]

Edmund of Langley. See Edmund of Langley, 1st duke of YORK.

education. Shakespeare's schooling, like that of other Stratford boys, probably began in a petty school (pre-grammar school), when he was about five years old. John and Mary Shakespeare did not need to employ a tutor to teach William to read. There were both private and public petty schools in Stratford which provided for the first step in a child's education. A petty school was probably attached to the Stratford grammar school. There a child could master his hornbook and his abc book.

The hornbook was so called because it consisted of a sheet of paper placed on a wooden board protected by a sheet of transparent horn (a tough, fibrous material). On the board was printed the alphabet, first in small letters, and then in capitals; next the five vowels, then simple syllables; and finally the Lord's Prayer. After the child had mastered these simple fundamentals, he went on to the abc book, an elementary book for teaching reading, i.e., a primer. At the same time he learned writing from a copybook. The style of writing taught when Shakespeare was in school was the old English script, resembling modern German script, and sharply different from the Italian hand that was just coming into use in Elizabethan England. Persons unfamiliar with old English script make the mistake of pronouncing Shakespeare's signatures illegible, those of an illiterate man. As a matter of fact, his handwriting was quite legible. See HANDWRITING.

The Stratford grammar school had been established by the corporation of the town in 1553, to serve as a direct successor to the medieval Guild school, and was housed in the Guild Hall. It was one of the best in England. The master's salary, including what are now called "fringe benefits," amounted to about £40 a year, a compensation not much less than that of the provost of Eton. We have no proof that William attended this school, but the son of a man as prominent as his father in town affairs would certainly have been sent there. If he had entered the school at the usual age of seven, he would have begun his formal education in 1571.

The main business of the 300 grammar schools of Shakespeare's England in the first four forms was the teaching of Latin grammar. At this dreary task the small boys labored summer and winter from 7 to 11 in the morning and returned at one o'clock to stay until 5. The discipline was harsh. The master hung up his rod where all the children could see it and used it often in merciless beatings. The small scholars were first put through William Lily's *Grammatica Latina*, 10,000 copies of which were sold each year in Elizabethan England. Every word of this official schoolbook the boys had to commit to memory. Sir Hugh Evans, the Welsh schoolmaster in *The Merry Wives of Windsor*, gives the boy William a quiz that is doubtless a replica of many that the master of the Stratford school gave William Shakespeare:

Evans . . . . What is he, William, that does lend articles?

AN ELIZABETHAN SCHOOLROOM. WOODCUT FROM A BALLAD.

William. Articles are borrowed of the pronoun and be thus declined, Singulariter, nominativo hic, haec, hoc . . . .
Evans. What is your genitive case plural, William?
William. Genitive case!
Evans. Ay.
William. Genitive,—horum, harum, horum.
(IV, i, 39–63)

The next required text was a collection of Latin axioms called *Sententiae Pueriles*, which also had to be learned by heart (see Leonard CULMAN). It was followed by the so-called *Distiches* (proverbs) of Cato. The boys then went on to *Aesop's Fables* and the *Eclogues* of Baptista Spagnuoli Mantuanus (i.e. of Mantua). First printed in 1500, this work, much admired for its pure style, at once became a popular textbook. Holofernes, the schoolmaster in *Love's Labour's Lost*, expresses appropriate admiration for "Mantuan." He exclaims, "Old Mantuan, old Mantuan! who understandeth thee not, loves thee not" (IV, ii, 101–102).

From the fourth form on the boys read some of the great Latin classics, Cicero's *Letters*, Vergil's *Eclogues*, and, most of all, Ovid. Shakespeare refers to him more often than to any other ancient author. The source of nearly all the mythology that he seems to know is Ovid's *Metamorphoses*, especially the first two books. Although in school he read the work in Latin, he seems later to have turned more often to Arthur Golding's metrical English translation, the first four books published in 1565, the entire fifteen in 1567.

The students in the upper forms read Plautus and Terence, some of whose plays they used to act under the direction of the master. These productions gave the boys training in the correct and effective use of the voice and in the proper modulation and accentuation of expression in the recitation of dramatic speeches. This forensic experience was of undoubted benefit to the actor that Shakespeare was to become.

The studies in logic and rhetoric that formed the greater part of the curriculum of the grammar schools' upper forms were the subjects most useful to the future dramatist. From the Middle Ages to Shakespeare's day Cicero was held in high esteem principally for his works in rhetoric and morals. It is, therefore, no surprise to find that his *Topics* (prepared forms of argument) was given to the boys to serve as their grounding in logic. This was followed by Joannes Susenbrotus' *Epitome of the Topics and Figures of grammar and rhetoric* (*Epitome Troporum ac Schematum et grammaticorum et rhetorum*, c. 1540). This book contained the definitions and illustrations of 132 figures of speech. Then came Erasmus' explanation of the two ways of securing copiousness or amplification both of diction and of matter ("De duplici copia verborum"). He explained that the way to secure copiousness in diction was by means of the figures (the forms of syllogism) and a large vocabulary. To obtain amplification of matter, Erasmus recommended the use of the topic of logic. The boys in the upper forms devoted five or six hours a day to illustrating the proper use of these rhetorical figures in their own compositions. Finally they were required to compose epistles in Latin, first in prose, then in verse, following the rules laid down by Erasmus in "How to compose Epistles" ("Modus conscribendi Epistolas"). Of the Latin poets Ovid was most thoroughly studied. The boys memorized the *Metamorphoses* at the rate of 12 lines a week up to a total of 500. His *Heroides* (letters from heroines), which often reveal dramatic power, the boys used as models for their verses. Among other Latin poetical works read at school were Vergil's *Eclogues*, his *Georgics*, and the *Aeneid*. In the last two forms the study of Greek began. This summary of the rhetorical and poetic works taught in Elizabethan grammar schools is partial and selective. For a full treatment of the subject a student must go to T. W. Baldwin's *William Shakspere's Small Latine and Lesse Greeke*. In this context Jonson's famous phrase has ironical overtones. A dramatist saturated with this prolonged study of rhetoric and poetry during his formative years made abundant use of his lessons in his first plays. See RHETORIC; William SHAKESPEARE, HIS PLAYS AND POEMS: *The Early Years*.

One of the most important of school textbooks in Shakespeare's day was Quintilian's *De Institutione Oratoria*, a comprehensive description of the proper education, training, and technique of an orator. Shakespeare betrays some familiarity with this famous work.

Seneca's tragedies were usually studied in the last two years of school, along with the *Colloquies* of Erasmus. Some grammar schools introduced Greek grammar into the fifth form curriculum. In the light of this fact, Jonson's famous line "And though thou hadst small Latine and lesse Greeke" suggests that Shakespeare had acquired in school a smattering of Greek. Else why had Jonson not written "no Greek"?

The school curriculum in history consisted solely of Latin historians: Caesar's *Commentaries on the Gallic War*, Sallust's *Catiline's Conspiracy*, *The Jugurthan War*, and *Annales*, a history of Rome from 78 to 67 B.C., of which only fragments are extant, and Livy's *History of Rome*, from its foundation down to the death of Drusus (9 B.C.). These histories were studied for the lessons that experience taught, and their moral significance. When Shakespeare began to write the history of the Wars of the Roses from Henry VI through Richard III, he kept his audiences continually aware of the moral and political issues at stake.

The succession of headmasters of the Stratford grammar school during Shakespeare's boyhood could have acquainted him with the current struggle between the old faith and the new Protestantism. At the time William would have entered the school, the master was Walter ROCHE, an active Protestant. He first engaged Simon HUNT as an usher to help him with the teaching of the younger boys. When Roche resigned from the post in 1571, Hunt succeeded him. His sympathies were with the Catholics, and after his retirement in 1577 he became a professed Catholic, went to the Catholic seminary at Douay, to the English College for priests in Rome, and finally became a Jesuit. If Shakespeare was brought up in a Catholic household, as is probable (see John SHAKESPEARE), he must have found Hunt a sympathetic teacher. In 1577 Hunt was succeeded by a Welshman, Thomas JENKINS, who came to Stratford from the Warwick grammar school, one of England's best. His Welsh brogue may be ridiculed in the character of Sir Hugh Evans in *The Merry Wives of Windsor*, who makes fritters of the English language. In 1579, John Cottam succeeded Jenkins. Cottam retained the post until 1582. By that time Shakespeare had surely left the school. All these four masters were Oxford graduates and, by the standards of the day, well-educated men. But they taught nothing but Latin and rhetoric—no mathematics, no science. The French of which Shakespeare shows a little knowledge he must have learned from the many Frenchmen who came to London to teach their language. See John ELIOT.

Like all of his fellow grammar school pupils, Shakespeare was made familiar with the Bible. Up to about 1596–1597 his allusions are to the text of the Bishop's Bible (1568), which he would hear read in church. After that date, they are more frequently to the Geneva Bible (1560). In the plays there are scores of definite references to situations and characters in both Old and New Testament and in the Apocrypha. The Prayer Book was an equally important source of the poet's religious phrases and ideas. The Psalms he remembers in the Prayer Book versions. Phrases of morning and evening prayers are frequently echoed in the plays. Many of his political views were founded on the doctrines enunciated in *The Book of Homilies* (1563), many of which, particularly the sermons on "Obedience," "Disobedience," and "Wilful Rebellion," he heard read from the pulpit (see HOMILIES). Regular attendance at the parish church had played as important a part in the development of his mind and his permanent attitudes toward traditional learning, as did his studies at school. [Charles Hoole, *A New Discovery*, 1660; Foster Watson, *The Curriculum and Textbooks of English Schools*, 1901; H. R. D. Anders, *Shakespeare's Books*, 1904; Foster Watson, *The English Grammar Schools to 1660*, 1908; Sir Edward Maunde Thompson, *Shakespeare's Handwriting*, 1916; E. I. Fripp, *Shakespeare, Man and Artist*, 1938; T. W. Baldwin, *William Shakspere's Petty School*, 1943; T. W. Baldwin, *William Shakspere's Small Latine and Lesse Greeke*, 1944; Sister Miriam Joseph, *Shakespeare's Use of the Arts of Language*, 1947.]—O. J. C.

Edward, Prince of Wales. See EDWARD V.

Edward II (c. 1592). A tragedy by Christopher MARLOWE. Entered in the Stationers' Register in 1593, *Edward II* was first published in 1594 as "The troublesome raigne and lamentable death of Edward the second, King of England: With the tragicall fall of proud Mortimer. As it was sundrie times publiquely acted in the honourable citie of London, by the right honourable the Earl of Pembroke his servants. Written by Chri. Marlowe. Gent."

No play of Marlowe's is more closely related to one of Shakespeare's than is *Edward II* to *Richard II.* For decades scholars assumed that Marlowe's was the first significant English chronicle history play, and that therefore he taught Shakespeare much. Recently, however, it has been established that Shakespeare's *Henry VI* trilogy antedates *Edward II;* in other words, Shakespeare helped Marlowe; the combination of Shakespeare-Marlowe helped Shakespeare in *Richard II.* The intricacies of these interrelationships are detailed and complex.

The two plays in question concern Kings who, because of grievous personal weaknesses, are unable to maintain order in the realm and therefore find themselves in conflict with their peers. Edward is infatuated with Gaveston, a French upstart on whom the King lavishes abnormal attention and every available title of nobility and power. This infuriates the English lords and particularly Edward's Queen, Isabella, who, being familiar with the first act of Marlowe's *Dido,* describes the Edward-Gaveston relationship with pinpoint accuracy: "never doted Jove on Ganymede / So much as he on cursed Gaveston."

The noblemen, overbearing and seemingly interested in the welfare of their King, Queen, and country, force the exile of Gaveston. Edward suffers a prolonged fit of petulant desolation until Gaveston is returned. Infuriated again, the lords, apparently omnipotent, contrive the murder of Gaveston. Edward immediately takes a new favorite, Young Spencer, attacks the recalcitrant noblemen, defeats them, and decapitates Warwick and Lancaster, the senior leaders. Young Mortimer, the chief hope of the lords, escapes and joins the Queen, who has fled to her native France to raise a power. Together they invade England, defeat and capture Edward. Under pressure Edward "gives the crown" after his requests to "take my crown" are unavailing (this anticipates the finest ambiguity in *Richard II:* the question is abdication or usurpation; both Kings recognize abdication as a foul crime; both abdicate and then persuade themselves that their crowns were usurped). Edward dies a wretched death: he is forced to stand 10 days in the sewer of Killingworth Castle, up to his knees in water and filth, with someone nearby beating a drum to make sleep impossible. Finally, he is placed on a feather bed and stomped to death with a table on top of him to prevent bruises.

Edward II discloses a radical change in Marlowe's style and dramatic organization. Gone is the "mighty line" and the superman in whose reflection all other characters live and have their being. Instead there is an approach to the give and take of ordinary characters conversing in this world, and Marlowe makes an effort to suit the speech to the person speaking it. In place of the great central character, the chief source of unity in the earlier plays, we have Young Mortimer and Edward in sharp contrast and mortal conflict. As Edward falls, Mortimer prospers; the wheel of fortune turns as it never did in *Tamburlaine,* as it does again for Richard and Bolingbroke in Shakespeare. But there is a difference. At the end of *Edward II,* Mortimer, who changes rapidly fro a patriot to a Machiavellian, is dead, and the King Edward's son, young Edward III, whose first reg actions, like those of Henry V, show that order wi be restored to England and the divinity of a kin respected. Marlowe's budding concern for order an degree marks the closest approach he made to Shake speare's view of the world.—G. W. M.

Edward III. An anonymous history play, regarde by many as having been at least partly written b Shakespeare. The play was entered in the Stationer Register in 1595 and published in the following yea by Cuthbert Burby as *The Raigne of King Edwar the Third.* The play was first ascribed to Shakespea by Humphrey Moseley in a catalogue of plays pub lished in 1656. The attribution was supported by th Shakespeare scholar Edward Capell in the 18t century, and in the 19th by the poet Tennyson an the scholars A. W. Ward and F. G. Fleay. Amon those who reject the attribution to Shakespeare there is a tendency to assign the play to Georg Peele.

A recent study of the imagery of the play b Kenneth Muir has demonstrated some interestin correspondences to Shakespeare's work, particularl to *Henry V* and *Measure for Measure.* The play als contains a line ("Lilies that fester smell far wors than weeds"), which serves as the concluding line o Sonnet 94. Large sections of the play, however, are s uncharacteristic of Shakespeare as to preclude an possibility of his having written it in its entirety Muir suggests that the play as we have it represent Shakespeare's hasty revision of the original, majo portions of which he left untouched. [Kenneth Muir *Shakespeare as Collaborator,* 1960.]

Edward IV (1442–1483). King of England, son o Richard, duke of York, and Cicely Neville. As th earl of March, Edward helped the Yorkists Warwic and Salisbury to defeat Henry VI's royal army a Northampton. After his father's death at Wakefiel in 1460, Edward was proclaimed king; he wa crowned after his victory over the Lancastrians a Towton. While Warwick was negotiating a matc for Edward with Bona of Savoy in 1464, the kin married Elizabeth Woodville (Lady Grey). Conse quently, the insulted earl began to plot against him After an attack in which Warwick was joined b Queen Margaret and the king's brother, the duke o Clarence, Edward overcame the rebels, killing War wick and Edward, prince of Wales, and capturin the latter's parents, Queen Margaret and Henry V

In *2 Henry VI,* Edward and his brother Richard Duke of Gloucester, are called in to stand bail fo their father on his arrest for treason. In *3 Henry VI* the two brothers press York to usurp the throne Yielding to them, York goes to battle against Mar garet at Wakefield, where he is murdered. Edward then defeats the Lancastrians at Towton, become King, and marries Lady Elizabeth Grey. Capture by the Lancastrians, he temporarily loses his crow to Henry. After his escape, however, Edward is vic torious at Barnet and Tewkesbury, and so regain the throne. His death occurs in *Richard III.*

Edward V (1470–1483). King of England, eldes son of Edward IV and Elizabeth Woodville. He wa born during Henry VI's temporary restoration t the throne. When his father regained the monarchy in 1471, young Edward became prince of Wales and was entrusted to the protection of his uncles Clarence, Gloucester, and Rivers. He became king at 13 and reigned for two months while the Woodvilles contended with Richard, duke of Gloucester. The latter gaining control of the kingdom, Edward was committed to the Tower, where he was soon joined by his younger brother Richard, duke of York. The boys were murdered (some say by order of the usurping king, Richard III), Edward having been deposed on the ground that his parents' marriage was invalid.

In *3 Henry VI,* the infant Edward appears with his nurse and is saluted by his uncles Clarence and Gloucester with a kiss. In *Richard III,* he and his brother are persuaded to stay at the Tower until Edward's coronation. There they are murdered on the instructions of their uncle Richard, who himself takes the crown.

Edward Plantagenet (1453–1471). Prince of Wales, the only son of Henry VI and Queen Margaret. When parliament named the duke of York heir to the throne in 1460, Edward was cut off from the succession, for on York's death, the duke's son became King Edward IV. In the meantime, Queen Margaret, who had rallied support for the royal house of Lancaster, suffered defeat at Towton, after which battle she fled with her son, first to Scotland, and then to France. After the earl of Warwick deserted the Yorkists for the Lancastrians, Prince Edward and Margaret joined him in his invasion of England in 1471. They were defeated at Tewkesbury, where Edward was captured and killed.

In *3 Henry VI,* King Henry, admitting that his claim to the throne is weak, names York as his heir, but Queen Margaret vows to maintain Edward's birthright. Later, after the reconciliation with Warwick, Edward is betrothed to that earl's eldest daughter. At the battle of Tewkesbury the Prince is stabbed to death by King Edward IV and his brothers.

Edwards, Richard (1524–1566). Dramatist. Educated at Oxford, Edwards became Master of the Children of the Chapel in 1561. Under his tutelage the Children prospered, giving a number of performances at court. In 1565 they acted in Edwards' *Damon and Pythias,* a play which marks a milestone in English drama because it presents a fusion of Latin comedy and tragedy with the native English comic tradition. Edwards, describing the play in the Prologue, coins the term "tragical comedy." Edwards is also the author of *Palamon and Arcite,* a lost, two-part play presented before Elizabeth at Oxford in 1566. The play, which is based on Chaucer's *Knight's Tale,* may have been a source of Shakespeare and Fletcher's *Two Noble Kinsmen.*

According to Thomas Warton's *History of English Poetry* (1774–1781), Edwards was also the author of a jest-book which contained a version of the Christopher Sly story in the Induction to *The Taming of the Shrew.*

Egeus. In *A Midsummer Night's Dream,* Hermia's father, who stubbornly insists that she marry Demetrius. Egeus threatens his daughter with death or an austere life in a nunnery if she denies his wishes. He is overruled by Theseus when Demetrius rediscovers his love for Helena.

Eglamour, Sir. In *The Two Gentlemen of Verona,* a courtly gentleman who has taken a vow of chastity on his wife's grave. Sir Eglamour accompanies Silvia in her flight to join Valentine but runs off when they encounter a band of outlaws.

Eglestone, William. See William Ecclestone.

Elbow. In *Measure for Measure,* a constable given to malapropisms. Elbow brings before the deputies two "notorious benefactors," Pompey and Froth, who are disreputable associates of Mistress Overdone. Elbow accuses Froth of abusing Mistress Elbow (II, i).

Eld or Elde, George (d. 1624). London printer of the first editions of the *Sonnets* (1609) and *Troilus and Cressida* (1609). An apprentice from 1592 to 1600, Eld was located at The Printer's Press, Fleet Lane. He printed the *Sonnets* for the publisher Thomas Thorpe and *Troilus and Cressida* for Richard Bonian and Henry Walley.

Eleanor or **Elinor of Aquitaine** (1122?–1204). Daughter of William X, duke of Aquitaine. Eleanor was married in 1137 to Louis VII of France and divorced from him in 1152. The same year she married Henry, count of Anjou and duke of Normandy, who became Henry II of England. It was a loveless marriage, and Eleanor consequently sided against her husband when her sons revolted against him in 1173. She was arrested and placed under guard until his death. On the accession of her son Richard I, Eleanor became extremely powerful in the affairs of state. When Richard died, she achieved the succession for his brother, John, thereby depriving her grandson, Arthur, whose claim to the throne was more valid than that of John.

In *King John,* Elinor appears as Henry II's widow. She is a dishonest and ignoble Queen, who, although aware of the tenuousness of her son John's claim to the English throne, nevertheless supports him in opposition to his young nephew, Arthur.

Elector Palatine's Men. See Admiral's Men.

Elgar, Edward. See music based on Shakespeare: *20th century.*

Eliot, John (b. 1562). A teacher of French and a possible acquaintance of Shakespeare. A native of Shakespeare's home county of Warwickshire, Eliot was educated at Oxford. He traveled throughout Europe in the 1580's, returning to England at the end of the decade and taking a position as a teacher of French. In 1593 he published his *Ortho-epia Gallica* or *Eliot's Fruits for the French,* a French-English conversation manual, enlivened by a number of parodies and humorous digressions. Traces of Eliot's book have been seen in some of the scenes in *2 Henry IV* and *Henry V* in which French is employed. More important, if true, however, is Frances Yates' argument that Eliot provides a significant clue to the veiled topical allusions in *Love's Labour's Lost.* According to Miss Yates, he was Shakespeare's source for the activities of the French aristocracy which provide the basis of that play. [Frances A. Yates, *A Study of Love's Labour's Lost,* 1936; J. W. Lever, "Shakespeare's French Fruits," *Shakespeare Survey 6,* 1953.]

Eliot, T[homas] S[tearns] (1888–1965). American-born poet, critic, and playwright. Born in St. Louis, Missouri, of a New England family, and educated at Harvard, the Sorbonne, and Merton College, Oxford,

Eliot was perhaps the most commanding literary figure of his generation. He became a British subject in 1927. His poetry, which is sophisticated and addressed to a highly literate audience, includes "The Love Song of J. Alfred Prufrock" (1915), *The Waste Land* (1922), "The Hollow Men" (1925), *Ash Wednesday* (1930), and *Four Quartets* (1943). It shows the influence of John Donne and the metaphysical poets, the French symbolists, and Ezra Pound. Eliot's verse dramas include *Murder in the Cathedral* (1935), *The Family Reunion* (1939), *The Cocktail Party* (1950), and *The Confidential Clerk* (1954). His influential critical essays examine the works of writers such as Andrew Marvell, John Dryden, Dante, and a number of Elizabethan dramatists. Among Eliot's critical studies are *The Sacred Wood* (1920), *For Launcelot Andrewes* (1929), *Dante* (1929), *The Use of Poetry and the Use of Criticism* (1933), *After Strange Gods* (1934), and *The Three Voices of Poetry* (1954). What now seems his most significant critical achievement is contained in *The Selected Essays* (1932).

Eliot's criticism deals essentially with aesthetic questions and matters of artistic technique. In early Eliot, a poet of the past is valued in proportion to the relevance of his diction and technical devices to 20th-century literature. By this standard Milton and, to some extent, Shakespeare had to give way to Donne, Dryden, and Dante. Despite his espousal of classicism, Eliot is often subjective and romantic in his approach. Shakespeare, he wrote, is "occupied with the struggle—which alone constitutes life for a poet—to transmute his personal and private agonies into something rich and strange, something universal and impersonal."

Eliot's best-known treatment of Shakespeare is his celebrated essay "Hamlet and His Problems" (in *Selected Essays*), an attempt to explain why *Hamlet* "is most certainly an artistic failure." In the course of his presentation, he invokes the famous dictum of the "objective correlative," which subsequently came to be regarded as a critical principle of great significance. The "objective correlative," according to Eliot, is "the only way of expressing emotion in art." This is achieved by employing an external object or event which will evoke in the reader an emotion equivalent to the state of mind of a given character. *Hamlet* is a failure because there are no adequate objective equivalents to Hamlet's emotion: "Hamlet [the man] is dominated by an emotion . . . [which] is in excess of the facts as they appear." See HAMLET: *Selected Criticism* for an extract from this essay.

A more general exposition is Eliot's "Shakespeare and the Stoicism of Seneca," also in *Selected Essays*, in which he argues that Shakespeare adapted from Seneca "an attitude of self-dramatization assumed by Shakespeare's heroes at moments of tragic intensity." As an example of the self-dramatizing hero, Eliot cites Othello, thus inspiring a new and controversial critical attitude toward that character. See OTHELLO, character entry and OTHELLO: *Selected Criticism*.

Toward the end of his life, Eliot gave evidence of having changed some of his views in regard to Shakespeare. In 1955, rereading his essays on Elizabethan playwrights, he was pleased with those concerned with minor figures, while the two concerned with Shakespeare "embarrassed" him because of their "callowness." Eliot suggested that consistency in one's view of Shakespeare is the hallmark of a little mind: "A lifetime is not too long" for the study of Shakespeare, and "the development of one's opinion may be the measurement of one's development in wisdom." See CRITICISM—20TH CENTURY.

Elizabeth (c. 1437?–1492). Queen of Edward IV daughter of the 1st Earl Rivers and Jacquetta of Luxembourg. Elizabeth married Sir John Grey, who was killed at the second battle of St. Albans in 1461 Because of her family's alliance with the Lancastrian party, Elizabeth forfeited her inheritance when Edward IV became king. When she appealed personally to him for help, he fell in love with her, and in 1464 they were secretly married. After Edward's death and the accession of Richard III, Elizabeth was persuaded by the king to deliver her daughters into his care. This action so angered the earl of Richmond, who had proposed to marry her daughter Elizabeth, that when he became King Henry VII, he took the queen dowager's lands from her. Henry did marry the young Elizabeth, and her mother withdrew to the Abbey of Bermondsey, where she subsequently died.

In *3 Henry VI*, Elizabeth first appears as the widowed Lady Grey. King Edward falls in love with her, and they are married just as negotiations are being completed for his marriage to Bona of Savoy In *Richard III*, she is Edward's queen. After her husband dies, and on hearing that her supporters have been imprisoned by Richard, Elizabeth seeks sanctuary for herself and for her younger son, Richard duke of York. Later, she finds it expedient to agree to convey Richard's proposal of marriage to her daughter.

Elizabeth I (1533–1603). Queen of England (1558-1603). The daughter of Anne Bullen and Henry VIII Elizabeth inherited her mother's flirtatious charm and her father's ruthlessness. To this combination she brought her own distinctive characteristics of intelligence and a capacity for hard work. The early years of her life were spent in an atmosphere of intrigue and terror (on at least one occasion she narrowly escaped execution) which had a strong impact on her later life. She came to the throne in 1558, six years before the birth of Shakespeare. A young woman of 25, she inherited a series of social, religious, political, and economic problems that threatened to topple England into chaos. Her own claim to the throne was disputed by many of her countrymen, political intrigues and plots were commonplace and the threat of invasion by her Spanish brother-in-law, Philip II, was imminent. In this potentially anarchic situation she steered a course which was to leave England one of the strongest and most prosperous nations in Europe by the end of her reign.

It is still a matter of debate whether the principal credit for this achievement lies with Elizabeth herself, or with her able and devoted administrators led by William Cecil, Lord BURGHLEY. In any case the credit for the selection of those subordinates belongs to her; her appointments are all the more commendable when it is realized that in making them she frequently disregarded her personal favorites Thus in spite of her long, intense involvement with the earl of LEICESTER, he was never able to unseat Burghley as her principal political adviser. This is

ELIZABETH I. PORTRAIT BY AN UNKNOWN ARTIST. (NATIONAL PORTRAIT GALLERY)

ven more applicable to her last great favorite, the eadstrong, impulsive earl of ESSEX, whose ambitions he continually frustrated.

Whatever her actual role in the emergence of ngland as a great world power, probably her greatst achievement lay in the symbolic value with which he invested herself. The image she projected to ngland and the world of the "Virgin Queen" (the ccuracy of this epithet remains one of the great ysteries about her) not only generated a sincere lolatry among the English people but also served as useful aid to her foreign policy. Elizabeth continully dangled her marriageability before the princes f Europe, thereby gaining a distinct advantage in iplomatic maneuvering. In the eyes of most of her ountrymen she was the paragon represented by the ymbolic figure of Gloriana in Spenser's *Faerie ueene*. To this role she was ideally suited, and beame the subject of paeans by most of the poets of er age, a fact which renders inscrutable Shakeeare's apparent absence from the ranks of those ho sang her praise.

As an actor and playwright Shakespeare would ave reason to be particularly grateful to Elizabeth, or she was an active and generous patron of the heatre. She not only cultivated her own acting ompany (the Queen's Men), but she stood as a ulwark against the opposition of the puritanical city athers to the players. Without this active support rom the crown, the Elizabethan theatre would never ave survived. Her attraction to the theatre was ooted in a love of spectacle and excitement, to hich she gave free reign in the years following the riumph over the Armada in 1588. In the 1590's the ourt revels became more elaborate and court perormances by the acting companies more frequent. Not surprisingly, Shakespeare's company was selected for these court performances more than any other. Despite this patronage, Shakespeare's references to Elizabeth are surprisingly meager. The only allusion generally accepted as referring directly to the queen is in *A Midsummer Night's Dream*, where Oberon describes Cupid's vain attempt to ensnare "a fair vestal throned by the west":

> But I might see young Cupid's fiery shaft
> Quench'd in the chaste beams of the watery
> moon,
> And the imperial votaress passed on,
> In maiden meditation, fancy-free.
> (II, i, 161–164)

There is also an open reference in the famous culminating speech in *Henry VIII* where, on the occasion of the infant Elizabeth's baptism, it is said of her that

> she shall be—
> But few now living can behold that goodness—
> A pattern to all princes living with her,
> And all that shall succeed: Saba was never
> More covetous of wisdom and fair virtue
> Than this pure soul shall be . . . .
> truth shall nurse her,
> Holy and heavenly thoughts still counsel her:
> She shall be loved and fear'd: her own shall
> bless her:
> Her foes shake like a field of beaten corn,
> And hang their heads with sorrow: good
> grows with her;
> In her days every man shall eat in safety,
> Under his own vine, what he plants; and sing
> The merry songs of peace to all his neighbours.
> (V, v, 21–26; 29–36)

The unqualified admiration in the foregoing speech appears to be a clear indication of its author's attitude, but most scholars believe the speech to have been the work not of Shakespeare, but of his collaborator, John Fletcher. See HENRY VIII: *Text*.

There are also several theories (of varying degrees of credibility) which suggest that Shakespeare made veiled or disguised allusions to Elizabeth. Elizabeth herself was apparently intensely aware of parallels between events in her reign and those portrayed in *Richard II*, an awareness shared by the Essex conspirators who ordered the performance of that play on the eve of their abortive rebellion (see William LAMBARDE). Then, too, there is a striking similarity between the details of Elizabeth's execution order for Mary, Queen of Scots, and John's order for the death of Arthur in *King John* (see William DAVISON). In any case these references, if they are references, are ambiguous tributes, at best. At Elizabeth's death Shakespeare wrote no elegy for her, a lapse for which he was censured by his contemporary Henry CHETTLE.

One suggestion which attempts to account for Shakespeare's apparent lack of enthusiasm for his sovereign is that he and his patron Southampton were adherents of the Essex faction. However, there is no real evidence to support this view.

Of the many legends and anecdotes related about Shakespeare and Elizabeth the most credible is that recorded by Nicholas Rowe in his *Life of Shakespeare* (1709):

> Queen Elizabeth had several of his plays acted before her, and without doubt gave him many gracious marks of her favour. It is that maiden princess plainly whom he intends by—"a fair vestal, throned by the west." And that whole passage is a compliment very properly brought in, and very handsomly apply'd to her. She was so well pleas'd with that admirable character of Falstaff in the two parts of Henry the Fourth, that she commanded him to continue it for one play more, and to shew him in love. This is said to be the occasion of his writing the Merry Wives of Windsor. How well she was obey'd, the play it self is an admirable proof.

This tradition about the origin of *The Merry Wives of Windsor* has received some modern confirmation; the now prevalent belief is that the play was written for a performance before Elizabeth in 1597. See THE MERRY WIVES OF WINDSOR: *Sources*.

Considerably less credible is the 19th-century anecdote by Richard RYAN describing Shakespeare's acknowledgment of Elizabeth's presence at a performance while maintaining the role he was playing. [Tucker Brooke, "Shakespeare's Queen," *Essays on Shakespeare and Other Elizabethans*, 1948.]—E.Q.

Elizabethan life in the plays. To call Shakespeare "myriad-minded" is one way of saying that nothing was ever lost upon him or escaped his notice. Like Keats, who wrote, "If a sparrow come before my window I take part in its existence and pick about the gravel," Shakespeare so identifies himself in the moment of apprehension with the thing felt, seen, or heard, that it becomes a part of his experience of life and incorporates itself spontaneously, when he feels and thinks and writes, in metaphor, simile, verb, or adjective. In consequence, the word he chooses, the language his characters speak, and especially the imagery that informs it throughout have tremendous aural, visual, and sensual impact, so that for every scene of daily life actually pictured on his stage there are a hundred allusions that flash a vivid impression of it to our senses.

Except in its reach and quality Shakespeare's was not a unique power of receptivity. Free of the devitalizing high-pressure attack forced today upon the ordinary man's natural sensitivity by mass-media of entertainment, instruction, and solicitation, the Elizabethan eye and ear had an alertness of response that we now dull or dissipate by over-stimulation. To jog another's forgetfulness men would recreate the living detail of setting and circumstances to recall exactly what had happened or had been said, because they had really seen and heard. But with Shakespeare this trick of the time is raised to its nth power: he has the gift of making such narrative appear as vivid as dramatic action. It is this that makes people speak of the "scene" of Hamlet's voyage to England, and the "scene on the pirate ship," because these recounted episodes make us see Hamlet in action as vividly as the First Player made Hamlet—and himself—*see* the sack of Troy and weep for Hecuba. The scene that Mistress Quickly stages for us in the mind's eye, when she endeavors to have Falstaff arrested, is more intensely Elizabethan in quality than the actual encounter in Eastcheap in which it occurs.

> Thou didst swear to me upon a parcel-gilt goblet sitting in my Dolphin-chamber, at the round table by a sea-coal fire, upon Wednesday in Wheeson week, when the Prince broke thy head for liking his father to a singing-man of Windsor, thou didst swear to me then, as I was washing thy wound, to marry me, and make me my lady thy wife. Canst thou deny it? Did not goodwife Keech, the butcher's wife, come in then and call me gossip Quickly? coming in to borrow a mess of vinegar; telling us she had a good dish of prawns; whereby thou didst desire to eat some; whereby I told thee they were ill for a green wound? And didst thou not, when she was gone down stairs, desire me to be no more so familiarity with such poor people; saying that ere long they should call me madam?
>
> (*2 Henry IV*, II, i, 92 ff.)

We may well be forgiven if we find this scene in her Dolphin-chamber taking the firmer hold upon our memories.

Unlike Ben Jonson or Thomas Middleton, Shakespeare never once sets his scene in Elizabethan London. It is Illyria or Vienna, ancient Rome or Athens Ephesus, Egypt, or the sea coast of Bohemia—anywhere but England, except when he goes back in point of time to the 14th and 15th centuries or earlier. Yet life as he knew it, the contemporaneous, is the very stuff of his writing—a rich lode of natural casual, Elizabethan allusiveness; whether the characters are ancient British or Scottish kings, gentlemen of Navarre, ladies of France, Greek and Trojan warriors, Roman statesmen, Athenian workmen, they are all Elizabethans—or Jacobeans—together. Macbeth keeps "a servant fee'd" in every noble household, as English statesmen and noblemen did throughout the Tudor century. Nowadays, to get the full impact of this kind of allusiveness, we need some historical acquaintance with the ways of Elizabethan life. Similarly, if we have never given a thought to the nature of a 16th century execution for treason, when the victim was hanged, cut down alive, and dismembered and disemboweled, we shall hardly recognize the horror of Macbeth's reference to his own "hangman's hands" as he gazes upon them after he has murdered Duncan, though experience may give us the intended shudder of revulsion conveyed by the implicit reference to blood, when Angus says of the tyrant, "Now does he feel his secret murders *sticking* on his hands." Again, unless we remember that Shakespeare's actors mostly wore contemporary dress, so that in fact Cleopatra does have a lace for Charmian to cut, we may not catch the full Elizabethan value of Enobarbus' description of her barge To those Londoners, who in the great days "had seen some majesty," it recalled another royal barge often to be seen on the Thames, between Westminster and Greenwich or Richmond—

> the Royal Barge of England . . . its cabin-tilt decorated with the Royal Arms in the blue and gold circle of the Garter, the watermen and Gentlemen Pensioners in their coats of scarlet and gold, the beauty and bright colours of the ladies-in-waiting and, in the middle of it all, a glimpse of the pale face and red-gold hair of the indomitable, incalculable old Queen . . . That was the Elizabeth they remembered . . . the grimly humorous, bejewelled figure, relentlessly unwithered by the time

her tirewomen had fitted her to appear in public, quelling men with her eye, scarifying them with her tongue, charming them with unexpected insight and graciousness and always, always keeping their interest alive by the sheer impossibility of foretelling what she would do next.

(Martin Holmes, *Shakespeare's Public*, 1960)

These examples of the allusive vein for which we require some background knowledge of history or social life, if we are to appreciate Elizabethan associative values and the associations of words in particular contexts, will suggest that it is not always easy for the unhistorically-minded reader, primarily interested in the characters and their stories, to grasp the full import of descriptive passages, casual references and even the actual language. We know Cleopatra's barge comes from Plutarch: we need to use our imaginations to see how it might have struck Shakespeare's contemporaries. So casual are some of the references to daily life, so minute the Elizabethan touches, that often enough we hardly notice them and do not consciously add them to our stock of Elizabethan information, but take them for granted, as the contemporary audience did; for we, too, are often genuinely familiar with the Elizabethan scene as it survives in its architecture, its furniture, and its portraiture. Familiarity as well as unrecognized significance can make us miss details. If asked what an Elizabethan household sent to the wash we might perhaps remember that Falstaff was rammed into the buck-basket with "foul shirts and smocks, socks, foul stockings, greasy napkins" and carried to the laundress in Datchet-mead; but if we have ever thought about his description of these "stinking clothes" and their greasiness we are more likely to have related it to Shakespeare's acute personal dislike of foul smells and grease, or to have let it sink without trace into a vague, general, and often exaggerated impression of the unhygienic aspects of the life of the time. And in connection with foul smells, how many of us, if asked what Borachio was doing when he overheard the Prince and Claudio discussing the wooing of Hero, would remember that Borachio could "whip me behind the arras" to eavesdrop because, "being entertained for a perfumer," he was "smoking a musty room"? Do those who remember how we used to clear the stale air by the burning of scented pastilles or joss-sticks take this Elizabethan glimpse for granted and forget it because familiar? Will the present day remember it by reason of its strangeness?

In another category are the contemporary touches usually discussed as "anachronisms," though strictly speaking the formal, functional architectural background of the Elizabethan stage and its general use of contemporary costume and properties make the term practically meaningless. Inevitably, with Elizabethan dress went such fashionable or necessary things as gloves, shoe-rosettes, rapiers, ruffs, farthingales—all matter of everyday life and reference. It might be wiser to drop the term and think of them only as Shakespeare's sense of the "here and now" of his characters, and therefore, by necessary extension, of scenes and events. Given the theatrical convention of his time, they were not merely logically admissible but essential for adding the last touch of verisimilitude. Moreover, it is not only the Elizabethan audience that was made to feel at home, in what were nominally ancient times and foreign climes, by clocks that strike for dinner in Ephesus and the sale of Elizabethan ballads and knick-knacks at the sheep-shearing feast in Sicilia where the guests are given posies of English garden flowers. We too are more at home with doublet and hose than toga

A FASHIONABLE JACOBEAN LADY AND GENTLEMAN. THESE DRAWINGS ARE FROM A PICTORIAL COMMONPLACE BOOK OF C. 1608. (FOLGER SHAKESPEARE LIBRARY)

and tunic, and a tiny episode such as the glimpse of Brutus slipping on his gown, feeling in its pocket and finding there the book he thought he had lost, gains enormously in Elizabethan dress; and though we are accustomed to *seeing* all the Falstaff scenes at the Boar's Head, or with Master Shallow in Gloucestershire, staged in medieval costume, we invariably *think* of them and discuss them as what they are—scenes from Elizabethan life.

Approaching thus, in scenes and descriptions and through Shakespeare's language and its imagery, we can picture England itself, the whole countryside, its gardens, fields, rivers, woods and highways; can people its towns, streets and houses, and observe all the multifarious activities of Elizabethan man. But if we are to understand certain ideas the age took for granted and habits of thought and assumptions which differ from our own, we must also acquire from the social historian some knowledge of the patterns of social relationships and behavior. When the context is everyday life, the relationships between parent and child, man and woman, master and servant, between equals and those in different ranks of society, are clearly the first matters to be examined, as being most central to the study of the plays. Lack of elementary knowledge can lead in stage production to misunderstanding and miscasting, and to would-be bright ideas which destroy the reality of character and situation. We should see characters appropriately and significantly dressed, as in a modern play, and the actor should be aware of the implications and niceties of behavior and manners dictated by social position or relationship. Rosencrantz and Guildenstern, for example, regarded as poor scholars and got up like two of the Marx Brothers in fancy dress and behaving accordingly, are embarrassing in themselves and a worse embarrassment to the plot. Turn them, as Guthrie did in his modern-dress *Hamlet,* into sucking diplomats, young Foreign Office attachés, and they are possible companions for the Prince. They are *in* the court picture: dress and behavior indicate the similar educational background. They immediately have status—the particular status which is essential if they are to be employed by the King. Unless we can accept them as appropriate and likely tools for this clever enemy, who has the quickest and most astute mind in the play, Claudius appears a fool and the credibility of the whole Claudius-Hamlet relationship is consequently undermined.

Equally important is the behavior due to rank and age, or the relationship between parent and child, or the subordinate and those in authority. It is preposterous, to cite a fairly recent instance, to find Beatrice in the opening scenes of *Much Ado,* "lolling," as Lady Wishfort would say, upon a *chaise-longue* in the presence of her uncle Leonato, the Governor of Messina, and later to have Claudio perching himself upon it while Don Pedro, his lord and commander, stands to talk to him. Formal behavior expressed the respect given to one's superiors in every rank in life. On greeting the parent the child knelt for a blessing: Henry VIII's children knelt while they spoke with him; and noblemen who spoke to Queen Elizabeth knelt until they were bidden to rise. Launce, saying goodbye to his family, so he tells us, asks his father's blessing and then kisses him and his mother (*Two Gentlemen of Verona,* II, iii), just as Laertes kneels for his father's blessing at the moment of leave-taking. The form of address between husband and wife was "my lord," "my lady;" "Sir," "Madam;" "husband," "wife." Juliet invariably speaks to her mother as "madam"; Goneril, Regan, and Cordelia say "my lord" or "sir" to Lear. The normal salutations are "uncle," "nephew," "niece," "cousin," "son," "daughter"; "father" and "mother" on the whole are less frequent than "sir" and "madam."

The marriage relationship is another which needs to be looked at as the Elizabethans saw it. *The Merchant of Venice* provides a straightforward illustration of the harm we do to the play if, because the bond story and the caskets story are fairy-tale material, we ignore the realities of Elizabethan life and adopt towards Bassanio the attitude—still current—which was made fashionable some 40 years ago by one of our most popular dramatic critics, who wrote him off as an unscrupulous fortune-hunter. It is true that some of Shakespeare's eligible young bachelors of the nobility and gentry, such as Bassanio and Bertram and Hero's Claudio, seem to us not good enough for the heroines they marry, and we can suspect that the author himself may also have felt his Portia was worth several Bassanios. But to the Elizabethan mind matrimony was a matter of business. It was a young man's duty to himself, his family, and friends to make a good match; and it was still more urgent that a young woman, especially an heiress and an orphan, should be found a suitable husband as quickly as possible. If love comes into the transaction, that is the happy accident which provides pleasant matter for a play; and we know that young men could and did borrow the necessary money to go a'wooing, and that respectable wealthy merchants and older friends of gravity and discretion aided and abetted them. Once married, all the lady possesses is his, not because this is a romantic play, but because marriage makes her feme covert and submerges her legal personality in her husband's. As a wife she then takes the social position that her talents, her beauty and her wealth deserve.

Shakespeare's spirited heroines—Portia, Beatrice, Rosalind, Helena—had their counterparts in real life, as did his older and more masterful women like Volumnia or Paulina or the Countess of Rousillon. They built houses, ran estates, were strict overseers—like the Queen—of the economy of their great households, and of the manners and morals of their gentlemen-servitors and waiting-gentlewomen. They engineered daughters' marriages, even at the risk of the Queen's displeasure; did their own business with ministers of state like Burghley; and ran their husbands and sons. The famous Bess of Hardwick built eight houses and had four husbands in her long life of 90 years, and also dominated the lives of her stepchildren and grandchildren. Anne, one of the three learned daughters of Sir Anthony Cooke, second wife of Sir Nicholas Bacon and mother of the great Francis Bacon, domineered over both her sons, and was as ready to rebuke the earl of Essex for his rumored "carnal dalliance" with one of her own relatives as to produce a translation of Bishop Jewel's Latin *Apologia Ecclesiae Anglicanae*, of which C. S. Lewis says, "If quality without bulk were enough, Lady Bacon might be put forward as the best of all 16th-century translators." Like these good ladies

Portia, Helena, Paulina, and the Countess and Shakespeare's other outstanding women make it quite clear where the initiative and organizing ability lies. In the concerns of human beings they call the tune and get their own way, while preserving outwardly the decorum of being subdued "even unto the very quality" of their lords and masters and accepting their nominally helpless position in society in relation to the male sex. Anne Bacon, reluctantly allowing a sale of land to pay her son's debts, insists that he must "make and give me a true account of all his debts and leave to me the whole order and receipt of all his money for his land," Francis being then in his 30's and a member of Parliament. The matriarch was not going to risk his squandering the money elsewhere. In the Tudor century the educated woman and the clever woman were both tough: witnesses—history itself, the drama, and notably William Shakespeare, whose heroines and great ladies illustrate a contemporary attitude to an important subject. Love may be central to the plot of a play, but it is not love that makes the world go round and it is not central to the pattern of the marriage relationship. Women's legal entities were submerged, but not their personalities or their sense of values. Nor were they as helpless and unprivileged as they might seem to us. Normally, a woman brought a dowry to her marriage, and whether it was in money or lands, or both, it became her husband's property, as Portia's inheritance did. But the corresponding jointure or settlement made upon her by the husband to provide for possible widowhood, chargeable as a rule upon his revenues and rents, could leave the son and heir largely dependent upon her until she died, thus giving a matriarch great power. There is sober reality in Shakespeare's image of the old moon's slow waning, which "lingers" Theseus' desires for his nuptial day,

> Like to a step-dame or a dowager
> Long withering out a young man's revenue.
> (*A Midsummer Night's Dream*, I, i, 5–6)

—another Elizabethan glimpse, which we can miss for lack of knowledge of contemporary life.

The relationship between master and man, mistress and maid, is simple enough at the middle-class level. Servants were hired at the annual hiring fairs and the wages they received were fixed by law. Launce in *Two Gentlemen of Verona* lists the qualifications of the maid upon whom he has cast a loving eye: she can fetch and carry, milk, brew good ale, sew, knit, wash and scour, and spin, and Shakespeare's imagery is full of references to women's kitchen and household work of this kind. Above this level of menial employment, however, we encounter the institution of "service," which it is necessary to understand when studying the relationships of servant and employer in the plays, as this system, which had formerly provided a scheme of life and social security for the gently-born, had already begun to decay before Shakespeare's time. Service realized in social life the concept of order, which in medieval and 16th-century thought gave every man his place—equal, superior, or inferior. Personal, intimate service was given to those of noble and gentle birth by their own kind: the duke's son was page to the prince, the gentleman's son served the esquire. It was part of the gentleman-servingman's and the waiting-gentlewoman's business to be companions to their lord or lady, to wait upon them at table, act as confidential secretary and letter-writer, conduct private negotiations for them, help them to dress, read, sing, and play to them. The servingmen would hawk, hunt, ride, play bowls or cards or chess with their masters and organize and take part in their amusements, while the women shared in the management of the household and joined their ladies in their great feats of embroidery and helped to educate the daughters of the house in the manners and accomplishments proper to a gentlewoman.

Already in the 1530's this convenient social contract, by which younger sons and daughters were placed in households of either better or equal standing to their parents', had been undermined by the rampant inflation which forced noblemen to cut down their vast households and try to place redundant servants with better-circumstanced friends. Service was ceasing to be a satisfactory whole-time employment to start a gentleman on a career; and from the lower ranks of society, as yeoman farmers and small-holders prospered, came their sons to seek advancement by this kind of personal service with the gentry. Where "Robin Rush, my gaffer Russetcoat's second son," mentioned in *A health to the gentlemanly profession of seruingmen* (1598), had formerly ploughed or carted, now he sought employment as personal servant to a gentleman, and though in the plays we find certain households where the old pattern still obtained, there are characters, such as Launce and Speed, Lancelot Gobbo, and the various sets of servants in *The Taming of the Shrew* or *The Comedy of Errors* to suggest that many of the servants who follow the young gentlemen of Shakespeare's plays are not gentlemen-servitors but rather this yeoman type, with whom, also, we find the merchant or the prosperous tradesman moving on pleasantly free and easy terms. Even the servants in the Capulet household are all of this rougher kind. It is true that, like the servants in the household of Aufidius, they are all menials; but the absence of any gentleman-servant is noticeable. That such individuals provided better opportunities for clowning may be part of their dramatic *raison-d'être*, but they give us a good idea of Robin Rush and his fellows, and like Speed and Launce reflect changing conditions. It is wrong, however, in presentation, to demote gentlemen like Fabian or Conrade or Borachio to the level of yeomen-servants, and there are still producers of *Twelfth Night* who ignore the setting of the action within the normal scheme of the personal relationships obtaining in great English households of Shakespeare's time. Even when Malvolio is faithfully presented as the chief officer of household to a great lady, Maria is still too often equated with the *soubrette* of musical comedy cap-and-apron tradition, while Signor Fabian, the gentleman-servitor, is given no recognizable status of any kind and in one post-war production was reduced to the indignity of the rags and tatters of a loafer in a Mediterranean fishing village. Similar complaints were continually urged by William Poel, and the misinterpretation of Malvolio as "the eternal old, low steward of comedy" distressed Charles Lamb: but even in 1964 yet another "servants' hall" production of the play was properly trounced by the London *Times*.

Besides the pictures of the great households of Duke Orsino and the Countess Olivia, Shakespeare has some delightful and nostalgic glimpses of

> The constant service of the antique world,
> When service sweat for duty, not for meed!
> (*As You Like It*, II, iii, 57–58)

as Orlando says of old Adam, who had served his father, Sir Rowland de Boys, "from seventeen years till now almost fourscore," and in his service saved the 500 crowns that he offers Orlando. In the Induction to *The Taming of the Shrew* the Lord's servants are his companions in the chase and can entertain him with the trick played on Sly, the drunken tinker. Bartholomew, his page, takes the part of Sly's lady wife, and his fellow servitors perform all the offices of gentlemen and grooms of the chamber.

> Let one attend him with a silver basin
> Full of rose-water, and bestrew'd with flowers;
> Another bear the ewer, the third a diaper,
> And say "Will't please your lordship cool your hands?"
> Some one be ready with a costly suit
> And ask him what apparel he will wear;
> Another tell him of his hounds and horse.
> (Induction, i, 55–61)

The Lord addresses them as "gentle sirs," instructs them to "burn sweet wood to make the lodging sweet," to have "music ready when he wakes," and to perform all their duties "kindly"—that is, exactly as gentlemen do when waiting on a lord. Ariel bringing Prospero his hat and rapier from his cell, helping him to "discase" himself of his magician's garment and to robe himself as Duke of Milan, is performing the same kind of office for his master (*The Tempest*, V, i, 82–86); and Timon's steward, Flavius, is an outstanding example of faithful, old-fashioned service, doing his utmost to check his master's reckless extravagance. To cut the little scene in which he tells Timon's servants of their master's downfall is to lose a moving valediction for the older order that was passing away. The Third Servant, speaking for all, says,

> Yet do our hearts wear Timon's livery;
> That see I by our faces; we are fellows still,
> Serving alike in sorrow.
> (IV, ii, 17–19)

And Flavius, dismissing them, parts the last of his own savings between them, saying,

> Wherever we shall meet, for Timon's sake,
> Let's yet be fellows; let's shake our heads, and say,
> As 'twere a knell unto our master's fortunes,
> "We have seen better days."
> (IV, ii, 24–27)

There is a wryly humorous reflection of the way this change was affecting society at all levels when, in *The Merry Wives of Windsor* (I, iii), Falstaff complains that his followers cost him £10 a week, and that he must turn some of them away, whereupon the Host of the Garter Inn offers to "entertain" Bardolph as his tapster. In the conversation that follows we then get one of those touches of nature that makes us kin with our Elizabethan ancestors, if we have an ear for words and for the way they reflect on men's manners and morals. Falstaff explains to Nym and Pistol that he was glad to get rid of Bardolph because "his thefts were too open." Nym agrees that one must steal at the right moment: Pistol deprecates the use of the word "steal"—"'Convey,' the wise it call"; and Falstaff caps them with, "There is no remedy; I must cony-catch; I must shift." It is a passage which shows Elizabethan speech as the living, growing, changing thing it was, and which must strike an answering chord in the generation which learned to "scrounge" in the First World War, and to "win" and finally to "liberate" in the Second.

We get a good idea of the social equality implicit in the mistress–waiting-gentlewoman relationship, at different levels in society, in the scenes between Julia and Lucetta in *Two Gentlemen;* Portia and Nerissa in *The Merchant of Venice;* between Cleopatra and Iras and Charmian; the Queen and her ladies in the gardeners' scene in Richard II; and especially in the *Much Ado About Nothing* scenes involving Margaret and Ursula, Hero's waiting-gentlewomen. The Queen's ladies, to beguile her of her sadness, suggest that they should play at bowls, or dance, or tell stories, and one of them offers to sing. Margaret and Ursula take part in the dancing with the Prince and his gentlemen; Don Pedro suggests that they must help in the gulling of Beatrice; and in the light-hearted jesting, while they help Hero dress for her wedding, we hear the same easy familiarity as in the discussions of their suitors between Portia and Nerissa and Julia and Lucetta. In contrast, however, to this gay companionship between these young women of similar age, and equally true to life, is the deeper quality of the relationship between the Countess of Rousillon and Helena in *All's Well That Ends Well.* As the Steward says to the Countess, "You love your gentlewoman entirely," and she replies,

> Faith, I do: her father bequeathed her to me; and she herself, without other advantage, may lawfully make title to as much love as she finds: there is more owing her than is paid; and more shall be paid her than she'll demand.
> (I, iii, 104–109)

There is no more exquisitely moving scene between two women in any of the plays than the one that follows, in which she draws from Helena the avowal of her love for Bertram. It is the nearest thing in literature to what is, in real life, the most beautiful tribute ever paid to the "constant service of the antique world." This occurs in a letter from an Englishwoman, Jane Dormer, who married Philip II's ambassador, the Count de Feria, and took with her to Spain her gentlewoman Damasyn Stradlyng. She wrote to Sir Thomas Stradlyng, when Damasyn died in 1567,

> . . . If you have lost a daughter by nature . . . I have lost one by election . . . In her time I knew not what troubles meant: all my cares, all my business, all my lusts were discharged upon her back; she honoured me like her mother, she loved me as a sister, and served me with such fidelity and pains, as not woman living, I am sure, could vaunt themselves of so wise, noble, virtuous, loving, careful nor able a servant as I.

There is, of course, no end to the subject of contemporary life when the text in which it is studied is Shakespeare's, and the aspects discussed here are only two among many. But the more we realize how the goings-on of life around Shakespeare colored his dialogue and were caught up by his imagery into the very texture of his writing, the more rewarding will be our perception of the Elizabethan scene. As Professor Raleigh says of him, "He is at home in the world" that we find too large for us; and the range of his imagination sets him beyond all other dramatists as "not for an age but for all time." Such, however, is the paradox of supreme genius, that the more we bring knowledge of the life of his age to the study of his plays, the more surely do we realize how deep his roots were driven into that life, so that he himself might have said with Walt Whitman, "I stand in my place with my own day here." [M. St. Clare Byrne, *Elizabethan Life in Town and Country*, 1961.]—M.St.C.B.

Elizabeth of Bohemia (1596–1662). Daughter of James I and wife of Frederick V, Elector Palatine. Elizabeth and Frederick were betrothed on December 27, 1612 and married shortly thereafter on February 14, 1613. During the period of their betrothal and until the couple's departure for Europe on April 10, 1613, there were numerous celebrations at court. The King's Men gave 20 court performances during this time. Among the plays offered were *Julius Caesar* and *The Tempest*.

Elizabeth's Men. See LADY ELIZABETH'S MEN; QUEEN'S MEN.

Ellis-Fermor, Una [Mary] (1894–1958). Scholar. Educated at Somerville College, Oxford, Miss Ellis-Fermor taught at Bedford College, London University, from 1918 to 1947. Her first book was *Christopher Marlowe* (1927), followed by an edition of the two parts of Marlowe's *Tamburlaine* (1930). In *The Jacobean Drama* (1936; 4th ed., 1958) she devoted a chapter to each of the 10 major playwrights and concluded with a consideration of Shakespeare's relationship to his fellow dramatists. Other works include *The Irish Dramatic Movement* (1939; 2nd ed., 1954); *The Frontiers of Drama* (1945; 3rd ed., 1948), which contains material on Shakespeare; and translations from Ibsen (1950 and 1958). Among several lectures given by her are "Some Recent Research in Shakespeare's Imagery," in *The Shakespeare Association Papers* No. 20 (1937); "Shakespeare the Dramatist," the British Academy Annual Shakespeare Lecture for 1948; and "The Study of Shakespeare" (1948), an Inaugural Lecture at Bedford College. Miss Ellis-Fermor served on the advisory board of *Shakespeare Survey* and for the first three volumes (1948–1950) reviewed the year's critical studies of Shakespeare. In 1946 she assumed the general editorship of The New Arden Shakespeare and set forth a statement of her policy in the edition of *Macbeth* (1951). At the time of her death Miss Ellis-Fermor was working on a full-length study of Shakespeare. In *Shakespeare the Dramatist and Other Essays* (1961) Kenneth Muir gave an outline of this projected book and reprinted several lectures and articles, together with some unpublished material, which would have made up a portion of Miss Ellis-Fermor's book.

Elliston, Robert William (1774–1831). Actor. Although destined by his family for the church, Elliston became involved in the theatre through participation in amateur productions. In 1796 he made his London debut and became one of the most popular actors of his time. In his line—Romeo, Hamlet, and Hotspur, the young romantic Shakespearean heroes—he was considered as good as Garrick. One of his successes in later life was as Falstaff. Though personally eccentric and alcoholic, Elliston became one of the most successful theatre managers of his day. His reputation was such that Lamb said, "Wherever Elliston walked, sat, or stood still, there was the theatre." [*Oxford Companion to the Theatre*, Phyllis Hartnoll, ed., 1951.]

Ely, John Fordham, bishop of (d. 1425). Canon of York and secretary to Richard II. In 1382 Fordham was made bishop of Durham, but by 1390 he had become so unpopular with the party opposed to the king that he was removed from his bishopric to the lesser one of Ely. In *Henry V*, Ely listens to Canterbury's account of Henry's change in character and to his cynical plan to urge the King to make war on France, thus benefiting the church (I, i). [W. H. Thomson, *Shakespeare's Characters: A Historical Dictionary*, 1951.]

Ely, John Morton, bishop of (1420?–1500). An ardent Lancastrian who, after the battle at Towton, accompanied Queen Margaret into exile. Nevertheless, Morton acquiesced in Edward IV's accession after the Lancastrian defeat at Tewkesbury (1471) and played an important role in that king's reign. Morton became bishop of Ely in 1479. When, after Edward's death, Richard, duke of Gloucester, usurped the throne, the bishop was imprisoned in the charge of Buckingham, whom Morton emboldened to rebel against Richard III. After escaping the country, Morton warned Richmond of the king's plan to capture him, thereby saving the earl's life. On Richmond's accession as Henry VII, the bishop became one of his chief counselors. In 1486 he was made archbishop of Canterbury, later becoming lord chancellor and cardinal.

In *Richard III*, Ely attends a council called to determine the day of young Edward V's coronation. Gloucester asks him to send for strawberries from his garden. Subsequently arrested, Ely escapes and joins Richmond's party.

Elyot, Sir Thomas (c. 1490–1546). Author and humanist. Trained as a lawyer, Elyot combined public service with humanistic studies. He represented Henry VIII at the court of Charles V (1531–1532, 1535) and was a commissioner for the visitation of religious houses. His views on the necessity of a strong monarch led him to take the Oath of Supremacy and to break with Sir Thomas More, whose circle he once frequented. Elyot wrote on a variety of subjects: political philosophy, translations from Plutarch and other classical moralists, a medical treatise, and the first Latin-English dictionary (1538). His most important work is *The Boke of the Governour* (1531).

The Governour is dedicated to Henry VIII as a manual treating of "the education of them that hereafter may be deemed worthy to be governours of the public weal under your highness." The first of its three books opens with an exposition of the public weal as a living body composed of various estates and degrees governed by the rule of moderation and reason; hierarchical order is necessary for order and stability; the best government is the rule of a single monarch or prince in the interests of the people. The remainder of the first book sets forth Elyot's educational ideal for the ruler and his advisors: a foundation in the classics, a strong moral bias, and due attention to physical education. The second book consists of practical advice to the ruler on his initial exercise of authority. Book three is a moral treatise of a more abstract nature: stress is on the four cardinal virtues and their numerous subdivisions, along with such considerations as the importance of history as a means of teaching by example. *The Governour* is in the tradition of the Renaissance handbook for the Christian ruler and shows the influence of similar treatises of the period by Erasmus, Juan Vives, Giovanni Pontano, and Francesco Patrizzi. It in turn influenced subsequent works such as those by Roger Ascham and Richard Mulcaster. The concept of order in *The Governour* is echoed in Ulysses' famous speech on degree in *Troilus and Cressida* (I, ii). Shakespeare may also have derived the notion of Caesar's hybris in *Julius Caesar* from Elyot's account of Caesar's pride.

Shakespeare is possibly indebted to *The Governour* for the concept of male friendship in *The Two Gentlemen of Verona*, which is one of the major themes of that play. See THE TWO GENTLEMEN OF VERONA: *Sources*. [D. T. Starnes, "Shakespeare and Elyot's Governour," *University of Texas Studies in English*, 7, 1927; Ralph M. Sargent, "Sir Thomas Elyot and the Integrity of *The Two Gentlemen of Verona*," *PMLA*, LXV, 1950.]

Ely Palace portrait. See PORTRAITS OF SHAKESPEARE.

emendation. In TEXTUAL CRITICISM, a conjectural correction inserted in a Shakespearean text by an editor in an attempt to restore the original meaning. Shakespeare's plays were often carelessly printed and there is no evidence that he ever concerned himself with seeing them accurately reproduced. As a result there are a large number of errors in the early editions of his plays which scholars through the centuries have struggled to correct. W. W. Greg defines an acceptable emendation as "one that strikes a trained intelligence as supplying exactly the sense required by the context, and which at the same time reveals to the critic the manner in which the corruption arose."

Errors based on obvious misprints are easily emended, but proper emendation of less obvious errors frequently requires an intimate knowledge of such recondite and varied material as Elizabethan printing techniques, Renaissance handwriting, contemporary history and literature, and local English place names. To these attributes must frequently be added a poetic imagination. Two of the most famous emendations in Shakespearean texts—one in *Henry V*, the other in *Hamlet*—are still disputed by scholars.

The example in *Henry V* occurs in the hostess' description of the dying Falstaff (II, iii, 16–17). The First Folio text of these lines reads "for his nose was as sharp as a pen, and a Table of greene fields." Lewis THEOBALD emended the line to read ". . . and a' [he] babbled of green fields," thus transforming an apparently meaningless phrase into one which suits the context. However, subsequent 18th-century editors ridiculed Theobald's emendation, offering in its place such fanciful explanations as Alexander Pope's conjecture that "and a Table of greene fields" was not part of the text but a stage direction indicating that a table was to be brought on stage at this point and that "Greenfield" was the name of the property man in Shakespeare's company.

Eventually, Theobald's emendation came to be accepted by the great majority of scholars, although there has been an attempt to restore the essential Folio reading based on the emendation "on" for "and." According to this view, "his nose was as sharp as a pen on a Table of green fields" carries a number of sexual puns which would not have been lost on an Elizabethan audience. Others have suggested that "Table" is merely a misprint for "Talk'd."

The other disputed emendation occurs in the opening lines of Hamlet's first soliloquy (I, ii, 129) which in the version of the First Folio reads "O that this too too solid flesh would melt" while both Quartos read "sallied flesh." Editors were traditionally inclined to accept "solid" without an emendation until J. Dover Wilson advanced the theory that the "sallied" of the Quartos is a misprint for "sullied," the "a" and the "u" being easily mistaken in Elizabethan handwriting. Also the idea that Hamlet considers his flesh "sullied" as a result of his mother's incestuous relationship with Claudius is a more effective one in the context of the play. Thus in this case a combination of a knowledge of Elizabethan handwriting with a sensitive reading of the line produced an emendation which has had increasing acceptance by modern editors. [W. W. Greg, *Principles of Emendation in Shakespeare*, 1928.]

Emerson, Ralph Waldo (1803–1882). American essayist, poet, and lecturer. Though neither an original philosopher nor a great poet, Emerson was the most influential spokesman of the New England transcendentalists. His frequently anthologized essays include "Nature" (1836), "The American Scholar" (1837), "Self Reliance" (1841), and selections from *Representative Men* (1850). Among his more familiar poems are "Each and All" (1839), "Concord Hymn" (1837), "Hamatreya" (1846), "Days" (1857), and "Brahma" (1857).

In "Shakspere; or, the Poet" from *Representative Men* Emerson appears to condemn Shakespeare, calling him the "master of revels" who shared the "halfness and imperfections of humanity." The American transcendentalist regretted that Shakespeare's life was not more exemplary and his plays more edifying. "Other admirable men," he notes, "have led lives in some sort of keeping with their thought; but this man in wide contrast." Regretfully, Emerson observes, "the best poet led an obscure and profane life, using his genius for the public amusement." In these remarks Emerson reveals his moral bent and a Puritan's suspicion of the theatre.

R. P. Falk has suggested that far too much has been made of Emerson's apparent condemnation of Shakespeare. Emerson called Shakespeare "the first poet of the world," selected him to exemplify the poet in *Representative Men*, and wrote "frequent and generous" comments on Shakespeare in his journals. Ranking Shakespeare above Milton, Dante, and Homer, Emerson delighted in "persons who clearly perceive the transcendent superiority of Shakespeare to all other writers." Not only did Shakespeare "dwarf all writers without a solitary exception," but he was the world's greatest artist as well. No man, Emerson suggested, could "produce anything comparable to one scene in *Hamlet* or *Lear*." He maintained that nothing, "no Parthenon, no sculpture, no picture, no architecture," is comparable to Shakespeare. Emerson, then, rather than being a detractor, would appear to be a member in good standing of the cult of Shakespeare worshipers.

In his adulation of Shakespeare, Emerson tended to praise his "wisdom" and his "poetry" and to neglect his merit as a playwright. He managed ultimately to praise Shakespeare's "inviolable . . . innocency" and to believe that Shakespeare was a "king of men" who would lead the good life "in whatever company" he found himself.

Although Emerson read the publications of the Shakespeare Society, the Shakespearean criticism of Goethe, Coleridge, and Malone, and articles by Collier and Dyce in the *Westminster Review* and the *London Quarterly*, his approach to Shakespeare was intuitive rather than scholarly. He thought that "it is not by discovery of contemporary documents, but by more cunning reading of the Book itself, that we shall at last illuminate the true biography of Shakspeare." Although he was "inquisitive of all possible knowledge concerning Shakspeare," Emerson felt that there were few valuable criticisms which he could treasure besides his own.

Emerson believed that Shakespeare as a poet possessed "above all men the essential gift of the imagination, the power of subordinating nature for the purposes of expression." In the works of Shakespeare nature is "put under contribution to give analogies and semblances that she has never yielded before." Emerson in his essay "Nature" described the quality of Shakespeare's imagery strikingly: "His imperial muse tosses the creation like a bauble from hand to hand, and uses it to embody any caprice of thought that is uppermost in his mind. The remotest spaces of nature are visited, and the farthest sundered things are brought together, by a subtile spiritual connection." [Robert P. Falk, "Emerson and Shakespeare," *PMLA*, LVI, 1941; Thomas A. Peery, "Emerson, the Historical Frame, and Shakespeare," *Modern Language Quarterly*, IX, 1948.]

Emilia. In *Othello*, Iago's wife and the servant of Desdemona. Frank and forthright, Emilia is easily duped by her husband. Her furious indignation upon the discovery of his plot (V, ii) provides the audience with an emotional outlet from the tragic tension.

Emilia. In *The Two Noble Kinsmen*, sister of Hippolyta and sister-in-law of Theseus, Duke of Athens. Emilia is the object of rivalry between Arcite and Palamon, but is unable to choose between them; following their contest for her hand and Arcite's death, she is betrothed to Palamon.

Emilia. In *The Winter's Tale*, a lady attending on Hermione. Emilia informs Paulina that Hermione has given birth to a daughter in prison (II, ii).

Empson, William (1906–). Critic and poet. Educated at Cambridge and lecturer in English at Peking National University, Empson published *Poems* (1935) and *The Gathering Storm* (1940), another book of poetry. His criticism includes *Seven Types of Ambiguity* (1930), *Some Versions of Pastoral* (1935), and *The Structure of Complex Words* (1951). This last book draws attention to the implications of key words in plays like *King Lear, Timon of Athens, Othello*, and *Measure for Measure*. For instance, in discussing *King Lear* Empson dwells upon the various meanings of the word "fool" as it is used in the play.

enclosure. A reorganization of agriculture that took place in the 15th, 16th, and 17th centuries. The medieval "open field" system of farming in long, narrow, nonadjacent strips of land came to be regarded as wasteful. By enclosing or consolidating scattered strips of land, the lord of the manor might be said to have performed a public service, providing the individual peasant with one large holding, instead of several smaller ones, to farm. However, much of the enclosure of the period was for the purpose of consolidating sheep pasture land. This tended to benefit the lord, who thus required fewer shepherds to look after his flock and could profit from the high prices the wool brought in the market; but for the peasants it was disastrous. The dispossession of large numbers of peasants from their land was the most serious economic problem of the period, and provoked a great deal of discontent among the poor who suffered the consequences of it.

In September 1614 Arthur Mainwaring and William Replingham began to explore the possibility of the enclosure of certain lands in the neighborhood of Stratford, particularly in Welcombe, a small hamlet where in 1605 Shakespeare had purchased a portion of the tithes (see STRATFORD TITHES). In order to secure Shakespeare's permission to enclose the lands, the promoters entered into an agreement in which they promised to "make recompence" for any loss of income which Shakespeare might sustain as a result of enclosure. See William REPLINGHAM.

In the meantime the Stratford corporation had voted to oppose enclosure and commissioned Thomas Greene (see GREENE FAMILY), the town clerk and a relative of Shakespeare, to negotiate with the promotors in an attempt to dissuade them. On November 16, while in London, Greene interviewed Shakespeare and his son-in-law Dr. John Hall, who assured Greene that the enclosure would not even begin until April of the following year, if at all:

> . . . they meane in Aprill to servey the Land & then to gyve satisfaccion & not before & he & Mr Hall say they think there will be nothyng done at all . . .

On December 10, Greene recorded that he had tried unsuccessfully to make contact with Replingham at New Place, Shakespeare's house, and on December 23 noted that letters were written to Mainwaring and "Mr Shakspeare with almost all of the com[panies] hands [i.e., the members of the Stratford corporation]." Greene also noted that he had personally written "to my Cosen Shakespeare" detailing the "Inconvenyences which wold grow by the Inclosure." At this time Mainwaring and Replingham were joined in the attempt to enclose by William Combe, one of the largest landholders in the area. In January 1615 Combe began to have a ditch dug on his property as the first step toward enclosure. Members of the corporation attempted to interfere with the digging, with the result that a brawl took place between Combe's men and those of the corporation. In March 1615 the corporation secured a court order, preventing enclosure until good cause could be shown. By this time Mainwaring and Replingham had apparently given up attempts to enclose, but Combe persisted. The battle continued for the next year, until April 1616, when Sir Edward Coke, chief justice of the king's bench, ruled against enclosure. Subsequently Combe attempted to offer a compromise arrangement with the corporation which was also turned down. The controversy was still in the courts as late as 1619.

Some particulars of the dispute are known to us from Thomas Greene's notes, one of which, dated September 1615, relates "W Shakspeares tellyng J Greene that J was not able to beare the encloseinge of Welcombe." This reference is a puzzling one. "J Greene" is evidently John Greene, Thomas' brother. The second "J" (i.e., "I") has been taken by some to refer to Shakespeare, and to mark the beginning of a direct quotation of Shakespeare, thus revealing his attitude toward enclosure, but the more likely meaning is that "J" refers to Thomas Greene. The word "beare" might mean either "justify" or "endure" and this adds to the ambiguity of the note. Shakespeare's role in the controversy was evidently not a significant one, but it is clear from the part he did play that he was a shrewd and careful businessman. [C. C. Stopes, *Shakespeare's Environment*, 1914; E. K. Chambers, *William Shakespeare*, 1930.]

enemies of the stage. Foes of the stage in any period are not necessarily hostile to other forms of art and entertainment, but its most vehement and implacable enemies have usually been so. They are persons who confidently undervalue the role of the feelings in life and overemphasize the powers of human reason. They presume to know the true from the false, and since all art is inevitably "false" in so simply two-valued a system, they condemn it as such. Since they view life as a grimly earnest affair, they would require all men to spend their time in demonstrably utilitarian ways. In order to maintain these attitudes, they find it necessary to deny the more tolerantly humane view that life is neither more nor less serious than a game. They deny the values of "play," in the various senses of that word. This may be one reason for their particular hostility to the theatre in all its forms, whether they demand its total suppression or some large degree of control over its activities.

Since the enemies of the arts are primarily concerned with questions of moral value and social utility, it is not surprising that the best-known early attacks on poetry should be found in Plato's *Republic*. The best-known early defense is Aristotle's *Poetics*, probably written in order to controvert Plato's arguments, and therefore couched in terms of probability (truth to reality), moral value (hamartia), and social utility (catharsis), as the attack had been. The controversy, which shows no signs of dying out, is still couched in these terms, as it was blatantly in some of the major periods of influential attacks on the stage: the denigration of the theatre of Imperial Rome by the early Christian fathers, and the condemnation of the theatre of Elizabethan and Stuart England by the so-called Puritans.

Just as the church fathers cited Plato, and each other, as authorities in their attacks on the stage, so the 17th-century Puritans, along with their predecessors and successors, copiously and repeatedly cited the church fathers as authorities for a right-minded view of such goings-on. In both periods, the attackers belonged to ardent minority groups that were rebellious toward the authorities in their societies, and both groups finally triumphed, however temporarily.

In the earlier Tudor period, theatrical activity, whether popular, academic, or courtly, whether professional or amateur, whether presented by companies of men or boys, was subject to censorship by officials both of the state and of the church, and there exist a number of early Tudor comments that indicate the desire for more stringent controls than were generally exercised. It is not until the English Reformation, however, when the claims of church and state more nearly coincided than they previously had, that we begin to find evidences both of a more careful censorship and of demands for the total suppression of various kinds of drama. The medieval popular drama was effectually suppressed in the course of the generation between the birth of Elizabeth (1533) and the immediate aftermath of the Northern Rebellion of 1569, despite sporadic attempts to resuscitate it, particularly during the last years of Henry VIII and the short reign of Mary Tudor.

The drama was specifically enlisted in the service of anti-Papal propaganda under the patronage of Thomas Cromwell, one of the most influential of Henry's Protestant advisors until his sudden fall from power in 1540. The most prolific of the playwrights he supported was John Bale, whose hostility to the pre-Reformation drama was as energetically outspoken as his contributions to the new Protestant drama. Bale's attitudes are sufficiently clear from a statement published from exile in 1544: "So long as they [players of interludes] played lies, and sang bawdy songs . . . and corrupted men's consciences, you [English ecclesiastical authorities] never blamed them, but were very well contented. But since they persuaded people to worship their Lord God aright . . . without your lousy legerdemains, you never were pleased with them." Bale's specification of lies, bawdry, and the corruption of the people were time-honored commonplaces that were to be endlessly reiterated by later writers and preachers against the stage.

The most influential of these attacks in Shakespeare's lifetime were triggered by the construction in 1576 of the first permanent public theatres in the northern suburbs of London. This wave of attacks should, perhaps, be seen as part of the attempt of Puritans and other dissidents, along with the London Corporation, to protest against certain of the policies of the central government, particularly during the 1570's and 1580's. The most vociferous of the enemies of the stage during Elizabeth's reign were to be found among those Protestant extremists who were dissatisfied with the Elizabethan religious settlement because, in their eyes, it retained too many vestiges of Roman Catholic liturgical practices. These discontented extremists, who are too easily lumped together under the vague term "Puritan," included a wide variety of Elizabeth's loyal but deeply anti-Catholic subjects. For all of them, in one way or another, the English Reformation had not gone far enough, but they were by no means exclusively Calvinists. In fact, at the height of the "Puritan" protests against Elizabeth's policies of moderation—from the time of the Ridolfi Plot (1571) to that of the execution of Mary Stuart (1587) and the seemingly providential defeat of the Spanish Armada (1588)—the disaffected Protestant extremists showed themselves to be quite as diverse in their opinions as did their Puritan descendants during the Commonwealth some two generations later. The fact that some of them agreed in their attacks on the stage should not be taken as symptomatic of any widespread agreement on an organized program for political action. Indeed, some of their pro-Episcopal, Anglican fellow citizens agreed with them in this and in other respects.

The extreme Protestants urged their policies for the reform of abuses in the English Church and in the daily lives of their less zealous brethren from sincere patriotic and religious motives. The promulgation of the Bull of Excommunication against Elizabeth (1570) and the St. Bartholomew's Massacre in France (1572) increased their eagerness for "Reformation without Tarrying." When, a few years later, professional companies of players began to withdraw from the inn yards of London to new playhouses in the suburbs in order to avoid the hostile control of the lord mayor and his council, both preachers and pamphleteers hastened to demand their suppression as sources of corruption. In doing so they exaggerated and extended the arguments that the London Corporation had been accustomed to using in its protests to the queen's privy council against allowing public performances by the players. Those arguments had centered primarily around the competition between players and preachers on Sundays and holy days and the danger of infection in plague-times. As one preacher now put it (1577): "Behold the sumptuous theater houses, a continual monument of London's prodigality and folly . . . . The cause of plagues is sin, if you look to it well; and the cause of sin are plays; therefore the cause of plagues are plays." Within the year another preacher was complaining: "Will not a filthy play, with the blast of a trumpet, sooner call thither a thousand, than an hour's tolling of a bell bring to the sermon a hundred?"

In the same year, one of the earliest pamphleteers, John Northbrooke (fl. 1568–1579), a nonconforming clergyman, reproved not only "vain plays or interludes" but also dancing, dicing, and "other idle pastimes . . . commonly used on the Sabbath day." Like many others, he condemns theatres as tempting schools of vice: "Many can tarry at a vain play two or three hours, when as they will not abide scarce one hour at a sermon . . . . In their plays you shall learn all things that appertain to craft, mischief, deceits, and filthiness, etc." Among the numerous vices that one is allured to practice by seeing plays are "how to be false . . . how to beguile, how to betray, to flatter, lie, swear, forswear . . . how to murder, how to poison, how to disobey and rebel against princes . . . to blaspheme, to sing filthy songs of love . . . to be proud, how to mock, scoff, and deride any nation . . . ."

Although Northbrooke's "Treatise" was reprinted in 1579, it was not so influential as the attacks by Stephen Gosson, a young Oxford graduate. Gosson, who later became a clergyman, had himself written plays. Indeed, he seems to have come to London with literary ambitions similar to those of his contemporary Oxonian Wits, Lyly, Lodge, and Peele. His best-known work, *The School of Abuse* (1579), is subtitled "a pleasant invective" and is written in Lyly's euphuistic style. Like Northbrooke, he does not confine his attack to plays; he also attacks poetry (and thereby stimulated Sidney, to whom the book was dedicated, to reply to this part of it), music, dancing, dicing, and fencing, among other "abuses." Although almost half of his text is devoted to the theatre, Gosson's attack on plays is far milder than Northbrooke's; he even allows that "as some of the players are far from abuse, so some of their plays are without rebuke," but he adds that these few "are as easily remembered as quickly reckoned."

Gosson's little pamphlet stimulated controversy out of all proportion to its rather mild attacks. In 1582 he published a more serious and considerable denunciation of the stage, *Plays Confuted in Five Actions.* In

TITLE PAGE OF GOSSON'S *Schoole of Abuse* (1579).

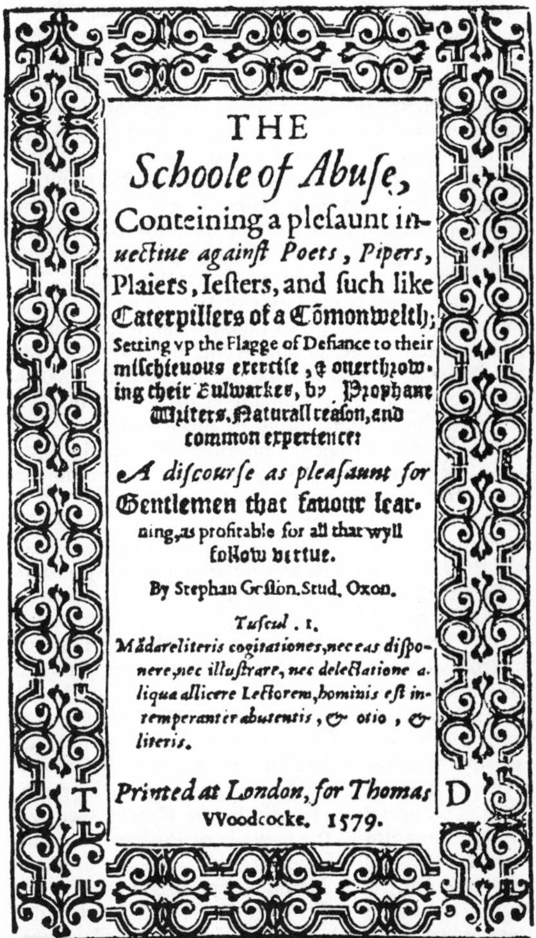

THE

Schoole of Abuse,

Conteining a plesaunt in-*uectiue against Poets, Pipers,* Plaiers, Iesters, and such like Caterpillers of a Cōmonwelth; Setting vp the Flagge of Defiance to their mischieuous exercise, & ouerthrowing their Bulwarkes, by Prophane Writers, Naturall reason, and common experience:

A discourse as pleasaunt for Gentlemen that fauour learning, as profitable for all that wyll follow vertue.

By Stephan Gosson. Stud. Oxon.

Tuscul. 1.

Mādare literis cogitationes, nec eas dispo-nere, nec illustrare, nec delectatione a-liqua allicere Lectorem, hominis est in-temperanter abutentis, & otio, & literis.

T *Printed at London, for Thomas* D
Woodcocke. 1579.

this work, he cites the Bible and the church fathers as well as classical authors. Now the Efficient Cause of plays is the Devil himself, the Final Cause is sinful delight, and theatres are "markets of bawdry." As for subject matter: "The argument of Tragedies is wrath, cruelty, incest, injury, murder either violent by sword or voluntary by poison . . . . The groundwork of Comedies is love, cozenage, flattery, bawdry, sly conveyance of whoredom." Obviously plays are no "Schoolmistress of life."

The year 1583 was climactic for Elizabethan attacks on the stage. On a Sunday afternoon in January of that year, a scaffold at Paris Garden collapsed, killing and maiming some of the spectators at a bear-baiting. The preachers lost no time in hailing the event as "an extraordinary judgment of God" and as a fair warning of what would surely happen to the spectators of "Heathenish Interludes and Plays" at "the Theatre, the Curtain, and such like" unless "they may be utterly rid and taken away." Later that year, Philip STUBBES' *The Anatomy of Abuses* was first published. Stubbes is concerned with all varieties of abuses, from music and dancing to extravagant dress, and he is particularly severe on the profanation of the Sabbath. He devotes only a few pages to the wickedness of stage plays, but his condemnation of them is virulent. He appropriates the most telling passages he can find in Northbrooke and Gosson (among them, the longest passages quoted above from each of these authors) and adds his thunder to them. Theatre audiences, he asserts, "go to Venus' palace and Satan's synagogue to worship devils and betray Christ Jesus." *The Anatomy* attained its fourth revised and enlarged edition in 1595. Its pages on the stage anticipate the tone and manner that William PRYNNE maintains throughout the thousand pages of his notorious *Histriomastix* (1633), that encyclopedic compilation from authorities and predecessors that played so significant a part in the events that led to the suppression of the stage in 1642.

Stubbes' book is the latest of the major attacks on the popular theatre in Elizabeth's reign and Shakespeare's lifetime. After the events of 1587 and 1588, the Puritans, even with the aid of Martin MARPRELATE, found it more difficult than it had been to persuade the general public of the urgency of their causes. Except during plague-times (when the theatres were in any event closed to prevent infection) it had come to seem more and more, to all but the extremists, that God could not be greatly dissatisfied with the ways of the English. It may be significant that the last major outburst by an enemy of the stage in Elizabeth's later years appeared in the form of an academic question. This was *The Overthrow of Stage Plays*, apparently printed in the Netherlands in 1599. John Rainolds (1549–1607), who probably edited and surely released its contents to the Dutch Puritan printer, may have been moved to do so at that time because of the current governmental suppression of nondramatic Juvenalian satire, written in a vein that was already finding its way to the public stage. The prefatory Epistle to the Reader seems, at any rate, to point to the ridicule of Puritans in comedies of "humours" of the sort that Jonson and Chapman and probably Nashe (one of the suppressed satirists) had recently introduced to the London stage. It refers to "those men . . . that have not been afraid of late days to bring upon the Stage the very sober countenances . . . gestures, and speeches of men and women to be laughed at as a scorn and reproach to the world," and it specifically condemns "the bad humour of such humourists as these [playwrights], who in their discovery of humours do withal foully discover their own shame and wretchedness to the world . . . ."

The Overthrow consists of two letters written in 1592 and 1593 by Rainolds, an eminent Oxford theologian, to William Gager (fl. 1580–1609), an Oxonian neo-Latin dramatist, and an exchange of four letters from the same period between Rainolds and Gager's champion, Albericus Gentilis, the Regius professor of civil law. The controversy is focused primarily on the propriety of amateur academic performances of plays in Latin. Rainolds, who had himself in his undergraduate days acted a woman's role in a college play (in English) on the occasion of the first of Elizabeth's two visits to Oxford (1566), makes much of such standard Puritan arguments against any play-acting as the violations of the Biblical injunctions against transvestism (Deuteronomy 22:5) and the profanation of the Sabbath (Exodus 20:8) and the wasteful prodigality of time and money involved in putting on such shows. All but the first of the six letters that constitute *The Overthrow* were written after Elizabeth's second visit to Oxford (1592), in the course of which she had attended a performance of one of Gager's plays and, on the morning of her departure, is reported to have "schooled Dr. John Rainolds for his obstinate preciseness, willing him to follow her laws, and not run before them."

Elizabeth's "schooling" of Rainolds is nowhere mentioned in *The Overthrow*, and it may have had nothing to do with his attitude toward the stage. It is nonetheless significant that she is said personally to have rebuked the learned Puritan for his inflexibility, because it was finally the queen's pleasure that, during the critical years of the attacks on the stage, had shielded and continued to shield the professional players from the hostility of the London Corporation. Again and again the privy council, in replies to the frequent protests of the lord mayor against the "inconveniencies" arising from the public performance of plays, had to resort to the ultimate argument that such performances were in the nature of exercise for the players and rehearsal of their plays for production at court during the Christmas revels, at which time their supreme justification was "the Queen's solace." It was this "convenient fiction," as it has been called (one might better call it the royal prerogative), that defenders of the stage held as their incontrovertible trump card in the continuing quarrel with the obstinate "precisians" and those of their sympathizers who wished to see the practice of public playing and the profession of common player abolished entirely. [Further readings: The most fruitful remain Appendices C and D of E. K. Chambers' *The Elizabethan Stage* (4 vols., 1923), which contain extracts from the primary documents. J. Dover Wilson's chapter "The Puritan Attack upon the Stage" in the *Cambridge History of English Literature* (Vol. VI, 1910) has not been superseded. More specialized but relevant works are Johan Huizinga's *Homo Ludens* (1944, Eng. trans. 1949), Wiliam Haller's various studies in Puritanism, and J. E. Neale's books on the Elizabethan parliaments.]—S.F.J.

England's Helicon. See John BODENHAM.

English Traveler, The. See Thomas HEYWOOD.

engravings of London. Tudor and Stuart views ınd maps of London, valuable as a source of information about the size, shape, and location of Elizabethan playhouses. Unfortunately, however, nany of these engravings are either inaccurate or lerivative in various details, and must be carefully tudied before being used as the basis for a recontruction of the Elizabethan theatre. See PLAYHOUSE STRUCTURE.

The earliest of the engravings which give a view of the predecessors of the London theatre, the bull and bearbaiting rings, is the so-called HOEFNAGEL MAP, first published in 1572 and probably drawn ometime after 1554. It served as the basis of a number of later maps, including those of Ralph AGAS and Claes Janszoon de VISSCHER. Later views of ome importance are those of Jodocus HONDIUS, Francis Delaram, and Wenceslas HOLLAR. Probably the most accurate of all the Elizabethan maps is the *Civitas Londini* of John NORDEN. Its distinguishing feature is that it shows the Globe, Swan, and Rose theatres as round buildings rather than as he polygonal structures usually pictured. [I. A. Shapiro, "The Bankside Theatres: Early Engravings," *Shakespeare Survey 1*, 1948.]

Enobarbus, Domitius. In *Antony and Cleopatra*, a trusted officer of Antony. Enobarbus deserts Antony after the defeat at Actium, but when the latter magnanimously sends him his treasure, Enobarbus is so overcome by remorse that he commits suicide. His part contains many witty and astute observations on he behavior of Antony and Cleopatra.

Epicoene. A comedy by Ben JONSON. Subtitled *The Silent Woman*, *Epicoene* was first acted in 1609 by the Children of the Queen's Revels. Regarded as one of Jonson's best plays, the comedy has a larger element of farce than is usual in his work. *Epicoene* is thought to contain an allusion to *Coriolanus*. See CORIOLANUS: *Date*.

epilogue. In drama, the formal address to the audience at the conclusion of a play. Ten of Shakespeare's plays have epilogues. These are listed below with the name of the character who delivers the epilogue:

A Midsummer Night's Dream—Puck
As You Like It—Rosalind
Henry V—Chorus
Twelfth Night—Feste
All's Well—King of France
Troilus and Cressida—Pandarus
Pericles—Gower
The Tempest—Prospero
2 Henry IV—Unidentified performer, probably a dancer
Henry VIII—Unidentified actor

Of these epilogues the best known are those from *Twelfth Night* and *2 Henry IV*. The *Twelfth Night* epilogue is the song of the clown Feste ("When that I was and a little tiny boy/With hey, ho, the wind and the rain"); the epilogue to *2 Henry IV* includes a disclaimer of the accusation that Falstaff was designed to resemble the historical Sir John Oldcastle: "for Oldcastle died a martyr, and this is not the man." See PROLOGUE.

PART OF HOEFNAGEL'S VIEW OF LONDON SHOWING BANKSIDE AND THE BEARBAITING AND BULLBAITING ARENAS.

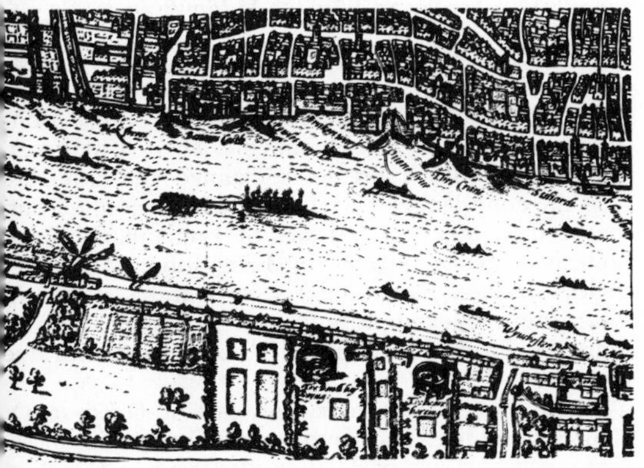

epitaphs. Term referring to two sets of verses, one on the gravestone in the floor of the chancel, the area around the altar, of Holy Trinity Church in Stratford and the other on the Shakespeare monument within the same church (for the text of the latter, see MONUMENT). The verse on the gravestone is as follows:

GOOD FREND FOR IESVS SAKE FORBEARE,
TO DIGG THE DVST ENCLOASED HEARE!
BLESTE BE Y^{E} MAN Y^{T} SPARES THES STONES,
AND CURST BE HE Y^{T} MOVES MY BONES.

According to a Mr. DOWDALL, who transcribed the verses in 1693, Shakespeare's epitaph was "made by himselfe a little before his Death." The attribution does no credit to the poet and is generally rejected. The curse in the epitaph was probably designed to ward off any future sextons who might be tempted to dig a new grave where Shakespeare's was and remove his bones to the charnel house.

J. O. Halliwell-Phillipps asserts that the gravestone is not the original one, but that it was laid to replace the original in the middle of the 18th century. The curse is said to have had such a powerful effect that the grave was never opened, not even to include the bodies of Shakespeare's wife and daughters. See William HALL. [J. O. Halliwell-Phillipps, *Outlines of the Life of Shakespeare*, 1881; E. K. Chambers, *William Shakespeare*, 1930.]

equivocation. Theory advanced by some 16th-century Catholic theologians who upheld the morality of giving false or misleading answers under oath. The equivocation theory caused considerable controversy among English Catholics in the period 1600 to 1606. The Jesuits, under the leadership of Robert PARSONS, argued for its validity while the regular Catholic clergy, aided by Archbishop Whitgift and the Anglicans, opposed it. Shakespeare's first reference to the term occurs in *Hamlet* (V, i, 149) when, in response to the riddling replies of the gravedigger, Hamlet remarks that "we must speak by the card, or equivocation will undo us." In *Macbeth* the Porter's references to equivocation (II, iii, 9–14) are allusions to the trial of Henry GARNET, a Jesuit convicted of complicity in the Gunpowder plot who invoked the theory in defending himself (see MACBETH: *Date*). F. L. Huntley has shown that the doctrine supplies *Macbeth* with one of the play's sustaining motifs. Equivocation is a prominent feature of the play, not only in the ambivalent utterances of the Weird Sisters, but in the language of Macbeth himself. The theory was ultimately condemned by Pope Innocent XI in 1679. [Frank L. Huntley, "Macbeth and Jesuitical Equivocation," *PMLA*, LXXIX, 1964.]

Erasmus, Desiderius (c. 1466–1536). Dutch humanist and influential scholar who was one of the chief agents in the development of HUMANISM in England. The illegitimate son of a priest, Erasmus was educated in monastic schools and at the University of Paris. In 1499 he visited England for the first time and made the acquaintance of the Oxford Reformers, particularly Sir Thomas More. In 1516 he published his most important work, an edition of the New Testament which provided a more accurate text than the Vulgate, the version which had been generally accepted throughout the Middle Ages. Although hailed by the Protestant reformers as a prophet of the Reformation, he never accepted the new religion, and remained a faithful, but critical, Catholic to the end. His best-known work is *Moriae Encomium* (1509; trans., *The Praise of Folie*, 1549), a satire on the pretensions of human knowledge. T. W. Baldwin (*William Shakspere's Small Latine and Lesse Greeke*, 1944) has cited Erasmus' *Adagia*, *Copia*, *Colloquia*, and *De Conscribendis* as among the probable school texts studied by Shakespeare. The *Adagia*, translated into English in 1539, is the source of the address to opportunity in *The Rape of Lucrece* (876–924). In the *Adagia* Shakespeare might also have found the famous "honorificabilitudinitatibus" of *Love's Labour's Lost* (V, i, 44), which has been made so much of by the advocates of the BACONIAN THEORY. Some scholars have argued that *The Praise of Folie* is the source of elements in *Troilus and Cressida* as well as of Jaques' speech on the seven ages of man, Touchstone's comments, and Rosalind's complaint against Cupid in *As You Like It*.

Eros. In *Antony and Cleopatra*, a faithful soldier to Antony. Commanded by Antony to kill him, Eros commits suicide rather than take his master's life (IV, xiv).

Erpingham, Sir Thomas (1357–1428). An English soldier who won the confidence of both Henry IV and Henry V. In *Henry V*, on the eve of the battle of Agincourt, the King borrows Erpingham's cloak and speaks of him with affection (IV, i).

Escalus. In *Measure for Measure*, a humane old counselor who is appointed by the Duke to assist Angelo, the Deputy, in his reform program. Publicly accepting the severe justice meted out to Claudio but personally disposed to clemency, Escalus intercedes unsuccessfully with the Deputy for Claudio's life. Toward the end of the play when the disguised Duke appears as a witness for Isabella and Mariana, the counselor accepts Lucio's testimony and unwittingly orders the Duke to prison for slander to the state.

Escalus. In *Romeo and Juliet*, the Prince of Verona. A sage ruler who attempts to avert the tragic folly of the Montague-Capulet quarrel, Escalus' three appearances on stage mark three significant points in the development of the play. He appears each time immediately following an outburst of violence, representing in his person the principles of order and reason which have been violated. At the play's end, Escalus' final disposition and judgment reinforce the theme that knowledge is acquired through suffering. [H. S. Wilson, *On the Design of Shakespearian Tragedy*, 1957.]

Escanes. In *Pericles*, a lord of Tyre who speaks only in II, iv. Escanes is left to govern in Tyre while Pericles and Helicanus travel to Tarsus (IV, iv).

Essay against too much Reading (1728). An anonymous pamphlet which attempted to illustrate the superiority of "natural wit" to acquired knowledge. Not surprisingly, one of the author's examples was Shakespeare, whose reputation as an untutored genius had been developing since his death. The tract purports to account for Shakespeare's historical knowledge.

> I will give you a short Account of M[r] *Shakespear*'s Proceeding; and that I had from one of his intimate Acquaintance. His being imperfect in some Things, was owing to his not being a Scholar, which obliged him to have one of those chuckle-pated Historians for his particular Associate, that could scarce speak a Word but upon that Subject; and he maintain'd him, or he might have starv'd upon his History. And when he wanted anything in his Way, as his plays were all Historical, he sent to him, and took down the Heads of what was for his Purpose in Characters, which were thirty times as quick as running to the Books to read for it: Then with his natural flowing Wit, he work'd it into all Shapes and Forms, as his beautiful Thoughts directed. The other put it into Grammar; and instead of Reading, he stuck close to Writing and Study without Book. How do you think, Reading could have assisted him in such great Thoughts? It would only have lost Time. When he found his Thoughts grow on him fast, he should have writ for ever, had he liv'd so long.

The pamphlet is an interesting foreshadowing of later developments in Shakespearean studies: the disintegration theory, which casts doubt on Shakespeare's sole authorship of many of the plays in the canon, and the anti-Stratfordian theories, which seek to prove that someone other than Shakespeare wrote the plays. [E. K. Chambers, *William Shakespeare*, 1930.]

Essex, earl of (*Henry VIII*). See Thomas CROMWELL.

Essex, Geoffrey Fitzpeter, earl of (d. 1213). Son-in-law of Geoffrey de Mandeville, 1st earl of Essex, upon whose death Fitzpeter claimed the title. He held the confidence of Richard I, who appointed him to the high office of justiciar of England. This appointment was confirmed by King John, who nonetheless disliked Essex and rejoiced at his death. In *King John*, Essex appears in only I, i, where he presents the brothers Philip and Robert Faulconbridge to John.

Essex, Robert Devereux, 2nd earl of (1566–1601). Courtier, soldier, and favorite of Queen Elizabeth. Essex was the son of Walter Devereux, 1st earl of Essex (d. 1576) and Lettice Knollys (1541–1634).

ROBERT DEVEREUX, 2ND EARL OF ESSEX. PORTRAIT BY AN UNKNOWN ARTIST. (NATIONAL PORTRAIT GALLERY)

vho married Robert Dudley, earl of LEICESTER, two rears after her husband's death. Essex soon became iis stepfather's protégé and was his chief heir. Intel-igent, well educated, handsome, generous, and cour-geous, Essex was, as Ophelia said of Hamlet, "the xpectancy and rose of the fair state." He soon won he heart, if not the mind, of the aging queen and vas in constant attendance upon her. As one report ad it, "my Lord is at cards, or one game or another vith her, that he cometh not to his own lodging til irds sing in the morning."

Essex became a member of the privy council nd gathered about him a following of brilliant oung men, including Shakespeare's patron Henry Vriothesley, earl of SOUTHAMPTON, Francis BACON, and Bacon's brother Anthony (1558–1601). At the same ime, however, he was making enemies at court, chief mong whom was Robert Cecil, 1st earl of SALISBURY, he son of William Cecil, Lord Burghley. In 1596, Essex' brilliant career reached its apex in the capture f Cadiz. His popularity now soared to unbounded evels, threatening to eclipse that of the queen her-elf. Partly as a result of this popularity, and partly s a result of his hot temper and refusal to compro-nise, relations between Essex and the queen became trained. In 1599 he inadvertently talked himself into aking command of the troops charged with quelling he Irish rebellion. (See IRELAND.) With an army of 5,000 men, he landed in Dublin in April 1599. The onfidence in which the English nation held the oung earl is expressed by Shakespeare in *Henry V:*

> Were now the general of our gracious empress,
> As in good time he may, from Ireland coming,
> Bringing rebellion broached on his sword,
> How many would the peaceful city quit,
> To welcome him!
>
> (V, Prologue, 30–34)

The expedition, however, proved a fiasco, and Essex concluded a dishonorable truce with the Irish leaders. With a small group of his most trusted lieutenants, he hurriedly left Ireland and, returning to England, dramatically strode into Elizabeth's private chamber. At first she received him with pleasure, but upon reflection, she had him placed in confinement and banished from court. Exiled from the royal presence, he and his band of malcontent followers (see Henry CUFFE), in an atmosphere of discontent and intrigue, conceived a plot to overthrow the queen and replace her with James VI of Scotland. On February 6, 1601 Sir Charles PERCY and a number of other Essex followers arranged for the performance of *Richard II* by Shakespeare's company on the following day, hoping the precedent of the deposing of a king would be fresh in the minds of the citizenry. The play was performed, and on the following day, Essex and his friends stormed into London, vainly expecting to arouse the populace against the queen. The uprising proved a spectacular failure. Essex was captured and tried: the chief prosecuting attorney was his former follower Francis Bacon. He was convicted of treason and executed on February 25, 1601.

That Shakespeare was an ardent admirer of Essex seems almost certain. Aside from the fact that his patron Southampton was Essex' closest friend, there are a number of apparent allusions in the plays to the young earl's career. The most direct of these, cited above, appears in *Henry V* (see HENRY V: *Date; Comment*). Others include a reference to the CADIZ expedition in *The Merchant of Venice* and possibly also in *King John.* There is a possible reference to the Elizabeth-Essex relations in THE PHOENIX AND THE TURTLE, and an alleged portrait of Essex as Achilles in *Troilus and Cressida* (see TOPICAL REFERENCES). But a number of scholars, most notably J. Dover Wilson, argue that the profound impact that Essex' career had on Shakespeare is not to be found in these scattered allusions, but in the psychological portrait of Shakespeare's greatest creation, Hamlet. Wilson argues that Hamlet is Shakespeare's attempt to understand Essex, who, in 1600 (the probable date of the writing of the play), was subject to the same fits of melancholy and depression that we see in the portrait of the Dane. [J. Dover Wilson, *The Essential Shakespeare,* 1932.]

Essex' Men. Elizabethan acting company, maintained by the earls of Essex since the 15th century. Under the patronage of Robert Devereux, 2nd earl of Essex and Queen Elizabeth's favorite, Essex' Men toured the provinces, but apparently never ventured to play in London. In 1587 they appeared on a number of occasions in Stratford. It is to be assumed that at the execution of Essex on February 25, 1601 the acting company disbanded.

Etkyns, Thomas. See Thomas EDKINS.

Eton College. School whose boys performed plays in the Elizabethan and Tudor periods. Boys from Eton had taken part in the BOY-BISHOP ceremonies as early as 1444. Although this custom was abandoned before the last half of the 16th century, the boys continued to give plays at Christmas. In 1538 the boys gave a play before Thomas Cromwell; their director was Nicholas Udall, whose play *Ralph Roister Doister* might be dated from his period (1534–1541) as master at Eton. The only court performance given by the Eton boys is recorded for January 6, 1573; the payee was William Elderton, presumably the same man who directed the boys of the WESTMINSTER SCHOOL at court in 1574. [E. K. Chambers, *The Elizabethan Stage*, 1923.]

Euphronius. In *Antony and Cleopatra*, an ambassador. After his defeat at Actium, Antony sends Euphronius to request Octavius Caesar that he be permitted to live in Egypt or Athens, and that Cleopatra remain queen of Egypt. Euphronius' mission is unsuccessful.

Evans, Dame **Edith** (1888–). Actress. Born in London, Dame Edith Evans was educated at St. Michael's School. In 1912 she appeared as Cressida in a revival of Shakespeare's play by the Elizabethan Stage Society. In 1914 she appeared as the Queen in *Hamlet*. In 1918 she toured with Ellen Terry in variety theatres as Mrs. Ford and Nerissa in scenes from Shakespeare's plays, repeating Nerissa in *The Merchant of Venice* at the Royal Court Theatre the following year. In 1923 she played Mistress Page at Hammersmith, and then joined the Birmingham Repertory Company, originating many parts with them, including the She Ancient and the Serpent in Shaw's *Back to Methuselah*.

After playing Helena in a Drury Lane production (1924) of *A Midsummer Night's Dream*, she joined (1925) the Old Vic, appearing (1925/6) as Portia, Margaret (*Richard III*), Katharine, Mariana, Cleopatra, Mistress Page, Beatrice, Rosalind, and the Nurse in *Romeo and Juliet*. In 1932 she again played with the Old Vic, as Emilia and Viola, and in 1934/5 she played the Nurse in Katharine Cornell's *Romeo and Juliet* in New York. In 1936 at the Old Vic she again played Rosalind, and in 1937 did Katharina in *The Taming of the Shrew*. She appeared in 1946 as Cleopatra and in 1950 spoke the prologue at the reopening of the Old Vic. In 1958 she played Queen Katharine in *Henry VIII* at the Old Vic and on the company's continental tour. In 1959 she played Countess Rousillon and Volumnia at the Shakespeare Memorial Theatre, Stratford-upon-Avon. She has appeared in many movies and on television. [*Who's Who in the Theatre*, 1961.]

Evans, Henry (fl. 1582–1608). Lessee of the Blackfriars theatre (1600–1608) and manager of the Children of the Chapel from 1600 to 1603. Evans held his lease from Richard and Cuthbert Burbage, the owners of the theatre. He relinquished his lease in 1608, thus enabling the King's Men to occupy the Blackfriars at that time. Evans and the King's Men were then sued by Robert KEYSAR, Evans' partner, but the outcome of the case is not known.

Evans, Sir **Hugh.** In *The Merry Wives of Windsor*, a Welsh parson. Sir Hugh is challenged to a duel by Doctor Caius when the latter learns that the parson favors Slender's suit to Anne Page. The merry Host of the Garter Inn directs each opponent to a different place to await the other, then reveals his deception, explaining that he did not want to lose either his doctor or his parson. The two adversaries, realizing that they have been made sport of, join forces against the Host. Sir Hugh is later delighted to assist at the public humiliation of Falstaff and volunteers to instruct the children in their roles. He disguises himself as a satyr to take part in the revel.

Evans, Maurice (1901–). British-American actor, producer, and director. Born in Dorchester, Dorset, Evans began to act professionally in 1926 at the Cambridge Festival Theatre as Orestes in Aeschylus' *Oresteia*. He made his London debut the following year, and in 1934 joined the Old Vic-Sadler's Wells company, with which he played Octavius Caesar (*Antony and Cleopatra*), Richard II, Benedick, Petruchio, Iago, Silence, and Hamlet. Before becoming a United States citizen in 1941, he appeared as Romeo in Katharine Cornell's *Romeo and Juliet* (1935) and as Malvolio with Helen Hayes in *Twelfth Night* (1940/1). In 1941 he presented *Macbeth* in New York under his own management and with himself as Macbeth. He also appeared with phenomenal success as John Tanner in Shaw's *Man and Superman* in 1947. For television, Evans directed and appeared as Hamlet, Richard II, and Macbeth, and directed *Twelfth Night*, *The Taming of the Shrew*, and *The Tempest*, in which he played Prospero. [*Who's Who in the Theatre*, 1961.]

Every Man In his Humour (1598). A comedy by Ben JONSON, originally acted by the Chamberlain's Men in 1598 with Shakespeare in one of the leading roles. *Every Man In his Humour* was entered in the Stationers' Register, along with three of Shakespeare's plays, in 1600 with the notation "to be staied" (see BLOCKING ENTRY). It was published the following year in quarto, and appeared in the Folio edition of Jonson's collected plays in 1616 in a much-revised form. It was performed before King James in 1605, at which time the revision, which included changing the scene of the play from Italy to England, may have taken place, although Jonson's editors, Herford and Simpson, suggest 1612. The 1616 edition of the play contains the following postscript:

This Comoedie was firſt
Acted, in the yeere
1598.

By the then L. CHAMBERLAYNE
his Seruants.

The principall Comœdians were,

WILL SHAKESPEARE.	RIC. BVRBADGE.
AVG. PHILIPS.	IOH. HEMINGS.
HEN. CONDEL.	THO. POPE.
WILL. SLYE.	CHR. BEESTON.
WILL. KEMPE.	IOH. DVKE.

With the allowance of the Maſter of REVELLS.

It is generally assumed that Shakespeare's role in the play was that of Elder Knowell (Lorenzo senior in the Italian version). Despite Shakespeare's participation in the play, Jonson's verse Prologue to the 1616 edition contains a number of satiric side-glances at Shakespeare's plays, specifically at *Henry VI,* in the reference to York and Lancaster, *Henry V,* in the allusion to the Chorus, and possibly at *Cymbeline,* in the reference to the "creaking throne":

Though neede make many *Poets,* and some such
As art, and nature haue not betterd much;
Yet ours, for want, hath not so lou'd the stage,
As he dare serue th'ill customes of the age:
Or purchase your delight at such a rate,
As, for it, he himselfe must iustly hate.
To make a child, now swadled, to proceede
Man, and then shoote vp, in one beard, and weede,
Past threescore yeeres: or, with three rustie swords,
And helpe of some few foot-and-halfe-foote words,
Fight ouer *Yorke,* and *Lancasters* long iarres:
And in the tyring-house bring wounds, to scarres.
He rather prayes, you will be pleas'd to see
One such, to day, as other playes should be.
Where neither *Chorus* wafts you ore the seas;
Nor creaking throne comes downe, the boyes to please;
Nor nimble squibbe is seene, to make afear'd
The gentlewomen; nor roul'd bullet heard
To say, it thunders; nor tempestuous drumme
Rumbles, to tell you when the storme doth come;
But deedes, and language, such as men doe vse:
And persons, such as *Comoedie* would chuse,

In the Prologue to *Bartholomew Fair* Jonson displays a similar displeasure with Shakespeare's disregard of the classical rules of dramaturgy. [*Ben Jonson,* C. H. Herford and Percy Simpson, eds., 11 vols., 1925–1952.]

Every Man Out of his Humour (1599). A "Comicall Satyre" by Ben JONSON, entered in the Stationers' Register on April 8, 1600 and printed three times that year. In the First Folio of Jonson's works (1616), *Every Man Out of his Humour* was reprinted with the following postscript:

This Comicall Satyre was first acted in the yeere 1599. By the then Lord Chamberlaine his Seruants. The principall Comoedians were, Ric. Burbadge, Ioh. Hemings, Aug. Philips, Hen. Condel, Wil. Sly, Tho. Pope. With the allowance of the Master of the Revels.

Attempts have been made to argue that the characters in the play are veiled portraits of Jonson's contemporaries, but the prevailing view is that Jonson was more concerned with presenting careful, accurate descriptions of conventional satiric character types rather than with satirizing individuals. There may, however, be a barb directed against Shakespeare's newly acquired COAT OF ARMS with an apparent parody of Shakespeare's motto, "*non sanz droict,*" in the play referred to as "*Not without mustard.*" [*Ben Jonson,* C. H. Herford and Percy Simpson, eds., 11 vols., 1925–1952.]

Executioner. In *The Two Noble Kinsmen,* a non-speaking role. Just before Palamon is to be executed, Pirithous brings word that Arcite with his dying breath has given Emilia to Palamon, thus saving his cousin's life (V, iv).

Exeter, Henry Holland, duke of (1430–1473). Although he was married to a daughter of Richard, duke of York, Exeter supported Henry VI and was consequently attainted by Edward IV. In *3 Henry VI,* Exeter appears briefly as a follower of King Henry. He admits, however, that York is the lawful king of England (I, i).

Exeter, Thomas Beaufort, duke of (c. 1375–1427). Youngest son of John of Gaunt by his third wife, Catherine Swynford. In 1405 Beaufort commanded the army of his half brother King Henry IV in the war against the northern rebels, and in 1412 he took part in the French expedition. When Henry V became king, Beaufort was appointed lieutenant of Normandy, and on the surrender of the town of Harfleur, he was appointed its governor. In 1416 he was made duke of Exeter for life. After helping to negotiate the treaty of Troyes, he was present at its ratification in 1420.

In *Henry V,* Exeter appears as the King's uncle. He urges Henry to claim the French throne, and is subsequently sent to demand the submission of King Charles of France. Exeter is with Henry on the Harfleur-Agincourt campaign. In *1 Henry VI,* he is the King's great-uncle and his personal guardian.

Exton, Sir Pierce, or **Piers,** of. Sir Pierce is thought to have been a near relation of Sir Nicholas Exton, sheriff of London in 1385, who strongly opposed Richard II in parliament. In *Richard II,* Sir Pierce is a friend of Henry IV. Overhearing Henry express a wish for Richard's death, Exton commits the murder to please him. Henry, however, is not grateful (V, iv–vi). [W. H. Thomson, *Shakespeare's Characters: A Historical Dictionary,* 1951.]

F

Fabian. In *Twelfth Night,* a servant in Olivia's household. Having lost favor with his mistress owing to Malvolio's report of a bear-baiting, Fabian exults in that steward's downfall during the course of the play. In the final scene, it is Fabian who confesses to Olivia his and Sir Toby's part in the "sportful malice" against Malvolio.

Fabyan, Robert (d. 1513). Chronicler. A clothier active in civic affairs, Fabyan became sheriff of London in 1493. He was also an amateur historian who expanded his private diary into a full-blown history of England, published in 1516, after his death. It ran through several editions and was edited and published as *The new chronicles of England and France* in 1811 by Sir Henry Ellis. Fabyan's work was frequently used by later historians of the 16th century and possibly by Shakespeare as one of the minor sources of his Henry VI plays and *Henry V*. [Geoffrey Bullough, *Narrative and Dramatic Sources of Shakespeare,* Vol. II, 1957.]

Faerie Queene, The (Books I–III, 1590; Books IV–VI, 1596). An allegorical epic poem by Edmund SPENSER. In a prefatory letter to Sir Walter Raleigh, Spenser outlined the general plan of the poem. He conceived that the work would consist of 12 books, each of which would portray the adventures of a knight who would embody an abstract virtue. Spenser finished only six books and a portion of the seventh before his death. Even in its incomplete state, however, the poem stands as the greatest nondramatic achievement of its age. Shakespeare is directly indebted to *The Faerie Queene* for some details of the deception episode in *Much Ado About Nothing,* but the thematic influence of the poem, while less tangible, is more pervasive. [W. B. C. Watkins, *Shakespeare and Spenser,* 1950; A. F. Potts, *Shakespeare and The Faerie Queene,* 1958.]

fair copy. Term used to describe the corrected copy of an Elizabethan play manuscript submitted to an acting company. An author would presumably make a rough copy of a play (see FOUL PAPERS), which would then be corrected and revised either by himself or by a professional scribe. The process is described by the playwright Robert Daborne to Philip Henslowe in a letter recounting his revision of his foul papers: "I will not fail to write this fair and perfit the book." The fair copy would presumably be annotated by the prompter, with appropriate notes for properties, stage effects, etc., and then be transcribed into the company's PROMPT-BOOK.

Shakespeare apparently did not make fair copies, his fluency being such that his revisions and corrections could be made in his original draft. [W. W. Greg, *The Editorial Problem in Shakespeare,* 1942.]

Fair Em. An anonymous play attributed to Shake-speare on the basis of its inclusion in a volume of plays in Charles II's library under the collective title "Shakespeare. Vol. I." The play was published, without date, with the following title page:

> A Pleasant Comedie of Faire Em, the Millers Daughter of Manchester. With the love of William the Conqueror. As it was sundry times publiquely acted in the Honourable Citie of London by the right Honourable the Lord Strange his Seruants.
>
> For T. N. and I. W.

Attempts to view the play as containing topical allusions to the activities of the acting companies in the 1590's have not met with acceptance, and virtually every critic rejects the ascription to Shakespeare.

TITLE PAGE OF THE SECOND QUARTO OF *Fair Em,* A COMEDY ONCE ASCRIBED TO SHAKESPEARE.

A Pleaſant
COMEDIE
OF
FAIRE EM,
The Millers Daughter of
Mancheſter:
With the loue of *William* the Conqueror.
As it was ſundry times publiquely acted in the Honourable Citie of London, by the right Honourable the Lord *Strange* his Seruants.

LONDON,
Printed for *Iohn Wright,* and are to be ſold at his ſhop at the ſigne of the Bible in Guilt-ſpur ſtreet without New-gate. 1631.

Fairholt, Frederick William (1814–1866). Engraver and antiquarian. Fairholt provided illustrations for numerous works on pageantry, costumery, silverware, plate, and numismatics. Because of Fairholt's extensive knowledge of costumery, Halliwell-Phillipps commissioned him to illustrate his *Life of William Shakespeare* (1848) and his folio edition of the *Works* (16 vols., 1853–1865). Fairholt's interest in Shakespeare led him to assemble an extensive collection of material which he bequeathed to the Stratford Library. He drew upon this material for his *Home of Shakespeare* (1847), illustrated with 33 engravings. Fairholt also served on the committee which purchased (1847) the "birthplace," the house traditionally regarded as the place of Shakespeare's birth. For the Percy Society he edited Lyly's *Dramatic Works* (2 vols., 1858).

fairies. Traditional popular belief in the existence of fairies had begun to fade by the end of the 16th century, although credence was still given popular spirits like Robin Goodfellow (see PUCK). This growing disbelief was probably increased, ironically enough, by the picture of fairy land in *A Midsummer Night's Dream.* For in that play, Shakespeare altered the folk concept of fairies, converting them into benevolent, ethereal, dream-like creatures instead of the more substantial, often malign, spirits of popular lore. Shakespeare also reduced the size of the fairies both in *A Midsummer Night's Dream* and in Mercutio's famous description in *Romeo and Juliet* of Queen Mab:

> She is the fairies' midwife, and she comes
> In shape no bigger than an agate-stone
> On the fore-finger of an alderman,
> Drawn with a team of little atomies
> Athwart men's noses as they lie asleep.
> (I, iv, 54–58)

Shakespeare's influence has been such that his imaginative conception of fairies has come to replace the traditional spirits of folklore. [M. W. Latham, *The Elizabethan Fairies*, 1930.]

Fairies, The. An operatic adaptation of *A Midsummer Night's Dream* by David GARRICK. *The Fairies*, advertised as a "new English opera," opened on February 3, 1755 at the Drury Lane. It consisted of an abridged version of the first four acts of Shakespeare's play to which were added 28 songs with music provided by John Christopher SMITH. The play, which ran for nine performances, featured a number of Italian operatic stars of the day. [John Genest, *Some Account of the English Stage*, 1832; C. B. Hogan, *Shakespeare in the Theatre, 1701–1800*, 2 vols., 1952–1957.]

Fair Youth. See MR. W. H.

Faithful Shepherdess, The. See John FLETCHER.

falconry. The sport of hunting with hawks. Falconry was so popular in Elizabethan days that its specific vocabulary came into the everyday language of the times. Some of Shakespeare's imagery is derived from the sport, as for example, when Juliet, longing for the departed Romeo, wishes "for a falconer's voice, / To lure this tassel-gentle back again" (II, ii, 159–160). This refers to the peregrine falcon, a type of hawk most commonly used for falconry; the female was called the falcon and the male the tercel gentle or tassel-gentle.

QUEEN ELIZABETH ON A HAWKING EXPEDITION. WOODCUT FROM TURBERVILE'S *The booke of faulconrie* (1575).

In his famous reference to the popularity of the children's acting companies over the adult companies, Shakespeare again borrows from the vocabulary of falconry:

> . . . but there is, sir, an eyrie of children, little eyases, that cry out on the top of question and are most tyrannically clapped for't: these are now the fashion . . .
> (*Hamlet*, II, ii, 354 ff.)

The eyas is the young hawk taken from its nest for training; the eyrie (or aerie) is a high nest and used also to mean the brood of birds of prey.

Shakespeare uses the term "haggard" frequently to denote wildness and intractability:

> If I do prove her haggard,
> Though that her jesses were my dear heartstrings,
> I'ld whistle her off and let her down the wind,
> To prey at fortune.
> (*Othello*, III, iii, 260–263)

The haggard is a hawk caught when fully moulted at least once. Accustomed to prey for themselves, they were naturally more difficult to train than birds caught at earlier stages of development. They proved to be highly skillful when trained, but they were often untrainable. The "jesses" referred to in the passage are short leather straps attached to the legs of a hawk for the purpose of holding it.

When caught, a wild hawk has its eyes seeled by means of a fine thread attached to the lower eyelid, drawn over the top of the head, and fixed to the lower eyelid of the other eye. When the thread is pulled fairly tight the lower lids are pulled up and the eyes nearly closed; as training progresses, the thread is loosened gradually, and more daylight admitted, until there is no longer any need for it and the thread can be removed. In addition to the seeling, a hood is used to blindfold the hawk to guarantee its quiescence. The rather technical term "seel" often occurs in Shakespeare:

the wise gods seel our eyes;
In our own filth drop our clear judgements; make us
Adore our errors.
(*Antony and Cleopatra*, III, xiii, 112–114)

The process of taming or manning a wild hawk includes taking it on the fist and gently stroking it until it becomes accustomed to being handled; at first the bird flutters or "bates," and is sometimes recalcitrant; the bird is made docile through fatigue. Shakespeare has Petruchio describe his taming of Kate with the metaphor of the manning of the falcon:

Another way I have to man my haggard,
To make her come and know her keeper's call,
That is, to watch her, as we watch these kites
That bate and beat and will not be obedient.
She eat no meat to-day, nor none shall eat;
Last night she slept not, nor to-night she shall not.
(*The Taming of the Shrew*, IV, i, 196–201)

Bells are sometimes fastened to the legs of the newly trained hawk in order that it might be easily found if it should bring down quarry (the prey) in thick cover. Apparently in Shakespeare's time it was believed that the sound of a falcon's bells terrified the quarry:

Harmless Lucretia, marking what he tells
With trembling fear, as fowl hear falcon's bells.
(*The Rape of Lucrece*, 510–511)

There are two basic types of hawking: the flight at the high mounty—that is, the pursuit of a high-flying quarry such as the heron or bittern; and the flight at the river, in which the hawk swoops down on quarry flushed from the ground. The greater the height, or pitch, of the waiting bird, the more ground it is able to cover, and the swifter its stoop, or descent. Shakespeare uses this term for the hawk's height as a metaphor in *Richard II*:

How high a pitch his resolution soars!
(I, i, 109)

[Gerald Lascelles, "Falconry," *Shakespeare's England*, 1916.]

Falstaff, Sir John. The comic hero of *1* and *2 Henry IV* and *The Merry Wives of Windsor*. Second only to Hamlet as Shakespeare's most famous creation, Falstaff has from his very inception been a source of comment and controversy. The earliest argument arose from the commotion caused by his original name (see Sir John OLDCASTLE) and by the fact that "Falstaff" came to be used as a nickname for a powerful Elizabethan nobleman (see William Brooke, 7th Lord COBHAM; Henry Brooke, 8th Lord COBHAM). On his appearance in the *Henry IV* plays, Falstaff's popularity became such that *The Merry Wives of Windsor* was created as a vehicle for him at the special request, according to tradition, of Queen Elizabeth I herself (see THE MERRY WIVES OF WINDSOR: *Date*). Since that time, he has been delighting audiences and inciting critics to probe the mystery of his universal appeal.

Falstaff's famous remark that he is not only witty in himself "but the cause that wit is in other men" has proven to be prophetic, for his character has provoked some of the finest Shakespearean criticism ever written. The earliest was Dryden's description of him as the "best of Comical Characters." Considerably less enthusiastic was Dr. Johnson's analysis of Falstaff as "a thief, a glutton, a coward and a boaster," but one whose faults we are all willing to forgive because of his "perpetual gaiety." This rather stern view of the old knight was sharply corrected in Maurice MORGANN's *Essay on the Dramatic Character of Falstaff* (1777). Morgann's *Essay*, justly famous as the 18th-century forerunner of Romantic criticism, argued that the view of Falstaff as a coward was an erroneous one, contradicted by various characters in the play who testify to Sir John's valor in his youth. The defense of Falstaff's courage prompted the skeptical reply from Dr. Johnson that having proved Falstaff to be courageous, Morgann should now attempt to "prove Iago a very good character." Morgann's vindication of Falstaff rested on a distinction which he drew between the action of a character and the impression that the character leaves on the audience. Thus the largely favorable impact of Falstaff on the audience was the final evidence of Falstaff's virtue.

Morgann's view of Falstaff's nature prevailed generally throughout the 19th century. Coleridge saw Falstaff as "no coward" but as one who pretends to cowardice "for the sake of trying experiments on the credulity of mankind." Hazlitt employed Morgann's argument in making an invidious comparison with Henry V; he concluded that ". . . to the readers of poetry at present, Falstaff is the better man of the two." The Romantic view achieved its finest expression, however, in A. C. Bradley's "The Rejection of Falstaff" (*Oxford Lectures on Poetry*, 1909). Bradley's essay focuses on Falstaff's relationship with Prince Hal and the subsequent repudiation of the old knight by his former companion (see HAL). For Bradley, Falstaff represented "the bliss of freedom gained in humour."

The reaction to Bradley, on this as on so many other points, was set in motion by E. E. Stoll. Stoll's "Falstaff" (reprinted in *Shakespeare Studies*, 1927) argued that the old knight was the Elizabethan incarnation of the *miles gloriosus* of Roman comedy. As such, Stoll argued, Falstaff was designed as a comic butt, not as the sympathetic, transcendent figure imagined by Bradley and the Romantic critics. Stoll pointed out that the glorifiers of Falstaff had concentrated on his roles in *Henry IV* to the exclusion of that in *The Merry Wives of Windsor*, but his opponents were quick to reply that the ludicrous Falstaff of *The Merry Wives of Windsor* bore little resemblance to the brilliant character of the *Henry IV* plays.

Stoll's view received unexpected support in 1943, however, with the publication of Dover Wilson's *The Fortunes of Falstaff*. Although formerly a confirmed Bradleyite in his attitude toward Falstaff, Wilson, adopting the methods of HISTORICAL CRITICISM employed by Stoll, revealed a new interpretation of the knight. For Wilson, Falstaff represents the development of the Vice of the morality play and the figure of Riot (leading Youth astray) in the allegorical drama of the early 16th century (see 1

HENRY IV: *Comment*). Thus Wilson argued that for the Elizabethans Falstaff was seen in a specifically moral context which demanded his expulsion and repudiation. Wilson's view of Falstaff as a Lord of Misrule who is ultimately overthrown was taken up and developed by mythic critics who have seen the character as an archetypal scapegoat figure (see MYTHIC CRITICISM). The Romantic view of Falstaff as one who transcends petty human laws in glorious amorality has been discredited. Nevertheless, most modern readers still give their hearts to Falstaff in a manner which suggests that the last word has not been said. [*1 Henry IV:* New Variorum Edition, Samuel B. Hemingway, ed., 1936; *2 Henry IV:* New Variorum Edition, M. A. Shaaber, ed., 1940; Samuel B. Hemingway, "On Behalf of that Falstaff," *Shakespeare Quarterly*, III, 1952.]—E.Q.

Family of Love, The. A play by Thomas MIDDLETON entered in the Stationers' Register in 1607 and published in the following year as: *The Famelie of Love. Acted by the Children of His Maiesties Reuells. The Family of Love* is Middleton's earliest known work, and the author's inexperience is attested to by his frequent imitations and parodies of older writers, particularly of Marlowe and Shakespeare. The play contains a balcony scene borrowed from *Romeo and Juliet* and a parody of Ulysses' speech on degree in *Troilus and Cressida.* The last parallel is important in establishing the date of *Troilus and Cressida* since *The Family of Love* is generally dated about 1602/3. [Richard H. Barker, *Thomas Middleton*, 1958; Robert Kimbrough, "The Origins of *Troilus and Cressida*," *PMLA*, LXXVII, 1962.]

Famous Victories of Henry V, The. An anonymous play used by Shakespeare as a minor source of the *Henry IV* and *Henry V* plays. *The Famous Victories of Henry V* was entered in the Stationers' Register on May 14, 1594, but the earliest extant edition is dated 1598. Some scholars have suggested that the play as it has survived is a "bad quarto," a bungled MEMORIAL RECONSTRUCTION of a lost play, and that it was the lost play and not *The Famous Victories* which served as a source of Shakespeare's plays.

This position has been challenged recently by Seymour Pitcher, who has argued that *The Famous Victories* was in fact written by Shakespeare in 1586 for Queen Elizabeth's Men. Pitcher's thesis rests in part on the argument of Allan Keen and Roger Lubbock that Shakespeare's youthful hand can be detected in the annotations of a copy of Halle's chronicles (see Edward HALLE). Pitcher argues that the annotations bear a close enough resemblance to the text of the play to suggest that the annotator and the author of *The Famous Victories* were identical. [Alan Keen and Roger Lubbock, *The Annotator*, 1954; Seymour Pitcher, *The Case for Shakespeare's Authorship of "The Famous Victories,"* 1961.]

fanfare. Three trumpet blasts sounded to announce the commencement of a play (or the beginning of an act should there be an "intermission"); the fanfare also may have been used (in addition to the flag atop the Elizabethan theatres) to signal townspeople that a performance would be given in the public theatres. It is believed that the trumpeter was stationed in the hut (indicated in DeWitt's sketch of the Swan), and that upon the third blast of the trumpet, the action commenced. In Marston's *What You Will* (1601), a stage direction reads, "Before the music sounds for the Act" and in *Antonio and Mellida* (1599), "The music will sound straight for entrance." The fanfare was also used to announce regal entrances within the action of the play.

When the practice of sounding the three blasts evolved into the more general phrasing, "music sounds," is uncertain, though it may be assumed that the use of more elaborate musical preparation and devices appeared about 1608 under the influence of the musical intervals in the private theatres. A similar device may be found in the later French theatre, with the three-time knocking substituted for the trumpet blasts to signal the beginning of a performance. [E. K. Chambers, *The Elizabethan Stage*, 1923; Bernard Beckerman, *Shakespeare at the Globe*, 1962.]

Fang. In *2 Henry IV*, a sheriff's officer who arrests Falstaff at the suit of Mistress Quickly (II, i).

Farjeon, Herbert (1887–1945). Actor, author, and dramatic critic. Farjeon wrote and produced many intimate revues which were staged at the Little Theatre in London. He also edited the Nonesuch and other editions of Shakespeare's works, as well as the *Shakespeare Journal* from 1922 to 1925. His grandfather was the famous actor Joseph Jefferson (1829–1905). [*Oxford Companion to the Theatre*, Phyllis Hartnoll, ed., 1951.]

Farmer, Richard (1735–1797). Scholar. Educated at Emmanuel College, Cambridge, Farmer eventually became master of Emmanuel and vice chancellor of the university. He compiled both a rich collection of Shakespeareana and other books related to early English literature. His only published work is the well-known *Essay on the Learning of Shakespeare* (1767), in which he demonstrated that Shakespeare's knowledge of classical literature was derived from English translations of the original sources.

Farnham, Willard (1891–). American scholar, professor emeritus at the University of California. Farnham's *Medieval Heritage of Elizabethan Tragedy* (1936) is a study of the medieval concept of tragedy and its development into the Renaissance historical narrative, as exemplified by such works as *A Mirror for Magistrates.* This development has relevance to the histories as well as the tragedies of Shakespeare. *Shakespeare's Tragic Frontier: The World of his Final Tragedies* (1950) is a detailed study of *Timon of Athens, Macbeth, Antony and Cleopatra,* and *Coriolanus.* Farnham has also edited *Hamlet* for the Pelican Shakespeare series.

Farrant, Richard (c. 1530–1580). Composer, choirmaster, and director of children's acting companies. Farrant, who was a distinguished composer of songs and services, became the organist and master of the choristers at St. George Chapel, Windsor, in 1564. From this nucleus, he developed the choir boys into a company known as the CHILDREN OF WINDSOR, who were soon making annual appearances before the court as part of the "twelfth night" festivities. By 1576 the Children of Windsor had combined with the CHILDREN OF THE CHAPEL for some performances and in that year Farrant leased six rooms in the dissolved Blackfriars monastery with the purpose of converting them into a theatre (see BLACKFRIARS THEATRE). Farrant apparently managed to circumvent city ordinances against plays by characterizing the performances which the Children gave at Blackfriars as public "rehearsals." He directed his company in court, as well as public, performances (for which Farrant was always paid the fee—£6 13s. 4d.) until his death in 1580. [Robert K. Sarlos, "Development and Operation of the First Blackfriars Theatre" in *Studies in the Elizabethan Theatre*, C. T. Prouty, ed., 1961.]

Fastolfe, Sir John (c. 1378–1459). Fastolfe fought under Henry V in the French campaign, and after the capture of Harfleur in 1415 was made governor of the city along with Thomas Beaufort, duke of Exeter. After the king's death, Fastolfe served under the duke of Bedford, eventually becoming regent of Normandy and governor of Anjou and Maine. In 1429 he successfully brought provisions to the English army beseiging Orléans, after heroically fending off a French army in the "Battle of the Herrings." The same year, while serving under John Talbot, earl of Shrewsbury, Fastolfe was put to flight at Patay by Joan of Arc.

In *1 Henry VI*, Fastolfe is represented as a cowardly English captain who deserts Talbot, first at Patay, then again at Rouen. For his faint-heartedness he is deprived of the Garter and banished. It is generally assumed that Shakespeare derived the name Falstaff from Fastolfe. This conjecture has received support from the discovery that the historical Fastolfe had a man named "Bardolph" under his command. Added to this is the fact that in the 17th century Fastolfe and Falstaff were regarded as identical. See Richard JAMES.

Father that has killed his son. In *3 Henry VI*, he drags on the body of a boy whom he has killed in battle and is horrified to discover that his opponent is his only son (II, v).

Faucit, Helen. Real name **Helena Saville** (1817–1898). Actress. Helen Faucit made her debut as Juliet in Norwich, where she met Edmund Kean. In 1836 she made her London debut, attracting the interest of Charles Kemble, who was seeking a replacement for Fanny Kemble; during her resulting three years' engagement at Covent Garden, she acted with Macready. During the ensuing years she added to her repertory many leading Shakespearean roles, which she played in Dublin, Edinburgh, and Glasgow as well as in London. She married Theodore Martin in 1851. Her last stage appearance was as Rosalind at Manchester in 1879. Her acting style was characterized by imagination, and she excelled in both comic and tragic roles. A biography, *The Life of Helena Faucit, Lady Martin*, by her husband, was published in 1900. Earlier, she herself had written *On Some of Shakespeare's Female Characters* (1885), which was dedicated to Queen Victoria, with whom she maintained a warm personal relationship. The studies, in the form of letters to famous literary men, deal with Ophelia, Portia, Rosalind, Beatrice, Hermione, Desdemona, Juliet, and Imogen. [*Dictionary of National Biography*, 1885– .]

Faukes de Brent. See Faukes de BRENT.

Faulconbridge, Lady. In *King John*, the mother of Robert Faulconbridge and Philip the Bastard. Philip forces her to admit that he was fathered by Richard Coeur de Lion, who had seduced her during her husband's absence (I, i).

Faulconbridge, Philip. Called the Bastard. In *King John*, the cynical, witty illegitimate son of Richard Coeur de Lion. His vivid, lively commentary on the action of the play has been compared by some to that of the chorus in Greek tragedy. However, the Bastard has a more significant role to play than that of commentator. Indeed, many critics regard him as the hero of the play—the representative of the spirit of England, burdened with an unworthy King and yet faithful to him as a national symbol. To the Bastard is given the most famous speech in the play, the scathing denunciation of power politics as "Commodity" (II, i, 561–598).

E. A. J. Honigmann, who believes that *John* was written in 1590 for the combined Strange's-Admiral's Men at The Theatre, argues that the role of the Bastard was created for Richard Burbage and that for certain incidents the playwright drew on an affair which occurred at that playhouse in 1590 (see THE THEATRE). Other scholars think that Faulconbridge may be a portrait of Faukes de BRENT.

Faulconbridge, Robert. In *King John*, the legitimate son of Sir Robert and Lady Faulconbridge. When it is disclosed that his older brother, Philip, is illegitimate, Robert is granted his father's inheritance (I, i).

Feeble, Francis. In *2 Henry IV*, a ladies' tailor. Of the men conscripted by Justice Shallow, Feeble is one of the three selected by Falstaff for service in the army (III, ii).

Felix and Philiomena, The History of. A lost play, based on Jorge de Montemayor's pastoral play *Diana Enamorada*. *Felix and Philiomena* was performed at court by the Queen's Men in 1585, and may have been a source of Shakespeare's *Two Gentlemen of Verona*. See THE TWO GENTLEMEN OF VERONA: *Sources*.

Felton portrait. See PORTRAITS OF SHAKESPEARE.

fencing and dueling. Fencing is, strictly speaking, the practice of the art of self-defense. The noun "fence" is merely a shortened form of "defence," and both words were used interchangeably in Shakespeare's time. The rapier, a two-edged, pointed sword, was introduced into England toward the middle of the 16th century and became so popular that it almost completely superseded earlier weapons. While the rapier remained a dangerous weapon, fencing in the 16th century had grown to be an art indulged in for the demonstration of one's skill, as well as for the vindication of one's honor.

Early in Elizabeth's reign, the foil, a light sword bated, or blunted, with a button, came into use. In *Much Ado About Nothing* Benedick's wit is described as "blunt as the fencer's foils, which hit, but hurt not" (V, ii, 13–14). In *Hamlet* Claudius arranges a supposedly innocent fencing match as a test of skill between Hamlet and Laertes; but Laertes is to have

> A sword unbated, and in a pass of practice
> Requite him for your father.
>
> (IV, vii, 139–140)

Shakespeare uses some of the jargon of fencing in the following passage from *The Merry Wives of Windsor:*

> To see thee fight, to see thee foin, to see thee traverse; to see thee here, to see thee there; to see thee pass thy punto, thy stock, thy reverse, thy distance, thy montant.
>
> (II, iii, 24–27)

Foin, punto, and stock (or stoccata) are roughly syn-

THE *en garde* POSITION FOR DUELLING WITH RAPIER AND DAGGER. WOODCUT FROM GEORGE SILVER'S *Paradoxes of defence* (1599).

onymous with thrust; and montant (or montanto) is an upright thrust.

Professional fencers in Elizabethan times were of the same category as players, minstrels, and other wanderers who followed no recognized "merchandise, craft, or mystery" from which to gain a living; hence, in the eyes of the law, they were accounted vagabonds. Perhaps related to the legal disrepute in which fencers were held was the degradation of the duel. In medieval times the duel was conceived as judicial combat which was held to determine legal right and wrong; the victor of such a duel was either proved innocent of whatever charge he had been accused of, or vindicated in his charge of wrongdoing against another. At the beginning of *Richard II*, a formal charge of treason is lodged against Mowbray by Bolingbroke, who sums up his initial accusation:

> With a foul traitor's name stuff I thy throat;
> And wish, so please my sovereign, ere I move,
> What my tongue speaks my right drawn sword
> may prove.
>
> (I, i, 44–46)

By Elizabethan times, however, the duel had degenerated into an overnice preoccupation with personal honor, a tendency which Shakespeare ridicules with his treatment of dueling in the plays. Thus, in *As You Like It,* Touchstone remarks that he "did dislike the cut of a certain courtier's beard"; however, they "measured swords and parted." He explains the rules for quarreling:

> O sir, we quarrel in print, by the book; as you have books for good manners: I will name you the degrees. The first, the Retort Courteous; the second, the Quip Modest; the third, the Reply Churlish; the fourth, the Reproof Valiant; the fifth, the Countercheck Quarrelsome; the sixth, the Lie with Circumstance; the seventh, the Lie Direct.
>
> (V, iv, 94–101)

Giving the lie was the final and irrevocable injury, and the stain upon the receiver's honor could be expunged only by a duel. The receiver had the right to challenge. The challenge was usually made by letter, which according to etiquette was to be couched in the plainest, most honorable language. Sir Toby's advice to Sir Andrew Aguecheek on the writing of such a letter hardly advocates the proper tone of plainness and honor:

> Go, write it in a martial hand; be curst and brief; it is no matter how witty, so it be eloquent and full of invention: taunt him with the license of ink: if thou thou'st him some thrice, it shall not be amiss; and as many lies as will lie in thy sheet of paper, although the sheet were big enough for the bed of Ware in England, set 'em down.
>
> (*Twelfth Night,* III, ii, 45–52)

[A. Forbes Sieveking, "Fencing," *Shakespeare's England,* 1916.]

Fenton. In *The Merry Wives of Windsor,* a young gentleman suitor of Anne Page. Fenton admits that he was originally moved by her father's wealth to woo her, but he has since come to value Anne for herself. Master Page refuses Fenton's suit because of the young man's high birth and reputation for equally high living. However, with the purchased assistance of the Host of the Garter Inn, Anne and Fenton elope, and the new husband is embraced by his bride's easygoing parents.

Fenton, Sir **Geoffrey** (c. 1539–1608). Translator and statesman. Fenton translated the *Histoires Tragiques* (c. 1559) of François de BELLEFOREST under the title *Certaine Tragicall Discourses written oute of Frenche and Latin* (1567) and dedicated the work to Lady Mary Sidney (later, countess of Pembroke). Fenton consciously strove for elegance of style but succeeded only in producing the strained, artificial, and ornate rhetorical flavor popular among Elizabethan prose stylists and often ridiculed by Shakespeare. Although Shakespeare undoubtedly knew Fenton's translation, there is no direct evidence that he used Fenton's work instead of the original in French. Fenton's translation, however, was used by a number of Elizabethan dramatists, including John Lyly in his *Love's Metamorphosis* (1589–1590).

Fenton's other works include a number of translations, including an English version of Francesco Guicciardini's *Storia d'Italia* (1561), *The Historie of Guicciardin . . . Reduced into English* (1579). Fenton spent the latter part of his life as an administrator in Ireland during the English occupation. [C. S. Lewis, *English Literature in the Sixteenth Century,* 1954.]

Fenton, Richard (1747–1821). Antiquarian and poet. In 1811 Fenton printed, and probably forged, extracts from what he claimed to be "a curious journal of Shakespeare, an account of many of his plays, and memoirs of his life by himself." An acquaintance of Dr. Johnson and David Garrick, Fenton was a native of Pembrokeshire, Wales, in which county he did most of his historical research. His Shakespearean fabrications appeared in a volume called *Tour in Quest of Genealogy* (1811), in which he claimed to have discovered in an old Welsh manor manuscripts written by Anne Hathaway. [E. K. Chambers, *William Shakespeare,* 1930; *Dictionary of Welsh Biography,* 1959.]

Ferdinand. In *Love's Labour's Lost,* the King of Navarre. Having vowed with three companions to study for three years and avoid contact with women during that period, King Ferdinand issues an edict forbidding any woman to come within a mile of the court. Despite his oath, he falls in love with the Princess of France before the three years have elapsed. The character of Ferdinand is loosely based on HENRY OF NAVARRE.

Ferdinand. In *The Tempest,* son of the King of Naples. Separated from the other survivors of the shipwreck, Ferdinand roams the island searching for his lost companions. Ariel's sweet music leads him to Prospero's cave, where Miranda's loveliness immediately enslaves his heart. To test Ferdinand's constancy, her father sets the youth to hard menial labor. After nobly bearing his trial, Ferdinand is rewarded with Prospero's consent to marry Miranda, and the couple are entertained with a pageant enacted by Ariel and his fellows.

Fergusson, Francis (1904–). American critic. Fergusson is best known as a critic of drama in general, but he has done distinguished work on Shakespeare particularly. His *The Idea of a Theatre* (1949) includes a well-known analysis of *Hamlet* (see MYTHIC CRITICISM), and in *The Human Image of Dramatic Literature* (1957) he presents cogent essays on *Macbeth* and Shakespearean comedy. Fergusson also served as general editor of the Dell Laurel paperback editions of Shakespeare's works.

Feste. In *Twelfth Night,* Olivia's clown. Because he "must observe their mood on whom he jests," the Clown's position is endangered by Olivia's melancholy disposition. He reinstates himself when he catechizes her, demonstrating the folly of her mournful pose. As a participant in the duping of Malvolio, Feste pretends to be Sir Topas, a curate, and professing to think the Steward possessed by the Devil, badgers him mercilessly.

In a final song, "When that I was and a little tiny boy," Feste shows that Illyria represents a longed-for dream world; the song signals a return to the real world where love is not always fulfilled. The part of Feste is thought to have been written for Robert Armin. [Joseph H. Summers, "The Masks of Twelfth Night," *University of Kansas City Review,* XXII, 1955.]

Feuillerat, Albert Gabriel (1874–1952). French scholar. Educated at several French universities, Feuillerat taught at the University of Rennes (1901–1927) and at Yale (1928–1943). Early in his career he conceived the plan of publishing the records of the Master of Revels from the reign of Henry VIII through that of Charles I. Two of the contemplated four volumes appeared: *Documents Relating to the Office of the Revels in the Time of Queen Elizabeth* (1908) and *Documents Relating to the Revels at Court in the Time of King Edward VI and Queen Mary* (The Loseley Manuscripts) (1911), both with notes and comprehensive indexes. *Le Bureau des Menus-Plaisirs* [Office of the Revels] *et la Mise en Scène à la Cour d'Élizabeth* (1910) is a brief volume supplying the historical background to the subject. Feuillerat also published, with notes and commentary, documents relating to the Blackfriars theatre in the *Shakespeare Jahrbuch* (1912) and in a volume of the Malone Society Collections, Vol. II, Pt. 1 (1913). Feuillerat's study of John Lyly (1910) is important for its contribution to the history of euphuism and for its extensive bibliography; his edition of the works of Sir Philip Sidney is standard (4 vols., 1912–1926). His Shakespearean studies include a series of articles on Shakespeare in France (*Shakespeare Jahrbuch,* 1910, 1911, 1912), an edition of the minor poems for the Yale Shakespeare (1927), and a French translation of selected plays with introductions and notes (1921–1925). At the time of his death he had completed *The Composition of Shakespeare's Plays,* the first volume in a projected three-volume study of the authorship, chronology, and text of the plays; this work was translated by Mrs. Charles Prouty and appeared posthumously in 1953. Feuillerat also wrote full-length studies of Baudelaire, Proust, and Bourget. [Henri M. Peyre, *Essays in Honor of Albert Feuillerat,* 1943.]

Ffrangcon-Davies, Gwen (1896–). Actress and singer. Born in London, Gwen Ffrangcon-Davies studied for the stage with Mrs. L. Manning Hicks and Agnes Platt before making her debut in 1911 in a walk-on part in *A Midsummer Night's Dream.* She has played with the Old Vic, the Birmingham Repertory Company, the Oxford University Dramatic Society, and the Shakespeare Memorial Theatre, Stratford-upon-Avon (1950, as Queen Katharine, Portia in *Julius Caesar,* Regan, and Beatrice). Her many other Shakespearean roles have included Cordelia and Titania (1924), Ophelia in the all-star *Hamlet* (1930) at the Haymarket, Chorus in *Henry V* (1938), and Lady Macbeth with Gielgud in 1942. She is well known on English and Canadian television. [*Who's Who in the Theatre,* 1961.]

Fidele. In *Cymbeline,* the name adopted by Imogen when she disguises herself as a boy in order to find her husband and escape the execution of his order that she be killed.

Field, Nathan ["Nat," "Nid"] (1587–1620). Actor and playwright. Field was the son of John Field, a Puritan minister and fierce enemy of the stage; he was also the brother of Theophilus Field, the bishop of Llandaff, and Nathaniel Field, a printer, with whom he has often been confused. Nathan Field was a student at St. Paul's Grammar School when, at some time about 1600, he was pressed into service as an actor with the Children of the Chapel. He was evidently quite talented, and achieved prominence with them as both actor and playwright. At this time he became the protégé of Ben Jonson, who was creating plays for the Children. William Drummond's *Conversations with Ben Jonson* (first pub. in 1833) contains the following account of their relationship:

> Nid Field was his Schollar, & he had read to him the Satyres of Horace & some Epigrames of Martiall.

Jonson's *Bartholomew Fair* (1614) contained an allusion to Field and Richard Burbage as the best actors on the stage (see Richard BURBAGE), and Jonson praised Field's acting skill in his verses to *Volpone*

(1605) and *Catiline* (1611). When the Children's company finally broke up, Field joined Lady Elizabeth's Men as a leading actor. By 1616 he was with the King's Men and was sharing the leads with Burbage. He is in the King's Men acting lists from 1616 to 1619. In 1619 his name appears in both the new patent granted the company and the list of actors receiving the king's livery, but in no company lists thereafter. He is, however, one of the "principall Actors" in the First Folio of Shakespeare's plays (1623).

According to T. W. Baldwin, Field often played a young lover cast as a foil to Burbage's elder lover, a not improbable suggestion, considering Field's popular reputation as a ladies' man, and the romantic, dark-eyed portrait of him which hangs in the picture gallery at Dulwich College. Field is known to have played the title role in *Bussy D'Ambois*. In the prologue to the 1634 revival of the play there is a lament for Field: "Field is gone, Whose Action first did give it name." Baldwin and others have also suggested that Field was taken into the company as a replacement for Shakespeare.

As a dramatist, Field wrote two comedies, *A Woman Is a Weather-cocke* (c. 1609), written for the Children of the Queen's Revels, and *Amends for Ladies* (1611), written for Lady Elizabeth's Men. He collaborated with Philip Massinger in *The Fatal Dowry* (1619). Both his comedies reveal indebtedness to Shakespeare in passages of comic dialogue and in individual scenes.

Field left the King's Men about 1619, conceivably because of a scandal over the birth of a child to Lady

TITLE PAGE OF FIELD'S COMEDY *Amends for Ladies* (1639).

AMENDS FOR LADIES.

With the merry prankes of Moll Cut-Purse: Or, the humour of roaring:

A Comedy full of honest mirth and wit.

As it was Acted at the *Blacke-Fryers*, both by the PRINCES Servants, and the Lady ELIZABETHS.

By *Nath. Field.*

LONDON,

Printed by *Io. Okes*, for *Math. Walbancke*, and are to be sold at his Shop, at *Grayes-Inne* Gate 1639.

Argyll and the attending attribution of its paternity to Field. (According to E. K. Chambers, Lady Argyll was Anne, daughter of Sir William Cornwallis of Brome.) The scandal elicited many contemporary epigrams, with titles such as *On Nathaniell Feild suspected for too much familiarity with his Mris Lady May*. In 1616 Field addressed *Feild the Players Letter to Mr Sutton, Preacher att St Mary Overs*, in which he replied to attacks by Thomas Sutton on him and other King's Men. Field remonstrated that Sutton's attempt to "hinder the Sacrament and banish me from myne owne parishe Churche" was "uncharitable dealing with your poore parishioners, whose purses participate in your contribution and whose labour yow are contented to eate."

An epigram, *De agello et Othello*, which alludes to Field as having acted Othello, is usually regarded as one of John Payne Collier's forgeries. [T. W. Baldwin, *The Organization and Personnel of the Shakespearean Company*, 1927; W. Peery, ed., *The Plays of Nathan Field*, 1950; G. E. Bentley, *The Jacobean and Caroline Stage*, 5 vols., 1941–1956.]

Field, Richard (1561–1624). Native of Stratford and printer of the first editions of *Venus and Adonis* (1593) and *The Rape of Lucrece* (1594). He was the son of Henry Field, a Stratford tanner whose goods were evaluated by Shakespeare's father in 1592. Richard Field left Stratford in 1579. On his arrival in London he entered a printer's apprenticeship under George Bishop (d. 1611) and, later, under Thomas Vautrollier (d. 1587). He married the widow of the latter in 1588, thus securing control of a thriving business, and became one of the leading members of the Stationers' Company. He was elected Master of the Company in 1619 and 1622. His shop was first in Blackfriars and after 1600 at the sign of the Splayed Eagle in the parish of St. Michael, Wood Street. During his 36-year career as a printer, he printed 295 books. His editions of *Venus and Adonis* and *Lucrece* are carefully printed, and his work was generally of a high order. He was also the printer of *Love's Martyr* (1601), the collection of verse which includes Shakespeare's *The Phoenix and the Turtle*. [R. B. McKerrow, ed., *A Dictionary of Printers and Booksellers . . . 1557–1640*, 1910.]

Fielding, Henry (1707–1754). Novelist and playwright, an important figure in the development of the English novel. Originally a dramatist, Fielding's satiric treatment of Robert Walpole's government helped to provoke the Licensing Act of 1737 which prohibited the use of the stage for political satire. Fielding abandoned the stage and studied law, eventually becoming a judge. Meanwhile, he turned to fiction and wrote *Joseph Andrews* (1742), *Jonathan Wild* (1743), *Tom Jones* (1749), and *Amelia* (1751). Fielding's masterpiece, *Tom Jones*, includes a comic episode describing a performance by David Garrick of the title role in *Hamlet*. Partridge, Tom's friend, constantly misunderstands the play and has to be corrected by Tom.

Fielding's interest in Shakespeare took two forms: a close reading of contemporary editions and attendance of current productions. He was often disturbed by the freedom with which some editors amended the text. In an article in *The Covent Garden Journal* (No. 31, April 18, 1752), he parodies this tendency with a burlesque reconstruction of Hamlet's soliloquy; with mock solemnity, he suggests that the opening line should be emended to read: "To be, or not. To be! that is the bastion." [F. Homes Dudden, *Henry Fielding*, 1952.]

films. Shakespeare's plays have been adapted and filmed almost from the inception of motion pictures. Many of the earliest efforts, however, were Shakespearean only in title; at best they offered very brief scenes from the plays, and some were but parodies or burlesques. The first known Shakespearean film (1899), no longer extant, featured Sir Herbert Beerbohm Tree as King John; it is thought to have consisted entirely of a tableau of the signing of Magna Carta, which Tree interpolated into the play. The following year, the great Sarah Bernhardt appeared as Hamlet in a three-minute version of the dueling scene from the last act. Another *Hamlet* of 1907 managed to encompass the entire action of the play in 10 minutes.

With the advent of sound films, more serious efforts were made. The American productions of *As You Like It* (1936), *A Midsummer Night's Dream* (1935), and *Romeo and Juliet* (1936) were all failures of taste—lackluster performances of badly edited plays—but marked by lavish and occasionally brilliant technical effects.

The 1944 production of *Henry V* by Laurence Olivier is a landmark in filmed Shakespeare. In its careful editing of scenes rather than lines, its fidelity to the original play, and its unwaveringly intelligent direction and performances, it set critical standards for future comparisons. Olivier's *Hamlet* (1947) and *Richard III* (1955) are equally careful in terms of cutting and performance, but critical and scholarly opinion is divided about the interpretation given the plays. Particularly, scholars have criticized Olivier, who was much influenced by Ernest Jones' *Hamlet and Oedipus*, for his Freudian interpretation of Hamlet.

Renato Castellani's *Romeo and Juliet* (1953) and Orson Welles' *Macbeth* (1948) and *Othello* (1950) shared a hostile critical reception. Scholars dismissed the efforts of both men as beneath serious consideration, and laymen familiar with the plays were disconcerted by the eccentric liberties taken by the directors, who seem to have been more concerned with sets, camera manipulations, and with placing a personal stamp on the plays than with fidelity to the originals.

In all, 30 of the plays have been partially or entirely filmed, most often in adaptations or drastically cut versions of Shakespeare's texts. The overwhelming majority have been aesthetic miscarriages.

Antony and Cleopatra had silent productions in France (1910 and 1913), Italy (1913), and in the U.S. (1909).

As You Like It was filmed in shortened silent versions by American companies in 1908 and 1912; in 1936 Paul Czinner directed a sound film that starred Laurence Olivier and Elisabeth Bergner. A modernized version is also known to have been made in England in 1916.

Cymbeline was produced in the U.S. in 1913.

Hamlet and *Romeo and Juliet*, with nearly two dozen screenings each, have been the most popular Shakespearean subjects with film-makers. In 1900, the year of *Hamlet's* camera debut, Sarah Bernhardt must have been over 55 years old when she played the Prince. She had only recently played the role on

CHORUS SPEAKING THE PROLOGUE IN OLIVIER'S FILM VERSION OF *Henry V*. (MUSEUM OF MODERN ART)

the stage, in the Dumas version. Other early French and Italian films have apparently become confused in the available bibliographies. An American silent is known to have been made in 1908, but an oft-printed report that the actress Nazimova starred in the title role of an early American *Hamlet* has not been substantiated. In 1964 John Gielgud's New York stage production starring Richard Burton and acted in present-day rehearsal clothes, was seen simultaneously in over 900 movie houses. The feat was made possible by the development of a photographic recording process called Electronovision. In England, aside from the 1947 production of Olivier already mentioned, there were also silent verisons in 1910, and, with Forbes-Robertson, in 1913. Kronborg castle served as the setting for a Danish *Hamlet* filmed in 1911. A German company produced the film in 1920. A stage production was filmed in India in 1935, and a 1954 production there (in Hindustani) featured the direction and acting of Kishore Sahu. The single Russian effort is a lavish color film made in 1964.

Henry V had its most notable production in the magnificent color film directed and acted by Laurence Olivier.

Henry VIII has had several screenings, the most interesting of which is the 1911 motion picture of Beerbohm Tree's London stage production.

Julius Caesar was filmed by French and English companies in 1907 and 1911, respectively, and Italian companies are credited with several more, including one in 1909 and another, which was only remotely Shakespearean, in 1914. A Northwestern University production in 1949 was directed by David Bradley and starred Charlton Heston. Joseph Mankiewicz directed a Hollywood spectacular, released in 1953, with a cast that included John Gielgud as Cassius, James Mason as Brutus, and Marlon Brando as Mark Antony.

King John appears to have had its only filming in the 1899 production, with Beerbohm Tree as the King.

King Lear had silent productions in the U.S. in 1909 and 1916 and in Italy in 1910 and 1912. Only parts of the play have been filmed with sound. A Yiddish *King Lear*, filmed in the U.S. in 1935, was a modern story based on a play by Jacob Gordon.

Macbeth was filmed first in America in 1905, although this, like the first *Hamlet* motion picture, consisted entirely of a dueling scene. Other early American films were made in 1908 and 1916, the latter a production supervised by David Griffith and starring Beerbohm Tree. In 1948 Orson Welles directed and acted in a badly edited version which had little artistic merit. Arthur Bourchier and Violet Vanbrugh headed the English cast of a five-reel production shot against natural backgrounds in Germany in 1913; another English silent version was made in 1911. It has also been filmed by several French companies, by one German (1913), and by a Japanese company in 1956. In Italy it was filmed in 1909 and, with the title *Lady Macbeth*, in 1917.

Measure for Measure was filmed by an Italian company in 1942. Its title, *Dente per Dente*, is known to have been used for an earlier film there, but the Shakespearean character of the first picture has not been established.

The Merchant of Venice has been produced in Italy (1910), England (1916), Germany (1923), the United States (1908, 1912, and 1914), and in France (a 1913 film called *Shylock* and a 1952 French-Italian effort directed by Pierre Billon).

The Merry Wives of Windsor has been screened more often than not in versions based on Nicolai's opera rather than on Shakespeare; such is the nature of German productions of 1918, 1935, and 1950. A French film of 1911 is entitled *Falstaff*. It was also screened at least once in the United States, in 1910.

A Midsummer Night's Dream had a silent production in America in 1909, and in 1935 Max Reinhardt directed a beautifully photographed but badly miscast Hollywood film. There were German productions in 1913 and 1925, French in 1909, and Czechoslovakian in 1958—with a cast composed entirely of puppets.

Othello has been especially popular with Italian film-makers. A 1907 film depicting the death of Othello was shown while a phonograph, undoubtedly the *pièce de résistance*, played appropriate music from the Verdi opera. It was also produced there twice in 1909, again in 1914, and last in 1950, when Orson Welles directed and starred in an Anglo-Italian venture. A company of virtual amateurs produced a 16-mm. film in England in 1946. Emil Jannings and Werner Krauss starred in a German film of 1922; an earlier silent was made there in 1918. The play was also produced in the U.S. in 1908, and in Russia Sergei Youtkevich directed a production in 1955. A 1910 Danish film entitled *Desdemona* is a modern story about an actor and his wife who play the leading roles.

Richard III has been filmed twice in the U.S. (1909 and 1913) and twice in England (1911; and the 1955 film directed by Olivier, starring him and John Gielgud).

Romeo and Juliet had American screenings in 1908, 1911 (with Theda Bara), and in 1936. Leslie Howard and Norma Shearer played the lovers in the last-mentioned film. George Cukor directed, and John Barrymore, who appeared in Shakespearean bits in other films, played Mercutio. There were Italian silent versions in 1908, 1911, and 1912, and in 1953 Renato Castellani directed an Anglo-Italian company in a picture that had little to recommend it beyond exquisite color photography of scenes of Verona and Mantua. In England the play was filmed in 1908 with Godfrey Tearle and Mary Malone. It has also been produced in Egypt (1944) and in India (1948).

The Taming of the Shrew was directed in the U.S. by David Griffith in 1908, and in 1929 the first "talkie" Shakespeare also featured the acrobatic Petruchio of Douglas Fairbanks, Sr., with Mary Pickford's Katharina. The story that the credits for this picture included the line "Additional dialogue by Sam Taylor" is apocryphal; it began as a joke. *The Shrew* was also made three times in Italy (1908, 1913, and 1942), twice in England (1911 and 1923), and once each in France (1911), Spain (1955), and India (1955).

The Tempest has the distinction of being the first "color" Shakespeare—in a 1905 film of the storm scene which captured the first two minutes of a Beerbohm Tree stage production. There were also silent versions in France (1912) and in the U.S. (1911).

Twelfth Night had an American production in 1910, and Jacob Frid directed a Russian film in 1955.

The Winter's Tale has never been made with dialogue. Silent screenings were made in the U.S. (1910), Italy (1913), and Germany (1914).

A bibliography of film titles and film criticism, with some errors and omissions, has been collected by Riccardo Redi and Roberto Chiti: "Shakespeare e il Cinema: Contributo a una Bibliografia," *Bianco e Nero*, XVIII, Rome, 1957. A comprehensive study of the subject, tentatively titled *Shakespeare on Film*, was being written as *The Reader's Encyclopedia of Shakespeare* went to press, by Robert Hamilton Ball, who contributed many details to the listing above. Some of Professor Ball's findings appear in "If We Shadows Have Offended," *Pacific Spectator*, Winter 1947; "The Shakespeare Film as Record: Sir Herbert Beerbohm Tree," *Shakespeare Quarterly*, July 1952; and "Shakespeare in One Reel," *The Quarterly of Film, Radio, and Television*, Winter 1953.

Fiorentino, Ser **Giovanni** (fl. 14th cent.). Italian writer. Fiorentino is the author of *Il Pecorone* (1558), a collection of tales and anecdotes in the manner of Boccaccio's *Decameron*. One of the tales may be the source of the elements of the duping of Falstaff in *The Merry Wives of Windsor*. More importantly *Il Pecorone* may have provided the main source of *The Merchant of Venice*. See MERCHANT OF VENICE: *Sources*.

First Folio. The earliest collected edition of Shakespeare's plays and one of the world's most famous books.

Text. The volume was published toward the end of 1623 with the following title page:

MR. WILLIAM SHAKESPEARES COMEDIES, HISTORIES, & TRAGEDIES.
Publiſhed according to the True Originall Copies.
LONDON
Printed by Iſaac Iaggard, and Ed. Blount. 1623.

There is also a head-title, which appears in different places in different editions:

> The Workes of William Shakespeare, containing all his Comedies, Histories and Tragedies: Truely set forth, according to their first Originall.

Despite the fact that the title page lists Edward Blount as one of the printers, the entire volume was printed at the shop of William Jaggard and his son Isaac. Blount, however, was one of the publishers of the joint venture along with Jaggard, John Smethwicke, and William Aspley. Their names appear in the colophon: "Printed at the Charges of W. Jaggard, Ed. Blount, I. Smethweeke, and W. Aspley, 1623." The volume contains 36 plays, exactly half of which had never been published before. Of these 18 previously unprinted plays, 16 were entered in the Stationers' Register on November 8, 1623 shortly before publication:

> Mr Blounte Isaak Jaggard. Entred for their Copie vunder the hands of Mr Doctor Worral and Mr Cole, warden, Mr William Shakspeers Comedyes Histories, and Tragedyes soe manie of the said Copies as are not formerly entred to other men. vizt. Comedyes. The Tempest. The two gentlemen of Verona. Measure for Measure. The Comedy of Errors. As you Like it. All's well that ends well. Twelft night. The winters tale. Histories. The thirde parte of Henry the sixt. Henry the eight. Coriolanus. Timon of Athens. Julius Caesar. Tragedies. Mackbeth. Anthonie and Cleopatra. Cymbeline.

The volume is printed in three separately paginated sections: Comedies, Histories, and Tragedies. The plays are not arranged in any particular order, except that the histories are set up chronologically.

The first preliminary page consists of the verse by Ben Jonson on the Droeshout Portrait (see PORTRAITS OF SHAKESPEARE):

To the Reader.

This Figure, that thou here seest put,
It was for gentle Shakespeare cut;
Wherein the Grauer had a strife
with Nature, to out-doo the life:
O, could he but haue drawne his wit
As well in brasse, as he hath hit
His face; the Print would then surpasse
All, that was euer writ in brasse.
But, since he cannot, Reader, looke
Not on his Picture, but his Booke.
B.I.

This is followed by the title page, which includes the portrait. The next item is the dedication to William Herbert, 3rd earl of Pembroke, and his brother Philip Herbert, earl of Montgomery:

> Right Honourable,
> Whilst we studie to be thankful in our particular, for the many fauors we haue receiued from your L.L. we are falne vpon the ill fortune, to mingle two the most diuerse things that can bee, feare, and rashnesse; rashnesse in the enterprize, and feare of the successe. For, when we valew the places your H.H. sustaine, we cannot but know their dignity greater, then to descend to the read-

ing of these trifles: and, while we name them trifles, we haue depriu'd our selues of the defence of our Dedication. But since your L.L. haue been pleas'd to thinke these trifles some-thing, heeretofore; and haue prosequuted both them, and their Authour liuing, with so much fauour: we hope, that (they out-liuing him, and he not hauing the fate, common with some, to be exequutor to his owne writings) you will vse the like indulgence toward them, you haue done vnto their parent. There is a great difference, whether any Booke choose his Patrones, or finde them: This hath done both. For, so much were your L.L. likings of the seuerall parts, when they were acted, as before they were published, the Volume ask'd to be yours. We haue but collected them, and done an office to the dead, to procure his Orphanes, Guardians; without ambition either of selfe-profit, or fame; onely to keepe the memory of so worthy a Friend, & Fellow aliue, as was our SHAKESPEARE, by humble offer of his playes, to your most noble patronage. Wherein, as we haue iustly obserued, no man to come neere your L.L. but with a kind of religious addresse; it hath bin the height of our care, who are the Presenters, to make the present worthy of your H.H. by the perfection. But, there we must also craue our abilities to be considerd, my Lords. We cannot go beyond our owne powers. Country hands reach foorth milke, creame, fruites, or what they haue: and many Nations (we haue heard) that had not gummes & incense, obtained their requests with a leauened Cake. It was no fault to approch their Gods, by what meanes they could: And the most, though meanest, of things are made more precious, when they are dedicated to Temples. In that name therefore, we most humbly consecrate to your H.H. these remaines of your seruant *Shakespeare;* that what delight is in them, may be euer your L.L. the reputation his, & the faults ours, if any be committed, by a payre so carefull to shew their gratitude both to the liuing, and the dead, as is

Your Lordshippes most bounden,
IOHN HEMINGE.
HENRY CONDELL.

Following this is the editors' (Heminges and Condell's) epistle "To the Great Variety of Readers":

From the most able, to him that can but spell: There you are number'd. We had rather you were weighd. Especially, when the fate of all Bookes depends vpon your capacities: and not of your heads alone, but of your purses. Well! it is now publique, & you wil stand for your priuiledges wee know: to read, and censure. Do so, but buy it first. That doth best commend a Booke, the Stationer saies. Then, how odde soeuer your braines be, or your wisedomes, make your licence the same, and spare not. Iudge your sixe-pen'orth, your shillings worth, your fiue shillings worth at a time, or higher, so you rise to the iust rates, and welcome. But, what euer you do, Buy. Censure will not driue a Trade, or make the Iacke go. And though you be a Magistrate of wit, and sit on the Stage at *Black-Friers,* or the *Cock-pit,* to arraigne Playes dailie, know, these Playes haue had their triall alreadie, and stood out all Appeales; and do now come forth quitted rather by a Decree of Court, then any purchas'd Letters of commendation.

It had bene a thing, we confesse, worthie to haue bene wished, that the Author himselfe had liu'd to haue set forth, and ouerseen his owne writings; But since it hath bin ordain'd otherwise, and he by death departed from that right, we pray you do not envie his Friends, the office of their care, and paine, to haue collected & publish'd them; and so to haue publish'd them, as where (before) you were abus'd with diuerse stolne, and surreptitious copies, maimed, and deformed by the frauds and stealthes of iniurious impostors, that expos'd them: euen those, are now offer'd to your view cur'd, and perfect of their limbes; and all the rest, absolute in their numbers, as he conceiued them. Who, as he was a happie imitator of Nature, was a most gentle expresser of it. His mind and hand went together: And what he thought, he vttered with that easinesse, that wee haue scarce receiued from him a blot in his papers. But it is not our prouince, who onely gather his works, and giue them you, to praise him. It is yours that reade him. And there we hope, to your diuers capacities, you will finde enough, both to draw, and hold you: for his wit can no more lie hid, then it could be lost. Reade him, therefore; and againe, and againe: And if then you doe not like him, surely you are in some manifest danger, not to vnderstand him. And so we leaue you to other of his Friends, whom if you need, can bee your guides: if you neede them not, you can leade your selues, and others. And such Readers we wish him.

IOHN HEMINGE.
HENRIE CONDELL.

After the epistle are two commendatory poems by Ben JONSON and Hugh HOLLAND. Next is a "Catalogue of the severall Comedies, Histories, and Tragedies contained in this Volume" from which *Troilus and Cressida* is omitted. This is followed by two more commendatory verses, those by Leonard DIGGES and the author, probably James Mabbe, who signed with his initials as "I. M." (See M., I.).

The last item is a list of the "Principall Actors" in the plays:

William Shakespeare.	Samuel Gilburne.
Richard Burbadge.	Robert Armin.
John Hemmings.	William Ostler.
Augustine Phillips.	Nathan Field.
William Kempt.	John Underwood.
Thomas Poope.	Nicholas Tooley.
George Bryan.	William Ecclestone.
Henry Condell.	Joseph Taylor.
William Slye.	Robert Benfield.
Richard Cowly.	Robert Goughe.
John Lowine.	Richard Robinson.
Samuell Crosse.	Iohn Shancke.
Alexander Cooke.	Iohn Rice.

Immediately after this list, the plays begin. The first is *The Tempest* and the last is *Cymbeline*, incorrectly classed as a "tragedy."

The text was obviously edited by someone familiar with the plays who would be responsible for eliminating profanity, making acting divisions, and other details. It is doubtful that Heminges and Condell would be qualified for this exacting work. W. W. Greg suggests that Edward KNIGHT, the book-keeper of the King's Men, would have been a logical choice for the task. [E. K. Chambers, *William Shakespeare*, 1930; W. W. Greg, *The Shakespeare First Folio*, 1955.]

History. There were probably about 1,000 copies of the Folio printed, of which something like 238 copies, in various stages of decomposition, are extant. The book consisted of a total of 907 pages, printed on good paper (see William PRYNNE) and offered for sale at a price of £1, the estimated modern equivalent of which is $45. Despite the high price the book sold well enough to warrant a second edition in 1632 (see SECOND FOLIO) and two more editions later in the century (see THIRD FOLIO; FOURTH FOLIO). The £1 selling price looks modest, however, in the light of the prices that subsequent generations have paid for the volume. The so-called Burdett-Coutts's copy of the Folio, for example, was sold in 1840 for £100, in 1864 for £716 2s., and in 1922 for $43,000. This last purchase was made by A. S. W. Rosenbach, a book dealer, who three years later purchased another Folio volume for $75,000. [Louis Marder, *His Exits and His Entrances: The Story of Shakespeare's Reputation*, 1963.]

Printing. The idea for a collected edition of the plays probably began with the Folio edition of Ben Jonson's plays in 1616. Since that publication was in preparation for a number of years while Shakespeare was still alive, it is not impossible that he had given at least some thought to a similar edition of his own plays. The terms of the *Address* of Heminges and Condell, who lament the fact that Shakespeare had not "liu'd to haue set forth, and ouerseen his owne writings . . ." suggest this possibility. In any event the major impetus for the edition was the publication by Thomas Pavier and William Jaggard of 10 Shakespearean and pseudo-Shakespearean plays in 1619. This corrupt and poorly planned edition, made up largely of reprints of the "stolne, and surreptitious copies" referred to by Heminges and Condell, may have stirred his fellow actors to prevent any further abuse and vulgarization of Shakespeare's name by printing a final authorized version.

Much new information about the printing of the Folio has come to light as a result of the exhaustive labors of Charlton Hinman. In his *The Printing and Proof-Reading of the First Folio of Shakespeare*, he has shown that the printing was begun early in 1622, interrupted during the summer of that year, resumed shortly thereafter, and completed in November 1623. A total of five compositors set the type for the book, almost half of the work being done by one man, "Compositor B" (see COMPOSITOR). Each gathering of the book consisted of 12 pages (3 "sheets") which were set by "formes," that is, not in the order in which they are read, but from the middle (pp. 6 and 7 of a gathering) toward either end. This procedure required the printer to "cast-off" copy, that is, to make a rough estimate as to the amount of copy that would be needed to occupy the first five pages of a gathering. If the estimate was incorrect the printer would then be forced to fill in blank space where he had overestimated the space required, or to crowd, or even cut, the text in those cases where he had underestimated the space requirements. The latter instance, particularly, lends itself to distortion, for it results in the printing of verse as prose and, in some cases in tampering with the text. Finally, the proofreading of the text was done with little or no consultation of the copy. Other evidence has also made it clear that in more cases than was formerly thought, the "copy" on which a Folio play was based was merely a copy of an earlier quarto. All of these recent disclosures tend to undermine the authority of the Folio and call for a greater eclecticism by future editors (see TEXTUAL CRITICISM). Four facsimiles of the First Folio have been published: in 1866, edited by Howard Staunton; in 1876, edited by J. O. Halliwell-Phillipps, in 1902, edited by Sir Sidney Lee; and in 1954, edited by Helge Kökeritz and Charles Tyler Prouty. [E. E. Willoughby, *The Printing of the First Folio of Shakespeare*, 1932; Alice Walker, *Textual Problems of the First Folio*, 1953; John W. Shroeder, *The Great Folio of 1623*, 1956; Charlton Hinman, *The Printing and Proof-Reading of the First Folio of Shakespeare*, 1963.]—E. Q.

First Part of the Contention. See CONTENTION PLAYS.

First Player. In *Hamlet*, the leader of the company of actors who visit the court. The First Player recites a speech for Hamlet based upon the description of Troy's destruction in the *Aeneid* and Hamlet arranges with him for the production of a "play-within-a-play" (II, ii). There is a tradition that Shakespeare played the role of the Ghost, and another, probably unrelated, tradition that the actor who plays the Ghost doubles as the First Player. The significance of the player's speech has been brilliantly demonstrated by Harry Levin. [Harry Levin "An Explication of the Player's Speech" in *The Question of Hamlet*, 1959.]

Fisher, Thomas (fl. 1600–1601). London publisher In 1600, Fisher published the First Quarto of *A Midsummer Night's Dream*. Fisher's shop was located in Fleet Street. In 1601 he entered John Marston's play *Antonio and Mellida* in the Stationers' Register. Nothing else is known of him. [R. B. McKerrow, ed., *Dictionary of Printers and Booksellers . . . 1557–1640*, 1910.]

Fitton, Mary (c. 1578–1647). The mistress of William Herbert, 3rd earl of PEMBROKE, and a candidate for the role of the DARK LADY of the *Sonnets*. Mistress Fitton's eventful story began with her arrival in London from Cheshire, when she was 17 years old. Her father, Sir Edward Fytton, had been knighted through the influence of Herbert's grandfather. It was therefore natural that Lady Pembroke, Herbert's mother, should welcome Mary to her estate at Wilton. She became fond of the girl and her son developed a passion for her. The queen found her charming and in 1596 made her one of her maids of honor. Sir William KNOLLYS, comptroller of the royal household and a friend of Mary's father, though promising to take a fatherly interest in her, fell hopelessly and foolishly in love with the irresistible girl. As soon as she discovered that she could attract any young courtier who took her fancy she broke completely with her ancient suitor. Armed with the assurance of her fatal attraction, she decided to take part in the gay life of the other maids of honor. She became Pembroke's favorite and her goings-on with him became a public scandal.

Early in the year 1601 Mary's intimacy with Pembroke had unfortunate results. She became pregnant.

Pembroke readily admitted his paternity of the unborn child, but, completely indifferent to Mary's plight, refused to marry her. In February 1601 she gave birth to a stillborn boy. The angry queen put her in the care of Lady Hawkins, the second wife of Sir John Edgerton. Pembroke she punished more severely. She sent him to Fleet Prison for a brief stay, and then banished him to the continent, whence he did not dare to return to England until after the queen's death in 1603. The history of Mary's career at court offers no actual proof that she was the Dark Lady. However, a woman of her easy virtue could without compunction carry on a love affair with two men at the same time. Her later history confirms this opinion. She had two bastard children by Sir Richard Leveson. Her later marriages to the commoners Captain William Polewhele and a Captain Lougher (d. 1636) suggest that she would not be socially above becoming the mistress of an ornament to the stage of which Pembroke was a generous patron, an actor who was also a famous playwright and poet, although far below her in the social scale. No evidence of any sort establishing a relationship between Mary and Shakespeare has ever been found, but Will Kempe's dedication of his *Nine Days Wonder* (1600) to Mistress Anne Fitton furnishes indirect evidence of that possibility, Kempe being a member of Shakespeare's company. His dedication reads, "To Mistress Anne Fitton, Mayde of Honor to the Mayde Royal" and proceeds, "To show my duty to your honourable self." Kempe must have intended his dedication not for Anne but for her sister Mary, for she alone was a maid of honor. Mary outlived all her keepers and husbands, dying in 1647. [F. J. Furnivall, "Shakespeare and Mary Fitton," *Theatre*, XXX, 1897; Lady Newdigate-Newdegate, *Gossip from a Muniment Room, being passages in the lives of Anne and Mary Fitton*, 1907.]—O. J. C.

Fitzwater, Walter, 5th Baron (c. 1368–1407). A descendant of Robert Fitzwater, general of the barons who rebelled against King John. In Henry IV's first parliament Fitzwater was the first to accuse the duke of Aumerle of Gloucester's murder. In *Richard II*, Lord Fitzwater supports Bagot's accusation of Aumerle, saying, "If thou deny'st it twenty times, thou liest" (IV, i). [W. H. Thomson, *Shakespeare's Characters: A Historical Dictionary*, 1951.]

Flaminius. In *Timon of Athens*, the servant sent by Timon to borrow money from Lucullus. When Lucullus offers Flaminius a bribe if he will pretend not to have found him, the servant hurls the coins back at his master's false friend (III, i).

Flavius. In *Timon of Athens*, Timon's wise and good steward. Flavius tries unsuccessfully to caution his master against foolish generosity, but, after Timon's ruin, the steward divides his own money with the other servants. When he goes to his master's cave, Flavius is the only man whom Timon does not revile.

Flavius and Marullus. In *Julius Caesar*, two tribunes who reproach the citizens for forgetting their former devotion to Pompey in their eagerness to honor Caesar (I, i). According to Plutarch, Flavius and Marullus won the applause of the people by imprisoning those who hailed Caesar as king during the Lupercalia; as a result, Caesar divested them of their offices.

Fleance. In *Macbeth*, the son of Banquo. In order to thwart the Witches' prophecy that Banquo shall be the ancestor of the Scottish kings, Macbeth arranges the murder of both Banquo and his son. Fleance, however, escapes the assassins.

Fleay, Frederick Gard (1831–1909). Scholar. Educated at Cambridge, where he received a B.A. (1853) and M.A. (1856), Fleay became a schoolmaster and published many books on grammar and phonetics. In 1874 he joined the New Shakspere Society and began a long and distinguished career devoted to Shakespeare and Elizabethan drama. His works include *A Chronicle History of the Life and Work of William Shakespeare* (1886), *A Chronicle History of the London Stage, 1559–1642* (1890), and a *Biographical Chronicle of the English Drama, 1559–1642* (2 vols., 1891). The two latter works are marred by Fleay's dogmatic insistence on identifying authors of anonymous plays, but they remain a valuable contribution to scholarship. His Shakespearean publications are distinguished by his pioneer work on VERSE TESTS, an effort which unfortunately led him to many hasty conclusions about the authorship of parts of Shakespeare's plays. See DISINTEGRATION.

Flemish productions. Although Shakespeare was slow in gaining a foothold in the Flemish-speaking theatre of Belgium, his plays are now part of its classical repertory. The Flemish theatre has not contributed innovations to the production of Shakespeare, but its directors and actors have created honest and sincere professional performances.

The largest of the Flemish-speaking theatres is at Antwerp. Shakespeare has been a regular part of this theatre's repertory since 1876, and one of his plays ordinarily opens the season. The theatre at Brussels and the touring *Volkstheater* each offers one or two productions of Shakespeare every season, so that at least three professional productions are given each year in the Flemish language.

The historical development of the Flemish and English theatres is similar. Flemish mystery and miracle plays were performed by amateurs as early as 1275. In the 15th century Petrus Dorlandus, a monk belonging to the Chartreuse cloister at Zeelem, wrote *Den Spieghel der Salichiet van Elckerlych*, a morality play which some scholars argue became *Everyman* in English. Until the middle of the 19th century, however, no professional theatre and no outstanding playwright appeared, and the Flemish stage was dominated by German, Spanish, and French influences. In 1853, three years after Belgium became an independent nation, two Flemish actors, Victor Driessens and Frans Van Doeselaer, founded a professional company which was subsidized by the town council of Antwerp. This theatre relied heavily on translations of French and German plays.

Shakespeare appeared on the Belgian stage in March of 1876 when Ernesto Rossi, the Italian tragedian, performed *Othello* and *Hamlet* in Italian. In 1884 Jan Dilis played Romeo in the first Flemish performance of a Shakespearean play. The duke of Saxe-Meiningen brought his acting company to Belgium in 1886 to perform *The Winter's Tale*, *Julius Caesar*, *The Merchant of Venice*, and *Twelfth Night* in German. These plays were so well received that the Royal Netherlands Theatre of Antwerp produced *Hamlet* in Flemish and revived *Romeo and Juliet*. Jan Dilis, who played Hamlet in this production, had traveled to England to study Henry Irving's interpretation of the role. Reviews suggest that the company did not use the play as a vehicle to display a star performance, as was common on the English stage. Dilis apparently aimed at a balanced interpretation of the whole play.

Between 1884 and 1914, 9 of Shakespeare's plays were staged in 23 productions with a total of 57 performances. The most popular play was *The Merchant of Venice,* with 10 productions.

Since World War I Shakespearean plays have been produced more systematically and for longer runs. During this time 18 plays were staged in 40 productions with a total of 298 performances to 1950. The most popular play again was *The Merchant of Venice,* which was performed 50 times. Other popular plays include *The Taming of the Shrew, Hamlet, Twelfth Night, As You Like It,* and *The Merry Wives of Windsor.* J. O. De Gruyter, who became director of the Royal Netherlands Theatre of Antwerp in 1921, and Charles Gilhuys, an actor and director, are largely responsible for the success of these productions. Recent Flemish productions of Shakespeare are known for their adherence to the text, the use of unit sets, and side lighting—called "Rembrandt Lighting."

The leading Flemish actor in Belgium, Jos Gevers, has been successful in the roles of Shylock, Richard III, Iago, Aguecheek, Angelo, and Leontes. [Henry De Vocht, *Everyman: A Comparative Study of Texts and Sources,* 1949; Lode Monteyne, *Over Shakespeare,* 1948; Lode Monteyne, *Drama en Tooneel,* 1949; J. O. De Gruyter and Wayne Hayward, "Shakespeare on the Flemish Stage of Belgium, 1876–1951," *Shakespeare Survey 5,* 1952.]

Fletcher, John (1579–1625). Playwright. The Lord Chamberlain's company of players (renamed the King's Men at James I's accession in 1603) had Shakespeare as its leading dramatist from the effective foundation of the company in 1594 until his retirement in, probably, 1612; then John Fletcher, working either alone or in collaboration, occupied that position until his death; his successor was Philip Massinger, whose reign lasted almost until the closing of the theatres in 1642. We know that Fletcher and Massinger worked together on a number of plays, and that Massinger, distinctive as his note was, wrote under Fletcher's influence. The relations between Fletcher and his predecessor, Shakespeare, are less clear but of inevitably greater importance.

First, there is the matter of possible collaboration between them; second, the indubitable influence of Shakespeare on Fletcher; third, a suggested influence of Fletcher on Shakespeare. We should note that Fletcher and his early collaborator, Francis Beaumont, came, unlike Shakespeare, from the upper middle classes. Fletcher's father was vicar of Rye in Sussex, and later was bishop of Bristol, Worcester, and London in turn. Beaumont came from the Leicestershire gentry, studied at Oxford and the Inner Temple, and retired from playwriting on his marriage into a county family of Kent in or about 1613. The social standing of these newer dramatists—Fletcher was 15 years younger than Shakespeare, Beaumont some 20 years younger—corresponds with the trend in the fortunes of the King's Men from around 1610. Increasingly, we have to think of Shakespeare's company as playing at the Blackfriars Theatre to a "select" and homogeneous audience. Previously, at the Theatre and the Globe, their public was near to being a cross section of the whol people of London.

The possibility of collaboration between Shakespeare and Fletcher involves three plays—*The Tw Noble Kinsmen,* the lost *Cardenio,* and *Henry VII. The Two Noble Kinsmen* was published in 163 with the assertion on its title page that it was writte by Fletcher and Shakespeare. It is generally agree that the play was written in 1613, since it made us of an antimasque from Beaumont's *Masque of th Inner Temple,* which was presented in that year. Th play contains a good deal of verbal reminiscence o Shakespeare, echoing of so close a kind that it i difficult to believe that Shakespeare was responsibl for the parts of the play in which it occurs. But vers tests, vocabulary tests, and the tracing of Shakespearean image clusters have together built up a formidable case for Shakespeare's authorship of certai scenes. Moreover, the use of Theseus' wedding as framework for the action takes us back to *A Midsummer Night's Dream,* just as the ending of *Pericle* takes us back to the framework action of *The Comedy of Errors,* and the Chaucerian source here is link with the use of Gower in *Pericles.* Thus ther are substantial grounds for accepting the statemen on the 1634 title page, and Kenneth Muir declare that *The Two Noble Kinsmen* has perhaps as muc right to inclusion in editions of Shakespeare as *Titu Andronicus, 1 Henry VI,* and *Pericles.* See The Tw Noble Kinsmen: *Text.*

Cardenio provides a more complex problem. W know that a play called *Cardenno* or *Cardano, Cardema,* or *Cardenna* was performed at court by th King's Men on two occasions in 1613. In 1653 th bookseller Humphrey Moseley entered in the Stationers' Register "The History of Cardennio by Mr Fletcher & Shakespeare." Probably this is the play performed at court; certainly it was a dramatizatio of the Cardenio story in *Don Quixote* (Part I, chaps XXIII–XXXVI). No edition appeared, but there wa a performance at Drury Lane in 1727, followed by publication in 1728, of a play by Lewis Theobald called *Double Falsehood; or, The Distrest Lovers* Theobald asserted that the play was originally Shakespeare's, though he admitted that some people ha found its style closer to Fletcher's. The versio acted and published was avowedly an adaptation by Theobald; its action derives from the Cardenio story There were skeptics in 1728, including Pope, who however, admitted ten years later that the play seemed to be of Shakespeare's time. Certainly th play as we have it, with its remote setting, its disguises and its pastoral motif, seems to belong wit Shakespeare's final romances and with the Beaumon and Fletcher tragicomedies of approximately th same date. Critical opinion now seems to be moving in the direction of seeing Theobald's version as dependent on a Shakespeare-Fletcher collaboration with Shakespeare's responsibility more for the beginning of the play and Fletcher's more for the ending See Cardenio.

The composition-year for *The Two Noble Kinsmen* and at least an acting-year for *Cardenio* wa 1613. This was also the year in which the Globe theatre was burned down during a performance of a new play which we can almost certainly identify as *Henry VIII.* But there is no contemporary o near-contemporary evidence that *Henry VIII* was a work of collaboration. It appeared in the 1623 Shakespeare Folio, and there was no questioning of Shakespeare's total authorship until J. Spedding in 1850 argued that the play was written jointly by Shakespeare and Fletcher. Spedding's argument depended largely on the frequency of feminine endings in the play's lines, but it has been supported by scholars who have investigated the variation in different parts of the play in the occurrence of certain forms of words (most notably by A. C. Partridge, *The Problem of Henry VIII Re-opened*, 1949). Further, it has been argued (*The John Fletcher Plays*) that in this play "we are not conscious of different layers of meaning, through which we penetrate one by one until we have a sense of a complexity that enfolds all the layers we have reached. Rather, we have the sense that at different moments we are offered differing views of the play's events and characters: these are irreconcilable and, in Fletcher's way, frankly so." (See HENRY VIII: *Text*.) Critical opinion on the authorship problem is today about equally divided.

While there are thus indications that Shakespeare and Fletcher worked together on two or three plays, there is no doubt that Shakespeare exerted an influence on what we have come to call the "Beaumont and Fletcher" writings. The two Beaumont and Fletcher Folios (1647 and 1679) give us 52 plays of an allegedly joint authorship. But Beaumont's collaboration with Fletcher lasted for only a few years. Their first notable joint work was, in all likelihood, *Philaster* (c. 1609), which set the tone for many tragicomedies between this time and the closing of the theatres. Beaumont seems to have given up playwriting in 1613, the year in which we have evidence that Fletcher found a new collaborator in Shakespeare. Later Fletcher was to work with Massinger and with several other writers of the later years of James' reign. Yet it is difficult to find a play in the 1647 and 1679 Folios having no clear indebtedness to Shakespeare. It is well known that *Philaster* uses a plot situation similar to that of *Hamlet*, both plays showing a rightful heir, with popular support, at the court of a usurper. And *Thierry and Theodoret* (c. 1617, probably by Fletcher and Massinger) inverts the *Lear* situation, showing two virtuous sons of a wicked mother, who changes her place of residence from the court of one to the court of the other, and attempts to create enmity between them. So in *A Wife for a Month* (1624, probably by Fletcher alone) there is a King ready to part with his wife in order to marry a lady of the court, as in *Henry VIII*, but again Fletcher varies the situation by making the lady unwilling. Earlier, it was probably Fletcher alone who wrote *The Woman's Prize, or The Tamer Tamed* (c. 1611), an ironic sequel to *The Taming of the Shrew*, in which we see Petruchio marrying for a second time and encountering a wife less amenable than Katherina. And in *The Custom of the Country* (c. 1619–20, probably by Fletcher and Massinger) there is an echo of the Angelo-Isabella situation of *Measure for Measure*, with the sexes reversed. Fletcher, with or without a collaborator, delighted in taking an initial idea from Shakespeare, making a variation upon it, and then seeing how the logic of event would work out.

But perhaps the closest relation between Shakespeare and his younger contemporary is to be found in the plays they were writing at the same time. That *Bonduca* (c. 1613) is a derivative from *Cymbeline* (c. 1609) is almost indubitable: both are set in Roman Britain, both show a final reconciliation between Romans and Britons, both include studies of remorse, both are curiously free from the complex attitude to the chief characters that generally marks both Shakespeare's and Fletcher's plays of approximately the same date. But the debt may not have been all one way. *The Faithful Shepherdess* (c. 1608) has a Satyr interestingly anticipatory of Ariel and, at its center, a human being with magical control over the action. Both this play and *The Tempest* show how the erring are brought to repentance, and Fletcher's Sullen Shepherd has something of the same obstinacy as Caliban. A. H. Thorndike argued that Shakespeare's last plays were written in imitation of Beaumont and Fletcher's tragicomedies, making a similar use of remote setting and romantic incident, but he did not sufficiently allow for the fact that *Pericles* almost certainly antedates *Philaster*. It would be more plausible to suggest that Shakespeare ventured into a revival of earlier romance themes in *Pericles*, and then in the following plays drew both on that and on the example of Fletcher in *The Faithful Shepherdess* and of Beaumont and Fletcher in *Philaster*.

Nevertheless, Shakespeare's last plays are essentially different in mood from the Beaumont and Fletcher tragicomedies. Although critical opinion is by no means uniform on the subject of *Cymbeline*, *The Winter's Tale*, and *The Tempest*, we can hardly doubt a depth of concern in them, a profound preoccupation with penance and pardon, with the relation of Nature and Art, and an increasingly evident fatigue. Beaumont and Fletcher, on the other hand, are young experimenters, preponderantly amused by the quirks of human conduct and basically skeptical concerning values. Though they learned much from Shakespeare, and delighted in taking his situations as their starting points, they differ from him in their noninvolvement with either character or situation. If their skill in language would not have been possible without his example, they nevertheless develop an easy courtliness and informality, a relaxed rhetoric, too, which puts less strain on the hearer than Shakespeare's mature style does. They usher in a dramatic mode both more courtly and more familiar than we find in their master. They cultivate the sophisticated shrug in a way that had not occurred to him. Yet the whole Fletcherian drama that continued after Beaumont's retirement, and indeed after Fletcher's death, was a derivative partly from the wide-ranging Shakespearean world and, in its later stages, partly also from the satiric impulse that Ben Jonson had given to the drama of the 17th century.

Shakespeare, Jonson, and Fletcher were the only early 17th-century dramatists to be honored with Folio printings of their work. They constituted "the Triumvirate of wit," as John DENHAM put it in his commendatory verses to the 1647 Beaumont and Fletcher Folio. For the 75 years after Fletcher's death, there was no question that these were the major dramatists of their time. And we have seen that Fletcher and Shakespeare were probably, at least on occasion, collaborators. That they, working in the same years for the same company of actors, influenced each other is something we can regard as nearly inevitable. Yet we have no direct evidence of a personal relationship between them, no document or literary allusion which brings their names closely together in the lifetime of either man. [J. Spedding, "On the Several Shares of Shakspere and Fletcher in the Play of Henry VIII," *Gentleman's Magazine*, n.s. XXXIV, August-October 1850, 115–124, 381–382; A. H. Thorndike, *The Influence of Beaumont and Fletcher on Shakspere*, n.d., 1901; Kenneth Muir, *Shakespeare as Collaborator*, 1960; Clifford Leech, *The John Fletcher Plays*, 1962; Paul Bertram, *Shakespeare and The Two Noble Kinsmen*, 1965.]—C. L.

Fletcher, Lawrence (d. 1608). Actor. Fletcher was among the actors enumerated as a member of the King's Men in the patent granted them by James I in 1603. Fletcher had been one of a group of "Inglis comedianis" who visited Scotland in 1594; apparently he had there become the personal favorite of James I who was then James VI of Scotland. There is no evidence, however, of Fletcher's having been an active member of the King's Men, although Augustine Phillips' will in 1605 named him as one of Phillips' "fellows." At his death in 1608 Fletcher was buried in St. Saviour's Church. [E. K. Chambers, *The Elizabethan Stage*, 1923.]

Florence, Duke of. In *All's Well That Ends Well*, a minor character. The Duke appears in two scenes: in the first to justify his war and to complain of France's refusal to give aid (III, i), in the second to appoint Bertram general of his cavalry (III, iii).

Florio, John (1554?–?1625). Translator and scholar. Florio was the English-born son of Michelangelo FLORIO. After graduation from Oxford, he completed a series of translations from Italian and two well-known Italian grammars, *Florio his Firste Fruites* (1578) and *Florio's Second Fruites* (1591). These were followed by his copious Italian-English dictionary *A World of Words* (1598).

If, as now seems probable, Shakespeare knew Italian, he undoubtedly learned it with the help of Florio's books. The Italian sentences in *The Taming of the Shrew* (I, ii) are taken from the *First* and *Second Fruites*. That Shakespeare knew Florio also seems extremely likely, since in 1591 Florio was appointed tutor to Henry Wriothesley, earl of Southampton and Shakespeare's patron. Florio is also alleged to have been a member of the so-called SCHOOL OF NIGHT and as such to be ridiculed in the person of Holofernes, the pedantic schoolmaster in *Love's Labour's Lost*. (The title of *Love's Labour's Lost* may be an echo of a line in *First Fruites*, ". . . it were labour lost to speake of love.")

It has also been suggested that it was from Florio's extensive library of Italian books that Shakespeare was able to secure the Italian authors and atmosphere which are so vital a part of his work. In 1603 appeared Florio's greatest work, his translation of the *Essays* of MONTAIGNE. His translation is frequently inaccurate, but it is characterized by a vitality and richness which have sometimes been described as Shakespearean. Shakespeare's debt to Florio's phrasing is most evident in *The Tempest* and *King Lear;* according to W. B. Henderson, there are over 100 words used for the first time in the latter play which are also found in Florio's translation. The strongest elements of Montaigne's thought are evident in the questioning and introspection of *Hamlet*. Florio's close association with the stage is further attested to by a copy of Ben Jonson's *Volpone* now in the British Museum. Written in Jonson's hand is the statement, "To his louing Father & worthy Freind Mr John Florio: The Ayde of his Muses. Ben: Jonson seales this testimony of Freindship, and Loue." See ITALY IN THE PLAYS; PHAETON SONNET. [F. A. Yates, *John Florio*, 1934; W. B. Henderson, "Montaigne's *Apologie of Raymond Sebond*, and *Lear*," *Shakespeare Association Bulletin*, XIV, 1939; Clara Longworth de Chambrun, *Shakespeare: A Portrait Restored*, 1955.]

Florio, Michelangelo (fl. mid-16th century). Italian author. The father of John Florio, Michelangelo Florio was a rather mysterious and mercurial figure. Of Jewish ancestry, he entered the Franciscan order as a young man but was soon unfrocked and imprisoned. He was later converted to Protestantism and made his way to England where he became the tutor of Lady Jane Grey. After her death he wrote a moving history of her life. In 1559 he was forced to leave England and spent the rest of his life at Soglio. He has recently received the dubious distinction of joining the list of claimants to the authorship of Shakespeare's works. This latest hypothesis is put forth by one Santi Paladino (*Un italiano autore delle opere shakespeariane*, 1955), who suggests that the plays were written by Florio in Italian and translated into English by his son. See CLAIMANTS.

Florizel. In *The Winter's Tale*, the Prince of Bohemia and the lover of Perdita. Although Florizel is cast in the conventional mold of the young swain of the popular Elizabethan prose romance, his character is sufficiently delineated to enable him to emerge as a distinctive, individual figure. He is an articulate and spirited hero, worthy of the hand of the matchless Perdita.

Florizel and Perdita (1756). An adaptation by David GARRICK of *The Winter's Tale*. *Florizel and Perdita* was first performed in 1756 and published in 1758. A year earlier at the Smock Alley Theatre in Dublin, McNamara Morgan had adapted *The Winter's Tale* under the title of *The Sheep-Shearing: or Florizel and Perdita*. Garrick's adaptation, however is independent of Morgan's. It is based primarily on the fourth and fifth acts of Shakespeare's play, compressing the early action of *The Winter's Tale* into a 150-line prologue narrative written by Garrick. The play, with Garrick playing Leontes, was a great success and was presented a number of times throughout the next decade. It sparked two other adaptations of *The Winter's Tale*, one by Thomas Hull, the other by George Colman. [C. B. Hogan, *Shakespeare in the Theatre, 1701–1800*, 1957.]

Flotow, Friedrich, Freiherr **von.** See MUSIC BASED ON SHAKESPEARE: *19th century, 1850–1900.*

Flower, Charles Edward. See ROYAL SHAKESPEARE THEATRE.

Flower portrait. See PORTRAITS OF SHAKESPEARE.

Fluellen. In *Henry V*, a Welsh officer serving in King Henry's French campaign. Though a well-trained and loyal soldier, Fluellen is totally humorless and is constantly involved in arguments. During the course of the play he quarrels with Captain Macmorris, with Pistol, and with Williams.

Fluellen has been seen variously as Shakespeare's portrait of Sir Roger WILLIAMS, a follower of Essex, r of Ludovic Lloyd, a well-known figure at the lizabethan court.

Fluellen, William. See recusancy.

Flute, Francis. In *A Midsummer Night's Dream,* n Athenian bellows mender who is assigned the role f Thisby in the dramatic interlude. Flute protests aving to play a woman because he has a beard comg, and so he is allowed to wear a mask (I, ii).

Folger, Henry Clay (1857–1930). American busiessman and collector of Shakespeareana. Born in rooklyn and educated at Amherst College, Folger ecame president of the Standard Oil Company. His ollection of folios, quartos, manuscripts, and other vidences of Shakespearean scholarship, which he egan in 1889, became the most valuable in the world. : was presented to the United States in 1932 and is oused in the Folger Shakespeare Library at Washgton, D.C.

Folger Shakespeare Library, The. The Folger hakespeare Library was presented to the American eople on April 23, 1932, when President Herbert Ioover accepted the keys from Mrs. Henry Clay olger. The library and its endowment are admintered by the trustees of Amherst College, where Ienry Clay Folger (1857–1930) received his college ducation and began to develop a serious interest in ie text of Shakespeare.

Descended from Peter Folger (1617?–1690) of Nanicket, Folger was reared in Brooklyn, and lived iere until he moved late in life to Glen Cove, Long sland. Upon graduating from Amherst, Folger stud-d law at Columbia College while working for the ratt Company, which had connections with Standrd Oil. Eventually he served as president and chairian of the board of the Standard Oil Company of Jew York. He died in 1930, two weeks after the layig of the cornerstone of the building that he had ommissioned. There were no children of his mariage with Emily Clara Jordan, who shared actively ith her husband in the collection of the Shakeoeare library. At her death in 1936, she added her state to the original endowment made by her husand.

the collections. In a period of great collectors, iany wealthier than himself, Folger was remarkable or his acumen and singleness of purpose. During iuch of his lifetime, scholars considered the First olio edition (1623) of the plays to be the chief auiority for Shakespeare's text, and so Folger brought nder one roof as many copies of the book as possible o facilitate minute study. Fortunately, the high auhority of certain quartos was recognized in time for im to acquire them in quantity. He did not secure copy of every first edition, or even of every 17thentury reprint. Some of the missing items exist in nly one or two copies in institutional libraries; thers did not come on the market during his lifeime. No library has a copy of every early edition of ie poems and plays. The British Museum, the Henry :. Huntington Library, and the Folger Shakespeare ,ibrary have approximately equal numbers of first ditions, but the Folger has an unmatched number f copies of the First (79 and fragments), Second 58), Third (24), and Fourth (37) Folios and of the 6th- and 17th-century quartos. Especially notable re the unique *Titus Andronicus* of 1594, the unique ragment of the first edition of *1 Henry IV,* the unique fragment of the first edition of *The Passionate Pilgrim,* and the copy of the First Folio presented by Isaac Jaggard, its publisher, to Augustine Vincent.

These early editions are supplemented by the most extensive collection in the world of the later editions and adaptations in English, both of the complete works and of the plays and poems published singly. The relatively few missing imprints—whether English, Scottish, Irish, or American—are sought systematically. Some of the Folger copies were owned and used by the great Shakespeare editors; many others have equally high associational value. Many early translations and most of the important ones are available here. This section of the library has expanded rapidly in recent years.

Materials for the study of Shakespeare's life and times consist of almost all of the documents containing allusions that were in print by 1700, and a quantity in manuscript, including the diary of the Reverend John Ward of Stratford, which has the only account of the poet's death. A signature in William Lambarde's *Archaionomia* (1568) may be genuine. There are Shakespeare's own copies of documents relating to the property that he bought in Blackfriars—their counterparts in English libraries bear his signature. The numerous notebooks and handsomely bound volumes of illustrations belonging to the scholar James O. Halliwell-Phillipps are rich in documents, prints, drawings, water colors, and printed extracts relating to Shakespeare's London and Warwickshire.

Folger searched indefatigably for Shakespeare source books, English and continental. He was no less assiduous in collecting the contemporary and later literary criticism and appreciation, wherever published, and also many essays in manuscript, some of them still unpublished.

For the study of Shakespeare on the stage, there are such early manuscript adaptations as the Dering *Henry IV;* a dozen prompt-books used before 1700 and hundreds of later date; thousands of London playbills, the earliest dated 1697, and a scattering from the English provincial theatres and from Ireland and Scotland. There are also rare items from theatres in the United States, important documents and a long run of account books of the Drury Lane Theatre (1766–1880) and Covent Garden (1740–1832), and many thousands of theatrical prints and photographs. Supplementing the elaborately illustrated prompt-books of Charles Kean are volumes of water-color designs of costumes. From actors like David Garrick and Edmund Kean there are quantities of letters, literary manuscripts and scraps, memorabilia, and collections of pictures.

Early in his career, Folger extended the limits of his library to include the dramatic and nondramatic literature of Tudor and Stuart England and also contemporary literary criticism. During his later years he enlarged the scope of the collection still further, until it was well on its way to becoming a general research library of the English Renaissance. He could not have anticipated the growth the library was to enjoy in its early decades.

During the depression years, Dr. Joseph Q. Adams, the director, was able to acquire a First Quarto of *Lear* (1608) and a quarto of *Lucrece* (1616), and hundreds of books published in English between

1475 and 1640. Then came the opportunity to secure from Loseley Hall in England first the great collection of manuscript records of Sir Thomas Cawarden, Master of the Office of Tents and Revels, and then the John Donne letters relating to his marriage. In a later decade, the second director, Dr. Louis B. Wright, added a great quantity of other manuscripts from Loseley.

In 1938, the collection of early English books was more than doubled by the purchase of a great portion of the library of the late Sir Leicester Harmsworth. The combined holdings were—and are—exceeded only by those in the British Museum. Among the Harmsworth books there was comparatively little drama, but the materials on Chaucer, Daniel, Donne, and Drayton, to name only a few, were formidable. Most of the early English presses are represented, including books printed by Caxton, Pynson, and Wynkyn de Worde. One of the most welcome and important sections is that containing Americana, though the early liturgical books are of equal or greater rarity.

About this time, Folger's extensive collection of John Dryden was enriched by the purchase of the extraordinary lot of plays, poems, and translations collected by P. J. Dobell.

At Folger's death, the continental books were largely Shakespearean sources and analogues, though there were quantities of emblem books, of Italian plays, and of neo-Latin plays. It has been possible for Dr. Wright to build the continental collection to the point where it includes works of such theologians as Luther and Calvin, and also representative volumes of Italian, French, Spanish, and Dutch literature, as well as many of the important Renaissance works in science, architecture, medicine, history, political theory, and agriculture. A notable purchase was the collection of some 200 volumes of the papers of the great Strozzi family.

The museum material includes pieces of Elizabethan furniture, coins, bric-a-brac, theatrical properties and a few costumes, early musical instruments to complement the manuscript and printed music, and statues and busts of Shakespeare in marble, bronze, and wood. The Elizabethan music, collected by Folger and Harmsworth, is supplemented by most of the 17th-century English song books and a remarkable amount of theatrical sheet music of the 17th and 18th centuries. There are many settings of Shakespearean songs, early and late, and some operatic scores. The small collection of paintings is made up of (1) so-called PORTRAITS of Shakespeare, among them the Ashbourne, Janssen, and Felton portraits, and a fine early copy of Kneller's copy of the Chandos portrait and (2) representations of characters and scenes in Shakespeare's plays, including canvases by George Romney and Henry Fuseli and a few from BOYDELL'S SHAKESPEARE GALLERY. Among the prints will be found practically all the engravings of Shakespeare, including two "proof" states of the Droeshout portrait in the First Folio. There are a few miniatures, two by Isaac Oliver.

Since 1948, there have been systematic additions to all of the basic collections and a vast expansion of the reference collections. Particular emphasis has been given to securing the non-literary publications between 1640 and 1715, especially those in theology, history, commerce and exploration, and all the new sciences. The nearly 1100 Bagot family papers provide contemporary information about domestic economy, local history, and other facets of life in England between 1560 and 1623, as does the smaller collection of Cavendish-Talbot correspondence and Wentworth papers from 1548–1658 and 1624–1705. These manuscripts supplement the collection of more than 1000 papers of Sir Nathaniel Bacon that Folger had bought. Politics, history, and gossip are recorded in the nearly 4000 manuscript news letters written by Sir Joseph Williamson to Sir Richard Newdigate between 1674 and 1715.

publications. Publications began with series of collotype cards and prints illustrating Shakespeare's London and Stratford, Shakespeare portraiture, the Elizabethan stage, and some of Shakespeare's works. Many other subjects have been added. Then came editions, with collotype facsimiles, of several unique books and manuscripts that had long been wanted by scholars (*Titus Andronicus*, 1594; *Oenone and Paris; The Ghost of Lucrece; Hengist, King of Kent* and others). In 1958 appeared the first of a continuing series of attractively printed and amply illustrated Folger Booklets on Tudor and Stuart Civilization. A hard-cover series of reprints began in 1962, Folger Documents of Tudor and Stuart Civilization. These are both literary and historical, as indicated by the first two volumes: *Advice to a Son, Precepts of Lord Burghley, Sir Walter Raleigh, and Francis Osborne*, and *William Lambarde and Local Government: His "Ephemeris" and Twenty-nine Charges to Juries and Commissions.*

the building. Situated in proximity to the Capitol and the Supreme Court, which are classical in style, the Folger Library is built of white Georgia marble in a style that harmonizes with them. However, its modern design by Paul Philippe Cret and Alexander Trowbridge, the consulting architect, features glass and aluminum instead of columns. Along the north façade are bas-reliefs by John Gregory with scenes from nine of Shakespeare's plays. In the garden at the west end of the building, a figure of Puck by Brenda Putnam looks out across a fountain. To house appropriately the Tudor and Stuart books and manuscripts, the interior of the building derives its inspiration from Shakespeare's England. Along the north front is a lofty Exhibition Gallery with a ceiling of strapwork in low relief, oak-paneled walls, and an Enfield tile floor. Here are displayed books, manuscripts, paintings, and museum pieces for the visitors who come daily. At the east end of the building is an auditorium designed to suggest an Elizabethan public playhouse. It is used for lectures, concerts, and conferences. The Reading Room is like a Tudor great hall, with a west window of stained glass, designed by Nicola D'Ascenzo, representing the Seven Ages of Man.

services to scholarship. The first fellowships were awarded in 1936. They are made for short or longer periods, depending on the nature of the project, the library's holdings, and the qualifications of the applicant. Fellows have come from most of the states of the union and many foreign countries.

The Folger is a research library in which properly qualified readers are given ready access to the collections. It is prudent to inquire in writing about particular holdings before seeking admittance. The library is equipped to furnish photographic, photostatic, microfilm, and Xerox copies of its holdings.

In response to requests for loans of early editions of Shakespeare, a traveling exhibit was prepared in 1952 (the founder had forbidden interlibrary loans). It consisted of a set of the first four Folios, two Quartos of 1619, and certain reprints and minor library publications. This widely traveled exhibit was supplemented by six others during the celebrations of Shakespeare's quatercentenary in 1964. Two of the exhibits contain a play abstracted from the First Folio, a 1619 Quarto, and sets of Folger booklets, prints, cards, and photographs. The other four differ only in lacking original editions of the plays. These seven exhibits were in continuous use by universities, colleges, preparatory and high schools, and public libraries throughout 1964, and the demand for them remains constant.—J. G. M.

folio. A printing term referring to a book made up of sheets folded once to form 2 leaves (4 pages) ranging in size from 11 to 16 inches in height and from 8 to 11 inches in width. The abbreviations commonly used for the four 17th-century Shakespearean Folios are F1, F2, F3, and F4.

folk festivals. Hamlet's words "For, O, for, O, the hobby-horse is forgot" (III, ii, 144–145) sum up the decline of the folk festival which Shakespeare witnessed in his own lifetime. Linked with the Church's festive year, and with the four seasons, many of these occasions came under an early ban from the reformers as "Popish"; and this, coupled with rapid changes in traditional agricultural life, more especially ENCLOSURES, weakened the hold of old custom—except in such remote parts as Catholic Lancashire or Cornwall, far from the centers of drama. The more prosperous farming areas were those where the reformed faith flourished, so that where the community might well have sustained old festivities, there was least inclination to do so. Town sports withered with the extinction of many religious guilds and fraternities, or took on a national, secular coloring.

Not far from Stratford-upon-Avon, Coventry had provided a great center not only for guild plays but for a popular festive game. On Hock Monday (the second Monday after Easter) men went out and "captured" women, who, before they were released, had to pay a small ransom; on Tuesday the women retaliated and went out to capture the men. This game became related to the legend of a battle between the English and the Danes in which the Danes were held captive by English women, and also to the annual muster of the city trained-bands, who in the 1570's were led by one Captain Cox, a mason by trade and a lover of ballads and plays. When in July 1575 Queen Elizabeth visited Kenilworth Castle, the Coventry men brought their show to Kenilworth in an attempt to revive it—for the local preachers had issued a ban. Shakespeare, then a boy of 11 years, may have seen this mixture of mumming and folk sport; the linking of combats with English history may have suggested the germ of his first great popular success, the plays on King Henry VI. "York and Lancaster's long jars" are really a series of combats, with women leading the enemy troops—first Joan of Arc, then that other she-wolf of France, Margaret of Anjou. The mock crowning of Richard of York by Margaret recalls the savage kind of folk sport which a town mob could mete out to condemned characters. To a London audience, who had their own spectacular musters at Mile-end, the tradition would be familiar.

But it was not long before London town sports became a subject for good-natured mockery with Shakespeare. The leaders of the trained-bands had taken the name of Prince Arthur's Knights, and in *2 Henry IV* Justice Shallow recalls that he played the part of Sir Dagonet, Arthur's court fool:

> I remember at Mile-end Green, when I lay at Clement's Inn,—I was then Sir Dagonet in Arthur's show,—there was a little quiver fellow, and a' would manage you his piece thus . . . .
>
> (*2 Henry IV*, III, ii, 298–301)

In some places the muster men became "Robin Hood's men"; and in many popular Robin Hood plays, the outlaw was shown exchanging a buffet with King Richard Coeur de Lion in disguise. The memory of such folk plays is perhaps behind the challenge between the King and Williams in *Henry V*, where the King in disguise accepts his subject's glove, but later sends Fluellen off with the glove in his cap to meet the challenger. Fluellen next wears a leek in his cap and challenges Pistol, making him eat it; the wearing of the leek is defended by Captain Gower as an old custom:

> Will you mock at an ancient tradition, begun upon an honourable respect, and worn as a memorable trophy of predeceased valour . . . ?
>
> (V, i, 74–76)

The wearing of badges by the followers of "summer lords" was a jesting echo of such custom.

Robin Hood, Maid Marian, Friar Tuck, the Fool, and the Hobby Horse all figured in the morris dance (see Will KEMPE), May Day sport of villages from the early 16th century. Shakespeare makes little use of these figures directly—*As You Like It* shows the banished Duke and his followers living "like old Robin Hood of England"—but the whole play, shot through with satire and irony, is far from simple folk-life. In the scene celebrating the death of the deer there could be a recollection of the famous Horn Dance at Abbot's Bromley. The forester is decked with horns and a ribald song is sung:

> What shall he have that kill'd the deer?
> His leather skin and horns to wear . . . .
>
> (IV, ii, 11–12)

The sport of hunting was clearly Shakespeare's favorite, whether or no there is any foundation for the old story of his poaching activities.

On May Day, the London populace went out to the fields, with the lord mayor leading the procession, and "the mob began to wrestle before him, two at a time!" The playhouses also stood in the fields and they may have been used for other activities than those of the actors. Perhaps for this very reason, Shakespeare dissociates himself from the city sports; it is paradoxically in his most courtly plays that elegant parody of country festivities appears. *A Midsummer Night's Dream* may have been intended for a court wedding, and it is here that Hermia and Lysander plan to meet

> . . . in the wood, a league without the town,
> Where I did meet thee once with Helena,
> To do observance to a morn of May.
> (I, i, 165–167)

When Theseus finds the lovers sleeping in the woods at the end of their night's adventure he says:

> No doubt they rose up early to observe
> The rite of May.
> (IV, i, 136–137)

To ride to the woods and come home with the May boughs was a sport that Queen Elizabeth herself indulged in at the very end of her life; in 1602 she went Maying. The humbler folk who stole off to the greenwood would plight troth with rush rings, and, as the angry Puritan Philip Stubbes averred, they would spend the night there. To give a country lass "a green gown" was a proverbial phrase for tumbling her.

Theseus greets the lovers with a reference to a festivity of the same sort:

> Good morrow, friends. Saint Valentine is past;
> Begin these wood-birds but to couple now?
> (IV, i, 143–144)

St. Valentine's Day, February 14, was the day when birds were supposed to choose their mates, and from Chaucer's *Parliament of Fowls* it can be learned how the court celebrated it too. Seasons combine in a magic way within this enchanted wood of Shakespeare; the flowers are those of early May (cowslips) to late June (honeysuckle and moss rose). On Midsummer Night, young women practiced charms to make the form of their future husbands appear to them in their dreams. The spirits of the Woodland here enchant Bottom by putting on him the ass's head, which was the traditional disguise of a country mummer, and in this disguise he is courted by the Fairy Queen. At his waking he treats it all as a midsummer night's dream. In this play rural sports, fairy lore, and courtly wit combine to form a very delicate and complex whole. A similar pattern can be traced in *Love's Labour's Lost,* which ends with a traditional rural singing contest, the song of the Owl and Cuckoo, Winter and Spring. In *Summer's Last Will and Testament,* Nashe built a whole show—it can hardly be called a play—upon the festive calendar; but Shakespeare keeps such passages for interludes only.

Twelfth Night sports contribute very indirectly to the play that bears the name of this last great Christmas feast. On January 6 the Twelfth Night cake was baked, with a bean inside, to determine which of the company should rule over the feast as King of the Bean. Sir Toby Belch has some characteristics of a Lord of Misrule—who, however, might be elected for the whole Christmas season. The chief claimant for the title, of course, is Falstaff in *1* and *2 Henry IV;* the case for considering him as Lord of Misrule has been set out by J. Dover Wilson in *The Fortunes of Falstaff* (1943). His riotous train of followers, his mock state at the Boar's Head (itself an emblem of Christmas revelry) are ironically overshadowed by the presence of the true Prince. Falstaff includes also some element of Robin Hood's follower, jolly Friar Tuck, who appears in the old play of *Robin Hood and the Friar* (c. 1550) with his wench, singing:

> Here is a huckle duckle,
> An inch above the buckle,
> She is a trull of trust to serve a friar at his lust,
> A pricker, a prancer, a tearer of sheets.

When the rival company produced a play to rival this one, they put in a fat priest, Sir John of Wrotham, and his doxy Doll (see Sir John Oldcastle). Falstaff's appearance at the Battle of Shrewsbury, with a bottle of sack for a weapon, recalls the fooling of the mummer's play, as does his miraculous "revival" after being "killed" by Douglas. Falstaff is the most complete embodiment of Merry England; and ultimately, of course, he is rejected, as, in fact, both Court and City had discontinued their Lords of Misrule.

In *The Merry Wives of Windsor,* Falstaff reappears as victim of a local merriment. When he stands under Herne the Hunter's oak in Windsor Forest, wearing the magic horns and buck's head of a country mummer, he is attacked and pinched by the fairies. The legend of Herne the Hunter, who is supposed to be seen galloping across the clouds in stormy weather with his hounds, is rather a terrifying one, and belongs to primitive Germanic stock. But here again a popular tale is made part of a courtly compliment, for the scene includes praise of Elizabeth ("Our radiant queen hates sluts and sluttery") and of the Garter Knights, whose chapel is at Windsor.

The tragedies have, naturally, little trace of popular festivities, but in *Hamlet,* Yorick, a jester in the old style, is mourned by Prince and Gravedigger alike. The old customs are seen nostalgically across the years. Yorick's place is in the hall, not on the stage.

In the romances there is a return to folk materials, and Jonson was to speak scornfully of "Tales, tempests and such drolleries" (or popular dumb shows) in the Induction to *Bartholomew Fair*—itself a celebration of a great popular festivity.

In *Pericles,* the poet Gower comes "to sing a song that old was sung"—

> It hath been sung at festivals,
> On ember-eves and holy-ales . . .
> (I, i, 5–6)

—and much of the tale to which he acts as "Presenter" is in dumb show. It resembles in outline some of those popular romances that Sidney was complaining of in *The Defence of Poetry,* more than a quarter of a century before, and that Beaumont had parodied so gaily in *The Knight of the Burning Pestle.*

The sheep-shearing scene of *The Winter's Tale,* which is not in his source, is Shakespeare's most complete depiction of a popular festivity, but again it shows a complex superimposing of the courtly upon the rural scene. Drayton, Shakespeare's friend, was doing the same thing in the Ninth Eglog of his *Poems Lyrick and Pastorall* (1606?). Perdita, the Queen of the feast, is "most goddess-like prankt up"; she is half a princess and half a country girl. The group of 12 countrymen who come in to dance may have been identical with a group that had danced at court in Ben Jonson's own *Masque of Oberon,* and their claim to have "danced before the King" is a pretty piece of dramatic irony; they are (in the play) dancing before King Polixenes in his disguise, and they may have also danced before King James.

In *The Tempest*, the "sunburnt sicklemen of August weary" who come to dance "in country footing" for the delight of Ferdinand and Miranda are partnered by water nymphs, demigoddesses. So that from the beginning to the end of his career, Shakespeare combines recollection of folk festivals with courtly ceremony, with magic and dream, with wit and satire. The true folk elements of the Elizabethan stage, such as the clown's improvised jests, were not to his taste and he condemns them in *Hamlet*. What he keeps, as C. L. Barber shows in *Shakespeare's Festive Comedy* (1959), is the spirit of revelry and not its substance.—M.C.B.

food and drink. Meals in Elizabethan times were by modern standards very heavy, and with the general increase in prosperity during the period there was an increased demand for gastronomic luxuries. Breakfast was taken about six-thirty, and was usually a substantial meal which sometimes included several different meat dishes. By the time of Elizabeth, the first meal had become considerably lighter than it was in the reign of her father, Henry VIII. Dinner, the main meal of the day, was served between 11 and 12 and sometimes lasted until 2 or 3 in the afternoon. A typical gentleman's dinner might include a piece of beef, a loin of veal, two chickens (with accompanying sauces), and oranges. Supper, between five-thirty and seven o'clock, was a somewhat lighter version of dinner.

Shakespeare mentions salads, green peas, and potatoes, by which he means sweet potatoes, or yams. The latter, introduced to England by John Hawkins, were thought to possess aphrodisiac qualities, as Thersites describes them in *Troilus and Cressida:*

> How the devil Luxury, with his fat rump and potato-finger, tickles these together! Fry, lechery, fry!
>
> (V, ii, 55–57)

The "Virginian," or white potato, was a rare, expensive luxury at the time; a bill charged to Anne of Denmark priced them at 2 s. the pound.

Fruit was much in demand, and many varieties were cultivated in England, including apples, pears, cherries, strawberries, plums, apricots, muskmelons, figs, and grapes. Oranges, most of which were imported, were commonly sold by "orange-wives" who hawked their wares in the streets. The orange-wife is mentioned at one point in *Coriolanus:*

> you wear out a good wholesome forenoon in hearing a cause between an orange-wife and a fosset-seller.
>
> (II, i, 77–79)

In *Much Ado About Nothing*, Beatrice puns on the bitter Seville variety of orange:

> The count is neither sad, nor sick, nor merry, nor well; but civil count, civil as an orange, and something of that jealous complexion.
>
> (II, i, 303–305)

An attempt to make wine in England early in the 16th century had proved to be a failure, and as a result wines were imported from Europe. Popular wines were alicant, a dark red wine from Alicante, Spain; claret; charneco, a kind of port; muscadine; Rhenish; and sack. Sack (from *sec*, meaning dry) was the generic name of wines from Spain and the Canaries and was the most popular wine with all classes in England. In the following tavern bill from *1 Henry IV*, an exaggerated consumption of sack is attributed to Falstaff:

> Item, A capon, ... 2s. 2d.
> Item, Sauce, ... 4d.
> Item, Sack, two gallons, ... 5s. 8d.
> Item, Anchovies and sack after supper, . 2s. 6d.
> Item, Bread, ... ob.
>
> *Prince.* O monstrous! but one half-penny worth of bread to this intolerable deal of sack!
>
> (II, iv, 585–592)

Both white and dark breads were evidently known; humble folk, however, made do with barley and rye brown bread. A contemporary observation noted that the latter was preferred to white bread because it was thought to remain undigested in the stomach for the duration of whatever labor the trencherman had to perform.

Sweets and cakes were popular and of great variety. One servant in *Romeo and Juliet* asks another to save him a piece of marchpane after a banquet; marchpane was a confection of pounded almonds, pistachio nuts, sugar, flour, and various essences. In *The Merry Wives of Windsor*, Falstaff refers to "kissing-comfits and eringoes"; the former confections were perfumed in order to sweeten the breath, and the latter were candied sea-holly roots, popularly believed to be aphrodisiac.

Cooking was accomplished in a large open fireplace equipped with spits upon which meats were roasted, and rods and chains on which stewpots were hung. The most menial kitchen task was the turning of the spit; thus, Benedick says of Beatrice:

> she would have made Hercules have turned spit, yea, and have cleft his club to make the fire too.
>
> (*Much Ado About Nothing*, II, i, 260–262)

Forks were used only by the eccentric at this time. Knives, spoons, and fingers were the common utensils, and ewers and basins were essential for use both before and after the meal. For drinking, glasses, originating in Venice, became increasingly popular, replacing metal and stoneware cups. English silver plate was of very fine quality and much in demand in Europe in the 16th century. [Percy Macquoid, "The Home," *Shakespeare's England*, 1916.]

Fool. In *King Lear*, the court jester and the ironic commentator on the tragic action of the play. One of the most remarkable of Shakespeare's creations, the Fool's role has been compared to that of the chorus in Greek tragedy. His speeches, delivered in a picturesque jumble of disjointed images and snatches of songs and proverbs, are the touchstones of the audience's reaction to the play's events. His bitter insights into the motives and designs of Goneril and Regan are alternated with his ironically expressed compassion for the old King; as he desperately attempts to restore Lear to sanity, he assumes the role of a tragic Sancho Panza.

One aspect of the Fool which has troubled commentators is his unexplained departure from the play in III, vi. One of the many explanations for this apparent lapse is the suggestion that the same boy actor who originally played Cordelia doubled as the Fool, thus requiring the elimination of his part before the return of Cordelia in Act IV (see DOUBLING). This hypothesis at least accounts for Lear's puzzling line over the dead body of Cordelia: "And my poor fool is hanged" (V, iii, 305).

Forbes-Robertson, Sir Johnston (1853–1937). Actor. A student of Samuel Phelps, Sir Johnston was one of the finest actors of his time. Although well respected in England, where he played Claudio in *Much Ado About Nothing* as well as many non-Shakespearean roles, he did not receive real acclaim until his 1885 tour of the United States, where he performed with great success in *As You Like It* and *Romeo and Juliet*. His London production of *Hamlet* in 1897 showed English audiences that he was a great tragedian. His "sane" Hamlet was considered one of the finest interpretations of that role, which he repeated in the United States, Canada, and on the continent. He also produced and starred in *Romeo and Juliet*, *Macbeth*, and *Othello*. He retired from the stage in 1914. [*Dictionary of National Biography*, supp., 1949; *Oxford Companion to the Theatre*, Phyllis Hartnoll, ed., 1951.]

Ford, John (1586–post 1640). Dramatist. Ford's name first appears in the records of the Middle Temple, from which he was expelled in 1605/6 for failure to pay his bills. He probably began his dramatic career in collaboration with Thomas Dekker; with the latter and William Rowley he wrote *The Witch of Edmonton* (1621). Ford's own plays are among the most distinguished tragedies in Stuart drama. They are characterized by a brooding, melancholic strain and an intense psychological probing of character. These elements are evident in his best plays, *'Tis Pity She's A Whore* (c. 1626), *Love's Sacrifice* (c. 1630), and *The Broken Heart* (c. 1632). Ford lacks Shakespeare's capacity to integrate comedy and tragedy, but Shakespeare's influence can be seen in most of Ford's work, most strikingly in *Love's Sacrifice*, where the character D'Avolos deceives the Duke in much the same language and manner that Iago employs on Othello. Ford draws on Shakespeare for certain techniques, such as the presentation of madness to evoke pathos instead of laughter. He also shares with his great predecessor a concern with a theme that is particularly pervasive in Shakespeare's last plays—the relationship of father and daughter. [M. Joan Sargeaunt, *John Ford*, 1935; Clifford Leech, *John Ford and the Drama of His Time*, 1957.]

Ford, Master Frank. In *The Merry Wives of Windsor*, a gentleman of Windsor. Warned by Pistol that Falstaff is wooing Mistress Ford, the jealous Ford resolves to test his wife's fidelity. He disguises himself as Master Brook and, pretending to be in love with Mistress Ford, secures Falstaff's services as go-between. When Falstaff boasts that he himself has an appointment with the lady for that evening and assures Brook that he shall soon see Ford as a cuckold, the tormented husband resolves to prevent the encounter. Accompanied by some friends, he arrives home at the trysting hour, but Falstaff is spirited away in a laundry basket and Ford's companions mock his jealousy. When the same scene is repeated with variations the next evening, Mistress Ford reveals to her husband the game being played at Falstaff's expense. Ford promises her to "rather suspect the sun with cold than thee with wantonness." (See William Brooke, 7th Lord COBHAM).

Ford, Mistress. In *The Merry Wives of Windsor*, a merry, yet honest, wife. Determined to be revenged upon Falstaff for his presumptuous love letter, Mistress Ford encourages the old lecher to visit her. With the help of Mistress Page, she plays him for the fool and, at the same time, confounds her jealous husband's attempts to surprise her in a compromising situation.

Ford, Thomas (d. 1648). Composer and lutenist, in which capacities he served Henry, prince of Wales, and Charles I. Ford's only published work, *Musicke of Sundrie Kindes* (1607), includes what is perhaps the best known of all English lute songs, "Since first I saw your face." Ford also set to music the lyric "Sigh no more, ladies," from *Much Ado About Nothing* (II, iii, 64–76).

Forman, Simon (1552–1611). Astrologer. Educated at Oxford, Forman made his living first as a schoolmaster, then turned to astrology and medicine after "discovering" in himself miraculous prophetic and curative powers. Though frequently jailed by the authorities as a quack, Forman had many powerful friends among the ladies of the court, whom he provided with love potions and advice on the conduct of their intrigues, and in 1603 he was granted a license to practice medicine. He correctly predicted the day of his own death (September 12, 1611), an indication that he may have committed suicide.

Among Forman's papers there is a folio manuscript titled "The Bocke of plaies and Notes herof & formans for Common pollicie." It contains the earliest extant account of the performances of three of Shakespeare's plays on the days that Forman attended them: *Macbeth* (April 20, 1611), *The Winter's Tale* (May 15, 1611), and *Cymbeline* (no date given). The manuscript also records Forman's attendance at a performance at the Globe on April 30, 1611 of a play about Richard II, but from the description of the plot it is clearly not the Shakespearean play. The "Bocke of plaies" was first discovered in 1836 by John Payne Collier, a notorious forger. As a result, the authenticity of the book has been questioned, particularly by the American scholar Samuel Tannenbaum and by Sydney Race (*Notes & Queries*, 203, 1958), but the entries are still regarded as genuine.

Forrest, Edwin (1806–1872). American actor. Born in Philadelphia, Forrest overcame the disadvantages of a poverty-stricken childhood to become the earliest American actor of first rank. He made his debut in 1820 in Philadelphia. After several years in various frontier theatres on the Ohio River, he appeared in 1825 as Iago with Edmund Kean in Albany; his Iago was a gay and dashing fellow, quixotic and given to passionate climaxes. The experience of working with Kean also served to enhance Forrest's own acting technique. The next year, at the Park Theatre, Forrest made his first appearance in New York as Othello with great success. At the less fashionable Bowery Theatre he won popular acclaim in the role of Mark Antony. More critical audiences, however, preferred the Park Theatre and the English actor Macready, whose rivalry with Forrest was later to prove disastrous. At $200 per night, Forrest was the best-paid actor in America. Later at the Park Theatre, Forrest encouraged native playwriting by offering prizes for the best American plays. In 1834 he visited London, where his roughhewn Spartacus at the Drury Lane captivated supposedly sophisticated London audiences. In 1837 Forrest married Catherine Norton Sinclair, an English girl. Again in London in 1845, Forrest was hissed as Macbeth. Erroneously or not, he blamed Macready, and in turn hissed Macready's Macbeth in Edinburgh. Macready's visit of 1849 to New York resulted in the tragic Astor Place riots, for which popular sentiment blamed Forrest. A man of animal vigor and colossal, heroic energy, he was most effective in strong-willed roles, such as Richelieu, Lear, or Coriolanus. [*Dictionary of American Biography*, 1927– .]

Fortinbras. In *Hamlet*, nephew of the King of Norway and son of the former King. Fortinbras' father was killed by King Hamlet. Thus Fortinbras, like Hamlet, is a king's nephew and the avenger of his father's death. By undergoing this experience analogous to Hamlet's own, Fortinbras is qualified to assume, at the end of the play, the throne that would have been Hamlet's.

Fortune's Tennis. A lost play in two parts belonging to the Admiral's Men, which derives its importance from the fact that a fragment of the "plot" or outline of the second part of the play is extant. Nothing is known of *Fortune's Tennis* itself except that it was probably revised by Thomas Dekker in 1600. The plot is written in the same hand as that of *2 Seven Deadly Sins* and of that designated as "Hand C" in SIR THOMAS MORE, a manuscript play, three pages of which are generally thought to have been written by Shakespeare. The occurrence of this scribe's hand in *2 Fortune's Tennis*, dated about 1597 and known to belong to the Admiral's Men, is one of the complicating factors in attempting to date *Sir Thomas More*. If *Sir Thomas More* is an Admiral's play, it becomes extremely difficult to explain Shakespeare's revision, in view of the fact that the Admiral's Men were his company's chief rivals. [W. W. Greg, *Dramatic Documents from the Elizabethan Playhouses*, 1931.]

Fortune theatre. An Elizabethan playhouse located to the north of London outside of Cripplegate. The Fortune theatre was built in 1600 by Edward ALLEYN and Philip Henslowe as a home for the Admiral's Men, the company of which Alleyn was the leading actor. The contract for building the Fortune was given to Peter Street, the same contractor who had built the Globe. The contract is important for it provides us with the only accurate record of the specifications of an Elizabethan theatre (see PLAYHOUSE STRUCTURE). The Fortune was modeled on the Globe. Unfortunately, we are deprived of an accurate picture of many details, particularly the design of the stage, because the contract merely states "like unto the Globe" or a similar phrase:

> This Indenture made . . . betwene Phillipp Henslowe and Edwarde Allen of the parishe of Ste Saviours in Southwark in the Countie of Surrey, gentlemen, on thone parte, and Peeter Streete, Cittizen and Carpenter of London . . . ; The frame of the saide howse to be sett square and to conteine ffowerscore foote of lawfull assize everye waie square withoutt and fiftie fiue foote of like assize square everye waie within, with a good suer and stronge foundacion of pyles, brick, lyme and sand bothe without & within, to be wroughte one foote of assize att the leiste aboue the grounde; And the saide fframe to conteine three Stories in heighth, the first or lower Storie to conteine Twelue foote of lawfull assize in heighth, the second Storie Eleaven foote of lawfull assize in

THE FORTUNE THEATRE AS RECONSTRUCTED BY C. WALTER HODGES. (COURTESY OF COWARD-MC CANN, INC.)

heigth, and the third or vpper Storie to conteine Nyne foote of lawfull assize in height; . . . With a Stadge and Tyreinge howse to be made, erected & settupp within the saide fframe, with a shadowe or cover over the saide Stadge, which Stadge shalbe placed & sett, as alsoe the stearecases of the saide fframe, in suche sorte as is prefigured in a plott thereof drawen, and which Stadge shall conteine in length Fortie and Three foote of lawfull assize and in breadth to extende to the middle of the yarde of the saide howse; The same Stadge to be paled in belowe with good, stronge and sufficyent newe oken bourdes, and likewise the lower Storie of the saide fframe withinside, and the same lower storie to be alsoe laide over and fenced with stronge yron pykes; And the saide Stadge to be in all other proporcions contryved and fashioned like vnto the Stadge of the saide Plaie howse called the Globe; With convenient windowes and lightes glazed to the saide Tyreinge howse; And the saide fframe, Stadge and Stearecases to be covered with Tyle, and to haue a sufficient gutter of lead to carrie & convey the water frome the coveringe of the saide Stadge to fall backwardes . . . .

The theatre opened in the autumn of 1600 and remained for the next two decades one of the best and most popular playhouses, where foreign visitors were frequently entertained.

In 1616 Henslowe died and the property came under the sole ownership of Alleyn, who in 1619 leased the building to his former acting company, the Admiral's Men, then known as the Elector Palatine's Men. Two years later, in 1621, the theatre was burned to the ground.

It was rebuilt in the following year, this time as a brick building circular in shape. The playhouse never regained its former eminence, however, and by the 1630's had a poor reputation. The building was wrecked by commonwealth soldiers in 1649 and totally demolished by 1662. [J. Q. Adams, *Shakespearean Playhouses,* 1917; E. K. Chambers, *The Elizabethan Stage,* 1923.]

foul papers. An author's original, uncorrected play manuscript. The foul papers presumably contained the essential text of the play with the author's corrections, interlineations, and deletions on the manuscript. This manuscript would then be copied on a clean sheet for the use of the acting company which had purchased the play (see FAIR COPY). All the available evidence seems to indicate that some of the early Shakespearean quartos were printed from his foul papers, a fact which accounts for the numerous errors and inconsistencies in these texts. Among the quartos thought to be derived from the foul papers are the First Quartos of *Much Ado About Nothing, Love's Labour's Lost, Midsummer Night's Dream, Richard II, 1* and *2 Henry IV,* and the First Folio versions of *The Comedy of Errors, The Taming of the Shrew,* and *Coriolanus.*

The term "foul papers" was used in 1625 by the scribe of the King's Men, explaining the absence of a scene from a transcript of Fletcher's play *Bonduca* (c. 1613): "the book whereby it was first Acted from is lost: and this hath beene transcrib'd from the fowle papers of the Authors whch were founde." Evidently, the company preserved in its archives all available copies of a play which they owned in order to prevent its falling into the hands of a rival company or a printer. Shakespeare, who was well known for fluency and ease in composition, apparently wrote only foul papers; nevertheless, if, as some scholars contend, the handwriting in a portion of the manuscript of *Sir Thomas More* is Shakespeare's, he evidently was in the habit of correcting his draft. Thus the statement of Heminges and Condell in the Preface to the First Folio "that wee have scarce receiued from him a blot in his papers" is now regarded as an understandable exaggeration, but an exaggeration, nevertheless. [W. W. Greg, *The Editorial Problem in Shakespeare,* 1942; E. A. J. Honigmann, *The Stability of Shakespeare's Text,* 1965.]

Fourth Folio. The fourth collected edition of Shakespeare's plays, published in 1685.

> Mr. William Shakespear's Comedies, Histories, And Tragedies. Published according to the true Original Copies. Unto which is added, Seven Plays, Never before Printed in Folio: viz. Pericles Prince of Tyre. The London Prodigal. The History of Thomas Lord Cromwel. Sir John Oldcastle Lord Cobham. The Puritan Widow. A Yorkshire Tragedy. The Tragedy of Locrine. The Fourth Edition. London, Printed for H. Herringman, E. Brewster, and R. Bentley, at the Anchor in the New Exchange, the Crane in St. Pauls Church-Yard, and in Russel-Street Covent-Garden. 1685.

The Fourth Folio is a reprint of the Third (1664) with a good deal of correction and modernization, apparently made by three different persons. There are 751 editorial changes in F4, most of them designed to make the text easier to read and comprehend. Often regarded as the worst of the four folios, it has been seen by its later close students, M. W. Black and M. A. Shaaber, as a workmanlike and often valuable addition to the standard Shakespearean text. [M. W. Black and M. A. Shaaber, *Shakespeare's Seventeenth-Century Editors,* 1937.]

fowling. See HUNTING, COURSING, AND FOWLING.

Foxe, John. See BOOK OF MARTYRS.

France. Knowledge of Shakespeare outside Britain was very scant in the 17th century, France being no exception. In fact, none of the available evidence seriously disproves Voltaire's claim that it was he who first (c. 1730) focused continental attention upon the poet. Voltaire achieved this with a great economy of means; nevertheless, he managed to set the prevalent motif of French Shakespearean criticism. Plainly to be seen even today, underneath that criticism and its bewildering variations, is the old Voltairian belief that Shakespeare, on his journey across the Channel, must undergo some process of naturalization. (See VOLTAIRE.) To be sure, modern academic methods have bred a generation or two of French scholars (translators or literary historians) who strove and strive for the dispassionate approach. Much louder than theirs, however, are the voices which maintain that the essence of Shakespeare's art, of his language itself, becomes lost in translation; or again, that what is unfathomable about him—his outlook on life, his poetry, his shadowy personality—raises him to the status of a symbol. For the most part it is in an oblique way—not as a subject for sedate study, but as an emanation of the monstrous or the sublime, as a flag or a weapon, as a spur to soul-searching, as a pretext for experimental stagecraft—that the French have embraced Shakespeare.

Not that the original issues were overly complicated. In literary matters, 18th-century France wavered between its allegiance to classical "rules" and a keen awareness that new inspirations required new techniques. Of crucial importance was the fate of tragedy, by all odds the proudest and most cumbersome legacy of the preceding age. The question was, how could French tragedy, which Racine had brought to almost inimitable perfection, move forward, perhaps away from the rules, without losing its identity? Shakespeare provided the answer. Obviously not Shakespeare in the rough, nor the whole of Shakespeare, since straight transfusions would defeat their own purpose; but Shakespeare in distilled, assimilable quantities. This policy of "reasonable" quotas, truly the burden of Voltaire's campaign, went unopposed for several decades; instead, what gave rise to hot dispute was the level of the quotas. From Abbé Jean-Bernard Le Blanc (*Lettres d'un Français à Londres*, 1745) to François de La Harpe (*De Shakespeare*, 1799), a long line of "moderates," following Voltaire's lead, advocated restraint and cautiousness. "Anglomaniacs," for their part, insisted on bold remedies, thereby destroying Voltaire's equanimity and precipitating a noticeable increase of Shakespearean fervor. Genuine warmth, despite some guarded notes, suffused Abbé Prévost's articles in *Le Pour et le Contre* (1738) and the *Discours sur le théâtre anglais* (1745) of Pierre-Antoine de La Place (1707–1793). The *Discours* ushered in 23 plays in translation, 10 of them by Shakespeare, which afforded French readers their first taste, however adulterated, of Elizabethan drama. No more, at any rate, was needed to fire the imagination of Jean-François Ducis. This mediocre craftsman, who knew no English, used La Place's and subsequent translations as a starting point for six adaptations in verse (the first, *Hamlet*, 1769; the last, *Othello*, 1792); and their successful performance at the Comédie Française made him, implausibly enough, a potent factor in the French fortunes of "le grand Guillaume." By the time he finished his labor of love, Pierre Le Tourneur (1736–1788) had long since entered and departed the scene, leaving behind him a complete translation of Shakespeare's dramatic works (20 vols., 1776–1782). A trained student of English literature, sometimes called the first modern translator, Le Tourneur threw La Place into oblivion. Quite significantly, too, his prefatory statement was anti-Voltairian and pre-Romantic in spirit.

Ever since the 1750's the wind of the *Aufklärung* had been blowing from Germany. It was a Shakespearean wind, in the literal sense that Lessing and his disciples, no longer willing to be beholden to Corneille and Racine, called upon the Stratfordian—a blood brother, or so they said—to "liberate" the German theatre for them (see Germany). Gallic reaction was one of pique, naturally; but shrewd minds, knowing a lost cause when they saw one, undertook to steal Lessing's thunder. All being fair in war, Lessing had based much of his appeal to Shakespeare on Denis Diderot's (1713–1784) defense of the forces of nature ("genius") against artificial refinements ("taste"); whereupon Diderot and, above all, Louis-Sébastien Mercier (1740–1814) felt bound, under German pressure, to intensify their own search for new dramatic formulae. This give-and-take caused Mercier to write his *Nouvel essai sur la poésie dramatique* (1773), three adaptations from Shakespeare, and original plays (e.g., *La Mort de Louis XI*, 1783) which clearly heralded one of Stendhal's pet schemes—a topically national theatre patterned after *Richard III* and other "histories."

Classical resistance was stout and lasted into the 1820's. It even drew renewed strength from the upheavals of the Revolution and the Empire, so compelling, in those times, were the memories and examples of antiquity. Chateaubriand and Madame de Staël, variously hampered by their backgrounds, contributed little to the greater glory of the poet. All things considered, three men, under the Bourbon Restoration, were responsible for passing on the Shakespearean torch: Charles Nodier (1780–1844), who "discovered" for the French the magic world of Puck and Titania, of Ariel and Caliban, and was Hugo's initiator; François Guizot (1787–1874), the future statesman, who revised Le Tourneur's translation, prefacing it with a substantial *Etude sur Shakespeare* (1821); and then—Stendhal. The anatomist of love, who described it as a crystallization, had begun "crystallizing" around Shakespeare at the turn of the century. On the morrow of Waterloo, he knew in his heart the why and wherefore of his passion. The Napoleonic world had been that of the Renaissance, of Shakespeare, of his characters, brought to life once again: a world of risk and highly individual prowess—generous or criminal, who cared? Now that the last of the *condottieri* was gone, nothing remained but the prospect of bleak mediocrity. Could the fires be rekindled? Stendhal doubted it; he, one day, was to send his Julien Sorel to the scaffold for the sin of believing it; but his doubts flared into anger when he saw the Parisian public, led or misled by a political clique, shout down a British troupe who had come to play Shakespeare in the original (1822). He then wrote the first part of his *Racine et Shakespeare* (1823) as a lesson in spiritual rejuvenation. Do not ape Shakespeare, he admonished his readers, as you copy Racine who himself copied the ancients; live in your own flesh and, if you write, write in your own blood—as, indeed, Shakespeare did. The warning having chanced upon the ears of Louis-Simon Auger (1772–1829), that member of the conservative French Academy delivered himself of an oration (1824) in which he derided the "romantic" avant-garde. Stendhal clutched at the word, made it the defiant leitmotif of his second *Racine et Shakespeare* (1825)—and the Romantic battle was on.

A man of prose, though not a prosaic man, Stendhal equated Shakespeare with a way of life, not so much with a form of art; the master's eminence rested on his having been the incomparable mirror of his times—the Elizabethan of Elizabethans. If this was romanticism, it was romanticism in a historical, or *realistic*, context. To Victor Hugo, on the contrary, Shakespeare represented poetry incarnate: a mirror, yes, but a cosmic one, reflecting all the sunbeams and all the shadows, all the harmonies and contradictions that have gone into nature itself—hence into human nature—since the beginning of time. Such a remote, nearly abstract quality called for a manner of worship entirely foreign to Stendhal's ways, yet not unmixed with opportunistic considerations. Hugo's first Shakespearean pronouncement, the *Préface* to his unplayed *Cromwell* (1827), exploited, in a bid for leadership, the triumph of another British troupe (Kemble-Macready-Harriet Smithson), whose performances at the Odéon had recently avenged the 1822 fiasco. The miracle of it is that, even to this day, the *Préface* retains the radiance and the all-redeeming grace of youth. Hugo never quite recaptured that blessed mood. Giving free rein to his taste for the oracular, he thought of himself, more and more, as "the poet of France" judging, and communing with, "the poet of England." This lofty *entente cordiale*, at work in Hugo's mature writing (including the posthumous *Théâtre en liberté*, 1886), became sanctified, as it were, when his bulky *William Shakespeare* (1864), ostensibly a foreword to his son's new translation, lifted the poet onto the promontory of Dream—i.e., of Supreme Contemplation. Only 13 others preceded Shakespeare in that lonely spot, reserved for universal prophets and geniuses; no one—so far—had followed him. Neither a biography nor, on the whole, a critical study, the book has variously been called epic, titanic, oceanic, apocalyptic; to the author, in his own words, it was nothing less than "the manifesto of the century."

Both Romantic traditions—Hugo's and Stendhal's—accounted for an extraordinary surge of pro-Shakespeare sentiment. However sharp the cleavage between them, they concurred in making the man or the dramatist larger than his medium. Shakespeare began bursting at the seams; in no time at all, artists and writers of every stripe would take him out of the theatre altogether.

Members of Hugo's *cénacle*, almost to a man, returned moonstruck from the Odéon performances of 1827 and ready to embark upon Shakespearean rituals of their own. If the scruples of Alexandre Dumas *père* (1802–1870) had matched his ebullience, his *Hamlet*, produced at a late date (1846) in collaboration with Paul Meurice (1820–1905), would have been a masterpiece. Alfred de Vigny (1797–1863), on the other hand, having earned a resounding success with *Othello* (Comédie Française, 1829), turned to brooding over man's destiny in general and the poet's in particular, his *Journal* for 1834 testifying to a close link between that basic theme of his and Hamlet's "To be or not to be." Memories of the melancholy Dane likewise haunted Théophile Gautier's and Gérard de Nerval's more esoteric writing. And then, what of Hector Berlioz? Through his love for Harriet Smithson (or was it for her in the part of Ophelia?) he let Shakespeare invade both his private life and his musical world. New vistas opened before the composer of composers who, contrary to Beethovenian practice, relied on literary sources for his inspiration. *Lélio* (1832) was one of several pieces derived from *Hamlet; Much Ado About Nothing* supplied the libretto of *Béatrice et Bénédict*, written around 1833 by Berlioz himself (first performance, 1862); *Romeo and Juliet* inspired the well-known "dramatic symphony" (1839) of the same name. Those by no means represented Shakespeare's first (or last) appearances in French music; Berlioz alone however, achieved the miracle of idiomatic transference through the right admixture of intuition and skill.

There were no Stendhalians as such—unless a case be made for Ludovic Vitet (1802–1873), the author of several "national tragedies," or "histories," in prose (such as *Les Barricades*, 1826); or again, Prosper Mérimée (1803–1870) who, before writing *La Jacquerie* in the same vein (1828), concocted a spicy blend of Shakespearean realism and pseudo-Spanish comedy (*Théâtre de Clara Gazul*, 1825). It is a moot question, however, whether Stendhal may not claim for his own any and all contemporaries, including some of Hugo's early associates, whose unmystical bent prevented them from joining in the Shakespeare liturgy. Alfred de Musset (1810–1857), for instance delightful midsummer-daydreamer though he was, belonged at heart to the "no nonsense" school: he pointedly referred to "my good friend Shakespeare," and *Lorenzaccio* (1834) lives up to Stendhalian precepts in that it is an original French drama that the author of *Hamlet* might not have disowned. Turning to Eugène Delacroix (1799–1863) and the 75 Shakespeare entries in his *Journal*, one sees him stealing a hard look at the 16th-century colossus. No Berlioz he, share as he might the "literary" proclivities of that fellow artist. His approach was neither impulsive nor intuitive; "identification," if any, would not come through adoration but through understanding. A tortured spirit of inquisitiveness informs the collection of *Hamlet* lithographs that he put out in 1843: a work touched with genius, whereas similar efforts by Théodore Chassériau (*Othello* series, 1844) and Gustave Doré (various subjects, c. 1865) show only considerable talent. Charles Baudelaire (1821–1867) in his *Curiosités esthétiques* described Delacroix's *Hamlet* as a study in restlessness and a quasi-clinical probe into the new *mal du siècle:* a safe enough guarantee that Baudelaire's own Shakespeare owed much to Delacroix's and, albeit tortuously, to Stendhal's.

Come 1850, middle-of-the-road critics began clamoring for more judicial views than had prevailed during the Romantic extravaganza. Philarète Chasles (1798–1873) wrote *Etudes sur Shakespeare* in 1852; he and others undertook an "objective" re-examination. How objective remains open to question; they did not find it easy to shed every vestige of the old impressionism. Nor did, for that matter, Hippolyte Taine (1828–1893). His portrait of Shakespeare (1856; reprinted in his *Histoire de la littérature anglaise*, V. II), though subordinated, one may be sure, to the unyielding factors of his theory of *race, milieu, moment*, carried over many of the moralistic assumptions that he had found in Carlyle's criticism. Meanwhile, partly in protest, the Romantic diehards were uttering some of their more flamboyant pronouncements. Hugo's *William Shakespeare*, it will be remembered, escorted with full regalia the new, 18-volume translation (1859–1866, *Sonnets* and apocrypha included) by his son François-Victor (1828–1873)—an achievement which retains the esteem of modern competitors and may, indeed, be more genuinely poetic than theirs. Many a Flaubert letter enlisted old man Shakespeare into the writer's war against the Philistines. Barbey d'Aurevilly, in one of the most striking French tributes ever paid the Elizabethan (1864; in his *Portraits politiques et littéraires*, 1898), argued that Balzac, incidentally no great Shakespearean himself, was the only Frenchman worthy of comparison with the "black genius of England"—and that the black genius of England, were he to return among us, would renounce the limitations of the stage and sprawl at ease in the novel. It is at least a fact that the symbolists made him sprawl at ease across the length and breadth of their poetry. True enough, they concentrated on Hamlet, the spiritually embattled hero *par excellence*, with something approaching flippant disregard for *Hamlet* the play, or even Shakespeare himself; but that exclusive absorption colored, or let us say tinted, their every mood. *Hamletism* signified, at will, "the enigma of us all" or the far more specific one of the *fin-de-siècle* decadent. It remained almost protoplasmic at the hands of Mallarmé, whose quintessential hero Igitur "descends the stairs of the human mind to the bottom of things" (*Igitur, ou la Folie d'Elbehnon*, a dramatic monologue, post. pub., 1925). Jules Laforgue (1860–1887), on the contrary, made Hamlet his identical twin, the better to mock his personal doubts and conflicts: the result being one of the first incarnations of the "absurd" and, as such, a marvelously original creation ("Hamlet, ou les Suites de la piété filiale," in *Moralités légendaires*, 1887).

Shakespeare in France in our century, when cultural advances bred new curiosities—the subject would, of itself, require a separate article. The period supplied serious-minded specialists in abundance, the first in time being Jean-Jules Jusserand (1855–1932); one prominent anti-Stratfordian (Abel LEFRANC); at least one commentator of uncommonly perceptive ability (André Suarès, *Poète tragique: essai sur Prospéro*, 1921); any number of faithful or foolish adapters; and, not least of all, a vastly more enlightened public.

The fact is that, in the last analysis, and with the customary percentage of exceptions, the 20th century's main order of business appears to have been the de-hugolization, de-stendhalization, and de-hamletization of Shakespeare. In simpler terms, our contemporaries restored him to the theatre. The break with the old order was smooth: as late as 1934 the performance of *Coriolanus* could carry political overtones; even closer to us, Jean-Louis BARRAULT, in truly Stendhalian fashion, hails Shakespeare as a fellow sufferer in an "age of transition" similar to our own (*A propos de Shakespeare et du théâtre*, 1949). Nor does Shakespeare's emergence as an all-around professional man (playwright, manager, stage director, actor) in any way obliterate the tangential aspect of his value to the French. Forever a symbol, or a springboard, he leads on to technical adventure, that is all. He sponsored, so to speak, the reintroduction of the open (Greek, medieval, Elizabethan) stage, as opposed to the closed (Italian-type) box which had encased and, to an extent, determined dramatic production since the Renaissance; in the words of producer Jacques Copeau (1879–1949), he helped reestablish "an authentic theatrical universe," no longer a compromise between realism and convention but possessed of its own style and its own laws. A long story, this, which may have had its beginnings in the presentation of *King Lear* (1904) by André Antoine (1858–1943), whose efforts, geared to the spectacular, were amplified by Firmin Gémier, whose godchild is the present Théâtre National Populaire under the direction of Jean Vilar. The productions of Gaston Baty (1885–1952), on the other hand, while still wedded to the formula of elaborate stage effects, marked a progress in sophistication which was undoubtedly due to Copeau's influence. Copeau's "workshop," the famous Vieux-Colombier, stressed the virtues of refined intimacy (as, for example, in its offering of *Twelfth Night*, memorably ensconced in French dramatic annals as *La Nuit des Rois*, 1914). This sober though far from simple approach was adopted by Georges PITOËFF and used, to great advantage, in Charles Dullin's (1885–1949) staging of *Richard III* (1933). With Jean-Louis Barrault, as formerly with Gaston Baty, the pendulum oscillates between lavishness and austerity; but it does so in different productions (toward the former in *Antony and Cleopatra*, 1945; toward the latter in *Hamlet*, 1946), each play being considered a self-contained unit—an instance of "total theatre" unrelated to any others.

What with the growing spate of Shakespeare performances in Parisian art houses and autonomous provincial centers (Théâtre de la Cité de Villeurbane, Comédie de Saint-Etienne, Grenier de Toulouse, etc.), the conclusions seem inescapable that, while the French 20th century never gathered around Shakespeare the wealth of ratiocinations accumulated by the 19th, it promises to achieve a plainer, perhaps more satisfying result by driving him into every man's consciousness. See Paul CLAUDEL; André GIDE. [J.-J. Jusserand, *Shakespeare en France sous l'ancien régime*, 1898 (English tr., 1899); F. W. M. Draper, *The Rise and Fall of the French Romantic Drama*, 1923; Margaret Gilman, *Othello in French*, 1925; C. M. Haines, *Shakespeare in France. Criticism: From Voltaire to Victor Hugo*, 1925; Paul Van Tieghem, *La Découverte de Shakespeare sur le Continent*, in Vol. III of his *Le Préromantisme*, 1947; Henri Fluchère, "Shakespeare in France, 1900–1948," *Shakespeare Survey 2*, 1949; "Shakespeare en France," *Etudes Anglaises*, XIII, 2, 1960; Jean Chatenet, *Shakespeare sur la scène française depuis 1940*, 1962; Helen P. Bailey, *Hamlet in France*, 1964; Jean Jacquot, *Shakespeare en France: mises en scène d'hier et d'aujourd'hui*, 1964.]—J-A.B.

France, King of. In *All's Well That Ends Well*, Bertram's patron. Although theoretically democratic, the King is emphatic in demanding his royal prerogative. He is aware of the contradiction in his personality and describes himself, "thou mayst see a sunshine and a hail in me at once."

Considered fatally ill, the King allows Helena to try her cure, and when she is successful gratefully fulfills a promise to let her choose a husband from among the bachelors at court. When Bertram, Helena's choice, resentfully protests because of her humble station, the King wrathfully threatens the Count with disfavor if he does not submit to the marriage.

France, King of. In *King Lear*, the suitor of Cordelia. The King agrees to marry Cordelia even though her father has given her nothing for a dowry but his curse. After the first scene, he does not appear again in the play, though he brings his army to Lear's rescue in Act IV. In IV, iii, it is reported that state business has called him back to France.

France, Princess of. In *Love's Labour's Lost,* she travels to Navarre on a diplomatic mission. The Princess arrives just as King Ferdinand has compacted with three courtiers to give up the society of women for three years. She engages the King's romantic interest but, on learning of her father's death, she defers his suit for her hand and returns home. The diplomatic mission in this play is based on history, and the Princess of France has her historical counterpart in Marguerite de Valois. See LOVE'S LABOUR'S LOST: *Sources.*

Francis, Friar. In *Much Ado About Nothing,* an advisor to Leonato. Having beheld the fire of innocence in the dishonored Hero's eyes, Friar Francis suggests that she is the victim of "some biting error." It is Friar Francis' counsel to pretend that Hero is dead and thus convert slanderousness to remorse (IV, i). His plan is successful and, when Hero is vindicated, Friar Francis officiates at her and Claudio's new wedding ceremony.

Francisca. In *Measure for Measure,* a nun who instructs Isabella regarding the rule of the order of Saint Clare (I, iv).

Francisco. In *Hamlet,* a soldier. He appears only in I, i, where he guards the battlements but is relieved by Bernardo.

Francisco. In *The Tempest,* one of the lords attending the King of Naples. Francisco joins Gonzalo in the attempt to console Alonso, who fears that his son Ferdinand is dead. Francisco thereafter speaks only three words, "They vanished strangely," referring to the island spirits who set a banquet before the weary courtiers (III, iii).

Francis the Drawer. In *1 Henry IV,* a butt of humor. While Prince Henry questions Francis, Poins, hidden in a nearby room, calls out the Drawer's name, so that he answers "Anon, anon," to most of Prince Henry's queries (II, iv).

Frederick. In *As You Like It,* the envious younger brother of the exiled Duke and the usurper of his title. Frederick admires Orlando's mastery over his court wrestler, Charles, but becomes annoyed on learning that Orlando is the son of Rowland de Boys, a close friend of the banished Duke. Angered by this reminder of his brother, Frederick expels his niece Rosalind from the court. When his daughter Celia decides to accompany her cousin into exile, Frederick suspects Orlando of joining them. Holding Orlando's brother Oliver responsible, he charges the latter to find Orlando within 12 months or suffer banishment. On an expedition into the Forest of Arden to kill his own brother, Frederick meets an old hermit who converts him to the religious life. He thereupon relinquishes his dukedom to its rightful owner and restores the lands which he had provisionally seized from Oliver.

Freeman, Thomas (fl. 1607–1614). Poet. Freeman was a native of Gloucestershire and a graduate of Magdalen College, Oxford (1611). In 1614 he published a collection of epigrams in two parts under the titles *Rubbe and a Great Cast* and *Runne and a Great Cast,* which contain verses on Shakespeare, Samuel Daniel, Donne, and others. The poem on Shakespeare suggests that even at this late date in his career he was still best known for his early nondramatic works, *Venus and Adonis* and *Lucrece*:

> *Shakespeare,* that nimble *Mercury* thy braine,
> Lulls many hundred *Argus*-eyes asleepe,
> So fit, for all thou fashionest thy vaine,
> At th' *horse-foote* fountaine thou hast drunk full deepe,
> Vertues or vices theame to thee all one is:
> Who loues chaste life, there's *Lucrece* for a Teacher:
> Who list read lust there's *Venus* and *Adonis,*
> True modell of a most lasciuious leatcher.
> Besides in plaies thy wit windes like *Meander:*
> Whence needy new-composers borrow more
> Then *Terence* doth from *Plautus* or *Menander.*
> But to praise thee aright I want thy store:
> Then let thine owne works thine owne worth upraise,
> And help t'adorne thee with deserued Baies.

[E. K. Chambers, *William Shakespeare,* 1930.]

Freud, Sigmund (1856–1939). Austrian psychiatrist, founder of psychoanalysis. Freud's psychoanalytic theory has had an incalculable impact—manifested particularly in the fine arts, literature, and the social sciences—on 20th-century culture and has radically modified man's conception of himself. Among his more influential works are *The Interpretation of Dreams* (1900), *Three Contributions to the Theory of Sex* (1910), and *Totem and Taboo* (1918).

Freud's esteem for Shakespeare is attested to by the more than 100 quotations from the poet in the psychiatrist's writings. More significant, however, than the instances in which Freud cites Shakespeare to illuminate a point of psychoanalytic doctrine is the body of his work that deals directly with Shakespeare, his plays, and his characters. Freud's criticism of Shakespeare is marked by two traits: he took a 19th-century view of Shakespeare's characters and plots, treating them as though they were essentially people and events from life; he sought in Shakespeare—and almost invariably found—support for his own theories. Analyzing the characters in the plays, Freud applied many of the same principles that he used in the therapeutic situation; likening art to dreams, he attempted to demonstrate that a given play dramatized a type of repressed, infantile desire common to all men and then sought the event in the playwright's life which stimulated the desire and led him to express it in drama. Freud's most widely known interpretation of Shakespeare is his explanation of Hamlet's procrastination in avenging his father's death. The situation in the play—his father dead at Claudius' hand and Claudius in possession of his mother—evokes Hamlet's early Oedipal conflict: his infantile wish to kill his father and marry his mother. The wish persists, repressed, into adulthood and renders Hamlet incapable of killing the man who has achieved what Hamlet himself wishes to do. Thus Hamlet dispatches Rosencrantz, Guildenstern, and Polonius with untroubled conscience, since none of them arouses Hamlet's paralyzing Oedipal wish. Freud's analysis of Hamlet's delay was enlarged and developed by his disciple Ernest JONES.

In his examination in 1934 of *King Lear*, Freud again found manifestations of the Oedipus complex. The fact that the girls' mother is absent and unmentioned led Freud to suggest that the play dealt with Lear's repressed incestuous love for his daughter Cordelia; when he rejects her, he rejects his own incestuous desire. In an earlier, more mythological approach to the play ("The Theme of the Three Caskets," 1913), Freud considered the love-contest in the first scene of *King Lear* and the lottery in *The Merchant of Venice*. He deduced from the fact that Cordelia is virtually mute in the one scene and that Portia is represented by a leaden casket in the other that both stand for death, which, in folklore, is often represented by leaden or mute figures. The fact that Cordelia and Portia are antitheses of death's grimness is explained by the mechanism of "replacement by the opposite," which Freud often refers to in his purely psychoanalytic writings; in this process dreams, stories, and legends reverse realities too painful to be consciously admitted. Lear's love-contest and his choice of Goneril and Regan over Cordelia indicate his refusal to accept death, as well as his desire for a woman's love. His last entrance, carrying Cordelia's corpse, is a reversal of the fact that he himself is about to be carried away by death.

Turning to *Macbeth*, Freud posed the problem: why does Lady Macbeth, having succeeded in her plans, suffer nervous collapse, when neurosis as we understand it is the expression of frustration? Freud offered several solutions. He observed that Lady Macbeth and Macbeth switched roles after the crime, she assuming the guilt and madness that Macbeth had feared before the murder, he assuming the remorselessness and defiance that had earlier characterized her. He suggested that "together they exhaust the possibilities of reaction to the crime, like two disunited parts of the mind of a single psychical individuality." Freud also suggested that Lady Macbeth's disintegration might be explained in terms of her Oedipus complex, her overpowering remorse being triggered by having helped to kill a man who resembled her father.

In approaching the characters of Falstaff and Richard III, Freud attempted to determine why characters whose immorality ought to revolt us in fact appeal to us. In the case of Falstaff, Freud concluded that because the man is basically harmless in his mischief and finally becomes a virtual plaything in the hands of Hal, and moreover, because the demands of morality and honor "must rebound from so fat a stomach," we are delighted rather than disgusted with the character. In the case of Richard, Freud finds the explanation in the character's attitude toward his own physical defect. Richard reproaches nature for his own lack of perfection and excuses his actions with the suggestion that they are demands for reparation for the pain his deformity has caused him and for the irreparable damage it has inflicted on his early self-love. We are drawn into sympathy with Richard through our own similar resentment at our lack of perfection.

Much to the chagrin of many of his followers, Freud did not believe Shakespeare to be the real author of Shakespeare's works. He rested finally on the view that Edward de Vere, 17th earl of Oxford, had written Shakespeare's works. However, Freud's theories as to Shakespeare's identity have in no way impeded serious consideration, both among scholars and actors, of his speculations on the plays and on the man himself. [Norman N. Holland, "Freud on Shakespeare," *Show*, February 1964.]

Friar. See Friar FRANCIS; Friar JOHN; Friar LAURENCE; Friar LODOWICK; Friar PETER; Friar THOMAS.

Friendly Admirer, The. Epithet for the anonymous author of the long poem prefixed to the Second Folio (1632) of Shakespeare's plays. The poem is entitled "On Worthy Master Shakespeare and His Poems." It is signed "The friendly admirer of his Endowments," after which are inserted the cryptic initials "I. M. S." Some take I. M. S. to be the initials of the author of the poem, suggesting as possible candidates John Milton, Student; John Marston, Satirist; Jasper Mayne, Student. Others argue that the three letters merely signify *In Memoriam Scriptoris* and that the author is a distinguished contemporary of Shakespeare, possibly Chapman or Donne. The quality of the poem is of such a high order as to suggest a poet of the first rank:

A Mind reflecting ages past, whose cleere
And equall surface can make things appeare
Distant a Thousand yeares, and represent
Them in their lively colours just extent.
To outrun hasty time, retrive the fates,
Rowle backe the heavens, blow ope the iron gates
Of death and Lethe, where (confused) lye
Great heapes of ruinous mortalitie.
In that deepe duskie dungeon to discerne
A royall Ghost from Churles; By art to learne
The Physiognomie of shades, and give
Them suddaine birth, wondring how oft they live.
What story coldly tells, what Poets faine
At second hand, and picture without braine
Senselesse and soullesse showes. To give a Stage
(Ample and true with life) voyce, action, age,
As Plato's yeare and new Scene of the world
Them unto us, or us to them had hurld.
To raise our auncient Soveraignes from their herse
Make Kings his subjects, by exchanging verse
Enlive their pale trunkes, that the present age
Joyes in their joy, and trembles at their rage:
Yet so to temper passion, that our eares
Take pleasure in their paine; And eyes in teares
Both weepe and smile; fearefull at plots so sad,
Then, laughing at our feare; abus'd, and glad
To be abus'd, affected with that truth
Which we perceive is false; pleas'd in that ruth
At which we start; and by elaborate play
Tortur'd and tickled; by a crablike way
Time past made pastime, and in ugly sort
Disgorging up his ravaine for our sport—
——While the *Plebeian* Impe, from lofty throne,
Creates and rules a world, and workes upon
Mankind by secret engines; Now to move
A chilling pitty, then a rigorous love:
To strike up and stroake down, both joy and ire;
To steere th' affections; and by heavenly fire
Mould us anew. Stolne from ourselves——

This, and much more which cannot be exprest,

But by himselfe, his tongue and his owne brest,
Was *Shakespeares* freehold, which his cunning braine
Improv'd by favour of the ninefold traine.
The buskind Muse, the Commicke Queene, the graund
And lowder tone of Clio; nimble hand,
And nimbler foote of the melodious paire,
The Silver voyced Lady; the most faire
Calliope, whose speaking silence daunts.
And she whose prayse the heavenly body chants.
These joyntly woo'd him, envying one another
(Obey'd by all as Spouse, but lov'd as brother)
And wrought a curious robe of sable grave
Fresh greene, and pleasant yellow, red most brave,
And constant blew, rich purple, guiltlesse white
The lowly Russet, and the Scarlet bright;
Branch'd and embroydred like the painted Spring
Each leafe match'd with a flower, and each string
Of golden wire, each line of silke; there run
Italian workes whose thred the Sisters spun;
And there did sing, or seeme to sing, the choyce
Birdes of a forraine note and various voyce.
Here hangs a mossey rocke; there playes a faire
But chiding fountaine purled: Not the ayre,
Nor cloudes nor thunder, but were living drawne,
Not out of common Tiffany or Lawne.
But fine materialls, which the Muses know
And onely know the countries where they grow.
Now, when they could no longer him enjoy
In mortall garments pent; death may destroy
They say his body, but his verse shall live
And more then nature takes, our hands shail give.
In a lesse volumne, but more strongly bound
Shakespeare shall breath and speake, with Laurell crown'd
Which never fades. Fed with Ambrosian meate
In a well-lyned vesture rich and neate.
So with this robe they cloath him, bid him weare it
For time shall never staine, nor envy teare it.

The friendly admirer of
his Endowments.
I. M. S.

Friends to the Jailer. In *The Two Noble Kinsmen,* minor characters. The first Friend can bring the Jailer no news concerning Palamon's escape, but the second arrives to report that the Jailer has been pardoned of all responsibility in the event; he reveals also that the Jailer's Daughter has been forgiven her complicity in aiding Palamon (IV, i).

Fripp, E[dgar] I[nnes] (d. 1931). Antiquarian. Fripp's most important work was the assembling of documents under the title *Minutes and Accounts of the Corporation of Stratford-upon-Avon* (4 vols., 1921–1929), covering the period 1553–1620. His antiquarian interests are indicated by the titles of several of his books: *Shakespeare's Stratford* (1928); *Shakespeare's Haunts Near Stratford* (1929); and *Master Richard Quyny* (1924), a biography of a bailiff of Stratford and friend of Shakespeare. His *Shakespeare Studies, Biographical and Literary* (1930) and *Shakespeare, Man and Artist* (2 vols., 1938) are more general studies.

Froissart, Jean (1333?–?1400). French historian and poet. Born at Valenciennes in Hainault, Froissart visited England in 1361 and traveled extensively there under the protection of Queen Philippa, the wife of Edward III. He returned to France in 1369 and began work on the first book of his *Chroniques,* an account of the Hundred Years War (c. 1325–c. 1425). The *Chroniques* (which in its completed version comprises four volumes) is a vivid narrative of the major battles, sieges, and atrocities of the war. Froissart's emphasis, in the later volumes of his work at least, is on the splendid panoply of late medieval chivalry in England and France. His account has such a strikingly vivid, pictorial quality that it has often been likened to a brilliant medieval tapestry. Froissart's *Chronicles* were translated (1523–1525) into English by Lord BERNERS, and in the English version were used by Shakespeare for a number of details in *Richard II.* The *Chronicles* may be partially responsible for the striking and colorful imagery of that play. Froissart was also a poet of some competence. He is the author of several verse romances in the courtly love tradition. Froissart revisited England in 1395 where he recorded with grief the deposition of Richard II (1399). His *Chronicles* end with the year 1400 and nothing is known of his later years. See RICHARD II: *Sources.*

Froth. In *Measure for Measure,* a foolish gentleman and habitué of Mistress Overdone's house. With his associate Pompey, Froth is brought before the deputies by Elbow, who accuses Froth of abusing Mistress Elbow. This gentleman of "fourscore pounds a year," who never voluntarily enters a taphouse but is "drawn in," is dismissed by Escalus with a warning (II, i).

Frye, Northrop (1912–). Canadian critic. Although not a specialist in Shakespeare, Frye frequently refers to him in order to elucidate a general point and, in so doing, often throws light on otherwise neglected aspects of Shakespeare's work. His *Anatomy of Criticism* (1957), for example, is an ambitious attempt to locate all of literature within a series of broad classifications and to relate these categories to their sources in myth and ritual. Thus in his analysis of the structure of comedy, which he views as a reenactment of the ritual of death and revival, he uses the patterns of Shakespearean comedy in order to establish his argument. His analysis provides a number of insights into the "romantic comedies" in particular and the function of characters like Falstaff and Shylock. Frye also wrote a book on the romances titled *A Natural Perspective: The Development of Shakespearean Comedy and Romance* (1965). See MYTHIC CRITICISM.

Fuller, Thomas (1608–1661). Biographer and historian. After graduating from Cambridge, Fuller enjoyed a successful career as an Anglican minister until the outbreak of the Civil War. At the Restoration he was named a royal chaplain and died the following year. His works include *The Holy State and the Profane State* (1642), a book on moral conduct punctuated with numerous proverbs and biographical sketches; and *The Church History of Britain* (1655), an account of the English church which ends with the death of Charles I. His best-known work is his lively and erratic *The History of the Worthies of England,* published posthumously in 1662. Fuller's *Worthies,* a dictionary of the famous people and places of English history, is the source of many hallowed anecdotes, including that of Sir Walter Raleigh's cloak. His account of Shakespeare states that he was a compound of the spirit of three Roman poets—Martial, Ovid, and Plautus—and goes on to record a number of traditions:

> He was an eminent instance of the truth of that Rule, *Poeta non fit, sed nascitur*, one is not *made*, but *born* a Poet. Indeed his Learning was very little, so that as *Cornish diamonds* are not polished by any Lapidary, but are pointed and smoothed even as they are taken out of the Earth, so *nature* it self was all the *art* which was used upon him.
>
> Many were the *wit-combates* betwixt him and *Ben Johnson*, which two I behold like a *Spanish great Gallion* and an *English man of War;* Master *Johnson* (like the former) was built far higher in Learning; *Solid*, but *Slow* in his performances. *Shake-spear*, with the *English-man of War*, lesser in *bulk*, but lighter in *sailing*, could turn with all tides, tack about and take advantage of all winds, by the quickness of his Wit and Invention. He died *Anno Domini* 16 . . , and was buried at *Stratford* upon *Avon*, the Town of his Nativity.

[E. K. Chambers, *William Shakespeare*, 1930.]

Fulman, William (1632–1688). Antiquary. Educated at Oxford, Fulman received an M.A. from Corpus Christi College in 1660, and became rector of Meysey Hampton in 1669. A scholar of repute, he published *Academiae Oxoniensis Notitia* (1665); Vol. I of *Rerum Anglicarum Scriptorum Veterum* (1684); *Works of Henry Hammond* (1684); and was the real editor of Richard Perrinchief's *Works of Charles I* (1662). In addition, Fulman started a collection of biographical notes of English poets, which he bequeathed to his friend Richard DAVIES, the complete collection eventually being given to Corpus Christi College.

funeral customs. See MARRIAGE AND FUNERAL CUSTOMS.

Furness, H[orace] H[oward] (1833–1912). American scholar. Born in Philadelphia, Furness graduated from Harvard in 1854 and was admitted to the bar in 1859, but abandoned the law in order to devote himself to Shakespeare scholarship. In the early 1860's he made for his personal use a variorum *Hamlet* by pasting together notes from several editions. He became convinced that a new variorum edition was needed, and encouraged by the Shakespeare Society of Philadelphia to which he had been elected in 1860, he planned such an edition based on the Boswell-Malone, or Third Variorum, of 1821. See VARIORUM EDITIONS.

Furness' first volume, *Romeo and Juliet*, appeared in 1871; for this he made his own text, but as time went on he leaned more and more on the First Folio. The New Variorum, as this series was called, became valued for the extensive textual, critical, and annotative notes drawn from the best authorities in all languages. In all, 18 volumes appeared under his editorship, the last being the posthumous *Cymbeline* (1913). His wife, ***Helen Kate Furness*** (1837–1883), collaborated with him and compiled *A Concordance to the Poems of Shakespeare* (1874). In his later years Furness was joined by his son, ***Horace Howard Furness, Jr.*** (1865–1930), who served as co-editor and devoted himself to the history plays. On the death of his father, the younger Furness carried on the work as an act of filial piety. The subsequent volumes were welcomed, but they were not up to the standards set by the senior Furness. The editorship fell to various hands and eventually was assumed in 1936 by a committee of the Modern Language Association of America. [*Letters of H. H. Furness*, H. H. Furness, Jr., ed., 2 vols., 1922.]

Furnivall, Frederick James (1825–1910). Scholar and philologist. One of the giants of 19th-century scholarship, Furnivall's activities were by no means limited to Shakespeare. He was active in the Christian Socialist movement, served as an editor of the monumental *Oxford English Dictionary*, and founded the Early English Text Society, an organization which for the past century has rendered invaluable service by publishing medieval and Renaissance texts. Furnivall began as a Chaucer scholar, founding the Chaucer Society and publishing the famous "Six Text" edition of the *Canterbury Tales*.

Turning his hand to Shakespearean scholarship, Furnivall founded the New Shakspere Society, which made the first systematic attempt to introduce the principles of scientific investigation to the study of Shakespeare. The Society soon became the focus of a flurry of activity designed to measure Shakespeare's poetic and dramatic growth by means of VERSE TESTS —detailed examinations of variations in the metrical features of Shakespeare's poetry. The verse tests were the subject of considerable controversy and involved Furnivall in a number of intensely acrimonious disputes, including a famous battle with the poet Swinburne which in the course of four years developed into a "grotesque warfare" about as scholarly and dignified as a street brawl.

Furnivall's edition of Shakespeare, the Leopold Shakespeare (1877), includes his valuable Introduction. He also supervised, from 1880 to 1889, the publication of photolithographic facsimiles of Shakespearean quartos in 44 volumes. Furnivall's work is indicative of the incursions which late 19th-century scientism had made in the field of literary scholarship: "The study of Shakespeare's work must be made natural and scientific . . . and I claim that the method I have pursued is that of the man of science."

Fuseli, Henry. Born **Johann Heinrich Füssli** (1742–1825). Painter. Of Swiss origin, Fuseli was English in his taste and education, and many of his works were inspired by the poetry of Shakespeare and Milton. He came to England in 1764 and became part of the circle of artists, writers, and actors which included David Garrick and Sir Joshua Reynolds. In 1770 he visited Italy and devoted most of the next eight years to the study of Michelangelo. Some of his best drawings from Shakespeare were produced in Rome. Returning to England in 1779, he exhibited at the Royal Academy, where he became a professor in 1799. By 1786 he was an important member of the Boydell project, to which he contributed several paintings. See ART; BOYDELL'S SHAKESPEARE GALLERY.

Fuseli's work reflects a romantic, even melodramatic temperament, and he usually chose Shakespeare's most frenzied or pathetic scenes as his subject matter. Many of his most effective works are sketches and watercolors which emphasize the mood of the scenes and the passions of the characters. "Macbeth and the Armed Head," for example, which was developed into an Academy study in 1811, vividly suggests the power of the witches by extending their pointing fingers into sword flashes.

Two early drawings, "Garrick as the Duke of Gloucester" and "Garrick and Mrs. Pritchard in *Macbeth*" are drawn with a painstaking detail (which Fuseli later abandoned); they provide precise information about Garrick's settings. One of Fuseli's finest Shakespeare drawings is "Lear Embracing the Dead Cordelia," done in Rome in 1774 and engraved 30 years later for the Chalmers edition of Shakespeare.

Fuseli also produced well-composed and fully developed oil paintings on Shakespearean themes: "Lady Macbeth in the Sleep-walking Scene," his Academy picture of 1784, and "Titania and Bottom" are perhaps the best of his full-dress Shakespearean studies. [W. M. Merchant, *Shakespeare and the Artist*, 1959.]

Fylde College Theatre Group. The Fylde College Theatre Group in Blackpool, England, was formed in January 1950 under the general direction of Frank Winfield, lecturer at the college. At regular intervals the group presented a varied selection of plays, mostly contemporary, which consistently ran at a loss. It was not until the first Shakespeare production, *Richard II*, that the financial fortunes of the group improved. Since that production in January 1955, Shakespeare plays have become a regular part of the repertoire, and two are presented each year.

The Group's Shakespeare productions are of two types: the more intimate and technically equipped productions which take place in the small Fylde College Theatre, and the more panoramic and sweeping productions performed in the Circus. The Circus is a structure built under the four legs of the famous Blackpool Tower, and it provides a circle of seats around the circus-ring, and balconies between each two legs, seating 1789 people in all.

Some of the outstanding Shakespearean productions of the Group are *Julius Caesar*, *Macbeth*, *As You Like It*, *Henry V*, *Twelfth Night*, *King Lear*, and *A Midsummer Night's Dream*.

G

Gadshill. In *1 Henry IV,* a collaborator with Bardolph, Falstaff, and Peto in the robbery of the travelers at Gadshill (a place). It is Gadshill who discovers the hour of the travelers' departure from the Rochester inn (II, i). After the robbers have themselves been robbed by Prince Henry and Poins, both disguised, Gadshill spurs Falstaff on to offering a fictitious account of their misadventure to the patrons of the Boar's Head Tavern.

Gager, William. See ENEMIES OF THE STAGE.

Gallus. In *Antony and Cleopatra,* a friend to Octavius Caesar. Gallus is among the group sent by Caesar to remove Cleopatra from the monument where she has taken refuge after the death of Mark Antony (V, ii).

Game At Chesse, A. A political satire by Thomas MIDDLETON acted at the Globe by the King's Men in 1624. *A Game At Chesse* was produced in the wake of the attempt by the Spanish ambassador, Gondomar, to promote a marriage between Prince Charles (later Charles I) and the infanta of Spain. The match, however, was broken off, to the undisguised relief of the English populace. Middleton's play presented the machinations of Gondomar allegorically, with all of the characters representing various chess pieces. The first performance was given on August 8, 1624 and ran for the next nine days, playing to packed houses and achieving an unheard-of success, until it was suppressed by order of the king on August 17. The King's Men were forbidden to act any plays, but the prohibition was short-lived, partly as a result of intervention on behalf of the players by William Herbert, 3rd earl of Pembroke and lord chamberlain, who the year before had been a dedicatee of Shakespeare's First Folio. [G. E. Bentley, *The Jacobean and Caroline Stage,* 5 vols., 1941–1956.]

Ganymede. In *As You Like It,* the name adopted by Rosalind when she disguises herself as a boy.

Gardiner, Stephen, bishop of **Winchester** (1483?–1555). Protégé first of the duke of Norfolk, then of Wolsey, Gardiner became secretary to Henry VIII and was made bishop in 1531. He supported the king's divorce of Catherine, but opposed the radical Protestantizing of Cranmer and Cromwell and later became a loyal supporter of the Catholic Mary Tudor. In *Henry VIII,* Wolsey strengthens his own position by arranging that Gardiner become Henry's secretary (II, ii). In Act V, Gardiner, now Bishop, conspires with several nobles to imprison Cranmer, but the King, loyal to Cranmer, tells Gardiner "Thou hast a cruel nature and a bloody" (V, iii).

Gardiner, William (1531–1597). Justice of peace of Southwark and, according to Leslie Hotson, the original of Robert SHALLOW in *The Merry Wives of Windsor* and *2 Henry IV.* Gardiner inherited a substantial estate in Bermondsey, near Southwark, and increased his wealth in 1558, when he married Frances Wayte, the widow of Edmund Wayte, a dealer in leather goods. Gardiner's career has been reconstructed by Hotson from extant records; it is a career marked by usury, malice, fraud, and perjury. Nevertheless, in 1580 he was elevated to the rank of esquire and named a justice of peace for Brixton Hundred, an area which included Southwark and Paris Garden. In 1594/5 he served as high sheriff of Sussex and Surrey. In 1596 Francis LANGLEY, the owner of the Swan theatre, claimed sureties of the peace against William Gardiner and William WAYTE, Gardiner's stepson. Shortly thereafter, Wayte retaliated by claiming sureties of the peace against Langley and William Shakespeare. Sureties of the peace claims were petitions presented to a judge of the queen's bench in which the deponent swore that his life or limb was endangered by certain parties. If, upon examination, this was found to be the case, the parties cited were required to post bonds as assurance that they would keep the peace within a specified time or forfeit the bond money. Gardiner and Langley had been old enemies, and in this quarrel Wayte had apparently acted as an agent of Gardiner. Shakespeare's residence in Southwark at this time (1596) and his association with Langley have led Hotson to conclude that Shakespeare's company was occupying the Swan during this period. Hotson also argues that the reference in *The Merry Wives of Windsor* to Justice Shallow's coat of arms (I, i, 16), traditionally thought to be an allusion to Sir Thomas LUCY, is in reality a reference to Gardiner's coat-of-arms, which includes three luces by virtue of Gardiner's marriage into the family of Sir Robert Luce. The character of Slender is identified by Hotson with Wayte. [Leslie Hotson, *Shakespeare Versus Shallow,* 1931.]

Gargrave, Sir Thomas. An English officer who served under the earl of Salisbury at the siege of Orléans. In *1 Henry VI,* Gargrave and Salisbury are killed during the same siege (I, iv). [W. H. Thomson, *Shakespeare's Characters: A Historical Dictionary,* 1951.]

Garnet, Henry (1555–1606). Jesuit, implicated in the GUNPOWDER PLOT. Educated at Winchester, Garnet later studied law in London. His upbringing had been in the Church of England but by the time he was 20 he had embraced Roman Catholicism. In 1575 he left England to travel to Italy where he joined the Society of Jesus. He returned to England in 1586 as a missionary priest, and a year later was made superior of the English province. For a period of 20 years he was instrumental in promoting the cause of Catholicism in England, with the number of Jesuits increasing from one to 40.

Garnet's activities came to an end with the disclosure of the Gunpowder Plot. The extent of his complicity is still uncertain. He was clearly not an active conspirator, but he apparently knew, at least in a general way, that something was afoot. At his trial he stated that he attempted to dissuade the plotters when he learned of some of the details, but, since this information was given under the seal of confession, he could not warn the government. He was tried on March 28, 1606, found guilty, and executed on May 3.

During the interrogation and trial the subject of EQUIVOCATION came up. Garnet had in his possession a manuscript entitled *A Treatise of Equivocation* (David Jardine, ed., 1851) which contained some notations and alterations in his hand. During his trial he had given an equivocal answer to at least one question, which, however, was on an immaterial point —about a conversation with a fellow prisoner. In his charge to the jury, Lord Chief Justice Coke dwelt at length upon the subject of equivocation. And after the sentencing, the execution was delayed for five weeks during which time Garnet was further interrogated on this and related questions.

The widespread interest in the trial of the Jesuit superior made the public conscious of equivocation. This awareness is reflected in the words of the Porter in *Macbeth:* "Faith, here's an equivocator, that could swear in both the scales against either scale; who committed treason enough for God's sake, yet could not equivocate to heaven" (II, iii, 10–14). The Porter's earlier words about "a farmer that hanged himself" (II, iii, 5–6) may also refer to Garnet, since Garnet had used the name "Farmer" as one of his aliases. The references to Garnet and the Gunpowder Plot are an aid in establishing a date for Macbeth. See MACBETH: *Date*. [Philip Caraman, S.J., *Henry Garnet and the Gunpowder Plot*, 1965.]

Garnier, Robert (c. 1534–1590). French dramatist and poet. The foremost French dramatic writer of the 16th century was also a lawyer and magistrate. His work, influenced strongly by Seneca, is predominantly literary and elegiac. His *Marc-Antoine* (1578) was translated into English in 1592 by Mary Herbert, countess of PEMBROKE. Shakespeare may have consulted this play for minor details in his *Antony and Cleopatra*.

Garrick, David (1717–1779). Actor and producer. The son of an army officer and one of a family of six children, Garrick was born February 19, 1717 in Hereford and was reared in Lichfield. He and his brother George were the two and only pupils of Samuel Johnson's attempt at schoolmastering in nearby Edial. As a young man Garrick was destined for the wine trade along with his older brother Peter. They set up in London, whither David had gone with Johnson in 1737. But there the theatre so attracted him that, with the promptings of a fine actor and experienced theatre manager, Henry Giffard, he was given a chance to appear, first in the summer of 1741 at Ipswich, and later at Goodman's Fields in London (October 19, 1741).

By law actors were still classed with vagabonds and sturdy beggars, despite the long train of excellent people, both men and women, who had taken up the profession. And Goodman's Fields Theatre was an unlicensed one as a result of the Licensing Act of 1737. So Garrick, as protection for his family, appeared in his Ipswich performance under the name of Lydall (Giffard's wife's maiden name), and in his first London performance of *Richard III* as "a Gentleman who never appeared on any Stage." His presentation of that Shakespearean monarch was so different and so fine that it took the town by storm and put the stamp of probable success on his career at the outset. His novelty lay in his naturalness in acting. A journalist in 1742 described this in a single paragraph:

> Mr Garrick is but of middling stature, yet, being well-proportioned and having a peculiar happiness in his address and action is a living instance that it is not essential in a theatrical hero to be six foot high. His voice is clear and piercing, perfectly sweet and harmonious, without monotony, drawling, or affectation; it is capable of all the various passions which the heart of man is agitated with, and the Genius of Shakespeare can describe; it is neither whining, bellowing or grumbling, but in whatever character he assimilates perfectly easy in its transition, natural in its cadence, and beautiful in its elocution. He is not less happy in his mien and gait, in which he is neither strutting nor mincing, neither stiff nor slouching. When three or four are on the stage with him he is attentive to whatever is spoke and never drops his character when he has finished a speech, by either looking contemptibly on an inferior performer, unnecessary spitting, or suffering his eyes to wander through the whole circle of spectators. His action corresponds with his voice, and both with the character he is to play.

Letters of congratulation, praise, and suggestion poured in upon him. He wrote diplomatically to his family announcing his determination to stick with the stage, where he continued to act brilliantly for the next 35 years. During this span he undertook 20 Shakespearean roles and 78 characters in non-Shakespearean plays. At the time of Garrick's death Burke noted that he had raised the profession of acting to that of a liberal art, and Dr. Johnson lamented that his death had eclipsed the gaiety of nations.

From the perspective of 200 years, it is clear that Shakespeare's plays provided sources of increasing activity and delight for 18th-century Londoners and the world in fields dominated by five creative sorts of persons—actors, editors, critics, novelists, and pictorial artists. Books about them and their professions weigh down the library shelves. It is not surprising, however, to see the actor at the center of this widespread activity, because the interplay between the participants returned to base again and again for the refreshment provided by the performance of Shakespeare's plays onstage. A rule of thumb in English theatrical history classes is that the 17th century is the period of great creative work in drama, the 18th that of great actors, the 19th that of improved stage effects (lighting, scenery, sets, and the like), and the 20th that of experimentation in new forms. Particuarly pertinent then is it amid an age of fine actors to focus upon the one considered by his 18th-century contemporaries as the greatest portrayer of Shakespearean roles.

An anonymous author for Dodsley's *Museum* in 1747 wrote:

> As for Garrick, he has given me so many new ideas in acting that I am not sure you will understand what I now write . . . till you have seen him. His action is an excellent comment upon Shakespeare, and with all the pains which you have taken with your favourite author, you don't understand him so well as if you knew the supplemental lights which Garrick throws upon him.

Twenty years later the Shakespearean editor George Steevens wrote to Garrick (presenting him with a copy of his edition):

> I hope you will oblige me so far as to accept of a work which I could never have carried into execution but for the assistance you lent me . . . . I am contented with the spirit of the author you first taught me to admire, and when I found you could do so much for him I was naturally curious to know the value of the materials he had supplied you with; and often when I have taken my pen in hand to try to illustrate a passage I have thrown it down again with discontent when I remembered how able you were to clear that difficulty by a single look, or a particular modulation of voice, which a long and laboured paraphrase was insufficient to explain half so well.

Garrick's impact on his time was increased a hundredfold by the fact that he became co-manager of Drury Lane Theatre in 1747, and thus held as his particular responsibility the production of all plays. Powerful by personal example, as well as by managerial position, he enforced more regularity on the resident company than it had known before. Rehearsals were careful, standards of individual performance were raised, and above all the concept of ensemble acting came into its own. He strove to surround himself with an excellent company and demanded that they work together onstage. Study of his adaptations of earlier plays, as well as of plays of his own, indicates his care that all actors onstage should be occupied with business pertinent to the whole scene. Not having to worry about being a star, his concern was that all should present a well-balanced performance. He took minor roles as well as major ones. The cuts he made in Shakespeare's plays are particularly worth study, made as they were, not to aggrandize the leading role, but to increase pace or achieve novelty for the whole performance. In 1772 he adapted *Hamlet* and eliminated the gravediggers, but at the same time restored to the earlier scenes of the play over 600 lines which no audience had heard on the stage for more than 100 years.

One of his greatest contributions in producing Shakespeare's plays lay in his gradual and subtle restoration of Shakespeare's text for the "improved" versions current on the stage when he appeared. He sensed the poetic imagery and felicity of speech in Shakespeare's lines in *Macbeth, King Lear, A Midsummer Night's Dream, The Tempest, Cymbeline,* and *Othello.* So more and more of Shakespeare's exact wording appeared in Garrick's prompt copies —even in situations where, with the speed with which words travel over the footlights, contemporaries might have thought it unnecessary. And in 1759 he produced the first performance of *Antony and Cleopatra* since Shakespeare's time.

The success of his management financially is attested by the fact that for a quarter of a century he and his partner James Lacy made annual profits of from £4000 to £6000 and that he sold his portion of the patent in 1776 to Richard Brinsley Sheridan for four times what he had paid for it. During his regime he gave special attention to text, to ensemble performance, to brilliance and appropriateness of costume, to lighting and scenic effect, and he improved the facilities of his theatre for the physical comfort of the spectators.

An extremely busy and dynamic man, he also wrote 20 plays and adapted dozens of others for the stage, all of which were popular. He excelled in the light farce and comedy of manners. In addition he carried on one of the most voluminous of 18th-century correspondences with all sorts of people in England and abroad, traveled twice to France and Italy, and wrote diaries commenting on the trips. His more than 1300 letters show his warmth as a family man, the nervous energy of his managerial career, the geniality of his relations with his French friends, and with the business, intellectual, and aristocratic communities of London. He was easily hurt, but easily made happy. He had a temper, but exercised judgment and patience. His appetite for news at all times in his life—political (he was friend to Burke, Wilkes, and Generals Howe and Burgoyne), theatrical (from actors, actresses, managers, and spectators), literary and journalistic (from England when in France, and from France when in England)—was insatiable. The letters reveal him to have been a sensitive person, intense and thin-skinned beneath what must have seemed a charmingly extroverted character. They also reveal that he was generous to a fault. His spirits always revived under praise, and his balancing, agreeable sense of humor served him well. As an actor he was praised by all. As a manager he was constantly engaged in controversy.

He moved in the highest social circles of his time, was a member of the club which included intellectuals and artists, such as Dr. Johnson, Sir Joshua Reynolds, Oliver Goldsmith, Edmund Burke, and Edward Gibbon. He often entertained at his house in Southampton Street, or later in Adelphi Terrace in London, as well as at his estate at Hampton. To this last place came many from all classes, both from England and abroad, to dine at the villa, to visit, and to see his famed temple to Shakespeare. The marble statue which it enshrined now stands in the British Museum, where is also deposited his dramatic library, the greatest in England. In 1769, with his Stratford Jubilee, he called the attention of the world to Shakespeare's birthplace and gave an injection to the "Shakespeare business" which has moved at an increasingly lively tempo ever since.

Dramatic criticism of great insight gradually emerged from 18th-century pamphlets, but it began with theatrical criticism, which in turn focused upon the actors. They and in particular Garrick, as visible examples of ideas in the texts, were viewed in terms of their effectiveness on stage. This close scrutiny led to a fresh examination of the plays themselves, to a review of the accuracy of the playing texts, to the intentions of the original author, to comparative values of different treatments of similar themes, and to all that we now consider valid critical interest in drama as opposed to mere theatre.

The actor's was the most ephemeral of all the arts until the motion picture arrived to give it a kind of permanence. Yet some of the greatest English and foreign painters sought to perpetuate in "still" scenes what had most impressed spectators in the theatre. Garrick, never one to shun publicity, sat to Hogarth, to Reynolds, to Francis Hayman, to Gainsborough, to Sir Nathaniel Dance-Holland, to Johann Zoffany, as well as to Jean-Baptiste Van Loo, Jean Liotard, Batoni, and Cochin, and thus enabled many engravers to spread the scenes in hundreds of prints throughout the land.

The new and popular novel, molded so skillfully in the hands of Fielding, Richardson, Smollett, Sterne, and half a hundred others in the century, gained some of its unforgettable scenes and episodes by describing visits of, or reactions by, its characters to plays, as amply demonstrated in two books by Robert Gale Noyes (*The Thespian Mirror*, 1953, and *The Neglected Muse*, 1958). Garrick and Drury Lane Theatre became sources upon which the novelists drew.

One wishes not to make too much of the matter, but it becomes apparent that for Shakespeare the actors, with Garrick as the ostensible leader, went a great way toward making the age Shakespeare-conscious, thus providing a market of interest for the new editions of the plays, and for the volume of critical pamphlets that issued from the presses. Editors and critics owed Garrick more than the market, for they used his dramatic library. The moralists owed Garrick the maintenance of a clean stage. He had, for example, substituted *The Merchant of Venice* for the bawdy *London Cuckolds* (1681) as the customary play for Lord Mayor's Day, and many a clergyman complimented him for his thoughtfulness in preparing his repertory. His marriage to the dancer Eva Maria Violetti was a model one, both in and out of his profession.

Painters and novelists drew upon him and his theatre for subjects the public liked. He had his critics, especially among disappointed authors whose plays he had had to reject, even though his rejections were carefully explained and soundly reasoned. Men of taste and judgment owed to him in his conversation offstage, as well as to his action on, an enlightened view of Shakespeare. The London populace owed to him a quarter of a century of lively entertainment in the best humanistic tradition. His fellow actors owed to him, not only years of friendship and a sound stage business, but the establishment of one of the early insurance funds against old age and illness. The Theatrical Fund, towards which Drury Lane by 1766 was devoting its largest benefit night each season, gained through his efforts the right to incorporate in 1777.

Garrick sensibly retired from the stage in 1776, while his powers were still excellent. He died in 1779 and was buried with great pomp in the Poets' Corner of Westminster Abbey. Actor, manager, author, letter writer, businessman, humanitarian, interested in art, music, architecture, landscape gardening, traveling, book collecting, and gracious sociability—such was this man who claimed and, despite his 19th century critics, rather well demonstrated that Shakespeare was the "god of his idolatry." [*The Private Correspondence of David Garrick with the most Celebrated Persons of his Time*, James Boaden, ed. 2 vols., 1831–1832; Alan S. Downer, "Nature to Advantage Dressed," *PMLA*, December 1943; Dougald Macmillan, "David Garrick Manager," *Studies in Philology*, LXV, 1948; Carola Oman, *David Garrick* 1958; *The Letters of David Garrick*, D. M. Little and George Kahrl, eds., 1963. Detailed studies by G. W. Stone: "Garrick's Long Lost Alteration of *Hamlet*," *PMLA*, September 1934; "Garrick's Presentation of *Antony and Cleopatra*," *Review of English Studies* January 1937; "*A Midsummer Night's Dream* in the Hands of Garrick and Colman," *PMLA*, June 1939 "An Unknown Operatic Version of *Love's Labour's Lost*," *Review of English Studies*, June 1939; "Garrick's Handling of *Macbeth*," *Studies in Philology* October 1941; "Garrick's Production of *King Lear*," *Studies in Philology*, January 1948; "David Garrick's Significance in the History of Shakespearean Criticism," *PMLA*, March 1950; "Shakespeare's *Tempest* at Drury Lane During Garrick's Management," *Shakespeare Quarterly*, VII, 1956.]—G.W.S., Jr.

Garter King-at-Arms. In *Henry VIII*, he appears in the procession at the coronation of Anne Bullen and at the christening of the baby Elizabeth. This character was Sir Thomas Wriothesley (originally Writh; died 1534), who held important ceremonial posts under Henry, as did his elder brother, William. William's son Thomas was created 1st earl of Southampton under Edward VI. William's great grandson Henry Wriothesley, the 3rd earl, was Shakespeare's patron.

Gascoigne, George (1542–1577). Author. During his brief turbulent career as a soldier and adventurer, Gascoigne wrote extensively and pioneered in several literary fields. In collaboration with Francis Kinwelmershe (fl. 1566–1580), he produced *Jocasta* (1566), based on an Italian version of Euripides' *Phoenician Women*, the first recorded English translation of a Greek drama. His *Supposes* (1566), a loose paraphrase of Ariosto's *I Suppositi*, is the earliest extant prose comedy in English and the source of the subplot of Bianca and her suitors in *The Taming of the Shrew*. The two plays, together with a miscellany of verse by Gascoigne and others, were published in *A Hundreth Sundry Flowers* (1573). Gascoigne, who at the time was serving as a soldier in Holland, disclaimed responsibility for this volume and two years later issued a revision under the title *The Posies of George Gascoigne*. He included an essay entitled "Certain Notes of Instruction," the earliest surviving treatise on English prosody. *The Steel Glass* (1576) is one of the earliest formal satires in English and the first original nondramatic poem to use blank verse. Other works are *The Adventures Passed by Master F.J.* (1573), claimed by some to be the first English novel; *The Complaint of Philomene* (1576), a narrative poem; and *The Grief of Joy* (1577), a series of reflective poems presented in manuscript to Queen Elizabeth.

PART TITLE OF *The Steele Glas* FROM GASCOIGNE'S *Whole Workes* (1587).

Gascoigne, William (fl. 1624–1642). Stagehand with the King's Men in 1624, when he was last in a list of 21 "Musitions and necessary attendants" of the company exempted from arrest. Gascoigne is mentioned in the prompt-book of the King's Men play *Believe as You List* (1631) where, at the beginning of Act IV, the stage directions call for "Gascoigne and Hubert" to open the trap door on the floor of the stage. He is probably the same William Gascoigne whose daughter was buried from St. Giles in the Fields Church in 1642. See HIRED MEN. [G. E. Bentley, *The Jacobean and Caroline Stage*, 5 vols., 1941–1956.]

Gastrell, Francis (fl. 1756–1758). Vicar of Frodsham in Cheshire. In 1756, Gastrell purchased New Place, a house built in 1702 on the site of the original New Place, Shakespeare's home. In 1758, irritated by tourists, he ordered the removal from the property of a mulberry tree which had allegedly been planted by Shakespeare. The following year, Gastrell had the entire building destroyed, to the dismay and outrage of the citizens of Stratford and other Shakespeare idolators, who seem to have been in evidence even at this early date.

Gates, Sir Thomas (fl. 1596–1621). Governor of Virginia from 1611 to 1614. In 1609 Gates was named the chief official of the Virginia Company and in May of that year set sail for the American colony with a fleet of nine ships. The ship on which Gates was sailing, the *Sea Venture*, was wrecked off the coast of Bermuda. Accounts of the disaster were written by William Strachey and Sylvester Jourdain, both of which accounts furnished Shakespeare with material for *The Tempest*. See THE TEMPEST: *Sources*.

Gaunt, John of. See JOHN OF GAUNT.

General of the French forces in Bordeaux. In *1 Henry VI*, he defies Talbot's demand that the city open its gates, saying, "These eyes, that see thee now well coloured, / Shall see thee wither'd, bloody, pale and dead" (IV, ii).

Gentillet, Innocent. See Niccolò MACHIAVELLI.

Gentleman. In *The Two Noble Kinsmen*, he informs Emilia that her two suitors have arrived for their combat (IV, ii).

Gentleman attendant on Cordelia. In *King Lear*, a minor character. In IV, vii, in answer to Cordelia's inquiry, he states that the sleeping Lear has been dressed in fresh clothes. At the end of the scene he asks Kent if the Duke of Cornwall is slain and reports that Edgar is with the Earl of Kent in Germany.

Gentleman, Francis. See ADAPTATIONS.

Gentlemen, Two. In *2 Henry VI*, they are captured, along with the Duke of Suffolk, by pirates. Begging for their lives, the two promise to pay ransom (IV, i).

Geoffrey of Monmouth (d. 1154). Medieval chronicler. Probably of Welsh origin, Geoffrey was for most of his life a canon at Oxford. His *Historia Regum Britanniae* (c. 1137) is a legendary account of the early history of Britain, beginning with the founding of the nation by Brut, great-grandson of Aeneas, the founder of Rome. The chronicle continues to the reign of Arthur and gives a detailed account of the Arthurian myth. The *Historia* was one of the most popular books in England in the Middle Ages and exerted a strong influence on later literature. In the 16th century it was accepted as a legitimate historical chronicle and it was used by Holinshed and other historians for the early sections of their histories. Shakespeare is indirectly indebted to Geoffrey (through Holinshed) for the legendary accounts of the reigns of King Lear and Cymbeline.

German, Edward. See MUSIC BASED ON SHAKESPEARE: *19th century, 1850–1900*.

Germany. ***English Players in Germany, 1590–1620.*** During the latter part of the 16th century, English actors, as well as musicians and acrobats, played at the courts of various princelings in the German-speaking states. Such performers had generally entered the continent by way of the Scandinavian countries or the Netherlands. In the early 1590's well-organized, professional English theatrical companies invaded Germany in force. In 1591 a troupe headed by Robert Brown, who had been a member of the Earl of Worcester's Men, played at Leyden. The following year the troupe, augmented by seasoned actors such as John Bradstreet, Thomas Sackville, and Richard Jones, established itself at Wolfenbüttel at the court of Duke Heinrich Julius of Brunswick, who was a playwright as well as a patron. The duke's dramas, 10 of which were in print by 1594, occasionally reflect some features of the plots that Shakespeare used in *Titus Andronicus*, *Richard III*, and *The Merry Wives of Windsor*. Subsequent patrons of the English visitors included the landgraves of Hesse-Cassel and Brandenburg.

Brown's company visited Frankfurt in August 1592, performing, among others, plays by "the celebrated Herr Christopher Marlowe," and then moved on to Cologne and Nuremberg. Its principal clown was John Green, who soon displaced Brown as leader and led the company over the entire length and breadth of the German-speaking states. Presently other English actors streamed in, splinter companies were formed and re-formed, and in the following years, up to the outbreak of the Thirty Years' War in 1618, they ranged through all of central Europe and Poland.

The English found many well-equipped theatres in which to perform, especially at the courts of the nobility. Germany had also anticipated England in the erection of public playhouses. In 1550 the city of Nuremberg had built its theatre for the accommodation of visiting troupes, and Augsburg followed its example shortly thereafter. These structures featured a large platform and a deep inner stage, surrounded by an unroofed amphitheatre for the spectators. This was 27 years before James Burbage built his first playhouse, the Theatre, in Shoreditch.

At this time German dramaturgy was crude. In private mansions and at the courts of the princelings the vulgar Shrovetide plays were regularly performed. Religious plays could be seen in churches and in public squares, as performed by the artisans' guilds. Hans Sachs of Nuremberg had written no less than 208 playlets on a wide variety of subjects; they were all very slight, and crude in construction. Classical and neoclassical dramas were produced in Latin at the schools and universities. German acting was not yet a profession; untrained mechanics and schoolboys were the performers.

The immediate success of the English companies is therefore easy to understand. Plagues, poverty, unemployment, as well as adventurous ambition, had driven them to seek careers abroad. They carried with them elaborate costumes and properties and a rich repertory of dramatizations of stories both old and new. What was even more significant was that German audiences for the first time were able to witness professional acting. The English clowns became immensely popular, especially the actor Robert Reynolds (fl. 1610–1640), originally a Queen Anne's man, who succeeded John Green as leader of the continental troupe. His clown-name was Pickelherring, and he appeared in play after play. He took the part of Peter in the German version of *Romeo and Juliet.* Since the actors made their effects largely through pantomime and concentrated on the lowest kind of slapstick and gory, action-packed melodrama, the language barrier was of no great consequence. The visitors at first used only English, the earliest companies requiring the services of an interpreter on their travels. The clowns, however, soon learned a few German expressions and amused the spectators with their mispronunciations. By 1600 all the players acted in German, and several leading performers even Germanized their names. John Bradstreet became known as "Johann Breitstrass" and Andrew Rudge as "Andreas Rötsch." But the companies continued to be billed as *Die Englische Comödianten.*

The English influence on German playwriting, first faintly indicated in the plays of Duke Heinrich Julius, became slightly more marked in the works of Jacob Ayrer of Nuremberg, whose *Opus Theatricum* was published in 1618. His *Schöne Sidea* shows certain resemblances in plot to Shakespeare's *Tempest,* his *Schöne Phänicia* to *Much Ado About Nothing,* and Ayrer elsewhere exhibits echoes of both *The Spanish Tragedy* of Kyd and Shakespeare's *Comedy of Errors.*

In 1620 there was published, perhaps at Leipzig, a volume of 384 unnumbered pages entitled *Englische Comedien und Tragedien* described as "the plays acted by the English in Germany." It contains the Biblical episodes of Esther and the Prodigal Son, many Pickelherring farces, *Fortunatus* (related to Dekker's *Old Fortunatus*), *Julius und Hippolyta* (resembling Shakespeare's *Two Gentlemen of Verona*) and *Titus Andronicus,* certainly derived either from Shakespeare or from Shakespeare's source.

German Performances of Shakespeare, 1620–1700. The ravages of the Thirty Years' War greatly curtailed all dramatic activity in Germany, but after its conclusion in 1648 the English companies, now augmented by German actors and even actresses, continued to flourish. Except for that unfortunate interval, many of Shakespeare's plays, in one bizarre form or another, held the stage throughout the 17th century. There are records of German performances of *Julius Caesar, The Comedy of Errors,* and *Othello.* A scenario of the German *King Lear* (with a happy ending) was until recently preserved in the University Library at Wroclaw (Breslau). Among the garbled acting versions of other plays which survive in manuscripts and early printed editions, besides *Titus Andronicus,* there are *Romeo and Juliet* (unquestionably derived directly from Shakespeare), *The Taming of the Shrew,* the Pyramus and Thisbe burlesque from *A Midsummer Night's Dream, The Merchant of Venice, Twelfth Night,* and *Hamlet.*

Not one of these German variants is a really finished composition. Most of them give evidence of multiple authorship. The passages which may have been written by English visitors display the characteristics typical of writers working in a newly learned foreign language; they are full of ill-digested German idioms and clumsy Anglicisms. Those composed by German writers are full of obvious misunderstandings of the English vocabulary. These plays are evidently transcripts of PROMPT-BOOKS, valuable and effective enough for stage purposes, like some of the "bad" Shakespeare quartos. Unfortunately, there seems to have been not a single writer, equally competent in both languages, who was able and willing to turn an English script into acceptable German.

It follows that any fine linguistic flights which the English originals might have contained could not possibly be used in Germany. Blank verse was generally reduced to flat German prose. The great set speeches and soliloquies had to be sacrificed; Portia on mercy, Mercutio on Queen Mab, Hamlet's soliloquies—all gave way to the immediate display of demonstrable high passions and low slapstick.

Some of these German distortions call for special comment. The Pyramus and Thisbe burlesque, for instance, expanded into an autonomous comedy, ent through a number of transformations, includ-ng versions described by Johann Balthasar Schupp 1610–1661) and Johannes von Rist (1607–1667), and e "Absurda Comica," *Herr Peter Squenz*, of An-reas Gryphius, one of the least illiterate of this roup of adaptations. In these the low comedy is xaggerated, the Lion's role sometimes being enacted y a "Lioness" who is seen giving birth to her cubs played by live kittens) on Thisbe's mantle. One of e leading clowns, Bulla-Butain, turns out to be ully Bottom.

Between 1607 and 1674 there were many German erformances of "Jew of Venice" plays. Some of em may have stemmed at least partially from the st play mentioned by Stephen Gosson in 1579 as the Jew . . . shown at the Bull," and from Dekker's st *Jew of Venice*. But most of them were certainly erived from either Marlowe's *Jew of Malta* or hakespeare's *Merchant of Venice*, or both. One ersion only has survived, in two separate manu-cripts preserved at Karlsruhe and at Vienna, entitled *he Well-spoken Judgement of a Female Student, r The Jew of Venice*. It appears to be an amalgama-on of four distinct sets of materials: borrowings rom Marlowe; the insertion of Pickelherring's role, astly expanded from the parts of Shakespeare's Gratiano and Launcelot Gobbo; a courtship in dis-uise, possibly suggested by the wooing of Bianca in hakespeare's *The Taming of the Shrew;* and direct nitations of Shakespeare's *Merchant of Venice* in s Acts IV and V. The great trial scene was one which the English comedians could not afford to mit.

On October 30, 1677 a play called *The Conflict of ove and Virtue, or What You Will* was performed y the court players of the duke of Brunswick in his ewly built theatre at the castle of Bevern, in honor f his duchess's 30th birthday. Its text was published n the same year, and its derivation from Shake-peare's *Twelfth Night* is unmistakable. Some of he names of its characters, especially Apolonius and illa, suggest that its source was Barnabe Rich's tale f the same title in *Riche his Farewell to Militarie rofession* (1581). A comparison of this play with Riche's story and Shakespeare's *Twelfth Night* leads o the certain conclusion that the Anglo-German uthors of the script used a lost play based on Riche, hakespeare's own text, and a number of improvisa-ions provided by the touring companies in Ger-many. Sir Toby Belch, Sir Andrew Aguecheek, and Malvolio do not appear here, but Pickelherring mag-ifies the part of Feste into that of a vulgar clown without a trace of subtlety.

Fratricide Punished. By far the most interesting of he early German adaptations is that of *Hamlet*, alled BESTRAFTE BRUDER-MORD (*Fratricide Punished*), which appears to be an amalgamation of pre-Shake-pearean material from the lost UR-HAMLET with erivations from Shakespeare himself and obvious ater German overlays. This version seems to have een taken into the repertory of a German company eaded by Carl Andreas Paul (fl. 1654–1695) and re-erred to as "Carl's Comedians." Between the 1660's nd 1680's Carl's company was active in Schleswig-Holstein, Denmark, Sweden, Lübeck, Hamburg, Dresden, and Prague. It is interesting to note that he principal actor in the company which performs the "mousetrap" dumb show in the *Bestrafte Bruder-mord* (hereafter abbreviated as the *BB*) is named Carl.

Another important actor-impresario of the late 17th century was one Spiegelberg, who eventually headed his own company. His son-in-law was the celebrated actor Conrad Ekhof, who owned what was apparently a prompter's copy of the *BB* and may have played its principal role. Ekhof's final appear-ance on the stage was in 1778 in the part of the Ghost in Wieland's translation of the Shakespeare play. Some time before his death Ekhof presented the *BB* manuscript, dated October 1710, to H. A. O. Rei-chard, editor of the *Gotha Theater-kalendar*, in which an abstract of it appeared in 1779. Reichard issued the complete text in his *Olla Podrida* in 1781. By this time Shakespeare's *Hamlet* was gaining popularity in Germany. The *BB* and the genuine Shakespeare seem to have been confused during the 1770's. In 1779 the famous actor-director Friedrich Ludwig Schröder played a version of *Hamlet* which is said to have in-cluded echoes of the *BB*.

The manuscript of the *BB* has disappeared, but the Reichard transcript is available and has been trans-lated into both English and French. Its language and style are basically mid-17th century, but not uniform in vocabulary or idiom. Some passages are in high, some in low German, some expressions are relatively early, some late. Save for a few couplets in the curi-ous prologue, the work contains nothing that could be called poetry.

It is nevertheless a document of immense interest and importance. One of the most vexing problems in Shakespearean scholarship is that of the lost play which was certainly Shakespeare's immediate source. Did the *Ur-Hamlet* find its way into Germany be-fore any version of Shakespeare's own work? The first recorded performance of any *Hamlet* in Ger-many is one by Green's company of *Engländer* at Dresden on June 21, 1626. Other *Hamlets* followed; the surviving descriptions of them indicate only that they presented some of the features of the play as we know it, such as the drunken revels of the Prince's uncle and the visit of the foreign players. The question which chiefly concerns Shakespeare scholarship is, in what respects does the *BB* provide evidence as to the content of the lost *Hamlet*?

That the *BB* is at least partially descended from the Shakespeare play is obvious enough. It contains the opening scene on the battlements, a paraphrase of the King's first speech to the court, of Hamlet's soliloquy while the King is at prayer (none of the other soliloquies is used), and the play-within-the-play in dumb show only. There are obvious late German overlays: the sentries carrying muskets rather than partisans, the Ghost boxing a sentry's ears, the appearance of Carl's company with women actors, Hamlet's companions shooting each other while attempting to assassinate him, the peasant clown Jens appealing for the protection of Phan-tasmo (Osric), who is pursued by a comically mad Ophelia.

There remain the following contents of the *BB* which have persuaded some scholars to conclude that it partially reflects the lost *Hamlet*. It opens with a prologue in verse, in which Night commands the three Furies to sow dissension and strife between the new King and his wife, his brother's widow. This resembles the Induction to Kyd's *Spanish Tragedy*, and may point to Kyd's authorship of the *Ur-Hamlet*. In the *BB* the name of the councillor slain by Hamlet is Corambus. He is Corambis in the Shakespeare First Quarto. He is of course the Polonius of the Second Quarto and the Folios. This has sometimes been taken to intimate that both Shakespeare and the authors of the *BB* drew upon a common source. Hamlet's aversion to women's use of cosmetics and his story of a murderess whose conscience was awakened by her witnessing a tragedy, elaborately set forth in the *BB*, may represent the old materials which Shakespeare assimilated and condensed. In the *BB*, when the King informs him that he is to be dispatched to England, Hamlet replies, "Only send me to Portugal, so that I may never return." Since the earliest reference to the lost *Hamlet* is dated 1589, this seems to be a clear allusion to Drake's disastrous expedition to Portugal in that very year, in which only 350 out of 1100 volunteer gentlemen survived. As to Ophelia's death, in the *BB* the Queen announces briefly that the maid has thrown herself down from a high hill. This is perhaps the simple version of the incident that stemmed from the *Ur-Hamlet*. Shakespeare, perhaps doubtful about the way to treat the end of the distracted maid, may have remembered the accidental drowning of a Katherine Hamlett at Tiddington-on-Avon when he was 15 years old and substituted it for the older story which appears in the *BB*. Such speculations have caused much throwing about of brains.

Earliest Translations and Criticisms. Fantastic as were all these distortions of Shakespeare, they opened up a new vista during the 17th and early 18th centuries to serious German dramatic and literary enthusiasts and began to deflect German attention from the theatre of the ancients and the French to that of England. They served to prepare the German people, by the mid-18th century, to receive Shakespeare in his purity and to make him the foundation of their own national drama.

The first translation from Shakespeare's actual text was that of the Baron von Borck, Prussian ambassador to London. In 1741 he published a *Julius Caesar* in Alexandrine verses, including even the prose passages. This immediately received critical attention from Johann Christoph Gottsched and Johann Elias Schlegel, who deplored Shakespeare's ignorance or disregard of the classical rules and unities, but admired his "natural" powers of characterization. Thus they were the first to suggest the nature of the controversial discussions that were to inspire much fruitful appreciation by the German leaders of the Romantic and *Sturm und Drang* movements during the next few decades. The disputes roughly followed the lines drawn by Dryden (ancients versus neoclassicists versus moderns) in his *Essay of Dramatic Poesy* in 1668, and later by Pope and Johnson. The followers of Gottsched and J. E. Schlegel were able to turn to Shakespeare in his original English, but with the ensuing proliferation of translations and the increasing rate of popular stage productions, critical excitement soon mounted to an explosion of bardolatry—the earlier stages of which may be summarized as follows.

In 1753 there was established a monthly periodical called *Neue Erweiterungen der Erkenntniss und de Vergnügniss*, which from time to time printed elaborate reviews of Shakespeare's principal works, th anonymous critics using mainly Pope's edition o 1728. In 1755 Friedrich Nicolai carried on the discussion in his *Briefe über den jetzigen Zustand de schönen Wissenschaften in Deutschland*. In 175 *Neue Erweiterungen* offered an anonymous translation of four scenes from *Richard III*. In the sam year there appeared a play called *Der Sturm*, a translation of Destouches's French *Tempest*, based on th fantastic version by Davenant and Dryden.

In 1762 Christoph Martin Wieland, a poet who ha been prompted by his studies of Voltaire to examin Shakespeare in the original, began to publish faithfu prose translations of 22 of the plays, a task which h completed in 1766. His versions were widely ac cepted for stage performances, and provided Germa commentators with an easily available body of au thentic reference.

Shakespeare Worship. Gotthold Ephraim Lessing dramatist, critic, and producer, may be regarded a the founder of the Shakespeare cult in Germany Early in his career, in his periodical *Beiträge zu Historie und Aufnahme des Theaters* (1750), h wrote, "Shakespeare, Dryden, Wycherly, Vanbrugh Cibber, and Congreve are dramatists whose ver names we hardly know, but they deserve recognitio equal to that which we accord to the French drama tists." This enthusiasm for the English was mani fested in his domestic tragedy *Miss Sara Sampson* (1755), an imitation of George Lillo's *The Merchan of London, or George Barnwell* (1731). He becam convinced that the works of Shakespeare met th real need for fresh dramatic impetus in Germany which had as yet no national tradition. Taking issu with Voltaire, who had recognized Shakespeare as genius but had deplored his "irregularities," Lessing defended Shakespeare as one who did *not* break th Aristotelian rules, "if rightly understood." Hi common-sense arguments resembled those of Samue Johnson. They were explicitly stated in his *Briefe die neueste Litteratur betreffend* in 1759–1765 and i his *Die Hamburgische Dramaturgie*, 1767–1768. A the first important German dramatist and in his position as spokesman for the first German "Nationa Theatre," Lessing gave generous credit to Shakespeare. In his last important play, *Nathan der Weise* (1779), he modeled his blank verse on that of Shakespeare.

On the stage, beginning in 1776, F. L. Schröder introduced his own adaptations of *Hamlet, Othello, The Merchant of Venice, Comedy of Errors, Measure for Measure, Lear, Richard II, Henry IV, Macbeth*, and *Much Ado* into the regular program of his theatre in Hamburg. In 1782 he presented *Cymbeline* to audiences in Vienna. His performances in the roles of Macbeth, Hamlet, Lear, and Othello in Hamburg, Berlin, and Vienna were greeted with tumultuous acclaim. Women screamed and fainted upon witnessing his Othello. It may be said that Schröder firmly entrenched Shakespeare in the classical repertory of the German stage.

Lessing's efforts inspired further German translations. Between 1775 and 1782 Johann Joachim Eschenburg of Brunswick completed Wieland's work and provided the first definitive German version of all the plays, in prose. He was followed by August Wilhelm von SCHLEGEL, the leader of the German Romantic movement, who translated 16 Shakespeare plays into appropriate verse as well as prose, and added a 17th in 1810. This monumental work was completed in 1825–1833, under the supervision of Johann Ludwig TIECK, by Graf Wolf Heinrich Baudissin and his wife, Tieck's daughter Dorothea. Between them they added 19 plays, including *Macbeth, Othello,* and *King Lear,* all of which then constituted the poetic version that for more than a century afterward inspired Germany to claim the Swan of Avon as *unser Shakespeare.* Between 1770 and 1860 there were also innumerable "adaptations" and quasi-translations.

Johann Gottfried HERDER, a leader of the Romantic movement, an admirer of Ossian as well as of Homer, an enthusiast for the renascence of folk poetry, was inspired by Lessing to turn to the study of Shakespeare. It was not Lessing's logical criticism or stagecraft that appealed to him but rather the intoxicating effect of Shakespeare's poetry. He wrote about "Shakespearean wildfire"; he referred to his favorite character as "my noble, good, moody, mad Hamlet"; he described *Romeo and Juliet* as "the only love-tragedy that exists in the whole world." Every one of Shakespeare's pieces, he asserted, "contains a complete philosophy of the passion with which it deals." In his essay *Von deutscher Art und Kunst* (1773) he described "a man seated on a rocky pinnacle—at his feet storm, tempest, and a raging sea—but his head in the effulgence of heaven—that is Shakespeare!" In such a spirit he anticipated the English school of impressionistic appreciation, autobiographical rather than critical. At Strasbourg in 1770 he met the young Goethe, and the two poets became united in their obsession with Shakespeare.

Johann Wolfgang von Goethe (1749–1832), inspired by Herder, planned to write a *Caesar* in 1771. His was a more balanced attitude, combining Herder's mania with an assimilation of Lessing's critical ideas. But in one of his earliest statements he declared, "The first page of Shakespeare that I read made me aware that he and I were one . . . . I had been as one born blind who first sees the light . . . . I did not hesitate for a moment to renounce the rule-ridden theatre of the ancients . . . . I leaped into free air and for the first time was aware that I possessed hands and feet . . . . In the face of Shakespeare I acknowledge that I am a poor sinner, while he prophesies through the pure force of nature."

In 1773 Goethe composed his *Götz von Berlichingen,* under direct Shakespearean influence and with a deliberate defiance of the traditional "rules." In *The Sorrows of Young Werther* (1774) he continued his Shakespeare-inspired sentimentalism. In *Wilhelm Meisters Lehrjahre* (1795–1796) he indicated that he was still aware of the virtues of classicism, which he had exhibited in his *Egmont* (1788) and *Iphigenie auf Tauris* (1779, 1787), but he persisted in his subjective interpretation of the character of Hamlet: "An oak tree planted in a costly jar, which should have borne only pleasant flowers in its bosom; the roots expand—the jar is shivered." The appearance of *Faust,* Part I, in 1808, showed how deeply he had been influenced by the loose structure of Shakespeare's histories; and in its details it exhibited Shakespearean echoes again and again. His "Erdgeist" was suggested by Caesar's ghost; Faust's brawling with the students, by Prince Hal and his companions; Margaret's widow-companion, by Juliet's Nurse; Faust's duel with Valentine, by Romeo's with Tybalt; Margaret's insanity, by Ophelia's. Goethe's "concentrated" adaptation of *Romeo and Juliet,* in which he took many liberties, was unsuccessful when it was produced at Weimar in 1812. But in the four volumes of autobiographical fragments, printed under the title *Dichtung und Wahrheit* between 1811 and 1833, he included scattered passages that reaffirmed his balanced admiration of Shakespeare from both the classical and the Romantic points of view.

J. C. Friedrich von Schiller (1759–1805) studied Shakespeare early in his career. In his essay *On the Animal and Spiritual Nature of Man (Ueber die Zusammenhang der thierischen Natur des Menschen mit einer geistigen,* 1780) he alluded to Cassius, Richard III, Lady Macbeth, Lear, and Othello as faithful representations of humanity. In the following year his play *Die Räuber* exhibited a character, Franz Moor, which bears striking resemblances to Richard III. Then, like Lessing, he turned to contemporary English "bourgeois tragedy" in composing his *Kabale und Liebe.* At the same time he planned adaptations of *Timon of Athens,* which he admired inordinately, and of *Macbeth,* which finally appeared in 1801. He met Goethe in 1788 and maintained a close friendship with him for the rest of his life. The Goethe–Schiller correspondence indicates that the two poets agreed on nearly all Shakespearean questions, such as the opinion that the Aristotelian rules had to be reinterpreted. Schiller also considered making adaptations of the principal histories as a great "epochal" spectacle. This intention may have combined with his concentration on Greek tragedy to inspire his *Wallenstein* trilogy in 1798–1799. Finally, the influence of *Julius Caesar* may be observed in his last play, *Wilhelm Tell,* in 1804.

The span of less than a half century from Lessing through Schiller witnessed one of the most violent cultural explosions ever ignited by Shakespeare. With regard to this renascence of the German theatre, Herder remarked, "We arrived late, but we are just so much younger." It has been pointed out that one reason why German audiences responded to Shakespeare with such fanatic enthusiasm at this time was that the German translations were in the language then in common use, whereas in England Shakespeare's vocabulary, idiom, and style were already obsolescent.

The 19th Century. Heinrich Heine (1797–1856) as a student at Bonn in 1819 had as one of his teachers A. W. von Schlegel, from whom he absorbed the current Romantic tendencies but no immediate incentive to engage upon Shakespearean studies, although he could find no fault with Shakespeare "except that he was an Englishman." In 1827 he visited England and was impressed by the London theatres. Ten years later he published his *Shakespeares Mädchen und Frauen,* originally designed as a commentary on a series of illustrations but including certain remarks on Shylock which served to reorient the general interpretation of that character. "When I saw a performance of that play [*The Merchant of*

Venice] at Drury Lane," he wrote, "a pale, beautiful Englishwoman was standing behind me in the box. She wept profusely at the end of the fourth act and called out repeatedly, 'The poor man is wronged!' . . . I have never been able to forget those big dark eyes that wept for Shylock."

Heine went on to clear Shakespeare of the charge of anti-Semitism: "He intended, perhaps for the amusement of 'the general,' to present a tormented werewolf, a hateful creature that thirsts for blood. But the genius of the poet and of humanity that reigned in him stood ever above his private will; and so it happened that the poet vindicates an unfortunate sect which has been burdened by Providence with the hate of the rabble, both high and low . . . . The drama shows us neither Jew nor Christian exclusively, but oppressor and oppressed . . . . In truth, with the exception of Portia, Shylock is the most respectable person in the whole play."

Important German translations continued to be produced, among which there may be mentioned those of J. W. O. Benda (1825–1826), J. H. Voss (1818–1829), E. Orlepp (1838–1839), and that of Friedrich Bodenstedt, N. Delius, and others (1867–1871). The most significant dramatists of this period, such as Kleist and Grillparzer, although sharing in the general veneration for Shakespeare, displayed little of his direct influence in their work. Friedrich Hebbel (1813–1863), however, not only expressed enthusiasm but also planned adaptations of *Coriolanus, Richard III,* and *Julius Caesar* as political edification for the reactionary Viennese during the revolutionary disturbances of 1848. He also intended them as acting vehicles for his wife, the actress Christina Hebbel-Enghaus. He completed only the *Julius Caesar,* basing it on the Schlegel translation, which he altered so as to make it "intelligible"; he found this task troublesome and time-consuming. It was not produced, and only a few fragments have survived.

In the mid-century there was also a marked tendency to supplement Shakespeare's impact on the stage by bringing him to the attention of those who did not frequent the theatre. In 1849, for instance, one D. L. B. Wolff brought out his *Familien-Shakespeare,* "a selection in German verse for school and home, especially for the female world and that of growing youth." Thomas Bowdler had thus invaded Germany. Again, between 1800 and 1875 *Shakespeare-Recitatoren* became very popular. Ludwig Tieck lectured and recited frequently, and was followed by Pius Alexander Wolff, who founded the *Rezitationskunst* in Dresden between 1820 and 1830. Among his intimate groups of 30 to 50 persons there were such distinguished auditors as Hegel, Ranke, Jean Paul, and Grillparzer. The vogue continued in Berlin, Jena, and Munich.

Shakespearean acting was now recognized as an important profession. In the course of the century the public became familiar with the brilliant interpretations of such actors as Joseph Schreyvogel, Carl Seydelmann, and Theodor Döring and actresses such as Frederike Bethmann-Unzelmann, Sophie Schröder, and Charlotte von Hagn. All these excelled in both tragic and comic parts, and the "star system" was established. Producers, managers, and directors also floated to profit and glory on the Shakespearean flood tide. August Wilhelm Iffland (1759–1814), a protégé of Hans Ekhof, became director of the National Theatre of Prussia at Berlin and also distinguished himself as a critic and as a prolific, but mediocre, playwright. His successor, Ludwig Devrient (1784–1832), after acting the major roles in the Schiller dramas, became an idolized Shakespearean actor-manager. His three nephews, Karl August, Philipp Eduard, and Gustav Emil, also succeeded in this profession. When G. E. Devrient played Hamlet in London, his performances were compared favorably with those of Edmund Kean. Heinrich Laube (1806–1884) was influential as director of the Hofburgtheater at Vienna. The most brilliant of them all was Franz Dingelstedt (1814–1881), who was active in Stuttgart, Munich, Weimar, and Vienna. He produced the entire cycle of the Shakespearean histories, from *Richard II* through *Richard III,* at the Weimar tercentenary festival in 1864. The success of this and other festivals throughout Germany led to the foundation of the *Deutsche Shakespeare Gesellschaft* in the following year, which proved to be one of the most notable events in the whole history of Shakespeare in Germany.

The founder of the *Gesellschaft* was Friedrich von Bodenstedt (1819–1892), a professor at Munich. In 1862 he had published a translation of the *Sonnets,* and was already engaged in a complete translation of the plays, with several collaborators. The Society began with a membership of 30 enthusiasts. Its first *Jahrbuch* appeared in 1865. Its leading article was the lecture *Shakespeare in Deutschland,* which had been delivered by Dr. August Koberstein, "*zur Shakespeare-feier in Pforta,* 23. April, 1864," a competent summary of German Shakespeare activity through Schiller. The *Jahrbuch* also reviewed current events and provided an exhaustive bibliography and a statistical review of performances from the beginning of 1864 through July 1865. This scheme was carefully carried out through the following century, year by year. The 100-odd volumes of the *Jahrbuch* remain a storehouse of invaluable information.

The issue of 1865 contained a critical review of Albert Cohn's important work *Shakespeare in Germany in the 16th and 17th centuries,* which gave a fresh impetus to serious scholarship on Shakespeare's influence outside of England. Cohn's contribution was followed by an increasing harvest of investigations and criticisms which continue to the present day. Among the most important which appeared in Germany before the outbreak of World War I were those of Wilhelm Creizenach, Rudolf Genée, Hans Hartleb, Emil Herz, Johannes Meissner, Julius Tittmann, and Anna Baesecke. Performances and general enthusiasm continued to increase and multiply.

The 20th Century. On July 1, 1913 Professor Alois Brandl of Berlin University, president of the German Shakespeare Society, delivered a lecture, "Shakespeare and Germany," before the British Academy. In it he reviewed the benefits which Germany had long enjoyed from Shakespeare. He observed that 180 German companies then maintained a repertory of 25 Shakespeare plays, that throughout the nation 3 or 4 Shakespeare plays were performed every evening, that in Berlin alone it sometimes happened that on 5 or 6 successive evenings as many different

Shakespeare plays might be seen. Shakespearean phraseology had permeated ordinary German speech. Shakespeare had in fact become a German national hero. He presented an opportunity for both nations "to stand up as one man" and hail him as the greatest of international literary creators. Dr. Brandl's peroration must be quoted:

> Such an opportunity will present itself in a short time, when we shall celebrate the 300th anniversary of his death—his first three centuries of immortality. If, on April 23, 1916, the world's homage to the poet of Hamlet and Lear will be rendered, as is hoped, here, in the capital of his country, the scene of his literary activity, it will be an assertion of the harmonizing power of poetry over distinctions of race, it will demonstrate the empire of Shakespeare of which Carlyle perhaps spoke even in too modest terms, and it will help us to realize that, after all, humanity is larger than nationality.
> *Au revoir* till Shakespeare Day, in 1916!

"Shakespeare Day, 1916," as Dr. Brandl anticipated it, never arrived. In the 50th volume of the *Jahrbuch*, published in 1914, his *Festrede* for 1913–1914 presented only the familiar review of recent events and pointed out that membership in the Society had increased to 680. The 51st *Jahrbuch* was issued late in 1915, and contained a *Jahresbericht* for 1914–1915. A general meeting of the Society had been held on April 23, 1915. The sentiments expressed on that occasion were moderate and rather sad in tone. "Shakespeare still belongs to us," the speakers insisted, "although our loyalty must be devoted to our Fatherland." The financial income of the *Gesellschaft* had been turned over to war relief. The leading article was contributed by Gerhart Hauptmann: "*Deutschland und Shakespeare*." It answered the question which was disturbing the Germans at this time: "Is the cult of a poet born of an English mother to be tolerated in Germany?" Hauptmann's answer was unequivocal: "Yes! Not only permitted, but demanded!" The result was that throughout World War I there was no diminution of Shakespearean activities in Germany. The 52nd issue of the *Jahrbuch* in 1916 modestly announced that "we simply carry on." The leading article was contributed by Dr. Rudolf Brotennek; it was a calm interpretation of Shakespeare's presentations of warlike activities: "*Shakespeare über den Krieg*." The only jingoistic item was a *Prolog* composed by one Ernst Hardt and recited at various performances of *Twelfth Night*. Feste appeared and stated that he was really no fool; that since Shakespeare had been forced to flee from the land of his birth, he had now found refuge in "his second home."

Hauptmann (1862–1946) called Hamlet "my lifelong, deathless friend," but found it impossible to accept as Shakespeare's the weak-willed, melancholy, and vacillating character portrayed in the early quartos and the First Folio. These publications he believed to be corruptions of Shakespeare's genuine but lost *Ur-Hamlet*, which had been based on a lost play by Kyd. He conceived the original Hamlet as a tough and resolute man of action. Accordingly, in 1929 and 1930, he radically recast Schlegel's version of the play and composed five substantial insertions of his own, emphasizing the Norwegian war-threat, adding a confrontation of Claudius and the English ambassador, and actual invasion of Denmark by Fortinbras, and a reconstruction of Act IV to rid it of what he considered "stagnation." He made Hamlet, rather than Laertes, the leader of the uprising against the King; he interchanged some of the speeches of Hamlet and Laertes in the churchyard scene and placed the "To be or not to be" soliloquy immediately before the final duel. As a supplement to this recension he produced a fresh play in 1936, *Hamlet in Wittenberg*, for which he invented stormy episodes in the career of the youthful Prince. He needlessly disclaimed any intention to rival Shakespeare himself. His considered opinions on *Hamlet* were expressed in his "Shakespeare romance," *Im Wirbel der Berufung*, which also appeared in 1936.

The long career of Max Reinhardt of Vienna (1873–1944), a spectacular producer, served to enlarge audiences for Shakespeare everywhere, not only on the legitimate stage but also in cinema.

World War II, like the Thirty Years' War three centuries in the past, damaged, but failed to extinguish, Shakespearean activity in Germany. The German *Gesellschaft* survived. The *Jahrbuch*, still published in Weimar, appeared as a double volume (78/79) in 1943, again as a double but poor shrunken thing (80/81) in 1946, then somewhat revivified (82/83) with the support of the Russian military government in 1948. In 1950 the publication was transferred to Heidelberg, where, after two additional double numbers, it has now resumed its place as the indispensable German record of Shakespearean activity. At the meeting of the Society on April 23, 1950, it was announced that membership had risen to more than 2000. In 1960 Shakespeare remained the most popular playwright in Germany, with 22 plays produced in 74 theatres—2224 performances altogether.

Professor Rudolf Alexander Schröder, who had been president of the *Gesellschaft* since 1951, died on August 22, 1962. This event brought into the open a long-standing dispute as to whether the policies of the East German or the West German membership of the Society should dominate its activities. On October 27 the directors, meeting in Frankfurt-am-Main, elected as the new president Dr. Werner Schütz of Düsseldorf, a retired cabinet minister, who accepted the post with reluctance in the face of opposition from the eastern, or Weimar, group. A "gentlemen's agreement" was reached, by which Professor Otto Lang, *Generalintendant* and a political spokesman for the Socialist Unity party (SED), was elected to a vice-presidency, Dr. Wolfgang Clemen of Munich voluntarily turning over that office.

The controversy nevertheless developed into a trial of strength. In less than 8 weeks more than 800 new members, mostly functionaries of the SED, were inducted into the eastern division, and President Schütz, feeling unable to commit the entire *Gesellschaft* to a Soviet-oriented political policy, withdrew western participation from the Weimar festival of 1963, which was presided over by the city *Oberbürgermeister* and featured an address by Dr. Martin Lehnert of East Berlin's Humboldt University. Vice President Lang declared in a manifesto that the Society in the German Democratic Republic would be dedicated to the ideals of "socialistic realism," and a performance of *Troilus and Cressida* by the Dresden State Theatre was designed to demonstrate Shakespeare's "correct" attitude toward war and peace.

On October 25–26 the *Gesellschaft* met under President Schütz at Bochum in the Ruhr, and it was decided to hold the quatercentenary festival in that town. The Bochum group established itself independently as the *Gesellschaft-West.* It was hoped that this estrangement from Weimar, a tragic illustration of the political division of Germany, would not be permanent. The split was emphasized, however, on January 10, 1964 by the formation of the Shakespeare Committee of the German Democratic Republic in the east. Dr. Alexander Abusch, deputy prime minister of the Soviet Zone, was appointed chairman, and as committee members Kurt Hager (chairman of the ideological commission of the SED central committee), Hans Bentzien (minister of culture in East Berlin), Professor Lehnert, and Gerhart Eisler (radio-propagandist). This group organized the April festival in Weimar, which included 5 Shakespeare performances, an address by Dr. Abusch on "Shakespeare, Realist and Humanist," a dinner for 750, including the Russian ambassador, the laying of a wreath on the monument by President Ulbricht of East Germany, and the publication of a volume of criticism and essays and a history of the *Gesellschaft* by Dr. Lehnert.

Meanwhile the *Gesellschaft-West* issued the 100th volume of the *Jahrbuch* in Heidelberg. The festival at Bochum took place on May 8–10 and included the usual addresses, performances of *Troilus and Cressida, King Lear,* and *All's Well That Ends Well,* a "Shakespeare Garden" like the one at Stratford-upon-Avon, and an exhibit of 555 items in the art gallery, which was then sent to Schloss Heidelberg to remain on view until October.

In spite of the bitter charges and countercharges of "propaganda" on both sides, occasioned by the east-west division, Shakespearean activities continue to flourish in Germany, perhaps even more vigorously than before. The Schlegel-Tieck-Baudissin translation, having nobly served its purpose, no longer monopolizes the stage. To counteract what recent critics have called its "romantic vagueness," there is a tendency to return to Wieland's prose and to the renditions into more colloquial present-day German by Hans Rothe, Richard Flatter, and the late R. A. Schröder. Many daring experiments and innovations in interpretation, criticism, and production continue to keep Shakespeare alive in Germany. [Albert Cohn, *Shakespeare in Germany,* 1865; Rudolf Genée, *Geschichte der Shakespeare'schen Dramen in Deutschland,* 1870; Wilhelm Creizenach, *Die Schauspiele der englischen Komödianten,* 1889; Ernst Leopold Stahl, *Shakespeare und das deutsche Theater,* 1947; E. and H. Brennecke, *Shakespeare in Germany, 1590–1700,* 1964.]—E.B.

Gerrold. In *The Two Noble Kinsmen,* a schoolmaster. He teaches a group of country folk a morris dance, which they perform in the woods before the royal company; he also delivers a humorous monologue which amuses the Duke of Athens (III, v).

Gertrude. In *Hamlet,* Queen of Denmark and Hamlet's mother. Although probably guilty of adultery with Claudius, Gertrude is apparently not an accomplice in the murder of King Hamlet. She is portrayed as a venal and easily dominated woman. Nevertheless, within the limits of her own weakness she appears to be genuinely concerned for her son. In a famous essay on the play ("Hamlet and His Problems") T. S. Eliot argues that Gertrude is not a significant enough figure to justify Hamlet's passionate reaction to her infidelity. See HAMLET: *Selected Criticism.*

Gervinus, Georg Gottfried (1805–1871). German historian and literary scholar. After some years of travel and teaching, in 1844 Gervinus settled at Heidelberg and was appointed honorary professor at the university there. Between 1849 and 1852 he published in four volumes his *Shakespeare,* translated by F. E. Bunnett as *Shakespeare Commentaries* (1863). Gervinus gave an exhaustive analysis of the individual plays with special stress on the unity of plot; furthermore, by means of verse tests he divided the works of Shakespeare into three distinct periods and traced the development of the poet's art. F. J. Furnivall was influenced by this use of verse tests and in later editions of the English translation of Gervinus' work supplied an Introduction in which he set forth his views on the subject. Gervinus also wrote *Händel und Shakespeare* (1868), parallel studies of the musician and the playwright.

Gesta Grayorum. Records of Gray's Inn, printed in 1688. They include a contemporary account of the revels held there on December 27 or 28, 1594, during which a "comedy of errors," undoubtedly Shakespeare's, was performed. For an account of this performance, see INNS OF COURT.

Gesta Romanorum (Deeds of the Romans) (c. 1340). A collection of medieval Latin prose tales relating the legends of classical figures and Christian saints as well as many stories of Eastern origin. The complete edition of *Gesta Romanorum* consists of 181 tales. The collection, a rich source of plots for later writers, was translated into a number of languages. The "Man of Law's Tale" in *The Canterbury Tales* is based on a tale in the collection, and John Gower derived his version of the story of Apollonius of Tyre, the source of Shakespeare's *Pericles,* from the collection. The story of the three caskets in *The Merchant of Venice* is probably derived from the English translation of a tale in the *Gesta,* published by Wynkyn de Worde (1524?) and revised anonymously in 1557 and by Richard Robinson in 1595. See THE MERCHANT OF VENICE: *Sources.*

Ghost. In *Hamlet,* the spirit of Hamlet's father, King Hamlet, who orders the son to avenge his murder (I, v). The ghost who demands satisfaction is a familiar staple of Elizabethan revenge tragedy adapted from Seneca. Recent discussion of King Hamlet's Ghost, however, has centered on his particular characteristics in order to determine whether he conforms in a very specific and systematic manner to Renaissance Catholic teaching on spirits or whether he is merely the dramatic embodiment of the popular Elizabethan conception of spirits.

There is a tradition, traceable to Nicholas Rowe, Shakespeare's first editor, that the part of the Ghost was played by Shakespeare. [Sr. Miriam Joseph

"Discerning the Ghost in Hamlet," *PMLA*, 1961; Paul Siegel, "Discerning the Ghost in Hamlet," *PMLA*, 1963.]

ghosts and apparitions. Ghosts, in the sense of spirits of the deceased, appear in five of Shakespeare's plays. In *Richard III*, V, iii, the ghosts of Prince Edward, Henry VI, Clarence, Rivers, Grey, Vaughan, Hastings, the two young princes, Lady Anne, and Buckingham appear to the sleeping Richard and Richmond as they lie dreaming on the eve of battle. After taunting Richard for having murdered them, the ghosts urge him to despair and die, then turn to Richmond and wish him victory and life. In *Julius Caesar*, IV, iii, the ghost of Caesar appears to Brutus, claiming to be his evil spirit, and promises to meet him at Philippi. In *Macbeth*, III, iv, the ghost of the murdered Banquo takes Macbeth's seat at the banquet, throwing Macbeth into guilty panic in front of the other guests. In each of these three instances, a murderer is confronted with the ghost of his victim or victims.

In *Hamlet*, I, i, and I, iv, the ghost of Hamlet's murdered father appears on the castle battlements, speaking to Hamlet on his second appearance and urging the Prince to avenge his murder. In *Cymbeline*, V, iv, the ghosts of Posthumus' father, mother, and two brothers appear to him in prison, appealing to Jupiter to help Posthumus. Jupiter appears and promises his aid. The ghosts are referred to as "apparitions," and they and Jupiter appear to Posthumus in a dream, the brothers still bearing the battle wounds of which they died.

Apparitions of various sorts, both speaking and silent, appear in several of the historical plays. In *1 Henry VI*, V, iii, fiends appear to La Pucelle before Angiers. She refers to them as familiar spirits that she has fed with her blood; she offers them her body and soul if they will help France expel the English, but they do not answer her. In *2 Henry VI*, I, iv, the witch Margaret Jourdain and the priests Southwell and Bolingbroke conjure the spirit Asnath, who foretells the fates of Henry, Suffolk, and Somerset. In *Henry VIII*, IV, ii, the sick dowager Katharine has a vision of six white-clad personages who dance and vanish, and whom she calls "spirits of peace"; her attendants, though present, do not see them. In *Macbeth*, IV, i, the three witches conjure three apparitions: an armed head, warning Macbeth against Macduff; a bloody child, telling Macbeth that none of woman born shall harm him; and a child crowned, with a tree in his hand, assuring Macbeth that he shall not be vanquished till Birnam wood comes to Dunsinane. The apparitions are followed by a show of eight future kings, Banquo's descendants, followed by the ghost of Banquo himself. For supernatural elements in these and other plays, see the SUPERNATURAL.

Gibbons' Tennis Court. A playhouse located in Vere Street, southwest of Lincoln's Inn Fields. Gibbons' Tennis Court was built in 1633 as an indoor tennis court. By 1653 it was already being used as a theatre, and was raided by commonwealth soldiers during a performance of Thomas Killigrew's *Claracilla*. In 1656 Davenant used the court for presentations of his "operas." On November 8, 1660 it was occupied by Killigrew's King's Company who continued there until the opening of their new theatre in Drury Lane. Among the plays performed at the theatre during the occupation of the King's Company were *Henry IV*, *The Merry Wives of Windsor*, *Othello*, and *A Midsummer Night's Dream*. [Leslie Hotson, *The Commonwealth and Restoration Stage*, 1928.]

Gide, André (1869–1951). French novelist. Gide's *Journals* (1889–1949) demonstrate a lifelong interest in Shakespeare. In 1921 he translated *Antony and Cleopatra* and the following year began work on his famous translation of *Hamlet*. After six months of arduous work he put aside the translation, complaining that "in order to write good French one has to get too far away from Shakespeare." In 1942 he returned to his translation at the insistence of the young French actor Jean-Louis BARRAULT, completing the task in three months. Gide's *Hamlet*, with Barrault in the title role, opened at the Théâtre Marigny in 1946 and is recorded as one of the great achievements of the postwar French theatre.

Gielgud, Sir **[Arthur] John** (1904–). Actor. Regarded as one of the greatest Shakespearean actors of this century, Gielgud was educated at Westminster and began his career in 1921 with the Old Vic as the Herald in *Henry V*. After a number of years with different repertory groups, he rejoined the Old Vic in 1929, appearing as Romeo, Antonio in *The Merchant of Venice*, Richard II, Mark Antony, Orlando, Macbeth, and Hamlet. At the reopening of the Sadler's Wells Theatre in 1931, he played Malvolio in *Twelfth Night*, but it was his Hamlet (1930) which first brought him to national prominence. He repeated Hamlet in 1934 and in a 1936 tour of the United States, emphasizing the aristocracy and wit of the Prince. His Richard II in 1938 was hailed as the finest of the century.

In 1940 he returned to the Old Vic in *King Lear* and in *The Tempest* as Prospero. During World War II he was active as both producer and player. Since the end of the war, Gielgud's production of *Much Ado About Nothing* (1950, 1952, and 1955), in which he played Benedick, has been hailed as "a shining landmark in the theatre of our century." He also scored a great success as Angelo in *Measure for Measure* (1950) and Leontes in *The Winter's Tale* (1951). He has appeared in motion pictures as Cassius in *Julius Caesar* (1952) and as the Duke of Clarence in Laurence Olivier's *Richard III* (1955). His series of readings, *The Ages of Man* (1959/60), based on a Shakespearean anthology compiled by George Rylands, won wide acclaim in England and the United States. In 1961 he played Othello at Stratford-upon-Avon and in 1964 directed a New York production of *Hamlet* which starred Richard Burton. Among his recent non-Shakespearean successes has been a presentation of *The School for Scandal* (1962/3), which he produced and in which he took the role of Joseph Surface. He has published two volumes of his autobiography: *Early Stages* (1938) and *Stage Directions* (1964). Gielgud was knighted in 1953. [*Who's Who in the Theatre*, 1961.]

Gilburne, Samuel (fl. 1605). Actor. Gilburne's name appears in the First Folio list of actors playing with the King's Men, Shakespeare's company. Augustine Phillips, in his will of 1605, mentioned Gilburne as "my late apprentice" and left him a bass viol and various garments. A copy of the First Folio which may have once belonged to Gilburne is now in the Folger Library. Gilburne's name, presumably inscribed by himself, appears on the page of the Folio in which the actors' names are enumerated. [G. E. Bentley, *The Jacobean and Caroline Stage*, 5 vols., 1941–1956.]

Gild of the Holy Cross. The Stratford fraternal organization which had an important voice in the town's affairs until its dissolution during the Reformation. The organization was in existence as early as 1269, at which time it was actively engaged in religious and charitable activities. During the 15th century, it built in Stratford a guildhall; a grammar school, which eventually became the King Edward School of Shakespeare's day; and a number of almshouses for the poor. The Gild was essentially, however, a religious organization, and for this reason was dissolved in 1547 during the Protestant reign of Edward VI. [Levi Fox, *The Borough Town of Stratford-upon-Avon*, 1953.]

Gildon, Charles (1665–1724). Dramatist and essayist. A man of "great literature but mean genius" who squandered his family inheritance at an early age, Gildon led a hand-to-mouth existence as a hack writer. His diverse activities included editing and enlarging *The Lives and Characters of the English Dramatick Poets* (1698) by Gerard LANGBAINE. The entry on Shakespeare included Gildon's comment ". . . that he writ the scene of the Ghost in *Hamlet*, at his house which bordered on the Charnal-House and Church-Yard." His "Remarks on the Plays of Shakespear" were prefixed to a volume of Shakespeare's poems, fraudulently designed to look like the seventh volume of Rowe's Shakespeare (6 vols., 1709). The "Remarks" included the following tradition about *The Merry Wives of Windsor:*

> The *Fairys* in the fifth Act . . . makes a Handsome Complement to the Queen, in her Palace of *Windsor*, who had oblig'd him to write a Play of *Sir John Falstaff* in Love, and which I am very well assured he perform'd in a Fortnight; a prodigious Thing, when all is so well contriv'd, and carry'd on without the least Confusion.

Gildon was also responsible for the tradition that the actor who originally played Iago was a comedian.

In 1700, he published *Measure for Measure, or Beauty the Best Advocate*, an adaptation that relies as heavily on Davenant's adaptation, *The Law Against Lovers*, as on Shakespeare's play, although he does not adhere too closely to either. Following Davenant, he sets the scene in Turin, rather than Vienna, eliminates Benedick and Beatrice and all the clowns, and restores the Mariana plot. He also offers one interesting change: in his version, Claudio and Julietta are secretly married and only lack proof. Gildon, or his audience, evidently could not accept the Elizabethan view on premarital union. He maintains consistency in the alteration: in his version, Angelo is married to Mariana before he deserts her.

Except for these liberties, Gildon followed Shakespeare's story rather closely, referring to Davenant frequently in rewriting speeches. There was, however, one other major change, inspired, no doubt, b the success of the operatic versions of *The Tempe* and *A Midsummer Night's Dream:* Escalus presen for Angelo's benefit a series of entertainments dealin with "The Loves of Dido and Aeneas," includin solo and part songs and dances. There are four c these operatic passages in the play, including a gran finale following the reappearance of the Duke; th music was derived from Henry Purcell. This versio of *Measure for Measure* was first produced in 1699 1700 at Lincoln's Inn Fields with Betterton as Angel Verbruggen as Claudio, and Mrs. Bracegirdle a Isabella. [Hazelton Spencer, *Shakespeare Improve* 1927.]

Giles, Nathaniel (c. 1559–1634). Master of th Children of the Chapel and the Children of Windso Giles was educated at Magdalen College, Oxfor and was highly esteemed as a musician. Extant in th Ashmole papers is Giles' indenture of appointmen October 1, 1595 by the Windsor chapter as Maste of the Children of Windsor. The indenture grante him to the end of his life

> the Roome and place of a Clerk within the sai ffree Chappell and to be one of the Players on th Organes there, and also the office of Instructo and Master of the ten Children or Choristers o the Same ffree Chappell, And the office of tuto creansor, or governor of the same tenn Childre or Coristers.

He received an annuity of £81 6s. 8d. and a hous his predecessor Richard Farrant had used at a ren of £1 6s. 8d. He was also to receive

> all such giftes, rewardes or benevolences as fron tyime to time during the naturall lief of him th said Nathanell Gyles shall be given bestowed o ymployed to or vpon the Choristers for singing of Balattes, playes or for the like respects whatso ever.

In July 1597 he became Master of the Children o the Chapel. Under Giles the Children of the Chape benefited from the revival of interest in children' acting companies at the turn of the century. Gile with Henry Evans, put the Children of the Chape on a business footing. They purchased an interest i the Blackfriars theatre and were accused of usin the place as a public theatre rather than, as they ha ostensibly intended, as a place to rehearse the Chil dren for their court performances. Giles was paye for the children's performances at court on thre occasions. On January 6, 1601 he received £5 fo "a showe wth musycke and speciall songes p'pare for the purpose," and on February 22, received £1 "for a play." The Children also received £30 fo three performances at the revels in 1601/2. In 160 the Children and Giles provided the music at dinner given for King James and Prince Henry a the Merchant Taylors' hall, where several member of Shakespeare's company, the King's Men, als performed in a tableau.

Giles was accused of violating his royal commis sion for impressing boys into the service of chapel a singers; a father of one of the impressed boy charged that Giles had taken boys who could nc sing and made actors of them. Despite censure b e Star Chamber, Giles kept his posts as Master of e CHILDREN OF THE CHAPEL and CHILDREN OF 'INDSOR until his death. [E. K. Chambers, *The 'izabethan Stage*, 1923.]

Giraldi, Giovanni Battista. See CINTHIO.

Giustinian, Zorzi or **Giorgio** (fl. 1606–1608). Vene-n ambassador to England from January 5, 1606 to ovember 23, 1608. *The Calendar of State Papers 'd Manuscripts relating to English Affairs existing the Archives and Collections of Venice. 1202–1603* 2 vols., 1864–1890); *1603–1666* (25 vols., 1900–1933) cords testimony given in 1617 concerning the play-ing activities of foreign ambassadors in England:

> All the ambassadors, who have come to England have gone to the play more or less. Giustinian went with the French ambassador and his wife to a play called *Pericles*, which cost Giustinian more than 20 crowns. He also took the secretary of Florence.

he allusion is important in the dating of *Pericles*. . K. Chambers, *William Shakespeare*, 1930.]

Glansdale, Sir William. An English officer who owned in the Loire at Orléans after a drawbridge oke. In *1 Henry VI*, Glansdale is present at the ge of Orléans, where he stations himself "at the lwark of the bridge" (I, iv). [W. H. Thomson, *akespeare's Characters: A Historical Dictionary*, 51.]

Glendower, Owen (1359?–?1416). A Welsh rebel. 'hen Henry IV became king, Glendower led orth Wales in revolt against him, and in 1401 he vaded South Wales, where he was defeated by otspur. When rebellion flared anew, the king and ince Henry invaded North Wales. Glendower, maining undefeated, took as prisoner Sir Edmund ortimer, who married his daughter. After signing e famous treaty with Mortimer and Hotspur in hich England and Wales were equally divided nong them (probably 1405), Glendower began to ffer defeat at the hand of Henry. His influence clined, and he is thought eventually to have died starvation in the mountains of North Wales.

In *1 Henry IV*, Glendower, meeting his allies in der to divide the country into three parts, is baited Hotspur for his belief in portents. They also arrel over their prospective shares of the kingdom I, i).

Gl' Ingannati. See TWELFTH NIGHT: *Sources*.

Globe Shakespeare, The (1864). A one-volume ition by W. G. Clark, J. Glover, and W. A. 'right. The text is that of The Cambridge Shake-eare (1863–1866). The Globe has long been ac-pted as the standard for line numbering. See HOLARSHIP—19TH CENTURY.

Globe theatre. An Elizabethan playhouse located the Bankside near Maiden Lane and the home of akespeare's company, the Chamberlain's (later the ng's) Men. In February 1597 James Burbage, vner of the Theatre, died and in his will be-eathed the building to his sons Cuthbert and Rich-d. The land on which the Theatre stood, however, longed to Giles Alleyn, who refused to renew the se for the building. In December 1598 the Bur-ges arranged to have the building torn down and e lumber transported to the other side of the hames in order to be used in the construction of a new theatre, the Globe. This rather daring exploit was described by the outraged Alleyn in the suit he brought before the local court (*Allen v. Burbadge*, 1602):

> . . . the sayd Cuthbert Burbage . . . wth the sayd Richard Burbage and one Peeter Streat, William Smyth and diuers other persons to the number of twelve to your Subiect vnknowne did aboute the eight and twentyth daye of December in the one and fortyth yeere of your highnes Raygne . . . ryoutouslye assemble themselves together and then and there armed themselves wth divers and manye vnlawfull and offensive weapons, as namelye swordes daggers billes axes and such like And soe armed did then repayre vnto the sayd Theater And then and there armed as aforesayd in a verye ryotous outragious and forcyble manner and con-trarye to the lawes of your highnes Realme at-tempted to pull downe the sayd Theater . . . And having so done did then also in most forcible and ryotous manner take and carrye awaye from thence all the wood and timber therof vnto the Banckside in the parishe of St Marye Overyes and there erected a newe playe howse wth the sayd Timber and wood.

In order to finance the construction and upkeep of the new theatre, the Burbages retained half the ownership of the theatre and divided the other half among five members of the Chamberlain's Men. These five were Shakespeare, John Heminges, Au-gustine Phillips, Thomas Pope, and Will Kempe. In order to have this moiety (or half-ownership) di-vided equally among the five actors, it was necessary to assign the property to two interested friends, Wil-liam LEVESON and Thomas SAVAGE, who in turn re-assigned the moiety to the players in equal fifths. The transaction was described by Heminges and Condell many years later in connection with a dis-pute with John Witter over certain shares of the theatre:

> The said Def[endants] . . . do say . . . the said gardens and groundes wherevpon the said Play-howse & galleryes were afterwardes builded were demised & letten by the said Nicholas Brend by his Jndenture of lease tripartite bearing date in or about the xxj^th^ day of ffebruary in the xlj^th^ yeere of the raigne of the late Queene Elizabeth [1599] . . . vnto Cuthbert Burbadge Richard Burbadge William Shakespeare the said Augustine Phillipps Thomas Pope the said John Heminges one of the said def[endants], and William Kempe . . . from the ffeast of the birth of our Lord God Last past . . . before the date of the said Jndenture vnto thend & terme of xxxj yeeres from thence next en-suing for the yeerely rent of seaven poundes & five shillinges . . . Which said W Shakespeare Augustine Phillipps Thomas Pope John Heminges & William Kempe did shortlie after graunte & assigne all the said Moitie of & in the said gardens & groundes vnto William Levison and Thomas Savage, who regraunted & reassigned to euerye of them seuer-ally a fift parte of the said Moitie of the said garden & groundes, Vpon w[hich] premisses or some parte thereof there was shortly after built the said then playhowse.

The land was leased from Nicholas Brend, whose father, Thomas BREND, owned property in the area in which Shakespeare was residing in 1599.

The seven owners of the theatre were known as HOUSEKEEPERS and each one was responsible for a proportionate share of the ground rent and the maintenance of the theatre. In return for this he received a share of the gate receipts. Thus Shakespeare's income derived from two sources: as actor-sharer in the company and as housekeeper or landlord of the Globe.

For the next ten years the Globe was the exclusive home of Shakespeare's company and it was during this period that his greatest plays were produced. In 1609 the company acquired the Blackfriars theatre which it began to use as its winter home, the Globe remaining in use during the summer. In 1613, however, the Globe was destroyed by fire during a performance of *Henry VIII*. A number of descriptions of the fire are extant (see Henry WOTTON, Thomas LORKINS, Edmund HOWES, and John CHAMBERLAIN), but the most amusing is to be found in a contemporary ballad titled *A Sonnett upon the pittiful burneinge of the Globe playhowse in London:*

This fearfull fire beganne above,
  A wonder strange and true,
And to the stage-howse did remove,
  As round as taylors clewe;
And burnt downe both beame and snagg,
And did not spare the silken flagg.
  Oh sorrow, pittifull sorrow, and yett all
    this is true.

Out runne the knightes, out runne the lordes,
  And there was great adoe;
Some lost their hattes, and some their swordes;
  Then out runne Burbidge too;
The reprobates, though druncke on Munday,
Prayd for the Foole and Henry Condye.
  Oh sorrow, pittifull sorrow, and yett all
    this is true.

The perrywigges and drumme-heades frye,
  Like to a butter firkin;
A wofull burneing did betide
  To many a good buffe jerkin.
Then with swolne eyes, like druncken Flemminges,
Distressed stood old stuttering Heminges.
  Oh sorrow, pittifull sorrow, and yett all
    this is true.

No shower his raine did there downe force
  In all that Sunn-shine weather,
To save that great renowned howse;
  Nor thou, O ale-howse, neither.
Had itt begunne belowe, sans doubte,
Their wives for feare had pissed itt out.
  Oh sorrow, pittifull sorrow, and yett all
    this is true.

Bee warned, yow stage-strutters all,
  Least yow againe be catched,
And such a burneing doe befall,
  As to them whose howse was thatched;
Forbeare your whoreing, breeding biles,
And laye up that expence for tiles.
  Oh sorrow, pittifull sorrow, and yett all
    this is true.

Goe drawe yow a petition,
  And doe yow not abhorr itt,
And gett, with low submission,
  A licence to begg for itt
In churches, sans churchwardens checkes,
In Surrey and in Midlesex.
  Oh sorrow, pittifull sorrow, and yett all
    this is true.

The Globe was rebuilt in the next year and wa declared by John Chamberlain to be "the fairest tha ever was in England." At first there had been hesi tation about rebuilding because of some doubt as t the security of the lease, but the players were abl to secure an extension to the old lease which guaran teed their occupancy until 1644. The rebuilding wa financed by the housekeepers at a total cost of £140 (see John WITTER). The theatre opened on June 30 1614 and remained standing until 1644 when it wa "pulled downe to the ground . . . to make tenement in the room of it."

The physical characteristics of the first Globe an the design and shape of its stage have long been th subject of scholarly inquiry. Nevertheless, despit the ingenious and often plausible efforts of men lik John Cranford Adams, C. Walter Hodges, and Les lie Hotson to reconstruct the Globe (see PLAYHOUS STRUCTURE), all that we know of the playhouse fo certain is that it had a thatched roof over the uppe gallery and that certain of its dimensions were th same as those of the FORTUNE THEATRE. Beyond that every attempt to reconstruct the theatre lies in th area of more or less reasonable conjecture. Even th

PART OF HOLLAR'S "LONG VIEW" OF LONDON (1647). IT HAS BEEN DISCOVERED THAT THE NAMES OF THE GLOBE AND THE "BEERE BAYTING" (THE HOPE) HAVE BEEN REVERSED.

mous reference in *Henry V* (in the Prologue to ct I, line 13) to the theatre as a "wooden O" is now garded as a reference not to the Globe but to the urtain. [J. C. Adams, *The Globe Playhouse*, 1942; . Walter Hodges, *The Globe Restored*, 1953; A. M. agler, *Shakespeare's Stage*, 1958; Leslie Hotson, *akespeare's Wooden O*, 1959; G. E. Bentley, *akespeare, A Biographical Handbook*, 1961.]

Gloucester, Earl of. In *King Lear*, the father of dmund and Edgar, who suffers a fate parallel to at of Lear. Although Gloucester lacks the tragic ature of the main character, he is the more pathetic gure. His total despair is registered in his famous ie "Like flies to wanton boys are we to the gods," it before his death he is rescued from this despair rough the loving care of Edgar.

Gloucester, Eleanor Cobham, duchess of (d. 446). Mistress, then wife, to Humphrey of Glou- ster, whom she married in 1431. In 1441 her hus- and's enemies brought the duchess to trial on arges of witchcraft and treason. First imprisoned Chester and Kenilworth, she was transferred in 46 to the Isle of Man. There she is thought to have ed some time later.

In *2 Henry VI*, Eleanor, aspiring to be queen, ar- nges for sorcerers to reveal the future to her. For is traitorous act she is banished.

Gloucester, Eleanor de Bohun, duchess of (1359 or 65–1399). Widow of Thomas of Woodstock, duke Gloucester. In *Richard II*, she urges her brother- -law John of Gaunt to avenge her husband's death, it he replies that she must address her pleas to God. ie then states her intention of retiring to her coun- y house in Essex (I, ii).

Gloucester, Humphrey, duke of (1391–1447). ourth son of Henry IV and Mary de Bohun. He as made duke by his brother Henry V. Gloucester companied the king on two invasions of France. n Henry's death, he was made deputy in England r the duke of Bedford, but, on attempting to claim e regency for himself, Gloucester failed. His career as marked by bitter quarrels with his brother Bed- rd and with Henry Beaufort, bishop of Win- iester. When Bedford's death left Gloucester heir esumptive to the throne, Henry VI, distrusting his ncle, diminished his power. In 1441, the duchess of loucester was prosecuted for practicing witchcraft n the king, and the duke himself was subsequently ommitted to prison, where he died.

In *2 Henry IV*, Prince Humphrey of Gloucester tends the King in the Jerusalem chamber (IV, iv) nd at his bedside (IV, v). In *Henry V*, he is the uke of Gloucester and takes part in the battle of gincourt. In *1 Henry VI*, he is Henry's protector. is quarrel with Winchester is depicted at length. *2 Henry VI*, Gloucester's wife is banished as a itch, he loses his protectorship, and his enemies Cardinal Beaufort, Queen Margaret, and the Dukes f Suffolk and York) cause his arrest and arrange his urder.

Gloucester, Richard, duke of. See RICHARD III.

Gobbo, Launcelot. In *The Merchant of Venice*, a own. A quibbler and practical joker, Launcelot's it consists mainly in misuse and mispronunciation f words: he informs his father, "I am famished in hylock's service; you may tell every finger I have ith my ribs." Leaving his master, Launcelot be- comes an attendant to Bassanio (II, ii). At Portia's residence in Belmont, he serves as messenger and as- sumes the role of favored jester.

Gobbo, Old. In *The Merchant of Venice*, Launce- lot's half-blind father. At his son's suggestion, Gobbo presents to Bassanio a dish of doves originally in- tended for Shylock, with the request that Bassanio take Launcelot into his service.

Goethe, Johann Wolfgang von. See CRITICISM—19TH CENTURY; GERMANY.

Goffe, or **Gough, Matthew** (d. 1450). A distin- guished English soldier who was killed by Jack Cade's rebels on London Bridge. In *2 Henry VI*, Goffe appears but does not speak. Sent to Smithfield by Lord Scales to oppose the rebels, he is killed by them. [W. H. Thomson, *Shakespeare's Characters: A Historical Dictionary*, 1951.]

Goffe, Robert. See Robert GOUGHE.

Golding, Arthur (1536?–?1605). Translator. One of the most prolific translators of the age, Golding was apparently educated at Cambridge, although his name is not listed in the university register. His half sister was the mother of Edward de Vere, earl of Oxford, and probably as a result of this connection, he made the acquaintance of the powerful Sir Wil- liam Cecil (Lord Burghley) to whom he dedicated his translation of Caesar's *Commentaries* (1565). He is best known for his translation of Ovid's *Meta- morphoses* (1567), which he converted into English "fourteeners" (a verse form of 14 syllables to a line). Golding's translation was highly regarded in its own time (and applauded in ours by Ezra Pound, who prefers it to *Paradise Lost*). That Shakespeare knew and used Golding is evidenced by echoes in a number of plays; the line from *The Tempest*, "Ye elves of hills, brooks, standing lakes" (V, i, 33), is derived from Golding's ". . . ye elves of Hills, of Brookes, of/ Woods alone/ Of Standing lakes."

A man of strong Puritanical sympathies, Golding was also the author of *A Discourse upon the Earth- quake* [*that hapned throughe this realme of England*] (1580), in which he argues that the earthquake which shook England in 1580 was a result of the sinfulness and decadence of the time. He cites as a particularly heinous example of this moral dissolution the per- formance of plays on Sundays. [L. T. Golding, *Eliza- bethan Puritan: Arthur Golding*, 1937.]

Goldoni, Carlo. See ITALY.

Gollancz, Sir Israel (1863–1930). Scholar. Born in London, Gollancz graduated from Christ's College, Cambridge. From 1894 to 1896 he edited the popular Temple Edition (see SCHOLARSHIP—19TH CENTURY) of Shakespeare's works and was active in collecting the massive *A Book of Homage to Shakespeare* (1916), an extensive series of essays on Shakespeare by the greatest literary and scholarly figures of the day. He was also the editor of *Studies in the First Folio* (1924) and *The Sources of Hamlet* (1926). He was the principal founder of the British Academy and of the Shakespeare Association. He was knighted in 1919.

Goneril. In *King Lear*, the eldest daughter of the King. The fiercer and more savage of the two un- natural daughters, Goneril is also the more sensual. There are strong indications in the play that before her affair with Edmund, she had an illicit relationship with her servant Oswald.

Gonzalo. In *The Tempest*, an honest old Counselor to Alonso, the King of Naples. Gonzalo, a loyal noble, shared no direct responsibility for Prospero's deposal but charitably provisioned his boat, thus becoming the overthrown Duke's savior. Gonzalo attempts to console the distressed Alonso despite the cynical jests of Sebastian and Antonio, and when he bothers to notice their taunts, Gonzalo proves himself a surprising match for their wit. After the reconciliations and Alonso's reunion with his son, the Counselor judges the misadventures, finding "all of us ourselves when no man was his own." Gonzalo's description of the ideal commonwealth is based on a passage in John Florio's translation of the *Essays* of Montaigne. See THE TEMPEST: *Sources*.

Goodhall, James. See ADAPTATIONS.

Goodman's Fields Theatre. (1) A London theatre, built about 1703, of which the only record is in *The Observator* for that year:

> The great playhouse has calved a young one in Goodman's Fields, in the passage by the Ship Tavern, between Prescot Street and Chambers Street.

(2) A theatre in Leman Street, Whitechapel, which was converted from a shop in 1729 by Thomas Odell, who hired an Irish actor, Henry Giffard (1694–1772), as manager. After Giffard left Odell's Goodman's Fields, it continued to present acrobatics, plays, and other entertainments until 1751, when it became a warehouse. It burned down in 1802.

(3). A theatre built in 1733 by Giffard in Ayliffe Street, and home to an excellent company of actors, including Richard Yates and Henry Woodward. It was at this Goodman's Fields in 1741 that *The Winter's Tale* received its first revival in 100 years. Giffard avoided the necessity of applying for a license to give plays by selling tickets to "concerts" and presenting plays between the pieces of music. The theatre was also the scene of David Garrick's debut as Richard III in 1741, while understudying Yates. The theatre was closed, however, the following year. [*The Oxford Companion to the Theatre*, Phyllis Hartnoll, ed., 1951.]

Googe, Barnabe (1540–1594). Poet and translator. *The Zodiake of Life* (1560–1565) is Googe's translation of the *Zodiacus Vitae* (1543) of Marcellus Palingenius, a popular compendium of astronomical, moral, and philosophical lore in dialogue form. Shakespeare may have borrowed from this work for miscellaneous images and themes (see IMAGERY). The most striking analogue is the marginal comment in the 1576 edition —"The world a stage play"—which recalls the words of Jaques in *As You Like It* (II, vii, 139). Googe's only independent work was the *Eglogs, Epytaphes and Sonnettes* (1563), a collection of eight eclogues, two sonnets, some descriptive verse, and epitaphs on such contemporaries as Nicholas Grimald and Thomas Phaer. [John E. Hankins, *Shakespeare's Derived Imagery*, 1953.]

Gorbuduc (1561). A tragedy by Thomas Norton (1532–1584) and Thomas Sackville (1536–1608). *Gorbuduc* was written in 1561 for the Christmas revels at the Inner Temple, one of the inns of court. The play, heavily indebted to Seneca, was the first English tragedy in blank verse and its successful reception set the standard for a series of Senecan dramas in English. It tells the story of old King Gorbuduc, who divides his kingdom, thus precipitating a series of catastrophic events. It has been argued that there is a direct relationship between *Gorbuduc* and *King Lear*, particularly in the tragic tone of the latter, not present in any of the known sources of the play. [Barbara Heliodora Carneiro De Mendonca, "The Influence of *Gorbuduc* on *King Lear*," *Shakespeare Survey 13*, 1960.]

Gosson, Henry (fl. 1601–1640). London publisher of the first two editions of *Pericles*. Gosson was admitted to the Stationers' Company as a freeman in 1601. In 1609 he published *Pericles*, although it had been registered in the previous year by Edward Blount. This, together with the corrupt state of the text, is an indication that Gosson's *Pericles* is one of the "stolne and surreptitious copies" referred to by Heminges and Condell in the Preface to the First Folio (1623). In any case Gosson's Quarto sold so well—even in its corrupt state—that it was reprinted in the same year. See PERICLES: *Text*. [R. B. McKerrow, ed., *A Dictionary of Printers and Booksellers . . . 1557–1640*, 1910.]

Gosson, Stephen (1554–1624). Pamphleteer. After graduating from Oxford in 1576, Gosson came to London and began an unsuccessful attempt to write for the theatre. His initial attraction turned to revulsion, and in 1579 he published an attack on the contemporary stage entitled *The School of Abuse*. Several replies were made. Sir Philip Sidney, to whom Gosson had dedicated his pamphlet without permission, was stimulated to make a general defense of letters in his *Apology for Poetry*. Thomas Lodge answered Gosson in his *Reply to Stephen Gosson Touching Plays* (1579). Gosson continued the attack in an appendix to *The Ephemerides of Phialo* (1579) and in *Plays Confuted in Five Actions* (1582), the latter of which was specifically directed against Lodge. Gosson, who eventually took orders, is in the tradition of English Puritanism with its distrust of the stage. Numerous contemporaries voiced protests similar to his, and in the next century he was succeeded by such critics as Philip Stubbes and William Prynne. In addition to the moral strictures, *The School of Abuse* gives much incidental information about the Elizabethan theatre-going public. See ENEMIES OF THE STAGE.

Götz, Hermann. See MUSIC BASED ON SHAKESPEARE: *19th century, 1850–1900*.

Goughe or **Goffe, Robert** (d. 1624). Actor. Goughe was a member of Shakespeare's company, the Chamberlain's Men, probably from an early date. He was probably the "R. Go." cast as Aspasia in the *Sloth* episode of Tarlton's *Seven Deadly Sins* when that play was revived by the combined Admiral's-Strange's company in 1590/1. Goughe was one of the "principall Actors" listed in the First Folio (1623) of Shakespeare's plays, and he was cited in the official lists of the King's Men for 1619 and 1621. His known roles include Memphonius in *The Second Maiden's Tragedy* (1611) and Leidenberch in *Sir John Van Olden Barnevelt* (1619).

In Thomas Pope's will, executed in 1603, Goughe is named a legatee, and he was a witness to the will made by Augustine Phillips in 1605. He was probably married to Phillips' sister Elizabeth. His son Alexander also became an actor. He lived in the parish of St. Saviour's, Southwark, where the births and deaths of his children are recorded. [E. K. Chambers, *The Elizabethan Stage*, 1923.]

Gounod, Charles François (1818–1893). French composer. Gounod's *Roméo et Juliette*, next to his *Faust*, is his most successful operatic work, though less popular than formerly. It was first presented at the Théâtre-Lyrique, Paris, in 1867. On the whole, the libretto is faithful to the play, though two minor characters are added. [Christopher Wilson, *Shakespeare and Music*, 1922.]

Governor of Harfleur. In *Henry V*, chief commander of the city during its siege. Failing to receive help from the Dauphin, he surrenders Harfleur to the English. Historically there were two governors of Harfleur at this time. Initially Jean Lord D'Estouteville held the office, but Raoul Sieur de Gaucort seems to have taken it over when reinforcements were sent in under his command. The latter represented the city on its surrender, in 1415, after 36 days of siege. [W. H. Thomson, *Shakespeare's Characters: A Historical Dictionary*, 1951.]

Governor of Paris. In *1 Henry VI*, a minor character who, at Henry's coronation, is charged to "elect no other king but him" (IV, i). Historically, the governor of Paris may have been John of Luxembourg, who was appointed to that post when Paris was captured by the English. [W. H. Thomson, *Shakespeare's Characters: A Historical Dictionary*, 1951.]

Gower. In *2 Henry IV*, an officer of Henry's army who, in II, i, announces to the Lord Chief Justice that "The king, my lord, and Harry Prince of Wales / Are near at hand." In *Henry V*, Gower is a captain at the battle of Agincourt. As Fluellen's "dear friend," he listens to that gentleman's fiery outpourings. When Fluellen quarrels with Pistol, Gower takes his friend's part, calling Pistol a "counterfeit cowardly knave" (V, i). Historically, Gower may have been Thomas Gower, who accompanied Henry V on his French campaign. [W. H. Thomson, *Shakespeare's Characters: A Historical Dictionary*, 1951.]

Gower, John (c. 1325–1408). English poet. He was termed "the moral Gower" by his friend Chaucer. His principal works are the *Miroir de l'Omme* or *Speculum Meditantis* (French, c. 1378), a moral allegory condemning the vices of society; *Vox Clamantis* (Latin, c. 1382), another allegory, which gives much information about the Peasants' Revolt and the social unrest of the day; and *Confessio Amantis* (English, 1390, 1393), a collection of tales illustrating the Seven Deadly Sins. Gower's version in this book of the story of Apollonius of Tyre (VIII, 271–2008) provided Shakespeare with one of the sources for his *Pericles*, and the figure of Gower appears in the play. There is no evidence to connect the poet with the Thomas Gower who appears briefly in *2 Henry IV* and *Henry V*.

In *Pericles*, Gower acts as Chorus. Imitating the poet's style, and speaking for the most part in the octosyllabic verse of the *Confessio Amantis*, he presents the drama and recounts the action of the play. Before each act he bridges the years by describing intervening events; in II, III, and IV, iv, his speeches are enacted with dumb shows. He also appears in V, ii and summarizes the play in the Epilogue.

There is some dispute as to the authorship of Gower's part. Some critics hold that Shakespeare did not write the role, while others assign to him only the decasyllabic passages in his second appearance.

Grabu, Louis. See MUSIC BASED ON SHAKESPEARE: *17th century*.

Grafton, Richard (c. 1513–c. 1572). Printer and chronicler. A wealthy merchant, Grafton financed the publication of one of the earliest versions of the Bible in English, the so-called Matthew Bible of 1537. Becoming directly involved in printing, he printed an enlarged English version of the Bible in 1539, the "Great Bible," which became the official version used in the English church for the next 20 years. Subsequently Grafton secured the position of the king's printer. In 1548 he edited and published the posthumous *Union of the Two Noble and Illustre Famelies of Lancastre and York* by Edward HALLE. By judiciously borrowing materials from earlier histories, particularly Halle's, Grafton began to piece together his own chronicles under the titles *An Abridgement of the Chronicles of England* (1562), *A Manuell of the Chronicles of Englande* (1565), and *A Chronicle at Large and Meere History of the Affayres of England and Kinges of the Same* (1568). Grafton often is so closely indebted to Halle that in some cases it is impossible to determine whom Shakespeare is using. However, Shakespeare did use Grafton for isolated elements in the histories, such as the false miracle of Simpcox in *2 Henry VI*. [Geoffrey Bullough, *Narrative and Dramatic Sources of Shakespeare*, Vol. III, 1960.]

grammar. Shakespeare's grammar is not substantially different from that of modern English; the old inflectional endings had, in most cases, been dropped, and the *-eth* ending of the third person present was already becoming an archaism found more frequently in elevated prose than in colloquial speech; except for words like "saith," "hath," and "doth," Shakespeare tends to use the *-s* or *-es* form.

The fluid state of the language was reflected in the conjugations of verbs; Shakespeare used many forms which were then evolving but which have since been replaced in favor of older forms. Thus he makes a regular (weak) verb out of "shake" and gives its past tense as "shaked," while modern English goes back to the older irregular (strong) forms "shook" and "shaken." Following the similarity of preterite and past participle in weak verbs (he lived, he had lived), Elizabethan writers tended to use the preterite for the past participle in strong verbs, resulting in some permanent changes in the language (we now say "held" instead of "holden" and "stood" rather than "standen") as well as some Shakespearean solecisms: "had gave over," "might have took," "hath wrote." In Elizabethan times there was also extraordinary freedom in using one part of speech for another; Shakespeare makes nouns of verbs, adjectives, adverbs, and pronouns; puts nouns and adjectives to service as verbs; and uses nouns, adverbs, verbs, and even prepositional phrases as adjectives. See COLLOQUIALISMS; PRONUNCIATION. [E. A. Abbott, *Shakespearean Grammar*, 1869; Henry Bradley, "Shakespeare's English," *Shakespeare's England*, 1916.]

Grandpré, Lord (d. 1415). A leader in the French force at Agincourt. In *Henry V*, Grandpré ridicules the English before the battle (IV, ii). Grandpré is later listed among the casualties.

Granville, George. See Lord LANSDOWNE.

Granville-Barker, Harley (1877–1946). Actor, playwright, director, and critic. Granville-Barker made his first stage appearance in 1891 and continued acting until 1910. His preference was for Elizabethan rather than contemporary drama, and he played Shakespearean roles with the companies of William Poel and Ben Greet. Combining an acting career with producing and directing, in 1904 he undertook, in collaboration with J. E. Vedrenne, the management of the Court Theatre. There they offered fine productions of Ibsen, Maeterlinck, Galsworthy, Masefield, Shaw, and others; several of Granville-Barker's own plays were also produced at the Court.

Granville-Barker initiated a theatrical revolution with his productions of Shakespeare. He extended the apron stage and accelerated the pace with a continuous flow of action and rapid, lightly stressed lines. His production of *A Winter's Tale* (1912), long neglected on the London stage, created a sensation with its use of the full text (only six lines were eliminated), its single intermission of 15 minutes, and its brilliant costumes. Also in 1912 Granville-Barker produced *Twelfth Night,* which proved an immediate success; the continuous action, black-and-silver setting, and fresh interpretations pleased both audience and critics. A more mixed reception was accorded *A Midsummer Night's Dream* (1914) with its fairies gilded from head to foot and the unearthly atmosphere created by the play of light and color. Productions of *Macbeth* and *Antony and Cleopatra* were planned but never carried out.

After World War I, in which he served with the Red Cross, Granville-Barker found himself out of sympathy with current theatrical trends. He settled in Paris and devoted himself to various activities. The fruits of this period were the various prefaces and lectures ultimately published as *Prefaces to Shakespeare* (5 series, 1927–1947). These prefaces, coming as they did from a man conversant with several aspects of the theatre, have been widely acclaimed as inaugurating a new approach to Shakespeare. However, there has been some exaggeration on this point; Granville-Barker was writing at a time when his theatrical career lay behind him, and he was increasingly influenced by academic critics, such as A. C. Bradley, whom he greatly admired. In 1930 he succeeded Sir Israel Gollancz as president of the Shakespeare Association, and in that capacity was instrumental in bringing about compilation of a general index to the works of E. K. Chambers. During this period he also collaborated with G. B. Harrison in editing *A Companion to Shakespeare Studies* (1934). Although a composite work, it bears the stamp of Granville-Barker: he carefully selected the contributors, gave specific instructions as to what was desired, and frequently insisted upon revisions. His own contribution was an essay entitled "Shakespeare's Dramatic Art."

Gratiano. In *The Merchant of Venice,* a volatile, garrulous friend of Bassanio and Antonio. Gratiano is allowed to travel with Bassanio to Belmont after promising his friend that he will "put on a sober habit, talk with respect and swear but now and then" (II, ii). At Belmont he courts and marries Nerissa.

Gratiano. In *Othello,* the brother of Brabantio and uncle of Desdemona. Gratiano announces Brabantio's death in V, ii.

Gravediggers. In *Hamlet,* two clowns who appear in V, i, underscoring the inevitable tragic movement of the drama with an earthy humor. In the neoclassical period this scene was regarded as a blemish and was omitted. It is now regarded as a significant and intensifying ironic commentary on the main action.

Gravelot, Hubert François. Real surname **Bourguignon** (1699–1773). French painter, engraver, and designer. Born of a distinguished French family, Gravelot was something of a black sheep in his youth. He was poor when he opened his art school in London, but he had studied with François Boucher and had learned his craft well. He grew prosperous and influential, "discovered" and befriended Thomas Gainsborough, and moved in the artistically progressive circle which included William Hogarth and David Garrick.

The large body of work he produced (illustrations of John Gay's *Fables* and Edward Young's *Poetical Works* as well as many Shakespeare plates) carried French traditions directly into the mainstream of English book illustration. He was one of the first caricature artists in England, and his work helped define the characteristics of comic illustration, a genre that was to flourish in England for a hundred years. In addition to his rococo lightness, he maintained the solid qualities of the French Academy.

Gravelot designed 36 plates for Lewis Theobald's 1740 edition of Shakespeare and collaborated with Francis Hayman on the Thomas Hanmer edition of 1744. This was one of the handsomest editions of Shakespeare printed in the 18th century, and Gravelot contributed designs for 5 plates, 3 fine tailpieces, the portrait and vignette of the title page, and the engraving of all 36 plates. See ART. [W. M. Merchant, *Shakespeare and the Artist,* 1959.]

Great Lakes Shakespeare Festival. An annual dramatic festival held at Lakewood, Ohio. It is one of the more recently established of the American Shakespeare festivals, but its director, Arthur Lithgow, is no stranger to such celebrations, having guided the Antioch Area Shakespeare Festival when that festival existed during the 1950's at Yellow Springs, Ohio. In the 2000-seat civic auditorium at Lakewood, a suburb of Cleveland, the festival opened in 1962. On the proscenium stage a superstage was erected which incorporated features of the Elizabethan stage. It was similar to that at Antioch, where the entire canon had been offered. The Great Lakes festival plays have impressed audiences and critics as productions that convey the spirit of the plays and avoid "gimmicks." The comedies are joyous, but not "guyed," and their serious passages—such as Aegeon's long account of his adventures in *The Comedy of Errors*—are delivered seriously and effectively. The comparatively large number of plays offered in the first two seasons—the opening season included *Richard II, 1* and *2 Henry IV, The Merchant of Venice, As You Like It,* and *Othello,* starring Earle Hyman—may account for the fact that some of these productions seemed insufficiently prepared. Another problem is that of achieving a sense of intimate rapport between actor and audience in so large an auditorium. However, the festival has been well supported, drawing statewide as well as local audiences. —A.G.

Greek Anthology. A collection of about 4500 fugitive pieces of Greek poetry called epigrams (inscriptions). The earliest extant compilation is that in 15 books made at the beginning of the 10th century by a Byzantine scholar, Constantinus Cephalas. It is also called the Palatine Anthology for the place of its rediscovery in the 17th century. The anthology is the source of Shakespeare's Sonnets 153 and 154. It is doubtful that the poet translated them from the original Greek, but no intermediate source is known. T. W. Baldwin believes that Sonnet 154 is not by Shakespeare, but that it was used by him as the source of Sonnet 153. [T. W. Baldwin, *On the Literary Genetics of Shakspere's Poems and Sonnets*, 1950.]

Greek romances. The exotic romances written in Greek during the early Christian era. The structure of Shakespeare's "romances" and fiction such as Sir Philip Sidney's bear a resemblance to the plots of Greek romances. These stories generally involve the fortunes of a pair of royal lovers, one or both of whom is disguised, whose union is thwarted as a result of parental interference. The stories invariably end happily, with the last-minute revelation of the hero's or heroine's true identity. Typical of the genre is the *Aethiopica* of Heliodorus (fl. 3rd cent. A.D.), translated by Thomas Underdowne (fl. 1566–1587) as *An Aethiopian Historie* (c. 1569). Underdowne's translation is one of the minor sources of *Cymbeline*.

Green, Sir Henry (d. 1399). A favorite of Richard II. On Bolingbroke's invasion of England, Green fled with Sir John Bushy and the earl of Wiltshire to Bristol, where they were seized and executed without trial by Bolingbroke's followers. In *Richard II*, Green and his fellow courtier Bushy flee to Bristol, where Bolingbroke captures and executes them. Green is included in Bolingbroke's reference to "Bushy, Bagot and their complices, / The caterpillars of the commonwealth, / Which I have sworn to weed and pluck away" (II, iii). [W. H. Thomson, *Shakespeare's Characters: A Historical Dictionary*, 1951.]

Green, John (fl. 1607–1627). Actor. Green was the leader of a troupe of English actors who toured Germany between 1607 and 1627. Among the plays in the repertoire of Green's company were *Titus Andronicus, Julius Caesar, Hamlet, Lear King of England*, and *Romeo and Juliet*. See GERMANY.

Greene, Joseph (1712–1790). Master of Stratford grammar school and the discoverer in 1747 of Shakespeare's will. Greene was also the first person to suggest that Shakespeare's BIRTHDAY was April 23.

Greene, Robert (1558–1592). Playwright, novelist, poet, pamphleteer. A native of Norwich, Greene received his first degree from Cambridge in 1575. Shortly thereafter he apparently left England to travel in Italy. There, if we are to believe his later, rather sensational, "autobiographical" accounts, he led a life of unrestrained debauchery, becoming a model of the dissolute "Italianate Englishman" against whom Puritan preachers frequently railed. On his return he began the perilous career of free-lance Elizabethan writer. His earliest works were a series of prose romances written in imitation of the style and subject of John Lyly's *Euphues*. These included *Mamillia* (1583?), *Euphues, his Censure to Philautus* (1587), *Pandosto, the Triumph of Time* (1588), and *Menaphon* (1589). Shakespeare found the main plot of *The Winter's Tale* in *Pandosto*, the best of these works and the most popular (see THE WINTER'S TALE: *Sources*). *Euphues, his Censure to Philautus* may have been the source of incidents in *Troilus and Cressida*. *Menaphon* is best known for a prefatory epistle by Thomas Nashe, in which he makes an allusion to the UR-HAMLET, and for the lovely songs that are interspersed throughout the story.

Greene returned to London, received an M.A. from Oxford, and began a new career as playwright. His first effort was *Alphonsus, King of Aragon* (c. 1587). An inept imitation, or travesty, of Marlowe's *Tamburlaine*, it is noteworthy only for its stage directions, which provide some clues about the structure of the Elizabethan stage. See INNER STAGE.

After this false start, Greene developed the dramatic mode of romantic comedy, which was more suited to his talents and which was later perfected by Shakespeare. In two plays, *James IV* (c. 1591) and *Friar Bacon and Friar Bungay* (c. 1591), Greene set the stage for Shakespeare's later achievements in that genre. *James IV*, a hybrid of history, fantasy, and romance, is notable for its setting—rural England—and its charming, gifted heroines, Dorothea and Ida, the forerunners of the feminine characters in *As You Like It, Twelfth Night*, and the romances. In *Friar Bacon and Friar Bungay*, Greene created another memorable heroine, Margaret, whose love affair was set against a background of the magical feats of the legendary Friar Bacon, an old folk hero. The play, which was extremely popular in its day, bears some primitive and remote resemblance to *The Tempest* and is one of the earliest examples of the successful interweaving of a subplot with the main story. Greene also wrote ORLANDO FURIOSO, a play based on Ariosto's epic poem.

Although Greene's literary output was considerable, he continued to lead a life of dissipation. He deserted his wife and began to frequent the Elizabethan underworld. His unsavory associations, however, did not deter ecclesiastical authorities from commissioning him to answer the attacks of the Puritan pamphleteer Martin Marprelate. The irony of Greene in the role of defender of the faith was noted by Richard Harvey in his pamphlet *Plaine Percevall the Peace-Maker of England* (1590). Greene responded in turn with an attack on the Harvey family in his *Quip for Upstart Courtier* (1592). It was this exchange that provoked the famous quarrel between Greene's protégé, Thomas Nashe, and Richard Harvey's brother, Gabriel. Greene's acquaintance with the underworld resulted in his most popular work, the famous CONY-CATCHING PAMPHLETS. At the same time, writing at a furious pace, he was issuing his "repentance" pamphlets, exaggerated autobiographical accounts of his past sins and present remorse. Although ostensibly moral tracts designed to point up the wages of sin, the pamphlets derived their popularity from sensational disclosures of the wickedness of Greene and his cohorts, "that unclean generation of vipers." The repentance pamphlets included *Greenes mourning garment* (1590), *Greenes never too late* (1590), his *The Re-*

pentance of Robert Greene Maister of Artes (1592), and his GROATS-WORTH OF WIT (1592)—the latter containing a well-known attack on Shakespeare. The *Groats-worth* was published shortly after Greene's death. He died, according to his enemy Gabriel Harvey, after a meal in which he had overindulged in wine and pickled herring. At the conclusion of the *Groats-worth* is Greene's final letter to his wife. It reveals that his repentance, despite its attendant publicity, was probably sincere:

> That I have offended thee highly I know, that you canst forget my injuries I hardly believe; yet persuade I myself, if thou saw my wretched estate thou couldst not but lament it, nay, certainly I know thou wouldst. All my wrongs muster themselves before me, every evil at once plagues me. For my contempt of God I am contemned of men; for my swearing and forswearing no man will believe me; for my gluttony I suffer hunger; for my drunkenness, thirst; for my adultery, ulcerous sores.

There has been considerable disagreement among scholars as to the relationship of Greene and Shakespeare. If, as many scholars have believed, Shakespeare began his career by revising other men's plays, then it is probable that some of these plays were at least partly Greene's. Greene has been viewed variously as the original author of, or one of a group of original collaborators on, the Henry VI plays, *The Comedy of Errors, Two Gentlemen of Verona,* and several other early Shakespeare plays. Many modern scholars, however, reject the idea that Shakespeare's earliest writing was revision of other men's work. Much of the evidence, pro and con, on this question hinges on the interpretation of the language of Greene's attack in the *Groats-worth of Wit.* [J. Dover Wilson, "Malone and the Upstart Crow," *Shakespeare Survey 4,* 1951.]

Greene Family. Neighbors and kinsmen of Shakespeare. On March 6, 1590 "Thomas Greene, alias Shakspere" was buried in the Stratford churchyard. The significance of the "alias" is unknown, as is the identity of the "Thomas Greene" here referred to. However, he may have been a cousin of ***Thomas Greene*** of Warwick (d. 1590), two of whose sons settled in Stratford.

The elder of the two sons, ***Thomas Greene*** (d. 1640), was educated at Middle Temple. In 1601 he was solicitor for Stratford in London. He is also the same Thomas Greene who contributed a commendatory poem to the 1603 edition of Michael Drayton's long narrative poem *The Baron's Wars.* From 1603 to 1617 he served as town clerk of Stratford. He married Lettice Tutt, by whom he had six children, one of whom was named ***Anne*** (b. 1604) and another, ***William*** (b. 1608), an indication that the Shakespeares may have served as the children's godparents. In 1609 Greene and his family were living at New Place while waiting to move into his own house, which the old tenant was slow in vacating. Greene explained the delay in a letter to Sir Henry Rainsford:

> He doubted whether he might sowe his garden, untill about my goinge to the Terme. (seing I could gett noe carryages to help me here with tymber) I was content to permytt yt without contradiccion. & the rather because I perceyued I mighte stay another yere at newe place.

In 1609 he also purchased an interest in the STRATFORD TITHES of which Shakespeare was a part owner. When the possibility of the ENCLOSURE of these lands arose, Greene—as an agent of the Stratford corporation which opposed the enclosure—was faced with a conflict of interest. Nevertheless, despite the fact that he would have profited by enclosure, he faithfully upheld the corporation's position. In connection with the tithes, Greene recorded references to "my Cosen Shakespeare" in 1614 and 1615:

> At my Cosen Shakspeare commyng yesterday to towne I went to see him howe he did he told me that they assured him they ment to inclose noe further then to gospell bushe & so vpp straight (leavyng out part of the dyngles to the ffield) to the gate . . . I alsoe wrytte of myself to my Cosen Shakespeare the Coppyes of all our oathes m[a]de then alsoe a not of the Inconvenyences wold gr[ow] by the Inclosure . . . .

Shortly after Shakespeare's death Greene gave up his post as town clerk and moved to London. There he served as reader at Middle Temple until his death in 1640.

Thomas' brother, ***John Greene*** (c. 1575–1640), served as solicitor for the Stratford corporation in 1612, and in 1613 as deputy town clerk. He negotiated with Shakespeare in 1615 in connection with the enclosure controversy, and in 1618 was a trustee of Shakespeare's Blackfriars Gate-House, acting as an agent of Shakespeare's daughter Susanna. [E. K. Chambers, *William Shakespeare,* 1930; Mark Eccles, *Shakespeare in Warwickshire,* 1961.]

Greene's Funeralls (1594). A collection of poems. It was entered in the Stationers' Register on February 1, 1594 and published in the same year. The author of the poems, R. B., has been identified as either Richard BARNFIELD or Barnabe RICH. In the ninth poem of the collection there is an apparent reference to Robert Greene's famous attack on Shakespeare in his GROATS-WORTH OF WIT (1592).

> Greene, is the ground of euerie Painters die:
> Greene, gaue the ground, to all that wrote vpon him.
> Nay more the men, that so Eclipst his fame:
> Purloynde his Plumes, can they deny the same?

[E. K. Chambers, *William Shakespeare,* 1930.]

Greet, Sir [Philip Barling] Ben (1857–1936). Actor and manager. Intended for a naval career, Greet attended the Royal Naval School and was for a time master in a private school at Worthing. He made his first stage appearance in 1879 in a stock company at Southampton, then joined Sarah Thorne's company in Margate. In 1883 he made his London debut as Caius Lucius in *Cymbeline.* In Mary Anderson's 1884 production of *Romeo and Juliet,* Greet played the Apothecary and embarked on what was to be a lifelong friendship with the great actress. In 1886 he began to manage open-air productions of Shakespeare which he referred to as "pastoral." He toured the United Kingdom and the United States with a company of actors, of whom many became quite famous.

The Greene Family

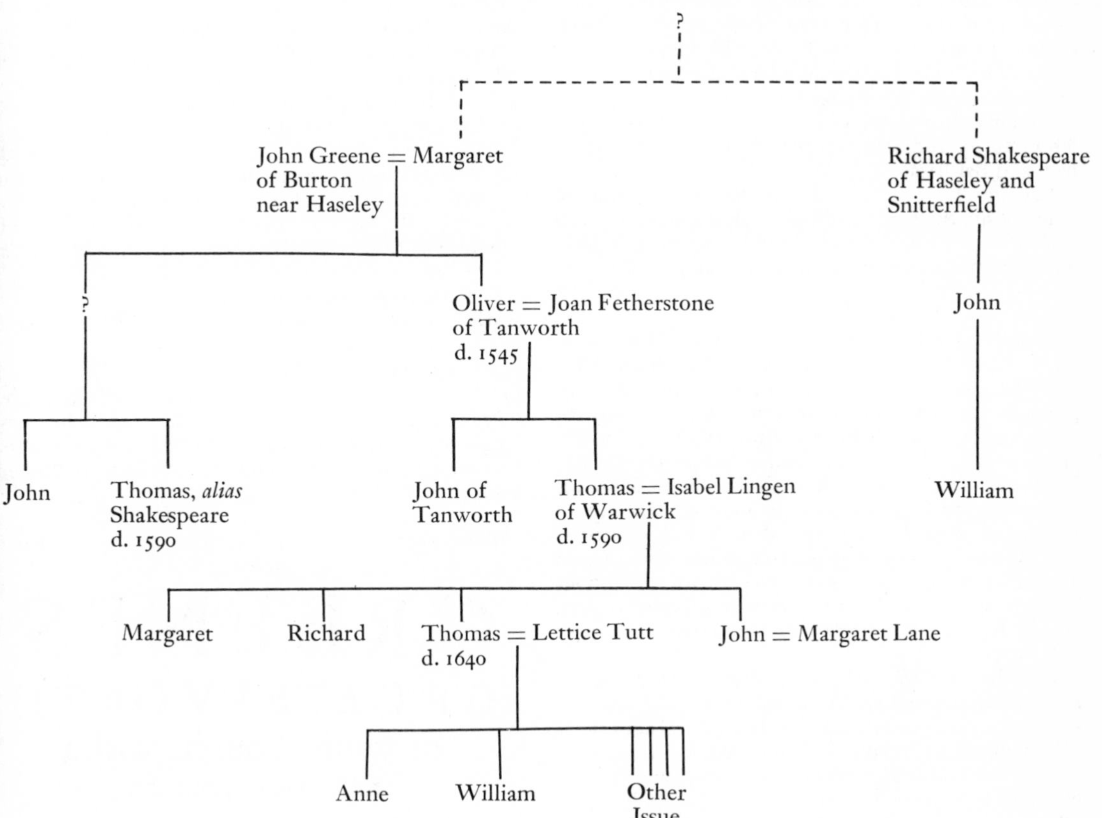

Note: The relationship between Richard Shakespeare and Margaret Greene was suggested by E. I. Fripp. However, Chambers points out that there is no evidence that the Richard Shakespeare of Snitterfield and the Richard Shakespeare of Haseley are the same person. Nor can it be established that Margaret Greene was born a Shakespeare.

It was Thomas Greene (d. 1640) who three times referred to William Shakespeare as his cousin and gave his first two children the Christian names of Shakespeare and his wife. His brother John became a trustee of Shakespeare's house in Blackfriars, acting for Susanna Hall.

In 1902 a production of *Everyman* at the Imperial signaled the beginning of a special interest for Greet in the pre-Shakespearean drama. He was a constant visitor to the United States between 1902–1914 and 1929–1932. In 1914 he joined Lillian Baylis at the Old Vic, where his company became the nucleus of the Old Vic-Sadler's Wells companies. In 1918 he formed a company to give performances of Shakespeare for London area schoolchildren; in four years, more than one million children witnessed Greet's productions. From 1924 to 1926 he presented English plays in Paris. In 1929 he was knighted. As an actor, Greet had some success in character roles, and as a producer his reputation was for patient, painstaking, and practical presentations in good taste. [*Dictionary of National Biography*, supp., 1949.]

Greg, Sir W[alter] W[ilson] (1875–1959). Scholar and bibliographer. A graduate of Trinity College, Cambridge, in 1898, Greg returned there in 1907 as college librarian. He founded the Malone Society in 1906, serving as its general editor until 1939 and as its president from 1939 to 1959. In 1928 he was made a fellow of the British Academy and was knighted in 1950.

Greg, together with his Cambridge classmate R. B. McKerrow and A. W. Pollard, is among the giants of modern bibliographical scholarship. He formulated the general principles and high standards that have been applied to the study of Shakespeare's text in this century. (See TEXTUAL CRITICISM.) One of Greg's major achievements was his edition (1911) of SIR THOMAS MORE. Among the many books he wrote and edited are an edition of *Henslowe's Diary* (1904–1908); *Pastoral Poetry and Pastoral Drama* (1906); *Calculus of Variants: An Essay on Textual Criticism* (1927); *Dramatic Documents from the Elizabethan Playhouses* (2 vols., 1931); *The Editorial Problem in Shakespeare* (1942); the massive four-volume *Bibliography of the English Printed Drama to the Restoration* (1940–1959); and *The Shakespeare First Folio* (1955). He also edited a large number of Elizabethan plays for the Malone Society.

Gregory. In *Romeo and Juliet,* a servant to Capulet. Gregory and Sampson pick a quarrel with Abraham and Balthasar (I, i).

Gremio. In *The Taming of the Shrew,* one of Bianca's suitors. Gremio unwittingly engages his rival Lucentio as Bianca's tutor, thereby losing her himself. Gremio describes Petruchio's and Katharina's marriage in III, ii.

Gresham, Thomas. See London.

Greville, Curtis (fl. 1615–1634). Actor. First with Lady Elizabeth's and the Elector Palatine's Men, Greville joined the King's Men around 1625. He appears in the stage direction of the First Quarto of Shakespeare and Fletcher's *Two Noble Kinsmen* (pub. 1634) as a messenger and an attendant (IV, ii; V, iii). In 1631 he was still with the King's Men, his name appearing in the prompt-book of Massinger's *Believe as You List.* Dover Wilson has suggested that "Curtis," the name given to a minor character in *The Taming of the Shrew,* is actually the bookkeeper's note indicating that Greville played the part. [G. E. Bentley, *The Jacobean and Caroline Stage,* 5 vols., 1941–1956.]

Greville, Fulke. 1st Baron **Brooke** (1554–1628). Poet and biographer. A member of one of the wealthiest families in Shakespeare's native county of Warwickshire, Greville was educated at Shrewsbury School and Cambridge. While at Shrewsbury School, he became a close friend of Sir Philip Sidney, of whom he wrote a famous biography, *Life of the Renowned Sr Philip Sidney* (1610–1612). He served as secretary for the principality of Wales (1583–1628) and chancellor of the exchequer (1614–1621) and was a prominent member of Elizabeth's court. His extant literary output consists of two closet dramas, *Alaham* (c. 1600) and *Mustapha* (1603–1608), and a sonnet sequence, *Caelica* (1580–1600).

Rosemary Sisson's study of Shakespeare's early life has suggested that he was a page at Greville's estate in Beauchamp Court, near Stratford. One source of this hypothesis is the statement of David Lloyd, in *Statesmen and Favourites of England* (1665), that Greville desired "to be known to posterity under no other notions than of Shakespear's and Ben Johnson's Master . . . ." The only other explanation of this allusion that has been suggested is that it may possibly refer to Greville's role, from 1606 to 1628, as recorder of the town of Stratford, a position in which he was expected to exert his influence in high places in the interests of the town. [Rosemary A. Sisson, *The Young Shakespeare,* 1960.]

Grey, Sir **Richard** (d. 1483). Younger son of Sir John Grey and Elizabeth Woodville, and brother of the marquis of Dorset. After Edward IV died, Grey, Earl Rivers, and Sir Thomas Vaughan were escorting the young King Edward V to London for his coronation when they were arrested by Richard, duke of Gloucester. The three men were subsequently executed for treason. In *Richard III,* Lord Grey exclaims, just before his death at Pomfret Castle: "God keep the prince from all the pack of you! / A knot you are of damned blood-suckers" (III, iii). [W. H. Thomson, *Shakespeare's Characters: A Historical Dictionary,* 1951.]

Grey, Sir **Thomas** (d. 1415). Second son of Sir Thomas Grey of Berwick. Grey was condemned and beheaded for his part in the conspiracy with the earl of Cambridge and Lord Scrope to murder King Henry V. In *Henry V,* Grey is a traitor who, with Cambridge and Scroop, has been bribed by the French to murder the King. When the plot is discovered (II, ii), the three are executed. [W. H. Thomson, *Shakespeare's Characters: A Historical Dictionary,* 1951.]

Griffith. In *Henry VIII,* gentleman-usher to Queen Katharine. Griffith is present with her at her divorce trial (II, iv) and in her last illness (IV, ii).

Groats-worth of Wit. A pamphlet by Robert Greene containing a famous attack on Shakespeare. Greene's pamphlet was entered in the Stationers' Register on September 20, 1592, three weeks after Greene's death on September 3. It was published shortly thereafter with the following title page:

TITLE PAGE OF GREENE'S *Groats-worth of Wit* (1592).

GREENES,
GROATS-VVORTH
of witte, bought with a
million of Repentance.

Describing the follie of youth, the falshood of makeshifte flatterers, the miserie of the negligent, and mischiefes of deceiuing Courtezans.

Written before his death and published at his dyeing request.

Fœlicem fuiſſe infauſtum.

LONDON
Imprinted for William Wright.
1592.

The *Groats-worth* was one of Greene's repentance pamphlets, pseudo-autobiographical accounts of his dissolute life and subsequent remorse. The passage on Shakespeare occurs in a section titled:

To those Gentlemen his Quondam acquaintance, that spend their wits in making plaies, R. G. wisheth a better exercise, and wisdome to preuent his extremities.

The "Gentlemen" addressed are Christopher Marlowe, Thomas Nashe, and George Peele, who are warned not to trust actors, and one actor in particular who fancies himself "the onely Shake-scene in a countrey":

Base minded men all three of you, if by my miserie you be not warnd: for vnto none of you (like mee) sought those burres to cleaue: those Puppets (I meane) that spake from our mouths, those Anticks garnisht in our colours. Is it not strange, that I, to whom they all haue beene beholding: is it not like that you, to whome they all haue beene beholding, shall (were yee in that case as I am now) bee both at once of them forsaken? Yes trust them not: for there is an vpstart Crow, beautified with our feathers, that with his *Tygers hart wrapt in a Players hyde,* supposes he is as well able to bombast out a blanke verse as the best of you: and beeing an absolute *Iohannes factotum,* is in his owne conceit the onely Shake-scene in a countrey. O that I might intreat your rare wits to be imploied in more profitable courses: & let those Apes imitate your past excellence, and neuer more acquaint them with your admired inuentions.

That Shakespeare is the "Shake-scene" here referred to is made all but certain by the epithet "*Tygers hart wrapt in a Players hyde,*" which is a parody of a line in *3 Henry VI:* "O tiger's heart wrapt in a woman's hide" (I, iv, 137). What Greene meant by the phrase "vpstart Crow, beautified with our feathers" is considerably less certain. Since the late 18th century, scholars have analyzed the phrase in an attempt to determine its significance. Some have concluded that Greene was charging Shakespeare with plagiarism. This has been the view of many scholars from Edmund Malone to Dover Wilson, who have used Greene's attack to support the thesis that certain of Shakespeare's plays, chiefly the Henry VI trilogy, were his revisions of plays originally written by Greene and others. This position was dominant during the last years of the 19th century and the first two decades of the 20th century, particularly among those who held the so-called disintegrationist view of the Shakespeare canon. See DISINTEGRATION.

The plagiarism argument as advanced by Dover Wilson has a threefold basis: the first is the apology that Henry Chettle, Greene's editor, delivered in the epistle to Chettle's own *Kind-Harts Dreame*, published shortly after the *Groats-worth:*

About three moneths since died M. *Robert Greene,* leauing many papers in sundry Booke sellers hands, among other his Groatsworth of wit, in which a letter written to diuers play-makers, is offensiuely by one or two of them taken; and because on the dead they cannot be auenged, they wilfully forge in their conceites a liuing Author: . . . With neither of them that take offence was I acquainted, and with one of them I care not if I neuer be: The other, whome at that time I did not so much spare, as since I wish I had, for that as I haue moderated the heate of liuing writers, and might have vsed my owne discretion (especially in such a case) the Author beeing dead, that I did not, I am as sory as if the originall fault had beene my fault, because my selfe haue seene his demeanor no lesse ciuill than he exelent in the qualitie he professes: Besides, diuers of worship haue reported his uprightnes of dealing, which argues his honesty, and his facetious grace in writting, that aproues his Art.

The fact that Chettle's vindication of Shakespeare, if indeed it is Shakespeare he is referring to, stressed the poet's "honesty" is cited as evidence that Greene was charging Shakespeare with plagiarism.

The second point is that "R. B.," the author of GREENE'S FUNERALLS, published in February 1594, made an apparent reference to the plagiarizing of Greene's work. The third argument advanced by Wilson traces the term "crow" back to Horace's *Epistles* where it was used with the implication of plagiarism.

Despite the cogency of these arguments, most modern scholars, including W. W. Greg, Peter Alexander, and E. K. Chambers, have seen in Greene's charges, not an accusation of plagiarism, but merely an assertion that Greene considered Shakespeare presumptuous in fancying himself a writer. The latter group of critics have pointed out that while Chettle may have interpreted Greene's charge as plagiarism, it does not necessarily follow that it actually was. They have also suggested that R. B.'s lines in *Greene's Funeralls* referred, not to Shakespeare, but to Gabriel Harvey, who had slandered Greene while capitalizing on his name. [J. Dover Wilson, "Malone and the Upstart Crow," *Shakespeare Survey 4,* 1951; Warren B. Austin, "A Supposed Contemporary Allusion to Shakespeare as a Plagiarist," *Shakespeare Quarterly,* VI, 1955.]

grooms of the chamber. See ACTORS.

Groto, Luigi (1541–1585). Italian dramatist and poet. Groto is the author of *La Hadriana* (1578), a tragedy which retells the story of *Romeo and Juliet.* There is some slight evidence to indicate that Shakespeare may have known Groto's play, but it is unlikely that it served as one of the sources of his own.

groundlings. See AUDIENCES.

Grumio. In *The Taming of the Shrew,* one of Petruchio's servants. Grumio describes his master and Katharina's trip from Padua to the country in a humorous speech in IV, i.

Guiderius. In *Cymbeline,* the King's elder son. Guiderius is kidnapped with his brother, Arviragus, by Belarius and reared as Belarius' son under the name of Polydore. Guiderius is an outstanding product of his rugged environment but with the difference that he has royal blood in his veins. When this noble savage is set against the barbaric nobleman, Cloten, in an ironic confrontation between the true heir to the throne and the would-be usurper, Guiderius remains unimpressed by his antagonist's rank and kills him.

There is an element of simplicity run rampant in his proposal to throw the severed head into a creek "and tell the fishes he's the Queen's son, Cloten." The same is true when he announces, "I have sent Cloten's clotpoll down the stream in embassy to his mother." [Harley Granville-Barker, "Cymbeline," in *Prefaces to Shakespeare*, 1946.]

Guido delle Colonne (1215?–?1290). Italian poet and translator. Guido's Latin adaptation, *Historia Troiana* (1287), of the French poem *Roman de Troie* was one of the sources of Chaucer's *Troilus and Criseyde*. Chaucer's poem is one of the chief sources of Shakespeare's *Troilus and Cressida*.

Guildenstern. See ROSENCRANTZ AND GUILDENSTERN.

Guildford, Sir **Henry** (1489–1532). Master of the horse to Henry VIII. In *Henry VIII*, Guildford is controller of the royal household and greets the guests of Wolsey (I, iv).

Guinness, Sir **Alec** (1914–). Actor. Sir Alec was born in London, studied for the stage at Fay Compton's Studio of Dramatic Art, and made his debut in 1934 at the Playhouse. His earliest Shakespearean roles were Osric and the Third Player in *Hamlet* and Sampson and the Apothecary in *Romeo and Juliet* (1935). In 1936/7 he joined the Old Vic, taking the roles of Boyet, Le Beau, William, Osric, Aguecheek, and Exeter. In 1937 he played Osric at Elsinore with the Old Vic, and then joined Gielgud's company in the roles of Aumerle and the Groom (*Richard II*) and Lorenzo (*The Merchant of Venice*). He rejoined the Old Vic the following year to play Hamlet. He played the Chorus in *Henry V* and Hamlet again on the Old Vic's tour of the continent and Egypt in 1939, and Romeo in Perth in the same year. Guinness has also portrayed Ferdinand, Lear's Fool, Richard II, Menenius Agrippa, Richard III, and the King in *All's Well That Ends Well*. In 1948 he produced *Twelfth Night* for the Old Vic and played and directed *Hamlet* in 1951. His film roles include many memorable portrayals. He was knighted in 1959. [*Who's Who in the Theatre*, 1961.]

Guls Horne-booke. A pamphlet by Thomas DEKKER first published in 1609. A satiric portrait of a provincial young man who comes to London to make his mark, *Guls Horne-booke* provides a lively and detailed portrait of Jacobean London. Dekker's ironic account of the way to behave in the playhouse affords one of the best, if somewhat exaggerated, descriptions of the behavior of the young gallants who sat on the stage in the public theatres and made themselves a general nuisance:

> By spreading your body on the stage, and by being a Justice in examining of plaies, you shall put your selfe into such true *Scaenical* authority, that some Poet shall not dare to present his Muse rudely vpon your eyes, without hauing first vnmaskt her, rifled her, and discouered all her bare and most mysticall parts before you at a Tauerne, when you most knightly shal for his paines, pay for both their suppers.
>
> By sitting on the stage, you may (with small cost) purchase the deere acquaintance of the boyes: haue a good stoole for sixpence: at any time know what particular part any of the infants present: get your match lighted, examine the play-suits lace, and perhaps win wagers vpon laying tis copper, &c. . . .
>
> Now sir, if the writer be a fellow that hath either epigramd you, or hath had a flirt at your mistris, or hath brought either your feather or your red beard, or your little legs, &c. on the stage, you shall disgrace him worse then by tossing him in a blancket, or giuing him the bastinado in a Tauerne, if, in the middle of his play (bee it Pastoral or Comedy, Morall or Tragedie), you rise with a skreud and discontented face from your stoole to be gone: no matter whether the Scenes be good or no, the better they are the worse do you distast them: and, beeing on your feet, sneake not away like a coward, but salute all your gentle acquaintance, that are spred either on the rushes, or on stooles about you, and draw what troope you can from the stage after you: the *Mimicks* are beholden to you, for allowing them elbow roome: their Poet cries perhaps a pox go with you, but care not you for that, theres no musick without frets.

[E. K. Chambers, *The Elizabethan Stage*, 1923.]

Gunpowder Plot (1605). An attempt on the part of a group of Roman Catholic conspirators to blow up the English parliament. The plot was conceived and directed by Robert Catesby, a native of Warwickshire and a distant relative of Shakespeare (see CATESBY FAMILY). The conspiracy had begun as early as 1603 as a result of increased government repression against Catholics at that time. Other leading members of the conspiracy included Guy Fawkes, a professional soldier, and Thomas Percy, who had been a friend of the earl of Essex and who was the second cousin of Henry Percy, 9th earl of Northumberland. The conspirators rented a vault directly underneath the house of lords where they stored 36 barrels of gunpowder. The plan was to blow up the house of lords on the opening day of parliament, November 5, 1605, when the king would be in attendance. Shortly before the designated day, however, one of the conspirators revealed the plot to Lord Monteagle in order to prevent his appearance in parliament on that day. Monteagle informed the government authorities and the plotters were apprehended and executed.

Leslie Hotson has shown that a number of the conspirators, including Catesby, were natives of the area around Stratford and habitués of the Mermaid Tavern in London. Shakespeare undoubtedly knew some of them. J. Dover Wilson believes that the line in Sonnet 124 alluding to ". . . the fools of time, / Which die for goodness, that have lived for crime" is a reference to the conspirators. A more generally accepted allusion is the reference in *Macbeth* (II, iii, 12) to the trial of Henry Garnet, a Jesuit priest implicated in the plot although not himself a conspirator. See EQUIVOCATION. [Leslie Hotson, *I, William Shakespeare*, 1937; J. Dover Wilson, *An Introduction to the Sonnets of Shakespeare*, 1964.]

Gurney, James. In *King John*, a servant to Lady Faulconbridge (I, i).

Guthrie, Sir **[William] Tyrone** (1900–). Director. Born at Tunbridge Wells, Guthrie was educated at Oxford. In 1924 he made his first professional appearance in repertory at Oxford, and in 1926 began directing the Scottish National Players. He also had directorial engagements at the Cambridge Festival in 1929/30. His first London production was in 1931, and he directed at the Old Vic in 1933/4 and gain in 1936. From 1939 to 1945 he acted as administrator of the Old Vic. After resigning from the Old Vic, Guthrie displayed amazing directorial versatility, staging everything from classical plays to operas and musical comedies all over the world. He has directed *The Taming of the Shrew* (Helsingfors, 1949; Stratford, Ontario, 1954); *Hamlet* (Dublin, 1950); *A Midsummer Night's Dream* (Old Vic, 1952); *Henry VIII* (Old Vic, 1953); *All's Well That Ends Well* (Stratford, Ontario, 1953; Shakespeare Memorial Theatre, Stratford-upon-Avon, 1959); *Troilus and Cressida* (New York and London for the Old Vic, 1956); *Twelfth Night* (Stratford, Ontario, 1957); and *The Merchant of Venice* (Habimah Theatre, Israel, 1959). Guthrie was knighted in 1961. He founded the Tyrone Guthrie Theater in Minneapolis in 1963. [*Who's Who in the Theatre*, 1961.]

Guy of Warwick. An anonymous play published in 1661, possibly the same play entered in the Stationers' Register in 1620 as *The Life and Death of Guy of Warwick*. Alfred Harbage has suggested that the play might be dated as early as 1593, a theory which if true lends particular interest to a passage in Act V in which the character Sparrow describes himself as a native of Stratford:

Sparrow. I faith Sir I was born in England at Stratford upon Avon in Warwickshire.
Rainborne. . . . What's thy name?
Sparrow. Nay I have a fine finical name, I can tell ye . . .

If Harbage's theory concerning the early date of *Guy of Warwick* could be proved, it would seem at least probable that the character who is a native of Stratford and the possessor of a "fine finical name" is a satiric portrait of Shakespeare. Shakespeare alludes to the adventures of Guy of Warwick and his servant, Philip Sparrow, in *King John* (I, i, 225–232). [Alfred Harbage, "A Contemporary Attack Upon Shakespeare?" *Shakespeare Association Bulletin*, XVI, 1941; *King John*, New Arden Edition, E. A. J. Honigmann, ed., 1954.]

Gwinne or **Gwynne, Matthew** (c. 1558–1627). Physician and dramatist. Gwinne was for many years associated with Oxford University where he took part in a number of performances and festivals in honor of visiting nobility. An author of several academic plays in Latin, Gwinne was friendly with many literary figures, particularly John Florio. On August 27, 1605 James I visited Oxford where he listened to a debate between Gwinne and another physician on such topics as the beneficial effects of tobacco and whether a baby might derive its morals from the milk of its nurse. In the evening James attended a performance of a brief playlet, *Tres Sibyllae*, written both in Latin and in English by Gwinne, in which three sibyls predict "an empire without end" to the descendants of Banquo. The playlet was designed to flatter James, who was inordinately proud of his ancestry, which he traced back to Banquo (see MACBETH: *Sources*). Shakespeare either attended this performance or, as is more possible, heard a report of it and was then able to incorporate this element in *Macbeth*. [H. N. Paul, *The Royal Play of Macbeth*, 1950.]

H

Haberdasher. In *The Taming of the Shrew,* a minor speaking role in IV, iii. To torment Katharina, Petruchio has the Haberdasher show her a fine hat but, calling it ugly, Petruchio refuses to let her have it.

Hackett Family. American actors and managers. ***James Henry Hackett*** (1800–1871) was born in New York and spent a year at Columbia University. Later, failing in the grocery business, he followed his wife, a former singer, on the stage. They appeared unsuccessfully in 1826 in New York, but his later imitations of actors and miscellaneous characters delighted the public in New York, though not in London. In 1828 he played Falstaff in *1 Henry IV* for the first time, and, in search of novelty, added a dramatization of Rip Van Winkle. He also began offering prizes for original American dramas. Later appearances in London established him as one of the prime interpreters of Falstaff, though he was inadequate as Lear and Hamlet. Although Joseph Jefferson in his *Autobiography* (1890) called the elder Hackett an amateur, he was effective as a dry, sardonic Falstaff, and although he was at his best portraying native American character types—realistic, broadly humorous, and crude—he had a lifelong interest in Shakespeare. In 1863 he published *Notes and Comments upon Certain Plays and Actors of Shakespeare, with Criticisms and Correspondence;* the correspondence was with John Quincy Adams.

Hackett's son by his second wife, ***James Keteltas Hackett*** (1869–1926), was born in Ontario and educated at the College of the City of New York. He abandoned law for the stage, making his debut in 1892 as an amateur. After a short stint in Philadelphia, he joined Daly's company and appeared in *The Taming of the Shrew* and *Twelfth Night.* In 1894 he managed his own touring company and in 1897 played a scene from *Romeo and Juliet* with Olga Nethersole as Juliet. He joined Maude Adams' company in 1899 as Mercutio. In 1914 he played Othello on tour and in 1916 produced *Macbeth* with himself in the title role in New York. He made his first London appearance in 1920, also as Macbeth, following this with a visit to Paris. In 1922 he played Othello at Stratford-upon-Avon. [*Who's Who in the Theatre*, 1925; *Dictionary of American Biography*, 1927– .]

Hakluyt, Richard (1552?–1616). Clergyman and geographer. While still a student at Oxford, Hakluyt read widely in the field of travel and exploration. In 1582 he dedicated to Sir Philip Sidney his *Divers Voyages Touching the Discovery of America,* written with the hope of stimulating English colonization for both commercial and religious reasons. From 1583 to 1588, while serving as chaplain to the English ambassador at Paris, Hakluyt began his extensive collection of English voyages which he published under the title *The principall Navigations, Voiages and Discoveries of the English nation, made by Sea or over Land, to the most remote and farthest distant Quarters of the earth* (1589). He later expanded the work to three volumes (1598–1600). After his death in 1616 Hakluyt's manuscripts passed into the hands of Samuel Purchas who included them in his *Pilgrims* (1625). Publication of similar voyages was resumed with the founding of the Hakluyt Society in 1846. Hakluyt's accounts are imbued with the spirit of English nationalism and Protestant missionary zeal, a fact which led J. A. Froude to term the *Navigations* "the prose epic of the English nation." Among the voyages printed by Purchas was William Strachey's "A True Account of the Wrack," a report of the shipwreck of the *Sea Venture* in Bermuda in 1609. Strachey's letter has been mentioned as a source for *The Tempest* (see THE TEMPEST: *Sources*). The manuscript circulated among Shakespeare's friends who could have easily shown it to him. Shakespeare seems to have drawn upon Strachey for the opening scene and for miscellaneous facts and suggestions elsewhere. [J. A. Froude, *History of England from the Fall of Wolsey to the Death of Elizabeth,* 12 vols., 1856–1870.]

Hal. Nickname of **Henry, Prince of Wales.** Son of Henry IV by Mary de Bohun; in *1* and *2 Henry IV,* "the madcap Prince of Wales." (For historical background, see HENRY V, King of England.) Hal's scapegrace existence as boon companion to FALSTAFF belies his underlying seriousness and pragmatic grasp of the realities of political power. These paradoxical elements of Hal's character have elicited a wide variety of responses from readers and actors, ranging from unqualified acceptance of the Prince as a paragon of kingly virtue to a total repudiation of him as a hypocritical Machiavellian devoid of genuine human emotion. The wide disparity of views rests on the famous rejection of Falstaff at the end of *2 Henry IV.* Hal's disparagers assert that only a Puritan moralist of the type that wished to suppress all plays could approve Hal's callous dismissal of the old knight at the end of *2 Henry IV:*

> I know thee not, old man: fall to thy prayers;
> How ill white hairs become a fool and jester!
>
> . . . . .

Reply not to me with a fool-born jest:
Presume not that I am the thing I was;
For God doth know, so shall the world perceive,
That I have turn'd away my former self.
(V, v, 51–52, 59–62)

Hal's defenders argue that the tears shed for Falstaff are those of the modern sentimentalist, not of Shakespeare and his audience. For, they assert, the subjects of Queen Elizabeth invested the notion of kingship with an awesome solemnity that precluded the possibility of simple human choice. They cite the example of Elizabeth herself, who rejected, despite her personal inclinations, a number of "Falstaffs"—notably the earls of Leicester and Essex—because she recognized the potentially disastrous consequences of placing royal authority in their hands. Another argument in their favor is that in Hal the Elizabethans recognized the figure who was to emerge in their eyes as England's greatest and most heroic king. See HENRY IV: *Comment.*

Nevertheless, such notably unsentimental figures as George Bernard Shaw, William Butler Yeats, and E. E. Stoll are among Hal's detractors. Shaw describes him as "an able young Philistine"; Yeats views him as an exemplar of the doctrine that "the commonplace shall inherit the earth . . ."; and Stoll, who argues that Shakespeare was deliberately undercutting the popular Elizabethan view of Henry V, calls attention to "his bragging, his priggishness and cant."

More recent criticism has tended to view the problem of Falstaff's rejection less in terms of Hal's character than as a manifestation of the archetypal structure of the play. Thus Falstaff has been seen as the expression of the spirit of Misrule, whose ultimate conversion into a scapegoat figure is an inevitable condition of the underlying ritualistic pattern of the play (see MYTHIC CRITICISM). A similar though less controversial view is one which presents Falstaff as a development of the figure in medieval drama known as Riot, who attempts to lead youth astray, is successful for a while, but is ultimately rejected. From another standpoint, the conflict between Hal and Falstaff is the outgrowth of the opposing values of the dramatic genres of comedy and history.

These latter perspectives, however, direct the problem away from the character of the Prince, thereby failing to resolve Shakespeare's underlying attitude toward Hal himself. He is clearly presented, at least in some aspects, as an admirable figure. What is less clear is the nature and extent of his limitations and flaws. One resolution that raises more questions than it answers is William Empson's brilliant suggestion that Sonnet 94 ("They that have power to hurt") might serve as a gloss on the Hal-Falstaff relationship. The difficulty here is that the same ambivalent attitude toward the wielders of power ("That do not do the thing they most do show, / Who, moving others, are themselves as stone") is evidenced in the poem as is present in the play. [A. C. Bradley, "The Rejection of Falstaff," in *Oxford Lectures on Poetry*, 1909; William Empson, *Some Versions of Pastoral*, 1935; *1 Henry IV:* New Variorum Edition, S. B. Hemingway, ed., 1936; J. Dover Wilson, *The Fortunes of Falstaff*, 1943; John Palmer, *Political Characters of Shakespeare*, 1945; C. L. Barber, *Shakespeare's Festive Comedy*, 1959; Jonas Barish, "The Turning Away of Hal," address before the Modern Language Association of America, December 28, 1964.]—E. Q.

Hales, Bartholomew (fl. 1560–1580). Owner of the manor in Snitterfield occupied by Richard Shakespeare, the grandfather of the poet. Hales assumed ownership of the property about 1560. He is also indirectly connected with Shakespeare through his relationship with the Arden family. In 1580 he served as an agent of the local court by taking the testimony of Agnes Arden, the widow of Robert Arden, Shakespeare's maternal grandfather, in a property dispute. See Thomas MAYOWE.

Hales, John, of Eton (1584–1656). Scholar and divine. Born in Bath and educated at Oxford, where he was a distinguished student of Greek and philosophy, Hales was made a fellow of Eton in 1613. He published numerous sermons and polemical tracts directed against the Puritans. An anecdote concerning Hales and Shakespeare was repeated at the end of the 17th century in a number of versions, among which were those by John Dryden, Nahum Tate, Charles Gildon, and Nicholas Rowe. The story as given by Rowe involves Hales' rebuking of Ben Jonson:

> In a Conversation between Sir *John Suckling*, Sir William *D'Avenant*, *Endymion Porter*, Mr. *Hales of Eaton*, and *Ben Johnson;* Sir *John Suckling*, who was a profess'd admirer of *Shakespear*, had undertaken his Defence against *Ben Johnson* with some warmth; Mr. *Hales*, who had sat still for some time, hearing *Ben* frequently reproaching him with the want of Learning, and Ignorance of the Antients, told him at last, That if Mr. *Shakespear* had not read the Antients, he had likewise not stollen any thing from 'em; (a Fault the other made no Conscience of) and that if he would produce any one Topick finely treated by any of them, he would undertake to shew something upon the same Subject at least as well written by *Shakespear*.

[E. K. Chambers, *William Shakespeare*, 1930.]

Hales, John Wesley (1836–1914). Scholar. Professor of English at King's College, London, Hales prepared textbooks and edited for school use works by such authors as Malory, Spenser, Milton, Gray, Goldsmith, Thomas Percy, and Johnson. He served as general editor of the 10-volume *Handbooks of English Literature* (1895–1903) and wrote the Introduction to the first volume in that series, *The Age of Shakespeare* by Thomas Seccombe and J. W. Allen. Hales also contributed literary essays on a variety of topics to general periodicals. Several on Shakespeare were collected and published under the title *Essays and Notes on Shakespeare* (1884).

Hall, Arthur, of Grantham (c. 1540–1604). Translator and politician. A ward of William Cecil, Lord Burghley, Hall had an early introduction to politics. He served in parliament from 1571 to 1581, but was expelled in the latter year for "lewd speaking." Hall's *Ten Books of Homers Iliades, translated out of French* was published in 1581. The first English translation of Homer, Hall's work was translated from the French version of Hugues Salel. Hall's translation may have been one of the sources of *Troilus and Cressida*, although it is more probable that Shakespeare used George Chapman's infinitely superior translation.

Hall, Edward. See Edward HALLE.

Hall, Elizabeth (1608–1670). Shakespeare's granddaughter, the only child of John Hall and Shakespeare's daughter Susanna. Elizabeth was born on February 8, 1608 and was christened three weeks later on the 28th. In his will Shakespeare bequeathed her all of his plate. In 1626 she married Thomas Nash, the son of Shakespeare's friend Anthony Nash. (See NASH FAMILY.) After her father's death in 1635, Elizabeth and her husband went to live with her mother at New Place. Her husband died in 1647; in his will he left to his cousin, Edward Nash, New Place and other property of the Shakespeare inheritance which had passed to Elizabeth. The will was contested by Susanna and Elizabeth who apparently succeeded in retaining control of the property. On June 5, 1649 Elizabeth married John, later Sir John, BERNARD. Shortly thereafter her mother died and she left New Place to live at Bernard's ancestral estate in Abington, where she died in 1670. There were no children from either of her two marriages. On April 18, 1653 she made a deed offering for sale the Shakespeare property to persons she might nominate at a future date. In her will of January 29, 1670 she stipulated that after the decease of her husband, the property was to be offered to her cousin Edward Nash or to her "kinsman" Edward Bagley. The will is reprinted below:

> In the name of God, Amen, I, Dame Elizabeth Barnard, wife of Sir John Barnard of Abington in the county of Northampton, knight, being in perfect memory,—blessed be God!—and mindfull of mortallity, doe make this my last will and testament in manner and forme following. Whereas by my certaine deed or writeing under my hand and seale dated on or about the eighteenth day of Aprill, 1653, according to a power therein mencioned, I, the said Elizabeth, have lymitted and disposed of all that my messuage with th'appurtenances in Stratford-upon-Avon, in the county of Warwicke, called the New Place, and all that foure yard land and a halfe in Stratford, Welcombe and Bishopton in the county of Warwick, after the decease of the said Sir John Barnard and me, the said Elizabeth, unto Henry Smith of Stratford aforesaid, gent., and Job Dighton of the Middle Temple, London, esquire, sithence deceased, and their heires, upon trust that they and the survivor of them, and the heirs of such survivor, should bargaine and sell the same for the best value they can gett, and the money thereby to be raised to bee imployed and disposed of to such person and persons, and in such manner, as I, the said Elizabeth, should by any writing or note under my hand, truly testified declare and nominate, as thereby may more fully appeare. Now my will is, and I doe hereby signifie and declare my mynd and meaning to bee that the said Henry Smith, my surviving trustee, or his heires, shall with all convenient speed after the decease of the said Sir John Bernard, my husband, make sale of the inheritance of all and singuler the premisses, and that my loving cousin, Edward Nash, esq., shall have the first offer or refusall thereof according to my promise formerly made to him; and the moneys to be raised by such sale I doe give, dispose of and appoint, the same to be paid and distributed as is hereinafter expressed, that is to say, to my cousin Thomas Welles of Carleton, in the county of Bedford, gent., the somme of fifty pounds to be paid him within one yeare next after such sale; and if the said Thomas Welles shall happen to dye before such time as his said legacy shall become due to him, then my desire is that my kinsman, Edward Bagley, cittizen of London, shall have the sole benefitt thereof. Item, I doe give and appoint unto Judith Hathaway, one of the daughters of my kinsman, Thomas Hathaway, late of Stratford aforesaid, the annuall somme of five pounds of lawfull money of England, to be paid unto her yearely and every year from and after the decease of the survivor of the said Sir John Bernard and me, the said Elizabeth, for and during the natural life of her, the said Judith, att the two most usuall feasts or dayes of payment in the yeare, videlicet, the feast of the Annunciacion of the Blessed Virgin Mary and St. Michaell the Archangell, by equall porcions, the first payment thereof to beginne at such of the said feasts as shall next happen after the decease of the survivor of the said Sir John Bernard and me the said Elizabeth, if the said premisses can be soe soone sold, or otherwise soe soone as the same can be sold; and if the said Judith shall happen to marry, and shal be mynded to release the said annuall somme of five pound, and shall accordingly release and quitt all her interest and right in and to the same after it shall become due to her, then and in such case I doe give and appoynte to her the somme of forty pounds in liew thereof, to bee paid unto her at the tyme of the executing of such release as aforesaid. Item, I give and appointe unto Joane, the wife of Edward Kent, and one other of the daughters of the said Thomas Hathaway, the somme of fifty pounds to be likewise paid unto her within one yeare next after the decease of the survivor of the said Sir John Bernard and me the said Elizabeth, if the said premisses can be soe soone sold, or otherwise soe soone as the same can bee sold and if the said Johan shall happen to die before the said fiftie pounds shal be paid to her, then I doe give and appoynt the same unto Edward Kent, the younger, her sonne, to be paid unto him when he shall attayne the age of one-and-twenty yeares. Item, I doe alsoe give and appoynt unto him, the said Edward Kent, sonne of the said Johan, the somme of thirty pounds towards putting him out as an apprentice, and to be paid and disposed of to that use when he shall be fitt for it. Item, I doe give, appoynte, and dispose of unto Rose, Elizabeth and Susanna, three other of the daughters of my said kinsman, Thomas Hathaway, the somme of fortie pounds a-peece to be paid unto every of them at such tyme and in such manner as the said fiftie pounds before appointed to the said Johan Kent, their sister, shall become payable. Item, all the rest of the moneys that shal be raised by such sale as aforesaid I give and dispose of unto my said trustee, Henry Smith, for his paines; and if the said Edward Nash shall refuse the purchase of the said messuage and foure yard land and a halfe with the

appurtenances, then my will and desire is that the said Henry Smith, or his heires, shall sell the inheritance of the said premisses and every part thereof unto the said Edward Bagley, and that he shall purchase the same; upon this condicion, nevertheles, that he, the said Edward Bagley, his heyres, executors or administrators, shall justly and faithfully performe my will and true meaning in making due payment of all the severall sommes of money or legacies before-mencioned in such manner as aforesaid. And I doe hereby declare my will and meaning to be that the executors or administrators of my said husband, Sir John Bernard, shall have and enjoy the use and benefit of my said house in Stratford, called the New Place, with the orchard, gardens and all other thappurtenances thereto belonging, for and dureing the space of six monthes next after the decease of him, the said Sir John Bernard. Item, I give and devise unto my kinsman, Thomas Hart, the sonne of Thomas Hart, late of Stratford-upon-Avon aforesaid, all they my other messuage or inne, situate in Stratford-upon-Avon aforesaid, commonly called the Maydenhead, with the appurtenances, and the next house thereunto adjoyning, with the barne belonging to the same now or late in the occupacion of Michaell Johnson or his assignes, with all and singuler the appurtenances, to hold to him, the said Thomas Hart, the sonne and the heires of his body; and for default of such issue, I give and devise the same to George Hart, brother of the said Thomas Hart, and to the heires of his body; and for default of such issue, to the right heires of me, the said Elizabeth Bernard, for ever. Item, I doe make, ordayne, and appoynte my said loving kinsman, Edward Bagley, sole executor of this, my last will and testament, hereby revokeing all former wills; desireing him to see a just performance hereof according to my true intent and meaning. In witnes whereof I, the said Elizabeth Bernard, have hereunto sett my hand and seal the nyne-and-twentieth day of January, anno domini one thousand six hundred sixty-nyne.—Elizabeth Barnard.—Signed, sealed, published and declared to be the last will and testament of the said Elizabeth Bernard, in the presence of—John Howes, rector de Abington, Francis Wickes.

[J. O. Halliwell-Phillipps, *Outlines of the Life of Shakespeare*, 1881.]

Hall, John (1575–1635). Physician who married Shakespeare's elder daughter, Susanna, in 1607. The son of a medical practitioner, Hall attended Queens College, Cambridge. After graduation in 1597 he studied medicine in France, returning to England in 1600 where he established a practice at Stratford. Seven years later he married Susanna SHAKESPEARE, who bore him a daughter, Elizabeth, in 1608.

Hall was a prosperous and highly regarded physician. His medical notes, written in Latin, on the illnesses of the patients he attended were translated into English and published in 1657 as *Select Observations on English Bodies*. The translator, James Cooke, in his Introduction describes Hall as a physician who won "great fame for his skill, far and near."

Hall was also noted for his intense interest in religious matters. He was the staunch friend and asso-

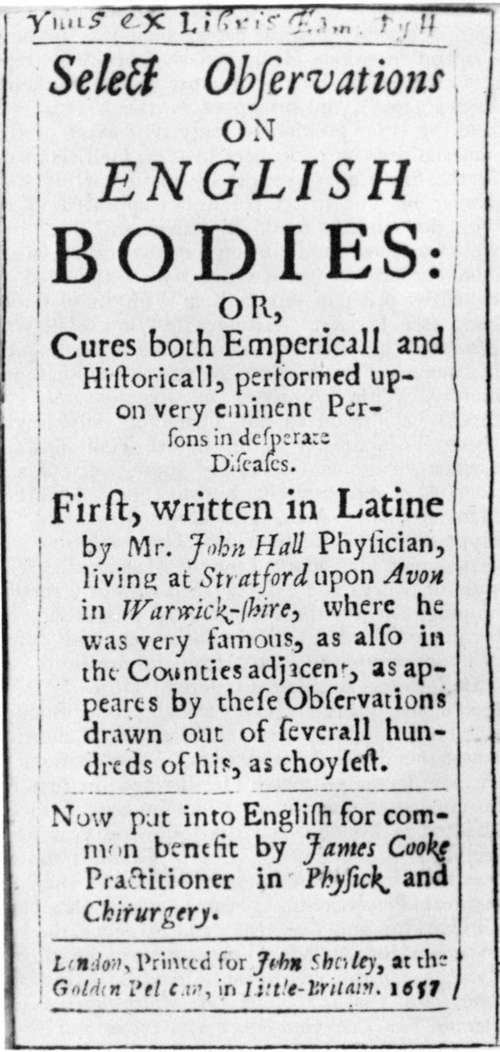

Select Obſervations
ON
ENGLISH
BODIES:
OR,
Cures both Empericall and Hiſtoricall, performed upon very eminent Perſons in deſperate Diſeaſes.

Firſt, written in Latine by Mr. *John Hall* Phyſician, living at *Stratford* upon *Avon* in *Warwick-ſhire*, where he was very famous, as alſo in the Counties adjacent, as appeares by theſe Obſervations drawn out of ſeverall hundreds of his, as choyſeſt.

Now put into Engliſh for common benefit by *James Cooke* Practitioner in *Phyſick* and *Chirurgery*.

London, Printed for *John Sherley*, at the *Golden Pelican*, in *Little-Britain*. 1657

TITLE PAGE OF HALL'S *Select Observations* (1657).

ciate of Thomas Wilson, a Stratford preacher of strong Puritan sympathies. Hall's Puritanism, however, is not easily reconciled with his wife's apparently Catholic leanings (see RECUSANCY).

Hall and his wife, who occupied New Place after Shakespeare's death, are generally regarded as the literary executors of Shakespeare's will, and it has been suggested on no substantial basis other than Hall's Puritanism that he may have destroyed any Shakespearean manuscripts that were in his possession. In his own will, made in 1635, Hall left his "study of Books" and his manuscripts to his son-in-law Thomas Nash.

R. R. Simpson's recent study of Shakespeare's use of medical terms concludes that "there is no evidence that Hall influenced the medical references to be found in the plays of Shakespeare, [but] there is some evidence to suggest that, in the portrayal of doctors as doctors in the plays, Shakespeare might have been influenced by . . . his own doctor son-in-law." [Simpson, *Shakespeare and Medicine*, 1959.]

Hall, Joseph (1574–1656). Churchman and author. During his ecclesiastical career Hall was appointed chaplain to Prince Henry (1608), the king's representative at the Synod of Dort (1618), bishop of Exeter (1627), and bishop of Norwich (1641). He held the latter position for only two years, until his impeachment by parliament in 1643. Hall claimed to be the first English satirist by reason of his *Virgidemiarum.* The first three books appeared in 1597 with the subtitle "toothless satires" and three more were published the following year as "biting satires." The outburst of verse satire which followed was halted by order of Archbishop Whitgift of Canterbury (see JUVENAL). Around this time Hall wrote *Mundus Alter et Idem* (1605), a Latin burlesque of the themes of the fabulous voyage and utopian community. With *Characters of Vertues and Vices* (1608) he introduced the "character" into English. Using Theophrastus as his model, Hall illustrated various virtues and vices by short, self-contained sketches of representative human types—An Honest Man, A Happy Man, The Good Magistrate, The Hypocrite, The Vainglorious, The Ambitious, The Malcontent. Hall adopted the then-fashionable "curt" style of Seneca and used neo-Stoicism as a standard of judgment. As the 17th century progressed, Hall became involved in religious controversy; his defense of episcopacy drew attacks from John Milton.

Hall, Peter [Reginald Frederick] (1930–). Director and manager. Hall was born at Bury-St.-Edmunds, Suffolk, and educated at Cambridge, where he directed more than 20 productions for various dramatic groups. He directed his first professional production in 1953 in Windsor; in 1955 he directed in London, and the following year he directed a production of *Love's Labour's Lost* at Stratford-upon-Avon. In 1957 he formed the International Playwrights' Theatre, which has given *Camino Real* and *The Moon and Sixpence*, the latter an opera for Sadler's Wells. In 1957 he directed *Cymbeline* at the Shakespeare Memorial Theatre and, later, also *Twelfth Night, A Midsummer Night's Dream, The Two Gentlemen of Verona*, and *Troilus and Cressida.* In January 1960 he was appointed director of the Royal Shakespeare Company at the Stratford Memorial Theatre. [*Who's Who in the Theatre*, 1961.]

Hall, William. Stationer's assistant and Sidney Lee's candidate for the MR. W. H. of the *Sonnets.* Lee identifies him with the W. H. who was active during the 1590's and early 1600's in securing manuscripts for London publishers; for example, this W. H. was responsible for procuring a manuscript (*Foure-fold Meditation*) printed in 1606 as Robert Southwell's, and wrote a dedication to it, signing himself as W. H. Lee identifies this W. H. with Mr. W. H., assuming that the latter procured the *Sonnets* for Thomas Thorpe. Both W. H.'s are identified by Lee with a William Hall who was a printer in 1609.

Hall, William (fl. 1694). Clergyman. The son of a Lichfield innkeeper, Hall was graduated from Queen's College, Oxford, in 1694, and ultimately became prebendary of St. Paul's, London. Upon his graduation from Queen's, however, he wrote a letter (dated January 2, 1694) to a former classmate, Edward Thwaites (1667–1711), in which he described a visit he had made to Shakespeare's tomb at Holy Trinity Church in Stratford. The letter related one version of the famous admonition in the poet's epitaph. For another version, see EPITAPHS. The text of the letter follows:

> Dear Neddy,
>
> I very greedily embraced this occasion of acquainting you with something which I found at Stratford upon Avon. That place I came unto on Thursday night, and ye next day went to visit ye ashes of the Great Shakespear which lye interr'd in that Church. The verses which in his life-time he ordered to be cut upon his tomb-stone (for his Monument have others) are these which follow;
>
> Reader, for Jesus's Sake forbear
> To dig the dust enclosed here:
> Blessed be he that Spares these Stones,
> And cursed be he that moves my bones.
>
> The little learning these verses contain, would be a very strong argument of ye want of it in the Author; did not they carry something in them which stands in need of a comment. There is in this Church a place which they call the bone-house, a repository for all bones they dig up which are so many that they would load a great number of waggons. The Poet being willing to preserve his bones unmoved, lays a curse upon him that moves them; and haveing to do with Clarks and Sextons, for ye most part a very [i]gnorant sort of people, he descends to ye meanest of their capacitys; and disrobes himself of that art, which none of his Co-temporaryes wore in greater perfection. Nor has the design mist of its effect; for lest they should not onely draw this curse upon themselvs, but also entail it upon their posterity, they have laid him full seventeen foot deep, deep enough to secure him . . . .

The "bone-house" or charnel house was formerly located next to the church. It has since been demolished. [E. K. Chambers, *William Shakespeare*, 1930.]

Hallam, Lewis, Jr. (c. 1740–1808). American actor and theatre manager. Lewis Hallam was 12 years old when his family came to the United States as a practically complete acting company. During his first stage appearance, in *The Merchant of Venice*, he panicked. The troupe spent several years in Jamaica and then again visited the United States. As their leading actor, Hallam played what was probably the first Hamlet in America and acted as Romeo to his mother's Juliet. When the elder Hallam died, the company became the American Company, under the direction of David Douglass, who married Hallam's mother. In 1775 Hallam appeared as Hamlet in London. The players returned to the United States in 1785 and gained a following despite accusations of British sympathies. Hallam, at this point in charge of the company with John Hodgkinson, opened the Park Theatre in New York in 1798. [*Dictionary of American Biography*, 1927– .]

Halle or Hall, Edward (c. 1498–1547). Historian. Halle occupied a number of legal and governmental posts under Henry VIII, of whom he was an ardent supporter. Probably at some time about 1530 he began work on his chronicles, completed and published posthumously in 1548 by Richard GRAFTON as *The Union of the Two Noble and Illustre Famelies* *of Lancastre and York.* A number of stylistic inconsistencies in Halle's work have led scholars to conjecture that initially the work was in the nature of a journal of contemporary events to which he was himself an interested spectator. The publication in 1534 of Polydore Vergil's *Anglicae Historiae Libri XXVI,* however, inspired Halle to attempt a full-scale history of England from the reign of Henry IV. His account of the earlier reigns is based on Vergil and is rather undistinguished. Far more interesting is the portion concerning events occurring during the reign of Henry VIII, up to the year 1532.

Halle's chronicle is a good example of the fiercely didactic Renaissance view of history as the "mirror of policy" and "warning to princes." His work was used to some extent by all subsequent Tudor historians, particularly by Raphael Holinshed for the English section of his *Chronicles.* Halle is now recognized as being a more important source than Holinshed for Shakespeare's earlier histories. Alan Keen and Roger Lubbock have asserted in *The Annotator* (1954) that annotations made in a copy of Halle's chronicle are in Shakespeare's handwriting. See William SHAKESHAFTE. [Geoffrey Bullough, *Narrative and Dramatic Sources of Shakespeare,* Vol. III, 1960.]

Halliwell, later **Halliwell-Phillipps, James Orchard** (1820–1899). Bibliophile and scholar. Son of a well-to-do London businessman, Halliwell-Phillipps began collecting books at the age of 15, published his first book at 18, and was elected a fellow of the Royal Society at 19. He studied at Jesus College, Cambridge, and acted as librarian, but in 1840 he left without taking a degree. He then began publishing catalogues of books and manuscripts for various antiquarian societies.

He soon turned his attention to Shakespeare and began his Shakespeare collection; he wrote short monographs on various plays, and published *Shakesperiana* (1841), a catalogue of early editions. Halliwell-Phillipps was the first to make extensive use of the town records at Stratford, presenting much of this material in his *Life of William Shakespeare* (1848). Of his several editions of Shakespeare, the most important were the *Works* (16 vols., 1853–1865), an elaborate edition with notes, critical apparatus, and wood engravings by J. W. Fairholt; the lithographed facsimile of the quartos (48 vols., 1862–1871); and the reduced facsimile of the First Folio (1876). As time went on, he shifted his interest from textual and critical problems to those of historical background. He published several volumes of records and documents relating to Stratford, the bulk of which he incorporated into his *Outlines of the Life of Shakespeare.* He issued a private printing of this book in 1881 and a public edition in the following year, continuing to add new material in subsequent editions; that of 1887 was the last to appear during his lifetime. In 1872 Halliwell-Phillipps added the surname of his first wife to form the compound by which he was known in later years. On the basis of his own experience as a biographer of Shakespeare, Sir Sidney Lee (in the *Dictionary of National Biography*) made the following tribute: "As a biographer of Shakespeare Halliwell deserves well of his country, and his results may for the most part be regarded as final. The few errors detected in his transcription of documents do not detract from the value of his labor." [Justin Winsor, *Halliwelliana: a Bibliography of the Publications of James Orchard Halliwell-Phillipps,* 1881.]

Hamilton, William (1751–1801). Illustrator, history and portrait painter. Hamilton was the second largest contributor to BOYDELL'S SHAKESPEARE GALLERY, with 23 paintings in the collection. A conventional, uninteresting painter, Hamilton's work is marked by a tendency to overdramatic gesture. His scenes from the comedies are brisker than the scenes from the histories, but only "The Discovery of Hermione" from *The Winter's Tale* carries some of the domestic warmth that the dramatic moment requires. [W. M. Merchant, *Shakespeare and the Artist,* 1959.]

Hamlet. The hero of the tragedy that bears his name. Hamlet has inspired more speculation and comment than any other figure in Western literature. A history of the interpretations of his character reads like an account of the development of critical taste and aesthetic theory since the Renaissance. Actors and critics, exploring every possible interpretation within, and occasionally beyond, the borders of sanity, have been unable as yet to answer the challenge—first put forth by Hamlet himself—to "pluck out the heart of my mystery" (III, ii, 382).

The major source of the overwhelming mountain of material on his character is the famous problem of his "delay": Why does Hamlet fail to obey the injunction of the Ghost to avenge his father's murder? This problem was first discussed in the latter part of the 18th century and its echoes are still reverberating. Of the countless explanations offered, the most famous are those associated with the great critical names of Goethe, Coleridge, Bradley, and Freud (see HAMLET: *Selected Criticism*). Goethe suggests that Hamlet is too delicate, too exquisitely sensitive a figure to engage in the bloody business of revenge. Coleridge proposes that Hamlet's overly reflective, intellectual approach to life leaves him unable to engage in any sort of meaningful action ("the native hue of resolution is sicklied o'er with the pale cast of thought"). A. C. Bradley argues that Hamlet's inaction results from a deep-seated melancholy which periodically paralyzes him. The Freudian explanation, most ably presented by Ernest JONES, describes a Hamlet victimized by an Oedipal fixation, unable to kill his uncle because of an intense, unconscious identification of himself with Claudius, the lover of his mother and murderer of his father. While these and other views have gained some acceptance for a time, they have invariably been rejected by succeeding generations as fragmentary or oversimplified.

Although the heaviest emphasis has fallen on the problem of Hamlet's delay, on the ground that it is the key to the solution of his character, there are a number of other perplexing elements in his makeup: his intense self-consciousness, the nature and degree of his antic disposition, his behavior toward Ophelia, and his often-overlooked sardonic wit. All of these and many other features have been cited in the attempt to reduce the complexity and magnitude of his personality to manageable proportions, but a fully comprehensive and definitive synthesis seems to be beyond the ability of even the most talented critics and actors. Then, too, later critics have pointed out the oversimplifications which result when a character is removed from his dramatic context, a practice to which the 19th-century critics were particularly prone. They argue that *Hamlet* must be seen, in Caroline Spurgeon's words, "not as the problem of an individual at all but as something greater and even more mysterious, as a condition . . ."

Thus it becomes necessary to consider Hamlet's character in its relationship to the structure of the entire play, including such elements as imagery and rhetorical design. In the light of these strictures, the most generally accepted view of Hamlet is that of the "scourge and minister," the sacrificial agent whose role it is to redeem the rottenness of Denmark, to set right the time that is out of joint, and whose delay springs from his reluctance to accept the inevitable, tragic consequences of his fate. This approach is particularly favored by those critics who wish to emphasize the mythic experience in the play, thus presenting us with a Hamlet whose prototype can be found in the scapegoat figure of primitive ritual. Here, too, there is nothing like a unanimity of opinion, but there is an awareness that each age manages to find in him its own conception of the tragic hero, an indication that in the figure of Hamlet we are given, in Maynard Mack's words, "a paradigm of the life of man." (For a discussion of Hamlet as Essex, see Robert Devereux, 2nd earl of ESSEX.) [Claude C. Williamson, *Readings on the Character of Hamlet*, 1950.]—E.Q.

The Tragedy of HAMLET,
Prince of Denmark.

Hamlet. A tragedy by Shakespeare.

Text. The play was entered in the Stationers' Register on July 26, 1602: "James Robertes. Entred for his Copie vnder the handes of master Pasfield and master Waterson warden A booke called the Revenge of Hamlett Prince Denmarke as yt was latelie Acted by the Lord Chamberleyne his servantes." There are three different texts of the play: that of the First Quarto (1603), of the Second Quarto (1604), and of the First Folio (1623). The First Quarto was advertised as "The Tragicall Historie of Hamlet Prince of Denmarke By William Shakespeare. As it hath beene diuerse times acted by his Highnesse seruants in the Cittie of London: as also in the two Vniuersities of Cambridge and Oxford, and else-where. At London printed for N. L. [Nicholas Ling] and Iohn Trundell. 1603." The printer was Valentine Simmes. This is a BAD QUARTO, clearly a pirated edition. It differs greatly from the two later, authoritative editions. Its text frequently distorts the meaning and mutilates the verse. The most generally accepted theory of its origin is that it is a MEMORIAL RECONSTRUCTION by the actor who played Marcellus and Lucianus. When his memory failed him, he filled in with scraps of the speeches remembered from other parts of *Hamlet*, or even from the UR-HAMLET.

The Second Quarto is advertised as "The Tragicall Historie of Hamlet, Prince of Denmarke. By William Shakespeare. Newly imprinted and enlarged to almost as much againe as it was, according to the true and perfect Coppie. At London, Printed by I. R. [James Roberts] for N. L. [Nicholas Ling] and are to be sold at his shoppe vnder Saint Dunstons Church in Fleet-street. 1604." This is the longest of the three versions, containing nearly 4000 lines. It was printed partly from a corrected copy of the bad First Quarto, at least for Act I, and partly from Shakespeare's FOUL PAPERS. The copy for the Folio text appears to have been a transcript of the PROMPT-BOOK made, with occasional reference to Q2, by a professional scribe. It is about 200 lines shorter than the Q2 text, eliminating many passages of a philosophizing or moralizing quality, such as the last long soliloquy (IV, iv, 32–66) beginning, "How all occasions do inform against me."

Date. The date of the composition and first performance of *Hamlet* is probably 1601–1602. In his *William Shakespeare*, E. K. Chambers writes, "On the whole, any date from 1598 to the opening week of 1601 seems to me possible." There are two reasons for believing that the play was not written before 1598: it does not appear in Meres' list of plays in his *Palladis Tamia*, published in that year, and the reference to child actors—an "aery of children" (II, ii, 354–355), undoubtedly the Children of the Chapel Royal—could not have been made before 1598, in which year the children's company began acting at the Blackfriars theatre. Furthermore, Shakespeare would hardly have made his slurring reference to the children until sometime between 1599 and 1601, when they were a serious threat to the popularity of the Chamberlain's Men.

The most precise information about the date, however, derives from a marginal note made by Gabriel

THE

Tragicall Hiſtorie of

HAMLET

Prince of Denmarke

By William Shake-ſpeare.

As it hath beene diuerſe times acted by his Highneſſe ſeruants in the Cittie of London : as alſo in the two Vniuerſities of Cambridge and Oxford, and elſe-where

At London printed for N.L. and Iohn Trundell. 1603.

TITLE PAGE OF THE BAD QUARTO (Q1) OF *Hamlet* (1603). (HUNTINGTON LIBRARY)

Harvey in an edition of Chaucer first published in 1598:

> The Earle of Essex much commendes Albions England .... The younger sort takes much delight in Shakespeares Venus, & Adonis: but his Lucrece, & his tragedie of Hamlet, Prince of Denmarke, haue it in them, to please the wiser sort.

Essex was executed in February 1601, and Harvey's reference to him in the present tense in the same passage in which he refers to *Hamlet* is an indication that the play must have been written and performed by that time.

Sources. Shakespeare's immediate source was an earlier English play telling Hamlet's story. Thomas Nashe alludes to it in his *Epistle to the Gentlemen Students of Both Universities,* prefixed to Robert Greene's novel *Menaphon,* 1589. From some of Nashe's phrases we can infer certain facts about this pre-Shakespearean *Hamlet,* now usually called the UR-HAMLET, meaning "original *Hamlet.*" "Yet English *Seneca* read by Candle light," writes Nashe, "yields many good sentences [maxims], as *Blood is a beggar,* and so forth; and if you intreate him faire in a frostie morning, hee will affoord you whole *Hamlets,* I should say handfuls of Tragicall speeches." A punning reference in Nashe's passage to "Seneca's famished followers" imitating "the Kidde in Æsop," makes it probable that Thomas KYD was the author of the *Ur-Hamlet* and the fact that the author has left the trade of noverist (notary) also points to Kyd, for he had been trained to become a notary, his father's profession. Kyd was the author of the enormously popular *Spanish Tragedy* (c. 1589). In *Hamlet* Shakespeare adopts some of the devices that Kyd exploits in his famous work.

The *Ur-Hamlet* must have been well known in London as early as 1589. Philip Henslowe, the famous manager of the Admiral's Company, records a performance of a *Hamlet* on June 11, 1594 at the theatre at Newington Butts, when it was jointly occupied by the Admiral's Men and the Chamberlain's Men. Henslowe failed to mark it "ne" (new), so it was probably old stuff. A sentence in Thomas Lodge's *Wits Miserie, and The World's Madnesse* (1596) makes it certain that the play belonged to the Chamberlain's Men. Lodge describes a devil as looking as pale as "the Vizard of ye ghost which cried so miserably at ye Theatre, like an oister wife, Hamlet, revenge." Since the theatre, up to 1596, was occupied by Shakespeare's company, *Hamlet* was obviously one of its plays.

Some indication of what the *Ur-Hamlet* was like can be gleaned from the extant 17th-century German play DER BESTRAFTE BRUDER-MORD (*Fratricide Punished*), which is apparently derived from Shakespeare's source play. From available evidence it appears that Shakespeare followed the plot of his source fairly closely. It is of some importance to establish the relation of this *Ur-Hamlet* to other parts of the saga. We know that the story was told in primitive Scandinavian times, but we are ignorant of the precise place of its origin and of its wanderings in oral tradition. The name in its Old Norse or Icelandic form, *Amlothi,* first turns up in a fragment of the Prose Edda (c. 1230). "Amele" was a common Scandinavian given name and "Othi" means both "brave in battle" and, later, "mad"; therefore, the feigned madness was probably an important feature of the original story. The Danish historian Saxo Grammaticus (1150?–?1206) was the first to give the folk tale literary form. He introduced it into his *Historiae Danicae* (c. 1200), a pseudohistorical work composed as much of popular legends and folk traditions as of authentic historical material. Even in this early version, the important elements of the plot are much like those of Shakespeare's tragedy. There is the fratricide, the incest, the antic disposition, the hero's relationship to the original of Ophelia, to Horatio, Polonius, Rosencrantz, and Guildenstern. Yet there are important differences. For example, in Saxo everyone knows that Amleth's uncle Feng is the murderer of the youth's father and that Amleth is the foreordained avenger of the crime. In order to protect himself from Feng's threatening designs, Amleth pretends to be an idiot. He eats dirt and talks what superficially seems to be complete nonsense, though beneath its surface there is often hidden a sinister meaning. Another important difference from *Hamlet* is the manner of Amleth's revenge. When he returns from England, where he has married the king's daughter, he finds Feng and his retainers riotously celebrating Amleth's supposed death. Still playing the fool, he gets the celebrators

THE

Tragicall Hiſtorie of

HAMLET,

Prince of Denmarke.

By William Shakeſpeare.

Newly imprinted and enlarged to almoſt as much againe as it was, according to the true and perfect Coppie.

AT LONDON,
Printed by I. R. for N. L. and are to be ſold at his ſhoppe vnder Saint Dunſtons Church in Fleetſtreet. 1604.

TITLE PAGE OF THE GOOD QUARTO (Q2) OF *Hamlet* (1604).

dead drunk, sets fire to the hall, and kills Feng. Then he proclaims himself king of Jutland.

This typically savage tale of Old Norse times appears as one of the "histories" in the fifth volume of François de Belleforest's *Histoires Tragiques, Extraicts des Oeuvres Italiennes de Bandel* (7 vols., 1559–1580). This tale of Hamlet, Belleforest found, not in Bandello, but in Saxo. He expanded the tale a little, the most important addition being the adultery of Amleth's mother and his uncle before the murder. Shakespeare, or possibly the author of the *Ur-Hamlet*, owed something to both Belleforest and Saxo, more to the former than to the latter. An English translation of Belleforest's history, *The Historie of Hamblet* (1608), was slightly influenced by Shakespeare's play.

For certain details of Hamlet's character, Shakespeare used Timothy Bright's *Treatise of Melancholy* (1586). Hamlet's comments on the bibulous Danes apparently echo those in *Pierce Pennilesse* (1592), a pamphlet by Nashe. Polonius' advice to Laertes may be derived from Isocrates' *Ad Demonicum*, a familiar Elizabethan textbook. Certain features of the Ghost and of Ophelia's burial may have been taken from the Catholic burial service. The general debt to MONTAIGNE's *Essais* (1580), though nebulous, may be reflected in the skeptical temper of Hamlet's mind. Finally, the character and career of the earl of Essex may have been the real-life model for Shakespeare's greatest creation.—O.J.C.

Plot Synopsis. Act I. The Ghost of Hamlet, late King of Denmark, has on two successive nights terrified officers guarding the royal castle at Elsinore. Horatio, friend of the younger Hamlet, the dead King's son, joins the watch on the third night. The Ghost appears, but will not speak, and Horatio fears that the apparition bodes ill for Denmark. The kingdom is already on the brink of war. Fortinbras, rash young Prince of Norway, is raising an army with which, it is expected, he will try to recover lands forfeited to Denmark after his father had been killed in battle by the elder Hamlet.

In a room of state, Claudius thanks the assembled courtiers for their acquiescence in his succession to the throne of his brother and in his admittedly hasty marriage to Gertrude, the widowed Queen. Claudius sends emissaries to the aged uncle of Fortinbras, asking him to restrain his nephew. The King and Queen then chide Hamlet: he has been unduly melancholy since the death of his father about two months before. Left alone, the Prince gives vent to a paroxysm of grief and of outrage over his mother's "incestuous" remarriage. When Horatio tells him about the Ghost, Hamlet arranges to stand watch himself.

Hotheaded Laertes, about to return to school in France, warns his sister Ophelia not to give credence to Hamlet's proffers of love; a prince, he says, is not free to choose a wife. Their father Polonius, chief counselor to Claudius and a foolish meddler, gives Laertes some parting advice and forbids Ophelia to meet Hamlet again.

That night on the battlements of the castle the Ghost returns and, drawing Hamlet apart, tells him that he has returned to demand revenge for his death, a foul and unnatural murder. The Prince begs to know the criminal's name, so he may sweep to his revenge. He is horrified when the Ghost tells him that the murderer is Claudius, who had debauched his wife and poured poison in his ear while he slept; the King had died, therefore, without even the opportunity to confess his sins. He appeals to his son not to let the royal bed of Denmark be a couch of lust and "damned incest." Hamlet promises to think of nothing else until he has accomplished his father's wishes.

Act II. Weeks pass, and Hamlet cannot bring himself to act: he does not relish the role of avenger, and is not certain the Ghost is a benevolent spirit. While he awaits an opportunity to confront his uncle, he feigns madness. In this guise he frightens Ophelia, who has dutifully refused to either see him or accept his notes. Polonius tells Claudius that Hamlet's insanity is the "very ecstasy of love"; to prove it, he says he will contrive to have the pair meet where he and the King can spy upon them. Claudius first sends two friends of the Prince, Rosencrantz and Guildenstern, to him to see if they cannot discover the reason for his strange conduct. The King has learned, meanwhile, that his appeal to Norway has been successful. Fortinbras has been deterred and now asks for and receives permission to march through Denmark to attack Poland.

A troupe of players comes to the castle, and Hamlet resolves to have them act before the court a tragedy containing an incident very like the alleged murder of his father. If the King reacts guiltily, Hamlet will know that the Ghost is not an agent of the devil.

Act III. The following day the Prince meets Ophelia and shocks her with wild denunciations of women and marriage. Claudius and Polonius hear the tirade from a hiding place and the King, fearful of what it portends, determines to send Hamlet away. Polonius suggests that the Prince confide in his mother; he proposes a meeting between them, at which he intends to eavesdrop.

When the players present the tragedy, Claudius flees the hall in consternation. He orders Rosencrantz and Guildenstern to take his lunatic nephew to England. Alone, the King tries to pray. Hamlet observes him and, now convinced of his guilt, draws his sword to kill him, but restrains himself, musing ironically that by dispatching the King at prayer, he may send his soul to heaven.

The Prince goes to his mother's chamber and denounces her so ferociously that she cries out in alarm. Polonius, hidden behind the arras, shouts also. Hamlet, believing the spy to be Claudius, stabs through the arras and kills the aged counselor. He renews his scalding indictment of his mother, but the Ghost, unseen by Gertrude, intervenes to remind the Prince of his mission. After begging his mother to repent and warning her not to side against him, Hamlet drags away the body of Polonius.

Act IV. Now convinced of her son's madness, the Queen tells Claudius of Polonius' death and the King, suspecting that he will be blamed for not confining the insane Prince, orders him dispatched immediately to England. Rosencrantz and Guildenstern carry documents which order Hamlet's execution there. En route, Hamlet sees Fortinbras' army bivouacked, and comparing his own grievances with those that have led to the forthcoming slaughter over a worthless piece of land, he resolves hereafter to be bloody.

Laertes returns to Elsinore and demands of the royal couple an explanation for the murder and secret burial of his father. Ophelia, desolate and deranged, wanders about singing distractedly. Claudius tells Laertes how Polonius was killed and explains that he dare not punish the Prince because Gertrude dotes upon him, as do the people of Denmark. Sailors arrive, bearing letters from Hamlet. To Horatio he writes that pirates attacked the ship bound for England and that they have helped him return to Elsinore. The Prince's note to the King simply announces his return and promises an early explanation.

Claudius suggests to Laertes that they arrange an "accidental" death for Hamlet, and Laertes readily agrees to a display of swordsmanship, in which he will wield a foil tipped with a lethal poison. The Queen enters and tells them tearfully that Ophelia has drowned herself.

Act V. Hamlet meets Horatio in the graveyard at Elsinore and exchanges quips with a gravedigger. The Prince and Horatio hide when a funeral procession approaches. They hear a priest tell Laertes that only a perfunctory service is allowed for the deceased because her death was "doubtful" (that is, probably suicidal). Laertes leaps into the grave for a final embrace with his sister, and Hamlet, when he hears that the funeral is Ophelia's, emerges to assert that his great love entitles him to the honor of first mourner. He jumps into the grave with Laertes, and they fight.

Later, Hamlet tells Horatio how he had discovered the plot to kill him and escaped, after forging an order that insured the deaths of Rosencrantz and Guildenstern. Osric, a foppish courtier, tells the Prince of the proposed match with Laertes and of a heavy wager that the King has made on his nephew.

As the two fence before the court, Claudius drops a poisoned pearl into a drink intended for Hamlet. Unwittingly, the Queen intercepts the cup and drinks from it. Laertes wounds Hamlet, then in a furious exchange they switch foils. Before Claudius can interfere, Laertes is mortally wounded; the Queen, swooning, warns her son about the cup.

Dying, Laertes begs Hamlet's forgiveness and blames the King. Hamlet rushes to Claudius, runs him through, and forces him to drink the poison. Horatio, distraught at the sight of his stricken friend, attempts to take the cup also. Hamlet wrenches it from him, bidding him to live and tell the true account of these events, and then dies in his arms. His last wish is that Fortinbras succeed to the throne of Denmark. Ambassadors from England arrive with news of the deaths of the courtiers. Fortinbras, returning victorious from Poland to claim the crown, orders military honors for the dead Prince.—P.B.

Comment. *Hamlet* is undoubtedly the world's most famous play. Equally undeniable is the fact that the source of that fame is the play's enormously attractive, profoundly puzzling hero. However, the wealth of commentary that has been devoted to the Prince (see HAMLET, the entry for the character) has frequently resulted in a tendency to overlook the play in which he appears. Hamlet has too often been extracted from his tragedy and made to serve an independent existence as the prototype of the modern man, the Romantic poet, or merely the eternally irresolute man. These and other universal aspects of the Prince's character are not to be denied. However, it is important to remember that his character must always be seen within that total dramatic and poetic structure which we know as *The Tragedy of Hamlet, Prince of Denmark*. For this play marks a high point in Shakespeare's development, not only as a creator of character, but as a dramatic artist. He achieved this artistic maturity through the transformation of his source, the so-called *Ur-Hamlet*. We can infer enough about the nature of this early drama to be fairly sure that it was a revenge tragedy, the same type of play as *Titus Andronicus*, a melodrama full of blood and horror. But by 1600–1601, while the poet was devising *Hamlet*, he had lost interest in creating another outmoded, sensational *jeu de théâtre*. So he turned from the invention of deeds of violence to dramatizing a struggle in the avenger's mind and moral nature. He began by substituting for the traditional avenger—a man with an irresistible thirst for vengeance—a noble and sensitive hero, an ideal Renaissance gentleman, whom Ophelia might call

> The courtier's, soldier's, scholar's, eye, tongue,
> sword;
> The expectancy and rose of the fair state,
> The glass of fashion and the mould of form.
> (III, i, 159–161)

He is a man whose nobility is shown in his moral integrity.

When the play opens, Hamlet is in a state of deep melancholy—"sore distraction" he calls the woe caused by his loved father's death, which he suspects was murder, and by his mother's overhasty, incestuous marriage. This persistent melancholy was one element in the role of another Elizabethan stage type, the malcontent. The play may profitably be taken as a struggle between Hamlet's nature and the demands of the two uncongenial roles in which fate has cast him. His sensitive nature and the imperatives of his religious faith revolt against the Ghost's sacred injunction to avenge this most foul and unnatural murder. It demands that Hamlet perform an act alien to his nature that bids fair to endanger his life and even to jeopardize his immortal soul. For Hamlet is no pagan avenger of Icelandic saga, but a Christian Elizabethan who adopted the current confused beliefs of his age about ghosts. The apparition is in type a Senecan ghost, come from an afterworld of punishment—in this case from purgatory—to urge revenge on his murderer. The Protestants, having banished purgatory from their theology, held that a man once dead could find no exit from heaven or hell. Therefore, such spectres as the ghost of Hamlet's father were either illusions of minds unhinged by melancholy or devils masquerading as spirits of the departed in order to lure the persons they address to damnation. Hamlet vacillates between the conviction that the Ghost is actually his father's spirit and the fear that it is a devil. Hamlet's opinion of the phenomenon reflects the confused thinking of Tudor England and should not be regarded as his trumped-up excuse for inaction. Shakespeare only occasionally hints at the cause of Hamlet's delay: his interest lay in the conflict in Hamlet's mind between obedience to the Ghost's solemn injunction and the dictates of his own temperament. Shakespeare devotes the first part of the tragedy to demonstrating the thoughts and feelings that he assumed would pass through the mind of this new sort of avenger. Hamlet vacillates between brooding over his fate and headlong bursts of activity. This fluctuation constitutes the rhythm of his conduct.

The soliloquies are the passages that most clearly reveal Hamlet's struggle on the one hand to obey the Ghost's sacred injunction and on the other to follow the dictates of his own nature. They are the first example of Shakespeare's method of acquainting an audience with the drama taking place in the minds and souls of his tragic protagonists. These soliloquies are different in kind from those of characters in his earlier tragedies. The famous soliloquy of Gloucester that opens *Richard III* is a good example of the playwright's earlier practice. Gloucester comments with bold-faced irony on his situation and announces the program for his villainy. The poet informs Hamlet's soliloquies with a much more sophisticated artistic purpose. They relate what is passing through his mind to moral imperatives and religious principles. In the "To be or not to be" speech Hamlet considers the implications of his undertaking the career of an avenger to which he has just dedicated himself.

The avenger's role is the structural determinant of the play. Superimposed on it are the images of disease and disorder and the atmosphere of death which pervade the play. Embodied within it is the human experience, rooted in ancient ritual drama, through which man has attempted to come to terms with the absolute fact of death. For *Hamlet*, as Gilbert Murray and others have shown, is a reenactment of a worldwide myth of a hero born to "set right" a world out of joint, reluctant at first to undergo the trial and ultimately accepting his fate in order to expiate the sins of society. But *Hamlet* is not just a ritual. It is primarily and supremely a work of art, generating a proliferation of meanings and interpretations, no one of which is able to contain or finally define its richness. It is a play which has a private as well as a public dimension. From this point of view the drama is a domestic tragedy, probing the conflicts within a family or within a group of families, if we consider the Polonius-Laertes-Ophelia relationships and the muted but important role of Fortinbras and his father, who was slain by Hamlet's father. The play also has a philosophical complex in which the themes of appearance and reality, of the relationship of the self to the world, and of the nature of action are but a few of the many which scholars and philosophers have discerned. The play has all of this and more, for its essential characteristic is an inexhaustible and infinite variety.—O.J.C.

Stage History: England. Undoubtedly Richard Burbage, the star of Shakespeare's company, created the title role of *Hamlet*, and tradition credits Shakespeare himself with originating the part of the Ghost. An allusion by a contemporary writer, Anthony SCOLOKER, is interesting for the light it sheds on Hamlet's costume in what was probably the original production of the play. There is no record of an early performance at court, a fact that may lend support to the thesis that the play contains veiled allusions to prominent and controversial political figures, notably the earl of Essex. The earliest recorded but improbable performance is that given on board the H.M.S. *Dragon* at Sierra Leone on September 5, 1607 (and probably repeated the following March) for the entertainment of Portuguese and English guests (see William KEELING). For a court performance during the winter of 1619/20, it is safe to assume that the title role was portrayed by Joseph Taylor, the successor to Burbage, who died on March 13, 1619. Taylor most likely could still be seen in the part when *Hamlet* was presented at Hampton Court on January 24, 1637.

At the Restoration, Sir William Davenant's DUKE'S COMPANY presented the tragedy in the summer of 1661 at Lincoln's Inn Fields. Although his omissions were extensive, Davenant spared *Hamlet* the usual distortions and presented a structurally faithful acting version of the original text. Samuel PEPYS was delighted with the production, which he first saw on August 24, pronouncing Betterton's acting of Hamlet "beyond imagination." Betterton was about 26 at the time he began playing the Prince, and he continued to take the part for almost 50 years.

After Betterton and other leading actors withdrew from Drury Lane to form their own company in 1695, Robert Wilks assumed the part of Hamlet. Some commentators considered his interpretation misguided and too restless, but Wilks was commended for excellently rendering the "To be or not to be" soliloquy and was undoubtedly accepted by audiences, for the tragedy was presented every season but two from 1710 to 1733. Wilks restored Hamlet's advice to the actors. When the companies reunited, he played the title role at Drury Lane on

THOMAS BETTERTON.

January 15, 1709. There were many Hamlets by this time, but probably the best was Lacy Ryan, who first took the role in 1719.

David Garrick played the Ghost opposite Henry Giffard's Hamlet at Goodman's Fields on December 9, 1741. The following August he acted the title role in Dublin, opposite Peg Woffington's Ophelia, and that November made his first London appearance in the part at Drury Lane, with Kitty Clive as Ophelia, Hannah Pritchard as the Queen, and Charles Macklin as the First Gravedigger. Garrick played the Prince 13 times that season, and thereafter appeared in the role almost every year until his final performance on May 30, 1776. His representation of a sane man feigning insanity was one of his most popular roles.

At first Garrick produced the tragedy as Shakespeare had written it, but in 1772 he laid violent hands on its structure. G. C. D. Odell suggests that he became nervous under Voltaire's strictures on the play and tried to make it "regular" according to 18th-century critical standards (see VOLTAIRE). He omitted scenes of low humor, such as that of the gravediggers, and "barbarous" encounters, such as the struggle of Hamlet and Laertes over Ophelia's grave; in fact, the funeral is entirely omitted. Moreover, the Senecan ending is greatly modified. The Queen, for example, is not poisoned on the stage but is led off and the audience is informed that her sense of guilt has driven her insane. The King defends himself with his sword and is killed in a duel with Hamlet. This unpublished version, although disapproved by some, held the stage at Drury Lane until October 30, 1779, then apparently disappeared from London, to be seen again only at Bath in 1781. About this same time, the Germans allegedly laid hands on the original, astonishingly effecting a happy ending, as did Ducis' *Hamlet*, first produced in Paris in 1769. Professor Odell quotes Crabb Robinson, who saw the latter version at Rouen in 1814; in it "the unities are preserved, and Hamlet is victorious."

After Garrick, William Smith, who had acted the Prince in many Covent Garden productions from 1757 to 1773, transferred to Drury Lane in 1774, where he appeared regularly in the title role until 1783, vying with John Henderson for the honors as Hamlet. Henderson's first London performance in the part was at the Haymarket on June 26, 1777. That September, he acted Hamlet at Drury Lane and again in the following two seasons, whereafter he transferred to Covent Garden, taking the role each season up to September 20, 1784. While Henderson exhibited unique tenderness in the role, his performances displayed little greatness, and the tragedy awaited the Romantic movement, with John Philip Kemble's introspective and melancholy Dane. On September 30, 1783 Kemble made his first Drury Lane appearance in the part, wearing black velvet court dress. His powdered hair was disheveled in the scenes of feigned insanity; when he spoke the word "father" to the Ghost, he sank to his knees, repeating the gesture on the Ghost's disappearance. The production was given 12 times that season. After his initial triumph, Kemble staged the play often, but irregularly, presenting it every year of that decade except the last, and resuming its production from 1796 to the end of the century.

In 1786, Sarah Siddons portrayed Ophelia for one performance at Drury Lane and another in Liverpool. Ten years later, on April 29, she played the Queen—her only London appearance in that role—with Wroughton as Hamlet. Earlier, she had acted the title role at both Manchester and Liverpool in 1777, at Bath the following year, and at Bristol in 1781. Her final appearance as Hamlet came as late as 1802, when she played the Prince in Dublin. Another female impersonator of the part at that period was Mrs. William Powell, who added Hamlet to her repertoire in 1796 and repeated the role in 1797, both times opposite Dorothy Jordan's Ophelia. According to C. B. Hogan, the tragedy ranked first in popularity throughout the 18th century, totaling 601 performances.

For his Covent Garden productions from 1803 until his final appearance as Hamlet just before his retirement in 1817, Kemble's acting version contained several omissions. Fortinbras, the Ambassadors, and Reynaldo are eliminated, as well as the dumb show, the King's prayer, with Hamlet's soliloquy on it, and Polonius' advice to Laertes. Certain passages are shortened, such as the "O what a rogue" soliloquy and the description of Ophelia's death, while Hamlet's final speeches to the Queen in the closet scene are severely curtailed. Charles Kemble played Laertes at the Haymarket Theatre in 1795 and first acted Hamlet in 1803, his interpretation that of a truly distracted Prince. Charles Mayne Young gained some success with his classical portrayal of Hamlet from his initial performance on June 22, 1807 to his farewell benefit in 1832, when William Charles Macready was the Ghost.

Edmund Kean's romantic genius exercised itself in *Hamlet* first on March 12, 1814 at Drury Lane. His inconsistent interpretation allowed for a series of impressive dramatic flashes but neglected the character as a whole. The emphasis often fell in the wrong places, and Kean's exaggerated mannerisms denied Hamlet his introspective qualities. However, succeeding actors who approved his treatment of Ophelia—he ignored the traditional roughness and cruelty and kissed her hand after the "nunnery" speech—also imitated his ready confidence in following the Ghost after the first meeting. Macready followed Kean's lead in abandoning the extreme physical terror at meeting the Ghost, replacing it with a tender wonderment. While his Hamlet was labored, Macready achieved in good measure the intellectual power and dramatic force of the play. From his early performances in 1821 until his own Covent Garden production in 1837, he worked to convey more of the tender, earnest dignity of Hamlet, his conception that of an amiable, loving gentleman before learning of his father's murder. Macready's acting version cut Fortinbras, the Ambassadors, and the dumb show, and ended the play with "The rest is silence." In 1845 *Hamlet* was included in a repertoire which Macready brought to Paris; when he acted the tragedy before the king and queen at the Tuileries, he also eliminated the gravediggers.

Charles Kean honorably acquitted himself as Hamlet, his performance owing much to his father's, underlining moments of highest dramatic value and neglecting the full portrait. He performed the Prince at Drury Lane in 1838, at the Haymarket in 1843, and staged the tragedy conscientiously, elaborately, and successfully at the Princess' Theatre in 1850, bringing nothing that was original to the conception of the play. From time to time, Samuel Phelps had acted the Ghost opposite Macready's Hamlet. In 1837 he appeared at the Haymarket in the title role. His first Sadler's Wells production of the tragedy was introduced in July 1844.

On February 7, 1852 Barry Sullivan made his first London appearance, playing Hamlet at the Haymarket. His completely sane, intellectual, unpoetic Prince, wearing black and purple and a curly, light brown, flowing wig, was most effective when expressing the bitter humor of his speeches. Quite unorthodox was his introduction of the exclamation "Pshaw," with which at one reading he expressed his contempt for Rosencrantz and Guildenstern. In 1860 at the St. James, Sullivan's Hamlet was less explosive. The next Hamlet to arouse popular interest was the naturalistic, nonchalant, professionally expert representation by the Frenchman Charles Fechter, first seen by London audiences at the Princess' in March 1861. His delivery was colloquial, indicating neither terror nor tenderness in the Ghost scene, and speaking the "To be or not to be" soliloquy rapidly and unexpressively, while numerous innovations of stage business seemed to monopolize attention. The depth of true tragedy was missing from his performance, but his style did set an example for those who may have hesitated to defy the traditions.

Before Fechter's and a few months after Sullivan's first London Hamlet, a German company appeared at St. James Theatre during a season which introduced Emil Devrient's foreign-language Dane, noted for underlining the Prince's love for his mother. Another visiting Hamlet from Germany played at the Princess' in 1873. Unlike his preceding conservative countryman, however, Daniel Edward Bandmann diligently strove for originality, with erratic innovation. In the closet scene, for example, Hamlet, on seeing the Ghost, falls backward, and thereafter recites from a supine position. London saw the Italian Hamlets of Tommaso Salvini in 1875 and Ernesto Rossi in 1876, both at the Drury Lane. Neither performer, though technically expert and dramatically impressive, was convincing in the role, for both made Hamlet seem competent and energetic, instead of thoughtfully hesitant.

Henry Irving had worn a flaxen wig after the style of Fechter at Manchester in 1864. Ten years later, he had discarded the wig, but retained a naturalistic approach for his initial Lyceum appearance in the role on October 31, 1874. The production, which ran for an unprecedented 200 performances, depended almost exclusively on Irving's performance. But when he staged his own Hamlet on December 30, 1878, for a run of 108 nights, credit for his success must be shared by Ellen Terry, the most exquisite of Ophelias.

Wilson Barrett's version, presented at the Princess' in October 1884, created more discussion for his scene rearrangement and novel reading than for his conception of the character of Hamlet. Possibly his greatest contribution to the play was the restoration of Claudius to his position of chief villain for the first time in 200 years. E. S. Willard was widely acclaimed for his brilliant interpretation of what became for the first time a great character part. Barrett envisioned Hamlet as a sane, passionate, impetuous youth of 18 who, according to one critic, "would have killed Claudius without more ado, and there would have been no need for the play to proceed beyond the second act." The production was overburdened with unnecessary innovations, such as presenting the mock play in a garden that attracted more attention than its dramatic value warranted.

In 1892 Beerbohm Tree's Hamlet, alternating between sanity and madness, bowed in an elaborate Haymarket production which censored important words from the First Gravedigger, cut the part of Laertes, eliminated Osric, and concluded with an angelic choir singing the dead Prince to his rest. As manager of His Majesty's Theatre, Tree presented the tragedy in his annual Shakespeare Festivals each year from 1905 to 1909, and gave a guest performance in the title role during the Shakespeare birthday celebration at Stratford-upon-Avon in 1909. After several centuries, Fortinbras was finally restored when Johnston Forbes-Robertson added *Hamlet* to his repertory in 1897. To him, the young Prince was a meditative philosopher whom life had thrust into uncongenial action. His Hamlet never passed beyond love for Ophelia and never crossed the limits of sanity. Though he lacked tragic force at the end, the poetic beauty of this rendition set a standard for succeeding actors. The soliloquy during the King's prayer was retained, along with some portions of Reynaldo's part, but otherwise the traditional cuts were followed. Forbes-Robertson became identified with Hamlet, and played the role during his Drury Lane farewell in 1913. Before closing the history of Hamlet productions in the 19th century, a brief note on two theatrical events in 1899 should be included. One was Sarah Bernhardt's assumption of the title role in Paris on May 20 and in London at the Adelphi the following month. Miss Bernhardt's stage business included such novelties as knocking Rosencrantz' and Guildenstern's heads together and kicking Polonius in the shins. The other event was the uncut

Hamlet of Frank R. Benson, who had staged the tragedy in five previous years at Stratford. This unprecedented presentation was repeated in March 1900 at the Lyceum Theatre, in an afternoon and evening session interrupted by a dinner recess.

In addition to the complete *Hamlet*, Benson produced standard versions at Stratford every year from 1902 to 1916. Guest Hamlets at special performances for the Memorial Theatre included Forbes-Robertson in 1908, Matheson Lang in 1909, and John Martin Harvey in the spring of 1910. Harvey had first acted the title role in London in May 1905 at the Lyric, during a period when a surfeit of Hamlets made the tragedy a topical joke for satirists. His archaeologically correct, 11th-century production had to be withdrawn because of meager attendance. When his romantic and passionate Hamlet was brought to Stratford, Harvey was beginning to yield to the influence of Gordon Craig, and his setting for the 1910 production relied less on accurate costumes and scenery and more on the suggestion of a period and environment. Large, triangular, prism-shaped revolving pillars were decorated with simple designs designating various locations. Although this set was attractive, it was restrictive and provided little of the expanse that Harvey desired for the battlements, so his revival in 1916 at His Majesty's introduced further simplified sets. An enormous, concave white canvas effectively represented the horizon, against which curtains were arranged with no distracting details evident. Harvey's fourth *Hamlet* in 1919 was somewhat overshadowed on the massive stage of the Royal Opera House, Covent Garden, and must be counted among the ambitious failures. Another Stratford guest Hamlet, Henry Irving's son, H. B. Irving, in the spring of 1914, played Hamlet in London at the Adelphi, but he suffered from Hamlet's overexposure that season and had only a short run. He saw the character as a reasonable, essentially amiable but weak noble burdened by an intuitive hatred for his uncle that was strengthened by love for his father. Over the years, Irving refined his Hamlet performances. In 1910 he appeared in the tragedy at the Queen's followed by the Memorial Theatre engagement. His final effort with the part, an artistic success, was displayed on the stage of the Savoy in the spring of 1917. E. H. Sothern and his wife, Julia Marlowe, brought from America a repertory including *Hamlet* presented at the Waldorf in 1907. On May 1, Mr. Sothern's Hamlet, although admired by many, failed to win the enthusiasm accorded it in the United States.

On January 27, 1914 William Poel, who had presented the Elizabethan Stage Society in a reading of the First Quarto text at St. George's Hall in 1881 and again at Carpenter's Hall in 1900, produced a *Hamlet* edited "to show scenes never acted in versions given on the modern stage." Esme Percy gave a forceful performance in his first Hamlet. He later starred in the version of DER BESTRAFTE BRUDER-MORD, titled *Fratricide Punished*, which Poel staged in 1924 at the New Oxford Theatre.

In April 1916 the Old Vic under Ben Greet acted the full text of the Second Quarto and that summer sustained the Stratford Festival with a repertory including William Stack's Hamlet. Stack re-created his impersonation for W. Bridges-Adams in the 1922 Memorial Theatre production. For Greet's second Old Vic production of the tragedy during 1916/7, Russell Thorndike acted the title role. Thorndike presented the play when he assumed the direction of the Old Vic jointly with Charles Warburton in 1919. He appeared as Hamlet at the Lyceum in 1926, and again during a week's repertory season at the Kingsway under producer Peter Dearing in 1932. Throughout this period of Thorndike's efforts with the play, numerous actors essayed the Prince with varying effects. Henry Baynton presented a vividly passionate Hamlet to the provinces in a somber set of black velvet drapes during the autumn tour of 1920. Ernest Milton, a less histrionic but equally passionate Hamlet, starred in several Old Vic productions in a decade. The first was under George R. Foss in the 1918/9 season. Three were directed by Robert Atkins, the earliest of which traveled to Brussels, where Milton appeared at the Théâtre du Parc in June 1921. He played another Hamlet under Andrew Leigh in 1928. Other Old Vic Hamlets at this time included Ion Swinley's agonized, poetic Prince in Atkins' presentation during April 1924, Baliol Holloway's in 1927; and John Laurie's in 1929. Laurie had previously acted the role for Bridges-Adams at Stratford in 1927. He was succeeded at the Memorial Theatre by George Hayes in 1928 and 1929.

Four Hamlets were displayed in 1925. In February John Barrymore arrived at the Haymarket with an extravagantly cut text which lumbered slowly along despite the excellent support of Constance Collier as Gertrude and Fay Compton as Ophelia. The scenery created by Robert Edmond Jones, an American designer, generated more discussion than the performance. Dominated by a vast staircase intersected by two levels on which indoor scenes were enacted, the setting was alternately praised for its beauty and condemned as perilous. That year Milton starred in his third Hamlet under Atkins (his fourth at the Old Vic), with Marie Ney as Ophelia. In May Godfrey Tearle played a straightforward Prince for the Fellowship of Players. But the most significant contribution to the drama that year was Barry Jackson's modern-dress production by H. K. Ayliff, presented at the Kingsway on August 5. The experiment created a renewed interest in a contemporary Hamlet divested of the classical Scandinavian apparel.

There were an unprecedented four separate revivals in 1930. Esme Percy re-created the title role in the first of these with pathos, tenderness, and energetic passion. The fast-moving production by Peter Godfrey opened at the Court on February 12. Henry Ainley's Hamlet was part of an "all-star" production at the Haymarket by Charles La Trobe, under the supervision of Johnston Forbes-Robertson. Ainley's frenzied, poetic portrayal after the old tradition received support from a cast including Irene Vanbrugh as Gertrude, Malcolm Keen as Claudius, Gwen Ffrangcon-Davies as Ophelia, and Godfrey Tearle as Horatio. On April 28 John Gielgud's portrayal thrilled audiences at the Old Vic, as he acted in both the cut and the complete versions of the tragedy under Harcourt Williams' direction. Maurice Browne arranged a transfer of the production to the Queen's Theatre a month after the initial performance.

Gielgud fulfilled the promise of his 1930 characterization four years later in a revival that ran for 155 performances, a record second only to Irving's first

Lyceum production. With a scrupulous text arranged in 14 scenes, interrupted only once, the action moved at an even pace in Motley's multilevel set, which revolved on a turntable. Gielgud transported this production to the St. James Theatre in New York in October 1936, where *Hamlet* enjoyed its longest American run of 132 performances. In 1935 there was a Liverpool Playhouse production starring Geoffrey Edwards; and the Dublin Gate Theatre company's romantic Hamlet, acted by Michael MacLiammoir under producer Hilton Edwards, filled an engagement at the Westminster. The same year Maurice Evans assumed the title role at the Old Vic. Evans presented a vigorous, amiable young man somewhat lacking in depth. Later in 1938, Evans presented *Hamlet* in its entirety at the St. James in New York, giving 98 performances, and the following year acted the title role at the 44th Street Theatre. His conception of the role was emphasized in his so-called G.I. *Hamlet*, presented first to the armed forces in Hawaii and in 1946 in New York, with costumes and settings of the 19th century.

Another successful Hamlet, Donald Wolfit, had been first seen in the tragedy as Claudius in the 1930 Old Vic production. He graduated to the title role in a First Quarto rendition at the Arts Theatre Club in 1933. On joining the Stratford company in 1936, he began his regular appearances in the part, both in London and on his world-wide tours, which took him to the provinces, Europe, Asia, Africa, and America.

Few people were aware that Laurence Olivier was endeavoring to apply the theory that Hamlet suffered from an Oedipus complex to his interpretation of the role when he appeared in Tyrone Guthrie's Old Vic production in January 1937. None, however, failed to admire the surging force of his performance. In late spring, the Old Vic company with a new Ophelia, Vivien Leigh, and including Alec Guinness as Osric, Reynaldo, and the Player Queen; Anthony Quayle as Laertes; John Abbott as Claudius; and Leo Genn as Horatio, journeyed to Elsinore to act the play on a replica of the Old Vic's set in the courtyard of Kronborg Castle. Heavy rain prevented the outdoor performance, but an improvised stage in the cabaret of the nearby Marienlyst Hotel served uniquely and admirably. Guthrie considered the unorthodox setting in many ways an effective staging method which served to heighten the audience's involvement in the drama.

In 1947 Olivier added his own production to the 17 *Hamlets* already on film. The heavily edited motion picture offered less of Shakespeare and seemed more a showpiece for Olivier. Although he was still a vigorous Hamlet, some of the most stirring moments of his early performance were missing.

Michael MacOwan, producing the play at the Westminster in 1937, limited himself to the "resources of the Globe Theatre company" and presented an unexciting *Hamlet* on a bare stage, without the benefit of lighting effects. Christopher Oldham's Prince added nothing to the part, but two performances did excel: Cecil Trouncer's Polonius and Mark Dignam's Ghost.

Guthrie's next innovations with the play came in a 1938 Old Vic production of a complete version in modern dress. The costumes, designed by Robert Furse, retained formality, with uniforms and long dresses. Alec Guinness played Hamlet in this revival. A presentation in Greek, with Alexis Minotis leading the Royal Theatre of Greece company, was given at His Majesty's Theatre on June 20, 1939. On the 28th Gielgud acted the last Lyceum production before that theatre's scheduled demolition. In October 1944 Gielgud gave his fourth Hamlet in George Ryland's careful production, this time surpassing himself in clarity, eloquence, and bitterness. Peggy Ashcroft was Ophelia and Leslie Banks, Claudius. Earlier, Tyrone Guthrie and Michael Benthall had produced the play with an Old Vic company headed by Robert Helpmann at the New Theatre in February. Benthall was sole director for three more major *Hamlet* productions, one at Stratford (1948), and two for the Old Vic (1953 and 1957). Helpmann was again his Hamlet at the Memorial Theatre, but this time he alternated in the role with Paul Scofield, whose dynamic, tormented hero, who saw through the other characters as well as himself and discovered refuge only in death, made Helpmann seem merely fastidious. Benthall selected a mid-19th-century setting, which, however, never clouded the play's contemporary significance. Anthony Quayle was Claudius; Diana Wynyard, Gertrude; and Claire Bloom, Ophelia. Three wartime Hamlets had preceded Scofield at Stratford: Basil Langton and George Hayes in B. Iden Payne's 1940 and 1942 productions, and John Byron in Robert Atkins' 1944 production. All turned in standard, respectable performances, adding no new excitement to the character. Alec Clunes was a tender and very sane Prince at the Arts Theatre in 1945, and Robert Eddison with the Bristol Old Vic acted a haunted, impassioned Hamlet in Hugh Hunt's production at the St. James in 1948. Hunt's next *Hamlet*, for the London Old Vic, opened in February 1950 at the New, with Michael Redgrave as a sensitive noble of keen mind and agile wit, who struggles, not always successfully, to control the madness within. In June the company, which included Yvonne Mitchell as Ophelia, presented the play at the Zurich and Holland festivals and at Kronborg Castle, Elsinore. When Redgrave appeared again in the tragedy in 1958 at Stratford, his portrayal had gained richness and conveyed even more clearly the mental processes of an anguished soul. Glen Byam Shaw directed; Cyril Luckham was Polonius; Dorothy Tutin, Ophelia; Googie Withers, Gertrude; and Mark Dignam, Claudius. In the winter the company visited Leningrad and Moscow with the production. Previously, in 1955, an Old Vic *Hamlet* appeared at the Moscow Art Theatre, having filled touring dates at Oxford and Birmingham. This was Peter Brook's production, with Paul Scofield expressing anguish with restraint and Diana Wynyard and Alec Clunes impressive as Gertrude and Claudius.

Alec Guinness performed the drama on a flat, square stage at the New in 1951. A herald of the anti-hero vogue, his Hamlet was an introspective, passionless characterization, droned away in monotone further emphasized by the drab surroundings. Other London Hamlets of the decade included David Markham at the New Boltons in John Harrison's production (1951); Laurence Payne at the Embassy (1953); Michael Croft's Youth Theatre presen-ation at the Queen's (1959) and later in repertory at Scala (1963). The first of two revivals directed by Michael Benthall for the Old Vic starred Richard Burton, performing with care and resolution but little fire, supported by Michael Hordern (Polonius), Claire Bloom (Ophelia), and Fay Compton (Gertrude) in 1953. The Hamlet of the second production (1957) was John Neville. Michael Langham directed the tragedy both in 1956, with Alan Badel in the title role, and in the following year for the Stratford Shakespearean Festival in Ontario, with Christopher Plummer as Hamlet, Douglas Campbell as Claudius, and Joy Lafleur and Frances Hyland as Gertrude and Ophelia. In a Memorial Theatre production in 1961, Ian Bannen's neurotic Prince developed somewhat with practice in a generally mediocre presentation under Peter Wood.

On October 22, 1963 the newly organized National Theatre, temporarily housed at the recently dissolved Old Vic company's theatre, presented *Hamlet* as its initial production. Olivier directed and Peter O'Toole (who at the Bristol Old Vic in 1958 had been an angry-young-man Hamlet) spoke the title part in harsh tones. Others in the cast included Michael Redgrave and Diana Wynyard, exceptional as Claudius and Gertrude, and Rosemary Harris as Ophelia.

Stage History: America. The first Hamlet in America was Lewis Hallam, the younger, who first acted the role on July 27, 1759 at Philadelphia after David Douglass assumed control of the American company. On this occasion, Douglass played the Ghost. Hallam repeated his impersonation on November 26, 1761 at the Chapel Street Theatre in New York and this time Douglass took the role of Claudius while Polonius and Ophelia were played by Owen Morris and Mrs. Morris. The same cast, with the exception of Ophelia, who was played by Margaret Cheer, presented the play at the Southwark in Philadelphia on January 9, 1767 and at the John Street in New York on December 21 of that year. Up to this time, Shakespeare's text supplied the acting version; in 1788, however, eight years after London abandoned it, Garrick's adaptation was performed. During the 1790's several new Hamlets appeared: Charles Stuart Powell (from Covent Garden) in Boston on November 30, 1792; James Fennell at the New in Philadelphia in April 1794; John P. Moreton, the first American-trained actor other than Hallam to play the part, on April 13, 1796; and Chalmers in 1797.

Thomas Abthorpe Cooper played the Prince during 1798 at the Park when he was just 21 and achieved the reputation of being up to that time the best Hamlet seen in New York. A review of a performance on December 4, 1799 commends Cooper as unrivaled in the closet scene but criticizes Ophelia's funeral scene for its lack of decorum. Mrs. Hodgkinson's Ophelia, however, drew excellent notices praising especially her mad-sweet singing. Regard for Hallam's Ghost and Joseph Jefferson's Polonius was high.

Of the many subsequent Hamlets on the American stage, notice can be given only the most renowned. James William Wallack acted the Prince during his American debut season in 1818; he continued to appear in the role for many years, giving several performances during the last half of the 1830's with Charlotte Cushman as Gertrude. William Augustus Conway, a morbidly sensitive actor who, despite popular acclaim, abandoned his career in England because of one critic's adverse review, was persuaded to resume on the American stage. His Park debut on January 12, 1824 presented a tender Hamlet absorbed by the intensity of his melancholy. Four years later his mental depression, undispelled by theatrical success, overcame him and Conway committed suicide. Junius Brutus Booth also included his portrayal of Hamlet in his debut season at the Park in 1821, playing the part in New York and on tours throughout the country for almost 30 years.

Invariably, the famous British actors elected to play Hamlet for their first performance on the American stage. Thomas Hamblin acted the role for his Park debut on November 1, 1825, making an initial impact as a tragedian in the Kemble tradition. Though Hamblin preferred melodrama, *Hamlet* remained in his repertory throughout his more than 25-year career in this country. James Barton's first performance (March 9, 1831) on the New York stage was as the Prince, and Charles Kemble, despite a weak voice, won immediate approval on his first visit to the United States, essaying Hamlet for his Park debut on Sepember 7, 1832. John Vandenhoff acted the role during his initial season at the National Theatre, New York, in 1837 and repeated the impersonation in 1841, his last year in the United States. His son, George Vandenhoff, gave a dignified and studious representation of Hamlet, which, though lacking somewhat in passion, was considered close to perfect. He played the part for his American debut at the Park on September 21, 1842.

Philadelphia-born James E. Murdoch, after a temporary withdrawal from the stage in 1842, returned in 1845, playing Hamlet for the first time, and on November 22, 1858 Barry Sullivan, whose first London appearance had been as the Prince, made his New York debut in the same role, presenting it again during his last American tour in 1875.

In 1829 Edwin Forrest joined the Park company, portraying Hamlet in October. Although Forrest was not the first native American to essay the role (John Howard Payne achieved that distinction in 1809), he most certainly was the first major tragedian born in the United States to gain esteem with his representation of the Prince. His acting always aroused controversy among critics, many of whom considered his sporadic effectiveness accidental, claiming Forrest unsuited temperamentally and physically for the part and his Hamlet divested of any tenderness or grace. William Winter describes his Prince as menacing rather than melancholy. Edward Loomis Davenport's Hamlet, first assumed around the middle of the 19th century and acted almost up to his death in 1877, possessed just those qualities missing in Forrest's, but he never ranked above an eminently respectable second best.

It was Edwin Booth who captured the honors for being the foremost interpreter of the Prince on the American stage. His first appearance in the role occurred on April 25, 1853 in San Francisco, and after his debut in New York in 1857 he filled repertory engagements there and in many cities throughout England and the United States. Booth's most conspicuous success as the Dane was accomplished in his series of magnificent revivals at the Winter Garden in New York. *Hamlet* was the first production in the series, opening on November 26, 1864 and running for 100 consecutive performances, thus establishing a Shakespearean record in America. The day his brother, John Wilkes Booth, assassinated Lincoln —April 14, 1865—Booth was acting Hamlet during a Boston engagement. His subsequent brief withdrawal from the stage ended with a performance in the tragedy at the Winter Garden on January 3, 1866. From then on, he effected numerous revivals of *Hamlet*—one of the best at Booth's Theatre in New York on January 5, 1870, its first production there—and for his farewell from the stage on April 4, 1891 at the Brooklyn Academy of Music, he elected to play Hamlet. In his eloquent portrayal, Booth's characterization embodied a princely dignity, haunting affection for his dead father, and anguished devotion for his sinning mother.

Other respectable Hamlets of the period include Lawrence Barrett, John McCullough, and Walter Montgomery. Foreign Hamlets appearing in the United States during Booth's time were: Daniel Edward Bandmann (1863), Tommaso Salvini (1873), Ernesto Rossi (1881), Adolf von Sonnethal (1885), Ludwig Barnay (1888), and Jean Mounet-Sully (1894).

Edward H. Sothern began his Shakespearean career acting Hamlet at the Garden Theatre on September 17, 1899 and continued to give intelligent but unauthoritative performances in repertory seasons with his wife, Julia Marlowe, as Ophelia, for more than two decades. His contemporary, Robert Mantell, who returned to the New York stage in 1904 with a large Shakespeare repertory including *Hamlet,* acted the Prince regularly up to 1918. In 1912 John E. Kellerd, having essayed Hamlet the previous year at the Irving Place Theatre, achieved a run of the tragedy to equal Booth's. He began at the Garden Theatre on November 18 and transferred to the Harris on January 13, 1913, breaking his predecessor's record with 102 performances. Earlier that year, on April 23, Wallack's presented a birthday celebration performance of the tragedy starring Ian Maclaren, but probably the most proficient Hamlet seen in America during the early 1900's was a visitor from England, Johnston Forbes-Robertson, who first acted it in New York on March 7, 1904, then again the following year, and later in 1913.

On May 20, 1919 Walter Hampden, who had been making appearances as the Prince for a few years, revived *Hamlet* at the 39th Street Theatre for 23 performances. Critical opinion of his anything but melancholy Dane praised Hampden's earnest, intelligent interpretation but found his exceedingly energetic performance somewhat inconsistent with the more thoughtful aspects of the character.

Critics hailed John Barrymore's Hamlet debut as the finest of all impersonations of the Prince in this country in the present century. His colloquial, low-keyed presentation infused a meditative, sensitive personality with grace, wit, and energy, carefully preserving the poetic beauties of the verse. Particularly interesting in his interpretation was his relationship with the Queen—the confrontation played as a love scene. Alexander Woollcott styled Barrymore "the realest Hamlet we have known" and hi colleagues were no less enthusiastic. The productio opened on November 16, 1922 at the Sam H. Harri Theatre and ran for 101 performances. Even Joh Gielgud could not replace Barrymore, forever es teemed in the memories of his countrymen, when h brought his *Hamlet* to New York on October 1936. Most thought him an intelligent and stirrin Prince but missed the fire of their American Dan The production, staged by Guthrie McClintic at th Empire, included Lillian Gish as Ophelia, Judith An derson as Gertrude, and Malcolm Keen as Claudiu and was acted 132 times.

In between Barrymore and Gielgud, several worth Hamlets appeared. Fritz Leiber had acted Laerte opposite Robert Mantell at Daly's in 1911 and durin the 1920/1 season took the title role at the Lexingto Opera House. Criticized for poor phrasing in th soliloquies, Leiber was commended, in later appear ances with the Chicago Civic Shakespeare Society a the Shubert (1930) and the Ambassador (1931), fo straightforward personations indicating respect fo the integrity of the play. Unity and honesty, how ever, could not elevate the presentations above th pedestrian.

In 1925 Hampden reappeared in the title role an achieved a more profound characterization than h had in 1919; he was aided by an appealing Ophelia Ethel Barrymore, at his own theatre. He revived th tragedy again in 1928 and at the 44th Street Theatr in 1934, always improving his presentation. Raymon Massey attempted Hamlet at the Broadhurst in 193 acting in a compressed version adapted by Norma Bel Geddes. Massey was no sweet prince; his ener getic performance left little doubt about his deter mination to avenge his father's death. However, th mutilated and rearranged text (a striking eccentricit assigned the Ghost's speeches, during the first en counter, to Hamlet) failed to justify the Prince' behavior.

One month after Gielgud's production opene another *Hamlet* bowed in New York. Leslie How ard, staging and starring in a costly production a the Imperial, came in a poor second to the rival re vival. His amiable, unneurotic gentleman caught in difficult situation lacked most of the qualities tha make Hamlet a commanding figure, and certainl this Prince suffered misgivings over exacting ven geance. The best characterization in this presenta tion was Wilfrid Walter's admirably drawn Claudiu On October 12, 1938 Maurice Evans began a lon run of 98 performances in New York in an uncu version of the tragedy. Determined to present a ma and not a critic's problem child, he divested Hamle of all his deeper qualities to present a pleasant youn man who played with zest the principal part in a Elizabethan melodrama. This conception he empha sized in his so-called G.I. *Hamlet*—presented first t the armed forces in Hawaii and later, in Decembe 1945, in New York for 131 performances.

The New York Repertory Group presented *Ham let*, staged by Robert T. Eley at the Cherry Lane i December 1948. Bill Butler in the title role, whil often too rushed, showed ability in some parts, espe cially the closet scene. Despite good directing, how ever, the revival was ruined by poor speaking. I December 1952 Jean-Louis Barrault staged an starred in André Gide's French translation of the tragedy at the Ziegfeld Theatre, revealing a macabre-looking Prince enveloped in existentialist gloom.

A physically vigorous, but not especially penetrating, portrayal of the Dane was that of Philip Lawrence playing with the Shakespearewrights. A two-act revival by Donald H. Glodman under Mitchell Jason's direction, it was presented in October 1956. Although the Hamlet of the production proved unsuccessful, two other performances excelled: Lester Rawlins' less-doddering-than-usual Polonius and Joseph Ruskin's authoritative Claudius. The following January an experimental version conceived and directed by Henry Hewes featured Siobhan McKenna as the Prince alone on the stage while the other roles were read by actors hidden behind the arras. General opinion of this offering by the American National Theatre and Academy at the Theater de Lys considered the presentation impressive as a tour de force but essentially an unnecessary stunt. The conventional Old Vic *Hamlet*, directed by Michael Benthall and starring John Neville, displayed at the Broadway during December 1958 was just as poorly received but perhaps preferred to the American Shakespeare Festival production at Stratford, Connecticut, the preceding summer. In a cast which included Fritz Weaver as the Prince, Morris Carnovsky as Claudius, Geraldine Fitzgerald as Gertrude, Earle Hyman as Horatio, Hiram Sherman as Polonius, and Inga Swenson as Ophelia, only Laertes, portrayed by John Colicos, won unqualified approval.

First-night predictions of inevitable improvement by Donald Madden at the Phoenix in 1961 were proven correct. His hurt, innocent youth corrupted by the knowledge of evil was a bit too breathless and occasionally so overwrought as to blur meaning. But the over-all well-integrated conception strengthened with repetition, and Madden's impressive Hamlet grew into one of the more significant representations of the character on the modern stage. The tragedy's fortunes rose still higher when, in 1964, John Gielgud directed a rehearsal-clothes production at the Lunt-Fontanne, achieving popular and financial success. Critics almost unanimously agreed that Richard Burton's Dane was never dull and, while sometimes hurried, his impersonation was imbued with skill and intelligence. The supporting cast, except for Hume Cronyn's assertive, senile Polonius, disappointed—especially the bland Claudius of Alfred Drake and an Ophelia badly played by Linda Marsh.—M.G.

Bibliography. TEXT: *Hamlet*, New Cambridge Edition, J. Dover Wilson, ed., 1934; H. De Groot, *Hamlet, Its Textual History*, 1923; J. Dover Wilson, *The Manuscript of Shakespeare's Hamlet*, 1934; Alice Walker, "The Textual Problem of *Hamlet*," *Review of English Studies, II*, 1951; Clifford Leech, "Studies in *Hamlet*, 1901–1955," *Shakespeare Survey 9*, 1956. DATE: E. K. Chambers, *Shakespearean Gleanings*, 1944; E. A. J. Honigmann, "The Date of *Hamlet*," *Shakespeare Survey 9*, 1956. SOURCES: Israel Gollancz, *The Sources of Hamlet*, 1926; Kenneth Muir, *Shakespeare's Sources*, Vol. I, 1957. COMMENT: A. C. Bradley, *Shakespearean Tragedy*, 1904; E. E. Stoll, *Hamlet: An Historical and Comparative Study*, 1919; J. Dover Wilson, *What Happens in Hamlet*, 1935; C. S. Lewis, *Hamlet: The Prince or the Poem?*, 1942. STAGE HISTORY: New Cambridge Edition; William Winter, *Shakespeare on the Stage*, 3 vols., 1911–1916; G. C. D. Odell, *Shakespeare from Betterton to Irving*, 1920; J. C. Trewin, *Shakespeare on the English Stage, 1900–1964*, 1964.

Selected Criticism

SAMUEL JOHNSON. If the dramas of *Shakespeare* were to be characterised, each by the particular excellence which distinguishes it from the rest, we must allow to the tragedy of Hamlet the praise of variety. The incidents are so numerous, that the argument of the play would make a long tale. The scenes are interchangeably diversified with merriment and solemnity; with merriment that includes judicious and instructive observations, and solemnity, not strained by poetical violence above the natural sentiments of man. New characters appear from time to time in continual succession, exhibiting various forms of life and particular modes of conversation. The pretended madness of *Hamlet* causes much mirth, the mournful distraction of *Ophelia* fills the heart with tenderness, and every personage produces the effect intended, from the apparition that in the first act chills the blood with horror, to the fop in the last, that exposes affectation to just contempt.

The conduct is perhaps not wholly secure against objections. The action is indeed for the most part in continual progression, but there are some scenes which neither forward nor retard it. Of the feigned madness of *Hamlet* there appears no adequate cause, for he does nothing which he might not have done with the reputation of sanity. He plays the madman most, when he treats *Ophelia* with so much rudeness, which seems to be useless and wanton cruelty.

Hamlet is, through the whole play, rather an instrument than an agent. After he has, by the stratagem of the play, convicted the King, he makes no attempt to punish him, and his death is at last effected by an incident which *Hamlet* has no part in producing. [*The Plays of William Shakespeare*, 1765.]

GOETHE. "Figure to yourselves this youth," cried he, "this son of princes: conceive him vividly, bring his state before your eyes, and then observe him when he learns that his father's spirit walks; stand by him in the terrors of the night, when the venerable ghost itself appears before him. A horrid shudder passes over him; he speaks to the mysterious form; he sees it beckon him; he follows it, and hears. The fearful accusation of his uncle rings in his ears; the summons to revenge, and the piercing oft-repeated prayer, Remember me!

"And when the ghost has vanished, who is it that stands before us? A young hero panting for vengeance? A prince by birth, rejoicing to be called to punish the usurper of his crown? No! trouble and astonishment take hold of the solitary young man; he grows bitter against smiling villains, swears that he will not forget the spirit, and concludes with the significant ejaculation:

> The time is out of joint: O cursed spite,
> That ever I was born to set it right!

"In these words, I imagine, will be found the key to Hamlet's whole procedure. To me it is clear that Shakespeare meant, in the present case, to represent the effects of a great action laid upon a soul unfit for the performance of it. In this view the whole piece seems to me to be composed. There is an oak-tree planted in a costly jar, which should have borne only pleasant flowers in its bosom; the roots expand, the jar is shivered.

"A lovely, pure, noble and most moral nature, without the strength of nerve which forms a hero, sinks beneath a burden which it cannot bear and must not cast away. All duties are holy for him; the present is too hard. Impossibilities have been required of him; not in themselves impossibilities, but such for him. He winds, and turns, and torments himself; he advances and recoils; is ever put in mind, ever puts himself in mind; at last does all but lose his purpose from his thoughts; yet still without recovering his peace of mind." [*Wilhelm Meister's Apprenticeship*, 1795–1796; translated by Thomas Carlyle, 1824.]

SAMUEL TAYLOR COLERIDGE. Shakespeare's mode of conceiving characters out of his own intellectual and moral faculties, by conceiving any one intellectual or moral faculty in morbid excess and then placing himself, thus mutilated and diseased, under given circumstances. This we shall have repeated occasion to restate and enforce. In Hamlet I conceive him to have wished to exemplify the moral necessity of a due balance between our attention to outward objects and our meditation on inward thoughts—a due balance between the real and the imaginary world. In Hamlet this balance does not exist—his thoughts, images, and fancy [being] far more vivid than his perceptions, and his very perceptions instantly passing thro' the medium of his contemplations, and acquiring as they pass a form and color not naturally their own. Hence great, enormous, intellectual activity, and a consequent proportionate aversion to real action, with all its symptoms and accompanying qualities . . . .

Even after the scene with Osrick, we see Hamlet still indulging in reflection, and hardly thinking of the task he has just undertaken: he is all dispatch and resolution, as far as words and present intentions are concerned, but all hesitation and irresolution, when called upon to carry his words and intentions into effect; so that, resolving to do everything, he does nothing. He is full of purpose, but void of that quality of mind which accomplishes purpose.

Anything finer than this conception, and working out of a great character, is merely impossible. Shakespeare wished to impress upon us the truth, that action is the chief end of existence—that no faculties of intellect, however brilliant, can be considered valuable, or indeed otherwise than as misfortunes, if they withdraw us from, or render us repugnant to action, and lead us to think and think of doing, until the time has elapsed when we can do anything effectually. In enforcing this moral truth, Shakespeare has shown the fullness and force of his powers; all that is amiable and excellent in nature is combined in Hamlet, with the exception of one quality. He is a man living in meditation, called upon to act by every motive human and divine, but the great object of his life is defeated by continually resolving to do, yet doing nothing but resolve. [The first paragraph above is from notes for a lecture on *Hamlet*, 1813; the remaining material is from a Collier report of the twelfth lecture of 1811–12; both are reprinted in *Shakespearean Criticism* by S. T. Coleridge, T. M. Raysor, ed., Everyman Library Edition, 1960.]

WILLIAM HAZLITT. The character of Hamlet stands quite by itself. It is not a character marked b strength of will or even of passion, but by refine ment of thought and sentiment. . . . He is the princ of philosophical speculators; and because he canno have his revenge perfect, according to the most re fined idea his wish can form, he declines it alto gether. . . . His ruling passion is to think, not to act and any vague pretext that flatters this propensity in stantly diverts him from his previous purposes. [*Th Characters of Shakespear's Plays*, 1817.]

ABRAHAM LINCOLN. Some of Shakespeare's plays have never read; while others I have gone over per haps as frequently as any unprofessional reade Among the latter are "Lear," "Richard III," "Henr VIII," "Hamlet," and especially "Macbeth." I thin nothing equals "Macbeth." It is wonderful. Unlik you gentlemen of the profession I think the soliloqu in "Hamlet" commencing "Oh, my offense is rank, surpasses that commencing "To be or not to be. But pardon this small attempt at criticism. [Letter t James K. Hackett; reprinted in *American Shake spearean Criticism*, A. V. Westfall, ed., 1939.]

IVAN SERGEYEVICH TURGENEV. . . . On the one sid stand the Hamlets—reflective, conscientious, ofte all-comprehensive, but as often also useless an doomed to immobility; and on the other the hal crazy Don Quixotes, who help and influence man kind only to the extent that they see but a singl point—often nonexistent in the form they see it. Un willingly the questions arise: Must one really be lunatic to believe in the truth? And, must the min that has obtained control of itself lose, therefore, a its power? . . .

The Don Quixotes discover; the Hamlets develo But how, I shall be asked, can the Hamlets evolv anything when they doubt all things and believe i nothing? My rejoinder is that, by a wise dispensatio of Nature, there are neither thorough Hamlets no complete Don Quixotes; these are but extreme mani festations of two tendencies—guideposts set up b the poets on two different roads. Life tends towar them, but never reaches the goal. We must not forg that, just as the principle of analysis is carried i Hamlet to tragedy, so the element of enthusias runs in Don Quixote to comedy; but in life th purely comic and the purely tragic are seldom en countered . . . .

Both Hamlet and Don Quixote die a touchin death; and yet how different are their ends! Hamlet last words are sublime. He resigns himself, grow calm, bids Horatio live, and raises his dying voice i behalf of young Fortinbras, the unstained represen tative of the right of succession. Hamlet's eyes ar not turned forward. "The rest is silence," says th dying skeptic, as he actually becomes silent foreve The death of Don Quixote sends an inexpressib emotion through one's heart. In that instant the fu significance of this personality is accessible to al When his former page, trying to comfort Do Quixote, tells him that they shall soon again sta out on an expedition of knight-errantry, the expirin knight replies: "No, all is now over forever, and ask everyone's forgiveness; I am no longer Do Quixote, I am again Alonzo the good, as I was on called—Alonso el Bueno." ["Hamlet and Don Qui ote—the Two Eternal Human Types," *Current Li erature*, January, 1907. Tr. by David A. Modell.]

A. C. BRADLEY. And therefore the Schlegel-Col

dge view (apart from its descriptive value) seems to e fatally untrue, for it implies that Hamlet's pro-astination was the normal response of an over-eculative nature confronted with a difficult prac-cal problem.

On the other hand, under conditions of a peculiar ind, Hamlet's reflectiveness certainly might prove angerous to him, and his genius might even (to ex-ggerate a little) become his doom. Suppose that vio-nt shock to his moral being of which I spoke; and ppose that under this shock, any possible action eing denied to him, he began to sink into melan-holy; then, no doubt, his imaginative and generalis-g habit of mind might extend the effects of this ock through his whole being and mental world. nd if, the state of melancholy being thus deepened nd fixed, a sudden demand for difficult and decisive ction in a matter connected with the melancholy rose, this state might well have for one of its symp-ms an endless and futile mental dissection of the re-uired deed. And, finally, the futility of this process, nd the shame of his delay, would further weaken im and enslave him to his melancholy still more. hus the speculative habit would be *one* indirect ause of the morbid state which hindered action; and would also reappear in a degenerate form as one of e *symptoms* of this morbid state . . . .

'Melancholy,' I said, not dejection, nor yet insan-y. That Hamlet was not far from insanity is very robable. His adoption of the pretence of madness ay well have been due in part to fear of the real-y; to an instinct of self-preservation, a fore-feeling at the pretence would enable him to give some tterance to the load that pressed on his heart and rain, and a fear that he would be unable altogether repress such utterance. And if the pathologist alls his state melancholia, and even proceeds to de-ermine its species, I see nothing to object to in that; am grateful to him for emphasizing the fact that Iamlet's melancholy was no mere common depres-ion of spirits; and I have no doubt that many read-rs of the play would understand it better if they ead an account of melancholia in a work on mental iseases. If we like to use the word 'disease' loosely, Iamlet's condition may truly be called diseased. No xertion of will could have dispelled it. Even if he ad been able at once to do the bidding of the Ghost e would doubtless have still remained for some ime under the cloud. It would be absurdly unjust to all *Hamlet* a study of melancholy, but it contains uch a study . . . .

I have dwelt thus at length on Hamlet's melan-holy because from the psychological point of view, is the centre of the tragedy, and to omit it from onsideration or to underrate its intensity is to make hakespeare's story unintelligible. But the psycholog-al point of view is not equivalent to the tragic; and, aving once given its due weight to the fact of Ham-et's melancholy, we may freely admit, or rather ay be anxious to insist, that this pathological con-ition would excite but little, if any, tragic interest it were not the condition of a nature distinguished y that speculative genius on which the Schlegel-oleridge type of theory lays stress. Such theories isinterpret the connection between that genius and Iamlet's failure, but still it is this connection which ives to his story its peculiar fascination and makes appear (if the phrase may be allowed) as the symbol of a tragic mystery inherent in human nature. Wherever this mystery touches us, wherever we are forced to feel the wonder and awe of man's godlike 'apprehension' and his 'thoughts that wander through eternity,' and at the same time are forced to see him powerless in his petty sphere of action, and powerless (it would appear) from the very divinity of his thought, we remember Hamlet. And this is the reason why, in the great ideal movement which began towards the close of the eighteenth century, this tragedy acquired a position unique among Shakespeare's dramas, and shared only by Goethe's *Faust*. It was not that *Hamlet* is Shakespeare's greatest tragedy or most perfect work of art; it was that *Hamlet* most brings home to us at once the sense of the soul's infinity, and the sense of the doom which not only circumscribes that infinity but appears to be its offspring. [*Shakespearean Tragedy*, 1904.]

GEORGE SANTAYANA. The psychology of Hamlet is like that which some German metaphysicians have attributed to their Spirit of the World, which is the prey to its own perversity and to what is called romantic irony, so that it eternally pursues the good in a way especially designed never to attain it. In Hamlet, as in them, beneath this histrionic duplicity and earnestness about the unreal, there is a very genuine pathos. Such brilliant futility is really helpless and sick at heart. The clouded will which plays with all these artifices of thought would fain break its way to light and self-knowledge through this magic circle of sophistication. It is the tragedy of a soul buzzing in the glass prison of a world which it can neither escape nor understand, in which it flutters about without direction, without clear hope, and yet with many a keen pang, many a dire imaginary problem, and much exquisite music. [Introduction to *Hamlet*, The University Press Shakespeare, Renaissance Edition, 1908.]

T. S. ELIOT. The upshot of Mr. [J. M.] Robertson's examination is, we believe, irrefragable: that Shakespeare's *Hamlet*, so far as it is Shakespeare's, is a play dealing with the effect of a mother's guilt upon her son, and that Shakespeare was unable to impose this motive successfully upon the "intractable" material of the old play . . . .

It is not merely the "guilt of a mother" that cannot be handled as Shakespeare handled the suspicion of Othello, the infatuation of Antony, or the pride of Coriolanus. The subject might conceivably have expanded into a tragedy like these, intelligible, self-complete, in the sunlight. *Hamlet*, like the sonnets, is full of some stuff that the writer could not drag to light, contemplate, or manipulate into art. And when we search for this feeling, we find it, as in the sonnets, very difficult to localize . . . .

The only way of expressing emotion in the form of art is by finding an "objective correlative," in other words, a set of objects, a situation, a chain of events which shall be the formula of that *particular* emotion; such that when the external facts, which must terminate in sensory experience, are given, the emotion is immediately evoked. If you examine any of Shakespeare's more successful tragedies, you will find this exact equivalence; you will find that the state of mind of Lady Macbeth walking in her sleep has been communicated to you by a skilful accumulation of imagined sensory impressions; the words of Macbeth on hearing of his wife's death strike us as if, given the sequence of events, these words were automatically released by the last event in the series. The artistic "inevitability" lies in this complete adequacy of the external to the emotion; and this is precisely what is deficient in *Hamlet*. Hamlet (the man) is dominated by an emotion which is inexpressible, because it is in *excess* of the facts as they appear. And the supposed identity of Hamlet with his author is genuine to this point: that Hamlet's bafflement at the absence of objective equivalent to his feelings is a prolongation of the bafflement of his creator in the face of his artistic problem. Hamlet is up against the difficulty that his disgust is occasioned by his mother, but that his mother is not an adequate equivalent for it; his disgust envelops and exceeds her. It is thus a feeling which he cannot understand; he cannot objectify it, and it therefore remains to poison life and obstruct action. None of the possible actions can satisfy it; and nothing that Shakespeare can do with the plot can express Hamlet for him. And it must be noticed that the very nature of the *données* of the problem precludes objective equivalence. To have heightened the criminality of Gertrude would have been to provide the formula for a totally different emotion in Hamlet; it is just *because* her character is so negative and insignificant that she arouses in Hamlet the feeling which she is incapable of representing. ["Hamlet and His Problems" (1919) in *Selected Essays: 1917–1932*, 1932.]

GILBERT MURRAY. ... *Hamlet*, like most of the great Elizabethan plays, presents itself to us as a whole that has been gradually built up, not as a single definitive creation made by one man in one effort. There was an old play called *Hamlet* extant about 1587, perhaps written by Kyd. It was worked over and improved by Shakespeare; improved doubtless again and again in the course of its different productions. We can trace additions; we can even trace changes of mind or repentances, as when the Folio of 1623 goes back to a discarded passage in the First Quarto. It is a live and growing play, apt no doubt to be slightly different at each performance, and growing steadily more profound, more rich, and more varied in its appeal.

And before it was an English play, it was a Scandinavian story; a very ancient Northern tale, not invented by any person, but just living, and doubtless from time to time growing and decaying, in oral tradition. It is recorded at length, of course with some remodelling, both conscious and unconscious, by Saxo Grammaticus in his great *History of the Danes* (*Gesta Danorum*), Books III and IV. Saxo wrote about the year 1185; he calls his hero Amlethus, or Amloði, Prince of Jutland, and has worked in material that seems to come from the classical story of Brutus—Brutus the Fool, who cast out the Tarquins—and the deeds of Anlaf Curan, King of Ireland. But the story of Hamlet existed long before Saxo; for the prose *Edda* happens to quote a song by the poet Snaebjørn, composed about 980, with a passing reference to "Amloði." And it must mean our Amloði; for our Amloði in his pretended madness was a great riddle-maker, and the song refers to one of his best riddles. He speaks in Saxo of the sand as meal ground by the sea; and in Snaebjørn's song calls the sea "Amloði's meal-bin."

Besides Saxo we have a later form of the same legend in the Icelandic *Ambales Saga*. The earliest extant manuscripts of this belong to the seventeenth century.

Thus our sources for *Hamlet* will be (1) the various versions of the play known to us, (2) the story in *Saxo Grammaticus* and the *Ambales Saga*, and (3) some occasional variants of these sagas.

... we finally run the Hamlet-saga to earth in the same ground as the Orestes-saga: in that prehistoric and world-wide ritual battle of Summer and Winter, of Life and Death, which has played so vast a part in the mental development of the human race and especially, as Mr. E. K. Chambers has shown us, in the history of mediaeval drama. Both heroes have the notes of winter about them rather than summer, though both are on the side of right against wrong. Hamlet is no joyous and triumphant slayer. He is clad in black, he rages alone, he is the Bitter Fool who must slay the King....

In plays like *Hamlet* or the *Agamemnon* or the *Electra* we have certainly fine and flexible character study, a varied and well-wrought story, a full command of the technical instruments of the poet and the dramatist; but we have also, I suspect, strange unanalyzed vibration below the surface, an undercurrent of desires and fears and passions, long slumbering yet eternally familiar, which have for thousands of years lain near the root of our most intimate emotions and been wrought into the fabric of our most magical dreams. How far into past ages this stream may reach back, I dare not even surmise; but it seems as if the power of stirring it or moving with it were one of the last secrets of genius. ["Hamlet and Orestes" in *The Classical Tradition in Poetry*, 1927.]

CAROLINE F. E. SPURGEON. To Shakespeare's pictorial imagination, therefore, the problem in *Hamlet* is not predominantly that of will and reason, of a mind too philosophic or a nature temperamentally unfitted to act quickly; he sees it pictorially *not as the problem of an individual at all*, but as something greater and even more mysterious, as a *condition* for which the individual himself is apparently not responsible, any more than the sick man is to blame for the infection which strikes and devours him, but which, nevertheless, in its course and development, impartially and relentlessly, annihilates him and others, innocent and guilty alike. That is the tragedy of *Hamlet*, as it is perhaps the chief tragic mystery of life. [*Shakespeare's Imagery*, 1935.]

ERNEST JONES. For some deep-seated reason, which is to him unacceptable, Hamlet is plunged into anguish at the thought of his father being replaced in his mother's affections by someone else. It is as if his devotion to his mother had made him so jealous for her affection that he had found it hard enough to share this even with his father and could not endure to share it with still another man. Against this thought, however, suggestive as it is, may be urged three objections. First, if it were in itself a full statement of the matter, Hamlet would have been aware of the jealousy, whereas we have concluded that the mental process we are seeking is hidden from him. Secondly, we see in it no evidence of the arousing of an old and forgotten memory. And, thirdly, Hamlet is being deprived by Claudius of no greater share in the Queen's affection than he had been by his wn father, for the two brothers made exactly nilar claims in this respect—namely, those of a ved husband. The last-named objection, however, ads us to the heart of the situation. How if, in ct, Hamlet had in years gone by, as a child, bitrly resented having had to share his mother's afction even with his own father, had regarded him a rival, and had secretly wished him out of the ay so that he might enjoy undisputed and undisrbed the monopoly of that affection? If such oughts had been present in his mind in childhood ys they evidently would have been "repressed," d all traces of them obliterated, by filial piety and her educative influences. The actual realization of s early wish in the death of his father at the hands a jealous rival would then have stimulated into tivity these "repressed" memories, which would ve produced, in the form of depression and other ffering, an obscure aftermath of his childhood's nflict. This is at all events the mechanism that is tually found in the real Hamlets who are investited psychologically.

The explanation, therefore, of the delay and selfustration exhibited in the endeavour to fulfil his ther's demand for vengeance is that to Hamlet the ought of incest and parricide combined is too inlerable to be borne. One part of him tries to carry it the task, the other flinches inexorably from the ought of it. How fain would he blot it out in that estial oblivion" which unfortunately for him his nscience contemns. He is torn and tortured in an soluble inner conflict. [*Hamlet and Oedipus*, 1949.]

MAYNARD MACK. In the last act of the play (or so seems to me, for I know there can be differences this point), Hamlet accepts his world and we disver a different man. Shakespeare does not outline r us the process of acceptance any more than he d done with Romeo or was to do with Othello. it he leads us strongly to expect an altered Ham-, and then, in my opinion, provides him. We must call that at this point Hamlet has been absent from e stage during several scenes, and that such abnces in Shakespearean tragedy usually warn us to on the watch for a new phase in the development the character. It is so when we leave King Lear Gloucester's farmhouse and find him again in over fields. It is so when we leave Macbeth at the itches' cave and rejoin him at Dunsinane, hearing the armies that beset it. Furthermore, and this is important matter in the theatre—especially imrtant in a play in which the symbolism of clothg has figured largely—Hamlet now looks different. e is wearing a different dress—probably, as ranville-Barker thinks, his "seagown scarf'd" out him, but in any case no longer the disordered stume of his antic disposition. The effect is not tirely dissimilar to that in *Lear*, when the old king akes out of his madness to find fresh garments on m.

Still more important, Hamlet displays a considerle change of mood. This is not a matter of the ay we take the passage about defying augury, as r. Tillyard among others seems to think. It is a atter of Hamlet's whole deportment, in which I el we may legitimately see the deportment of a an who has been "illuminated" in the tragic sense. adley's term for it is fatalism, but if this is what we wish to call it, we must at least acknowledge that it is fatalism of a very distinctive kind—a kind that Shakespeare has been willing to touch with the associations of the saying in St. Matthew about the fall of a sparrow, and with Hamlet's recognition that a divinity shapes our ends. The point is not that Hamlet has suddenly become religious; he has been religious all through the play. The point is that he has now learned, and accepted, the boundaries in which human action, human judgment, are enclosed.

Till his return from the voyage he had been trying to act beyond these, had been encroaching on the role of providence, if I may exaggerate to make a vital point. He had been too quick to take the burden of the whole world and its condition upon his limited and finite self. Faced with a task of sufficient difficulty in its own right, he had dilated it into a cosmic problem—as indeed every task is, but if we think about this too precisely we cannot act at all. The whole time is out of joint, he feels, and in his young man's egocentricity, he will set it right. Hence he misjudges Ophelia, seeing in her only a breeder of sinners. Hence he misjudges himself, seeing himself a vermin crawling between earth and heaven. Hence he takes it upon himself to be his mother's conscience, though the ghost has warned that this is no fit task for him, and returns to repeat the warning: "Leave her to heaven, And to those thorns that in her bosom lodge." Even with the king, Hamlet has sought to play at God. *He* it must be who decides the issue of Claudius's salvation, saving him for a more damnable occasion. Now, he has learned that there are limits to the before and after that human reason can comprehend. Rashness, even, is sometimes good. Through rashness he has saved his life from the commission for his death, "and prais'd be rashness for it." This happy circumstance and the unexpected arrival of the pirate ship make it plain that the roles of life are not entirely self-assigned. "There is a divinity that shapes our ends, Roughhew them how we will." Hamlet is ready now for what may happen, seeking neither to foreknow it nor avoid it. "If it be now, 'tis not to come; if it be not to come, it will be now; if it be not now, yet it will come: the readiness is all."

The crucial evidence of Hamlet's new frame of mind, as I understand it, is the graveyard scene. Here, in its ultimate symbol, he confronts, recognizes, and accepts the condition of being man. It is not simply that he now accepts death, though Shakespeare shows him accepting it in ever more poignant forms: first, in the imagined persons of the politician, the courtier, and the lawyer, who laid their little schemes "to circumvent God," as Hamlet puts it, but now lie here; then in Yorick, whom he knew and played with as a child; and then in Ophelia. This last death tears from him a final cry of passion, but the striking contrast between his behavior and Laertes's reveals how deeply he has changed . . . .

After the graveyard and what it indicates has come to pass in him, we know that Hamlet is ready for the final contest of mighty opposites. He accepts the world as it is, the world as a duel, in which, whether we know it or not, evil holds the poisoned rapier and the poisoned chalice waits; and in which, if we win at all, it costs not less than everything. I think we understand by the close of Shakespeare's *Hamlet* why it is that unlike the other tragic heroes he is given a soldier's rites upon the stage. For as William Butler Yeats once said, "Why should we honor those who die on the field of battle? A man may show as reckless a courage in entering into the abyss of himself." ["The World of Hamlet," *Yale Review*, Vol. 41, 1952.]

WYLIE SYPHER. When Coleridge lectured on *Hamlet* and *Lear* he pointed out that terror is closely joined with what is ludicrous, since "The laugh is rendered by nature itself the language of extremes, even as tears are." Thus *Hamlet* "will be found to touch on the verge of the ludicrous," because "laughter is equally the expression of extreme anguish and horror as of joy." The grimace of mirth resembles the grimace of suffering; comic and tragic masks have the same distortion. Today we know that a comic action sometimes yields tragic values....

Young Hamlet, late from Wittenberg, stands alone on the brink of this abyss, sees himself as a ridiculous fellow crawling between heaven and earth with more sins at his beck than he has time to act. So he puts on the antic disposition of the fool. And if a sense of contradiction and absurdity is a cause of comedy, then Hamlet is a profoundly comic character. He encounters what Kierkegaard calls either/or choices, the extremes that cannot be mediated but only transcended. That is, the comic hero and the saint accept the irreconcilables in man's existence. Both find themselves face to face with the Inexplicable and the Absurd....

The tragic hero, noble and magnified, can be of awesome stature. The comic hero refuses to wear the trappings of moral or civil grandeur, usually preferring motley, or the agility of the clown. He is none the less man, and Hamlet more than once rouses our suspicion that the tragic hero is eligible for comic roles: or is it the other way round, that Hamlet is a comic hero who generates tragic values? The Prince touches his deepest meanings when he has on his antic humor. ["The Meanings of Comedy," appendix to *Comedy*, 1956.]

HARRY LEVIN. With Shakespeare the dramatic resolution conveys us, beyond the man-made sphere of poetic justice, toward the ever-receding horizons of cosmic irony.

This is peculiarly the case with *Hamlet*, for the same reasons that it excites such intensive empathy from actors and readers, critics and writers alike. There may be other Shakespearean characters who are just as memorable, and other plots which are no less impressive; but nowhere else has the outlook of the individual in a dilemma been so profoundly realized; and a dilemma, by definition, is an all but unresolvable choice between evils. Rather than with calculation or casuistry, it should be met with the virtue of readiness; sooner or later it will have to be grasped by one or the other of its horns. These, in their broadest terms, have been—for Hamlet, as we interpret him—the problem of what to believe and the problem of how to act. Hamlet is unwittingly compelled to act as if life were a duel, with unbated swords and against a series of furtive assailants. He is unwillingly led to believe that death comes as a cup, filled with poisonous wine and containing a flawless pearl. His doom is generalized in Fulke Greville's chorus:

> Oh, wearisome condition of humanity,
> Born under one law, to another bound . . .

Irony cannot solve the incalculable contradiction between the personal life and the nature of things Yet it can teach us to live with them; and that is n mean achievement; for Hamlet's knowledge was no idle reflection, according to Nietzsche. It was an in sight which hindered action by stripping the veil o illusion from the terrible truth, the terror or th absurdity of existence. This would be intolerable were it not for the transformations of art, whicl asserts man's conquest over his fears, and whicl thereby allays his vexation of spirit. Thus Hamlet' limited victory commences with the play-within-the play, a working-model of the play itself, which re peats the lesson in mastery on a larger scale withi our minds. From its very commencement, after th stroke of midnight, we are brought face to face wit the supernatural. Volleys of gunfire augment an accelerate the sound effects until, at the conclusio of the dead march, '*a peal of ordinance*' signalizes battle lost and won. [*The Question of Hamlet* 1959.]

Hamlet, Katharine (d. 1579). A resident of Tid dington, about two miles from Stratford, who wa drowned in the Avon on December 17, 1579. Th inquest, which declared that the death was an acci dent and not a suicide, was held in the office of th Stratford town clerk. The conjunction of the nam "Hamlet" with an incident similar to that of Ophelia' death has been regarded by some as more tha coincidental. [E. I. Fripp, *Shakespeare, Man an Artist*, 1938.]

Hamlet, King. See GHOST.

Hammond, Lieutenant (fl. 1634). The unidentifie author of *A Relation of a Short Survey of 26 Coun ties . . . By a Captaine, a Lieutennant and an Ancient All three of the Military Company of Norwich.* Th manuscript is an account of a tour begun August 1 1634, which reached Stratford September 9. Th *Relation* contained the first recorded reference t Shakespeare as the alleged author of an epitaph o John Combe, his Stratford neighbor (see COMB FAMILY):

> In that dayes trauell we came by Stratford vpo Auon, where in the Church in that Towne ther are some Monuments which Church was built b Archbishop Stratford; Those worth obseruing an of which wee tooke notice of were these . . . A neat Monument of that famous English Poet, M William Shakespeere; who was borne heere.
>
> And one of an old Gentleman a Batchelor, M Combe, vpon whose name, the sayd Poet, did mer rily fann vp some witty, and facetious verse which time would nott giue vs leaue to sacke v

[E. K. Chambers, *William Shakespeare*, 1930.]

Hampton Lucy. A hamlet about four miles east c Stratford. In 1537 a sermon preached there by Ed ward Large stirred a controversy between Prote tants and Catholics which involved the two powerfu families of the Cloptons and the Lucys. The haml of Ingon, where Henry Shakespeare, the poet's uncl tenanted a farm, was in the parish of Hampton Luc

handbills. Brief printed announcements of play Handbills were set up on posts in conspicuous loc tions about the city; they were also circulated b hand and affixed to the door or gate of the theatr or other place where a play was to be given. The earliest extant English bill, dating from the late 17th century, is described by W. J. Lawrence and reads as follows:

> At the Theatre Royall, in Drury Lane, this present Wensday being the nineth day of November, will be presented, a new play called, Henry the Second of England.

Neither the names of the playwright nor the actors are mentioned in the handbills (see TITLES). The bills were used in addition to a simpler method of advertising a coming play, that is, by means of an epilogue appended to a play currently being viewed by an audience. The printing of playbills was regularized by a license, entered in the Stationers' Register on October 30, 1587, whereby John Carlwood was made responsible for the "onely ympryntinge of all manner of billes for players." The same privilege passed first to James Roberts and then to William Jaggard on October 29, 1615.

An early allusion to playbills or handbills occurs in a letter from Edmund Grindal to Sir William Cecil (February 23, 1564). Grindal, the bishop of London, was concerned about the plague, which spread rapidly whenever a crowd gathered, and he inveighed against the gathering of audiences for "lewd enterludes" by "these Histriones, common playours; who now daylye, butt speciallye on holydayes, sett vp bylles." A Gloucester minister, John Northbrooke, similarly mentions the practice of posting bills in his *Treatise . . .* [against] *Dicing, Dauncing, Vaine playes, or Enterluds, with other idle pastimes . . .* (1577):

> They vse to set vp their billes vpon postes certain dayes before, to admonishe the people to make their resort vnto their theatres, that they may thereby be the better furnished, and the people prepared to fill their purses with their treasures.

A line in Marston's *Scourge of Villainy* (1598) advises a playgoer to "Go read each post, view what is play'd to-day," and the Puritan George Wither's *Abuses Stript and Whipt* (1613) contains the lines: "But, by the way, a Bill he doth espy,/ Which showes theres acted some new Comedy."

The war between the city of London and the London stage is documented in one instance by a "preceptt" of the lord mayor (November 14, 1581) "agaynste foote-ball playe and stage playes" in which he indicated that he would not

> . . . suffer anye person or persons whatsoeuer, to sett vpp or fixe anye papers or beriefes vppon anye postes, houses, or other places within your warde, for the shewe or settynge out of anye playes, enterludes, or pryzes . . .

in the city of London, its liberties, suburbs, or other locations within two miles of the city. [W. J. Lawrence, *The Elizabethan Playhouse and Other Studies,* 2nd Series, 1913; E. K. Chambers, *The Elizabethan Stage,* 1923; Leslie Hotson, *The Commonwealth and Restoration Stage,* 1928.]

handwriting. During Shakespeare's lifetime the national handwriting of England was still undergoing the gradual but revolutionary changes imparted by the influence of the Italian style in the 16th century.

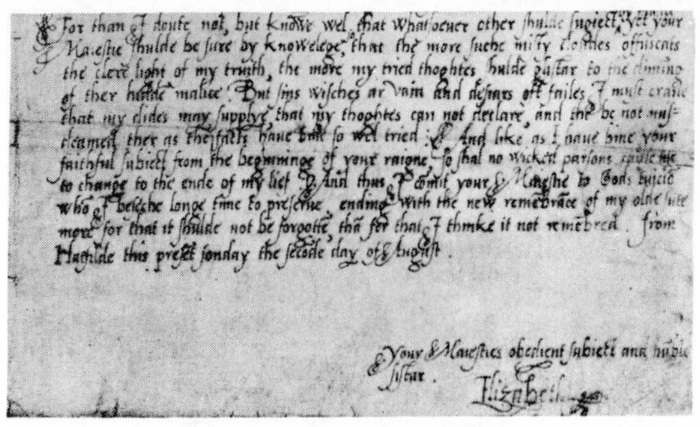

For than I doute not, but knowe wel, that whatsoeuer other shulde suggest, yet your Maiestie shulde be sure by knowelege, that the more suche misty clowdes offuscats the clere light of my truthe, the more my tried thoghtes shulde glistar to the dimming of their hidden malice. But sins wisches ar vaine and desyrs oft failes, I must craue that my dides may supply that my thoghtes can not declare, and they be not misdemed ther as the factes haue bine so wel tried. And like as I haue bine your faithful subiect from the beginning of your raigne, so shal no wicked parsons cause me to change to the ende of my life. And thus I comit your Maiestie to Gods tuicion, who I beseche longe time to preserue, ending with the new remembrance of my olde sute more for that it shulde not be forgotten, than for that I thinke it not remembred. From Hatfilde this present sonday the seconde day of August.

Your Maiesties obedient subiect and humble sistar.
Elizabeth

PART OF A LETTER WRITTEN BY ELIZABETH I TO QUEEN MARY IN 1556 WHEN ELIZABETH WAS 22 YEARS OLD. IT IS AN INTERESTING EXAMPLE OF A STUDIED ITALIAN HAND. (BRITISH MUSEUM)

The angular medieval hand which had been dominant in England since the Norman Conquest was very slowly replaced, though it did leave its impress on the new style. The resultant hand of the late Renaissance was a more graceful and legible one, though these qualities varied with the strata of society. The court of Henry VII employed an Italian cleric, Pietro Carmeliano, to write the Italian script in letters addressed to foreign courts, and by the early 16th century children of the higher classes were taught the new style. (Hamlet, in intercepting a letter to the King of England and substituting a false one (V, ii, 31–53), knew the Italian calligraphy by virtue of his education as a prince.) *A Booke containing Divers sortes of Hands* (first English edition, 1570) by the French writing master John De Beauchesne was a model for English writing books that appeared later, chief among them Peter Bales' *The Writing Schoolemaster* (1589; 2nd edition 1597) and John Davies' *Writing Schoolemaster* (1636). There was high regard for writing masters in Shakespeare's day and they often gave public exhibitions of their skill. As more and more books appeared the number of styles increased and handwriting became more pedantic and specialized.

The major writing styles of Elizabethan England comprised two of foreign origin, Italian and Roman, and four which developed from a combination of the Italian and native English script: secretary, chancery, court, and text. The secretary style was the most widely used for cursive writing and the principal business hand. The chancery and court hands were more artificial and used in official documents and records. The text hand was a larger upright lettering used for texts of books.

In Stratford schools only the native English hand was taught until the end of the 16th century, but Richard QUINEY, in the only extant letter addressed to Shakespeare, employed a rather fine and legible handwriting, and the poet's granddaughter, Elizabeth Hall, wrote a good Italian script, evidence that by the early 17th century the native English hand was disappearing.

Shakespeare undoubtedly wrote the native English hand that he had learned in school; it is unlikely that he had much practical experience in the fashionable Italian style, though probably a degree of fluency was worked by practice into his natural hand. Of his

THE BELOTT-MOUNTJOY DEPOSITION. (PUBLIC RECORD OFFICE)

GATEHOUSE CONVEYANCE. (GUILDHALL LIBRARY)

GATEHOUSE MORTGAGE. (BRITISH MUSEUM)

handwriting there are six known examples of undisputed authenticity, each of them signatures and one of which is preceded by two words:

(1)	Willm Shakp	Disposition in a suit brought by Stephen Belott vs. his father-in-law, Christopher Mountjoy, 11 May 1612
(2)	William Shakspēr	Conveyance of a house in Blackfriars, London, purchased by Shakespeare, 10 March 1613
(3)	Wm Shakspē	Mortgage deed of Blackfriars house, 11 March 1613
(4)	William Shakspere	Signature at foot of page 1 of poet's will, 25 March 1616
(5)	Willm Shakspere	Signature of same, page 2
(6)	By me William Shakspeare	Signature of same, page 3

The first three signatures may be taken as the more reliable indication of Shakespeare's handwriting, as the signatures on his will were undoubtedly executed while the poet was in the throes of a mortal illness. The earlier signatures are clearly of the native English script, but with certain traces of the more graceful Italian style. The noted scholar and calligraphy expert Sir Edward Maunde Thompson describes it as "a free and rapid, though careless hand, sufficiently legible and business-like for practical purposes," and notes the poet's "liberal use of abbreviation," concluding that Shakespeare "made no pretense to be an elegant penman." The variant abbreviations of the surnames is not unusual, and probably have to do with the fact of the limited space afforded by the seal labels, which fact probably accounts for a certain constrainment in the writing as well.

Each of the signatures on the will indicates, in Thompson's words, "the unsteady action of a tremulous hand." The fact that the signatures are dissimilar can probably be accounted for by the writer's illness, the last signature (the most important as it comes at the end of the will, and probably written before the other two) being the best, and the only one of the six in which the poet wrote his full surname.

The authenticity of signatures of Shakespeare in W. Hall's Copy of Ovid's *Metamorphoses* (1502), in a copy of Florio's translation of MONTAIGNE's *Essays* (1603), and in a copy of William LAMBARDE's *Archaionomia* (1568) is disputed.

Shakespeare has been identified by some as Hand D in the manuscript of SIR THOMAS MORE on the basis of certain peculiarities common to both: Shakespeare and Hand D use abnormal forms of "a," "k," "p," and "s," one of which, the "spurred a," is not exactly duplicated elsewhere; they use the same three normal forms of "a" and "k" and the same two of "e," "h," and "p"; both use the dotted "w" and the looped *per* symbol, and habitually begin certain initial letters with a long, fine upstroke. In the latter, there is an example in both hands of a needle-like eye at the base. [Sir Edward Maunde Thompson, "Handwriting," *Shakespeare's England*, 1916; A. W. Pollard and others, *Shakespeare's Hand in the Play*

THE WILL, FIRST SHEET. (PUBLIC RECORD OFFICE)

THE WILL, SECOND SHEET. (PUBLIC RECORD OFFICE)

THE WILL, THIRD SHEET. (PUBLIC RECORD OFFICE)

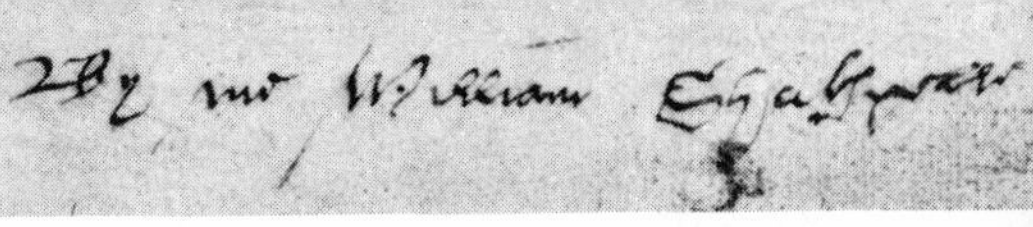

of Sir Thomas More, 1923; S. A. Tannenbaum, *Problems in Shakespeare's Penmanship*, 1927; *A Companion to Shakespeare Studies*, Harley Granville-Barker and G. B. Harrison, eds., 1934.]

Hanmer, Sir Thomas (c. 1676–1746). Scholar. After a political career that carried him to the speakership of the House of Commons in 1715, Hanmer published a six-volume edition of Shakespeare's plays in 1743/4. He used Alexander Pope's text, correcting it by Lewis Theobald's edition and his own intuitive judgment. William Warburton had entrusted Hanmer with the notes and emendations for his own projected edition, and claimed they had been used without authorization. Hanmer's edition is one of the poorest of the 18th century, largely dependent on earlier editions and marred by frequent arbitrary judgments, such as his omission of the courtship scene in *Henry V*, which he deemed ribald and unintelligible. It is valuable chiefly for the elegance of its illustrations, engraved by F. Gravelot after Francis Hayman's designs. [D. Nichol Smith, *Shakespeare and the Eighteenth Century*, 1928.]

Harbage, Alfred (1901–). American scholar, Cabot professor of English literature at Harvard. Harbage's earlier works include monographs on Thomas Killigrew and Sir William Davenant and a study of the Cavalier drama. There followed *Annals of English Drama, 975–1700* (1940; rev. by S. Schoenbaum, 1964). *Shakespeare's Audience* (1941) is a study of the social and intellectual background of the Elizabethan playgoing public. *As They Liked It* (1947), subtitled "an essay on Shakespeare and morality," considers the moral assumptions shared by Shakespeare and his audience. *Shakespeare and the Rival Traditions* (1952) discusses the differences between the public and private theatres, with their respective appeals to a popular and to a coterie audience. The author's Alexander Lectures at the University of Toronto have been published as *Theatre for Shakespeare* (1955). *William Shakespeare: A Reader's Guide* (1963) is a detailed consideration of the plays. *Shakespeare: The Tragedies* (1964) is a selection from critics of the 20th century. Harbage is also general editor of The Pelican Shakespeare, and for that series he has edited *King Lear*, *Macbeth*, and *Love's Labour's Lost*.

Harcourt. In *2 Henry IV*, an officer in Henry's army. In IV, iv, he reports to the King that the Earl of Northumberland and Lord Bardolph have been overthrown. Historically, this character may have been Sir Thomas Harcourt, who was sheriff of Berkshire in 1407. [G. R. French, *Shakespeareana Genealogica*, 1869.]

Hardwicke, Sir Cedric (1893–1964). Actor. Born in Worcestershire, Sir Cedric studied at the Royal Academy of Dramatic Art before making his first stage appearance in 1912. In the following year he acted with the Benson company, and in 1914 appeared at the Old Vic as Malcolm, Tranio, and the First Gravedigger in *Hamlet*. In 1922 he joined the Birmingham Repertory Company, appearing as Iachimo and Sir Toby Belch and in many non-Shakespearean productions. In 1925 at the Kingsway he acted Caesar in Shaw's *Caesar and Cleopatra*, the Gravedigger, and Iago. In 1928 he began directing at the Lyric and appeared in an all-star *Hamlet* as the First Gravedigger. From 1938 to 1944 he lived in Hollywood, where he made many films. In 1948 he again acted with the Old Vic as Sir Toby and as Dr. Faustus. In 1936 he presented the Rede lectures at Cambridge, and in 1934 he was knighted. [*Who's Who in the Theatre*, 1961.]

Hardy, Thomas (1840–1928). Novelist and poet. Hardy turned from poetry, for financial reasons, to fiction, producing several novels, including *The Return of the Native* (1878), *Tess of the D'Urbervilles* (1891), and *Jude the Obscure* (1895). Accused of amorality, especially in regard to the latter work, Hardy returned to poetry and published *Wessex Poems* (1898), which included many of his earlier works.

Hardy's knowledge of English literature was vast, and his greatest love was Shakespeare. According to his biographer, Carl J. Weber, Hardy's mind was saturated with Shakespearean lines, themes, situations, and characterizations (especially his rustics). Professor Weber notes over 100 quotations from, and references to, Shakespeare's plays in Hardy's novels and poems. Allusions to no fewer than 26 of the plays are recognizable, with *Hamlet* the most frequently echoed. When readers criticized the "amorality" of *Tess of the D'Urbervilles*—especially the blasphemous outburst against the President of the Immortals at the end—Hardy replied (in a Preface to the 1892 edition) by referring them to Gloucester's similar complaint to Lear: "As flies to wanton boys, are we to th' gods,/ They kill us for their sport" (IV, i, 38–39). His poem "The Two Rosalinds" was inspired by a performance of *As You Like It*, and in 1916, at the age of 75, he wrote "To Shakespeare," a poem commemorating the tercentenary of the poet's death. [Carl J. Weber, "Hardy's Debt to Shakespeare," *Hardy of Wessex*, 1940.]

Harington, Sir John (1561–1612). Courtier and translator. Harington was the son of John Harington (fl. 1550), a friend and relative of Queen Elizabeth, who acted as godmother at the younger Harington's baptism. He was educated at Cambridge and Lincoln's Inn, where he developed a reputation as a wit. At court his epigrams were frequently quoted, and he became one of the lively young men in the entourage of the earl of Essex. As a disciplinary measure the queen ordered him to retire from court and translate the *Orlando Furioso* of Lodovico Ariosto. He completed the work in 1591, and it may have provided the source of the Hero-Claudio story in *Much Ado About Nothing*. In 1596 he published, under a pseudonym, two celebrated essays in scatology, *The Metamorphosis of Ajax* and *Ulysses upon Ajax*, the word Ajax here being a pun, as it is in Shakespeare, on "a jakes," or privy.

Harington served under Essex on the disastrous expedition to Ireland in 1599. When the earl made his dramatic return to England, Harington accompanied him, an act for which the queen banished him from court. He was not involved in the Essex rebellion because Elizabeth had seen to it that her "witty nephew" was kept out of trouble. In the reign of James I, he acted as tutor to James' oldest son, Prince Henry, but he was unhappy with the dissolute character of Jacobean court life. Harington is perhaps best known for his letters and miscellaneous verse, collected and published under the title *Nugae Antiquae* (2 vols., 1769–1775), which provide a

VLISSES
vpon Aiax.

Written by *Misodiaboles* to his friend Philaretes.

AT LONDON
Printed for *Thomas Gubbins*:
1596.

TITLE PAGE OF HARINGTON'S *Ulysses upon Ajax* (1596).

fascinating and intimate view of court life in the age of Shakespeare.

Harington, Lucy. See Lucy Harington, Countess of BEDFORD.

Harriot, Thomas. See SCHOOL OF NIGHT.

Harris, Frank (1856–1931). Irish-born author and journalist. Harris emigrated to the United States, studied at the University of Kansas, and became an American citizen. Later he became a journalist in London. Among his books are collections of short stories, five volumes of *Contemporary Portraits* (1915–1927), and biographies of Oscar Wilde and G. B. Shaw. *My Reminiscences as a Cowboy* (1930) and *My Life and Loves* (3 vols., 1923–1927) are highly romanticized autobiographical accounts which need to be accepted with caution. *The Man Shakespeare and His Tragic Life-Story* (1909) is a fanciful attempt to read the plays as Shakespearean autobiography with characters such as Hamlet and Jaques reflecting the nature of their author. In *The Women of Shakespeare* (1911), Harris speculates on Shakespeare's mother, wife, daughter, and mistress, relating them to the various female characters in the plays. Thus Harris claims that traits of Shakespeare's mother appear in Volumnia, that the shrewish Kate of *The Taming of the Shrew* is drawn from his wife, and that Perdita is derived from his daughter. With the mistress, the situation is more complex. Harris believes that the various phases of her personality are reflected in a variety of women: Juliet, Portia, Beatrice, Rosalind, Cleopatra, and Cressida; he is most intrigued by the Dark Lady of the *Sonnets* and by the Rosaline who is described as the earlier love of Romeo. He identified Mary FITTON as the Dark Lady. Harris was indebted to Georg Brandes for many of his ideas, but he carried the Danish critic's speculations to an exaggerated length.

Harris, Henry (1630?–?1682). Actor. Harris was one of the original members of William Davenant's Duke's Company, formed at the Restoration. As an actor he was eclipsed by his colleague Thomas Betterton, but he was nevertheless distinguished for his Shakespearean roles, including those of Romeo, Macduff, Sir Andrew Aguecheek, and Cardinal Wolsey, the last his most famous role. After the death of Davenant, Harris and Betterton became the directors of the DUKE'S COMPANY at the Dorset Garden Theatre. Harris died shortly before the union of the Duke's Company with the King's Company. [Hazelton Spencer, *Shakespeare Improved*, 1927.]

Harrison, G[eorge] B[agshawe] (1894–) Scholar, professor emeritus at the University of Michigan. English by birth and education, Harrison was for many years reader in English literature at London University before assuming positions at Queen's University, Ontario, and the University of Michigan. His books include the following: *Shakespeare's Fellows* (1923), *Shakespeare: The Man and His Stage* (1923), *The Story of Elizabethan Drama* (1926), *The Genius of Shakespeare* (1927), *England in Shakespeare's Day* (1928), *Shakespeare at Work* (1933), *Shakespeare Under Elizabeth* (1933), *Introducing Shakespeare* (1939), *Elizabethan Plays and Players* (1940), and *Shakespeare's Tragedies* (1951). With H. Granville-Barker he has edited *A Companion to Shakespeare Studies* (1934), a collection of introductory essays. He has also served as editor-in-chief of several series: The Bodley Head Quartos, The Shakespeare Association Facsimiles, The New Stratford Shakespeare, and The Penguin Shakespeare. His edition of the *Complete Works* appeared in 1952; subsequently, the text and annotations have been reprinted as separate titles in The Harbinger Shakespeare series. Harrison is perhaps best known for his Elizabethan and Jacobean journals. Drawing upon contemporary sources, he has created journals in the form of day-by-day accounts of events as they might have been noted and reflected upon by men of the period. *Elizabethan Journals, 1591–1603* appeared separately in three volumes from 1928 to 1933; in 1938 they were revised and reprinted as one volume. Two volumes covering the period following have also been published: *A Jacobean Journal . . . 1603–1606* (1941) and *A Second Jacobean Journal . . . 1607–1610* (1958). See TOPICAL REFERENCES.

Harrison, John (d. 1618). London bookseller. Harrison, whose shop was located at the sign of the Golden Anchor in Paternoster Row, was continually in trouble with the authorities of the Stationers' Company for violating its rules. On May 9, 1594 he entered *The Rape of Lucrece* in the Stationers' Register and published it in the same year, printed by Richard Field. Harrison also published four subsequent editions of the poem, two of which were printed by his son John Harrison III (d. 1604). The elder Harrison also published the second and third editions (1595, 1596) of *Venus and Adonis.* [*The Poems,* New Variorum Edition, Hyder Rollins, ed., 1938.]

Harrison, William (1534–1593). Topographer and historian. Educated at Cambridge and Oxford, Harrison was a clergyman whose avocations included history and topographical studies. His *An historicall description of the Islande of Britayne* (1577) was included as part of the first edition of Holinshed's *Chronicles,* one of the sources of Shakespeare's history plays. Harrison's "Description," a sort of geographical and sociological compendium, is one of the finest single sources of information about the life and times of 16th-century England. Harrison expanded the "Description" for the second edition of the *Chronicles* in 1587. For the same work Harrison also contributed "The Description of Scotlande," derived from Hector Boece's *Scotorum Historiae,* one of the sources of *Macbeth.*

Harsnett or **Harsnet, Samuel** (1561–1631). Prelate. Harsnett was educated at Cambridge, receiving his M.A. in 1584. In 1599 he was employed by the royal government as a licenser of books, responsible for the censorship of seditious matter. Inadvertently, he allowed the publication of a book which contained a dedication to Robert Devereux, 2nd earl of Essex, and hinted at his eventual accession to the throne. Essex was in disgrace at the time over the failure of the Irish campaign (see IRELAND) and Harsnett was threatened with imprisonment. He managed to exonerate himself and in 1603 published *A declaration of egregious popish impostors,* an attack on exorcism as practiced by the Jesuits. Lewis Theobald first pointed out that Edgar's catalogue of devils and his feigned lunacy in *King Lear* are derived from descriptions in Harsnett's pamphlet. Kenneth Muir has investigated Shakespeare's debt to Harsnett further and has given a detailed account of the use of the *Declaration,* not only in *King Lear,* but in *Pericles* and *The Tempest* as well. [Kenneth Muir, *Shakespeare's Sources,* Vol. I, 1957.]

Hart, Charles (d. 1683). Actor. Hart is thought by some to have been the son of William Hart, the grandson of Joan Shakespeare Hart, and thus the grandnephew of Shakespeare. According to James Wright's *Historia Histrionica,* he was apprenticed to Richard Robinson, one of Shakespeare's fellow King's Men, and played women's parts during his early years. During the period of the closing of the theatres (1642–1660), Hart acted first at the Cockpit and then in private performances at the homes of the nobility. At the Restoration he joined Killigrew's company, remaining with them until he retired on a pension in 1682. The occasion for his retirement was the amalgamation of Killigrew's company with that of Betterton's; Hart was said to be afraid of Betterton's competition as an actor.

Hart originated many of the leads in Dryden's plays, including Antony in *All for Love* (1677) and Celadon in *Secret Love,* in which Nell Gwynn played Florimel. Among his other parts were characters in plays by Ben Jonson and Beaumont and Fletcher, as well as Shakespeare's Othello, Cassio, Brutus, and Hotspur. Downes, in his *Roscius Anglicanus* (1708), places Hart among the best actors of his day:

> *First,* Mr. *Hart,* in the Part of *Arbaces,* in King and no King; *Amintor,* in the Maids Tragedy; *Othello; Rollo; Brutus,* in *Julius Caesar; Alexander,* towards the latter End of his Acting; if he Acted in any one of these but once in a Fortnight, the House was fill'd as at a New Play, especially *Alexander,* he Acting that with such Grandeur and Agreeable Majesty, That one of the Court was pleas'd to Honour him with this Commendation; That *Hart* might Teach any King on Earth how to Comport himself: He was no less Inferior in Comedy; as *Mosca* in the Fox; *Don John* in the Chances, *Wildblood* in the Mock Astrologer; with sundry other Parts. In all the Comedies and Tragedies, he was concern'd he Performed with that Exactness and Perfection, that not any of his Successors have Equall'd him.

[*Dictionary of National Biography,* 1885– ; *Oxford Companion to the Theatre,* Phyllis Hartnoll, ed., 1951; *The Restoration Stage,* John I. McCollum, Jr., ed., 1961.]

Hart, Joan. Born **Joan Shakespeare** (1569–1646). Shakespeare's younger sister. Christened on April 15, 1569, Joan was the only one of Shakespeare's sisters to survive childhood. Sometime before 1600 she married William HART, by whom she had four children. She and her family resided in the western house, the BIRTHPLACE, in Henley Street. In his will, Shakespeare bequeathed her £20, his wearing apparel, as well as the tenancy of the house ". . . wherein she dwelleth for her naturall lief vnder the yearelie Rent of xijd." [Mark Eccles, *Shakespeare in Warwickshire,* 1961.]

Hart, William (d. 1616). The husband of Shakespeare's younger sister Joan. Hart was a hatter about whom little is known other than that he was sued for debts in 1600 and again in 1601. He died shortly before Shakespeare and was buried April 17, 1616. He and his wife had four children: William (1600–1639), Mary (1603–1607), Thomas (1605–1661), and Michael (1608–1618). William has been confused with William Hart, an actor with the King's Men who died in 1650. Thomas succeeded to the ownership of the BIRTHPLACE in Henley Street, and his son Thomas (b. 1634) became owner of the birthplace and the WOOLSHOP, which remained in the Hart family until 1806.

William Hart's initials qualify him as yet another candidate for the title MR. W. H. [Mark Eccles, *Shakespeare in Warwickshire,* 1961.]

Harvey, Gabriel (c. 1550–1631). Scholar. While a fellow at Cambridge, Harvey became a close friend of Edmund Spenser. The friendship is celebrated in the latter's *Shepheardes Calendar* (1579) through the characters Colin Clout (Spenser) and Hobbinol (Harvey). Further material on the friendship is found in *Three Proper, and Wittie, Familiar Letters* (1580), consisting of two letters by Spenser and three by Harvey. A controversy with Thomas Nashe, the origins of which are only partially known, resulted in Harvey's *Four Letters and Certain Sonnets* (1592). Harvey's allusion to Shakespeare (see HAMLET: *Date*) occurs as a marginal note in his copy of *Chaucer:*

> The younger sort take much delight in Shakespeares Venus, & Adonis: but his Lucrece, & his tragedie of Hamlet, Prince of Denmark, haue it in them, to please the wiser sort.

Harvey, Sir **John Martin.** See Sir John Martin MARTIN-HARVEY.

Harvey or **Hervey, William.** Lord **Harvey of Kidbrooke** (d. 1642). Soldier and courtier. Harvey served under the earl of Essex in the expedition to Cadiz, for which service he was knighted in 1596. In 1598 he married Mary, the widow of the 2nd earl of Southampton, over the strenuous objections of her son, Shakespeare's patron, Henry Wriothesley, 3rd earl of Southampton. On the basis of his relationship with Southampton, some scholars have suggested Harvey as the MR. W. H. of the *Sonnets*. They argue that if the sonnets were addressed to Southampton, it would have been relatively easy for Harvey, who in 1607 became the sole executor of the will of Southampton's mother, to have come into possession of a copy of them and to have sold or given them to Thomas Thorpe, the printer of the First Quarto of the *Sonnets*.

Harvey may also be connected with Shakespeare as the "W Har" who made an early allusion to the *Rape of Lucrece*. The allusion occurs in a poem entitled *Epicedium. A funeral Song upon . . . the Lady Helen Branch* (1594):

> You that have writ of chaste Lucretia,
> Whose death was witnesse of her spotlesse life: . . .
> Hither unto your home direct your eies,
> Whereas, unthought on, much more matter lies.

After the death of his first wife, Harvey married Cordell, the daughter of Sir Brian ANNESLEY, in 1608. [A. L. Rowse, *William Shakespeare*, 1963.]

Hastings, Lord. In *2 Henry IV*, a leader of the rebel army. Hastings is in favor of accepting Prince John's treacherous offer of peace, but when his army has been dismissed, Hastings is arrested and executed, as are Archbishop Scroop and Lord Mowbray. The historical model for this character is Sir Ralph Hastings. According to some authorities, his life was spared. [W. H. Thomson, *Shakespeare's Characters: A Historical Dictionary*, 1951.]

Hastings, William, Baron (1430?–1483). A devoted supporter of Edward IV, who made Hastings a peer in 1461. After helping the king to escape to Holland before Warwick's attack of 1470, Hastings raised Yorkist support against the invading Lancastrian. When the king died, Hastings championed the claims of Edward's children to the throne, thus becoming a hindrance to Richard, duke of Gloucester, who wished to be king. In 1483, while attending a council in the Tower, Hastings was charged by Gloucester with treason and was beheaded without trial.

In *3 Henry VI*, it is Lord Hastings who helps King Edward to escape after his capture by Warwick. In *Richard III*, despite his enmity toward Queen Margaret, Hastings refuses to encourage Gloucester's usurpation of the throne. Accordingly Richard, accusing Hastings of being a traitor and protecting a witch, orders his execution.

Hatcliffe, William (1568–?1631). Leslie Hotson's candidate for the MR. W. H. and Fair Youth of the *Sonnets*. A native of Lincolnshire, Hatcliffe studied at Jesus College, Cambridge, and Gray's Inn, to which he was admitted on November 4, 1586. While at Gray's Inn he was chosen during the Christmas revels of 1587/8 as Prince of Purpoole, the mock king who acted as a Lord of Misrule during the festive season. This title, Hotson argues, explains the royal metaphors which are used to address the Fair Youth of the *Sonnets*. With this conjecture as his basis Hotson proceeds to discover Hatcliffe's name, in a number of variant spellings such as Hatlin, Hatlyff, Hatelyffe, etc., embedded in the text of the poems as well as in Thomas Thorpe's epistle to the 1609 edition. In the course of developing his thesis he asserts that *Love's Labour's Lost* was written for Gray's Inn in 1588, that Hatcliffe is being gently satirized in the figure of Pompey in that play and that Hatcliffe's portrait can be seen in the famous Elizabethan miniature by Nicholas Hilliard, "Portrait of a Young Man Leaning Against a Tree."

Aside from this early ostensible connection Hotson is unable to discover any connection between Shakespeare and Hatcliffe. He suggests that the friendship must have ended shortly after the supposed composition of the *Sonnets* in 1589.

A chronic debtor, Hatcliffe in 1597 married Dorothy Kay, daughter of John Kay of Hackney (d. 1589), a royal clerk. The couple lived in Lincolnshire where Hatcliffe frittered away his inheritance, and from which, according to Hotson, he traveled to London in 1609 to sell the manuscript of the *Sonnets* to Thomas Thorpe. Hotson's lively and provocative theory has generated a great deal of discussion in literary circles as well as in the more restricted area of Shakespearean scholarship. The general consensus, however, is inclined to reject the claim. [Leslie Hotson, *Mr. W. H.*, 1964.]

Hathaway Family. The family of Shakespeare's wife. The Hathaways were landowners in Shottery, a small village near Stratford. ***John Hathaway*** (fl. 1556) is cited in local records as the owner of a house called "Hewlands." The house is presumably the one now known as ANNE HATHAWAY'S COTTAGE. John's son was probably ***Richard Hathaway*** (d. 1581), the father of Shakespeare's wife, Anne. In his will, dated September 1, 1581, Richard alludes to his wife, Joan (d. 1599), and seven children: Agnes (Anne), Catherine (d. 1563), Margaret (b. 1564), Bartholomew (d. 1624), Thomas (b. 1569), John (b. 1575), and William (b. 1578). Richard was apparently a well-to-do farmer, for in his will he left legacies for all of his children, including 10 marks to his daughter Anne to be paid on the day of her marriage. Extracts of the will are given below:

> . . . I, Richard Hathway of Shottree in the parrishe of Stratforde-uppon-Avon in the countie of Warwicke, husbandman, beinge sicke in bodye but of perfect memorye, I thancke my Lord God, doe ordaine and make this my last will and testamente in manner and forme followinge. Firste, I bequeathe my sowle unto Allmightie God, trustinge to be saved by the merittes of Christes Passion, and

my bodye to be buried in the churche or churcheyarde of Stratforde aforesaide . . . Item, I give and bequeathe unto Agnes, my daughter, sixe poundes thirtene shillinges fower pence, to be paide unto her at the daie of her marriage . . . And I desier my trustie frende and neighbours, Stephen Burman and Fowlke Sandelles, to be my supervisors of this my last will and testamente, and theie to have for theire paynes therin to be taken twelve-pence a-peece of theme. Witnesses, sir William Gilbarde, clarke and curate in Stretforde, Richard Burman, John Richardson, and John Hemynge, withe others . . . .

Bartholomew Hathaway, Anne's older brother, succeeded to his father's copyhold estate upon the death of his mother in 1599. In 1610 he bought the estate outright for the sum of £200. In his will he left the property to his son ***John*** (b. 1584), naming as one of the overseers Dr. John Hall, Shakespeare's son-in-law.

Anne Hathaway's name is not recorded in the baptism registry of the parish church because she was born before the first registry was begun (1588). The inscription on her grave, however, indicates that she was 67 at the time of her death in 1623, thus placing the year of her birth as 1555 or 1556. She married Shakespeare on November 27, 1582 when she was 26 and he 18.

Two extracts from Shakespeare's plays have been adduced to prove that the marriage was unhappy. The Duke in *Twelfth Night* advises Viola:

> let still the woman take
> An elder than herself; so wears she to him,
> So sways she level in her husband's heart.
> (II, iv, 30–32)

And Prospero in *The Tempest* warns Ferdinand that prenuptial intimacy will produce "sour-eyed disdain and discord" (IV, i, 20), an alleged reference to Shakespeare's premarital relations with Anne (see MARRIAGE). But it is perilous business to discover the dramatist's opinions in the lines of any of his characters.

Shortly after the birth of his twins Hamnet and Judith, Shakespeare left Stratford for London, and began what many biographers refer to as a lifelong estrangement from Anne. It is true that Anne and her babies did not accompany her husband to London, but in 1596, about 10 years after his arrival in the city, we find him living in the parish of St. Helen's, near the Theatre, in what seems to have been a large house. At least, the taxes assessed on the property were larger than those paid by either Richard or Cuthbert Burbage, both rich men. Near the close of 1596 the boy Hamnet died and Shakespeare moved into lodgings in Southwark. The next year he bought New Place, one of the largest estates in Stratford. After repairing the house and restoring its garden, he installed his wife and children in it. She continued to reside there until her death in 1623. There is evidence that Shakespeare often visited his family at New Place during the years of his active career in the theatre. And he lived there with Anne from the time of his retirement in 1611 to his death in 1616. The fact that he willed his second-best bed to her has been interpreted as a gesture of contempt. But the bequest may have possessed the opposite significance, for the best bed would have been hers as a part of a widow's dower rights.

In truth, there is no warrant for the assumption that Shakespeare's marriage was a failure or that he and Anne Hathaway were incompatible. On August 6, 1623 Shakespeare's widow died at New Place at the age of 67. According to the clerk interviewed by Mr. DOWDALL, Anne "did Earnestly Desire to be Layd in the same Graue" with her husband. But in view of the warning verses on Shakespeare's grave, the sexton did not dare to open the grave, and Anne was buried in the churchyard. [Mark Eccles and C. C. Stopes, *Shakespeare's Family*, 1901.]

Hawkins, Richard (fl. 1613–1636). London bookseller. Hawkins, whose shop was located in Chancery Lane, was chiefly a publisher of plays. He was one of a group of publishers, including Robert Allot, John Smethwicke, William Aspley, and Richard Meighen, who published the Second Folio (1632) of Shakespeare's plays.

Hawkins, William (1722–1801). Hawkins is the author of an adaptation of *Cymbeline*, first produced on February 15, 1759. Hawkins' version, which has the same title as the Shakespeare play, had seven performances. Acts IV and V are completely rewritten and the character of Iachimo is eliminated. Hawkins was a professor of poetry at Oxford, and the liberties he took with Shakespeare's text indicate that even in conservative circles in the mid-18th century it was common practice to "improve" upon Shakespeare's originals. See CYMBELINE: *Stage History*. [John Genest, *Some Account of the English Stage*, 1832.]

Haydn, Franz Josef. See MUSIC BASED ON SHAKESPEARE: *18th century*.

Hayes, George (1888–). Actor. Born in London, Hayes made his acting debut at the Nottingham Theatre Royal in 1912. Later that year he played Osric in Sir Johnston Forbes-Robertson's *Hamlet* and Roderigo in *Othello;* in 1913 he accompanied Sir Johnston's company to Drury Lane (as Osric) and to New York as Laertes. In 1915/6, in the United States with Sir Herbert Beerbohm Tree's company, he portrayed the Prince of Arragon and Launcelot Gobbo in *The Merchant of Venice* and Slender in *The Merry Wives of Windsor*. In 1919 he added the role of Gratiano to his repertory. In the following year he joined the Everyman Repertory Company at Hampstead and in 1923 began acting with the Old Vic, playing Don Adriano, Aaron, Ajax, Valentine, Tullus Aufidius, Iago, and Bottom. He played with the New Shakespeare Company at Stratford-upon-Avon from 1928 to 1930 as Demetrius, Apemantus, King Henry (*1 Henry IV*), Richard III, Doctor Caius, Shylock, and Hamlet. Hayes made other appearances in subsequent years at the Stratford Festival and other theatres as Brutus, Claudio, Romeo, Macbeth, Richard II, Benedick, Clown (*Antony and Cleopatra*), Malvolio, Prospero, and Jaques. He has also appeared in films since 1935. [*Who's Who in the Theatre*, 1957.]

Hayes or **Heyes, Laurence** (fl. 1603–1637). Publisher. Hayes was the son of Thomas Hayes (d. 1603), the publisher of the 1600 Quarto of *The Merchant of Venice*. Hayes inherited the copyright of the play and re-entered it in the Stationers' Register in 1619 after the unauthorized printing of the play in that year by William Jaggard. Hayes printed another quarto of *The Merchant* in 1637.

Hayes or **Heyes, Thomas** (d. 1603). London bookseller. Hayes, whose shop was located at St. Paul's Churchyard, was the publisher of the First Quarto (1600) of *The Merchant of Venice*. After Hayes' death, the copyright of the play passed to his son Lawrence (fl. 1600–1637), who confirmed the copyright in 1619 after William Jaggard had printed the play without obtaining copyright. In 1637 Lawrence Hayes printed another edition of the play.

Hayman, Francis (1708–1786). Artist, theatrical scene painter, and illustrator. The range of Hayman's artistic activities makes him an important figure in relation to Shakespeare.

A pupil of the portraitist Robert Brown (d. 1753), Hayman was a very young man when he came to London and found employment as a scene painter at Drury Lane. His reputation grew, and he contributed four large figure compositions to the decoration of Vauxhall Gardens, three of which have been lost. The fourth, a study of the play scene from *Hamlet*, is particularly interesting because it departs from the common practice of making Hamlet the central figure in any illustration of the play. Hamlet is not even shown; attention is focused instead on the King, who watches the players in apparent alarm. The dramatic and economic disposition of the figures is characteristic of Hayman's artistic virtues. Considered the finest history painter of his day, he excelled in compositions involving a number of figures. Although his color was weak and his figure drawing somewhat mannered, he was a good draftsman and could treat complicated subject matter with clarity and verve.

Hayman was a founding member of the Royal Academy and contributed paintings of scriptural subjects to its exhibitions. A *bon vivant* and a member of Hogarth's circle, he was also one of the most important book illustrators of his time, and his collaboration with Hubert Gravelot in the Hanmer edition of 1744 produced the finest of the early illustrated editions of Shakespeare. See ART; BOYDELL'S SHAKESPEARE GALLERY. [W. M. Merchant, *Shakespeare and the Artist*, 1959.]

Haymarket Theatre. Playhouse. Built in 1720 by John Potter, a carpenter, the Haymarket is the second oldest playhouse still in use in London. In 1747 it was taken over by Samuel Foote (1720–1777), a playwright and actor with a great gift for mimicry. Foote was succeeded by George Colman and his son. Early in the 19th century, Ira Aldrich appeared at the Haymarket as Aaron and Othello.

In 1820, the old theatre was demolished and the Modern Haymarket was constructed. Samuel Phelps made his successful debut as Shylock there in 1837. Among other successes at the theatre in the 1850's and 1860's was the London debut of Edwin Booth. In 1887 the Haymarket's lessee was Herbert Beerbohm Tree, who, during the next 10 years, presented a series of lavish Shakespearean productions. [W. J. Macqueen-Pope, *Haymarket: Theatre of Perfection*, 1948.]

Hayward, Sir **John** (c. 1564–1627). Elizabethan historian. Hayward's account of the deposing of Richard II and the subsequent rule of Henry IV (*The First Part of the Life and Raigne of King Henrie the IIII*) was widely regarded as a veiled allegory supporting the earl of Essex in his rivalry with the queen. As a result of the publication, Hayward was brought to trial in 1600 and imprisoned for at least two years. After the death of Elizabeth, he was released and devoted the remainder of his life to historical research.

Attempts have been made to connect Hayward's work with Shakespeare's *Richard II*. The history was published in 1599, two years after the printing of the First Quarto of *Richard II*. In its original form the book contained a dedication to the earl of Essex. The dedication was removed from later copies of the book, either at the request of Essex or of the government authorities, but this did not prevent the subsequent suppression of the book and imprisonment of Hayward. He was convicted of writing a pointed political allegory in which Bolingbroke is equivalent to Essex and Richard II to Elizabeth. That Elizabeth was already sensitive to this comparison is known from another source (see William LAMBARDE). From the standpoint of Shakespeare, the interesting aspect of the book is that it has a number of verbal parallels with *Richard II*. On this basis some commentators have attempted to see the Shakespeare play as another, earlier example of political allegory, written to support the Essex faction. The conjecture is, of course, supported by the special performance of *Richard II* given at the request of the Essex followers on the eve of the rebellion. Nevertheless, the evidence of dates seems to indicate that Shakespeare's play was merely the source of Hayward's work and did not necessarily share in any allegorical scheme which that work might have had. [*Richard II*, Arden Edition, Peter Ure, ed., 1956.]

Hazlitt, William (1778–1830). Essayist and critic. Born at Maidstone, Kent, and educated at Hackney College, a Unitarian seminary, Hazlitt remained loyal to liberal political and philosophical principles throughout his life. In 1802 he went to Paris to study painting, but soon turned to free-lance writing. His essays cover a variety of subjects, from art and literary criticism to economics, politics, and philosophy. His most important critical works are *The Characters of Shakespear's Plays* (1817), *The English Poets* (1818), *The English Comic Writers* (1819), and *The Dramatic Literature of the Age of Elizabeth* (1820). *A View of the English Stage* (1818) is a collection of his reviews. Although his continuing interest in politics and art is reflected in his *Life of Napoleon Bonaparte* (4 vols., 1828–1830) and his *Life of Titian* (1830), Hazlitt is best known for the familiar essays which he published in the *Examiner* and the *London Enquirer*. These were collected in *The Round Table* (1817), *Table Talk* (2 vols., 1821–1822), *The Plain Speaker* (1826), *Sketches and Essays* (1839), and *Winterslow* (1850).

In his Shakespearean criticism Hazlitt manages to convey his experience of the plays, often in a manner suggestive of the close attention modern critics give to the text. He points to the personality and particularity of Shakespeare's characters, who "speak like men, not like authors." Hazlitt's appreciation of Shakespeare's metaphors and his language challenges the neoclassical view, propounded by Dryden, that Elizabethan taste and Shakespeare's style were unrefined or unnatural. "His language is hieroglyphical," Hazlitt writes. "It translates thoughts into visible images." Hazlitt clearly admires Shakespeare's metaphysical imagery: "The more the thoughts are strangers to each other, and the longer they have been kept asunder, the more intimate does their union seem to become. Their felicity is equal to their force. Their likeness is made more dazzling by their novelty. They startle, and take the fancy prisoner in the same instant."

The Characters of Shakespear's Plays is essentially a commentary in the manner of A. W. von Schlegel's criticism, which Hazlitt believes "by far the best account of the plays of Shakespeare that has hitherto appeared." Hazlitt pays close attention to poetic elements in Shakespeare which he feels Samuel Johnson was unable to appreciate. He claims to improve upon Schlegel by "avoiding an appearance of mysticism in his style" and by providing "illustrations from particular passages of the plays themselves, which Schlegel's work, from the extensiveness of his plan, did not admit." [Herschel Baker, *William Hazlitt*, 1962.]

Hazlitt, William Carew (1834–1913). Bibliographer and man of letters, grandson of the essayist. Educated at the Merchant Taylors' School, Hazlitt was called to the bar in 1861. His activities as a book collector led to the publication of numerous notes, lists, and miscellaneous bibliographical information. He later became involved in editing many of the works that came to his attention. *Old English Jest-Books* (3 vols., 1864) is a reprint of early jest books supposedly used by Shakespeare. *The English Drama and Stage Under the Tudor and Stuart Princes, 1543–1664 . . .* (1869) contains primary source material relating to the theatre, including legal documents, descriptions of playgoing, and attacks against the theatre. *Shakespeare's Library* (6 vols., 1875) is a collection of the principal sources used by Shakespeare; it is based on John Payne Collier's edition of 1843 and includes the notes of Collier and Halliwell-Phillipps. Hazlitt also issued new editions of Thomas Wharton's *History of English Poetry* (1871) and Robert Dodsley's *A Select Collection of Old English Plays* (15 vols., 1874–1876). His *Shakespeare, the Man and the Work* (1902) is a general study.

Hearne, Thomas (1685–1735). Scholar and antiquary. Hearne's private diary recorded the apocryphal story of Shakespeare as the godfather (and possibly the father) of William Davenant. Hearne, whose chief interest lay in English history, published a series of editions of the early English chroniclers. His diary, not published until the 19th century, contained Hearne's private opinions of a number of eminent people. The Shakespeare allusion was in a section dated 1709:

> 'Twas reported by Tradition in Oxford that Shakespear as he us'd to pass from London to Stratford upon Avon, where he liv'd & now lies buried, always spent some time in ye Crown Tavern in Oxford, which was kept by one Davenant who had a handsome Wife, & lov'd witty Company, tho' himself a reserv'd and melancholly Man. He had born to him a son who afterwards Christen'd by ye Name of W[m]. who prov'd a very Eminent Poët, and was knighted (by ye name of S[r]. William Davenant) and ye said M[r]. Shakespear was his God-fàther & gave him his name. (In all probability he got him.) 'Tis further said that one day going from school a grave Doctor in Divinity met him, and ask'd him, *Child whither art thou going in such hast?* to wch the child reply'd, *O Sir my God-father is come to Town, & I am going to ask his blessing.* To w[ch] the D[r]. said, *Hold Child, you must not take the name of God in vaine.*

[E. K. Chambers, *William Shakespeare*, 1930.]

Heath, Benjamin (1704–1766). Author. In 1765 Heath published his notes to the various plays under the title *A Revisal of Shakespeare's Text, wherein the Alterations introduced into it by the more modern Editors and Critics are particularly considered.* As the title indicates, Heath took issue with previous editors, especially William Warburton. Warburton is also the object of an abusive attack in the preface, and the book proper begins with the heading "A Revisal of Shakespeare's Text, as Published by Mr. Warburton." Heath also published some notes on the Greek tragedies in 1762.

heavens. See playhouse structure.

Hecate. In Greek mythology, a goddess of the moon, earth, and underworld, and, in later times, a goddess of dark magic. In *Macbeth*, III, v and IV, i, Hecate chides the three witches for having acted without consulting her. It is thought that her lines were inserted into Shakespeare's play by another writer, possibly Thomas Middleton.

Hecatommithi. See Cinthio.

Hector. In Greek mythology, a Trojan hero and the eldest son of Priam. As treated in Homer's *Iliad*, Hector is the most magnanimous of all the Trojan chieftains, but, after holding out for 10 years, he is slain by Achilles, lashed to the victor's chariot, and dragged three times round the walls of Troy. In *Troilus and Cressida*, Hector appears as Troy's most illustrious warrior.

For the Elizabethan audience, who regarded the Trojans as ancestors, Hector, and not Achilles, was the hero of the Trojan War. In the play he is presented as the most truly noble of the legendary figures in both camps. In keeping with the ironic, ambiguous tone of the play, however, even the portrait of Hector is not without a hint of satire. In his debate with Troilus over the possibility of surrendering Helen to the Greeks and thereby restoring peace (II, ii), Hector is a model of sanity and reason:

> . . . these morall lawes
> Of Nature, and of Nation, speake alowd
> To have her back returned.

Nevertheless, at the end of the debate, he falls in with Troilus' argument that by retaining Helen the Trojans will be spurred to "valiant and magnanimous deeds," thus adding to their glory and renown, and reveals that he has challenged "the dull and factious nobles of the Greeks" to individual combat.

Hegel, Georg Wilhelm (1770–1831). German philosopher. Born at Stuttgart and educated at the University of Tübingen, Hegel became a private tutor, a lecturer at the University of Jena, and a professor at the universities of Heidelberg and Berlin. Among his philosophical publications are *Die Phänomenologie des Geistes* (1807), his first influential book, and *Enzyklopädie der Philosophischen Wissenschaften im Grundrisse* (1817), a description of his system as a whole. At Berlin Hegel lectured on aesthetics, the philosophy of religion, and the philosophy of history.

A. C. Bradley suggested in his *Oxford Lectures on Poetry* (1909) that Hegel was the only philosopher since Aristotle to have treated tragedy "in a manner both original and searching." Hegel's theory of tragedy, like his dialectic, is based on the principle of conflict. He argues that the tragic situation is one in which two spiritual or ethical imperatives come into collision, such as duty to family and duty to the state in Sophocles' *Antigone*, a play which to Hegel was the "perfect exemplar of tragedy." The tragic hero, according to this view, single-mindedly identifies himself with one of these imperatives at the expense of the other or is internally divided between the two. In the modern tragedy the hero is often a unique individual as opposed to the "type" represented in the Greek drama. The collision of forces in the modern tragedy is often internal.

Anne Paolucci has recently suggested, contrary to Bradley's suggestion, that Hegel did not prefer the Greek tragedy to the modern. For modern tragedy Hegel particularly admired the English, whom he considered "exceptionally distinguished" in their delineation of "fully developed characters and personality." To Hegel, "soaring above the rest at an almost unapproachable height, stands Shakespeare." [Anne Paolucci, "Bradley and Hegel on Shakespeare," *Comparative Literature*, 1964.]

Helen. In *Cymbeline*, an attendant on Imogen. In II, ii, Imogen asks Helen to "fold down the leaf" where her mistress has left off reading, and to call her at four o'clock.

Helen. In Greek mythology, the daughter of Zeus and Leda and wife of Menelaus; her abduction by Paris led to the Trojan War. In the *Iliad* of Homer and *The Trojan Women* of Euripides, Helen appears as a shallow and self-centered woman, unconcerned with the havoc that her infidelity has wrought. The subject of much rhapsodizing by classical and Renaissance poets, who saw her as a symbol of womanly beauty and sexual attraction, Helen suffers a sharp comedown in Shakespeare. In *Troilus and Cressida*, she is pictured as a vacuous and rather insipid creature, entirely unworthy of the idealism of Troilus and Paris, a fact which is itself a telling commentary on the illusionary nature of that idealism.

Helena. In *All's Well That Ends Well*, the orphaned ward of the Countess of Rousillon. Because of her love for the Countess' son, Bertram, the beautiful and accomplished Helena follows him to the court of the King of France. Equipped with a rare prescription bequeathed to her by her father, a famous physician, Helena offers to cure the mortally ill King. Courageously submitting her life should she fail, but exacting as a fee the choice of a husband from among the courtiers if successful, Helena chooses Bertram upon the patient's recovery. Reluctantly Bertram accedes to the marriage, which he considers a misalliance, then abandons his bride of low rank.

Repenting her "ambitious love," Helena goes into self-exile but, through a ruse, is able to win her husband's acceptance on his own terms, namely, that she must get from his finger his family ring and conceive his child. At the end of the play, when Helena asks her husband, "Will you be mine now you are doubly won?" Bertram's reply demonstrates his change of heart.

Despite her obvious virtue and charm, Helena has encountered considerable resistance among Shakespearean critics. Many of them have viewed her deception of Bertram as indicative of an unbecoming deviousness. Others have come to regard this feature of her personality as an example of the ambivalence with which Shakespeare treats all of the characters in his PROBLEM PLAYS. Helena's most articulate defender has been Edward Dowden, who saw Helena as the healing "providence of the play." See ALL'S WELL THAT ENDS WELL: *Selected Criticism*. [Edward Dowden, *Shakespeare: A Critical Study*, 1875.]

Helena. In *A Midsummer Night's Dream*, an Athenian maid who is in love with Demetrius. Attempting to remedy a situation in which both Demetrius and Lysander love Hermia, Puck casts a spell which goes awry and causes them both to be enamored of Helena. Eventually Puck corrects his error and, casting a fresh spell, arranges for Helena to win Demetrius and Lysander to win Hermia.

Helenus. In Greek legend, a son of Priam and Hecuba of Troy, famous as a prophet; in *Troilus and Cressida*, a son of Priam. Helenus argues with Troilus over the advisability of returning Helen to the Greeks (II, ii).

Helicanus. In *Pericles*, a lord of Tyre. Entrusted by Pericles with the government of Tyre, the good Helicanus refuses to accept the sovereignty, but instead urges the noblemen of Tyre to search for their long-absent prince. In the Epilogue, Gower describes Helicanus as "a figure of truth, of faith, of loyalty."

hell. See PLAYHOUSE STRUCTURE.

Helmes, Henry. See INNS OF COURT.

Helpmann, Robert (1909–). Actor and dancer. Helpmann, born and educated in Australia, began his professional career as a dancer there in 1922 and made his London debut in 1933 with the Vic-Wells ballet and as an actor at the Gate Theatre. Since that time he has had a considerable impact on both the theatre and ballet. His Shakespearean roles have included Oberon (1937), Gremio and Nicholas (1939), Hamlet (1944), King John, and Shylock (Shakespeare Memorial Theatre, 1948). He became associated with Michael Benthall in 1947 as artistic director of the Duchess Theatre and has since directed several Old Vic productions: *The Tempest* (1954), *As You Like It* (1955), *Romeo and Juliet* (1956), and *Antony and Cleopatra* (1956/7). Helpmann is a noted choreographer; for the Sadler's Wells he did *Comus* and *Hamlet*. Among his dancing parts have been the leads in the Royal Ballet's productions of *The Rake's Progress*, *Coppélia*, and *Hamlet*. [*Who's Who in the Theatre*, 1961.]

Heminges, John (d. 1630). Actor and business manager of Shakespeare's acting company. Heminges' origin, if the evidence on the confirmation of arms granted to him in 1629 is to be credited, is as the "Sonne and Heire of George Hemings of Draytwiche in the Countye of Worcester Gent." The confirmation describes him as "long tyme Servant to Queen Elizabeth of happie Memory, also to King James hir Royal Successor and to King Charles his

Sonne." He began his career as an actor with the Queen's Men. By 1593 he was with Strange's Men and was listed with them in their license to travel for that summer. A year later he had become one of the newly formed Chamberlain's Men, with whom he remained until his death. He is in the acting lists of the King's Men's productions of *Every Man In his Humour* (1598), *Every Man Out of his Humour* (1599), *Sejanus* (1603), *Volpone* (1605), *The Alchemist* (1610), and *Catiline* (1611). The type of roles he played can only be guessed at. John Roberts, an unreliable source, in *An Answer to Mr. Pope's Preface to Shakespeare* (1729) refers to him as a tragedian, while Malone (in the 1821 Variorum) alluded to Heminges as Falstaff, citing as evidence a tract the title of which he had forgotten. A couplet from the ballad on the burning of the Globe in 1613 describes him as follows:

> Then with swolne eyes, like druncken
> Flemminges,
> Distressed stood old stuttering Heminges.

Most scholars assume that Heminges ceased acting at some time after 1611 and devoted himself exclusively to the company's business affairs; he was also quite active in the affairs of his parish, St. Mary's Aldermanbury, from 1608 to 1619, according to that parish's minute book.

Heminges' reputation for business acumen is evidenced in many ways. Especially significant is his appointment as executor or overseer in many of the wills executed by his fellow actors, including those of Augustine Phillips (as legatee and overseer), Alexander Cooke (trustee), Richard Cowley (witness), Shakespeare (legatee), and John Underwood and Henry Condell (overseer). When Phillips' widow remarried, Heminges also became executor of the will, and he was the trustee for Shakespeare's Blackfriars property in 1613. His greatest fame, however, has derived from his joint editorship with Condell of the FIRST FOLIO of Shakespeare's plays in 1623.

Heminges amassed considerable financial interests in the Globe and Blackfriars. His original share was one seventh of the actors' moiety of the Globe lease (acquired in 1599), and one seventh of moiety of the Blackfriars (acquired in 1608). As executor of his fellow actors' wills, Heminges was also able to add to his shares by purchasing the interests of actors' heirs who were either uninterested or not associated with the King's or Chamberlain's Men. At the time of his death, according to the SHARERS' PAPERS, he had come into possession of four-sixteenths shares in the Globe, and two-eighths shares in the Blackfriars over a period of 30 years. The suit *Witter* v. *Heminges and Condell* (1619) alluded to him as a man of "greate lyveinge wealth and power."

There is, in addition, some evidence which suggests that he was of more importance to the company than a mere listing of his assets would lead us to believe. G. E. Bentley surmises that Heminges was the man who dealt with government authorities on behalf of the company, and occasionally on behalf of all the London acting groups. This was especially important when control of the theatre was so centralized. Heminges was apparently able to secure special favors for his company from Sir Henry Herbert, the Master of the Revels. Bentley cites the following, based on entries in Herbert's office-book:

> 1623, Aug. 19—Herbert reallowed *The Winter's Tale* 'on Mr. Hemmings his worde that there was nothing profane added or reformed, thogh the allowed booke was missinge.'
>
> 1627, Apr. 11—'[Received] from Mr. Hemming, in their company's name, to forbid the playing of Shakespeare's plays, to the Red Bull Company, this 11 of April, 1627,—*5l*. 0. 0.'

John Heminges was named the recipient of the £100 which the king authorized for the relief of the players on September 20, 1630. In addition, Bentley has suggested that Heminges was named to a special post as a quasi assistant to the lord chamberlain.

After Heminges' death his son William, the executor of his will, sold one of Heminges' Globe shares to Joseph Taylor and John Lowin and one share in the Globe and one in Blackfriars to John Shank in 1633 for £156. The remaining shares he sold Shank in 1634 for £350. William Heminges' sale of the shares to Shank was the original cause of the players' 1635 petition to the lord chamberlain (see SHARERS' PAPERS). John Heminges had also been involved in a dispute with his daughter Thomasina over the disposal of her dead husband, Will Ostler's, shares. See Thomasina OSTLER. [E. K. Chambers, *The Elizabethan Stage*, 1923; G. E. Bentley, *The Jacobean and Caroline Stage*, 5 vols., 1941–1956.]

Henderson, John (1747–1785). Actor. Henderson began his career as an actor at Bath under the name of Courtney. He scored a great success there as Hamlet in 1772 and later as Macbeth. A portrait of him in the latter role was painted by Gainsborough. In 1777 he made his first appearance in London as Shylock and won immediate acclaim. Among the many other Shakespearean roles in which he excelled were Benedick, Falstaff, Iago, King John, Lear, Leontes, Richard III, Cardinal Wolsey, and Jaques. His death came at the height of his career. A multitalented man, he was also distinguished as a poet and musician.

Henderson, Robert. See Robert HENRYSON.

Heneage, Sir **Thomas** (d. 1595). Vice-chamberlain of Queen Elizabeth's household from 1589 to 1595. The vice-chamberlain was chief assistant to the lord chamberlain and his duties included the disbursement of funds for court entertainments. Heneage was, in addition, one of Elizabeth's favorite courtiers and was frequently employed on important diplomatic missions. In 1594, Heneage married Mary, countess of Southampton, widow of the 2nd earl of Southampton and mother of Shakespeare's patron Henry Wriothesley, 3rd earl of Southampton. Their wedding on May 2, 1594 has been one of those suggested as the occasion of the première performance of *A Midsummer Night's Dream*. As stepfather of Shakespeare's patron and one of the individuals responsible for the selection of the plays to be given at court during the Christmas Revels, Heneage would have represented an important figure to the dramatist and his company. See MIDSUMMER NIGHT'S DREAM: *Date*.

Henley, William Ernest (1849–1903). Poet and editor. Best known for his poem "Invictus," Henley first achieved recognition with his impressionistic free-verse sketches. He became prominent as an editor in the 1890's. Purchasing the *Scots Observer* (Edinburgh) in 1889, he renamed it the *National Observer* when he moved it to London one year later. Hardy, Kipling, Stevenson, Wells, and Yeats were among the contributors.

Henley's admiration for Elizabethan literature led him to sponsor the Tudor Translations series, a reprint of all the major translations of the English Renaissance. Of his dealings with Shakespeare, the most important was his editing the Edinburgh Folio Shakespeare and his Introduction to *Othello* in the Caxton Shakespeare. In the latter he stressed the fact that Shakespeare wrote for a living stage and that he conformed to the theatrical conventions of the age. Henley suggested that the characterizations of some major figures were shaped to fit the requirements of certain actors, such as Burbage, for example. E. E. Stoll has stated that Henley presented a concept similar to his own. [Jerome H. Buckley, *William Ernest Henley*, 1945.]

Henley-in-Arden. A town eight miles northwest of Stratford and its closest rival as an important market town. Originally known as Henley in the Forest of Arden, it was connected to Stratford by the main thoroughfare, Henley Street, the location of John Shakespeare's house. A number of important families in Stratford were originally from Henley-in-Arden.

Henrietta Maria (1609–1669). Queen Consort of Charles I, king of England, and daughter of Henry IV, king of France. She married Charles in 1625, the year of his coronation. As a Catholic and a foreigner she was never popular with the English people and her attempts to bring aid to her husband from foreign governments were instrumental in bringing about his execution. At the Restoration she returned to England where she remained until 1665.

From 1625 to 1642 Henrietta's patronage of the drama was lavish, particularly in the presentation of court masques, in which she loved to take a leading part. Her performance in these entertainments shocked the English public and elicited a rebuke from the Puritan William PRYNNE, for which offense his ears were cut off. There is evidence that her interest extended to the point of attending public performances of plays, an act hitherto unheard of for royalty.

There is a tradition that during the civil war the queen stayed at New Place, Shakespeare's house, while visiting Stratford.

Henry III (1207–1272). King of England, eldest son of King John and Isabella of Angoulême. On his father's death, Henry inherited the crown when he was only nine years old. William Marshall, earl of Pembroke, was accordingly appointed regent, and after Pembroke's death, Hubert de Burgh became greatly influential. In 1223, because of a rebellion among the barons, Henry was required to confirm the Magna Carta signed by his father in 1215. In *King John,* he appears as Prince Henry. Weeping over his dying father, he exclaims: "O that there were some virtue in my tears,/That might relieve you!" (V, vii, 44–45).

Henry IV (1367–1413). King of England; in *Richard II,* he is Henry Bolingbroke, the successful usurper of Richard's crown, and in *1* and *2 Henry IV*, the troubled, ailing King. Henry was the son of John of Gaunt and cousin of Richard II. An early supporter of Richard, he was named duke of Hereford in 1397. A year later, however, he suffered banishment as a result of a quarrel with Thomas Mowbray, duke of Norfolk. Returning to England in 1399 he rallied overwhelming forces behind him to compel the abdication of Richard and gain his own coronation. Henry's reign (1399–1413) was a troubled one, and his health deteriorated. In his latter days he was conscience-stricken over the deposition and murder of Richard but was never able to realize his dream of expiation—the formation of a new crusade to rescue Jerusalem.

Shakespeare's picture of Henry alters considerably in the two plays in which he has a significant role. As Bolingbroke in *Richard II,* he is a robust, chivalrous, occasionally impulsive young challenger; as Henry IV, he is a suspicious, weary, disenchanted old man. In both roles, however, Henry is less exciting than his predecessor, Richard II, and his successor, Prince Hal. See RICHARD II: *Comment*; 1 HENRY IV: *Comment;* and 2 HENRY IV: *Comment.*

HENRY IV. PORTRAIT BY AN UNKNOWN ARTIST. (NATIONAL PORTRAIT GALLERY)

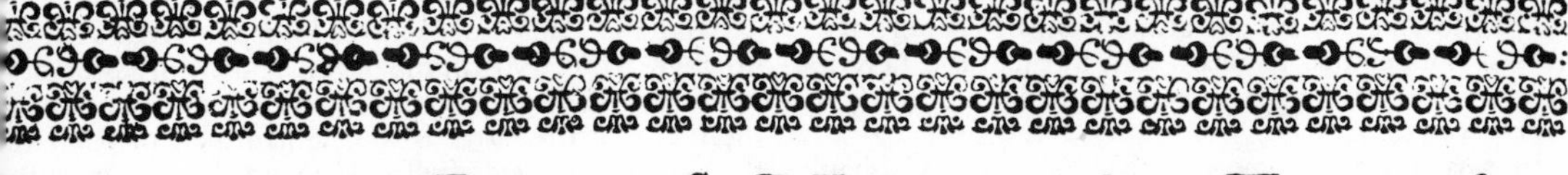

The First Part of Henry the Fourth, with the Life and Death of HENRY Sirnamed HOT-SPURRE.

Henry IV, Part One. A history play by Shakespeare.

Text. *1 Henry IV* was entered in the Stationers' Register on February 25, 1598 as "The historye of Henry the IIIJth with his battaile of Shrewsburye against Henry Hottspurre of the Northe with the conceipted mirthe of Sir John ffalstoff."

The authoritative text of the play is that of the First Quarto, issued in 1598 under the title "The History of Henrie the Fourth; With the battell at Shrewsburie, betweene the King and Lord Henry Percy, surnamed Henrie Hotspur of the North. With the humorous conceits of Sir Iohn Falstalffe. At London, Printed by P.S. [Peter Short] for Andrew Wise, dwelling in Paules Churchyard, at the signe of the Angell 1598." Q1 was based on an even earlier quarto (usually designated Q0), of which only an eight-page fragment survives. The Quarto was reprinted in 1599 and advertised as "Newly corrected by W. Shakespeare." This statement is not true, for there are only very small differences between the texts of the two quartos. Other editions appeared in 1604, 1608, 1613, and 1622. The text of the First Folio was set up from the 1613 Quarto, from which the oaths had been scrupulously removed. Some scholars believe that the extant text is a revision of an earlier version in which the comic scenes were originally written in verse and were later expanded when the name "Oldcastle" was changed to "Falstaff," as explained below.

Date. In this play the poet takes up the historical story from exactly the point where he dropped it at the end of *Richard II*, probably written in 1595. Meres, in the list of plays in his PALLADIS TAMIA, completed by October 19, 1598, includes the play among Shakespeare's "excellent tragedies." If, as seems likely, *The Merry Wives of Windsor* was written in the early months of 1597, and if *1 Henry IV* was written shortly before that comedy, as the available evidence seems to indicate, then the latter part of 1596 would appear to be the best date for the history play.

Sources. Shakespeare drew his historical material from the second edition of HOLINSHED's *Chronicles of England, Scotland and Ireland* (1587), and also from Samuel Daniel's epic, *The First Fowre Bookes of The Civile Wars between the two houses of Lancaster and York* (1595) (see CIVIL WARS). Prince Hal's wild youth had by 1597 enjoyed a long life in popular tradition. It had been dramatized in the anonymous play *The Famous Victories of Henry V*. This crude old play was entered in the Stationers' Register in 1594, the first surviving copy bearing the date 1598. From this work Shakespeare took many details of Prince Hal's riotous conduct. In it he found the name of Sir John Oldcastle, which he originally gave the character who became Falstaff. Traces of this name appear in *1 Henry IV*. The Prince addresses him as "my old lad of the castle" (I, ii, 47). The poet's use of the name caused him a good deal of trouble. The real Sir John was quite a different sort of person from the old tavern-haunter. Holinshed describes Sir John, Lord Cobham (the title he

TITLE PAGE OF THE FIRST QUARTO OF *1 Henry IV* (1598).

THE
HISTORY OF
HENRIE THE
FOVRTH;

With the battell at Shrewsburie,
betweene the King and Lord
Henry Percy, surnamed
Henrie Hotspur of
the North.

With the humorous conceits of Sir
Iohn Falstalffe.

AT LONDON,
Printed by P. S. for *Andrew Wise*, dwelling
in Paules Churchyard, at the signe of
the Angell. 1598.

acquired from his marriage to Joan, heiress of Cobham), as a "valiant captain and a hardy gentleman." Accused of heresy by the archbishop of Canterbury, he was condemned to death and burned as a heretic in 1417, thus winning a place in John Foxe's *Book of Martyrs* (1563).

In Shakespeare's day the title of Lord Cobham passed to William Brooke (see 7th Lord COBHAM). He was apparently offended at the poet's presenting his martyred ancestor in so disreputable a guise and was powerful enough to force Shakespeare to change the old rogue's name. So for a substitute he took from *1 Henry VI* the name of an allegedly cowardly character called Sir John Fastolfe and by a shift of vowels came up with Falstaff. He was the character most often mentioned and quoted by Shakespeare's contemporaries and remains today one of the most popular of all the characters in the plays.

Shakespeare also apparently had recourse to a number of minor sources for his drama. His characterization of Owen Glendower is based on the account of that figure given by Thomas PHAER in *A Mirror for Magistrates* (1559). Details of Hal's behavior may derive from *The Chronicles of England* (1580) or *The Annales of England* (1592), both recorded by John STOW. Falstaff's speech on honor (V, i, 127 ff.) is probably a parody of a similar speech in the anonymous play SOLIMAN AND PERSEDA. —O.J.C.

Plot Synopsis. Act I. King Henry's plans to lead a crusade to the Holy Land as penance for the murder of Richard II are frustrated when he learns from the Earl of Westmoreland that the Welsh chieftain Owen Glendower has recently defeated a large English army under Edmund Mortimer, Earl of March, who has himself been taken prisoner. Henry also reveals that in an engagement at Holmedon, Harry Percy, usually known as Hotspur, has triumphed over a Scottish host led by Archibald, Earl of Douglas, but has refused to surrender his prisoners to the King. Thinking of his own wayward son Hal, the Prince of Wales, the King admits that he envies the Earl of Northumberland, Hotspur's father.

Meanwhile, Prince Hal has been disporting himself with Sir John Falstaff, a corpulent knight whose taste for merriment and sack has not been blunted by his white hairs and empty purse. Ned Poins, one of Falstaff's cronies, exhorts them to take part in a robbery at Gadshill, where pilgrims and traders abound, and persuades the reluctant Hal by secretly unfolding a scheme that will reveal Falstaff as the coward that he is. Alone, the Prince reflects on his conduct, likening himself to the sun, who permits himself to be hidden by the clouds, only to seem more radiant when he emerges from the mists.

Relations between King Henry and the Percy family become even more strained as the Earl of Worcester, brother of the Earl of Northumberland and Hotspur's uncle, reminds the King that they had seated him on his throne. Although Hotspur maintains that his attitude in denying the Scottish prisoners has been misrepresented, he angers Henry by refusing to surrender them unless the King in turn ransoms Hotspur's brother-in-law, Mortimer, who had recently wed the daughter of his captor, Glendower. "Shall our coffers, then, / Be emptied to redeem a traitor home?" the King demands. Refusing to heed Hotspur's ardent defense of Mortimer's loyalty, Henry warns, "Send us your prisoners, or you will hear of it."

After the King's departure, Hotspur gives vent to his rage while Northumberland and Worcester observe that Henry's hostility to Mortimer stems from the fact that the latter is the rightful heir of Richard II. When Hotspur finally recovers his composure his uncle proposes that they launch a rebellion against the King, counting on the support of Mortimer, Glendower, Douglas, and Richard Scroop, the Archbishop of York.

Act II. As arranged, Falstaff, Prince Hal, and Poins abetted by Gadshill, Bardolph, and Peto, attack some hapless travelers and relieve them of their gold. The Prince and Poins then slip away from the others, don disguises, and set upon their accomplices, who hastily flee, leaving the loot behind. Later, at the Boar's Head Tavern in Eastcheap, Hal and Poins are joined by Falstaff, who describes in vivid, if inconsistent, detail the heroic manner in which he had fought off his assailants, displaying his tattered doublet and hose as proof. When Hal at last reveals the deception, Falstaff is undismayed. He had, of course, recognized the Prince; but, he asks, "was it for me to kill the heir-apparent? should I turn upon the true prince?" When the King sends for Prince Hal, Falstaff suggests that he rehearse the explanation he will give to his irate parent. Taking the part of the King, Falstaff condemns Hal's associates, except for one portly man of virtue often seen in his company. When the roles are reversed and Hal plays the King, he has harsh words for "that villanous abominable misleader of youth, Falstaff." The "prince," on the other hand, speaks amiably of "sweet Jack Falstaff, kind Jack Falstaff, true Jack Falstaff, valiant Jack Falstaff."

Act III. Hotspur's impetuous tongue brings him into conflict with Owen Glendower, when the conspirators gather at Bangor, in Wales. He scoffs at Glendower's account of the portents that heralded his birth and at his belief in his supernatural powers. They also quarrel over their shares in the kingdom they hope to win. Both Mortimer and Worcester scold Hotspur for baiting the Welshman, whom Mortimer describes as "a worthy gentleman, / Exceedingly well read." Their thoughts are temporarily deflected from politics by the arrival of Hotspur's high-spirited wife, Kate, and Mortimer's Welsh bride, whose inability to speak English does not dampen her husband's ardor.

Meanwhile, the King upbraids Prince Hal for his misconduct, contrasting his son's character with that of Hotspur and with his own behavior as a young man. He recalls that, unlike Richard, who had "enfeoff'd himself to popularity," he had held himself aloof from the public, becoming a mysterious and attractive figure in their eyes. In reply the chastened Prince vows to outstrip Hotspur's achievements.

Act IV. In their camp near Shrewsbury, the rebels learn that the Earl of Northumberland is prevented by illness from taking part in the campaign. Though Worcester points out that Northumberland's absence will lead some to believe that he has abandoned their cause, Hotspur, seconded by Douglas, insists that they are not seriously weakened. He remains optimistic even when it is reported that royal troops are on their way, and that Glendower's forces will be delayed for a fortnight.

Hotspur is anxious to engage in hostilities as soon

as the King's army reaches Shrewsbury. Worcester and Sir Richard Vernon, however, advise caution. Their discussion is cut short by the arrival of an emissary from the King, Sir Walter Blunt, who asks the insurgents to state their grievances and promises pardon. Hotspur replies by assailing Henry's ingratitude to the Percy clan.

Act V. Worcester and Vernon parley with the King, who indicates his willingness to forgive the rebels if they will disband their forces, while Prince Hal offers to meet Hotspur in single combat. One of the less intrepid spirits in the King's army is Falstaff, who has recruited a company of bedraggled incompetents. When the Prince reminds him that he owes God a death, Falstaff protests that " 'tis not due yet." And, realizing that honor might prick him on to an early encounter with death, he condemns that sentiment as "a mere scutcheon," of little use to the living or the dead.

Convinced that Henry will always be suspicious of the rebels, Worcester decides to conceal the King's generous terms from Hotspur and declares instead that Henry has been harsh and unyielding. This news goads Hotspur into seeking battle immediately.

In the ensuing engagement, Prince Hal acquits himself with distinction; he saves his father from the sword of Douglas and kills Hotspur. Falstaff, who has lain nearby feigning death, later claims to have killed Hotspur himself, and remains imperturbable when contradicted by Hal. The victorious King orders the execution of Worcester and Vernon, while the Prince frees Douglas as a tribute to his valor. Henry then announces his plans for terminating the rebellion.—H.D.

Comment. In the two parts of *Henry IV*, Shakespeare presents a field of military action broader than any which he dramatizes in his other chronicle history plays. The events of Part I all concern what may be called Hotspur's Rebellion, which was the first of three revolts against the throne. The action begins in late 1402 and ends with the battle of Shrewsbury, July 2, 1403. The leader of the rebellion was Lord Henry Percy, eldest son of the earl of Northumberland. Holinshed gave him the name Hotspur, appropriate for a man so eager for action that he kept his spurs hot in the flanks of his horse. In the battle of Holmedon Hill, Hotspur defeated and took prisoner the earl of Douglas and other rebel Scotsmen. These prisoners Hotspur refused to deliver to the king, an act of insubordination that seriously strained the alliance between the monarch and his fiery subject. That alliance reached its breaking point at Henry's refusal to secure the release of Hotspur's brother-in-law, Sir Edmund Mortimer, from the prison into which the Welsh rebel Owen Glendower had thrust him. Regarding Mortimer as a dangerous rival claimant to the thorne, Henry was suspicious of his every act.

An added source of concern to the king—at least in the popular tradition—was the profligacy of his son and heir to the throne, Prince Hal. These anxieties plunged Henry for long periods into deep melancholy. He attributed his troubles to his sin in having forced the deposition of Richard II and often expressed his determination to do penance for the deed (see RICHARD II: *Plot Synopsis* and *Comment*). In the play he believes that his son's wild behavior is proof that he is marked

> For the hot vengeance and the rod of heaven
> To punish my mistreadings.
> (III, ii, 10–11)

In this way Shakespeare relates the political theme of the plays to the moral flaw in the king's nature. Henry's usurpation of Richard's throne is represented as an evil act that brings about the subsequent disruption in the state. Henry could not, therefore, be presented as a sympathetic character. Rather, he is shown as calculating and cold, always a political manipulator, seldom an understanding father.

The character of Hotspur is almost entirely Shakespeare's invention. He is a spiritual descendant of the knights errant of medieval romance. He regards warfare, not as an instrument of policy, but as a highway to honor, which he glorifies in a speech compounded of extravagant metaphors (I, iii, 201–207). Yet he is even more clearly a representative of the turbulent barons from whom the monarch had to wrest power before he could establish a strong central government. He is always in an agony of impatience. Everything he does is the product of disgust or anger. He thus is an easy victim of the crafty King. Prince Hal refers contemptuously to Hotspur's reputed feverish energy: the "Hotspur of the north; he that kills me some six or seven dozen of Scots at a breakfast, washes his hands, and says to his wife 'Fie upon this quiet life! I want work' " (II, iv, 115–119). However, Shakespeare does not devote all the Hotspur scenes to this side of his nature. He shows him in two scenes with his wife in which he displays reluctant tenderness. After the firebrand has been mortally wounded by the Prince, Shakespeare enlists our respect for Hotspur: Hal covers the mangled face of his fallen adversary with the plume from his helmet. Shakespeare thus bids for us a tender farewell to the dying age of chivalry.

Shakespeare's sources represented Prince Henry as a royal prodigal. It was natural, then, for Shakespeare to model the adventures of his wild Prince upon those of the Prodigal Son of the Gospels as pictured in the morality plays treating his career. Although ostensibly dramas devoted to ethical instructions, these plays were largely given over to the depiction of the taverns and brothels in which the Prodigal wasted his substance. Because Shakespeare chose to retain the emphasis on this phase of the Prodigal's dissipation, he was able to paint for us the immortal pictures of the gatherings in the Boar's Head Tavern. Although Hal does take part in the Gadshill robbery, Shakespeare contrives to transform the ruffian of *The Famous Victories* into a likable mapcap whose dissipation did not degrade him beyond the hope of eventual reform. His speech at the end of Act I, scene ii, in which he explains that he is only posing as a wastrel so that he can add luster and surprise to his eventual reformation, should not establish him as a scheming prig in the eyes of the spectator. This speech is Shakespeare's way of calming the anxiety of his audiences by assuring them that the Prince is going to give up his wild ways and become a responsible king.

Elizabethans went to the theatre knowing that they were to see a dissipated prince, but eager to learn the playwright's version of why Hal became a profligate and what form his profligacy assumed. Falstaff provided the answer to both questions. His gaiety lured the youth away from his father's gloomy court into one of the low resorts over which Falstaff presided as the Lord of Misrule.

Falstaff is on the surface a representative of a contemporary type, the soldier who between the wars joined with others of his ilk to swarm into London where he haunted taverns, brothels, and other unsavory places of amusement. He is, however, in large measure a dramatic figure in which many stage traditions of comedy unite to form his complex personality. Though he is "gross as earth," his wit gives him wings. This imprisonment of a lively mind in a great hulk of a body is the most ridiculous of all the incongruities that Nature imposes on man. And Falstaff is the most ridiculous utterance of her favorite jest. He is also a Puritan fallen from grace, delighted to put into inappropriate contexts pious tags that he remembers from the days when he used to go to church. For example, when Poins promises Falstaff that he will persuade the Prince to take part in the Gadshill robbery, Sir John replies in the language of the Puritans: "Well, God give thee the spirit of persuasion and him the ears of profiting, that what thou speakest may move and what he hears may be believed" (I, ii, 170–173). And in *2 Henry IV* he assures the lord chief justice that he has lost his voice by singing anthems (I, ii, 213). Although he is a tavern-haunter and the leader of a crew that tempts the prodigal Hal to waste his substance in the Boar's Head Tavern, he pretends to be a sanctified spirit whom the wild Prince has led astray.

Falstaff is also a late incarnation of the *miles gloriosus*, or braggart soldier, who, with all his marks of identification, came from Latin comedy into the Renaissance drama. Wherever this traditional character appears, he is a fantastic boaster, bragging of his military exploits and his amorous conquests. But, brought to a test, he proves to be a grotesque coward and a lover easily led by the nose. When on Gadshill Falstaff roars and runs away, and later when he smears his jerkin with blood, he is adopting some of the conventional business of the braggart. His farcical antics at the battle of Shrewsbury give even more striking evidence of his descent from the *miles gloriosus*. Shakespeare has transformed this antipathetic character into a figure of fun, a source of inexhaustible laughter who easily charms Prince Hal into spending long, merry hours in his company.

1 Henry IV is today the most popular of all Shakespeare's chronicle history plays. It brings to life famous warlords of England's storied past, it feasts the eye with the pageantry of chivalric combats, it charms the ear with the stirring music of the best blank verse that Shakespeare had so far written. In its own time it fed the patriotism of Elizabethan audiences by showing a dissipated prodigal on his way to becoming an ideal English warrior king.—O.J.C.

Stage History. It is generally accepted that the first production of *1 Henry IV* was given in 1596 or 1597. The first recorded performance of the play was a private one, having been commissioned by the lord chamberlain as part of the entertainment of the Flemish ambassador in 1600. Among the 20 plays presented at court as part of the wedding festivities of Princess Elizabeth and the elector palatine (1612/3), the titles *The Hotspurre* and *Sir John Falstaffe* appear. Sir Edmund Chambers guesses that these were, respectively, *1 Henry IV* and *2 Henry IV*. The two plays were combined for a private performance at the home of Sir Edward Dering about 1623. (See DERING HENRY IV.) On New Year's night 1625 *The First Part of Sir John Falstaff* was played at Whitehall, and on May 29, 1638, the evening of the prince's birthday, *Ould Castel* was acted by the King's Men at the COCKPIT AT COURT. There is no way of telling whether this title referred to the first or second part only, or to both parts. We do not know what actors composed the original cast of *1 Henry IV*. Edmund Malone remembered reading somewhere that John Heminges created the role of Falstaff. Some critics guessed that Will Kempe or Thomas Pope played the part, and that Richard Burbage, most probably, was Prince Hal. In *Historia Histrionica* (1699) James Wright remarked, "In my time before the Wars Lowin used to act, with mighty applause Falstaff." Contemporary references attest to the play's enormous popularity during the first half of the 17th century, but the actual record of performances before the extinction of the stage by parliament in 1642 is meager.

1 Henry IV was one of the first plays to be staged by Thomas Killigrew's King's Company. Its initial performance took place on November 8, 1660 at the company's first theatre, Gibbons' Tennis Court in Vere Street. Samuel Pepys saw it there on December 31, 1660, but the performance disappointed his expectations. At later productions, in 1661 and 1667, however, he found it "a good play." John Downes lists the actors in these productions as follows: William Cartwright as Falstaff, Burt as the Prince, Charles Hart as Hotspur, William Wintersel as the King. John Lacy also acted Falstaff successfully. In 1682, when the King's Company and the Duke's Company were amalgamated, Thomas Betterton took the role of Hotspur. When he revived the play in 1700 at Lincoln's Inn Fields, he appeared as Falstaff for the first time, thus establishing the tradition of casting a company's leading actor in the role of Falstaff. Later producers would extensively cut the historical portions of *1 Henry IV* in order to elevate Falstaff's role, but Betterton confined himself to making minor cuts and transposing scenes; he made no attempt to rewrite Shakespeare. The great popularity that he enjoyed with his impersonation of the fat knight was rivaled by that of James Quin, who began his career as a Shakespearean actor playing Hotspur at Lincoln's Inn Fields in 1718/9. Two seasons later he essayed the King and another two seasons after that, Falstaff. In 1734 Quin moved to Covent Garden, where he continued to play a Falstaff endowed with breeding and intellectuality, a portrait considered unequaled until Quin's retirement in 1753. Barton Booth often acted Hotspur opposite Quin. A favorite Falstaff during the latter part of the 18th century was John Henderson, who played the role from 1777 to 1785.

Among John Philip Kemble's careful and effective Shakespeare revivals was a *1 Henry IV* produced during his first season as manager of Covent Garden (1803/4). Re-creating a role he had played notably since 1791, Kemble took the part of Hotspur, supported by George Frederick Cooke's Falstaff, an impersonation fashioned after Henderson's. Kemble's brother Stephen, whose only apparent qualification for the role was the corpulence which enabled him to play the part without padding, was Drury Lane's Falstaff from 1802 to 1820. In 1824 the youngest of Kemble's brothers, Charles staged a *1 Henry IV* noted more for the historical accuracy of the costumes than for the excellence of the acting. The failure of this production was largely attributable to Charles Kemble's interpretation of Falstaff, a role for which he was ill-suited. William Charles Macready, a contemporary of the Kembles, began his career as an actor at Bath, where he played Hotspur in 1815. He later continued to take the part at Covent Garden and Drury Lane until December 1847. Samuel Phelps, a distinguished actor of tragedy, opened his third season as manager of Sadler's Wells (1846/7) with *1 Henry IV*, playing first Hotspur and afterward Falstaff. In 1864, during the tercentenary of Shakespeare's birth, the Falconer-Chatterton management at Drury Lane presented an almost complete text of the play. Phelps re-created his Falstaff in an excellent cast which included Walter Montgomery as Hotspur, Walter Lacy as the Prince, John Ryder as the King, and Mrs. Edmund Falconer as the Hostess. An outstanding scenic feature of this revival, which ran successfully for several months, was the representation of the battle of Shrewsbury created by William Beverley.

The Romantics, and even more the Victorians, found Falstaff too coarse for their refined tastes. Toward the end of the century London's interest in *Henry IV* lagged, but, in 1885, there were performances by the Oxford University Dramatic Society and at Cambridge. The Oxford cast had Arthur Bourchier acting Hotspur, the second Lord Coleridge as Falstaff, Alan Mackinnon and Holman Clark as the Prince and Glendower. The prologue was spoken by the future archbishop of Canterbury, C. Gordon Lang.

On the basis of the acclaim he won for his Falstaff in *The Merry Wives of Windsor*, Beerbohm Tree revived *1 Henry IV* at the Haymarket Theatre on May 8, 1896, and gained some kindly critical reviews (George Bernard Shaw's excepted) for his impersonation of the fallen gentleman. Lewis Waller was Hotspur and Lady Helen Tree was Lady Percy in this handsome production. Tree staged the play again during His Majesty's second annual Shakespeare Festival in 1906 and played Falstaff in 1914, supported by Matheson Lang's stammering Hotspur. One elaborate feature in this otherwise unspectacular presentation was the King, acted by Basil Gill, atop a white horse leading a victorious army on to the battlefield of Shrewsbury after Hotspur's death. Frank Benson all but ignored *1 Henry IV* in favor of *Part 2*, but he did offer productions at Stratford-upon-Avon in 1905 and later in 1909, with Lewis Waller believable as Hotspur; Louis Calvert, a fat, intelligent Falstaff; and Robert Loraine as Prince Hal. The latter production was also presented at the Lyric in May 1909.

The first full text of the drama with no transposed scenes was staged by the Birmingham Repertory Company under Barry Jackson on October 11, 1913. Jackson was also the first to present both parts of *Henry IV* in one day, April 23, 1921. Another repertory company, the Norwich Players, staged an Elizabethan-style *1 Henry IV* the following year at Maddermarket. The Old Vic staged George Foss' production in 1919 and, in 1920, Russell Thorndike played Falstaff in performances coproduced with Charles Warburton. Robert Atkins presented the drama during the Vic's 1922/3 season, with Wilfrid Walter as Falstaff and Douglas Burbidge as Hotspur. In the next London production Falstaff took a back seat. Harcourt Williams began his second season at the Old Vic (1930/1) casting John Gielgud as Hotspur and Ralph Richardson as Prince Hal; Henry Wolston's Falstaff ran a poor third in this extraordinary cast, which also featured Dorothy Green as Lady Percy. W. Bridges-Adams staged the play at Stratford in 1923 and 1928; in 1932 he followed Jackson's lead in presenting both parts of *Henry IV* in one day. The Prince of Wales had flown down for the event, the ceremonial opening of the new Memorial Theatre on April 23, but the production suffered in the strange surroundings. Randle Ayrton's stilted Henry set the pace for a company perhaps overawed by the occasion, and the play went poorly.

The much-heralded experimental casting of George Robey, 65-year-old vaudeville-trained master comedian of the variety stage, as Falstaff assured a full house for the premiere of Robert Atkins' production at His Majesty's Theatre on February 28, 1935. Robey's performance merited critical praise from James Agate, who commended his "authentic geniality"; Herbert Farjeon, who considered the impersonation promising; and W. A. Darlington, who thought Robey would probably develop into one of the best Falstaffs of the theatre. *The Times*, dissenting, found the portrayal a "diverting . . . but not a comfortable one," while the *New Statesman* described Robey as too much "the old soak rather than the fallen gentleman." The interest created by Robey overshadowed the rest of the cast and excellent performances by Lewis Casson as Glendower and John Laurie as Douglas were practically ignored. Edmund Willard was too old for Hotspur and John Drinkwater's King was a bit too cautious. At Stratford that year Roy Byford, a physically natural Falstaff who burst into convulsive laughter, surpassed Robey's impersonation with considerably less fanfare in B. Iden Payne's production. When Robert Atkins next staged the play, he himself acted a Falstaff who, at times quiet and thoughtful, betrayed nostalgia for the past; Esme Percy played Hotspur. This revival at the Vaudeville in 1940 failed commercially. Atkins tried his deliberate Falstaff again at the Westminster, in 1942, but was hindered by a weak cast.

Probably the most accomplished Falstaff of modern times was Ralph Richardson, who took the part in John Burrell's Old Vic production of *1* and *2 Henry IV* at the New Theatre in 1945. Although his was the least gluttonous and sensual of contemporary portrayals of the fallen knight, Richardson most completely personified the mental agility and wisdom of the man, delivering his speech in dry tones. Laurence Olivier played Hotspur, blazing, vulgar, stammering on the letter "w," his death agony masterful. For one of the first times, Henry was allotted his full proportion in Nicholas Hannen's effective interpretation, but Prince Hal suffered from a weak performance by Michael Warre. Sybil Thorndike, who in her first years with the Vic had attempted

Prince Hal, played Mistress Quickly in this almost perfect presentation.

In June 1947 the close quarters of the Harrow School speech room was the scene of Ronald Watkins' revival of *1 Henry IV*. When the play was again staged at Stratford, the void between audience and actors which had inhibited the cast of the 1932 production had been eliminated by the remodeling of the interior of the Memorial Theatre. *1 Henry IV*, the second production of the 1951 season, was codirected by John Kidd and Anthony Quayle, who also acted Falstaff; Michael Redgrave was an awkward, unromanticized, thick-tongued Hotspur; Richard Burton's unlyrical but rhythmic Hal was reflective, conscious even in comedy scenes of being a future king; Harry Andrews' Henry IV and Hugh Griffith's Glendower were memorable portraits. *1 Henry IV* was given again in November of the following year, and the play was also performed during Donald Wolfit's 1953 repertory season at King's Theatre, at Hammersmith.

Paul Rogers was the Old Vic's Falstaff during the 1954/5 season, deliberately gullible yet apprehensive, anxious to recapture his youth. Others in the cast of Douglas Seale's production were John Neville as a coarse Hotspur, Ann Todd as Lady Percy, and Robert Hardy as Prince Hal. Dennis Vance staged *1 Henry IV* for the Old Vic during 1960/1, Douglas Campbell re-creating the Falstaff he had played at Stratford, Ontario, in 1958 opposite the Hotspur of Jason Robards, Jr. In the latter production, Tony Britton acted Hotspur; Robert Harris, Henry IV; and John Stride, Prince Hal.

The future of the drama brightened considerably when Peter Hall presented it at Stratford in 1964 with an excellent cast. Hugh Griffith humanized but never sentimentalized Falstaff; all his faults were revealed in a realistic and, at the same time, larger-than-life performance. Ian Holm as Prince Hal was shrewd and serious. This production emphasized the father-son relationship between Falstaff and Hal, as well as the obsessive guilt of Henry (as portrayed by Eric Porter) over the deposition of Richard II. Hall was assisted in this production by John Barton and Clifford Williams.—M. G.

Bibliography. TEXT: *Henry the Fourth, Part I*, New Variorum Edition, S. B. Hemingway, ed., 1936; Supplement to the New Variorum Edition, G. B. Evans, ed., *Shakespeare Quarterly*, VII, 1956; *The First Part of the History of Henry IV*, New Cambridge Edition, J. Dover Wilson, ed., 1946; *The First Part of King Henry IV*, New Arden Edition, A. R. Humphreys, ed., 1960; A. E. Morgan, *Some Problems of Shakespeare's "Henry the Fourth,"* 1924. DATE: New Variorum Edition; New Arden Edition. SOURCES: New Variorum Edition; New Arden Edition; Geoffrey Bullough, *Narrative and Dramatic Sources of Shakespeare*, IV, 1962. COMMENT: J. Dover Wilson, *The Fortunes of Falstaff*, 1943; D. A. Traversi, *Shakespeare from Richard II to Henry V*, 1957. STAGE HISTORY: New Variorum Edition; New Cambridge Edition; G. C. D. Odell, *Shakespeare from Betterton to Irving*, 1920; J. C. Trewin, *Shakespeare on the English Stage, 1900-1964*, 1964.

Selected Criticism. See HENRY IV, PART TWO: *Selected Criticism*.

The Second Part of Henry the Fourth,

Containing his Death : and Coronation of King Henry the Fift.

Henry IV, Part Two. A history play by Shakespeare.

Text. *2 Henry IV* was entered in the Stationers' Register on August 23, 1600, and the Quarto appeared in the same year, with the following on the title page: "The Second part of Henrie the fourth, continuing to his death, and coronation of Henrie the fift. With the humours of sir Iohn Falstaffe, and swaggering Pistoll. As it hath been sundrie times publikely acted by the right honourable, the Lord Chamberlaine his seruants. Written by William Shakespeare." The text was reissued, probably in the same year, with the addition of Act III, scene i, which had been omitted in the first printing. The play was not printed again until it appeared in the First Folio (1623). The Quarto offers a good text. It was apparently set up from Shakespeare's own manuscript. But both issues lack several striking passages which first appear in the Folio. The most important of these are the following: (1) Morton's speech to Northumberland (I, i, 166–179), urging him to proceed with the organization of his plot, despite its dangers to his son; (2) Lord Bardolph's explanation of the best way to plan a rebellion (I, iii, 36–

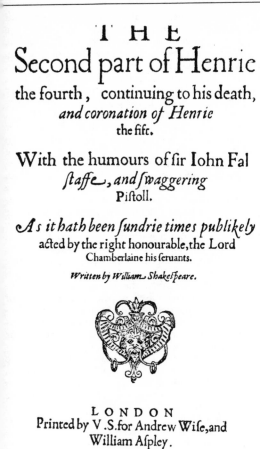

THE
Second part of Henrie
the fourth, continuing to his death,
and coronation of Henrie
the fift.

With the humours of sir Iohn Fal
staffe, and swaggering
Pistoll.

As it hath been sundrie times publikely
acted by the right honourable, the Lord
Chamberlaine his seruants.

Written by William Shakespeare.

LONDON
Printed by V. S. for Andrew Wise, and
William Aspley.
1600.

TITLE PAGE OF THE FIRST QUARTO OF *2 Henry IV* (1600).

55); (3) Lady Percy's speech calling to mind the virtues of her dead husband (II, iii, 23–45); (4) the Archbishop's enumeration of the rebels' grievances (IV, i, 54–79); (5) a conversation between Mowbray and Westmoreland in which the latter attempts to persuade Mowbray that his grievances are groundless (IV, i, 103–139). It is generally assumed that the cuts were made by the official censor, who saw some uncomfortably close parallels in the stricken passages to the relationship between the court and the Essex faction—a relationship which, shortly after the publication of the play, was to erupt in the Essex revolt of February 1601. One strong warrant for this assumption is the fact that much of the excised material alluded to the fate of Richard II, a monarch with whom Elizabeth frequently identified herself (see William LAMBARDE).

The Folio text was printed either from a transcript of the company's PROMPT-BOOK or from a copy of Q1 which had been collated with a manuscript version of the play. It was also cut, this time in obedience to an act of parliament in 1606 which forbade the use of the names of "God, Jesus Christ, The Holy Ghost or The Trinity in any stage play." Throughout this drama "Heaven" is substituted for "God," "in good earnest" for "God save me," etc.

The best authority for a modern text of *2 Henry IV* is the Quarto, with passages deleted there added from the First Folio.

Date. The great success of *1 Henry IV* set Shakespeare at once to work on a sequel that would capitalize in particular on Falstaff's popularity. If he wrote *2 Henry IV* before his other Falstaff play, *The Merry Wives of Windsor*, which is now generally thought to have been written in the spring of 1597, then *2 Henry IV* must have been written in late 1596 or early 1597. If he wrote *Part 2* after *The Merry Wives*, then the play would have first reached the stage late in 1597. *Part 2* is alluded to in a letter written in 1600 by Sir Charles PERCY, a follower of Essex.

Sources. The sources of this play were the same as those of *1 Henry IV* (see 1 HENRY IV: *Sources*): the 1587 edition of Holinshed's *Chronicles* and *The Famous Victories of Henry the Fifth* (registered May 14, 1594). However, fewer scenes in this play are devoted to historical events and more to the poet's fictional account of the adventures of Falstaff and his familiars. The story of Hal's offense to the Chief Justice is recounted in Sir Thomas Elyot's *Governour* (1531) and reprinted in John Stow's *Annales* (1592). The picture of Henry IV, plagued by sickness and a bad conscience, was probably derived from Samuel Daniel's epic *Civile Wars* (1595), a work which Shakespeare knew and apparently admired.—O. J. C.

Plot Synopsis. *Act I.* After hearing false reports of victory, the Earl of Northumberland learns that his son Hotspur has been slain at the battle of Shrewsbury and that a royal army under Prince John of Lancaster, the King's second son, and the Earl of Westmoreland is marching against him. Stirred to action by the ill tidings, the Earl considers uniting his forces with those of the Archbishop of York.

Act II. In London, Mistress Quickly, hostess of the Boar's Head Tavern in Eastcheap, orders the arrest of Sir John Falstaff for debt, but he succeeds in wheedling another loan from her, as well as an invitation to supper. Determined to see Falstaff "in his true colours," Prince Hal and Ned Poins plan to disguise themselves as drawers and wait on him as he sups.

As Falstaff, Mistress Quickly, and Doll Tearsheet are enjoying a convivial evening in Eastcheap, they are joined by Bardolph's and Falstaff's bombastic ensign, Pistol, who is quickly removed from the premises. The Prince and Poins, in the garb of drawers, witness an affecting scene between Falstaff and Doll and hear him describe Hal as "a good shallow young fellow," who would have made a good pantry servant. When Hal and Poins reveal their identity, Falstaff explains that he had disparaged the Prince before the "wicked" company so "that the wicked might not fall in love with him; in which doing, I have done the part of a careful friend and a true subject." The festivities end abruptly, as both Hal and Falstaff are called to arms against the northern rebels.

Act III. Meanwhile, in the palace at Westminster, a weary King Henry reflects on the sleepless nights that are the lot of every king and remembers that Richard II had foreseen the rupture between him and Northumberland. In an effort to rouse the King's flagging spirits, the Earl of Warwick deprecates the strength of the rebel army and informs him of the death of Owen Glendower, the refractory Welsh lord.

Arriving at Gloucestershire, Falstaff, who is recruiting soldiers for the King's army, is greeted by Justice Shallow, a comrade of his youth. After interviewing several candidates, Falstaff excuses the likeliest fellows—for a consideration—and chooses the unprepossessing Feeble, Shadow, and Wart.

Act IV. In Yorkshire's Gaultree Forest, the Archbishop of York informs Lord Mowbray and Lord Hastings that they have been abandoned by Northumberland, who, bowing to the pleas of his wife and widowed daughter-in-law, has retired to Scotland. The Earl of Westmoreland arrives and, belittling their reasons for rebelling against the King, urges them to make peace with Prince John. Though Mowbray doubts that a permanent settlement can be reached, the Archbishop and Hastings believe that the King is eager to see tranquility restored to the kingdom. At a meeting with the rebels, Prince John promises that their grievances shall be redressed; the insurgents then disperse their forces, only to be arrested for treason by the perfidious Prince.

The King is in the Jerusalem chamber at Westminster when Westmoreland brings word that Prince John has crushed the revolt and Harcourt reports that Northumberland has been defeated by the sheriff of Yorkshire. Despite the good news, the King falls ill and is taken to bed. As he lies asleep in another chamber, Prince Hal enters and, in the belief that his father has died, sadly removes the crown from the King's pillow. Henry, awaking to find the crown gone and learning that the Prince had been in the room, bitterly accuses him of desiring his death. "Thy life did manifest thou lovedst me not," he says, "And thou wilt have me die assured of it." The Prince hastens to explain his act, assuring his father that he was not prompted by disloyal or unfilial motives. Touched by his son's eloquence, the King beckons him to his bedside. Recalling the devious means by which he won the crown, he observes that the Prince's position is comparatively secure, but warns him to protect himself against domestic strife. "Be it thy course to busy giddy minds / With foreign quarrels," he counsels. When the King realizes that he has been taken ill in the Jerusalem chamber, he remembers a prophecy that he should not die but in Jerusalem, words that he thought referred to the Holy Land. Now he asks to be taken to that room again: "In that Jerusalem shall Harry die."

Act V. After Henry's death, the new King assures his brothers that they have no cause for trepidation about their fate under his rule. Although the Lord Chief-Justice is also fearful, because he had once jailed the King during his madcap days as prince of Wales, he stoutly defends his conduct in upholding "the majesty and power of law and justice." The King praises the Chief-Justice, vowing always to heed his "well-practised wise directions," and explains that his youthful wildness has died with his father.

Falstaff and Bardolph are still in Gloucestershire with Shallow when Pistol brings them news of the King's death. Dazzled by their prospects now that their old crony is king, they rush to London and station themselves in a prominent spot during the coronation procession. When Falstaff addresses the newly crowned monarch with a familiar greeting, Henry's response is forbidding: "I know thee not, old man: fall to thy prayers; / How ill white hairs become a fool and jester!" He banishes his former companions from his presence, granting them pensions to keep them from resorting to crime. Though Falstaff insists that the King will surely send for him privately, he and his friends are hustled off to Fleet prison by the Chief Justice. As he surveys the scene with satisfaction, Prince John foresees an expedition to France before the end of the year.—H.D.

Comment. The historical events dramatized in *2 Henry IV* do not form a coherent whole. They consist of only 8 loosely connected scenes. Shakespeare devotes the most significant of these to the new rebellion in the north instigated by Northumberland and the Archbishop and its suppression through the Machiavellian cunning of Prince John. Even in this small compass, the dramatist was able to give this second rebellion against the King a strong resemblance to the revolt raised by the Catholic lords of the northern counties in 1569 against Queen Elizabeth. This likeness of an historical crisis to a contemporary political situation enhanced the interest for Elizabethan spectators; their acceptance of the concept of history's cyclic movement enabled them to judge a present crisis through study of its replica in the past. Throughout the play, Shakespeare shows the King as paying the penalty for his part in the dethroning and death of Richard II, plotting that to an orthodox Elizabethan was sacrilegious (see RICHARD II: *Comment*). The King first appears in the first scene of the third act. There, suffering from insomnia, always in Shakespeare the sign of a guilty conscience, he utters an apostrophe to sleep beginning:

> How many thousand of my poorest subjects
> Are at this hour asleep! O sleep, O gentle sleep,
> Nature's soft nurse, how have I frighted thee?
> (III, i, 4–6)

The melancholy, resulting from his sleeplessness, induces a profound pessimism and a sense of foreboding. He finds the book of fate so filled with examples of changes for the worse that

> The happiest youth, viewing his progress through,
> What perils past, what crosses to ensue,
> Would shut the book, and sit him down and die.
> (III, i, 54–56)

On his deathbed these fears assail the King with increased intensity. They are complicated by his concern for the future of the realm after the wild Prince has succeeded him. In this state of profound anxiety, he takes the crown from his head, places it on a pillow beside him and lapses into a coma. The Prince, thinking that his father has died, puts the crown on his own head and walks into an adjoining room full of grief and misgiving. But the King, regaining consciousness, misconstrues his son's motive in walking off with the crown. He thinks it proof that Prince Hal is impatient to become king and free from any restraint upon his wild impulses. Thus suspicion and dismay poison the last moments of the King's life. It is the punishment inflicted upon him by God for his political crimes. But Prince Hal, summoned by his father, convinces him that he is resolved to reform. Then the King utters a prophecy of great importance for understanding the real reason for Hal's reclamation: God has punished the monarch for the "indirect crooked ways" by which he has gained the crown by making his reign a time of civil strife and personal anxiety. But Hal's reformation will prove to be authentic because his profligacy is an important part of the divine punishment visited upon the guilty father. After the King's death the reason for this phase of his chastisement disappears.

When Shakespeare began to plan the structure of *2 Henry IV*, he at once realized that he had to prepare his audience for the Prince's repudiation of Falstaff. He systematically debases Sir John in order to destroy the audience's affection for the old rogue. However, to meet the demand of his public for more of Falstaff, Shakespeare creates new scenes like those of *1 Henry IV* that had provoked the most laughter. But far from being harmlessly funny, the Falstaff scenes in the new play are touched with vulgarity, meanness, or downright evil. The change is typified in some of the fat knight's new cronies, introduced in order to increase the number of scenes in which Falstaff appears. Instead of the merry Prince, Falstaff's companions are now Pistol, the swaggering humbug, and the tipsy whore, Doll Tearsheet. Pistol is his ancient (ensign), a triumphant variation of the boastful soldier, the *miles gloriosus* of Plautus. His bombastic speeches are pure cannonfire and bounce. In his garbled quotations from the tragedies of Marlowe and less successful inventors of rant he is doubtless parodying the empty bluster that disfigured those old-fashioned plays that formed the stock-in-trade of the Admiral's Men, at that time the only serious rival of Shakespeare's company.

Another new crony is the imbecile country justice, Master Shallow. He presents an exaggerated contrast to Falstaff. He is so thin that he seems the very genius of famine, and his mind is a perfect match for his starveling figure. He meanders in his talk, which is interspersed with fictitious reminiscences of his wild youth at Clement's Inn. Shallow probably embodies a Londoner's idea of a country justice: stupid, self-important, and corruptible.

In the last act (V, iv) we are hardly surprised to learn that two of Falstaff's intimates have become criminals. The beadles who arrest Doll report that "there hath been a man or two lately killed about her" and warn her that "the man is dead that you and Pistol beat amongst you." Thus, Falstaff is already heavily burdened with the spectator's hard opinion before his fatal appeal to his old royal companion. He could not have chosen an occasion or a moment less favorable to his fortunes, or more embarrassing to Henry. He confronts the young King as he comes from his coronation, while the streets are lined with his cheering subjects. He thus forces his monarch to choose in public between the symbol of his youthful dissipation and his just solemnly sworn duties to the throne. And Henry chooses without an instant of hesitation to be faithful to the demands of his high office. It is largely Falstaff's ineptitude that forces Henry to reject him in the hard, self-righteous manner that has broken the hearts of most commentators on this scene. It is safe to say that no heart of a spectator in the Globe theatre would have been thus tormented (see HAL).

Yet the author's epilogue to the play shows that he still hoped to capitalize on Falstaff's popularity. He promises to continue the story with Sir John in it, "where, for any thing I know, Falstaff shall die of a sweat." This promise he did not keep, probably because he did not wish to sully the hero King or his victories in France with sordid memories of Eastcheap and the Boar's Head Tavern—O. J. C.

Stage History. The second part of *Henry IV* has always been less popular with producers and actors than the first part. Falstaff of *Part 2*, therefore, was less often acted than the Sir John of *Part 1*. *2 Henry IV* was evidently staged immediately after the mounting of *1 Henry IV* and its cast was probably the same as that of the earlier play, with John Heminges or Thomas Pope in the role of Falstaff. As part of the wedding festivities of Princess Elizabeth, the daughter of King James I, to the elector palatine on February 19, 1613 there were productions of *The Hotspurre* and *Sir John Falstaffe*, which were probably the titles respectively of *1* and *2 Henry IV*. But there is no evidence as to whether the drama entitled *Oldcastle*, performed in 1600 and 1638, was *Part 1* or *Part 2*, or possibly a compilation of Falstaff's scenes from both. Such a compilation was staged about 1623 at the home of Sir Edward Dering in Surrenden, Kent (see DERING HENRY IV).

A production of *2 Henry IV* took place on December 17, 1720 at Drury Lane. A printed acting edition of the text used at this performance was entitled "The Sequel of Henry the Fourth: with the Humours of Sir John Falstaffe and Justice Shallow. As it was acted by his Majesty's Company of Comedians at the Theatre Royal in Drury Lane. Altered from Shakespeare by the late Mr. Betterton." It is considered doubtful that Thomas Betterton was responsible for this alteration, since it in no way compares with the respectful treatment he accorded Shakespeare's *1 Henry IV*. The dialogue is severely cut and the Induction of the first scene omitted. The King's soliloquy on sleep is mangled and transposed from III, i, to before the deathbed scene in Act IV. Other omissions include Northumberland's farewell and the arrest of Doll and the Hostess. At the end of the play is part of the first act of *Henry V*. In the cast of this production were Barton Booth as the King, John Mill as Falstaff, Robert Wilks as the Prince of Wales, and Colley Cibber as Shallow.

From 1720 to 1750, 80 London performances of *2 Henry IV* are recorded and from 1710 to September 1747, when David Garrick assumed the management of Drury Lane, the play was performed at that theatre 45 times. Garrick cared even less for *2 Henry IV* than for *Part 1*, but he did stage it on March 13, 1758, and by 1770 had offered seven productions, in four of which he acted the role of King Henry. James Quin's Falstaff seriously rivaled Betterton's and he played the part in both *1* and *2 Henry IV* until his retirement in 1751, acting the Falstaff of *Part 2* less often than that of *Part 1*. Another famous characterization from the play was Theophilus Cibber's Pistol. When Cibber presented his two-act adaptation, *The Humorists,* in 1754, the cast list indicates that the play consisted largely of Act II, scene 4, and Act III, scene 2 of *2 Henry IV*. Covent Garden, lacking a memorable Falstaff, nevertheless staged *2 Henry IV* at regular intervals during the 18th century, mounting a showy production during 1761/2 to honor the coronation of King George III. The first notable successor to Quin's Falstaff was John Henderson's. Henderson first played the part in 1777 at Drury Lane and appeared in four productions of *2 Henry IV*, acting in the play for the last time at Covent Garden in 1784. After this, *Part 2* disappeared from the stage until John Philip Kemble revived it 20 years later.

Another coronation production was presented at Covent Garden in 1821, this time to commemorate the accession of George IV. The play, brilliantly staged with spectacular pageant and procession, was first performed on June 25, with William Charles Macready as the King and Charles Kemble as the Prince. By royal command the theatre was opened free for a second performance of the production on coronation day, July 19. Later, in 1827, Macready brought the production to New York's Park Theatre.

Samuel Phelps displayed his remarkable versatility when at Sadler's Wells he doubled in the roles of the King and Shallow, performing these parts first from March 17 to April 13, 1853 and repeating them on two occasions in 1861. This triumph was again exhibited at Drury Lane in 1864 and at Manchester in 1874.

Frank Benson preferred *Part 2* to the generally more popular *Part 1*, perhaps because it fitted more naturally into the production of his famous cycle of the histories in 1901 and 1906 as an induction to *Henry V*. He produced the play at Stratford-upon-Avon on 12 different occasions from 1894 to 1916, and his company performed it twice more after W. Bridges-Adams assumed direction of the Memorial Theatre. George Weir played Falstaff in Benson's productions until his death in 1909.

2 Henry IV preceded *Part 1* at the Old Vic by a year and a half; its first production at that theatre was directed by Ben Greet in October 1917. Russell Thorndike, coproducing with Charles Warburton, played Falstaff in the Old Vic's 1920 *2 Henry IV*, given two weeks after that season's first performance of *Part 1*. Under Robert Atkins, the last dramatization of the second part to be staged at the Vic for more than 12 years was presented in October, 1922, with Wilfrid Walter in the role of Falstaff. Alfred Clark acted that part in J. B. Fagan's 1921 Court Theatre presentation of a cut version in which H. O. Nicholson's portrayal of Shallow was notable. There was one other West End *2 Henry IV* during the 1920's, that in 1925 at the Regent acted by the Fellowship of Players, with Alfred Clark again as Falstaff.

The opening of the New Memorial Theatre at Stratford on April 23, 1932 was the occasion of the presentation of both *1* and *2 Henry IV* in a single day. Barry Jackson had led the way 11 years earlier when he staged the 2 parts at the Birmingham Repertory Theatre on April 23, 1921. Randle Ayrton, who had been Stratford's Falstaff in *2 Henry IV* in 1926, repeated the characterization for W. Bridges Adams in an uninspiring performance. The only other major theatre production during this period was Henry Cass' at the Old Vic in 1935, with George Merritt as Falstaff, Abraham Sofaer as King Henry and Maurice Evans playing Silence.

Robert Atkins, whose production of *2 Henry IV* in November 1942 followed by a month his presentation of *Part 1*, impersonated a quiet, deliberate nostalgic Falstaff in both parts. Early the next spring an amateur performance of *Part 2* was given by the King's Scholars of Westminster School at Whitbourne Court, Worcestershire.

The most memorable moments in John Burrell's Old Vic production of *1* and *2 Henry IV* at the New Theatre in 1945 were attributable to Ralph Richardson's matchless portrayal of Falstaff. High moments of *Part 2* were the tavern scene, where first glimpsing his fate, he quietly bade Doll not to remind him of his end, and later, during Hal's rebuke, which left him only a tired, old man. Laurence Olivier was Shallow in this production; Nicholas Hannen was Henry IV; Michael Warre, Prince Hal and George Relph, Pistol. Joyce Redmond was Doll Tearsheet. Michael Redgrave directed *2 Henry IV* presented in sequence with *Richard II, 1 Henry IV* and *Henry V* at Stratford in 1951. In his cast were Anthony Quayle as Falstaff, Richard Burton as Prince Hal, Harry Andrews as Henry IV, Alan Badel as Shallow, and Heather Stannard as Doll Tearsheet.

During the Old Vic's 1954/5 season, Douglas Seale staged a *Henry IV* with Paul Rogers playing a notable Falstaff in both parts, John Neville in an excellent, coarse-voiced portrayal of a swaggering Pistol and Paul Daneman as Shallow. There was a production in August 1961 at the Apollo performed by the Youth Theatre under Michael Croft. In 1964, at Stratford, Peter Hall, with John Barton and Clifford Williams, staged *2 Henry IV* in a series of historical plays beginning with *Richard II* and ending with Hall's *The Wars of the Roses* trilogy. Hugh Griffith was an outstanding Falstaff in this production, which had Eric Porter in the title role and Ian Holm as Prince Hal.—M. G.

Bibliography. TEXT: *The Second Part of Henry the Fourth*, New Variorum Edition, M. A. Shaaber ed., 1940; Alice Walker, *Textual Problems of the First Folio*, 1953; M. A. Shaaber, "The Folio Text of *2 Henry IV*," *Shakespeare Quarterly*, VI, 1955. DATE: New Variorum Edition; William Green, *Shakespeare's Merry Wives of Windsor*, 1962. SOURCES: Geoffrey Bullough, *Narrative and Dramatic Sources of Shakespeare*, Vol. IV, 1962. COMMENT: J. Dover Wilson, *The Fortunes of Falstaff*, 1943; Lily B. Campbell, *Shakespeare's Histories*, 1947. STAGE HISTORY: New Variorum Edition; G. C. D. Odell, *Shakespeare from Betterton to Irving*, 1920; J. C. Trewin, *Shakespeare on the English Stage, 1900–1964*, 1964.

Selected Criticism

SAMUEL JOHNSON. . . . *Falstaff* unimitated, unimitable *Falstaff*, how shall I describe thee? Thou compound of sense and vice; of sense which may be admired but not esteemed, of vice which may be despised, but hardly detested. *Falstaff* is a character loaded with faults, and with those faults which naturally produce contempt. He is a thief, and a glutton, a coward, and a boaster, always ready to cheat the weak, and prey upon the poor; to terrify the timorous and insult the defenceless. At once obsequious and malignant, he satirises in their absence those whom he lives by flattering. He is familiar with the prince only as an agent of vice, but of this familiarity he is so proud as not only to be supercilious and haughty with common men, but to think his interest of importance to the duke of *Lancaster*. Yet the man thus corrupt, thus despicable, makes himself necessary to the prince that despises him, by the most pleasing of all qualities, perpetual gaiety, by an unfailing power of exciting laughter, which is the more freely indulged, as his wit is not of the splendid or ambitious kind, but consists in easy escapes and sallies of levity, which makes sport but raises no envy. It must be observed that he is stained with no enormous or sanguinary crimes, so that his licentiousness is not so offensive but that it may be borne for his mirth.

The moral to be drawn from this representation is, that no man is more dangerous than he that with a will to corrupt, hath the power to please; and that neither wit nor honesty ought to think themselves safe with such a companion when they see *Henry* seduced by *Falstaff*. [*The Plays of William Shakespeare,* 1765.]

MAURICE MORGANN. To me then it appears that the leading quality in *Falstaff's* character, and that from which all the rest take their colour, is a high degree of wit and humour, accompanied with great natural vigour and alacrity of mind. This quality so accompanied, led him probably very early into life, and made him highly acceptable to society; so acceptable, as to make it seem unnecessary for him to acquire any other virtue. Hence, perhaps, his continued debaucheries and dissipations of every kind.—He seems, by nature, to have had a mind free of malice or any evil principle; but he never took the trouble of acquiring any good one. He found himself esteemed and beloved with all his faults; nay *for* his faults, which were all connected with humour, and for the most part, grew out of it. As he had, possibly, no vices but such as he thought might be openly professed, so he appeared more dissolute thro' ostentation. To the character of wit and humour, to which all his other qualities seem to have conformed themselves, he appears to have added a very necessary support, *that* of the profession of a *Soldier*. He had from nature, as I presume to say, a spirit of boldness and enterprise; which in a Military age, tho' employment was only occasional, kept him always above contempt, secured him an honourable reception among the Great, and suited best both with his particular mode of humour and of vice. Thus living continually in society, nay even in Taverns, and indulging himself, and being indulged by others, in every debauchery; drinking, whoring, gluttony and ease; assuming a liberty of fiction necessary perhaps to his wit, and often falling into falsity and lies, he seems to have set, by degrees, all sober reputation at defiance; and finding eternal resources in his wit, he borrows, shifts, defrauds, and even robs, without dishonour.—Laughter and approbation attend his greatest excesses; and being governed visibly by no settled bad principle or ill design, fun and humour account for and cover all. . . . a butt and a wit, a humourist and a man of humour, a touchstone and a laughing stock, a jester and a jest, has Sir *John Falstaff*, taken at that period of his life in which we see him, become the most perfect Comic character that perhaps ever was exhibited. ["An Essay on the Dramatic Character of Sir John Falstaff," 1777.]

WILLIAM HAZLITT. Wit is often a meagre substitute for pleasurable sensation; an affusion of spleen and petty spite at the comforts of others, from feeling none in itself. Falstaff's wit is an emanation of a fine constitution; an exuberance of good-humour and good-nature; an overflowing of his love of laughter and good-fellowship; a giving vent to his heart's ease, and over-contentment with himself and others. He would not be in character, if he were not so fat as he is; for there is greatest keeping in the boundless luxury of his imagination and the pampered self-indulgence of his physical appetites. . . . He is represented as a liar, a braggart, a coward, a glutton, etc., and yet we are not offended but delighted with him; for he is all these as much to amuse others as to gratify himself. He openly assumed all these characters to shew the humorous part of them. . . .

The secret of Falstaff's wit is for the most part a masterly presence of mind, an absolute self-possession, which nothing can disturb. His repartees are involuntary suggestions of his self-love; instinctive evasions of everything that threatens to interrupt the career of his triumphant jollity and self-complacency. His very size floats him out of all his difficulties in a sea of rich conceits; and he turns round on the pivot of his convenience, with every occasion and at a moment's warning. His natural repugnance to every unpleasant thought or circumstance, of itself makes light of objections, and provokes the most extravagant and licentious answers in his own justification. His indifference to truth puts no check upon his invention, and the more improbable and unexpected his contrivances are, the more happily does he seem to be delivered of them, the anticipation of their effect acting as a stimulus to the gaiety of his fancy . . . .

The truth is, that we never could forgive the Prince's treatment of Falstaff; though perhaps Shakespeare knew what was best, according to the history, the nature of the times, and of the man. We speak only as dramatic critics. Whatever terror the French in those days might have of Henry V, yet, to the readers of poetry at present, Falstaff is the better man of the two. [*Characters of Shakespear's Plays,* 1817.]

A. C. BRADLEY. The bliss of freedom gained in humour is the essence of Falstaff. His humour is not directed only or chiefly against obvious absurdities; he is the enemy of everything that would interfere with his ease, and therefore of anything serious, and especially of everything respectable and moral. For these things impose limits and obligations, and make us the subjects of old father antic the law, and the categorical imperative, and our station and its duties, and conscience, and reputation, and other people's opinions, and all sorts of nuisances. I say he is therefore their enemy; but I do him wrong; to say that he is their enemy implies that he regards them as serious and recognizes their power, when in truth he refuses to recognize them at all. They are to him absurd; and to reduce a thing *ad absurdum* is to reduce it to nothing and to walk about free and rejoicing. This is what Falstaff does with all the would-be serious things of life, sometimes only by his words, sometimes by his actions too. He will make truth appear absurd by solemn statements, which he utters with perfect gravity and which he expects nobody to believe; and honour, by demonstrating that it cannot set a leg, and that neither the living nor the dead can possess it; and law, by evading all the attacks of its highest representative and almost forcing him to laugh at his own defeat; and patriotism, by filling his pockets with the bribes offered by competent soldiers who want to escape service, while he takes in their stead the halt and maimed and the gaol-birds; and duty, by showing how he labours in his vocation—of thieving; and courage, alike by mocking at his own capture of Colevile and gravely claiming to have killed Hotspur; and war, by offering the Prince his bottle of sack when he is asked for a sword; and religion, by amusing himself with remorse at odd times when he has nothing else to do; and the fear of death, by maintaining perfectly untouched, in the face of imminent peril and even while he *feels* the fear of death, the very same power of dissolving it in persiflage that he shows when he sits at ease in his inn. These are the wonderful achievements which he performs, not with the discontent of a cynic, but with the gaiety of a boy. And, therefore, we praise him, we laud him, for he offends none but the virtuous, and denies that life is real or life is earnest and delivers us from the oppression of such nightmares, and lifts us into the atmosphere of perfect freedom . . . .

To show that Falstaff's freedom of soul was in part illusory, and that the realities of life refused to be conjured away by his humour—this was what we might expect from Shakespeare's unfailing sanity, but it was surely no achievement beyond the power of lesser men. The achievement was Falstaff himself, and the conception of that freedom of soul, a freedom illusory only in part, and attainable only by a mind which had received from Shakespeare's own the inexplicable touch of infinity which he bestowed on Hamlet and Macbeth and Cleopatra, but denied to Henry the Fifth. ["The Rejection of Falstaff," *Oxford Lectures on Poetry*, 1909.]

MADELEINE DORAN. On reading the First Part of *Henry IV* immediately after *Richard II* one is struck, along with evidences of greater maturity in other matters, by the difference in the handling of the images. I shall begin with a general statement which will obviously need qualification and if pushed too far will distort the picture, but which, for convenience, has nevertheless to be made at the outset. It may be said that the images in *Richard II* tend to be direct or explicit, complete, correspondent, point by point, to the idea symbolized, and separate one from another; whereas the images in *1 Henry IV* tend to be richer in implicit suggestion and in ambiguity, not fully developed, fluid in outline and fused with one another . . . .

But *1 Henry IV* is a stage beyond *Richard II* in the welding of poetic imagination to dramatic need. This is best illustrated in the case of Hotspur. Dr. Tillyard says that there is no profound obliquity in Richard's character and that a good deal of the pla is the poetry of statement. Richard's character i exhibited directly. He is a poet and he speak poetically. But Hotspur is a hater of poetry wh speaks some of the most vivid and the most beautifu poetry in the play. In all of Richard's poetica speeches, he has nothing like Hotspur's speech o honour, so loaded with unexpressed meaning. Ye Hotspur's animadversions on poets and poetry re main convincing. It will not do to say that we do no take him at his word. That is a very superficial vie of his character and of Shakespeare's art. We do tak him at his word if we pay attention to the play. H is an entire man of action, as he says he is, withou artistic habits or interests. He is intensely imagina tive, certainly, but imagination is not enough to mak a poet. Whereas Richard's speeches are the poem that Shakespeare puts into his mouth as his ow compositions, Hotspur's speeches are Shakespeare poetry to express the mind of a character wh could not himself compose a poem at all. This is very high degree of obliquity in the use of artisti means. It is accomplishment of an altogether differ ent order from the minor perfection of *Richard I* ["Imagery in *Richard II* and in *Henry IV*," *Moder Language Review*, XXXVII, April, 1942.]

J. DOVER WILSON. . . . Shakespeare's *Henry IV* is Tudor version of a time-honoured theme, alread familiar for decades, if not centuries, upon th English stage. Before its final secularization in th first half of the sixteenth century, our drama wa concerned with one topic, and one only: huma salvation. It was a topic that could be represente in either of two ways: (i) historically, by means c miracle plays, which in the Corpus Christi cycl unrolled before spectators' eyes the whole schem of salvation from the Creation to the Last Judge ment; or (ii) allegorically, by means of moralit plays, which exhibited the process of salvation in th individual soul on its road between birth and deat beset with the snares of the World or the wiles c the Evil One. In both kinds the forces of iniquit were allowed full play upon the stage, including good deal of horse-play, provided they were broug to nought, or safely locked up in Hell, at the en Salvation remains the supreme interest, howev many capers the Devil and his Vice may cut c Everyman's way thither, and always the powers darkness are withstood, and finally overcome, by th agents of light. But as time went on the religio drama tended to grow longer and more elaborat after the encyclopaedic fashion of the Middle Age and such development invited its inevitable reactio With the advent of humanism and the early Tud court, morality plays became tedious and gave pla to lighter and much shorter moral interludes de ing, not with human life as a whole, but with yout and its besetting sins . . . .

All this . . . gave the pattern for Shakespeare *Henry IV*. Hal associates Falstaff in turn with t Devil of the miracle play, the Vice of the moralit and the Riot of the interlude, when he calls him 'th villainous abominable misleader of Youth, that o white-bearded Satan', 'that reverend Vice, that gre Iniquity, that father Ruffian, that Vanity in year and 'the tutor and the feeder of my riots'. 'Rio again, is the word that comes most readily to Ki

Henry's lips when speaking of his prodigal son's misconduct. And, as heir to the Vice, Falstaff inherits by reversion the functions and attributes of the Lord of Misrule, the Fool, the Buffoon, and the Jester, antic figures the origins of which are lost in the dark backward and abysm of folk-custom. We shall find that Falstaff possesses a strain, and more than a strain, of the classical *miles gloriosus* as well. In short, the Falstaff-Hal plot embodies a composite myth which had been centuries amaking, and was for the Elizabethans full of meaning that has largely disappeared since then: which is one reason why we have come so seriously to misunderstand the play. [*The Fortunes of Falstaff*, 1943.]

E. M. W. TILLYARD. The structure of the two parts is indeed very similar. In the first part the Prince (who, one knows, will soon be king) is tested in the military or chivalric virtues. He has to choose, Morality-fashion, between Sloth or Vanity, to which he is drawn by his bad companions, and Chivalry, to which he is drawn by his father and his brothers. And he chooses Chivalry. The action is complicated by Hotspur and Falstaff, who stand for the excess and the defect of the military spirit, for honour exaggerated and dishonour. Thus the Prince, as well as being Magnificence in a Morality Play, is Aristotle's middle quality between two extremes. Such a combination would have been entirely natural to the Elizabethans, especially since it occurred in the second book of the *Fairy Queen*. Guyon is at once the Morality figure fought over by the Palmer and Mammon and the man who is shown the Aristotelian allegory of Excess Balance and Defect in Perissa Medina and Elissa. Near the end of the play the Prince ironically surrenders to Falstaff the credit of having killed Hotspur, thus leaving the world of arms and preparing for the motive of the second part. Here again he is tested, but in the civil virtues. He has to choose, Morality-fashion, between disorder or misrule, to which he is drawn by his bad companions, and Order or Justice (the supreme kingly virtue) to which he is drawn by his father and by his father's deputy the Lord Chief Justice. And he chooses Justice. [*Shakespeare's History Plays*, 1944.]

J. I. M. STEWART. . . . anthropologists are always telling us of countries gone waste and barren under the rule of an old, impotent and guilty king, who must be ritually slain and supplanted by his son or another before the saving rains can come bringing purification and regeneration to the land. Is not Henry IV in precisely the situation of this king? . . .

Perhaps, then, we glimpse here a further reason why the rejection of Falstaff is inevitable—not merely traditionally and moralistically inevitable but symbolically inevitable as well. And this may be why, when in the theatre, we do not really rebel against the rejection; why we find a fitness too in its being sudden and catastrophic. As long as we are in the grip of drama it is profoundly fit that Hal, turning king and clergyman at once, should run bad humours on the knight, should kill his heart. For the killing carries something of the ritual suggestion, the obscure *pathos*, of death in tragedy.

I suggest that Hal, by a displacement common enough in the evolution of ritual, kills Falstaff instead of killing the king, his father. In a sense Falstaff *is* his father; certainly is a "father-substitute" in the psychologist's word; and this makes the theory of a vicarious sacrifice the more colourable. All through the play there is a strong implicit parallelism between Henry Bolingbroke and his policies and Falstaff and *his* policies; and at one point in the play the two fathers actually, as it were, fuse (like Leonardo's two mothers in his paintings of the Virgin and St. Anne), and in the Boar's Head tavern King Falstaff sits on his throne while his son Prince Henry kneels before him. And Falstaff, in standing for the old king, symbolises all the accumulated sin of the reign, all the consequent sterility of the land. But the young king draws his knife at the altar—and the heart of that grey iniquity, the father ruffian, is as fracted and corroborate as Pistol avers. Falstaff's rejection and death are very sad, but Sir James Frazer would have classed them with the Periodic Expulsion of Evils in a Material Vehicle. . . .

If this addition of another buried significance to the composite myth of Hal and Falstaff should seem extravagant, or an injudicious striving after Morgann's "lightness of air," let it be remembered that drama, like religious ritual, plays upon atavic impulses of the mind. All true drama penetrates through representative fiction to the condition of myth. And Falstaff is in the end the dethroned and sacrificed king, the scapegoat as well as the sweet beef. [*Character and Motive in Shakespeare*, 1949.]

WILLIAM EMPSON. The sort of ruler you can trust, you being one of the ruled, the sort that can understand his people, can lead them to glory, is one who has learned the world by experience, especially rather low experience; he knows the tricks, he can allow for human failings, and somehow between the two he can gauge the spirit of a situation or a period. The idea is not simply that Falstaff is debauched and tricky, though that in itself made him give Hal experience, and hardly any price was too high to pay for getting a good ruler, but that he had the breadth of mind and of social understanding which the Magnanimous Man needed to acquire. It seems a lower-class rather than upper-class line of thought (it is, of course, militantly anti-puritan, as we can assume the groundlings tended to be) and Falstaff can be regarded as a parody of it rather than a coarse acceptance of it by Shakespeare; but surely it is obviously present; indeed I imagine that previous critics have thought it too obvious to be worth writing down—there was no need to, until Mr. Dover Wilson began preaching at us about his Medieval Vice and his Ideal King . . . .

The real case for rejecting Falstaff at the end of Part II is that he was dangerously strong, indeed almost a rebel leader; Mr. Dover Wilson makes many good points here, and he need not throw the drama away by pretending that the bogey was always ridiculous. He is quite right in insisting that the Prince did not appear malicious in the rejection, and did only what was necessary; because Falstaff's expectations were enormous (and were recklessly expressed, by the way, to persons who could shame him afterwards); the terrible sentence "the laws of England are at my commandment, and woe to my Lord Chief Justice" meant something so practical to the audience that they may actually have stopped cracking nuts to hear what happened next. A mob would enter the small capital to see the coronation, and how much of it Falstaff could raise would be a reasonable subject for doubt; he could become "protector" of the young king; once you admit that he is both an aristocrat and a mob leader he is a familiar very dangerous type ["Falstaff and Mr. Dover Wilson," *Kenyon Review,* XV, Spring, 1953.]

CLIFFORD LEECH. . . . it has been apparent, I think, that *2 Henry IV* differs from Part I in its dominant tone. Of course, there are sharp incidental things in the earlier play, but they do not weigh heavily on the spectator's mind. Falstaff abuses the press in both Parts, but his activities in this direction are shown at closer quarters in Part II. And there is broad merriment in the later play, but it is worked into a pattern where good humour is not the main theme. Towards the end of Part II there is, indeed, a strong measure of simplification. From the Prince's last interview with his father to the rejection of Falstaff, Shakespeare strives to make the morality-element all-pervading, until we have the curious spectacle of Henry V urging repentance on his old companions: banishment was, of course, required, but he is an odd preacher to men whom kingship did not call to the disciplined life. And, as we have seen, the prose epilogue pretends that, after all, merriment is the prime concern of this play and the one to come. But, until Henry IV's death-scene, the delicate balance between the two layers of meaning is skilfully maintained . . . .

He [Shakespeare] was an Elizabethan certainly: he made assumptions about kingship and "degree" and incest and adultery that perhaps we may not make. But he was also a human being with a remarkable degree of sensitivity: it is indeed for that reason that he can move us so much. If he merely had skill in "putting over" characteristic Tudor ideas, we could leave him to the social and political historians. Because his reaction to suffering, his esteem for good faith, his love of human society, his sense of mutability and loss, his obscure notion of human grandeur, his ultimate uncertainty of value, are not basically different from ours—though more deeply felt and incomparably expressed—he belongs supremely to literature. We do him, I think, scant justice if we assume that he could write complacently of Prince John of Lancaster, and could have no doubts about Prince Hal. ["The Unity of 2 Henry IV" in *Shakespeare Survey 6,* 1953.]

C. L. BARBER. It is in the Henry IV plays that we can consider most fruitfully general questions concerning the relation of comedy to analogous forms of symbolic action in folk rituals: not only the likenesses of comedy to ritual, but the differences, the features of comic form which make it comedy and not ritual. Such analogies, I think, prove to be useful critical tools: they lead us to see structure in the drama. And they also raise fascinating historical and theoretical questions about the relation of drama to other products of culture. One way in which our time has been seeing the universal in literature has been to find in complex literary works patterns which are analogous to myths and rituals and which can be regarded as archetypes, in some sense primitive or fundamental. . . . such analysis can be misleading if it results in equating the literary form with primitive analogues. When we are dealing wit so developed an art as Shakespeare's, in so comple an epoch as the Renaissance, primitive patterns ma be seen in literature mainly because literary imagination, exploiting the heritage of literary form, dis engages them from the suggestions of a comple culture. And the primitive levels are articulated i the course of reunderstanding their nature—indee the primitive can be fully expressed only on condi tion that the artist can deal with it in a most civilize way. Shakespeare presents patterns analogous t magic and ritual in the process of redefining magi as imagination, ritual as social action . . . .

In *Part One,* Falstaff reigns, within his sphere, a Carnival; *Part Two* is very largely taken up wit his trial. To put Carnival on trial, run him out c town, and burn or bury him is in folk custom a wa of limiting, by ritual, the attitudes and impulses se loose by ritual. Such a trial, though conducted wit gay hoots and jeers, serves to swing the mind roun to a new vantage, where it sees misrule no longer a a benign release for the individual, but as a sourc of destructive consequences for society. This sort o reckoning is what *Part Two* brings to Falstaff.

But Falstaff proves extremely difficult to brin to book—more difficult than an ordinary mummer king—because his burlesque and mockery are de veloped to a point where the mood of a momen crystallizes as a settled attitude of scepticism. As w have observed before, in a static, monolithic societ a Lord of Misrule can be put back in his place afte the revel with relative ease. ["Rule and Misrule i *Henry IV,*" *Shakespeare's Festive Comedy,* 1959

HENRY V. PORTRAIT BY AN UNKNOWN ARTIST. (NATIONAL PORTRAIT GALLERY)

Henry V (1387–1422). King of England (1413–1422). Titular hero of *Henry V*. (For Shakespeare's treatment of his youth in *1* and *2 Henry IV*, see FAL.) In the eyes of Elizabethans, Henry V ranked among the greatest and noblest kings of English history. The 16th-century historian Edward Halle, whose work provided one of the sources of the play, describes Henry as a king "whom all men loved." "All men" did not include his enemies, chief among whom were the French. Henry's attack on France, culminating in his victory at Agincourt (1415), was politically expedient but ultimately unwise. The French campaign was designed to unite England in a common cause and consequently to divert attention from the tenuousness of Henry's claim to the throne. In the end, however, it served only to undermine the nation, resulting in the disastrous Wars of the Roses in the latter half of the century. Nevertheless the king was a brilliant, if often cruel, general and had achieved by Shakespeare's time the status of an epic hero.

This is the picture of him given in *Henry V*, and it accounts for the character's lack of "inner life." Henry, like all epic heroes, is seen less as an individual than as the embodiment of his nation's ideals. See HENRY V: *Comment*.

The Life of King HENRY the Fifth.

Henry V. A history play by Shakespeare.

Text. "Henry the ffift, a booke" was entered in the Stationers' Register along with *Much Ado About Nothing*, *As You Like It*, and Jonson's *Every Man In his Humour* on August 4, 1600 by the printer James Roberts. A notation accompanying the entry reads "to be staied." This was evidently a BLOCKING ENTRY, the registration of a work not actually intended for publication, in order to prevent unauthorized persons from producing pirated editions. In this case the effort failed, for in the same year (1600) the First Quarto was published, entitled, "The Chronicle History of Henry the fift, With his battel fought at Agin Court in France. Togither with Auntient Pistoll. As it hath bene sundry times playd by the Right honorable the Lord Chamberlaine his seruants. London Printed by Thomas Creede, for Tho. Millington, and Iohn Busby. And are to be sold at his house in Carter Lane, next the Powle head. 1600."

This edition is a BAD QUARTO, probably based on a MEMORIAL RECONSTRUCTION of a cut version of the play used by the company while on tour. The reporters of the text were probably the actor or actors who played Gower and the Duke of Exeter. This corrupt text was reissued in 1602 and again in 1619, under the false date 1608, by Thomas Pavier and William Jaggard, who antedated the play in order to circumvent the lord chamberlain's injunction (1619) against the printing of the King's Men's plays without their permission. Therefore, the First Folio text (1623), set up either from Shakespeare's FOUL PAPERS, with occasional reference to the 1619 Quarto, or from a corrected copy of that Quarto, is the only authoritative text.

One line in the Folio text was subjected to the most famous emendation in Shakespeare's works. It occurs in the Hostess' description of the death of Falstaff. The Folio reading is "and a Table of green fields" (II, iii, 17). Lewis Theobald, one of Shakespeare's earliest editors, emended this phrase to "and a' babbled of green fields." Theobald's alteration was ridiculed by later 17th-century editors, but it has come to be generally accepted by modern editors. Recently, however, there have been some attempts to discredit the emendation and reinterpret the Folio reading. See EMENDATION.

Date. The date can be fixed with unusual exactness by a reference to the earl of Essex' campaign in Ireland. The lines read:

> Were now the general of our gracious empress,
> As in good time he may, from Ireland coming,
> Bringing rebellion broached on his sword,
> How many would the peaceful city quit,
> To welcome him!
>
> (V, prologue, 30–34)

Essex left London on March 27, 1599, reached Dublin in April, and, after conducting a completely unsuccessful campaign, returned to England on September 28 of the same year. Shakespeare must therefore have worked on the play sometime between March 27 and September 28, 1599. Meres' PALLADIS TAMIA, published in the autumn of 1598, lists among Shakespeare's plays a *Henry IV*, but not *Henry V*. The reference in the first prologue to "this wooden O" supports the date of 1599. This phrase is usually taken to allude to the new Globe theatre, first occupied by Shakespeare's company in 1599, although J. Dover Wilson and others argue that the allusion is to the Curtain theatre, not the Globe.

Sources. Henry V (1387–1422) came to the throne

THE

CRONICLE

Hiſtory of Henry the fift,

With his battell fought at *Agin Court* in *France*. Togither with *Auntient Piſtoll*.

As it hath bene ſundry times playd by the Right honorable the Lord Chamberlaine his ſeruants.

LONDON

Printed by *Thomas Creede*, for Tho. Millington, and Iohn Busby. And are to be ſold at his houſe in Carter Lane, next the Powle head. 1600.

TITLE PAGE OF THE BAD QUARTO OF *Henry V* (1600).

in 1413. Shakespeare drew the events of his reign from the 1587 edition of HOLINSHED's *Chronicles*, from Edward HALLE's history *The union of the two noble and illustre famelies of Lancastre and York* (second issue, 1548), and, in a few details, from Robert Fabyan's (d. 1513) *New Chronicles of England and France* (1516). An anonymous play, THE FAMOUS VICTORIES OF HENRY V, entered in the Stationers' Register on May 14, 1594, had until recently been thought to be a dramatic source. In it the poet could have found the Dauphin's satiric gift of tennis balls to the young King, Pistol's capture of M. de Fer, and Henry's wooing of Princess Katharine. Now, however, evidence has been adduced that there was an earlier play than *The Famous Victories*, that it was owned by the Queen's Men and referred to by Henslowe as "Henry the Fifth" and "harey the Vth" in entries in his diary from November 1595 to July 1596. It is this earlier play, or a brace of Queen's Men's plays, that is now thought to be the source of *Henry V*. Scholars consider *The Famous Victories* to be an abridged and degraded version of the Queen's company's plays, reported from memory and published in 1594. It is, therefore, in no sense a source of *Henry V*.

Various attempts have been made to uncover topical allusions in the play. Of these the most convincing are the theories that the Welsh soldier Fluellen is a portrait of Sir Roger WILLIAMS or of Ludovic LLOYD and that Pistol is intended as a parody of Marlowe's bombastic hero Tamburlaine. —O. J. C.

Plot Synopsis. Act I. Alarmed by a proposed bill that would confiscate ecclesiastical property, the Archbishop of Canterbury and the Bishop of Ely are hopeful that King Henry will oppose the measure. The prelates remark that, since his accession to the throne, Henry has been transformed from a riotous idler to a ruler of uncommon sagacity, learning, and grace. The Archbishop adds that he has promised the King a generous contribution from the clergy if he embarks upon a campaign to claim the French crown, his by virtue of descent from Isabella of France, mother of his great-grandfather, Edward III.

At the request of the King, who wishes to ascertain whether his claim is just, the Archbishop expounds the history of the Salic Law, which supposedly bars succession to the French throne through the female line, pointing out that it had often been violated by the French themselves. He assures Henry that he can press his claim with a clear conscience. Summoned to the King's presence, ambassadors from France present him with a gift which the Dauphin considers in keeping with his character: tennis balls. The

TITLE PAGE OF THE 1619 *Henry V* QUARTO PUBLISHED ILLEGALLY BY THOMAS PAVIER. THE PUBLISHER PREDATED THE QUARTO TO AVOID A 1619 BAN ON THE PUBLICATION OF THE KING'S MEN'S PLAYS WITHOUT THEIR CONSENT.

THE

Chronicle Hiſtory

of Henry the fift, with his battell fought at *Agin Court* in France. Together with ancient *Piſtoll*.

As it hath bene ſundry times playd by the Right Honorable the Lord Chamberlaine his Seruants.

Printed for *T. P.* 1608.

angry King retorts that many French widows and mothers will curse the Dauphin's jest.

Act II. As preparations for the invasion of France get under way, two members of the expedition—Corporal Nym and the red-nosed Lieutenant Bardolph—meet on a London street. They are joined by Mistress Quickly and her new husband Pistol, who has won her from Nym, thereby incurring the latter's enmity. After the two are grudgingly reconciled by Bardolph, they are summoned to the bedside of the ailing Falstaff, whose "heart is fracted and corroborate" because of the King's rejection of him.

In Southampton, Henry converses with three courtiers—the Earl of Cambridge, Lord Scroop, and Sir Thomas Grey—who are in league with the French and have conspired against the King's life. Unaware that their treason has been detected, they advise Henry not to pardon a poor wretch who has spoken against him. In their turn, they plead for mercy when the King orders their arrest. Stating that he does not seek revenge for the attempt on his person, but that the safety of the kingdom must be protected, Henry sentences them to death.

As they prepare to leave for Southampton, Pistol, Nym, and Bardolph lament the death of Falstaff. When Bardolph wishes that he were with him, "wheresome'er he is, either in heaven or in hell," Mistress Quickly assures him that the old knight is undoubtedly in "Arthur's bosom," since he had made a most Christian end. Nym and Falstaff's servant, however, express reservations on the latter point.

In the palace of King Charles of France, the Dauphin ridicules Henry as "a vain, giddy, shallow, humorous youth," but the Constable warns him not to underestimate the English King. Their discussion is interrupted by the arrival of the Duke of Exeter, who voices Henry's demand that Charles give up his throne.

Act III. Unappeased by Charles' offer of his daughter Katharine and a few minor dukedoms, Henry sails for France, where he lays siege to the town of Harfleur. Fluellen, a doughty Welsh captain, spurs on the laggardly Nym and Bardolph; later, to the amusement of Captain Jamy, a Scot, he attempts to enlist Captain Macmorris, a truculent Irishman, in a discussion of the "disciplines of the war." When the Governor of Harfleur learns that the Dauphin is unable to send help, he is forced to surrender.

In the French palace, Princess Katharine receives an English lesson from Alice, her attendant, while the King and his court discuss the advance of the English who, undeterred by hunger or fatigue, have crossed the Somme and are marching toward Calais. Ordering his nobles to gird themselves for battle, the King dispatches the herald Montjoy to the English camp in Picardy. There Fluellen remarks to Captain Gower on the valor of one Pistol during a skirmish on a nearby bridge. Pistol himself appears and, explaining that Bardolph is to be hanged for looting a church, asks Fluellen to intercede for him with the Duke of Exeter, roundly cursing the Welshman when he refuses. Seeing the King, Fluellen announces that Exeter has successfully defended the bridge. A trumpet announces the arrival of Montjoy, who haughtily bids Henry to consider the huge ransom he will have to pay if he is captured in battle. The King replies that he had planned to proceed directly to Calais but that, despite the weakness of his forces, he is prepared to give battle.

At Agincourt, the French and English camps lie within 1500 paces of each other. The Dauphin impatiently waits for dawn to signal the start of the battle, though the Constable remarks to the Duke of Orléans that the Dauphin's valor is a "hidden virtue," seen only by his lackeys.

Act IV. Meanwhile, the "poor condemned" English huddle by their fires, cheered by the King, who gives to each "a little touch of Harry in the night." Borrowing a cloak and dismissing his counselors, Henry wanders unrecognized through the camp. To one Williams, who asserts that the King will have to answer for the sins of those who fall in the battle if his cause is not just, Henry replies that a monarch cannot be held to account for the souls of his soldiers. As a result of an altercation, he and Williams exchange gloves that they will wear in their caps so as to be able to recognize each other and continue the quarrel. Alone, Henry reflects on the cares of kingship, noting that the only advantage he derives from his position is the "idol ceremony." Imploring divine aid, he hopes that God will overlook, for one day, his father's sin in wresting the crown from Richard II.

At daybreak, the French confidently prepare to meet the "island carrions." In the opposing camp, Henry buoys up his men's sinking spirits by describing the pride with which the survivors will be able to point to their scars and say that they had been won on this Saint Crispin's day.

In the battle that follows, the English cover themselves with glory, while the French forces scatter in disorder. A humble Montjoy asks Henry to permit the French to bury their dead, conceding that the English have triumphed. After encountering Williams, who is wearing the King's glove in his cap, Henry, jocular even on the battlefield, gives the soldier's gage to Fluellen, solemnly explaining that any man who challenges it is an enemy of his. When Williams accosts Fluellen and strikes him, the Welshman orders the arrest of the soldier, who is freed by the King and given a glove filled with money for his pains.

Act V. After returning to England in triumph, Henry again sets sail for France to conclude a treaty of peace. In the English camp, Fluellen encounters his old enemy Pistol and thrashes the "scurvy, lousy knave" when the latter derides the Welsh nation. Pistol, now a widower, decides to resume his larcenous career in England.

In an interview between Henry and King Charles, the Duke of Burgundy expresses his desire for the restoration of peace, that "dear nurse of arts, plenties and joyful births," to France, which is in dire need of her husbandry. During the negotiations, Henry woos Katharine, offering himself as "a fellow of plain and uncoined constancy." When he wins her consent, he seals the compact with a kiss, ignoring her protests that it is a breach of French custom. Acceding to the English peace terms, King Charles gives his daughter to Henry, and declares him heir to the throne of France.—H. D.

Comment. *Henry V* is, first of all, a nationalistic play, in which Shakespeare dramatizes the enthusiastic cooperation of the various peoples of a Greater Britain—Scots, Irish, Welsh, and English—in fighting a foreign war. This was the national policy advocated by the earl of Essex and applied disastrously to his campaign against the Irish, whom he wished not to conquer but to woo. This resemblance of the drama to Essex' policies has led some critics to the unwarranted assumption that Shakespeare was an active partisan of Essex' program and that he designed Henry to be an idealized portrait of Essex.

Henry V is also an epic of a great conqueror and a national hero. The young King's patriotism is often frank chauvinism. He is contemptuous of the French and of the Dauphin in particular. They are boasters, trivial in their attitude toward warfare. The Dauphin is almost insanely volatile, given to incessant gesticulation and shameful bragging. He is described by his companions as longing to devour his English foes and his soldiers are sure that he will eat all that he can kill. Henry, on the other hand, is magnanimous to his foe. He warns his soldiers against all forms of pillage. And, when Bardolph is convicted of the sacrilegious crime of robbing a church, Henry orders him hanged. Nor does he permit his troops to use disdainful language to the French populace, "for when levity and cruelty play for a kingdom, the gentler gamer is the surest winner." He is at once modest and deeply religious, attributing the seemingly miraculous victory at Agincourt, not to his valiant leadership, but to God's help.

As a general he will enter upon a war only after being assured of the legal and moral right of his cause. So important did Shakespeare think it to assure his audience that Henry's claim to French provinces was justified that he took from Holinshed a long statement of the legal and genealogical evidence supporting Henry's right and gave it 63 lines of the first act of his play. When embarked upon actual fighting, the King becomes resolute and fierce. Elizabethans would have thought any other attitude effeminate. His famous exhortation of his troops drawn up in battle array for their assault upon Harfleur, beginning "Once more unto the breach, dear friends" (III, i, 1), is an admission that the attack will be cruel and bloody. His horrible threats to the citizens of Harfleur of slaughter of their infants and rape of their fair fresh maidens (III, iii, 1–41) are designed to frighten the garrison into surrender, as they do. J. Dover Wilson suggests that Shakespeare composed this hideous tirade in order to "bring home to his audience the meaning of war in terms of human agony." Henry's own conduct of war in no way resembles the violence of his threats. Harfleur once having yielded, he instructs Exeter, who is to take charge of the town and its citizens, to "use mercy to them all."

This paragon is so miraculous a development of the wild Prince Hal of the Henry IV play that the poet puts into Canterbury's mouth expressions of surprise at its suddenness: "Never came reformation in a flood, / With such a heady currance, scouring faults" (I, i, 33–34). Shakespeare gives us to understand that Hal's dissipation was one of God's punishments of Henry IV for his causing the dethronement and death of God's anointed, Richard II. Henry IV had taken all the soil of this achievement into h grave with him and so Hal's riotous living abrupt ceased.

"This pattern of princehood," "this mirror magnificence" Shakespeare could not allow to l smirched by association with his old companions Eastcheap, so he cleared the stage of all of ther beginning with Falstaff. He fails to keep the promi made in the epilogue of *2 Henry IV* to "continue th story with Sir John in it." Instead he writes fo Mistress Quickly a report of Falstaff's death in mixture of pathos and absurdity that characteriz them both and forms one of the most striking ex amples of the poet's sheer genius (II, iii, 8–28).

Some of the gang of rogues do appear in the earl scenes of *Henry V*, only to be summarily ejecte Pistol of the resonant rodomontade and Bardolph the bulbous nose are joined by a rogue called Nyr The name means "take" and suggests the thieving h is to practice. Nym has heard that men of the fewe words are the most formidable. Therefore, he merel hints through understatements at dark deeds he wi do when occasion is ripe. He has picked up th newly popular term "humour," in the sense of whin probably derived from Ben Jonson's *Every Man I his Humour*. He becomes sworn brother to Bardolp in filching, which leads to the gallows for both them. Pistol, in spite of his adoption of the bomba of the hero in a tragedy of blood, is a poltroo After Fluellen has shown him to be a craven, di graced, he creeps back to England to turn cutpur and bawd. The place of these reprobates is taken by group of characters who, though humorous, hav political significance. They are Fluellen, a Welsh man; Captain Jamy, a Scotsman; Macmorris, a Irishman; and two English soldiers, Bates and Wi liams. Each speaks a dialect and each illustrates a amusing social peculiarity. Together they prophes a time when the Welsh, the Scots, and the Irish wi join the English in happy military fellowship.

Williams serves a different purpose. It is he wit whom the disguised King discusses some of th moral and religious questions raised by war th were asked at the time, particularly by the Catholic Is it ever right for a Christian state to make w upon another? How much responsibility for killin does the individual private soldier incur while figh ing in the king's quarrel? How much responsibilit has the king for the damnation of a soldier slain i battle before he has made peace with God? The questions, boring to a modern audience, were of th greatest concern to Elizabethan soldiers preparing t fight on the morrow.

Henry's wooing of Katharine, from Dr. Johnso down to the present, has been stamped as gros displaying the King's ignorance of the simplest rul of courtly behavior. But Henry is amused at findin himself in a situation outside his experience, con plicated by a language difficulty, and, moreove Shakespeare wished Henry's simplicity and rust plainness to form a strong contrast to the artf coquetry of the French Princess. His artless wooin wins her so that the play can end with a roy betrothal bringing peace to the traditional foes.

In the end, *Henry V* celebrates, not a chauvinist patriotism, but a noble conception of England destiny. From his invocation of a Muse of Fir rough the paeans of the later choruses, through e revelation of the qualities of an ideal king, iakespeare produces the effects of an epic poem. It a dramatic lyric glorifying the most forward-oking national ideal conceived in Elizabethan ngland—O. J. C.

Stage History. As explained above under *Date,* the rst performance of *Henry V* was given sometime etween March 27 and September 28, 1599. Richard urbage probably created the title role and acted e part in the first recorded performance given at ourt on January 7, 1605, during the Christmas evels. There is no record of another presentation of iakespeare's *Henry V* until 1735; An adaptation of *enry V* composed by Aaron Hill in 1723 omitted l the comic characters and added a sentimental ıbplot. Hill's version supplanted Shakespeare's rama for a time. On November 26, 1735 the ıthentic *Henry V* was restored to the stage at oodman's Fields, and thereafter was performed at egular intervals. Covent Garden staged the play 10 mes between 1731 and 1739, 3 times in 1750, and very year but 4 from 1752 to 1773. Spranger Barry ayed the King at Drury Lane in 1747 (while David arrick appeared as the Chorus) and in three ovent Garden productions. An even more popular lenry at the time was William Smith, who acted ie part during 17 seasons from 1755 to 1779. On ctober 1, 1789 John Philip Kemble revived *Henry* at Drury Lane; he gave 10 performances as the ing that year and acted the part in 5 consecutive easons from 1790. Pageantry and elaborate settings ecame a permanent feature of these presentations. or one particular performance on September 22, 767, Covent Garden advertised a "procession from ie *Abbey* at the *Coronation,* with the Representa-on of *Westminster Hall,* and the *Ceremony of the hampion.*"

By the time Charles Macready staged *Henry V,* pectacle was *de rigueur.* About to withdraw from ovent Garden, he closed his second and last season s manager of that theatre with an elaborate revival n June 10, 1839, exploiting every available scenic ffect. He also restored the Chorus, which had been ut from all acting versions since the Restoration vith the possible exception of Garrick's 1747 pro-uction. George Vandenhoff spoke the lines in the haracter of Time, indicating a succession of illus-rations painted by Clarkson Stanfield, including a ioving diorama tracing the English fleet's voyage rom Southampton to Harfleur. This production was he crowning achievement of Macready's managerial areer. Charles Kean also signaled his retirement rom theatrical management with a production of *lenry V,* this one at the Princess' Theatre in 1859. ean's wife, Ellen Tree, chanted the Chorus in the haracter of Clio, setting a precedent in the casting f a role always previously assigned to a male. Still nother of the famous actor-managers closed his areer in *Henry V.* Samuel Phelps, who played the ing in the memorable Sadler's Wells revival of 852, lent his talent to John Coleman for a produc-ion at the Queen's Theatre in 1876. Coleman, a econd-rate actor, assumed the leading role himself nd assigned to Phelps the part of Henry IV in pisodes from *2 Henry IV* that he included as a rologue.

MACREADY AS HENRY V.

Henry V was chosen by Augustus Harris to inaugurate his management of Drury Lane in 1879. Earlier in the decade Charles Calvert had revived the piece in Manchester and sold the production rights to the managers of Booth's Theatre in New York where, in 1875, George Rignold had magnificent success with his portrayal of Henry. Harris enlisted the services of this dashing actor in his opening production and adopted Calvert's acting version of the play. This production, in the manner of a "grand revival," was later taken to Australia, winning for Rignold unequaled world renown as one of the most vigorous, commanding impersonators of Henry V.

When Frank Benson brought his company to the Lyceum in 1900, while Henry Irving toured the United States, he opened the season with *Henry V.*

On February 15 the London audience heard the bells ringing for the feast of Crispin and saw Benson, re-creating his Stratford impersonation of a youthful Henry, vault the walls of Harfleur in full armor. At that time the talented company included Leslie Faber (Westmoreland), H. H. Ainley (Duke of Gloucester), Harcourt Williams (Grey), A. M. Lang (Montjoy), Lily Brayton (Alice)—and Isadora Duncan playing a French camp follower. In December of that year Lewis Waller selected the play as his first managerial offering at the Lyceum. The patriotic fervor of *Henry V* heightened its popularity whenever England was at war. At that time, with the Boer War in progress, Waller's highly theatrical rendition of the King seemed most appropriate. The house stood and cheered when Henry, with his back to the audience, finished the Crispin speech. In 1905 at the Imperial, in 1908 at the Lyric, and in 1910 for Beerbohm Tree's sixth annual Shakespeare festival at His Majesty's, Waller gave his stirring impersonation of the King. Meanwhile, in 14 seasons between 1901 and 1916, Benson staged the drama at Stratford-upon-Avon, and also dashed to London's Shaftesbury Theatre during the turbulent Christmas of 1914 to recover his youth in the patriotism of *Henry V*. John Martin-Harvey acted the title role in May 1916 at His Majesty's. The next month Marie Slade's all-woman company gave a matinee performance at the Queen's; this strange presentation, with Miss Slade as Henry, was staged again on April 26, 1921 at the Strand. *Henry V* was included in the Old Vic repertoire and produced every season from 1915 to 1920. While Sybil Thorndike was in the company, she played the Chorus and Princess Katharine. Robert Atkins presented *Henry V* during the 1921/2 and 1923/4 seasons, the latter production featuring Ion Swinley as the King. Under Andrew Leigh, the Vic staged the play twice, first in 1926, with Baliol Holloway; second, at the Lyric, Hammersmith, in January 1928, with Sybil Thorndike costumed as an Elizabethan boy to act the Chorus, and Lewis Casson in the title role.

At Stratford W. Bridges-Adams allowed only one short interval to separate 19 scenes; this pictorial presentation in the summer of 1920 was brought to the Strand the following October. Stratford had another production under Bridges-Adams in 1927. In 1934 Robert Atkins produced the drama at the Memorial Theatre, starring John Wyse. Other Stratford productions were B. Iden Payne's in 1937; Milton Rosmer's in 1943, with Baliol Holloway in the title role; and Dorothy Green's 1946 production, which had Paul Scofield as the King.

In November 1931 Harcourt Williams presented *Henry V*, with Ralph Richardson as the King. Godfrey Tearle took the role in Stanley Bell's production at the Alhambra in 1934. In 1936, under the glare of white lights at the Ring, Blackfriars, Robert Atkins staged the play, with Hubert Gregg as Henry. Tyrone Guthrie directed a coronation year *Henry V* in April 1937 at the Old Vic; Harcourt Williams was a nervous and brooding Charles VI; Leo Genn brought attention to the often neglected Duke of Burgundy, and Laurence Olivier was King Henry. Lewis Casson produced a spectacular but short-lived *Henry V* at Drury Lane in 1938; Patrick Kinsella performed vigorously as Henry on a rainy August 19, 1941 at the Open Air to an audience o less than 50.

Laurence Olivier successfully combined poetr and scenic splendor in a film version of *Henry V* first released in London on November 27, 194 Under Olivier's direction, the motion picture, prob ably the finest of all Shakespeare films, set creativ standards for future productions. A bird's-eye view of Shakespeare's London introduced the first tw acts set on a replica of the original Globe theatr stage. Magnificent scenes of the siege of Harfleu and the battle of Agincourt followed. Intelligentl performed, with Olivier as Henry, carefully edite with a sense of truth to the original, the film wo acclaim on both sides of the Atlantic, appearing i New York for the first time during the 1946/ dramatic season.

Both the Old Vic and Stratford presented *Henr V* during 1951. Glen Byam Shaw directed the excit ing Old Vic production, with Alec Clunes' softene impersonation of the King. Richard Burton was serious, heroic, and somewhat colorless Henry i Anthony Quayle's presentation at the Memori Theatre. During the 1952/3 season, the Bristol com pany performed *Henry V* at the Old Vic, wit Denis Carey in the title role. In July 1953 the firs West End presentation of the play in 12 years wa produced by John Barton and acted by the Eliza bethan Theatre Company at the Westminste Burton re-created his Henry in 1955 at the Old Vi this time in Michael Benthall's production, whic featured John Neville as Chorus. In May 196 Neville assumed direction of an Old Vic *Henry V* which starred Donald Houston. Three months be fore, on February 25, a modern-dress *Henry V* adapted by Julius Gellner and Bernard Miles, bowe at the Mermaid, Blackfriars; the Chorus introduce the second half of the drama by attempting harmonica rendition of "Roses of Picardy," and th King, portrayed by William Peacock, wore flann knickers for a scene with the Archbishop o Canterbury.

There was a performance by the Youth Theatr under Michael Croft at Sadler's Wells in Augu 1962 and an ensemble production at Stratford i 1964 by Peter Hall, with John Barton and Cliffor Williams. In the later presentation, Ian Holm im personated a youthful King, a commander of th army rather than a glorious hero.

One of the most stirring performances of Shake speare's plays given at the Stratford, Ontario, festiv was a production of *Henry V* during the 1956 seaso Christopher Plummer, the Canadian actor, was a excellent King, and French-Canadian actors ap peared as elegant and graceful French soldier *Henry V* was included in Gilmor Browne's 19 festival of all the Shakespeare histories at the Pas dena Community Playhouse in California, and i Peter Dews' television series, entitled *An Age o Kings*, produced for the British Broadcasting Com pany in 1961.—M. G.

Bibliography. Text: *Henry V*, New Cambridg Edition, J. Dover Wilson, ed., 1947; *King Henry V* New Arden Edition, J. H. Walter, ed., 1954; A. Cairncross, "Quarto Copy for the Folio *Henry V*, *Studies in Bibliography*, VIII, 1956. Date: Ne Cambridge Edition; New Arden Edition. Source

New Cambridge Edition; New Arden Edition; Geoffrey Bullough, *Narrative and Dramatic Sources of Shakespeare*, Vol. IV, 1962. COMMENT: J. Dover Wilson, *The Fortunes of Falstaff*, 1943; Lily B. Campbell, *Shakespeare's Histories*, 1947. STAGE HISTORY: New Cambridge Edition; G. C. D. Odell, *Shakespeare from Betterton to Irving*, 1920; C. B. Hogan, *Shakespeare in the Theatre, 1701–1800*, 2 vols., 1952, 1957; J. C. Trewin, *Shakespeare on the English Stage, 1900–1964*, 1964.

Selected Criticism

WILLIAM HAZLITT. Henry V. is a very favourite monarch with the English nation, and he appears to have been also a favourite with Shakespear, who labours hard to apologise for the actions of the king, by shewing us the character of the man, as 'the king of good fellows.' He scarcely deserves this honour. He was fond of war and low company:—we know little else of him. He was careless, dissolute, and ambitious;—idle, or doing mischief. In private, he seemed to have no idea of the common decencies of life, which he subjected to a kind of regal licence; in public affairs, he seemed to have no idea of any rule of right or wrong, but brute force, glossed over with a little religious hypocrisy and archiepiscopal advice. His principles did not change with his situation and professions. His adventure on Gadshill was a prelude to the affair of Agincourt, only a bloodless one; Falstaff was a puny prompter of violence and outrage, compared with the pious and politic Archbishop of Canterbury, who gave the king *carte blanche*, in a genealogical tree of his family, to rob and murder in circles of latitude and longitude abroad—to save the possessions of the church at home. This appears in the speeches in Shakespear, where the hidden motives that actuate princes and their advisers in war and policy are better laid open than in speeches from the throne or woolsack. Henry, because he did not know how to govern his own kingdom, determined to make war upon his neighbours. Because his own title to the crown was doubtful, he laid claim to that of France. Because he did not know how to exercise the enormous power, which had just dropped into his hands, to any one good purpose, he immediately undertook (a cheap and obvious resource of sovereignty) to do all the mischief he could. [*Characters of Shakespear's Plays*, 1817.]

CHARLES KNIGHT. In the case of the 'Henry V.' it appears to us that our great dramatic poet would never have touched the subject, had not the stage previously possessed it in the old play of 'The Famous Victories.' 'Henry IV.' would have been perfect as a dramatic whole, without the addition of 'Henry V.' The somewhat doubtful mode in which he speaks of continuing the story appears to us a pretty certain indication that he rather shrunk from a subject which appeared to him essentially undramatic. It is, however, highly probable that, having brought the history of Henry of Monmouth up to the period of his father's death, the demands of an audience, who had been accustomed to hail "the madcap Prince of Wales" as the conqueror of Agincourt, compelled him to "continue the story." That he originally contemplated lending to it the interest of his creation of Falstaff is also sufficiently clear. It would be vain to speculate why he abandoned this intention; but it is evident that, without the interest which Falstaff would have imparted to the story, the dramatic materials presented by the old play, or by the circumstances that the poet could discover in the real course of events, were extremely meagre and unsatisfying. It is our belief, therefore, that, having hastily met the demands of his audience by the first sketch of 'Henry V.,' as it appears in the quarto editions, he subsequently saw the capacity which the subject presented for being treated in a grand lyrical spirit. . . . The 'Henry V.' constitutes an exception to the general rules upon which he worked. "High actions" are here described as well as exhibited; and "high passions," in the Shaksperean sense of the term, scarcely make their appearance upon the scene. Here are no struggles between will and fate; no frailties of humanity dragging down its virtues into an abyss of guilt and sorrow,—no crimes,—no obduracy,—no penitence. We have the lofty and unconquerable spirit of national and individual heroism riding triumphantly over every danger; but the spirit is so lofty that we feel no uncertainty for the issue. We should know, even if we had no foreknowledge of the event, that it must conquer. We can scarcely weep over those who fall in that "glorious and well-foughten field," for "they kept together in their chivalry," and their last words sound as a glorious hymn of exultation. The subject is altogether one of lyric grandeur; but it is not one, we think, which Shakspere would have chosen for a drama. [*Studies of Shakspere*, 1849.]

THOMAS KENNY. We do not know any other work of his [Shakespeare's] in which his national or personal predilections have made themselves so distinctly visible: and yet it is impossible to class this play among the great productions of his genius. In all the higher conditions of the dramatic representation of life—in freedom, in variety, in depth, in truthfulness, in imaginative power—it is decidedly inferior not only to his more famous tragedies, but to some even of his mixed dramas. It contains hardly a single passage which can be said absolutely and unmistakably to reveal his distinctive ease and splendour or form, or his distinctive insight into character and passion. The truth is, that the subject itself did not admit of perfect dramatic treatment. It is a heroic history, and such a history, to be dealt with effectively, should be dealt with epically or lyrically. Henry V. is here exhibited as a complete, harmonious, self-possessed character; but such characters are not dramatic. In the epic delineation of great personages and great exploits we are dominated by them. In dramatic representation we are comparatively independent of the agents in the scene. We see them caught in the struggle of passions which we know to be but distant and latent elements in our own nature. In epic narration it is our admiration that is mainly or exclusively awakened; in the dramatic exhibition of life it is our critical, discriminating, illuminating sympathy that is called into action. The play of "King Henry V." is the representation, not of great passions, but of great events, and it naturally fails to attain the highest dramatic vitality and movement. [*The Life and Genius of Shakespeare*, 1864.]

BARRETT WENDELL. In the honestly canting moods which we of America inherit with our British blood we gravely admire *Henry V.* because we feel sure that we ought to. In more normally human moods, most of us would be forced to confess that, at least as a play, *Henry V.* is tiresome.

If it be a dull play, however, it is just as surely the dull play of a great artist; it is full of excellent detail. In the distinctly historical parts, the excellent detail is chiefly rhetorical; as such, it is almost beyond praise. The eloquence of Henry's great speeches everybody recognizes. Perhaps an even more notable example of Shakspere's now consummate mastery of style may be found in the Archbishop of Canterbury's exposition of the Salic law. The passage—one of the kind which sometimes makes superficial readers marvel at the learning of Shakspere—actually states the law in question, along with many historical details, about as compactly as any lawyer could have stated it under Queen Elizabeth . . . .

The excellence of detail in the comic scenes of *Henry V.* is perhaps more notable still. While in substance all the comic characters are what an Elizabethan would have called "humourous," and what we should now call "eccentric comedy," they are almost all human, too. Comic dialect, to be sure, already proved effective in the *Merry Wives of Windsor,* is repeated in the speeches of Jamy, Macmorris, and Fluellen; repeated, too, is the broad burlesque on the execesses of Elizabethan ranting which pervades the speech of Pistol everywhere. For all this conventional humor, however, one grows to feel of the comic characters in *Henry V.*, as of all the characters in *Henry IV.*, that these are real people. [*William Shakspere, A Study in Elizabethan Literature,* 1894.]

WILLIAM BUTLER YEATS. To pose character against character was an element in Shakespeare's art, and scarcely a play is lacking in characters that are the complement of one another, and so, having made the vessel of porcelain Richard II., he had to make the vessel of clay Henry V. He makes him the reverse of all that Richard was. He has the gross vices, the coarse nerves, of one who is to rule among violent people, and he is so little "too friendly" to his friends that he bundles them out of doors when their time is over. He is as remorseless and undistinguished as some natural force, and the finest thing in his play is the way his old companions fall out of it broken-hearted or on their way to the gallows; and instead of that lyricism which rose out of Richard's mind like the jet of a fountain to fall again where it had risen, instead of that phantasy too enfolded in its own sincerity to make any thought the hour had need of, Shakespeare has given him a resounding rhetoric that moves men, as a leading article does to-day. His purposes are so intelligible to everybody that everybody talks of him as if he succeeded, although he fails in the end, as all men great and little fail in Shakespeare, and yet his conquests abroad are made nothing by a woman turned warrior, and that boy he and Katherine were to "compound," "half French, half English," "that" was to "go to Constantinople and take the Turk by the beard," turns out a Saint and loses all his father had built up at home and his own life.

Shakespeare watched Henry V. not indeed as he watched the greater souls in the visionary procession, but cheerfully, as one watches some handsome spirited horse, and he spoke his tale, as he spoke a tales, with tragic irony. ["At Stratford on Avon," i *Ideas of Good and Evil,* 1903; reprinted in *Essay and Introductions,* 1961.]

CHARLES WILLIAMS. With *Henry V,* therefor Shakespeare reached the climax of exterior life; it at once a conclusion and a beginning. It is not pri marily a patriotic play, for the First Chorus know nothing of patriotism nor of England, but only of *Muse* of fire which would ascend the brightes heaven of invention by discovering a challenge be tween mighty monarchies. Patriotism certainly keep breaking in, but rather like the army itself: the ma behind Henry is dramatically an English mass, an as the play proceeds he becomes more and more a English king. So much must be allowed to th patriots; it is, however, for them to allow that he be comes something else and more as well, and it is i that something more that his peculiar strengt lies . . . .

It is Falstaff's greatness that we are delighted t feel heaven give way to him; Henry's that we ar eased by his giving way to heaven. But the artisti difference is that there is no more to be done in th method of Falstaff—he is complete and final. He ca be continually varied and repeated, but he cannot b developed. Henry is complete, but not final. For h in whose honour there is no self-contradiction, coul love his pains simply because there was nothing els to do except run away, and that the same honou forbade. [*Shakespeare Criticism: 1919–1935,* A. Brad bey, ed., 1936.]

ROSE A. ZIMBARDO. *Henry V* is an almost perfe realization of meaning in form. Its thematic essenc is to be found in the formalism of its style and arch tecture. In movement the play resembles a statel ceremonial dance, each figure of which calls to life different aspect of the hero's excellence. These fi ures, each retaining a degree of independence, eac preserving its own boundaries, move in measure order to complete the design of the whole. The e fect is of a universal harmony wherein each plane exactly placed, has its proper movement and fun tion. The thematic relevance of such a structure obvious: the ideal king embodies in himself and pr jects upon his state the ideal metaphysical order. harmonious operation of parts in an ordered whole the design of the cosmos, of the state, of the perfe king,

> For government, though high and low and lower,
> Put into parts, doth keep in one consent,
> Congreeing in a full and natural close,
> Like music.
>
> (I, ii, 180–183)

And, as the object of art is to imitate such ide forms as "nature often erring yet shewes she wou faine make," this is the design too of the imitati rhetorical construct, the play itself . . . .

The trappings of war that deck the play functi as ornament, heroic conceit. There is no warli clamor in the play; there is indeed no motion at that is not controlled and measured. No moral te sion is created by the war, for one knows from t beginning that God is with Henry. One knows b fore the battle that the English will win and wou be no less confident had he never heard of Agi ourt. Even the conspiracy, so quietly discovered nd handled, on Henry's part with control and on ne conspirators' with an almost grateful admission f guilt, creates no impression of faction. The army ; displayed only that the comparison may be struck etween its harmonious order and the disorder of the rench army. The characters in the scene are types; ke all the characters in the play they have no existnce in themselves but serve only to illustrate some race of Henry's. For example, the captains in Ienry's army, Jamy, the Scot, Macmorris, the Irishıan and Fluellen, the Welshman, are by design exagerated almost into music-hall types. Their function ; to illustrate the *concors discordia* which the ideal ing makes of his state, and which is comparable to he *concors discordia* of the natural universe under God . . . .

Henry V is a study in order and harmony; it does ot record, but rather it celebrates the victory of orm over disorder and chaos. As form governs very attribute of the king, so does it every aspect of he play that celebrates him—structure, characterizaıon, style. Finally, it reaches beyond the limits of ne play to invest the tetralogy with new meaning nd to draw the circle closed. ["The Formalism of Ienry V," *Shakespeare Encomium*, Anne Paolucci, d., The City College Papers I, 1964.]

Henry VI (1421–1471). King of England; in *1*, *2*, nd *3 Henry VI*, the pious, often pathetic, always neffectual King. Despite the title of the trilogy, Ienry is never the major protagonist in the plays, s in fact he never was in history. Proclaimed king t the age of nine months, Henry unfortunately ever did acquire the habit of acting like one. 'hysically frail and subject to fits of insanity, he was ominated by Cardinal Beaufort and the earl of uffolk and, after his marriage, by his wife, Margaret f Anjou. In less turbulent times Henry VI, as evoted to peace as his father, Henry V, was evoted to war, might have ruled successfully. Nevertheless, it was this gentle, irresolute king who recipitated the dynastic struggle known as the Wars f the Roses. In 1453 Henry became temporarily nsane, and Richard, duke of York, was appointed rotector of England. Under York's firm and efficient rule, order was restored in the kingdom. When the king regained his reason, however, he sided with York's enemies, thus provoking the march on London by the Yorkist faction in 1455. After the Yorkist victory at the first battle of St. Albans that year, Henry again lost his reason and was taken prisoner. As the fortunes of the war ebbed and flowed, Henry spent his life alternately as prisoner and king, miserable in both roles. This existence came to an end in 1471 after the defeat of Queen Margaret at the battle of Tewkesbury. Henry may have been murdered, and Elizabethan historians had no qualms about attributing the alleged murder to their favorite villain, Richard III.

HENRY VI. PORTRAIT BY AN UNKNOWN ARTIST. (NATIONAL PORTRAIT GALLERY)

The firſt Part of King HENRY the Sixth,

Henry VI, Part One. A history play by Shakepeare.

Text. The only authoritative text for *1 Henry VI* ; that of the First Folio. It was entered in the tationers' Register, along with all of Shakespeare's previously unpublished plays, on November 8, 1623 as ". . . The thirde parte of Henry ye Sixt . . . ." The misnaming of *1 Henry VI* in the register was doubtless a result of the fact that *2* and *3 Henry VI* had already been published in quarto, thereby making the entries of those plays unnecessary. Therefore, in the publisher's mind at least, *1 Henry VI* was conceived of as "The thirde parte."

A number of inconsistencies and contradictions in the text have been attributed by scholars either to composite authorship or to revision. Dover Wilson argues that most of the play was written by the "University Wits" Thomas Nashe and Robert Greene and completed by Shakespeare, and that the work is identical with the drama identified in Henslowe's diary as "Harey the vj." Other scholars, following Peter Alexander, have argued for Shakespeare's sole authorship of the play and explain the inconsistencies, as does A. S. Cairncross, as a result of the fact that the COPY for the text was derived from Shakespeare's own uncorrected manuscript, with some minor adaptations by a "stage-adapter." For a discussion of theories disputing Shakespeare's authorship of the Henry VI plays, see GROATS-WORTH OF WIT.

Date. The problems of the dates and chronology of the three Henry VI plays are difficult ones. Many scholars argue that *2* and *3 Henry VI* were written before *1 Henry VI;* other believe that the plays were written in their natural order. Later scholarship has tended to follow the latter course, basing its position on the fact that the CONTENTION PLAYS, "bad quartos" of *2* and *3 Henry VI,* contain echoes of *1 Henry VI.* Added to this argument is the fact that *The Troublesome Raigne of King John* (1591) also gives evidence of borrowing from *1 Henry VI,* thus pushing the date of that play back to about 159

On the other hand, J. Dover Wilson and other argue that *1 Henry VI* is the same play as th "Harey the vj" cited as "ne" [new] by Henslowe i his diary for March 3, 1592. They contend tha Henslowe's entry alludes to a revision by Shake speare of a play written by one of the Universit Wits mentioned above. Still others argue that Shake speare revised his own play in 1592, at which poir he would have added the last scene in order to lin the drama to *2 Henry VI,* when he had decided t make his first four chronicle plays into a connecte saga of the Wars of the Roses. The crux of th argument rests upon the identity of "Harey the vj and *1 Henry VI.* Henslowe's entry states that "Hare the vj" was performed by Strange's Men. There no evidence to support the assumption that Shake speare was writing for this company in 1592, an until some evidence of the dramatist's theatric affiliations before 1594 is discovered the issue wi remain in doubt.

Sources. Shakespeare found his historical materi in Raphael HOLINSHED's *Chronicles of England, Sco land and Ireland* (1587 ed.) and Edward HALLE *The union of the two noble and illustre famelies c Lancastre and York* (1548). The poet altered th strict chronology to suit his dramatic purpose. Fc example, although Joan of Arc was executed i 1431, Shakespeare keeps her alive to take part in th battle of 1451 in which Talbot was slain. Th episode of Talbot's ruse, by which he defeats th

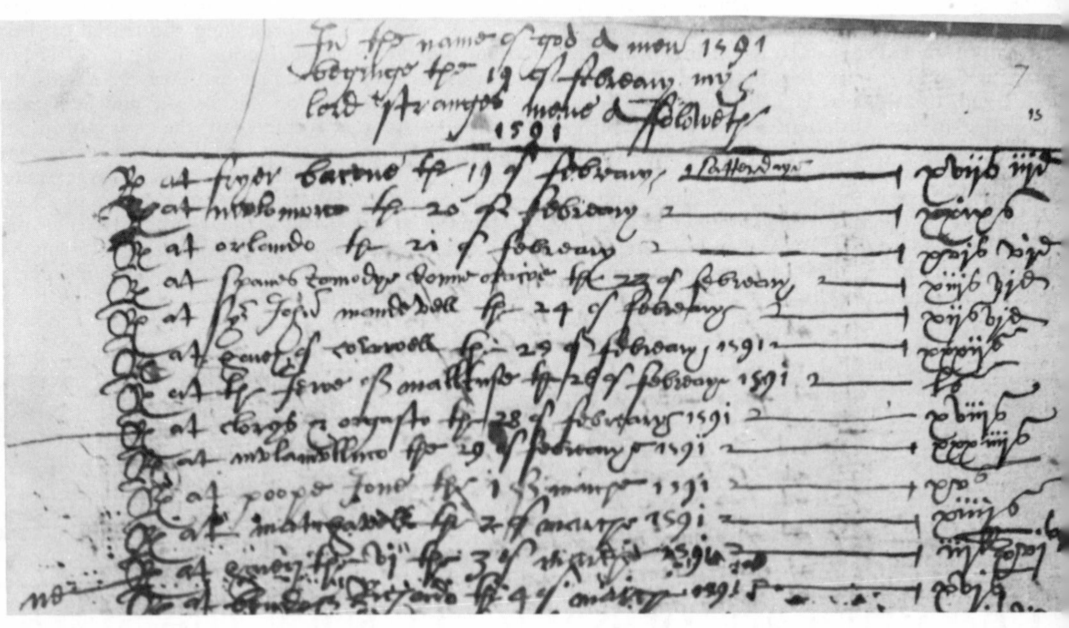

HENSLOWE'S DIARY FOR FEBRUARY AND MARCH 1592 (1591 OLD STYLE). AT THE TOP OF THE PAGE HENSLOWE HAS WRITTEN, "IN THE NAME OF GOD A MEN 1591 BEGININGE THE 19 OF FEBREARY MY LORD STRANGES MENE AS FFOLOWETH." THE PLAYS LISTED ARE *Fryer Bacune, Mulomurco, Orlando, Spanes comodye, Syr John Mandevell, Harey of Cornwell, the Jewe of Malltuse, Clorys & Orgasto, Mulamulluco, Poope Jone, Matchavell, Harey the vj, Bendo & Richardo.* IN THE MARGIN IN FRONT OF *Harey the vj* HENSLOWE HAS NOTED "NE" MEANING THIS WAS A NEW PLAY. IT WAS THE MOST SUCCESSFUL PRODUCTION OF THAT SEASON ACCORDING TO HENSLOWE'S GATE RECEIPTS OF £ 3. 16. 8. (DULWICH COLLEGE, BY PERMISSION OF THE GOVERNORS)

Countess of Auvergne's plot to hold him captive, has not been well integrated into the plot. It reads like an adventure out of a Robin Hood ballad. G. L. Kittredge points out that the episode is "in some way related to a popular romance in which Caloman, Don Ranier of Leon, or the Bastard of Bouillon appears as the hero in different versions of the trick." Much of the rest of the drama, even the famous scene in the Temple Garden (II, iv) is fiction, the product of Shakespeare's invention.

The superpatriotism of the drama is the playwright's personal expression of the national pride and exultation that swept over all England with the defeat of the Armada in 1588. This chauvinism explains the fervid response of Elizabethan audiences to Talbot's heroism. Thomas Nashe in his *Pierce Pennilesse* (1592) exclaims: "How would it have ioyed braue Talbot (the terror of the French) to thinke that after he had lyne two hundred yeares in his Tombe, hee should triumphe againe on the Stage, and haue his bones newe embalmed with the teares of ten thousand spectators at least, (at seuerall times) who, in the Tragedian that represents his person, imagine they behold him fresh bleeding?"

Shakespeare did not originate the conception of Joan as a witch and a harlot. He found this view fully developed in Holinshed, whose authority he rarely questioned. Her scene with the fiends (V, iii) betrays the author's acquaintance with Reginald Scot's *Discoverie of Witchcraft* (1584) and with the folklore of demonology, particularly the reference to Joan's feeding the fiends with her blood. In return for the power given by the devil through his emissary, a familiar spirit, the adept surrenders to him body and soul. The play is so strange a medley that it is little wonder that critics formerly thought it a joint project. However, traces of the manner of Greene and Nashe in *1 Henry VI* can be explained as a young writer's natural imitation of the work of more experienced hands in the genre at which he was making his first essay.—O. J. C.

Plot Synopsis. Act I. The untimely death of Henry V and the accession of Henry VI while still a boy have left England at the mercy of its contentious nobles. As a result of the dissension at home the English are gradually being driven from their French possessions, despite the able leadership of the valiant Lord Talbot. The bitterest rivalry is between the Duke of Gloucester, the King's uncle and Protector of the Realm, and the ambitious Henry Beaufort, great-uncle of the King and Bishop of Winchester. Such is their animosity that when the Duke is refused admission to the Tower of London by order of the Bishop, Gloucester's followers come to blows with the tawny-coated servants of Winchester.

In France, meanwhile, Joan la Pucelle, a shepherdess who claims that the mother of God has appeared to her in a vision and ordered her to free her country from the English, awes King Charles and his court by her mysterious powers and military prowess. With her aid, they are able to raise the English siege of Orleans.

Act II. The French triumph is short-lived, for a daring night attack by Talbot and the Duke of Burgundy, an ally of the English, so surprises the French that they must flee, clad only in their shirts. Invited to the castle of the Countess of Auvergne, Talbot finds himself a prisoner of the lady, who taunts him as a "weak and writhled shrimp" until the old soldier reveals that he has taken the precaution of bringing along an armed force.

In London's Temple Garden, a new quarrel is brewing between Richard Plantagenet and the Earl of Somerset. When the Earl of Warwick, asked to judge between them, is reluctant to state his opinion, Plantagenet invites those who support him to join him in plucking a white rose from a briar; Somerset responds by plucking a red rose. Warwick eventually chooses a white rose, while the Earl of Suffolk sides with Somerset. To humiliate Plantagenet, Somerset recalls that Richard's father, the Earl of Cambridge, had been executed for treason by Henry V and his heirs attainted. Plantagenet retorts that his father was no traitor and vows to avenge the insult. Warwick, who assures Plantagenet that he will secure a reversal of the attainder at the next session of parliament, predicts that many men will lose their lives because of the conflict between the red rose and the white.

Hoping to learn the real reason for his father's execution, Plantagenet visits his aged uncle, Edmund Mortimer, for many years a prisoner in the Tower. Mortimer explains that he is the rightful heir of Richard II, who was deposed by Henry Bolingbroke, grandfather of the present King; Plantagenet's father, who was married to Mortimer's sister, was executed for conspiring to place him on the throne. Mortimer, who has no issue, now names Plantagenet as his heir and dies after advising him to press his claims with caution.

Act III. The enmity between Gloucester and Winchester flares anew at the meeting of parliament, to the dismay of young Henry, who warns that "Civil dissension is a viperous worm / That gnaws the bowels of the commonwealth." Even the attendants of the feuding nobles are still at odds and, forbidden by the Mayor of London to carry arms, have resorted to pelting each other with stones. At the insistence of Warwick and the King, Gloucester and the Bishop reluctantly reach a truce, though the haughty prelate has no intention of abiding by it. The King generously restores to Plantagenet the title and the property that are his as the scion of the House of York. After Henry departs for France, where he is to be crowned, the old Duke of Exeter sadly recalls a prophecy that this Henry would lose all that Henry V had won.

Though the French, led by Joan and King Charles, manage to capture Rouen by a ruse, they are soon evicted by Talbot. During the fray, Sir John Fastolfe repeats an earlier act of cowardice by taking flight. Undismayed by the setback, Joan resolves to separate the Duke of Burgundy from the English cause; at a parley with him, she appeals to his patriotism and self-interest with such eloquence that he immediately decides to join the French.

Act IV. Immediately after Henry's coronation in Paris, Fastolfe arrives with a letter from the Duke of Burgundy. Talbot, recognizing Fastolfe, rips the badge of the Order of the Garter from the leg of the pusillanimous knight. After learning from the letter that Burgundy has forsaken the English, Henry orders Talbot to chastise him for his treason. His attention now directed to the quarrel between

York and Somerset, the King exhorts them to make peace and observes that their squabbling will harm the English campaign in France. He puts on a red rose, declaring that it does not indicate that he prefers Somerset, for both he and York are his kinsmen and he loves them both.

Talbot, trapped by the French near Bordeaux, sends a desperate request for help to the Duke of York, who has been named Regent of France, but the latter, denouncing Somerset for refusing some badly needed horsemen, declares that he is powerless. Somerset, however, insists that York could have sent reinforcements to Talbot.

Meanwhile, Talbot urges his son John, with whom he has just been reunited after seven years, to flee before the fighting starts, but the youth scorns to play so ignoble a role. In the battle John is killed and Talbot, mortally wounded, dies with his arms about the lifeless body of his son.

Act V. In London, Gloucester informs the King that the Pope and other magnates are anxious to see peace restored between England and France, adding that Henry's marriage to the daughter of the Earl of Armagnac, a close relative of King Charles, would cement the agreement. Though the King protests that he is too young for marriage, he acquiesces for the sake of his kingdom. He orders Winchester, who has secured a cardinal's hat by bribing the Pope, to go to France to arrange the treaty of peace.

Before Angiers, Joan, deserted by her fiendish spirits, is captured by the Duke of York. Suffolk also takes a prisoner, Margaret, daughter of Reignier, the titular King of Naples. Instantly attracted to her, Suffolk, who is already married, decides to wed her to King Henry, a proposal to which both Margaret and her father consent.

Joan, condemned to be burned as a witch, angrily rebuffs an old shepherd who claims to be her father, declaring that she is descended from kings. As the moment of execution approaches, she begs for her life and pretends to be with child, though she is uncertain as to the identity of the father. When York and Warwick reply with ribald jests, she utters a final curse on them and on England. Learning that Cardinal Beaufort has arrived to make peace with the French, York is chagrined. "Is all our travail turn'd to this effect?" he asks in dismay. After some initial reluctance, King Charles accedes to the English terms, agreeing to wear his crown as Henry's viceroy.

Meanwhile, in London, Suffolk has dazzled the impressionable King with his description of Margaret's beauty and virtue. Ignoring Gloucester's reminder that he is already betrothed to Armagnac's daughter, Henry declares his intention of marrying Margaret. Suffolk, entrusted with the task of bringing her to England, is exultant. "Margaret shall now be queen, and rule the king," he reflects, "But I will rule both her, the king and realm."—H.D.

Comment. This play is the first of a tetralogy, composed of *1, 2,* and *3 Henry VI* and *Richard III,* which dramatizes the Wars of the Roses. *1 Henry VI* is, however, only indirectly concerned with that civil war. As Tillyard suggests, a more appropriate title for the work might be "The Tragedy of Talbot." On the surface it is a chronicle of Talbot's heroic exploits as leader of an expeditionary English force at war with a French army marshaled by Joan of Arc. But his defeat and death are caused as much by the struggle between the Houses of York and Lancaster, dramatically illustrated in the Temple Garden scene. In spite of his many glorious victories he is in the end conquered and slain through the disloyalty of England, not the might of France.

The poet's conception of Joan as a harlot and a witch is repulsive to many, accustomed as they are to regard her as a saintly figure. But the playwright's design for the drama made it necessary for her to be an agent of the devil. He makes it clear that Talbot, too, is the creature of supernatural forces to which God allows free play. The chief of these are the "bad revolting stars" and the powers of hell. Even Joan realizes that she has been cast in the role of England's scourge. For Talbot is made the scapegoat for the sins of the royal house. The direst of these was Bolingbroke's contrivance of the deposition and death of Richard II, God's deputy on earth. His punishment through the wildness of Prince Hal was only a partial expiation. During Henry V's reign, because of the King's piety, God had held in abeyance the retribution still due, but the curse, operative again at his early death, falls upon Talbot.

The play is filled with naïve chauvinism. In Elizabethan times, France was England's traditional and very present enemy. The French were seen as plotters of the massacre of Saint Bartholomew and of incessant wars against England. Of the many examples of French wickedness that Shakespeare presents in his chronicle history plays, Joan is but the most fearsome. The French are unstable and treacherous. Even Joan herself cynically accepts as true the English opinion of her countrymen. When Burgundy breaks his union with the English army and joins the French, she remarks,

> Done like a Frenchman: turn, and turn again!
> (III, iii, 85)

The positive side of Shakespeare's jingoism is Talbot's incredible heroism. His deeds in battle are like those of a primitive folk hero. He lists his superhuman achievements to Henry VI when the young King comes to Paris for his coronation. He has reclaimed to his sovereign's obedience 50 fortresses, 12 cities, and 7 walled towns, besides capturing 500 "prisoners of esteem." No wonder that the King creates him Earl of Shrewsbury on the spot. The mere sight of this paragon terrifies the French. When his guards display him as a captive to the French populace, he breaks from them, digs stones from the pavement with his nails, and hurls them at the gaping crowd. While he is thus rapt in anger, his "grisly countenance" makes everyone flee. Shakespeare naturally did not allow Joan to kill Talbot. He dies from wounds received in battle and falls upon heaps of dead Frenchmen whom he has himself slain. It was doubtless his death that called for the "tears of ten thousand spectators" recorded above.

1 Henry VI reveals a young dramatist's great and growing power. To be sure, his verse is not that of a master poet; most of it is little better than an imitation of the blank verse that the University Wits had made the conventional dramatic medium. On occasion it rises to turgidity rather than to eloquence. In certain passages Shakespeare gave the verse a ritualistic solemnity by casting it in mechanically wrought rhymed couplets. This is true of Talbot's address to the son after rescuing him from foes that press around him (IV, vi). The formal rhythm of his speech is appropriate to what is, in effect, a last will and testament. The form is also fitting for Talbot's funeral oration over his son's body (IV, vii, 1–16, 18–32).

In the first of his history plays the poet shows his dramatic skill in converting events recorded by Holinshed and Halle into a unified movement of the characteristic deeds of a central figure toward a series of climaxes. In so doing he fits the play securely into the sweep of incidents that combine to create the Wars of the Roses. He also creates many scenes thrilling to an Elizabethan audience. Such is the episode in which Joan offers to a crowd of ominously silent fiends her members, her whole body, and finally, "my body, soul and all" (V, iii, 22). Other scenes arouse glee at the grotesque cowardice of the French soldiers. When the English enter Orleans crying "St. George" and "A Talbot, A Talbot," the French leap over the walls in their shirts, and the Bastard of Orleans, Alençon, and Reignier rush in with their clothes half off (II, i, 38–39). At the end of the scene the French flee, "leaving their clothes behind." The battle scenes and those of defiance and loud-mouthed threats, written here for the first time in Shakespearean idiom, gained at once the popularity that they continued to hold in his later chronicle histories. More significant than all these virtues is the fact that in *1 Henry VI* Shakespeare first enunciates the philosophy of history that is embodied in all his English chronicle plays. It is based on the assumption of divine interference in the political affairs of his country. The hero of this, as of the other Henry VI dramas, is, as E. M. W. Tillyard makes clear, Res Publica, the State. God intervenes in the life of the English state to make sure that the order of legitimacy triumphs over the disorder created by attacks upon it both from without and within. Thus He assures the triumph of His will on the strife-torn soil of England.—O. J. C.

Stage History. If *1 Henry VI* is the *Harey the vj* performed on March 3, 1592 by the Lord Strange's Men at the Rose theatre (see *Date* above) it was evidently popular, for that play was presented 13 more times that year and twice the following January. Since that time, however, *1 Henry VI* has been acted most infrequently. It was staged at Covent Garden on March 13, 1738 for the pleasure of some unnamed "Ladies of Quality," but this single performance failed to renew interest in the play. The cast included Denis Delane as Talbot and Lacy Ryan as Gloucester. This was the only 18th-century revival of *1 Henry VI*. On December 22, 1817 Edmund Kean played York at Drury Lane in an adaptation entitled *Richard Duke of York; or the Contention of York and Lancaster*, purporting to be an alteration from "Shakespeare's Three Parts of Henry VI." Actually only fragments of *Part 1* are incorporated into this confused version, which consisted mainly of *Part 2*. John Herman Merivale wrote this mutilation, which, although criticized for a complete lack of dramatic unity, was performed seven times during the 1817 season.

When Osmond Tearle revived Shakespeare's *1 Henry VI* at the Memorial Theatre, Stratford-upon-Avon, more than 150 years had elapsed since the Covent Garden performance. For this lavish production, staged in 1889, Tearle had borrowed props and costumes from Henry Irving and draped a mock Westminster Abbey in black for the opening funeral scene. He himself took the role of Talbot. In 1906 Frank Benson produced the trilogy on consecutive evenings at Stratford, beginning on May 2. Benson played Talbot opposite Constance Benson's Margaret.

London had completely ignored the play since 1738 until Robert Atkins staged his productions of all the Folio plays except *Cymbeline* at the Old Vic. On January 29, 1923 he presented *Part 1* with the first half of *Part 2* in this revival of the entire trilogy. Critical notice of the play is almost nonexistent. The *Times* failed to print a review of the Old Vic's effort that would create interest in the drama with its talented cast. Ernest Meads acted Talbot, Wilfrid Walter impersonated Gloucester, Maxwell Gray was Winchester, and Rupert Harvey, York. D. Hay Petrie took the roles of Mortimer and Basset, while Douglas Burbidge played Buckingham and the Dauphin, and John Laurie, Suffolk.

1 Henry VI vanished from the London stage for another 30 years, but in the United States during the summer of 1935 Gilmor Browne, director of the Pasadena Community Playhouse, presented a festival season of all the historical plays. *1 Henry VI* was acted (in what was probably the only American production of the drama) from July 25 to 27, and won immediate popularity with the audience. Then, in 1953, Douglas Seale produced the first part of the history at the Birmingham Repertory Theatre, using Barry Jackson's amplified text. This production was brought to the Old Vic in July of that year introducing the complete trilogy to be presented in chronological sequence. (*Part 2* and *Part 3* had been staged at Birmingham in 1951 and 1952, respectively.) Critical approval of this forceful, well-paced, uncluttered production in Finlay James' Gothic arch setting was unanimous. Alan Bridges played Talbot and Nancie Jackson, Joan. Seale restaged the complete *Henry VI* at the Old Vic during October 1957.

Henry VI in Peter Hall's *The Wars of the Roses* was constructed by John Barton from *1 Henry VI* and the first half of *2 Henry VI*. This coherent narrative was first seen at Stratford in 1963 and transferred to the Aldwych in London, where, on January 11, 1964, the three parts of *Henry VI* and *Richard III* were acted in one day. Later the plays were given at consecutive performances, and returned to Stratford for the 1964 season. Fiercely dramatic and free-moving, the disintegration at court and on the battlefield was stressed as a result of the sin of the deposition of Richard II. David Warner played an indecisive King, dependent on advisors. Roy Doltrice acted Bedford, Donald Sinden was the Duke of York, and Peggy Ashcroft appeared as Margaret of Anjou.

An Age of Kings, produced by Peter Dews on television for the British Broadcasting Company in 1961, spanned the Shakespeare histories, from *Richard II* to *Richard III*. As acted by members of several of the repertory companies, the series was considered a great artistic success and was broadcast in

New York and Washington, as well as in Great Britain.—M. G.

Bibliography. TEXT: *Henry VI, Part I*, New Cambridge Edition, J. Dover Wilson, ed., 1952; Leo Kirschbaum, "The Authorship of *1 Henry VI*," *PMLA*, LXVII, 1952; *The First Part of King Henry VI*, A. S. Cairncross, ed., New Arden Edition, 1962. DATE: New Cambridge Edition; New Arden Edition. SOURCES: Geoffrey Bullough, *Narrative and Dramatic Sources of Shakespeare*, III, 1960. COMMENT: New Cambridge Edition; New Arden Edition; E. M. W. Tillyard, *Shakespeare's History Plays*, 1944; Lily B. Campbell, *Shakespeare's Histories*, 1947; J. P. Brockbank, "The Frame of Disorder—'Henry VI'," *Early Shakespeare*, Stratford-Upon-Avon Studies 3, 1961. STAGE HISTORY: New Cambridge Edition; G. C. D. Odell, *Shakespeare from Betterton to Irving*, 1920; J. C. Trewin, *Shakespeare on the English Stage, 1900–1964*, 1964.

Selected Criticism. See HENRY VI, PART THREE: *Selected Criticism.*

The ſecond Part of King HENRY the Sixth

With the Death of the good Duke HUMPHREY.

Henry VI, Part Two. A history play by Shakespeare.

Text. One of the thornier problems of Shakespeare scholarship is the determination of an authoritative text for this play. The basic source of the text is that found in the First Folio (1623), but this is complicated by the existence of a similar play published in quarto in 1594 and 1600 and reprinted in an amalgamated form in 1619. This Quarto bears the title: "The First part of the Contention betwixt the two famous Houses of Yorke and Lancaster, with the death of the good Duke Humphrey: And the banishment and death of the Duke of Suffolke, and the Tragicall end of the proud Cardinall of Winchester, with the notable Rebellion of Iacke Cade: And the Duke of Yorkes first claime vnto the Crowne. London. Printed by Thomas Creed, for Thomas Millington, and are to be sold at his shop vnder Saint Peters Church in Cornwall." See CONTENTION PLAYS.

From the time of the great 18th-century Shakespeare scholar Edmund Malone until comparatively recently, this Quarto was regarded as an earlier version of the play which was printed in the Folio. In the 20th century, however, there has been a general acceptance of the view, derived from the work of Peter Alexander, that the Quarto represents a MEMORIAL RECONSTRUCTION of the play which appears in the Folio, made by actors who had played in an abridged version of the play (see BAD QUARTOS). Added to this view are the suggestions of A. S. Cairncross that certain passages in the Quarto were deleted or altered in the Folio as a result of the increasingly rigid theatrical censorship of the period and that the Folio text was partially printed from a corrected copy of the 1619 edition of the Quarto. The tentative acceptance of this theory has led to a renewed endorsement of the view that Shakespeare should be accepted as the author of the entire play. For a discussion of the theories disputing Shakespeare's authorship of the Henry VI plays, see GROATS-WORTH OF WIT.

Date. If we assume that *2 Henry VI* was written before *3 Henry VI*, the play must be dated prior to September 1592, the date of the publication of Robert Greene's *Groats-worth of Wit*, which included the famous attack on Shakespeare and the parody of a line from *3 Henry VI*. The generally accepted date is 1590–1591.

Sources. The sources of the historical facts are Raphael Holinshed's *Chronicles* and Edward Halle's *Union of the two noble and illustre famelies of Lancastre and York*. The incident of Simpcox's feigned miracle (II, i) is recounted in Thomas More's *Dialogue of the Worship of Images* (1529), reprinted by Richard Grafton in his *Chronicle* and in Foxe's *Book of Martyrs* (1563). Other minor sources may have included the *English Chronicle* of John Hardyng (1378-?1465) and *The New Chronicles of England and France* (1516) of Robert Fabyan. As in his other history plays, Shakespeare does not scruple in altering the historical facts in his sources in order to suit the dramatic requirements of the play.—O. J. C.

Plot Synopsis. Act I. The factionalism besetting England erupts anew when it is revealed that the Duke of Suffolk, sent to France to arrange the King's marriage to Margaret, has conceded Anjou and Maine to the father of the dowerless bride with whom he is enamoured. Though Henry declares himself pleased by the marriage contract, his uncle Humphrey, Duke of Gloucester and Protector, who is heir apparent to the throne, casts doubt upon Suffolk's loyalty to the King. Cardinal Beaufort ishop of Winchester, opposes Gloucester and joins vith Suffolk, the Duke of Buckingham, and the uke of Somerset in a pact to topple him from ower. The old Earl of Salisbury, the Duke of York, nd Salisbury's son, the Earl of Warwick, agree, on ne other hand, to oppose the schemes of Gloucester's enemies. The crafty York, however, is bent nly on winning the crown and will support loucester only so long as it suits his purpose.

Despite Gloucester's admonitions, his wife, Eleaor, cannot stifle her ambition for the crown. After er husband leaves for St. Alban's to go hawking ith the royal couple, she arranges with the priest Iume for conjurors to reveal the future to her, gnorant of the fact that Hume is in the pay of uffolk and the Cardinal. The Spirit that the conurors invoke declares that Henry will be deposed y a duke, that Suffolk will die by water, and that omerset should shun castles. Suddenly, York and uckingham break in and arrest Eleanor for treason.

Act II. At St. Alban's, meanwhile, the Protector xposes a sanctimonious rogue, Simpcox, who has ersuaded the credulous King that his eyesight has een miraculously restored at a nearby shrine after lifetime of blindness. When Buckingham arrives ith the news of Eleanor's arrest, Gloucester proests his own innocence, rejecting his wife for having ishonored his name.

The King subsequently banishes Eleanor to the le of Man, while her husband is deprived of his ffice as Protector. No one is more pleased than ueen Margaret, who loathes the once-haughty uchess.

As she performs public penance, Eleanor reroaches Gloucester for enduring her shame so eekly. She warns him that his enemies are deterined to destroy him, but he insists that he cannot e harmed as long as he is innocent of any wrongoing.

Act III. At a session of parliament in Bury-St.-Edund's, the Queen complains to Henry about loucester's pride and insolence. Noting his nearness the King in descent and his popularity with the ommoners, she advises her husband to keep him at rm's length. Her suspicions are echoed by Suffolk, ho arrests Gloucester for treason as soon as he arves. Grief-stricken, the King expresses his hope at Gloucester will be able to clear himself of all ispicion.

After Henry's departure, the Queen, deriding her usband's "foolish pity," declares that Gloucester ust be put out of the way, an opinion in which uffolk and the Cardinal concur, the latter offering provide the executioner. When a messenger brings ews of a revolt in Ireland, York agrees to the ardinal's suggestion that he lead an expedition ere. Alone, York gloats over the fact that the ther nobles, in their eagerness to be rid of him, ave agreed to supply him with the army that he cked. He also decides to prevail upon a Kentishan named Jack Cade to foment an insurrection, uring his absence, that will reveal the public temper garding the Yorkist claim to the throne and give im a pretext for deposing Henry.

When Suffolk reports that Gloucester is dead, enry faints and, to the dismay of Margaret, reoils from the ministrations of the Duke. Warwick and Salisbury arrive, followed by a crowd of irate commoners, who accuse Suffolk and the Cardinal of murdering Gloucester, and demand Suffolk's exile. Though Suffolk is disdainful of the mob, Henry banishes him, sternly reproving Margaret for her pleas in his behalf.

Bidding Suffolk a sorrowful farewell, the Queen promises to secure his recall or to follow him into exile. Meanwhile, the King and Warwick are summoned to the bedside of the dying Beaufort, who, in his delirium, betrays his complicity in Gloucester's murder. Warwick observes that "So bad a death argues a monstrous life," but the King says, "Forbear to judge, for we are sinners all."

Act IV. Suffolk, captured by pirates as he sailed to France, is killed by one Walter Whitmore, thus fulfilling the prophecy made to the Duchess of Gloucester.

Jack Cade, who claims to be John Mortimer and the rightful heir of Richard II, launches his rebellion in Blackheath, promising that when he is king seven half-penny loaves shall be sold for a penny and it will be a felony to drink small beer. As they make their way toward London, the rebels hang a clerk because "he can write and read and cast accompt." They also behead Lord Say, who was involved in Suffolk's negotiations in France and who is further accused of associating with men "that usually talk of a noun and a verb, and such abominable words as no Christian ear can endure to hear." In Southwark, the mob is met by Buckingham and Lord Clifford, who reminds them of the deeds of Henry V and urges them to vent their fury on the French instead of on the King, Henry's son. Abandoned by his followers, Cade asks in disgust: "Was ever feather so lightly blown to and fro as this multitude?" He flees to Kent and is killed by an esquire called Alexander Iden, whose garden he had entered in a search for food. Cade dies affirming that "famine and no other hath slain me."

Act V. York, who has returned to England with a large number of Irish troops, asserts that he has brought his army only to remove the seditious Somerset from the King's circle. After Buckingham assures him that Somerset is in the Tower, York agrees to disband his forces. But when the King and Queen arrive, accompanied by Somerset, the infuriated York denounces Henry as one more fit "to grasp a palmer's staff" than "to grace an awful princely sceptre." Supported by Warwick and Salisbury, he openly demands the crown.

The conflict between King Henry and York flares into open warfare at St. Alban's. During the battle, Warwick kills old Clifford, whose son vows to avenge himself on the sons of York. Somerset is slain near an alehouse, the Castle, by Richard, the crookbacked son of York. Their forces routed, the King and Queen flee to London, closely pursued by York and Warwick.—H. D.

Comment. The action of the play begins in the year 1445 with Margaret of Anjou's arrival at the English court to marry Henry. All of the succeeding disasters are the result, direct or indirect, of this fatal marriage, for Margaret drives the dissident nobles into more and more successful efforts to undermine the authority of the throne. Henry is a pious weakling, who is unable to function as the head of the state. The result is England's loss of territory abroad and social chaos at home. He is so incompetent that he cannot keep the church in proper subjection to the state. The Cardinal, no longer a faithful priest, plots to gain political power and acts more like a soldier than a man of the church.

The disruption of proper social relationships descends step by step much lower in the social scale. For example, Peter, the apprentice of Horner, an armourer, seeking revenge upon his master for just punishment, rightly accuses Horner of saying that the Duke of York was rightful heir to the crown. Since this brings York under suspicion, the King orders the two to meet in single combat. In a farcically conducted duel, Peter kills Horner. The social structure of a realm in which an apprentice dare rebel against his master and finally kill him has turned topsy-turvy.

The most ominous manifestation of Henry's incompetence is Cade's rebellion, in which the lowest classes rise, briefly to be sure, to the top. Shakespeare seems to be either ignorant of the injustices that sparked the peasants' insurrection or simply unsympathetic. He merely follows the chroniclers in making of Cade a grotesque ignoramus who incites his vagabonds to burn, kill, and destroy, first of all, those who can read and write. His followers are a wild muddled mob. Some of the episodes in other parts of the play, like Margery Jourdain's practice of witchcraft (I, iv), though having little to do with the theme of the play—social disintegration—must have aroused in an Elizabethan audience a peculiar mixture of excitement and terror.

Shakespeare gives the clearest view of his growing powers of characterization in his picture of the pathetic and futile King, and of Margaret and her pack of ferocious lords. Of these the most vivid are those of the good Humphrey, Duke of Gloucester, who displays all the qualities of kingship except cunning, and of Richard Plantagenet, Duke of York, wily and unscrupulous in his efforts to seize the throne. The most sinister of all is York's son, the hunchbacked Richard, who begins to display in this drama the fierceness of a lion yoked to the guile of a fox. He will soon become, as Richard III, a veritable cacodemon.

The speeches of these schismatics are declamator and resoundingly rhetorical. They are sustained an ennobled by the poetic images appropriate to th speaker. As Andrew Cairncross points out, *2 Henr VI* is full of "the imagery of the jungle, the chas and the slaughterhouse. . . . images of beasts an birds of prey and . . . creatures of ill omen, like th raven and the screech-owl, and all ugly and venom ous creatures like the toad, the serpent, the lizar and the spider."

In other passages the images more subtly emph size the emotion and elevate it. Such are the imag to be found in Young Clifford's angry lament at th discovery of his slain father:

> York not our old men spares;
> No more will I their babes: tears virginal
> Shall be to me even as the dew to fire,
> And beauty that the tyrant oft reclaims
> Shall to my flaming wrath be oil and flax.
> Henceforth I will not have to do with pity:
> Meet I an infant of the house of York,
> Into as many gobbets will I cut it
> As wild Medea young Absyrtus did.
> (V, ii, 51–59)

2 Henry VI is by far the best of the three Henr VI plays and one of the most expertly composed all Shakespeare's tragic histories.—O. J. C.

Stage History. See HENRY VI, PART THREE: *Stag History.*

Bibliography. TEXT: *Henry VI, Part 2,* New Can bridge Edition, J. Dover Wilson, ed., 1952; *The Se ond Part of King Henry VI,* New Arden Edition, A S. Cairncross, ed., 1957; Peter Alexander, *Shakespeare Henry VI and Richard III,* 1929; C. T. Prouty, *Th Contention and Shakespeare's 2 Henry VI,* 195 DATE: New Cambridge Edition, New Arden Editio SOURCES: R. A. Law, "The Chronicles and *1, 2, Henry VI,*" *Texas Studies in English,* XXXIII, 195 Geoffrey Bullough, *Narrative and Dramatic Sourc of Shakespeare,* III, 1960. COMMENT: E. M. W. Til yard, *Shakespeare's History Plays,* 1944; M. M Reese, *The Cease of Majesty,* 1961.

Selected Criticism. See HENRY VI, PART THRE *Selected Criticism.*

The third Part of King HENRY the Sixth

with the death of the Duke of YORK.

Henry VI, Part Three. A history play by Shakespeare.

Text. The sole authoritative text is that of the First Folio. Like the second part of the chronicle, *3 Hen VI* appeared first in a corrupt text. This text—t First Quarto, but really an octavo—appeared

595, and again in 1600, with the title "The true ragedie of Richard Duke of Yorke, and the death f good King Henrie the Sixt, with the whole conention betweene the two Houses Lancaster and orke, as it was sundrie times acted by the Right Ionourable the Earle of Pembrooke his seruants. rinted at London by P[eter] S[hort] for Thomas Iillington, and are to be sold at his shoppe vnder aint Peters Church in Cornwal." The source of the Quarto is now generally considered to be a MEMO-AL RECONSTRUCTION on the part of an actor or group f actors. For a discussion of earlier controversy oncerning authorship of the Henry VI plays, see ROATS-WORTH OF WIT.

In 1619 Jaggard printed for Pavier the combined bad quartos" of *2* and *3 Henry VI* under the title *he Whole Contention betweene the Two Famous Iouses, Lancaster and Yorke*. The title page claimed at the plays were "newly corrected and enlarged," ut in reality the text was a reprint of the Contenon plays.

Date. The generally accepted date for *3 Henry VI* 1590–1592. One line in Robert Greene's *Groatsvorth of Wit* fixes the latest limit at 1592. In this amphlet, composed shortly before his death in eptember 1592, Greene wrote: "There is an upstart row, beautified with our feathers with his *Tyger's eart wrapt in a Player's Hyde*." The italicised hrase parodies a line in York's diatribe against Queen Margaret: "O tiger's heart wrapt in a voman's hide" (I, iv, 137). This contemptuous ference to *3 Henry VI* makes it certain that it was rst played before September of the year 1592.

TITLE PAGE OF *The Whole Contention.*

THE

Whole Contention

betweene the two Famous

Houſes, LANCASTER and

YORKE.

With the Tragicall ends of the good Duke

Humfrey, Richard Duke of Yorke,

and King Henrie the

ſixt.

Diuided into two Parts: And newly corrected and enlarged. Written by *William Shake-ſpeare*, Gent.

Printed at LONDON, for T. P.

Sources. The sources for all the historical material dramatized are Holinshed's *Chronicles* and Edward Halle's *The union of the two noble and illustre famelies of Lancastre and York*. The action of the drama is so closely connected with that of *2 Henry VI* that one may guess that the author designed the two histories to be performed on successive days. The first scene of *3 Henry VI* records the events immediately following the battle of St. Alban's—May 22, 1452—to which the last two scenes of *2 Henry VI* are devoted. Yet, once launched, *3 Henry VI* is intelligible by itself.

For the details of Richard's alleged murder of Henry, Shakespeare may have drawn upon the accounts of the two kings in the 1559 edition of A MIRROR FOR MAGISTRATES.—O. J. C.

Plot Synopsis. Act I. After his triumph over King Henry at St. Alban's, the Duke of York pursues the King to London, accompanied by his sons Edward and Richard and by the Earl of Warwick. In parliament, he mounts the throne, where he is found by Henry and the leaders of the Lancastrian party. A heated exchange ensues, during which Henry admits that his title to the crown is weak. To the disgust of his followers, he names York as his heir, disinheriting his own son, Edward, Prince of Wales, on the condition that he be permitted to reign in peace during his lifetime. Queen Margaret, determined to preserve her son's birthright, vows to continue the fight against the Yorkists, with the help of the northern barons.

Even as York, at the instigation of his sons, decides to break his oath to Henry, he learns that the Queen and her allies are approaching with an army of 20,000 men. In the battle that follows, the bloodthirsty Lord Clifford avenges his father's death by killing the Earl of Rutland, York's youngest son. Though his other sons manage to escape, York himself is taken prisoner and is forced to submit to the cruel gibes of his captors, who put a paper crown upon his head. When Margaret bids him weep and offers him a handkerchief stained with Rutland's blood, he utters an anguished protest, assailing the Queen as the "She-wolf of France" whose "tongue more poisons than the adder's tooth." The Earl of Northumberland confesses himself unmanned by York's outburst, but Margaret and Clifford, pitiless in their rancor, stab him to death.

Act II. Some days later, while Edward, Earl of March, York's eldest son and heir, and his brother Richard are marching across a plain in Herefordshire, they are startled by what appear to be three suns in the eastern sky. As they watch the suns unite to form a single sphere, Edward observes that the sight may be an omen of success and promises henceforth to bear three suns on his shield. No sooner have they learned of the deaths of York and Rutland than Warwick arrives with the news of fresh disasters. Their spirits unbowed, all three renew their pledge to drive Henry from the throne.

The rival Houses of Lancaster and York again meet, at Towton in Yorkshire. Henry, having been dismissed from the battlefield by Margaret and Clifford, sits on a hill to await the outcome, envious of the tranquil existence of the "homely swain" who tends his flocks untroubled by royal cares. As he realizes that the war has pitted father against son, he wishes that his death would end the struggle between the red rose and the white. The King's mournful reverie is interrupted by Margaret and Prince Edward, who urge him to flee toward the Scottish border. Clifford, who has been fatally wounded, is spared the humiliation of hearing the taunts of the victorious Yorkists. York's son Edward agrees to Warwick's suggestion that Warwick be sent to France to arrange for the former's marriage to the Lady Bona, sister-in-law of King Lewis. After naming Richard Duke of Gloucester and giving the title of Duke of Clarence to another brother, George, he sets out for London to be crowned.

Act III. Henry, having left his place of refuge in Scotland for a glimpse of his beloved England, is captured by two gamekeepers. When he reminds them that they had once taken an oath of fealty to him, they reply that their allegiance is now with the new King, Edward IV.

Edward, meanwhile, is attracted by a widow, Lady Elizabeth Grey, who is seeking the restoration of her husband's lands. Though compliance would ensure the success of her suit, she rejects his blunt advances. Edward resolves to make her his queen, to the surprise of Clarence and Gloucester. The latter, rendered unfit for romantic conquests by his crooked back and shriveled arm, longs to be king himself. To attain his goal, he is prepared to "add colours to the chameleon" and "set the murderous Machiavel to school."

Arriving at King Lewis' court, Warwick finds that Margaret and Prince Edward have already prevailed upon the French King to aid the Lancastrian cause, but by dangling the prospect of an alliance with England, the Earl secures his consent to the marriage of Bona and King Edward. Margaret's hopes revive when it is learned that Edward has wed the Lady Grey. Angered by the insult to him and to his sister-in-law, Lewis promises his support to Margaret. Even Warwick, outraged by the King's duplicity and ingratitude, makes peace with Margaret, and, as a pledge of his fidelity, offers his eldest daughter as a wife to Prince Edward.

Act IV. The Duke of Clarence is also offended by King Edward's marriage and, hearing of Warwick's defection, decides to ally himself with the Lancastrians. Gloucester, his mind still fixed on the crown, remains loyal to the King. Warwick invades England and, in a surprise raid on the King's camp, takes Edward prisoner. Henry, released from confinement in the Tower of London, is again hailed as King, though he is content to let Warwick and Clarence direct the government. Meanwhile, Edward, who has escaped from captivity with Gloucester's help and has obtained reinforcements in Burgundy, returns to England; after taking possession of the city of York, he marches to London and once more seizes Henry.

Act V. In a parley before Coventry, Edward offers to pardon Warwick if he will yield. In reply, Warwick angrily reminds Edward that he had made him king. Arriving with his troops, Clarence declares himself unwilling to fight against his brothers and rejoins the Yorkists.

Another battle between the opposing parties takes place at Barnet, during which Warwick is mortally wounded. Queen Margaret, having landed with a powerful French force, is defeated at Tewkesbury and is captured, together with Prince Edward. Before his mother's horrified eyes, the young prince stabbed to death by Edward, Gloucester, and Cl ence. Although she begs to share her son's fate, s is spared. Gloucester, meanwhile, has sped to t Tower of London, where Henry is confined. Su pecting his visitor's intention, Henry prophesies th multitudes will rue the day that Gloucester had co into the world, "an indigested and deformed lump Richard replies by stabbing him to death. He d not deny the truth of Henry's words, but he co cludes that "since the heavens have shaped my bo so, / Let hell make crook'd my mind to answer i —H. D.

Comment. *3 Henry VI* carries the story of t Wars of the Roses from 1455 to the battle Tewkesbury on May 4, 1471. The tragic results that conflict are the capture of Queen Margaret a her son, the young Prince Edward, and his murd by the three sons of the Duke of York. As for Ki Henry, history records only that he died in t Tower after his defeat at Tewkesbury; but Shak speare, accepting as fact a popular tradition, h Richard force his way into the King's prison a there murder him.

3 Henry VI is a logical sequel to *2 Henry VI.* paints in blacker and blacker colors the picture chaos and crime sketched in the earlier drama. It the most tiresomely episodic of any of the Hen VI plays, suggesting that it represents the poe hurried dramatization of history with which he h recently become acquainted in Holinshed's a Halle's *Chronicles.* Yet every episode has somethi to do with the struggle. The resulting comple anarchy fulfills the author's larger purpose. For th culminating phase of the disorder bred by the d nastic rivalry is the situation pre-eminently respo sible for the emergence of the tyrant Richard Gloucester. His ominous rise to power is one of t motifs that gives unity to the almost unbroken su cession of battles and murders. All the embattl lords, except Richard, are types of personificati in the manner of the morality plays; of lust, in E ward IV; of perjury, in Clarence; of revenge, Clifford, and so on. Though Richard is excessive ambitious and excessively deceitful, he is more th a mere impersonation of either of these vices. Shak speare makes his characteristic mental attitude bo cruel irony. The first expression of this mixture humor and contempt that becomes his fixed attitu toward all that happens occurs when the Yo brothers gather to boast of their achievements in t battle of St. Alban's. Instead of recounting his tr umphs, as his brothers have done, he throws dow the severed head of the Duke of Somerset, exclai ing, "Speak thou for me and tell them what I di (I, i, 16). His scornful irony reaches its most me orable expression at the end of the play after he h stabbed the King to death. Seeing the pool of t King's blood covering the ground, he cries,

> What, will the aspiring blood of Lancaster
> Sink in the ground? I thought it would have
> mounted.
> See how my sword weeps for the poor king's
> death!
>
> (V, vi, 61–63)

This is the voice of a new kind of villain who is gain his full status in *Richard III.*

Another theme newly and fully developed in the lay is the character of the weak King. As the rep-esentative of legitimacy in a time of revolution, he fated to be thwarted and disgraced at every turn f the plot. Seen through the eyes of the fierce obles, he is a poltroon who disinherits his son in eturn for permission to continue to rule, by the ufferance of York, as long as he lives. His Queen so disgusted with his faint heart that she forth-ith divorces herself from his table and his bed ntil an act of parliament repeals the law that has isinherited his offspring. Yet Shakespeare has not esigned him to be only an object of scorn. He be-omes more and more clearly a representative of eace and its blessings, as the warriors are of war nd its horrors. He sits upon a hill, withdrawn from ne battle from which Margaret and Clifford have chid" him, and gives voice to his longing to be a nepherd, a Renaissance symbol of peace. He tells ow much he wants quiet for contemplation in lines nat approximate the tone and cadence of a litany:

> O God! methinks it were a happy life,
> To be no better than a homely swain; . . .
> So many hours must I tend my flock;
> So many hours must I take my rest.
> (II, v, 21–22, 31–32)

His moment of meditation is interrupted by a dread-ul tableau: "a son that hath killed his Father, with ne body in his arms," followed by "a Father that ath killed his son, with the body in his arms." At ais point the drama becomes definitely an antiwar lay.

Thus *3 Henry VI,* in spite of its crowding of only artly digested facts, proves to be much more than n inexpert transfer of chronicle into play, more lso than a dress rehearsal for *Richard III.* It is hakespeare's vivid comment upon the desperate ate of England when racked by civil war.—O. J. C.

Stage History. The history of *Henry VI, Parts 2* nd *3,* is almost as meager as that of *Part 1.* There no record of a single performance of the plays nder those titles before the Restoration.

John CROWNE (d. 1703) was the first to adapt the aterial of the three parts of *Henry VI* to the de-nands of the Restoration stage and its audiences. He educed their multitudinous scenes into two parts. His first part, "with the murder of Humphrey, Duke f Gloucester," is composed of materials drawn from ne first three acts of *2 Henry VI,* comprising the evelopment of the conspiracy of Beaufort, York, uffolk, and Queen Margaret against Humphrey nd his proud Duchess. Crowne thus gives some of he important events of the Wars of the Roses struc-ural unity, but greatly weakens their effectiveness y diluting the substance of Shakespeare's three acts nd stretching them into the five acts that critical rthodoxy and theatrical custom then demanded.

Crowne named his second part *The Misery of Civil War.* Except for fragments concerning Cade's ebellion, lifted from *2 Henry VI,* its facts come rom *3 Henry VI.* To exploit the obsession with sex nat afflicted Restoration audiences, Crowne in-ented a Lady Elinor Butler to serve as one of Ed-ard IV's mistresses. Her encounters with the King ust have given Crowne's hodgepodge what little iccess it enjoyed. Records indicate that both parts ere first produced at the Duke's Theatre in 1681. Thomas Betterton acted Gloucester opposite Mrs. Betterton's (Mary Saunderson) Duchess of Gloucester in the first part and Warwick to her Lady Grey in the second. Joseph Williams played King Henry in both plays.

In 1723 Drury Lane presented two plays based on *Henry VI.* Ambrose Philips' *Humfrey Duke of Gloucester,* vaguely resembling Shakespeare's historical drama but with only about 35 lines taken from the first three acts of the original *2 Henry VI,* was produced on February 15. Colley Cibber played Cardinal Beaufort, while Barton Booth took Gloucester's role in this inferior work, which was acted no more than nine times and disappeared. On July 5 *An Historical Tragedy of the Civil Wars in the Reign of King Henry 6th* was given its first and only performance. This was Theophilus Cibber's alteration which, in addition to material from Shakespeare's *2 Henry VI,* Act V, and *3 Henry VI,* includes generous appropriations from Crowne's *Misery of Civil War.* For the fourth and fifth acts, Cibber relied largely on his own invention, but lifted lines from Henry V's speech before Harfleur (III, i, 7–33) and inserted them into Queen Margaret's speech in V, iv.

The next adaptation of *Henry VI* was performed on December 22, 1817, again at Drury Lane. Edmund Kean played the lead in this version by J. H. Merivale, entitled *Richard, Duke of York; or the Contention of York and Lancaster.* Although drawn from all three parts of Shakespeare's *Henry VI,* the greater share is composed of matter from *Part 2* and *Part 3.* Despite harsh criticism for the complete absence of dramatic continuity, the play was performed seven times during December and the following January.

The only 19th-century production of *2 Henry VI* in London was a tercentenary performance on April 23, 1864, at the Surrey Theatre. The revival of the original drama, probably the first since the late 16th century, ran for a week. A notice in the *London Illustrated News* commends this "noblest effort," citing for special praise the fight in which Iden kills Jack Cade. James Anderson, a popular actor, doubled in the roles of the Duke of York and Jack Cade, while James Fernandez acted both Suffolk and Iden. Meanwhile, the genuine *3 Henry VI* remained buried.

At Stratford-upon-Avon Frank Benson staged *2 Henry VI* in 1899, 1901, and 1909, and the complete trilogy in a cycle of seven histories in 1906. Benson acted the Cardinal in the revivals of *Part 2;* in *Part 3* in 1906 he played Richard of Gloucester. Constance Benson was Queen Margaret in all of these productions and was praised for her forceful, spirited portrayal. In 1899 and 1901 Frank Rodney impersonated Gloucester; Oscar Asche, Jack Cade; and Matheson Lang, Bolingbroke. Harcourt Williams, who was Young Clifford in 1899, transferred to the part of Salisbury in the 1901 *2 Henry VI,* while Henry Ainley was that year's Buckingham. In 1906 H. O. Nicholson was Gloucester in *Part 1* and *Part 2* and Edward IV in *Part 3;* George Buchanan acted the King; Murray Carrington, Young Clifford.

The first half of *Part 2* was joined to *Part 1* when Robert Atkins staged *Henry VI* at the Old Vic in 1923. This revival on January 9 was followed by the performance on February 12 of the second half of *Part 2,* together with *Part 3.* It had been 60 years since London saw any part of the historical trilogy. The cast included Atkins as Richard, Wilfrid Walter as Gloucester and Jack Cade, D. Hay Petrie portraying Simpcox and Dick the Weaver, Douglas Burbidge playing Buckingham, and Rupert Harvey in the role of York.

Part 2 was the first of the three parts to reappear. In April 1951 the Birmingham Repertory Company began its cycle of the *Henry VI* plays, to be staged singly in consecutive years, with the presentation of *2 Henry VI. Part 3* followed the next April and paid a short visit to the Old Vic in July of that year. In 1953, after the presentation of *Part 1* at Birmingham in June, the complete trilogy, performed in chronological sequence, achieved a triumph in Finlay James' setting on the Old Vic stage. Douglas Seale directed these productions, using Barry Jackson's amplified text. The entire trilogy was again performed at the Old Vic under Seale's direction during October 1957.

In August 1961 Valery Hovenden presented *Part 2* at the Hovenden Theatre Club while that same year the Marlowe Society staged *Part 2* and *Part 3* at Cambridge under the title *Alarums and Excursions*. Then, at Stratford in 1963, Peter Hall staged *The Wars of the Roses* trilogy, which consisted of *Henry VI* (including *1 Henry VI* and the first half of *2 Henry VI*), *Edward IV* (composed of the second half of *2 Henry VI* and *3 Henry VI*), and *Richard III*. A cohesive narrative arranged by John Barton cleverly bridged the chronicles. Ian Holm acted an unsatanic Richard of Gloucester, trapped by a power struggle; David Warner was the detached, monklike King; and Peggy Ashcroft, a Margaret who, hardened by ambition and strengthened by despair, was transformed from the French Princess of *Part 1* to a bloodthirsty fiend on the battlefield, taunting Richard of York at his death. Donald Sindon played the Duke of York, and Roy Doltrice, Edward IV. This production was transferred to the stage of the Aldwych where the entire trilogy was acted in one day on January 11, 1964, and later at consecutive performances. That spring *The Wars of the Roses* returned to Stratford for the 1964 season.

The first American revival of *2* and *3 Henry VI* was at the Pasadena Community Playhouse in 1935. That summer Gilmor Browne directed all 10 of Shakespeare's history plays in continuous sequence. *Part 2* of *Henry VI* appeared on July 29 and *3 Henry VI* followed on August 1. Television audiences in New York and Washington, as well as in Great Britain, saw the chronicle in Peter Dews' production for the British Broadcasting Company in 1961 of Shakespeare's "king plays" in their chronological order. The series, entitled *An Age of Kings*, was presented in 1961 and considered a great artistic success.—M. G.

Bibliography. TEXT: *Henry VI, Part 3*, New Cambridge Edition, J. Dover Wilson, ed., 1952; *The Third Part of Henry VI*, A. S. Cairncross, ed., New Arden Edition, 1964; Peter Alexander, *Shakespeare's Henry VI and Richard III*, 1929. DATE: New Cambridge Edition; New Arden Edition. SOURCES: Geoffrey Bullough, *Narrative and Dramatic Sources of Shakespeare*, III, 1960. COMMENT: Hereward T. Price, *Construction in Shakespeare*, 1951; F. P. Wilson, *Marlowe and the Early Shakespeare*, 1953. STA[GE] HISTORY: New Cambridge Edition; G. C. D. Ode[ll], *Shakespeare from Betterton to Irving*, 1920; J. [C.] Trewin, *Shakespeare on the English Stage, 190[0]–1964*, 1964.

Selected Criticism

SAMUEL JOHNSON. The three parts of *Henry VI* a[re] suspected, by Mr. *Theobald*, of being suppositio[us] and are declared, by Dr. *Warburton*, to be *certain[ly] not Shakespeare's*. Mr. *Theobald's* suspicion aris[es] from some obsolete words; but the phraseology [is] like the rest of our authour's stile, and single word[s] of which however I do not observe more than tw[o] can conclude little.

Dr. *Warburton* gives no reason, but I suppose hi[m] to judge upon deeper principles and more compre[hensive] hensive views, and to draw his opinion from th[e] general effect and spirit of the composition, whic[h] he thinks inferior to the other historical plays.

From mere inferiority nothing can be inferred; i[n] the productions of wit there will be inequalit[y]. Sometimes judgment will err, and sometimes th[e] matter itself will defeat the artist. Of every authour[s] works one will be the best, and one will be th[e] worst. The colours are not equally pleasing, nor th[e] attitudes equally graceful, in all the pictures [of] *Titian* or *Reynolds*.

Dissimilitude of stile and heterogeneousness [of] sentiment, may sufficiently show that a work do[es] not really belong to the reputed authour. But i[n] these plays no such marks of spuriousness are foun[d]. The diction, the versification, and the figures, ar[e] *Shakespeare's*. These plays, considered, without re[gard] gard to characters and incidents, merely as narrative[s] in verse, are more happily conceived and mor[e] accurately finished than those of king *John, Richar[d]* II., or the tragick scenes of *Henry* IV. and V. If w[e] take these plays from *Shakespeare*, to whom sha[ll] they be given? What authour of that age had th[e] same easiness of expression and fluency of numbers[?]

Having considered the evidence given by th[e] plays themselves, and found it in their favour, let u[s] now enquire what corroboration can be gained fro[m] other testimony. They are ascribed to *Shakespear[e]* by the first editors, whose attestation may be re[ceived] ceived in questions of fact, however unskilfully the[y] superintend their edition. They seem to be declare[d] genuine by the voice of *Shakespeare* himself, wh[o] refers to the second play in his epilogue to *Henry* V. and apparently connects the first act of *Richard* II[I.] with the last of the third part of *Henry* VI. If it b[e] objected that the plays were popular, and therefor[e] he alluded to them as well known; it may b[e] answered, with equal probability, that the natur[al] passions of a poet would have disposed him t[o] separate his own works from those of an inferio[r] hand. And indeed if an author's own testimony is t[o] be overthrown by speculative criticism, no man ca[n] be any longer secure of literary reputation.

Of these three plays I think the second the bes[t]. The truth is, that they have not sufficient variety o[f] action, for the incidents are too often of the sam[e] kind; yet many of the characters are well discrim[i]nated. King *Henry*, and his queen, king *Edwar[d]*, the duke of *Gloucester*, and the earl of *Warwic[k]* are very strongly and distinctly painted.

The old copies of the two latter parts of *Henr[y]*

I. and of *Henry* V. are so apparently imperfect id mutilated, that there is no reason for supposing iem the first draughts of *Shakespeare*. I am inclined believe them copies taken by some auditor who rote down, during the representation, what the me would permit, then perhaps filled up some of is omissions at a second or third hearing, and when e had by this method formed something like a play, nt it to the printer. [*The Plays of William Shakeeare*, 1765.]

WILLIAM HAZLITT. The characters and situations of oth these persons [Richard II and Henry VI] were nearly alike, that they would have been cometely confounded by a commonplace poet. Yet ey are kept quite distinct in Shakespear. Both were ings, and both unfortunate. Both lost their crowns wing to their mismanagement and imbecility; the ne from a thoughtless, wilful abuse of power, the ther from an indifference to it. The manner in hich they bear their misfortunes corresponds xactly to the causes which led to them. The one is lways lamenting the loss of his power which he has ot the spirit to regain; the other seems only to egret that he had ever been king, and is glad to be d of the power, with the trouble; the effeminacy f the one is that of a voluptuary, proud, revengeful, npatient of contradictions, and inconsolable in his isfortunes; the effeminacy of the other is that of n indolent, good-natured mind, naturally averse to e turmoils of ambition and the cares of greatness, nd who wishes to pass his time in monkish indolence nd contemplation.—Richard bewails the loss of the ingly power only as it was the means of gratifying is pride and luxury; Henry regards it only as a neans of doing right, and is less desirous of the dvantages to be derived from possessing it than fraid of exercising it wrong. [*Characters of Shakepear's Plays*, 1817.]

G. G. GERVINUS. Duke Humphrey of Gloster, who ppears in the second part totally different to the loster of the first, is invested with the great qualiies of consummate mildness and benevolence, with Solomon-like wisdom, with freedom from all mbition, and with severe Brutus-like justice towards everyone, even towards his wife, in whose last ishonour he notwithstanding shares as a private haracter. The greatness of his self-command, which contrasted with the unbridled passion of his wife, as been rendered prominent by Shakespeare in one f his happy touches. In the passionate scene (Part I. Act I. sc. 3), preparatory to his own fall and that f his Duchess, he goes out and returns without eason; Shakespeare explains this as an intentional novement, with which the loyal man endeavoured o suppress his excitement and choler. There is too nuch noble and quiet grandeur in Humphrey for us ot to be grieved at his fall, which appears merely n exemplification of the fable of the lamb that had roubled the wolf's water. It is Shakespeare's addiion that he entwined in the garland of his virtues hat foolish reliance upon his innocence which leads im to destruction, and which renders him careless mid the persecutions of his enemies, although he new that York's 'overweening arm was reaching at he moon.' At the moment of his fall, he too late ecomes keen-sighted, and predicts his own ruin nd that of his king. That weakness is a crime is indicated by Shakespeare in this character, and is more closely worked out in Henry VI. This character, indeed, is entirely due to him; Greene placed the king as a cypher silently into the background, but Shakespeare drew him forth and delineated his nothingness. A saint, 'whose bookish rule had pulled fair England down,' formed rather for a pope than a king, more fit for heaven than earth—a king, as Shakespeare adds, who longed and wished to be a subject more than any subject longed to be a king—he is in his inaction the source of all the misdeeds which disorder the kingdom. [*Shakespeare*, 1849-1850; tr. 1863 as *Shakespeare Commentaries*.]

THOMAS KENNY. We shall now proceed to state a number of additional reasons which induce us to adhere to the opinion that Shakespeare was substantially the author of the "First Part of the Contention" and of the "True Tragedie," however imperfectly his work may have been copied in those two publications.

It is evident that the smaller details of the controversy are strangely involved, and some persons may think that they are still inconclusive. We shall, therefore, pass at once to a consideration of those more obvious characteristics of the two works by which this question will perhaps be best decided. We believe that those characteristics distinctly reveal the hand of Shakespeare. On any large review of these two dramas, we are at once struck by the close connection which exists, not only between them and the "First Part of King Henry VI.," but also between them and "King Richard III." The unity of design which seems to connect the four works naturally leads us to think that they must all have proceeded from one and the same mind; and this impression is considerably strengthened by the completeness with which the identity of character is preserved in the dramatic personages, and more especially in Margaret and Richard, the two most striking figures in the whole scene. The very vigour with which these most distinguishing personages are presented, even in single passages, seems decidedly Shakespearian, and we are strongly disposed to believe that no such characterisation was within the reach of any other dramatist of that generation....

We do not of course consider it at all impossible that some of the actors in the original dramas may have been tempted to aid in furnishing more complete versions of the parts they had sustained, or even that more or less imperfect playhouse copies may have been used in the construction of these singular volumes....

But if these two old plays are, as we believe them to be, mere mutilated copies of Shakespeare's dramas, they are undoubtedly in their way very remarkable productions. [*The Life and Genius of Shakespeare*, 1864.]

EDWARD DOWDEN. . . . He [Henry VI.] only, who most should have treasured and augmented his inheritance of glory and of power, is insensible to the large responsibilities and privileges of his place. He is cold in great affairs; his supreme concern is to remain blameless. Free from all greeds and ambitions, he yet is possessed by egoism, the egoism of timid saintliness. His virtue is negative, because there is no vigorous basis of manhood within him out of which heroic saintliness might develop itself. For fear of what is wrong, he shrinks from what is right. This is not the virtue ascribed to the nearest followers of "the Faithful and True" who in his righteousness doth judge and make war. Henry is passive in the presence of evil, and weeps. He would keep his garments clean; but the garments of God's soldier-saints, who do not fear the soils of struggle, gleam with a higher, intenser purity. "His eyes were as a flame of fire, and on his head were many crowns; . . . And the armies which were in heaven followed him upon white horses, clothed in fine linen, white and clean." These soldiers in heaven have their representatives in earth; and Henry was not one of these. Zeal must come before charity, and then when charity comes it will appear as a self-denial. But Henry knows nothing of zeal; and he is amiable, not charitable. [*Shakspere: A Critical Study of His Mind and Art*, 1875.]

FRANK HARRIS. Shakespeare might have painted the traditional Joan of Arc of Holinshed as he painted the traditional Margaret, and no one would have been able to deduce much more than youth from his subservience. He began by doing this, then out of patriotism he went on to idealize Talbot, and consequently is almost compelled to diminish Joan's triumphs; he makes her take Rouen (which was never taken, but opened its gates seventeen years after her death) by a trick because he wants to give Talbot the glory of retaking it by sheer English courage. He puts down all her successes to witchery and sorcery, as Holinshed did, and when she is captured, he not only repeats the usual libel on her that she pretended to be with child by this and that noble in order to prolong her life, but he blackens this libel by a suggestion made in the first act. When the Dauphin presses her to marry him, Shakespeare makes her half-promise to yield to him and talk of her "recompense," and this half-promise and the desire of reward deepen the bad impression made by her pretended confessions in the last act . . . .

This invention does not surprise me in Shakespeare; it is all in character: Shakespeare, forgetting the previous confession and making Joan brag that she is of "nobler birth" and "issued from the progeny of kings," it is, I repeat, all in keeping and just such a boast as would first suggest itself to Shakespeare's snobbishness. [*The Women of Shakespeare*, 1911.]

MARK VAN DOREN. Here all is explicit. The spring of every action is exposed; each person tells the audience at the top of his voice both what he privately intends and what he means publicly to be understood as intending. Enmities are confessed and clear. Conflicts are obvious, as of large bodies moved up to each other and palpably colliding on an open field. There is no mystery or ambiguity of purpose, there are no uninterpretable acts. The fifteenth century is for Shakespeare a time filled solidly with faction; parties split, feuds rage, and oversized heroes growl at one another's tough throats. Hatred is elementary and theatrical, whether it is the hatred of Gloucester for Winchester, Talbot for Joan of Arc, Margaret for the Duchess of Gloucester and the house of York, Suffolk for Gloucester, York for Clifford, Somerset for York, Warwick for Edward IV, Jack Cade for the nobility, Vernon for Basset, or Red for White. No sounder apprenticeship could have been served by a playwright whose destiny it was to b subtle. Subtlety counts most in one who is capabl of plainness. Shakespeare was to have had his plair ness, as indeed he was to keep a necessary portion c it to the end. He could have traveled toward h later plays from no better direction than "Henr VI." Toward, for example, "Othello," where th theme of witchcraft taints a whole play from source somehow hidden, and is not, as here in the persor of Joan and the Duchess of Gloucester, merely a aspect of intrigue or an excuse for calling name [*Shakespeare*, 1939.]

E. M. W. TILLYARD. . . . this tetralogy to an equ extent with the later tetralogy and more powerfull than the most civilised of the Chronicle Plays show Shakespeare aware of order or degree. Behind a the confusion of civil war, and the more preciou and emphatic because of the confusion, is the beli that the world is a part of the eternal law and th earthly mutability, as in Spenser's last cantos, is itse a part of a greater and permanent pattern. Furthe human events as well as being subject to the etern law are part of an elaborate system of correspond ences and hence the more firmly woven into th total web of things. The very first words of the fir of the four plays will illustrate. They are spoken b the Duke of Bedford at the funeral procession of h brother Henry V.

> Hung be the heavens with black, yield day to night,
> Comets, importing change of times and states,
> Brandish your crystal tresses in the sky
> And with them scourge the bad revolting stars
> That have consented unto Henry's death!

Here the stars that have "consented unto," whic means "conspired to procure," the death of Henr are intended to be the counterpart in the heavens c the English nobility who have already fallen int discord. The universe, in fact, was so much of unity that the skies had to re-enact the things th happened in the human polity. It is the same corre spondence that occurs in the speech on "degree" i *Troilus and Cressida*.

> But when the planets
> In evil mixture to disorder wander,
> What plagues and what portents, what mutiny,
> What raging of the sea, shaking of earth,
> Commotion in the winds, frights, changes, horrors,
> Divert and crack, rend and deracinate
> The unity and married calm of states
> Quite from their fixure!

[*Shakespeare's History Plays*, 1944.]

IRVING RIBNER. In this episodic treatment of a lon series of tragic events, the *Henry VI* plays carry o the dramatic tradition of the miracle drama as it ha been developed through the Digby *Mary Magdalene Cambises* and *Tamburlaine*. The relation of the play to *Tamburlaine* is particularly close in Parts II an III, for just as in Marlowe's play we have the figur of Tamburlaine steadily expanding through an epi sodic series of battles, here we have the figure o Richard, Duke of York, steadily expanding in th same episodic manner. An important difference however, is that York falls before he reaches the summit of his glory, whereas Tamburlaine is triumphant to the end. There is little in Shakespeare of Marlowe's humanistic philosophy of history. Richard's personal abilities avail him nothing in the face of a hostile fortune which destroys him in retribution for his sins. Stylistic similarities between the *Henry VI* plays and *Tamburlaine*, and particularly the numerous verbal parallels, have been offered as evidence of Marlowe's hand in the *Henry VI* plays, but certainly if there were any dramatist Shakespeare would be likely to imitate at this stage of his career, it would be Marlowe. The author of all three parts of *Henry VI* clearly had *Tamburlaine* as a model before him; he imitated its blank verse, its rhetorical trappings, and its episodic structure. He did not, however, share the political and philosophical principles espoused in Marlowe's play . . . .

History for Shakespeare was never mere pageantry. He saw significant meaning in it, and he seized upon morality devices to make its meaning clear, clearer than the factual method of the chronicles themselves could make it. But the morality tradition is not limited to the third part of Shakespeare's first historical trilogy; there is far more of this than Rossiter has perceived. . . . For if there is any hero who emerges from the vast panorama of events, it can be only England itself. The *Henry VI* plays, in spite of their unintegrated, episodic structure, carry on the dramatic tradition of such political morality plays as *Respublica*. The three plays, with *Richard III*, embody one vast scheme in which England, like a morality hero, brings evil upon herself; she suffers degradation in the Wars of the Roses, loses her conquests in France, and is brought almost to total destruction under the tyranny of Richard III. But God pities England, shows her his grace, and, through the person of Henry of Richmond, allows her to make a proper choice upon which the factions among her nobles can unite. Thus England attains a new and greater felicity to be exemplified in the reign of the Tudors. This scheme of salvation for England is at the heart of the four plays. ["The Early Shakespeare," *The English History Play in the Age of Shakespeare*, 1957.]

J. P. BROCKBANK. The three parts of *Henry VI* express the plight of individuals caught up in a cataclysmic movement of events for which responsibility is communal and historical, not personal and immediate, and they reveal the genesis out of prolonged violence of two figures representing the ultimate predicament of man as a political animal—Henry and Richard, martyr and machiavel. But one would not wish to over-stress whatever analogues there may be between the fifteenth century and the twentieth, since these might be proved quite as striking for ages other than our own. If we are now more sympathetically disposed towards Shakespeare's history plays than were the readers and audiences of seventy years ago, it is largely because we have more flexible ideas about the many possible forms that history might take. We are less dominated by the Positivist view that the truth is co-extensive with, and not merely consistent with, the facts. . . . For Shakespeare was peculiarly sensitive to the subtle analogues between the world and the stage, between the shape of events and the shape of a play, between the relationship of historical process to individuals and that of the playwright to his characters. He tried from the beginning to meet the urgent and practical problem of finding dramatic forms and conventions that would express whatever coherence and order could be found in the 'plots' of chronicle history. Where narrative and play are incompatible, it may be the record and it may be the art that is defective as an image of human life, and in the plays framed from English and Roman history it is possible to trace subtle modulations of spectacle, structure and dialogue as they seek to express and elucidate the full potential of the source material. A full account would take in *The Tempest,* which is the last of Shakespeare's plays to be made out of historical documents and which has much to do with the rule of providence over the political activities of man. But from these early plays alone there is much to be learned about the vision and technique of historical drama, and these are the plays that are submitted most rigorously to the test of allegiance to historical record. ["The Frame of Disorder—'Henry VI'," *Early Shakespeare,* Stratford-Upon-Avon Studies 3, 1961.]

Henry VII (1457–1509). King of England; posthumous and only son of Edmund Tudor, earl of Richmond, and Margaret Beaufort. When in 1470 Henry VI was temporarily restored to the throne, Richmond's uncle Jasper Tudor presented him to the king, who prophesied that the boy would one day possess the crown. Richmond became head of the house of Lancaster after the deaths of Henry VI and his son, Edward. When Richard, duke of Gloucester, usurped the throne in 1483, Richmond, in order to unify the quarreling houses of York and Lancaster against the new king, agreed to marry Elizabeth of York on his own accession. Meeting Richard in combat at Bosworth in 1485, Richmond defeated him and was proclaimed King Henry VII. The following year he married Elizabeth of York.

In *3 Henry VI*, he appears as the young earl of Richmond, of whom King Henry says: "This pretty lad will prove our country's bliss." In *Richard III,* as in history, Richmond battles Richard for the crown, kills him, and is proclaimed king. Announcing his intention to marry Elizabeth, daughter of Edward IV, he declares: "We will unite the white rose and the red."

Henry VIII (1491–1547). King of England (1509–1547); titular hero of *Henry VIII.* Henry's tumultuous reign was marked by the establishment of the Anglican church, the seizure of church lands and monasteries, the consolidation of royal power, the development of the English navy, and the creation of a new aristocracy composed of men of talent, wealth or ambition, regardless of birth. These achievements derived directly from the character and temperament of the monarch himself. Self-indulgent and ruthless, Henry was nevertheless a shrewd and capable administrator. In the early years of his reign, he relied heavily on his chief minister, Cardinal Wolsey. After Wolsey's fall, Henry assumed increasingly greater power, delegating authority to a number of able ministers such as Sir Thomas More and Thomas Cromwell. The other aspect of Henry's character, however, is revealed in the fact that More and Cromwell were ultimately executed.

In *Henry VIII*, Shakespeare's portrait of the King is diplomatically complimentary. Henry is carefully characterized as a stern champion of England but one who is too easily manipulated by the guileful Wolsey. Thus his character emerges in an ambiguous light which suggests, without directly asserting, that as a king Henry was something less than ideal.

The Famous Hiſtory of the Life of King *Henry* the Eighth.

Henry VIII. A history play by Shakespeare.

Text. *King Henry VIII* was first published in the First Folio (1623), which is the sole authority for the text. It is generally thought to be of divided authorship, a collaborative effort of Shakespeare and John Fletcher. Although no direct evidence exists to connect Fletcher with the composition of *Henry VIII*, there are good reasons for believing that he cooperated with Shakespeare in the composition of *The Two Noble Kinsmen*, which was probably written at about the same time as *Henry VIII*. The case for Fletcher and the assignment of the shares to each author were first authoritatively presented by James Spedding in 1850. He gave Shakespeare only the first two scenes of Act I, the third and fourth scenes of Act II, lines 1–203 of the first scene of Act IV and the first scene of Act V. Although other scholars have made different assignments, Spedding's allotment of shares has been generally accepted as approximately correct. His division takes from Shakespeare two of the most famous passages in the drama: Wolsey's farewell to his greatness (III, ii, 351–372) and his advice to Cromwell (III, ii, 428–457). Scholars have continued to speculate about the nature of the collaboration. Spedding, followed by many recent scholars, believed that the original design was Shakespeare's. F. G. Fleay conjectured that the poet wrote a complete play, but that some parts of his manuscript were destroyed in the 1613 burning of the Globe and that Fletcher supplied the lost pages. The most acceptable theory is that advanced by Edward Dowden, namely that the two authors worked together, Shakespeare agreeing to supply the beginning of the drama and the scenes introducing the principal characters and Fletcher contributing the rest. The chief objection to this analysis is that at the time of the play's composition, Shakespeare was living in Stratford and Fletcher in London. Moreover, the piece is loosely constructed. It has no center of interest, no continuous movement toward a designated goal, and no logical culmination. Could Shakespeare at the end of his career have been so inexpert in designing a play? It is hard to believe. Yet recently there has been a revival of the belief in Shakespeare's sole authorship, but the prevailing view of scholars is that Fletcher was a collaborator and probably the major contributor to the play.

The copy for the Folio text appears to have been a transcript of the author's FOUL PAPERS, made by a professional scribe.

Date. *King Henry VIII* must have been written shortly before June 29, 1613, for on that date, during the first performance of the drama, referred to as *All is True*, the GLOBE theatre burned to the ground, set afire by a cannon fired in the royal salute at the entrance of the King in the fourth scene of Act I.

Sources. For the principal part of the play Shakespeare used HOLINSHED's *Chronicles*, supplemented now and then by material from Halle's older chronicle, *Union of the two noble and illustre famelies of Lancastre and York*, 1548. The source of the Cranmer story as developed in Act V was Foxe's BOOK OF MARTYRS (1563). Samuel Rowley's *When You See Me You Know Me*, an earlier drama (between 1603 and 1605) dealing with Henry's reign, served as an auxiliary, but unimportant source. Shakespeare had little reason to augment the story told in the *Chronicles* with dramatic accounts of Wolsey's fall, for the action is comparatively simple, covering only a part of Henry's reign. It begins with Norfolk's description of the splendor of the "Field of the Cloth of Gold" (1520) and ends with the christening of Princess Elizabeth (1533). But there are some anachronisms in the play. For example, the death of Queen Katharine, which actually occurred in 1536, is imminent at the end of Act IV. The accusation of Cranmer before the council (V, iii) did not take place until after 1540, but in the play it precedes the christening of Elizabeth. Such minor liberties taken with chronology, resulting in essentially nothing unhistorical, have no effect upon the play's dramatic values.—O. J. C.

Plot Synopsis. Act I. In an antechamber of the royal palace, the Duke of Norfolk describes the recent meeting of King Henry and Francis I of France on the Field of the Cloth of Gold. Unimpressed by Norfolk's account of the magnificent scene, the

Duke of Buckingham and his son-in-law, Lord Abergavenny, inveigh against the pride and extravagance of the Lord Chancellor, Cardinal Wolsey, who had arranged the French alliance. As Buckingham informs Norfolk of his plan to denounce Wolsey to the King, the Cardinal himself enters and arrests Buckingham for high treason.

As the King prepares to hear Buckingham's defense, Queen Katharine interrupts with a plea that Henry reduce the taxes that Wolsey has imposed on the clothiers of the realm. Henry grants his wife's petition, but Wolsey sees to it that he, rather than the King, is given credit for the reduction. When Buckingham's Surveyor accuses the Duke of coveting the crown, Katharine points out that the Surveyor had been dismissed by Buckingham on complaint of his tenants. The Surveyor's allegations, however, convince the King.

Act II. Condemned to death through the machinations of Wolsey, Buckingham maintains his innocence as he is led to execution. He forgives those who conspired against him and recalls that, like his father, he has been betrayed by his own servants.

According to Norfolk, Wolsey has also succeeded in persuading the King to question the legality of his marriage to Katharine. Previously betrothed to Henry's older brother, Prince Arthur, she had wed Henry only after obtaining a papal dispensation. Now, 20 years later, Wolsey, reportedly to avenge a slight from the Emperor Charles, Katharine's nephew, has advised Henry to divorce his wife and marry the Duchess of Alençon, sister of the King of France. Accordingly, the King has invited Cardinal Campeius from Rome to judge the case.

Meanwhile, at a gala banquet at Wolsey's residence, the King's fancy has lighted on Anne Bullen, one of the Queen's ladies. Anne sympathizes with Katharine's plight and believes that it is better to be humbly born than to fall from so lofty a height. But when she remarks that she has no desire to be a queen, a lively old lady with whom she converses is skeptical. They are interrupted by the Lord Chamberlain, who announces that the King has made Anne Marchioness of Pembroke, with an annual income of £1000. Observing her reaction, the Chamberlain is not surprised that her beauty and honor have captivated the King.

Before an imposing assembly of prelates, gathered to decide on the legality of the King's marriage, Queen Katharine reminds Henry that she has been "a true and humble" wife for 20 years and refuses to acknowledge Wolsey as her judge. Wolsey protests that he bears her no ill will. She replies that she is a simple woman who is no match for his cunning and denounces his arrogance and neglect of his holy calling. After stating that she will appeal to the Pope, she angrily leaves the chamber. Although the King extols his wife's virtues, he explains that his conscience had first been stirred with respect to the validity of his marriage when the legitimacy of his daughter, Mary, had been questioned. The fact that none of his male children has survived might also be a sign of heavenly disfavor. Now he asks only that his marriage be proved lawful, but Campeius, to Henry's annoyance, adjourns the meeting because of the Queen's absence.

Act III. The Queen remains intransigent despite the pleas of Wolsey and Campeius, who advise her to put herself under the King's protection. She condemns the two Cardinals for offering her such meager comfort and insists that she will never give up her title as queen.

Wolsey's schemes go awry as a result of Henry's decision to wed the Protestant Anne Bullen instead of the Duchess of Alençon. The Cardinal writes to Rome, urging the Pope to delay his decision regarding the King's first marriage, but the letters fall into Henry's hands. When Henry, obtaining by chance an inventory of Wolsey's property, becomes aware of the extent of his wealth, Wolsey's downfall is assured. Acting on the King's orders, Norfolk commands Wolsey to surrender the great seal. He must also endure the abuse of the Earl of Surrey, Buckingham's son-in-law, who reviews the Cardinal's offenses against his family and the kingdom. When the Duke of Suffolk reveals that the King has ordered Wolsey's property confiscated, the Cardinal realizes that his "high-blown pride" has destroyed him. "O, how wretched / Is that poor man that hangs on princes' favours!" he reflects. His servant, Thomas Cromwell, reports that Cranmer, a cleric of dubious orthodoxy, has been named Archbishop of Canterbury and that Henry has secretly married Anne.

Act IV. Anne is crowned Queen of England in an impressive ceremony at Westminster Abbey, while Katharine, now known as the Princess Dowager, lies ill at Kimbolton. Hearing of Wolsey's death, Katha-

HENRY VIII. PORTRAIT POSSIBLY BY HANS HOLBEIN. (NATIONAL PORTRAIT GALLERY)

rine recalls his faults, but when her attendant Griffith reminds her of his learning and liberality, she wishes him peace. Falling asleep, she sees a vision in which six figures, robed in white, appear before her with garlands and bid her a solemn farewell. After she awakens, she receives Capucius, an emissary from the Emperor, and expresses her hope that she will arrange an honorable marriage for her daughter. Her strength failing, she is taken to bed.

Act V. While Queen Anne undergoes the ordeal of childbirth in the palace, Gardiner, the Bishop of Winchester, and Sir Thomas Lovell air their criticism of the royal favor shown to Cromwell and Cranmer. Gardiner reveals that the lords of the council have prevailed upon the King to summon the Archbishop to a meeting that day. The King himself, however, has confidence in Cranmer's integrity and gives him a ring as a token of royal favor. The King learns that the Queen has given birth to a daughter.

Cranmer is kept waiting before the council chamber like a lackey, a sight which angers Dr. Butts, the King's physician, who invites Henry to observe the scene from a window. During the ensuing council meeting, the Lord Chancellor and Gardiner accuse Cranmer of spreading heresy throughout the realm, ignoring his request that he be allowed to confront his accusers. When he is ordered to the Tower of London, Cranmer produces Henry's ring, and the King himself appears, reprimanding the nobles for their discourtesy toward the Archbishop, whom he selects as godfather to his daughter. The child is christened Elizabeth, and Cranmer foresees that the royal infant will bring to England "a thousand thousand blessings" and that she will be "a pattern to all princes living with her, / And all that shall succeed." —H. D.

Comment. This history play differs widely from those attributed entirely to Shakespeare both in plan and in purpose. The architecture of his histories was moral and religious, revealing a divine purpose in the ordering of the events of English history. They often dramatized the punishment meted out to English kings for flouting God's will. Henry IV's sacrilege in deposing God's anointed, his earthly deputy Richard II, was paid for by Henry's descendants to the third and fourth generations, culminating in the death of Henry VI and the ruin of the House of Lancaster. *Henry VIII* is built on no such plan. It has been aptly described as a dramatized *Mirror for Magistrates*, representing the falls of Buckingham, Katharine, Wolsey, and Cranmer—interrupted by five gorgeous pageants. Frank Kermode has characterized the drama as a "late morality . . . showing the state from which great ones may fall and the manner of their falling." Each ruined figure comments on his fall in Fletcher's characteristic verse. Although these successive tragedies, each the result of Henry's tyranny, form a loose unity, the drama as a whole is episodic. Moreover, the intrusion of these and other scenes of elaborate pageantry breaks the continuity of the action. This splendid procession of gorgeously arrayed churchmen, each with his attendant gentleman bearing the insignia of his office, must have held the exclusive attention of the audience for at least 10 minutes. These shows of splendor were the commoners' equivalent of the masques given at court at the same time. Edward Dowden suggests that it may have occurred to the King's Men that the London populace, which could not gain admission to Whitehall, would be glad to see at the Globe a coronation, a masque, and a royal baptism on the stage—all for the price of a shilling.

Fletcher, the probable author of the prologue, explains just how his play is to differ from the conventional English "histories." He announces that those who expect the old standbys: "noise of targets" [a clash of shields], that is, the battle scenes with their alarums and excursions, their defiances, their boasts and threats, their single combats, and the antics and chop-logic of the fool in his long yellow coat, will be disappointed. To give an audience a "fool and fight" show would be to insult his own intelligence and to disavow his determination to give the spectators the whole historical truth of Henry VIII's reign and nothing but that. Some of these royal affairs, he continues, are so serious and, indeed, so distressing that they may provoke his audience to tears.

Although the author does discard most of the features of the old-fashioned "history," he develops an artificial method of his own. He invents scenes and situations primarily in order to provide the characters with opportunities for declamation. By far the most famous of these formal speeches is Wolsey's "Farewell! a long farewell, to all my greatness!" since spouted by generations of schoolboys at oratorical contests. Not far behind in popularity is Wolsey's advice and confession to Cromwell (III, ii, 428–457), ending with the impressive lines:

O Cromwell, Cromwell!
Had I but served my God with half the zeal
I served my king, he would not in mine age
Have left me naked to mine enemies.
(III, ii, 454–457)

An experienced actor can let these lines come trippingly from his tongue. They are self-contained; and, though they are not all end-stopped, there is an inevitable pause for breath at the end of each line. The movement of the thought is straightforward, lacking all complication or subtlety. This artful simplicity renders the declamation fluent and elegant. Since the author's main concern seems to have been the rhetorical features of the play, he shows little interest in the development of the characters of the principal dramatis personae. Indeed, Queen Katharine is the only one fully drawn. To the courtiers she is a paragon of royal propriety and wifely devotion. According to Norfolk, it is the King-Cardinal who counsels the divorce:

a loss of her
That, like a jewel, has hung twenty years
About his neck, yet never lost her lustre;
Of her that loves him with that excellence
That angels love good men with.
(II, ii, 31–35)

Henry, who, although troubled by his possible sin in marrying his older brother's widow, is still a slave to Katharine's charm, describes her with apparent sincerity as "the queen of earthly queens" and professes eagerness to live with her through all eternity. The fall of so blameless and glorious a creature awakens deep pity. And Katharine is eloquently pathetic. She cries:

> I am the most unhappy woman living.
> Alas, poor wenches, where are now your fortunes!
> Shipwreck'd upon a kingdom, where no pity,
> No friends, no hope; no kindred weep for me;
> Almost no grave allow'd me.
>
> (III, i, 147–151)

She is more than a sentimental heroine, the victim of man's cruelty to woman. She defends herself with dignity and spirit against both Henry and Wolsey, winning as much admiration as pity, and occupies an honorable place among Shakespeare's sympathetically portrayed women of charm and brain. Katharine is the most effectively realized of all his characters in *Henry VIII*. The epilogue refers only to her, and as a representative of good women:

> All the expected good we're like to hear
> For this play at this time, is only in
> The merciful construction of good women;
> For such a one we show'd 'em.
>
> (Epilogue, 8–11)

None of the other characters attain recognizable human stature. They play their parts convincingly only in the separate scenes.

Fletcher found it hard to draw a consistent picture of Henry. In portraying him he found himself in a ticklish position, particularly in defining Henry's attitude toward the divorce. He could not have the King definitely oppose it, for it was a necessary preliminary to his marriage to Anne Bullen and the birth of Queen Elizabeth. Yet, if Henry had been made actively to further it, as he did in real life, the playwright would have completely lost sympathy for Henry; sympathy which it was essential to maintain for political-historical reasons, no less than for subsequent events in the play. It is no wonder that the King's attitude toward his separation from Katharine is ambiguous. The author tried to escape from the horns of his dilemma by showing the King struggling between his expressed love and admiration for Katharine and his fear that his marriage to his brother's affianced wife had been unlawful and his daughter by her illegitimate. His conscience, therefore, demands that he break the wicked tie. His exclamation "But, conscience, conscience! / O, 'tis a tender place; and I must leave her" (II, ii, 143–144) may have relieved him of the opprobrium of an Elizabethan audience, but it sounds hypocritical to us. And there is at least one indication that it had a hollow sound to the courtiers in the play. The Second Gentleman, after describing the physical charms of Anne, remarks sardonically, "I cannot blame his conscience."

The treatment of Wolsey betrays the limitations of the divided authorship. In the early part of the drama Wolsey bids fair to become the principal character. We thus have the right to expect that his overthrow become a moving tragedy. But nothing of the sort happens. No one of his powerful enemies at court has a hand in his downfall. None of them represents a mounting threat to his political survival. For suspense and mounting apprehensions, the author substitutes surprise. In one scene Henry employs Wolsey in a delicate negotiation; in the next, the Cardinal falls, never to rise again, but his disgrace is the result of sheer accident—of a letter gone astray. This is a striking example of the authors' failure to make the characters and the individual scenes contribute their share to the creation of a coherent plot or to the progress of a dramatic action. Each scene is usually self-contained. It points neither before nor after. For this reason *Henry VIII* impresses most thoughtful critics as a collection of loosely joined, often beautiful and moving, shreds and patches, more a diversified entertainment, a superior variety show, than a unified play. Yet, in spite of this basic weakness, except for Shakespeare's greater "histories," *Henry VIII* is one of the most historically effective of all the chronicle histories produced on the Elizabethan and Jacobean stage.—O. J. C.

Stage History. *Henry VIII*, since it was first staged on the fateful afternoon of June 29, 1613 (see above under *Date*), has frequently been produced both in England and America. However, the only other pre-Restoration performance in the records is one mounted in the rebuilt Globe on July 29, 1628 (see George Villiers, duke of BUCKINGHAM). At the Restoration, Thomas Betterton played the King. John DOWNES reports that Betterton was instructed in the part by William Davenant "from what he had heard from old Mr. Lowen [John Lowin] that had his instructions from Mr. Shakespear himself." He continued to play the part until 1709, the year before his death.

There were many revivals during the 18th century, first at Drury Lane, later also at Lincoln's Inn Fields and Covent Garden. In 1707 Wolsey was played by John Verbruggen. Barton Booth played the King in the Drury Lane production of 1727, staged in honor of the coronation of George II. A highlight of this spectacle was the inclusion of a lavish coronation scene which would burden many later productions. In 1744 James Quin played the King at Covent Garden opposite Hannah Pritchard's Katharine. Peg Woffington was Quin's Queen in 1751 while, at Drury Lane, Mrs. Pritchard re-created the role every year from 1752 through 1761.

By the time John Philip Kemble revived the play at Drury Lane under Thomas Sheridan on November 25, 1788, elaborate pageantry had become essential to the staging of *Henry VIII*, and the parts of Wolsey and Katharine had been established as the leading roles. It was in this production that Sarah Siddons first appeared as the Queen, excelling in this portrayal. She acted Katharine in Drury Lane productions until the end of the century and re-created the role opposite Kemble's Wolsey in nine Covent Garden presentations from 1806, appearing for the last time in the part on June 29, 1816. William Charles Macready first appeared as Wolsey at Covent Garden on January 15, 1823. He played the Cardinal, again with notable success, in his own production in 1837, with Helen Faucit as Katharine and John Vandenhoff as Henry. In 1847, he was Wolsey again at the Princess' Theatre, opposite Charlotte Cushman's Queen. Samuel Phelps opened his second year at Sadler's Wells (1845) acting Wolsey, at first ending the play with the fall of Wolsey but, later, adding the fourth act. When

Charles Kean produced *Henry VIII* at the Princess' Theatre in 1855, he took advantage of every opportunity for pageant and procession available in the play. He included a fifth act, which had "of late years been entirely omitted," consisting of little more than the christening of Princess Elizabeth. A moving barge and an historically accurate panoramic view of London "as it then appeared" were among the elaborate stage effects which necessitated dropping the curtain for scene changes. This production, in which Kean played Wolsey and his wife, Ellen Tree, Katharine, ran for an unprecedented 100 performances and was reproduced in 1858.

In 1892 Henry Irving mounted *Henry VIII* at the Lyceum Theatre. His cast was superb: Ellen Terry played Katharine; Violet Vanbrugh, Anne; Johnston Forbes-Robertson, Buckingham; William Terriss, the King. Irving's version gave the first three acts practically uncut, but only parts of Act IV. Act V consisted solely of Cranmer's prophecy speech and the christening ceremony. Although this production surpassed Kean's in sumptuous display (the Church of the Grey Friars at Greenwich was exquisitely reproduced) and ran for 203 performances, the cost of the spectacle was even greater than the receipts, discouraging later producers from equaling Irving's extravagance.

However, the tradition of historically accurate dress has remained into the 20th century. With possibly only one exception, Holbein's portrait of the King has been used as the guide for costuming *Henry VIII.* Arthur Bourchier, playing Henry in Beerbohm Tree's 1910 production at His Majesty's, represented a detailed imitation of the picture. This presentation, in three acts, ended with Anne Bullen's coronation. Tree drastically cut the dialogue, but the performance nevertheless lasted four hours, the time largely filled with elaborate processions and the changing of gorgeous settings behind a dropped curtain. Violet Vanbrugh was a successful Katharine, and Tree played Wolsey in this production, which was repeated for the seventh and eighth annual Shakespeare Festivals at His Majesty's Theatre in 1911 and 1912, and four years later presented on the American stage.

Ellen Terry visited Stratford-upon-Avon in 1902 to play Katharine and, in the summer of 1916, Philip Ben Greet's Old Vic company performed *Henry VIII* at the Festival Theatre, with the producer in the role of Wolsey. This production was transferred to the stage of the Old Vic the following September. Two years later, during his second season with the Old Vic, Russell Thorndike played Wolsey opposite Sybil Thorndike's Katharine. The next *Henry VIII* at the Old Vic was in early 1924 with producer Robert Atkins and Ion Swinley as Wolsey and Buckingham, Wilfrid Walter as the King, and Florence Saunders as Katharine. This was followed by a West End production at the Empire Theatre in December 1925. Under Lewis Casson's direction, the play was divided into 13 scenes within 4 acts. The sets were uncluttered, but the splendor of the pageantry was retained most effectively, particularly in the magnificent spectacle of the coronation. Sybil Thorndike's perfectly conceived portrayal of a dignified, heroic Katharine was ably supported by the notable performances of E. Lyall Swete as Wolsey and Norman V. Norman as Henry. The part of the First Serving Man in this production was played by the young Laurence Olivier.

Terence Gray took exception to the traditional dress and decor for *Henry VIII* when he staged the play at the Cambridge Festival Theatre in 1931. His set consisted of an enormous, curved aluminum ramp and the costumes were fashioned after playing-card figures. This production managed to provoke loyal Shakespeareans when, in the christening scene, Gray had the baby, a miniature Queen Elizabeth, thrown into the audience. Tyrone Guthrie first produced *Henry VIII* at Sadler's Wells in November 1933, with Charles Laughton as the King and Flora Robson as Katharine. The first Open Air Theatre (Regent's Park) *Henry VIII* was staged in 1936 and acted by Lyn Harding (King), Baliol Holloway (Wolsey), and Phyllis Neilson-Terry (Katharine). B. Iden Payne directed a Stratford production in 1938 with Miss Neilson-Terry again playing Katharine. Stratford presented another *Henry VIII* under Robert Atkins in 1945 and, in 1949, staged Guthrie's second, and perhaps best, production of the play. On Tanya Moiseiwitsch's expansive permanent set, Guthrie utilized uncolored lighting and quickened the pace of the pageantry. Minor characters were given a dramatic importance never previously realized, while the major roles were acted in the traditional manner. Overinventiveness often marred the production with unnecessary distractions, but, on the whole, Guthrie succeeded.

Michael Benthall's 1958 production of the play preserved the balance between the pageantry and private drama. This Old Vic presentation returned John Gielgud to the stage on Waterloo Road in the role of Wolsey. Edith Evans gave a controlled and properly regal portrait of Katharine and Harry Andrews played Henry. In 1963 there was a Birmingham Repertory Company *Henry VIII,* directed by David Buxton, included in a season of three plays.—M. G.

Bibliography. TEXT: *King Henry VIII,* New Arden Edition, R. A. Foakes, ed., 1957; *King Henry VIII,* New Cambridge Edition, J. C. Maxwell, ed., 1962; James Spedding, "On the Several Shares of Shakespere and Fletcher in the Play of *Henry VIII,*" *Gentleman's Magazine,* XXXIV, 1850; A. C. Partridge, *The Problem of "Henry VIII" Reopened,* 1949; Marco Mincoff, "*Henry VIII* and Fletcher," *Shakespeare Quarterly,* XII, 1961. DATE: New Cambridge Edition. SOURCES: New Cambridge Edition; Geoffrey Bullough, *Narrative and Dramatic Sources of Shakespeare,* Vol. IV, 1962. COMMENT: Edward Dowden, *Shakspere: A Critical Study of His Mind and Art,* 1875; Frank Kermode, "What is Shakespeare's *Henry VIII* About?" *Durham University Journal,* IX, n.s., 1948; E. M. W. Tillyard, "Why Did Shakespeare Write *Henry VIII?*" *Critical Quarterly,* III, 1961. STAGE HISTORY: New Arden Edition; New Cambridge Edition; G. C. D. Odell, *Shakespeare from Betterton to Irving,* 1920; J. C. Trewin, *Shakespeare on the English Stage, 1900–1964,* 1964.

Selected Criticism

SAMUEL JOHNSON. The play of *Henry* the eighth is one of those which still keeps possession of the stage, by the splendour of its pageantry. The coronation about forty years ago drew the people together in multitudes for a great part of the winter. Yet pomp is not the only merit of this play. The meek sorrows and virtuous distress of *Catherine* have furnished some scenes which may be justly numbered among the greatest efforts of tragedy. But the genius of *Shakespeare* comes in and goes out with *Catherine*. Every other part may be easily conceived, and easily written.

Though it is very difficult to decide whether short pieces be genuine or spurious, yet I cannot restrain myself from expressing my suspicion that neither the prologue nor epilogue to this play is the work of *Shakespeare; non vultus, non color*. It appears to me very likely that they were supplied by the friendship or officiousness of *Johnson*, whose manner they will be perhaps found exactly to resemble. There is yet another supposition possible: the prologue and epilogue may have been written after *Shakespeare*'s departure from the stage, upon some accidental revisal of the play, and there will then be reason for imagining that the writer, whoever he was, intended no great kindness to him, this play being recommended by a subtle and covert censure of his other works. There is in *Shakespeare* so much of *fool and fight*,

> the fellow
> In a long motley coat, guarded with yellow,

appears so often in his drama, that I think it not very likely that he would have animadverted so severely on himself. All this, however, must be received as very dubious, since we know not the exact date of this or the other plays, and cannot tell how our authour might have changed his practice or opinions. [*The Plays of William Shakespeare*, 1765.]

G. G. GERVINUS. In the King Henry VIII, the poet had to paint a portrait which must be flattered and must yet be like; he must not shake the moral respect or excite the kingly jealousy of James I, and yet he would not be untrue to history, which presented to his view a repulsive despotic character, not even idemnified by the fearful magnitude of the crime of a Richard III. Shakespeare portrayed him, without misrepresenting or disguising his cruelty, his sensuality, his caprice, his semi-refinement united with natural coarseness, but he kept them in the background and there is great field for an actor between the vague generality with which this portrait is sketched, and the few features of complete individual peculiarity which the poet has admitted; and indeed the character of Henry VIII, originally played by Lowin, and from his conception of it transmitted through Davenant to Betterton, has always been a favourite part for the English actor. His dependence upon flatterers, together with his jealous desire to rule alone; the ease with which he is deceived, together with his resentful bitterness when he sees himself deluded, and his deceitful dissimulation in suppressing malice and revenge; his caprice, together with his impetuosity, his unwieldy clumsy appearance, together with a certain mental refinement; his lack of feeling, together with isolated traits of good-nature; his sensuality under the transparent mask of religion and conscience; his manner, condescending even to vulgarity; all these are so many delicate contrasts, in which the player has to hit the fine line of contact. Held in magic fetters by so great a man as Wolsey, surrounded throughout by devoted instruments, and humored in every wish and every caprice by the most yielding and devoted wife, the king appears as one of the princes who

> kiss obedience,
> So much they love it, but to stubborn spirits
> They swell, and grow as terrible as storms,

and who are implacable when crossed; he is jealous, even to bloody severity, of every threated self-exaltation in a subject, as in Buckingham. He is the slave of his nature, and of all the passion and self-will which belong to it. [*Shakespeare*, 1849–1850; tr. as *Shakespeare Commentaries*, 1863.]

G. WILSON KNIGHT. There is nothing in Shakespeare more remarkable than these three similar falling movements, of Buckingham, Wolsey, and Queen Katharine. The two first conform to the two main types of Shakespearian tragedy involving (i) betrayal and (ii) the power-quest; while the Queen sums all Shakespeare's feminine sympathies. The Tragedies culminating in *Timon of Athens* and *The Tempest* (for man) and *Antony and Cleopatra* and the remaining Final Plays (for woman) have developed the Shakespearian humanism to its limit, though with no severing of Christian contacts. Here we face the limits of even that, purified, humanism . . . .

King Henry is the one king in Shakespeare in whom you cannot dissociate man from office. In Henry VI, Richard II, Richard III, King John and Prince Hal there are clear divergences; while Henry V shows as king an idealized literary heroism as national hero followed by an equally literary bluffness as a private person; nor do the national heroism and the bluffness quite coalesce. Claudius is a baffling example of resolute kingship backed by crime. In the tragedies temporal kingship pales before the advance of spiritual powers; and we have our impractical governors of philosophic insight. King Cymbeline is scarcely a personal study at all. Now Henry VIII shows something of the rough manliness, the tough royal essence, of Coeur de Lion's son, the Bastard (and Richard III, too, in his oration), together with the official lustre of Richard II; and here the identity is always exact. He has, if not spiritual understanding, yet clear spiritual sympathies. He is all Shakespeare's more practical royalty rolled into one, and is thus kingliness personified. But it is an eminently human kingliness. He is neither faultless, nor austere: his is not quite the kingliness in whose name Henry V rejects Falstaff—he has almost as much of Falstaff in him as of Hal—nor has he the remote austerity of Prospero. He is to be aligned more nearly with our humour than with our religious inwardness. He is, like everyone here, religious, but his personality is not subdued to religion, he takes it, as it were, in his stride. [*The Crown of Life*, 1947.]

FRANK KERMODE. . . . one should beware of regarding the play as episodic. It is called *Henry VIII* and it is about Henry VIII. Notoriously, kings were men as well as divine agents. Here is a king susceptible to flattery, to adulterous passions, choleric and extravagant. His rejection of Katharine is influenced by some of those human flaws; but it is not quite unconnected with a proper kingly concern over the health of the state. The result is the tragedy of a good woman, a type well understood, and for which the dramatist had exemplars. Human justice lacks the certainty of its divine counterpart; so, in spite of a fair trial, Buckingham, not without sin, falls. The man who caused this tragedy falls as a result of his treachery in the treatment of the affair of the Queen; he knows very well what the moral of his tragedy is, and urges it on Cromwell at some length. "Fling away ambition," he says, already seeing himself as an example or a Mirror. He was never happy until the fall occurred, for God has so disposed it that the evildoer has that in his own breast which destroys his peace. Here punishment is visited on the offender through the King; he is the agent of the divine retribution. As Wolsey falls in sin, Cranmer rises in virtue, and they clearly represent Popery and the English Church as much as they do great men vicious and virtuous. In his turn, Cranmer falls, and we have a pattern whereby to understand the nature of his tragedy; but there is no need for it; Mercy intervenes, and virtue is saved from such a tragedy by the King himself. The guilt or virtue of the King in respect of these happenings should be judged primarily by their fruits. These are the birth of a great queen and the establishment of the reformed church. It is unthinkable that these should be dismissed as the workings of chance; such a position would be both heterodox and treasonable. The play may be regarded as a late morality, showing the state from which great ones may fall; the manner of their falling, be they Good Queen, Ambitious Prelate, Virtuous Prelate, or merely Great Man; and the part played in their falls for good or ill by a King who, though human, is *ex officio* the deputy of God, and the agent of divine punishment and mercy. ["What is Shakespeare's *Henry VIII* About?" *Durham University Journal*, n.s., IX, 1948.]

IRVING RIBNER. The difference between *Henry VIII* and the earlier Lancastrian plays may be accounted for most readily, I believe, by the general decline in the history play which had taken place by the time that *Henry VIII* was written. The great age of the history play was now over. The weakness of *Henry VIII* results from its failure to embody an over-all consistent philosophical scheme such as makes cohesive unities out of all of Shakespeare's earlier histories, including *King John*. When didactic purpose was abandoned, much of the consistent design and cohesiveness which make for great drama began to disappear. That Fletcher had a hand in the play, although certainly possible, has yet to be definitely established.

What we have in *Henry VIII* is a patriotic pageant, and fortunately the well-preserved stage directions in the folio text give us ample indication of the display and fanfare with which the play was staged. In it Shakespeare almost slavishly follows Holinshed for the first four acts; for his final act he turns to John Foxe's *Acts and Monuments*. He follows his sources with a greater fidelity than he had ever before observed in an English history play, but with a strange unawareness of the basic inconsistencies within his sources, inconsistencies which he carried over into his play and which make his portrait of Wolsey in particular almost incomprehensible. ["The History Play in Decline," *The English History Play in the Age of Shakespeare*, 1957.]

Henry, Prince. See HENRY III.

Henry, Prince of Wales (in *1* and *2 Henry IV*). See HAL.

Henry, prince of **Wales** (1594–1612). The eldest son and heir of James I. A figure of some promise, Henry died at the age of 18 from typhoid fever. As a result of Henry's early demise, his younger brother, the ill-fated Charles I, eventually succeeded to the throne. At an early age Henry revealed a fondness for the theatre, attending performances with his sister Elizabeth and brother Charles at a theatre constructed primarily for their use (the cockpit at court). Henry was also patron of the Admiral's Men, who, from late 1603 until his death, were known as Prince Henry's Men.

Henry of Navarre. Henry IV of France (1553–1610). King of Navarre (1572–1589) and king of France (1589–1610). The founder of the Bourbon line of kings, Henry was one of the greatest rulers in French history. Despite his conversion to Catholicism in 1593, his relations with England were generally warm and friendly, particularly with regard to their common hostility to Spain.

Henry was a patron of scholarship and learning; in 1582 he established a "royal academy" devoted to the study of philosophy and the arts. Navarre's enthusiasm for learning, together with the embassy which his separated wife, MARGUERITE DE VALOIS, made to him in 1578, might have provided the chief historical basis of *Love's Labour's Lost* (see LOVE'S LABOUR'S LOST: *Sources*). Another Shakespearean allusion to Henry is regarded as an important clue in the dating of *The Comedy of Errors* (see COMEDY OF ERRORS: *Date*). In 1599 Henry divorced Marguerite and the following year married Marie de Médicis. Marie bore him six children, one of whom, Henrietta Maria, became the wife of Charles I of England.

Henry's Men. See ADMIRAL'S MEN.

Henryson or **Henderson, Robert** (1425?–?1500). Scottish poet. Henryson, one of the so-called Scottish Chaucerians, is the author of a remarkable sequel to Chaucer's *Troilus and Criseyde* titled *The Testament of Cresseid* (1593). In Henryson's version Cressida is a victim of leprosy and has one last ironic encounter with Troilus. There is no conclusive evidence that Shakespeare knew this version of the legend, but Henryson's poem was generally printed as a sequel to *Troilus and Criseyde* in the 16th-century editions of Chaucer. [Kenneth Muir, *Shakespeare's Sources*, Vol. I, 1957.]

Henry the Sixth, The First Part. See John CROWNE.

Henslowe, Philip (d. 1616). Theatre owner and manager. Philip Henslowe came of a family of Devonshiremen who settled in Sussex. His father was the master of the game in Ashdown Forest and Brill Park. Philip apparently received very little education and until the time of his marriage in the 1570's to a rich widow, Agnes Woodward, he was rather poor. In London papers of 1584–1587 he is mentioned as a "citizen and dyer." From 1587, and probably before that date, he began to acquire interests in theatrical property. From 1593 to 1596 he conducted, through agents, a pawnbroking business.

By 1592 he had been named a groom of the chamber at court, and in 1603 he became a gentleman sewer of the chamber to King James. In 1594 he was financing the sport of bearbaiting on the Bankside, under license by the master of the royal game of

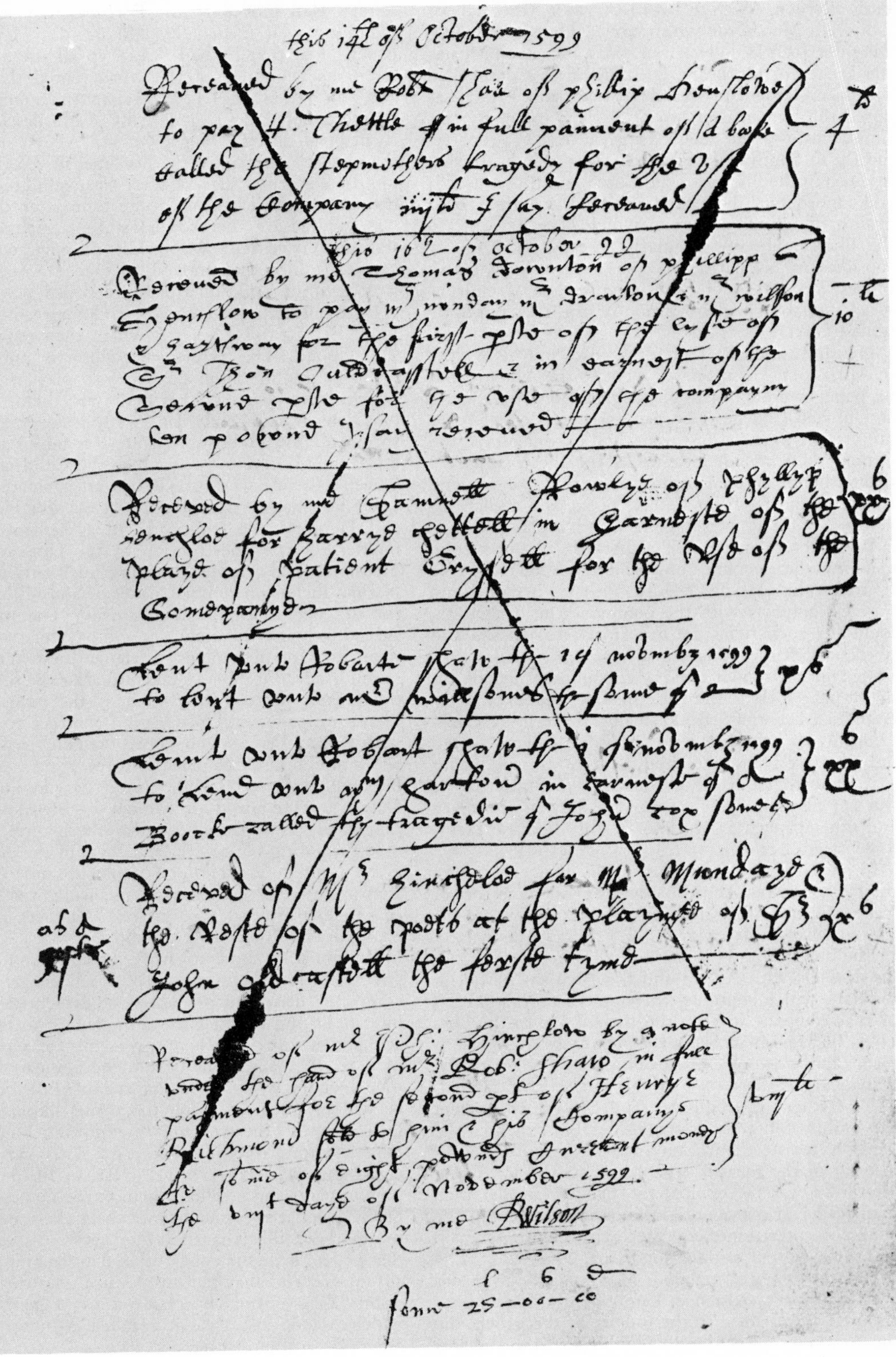

A PAGE FROM HENSLOWE'S DIARY, ONE OF THE MOST IMPORTANT DOCUMENTS OF THE ELIZABETHAN PLAYHOUSES. THIS PAGE CONTAINS A RECORD OF SOME OF HENSLOWE'S FINANCIAL DEALINGS WITH HIS ACTORS AND PLAYWRIGHTS. FOR A TRANSCRIPT SEE APPENDIX. (DULWICH COLLEGE, BY PERMISSION OF THE GOVERNORS)

Paris Garden. With Edward ALLEYN (the famous Admiral's Men actor who married Henslowe's stepdaughter Joan Woodward in 1592) and Jacob MEADE, the keeper of the bears, he more or less controlled the Bear Garden. In 1604 Henslowe and Alleyn secured the joint mastership of Paris Garden. By this time Henslowe had amassed a great deal of property, mostly in Southwark. Records of 1577 indicate that he lived in the liberty of the Clink, and those of 1593 still record him there, "on the bank sid right over against the clink" or prison which gave its name to the liberty. He was regularly assessed at £10 for subsidies in his parish and he held various parish offices: vestryman of St. Saviour's (1607), churchwarden (1608), and governor of the free grammar school (1612).

Henslowe died on January 6, 1616, and his widow in April 1617. His property went to the Alleyns, and his papers were ultimately amalgamated with Alleyn's at Dulwich College. The papers have been of great importance to social historians and chroniclers of the drama: they include title-deeds for theatres; agreements; bonds entered into by companies of players; letters to and from his family, poets, and actors; inventories of costumes; "plots"; and the famous so-called diary, which is not a diary at all but a folio memorandum account book which he kept from 1592 to 1603. The accounts record both his personal and business contacts with the companies he dealt with, including such items as loans made to players and poets, which they themselves wrote, signed, or witnessed in their own hands. The importance of his diary and papers to dramatic history cannot be overemphasized. Bernard Beckerman's *Shakespeare at the Globe* (1962) presents a comparison of plays known only because Henslowe cited them in his papers with plays known from other sources. He finds that of the 113 plays in the performance lists in the diary and other papers, 67 are known only because Henslowe mentions them.

In his earlier years he was mainly concerned with the ROSE THEATRE; he probably also had some sort of interest in the NEWINGTON BUTTS THEATRE, where the CHAMBERLAIN'S MEN played for a short while in 1594. In the autumn of 1594 his diary begins a record of his dealings with Alleyn and the ADMIRAL'S MEN at the Rose which continues through the reorganization of that company in 1597 and their move to the FORTUNE THEATRE in 1600. As the Admiral's Men's landlord, Henslowe took his profits from a share of the daily receipts; he took half the proceeds of the galleries (rather than the outer gate). In return he kept the building in repair, at considerable expense, and paid the fees to the Master of the Revels for the licensing of the theatre. According to W. W. Greg, Henslowe was the company's "banker," rather than their leader or manager. The individual actors of the company entered into contracts with Henslowe, who had the option of terminating them.

The company depended inordinately upon his good will for its existence. Undoubtedly Alleyn contributed a great deal to the morale of the group. To the Admiral's Men Henslowe advanced the sums of money necessary to pay playwrights and tradesmen, and he maintained a running account of his outlay. He occasionally supplied the money necessary for an actor to purchase a share in the company and took his repayment in small installments. After the Admiral's Men moved to the Fortune, they evidently did quite well financially, and in 1604 Henslowe's papers note that he had "caste vp all the acowntes from the beginingе of the world vntell this daye" and "all reconynges consernynge the company in stocke generall descarged & my sealfe descarged to them of al deates." Henslowe and Alleyn shared in the "house" interest of the Fortune; in 1608 the Admiral's company sharers were also admitted to an interest as housekeepers. Some time after the Rose was vacated by the Admiral's Men, Henslowe installed WORCESTER'S MEN. His dealings with that company until they moved, as Queen Anne's Men, in 1604 to the Red Bull are also recorded.

In 1611 Henslowe entered into an agreement with LADY ELIZABETH'S MEN for which they gave him a £500 bond. The agreement, which is not extant, probably required the company to play at a house which Henslowe would provide for them. Initially that house was possibly the Swan theatre, but by the spring of 1613 Henslowe also had acquired an interest in the WHITEFRIARS, at which the Children of the Queen's Revels were playing in amalgamation with Lady Elizabeth's. By the autumn of 1613 Henslowe and Jacob Meade had made an agreement with a builder for the construction of the HOPE THEATRE. Henslowe and Meade also concluded articles with Nathan Field, the nominal leader of Lady Elizabeth's, for the operation of the company. The managers agreed to house the company and pay for costuming them, and for their plays. In return they were to be reimbursed with moneys taken in after the second or third day's performance. One of the items in the Henslowe papers at Dulwich is a contract concluded with Robert Dawes who joined the company in 1614 and bound himself to play for three years as a player in any company Henslowe and Meade indicated; Dawes was required to consent to Henslowe's arrangements over the disposal of the profits as well.

In the spring of 1615 the members of the company drew up their "Articles of Grieuance [and] Oppression against Mr. Hinchlowe," probably for submission to an arbiter such as the lord chamberlain. They charged Henslowe with definite acts of dishonesty in manipulating the company's accounts, and oppressive use of his legal position to his advantage and the company's disadvantage. They also evidently accused him of having cheated them by failing to make an account of sums due them, by taking for repayment of personal loans money from the company's common account, by overcharging them for the costumes he had supplied, by using too many admission collectors at the theatres, and by offering bonuses to outside actors to join his company. They further accused him of having bribed Nathan Field and of buying plays and reselling them to the company at a profit (a letter is extant from Robert Daborne which substantiates this charge). The actors also insisted that he had kept the company in debt to him personally in order to maintain his control over them. The dispute was ultimately resolved by a compromise which Meade and Alleyn reached with the actors after Henslowe's death.

At various times in the past it has been suggested that Henslowe's apparently ruthless business conduct makes him an ideal model for Shakespeare's character Shylock, but the suggestion has generally been rejected by modern scholars. Henslowe's career is not an extraordinary one; it resembles that of many businessmen and self-made men whether Elizabethan or modern. [W. W. Greg, *Henslowe Papers*, 1907; E. K. Chambers, *The Elizabethan Stage*, 1923; *Henslowe's Diary*, R. A. Foakes and R. T. Rickert, eds., 1961.]

Hentzner, Paul (fl. 1600). German traveler. Hentzner visited England, France, and Italy in 1598 and left a record of his travels in his *Itinerarium Germaniae, Galliae, Angliae, et Italiae* (1612). As tutor to a young German nobleman, Hentzner visited with his pupil the outstanding points of interest in England, including the London theatres. His account, which gives an interesting picture of the Elizabethan audience, is written in Latin; the following translation is from W. B. Rye's *England as seen by Foreigners in the Days of Elizabeth and James I* (1865).

> Without the city are some theatres, where English actors represent almost every day comedies and tragedies to very numerous audiences; these are concluded with variety of dances, accompanied by excellent music and excessive applause of those that are present. . . . At these spectacles and everywhere else, the English are constantly smoking the Nicotian weed which in America is called Tobaca —others call it Paetum—and generally in this manner; they have pipes on purpose made of clay, into the farther end of which they put the herb, so dry that it may be rubbed into powder, and lighting it, they draw the smoke into their mouths, which they puff out again through their nostrils, like funnels, along with it plenty of phlegm and defluxion from the head. In these theatres, fruits, such as apples, pears and nuts, according to the season, are carried about to be sold, as well as wine and ale.

Hepburn, Katharine (1909–). American actress. Born in Connecticut, Miss Hepburn made her professional stage debut in Baltimore in 1928. Though best known for her films, she has appeared in a number of notable Shakespearean productions. Her roles include Rosalind in *As You Like It* (New York, 1950); Portia, Katharina, and Isabella (*Measure for Measure*) on the Old Vic company's tour of Australia in 1955; and appearances as Portia, Beatrice, Viola, and Cleopatra at the American Shakespeare Festival Theatre, Stratford, Connecticut, in 1957 and 1960. [*Who's Who in the Theatre*, 1961.]

Heptameron of Civil Discourses. See George Whetstone.

Herald. In *Henry V*, a minor character identified in the play as an English herald. In IV, viii, he brings King Henry two lists, one indicating the 10,000 French that have fallen in battle, the other the 29 English.

Herald. In *King Lear*, a minor character. In V, iii, the Herald summons any man maintaining Edmund a traitor to appear before the third sound of the trumpet. Edgar appears, draws swords with Edmund, and kills him.

heraldry. A legacy of medieval wars when knights rode under blazoned banners, heraldry assumed a new social importance in Tudor times when possession of a coat of arms came to be held as the mark of a gentleman. The Herald's College was given a second charter by Mary Tudor in 1555 (the first was granted in 1483 by Richard III), and it was to this august body that men petitioned for arms instead of simply designing arms for themselves as they had in earlier times. In addition to granting arms, the duties of the heralds included the registration of pedigrees and the supervision of funerals; from the latter they derived a substantial part of their revenue. Headstones and hatchments over tombs bore the escutcheon of the late owner, and the heralds, wearing their traditional tabards (short, sleeveless smocks blazoned with arms), marshaled the procession at a nobleman's funeral and proclaimed the deceased's rank and station at the graveside. Shakespeare referred to this custom in *Coriolanus* (V, vi, 145–146) where the dead Coriolanus is hailed "As the most noble corse that ever herald/ Did follow to his urn."

A 16th-century gentleman's education was not complete unless he knew at least enough about heraldry to blazon his own coat, that is, to describe his armorial bearings in the correct technical language. The escutcheon which bore the arms was usually shield-shaped (occasionally, a woman's arms was in the shape of a diamond). The surface of the escutcheon was known as the field, and its tincture, or color, was the first attribute mentioned in blazoning. Two or more different coats could be borne on one shield by dividing the shield into four or more sections, a process known as quartering. The crest, a figure set above the shield, could be used separately as an emblem on plate, liveries, and the like.

The coat of arms acquired by Shakespeare for his father had simplicity:

> This sh[ield] or [cote of] Arms, viz. Gould, on a Bend Sables, a Speare of the first steeled argent. And for his creast or cognizaunce a falcon his winges displayed Argent standing on a wrethe of his coullers: suppo[rting] a Speare Gould steeled as aforesaid sett vppon a helmett with mantelles & tasselles as hath ben accustomed and doth more playnely appeare depicted on this margent:

Translated from the language of heraldry, the shield was described as gold with a black band crossing it diagonally from top right to bottom left (the right and left sides being determined by the wearer, not the observer), and upon the black band a gold spear with a silver tip. Above the shield is a silver wreath upon which is perched a silver falcon holding an upright gold spear in one of his pinions.

A certain amount of heraldic vocabulary is found in Shakespeare's plays. A play on the word "difference," which in heraldry refers to a marking which distinguishes the arms of a son or collateral relative from those of the main branch of the family, occurs in *Much Ado About Nothing* (I, i, 68–70). Here, Beatrice is discussing Benedick and remarks, "if he have wit enough to keep himself warm, let him bear it for a difference between himself and his horse . . ."

More armorial puns occur in the opening scene of *The Merry Wives of Windsor*. Shallow's pride in his 300-year-old coat of arms with its bearing of a dozen white luces (fresh-water fish often used in heraldry) provokes Parson Evans' punning taunt:

> The dozen white louses do become an old coat well; it agrees well, passant; it is a familiar beast to man, and signifies love. (I, i, 19–21)

Shakespeare frequently used the term "gules," the heraldic term for red, when describing blood. Timon advises Alcibiades "With man's blood paint the ground, gules, gules." (*Timon of Athens*, IV, iii,

59.) And in *Hamlet* (II, ii, 478–479), the First Player, describing the slaughtered Pyrrhus, cries, "head to foot/ Now is he total gules." [Oswald Barron, "Heraldry," *Shakespeare's England*, 1916.]

Herbert, Sir **Henry** (1595–1673). Master of the Revels from 1623 to 1642. A member of a distinguished family, Herbert was a younger brother of the philosopher Lord Herbert of Cherbury (1583–1648) and of the poet George Herbert (1593–1633). He was also a relative of William Herbert, earl of Pembroke, through whom he obtained a court appointment in 1622 as a servant of King James. He was knighted by the king in 1623, and in that same year he bought the office of MASTER OF THE REVELS from Sir John Astley (or Ashley). He continued in the post, claiming the right to license every kind of public entertainment, until the closing of the theatres. Although he did not succeed in extending his sway over all public entertainment, Herbert's major work involved the arrangement of dramatic performances at court and in licensing plays (see CENSORSHIP) for the public theatres; for the latter he exacted a fee of £2 for every new play and £1 for every revival of an old play. He carefully checked all plays that were submitted to him, censoring "all prophaneness, oathes, ribaldry and matters reflecting piety and the present government."

During this period Herbert kept a record of his activities in his office-book, the most important source of information on the theatre of the period. The office-book contained dated entries of plays licensed by him and plays and other entertainment which he arranged for court performances. The book also details valuable information about the relationship between the players and the government. For example, in 1624 the King's Men had apparently attempted to act in an unlicensed play, *The Spanish Viceroy*. Sir Henry's threatened punishment for this offense must have been severe indeed, for the office-book records the following abject apology from the players:

> To Sir Henry Herbert, K^t. master of his Maties Revels.
>
> After our humble servise remembered unto your good worship, Whereas not long since we acted a play called *The Spanishe Viceroy*, not being licensed under your worships hande, nor allowd of: wee doe confess and herby acknowledge that wee have offended, and that it is in your power to punishe this offense, and are very sorry for it; and doe likewise promise herby that wee will not act any play without your hand or substituts hereafter, nor doe any thinge that may prejudice the authority of your office.

The office-book is also a valuable source for determining the identity of the players in the various companies, as in the following list from a patent issued to the King's Men in 1625:

John Hemings
Henry Coudall
John Lowen
Joseph Taylor
Richard Robinson
Robert Benefeild
John Shanck
William Rowley
John Rice
Elliart Swanston
George Birch
Richard Sharpe
And *Thomas Pollard*

The original manuscript of the office-book is lost, but many extracts from it were printed by Malone and Chalmers. These were collected and published by Joseph Quincy Adams as *The Dramatic Records of Sir Henry Herbert* (1917).

Herbert himself lived on into the Restoration period, resuming his office of Master of the Revels. However, he was never able to exert his former authority over the Restoration acting companies. By the authority of Charles II, Thomas KILLIGREW and William DAVENANT received permission to license their own plays, and Herbert, after a series of numerous unsuccessful court petitions, abandoned the office to two of his deputies. [G. E. Bentley, *The Jacobean and Caroline Stage*, 5 vols., 1941–1956.]

Herbert, Mary. See Mary Herbert, countess of PEMBROKE.

Herbert, Philip. See Philip Herbert, 4th earl of PEMBROKE.

Herbert, Sir **Walter.** Son of William Herbert, earl of Pembroke, who appears in *3 Henry VI*. In *Richard III*, Sir Walter, "a renowned soldier," supports Richmond at Bosworth Field.

Herbert, William. See William Herbert, 3rd earl of PEMBROKE.

Herder, Johann Gottfried von (1744–1803). German poet and critic. Born in East Prussia, Herder studied at the University of Königsberg, where he became acquainted with Immanuel Kant. Herder's interest in legends and folk literature influenced the German Romantics.

In his critical works, *Fragmente über die neuere deutsche Literatur* (1767) and *Kritische Wälder* (1769), Herder is concerned with the relation of poetry to race and environment, and in other questions which were to become central in Romantic criticism. A leader of the *Sturm und Drang* movement, Herder wished to free German literature from the influence of France and classical antiquity. To Herder, Shakespeare was essentially a folk poet with roots in the Middle Ages. More interested in Shakespeare as lyric poet than as playwright, Herder conveyed his enthusiasm for Shakespeare to the young Goethe, whom he met at Strasbourg in 1771.

Hermia. In *A Midsummer Night's Dream*, the willful daughter of Egeus. Hermia defies her father's command that she marry Demetrius, and runs off with Lysander. When Puck misapplies his magic, both Demetrius and Lysander fall in love with Helena. The spell is undone, however, and Hermia marries Lysander.

Hermione. In *The Winter's Tale*, the Queen of Sicilia, falsely accused of adultery by her husband, Leontes. The gaiety and wit which Hermione displays in the opening scene are permanently destroyed by Leontes' folly, but nothing can alter the profounder aspects of her personality. The majesty of her bearing lends a classical quality to her ordeal and evokes less pity than admiration. During her trial, her serene dignity not only remains intact but is enhanced by the intensity and ferocity of her husband's accusations. Hermione's speech in her own defense (III, ii) is an eloquently restrained expression of the injustice of the gross charges against her. The beauty of her character is such that the audience is unconsciously prepared to accept the symbolic, semidivine status attributed to her by Paulina and dramatically realized through her miraculous "resurrection" in the statue scene (V, iii).

Hero. In *Much Ado About Nothing*, daughter of Leonato and a foil to her cousin Beatrice. Hero is described by Benedick as "too low for a high praise, too brown for a fair praise, and too little for a great praise," or briefly, "Leonato's short daughter." After her own unspectacular betrothal to Claudio, the modest Hero is a willing accomplice in Don Pedro's innocent conspiracy to bring about a marriage between Beatrice and Benedick. However, she becomes the victim of Don John's vicious intrigue and is humiliated by Claudio, who denounces her before the wedding assembly as "an approved wanton." Hero's innocence receives support from Friar Francis and, when the accusation is proved false, she marries the repentant Claudio. At the play's end, it is Hero who produces the evidence of Beatrice's affection for Benedick by presenting a poem stolen from her cousin's pocket.

Her or **His Majesty's Theatre.** London playhouse. It was opened by Herbert Beerbohm TREE in 1897, at which time it was known as Her Majesty's. For the next two decades, under Tree's leadership, the theatre was the scene of a number of brilliant Shakespearean productions, including *Julius Caesar* (1898), *King John* (1899), *A Midsummer Night's Dream* (1900), *Henry VIII* (1910), and *Macbeth* (1911), all marked by elaborate and extravagant pageantry. After Tree's departure in 1915 His Majesty's became less well known for Shakespearean productions and was increasingly used for contemporary drama. In 1916, however, John Martin-Harvey produced *Richard III*, *The Taming of the Shrew*, *Hamlet*, and *Henry V* during a notable engagement.

Hertford's Men. Acting company under the patronage of Edward Seymour (1539–1621), earl of Hertford. A rather obscure group, Hertford's Men are mentioned traveling in the provinces from 1582 to 1591. In 1591 they entertained Queen Elizabeth at Elvetham, one of Hertford's mansions, on her progress. The queen's visit had political overtones, for Hertford's first wife, whom he had married against the queen's will, had been Lady Catherine Grey, the heiress to Elizabeth's throne under the terms of Henry VIII's will; Elizabeth's visit was the occasion for a reconciliation. Hertford's Men took part in the elaborate entertainment offered the queen and incidentally earned an appearance at court, their only one, in January 1592. The incident, according to E. K. Chambers, could have been the source of the episode of the play within a play in *A Midsummer Night's Dream*, with Bottom and his fellows satirizing Hertford's Men. See A MIDSUMMER NIGHT'S DREAM: *Comment*.

In 1595 Hertford was in disgrace again. That circumstance and a serious visitation of the plague in 1592–1594 probably meant the demise of the acting company. From 1596 to 1602, a provincial group calling themselves Hertford's Men appears intermittently in the records. They gave one performance at court in January 1603. After that they continued to be active for a period in the provinces. [E. K. Chambers, *The Elizabethan Stage*, 1923.]

Heseltine, Philip ("Peter Warlock"). See MUSIC BASED ON SHAKESPEARE: *20th century*.

Hesketh, Sir **Thomas.** See William SHAKESHAFTE.

Hewlands. See ANNE HATHAWAY'S COTTAGE.

Heyes, Thomas. See Thomas HAYES.

Heywood, Thomas (c. 1570–1641). Dramatist and actor. Educated at Cambridge, where he acquired an interest in the drama and a fairly extensive knowledge of the classics, Heywood is mentioned in Philip Henslowe's diary in 1596 as receiving an advance payment for a play. In 1598 he bound himself to play exclusively in Henslowe's theatre for a period of two years. His career as an actor apparently lasted until 1619. Most of this time was spent with Worcester's (Queen Anne's) Men. According to his own calculation he had a hand, "or at least a main finger," in some 220 plays. His dramatic output ranges from elaborate dramatizations of classical myth to realistic portraits of the Elizabethan middle class.

Taken together, Heywood's *The Golden Age* (c. 1611), *The Silver Age* (c. 1612), *The Brazen Age* (c. 1613), and *The Iron Age* (c. 1613) represent an extraordinary attempt to dramatize the major elements of Greek mythology up to the Trojan War. *The Iron Age* reveals a number of similarities with *Troilus and Cressida* and there is one scene in Heywood's play which appears to be directly borrowed from *Hamlet*. This occurs when the ghost of Agamemnon appears to his son, Orestes, but is not perceived by Clytemnestra, the mother of Orestes, who is present—a situation clearly derived from the "closet scene" in *Hamlet* (III, iv).

Other plays of Heywood reveal frequent borrowing from Shakespeare. His *The Rape of Lucrece* (1608) was an attempt to capitalize on the popularity of Shakespeare's poem. His *English Traveler* (1632) is indebted to *Macbeth*, and his other plays are sprinkled with verbal echoes of Shakespeare. If, as seems highly probable, Heywood is the "T. H." who wrote *Oenone and Paris* (1594), he is also the first and closest imitator of *Venus and Adonis*.

Heywood's finest drama is *A Woman Killed With Kindness* (1603), an excellent example of the genre known as "domestic tragedy." Dealing with the theme of marital infidelity, it bears an interesting contrast to *Othello*. It has nothing like the tragic intensity and power of the latter play, but it does display enough merit to justify, at least partially, Charles Lamb's characterization of Heywood as "a sort of prose Shakespeare."

Besides his plays, Heywood wrote many nondramatic compositions. His APOLOGIE FOR ACTORS (1612) is, in Tucker Brooke's words, "one of the most successful apologias in the language." His long poem *Troia Britannica or Great Britain's Troy* (1609) is a lively account of the story of Troy with frequent digressions on English history. His *Hierarchy of the Blessed Angels* (1635) includes a brief reference to recent English poets who suffered from having their first names shortened. Among the group is "Mellifluous *Shake-speare*, whose inchanting Quill/ Commanded Mirth or Passion, was but *Will*." [F. S. Boas, *Thomas Heywood*, 1950.]

Hiccox Family. Natives of Stratford and the surrounding region. Thomas and Lewis Hiccox were tenants of the land in Old Stratford purchased by Shakespeare in 1603. The names were common in the area, thus making it difficult to establish identification. Thomas was probably the Thomas Hiccox (d. 1607) described as a husbandman of Welcombe. Another Thomas Hiccox (d. 1611) occupied a house in Henley Street. Lewis Hiccox (d. 1627) was apparently the same man who in 1603 opened an inn in Henley Street, on the site of what was probably one of the two houses owned by John Shakespeare. In 1642 the inn was known as "The Maidenhead" and was located next door to the building known as the "birthplace." [Mark Eccles, *Shakespeare in Warwickshire*, 1961.]

Higford, Henry (fl. 1566–1578). Steward of Stratford from 1566 to 1570. In 1573 he sued John Shakespeare for a debt of £30. By 1578 he had still not been paid and revived his suit. It is known that shortly thereafter Shakespeare mortgaged some of his wife's property, possibly to pay Higford.

highways subscription. A collection taken up in Stratford in 1611 to pay the costs of prosecuting a bill in parliament for the repairing of Stratford highways. Shakespeare's name appeared among a list of 72 prominent citizens of Stratford who agreed to pay the subscription. Shakespeare's name was not in the regular list, but in the right-hand margin, which suggests that he might have been in London when the list was originally drawn up. The relevant sections are as follows:

> Wednesdaye the xj[th] of September, 1611. Colected towardes the charge of prosecutyng the Bill in parliament for the better Repayre of the highe waies and amendinge diuers defectes in the Statutes alredy made.
> of m[r] Johne Smithe
> of m[r] William wyatt   M[r] Willia shacksper
> of m[r] Henry walker

[B. Roland Lewis, *The Shakespeare Documents*, 1940.]

Hill, Aaron (1685–1750). Dramatist, editor, and poet. A prolific, if generally undistinguished, writer, Hill is best known for his interesting correspondence with Alexander Pope and others. His life, however, was devoted to the stage. In addition to writing a number of plays he acted as stage manager at the Drury Lane and Haymarket theatres. Hill's adaptations included a version (1723) of *Henry V* in which he added another female character in order to complicate the courtship of Henry and Katharine. See ADAPTATIONS. [C. B. Hogan, *Shakespeare in the Theatre, 1701–1800*, 2 vols., 1952, 1957.]

Hilliard, Nicholas (1537–1619). Foremost miniature painter of his day. Hilliard began as a goldsmith, but his skill in painting miniatures soon brought him to the attention of Queen Elizabeth, who engaged him as her personal goldsmith and limner. He retained the post under James I. His miniatures include four portraits of the queen, as well as portraits of Sir Philip Sidney, Sir Francis Drake, Edward de Vere, 17th earl of Oxford, and of a number of other well-known figures of the time. One of his best-known miniatures is his "Portrait of a Young Man Leaning Against a Tree." Leslie Hotson believes that the unidentified figure in the portrait is William HATCLIFFE, whom he takes to be the Mr. W. H. and Fair Youth of the *Sonnets*. The basis of his argument is that Sonnet 16 makes a reference to the Fair Youth's "painted counterfeit" by "this Time's pencil." Hotson argues that "this Time's pencil" is a reference to Hilliard. A miniature portrait of Shakespeare has been attributed to Hilliard. See Sir William SOMERVILLE. [Leslie Hotson, *Mr. W. H.*, 1964.]

Hilton, John (1599–1657). Composer and organist. It is recorded that in 1628 Hilton served as parish clerk and organist of St. Margaret's, Westminster. In addition to composing church music and fancies for viols, he edited *Catch that Catch Can* (1652), a collection of catches, including several of his own, which is credited with having initiated the vogue of the catch in England. For the lyric "What shall he have that killed the deer?" in *As You Like It* (IV, ii, 11–19), he composed a catch for men's voices.

Hinman, Charlton K. (1911–). American scholar, professor of English at the University of Kansas. Hinman has specialized in the collation of the First Folio texts, inventing for that purpose a machine which collates texts mechanically. Preliminary reports have appeared in various bibliographical journals and the final results in *The Printing and Proof-Reading of the First Folio of Shakespeare* (2 vols., 1963). Hinman is also editing, with new introductions, a reissue of the *Shakespeare's Quartos in Collotype Facsimile*. See COMPOSITOR; FIRST FOLIO.

Hippolyta. In ancient Greek legend, an Amazon queen, attacked by Attica and defeated with her Amazons by Theseus, who took her as his concubine. In *A Midsummer Night's Dream*, Hippolyta is betrothed to Theseus, Duke of Athens. In I, i, she cheers her impatient fiancé by reminding him that "Four nights will quickly dream away the time." As a member of the court subjected to the performance of "Pyramus and Thisby," Hippolyta engages in the general banter at the actors' expense. In *The Two Noble Kinsmen*, she is Theseus' bride. Their wedding celebration is interrupted by the appearance of three Queens who, with Hippolyta's aid, persuade Theseus to avenge them against King Creon of Thebes. Later Hippolyta implores her husband to spare the lives of Arcite and Palamon, who are rivals for the hand of her sister, Emilia.

hired men. Members of 16th- and 17th-century acting companies who were neither actor-sharers (see SHARERS) nor boy apprentices. The hired men included the musicians; actors hired by the week and paid a wage; the TIREMAN, or wardrobe-keeper; the book-keeper, or prompter; the stage-keeper, who moved properties and swept the stage; callboys, who communicated to the actors the orders of the book-keepers for men, properties, or machines. All the hired men were available to perform as supers except the book-keeper, who, as seen from the vantage of modern stagecraft, must have been a most important member of the company. See BOOK-KEEPER.

In the 1821 edition of Nicholas Rowe's biography (1709) of Shakespeare, Edmund Malone records the stage tradition that Shakespeare began his theatrical career as a callboy, or prompter's attendant, who was responsible for notifying the players of their entrance cues. The tradition was first related by a "Mr. Dowdall" in 1693, who recalled his visit to Stratford and remembered being told that Shakespeare ran away to London, "and there was Rec[d] Into the playhouse as a serviture." Nicholas Rowe records a similar tradition, that is, that Shakespeare "made his first acquaintance in the playhouse. He was received into the company then in being, at first in a very mean rank . . . ." An anonymous manuscript note discovered by J. O. Halliwell-Phillipps in the Edinburgh University library, dated c. 1748, attributes to William Davenant a story about Shakespeare as an attendant who took care of the horses belonging to fashionable members of the theatre audience, much as a modern carpark or garage attendant sees to motor vehicles:

> Shakespear, when he first came from the country to the play-house, was not admitted to act; but as it was then the custom for all the people of fashion to come on horseback to entertainments of all kinds, it was Shakespear's employment for a time, with several other poor boys belonging to the company, to hold the horses and take care of them during the representation;—by his dexterity and care he soon got a good deal of business in this way, and was personally known to most of the quality that frequented the house, insomuch that, being obliged, before he was taken into a higher and more honorable employment within doors, to train up boys to assist him, it became long afterwards a usual way among them to recommend themselves by saying that they were Shakespear's boys.

A list of the hired men of the King's Men is given in a protection from arrest issued by the Master of the Revels in 1624. The list included all but the apprentices and principal actor-sharers at that date. The nature of the offense which warranted such a protection is tantalizingly unknown, but it probably had something to do with anti-Spanish plays which the King's Men had given:

> Theise are to Certefie you That Edward Knight, William Pattrick, William Chambers, Ambrose Byland, Henry Wilson, Jeffery Collins, William Sanders, Nicholas Vnderhill, Henry Clay, George Vernon, Roberte Pallant, Thomas Tuckfeild, Roberte Clarke, [George Rickner *del.*], John Rhodes, William Mago, [and *del.*] Anthony Knight, [in the margin: and Edward Ashborne, Will: Carver, Allexander Bullard, William Toyer, William Gascoyne] are all imployed by the Kinges Maties servantes in theire quallity of Playinge as Musitions and other necessary attendantes, And are att all tymes and howers to bee readie with theire best endevo^rs^ to doe his Maties service (dureinge the time of the Revells) Jn Which tyme they nor any of them are to bee arested, or deteyned vnder arest, imprisoned, Press'd for Souldiers or any other molestacon Whereby they may bee hindered from doeing his Maties service, Without leaue firste had and obteyned of the Lo^r^: Chamberlyne of his Maties most hono^ble^ houshold, or of the Maiester of his Maties Revells. And if any shall presume to interrupt or deteyne them or any of them after notice hereof given by this my Certificate hee is to aunswere itt att his vtmost p[er]ill. Given att his Maties Office of the Revells vnder my hand and Seale the xxvij^th^ day of Decemb^r^. 1624.
>
> H. Herbert
>
> To all Mayo^rs^, Sheriffes, Justices of the Peace, Bayleiffes, Constables, knight Ma^r^shalls men, and all other his Maties Officer^s^ to whom it may or shall apperteyne.

Of the above, Edward or Anthony Knight was the group's book-keeper, John Rhodes was the tireman, or wardrobe-keeper; William Gascoigne was a stagehand; Henry Wilson and William Toyer were musicians. George Vernon later became a sharer; Robbert Pallant, Thomas Tuckfield, Henry Clay, William Patrick, William Mago, and Nicholas Underhill are all traceable as actors. Of the rest, there is no indication whether they were musicians, actors, or stagehands, but all were probably available to take minor parts on occasion.

The status of a hired man, or hireling, as they were also called, was not high. Their salaries, paid for from the common stock of the company, do not seem to have varied much over the years from the 6s. per week they received in 1579, as noted below by Gosson; in 1597, manager Philip Henslowe paid hired men (under contract to him specifically) either 5s., 6s. 8d., or 8s. per week; they were required to sign a contract for a minimum of two years' service and had to post a bond of £40 as a guarantee. The King's Men, in 1635, account for £3 spent weekly on hired journeymen, boys, music, and lights, over the other expenses they had to meet for costumes and plays.

Stephen Gosson, in *The Schoole of Abuse, Containing a pleasaunt inuective against Poets, Pipers, Plaiers, Iesters and such like Caterpillers of a Commonwelth* . . . (pub. 1579), inveighed against the airs assumed by the hired men, who dressed in elaborate costume and paraded themselves about. E. K. Chambers suggests that such practice was in the nature of advertisement for theatrical activities and that the practice of wearing apparel belonging to the acting company outside the theatre was no longer permitted by 1615. In any case, Gosson is a source of information both about the Puritan disgust with the stage and the practices of the stage:

> Ouerlashing in apparel is so common a fault, that the very hyerlings of some of our players, which stand at reuersion of vi.s by the weeke, iet vnder gentlemens noses in sutes of silke, exercising themselues too prating on the stage, and common scoffing when they come abrode, where they looke askance ouer the shoulder at euery man, of whom the Sunday before they begged an almes.

Most of the hired men could be counted on to act minor roles or be supernumeraries; they made up the armies in battle scenes and the crowds collected for every sort of occasion. Some of them were the "gatherers," or collectors, of admission fees at the various entrances to the playhouse and galleries. They also formed the backstage crews and supplied sound effects. At the cue of "thunder," for example, some of the hired men rolled an iron bullet down an inclined wooden trough; a "thunder-clap" meant someone had to give a shove to a barrel half-filled with stones. [E. K. Chambers, *The Elizabethan Stage*, 1923; W. J. Lawrence, *Pre-Restoration Stage Studies*, 1927; G. E. Bentley, *The Jacobean and Caroline Stage*, 5 vols., 1941–1956; John Cranford Adams, *The Globe Playhouse*, 1942.]

His Majesty's Theatre. See HER MAJESTY'S THEATRE.

Histoires Tragiques. See François de BELLEFOREST.

Historia Histrionica. See James WRIGHT.

Historia Regum Britanniae. See GEOFFREY OF MONMOUTH.

historical criticism. A critical movement which seeks to place Shakespeare in his own time and to see his plays as the expressions of the literary, philosophical, ethical, and dramatic traditions, beliefs, and conventions of the Elizabethan age. It is a critical mode closely related to and reliant on scholarly research and for that reason it remains, with various modifications, the basic critical approach of most American and many English scholars. The movement began in the early part of the 20th century as a "realist" reaction against the excesses of Romantic and Victorian criticism which had assumed that there was a psychological consistency to the presentation of character in Shakespearean drama (see CHARACTER CRITICISM). This approach had achieved its profoundest expression in A. C. Bradley's *Shakespearean Tragedy* (1904), a work which left its admirers with the faintly despairing sensation that the last word had been said.

In countering the approaches of their predecessors, the historical critics, led by E. E. Stoll and Levin L. Schücking, began their assault on the tendency to mistake art for life. They argued that, although Shakespeare was a universal genius, he was also a practicing Elizabethan-Jacobean playwright with an audience to please and a dramatic tradition to conform to (see CRITICISM—20TH CENTURY). They called attention to the conditions and conventions of the Elizabethan theatre in an attempt to solve some famous 19th-century critical dilemmas, such as Iago's apparent lack of motivation (see IAGO) and Lear's division of his kingdom. They prided themselves on the epithets "realist" and "hard-boiled," but did not attempt to rationalize every inconsistency in the plays; rather, they recognized in those "irrational" elements the hand of a busy, often harassed "artificer," who knew that such inconsistencies would never be noticed in a theatre.

From a focus on dramatic convention, the historical critics expanded their view to relate the philosophical and social commonplaces of the age to Shakespeare. Thus Hardin Craig's *The Enchanted Glass* (1936) and E. M. W. Tillyard's *The Elizabethan World Picture* (1943) presented to the modern reader the Elizabethan view of the universe as an ordered, harmonious, hierarchical structure; and Theodore Spencer's *Shakespeare and the Nature of Man* (1942) demonstrated how this world view operated in Shakespeare's plays. Similar studies of Elizabethan psychology, theology, language, and social attitudes have endeavored, in Stoll's words, "to ascertain . . . the author's intention, and to gauge and measure the forces and tendencies of his time."

Despite its endorsement by scholars, historical criticism has been less influential than its chief rival inside and outside the academy—the so-called new criticism. The new critics argue that historical criticism is flawed by its concentration on the specifically Elizabethan character of the work to the exclusion of its universal character. (Doubtless many new critics would add that the attempt to discover "the author's intention" is based on a naïve misconception of the nature of literature.) The result of the exchange between these two schools—exemplified by Cleanth Brooks' essay on *Macbeth*, "The Naked Babe and the Cloak of Manliness" in *The Well-Wrought Urn* (1947); Helen Gardner's "A Reply to Cleanth Brooks" (1953); and O. J. Campbell's "Shakespeare and the New Critics" (1948)—has been beneficial. It has fostered a greater awareness among its various practitioners that no one particular critical approach can exhaust the infinite possibilities of Shakespearean drama.

Beyond the polemics, however, remains the substantial achievement of historical criticism. It consists of a reconstruction of Shakespeare's age, its values and attitudes, and Shakespeare's response to those forces. [Robert Ornstein, "Historical Criticism and the Interpretation of Shakespeare," *Shakespeare Quarterly*, X, 1959.]

History of King Lear, The. See Nahum TATE.

History of King Richard the Second, The. See Nahum TATE.

History of King Richard III, The. See Thomas MORE.

Histriomastix. See WAR OF THE THEATRES.

Histrio-mastix, The Players Scourge. See William PRYNNE.

Hoby, Sir Edward (1560–1617). Diplomat. The eldest son of Sir Thomas Hoby, the translator of Castiglione's *Courtier* (*Il Cortegiano*), Hoby married a daughter of Henry Carey, Lord Hunsdon, the patron of Shakespeare's company, the Chamberlain's Men. On December 7, 1595 Hoby wrote to Sir Robert Cecil inviting him to attend a private performance of a play about "K. Richard." The play in question is generally thought to be either *Richard III* or *Richard II:*

> Sir, findinge that you wer not convenientlie to be at London to morrow night I am bold to send to knowe whether Teusdaie (Dec. 9) may be anie more in your grace to visit poore Channon rowe where as late as it shal please you a gate for your supper shal be open: & K. Richard present himselfe to your vewe.

Hoby, Sir Thomas. See THE COURTIER.

Hodges, William (1744–1797). Artist and painter for the theatre. Hodges was an errand boy in London when he came to the attention of Richard Wilson (1714–1782), a member of the Royal Academy who specialized in classical landscape. He absorbed his patron's formulae and became a scene painter at the Drury Lane. He also served as staff artist and draftsman on Captain James Cook's second expedition to the Pacific (1772–1775).

Hodges contributed two paintings to BOYDELL'S SHAKESPEARE GALLERY: "Portia's Garden" and "Jaques and the Wounded Stag." They are primarily landscape pieces, scarcely disturbed by the presence of Shakespearean characters. [W. M. Merchant, *Shakespeare and the Artist*, 1959.]

Hoefnagel map. A map of London valuable as a source of information about the position and shape of early Elizabethan theatres. (See ENGRAVINGS OF LONDON.) The map was included in *Civitates Orbis Terrarum*, a collection of maps published in 1572. The Hoefnagel map derives its name from the unverified assumption that it was drawn by a German mapmaker, Georg Hoefnagel. It presents an unusually detailed picture of London, but its accuracy, at least in reference to Southwark, has been questioned. It served as the basis for a number of later maps including that of Ralph AGAS. [I. A. Shapiro, "The Bankside Theatres: Early Engravings," *Shakespeare Survey 1*, 1948.]

Hofstra College Shakespeare Festival. A dramatic festival held annually at Hofstra College, Hempstead, Long Island. It was inaugurated in 1950 on a unique replica of an Elizabethan stage. Constructed with student aid, the stage was based on the dimensions of the Globe as set forth by John Cranford Adams in *The Globe Playhouse* (1942). It was assembled each spring in the gymnasium until a new playhouse was erected in 1958. Varicolored, diamond-shaped insets ornament the pillars supporting the "heavens"; inner and upper stages are hung with tapestries; the half-timbered stage wall resembles an Elizabethan house. The structure allows scenes to follow each other without interruption, as in Shakespeare's theatre. Dr. Bernard Beckerman, formerly chairman of the college drama department, directs the plays, which demonstrate the advantage of presenting Shakespeare's plays on the type of stage for which they were written. Among his outstanding productions have been *1 Henry IV*, *Twelfth Night*, and *Romeo and Juliet*, with imaginative use of the three main playing areas. The week-long events of the spring festival include, in addition to the play, lectures, symposia, concerts, demonstration scenes, and early Tudor plays. Other productions have included *The Merry Wives of Windsor* and *Hamlet*, in which William Hutt of Stratford, Canada, appeared as guest star.—A. G.

Hogarth, William (1697–1764). Engraver, painter, and social satirist. Hogarth's gift for vigorous portrayal of the contemporary scene led him to create the series of engravings for which he is best known: *The Harlot's Progress* (1731), *The Rake's Progress* (1735), and *Marriage à la Mode* (1745). Their moral purpose in depicting society's progressive moral decay conformed in a large measure with contemporary official ideas of the purpose of art. Hogarth's personal talents and interests are characterized by a revolutionary truthfulness and immediacy of expression which were then also becoming increasingly evident in the theatre's more naturalistic style of staging. This new concept had come to dominate theatrical practice, largely through the influence of David Garrick. The temperamental sympathy between Hogarth and Garrick probably contributed to the quality of the artist's portrait of "Garrick as Richard III," produced sometime between 1742 and 1746, which is considered one of the finest theatre portraits painted in England.

The novel attention Hogarth pays to the individual characteristics and gestures of his subject makes his earlier drawing of "Falstaff examining his troops" (c. 1728) important. For the first time a Shakespearean character is drawn as if he were a real person in a real world; yet the sketch, a swift and vivid presentation of a single dramatic moment, cannot be separated from the stage which gives it life.

Hogarth's work marks a new impulse in illustration of the plays: the full interplay of theater and subject picture. His Shakespearean studies, however, are few. Paintings he contributed to the decoration of Vauxhall Gardens are known chiefly through prints, but "A Scene from *The Tempest*," still extant, may be one of the original pictures. [W. M. Merchant, *Shakespeare and the Artist*, 1959.]

Holinshed, Raphael (d. c. 1580). Chronicler. Holinshed began his career as a translator for a London publisher, Reginald Wolfe (d. 1573). He was soon given the task of compiling and editing for Wolfe a proposed history of the world ranging from the time of the Flood to the reign of Queen Elizabeth. The ambitious project was never realized, but a portion of the work, limited to England, Scotland, and Ireland, was published in 1577 as *The firste volume of the chronicles of England, Scotlande and Irelande . . . conteyning the description and chronicles of England from the first inhabiting unto the Conquest* . . . . In addition to a history of each nation, the work included a "description" or geographical and social survey for each of the three countries. The "description" of England was written for Holinshed by William HARRISON and provides an invaluable source of information about the England of Shakespeare's time.

Holinshed's *Chronicles*, as the work is now known, was reprinted and enlarged in 1587. This second edition was the one used by Shakespeare as one of the major sources of his English history plays. Shakespeare's indebtedness to Holinshed is well known. Although for his Henry VI plays the dramatist relied more heavily on the *Chronicles* of Edward Halle, Holinshed remains the principal source of the history plays as a whole as well as for one of his greatest tragedies, *Macbeth*. Shakespeare also used Holinshed for parts of *King Lear* and *Cymbeline*. The *Chronicles* stand with North's translation of Plutarch's *Lives* as the two greatest sources of Shakespeare's plays. For Shakespeare's use of Holinshed see the *Sources* section of the individual history plays. [*Holinshed's Chronicle as Used in Shakespeare's Plays*, Allardyce and Josephine Nicoll, eds., 1927.]

Holland, Hugh (d. 1633). Poet. Educated at Cambridge, Holland traveled abroad where he was converted to Catholicism. He is the author of *Pancharis* (1603), a historical romance in verse, and *A Cypres Garland* (1625). Holland frequented the Mermaid Tavern. There he doubtless met Shakespeare, for whom he wrote the following commendatory verse affixed to the First Folio (1623):

Vpon the Lines and Life of the Famous
Scenicke Poet, Master WILLIAM SHAKESPEARE.

Those hands, which you so clapt, go now, and wring
You *Britaines* braue; for done are *Shakespeares* dayes:
His dayes are done, that made the dainty Playes,
Which make the Globe of heau'n and earth to ring.
Dry'de is that veine, dry'd is the *Thespian* Spring,
Turn'd all to teares, and *Phoebus* clouds his rayes:
That corp's, that coffin now besticke those bayes,
Which crown'd him *Poet* first, then *Poets* King.
If *Tragedies* might any *Prologue* haue,
All those he made, would scarse make one to this:
Where *Fame*, now that he gone is to the graue
(Deaths publique tyring-house) the *Nuncius* is.

For though his line of life went soone about,
The life yet of his lines shall neuer out.

[E. K. Chambers, *William Shakespeare,* 1930.]

Holland, John. In *2 Henry VI,* one of the men who join the rebel band of Jack Cade and follow him on his plundering, murdering march to London.

Holland, Philemon (1552–1637). Translator. After years at Cambridge both as student and fellow, Holland received a medical degree and, about 1595, settled at Coventry to practice medicine and to teach. It was during this period that he made his famous translations: Livy (1600), Pliny's *Natural History* (1601), Plutarch's *Moralia* (1603), Suetonius (1606), Ammianus Marcellinus (1609), and Xenophon's *Cyropaedia* (1632). Besides the classics, Holland translated several medical treatises and, with additions, the *Britannia* (in two parts, 1610–1637) of his friend William CAMDEN. Shakespeare drew upon Holland's translation of Pliny's *Natural History* for Othello's defense against the charge of witchcraft (I, iii).

Hollar, Wenceslaus or **Wenzel** (1607–1677). Bohemian engraver. A native of Prague, Hollar came to England in 1637, and in 1640 he was appointed art tutor to Prince Charles, later Charles II. During the civil war he was a member of the king's army and was captured by the parliamentary forces. In 1645 he escaped to Antwerp where in 1647 he published his best known map, a panoramic view of London. His "Long View of London," as it is called, is based partly on his own sketches and partly on an earlier view by Janzoon de Claes Visscher. Hollar's "Long View" is generally regarded as an accurate picture of the London theatres about 1640. Its accuracy is marred, however, by one detail. He seems to have mislabeled the Globe and the bearbaiting ring. Thus the building labeled "the Beere bayting" is in fact the Globe. See PLAYHOUSE STRUCTURE. [I. A. Shapiro, "The Bankside Theatres: Early Engravings," *Shakespeare Survey 1,* 1948.]

Holloway, John (1920–). Critic and poet. Although he has written only one book of Shakespearean criticism, Holloway has established himself in the front rank of contemporary Shakespearean critics. His *The Story of the Night* (1961), a study of the major tragedies, has been hailed in some quarters as the manifesto of a new school of Shakespearean criticism. Holloway rejects the prevailing interpretation of Shakespeare, which he characterizes as an attempt, in essentially metaphorical language, to define the moral values inherent in the plays. His own approach, admittedly tentative, derives from the consideration of the ritual origins of drama, and focuses on the collective psychological reaction of the audience. Each play, in his view, is a uniquely revitalizing experience. His book is generally regarded as an attack on the aesthetic principles associated with the influential critic F. R. Leavis. See MYTHIC CRITICISM.

Holman, Joseph George. See ADAPTATIONS.

Holofernes. In *Love's Labour's Lost,* a dogmatic village schoolmaster, who corresponds to the standard pedant of Italian comedy (see LOVE'S LABOUR'S LOST: *Sources*). It is at Holofernes' suggestion that a dramatic representation of the Nine Worthies is presented for the Princess' entertainment, with himself cast as Judas Maccabaeus. Holofernes has spoken only his first lines when the taunting audience forc him to retire. Commentators have suggested sever contemporaries whom Shakespeare may have bee satirizing in his characterization of Holofernes John Florio, Thomas Harriot, Gabriel Harvey, an Alexander ASPINALL, a schoolmaster at the Stratfor grammar school.

Holy Trinity Church. The local church of Strat ford in which Shakespeare was buried. The buildin is an ancient one, dating in some of its parts to th beginning of the 13th century. In the 15th centur the church was enlarged and the chancel, the sectio in which Shakespeare is buried, was rebuilt. Th church has a cruciform design; the chancel an nave running east and west are intersected by th north and south transept. In addition to Shakespeare tomb and MONUMENT, the church houses the paris registers of Stratford which contain the entries fo Shakespeare's baptism and burial. [J. H. Bloon *Shakespeare's Church,* 1902.]

Home, Henry. See Lord KAMES.

Homer (fl. c. 10th cent. B.C.). Greek poet. For th greater part of the 16th century the supreme poe of the classical age was considered to be, not Home but Vergil. This situation was due largely to th fact that relatively few Englishmen had mastere Greek whereas Vergil was read in the public gram mar schools. In 1581 Arthur Hall of Grantham (f 1563–1604) produced a translation of the *Iliad* i lumbering "fourteeners," which were not calculate to enhance Homer's reputation. In 1598, howeve George Chapman produced the first of his famou Homeric translations, *Seaven Bookes of the Iliade* from which Shakespeare derived a number of ele ments in his *Troilus and Cressida,* notably the char acter of Thersites. There is no evidence that Shake speare read Homer in the original Greek.

homilies. Admonitory discourses on moral or re ligious themes. Upon the death of Henry VIII i 1547, a Council of Regency was established to rul in the name of the young Edward VI. A part of it program to enforce religious conformity was t forbid independent preaching; instead, pastors wer to read from the pulpit officially prepared texts. Fo this purpose Thomas Cranmer edited *Certaine Ser mons or Homilies* (1547), consisting of 12 such dis courses, 4 of which are believed to have been writte by him. During the reign of Mary the book wa suppressed, but it was reissued soon after the acces sion of Elizabeth. In 1563 there appeared a secon volume, *The Seconde Tome of Homilies,* with 2 additional sermons. A lengthy sermon against dis obedience and rebellion (also issued independently was added in 1571. The collection now consisted o 33 titles, most of them with several parts which wer in fact separate sermons. The sermons continued t be issued throughout the reigns of Elizabeth, James and Charles, and were gathered into one volume *Certain Sermons or Homilies Appointed to be rea in Churches,* in 1623.

The sermons are varied in subject matter wit ample treatment of moral, doctrinal, and liturgica questions. Several contain political implications o major importance, especially "An Exhortation t Obedience" in three parts and "An Homily Agains Disobedience and Wilfull Rebellion" in six. Th latter reflects the activities of the years immediatel preceding its appearance in 1571: the rebellion in the North in 1569, the excommunication of Elizabeth by Pope Pius V shortly afterward, and the various plots which followed. Each of the six parts concludes with a prayer to be said by the congregation for the safety of the queen, and the book itself ends with "A Thanksgiving for the Suppression of the Last Rebellion." The two sermons, comprising nine parts or separate sermons, cover such subjects as hierarchy, the divine right of kings, nonresistance, passive obedience, and the evils of rebellion. Hence for nine Sundays and holy days, congregations received exhortations concerning their civil obligations. Since church attendance was required by law and permission to deviate from the official sermons was rarely granted, these sermons had an incalculable effect on the minds of the age. They contained analogues and probable sources for political ideas expressed by many of Shakespeare's characters. The 1547 sermon on obedience, for example, opens with the following words: "Almighty God hath created and appointed all things in heaven, earth and waters, in most excellent and perfect order." This order is then traced throughout all creation: in the heavenly hierarchy, among the elements, in the four seasons, and in the ranks of society. The thought and at times the phraseology of this sermon are echoed in the speeches of such characters as Ulysses (*Troilus and Cressida*, I, iii, 85–137; see DEGREE), Titania (*A Midsummer Night's Dream*, II, i, 81–117); Northumberland (*2 Henry IV*, I, i, 153–160); Canterbury (*Henry V*, I, ii, 183–213); and Coriolanus (*Coriolanus*, III, i, 142–149). Similar analogues can be found on the topics of divine right of kings, passive obedience, and the evils of rebellion. [Alfred Hart, *Shakespeare and the Homilies*, 1934.]

homosexuality. The idea that Shakespeare was a homosexual is based upon the suspicion that the relationship recorded in the SONNETS between the poet and the Fair Youth is a homosexual one. The charge had been vaguely hinted at throughout the 19th century and was openly asserted by Samuel Butler in his edition of the *Sonnets* (1899). Butler described the relationship of the two men as "more Greek than English." Later writers have alternately attacked and defended the theory. Evidence in support of it is slight and tenuous, involving an always dangerous, literal, biographical interpretation of the *Sonnets*. Using the same criterion, one might find that the poet's consuming sexual passion for the Dark Lady in the later sonnets is inconsistent with a theory of his homosexuality. As early as 1790 Edmund Malone pointed out that the Renaissance cult of male friendship employed the convention of using amatory terms in addressing one another. A detailed study of the problem has been made by H. M. Young (*The Sonnets of Shakespeare: A Psycho-Sexual Analysis*, 1937), who concludes that no homosexual would ever urge his lover to marry (Sonnets 1–17), nor be attracted to the friend by virtue of his "woman's face" (Sonnet 20). G. Wilson Knight (*The Mutual Flame*, 1955) has argued that the basic theme of the *Sonnets* is that of "bisexual integration," a fusion of the feminine and masculine which has its roots in physical attraction of the poet for the youth, but which finally transcends the merely sensual experience.

In the plays there is only one reference (*Troilus and Cressida*, V, i, 15–17) to homosexuality, and that is a disparaging one.

Hondius, Jodocus. Real name **Joos de Hondt** (1563–1611). Engraver. Born in Flanders, Hondius came to London in the late 1580's, setting up business as an engraver. In 1594 he left England for Amsterdam where he remained for the rest of his life. His best-known works are the engravings which he drew for John Speed's *Theatre of the Empire of Great Britain* (1611), one map of which contains an inset showing the Globe as a circular building. The Hondius View is an important pictorial source of information about the shape and location of Shakespeare's theatre. See PLAYHOUSE STRUCTURE. [I. A. Shapiro, "The Bankside Theatres: Early Engravings," *Shakespeare Survey 1*, 1948.]

Honegger, Arthur. See MUSIC BASED ON SHAKESPEARE: *20th century*.

Hooker, Richard. See LAWS OF ECCLESIASTICAL POLITY.

Hope theatre. Combination playhouse and bear garden on the Bankside in Southwark. The Hope was constructed in fulfillment of an agreement which Phillip HENSLOWE and Jacob MEADE had concluded with LADY ELIZABETH'S MEN, requiring them to provide that troupe with a suitable playhouse. It was to replace the earlier Bear Garden on the same site; the reconstructed theatre was to serve as a bearbaiting ring on the days that sport was allowed. See BEARBAITING, BULLBAITING, AND COCKFIGHTING.

The contract for the construction of the building is dated August 29, 1613; in it Henslowe and Meade agree to pay Gilbert Katherens, a carpenter, the sum of £360 by the end of the work. Construction was to be completed by the following November. The date of completion, however, seems to have been delayed. The contract is an important document in itself, for it has provided scholars with clues to the structure of the Jacobean theatres. The Hope was to be modeled on the Swan theatre. It was to have a

THE HOPE THEATRE AS RECONSTRUCTED BY C. WALTER HODGES. (COURTESY OF COWARD-MC CANN, INC.)

covered roof (a circumstance not entirely advantageous, however, for the stench of the place resulting from the bearbaiting was likely to offend the nose of the staunchest London theatregoer).

Under the terms of the contract, Katherens was to tear down the Bear Garden and replace it with a theatre suitable for players to act in and for bullbaiting and bearbaiting, with a tiring-house and a portable stage. The stage was to be on trestles heavy enough to bear its weight. The details of construction are set forth in the following portions of the original contract:

> And to builde the same of suche large compasse, fforme, widenes, and height as the Plaie house called the Swan . . . And shall also builde two stearecasses without and adioyninge to the saide Playe house in such convenient places, as shalbe moste fitt and convenient for the same to stande vppon . . . And shall also builde the Heavens all over the saide stage, to be borne or carryed without any postes or supporters to be fixed or sett vppon the saide stage, and all gutters of leade needfull for the carryage of all suche raine water . . . And shall also make two Boxes in the lowermost storie fitt and decent for gentlemen to sitt in; And shall make the particions betwne the Rommes as they are at the saide Plaie house called the Swan; And to make turned cullumes vppon and over the stage; The inner principall postes of the first storie to be twelve footes in height and tenn ynches square, the inner principall postes in the midell storie to be eight ynches square, the inner most postes in the vpper storie to be seaven ynches square; The prick postes in the first storie to be eight ynches square, in the seconde storie seaven ynches square, and in the vpper most storie six ynches square; Also the brest sommers in the lower moste storie to be nyne ynches depe, and seaven ynches in thicknes, and in the midell storie to be eight ynches depe and six ynches in thicknes; The byndinge jostes of the firste storie to be nyne and eight ynches in depthe and thicknes, and in the midell storie to be viij and vij ynches in depthe and thicknes, . . . to make a good, sure, and sufficient foundacion of brickes for the said Play house or game place, and to make it xiij^teene ynches at the leaste above the grounde . . . . to new builde, . . . the saide Bull house and stable with good and sufficient scantlinge tymber, plankes, and bordes, and particions of that largnes and fittnes as shalbe sufficent to kepe and holde six bulls and three horsses or geldinges, with rackes and mangers to the same, and also a lofte or storie over the saide house as nowe it is. And shall also . . . new tyle with Englishe tyles all the vpper rooffe of the saide Plaie house, game place, and Bull house or stable, . . .

The Hope was in use before the autumn of 1614. Its company, probably Lady Elizabeth's Men, performed Ben Jonson's *Bartholomew Fair* that fall before presenting it at court during the Christmas season. In the play's Induction, Jonson describes the Hope as "durty as *Smithfield*, and as stinking euery whit."

Meade and Henslowe inserted in their agreement with Lady Elizabeth's Men a stipulation that the Hope would be reserved for bearbaiting one day every two weeks. Both Henslowe and Meade were aware that the bearbaiting was even more profitable than stage plays, and the actors eventually accused the two managers of taking more time for the bears than they were entitled to.

The Hope was apparently used only by some minor companies after 1617; at that point it seems to have been left to the bears. The location was not convenient for London playgoers, who were patronizing the playhouses in the Middlesex area, and the place apparently again became known by its older name of the Bear Garden.

The sport continued to be popular with Londoners, even after the closing of the theatres in 1642. In 1647 and 1648 parliament ordered the bearbaiting to cease; the order was evidently disobeyed. Finally, in 1655 and 1656 a series of horrible accidents, one involving a child killed in the ring, caused the authorities to order the bears shot and the place closed According to a manuscript addendum to a copy of John Stow's *Annales* (1631), the Hope was

> pulled downe to make tennementes, by Thomas Walker, a peticoate maker in Cannon Streete, on Tuesday the 25 day of March 1656. Seuen of Mr Godfries beares, by the command of Thomas Pride, then hie Sheriefe of Surry, were then shot to death, on Saterday the 9 day of February 1655 by a company of souldiers.

In 1663, however, with the evident sanction of Charles II, the sport was reallowed and the Hope reopened. [E. K. Chambers, *The Elizabethan Stage*, 1923; Leslie Hotson, *The Commonwealth and Restoration Stage*, 1928.]

Horatio. In *Hamlet*, the Prince's friend and schoolmate. Horatio tells Hamlet of the appearance of his father's ghost and is Hamlet's trusted confidant throughout the play. Hamlet dies in his arms while instructing him to "report my cause aright." Horatio functions in the drama in a manner similar to that of the chorus in Greek tragedy. He is the spokesman of the audience and his intelligence, moderation, and restraint define the limits of experience which the tragic hero is fated to transgress.

Hordern, Michael (1911–). Actor. Hordern made his first stage appearance as Lodovico in *Othello* (1937). Subsequent Shakespearean roles have included Macduff in *Macbeth* (1950), Menenius in *Coriolanus* (1952), Jaques in *As You Like It* (1952), Polonius in *Hamlet* (1953), Parolles in *All's Well That Ends Well* (1954), Prospero in *The Tempest* (1954), and Cassius in *Julius Caesar* (1958).

hornbook. See EDUCATION.

Horner, Thomas. In *2 Henry VI*, an armorer. His apprentice, Peter Thump, accuses Horner of traitorously declaring the Duke of York to be the rightful heir to the English crown. Denying the charge, Horner accuses Peter of spite (I, iii). In a trial by combat fought with sandbags before the King, Peter dispatches his drunken master who, before he dies, confesses his treason (II, iii). A similar incident actually occurred at Smithfield in 1446 when William Catur, an armorer, was accused of treason by his servant, John David. The servant killed his master in combat, but later admitted that the accusation was false. [W. H. Thomson, *Shakespeare's Characters. A Historical Dictionary*, 1951.]

horsemanship. There were about a dozen distinct

breeds of horses in England in Elizabethan times, the most popular riding horses being the Turkey horse, the Barb, the Neapolitan, and the Spanish Jennet. Shakespeare frequently refers to the Barb or Barbary horse, a relatively small animal somewhat like the modern Arabian, which was valued for its speed and endurance. In *Richard II*, the King's groom refers to the coronation day:

> When Bolingbroke rode on roan Barbary,
> That horse that thou so often hast bestrid,
> That horse that I so carefully have dress'd!
> (V, v, 78–80)

In *Hamlet*, the King wagers six Barbary horses against six French rapiers and poniards on Hamlet's ability to win a fencing match with Laertes (V, ii, 154–157). Iago raffishly describes Othello as a Barbary horse, an allusion based on both the Barbary's Moorish origins and the common practice of breeding a Barbary to an English mare (*Othello*, I, i, 112).

The temperament of a horse, like that of a man, was determined by whichever of the four elements or humours predominated in him; earth made a melancholy horse, water a phlegmatic one; a horse dominated by air was sanguine and nimble; and one dominated by fire was choleric, hot, and fiery. The perfect horse, of course, was one in which all the elements mingled equally. In *Henry V* the Dauphin boasts that his horse is "pure air and fire; and the dull elements of earth and water never appear in him" (III, vii, 22–24). Bay was considered the best color, particularly if there were a white star on the horse's forehead. A horse without a star was considered to have a cloud in its face and was supposedly furious and full of mischief. Shakespeare alludes to this belief in *Antony and Cleopatra:*

> *Enobarbus.* Will Caesar weep?
> *Agrippa.* He has a cloud in 's face.
> *Enobarbus.* He were the worse for that, were he a horse;
> So is he, being a man.
> (III, ii, 50–53)

The basic technical terms of horsemanship were familiar to an Elizabethan audience and appear frequently and metaphorically in Shakespeare's works. An important part of a horse's schooling, or manage, concerned the art of pacing. In *Pericles*, the Bawd says of Marina:

> My lord, she's not paced yet: you must take some pains to work her to your manage.
> (IV, vi, 68–69)

In Elizabethan times the accepted paces were the trot, rack, amble, and gallop, the amble being a favorite gait because of its smoothness. In the more jarring trot, the legs move in diagonal pairs; in the amble the fore and hind legs on each side move at the same time, producing a comfortable and easy gait. In *Much Ado About Nothing* Benedick observes to Claudio: "Sir, your wit ambles well; it goes easily" (V, i, 159). In *As You Like It*, Rosalind tells Orlando her metaphor of Time (III, ii, 326–351), who "travels in divers paces with divers persons." Time

> . . . trots hard with a young maid between the contract of her marriage and the day it is solemnized.

Time ambles

> . . . with a priest that lacks Latin and a rich man that hath not the gout, for the one sleeps easily because he cannot study and the other lives merrily because he feels no pain.

Time gallops with "a thief to the gallows" and stands still with "lawyers in the vacation."

Horses are notoriously subject to ailments, as the Fool in *King Lear* observes:

> He's mad that trusts in the tameness of a wolf, a horse's health, a boy's love, or a whore's oath.
> (III, vi, 19–21)

Shakespeare catalogues a number of diseases peculiar to horses in his description of the nag on which Petruchio rode to fetch Katharina on their wedding day. This unfortunate beast was

> . . . possessed with the glanders and like to mose in the chine; troubled with the lampass, infected with the fashions, full of windgalls, sped with spavins, rayed with the yellows, past cure of the fives, stark spoiled with the staggers, begnawn with the bots, swayed in the back and shoulder-shotten.
> (*The Taming of the Shrew*, III, ii, 51–57)

In *1 Henry IV* there is a bit of realistic dialogue on horse-care; an ostler is told to pad with locks of wool the part of the ill-fitting saddle which had been pinching or galling the horse's shoulders:

> I prithee, Tom, beat Cut's saddle, put a few flocks in the point; poor jade, is wrung in the withers out of all cess.
> (II, i, 6–8)

[A. Forbes Sieveking, "Horsemanship, with Farriery," *Shakespeare's England*, 1916.]

Hortensio. In *The Taming of the Shrew*, a friend of Petruchio's. Hortensio tempts Petruchio to court Katharina by revealing her large dowry, so that he may press his own suit for Bianca. Disguised as a music teacher, Hortensio gains access to Bianca, but when he loses her to Lucentio, he consoles himself with a widow.

Hortensius. In *Timon of Athens*, a servant of one of Timon's creditors. Hortensius sues unsuccessfully for payment (III, iv).

Host. In *The Two Gentlemen of Verona*, the old man who, in IV, ii, leads Julia to the Duke's palace in time to witness the serenade at Silvia's window and Proteus' courting of her. The Host later reveals that Proteus is a lodger at his house.

Hostess. In the Induction to *The Taming of the Shrew*, the Hostess goes to get the constable to arrest the drunk, Sly, for refusing to pay for broken glasses.

Host of the Garter Inn. In *The Merry Wives of Windsor*, the high-spirited and sportive innkeeper. He gives contradictory directions to Dr. Caius and Sir Hugh Evans when they plan to meet for their duel. When the Host merrily reveals this ruse, the two antagonists join forces in retaliation and rob him of his horses. The Host's spirits are dampened until Fenton offers to pay him £100 more than his loss if the Host will assist him in his elopement scheme. Happily renewed, the Host provides the priest to perform the marriage ceremony for Fenton and

Anne Page. The actor who originally played this role is thought to have been the reporter of the "bad quarto" of the play. See MEMORIAL RECONSTRUCTION.

Hotson, [John] Leslie (1897–). Canadian-born scholar and researcher. Hotson's scrutiny of Elizabethan documents and records has resulted in some of the 20th century's most important discoveries concerning Shakespeare's biography. He began his career with the publication of *The Death of Christopher Marlowe* (1925), a book which solved the mystery surrounding Marlowe's death. In 1928 he published *The Commonwealth and Restoration Stage,* bringing new light to bear on a then neglected area of study.

His Shakespearean studies include *Shakespeare Versus Shallow* (1931), based on the discovery of a document naming Shakespeare in a court order (see William GARDINER; William WAYTE); *I, William Shakespeare* (1937), an account of Shakespeare's relationship with Thomas RUSSELL, the overseer of his will; *Shakespeare's Motley* (1952); and *The First Night of Twelfth Night* (1954), a brilliant conjectural reconstruction of the first performance of Shakespeare's comedy. See TWELFTH NIGHT: *Date.*

Hotson's evidence sometimes leads to conjectures which have aroused a great deal of controversy. His *Shakespeare's Sonnets Dated* (1949) is an attempt, on the basis of his reading of Sonnet 107, to move the dating of the *Sonnets* back to 1589. *Shakespeare's Wooden O* (1960) represents his effort to present the original Globe as a theatre-in-the-round, and *Mr. W. H.* (1964), his attempt to identify that enigmatic figure of the *Sonnets* with William HATCLIFFE. The theories upon which these three books rest have not generally been accepted by scholars although even here much useful information has been unearthed by this eminent "literary detective."

Hotspur. Nickname of **Henry Percy** (1364–1403). Eldest son of the 1st earl of Northumberland; in *Richard II* and *1 Henry IV,* a fiery leader in the rebellious forces. When Bolingbroke returned to England to claim his inheritance, Hotspur and his father were instrumental in placing him on the throne. In 1402, he defeated the Scots at Homildon Hill; the prisoners taken were Hotspur's by law of arms. When the king demanded them for himself and forbade Hotspur to ransom his brother-in-law, Sir Edmund Mortimer, Hotspur refused to deliver to the king the earl of Douglas. In 1403 the dispute turned to rebellion, which is recorded more or less accurately in *1 Henry IV,* with one notable divergence from historical fact: Hotspur was 23 years older than Hal, but Shakespeare, in order to contrast the two characters, gave them the same age.

Hotspur is one of Shakespeare's most interesting secondary characters. His passionate, fearless, extravagant nature is at once endearing and exasperating. Audiences have never failed to respond to his reckless courage, his blunt honesty, and his inexhaustible vitality. Added to these qualities are his wit and eloquence, all combining to make him a most formidable adversary to Hal, both on the battlefield and in the mind of the spectator. Indeed, his virtues have seemed to some to overshadow those of the Prince. For, while matching Hal in positive attributes, Hotspur displays none of the craft and guile which are characteristic of Bolingbroke's son. Accordingly, it is perhaps significant that Shakespeare supplies a glimpse of Hotspur's home life (with its revelation of his humanity and underlying tenderness) without providing a corresponding scene in which Hal is humanized.

Nevertheless, it is precisely Hotspur's guilelessness that renders him dangerous in the world of political reality. His commitment to honour is extravagant in itself and more so in that it is based on an illusionary and simplistic view of the operation of that value in the world. In this respect, Hotspur's adversary is not Hal but Falstaff, whose famous pronouncement on honor ("Honour is a mere scutcheon") stands in marked contrast to Hotspur's conviction. Both these attitudes represent opposite extremes, between which Hal stands as the exemplar whose concept of honor is tempered by his awareness of the complexity of human motives and the impossibility of realizing ideals. See 1 HENRY IV: *Comment.*

Houghton, Alexander. See William SHAKESHAFTE.

housekeeper. In the Elizabethan theatre, a term used to describe the owner of an interest in the theatre building itself. A housekeeper is to be distinguished from a SHARER, a part-owner of an acting company, although in Shakespeare's company (the Chamberlain's Men) the major sharers were generally also the housekeepers. In 1599 the original housekeepers of the Globe were Richard and Cuthbert Burbage, who owned one half of the building and Shakespeare, Augustine Phillips, Thomas Pope John Heminges, and Will Kempe, who together owned the other half. When the BLACKFRIARS THEATRE was purchased in 1608 there were seven equal housekeepers: Richard and Cuthbert Burbage, Shakespeare, John Heminges, Henry Condell, William Sly, and Thomas Evans.

This arrangement, whereby the actor-sharers were also housekeepers, was unique to Shakespeare's company. The usual procedure was to have a sole owner or housekeeper, such as Philip HENSLOWE, who rented his theatre to an acting company and received a proportion of the receipts in return. [E. K. Chambers, *The Elizabethan Stage,* 1923.]

Housman, A[lfred] E[dward] (1859–1936). Poet Housman's native district is the scene of his lyrics *A Shropshire Lad* (1896), *Last Poems* (1922), and the posthumously published *More Poems* (1936). In his lecture "The Name and Nature of Poetry" (1933), Housman characterized the songs in Shakespeare's plays as ravishing nonsense and "the very summit of lyrical achievement." He cited the Border Ballads, Heine's lyrics, and Shakespeare's songs as the dominating influences on his own poetry. The somber melancholy of many of the songs naturally appealed to him, most clearly the dirge from *Cymbeline,* "Fear no more the heat o' the sun" (IV, ii 258–281), lines from which he used in *A Shropshire Lad* (XLIII and XLIV) and *Last Poems* (II and XXXVII). Many such borrowings are listed in Laurence Housman's biography of his brother [Laurence Housman, *My Brother, A. E. Housman* 1938; Tom B. Haber, "What Fools These Mortals Be! Housman's Poetry and the Lyrics of Shakespeare," *Modern Language Quarterly,* VI, 1945.]

Howard, Charles. See Charles Howard, 1st earl of NOTTINGHAM.

Howard, Henry. See Henry Howard, earl of SURREY.

Howard, James. See ADAPTATIONS.

Howard, Thomas. See duke of NORFOLK; earl of SURREY.

Howard's Men. See ADMIRAL'S MEN.

Howes, Edmund (d. 1640). Chronicler. Howes edited and expanded two chronicles of the English antiquary John Stow, after Stow's death. In 1607 he continued Stow's *A Summarie of Englyshe Chronicles* and in 1615 he edited Stow's *Annales*. In the latter work, Howes cited among a list of noted contemporary poets "*M. Willi Shakespeare* gentleman."

Another enlarged edition was published in 1631, including a list of all the playhouses which had been erected in London to date and an account of the burning of the Globe in 1613.

> Upon S. Peters day last, the play-house or Theater, called the Globe, upon the Banck-side near London, by negligent discharging of a peal of ordinance, close to the south-side thereof, the thatch took fire, and the wind sodainly disperst the flame round about, and in a very short space the whole building was quite consumed, and no man hurt; the house being filled with people to behold the play, viz. of Henry the Eighth. And the next spring it was new builded in far fairer manner than before.

One extant copy of that edition also contained a handwritten account—not by Howes, who died in 1640—of the destruction of the theatres during the Commonwealth period. The account records the interior destruction of the Fortune, Salisbury Court, and Phoenix theatres in 1649 by government soldiers and the demolition of the Globe in 1644, of Blackfriars in 1655, and of the Hope in 1656. [Joseph Quincy Adams, *Shakespearean Playhouses*, 1917.]

Hubaud or **Huband, Ralph** (d. 1605). Warwickshire official and tithe-holder who in 1605 sold his interest in the STRATFORD TITHES to Shakespeare for £440. Hubaud had inherited the tithes in 1583 on the death of his brother, Sir John Hubaud, constable of Kenilworth Castle, the home of the earl of Leicester. Ralph was sheriff of Warwickshire in 1592. He died shortly after the sale of the tithes, and an inventory of his estate made in January 1606 indicated an unpaid debt of £20 "Owinge by Mr. Shakespre." [Mark Eccles, *Shakespeare in Warwickshire*, 1961.]

Hubert de Burgh (d. 1243). A vastly influential minister to King John and Henry III. After the death of William Marshall, earl of Pembroke, who was regent for the young Henry III, Hubert gained almost complete sway over the kingdom. In *King John*, the King entrusts his nephew, Arthur, to Hubert to be put to death. Unable to bring himself to blind the boy, as John's written instructions require, Hubert hides him and informs the King that Arthur is dead. When Arthur dies while trying to escape Hubert's custody, Hubert is thought to have murdered him.

Hudson, George. See MUSIC BASED ON SHAKESPEARE: *17th century*.

Hudson, Henry Norman (1814–1886). American scholar and clergyman. After a period of teaching and lecturing, Hudson was ordained an Episcopalian minister and served as a pastor, editor of several religious journals, and Civil War chaplain. After 1865 he settled at Cambridge, Massachusetts, and devoted himself to lecturing and writing. Hudson gained an early popularity for his lectures on Shakespeare, the substance of which was published as *Lectures on Shakespeare* (2 vols., 1848). He then turned to editing and in the period 1851–1856 issued the plays in 11 volumes. His *Shakespeare, His Life, Art, and Character* (2 vols., 1872) shows an advance over the earlier work with regard to both scholarship and criticism. An advance in scholarship is also evident in his Harvard edition of Shakespeare (20 vols., 1880–1881). Through his ability to communicate his enthusiasm, Hudson contributed substantially to the spread of Shakespeare's popularity. His editions of the plays, revised and edited by later scholars, appeared under the title The New Hudson Shakespeare. For generations they were widely used in American schools and exerted a widespread influence. See SCHOLARSHIP—19TH CENTURY. [J. E. Rankin, *The Shakespearean Interpreter*, 1886.]

Hughes, John (1677–1720). Critic and dramatist. Hughes, an occasional contributor to the *Spectator* and *Guardian*, was one of the first critics to focus attention on Shakespeare's characters rather than on the plays as units. His comments on *Othello* in an essay (1713) include character sketches of Othello and Iago which emphasize the complexity of their personalities and the supremacy of the talent that could create them. Hughes notes some minor flaws in plot construction, but he argues that to emphasize them would be to ignore the obvious excellence of the play as a whole.

Hughes also used exemplary passages from Shakespeare's plays in his essays on religion and on Cicero's laws of oratory. For instance, he regarded Hamlet's "To be or not to be" soliloquy, delivered gravely but calmly, as the model for the proper representation of perplexity. [Herbert Spencer Robinson, *English Shakespearian Criticism in the Eighteenth Century*, 1932.]

Hughes, William. A candidate for the title MR. W. H. of the *Sonnets*. Hughes' candidacy dates from the 18th century and is based on the assumption that the 7th line in Sonnet 20 ("A man in hue, all 'hues' in his controlling") is a pun on the last name of W. H. The theory achieved its most popular expression in Oscar WILDE's fictional account *The Portrait of Mr. W. H.* (1889). Wilde presents William Hughes as a boy actor, "of great beauty," who performed the leading female roles in the plays and who abandoned Shakespeare's company in order to play at a rival theatre. There is no record of an actor of this name, however. Samuel Butler in his edition of the *Sonnets* (1899) discovered a man named William Hughes who had served as a cook on several vessels. Another "William Hewes," who was a musician attached to the earl of Essex, is a more likely candidate except that his name usually appears as "Howes." In any event there is no evidence that Shakespeare ever knew anyone of that name. [*The Sonnets*, New Variorum Edition, Hyder Rollins, ed., 1944.]

Hugo, Victor [Marie] (1802–1885). French novelist and poet. After the success of *Les Misérables* (1862) Hugo agreed to write a preface to his son's (François Victor's) monumental translation of Shakespeare (1859–1866). When he began work he discovered that he had sufficient material to work into a book on the subject. In 1865 he published *William Shakespeare*.

The book is a long essay on a number of geniuses

which Western civilization has produced. In it, Hugo almost literally maintains that Shakespeare is a reincarnation of Aeschylus. He distinguishes the normal man from the poet-seer who ventures "out on that fearful promontory of thought from which one perceives the shadows." Hugo draws attention to Shakespeare's use of the supernatural and maintains that the poet "believed profoundly in the mystery of things." See FRANCE; LOVE'S LABOUR'S LOST: *Selected Criticism;* OTHELLO: *Selected Criticism;* THE TEMPEST: *Selected Criticism;* THE WINTER'S TALE: *Selected Criticism.*

Hull, Thomas (1728–1808). Dramatist and actor. For 48 years Hull was an actor at Covent Garden, where he also served as manager from 1775 to 1782. As an actor he generally played secondary parts, appearing as Horatio, Friar Lawrence, Macduff, and Gloucester (*King Lear*). One of his rare starring roles was that of Prospero in *The Tempest.* Hull was also a prolific playwright, and at least two of his dramas were adaptations of Shakespearean plays. *The Twins*, an adaptation of *The Comedy of Errors* performed in 1762 and never published, has been doubtfully attributed to Hull. Another slight alteration of *The Comedy of Errors* was published under Hull's name in 1793. He also adapted *Timon of Athens* for the stage in 1786.

humanism. A Renaissance term describing the recovery and study of the literature of Greece and Rome. Originating in Italy in the 14th and 15th centuries, humanism had spread to England by the beginning of the 16th century. Here, under the influence of such scholars as Sir Thomas More and Erasmus, the great synthesizing task of fusing pagan culture with Christian ethics was begun. In drama this fusion was evidenced by the so-called Christian Terence, a phenomenon beginning about 1530 in Holland in which the structure of the comedies of Terence was applied to subject matter from the Bible. The plays were written in Latin and were forerunners of the university drama of the later Tudor period. The tradition of drama as a mode of religious edification went back to the Middle Ages, but the advent of humanism brought about the view of drama as a legitimate cultural enterprise and a worthy adjunct to the Latin curriculum in the schools.

Viewed in a less benign light, humanism contributed to the development of NEOCLASSICISM with its strict censures and literal interpretation of Aristotle's *Poetics.* This aspect of humanism, formulated in Italy and France in the 16th century and expressed in England in Sir Philip Sidney's *Apologie for Poetrie* (1595), tended to retard the development of English drama. It subordinated to the ideals of correctness and regularity such native elements as the mixture of comedy and tragedy. Fortunately, Shakespeare and his fellow dramatists absorbed humanist critical theory only in a diluted form, retaining, for example, the five-act structure of classical drama without succumbing to the strangulating restrictions of the unities of time, place, and action. The result was a drama that at its best expressed vitality and flexibility within a generally coherent formal structure—in Elizabethan terms, an ideal blend of "nature" and "art" (see MEDIEVALISM IN SHAKESPEARE).

Hume, John. A priest who was advisor to the duchess of Gloucester. In 1441 Hume was charged with treason, but was later pardoned. In *2 Henry VI* Hume is paid by Cardinal Beaufort and Suffolk to assist the Duchess in her use of sorcery to discover the future. The conjurors are surprised at their ceremonies by York and Buckingham, and Hume is condemned to hang. [W. H. Thomson, *Shakespeare's Characters: A Historical Dictionary*, 1951.]

Humfrey, Pelham. See MUSIC BASED ON SHAKESPEARE: *17th century.*

humors. See PSYCHOLOGY.

Humperdinck, Engelbert. See MUSIC BASED ON SHAKESPEARE: *20th century.*

Hungary. The introduction of Shakespeare to the Hungarian reading and theatregoing public followed much the same pattern as it had among other subject peoples within the German sphere of influence; that is, it was an integral part of the general development of Hungarian nationalism and the rehabilitation of the Hungarian language. During the 18th century, the Hungarian language was moving toward extinction. It had passed into disuse among the aristocracy, who preferred the German used at the court, and among the middle classes, who preferred the Latin of public life. Only among the peasantry had the Hungarian language retained its predominance. By 1776, the year in which Hungarians had their first taste of Shakespeare in Heufeld's German adaptation of *Hamlet,* performed at Buda, the Hungarian language had declined to the point where it was unquestionably an inadequate medium for the sustenance of a sophisticated culture. However, this performance marked the beginning of a literary revival which was to come to full flower under Ferencz Kazinczy (1759–1831) in the 1780's.

Although Kazinczy was responsible for the first full-length translation of a Shakespearean play, a rendering of *Hamlet* (1790) from Fr. L. Schröder's German prose adaptation, of far greater significance to the later course of Shakespeare translation was his call for a reformation of the Hungarian language. During the years between 1780 and 1820, Kazinczy's group of young "neologists" addressed themselves to the task set for them by "the Master," radically expanding and reforming the language. Even before this reformation was completed, and for some 20 years after, Hungarian poets experimented with this new language, perfecting their technique. The 1830's saw the development of the language, the theatre, and poetic technique converging upon and crystallizing into a demand for the translation of the complete works of Shakespeare.

Before the 1830's, virtually all Shakespearean translations were written expressly for the touring theatre companies for performance in the provinces, the urban theatre being for the most part dominated by German productions. The touring companies, eager to raise the taste of their audiences and to add to their own prestige, gave frequent benefit performances of Shakespeare. However, the general quality of the translations was low. With the sole exception of the *Macbeth* (1830) of Gábor Dobrentei (1786–1851), these translations were loose renderings of German adaptations. They were further limited by the inexperience of the companies for which they were written and by the narrow resources of the unreformed Hungarian language. The translators were often amateurs with few literary qualifications beyond their love of Shakespeare. Yet the activity of the touring companies was not without value. By training actors and building an audience for Hungarian theatre, these companies helped to bring about the establishment, in 1837, of the National Theatre. The National Theatre, in turn, commissioned Shakespearean translations of increasing quality, at first in collaboration with the National Academy (founded in 1831) and later independently. Conditions were ripe for the translation of the complete works.

Translation. In 1847, the three major Hungarian poets of the day, Mihály Vörösmarty (1800–1855), Alexander Petőfi (1823–1849), and János Arany (1817–1882), agreed to collaborate on a translation of the complete works of Shakespeare. Vörösmarty had published a translation of *Julius Caesar* in 1839 and now agreed to start work on *King Lear*. Meanwhile, Petőfi translated *Coriolanus,* which appeared in print in February 1848, the first fruits of the collaboration. A few days before the publication of *Coriolanus,* Gabriel Egressy, one of the greatest Shakespearean actors in Hungary, published an article entitled "Proposal for the Magyar Shakespeare" in which he urged national subsidization of the project. Three weeks later the Revolution of 1848 broke out and the project collapsed, but the basis for the future Kisfaludy Edition, the standard Hungarian translation, was established.

Ten years elapsed before serious efforts toward a complete Shakespeare could be resumed. Neither the Academy nor the Theatre was prepared to undertake the task alone and a quarrel over the revision of Lajos Lukács' translation of *The Merchant of Venice,* in 1839, made cooperation between the two national institutions impossible. Finally, in 1858, Anasztáz Tomori, a former professor who had inherited a fortune, offered to finance the translation and succeeded in interesting a former colleague, Arany, in editing it.

In 1860, the project, with Arany at its head, was placed under the auspices of the Kisfaludy Society, a literary group. The translation progressed smoothly from 1864, when the first volume appeared, until 1878, when it was successfully completed. Translations by Vörösmarty, Petőfi, and Arany, which have become classics of Hungarian Shakespeare translation, were included in the edition. Most of the other translations were executed by Charles Szász, Joseph Lévay, William Györi, Eugene Rakósi, and László Arany, János Arany's son.

With the development of the language and a period of reaction at the end of the 19th century, during which many of the neologisms were weeded out of the language, the original Kisfaludy Edition underwent a number of changes, in some cases involving the substitution of a completely new translation for an old one. However, after World War II, it became apparent that a full-scale, systematic revision was necessary. In 1953, the publishing house of Uj Magyar Könyvkiadó entrusted the responsibility to a committee of four: Endre Illés, critic; Gyula Illyés, writer; László Kardos and Tibor Lutter, professor of world literature and chairman of the English department at the University of Budapest, respectively. This committee, drawing on the services of 16 poets and 16 scholars and critics, replaced some of the translations in the Kisfaludy Edition, altered others (though retaining, with few changes, the work of Vörösmarty, Petőfi, and Arany), and added critical notes of a Marxist persuasion. In 1955, the completed revision appeared in the bookstores, representing the work of 24 translators, living and dead.

Influence and Criticism. The critical literature concerned with Shakespeare and the drama and fiction manifesting his influence are so extensive that only a few outstanding examples can be noted here. Among the critics, George Szerdahelyi wrote the first sketch of Shakespeare's life and works in Hungarian in *Ars Poetica* (1784) and Gabriel Egressy published a series of articles in the *Athenaeum* between 1839 and 1842, which were later incorporated into his *Book of Acting*. The first full Hungarian bibliography of Shakespeare was Joseph Bayer's *Shakespeare Drámái Hazánk Ban* ("Shakespeare's Drama in Our Country"; 2 vols., 1909). A *Hungarian Shakespeare Yearbook* was published by the Kisfaludy Society between the years 1908 and 1920.

Several notable Hungarian authors were influenced by Shakespeare. Joseph Katona's play *Bánk bán* (1821) uses characterization, plot devices, and themes similar to those found in *Richard III*. Katona's earlier plays show the influence of several Shakespearean tragedies. He is regarded by many as one of the two greatest Hungarian playwrights. Vörösmarty's *Csongor and Tünde* (1830) is a fantasy play with echoes of *A Midsummer Night's Dream, The Tempest,* and *The Winter's Tale.* Vörösmarty also wrote two history plays modeled on Shakespeare. Petőfi's two poems *Az Örült* ("The Madman" and "Light") were clearly influenced by the soliloquies in *King Lear* and *Hamlet.* A character in János Arany's epic poem *Buda Halála* ("The Death of Buda") resembles Iago. His *Toldi,* a three-part epic, has scenes suggestive of *As You Like It* and *Romeo and Juliet.* The characters in his ballads are frequently based on Shakespearean characters. A fuller account of critical works and influences can be found in Zoltán Haraszti's *Shakespeare in Hungary* (1929). [Tibor Lutter, "The New Hungarian Edition of Shakespeare's Plays and the Hungarian Shakespeare Tradition," *ZAA,* IV, 1956; Thomas Raymond Mark, "Shakespeare in Hungary: A History of the Translation, Presentation, and Reception of Shakespeare's Dramas in Hungary, 1785–1878," doctoral dissertation submitted to Columbia University, *Dissertation Abstracts,* XVI, 1955.]—A.B.

Hunnis, William (d. 1597). Poet and musician. In 1566 Hunnis was appointed Master of the Children of the Chapel Royal, the boys' acting company which regularly gave performances at court during the Christmas revels. Hunnis contributed verses to the entertainment of the queen at Kenilworth in 1575, and was probably the author of some of the plays performed by the children under his direction at the Blackfriars playhouse. Hunnis is the author of numerous verse renderings of the Psalms, including *Seven Sobs of a Sorrowful Soule for Sinne* (1585), a translation of the Penitential Psalms and one of the most popular books of the day.

Hunsdon, George Carey, 2nd Lord. (1547–1603). Patron of Shakespeare's company, Chamberlain's Men, from 1597 to 1603. The eldest son and heir of Henry Carey, 1st lord Hunsdon, he succeeded Lord Cobham in 1597 as lord chamberlain, a position which Carey's father had held until his death in 1596. Both Carey and his wife Lady Elizabeth Carey were active and generous patrons of poets. Lady Carey was one of the dedicatees of Spenser's *Faerie Queene* and the sole dedicatee of his *Muipotmos*. Their daughter Elizabeth Carey was betrothed to William Herbert, but the betrothal was broken off. Scholars who identify Herbert with the Fair Youth of the *Sonnets* have argued that this was the occasion of the group of sonnets urging the Fair Youth to marry and beget children. See MR. W. H.

During most of his tenure as lord chamberlain, Carey was in poor health and often unable to perform his duties. With the accession of James in 1603 he was relieved of his office and in September of that year he died. It is not known whether he took an active part in the affairs of the Chamberlain's Men, but it can be assumed that their success and prosperity from 1597 to 1603 was due in some part, however small, to his assistance. See MERRY WIVES OF WINDSOR: *Date*.

Hunsdon, Henry Carey, 1st Lord (c. 1524–1596). Lord chamberlain. Despite his title of lord chamberlain of the queen's household, Hunsdon spent comparatively little time at court, his chief duties being related to his activities as Elizabeth's personal representative in northern England and as the principal negotiator within Scottish affairs.

In 1594 when a new company of players, derived chiefly from the old Strange's Men, were assembled in London, Hunsdon became their patron. It was this company, the Chamberlain's Men, of which Shakespeare became a member at this time. Hunsdon's intervention on behalf of the players is recorded in a request, dated October 8, 1594 and addressed to the lord mayor of London, to allow his company the right to perform at the Cross Keys Inn within the city. After Hunsdon's death in 1596 the patronage of the company passed to his son George Carey, 2nd Lord Hunsdon.

Hunsdon's Men. See CHAMBERLAIN'S MEN.

Hunt, Simon (d. c. 1585). Schoolmaster at the Stratford grammar school from 1571 to 1575. Hunt is probably the same Simon Hunt who in 1575 attended the University of Douai in France, the home of English Catholic refugees, and who in 1578 became a Jesuit. If the schoolmaster and the Jesuit are the same man, it is evidence of an early Catholic influence on Shakespeare (see RELIGION). There was, however, another Simon Hunt in Stratford who died in 1598 and who may have been the schoolmaster. [Mark Eccles, *Shakespeare in Warwickshire*, 1961.]

Hunter, Joseph (1783–1861). Antiquary. While serving as Presbyterian minister at Bath (1809–1833), Hunter gathered and published material on local history that was primarily concerned with his native Hallamshire. He also made discoveries concerning the first settlements in New England which attracted attention on both sides of the Atlantic. In 1833 he moved to London and entered the public records office. He published several volumes of records and, in 1836, an edition of the *Towneley Mysteries*. His interest in genealogy led him to undertake one of the earliest thorough investigations of the Shakespeare and allied families. In *New Illustrations of the Life, Studies and Writings of Shakespeare* (2 vols., 1845) he published the results of these investigations, together with textual and critical notes to the plays. Hunter also wrote a series of lives of the English poets which, however, still remains in manuscript.

hunting, coursing, and fowling. The "noble arte of venerie or hunting" was pursued with enthusiasm in Elizabethan times. Shakespeare frequently employs metaphors drawn from the hunting of deer and other animals. There were various methods of pursuing deer. Of the chase with dogs alone, Shakespeare says almost nothing, but he was obviously familiar with the practice of driving deer into nets or enclosures from which they could not escape. In *1 Henry VI* John Talbot, surrounded on the field of battle, compares his soldiers to "a little herd of England's timorous deer" that have been "park'd and bounded in a pale"; he charges them "not rascal-like to fall down with a pinch"—not, like young deer, to fall after being bitten once—

> But rather, moody-mad and desperate stags,
> Turn on the bloody hounds with heads of steel
> And make the cowards stand aloof at bay.
> (IV, ii, 50–52)

In *3 Henry VI* Shakespeare describes the shooting of deer with the crossbow; the hunters hide themselves near the deer-trail and await the passing of the herd (III, i, 1–8).

Shakespeare occasionally uses technical names for various types of deer: he uses the word "hart" (the male red deer, synonymous with stag) in reference to both Achilles (*Troilus and Cressida*, II, iii, 269) and to Julius Caesar (*Julius Caesar* III, i, 204). In a riot of alliterative punning in *Love's Labour's Lost* Holofernes plays on the words "pricket," "sorel," and "sore" (technical terms for a buck in its second, third, and fourth years) and delivers an "extempora[l] epitaph on the death of the deer":

> The preyful princess pierced and prick'd a
> pretty pleasing pricket;
> Some say a sore; but not a sore, till now made
> sore with shooting.

WOODCUT FROM AN ELIZABETHAN BALLAD ABOUT FOX HUNTING.

The dogs did yell; put L to sore, then sorel
  jumps from thicket;
Or pricket sore, or else sorel; the people fall
  a-hooting.
If sore be sore, then L to sore makes fifty sores
  one sorel.
Of one sore I an hundred make by adding but
  one more L.
(IV, ii, 58–63)

Hart, hind, hare, boar, and wolf were animals included in the medieval classification of beasts of venery. The fox, incidentally, was considered mere vermin and not part of this glorious company, but it, too, was sometimes hunted for sport. Shakespeare gives a lengthy account of the hunt for the hare in *Venus and Adonis* (679–708) and a rather technical description of hounds returning from a hunt, presumably for hare, in the Induction to *The Taming of the Shrew* (16–29).

Coursing, as distinguished from hunting, refers to the pursuit of the hare by greyhounds, dogs which hunt by sight rather than scent. Thus in *3 Henry VI* Queen Margaret, urging flight, cries that

Edward and Richard, like a brace of greyhounds
Having the fearful flying hare in sight, . . .
Are at our backs.
(II, v, 129–133)

Whereas dogs were customarily used in hunting beasts of venery, a variety of mechanical contrivances were used against birds in fowling. Shakespeare often refers to the springe, a birdtrap probably akin to the bent-sapling-and-noose trap and used for snaring woodcock and snipe. The woodcock was proverbially a dim-witted creature with a propensity for falling in traps. "Now is the woodcock near the gin" (*Twelfth Night*, II, v, 92), exclaims Fabian as Malvolio picks up Maria's counterfeit letter. The gin may have been either similar to the springe, or possibly a steel contraption resembling a modern rattrap. Most of the common birdtraps of Shakespeare's time are included in Lady Macduff's words to her young son:

Poor bird! thou'ldst never fear the net nor lime,
The pitfall nor the gin.
(*Macbeth*, IV, ii, 34–35)

The use of birdlime, a sticky substance smeared on twigs, was the most widely practiced method of trapping small birds. [A. Forbes Sieveking, "Coursing, Fowling, and Angling," and J. W. Fortescue, "Hunting," *Shakespeare's England*, 1916.]—D.T.

Huntington Library. Popular name of the library officially known as the Henry E. Huntington Library and Art Gallery in San Marino, California. The library was part of the estate of an American businessman, Henry E. Huntington (1850–1927), which was placed (1919–1922) with trustees to be administered for the benefit of the public after his death. The Huntington Library is particularly rich in its collection of English Renaissance literature. Its Shakespearean items include copies of all the first editions of Shakespeare's plays published in quarto, except *Titus Andronicus*. It also contains 4 copies of the First Folio, 10 copies of the Second Folio including the Perkins Folio with the forged notes of John Payne Collier, 7 copies of the rare Third Folio, and 8 copies of the Fourth Folio. The library also contains a large collection of pictorial items, including a collection of more than 300 engraved portraits of Shakespeare. [Godfrey Davies, "The Huntington Library," *Shakespeare Survey 6*, 1953.]

Huntsmen. In the Induction to *The Taming of the Shrew,* companions in the Lord's amusements with Sly.

Huon of Bordeaux, The Famous Exploits of. See A MIDSUMMER NIGHT'S DREAM: *Sources.*

Huxley, Aldous [Leonard] (1894–1963). Author. Huxley's principal novels are *Crome Yellow* (1921), *Antic Hay* (1923), *Point Counter Point* (1928), *Brave New World* (1932), and *Eyeless in Gaza* (1936). He also published several volumes of essays, travel sketches, and miscellaneous prose.

Brave New World is an anti-Utopian satire which depicts the world as it might exist some six centuries in the future should present-day tendencies towards technological control continue to develop. The title is taken from Miranda's words near the conclusion of *The Tempest:* "O brave new world, / That has such people in't" (V, i, 183–184). Prospero's reply—"'Tis new to thee"—can be taken ironically: Miranda is unaware that this world is peopled by usurpers, murderers, drunkards, lechers, and monsters. Other affinities to *The Tempest* are suggested. Just as Prospero has controlled his island with white magic, so science controls this new world, also in an attempt to bring about human happiness. But a part of this world still untouched by scientific control is the Savage Reservation in New Mexico where a wild tract has been preserved in order to study primitive forms of life. Into the Reservation come Bernard and Lenina, the Ferdinand and Miranda of the novel. They meet their Caliban in John, the wild "savage" who has educated himself with an old copy of Shakespeare's plays. John is brought to London where he is appalled by what he sees; he prefers a world in which humanism and freedom exist, even at the price of suffering. The novel concludes with John, in a savage fury, killing Lenina and then committing suicide after he realizes what he has done. His tragic end is in contrast to the conclusion of *The Tempest* where Caliban is left behind on his island. One of Huxley's last works before his death was an essay, "Shakespeare's Religion," published in *Show* magazine (February 1964).

Hymen. The ancient Greek god of marriage. In *The Two Noble Kinsmen,* he appears in the wedding procession of Theseus and Hippolyta. In *As You Like It,* he restores Rosalind to her father and performs the nuptial ritual.

I

Iachimo. In *Cymbeline,* the villainous Italian who wagers that he can seduce Posthumus' wife, Imogen. Failing in the seduction attempt, Iachimo manages to smuggle himself into Imogen's chamber, observe her at sleep, and take inventory of her charms. When he falsely claims success, Iachimo's report is so slyly touched with erotic reminiscence that Posthumus is easily convinced of Imogen's infidelity. At the play's conclusion, a repentant Iachimo confesses his vile deception and is pardoned by his victim.

Iago. In *Othello,* a supreme villain whose commitment to evil is so absolute as to defy rational explanation. Iago's apparently "motiveless malignity" has puzzled critics and readers for centuries. The phrase was coined by Coleridge, who argued that Iago's self-expressed motives for his villainy—anger resulting from his being passed over for promotion and his suspicion that Othello had cuckolded him—are rationalizations by which Iago attempts to provide a plausible reason for the deeply-rooted, inexplicable evil in his nature. Other critics, equally dissatisfied with Iago's explanations, have supplied their own interpretations of his behavior. These range from lust for Desdemona to a will-to-power, a desire to control other people's lives. Implicit in these latter views is the modern assumption that a dramatic character must be motivated, something which was not always true of the Elizabethan theatre with its rich tradition of dramatic convention. In this connection, Iago is perhaps best explained in terms of the conventional part of the VICE in medieval drama, a familiar figure to an Elizabethan audience (see OTHELLO: *Comment*). He is also, however, a cynical rationalist who denies the existence of any values other than those of self-interest. His polar opposite is Desdemona, whose life (and death) is a refutation of Iago's creed. [Bernard Spivack, *Shakespeare and the Allegory of Evil,* 1958.]

Ibsen, Henrik (1828–1906). Norwegian playwright. Generally regarded as the father of modern drama, Ibsen made striking contributions in two divergent areas of drama. To his dramas of psychological naturalism such as *A Doll's House* (1879) or *An Enemy of the People* (1882) he brought a concern with important social themes which revolutionized the 19th-century theatre. In later symbolic dramas (*The Wild Duck,* 1884; *The Master Builder,* 1892) he pointed the way to the future development of the theatre.

The Shakespearean influence on Ibsen's work was evident fairly early in his career. The first indication of Shakespearean traits appeared in his *Lady Inger of Östråt* (1855), a tragedy whose heroine resembled Lady Macbeth. The influence of *Othello* is traceable in his historical tragedy *The Pretenders* (1864), an *Coriolanus* provided some hints for the main character in *Brand* (1866), as well as being the source o the title *An Enemy of the People*. In 1855 Ibsen delivered a lecture on "Shakespeare and His Influenc on Nordic Art" but the text of the lecture is not extant. [Halvdan Koht, "Shakespeare and Ibsen," *Journal of English and Germanic Philology*, Januar 1945.]

I. C. See C., I.

Iden, Alexander. Sheriff of Kent during the reig of Henry VI. Iden discovered the rebel leader Jac Cade who, deserted by his men, had hidden in field. Iden won the reward offered for the rebel' capture. In *2 Henry VI,* Iden finds Cade hiding i his garden and, when attacked, kills him. On learning whom he has killed, Iden takes Cade's head t the King and is knighted. [W. H. Thomson, *Shakespeare's Characters: A Historical Dictionary,* 1951.

I. M. See M., I.

imagery. The present wave of studies in Shakespeare's imagery first took definite shape about th year 1930. Its origins, however, go back to the lat 18th century, for all contemporary interest in poeti or dramatic imagery is a particular manifestation o modern Romanticism, with its probing of associational psychology, its ideal of organic unity, and it willingness to find prophetic significance in art.

The term "imagery" as it is now used includes an word or group of words conceived as an analogica unit of thought or physical sensation. Thus ever figure of speech (simile or metaphor) is an "image" and one may speak of "sickness" or "disease" imager in *Hamlet* as introduced by Francisco's remark: "'Ti bitter cold, / And I am sick at heart" (I, i, 8–9). Thi survey will include three general kinds of imager studies. First, those that show a primary interest i discovering the personality of the man who chos the imagery. Second, those that develop an argumen of symbolic or moral "vision" from the imagery And third, those that use imagery as an essentia means of discussing dramatic theme or atmospher moral sensibility or "vision," and meaning or statement. The distinction between the second and thir categories is most often a matter of degree, but i actual practice that difference is very important. shall of course be unable to describe or even mentio all the lengthy and detailed studies of imagery tha have been written. My purpose is to discuss only th major representative examples.

Attempts to classify or interpret imagery are face with considerable difficulties that cannot be displayed at length here. But one central aspect of th problem which has been widely recognized should be illustrated. In an article ("Suggestions for a New Approach to Shakespeare's Imagery," *Shakespeare Survey 5*, 1952) that has yielded good results, R. A. Foakes uses the following example:

> Sleep that knits up the ravell'd sleave of care.
> (*Macbeth*, II, ii, 37)

This may be classified as an image of a "ravell'd sleave" (what Foakes calls the *subject-matter*) or as an image giving force to the "idea of sleep" (the *object-matter*). That is to say, every image is or implies a comparison offering two directions of inquiry. Several students of imagery have noted this problem and have given the two halves of the image special names. H. W. Wells in *Poetic Imagery* (1924) calls the *subject-matter* the "minor term" and its companion the "major term." I. A. Richards calls the *subject-matter* the "vehicle" and its companion the "tenor." Several general facts may be kept in mind in relation to this distinction. Students interested in the personality of Shakespeare tend to classify and analyze imagery in terms of the *subject-matter*. Those interested in symbolic significances tend to stress the *object-matter*, and of the two the *object-matter* has been by far the more important in recent studies.

The central figure in the emergence of this literary activity was undoubtedly Caroline F. E. Spurgeon. Her Shakespeare Association lecture of 1930 was "Leading Motives in the Imagery of Shakespeare's Tragedies," in which she showed how "recurrent images" have the effect of a "motif" in a Wagner opera or—more accurately—the "peculiar quality" of "Blake's illustrations to his prophetic books." By observing these patterns Miss Spurgeon expected to find how Shakespeare "sees and feels the main problem or theme of the play, thus giving us an unerring clue to the way he looked at it, as well as a direct glimpse into the working of his mind." Miss Spurgeon also distinguished between the imagery of the earlier plays, which is decorative, occasional, and frequently tied to a source, and the imagery of the mature plays, which is subtle, complex, and all-pervading. The following year she addressed the British Academy on "Shakespeare's Iterative Imagery (i) As Undersong (ii) As Touchstone in His Work." Here she concentrated on what was essentially her main interest, the discovery of Shakespeare's personality, by studying "clusters of certain associated ideas" that reveal what "the psychoanalyst would call 'complexes.'" One of the most striking of these "clusters" was that of fawning dogs, candy, and melting. Hamlet, for example, in assuring Horatio that he is not flattering him says:

> Why should the poor be flatter'd?
> No, let the candied tongue lick absurd pomp,
> And crook the pregnant hinges of the knee
> Where thrift may follow fawning.
> (III, ii, 64–67)

This chain of association had in fact been noticed by Walter Whiter at the end of the 18th century. Miss Spurgeon, however, gave the rediscovery a new significance, interpreting the imagery in a context of dramatic intensity that betrayed Shakespeare's deep personal disgust at "feigned love and affection assumed for a selfish end." She thought it "as certain as anything can be, short of direct proof, that he had been hurt, directly or indirectly, in this particular way." But most of her observations gave us a picture of Shakespeare the quiet and sensitive country man, long remembering the crafts, trades, and sports of rural England. All in all, there was little surprising in Miss Spurgeon's analysis of Shakespeare's personality. It was her method that was questionable, in proceeding so easily from dramatic imagery to biographical experience and convictions.

Miss Spurgeon had planned to write three major studies based on imagery. The first was intended to examine Shakespeare's "personality, temperament, and thought," together with the "themes and characters of the plays." Her early essays accomplish this aim in part, and it was completed in *Shakespeare's Imagery and What It Tells Us* (1935). She did not live to complete the other two, which would have dealt with problems of authorship and "the background of Shakespeare's mind and the origins of his imagery." Although the major part of *Shakespeare's Imagery* is directed towards her most disputable conclusions about Shakespeare the man (for example, that Shakespeare blushed easily and disliked noise), we must not forget that she established the thematic structure of the plays on the basis of imagery. Although some may disagree with her classification of the images or her count, almost everyone gives serious credit to her method of determining a play's atmosphere or thematic structure.

That Miss Spurgeon's view of Shakespeare's poetry was very much a Romantic one is indicated by her comparisons, in *Shakespeare's Imagery*, between Shakespeare, Keats, and Wordsworth. She was therefore insensitive to the rhetorical artistry that would have struck Shakespeare's contemporaries as strongly as his suggestive powers. See RHETORIC.

On the thematic relations of Love and Time, Miss Spurgeon quotes with approval from G. Wilson Knight's *The Wheel of Fire* (1930), but his work was already developing in a direction very different from hers. Perhaps Miss Spurgeon's most distinguished follower was Una Ellis-Fermor, who used her methods in *Jacobean Drama* (1936) and *The Frontiers of Drama* (1945). By 1937 it had become apparent that a new movement in criticism was established, and a backward look at this phenomenon was taken by Miss Ellis-Fermor in *Some Recent Research in Shakespeare's Imagery* (1937). Among other pioneers of imagery study, Miss Ellis-Fermor cited Henry W. Wells for *Poetic Imagery . . . from Elizabethan Literature* (1924), Stephen J. Brown for *The World of Imagery* (1927), and Elizabeth Holmes for *Aspects of Elizabethan Imagery* (1929). Special note should also be made of George Rylands' *Words and Poetry* (1928), which looked closely at the diction and figurative language of the early Shakespeare as opposed to the mature work. In 1930 another study of Shakespeare's diction by F. C. Kolbe, *Shakespeare's Way*, emphasized the importance of key words repeated in relation to thematic ideas. And as early as 1928, G. Wilson Knight had made public his position. I shall discuss Knight and a number of other important persons below.

One of Miss Spurgeon's more scientific followers was Edward A. Armstrong, ornithologist and psychologist. In *Shakespeare's Imagination, A Study of the Psychology of Association and Inspiration* (1946), Armstrong diagramed a number of "clusters": a kite-bed-death-spirits-birds-food "cluster"; a beetle-crow-mice-night-death-madness-fairies-cliff "cluster"; a drone-weasel-(king-creature)-creeping-cat-mood-sucking-music "cluster"; and the like. These were and are interesting patterns, but Armstrong's conclusions were not revelatory. The following, for example, from *Shakespeare's Imagination*, is what one would get as a general impression from the plays:

> The foundation of Shakespeare's imaginative thought . . . is the realisation and expression of life's dualism. His mind was dominated by the warring opposites disclosed by experience. Here we have one of the many indications of the "primitive" or "universal" mould of his mentality.

In the study of imagery as evidence of authorship, Miss Spurgeon did make a start with "Imagery in the *Sir Thomas More* Fragment" (*Review of English Studies*, VI, 1930) and in two chapters of *Shakespeare's Imagery*. The fullest development of this and other aspects of the *Sir Thomas More* problem was accomplished by R. W. Chambers in *Man's Unconquerable Mind* (1939). An even more extensive use of Miss Spurgeon's work in a parallel area was Marion Bodwell Smith's *Marlowe's Imagery and the Marlowe Canon* (1940). Generally it is safe to say that no question of authorship in the Elizabethan age could be argued today without attention to the imagery of those artists in question.

Every editor and critic of Shakespeare has been inevitably a student of his imagery. What is done with the text depends of course on the taste and aesthetic assumptions of the person at work. The term "imagery" was familiar to rhetoricians from Aristotle on and was applied critically to English poets before Shakespeare's day. John Dryden and Joseph Addison used the term to describe vivid poetic passages, and Dr. Johnson thought it worth defending his tragedy *Irene* on the strength of its imagery (*OED, imagery*, sb.; *image*, v.; and *icon*). But the Renaissance and 18th-century taste in imagery favored logical precision and the decorum of the classical epic or its imitations. Today's taste is for vagueness and ambiguity of reference, for richness of connotation and atmosphere. In his *Troilus and Cressida* (1679), Dryden "improved" upon Shakespeare's method of saying "nothing without a Metaphor, a Simile, an Image, or description," as he described it in his Preface, by removing them. In so doing, of course, Dryden revealed that he did not grasp the essential nature of Shakespeare's dramatic art. However, it is a mistake to believe that we can ignore the decisions of 18th-century editors because they had an alien view of Shakespeare's imagery. The editions of Nicholas Rowe, Alexander Pope, and the later editors are still useful and powerful authorities, and their usefulness ought to remind us that the cycles of changing taste never end.

One notable example will suffice to show that the imagery of Shakespeare's plays as we now read them is strongly affected by the taste and decisions of 18th-century editors. In his edition of 1725 Pope saw no reason to depart from the Quarto and Folio reading of *Richard II* (III, iii, 100). The context is the King's warning to Bolingbroke and those with him that the rebellion will bring a plague of civil war upon England.

> But ere the crown he looks for live in peace,
> Ten thousand bloody crowns of mothers' sons
> Shall ill become the flower of England's face,
> Change the complexion of her maid-pale peace
> To scarlet indignation, and bedew
> Her pastor's grass with faithful English blood.
> (III, iii, 95–100)

So line 100 reads—along with Pope—in the recent edition of Matthew W. Black (Penguin Edition, 1957), while the edition of Peter Ure (New Arden Edition, 1956) reads:

> Her pastures' grass with faithful English blood.

In so emending his text Ure follows the innovation of Edward Capell, a later editor of the 18th century. The basis of the emendation must be a sense of what seems more suitable to the dramatic and poetic context, i.e., more "Shakespearean." Both 20th-century editors have digested the historical scrutiny of the play and then decided upon images of markedly different traditions of poetic quality. What is particularly interesting in this instance is that Black's (and Pope's) reading of the passage as an image of Richard as England's "shepherd" suits admirably Ure's general interpretation of the play. For in Ure's view the last part of the play "trenches upon a sacred tragedy, the divesting of royalty of its mysterious panoply." The "shepherd" image here then would appear to be part of the "cluster" of images in the play associating the King with Christ. These divisions and chance agreements among editors should serve as a caveat against our deciding that we have caught the definitive sense of Shakespeare's art. Every scrupulous reader of Shakespeare will find himself baffled by similar decisions at important moments in the plays. Incidentally, the reading "pastures'" is the dominant modern one, being adopted in the texts of G. L. Kittredge, W. A. Neilson and C. J. Hill, G. B. Harrison, and Peter Alexander. Kittredge also credits Lewis Theobald with the reading "pastures'" in his separate volume text of *Richard II* (1941).

As I have noted, Miss Spurgeon's discovery of significant "clusters" was anticipated at the end of the 18th century in the work of Walter Whiter (1758–1832). The title of his book was: *A specimen of a Commentary on Shakespeare. Containing I. Notes on "As You Like It." II. An Attempt to Explain and Illustrate Various Passages, on a New Principle of Criticism, Derived from Mr. Locke's Doctrine of the Association of Ideas* (1794). Whiter's value as an annotator was recognized in the 19th century, but the general direction of Shakespearean criticism did not encourage the development of his method.

One purpose Whiter had in mind was the defense of readings that "have perhaps been too hastily condemned, as quaint, remote, or unintelligible." He pointed out that Shakespeare sometimes employs a particular image, not because it logically suits the thought he is developing, but because the originating word or circumstance suggested the image by independent association. For example, in the following passage the word "moist" is actually Shakespearean although it had been emended by Sir Thomas Hanmer and Edmund Malone to "moss'd":

> What, think'st
> That the bleak air, thy boisterous chamberlain,
> Will put thy shirt on warm? Will these moist
> trees,
> That have outliv'd the eagle, page thy heels
> And skip when thou point'st out?
> (*Timon of Athens*, IV, iii, 221–225)

Whiter explained that the image of the chamberlain putting the "shirt on warm" led by association to the adjective "moist" for the trees, because in Shakespeare's day the distinction between a "warm" and a "moist" shirt was what later came to be phrased as that between an "aired" and a "damp" (unaired) shirt. In "Shakespeare and the Diction of Common Life" (printed in *Shakespeare Criticism 1935–1960*, Anne Ridler, ed., 1963), F. P. Wilson noted Whiter's originality and also his failure to see in this instance that "moist" could mean "full of sap" or "pithy" in relation to trees. Shakespeare's chain of association is therefore supported by logic.

Whiter also illustrated the existence of puns created by the chance association of sound with sense, puns hidden from the conscious mind of Shakespeare himself. His aim in so doing was to excuse Shakespeare from the accusation that he was too fond of quibbles. Apparently, it did not occur to Whiter that an unconscious habit was evidence of a deeply engrained trait and therefore—even if reprehensible—all the more central to the artist's work.

The outstanding parallel between Whiter's observations and those of 20th-century critics is the instance of Shakespeare's associating "fawning obsequiousness" with dogs and melting candy or sweets. Whiter cited four such passages and successfully explained a fifth by knowledge of the pattern. In his *Suggestions* (1923) E. E. Kellett noticed two of the group; while George Rylands in *Words and Poetry* (1928) examined four. Miss Spurgeon discussed five such passages, including two Whiter had not noticed but also omitting two that he had. Whiter could not account for the origin of this image "cluster," while Rylands suggested that dogs must have been constantly present at Elizabethan meals, begging for sweets and licking the hands of the eaters who offered them.

Although Whiter stressed the unconscious nature of most of the links in the image patterns, he was not drawn into the analysis of the personality behind the associations. He was especially interested, however, in Shakespeare's theatrical environment as a source of metaphors in the plays. He also examined the wider expanse of theatrical activity in the court masque and pageant. Only now, in the work of Glynne Wickham is the significance of this environment becoming evident. In *Early English Stages 1300–1660* (2 vols., 1959–1963), for example, Wickham describes pageants that treated the audience to hailstones and snow which "were clearly sweets." This custom cannot be ruled out as a source of the melting candy imagery. Of course, there would be egregious fawning and feigned love during public pageants.

The explicit similarities between the work of Whiter and the works of Rylands and Spurgeon are less important than they are surprising. For the criticism of the 1930's has a stronger affinity to the Platonic aspects of Romantic thought, particularly as expressed by Coleridge and Keats. The most important of Keats' observations about Shakespeare was undoubtedly his conception—which he articulated in a letter of December 21, 1817—of the artist's "Negative Capability," the ability "of being in uncertainties, mysteries, doubts, without any irritable reaching after fact and reason." This idea underlies most of the systematic verbal analyses that have been done on imagery. It frees the critic to construct inductively a temperament characteristic of each play. Coleridge has proved to be the point of departure for all succeeding attempts to analyze Shakespeare's imagination through imagery. The central principle Coleridge illustrated from Shakespeare was the fusion of multiple significances into a unity. If there is any dominant impetus in the criticism of the last 30 years it is that.

The passages in the *Biographia Literaria* and the lectures which show Coleridge working on this principle are too familiar to require repetition. Less known is this passage cited in a recent collection of his Shakespearean writings (*Coleridge's Writings on Shakespeare*, T. Hawkes, ed., 1959):

> Each scene of each play I read, as if it were the whole of Shakespere's Works—the sole thing extant. I ask myself what are the characteristics—the Diction, the Cadences, and Metre, the character, the passion, the moral or metaphysical Inherencies, & fitness for theatric effect, and in what sort of Theatres—all these I write down with great care & precision of Thought and Language—and when I have gone thro' the whole, I then shall collect my papers, & observe, how often such & such Expressions recur & thus shall not only know what the Characteristics of Shakespere's Plays are, but likewise what proportion they bear to each other.

These words are from a letter to Sir George Beaumont dated 1804; yet they could serve as a description of the analytical procedure employed in numerous essays of the last few decades. A good example of how Coleridge still sets the limits of thinking about imagination through imagery is the essay on "Metaphor" by John Middleton Murry, printed in *Shakespeare Criticism 1919–1935* (Anne Ridler, ed., 1941). Murry demonstrates impressively that Shakespeare's poetry gives his plays a rich harmony of effects within a unity. The play in question is *Antony and Cleopatra*, and the whole argument is presented as a gloss on Coleridge's idea that images (in Murry's following words)

> become proofs of original genius only so far as they are modified by a predominant passion, or by associated thoughts and images awakened by that passion; or when they have the effect of reducing multitude to a unity; or succession to an instant; or lastly when a human and intellectual life is transferred to them from the poet's own spirit.

More difficult to estimate is the indirect influence of Coleridge through rhetoricians like I. A. Richards and his pupil William Empson. In any case one may say that their work is essentially Coleridgean in spirit and that it has had considerable effect. In 1930, when Miss Spurgeon published her first study, William Empson published *Seven Types of Ambiguity,* a book which—together with Richards' *Practical Criticism* (1929)—has served as a handbook for students of imagery.

But the critics of Shakespeare who immediately followed Coleridge did not find his observations useful—however much they may have admired them—in developing their main interest. Characterization, worked out on the basis of a rationalistic calculus of motivation and moral choice, was the dominant interest between Coleridge and A. C. Bradley at the end of the century. One may see this in *A History of Shakespearian Criticism* (2 vols., 1932) by Augustus Ralli, who notes that by 1840 there is an "advance"

> in appreciating Shakespeare's power to draw the characters of women—and also growing consciousness of the nature of his creative power in the insistence that his characters are real men and women, though produced by imagination, not observation.

That Shakespeare's characters are "real men and women" (see CHARACTER CRITICISM) or can be adequately conceived as such is just what criticism since the 1930's has insisted upon challenging. Instead, the plays are treated as vast lyric poems in which characterization is inseparable from thematic structure based primarily on imagery. While there was a growing fascination in the 19th century with Shakespeare as moralist, the mystery of his convictions was never long discussed without reference to the manners and motives of his characters as "real" people.

A little-known work at the end of the 19th century may be examined to discover what the study of imagery meant at that time. Its title was *Metaphor and Simile in the Minor Elizabethan Drama* (1895), a University of Chicago dissertation by Frederic I. Carpenter. Although Shakespeare is not directly studied in this book, his imagery is taken as the standard of greatness in Elizabethan drama. Carpenter thought a classification of Shakespeare's imagery to be unnecessary, since Schmidt's lexicon had made reference to "single metaphors" easy.

The central question that directs Carpenter's study of imagery is whether the Elizabethan dramatists are primarily poets of nature or of human life. He easily demonstrates that the latter is the case, and in this connection he stresses that visual or conceptual vividness is not of particular value in imagery. Rather, the "emotional association and the representative realization of human pathos and passion are far more important." By contrast, the exemplary poet of nature is Wordsworth. Carpenter states in a note that a recent study of Wordsworth's imagery had shown 258 images (or over 50 per cent) illustrating human things by natural; 46 natural by human; 136 human by human; and 59 natural by natural. This count and classification had been made by Vernon P. Squires, also of the University of Chicago. Thus Shakespeare and Wordsworth were viewed as the two great opposites of English poetry as defined by their imagery.

At several points Carpenter anticipates the conclusions of some 40 years later. He observes, fo[r] example, that

> the fundamental ethical questions connected wit[h] the life of the individual and the welfare of th[e] human soul are perpetually touched upon an[d] made prominent in the favorite comparisons an[d] metaphors of the Elizabethan playwrights.

This impression has been thoroughly documented i[n] works like A. O. Lovejoy's *The Great Chain o[f] Being* (1936) and E. M. W. Tillyard's *The Eliza[bethan] World Picture* (1943). Carpenter also stresse[s] what he calls the "Sombre Criticism of Life" in Eliza[bethan] drama, and especially in the plays of Joh[n] Webster. Of Webster's morbid quality he exclaim[s] "Such is Webster's world!" prefiguring the presen[t] critical habit of describing a play as a "world" con[structed] in its own terms. (Carpenter also led th[e] way in seeing a similarity between Shakespeare[’s] imagery and some of "Chapman's obscured bu[t] colossal metaphors.")

In 1928 G. Wilson Knight published an essay o[n] "The Principles of Shakespeare Interpretation[,"] which he has reprinted in his climactic work *Th[e] Sovereign Flower* (1958). The following passage wi[ll] show in embryo his approach (see SYMBOLISM) an[d] its relation to imagery:

> It will be found that each play thus expresses [a] particular and peculiar vision of human existenc[e] and that this vision determines not alone the choic[e] of the main plot, but the selection or invention o[f] subsidiary scenes and characters, the matte[r] brought up for discussion within the scenes, an[d] the very fibre of the language in allusion, choic[e] of imagery, metaphor and general cast of though[t].

Beginning with *The Wheel of Fire* (1930), Knigh[t] presented an "interpretation" of each play as a vi[sionary] unit based upon a self-consistent pattern o[f] words, imagery, and events. With this metho[d] Knight has been broadly influential among critics o[f] Shakespeare. However, he is unique in viewing th[e] plays as forming a single vast design concentrate[d] between 1599 and 1611 and working out Shake[speare's] "vision" of transcendent humanism.

Although the term "vision" has become commo[n] among critics of Shakespeare, poetry, and the mod[ern] novel, Knight uses it in a specifically metaphysi[cal] sense shown by this comment from "The Shake[spearian] Integrity" in *The Sovereign Flower:*

> His [Shakespeare's] recognition of the significan[t,] the apparently romantic, directions, is one with hi[s] nature-quality, since he uses mainly, and with un[swerving] insight, only what has positive strengt[h] and survival-value. That is, he is prophetic. To rec[ognize], explore, and express what was most signifi[cant] in England during the medieval-Renaissanc[e] transition was necessarily to be prophetic, since w[e] still, as a nation, as men, move by the momentu[m] then generated.

More specifically, Knight sees Shakespeare as th[e] poet of an optimistic royalism. He emphasizes th[e] centrality of kingly figures who define manliness an[d] fatherhood for humankind either by positive strengt[h] or individual failure. And tragedy is seen as a sacri[ficial] experience that generates new strength amon[g] those involved. All of these views are close to th[e] truth—or one important aspect of it—in Shakespeare. Often, however, one recognizes that Knight's "vision" is a mosaic of lines of events better limited to their original context. Notice, for example, how the passage from *King Lear* is given a special force in the following:

> But the evil also throws up more life, denying itself, as in the child-apparitions of *Macbeth*. And the worst conflicts are never depressing: they reflect a health and sense of energic being denied to the horror-paralysis and nightmare harmonies of *The Duchess of Malfi*. Lear's "No, I'll not weep" (*King Lear*, II, iv, 286) is a key passage in the Shakespearian victory. Moreover, spiritual conflict tends to objectify itself into armed opposition and the wound contributes to its own closure.

The three plays mentioned here are actually observed in distinct degrees of generalization. The description of *The Duchess of Malfi* is accurate. The inference about the relation of evil to good in *Macbeth* is at least arguable as one of two or more possible positions, while the weight of significance given to Lear's four words is beyond all reason unless one interprets the entire play in a limited way. One frequently has this experience in reading Knight's work. However, his very personal style has enabled him to do fundamentally redeeming work on formerly neglected or maligned plays such as *Measure for Measure, Troilus and Cressida*, and *Timon of Athens*. I have already noted that his view of the last two of these plays was adopted by Miss Spurgeon.

Knight has acknowledged a debt to the work of John Middleton Murry. His "manifesto" of 1928 also praised the work of A. C. Bradley; in fact, Knight has thought of his work as an extension of Bradley's. Although it is not likely that Bradley would have viewed the plays quite as Knight does, it is understandable that Bradley's work should have inspired Knight to develop his method of interpretation. Bradley remains unequaled for depth and range of observation, having anticipated much of the psychological, moral, and poetic views of today.

An event marking a sharp break with Bradley's emphasis on "real" characters was the publication of "How Many Children had Lady Macbeth?" (1933) by L. C. Knights. Bradley, in an appendix to his *Shakespearean Tragedy* (1904), had attacked the question seriously. And Knights seized upon the issue as an example of irrelevant concern resulting from a wrong approach to the plays. Evidence of characterization—in Knights' view—must be limited to what is said and done onstage, without regard for a hypothetical past or existence between the scenes. Further, characters must be viewed within the "world" of the play, which has its special laws and values determined by the lyric design of the whole. As a result, character tends to become an embodiment of the play's atmosphere or tone. In so proceeding, Knights exemplifies the critic who studies imagery indirectly as a measure of moral and aesthetic sensibility. His essays and lectures have been collected in *Explorations* (1946), *Some Shakespearean Themes* (1959), and *An Approach to Hamlet* (1960). See CRITICISM—20TH CENTURY.

After Miss Spurgeon's book, the most comprehensive study of Shakespeare's imagery that has yet appeared is *The Development of Shakespeare's Imagery* (1951) by Wolfgang Clemen. This is a revised and expanded version of the earlier book *Shakespeares Bilder* (1936). The appearance of the book in English is largely due to the encouragement of Una Ellis-Fermor and her interest in imagery studies. The general development of imagery that Clemen finds in the plays is familiar but unusually well documented. The imagery of the early plays is rhetorical, "inserted," and "inorganic," closer to the detached simile of the epic. That of the mature plays is highly complex and interrelated, reaching a pitch of complexity in *King Lear*. However, Clemen stresses that the plays of the great tragic period have *different* kinds of organization rather than advancing qualitatively one over another. Clemen's primary focus is upon character and the way imagery connects character with atmosphere.

The common principle among these students of imagery I have described is not their agreement as to Shakespeare's "vision" of reality or society. It is rather their Coleridgean and Platonic sense that the essential quality of Shakespeare's art is the fusion of multiplicities within unity. The most concentrated of such studies are two by Robert B. Heilman, *This Great Stage, Image and Structure in King Lear* (1948) and *Magic in the Web, Action and Language in Othello* (1956). The first chapter of the second book is a learned summation of arguments for and against the study of imagery and theme in their structural implications. Heilman's work has the advantage of a system applied to one end and carried out in careful and exhaustive detail. While he is carrying on the demonstration of interrelatedness his work is illuminating. One is always rather surprised to find that he thinks a play has a final "statement" to make.

Those who wish to keep Shakespeare within an Elizabethan perspective have not found imagery such fertile material as have those who explore the "inner world" of the play. In 1953 John E. Hankins published a study of *Shakespeare's Derived Imagery*, which made the mistake of arguing that Shakespeare got his images from particular sources. A special indebtedness was claimed to the *Zodiacus Vitae* of Palingenius as translated by Barnabe Googe (1561–1565). A much wiser strategy was used by Russell A. Fraser in *Shakespeare's Poetics in Relation to King Lear* (1962), which shows that Shakespeare's imagery can be found in a wide range of sermons, pageants, proverbs, emblematic illustrations, allegories, and traditional motifs of many kinds. Thus Shakespeare's centrality in his age is once again confirmed.

Although little has been done in comparing Shakespeare's imagery with that of his contemporaries, questions of authenticity have occasioned the use of imagery as a key. K. Wentersdorf argued for the authenticity of *The Taming of the Shrew* on the basis of its characteristic imagery in *Shakespeare Quarterly*, V (1954). And Alvin Kernan has made a case for *3 Henry VI* and against *The true Tragedy of Richard Duke of Yorke* on similar grounds in *Studies in Philology*, LI (1954). The soundness of imagery as a test of authorship was challenged by Moody E. Prior in *Shakespeare Quarterly*, VI (1955); however, Prior in turn was challenged on the basis of his own evidence by Kenneth Muir in

Shakespeare Survey 10 (1957). It is certain that imagery will be studied with even greater care in problems of authorship as they arise. One hopes that the comparative study of Shakespeare's imagery with that of his contemporaries will not continue to be neglected.

Only one of the recent books on imagery has developed a new dimension in such studies. I refer to Maurice Charney's *Shakespeare's Roman Plays: The Function of Imagery in Drama* (1961). Charney takes as a point of departure the criticism expressed by R. A. Foakes, who argued that dramatic and theatrical imagery should not be conceived in purely verbal terms. Therefore Charney's discussion of the Roman plays relates the verbal themes to presentational effects of staging, gesture, and spectacle. The advantage of this more physical approach to imagery is in confirming one's sense of a dominant impression suggested by the imagery. It puts the critic and the reader in more direct contact with the dramatic life of the play as it happens.

I have necessarily omitted from this survey many studies of imagery, such as R. D. Altick's "Symphonic Imagery in *Richard II*," *PMLA*, LXII (1947), or D. A. Stauffer's *Shakespeare's World of Images: The Development of his Moral Ideas* (1949). But what I have said indicates the main lines of procedure and interpretation. A look at the "Annotated Bibliography for 1963" in *Shakespeare Quarterly*, XV (No. 3) will show that imagery studies are still prominent in a year's work. In general the continuing impetus among critics is to establish some kind of thematic unity for each play.

The emphasis upon imagery and theme as the bases of Shakespearean dramatic structure has undoubtedly given the plays a new life. But like every kind of criticism it has its pitfalls. The most serious of these has probably been the forcing of particular meanings or "statements" upon the major plays. We have to go back as far as A. C. Bradley to find a critic who writes consistently from the conviction that the plays are human events. And that conviction is essential to sound criticism. At the same time, it is obvious that Shakespeare is discussed far too much in terms suited to modern poetry and the novel. But the study of imagery carried on with such energy in the last four decades has also given us a clearer view of the problem. [I. A. Richards, *Principles of Literary Criticism*, 1924; *The Arte of English Poesie*, Gladys D. Willcock and Alice Walker, eds., 1936; M. M. Morozov, "The Individualization of Shakespeare's Characters through Imagery," *Shakespeare Survey 2*, 1949; Kenneth Muir, "Fifty Years of Shakespearian Criticism," *Shakespeare Survey 4*, 1951; Muriel C. Bradbrook, "Fifty Years of the Criticism of Shakespeare's Style," *Shakespeare Survey 7*, 1954; *Coleridge's Writings on Shakespeare*, Terence Hawkes, ed., 1959; Sailendra Kumar Sen, "A Neglected Critic of Shakespeare: Walter Whiter," *Shakespeare Quarterly*, XIII, 1962; Caroline Spurgeon, "Shakespeare's Iterative Imagery," reprinted in *Studies in Shakespeare: British Academy Lectures*, Peter Alexander, ed., 1964; for a criticism of Miss Spurgeon's work, see W. T. Hastings, "Shakespeare's Imagery," *Shakespeare Association Bulletin*, XI, 1936 and Lilian H. Hornstein, "The Analysis of Imagery," *PMLA*, LVII, 1942.]—R. H.

Imogen. In *Cymbeline*, the King's daughter. Long acknowledged as one of Shakespeare's loveliest heroines, Imogen is also one of his most complex and detailed characters. Her virtues extend over the widest possible range—from tenderness and purity to courage and forbearance. Rejected by her father, pursued by villains, and despised by a husband who is witlessly convinced of her infidelity, she manages to endure her trials with a hardiness and strength which belie the seeming simplicity of her nature.

She thus emerges as a far more complex and, consequently, more credible character than would appear at first glance. Imogen exhibits a greater versatility than her literary ancestors, the stock heroines of the prose romances, of whom it was required only that they be pure and put upon. Her high spirits and wit enable her to overcome this passive conception of the female role and at the same time they represent a complicated and more fully realized woman. This complexity has drawn some adverse reaction, such as George Bernard Shaw's description of Imogen as "a double image . . . a natural aristocrat, with a high temper and perfect courage [as well as] an idiotic paragon of virtue." Shaw's iconoclasm notwithstanding, Imogen continues to be regarded as one of Shakespeare's most radiant creations.

imprint. See COLOPHON.

India. The growth of Indian nationalism after World War I placed Shakespeare in the ranks of an alien civilization imposing itself upon India, and consequently there grew a tendency to exalt Sanskrit literature and drama at the expense of the English classics. Nevertheless, since 1890 many of Shakespeare's plays have been published and produced in India in vernacular adaptations. The best known of these is Harana Chandra Rakskit's four-volume translation of the complete works into Bengali (1896–1902). At the present time the Sahitya Akademi of India is sponsoring an ambitious series of translations of the plays into a variety of Indian languages. Each of the volumes contains a special introduction in English by J. Dover Wilson. Among the volumes completed thus far are editions of *Hamlet* in Tamil and Telugu; *Macbeth* in Malayalam, Punjabi, Tamil, and Telugu; *Othello* in Hindi, Oriya, Tamil, and Telugu; and *King Lear* in Malayalam and Urdu. The most popular Shakespearean play with Indian audiences is *Othello*, which is regarded as a "tragedy of caste."

Indian scholars have made important contributions to Shakespeare studies. Among these have been Rentala Venkata Subbarau, whose *Othello Unveiled* (1906) and *Hamlet Unveiled* (1909) are highly regarded critical works. More recent work of note has been accomplished by S. C. Sen Gupta in his *Shakespearean Comedy* (1951) and *The Whirligig of Time: the Problem of Duration in Shakespeare's Plays* (1964). [K. R. Srinivasa Iyengar, "Shakespeare in India," *Indian Literature*, VII, 1964.]

Inganni. See TWELFTH NIGHT: *Sources*.

Ingleby, Clement Mansfield (1823–1886). Scholar. Educated at Cambridge, Ingleby was for many years a practicing attorney before abandoning law to devote his time entirely to scholarship. In the 1850's he became interested in the controversy regarding the authenticity of John Payne Collier's publications. In

The Shakspere Fabrications (1859) and *A Complete view of the Shakspere Controversy* (1861) he exposed Collier's forgeries and summed up the case against him in the manner of a lawyer. *Shakespeare Hermeneutics* (1875) consists of suggestions for the restoration of Shakespeare's text. *Shakespeare's Centurie of Prayse* (1874) is an anthology of allusions to Shakespeare from 1591 to 1693. Much of its contents became incorporated into the *Shakspere Allusion-Book* edited by John Munro (1909). *Shakespeare, The Man and the Book* (2 vols., 1877 and 1881) is a general survey. *Shakespeare's Bones* (1883) is a proposal to disinter the poet's body in order to examine the skull. Ingleby also served as a trustee of Shakespeare's birthplace and as vice president of the New Shakspere Society.

Ingratitude of a Common-wealth. See Nahum TATE.

Injured Princess, The, or the Fatal Wager. See Thomas D'URFEY.

inner stage. An interior acting area at the rear of the stage, believed by some to have been a feature of the Elizabethan theatre. A great deal of controversy has been generated over the nature and existence of the inner stage.

The stoutest defender of its existence is John Cranford Adams, whose reconstruction of the Globe places the inner stage (called "the Study" by Adams) between the tiring-house doors. Adams conjectures that the area was 7 or 8 feet deep, 23 feet wide, and 12 feet high and that it could be separated from the outer stage by curtains. Although for many years the theory positing an inner stage was accepted, its existence has in recent years come increasingly under doubt. See PLAYHOUSE STRUCTURE.

The two most important suggested alternatives to the inner stage are that of a curtained booth or pavilion set up against the tiring-house façade and that of a DISCOVERY SPACE behind the curtains at the rear of the stage. Advocates of these possibilities argue that the action in an inner stage as conceived by Adams would not be visible to a large portion of the audience in an Elizabethan public theatre.

No extant stage directions refer to an "inner stage." There is a direction in Robert Greene's *Alphonsus King of Aragon* indicating an action as occurring in "the place behind the stage," but the action called for would not require any significant amount of space. There are, however, fairly frequent directions calling for "discoveries," the exposing of interior scenes by the drawing back of curtains.

inns and taverns. See LONDON.

inns of court. Legal societies which trained young gentlemen in the law and in refined accomplishments such as dancing, singing, and playing musical instruments. In Shakespeare's time there were four inns of court: Lincoln's Inn, Gray's Inn, Middle Temple, and Inner Temple. The activities of the inns of court led naturally to the production of masques and plays, forms of entertainment so popular among these societies that they sometimes employed professional troupes to present them. Documentary evidence indicates that *The Comedy of Errors* was presented at Gray's Inn, and *Twelfth Night* at the Middle Temple. Whether *Troilus and Cressida* was also played at an inn of court has remained a matter of dispute.

On December 28 (Innocents' Day, the traditional date for the Feast of Fools), 1594, Gray's Inn held a revel presided over by the Prince of Purpoole, or Lord of Misrule who, for the 1594/5 revels was Henry Helmes. The revels had been suspended because of the plague, and the students now resumed them with gusto. The confusion and disorder grew so great that the planned entertainment could not be presented; the ambassador from the Inner Temple, especially invited for the occasion, was displeased and withdrew, taking his retinue with him. The *Gesta Grayorum*, the records of Gray's Inn, gives a contemporary account of the scene:

> After their Departure the Throngs and Tumults did somewhat cease, although so much of them continued, as was able to disorder and confound any good Inventions whatsoever. In regard whereof, as also for that the Sports intended were especially for the gracing of the *Templarians*, it was thought good not to offer any thing of Account, saving Dancing and Revelling with Gentlewomen; and after such Sports, a Comedy of Errors (like to *Plautus* his *Menechmus*) was played by the Players. So that Night was begun, and continued to the end, in nothing but Confusion and Errors; whereupon, it was ever afterwards called, *The Night of Errors*.

This presentation of *The Comedy of Errors* was doubtless planned in advance; there is no support for the suggestion that it was a last-minute substitution for the canceled entertainment. The Chamberlain's Men had earlier that day presented a play before Elizabeth (nothing supports the contention that the date of December 27 or 28 in the treasurer of the chamber's records is erroneous); this play was quite possibly *The Comedy of Errors* (see COMEDY OF ERRORS: *Date*). In any case, the gentlemen of Gray's Inn were probably not the first to see the play, since the private presentation of an untried piece was a risky matter: plays were tested in front of a public audience before they were given in private. However, it has been argued that the play was expressly written for Gray's Inn on the grounds that it is short, does not require an inner stage, and employs a large number of legal puns and references.

The diary of John MANNINGHAM, a law student, records that *Twelfth Night* was presented in the Middle Temple on February 2 (Candlemas), 1602: "At our feast wee had a play called 'Twelue Night, or What You Will,' much like the Commedy of Errores, or Menechmi in Plautus, but most like and neere to that in Italian called *Inganni*." The entry goes on to praise the "practise" of the plot laid against Malvolio. It is generally accepted that the passage is authentic, despite some doubts raised by the fact that one of the first persons to have worked with the manuscript was the notorious forger John Payne Collier, who was responsible for the spurious corrections in the Second Folio.

The suggestion that *Twelfth Night* was written expressly for an inn of court is based on the numerous legal jests in the play. The ironic reference to "bay windows transparent as barricadoes, and clerestories towards the south-north . . ." (IV, ii, 40–41) has been taken to refer to the oriel windows in Middle Temple Hall. It has also been suggested

MIDDLE TEMPLE HALL. JOHN MANNINGHAM RECORDED A PERFORMANCE OF *Twelfth Night* HERE ON FEBRUARY 2, 1602. (RADIO TIMES HULTON PICTURE LIBRARY)

that the saturnalian spirit of the Feast of Fools, with its inversion of normal relationships and its destruction of conventional order, inspired the account of the follies of Sir Andrew, Sir Toby, Feste, and Malvolio.

The scurrility running throughout *Troilus and Cressida*, and particularly the reference in the epilogue to the bawds and panders in the audience, render it unlikely that the play was ever presented at court. Peter Alexander has suggested that the witty obscenity of the play would have appealed to the young sophisticates of the inns of court, and that the tone of the play would have suited the atmosphere of their revels. Those who support this hypothesis point out that the play does not require an inner stage or a balcony; that Pandarus makes a number of legal references; that Hector's statements on law reveal a knowledge of the jurist Alberico Gentili; that the satirical elements in the play would have been appreciated by the wits of the law schools; that its undramatic, philosophical tone would have appealed only to an educated audience; that the large cast demanded by the play could better be supplied by a large amateur group than by Shakespeare's company; and that an allusion dated 1635 refers to Shakespeare and Marston as the favorite dramatists of the Middle Temple.

However, objections have been raised against Alexander's theory. It has been pointed out that during Shakespeare's lifetime there is no evidence that a private audience supported the production of a play exclusively for their own enjoyment. Such a procedure would have been considerably more expensive than simply hiring a company to perform a play already in its repertoire. It has been further objected that the allusions to the panders and bawds in the audience would have been equally out of place in both court and law school, and that such allusions rather indicate public performance. Finally, it has been argued that actually very little is known about the dramatic tastes of the law students, and that the statutes of the inns of court enforce a decorum and refinement inimical to the bawdy tone of *Troilus and Cressida*. This last argument, however, perhaps ignores the fact that the temporary suspension of decorum was the salient characteristic of the Feast of Fools. See TROILUS AND CRESSIDA: *Comment*. [*Diary of John Manningham*, John Bruce, ed., 1868; *Gesta Grayorum*, W. W. Greg, ed., 1914; Peter Alexander, "'Troilus and Cressida,' 1609," *The Library*, N. S., IX, 1928; A. Wigfall Green, *The Inns of Court and Early English Drama*, 1931; Oscar J. Campbell, *Comicall Satyre and Shakespeare's Troilus and Cressida*, 1938; Sidney Race, "Manningham's Diary," *Notes and Queries*, N. S., CXCIX, 1954; G. P. V. Akrigg, "*Twelfth Night* at the Middle Temple," *Shakespeare Quarterly*, IX, 1958; L. G. Salingar, "The Design of *Twelfth Night*," *Shakespeare Quarterly*, IX, 1958.]—E.G.

inn yards. Open areas of inns (hostels and taverns) used as theatres in London from the last half of the 16th century. Owners of inns appear to have been particularly eager to attract public entertainment (and, consequently, an enlarged clientele) to their houses; they entered into contracts with players and even undertook the structural changes necessary to construct stages on trestles or scaffolds.

The yards of the inns were entered from one or more streets through archways built under the inn buildings. The spacious yards were surrounded by galleries or balconies on which some spectators, sitting or standing, could be accommodated. Most of the audience, however, stood in the courtyard proper in front of a rough stage laid on trestles which had been erected between the pillars supporting the galleries. A gallery located directly above the stage might be used as an upper stage for balcony scenes or as battlements, for example. External stairways led to the upper floors. To the rear of the stage or at the sides were chambers which could be used by the actors as dressing- or tiring-rooms. The stage was equipped with no scenery and with few properties.

Inn yards had been used for performance of interludes and the like since early Tudor times; they were in regular use for the presentation of plays by the time of Elizabeth. The earliest London performance took place at the Saracen's Head Inn, Islington, and the BOAR'S HEAD INN, Aldgate, in 1557. In 1559, however, a proclamation prohibited plays in hostels and taverns, and by 1574, in response to Puritan critics of the stage, the city of London had instituted regulations directed against plays given in "greate innes, havinge chambers and secrete places adjoyninge to their open stagies and gallyries." The inns were probably considered too convenient for their audiences; certainly they afforded several advantages not available in the great public halls which had also been used for plays upon occasion. The inns offered refreshments of sack and ale and, as the Puritans were wont to argue, they had chambers for "deeds of darkness" after the play.

The RED LION INN, located outside the city's jurisdiction, was used as a theatre as early as 1567, according to an extant contract for the erection of scaffolding there that year. The BELL INN and CROSS KEYS INN in Gracechurch Street (where the Chamberlain's Men, Shakespeare's company, later performed), the BULL INN in Bishopsgate, and the BEL SAVAGE INN on Ludgate Hill were not used as theatres before 1575. Although civic regulation curtailed their activity, the inns remained in use to some extent for another 20 years, mainly because the theatres built in the suburbs could be rather uncomfortable in inclement weather. Despite this disadvantage, with the construction of James Burbage's Theatre in 1576 the dramatic focus in London shifted to playhouses constructed specially for plays. [J. Q. Adams, *Shakespearean Playhouses*, 1917; E. K. Chambers, *The Elizabethan Stage*, 1923.]

interludes. An ambiguous term used to describe dramatic entertainments in the late 15th and early 16th centuries. There is a lack of agreement among scholars as to whether interludes were playlets presented in the interval of a longer entertainment or feast, or short plays presented at the hall of a great noble. In either case the defining characteristics of interludes were brevity and wit.

The earliest extant English interlude is *Fulgens and Lucres* (c. 1496) by Henry Medwall. Other successful practitioners of the art were John Heywood (1497?–?1580) and John Rastell (c. 1475–1536), both of whom were related to and companions of Sir Thomas More. Heywood's interludes include *The Four P's*, *The Play of the Weather*, and *John John The Husband, Tyb his Wife and Sir John the Priest* (all first published in 1533). Rastell's best-known interlude is *The Nature of the Four Elements* (1519). Another important interlude is John Bale's KYNGE JOHAN, the earliest play dealing with English history.

Interludes were generally acted by a company of four. A royal company of interluders is traceable to the reign of Henry VII (c. 1493). By the time of the accession of Elizabeth (1558), however, interludes had given way to the newly developing dramas favored by the queen and presented at court by companies of boys.

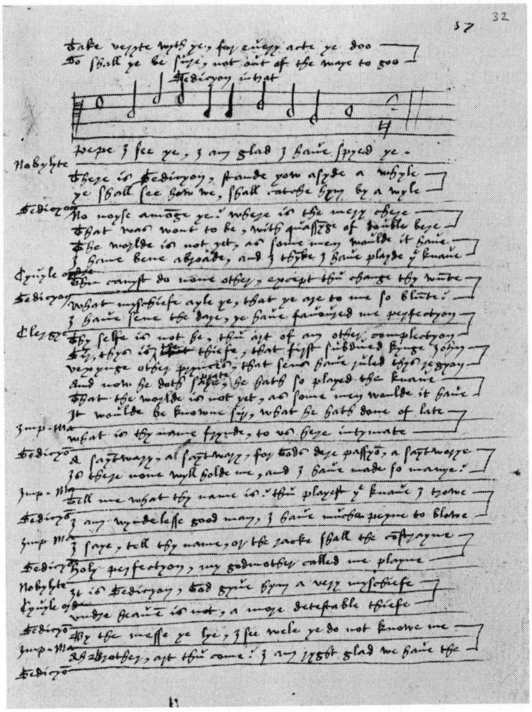

A PAGE OF THE MANUSCRIPT OF BALE'S *Kynge Johan.* IT IS OF PARTICULAR INTEREST BECAUSE OF THE MUSICAL NOTATION WRITTEN WITH THE TEXT. (HUNTINGTON LIBRARY)

Interludes are important in the development of English drama, for they represent a transition from the morality plays of the 15th century to the rich dramatic literature of the late 16th century. They facilitated the movement away from the abstract allegory of medieval drama and provided a concrete and particularized focus for succeeding drama.

The Puritans used the term "interlude" from a very early date to describe, pejoratively, any kind of play.

Invader of His Country, The. See John DENNIS.

Iphis and Iantha. A lost play ascribed to Shakespeare. It was entered in the Stationers' Register June 29, 1653 by Humphrey Moseley, a bookseller, as "Iphis & Iantha or a marriage without a man, a Comedy. By Will: Shakspeare."

Iras. In *Antony and Cleopatra*, an attendant on Cleopatra. Iras falls dead a moment after her mistress kisses her attendants farewell (V, ii).

Ireland. In Shakespeare's time, Ireland was an unwilling and unyielding colony of England. The attempts of the Tudor governments to administer and govern the Irish resulted in continual failure. The failure cost the English dearly in money and manpower, both of which were needed to quell the repeated uprisings of the Irish clans in the north and west. The situation reached its most critical point when the leader of the Irish rebels, Hugh O'Neill, earl of Tyrone (c. 1540–1616), entered into negotiations with England's powerful enemy, Philip II of Spain. Every English general who sought to subdue the rebels failed and in 1599 the unhappy task fell to the earl of ESSEX; accompanied by Shakespeare's patron, the earl of Southampton, Essex left England in command of a large army. In *Henry V* Shakespeare expressed the hopes of the English in a reference to Essex' expected return, "bringing rebellion broached on his sword."

However, the impetuous Essex was as unsuccessful as his predecessors in bringing Tyrone to heel, and he suffered a humiliating defeat from which he never recovered. Essex' successor, Sir Charles Blount, Lord Mountjoy (1563–1606), was more successful however. In 1603, Tyrone finally surrendered, and the subjugation of the Irish was achieved.

Shakespeare's portrait of an Irishman is given in *Henry V* in the figure of Captain Macmorris, whose hot temper and national pride mark him as the first "stage Irishman." To the Elizabethans, the Irish were essentially barbarians, a conception on which Shakespeare capitalizes when he has Macmorris lament any inactivity as long as "there is throats to be cut."

Shakespeare in Ireland. During the Puritan interregnum, theatres were closed in Ireland as well as in England. With the Restoration, however, a Theatre Royal was established in Dublin which came to be known as the Smock Alley Theatre. Here were played a surprisingly large number of Shakespearean plays. Evidence of the Smock Alley's Shakespearean repertoire derives from a copy of the Third Folio, used by the company as a prompt-book. This and other extant evidence reveal that the company played at least 14 Shakespearean plays, at a time when the London companies were presenting few Shakespearean plays that had not been subjected to adaptations. The plays at the Smock Alley were *The Merry Wives of Windsor, Twelfth Night, The Winter's Tale, Henry VIII, 1* and *2 Henry IV, Timon of Athens, Macbeth, King Lear, Othello, Hamlet, A Midsummer Night's Dream, Troilus and Cressida, Julius Caesar,* and possibly *The Comedy of Errors.*

During the 18th century the Smock Alley was the center of Irish theatrical life. Shakespeare's plays, both in their adapted and original forms, were frequently played by many distinguished English actors on tour as well as by the native Dublin company. Members of this company who were later to win fame in London as Shakespeareans were James QUIN, Peg WOFFINGTON, and Thomas SHERIDAN, who was also the manager of the theatre for 10 years. In 1758 two other distinguished Irish actors, Spranger BARRY and Charles MACKLIN, opened up a second theatre in Dublin, known as the Crow Street Theatre. Unfortunately, the resultant competition proved unprofitable for both theatres, and they were eventually combined under the leadership of another Shakespearean actor, Henry MOSSOP.

In the latter half of the 18th century the Irish, following the English example, altered Shakespeare's plays in order to cater to the tastes of their audiences. MacNamara Morgan (d. 1762) adapted *The Winter's Tale* as *The Sheep-Shearing or Florizel and Perdita* (1755). Robert Jephson (1736–1803) adapted *Much Ado About Nothing* as *The Law of Lombard* (1779), and Frederick Pilon (1750–1788) in 1785 pr pared an adaptation of *All's Well That Ends We* while retaining Shakespeare's title. In the 19th cen tury both the Crow Street and Smock Alley theatr were replaced by the new Theatre Royal as the Iris home of Shakespearean theatre. In the 20th centur Dublin's Gate Theatre has frequently been the scen of Shakespearean production.

Two of the most distinguished Shakespearea scholars and critics are Irishmen, Edmund Malor and Edward Dowden, and some of Ireland's greate literary figures, including James JOYCE, G. B. SHAW and W. B. YEATS, have demonstrated a lively critic interest in Shakespeare. [William Smith Clark, *Th Early Irish Stage*, 1955.]

Ireland, John. See MUSIC BASED ON SHAKESPEAR *20th century.*

Ireland, William Henry (1777–1835). Forger c Shakespearean manuscripts. Ireland was the son c Samuel Ireland (d. 1800), a well-known London en graver. Both father and son shared an intense intere in rare books and antiquarian studies. In 1794 the visited Stratford, where they employed as a guide a imaginative, but rather unreliable, resident, Joh JORDAN. Jordan's "traditional" anecdotes, some c them concocted especially for his visitors, were in corporated by the elder Ireland in *Picturesque View on the Warwickshire Avon* (1795).

At the age of 19, William Henry Ireland was em ployed as a conveyancer's clerk, a position whic brought him into contact with early deeds and othe documents. He used these as models when he bega to create his own forgeries. Copied in ink, in imita tion of the poet's handwriting, were a great numbe of papers allegedly dealing with Shakespeare's ca reer: licenses, contracts with actors, notes, receipt a profession of faith, a letter to Anne Hathawa (containing a lock of her hair), a mortgage dee signed by Shakespeare, and snippets of verse. Ac cording to Ireland the source of the documents wa a wealthy friend who wished to maintain a secre identity and who was known simply as "M. H." I 1796 the "documents" were published as *Miscellane ous Papers and Legal Instruments under the Han and Seal of William Shakespeare.* The year befor their publication Samuel Ireland had placed his son "discoveries" on exhibition at his home, where the were examined and pronounced genuine by some o the leading literary figures of the day. At least thre prominent Shakespearean scholars, however—Josep Ritson, George Steevens, and Edmund Malone—per ceived the deception. Malone, indeed, was convince that the documents were spurious without havin even examined them. Malone's arguments in his *A Inquiry into the Authenticity of Certain Papers at tributed to Shakespeare, Queen Elizabeth, an Henry, Earl of Southampton* (1796) convinced man that the papers were forged. Encouraged neverthe less by the success of the published "manuscripts, Ireland announced the same year that he had discov ered a lost play, *Vortigern and Rowena,* which h attributed to Shakespeare. The claim did not go un challenged, and the production at the Drury Lane or April 2, 1796 elicited ridicule and laughter from th audience with its crude action and inept dialogue (Still convinced that his son had made an authenti discovery, Samuel Ireland had it published in 1799 as *Vortigern, an Historical Tragedy*, coupled with another "Shakespearean" vehicle titled *Henry the Second, an Historical Drama, supposed to be written by the Author of Vortigern.*) Toward the end of 1796, however, the younger Ireland confessed his forgeries in *An Authentic Account of the Shakesperian Manuscripts,* completely absolving his father of any complicity. Still, Samuel Ireland was widely and unjustifiably regarded as having had a hand in the deceit. He died in 1800, protesting his innocence to an incredulous public. The son wrote a detailed account of the affair later in his *Confessions of William Henry Ireland* (1805). He spent the rest of his life as a hack writer, engaged in producing a number of novels and volumes of verse. In 1827 he edited, anonymously, *Shakespeariana: Catalogue of all the Books, Pamphlets . . . relating to Shakespeare.*

One of the positive results of the scandal was the publication by George Chalmers of *An Apology for the Believers in the Shakespeare Papers* (1797), a defense of his own credulity and an important contribution to Shakespeare scholarship. [Sidney Lee, 'William Henry Ireland," *Dictionary of National Biography*, 1892; Bernard Grebanier, *The Great Shakespearean Forgery*, 1965.]

Iris. In *The Tempest,* a role assumed by one of the island's spirits in the masque arranged to entertain Ferdinand and Miranda. Iris is the messenger of the gods, especially Juno. She summons Ceres to celebrate "a contract of true love" (IV, i).

Iron Age, The. See Thomas HEYWOOD.

Irving, Sir **Henry.** Real name **John Henry Brodribb** (1838–1905). Actor and manager. Irving was generally regarded as the greatest Shakespearean performer of his day. Born in Somerset, he was educated at the local grammar school, after which he worked as a clerk for four years. He began his theatrical career at the age of 18, one of his first parts being that of Cleomenes in *The Winter's Tale.* Irving's first great success was in a production (1874) of *Hamlet;* his portrayal introduced the plaintive, frail, and introspective figure popularized by 19th-century Shakespearean critics. The play ran for 200 performances. The following year he presented a controversial portrait of Macbeth and in 1876 played Othello to a mixed critical reaction. In 1877 he presented for the first time since the early 18th century Shakespeare's version of *Richard III*, instead of Colley Cibber's adaptation of that play, which had until then held the stage.

In 1878 he bought the Lyceum Theatre where for the next 24 years he triumphed in a series of Shakespearean roles including Shylock (1879), Benedick (to Ellen Terry's Beatrice, 1881), and Lear (1892). In 1889 he played Shylock before Queen Victoria and in 1895 received the outstanding honor of becoming the first actor to be knighted. Despite severe illnesses and financial setbacks, he continued acting up to the day of his death. He was buried in Westminster Abbey.

Irving's acting was marked by a slowness of speech and an intellectual conception of the roles he portrayed. His proclivity for elaborate, even sumptuous productions left him open to a charge of obscuring Shakespeare with scenery. He was, nevertheless, the most important single force in the presentation of serious Shakespearean drama in the latter half of the 19th century. [*Dictionary of National Biography*, 1885- .]

Irving, Washington (1783–1859). American essayist, short story writer, and biographer; author of *Knickerbocker's History of New York* (1809) and *The Sketch Book* (1819–1820). Irving felt that Shakespeare had "a phrase for everything" and apparently quoted him more than he quoted any other author. In *The Sketch Book* Irving describes his visits to Shakespeare's birthplace at Stratford and to the site of the Boar's Head Tavern, where Shakespeare located the revels of Falstaff and Prince Hal. These sketches, according to Edward Wagenknecht, reveal "affection for and familiarity with Shakespeare, but little erudition."

"The Boar's Head Tavern, Eastcheap: A Shakspearian Research" opens with a humorously condescending attack upon Shakespearean commentary. Irving suggests that Shakespeare is obscured by his commentators just as the statue of a saint is obscured by the smoke from candles lighted by devotees. "Every writer considers it his bounden duty to light up some portion of his character or works, and to rescue some merit from oblivion." Specifically, "the commentator, opulent in words, produces vast tomes of dissertations; the common herd of editors send up mists of obscurity from their notes at the bottom of each page; and every casual scribbler brings his farthing rushlight of eulogy or research, to swell the cloud of incense and of smoke." Instead of contributing to this haze of smoke, in which "Every doubtful line has been explained a dozen different ways," Irving prefers to recount his experiences and musings at Eastcheap.

Irving found the site of the Boar's Head Tavern disenchanting. "The madcap roister has given place to the plodding tradesman," he notes, and no song is heard except "the strain of some siren from Billingsgate, chanting the eulogy of deceased mackerel." The only relic of the tavern was its sign, a boar's head carved in relief on stone. The tavern, Irving informs the reader, had been destroyed during the great fire of London. Rebuilt, it was left to St. Michael's Church, and later turned into a shop. Irving recounts a yarn about the ghost of Robert Preston, a former bartender, who is supposed to have appeared at a vestry meeting one evening. At a neighborhood tavern Irving is shown a picture of the old tavern itself on a metal tobacco box, and an antique goblet, which he suggests may be the "parcel-gilt goblet" of the play. The sketch, though whimsical, is not altogether successful.

In "Stratford-on-Avon" Irving describes the cottage traditionally cited as Shakespeare's birthplace as "a small, mean-looking edifice of wood and plaster, a true nestling-place of genius, which seems to delight in hatching its offspring in by-corners." He pokes fun at the "relics" of Shakespeare and draws an uncomplimentary sketch of Mrs. Hornsby, who displayed the relics. Later he tells of meeting a sexton and his companion who had been "employed as carpenters on the preparations for the celebrated Stratford jubilee." They remembered Garrick, "the prime mover of the fete."

Finally Irving describes his visit to Charlecote, a mansion owned by the Lucy family. He recounts the anecdote of Shakespeare's poaching on the Lucy estate and he argues that Justice Shallow of *The Merry Wives of Windsor* was modeled on Sir Thomas Lucy. Irving concludes by noting that "under the wizard influence" of Shakespeare he "had been walking all day in a complete delusion." [Edward Wagenknecht, *Washington Irving: Moderation Displayed*, 1962.]

Isabella. In *Measure for Measure*, Claudio's sister and an aspirant to the sisterhood of Saint Clare. "I hold you as a thing ensky'd and sainted" is the corrupt Lucio's sincere tribute to her. When Claudio is imprisoned for immorality, Isabella intercedes with Angelo, the deputy, on his behalf, though deploring her brother's vice. On Angelo's proposal that she surrender her virginity to free Claudio, Isabella goes to prepare Claudio's mind for death, holding the conviction that "more than our brother is our chastity."

Of all of Shakespeare's female characters, none has evoked a wider range of reaction than Isabella. Her refusal to sacrifice her virginity in order to save her brother's life has always evoked mixed comments. She has been alternately condemned as an "icicle" or lauded as a saint. Una Ellis-Fermor has seen her as the embodiment of "pitiless, unimaginative self-absorbed virtue"; R. W. Chambers has viewed her as a type of Christian martyr. Between these two extremes lies the view of her as an attractive figure whose chastity is presented as admirable but which is not the highest value in the play. According to this interpretation, Isabella's suffering enables her to emerge with a stronger sense of the importance in life of mercy and charity. [Una Ellis-Fermor, *The Jacobean Drama*, 1936; R. W. Chambers, *Man's Unconquerable Mind*, 1939.]

Isabella, or **Elizabeth, of Bavaria** (1370–1435). Queen of Charles VI of France. In *Henry V*, Isabel invokes God's blessing on the coming marriage of her daughter Katharine to King Henry (V, ii).

Isabella of Valois (c. 1389–1409). Daughter of Charles VI of France and the second wife of Richard II of England, to whom she was married as a child in 1396. Richard was strongly attached to his queen, but did not see her again after his departure for Ireland in 1399. When Bolingbroke overthrew her husband, Isabella was for a time imprisoned; in 1401 she returned home. In 1406 she was married to her cousin Charles, count of Angoulême, and three years later she died in childbirth.

In *Richard II*, Isabella appears as Richard's adult wife. When he is taken to Pomfret Castle, she bids him a sad farewell (V, i).

Isle of Dogs (1597). A satiric comedy by Thomas NASHE and Ben JONSON. The *Isle of Dogs,* no longer extant, contained such explosive political satire that its performance at the Swan by Pembroke's Men on July 28, 1597 resulted in the closing of all the London theatres and the subsequent imprisonment of three performers, including Jonson, the co-author. The exact nature of the play is not known, but, as the product of the two greatest satirists of the age, it doubtless contained what the suppression order from the privy council described as "very seditious and sclanderous matter." See PEMBROKE'S MEN.

Italy. Shakespeare became popular in Italy at the beginning of the 19th century when Italian Romanticism began to be influenced by English writers. His name is mentioned quite early, however, by Antonio Conti of Padua in the Preface to his play *Il Cesare* (1726). Conti, a man of letters and a scholar, traveled to England in 1715 where he met Newton and apparently talked with John Sheffield, duke of Buckingham, about Shakespeare's plays. Conti's own play observes the unities strictly and gives no evidence of having been influenced by Shakespeare's *Julius Caesar.*

Paolo Rolli, who also came to England in 1715 was the first Italian to comprehend and appreciate Shakespeare. A lyric poet himself, and a translator of Milton, Rolli compared Shakespeare to Dante and suggested that Shakespeare had "raised the English theatre to heights which can never be surpassed . . . ." In his *Remarks upon M. Voltaire's Essay on the Epick Poetry of the European Nations* (1728) Rolli praises Shakespeare's histories and argues that Voltaire had never read *The Tempest* or *Macbeth*, the tragedy which Rolli considered Shakespeare's greatest. When he returned to Italy, however, Rolli did nothing to introduce Shakespeare to the Italian literary world.

In Italy, as in the rest of Europe, French taste was in command. The Italian playwrights Pietro Metastasio, who may have read Shakespeare in translation, and Carlo Goldoni, his contemporary, protested against the neoclassical interpretation of Aristotle's *Poetics,* but they realized it was useless to go against the climate of opinion. Lacy Collison-Morley in his *Shakespeare in Italy* (1916) argues that "there was no chance of Shakespeare becoming known at all in Italy until he had aroused the interest of a Frenchman of sufficient standing in the world of letters to command attention." The figure admirably suited for the role was VOLTAIRE.

In his *Lettres Philosophiques* (1734) Voltaire drew Shakespeare to the attention of literary men throughout Europe. Voltaire's views of Shakespeare dominated Italian opinion until the end of the century. Voltaire recognized that Shakespeare had a forceful and fertile genius, but he condemned the plays for their bad taste and their failure to conform with the rules. He felt that Shakespeare's tragedies were "monstrous farces" and was astonished to find that an audience familiar with Addison's *Cato* could endure them. Francesco Algarotti, a cultivated protégé of Frederick the Great and a disciple of Voltaire, notes in a letter generally prefixed to Voltaire's *Jules César* that in this work his master adopted the severity but not the barbarity of Shakespeare. Although Algarotti saw *Julius Caesar* in London in 1736 and probably knew more of Shakespeare, he was apparently unable to appreciate him.

The first Italian history of literature to mention Shakespeare is Francesco Saverio Quadrio's *Della Storia e della Ragione d'Ogni Poesia* (1743), but the author merely transcribes Voltaire. Other Italian critics who echo Voltaire are Luigi Riccoboni in his *Réflexions Historiques et Critiques* (1740), Carlo Denina in his *Discorso sopra le Vicende della Letteratura* (1760), and the Jesuit Saverio Bettinelli in his *Dialoghi sopra il Teatro Moderno* (1788). Francesco Milizia, Pietro Signorelli, and Aurelio Bertola in books appearing during the last quarter of the

18th century agree in condemning Shakespeare for his neglect of the unities, for his lack of good taste, and for his fondness for horror.

Voltaire's visit to England triggered an Anglomania which spread throughout Europe during the second half of the 18th century. English life, manners, science, government, and industry were eagerly studied by the Italians. Although English literature did not play a leading role in this craze, it was not overlooked. With the exception of Milton, who had been appreciated even earlier, the writers who found an audience in Italy were relative contemporaries, such as Pope, Addison, and Swift. Alessandro Verri, in his *Caffè*, and Gaspare Gozzi in the *Osservatore* imitated the English periodical the *Spectator*, and Giuseppe Baretti, who modeled his *Frusta Letteraria* on it, told Dr. Johnson that admiration for the *Spectator* was his principal reason for wanting to visit England. When pre-Romantic English poetry began to make its way to Italy, the stage was set for a defense of Shakespeare against the dictates of Voltaire.

Giuseppe Baretti, who became Dr. Johnson's friend and correspondent, was thoroughly familiar with Shakespeare and admired him. "Should anybody weigh, for instance, Shakespeare in the Aristotelian scales," he observes in the *Italian Library* (1757), "he would find him defective; yet was not Shakespeare at least as great a tragic poet as any Grecian? . . . Consult your heart rather than Aristotle when you read." Baretti had attacked the three unities in his second Preface to his translation of Corneille (1747–1748), and in his *Frusta*, No. 8, he argues that Shakespeare, "both in tragedy and comedy, is by himself a match for all the Corneilles, all the Racines and all the Molières of Gaul." Shakespeare, he maintains, is a "transcendent poet" whose genius soars beyond the reach of art. When in 1776 Voltaire sent his famous letter to the French Academy attacking Shakespeare, Baretti replied with his *Discours sur Shakespeare et sur Monsieur de Voltaire* (1778), an essay which defends Shakespeare and violently attacks Voltaire. Baretti claims that Voltaire did not know English and that his translations of Shakespeare are often faulty or so literal as to make the poet seem ridiculous. Voltaire's attempt to translate Shakespeare into French blank verse Baretti finds unfortunate, for, he suggests, the meter is utterly foreign to the spirit of the French language. The English were surprised to find their poet defended by an Italian critic writing in French, but Baretti's work went largely unnoticed.

Other Italian writers of the time shared Baretti's enthusiasm for England and for Shakespeare. Vittorio Alfieri, the only great writer of tragedy Italy has produced, admired Shakespeare though he was unable to read him in the original. Vincenzo Monti, the most popular Italian poet of the Napoleonic era, praised and imitated Shakespeare though, like Manzoni and many another contemporary, he used Le Tourneur's French translation. Ugo Foscolo, though a classicist, proclaimed Shakespeare "the master of all superhuman geniuses."

The Romantic revolution had a great effect upon the position of Shakespeare in Italy. Shakespeare came to Germany as a liberator. Italy, however, was too completely dominated by France and by sympathy with classical dicta to respond completely at this time to Shakespeare. However, after the fall of Napoleon, who had encouraged a classical revival in Italy, the way was opened to a reappraisal of the English poet. The leader of this movement was Alessandro Manzoni, the greatest name in Italian literature of the 19th century and an unqualified admirer of Shakespeare.

The word Romantic came to Italy in Mme. de Staël's *De l'Allemagne* (1813), which Napoleon would not allow to be printed in France. In this book Mme. de Staël argued that literature must be as free as man and that all nations had a right to intellectual equality. Thus the attack on the French hegemony in literature and politics was launched.

Though his own plays were rather classical, Manzoni called Shakespeare a "great and unique poet" with superhuman genius. "Anyone who wants to write," he once said in the Countess Maffei's drawing room, "must read Shakespeare." Considering Vergil and Shakespeare the greatest of poets, Manzoni praised the English playwright throughout his critical works and freely admitted the debt his own plays owed to Shakespeare. Shakespeare's influence upon Manzoni was recognized and the attention of contemporary Italian writers was turned to the English poet. Among these writers were Giovanni Berchet, the poet of the Italian *Risorgimento;* Silvio Pellico, one of the editors of *Conciliatore*, a journal founded by liberals in 1818; and Niccolo Tommaseo, one of the leading Romantic critics of the next generation.

The majority of Italian literary men of the age did not understand English well enough to read Shakespeare in the original. Manzoni read Le Tourneur's translation again and again until he became steeped in this French version of Shakespeare. During the years of the controversy between Romantics and classicists, the need for an Italian translation of Shakespeare was clearly felt. Mme. de Staël in her *Sulla Memoria e l'utilità delle traduzioni* (1816) argued that "the best cure for the wretched state of literature in the country was to be found in the translating of recent English and German poets." Thanks to Schlegel's translation, she suggested, Shakespeare was treated as a German author in Germany. The same thing, it was hoped, might be possible in Italy. In his *Lettera Semiseria di Grisostomo* (1816), which Collison-Morley calls "the real manifesto of Romanticism in Italy," Giovanni Berchet called for effective translations of Shakespeare's plays.

Michele Leoni devoted himself to the task of translating English writers. After translating *Paradise Lost*, Pope's *Essay on Man*, Sheridan's *School for Scandal*, Byron's *Lament of Tasso*, and Hume's *History of England*, Leoni turned his attention to Shakespeare. The *Tragedie di Shakspeare* appeared in 14 volumes, 1819–1822. The first volume contained a version of Johnson's *Essay on Shakespeare* and Rowe's *Life*. Each play was prefixed by Schlegel's Introduction and copious notes were provided by the translator. *The Tempest*, *King John*, *A Midsummer Night's Dream*, *Othello*, *Macbeth*, *Julius Caesar*, *Romeo and Juliet*, *Richard III*, *Cymbeline*, and *Hamlet*, revisions of earlier translations, were done in blank verse. *King Lear*, *Richard II*, and the two parts of *Henry IV* were rendered in prose for greater accuracy and because Leoni found English historical names difficult to manage in Italian verse. These translations are rather free and at times bowdlerized, Leoni often following Le Tourneur's omissions.

Leoni was not the first to undertake an Italian translation of Shakespeare. As early as 1756 Domenico Valentini translated *Julius Caesar* into the Tuscan dialect. Although his Preface discusses at length the qualifications of a translator, Valentini's own were less than ideal. Owing to a "natural impatience," Valentini did not understand English. This difficulty, he explains, was overcome by the willingness of his English friends at Sienna to explain the tragedy to him. Valentini's prose translation, though undistinguished, is surprisingly accurate. Considerable effort was taken to reproduce the puns in the first scene, for instance. Valentini's translation did not receive the encouragement he had expected and he did not continue the task. Toward the end of the century Giustina Renier-Michiel, the niece of the last doge of Venice, published her translations of *Othello*, *Macbeth*, and *Coriolanus*. These translations of Le Tourneur's French Shakespeare, though unimpressive, won considerable fame for her.

By the time Leoni's translations appeared the victory of the Romantics had been assured. Critics might not approve of Shakespeare's methods, but it was impossible for them to ignore him. He was universally recognized as one of the world's great writers. Evidence of the change in attitude is afforded by an article which appeared in the October 1821 issue of *Biblioteca Italiana*, a stronghold of the anti-Romantics. This long review of Leoni's translation echoes Johnson's justification of Shakespeare and goes so far as to suggest that Aristotle's "rules" would have been different had the philosopher read Shakespeare. Count G. U. Pagani-Cesa's *Sopra Il Teatro Tragico Italiano* (1825), the last serious attempt to buttress the position of the classicists, is significant primarily for the criticism it provoked. Reviewers claimed that Pagani-Cesa belonged to "another epoch" and affirmed Shakespeare's greatness.

In 1830 Giuseppe Mazzini contributed three articles to *Antologia*, a liberal paper which played an important part in the *Risorgimento*. These articles, which were to affect Italian opinion profoundly, argue that Shakespeare, though perhaps the greatest creator of characters in all literature, had no great guiding moral principle. The prophet of a new Italy regretted that Shakespeare had reproduced a past epoch instead of proclaiming a new one.

During 1830 and 1831 four translations of the English poet were published, culminating his triumph in Italy. Giuseppe Niccolini's *Macbeth* (1830) was perhaps the most successful Italian version of a Shakespearean play to have appeared to date. In 1839 Carlo Rusconi produced the first complete translation of Shakespeare's plays. This prose translation, in two volumes with continuous pagination, is far more accurate than Leoni's. His *Hamlet* remained standard in Italy into the 20th century. The most important Italian translation of Shakespeare is that of Giulio Carcano, who spent much of his life on the task and published the complete works in 12 volumes (1875–1882). Carcano's translation is in blank verse. Collison-Morley argues that "his lines often catch something of a Shakespearean ring, especially in the more rhetorical and poetical passages," but Guido Ferrando in a more recent study avers that the "Italian verse is rather too redundant, and the rendering of some of the most poetical passages is unsatisfactory."

More recently Diego Angeli embarked upon a new translation of the complete plays, the first of which, *The Tempest*, appeared in 1911. Ferrando judged them to be of "very unequal merit" and generally inferior to Carcano's translations. Recent single-play translations were provided in the *Biblioteca Sansoniana Straniera*. Each volume of this edition has a scholarly Preface, the English and Italian are given on opposing pages, and recent interpretations and clarifications are provided by copious notes. In this series the commentary of Aldo Ricci, Raffaello Piccoli, and G. S. Gargano is of particular interest. Salvatore Quasimodo has done sensitive translations of *Romeo and Juliet*, *Richard III*, *Othello*, *Macbeth*, and *The Tempest*. The first scholarly translation is being completed under the editorship of Mario Praz.

According to Guido Ferrando the contribution of Italy to sound Shakespearean criticism has been almost negligible. Worthy of note, however, is Giuseppe Chiarin's *Studi Shakespeariani* (1897), which contains an interesting study of the Italian sources of *The Merchant of Venice* and *Romeo and Juliet* and an essay on women in Dante and Shakespeare. Federico Garlanda's extensive monograph *Guglielmo Shakespeare; il poeta e l'uomo* (1900) is accurate and sound but it adds nothing to our knowledge of Shakespeare's life or the interpretation of his works. Benedetto Croce's essay on Shakespeare, which first appeared in *La Critica* (1919), is more significant as a statement of his critical position than as a contribution to Shakespearean scholarship. G. S. Gargano, a serious Italian Shakespeare scholar, has written provocatively of life in England in the late 16th and early 17th centuries in his *Scapigliature Italiane a Londra sotto Elisabetta e Giacomo I* (1923).

After World War I English was substituted for French in many of Italy's secondary schools and chairs in English literature were founded in the Italian universities. Florence, which has become the center of English studies in Italy, offers a course in Shakespeare each year. Shakespeare, in the original and in translation, has become a textbook in many Italian secondary schools. Recently many of the plays, especially *Othello*, *The Merchant of Venice* and *Macbeth*, have become popular and draw large audiences when they are played.

Although Shakespeare was accepted in Italy as a great writer in the 1830's, his plays were not performed on the Italian stage until considerably later. In the 18th century there were a number of adaptations of Shakespeare's plots, and audiences continued to show interest in ballets and operas based upon Shakespeare and even in plays that had been adapted to conform with the unities and with the classical view of decorum. Yet Italian producers hesitated when it came to playing Shakespeare straight. Their doubts were justified, for when Gustave Modena, the greatest Italian actor of the 19th century, attempted to play Othello at Milan in 1845, the curtain had to be lowered during the first scene amid a storm of hisses and whistles. Brabantio's appearance on the balcony half-asleep and with his clothes disordered 'as too much for an audience which had come to iew a "tragedy." Alemanno Morelli played Hamlet t Padua in 1850. Though no great success, Morelli's *Hamlet* fared better than had Modena's *Othello.* rnesto Rossi was the first Italian to interpret Shakespeare successfully on the stage. In 1855 he saw harles Kean's Richard III and received from him cting versions of *Hamlet, Othello,* and other plays. n the spring of 1856 Rossi played Othello at the 'eatro Re in Milan, a performance which was repeated several times. Rossi became famous in Italy as n interpreter of Shakespeare. In addition to Othello, hroughout his career he played Hamlet, Macbeth, ear, Coriolanus, Shylock, and Romeo. Garibaldi was o moved by Rossi's Hamlet, which he saw at Genoa n 1866, that he was unable to sleep after the perormance. Among the best interpreters of Shakespeare in Italy were Tommaso SALVINI, who played Othello, Hamlet, and Lear; Adelaide Ristori, known or her Lady Macbeth; Eleonora Duse, a delightful uliet; and Ermete Novelli, an excellent Shylock and 'etruchio.

Though Shakespeare has never been as successful n Italy as he has been in Germany, the Italians have een more receptive to him than have the French. hakespeare is played regularly on the Italian stage, ven in the inexpensive popular theatre. The average talian, Collison-Morley suggests, thinks of Shakespeare as primarily a writer of tragedies. Until reently his comedies were largely unread and rarely cted in Italy. Though the Latin sensibility perhaps eels that *Hamlet* and *Lear* are grotesque and incomrehensible, *Othello* and *Romeo and Juliet* go traight to the heart of an Italian audience. These lays combine Italian settings with a central concern or love and jealousy. It is not surprising that Giueppe VERDI based his great opera on *Othello,* perennially the most popular of Shakespeare's plays in taly. [Paul Hazard, *La Révolution Française et les Lettres Italiennes,* 1910; Lacy Collison-Morley, *Shakespeare in Italy,* 1916; Guido Ferrando, "Shakespeare n Italy," *Shakespeare Association Bulletin,* V, 1930.]

Italy in the plays. From one of his earliest plays, *The Two Gentlemen of Verona,* to the one which s his last finished work, *The Tempest,* Shakespeare requently brought Italian characters on the stage; ll or a part of the action of six of the plays was set n Italy. Yet it is not the Italy of the average Elizabethan dramatist—a place of dark violence and criminality—that he represents. Horrible murders and treasons occur in Shakespeare's plays, but, oddly enough, not as a rule in the plays whose action takes place in Italy. It is a matter of no little surprise to see how Shakespeare's Italian plays are comparatively free from the usual horrors and thrills. He evidently took a more sober view of Italian society than the current one circulated by religious or conservative fanatics and cherished by the thrill-seeking crowd. Indeed, his conception is near to that idyllic Italy which we can picture from Ariosto's and Castiglione's works. How are we to account for this view when everybody around the young playwright was spellbound by the myth of Italian wickedness?

It has been suggested that Shakespeare may have traveled to northern Italy, for some of his plays show a remarkable acquaintance with the local topography of certain northern Italian towns. By 1592 he was already a successful actor and playwright. The years 1592–1594 marked a critical phase in the history of London players: seasons were short in consequence of the plague, short-lived regroupings of companies took place. When theatrical life was in full swing again after the plague, Shakespeare produced a number of plays with an Italian background. Had he visited Italy in the interim?

Before coming to the actual question about the way in which Shakespeare may have become acquainted with Italian things, let us make a rapid survey of his Italian plays. The scenes of *The Two Gentlemen of Verona* are Verona and Milan. The names of the chief characters are more or less Italianate, but those of the two servants, Speed and Launce, are English. There are several inconsistencies about places (for instance, in II, v, which is supposed to take place in Milan, Speed is heard welcoming Launce "to Padua"; elsewhere we find Verona where we should expect Milan). These errors have led critics to think that Shakespeare had written the whole of the play before he had settled where the scene was to be laid. At any rate the plot structure of *Two Gentlemen* is modeled on that of a typical Italian *commedia dell' arte;* and the influence of the *commedia dell' arte* is already evident in Shakespeare's first comedy, *Love's Labour's Lost,* where the characters of Armado and Holofernes, respectively, correspond to the Spanish Captain and the Pedant of the Italian comedy. *Lazzi* and other proceedings familiar to the *commedia dell' arte* are so frequent in Shakespeare that Valentina Capocci (in *Genio e mestiere, Shakespeare e la commedia dell' arte,* 1950) has jumped to the conclusion that most of the prose of the plays must be due to the collaboration of the actors themselves.

In *Two Gentlemen* Valentine's father "at the road / Expects my coming, there to see me shipp'd" to Milan; in Act II, scene iii, Verona is imagined on a river with tides that ebb and flow, connected to Milan by a waterway. In *The Tempest* (I, ii, 144 ff.) Prospero tells how he was put aboard a bark at the gates of Milan together with his little daughter. Milan, therefore, is imagined as being on a waterway communicating with the sea. Again, in *The Taming of the Shrew* (I, i, 42), where the scene is Padua, we hear Lucio saying: "If, Biondello, thou wert come ashore," and later on: "Since I have come ashore." Gremio, a citizen of Padua, boasts (II, i, 376) of being the owner of a large merchant vessel, an argosy. Farther on (IV, ii, 81 ff.) we hear of Mantuan ships which are stayed at Venice because of a quarrel between the two towns. Finally, we are told of a sailmaker in Bergamo, another inland town.

Sir Edward Sullivan, in an article ("Shakespeare and the Waterways of North Italy") published in *The Nineteenth Century* (LXIV, 1908) was at great pains to show that those seeming inaccuracies, far from revealing Shakespeare's ignorance of Italian geography, show an intimate acquaintance with it, since it can be proved by quotations of Italian writers of, and prior to, the 17th century, and with the aid of a map of Lombardy of the time, that the highroad from Milan to Venice was by water, and a journey from Verona to Milan could be made by water. At a date much nearer to us, in 1755, Winckelmann traveled from Venice to Bologna by water, employing three nights and three days. G. Lambin in *Voyages de Shakespeare en France et en Italie* (1962) has added some further considerations in order to show that the navigation of the two gentlemen and their servants is not "an ignorant invention of the playwright. It exactly corresponds to what was taking place in his time. A boat was the only comfortable conveyance from Verona to Milan. But one must have made use of it oneself to be so well informed." But even if we agree with Sir Edward Sullivan and Lambin about the possibility, nay, the advisability, of traveling from Verona to Milan by water in Shakespeare's time, so far as the dramatist is concerned their demonstration seems wide of the mark.

There are other allusions in these plays which bear on the matter of local color, but, while some of those allusions point to Italy, most of them point to England, specifically to London. In *The Merchant of Venice*, for instance (II, ii, 99–101), Old Gobbo says to Launcelot: "Thou hast got more hair on thy chin than Dobbin my fill-horse has on his tail." Those who maintain that *The Merchant of Venice* shows a strong Venetian local color will not find it easy to reconcile with the town of the canals and gondolas the fact that Gobbo possesses a horse, and a horse which has such an English name as Dobbin (cf. Samuel Johnson: "A tree might be a show in Scotland as a horse in Venice"), although there are proofs that one found horses in Venice well into the 16th century. But the obvious explanation is that, although Shakespeare speaks of gondolas and the Rialto and the "tranect," when he mentions the fill-horse Dobbin he is thinking of England and of his characters as English characters. And the same is true when he speaks in *The Two Gentlemen* and in *The Taming of the Shrew* of alehouses and of festivals and ballads peculiar, not to Italy, but to England. Therefore, the only reasonable conclusion we can draw is that, in conceiving of the towns in which the plays take place as situated on tidal rivers that connect them with the sea, Shakespeare was thinking of London, and using Milan and Verona as mere labels.

The second of Shakespeare's Italian dramas, *Romeo and Juliet*, displays a much stronger local color than *The Two Gentlemen*. Romeo's love expresses itself in the metaphors of the school of Serafino Aquilano, that school of sonneteering which anticipated the *concetti* of the 17th century. In fact Shakespeare succeeds so well in imitating the language of the Italian Petrarchists that in two passages his similes coincide with those used by Romeo's counterpart, Latino, in a tragedy by Luigi Groto, *La Adriana* (pub. 1578), which is also inspired by the story of Juliet and Romeo. The resemblance between these passages (see my essay on "Shakespeare's Italy" in *The Flaming Heart*, 1958), and the mention of the nightingale in the parting scene between the lovers, led some critics to conclude that Shakespeare knew Groto's tragedy, though the two plays are as different as they could be in the treatment of the story and in the study of the characters. The resemblances prove only that Shakespeare succeeded so well in depicting an Italian lover that the language he puts into his mouth may occasionally appear derived from that extremely artificial poet of the Petrarchan school, Luigi Groto.

The local color of *The Merchant of Venice* ha been declared well-nigh astonishing. Accurate sailor expressions are put into the mouths of Salanio an Salerio, mention is made of the "tranect," or *tra ghetto*, the ferry which connects Venice to th mainland, and of the correct distance that Portia an Nerissa would have to travel from Belmont, i.e Montebello, to Padua. Shakespeare knows about "th liberty of strangers" which formed one of the point of the Venetian constitution, and, in *Othello* (I, 183), he mentions the "special officers of night," i.e the *signori di notte*. Against the considerable amour of accurate information in *The Merchant of Venice* we may record as mere slips Gobbo's mention of hi horse Dobbin, and Launcelot's objection to the con version of the Jews: "If we grow all to be pork eaters, we shall not shortly have a rasher on the coal for money," which alludes to that peculiarly Englis dish, a fried slice of bacon. As for the character themselves, one cannot say that they are mor Venetian than anything else. They seem to fit th setting so well because they are lifelike in the broad est sense of the word; their type is universa whereas the Italian characters of the blood-and thunder school of Elizabethan drama are generall caricatures of the seamy side of Italian life.

But what about the sinister Italian knave, Iago This seemingly accomplished Machiavellian seems t be a refinement of the *alfiero* in the seventh *novell* of the third Decade of Giraldi Cinthio's *Hecatom mithi*. When his malicious hints have driven Othell into an epileptic seizure, he says,

> Thus credulous fools are caught;
> And many worthy and chaste dames even thus,
> All guiltless, meet reproach.
>
> (IV, i, 46–48)

These words echo almost literally the moral o Cinthio's story: "*Aviene talhora che senza colpa fedele et amorevale donna per insidie tesele da anim malvagio, et per leggierezza di chi più crede che no bisognerebbe, da fedel marito riceve morte.*" Th ostensible plot of the play would make Iago appea actually incensed by the public report that Othell has cuckolded him: if so, Iago's story, as told b Shakespeare, would find parallels in many cases o retaliation instanced by Italian *novelle*. Needless t say, the character of Iago does not imply any direc acquaintance with Machiavelli's writings. Wha Machiavellism is displayed in Shakespeare's drama seems either to be already present in the historica sources (as in the case of *Richard III*), or to be de rived from the current popular legend.

Finally, an unusual case among Shakespeare's plays *The Tempest*, whose Italian inspiration has bee convincingly traced by Ferdinando Neri (*Scenar delle maschere in Arcadia*, 1913), introduces tw clowns who, instead of being portrayed as Eliza bethan Londoners as in Shakespeare's other plays seem to have been borrowed from a Neapolita farce. (B. Croce, "Shakespeare, Napoli, e la comme dia napoletana dell' arte," in *La Critica* for May-July 1919.)

Shakespeare's persuasive sense of locale can b misleading indeed when it is emphasized unduly, a several scholars have shown. Madame Clara Long worth de Chambrun (in *Giovanni Florio, Un apôtr* de la Renaissance en Angleterre à l'époque de Shakespeare,* 1921) wrote, "What strikes us above all in Shakespeare's works, is to see how the dramatist has succeeded in giving us a true impression of Italian culture whereas, all things considered, one finds in him very little real knowledge. Shakespeare, though having a very slight acquaintance with the Italian language, gives to the spectator or the reader a very strong illusion of local colour." On the same theme Professor F. E. Schelling warns: "Much nonsense has been written about Shakespeare's power of local colouring. This power he undoubtedly possesses in a high degree, but it comes from the suggestions of his sources and only the unimaginative commentator can think it needful to send him to Italy for the colouring of *The Merchant of Venice* and *Othello*, or to Denmark for his *Hamlet*. Shakespeare's personages are seldom foreigners" (*Elizabethan Drama*, 2 vols., 1908).

As for Shakespeare's knowledge of Italian, besides the passage of *Othello* quoted above, which seems to go back directly to the Italian source, it appears that in *Measure for Measure* Shakespeare may have taken the idea of the substitution of the bodies of Claudio and Barnardine from Cinthio's drama *Epitia*, since the substitution does not occur in the story of the *Hecatommithi* (Deca VIII, Novella 5), of which *Epitia* is a dramatic version. Neither does it occur in Whetstone's rehandling of Cinthio's story. Since Italian books were widely read in the society in whose midst Shakespeare lived, there is nothing extraordinary in his acquaintance with Italian literature; rather, the contrary would be surprising. What seems to be more puzzling is Shakespeare's accuracy in certain local allusions. Some of them have already been mentioned, and even if Lambin has overstated the case of Shakespeare's knowledge of the topography of Milan, the mention of St. Gregory's well near that town, in *The Two Gentlemen,* seems definite enough. We find, moreover, Bellario as a Paduan name in *The Merchant of Venice,* which in fact it is, and in *Romeo and Juliet,* details about Juliet's funeral (found, however, already in Brooke's poem) and about the evening mass in Verona.

An important fact is that these allusions are confined to a very definite part of Italy: Venice and the neighboring towns of Verona, Padua, Mantua, and Milan. There are two possible alternatives: either Shakespeare traveled to the north of Italy, or he got this information from intercourse with some Italian in London. There is no evidence for the first alternative. As for the second, Shakespeare may have had frequent occasions to meet Italian merchants. The Elephant Inn (which he mentions with praise as the one where it was "best to lodge" in the unknown Illyrian town of *Twelfth Night,* but which was nothing else but the inn called "The Oliphant" on Bankside) was patronized by Italians (see G. S. Gargano, *Scapigliature Italiane a Londra sotto Elisabetta e Giacomo I,* 1923). But whatever his relations may have been with these Italian tradesmen and adventurers (many of whom were northern Italians and chiefly, as is natural, from the commercial town of Venice), it is today well established that Shakespeare must have come across, at least, John Florio, the apostle of Italian culture in England (Madame de Chambrun was the first to discuss this connection). Florio and Shakespeare moved in the same circle; Florio, at least, was a member of Southampton's household. Florio supplied Ben Jonson with whatever information the dramatist shows about Venice in *Volpone:* a copy of this play in the British Museum has this autograph dedication: "To his louing Father, & worthy Freind Mr. John Florio: The ayde of his Muses. Ben: Jonson seals this testemony of Freindship, & loue." Florio's vocabulary has a prevailing Lombardo-Venetian character (see my essay on "Ben Jonson's Italy" in *The Flaming Heart*), and Venice is for him the foremost Italian town, as can be seen in the eighth chapter of the *First Fruites.* This may help us to understand why the local allusions in Shakespeare's Italian plays are limited to Venice and the neighboring towns. Florio had also made a translation (1603) of Montaigne, which, plethoric as it is with pretended elegances, has become a classic, and was a source for Elizabethan dramatists, first of all Shakespeare, who bred his Hamlet on it. Florio's manuals of conversation and his Italian dictionary were responsible for most of the knowledge of Italian of Shakespeare's contemporaries. He was called "the ayde of his Muses" by Ben Jonson. Probably he would have deserved a similar appellation from Shakespeare.—M.P.

J

Jackson, Sir Barry Vincent (1879–1961). Director and playwright. Born in Birmingham, Jackson was the founder and director of the highly respected Birmingham Repertory Company in 1913. In its first season the company undertook productions of *Twelfth Night, King John,* and *The Merry Wives of Windsor,* as well as plays by Shaw. Jackson directed the group from 1914 to 1918. Among the group's later Shakespearean productions were *Romeo and Juliet* (1924) and modern-dress versions of *Hamlet* (1925/6), *Macbeth* (1928), and *The Taming of the Shrew* (1928). For his work at Birmingham, Jackson received many honors. In 1945 he became the director of the Shakespeare Memorial Theatre at Stratford-upon-Avon, a post he held until 1948. He was the author or co-author of many plays, most of them adaptations and translations of the dramatic literature of the past several hundred years. [*Who's Who in the Theatre,* 1961.]

Jackson, John (c. 1575–1625). London merchant and shipping magnate who acted as a trustee in Shakespeare's purchase of the Blackfriars Gate-House. A native of Yorkshire, Jackson was a businessman who preferred the company of poets. He frequented the Mermaid Tavern and contributed verses to Thomas Coryate's *Crudities* (1611). Another apparent connection of Jackson with Shakespeare derives from the fact that Jackson married the widow of Jacob James, whose brother Elias James is the subject of an epitaph ascribed to Shakespeare. [Leslie Hotson, *Shakespeare's Sonnets Dated,* 1949.]

Jaggard, William (1569–1623). London bookseller and printer. With his son **Isaac Jaggard** (1595–1627), he printed the First Folio (1623). William Jaggard was admitted to the Stationers' Company as a freeman in 1591. In 1599 he collected a number of poems by a variety of authors which he published under the title *The Passionate Pilgrime,* "by W. Shakespeare." In 1609 he published Thomas Heywood's *Troia Britanica,* and when in 1612 he printed a third edition of *The Passionate Pilgrime,* he included some selections from Heywood's poem. This blatant piracy incited Heywood to attack Jaggard in his Apologie for Actors, in which he alluded to Shakespeare's displeasure with Jaggard's tactics. (See The Passionate Pilgrim.) Jaggard, however, continued to prosper despite Heywood's criticism and despite the blindness with which he was beginning to be afflicted. In 1610 Jaggard took as an apprentice a John Shakespeare (d. 1646), who, like the dramatist, was a native of Warwickshire and possibly a distant relative. In 1619, possibly inspired by the folio edition of Ben

A

Most pleasant and excellent conceited Comedy, of Sir Iohn Falstaffe, and the merry VViues of VVindsor.

VVith the swaggering vaine of Ancient Pistoll, and Corporall Nym.

Written by W. Shakespeare.

Printed for Arthur Iohnson, 1619.

TITLE PAGE OF THE SECOND QUARTO OF *The Merry Wives of Windsor* (1619). THIS IS ONE OF TEN SHAKESPEAREAN PLAYS PRINTED IN 1619 BY JAGGARD, MANY OF WHICH ARE FALSELY DATED.

Jonson's plays (1616), Jaggard and the publish Thomas Pavier decided to issue a collected editi of Shakespearean and pseudo-Shakespearean play probably to be sold in sets of nine quarto volume Apparently he first printed four of these volume *The Whole Contention betweene the two Famo Houses, Lancaster and Yorke* (a combined edition *2* and *3 Henry VI*), *Pericles, A Yorkshire Traged* and *The Merry Wives of Windsor,* all of which a dated 1619. At this time, however, an order arriv from the lord chamberlain to the Stationers' Com pany prohibiting the printing of any of the plays the King's Men without their consent. In order circumvent this order Jaggard then issued the r maining plays in the collection with false title date so as to make them appear to have antedated the prohibiting order. These include *A Midsummer Night's Dream, The Merchant of Venice,* and *1 Sir John Oldcastle,* all misdated on the title page, 1600; and *Henry V* and *King Lear,* misdated 1608. Jaggard was apparently successful in the use of these antedated quartos. It was not until the 20th century, with the work of A. W. Pollard, W. W. Greg, and other bibliographical scholars, that the ruse was detected. Whatever the reaction of the players to this piracy, two years later they permitted Jaggard, whose business at this time was largely run by his son Isaac, to be the printer of the FIRST FOLIO. The printing was begun in 1622 and apparently interrupted for some time before its completion in 1623. The previously unregistered plays were entered in the Stationers' Register on November 8, 1623 to "Master Blounte and Isaac Jaggard." By this time William Jaggard, whose will was proved in court on November 17, 1623, was apparently dead. In 1627 Isaac died and his wife sold the business to Thomas and Richard COTES. [E. E. Willoughby, *A Printer of Shakespeare*, 1934.]

Jahrbuch der Deutschen Shakespeare-Gesellschaft, generally known as the **Shakespeare Jahrbuch.** The annual publication of the German Shakespeare Society. The *Jahrbuch,* the oldest Shakespeare periodical still in existence, was first published in 1865. Each issue contains an annual bibliography of Shakespearean studies.

Jailer. In *The Two Noble Kinsmen,* keeper of the Athenian prison. After the victory over Thebes, he guards Arcite and Palamon. When Arcite is banished and Palamon imprisoned, the Jailer's Daughter, who is in love with the latter, helps him to escape. Later the Jailer and his daughter's Wooer engage a doctor to cure her madness.

Jailer's Daughter. In *The Two Noble Kinsmen,* she is loved by the Wooer. Falling in love with Palamon, who has been imprisoned, she effects his escape but goes mad searching for him in the woods. Her madness is cured when the Wooer addresses himself to her disguised as Palamon.

James I (1566–1625). King of England (1603–1625) and, as James VI, of Scotland (1567–1625). The son of Mary Stuart (Mary, Queen of Scots), James was proclaimed king of Scotland after his mother's forced abdication in 1567. James' rule of Scotland was a successful and, on the whole, unspectacular one. In 1598 he married Princess Anne of Denmark, under whose influence he began to indulge in a taste for the drama.

By the time of his accession to the English throne he was, in his own words, "an experienced king, needing no lessons." Discernible in the arrogance of that phrase is James' major flaw, one which was to involve him in a series of disputes with parliament and which ultimately would end in disaster for his son Charles I. A man of considerable learning, James was unfortunately also pedantic and garrulous, qualities that won him the famous epithet "the wisest fool in Christendom."

James' taste in drama, however, was above reproach. He lost no time in becoming the patron of Shakespeare's company, proclaiming their status in a royal patent in 1603 (see CHAMBERLAIN'S MEN). Shakespeare reciprocated by tailoring at least one of his plays—*Macbeth*—to the interests and tastes of his sovereign (see MACBETH: *Sources*). It has also been suggested that James' concept of kingship is mirrored in some of Shakespeare's Jacobean plays, such as *King Lear* and *Coriolanus.*

Another, less tenable, connection between James and Shakespeare has been suggested with regard to *A Midsummer Night's Dream:* namely, that James' claim to the English throne is satirized in the character of Bottom. This conjecture has not been generally accepted, however, especially in view of the fact that *A Midsummer Night's Dream* was probably one of the first plays revived for performance before James at court. See A MIDSUMMER NIGHT'S DREAM: *Comment.*

The king's admiration, according to a story in an "advertisement" appended to a collection (1709) of Shakespeare's poems, was expressed in a letter written to Shakespeare:

> That most learn'd Prince, and great Patron of Learning, King James the First, was pleas'd with his own Hand to write an amicable Letter to Mr Shakespeare; which Letter, tho now lost, remain'd long in the Hands of Sir William D'avenant, as a credible Person now living can testify.

The "credible Person" referred to here has been identified as John Sheffield, duke of Buckingham (1648–1721).

James, Elias (c. 1578–1610). London brewer whose verse epitaph may have been written by Shakespeare. James was the son of one Dericke James (d. 1590), who owned a brewery in the Blackfriars district. Elias took over the business in 1600, continuing as owner until his death in 1610. Another connecting link with Shakespeare is to be found in the fact that James' sister-in-law married John Jackson, one of Shakespeare's trustees in his purchase of the Blackfriars Gate-House.

The epitaph on James is to be found among the Rawlinson manuscripts in the Bodleian Library, dated c. 1630–1640:

An Epitaph

When god was pleas'd ye world vnwilling yet
Elias James to nature payd his debt
And here reposeth; as he liv'd he dyde
The saying in him strongly verefi'de
Such life such death yen ye known truth to tell
He liv'd a godly life and dy'de as well.
Wm: Shakespeare.

[Leslie Hotson, *Shakespeare's Sonnets Dated,* 1949.]

James, Henry (1843–1916). American novelist. Author of an imposing array of novels, novelettes, and short stories, James exercised his critical faculties in essays like "The Art of Fiction" (1884) and in the prefaces (collected in *The Art of the Novel: Critical Prefaces,* R. P. Blackmur, ed., 1934) which he prepared for the New York edition of his novels. William T. Stafford points out that the novelist "has much to say explicitly" about Shakespeare. "His autobiographical memoirs, his published letters, his critical prefaces, his notebooks, and his literary and dramatic criticism, when taken collectively, reveal a surprisingly large body of both casual and critical comment on Shakespeare."

Between April of 1873 and September of 1896 James reviewed 11 Shakespearean plays: 2 histories,

Henry V and *Richard III;* 4 comedies, *As You Like It*, *The Merchant of Venice*, *The Merry Wives of Windsor*, and *Cymbeline;* and 5 tragedies, *Romeo and Juliet*, *Macbeth*, *Hamlet*, *Othello*, and *King Lear*. During this time James commented on *Richard III*, *Macbeth*, and *Othello* twice. Although these reviews are concerned primarily with acting and production, James reveals a working knowledge of Shakespeare and well-informed (if not original) interpretations of the plays. Admitting, for instance, that there is evidence in the text for Henry Irving's interpretation of Macbeth as "so spiritless a plotter before his crime, and so arrant a coward afterwards," James prefers Tommaso Salvini's Macbeth, who is "simple, demonstrative, easily tempted, pushed and bitten by the keener nature of his wife; dismayed, overwhelmed, assailed by visions, yet willing to plunge deeper into crime, and ready after all to fight and die like a man." He suggests, however, that Salvini should have read De Quincey's "On the Knocking at the Gate in *Macbeth*."

In his prefaces to *The Portrait of a Lady* (1881), *The Princess Casamassima* (1886), and *The Tragic Muse* (1890), James refers to Shakespearean characters "as precedent." His tale, *The Birthplace* (1903), which seems to be an allegory of the artist and his audience, deals with the caretakers of a Shakespeare-like shrine at Stratford. When Morris Gedge becomes its custodian, he tells tourists only the truth and is threatened with dismissal. When he fabricates elaborate anecdotes, his salary is doubled. In August of the year this story appeared, James wrote that he was haunted by the conviction that Shakespeare was the "biggest fraud" ever practiced on the world and that he found it "almost as impossible" to believe the plays were written by Bacon as to believe they were written by the man from Stratford.

In a 1907 introduction to *The Tempest,* James presents a somewhat nebulous discussion of the nature of Shakespeare's genius. He argues against symbolic interpretations which view the plays as "lights of philosophic and political truth." Shakespeare's particular genius is "the instant sense of some copious equivalent of thought for every grain of the grossness of reality." In *The Tempest* Shakespeare "plays for his own ear, his own hand, his own innermost sense, and for the bliss and capacity of his instrument." James obliquely attacks the problem of Shakespeare's silence in his last years. With his sacerdotal view of the artist, James seems unwilling to admit that the greatest poet of them all may have quit when he had made enough money.

In a revealing metaphor, James asserts that Shakespeare the man remains a mystery which may be got at only indirectly. "The figured tapestry, the long arras that hides him, is always there, with its immensity of surface and its proportionate underside. May it not then be but a question, for the fulness of time, of the finer weapon, the sharper point, the stronger arm, the more extended lunge?" [William T. Stafford, "James Examines Shakespeare: Notes on the Nature of Genius," *PMLA,* LXXIII, 1958.]

James, Richard (1592–1638). Scholar. A nephew of Thomas James (c. 1573–1629), the first librarian of the famous Bodleian Library, Richard James was educated at Oxford. After traveling extensively on the continent, he became the librarian of Sir Robert Cotton (1571–1631). He was friendly with Ben Jonson, to whom he dedicated a poem, and with a number of other celebrated figures in England. In 1625 he wrote an Epistle to Sir Harry Bourchier in which he explains the Fastolfe-Falstaff problem (see Sir John FASTOLFE):

> A young Gentle Lady of your acquaintance, having read ye works of Shakespeare, made me this question. How Sr John Falstaffe, or Fastolf, as he is written in ye Statute book of Maudlin Colledge in Oxford, where everye day that society were bound to make memorie of his soul, could be dead in ye time of Harrie ye Fift and again live in ye time of Harrie ye Sixt to be banished for cowardice: Whereto I made answear that it was one of those humours and mistakes for which Plato banisht all poets out of his commonwealth. That Sr John Falstaffe was in those times a noble valiant souldier, as apeeres by a book in ye Heralds Office dedicated unto him by a Herald who had binne with him, if I well remember, for the space of 25 yeeres in ye French wars; that he seems also to have binne a man of learning, because, in a Library of Oxford, I find a book of dedicating Churches sent from him for a present unto Bishop Wainflete and inscribed with his own hand. That in Shakespeares first shew of Harrie the fift, the person with which he undertook to playe a buffone was not Falstaffe, but Sir John Oldcastle, and that offence beinge worthily taken by Personages descended from his title (as peradventure by many others allso whoe ought to have him in honourable memorie) the poet was putt to make an ignorant shifte of abusing Sir John Falstophe, a man not inferior of Vertue, though not so famous in pietie as the other, who gave witnesse unto the truth of our reformation with a constant and resolute Martyrdom, unto which he was pursued by the Priests, Bishops, Moncks, and Friers of those days.

Jamy, Captain. In *Henry V*, a Scottish captain in the English army at Harfleur. In III, ii, Jamy has a conversation with the Welshman Fluellen and the Irishman Macmorris. Jamy's historical counterpart may have been King James I of Scotland, who was taken prisoner during the reign of Henry IV. Kept for a time at Windsor Castle, he was later released by Henry V to serve the king as a private knight. [W. H. Thomson, *Shakespeare's Characters: A Historical Dictionary*, 1951.]

Janssen, Gheerart. Anglicized name **Gerard Johnson** (fl. 1600–1623). The tombmaker who built the Shakespeare MONUMENT some time between 1616 and 1623. Janssen was the son of a Dutch sculptor who emigrated to London in 1567 and set up his trade in Southwark. After the retirement of the elder Janssen in 1605, the business was conducted by his sons. The information that Gheerart was responsible for Shakespeare's bust derives from the *Diary* of Sir William Dugdale:

> Shakespeares and John Combes Monum^{ts}, at Stratford sup Avon, made by one Gerard Johnson.

Japan. Like that of everything else Western, the history of Shakespeare in Japan is a remarkably recent one. Although the country had had brief contact with England in the early 17th century, this was ɔruptly terminated by Japan's isolationist Tokugawa ɔvernment, which effectively barred European cul-ɪral exchange with the island nation for more than ɔo years. Thus Shakespeare, together with all the ɛher great and lesser names of Western culture, was irtually unknown in Japan until the latter part of ıe 19th century, with the consequence that at the eginning of his Japanese career his rivals were ulwer-Lytton and Disraeli rather than Marlowe nd Jonson. In fact, the first of Shakespeare to be ublished in Japan was the "Neither a borrower nor lender be" fragment which appeared as the motto ɔr the chapter on "Money—Use and Abuse" in an 871 translation of Samuel Smiles' *Self-Help.* From ıere the admonition made its way into *Western Vords of Wisdom* published in 1874. Also in 1874, he *Yellow Yokohama Punch* magazine featured an Extract from the new Japanese Drama Hamuretu an, 'Danumark no Kami' proving the plagiarisms of :nglish literature of the 16th century," illustrating it ⁄ith a drawing of a thoughtful samurai. The "ex-ract" was, of course, the "To be or not to be" oliloquy, and, as translated into Japanese by a resi-ent Englishman, it was a superb parody whose amous opening line had now become the Japanese quivalent of "There is; there is not: What is that?"

Translation. About this time, Shakespeare began to njoy wide fame in Japan. The first "translations" vere free adaptations for the most part, the writers n effect composing a new work in Japanese based on he Shakespeare plot. One of the first to be so han-lled was the 1877 Japanese version of *The Merchant f Venice,* written as a prose tale rather than a lay. The author had thoroughly naturalized all the cenes and characters of his story, which he called *Cyōniku-no Kishō,* literally, "A Strange Litigation bout the Flesh of Chest." It is understandable, then, hat for these early Shakespeareans, who were just eginning to discover the English language and its iterature, the single most helpful book was Charles nd Mary Lamb's *Tales from Shakespeare* (1807).)uring the last decades of the century, various ranslations of the *Tales* appeared in books and eriodicals, many of them very faithful to the Lambs' ɔriginal. Often, of course, these stories were taken 'or Shakespeare's own works and as such provided he basis for stage versions. The *Tales* continued trong in the 20th century, perhaps stronger upon heir return to their intended audience of young ɔeople. By 1930 the *Tales* had appeared in at least 00 different books or collections.

Though Shakespeare's fame was greatly assisted y these popularizing efforts, rigorous versions of the ɔriginal plays were slow in coming. The first such ttempt, made in 1883, was Kawashima Keizō's com-ɔlete translation of *Julius Caesar,* a play having great ɔolitical significance for an Imperial generation vhose accomplishments were being undermined by a eries of assassinations. *Romeo and Juliet* and *The Comedy of Errors* followed in the 1880's. However, ıothing in the way of a systematic program for ranslation of the plays appeared before the first lecade of this century, when Tozawa Masayasu and Asano Wasaburō set to work and between them fin-shed 10 plays. Tsubouchi Shōyō (1859–1935), the giant of Shakespeare translators, was also hard at vork at this time. Playwright as well as scholar, Tsubouchi brought out the entire Shakespearean canon in Japanese between 1909 and 1928. Then, not altogether satisfied with this work, which he felt depended too heavily on Deighton's annotations, he started a new version—this time with the help of all the available Western scholarship—and at the time of his death had almost completed it. Tsubouchi's feat stimulated many attempts at Shakespeare transla-tion. In the postwar period, almost 50 translations of individual plays have appeared, and Fukuda Kōzon has been engaged in a new translation of the com-plete works.

Since the very nature of Japanese metric form (alternating five- and seven-syllable verses) deters any attempt at rendering a complete play in poetry, the translations have all been in prose. This did not, however, make the task very much easier for the early translators since prose translation raised other formidable problems, particularly in the matter of diction: namely, which style to use, literary or col-loquial. Of the several highly developed native literary styles, perhaps *jōruri,* often used in Kabuki plays, would seem the most natural for a theatre work. But *jōruri,* at one time easily understood by its audience, was becoming increasingly more difficult to follow, whether in spoken or written form. The translator had another choice, the style in which Chinese classics had been rendered into Japanese. This style, more refined than *jōruri,* was even more difficult to understand. Finally, there was the lan-guage of the *nō* drama, utterly elegant and utterly archaic. As for the literary possibilities of colloquial speech, on the other hand, these were recognized and promoted, at least from the 1880's on, by many university-educated writers, but since the colloquial Japanese of the time could not provide a large or expressive enough vocabulary for Shakespeare, the writers had to make do with an uneasy marriage of new and old, colloquial and classical, both as to style and vocabulary. A comparison of Tsubouchi's two versions makes clear, however, that translation, in common with other types of Japanese writing, was tending increasingly toward the colloquial style.

In the years since the first translations, Japanese has greatly developed its vocabulary for Western things and concepts (100 years ago, there was not even a Japanese word for fork and spoon!), and it is now-adays a much more flexible and "worldly" instru-ment in the hands of capable writers. The translators' scholarship is now sufficient for them to discern the finer aspects of Shakespearean style, and their efforts are directed toward re-creating these same, or cor-responding, effects in Japanese.

Stage Production. The first staging of Shakespeare in Japan was the Nakamura Sōjurō Kabuki com-pany's production of *The Merchant of Venice* in 1885. Entitled *Sakura-doki Kane-no Yononaka* ("The Season of Cherry-Blossoms, The World of Money") and set in the Osaka of the Tokugawa period, it was quite a free adaptation of the Lamb tale. In fact, although it handles the casket theme and the trial scene cleverly, the play as a whole was hardly Shakespeare's. At the turn of the century similar loose adaptations of *Julius Caesar* and *King Lear* were performed. In 1903 the Shimpa (revisionist Kabuki) actors Takada Minoru, Kawakami Otojirō, and Kawakami Sadayakko played the roles of, respectively, "Lieutenant Iya Gōzō," "Muro Washihiro, Governor-general of Formosa," and "Tomone, Governor's Wife," in a famed Tokyo production of *Osero* (*Othello*). The situation was thus completely naturalized to the Japan of the age of *Madama Butterfly*, the director even providing a new ending to satisfy the audience's demand for poetic justice. It wasn't long, however, before groups were formed which were concerned with developing production styles more faithful to the Shakespearean spirit. In 1911, after a great deal of experimentation, the Bungei Kyōkai (Literary Art Association), with Tsubouchi as director, performed authentic translation versions of *Hamlet* and *The Merchant of Venice* at the new Imperial Theatre in Tokyo. Unfortunately, soon afterward, the Bungei Kyōkai, unable to withstand pressures coming from both the conservative Kabuki and the progressive Free Theatre movement, split into several schools, each interpreting Shakespeare in its own way. This probably contributed to the temporary decline in the number of Shakespeare productions that followed. Japanese theatregoers—perhaps overexposed to such Victorians as Ibsen, Hauptmann, Strindberg, *and* Shakespeare!—turned their attention to Pirandello and other new European playwrights. However, in 1924, with the founding of the Tsukiji Little Theatre, good authentic Shakespeare was again available and, except for the war years 1939–1945, the plays, directed by such men as Tsubouchi, Osanai, and Hijikata, have been in continuous production.

The "Japanese" Shakespeare was thus very well established in the commercial theatre at a time when the "English" Shakespeare there was, understandably, a rarity. Then, with interest in the English language stimulated by the American Occupation, school productions in English as well as Japanese became fairly commonplace. Young people's interest in Shakespeare has also been encouraged by the performances of the touring Youth Theatre of the Zenshinza Company.

As for the Kabuki style of Shakespeare production, it should be said that despite the peculiarities and distortions it introduced into the plays, without it, there is little likelihood that Shakespeare would have been so readily accepted by the Japanese. It was only gradually, as a more knowledgeable audience came to appreciate a more authentic Shakespeare, that the Kabuki idiom and convention and, more specifically, the severe limitation of its actors in the matter of voice modulation, were seen as problems intrinsic to the whole enterprise of Shakespeare in Japan, problems that perhaps only a more thoroughly bilingual culture will finally overcome.

Scholarship. It is natural, given the recency of Japan's contact with the West and its rapidly developing international commerce, that Japanese scholarly efforts in English were directed at first to problems of translation. Gradually, the more intrinsically scholarly interests—such as the production of annotated editions of English classics and the like—were served by school and university professors devoted to literary studies. Special mention must be made here of the several visiting English and American professors—Edward H. House, James Summers, William A. Houghton, and of course Lafcadio Hearn—who from the 1870's on helped develop the first generation of native scholars (Okakura Kakuz[o], Wadagaki Kenzō, Inoue Tetsujirō, Niitobe Inaz[o], Uchimura Kanzō, Tsubouchi Shōyō, Takata Sana[e], and the well-known novelist Natsume Sōseki), man[y] of whom became noted Shakespeareans and disti[n]guished educators. Hearn's great importance as [a] teacher lies in his insistence on colloquial translatio[n] of Shakespeare and his demonstration of the similar[i]ties between Elizabethan England and Meiji Japa[n]. Tsubouchi, too, in his writing and teaching dre[w] interesting parallels between the Kabuki tradition [as] exemplified especially by Chikamatsu and the Shake[s]speare of the Elizabethan theatre. Whether or n[ot] such comparisons will bear close analysis, it is un[]deniable that by such methods Shakespeare wa[s] rapidly domesticated.

In 1910 Japanese criticism came abreast of Wester[n] Shakespeare scholarship with the publication o[f] Hirata Motokichi's study of *Hamlet*, which showe[d] his familiarity with the work of Furness, Kun[o] Fischer, Karl Werder, Richard Löning, Sidney Le[e], Bradley, and others. Since then, the writings of Stol[l], Dover Wilson, Eliot, and others have been intro[]duced in Japan almost as soon as they are publishe[d] in England and in the United States. Foremost amon[g] the scholars who have published studies in Japanes[e] on various aspects of Shakespeare and his works ar[e] Saitō Takeshi, Ichikawa Sanki, Nakanishi Shintarō, Toyoda Minoru, Nakano Yoshio, Kashikura Shunzō, Yamamoto Tadao, Ōyama Toshikazu, and Ōyam[a] Toshiko. Although Japanese scholarship has not ye[t] produced a study that commands the notice of West[]ern Shakespeareans, looking back, we see such a[n] enormous amount of work done in such a sho[rt] period of time that it is surely not too optimistic t[o] look ahead to one in the not too distant futur[e]. [Toyoda Minoru, *Shakespeare in Japan*, 1940; *Sōg[ō] Kenkyū Shakespeare*, Nakano Yoshio and Ozu Jirō, eds., 1960; Nishizaki Ichirō, "Nippon-niokeru Shake[]speare," *Eibei Bungakushi Kōza*, III, 1961; Yanagid[a] Izumi, *Meiji Shoki Honyaku Bungaku-no Kenky[ū]*, 2nd ed., 1961.]—M.M.

Jaquenetta. In *Love's Labour's Lost*, a countr[y] wench. Jaquenetta is courted by both Don Adrian[o] de Armado and Costard. Don Armado challenge[s] Costard in V, ii, and they almost duel over her.

Jaques. In *As You Like It*, a melancholy lord at[]tending the banished Duke in the Forest of Arden. In his famous "seven ages" speech (II, vii), thi[s] cheerless philosopher cynically disparages the huma[n] race. Although Jaques is detached from his fellow creatures, he is spied weeping over a wounded dee[r], decrying the cruelty of man. At the play's en[d], Jaques leaves the rejoicing company to join Fred[]erick in his religious life. See As You Like It: *Com[]ment.*

Jaques de Boys. In *As You Like It*, second son o[f] Sir Rowland and brother of Oliver and Orlando. I[n] V, iv, Jaques brings news that Duke Frederick, hav[]ing set out with an army to kill his banished brother had met a hermit, been converted to the religiou[s] life, and restored the mistreated Duke to his land and title.

Jealous Comedy, The. See The Merry Wives o[f] Windsor: *Sources;* The Comedy of Errors: *Sources*.

Jenkins, Harold (1909–). Scholar. Professor o[f] English at the University of London, Jenkins is th[e] uthor of *The Life and Work of Henry Chettle* 1934) and *The Structural Problem in Shakespeare's Ienry the Fourth* (1956). With Harold Brooks, he the general editor of the New Arden Edition of he plays.

Jenkins, Thomas (fl. 1566–1579). Master of the tratford grammar school from 1575 to 1579. Jenkins vas not a native of Wales as has been previously hought. He was born in London and attended St. ohn's College at Oxford from which he received a 3.A. in 1566 and M.A. in 1570. Prior to his assumption of the mastership at Stratford, he was a fellow t St. John's. He was succeeded at Stratford by his riend John Cottam in 1579. See EDUCATION OF SHAKEPEARE. [Mark Eccles, *Shakespeare in Warwickshire*, 961.]

Jennens, Charles (1700–1773). Patron. Educated at Oxford, Jennens inherited the family estate at Gopall in 1747 and set about becoming a patron of the rts and a man of letters. He is remembered as a enefactor of Handel; not only did he support the musician on many occasions, he also wrote the vords for several of the oratorios and selected the criptural passages for the *Messiah*. He assembled an mpressive collection of books and objects of art; 28 Shakespeare quartos were included in the collection. ate in life he began to edit Shakespeare. His *King ear* (1770) became a subject of controversy, with George Steevens his principal critic. An attempt was nade to establish a correct text and to present variant eadings, but the result was an unsightly page and a nethod that was awkward to use. He invited critiism by pointing to the errors of earlier editors. ennens answered his critics with a pamphlet entitled *The Tragedy of King Lear, as lately published, indicated from the Abuse of the critical Reviewers* 1772). He proceeded to publish editions of four nore plays: *Hamlet, Macbeth, Othello* (all 1773), nd *Julius Caesar* (posthumous, 1774). [Gordon Crosse, "Charles Jennens as Editor of Shakespeare," *The Library*, 4th Series, XVI, Sept. 1935.]

Jephson, Robert. See ADAPTATIONS; IRELAND.

Jessica. In *The Merchant of Venice*, Shylock's ivacious but amoral daughter. Ashamed of her ather and loathing the dreary atmosphere of her ome, Jessica disguises herself as a page and elopes vith Lorenzo. With her Jessica takes a casket of Shylock's valuables.

Jesuits. Priests of the Roman Catholic order of the Society of Jesus. The organization was founded in 534 by St. Ignatius Loyola and quickly became the pearhead of the Counter-Reformation, the Catholic ttempt to turn back the tide of Protestantism. The esuits' work in England began in 1580 when they ttempted to place Mary, Queen of Scots, on the hrone. Officially banished in 1585, they continued heir political-religious activities throughout the rest f Elizabeth's reign, often coming in conflict with he regular English Catholic clergy over such quesions as EQUIVOCATION. In 1606 the Jesuit Henry GARNET was tried and executed as an accomplice in the GUNPOWDER PLOT. Among English Jesuits of the age vere the polemicist Robert PARSONS; the poet Robert Southwell; Jasper Heywood, the translator of Seneca; nd Simon HUNT, the schoolmaster at the Stratford rammar school from 1572 to 1575, the years during vhich Shakespeare probably attended there.

Jew, The. A lost play which may have been the source of *The Merchant of Venice.* The only information about *The Jew* is found in Stephen Gosson's *Schoole of Abuse* (1579), a Puritan pamphlet attacking stage plays:

> The *Iew* and *Ptolome*, showne at the Bull, the one representing the greedinesse of worldly chusers, and bloody mindes of usurers: the other very liuely descrybing how seditious estates, with their owne deuises, false friendes, with their own swoordes, and rebellious commons in their owne snares are owerthrowne: neither with amorous gesture wounding the eye: nor with slouenly talke hurting the eares of the chast hearers.

The reference to the "worldly chusers" and "bloody . . . usurers" has been argued by some as evidence of the existence in *The Jew* of the "casket plot" as well as the Shylock story (see MERCHANT OF VENICE: *Sources*).

Another possible model of *The Jew* is the story in Book Three of Anthony Munday's *Zelauto* (1580), which gives some indication of having been adapted from a play. *The Jew* may have been the source of Munday's story. If so it probably bears only a slight resemblance to Shakespeare's play and does not constitute a major source of *The Merchant of Venice.* [*The Merchant of Venice*, New Arden Edition, John Russell Brown, ed., 1955.]

Jewel, John (1522–1571). Churchman and author. Educated at Oxford, Jewel was university orator at the time of Mary's accession (1553). In this capacity he composed a congratulatory epistle to Mary and later signed a series of Catholic articles. However, he was suspected of Protestant sympathies and fled to the continent, where he remained until the death of Mary. Upon the accession of Elizabeth, he returned to England, was made bishop of Salisbury (1560), and became an active apologist for the Elizabethan church settlement (see ACT OF SUPREMACY). The *Apologia Ecclesiae Anglicanae* (1562) was the principal result of his efforts, a work which has been described as "the first methodical statement of the position of the Church of England against the Church of Rome, and [the one which] forms the groundwork for all subsequent controversy." A dispute followed with Thomas Harding, a recusant who had been deprived of his position at Salisbury Cathedral by Jewel; *A Defence of the Apology* (1567) was Jewel's rejoinder against Harding. In later controversies Jewel found himself defending the Elizabethan settlement against Puritan attacks, and consequently he adopted a more conservative position.

Jeweller. In *Timon of Athens,* a minor character who, in I, i, enjoys Timon's generous patronage.

Jew of Malta, The (c. 1589). A tragedy by Christopher MARLOWE. It was entered in the Stationers' Register in 1594 and first published in 1633 as "The Famous Tragedy of the Rich Iew of Malta. As it was played before the King and Queene, in his Majesties Theatre at White-Hall, by her Majesties Servants at the Cock-pit. Written by Christopher Marlo."

The Jew of Malta concerns the degeneration and final destruction of Barabas, a usurer and merchant of untold wealth. After a prologue spoken by a figure called "Machiavel," Barabas is seen in his counting house gloating over his "infinite riches in a little room." News arrives that all of his richly laden ships have returned to port safely, and Barabas stands at the peak of his mercantile prosperity. Then, however, a Turkish fleet appears off Malta, and all the Jews in Malta are summoned to the senate house. There they learn that by order of Ferneze, the Governor, half of their estates will be confiscated to enable Malta to pay the Turks long-overdue tribute. When Barabas protests, all of his holdings are seized, and his house is converted to a nunnery. Barabas determines to get revenge on the treacherous Christians; from this point on, the play is little more than a loosely connected series of episodes designed to exhibit the Jew's Machiavellian trickery and ruthlessness.

Barabas reveals to his only child, Abigail, that he has hidden a great store of gold and jewels under a floor in the house. Abigail gains entry by persuading the nuns that she wishes to become one of them and repossesses her father's wealth, throwing moneybags from the window as Barabas below hugs them in ecstasy: "O girl! O gold! O beauty! O my bliss!" Barabas then buys a sickly Levantine slave, Ithamore, to help him in his attack against Ferneze and the Christian world.

His first move is to forge a challenge that causes a duel between Don Lodowick, Ferneze's son, and one Don Mathias, in which both are killed. When Abigail learns that her father was responsible for the deaths of these men, both of whom were courting her, she abandons him and joins the nunnery in earnest. Outraged at her apostasy, Barabas prepares a pot of poisoned rice which Ithamore carries to the nuns for their supper. Before she dies, Abigail reveals to two friars the secret of the duel. They attempt to blackmail Barabas who, by means of another device, soon sees them dead.

Ithamore, meanwhile, has become enamored of Bellamira, a courtesan. She and her pander, Pilia-Borsa, persuade Ithamore to pressure Barabas for money. Barabas, fearing that Ithamore will confess, at first complies by sending the slave 10 crowns. When he asks for more, Barabas appears dressed as a French fiddler with a flower in his hat. Bellamira asks for the flower, which of course is poisoned. She and Pilia-Borsa survive until they have told all to Ferneze. Barabas is arrested, but before he can be punished he drinks of "poppy and cold mandrake juice." Ferneze, thinking him dead, has his body thrown from the walls.

Barabas revives just as the Turkish fleet, led by Selim Calymath, returns to collect its tribute or lay siege to Malta. Barabas, a one-man fifth column, leads them through a secret passage under the walls; the Turks surprise the town and name Barabas governor. In an extraordinary about-face Barabas suddenly abandons his Machiavellian policy and attempts to make friends with Ferneze by showing him how he will undo the Turks. He has invited Calymath to dinner at a table that is trapped. When Ferneze understands the mechanism of the trap, he springs it, and Barabas falls into a cauldron of boiling oil. Crying in vain for Christian mercy, he dies, cursing "Damn'd Christians, dogs, and Turkish infidels!" all alike.

It is curious that this play, which T. S. Eliot justifiably described as a "farce" and a "prodigious cari cature," should have elicited as much interest amon literary scholars as any other of Marlowe's plays. Ye the reasons are not far to seek. In the prologue Mar lowe formally introduced to the London stage a typ known as "Machiavel." How much Marlowe kne of the historical Machiavelli is not demonstrable, bu it is reasonably certain that his audience, and Shake speare's, knew next to nothing at firsthand abou the Italian political theorist. As a result the popula idea of the Machiavellian was that of a self-seekin atheist who, believing that the end justifies th means, employed the cunning of the fox with th strength of the lion to gain his ends, however fou The Massacre of St. Bartholomew, 1572, in whic Catherine and the Duc de Guise attempted to wip out the Huguenot sect, seemed to confirm thes views. At any rate, Marlowe, recognizing the dra matic potentialities of the image, produced, howeve crudely, in Barabas the prototype of the Elizabetha "Machiavellian villain," a hybrid character that, lik the old morality Vice, took infinite delight in deceiv ing men. The descendants of Barabas were many an memorable; they included, among others, Shake speare's Aaron the Moor, Richard III, Iago, an Edmund. See Niccolo MACHIAVELLI.

The similarities between Marlowe's play an Shakespeare's *Merchant of Venice* have attracte much attention, but they are more obvious than sig nificant. Each play of course concerns a wealth Jew who has a daughter and grievances agains Christians. But Barabas is an egocentric, unfeelin monster from the beginning. His motivation is neve adequate, and it is clear that he learned his Hallowee tricks and lost all sense of acceptable values long be fore he came to Malta. Shylock, although villainou we understand as a human being. His hatred of th Christians develops before our eyes, and we feel sympathy for him that is never granted Baraba Jessica and Abigail have nothing in common but se and race; Abigail loves her father, until he kil Lodowick and Mathias; Jessica conspires with Chris tians to humiliate and rob Shylock. In Marlowe w find no Belmont, no Portia, and nothing equivaler to the Gobbos. The revival of Marlowe's *Jew* i 1594, the year of the execution of Roderigo Lópe may well have triggered Shakespeare's compositio of *The Merchant of Venice* and provided him wit a model to surpass. That is about all.

The Shakespeare play most clearly reflecting th influence of *The Jew* is *Richard III*. Richard inform us in *3 Henry VI* that he can "set the murtherou Machiavel to school," and thus places himself in th line of Barabas. In structure, unlike *The Merchan of Venice* with its delicately intertwined quadrup plot, *Richard III* follows the simple, straight-line o ganization of *The Jew*. Barabas craves reveng Richard wants the crown. Each plot provides th opportunity for the great central character to di play in episode after episode his distinctive power In the comparison of these powers we see one of th differences between Marlowe and Shakespear Barabas perpetrates crass physical destruction on h victims; Richard, willing to use the lion's pow when necessary, works skillfully on the minds c those who stand in his way.—G.W.M.

Jew of Venice, The. See George Granville, Lord ANSDOWNE.

jig. A skit accompanied by songs and dances. The :igin of the word "jig," though said to be of un- ertain derivation, has perhaps a close relation to its istory as a form of art. It recalls a group of words f French origin which associate dancing in England ith dancing in France. This group includes the alliard, the pavan, the jig, and the brawl, which are nked together, in that order, in William Webbe's *iscourse of English Poetry* in 1586. The jig, in fact, ay have taken its name from the instrument used accompany the dance, the *gigue*, a stringed instru- ent, and the frequent spelling *gig* may preserve is origin.

The jig, in its earliest occurrence, is generally as- ciated with the descriptive epithets "Scottish" or Northern," and we should bear in mind the close :lationship between Scotland and France in the ter 16th century, when the word first occurs. It was rst used, in fact, by the Scottish poet Alexander cott, about 1560. Shakespeare, referring to a "Scotch g," uses its movement as an image of "hot and asty" wooing. But the term is used not only for the ance, but also for the type of sung verse-composi- on in dialogue to which the dance was an accom- animent. Here again Shakespeare offers a clue in the ords, "He's for a jig or a tale of bawdry," which iggests the kind of content proper to the type. In is latter sense, the jig is indeed a forerunner of the omic opera. In a few extant specimens of the genre its full development, each section of the jig is sung a different tune, which is named at the opening f the section. These tunes mark off successive scenes the action.

Alexander Scott's reference to the jig suggests learly its general character:

> Some loves, new come to town,
> With jigs to make them jolly,

nd a further clue to its nature is the title of the oem, *A Ballad made to the Derision and Scorn of anton Women*. The jig was, in fact, a humorous, atirical form of public entertainment in sung dia- gue, accompanied by dancing. The satire was nainly directed against the frailty of women, a pro- fic theme of comment and a source of mirth. The g appears to belong to the underworld of literature nd drama. We can now fully understand Marlowe's ontemptuous dismissal of "the jigging vein of hyming mother-wits" as the antipodes of "high stounding tragedy" in the prologue to *Tamburlaine*. hakespeare shared Marlowe's contempt, as in Ham- et's reference to a "jigmaker." In stage history, how- ver, two outstanding "clowns" were associated with g-making and jig-dancing: Tarlton and Kempe, the atter a member of Shakespeare's company, famous or his morris-dancing journey from London to Norwich on foot with pipe and tabor.

Professor C. R. Baskervill's standard work, *The Elizabethan Jig* (1927) dismisses as fortuitous any ssociation of the genre with Scotland and the North nd includes in his definition all forms of song with ance, and even monologues, that were found in England from the Middle Ages onwards. He regards his broad group as one of many types of folk-play. In his view, the type includes poems described as "ballads" before the emergence of the term "jig." But this survey casts a very wide net, beyond any relevance to the jig as a definable form of literature. The first of the 36 specimen texts of jigs reproduced in his book is entitled "A Jigge for the Ballad-monger to sing." It dates from 1595 and is spoken by one person, without mention of any tune or any accompanying dance. It is, in fact, a ballad, as distinguished from a jig.

The jig, as an afterpiece of a play, was known in Germany as a *Sing-spiel* and was applied to public performances given by visiting English companies of actors. A number of these have been preserved in German translation. The most striking of these is *Die Tügende Bawrin*, which is the German counterpart of what is known as *Mr. Attowel's Jigge* in English. The English version was printed in 1595, under the title *Frauncis new Jigge . . . to the tune of Walsingham*, and ends with the printed signature of George Attewell. It may have been performed by the visiting company to which Attowel belonged, Strange's Men.

Mr. Attowel's Jigge (Baskervill No. 22) is an entirely moral anecdote concerning Bess' resistance under temptation by Francis, a gentleman neighbor of her husband Richard, a farmer. An assignation is made, but Francis' wife impersonates Bess, and Francis learns his lesson. In *Rowland's Godson* (Baskervill No. 20), however, Bess has an intrigue with her husband's servant, John. Bess plans that the husband, disguised as Bess, shall meet him and be told of his faithfulness to his master, incurring a beating as John's expression of his contempt for a wanton wife. The way is now clear for the lovers, as the husband is convinced of John's good faith.

That *Attowel's Jig* was an authentic example of the genre is made clear by the recent discovery of the first known play to be certified as a jig in contemporary records, with details of its origin and performance: the play of *Michael and Frances*. (See C. J. Sisson, *Lost Plays of Shakespeare's Age; The Jig of a Horse load of Fools*, ascribed to Tarlton, is a forgery of John Payne Collier's.) This has survived in a copy attached to a bill of complaint in the court of Star Chamber, without title, as an exhibit in a libel suit of June 1602. It was written by Francis Mitchell just before Christmas 1601, and received many private performances in local houses in the North Riding of Yorkshire. A year later it was produced professionally by Simpson's Men as an afterpiece of their play at Osmotherly. The company was charged with having "at the ending of their plays sung the same as a Jig." Their audiences "called for the Jig at the end of any play."

The plot of this jig concerns the relations of Michael Steel of Skelton with his maidservant, Frances Thornton. He pretends illness as an excuse for lying alone, in order to enjoy the visits of Frances. His wife and Frances' brother John, who is the wife's cousin, are suspicious, but Frances escapes and pretends sleep in the hall, where they find her and apologize for their suspicions. There are six short scenes, each headed by the name of the tune to which it was sung. Two well-known families were involved in the affair, the Meynells of Hawnby and the Bowes of Ellerbeck, who had some local feud with Steel over his treatment of his wife and supervised the making and performance of the jig. There is no record of the outcome of Steel's action against his tormentors.

Attowel's Jig alone has some stage directions. *Rowland's Godson,* unlike the other two, is all sung to the one tune "Loth to Depart." None of the three gives any direction for dancing.

The jig as a term of art had no relation to the surviving afterpieces of Shakespeare's plays. Feste's concluding song in *Twelfth Night* was certainly not a jig. The vogue of the jig in stage history was confined to theatres of lesser repute in the suburbs, the Fortune, the Curtain, and the Red Bull. In 1612 the Middlesex justices made an "Order for suppressing Jigs at the end of Plays" because of their lewdness, saying they gave rise to tumults and breaches of the peace, and naming the Fortune theatre in particular.

The history of the jig ends as it began. Scott's reference to "Jigs to make them jolly" describes its purpose when the word first occurs, and it is applicable to the genre as a whole. An importation from Scotland developed in England in the repertory of the suburban theatres as a satirical comment on current affairs of notoriety. It is small wonder that the texts of these jigs have so rarely survived. [*The Shirburn Ballads 1585–1616,* Andrew Clark, ed., 1907; C. R. Baskervill, *The Elizabethan Jig,* 1929; C. J. Sisson, *Lost Plays of Shakespeare's Age,* 1936.]—C.J.S.

Joachim, Joseph. See MUSIC BASED ON SHAKESPEARE: *19th century, 1850–1900.*

Joan of Arc. Called **La Pucelle** (c. 1412–1431). French saint and heroine. Joan was the daughter of Jacques d'Arc, a peasant of Domrémy. Hearing the voices of St. Michael, St. Margaret, and St. Catherine commanding her to rid France of the English invaders, Joan went, in 1429, to see the dauphin Charles. With his approval and with that of the church, she marched on Orléans with an army and routed the enemy. The next year, while defending Compiègne against the Burgundians, who were allied with the English, Joan was taken prisoner. The ungrateful Charles having made no attempt to bring about her release, she was sold by the Burgundians to the English, tried for witchcraft and heresy, and burned at the stake in Rouen.

In *1 Henry VI,* Joan, called La Pucelle, wins the love and respect of the Dauphin. She raises the siege of Orléans and takes Rouen, losing the latter city almost immediately to the English forces under Talbot. In a scene with the Duke of Burgundy, she succeeds in persuading him to forsake the English in favor of his own countrymen. Joan is captured by York at the battle of Angiers and is subsequently burned at the stake. Following Holinshed, Shakespeare represents Joan as a witch and a harlot. See 1 HENRY VI: *Sources, Comment.*

Jodelle, Etienne (1532–1573). French dramatist and poet. A literary prodigy, Jodelle wrote his best-known work at the age of 20. His *Cléopâtre captive* (1553) is not so much a drama in the modern sense of the term as a series of long declamations in verse spoken by various characters. It is not likely to have been known by Shakespeare directly, but it was influential in conveying popular attitudes toward the lovers. [*Antony and Cleopatra,* New Variorum Edition, H. H. Furness, ed., 1907.]

John (1167?–1216). King of England; in *King John,* the titular hero. The younger brother of Richard the Lionhearted (1157–1199), John managed to supplant Richard as king during the latter's absence in the Holy Land. On Richard's return to England in 1194, John was deposed, but when his brother died in 1199, he again ascended the throne. Soon establishing himself as an unscrupulous tyrant, he alienated the two most powerful groups in England the church and the nobility. John's conflict with the church led to his excommunication by the powerful medieval pope, Innocent III, and his dispute with the barons led to the most famous event of his reign, the signing of the Magna Carta (1215).

For a long time John was the most unpopular king in English history. During the Reformation, however, his opposition to the Roman Church resulted in his regeneration as a proto-Protestant, making him forerunner of Henry VIII. This aspect of John' character is given us in KYNGE JOHAN (1548), an early Tudor interlude by John Bale. Shakespeare' John, however, is the more traditional figure—a cynical, selfish tyrant and a not very successful one a that.

John, Don. In *Much Ado About Nothing,* the bastard brother of Don Pedro and "a plain-dealing villian." This malcontent, Don John, spitefully revenges himself upon Claudio, "that young upstar who hath all the glory of my overthrow," by slandering Hero to him and Don Pedro. Although hi only gain is the pleasure of misusing the Prince and making Claudio and Hero unhappy, for this Don John "will endeavor anything." After perpetrating his crime, the scoundrel flees, but is captured and brought back to Messina for punishment. [W. H Auden, "The Joker in the Pack," in *The Dyer' Hand and Other Essays,* 1962.]

John, Friar. In *Romeo and Juliet,* the Franciscan brother dispatched by Friar Laurence to tell Romeo that Juliet is alive in her tomb. Suspected by the constabulary of being a plague carrier, Friar John is detained and is unable to transmit the message (V, ii)

John of Gaunt, duke of **Lancaster** (1340–1399) Fourth son of Edward III; by his first wife father o Henry Bolingbroke, who became Henry IV; and by his third wife progenitor of the Beaufort-Tudor line When in 1387 his brother the duke of Gloucester formed an alliance with Arundel and Warwick against the king, Gaunt and his son Henry fough for Richard II, participating in the arrest and tria of the rebels. A quarrel subsequently led to Henry's banishment, and his father died shortly thereafter.

In *Richard II,* Gaunt, on his deathbed after Bolingbroke's disgrace, praises England as "This roya throne of kings, this sceptr'd isle." After Gaunt' death, Richard confiscates his estates, thus provoking Bolingbroke's return and his own fall.

John of Lancaster. See John of Lancaster, duke o BEDFORD.

Johnson, Arthur (d. 1630). Bookseller in London and Dublin. Johnson was admitted to the Stationers Company in 1601. In the 1620's he moved to Dublin where he established himself as a stationer. In 160 he published a "bad quarto" of *The Merry Wives o*

Windsor, the copyright for which was assigned to him by John Busby. [R. B. McKerrow, ed., *A Dictionary of Printers and Booksellers . . . 1557–1640*, 1910.]

Johnson, Charles (1679–1748). Dramatist. A friend of the actor Robert Wilks and an enemy of Alexander Pope, who satirized him in the *Dunciad*, Johnson was the author of two Shakespearean adaptations. His The Cobler of Preston (1716) was an adaptation of the Induction to *The Taming of the Shrew*. Johnson's version was produced at Drury Lane in February 1716 at the same time that another adaptation with the same title was produced at Lincoln's Inn Fields. Johnson's adaptation proved to be less successful.

In 1723 Johnson adapted *As You Like It* as *Love in a Forest*. His chief alteration seems to have been the insertion in Act V of the mock play, "Pyramus and Thisbe," from *A Midsummer Night's Dream*. Johnson also added bits of dialogue from other Shakespearean plays, including *Much Ado About Nothing* (I, i, 245–282), *Love's Labour's Lost* (III, i, 183–215), and *Twelfth Night* (II, iv, 107–117). The play was first produced on January 9, 1723, with Colley Cibber as Jaques. It was not very well received, however, and ran for only six performances. See As You Like It: *Stage History*. [C. B. Hogan, *Shakespeare in the Theatre, 1701–1800*, 2 vols., 1952–1957.]

Johnson, Gerard. See Gheerart Janssen.

Johnson, Joan (fl. 1604–1612). A maid in the house of Christopher Mountjoy who testified as to Shakespeare's involvement in the Belott-Mountjoy suit.

Johnson, John (fl. 1641). Poet. Johnson is the author of a thin volume of prose fiction entitled *The Academy of Love, describing ye folly of younge men & ye fallacy of women* (1641). The volume is noteworthy only for its reference to Shakespeare's popularity as an author with "young sparkish Girles":

> There was also *Shakespeere*, who (as *Cupid* informed me) creepes into the womens closets about bed time, and if it were not for some of the old out-of-date Grandames (who are set over the rest as their tutoresses) the young sparkish Girles would read in *Shakespeere* day and night, so that they would open the Booke or Tome, and the men with a Fescue in their hands should point to the Verse.

[*The Shakspere Allusion-Book*, J. Munro, ed., 1909.]

Johnson, Robert (d. 1611). Stratford neighbor of Shakespeare. Johnson, an innkeeper, lived in Henley Street near the poet's "birthplace." He kept an inn there, later known as the White Lion, from 1591 until his death. An inventory of his goods, dated October 5, 1611 and written by Alexander Aspinall, Stratford schoolmaster, listed among Johnson's possessions, "A lease of a barne that he holdeth of Mr Shaxper, xxli." In 1670 this barn was mentioned in the will of Elizabeth Hall, Shakespeare's granddaughter, as part of her Henley Street property. [Mark Eccles, *Shakespeare in Warwickshire*, 1961.]

Johnson, Robert (1583?–?1633). Lutenist and composer. In 1596 Johnson became a "covenant servant" for the 2nd Lord Hunsdon, patron of Shakespeare's company, and from 1604 to 1633 he was a lutenist at the courts of James I and Charles I; he was, in addition, a member of the private chapels of Prince Henry and of the Prince of Wales.

Composing regularly for the masques of the King's Men at the Globe and Blackfriar theatres, Johnson wrote incidental music for plays of Thomas Middleton, Ben Jonson, Shakespeare, Beaumont and Fletcher, John Webster, and John Day. His settings of "Full fathom five" and "Where the bee sucks" from *The Tempest* were probably composed for a 1612 or 1613 court performance given in connection with Lady Elizabeth's marriage, and are preserved in John Wilson's anthology *Cheerfull Ayres or Ballads* (1660). Johnson's songs for *The Tempest* and for Beaumont and Fletcher's plays are essential documents in the study of Elizabethan incidental music.

Johnson, Samuel (1709–1784). Journalist, lexicographer, and literary figure. In any discussion of Shakespearean critics Samuel Johnson deserves a distinguished place. He was born September 18 [n.s.], 1709 in Lichfield, Staffordshire, the son of a provincial bookseller, and died in London December 13, 1784, after a long life as a journalist, distinguished man of letters, and center of a famous literary circle. Today he is remembered as a poet (*London*, 1738; *The Vanity of Human Wishes*, 1749), essayist (*The Rambler*, 1750–1752; *The Idler*, 1758–1760), lexicographer (compiler of the first complete dictionary of the English language, 1755), editor (Shakespeare, 1765), biographer and critic (*The Lives of the Poets*, 1779–1781). Called "the Great Cham" of literature, he was given a pension by the king in 1762, and devoted most of his later life to conversation which was admirably set down by James Boswell.

Even as a boy Johnson was emotionally involved with Shakespearean characters. The story is told that in his ninth year, while reading *Hamlet* in the basement kitchen of his home in Lichfield, he was so powerfully moved by the ghost scene that he had to rush upstairs to the street door to see people about him. His shock at the death of Cordelia in *King Lear* was so great that he refused to reread the last scenes of the play until forced to do so years later. As a young man beginning his career as a hack writer in London, one of his first unrealized projects was an edition of Shakespeare. None of the earlier editors—Rowe, Pope, Theobald—he thought, had been satisfactory. While they played the game of emendation, the text was still corrupt, and there were many fascinating problems to be settled. Consequently, early in 1745 Johnson began to plan his own version. To show the world what he could do, in April he published *Miscellaneous Observations on the Tragedy of Macbeth*. Tucked away at the back of this 64-page pamphlet was a separate sheet of *Proposals* for printing a completely new edition of all of the plays of Shakespeare. Unfortunately, copyright considerations stood in the way, and the threat of a chancery suit by Jacob Tonson, the well-known bookseller, put an end to the project. Instead, the next year Johnson began work on a *Dictionary of the English Language*, which was to bring him fame.

Although the *Observations* at the time led to nothing, it did show clearly the basic patterns of Johnson's critical approach—his skepticism, his doubts about Romantic illumination, his willingness to examine both sides of a question, his desire to adjudicate between conflicting theories. His purpose was obviously to act as an interpreter, always stressing the effect of the work on the general reader.

During the next few years, though busy with other matters, Johnson's interest in Shakespeare did not flag. He wrote about him in *The Rambler,* and Shakespeare is the most quoted author in the *Dictionary* (almost 8700 quotations in the first volume alone). After the appearance of the *Dictionary* in 1755, Johnson again turned to his earlier plan, and in June 1756 he issued elaborate proposals for a new edition. With characteristic overconfidence he promised publication of the whole work on or before Christmas 1757. But year after year dragged on, as he collected the money from subscriptions, and nothing appeared. Finally, after much zealous pushing from friends, the set of eight volumes was published in October 1765.

Textually Johnson's edition proved something of a disappointment. Although from references in the notes and in the Preface it is evident that he knew exactly what ought to be done, he had neither the inclination nor the proper materials to do a thorough job of collation. Moreover, he disappointed the readers of his day by refusing to make extensive emendations in the text, in the manner of his predecessors. "As I practiced conjecture more," he confessed, "I learned to trust it less; and after I had printed a few plays, resolved to insert none of my own readings in the text." Despite his unwillingness to change words or meanings, Johnson did consider punctuation and arrangement within his province, and made numerous minor alterations—inserting dashes and periods and removing excess commas and colons. Also added were some new stage directions. His goal was always clarity—whatever was necessary to make the text easier and more vivid for the lay reader. Basically he wanted to prepare a version which could be easily read, yet which also would be as close as possible to the original.

Although as a work of textual scholarship it was soon superseded by the work of George Steevens, Edmund Malone, and the later more rigorous scholars, Johnson's edition has remained a high point in Shakespearean criticism. In his explanations of difficult passages, in his factual notes, and appreciative comments, Johnson always has something pertinent to say. His experience as a dictionary-maker had made him expert in succinct, accurate explication. Modern students using the Variorum volumes for help on particular points soon learn to look first to see what Johnson has to say. If shrewd common sense can probe to the bottom of the problem, Johnson will give the answer. But what is most astonishing is Johnson's lack of pedantry. He did not show off his immense learning. "Notes are often necessary," he commented, "but they are necessary evils." And he added, "Let him, that is yet unacquainted with the powers of *Shakespeare,* and who desires to feel the highest pleasure that the drama can give, read every play from the first scene to the last, with utter negligence of all his commentators."

When in his notes Johnson occasionally falters, it is usually through an inadequate knowledge of Elizabethan customs and historical details or through an unwillingness to follow an extended Elizabethan metaphor. As Meyer H. Abrams points out, "What Johnson did was to analyze the passage in the very process of reading it; he habitually interposed the demand that he understand how a figure works, and the qualification that its foundation be neither far-fetched nor difficult to discover, before allowing it to become poetically effective." The result was to limit for him the kind of metaphoric structure he found acceptable. But despite this self-imposed restriction one finds in Johnson's commentary the evidence of an astute critical mind working firsthand on literature. He is at his best when describing human motives and psychological traits. Thus Johnson's shrewd analyses of Polonius and Falstaff, among others, herald the study of Shakespeare through his characters, which was to become the preoccupation of following generations of critics.

It is largely because of his 68-page Preface, however, that Johnson takes his place among the major Shakespearean critics. Some 20th-century authorities (recently Frank Kermode) insist that the Preface is the best single long estimate of Shakespeare ever written. It is not that it embodies any new discoveries or novel suggestions; as recent scholars have clearly shown, almost everything in it had been said before, though never so effectively. What Johnson did was to embody in one admirably phrased essay all the important problems which had occupied the thoughts of earlier critics. In places it almost becomes a dialogue between Johnson and former commentators. Essentially, he sums up what seem to him to be the major considerations for the 18th-century reader of Shakespeare. And many are still pertinent.

In his *Dictionary* Johnson defined a critic as "a man skilled in the art of judging of literature; a man able to distinguish the faults and beauties of writing." He must do more than merely appreciate and explain. He is to be a judge who says what he thinks about a work of art. Johnson was convinced that nothing on earth could be perfect. Even the finest creation must have some human imperfections, and it is the duty of the impartial critic to point them out. Moreover, he must set right false impressions of earlier critics.

To be sure, praise and blame need not exactly balance. In his Preface the ratio is about three to one on the positive side. Some Romantic authors, horrified at finding anyone with the temerity to denigrate Shakespeare in any way, quoted his adverse remarks out of context and failed to see how they were overbalanced by the highest praise. Actually, the overwhelming effect of the Preface is one of intense admiration.

In essence, Johnson's is a frank, honest attempt to explain Shakespeare's continuing appeal. He approaches the earlier writer not with reverence but as he would any other man of letters. The Preface begins by recognizing Shakespeare's undoubted greatness. His plays have stood the test of time. His supreme excellence is that he is the poet of general nature, who holds the mirror up to life and manners. Shakespeare pictures all the emotions, not only those of love. His characters are recognizable types. Johnson then defends Shakespeare from what he thinks are the unjustified carping attacks by 17th-century critics in the French tradition—for his independence of traditional rules, for his violations of the doctrine of "decorum," for his mixtures of comic and tragic. Denying categorically the whole notion of dramatic illusion, he sees no need for observing the unities. Later in the Preface he comes back to this point and provides the most convincing exposure of the weakness of the strict classical position.

But after this enthusiastic praise and partisan defense, Johnson frankly admits that Shakespeare had some weaknesses. "We must confess the faults of our favorite," Johnson once commented in a letter, "to gain credit to our praise of his excellencies." Patiently, one after another, Johnson lists what he does not like—to be sure, not all defects of equal importance. Shakespeare, he says, occasionally sacrifices virtue to convenience, being often more anxious to please than to instruct; his plots are loosely constructed; the endings are often poorly devised; there are occasional anachronisms (such as Hector quoting Aristotle); some jests are too gross; in tragedy Shakespeare at times becomes obscure and strains too hard; in narration he is sometimes wordy and cumbersome; the declamatory and set speeches can be cold; when entangled in unwieldy sentiment he may become obscure, leaving the reader to disentangle the words; he uses conceits and puns in serious passages.

For modern readers some of the objections may easily be assented to. It would be useless to deny that Shakespeare does make historical slips, that his plots are designedly loose (most modern productions prune the plays for effectiveness), and that at times the low comedy may seem out of place. On the other hand, most 20th-century readers are not upset by the conceits or the puns, possibly because most of the double meanings go unrecognized, and we now recognize that punning can be a metaphorical device, as well as a form of wit. Perhaps the objection which is most difficult for us to accept is Johnson's complaint about the lack of moral point to the plays. Johnson always tended to judge on ethical grounds. But although moral considerations were paramount, and he felt obliged to point out deficiencies, it may be significant that there is no evidence that Johnson ever wished Shakespeare's plays to be radically different.

In the latter part of the Preface Johnson shows the necessity of considering Shakespeare in the framework of his own age, and there are perceptive comments on his realism, invention, and use of language. To be sure, Johnson finds him too easily satisfied, too ready to pander to the low tastes of his time, his style often mixed and ungrammatical. But, unlike Pope, Johnson does not try to shift the blame to Shakespeare's early editors. Then follows a judicial summary of the achievements of the earlier editors, in which Johnson defends Rowe, is respectful of Pope, is somewhat unfair to Theobald (or so the 20th century thinks), is complimentary to Hanmer, and equivocal on Warburton. At the end comes a candid explanation of his own procedure.

It has been customary in some circles to speak of Johnson as the last of the rigid neoclassic critics, but this is completely to misunderstand his method. Actually Johnson is scornful of stale tradition. He once referred to "the cant of those who judge by principles rather than perception." His criticism usually represents a personal reaction. Indeed he is fundamentally subjective. How, he asks, does this work strike me? To be sure, he often attempts to justify his personal reaction by recourse to abstract theory, but if the two fail to agree he stands by his own opinion. He is always impatient with slavish following of old rules or themes. All that he insists upon is that a work of art instruct as well as please. As Walter Jackson Bate puts it, Johnson's entire career as a critic might be described as a "restless search for novelty, not only in subject but approach." He refused, however, ever to tolerate novelty which strained too hard or which transcended reason. And he always rejected the emotional quality of pure rhetoric.

It is this last insistence on the restricting control of common sense that remains for many modern readers Johnson's chief weakness, as well as his strength, as a critic. Because the 20th century stresses subtle types of metaphor and ambiguity of a kind that Johnson found reprehensible, it is natural for us to consider him too rigorous in his point of view. But on his own ground one might go far to find a more perceptive critic. [Johnson's Shakespearean criticism is easily available in *Johnson on Shakespeare*, Walter Raleigh, ed., 1908; *Johnson's Notes to Shakespeare*, Arthur Sherbo, ed., 1956–1958; *Samuel Johnson on Shakespeare*, W. K. Wimsatt, Jr., ed., 1960. For appraisals of his edition see Walter Raleigh, *Six Essays on Johnson*, 1910; D. Nichol Smith, *Shakespeare in the Eighteenth Century*, 1928; Joseph Wood Krutch, *Samuel Johnson*, 1944; Arthur M. Eastman, "Johnson's Shakespeare and the Laity," *PMLA*, LXV, December 1950; Arthur Sherbo, *Samuel Johnson, Editor of Shakespeare*, 1956; Arthur M. Eastman, "In Defense of Dr. Johnson," *Shakespeare Quarterly*, VIII, Autumn 1957; Robert E. Scholes, "Dr. Johnson and the Bibliographical Criticism of Shakespeare," *Shakespeare Quarterly*, XI, Spring 1960. Important analyses of his method may be found in W. R. Keast, "The Theoretical Foundations of Johnson's Criticism," *Critics and Criticism*, R. S. Crane, ed., 1952; Jean H. Hagstrum, *Samuel Johnson's Literary Criticism*, 1952; Walter Jackson Bate, *The Achievement of Samuel Johnson*, 1955; T. S. Eliot, *On Poetry and Poets*, 1957; Meyer H. Abrams, "Dr. Johnson's Spectacles," *New Light on Dr. Johnson*, F. W. Hilles, ed., 1959.]—J. L. C.

Johnson, William (c. 1575–1616). Vintner who acted as a trustee in Shakespeare's behalf during the latter's purchase of the Blackfriars Gate-House in 1613 and who, according to Leslie Hotson, was the host of the MERMAID TAVERN. The fact that Johnson acted in a position of trust for Shakespeare lends substance to the legend that Shakespeare frequented the Mermaid Tavern, along with Ben Jonson and other poets and playwrights of the day. [Leslie Hotson, *Shakespeare's Sonnets Dated*, 1949.]

Jolly, George (fl. 1648–1673). Actor. Jolly was one of the group of English actors who toured Europe as strolling players after the closing of the theatres in 1642. From 1648 to 1659 he was the leader of a troupe of players in Germany. In 1655 he performed at Frankfort, where he met Charles II.

At the Restoration, Jolly returned to England, where in 1660 he received permission, probably as a result of his personal acquaintance with the king, to open a theatre. Jolly's license was a direct contradiction of an earlier patent in August which had given Thomas Killigrew and William Davenant the exclusive monopoly in producing plays. Jolly's company, which played from 1661 to 1667 at the Phoenix Theatre, proved a thorn in the side of the two major companies under Killigrew and Davenant. Although a number of Elizabethan plays, including Marlowe's *Dr. Faustus* and Ford's *'Tis Pity She's A Whore,* were produced by Jolly's company, there is no record of a Shakespearean play in its repertory.

In 1667 Jolly was deprived of his license as a result of the chicanery of Killigrew and Davenant, and in compensation was named manager of the so-called Nursery, a company of young actors of distinctly inferior status. Jolly remained as manager of this troupe until 1673. [Leslie Hotson, *The Commonwealth & Restoration Stage*, 1928.]

Jones, Ernest (1879–1958). Psychoanalyst and author. Receiving his M.D. at the age of 21, Jones later studied with Freud in Vienna. His definitive biography *The Life and Work of Sigmund Freud* (3 vols., 1953–1957) received wide acclaim. Jones' most significant contribution to literary criticism are his studies of *Hamlet,* the best known of which is *Hamlet and Oedipus* (1949). Shakespeare, he suggests, was himself unable to explain Hamlet's delay, the motive being hidden in the unconscious mind of the author. Hamlet's inability to do the things he sees he must do is derived from an Oedipal conflict: Claudius, who murdered Hamlet's father and married his mother, has done precisely what Hamlet, in his incestuous love for his mother, has unconsciously wished to do. Hamlet's guilt over his own wish paralyzes his will and renders him incapable of avenging his father's death. See Sigmund FREUD.

Jones, Inigo (1573–1652). Stage designer and architect. Jones, a native of London, studied in Denmark and Italy, where he developed such an outstanding reputation that he was appointed as Queen Anne's personal architect. Jones' first assignment on his return to England was the staging of a royal masque, Ben Jonson's *The Masque of Blackness,* given on January 6, 1605. Jones brought to the design of this masque the knowledge he had acquired from a study of Sebastiano SERLIO and other designers for the Italian stage. He introduced into England on this occasion the use of painted perspective scenery and of a proscenium frame and front curtain. From these and later innovations introduced in such masques as *The Hue and Cry after Cupid* (1608), *The Masque of Queens* (1609), and *Salmacida Spolia* (1640), Jones developed a scenic technique which was to have a profound effect on the development of the English stage in the 17th century.

His collaborations with playwrights in the production of masques were often stormy, particularly those with his most celebrated collaborator, Ben Jonson. Jonson satirized Jones in a number of his plays, most effectively as Lanthorn Leatherhead, the puppeteer in *Bartholomew Fair.*

Jones, Robert (c. 1575–1615). Musician and composer. Jones' *The first booke of Songs & Ayres of foure parts* (1600) contains a setting of the lyric "Farewell, dear heart," sung by Sir Toby and Feste in *Twelfth Night* (II, iii, 110–121).

Jonson, Ben[jamin] (1572–1637). Dramatist and poet. Jonson was raised by his stepfather, a bricklayer, and briefly followed the same trade, after some years as a scholarship student at Westminster School. He was for a short time a soldier in the Netherlands. On his return, he probably supported himself by acting and reworking old plays until the performance of his first original play, *Every Man In his Humour* in 1598. In spite of this seemingly inadequate preparation, he became the literary arbiter of Jacobean London. He was perhaps Shakespeare's closest rival among the age's writers of comedy, yet the evidence suggests that the two dramatists were also friends.

BEN JONSON. PORTRAIT BY AN UNKNOWN ARTIST. (NATIONAL PORTRAIT GALLERY)

One evidence of this association is in the great encomium to his dead friend which Jonson prefixed to the First Folio of 1623: "To the memory of my beloved, The Author Mr. William Shakespeare: And what he hath left us."

To draw no envy (*Shakespeare*) on thy name,
Am I thus ample to thy Booke, and Fame:
While I confesse thy writings to be such,
As neither *Man,* nor *Muse,* can praise too much.
'Tis true, and all mens suffrage. But these wayes
Were not the paths I meant unto thy praise:
For seeliest Ignorance on these may light,
Which, when it sounds at best, but eccho's right;
Or blinde Affection, which doth ne're advance
The truth, but gropes, and urgeth all by chance;
Or crafty Malice, might pretend this praise,
And thinke to ruine, where it seem'd to raise.
These are, as some infamous Baud, or Whore,
Should praise a Matron. What could hurt her more?
But thou are proofe against them and indeed
Above th'ill fortune of them, or the need.
I, therefore will begin. Soule of the Age!

The applause! delight! the wonder of our Stage!
My *Shakespeare,* rise; I will not lodge thee by
Chaucer, or *Spenser,* or bid *Beaumont* lye
A little further, to make thee a roome:
Thou art a Moniment, without a tombe,
And are alive still, while thy Booke doth live,
And we have wits to read, and praise to give.
That I not mixe thee so, my braine excuses;
I meane with great, but disproportion'd *Muses:*
For, if I thought my judgement were of yeeres,
I should commit thee surely with thy peeres,
And tell, how farre thou didstst our *Lily* outshine,
Or sporting *Kid,* or *Marlowes* mighty line.
And though thou hadst small *Latine,* and lesse *Greeke,*
From thence to honour thee, I would not seeke
For names; but call forth thund'ring *Æschilus,*
Euripides, and *Sophocles* to us,
Paccuvius, Accius, him of *Cordova* dead,
To life againe, to heare thy Buskin tread,
And shake a Stage: Or, when thy Sockes were on,
Leave thee alone, for the comparison
Of all, that insolent *Greece,* or haughtie *Rome*
sent forth, or since did from their ashes come.
Triúmph, my *Britaine,* thou hast one to showe,
To whom all Scenes of *Europe* homage owe.
He was not of an age, but for all time!
And all the *Muses* still were in their prime,
When like *Apollo* he came forth to warme
Our eares, or like a *Mercury* to charme!
Nature her selfe was proud of his designes,
And joy'd to weare the dressing of his lines!
Which were so richly spun, and woven so fit,
As, since, she will vouchsafe no other Wit.
The merry *Greeke,* tart *Aristophanes,*
Neat *Terence,* witty *Plautus,* now not please;
But antiquated and deserted lye
As they were not of Natures family.
Yet must I not give Nature all: Thy Art,
My gentle *Shakespeare,* must enjoy a part.
For though the *Poets* matter, Nature be,
His Art doth give the fashion. And, that he,
Who casts to write a living line, must sweat,
(such as thine are) and strike the second heat
Upon the *Muses* anvile: turne the same,
(And himselfe with it) that he thinkes to frame;
Or for the lawrell, he may gaine a scorne,
For a good *Poet's* made, as well as borne.
And such wert thou. Looke how the fathers face
Lives in his issue, even so, the race
Of *Shakespeares* minde, and manners brightly shines
In his well torned, and true filed lines:
In each of which, he seemes to shake a Lance,
As brandish't at the eyes of Ignorance.
Sweet Swan of *Avon!* what a sight it were
To see thee in our waters yet appeare,
And make those flights upon the bankes of *Thames,*
That so did take *Eliza,* and our *James!*
But stay, I see thee in the *Hemisphere*
Advanc'd, and made a Constellation there!
Shine forth, thou Starre of *Poets,* and with rage,
Or influence, chide, or cheere the drooping Stage;
Which, since thy flight frõm hence, hath mourn'd like night,
And despaires day, but for thy Volumes light.
Ben: Jonson.

This well-known poem is not merely a conventional tribute. The deep sincerity of Jonson's admiration and his true love for the dead Shakespeare are everywhere apparent. He salutes Shakespeare as "Soule of the Age!" He places him above all contemporary poets and, in spite of his "small Latine and less Greeke," in the company of "thund'ring Æschylus, Euripides, and Sophocles"; he is the one genius with which Britain may rival the classical writers of old, and Jonson envisages him transported to heaven to reign as a "star of poets" to inspire his successors.

Shakespeare's acquaintance with Jonson probably began shortly before *Every Man In his Humour* was staged by the Lord Chamberlain's Men with Shakespeare himself in a major role. Nicholas Rowe reported that it was Shakespeare who urged his company to put on this play by the then unknown Jonson, when other members of the company to whom Jonson had offered it were about to return it to him "with an ill-natured answer." We have little reason to doubt Rowe's account, and it is true that when Jonson printed a revised version of the play in his folio volume of 1616, followed by a list of actors who had appeared in the first performance, the name of Shakespeare led all the rest. Shakespeare's name appears also among the actors who performed in Jonson's less successful play *Sejanus* (1603), and it has been suggested that Shakespeare may have been the unknown collaborator with whom Jonson worked on the earliest version of the play, although we have no real evidence to support this supposition. Many scholars have argued, however, that Shakespeare was influenced by Jonson's invention of the COMICAL SATIRE and adopted several of its features in his own dark comedies.

In the year following the staging of *Every Man In his Humour* Jonson became involved in a sensational struggle which has come to be known as the poetomachia or WAR OF THE THEATRES and which, before it subsided around 1602, had come to involve many of the leading writers for the London stage. If Shakespeare was among these, it is clear that Jonson harbored no animosity for any part he may have had in the affair.

Many legends have survived which attest to the close relations Ben Jonson and William Shakespeare continued to maintain. They are reported to have engaged in wit combats in various taverns at which the heavier-handed Jonson was reputedly often put down by Shakespeare's more nimble wit. Anecdotes involving their friendship and their rivalry continued to appear throughout the 17th and 18th centuries, and although we cannot give credence to all of this apocryphal matter, we cannot doubt the reality of the relationship which gave rise to so much legendry and gossip. One story which appears in several versions records that Shakespeare was godfather to Jonson's child (see Nicholas L'ESTRANGE).

Ben Jonson was his age's greatest literary critic,

and during his long career he handed down pronouncements on the work of the best of his contemporary poets. In spite of what friendship may have existed between them—perhaps because of it—Jonson never hesitated to criticize the plays of Shakespeare, and some of Jonson's strictures upon them are extremely interesting. Probably the most notable appears in Jonson's *Timber, or Discoveries* (pub. post., 1640), actually a set of notes which he prepared for his lectures at Gresham College, London:

> I *remember*, the Players have often mentioned it as an honour to *Shakespeare*, that in his writing, (whatsoever he penn'd) hee never blotted out a line. My answer hath beene, would he had blotted a thousand. Which they thought a malevolent speech. I had not told posterity this, but for their ignorance, who choose that circumstance to commend their friend by, wherein he most faulted. And to justifie mine owne candor, (for I lov'd the man, and doe honour his memory (on this side Idolatry) as much as any.) Hee was (indeed) honest, and of an open, and free nature: had an excellent *Phantsie;* brave notions, and gentle expressions: wherein hee flow'd with that facility, that sometime it was necessary he should be stop'd; *Sufflaminandus erat;* as *Augustus* said of *Haterius.* His wit was in his owne power; would the rule of it had beene so too. Many times hee fell into those things, could not escape laughter: As when hee said in the person of *Caesar*, one speaking to him; *Caesar thou dost me wrong.* Hee replyed: *Caesar did never wrong, but with just cause* and such like: which were ridiculous. But hee redeemed his vices, with his vertues. There was ever more in him to be praysed, then to be pardoned.

Since the line in question from *Julius Caesar* does not appear in our text of that play, which was first printed in the First Folio of 1623, we have the interesting possibility that Shakespeare may have revised his play in the light of Jonson's criticism—that is, if Jonson made the comment to Shakespeare while he was still alive, for the notes in *Timber* were written after Shakespeare's death.

There is a slighting reference to *Titus Andronicus* in Jonson's *Bartholomew Fair* of 1614, but this merely criticizes the play, along with Kyd's *Spanish Tragedy* —in which there is good reason to suppose that Jonson himself had acted, and to which he was paid by Philip Henslowe to make additions—as old and out of fashion. Jonson seems to have been very critical of Shakespeare's final romances, plays in a tradition utterly alien to that in which Jonson himself wrote. William Drummond of Hawthornden, who kept careful record of Jonson's conversations when he was visited by the poet in December and January of 1618/9, reports Jonson as saying that Shakespeare "wanted art," one of the reasons being that "Shakespeare in a play brought in a number of men saying they had suffered shipwreck in Bohemia, where there is no sea near by some one hundred miles." The reference, of course, is to Shakespeare's *Winter's Tale.* It is virtually certain that Jonson is thinking of Shakespeare's play when he refers to "some mouldy tale like *Pericles*" in his *Ode to Himself.*

That Jonson may have felt some sense of rivalry with Shakespeare is likely, but there is no reason to

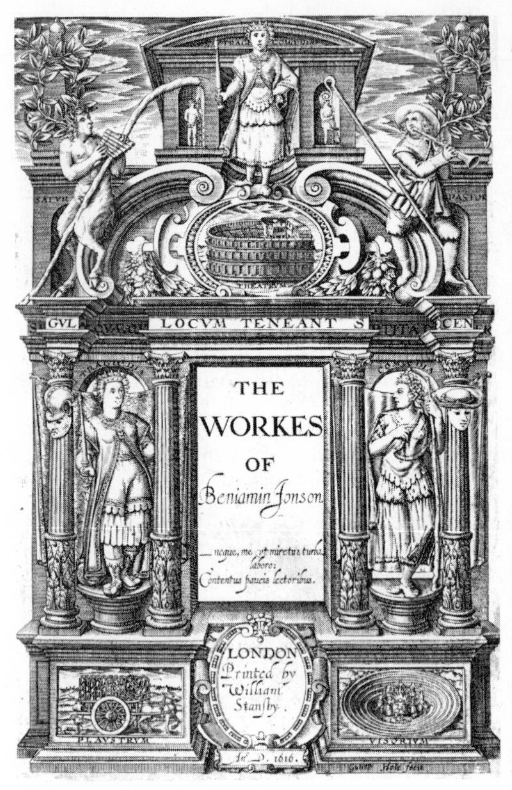

TITLE PAGE OF JONSON'S *Workes* (1616).

assume that their personal relations were in any way impaired. We have good reason to believe that ever after Shakespeare retired from the theatre and went to live in his native Stratford his association with Jonson continued. In the notebooks kept by the Reverend John Ward, who served as vicar of Holy Trinity Church, Stratford, from 1662 to 1681, appears the following entry: "Shakespeare, Drayton, and Ben Jonson had a merry meeting, and it seems drank too hard, for Shakespeare died of a fever there contracted." There is little reason to doubt that Ward was recording some 40 years after Shakespeare's death the event as it was then recalled by many Stratford villagers.

There is thus no reason to question Jonson's sincerity when he says that he "lov'd the man, and doe honour his memory (on this side Idolatry) as much as any." In the many tributes to Shakespeare's memory which followed his death, the praise of no other poet is greater than that offered to him by Ben Jonson. [G. E. Bentley, *Shakespeare and Jonson: their Reputations in the Seventeenth Century Compared*, 1945.]—I.R.

Jordan, Dorothea or **Dorothy** (1762–1816). Irish-born actress. Mrs. Jordan was the illegitimate daughter of Francis and Grace Phillips. In 1777 she appeared as Phoebe in *As You Like It* in Dublin. In 1758 she made an inconspicuous debut at Drury Lane, but during her first season there she established herself in public favor, playing Viola and Imogen. She was exceptionally good in Shakespearean comedy roles: Rosalind, Beatrice, and Helena

All's Well That Ends Well), but she also played uliet, Ophelia, and Dorinda in Kemble's version of *'he Tempest*. She was praised by Hazlitt, Leigh Hunt, Lamb, Byron, and Sir Joshua Reynolds. However, her scandalous private life sometimes provoked iots at her appearances on stage, especially during he political ferment of 1790. [*Dictionary of National Biography*, 1885– ; Charles Beecher Hogan, *'hakespeare in the Theatre, 1701–1800*, 2 vols., 1952, 957.]

Jordan, John (1746–1809). Antiquarian. Born in Tiddington, a few miles from Stratford, Jordan, a elf-educated man, early became interested in Shakespeare. His first literary effort was a poetic epistle to David Garrick on the occasion of the Stratford Jubilee of 1769. In 1780 he completed his *Original Collections on Shakespeare and Stratford-on-Avon*, and in 790 his *Original Memoirs and Historical Accounts of the Families of Shakespeare and Hart*, neither of which was published during Jordan's lifetime. Both olumes contain material which Jordan presented as amiliar Stratford legends and tradition. At least ome of these tales, however, are thought to have een invented by Jordan himself, who at this time vas acting as a self-appointed guide to visitors who had begun to be attracted to Shakespeare's native own.

Among the stories recorded by Jordan was that of Shakespeare's drinking bout with the men of BIDFORD. Another of his stories was a version of the deer-stealing episode (see Sir Thomas LUCY). He lso supplied biographical information to the scholar Edmund Malone, who was properly skeptical of Jordan but attentive to his accounts. Probably the most mportant and most disputed of Jordan's work is the ublication of John Shakespeare's religious testament, which suggests that the poet's father was an adherent of the old faith (see John SHAKESPEARE). Jordan is esponsible for the identification of the farmhouse in Wilmcote, now known as "Mary Arden's House," nd was also the source of some of the imagined 'legends" reprinted by Samuel Ireland. See William Henry IRELAND.

Jourdain, Margery or **Margaret** (fl. 1433). A sorceress who was popularly known as the witch of Eye. She was burned at Smithfield for her complicity in he alleged treason of the duchess of Gloucester. In *2 Henry VI*, she helps to conjure up a spirit for the Duchess (I, iv) and is arrested and sentenced to be 'burn'd to ashes" (II, iii). [W. H. Thomson, *Shakespeare's Characters: A Historical Dictionary*, 1951.]

Jourdain, Sylvester (d. 1650). Traveler. In 1609 Jourdain was a passenger on a ship bound for Virginia which was wrecked on the coast of Bermuda. Subsequently rescued, Jourdain returned to England n the following year and published an account of his experiences on the uninhabited island as *A Discovery of the Barmudas, Otherwise called the Ile of Divels*. Shakespeare may have made use of this pamphlet for the description of the storm and the atmosphere of Prospero's island in *The Tempest*. See THE TEMPEST: *Sources*.

Joyce, James (1882–1941). Irish author. His principal works are *Dubliners* (1914), *A Portrait of the Artist as a Young Man* (1916), *Ulysses* (1922), and *Finnegans Wake* (1939). Given the allusive and evocative nature of Joyce's work, it was inevitable that Shakespeare would be among the numerous authors upon whom he drew.

Using the structure of the *Odyssey* in his *Ulysses*, Joyce depicts one day in Dublin as a microcosm of the contemporary world. "Scylla and Charybdis," the ninth episode, takes place in the office of the National Library, where the protagonist, Stephen Dedalus, gives a fanciful reconstruction of the Shakespeare story. The young Shakespeare is seduced by the older woman, Anne Hathaway. He later departs for London where he becomes the successful playwright; Anne remains in Stratford where she has a liaison with one of his brothers. In Joyce's version Shakespeare never recovers from the psychic wound inflicted by the seduction and cuckolding, and his life and works are profoundly affected. The frequent occurrence of the treacherous brother in the plays, for example, is but one reflection of his personal situation.

To substantiate his theory, Dedalus goes beyond established facts and draws upon *Hamlet*, which he considers a projection of Shakespeare's own life. Thus King Hamlet is identified with Shakespeare, Gertrude with Anne Hathaway, Claudius with the brother, and Hamlet with Shakespeare's son Hamnet. Dedalus not only sets forth a theory of Shakespeare but, it becomes increasingly clear as the episode progresses, he identifies himself with Shakespeare and Hamlet—as seen through the eyes of the Romantic critics. Thus Dedalus regards himself as a solitary figure, as the artist cut off from, and antagonistic to, society, and as the man without roots, searching for a father. In *A Portrait of the Artist as a Young Man*, where Dedalus appears in his earlier years, the Shakespeare-Hamlet parallel is in embryonic form, but the identification is not as pronounced as in *Ulysses*. Throughout this episode Joyce weaves a pattern of Shakespearean allusions, quotations, and puns ("If others have their will, Ann hath a way"). Joyce also shows his familiarity with the writings of such contemporary scholars and critics as Sydney Lee, Georg Brandes, and Frank Harris.

In "Ithaca," the 17th episode in *Ulysses*, a parallel is drawn between Leopold Bloom and Shakespeare, a parallel which depicts both similarities and marked contrasts. *Finnegans Wake* depicts the complex state of the mind between the states of sleep and waking. In this world of dreams and reverie, Shakespearean allusions and evocations are numerous. [William M. Schutte, *Joyce and Shakespeare: A Study in the Meaning of Ulysses*, 1957.]—R.C.F.

Jubilee of 1769. Name given to the series of ceremonies at the first Stratford Shakespearean Festival. The idea for the celebration was conceived by the members of the Stratford corporation, who invited the noted actor David Garrick to organize and direct the festival.

The festival opened on September 6, 1769 after much hectic preparation which involved the overhauling of virtually every building in the town. The festivities lasted three days, during which time the town was filled with hundreds of visitors including the leading nobles of the land. The ceremonies began with the firing of a cannon at dawn. This was followed in the next three days by a series of parades, masquerade balls, and displays of fireworks lending a carnival atmosphere, only slightly allayed by the

FIRST DAY,

Wedneſday, the 6th of *SEPTEMBER,*

Shakeſpeare's Jubilee.

The STEWARD of the JUBILEE begs Leave to inform the COMPANY, that at Nine o'Clock will be

A PUBLIC BREAKFAST

At the TOWN-HALL;

Thence to proceed to the CHURCH to hear

The ORATORIO of *JUDITH,*

Which will begin exactly at ELEVEN.

From Church will be a full CHORUS of VOCAL and INSTRUMENTAL MUSIC to the AMPHITHEATRE; where, at Three o'Clock, will be

An ORDINARY for Gentlemen and Ladies.

About Five o'Clock, a Collection of NEW SONGS, BALLADS, ROUNDELAYS, CATCHES, GLEES, &c. will be performed in the AMPHITHEATRE; after which the Company is deſired to prepare for the BALL, which will begin exactly at Nine, with NEW MINUETS, (compoſed for the Occaſion) and played by the whole Band.

The SECOND DAY'S ENTERTAINMENTS will be publiſhed To-morrow.

N. B. As the PUBLIC BREAKFASTS and ORDINARIES are intended for thoſe Ladies and Gentlemen who have taken the Guinea Tickets, no Perſon can be admitted without firſt ſhewing ſuch Ticket. Should there be Room for more than the Proprietors of thoſe Tickets, Ladies and Gentlemen will be admitted to the ORATORIO and FIREWORKS, at *Five Shillings* each; and to the DEDICATION, ODE, and BALL, at *Half a Guinea* each.

_ The STEWARD hopes that the Admirers of *Shakeſpeare*, will, upon this Occaſion, wear the Favors which are called the *Shakeſpeare Favors.*

☞ As many Ladies have complained of the Fatigue they ſhall undergo, if the Ball and Maſquerade are on two ſucceſſive Nights, there will be only the FIREWORKS on *Thurſday* Night, and the MASQUERADE on *Friday* Night, the 8th Inſt. which will conclude the Entertainments of the Jubilee.

STRATFORD: Printed by FULK WEALE, next Door to the Coffee-Houſe,

POSTER ANNOUNCING EVENTS AT THE GARRICK JUBILEE OF 1769. (SHAKESPEARE BIRTHPLACE TRUST)

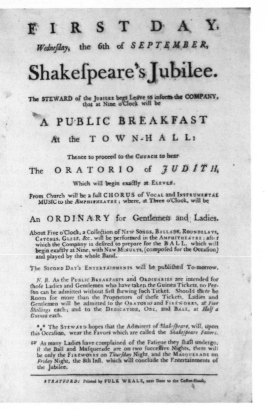

almost continuous rain which fell during the festivities. The highlight of the proceedings was Garrick's rendition, in a specially built amphitheatre designed to hold 1000 people, of his *Ode upon Dedicating a Building, and Erecting a Statue, to Shakespeare.* In general the visitors, and Garrick in particular, enjoyed themselves immensely. Only after the Jubilee ended was it observed that not one line of Shakespeare's had been spoken during the proceedings.

The extravagance and gaudiness of the Jubilee evoked considerable satire in the press and on the stage. Garrick himself produced an enormously successful, mildly satiric version of the festival, titled *The Jubilee* (1769). Despite its frivolous nature, the Jubilee has gained some historical importance as the earliest expression of the Romantic conception of Shakespeare as a supreme creator of character. See CHARACTER CRITICISM.

Julia. In *The Two Gentlemen of Verona,* Proteus' fiancée. She disguises herself as a boy to journey to Milan to see Proteus. When she discovers that her betrothed has become infatuated with Silvia, she enters his service as the page Sebastian. Proteus regrets his actions and the lovers are reconciled.

Juliet. In *Measure for Measure,* Claudio's betrothed. Juliet and Claudio have anticipated matrimony and, as a result, Juliet is pregnant and her beloved condemned to death. She acknowledges that the act was "mutually committed" and accepts the heavier burden of the sin (II, iii).

Juliet. The heroine of *Romeo and Juliet.* In Shakespeare's source Juliet is 16, and in the play 14; her extreme youth helps to account for the vitality and purity of her spirit. Her innocence, however, is never cloying, seasoned as it is with sensuality and wit. To these are added a boldness of spirit, not native to Juliet but infused by love, which enables her to withstand every convention of her life and to confront the overwhelming reality of death. Both her fear and courage vie for mastery in the scene in which she drinks the potion after envisioning the terrors of awakening alone in the tomb. Her irresolution lasts but a moment, however, as her commitment to love achieves its finest expression.

Juliet is not, as is Romeo, transformed and matured in the course of the play. Rather, her essential qualities of youth and innocence remain intact until the end, serving to represent the suffering and death of the innocent, which is an essential aspect of tragedy.

THE TRAGEDY OF JULIUS CÆSAR.

Julius Caesar. A tragedy by Shakespeare.

Text. The First Folio offers the only authoritative text. Its shortness, combined with its excellence, suggests that it was set up from an acting script long used by Shakespeare's company. There is strong evidence of revision in the Folio text. Brents Stirling has pointed out that inconsistent abbreviation of the speech headings (II, i, 86–228) and such details as the repetition of the news of Portia's death (IV, iii, 143–195) indicate that Shakespeare revised his text at these points in order to speed up the action of the play. Because of the immediate and continued popularity of the drama on the stage, no edition of *Julius Caesar* was printed before that of the Folio. No quarto editions were published until the latter half of the 17th century.

Date. John WEEVER, whose *Epigrammes* (1599) contains a complimentary poem addressed to "Honie-tong'd Shakespeare," refers to *Julius Caesar* in *The Mirror of Martyrs or The Life and Death of Sir John Oldcastle.* This work was not published until 1601, but, according to Weever, it was "ready for the Press some two years agoe," that is, in 1599. The lines read:

The many-headed multitude were drawne
By *Brutus* speach, that *Caesar* was ambitious,
When eloquent *Mark Antonie* had showne
His vertues, who but *Brutus* then was vicious?

Thomas Platter, a doctor of Basle, Switzerland, kept a notebook describing his travels during the years 1595–1600, which included a visit to England in 1599. While there he saw two plays, one of them a tragedy, "*Vom Ersten Keyser,*" which he witnessed on September 21, 1599 in a theatre on the south side of the Thames. This play can only have been Shakespeare's, and Platter's note is a confirmation of the date 1599 for its presentation. Another confirmation is the fact that the title does not appear in Meres' list in his *Palladis Tamia* (autumn of 1598).

Sources. The principal source of the historical events dramatized in *Julius Caesar* was the lives of Caesar, Brutus, and Antony in the English translation (1579) of Plutarch's *Lives of the noble grecians and Romanes* made by Sir Thomas NORTH, probably by way of Amyot's French translation, *Vies des hommes illustres* (1559–1565). Caesar had appeared more than once on the Elizabethan stage before Shakespeare's drama. A somewhat doubtful entry in Henry Machyn's diary (1561–1562) refers to what was probably a Caesar play in the following terms: "The first day of February [1562] at nyght was the goodlyest maske and divers goodly men of armes in gylt harnes and Julyes Sesar played." According to Henslowe's diary, during the year 1594, his company staged a two-part play about Caesar, of which Shakespeare must have had some knowledge. We can only guess as to what sort of drama this was. Polonius (*Hamlet*, III, ii, 108–109) boasts that he once acted Julius Caesar at the university. The profusion of pre-Shakespearean English dramas about Caesar establishes the vitality of a dramatic tradition, but does not enable scholars to find a direct source for Shakespeare's work. The arrogant, self-assured boaster that his Caesar is, however, is a representative of the tradition developed in the 16th century in the style of Seneca's *Hercules Oetaeus.* A Caesar of this type appears first in Marc-Antoine Muret's *César* (1544). In 1559 Jacques Grévin wrote a French vernacular play, *La Mort de César,* in which the hero, a replica of Muret's character, is also a braggart. Even closer to Shakespeare's work is Robert Garnier's (1534–1590) *Cornélie*, which the poet must have read in Kyd's English translation of 1594. Garnier fills Caesar's role with long bombastic speeches in Hercules' vein. In creating a Caesar who struts to his doom Shakespeare follows a well-established and popular stage tradition. Another contemporary Caesar play is the anonymous *Caesar's Revenge*, registered in 1606 and printed in 1607. It probably antedated Shakespeare's play, however.—O.J.C.

Plot Synopsis. Act I. Caesar has returned to Rome in triumph after crushing the forces of Pompey, but many are displeased by his ascendancy, among them Cassius, who expresses amazement that a man of such "feeble temper" should rule the world. Cassius addresses his remarks to his brother-in-law, Marcus Brutus, a patrician who loves Caesar, but who is concerned about the possible consequences of his vast power. As they converse, they hear shouts from the place where Caesar is observing the feast of Lupercal. From the plain-speaking Casca they learn that Caesar's lieutenant, Antony, has offered him the crown three times; Caesar has refused it thrice, each time more reluctantly than the last, and has finally suffered an attack of the falling-sickness. Confident that he can win Brutus' support, Cassius decides to throw in Brutus' windows letters purporting to come from citizens fearful of Caesar's ambition.

Meeting Casca during a fearful storm, marked by ominous disturbances of nature, Cassius declares that these signs should be interpreted as a heavenly warning against the pretensions of Caesar, who "would not be a wolf, / But that he sees the Romans are but sheep." After Casca has stated that he will cooperate with Cassius, they betake themselves to the house of Brutus.

Act II. Brutus, meanwhile, is torn between his affection for Caesar and his fear that he may prove a tyrant if he is crowned. It would be best, he concludes, to kill him before any of the forebodings can be realized. Brutus' nocturnal meditations are interrupted by the arrival of Cassius, Casca, and their fellow-conspirators, Decius Brutus, Trebonius, and Metellus Cimber. When Cassius suggests that they swear to their resolution, Brutus demurs, stating that their lofty motives are sufficient guarantee of their fidelity. Neither does he agree with Cassius' proposal that Antony be slain together with Caesar, for he is convinced that the frivolous Antony will prove powerless once Caesar is dead. After the meeting ends, Portia, Brutus' wife, pleads with him to unfold to her the cause of his perturbation, but he promises only that he will satisfy her by and by.

The strange events of the turbulent night have alarmed Calpurnia, Caesar's wife, who has dreamed of his death and begs him not to leave the house that day. Her warning is confirmed by the findings of the augurers. Although Caesar scoffs at her fears, he is willing to humor her until Decius Brutus, who has arrived to escort him to the Capitol, gives her dream a favorable interpretation and observes that the senators may believe that Caesar is afraid if he does not appear.

Act III. As he makes his way to the Capitol in the company of Antony, Brutus, Cassius, and other conspirators, Caesar espies a soothsayer who had warned him to beware the ides of March; since it is now the 15th of March, he remarks that the ides have come, to which the soothsayer replies that they have not gone. Artemidorus, a teacher of rhetoric who has written a letter warning Caesar of the plot, urges him to read the scroll, but he brushes it aside.

In the senate house, Trebonius draws Antony

aside, while Caesar listens to a petition concerning the banished brother of Metellus Cimber, which he rejects. Crowding about him, as if to plead for Metellus, the conspirators stab him one by one, Brutus giving him the final thrust. As the onlookers flee in panic, the assassins bathe their hands in Caesar's blood. Antony, recovering from his initial shock, states his willingness to come to terms with the conspirators; despite Cassius' misgivings, he obtains from Brutus permission to speak at Caesar's funeral. When he is alone with the mutilated corpse, however, Antony vows revenge on the assassins and prophesies that "domestic fury and fierce civil strife" shall ravage Italy.

At Caesar's funeral, Brutus explains to the citizens that Caesar has been slain because his ambition was a threat to their liberties. Having won the approbation of the crowd, Brutus makes way for Antony. Although he refrains from denouncing the assassins, Antony reminds his listeners of Caesar's virtues and points out that he had thrice refused the crown; he tantalizes them with references to Caesar's will and, as their sentiments waver, holds up Caesar's mantle, rent by the daggers of his murderers. The crowd becomes wholly his when he at last reads Caesar's will, which reveals that he had bequeathed his gardens to Rome and left to each citizen 75 drachmas. The people are so inflamed that they kill a poet called Cinna merely because he bears the same name as one of the conspirators. Meanwhile, Brutus and Cassius have had to flee the city.

Act IV. Antony's allies in the impending war against Brutus and Cassius are young Octavius, Caesar's grandnephew, and Lepidus. During a conference of the triumvirs, Lepidus agrees to the proscription of his brother, and Antony to that of his nephew. Antony later confides to Octavius his opinion that Lepidus is "a slight unmeritable man," unfit to share in the threefold division of the world.

Cassius arrives in Brutus' camp near Sardis, aggrieved because Brutus has ignored his pleas on behalf of a man convicted of bribery. After pointing out that Cassius is noted for "an itching palm," Brutus then reminds Cassius that he has denied Brutus' requests for gold. Cassius reproaches his friend for magnifying his infirmities instead of tolerating them; he bares his breast and offers him his dagger, but by now Brutus' anger has disappeared, and they are reconciled. When Brutus reveals that Portia has killed herself by swallowing hot coals, Cassius can only admire his stoicism.

They now turn to a discussion of the military situation. Overruling Cassius' objections, Brutus decides to meet the forces of Octavius and Antony at Philippi. After Cassius leaves, Brutus asks his young servant Lucius to play the lute, but the lad falls asleep, and his master gently takes the instrument from him. He sees the ghost of Caesar, who declares that they will meet again at Philippi.

Act V. After exchanging angry words with Antony and Octavius at Philippi, Cassius and Brutus bid each other an "everlasting farewell." During the battle, Cassius, hard pressed by Antony's soldiers, sends Titinius to learn the identity of some nearby troops. When Cassius' slave Pindarus mistakenly reports that Titinius has been captured, his master despairs of victory and, giving Pindarus his freedom, persuades him to stab him. Titinius learns from Messala that Brutus has defeated the legions of Octavius. Returning too late to Cassius' tent, he joins Cassius in death.

When his troops are defeated in another part of the field, Brutus asks his servants Clitus and Volumnius to kill him, but they refuse. At last Strato consents to hold the sword while Brutus runs on it. Upon finding the body, Antony expresses his esteem for the fallen patrician, who was guided only by his concern for the welfare of Rome. Octavius orders that he be buried with full honors.—H.D.

Comment. *Julius Caesar* is unique among the poet's dramas in that it presents two parallel and contrasting tragedies. Caesar's fall is the time-honored story of the fall of a prince, which reaches its climax at the end of Act III with the assassination. The character of Caesar has provoked considerable controversy among readers of the plays. Some feel that he is portrayed as the tyrannical braggart of 16th-century tradition. Others argue that, despite some very human failings, Caesar's greatness is clearly established in both plays. In both instances, however, there is agreement that Caesar is guilty of the sin of *hybris* (overweening self-assurance) which had by Shakespeare's time become conventional in portrayals of Caesar's fall (see above under *Source*). Calpurnia makes this clear in her warnings to her husband. His seemingly self-confident reply is really an act of bravado that betrays his inner anxiety. It is precisely this anxiety, the fear of public opinion, that betrays him into going to the Capitol—despite the ominous portents of the soothsayers. Shakespeare's picture of Caesar not only intensifies the tragic impact of his fall, it serves to humanize an historical figure of enormous stature.

The second tragedy, dramatized in the last two acts of the play, is that of Brutus, and it represents an innovation in Shakespeare's art. Brutus is a noble character, a dedicated Stoic. As a philosopher of that school, he finds the only beneficent force in an evil world to be a disciplined soul and the serenity that it creates. His famous quarrel with Cassius is the result of their different reasons for striking down Caesar. Cassius is motivated by envy; Brutus by what he conceives as his painful duty to rid Rome of a tyrant. His failure is the defeat of an idealist frustrated by the revolutionary forces that the murder of Caesar has loosed. His Stoical principles produce the calmness that he displays in every difficult situation, even upon receiving news of his wife's death. His cool self-control is mitigated by the sweetness of his nature and his consideration, even of his social inferiors—of the tired boy Lucius, for example, who falls asleep while playing and singing to his master. Instead of chiding him, Brutus bends tenderly over him, takes his lute from him and in this gentle fashion bids him good night. His reasons for committing suicide are in accord with his Stoical principles. He takes his life not in order to escape the fate that Providence has chosen for him, but to avoid the dishonor of capture and being taken a bound prisoner to Rome. Before and during the battle of Philippi he is haunted by Caesar's ghost, a symbol of his sense of guilt over having slain the head of the state. This is Shakespeare's way of enforcing the political lesson of the drama. Even idealistic motives do not cleanse a noble creature of the guilt of an almost sacrilegious murder. This moral dichotomy gives Shakespeare a chance to sound for the first time the note of irony which accompanies the sweep of his action toward inevitable catastrophe.—O.J.C.

Stage History. The earliest reference to a production of Julius Caesar is that of Thomas Platter, who attended a performance at the Globe theatre on September 21, 1599 (see above under *Date*). The play continued to be a favorite of London audiences up to the closing of the theatres in 1642. Leonard DIGGES in his commendatory verse to Shakespeare's *Poems* (1640) noted its great popularity. It was presented at court during the festivities marking the marriage of Princess Elizabeth and the elector palatine in 1612/3, and also on January 31, 1637, as well as on November 13, 1638.

The tragedy was one of the plays assigned to Thomas Killigrew's KING'S COMPANY and thus escaped the wholesale disfigurement of William Davenant's adaptations. A performance dated about 1671 includes in the cast of a production at the Theatre Royal, Drury Lane, the following: Edward Kynaston (Mark Antony), Charles Hart (Brutus), Michael Mohun (Cassius), and Richard Bell (Caesar). There is a record of a performance in 1676 and another in 1684 after the King's and Duke's Companies combined at Drury Lane. In the latter, Thomas Betterton played Brutus, Cardell Goodman was Caesar, William Smith was Cassius, while Kynaston remained Antony. Except for slight alterations, such as Casca's assumption of Marullus' part in the first scene, the acting version faithfully followed the original text.

When the companies redivided, Betterton produced the tragedy regularly, and presentations with himself as Brutus are noted in 1704 at Lincoln's Inn Fields and in 1706 at the Haymarket Theatre. They were followed in January 1707 with a remarkable cast which included John Verbruggen as Cassius, Robert Wilks as Antony, Barton Booth as Caesar, Anne Bracegirdle as Portia, and Elizabeth Barry as Calpurnia. Betterton gave way to Booth at the close of 1709, and his death the next year saw his successor as Brutus every season, except one, up to 1715. In those years Booth played opposite George Powell's Cassius, while Wilks appeared as Antony, and William Mills portrayed Caesar. Thereafter, Thomas Elrington played Cassius in annual productions until Mills transferred to that role in 1722.

Drury Lane staged *Julius Caesar* continuously to 1728, when the play disappeared from its lists for seven years, probably because Booth no longer acted Brutus. An acting version, published in 1719 and used at Drury Lane, purports to be an alteration authored by Davenant and Dryden; this claim, however, is probably false. In it Casca, still taking Marullus' lines, is also assigned those of Titinius, while Popilius combines his own role with that of Volumnius. The Soothsayer and Artemidorus are united and the nameless Poet omitted. Brutus is given some uncharacteristic, rather flourishing lines after the visit of Caesar's ghost, and this spirit is allowed a reappearance in the last act. Some of these changes, along with additions to Brutus' dying speech, persisted throughout the age of John Philip Kemble.

Eleven separate productions were staged at the rival Lincoln's Inn Fields during the period from 1716 to 1729. Theophilus Keen was Brutus in the first of them. When he played the part again in March, 1718, James Quin, subsequently Booth's rival Brutus, acted Antony. The tragedy was revived in 1734 when Quin, now at Drury Lane, appeared as Brutus to Mills' Cassius and was seen again every year (except 1737) from 1736 to 1741.

In March 1747 Spranger Barry was Drury Lane's Antony and Dennis Delane played Brutus. That autumn David Garrick succeeded to the management of the theatre and *Julius Caesar* was not seen there again for 33 years. Meanwhile, Covent Garden continued with regular productions, showing 11 revivals from 1742 to 1758. Quin, having transferred to this theatre, was Brutus until 1751. His part was assumed by Thomas Sheridan in 1744 and 1755, while Sparks played Brutus in 1753, 1754, and 1758. There were no further revivals until 1766, when the play was performed four times with Walker, William Smith, and David Ross as Brutus, Cassius, and Antony. In a production on April 25, 1767, Thomas Hull replaced Ross. The play was acted only eight more times that century: once at the Haymarket in 1769, with Sheridan again as Brutus; once at Covent Garden in 1773; and six times in the Drury Lane revival of 1780. On April 27 that year, the tragedy was shown for the last time before vanishing from the London stage for 32 years.

John Philip Kemble restored the drama on February 29, 1812 at Covent Garden, where he staged a scenically splendid production with careful attention to historical accuracy. He followed John Bell's acting version of 1773 in doubling minor characters and omitting Ligarius and Cinna the Poet, but rejected the interpolated lines at the end of the ghost scene. The cast for this revival was exceptionally strong, Kemble giving an excellent impersonation of Brutus; his brother Charles, an adequate performance of Antony's role; and Charles Mayne Young, a most convincing portrayal of Cassius. This *Julius Caesar* was revived at Covent Garden each year until 1817. In 1819 at Covent Garden, Young played Brutus, a role he repeated in five seasons until 1827, and for the last recorded time in October 1829 at Drury Lane.

William Charles Macready's first role in the play was as Cassius in the 1819 revival. In May 1836 he portrayed Cassius at Covent Garden, and Charles Kemble, who had appeared regularly as Antony, took that part again, while Sheridan Knowles played Brutus. Macready portrayed Brutus in 1838 (when Samuel Phelps first played Cassius) and in 1850, when he performed at Windsor Castle before Queen Victoria and Prince Albert. His final appearance in the part was at the Haymarket Theatre in 1851. When Phelps presented his Sadler's Wells revival in 1846, he himself played Brutus, continuing in that role even after he had concluded his career as manager of that theatre with a production of *Julius Caesar* (November 6, 1862). In 1865 Phelps played Brutus again at Drury Lane opposite J. R. Anderson's Antony.

After the mid-19th century, the tragedy suffered neglect in London except for two revivals. One, staged by Ludwig Barnay and the Saxe-Meiningen company at Drury Lane in 1881, was noted for the handling of the mob scenes; it was criticized for excesses at Caesar's first entrance, but praised for effectiveness during Antony's speech. The other revival was staged by Edmund Tearle at the Olympic Theatre in 1892.

Beerbohm Tree re-established the tragedy's vogue with an opulent end-of-the-century production. On January 22, 1898 Tree initiated his Shakespeare epoch at Her Majesty's Theatre with a magnificently staged *Julius Caesar* centered on Mark Antony, the role he elected for himself. Cinna the Poet was restored, as was Ligarius, in a three-act version praised particularly for the effective management of the mob scenes. Lewis Waller's Brutus and Frank McLeay's Cassius were exceptional impersonations. The production ran for 100 nights, was revived on September 6, 1900, and staged at His Majesty's annual Shakespeare festivals every year but two (1908 and 1912) from 1905 to 1913.

At Stratford-upon-Avon Osmond Tearle had managed a production of the tragedy in 1889, and, under Frank Benson, *Julius Caesar* was revived during 11 seasons from 1892 through 1915. On May 2, 1916 a Drury Lane matinee commemorating the tercentenary climaxed Benson's appearances in the play. Standard performances were rendered by Henry Ainley as Mark Antony, Arthur Bourchier as Brutus, and H. B. Irving as Cassius. But the moment of highest emotion came between acts when Benson, still in the costume of the assassinated Caesar, was knighted by King George.

The Old Vic Theatre presented the play every year from 1914 to 1921, when Robert Atkins (Cassius during the 1915/6 season and before that Metellus Cimber for Tree) produced the tragedy with Ernest Milton as Antony. Milton had appeared as Decius Brutus in January 1920 at the St. James Theatre, where Henry Ainley repeated his portrayal of Antony and Basil Gill played Brutus. Claude Rains took the part of Casca. When the production was taken on tour in May, he was promoted to Cassius, originally Milton Rosmer's role. A month's repertory season of matinees at the Savoy in 1922 produced by Henry Baynton included a staging of the tragedy with Baynton as Brutus in the final West End *Julius Caesar* for 10 years.

Meanwhile Atkins directed another *Julius Caesar* for the Old Vic during the 1922/3 season, and, in 1926, Andrew Leigh presented the tragedy with Frank Vosper (Antony), Duncan Yarrow (Brutus), Baliol Holloway (Cassius), and Edith Evans (Portia). Harcourt Williams played Brutus in his own production for the Old Vic in 1930, which also featured John Gielgud as Antony, Donald Wolfit as Cassius, and Martita Hunt as Portia. Stratford saw six productions staged by W. Bridges-Adams from 1919 to 1934.

In addition to a performance at Stratford in 1932, *Julius Caesar* figured in three major productions that year. Two opened on January 25. The one at the Old Vic starred Ralph Richardson as Brutus, "the best . . . since Waller," according to Gordon Crosse; Robert Speaight played an impassioned Cassius, while this time producer Harcourt Williams portrayed Caesar and Robert Harris, Antony. The other production at the "Q" included Victor Lewisohn (Antony) and J. St. Barbe West (Cassius). Basil Gill took the part of Brutus in this as well as in the third production at His Majesty's Theatre; this one opened on February 8 and reverted to Tree's spectacular staging methods. It was managed by Oscar Asche, and its interpolated scenes, which were harshly criticized, included one of Portia discovering a document revealing the murder plot and another of Calpurnia weeping over Caesar's body. The cast, however, was talented and, in addition to Basil Gill, included Godfrey Tearle as Antony, Baliol Holloway as Cassius, Dorothy Green as Portia, and Lily Brayton as Calpurnia. Tearle's virile Antony and Gill's Brutus were seen again two years later at Oswald Stoll's Alhambra Theatre with Frank Dyall's Cassius.

In 1935 Henry Cass produced *Julius Caesar* for the Old Vic, where Ion Swinley played a successful Antony, and Leo Genn and William Devlin staged a more than usually vigorous quarrel scene as Brutus and Cassius. Antony was one of Swinley's last major roles; he played it at the Open Air Theatre in July 1937, two months before his untimely death. In that production Eric Portman played Brutus; Laidman Browne, Cassius; Phyllis Neilson-Terry, Portia; and Fay Compton, Calpurnia. When Henry Cass directed his next *Julius Caesar*, Portman took the role of Antony. This was in a modern-dress version staged first at the Embassy in November 1939, and after good notices transferred the next month to His Majesty's Theatre where, however, West End audiences remained unmoved. The costumes were those of Mussolini's army, the warring commanders communicated by telephone, and Caesar, portrayed by Walter Hudd, was a bespectacled hypochondriac. Others in the cast were Godfrey Tearle as Brutus, Clifford Evans as Cassius, and Vivienne Bennett and Marjory Clark as Portia and Calpurnia.

After Bridges-Adams' production, Stratford saw one by John Wyse (1936) in which Donald Wolfit played Cassius; James Dale, Brutus; and Peter Glenville, Antony. It was followed five years later by Andrew Leigh's with classic performances by another frequent impersonator of Cassius, Baliol Holloway. George Hayes played Brutus and Godfrey Kenton portrayed Antony. In 1950 John Gielgud, surprisingly dynamic as Cassius, dominated the quarrel scene despite the directors' (Anthony Quayle and Michael Langham) stifling arrangement whereby the commanders were kept seated at a table. Quayle took the part of Antony for himself in this Stratford production.

A second modern-dress *Julius Caesar* was staged at the King's Theatre at Hammersmith in 1949 with Bryan Johnson as Antony, Nigel Clarke as Cassius, and Donald Wolfit this time playing Brutus while his wife, Rosalind Iden, was Portia. Later in 1952, a production entirely Elizabethan in speech was presented by the anonymous actors of the Marlowe Society.

During the 1952/3 season, Hugh Hunt produced the first Old Vic *Julius Caesar* in more than a decade and a half, with Paul Rogers, William Devlin, and Robin Bailey as Cassius, Brutus, and Antony. Michael Benthall's cast for a production during 1955/6 included Paul Rogers, who this time took the part of Brutus, while John Neville played Antony. Two final Vic productions complete that company's record with the tragedy. Douglas Seale directed the play in 1958 with Michael Hordern as Cassius, John Phillips as Brutus, and Ronald Lewis as Antony. And in 1962 the Greek director Minos Volanakis dressed Rome's citizens in shabby garments while his designer, Nicholas Georgiadis, fitted Caesar's world with rusted scaffolding. This presentation was noted for the excellent portrayal by Robert Eddison of a murderously bitter Cassius. Maurice Good and John Gregson were Antony and Brutus.

Michael Croft's Youth Theatre was responsible for hree of the West End's five later performances of *ulius Caesar*. During August 1960, the group was at he Queen's Theatre with a modern-dress producion, and on August 30, 1962 the company staged another presentation at Sadler's Wells. The following ear, from August to September, during a season at he Scala Theatre which also included *Richard III* nd *Hamlet*, Croft revived the modern-dress *Julius Caesar*. These three productions spanned that of Aichael Macowan at the Westminster in 1963 perormed by the Elizabethan Theatre Company (with Toby Robertson as Antony) and John Franklyn-Robbins' matinee presentation at the Comedy Theare in February 1964 (with Barry Boys in that role).

Stratford offered two more productions in the next ew years. One took place in 1957 under Glen Byam Shaw, with Alec Clunes as Brutus, Richard Johnson s Antony, and Geoffrey Keen as Cassius. The second, in 1963, was directed by John Blatchley. In this nediocre presentation Caesar, portrayed by Roy Doltrice, was given some perspective; the other parts, however, were played without distinction. Tom Fleming portrayed Brutus; Cyril Cusack, Cassius; and Kenneth Haigh, Antony.

In America, Lewis Hallam the younger first produced *Julius Caesar* in Charleston, South Carolina, in 1774. During the 19th century, it was staged in 51 different years in New York. In the 1830's, Thomas Hamblin and Junius B. Booth regularly played Brutus and Cassius at the Bowery Theatre. Later that century, Edwin Booth and Laurence Barrett took those roles, thrilling audiences in every part of the United States. On November 25, 1864 the tragedy was staged at the Winter Garden in an effort to raise funds for a statue of Shakespeare in Central Park. The three Booths performed: Edwin portrayed Brutus, Junius was Cassius, and John Wilkes, who in the next year assassinated Lincoln, was Antony. Laurence Barrett played Cassius in two long-run presentations, once opposite Edwin Booth for 85 nights during 1871/2, and later in 1875/6 opposite E. L. Davenport's Brutus, when the drama was given 101 performances.

LAWRENCE BARRETT AS CASSIUS.

Orson Welles' highly original production in 1937 was the 17th New York revival of *Julius Caesar* in this century. Recognizing the contemporary relevance of the tragedy, Welles used modern dress and colored the conspiracy with anti-Fascist tones. The revival, which was presented without scenery, was immediately successful and played for 157 consecutive performances, with Welles taking the part of Brutus. Of the eight *Julius Caesar* films, half have been American productions, two of which were silent versions released in 1908. In 1949 David Bradley directed a motion picture of the tragedy for Northwestern University which starred Charlton Heston. The last, released in 1952 by Metro-Goldwyn-Mayer, was directed by Joseph Mankiewicz. In it John Gielgud repeated his successful Stratford Cassius, James Mason played Brutus, and Marlon Brando was Antony.—M. G.

Bibliography. TEXT: *Julius Caesar*, New Cambridge Edition, J. Dover Wilson, ed., 1949; *Julius Caesar*, New Arden Edition, T. S. Dorsch, ed., 1955; Brents Stirling, "*Julius Caesar* in Revision," *Shakespeare Quarterly*, XIII, 1962. DATE: New Arden Edition. SOURCES: C. F. Tucker Brooke, *Shakespeare's Plutarch*, 1909; M. H. Shackford, *Plutarch in Renaissance England*, 1929; Geoffrey Bullough, *Narrative and Dramatic Sources of Shakespeare*, Vol. V, 1964. COMMENT: H. M. Ayres, "Shakespeare's Julius Caesar in the Light of Some Other Versions," *PMLA*, 1910; M. W. MacCallum, *Shakespeare's Roman Plays and their Background*, 1910; John Palmer, *Political Characters of Shakespeare*, 1945; Maurice Charney, *Shakespeare's Roman Plays*, 1961. STAGE HISTORY: New Cambridge Edition; G. C. D. Odell, *Shakespeare from Betterton to Irving*, 1920; J. C. Trewin, *Shakespeare on the English Stage, 1900–1964*, 1964.

Selected Criticism

LEIGH HUNT. *Julius Caesar*, with the exception of *Coriolanus*, has perhaps less of the poetical in it than any other tragedy of Shakespeare; but fancy and imagination did not suit the business of the scene; and what is wanting in colour and ornament, is recompensed by the finest contrasts of character. It is of itself a whole school of human nature. The variable impotence of the mob, the imperial obstinacy of *Caesar*, the courtly and calculating worldliness of *Anthony*, the vulgar jealousy of *Casca*, the loftier jealousy and impatient temper of *Cassius*, the disinterestedness and self-centered philosophy of *Brutus*, seem to bring at once before us the result of a thousand different educations, and of a thousand habits, induced by situation, passion, or reflection. *Brutus*, however, is clearly the hero of the story, and as Gildon observes, should have given his name to the piece; for *Caesar* appears but in two short scenes and is dispatched at the beginning of the third act; whereas *Brutus*, after his first interview with *Cassius* in the commencement of the play, is the arbiter of all that succeeds, and the predominant spirit to the last. [Comment, 1812; reprinted in *Leigh Hunt's Dramatic Criticism, 1808–1831,* L. H. and C. W. Houtchens, eds., 1949.]

R. G. MOULTON. The passion in the play of *Julius Caesar* gathers around the conspirators, and follows them through the mutations of their fortunes. If however we are to catch the different parts of the action in their proper proportions we must remember the character of these conspirators, and especially of their leaders Brutus and Cassius. These are actuated in what they do not by personal motives but by devotion to the public good and the idea of republican liberty; accordingly, in following their career we must not look too exclusively at their personal success and failure. The exact key to the movement of the drama will be given by fixing attention upon the *justification of the conspirators' cause* in the minds of the audience; and it is this which is found to rise gradually to its height in the center of the play, and from that point to decline to the end . . . .

The stoicism of Brutus, with its suppression of the inner sympathies, arrives practically at the principle —destined in the future history of the world to be the basis of a yet greater crime—that it is expedient that one man should die rather than that a whole people should perish. On the other hand, Antony trades upon the fickle violence of the populace, and uses it as much for personal ends as for vengeance. This demoralisation of both the sides of character is the result of their divorce. Such is the essence of this play if its action be looked at as a whole: but it belongs to the movement of dramatic passion that we see the action only in its separate parts at different times. Through the first half of the play, while the justification of the conspirators' cause is rising, the other side of the question is carefully hidden from us; from the point of the assassination the suppressed element starts into prominence, and sweeps our sympathies along with it to its triumph at the conclusion of the play. [*Shakespeare as a Dramatic Artist,* 1885.]

BERNHARD TEN BRINK. But though Brutus is the chief character in the tragedy, it bears its title "Julius Cæsar" not in vain. Mightier than all the personages of the drama does the idea prove that was projected into the world by Cæsar and represented by him. In vain do Brutus and his friends combat against it; they are annihilated in the struggle. And the less adequate its embodiment, the more distinctly does the full significance of the idea as such stand out. Or, to be more explicit, it is embodied not so much in Cæsar's person as in his position, his power, in the judgment, the mood, the character, of the people. Hence the significance in this tragedy of the gatherings of the populace, scenes which are at once eminently characteristic and intensely dramatic. If Shakespeare be guilty of serious errors as to the outward usages, nay, in individual instances as to the views, the manners, of the Romans, that which is really typical of the time and situation he reproduces with historic fidelity. ["Shakespeare as Tragic Writer," *Five Lectures on Shakespeare,* 1895.]

MARY MCCARTHY. The purpose of the Mercury Theatre *Caesar* . . . was to say something about the modern world, to use Shakespeare's characters to drive home the horrors and inanities of present-day fascism . . . .

Julius Caesar is about the tragic consequences that befall idealism when it attempts to enter the sphere of action. It is perhaps also a comment on the futility and dangerousness of action in general. In a non-political sense it is a "liberal" play, for it has three heroes, Caesar, Antony, and Brutus, of whom Brutus is the most large-souled and sympathetic. Shakespeare's "liberal" formula, which insists on playing fair with all its characters, is obviously in fearful discord with Mr. [Orson] Welles's anti-fascist formula, which must have heroes and villains at all costs. . . . Mr. Welles has cut the play to pieces; he has very nearly eliminated the whole sordid tragic business of the degeneration and impotence of the republican forces; he has turned the rather shady Cassius into a shrewd and jovial comedian whose heart is in the right place; he has made Caesar, whose political stature gave the play dignity and significance, into a mechanical, expressionless robot; he has transformed the showy, romantic, buccaneering Antony into a repulsive and sinister demagogue. If he could do all this and still come out with a play that was consistent and uniformly forceful, the experiment might be forgivable. There were some things, however, which could not be cut or distorted, and these by their very incongruous presence, destroyed the totality of the play's effect. The most prominent of these unassimilated chunks of Shakespeare was Antony's final speech ("This was the noblest Roman of them all" —too famous, doubtless, to be cut), which in the mouth of the blackshirt monster of the Welles production seemed an unconvincing and even tasteless tribute to the memory of Brutus. [Comment (1938) on Orson Welles' modern-dress production of 1937; reprinted in *Mary McCarthy's Theatre Chronicles, 1937–1962,* 1962.]

G. WILSON KNIGHT. The human element in *Julius Cæsar* is charged highly with a general eroticism. All the people are 'lovers'. This love is emotional, fiery, but not exactly sexual, not physically passionate: even Portia and Brutus love with a gentle companionship rather than any passion. Though the stage be set for an action 'most bloody, fiery, and most terrible', though the action be fine, spirited, and adventurous, and noble blood be magnificently spilt in the third act, yet the human element is often one of gentle sentiment, melting hearts, tears, and the soft fire of love. There are many major and minor love-themes. There is love expressed or suggested between Brutus and Cassius, Brutus and Cæsar, and Antony and Cæsar; Brutus and Portia, Brutus and Volumnius, Brutus and Lucius; Cæsar and Decius, Cassius and Lucius Pella, Cassius and Titinius; Ligarius and Brutus, Artemidorus and Cæsar. Probably there are other instances. The word 'lover' is strangely emphatic, sometimes meaning little more than 'friend', but always helping to build a general atmosphere of comradeship and affection. Love is here the regal, the conquering reality: the murder of Cæsar is a gash in the body of Rome, and this gash is healed by love, so that the play's action emphasizes first the disjointing of 'spirit' from 'matter' which is evil, fear, anarchy; and then the remating of these two elements into the close fusion which is love, order, peace. ["The Eroticism of *Julius Caesar,*" *The Imperial Theme,* 1954.]

BRENTS STIRLING. Shakespeare never presents Brutus

as a demagogue, but there are ironical traces of the politician. . . . It is curious, in fact, that although Brutus is commonly thought to be unconcerned over public favor, he expresses clear concern for it in the passage just quoted and in III.i.244–51, where he sanctions Antony's funeral speech only if Antony agrees to tell the crowd that he speaks by generous permission, and only if he agrees to utter no evil of the conspiracy. Nor is Brutus' speech in the Forum wholly the nonpolitical performance it is supposed to be; certainly Shakespeare's Roman citizens are the best judges of it, and they react tempestuously. Although compressed, it scarcely discloses aloofness or an avoidance of popular emotive themes.

Act II, scene ii now shifts to the house of Caesar, but the emphasis on ritual continues as before. With dramatic irony, in view of Brutus' recent lines on sacrificial murder, Caesar commands, "Go bid the priests do present sacrifice." Calpurnia who has "never stood on ceremonies" (omens) is now terrified by them. News comes that the augurers, plucking the entrails of an offering, have failed to find a heart. Calpurnia has dreamed that smiling Romans have laved their hands in blood running from Caesar's statue, and Decius Brutus gives this its favorable interpretation which sends Caesar to his death.

The vivid assassination scene carries out Brutus' ritual prescription in dramatic detail, for the killing is staged with a formalized approach, ending in kneeling, by one conspirator after another until the victim is surrounded. This is met by a series of retorts from Caesar ending in "Hence! Wilt thou lift up Olympus," and the "sacrifice" is climaxed with his "Et tu Brute!" The conspirators ceremonially bathe their hands in Caesar's blood, and Brutus pronounces upon "this our lofty scene" with the prophecy that "it shall be acted over / In states unborn and accents yet unknown!" [*Unity in Shakespearian Tragedy*, 1956.]

WILLIAM AND BARBARA ROSEN. In dramatizing the complex issues of power politics, *Julius Caesar* offers no easy solution to problems that are no less baffling to our own age. Many will find that this work is one of Shakespeare's most perplexing, for it is disconcerting when a play—or history itself—appeals to man's earnest desire to judge actions in terms of simple, personal standards of right and wrong and then betrays and mocks his deepest convictions by suggesting that Power is better than Virtue, that efficiency may be preferable to goodness, or that conscience may be dangerously inadequate in determining political action.

An individual's scrupulous concern for morality may, indeed, be disastrously impolitic. Cassius leads Brutus to an abhorrent deed, but when the consequences involve Brutus in the exercise of power, Brutus continues to think and act in accordance with private morality. His scruples about killing Antony or about unjustly raising money hinder the success of the conspiracy. His wish to fight a pitched battle, to decide the matter once and for all, instead of following stratagems and winning by attrition, is also the decision of a man who refuses to take on the role of politician. It is noteworthy that Cassius, after his initial victory, consistently defers to Brutus' moral scruples; knowing him to be wrong in his strategy, he is still swayed by the very image of nobility for which Brutus was chosen as the figurehead of the conspiracy. The irony is unmistakable: the politic man sets up an image of virtue, dissociated from politics, to serve his own purposes, to endear him to the populace; but once that image is established, his freedom to act without it is curbed, and he is hampered in the achievement of his political ends by the very image he has fostered.

The spirit of Caesar that dominates the play is to be associated, finally, with the exercise of supreme power. When Caesar dies, power is without a master, and as such, indiscriminately destructive. Each man in his turn tries to grasp the lightning that has been set free, and is fearfully transformed, until finally it comes to rest upon the man who alone, by gift of personality and legitimate succession, may wield it unscathed.

Shakespeare fully delineates the intriguing pattern of shifting power as an old Caesar is succeeded by a young one. The politic Cassius gives in to an impolitic Brutus and both fail as a result. Antony, Octavius, and Lepidus begin with complete ruthlessness; however, this does not guarantee them power or even win the battle for them—their opponents defeat themselves through mistakes. Lepidus, the "straw man," is first burdened with responsibility, then eliminated; and afterward, effortlessly, Antony, the ruthless and emotional partner, is displaced by the man without a temperament, the personification of impersonal rule. [Introduction to *Julius Caesar*, the Signet Classic Shakespeare Edition, 1963; Sylvan Barnet, gen. ed.]

Juno. In *The Tempest*, a role assumed by one of the island's spirits in the masque arranged by Prospero to celebrate the betrothal of Ferdinand and Miranda. Queen of the sky and wife of Jupiter, Juno comes, accompanied by Ceres, to bless the couple (IV, i).

Juvenal. Full Latin name **Decimus Junius Juvenalis** (60?–?140). Roman satirist. Juvenal, the details of whose life remain obscure, was the author of 16 satires, all distinguished by their ferocity, stylistic polish, and cryptic allusions to contemporary people and events. Towards the end of the 16th century in England, he enjoyed a great vogue and became the *locus classicus* for the growing disillusion which had begun to set in. A number of "English Juvenals" began to spring up, sparked by Joseph Hall's *Virgidemiarum* (1597), Edward Guilpin's *Skialetheia* (1598), and John Marston's *The Scourge of Villanie* (1598). Satiric productions were so frequent and so fierce that the authorities found it necessary to suppress all satires and to burn publicly those books which had been most offensive (see John WHITGIFT). Juvenal is generally thought to be the "satirical rogue" whom Hamlet claims to be quoting while he mocks Polonius (II, ii, 198).

K

Kames, Henry Home, Lord (1696–1782). Scottish philosopher and jurist. Kames referred frequently to Shakespeare in his *Elements of Criticism* (1762), using passages from the plays either as examples for his criticism or as authority for his theories. He considered Shakespeare's greatest talent his ability to express, not merely describe, the most intense and diverse emotions. He praised the psychological insight behind many passages, such as Antony's funeral oration and Hamlet's soliloquies. Kames contrasted these scenes to similar passages in Corneille and Racine which he found, by comparison, cold and ineffectual.

Kames praised Shakespeare for the vividness of his descriptions, an effect achieved by his use of concrete terms rather than generalities, and for his ability to define characters in a few words. He commented on the naturalness of Shakespeare's dialogue and approved the way he mixed verse and prose, depending on the speaker.

Kames briefly criticized Shakespeare for several faults: occasional exaggerations of sentiment beyond the limits of reality or good taste; frequent punning and playing with words; a large element of chance in some of the tragedies; subplots insufficiently related to the main action; and at least one villain, Iago, who is too horrible to be accepted. He pointed out, however, that most of Shakespeare's flaws were technicalities, and did not seriously detract from his creative genius. [Herbert Spencer Robinson, *English Shakespearian Criticism in the Eighteenth Century*, 1932.]

Katharina. In *The Taming of the Shrew*, the fiery-tempered older daughter of Baptista of Padua. He has settled a handsome dowry on Katharina, insisting that she be married before her much-sought-after younger sister. Petruchio, who is attracted by the dowry and anxious to help a friend gain her sister, marries Katharina. He then removes her to the country, maltreats and so adroitly starves her into submission that, at the comedy's end, Katharina is deemed the most submissive of the three brides in the play.

Katharine. In *Love's Labour's Lost*, a lady attending the Princess of France. Katharine is wooed by Dumain, falls in love with him, and, when required to return to France with the Princess, promises that if Dumain will wait a year in isolation for her, she will be his.

Katharine of Aragon (1485–1536). First wife of Henry VIII and Queen of England. Daughter of Ferdinand and Isabella of Spain, Katharine married Henry in 1509, shortly after her unconsummated marriage to his elder brother Arthur had ended with Arthur's death. Only one daughter, Mary Tudor, survived of the five children she bore to Henry in their 20 years of marriage. She refused to consent to a divorce and became princess-dowager when Henry married Anne Bullen in 1533, but her marriage was nullified by Cranmer, the archbishop of Canterbury. She died a year later.

In *Henry VIII,* Katharine is high in the King's favor and successfully pleads with him to grant tax relief for the people (I, ii). Not long afterward, Henry having meanwhile met Anne Bullen, Katharine is haled before the papal legates, Wolsey and Campeius, appointed to try Henry's divorce case against her. She refuses to remain at the trial (II, iv). Later the legates visit her (III, i) and try vainly to persuade her to accept the King's wishes. After Anne's marriage and coronation, Katharine is shown in her final illness; she sends a letter of forgiveness to Henry (IV, ii).

Katharine of Valois (1401–1437). Youngest daughter of Charles VI and Queen Isabella of France. In accordance with the treaty of Troyes, Katharine was married in 1420 to Henry V of England. The following year she gave birth to a son, who became Henry VI. Several years after her husband's death in 1422, Katharine secretly married Owen Tudor, subsequently becoming the mother of Edmund, who was later earl of Richmond, and Jasper, who became earl of Pembroke. In *Henry V*, she is wooed by Henry, who says: "O fair Katharine, if you will love me soundly with your French heart, I will be glad to hear you confess it brokenly with your English tongue" (V, ii).

Kean, Charles [John] (c. 1811–1868). Actor. The son of the famous actor Edmund Kean, Charles Kean was born in Waterford and educated at Eton, which he left when his father's fortunes declined. He took to the stage, where, though inexperienced, he was given jobs because of his name. He made his debut in 1827 at the Drury Lane. In 1828 he joined his father and later that year failed ignominiously as Romeo. In 1830 he played *Richard III* in New York, and in 1833 the two Keans gave their single London performance together in *Othello* at Covent Garden, with Charles as Iago and Edmund as Othello.

Charles Kean's acting during his earlier years evoked nothing but depreciation from the critics. The *Dramatic Spectator's* critic, for example, termed his Hamlet a "boisterous piece of mere acting," his Richard III a "failure," and his Othello "a fine piece of low comedy." After 1838, however, Kean began to gain in stature as an actor, and earned critical esteem. In 1840 he played in *Romeo and Juliet* and *Macbeth* opposite his future wife, Ellen Tree. In 1850 he embarked upon a managerial career, becoming co-lessee of the Princess' Theatre with Robert Keeley. Under his own management he did *Hamlet* (with himself in the title role), *As You Like It,* and *1 Henry IV.* After Keeley's retirement, Kean's taste for spectacle was evident in the revival of *King John* in 1852; with Kean in the title role, it enjoyed a huge success. The *Macbeth* which followed in 1853 was equally successful, unlike his later revival of Cibber's *Richard III.* In 1855 Kean apparently reached the climax of his success as an actor with the part of Wolsey in *Henry VIII.* In later years he produced *The Winter's Tale* (1856), *A Midsummer Night's Dream* (1856), *Richard II* (1857), and *King Lear* and *The Merchant of Venice* (1858). His last Shakespearean production, *Henry V,* was presented in 1859. Kean's best Shakespearean roles were Hamlet and Richard III, but he showed versatility in his comic roles as well, especially as Ford. [*Dictionary of National Biography,* 1885– .]

Kean, Edmund (1787–1833). Actor. Kean was one of the most flamboyant of the great tragedians. With his debut performance of Shylock at Drury Lane in 1814, he established a new school of Shakespearean interpretations, one which portrayed elemental passions. Among Kean's greatest successes were Richard III, Othello, Iago, and Macbeth, but his portrayals of Hamlet and Lear rivaled those of John Philip Kemble. By 1815, Kean was the outstanding actor of the London stage.

Kean's origins are obscure, and almost certainly humble. Evidence indicates that he was the illegitimate son of itinerant traveling players and was reared at Drury Lane, where he absorbed the subtleties of his art. Under severe hardships, he traveled with provincial companies for six years before his Drury Lane triumph.

In 1820 Kean embarked on a tour of America and was applauded in New York and Philadelphia. His arrogance angered Boston audiences, however, and he returned to England. Nevertheless, Kean had given America its first genuinely good theatre in his performances of Lear and Richard III.

During a performance of *Othello* at Covent Garden in 1833, Kean collapsed into the arms of his son, Charles Kean, and died two months later. [*Dictionary of National Biography,* 1885– .]

Keats, John (1795–1821). Romantic poet. Born in London, Keats was trained to be an apothecary, but turned to poetry instead. In his short life he produced a surprisingly large body of poetry, including several poems that are often considered among the finest examples of English lyric poetry. He died in Italy of tuberculosis at the age of 25.

In 1817 Keats wrote that he felt a "good Genius" presiding over his life and fancied that it was Shakespeare. This was the time he was writing *Endymion* (1818) and from his letters and his personal copy (7 vols., 1814) of Shakespeare, as well as internal evidence in the poem, it is clear that he was indeed steeped in the plays. The condition of and annotations in his edition of Shakespeare—which is extant—testify to the depth of Keats' reading and his impatience with Samuel Johnson's notes. Keats wrote that he responded especially to the intensity of Shakespeare's poetry and to the "negative capability" of his character, his ability to be in "uncertainties, Mysteries, doubts, without any irritable reaching after fact and reason." *Endymion* reflects this influence and seems particularly indebted to *The Tempest* and *A Midsummer Night's Dream.* Shakespearean echoes are to be found in the later poems as well, to a somewhat lesser extent, most noticeably in "The Eve of St. Agnes" (1820). Letters and markings in his text show that Keats thought of his courtship of Fanny Brawne in terms of Troilus and Cressida. He wrote a sonnet on *King Lear,* and as early as 1817 considered the Beauty-Truth relationship with reference to *Lear.* The sonnet "Bright Star" was written at sea en route to Italy, on a blank page in his copy of Shakespeare's *Poems.* [John Middleton Murry, *Keats and Shakespeare,* 1925; Caroline Spurgeon, *Keats's Shakespeare,* 1928.]

Keeling, William (d. 1620). Naval commander. Keeling kept a journal during a voyage to the East Indies, and recorded shipboard performances of *Hamlet* and *Richard II.* On March 12, 1607, Keeling set forth from England in command of the East India Company's ship the *Dragon,* accompanied by another ship, the *Hector,* under the command of Captain William Hawkyns (d. 1613). While anchored off the coast of Sierra Leone in September 1607, the ship's company presented two performances, recorded in Keeling's journal as follows:

> 1607, Sept. 5. I sent the interpreter, according to his desier, abord the Hector whear he brooke fast, and after came abord mee, wher we gaue the tragedie of Hamlett.
>
> 30. Captain Hawkins dined with me, wher my companions acted Kinge Richard the Second.

Six months later on the same voyage, the company repeated its performance of *Hamlet:*

> [1608, Mar. 31]. I envited Captain Hawkins to a ffishe dinner, and had Hamlet acted abord me: which I permitt to keepe my people from idlenes and unlawful games, or sleepe.

The authenticity of this entry has been questioned in the past because the original document was lost, but it is now generally accepted as reliable.

The *Dragon* returned to England in 1610. Keeling made one more voyage to the East Indies in 1615, returning in 1617. His will, dated October 16, 1620, describes him as a resident of the Isle of Wight. [E. K. Chambers, *William Shakespeare,* 1930.]

Keightley, Thomas (1789–1872). Irish author. Educated at Trinity College, Dublin, Keightley settled in London to make a living by his pen. He published a number of works in the field of mythology, history, and the ancient classics, with some of his works appearing under the imprint of the Bohn Library. Later in his life he turned to English literature. His *Account of the Life, Opinions, and Writings of John Milton, with an Introduction to Paradise Lost* (1855) and *The Poems of John Milton* (2 vols., 1859) were popular, the latter containing excellent notes. He was less successful with his edition of Shakespeare (6 vols., 1864); the text was poorly emended and no notes were provided. But with his *The Shakespeare Expositor* (1867) he once again was able to provide his audience with a useful introduction and guide.

Kemble Family. Actors. The foremost member of a distinguished acting family, ***John Philip Kemble*** (1757–1823), began his acting career at the Drury

Lane with a portrayal of Hamlet in 1783, and in 1788 he fell heir to the Garrick tradition with his performance of Lear. During the intervening formative years his characterizations of Richard III, King John, Othello, and Coriolanus won him the increasing attention of London audiences. After 1788 he tried a number of new roles and new approaches to old ones, including Macbeth, an unsuccessful Romeo, Iago, Prospero, and Petruchio. He won particular acclaim for his Henry V, which he restored to the London stage in 1789. His crowning achievement was a portrayal of Coriolanus, which he played many times and with which he closed his career in 1817.

Kemble was successively manager of Drury Lane and Covent Garden and was responsible for introducing historically accurate settings and costumes to Shakespearean performances.

Kemble wrote adaptations of Shakespeare's plays, which are characterized by omissions, transpositions, and new readings of the original lines. His alteration of *All's Well That Ends Well* was first performed at Drury Lane in 1793. *Coriolanus . . . Altered from Shakespeare and Thompson*, performed in 1789, had only minor omissions and three brief new speeches. He adapted *Hamlet* twice, in 1796 and again in 1800, with further omissions (including the first third of the second soliloquy). In his alteration of *Henry V*, performed in 1789, IV, iv was omitted and IV, ii was written entirely in prose. *King John*, performed at Drury Lane in 1800, contains some omissions from Shakespeare, but restores lines that earlier adaptations omitted. In his *Macbeth* (1794), speeches are transposed to different characters, the singing witches of Davenant's adaptation are included, and there are minor omissions and new readings dependent upon varying punctuation. The adaptation of *Measure for Measure*, first given in 1795, suffered omissions, including the entire first scene of Act IV, and two transpositions. *The Merry Wives of Windsor*, given in 1797, restores some lines to earlier adaptations, makes some further omissions, and transposes some lines. *Much Ado About Nothing*, performed at Drury Lane in 1797, omits more lines than earlier adaptations, while a version of *The Tempest* (1798; printed with the subtitle, *With Additions from Dryden: Compiled by J. P. Kemble*) keeps Dryden's characters Dorinda and Hippolito, and shortens Acts III and V. Kemble's *Memoranda*, in a British Museum manuscript, and an assortment of contemporary playbills which he collected have been important sources for students of 18th-century drama history.

Charles Kemble (1775–1854), younger brother of John Philip, was born in South Wales and educated by his brother, who opposed his debut, in 1792 or 1793, as Orlando in a Sheffield theatre. The elder Kemble's influence secured him an engagement at Drury Lane, where in 1794 he played Malcolm, followed by several other, relatively unsuccessful, performances. After the age of 30, however, he demonstrated a marked improvement as an actor and played for many years with his brother and their sister, Sarah SIDDONS, in a large variety of roles, including many Shakespearean parts. His Mercutio, played for the first time in 1829, is often considered his greatest part.

In 1806 he married an actress, Maria Theresa de Camp, who acted under the name of Mrs. Charles Kemble, and who bore him a daughter, ***Frances Ann Kemble*** (1809–1893) who, as Fanny Kemble, became an actress in her own right. Fanny Kemble helped her father recoup the losses he had suffered managing Covent Garden. She became, at the age of 19, an overnight success as Juliet. In 1832 she and her father toured the United States, playing to enthusiastic crowds. While in the United States, she married a Georgia plantation owner and retired from the stage but left her husband in 1847 because of her growing antipathy to slavery. In 1848 she began a series of Shakespearean readings in England and the United States which reestablished her popularity. She wrote a number of books, including *Notes Upon Some of Shakespeare's Plays* (1882).

Charles Kemble announced his nominal retirement from the stage in 1836, but continued to give command performances and readings from Shakespeare until his death. He was one of the most important actors of his time and played a greater range of parts than any other actor except Garrick. The less sentimental critics, however, wrote that he looked his parts, rather than acted them. [*Dictionary of National Biography*, 1885– .]

Kempe, Will[iam] (d. post 1603). Actor. Kempe was the low-comedy actor in Shakespeare's company, the Chamberlain's Men, from 1594 to 1599 and is cited as one of the "principall Actors" in the 1623 Folio of Shakespeare's plays. He first appears on record as one of LEICESTER'S MEN visiting the Low Countries and Denmark about 1585–1586. By 1590 he had acquired an international reputation for comedy in the style of Richard Tarlton, with whom Thomas Nashe compares him in *An Almond for a Parrat* (1590). Nashe's dedication is "To that most Comicall and conceited Caualeire Monsieur du Kempe, Jestmonger and Vice-gerent generall to the Ghost of Dicke Tarlton." In the work, the author adds that he had been asked by "that famous Francatrip Harlicken" at Bergamo the summer before whether he knew "any such Parabolano here in London as Signior Chiarlatano Kempino" of whose "pleasance" Harlicken had heard report.

Kempe became one of Strange's Men, evidently going on tour with them and Edward Alleyn in the summer of 1593 after appearing in their production of *A Knack to Know a Knave* (1592). He had become by this time famous in his own right for his jigs (see JIG).

Kempe was one of the original Chamberlain's Men, joining the company in 1594/5 (see CAST). He appears in the stage directions to the Second Quarto of *Romeo and Juliet* in the role of Peter, and in *Much Ado About Nothing* as Dogberry. He is in the acting list of *Every Man In his Humour* (1598), but not in the list for *Every Man Out of his Humour* of 1599, leading E. K. Chambers and others to conclude that he had left Chamberlain's Men by that time.

In 1600 Kempe undertook to perform, for a wager, a morris dance from London to Norwich (almost 100 miles). He left London on February 11 and on March 11 arrived in Norwich. There are many contemporary references to his extraordinary feat, including an allusion to "Kemps morice" in *Jack Drum's Entertainment* (1600). In his own story of the morris dance, recorded in the Stationers' Register April 22, 1600, entitled "Kemps morris to Norwiche," he says "I haue daunst my selfe out of the world," perhaps alluding as well to his departure from the Globe.

He toured Europe again in 1601, returning to England by September of that year. In *3 Parnassus* there is an allusion to Kempe "dancing the morrice ouer the Alpes" (see PARNASSUS PLAYS). Chambers conjectures that for a short time he rejoined the Chamberlain's Men. By 1602, however, he was associated with Philip Henslowe (a loan from Henslowe to Kempe is on record in Henslowe's diary), and in 1602/3 he was one of Worcester's Men.

Kempe is not traceable after 1603. In Thomas Heywood's *An Apologie for Actors* (c. 1608) he is mentioned as one of those "being before my time" and he is again compared with Tarlton:

> Here I must needs remember Tarleton, in his time gratious with the queene, his soveraigne, and in the people's generall applause, whom succeeded Wil. Kemp, as wel in the favour of her majesty, as in the opinion and good thoughts of the generall audience.

He is considered to have been either dead or retired in Dekker's *Gull's Hornbook* (1609). Citing as evidence an epitaph on Kempe, published in R. Braithwaite's *Remains after Death* (1618), Chambers speculates that it is likely that Kempe died shortly after his morris dance. [E. K. Chambers, *The Elizabethan Stage*, 1923.]

Kenrick, William (c. 1725–1779). Author. Born near Waterford, Kenrick came to London with literary ambitions. He supported himself by pamphleteering, often writing in support of both sides in a particular controversy. He wrote several plays, one of which, *Falstaff's Wedding* (1760), was a continuation of *2 Henry IV* written in Shakespeare's style. For the most part Kenrick was unsuccessful, a fact which led to abusive attacks by him on such contemporaries as Oliver Goldsmith, Samuel Johnson, James Boswell, and David Garrick. When Johnson's edition of Shakespeare appeared, he assailed it with *A Review of Doctor Johnson's New Edition of Shakespeare: In which the Ignorance, or Inattention of that Editor is exposed* (1765). Johnson ignored the attack, but a young student came to his defense; Kenrick then issued an anonymous rejoinder supposedly written "by a friend." He announced his intention of bringing forth an edition of his own and even succeeded in attracting a few subscribers, but nothing came of the project. After a delay of eight years, Kenrick informed his subscribers that he was setting aside his original plans because of George Steevens' projected edition. To placate them, he gave a series of lectures which were published as *Introduction to the School of Shakespeare . . . To which is added a Retort Courteous to the Criticks* (1774). Though hardly to be taken seriously as a critic, Kenrick nevertheless raised one or two valid points: he defended Shakespeare's versification, insisting that mechanical syllable-counting was not a sound critical method; and, in answer to Johnson's charge that Shakespeare was ungrammatical, countered with the assertion that the poet was idiomatic. (Herbert Spencer Robinson, *English Shakesperian Criticism in the Eighteenth Century*, 1932.)

Kent, Earl of. In *King Lear*, the blunt-spoken, faithful follower of the king. Disguising himself as the servant Caius, Kent renders devoted service to Lear. Hot-tempered and rash, he is frequently seen in opposition to Oswald, the equally devoted servant of a bad cause.

Kesselstadt death mask. See PORTRAITS OF SHAKESPEARE.

Keysar, Robert (fl. 1605–1613). Manager of the Children of the Queen's Revels at the Blackfriars theatre who, in 1610, brought suit against the housekeepers of Blackfriars, Shakespeare, and his fellow actors. A goldsmith by profession, Keysar became involved in theatrical activities around 1605 when he purchased an interest in the Children of the Queen's Revels. At the time the Children had been suspended as a result of a performance of *Eastward Ho!* which had directly insulted King James. Keysar reconstituted the Children, then no longer under the patronage of the queen, and called simply the Children of Blackfriars. He managed the troupe without further difficulty until 1608 when they again gave an offensive performance, this time in George Chapman's *Conspiracy . . . of Charles, Duke of Byron.* Although the company was forbidden to play, Keysar managed to hold them together.

In the meantime, however, Henry Evans, the lessee of the Blackfriars, surrendered his lease to the King's Men, who began to occupy the theatre in 1609. Keysar was then forced to move the Children's company to the Whitefriars theatre. In 1610 he brought a suit against Evans and the King's Men, charging that the surrender of the lease had occurred without his consent as owner of one sixth of the property. He claimed a share in the theatre's profits, which he estimated at £1500. In their reply to the suit, the King's Men asserted that they had had no knowledge of Keysar's interest in the theatre and that his share of the stock should be recovered from Evans. They also denied that their profits for the period had amounted to £1500. The outcome of the case is not known. Keysar continued as manager of the Children at Whitefriars until at least 1613. See CHILDREN OF THE CHAPEL. [C. W. Wallace, *Shakespeare and his London Associates*, 1910.]

Khachaturian, Aram. See MUSIC BASED ON SHAKESPEARE: *20th century*.

Killigrew, Thomas (1612–1683). Dramatist and theatre manager. As a boy, Killigrew was a page at court. During the 1630's he became a member of the literary circle that formed around Queen Henrietta Maria; he wrote two plays at this time, *Claracilla* (1636) and *The Princess* (1637, pub. 1664). During the interregnum, he served the royal family as a messenger on the continent. At the Restoration he accompanied Charles II on his return to England and was rewarded for his long service by receiving, with William Davenant, the patent monopoly for the London theatre. Killigrew became the manager of the KING'S COMPANY, a troupe for which he built the famous Drury Lane Theatre in 1663. The company was a distinguished one, but Killigrew was unsuited to the job of managing and he eventually gave up control of the company to his son, Charles (1665–1725). In 1673 Killigrew succeeded Sir Henry Herbert as Master of the Revels. He remained a close friend of the king all of his life, and upon his death was buried in Westminster Abbey. [Alfred Harbage, *Thomas Killigrew, Cavalier Dramatist*, 1930.]

Kind-Harts Dreame. See Henry CHETTLE; GROATSWORTH OF WIT.

The Life and Death of King John.

King John. A history play by Shakespeare.

Text. The only authoritative text is that of the First Folio (1623), the copy for which is now thought to have been Shakespeare's FOUL PAPERS, that is, his holograph before a fair copy of the manuscript was made. The title in the First Folio reads "The Life and Death of King John."

Date. There has been considerable disagreement as to the date of the play, which, until recently, was generally thought to be 1594–1597. The most recent editors of the play, however (E. A. J. Honigmann and J. Dover Wilson), argue for dates of 1590–1591. The basis of Honigmann's argument is that an anonymous play called *The Troublesome Raigne of John, King of England* (pub., 1591) is not, as it is generally regarded, the source of Shakespeare's play, but that it, in fact, derives from the Shakespearean *King John*.

King John appears in Meres' list in his PALLADIS TAMIA (1598). The reflection of political events in England is not precise enough to be of much value in fixing the date of composition. The most convincing evidence for the earlier date is an echo in *King John* of the following lines in Kyd's *The Spanish Tragedy* (1589):

> He hunted well that was a lion's death,
> Not he that in a garment wore his skin;
> So hares may pull dead lions by the beard.
> (I, i)

These lines, containing a definite allusion to the Duke of Austria's wearing Richard Coeur de Lion's "lionskin," are, in substance and phraseology, somewhat like those of *King John* in which the Bastard taunts Austria:

> You are the hare of whom the proverb goes,
> Whose valour plucks dead lions by the beard.
> (II, i, 137–138)

Shakespeare was in this case almost surely the borrower. However, the likeness of the two passages is not close enough to prove that Shakespeare wrote his lines immediately after Kyd's play was first produced, in 1589. The play was so popular that phrases from it could have rung in a retentive mind like Shakespeare's for a long time.

King John also contains an allusion to an anonymous Elizabethan play, SOLIMAN AND PERSEDA, which dates from sometime around 1589.

The more widely accepted view of the play is that it was written at approximately the same time as *Richard II*, with the disagreement centered on the problem of which came first. The superiority of *Richard II* in originality, character portrayal, and lyrical power argues for its being the later play, but some literary historians cling to the belief that Constance's lament for her child Arthur (III, iv, 93–105) reflects the poet's grief over the death of his son Hamnet, in August 1596. Adherents of this view are forced to date the play in late 1596 or early 1597.

Sources. *King John* is generally believed to be a revamping and condensation of an anonymous two-part play called *The Troublesome Raigne of John King of England*, published in two separate quartos in 1591. E. A. J. Honigmann's argument, mentioned above, that this play is merely a BAD QUARTO of Shakespeare's play, rather than its source, is not generally accepted. The title page of *The Troublesome Raigne* reads:

> The Troublesome Raigne of Iohn King of England, with the discouerie of King Richard Cordelions Base sonne (vulgarly named, The Bastard Fawconbridge): also the death of King Iohn at Swinstead Abbey. As it was (sundry times) publikely acted by the Queenes Maiesties Players, in the honourable Citie of London. Imprinted at London for Sampson Clarke, and are to be solde at his shop, on the backeside of the Royall Exchange. 1591.

The title page of Part II reads:

> The Second part of the troublesome Raigne of King Iohn, conteining the death of Arthur Plantaginet, the landing of Lewes, and the poysning of King Iohn at Swinstead Abbey. As it was (sundry times) publikely acted by the Queenes Maiesties Players, in the honourable Citie of London. Imprinted at London for Sampson Clarke, and are to be solde at his shop, on the backeside of the Royall Exchange. 1591.

The play was reprinted in 1611 as written by "W. Sh." and again in 1622 as written by "W. Shakespeare." Thus the confusion about the relationship of the two King John plays has existed from their inception. Shakespeare's play, like its source, covers the entire reign of the monarch, 1199–1216, deals with the same events, and presents the same characters. Neither play mentions the signing of the Magna Carta in 1215. However, the spirit of the two dramas is completely different. The *Troublesome Raigne* is a violently anti-Catholic play. In toning down its Protestant bias, Shakespeare cut incidents and whole episodes. He even omitted some scenes necessary for a complete understanding of the action. Examples of such cuts are a soliloquy of a monk of Swinstead, in which he sets forth his purpose to murder the King as suitable punishment for his sacking of the monasteries, and the scene of the actual poisoning, in which the King and the monk who serves as his "taster" drink from a poisoned wassail cup. For the same political reason Shakespeare cuts the scene of John's death, in which his pangs become sheer Senecan melodrama, and a comic scene in which Faulconbridge ransacks a monastery and finds a nun in hiding there. Shakespeare reduces this incident to two lines in one of Pandulph's speeches:

> The bastard Faulconbridge
> Is now in England, ransacking the church,
> Offending charity.
>
> (III, iv, 171–173)

The two plays share one line in common (V, iv, 42), and *King John* is about 300 lines shorter. The authorship of the *Troublesome Raigne* has been variously ascribed to Christopher Marlowe, George Peele, Robert Greene, and Thomas Lodge. Both plays had been preceded on the stage by an interlude, *Kynge Johan*, written by the Protestant apologist John Bale. It is unlikely that Shakespeare made any use of Bale's play. If the thesis that *The Troublesome Raigne* is not the source of Shakespeare's play gains acceptance, however, a number of hitherto disregarded source possibilities, including the historical accounts, will have to be reconsidered.—O. J. C.

Plot Synopsis. Act I. In England, King John receives Chatillon, an ambassador from King Philip of France, who demands that John give up his throne to Arthur, Duke of Bretagne and son of Geoffrey, the King's elder brother, now dead. Angrily dismissing Chatillon, John announces his intention of responding to Philip's threats with armed force, much to the satisfaction of his mother, Queen Elinor. The attention of the court is now directed to two young men, Robert Faulconbridge and Philip the Bastard, who are supposedly the sons of the late Sir Robert Faulconbridge. When it is revealed that the Bastard is in reality an illegitimate son of Richard Coeur de Lion, King John's older brother and predecessor on the throne, the Bastard readily forfeits his claim to the Faulconbridge inheritance, is dubbed Sir Richard Plantagenet, and becomes a loyal follower of the King.

Act II. Before the city of Angiers in France, King Philip, accompanied by Arthur and Arthur's mother, Constance, parleys with John and his court, accusing him of usurping his nephew's rights. Simultaneously, the Bastard baits Lymoges, Duke of Austria and an ally of the French King, who was responsible for the death of Richard. John offers to make peace with Arthur, but Constance bitterly spurns any attempt at conciliation. The leading citizens of Angiers refuse to commit themselves to either party until they are satisfied as to the identity of the rightful king. Philip and John, at the Bastard's suggestion, agree to make a joint attack on the city and to settle its disposition afterward. At this point, the citizens propose that peace be restored by means of the marriage of Lewis, the Dauphin of France, to Blanch of Spain, who is King John's niece.

Act III. To the dismay of Constance, the marriage soon takes place. The wedding festivities are interrupted by Cardinal Pandulph, legate of the Pope, who upbraids John for keeping Stephen Langton, newly chosen archbishop of Canterbury, from taking possession of his see. When John rejects the Pope's demands, Pandulph excommunicates him and prevails upon the reluctant Philip to break his compact with the English king.

A battle takes place in which the English are victorious, the Bastard kills the Duke of Austria, and young Arthur is captured by John, who puts him into the custody of Hubert de Burgh. In the French camp, Constance is disconsolate. Pandulph, on the other hand, points out to Lewis that, with Arthur out of the way, he can now, as Blanch's husband, lay claim to John's possessions.

Act IV. On John's orders, Hubert prepares to have Arthur blinded, but the young Duke so moves him by his entreaties that his heart softens. He decides to let John think that Arthur is dead. The Earls of Pembroke and Salisbury, already dubious as to the wisdom of John's policies, are further disenchanted when they hear his version of Arthur's supposed demise.

A messenger brings word to King John that both his mother and Constance have died in France and that a French army has invaded England. Because the report of Arthur's death is causing unfavorable comment, John is relieved to learn from Hubert that the Duke is still alive. Neither of them knows that the unfortunate youth has killed himself while trying to escape from the castle in which he was confined. His body is found by Pembroke, Salisbury, and Hugh Bigot, who assume, despite Hubert's protestations of innocence, that he was murdered at the King's command.

Act V. Having yielded to the Pope, John secures Pandulph's promise that he will persuade the French to lay down their arms. The Bastard informs him that the Dauphin's army has been welcomed by the English citizenry and that the nobles have deserted the King's cause; he urges John to take defensive measures, despite Pandulph's assurances.

In the French camp at St. Edmundsbury, Pandulph informs the Dauphin that John has made his peace with the church, but Lewis refuses to abandon his plan to win the English crown. The Bastard, learning of the Dauphin's intransigence, assures the invaders that these "boyish troops / The king doth smile at; and is well prepared / To whip this dwarfish war, these pigmy arms." In the ensuing battle, Melun, a French lord who has been mortally wounded, reveals to the defecting English nobles that the Dauphin intends to kill them all once his purpose is accomplished. At this news they decide to return to the King's camp. The Dauphin's position becomes even more precarious when some badly needed supplies are destroyed near the coast.

Having been felled by a fever during the battle, King John is taken to Swinstead Abbey, where he is poisoned by a monk and dies, leaving his crown to his son Henry. The Bastard, still anxious to press the campaign against the Dauphin, is mollified when he learns that Pandulph is engaged in negotiating an honorable peace. His verdict on the struggle is that England will ever be invulnerable to attack unless "it first did help to wound itself."—H. D.

Comment. The historical material that Shakespeare dramatizes concerns John's defense of his throne against the united Catholic powers of Philip, king of France, and the duke of Austria. They both support the legitimate claim to the throne of Prince Arthur,

John's young nephew. When the armies of these foreign potentates are defeated, John ridicules the threats of Pandulph, the papal legate, to excommunicate Philip if he forms an alliance with an archheretic like John. John's vigorous denial of Pandulph's authority is the only strongly anti-Catholic speech in the play (III, i, 147–171). This aspect of John's policy would have interested, even excited, an Elizabethan audience, for there are striking parallels between John's reign and that of Elizabeth. In particular, Elizabeth's order for the death of Mary, Queen of Scots, mirrors John's desire for the death of Arthur (see William DAVISON). But an Elizabethan, however patriotic, would have been outraged at John's part in bringing about Arthur's death.

Shakespeare applied much of his poetic energy to the characterization of Faulconbridge, the illegitimate son of Richard Coeur de Lion. He is not what some critics, searching for a hero-protagonist in the drama, take him to be: the embodiment of the soul of England, the man who should have been king. He is rather a satiric commentator, a dissimulator, intriguer, and scoffer. He scoffs at every sort of pretension. After being knighted, he ridicules the snobbery and affectation of the high society to which he has just gained admission (I, i, 182–219). He derides the speech of a citizen on the walls of Angiers, who urges the marriage of Blanch, King John's niece, to the Dauphin. The fellow's harangue is so absurd a mixture of wordplay, conceits, and mouthfilling metaphors that the Bastard protests: "Zounds! I was never so bethump'd with words / Since I first call'd my brother's father dad" (II, i, 466–467). A moment later he parodies the Dauphin's inane praise of Lady Blanch's beauty by twisting his conceits until they become nonsense (II, i, 504–509). After the Kings have accepted the proposal of the citizens of Angiers and made peace, the Bastard delivers his famous ironical panegyric on Commodity (expediency). But at the close of the sarcastic eulogy, he returns to scoffing—this time at himself:

> And why rail I on this Commodity?
> But for because he hath not woo'd me yet.
> (II, i, 587–588)
>
> Well, whiles I am a beggar, I will rail
> And say there is no sin but to be rich.
> (Ibid. 593–594)

As the action develops, the Bastard becomes more and more clearly the embodiment of the orthodox political opinions of the age. The poet awards him the honor of making the final patriotic comment on the significance of the history:

> This England never did, nor never shall,
> Lie at the proud foot of a conqueror,
> But when it first did help to wound itself.
> (V, vii, 112–114)

Shakespeare assigns him this important function, not to show that he considers the Bastard the only man in the play fit to be king and so worthy of making the final speech (which is usually given to the character of highest rank), but because this is the culminating speech in his role of commentator or, if one prefers, of chorus.—O. J. C.

Stage History. There is no record of a production of *King John* until John Rich revived it at Covent Garden on February 26, 1737. It was acted seven times before the end of March of that year. Arthur was played by Elizabeth Bircks, thus establishing a tradition of casting actresses in the role. By 1737 Colley Cibber had made his adaptation of the play, *Papal Tyranny in the Reign of King John*, but it was not staged until February 15, 1745, when the threatened Jacobite rebellion lent it topical significance. Cibber revived and intensified the anti-Catholic bias of *The Troublesome Raigne* mentioned above under *Sources*. Five days after Cibber's first night at Covent Garden, David Garrick staged Shakespeare's *King John* at Drury Lane. His cast was an extraordinary one. Garrick played the King; Susannah Cibber, Constance; Denis Delane, Faulconbridge; Charles Macklin, Pandulph; and Miss Macklin, Arthur.

The Reverend Richard Valpy, headmaster of the Reading School, altered *King John*, "refining" Shakespeare's language for the edification of his young students. This innocent version was displayed at Covent Garden for the first time on May 20, 1803, and played a few performances that season. Its minor success was probably due to the insertion of anti-French sentiments conforming with contemporary political bias. Almost all of the famous actor-producers of the 19th century mounted the play. John Philip Kemble's production every year from 1804 to 1817 featured Sarah Siddons as Constance, a role in which she was at her best; it took its place beside her extraordinary impersonation of Lady Macbeth.

The best-known production of *King John* was that which opened at Covent Garden on November 24, 1823. Charles Kemble had commissioned J. R. Planché to design costumes in the precise fashion of the period of the drama. To the actors this clothing was merely cumbersome, but the public found it at once beautiful and educational. *Bell's Weekly Messenger*, dated November 30, 1823, echoed the enthusiasm of the public: "Charles Kemble never more distinguished himself than by his powerful personation of the bastard Falconbridge. His first and second dresses were particularly graceful and picturesque." William Charles Macready staged an equally elaborate spectacle at Drury Lane in 1842, with an exceptional cast that proved better able to hold its own against the scenic splendor. Macready played the King; Samuel Phelps, Hubert; James R. Anderson, Faulconbridge; Helen Faucit, Constance. The height of historical exactitude in King John productions was reached in Charles Kean's revival at the Princess' Theatre on February 9, 1852. This producer's passion for detailing with minute accuracy the scenery and costumes of the play's period would be considered less than necessary today. By that time it had become the established custom for the star to act the Bastard and an actress to play Arthur. In this production Kean and Ellen Terry assumed those roles. However short, the text of *King John* was almost always cut further, while producers introduced many novelties to the play. Beerbohm Tree, for example, interpolated an elaborate dumb show of the granting of Magna Carta in his 1899 presentation.

Although it has not enjoyed great popularity in this century, *King John* has been produced occasionally. London ignored the play during the very early 1900's, but in 1901, 1909, and 1913, productions were staged at Stratford-upon-Avon. It was included in the 1917–1918 season at the Old Vic with Russell Thorndike as King John and his sister Sybil playing Constance. Another Old Vic production followed in 1920; staged by Robert Atkins, it starred Ernest Milton as King John and Rupert Harvey as the Bastard. Milton repeated his John in 1924 at the Strand, and the next year Randle Ayrton played the King at Stratford.

Ralph Richardson played the Bastard at the Old Vic in 1931/2, but it was 10 years before another *King John* was staged at a major London theatre. In July 1941 an Old Vic touring company, directed by Tyrone Guthrie and Lewis Casson, brought a revival to the New Theatre, after a series of engagements all over Britain. The cast was superlative: Sybil Thorndike as Constance; Lewis Casson, Pandulph; George Hagan, the Bastard. But the play belonged to the decadent John as acted by Ernest Milton.

The Birmingham Repertory Theatre in 1945 focused on the Bastard of Paul Scofield, as directed by Peter Brook, but in three later presentations the role of the King regained prominence. Robert Helpmann played the part at Stratford in 1948, looking to Eric Keown of *Punch* like "an emaciated King of Diamonds." That same year, David Read took the role at the Open Air Theatre and Donald Wolfit on television in 1952. When George Devine produced the drama for the Old Vic in 1953, his cast included Richard Burton as the Bastard, Michael Hordern as King John, and Fay Compton as Constance. Douglas Seale's production (1957) at Stratford starred Alec Clunes as the Bastard, and for the 1961/2 season at the Old Vic Peter Potter staged the play, with Paul Daneman and Maurice Denham as the Bastard and King John.—M. G.

Bibliography. TEXT: *King John*, New Cambridge Edition, J. Dover Wilson, ed., 1936; *King John*, New Arden Edition, E. A. J. Honigmann, ed., 1954. DATE: New Arden Edition; T. M. Parrott, "*King John:* the Arden Edition," *Journal of English and Germanic Philology*, LV, 1956; R. A. Law, "On the Date of *King John*," *Studies in Philology*, LIV, 1957. SOURCES: New Arden Edition; Geoffrey Bullough, *Narrative and Dramatic Sources of Shakespeare*, IV, 1962. COMMENT: Lily B. Campbell, *Shakespeare's Histories*, 1947; Adrien Bonjour, "The Road to Swinstead Abbey," *ELH*, XVIII, 1951. STAGE HISTORY: New Cambridge Edition; G. C. D. Odell, *Shakespeare from Betterton to Irving*, 1920; J. C. Trewin, *Shakespeare on the English Stage, 1900–1964*, 1964.

Selected Criticism

LEIGH HUNT. The *Constance* of Mrs. Siddons is an excellent study for young actresses, to whom it will shew the great though difficult distinction between rant and tragic vehemence. In an inferior performer, the loudness of *Constance's* grief would be mere noise; but tempered and broken as it is by the natural looks and gestures of Mrs. Siddons, by her varieties of tone and pauses full of meaning, it becomes as grand as it is petrifying. Mr. Kemble's *King John*, with its theatrical tone of dignity and its mixture of confidence and whining, is one of his happiest performances: in the scene with *Hubert* he displays much knowledge of effect, and has in particular one excellent expression of the mouth, which, while he is anxiously looking for *Hubert's* reply to his dark hints, is breathlessly opened and gently dropped at the corners; but there is too much pantomimic rolling of the eyes. Charles Kemble, always elegant, with a chivalrous air, and possessing a strong taste for contemptuous irony, is as complete a *Faulconbridge* as one can desire. The effect of this and other tragedies of Shakspeare must give Mr. Kemble great satisfaction. Every person, indeed, who has a regard for the spirit and dignity of this country's literature must be gratified to see that these endeavours, founded on so just an enthusiasm, are properly rising in the public estimation. [Comment on Covent Garden production, June 3, 1810; reprinted in *Leigh Hunt's Dramatic Criticism, 1808–1831*, L. H. and C. W. Houtchens, eds., 1949.]

CHARLES KNIGHT. Up to the concluding scene of the third act we have not learnt from Shakspere to hate John. We may think him an usurper. Our best sympathies may be with Arthur and his mother. But he is bold and confident, and some remnant of the indomitable spirit of the Plantagenets gives him a lofty and gallant bearing. We are not even sure, from the first, that he had not something of justice in his quarrel, even though his mother confidentially repudiates "his right." In the scene with Pandulph we completely go with him. We have yet to know that he would one day crouch at the feet of the power that he now defies; and he has therefore all our voices when he tells the wily and sophistical cardinal

That no Italian priest
Shall tithe or toll in our dominions.

But the expression of *one thought* that had long been lurking in the breast of John sweeps away every feeling but that of hatred, and worse than hatred; and we see nothing, hereafter, in the king, but the creeping, cowardly assassin, prompting the deed which he is afraid almost to name to himself, with the lowest flattery of his instrument, and showing us, as it were, the sting which wounds, and the slaver which pollutes, of the venomous and loathsome reptile. [*Studies of Shakspere*, 1849.]

BARRETT WENDELL. . . . what has happened in *King John* is what happened in *Romeo and Juliet*. Creative imagination, to all appearances spontaneous, has made real, living people out of what had previously been stage types.

In this very fact lies the reason why *King John* generally impresses one as more archaic, or at least as more queer, than *Richard II*. Such a phrase as Richard's

"Old John of Gaunt, time-honour'd Lancaster,"

could never have been uttered by any real man; such a phrase as John's

"Now say, Chatillon, what would France with us?"

might be uttered by anybody still. In *Richard II*, then, the consistent conventionality of everything makes us accept the whole play if we accept any part of it. In *King John* the continual confusion of real, human vitality with the old quasi-operatic conventions combines with the general carelessness of construction to make each kind of thing seem more out of place than it would seem by itself. Like any other transitional incongruity, *King John* is often harder to accept than the consistent conventions from which it departs. Its very excellences emphasize its faults and its oddities. [*William Shakespeare, A Study in Elizabethan Literature*, 1894.]

G. P. BAKER. In *King John*, though Shakespeare gains decidedly in dramatic skill, some of the old weakness persists. Again we face in John a weakling who can only slightly command our sympathy and whose death is far less touching than it would be had he in the earlier scenes been of larger mould. There can be no question that Faulconbridge is the strength of the play. As any reader knows who has compared Shakespeare's *John* with the earlier play in two parts, from which he skilfully condensed it, *The Troublesome Raigne of King John*, and with the historical material in Holinshed, Faulconbridge is Shakespeare's creation from vague and inadequate suggestions. But it is not merely the courage, resourcefulness, and wit of Faulconbridge—in a word, his characterization—which make him memorable: it is he who passes straight through the play, carrying our sympathies and affection with him and giving to it a kind of unity. But he cannot give it that essential unity which would come from a compelling central figure indispensable to all the important scenes, without whom the play could have no being. Particularly noticeable is the development of the comic in this play. Part I. of *Henry VI.* showed only touches, and those coarse; Part III. lacked it; and in Part II. Cade's followers provided comic relief. *Richard II.* lacks it, and in *Richard III.* its place is taken by the sardonic irony of the king himself. In *Henry V.*, as it stands, the comic alternates with the graver scenes. Thus far, then, the really comic has come almost entirely, if present at all, from people not closely involved with the main plot. In *King John* it is Faulconbridge himself, an important person in nearly all the main scenes, who brings the comic relief. This recognition that the comic is desirable for contrast and that it may relax tense motion till a hearer may again be wrought upon with effect, Shakespeare, in part, owes the author of the *Troublesome Raigne;* but a few years later in the *Merchant of Venice* he will show us in the trial scene that the comic and the tragic depend not upon the person who is looked at, but the sympathies of the person who looks at him. Growing maturity is seen also in *King John* in the scene of Arthur and Hubert, by the subordination of mere physical horror to working upon us through sympathies with the lad himself. There are, too, repeated instances which show increasing sureness of theatrical knowledge. In the original of the Hubert-Arthur scene, the murderers enter shortly after Hubert begins to speak with the lad and seize upon the boy. Shakespeare holds them back till just as Hubert is beginning to yield. Their coming fills an audience with dread lest it strengthen Hubert's weakening purpose. Our eager watching of Hubert relaxes only when he orders out the murderers, for then we know that he will yield. The earlier dramatists seem not to have understood how to make an entrance or an exit dramatically effective. Here Shakespeare proves that he knows how to make both significant for their scene. [*Development of Shakespeare as a Dramatist*, 1907.]

JOHN MASEFIELD. Like the best Shakespearian tragedies, *King John* is an intellectual form in which a number of people with obsessions illustrate the idea of treachery. The illustrations are very various. Perhaps the most interesting of them are those subtle ones that illustrate treachery to type, or want of conformity to a standard imagined or established. In the historical plays Shakespeare's mind broods on the idea that our tragical kings failed because they did not conform to a type lower than themselves. . . King John presents that most subtle of all the images of treachery, a man who cannot conform to the standard of his own ideas. He fails as a king because his intellect prompts him to attempt what is really beyond the powers of his nature to perform. By his side, with an irony that is seldom praised, Shakespeare places the figure of the Bastard, the man who ought to have been king, the man fitted by nature to rule the English, the man without intellect but with a rough capacity, the man whom we meet again, as a successful king, in the play of *Henry V*. King John is placed throughout the play in treacherous relations with life. He is a traitor to his brother's son, to his own ideas, to the English idea, and to his oath of kingship. He has a bigger intellect than anyone about him. His brain is full of gusts and flaws that blow him beyond his age, and then let him sink below it. Persistence in any one course of treachery would give him the greatness of all well-defined things. He remains a chaos shooting out occasional fire. [*William Shakespeare*, 1911.]

J. MIDDLETON MURRY. The Bastard is a cynic, and not a cynic at all. He is realist and idealist at once yet he is not divided. He is the natural Man, in whom the gift of consciousness has served only to make nature more truly itself. He is detached from the world only to be more effectively a part of it. A new *kind* of experience, different from any that had hitherto found utterance in Shakespeare's plays speaks in him. He is conscious, as no Shakespearian character has been conscious before . . . .

The Bastard's cynicism about himself is simply that of a man who hates to strike an attitude in his own eyes. He can afford to be cynical about himself, because he knows he cannot do anything base. He has no need of virtue, because he has no vice to conceal.

The raw material of the Bastard is the crude character in *The Troublesome Raigne of King John*. Shakespeare simply took him and made him live. His one trait in the old play was that at the critical moment he preferred to sacrifice his lawful inheritance for the honour of being known to be the bastard of Cœur de Lion. With this one trait—no slight one—to build on, Shakespeare made him into the likeness of a King of England, by 'sovereignty of nature'. He becomes the champion of English unity, and the victorious assailant of Papal pretensions: the healthy substance of the corrupt shadow which is King John. But his political function, though glorious, is subordinate to his function of being himself. He is the first of Shakespeare's great characters, who speaks with a voice of his own, sentiments of his own. He is *the* Englishman, the 'madcap' revolutionary Englishman. [*Shakespeare*, 1936.]

ADRIEN BONJOUR. To the split in the body politic corresponds a fission in the King's soul; in that sense the personal tragedy of John could be termed "les nains sales." The Bastard, on the other hand, spontaneously sets the interest of the nation above his self-interest; he remains unstained by Commodity and, having kept a total integrity in the most trying circumstances, finally proves to be himself the natural ruler that John had ceased to be. When everything seems to crumble about him in a crisis decisive for the future of the kingdom, he "alone upholds the day," prevents a complete disaster before the enemy and makes the reconciliation between lords and crown possible. Such is the reward of his unswerving loyalty. Nothing is clearer in that respect than his attitude towards Prince Henry, which critics have curiously passed over. When at the very apex of his career, when holding in his hands strength, authority and the future of the kingdom, he naturally, and as a matter of course, offers his oath of allegiance to the young Prince, by much his junior not only in years but in experience. Thus, at Swinstead Abbey, close upon the death of John, he presides over the transmission of power to Henry who, thanks to him, has now become the new King, "born to set a form upon that indigest" which John had "left so shapeless and so rude." This is the final illustration of the governing idea of the play. ["The Road to Swinstead Abbey," *ELH*, XVIII, 1951.]

JAMES L. CALDERWOOD. The view I am proposing is that *King John* represents a dramatic crucible in which Shakespeare explores and tests two antagonistic ethical principles, Commodity and Honour. The opposition between Commodity, or scheming self-interest, and Honour, loyalty in general but in its highest form loyalty to the good of England, comprises a basic theme to which almost every action and character of the play is vitally related. In its political implications the theme explores the qualities demanded of the kingly character; in its general pervasiveness and in its specific application to John and the Bastard, it imparts to the play a unity of structure generally denied it . . . .

If John has sunk to contemptible depths of Commodity, even to the point of shaming An English King, the Bastard has steadily risen towards the genuine Honour befitting An English King . . . .

Yet if the Bastard has committed himself to Honour, it is no such ingenuous Honour as that which precipitated Blanche to destruction. It has at least once already withstood the severest inner tests of Commodity, and it has proven shrewdly adept at discerning Commodity in others . . . .

It is, therefore, perfectly appropriate that the Bastard is given the concluding speech of the play, which is usually reserved for the king. He has confirmed his loyalty to England and to the soon-to-be King Henry III in this final scene. Yet this final speech of his, with its conspicuously qualifying "if" —". . . Naught shall make us rue, / If England to itself do rest but true"—is not just a set piece of perfunctory patriotism with which to conclude the play. The Bastard is too perspicacious and he has had too much experience with the renegade nobles not to be suspicious of their professions of Honour in this last scene. His closing speech is both a stirring proclamation of an ideal—but not, he realizes, untempered—national unity, and also his declaration to the nobles of the standards by which he has been governed and by which he expects them to be governed in the future. Thus, with what we might call "experienced" Honour dictating the terms to Commodity, *King John* concludes upon the same theme with which it began. ["Commodity and Honour in *King John*," *University of Toronto Quarterly*, XXIX, 1960.]

The Tragedy of King LEAR.

King Lear. A tragedy by Shakespeare.

Text. The play was entered in the Stationers' Register on November 26, 1607: "Nathanael Butter John Busby. Entred for their Copie under thandes of Sir George Buck knight and Thwardens A booke called. Master William Shakespeare his historye of Kinge Lear, as yt was played before the Kinges maiestie at Whitehall vppon Sainct Stephens night at Christmas Last, by his maiesties servantes playinge vsually at the Globe on the Banksyde vj[d]."

The First Quarto appeared in 1608, entitled: "M. William Shak-speare: His True Chronicle Historie of the life and death of King Lear and his three Daughters. With the vnfortunate life of Edgar, sonne and heire to the Earle of Gloster, and his sullen and assumed humor of Tom of Bedlam: As it was played before the Kings Maiestie at Whitehall vpon S. Stephans night in Christmas Hollidayes. By his Maiesties seruants playing vsually at the Gloabe on the Bancke-side. London, Printed for Nathaniel Butter, and are to be sold at his shop in Pauls Church-yard at the signe of the Pide Bull neere St. Austins Gate. 1608."

Although the "Pied Bull" Quarto was apparently

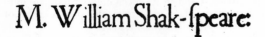

M. William Shak-speare:

HIS

True Chronicle Historie of the life and death of King LEAR and his three Daughters.

With the vnfortunate life of Edgar, *sonne* and heire to the Earle of Gloster, and his sullen and assumed humor of TOM of Bedlam:

As it was played before the Kings Maiestie at Whitehall vpon S. Stephans night in Christmas Hollidayes.

By his Maiesties seruants playing vsually at the Gloabe on the Bancke-side.

LONDON,
Printed for *Nathaniel Butter*, and are to be sold at his shop in *Pauls* Church-yard at the signe of the Pide Bull neere St. *Austins* Gate. 1608.

TITLE PAGE OF THE FIRST QUARTO OF *King Lear* (THE PIDE OR PIED BULL QUARTO, 1608).

an authorized edition, the text is in many places corrupt. There is some disagreement as to whether the Q1 is to be classified as a BAD QUARTO, but it shows many of the characteristics of bad quartos. Various attempts have been made to explain this corruption. Leo Kirschbaum has argued that the copy for the text was provided by a reporter, possibly the BOOK-KEEPER, who had access to the PROMPT-BOOK and imperfectly memorized what he saw. G. I. Duthie at one time suggested that the text represents a MEMORIAL RECONSTRUCTION made by the entire company during a provincial tour. Some scholars were of the opinion that the text represented a stenographic report surreptitiously taken down during a performance of the play. Alice Walker has developed a theory (which has come to be generally, though tentatively, accepted) that the text was derived from a combination of memorial reconstruction and dictation. She argues that the two boy actors who played Goneril and Regan had access to Shakespeare's FOUL PAPERS, from which they dictated to a printer's agent the text of the play, supplementing this dictation with their own recollection of lines. The Second Quarto, issued by William JAGGARD in 1619, but fraudulently dated 1608, is a reprint of Q1.

Like the 1608 Quarto, the copy for the text of the First Folio has provoked a great deal of speculation. The best guess that scholars have made is that the Folio text was printed from pages of Q1 (and possibly Q2) which had been edited and corrected through reference to the company's prompt-book Thus, the attempt to establish a definitive text o this most important play is a formidable task. Th Folio contains 100 lines not in Q1. The Quartc however, contains about 300 lines not in the Folio Neither alone constitutes the authoritative text, an editing the play requires the capacity to produce judicious combination of both. For example, th Fool's mock prophecy (III, ii, 80–95), which appear in the Folio and not in the Quarto, is regarded b some as spurious, although it is generally retained i the text.

Date. *King Lear* was probably written in late 160 or early 1606. It was performed at court on Decem ber 26, 1606. "These late eclipses in the sun an moon" to which Gloucester refers (I, ii, 112 occurred in September and October 1605. Narrowe limits for the time of the first production of th tragedy can perhaps be fixed by the history of th publication of the old *King Leir* (see *Sources* be low). It had been entered in the Stationers' Registe in 1594, but published only in May 1605, probably t capitalize on the new interest in the Lear stor aroused by Shakespeare's play and incidentally t deceive purchasers into believing that the publicatio contained the text of the recent hit. If the specula tion is valid, *King Lear* must have been first stage sometime before May 1605.

Sources. GEOFFREY OF MONMOUTH (d. 1154) in hi *Historia Regum Britanniae* (c. 1137) was the firs to tell a connected story of Lear and his daughter Lyr or Ler before this history was a shadowy figur in ancient British mythology. For his work Geoffre drew partly on confused Celtic tradition, partly o accepted authorities for early British history, an partly on his own powers of invention. Holinshe took over the story from Geoffrey and inserted i into his *Chronicles*, as did Spenser in *The Faeri Queene* (II, x) and John Higgins in *A Mirror fo Magistrates* (1574).

The principal direct source is *The True Chronicl History of King Leir and his three daughter Gonerill, Ragan and Cordella* (pub. 1605). This ol play has a happy ending. With the help of a Frenc army Cordella's forces are victorious and Leir i restored to his throne, where he reigns for a fe years, then dies peacefully. This close of Leir' career is appropriate, because, instead of bein dominated by wild, insane passion, he is patien under affliction. Although his daughters constantl harass him, he remains "the mirror of mild patience puts up all wrong and never gives reply." Lear' madness was not a part of the original story, but i the poet's invention. Gloucester's tragic story Shake speare took and adapted with all its important fea tures from "The Tale of the Blind King of Paphla gonia" in Sir Philip Sidney's *The Countess o Pembroke's Arcadia*. For many modern audience this second story of children's cruelty to an age father (often called an echo plot) fills the pla overfull of horror and overcomplicates the plo The relation between the two stories depends on th interpretation of Lear's story. Whatever the relation ship, Shakespeare had a dramatist's reason for addin the Gloucester plot. The action of the Lear stor rises to a climax in the first act. The rest of this pl is a psychological denouement, an exhibition of a inner struggle against madness, a series of ment ates growing more and more turbulent. To satisfy very audience's demand for action moving from risis to crisis and for tension finally exploding into atastrophe the playwright attached the Gloucester ory to that of Lear.

Two other important sources were John Florio's anslation of Montaigne's *Essays* and Samuel Harsnett's *A Declaration of Egregious Popish Impostures.* It has been pointed out that over 100 words ever used by Shakespeare before *King Lear* are n Florio's translation, and that Montaigne's most amous essay—the "Apology for Raymond Sebonde" -has references to the major themes of the play. Harsnett's *Declaration* provided the names of the ends enumerated by Tom o' Bedlam (IV, i), as ell as many other features of the storm scenes. inally, the story of Sir Brian ANNESLEY, unjustly eated by two of his daughters and defended by a iird, named Cordell, bears a striking resemblance o the main plot.—O. J. C.

Plot Synopsis. Act I. Old King Lear of Britain, ager to divest himself of the cares of kingship, roposes to divide his realm among his three daughters, giving the largest share to the one who describes her love for him most eloquently. The two lder daughters, Goneril and Regan, vie with each ther in declaring their devotion, but Cordelia, the oungest and Lear's favorite, says simply that she ears him the love due him as her father. Disappointed and enraged by her answer, the King disowns Cordelia and bestows his royal power and ossessions on her sisters and their husbands, retaining only his title. Henceforth, he and his retinue of 00 knights will live in turn with Goneril and Regan. When the Earl of Kent upbraids Lear for his mpetuosity in disinheriting Cordelia, he is banhed by the angry King. Having been summoned to he royal presence, the Duke of Burgundy and the ing of France, both candidates for Cordelia's hand, arn that she has no dowry. Burgundy refuses to ed her under such conditions, but France declares hat her plight has kindled his love. Before she leaves or France with her prospective husband, Cordelia rges her sisters to treat their father well, but they eceive her admonition coldly, for they have little onfidence in the discretion of the King, who even n "the best and soundest of his time hath been but ash."

Meanwhile, Edmund, illegitimate son of the Earl f Gloucester, is bitterly resentful of the low estate o which his bastardy condemns him. Determined to upplant his legitimate older brother, Edgar, in his ather's affections, he contrives to persuade Gloucester that Edgar wishes to kill him.

Goneril, who is married to the Duke of Albany, roves a reluctant hostess to her father and orders er steward, Oswald, to show him scant respect. Offended by Oswald's insolence, Lear strikes him, nd Kent, who has re-entered Lear's service in isguise, trips him. Goneril then complains of the oisterous behavior of her father's knights and suggests that he dismiss 50 of them. Damning Goneril or her ingratitude and already regretting his behavior toward Cordelia, Lear decides to go to Regan's castle.

Act II. In Gloucester's castle, Edmund continues s machinations against his brother and convinces he Earl that he had tried to dissuade Edgar from his

M. VVilliam Shake-ſpeare,
HIS
True Chronicle Hiſtory of the life and death of King *Lear*, and his *three Daughters.*

With the vnfortunate life of EDGAR, ſonne and heire to the Earle of *Glocester*, and *his ſullen and aſſumed humour of* TOM of Bedlam.

As it was plaid before the Kings Maieſty at White-Hall, vpon S. Stephens night, in Christmas Hollidaies.

By his Maieſties Seruants, playing vſually at the *Globe* on the *Banck-ſide.*

Printed for *Nathaniel Butter.*
1608.

TITLE PAGE OF THE SECOND QUARTO OF *King Lear.* ACTUALLY PUBLISHED IN 1619, IT WAS FALSELY DATED.

plot against his father's life, and was wounded in the attempt. Kent, bearing a letter for Gloucester from King Lear, encounters Oswald near the castle and quarrels with him. Oswald's shouts bring Gloucester, Regan, and her husband, the Duke of Cornwall, to the scene. Upon hearing Oswald's account of the dispute, Cornwall orders that Kent be placed in the stocks. When Lear arrives, he is outraged by the indignity inflicted on his servant. He complains to Regan of the unfilial conduct of Goneril, who herself arrives and joins her sister in demanding that Lear dismiss his followers. They insist that Lear has no need of them, but Lear replies, "O, reason not the need: our basest beggars / Are in the poorest thing superfluous." Fighting against tears and vowing revenge on the two "unnatural hags," he rushes out into a wild and stormy night. Regan and Cornwall advise Gloucester to bar his doors to the King, who may be driven to desperate measures.

Act III. Standing bareheaded on a heath as the tempest rages, Lear calls on the "all-shaking thunder" to smite the world and crack the molds of nature "that make ungrateful man." At Kent's urging, he and the Fool seek shelter in a hovel, and the King feels for the first time pity for "poor naked wretches." In the hovel, they meet with Edgar, who, having been declared an outlaw, has disguised himself as a mad beggar. In defiance of Cornwall's edict,

Gloucester conducts Lear and his little band to a farmhouse, where the King, who is by now mad, arraigns his daughters at an imaginary bar of justice. Gloucester tells Kent that Lear's life is in danger and bids him take the King to Dover, where he has friends.

Having learned from Edmund that his father intended to aid Lear, Cornwall orders the arrest of Gloucester and, while Regan cries encouragement, gouges out one of his eyes. He is about to put out the other when a servant tries to stop him; the servant is killed by Regan, but not before he can wound Cornwall. The Duke then completes his gruesome task and informs Gloucester that it was Edmund who betrayed him. The Earl now laments the folly that led him to mistreat Edgar.

Act IV. Gloucester engages Edgar, still posing as a lunatic, to lead him to a high cliff near Dover, from which he plans to throw himself. Edgar takes him instead to a plain and after Gloucester has jumped without harm from an imagined height, succeeds in persuading him that his life has been saved by a miracle. Suddenly the King appears, dressed fantastically with wild flowers. He and Gloucester recognize each other, despite the madness of one and the blindness of the other. Oswald, acting on Regan's instructions, tries to kill Gloucester, but is himself slain by Edgar. Lear is then taken to the camp of the King of France, who has invaded England to avenge the wrongs done his father-in-law. He awakens from a long sleep to find Cordelia at his side. At first he can scarcely believe his eyes, for, as he explains, he is "a very foolish fond old man" and fears that he is not in his right mind.

Act V. Meanwhile, Cornwall has died of the wounds inflicted by his servant, and Edmund has become the paramour of Regan, though Goneril is also in love with him. Goneril's husband, the Duke of Albany, who has come to hate his wife, declares that he will take arms against the French because they have violated British soil, not because they seek to help Lear. Edgar, wearing the garb of a peasant, gives Albany a letter, found in Oswald's pocket, in which Goneril declares her love for Edmund and her desire to be rid of her husband.

In a battle between the French and British forces, the latter are victorious and Lear and Cordelia are taken prisoner. Unknown to Albany, Edmund orders their execution. While Goneril and Regan dispute their claims to Edmund, Albany arrests him for treason, whereupon he offers a challenge to anyone who calls him a traitor. Still wearing a disguise, Edgar takes up the challenge and mortally wounds his brother. After Albany discloses his awareness of the adulterous relationship between Edmund and Goneril, Edgar reveals himself and reports that Gloucester's heart had "burst smilingly" when he learned the identity of his guide; he adds that Kent had told him the story of his own masquerade. Meanwhile, Goneril, who has poisoned Regan, kills herself. The dying Edmund, who declares his desire to do some good, countermands his order for the deaths of Lear and Cordelia, but he is too late. Lear enters, bearing the body of Cordelia, and after a vain effort to revive her, dies himself. Thus Albany, with Edgar and Kent, is left to mourn and to heal the wounds of "the gored state."—H.D.

Comment. *King Lear* is both the tragic history a slave of passion, of the ravages of uncontroll anger, and a vehicle of general philosophical a moral significance. Sheer fury drives Lear relen lessly toward madness, yet during its gradual ons he struggles to gain control of his passion—the stor in his mind. Shakespeare's preparation of his audien for Lear's insanity had to be skillful and thoroug because, as Josephine Bennett has pointed out, it w an innovation, not found in any earlier versions the story. Lear's violent reaction to Cordelia's r fusal to express her love may seem extreme until v remember Goneril's explanation that her father h always been hasty and the victim of freakish sudd impulses. Furthermore, like any other of the pa sions, anger, once liberated from the control reason, is much greater than the situations that ha aroused it. Feeding on itself, it continues to gro until it issues in madness. Shakespeare's portrayal each stage of Lear's tragic journey to insanity r veals his surprising knowledge of the onset of co plete derangement. Kent first puts the idea into t minds of the spectators when he implies that Lear crazy to banish Cordelia from his heart and h realm. He defends his scolding of Lear for his fo with the blunt words ". . . be Kent unmannerly, When Lear is mad" (I, i, 147–148). After Lear h had his first experience of Goneril's hard heart, cries "O, let me not be mad, not mad, sweet heave (I, v, 50). He flies first to Goneril and then to Reg pathetically seeking to retain the emotional founc tions upon which he had built his little univer Finding no center of security in their false love, abandons hope of a haven of emotional safety an where in the protected world in which he has alwa lived. Then he realizes that the bare necessities living have never been enough for him, or for a other human being, for

> our barest beggars
> Are in the poorest thing superfluous:
> Allow not nature more than nature needs,
> Man's life's as cheap as beast's.
>
> (II, iv, 267–270)

Lear thus voluntarily gives up the protection giv him by his regal position, the trappings that ha insulated him from a firsthand knowledge of li From now on he will have to face reality as a pl "unaccommodated" man.

The culmination of Lear's passion occurs in t scene on the storm-swept heath. The destructi power of the tempest is a manifestation of the for of evil that have invaded Lear's mind. The storm thus more than an adjunct to the old man's fury; elevates his passion to the awesome dignity of natural portent. As Theodore Spenser has point out, Lear's language universalizes his private expe ence. He calls upon the elements of the storm— rain, the thunder, and the lightning—to wreak kind of destruction upon all human creatures that his violent anger he would like to inflict upon "pelican daughters." He demands that ruin

> Smite flat the thick rotundity o' the world!
> Crack Nature's moulds, all germens spill at once
> That make ingrateful man!
>
> (III, ii, 7–9)

Also a revelation of Lear's notion of the correspondence between the microcosm of man and the macrocosm of nature is his appeal to the elements to punish sexual incontinence—often a matter of obsessive concern to persons whose failure of emotional control releases all the buried vagaries of their subconscious minds. It is after this invocation of divine justice, at the moment when Kent begs Lear to take refuge in the hovel, that he replies "My wits begin to turn." This is a signal to the audience to watch for symptoms of madness. However, Lear does not become completely deranged until Edgar appears disguised as Tom o' Bedlam, one of the harmlessly insane creatures who were released from confinement in order to go about London begging for money to pay for their keep.

It is important to note in passing that to Lear the storm has no symbolic significance; it is the cause of the cold and other physical ills that plague him, and he finds in them a way to counteract the tumult in his mind. He tells Kent:

> Thou think'st 'tis much that this contentious storm
> Invades us to the skin: so 'tis to thee;
> But where the greater malady is fix'd,
> The lesser is scarce felt.
> . . . . .
> . . . the tempest in my mind
> Doth from my senses take all feeling else
> Save what beats there.
>
> (III, iv, 6–9, 12–14)

After the arrival of poor Tom, Shakespeare employs an effective method of presenting the growth and manifestation of Lear's insanity. He contrasts it with the mock madness of Edgar. Incoherence is the form that Tom's mental derangement takes, while Lear betrays most of the symptoms that a modern alienist would recognize as typical. His idea of cruel daughters has become so firm a fixation that he refers to Tom's daughters with obsessive repetition. His attempt to strip off his clothes is another symptom of insanity.

Kent and the Fool are both utterly devoted to Lear. Yet they aggravate his anger and hurry him along the road to madness. Kent is a faithful counselor, an old man who cannot resist speaking the plain truth whatever the consequences. His bluntness forms a striking contrast to the initial flattery of Goneril and Regan. His bursts of righteous indignation, designed to protect Lear from his hideous rashness, are such that they only raise the temperature of Lear's anger until he banishes Kent. But, returning almost at once disguised as a servant, Kent continues to encourage Lear's tyrannical impulses. Despite his continued provocation of new seizures of Lear's pathological anger, Kent remains at his master's side, even after he has become completely mad. He stays with his demented King through the storm with solicitude mixed with awe. For to him the mad creature remains "every inch a king," whose sad steps he follows even to the brink of the grave. His last speech voices a determination to attend his master through death:

> I have a journey, sir, shortly to go;
> My master calls me, I must not say no.
>
> (V, iii, 321–322)

Kent's loyalty serves as an example of the unswerving devotion expected of an English subject to his king that was the cornerstone of Tudor patriotism.

The Fool is also utterly devoted to Lear, yet his wise utterances, often on the edge of nonsense, serve only to stimulate Lear's wild regret for his past folly. A. C. Bradley describes the fool as "a faithful half-witted lad," who tries heroically to "outjest his master's injuries." J. W. Bennett accepts and develops this idea. He is a boy, she writes, "whose mind is sane but has failed to develop into maturity. He is full of riddles, like a ten-year-old, with a craze for morose jokes. He is child-like, unsophisticated, uninhibited rather than insane." Far from "outjesting his master's injuries," as Bradley suggests, the Fool deepens Lear's cognizance of his folly. Everything that the Fool says or does accords with the traditional role of a court jester. Exploiting his allowed impudence, he shoots his bolts of apparent nonsense. When he fears that he has gone too far, he darts away from his insolent interjection into irrelevance or sheer nonsense, as when he diverts Lear's anger by singing the refrain of an old song, "Whoop, Jug! I love thee." His dramatic function is to keep the spectators from forgetting for a moment Lear's guilty folly and thus ironically to become one of the principal forces that are driving his passion into madness. He disappears from the play with the line, "And I'll go to bed at noon," a proverbial expression meaning "I'll play the fool." A practical reason may account for the Fool's abrupt disappearance: a boy actor playing two roles had to vanish as the Fool in order to reappear at the end of the play as Cordelia. In any case, the Fool's service to the plot has been completed, and Shakespeare permits him quietly to disappear.

Lear's reunion with Cordelia through their mutual love allays his madness so that he goes off to prison with her with a moment of ecstasy. But her death carries him back to irrevocable madness. Snatching at the belief that the Cordelia in his arms whom he has just pronounced as "gone for ever" is really alive, he cries,

> If it be so,
> It is a chance which does redeem all sorrows
> That ever I have felt.
>
> (V, iii, 265–267)

It is not so; and Lear dies in the pathetic delusion that she still lives. The dramatist seems here to be saying that only in madness and death can a suffering soul find release from the tragedy of the human situation. This interpretation of *King Lear* makes the drama one of the most terrible expressions of pessimism in all literature.

If this is the meaning of Lear's fate, that of Gloucester must have a related significance. His story is usually described as forming an echo plot, a different version of the same situation. Lear and Gloucester are both victims of filial ingratitude and vindictiveness. Some critics see in the blinding of Gloucester a Senecan equivalent of Lear's madness. Others have suggested that the echo plot makes the tragedy more than a different treatment of the same sets of circumstances—that it raises the inhumanity of children to aged fathers into a declaration of moral and philosophical law of human behavior. Edmund's motives for his slander are not far to seek.

His father's snickering attitude toward his surreptitiously begotten son strips the man of every shred of human dignity. Why, he asks, should he be bound by a moral law his father had violated in begetting him? Furthermore, as a bastard he is deprived of the right to inherit any kind of property and is really an outcast from the social system. He is unnatural then in not being subject to the customs and rules of civilized conduct. The Nature that he worships is not the expression of reason that the Stoics and Christian humanists conceived her to be. Edmund's Nature is a deity of animal instincts untamed to the uses of society. The other evil characters in the tragedy are also worshipers of Edmund's goddess. Goneril and Regan, by seeking to dominate their father, turn upside down an important phase of the God-ordained social order—the submission of children to parents. To this phase of Lear's unnatural situation the Fool makes continual oblique reference, as when he asks, "May not an ass know when the cart draws the horse?" (I, iv, 244). In his plot to deceive Gloucester, Edmund adopts a much less subtle technique than that which Iago uses to dupe Othello. For Gloucester has always been afflicted with moral and spiritual blindness and so easily mistakes evil for good and good for evil. His credulity leads him through injustice to catastrophe. The blinding of Gloucester, in a scene of more than Senecan savagery and horror, is not to the taste of a modern audience, yet Shakespeare gives it an ironic symbolical value. The instant Gloucester's eyes are blinded, the eyes of his mind are opened, and he becomes aware of his blind folly in believing Edmund's malicious accusation of Edgar. The awful results of his tragic blindness produce despair and cosmic pessimism. He ceases to believe that gods keep a nice balance between desert and reward. To him they are really malign supernatural beings who toy with men in a way he describes in the famous lines, "As flies to wanton boys, are we to the gods, / They kill us for their sport" (IV, i, 38–39). This is not Shakespeare's pessimism that speaks, but Gloucester's while in the depths of despair, from which we shall see him painfully rise.

The conception of *King Lear* as an expression of radical pessimism is not accepted by many critics. Many take it to be a message of hope and faith—an exalted, half-Christian, half-Stoic morality play, a profound commentary on life set against a backdrop of eternity. It is a pilgrim's progress, mankind's agonized search for the true values of both of these religious systems. At his first appearance Lear shows that his love of power and ostentatious display has distorted his ideals. His possessions and his passions dictate his conduct. He is, therefore, the most unstoical of men. Philosophers of this school taught that love of possessions, shameful in men of any age, was detestable in the old. And they continually warned their disciples against the degradation of emotional intemperance. Lear, according to this interpretation of the tragedy, is purged of these unworthy impulses through suffering. This was the form of purgation advocated by Stoic teachers. Lear, however, does not attain Stoic peace of mind by recognizing the ultimate cruelty of things and then withdrawing from participation in life to the sanctuary of his untroubled soul. He gains instead the

A TOM O' BEDLAM.

Christian equivalent of that ancient pagan virtue love. It is unselfish Christian love that redeems Lea and prepares him, not for a Stoic nirvana, but for Christian heaven.

After he has lost the protection of his royal trappings that have always insulated him from direc contact with experience, he is forced to face realit as a plain "unaccommodated man"—one unprovide with any of the gifts of civilization. Only thus ca he discuss life's essence. Therefore, at the end of th first act, the plot becomes Lear's mad search for th spiritual truth that will enable him to surmount th blows of circumstance and to establish sanity an peace in his disordered nature.

The congruity which he recognizes between hi passion and the fury of the storm only aggravate the tumult in his breast. Yet, as he is about to see shelter from the tempest in a hovel, his mind clear for an instant and he feels a flash of social sympathy He pities poverty-stricken wretches whose "house-less heads" and "unfed sides" find no shelter fro pitiless storms like the one whose rain now pelts hin This impulse to pity, A. C. Bradley believes, is th first sign of Lear's redemption. But Shakespeare doe not permit him to find his answer in this train c thought. For his moment of control is at once shattered by the appearance of Edgar, whose feigne insanity drives Lear back into madness for good, an sets him again on the road of his frantic quest.

His first experiment is to tear off his clothes. Thi

; an important station in his search. He will dis-over what a naked man is worth when he faces the aked forces of Nature. The answer he receives is egative. Nature, he discovers, is no fostering nother, sustaining her errant child, but an enemy hose wind now lashes him, whose rain now pours orrents of water on his bare head, and whose orked lightning strikes him with terror. His quest annot come to rest in the bosom of Nature. Even 'om o' Bedlam remarks Lear's futility in seeking an nswer in Nature. Lear asks him, "What is your udy?" And Edgar answers, "How to prevent the end, and to kill vermin." Joseph Wood Krutch in-erprets this apparently meaningless remark to mean how to achieve both peace of mind and peace of ody." Both of these blessings Lear is obviously nable to secure in this cataclysm of the heavens. Iowever, the poet does not allow Lear to rest his ase in a gloomy denial of significance. He finds the nal answer for which he has been wildly searching Cordelia's devotion, a symbol of the love free to l men, even to those languishing in some form of nprisonment of mind and spirit. If this is the mean-g the author wished to convey to his listeners, how an we avoid interpreting what happens after the y of his moment of blessedness with Cordelia as essimism? The answer of those who insist that ear's sufferings are a purgation, a way to salvation, that to have Cordelia's life spared would have egated the diffused tragic temper of the work, and ade one of the greatest of tragedies of trivial gnificance. Worse still, it would have obscured its hristian revelation.

The two completely different interpretations of *ing Lear* outlined here present extremes of pessimism nd optimism among the commentators. Between ese explanations there are many others. Some of em lose the compulsive meaning in a scrutiny of e characters, some advance theories which apply onvincingly to only one or two of its aspects. None f them worthy of attention detract from the vast randeur of the stage upon which the action takes lace or from the universal significance of the pas-ons that plumb its depths.—O.J.C.

Stage History: England. The tragedy was probably resented at the Globe theatre in 1605, and on the tle page of the First Quarto reference is made to a ourt performance on December 26, 1606. Another rly mention of *King Lear* on the stage occurs in 609/10 when Sir Richard Cholmeley's company resented the play at Gowthwaite Hall in York-ire at Candlemas. (See CHOLMELEY'S MEN). John ownes includes *King Lear* in the list of stock ays acted by the Duke's Company from 1662 to 665 at Lincoln's Inn Fields; Thomas Betterton, in e title role, probably used a text relatively faithful the original. But Pepys makes no mention of the ay, and apparently the tragedy failed to compete ccessfully with many of the other Shakespeare ramas until, in 1681, Nahum Tate's mutilation was own at Dorset Garden. In his dedication Tate an-ounced that he had found in *King Lear* "a Heap Jewels unstrung and unpolish'd; yet so dazzling their disorder that I soon perceiv'd I had seized Treasure."

Tate's polishing resulted in three striking altera-ons:

1. By making Edgar and Cordelia lovers he provided Restoration audiences with the heroic love that they demanded in all their serious dramas. This change involved the elimination of the King of France, which in turn made it necessary that Cordelia be kept in England, where she was set to wandering on the heath with a confidante of Tate's invention called Arante. 2. Tate removed the Fool as being too low a figure for tragedy, and not until 1838 did this interesting character return to the stage. 3. Finally, Tate gave the play a happy ending, restoring Lear to his throne and permitting Cordelia to marry Edgar—though not before she has uttered some lines of Tate's invention in which she invokes revenge on her wicked sisters.

Although Tate writes that he was "wracked with no small fear for so bold a change," he need not have had any misgivings. This mangled thing, the more despicable for Tate's own verses which he had interpolated, held the stage for a century and a half, during which time Shakespeare's play was never once performed. Even Garrick's *Lear*, played in 1756 with "restorations from Shakespeare," retained all of Tate's changes in plot. About all that Garrick did was to substitute a good deal of the original poetry, particularly in the first three acts, for some of Tate's mutilations. Garrick's adaptation was performed at Drury Lane to 1788.

Tate's version continued to hold the Covent Garden stage throughout the century, except for six years from 1768 to 1773, during which time it was replaced by the version of George Colman the elder. This alteration left Shakespeare's first four acts virtually unchanged, except for the omission of the Fool, and eliminated the invented love story of Cordelia and Edgar. Although the happy ending remained, audiences preferred Tate's *Lear* and Colman's adaptation failed. When John Philip Kemble presented the tragedy in 1792, he revised Tate's alteration, making only a few relatively unimportant restorations such as Edmund's pretense that Edgar has wounded him (II, i) and his wish to rescue Lear and Cordelia (V, iii).

In 1820 Robert W. Elliston, then acting manager of Drury Lane, in a version closely resembling Kemble's, made two major restorations to the text. He used Shakespeare's language in the opening of the scene of Lear's ravings on the heath, and then in the scene of recognition. Edmund Kean made his first London appearance in the title role of this production on February 10, 1823. Three years later, on February 10, 1826, Elliston and Kean joined to make the first truly significant contribution to the restoration of the original play—its tragic ending. However, the love story was still preserved and the Fool still omitted until William Macready, somewhat apprehensively, eliminated the former and introduced the latter.

Macready's production on January 25, 1838 at Covent Garden brought the genuine *King Lear*, with some considerable cuts and some scene rearrangement, to the stage for the first time in more than 150 years. It succeeded in finally burying Tate's mutilation. Lear's curse was put at the end of Act I for greater theatrical effect, the details of Gloucester's blinding omitted, and his "jumping off the cliff" prevented by Lear's somewhat contrived entrance. During rehearsals Macready thought that he would have to abandon the introduction of the Fool, until it was suggested that a female play the role. Priscilla Horton, the illogical choice, won some approval for a "pleasing performance, giving evidence of deep feeling." Contemporary critics, however, generally felt that her "poor fool and knave" was not quite Shakespeare's. Macready himself played Lear, and Helen Faucit was Cordelia in a carefully executed production that was especially effective during the storm scene.

On November 5, 1845 Samuel Phelps, with no sacrifices to the presumed tastes of the public, staged *King Lear* at Sadler's Wells in an almost complete version. Only a few omissions were made, while the order of the scenes faithfully followed Shakespeare, and the Fool was assigned to a man. Charles Kean generally followed Macready's version when he produced and starred in the tragedy at the Princess Theatre on April 17, 1858, in a splendid setting which reproduced scenes and costumes of the 8th century. During this period, Fanny Stirling often appeared as Cordelia and was seen opposite both Edwin Forrest and Macready at the Princess in 1845. Fanny Kemble took the part opposite Macready in 1848, and Miss Cooper was the heroine in Phelps' first revival. Kean's Cordelia in 1858 was Kate Terry, and Edwin Booth, in one of his more successful ventures at the Princess during the 1880/1 season, played King Lear on February 14.

Henry Irving revived the tragedy in 1892, reducing the original 26 scenes to 16. He staged the play with its expected splendor, and Irving's Lear had tawny-gray hair and beard and rich, flowing robes. Although Lear's presence should have been one of regal authority, there is no evidence that Irving's performance was anything but ordinary; Ellen Terry, however, was a beautifully moving Cordelia. The production opened on November 10 and ran until February 6.

After Irving's effort, *King Lear,* widely considered unplayable, became a rarity in the West End. Even Frank Benson, the reliable producer of the entire approved Shakespeare repertory, offered only occasional productions of the tragedy. Before these, there had been two presentations at Stratford-upon-Avon, one in 1883 by Elliot Galer's company, and another under Osmond Tearle in 1890. Benson, a beardless Lear, gave the play at the Memorial Theatre during three seasons: 1902, 1904, and 1906. After 17 years, Herbert Trench, new manager of the Haymarket Theatre, chanced a West End production in September 1909. However, his Lear, Norman McKinnel, never did well with the part. Although the Haymarket company was invited to perform for Beerbohm Tree's 6th annual Shakespeare Festival at His Majesty's Theatre in 1910, the play was afterward consigned to another term in oblivion.

Ben Greet resurrected *King Lear* during his 4th season at the Old Vic (1917/8) with Russell Thorndike as Lear and his sister Sybil as the Fool. In his first season as director of the Vic (1920/1), Robert Atkins took the title role opposite Mary Sumner, with Rupert Harvey as Edmund and Florence Saunders as Goneril; for his second production during 1921/2, Atkins relinquished his role to Thorndike. Two minor presentations followed: one b Henry Baynton, with matinee performances at th Savoy Theatre between provincial tours in earl 1922; and another by the Phoenix Society at th Regent Theatre, with Hubert Carter in the title rol and Gwen Ffrangcon-Davies as Cordelia (Marc 1924).

Shortly afterward W. Bridges-Adams presente the tragedy at Stratford, the first *Lear* at the Memo rial Theatre in 18 years, starring Arthur Phillip However, the succession of impressive portraits o the old King began only with Ernest Milton's pow erful performance at the Old Vic in 1928, wit Jean Forbes-Robertson a lovely Cordelia. Joh Gielgud's initial appearance in the role came in 193 at the Vic under Harcourt Williams' direction; was admirably supported by Ralph Richardson' constant Kent and Dorothy Green's searing Goneri A sense of impending disaster was communicated a Gielgud strode to the high throne at the first en trance; but, for the most part, the portrayal offere just a glimpse of the stunning performance nin years away.

Meanwhile, Randle Ayrton and William Devli intervened to disprove the critical verdict that th tragedy was a "poor stage play." In 1931 Ayrton proud, authoritative, testy, maddened, and patheti old King, "a Lear of strange passions and familia things," fully commanded the Memorial Theat stage. Bridges-Adams, the director, designed th setting, which centered on a massive arcade of roug stone behind an inner proscenium. The productio toured America that winter and returned to Strat ford for another engagement the following sprin Stratford enjoyed another success with the traged when Ayrton again played the title role in Theodor Komisarjevsky's memorable *Lear* in 1936. The cas rehearsed only briefly, gave exceptional perform ances, with Barbara Crouper as Goneril and Donal Wolfit as Kent. This production was repeated a Stratford the following year.

At 22, Devlin astonished audiences with an excit ing performance at the Westminster Theatre in 193 His Lear, directed by Hugh Hunt, was a massiv powerful figure, aided by the evil Goneril of Doro thy Green. Devlin repeated his impressive por trayal for Henry Cass at the Old Vic two year later. At that time Vivienne Bennett's Cordelia, les meek than others, gratified those who looked for th strength that was her paternal inheritance. Io Swinley was a quietly loyal Kent, and Dorice For dred and Catherine Lacey were most corrosive a Goneril and Regan. In the mid-40's, Devlin playe Lear for the Bristol Old Vic; later, in 1950 an 1951, he impressed audiences at the Brattle Theat in Cambridge, Massachusetts, in the same role.

Harley Granville-Barker's "Preface" to *King Lea* provided the basis for Lewis Casson's 1940 produc tion at the Old Vic. It starred Gielgud and feature the director of the 1931 *Lear,* Harcourt Williams, i the role of Albany. Granville-Barker, in addition t giving personal advice, supervised 10 grueling re hearsals, in which the emphasis was placed on in telligent understanding of, and emotional identifica tion with, the character. Gielgud's controlled po trait of the arrogant King on his tortured pilgrima never lost strength.

Periodically, from 1943 to 1953, London saw Donald Wolfit's great performance as the intractable atriarch who was destroyed. Perhaps more than nyone before, Wolfit demonstrated that the tragedy ould be good theatre. Cordelia in each of these resentations was played by Rosalind Iden. Abraham ofaer, Stratford's Lear in 1943, seemed a character r too sensible to have relinquished his throne. At oments, however, he could be extremely convincing, but never more believable than his Kent, aliol Holloway. Laurence Olivier directed and cted in the title role for an Old Vic *King Lear* at e New Theatre in 1946. His stunning performance rove further into oblivion the acceptability of harles Lamb's pronouncement that Lear could not e acted. The most significant impersonation of that roduction, however, was Alec Guinness' Fool.

In 1950 John Gielgud codirected a Stratford production of the tragedy with Anthony Quayle portraying the King, while Peggy Ashcroft played Cordelia; Gwen Ffrangcon-Davies, Goneril; Harry Anrews, Edgar; and Andrew Cruickshank, Kent. ugh Hunt directed still another Old Vic *King Lear* uring the 1951/2 season which starred Stephen lurray. In 1953 Michael Redgrave played Lear for e first time at Stratford under George Devine, ith Harry Andrews as Kent and Yvonne Mitchell Cordelia. Devine's next production of the tragedy ith a Stratford company appeared at the Palace heatre in 1955. It was, according to its star, John ielgud, "little short of disastrous." The exotic production, designed by Isamu Noguchi, was Oriental decor and conceived with the intention of suggesting "the cosmic timelessness of Shakespeare's reatest tragedy." The audience reacted with "horfied expressions of dismay."

In 1958 Douglas Seale directed Paul Rogers as ear in the last Old Vic production of the tragedy ith a cast that included Paul Daneman (Fool), erek Godfrey (Edgar), John Humphry (Edund), Coral Browne (Goneril), and Rosemary Vebster (Cordelia). The following year Glen Byam haw staged the drama at Stratford, starring Charles aughton, who was supported by Angela Baddeley Regan, Cyril Luckham as Gloucester, Stephanie idmead as Goneril, Zoe Caldwell as Cordelia, Alert Finney as Edgar, Ian Holm as the Fool, and nthony Nicholls as Kent.

An existentialist interpretation of Lear's character, ased on the theories of Jan Kott, was represented y Paul Scofield in a revival at Stratford in 1962. Dicted by Peter Brook, the production was staged at e Aldwych Theatre during December of that year d was transported to New York in 1964.

Stage History: America. Malone was the first Lear America, acting in the tragedy on January 14, 754 at the Nassau Street Theatre in New York. Jahum Tate's version replaced Shakespeare's text in l the early productions in this country, which did ot see the original until Charles Macready presented it at the Park Theatre in New York on Sepmber 27, 1844. The cast of the first *King Lear* cluded Lewis Hallam, Sr., as Kent and Mrs. Hallam Cordelia. In 1759 David Douglass presented the rama in Philadelphia, with the former Mrs. Hallam, ow Mrs. Douglass, again as Cordelia. Lewis Hallam e younger first played Lear at the Southwark Theatre in Philadelphia in January 1767, then repeated the role at the John Street Theatre in New York in 1795, when his wife played Cordelia, and in 1798. On the latter occasion, a time when opposition to the stage inspired managers to disguise plays as "moral lectures," *King Lear* was billed as *The Crime of Filial Ingratitude.*

Several of the major tragedians active in the theatre during the early 19th century essayed the role of Lear, but apparently none made much impression in the part. Thomas Abthorpe Cooper's performance at the Park in 1824 created adverse reactions; James Fennell's in 1810 was generally ignored; and the usually fine George Frederick Cooke, who first acted the part in Liverpool in 1792, again in London in 1802, and in New York in 1811, was not good as Lear. Neither was Junius Brutus Booth when he appeared in Richmond, Virginia, during the summer of 1821. Even Edmund Kean's interpretation, which he brought to the Anthony Street Theatre in December 1820 and to the Boston Theatre the following February, was only occasionally effective.

The first actor on the American stage to distinguish himself with a portrayal of Lear was Edwin Forrest. He took the part on December 27, 1826, when he was only 20 years old, at the Bowery Theatre in New York, using David Garrick's emendation of Tate's version. He developed the role throughout his career, achieving a powerful representation that made relatively little use of tricks of stage business. Forrest continued as the supreme interpreter of Lear for more than four decades.

Augustus A. Addams in 1848 and James W. Wallack II in 1852 acted in condensations from Shakespeare's text. John Vandenhoff portrayed the character in 1837, Charles Walter Couldeck in 1849, Edward L. Davenport a year later, and James Stark in 1852. Others overshadowed by Forrest included James R. Anderson and James R. Scott in 1854, Joseph Proctor (1864), George Boniface (1865), and Charles Dillon (1867).

Edwin Booth adopted the role early in his career, using Tate's version, but discarded the part for several years in order to prepare for a revival of the original. This he presented first at McVicker's Theatre in Chicago in 1870 and again in New York at the Fifth Avenue on November 16, 1875. Though he was always an uneven actor, Booth's Lear ranks with his Hamlet, Othello, and Iago as a profoundly impressive interpretation possessing all the grandeur and authority of the patriarch in a highly intellectual portrayal which beautifully communicated the awakened humanity of the spirit suffering affliction.

Another effective Lear soon followed. John E. McCullough, having acted the role in San Francisco in 1873, appeared in the part for the first time in New York at Booth's Theatre on April 23, 1877. He presumably fashioned his early performances after Forrest, but, according to John Ranken Towse, McCullough "could assume a lofty dignity, in which Forrest was lacking, and had a notable mastery of virile pathos." His characterization of Lear embodied this natural majesty with a pitiable anguish; this was especially affecting during the mad scene, where he never completely forgot that he had once been king.

Lawrence Barrett acted in his own version of the tragedy which followed closely the original text. Barrett's Lear emphasized the quality of fatherly love and in his madness lost completely his former grandeur. William Winter characterized his ruin as typifying "a broken medallion rather than a fallen statue."

In the early part of the present century there was only one major portrayer of King Lear in America, Robert Mantell. He first acted in the tragedy at the Garden Theatre on November 27, 1905 and appeared in subsequent revivals in repertory throughout the first two decades of the 1900's. In the early scenes, Mantell carefully illuminated the varied facets of the character, revealing an authoritative, egotistical, and explosive king drifting into senility. Mantell's performance reached special poignance in the beautifully expressed desolation and abject realization of his decline during the lucid interval where he recognizes Cordelia.

During March 1923, Reginald Pole produced and starred in the tragedy for a special matinee season at the Earl Carroll Theatre. The setting was Elizabethan, the performances by Pole, Genevieve Tobin as Cordelia, and Lawrence Tibbett as Edgar were thoroughly inadequate, and the Fool, acted by a woman, completely unintelligible. Fritz Leiber, the Edgar of Mantell's 1918 presentation, acted Lear at the Civic Center in Chicago during the 1929/30 season, bringing his production to New York's Shubert on April 1, 1930 and to the Ambassador the following December. His impersonation, while done with conviction, lacked proper development, and Lear was not "every inch a king." In 1940 the German director Edwin Piscator, engaged by the Studio Theatre of the Dramatic Workshop of the New School for Social Research, presented for his first dramatic endeavor in America an experimental production in a setting of elevated stages on a revolving table. Sam Jaffe, though earnestly emotional in the role of Lear, could communicate little more than petulance and none of the tragic grandeur of the king. Louis Calhern, assuming the part in 1940 at the National Theatre under John Houseman's direction, presented a physically impressive Lear and a towering portrayal well received by most critics. However, a dissenting opinion was offered by George Jean Nathan, who observed that Calhern "doesn't seem to know whether he is Lear or Lahr." Supporting performances were commendable: Martin Gabel very capable as Kent; Nehemiah Persoff as Cornwall; Arnold Moss a resolute Gloucester; Edith Atwater a steadfastly evil Goneril, and Norman Lloyd a gently poignant Fool. Jo Van Fleet and Nina Foch acted with skill as Regan and Cordelia, but the production could not be extended beyond 48 nights and closed at a loss of $100,000. In 1956 another financially disastrous *Lear*, directed by and starring Orson Welles, lasted for only 27 performances at the New York City Center. Dogged by misfortune from the first, Welles had to play the role from a wheel chair.

Interest in the tragedy has grown in the last few years with productions of *King Lear* appearing more regularly than at any previous time in the United States. In 1959 the Players Theatre Company (formerly the Shakespearwrights) presented the drama as staged by Philip Lawrence, with Sidney Walke in the title role. The good intentions of this hones effort were evident, but with a few more rehearsal some of the early monotony of Walker's Lear migh have been relieved and the shouting reduced.

The New York Shakespeare Festival under Josep Papp brought *King Lear* to Central Park in Augus 1962, but, except for capturing the essence of th tragedy in the final scene, Frank Silvera's portra was devoid of kingly qualities. Throughout, how ever, flashes of brilliance illuminated several cha acterizations.

The finest interpretation of Lear by an America in this century was by Morris Carnovsky in 196 acting at the American Shakespeare Festival Theatr in Stratford, Connecticut, under Allen Fletcher's di rection. From the outset Carnovsky established th King as an old man no longer in full possession c his faculties, but never losing his regal magnificenc His finest moments were during the recognitio scene where, with almost inexpressible beauty, h evinced a touching humanity and later, with h "dear fool" dead in his arms. Nervous and cringin beside this massive Lear, Lester Rawlins, his Foo personified a true madman in whose hands the trut became frightening. Philip Bosco excellently po trayed a forthright Kent, and Gloucester achieve great pathos in a low-keyed performance by Patric Hines while Douglas Watson's Edmund was an el quent villain. The playing time of a very full te was three and a half hours. When, after touring wit the production, Carnovsky returned for another e gagement at Stratford in 1965, his performance ha grown both in humanity and tragic stature.—M. C

Bibliography. TEXT: *King Lear*, G. I. Duthie, ed 1949; *King Lear*, New Arden Edition, Kenneth Mui ed., 1952; *King Lear*, New Cambridge Edition, G. Duthie and J. Dover Wilson, eds., 1960; Madelai Doran, *The Text of King Lear*, 1931; Leo Kirsc baum, *The True Text of King Lear*, 1945; Alic Walker, *Textual Problems of the First Folio*, 1953; S. Cairncross, "The Quartos and the Folio Text *King Lear*," *Review of English Studies*, Vol. V 1955; Madelaine Doran, "King Lear" (Review of t New Cambridge Edition), *Shakespeare Quarterl* XII, 1961. DATE: New Cambridge Edition. SOURCE New Arden Edition; Wilfred Perrett, *The Story King Lear from Geoffrey of Monmouth to Shak speare*, 1904; Kenneth Muir, *Shakespeare's Source* Vol. I, 1957. COMMENT: A. C. Bradley, *Shakespea ean Tragedy: Lectures on Hamlet, Othello, Ki Lear, Macbeth*, 1904; Lily B. Campbell, *Shakespeare Tragic Heroes, Slaves of Passion*, 1930; E. E. Sto *Art and Artifice in Shakespeare: A Study in Co trast and Illusion*, 1933; Theodore Spencer, *Shak speare and the Nature of Man*, 1942; G. F. Kernodl "The Symphonic Form of *King Lear*," *Elizabetha Studies in Honor of George F. Reynolds*, 1945; Ha ley Granville-Barker, *Prefaces to Shakespeare*, 192 1947; Oscar James Campbell, "The Salvation Lear," *English Literary History*, Vol. XV, 194 H. B. Charlton, *Shakespearian Tragedy*, 1948; R. Heilman, *This Great State: Image and Structure King Lear*, 1948; Wolfgang H. Clemen, *The Deve opment of Shakespeare's Imagery*, 1951; D. James, *A Dream of Learning: An Essay on the A vancement of Learning, Hamlet and King Lear*, 195

. Sewall, *The Vision of Tragedy*, 1959; Josephine W. Bennett, "The Storm Within: The Madness of Lear," *Shakespeare Quarterly*, XIII, 1962. STAGE HISTORY: New Cambridge Edition; T. Alston Brown, *A History of the New York Stage . . . to 1901*, 1903; William Winter, *Shakespeare on the Stage*, 3 vols., 1911–1916; G. C. D. Odell, *Shakespeare from Betterton to Irving*, 1920; J. C. Trewin, *Shakespeare on the English Stage, 1900–1964*, 1964.

Selected Criticism

SAMUEL JOHNSON. The Tragedy of *Lear* is deservedly celebrated among the dramas of *Shakespeare*. There is perhaps no play which keeps the attention so strongly fixed; which so much agitates our passions and interests our curiosity. The artful involutions of distinct interests, the striking opposition of contrary characters, the sudden changes of fortune, and the quick succession of events, fill the mind with a perpetual tumult of indignation, pity, and hope. There is no scene which does not contribute to the aggravation of the distress or conduct of the action, and scarce a line which does not conduce to the progress of the scene. So powerful is the current of the poet's imagination, that the mind, which once ventures within it, is hurried irresistibly along . . . .

The injury done by *Edmund* to the simplicity of the action is abundantly recompensed by the addition of variety, by the art with which he is made to co-operate with the chief design, and the opportunity which he gives the poet of combining perfidy with perfidy, and connecting the wicked son with the wicked daughters, to impress this important moral, that villany is never at a stop, that crimes lead to crimes, and at last terminate in ruin.

But though this moral be incidentally enforced, *Shakespeare* has suffered the virtue of *Cordelia* to perish in a just cause, contrary to the natural ideas of justice, to the hope of the reader, and, what is yet more strange, to the faith of chronicles. Yet this conduct is justified by the Spectator, who blames *Tate* for giving *Cordelia* success and happiness in his alteration, and declares, that, in his opinion, *the tragedy has lost half its beauty*. *Dennis* has remarked, whether justly or not, that, to secure the favourable reception of *Cato*, *the town was poisoned with much false and abominable criticism*, and that endeavours had been used to discredit and decry poetical justice. A play in which the wicked prosper, and the virtuous miscarry, may doubtless be good, because it is a just representation of the common events of human life: but since all reasonable beings naturally love justice, I cannot easily be persuaded, that the observation of justice makes a play worse; or, that if other excellencies are equal, the audience will not always rise better pleased from the final triumph of persecuted virtue.

In the present case the publick has decided. *Cordelia*, from the time of *Tate*, has always retired with victory and felicity. And, if my sensations could add any thing to the general suffrage, I might relate, that I was many years ago shocked by *Cordelia's* death, that I know not whether I ever endured to read again the last scenes of the play till I undertook to revise them as an editor. [*The Plays of William Shakespeare*, 1765.]

CHARLES LAMB. So to see Lear acted,—to see an old man tottering about the stage with a walking-stick, turned out of doors by his daughters in a rainy night, has nothing in it but what is painful and disgusting. We want to take him into shelter and relieve him. That is all the feeling which the acting of Lear ever produced in me. But the Lear of Shakespeare cannot be acted. The contemptible machinery by which they mimic the storm which he goes out in, is not more inadequate to represent the horrors of the real elements, than any actor can be to represent Lear: they might more easily propose to personate the Satan of Milton upon a stage, or one of Michael Angelo's terrible figures. The greatness of Lear is not in corporal dimension, but in intellectual: the explosions of his passion are terrible as a volcano: they are storms turning up and disclosing to the bottom that sea, his mind, with all its vast riches. It is his mind which is laid bare. This case of flesh and blood seems too insignificant to be thought on; even as he himself neglects it. On the stage we see nothing but corporal infirmities and weakness, the impotence of rage; while we read it, we see not Lear, but we are Lear,—we are in his mind, we are sustained by a grandeur which baffles the malice of daughters and storms; in the aberrations of his reason, we discover a mighty irregular power of reasoning, immethodized from the ordinary purposes of life, but exerting its powers, as the wind blows where it listeth, at will upon the corruptions and abuses of mankind. What have looks, or tones, to do with that sublime identification of his age with that of the *heavens themselves*, when in his reproaches to them for conniving at the injustice of his children, he reminds them that 'they themselves are old.' What gesture shall we appropriate to this? What has the voice or the eye to do with such things? But the play is beyond all art, as the tamperings with it shew: it is too hard and stony; it must have love-scenes, and a happy ending. It is not enough that Cordelia is a daughter, she must shine as a lover too. Tate has put his hook in the nostrils of this Leviathan, for Garrick and his followers, the showmen of the scene, to draw the mighty beast about more easily. A happy ending!—as if the living martyrdom that Lear had gone through,—the flaying of his feelings alive, did not make a fair dismissal from the stage of life the only decorous thing for him. If he is to live and be happy after, if he could sustain this world's burden after, why all this pudder and preparation,—why torment us with all this unnecessary sympathy? As if the childish pleasure of getting his gilt robes and sceptre again could tempt him to act over again his misused station,—as if at his years, and with his experience, any thing was left but to die. [*The Reflector*, 1811; reprinted in *Lamb's Criticism*, G. M. W. Tillyard, ed., 1923.]

SAMUEL TAYLOR COLERIDGE. . . . in this tragedy the story or fable constrained Shakespeare to introduce wickedness in an outrageous form, in Regan and Goneril. He had read nature too heedfully not to know that courage, intellect, and strength of character were the most impressive forms of power, and that to power in itself, without reference to any moral end, an inevitable admiration and complacency appertains, whether it be displayed in the conquests of a Napoleon or Tamerlane, or in the foam and thunder of a cataract. But in the display of such a character it was of the highest importance to prevent the guilt from passing into utter monstrosity—which again depends on the presence or absence of causes and temptations sufficient to *account* for the wickedness, without the necessity of recurring to a thorough fiendishness of nature for its origination. For such are the appointed relations of intellectual power to truth, and of truth to goodness, that it becomes both morally and poetic[ally] unsafe to present what is admirable—what our nature compels us to admire—in the mind, and what is most detestable in the heart, as co-existing in the same individual without any apparent connection, or any modification of the one by the other. [*Shakespearean Criticism* by S. T. Coleridge, T. M. Raysor, ed., Everyman Library Edition, 1960.]

LEO TOLSTOY. [After describing the plot of *King Lear.*] Such is this celebrated drama. However absurd it may appear in my rendering (which I have endeavored to make as impartial as possible), I may confidently say that in the original it is yet more absurd. For any man of our time—if he were not under the hypnotic suggestion that this drama is the height of perfection—it would be enough to read it to its end (had he sufficient patience for this) to be convinced that far from its being the height of perfection, it is a very bad, carelessly composed production, which, if it could have been of interest to a certain public at a certain time, cannot evoke amongst us anything but aversion and weariness. Every reader of our time who is free from the influence of suggestion will also receive exactly the same impression from all the other extolled dramas of Shakespeare, not to mention the senseless dramatized tales, *Pericles, Twelfth Night, The Tempest, Cymbeline, Troilus and Cressida* . . . .

Dramatic art, according to the laws established by those very critics who extol Shakespeare, demands that the persons represented in the play should be, in consequence of actions proper to their characters, and owing to a natural course of events, placed in positions requiring them to struggle with the surrounding world to which they find themselves in opposition—and in this struggle should display their inherent qualities.

In *King Lear*, the persons represented are indeed placed externally in opposition to the outward world, and they struggle with it. But their strife does not flow from the natural course of events nor from their own characters, but is quite arbitrarily established by the author, and therefore cannot produce on the reader that illusion which represents the essential condition of art. [*Tolstoy on Shakespeare*, 1907; trans. V. Tchertkoff.]

G. WILSON KNIGHT. It may appear strange to search for any sort of comedy as a primary theme in a play whose abiding gloom is so heavy, whose reading of human destiny and human actions so starkly tragic. Yet it is an error of aesthetic judgement to regard humour as essentially trivial. . . . A shifting flash of comedy across the pain of the purely tragic both increases the tension and suggests, vaguely, a resolution and a purification. The comic and the tragic rest both on the idea of incompatibilities, and are also, themselves, mutually exclusive; therefore to mingle them is to add to the meaning of each; for the result is then but a new sublime incongruity.

King Lear is roughly analogous to Chekhov where *Macbeth* is analogous to Dostoevsky. The wonder of Shakespearian tragedy is ever a mystery—a vague yet powerful, tangible, presence; an interlocking of the mind with a profound meaning, a disclosure to the inward eye of vistas undreamed, and but fitfully understood. *King Lear* is great in the abundance and richness of human delineation, in the level focus of creation that builds a massive oneness, in fact, a universe, of single quality from a multiplicity of differentiated units; and in a positive and purposeful working out of a purgatorial philosophy . . . .

His purgatory is to be a purgatory of the mind, of madness. Lear has trained himself to think he cannot be wrong; he finds he is wrong. He has fed his heart on sentimental knowledge of his children's love: he finds their love is not sentimental. There is now a gaping dualism in his mind, thus drawn asunder by incongruities, and he endures madness. Thus the theme of the play is bodied continually into a fantastic incongruity, which is implicit in the beginning.

The core of the play is an absurdity, an indignity, an incongruity. In no tragedy of Shakespeare does incident and dialogue so recklessly and miraculously walk the tight-rope of our pity over the depths of bathos and absurdity . . . .

Sometimes we know that all human pain holds beauty, that no tear falls but it dews some flower we cannot see. Perhaps humour, too, is inwoven in the universal pain, and the enigmatic silence holds not only an unutterable sympathy, but also the ripples of an impossible laughter whose flight is not for the wing of human understanding; and perhaps it is this that casts its darting shadow of the grotesque across the furrowed pages of *King Lear*. ["*King Lear* and the Comedy of the Grotesque" from *The Wheel of Fire*, 1930.]

GEORGE ORWELL. [Tolstoy's] examination of *King Lear* is not "impartial," as he twice claims. On the contrary, it is a prolonged exercise in misrepresentation . . . .

If only, Tolstoy says in effect, we would stop breeding, fighting, struggling and enjoying, if we could get rid not only of our sins but of everything else that binds us to the surface of the earth—including love, then the whole painful process would be over and the Kingdom of Heaven would arrive. But a normal human being does not want the Kingdom of Heaven: he wants life on earth to continue. This is not solely because he is "weak," "sinful" and anxious for a "good time." Most people get a fair amount of fun out of their lives, but on balance life is suffering, and only the very young or the very foolish imagine otherwise. Ultimately it is the Christian attitude which is self-interested and hedonistic, since the aim is always to get away from the painful struggle of earthly life and find eternal peace in some kind of Heaven or Nirvana. The humanist attitude is that the struggle must continue and that death is the price of life. "Men must endure Their going hence, even as their coming hither: Ripeness is all"—which is an un-Christian sentiment. Often there is a seeming truce between the humanist and the religious believer, but in fact their attitudes cannot be reconciled: one must choose between this world and the next. And the enormous majority of human beings, if they understood the issue, would choose this world. They do make that choice when they continue working, breeding and dying instead of crippling their faculties in the hope of obtaining a new lease of existence elsewhere. ["Lear, Tolstoy, and the Fool" in *Shooting an Elephant And Other Essays,* 1945.]

HARLEY GRANVILLE-BARKER. Ought we . . . to assume —as Bradley seems to—that a play must necessarily make all its points and its full effect, point by point, clearly and completely, scene by scene, as the performance goes along? Not every play, I think. For the appreciation of such a work as *King Lear* one might even demand the second or third hearing of the whole, which the alertest critic would need to give to (say) a piece of music of like caliber. But leave that aside. No condoning of an ultimate obscurity is involved. And comedy, it can be admitted, demands an immediate clarity. Nor is the dramatist ever to be dispensed from making his story currently clear and at least provisionally significant. But he has so much more than that to do. He must produce a constant illusion of life. To do this he must, among other things, win us to something of a fellow-feeling with his characters; and even, at the play's critical moments, to identifying their emotions with our own.

Now the *significance* of their emotions may well not be clear to the characters themselves for the moment, their only certainty be of the intensity of the emotions themselves. There are devices enough by which, if the dramatist wishes, this significance can be kept currently clear to the audience. There is the Greek chorus; the earlier Elizabethans turned Prologue and Presenters to account; the *raisonneur* of nineteenth century comedy has a respectable ancestry. Shakespeare uses the *raisonneur* in varying guises. In this very play we detect him in the Fool, and in Edgar turned Poor Tom. But note that both they and their "reasoning" are blended not only into the action but into the moral scheme, and are never allowed to lower its emotional temperature by didactics—indeed they stimulate it. For here will be the difficulty in preserving that "dramatic clearness" which Bradley demands; it would cost—and repeatedly be costing—dramatist and actors their emotional, their illusionary, hold upon their audience. Lear's progress—dramatic and spiritual—lies through a dissipation of egoism; submission to the cruelty of an indifferent Nature, less cruel to him than are his own kin; to ultimate loss of himself in madness. Consider the effect of this—of the battling of storm without and storm within, of the final breaking of that Titan spirit—if Shakespeare merely let us look on, critically observant. From such a standpoint, Lear is an intolerable tyrant, and Regan and Goneril have a case against him. We should not side with them; but our onlooker's sympathy might hardly be warmer than, say, the kindly Albany's. And Shakespeare needs to give us more than sympathy with Lear, and something deeper than understanding. If the verity of his ordeal is really to be brought home to us, we must, in as full a sense as may be, pass through it with him, must make the experience and its overwhelming emotions momentarily our own. [*Prefaces to Shakespeare,* Vol. I, 1927.]

ARTHUR SEWELL. *King Lear* is the play in which Shakespeare returns once again to see man as a human soul, not in opposition to society, not rejecting society, but finding in society the sphere of fulfilment. Order is now seen, for the first time, and perhaps imperfectly, "not merely negative, but creative and liberating." It is a vision of society very different from that discovered in *Othello.* In *Othello* we cannot suppose that society is ever moral or good. Othello and Iago die, but future Othellos will find themselves betrayed in Venice, and future Iagos will still prey upon its profligates. In *King Lear* the conflict is no longer apprehended as a conflict between the individual and society; the conflict is now within society itself. Disorder in the human soul is both the agent and the product of disorder in society. Social order is the condition, as it is the resultant, of sweet and affirmative being, without which man relapses into a beastly and self-destructive individualism . . . .

Only through grace, perhaps, if at all, can man find blessedness; and Shakespearian tragedy is tragedy simply because in it Fallen Man seeks to find rehabilitation in "infiniteness"—but without grace. The tragedy is in the failure, and perhaps the failure is general to the case of Man. The tragic character (and in this there is no Senecan "cheering oneself up") will not resign himself to confinement in the secular world; but he has no certitude of status in a world more absolute. We cannot judge the tragic character in terms of our temporal moralities; neither can we schematize those mysteries of redemption which might at last exempt him from such judgments. He believes that he belongs to this world and he believes that he does not. He would jump the life to come—and yet he dare not. He comes to know that "the readiness is all," but that same ripeness, which releases him from the importunities of this world, discovers for him no other. Shakespearian tragedy is the product of the change in men's minds—the Renaissance change—by which men came to feel themselves separate from God; by which, indeed, the idea of God receded from men's habitual certitudes and became no more and often less than an intellectual construction, a merely credible hypothesis, a Being remote and not certainly just or beneficent, perhaps the Enemy. In a world where anarchism was of recent development and men had not yet resigned themselves to a disabling opportunism man's perennial hunger for metaphysical being prompted Shakespeare to create supreme drama out of the question, How shall man find the intersection between that which is in time and that which is out of time? Or, to put the matter simply, and I do not think too simply, What shall we do to be saved? ["Character and Society in *King Lear,*" *Character and Society in Shakespeare,* 1951.]

JOHN HOLLOWAY. . . . the king's end is like the end of the world: not the Day of Judgement, but the universal cataclysm which was to precede it . . . .

For the Elizabethans, the End of the World was a living conviction and even something of a current fear. . . . for Shakespeare's time collapse into universal chaos was not merely a permanent possibility in a fallen (though divinely created) Nature: it was a foreordained part of created Nature's route to salvation; and to envisage it, to dwell on it, to comprehend what it could be like, was part of what went to make up a comprehension of God's governance of the world . . . .

With these considerations in mind, one may incline to see the close of *Lear* in another light. . . . The ordeal has been unique in its protraction of torment, and the note is surely one of refusal to hide that from oneself, refusal to allow the terrible potentialities of life which the action has revealed to be concealed once more behind the veil of orthodoxy and the order of Nature. If there is such an order, it is an order which can accommodate seemingly limitless chaos and evil. The play is a confrontation of that, a refusal to avert one's gaze from that. Its affirmation is as exalted, humane and life-affirming as affirmation can be, for it lies in a noble and unflinching steadiness, where flinching seems inevitable, in the insight of its creator. ["King Lear," *The Story of the Night*, 1961.]

King Leir, The True Chronicle History of. An anonymous play, published in 1605, and the principal source of Shakespeare's *King Lear.* Although not published until 1605, *King Leir* was entered in the Stationers' Register as early as 1594. That same year Philip Henslowe also noted in his diary two performances of the play by the combined Queen Elizabeth's and Sussex' Men at the Rose theatre. The action of the play differs markedly from Shakespeare's, most notably in its happy ending. Its authorship has been the subject of considerable speculation, the leading candidates being George Peele, Thomas Lodge, and Robert Greene, with Peele generally considered the most likely author.

The play is also noteworthy as the object of one of the most celebrated iconoclastic statements in critical history: Tolstoy's declaration that it was superior to Shakespeare's play:

> . . . this old drama is incomparably and in every respect superior to Shakespeare's adaptation. It is so, firstly, because it has not got the utterly superfluous characters of the villain Edmund and the unlifelike Gloucester and Edgar, who only distract one's attention; secondly, because it has not got the completely false effects of Lear running about the heath, his conversations with the fool and all these impossible disguises, failures to recognize, and accumulated deaths; and above all, because in this drama there is the simple, natural, and deeply touching character of Leir and the yet more touching and clearly defined character of Cordella, both absent in Shakespeare. Therefore there is in the older drama—instead of Shakespeare's long drawn scene of Lear's interview with Cordelia and of Cordelia's unnecessary murder—the exquisite scene of the interview between Leir and Cordella, unequalled by any in all Shakespeare's dramas.

See King Lear: *Sources.* [*King Lear,* Arden Edition, Kenneth Muir, ed., 1952.]

King Richard III (1700). An adaptation of Shakespeare's *Richard III* by Colley Cibber. The most popular of all Shakespearean adaptations, Cibber's play is notable because, like Davenant in *The Law Against Lovers,* he borrows from several sources. Following the plot of *Richard III,* Cibber also incorporates scenes and speeches from *1 Henry VI, 3 Henry VI* (the scene of Henry's murder), *2 Henry IV* (the soliloquy on sleep), and *Henry V* (part of the "Once more into the breach" speech).

In Cibber's hands Richard becomes less completely a political figure. He woos Anne at least partly because of a real romantic attraction, and he later declares his passion for Elizabeth. On the other hand he is no less a monster for these changes; the greater part of the third act is given to a scene in which he coldly tells Anne that he has no further use or desire for her. The murder of the young princes is presented onstage, and in the final act the ghosts of Henry VI, the children, and Anne appear only to Richard. Clarence, Margaret, and Hastings do not appear in Cibber's play.

Cibber's use of Shakespeare's dialogue varies. Some speeches remain intact, some are drastically edited, some are rewritten. In the printed version of the play the direct quotations from Shakespeare are supposedly in italics, but Cibber falsely claims several of Shakespeare's passages as his own. With fewer characters and scenes than the original, Cibber's version is more easily played than Shakespeare's, but it is in no other way an improvement.

In 1700 Cibber's play was published and produced at the Drury Lane, with Cibber himself as Richard. It completely replaced the original, and bits and pieces continued to be played, even in "authentic" 20th-century productions. One of the most famous lines in the play, "Off with his head. So much for Buckingham," is Cibber's invention. [Hazelton Spencer, *Shakespeare Improved,* 1927.]

King's Company. A Restoration acting company under the patronage of Charles II formed by Thomas Killigrew in 1660. Killigrew took over a group of pre-civil war actors who had re-formed shortly before the Restoration and who were playing at the Red Bull theatre. The most prominent of the members of this company were Charles Hart, Michael Mohun, and John Lacy. When Killigrew and William Davenant of the Duke's Company received the royal patent for exclusive rights to perform plays in August 1660, Killigrew moved his players to Gibbons' Tennis Court. In 1662 Killigrew received a further charter from Charles II, designating his company as official members of the royal household and proclaiming his new theatre in Drury Lane, not completed until 1663, as the Theatre Royal (see Drury Lane Theatre).

Despite royal patronage, the company did not fare as well as its rival, the Duke's Company, and in 1682 the two companies merged under the leadership of Thomas Betterton of the Duke's Company. During its early years the King's Company was less interested in producing revivals of Shakespeare than of Jonson and Fletcher. It was Davenant's Duke's Company that tended to specialize in Shakespeare. The King's Shakespeare repertory was largely made up of adaptations despite the fact that the company, according to a list compiled by the lord chamberlain about 1669, had warrants to perform the following:

> *The Winters Tale, King John, Richard the Second, The Gentlemen of Verona, The Merry Wives of Windsor, The Comoedy of Errors, Loves Labour Lost, Midsomer Nights Dreame, The Merchant of Venice, As You like it, The Tameing of ye Shrew, Alls Well y^{t} ends well, Henry ye fourth, The Second part, Richard y^{e}*

Third, Coriolanus, Andronicus, Julius Caesar, The Moore of Venice, Anthony & Clopatra, and Cymbelyne.

Of its unadapted Shakespearean revivals the most successful were *Henry IV*, with Lacy as Falstaff; *Othello*, with Hart in the title role and Mohun as Iago; and *Julius Caesar*, with Hart as Brutus and Mohun as Cassius. [Hazelton Spencer, *Shakespeare Improved*, 1927.]

King's Men. See CHAMBERLAIN'S MEN.

King Stephen. A lost play ascribed to Shakespeare. It was entered in the Stationers' Register by Humphrey Moseley, a bookseller, on June 29, 1660 as "The History of King Stephen. by Will: Shakspeare."

Kirkman, Francis (fl. 1661–1674). Author and stationer. A lover of the theatre from his youth, Kirkman collected many plays which he used as the nucleus of a book store and lending library he established in 1661. In that year he also published his *Catalogue of all the Comedies, Tragedies . . . that were ever yet printed . . .*, all of which (609 plays) he offered for sale. The *Catalogue* was reprinted and expanded in 1671 to include 806 plays. It attributed 48 plays to Shakespeare, including such apocryphal items as *Thomas Lord Cromwell, Locrine, London Prodigal, Mucedorus, The Merry Devil of Edmonton, Puritan Widow, A Yorkshire Tragedy*, the two parts of *The Troublesome Raigne of King John, The Life and Death of Sir John Oldcastle*, and *Arraignment of Paris*. Kirkman assigned authorship of *The Birth of Merlin* to Shakespeare and William Rowley (in the following year he published that play as "Written by William Shakespear, and William Rowley"). Kirkman published *The Wits or Sport Upon Sport*, which included an extract from *A Midsummer Night's Dream* (see Robert COX; APOCRYPHA).

Kiss Me, Kate. See MUSIC BASED ON SHAKESPEARE: *20th century*.

Kittredge, George Lyman (1860–1941). American scholar. During his long career at Harvard (1888–1936), Kittredge acquired a reputation for being one of America's great teachers and scholars. To thousands of undergraduates he was the legendary "Kitty" whose course in Shakespeare was an arduous but rewarding experience. Kittredge's bibliography includes nearly 400 items of the greatest diversity: works on almanacs and witchcraft share company with the more traditional studies, but he is best known for his work on Chaucer, *Beowulf, Sir Gawain*, English and Scottish ballads, Malory and Shakespeare. Considering his reputation as a Shakespeare scholar, his publications in that area are not large. His *Shakespeare* (1916) was given as a lecture in which he described his critical method and set forth some interpretations. His edition of the *Complete Works* (1936) represents the textual studies of a lifetime; it lacks, however, the full annotation which appears in the *Sixteen Plays* (1946); several of the more popular plays included in the latter volume have been issued independently. Regret has been expressed that Kittredge never wrote a book on Shakespeare comparable to his *Chaucer and His Poetry* (1915), still one of the best general introductions to the subject. In lieu of such a work, attempts have been made to preserve some of his teachings. *New Lights on Romeo and Juliet* (1942) is the reconstructed text of a lecture which was given extemporaneously at a meeting of the Club of Odd Volumes on January 18, 1933. In a similar way, Kenneth Myrick has attempted to reconstruct Kittredge's thoughts on *Hamlet* by drawing upon his notes and recollections of the latter's classroom lectures, further amplified by the material included in the annotations of the play. [*The Kittredge Anniversary Papers*, 1913; *A Bibliography of the Writings of George Lyman Kittredge*, 1943; Clyde K. Hyder, *George Lyman Kittredge: Teacher and Scholar*, 1962; Kenneth Myrick, "Kittredge on *Hamlet*," in *Shakespeare 400*, James G. McManaway, ed., 1964.]

Knight, Charles (1791–1873). Author and publisher. The son of a bookseller and publisher, Knight devoted his life to the diffusion of popular knowledge through numerous books, periodicals, and serials. *The Penny Magazine* and *The Penny Cyclopaedia* were but two of the ventures by which he aided in the education of the Victorian working class. Among his several editions of Shakespeare, the Pictorial Edition (8 vols., 1839–1843) enjoyed a huge success thanks largely to its numerous illustrations. His *William Shakspere: A Biography* (1843) was designed to accompany this edition, and it likewise was profusely illustrated. Other editions were *The Library Shakspere* (12 vols., 1842–1844) and *The Stratford Shakspere* (6 vols., 1867). In *Studies in Shakspere* (2 vols., 1849) he gathered together for separate publication the notes to the *Pictorial* and *Library* editions. Although primarily a popularizer aiming for a mass audience, Knight showed some scholarly ability in his critical notes and was one of the founders of the first Shakespeare Society in 1840. [Charles Knight, *Passages of a Working Life During Half a Century*, 3 vols., 1864–1865.]

Knight, Edward (fl. 1624–1633). Book-keeper for the King's Men. In December 1624 Knight was listed with the "musitions and other necessary attendantes" by Sir Henry Herbert, the Master of the Revels, in a protection against arrest (see BOOK-KEEPER). Knight prepared the prompt-book of a play, *The Honest Man's Fortune*, licensed for acting on February 8, 1625, and in 1633 he was the recipient of a note from Herbert instructing him to "purge" from the actors' parts the passage which Herbert had censored in the prompt-book.

W. W. Greg suggests that Knight may have been the virtual editor of the First Folio, a volume on which a great deal of editorial work must have been expended. Heminges and Condell were, of course, the editors of the volume, but the task of rigorous supervision of the text is most likely to have fallen to someone like the book-keeper of the company. J. H. P. Pafford has strengthened Greg's suggestion by pointing out that the use of colons after a character's name, found, for example, in the Folio text of *The Winter's Tale*, was a distinctive characteristic of Knight's editing and an indication of his participation in the printing of the Folio. [W. W. Greg, *The Shakespeare First Folio*, 1955; *The Winter's Tale*, Arden Edition, J. H. P. Pafford, ed., 1963.]

Knight, G[eorge] Wilson (1897–). Critic, actor, and playwright. Formerly professor of English literature at the University of Leeds, Knight is the foremost expositor of symbolic interpretations of Shakespeare's plays. He has also directed and starred in a number of Shakespearean productions including *Timon of Athens*, *King Lear*, and *Othello*. His *Principles of Shakespearian Production* (1936, revised as *Shakespearian Production*, 1964) is a valuable discussion of the staging of the plays.

Knight's critical studies include *Myth and Miracle* (1929), *The Wheel of Fire* (1930), *The Imperial Theme* (1932), *The Shakespearian Tempest* (1932), *The Crown of Life* (1947), *The Mutual Flame* (1955), and *The Sovereign Flower* (1958). For a detailed account of Knight's work, see SYMBOLISM; IMAGERY; CRITICISM—20TH CENTURY.

Knight of the Burning Pestle, The (1607, pub. 1635). A comedy probably written entirely by Francis BEAUMONT, although published in 1635 as "by Francis Beaumont and John Fletcher." A burlesque of chivalric romance in the manner of Cervantes' *Don Quixote*, *The Knight of the Burning Pestle* is important for its incidental picture of an Elizabethan play audience.

At one point in the play a character is brought on to speak a "huffing part" and he delivers the following variation of Hotspur's famous speech (cf. *1 Henry IV*, I, iii, 201–205):

By heaven, me thinkes, it were an easie leape
To plucke bright honour from the pale-fac'd
    Moone,
Or dive into the bottome of the sea,
Where never fathome line touch't any ground,
And plucke up drowned honor from the lake of
    hell.

Another allusion in that play appears to be a reminiscence of the ghost of Banquo in *Macbeth:*

When thou art at the Table with thy friends,
Merry in heart, and fild with swelling wine,
Il'e come in midst of all thy pride and mirth,
Invisible to all men but thy selfe,
And whisper such a sad tale in thine eare,
Shall make thee let the Cuppe fall from thy
    hand.

Knights, L[ionel] C[harles] (1906–). Scholar and critic. Knights has written *Drama and Society in the Age of Jonson* (1937), *Shakespeare's Politics* (1957), *Some Shakespearean Themes* (1959), and *An Approach to Hamlet* (1960). His essay *How Many Children Had Lady Macbeth?* (1933) is an attack on the realistic character analysis found in such critics as A. C. Bradley (see CHARACTER CRITICISM). Knights suggests that this realistic approach obscures the unity of the play. He finds unity, not only in individual plays, but in Shakespeare's works as a whole. His *Some Shakespearean Themes* is "based on the belief that Shakespeare's plays form a coherent whole." According to this view, the great tragedies resolve "pressures and perplexities" discernible in the earlier plays. Questions such as the conflict between appearance and reality are raised in *Troilus and Cressida* and resolved in *King Lear*, a play which Knights considers "the great central masterpiece." This resolution contributes to the "assured judgment and the magnificent vitality" of *Macbeth*, *Antony and Cleopatra*, and *Coriolanus*. See CRITICISM—20T CENTURY.

Knights, Six. In *The Two Noble Kinsmen*, th knights accompanying Palamon and Arcite to the tournament, three to each man. Palamon's knigh have speaking parts in V, iv, where they are pr pared to follow him to the death.

Knight's Tale, The. See Geoffrey CHAUCER.

Knollys, Sir William (1547–1632). Comptroller o the royal household from 1596 to 1602. Knollys h been identified by Leslie Hotson as Shakespeare model for Malvolio in *Twelfth Night*. Like Malvoli he seems to have had strong Puritan sympathies, censorious disposition, and, paradoxically, a concep tion of himself as a ladies' man. This last aspect o his personality was revealed, according to Hotson, i his attempts to seduce Mary FITTON, his ward an one of the candidates for the so-called Dark Lad of the *Sonnets*. Knollys was also the uncle of th earl of Essex, among whose circle of friends he wa regarded as an obsequious and ambitious "tim server." [Leslie Hotson, *The First Night of Twelft Night*, 1954.]

Komisarjevsky, Theodore (1882–1954). Directo Born in Russia where he began his directing caree Komisarjevsky emigrated to England in 1919, becom ing a British subject in 1950. His directorial ca reer was noted for the unconventional and frequentl startling features which he inserted into his Shake spearean productions. His 1933 production of *Mac beth* was updated to World War I; his 1935 *Merr Wives of Windsor* was set in Vienna; his 1950 *Cym beline*, given at the Montreal Festival, was marked b the insertion of such non-Shakespearean lines a "We're off to see the wizard, the wonderful wizar of Oz." Despite these and other unsuccessful innova tions, Komisarjevsky's was a theatrical imaginatio of a high order. [J. C. Trewin, *Shakespeare on th English Stage, 1900–1964*, 1964.]

Kyd, Thomas (1558–1594). Playwright. Educated at the same time as Edmund Spenser at the Merchan Taylors' School, under headmaster Richard Mulcaster, Thomas Kyd received the classical training that played such an important role in his development as a dramatist. Although Kyd ranks with Marlowe as one of the creators of true Elizabethan tragedy, there is no direct evidence of his connection with the theatre because all the plays attributed to him were published anonymously. Among the contemporary allusions to Kyd is one by Ben Jonson in his Preface to the First Folio of Shakespeare's plays where he puns about "sporting Kyd," but tells us only that Shakespeare outshone him.

A reference in Heywood's *Apology for Actors* in 1612 identifies Kyd as the author of *The Spanish Tragedy* (c. 1589). The only other play known certainly to be Kyd's is a translation (1594) of Robert Garnier's *Cornélie*, a drama of the fashionable French Senecan school. Ascribed with more or less certainty to Kyd is SOLIMAN AND PERSEDA (c. 1589), which presents in five long acts the play that is supposed to be dramatized in the last act of *The Spanish Tragedy*. Shakespeare's knowledge of *Soliman and Perseda* is evidenced by his reference to Basilisco, one of its principal characters, in *King John* (I, i, 244) when Philip the Bastard, speaking to

The Spanish Tragedie:

OR,

Hieronimo is mad againe.

Containing the lamentable end of *Don Horatio*, and *Belimperia*; with the pittifull death of *Hieronimo*.

Newly corrected, amended, and enlarged with new Additions of the *Painters* part, and others, as it hath of late been diuers times acted.

LONDON,
Printed by W. White, for I. White and T. Langley, and are to be sold at their Shop ouer against the Sarazens head without New-gate. 1615.

TITLE PAGE OF THE 1615 EDITION OF KYD'S *The Spanish Tragedy*.

his mother, says, "Knight, knight, good mother, Basilisco-like."

Although 10 extant editions of *The Spanish Tragedy* were published between 1592 and 1633, the author's name does not appear on any of the title pages. This popular Elizabethan drama dealing with a father's delayed revenge for a murdered son is a remarkable counterpart to *Hamlet* which portrays a son's delayed revenge for a murdered father. Common to both tragedies are: the ghost, the grim pursuit of revenge, the madness of the hero, and the play within the play. While he may have preceded Marlowe in the use of blank verse in drama, Kyd owes his success primarily to his sense of theatre and his technical skill in plot construction. His wonderful sense of theatre enabled him to represent rather than narrate action as exemplified when Hieronimo discovers the body of his murdered son, Horatio. Moreover, Kyd motivates his characters so that they emerge as real people and not as allegorical symbols. Bel-Imperia, the proud and passionate heroine, and her brother Lorenzo, the first Machiavellian villain in Elizabethan literature, were soon to become part of the Shakespearean tradition.

Most critics believe that Kyd had some part in the writing of ARDEN OF FEVERSHAM. Published anonymously in 1592, this play, based on the murder of Ardern of Faversham in Kent in 1551 (recorded in Holinshed's *Chronicles*), marked the first of a series of domestic tragedies which drew their plots from contemporary murder cases. The value of the play lies in the skill of the dramatist in individualizing all characters, such as Arden, the weak and uxorious husband; Moshie, the low-born but fascinating steward; and Alice, the dominating wife. After the murder of Arden in which Alice has participated she cries, "Fetch water and wash away this blood," a line that foreshadows Lady Macbeth's "A little water clears us of this deed."

That Kyd's power as a playwright was recognized by his contemporaries is attested by the fact that in 1614 when Shakespeare's tragedies had been on the boards for years, Ben Jonson defined an old-fashioned playwright as one who would swear that "*Jeronimo* [*The Spanish Tragedy*] and *Andronicus* were the best plays yet."—S. G. M.

Kynge Johan (1534–1547). An interlude by the Protestant controversialist Bishop John Bale (1495–1563). *Kynge Johan*, in which literary merit is virtually nonexistent, derives its historical importance from the fact that it marks the earliest attempt on the English stage to dramatize English history.

L

Lacy, John (d. 1681). Actor and dramatist. Lacy began his career as a dancing master, but became an actor with the King's Company at the Restoration. He was the company's leading comedian, and Falstaff was one of his best roles. He is the author of four plays, including *The Dumb Lady* (1669), based on Molière's *Le Médecin malgré lui*, and *Sir Hercules Buffoon* (1684), a flimsy farce. In 1667 he adapted *The Taming of the Shrew* under the title of *Sauny the Scot*. See TAMING OF THE SHREW: *Stage History*.

Sauny the Scot is notable among the Restoration adaptations in that the main characters of the original are all reduced in importance in order to build up a comparatively minor figure. As the title suggests, the main interest of this altered version does not lie in the subjection of Katharina (here called Margaret), but in the peripheral activities of Petruchio's servant Grumio (Sauny), acted in the early years of production by Lacy himself.

The setting of Shakespeare's plays is changed to a nearly contemporary England. With corresponding changes in the characters, Lucentio becomes Winlove, a student from Oxford, and Sauny a typical British stage clown with a heavy "Scottish" accent. Since Petruchio is no longer the hero, Lacy feels under no obligation to make him admirable or sympathetic; consequently he emerges as something of a sadist, with none of the wit that made his pranks acceptable in Shakespeare's play. Margaret is also much more of a shrew than Katharina was. Both characters are important in Lacy's play only to the extent that they provide the right sort of comical setting for Sauny's comment and clowning. The tone of the Bianca subplot is less violently altered, with only those modifications added that were necessary to make it conform to the contemporary background. The play is in prose and is coarser and less witty than Shakespeare's.

Sauny the Scot is the final result of a series of changes that Lacy made in Shakespeare's play in the decade between 1660 and 1670. By some perverse logic, the most violent of the Restoration alterations, this play and Nahum Tate's *King Lear* (1681), won the greatest success. *Sauny the Scot* drove *The Taming of the Shrew* off the stage until Garrick finally brought back the original in a highly edited form. [Hazelton Spencer, *Shakespeare Improved*, 1927.]

Lady Capulet. See CAPULET, LADY.

Lady Elizabeth's Men [Queen of Bohemia's Men]. A company of actors organized in 1611 under the patronage of Elizabeth, daughter of James I. The company was controlled by Philip Henslowe, against whom the actors drew up a list of grievances in 1615. The playhouses at which the company performed probably included the Swan, the Rose, and Whitefriars. In 1615 they amalgamated (see AMALGAMATION) with PRINCE CHARLES' MEN. Upon the death of Henslowe (January 1616), the company lost its eight most prominent players, including Nathan Field, who joined the King's Men, possibly as a replacement for Shakespeare. These losses all but annihilated the company, reducing them to the status of a provincial troupe. They do not appear again in the records as a London company until 1622 when they played at the Phoenix in Drury Lane. This group was probably a newly organized company under the leadership of Christopher BEESTON. The new company enjoyed a few years of prosperity utilizing the services of such playwrights as Middleton, Massinger, Ford, Heywood, and Shirley. In 1625, however, London was struck by the worst plague in its history, a circumstance which, together with the death of King James, forced the closing of the theatres and the subsequent reorganization of many companies. It is probable that at this time Lady Elizabeth's Men assumed the title that had been given to Lady Elizabeth herself. (Elizabeth, the wife of Frederick V, the elector palatine, was crowned queen of Bohemia in 1619.) There is a record of a group known as the Queen of Bohemia's Men which appeared in London, probably at the Red Bull, at least until 1632. [G. E. Bentley, *The Jacobean and Caroline Stage*, 5 vols., 1941–1956.]

Lady Montague. See MONTAGUE, LADY.

Laertes. In *Hamlet*, the son of Polonius and brother of Ophelia. Laertes' impetuous haste in demanding revenge for his father's death is in marked contrast to Hamlet's indecision. Laertes is usually treated rather harshly by critics, who interpret his behavior at Ophelia's funeral (V, i) as flamboyant histrionics rather than sincere grief.

Lafeu. In *All's Well That Ends Well*, an old lord and friend of the Countess of Rousillon. Introducing Helena to the King at Paris, Lafeu becomes enraged with the courtiers who are impervious to her charms. The fiery Lafeu finds Bertram's companion Parolles completely detestable and misses no opportunity to censure him, referring to that knave as "a general offence." In the denouement, however, after Parolles has been exposed as a traitorous coward, it is Lafeu who deals with him compassionately.

Laforgue, Jules. See FRANCE.

Lamb, Charles (1775–1834). Essayist. Born in London and educated at Christ's Hospital, a charity school where he met Samuel Taylor Coleridge, Lamb ended his formal schooling at the age of 15 and in

1792 got a job as a clerk in the East India Company. His home became a gathering place for such distinguished people as Coleridge, William Wordsworth, Robert Southey, and Leigh Hunt. Lamb tried his hand at the theatre, writing *John Woodvil* (1802), a tragedy which has never been staged, and *Mr. H.* (1806), a farce which closed after its first performance. He did not come into his own until the age of 45, when he began to publish essays in the *London Magazine* under the pseudonym Elia. These were collected and published in *The Essays of Elia* (1823) and *Last Essays of Elia* (1833). These essays and the TALES FROM SHAKESPEARE (1807), written with Mary Lamb, are the works for which Lamb is chiefly remembered.

Lamb's critical writings, scattered through his letters, reviews, and essays, were collected by E. M. W. Tillyard in *Lamb's Criticism* (1923). Primarily descriptive in nature, Lamb's criticism deals with subjects that appealed to his friend Coleridge, such as Elizabethan drama, 17th-century prose, and contemporary poetry. George Watson in *The Literary Critics* (1962) suggests that Lamb is more conservative and less romantic than has been supposed, that he is "a sound Johnsonian. . . . partly romanticized by his reverence for Coleridge."

Lamb's "On the Tragedies of Shakespeare" (1811) argues that Shakespeare's plays suffer when they are represented on the stage. "It may seem a paradox," Lamb wrote, "but I cannot help being of the opinion that the plays of Shakespeare are less calculated for performance on a stage than those of almost any other dramatist whatever." To Lamb, Shakespeare as a great poet displays "absolute mastery over the heart and soul of man," in marked contrast to an actor's "low tricks upon the eye and ear." Thus he combines a Johnsonian contempt for the craft of acting with a Romantic veneration of Shakespeare as poet, rather than playwright. Lamb's application of this view to individual plays is often sentimental, as in the case of *Hamlet,* but it is sometimes telling. His discussion of *Lear* points to the ineptitude of supplying the play with a happy ending and the technical difficulties involved in staging certain scenes, such as the celebrated storm scene.

Lamb, George. See ADAPTATIONS.

Lambarde, William (1536–1601). Historian. A graduate of Lincoln's Inn, Lambarde was the author of several legal works as well as some antiquarian studies. In January 1601 he was appointed keeper of the records in the Tower of London. On August 4 of that year he presented the queen with an account of the records, and recorded a conversation referring to the attempt of Essex to depose the queen:

> . . . so her Majestie fell upon the reign of King Richard II. saying, 'I am Richard II. know ye not that?'
>
> *W. L.* 'Such a wicked imagination was determined and attempted by a most unkind Gent. the most adorned creature that ever your Majestie made.'
>
> *Her Majestie.* 'He that will forget God, will also forget his benefactors; this tragedy was played 40tie times in open streets and houses.'

Elizabeth's allusion to "this tragedy" was undoubtedly in reference to Shakespeare's *Richard II,* which the Essex faction had caused to be revived the day before the rebellion.

Lambarde's earliest published work was a collection and paraphrase of Anglo-Saxon laws, titled *Archaionomia* (1568). In 1938 the Folger Library secured a copy of this book which bears in the upper-right-hand corner of the title page the inscription "W. Shaksp.[ere]." The signature has not been universally accepted as Shakespeare's, but there is a case for its authenticity (see HANDWRITING).

THE DISPUTED SHAKESPEARE SIGNATURE IN A COPY OF LAMBARDE'S *Archaionomia* (1568). (FOLGER SHAKESPEARE LIBRARY)

Lambert Family. Relatives of Shakespeare. ***Edmund Lambert*** (d. 1587) of Barton-on-the-Heath married Shakespeare's aunt, Joan Arden (see ARDEN FAMILY), sometime before 1550.

In 1578 John and Mary Shakespeare borrowed £40 from Edmund Lambert. As security they mortgaged to their brother-in-law a house and land in Wilmcote which Mary Shakespeare had inherited. The loan was not repaid and Edmund Lambert retained ownership of the property, which was in turn inherited in 1587 by the Lamberts' only child, ***John*** (fl. 1597). John Lambert was then sued by the Shakespeares for allegedly failing to fulfill a promise to pay an extra £20 for outright ownership of the property. Lambert denied that he had agreed to the extra payment, and the court apparently decided in his favor. In 1597 the Shakespeares brought another suit to recover the property, this time alleging that they had offered to repay the original £40 but that the offer had been rejected, first by Edmund Lambert and later by his son. The Shakespeares' allegation is worded as follows:

> To the righte honorable Sir Thomas Egerton, knighte, lorde keper of the greate seale of Englande.—In most humble wise complayninge, sheweth unto your good lordshippe your dailye oratours, John Shakespere of Stratford-upon-Avon, in the county of Warwicke, and Mary his wief, that, whereas your saide oratours were lawfully seised in their demesne as of fee, as in the righte of the saide Mary, of and in one mesuage and one yarde lande with thappurtenaunces, lyinge and beinge in Wylnecote, in the saide county; and they beinge thereof so seised, for and in consideracion of the somme of fowerty poundes to them by one Edmounde Lamberte of Barton-on-the-Heath in the saide countie paide, your sayde oratours were contente that he, the saide Edmounde Lamberte, shoulde have and enjoye the same premisses untill suche tyme as your sayde oratours did repaie unto

him the saide somme of fowertie poundes; by reasone whereof the saide Edmounde did enter into the premisses and did occupie the same for the space of three or fower yeares, and thissues and profyttes thereof did receyve and take; after which your saide oratours did tender unto the saide Edmounde the sayde somme of fowerty poundes, and desired that they mighte have agayne the sayde premisses accordinge to theire agreement; which money he the sayde Edmounde then refused to receyve, sayinge that he woulde not receyve the same, nor suffer your sayde oratours to have the saide premisses agayne, unlesse they woulde paye unto him certayne other money which they did owe unto him for other matters; all which notwithstandinge, nowe so yt ys; and yt maye please your good lordshippe that, shortelie after the tendringe of the sayd fowertie poundes to the saide Edmounde, and the desyre of your sayde oratours to have theire lande agayne from him, he the saide Edmounde att Barton aforesayde dyed, after whose death one John Lamberte, as sonne and heire of the saide Edmounde, entred into the saide premisses and occupied the same; after which entrie of the sayde John your said oratours came to him and tendred the saide money unto him, and likewise requested him that he would suffer them to have and enjoye the sayde premisses accordinge to theire righte and tytle therein and the promise of his saide father to your saide oratours made, which he, the saide John, denyed in all thinges, and did withstande them for entringe into the premisses, and as yet doeth so contynewe still; and by reasone that certaine deedes and other evydences concerninge the premisses, and that of righte belonge to your saide oratours, are coumme to the handes and possession of the sayde John, he wrongfullie still keepeth and detayneth the possession of the saide premisses from your saide oratours, and will in noe wise permytt and suffer them to have and enjoye the sayde premisses accordinge to theire righte in and to the same; and he, the saide John Lamberte, hathe of late made sondrie secreate estates of the premisses to dyvers persones to your said oratours unknowen, whereby your saide oratours cannot tell againste whome to bringe theire accions att the comen lawe for the recovery of the premisses; in tender consideracion whereof, and for so muche as your saide oratours knowe not the certaine dates nor contentes of the saide wrytinges nor whether the same be contayned in bagge, boxe or cheste, sealed, locked or noe, and therefore have no remeadie to recover the same evydences and wrytinges by the due course of the comen lawes of this realme; and for that also, by reasone of the saide secreate estates so made by the saide John Lamberte as aforesaide, and want of your saide oratours havinge of the evidences and wrytinges as aforesaide, your oratours cannot tell what accions or against whome, or in what manner, to bringe theire accion for the recoverie of the premisses att the comen lawe; and for that also the sayde John Lamberte ys of greate wealthe and abilitie, and well frended and alied amongest gentlemen and freeholders of the countrey in the saide countie of Warwicke, where he dwelleth, and your saide oratours are of small wealthe and verey fewe frendes and alyance in the saide countie, maye yt therefore please your good lordshippe to graunt unto your saide oratours the Queenes Majesties moste gracyous writte of subpena, to be directed to the saide John Lamberte, comandinge him thereby att a certaine daie, and under a certaine payne therein to be lymytted, personally to appeare before your good lordshippe in Her Majesties highnes courte of Chauncerie, then and there to answere the premisses; and further to stande to and abyde suche order and direction therein as to your good lordshippe shall seeme best to stande with righte, equytie and good conscyence, and your sayde oratours shall daylie praye to God for the prosperous healthe of your good lordshippe with increase of honour longe to contynewe.

In his answer to the charge John Lambert asserted that the offer to repay the £40 had not been made within the time specified in the original agreement and that as a result the Shakespeares had forfeited their right to the property. The Shakespeares replied by asserting that they had offered the repayment shortly before the death of Edmund Lambert:

> The said complaynantes, for replicacion to the answere of the saide defendant, saie that theire bill of complaynt ys certayne and sufficient in the lawe to be answered; which said bill, and matters therein contayned, these complainants will avowe, verefie, and justifie to be true and sufficient in the lawe to be answered unto, in such sorte, manner and forme as the same be sett forthe and declared in the said bill: and further they saie that thanswere of the said defenndant is untrue and insufficient in lawe to be replied unto, for many apparent causes in the same appearinge, thadvantage whereof these complainantes praie may be to theym nowe and at all tymes saved, then and not ells; for further replicacion to the said answere they saie that, accordinge to the condicion or proviso mencioned in the said indenture of bargaine and sale of the premisses mencioned in the said bill of complaynt, he this complaynant, John Shakspere, did come to the dwellinge-house of the saide Edmunde Lambert, in Barton-uppon-the-Heathe, uppon the feaste daie of St. Michaell tharcheangell, which was in the yeare of our Lorde God one thousand fyve hundred and eightie, and then and there tendered to paie unto him the said Edmunde Lambert the said fortie poundes, which he was to paie for the redempcion of the said premisses; which somme the said Edmunde did refuse to receyve, sayinge that he owed him other money, and unles that he, the said John, would paie him altogether, as well the said fortie poundes as the other money, which he owed him over and above, he would not receave the said fortie poundes, and imediatlie after he, the said Edmunde, dyed, and by reason thereof, he, the said defendant, entered into the said premisses, and wrongfullie kepeth and detayneth and said premisses from him the said complaynant; without that, any other matter or thinge, materiall or effectuall, for these complaynantes to replie unto, and not herein sufficientlie confessed and avoyded, denyed and traversed, ys true; all which matters and thinges thes complaynantes are redie to averr and

prove, as this honourable court will awarde, and pray as before in theire said bill they have praied.

The decision of the court is not known, but by the latter half of the 17th century, the property had passed into the hands of the Edkins family, who were cousins of the Shakespeares and the Lamberts. [J. O. Halliwell-Phillipps, *Outlines of the Life of Shakespeare*, 1881; E. K. Chambers, *William Shakespeare*, 1930.]

lameness. The danger of interpreting the *Sonnets* literally is nowhere better demonstrated than in the notion, over which much ink was spilled in the 19th century, that Shakespeare was lame. The idea derives from a literal reading of the 3rd line of Sonnet 37 ("So I, made lame by fortune's dearest spite") and the 3rd line of Sonnet 89 ("Speak of my lameness, and I straight will halt"). The literal reading was first advanced in 1779 by Edward Capell, who connected these references to the apparent lameness of Adam in *As You Like It*, one of the acting roles traditionally assigned to Shakespeare. The idea received its greatest popularity, however, from Sir Walter Scott, himself lame, who depicts Shakespeare as suffering from the infirmity in his novel *Kenilworth* (1821). With this as a background it was only a short while before an enterprising reader "proved" that the injury was to the left leg and that it was suffered while acting at the Fortune theatre. The lameness lines have also been cited to show that "Shakespeare" was variously Sir Walter Raleigh, wounded at Cadiz in 1596, or Anthony Bacon, brother of Francis, who was deformed.

The often maligned 20th century can at least claim credit for not having pursued this question any further. [*The Sonnets*, New Variorum Edition, Hyder Rollins, ed., 1944.]

Lampe, John Frederick. See ADAPTATIONS.

Lancaster, John of. See John of Lancaster, duke of BEDFORD.

Lane Family. Neighbors and friends of Shakespeare. ***Nicholas Lane*** (d. 1595) was a successful landowner who in 1586 lent £20 to Henry Shakespeare, the poet's uncle, for which John Shakespeare gave surety. When Henry failed to pay, Lane sued John Shakespeare. Lane's son ***Richard*** (1556–1613) was part owner of the STRATFORD TITHES with Shakespeare, whom he joined in bringing a suit in chancery court about 1611. He married Joan Whitney, who in 1592 was cited in the same recusant list as John Shakespeare. Richard Lane died in 1613 and in his will named John Hall, Shakespeare's son-in-law, as the guardian of his children.

Richard's younger brother, ***John Lane*** (b. 1562), may have been one of Shakespeare's schoolfellows. He served on the Stratford town council from 1600 to 1604. His son ***John*** (1590–1640) was sued for defamation of character by Shakespeare's daughter Susanna in 1613. He failed to appear in court to answer the suit and was excommunicated (see Susanna SHAKESPEARE). Lane was sued in 1619 for attacking and libeling the vicar of Stratford. He was characterized in court as a drunkard. [Mark Eccles, *Shakespeare in Warwickshire*, 1961.]

Langbaine, Gerard (1656–1692). Biographer and historian of the theatre. Langbaine spent the early years of his life dissipating a substantial inheritance. He turned to literature as a means of making a living, producing his *Momus Triumphans: or the Plagiaries of the English Stage; exposed in a Catalogue of Comedies, Tragi-comedies . . .* (1688), an alphabetical account of English dramatists, under which are listed the various plays ascribed to them. Catalogued under Shakespeare's name are 41 entries, including the apocryphal *London Prodigal, Sir John Oldcastle, Locrine, The Puritan Widow, A Yorkshire Tragedy,* and *The Birth of Merlin.*

In 1691 Langbaine produced his *An Account of the English Dramatick Poets.* In this treatment of Shakespeare, he ascribes 46 plays to the dramatist, detailing Shakespeare's sources for many of the plays. An extract from the account is given below:

WilliaM SHAKESPEAR.

One of the most Eminent Poets of his Time; he was born at *Stratford* upon *Avon* in *Warwickshire;* and flourished in the Reigns of Queen *Elizabeth* and King *James* the First. His Natural Genius to *Poetry* was so excellent, that like those Diamonds, which are found in *Cornwall,* Nature had little, or no occasion for the Assistance of Art, to polish it. The Truth is, 'tis agreed on by most, that his Learning was not extraordinary; and I am apt to believe, that his skill in the *French* and *Italian* Tongues, exceeded his Knowledge in the *Roman* Language: for we find him not only beholding to *Cynthio Giraldi* and *Bandello,* for his Plots, but likewise a Scene in *Henry* the Fifth, written in *French,* between the Princess *Catherine* and her Governante: Besides *Italian* Proverbs scatter'd up and down in his Writings. Few Persons that are acquainted with *Dramatick Poetry,* but are convinced of the Excellency of his Compositions, in all Kinds of it: and as it would be superfluous in me to endeavour to particularise what most deserves praise in him, after so many Great Men that have given him their several Testimonials of his Merit; so I should think I were guilty of an Injury beyond pardon to his Memory, should I so far disparage it, as to bring his Wit in competition with any of our Age. 'Tis true Mr. *Dryden* has censured him very severely, in his Postscript to *Granada;* but in cool Blood, and when the *Enthusiastick* Fit was past, he has acknowledged him [in his *Dramatick Essay*] Equal at least, if not Superiour, to Mr. *Johnson* in *Poesie.* I shall not here repeat what has been before urged in his behalf, in that Common Defence of the Poets of that Time, against Mr. *Dryden's* Account of *Ben Jonson;* but shall take the Liberty to speak my Opinion, as my predecessors have done, of his Works; which is this, That I esteem his Plays beyond any that have ever been published in our Language: and tho' I extreamly admire *Johnson,* and *Fletcher;* yet I must still aver, that when in competition with *Shakespear,* I must apply to them what *Justus Lipsius* writ in his Letter to *Andrœas Schottus,* concerning *Terence* and *Plautus,* when compar'd; *Terentium amo, admiror, sed Plautum magis.*

There are numerous other Shakespearean references, particularly in Langbaine's account of Dryden, whom he attacks for the latter's alleged disparagement of Shakespeare. A later edition (1699) of Langbaine's work was enlarged and revised by Charles Gildon. Gildon's revision includes some additional information about Shakespeare:

> I have been told that he writ the Scene of the Ghost in *Hamlet,* at his House which bordered on the Charnel-House and Church-Yard. He was both Player and Poet; but the greatest Poet that ever trod the Stage, I am of Opinion, in spight of Mr. *Johnson,* and others from him, that though perhaps he might not be that Critic in Latin and Greek as *Ben;* yet that he understood the former, so well as perfectly to be Master of their Histories, for in all his Roman Characters he has nicely followed History, and you find his *Brutus,* his *Cassius,* his *Anthony,* and his *Caesar,* his *Coriolanus,* &'c., just as the Historians of those times describe 'em.

Two copies of the 1691 edition were annotated by Sir William Oldys. Oldys' notes are an interesting repository of legends relating to Shakespeare. [*The Shakspere Allusion-Book,* J. Munro, ed., 1909.]

Langham, Michael (1919–). Director. Born in Somerset and educated at the University of London, Langham studied for the bar until World War II, after which he began producing plays for the Arts Council, directing the Midland Theatre Company, Coventry, from 1946 to 1948. During this time he directed *Twelfth Night.* From 1948 to 1950 he was director of productions at the Birmingham Repertory Theatre, and in 1950 directed *Julius Caesar* at the Shakespeare Memorial Theatre, Stratford-upon-Avon. In 1951 he directed his first London play, as well as André Obey's French adaptation of *Richard III* in Brussels and *Othello* for the Old Vic in Berlin. He directed *The Merry Wives of Windsor* in Dutch at The Hague in 1952.

He directed *Julius Caesar* at the Stratford, Ontario, Shakespeare Festival in 1952, and was subsequently appointed artistic director and, two years later, general manager. There he has directed *Henry V* (also at the Edinburgh Festival), *The Merry Wives of Windsor* (1956), *Hamlet* (1957), *1 Henry IV, Much Ado About Nothing* (1958), and *Romeo and Juliet.* At Stratford-upon-Avon, the Old Vic, and in New York, he has directed *Hamlet* (1956), *Two Gentlemen of Verona* (1957), *The Merchant of Venice,* and *A Midsummer Night's Dream* (1960). [*Who's Who in the Theatre,* 1961.]

Langley, Edmund of. See Edmund of Langley, 1st duke of YORK.

Langley, Francis (1550–1601). A draper and goldsmith. Langley purchased the manor of Paris Garden in 1589. In 1594/5 he built on this site a playhouse called the "Swan." Leslie Hotson has discovered a writ of attachment naming Langley and William "Shakspere" in a petition for surety of the peace (see William WAYTE). On the basis of this association Hotson concludes that Shakespeare's company may have occupied Langley's theatre, the Swan, in 1596 before moving to the Globe. If the Chamberlain's Men were at the Swan in 1596, they were not there in 1597, for in February of that year Langley signed a contract with Pembroke's Men to play at his theatre for a year. In July of that year, however, Pembroke's Men gave a performance of Thomas Nashe's *Isle of Dogs,* which resulted in the closing of the theatres (see PEMBROKE'S MEN). When the theatres were reopened, the license of the Swan was not renewed. Langley tried to convince the Pembroke's Men to play without a license, but five of the leading members broke their contract and joined Henslowe's Admiral's Men. Langley sued them for violation of the contract. The outcome of the suit is not known.

Langley was the brother-in-law of Sir Anthony Ashley, a clerk to the privy council, and had himself been the alnager and searcher of cloth since 1582. (The office was an officially appointed sinecure which required the alnager to examine and attest the measurement and quality of woolen goods.) Langley was also the landlord of the Boar's Head theatre, the winter quarters of the Earl of Worcester's (Queen Anne's) Men. [Leslie Hotson, *Shakespeare Versus Shallow,* 1931.]

language and characterization. The Quatercentenary of 1964 succeeded in demonstrating one thing without the faintest shadow of doubt: Shakespeare stands absolutely unique among authors, not because of the profound esteem accorded to him by critics, but because of his wide general popularity—a popularity which, instead of declining with the passage of the centuries, is powerfully increasing year by year. Even if some spectators go to watch his plays out of a sense of duty or feel impelled by the force of social convention, clearly his success in the theatre could not be such as it is if his comedies and tragedies did not exercise a broad appeal among the theatregoing public. This fact itself requires no burden of proof, but it is important for us firmly to recognize its true source. In general, of course, the theatrical appeal of Shakespeare's greater plays derives from an unconscious appreciation on the part of the audience of their total artistic achievement, productive of a deep feeling of satisfaction even when the scope of their moving force cannot be precisely defined. While, however, the totality of each play makes its impact upon those who listen to the lines and see the actions unfolding, it seems obvious that fundamentally the average spectator thinks of these dramas in terms of their characters: the plots may be well known, and yet the manner in which the persons are delineated makes them appear perpetually new. As though the creatures of Shakespeare's imagination were endowed with eternal life, they continually reveal fresh aspects of their beings in successive productions. What delights the audience is the sense of meeting characters who somehow seem to be invested with a richer vitality than the living men and women encountered in our daily lives.

This is so far from being a novel observation that it might well be dismissed as a mere platitude. Platitudes, however, are often truths so basic, so much taken for granted, that we are led, through very familiarity, to ignore their true force; and this particular platitude needs to be heavily underlined in view of certain trends in modern Shakespearean criticism. In not a few critical circles "Bradleyism" has become a term of contempt, and opposition to Bradley's approach (see CHARACTER CRITICISM) has been carried to such an extent that attempts are made to argue that the characters drawn by Shakespeare must be looked upon as though they were nothing but symbols. It is assuredly true that symbolic elements do play a part in the total effect produced by Shakespeare's dramas, but the role of these symbols is by no means the chief one in giving these plays their unchallenged theatrical pre-eminence. The public would not flock night after night to watch walking shadows on the stage: if the figures presented in these comedies and tragedies were indeed simply symbols, the spectators would be left cold, whereas manifestly the impression created by the worlds of *Hamlet* and *Twelfth Night* is one of pulsating warmth.

Sense. This being so, we must clearly ask ourselves by what means—perhaps it might almost be said, by what magical potency—the author has infused into these fictional creatures, whom we are permitted to see only for a brief period of time and whose actual lines are comparatively few, such a vital spirit. Since drama basically consists in setting before an audience a group of persons who are made to move and speak, our first impulse might well be to assert that of course the vitality derives from what Shakespeare makes each one of his characters say. In the expression of thoughts and of such emotions as can be cast in terms of words Shakespeare exhibits to the full the typically paradoxical skill of the supreme dramatist, and he does this in two ways. First, if we read or listen to a passage from one of the mature plays, we usually can say to ourselves "That is Shakespearean," immediately recognizing a way of approach and a sequence of ideas which belong characteristically to the author: the passage possesses a distinct and individual quality, evasive perhaps and incapable of formal critical analysis, yet potent and palpable. At the same time, all audiences feel, as the words are spoken on the stage, that the passage itself is adjusted to and reveals the nature of the fictional person into whose mouth it has been put. The best way of explaining this paradox may be to say that in his greater plays Shakespeare gives to each of his major figures the ability to express himself, in terms somehow proper to his own being, which this character would have had if he had possessed the poet's command of word and of thought. Shakespeare is Hamlet, but he is also Claudius; he is Iago as much as he is Othello.

The second paradox is different in kind. An audience in the theatre unquestionably finds itself swayed more by emotion than by intellectual processes: a single member of that audience may be able easily to follow and appreciate a consecutive and logical argument if, by himself, he reads the sentences on a printed page, and yet, when he is in the playhouse, he will probably be incapable of grasping the significance of all that is being said. Partly this arises from the rapid speaking of the lines, which have, as it were, to be caught in their flight; chiefly it arises from the difference between audience approach and individual approach. One peculiar feature of Shakespeare's skill is the way in which he invests a passage, even a lengthy and complex passage, with what might be called a précis, or paraphrase, of itself. An audience in the theatre will not be able to trace, step by step, the course of Ulysses' argument when, in addressing Agamemnon, he starts with the "heavens themselves, the planets and this centre," and proceeds to his final vision, terrible in its intensity, of appetite, the universal wolf, consuming its own being (I, iii, 85–124). In precisely the same way, such a soliloquy of Hamlet's as that which is occasioned by his reflections upon Fortinbras' expedition (IV, iv, 32–66) cannot be expected to yield its entire content to spectators in the playhouse. Nevertheless, these spectators do not feel themselves simply overwhelmed by a spate of largely meaningless words: in addition to the complex argument, Shakespeare incorporates in the particular speech its own essential abstract, so that the audience can both comprehend its significance and perceive its appropriateness to the character who is speaking. It is this peculiar power which helps to explain the continuing popular appeal exerted by these plays: the meanings of many words are unknown, numerous other words, although still retained in our common speech, have altered their significance, and yet Shakespeare's language preserves its force against all Time's mutabilities.

Style. The first simple answer to the basic question, however, is not sufficient: in fact, its inadequacy may well lead us astray. What the characters say is important, but equally important is the way in which they express their thoughts and emotions. For an audience in the theatre sentences are not merely collections of words which, taken together, have perceptible meanings; they are also sounds which, like the sounds of music, create emotional responses in the minds of those who listen to them. Although an individual reader finds himself influenced by these sounds, basically his attention tends to be focused upon the meanings of the words themselves; this reader, when he sits in the auditorium, may well discover that the verbal music comes to assume predominance.

"Verbal music" possibly is not the most fitting and precise phrase to explain this particular aspect of Shakespeare's language; "style" might better comprehend the total amalgam of intellectual significance, imagery, rhythm, metrical form, and musical values which in the mature plays are closely and expertly adjusted to the qualities of the speakers and the emotional content of the scenes. Due stress here must be placed on the mature plays, since we are bound to admit that to the final consummation of his craft Shakespeare moved gradually through many years of experimentation. Indeed, if we compare scene with scene in different dramas written during these years we almost get the impression that often, with a deliberate sense of purpose, he kept alive in his mind verbal passages in the earlier plays so that he might, when occasion arose, eventually find the perfection of utterance which his imagination sought. As an apprentice in the writing of plays, he soon discovered that, in general, dramatic speech demands pithiness in expression, since a play, in contradistinction to a long poem or narrative, is restricted in its length and normally cannot bear digressions from its main path or leisurely meanderings during the course of its journey. An excellent example of the difference between nondramatic and dramatic verse was pointed out several years ago. Sonnet 73 begins with three lines reading,

> That time of year thou mayst in me behold
> When yellow leaves, or none, or few, do hang
> Upon those boughs which shake against the cold.

In *Macbeth* the same concept, even with the utilization of some of the original words, appears in a line and a half:

> My way of life is fallen into the sere,
> The yellow leaf.

It does not need to be emphasized that, while the former is poetically beautiful and effective, it lacks entirely the dramatic urge of the latter. This dramatic value derives not only from the condensation of Macbeth's utterance; the picture evoked in the sonnet's lines is passive and static, a still picture of leaves hanging and of boughs which do no more than faintly shiver in the chill, whereas the other picture, with its use of the words "way" and "fallen," creates an inner impression of movement.

Within some of the earliest dramas, passages of an undramatic sort certainly do occur, but very soon Shakespeare came to cast his language always in the dynamic style proper to the theatre. As he proceeded, however, he came to understand not simply the value of condensed directness, but also the effect that could be produced by means of expansion when such expansion was related to the nature of a particular speaker and was integrated within the prevailing symphony of the action. In *Troilus and Cressida* Ulysses could easily have been made to propound the essentials of his argument on degree concisely and tersely; actually, his long speech helps to establish both his character and the mood of the scene in which it is placed. Here, another example may be appropriate. In the early *Henry VI* Shakespeare had used two words, "antic death," epigrammatically evocative. When he came to write *Richard II* he remembered these words and enlarged them into a memorable passage of four lines:

within the hollow crown
That rounds the mortal temples of a king
Keeps Death his court, and there the antic sits,
Scoffing his state and grinning at his pomp.
(III, ii, 160–163)

The speech secures its dramatic quality partly because it so perfectly suits Richard's character and partly because even Death, the antic, has been made to live, a dynamically active person.

Finally, a third example may serve to illustrate the growing power of Shakespeare, not in his awareness of when to contract and when to expand, but in his verbal redesigning of a single line. In *King John,* the Bastard, confronted by another character who unsheathes his weapon, is made to say "Your sword is bright, sir; put it up again" (IV, iii, 79). The words are few, the command effectively abrupt, yet the command itself does not have any individual quality; another character than the Bastard might have uttered it. Many years later, however, Othello appears in a similar situation, confronted by several wrathful men; and when the line takes on a new shape as, "Keep up your bright swords, for the dew will rust them" (I, ii, 59), we immediately recognize how much more dramatic it has become: the allusion to the dew gives it individuality, and the whole sentence, not contemptuous but expressive of the consciousness of strength, becomes a reflection of Othello's personality.

The uses of meter. Exploration of the inner resources of Shakespeare's language is a subject which has attracted serious attention only within comparatively recent years, and the chief reason for its neglect rests probably in the difficulties inherent in discussing such an elusive theme as style. We are here not concerned with one single quality; rather a complex pattern, constantly varying in its elements, is set before us. The words are invested with meaning; but in addition full weight must be given to the measures (blank verse, couplets, quatrains, prose) employed, to the metrical forms of the lines, to the imagery and to the melodic texture of the passages in which the words appear. As yet, it would seem, this whole topic has received only tentative critical analysis, and maybe we shall be forced in the end to admit that it will defy complete explication.

Various obstacles hinder the path of those who might essay to work in this field. Apart from the fact that stylistic analysis inevitably tends toward the examination of the language as poetry divorced from its theatrical objective, the several elements contributing to the creation of Shakespeare's style are by no means all subject to intellectual assessment or statistical consideration. We can, it is true, easily observe and tabulate the measures used in the scenes; during recent years, indeed, several investigations of this aspect of Shakespeare's style have considerably enlarged our appreciation of the subtlety with which he has dealt with the various forms of speech then available for dramatic purposes. Yet, even though the study of these forms is a relatively simple task, yielding results which can be made subject to logical explanation, there still remains much to be done, particularly in the comparison of Shakespeare's practice and the practices of contemporary playwrights, and in the study of the long 16th-century tradition which familiarized both dramatists and audiences with an important series of dramatic principles and conventions. The measures apportioned to various Shakespearean characters must, therefore, be considered in relation to the metrical forms adopted for the play in which they appear, to the general conventions familiar to audiences at the time when the play was written, and to the traditional background against which they are set. The most important aspect of this subject is the connection between the forms and the characters to whom they are assigned, aiming at an understanding of the way in which these forms serve to distinguish and give individuality to the fictional speakers; but, in addition to that, we have to keep our minds alert to observe other ways in which conventional patterns, taken over by Shakespeare and adapted to his own purposes, are made to work. Those, for instance, who essay to support or to reject the authenticity of the vision scene in *Cymbeline* (V, iv, 30–122) need to examine the quatrains given to Jupiter in connection with a lengthy tradition carrying us back past the Jupiter of *The Rare Triumphs of Love and Fortune* in 1582 to the Jupiter of John Heywood's *A Play of the Weather* almost a half-century earlier, just as those who wish to appreciate the Elizabethans' acceptance of Friar Laurence's quatrains on his first appearance in *Romeo and Juliet* have to relate this friar's measures to the measures given to other friars, real or pretended, in such plays as *Robert Earl of Huntington* (1598), *The Turk* (1607), *The Welsh Ambassador* (1623), and *Grim the Collier of Croydon* (1600). It is true, of course, that the Elizabethans, familiar with conventions which are now largely lost, were able to get much more from these measures than audiences of today, yet even now it is perhaps not too much to assert that certain characters—Caliban, for example—assume living form in the modern theatre partly at least because the measures given to them operate unconsciously upon the minds of the spectators.

In a similar way, the metrical structure of Shakespeare's blank verse lines can be statistically examined; indeed, many of the conclusions reached concerning the dating of the plays have depended upon the counting of run-on lines and of varying kinds of metrical feet. This task, if laborious, is fairly easy; but it is vastly more difficult to observe and estimate the effect of patterns altering in accordance with the characters. Critically, we can grasp the over-all effect, recognizing that Shakespeare's blank-verse style in *Romeo and Juliet* is different from his over-all style in *Antony and Cleopatra;* we can readily segregate prose-speakers from verse-speakers or estimate the impression created in the theatre when the latter at moments turn from verse to prose; but any attempt to explain why and wherein the verse of one character varies from the verse of another character bears us into an area in which tabulation is of little avail—even although we may be prepared to agree that in the playhouse the variations in metrical form contribute toward giving to an audience the sense of individuality and vitality in the presentation of these characters.

Our judgments concerning the study of Shakespeare's imagery must also be somewhat the same. Much of the detailed work accomplished of late within this sphere (see IMAGERY) has been concerned with the general run of images exemplified by this play or that, and dissatisfaction with the results obtained has been expressed in certain circles by the use of the phrase "image-counting." Only a comparatively limited number of investigators have extended their observations to an examination of images expressive of the individualities of particular persons, and even here there is a tendency to concentrate solely upon the major figures. Naturally, these major figures, because they are the "heroes" of the dramas in which they appear and to which often they give their names, are predominantly important, yet an audience in the theatre does not come away from witnessing a Shakespearean tragedy with the impression that it has been confronted with one single vital personality surrounded by a group of lifeless puppets: the impression rather is that of being introduced to an entire world of living beings among whom one is of especial significance.

A pertinent example may be found in a contrast between the characters of Hamlet and Claudius. Wolfgang Clemen has excellently analyzed the nature of the Prince's imagery: "common and ordinary things," he notes, "familiar to the man in the street, dominate, rather than lofty, strange and rare objects," although at the same time Hamlet's training and quality of mind is expressed in his multitude of classical references; he thinks of Alexander and "imperious Caesar"; phrases such as "Hyperion to a satyr," "the front of Jove," "an eye like Mars," "a station like the herald Mercury," "like Niobe all tears," "no more like my father than I to Hercules," "as hardy as the Nemean lion's nerve," "my imaginations are as foul as Vulcan's stithy"—all testify to this. Other groups of images, typical of his nature, contribute toward giving him his stirring impression of livingness. In Clemen's study, however, Hamlet's imagery is considered in isolation, and no attempt has been made to relate this imagery to other features of the Prince's speech. What must be stressed here is that the impression of Hamlet's livingness arises in the theatre not only from what he says and from his characteristic imagery; both of these have to be considered alongside the form of his utterance. Actually, much of his speech is in prose, the easy familiar prose during his conversations with friends, the biting prose when he encounters those whom he doubts, and what might be called his philosophic prose. And here his words often assume a form congruent with his quickness of mind:

> A little more than kind, and less than kind. . . .
> (I, ii, 65)

> *Polonius*. What is the matter, my lord?
> *Hamlet*. Between who?
> (II, ii, 195–196)

> *Claudius*. Now, Hamlet, where's Polonius?
> *Hamlet*. At supper.
> *Claudius*. At supper! Where?
> *Hamlet*. Not where he eats, but where he is eaten: a certain convocation of politic worms are e'en at him.
> (IV, iii, 17–22)

In so far as his actual language is concerned, every listener in the theatre cannot but also catch his tendency toward a superfluity of synonyms:

> all forms, moods, shapes of grief . . . . melt, thaw and resolve itself into a dew . . . . weary, stale, flat and unprofitable . . . . pith and marrow of our attribute . . . . all saws of books, all forms, all pressures past . . . powerfully and potently believe . . . . very torrent, tempest and, as I may say, whirlwind of your passion.

The inserting of that phrase "as I may say" serves to give these synonyms their peculiar characteristic quality. Some persons in other plays also expand in words: Ulysses, for example, in *Troilus and Cressida*, with his

> degree, priority and place,
> Insisture, course, proportion, season, form,
> Office and custom . . .
> (I, iii, 86–88)

> For beauty, wit,
> High birth, vigour of bone, desert in service,
> Love, friendship, charity. . . .
> (III, iii, 171–173)

But instinctively we feel that the two expansions are of different kinds. Both Hamlet and Ulysses are intellectual characters, but whereas the latter expands deliberately in order to enforce his argument by a plenitude of words which, while they belong to the same general concept, are by no means synonymous, Hamlet appears to be searching out just the right word to express his meaning. With this goes his tendency toward repetition:

> too, too sullied flesh . . . . thrift, thrift, Horatio . . . . indeed, indeed, sirs . . . . very like, very like . . . . words, words, words . . . . except my life, except my life, except my life.

Efforts have been made to suggest that the same trend is to be found in more than one other drama, and some have even argued that the repetitions themselves may be due not to Shakespeare but to the actor Richard Burbage. Nevertheless, the particular force here cannot be ignored, nor can we ignore the fact that cumulatively they combine with the tendency toward expansion to create the image of a man keenly intellectual whose mind sometimes is rapt in thought even as he carries on a conversation and sometimes is anxiously bent on discovering the most appropriate words with which to express a thought. To all of these characteristic features may be added a metrical trick—not persistent, for that would have made the lines monotonous, yet definitely marked: this might be described as the starting of lines on a strong beat:

> "Séems," madam! Nay, it is; I know not
> seems . . . .
>
> Téars in his eyes . . . .
>
> Máke mád the guilty . . . .
>
> Plúcks off my beard . . . .
>
> Twéaks me by the nose . . . .
>
> Wítness this army, of such mass and charge,
> Léd by a delicate and tender prince . . . .
>
> Mákes móuths at the invisible event,
> Exposing what is mortal and unsure
> To all that fortune, death and danger, dare,
> Éven for an egg-shell.

All these qualities of Hamlet's speech aid, almost as much as the words themselves, in building up his personality; and it is important to observe that for most of the qualities we can find their opposites in the speech of Claudius. The King's prose utterances are cast in a form utterly unlike that of Hamlet's speeches. His images are of war and parts of the body:

> brow of woe . . . . visage of offence . . . . gilded hand shown by justice . . . . teeth and forehead of our faults . . . . reasons unsinew'd . . . . defeated joy . . . defeat my strong intent . . . as level as the cannon to his blank . . . sorrows come in battalions . . . . level to your judgments pierce . . . . arrows reverted.

He, too, indulges in repetitions, but his repetitions are different, taking shape either as extended explanations or as a hiding of thoughts behind mere words:

> The head is not more native to the heart,
> The hand more instrumental to the mouth . . .
> (I, ii, 47–48)
>
> your father lost a father;
> That father lost, lost his . . .
> (I, ii, 89–90)
>
> as 'twere with a defeated joy,—
> With an auspicious and a dropping eye,
> With mirth in funeral and with dirge in
> marriage,
> In equal scale weighing delight and dole . . .
> (I, ii, 10–13)
>
> A heart unfortified, a mind impatient,
> An understanding simple and unschool'd . . .
> (I, ii, 96–97)
>
> A fault against the dead, a fault to nature,
> To reason most absurd . . . .
> (I, ii, 102–103)

Throughout, his lines suggest a rounded emptiness and to this impression a different kind of rhythm makes its contribution:

> Though yet of Hamlet our dear brother's
> death
> The memory be green, and that it us
> befitted
> To bear our hearts in grief and our whole
> kingdom
> To be contracted in one brow of woe,
> Yet so far hath discretion fought with nature
> That we with wisest sorrow think on him,
> Together with remembrance of ourselves.
> Therefore our sometime sister, now our
> queen . . . .
> (I, ii, 1–8)

Sound. Even such a rough and cursory contrasting of the characteristic forms of speech given to Hamlet and to Claudius serves to demonstrate that the theatrical impressions of these two persons are wrought by combinations of diverse elements whereby what is said is enriched by the way it is said. Furthermore, we realize that, in order to appreciate the force which creates these theatrical impressions, the totality of the speeches must be examined as a whole: false, or at least wholly inadequate, conclusions may result if we confine ourselves to the meanings of the words, or to the measures employed, or to the imagery, or to the metrical structure of the lines.

Nor are these elements by any means all. In particular, there remains one which, although its potency is as great as the others, is the most elusive. Words, it has been said, come to an audience as sounds uttered by the actors, and the sounds impinge powerfully upon the sensibilities of the spectators. At one level, the lowest, the concatenation of certain sounds may be consciously appreciated. Sometimes, indeed, in an effort to secure emphasis, Shakespeare introduces alliterative compounds so pronounced that, divorced from their context, they might almost be deemed crude or absurd: the jingle chanted by the witches in *Macbeth* can be taken as an example:

> *F*air is *f*oul, and *f*oul is *f*air:
> Ho*v*er through the *f*og and *f*ilthy air.
> (I, i, 11–12)

Moving to a slightly higher level, audiences may also be conscious of the effects produced by somewhat similar emphatic alliterative devices within the course of longer speeches: here, as one example, we might refer to Hamlet's "*d*eath and *d*anger, *d*are" in his soliloquy after conversing with Fortinbras' captain, or we might note how Macbeth's "tomorrow" speech is stressed by "*p*etty *p*ace," "*d*usty *d*eath," "*p*oor *p*layer," "*t*ale *t*old by an idio*t*, full of *s*ound and *f*ury, *s*ignifying nothing."

Such emphatic alliteration, being palpable, may be

tabulated and statistically displayed; but the tabulations will in fact tell us very little. The final lines of Macbeth's soliloquy, indeed, amply warn us of the problems and difficulties involved. "*F*ull of *s*ound and *f*ury, *s*igni*f*ying . . ." is a clear instance of deliberate alternating alliteration, yet, when we consider Macbeth's lines carefully, we must realize that, instead of placing stress upon the alliterative words themselves, the heavy concatenation of like sounds throws tremendous weight upon the word which immediately follows; because this word, "nothing," is entirely different in sound, and because its first vowel flattens out, as it were, the rich *u* vowels in the preceding phrase, it comes to our ears like the dull echo of a cracked bell. No statistical analysis could possibly hope to reveal its force.

And even so we still stand on the lower levels of this territory. If we move higher, we realize that in Shakespeare's mature plays alliteration of a much subtler sort exerts its spell in the playhouse and that this alliteration depends for its prime power less upon the sound values themselves than upon their relationships. Some time ago Dame Edith Sitwell published a *Notebook on William Shakespeare* (1948) and many of her penetrating comments bear upon this perplexing theme: from among these comments a few of her remarks concerning the speeches of Macbeth and Lady Macbeth in the scenes before and after the murder may be selected as illustrative of her approach. "The very voices of these two damned souls," she observes,

> have a different sound. His voice is like that of some gigantic being in torment—of a lion with a human soul. In her speech invoking darkness, the actual sound is so murky and thick that the lines seem impervious to light, and, at times, rusty, as though they had lain in the blood that had been spilt, or in some hell-born dew. There is no escape from what we have done. The past will return to confront us. And that is even shown in the verse. In that invocation there are perpetual echoes, sometimes far removed from each other, sometimes placed close together. For instance, in the line
> 'And fill me from the crown to the toe, top-full,'
> 'full' is a darkened dissonance to 'fill'—and these dissonances, put at opposite ends of the line—together with the particular placing of the alliterative *f*'s of 'fill' and 'full' and the alliterative *t*'s, and the rocking up and down of the dissonantal *o*'s ('crown', 'toe', 'top') show us a mind reeling on the brink of madness, about to topple down into those depths, yet striving to retain its balance.

To present any comment upon such a commentary were otiose. All that need be said is that Dame Edith's remarkable analysis of the sound values of Lady Macbeth's speech makes us fully conscious of the complexities making up its pattern. Yet even she, like the students of imagery and prosody, has restricted herself to merely one single element in the total design. Reading her words, and thinking of them in relation to all the other interlocking qualities of Shakespeare's dramatic speech, we must indeed be confirmed in our belief that the forms assumed by the language used in his mature plays, even apart from its "meaning," are largely responsible for the impress which his characters make upon audiences; that the various aspects of these forms rarely can be subjected to statistical analysis; that, for a complete understanding of Shakespeare's dramatic skill, they have to be considered, not in isolation, but together; that, in a manner entirely proper to the theatre, a process of comparing and contrasting the speeches of different characters is likely to yield more fruitful results than an examination of individual parts; and, finally, that perhaps this is a realm wherein scholarly criticism, capable at its best of only vague definition and interpretation, must cede place to the imaginative interpretation of those who themselves are poets.—A. N.

Lansdowne, George Granville, Lord (1667–1735). Restoration dramatist who adapted *The Merchant of Venice* as a play called *The Jew of Venice* in 1701. Granville's dramatic works were written early in his career, his subsequent activities being largely political. In 1710 he was named secretary of war under Queen Anne and in the following year he was created a peer with the title of Lord Lansdowne. At the accession of George I (1714) he was deprived of his office and in 1715 was arrested for his complicity in the attempt of James II to regain the throne. Granville devoted the rest of his life to the composition of lyric poetry and polemical literature. His *The Genuine Works in Verse and Prose*, in two volumes, was published in 1732.

The Jew of Venice is a severely edited and somewhat rewritten version of Shakespeare's play. Morocco, Salanio, Salarino, and the two Gobbos are eliminated, and the number of scene changes is reduced. Shylock appears only four times: while making the bargain, at a feast in Bassanio's home, in a scene with the jailer, and at the trial. Bassanio's feast, an addition of Granville's, serves mainly to introduce a masque, supposedly an entertainment for the assembled merchants, but evidently a concession to the popular taste. The masque is not very elaborate, however; it does not include dancing or magic effects. Otherwise Shakespeare's story is reasonably closely followed.

Like Tate, Cibber, and most of Shakespeare's other adapters, Granville was no master of language, and his original and rewritten speeches are much inferior to Shakespeare's. In the editing of the play many passages were cut and mangled, including Portia's "quality of mercy" speech.

Granville's *Jew of Venice* has been a subject of particular interest because of his treatment of the title character. He cut Shylock's part but did not noticeably tamper with his personality. The role is known to have been played by Thomas DOGGET, a comedian, and this has been offered as evidence that Shakespeare conceived of Shylock's role as farcical. There are, however, no recorded productions of *The Merchant of Venice* between 1605 and 1701, when Granville's version was first played, so that the adaptation, however the title role was conceived, cannot be used as evidence that Shakespeare's Shylock was originally interpreted as a comic character. Granville's version maintained its popularity until 1741 when Charles MACKLIN electrified London with his performance of Shylock in the original Shakespearean version of the play. See MERCHANT OF VENICE:

Stage History. [Hazelton Spencer, *Shakespeare Improved,* 1927.]

La Place, Pierre-Antoine de. See FRANCE.

La Primaudaye, Pierre de (fl. 1577). Author of *L'Académie française* (1577), which may have provided Shakespeare with background material for *Love's Labour's Lost.* La Primaudaye's book, translated into English by Thomas Bowes in 1586, celebrates the practice in vogue at that time in the French court of withdrawing from the world in order to devote oneself to the pursuit of scholarship and learning. The work describes a model academy set up by four young idealists, not unlike those in Shakespeare's comedy (see LOVE'S LABOUR'S LOST: *Sources*). [Geoffrey Bullough, *Narrative and Dramatic Sources of Shakespeare,* Vol. I, 1957.]

Lartius, Titus. In *Coriolanus,* one of the generals who, with Coriolanus, lead the Roman army to victory against the Volscian town of Corioli. In I, ix, Cominius puts Titus Lartius in charge of the captured city; in III, i, Titus Lartius brings word to Coriolanus that Aufidius has withdrawn to Antium.

Laughton, Charles (1899–1962). British-American actor and director. Born in Scarborough and educated at the Royal Academy of Dramatic Art, Laughton was from the time of his debut in 1926 an imposing presence on the English and American stages. In 1936 he was the first English actor to act in French at the Comédie Française. In 1933 he played a season at the Old Vic-Sadler's Wells as Henry VIII, Angelo, Prospero, and Macbeth. In 1959 he appeared at the Shakespeare Memorial Theatre, Stratford-upon-Avon, as Bottom and King Lear. He was a successful stage director and gave memorable performances in many films. His wife, Elsa Lanchester, issued a volume of his biography, *Charles Laughton and I,* in 1938. [*Who's Who in the Theatre,* 1961.]

Launce. In *The Two Gentlemen of Verona,* Proteus' clowning servant. When he loses the dog that his master intended to give to Silvia, Launce offers her his dog Crab instead (IV, iv).

Laurence, Friar. In *Romeo and Juliet,* the Franciscan brother who devises a scheme for uniting the young lovers despite their families' mutual hatred and who performs their secret marriage ceremony. By a series of unhappy confusions, Friar Laurence's strategy is unsuccessful and results in Romeo's and Juliet's suicides.

Lavache (Lavatch). In *All's Well That Ends Well,* a clown in the service of the Countess of Rousillon. Expressing his desire to marry because of lust, Lavache delivers an elaborate justification of adultery and is consequently dismissed by his mistress as a "foul-mouthed and calumnious knave" (I, iii). Later, he proves to the Countess that the one answer, "O Lord, sir," will serve all questions and, having thus displayed good breeding, Lavache is then sent on an errand to the French court (II, ii).

Lavinia. In *Titus Andronicus,* daughter of Titus. When the Emperor Saturninus announces his intention to marry her, Lavinia is carried off by and married to the Emperor's brother Bassianus, who claims her as his betrothed. Her husband is subsequently murdered and she is raped and has her hands and tongue cut off by Tamora's sons, as part of a revenge scheme against Titus. She is able to reveal what has happened to her by turning her nephew Lucius' copy of Ovid's *Metamorphoses* to the story of Philomel. At the tragic banquet which brings the play to its gory climax, her father kills her to end her shame.

Law Against Lovers, The (1662). An adaptation of *Measure for Measure* and *Much Ado About Nothing* by William DAVENANT. *The Law Against Lovers* is essentially *Measure for Measure* with the interpolation of Benedick and Beatrice from *Much Ado.*

There are several major changes in the central *Measure for Measure* plot. Benedick, as Angelo's brother, and Beatrice, as "a great Heiress," take active roles in aiding Isabella and the lovers. Mrs. Overdone, Mariana, and the clowns are dropped, and the setting is changed from Vienna to Turin. The major scene between Isabella and Angelo is a radical innovation of Davenant's: after repeated efforts to corrupt her, Angelo suddenly announces that he had only been testing Isabella's virtue and that he never planned to kill Claudio.

The language of the play shows Davenant's desire prompted partly by adherence to the strictures of neoclassicism and partly by his personal inclinations against indecency, for clarity and propriety. Throughout the play even the most slightly involved metaphors are rephrased and, as a matter of course all impious and indecent remarks are censored. For the sake of uniformity, many of the passages which were written in prose in the original are converted into blank verse.

Davenant's interest in operatic spectacle appears in several interpolated songs and dances; in the fifth act, for instance, a quartet sings of Angelo's misuse of power.

The Law Against Lovers is the most radical of Davenant's adaptations of Shakespeare. During the Restoration it was considered to be Davenant's own play. It was the least successful of his adaptations and only two performances, both in 1662, have been recorded. [Hazelton Spencer, *Shakespeare Improved* 1927.]

Law or **Lawe, Matthew** (d. 1629). London bookseller who published some later editions of Shakespeare quartos. Originally a draper, Law transferred to the Stationers' Company in 1600. Three years later he took over from Andrew Wise the copyright privileges of *Richard II, Richard III,* and *1 Henry IV.* He published Q3 (the Third Quarto) of *1 Henry IV* in 1604 and three subsequent quartos of that play. In 1605 he published Q4 of *Richard III* and three subsequent quartos of that play. He published Q4 of *Richard II,* the first edition of that play to include the deposition scene (see RICHARD II: *Text*). The manifest errors in the scene as published by Law suggest that he secured the additional lines by stenographic report. Law published the Fifth Quarto of *Richard II* in 1615. [R. B. McKerrow, ed., *A Dictionary of Printers and Booksellers . . . 1557–1640,* 1910.]

Lawes, Henry. See MUSIC BASED ON SHAKESPEARE: *17th century.*

Lawrence, W. John (1862–1940). Irish-born scholar. Lawrence's most important volume is *The Physical Conditions of the Elizabethan Public Playhouse* (1927), a study of the physical aspects of the Elizabethan theatre and its influence on the structure of the drama. His other books are collections of essays on various aspects of the Elizabethan age with special emphasis on stagecraft: *The Elizabethan Playhouse and Other Studies* (two series, 1912, 1913), *Pre-Res-*

toration Stage Studies (1927), *Shakespeare's Workshop* (1928), *Those Nut-Cracking Elizabethans* (1935), and *Speeding Up Shakespeare* (1937).

Lawrence, William Witherle (1876–1958). American scholar. Lawrence wrote *Shakespeare's Problem Comedies* (1931), a work which initiated the modern revaluation of Shakespeare's so-called problem plays.

Laws of Ecclesiastical Polity, Of the (1593–1662). A classic defense of the Elizabethan church settlement by Richard Hooker (c. 1554–1600). By the 1580's, the Church of England was under heavy attack from such militant Puritans as Thomas Cartwright (1535–1603) and Walter Travers (c. 1548–1635) who advocated a radical change in church government along the lines of Geneva. Hooker, then Master of the Temple, was commissioned to answer these attacks. He completed the first four books in 1593; the fifth book appeared in 1597. Drafts of the three remaining books were left among his papers when he died in 1600 and were published posthumously (Books VI and VIII, 1648; Book VII, 1662). *Of the Laws of Ecclesiastical Polity* is a reasoned defense of the Church of England and a summation of traditional thought on political philosophy and natural law; it is set forth in a balanced and lucid style which has won for it acclaim as one of the masterpieces of English prose. The first book opens with a statement of Hooker's premises: that all creation is governed by a natural law which is supplemented and confirmed by Scriptures; that this natural law embodies the eternal law of God and as such is the supreme authority in both civil and ecclesiastical realms; and that as a consequence the Church must find its sanctions in both law and Scripture. The remainder of the work proceeds from these premises in a step-by-step series of arguments designed to win over the reader by cogent reasoning. This presentation is not unlike the speech on DEGREE by Ulysses in *Troilus and Cressida* (I, iii, 85–137).

Lawyer. In *1 Henry VI*, a minor character, who, in the Temple Garden, follows Vernon in plucking a white rose. He thus declares himself to be allied with Richard Plantagenet (II, iv).

Leake, William (d. 1633). Bookseller and printer. Leake was the printer of *The Passionate Pilgrim* (1599), an anthology of poetry ascribed to Shakespeare on the title page. He was also the publisher of Q5 (1599), Q6 (1599), Q7 (1602?), Q8 (1608?), Q9 (1609?) of *Venus and Adonis*. Leake was a prominent member of the Stationers' Company. He was succeeded by his son William (d. 1681) who in 1650 published a Quarto edition of *The Merchant of Venice* and in 1655 an edition of *Othello*. [Henry Plomer, *A Dictionary of Booksellers and Printers ... 1641–1667*, 1907; *The Poems:* Variorum Edition, Hyder Rollins, ed., 1938.]

Lear. In *King Lear*, the hero of the tragedy that bears his name. One of the towering figures of world drama and the central figure of what is often considered Shakespeare's greatest play, Lear is one character for whom the term "archetypal" would not be hyperbolic. He invites comparison with the great figures of the Bible and Greek tragedy, like them assuming a larger-than-life significance in the imagination of readers.

The tendency of some 19th-century critics to see Lear as in some sense "deserving" his fate has now been largely discredited. It is true that Lear's suffering and death issue from his initial blindness, but the disproportion between his initial error and his subsequent fate is far too great to be explained by any notion of reciprocal justice. The significant aspect of Lear's ordeal is that it is, in fact, an outrage, a symbol of the radically irrational nature of human experience. And it is the encounter with this experience which constitutes one aspect of tragedy. The other aspect of this experience, however—and the one which Lear best exemplifies—is the ability to emerge from this tragic encounter with grandeur and nobility.

learning in Elizabethan England. Elizabethan scholarship was pursued with the vigor and enthusiasm characteristic of the age. The spheres of learning fell into two main categories: history, and classical studies and translation. It was the latter category which occasioned considerable activity; interest in antiquity was high, and the urge to incorporate classical learning and literature into the English intellectual atmosphere accounted for the comparatively large amount of work done in translation.

Scholarship in Elizabethan England was to a certain extent crude and primitive. Though spirited, Elizabethan "scholars" cannot be considered professional in the modern sense (many of them were in fact men of other trades and professions), and inaccuracies and distortions abound in their work. Historians were for the most part uncritical, and many of the translators relied upon works which were themselves translations of the originals as the bases for their renderings. George Chapman, for example, an undisputed scholar and poet, took for his source a Latin commentary on Homer. The translator of Thucydides, Thomas Nicolls (fl. 1550), "citizeine and goldsmyth of London," used a French rendering of a Latin version of the original Greek. Though this method has obvious deficiencies where scholarship is concerned, the results could be described as new works with a new, and English, character and spirit, rather than sober and accurate renderings of original works from the past. In this regard, the question of Ben Jonson's learning and Shakespeare's apparent lack of it exemplifies the general spirit of Elizabethan scholarship. Jonson is precise and accurate in his portrayals of the externals of the Roman world, it has been argued, while Shakespeare's foreign settings are unrealistic and romantic. But as Goethe observed, "Shakespeare turns his Romans into Englishmen, and he does right, for otherwise his nation would not have understood him."

As we have noted above, the Elizabethans' familiarity with the classics was broadened through an increasing number of contemporary translations. A translation of the *Aeneid*, begun by Thomas PHAER and published in 1558, was completed after his death by Thomas Twyne in 1573. Terence was translated in 1598, and Horace's *Satires* in 1566; Plautus' *Menaechmi*, on which Shakespeare's *Comedy of Errors* is based, appeared in a translation by William WARNER in 1595. The Latin poets with the greatest influence on the Elizabethans were Seneca and Ovid. In 1581 there appeared a translation of *Seneca his tenne Tragedies* by Thomas Newton *et al.* It incorporated earlier translations of the individual plays by various translators. Seneca's influence on Elizabethan tragedy was considerable: many of the conventional trappings of his plays—the ghost, the chorus, and the graphic portrayal of horrors—are found in Elizabethan drama, and much that is considered typical of Elizabethan tragedy is derived from him.

The first edition of Arthur GOLDING's *The XV Bookes of P. Ovidius Naso, entytuled Metamorphosis, translated into English meeter* appeared in 1567. (It has been generally assumed that most of Shakespeare's knowledge of classical mythology came from Ovid.) In the field of Latin prose, the work of Philemon Holland (1552–1637) is important and his *The Romane Historie written by Titus Livius of Padua* (1600) a notable example of his contribution. Holland was described by one contemporary as the "Translator Generall of his age."

Translations of the works of the Greek dramatists were relatively rare. In 1566 George Gascoigne and Francis Kinwelmersh presented *Jocasta*, their translation and "digest(ion)" of Euripides' *Phoenissae*. Their source was an Italian adaptation by Lodovico Dolce.

Though there were various renderings of Homer, Chapman's *Iliad* (1598, 1611) and *Odyssey* (1615) superseded all other versions. The Greek prose writers were translated more often than the dramatists. Isocrates, Aesop, Diogenes Laertius, some of Plato, Aristotle's *Ethics* and *Politics*, Xenophon, Polybius, Diodorus Siculus, Demosthenes, and Dionysius were all known to the Elizabethans in English. Most important was Sir Thomas NORTH's English version of Plutarch's *The Lives of the noble Grecians and Romanes; translated into French by J. Amyot* (1579), used by Shakespeare in writing *Julius Caesar*, *Coriolanus*, and *Antony and Cleopatra*.

Translations of contemporary works from abroad were also available to the Elizabethans. William Painter's *The Palace of Pleasure* (2 vols., 1566–1567) included what he termed "Pleasaunt Histories and excellent Novelles," from French and Italian as well as Greek and Latin writers. Machiavelli was known in an English version, as were Du Bartas, Montaigne, Amadis de Gaule, and others.

Elizabethan historical writing may be said to begin with the work of Raphael HOLINSHED. Large portions of the work of earlier chroniclers, Polydore VERGIL and Edward HALLE, were absorbed into the *Chronicles of England, Scotlande, and Irelande, etc.* (1578) written by many persons under Holinshed's editorship. They are comprehensive indeed; beginning with the Flood, the history of England (with the last volume written by Holinshed) was brought to within four years of the date of publication.

John STOW, also known for an edition of Chaucer, wrote *A Summarie of Englyshe Chronicles* (1565), which appeared in various editions; and *A Survay of London* (1598). William CAMDEN published *Britannia sive florentissimorum regnorum, Angliae, Scotiae, Hiberniae Chorographica descriptio* (1586) and the *Annales Rerum Anglicarum, et Hibernicarum Regnante Elizabetha* (1615, 1625). Written in Latin, Camden's works were vigorous and patriotic. Sir John Hayward (c. 1564–1627) differs from most other chroniclers in being a relatively professional historian. The critical spirit of *The First Part of the Life and Raigne of King Henrie the IIII* (1599) displeased Elizabeth, and Hayward was imprisoned for several years. He then turned his attention to an earlier period and issued *The lives of the III Normans, Kings of England* (1613). Sir Walter Raleigh's *The History of the World* (1614), composed during his 13-year imprisonment in the Tower, was a remarkable work. It was not so much objective history as a series of soliloquies on mythology, magic, theology, law, war, and the ideal form of government. *The Historie of the Raigne of King Henry the Seventh* by Sir Francis Bacon was published in 1622. The sophistication of the work in style and general organization marks an enormous improvement in historical scholarship over the earlier efforts of Polydore Vergil, Halle, Holinshed, and Stow. [Sir John Sandys, "Scholarship," *Shakespeare's England*, 1916.]

Le Beau. In *As You Like It*, a pretentious courtier attending Duke Frederick. In I, ii, Le Beau recounts to Celia and Rosalind the victories of Charles, the court wrestler. After a match in which Charles is bested by Orlando, Le Beau kindheartedly warns the latter of Frederick's displeasure and advises the young man to leave court.

Lee, Anne. See William WAYTE.

Lee, John. See ADAPTATIONS.

Lee, Sir **Sidney** (1859–1926). Scholar. Educated at Oxford, Lee early became associated with the *Dictionary of National Biography*, serving as assistant editor from 1883 until he succeeded Sir Leslie Stephens as editor in 1891. Besides his editorial work, he contributed 820 articles, most of which are on Elizabethans. The article on Shakespeare was expanded to the full-length *Life of William Shakespeare* (1898), long the standard work on the subject. Another by-product of his research was *Stratford-on-Avon from the Earliest Times to the Death of Shakespeare* (1885). Upon completion of the *Dictionary*, he produced the facsimile edition of the First Folio, gave a series of lectures published as *Great Englishmen of the Sixteenth Century* (1904), and edited the complete *Works* (1910). Other works include *Shakespeare and the Modern Stage* (1906), *The French Renaissance in England* (1909), *The Principles of Biography* (1911), *and Shakespeare in the Italian Renaissance* (1915). A posthumous collection appeared under the title *Elizabethan and Other Essays* (1929), important for its emphasis on the impact which the discovery of America had upon the Elizabethan writers. Lee was knighted in 1911 and from 1913 to 1924 was professor of English at London University.

Lee, William. See William LEY.

Leech, Clifford (1909–). Critic. Professor of English at the University of Toronto, Leech is the author of a large number of critical studies of 17th-century drama, including *Shakespeare's Tragedies*... (1950) and *Shakespeare: The Chronicles* (1962). He is also the general editor of The Revels Plays, a distinguished series of Elizabethan plays.

Lefranc, Abel (1863–1952). French scholar. Lefranc was professor of French at the Collège de France between 1904 and 1937. In his *A la Découverte de Shakespeare* (2 vols., 1945, 1950) he argues that the author of Shakespeare's works was William Stanley, 6th earl of Derby (see DERBYITE THEORY). The work's real value, however, is that it provides historical background to *Love's Labour's Lost*.

Le Gallienne, Eva (1899–). American actress and producer. Born in London, Eva Le Gallienne was educated at the Royal Academy of Dramatic Art and made her debut in 1915. She came to America the following year and appeared in a succession of productions until 1926 when she founded the Civic Repertory Theatre in New York. With this group Miss Le Gallienne appeared as Viola and Juliet, and also gave notable productions of Ibsen. In 1946 she founded the American Repertory Theatre with Cheryl Crawford and Margaret Webster. Among Miss Le Gallienne's other Shakespearean roles have been Hamlet (1937) and Queen Katharine in *Henry VIII* (1946). She is the part-author of a dramatization of *Alice in Wonderland* and has translated several of Ibsen's plays, including *Ghosts* and *Hedda Gabler*. Two volumes of her autobiography have appeared: *At 33* (1934) and *With a Quiet Heart* (1953). [*Who's Who in the Theatre*, 1961.]

Legend of Good Women, The. See RAPE OF LUCRECE: *Sources*.

Legge, Thomas (1535–1607). Scholar and dramatist. One of the foremost scholars of his day, Legge served as vice chancellor of Corpus Christi College, Cambridge. He was also the author of two academic plays, one of which was a Latin tragedy, *Richardus Tertius* (c. 1579), based on the life of Richard III. The play bears interesting resemblances to Shakespeare's drama, since it is based on the same historical sources Shakespeare used. Legge's Richard, however, lacks the stature and depth of Shakespeare's villain.

Leicester, Robert Dudley, earl of (1532–1588). Courtier, soldier, and favorite of Queen Elizabeth. The fifth son of John Dudley, duke of Northumberland (c. 1502–1553), Robert Dudley was instrumental in the attempt in 1553 to place Lady Jane Grey (1537–1554), his sister-in-law, on the throne. With the accession of Elizabeth in 1558 he was appointed a member of the privy council and became intimately involved with the queen. In 1560 his wife, Lady Amy Dudley (c. 1532–1560), was found dead at the foot of a staircase in her home. Leicester was generally thought to have murdered her in order to marry Elizabeth. Although Elizabeth was apparently willing, the marriage never took place because of a number of political obstacles, chief among which was the opposition of Elizabeth's most trusted adviser, Lord Burghley.

Dudley was created earl of Leicester in 1564 and in 1578, having despaired of winning Elizabeth's hand, he married Lettice Knollys (1541–1634), the widow of the 1st earl of Essex. In 1585, with his stepson Robert Devereux, 2nd earl of Essex, he led an expedition to assist the Netherlands against Spain and was chosen absolute governor of the Netherlands in 1586. His move angered Elizabeth, but she ultimately relented. However, Leicester's performance as general in the Netherlands was very poor, and he was recalled in 1587. He died the following year.

Leicester was a great patron of literature and drama. In 1574 the actors under his patronage, Leicester's Men, were the first to receive a royal patent. In his castle at Kenilworth, a short distance from Stratford, he entertained the queen lavishly, particularly in the years 1572 and 1575. In the latter year the queen's visit lasted 19 days, and the entertainment included fireworks and an elaborate water pageant concerning the courting of Phoebe by Arion, who delivered his song from the back of a dolphin. This entertainment was attended by the local populace as well, and some scholars believe that Shakespeare may have seen it as a boy and alluded to it in *A Midsummer Night's Dream* (II, i, 146–168) or *Twelfth Night* (I, ii, 15–17).

ROBERT DUDLEY, EARL OF LEICESTER. MINIATURE BY NICHOLAS HILLIARD. (NATIONAL PORTRAIT GALLERY)

Leicester's Men. Elizabethan acting company under the patronage of Robert Dudley, earl of Leicester. Leicester's Men appeared at court during the Christmas seasons 1560/1 through 1562/3, and then did not return to London until December 1571. In the interim they are known to have traveled through the provinces. In 1572, in order to avoid entanglements with the law under the terms of the statutes against unlawful retainers, the players petitioned their patron:

> Vouchsaffe to reteyne us at this present as your houshold Servaunts and daylie wayters, not that we meane to crave any further stipend or benefite at your Lordshippes hands but our lyveries as we have had, and also your honors License to certifye that we are your houshold Servaunts when we shall have occasion to travayle amongst our frendes as we do usuallye once a yere, and as other noblemens Players do and have done in tyme past, Wherebie we maye enjoye our facultie in your Lordshippes name as we have done hertofore.

They signed themselves "Iames Burbage. Iohn Perkinne. Iohn Laneham. William Iohnson. Roberte Wilson. Thomas Clarke." In December 1571 they received a license to play in London "such matters as are alowed of to be played, at conventient howers & tymes, so that it be not in tyme of devyne service." On May 10, 1574 "Iacobo Burbage & allis" received a special patent from Elizabeth allowing the players greater scope and privileges than they had hitherto enjoyed (see LICENSING AND CENSORSHIP).

By this time the company was again playing at

court in the winter seasons, alternating with tours of the provinces to places such as Bristol, Beverley, Nottingham, and Stratford-on-Avon in the late summer and early fall, 1573. When Elizabeth paid an historic visit to Kenilworth in July 1575, it is likely that the company performed before her. They played at court December 28, 1575 and in the court payment account for March 4, 1576 are referred to as "Burbag and his company." When Burbage built THE THEATRE in 1576, they gained a London headquarters, but still toured the provinces regularly and continued to give performances at court.

In March 1583 several of Leicester's Men, including Laneham, Wilson, and Johnson, joined the newly formed QUEEN'S MEN. It has been conjectured that Queen's Men might then have taken over the Theatre and/or that Burbage might have given up acting altogether. A remnant of the company was recorded touring in 1584/5. This might have been either the old company reconstructed or a new one which was to accompany the earl to the low countries where he commanded the English forces aiding the Netherlands States-General against Spain. Related to the campaign is a controversy over the composition of the company and whether Shakespeare might not have been part of it on its visit abroad. A letter from Sir Philip Sidney to Sir Francis Walsingham (dated Utrecht, March 24, 1586) contains an allusion to a member of the company as follows:

> I wrote to yow a letter by Will, my lord of Lester's jesting plaier, enclosed in a letter to my wife, and I never had answer thereof . . . I since find that the knave deliverd the letters to my ladi of Lester.

It is considered most likely that the "jesting plaier" was William Kempe rather than Shakespeare, since Kempe was at the Danish court later that year with a group of players—Thomas Stevens, George Bryan, Thomas King, Thomas Pope, and Robert Percy—who have been identified as the English comedians commended by the earl to Frederick II of Denmark. There has been some confusion in identifying this or another group as Leicester's Men, since the comedians did not leave Europe until 1587, while a group calling themselves Leicester's Men were touring the English provinces in 1586. This remnant of the original company, if such they were, disbanded with the death of Leicester in 1588. [John Tucker Murray, *English Dramatic Companies, 1558–1642*, 1910; E. K. Chambers, *The Elizabethan Stage*, 1923.]

Leigh, Andrew (1887–1957). Actor and director. Leigh made his first stage appearance in *The Merry Wives of Windsor* in 1908. From that year until 1913 he was with F. R. Benson's Stratford troupe, assuming the chief clown's roles in most of the Shakespearean productions. In 1914 he joined the newly formed Old Vic company for which he played the leading comic roles. His directorial chores included productions of *The Merchant of Venice* (1930), *A Midsummer Night's Dream* (1938), *King John* (1940), and *Julius Caesar* (1941).

Leigh, Vivien. Real name **Vivien Mary Hartley** (1913–1967). Actress. Born in India, Vivien Leigh was trained at the Comédie Française and the Royal Academy of Dramatic Art. She made her first film in 1934 and her stage debut in 1935. The next year she played the first of many Shakespearean roles—the Queen in *Richard II* for the Oxford University Dramatic Society. Her other Shakespearean roles include Anne Bullen (1936), Ophelia (at Elsinore 1937, with the Old Vic), Titania (1937, at the Old Vic), Juliet (in New York, 1940), Lady Anne (with the Old Vic, 1949), Cleopatra (with Laurence Olivier, then her husband, New York, 1951), and Viola, Lavinia, and Lady Macbeth (at the Shakespeare Memorial Theatre, 1955 and 1957). She has made many memorable films. [*Who's Who in the Theatre*, 1961.]

Lena or **Laenas, Popilius.** In *Julius Caesar*, a senator. In III, i, Lena wishes Brutus and Cassius success in their enterprise. When they see him conversing with Caesar, they momentarily fear that he has betrayed them. The incident is recounted by Plutarch.

Lennox. In *Macbeth*, a Scottish nobleman. After the discovery of Duncan's murder, Lennox goes with Macbeth to the murdered man's room and is witness to Macbeth's murdering the supposedly guilty grooms. Observing Macbeth's terror when Banquo's ghost appears at the banquet, Lennox is convinced of the King's guilt and joins the rebellion against him.

Lennox, Charlotte Ramsay (1720–1804). American-born novelist and Shakespeare scholar. Mrs. Lennox was the daughter of Colonel James Ramsay, an English army officer and, at the time of his daughter's birth, lieutenant-governor of New York. She went to London in 1735, where she spent the rest of her life. Inheriting nothing from her father, she began to support herself by writing. She also had a brief, unsuccessful career as an actress. Her first important work was a novel, *The Female Quixote* (2 vols., 1752). Samuel Johnson developed an exaggerated admiration for her talents. Speaking of Elizabeth Carter, Hannah More, and Fanny Burney, he said: "Three such women are not to be found; I know not where to find a fourth except Mrs. Lennox, who is superior to them all . . . ." In 1753–1754 she published in three volumes a work entitled *Shakespear Illustrated; or the Novels and Histories, on which the Plays are founded, Collected and Translated*. In it she presented the text (in translation) of the sources, or extracts from them, of 22 of Shakespeare's plays and made some analyses of the way the poet used them. [Miriam Small, *Charlotte Ramsay Lennox*, 1935.]

Lennox' Men. A company of actors under the patronage of Ludovic Stuart, 2nd duke of Lennox (1574–1624). Lennox' Men apparently never played in London; their activities seem to have been confined solely to the provinces from 1604 to 1608. Among its members were two former Queen's Men: Francis Henslowe, the nephew of the manager Philip Henslowe, and John Garland. It is conceivable that Lennox' was the continuation of the Queen's Men following the death of Queen Elizabeth in 1603. After 1608 the name of the company disappears from the records. However, by 1610 John Garland had joined Prince Charles' Men (then known as the Duke of York's Men) which had been formed in 1608, and it is thought that Garland and others formed the nucleus of that company. [E. K. Chambers, *The Elizabethan Stage*, 1923.]

Leonardo. In *The Merchant of Venice*, Bassanio's servant. In II, ii, Leonardo is dispatched to purchase new livery for Launcelot Gobbo and to prepare a farewell supper for Antonio.

Leonato. In *Much Ado About Nothing*, governor of Messina and Hero's father. The hospitable Leonato, with vague expectations of a request from Don Pedro for his daughter's hand, nevertheless happily consents to the betrothal of Hero and Claudio. As Beatrice's guardian, the old man is anxious that his niece, too, find an acceptable husband. Although he is dubious about the outcome and believes that, were they married but a week, Beatrice and Benedick "would talk themselves mad," he enters Don Pedro's conspiracy to match the offish pair.

Leonatus, Posthumus. See POSTHUMUS LEONATUS.

Leoni, Michele. See ITALY.

Leonine. In *Pericles*, a servant to Dionyza. The latter orders Leonine to murder Marina (IV, i) and later poisons her servant.

Leontes. In *The Winter's Tale*, the King of Sicilia whose violent jealousy dominates the first three acts of the play. Leontes' apparently unmotivated jealousy has disturbed many readers, who recoil at the improbability of his behavior. Some critics have attempted to explain this phenomenon by pointing out that impulsiveness and lack of moderation, whether in anger or repentance, are the hallmarks of Leontes' character. Others, notably J. Dover Wilson, believe that ". . . the actor who plays him [Leontes] should display signs of jealousy from the very onset and make it clear that the business of asking Polixenes to stay longer is merely the device of jealousy seeking proof." Wilson's advice, it should be noted, has been successfully adopted in some recent performances of the play.

Leontes' jealousy has invited inevitable comparison with Othello, but whereas Othello's suspicions are externally motivated, Leontes' jealousy is an inner infection "begot upon itself." The images of infection and disease in reference to Leontes' mental state consistently reinforce this idea and help to explain his apparently motiveless passion, which, like a hidden cancer, pursues its frenzied course until it overwhelms his reason.

Leopold Shakespeare, The (1877). A popular one-volume edition of Shakespeare's works. The Leopold Shakespeare used the text established by Nikolaus Delius for his Berlin edition (1854–1861). F. J. Furnivall wrote the Introduction; in it he discussed the method of verse tests to indicate dating and development. The edition was named for Prince Leopold, duke of Albany, to whom it was dedicated. See SCHOLARSHIP—19TH CENTURY.

Lepidus, Marcus Aemilius (d. 13 B.C.). A member, with Octavius and Mark Antony, of the second triumvirate of Rome, but forced by the ambitious Octavius into retirement after having tried in 36 B.C. to seize Sicily. In *Julius Caesar*, Lepidus is a witness to the assassination of Caesar, and afterward, with Mark Antony and Octavius Caesar, forms the second triumvirate. In *Antony and Cleopatra*, Lepidus attempts to sustain harmonious relations between Octavius and Antony, but he is forcibly retired and imprisoned by Octavius.

Lessing, Gotthold Ephraim (1729–1781). German critic, playwright, and poet. Born at Kamenz in Saxony, and educated at the University of Leipzig, Lessing provoked controversy as a critic and dramatist. Among his plays are *Minna von Barnhelm* (1767) and *Emilia Galotti* (1772). His criticism includes *Laocoön* (1766), a fundamental contribution to aesthetics which defines the limits of poetry and the plastic arts, and *Hamburgische Dramaturgie* (1767–1769), essays which attacked the dictatorial influence of the French theatre. In his criticism of the drama, Lessing often praises the examples of Shakespeare and the Greeks.

His criticism in the *Hamburgische Dramaturgie* defends Shakespeare in Aristotelian terms by insisting that "unity of action was the first dramatic law of the ancients; unity of time and place were mere consequences of the former . . . ." The 19th-century German scholar G. G. Gervinus described Lessing as "the man who first valued Shakespeare according to his full desert."

L'Estrange, Sir Nicholas (d. 1655). Collector of anecdotes, one of which concerns Shakespeare and Ben Jonson. A member of a prominent royalist family, L'Estrange was knighted in 1629. His collection of anecdotes (in a manuscript in the British Museum) is titled *Merry Passages and Jests.* One story alleges that Shakespeare acted as godfather to one of Jonson's children; the point of the story is the double pun on the words "Lattin Spoones" (spoons made of a thin sheet of brass or other metal) and "translate" (the term in alchemy for the transformation of base metals to gold):

> Shake-speare was Godfather to one of *Ben:Johnsons* children, and after the christning being in a deepe study, Johnson came to cheere him vp, and askt him why he was so Melancholy? no faith *Ben:* (sayes he) not I, but I haue beene considering a great while what should be the fittest gift for me to bestow vpon my God-child, and I haue reaskt him why he was so Melancholy? no faith *Ben:* I'le e'en giue him a douzen good Lattin Spoones, and thou shat translate them.

The same anecdote, with the relationships reversed, is related in a manuscript of Thomas Plume. [E. K. Chambers, *William Shakespeare*, 1930.]

Le Tourneur, Pierre. See FRANCE.

Leveridge, Richard. See ADAPTATIONS.

Leveson, William (fl. 1599). Shipping merchant. In 1599 Leveson acted as trustee, along with Thomas Savage, for the Chamberlain's Men to enable the company to divide its half interest in the ground lease of the GLOBE THEATRE equally among the five actor-sharers, Shakespeare, John Heminges, Thomas Pope, Will Kempe, and Augustine Phillips. The other half interest was owned by Cuthbert and Richard Burbage.

Leveson was active in the Virginia Company, the organization which financed the colonization of Virginia. [Leslie Hotson, *I, William Shakespeare*, 1938.]

Levin, Harry (1912–). American critic. Irving Babbitt professor of comparative literature at Harvard University, Levin has published books on a variety of subjects including James Joyce, the French and American novel, and Christopher Marlowe. He has published one book on Shakespeare, *The Question of Hamlet* (1959), a study of the rhetorical structure of the play. The book includes in an appendix his well-known essay "An Explication of the Player's Speech." He has also edited *Coriolanus* for the Pelican Shakespeare series (1956).

Lewis the Dauphin. See LOUIS THE DAUPHIN.

Lewis, C[live] S[taples] (1898–1963). Scholar and author. Educated in Ireland and at Oxford, Lewis became professor of medieval and Renaissance English at Cambridge University in 1954. Lewis is recognized as a defender of the Christian tradition. *Out of the Silent Planet* (1938) and *The Screwtape Letters* (1942) are among his most popular books. In *The Allegory of Love* (1936) Lewis has interpreted central themes in medieval literature. In 1960 he published *The World's Last Night and Other Essays.*

Asked to deliver the annual Shakespeare Lecture to the British Academy in 1942, Lewis attempted to explain the failure of critics to solve the riddle of *Hamlet.* In his view critics have paid too much attention to Hamlet's character and not enough to the situation. In all of Shakespeare, he argues, "the first thing is to surrender oneself to the poetry and the situation." Character analysis along realistic lines has made a fairy tale like the *Merchant of Venice* seem a confused and irrelevant play. *Hamlet* is a play about ghosts and the idea of being dead. We are not interested in Hamlet's motives, he concludes, but in the situation and "that darkness which enwraps Hamlet and the whole tragedy and all who read or watch it."

Lewkenor, Sir Lewis (c. 1556–1626). Diplomat and translator. A native of Selsey, Sussex, Lewkenor studied at Middle Temple after which he traveled on the continent. His activities there included spying for Lord Burghley on the activities of English Catholics in Europe. These experiences are the basis of a book he published in 1595, *A Discourse of the Usage of English Fugitives by the Spaniard.*

In 1599 he translated Gasparo Contarini's *Della Republica et Magistrati de Venetia* as *The Commonwealth and Government of Venice.* The first book in English to deal exclusively with Venice, it may have been read in manuscript by Shakespeare and used for the legal background of Shakespeare's *Merchant of Venice.* The book was definitely used by the poet for *Othello,* not only for information about Venice, but for Othello's defense against the charge of witchcraft (I, iii).

Another relationship between Lewkenor and Shakespeare has been established on the basis of Lewkenor's remote kinship with the Combe family of Stratford with whom Shakespeare was friendly. [Christopher Whitfield, "Sir Lewis Lewkenor and *The Merchant of Venice,*" *Notes & Queries,* 209, 1964.]

Ley or **Lee, William** (fl. 1656). Bookseller who, in association with Richard Rogers, published a catalogue of plays in 1656. The catalogue, printed as an appendix to Thomas Goffe's *The Careless Shepherdess,* attributes to Shakespeare the authorship of *Edward II, Edward III, Edward IV,* and *The London Prodigal.* [W. W. Greg, *A List of English Plays Written before 1643 . . .,* 1900.]

Library Theatre, The. A repertory theatre in Manchester, England. Though the theatre, located in the basement of the Central Library Building in Saint Peter's Square, has been in operation in various forms since before the war, it has operated in its present location only since 1952. At that time the Libraries Committee decided to assume responsibility for the operation of the theatre itself, rather than to charge a nominal rental to other companies, as it had in the past. Since that time the Library Theatre has had its own director and repertory company functioning under the direct aegis of the city librarian.

The philosophy of the theatre is that the programing should have a sufficiently broad base to ensure fare for everyone, the plays should be high in entertainment and artistic value, and admission fees should be maintained at a nominal level to ensure that cost is no barrier to attendance. It is the policy of the theatre to present two Shakespearean productions in each season. One of the productions is normally presented at the beginning of the season, between September and Christmas, the second production following the Christmas season fairly closely.

Shakespeare productions since the 1952/3 season have been *Romeo and Juliet, A Midsummer Night's Dream, Macbeth, Richard II, Othello, Julius Caesar, The Tempest, Henry V, Twelfth Night, 1 Henry IV, The Merchant of Venice,* and *As You Like It.*

Lieutenant of the Tower. In *3 Henry VI,* King Henry's keeper. On the King's release by Warwick, the keeper begs Henry's pardon for having been obliged to hold him prisoner (IV, vi). Historically this character was probably John Tiptoft or Tibetoft (b. 1427), who was made 1st earl of Worcester in 1449. He was an ardent Yorkist who, on the accession of Edward IV, was appointed constable of the Tower. After hanging and impaling 20 followers of the duke of Clarence in 1470, he became known as "the butcher of England." On Edward's flight, the constable himself was committed to the Tower and executed. [W. H. Thomson, *Shakespeare's Characters: A Historical Dictionary,* 1951.]

Lieutenant to Aufidius. In *Coriolanus,* he turns his lord against Coriolanus by telling him that the Roman's successes have overshadowed those of Aufidius (IV, vii).

Ligarius, Caius. In *Julius Caesar,* a conspirator. Although he is ill, Ligarius joins the plot against Caesar, saying that he is not sick "if Brutus have in hand/ Any exploit worthy the name of honour" (II, ii). Plutarch recounts a similar episode.

Lillo, George (1693–1739). Dramatist. Lillo is best known as the author of the popular middle-class tragedy *The London Merchant: or, The History of George Barnwell* (1731). In 1738 he adapted *Pericles* under the title of *Marina.* Lillo's adaptation was derived almost entirely from Act IV of *Pericles,* together with new material which he interpolated. See ADAPTATIONS. [C. B. Hogan, *Shakespeare in the Theatre, 1701–1800,* 2 vols., 1952, 1957.]

Lily, William (1468?–1522). Scholar and humanist. A friend of Erasmus, Thomas More, and the dean of St. Paul's, John Colet, Lily was appointed master of St. Paul's school in 1510. He collaborated with Colet on the production of a Latin grammar, *Grammatices Rudimenta* (1534; known as *Lily's Latin Grammar* or *The Accidence*), which remained for the next 300 years the standard Latin text used in English schools.

Shakespeare's knowledge of the book is demonstrated in *The Merry Wives of Windsor* (IV, i) where Sir Hugh Evans asks William Page "some questions in his accidence." There are other borrowings from Lily in *Twelfth Night* (II, iii, 3), *Love's Labour's Lost* (IV, ii, 82), *The Taming of the Shrew* (I, i, 167), and an allusion to the grammar in *Titus Andronicus* (IV, ii, 20–23). [H. R. D. Anders, *Shakespeare's Books,* 1904.]

Lincoln, bishop of. **John Longland** (1476–1547). As confessor to Henry VIII, he was the first to uggest the possibility of divorce from Katharine, as ıe says in II, iv of *Henry VIII.*

Lincoln's Inn Fields Theatre. A theatre built in 695 on the site of the former LISLE'S TENNIS COURT THEATRE, in Portugal Street. The Lincoln's Inn Fields Theatre was closed on October 20, 1705, and then ebuilt and reopened in 1714. In 1732 the Lincoln's nn Fields company moved to a new theatre in Covent Garden, and for the next 11 years the old heatre witnessed a miscellany of plays, concerts, and peras. The theatre was permanently closed in 1744. After that date it was used as a guardroom (1745), a barracks (1756), a dancing academy (from 1770 to 778), a lecture hall (in the 1790's), and a china warehouse (early 19th century). The building was azed in 1848. [C. B. Hogan, *Shakespeare in the Thetre 1701–1800,* 2 vols., 1952, 1957.]

Lincoln's Men [Lord Clinton's Men]. A company of actors under the patronage of Edward Fiennes de Clinton, 1st earl of Lincoln (1512–1585), and Henry Fiennes de Clinton, 2nd earl of Lincoln (c. 1541–616). Lincoln's Men, led by Laurence Dutton, played at court during the Christmas festivities of 572/3 and 1574/5. After the death of their first patron in 1585, their activities declined, and they appeared only in the provinces.

Ling, Nicholas (fl. 1570–1607). Bookseller who published, in conjunction with John Trundell (fl. 589–1626), the "bad quarto" (Q1; 1603) of *Hamlet.* Ling was admitted as a freeman to the Stationers' Company in 1578. His publishing ventures were generally in collaboration with others. In 1597 he edited a collection of prose quotations called *Politeuphuia, or Wits Commonwealth* as part of the series of which Francis Meres' *Palladis Tamia: Wits Treasury* (1598) is the best-known volume. In 1607, the year in which he made his will, Ling received the copyrights of *Love's Labour's Lost, Romeo and Juliet,* and the anonymous *Taming of A Shrew* from Cuthbert Burby. Later the same year he transferred them, along with *Hamlet,* to John Smethwicke. One unusual aspect of Ling's publication of the bad quarto of *Hamlet* is that in the following year he also published the good quarto, apparently having received from the players an authoritative copy of the play. D. S. Savage, whose *Hamlet and the Pirates* (1950) argues that the pirate episode in *Hamlet* is Shakespeare's veiled attack on publishing "pirates," written after the publication of the bad quarto, asserts that these episodes in the play contain hidden allusions to Ling's name.

Lion. See SNUG.

Lisle's Tennis Court Theatre [Duke's House]. Restoration theatre initially built in 1656 as a tennis court by Thomas and Anne Lisle. Lisle's Tennis Court was located between the areas of Lincoln's Inn Fields and Little Lincoln's Inn Fields, abutting on what is now known as Portugal Street. In 1660 William Davenant contracted with Lisle to convert the tennis court into a theatre; the following year it was occupied by Davenant's Duke's Company which in August presented Thomas Betterton as Hamlet. See LINCOLN'S INN FIELDS THEATRE. [Leslie Hotson, *The Commonwealth and Restoration Stage,* 1928.]

Liszt, Franz. See MUSIC BASED ON SHAKESPEARE: *19th century, 1850–1900.*

Lives of the Noble Grecians and Romans. See Sir Thomas NORTH; PLUTARCH.

Livy. Latin name **Titus Livius** (59 B.C.–A.D. 17). Roman historian. A native of Padua, Livy went to Rome in his youth and gained the friendship and patronage of the Emperor Augustus. Livy's history of Rome (*Ab Urbe Condita,* literally "from the founding of the city") consisted of 142 books, of which only about a fourth are extant. His work has served subsequent generations as an invaluable source of information on the early history of Rome. Livy's account of the rape of Lucrece, translated into English by William Painter in *The Palace of Pleasure* (2 vols., 1566–1567), is one of the sources of Shakespeare's *The Rape of Lucrece.* It has also been suggested that *Coriolanus* may have been borrowed in part from Livy's history. See CORIOLANUS: *Sources.*

Lloyd, Ludovic (fl. 1573–1610). Welsh poet and courtier. Lloyd was a follower of Sir Christopher Hatton (1540–1591), Elizabeth's lord chancellor. Through the aegis of Hatton, Lloyd became a member of the English court where he quickly became a favorite. Edward Owen argues that Lloyd, known by members of the court as "Floyd," is the model for Shakespeare's Fluellen, the Welsh warrior in *Henry V.* Owen's thesis is put forth in contradiction to Dover Wilson's view that Fluellen is based on Sir Roger Williams. [Edward Owen, *Ludovic Lloyd,* 1931.]

Locrine. An anonymous tragedy, the authorship of which was ascribed to Shakespeare in the 17th century. The play was entered in the Stationers' Register in 1594 and published the following year.

TITLE PAGE OF *Locrine* (1595).

THE

Lamentable Tragedie of

Locrine, the eldest sonne of King *Brutus*, discoursing the warres of the *Britaines*, and *Hunnes*, with their discomfiture:

The Britaines *victorie with their Accidents, and the death of* Albanact. *No lesse pleasant then profitable.*

Newly set foorth, ouerseene and corrected, By *VV. S.*

LONDON

Printed by Thomas Creede.

1595.

It has been pointed out that the reference to "W. S." as one who has "newly set foorth, ouerseene and corrected" the play may not be a claim of authorship, but may merely refer to the fact that "W. S." revised and edited the play for publication. It was published in the Third (1664) and Fourth (1685) Folios as Shakespeare's.

Although no critic accepts the ascription to Shakespeare, some think that he may have been the play's editor. The editorship has also been attributed to another W. S., the poet William SMITH. It has been suggested that the play repeats historical data contained in Spenser's *Faerie Queene* (1590) and echoes many lines of Spenser's *Complaints* (1590). Smith, it has been noted, was an avowed disciple of Spenser.

The play has also been ascribed, on the basis of a note in an extant copy of the play, to Charles Tilney, executed for treason on September 20, 1586. The note, written in the hand of the Master of the Revels, George Buc, was discovered by John Payne Collier and is thought by some to be a further example of Collier's forgeries. W. W. Greg, however, has argued for its genuineness and restored the note to read as follows:

> Char. Tilney wrot[e a]
> Tragedy of this mattr [wch]
> hee named Estrild: [& wch]
> I think is this. it was [lost?]
> by his death. & now (?) [some]
> fellow hath published [it]
> I made dūbe shewes for it.
> wch I yet have. G.B.

There is no evidence that Tilney ever wrote a play named "Estrild" or that *Locrine* is "Estrild," although Estrild is an important character in the play.

E. K. Chambers believed that one of the University Wits was the author of the play, and the names suggested most frequently, although without any conclusive evidence, are George Peele and Robert Greene. [E. K. Chambers, *The Elizabethan Stage*, 1923; E. K. Chambers, *William Shakespeare*, 1930.]

Lodge, Thomas (1557/8?–1625). Writer. The son of the lord mayor of London, Lodge was educated at the Merchant Taylors' School and Trinity College, Oxford. He abandoned law in order to write and tried his hand at almost every form of literature. His treatise *A Defence of Poetry Music and Stage Plays* (1580) was a retort to Stephen Gosson's attacks on the stage in *School of Abuse*. The highly popular Elizabethan drama *Mucedorus* (pub. 1598, perf. c. 1589), which was once attributed to Shakespeare, has been ascribed to Lodge. Another popular work, a version of *King Leir* (c. 1594) with a happy ending, has also been attributed to Lodge. In his pamphlet *Wit's Miserie* (1596), Lodge refers to the UR-HAMLET when he speaks of the ghost which cried so miserably at the theatre "like an oister wife, 'Hamlet revenge!' "

Since Lodge in his later years repudiated his connection with the theatre, it is ironic that he is best remembered because Shakespeare based *As You Like It* on Lodge's *Rosalynde* (pub. 1590), written during a voyage to the Canaries in 1588. Lodge's work is a transformation of the old tale *Gamelyn* into a pastoral romance (see PASTORALISM). The story concerns Rosalynde and Rosader, who fall in love at a wrestling match that has been arranged by Rosader's wicked brother Saladyne. A short time later, Rosalynde and her cousin Alinda, having been banished by the usurping king, flee to the forest of Arden, Rosalynde disguised as the page Ganymede and Alinda posing as her sister, Aliena. Here they meet Rosader and, in her disguise, Rosalynde makes sport of his passion. She then tells him that she can cure it if he will woo her as if she were Rosalynde; this he does and they even go through a mock marriage ceremony. To make the pastoral complete, Lodge adds an amorous shepherd, Montanus, and a hardhearted shepherdess, Phoebe. Phoebe falls in love with Ganymede and agrees to marry Montanus only if Ganymede will not wed her. Meanwhile Rosader, finding his brother Saladyne asleep in the forest, saves him from a lion and then introduces him to Ganymede (Rosalynde) and Aliena. Saladyne promptly falls in love with Aliena and wins her love by saving her and Ganymede from a band of robbers. Saladyne and Aliena marry, and at their wedding Rosalynde reveals herself to her father, the banished king. Rosader and Rosalynde are then betrothed and Phoebe agrees to marry Montanus. The festivities are interrupted with the news that the 12 peers of France have risen against the usurper. Rosader and Saladyne join in the battle, the usurper is defeated, and Rosader is declared heir to the kingdom.

As this summary indicates, the plot of *Rosalynde* was a major source of *As You Like It*. With the addition of such characters as Touchstone and Jaques, Shakespeare gave a greater depth of reality to the plot. It should also be noted that while Lodge's Rosalynde does not rise above the traditional pastoral heroine, Shakespeare's Rosalind is one of the most charming women in the history of the drama.

The last literary reference to Lodge was made by Ben Jonson in *Cynthia's Revels* (1600) wherein he satirizes Lodge in the person of Asotus, the prodigal. —S. G. M.

Lodovico. In *Othello*, a kinsman to Brabantio. Lodovico brings Othello a letter recalling him to Venice and naming Cassio as his deputy in Cyprus (IV, i). Referring to Lodovico's good looks, Emilia says, "I know a lady in Venice would have walked barefoot to Palestine for a touch of his nether lip" (IV, iii).

Lodowick, Friar. In *Measure for Measure*, the name taken by Vincentio, Duke of Vienna, when he assumes his monk's disguise.

London. Shakespeare fashioned his entire professional career in London. For Londoners he wrote his plays, for them he and his fellow actors staged their productions. And the young man from a provincial town learned so quickly how to stimulate their interest and to appeal to their sympathies that he at once became their most popular playwright.

When Shakespeare arrived in London about the year 1588 he found it in many ways still a medieval town. The city proper was surrounded by walls through which entrance to the city could be made at a number of gates, but all of them were shut tight at nine o'clock curfew. Names like Billingsgate, Ludgate, Newgate, and Bishopsgate are still applied to districts of London adjacent to the old gates. The eastern anchor of the wall was the Tower, supposedly built by Julius Caesar and added to by each succeeding age. In Shakespeare's day it was fortress, armory, prison, and menagerie all in one.

In 1588 the population of London consisted of about 50,000 souls. It was the great commercial center of western Europe with a large foreign population. The residents of the great port city that London had become needed to gain all the knowledge they could of foreign nations, so that the city welcomed teachers of almost all the foreign languages of nations with which England traded. A whole colony of Frenchmen arrived in England to teach in particular their spoken language. Although London was then a cosmopolitan city, its citizens took a provincial view of foreigners, feeling superior to all of them, on some occasions actively resenting them. In 1565 Thomas Gresham (c. 1519–1579), a merchant and financial agent of the government, for the general good of English merchants built, at his own expense, the Royal Exchange. It had a hundred small shops in its upper corridor. His estate ultimately went to the founding of a London college in which law, medicine, geometry, rhetoric, and other practical subjects were to be taught. He specified that the lectures were to be given in English as well as Latin, since merchants and other citizens would be in the audience. This foundation marks the important place held by the merchants in the life of London.

The population of the city was growing so rapidly that it overflowed the narrow limits of the old town and spread out in all directions beyond the walls. These suburbs had come to have an unsavory reputation, for they harbored the notorious houses of prostitution, the bear pits, and the first of the London theatres, which had been built outside the city walls. There they were safely beyond the jurisdiction of the municipal authorities, who sought to hamper in every possible way the activities of the "common players." Fortunately the hostility of the merchants and tradesmen was offset by the generous support of the PRIVY COUNCIL and the court. Without their protection and patronage the Elizabethan theatre might have been stifled in its infancy and Shakespeare's plays never have been written.

Beyond the suburbs lay uncultivated meadows where the Londoners went for their sports. There they engaged in hawking and hunting on ground that now lies in the very heart of modern London. Even the city within the walls, covering only one-fortieth as much ground as the modern metropolis, boasted many gardens filled with trees and flowers. In it were only a few broad thoroughfares. Most of the streets were mere lanes. Even the smallest wheeled vehicles seldom attempted to make their way through those narrow alleys, and coaches, which had appeared only a few years before Shakespeare's arrival in London, found the broad avenues none too wide for their passage. All the streets were foul, with a channel in the center that served as an open sewer. Epidemics flourished in those dark and filthy streets and the plague existed in London during all the years that Shakespeare spent there. In 1593 and 1603 it broke out with especial virulence and devastated whole districts of the unsanitary town.

The Thames, a tidal river then swarming with fish, was London's principal thoroughfare. It was crossed by one bridge only, the famous London Bridge, accounted one of the wonders of the world. This span was lined with shops and houses along its entire length and was defended at its southern end by a gate and a tower. The river below was alive with small boats—the taxicabs or gondolas of the day—and the banks echoed the cries of the "watermen" who propelled their little craft and advertised the direction in which they were going by cries of "Westward Ho" or "Eastward Ho." See John TAYLOR.

The London of Elizabeth was a city of more than a hundred churches. Of these the great cathedral of St. Paul was by far the most famous, but not as a shrine or as a house of prayer. In the middle of the 16th century its spire had been struck by lightning and the entire structure gutted by fire, but, though the edifice had been promptly reconstructed, most of the interior was immediately given over to various commercial and social activities. It is true that religious services were regularly held in the choir, but the great central aisle, appropriately known as "Paul's Walk," became the resort of lawyers and merchants, who went there for conferences with clients and for the conduct of all sorts of business. On one of the pillars in another part of the cathedral jobless men advertised or posted up a list of their qualifications. The walled enclosure surrounding the edifice—the cathedral close—had become the center of the London book trade, which overflowed into certain of the adjoining lanes. Most of Shakespeare's plays published during his lifetime were issued from Paul's Churchyard.

The cathedral was also the approved place for social encounters and fashionable display. Gallants came to the nave to show off their clothes or their exquisite manner of "taking" tobacco or flourishing a toothpick. Social climbers wandered about to discover the latest fashion in men's attire, sometimes even bringing their tailors with them to copy some startling sartorial innovation. Convention had also fixed definite spots in Paul's Walk as the gathering places for persons of one sort or another. Duke Humphrey's tomb, for example, had become the rendezvous of penniless social climbers. There these upstarts waited eagerly for signs of social recognition, their most extravagant hope being an invitation to dinner. Sharpers infested the central aisle, lying in wait for some innocent country bumpkin or stupid city gull. Harlots and pimps mingled with the motley crowd, looking for victims. And the clergy, busy in its corner with prayer and praise, seemingly never thought of protesting against this desecration of their sacred edifice by graceless intruders.

The penetration of the bustling world into the very center of the house of God is in a sense symbolic of the spirit of the Renaissance. For Londoners of Shakespeare's day were the latest children of that great reawakening of the pagan world which had begun in Italy two centuries before. By the year 1588 the first enthusiasm of the movement had been tempered, even in England, by a spirit of criticism. Intellectual leaders had begun to question many of the time-honored views about man and the universe. Although most thinking men still believed that the earth was the center of a perfectly ordered little cosmos, some of the bolder speculative spirits in England had advanced the astounding idea that the

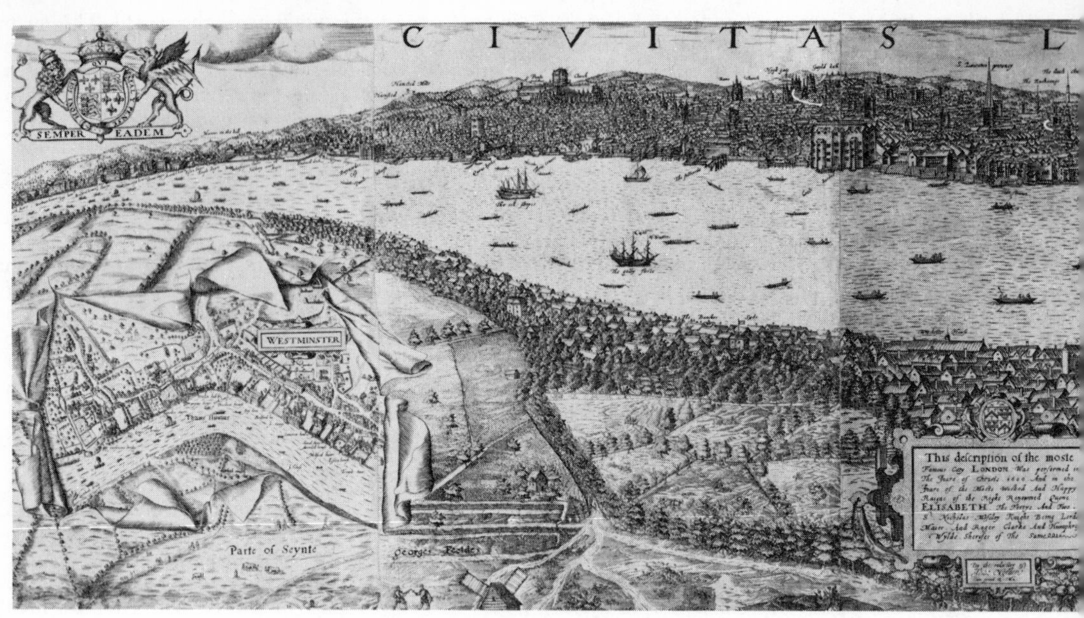

LONDON IN 1600. THIS PANORAMIC VIEW IS AN EXPANDED VERSION OF JOHN NORDEN'S MAP OF LONDON WHIC

universe might be infinite. In any case recent events in the heavens, such as the sudden appearance of blazing stars, had cast doubt upon an assumption basic to all traditional conceptions of the universe. It had been a cherished belief that all creation above the moon was changeless and incorruptible. If not even the heaven above was enduring, obviously there was no permanence anywhere. All creation was the slave of mutability. This dismal idea distressed thoughtful men to the depth of their souls. In particular it profoundly stirred Shakespeare's emotions and fired his imagination. The real subject of his *Sonnets* is the terrifying triumphs of Time—Time that ruthlessly destroys man and ultimately obliterates all his works.

The earth itself had also recently become an infinitely vaster place than the boldest minds of the Middle Ages had dared conceive it to be. The New World, the immensity of which no one as yet had even faintly imagined, was thought to be a domain of wealth beyond the wildest dreams of avarice, a region offering opportunities for romantic enterprise beyond the hopes of the most daring traveler or adventurer.

The new scientists, moreover, were beginning to urge direct experience of nature and subjective examination of the individual mind as being sounder sources of practical knowledge than the stores of tradition or the compilations of reason. This appeal to immediate experience stimulated, on the one hand, scientific inquiry and, on the other, probing self-analysis. Montaigne, the most famous of the new skeptics, expressed a revolutionary idea when he wrote, "I had rather understand myself well in myself than in Cicero." This view of human existence created a zest for new experience and greatly increased the importance and dignity of individual life on this earth. "What a piece of work is a man!" wa an exclamation that might have fallen from the lip of any thoughtful Elizabethan. This wonder at th heights and depths to be discovered in individu human beings, combined with an unparalleled powe of discriminating observation, enabled the genius o William Shakespeare to create his great company o immortal characters.

In England intense curiosity about man and enthu siasm for his achievements was wedded to a flamin patriotism. During the 16th century many of th countries of western Europe developed a strong na tional feeling. The firm centralizing policies of th Tudor monarchs from Henry VII to Queen Eliza beth brought this spirit to birth in England, and th defeat of the Spanish Armada in 1588 fanned smo dering patriotism into an inextinguishable flame. T be an Englishman was to be a citizen of the proude nation in the world. The virgin queen became th precious symbol of English power and glory.

This patriotic spirit penetrated into every corne of Shakespeare's London, for the metropolis had be come, as never before, the focus of all phases of Eng lish life. Its new importance was in part the result o fundamental changes in the economic life of th country. The worldwide demand for wool ha brought about the conversion of vast areas of culti vated land into pastures for sheep (see ENCLOSURE The withdrawal of large tracts of land from agricul ture drove thousands of farm laborers from thei customary occupations out upon the roads to wande as vagabonds in search of other work. For the mer chants, particularly the wholesalers and exporter the growth of the wool trade was a boon th greatly augmented their riches and their powe Such businessmen shared with the queen the ric profits from colonizing expeditions to the Ne

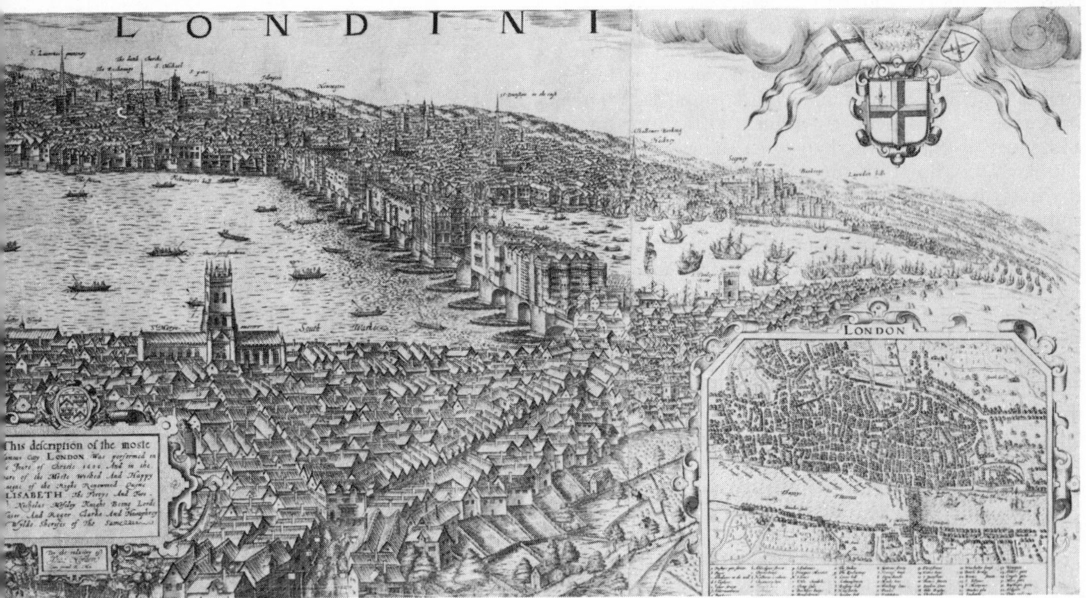

APPEARS ON THE RIGHT. (ROYAL LIBRARY, STOCKHOLM)

World and from plundering exploits on the high eas. Though some of them bought the estates of the old aristocracy and sought to become country gentlemen, most of them settled in London. It became their city and they enjoyed to the full its colorful life. They delighted in the progresses of the queen along the river to entertainments prepared for her by the lord mayor or some of the richest merchants. They stood in sober wonder at the gorgeous funeral processions which floated on barges down the Thames. And their love of display and of every sort of ritualistic celebration found ample satisfaction in the pageantry of Shakespeare's chronicle history plays.

Nor did the proudest citizens scorn to join with the humble in pastimes to be found in the open fields beyond the walls. There they played football or bowls or perhaps went to see a play in one of the new theatres.

Below the merchants in the social scale were the shopkeepers and the journeymen of the guilds of crafts, together with their apprentices. And on the fringes of this stable mercantile group was a motley floating population composed of the spendthrift sons of the new landed gentry. Upstart gentlemen, they had come up to London to discover the newest fashions, to display their finery, and to have a fling. Young men from the universities were also knocking about town, hoping to forge a career by their wits. And at the very bottom of the heap were runaway apprentices, masterless men, and impoverished farm laborers, all seeking asylum and a living in the hurly-burly of London.

The gathering places of all these groups were the many inns. Most famous of them was the Boar's Head Tavern in Eastcheap, where Sir John Falstaff is supposed to have taken his ease and drunk his deep potations of sack. These inns, besides serving as hotels for travelers, were also the city's restaurants. There a man might dine in the "ordinary," or public, dining hall, under the flirtatious eyes of the hostess, or in a private room where he and his intimates, male and female, were served by a special waiter, or "drawer." A "noise," or band of musicians, was usually on hand to furnish diversion.

The inns were also the disseminating point for news, rumor, and information of all sorts. To the great common room before the bar came men from every walk of Elizabethan life—to drink and to talk endlessly. The most picturesque tales undoubtedly were the reports of those who had sailed out into the western sea or perhaps circumnavigated the globe with Drake. But full of almost equally strange news

A TAVERN. WOODCUT FROM STUBBES' *The Anatomie of Abuses* (1583).

were the sailors who had recently returned from voyages to such faraway places as Sweden, Russia, or Persia. In the inns were gathered soldiers just back from wars in the low countries, and gentlemen newly returned from their grand tours to France, Navarre, and Italy, more familiar with the fashions and vices of the south than with the new learning. Scholars, too, up from the universities, dropped into the inns, as did the country squires agape at the stir and excitement of Bohemian life. And the disreputable taverns, then as now, were the resort of sharpers, harlots, and other riffraff of the slums. Any dramatist who frequented those ordinaries could find in them models for just about all the typical figures of the Elizabethan world.

Moreover, a playwright skilled in drawing a traveler out over a second glass of sack could glean from the cosmopolitan crowd gathered in one of those inns abundant information about the great world beyond the narrow seas. Shakespeare had no need to visit Elsinore himself, or Venice, or the court of Navarre at Nérac to collect necessary local color for the plays he set in foreign lands.

Learned and witty conversation flourished in the private rooms of the better inns, for there men with common interests assembled to form clubs. The most famous of these was the group which used to gather at the MERMAID TAVERN in Bread Street, to drink and to discuss the arts. Shakespeare and Ben Jonson belonged to this group. [T. Fairman Ordish, *Shakespeare's London*, 1897.]—O. J. C.

London Prodigal, The (pub. 1605). A play published as having been written by Shakespeare. The title page reads: "The London Prodigal. As it was plaide by the Kings Maiesties seruants. By William Shakespeare." Rejection of the ascription of the play to Shakespeare is all but universal among scholars. Drayton, Marston, and Dekker have all been suggested as the possible author. The play was reprinted, along with *Pericles* and five other apocryphal plays, in the Third Folio (2nd ed., 1664). [C. F. Tucker Brooke, *The Shakespeare Apocrypha*, 1908.]

Longaville. In *Love's Labour's Lost*, one of the three lords, companions of the King of Navarre, who vow to forswear the usual round of courtly pleasure. Nevertheless, Longaville becomes enamored of Maria and to her addresses the sonnet "Did not the heavenly rhetoric of thine eye." Longaville's counterpart in history was the duc de Longueville. See LOVE'S LABOUR'S LOST: *Sources*.

Longleat MS. An Elizabethan manuscript, presently in the library of the marquess of Bath at Longleat. The Longleat MS. contains an illustration of an episode purporting to be from *Titus Andronicus* with an accompanying text. The drawing depicts Tamora as she kneels before Titus. Behind her are her two sons, both kneeling, and behind them stands Aaron with a drawn sword. Beneath the picture are 40 lines of text extracted from various parts of the play which are connected in an attempt to provide a coherent commentary on the illustration. A marginal endorsement to the left of the text reads "Henricus Peacham Anno m^{o}q^{o}gq^{to}." This has been interpreted by a later scribe at another point in the manuscript to be "Henrye Peachams Hand 1595." The addition is strongly suspect; it is probably one of the ubiquitous forgeries of John Payne Collier. The date of the drawing depends on the interpretation of "m^{o}q^{o}gq^{to}," generally taken to be either 1594 or 1595. Presumably "Henricus Peacham" refers to Henry Peacham, the Elizabethan author and artist, although evidence is not available which would prove such an attribution.

THE LONGLEAT MANUSCRIPT OF *Titus Andronicus*. (LONGLEAT HOUSE, BY PERMISSION OF THE MARQUESS OF BATH)

The illustration itself does not faithfully depict any known incident in the play. In fact, there are a number of puzzling discrepancies between this illustration and the play as extant today. The drawing, for example, seems to show Tamora pleading for the lives of two sons, while in the play she pleads for only one, Alarbus. Dover Wilson attempts to explain this discrepancy by suggesting that the drawing was executed in 1595 by someone who had seen a production of the play and remembered some other scene in which Tamora might have had her two sons kneeling behind her. Wilson further speculates that the text was written a number of years later by a different person who had only a dim recollection of the play and who attempted to reconstruct what he thought the scene depicted. Wilson's argument is strengthened by the fact that the text seems to derive from either the 1611 Quarto or the 1623 Folio version of the play; this would clearly be impossible if the picture and text were the same date, i.e., 1595.

The drawing's importance, however, lies in the fact that it is the only extant depiction of a Shakespearean production in its own time. Thus, it provides a clue to the problem of costumes on the Elizabethan stage. In the drawing, the major characters seem to be wearing historical Roman attire, while the minor characters are dressed in contemporary Elizabethan garb. The drawing may offer additional information regarding the grouping of actors on the stage. The text, as reproduced by Wilson, is as follows:

Enter Tamora pleadinge for her sonnes going to execution

Tam. Stay Romane bretheren gratious Conquerors
Victorious Titus rue the teares I shed
A mother teares in passion of her sonnes
And if thy sonnes were ever deare to thee
Oh thinke my sonnes to bee as deare to mee
Suffizeth not that wee are brought to Roome
To beautify thy triumphes and returne
Captiue to thee and to thy Romane yoake
But must my sonnes be slaughtered in the streetes
for valiant doings in there Cuntryes cause
Or if to fight for kinge and Common weale
Were piety in thine it is in these

Andronicus staine not thy tombe with blood
Wilt thou drawe neere the nature of the Godes
Draw neere them then in being mercifull
Sweete mercy is nobilityes true badge
Thrice noble Titus spare my first borne sonne
Titus. Patient your self madame for dy hee must
Aaron do you likewise prepare your self
And now at last repent your wicked life
Aron. Ah now I curse the day and yet I thinke
few comes within the compasse of [your *deleted*]
my curse
Wherein I did not some notorious ill
As kill a man or els devise his death
Ravish a mayd or plott the way to do it
Acuse some innocent and forsweare my self
Set deadly enmity betweene too freendes
Make poore mens cattel breake theire neckes
Set fire on barnes and haystackes in the night
And bid the owners quench them with their
teares
Oft have I digd vp dead men from their graves
And set them vpright at theire deere frendes dore
Even almost when theire sorrowes was forgott
And on their brestes as on the barke of trees
Have with my knife carvd in Romane letters
Lett not your sorrowe dy though I am dead
Tut I have done a thousand dreadfull thinges
As willingly as one would kill a fly
And nothing greives mee hartily indeede
for that I cannot doo ten thousand more & cetera

[J. Dover Wilson, "Titus Andronicus on the Stage in 1595," *Shakespeare Survey 1*, 1948; W. M. Merchant, *Shakespeare and the Artist*, 1959.]

Look About You (c. 1600). An anonymous play which contains verbal echoes of *Romeo and Juliet* and *1 Henry IV*. *Look About You* was first published in 1600: *A Pleasant Commedie, Called Looke about you. As it was lately played by the right honourable the Lord High Admirall his seruants.* Authorship has been attributed to Anthony Wadeson (fl. 1600), a playwright in the employ of Philip Henslowe.

Lopez, Roderigo (d. 1594). Jewish physician to Queen Elizabeth who may have been the prototype of Shylock in *The Merchant of Venice*. Lopez' origins are obscure, but he was educated in Europe and came to England in the early years of Elizabeth's reign. He was a leading member of the College of Physicians and for some time the personal physician to the earl of Leicester in his palace at Kenilworth, not far from Stratford. In 1586 he became the queen's personal physician. When in 1588 Antonio Perez, pretender to the throne of Portugal, arrived in England in flight from his enemy, King Philip of Spain, Lopez was appointed his interpreter. In 1590 Lopez was drawn into a Spanish plot to assassinate Antonio and Queen Elizabeth. The plot was discovered by the earl of Essex, and Lopez was hanged on June 7, 1594. The news caused a sensation throughout England and reawakened a slumbering anti-Semitism among Londoners.

The idea that Lopez was the model for Shylock is based on several factors: the notion of revenge, said to be Lopez' motive, as it was Shylock's; the coincidence of the name Antonio as the enemy of both Lopez and Shylock; the reference in *The Merchant of Venice* to the "rack" (III, ii, 25, 32), the fear of which had brought about Lopez' confession; and the allusion to the wolf (Latin "lupus") hanged for human slaughter (IV, i, 134). All of these appear to indicate that Shakespeare had Lopez in mind to some degree in creating Shylock. See MERCHANT OF VENICE: *Sources*. [Sidney Lee, "The Jews in England," in *The Merchant of Venice*, New Variorum Edition, H. H. Furness, ed., 1888.]

Lord. In the Induction to *The Taming of the Shrew*, a nobleman. The Lord amuses himself and his companions by abducting the drunken Sly and engaging in the pretense that Sly is a nobleman who has suffered a fit of 15 years' insanity.

lord chamberlain. The official of the royal household in charge of lodgings in the royal palaces, the reception of ambassadors, the royal wardrobe, and all entertainments given before the sovereign. In the latter capacity he was the immediate superior of the MASTER OF THE REVELS, who was charged with furnishing dramatic entertainment at court.

Although the Master of the Revels eventually became the *de facto* ruler of the dramatic companies, he remained subordinate to the lord chamberlain, and on a few occasions the lord chamberlain exerted his authority directly in connection with theatrical matters. One particularly important occasion for the lord chamberlain's intervention occurred in 1619 when William Herbert, earl of Pembroke and the current lord chamberlain, issued an order prohibiting the printing of the King's Men plays without their consent.

The first lord chamberlain during Elizabeth's reign was Lord Howard of Effingham, her great-uncle, who served from 1558 to 1572. He was followed by Thomas Radcliffe, 3rd earl of Sussex, who served from 1572 to 1583. From 1583 to 1585 Lord Charles Howard held the office, vacating it in order to become lord admiral, under which title he served as patron of the Admiral's Men. His successor was Henry Carey, 1st Lord Hunsdon, who in 1594 established the great company with which Shakespeare was to be associated, the Chamberlain's Men. Carey died in July 1596 and was succeeded by William Brooke, 7th Lord Cobham, who some scholars believe was strongly opposed to the players. Lord Cobham served only six months; he died in March 1597. His successor was the 1st Lord Hunsdon's son, George Carey, 2nd Lord Hunsdon, who also inherited his father's patronage of the Chamberlain's Men. He was replaced in 1603, because of ill health, by Thomas Howard, earl of Suffolk, who remained in the post until 1614, resigning in order to become lord treasurer. The office was then given to Robert Carr, earl of Somerset and the personal favorite of James I. In the following year, however, Carr was convicted of complicity in the murder of Sir Thomas Overbury and sent to the Tower. His successor was William Herbert, 3rd earl of Pembroke and, many believe, the Mr. W. H., or Fair Youth, of the *Sonnets*. Herbert remained in office until 1626 and was succeeded by his brother Philip Herbert, earl of Montgomery, 4th earl of Pembroke, and the joint dedicatee, with his brother William, of the First Folio of Shakespeare in 1623. [E. K. Chambers, "The Elizabethan Lords Chamberlain," *Malone Society Collections*, I, 1907.]

Lord Chamberlain. In *Henry VIII*, he disapproves of continental fashions on his way to Wolsey's banquet, where he presides over the seating (I, iii and iv). Later he discusses rumors of Henry's divorce of Katharine with the Dukes of Norfolk and Suffolk (II, ii) and announces to Anne Bullen her elevation to Marchioness of Pembroke (II, iii). Shortly before Wolsey's fall, the Lord Chamberlain recommends caution to the nobles who hope to destroy the Cardinal (III, ii). Historically, it was Charles Somerset, earl of Worcester, who was lord chamberlain at the time of the meeting at the Field of the Cloth of Gold and the trial of Buckingham; Sir William Sands succeeded him on his death in 1526. Since the latter also appears as a character (Lord Sands) in *Henry VIII*, Shakespeare presumably intended Worcester to be the occupant of this office throughout the play. [W. H. Thomson, *Shakespeare's Characters: A Historical Dictionary*, 1951.]

Lord Chamberlain's Men. See CHAMBERLAIN'S MEN; SUSSEX' MEN.

Lord Chancellor. In *Henry VIII*, Sir Thomas More is named as successor to Cardinal Wolsey (III, ii, 393–399), but the Lord Chancellor who appears in the coronation procession and later presides over the council that attempts to imprison Cranmer (V, iii) is not named. Historically, Wolsey was Lord Chancellor from 1515 until his fall in 1529; he was succeeded by Sir Thomas More, who resigned in 1532; Sir Thomas Audley held the Seal until his death in 1544, and was chancellor during the coronation of Anne Bullen; Thomas Wriothesley succeeded Audley.

Lord Chief Justice. In *2 Henry IV*, he serves under both Henry IV and Henry V. Something of a moralist, he cautions Falstaff against the evils of his way of life and orders him to make amends to Mistress Quickly. He also imprisons the madcap Prince of Wales, and when the Prince becomes King Henry V, the Lord Chief Justice fears his possible revenge. The King, however, confirms him in his office and orders him to carry out Falstaff's banishment and imprisonment.

The historical model for this character, Sir William Gascoigne (1350–1419), was a judge made Lord Chief Justice in 1400. It is not certain whether he actually imprisoned Prince Hal. Gascoigne resigned his office soon after the accession of Henry V, probably on his own initiative. [W. H. Thomson, *Shakespeare's Characters: A Historical Dictionary*, 1951.]

Lord Clinton's Men. See LINCOLN'S MEN.

Lord Howard's Men. See ADMIRAL'S MEN.

Lord Hunsdon's Men. See CHAMBERLAIN'S MEN.

Lord Mayor of London. In *1 Henry VI*, the Mayor puts an end to the fighting between the factions of the Duke of Gloucester and the Bishop of Winchester in the streets of the city and requests that the King intervene in the dispute (I, iii and III, i). The fighting occurred in 1425, and the lord mayor at the time was John Coventry, who is reported to have put Winchester's men to flight. In *Richard III*, the Lord Mayor appears as a staunch supporter of the protagonist (III, v and vii). According to history, he was Sir Edmund Shaw (d.c. 1487). In *Henry VIII*, V, v, the Lord Mayor, historically Sir Stephen Pecocke, assists at the infant Elizabeth's christening.

lords' room. A gallery, probably located to the rear of and above the stage in an Elizabethan playhouse, comparable to a box in a modern theatre except for its location. The lords' room was probably reserved as seating for the lord under whose patronage the acting company was performing. It was, however, also available for the use of other individuals of equally high office, noble birth, or other distinction. Philip Henslowe's diary records the earliest mention of the lords' room in an entry concerning the repair of the lords' room roof at the Rose in 1592. By 1596, however, the lords' room had lost its earlier cachet and it had become fashionable for the great and near-great to view performances either from the lower side galleries or from the stage itself. The lords' room was probably then used by the actors as an additional UPPER STAGE. See PLAYHOUSE STRUCTURE; John De Witt's drawing at SWAN THEATRE. [E. K. Chambers, *The Elizabethan Stage*, 1923.]

Lord Strange's Men. See STRANGE'S MEN.

Lorenzo. In *The Merchant of Venice*, an artistic young friend of Bassanio. Eloping with Jessica, Lorenzo accompanies Bassanio to Belmont and is there entrusted with the management of Portia's household when she travels to Venice.

Lorkins or **Lorkin, Thomas** (d. 1625). A graduate of both Oxford and Cambridge, Lorkins worked as a secretary to the embassy in Paris, helping to arrange the marriage of Charles I and Henrietta Maria in 1623. He maintained a correspondence with Sir Thomas Puckering (1592–1636), and in one of his letters he recounted the destruction of the Globe in 1613:

> No longer since than yesterday, while Bourbege his companie were acting at Y^e Globe the play of Hen:8, and there shooting of certayne chambers in way of triumph; the fire catch'd & fastened upon the thatch of ye house and there burned so furiously as it consumed the whole house & all in lesse then two houres the people having enough to doe to save themselves.

Lorkins was drowned in a storm in the English Channel in November 1625. [*The Shakspere Allusion Book*, J. Munro, ed., 1909.]

Louis XI (1423–1483). King of France, son of Charles VII and Marie of Anjou. Ascending the throne in 1461, Louis so offended the nobles by his arrogant disregard of them that they revolted under the leadership of Charles the Bold of Burgundy. In 1465 the king was compelled to sign the treaty of Conflans, thereby giving up the "Somme towns" in Picardy which he had bought from Philip the Good. Determined to overcome his Burgundian enemy, who was supported by Edward IV of England, Louis gave help to the earl of Warwick and Queen Margaret in their effort to restore Henry VI to the throne. When Edward IV regained the monarchy, however, Louis bought his assistance, as well as that of the Swiss and the duke of Lorraine. His enemy Charles was defeated and killed at Nancy in 1477.

In *3 Henry VI*, King Lewis first agrees to assist Queen Margaret in her attempts to unseat Edward IV. Then, on Warwick's appearance to ask the hand of Bona, Lewis' sister-in-law, for King Edward, the French king accedes to Warwick's request.

Louis the Dauphin (1187–1226). Eldest son of Philip II of France. In 1216 Louis invaded England over the protests of the papal legate. Although he claimed the English throne in the right of his wife, Blanche of Castile, Henry II's granddaughter, it was Henry III who took the crown on King John's death. The dauphin succeeded his father in 1223 as Louis VIII of France.

In *King John,* Louis, called Lewis, marries Lady Blanch, daughter of John's sister Elinor, Queen of Castile, thereby temporarily settling the differences between France and England. On the excommunication of King John, Pandulph, the papal legate, prevails on King Philip to break his compact with England. After a battle on the continent in which the French are defeated, Lewis is persuaded by Pandulph to claim the English crown in the right of his wife and to invade that country.

Louis the Dauphin (1396–1415). Eldest son of Charles VI of France; in *Henry V,* the boastful young heir, called Lewis, who, in reply to Henry's demands for certain dukedoms in France, sends an insulting gift of tennis balls. With the Constable of France, Lewis subsequently leads the army at Agincourt, where he is badly defeated. Historically there were three dauphins during the time span of the play. Louis was dauphin at the time when the play begins, and it is he who is portrayed throughout. On Louis' death soon after the battle of Agincourt (at which he was not present), his brother Jean succeeded to the title. When Jean died the following year, the title was inherited by a younger brother, Charles, who later became Charles VII of France. [W. H. Thomson, *Shakespeare's Characters: A Historical Dictionary,* 1951.]

Lounsbury, Thomas Raynesford (1838–1915). American scholar. After serving in the Civil War, Lounsbury joined (1870) the staff of Yale and in the following year was appointed to a professorship in the Sheffield Scientific School, a position which he retained until his retirement in 1906. He also served as librarian at Sheffield from 1873 to 1906. His first book was *A History of the English Language* (1879), a popular but scholarly exposition which was followed by more specialized studies in pronunciation, usage, and spelling. His major scholarly work is *Studies in Chaucer* (3 vols., 1892), one of the most important of the 19th-century works on the subject. *Shakespearean Wars* is the collective title of three volumes which appeared separately as *Shakespeare as a Dramatic Artist* (1901), *Shakespeare and Voltaire* (1902), and *The Text of Shakespeare* (1906). The pervading theme of the three volumes is the "war" between the practice of Shakespeare and the theory of classicism. The first volume gives a survey of editions and of criticism with stress on classical theory, the second studies French neoclassical theory with emphasis on Voltaire, and the third traces the publication of the folios and quartos down through the editions of Pope and Theobald. Lounsbury also published full-length studies of Cooper, Browning, and Tennyson.

Loutherbourg, Philippe Jacques de (1740–1812). French-born painter and scene designer. In 1771 de Loutherbourg was only 31 years old (but already a member of the French Academy) when David Garrick invited him to settle in England and become the scene designer at the Drury Lane. He was a talented artist, specializing in battle, marine, and landscape paintings, but his inventiveness was most clearly demonstrated in the theatre. He collaborated with Garrick in improving lighting techniques for the stage and invented an elaborate Eidophusikon, which was exhibited at Spring Gardens in 1782. Like the dioramas popular a few years later, this was a large painted landscape scene which varied in appearance as different effects of color and light played over its surface. An ingenious use of gauzes, colored glass, and varying degrees of illumination provided the basis for this first "moving picture," which was extremely popular.

De Loutherbourg's innovations in stage design include the construction of set pieces (solid stage furniture) which permitted the actors to walk on and over the scenery, facilitating a more flexible use of the stage and a greater integration of action and set. His painted backdrops discarded formal symmetry in favor of natural, irregular, and picturesque forms, completely transforming the theatrical presentation of landscape. A set of de Loutherbourg's sketches for settings in *Richard III* have been used by Dr. Richard Southern in his attempts at reconstructing the original scenery. [W. M. Merchant, *Shakespeare and the Artist,* 1959.]

Love, James. See ADAPTATIONS.

Love Betray'd. See William BURNABY.

Lovel or **Lovell, Francis** Viscount (1454–?1487). One of Richard III's most trusted advisors. Lovel was created viscount in 1483. With Catesby and Ratcliff he was the target of William Collingbourne's couplet: "The catte, the ratte, and Lovell our dogge / Rulyth all England under a hogge." In *Richard III,* Lord Lovel appears as the usurper's lackey. At Richard's command he takes Hastings to execution and brings back his head (III, iv and v). [W. H. Thomson, *Shakespeare's Characters: A Historical Dictionary,* 1951.]

Lovell, Sir Thomas. Constable of the Tower under Henry VIII. Though the historical Lovell had withdrawn from public life six years before his death in 1524, he appears throughout *Henry VIII.* He is present at the false testimony of Buckingham's Surveyor, who claims that the Duke had marked Lovell for execution at the King's death (I, ii). Later, on their way to Wolsey's banquet, Lovell joins in the ridicule of continental fashions (I, iii and iv). Officiating at the execution of Buckingham, he asks the Duke's forgiveness (II, i). Though Lovell does not participate in the subsequent baiting of Wolsey (III, ii), he seems to have played a part in turning the King against him. Finally, he announces to Henry Anne's grave condition at Elizabeth's birth (V, i).

Lover's Complaint, A. A poem published in the first edition of the *Sonnets* (1609), where it was ascribed to Shakespeare. It was also included in John BENSON's 1640 edition entitled *Poems: Written by Wil. Shake-speare. Gent.*

The poem is written in rhyme royal, a seven-line stanza which Shakespeare employed in *The Rape of Lucrece.* In some respects it appears to be a labored and awkward imitation of Spenser, probably written in the 1580's or 1590's. Scholars have all but unanimously rejected any attribution of it to Shakespeare, while conceding that there is an occasional echo in it of Shakespeare's work.

Recently, however, Kenneth Muir has argued that

it is an authentic Shakespearean creation. The poem is largely a maiden's story, told to an old shepherd, of her seduction and abandonment by an irresistible youth. The subject is conventional, but the author's treatment is in many respects original. The girl is not a lovely young creature, but one who is "the carcass of a beauty spent and done." The setting is also unusual: the shepherd comes upon the girl by the side of a stream where she is weeping and tearing love letters to shreds. Muir's idea that the poem incorporates "a major Shakespearean theme," the relation of appearance to reality, seems forced and of no help in describing the nature of this awkward little pastoral. [Kenneth Muir, "A Lover's Complaint: A Reconsideration," *Shakespeare 1564–1964,* Edward Bloom, ed., 1964; Oscar James Campbell, "A Lover's Complaint," *The Sonnets, Songs and Poems of Shakespeare,* 1964.]

Love's Labour's loſt.

Love's Labour's Lost. A comedy by Shakespeare.

Text. The only authoritative text is the Quarto of 1598, probably set up from Shakespeare's FOUL PAPERS. It is the first of the published plays to bear Shakespeare's name. The title page reads: "A Pleasant Conceited Comedie Called, Loues labors lost. As it was presented before her Highnes this last Christmas, Newly corrected and augmented by W. Shakespere. Imprinted at London by W. W. [William White] for Cutbert Burby. 1598." It has no division into acts and scenes. The editors of the First Folio edition used the Quarto as COPY, correcting some errors and making some of their own. The Folio marks the acts, but not the scenes. The manuscript that Burby used for his Quarto had been much revised, sometimes carelessly. For example, the passage (IV, iii, 302) beginning "From women's eyes this doctrine I derive" is repeated, extended, and improved later (IV, iii, 350). Some scholars have attempted to account for these textual inconsistencies by postulating the existence of a lost "bad quarto" which, they believe, preceded the publication of the 1598 Quarto, but there is no evidence to support this view other than the phrase "newly corrected and augmented" on the title page of Q1. The stage directions are unusually elaborate and are descriptive rather than imperative.

Date. It has been suggested that the first version of the play was designed for a private performance, either in 1593 or 1594, for a hall in the country house of some great lord, conceivably the earl of Southampton. In support of this view is the argument that Shakespeare wrote the comedy at about the same time that he composed the two poems dedicated to Southampton, *Venus and Adonis* and *The Rape of Lucrece,* and the earliest of his sonnets. The three works bear remarkable similarities to *Love's Labour's Lost.* On the other hand, a convincing argument has been advanced by Alfred Harbage supporting the view that the play was written for a performance by a company of children in 1588 and that a thoroughly revised and augmented version was prepared for presentation before the queen at Christmas 1597. The play is mentioned in two volumes published in 1598: Meres' PALLADIS TAMIA and Robert Tofte's poem *Alba, or The Month's Mind of a Melancholy Lover.* The first two lines of this poem read:

> Loves' Labours Lost! I once did see a play
> Ycleped so, so called to my pain.

If by "once" Tofte meant "once upon a time," the word would suggest a considerable span of time.

Sources. The source of the enveloping action is some lost account of events dealing with a visit of Catherine de Médicis (1519–1589) and her daughter MARGUERITE DE VALOIS, wife of King HENRY OF NAVARRE, to Nérac in 1578. The ostensible purpose of the visit was to effect a reconciliation between Henry and Marguerite, who had been separated for years. But the real purpose was to negotiate with the king about Aquitaine.

The source containing an account of this diplomatic mission may have been a lost French or English play based on Marguerite's visit, accompanied, as she always was on such missions, by her "flying squadron" of ladies in waiting, beautiful and accomplished young women. Or, the source may have been an account of some young English lord who had been visiting Nérac at the time of the mission of the two queens.

The French atmosphere of *Love's Labour's Lost* is enhanced by the similarity in names between Shakespeare's characters—members of the "little Academe" —and their historical counterparts. The maréchal de Biron (in Shakespeare, Berowne) and duc de Longueville (in Shakespeare, Longaville) were two of Henry of Navarre's commanders in the French civil war that raged from 1589 to 1592. The duc de Mayenne (Dumain in Shakespeare) was the leader of the opposition. Biron was in particular favor with the English in 1592, because he became the military associate and adviser of the earl of Essex, leader of the English force that had come to Henry's aid.

In the play, Navarre's "little Academe" was like

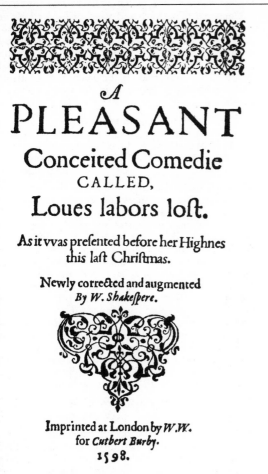

A

PLEASANT

Conceited Comedie

CALLED,

Loues labors lost.

As it vvas presented before her Highnes this last Christmas.

Newly corrected and augmented *By W. Shakespere.*

Imprinted at London by *W.W.* for *Cutbert Burby.* 1598.

TITLE PAGE OF THE FIRST QUARTO OF *Love's Labour's Lost* (1598). THIS IS THE FIRST TIME SHAKESPEARE'S NAME APPEARED ON A TITLE PAGE.

the real philosophical debating societies, called academes, established in Italy and France during the 16th century. Shakespeare could have learned about the intellectual movement from a popular account called *L'Académie française* by Pierre de LA PRIMAUDAYE.

The low-comedy characters all have their prototypes in the popular Italian comedy (*commedia dell' arte*). Berowne enumerates them as "The pedant, the braggart, the hedge-priest, the fool and the boy" (V, ii, 545). Holofernes, the pedant or schoolmaster, is, like his Italian prototype, prone to display his learning by larding his talk with proverbs and phrases in foreign tongues, particularly Latin. He becomes a typically English schoolmaster, his conversation derived from the routines of the English grammar school. One of the master's favorite methods of increasing his boys' mastery of an English vocabulary was to require them to find as many English synonyms of a Latin word as they possibly could. On many occasions he illustrates the proficiency he expects of his boys until his speech is like a Latin-English dictionary, as for example the following: "The deer was, as you know, sanguis, in blood; ripe as the pomewater [a sweet apple], who now hangeth like a jewel in the ear of caelo, the sky, the welkin, the heaven; and anon falleth like a crab [crab apple] on the face of terra, the soil, the land, the earth" (IV, ii, 3–7). These synonyms were called "epithets," and Nathaniel, the Latin parasite become an English curate or "hedge-priest," flatters Holofernes by assuring him that his epithets are "sweetly varied." It is possible that Shakespeare drew Holofernes on the model of some well-known learned men of his day, like John FLORIO or Gabriel HARVEY, but Shakespeare was amply capable of creating a bookish fool who had lost all contact with reality without making him a replica of any real pedant. Through touches of realism he was able to transform a stock figure of Italian comedy into a pompous, conceited, ignorant village schoolmaster.

Though Armado is called a "braggart" throughout the comedy, he displays none of the characteristics of Plautus' *miles gloriosus*. He does not boast of his military achievements or of his easy conquests of women. A closer prototype for Shakespeare's character is the Renaissance Italian idea of an offensive soldier—a Spaniard, typically a Castilian, vain, acrimonious, and grandiloquent. Berowne describes Armado as "a most illustrious wight, / A man of fire-new words, fashion's own knight" (I, i, 178–179). From the mint of phrases in Armado's brain comes such verbal stuff as "Dost thou infamonize me among potentates?" (V, ii, 684). In ridiculing Armado's bombast Shakespeare is joining the critics of his age who were determined to prevent the importation of words of Greek and Latin origin, usually polysyllables, into English.

Moth (Mote) is a transformation of a *zanni*, the buffoon of Italian popular comedy, into a quick-witted court fool who, many scholars believe, reflects Thomas Nashe. Costard represents the stupid servant who sets off the witty one in many Italian comedies. For a discussion of topical satire in the play, see below under *Comment*. See also John ELIOT.—O. J. C.

Plot Synopsis. Act I. Hoping to turn his court into "a little Academe," Ferdinand, King of Navarre, vows to dedicate himself to study and to shun women for three years. A similar oath is taken by Dumain, Longaville, and Berowne. The last named is skeptical as to the value of such an oath but boasts that he shall keep it longer than any of the others. Amusement will be provided by the antics of Don Adriano de Armado, a Spaniard "that hath a mint of phrases in his brain," and Costard, a slow-witted rustic.

Costard himself appears before the King as a prisoner of Constable Dull, who bears a letter from Armado. The Spaniard reports that he has caught Costard wooing a country wench, Jaquenetta, in defiance of a royal edict forbidding women to come within a mile of the court. The erring yokel is sentenced to fast for a week on bran and water and is remanded to the custody of Armado, who confesses to his page, Moth, that he is in love with Jaquenetta himself.

Act II. Meanwhile, the Princess of France has come to Navarre on a diplomatic mission for her father, who is in debt to Ferdinand. Because of the King's oath, she and her three companions, Rosaline, Maria, and Katharine, are obliged to lodge in a pavilion outside the royal park, where they are visited by Ferdinand and his lords.

Act III. Entrusted with a love letter for Jaquenetta from Armado, Costard is also given a note for Rosaline from Berowne. Although he had formerly scoffed at love, Berowne now finds that he has violated his oath by succumbing to the charms of "a wightly wanton with a velvet brow."

Act IV. By mistake Costard delivers Armado's letter to Rosaline, while Berowne's missive goes to Jaquenetta, who asks Sir Nathaniel, a curate, to read it to her. Nathaniel approves of the verses in the letter, but his friend, the schoolmaster Holofernes, himself blessed with a gift for poetry, finds them unimpressive.

As Berowne watches unobserved, Ferdinand reveals that, despite his vow, he has fallen in love with the Princess. Dumain and Longaville are also delinquent, for Dumain is smitten with Katharine and the latter with Maria. Berowne mocks his lovesick friends and chides them for their inconstancy. "When shall you see me write a thing in rhyme? / Or groan for love?" he asks. But he is forced to admit his infatuation for Rosaline when Costard and Jaquenetta bring him his letter. He claims, however, that, by abjuring women, they had foolishly foresworn knowledge, because all knowledge can be acquired through a lady's eyes, which "are the books, the arts, the academes, / That show, contain and nourish all the world." Convinced by Berowne's reasoning, his friends resolve to conquer the ladies' hearts, smoothing love's way with revels, masques, and dances.

Act V. While the Princess and her ladies are humorously dissecting the verses that their suitors have sent them, their attendant Boyet reports that the King and his lords are at hand, disguised as Russians. The Princess suggests that they have a little sport of their own by wearing masks and exchanging favors so as to conceal their identities. As a result, each man pays court to the wrong girl. When the gentlemen return to the pavilion in their own clothes, the ladies, forewarned by Boyet, speak scornfully of the Muscovite fools who had visited them. After the prank is disclosed, Berowne, who has learned his lesson, forswears affected and pedantic language, vowing to express his romantic ardor "in russet yeas and honest kersey noes."

The group is now treated to a dramatic representation of the Nine Worthies, in which Costard plays Pompey, Sir Nathaniel is Alexander, Holofernes is Judas Maccabaeus, Moth is the young Hercules, and Armado is Hector. The festivities end abruptly when the Princess learns that her father has died, and she is compelled to return to France immediately. In response to their wooers' suits, the ladies declare that Ferdinand and his companions must hie "to some forlorn and naked hermitage" and spend 12 months in seclusion, after which they promise to give them a favorable answer. Berowne is given the special task of visiting hospitals and using his quick wit to cheer the sick. The gentlemen grudgingly agree to these terms and offer to escort the ladies, delaying their departure only long enough to hear a dialogue composed by Holofernes and Sir Nathaniel in praise of the owl and the cuckoo.—H. D.

Comment. The warp and woof of *Love's Labour's Lost* is satire and, at certain points, burlesque. It is a court play, designed for the amusement of an audience of which Queen Elizabeth herself was doubtless a member. The comedy spreads a great feast of language. The conversations between the gentlemen and the derisive ladies form, in Berowne's opinion, a medley of

> Taffeta phrases, silken terms precise,
> Three-piled hyperboles, spruce affectation,
> Figures pedantical; these summer-flies
> Have blown me full of maggot ostentation.
> (V, ii, 406–409)

These are the verbal affectations that Berowne at the end of the play renounces for "russet yeas and honest kersey noes." Shakespeare at once ridicules John LYLY's euphuistic style and successfully imitates it. He creates a distinctive form of ridiculous speech for Armado, for Holofernes, for Moth, and even for Costard. In this play the arts, extravagances, and ingenuities of language have become the author's absorbing interest. He finds the varying moods of the speakers best expressed variously by rhyme, blank verse, couplets, quatrains, or sonnets. The comedy rejects the idea of cloistered study of philosophy and of leaden contemplation, and affirms direct experience of life in the society of women, where love is the supreme value. Shakespeare celebrates love in one of the most exquisite lyrical passages in the play with the lines beginning:

> For valour, is not Love a Hercules?
> (IV, iii, 340–345)

The play, then, is more than a collection of private jokes and satires of verbal affectation. It is a lively argument on the popular side of the widespread Renaissance conflict between art and nature.

Love's Labour's Lost is, above all, a topical play. Many of the references to contemporary jokes, events, and men have become unintelligible to modern audiences. However, one of the most puzzling problems has recently been solved to the satisfaction of many scholars. The crux is in the King's speech (IV, iii, 254–255) during an encounter with Berowne who had fallen in love with a "dark lady," Rosaline. Of her, the King remarks scornfully that she is "black as ebony" and a few lines later adds,

> O paradox! Black is the badge of hell,
> The hue of dungeons and the School of night.
> (IV, iii, 254–255)

Earlier commentators insisted that "school" was a misprint, and emended it to "suit," as it appears today in most editions. They suggested many alternatives, but the consensus of contemporary scholars is that Shakespeare applies the term "SCHOOL OF NIGHT" to a group of scientists and poets organized and patronized by Sir Walter Raleigh for the study of mathematics and the new astronomy of Copernicus (d. 1543). The speculations of these men led them to doubt some of the fundamental doctrines of Christianity and to earn the title that the Jesuit Father Robert Parsons (1546–1610) first applied to them: "The School of Atheism."

In addition to these allusions some scholars have seen in the low-comedy characters portraits of other of Shakespeare's contemporaries. Thus the character of Don Armado has been variously identified as Raleigh, Gabriel Harvey, Antonio Pérez, and Gervase Markham. Moth has been identified with Thomas Nashe and Holofernes with John Florio. However, a knowledge of these allusions is not necessary for a full enjoyment of the antics of Armado, Moth, and Holofernes, for these low-comedy characters are more than targets for satiric attack. Shakespeare cannot resist giving his audience a glimpse of the man behind each figure of fun. After Nathaniel, the toady to Holofernes, has forgotten his lines in the part of Alexander in the play of the Nine Worthies and has been baited so savagely by the gentlemen that he has left the stage discomfited, Costard speaks up for him:

> There, an't shall please you; a foolish mild man; an honest man, look you, and soon dashed. He is a marvellous good neighbour, faith, and a very good bowler: but, for Alisander,—alas, you see how 'tis,—a little o'erparted.
>
> (V, ii, 584–588)

Holofernes protests for himself against the ridicule the gentlemen rain on him: "This is not generous, not gentle, not humble" (V, ii, 632), and, for the moment at least, becomes a dignified and pathetic old man. Shakespeare contrives to render even Don Armado's exaggerated pride and folly touched with a pathetic madness like that of Don Quixote.

Shakespeare shows his originality most strikingly in the final *coup de théâtre*. Upon the strident gaiety of the courtiers' ridicule of the yokels, Mercade intrudes with the news that the Princess' father has died. At this stroke, the real world breaks in upon the retreat of the fantastics and blows it into thin air. The felicity of all the lovers is postponed for a year and the characters are ushered off the stage to the singing of two of the poet's most memorable songs, which carry us far away from the hothouse atmosphere of the court at Nérac to the countryside with its "daisies pied and violets blue" and to the winter's kitchen of Marian of the "red and raw" nose, while out of doors "all aloud the wind doth blow."—O. J. C.

Stage History. The first recorded performance of *Love's Labour's Lost* was that acted before Queen Elizabeth and her court during the Christmas season of 1597. A private performance of the play was also given during the Christmas revels of 1604/5 at the house of either the earl of Salisbury or the earl of Southampton (see Sir Walter COPE). In 1762 there was published, but apparently never staged, an adaptation of the comedy entitled THE STUDENTS. From Shakespeare's day through to the early 19th century no revivals of the play are recorded. On September 30, 1839 Elizabeth Vestris, manager of Covent Garden, put on an elaborate production of the comedy and drew effusive praise from the critics for her acting of Rosaline. This revival was ruined, however, by a riot on opening night caused by the new management's (Mathews-Vestris) decision to close the shilling gallery. On September 30, 1857 Samuel Phelps presented the comedy at Sadler's Wells, he himself taking the part of Armado, one of his choicest comic impersonations. This production had only nine performances. It was first staged at the Shakespeare Memorial Theatre in 1885 in celebration of Shakespeare's birthday on April 23. There was a production on July 2, 1886 at the St. James Theatre. In 1907 the comedy, almost unknown at Stratford-upon-Avon, was again chosen for the birthday play, this time by the F. R. Benson company, with Benson as Berowne.

There was an Old Vic production in 1918 with Ernest Milton playing Berowne, and another, produced by Robert Atkins, in 1923 with Ion Swinley as Berowne and George Hayes as Armado. The Birmingham Repertory Theatre staged a musical *Love's Labour's Lost* in 1919 and, in 1925, the Fellowship of Players, a group which often acted rarities, gave the comedy at the Apollo.

In 1932, Tyrone Guthrie, just 32, attracted attention with a bright, jaunty production of the play at the Westminster Theatre. When he staged it for the Old Vic in 1936, he was fortunate with his cast, which included Ernest Milton, a swaggering Armado, Alec Clunes as Berowne, and Michael Redgrave as Ferdinand of Navarre, but this elegant production was unsuccessful. The comedy was equally unpopular at Stratford, where, in 1934, W. Bridges-Adams produced it, using a single set. Baliol Holloway was an amusing Armado, but admittedly never cared for the part. The Open Air Theatre presented *Love's Labour's Lost* in 1935, 1936, and 1943, but it wasn't until 1946 that this comedy of youth would prosper. That year at Stratford, Peter Brook staged by far the most successful *Love's Labour's Lost* of the century. Aided considerably by Paul Scofield portraying a melancholy Armado, Brook captured the "sweet-sad mood of the play." This production was played at the Memorial Theatre again in 1947. It was followed by another excellent staging in 1949. This time the Old Vic company, playing at the New Theatre under producer Hugh Hunt, favored the comedy with ideal casting: Michael Redgrave, Berowne; Mark Dignam, Holofernes; Miles Malleson, Nathaniel; and Baliol Holloway, Armado.

Subsequent productions include two at the Open Air in 1953 and 1962, one during the Old Vic 1954/5 season in which John Neville portrayed Berowne and Paul Rogers played Armado, and another at Stratford produced by Peter Hall with Harry Andrews as Armado.—M. G.

Bibliography. TEXT: *Love's Labour's Lost*, New Cambridge Edition, Arthur Quiller-Couch and J. Dover Wilson, eds., 1923; *Love's Labour's Lost*, New Arden Edition, Richard David, ed., 1951. DATE: New Arden Edition; Alfred Harbage, "*Love's Labour's Lost* and the Early Shakespeare," *Philological Quarterly*, XLI, 1962. SOURCES: Abel Lefranc, *Sous le Masque de "William Shakespeare,"* 1919; Oscar James Campbell, "Love's Labour's Lost Restudied," *Studies in Shakespeare . . .*, 1925. COMMENT: New Cambridge Edition; Arthur Acheson, *Shakespeare and the Rival Poet*, 1903; Frances A. Yates, *A Study of Love's Labour's Lost*, 1936; Muriel C. Bradbrook, *The School of Night*, 1936. STAGE HISTORY: New Cambridge Edition; G. C. D. Odell, *Shakespeare from Betterton to Irving*, 1920; J. C. Trewin, *Shakespeare on the English Stage, 1900–1964*, 1964.

Selected Criticism

WILLIAM HAZLITT. If we were to part with any of

the author's comedies, it should be this. Yet we should be loth to part with Don Adriano de Armado, that mighty potentate of nonsense, or his page, that handful of wit; with Nathaniel the curate, or Holofernes the school-master, and their dispute after dinner on the 'golden cadense of poesy'; with Costard the clown, or Dull the constable. Biron is too accomplished a character to be lost to the world, and yet he could not appear without his fellow courtiers and the King; and if we were to leave out the ladies, the gentlemen would have no mistresses. So that we believe we may let the whole play stand as it is, and we shall hardly venture to 'set a mark of reprobation on it.' Still we have some objections to the style, which we think savours more of the pedantic spirit of Shakespeare's time than of his own genius; more of controversial divinity, and the logic of Peter Lombard, than of the inspiration of the muse. It transports us quite as much to the manners of the court, and the quirks of courts of law, as to the scenes of nature or the fairy-land of his own imagination. Shakespeare has set himself to imitate the tone of polite conversation then prevailing among the fair, the witty, and the learned, and he has imitated it but too faithfully. It is as if the hand of Titian had been employed to give grace to the curls of a full-bottomed periwig, or Raphael had attempted to give expression to the tapestry figures in the House of Lords. [*Characters of Shakespear's Plays*, 1817.]

SAMUEL TAYLOR COLERIDGE. I can never sufficiently admire the wonderful activity of thought throughout the whole of the first scene of the play, rendered natural, as it is, by the choice of the characters, and the whimsical determination on which the drama is founded. A whimsical determination certainly;—yet not altogether so very improbable to those who are conversant in the history of the middle ages, with their Courts of Love, and all that lighter drapery of chivalry, which engaged even mighty kings with a sort of serio-comic interest, and may well be supposed to have occupied more completely the smaller princes, at a time when the noble's or prince's court contained the only theatre of the domain or principality. This sort of story, too, was admirably suited to Shakspeare's times, when the English court was still the foster-mother of the state and the muses; and when, in consequence, the courtiers, and men of rank and fashion, affected a display of wit, point, and sententious observation, that would be deemed intolerable at present,—but in which a hundred years of controversy, involving every great political, and every dear domestic, interest, had trained all but the lowest classes to participate. Add to this the very style of the sermons of the time, and the eagerness of the Protestants to distinguish themselves by long and frequent preaching, and it will be found that, from the reign of Henry VIII. to the abdication of James II. no country ever received such a national education as England.

Hence the comic matter chosen in the first instance is a ridiculous imitation or apery of this constant striving after logical precision, and subtle opposition of thoughts, together with a making the most of every conception or image, by expressing it under the least expected property belonging to it, and this, again, rendered specially absurd by being applied to the most current subjects and occurrences. The phrases and modes of combination in argument were caught by the most ignorant from the custom of the age, and their ridiculous misapplication of them is most amusingly exhibited in Costard; whilst examples suited only to the gravest propositions and impersonations, or apostrophes to abstract thoughts impersonated, which are in fact the natural language only of the most vehement agitations of the mind, are adopted by the coxcombry of Armado as mere artifices of ornament. [*Shakespearean Criticism* by S. T. Coleridge, T. M. Raysor, ed., Everyman Library Edition, 1960.]

GEORG GOTTFRIED GERVINUS. In structure and management of subject, it is indisputably one of the weakest of the poet's pieces; yet one divines a deeper merit than is readily perceived, and which is with difficulty unfolded. . . . The whole turns upon a clever interchange of wit and asceticism, jest and earnest; the shallow characters are forms of mind, rather proceeding from the cultivation of the head than the will; throughout there are affected jests, high-sounding and often empty words, but no action, and, notwithstanding, one feels that this deficiency is no unintentional error, but that there is an object in view. There is a motley mixture of fantastic and strange characters, which for the most part betray no healthy groundwork of nature, and yet the poet himself is so sensible of this, that we might trust him to have had his reason for placing them together, a reason worth our while to seek. And indeed we find, on closer inspection, that this piece has a more profound character, in which Shakespeare's capable mind already unfolds its power; we perceive in this, the first of his plays, in which he, as subsequently is ever the case, has had one single moral aim in view, an aim that here lies even far less concealed than in others of his works. [*Shakespeare*, 1849–1850; tr. 1863 as *Shakespeare Commentaries*.]

VICTOR HUGO. Constrained by her [Elizabeth], the youngest and handsomest men of her court, Essex, Raleigh, and Southampton engaged themselves to worship none but the septuagenarian Madonna . . . .

Thus, of the three chief neophytes who had sworn, with the virgin queen, to observe the strictest celibacy, two had already broken their vows: Essex and Raleigh,—Essex to marry Lady Sidney, Raleigh to wed Mistress Throckmorton. One alone remained constant: Henry Wriothesley, Earl of Southampton, the same to whom Shakespeare had already dedicated two poems: *Venus and Adonis* and *Lucrece.* Handsome, young, learned, rich, and magnificent, Henry represented one of the great families of England. If *noblesse oblige,* paternity is its first demand. Respect for ancestors demands the desire for children. Just for the caprice of an old maid, should Henry suffer his lordly dynasty to expire in himself? Ought he barrenly to fritter away his haughty beauty which his ancestors had not given but merely lent him? 'Never!' said Shakespeare courageously in his *Sonnets*. . . . Only one opportunity was needed to convince the young Earl of the truth of the poet's words. Sweet verses are less potent to inspire love than sweet eyes. When listening to Shakespeare, Southampton doubted; when gazing on Mistress Elizabeth Vernon, he was persuaded . . . .

Then it was that Shakespeare, friend and confidant

of Southampton, devised the plot of the comedy, hitherto misunderstood, which now claims our attention.—To show all the absurdities to which diminutive human omnipotence exposes itself in braving supreme omnipotence, to prove the nothingness of the little codes of despotism when brought face to face with the unalterable laws of creation, victoriously to oppose primordial law to arbitrary statutes, to abolish, amid peals of laughter, visionary prohibitions which shackle the satisfaction of elemental needs and instincts, to denounce as grotesque all habits which social presumption attempts to impose on man in contempt of reason, in short to proclaim in the face of all tyrannies—the tyranny of power, the tyranny of fashion, the tyranny of false taste, the tyranny of vanity, the tyranny of success, —the imprescriptible sovereignty of nature, such was the thought of the poet in composing *Love's Labour's Lost*. The project of the author was more than audacious. A veritable satire was it, that Shakespeare was about to hurl against the Court, against its manners, against its most cherished affections. [*Oeuvres Complètes de Shakespeare*, 1859–1866; translation from *Love's Labour's Lost*, New Variorum ed., 1904.]

ALGERNON CHARLES SWINBURNE. . . . the real crown and flower of *Love's Labour's Lost*, is the praise or apology of love spoken by Biron in blank verse. This is worthy of Marlowe for dignity and sweetness, but has also the grace of a light and radiant fancy enamoured of itself, begotten between thought and mirth, a child-god with grave lips and laughing eyes, whose inspiration is nothing akin to Marlowe's. In this as in the overture of the play and in its closing scene, but especially in the noble passage which winds up for a year the courtship of Biron and Rosaline, the spirit which informs the speech of the poet is finer of touch and deeper of tone than in the sweetest of the serious interludes of *The Comedy of Errors*. The play is in the main a lighter thing, and more wayward and capricious in build, more formless and fantastic in plot, more incomposite altogether than that first heir of Shakespeare's comic invention, which on its own ground is perfect in its consistency, blameless in composition and coherence; while in *Love's Labour's Lost* the fancy for the most part runs wild as the wind, and the structure of the story is as that of a house of clouds which the wind builds and unbuilds at pleasure. Here we find a very riot of rhymes, wild and wanton in their half-grown grace as a troop of 'young satyrs, tender-hoofed and ruddy-horned'; during certain scenes we seem almost to stand again by the cradle of new-born comedy, and hear the first lisping and laughing accents run over from her baby lips in bubbling rhyme; but when the note changes we recognize the speech of gods. For the first time in our literature the higher key of poetic or romantic comedy is finely touched to a fine issue. The divine instrument fashioned by Marlowe for tragic purposes alone has found at once its new sweet use in the hands of Shakespeare. The way is prepared for *As You Like It* and *The Tempest;* the language is discovered which will befit the lips of Rosalind and Miranda. [*A Study of Shakespeare*, 1880.]

WALTER PATER. . . . modes of fashions are, at their best, an example of the artistic predominance of form over matter; of the manner of the doing of it over the thing done; and have a beauty of their own. It is so with that old euphuism of the Elizabethan age—that pride of dainty language and curious expression, which it is very easy to ridicule, which often made itself ridiculous, but which had below it a real sense of fitness and nicety; and which, as we see in this very play, and still more clearly in the Sonnets, had some fascination for the young Shakspere himself. It is this foppery of delicate language, this fashionable plaything of his time, with which Shakspere is occupied in *Love's Labour's Lost*. He shows us the manner in all its stages; passing from the grotesque and vulgar pedantry of Holofernes, through the extravagant but polished caricature of Armado, to become the peculiar characteristic of a real though still quaint poetry in Biron himself—still chargeable, even at his best, with just a little affectation. As Shakspere laughs broadly at it in Holofernes or Armado, he is the analyst of its curious charm in Biron; and this analysis involves a delicate raillery by Shakspere himself at his own chosen manner.

This 'foppery' of Shakspere's day had, then, its really delightful side, a quality in no sense 'affected,' by which it satisfies a real instinct in our minds—the fancy so many of us have for an exquisite and curious skill in the use of words. Biron in the perfect flower of this manner—'A man of fire-new words, fashion's own knight'—as he describes Armado, in terms which are really applicable to himself. In him this manner blends with a true gallantry of nature, and an affectionate complaisance and grace. He has at times some of its extravagance or caricature also, but the shades of expression by which he passes from this to the 'golden cadence' of Shakspere's own chosen verse, are so fine, that it is sometimes difficult to trace them. What is a vulgarity in Holofernes, and a caricature in Armado, refines itself in him into the expression of a nature truly and inwardly bent upon a form of delicate perfection, and is accompanied by a real insight into the laws which determine what is exquisite in language, and their root in the nature of things. He can appreciate quite the opposite style—'In russet yeas, and honest kersey noes'; he knows the first law of pathos, that—'Honest plain words best suit the ear of grief.' He delights in his own rapidity of intuition; and, in harmony with the half sensuous philosophy of the Sonnets, exalts, a little scornfully, in many memorable expressions, the judgement of the senses, above all slower, more toilsome means of knowledge, scorning some who fail to see things only because they are so clear—'So ere you find where light in darkness lies, Your light grows dark by losing of your eyes'—as with some German commentators on Shakspere. Appealing always to actual sensation from men's affected theories, he might seem to despise learning; as, indeed, he has taken up his deep studies partly in play, and demands always the profit of learning in renewed enjoyment; yet he surprises us from time to time by intuitions which can come only from a deep experience and power of observation; and men listen to him, old and young, in spite of themselves. He is quickly impressible to the slightest clouding of the spirits in social intercourse, and has his moments of extreme seriousness; his trial-task may well be, as Rosaline puts it—'To enforce the pained impotent to smile.' But still, through all, he is true to his chosen manner; that gloss of dainty language is a second nature with him; even at his best he is not without a certain artifice; the trick of playing on words never deserts him; and Shakspere, in whose own genius there is an element of this very quality, shows us in this graceful, and, as it seems, studied, portrait, his enjoyment of it.

As happens with every true dramatist, Shakspere is for the most part hidden behind the persons of his creation. Yet there are certain of his characters in which we feel that there is something of self-portraiture. And it is not so much in his grander, more subtle and ingenious creations that we feel this—in Hamlet and King Lear—as in those slighter and more spontaneously developed figures, who, while far from playing principal parts, are yet distinguished by a certain peculiar happiness and delicate ease in the drawing of them—figures which possess, above all, that winning attractiveness which there is no man but would willingly exercise, and which resemble those works of art, which, though not meant to be very great or imposing, are yet wrought of the choicest material. Mercutio, in *Romeo and Juliet,* belongs to this group of Shakspere's characters, versatile, mercurial people, such as make good actors, and in whom the 'Nimble spirits of the arteries,' the finer but still merely animal elements of great wit, predominate. A careful delineation of little, characteristic traits seems to mark them out as characters of his predilection; and it is hard not to identify him with these more than with others. Biron, in *Love's Labour's Lost,* is perhaps the most striking member of this group. In this character, which is never quite in touch with, never quite on a perfect level of understanding with the other persons of the play, we see, perhaps, a reflex of Shakspere himself, when he has just become able to stand aside from and estimate the first period of his poetry. [*Macmillan's Magazine,* December, 1885.]

C. L. BARBER. . . . That the play should end without the usual marriages is exactly right, in view of what it is that is released by its festivities. Of course what the lords give way to is, in a general sense, the impulse to love; but the particular form that it takes for them is a particular sort of folly —What one could call the folly of amorous masquerade, whether in clothes, gestures, or words. It is the folly of acting love and talking love, without being in love. For the festivity releases, not the delights of love, but the delights of expression which the prospect of love engenders—though those involved are not clear about the distinction until it is forced on them; the clarification achieved by release is this recognition that love is not wooing games or love talk. And yet these sports are not written off or ruled out; on the contrary the play offers their delights for our enjoyment, while humorously putting them in their place . . . .

In a world of words, the wine is wit. Festivity in social life always enjoys, without effort, something physical from the world outside that is favorable to life, whether it be food and drink, or the warmth of the fields when they breathe sweet. Exhilaration comes when the world proves ready and willing, reaching out a hand, passing a brimming bowl; festivity signals the realization that we *belong* in the universe. Now in wit, it is language that gives us this something for nothing; unsuspected relations between words prove to be ready to hand to make a meaning that serves us. All of the comedies of Shakespeare, of course, depend on wit to convey the exhilaration of festivity. But *Love's Labour's Lost,* where the word *wit* is used more often than in any of the other plays, is particularly dependent on wit and particularly conscious in the way it uses and talks about it. ["The Folly of Wit and Masquerade in *Love's Labour's Lost*" in *Shakespeare's Festive Comedy,* 1959.]

Love's Labour's Won. A play attributed to Shakespeare by Francis Meres in his *Palladis Tamia* (1598). There has been considerable speculation as to whether a play by this title actually existed. Meres may have erroneously titled a known play. In 1957 the discovery of another contemporary reference to "loves labor's won" in the fragments of a bookseller's accounts reinforced arguments for the play's authenticity. T. W. Baldwin, who made this discovery, nevertheless believes that *Love's Labour's Won* is the same play we know as *Much Ado About Nothing.* Others have argued that the play might conceivably refer to *The Taming of the Shrew.* Leslie Hotson opines that the title really means "love's pains earned" and that it refers to *Troilus and Cressida.* Probably the most reasonable of the conjectures is that the title is the alternate name of *All's Well That Ends Well,* a theory supported by the action of the play and the several references within it to "winning." See ALL'S WELL THAT ENDS WELL: *Text.* [Leslie Hotson, *Shakespeare's Sonnets Dated,* 1949; T. W. Baldwin, *Shakspere's Love's Labor's Won,* 1957.]

Love's Martyr (1601). An allegorical poem by Robert Chester (c. 1566–1640) which gives its name to a book in which Shakespeare's "The Phoenix and the Turtle" first appeared. The title page of the book reads:

> Loves Martyr: Or, Rosalins Complaint. Allegorically shadowing the truth of Loue, in the constant Fate of the Phoenix and Turtle. A Poeme translated out of the Italian by Robert Chester . . . . To these are added some new compositions of seuerall moderne Writers whose names are subscribed to their seuerall workes, upon the first subiect: viz. the Phoenix and Turtle. London Imprinted for E. B. [Edward Blount]. 1601.

The first half of the book is devoted to Chester's poem. The second half has a separate title page which reads as follows:

> Hereafter Follow Diuerse Poeticall Essaies on the former Subiect; viz: the Turtle and Phoenix. Done by the best and chiefest of our moderne writers, with their names subscribed to their particular workes: neuer before extant. And (now first) consecrated by them all generally, to the loue and merite of the true-noble Knight, Sir Iohn Salisburie.

The "moderne writers" referred to in the title included John Marston, George Chapman, Ben Jonson, and Shakespeare. All the contributors dealt with the subject of the Phoenix and the Turtle (see THE PHOENIX AND THE TURTLE). Of Robert Chester very little is known. He was apparently a protégé of Sir ohn SALISBURY, to whom the poem is dedicated. ;. Wilson Knight conjectures that the highly un- ven quality of *Love's Martyr* is the result of Shake- peare's having revised Chester's inept original. The ook was reissued with a new title in 1612 as *The nuals* [i.e., *Annuals*] *of Great Brittaine.* [*Poems,* lew Variorum Edition, Hyder Rollins, ed., 1938; ;. Wilson Knight, *The Mutual Flame,* 1955.]

Love's Sacrifice. See John FORD.

Lowin, John (1576–1653). Actor. Lowin, the son f a carpenter, was born in London and in 1593 was pprenticed to a goldsmith for an eight-year period. hortly after the term of his apprenticeship expired e appears for the first time as an actor, with Wor- ester's Men in 1602. In 1603 he first appears with ne King's Men, in the cast of Jonson's *Sejanus,* eginning what was to be a long career as one of the ompany's best-known leading actors. He held no nares as a housekeeper in the Globe or Blackfriars ntil after the death of John Heminges. At some me about 1630 Lowin and Joseph TAYLOR acquired Ieminges' four shares. He and Taylor also appar- ntly shared the responsibilities of managing the ompany after the death of Heminges.

From contemporary descriptions, lines referring o him directly in plays in which he appeared, and n engraving after a portrait in the Ashmolean Iuseum, it is apparent that Lowin was a huge, orpulent man. His roles, more than 12 of which are iven in extant cast lists, were those of the bluff, utspoken man who, according to T. W. Baldwin, layed an honest friend or a villain with equal con- iction. His size was also probably responsible for is appointment as a king's porter (confirmed in ocuments of 1625). Among his roles were Bosola in *'he Duchess of Malfi* (pub. 1623); Titus Flaminius 1 *Believe as You List* (1613); and Belleur "of a stout lunt humor . . . Most naturally Acted by Mr. *John owin,*" in the 1632 revival of *The Wild Goose 'hase.*

According to James Wright's *Historia Histrionica,* owin was acting at the Cockpit in 1648 when troops aided the theatre. Wright attributed to him many ther roles, including Falstaff (see James WRIGHT). 1 his *Roscius Anglicanus,* John Downes reported 1at Lowin might have been the original actor in the tle role of Shakespeare's *Henry VIII.*

Wright also referred to Lowin as "superannuated" : the outbreak of the civil war and added that owin

> in his latter days kept an inn (the Three Pigeons) at Brentford, where he dyed very old (for he was an actor of eminent note in the reign of King James the First), and his poverty was as great as his age.

owin's burial is registered in St. Clement Danes on ugust 24, 1653. [E. K. Chambers, *The Elizabethan tage,* 1923; T. W. Baldwin, *The Organization and ersonnel of the Shakespearean Company,* 1927; :. E. Bentley, *The Jacobean and Caroline Stage,* vols., 1941–1956.]

Lownes, Humphrey (d. c. 1629). Printer of the inth edition of *Venus and Adonis* (1602). Lownes 'as admitted to the Stationers' Company in 1587. In 4 he married the widow of the printer Peter hort and acquired Short's shop in Bread Street. He was appointed Master of the Stationers' Company in 1620/1 and 1624/5. In 1628 his copyrights included such distinguished items as Sir Philip Sidney's *Arcadia,* Edmund Spenser's *Faerie Queene,* and Ben Jonson's *Poetaster.* It has been suggested that Lownes' edition of *Venus and Adonis,* although dated 1602, was actually printed in 1608/9 and misdated in order to confuse the authorities, who from 1604 to 1610 tried to suppress the poem on the grounds of its "licentiousness." [*The Poems,* New Variorum Edition, Hyder Rollins, ed., 1938.]

Luce. In *The Comedy of Errors,* a servant of Adriana. Luce refuses to admit Antipholus of Ephesus to his own house (III, i).

Luce, Morton (1849–1943). Author. Luce dealt most extensively with Shakespeare and Tennyson. His *Handbook to the Works of William Shakespeare* (1906) presents the relevant background information followed by a critical discussion of each play. *Shakespeare: The Man and His Work* (1913) is a collection of seven essays. For the Shakespeare Library Luce edited Barnabe Riche's *Apolonius and Silla,* the probable source of *Twelfth Night.* For the original Arden Shakespeare he edited *The Tempest* and *Twelfth Night. Man and Nature* (1935) is a collection of literary essays, several of which are on Shakespeare.

Lucentio. In *The Taming of the Shrew,* Vincentio's son, a young student in Padua, and successful suitor of Bianca. Lucentio disguises himself as a tutor in languages to gain access to her.

Lucetta. In *The Two Gentlemen of Verona,* Julia's sharp-tongued waiting woman who favors Proteus' suit for her mistress. Nevertheless, Lucetta tries to discourage Julia's journey to Milan (II, vii).

Lucian. Greek name **Loukianos** (c. 120–200). Greek satirist. Frequently writing in the form of dialogues, Lucian constructed irreverent and witty commentaries on the follies of his time. One of his dialogues, *Timon Misanthropus,* either directly or in a French or Italian translation, provided Shakespeare with one of the sources of his *Timon of Athens.* See TIMON OF ATHENS: *Sources.*

Luciana. In *The Comedy of Errors,* the placid, unmarried sister of Adriana. Luciana is disconcerted when Antipholus of Syracuse, whom she mistakes for her brother-in-law, makes love to her. But after the errors are straightened out, it appears that she will marry him herself.

Lucilius. In *Julius Caesar,* a supporter of Brutus and Cassius. Upon being captured at Philippi, Lucilius at first claims to be Brutus. Antony, impressed by his devotion to his leader, orders that Lucilius be well treated (V, iv). This episode is recounted by Plutarch, who adds that Lucilius became a faithful friend to Antony.

Lucilius. In *Timon of Athens,* a servant of Timon's. The nobleman gives Lucilius money so that he can marry the girl who loves him.

Lucio. In *Measure for Measure,* a licentious fellow who confesses that he prefers the "foppery of freedom" to the "morality of prison." Expressing a passing sympathy for the condemned Claudio, Lucio persuades Isabella to petition Angelo to spare her brother's life. At the denouement, the Duke punishes Lucio by ordering him to marry the woman he has wronged.

Lucius. In *Julius Caesar*, a boy servant to Brutus. Brutus indicates a kind and tender affection for young Lucius. On two occasions when the boy falls asleep while on duty, Brutus is unwilling to disturb him, and on the night before the battle at Philippi promises: "if I do live, I will be good to thee" (IV, iv).

Lucius. In *Timon of Athens*, one of the flattering lords who take advantage of Timon's generosity but show him little in return. In I, ii, Lucius sends Timon four white horses with silver trappings, but later, when Timon's servant requests money for his ruined master, his false friend refuses it. In III, iv, Lucius' servant goes to collect a debt from Timon.

Lucius. In *Titus Andronicus*, the eldest son of Titus. In a series of schemes carried out by the empress Tamora and her Moorish lover, Aaron, Lucius' sister Lavinia is raped and mutilated, two of his brothers are executed, and his father has his hand chopped off. Lucius thereupon appeals to the Goths and secures their aid against the emperor Saturninus, whom he kills. After telling the Roman people of the crimes perpetrated against Titus, Lucius himself is chosen emperor. Tamora having been killed, Lucius orders Aaron buried breast-deep in earth and starved.

Lucius, Caius. In *Cymbeline*, General of the Roman forces. As Augustus Caesar's ambassador, Caius Lucius demands from Cymbeline the tribute due Rome and, when the payment is denied, pronounces war, sadly warning of a "fury not to be resisted." In defeat, this honorable soldier and gentleman asks that the disguised Imogen, whom Lucius has kindly taken into his service, be spared. When this request is granted and Imogen is offered a boon, Lucius assumes she will plead for his life but is astonished and somewhat indignant when she disappoints this expectation. However, the noble General is ultimately spared in Cymbeline's magnanimous pardon.

Lucius, Young. In *Titus Andronicus*, the young son of Lucius. His aunt Lavinia having been raped and mutilated by Tamora's sons, Demetrius and Chiron, she indicates to young Lucius what has happened to her by turning his copy of Ovid's *Metamorphoses* to the story of Philomel. Young Lucius thereupon takes to Tamora's sons a gift of arrows and a threatening letter from Titus.

Lucius' Servant. In *Timon of Athens*, the servant of a lord to whom Timon owes money. He tries vainly to collect the debt.

Lucullus. In *Timon of Athens*, one of the flattering lords who take advantage of Timon's generosity but show him little in return. In I, ii, Lucullus sends Timon two brace of greyhounds, but when Timon's servant Flaminius comes to request money for his ruined master, Lucullus tries to bribe the man into pretending that he could not be found.

Lucy, Sir Thomas (1532–1600). Owner of the great estate of Charlecote, near Stratford, where Shakespeare, according to a popular tradition, was caught poaching. The Lucys had owned the estate of Charlecote from the 12th century. Sir Thomas grew up there, assuming the mastership of the estate upon the death of his father in 1552. He was knighted in 1565 and served in parliament in 1577 and 1584. Lucy, a man of strong Puritan sympathies, took an active part in the affairs of Warwickshire and particularly of Stratford-upon-Avon. He had two sons, Thom (d. 1605) and Sir Richard Lucy (1592–1667 Thomas' eldest son, Sir Thomas Lucy (1586–164c eventually succeeded to the estate.

Lucy is best known for his alleged relationsh with Shakespeare. The poaching story was appa ently current in Stratford during the 17th centur It was first recorded by Richard Davies who, som time before his death in 1708, related it as follow

> William Shakespeare was born at Stratford up Avon in Warwickshire about 1563.4.
> much given to all unluckinesse in stealing venis & Rabbits particularly from Sr Lucy wl had him oft whipt & sometimes Imprisoned & last made Him fly his Native Country to his gre Advancemt. but His reveng was so great that he his Justice Clodpate and calls him a great man & in allusion to his name bore three lowses rampa for his Arms.

Davies' reference to "Justice Clodpate" is general considered to be an allusion to Justice SHALLOW, wl appears as a comic butt in *2 Henry IV* and *T Merry Wives of Windsor*.

The story is given at greater length in Nichol Rowe's life of Shakespeare (1709):

> He had, by a Misfortune common enough young Fellows, fallen into ill Company; ar amongst them, some that made a frequent practi of Deer-stealing, engag'd him with them mo than once in robbing a Park that belong'd to S *Thomas Lucy* of *Cherlecot*, near *Stratford*. F this he was prosecuted by that Gentleman, as l thought, somewhat too severely; and in order revenge that ill Usage, he made a Ballad upc him. . . .

The tradition has been rejected by some schola on the ground that there was no deer park at Charl cote. There were, however, deer in the woods ne the estate, and Sir Thomas was actively committed the preservation of game in Warwickshire. This is more reliable explanation than the one which asser that the incident refers to another estate which d have a deer park, that of Fulbrooke, Warwickshi Fulbrooke became the property of the Lucys onl some time after the death of Sir Thomas.

Two claims have been made to the discovery the ballad on Lucy that Rowe mentions in his a count. Malone printed one of these (see Josh BARNES) and another was recorded by Willia Oldys:

> A parliemente member, a justice of peace,
> At home a poor scare-crowe, at London an asse,
> If lowsie is Lucy, as some volke miscalle it,
> Then Lucy is lowsie whatever befall it:
>   He thinks himselfe greate,
>   Yet an asse in his state,
> We allowe by his ears but with asses to mate.
>   If Lucy is lowsie, as some volke miscalle it,
>   Sing lowsie Lucy, whatever befall it.

The most convincing argument for the truth the legend, however, remains the text of *The Merr Wives of Windsor* (I, i), where Justice Shallo wishes to treat Falstaff's deer-poaching as a "Sta chamber matter." Immediately following this ou burst is a reference to the "dozen white luces"

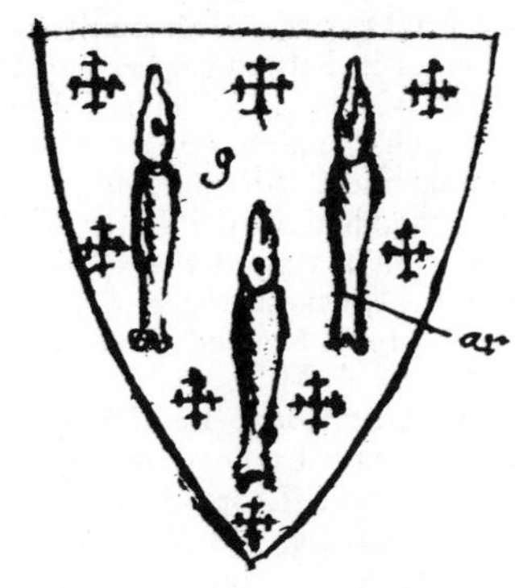

THE LUCY COAT OF ARMS EMBLAZONED WITH LUCES.

ıe coat of arms of Shallow's ancestors. The illustra- on of the Lucy coat of arms in Dugdale's *Antiqui- 'es of Warwickshire* (1656) shows three luces (pike sh) in each quarter, or a total of a dozen white ıces. Shallow also shares with Lucy some similarity f interests, such as a fondness for archery.

This conjecture has been challenged, however, by ,eslie Hotson, who argues that Shakespeare is attack- ıg another justice of the peace, William Gardiner. Iotson demonstrates that Gardiner's coat of arms an be similarly interpreted, since it too contains ıree luces. [Leslie Hotson, *Shakespeare versus Shal- ›w*, 1931.]

Lucy, Sir William. In *1 Henry VI*, an English ·ader. Lucy vainly asks York and Somerset to send ıd to the beleaguered Lord Talbot, blaming them or the latter's defeat (IV, iii and iv). The character as been identified with Sir William Lucy (1398– 466), a Yorkist who was sheriff of Warwickshire. W. H. Thomson, *Shakespeare's Characters: A His- ›rical Dictionary*, 1951.]

Lychorida. In *Pericles*, a nurse to the infant Ma- ına. Lychorida accompanies Pericles and Thaisa on ıe voyage to Tyre, during which Thaisa seemingly ıes while giving birth to Marina (III, i). Later she emains with Marina at Tarsus (III, iii). The poet Gower reports Lychorida's death in the Prologue o Act IV.

Lydgate, John (c. 1370–1451). Poet. One of the ıost prolific writers in English literature, Lydgate vas born at Lydgate in Suffolk and educated at the ıonastery school in Bury St. Edmunds. In 1397 he vas ordained a priest and spent the greater part of is life at Bury St. Edmunds. The best-known piece rom his enormous production is *The Troy Book* 1412–1420), an English metrical version of a Latin rose account of the Trojan War. Lydgate's version ıns to some 30,117 lines in decasyllabic couplets. *'he Troy Book*, the reputation of which was un- ccountably high in the 16th century, may have een Shakespeare's source for certain details in *'roilus and Cressida*.

Lydgate is also the author of *Falle of Princis* 1494), a 26,000-line collection of "tragedies" in erse based on Boccaccio's *De Casibus Virorum Il- ıstrium* by way of a French version by Laurent de remierfait. *Falle of Princis* eventually became the rototype of one of the most popular books of the lizabethan age, *A Mirror for Magistrates*.

Lyly, John (c. 1554–1606). Novelist and dramatist. ducated at Oxford, where he received the bachelor's degree in 1573 and the master's in 1575, Lyly was incorporated M.A. at Cambridge in 1579. The publication of his prose romance *Euphues, or the Anatomy of Wit* the previous year, followed by *Euphues and his England* in 1580 and the production of at least eight court comedies, made him the most famous and fashionable English writer for a decade. He long sought preferment at court, particularly the position of Master of the Revels, and he missed few opportunities to render homage and flattery (often through his dramatic characterizations) to the queen; but his efforts were doomed to failure. After 1590 his influence steadily declined.

Lyly's mannered romances involved courtly and pastoral characters and settings. Underlying the lengthy discourses in *Euphues* on women and love, education, religion, statesmanship—Renaissance ideas to which he gave popular currency—was an attack on female fickleness and the Italianate society of England. The outcry which followed prompted its sequel, *Euphues and his England*, a virtual retraction commending all things English. His comedies, also written to suit the taste of the court, were based on the theme of love and set in a classical or mythological background. Of these the best are probably *Sapho and Phao* (c. 1584), *Campaspe* (c. 1584), *Gallathea* (before 1588), and *Endimion* (c. 1588). The latter dramatizes the tale of a young shepherd who adores Cynthia the moon goddess and leaves unrequited the more earthly love of Tellus, and who for punishment is cast into a deep sleep from which nothing can awaken him except Cynthia's chaste kiss.

While Lyly can be generally credited with fathering the English comedy of courtship, he was indebted to two conventions. *Mother Bombie* (c. 1587), like Shakespeare's *Comedy of Errors*, borrows the stock figures of Latin comedy, such as the crafty servant, the duped parent, the braggart soldier, the aging lover, and the disguises and substitutions, while the humor springs more from earlier English buffoonery than from the Latin intrigues and imbroglios. From the medieval conventions of courtly love he borrows the attitudes of the lovesick youth with his melancholy sighs and fasting, his slovenly attire, his penchant for composing love songs—except that the mood is Platonic rather than adulterous. The foibles of lovers are treated as much with sympathy as with ridicule. All of this is enlivened by topical allegory and a fanciful imagination.

But Lyly's greater contribution to his period generally and to Shakespeare particularly was his advance in style over the awkwardness and crudity of 16th-century English through the conscious, often ostentatious, use of such devices as antithesis and balance, rhetorical question, metaphor and simile, personification and alliteration—all sustained by a nimble and aphoristic wit. This "euphuism" had a vast influence on contemporary dramatists like Greene, Lodge, and Nashe (the University Wits) and was brought to maturity in the rhythm, poise, and sparkle of the prose of Shakespeare's great comedies.

Being the most prominent comic writer among Shakespeare's predecessors, Lyly influenced Shakespeare's dramaturgic ideas as well. According to Mincoff, the Lylian strain is apparent in *The Comedy of Errors*, *The Two Gentlemen of Verona*, and *The*

Taming of the Shrew; reaches its height in *Love's Labour's Lost* and *A Midsummer Night's Dream;* and declines in *Much Ado About Nothing, As You Like It,* and *Twelfth Night.* More than 50 specific borrowings have been pointed out. Among these are the parallel and contrapuntal patterns of courtship and comedy characteristic of plays like *Gallathea;* Shakespeare echoed these in the farcical scenes between Moth, Armado, and Costard (*Love's Labour's Lost*) and between Launcelot and Old Gobbo (*Merchant of Venice*), contrasted with the wit combats between persons of rank: Boyet and the French ladies (*Love's Labour's Lost*) and Portia and Nerissa (*Merchant of Venice*), as well as the raillery between Katharine and Petruchio (*Taming of the Shrew*) and the contests between Beatrice and Benedick (*Much Ado About Nothing*). In *Love's Labour's Lost* particularly, Shakespeare caricatures the Italianate and pedantic fashions of the day—the strutting of the males and the coquetry of the ladies in the game of love. The aberrations of lovers are again lightly satirized in *A Midsummer Night's Dream.* Here and in *The Tempest* Shakespeare uses supernatural elements which are part of the mythology of love, although Shakespeare's fairies are less English than Lyly's.

In *Much Ado* and *As You Like It* there is open ridicule of Petrarchan sonneteering, particularly of the shepherd; but both Orlando and Benedick turn out more realistically human than their Lylian forebears. In *Twelfth Night* Viola's wooing of the Duke by indirection and the two pairs of lovers involving a girl disguised as a boy again repeat *Gallathea.* Even the late *King Lear* contains a parallel with *Euphues* in a situation involving a daughter's ingratitude toward an aged father, but there are of course many contemporary analogues.

While Lyly's influence dominated most of Shakespeare's comedies, Shakespeare's superior artistry transcended it and ultimately opposed it. He came to reject the nymphs and mischievous cupids, the mythology and artificiality, the intrigues and deceptions; and most of his lovers develop into real human beings who, overcoming their human contradictions, are moving toward marriage on a love soundly based. Moreover, Shakespeare's style reached heights to which Lyly's synthetic language could never aspire. Shakespeare's most pointed parody of Lyly's style comes in Falstaff's speech to Prince H (*1 Henry IV*, II, iv, 438–442): "Harry, I do not onl marvel where thou spendest thy time, but also ho thou art accompanied: for though the camomil the more it is trodden on the faster it grows, y youth, the more it is wasted the sooner it wears [Marco Mincoff, "Shakespeare and Lyly," *Shak speare Survey 14*, 1961; Kenneth Muir, *Shakespeare Sources*, Vol. I, 1957.]—M.H.

Lymoges. In *King John,* the Duke of Austri Shakespeare's character Lymoges is a combination of two historical persons: Leopold, second duke an first archduke of Austria; and Vidomar, viscount of Lymoges. Both were enemies of Richard Coeur d Lion. The archduke, whose standard Richard ha insulted at Acre, took his revenge by capturing an imprisoning the English king. The viscount o Lymoges, having discovered a treasure on h estate, refused to surrender it all to Richard, wh accordingly besieged Lymoges' castle and eventuall took it.

In *King John*, Lymoges, who was responsible fo the death of Richard Coeur de Lion, is an ally of th French King Philip II. He is killed by Philip Fau conbridge, the Bastard. [W. H. Thomson, *Shake speare's Characters: A Historical Dictionary*, 1951

Lysander. In *A Midsummer Night's Dream,* Her mia's beloved. On Hermia's refusal to marry he father's choice, Demetrius, the sweethearts fle Athens to escape Egeus' wrath. Waking in the fore after Puck has erringly administered his magi Lysander abandons Hermia to pursue Helena. Whe the mistake is corrected, the original lovers are rec onciled in matrimony.

Lysimachus. In *Pericles,* governor of Mytilene. A regular patron of the brothel, he joins the ranks o customers regenerated by the virtuous Marina an leaves that unhallowed place "saying his praye too." Lysimachus recognizes Marina's gentle breed ing and says that if he were certain of her nob parentage he would "wish no better choice" an consider himself "rarely wed." This assurance forthcoming when Marina is reunited with Pericle and it is revealed that she is in fact the daughter o a king.

M

M., I. The initials of the author of the commendatory verse affixed to the First Folio (1623) of Shakespeare's plays:

To the memorie of M. W. Shake-speare

Wee wondred (*Shake-speare*) that thou went'st so soone
From the Worlds-Stage, to the Graues-Tyring-roome.
Wee thought thee dead, but this thy printed worth,
Tels thy Spectators, that thou went'st but forthe
To enter with applause. An Actors Art,
Can dye, and liue, to acte a second part.
That's but an *Exit* of Mortalitie;
This, a Re-entrance to a Plaudite.

I. M.

"I. M." has been variously identified as John Marston, Jasper MAYNE, and James MABBE. Evidence showing that Mabbe was a friend of Leonard Digges, another contributor of verse to the Folio, has strengthened the case for Mabbe as the author. [E. K. Chambers, *William Shakespeare*, 1930.]

Mabbe, James (1572–1642). Translator and poet. A friend of Leonard Digges, the contributor of a commendatory verse to the First Folio, Mabbe is generally thought to be the I. M. (see M., I.) who also contributed a commendatory poem to that volume. Mabbe was a Spanish scholar at Oxford who upon graduation was made secretary to Sir John Digby the English ambassador to Spain. Mabbe is also the author of an extant drama, *The Spanish Bawd, represented in Celestina, or the Tragicke-Comedy of Calisto and Melibea* (1631), a translation of Fernando de Rojas' remarkable *La Celestina.*

Macbeth. (d. 1057). King of Scotland. In *Macbeth,* the tragic hero. Historically Macbeth was the son of Finlegh, Thane of Ross. Around 1040 he led a rebellion against King Duncan of Scotland whom he defeated in battle at Dunsinane. For the next 17 years Macbeth ruled Scotland, competently and justly, according to reliable accounts, until he was defeated and killed by rebel forces under Malcolm at the Battle of Lumphanan (1057). The distorted picture of Macbeth in Shakespeare's play derives from the inaccuracies of Renaissance Scottish historians (see MACBETH: *Sources*) who wished to represent Macbeth's reign as the only interruption in an unbroken dynasty of Scottish kings.

The Macbeth of Shakespeare's play is a figure of noble and heroic proportions, transformed in the course of the play into a monster of iniquity. Paradoxically, however, his villainy enhances rather than diminishes his stature. In this respect he is unique among Shakespeare's tragic heroes. Whereas they ascend the tragic heights, gaining the wisdom and insight which enables them to encounter their fate with resignation and with a renewed sense of purposefulness, Macbeth descends into the hell of himself, emerging with an overwhelming and unforgettable picture of life's meaninglessness and despair, as reflected in the "To-morrow, and to-morrow" speech (V, v, 19–28). It is a measure of Macbeth's peculiar greatness in the tragic order and total depravity in the moral order that the speech signifies not resignation but defiance hurled into the teeth of encroaching despair.

Many critics, disturbed by this attempt to transform a tyrant and murderer into a tragic hero, have argued that Macbeth's moral deterioration is unaccompanied by any dramatic enlargement. They see Macbeth tortured by doubt and indecision before the murder of Duncan and devastated by remorse after it. For the majority of modern commentators, however, this view, while a necessary corrective to the apocalyptic, Nietzschean view of the character, is too restrictive. They point out that Macbeth's greatness lies in his superhuman effort to control time, and by extension, his own fate. His speeches constantly allude to this struggle to move outside of the limitations of time, and in his effort to achieve this impossible goal, an effort in which he is the representative of the audience's unspoken aspirations, he is crushed. It is the greatness of the effort, however, which marks him as a tragic hero. [W. H. Thomson, *Shakespeare's Characters: A Historical Dictionary*, 1951; Leonard Dean, "Macbeth and Modern Criticism," *English Journal*, 1958.]—E.Q.

THE TRAGEDY OF MACBETH.

Macbeth. A tragedy by Shakespeare.

Text. The text of the FIRST FOLIO (1623) is the only authoritative one of *Macbeth.* It is short, consisting of only 2107 lines, as compared with the 3224 lines of *Othello* or the 3924 lines of the First Folio text of *Hamlet.* This text of *Macbeth* is probably based on the official PROMPT-BOOK of the play or on some transcript of it. It is the consensus of scholars either that Shakespeare did not finish the tragedy with his usual care or that it is largely the work of a collaborator, for the diction in the last act is often feeble and the rhymes either weak or forced. Critics also agree that this acting version of the Folio text has been somewhat changed from its original form. The activities and attitudes of Hecate are quite different from those of the Weird Sisters. Her harangue of the three witches (III, v) is an interpolation, as are a few lines of her second address to the same creatures (IV, i, 39–43) and the First Witch's invitation to her companions to a song and dance (IV, i, 127–132). Two stage directions in the Folio—"*Music and a song within:* 'Come away, come away,' &c." (III, v, 33) and "*Music and a song:* 'Black spirits,' &c." (IV, i, 43)—are calls for songs, the full text of which appear in Thomas Middleton's *The Witch* (first printed in 1778 from a unique manuscript now in the Bodleian Library). They suggest that Middleton was engaged to revise *Macbeth* in a manner designed to increase its operatic flavor.

The shortness of the text is a reason for suspecting that the piece was written for a court performance—perhaps one of the entertainments offered to King Christian IV of Denmark during his visit to the English court in the summer of 1606. Or it may be a version cut down from a play of normal length acted at the Globe. The comparative slackness of the writing in the last act may be due to the poet's hurry to complete the work for an important fixed date.

Date. Although no direct evidence exists to fix the date 1606 as the year for the first performance of *Macbeth,* references to certain contemporary events point to that year. The farmer who hanged himself "on the expectation of plenty" (II, iii, 5–6) is a stock figure, yet the price of wheat was so low in 1606 that Shakespeare's audience would think of the plight of the most recent speculators in wheat. The remarks of the Porter about equivocation refer to a famous contemporary trial. The drunken Porter, imagining that he is the keeper of the gate to hell, remarks about a figure seeking admittance, "Faith, here's an equivocator, that could swear in both scales against either scale; who committed treason enough for God's sake, yet could not equivocate to heaven: O, come in, equivocator" (II, iii, 10–14). This passage i clearly a reference to the trial and execution o Father GARNET for his complicity in the Gunpowde Plot. At Garnet's trial he admitted that he had lie to his accusers and had tried to justify his deceit b appealing to the doctrine of EQUIVOCATION. This doc trine justified, under certain circumstances, conceal ing the truth by dissimulation. It became one of th chief issues of the trial after March 28, 1606. Interes in this, as in every aspect of the Gunpowder Plo was widespread and intense throughout the yea 1606. The author's style and meter are also charac teristic of his writing in 1606 and thereabouts.

Sources. All the major elements of the plot o *Macbeth* are taken from Holinshed's *Chronicles o England, Scotlande and Irelande* (1577). Since Shake speare was not writing a chronicle history, but tragedy, he took some liberties with Holinshed's ma terial. For most of the facts in the history of Mac beth's career, he closely follows his source; but fo the murder of Duncan, he substitutes Holinshed' account of the murder of an earlier King Duff b Donwald. There he found the drugging of the cham berlains and the prodigies attending the attempte murder. Donwald, like Macbeth, was egged on by a ambitious wife. Since Shakespeare probably designe the play partly to please King James I, he may hav substituted Donwald's crime for Macbeth's in orde to make Duncan's murder more like Bothwell's mur der of Darnley, King James' father. Thus he coul involve more securely the king's horror and loathin of Duncan's murder.

The warning to "beware Macduff," according t Holinshed, was uttered by "certain wizards in whos words Macbeth put great confidence," and th prophecies that he need fear no man of woman bor and that of the moving of Birnam Wood were mad by "a certain witch in whom he had great trust. Holinshed derived Macbeth's story from Hecto Boece's Latin *History of Scotland,* published in 152 under the title *Scotorum Historiae,* in 17 books. Thi was translated into English by John Bellenden a *The Hystory and Croniklis of Scotland* (1535). Be hind this work of Boece was Andrew of Wyntoun' (1350–1420) metrical history of Scotland calle *Orygynale Cronykil of Scotland* (c. 1424), whic combined history and legend of the years 1040–105 with some out-and-out fictions, and the Lati *Scotichronicon* (c. 1384) of John Fordun. In Fordu there are no prophetic women, but in Wyntou there are three women who appear to Macbeth in dream, and by the fantasy of this dream he is incite to kill Duncan.

Shakespeare derived one of Macbeth's most striking encounters with the three witches from a pageant by Matthew GWINNE presented to King James, ıe queen, and the prince of Wales when they visited)xford in August 1605. At the gate of St. John's ;ollege, three youths "attired like nymphs or sybils" ppeared before the royal party. Reminding the king ıat once in the past they had prophesied power ·ithout end to Banquo's issue, they declared that ıey had now returned to predict for James and his escendants the same glorious destiny. The sybils ıen in turn saluted the king as follows:

First Sibyl: Hail, thou who rulest Scotland!
Second Sibyl: Hail, thou who rulest England!
Third Sibyl: Hail, thou who rulest Ireland!

[he details of this situation and even an echo of the .nes appear in *Macbeth* (I, iii, 48–56):

First Witch. All hail, Macbeth! hail to thee, thane of Glamis!
Second Witch. All hail, Macbeth! hail to thee, thane of Cawdor!
Third Witch. All hail, Macbeth, that shalt be king hereafter!

William Stewart's *Buik of the Croniclis of Scotland*, a long historical poem, may have been used by ;hakespeare, as well as George Buchanan's Latin history *Rerum Scoticarum Historia* (1582). Buchanan's .ccount of Macbeth's character as a man of "penerating genius and . . . unbounded ambition" is closer o Shakespeare's conception than is Holinshed's. It ıas also been suggested that Shakespeare may have nade use of still another Latin history of Scotland, ohn Leslie's *De Origine, Moribus, et Rebus Gestis ;cotorum* (1578), in his characterization of the vitches. Some passages in the play (the sense of ;uilt expressed in terms of blood-stained hands, the estorative quality of sleep) appear to echo passages n Seneca's *Agamemnon* and *Hercules Furens.* The ʼorter scene may have been derived from the docrine of the Harrowing of Hell as portrayed in medieval mystery plays. King James' own writings, paricularly his *Daemonologie* (1597), may have been :onsulted by Shakespeare. See below under *Comnent*.—O.J.C.

Plot Synopsis. Act I. Macbeth and Banquo, two ;cottish generals who have just crushed a revolt ıgainst King Duncan, are on their way to the King's ɔalace at Forres when they are startled by the sudlen appearance of three witches. Macbeth, who is Thane of Glamis, is told that he will become thane ılso of Cawdor and king of Scotland as well; Banquo s promised that his sons will be kings, though he ;hall never rule.

When he learns that the King has commanded the leath of the traitorous Thane of Cawdor, and will ɔestow that title on him, Macbeth begins to toy vith the thought that he might realize the whole of he prophecy, by force. Lady Macbeth has already resolved to do away with Duncan, who intends to :pend the night at their castle in Inverness. Scoffing ıt Macbeth's fears and scruples, she finally persuades ıer husband to murder Duncan that very night.

Act II. To avert suspicion, Macbeth stabs the leeping King with daggers belonging to his servants, ɔut he is so unnerved by the deed that he neglects to leave the weapons in the King's chamber, and the intrepid Lady Macbeth must finish the task alone. Despite his wife's confidence in their success, Macbeth senses that their troubles have just begun. When the murder is discovered, Malcolm, Duncan's eldest son and heir, and his brother Donalbain fear for their own lives and decide to flee, the former to England, the latter to Ireland. As a result, they are suspected of instigating the crime, and Macbeth is named king.

Act III. Although Macbeth's ambition has been satisfied, he is haunted by the witches' prophecy that Banquo's descendants would one day rule Scotland. He invites Banquo and his only son, Fleance, to a banquet and hires murderers to assassinate them on the way to his castle. As the guests are being seated at the feast, one of the murderers reports to Macbeth that Banquo has been killed but that Fleance escaped from the ambush. Macbeth approaches his own place at the table, speaking of his regret for the absence of their chief guest; he is terrified to find his chair occupied by the bloody Ghost of Banquo. None of the other guests can see the apparition, and as Macbeth's fearful cries continue, his wife sends the guests away. Determined now to be informed of whatever lies ahead, Macbeth arranges another meeting with the witches.

Act IV. The witches warn Macbeth to beware Macduff, the Thane of Fife, whose disloyalty Macbeth already suspects, and assure him not only that he will be safe until Birnam Wood moves to Dunsinane, but that no man born of woman will ever be able to harm him. He is, however, discomfited by the apparition of a line of eight kings followed by Banquo's ghost—a sight implying all too clearly that Banquo's issue will reign in Scotland. When he learns that Macduff has fled to England to join Malcolm, Macbeth storms his castle and orders the Thane's wife and children slain. In England, Macduff has some difficulty in convincing Malcolm of his trustworthiness, but when word reaches them of the massacre of Macduff's family, Malcolm invites him to join the army he has raised for an invasion of Scotland.

Act V. Lady Macbeth, driven mad by fear and guilt, walks in her sleep and tries to wash away the blood she imagines still stains her hands. Her physician can do nothing to ease her malady. Macbeth, as he awaits the invading army at Dunsinane castle, is confused and nervous, and clings almost desperately to the invulnerability promised by the witches. He is so surfeited with fear and horror that he remains impassive upon hearing of the death of his wife. For him, life has become "a tale told by an idiot, full of sound and fury, signifying nothing." When he learns that the enemy troops under Malcolm are moving against Dunsinane camouflaged by boughs from Birnam Wood, Macbeth is dismayed, but only momentarily. During the ensuing battle he comes face to face with the vengeful Macduff and boasts that he bears a charmed life that will yield only to one not born of woman. "Despair thy charm," his foe retorts, "Macduff was from his mother's womb untimely ripp'd." His last hope gone, Macbeth nevertheless fights on savagely until he is slain by Macduff. Macduff presents Macbeth's head to the triumphant Malcolm, who is proclaimed king of Scotland.—H.D.

Comment. In choosing and developing the story of Macbeth, Shakespeare sought to intrigue and flatter King James, before whom the tragedy was to be acted. James traced his title back to Banquo, an imaginary Scottish nobleman of the 11th century invented by the Scottish historian Hector Boece in order to provide the Stuarts with a suitably noble ancestry. Though the king's northern subjects may have been aware of the importance which their sovereign attached to the career of Banquo, the English had probably never heard of this worthy. So James must have been pleased at the staging of the ancient supernatural predictions of his glory and his extended sway—prophecies that he was fulfilling in 1606.

The witches who instigated Macbeth to sin also dramatized and justified one of King James' most cherished superstitions. He was certain that witchcraft had repeatedly delayed and thwarted his efforts to marry Anne of Denmark. Spells wrought by black magic, so he thought, had stirred up terrible storms at sea which had driven his bride's ship back to its Norwegian port of embarkation again and again.

These machinations of Satan's crew had driven James to ferret out women suspected of witchcraft throughout Scotland, to throw them into prison, to appear at their trials, and to take a sadistic delight in cross-examining the wretched creatures himself. Under torture, they had confessed to performing some of the impossible deeds of which the witches in *Macbeth* boast. For example, one of the pain-crazed old women admitted that she was one of 200 witches who had gone to sea, each in a sieve, in order to wreck a ship returning from Denmark to England, perhaps the very one bearing Princess Anne.

To a monarch convinced of the malign influence of witches upon his own private affairs, a book written by Reginald Scot in 1584, entitled *The discoverie* [Exposure] *of Witchcraft,* naturally seemed a thoroughly dangerous publication. For Scot asserted that the belief in witches was a foolish superstition and that the punishment inflicted on ugly old women accused of traffic with the devil was cruel and wicked. King James in 1597 composed a vigorous answer to Scot's contentions under the title of *Daemonologie,* venting his indignation upon a man "who is not ashamed in public print to deny that there can be such a thing as witchcraft."

Shakespeare's conception of the witches in *Macbeth* is not completely clear. Holinshed gives a picturesque account of Macbeth's and Banquo's first meeting with the witches:

> As they went sporting by the way together . . . passing through the woods and fields, when suddenly in the midst of a laund [open space] there met them three women in strange and wild apparel resembling the creatures of an elder world . . . . Afterwards the common opinion was that these women were either the wierd sisters, that is (as ye would say) the goddesses of destiny, or else some nymphs or fairies, imbued with knowledge of prophecy by their necromantical science, because everything came to pass as they had spoken.

In Shakespeare's day, "witch," "fairy," and "hag" each designated a female demon. To Macbeth, the witches are "secret, black, and midnight hags" (I[V] i, 48). Their supernatural powers over him are lin ited. They tempt him but never force him to pe form any act. They do not foretell any of his actu villainous deeds.

These witches conform exactly to King James' b liefs. Their every act confirms the truth of his su picions. Shakespeare, all but ignoring the supernatur elements of their nature, presents them as the witch of popular belief which the king passionately share They are wrinkled, ugly old women, or demons wh have taken their shape. They have sold their souls t the devil in return for the gift of powers half-awf and half-grotesque. By seeking and accepting the aid Macbeth becomes guilty, albeit indirectly, trafficking with the Prince of Darkness. This vivi way of dramatizing a man's bondage to evil has er thralled every spectator or reader of the tragedy, a in a peculiar sense, it must have enthralled Kin James.

Macbeth, like Richard III, is a victim of crimin ambition. Although at the end of the play he h become a monstrously wicked man, he is no villai hero, no virtuoso in villainy who deliberatel chooses evil for his god. Holinshed assures us tha until he yielded to the teasing of ambition, he ha been a loyal subject of the king and a brave warrio free from any taint of evil. The briefer view of h unspoiled nature that Shakespeare affords his au dience establishes the same virtues. Even after he h embarked upon his career of crime he is constantl plagued by conscience, whose warnings he disregard but cannot suppress. The outward manifestation c the inner voice of this monitor is fear that strangel forces him to loathe every one of his evil deeds a the very moment that he is performing it. But ambi tion, having once seized control of his little cosmo becomes an overwhelming passion that sweeps awa every moral restraint. Goaded on by his wife, h commits his first unspeakable crime. This murde leads inevitably to another, until Macbeth's mor nature lies in ruins and his spirit sinks into the lowe depths of pessimism and despair. In general term Macbeth's rapid moral decay is a telling illustratio of what the Elizabethans called "a chain of vice," th final link of which was "remorse of conscience." Bu Shakespeare has given his tale peculiar imaginativ intensity by putting Macbeth's retribution in term of more and more terrifying assaults of fear. Caution Lady Macbeth realizes, has always been the essenc of Macbeth's nature. In her first soliloquy she make us aware of the restraint that prudence exercise upon his ambition. She knows that her part is t sweep his mind clear of this unheroic quality. How ever, her first efforts to screw his courage to th sticking-place merely turn his caution to dread o punishment in this world. An onset of conscience in tensifies this anxiety. Recognizing the dastardl treachery of his intended deed, Macbeth feels a "din of pity" for the sweet-tempered old King and i loath to go further in the business. But Lady Mac beth banishes these hesitations by shaming away hi cowardice and making light of his fear of detection

Half-hypnotized by the strained intensity of hi wife, he commits the murder. But even while he i doing the deed his sick imagination completely un nerves him. The inner voice that he has heard crying "Sleep no more," sounding the last revolt of hi moral imperative, is a portent and a prophecy of the retribution that is to pursue him to his hour of death.

The knocking at the gate of the castle the morning after the murder, followed by Macduff's cry of "O horror, horror, horror" at the discovery of Duncan's dead body, signalizes the intrusion of the world of moral health into the little hell at the entrance to which the Porter has stood guard.

Thereafter, the increasing assaults of Macbeth's conscience throw his mind into disorder. His old impulsive courage is blotted out by undefined fear. His purely subjective terror, seeking an object, lights first on Banquo, whose assassination he can plan without his wife's help or her knowledge. He works through professional killers and this prevents his hands from being smeared with the horrifying color of blood. The ghost of Banquo, come to sit in Macbeth's place at the feast, is an awful projection of his persistent nameless dread. His first reaction to its appearance is like that of a naughty child caught in some forbidden situation: "Thou canst not say I did it: never shake / Thy gory locks at me" (III, iv, 50–51). But he soon summons the courage of desperation that becomes his settled refuge from fear. Since Macbeth is the only person in the company that sees the ghost, many critics believe it to be like the airborne dagger, a figment of an imagination half-crazed by fear. But Shakespeare clearly expected his audiences, if not the feasters, to see the apparition.

After Fleance's escape, Macbeth's fears and suspicions fall upon Macduff, whose wife and children he has murdered—a crime that signalizes his adoption of a headlong career of butchery which transforms him into what in the modern underworld is known as a "killer." His embarkation upon this orgy of crime is also a form of *hybris*, which carries his overweening confidence in the prophecies of the witches to the point of sheer fatuity. He throws away every sort of precaution. He refuses to listen to a messenger who reports the approach of 10,000 enemies, hurling violent curses upon him and the fear his news inspires. In spite of every consideration of sound military sense, he sallies forth from the protection of his castle to die at the hands of Macduff.

Shakespeare, however, makes us see that all these acts of sham boldness are but the cover of deep dejection and radical pessimism. Macbeth's wickedness has isolated him from all his kind and deprived his life of all its meaning until it seems to be a mere "tale / Told by an idiot, full of sound and fury, / Signifying nothing" (V, v, 26–28). Macbeth's tendency thus to philosophize at the crises of his career makes his individual death seem to be an important moment in the march of human destiny.

Lady Macbeth moves to her catastrophe by a course quite different from that taken by her husband. Her destruction is due to the revolt of her woman's nature, which has been forcibly suppressed. The strain of unsexing herself at first fills her with febrile exaltation. She longs to breathe her spirit of determination into Macbeth's will, too weak by itself to carry out her plan for murdering the King. She remains firm until Macbeth's killing of the grooms, not part of the original plan, arouses Macduff's suspicion. This exhibition of Macbeth's revolt from her carefully planned control, combined with his hollow explanation of the deed, deeply alarms her. Her consternation snaps her taut will. She sinks under the strain and swoons. This is the first intimation of the collapse of both her mind and body that is to bring on her catastrophe. In the sleepwalking scene, one of the greatest of Shakespeare's inventions, we see that it is not the fear of what is to come but the disheveled memory of the events crowding the dreadful night of the murder that has eaten away her nerves. A victim of utter devotion to her evil husband, in her death she arouses terror that is shot through with pity.

By this time Macbeth has become numb to any personal grief over the death of a wife, to whom he was bound by the strongest ties of common experience. Her end only turns his mind to the futility of his own and everyone else's life:

> Life's but a walking shadow, a poor player
> That struts and frets his hour upon the stage
> And then is heard no more.
>
> (V, v, 24–26)

Some critics have thought it a blemish on the tragedy that Shakespeare creates only two characters of importance. The rest reach only the threshold of his creative imagination. The structure of *Macbeth*, formed of but a single plot, is the simplest in all Shakespeare's plays. Except for the Porter's comic interlude, a scene filled with bitter irony, Shakespeare gives his spectators no relief from gripping tension. He holds their attention securely fixed on the crime and the doom of its perpetrators. Up to the banquet scene the action moves with a speed unmatched in any of Shakespeare's other tragedies. Thereafter the author reverts to the naïve narrative manner of his earlier chronicle history plays, and the last act, except for the sleepwalking episode, is composed of a series of separate conflicts in the final battle. Some of them, to be sure, transcend the chronicle type by revealing the tumult and dissolution of Macbeth's nature. This scenic disunity unduly relaxes the tension of a modern audience. Elizabethan spectators, familiar with the conventions of stage battles, doubtless felt more poignantly than we the slow closing-in of both outer and inner forces upon Macbeth's soul. They saw in the progress of the battle the development of both of these conflicts to a point where their only resolution lay in the catastrophe. And in Macbeth's death they saw the awesome spectacle of the triumph of supernatural powers of evil over a mortal who had become their willing servant.—O.J.C.

Stage History: England. Topical allusions in the play indicate that there were performances of *Macbeth* as early as 1606 (see above under *Date*). It is almost certain that it was one of the plays acted at Hampton Court during the visit of King Christian IV of Denmark on August 7 of that year. The earliest specific reference to *Macbeth* on the stage is in Simon FORMAN's *Bocke of plaies*, where is described a performance of the play at the Globe theatre on April 20, 1611. There is no further record of performances from then until the Restoration.

Samuel PEPYS saw the play at least nine times from 1664 to 1669. Thomas Betterton and Mrs. Betterton took the leading roles in the first of these presentations, at Lisle's Tennis Court. Some, at least, of these performances were probably of an adaptation of the play by Sir William DAVENANT, manager of the Duke's Company. Pepys was particularly pleased with the "divertissement" that had evidently been inserted. A professed admirer of Shakespeare, Davenant could not resist the temptation to make *Macbeth* "fit" for Restoration taste. His "improvements," printed in 1674, 1687, and 1710, were of two sorts. The first were those designed to add to the operatic splendor of the piece. Davenant's delight in scenic display led him to introduce much dancing and singing into the roles of the witches, who now flew through the air on machines. His second improvement was a change in structure designed to satisfy his passion for formal balance. He greatly enlarged Lady Macduff's part so that he could introduce a number of scenes between her and her lord to correspond to those between the two Macbeths. Lady Macbeth's wicked stimulation of her husband to crime is balanced by long speeches in which Lady Macduff warns her husband against the evil effects of ambition. Besides these changes, Davenant "refined" Shakespeare's language and set him a model in the insipid verse of the scenes he invented. Pepys' approval must have been widespread, for Davenant's travesty held the stage continuously until 1744. It was performed at the new Dorset Garden Theatre in 1672 and before the ambassador of Morocco in 1682. From 1685 to 1695, the united Duke's and King's Companies presented the play at Drury Lane and, after the companies redivided, annual revivals were seen at that theatre. Meanwhile, Betterton and Elizabeth Barry as Macbeth and Lady Macbeth dominated the Haymarket stage. In January 1708 the tragedy was the last play performed before the companies reunited. Thereafter, Drury Lane presented the play several times each season and *Macbeth* was shown more frequently than any other Shakespearean drama during the first half of the 18th century. The leading Macbeth after Betterton was James Quin, who acted the role at Drury Lane in 1717 and performed it at Lincoln's Inn Fields between 1718 and 1732. Quin played his final Drury Lane Macbeth in 1739, before transferring to Covent Garden, where he played the role during the 1742/3 and 1749/50 seasons. In 1751 he appeared in that century's last presentation of Davenant's version.

On January 7, 1744 David Garrick revived the play "as written by Shakespeare," causing a surprised Quin to remark, "What does he mean? Don't I play Macbeth as written by Shakespeare?" Garrick began by cutting the worst of Davenant's interpolations, in particular all of Lady Macduff's moral exhortations. But he kept the singing and dancing of the witches, to the immense satisfaction of his public. He still did not dare restore the drunken Porter or the murder of Lady Macduff's children. Having decided that Macbeth should die on the stage, he found it necessary to write a dying speech for him. This gave Garrick a chance to underline the moral meaning of the action by putting into the expiring criminal's mouth a confession of guilt and a realization of his certain punishment in the life to come. Garrick's original Lady Macbeth, Anna Giffard, was replaced by Hannah Pritchard in 1748, who, from then through 1768, completely surpassed her Covent Garden rivals, the most notable of whom was Peg Woffington. Even her successors, Mrs. Spranger Barry and Mary Ann Yates, could not eclipse Mrs. Pritchard's supremacy in the role. Garrick alternated with Henry Mossop as Macbeth up to 1759, then continued his portrayal at Drury Lane until 1763. He was only a little les successful than his leading lady in overshadowing hi contemporaries, Spranger Barry and Thomas Sheridan. In 1768 Barry appeared as Drury Lane's Macbeth, while William Powell took the role for Coven Garden, to be replaced at that theatre by Willian Smith in December 1769. Garrick's effectiveness i the tragedy was somewhat lessened by his costume a red British officer's coat and powdered wig. It wa not until Charles Macklin made his first appearanc as Macbeth on October 23, 1773 that realistic Scottis attire was introduced. At the same time, his Lad Macbeth exercised her feminine prerogative an dressed in contemporary style. Macklin played th role five times more at Covent Garden, the last o December 2, 1776, but apart from the service rendered in altering Macbeth's apparel, his performance were largely unimpressive.

John Philip Kemble fell heir to the role afte Smith's retirement in 1788. Directing his first seaso at Drury Lane, Kemble produced *Macbeth* in sumptuous style. When, on April 21, 1794, he presente the first dramatic offering of the newly enlarge Drury Lane, Kemble avoided all buffoonery and als eliminated the visible ghost of Banquo. Criticism o this last innovation caused Kemble to restore th apparition in his production at the new Coven Garden in September 1809, but this effort to pleas only annoyed the anonymous reviewer from th *Times*, who called for Banquo's ghost "to be laid and laid forever." At the opening performance, on of the most disastrous, the speech was rendered inaudible by a noisy audience protesting the price rise

The great producer's formal dramatic style wa adequate to Macbeth, but he never displayed th genius of his sister, Sarah Siddons, the most famou of all English Lady Macbeths. It was perfectly suite to her endowments. A great beauty, she was tall an of a commanding presence. Her Lady Macbeth wa a dignified, almost majestic, and desperately determined woman who so completely took captive he lord's will that he dared brave the dangers of detection and punishment and even the intimation o the hostility of supernatural powers. In the sleepwalking scene she betrayed the nature of the disaste that had overtaken her. In this scene Mrs. Siddon appeared wan and haggard, her sightless eyes fixe and burning. She walked rapidly across the stage put down her taper, and began frantically to g through the motions of washing her hands, preserving all the while her superb dignity. Her desperat suffering awakened awe and pity in every one of he audiences. Mrs. Siddons' acting of Lady Macbeth ha long been pronounced as one of the greatest exhibitions of histrionic art on the English stage. She i said to have first played the part when only 20 year old. In 1777 she played Lady Macbeth in Liverpoo followed by performances in Bath (1779) an Bristol (1780). Her first London performance in th role was on February 2, 1785. Kemble, who ha earlier played Macbeth in Dublin, gave his first London performance opposite Mrs. Siddons on March 3 1785, and the two continued to star in the dram until a final performance at Covent Garden on Jun 5, 1817.

Edmund Kean's first appearance as Macbeth a Drury Lane took place on November 5, 1814 op

›site Mrs. Bartley, and his magnificent performance ıallenged Kemble's supremacy in the role. Kean's ındling of the witch scenes was especially admira-le, and he is credited with having led the way in :storing the proper character of these malignant ›irits by cutting away "the rubbish" that had helped opularize the play from Davenant's time.

William Charles Macready first played Macbeth in 320 at Covent Garden. In 1837, as manager of that ıeatre, he revived the tragedy to critical acclaim, resenting the play 18 times that season. He appeared t Drury Lane in 1831 opposite Mrs. Warner, and in 835 with Ellen Tree, and presented the drama as ıe final play under his management of Drury Lane ı 1843. In 1846 and 1848 he was at the Princess' 'heatre, first opposite Charlotte Cushman and then › Fanny Kemble. Miss Cushman was one of the reat impersonators of Lady Macbeth in the first alf of the 19th century. She played this and other oles with Macready on one of his American tours, nd in 1845 first appeared in London, where she layed Lady Macbeth to the Macbeth of Edwin orrest. The English at once acclaimed her as the reatest tragic actress of her time. Possessing a esonant voice, a commanding figure, an expressive ountenance, and a temperament full of fire, she layed the role in a noble, heroic manner.

In 1844 Samuel Phelps presented his first Sadler's Vells *Macbeth,* appearing in the title role. When he taged another revival of the play on September 27, 847, the last traces of Davenant's version disap-›eared. The musical decorations of the witch scenes vere dropped and Lady Macduff and her son re-tored. Only one character was omitted—the English loctor (and his scene, V, iii). The *Times* praised 'helps for having "placed an impress of genius on he whole affair," and the special vanishing effects chieved by green gauze screens in the witch scenes mpressed several reviewers. In costuming, Phelps lispensed with the tartans introduced by Macklin in avor of dress considered more appropriate to an arlier period. Unfortunately, Charles Kean reverted o Davenant's operatic adaptation for his successful cenic revival at the Princess' on February 14, 1853, vhich was acted 60 times in 20 weeks.

Henry Irving's efforts with *Macbeth,* although cenically effective, were failures due to the pro-lucer's unsatisfactory impersonation of the hero. 'ossessing neither the stature nor the voice needed or the impersonation of a bluff warrior, Irving por-rayed Macbeth as a cowardly and neurasthenic :riminal continually plagued by the assaults of a ;uilty conscience. His manner, characterized as "fin-cky," and his delivery of the lines were harshly :riticized. His revivals at the Lyceum in 1875 op-›osite Kate Bateman, and in 1888 with Ellen Terry, ıad long runs, the last playing 151 nights, but this vas largely attributable to Irving's reputation and he splendid staging. Miss Terry played Lady Mac-›eth as a frail woman who became her husband's :onfederate out of wifely devotion; still, her acting eemed masterful compared with Irving's and was :onsidered a triumph of insight and histrionic skill.)uring this period, both Drury Lane, in 1876, and ;adler's Wells, in 1881, saw Hermann Vezin in the itle role, first opposite Genevieve Ward and, in the ater revival, alternating the parts of Macbeth and Macduff with Charles Warner. Vezin also substituted for an indisposed Irving in his second production from January 17 to 26, 1889. Irving's immediate successor as Macbeth was Johnston Forbes-Robertson.

Frank R. Benson directed *Macbeth* during 10 seasons at Stratford-upon-Avon from 1896 to 1916. In 1906 Arthur Bourchier and Violet Vanbrugh visited Stratford to play the leading roles and, in December of that year, acted in the drama at the Garrick. Bourchier and his wife repeated these portrayals for Beerbohm Tree's fifth annual Shakespeare Festival at His Majesty's in 1909; two years later, when Tree himself played Macbeth, Miss Vanbrugh was Lady Macbeth, while her husband assumed Macduff's role. Although the staging was less elaborate than most of Tree's efforts, a hazardous staircase might have caused some uneasy moments had Miss Vanbrugh been less graceful in her ascents.

The Old Vic under Ben Greet presented *Macbeth* each season from 1914 through 1917 and, when in 1916 it sustained the Stratford Festival, offered the tragedy with Mary Anderson as Lady Macbeth. During this time, Sybil Thorndike acted Lady Macbeth and, in 1915/6, Robert Atkins played Macbeth, followed the next season by Russell Thorndike in the role. Ernest Milton was Macbeth during 1918/9 in George Foss' production. Thorndike, coproducing with Charles Warburton for the next season, presented the Old Vic's fifth *Macbeth* of the decade. In 1920 the American tragedian James K. Hackett, wearing red hair and beard, was a resonant Thane at the Aldwych. His costar, Mrs. Patrick Campbell, was inadequate in her portrayal. *Macbeth* productions were often plagued by calamities. In 1926 at the Vic, Baliol Holloway, playing to Dorothy Massingham's Lady Macbeth, suffered injury during the final fight scene and had to be replaced for a time by Ernest Milton in the title role. Barry Jackson's disastrous experience with a modern-dress version produced by H. K. Ayliff at the Court in 1928 may have been attributable less to a fire in the dress circle the night before opening or the scenery collapse during the first week than to the difficulty of presenting the drama convincingly in contemporary dress. Cast in the leading role because other actors refused the part, Eric Maturin's deficiencies as a tragic hero became all the more obvious in tweeds.

Stratford, under W. Bridges-Adams' direction, presented the tragedy every season but four from 1920 through 1931. Edmund Willard was Macbeth in 1920. In 1923 and 1927, Dorothy Green acted Lady Macbeth opposite Frank Cellier, then Wilfrid Walter. Bridges-Adams' final *Macbeth* for Stratford in 1931 had Randle Ayrton in the title role. The Fellowship of Players acted the drama at the Strand in February 1924. At the Old Vic, Robert Atkins offered two productions, the last during 1924/5. Andrew Leigh followed with two more *Macbeths,* a final one in 1928/9 with John Laurie and Esme Church as Macbeth and Lady Macbeth.

John Gielgud's first attempt at *Macbeth* came in Harcourt Williams' Old Vic production in 1930. His sensitive, poetic characterization of the man tormented by ambition was a triumph. In Williams' next production, which opened in November 1932, Margaret Webster was Lady Macbeth, and several actors, including Malcolm Keen and Marius Goring, portrayed the title character during the season. Earlier that year, Russell and Eileen Thorndike appeared at the Kingsway in a week's repertory season produced by Peter Dearing that included *Macbeth.* Tyrone Guthrie refused to open his 1934 *Macbeth* at the Old Vic with the witches, wishing to remove any implication that the weird women controlled the tragic events. He used only those of their scenes which he considered essential to the plot. Charles Laughton, a pathological Macbeth, gave an erratic performance. Flora Robson played Lady Macbeth. In November 1935 Arthur Phillips and Maureen Shaw essayed the leading roles at the Lyric Theatre, Hammersmith, and at the close of that year Henry Cass presented another Old Vic *Macbeth* with Ion Swinley and Vivienne Bennett. This was followed two years later by Michel St. Denis' production with Laurence Olivier and Judith Anderson. Though powerful enough, Olivier gave only a sketch for his later full portrait of Macbeth, and Miss Anderson's Lady Macbeth seemed overdrawn. Audiences were large nonetheless, and the next month *Macbeth* was tranferred to the New Theatre, but it ran for only three more weeks.

In Theodore Komisarjevsky's Stratford production of 1933, supernatural elements were replaced by the merely nightmarish, the witches visited in a dream, and Banquo's ghost was only Macbeth's own shadow. B. Iden Payne's Stratford *Macbeth* of 1933 was more conventional. James Dale acted the title role; Phyllis Neilson-Terry, his lady; and Gyles Isham, Macduff. During this period, the Liverpool Repertory Company staged *Macbeth* in 1934, produced by William Armstrong, and the amateur Marlowe Society acted the tragedy at Cambridge under George Rylands in 1939.

During the early war years, Sybil Thorndike toured mining villages and towns, doubling as the First Witch and Lady Macbeth. The traveling company's sets were less elaborate than those in John Gielgud's *Macbeth;* his sets at the Piccadilly Theatre in 1942 were designed by Michael Ayrton and John Minton in subdued tones of blue, green, and gray. Gielgud's tragic hero, the prisoner of his own ambition, was another success; his Lady Macbeth, Gwen Ffrangcon-Davies, without the physical requirements for the part, gave an intense and convincing performance nonetheless. In 1946 a double staircase used in Michael MacOwan's *Macbeth* at Stratford dominated the action to such an extent that the power of the tragedy was reduced. Two years earlier, Robert Atkins had produced the tragedy for the Memorial Theatre with George Hayes and Patricia Jessel. Two years before that, B. Iden Payne had the gifted Margaretta Scott as Lady Macbeth opposite George Skillan. In 1949 another double stairway proved perilous at Stratford during the opening performance, when Diana Wynyard fell while maneuvering the sleepwalking scene. The actress continued bravely with barely a pause, but her Lady Macbeth seemed a bit too genteel, and Godfrey Tearle's Macbeth a bit too timid.

During the 1940's, the West End saw four *Macbeth* productions after Gielgud's. Ernest Milton essayed the hero once more at the Lyric, Hammersmith, in 1944 opposite Vivienne Bennett. In February 1945 and in 1946 Donald Wolfit, who had played Macbeth for the first time at the Malvern Festival i 1937, gave his successful characterization at th Winter Garden opposite Patricia Jessel. Wolfit re appeared as Macbeth opposite his wife, Rosalin Iden, during another season at the King's Theatr Hammersmith, from February to December 195 Finally, a presentation directed by Norris Houghtor starring Michael Redgrave and Ena Burrill, com pleted the decade's record of major London pro ductions.

Laurence Olivier fulfilled the promise of his earlie Macbeth in Glen Byam Shaw's masterfully directe Stratford presentation in 1955. Beginning quietly, th warrior's anguish mounted, revealing himself a guilty from the opening of desiring Duncan's deat

Bernard Miles experimented with speech in tw *Macbeths* produced by Joan Swinstead: the first, i 1952 at the Mermaid Theatre, St. John's Wood, em ployed early 17th-century speech patterns; the sec ond, in 1952 at the Royal Exchange Theatre, use contemporary accents. Both efforts costarred Jose phine Wilson and were considered legitimate ex periments. A less happy endeavor was a modern dress version in 1957 at Joan Littlewood's Theatr Workshop, Stratford East. The delivery was careles and, in seeming contradiction to her avowed inten to deliver the play from sentimentality, Miss Little wood interpolated a Highland lament sung over th murdered Lady Macduff and her son. A year late Douglas Seale was fortunate to have Michael Hor dern as a frightening Macbeth and Beatrice Lehman as a memorably wretched Lady Macbeth. The Strat ford *Macbeth* in 1962, carefully directed by Donal McWhinnie, gave first consideration to the verse and Shakespeare dominated the performances b Eric Porter and Irene Worth.

Stage History: America. Lewis Hallam the younge played Macbeth in Philadelphia in October 1759 an again in March 1767. His mother, Mrs. Davi Douglass, was his Lady Macbeth in the first per formance, but was replaced by Margaret Cheer i the second. The next year, 1768, the play had its firs New York performance. Its fifth revival is recorde in 1794, and from then until 1834, *Macbeth* was pro duced in three out of every four years. Thereafte up to the close of the 19th century, productions o the tragedy appeared almost annually. Edwin For rest was the most frequent impersonator of the her for 40 years (1828–1868) but sharply curtailed hi appearances in this role after performing opposit Charlotte Cushman in 1845 in London, where he Lady Macbeth completely obscured his robust war rior. Forrest, who had been coldly received in th English capital, was especially resentful toward Brit ish actor William Charles MACREADY. When the tw actors were giving rival performances of Macbeth o May 10, 1849, anti-British crowds at the Astor Plac Opera House, where Macready was appearing caused a riot that cost 22 lives.

Forrest's interpretation of Macbeth was undistin guished in contrast to that of his great compatriot Edwin Booth, which improved over the years fro a crude, melodramatic impersonation to a powerfu highly poetic, and imaginative characterizatio Booth also appeared with Miss Cushman and, in 188 opposite a less suitable Lady Macbeth, Helen Mod jeska. Another of Miss Cushman's associates in th tragedy, William Creswick, acted Macbeth at Booth's Theatre in 1871, giving a highly intellectualized and somewhat dispassionate portrayal. Tommaso Salvini played Macbeth, for the first time in America, at Booth's Theatre on February 10, 1881. His portrayal depicted Macbeth as a barbaric, rather than haunted, warrior, but his delivery, although in Italian, was highly commended. On January 21, 1889 Charles Coghlan and Lily Langtry presented the tragedy at the Fifth Avenue Theatre. In 1898 Joseph Haworth joined Mme. Modjeska, to be succeeded as her Macbeth the following year by John E. Kellerd; both leading men were as unequal to the tragedy as was their costar.

Early 20th-century Macbeths in the United States included Robert Mantell, who, having acted the part in the British provinces, played his first Macbeth in America at the Garden Theatre in New York on November 12, 1905, thereafter taking the part regularly through the first two decades of the 1900's. Edward H. Sothern appeared in the title role in repertory seasons with Julia Marlowe's Lady Macbeth at the Broadway Theatre and the Manhattan Opera House from 1910 through 1913, and John E. Kellerd played the part opposite Helena Modjeska at the Fifth Avenue in 1900 and later, in 1911, with Lillian Kingsbury at the Irving Place Theatre.

In 1916 Viola Allen staged a new treatment of the tragedy in which she herself played Lady Macbeth and James K. Hackett acted in the title role. The role of the supernatural in such events as Macbeth's encounter with the witches was minimized in this production at the Criterion, which ran for 40 performances. A three-act version of the drama produced by Arthur Hopkins opened at the Apollo in February 1921. It was designed by Robert Edmund Jones, who used futuristic settings suggesting a mood rather than a physical reality. Lionel Barrymore gave an intelligent portrayal of a bluff warrior, which, however, was marred by colloquial and at times monotonous speech. His Macbeth, a moral coward, was supported by the strictly feminine Lady Macbeth of Julia Arthur. In 1930 Fritz Leiber's Chicago Civic Shakespeare Society performed the tragedy at the Shubert Theatre, following with appearances the next season at the Ambassador Theatre. During the 1932/3 season, the Shakespeare Theatre Company acted *Macbeth* 27 times. That same season Florence Reed, who in 1928 had set a new record for the tragedy with 64 performances, played Lady Macbeth opposite Lynn Harding. In 1935 Gladys Cooper and Philip Merivale starred in the play. The Federal Theatre Project sponsored by the WPA presented an adaptation of *Macbeth* acted by Negroes, with Jack Carter in the title role and Edna Thomas as Lady Macbeth; it was given 59 consecutive performances in New York and 22 more on later tours. The greatest commercial success with the tragedy in America was achieved in 1941 when Maurice Evans and Judith Anderson played the principal roles for 131 performances at the National Theatre. In 1961 they repeated their characterizations for a highly acclaimed television presentation.

In October 1955 two productions of the tragedy appeared in New York. One at the Jan Hus Auditorium, staged by Brian Shaw, featured the well-spoken, vigorous Shakespearewrights in a direct, stimulating production with Pernell Roberts and M'el Dowd. Unfortunately much of the tragic beauty of the verse was lost in shouting and, while Roberts' masculine ruffian Macbeth conveyed urgent force and Miss Dowd was a handsome and unscrupulous Lady Macbeth, the motivations were cloudy. Nevertheless, this revival proved vastly superior to its rival staged by Ray Boyle at the Rooftop Theatre —a production burdened by an ineffectual impersonation of the title character alternately as a sneering scoundrel and a wild-eyed madman. Walter Kerr described Basil Langton's interpretation of Macbeth as "first cousin to Iago, second cousin to Jack the Ripper," and characterized the fast-moving presentation as "rapidly uninteresting." A somber production directed by Jack Landau was given at the American Shakespeare Festival, Stratford, Connecticut, in June 1961. Pat Hingle as an unpoetic, inconsistent Macbeth gave a one-dimensional interpretation with uneven force. But Jessica Tandy gave a compelling portrayal of a subdued Lady Macbeth, a study in controlled ambition and fury who revealed her burden of guilt in the sleepwalking scene, and a competent supporting cast delivered exceptional performances. James Ray was an effective Malcolm; Richard Waring, a handsome, impressive Macduff; and Donald Harron, an articulate, perceptive Banquo. Hiram Sherman provided welcome comic relief in this thoroughly gloomy presentation, taking full advantage of the Porter's speech, and Kim Hunter, Carla Huston, and Kathryn Loder were the Weird Sisters. In February 1962 an equally murky *Macbeth* staged by Michael Benthall and acted by an Old Vic Company visited the New York City Center. This strangely subdued production starred John Clements, somewhat casual in the title role, and Barbara Jefford as a remote, wistful, and oddly muted Lady Macbeth. That same year Christopher Plummer confused audiences as a Macbeth who became progressively more noble and self-aware; he appeared at the Stratford Shakespearean Festival in Canada under Peter Coe's direction. In New York Michael Higgins' Thane was unremittingly savage and cruel and Betty Miller's Lady Macbeth proud and pitiless in a production sponsored by the New York City Board of Education for school children. This gory *Macbeth*, in an edited version directed by Gladys Vaughan, played at the Heckscher Theatre and subsequently toured the city's schools.—M. G.

Bibliography. TEXT: *Macbeth*, New Cambridge Edition, J. Dover Wilson, ed., 1947; *Macbeth*, New Arden Edition, Kenneth Muir, ed., 1951; W. W. Greg, *The Shakespeare First Folio*, 1955. DATE: New Arden Edition; Henry N. Paul, *The Royal Play of Macbeth*, 1950. SOURCES: New Arden Edition; *The Royal Play of Macbeth*. COMMENT: A. C. Bradley, *Shakespearean Tragedy*, 1904; W. C. Curry, *Shakespeare's Philosophical Patterns*, 1937. STAGE HISTORY: New Cambridge Edition; T. Alston Brown, *A History of the New York Stage . . . to 1901*, 1903; William Winter, *Shakespeare on the Stage*, 3 vols., 1911–1916; G. C. D. Odell, *Shakespeare from Betterton to Irving*, 1920; J. C. Trewin, *Shakespeare on the English Stage, 1900–1964*, 1964.

Selected Criticism

SAMUEL JOHNSON. This play is deservedly celebrated for the propriety of its fictions, and solemnity, grandeur, and variety of its action; but it has no nice discriminations of character, the events are too great to admit the influence of particular dispositions, and the course of the action necessarily determines the conduct of the agents.

The danger of ambition is well described; and I know not whether it may not be said in defence of some parts which now seem improbable, that, in *Shakespeare's* time, it was necessary to warn credulity against vain and illusive predictions.

The passions are directed to their true end. Lady *Macbeth* is merely detested; and though the courage of *Macbeth* preserves some esteem, yet every reader rejoices at his fall. [*The Plays of William Shakespeare*, 1765.]

THOMAS DE QUINCEY. From my boyish days I had always felt a great perplexity on one point in *Macbeth*. It was this: the knocking at the gate, which succeeds to the murder of Duncan, produced to my feelings an effect for which I never could account. The effect was, that it reflected back upon the murder a peculiar awfulness and a depth of solemnity; yet, however obstinately I endeavored with my understanding to comprehend this, for many years I never could see *why* it should produce such an effect.

. . . my solution is this: Murder, in ordinary cases, where the sympathy is wholly directed to the case of the murdered person, is an incident of coarse and vulgar horror; and for this reason, that it flings the interest exclusively upon the natural but ignoble instinct by which we cleave to life; an instinct, which, as being indispensable to the primal law of self-preservation, is the same in kind (though different in degree) amongst all living creatures; this instinct, therefore, because it annihilates all distinctions, and degrades the greatest of men to the level of the 'poor beetle that we tread on,' exhibits human nature in its most abject and humiliating attitude. Such an attitude would little suit the purposes of the poet. What then must he do? He must throw the interest on the murderer. Our sympathy must be with *him;* (of course, I mean a sympathy of comprehension, a sympathy by which we enter into his feelings, and are made to understand them,—not a sympathy of pity or approbation.) In the murdered person, all strife of thought, all flux and reflux of passion and of purpose are crushed by one overwhelming panic; the fear of instant death smites him 'with its petrific mace.' But in the murderer, such a murderer as a poet will condescend to, there must be raging some great storm of passion,—jealousy, ambition, vengeance, hatred,—which will create a hell within him; and into this hell we are to look . . . .

Now apply this to the case of Macbeth. Here, as I have said, the retiring of the human heart, and the entrance of the fiendish heart, was to be expressed and made sensible. Another world has stept in, and the murderers are taken out of the region of human things, human purposes, human desires. They are transfigured: Lady Macbeth is 'unsexed'; Macbeth has forgot that he was born of woman; both are conformed to the image of devils; and the world of devils is suddenly revealed. But how shall this be conveyed and made palpable? In order that a new world may step in, this world must for a time disappear. The murderers, and the murder, must b insulated,—cut off by an immeasurable gulf from th ordinary tide and succession of human affairs,– locked up and sequestered in some deep recess; w must be made sensible that the world of ordinar life is suddenly arrested,—laid asleep,—tranced,– racked into a dread armistice; time must be annihi lated; relation to things without abolished; and a must pass self-withdrawn into a deep syncope an suspension of earthly passion. Hence it is, that whe the deed is done, when the work of darkness is per fect, then the world of darkness passes away like pageantry in the clouds: the knocking at the gate i heard; and it makes known audibly that the reactio has commenced; the human has made its reflux upo the fiendish; the pulses of life are beginning to bea again; and the re-establishment of the goings-on o the world in which we live, first makes us pro foundly sensible of the awful parenthesis that ha suspended them. ["The Knocking at the Gate," *Miscellaneous Essays*, 1851.]

EDWARD DOWDEN. Macbeth retained enough o goodness to make him a haggard, miserable criminal never enough to restrain him from a crime. His han soon became subdued to what it worked in—th blood in which it paddled and plashed. . . .

Yet the soul of Macbeth never quite disappear into the blackness of darkness. He is a cloud withou water, carried about of winds; a tree whose frui withers, but not, even to the last, quite plucked u by the roots. For the dull ferocity of Macbeth i joyless. All his life has gone irretrievably astray, an he is aware of this. His suspicion becomes uncon trollable; his reign is a reign of terror; and as h drops deeper and deeper into the solitude and th gloom, his sense of error and misfortune, futile an unproductive as that sense is, increases. He move under a dreary cloud, and all things look gray an cold. He has lived long enough, yet he clings to life that which should accompany old age, "as honor love, obedience, troops of friends," he may not loo to have. Finally, his sensibility has grown so dull tha even the intelligence of his wife's death—the deat of her who had been bound to him by such clos communion in crime—hardly touches him, and seem little more than one additional incident in the weary meaningless tale of human life. [*Shakspere: A Critica Study of His Mind and Art*, 1875.]

A. C. BRADLEY. A Shakespearean tragedy, as a rule has a special tone or atmosphere of its own, quit perceptible, however difficult to describe. The effec of this atmosphere is marked with unusual strengt in *Macbeth*. It is due to a variety of influences whic combine with those just noticed, so that, acting an reacting, they form a whole; and the desolation o the blasted heath, the design of the Witches, th guilt in the hero's soul, the darkness of the night seem to emanate from one and the same source. This effect is strengthened by a multitude of smal touches, which at the moment may be little noticed but still leave their mark on the imagination. We may approach the consideration of the characters and the action by distinguishing some of the ingredients of this general effect.

Darkness, we may even say blackness, broods over this tragedy. It is remarkable that almost all the

:enes which at once recur to memory take place ither at night or in some dark spot. The vision of 1e dagger, the murder of Duncan, the murder of anquo, the sleep-walking of Lady Macbeth, all ome in night-scenes. The Witches dance in the 1ick air of a storm, or, 'black and midnight hags,' ceive Macbeth in a cavern. The blackness of night to the hero a thing of fear, even of horror; and 1at which he feels becomes the spirit of the play. 'he faint glimmerings of the western sky at twi- ght are here menacing: it is the hour when 'light 1ickens,' when 'night's black agents to their prey do ouse,' when the wolf begins to howl, and the owl scream, and withered murder steals forth to his vork. Macbeth bids the stars hide their fires that his lack' desires may be concealed; Lady Macbeth calls n thick night to come, palled in the dunnest smoke f hell. The moon is down and no stars shine when anquo, dreading the dreams of the coming night, oes unwillingly to bed, and leaves Macbeth to wait or the summons of the little bell. When the next ay should dawn, its light is 'strangled,' and 'dark- ess does the face of earth entomb.' In the whole rama the sun seems to shine only twice; first, in the eautiful but ironical passage where Duncan sees he swallows flitting round the castle of death; and, fterwards, when at the close the avenging army athers to rid the earth of its shame. Of the many ighter touches which deepen this effect I notice nly one. The failure of nature in Lady Macbeth is 1arked by her fear of darkness; 'she has light by her ontinually.' And in the one phrase of fear that scapes her lips even in sleep, it is of the darkness of he place of torment that she speaks. [*Shakespearean Tragedy*, 1904.]

FRANCIS FERGUSSON. . . . I propose to attempt to llustrate the view that *Macbeth* may be understood s "the imitation of an action," in approximately Aristotle's sense of this phrase.

The word "action"—*praxis*—as Aristotle uses it in he *Poetics*, does not mean outward deeds or events, ut something much more like "purpose" or "aim." Perhaps our word "motive" suggests most of its 1eaning . . . .

I remarked that action is not outward deeds or vents; but on the other hand, there can be no action vithout resulting deeds. We guess at a man's action y way of what he does, his outward and visible leeds. We are aware that our own action, or motive, roduces deeds of some sort as soon as it exists. Now he plot of a play is the arrangement of outward leeds or incidents, and the dramatist uses it, as Aristotle tells us, as the first means of imitating the ction. He arranges a set of incidents which point to he action or motive from which they spring. You nay say that the action is the spiritual content of the ragedy—the playwright's inspiration—and the plot lefines its existence as an intelligible *play*. Thus, you annot have a play without both plot and action; yet he distinction between plot and action is as funda- nental as that between form and matter. The action s the matter; the plot is the "first form," or, as Aristotle puts it, the "soul" of the tragedy . . . .

The action of the play as a whole is best expressed n a phrase which Macbeth himself uses in Act II, cene 3, the aftermath of the murder. Macbeth is trying to appear innocent, but everything he says betrays his clear sense of his own evil motivation, or action. Trying to excuse his murder of Duncan's grooms, he says,

> *The expedition of my violent love* [for Duncan, he means]
> *Outran the pauser, reason.*

It is the phrase "to outrun the pauser, reason," which seems to me to describe the action, or motive, of the play as a whole. Macbeth, of course, literally means that his love for Duncan was so strong and swift that it got ahead of his reason, which would have coun- seled a pause. But in the same way we have seen his greed and ambition outrun his reason when he com- mitted the murder; and in the same way all of the characters, in the irrational darkness of Scotland's evil hour, are compelled in their action to strive be- yond what they can see by reason alone.

. . . The plot itself—"the arrangement or synthesis of the incidents"—also imitates a desperate race. This is partly a matter of the speed with which the main facts are presented, partly the effect of simultaneous movements like those of a race: Lady Macbeth is reading the letter at the same moment that her hus- band and Duncan are rushing toward her. And the facts in this part of the play are ambiguous in mean- ing and even as facts . . . .

"Outrunning reason" looks purely evil in the be- ginning, and at the end we see how it may be good, an act of faith beyond reason. ["*Macbeth* as the Imitation of an Action," *English Institute Essays 1951*, 1952.]

R. S. CRANE. . . . I will begin by considering what idea of the governing form of *Macbeth* appears to accord best with the facts of that play and the se- quence of emotions it arouses in us. I shall assume that we have to do, not with a lyric 'statement of evil' or an allegory of the workings of sin in the soul and the state or a metaphysical myth of de- struction followed by recreation, or a morality play with individualized characters rather than types, but simply with an imitative tragic drama based on his- torical materials. . . . The action of the play is two- fold, and one of its aspects is the punitive action of Malcolm, Macduff, and their friends which in the end brings about the protagonist's downfall and death. The characters here are all good men, whom Mac- beth has unforgivably wronged, and their cause is the unqualifiedly just cause of freeing Scotland from a bloody tyrant and restoring the rightful line of kings. All this is made clear in the representation not only directly through the speeches and acts of the avengers but indirectly by those wonderfully vivid devices of imagery and general thought in which modern critics have found the central value and meaning of the play as a whole; and our responses, when this part of the action is before us, are such as are clearly dictated by the immediate events and the poetic commentary: we desire, that is, the complete success of the counter-action and this as speedily as possible before Macbeth can commit further horrors. We desire this, however—and that is what at once takes the plot-form out of the merely retributive class—not only for the sake of humanity and Scot- land but also for the sake of Macbeth himself. For what most sharply distinguished our view of Macbeth from that of his victims and enemies is that, whereas they see him from the outside only, we see him also, throughout the other action of the play—the major action—from the inside, as he sees himself; and what we see thus is a moral spectacle, the emotional quality of which, for the impartial observer, is not too far removed from the tragic *dynamis* specified in the *Poetics* . . . .

We want him to be killed, as I have said, for his sake no less than that of Scotland; but we would not want him either to seek out Macduff or to flee the encounter when it comes or to 'play the Roman fool'; we would not want him to show no recognition of the wrongs he has done Macduff, or, when his last trust in the witches has gone, to continue to show fear or to yield or to fight with savage animosity; and he is made to do none of these things, but rather the contraries of all of them, so that he acts in the end as the Macbeth whose praises we have heard in the second scene of the play. And I would suggest that the cathartic effect of these words and acts is reinforced indirectly, in the representation, by the analogy we can hardly help drawing between his conduct now and the earlier conduct of young Siward, for of Macbeth too it can be said that 'he parted well and paid his score'; the implication of this analogy is surely one of the functions, though not the only one, which the lines about Siward are intended to serve. [*The Languages of Criticism and the Structure of Poetry*, 1953.]

MARY MC CARTHY. Macbeth "repents" killing the grooms, but this is strictly for public consumption. "O, yet I do repent me of my fury, That I did kill them." In fact, it is the one deed he does *not* repent (*i.e.*, doubt the wisdom of) either before or after. This hypocritical self-accusation, which is his sidelong way of announcing the embarrassing fact that he has just done away with the grooms, and his simulated grief at Duncan's murder ("All is but toys; renown and grace is dead; The wine of life is drawn," etc.) are his basest moments in the play, as well as his boldest; here is nearly a magnificent monster.

The dramatic effect, too, is one of great boldness on Shakespeare's part. Macbeth is speaking pure Shakespearean poetry, but in his mouth, since we know he is lying, it turns into facile verse, Shakespearean poetry parodied. The same with "Here lay Duncan, his silver skin lac'd with his golden blood . . ." If the image were given to Macduff, it would be uncontaminated poetry; from Macbeth it is "proper stuff"—fustian. This opens the perilous question of sincerity in the arts: is a line of verse altered for us by the sincerity of the poet (or speaker)? . . . My opinion is that Macbeth's soliloquies are not poetry but rhetoric. They are tirades. That is, they do not trace any pensive motion of the soul or heart but are a volley of words discharged. Macbeth is neither thinking nor feeling aloud; he is declaiming. ["General Macbeth" (1962); reprinted in *Mary McCarthy's Theatre Chronicles, 1937–1962*, 1962.]

Macbeth, Lady. In *Macbeth*, the tragic heroine. One of Shakespeare's greatest female characters, Lady Macbeth has been aptly described as "magnificent in sin." Imperious, bold, with a strength of conviction that denies her femininity, she is repr sented in the early part of the play as all but i human. Yet even in these scenes she is seen reflecti the tension and doubt which she fiercely repress as she steels herself for the dreadful deed whic faces her. Sensing the weakness of her own huma ity, she delivers an impious prayer for the diabolic strength necessary to carry out the murder of Du can (I, v, 41–55). This invocation of demonic spiri would doubtless have been regarded by an Eliz bethan audience quite literally, i.e., an invitation devils to take possession of her body. Yet despi the demoniacal possession, Lady Macbeth lacks th ultimate hardness of heart necessary to survive th torture of her conscience. The result is that she sin under the burden of remorse and anxiety so u forgettably pictured in the sleepwalking scen (V, i).

McCullough, John Edward (1832–1885). Irish-bor American actor. McCullough was born near Londo derry; his parents were peasants who emigrated t Philadelphia in 1847. Though at the age of 15 Mc Cullough could neither read nor write, he dete mined to become an actor. His apprenticeship w with a Philadelphia dramatic club, and in 1857 h made his debut there. Later joining the company le by Edwin Forrest, he in time played the leads an second leads in many plays of Shakespeare—Laerte Macduff, Iago, Edgar, Richmond, and Titus. Afte several seasons, he left Forrest to play in San Fran cisco for some years, part of that time as Lawrenc Barrett's partner. In 1881 he played in London.

McCullough's forte was mainly the "noble" char acters of Shakespeare's tragedies, classical Englis plays, and Forrest's melodramas. He was an effectiv actor, but less than inspired. [*Dictionary of Ameri can Biography*, 1927– .]

MacDowell, Edward. See MUSIC BASED ON SHAKE SPEARE: *20th century*.

Macduff. In *Macbeth*, the thane of Fife. Macdu discovers Duncan murdered and, suspecting Macbet of the deed, refuses to be present at his coronatio and feast, but joins Duncan's son Malcolm in Eng land. The witches warn Macbeth against Macduf though assuring him that "none of woman born sha harm Macbeth" (IV, i). Hearing of Macduff's fligh Macbeth has Lady Macduff and her children mu dered. Macduff returns to Scotland with an invadin army of Scottish nobles and English soldiers; meetin Macbeth on the battlefield, he states that he was no born, but "untimely ripp'd" from his mother' womb. He then kills Macbeth.

Macduff, Lady. In *Macbeth*, the wife of Macduf After Macduff's flight to England, Macbeth orde the murder of Lady Macduff and her childre (IV, ii).

Machiavelli, Niccolò (1469–1527). Italian autho and political philosopher. Machiavelli served as as sistant secretary of state of the Republic of Florenc from 1498 to 1512. In 1512 he was deprived of hi position and exiled from Florence. During his exil he wrote his major political works, *Il Principe* (*Th Prince*, 1513) and the *Discorsi* (*Discourses*, 1513 1517).

Machiavelli's political philosophy is an aspect o Renaissance humanism, insofar as the latter empha izes the return to origins. In the political sphere this was interpreted by Machiavelli as the need of a particular community or nation to renew itself by discovering its historical origins and recognizing the political reality out of which the community grew. Historical objectivity and political realism therefore constitute the basis of authentic Machiavellianism.

Two other aspects of Machiavelli's political doctrine are the concept of "fortuna," i.e., chance, which is a condition of political activity, and the connected concept of political commitment which demands that statesmen thrust themselves into events whose outcome, given the presence of chance, is never predetermined. These aspects of his doctrine imply, of course, choice, risk, and responsibility, hence freedom, and the problematic character of history.

Once the task has been accepted, the statesman cannot go halfway. The demands upon him derive from the sphere in which he moves. He cannot count on the good will of men, who, by nature, are neither good nor evil but can be one or the other. In order to achieve the security and well-being of the state, the statesman must wager that the worst will occur; he must presuppose that men are wicked and will show it at the first opportunity. The statesman cannot make a "profession out of goodness"; he should not divorce himself from good acts, but must be able, as situations demand, to enter into evil. Required of the effective statesman, then, are certain cruel expedients, contrary not only to Christian life but to human life, from which men ordinarily should flee. The man who cannot renounce his moral scruples is not fit to rule the state.

Machiavelli sees the limit of political activity as inherent in its very nature. The political act has no need to derive its morality outside itself. The norm that guides it is intrinsic to the demand of leading men to an ordered and free form of social living and it finds its limit in the possibility of success of the means employed.

Machiavelli, however, does not consider the state as an absolute end or invested with an existence superior to that of the individual as do Hegel and Marx. His sympathies lie with honesty and loyalty in personal and civil life. He admired, therefore, those societies which he believed rested on these virtues, such as Republican Rome and the Swiss. His aim, however, was to formulate rules of effective government on the bases of ancient, as well as current, political experiences. He considered, therefore, the effectiveness of these rules apart from their moral character. Those harsh actions which are employed for the common good of the citizens and which die away as the state settles down are well used.

This insistence upon certain amoral maxims of political conduct initiated the popular view of Machiavelli as a figure of diabolical stature. This conception of Machiavelli began in France and reached its culmination in the publication of Innocent Gentillet's *Contre-Machiavel* (1576), a savage attack upon the doctrines set forth in *The Prince*. Gentillet's work, translated into English in 1602, helped to spread the popular notion of Machiavelli in England, but Englishmen had had a firsthand knowledge of the Florentine's philosophy long before this. Henry VIII's lord chancellor, Thomas Cromwell, a supreme Machiavellian in every sense of the word, is known to have studied the Italian's works, as did Shakespeare's contemporaries Gabriel Harvey and Francis Bacon.

The popular view of Machiavelli, however, was the one which came to be so frequently expressed on the Elizabethan stage. Machiavelli became, in Wyndham Lewis' words, "the master figure of Elizabethan drama . . . at the back of every Tudor mind." "Machiavellism" is a prominent aspect of the dramas of Kyd, Marlowe, Chapman, and Webster. In Shakespeare, "Machiavellism" is a constituent part of the makeup of Iago and Richard III. The latter in *3 Henry VI* makes his affinity quite explicit by declaring that he will "set the murderous Machiavel to school" (III, ii, 193). Allusions to Machiavelli are also made in *The Merry Wives of Windsor* (III, i) and *1 Henry VI* (V, iv). But probably the nearest approach to authentic Machiavellianism is to be found in the Bastard's wryly cynical analysis of "commodity" in *King John* (II, i, 561–598). [Wyndham Lewis, *The Lion and the Fox*, 1927; Mario Praz, *The Flaming Heart*, 1958; N. Abbagnano, *Dizionario di Filosofia*, 1960.]—N. L.

Mackail, J[ohn] W[illiam] (1859–1945). Educator and scholar. Mackail served as a member of the staff of the ministry of education from 1884 to 1919, and was professor of poetry at Oxford from 1906 to 1911. Most of his Oxford lectures have been gathered into three volumes: *The Springs of Helicon* (1909), *Lectures on Greek Poetry* (1910), and *Lectures on Poetry* (1911). A lecture on the Sonnets and one on the romantic dramas have been included in the last-named volume. *The Approach to Shakespeare* (1930) is a general survey. Mackail also selected nine British Academy Lectures on Shakespeare for reprinting under the title *Aspects of Shakespeare* (1933).

Mackenzie, Henry (1745–1831). Scottish novelist and civil servant. An admirer of Shakespeare, Mackenzie engaged in critical discussions of his work, notably in four essays, two of which were published in *The Mirror* in 1780 and the other two in *The Lounger* in 1786.

In the 1780 essays Mackenzie explains Hamlet's erratic behavior by attributing to him an extreme sensitivity which is occasionally overcome by his situation. Mackenzie notes that Hamlet's indecision is his dramatic strength: had he acted purposefully and directly, as does Sophocles' Orestes, our interest would be in the action rather than the character. Mackenzie views Hamlet's madness as feigned throughout and explains some puzzling scenes in this light.

In the 1786 essays Mackenzie compares Shakespeare favorably with Homer and analyzes the character of Falstaff. He also argues that Shakespeare's plays should be judged by their total effect, not by individual passages, and he severely condemns the adaptations, or "improvements," of Shakespeare that were so prevalent in the 18th century. [Herbert Spencer Robinson, *English Shakesperian Criticism in the Eighteenth Century*, 1932.]

McKerrow, R[onald] B[runlees] (1872–1940). Bibliographer. After several years of teaching, McKerrow became associated with A. W. Pollard and W. W. Greg in the new field of descriptive and analytic bibliography. They were the pioneers in investigating such elements as manuscripts, handwriting, watermarks, prompter's copies, proofreading, and book production (see TEXTUAL CRITICISM). During most of his career, he was associated with the Bibliographical Society, which he joined in 1903 and whose joint secretary (with Pollard) he became in 1913; he contributed to the Society's journal, *The Library*, and edited it from 1934 to 1937. He also founded and edited, until his death, the *Review of English Studies*.

McKerrow first came into prominence with his edition of Thomas Nashe. When the three volumes of text appeared (1903–1904), scholars recognized in them a new standard of editorial excellence, especially with regard to the establishment of the text. After the edition was completed in 1910 with the two volumes of commentary and index, it was recognized as the best edition of any English writer. Among his important books are *A Dictionary of Printers and Booksellers in England, Scotland and Ireland, and Foreign Printers of English Books, 1557–1640* (1910) and *Printers' and Publishers' Devices in England and Scotland, 1485–1640* (1913). His *Introduction to Bibliography for Literary Students* (1927) sums up the results of his experience and is the standard guide. McKerrow devoted the last years of his life to planning a new edition of Shakespeare, but the only volume completed before his death was the *Prolegomena for the Oxford Shakespeare* (1939), in which he set forth his editorial principles. [W. W. Greg, "Ronald Brunlees McKerrow," *Proceedings of the British Academy*, XXVI, 1940; F. C. Francis, "A List of the Writings of Ronald Brunlees McKerrow," *The Library*, 4th series, XXI, 1940–1941.]

Macklin, Charles (c. 1700–1797). Irish-born actor. Macklin, whose real name was McLoughlin, had a tempestuous career marked by brawls and feuds, in one of which he killed a man, and in another assaulted the Shakespearean actor James Quin. His feud with Garrick lasted throughout his career.

Macklin's acting style was distinguished by its naturalness and gusto. His best roles included Touchstone and Iago, but he is remembered for his revolutionary interpretation of Shylock. Prior to his portrayal, it had been customary to play the role as low comedy, but Macklin created a figure of malevolence and intensity which bordered on the tragic. King George II attended a performance and reported that he could not sleep as a result of it.

Macklin was the first to inaugurate a series of public lectures on Shakespeare. Begun in 1754, they covered a wide range of Shakespearean studies; according to the handbills advertising them, they included an account of the plays' sources and "the Artificial or Inartificial Use, according to the laws of Drama, that Shakespeare has made of them. His Fable, Character, Passions, Manners will likewise be criticized and how his capital characters have been acted heretofore, are acted, and ought to be acted."

In 1748 Macklin claimed to have uncovered a Caroline pamphlet which related anecdotes about Shakespeare, Jonson, and John Ford. According to Macklin, the pamphlet was lost on a voyage from Ireland. The falsity of Macklin's claim, however, was demonstrated by Edmund Malone.

McManaway, James G[ilmer] (1899–). American scholar, editor of the *Shakespeare Quarterly* an consultant in literature and bibliography at th Folger Shakespeare Library. In collaboration wit others, McManaway compiled *A Check-List of English Plays, 1641–1700* (1945) and edited the *Joseph Quincy Adams Memorial Studies* (1948). He ha contributed a booklet, "The Authorship of Shakespeare," to *Life and Letters in Tudor and Stuart England* (1962), edited by Louis B. Wright an Virginia A. LaMar. In honor of the 400th anniversary of Shakespeare's birth, McManaway devoted a special issue of the *Shakespeare Quarterly* to essays b the most outstanding American scholars; with mino changes the issue was published in book form a *Shakespeare 400* (1964).

Macmorris. In *Henry V*, an Irish officer serving i King Henry's French campaign. He quarrels wit Fluellen in III, ii. See IRELAND.

Macready, [William] Charles (1793–1873). Acto and theatrical manager. Born in London, the son o actor-manager William Macready (d. 1829), Macready was intended for the bar and went to Rugb until 1808 when his father's financial difficultie forced him to turn to acting professionally. In 181 he made his debut at the Birmingham Theatre a Romeo, with considerable success, and for the nex four years acted principal roles with his father' company. In 1811 he made his first try at Hamlet a Newcastle, and of the experience later wrote: " total failure in that character is of rare occurrence. He played opposite Mrs. Siddons, who encourage and advised him, as well as with John Philip Kembl and other eminent actors of the day. In four year he had learned 74 parts, and was acting Faulconbridge, Antony, and Benedick. In 1814 at Bath h played Romeo, Hotspur, Hamlet, and Richard II. I 1816 he alternated with Charles Mayne Young a Othello and Iago. The critics were favorable excep for Hazlitt, who commented that Macready's performance was "effeminate," whimpering, and lachrymose. In 1819 his Richard III established him as rival to Kean, although he was unsuccessful in *Henr V*. His Coriolanus and Jaques were well received, a well as his Edmund. In 1822 he substituted a partia revision of *Richard III* for the Colley Cibber versio which had held the stage since 1700. In 1821 he signe a five-year contract with Covent Garden, but in 182 moved to Drury Lane, where he remained for 1 years. He added Macbeth and Leontes to his repertory, as well as the Duke in *Measure for Measure*. He married Catherine Frances Atkins, a leadin provincial actress, later that year. In 1826 and 182 he toured many American cities, performing Macbeth and other roles in New York. He appeared a Macbeth, Hamlet, and Othello in Paris in 1828.

Macready began his management of Covent Garden in 1837 with *The Winter's Tale*, playin Leontes. For the period of his management he engaged many famous actors and also opera an pantomime companies, the latter making up for h financial losses with elaborate Shakespearean productions. His 1838 production of *King Lear* restore the original play to the theatre for the first time sinc the 17th century. His *King Lear* was described "perhaps the most momentous in the entire histor of Shakespearean restorations." He concluded h management in 1843, having become famous for pr lucing the best available plays with the best com-anies. His policy of discouraging long runs of suc-essful productions, however, impaired his financial tability, and although he was generous to his com-anies, he was also known as vain, arrogant, and un-racious. In 1849 his New York appearance as Mac-eth set off the Astor Place riots (see Edwin FOR-EST).

He is generally considered to have been a man of ndisputable genius and scholarship with tragedy and haracter acting his forte; he was the "most romantic f actors," an impression enhanced by his thrilling oice. Numerous portraits of him are in existence, nd his *Diary and Reminiscences* was edited by Sir rederick Pollock in 1875. [*Dictionary of National Biography*, 1885– .]

Maddermarket Theatre. Playhouse in Norwich, England, founded in 1921 by Nugent MONCK. The eader of a group of amateur actors known as the Norwich Players, Monck acquired a dilapidated 8th-century building and converted it into the Maddermarket, a reconstructed Elizabethan play-ouse, on the model of the Fortune theatre. The Maddermarket opened on September 23, 1921 with a erformance of *As You Like It*. Since that time the Norwich Players, still amateur and remaining always nonymous, have performed all of Shakespeare's lays as well as a number of other Elizabethan ramas. They are considered the most successful mateur repertory group in England. [Nugent Monck, "The Maddermarket Theatre," *Shakespeare urvey 12*, 1959.]

madness. The Elizabethans believed that madness esulted from a pathological imbalance of the "hu-nours" (see PSYCHOLOGY). It was caused by a tem-eramental disposition toward such imbalance under ircumstances of a catastrophic nature, such as the iolent death of loved ones or unrequited love. It vas hardly distinguished from such terms as "mania" r pathological "melancholia." Both mania and mad-ess denoted an extraordinary degree of irrationality. Mania, however, could be classified according to two ypes: severe melancholia and pathological melan-holia.

Severe melancholia meant to Elizabethan audiences what severe neurosis would mean to a modern one. t closely resembled madness in its symptoms, but it vas considered primarily a disease of the imagina-ion. Jaques in *As You Like It*, Angelo in *Measure or Measure*, Hamlet, Timon, and Pericles exemplify n varying degrees the severe melancholiac. The sub-lass of love melancholiacs is best illustrated in hakespeare by Orsino in *Twelfth Night*. Tragic xamples of the love melancholiac are Giovanni in ohn Ford's *'Tis Pity She's a Whore*, Fernando in ord's *Love's Sacrifice*, Penthea in Ford's *The roken Heart*, the Spanish soldier in John Marston's *he Insatiable Countess*, and the old general in eaumont and Fletcher's *The Mad Lover*. The best ontemporary account of severe melancholia is Book of Robert Burton's *Anatomy of Melancholy* 1621).

Pathological melancholia is madness, an extreme egree of the former state; it meant to Elizabethans bout what psychosis means today. In contrast to the sser aberration, it was considered primarily a dis-ase of the reason. Its two commonest symptoms were frenzy and hallucinations. Frenzy was the result of an inflammation of the brain due to an invasion of choler. Hallucinations were the products of both a sick reason and a sick imagination; frequently, the victim imagined himself an animal, particularly a wolf. The principal cause of this type of madness was excessive grief, illustrated in Shakespeare by Ophelia; Lady Macbeth; Lear; Edgar, who assumes madness; and Lear's fool, who is, presumably, half mad.

Love madness was caused by uncontrollable jealousy. For Elizabethans, the moral problem involved with love madness centered on the belief that this passion's source was entirely internal. The problem of self-mastery or cure depended on self-knowledge. Thus, those who knew themselves least well were least prone to self-mastery and most open to this affliction. Othello and Leontes in *The Winter's Tale* best illustrate love madness. [Laurence Babb, *The Elizabethan Malady: A Study of Melancholia in English Literature from 1580 to 1642*, 1951.]—S.K.

Mainwaring, Arthur (fl. 1614). The owner of land in Welcombe near Stratford who in 1614, in association with William Replingham and William Combe, attempted to enclose lands in that area (see ENCLOSURE). The enclosure, which was bitterly opposed by the Stratford corporation, peripherally involved land owned by Shakespeare, but he apparently did not take an active part in the controversy.

Malcolm III, King of Scotland (d. 1093). Eldest son of Duncan I. On his father's death and Macbeth's accession to the throne in 1040, Malcolm fled to England. Later returning to Scotland, he defeated and killed Macbeth in 1057 and was himself crowned king. His reign was spent largely in warfare in order to insure the independence of the kingdom, and he was killed in battle near Alnwick. In *Macbeth*, Malcolm's father proclaims him Prince of Cumberland and heir to the throne. After Duncan's murder, however, Malcolm flees to England at the same time that his brother Donalbain flees to Ireland. Duncan's sons are accordingly suspected of being their father's assassins. [W. H. Thomson, *Shakespeare's Characters: A Historical Dictionary*, 1951.]

Malcontent, The. A play by John MARSTON published in three editions in 1604; the title page of the third edition describes it as

> The Malcontent. Augmented by Marston. With the Additions played by the Kings Maiesties servants.

The Malcontent is the best of Marston's cynical satires on human folly. It bears a slight resemblance to some of Shakespeare's plays of this period, notably *Measure for Measure*, and the leading character, Malevole, has traits similar to some of Hamlet's.

The Induction to the third edition of the play, written by John Webster, is important as a source of information concerning the rivalry in the early years of the 17th century between the children's companies and the adult companies who performed in the public theatres (see WAR OF THE THEATRES). Marston's play had originally been written for the Children of the Queen's Revels at Blackfriars; the King's Men, however, appropriated the play as their own, possibly as a retort to the Children's performance of *The Spanish Tragedy*. This at least appears to be the explanation given in the Induction, where one of the King's Men players, Henry Condell, describes how the company came by the play:

> *Condell*. Faith, sir, the booke was lost; and because 'twas pity so good a play should be lost, we found it and play it.
> *Sly*. I wonder you would play it, another company having interest in it?
> *Condell*. Why not Malevole in folio with us, as Jeronimo in decimo sexto with them? They taught us a name for our play; we call it *One for Another*.

The Induction is also valuable as evidence of the differences between the performances at the public and those at the private theatres. [O. J. Campbell, *Shakespeare's Satire*, 1943; Alfred Harbage, *Shakespeare and the Rival Tradition*, 1952.]

Malipiero, Gian Francesco. See MUSIC BASED ON SHAKESPEARE: *20th century*.

Malone, Edmund (1741–1812). Irish scholar. Born in Dublin, Malone was educated at Trinity and called to the bar; after the death of his father in 1774 he moved to London and became associated with such figures as Johnson, Boswell, Walpole, Reynolds, Burke, and Prime Minister Canning. For a while he collaborated with George Steevens on the latter's edition of Shakespeare. His *Attempt to ascertain the Order in which the Plays attributed to Shakespeare were written*, the first such chronological study, was included in Steevens' second edition of 1778 (see CHRONOLOGY). For the third edition of 1780 Malone was responsible for two additional volumes: one was a lengthy *History of the Stage* and the other contained the apocryphal plays of the Third and Fourth Folios and nondramatic poems. Malone thus became the first to make a critical edition of the sonnets and the first to write a history of the English stage based on extensive original sources.

In 1790 Malone issued his own edition of Shakespeare (10 volumes in 11). Steevens and Malone now were rivals rather than collaborators, for Steevens issued his 15-volume edition in 1793. At the time of his death Malone was working on a revision of his edition, the material for which passed into the hands of James Boswell, son of the biographer. "Boswell's Malone" or "The Third Variorum," as the work was variously called, appeared in 1821 with a biographical sketch of Malone in the "Prolegomena." Malone also edited an elaborate edition of Dryden (1800) with a memoir. His knowledge of primary sources led him to deny the antiquity of Thomas Chatterton's so-called Rowley poems and to expose the William Henry Ireland forgeries.

As the major Shakespearean editor of the 18th century, Malone's importance lies not so much in textual emendation as in his unrivaled knowledge of documentary material. David Nichol Smith has said that "he is representative of the main movement in English scholarship at his time. His edition of Shakespeare may be described as the summing up of the work of a century—a summing up in which everything is submitted to the test of his own investigations and controlled by a remarkable amount of new evidence. . . . no one has put the student of English literature under a greater debt." [D. Nichol Smith, "Edmond Malone," *Huntington Library Quarterl* III, 1939.]

Malone Society. A scholarly organization. Name in honor of Edmund Malone, it was founded b R. B. McKerrow and others at Trinity Colleg Cambridge, in 1896, but was inactive until its re organization in 1906 at University College, Londo where McKerrow was joined by W. W. Greg, F. Boas, E. K. Chambers, and A. W. Pollard. The pr mary objective of the Malone Society has been t reprint in type facsimile Elizabethan plays, ap proximately 100 of which have appeared to dat The Society also issues at irregular intervals i *Collections* which reprints such documentary ma terial as records, play lists, registers, journals, an letter books, as well as fragments of plays and dra matic compositions too brief for separate publicatio Volume IV (1956) of the *Collections* contains history of the Society during its first 50 years and complete list of its publications up to 1956.

Malvolio. In *Twelfth Night*, Olivia's steward, "a affection'd ass," whose gulling at the hands of Si Toby Belch and his friends provides one of th major elements in the action of the play. Sometim regarded as Shakespeare's portrait of a Purita Malvolio is not so much the representative of Pur tanism as he is the image of pomposity, hypocris and self-love. Added to these elements is a peculia joylessness which renders him particularly inimic in the world of comedy. Thus it is not surprisin that Malvolio, unlike many other unsympatheti characters, is not pictured as having gained the sel knowledge which would enable him to participat in the festivities that usually mark the end of Shak speare's comedies. The mortification which Malvoli undergoes fails to provide him with a new conce tion of himself, and he stalks off the stage vowin revenge, much in the manner of Shakespeare's oth great, equally irreconcilable comic creation, Shyloc

Leslie Hotson has argued with considerable effe tiveness that Malvolio is Shakespeare's portrait of S William KNOLLYS, the comptroller of Queen Eliz beth's household. Knollys shared many of the trai associated with Malvolio, including sympathy f Puritanism and a habit of interrupting revelers in h nightshirt. He was enamored of his ward Mar Fitton, the queen's maid of honor and one of th candidates for the title of Dark Lady of the Sonnet Knollys was also the uncle of the earl of Essex, whose faction he was at one time a member. He sul sequently abandoned it, and thus was characte ized by the followers of Essex as a "time server"– the same phrase which Maria uses to describe Ma volio. [Leslie Hotson, *The First Night of Twelft Night*, 1954.]

Mamillius. In *The Winter's Tale*, the young son Leontes and Hermione, a child who "makes o hearts fresh." Mamillius' insanely jealous father tak the boy from his mother. In II, iii, the gallant youn Prince, his thoughts "high for one so tender," reported ill; and when Leontes denies the judgme of Apollo's oracle, Mamillius dies from fear over th Queen's plight. His son's death brings the King to h senses and he repents his jealous suspicions.

Manners, Roger, 5th earl of **Rutland.** See RUTLAN THEORY.

Manningham, John (d. 1622). Diarist. Educate

or the law at Middle Temple, Manningham was alled to the bar in 1605. While a student at Middle 'emple he kept a diary for the period January 602 to April 1603. The journal provides a number f interesting insights into early 17th-century Lon- on life, including an account of a performance of 'welfth Night at Middle Temple on February 2, 602:

> At our feast wee had a play called "Twelve Night, or What You Will," much like the Commedy of Errores, or Menechmi in Plautus, but most like and neere to that in Italian called *Inganni.*

Ianningham goes on to describe the gulling of Ialvolio in that play, which he characterizes as "a ood practise." Manningham's diary is also the ource of the famous anecdote about Shakespeare nd Richard Burbage:

> Vpon a tyme when Burbidge played Rich. 3. there was a Citizen greue soe farr in liking with him, that before shee went from the play shee appointed him to come that night vnto hir by the name of Ri: the 3. Shakespeare overhearing their conclusion went before, was intertained, and at his game ere Burbidge came. Then message being brought that Rich. the 3.[d] was at the dore. Shakespeare caused returne to be made that William the Conquerour was before Rich. the 3. Shakespeare's name William.

The latter story shows some evidence of having een tampered with in the manuscript, and Sydney Race (*Notes & Queries*, 1954, 380–383) argues that he entire entry is a forgery inserted by John Payne Collier, who first called attention to the diary. [E. K. Chambers, *William Shakespeare*, 1930.]

Mansfield, Richard (1854–1907). American actor. Born in Berlin, where his mother, Erminia Ruders- orff, was then singing in opera, Mansfield spent most of his boyhood on tours. Finally, in 1872, sev- eral years after the death of his father, a London wine merchant, his mother settled in Boston as a inging teacher. Mansfield became involved in ama- eur theatrical enterprises and in 1876 went to Lon- on, giving entertainments and mimes in private ouses. A talented singer himself, he worked for a while with D'Oyly Carte in 1879. Until 1882 his areer consisted of small parts in provincial plays nd operettas. In that year, however, he returned to he United States and became famous in a role in *A Parisian Romance.* At the London Globe in 1889 Mansfield made his Shakespearean debut as Richard III, a production which he also brought to the United States, and which became one of his most mportant roles. In 1893 he played Shylock. He is oted for the first American performances of Shaw's *Arms and the Man* (1894) and *The Devil's Disciple* (1897). In 1900, Mansfield staged an elaborate *Henry V*, and in 1902 he played Brutus in *Julius Caesar.* His cting was in "the grand style" of repertory tradi- ion. A highly individual actor, he made full use of acial mimicry and eccentric speech effects. [William Winter, *Life and Art of Richard Mansfield,* 1910; *Dictionary of American Biography*, 1927– .]

Mantell, Robert Bruce (1854–1928). American actor. Born in Scotland, Mantell moved at an early age to Belfast, Ireland, where he began his stage career. In 1878 he emigrated to the United States, touring with an acting company headed by Helena Modjeska. His first part in America was that of Tybalt in *Romeo and Juliet.* During his long career he played a variety of Shakespearean roles, including Romeo, Hamlet, Othello, Macbeth, Richard III, Shylock, King Lear, and Iago. His acting was in the grand Victorian tradition, somber and slow-moving.

Mantuan. Real name **Baptista Spagnuoli** (1448–1516). Italian pastoral poet. A Carmelite monk (from Mantua) who eventually became general of the order, Mantuan is remembered for his Latin eclogues. These 10 poems, used as the basis for anticlerical and antiurban satire, broadened the scope of the pastoral form. They were extremely popular and influential in 16th-century England; they were imitated by Alexander Barclay (c. 1475–1552) in 1514 and translated by George Turberville (1540?–?1610) as *The Eglogs of the Poet Mantuan turned into English Verse* (1567). Mantuan's works, a basic part of the Elizabethan schools' curricula, were required reading for every schoolboy. Shakespeare pays tribute to him in *Love's Labour's Lost* (IV, ii, 101–102) with Holofernes' comment, "Old Mantuan, old Mantuan! who understandeth thee not, loves thee not."

Manzoni, Alessandro. See ITALY.

maps. See ENGRAVINGS OF LONDON.

Marcellus. In *Hamlet,* the officer who, with Bernardo, first saw the Ghost. After the spectre has twice appeared on the battlements, Marcellus and Bernardo bring Horatio to the scene of the apparition, and together the three inform Hamlet of the strange event they have witnessed (I, ii). When Hamlet speaks with the Ghost, Marcellus and Horatio are sworn to secrecy (I, v). The Elizabethan actor who first played Marcellus is thought to be the reporter of the "bad quarto" (Q1) of *Hamlet.* See MEMORIAL RECONSTRUCTION.

March, Earl of. See Sir Edmund de MORTIMER.

March, Edmund de Mortimer, 5th earl of (1391–1425). Son of Roger, 4th earl of March. Richard II having declared Roger heir to the throne, Edmund was widely regarded, after his father's death, as the future king. For this reason Henry IV put him under guard. Mortimer was later placed in custody of Prince Hal, whose loyal friend he remained, even after the prince became Henry V. Furthermore, refusing to cooperate in the 1415 plot of the earl of Cambridge to place him on the throne, Mortimer revealed the plot to Henry. He accompanied the king on the French campaign and subsequently retired to Ireland, where he died.

In *1 Henry VI,* Mortimer appears as an aged, failing prisoner in the Tower of London, where he has been confined since his youth. Having no issue, he names his nephew Richard Plantagenet his heir, after explaining the history of his imprisonment and his claim to the throne. Mortimer then wishes Richard prosperity, and dies (II, v). This incident did not occur in history. In *1 Henry IV* and *2 Henry VI* (II, ii), Shakespeare confuses the 5th earl of March with his uncle, Sir Edmund de MORTIMER.

March, Edward, earl of. See EDWARD IV.

Marcius. In *Coriolanus,* the son of the protagonist.

In V, iii, Marcius goes with Volumnia and Virgilia to his father's tent, where they plead with Coriolanus to spare Rome.

Marcus Andronicus. In *Titus Andronicus,* a tribune and the brother of Titus. He finds Titus' daughter Lavinia after she has been ravished and mutilated by Demetrius and Chiron. On discovering the perpetrators of this and other crimes against the family of Titus, Marcus joins with his brother in revenge on the family of the emperor Saturninus.

Mardian. In *Antony and Cleopatra,* a eunuch in attendance on Cleopatra. She sends Mardian to Antony with word that she has committed suicide (IV, xiii).

Margarelon. In *Troilus and Cressida,* an illegitimate son of King Priam of Troy. Margarelon challenges Thersites, who declares that he himself is "in every thing illegitimate" and will not fight another bastard (V, vii).

Margaret. In *Much Ado About Nothing,* a gentlewoman attending Hero, whose "wit is as quick as the greyhound's mouth." The saucy Margaret unintentionally becomes involved in the slander against Hero. Favoring Borachio, she contrives, at his bidding, to lean out her mistress's window while he woos her using Hero's name. Claudio and Don Pedro witness this encounter and are thus deceived into doubting Hero's virtue. When Borachio confesses his misdeeds, he vindicates Margaret of any willful wrongdoing. She is not, however, to be completely spared, for Leonato promises to have an explanation of "how her acquaintance grew with this lewd fellow."

Margaret, Queen. See MARGARET OF ANJOU.

Margaret of Anjou (1430–1482). Daughter of René Reignier, duke of Anjou. Betrothed to Henry VI of England after the peace negotiations at Tours in 1444, Margaret was married the following year, with the earl of Suffolk as proxy. She then traveled to London to be crowned. When her son, Edward, was born in 1453, the duke of York, who had hoped to succeed to the throne, became Margaret's bitter rival. Taking up arms against her, he defeated the royal army at St. Albans in 1455.

When parliament named York the protector and successor of the insane King Henry in 1460, Margaret arranged for her son's marriage to Mary, sister of James III of Scotland, and obtained the Scots' assistance in her cause. After York's death at Wakefield, however, his son Edward became king. With the help of the earl of Warwick, Edward IV delivered a crushing blow to Margaret's forces at Towton (1461), whereupon she fled with Henry to Scotland. Later, after a reconciliation with Warwick, Margaret was defeated at the battle of Tewkesbury in 1471, where her son was killed, and she and Henry were captured. On her release in 1476, Margaret was taken to France, where she died in poverty.

In *1 Henry VI,* Margaret is taken captive by Suffolk, who falls in love with her. Since he is already married, however, he brings her to England to become Henry's wife. In *2 Henry VI,* Margaret succeeds in having her rival, the Duchess of Gloucester, banished for sorcery, and arranges for the murder of the Duke. When Suffolk is subsequently ordered to be banished, Margaret openly avows her love for him. In *3 Henry VI,* Margaret raises an army against York when she hears that Henry has made him hi heir, bypassing her son, Edward. Defeating York a Wakefield, she stabs him to death. Edward anc Richard, York's sons, then rally forces and over come the Queen's army at Towton. Joined by War wick, Margaret is subsequently defeated in a battl near Tewkesbury and taken prisoner. She is ran somed by her father after the murder of Kin Henry. In *Richard III,* Margaret, Henry's widow curses the house of York and speaks of terribl things to come.

Marguerite de Valois (1553–1615). The daughte of Henry II of France and wife of HENRY O NAVARRE, whom she married unwillingly in 1572 In 1578, separated from her husband, she accom panied her mother, Catherine de Médicis, as ambas sadress of France in negotiations with Henry o Navarre. On this occasion she attempted to influ ence the outcome of the negotiations by employin the charms of her ladies-in-waiting on Henry and hi lords. The incident is generally regarded as th historical source of *Love's Labour's Lost* (see LOVE' LABOUR'S LOST: *Sources*). Like the princess in *Love' Labour's Lost,* Marguerite was witty and charming Her always tenuous relationship with Henry wa finally broken in 1599 when their marriage was dis solved by the pope.

Maria. In *Love's Labour's Lost,* a lady attendin the Princess of France. Maria is wooed by Longa ville, falls in love with him and, when required t return to France with the Princess, promises that i Longaville will wait a year in isolation for her, sh will be his.

Maria. In *Twelfth Night,* Olivia's gentlewoma a "most excellent devil of wit." The clever Maria, a originator of the intrigue against Malvolio and de viser of the love-letter scheme, so gratifies Sir Tob Belch that he marries her. She carefully tends "th fruits of the sport" with the duped steward, insinu ating his madness to Olivia, overseeing his "gentle care, and instigating Feste's imitation of a curate t further torment the misused Malvolio.

Mariana. In *All's Well That Ends Well,* a frien and neighbor of Diana's mother. Mariana warr Diana to beware of Bertram and Parolles (III, v).

Mariana. In *Measure for Measure,* Angelo's jilte fiancée. Though deserted by Angelo when he dowry was lost at sea, Mariana continues in her de votion and agrees to substitute for Isabella in a assignation with him. When Angelo's immorality exposed, the Duke orders him to marry Marian instantly, then sentences him to death. Quite sati fied with her knavish husband, Mariana is horrifie and appeals to Isabella to intercede on his behalf.

Marina. In *Pericles,* the lost daughter of the pro tagonist. Her adventures are the major elements Acts IV and V. A creature whose chastity is he outstanding characteristic, Marina was, not surpri ingly, one of the favorite heroines of the Victoria age. Her resistance to and conversion of the broth customers stirred the hearts of moralists who we at the same time repelled by the coarseness of th brothel scenes themselves. Moral aspects aside, hov ever, Marina's suffering and forbearance have a dr matic value, accounting for the sense of deliveranc which pervades the poignant and beautiful scene which she is reunited with her father (V, i).

Mariner. In *The Winter's Tale,* a sailor on th

ship that takes Antigonus to the "deserts of Bohemia" to abandon the child Perdita. The Mariner appears in III, iii, warning Antigonus that a storm is about to break and that there are beasts of prey on the shore.

Markham, Gervase or **Jervis** (c. 1568–1637). Author. Markham was a member of the circle of young men who in the early 1590's flocked under the banner of the earl of Essex. He served as an officer under Essex in Ireland. Apparently he turned to writing as a means of livelihood, for he eventually produced a great number of works on a variety of subjects: religious verse, dramas, translations, a con-inuation of Sidney's *Arcadia*, and practical hand-books on horsemanship, archery, agriculture, angling, nawking, military science, and other fields. His earli-st work is *A discourse of Horsmanshippe* (1593), which contains a description of a horse similar to hat in *Venus and Adonis*. In *The dumbe Knight* (1608), a play written in collaboration with Lewis Machin (fl. 1608), there is an allusion to and quota-ion from Shakespeare's *Venus and Adonis*, stanzas ; and 39. The plot of the play is indebted to *Othello* nd its villain is a direct imitation of Iago. In *Shake-peare's Rival* Robert Gittings gives a detailed pres-ntation of his theory that Markham is the Rival Poet of the *Sonnets*. Gittings also argues that in the haracter of Don Armado in *Love's Labour's Lost* Shakespeare first drew a satiric portrait of Antonio Perez, a well-known Spaniard, and later rewrote the art in order to have it correspond to Markham. Robert Gittings, *Shakespeare's Rival*, 1960.]

Marlovian theory. Term used to describe the heory that Christopher MARLOWE is the author of he works ascribed to Shakespeare. In the 19th cen-ury Marlowe's name was frequently listed among he "groups" and "schools" (see BACONIAN THEORY) whom various anti-Stratfordians had put forth as LAIMANTS, but Marlowe's sole authorship was not ggested until the publication of a novel, *It Was Marlowe: A Story of the Secret of Three Centuries* 1895), by Wilbur Ziegler. In 1901 Dr. Thomas Corwin Mendenhall gave support to this thesis as a esult of the application of his method of determin-g the authorship of the plays. Mendenhall's ap-roach consisted of counting the number of letters 400,000 words of Shakespeare, discovering that hakespeare's "word of greatest frequency was the our-letter word." Upon examining the writings of Marlowe, he discovered the same phenomenon. Un-rtunately Mendenhall's theory never took into ac-ount that he was using modern spelling editions of e plays. Interest in the theory was revitalized by e appearance of Calvin Hoffman's *The Murder of e Man Who Was Shakespeare* (1955), which aimed that Marlowe's so-called murder in 1593 was reality a staged affair which enabled Marlowe to cape to France. Here he wrote the plays which ere transmitted to England through Marlowe's omosexual lover, Sir Thomas Walsingham.

The proof of the theory was supposed to be con-rmed in Walsingham's tomb. In 1956 Hoffman ceived permission to open the tomb, where nothing as found—not even Sir Thomas. [Frank W. Wads-orth, *The Poacher from Stratford*, 1958.]

Marlowe, Christopher (1564–1593). Playwright and et. When William Shakespeare began to write for e London theatre, probably in 1589/90, by far the most distinguished English dramatist was Christopher Marlowe. Marlowe, a cobbler's son, was christened at St. George's Church in the great cathedral town of Canterbury on February 26, 1564 (the date of his birth, like that of Shakespeare, can only be conjectured). Little is known of Marlowe's education before January 14, 1579 when he took up a scholarship at the King's School in Canterbury, a few weeks before his 15th birthday, after which he would have been ineligible for consideration.

In March 1581 Marlowe proceeded to Corpus Christi College, Cambridge, the recipient of a scholarship established by Matthew Parker, archbishop of Canterbury. A condition of this scholarship was that he might keep it for six years if he studied divinity in preparation for taking orders, only three if he did not. Marlowe held his for the full term (B.A., November 1585; M.A., July 1587), but although he learned much theology at Cambridge, he clearly had no intention of entering the priesthood.

Marlowe completed the requirements for the M.A. in March 1587, but in June, when it was time for the degree to be conferred, he found himself in difficulty with his university. The later days of his academic career had been distinguished by frequent, extended, and unexplained absences from Cambridge. The problem created by Marlowe's errant behavior was resolved in an extraordinary way. On June 29, 1587 Queen Elizabeth's privy council addressed appropriate Cambridge officials in cryptic terms:

> Their Lordships thought good to certifie that . . . he had behauved him selfe orderlie and discreetlie wherebie he had done her majestie good service, and deserved to be rewarded for his faithfull dealings: Their Lordships' request was . . . that he should be furthered in the degree he was to take this next Commencement: Because it was not her majestie's pleasure that anie one employed as he had been in matters touching the benefitt of his Countrie should be defamed by those that are ignorant in th'affaires he went about.

Obviously Marlowe had powerful friends, and obviously he had been engaged in some government service that the privy council did not choose to describe. When he came down to London in 1587 Marlowe had many irons in the fire: he was learned in theology and the classics; in addition to translations of Lucan and Ovid, he had almost certainly written his first play, *The Tragedy of Dido, Queen of Carthage*, and perhaps outlined or written the first part of *Tamburlaine the Great;* he had or soon gained entree to the theatrical company known as the Admiral's Men, and he had somehow become associated with Thomas Walsingham, the director of a squad of international spies. Playwriting gave Marlowe immortality; espionage, in all probability, brought him an early grave.

In the six remaining turbulent years, Marlowe established his reputation as the first man of the London theatre by writing half a dozen successful plays: *Tamburlaine the Great*, Parts I and II (c. 1587); *The Tragical History of Doctor Faustus*, (c. 1588); *The Jew of Malta* (c. 1589); *The Massacre at Paris* (1593); and *Edward II* (c. 1592). He established simultaneously a reputation as a threat to the peace and order of the state. In 1589 Marlowe spent 13 days in Newgate charged with murder. He was exonerated, but he was clearly party to a brawl that resulted in the murder. In Newgate he met a fellow prisoner named Poole, skilled at counterfeiting. After his release Marlowe allegedly stated "That he had as good Right to Coine as the Queen of England . . . ." In May 1592 two constables of Shoreditch petitioned for a peace bond against Marlowe, swearing that they lived in terror because of his presence in the neighborhood. On May 18, 1593, 12 days before his death, the privy council issued a warrant for his arrest on suspicion of freethinking, blasphemy, and atheism. Charges of irreligion against Marlowe began in 1588, continued throughout his years in London, and culminated in June 1593 in a deposition made by one Richard Baines, a scurvy character, later hanged, who attributed the following opinions to the playwright: "That Christ was a bastard and his mother dishonest"; "That the woman of Samaria & her sister were whores & that Christ knew them dishonestly"; "That St John the Evangelist was bedfellow to Christ and leaned alwaies in his bosome, that he used him as the sinners of Sodoma"; "That all they that love not tobacco & Boyes were fooles." It was perhaps fortunate that Marlowe did not live to answer these charges, including the implication of homosexuality, for the weight of the evidence is on the side of the accusers.

Thanks to the researches of Leslie Hotson (*The Death of Christopher Marlowe*) we know the circumstances of Marlowe's death. He spent most of the day of May 30, 1593 with three men of unsavory reputation, Ingram Friser, Robert Poley, and Nicholas Skeres, all of them in some way connected with Thomas Walsingham. They met at the house of one Eleanor Bull of Deptford, a village near Walsingham's estate at Scadbury, Kent, where Marlowe had gone to escape the plague then raging in London. After the evening meal Marlowe lay down on a bed; his companions sat on a bench hard by and played backgammon. An argument arose over the payment of the bill (Marlowe supposedly was Friser's guest). Marlowe left the bed, came up behind Friser, whose freedom of movement was restricted by close quarters on the bench, seized Friser's dagger and inflicted two flesh wounds on the top of Friser's head. Friser wheeled, took Marlowe by the hand or wrist, and grappled with him. When the action was over, Marlowe had received "then & there a mortal wound over his right eye of the depth of two inches & of the width of one inch; of which mortal wound the aforesaid Christopher Morley then & there instantly died."

The circumstances of Marlowe's death have caused much conjecture. Had Marlowe become a security risk? Did he know something the revelation of which would have been disastrous to the state or to important private persons? Was his death a planned assassination? Why did not the three rascals he was with simply overpower him instead of killing him? Probably we will never know. This much is clear: Marlowe was the provocateur. Friser's reaction was instinctive, and his killing of the man who had just stabbed him might well be regarded as justifiable homicide (Friser was pardoned on June 28). In any case, the only English playwright who might have given Shakespeare serious competition in the 1590's was dead at the age of 29.

Marlowe came to London obsessed with fantasti aspiration. He and the chief characters of his plays all suffering from egomania, personified the positive forward-thrusting spirit of the English Renaissance Marlowe was 24 when England, with the defeat o the Invincible Armada, became pre-eminent on th seas. The world was expanding before men's eyes as it is again today, and there were few more curiou about it than Marlowe. He knew the maps of Abraham Ortelius, the German cartographer, and if h did not know Richard Hakluyt personally, and it i possible that he did, he shared the enthusiasm fo exploration and discovery that drove Frobisher Drake, Hawkins, and Raleigh, among others, on th principal voyages Hakluyt described in *The Principall Navigations Voyages and Discoveries of th English Nation* (1589).

His brain stuffed with the magic names of "strond afar remote," his imagination fired by histories an legends of characters not in the roll of common men Marlowe with his "mighty line" and his peculia penchant for the bizarre, the perverse, the outré wrote plays the likes of which had never before bee seen on any stage. His heroes are, or strive to b superhuman. They are driven by insatiable ambition a curiosity that scorns the limits of the know world, a compulsive lust for power and wealth tha transcends natural desire, and a susceptibility to passion, notably love (of whatever sort) and sadisti revenge, that reveal their contempt for tradition notions of law and order. The careers of these characters Marlowe presents in loosely constructe episodic-operatic plots in which the main line is occasionally broken by moments of comedy so griml grotesque that many critics, probably in error, believe them to be spurious interpolations penned b hacks or by bumptious actors eager for an extr laugh.

While the formative influence of Marlowe upo Shakespeare is usually overstated, an examination o Marlowe's work in this connection yields som parallels and echoings that are worthy, interesting and of note (see Dido, Queen of Carthage; Edward II; Jew of Malta; Massacre at Paris; Tamburlaine). There have even been suggestions tha the influence worked in the reverse, that Marlow was indebted to Shakespeare. Because the chronology of the composition of Marlowe's plays and thos of Shakespeare is uncertain, and because of th dearth of information about Shakespeare's activitie during the "seven lost years," it is impossible to discuss with precision the literary interrelationship o these two playwrights. We know enough, howeve to venture some conclusions on the basis of probability. *Tamburlaine*, almost certainly, antedated an play Shakespeare wrote and established Marlowe a London's most promising writer for the theatre. I is likely that an eager young Shakespeare woul somehow have made the acquaintance of Marlowe a an early date (they lived near one another, Shakespeare in Shoreditch, Marlowe in Norton Folgate) Whatever their personal relationship, it is demonstrable that Shakespeare knew Marlowe's plays an poetry. There are hundreds of verbal echoes an dozens of comparable scenes and situations in th works of the two men. Frequently it is difficult t guess who is echoing or borrowing from whom (fo

THE
HISTORIE
OF
THE DAMNABLE
LIFE, AND DESERVED
DEATH OF DOCTOR
IOHN FAVSTVS.

Newly printed, and in conuenient places, imperfect matter amended: according to the true Copie printed at *Frankfort*; and translated into English,
By *P. R.* Gent.

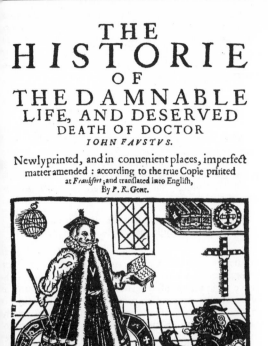

Printed at London for *Iohn Wright*, and are to be sold at the Sign of the *Bible* in *Giltspur-Street* without Newgate. 1636.

TITLE PAGE OF A TRANSLATION OF A GERMAN *Faustbuch* PUBLISHED IN 1587. THE GERMAN ORIGINAL IS THOUGHT TO BE A SOURCE OF MARLOWE'S PLAY.

example, did *Titus Andronicus* precede or follow *The Jew of Malta*? Which came first, *Richard III* or *The Massacre at Paris*?).

If we take the first part of *Tamburlaine* as the seminal document in the relationship, and there is no reason not to do so, several conclusions seem inevitable. The "mighty line" showed Shakespeare that King Cambyses' vein as the language of the theatre could be improved upon. The youthful Tamburlaine's successful defiance of all gods and fortune established a new basis for tragedy, one which had nothing, or little, to do with poetic justice. Marlowe helped create the mystery of Shakespeare's tragic world in which it is clear that although crime does not pay, neither necessarily does virtuous behavior. Goneril, Regan, Cornwall, and Edmund are dead at the end of *Lear*, but so are Lear and Cordelia. The epic scope of *Tamburlaine*, the geographical vastness of the scene and action, with its palpable rejection of the unities, opened vistas to Shakespeare's imagination that might not have come for years without the example of Marlowe.

Marlowe taught Shakespeare few tricks of stagecraft because there were few tricks possible on the stage they worked with. But Marlowe knew one thing that Shakespeare shared with him from the beginning of his career—the attention-getting value of a procession that included captives and/or coffins. *Tamburlaine* is exemplary; Shakespeare, after a few moments of exposition, opens *Titus Andronicus* with "two men bearing a coffin covered with black . . . then Titus Andronicus . . . then Tamora, the Queen of the Goths, and her two sons, Chiron and Demetrius, with Aaron the Moor and others, as many as can be . . . ." Especially effective was Marlowe's use of this device in the recessionals of *The Massacre at Paris* and *Edward II*. Shakespeare, with superior taste and sensitivity, outdid Marlowe in the final scenes of *Richard II* and *Hamlet*.

It is unlikely that Marlowe could have written Shakespeare's plays had he lived a thousand years (*pace* Calvin Hoffman). But Shakespeare would have been different, at least for a time, had Marlowe not lived. Shakespeare knew that he had learned from Marlowe; he also knew that he had gone beyond him. Shakespeare mocked the fustian bombast of Tamburlaine through the mouth of Ancient Pistol, and he ridiculed the senseless conjurations of Dr. Faustus with the hilarious contretemps between Owen Glendower and Hotspur. But in *As You Like It*, with obvious admiration and nostalgic affection, Shakespeare remembered his brilliant, if disturbed, colleague thus:

> Dead shepherd, now I find thy saw of might,
> 'Who ever lov'd that lov'd not at first sight?'
> (III, v, 81–82)

[Leslie Hotson, *The Death of Christopher Marlowe*, 1925; Una Ellis-Fermor, *Christopher Marlowe*, 1927; John E. Bakeless, *Christopher Marlowe, The Man in His Time*, 1937; F. S. Boas, *Christopher Marlowe, A Biographical and Critical Study*, 1940; Paul H. Kocher, *Christopher Marlowe, A Study of his Thought, Learning, and Character*, 1946; Harry Levin, *The Overreacher, A Study of Christopher Marlowe*, 1952; F. P. Wilson, *Marlowe and the Early Shakespeare*, 1954; J. B. Steane, *Marlowe, A Critical Study*, 1964.]—G.W.M.

Marlowe, Julia (1866–1950). American actress. Born in England, Julia Marlowe came to the United States at the age of five. She excelled in all the great Shakespearean female roles, including Juliet, Rosalind, Viola, Ophelia, and Lady Macbeth, and she is particularly remembered for her portrayal of Cleopatra. In 1911 she married the actor Edward Hugh Sothern, and their union was one of the most celebrated in American theatre history.

Marprelate, Martin. The pseudonym used by the authors of the Marprelate pamphlets, a series of seven Puritanical tracts attacking the Episcopal structure of the Anglican church. The identity of the author of the pamphlets remains unknown, but there was probably more than one; eligible candidates include John Penry (d. 1593), at whose press the pamphlets were printed, Sir Roger Williams, Job Throkmorton (1545–1601), and John Udall (1560?–1592). The Anglican authorities, led by the archbishop of Canterbury, John Whitgift, spared no effort in their attempt to suppress the pamphlets. Houses were raided, presses seized, and numerous suspects imprisoned and tortured. Nevertheless, the waspish "Martin" continued his attacks for two years (1588–1589). The bishops themselves attempted to counter the influence of the Marprelate tracts but their formal and sober replies were no match for the sprightly but scurrilous prose of Martin. In desperation the bishops turned to professional writers, including Thomas Nashe, John Lyly, and Robert Greene. At this point the controversy became even livelier, the quarrels being marked by references to the stage. The playwrights lost no time in castigating the Martinists in a number of plays, none of which is extant. One stage presentation must have won considerable fame, however, for it was frequently alluded to and credited with the "defeat" of Martin, as in the following anti-Martinist tract, *A Countercuffe given to Marin Iunior* . . . :

> The Anotamie latelie taken of him, the blood and the humors that were taken from him, by launcing and worming him at London vpon the common Stage . . . are euident tokens, that beeing thorow soust in so many showres, hee had no other refuge but to runne into a hole, and die as he liued, belching.

Of the series, probably the best of the Puritan pieces are *Hay any worke for Cooper* (1589), *The just censure and reproofe of Martin Junior* (1589), an ironic "reply" to an earlier Marprelate tract, and *The Protestacyon of Martin Marpelat* (1589). The best defenses of the bishops' position were Lyly's *Pappe with a Hatchet* (1589) and Nashe's *An Almond for a Parrat* (1590). The Marprelate controversy had a significant effect on the prose style of later English satirists.

J. Dover Wilson has put forth a dual hypothesis in connection with the authorship of the Marprelate tracts: first, that the major author was Sir Roger WILLIAMS, a Welsh soldier of Puritan sympathies, and second, that Sir Roger is Shakespeare's model for the character Fluellen in *Henry V*. [J. Dover Wilson, *Martin Marprelate and Shakespeare's Fluellen*, 1912.]

marriage and funeral customs. Betrothals had lost some of the strict legal importance of earlier times, but in the Elizabethan age they were still formally contracted. In *Twelfth Night*, Olivia asks Sebastian to go with her into the chantry and there, in the presence of a holy man, to "Plight me the full assurance of your faith" (IV, iii, 26). Betrothals were often considered as binding as marriage, particularly when the parties were unable to wed for some time because of external circumstances. Shakespeare himself was perhaps betrothed to Anne Hathaway before their marriage (see MARRIAGE). Rings were often exchanged as betrothal gifts, or two halves of a coin divided between the lovers. A gimmal, or jointed ring, which separated into two rings was sometimes used, each of the affianced parties wearing one until the marriage, when the two parts were joined to make the wedding ring. Other types of wedding rings included an enameled hoop set with small stones, or a ring formed of two hands clasping a heart made of a jewel. The plain gold wedding ring did not come into use until the time of the Puritans.

Brides usually wore white or russet (homespun cloth of a reddish-brown color) decorated with colored ribbons tied in love knots; these were customarily snatched by male guests after the ceremony and worn as trophies in their hats. The bride's hair was unbound and her head crowned with a garland of wheatears or flowers. The bridegroom customarily wore a bunch of rosemary tied with ribbons which was symbolic of his manliness. After the ceremony the wedding party drank a cup of muscatel with sops (cake) in it, as Petruchio after his mad marriage in *The Taming of the Shrew*

> quaff'd off the muscadel
> And threw the sops all in the sexton's face.
> (III, ii, 174–175)

A feast customarily followed the ceremony, with festivities sometimes lasting for many days.

Funerals were surrounded by many customs such as the use of the passing bell to signal a death in the parish, to which Shakespeare refers in *Venus and Adonis:*

> And now his grief may be compared well
> To one sore sick that hears the passing-bell.
> (701–702)

Mourners usually carried small branches of evergreens, such as bay or rosemary, to throw into the grave as symbols of the soul's immortality. Bunches of rosemary or yew were often tied to the side of the coffin, which was draped in black or, in the case of royalty, in purple. Flowers were strewn on the grave, and the biers of young unmarried women hung with garlands or "crants"; the priest says of Ophelia's burial,

> Yet here she is allow'd her virgin crants,
> Her maiden strewments.
> (*Hamlet*, V, i, 255–256)

When a nobleman was interred in a church it was customary to hang his sword and hatchment (a tablet with his armorial bearings) over his tomb; grieving Laertes speaks of his father's

> obscure funeral—
> No trophy, sword, nor hatchment o'er his bones.
> (*Hamlet*, IV, v, 213–214)

At the conclusion of the funeral there was an elaborate feast with various kinds of cold foods, wines, and ale. Like wedding feasts, funeral feasts often lasted for days. Hamlet sarcastically accounts for his mother's hasty marriage as being motivated by reasons of

> Thrift, thrift, Horatio! the funeral baked meats
> Did coldly furnish forth the marriage tables.
> (I, ii, 180–181)

[Percy Macquoid, "The Home," *Shakespeare's England*, 1916.]

marriage of Shakespeare. In November 1582 when Shakespeare was not quite 19 years old, he married Anne Hathaway (see HATHAWAY FAMILY), the daughter of a well-to-do farmer of Shottery, a hamlet about 2 miles north of Stratford-upon-Avon. The members of the two families had long been friends. John Shakespeare, a few years earlier, had gone surety for Hathaway in a suit for the collection of a debt.

It has been taken for granted, though it is by no means certain, that at the time of her marriage Anne was 26 years old. On a brass plate affixed to a slab over her grave (she died in 1623) the following words are inscribed: "Here lyeth interred the body of Anne, wife of William Shakespeare, who departed this life the 6th day of August, being of the age of 67 years." The arabic numerals 67 are now illegible. This inscription, along with others on the Shakespeare tombs, was copied for, or by, Sir William DUGDALE and first published in his *Antiquities of Warwickshire* (1656). An entry in this volume is the only evidence of Anne's age—and in other instances Dugdale's figures are wrong.

The circumstances under which Anne's marriage was contracted were somewhat unusual. An ecclesiastical ceremony of marriage was normally performed only after the banns were three times published; that is, notice given of the intended marriage of the espoused persons in their parish churches on three successive Sundays or holy days. But under unusual conditions a pair could marry after only one asking of banns, by obtaining a special license from the bishop of the diocese, in this case the bishop of Worcester. However, a special decree of the church forbade announcing of banns and the performance of the marriage ceremony between the first Sunday of Advent and the Octave of the Epiphany, eight days after January 6. In 1582 this period of prohibition began December 2. Hence, William and Anne would have been able to solemnize their marriage only after a lapse of two months from the time they instituted the proceedings. For reasons that will presently appear, they did not wish to be thus delayed. See Anne WHATELY.

Before the bishop could grant the special license, he was obliged to give valid reason for tendering it. Moreover, if either of the applicants was not of age, they had to make a formal allegation that the parents or guardians of each contracting party gave their consent. Since Shakespeare was only 18 this provision disposes of the notion that his parents were ignorant of his marriage, much less had actively opposed it. It also gives the lie to the often expressed opinion that their son's marriage was a runaway match.

A bond also had to be filed and signed by two financially responsible citizens protecting the bishop from any suits brought against him for ignoring possible impediments to the union on the grounds of "precontract, consanguinity, and affinity." Such a bond, filed and dated November 28, 1582, was signed by two substantial yeomen, long-time friends of the Hathaway family, Fulk Sandells and John Richardson. The filing of the bond was usually immediately followed by the delivery of the license to the clergyman who was to perform the ceremony. William and Anne lost no time in presenting themselves for the church wedding. It probably took place on the same day as the filing of the bond. Haste was clearly imperative, for their first child, Susanna, was baptized in Stratford on May 26, 1583.

These facts have often been taken as showing a discreditable sexual relationship between the pair; but this is not a necessary assumption. Marriage customs in Shakespeare's day were different from those now in vogue. Then the folk ritual of precontract or troth plight (pledge of betrothal) made a marriage legal in the eyes of both the church and the law. The man and woman adopted the prescribed rite of a betrothal before witnesses, often in a private house or even the room of an inn. No official record of a troth plight was made, but custom had established it as a quasi-legal agreement that conferred all the rights of marriage on the two participants in the informal solemnity, although the marriage had to be solemnized in order to prove the wife's right to dower or the offspring's right to inherit. We do not know that William and Anne made such a precontract, but it might well have happened. On February 2, 1585, less than two years after Susanna's birth, the twins Hamnet and Judith were baptized in Stratford.

Many biographers assume that the marriage was an unhappy one, that Shakespeare was forced or seduced into a union that he always regretted. It is gratuitous to assume that since Anne had no further children after the birth of the twins, Hamnet and Judith, that the two never afterward lived together as man and wife, or that Shakespeare, after leaving Stratford for London, neglected her and her children. For all we know, Anne Hathaway may have been an amiable woman and the poet a devoted husband. [J. O. Halliwell-Phillipps, *Outlines of the Life of Shakespeare*, 1881; Joseph William Gray, *Shakespeare's Marriage*, 1905.]—O. J. C.

Marsh, Charles. See ADAPTATIONS.

Marshall, William (fl. 1630–1650). Engraver who produced for the 1640 edition of Shakespeare's *Poems* a carefully wrought cut of the Droeshout Portrait in the First Folio. Marshall was the most prolific engraver of his day. Almost all of his work consisted of book illustrations. In addition to Shakespeare's portrait, he engraved portraits of John Donne (1635), Francis Bacon (1640), and John Milton (1645).

Marston, John (1576–1634). Dramatist and satirist. The son of a prosperous lawyer, Marston studied law at Middle Temple, after graduating from Oxford, but abandoned it in order to pursue a writing career. His strong satiric strain revealed itself in his first published works, *The Metamorphosis of Pygmalion's Image* (1598) and *The Scourge of Villanie* (1598), both written under the pseudonym, W. Kinsayder.

Marston began his career as a dramatist by writing for the Admiral's Men, but shifted to the Children of St. Paul's when that troupe was established in 1599. For that company he wrote *Antonio and Mellida*, (1599), *Jack Drum's Entertainment* (1600), and collaborated with Dekker in an attack on Jonson (see WAR OF THE THEATRES) in *Satiromastix* (1601). The dispute with Jonson was apparently more than literary. According to William Drummond's *Conversations of Ben Jonson with William Drummond of Hawthornden* (1842), "He had many quarrels with Marston, beat him and took his pistol from him, wrote his *Poetaster* on him; the beginning of them were, that Marston represented him on the stage." The quarrel was ultimately patched up, for in 1604 Marston dedicated his best-known play, THE MALCONTENT, to Jonson and collaborated with him and Chapman on EASTWARD HO! (1605). The truce was apparently short-lived, however, for in the epistle to his next play, *Sophonisba* (1606), Marston was again making sarcastic allusions to Jonson.

In 1608 Marston was jailed on an unknown charge. Sometime after, he quit the stage and entered the church. He secured the living at Christchurch,

Hampshire, where he lived until 1631. He died on June 25, 1634.

Marston's *Antonio and Mellida* bears a resemblance to *Hamlet*, particularly in the "closet scene" (III, iv) of the latter, but there is no certainty as to which play came first. Shakespeare may be indebted to *The Malcontent* for the incident of Gloucester's attempted suicide in *King Lear*. Marston alludes directly to *Romeo and Juliet* in *The Scourge of Villanie:*

> *Luscus*, what's playd to day? faith now I know
> I set thy lips abroach, from whence doth flow
> Naught but pure *Iuliat* and *Romio*.
> Say, who acts best? *Drusus* or *Roscio?*
> Now I have him, that nere of ought did speake
> But when of playes or Plaiers he did treate.
> H'ath made a common-place booke out of plaies,
> And speakes in print: at least what ere he sayes
> Is warranted by Curtaine plaudeties.

This allusion is usually cited as further evidence that Shakespeare's company was at the Curtain in 1598 before the building of the Globe.

Martext, Sir Oliver. In *As You Like It*, the vicar who proposes to marry Touchstone and Audrey. Jaques, however, advises Touchstone to find "a good priest that can tell you what marriage is" (III, iii).

Martin-Harvey, Sir John Martin (1863–1944). Actor and manager. Martin-Harvey began his career with Henry Irving's company and his subsequent career bore the mark of Irving's influence. In 1899 he took over the management of the Lyceum Theatre where in 1904 he produced and starred in *Hamlet*, one of his most successful roles. Other well-known Shakespearean productions included *Richard III* (1910) and *The Taming of the Shrew* (1913). During the tercentenary celebration in 1916, he revived these three plays along with *Henry V* at His Majesty's Theatre. Martin-Harvey was knighted in 1921 and received an honorary LL.D. from the University of Glasgow in 1938. His *Autobiography* was published in 1933.

Marullus. See FLAVIUS AND MARULLUS.

Martius. In *Titus Andronicus*, one of Titus' younger sons. With his brother Quintus, Martius falls into the pit where Tamora's sons have thrown the body of Bassianus. He and Quintus are accused of having murdered him and are executed.

Marxist criticism. Criticism of Shakespeare in the context of the Marxist view of literature has, naturally enough, been centered in the Soviet Union (see RUSSIA). There is, however, a substantial body of English and American criticism devoted to a Marxist analysis of the plays.

In general, Marxist critics view Shakespeare in the light of a Marxist interpretation of the social, political, and economic processes that took place in the reigns of Elizabeth and James. Elizabeth's reign is viewed as the culmination of the assimilation of the old nobility by the embryonic capitalists of the middle class who had risen to power under Henry VIII. This situation produced an intellectual and cultural climate uniquely favorable to art, permitting both the retention of traditional forms and a new freedom in selection of content. Thus, in his history plays Shakespeare is seen as celebrating the emerging nationalist spirit of the Renaissance. This national spirit temporarily breathed new life into th decaying class structure, a fact which enable Shakespeare to celebrate society in the optimisti manner of his joyous comedies. By 1599, howeve the inevitable conflict between the new bourgeoisi and the new nobility manifested itself and wa reflected in the political ambivalences and doubts c *Julius Caesar*, written in that year.

The Jacobean reign (1603–1625) is viewed as reassertion of medieval feudalism, to which Shake speare reacted with the unqualified disgust reflecte in his tragedies and problem plays. Shakespeare' social conscience and awareness, these critic acknowledge, is rarely directly expressed. Rathe it is to be seen in the profoundly personal transfor mation of individual characters and in the gener picture of humanity reflected in the plays, particu larly the tragedies.

Shakespeare's final period—the period of th romances—is seen as his attempt to compromis with the decadent aristocratic taste of the Jacobea court, a compromise dictated by economic pres sures. Even here, however, his profound awarenes of the processes of history is evident, particularl in his last great play, *The Tempest*.

In fine, Shakespeare is seen by the Marxists as "revolutionary humanist" whose nonreligious an materialist view of life incorporated the best feature of a revolutionary age, the Renaissance. To mos students of Shakespeare these views, howeve plausible in some details, add up to a distorte picture of Shakespeare and his plays. [A. A Smirnov, "Shakespeare: A Marxist Interpretation," *Approaches to Shakespeare*, Norman Rabkin, ed 1964; *Shakespeare in a Changing World*, Arnol Kettle, ed., 1964.]

Masefield, John (1878–). Poet. In 1930, upo the death of Robert Bridges, Masefield was appointe poet laureate. A substantial selection from his wor can be found in *Poems* (1951). Masefield has writte plays, essays, literary criticism, history, fiction, an autobiography as well as poetry. Several of his play show the influence of the Elizabethans. In *Th Tragedy of Pompey the Great* (1909) he followe Shakespeare in drawing upon Sir Thomas North' version of Plutarch's *Lives* for material. With *Th Faithful* (1915), set in 18th-century Japan, he acknowledges a debt to Granville-Barker's Shakespearean productions by constructing the play fo continuous action on a platform stage. *Philip th King* (1914) deals with Philip II of Spain, and *En and Beginning* (1933), with the last days of Mary Queen of Scots. For the Home University Library Masefield wrote a popular introduction, *William Shakespeare* (1911; rev., 1964). In 1924 he delivered the Romanes Lecture, "Shakespeare and Spiritual Life" (see SYMBOLISM), which was reprinted in *Recent Prose* (1933 ed.).

Mason, John Monck (1726–1809). Irish politician Educated at Trinity College, Dublin, Mason was admitted to the bar in 1752, and from 1761 he served intermittently in parliament. In 1779 he published an edition of Massinger's plays. A contemplated edition of Shakespeare was abandoned when he found that many of his emendations and comments had been anticipated in Isaac Reed's edition of 1785. His *Comments on the Last Edition of Shakespeare's Plays*

1785) is an abridged version of what he had intended as notes to his edition. George Steevens inserted many of Mason's notes into his own edition, giving him credit for being, "with all his extravagances," a person of some intelligence and erudition. In *Comments on the Plays of Beaumont and Fletcher* (1797) Mason included an appendix consisting of "some further observations on Shakespeare." He published a final volume entitled *Comments on the Several Editions of Shakespeare's Plays, extended to those of Malone and Steevens* (1807).

masque. A form of dramatic entertainment. The masque, like the drama itself, originates in primitive fertility rites. It enters the Elizabethan stage from two sources: as an importation from the court entertainments of 15th-century Italy, and as an elaboration of the native English tradition of mummery. The mummers were ordinary citizens who masked and disguised themselves, often as spirits or animals, on public holidays, particularly around Christmas, to serenade their neighbors and invade their houses in a spirit of revelry. The central elements of the masque were fantastic disguise, music, and dancing; its culmination was usually a revel or dance that united the players and the spectators.

As the masque developed, the original components of grotesqueness and sudden transformation of ordinary life by a party of celebrators became subdued, and more graceful elements predominated. Among the aristocracy the masque took the form of an unexpected visit to a friend's house, in which the visitors wore masks, brought gifts, and were accompanied by musicians and entertainers. Renaissance Italy introduced the masque into pastoral comedy, where the simple and idyllic plot provided a harmonious background for allegory, elaborate costuming, and dance. It is primarily in this nondramatic, spectacular form, part opera and part ballet, that Shakespeare uses the masque.

Under James I, arising in part from Queen Anne's taste for opulence and gaiety, the court masque entered the period of its greatest elaboration and importance. Enormous sums of money were spent on costumes, scenery, and mechanical pageant-effects, such as castles or ships mounted on wheels and moved into the performance hall. Inigo JONES, an artist trained in Italy, was responsible for the magnificence of the spectacles, and Ben Jonson must be credited with the high literary distinction achieved by the Jacobean masque. It was Jonson who "invented" the antimasque, a comic or grotesque contrast to the masque proper, which really constituted a re-introduction of some of the oldest elements of the masque tradition. Jonson's *Masque of Queens* (1609), for example, uses a dance of 12 hideous witches preliminary to the presentation of the 12 good queens in the House of Fame.

At the peak of its development, the masque retained the central theme of the culminating, all-embracing dance, set within a coherent poetic context. Lyric expressions by mythological characters or personified abstractions, such as Fame and Virtue, were combined with light, color, and movement to yield scenes of fairy-like beauty and charm.

Shakespeare introduces the masque into several of his plays. In *Love's Labour's Lost*, *Romeo and Juliet*, and *Much Ado About Nothing* the masque is used to set the mood of the scene and to enrich the stage spectacle. In *Timon of Athens* (I, ii) Timon's luxury is marked with the stage direction: "Re-enter Cupid, with a mask of Ladies as Amazons, with lutes in their hands, dancing and playing." The masque in *Henry VIII* is presented as an embodiment of Queen Katharine's dream. In the later plays, such as *A Midsummer Night's Dream*, the masque becomes a more pervasive influence, a structural element rather than an incidental diversion. Here the magical influence of mythological and fairy realms on more formal societies is integral to the plot and the meaning of the play.

Massacre at Paris, The (1593). A tragedy by Christopher MARLOWE. It was first published with no date as "The Massacre at Paris: With the Death of the Duke of Guise. As it was plaide by the right honourable the Lord high Admirall his Seruants. Written by Christopher Marlow."

A chronicle play, *The Massacre at Paris* covers the murder of Gaspard de Coligny and the Massacre of St. Bartholomew in 1572, the murder of the duke of Guise in 1588, the murder of Henry III and Henry of Navarre's accession in 1589.

F. P. Wilson suggests that what attracted Marlowe to this material was the character of Guise, "the character of a man who uses religion as a stalking-horse, and the game which he shoots at is absolute power, the crown of France." Guise's one extant soliloquy, like the opening soliloquy of Shakespeare's *Richard III*, is an avowed determination to be a villain.

In writing *Massacre*, Marlowe must have had Shakespeare's *3 Henry VI* in mind when he wrote the lines (1376–1377)

> Sweet Duke of Guise, our prop to lean upon
> Now thou art dead, here is no stay for us.

so closely do they parallel

> Sweet Duke of York, our prop to lean upon,
> Now thou art gone, we have no staff, no stay.
> (*3 Henry VI*, II, i, 68–69)

Further, line 953 of *Massacre*, "And we are graced with wreaths of victory," is the same as *3 Henry VI*, V, iii, 2. [E. K. Chambers, *William Shakespeare*, 1930; F. P. Wilson, *Marlowe and the Early Shakespeare*, 1953.]

Massinger, Philip (1583–1640). Dramatist. The son of a gentleman in the confidential service of Henry Herbert, 2nd earl of Pembroke, Massinger was educated at Oxford, which he left at the time of his father's death in 1606. In 1613, he, the actor Nathan Field, and playwright Robert Daborne were imprisoned, apparently for debt. They appealed to Philip Henslowe for a £5 advance on a play on which they were collaborating with John Fletcher. In 1616, Massinger and Fletcher collaborated in the writing of several plays for the King's Men. Massinger's first independent play was *The Duke of Milan* (1621/2), a drama bearing a strong resemblance to *Othello*. *The Bondman* (1623), one of a series of plays he wrote for Lady Elizabeth's Men, was dedicated to Philip Herbert (earl of Montgomery and co-dedicatee of the 1623 Shakespeare First Folio) and satirized Herbert's powerful enemy, the duke of Buckingham. At the death of Fletcher in 1625, Massinger became the chief playwright of the King's Men, remaining with them until his death.

Massinger's best-known play, *A New Way to Pay Old Debts* (1626), is a comedy of intrigue based on Thomas Middleton's *A Trick to Catch the Old One* (1608) and is noted for its chief comic character, Sir Giles Overreach. Overreach is based on a protégé of Buckingham's, Sir Giles Mompesson, and is one of the most popular roles in the English dramatic repertory. Overreach bears a strong resemblance to Shylock as well, and the play as a whole is indebted to *The Merchant of Venice*. There are other parallels evident between the two dramatists, and on the basis of these similarities an attempt has been made to prove that Massinger and not Shakespeare was Fletcher's associate in writing *Two Noble Kinsmen* and *Henry VIII*. Massinger's use of Shakespeare is undeniable and extensive; T. A. Dunn estimates that Massinger knew and echoed the language of at least 23 of Shakespeare's plays, his favorites being *Hamlet* and *Othello*. [T. A. Dunn, *Philip Massinger*, 1957.]

Master. In *2 Henry VI*, one of the crew of pirates who capture Suffolk. The Captain gives him a prisoner as his share of the booty (IV, i).

Master-Gunner of Orléans. In *1 Henry VI*, a French officer who aims his cannon at the secret grate through which the English observe the activities of the French in Orléans. His son fires the shot that kills the Earl of Salisbury and Sir Thomas Gargrave (I, iv).

Master of a Ship. In *The Tempest*, I, i, the captain whose vessel is endangered by Prospero's storm.

Master of the Revels. The official of the lord chamberlain's department who arranged, supervised, and paid for court entertainment. Originally the term of office was temporary, assigned to a household official for a particular court entertainment. However, as the theatre assumed a larger and more significant place in London life, the responsibility and power of the Master of the Revels increased. The sway of the office expanded greatly between 1579 and 1609 under Edmund Tilney, who obtained the right to read and license all plays before their performance; the Master thus became the official censor of plays. The precious copy containing the signed and stamped license of the Master of the Revels was bound into the prompt-book, or text of the play, and carefully preserved. Tilney considered it his duty to eliminate from texts submitted to him "all profaneness, oaths [even such mild ones as "faith," "death," and "slight"], ribaldry and matters reflecting upon piety and the present government." It was undoubtedly he who ordered the elimination of the deposition scene in *Richard II* (see censorship). In 1607 this privilege was increased to include the licensing of all plays before they could be printed. The Revels Office achieved its greatest power during the first 20 years (1623–1642) of the administration of Sir Henry Herbert, who endeavored to extend his power as censor to include all public entertainment. The radical nature of Sir Henry's censorship can be seen from a few examples from his office-book records: "This day, being the 11 of January 1630, I did refuse to allow a play of Massingers, because it did contain dangerous matter, as the deposing of Sebastian king of Portugal." . . . and June 8, 1648: "Received of Mr. Kirke, for a new play which I burnte for the ribaldr and offense that was in it" (£2). Sir Henry's dutie ended with the closing of the theatres (1642), an despite attempts to regain authority after the Resto ration the position fell into disuse.

The title of Master dates back to 1494 but the posi tion was not a permanent one until 1545 when Si Thomas Cawarden (d. 1559) was appointed. Cawar den held the office until his death, being succeede in turn by Sir Thomas Benger (d. 1572). At Benger' death no new appointment was made until 1579 whe Edmund Tilney succeeded to the title. Tilney serve until his death in 1609 and was succeeded in the fol lowing year by his deputy, Sir George Buc. Buc wa succeeded by Sir John Astley (Ashley), who shortl thereafter sold the office to Sir Henry Herbert, wh held the position into the Restoration period. [E. K Chambers, *Notes on the History of the Revels Offic under the Tudors*, 1906.]

Master's Mate. In *2 Henry VI*, one of the crew c pirates who capture Suffolk. In IV, i, he is offere his share of booty.

Masuccio Salernitano. Real name **Tommaso Gua dati** (1420–c. 1480). Italian novelist. The first of th horde of Italian imitators of Boccaccio's *Decamero* (1353), Masuccio of Salerno was probably also th best. His *Il Novellino* (1476), a collection of pros romances, includes the story of Mariotto and Gia nozza, a tale which bears a strong resemblance t *Romeo and Juliet*. Masuccio may also be the sourc of the romance of Lorenzo and Jessica in *The Me chant of Venice*. [Geoffrey Bullough, *Narrative an Dramatic Sources of Shakespeare*, Vol. I, 1957.]

Mathews, Charles James (1803–1878). Actor an playwright. The son of Charles Mathews (177 1835), Mathews was born in Liverpool. Although h was trained as an architect, he was involved in th theatre for many years both as an amateur actor an as a writer of songs and entertainments. At h father's death in 1835, he succeeded him as manag of the Adelphi Theatre, a short-lived, luckless ve ture. He then became a professional actor and w moderately successful. In 1838 he married his man ger, Elizabeth Vestris, and together they manage the Covent Garden Theatre. Their first seaso opened with an elaborate revised version of *Love Labour's Lost* which proved a failure and plunge the pair into debt. Subsequent productions, howeve drew in customers, particularly their *Beggar's Ope* and *The Merry Wives of Windsor*. (In the latte Mathews played Slender.) By 1842, when their ma agement of the theatre ended, they had produce over 100 plays, operas, and interludes, farces, mel dramas, and pantomimes; their Shakespearean offe ings had included *Hamlet, Romeo and Julie Twelfth Night*, and 70 performances of *A Midsum mer Night's Dream*. Mathews never recovered h financial stability and was even imprisoned for de in 1842 and again in 1856. After his wife's death, h left his country for America where he met his se ond wife, Mrs. Lizzie Davenport. He returned t England and in the 1870's toured Australia, Hon lulu, the United States, Canada, and India, as well his native English countryside. [*Dictionary of N tional Biography*, 1921–1922.]

Matthews, [James] Brander (1852–1929). Amer can scholar. For two decades Matthews was active i the literary, dramatic, and social life of New York; he contributed frequently to literary periodicals and wrote several plays. In 1900 he was made professor of dramatic literature at Columbia University, the first such position in an American university. Matthews continued to write extensively, his books reflecting his academic environment but never losing their popular appeal. Works of this period include two studies of the drama, a study of Molière, and *Shakspere as a Playwright* (1913). With A. H. Thorndike he edited *Shakespearean Studies* (1916), a collection of essays by members of the English department of Columbia on the occasion of the tercentenary of Shakespeare's death. Matthews' autobiography, *These Many Years* (1917), gives a vivid account of his many-sided activities.

Mayne, Jasper (1604–1672). Poet and divine. Mayne has been suggested as the "I. M." (see M., I.) who wrote a commendatory verse to the First Folio (1623) and as the "I. M. S." (Jasper Mayne, Student) who is the author (see FRIENDLY ADMIRER) of the admirable poem prefixed to the Second Folio (1632). Mayne's extant poetry, however, is of a quality considerably inferior to these two prefatory poems. He did contribute a poem to *Jonsonus Virbius* (1638), a collection of verses in memory of Ben Jonson. In it Mayne makes the following allusion to Shakespeare:

> Who without *Latine* helps had'st beene as *rare*
> As *Beaumont*, *Fletcher*, or as *Shakespeare* were:
> And like *them*, from thy *native Stock* could'st say,
> *Poets* and *Kings* are not *borne* every day.

[*The Shakspere Allusion-Book*, J. Munro, ed., 1909.]

Mayor of London. See LORD MAYOR OF LONDON.

Mayor of St. Alban's. In *2 Henry VI*, he presents the rogue Simpcox to the King. When Simpcox' trickery is exposed, the Mayor is ordered to send for a whip (II, i).

Mayor of York. In *3 Henry VI*, a "good old man" who at first refuses to open the city gates to King Edward but is persuaded to yield his keys. Historically, the mayor was Thomas Beverly. He allowed the king to enter on the understanding that Edward was merely trying to regain his dukedom. [W. H. Thomson, *Shakespeare's Characters: A Historical Dictionary*, 1951.]

Mayowe, Thomas (fl. 1580). Yeoman. In 1581 Mayowe brought a Chancery suit against the Arden family. Mayowe's suit was designed to recover the property in Snitterfield which his grandfather John Mayowe had sold to Mary Arden's grandfather Thomas in 1501. In 1582 John Shakespeare, the poet's father, was called as a witness in the case, but his testimony has not survived. [Mark Eccles, *Shakespeare in Warwickshire*, 1961.]

Mazzini, Giuseppe. See ITALY.

Meade, Jacob (d. 1624). Theatre owner. Meade was a resident of the parish of St. Olaves in Southwark, and a close associate in the various enterprises of Philip HENSLOWE. In the 1613 contract which he and Henslowe concluded to build the HOPE THEATRE, he is identified as "Jacobe Maide . . . waterman." In 1599 he was keeper of the bears and part manager, with Philip Henslowe and Henslowe's son-in-law Edward Alleyn, of the Bear Garden (Paris Garden), where Henslowe and Alleyn were licensed to conduct regular exhibitions of bear-baiting. After Henslowe's death, Meade continued to participate with Alleyn in the latter's business operations, including management of Prince Charles' acting company. [E. K. Chambers, *The Elizabethan Stage*, 1923; G. E. Bentley, *The Jacobean and Caroline Stage*, 5 vols., 1941–1956.]

MEASURE
For Meaſure.

Measure for Measure. A comedy by Shakespeare.

Text. The only authoritative text, that of the First Folio, is not a good one, being full of obvious mistakes and of puzzling passages. The usual explanation of these blemishes is that the copy which the editors gave to the printer was either a transcript by the scrivener Ralph Crane of the official PROMPT-BOOK, which had been jumbled by the insertion of frequent changes and revisions made during the company's many stagings of the play, or Crane's transcript of the author's FOUL PAPERS, which had been left in a fairly rough state.

Date. According to an account of the Revels Office, the authenticity of which has been disputed, the play was acted at court on St. Stephen's Night, December 26, 1604. Since the public theatres had reopened only in April of that year after having been closed for a year because of a severe epidemic of the plague, the play was probably first staged sometime between April and December 1604. A number of references in the play lend support to this conjecture: for example, an allusion to negotiations to end the war between the Netherlands and Spain. These negotiations took place between April and August of 1604.

Sources. The principal source is George WHET-

STONE's two-part play *Promos and Cassandra* (1578). Whetstone repeated the plot in his *Heptameron of Civill Discourses* (1582). He found the story in Giovanni Battista Giraldi's (called Cinthio) collection of tales entitled *Hecatommithi* (1565) where it appeared as the 5th novel of the 10th day. Later, Cinthio dramatized the story in a play (published 1583) called *Epitia,* the name of the heroine. Whetstone cannot have known this play. The facts which Cinthio slightly romanticized were those of a sordid Italian incident described in a letter written in 1547 by a Hungarian student. This is what he reported: "A citizen of a small Italian village was condemned to death for murder. His sister, a beautiful girl, begged the judge to pardon her brother. This he promised to do if she would yield her honor to him. Although she prostituted herself, the judge, nevertheless, had her brother beheaded. The girl appealed to the Emperor for redress. He responded by forcing the wicked judge to marry her and then having him executed." Traces of this tragedy in real life remain in all the reworkings of the plot, dramatic and nondramatic. They account for some of the melodramatic features of *Measure for Measure.* The civic corruption that seethes in Whetstone's Hungary, where he chose to set his play, Shakespeare converted into the low-comedy activities of the libertines, bawds, and whores who infested the houses of prostitution in the suburbs. His invention is at its best in the creation of Lucio, the sprightly patron of the bawdyhouses. In type he is a buffoon who adopts in his comments a careless, cynical tone that marks him as one of the most original creations in Shakespeare's figures of fun. Another character without a prototype in his source is the heavy-hearted Mariana of the Moated Grange, who rescues Isabella from an intolerable situation—i.e., submitting to Angelo in order to save her brother—by substituting herself for Isabella in Angelo's bed. For Mariana had been formally betrothed to Angelo and so is justified in consummating a virtual marriage with a reluctant husband by taking Isabella's place at night in Angelo's room.—O.J.C.

Plot Synopsis. Act I. Duke Vincentio of Vienna, who is about to leave for Poland, appoints Angelo as his deputy and names old Escalus to serve as his advisor. Angelo begins his administration by ordering the closure of all the bawdyhouses in the suburbs of Vienna, to the discomfiture of Mistress Overdone, who wonders what is to become of her. Another victim of Angelo's zeal is young Claudio, who is condemned to die for getting Juliet, his betrothed, with child in defiance of a long-neglected statute against lechery. As he is led off to prison, Claudio explains to his loquacious friend Lucio that his marriage to Juliet has been delayed because of complications over her dowry. At Claudio's request, Lucio goes to the convent of St. Clare, where Isabella, sister of the doomed man, has just become a novice, and persuades her to intercede for her brother with Angelo.

The Duke, meanwhile, has not left Vienna but has retired to a nearby monastery. There he reveals to one Friar Thomas the reason for his deception. During the 19 years of his permissive rule, he says, the city's laws have been universally flouted, and since he himself is too lenient to effect a change, he has entrusted the task to Angelo, "a man of stricture and firm abstinence." So that he may observe Angelo's conduct in office, the Duke plans to remain in Vienna disguised as a friar.

Act II. Escalus urges Angelo to spare Claudio, but the deputy is adamant: the laws must be enforced. Next they interview a constable called Elbow, who brings before them "two notorious benefactors," one Pompey Bum and a Master Froth, and accuses them of abusing his wife. Pompey, a bawd and tapster in Mistress Overdone's establishment, gives a lengthy explanation of the affair, after which Escalus lets them both off with a warning. Pompey, however, has no intention of giving up his trade.

Accompanied by Lucio, who whispers encouragement to her, Isabella calls on Angelo and beseeches him to show mercy to her brother. Her maidenly modesty stirs an unfamiliar passion in Angelo's breast. "O cunning enemy," he exclaims, "that, to catch a saint, / With saints dost bait thy hook." When she returns the next day, he tells her that he will save Claudio only if she gives herself to him. Isabella angrily rejects his proposal and threatens to expose him, but he replies that no one will believe her. Isabella then decides to disclose Angelo's shameful demand to her brother, in the belief that his outraged honor may reconcile him to death. Meanwhile, the Duke, visiting the prison in the guise of Friar Lodowick, has learned from the repentant Juliet the nature of Claudio's offense.

Act III. When Isabella enters her brother's cell she finds him accompanied by Friar Lodowick, who has been preparing him to meet death with tranquility. After the friar leaves, she informs Claudio of Angelo's proposal only to learn that her brother is afraid of dying and would prefer the most wretched earthly existence to the unknown terror that lie beyond the grave. He begs his sister to bow to Angelo's will, adding that she would not be guilty of any sin. As she berates him for his cowardice, she is called aside by Friar Lodowick who has overheard their conversation and sets forth a plan whereby she may save her brother without besmirching her honor. He explains that Angelo had once been formally betrothed to a lady called Mariana but had abandoned her when her dowry was lost. The friar proposes that Isabella feign compliance with Angelo's terms; at the time of the assignation, however, Mariana will take her place. Isabella readily agrees to the scheme.

On the street before the prison, the Duke, still disguised as Friar Lodowick, encounters Elbow and some officers guarding Pompey, who is accused of being a procurer. Pompey hopes that Lucio will provide him with bail, but that gentleman refuses. Catching the friar's ear, Lucio makes indelicate jests at Angelo's expense and slanders the absent Duke with whom he claims to be well acquainted.

Act IV. Isabella and Mariana put the Duke's plan into execution, but the faithless Angelo orders the provost of the prison to execute Claudio that very afternoon and send him his head. Friar Lodowick who is present when the provost receives Angelo's instructions, prevails upon him to execute another condemned man, the bibulous Barnardine, in his place. When Abhorson, the executioner, and his new assistant, who is none other than Pompey, summon Barnardine, he stoutly refuses to die that day and is saved by the timely demise of another prisoner, a pirate who resembles Claudio. The friar, however, tells Isabella that Claudio is dead and asks her to accuse Angelo before the Duke, who is to return on the morrow.

Act V. When the Duke makes his entrance to Vienna, he is greeted at the city gate by Angelo and Escalus. Isabella comes forward and accuses Angelo of fornication, but the Duke, feigning disbelief, orders her taken to prison. Mariana supports Isabella's charges and, removing the veil that hides her features, forces Angelo to admit that she is the woman he had deserted five years earlier, though he maintains that he has not seen her since then. Still professing to believe in Angelo's innocence, the Duke leaves and returns a moment later as Friar Lodowick in the company of Isabella. Escalus taxes the friar with having suborned the women to make false charges against Angelo and through him against the Duke. The friar retorts that he is not a subject of the Duke but merely a temporary resident of Vienna, where he has "seen corruption boil and bubble / Till it o'er-run the stew." Accusing the friar of having libeled the Duke in their conversation at the prison, Lucio pulls off his hood, only to discover the Duke himself. The Duke then orders the penitent Angelo to wed Mariana immediately and, after the ceremony has been performed, condemns him to death for the same transgressions that had brought Claudio to the block. Both Mariana and Isabella plead for Angelo's life, but the Duke remains obdurate until Barnardine and Claudio are brought in, and Isabella realizes that her brother has been saved after all. The Duke pardons Angelo, admonishing him to love his wife, and commands Lucio to marry a whore whom he had got with child. After ordering Claudio to wed Juliet, he himself commences a suit for Isabella's hand.—H. D.

Comment. Most modern critics define *Measure for Measure*, *Troilus and Cressida*, and *All's Well That Ends Well* as "problem plays" (see COMICAL SATIRE). In these plays sexual passion is substituted for the romantic love of the early comedies, and the dramas focus on the victims of this passion. In Elizabethan critical terminology *Measure for Measure* is a tragicomedy strongly infused with satire. The fact that the drama has a happy ending and that the characters in the subplot provoke laughter relates the play to comedy. But because Angelo's villainy launches the principal action and Claudio's cowardice precipitates the most important crisis in the plot, the drama is like a tragedy. Moreover the laughter that the characters in the subplot provoke is either ribald or derisive, much like that which satire aims to arouse. Indeed, the structure of *Measure for Measure* closely resembles that of one of Jonson's "comical satires." The Duke hints that he is going to conduct an experiment upon Angelo to determine and, if necessary, to expose the real nature of Angelo, whose blood appears to be "snow broth." In the Duke's words he

> scarce confesses
> That his blood flows, or that his appetite
> Is more to bread than stone: hence shall we see,
> If power change purpose, what our seemers be.
> (I, iii, 51–54)

The Duke clearly suspects that the emotional austerity of Angelo (the name itself is ironic) is not genuine. So he plans to test Angelo's moral sincerity, not through the wiles of an experienced temptress, but through the cold beauty of a woman "enskied and sainted," about to join the strict sisterhood of Saint Clare. Thus Shakespeare can present Isabella's dilemma in extreme terms. This is both a relic of the simple plotting of a medieval virtue story and an anticipation of the melodramatic situations that were to become the most striking feature of Beaumont and Fletcher's torrid romances. The resemblance to the methods of this new genre appears in Isabella's two great scenes with Angelo. The first (II, ii) is the one in which she begs him to spare her brother's life; the second (II, iv), the one in which she gradually understands, and finally rejects with horror, his offer to save Claudio at the expense of her honor. They are two of the most expertly planned and composed scenes that the poet ever wrote. Each mounts with an increasing crescendo to a thrilling climax. In these dialogues Isabella becomes Shakespeare's mouthpiece for some of the most eloquent pleas for mercy that he ever wrote. For the title of the play is ironic. "Measure" was a general term for apportionment of justice; hence, the title means "Justice for Justice"—but Angelo receives not justice for evil conduct, but mercy and forgiveness.

Isabella's interview with Claudio (III, i, 48–152), in which he begs her to meet Angelo's demands in order to release him from his craven fear of death, is constructed with the same consummate professional skill. But Isabella's violent denunciation of her brother has shocked many critics into stigmatizing her purity as "rancid." However, the intemperate language in which she spurns Claudio's appeal, though hateful to a modern reader, is appropriate to the situation if we accept Isabella's understanding of the issue involved. She states it passionately:

> Better it were a brother died at once,
> Than that a sister, by redeeming him,
> Should die for ever.
> (II, iv, 106–108)

For if she had consented to her prostitution she would have been guilty of a mortal sin and thus been in danger of everlasting damnation.

At the end of the third act we take leave of the moral and religious problems and those created by human frailty and become caught by what G. B. Harrison calls a thriller. The Duke becomes the author's agent in showing us with the proper suspense how Claudio is saved, Angelo forgiven, Isabella rewarded with a ducal husband, and a happy ending provided for all except Lucio, who is ejected from the play with no whip of steel, but with a smile for his incorrigibility. The Duke's forgiveness of Angelo has outraged many critics. Swinburne speaks for them when he cries, "Justice is buffeted, outraged, insulted, struck in the face." But such harsh critics seem to have forgotten that Shakespeare has planned the denouement as a manifestation of the triumph of mercy over legal justice. The greater the sin, the more complete the forgiveness must be.

Measure for Measure is one of Shakespeare's most original works. It is different in method and in spirit from most of his other plays. It deals with a subtly conceived problem of conduct treated partly in the mood of satire and partly in that of religious exaltation, as expressed in Isabella's sublime utterances. These often contradictory moods form the spiritual substance of a play masterfully exploiting all the artifices of the drama and all the crafts of the stage.—O. J. C.

Stage History. Except for a performance at court acted at Whitehall on St. Stephen's Night, December 26, 1604 by the King's Men, there is no record of a production before the Restoration. On February 18, 1662 Pepys saw at Lincoln's Inn Fields William Davenant's THE LAW AGAINST LOVERS, which combined elements of *Measure for Measure* and *Much Ado About Nothing*. Angelo undergoes drastic rehabilitation in the last act of this version and marries Isabella, after suffering punishment for his villainous behavior of the first four acts. Pepys thought it "a good play and well performed, especially the little girls (whom I never saw act before) dancing and singing." In 1699 Charles GILDON produced a version of the drama called *Measure for Measure or Beauty the Best Advocate*. A masque was incorporated into the drama and all the low-life and comic elements removed. Gildon's effort appeared at Lincoln's Inn Fields during the 1699/1700 season and was performed eight times with Thomas Betterton as Angelo, Anne Bracegirdle as Isabella, and John Verbruggen as Claudio.

By January 26, 1738 at Drury Lane, Shakespeare's play was restored. James Quin, who had previously acted the Duke at Lincoln's Inn Fields in 1720, took that role in this revival and again in 1742 at Covent Garden. In the last two performances, Mrs. Susannah Cibber was Isabella, one of her favorite impersonations. She chose the part for her benefit at Drury Lane on April 12, 1738. Hannah Pritchard attempted the part first in 1744 at Covent Garden and acted it again at Drury Lane on December 30, 1756, but neither actress did well as Isabella. Another Isabella of the period was Peg Woffington, who, in 1746, played opposite Spranger Barry's Duke and Charles Macklin's Lucio at Drury Lane.

The drama was neglected after Mrs. Cibber's retirement, until 1770, when a Covent Garden revival presented Robert Bensley as the Duke and Mrs. George Anne Bellamy as Isabella. Mary Ann Yates, taking over the heroine's role the next season, performed as Isabella at least six times at Covent Garden, and from 1775 appeared at Drury Lane each year up to October 20, 1778. In 1780 she resumed as Isabella at Covent Garden and was seen in the part during the two following seasons, having worthily filled the gap between Mrs. Cibber and the second of the great Isabellas, Sarah Siddons. During this time, William Smith was the most frequent Duke, essaying the role in every Drury Lane revival from 1775 through 1785, while John Henderson played the Duke at Covent Garden in 1780, 1781, and 1782.

Mrs. Siddons was first seen as Isabella at Bath on December 11, 1779 and again in the spring of 1782. On November 3, 1783 she made her first London appearance in the role at Drury Lane opposite Smith's Duke, performing in the play four times that month, once the next year, and twice more in 1785. Her next recorded performance as Isabella came in a Drury Lane revival on December 30, 1794, when John Philip Kemble played the Duke for the first time. Brother and sister continued in these roles at Drury Lane until 1802 and, transferring to Covent Garden, acted *Measure for Measure* during the winter of 1803 in the last revival for eight years. Then, in 1811, both resumed their portrayals during Mrs. Siddons' farewell season, giving eight performances opposite the Angelo of William Barrymore, a poor impersonator of the villain who had played the part since 1798 at Drury Lane, and Charles Kemble's Claudio, a role he had assumed at the same performance on October 27, 1798.

Mrs. Siddons' successor, Eliza O'Neill, played Isabella on February 8, 1816 at Covent Garden opposite Charles Mayne Young's Duke, while Charles Kemble re-created his Claudio; John Liston, John Emery, and Mrs. Davenport, the Pompey, Barnardine, and Mistress Overdone of 1811, reappeared in their roles. The last of the famous actors of this period to portray the Duke was William Charles Macready who on May 1, 1824 played that part for his first and last time.

Measure for Measure lost favor during the last half of the 19th century and revivals of the drama were rare. Samuel Phelps acted the Duke in his own production at Sadler's Wells on November 4, 1846. The next *Measure for Measure* in London was also noted for its Isabella, a superb portrayal by Adelaide Neilson who, having acted the role in the United States, appeared in a revival at the Haymarket Theatre on April 1, 1876 and again at that theatre in 1878. There were only two other major English productions in that century: that of Miss Ellen Lancaster Wallis, who played Isabella in the provinces and suburbs during the 1880's and 1890's and on March 27, 1899 at the Kennington, and that of the Charles Bernard and Miss Alleyn Company, which acted *Measure for Measure* at Stratford-upon-Avon in 1884 and 1885.

In 1906 the Oxford University Dramatic Society performed the drama, and that same year Oscar Asche staged the play at the Adelphi. His somewhat indistinct Angelo opposed the Isabella of Lily Brayton. One of the more memorable moments in this production was a guest performance by Ellen Terry, who, on April 28th, commemorated her golden jubilee in the theatre by playing Francisca, the nun.

Measure for Measure had been the first production of William Poel's Elizabethan Stage Society when, in November 1893, the company opened at the Royalty Theatre. In 1908 Poel presented the drama again at Manchester and later that year at Stratford, where a local group attempted to suppress the performance as unfit for public presentation. They failed, and the production succeeded in impressing critics with forceful and energetic portrayals, Poel as Angelo and Sara Allgood as Isabella, enhanced by the simplicity of the Society's Elizabethan platform stage.

George R. Foss introduced the play to Old Vic audiences with a production during the 1918/19 season. The next presentation was at Stratford, under the direction of W. Bridges-Adams in 1923, with Frank Cellier and Dorothy Green as Angelo and Isabella. Baliol Holloway appeared as Lucio in this and in a subsequent production of *Measure for Measure* by the Fellowship of Players on April 13, 1924 at the Strand, in which Ernest Milton acted Angelo. When the Vic staged its second production of the drama in 1925, Holloway took the part of

Angelo to Nell Carter's Isabella, while Edith Evans portrayed Mariana. Before the decade closed, Holloway impersonated the Duke for a Haymarket presentation which had Frank Cellier as Angelo opposite Jean Forbes-Robertson. In 1931 the distinguished actor resumed as Angelo for Robert Atkins at the Fortune, while Miss Forbes-Robertson re-created Isabella and Henry Oscar appeared as the Duke. That same year Randle Ayrton was Stratford's Duke; Gyles Isham, Angelo; and Hilda Coxhead, Isabella in Bridges-Adams' second *Measure for Measure* at that theatre.

Perhaps the most frequent producer of the drama has been Tyrone Guthrie, who began with a Cambridge Festival production during 1929/30 and proceeded to an impressive Vic-Wells revival in 1933, with Charles Laughton showing a frightening insight into the disordered mind of Angelo and Flora Robson excellent as Isabella. Guthrie's newest discovery, James Mason, played Claudio. After a preliminary appearance at Buxton's 1937 Summer Festival, Guthrie brought his next *Measure for Measure* to the Old Vic in October. Emlyn Williams impersonated a stern Angelo, with Marie Ney as Isabella and Sylvia Coleridge as Mariana. In 1954 the Stratford, Ontario, Shakespeare Festival, under Guthrie's direction, presented the drama with James Mason as Angelo, Frances Hyland as Isabella, Douglas Rain as Claudio, and Douglas Campbell as Pompey.

The Old Vic, except for a touring company which took the drama to Australia in 1955, abandoned the play for 20 years, and only Stratford continued to offer *Measure for Measure* during the interval. Holloway showed up as Lucio again for B. Iden Payne's production in 1940. Paul Scofield was Lucio in 1946 and 1947 at Stratford. A single permanent set designed by the director, Peter Brook, served the drama admirably when it next appeared at the Memorial Theatre in 1950. John Gielgud made Angelo more a tormented fanatic than a black villain; Harry Andrews was the Duke and Barbara Jefford, Isabella; George Rose portrayed Pompey. In 1956 Emlyn Williams re-created his Angelo in Anthony Quayle's production, which had Margaret Johnston and Alan Badel as Isabella and Lucio and Diana Churchill and Patrick Wymark as Mistress Overdone and Pompey. Another Stratford *Measure for Measure* was shown during 1962. Under John Blatchley's direction, Judi Dench's Isabella rang true.

Between Stratford's last productions, Margaret Webster had, in 1957, directed an Old Vic revival which starred John Neville and Barbara Jefford. Derek Godfrey played Lucio, Margaret Courtenay and Paul Daneman were Mistress Overdone and Pompey, while Judi Dench appeared here as Juliet. The final Old Vic performance before the company disbanded in favor of the National Theatre was of *Measure for Measure* on June 15, 1963. Produced by Michael Elliott and presented to an appreciative farewell audience, the drama ended with bells clanging and a cannon's boom.—M. G.

Bibliography. TEXT: *Measure for Measure*, New Cambridge Edition, Arthur Quiller-Couch and J. Dover Wilson, eds., 1922; *Measure for Measure*, New Arden Edition, J. W. Lever, ed., 1965; W. W. Greg, *The Shakespeare First Folio*, 1955. DATE: J. W. Lever, "The Date of *Measure for Measure*," *Shakespeare Quarterly*, X, 1959. SOURCES: Mary Lascelles, *Shakespeare's Measure for Measure*, 1953; Geoffrey Bullough, *Narrative and Dramatic Sources of Shakespeare*, Vol. II, 1958. COMMENT: W. W. Lawrence, *Shakespeare's Problem Comedies*, 1931; E. M. W. Tillyard, *Shakespeare's Problem Plays*, 1949; Ernest Schanzer, *The Problem Plays of Shakespeare*, 1963. STAGE HISTORY: New Cambridge Edition; G. C. D. Odell, *Shakespeare from Betterton to Irving*, 1920; J. C. Trewin, *Shakespeare on the English Stage, 1900–1964*, 1964.

Selected Criticism

A. W. SCHLEGEL. The piece takes improperly its name from punishment; the true significance of the whole is the triumph of mercy over strict justice; no man being himself so free from errors as to be entitled to deal it out to his equals. The most beautiful embellishment of the composition is the character of Isabella, who, on the point of taking the veil, is yet prevailed upon by sisterly affection to tread again the perplexing ways of the world, while, amid the general corruption, the heavenly purity of her mind is not even stained with one unholy thought: in the humble robes of the novice she is a very angel of light. When the cold and stern Angelo, heretofore of unblemished reputation, whom the Duke has commissioned, during his pretended absence, to restrain, by a rigid administration of the laws, the excesses of dissolute immorality, is even himself tempted by the virgin charms of Isabella, supplicating for the pardon of her brother Claudio, condemned to death for a youthful indiscretion; when at first, in timid and obscure language, he insinuates, but at last impudently avouches his readiness to grant Claudio's life to the sacrifice of her honour; when Isabella repulses his offer with a noble scorn; in her account of the interview to her brother, when the latter at first applauds her conduct, but at length, overcome by the fear of death, strives to persuade her to consent to dishonour;—in these masterly scenes, Shakespeare has sounded the depths of the human heart. [*A Course of Lectures on Dramatic Literature*, 1809–1811; trans. John Black, 1846.]

SAMUEL TAYLOR COLERIDGE. This play, which is Shakespeare's throughout, is to me the most painful —say rather, the only painful—part of his genuine works. The comic and tragic parts equally border on the hateful, the one disgusting, the other horrible; and the pardon and marriage of Angelo not merely baffles the strong indignant claim of justice (for cruelty, with lust and damnable baseness, cannot be forgiven, because we cannot conceive them as being *morally* repented of) but it is likewise degrading to the character of woman. Beaumont and Fletcher, who can follow Shakespeare in his errors only, have presented a still worse because more loathsome and contradictory instance of the same kind in their *Night-Walker*, in the marriage of Alathe to Algripe. Of the counter-balancing beauties of the *Measure for Measure* I need say nothing, for I have already said that it is Shakespeare's throughout. [*Shakespearean Criticism*, by S. T. Coleridge, T. M. Raysor, ed., Everyman Library Edition, 1960.]

R. W. CHAMBERS. Disguise and impersonation and misunderstanding are the very life of romantic comedy. The disguised monarch, who can learn the private affairs of his humblest subject, becomes a sort of earthly Providence, combining omniscience and omnipotence. That story has always had its appeal. 'Thus hath the wise magistrate done in all ages' [Jonson, *Bartholomew Fair*, II. i.]; although obviously to introduce into our daily life this ancient habit of the benevolent monarch would be to incur deserved satire. There is no doubt how Shakespeare meant us to regard the Duke. 'One that, above all other strifes, contended especially to know himself: a gentleman of all temperance', says Escalus. Isabel, in her moment of dire distress, remembers him as 'the good Duke'. Angelo, in his moment of deepest humiliation, addresses him with profound reverence and awe. Lucio (like our moderns) regards the Duke cynically; but he ends by admitting that he deserves a whipping for so doing.

The deputy, Angelo, is not so called for nothing. He *is* 'angel on the outward side'—an ascetic saint in the judgement of his fellow citizens, and despite the meanness of his spirit, nay, because of it, a saint in his own esteem. His soliloquies prove this, and Isabel at the end gives him some credit for sincerity . . . . *Measure for Measure* [is] an expression of 'the greatest discovery ever made in the moral world': the highly unpleasant discovery that there are things more important, for oneself and for others, than avoiding death and pain . . . .

Yet in Shakespeare's greatest plays, his greatest characters, for all their individuality, have also an imaginative, a symbolic suggestion. It is so in *The Tempest*, it is so in *Hamlet*. Thus also in the person of Lear, not only a helpless old man, but Paternity and Royalty are outraged; and 'Glamis hath murder'd Sleep'. No woman in Shakespeare is more individual than Isabel: silent yet eloquent, sternly righteous yet capable of infinite forgiveness, a very saint and a very vixen. But, first and last, she 'stands for' mercy. The Duke is shown to us as a governor perplexed about justice, puzzled in his search for righteousness, seeking above all things to know himself. It is altogether fanciful to remember once again that *Measure for Measure* was acted before the court at Christmas, 1604: that when Isabel at the beginning urges her plea for mercy (which she also makes good at the end) it is on the ground that

> He that might the vantage best have took
> Found out the remedy.

The day before *Measure for Measure* was acted, the finding out of that remedy was being commemorated. All sober criticism must remember the part which the accepted theology played in the thought of Shakespeare's day; that the Feast of the Nativity was—is—the union of Divine Mercy and of Divine Righteousness, and was—is—celebrated in the Christmas psalm:

> Mercy and truth are met together: righteousness and peace have kissed each other.

Shakespeare's audience expected a marriage at the end: and, though it may be an accident, the marriage of Isabel and the Duke makes a good ending to a Christmas play. ["Measure for Measure" in *Man's Unconquerable Mind*, 1939.]

M. C. BRADBROOK. This play is more theoretical than most of Shakespeare's writings, less easy, without his accustomed refusal to theorise or analyse. . . . In *Measure for Measure* the problems are ethical, and concern conduct rather than belief: the style is barer, sharper, and harder, the language simpler and plainer, and the characters allegorical rather than symbolical . . . .

Claudio and Juliet stand for human nature, original sin; Mariana for *eros* (as distinct from *agape*); Barnadine is contrasted with Claudio to show how much below panic-struck egoism is mere brute insensibility. Juliet, whom Claudio "wrong'd," is penitent from the first and therefore absolved by the Duke; nor apparently does she ever stand in peril of her life, and she is not given a judgment in the final scene as all the others are. In the last scene measure for measure is meted out to all; not, perhaps, their measure according to earthly law—for Barnadine is pardoned—but the measure best devised to save their souls. The main purpose of the scene is to bring Angelo to repentance, and to achieve it against so strong a character terrific pressure has to be brought to bear. The Duke, who is as ruthlessly efficient in his means as he is benevolent in his ends, proceeds to apply the third degree with the skill of a Grand Inquisitor: and to this end he is ready to inflict any temporary suffering on Mariana and Isabel. Had they known his purpose they would have accepted the situation readily—Isabel from charity and Mariana from affection. . . . He [the Duke] is naturally a merciful character; in theory he can condemn Barnadine, but when he actually sees the murderer, "A creature unpre-par'd, vnmeet for death," he realizes "To transport him in the minde he is, Were damnable" (IV. iii. 71–3). It is not Shakespeare's relenting before the miracle of his own creation, as the critics have sometimes stated, which reprieves Barnadine—in this play Shakespeare is hardly in a relenting mood—but the Duke's instinctive revolt from applying the penalties of the law without regard to their consequences. He gives Barnadine to Friar Peter to receive religious instruction, for he anticipates the maxim of Kant, and considers every human being as an end and never as a means, whether a means to the demonstration of the law or to other ends. ["Authority, Truth, and Justice in *Measure for Measure*," *Review of English Studies*, XVII, October, 1941.]

WILLIAM EMPSON. What is really offensive about the Duke is . . . that he should treat his subjects as puppets for the fun of making them twitch. But here, I suppose, the Character is saved by the Plot. It seems a peculiarly brutal flippancy that he should not only trick Isabella about Claudio unnecessarily but take pains to thrust the imagined death of Claudio upon her mind . . . But there is a question here of the mechanics of working on an audience; we forgive him for it because Isabella turns out not to care a rap about Claudio, and we wanted to know whether she would. The reasons why it seems all right, if you followed them up, would lead to quite a different view of the story.

. . . Mr. Wilson Knight was quite right to feel that there is a subtle ethic in the play somewhere, and that it is mixed up with Christianity. But I think there is a balancing idea to this, one that accounts for the unpleasantness of the two good characters. It is perhaps simply the idea that one must not act on these absolutes prematurely. Even granting that the conditions of life are inherently repulsive, a man makes himself actually more repulsive by acting on this truth; you cannot get outside the world and above justice, and a ruler who sets out to do this (except under very peculiar circumstances, by luck) is merely bad at his job. And the same ambivalence clings to the divine Isabella. In a way, indeed, I think this is a complete and successful work of the master, but the way is a very odd one, because it amounts to pretending to write a romantic comedy and in fact keeping the audience's teeth slightly but increasingly on edge. ["Sense in *Measure for Measure*," *The Structure of Complex Words*, 1951.]

FRANCIS FERGUSSON. . . . It is possible to read this act as an allegory of the descent of Mercy upon the scene of human judgment. The Duke, like God, comes not to destroy the Law—for he uses it to demonstrate everyone's guilt—but to transcend it. His role throughout the play is like that of Grace, in its various forms, as theologians describe it: he works through the repentant Mariana and Claudio to illuminate their motives and prevent their follies; and here at the end he answers Mariana's prayer after the intercession of Isabella. These relationships are worked out with theological scrupulousness, and I suppose that Shakespeare must have been aware of the possibility of this interpretation.

But at the same time he presents the Duke, not as God or as a mere symbol of a theological concept, but as a real human being; and Act V may be read, therefore, as the end of a *drama*. Mariana's love for Angelo had sharpened her insight: she was able to see through his actual savagery to the bewildered spirit within, which still had the potentialities of good; and the Duke, as Friar, had encouraged her in this strength, charity and understanding. Isabella had a wise *doctrine* from the first, but this doctrine remained helpless and disembodied until she was matured by suffering and appealed to by Mariana. In short, the play has shown how the wisdom of love proceeded from the Duke to the two women, to be finally confirmed by him when they reveal it at the end. Such is the *drama* of the growth of wisdom in Vienna, which finally reverses the tragic course toward anarchy. [*The Human Image in Dramatic Literature*, 1957.]

HANNS SACHS. The outstanding trait in his [Angelo's] character, constellating his attitude in all matters, small or great, is cruelty. To his subordinates he is gruff and unfriendly, always ready with a rebuke or a threat. . . . His cruelty is best demonstrated by the fact that he selects Claudio as the victim for the renewed enforcement of the laws against profligacy. In this Vienna of bawds and brothels it would have been easy to find a culprit whose transgressions were of a darker hue than those of Claudio. He seems to be singled out by Angelo just because he was the most innocent offender who came within the scope of the law; his betrothal gave him, according to custom, the right of a legitimate husband, especially since these things happened some time before the revival of the strict law. Indeed, this way of enforcing the old statute does nothing to give it renewed authority, but discredits it by making it appear fantastic and impossible . . . .

Through his office he finds an outlet for his dark desire in the form of a social function which has his own approval as well as that of society; in short, he shows what psychoanalysis calls a sublimation, although by no means a perfectly successful one, since his original nature looks through the rents in his gown. This sublimation breaks down with a sudden crash when he meets Isabella. The splendor of her purity, outshining everything to which he has been accustomed, together with the situation which delivers her into his hands, is too much for him . . . .

Thus stimulated and exposed to the storm of desire, his cruelty loses every aspect of sublimation and falls back, regressively, to its original source, revealing its primeval, sensual form. How near these two have dwelled together in Angelo's mind is illustrated by the identity he sees in murder and the sexual sin: " 'tis all as easy Falsely to take away a true life made As to put metal in restrained means To make a false one." The new temptation, against which Angelo fights in vain, is that of sadism. This psychological picture, the conflict caused by the regression to the sadistic stage of sensuality, would to us moderns who are concerned with the psychic processes in their immediate and intimate appearance, constitute an obsessional neurotic. Shakespeare who, as the true son of the Renaissance, projected his psychological intuition into the facts and forms of the world outside, made him a judge . . . .

Our play shows, at first glance, how in the judicial mind self-restraint for the sake of gaining the respect of others and self-respect break down when temptation takes the form of the suppressed sadistic wishes. The judge, by this resurrection of his primitive, unsublimated sensuality, is driven to repeating the act which he has censured, and thus changes place with the offender. ["The Measure in 'Measure for Measure,' " *The Creative Unconscious*, 2nd ed., 1951.]

Mecaenas. In *Antony and Cleopatra*, a friend to Octavius Caesar. In II, ii, Mecaenas questions Enobarbus about the splendors of Egypt and its Queen.

medicine. In the Elizabethan age the practice of medicine in general was carried on at a higher level than one might suppose. Practitioners were grouped under the control of two major bodies: the College of Physicians, founded in 1518, and the Company of Barber Surgeons, formed in 1540 by amalgamation of the Barbers' Company and the Fellowship of Surgeons. In 1546 regius professorships of medicine were established at Oxford and Cambridge, and when in 1597 Gresham College was founded, a professorship was instituted there as well.

The College of Physicians was initially a qualifying body responsible for the administration of examinations to medical candidates, under the control of a group of college censors. The College of Physicians was generally respected in its day, and Shakespeare reflected the public attitude when he referred to its members as "learned doctors" and "the congregated college" (*All's Well That Ends Well*, II, i, 120).

The most famous physician in Shakespeare's time was William Harvey (1578–1657). His studies at Padua, where he received his M.D. in 1602, led to the great revolutionary discovery of the circulation of the blood. He disproved the prevailing notion of his

AN ARMY SURGEON. WOODCUT FROM WILLIAM CLOWES' *A prooued practise for all young chirurgians* (1588).

time that the function of the heart was as a reservoir supplying the body. Although Harvey didn't demonstrate his theory until April 1616 (six days before Shakespeare's death), his hypothesis had gained some general credence even earlier. There are vague references to it in Shakespeare: in *Julius Caesar* a reference to "the ruddy drops / That visit my sad heart" (II, i, 289–290); and in *Coriolanus* in the famous "fable of the belly" in which the belly is "the store-house and shop of the whole body" sending "the general food . . . which you do live upon . . . through the rivers of your blood / Even to the court, the heart" (I, i, 135–140).

The career of a country doctor, such as Shakespeare's son-in-law, John HALL, was less spectacular, but it, too, had its rewards. Hall treated some noble patients, several with great success, and his reputation survived his death. James Cooke, a surgeon of Warwick, arranged for the publication of Hall's private treatment records as *Select Observations on English Bodies: or, Cures both Empiricall and Historicall, performed upon very eminent Persons in Desperate Diseases. First, written in Latine by Mr. John Hall Physician, living at Stratford upon Avon . . . where he was very famous* (1657).

Surgery, on the other hand, was not so greatly respected, and Shakespeare's few references to it are pejorative. In *Twelfth Night*, for example, Feste tells Sir Toby Belch that "Dick Surgeon" is too inebriated to attend to his duties (V, i, 203). The Barber Surgeons made much progress in the study of anatomy, making direct observations from the human body (using corpses of executed convicts) rather than perusing texts and plates. The Company maintained high standards of ethics and technical competence for surgical practitioners; they were constantly evaluating each other's work, particularly in the event of "mayme" or "dethe." References to anatomy and the practice of dissection in Shakespeare reflect the general knowledge of the work of the Barber Surgeons. In Elizabethan England the greatest surgeon was William Clowes, Sr. (c. 1540–1604). Clowes served in the army and was on the staff of St. Bartholomew's Hospital.

England, particularly London, was in Elizabethan times disease-ridden. The city was seldom free of the bubonic plague, of which there were particularly serious outbreaks in 1592 and 1603. Surprisingly, London did not have a special plague hospital, such as existed even in smaller foreign cities. London in Shakespeare's time did have three hospitals; all were originally religious houses that had been reorganized after the Reformation. St. Bartholomew's was the only one that had been originally intended for the sick. St. Thomas', originally an almonry, was established by the citizens of London as a hospital for the relief of the poor in 1552. Bedlam, originally the priory of the Hospital of St. Mary of Bethlehem, was made into a hospital for the insane after being taken over and given to the city of London by Henry VIII.

The most common and disruptive diseases of the time, in addition to the plague, were ague, gout, phthisis, and smallpox. Ague was inordinately common, for fields abounded that lacked irrigation and were fertile breeding grounds for the gnats or rat-fleas that are now thought to be the conveyors of the disease. Smallpox was a terrible scourge. The accepted treatment consisted of a course of suffumigation with cinnabar in a meat-pickling vat, referred to in *Henry V* as the "powdering-tub of infamy" (II, i, 79).

Shakespeare's plays mention several drugs; rhubarb and senna (*Macbeth*, V, iii, 55), bitter apple, colocynth or coloquintida (*Othello*, I, iii, 356) are a few. Poisons and narcotics are essential to the stories of *Romeo and Juliet* and *Cymbeline,* but doubt exists as to which poisons Shakespeare actually intended.

The contemporary popular terms for some diseases are listed in a lively catalogue in *Troilus and Cressida:*

> Now, the rotten diseases of the south, the guts-griping, ruptures, catarrhs, loads o' gravel i' the back, lethargies, cold palsies, raw eyes, dirt-rotten livers, wheezing lungs, bladders full of imposthume, sciaticas, limekilns i' the palm, incurable bone-ache, and the rivelled fee-simple of the tetter, take and take again such preposterous discoveries!
> (V, i, 20–28)

The modern counterparts of the above diseases would be syphilis, colic, hernias, catarrhs, pain in the loins ascribed to gravel or stone in the kidneys, apoplectic stroke with unconsciousness, permanent paralysis of the limbs, chronic inflammation of the lids with inverted lashes, diseases ascribed to the liver, asthma, chronic cystitis, lumbago or sciatica, psoriasis of the palm, bone-ache from any cause, and chronic ringworm. See ALCHEMY; PSYCHOLOGY. [Alban H. G. Doran, "Medicine," *Shakespeare's England*, 1916.]—P.G.

medievalism in Shakespeare. The medieval temper in England did not cease to have some part in shaping literature and other arts until after the age of Shakespeare, but its influence did not continue much beyond that time. By the middle of the 17th century it was possible for a new generation to look back with purely scornful high-mindedness upon the Elizabethan stage fool and all that he stood for in the medieval tradition. Like the gargoyle, this fool was dead. Shakespeare brought jester's foolery and much else from the Middle Ages into both comedy and tragedy. He did so, we realize, with little time to spare.

comedy. When we look at Shakespearean comedy in the setting of its age, we are always conscious that by its side stands Jonsonian comedy and that each reveals by contrast the peculiar greatness of the other. When we look onward from both, we know that it was not in vain that Jonson was younger than Shakespeare by some few years and lived beyond him for many years. Jonson was one of the "new men" of his period. His genius, particularly in comedy, had special authority for the immediate future. Jonson had "sons of Ben" who sensed the way the literary tide was running. Shakespeare had no "sons of Will" that we hear of, however much he may have been looked up to by younger poets for his recognized successes.

With reason, the Shakespeare of comedy can be called a dramatic poet of the old school in comparison with Jonson. It can be maintained, and has been by Professor Nevill Coghill supremely well, that in essence Shakespearean comedy is medieval whereas Jonsonian comedy is not (see COMEDY OF ERRORS: *Selected Criticism*). Jonson appeals to classic authority and makes his comedy morally corrective satire. In his revolt against what he finds established on the English stage in the line of the medieval tradition, he turns to a tradition even older than the medieval. This is not to say that there is never anything satiric within Shakespearean comedy, but it is to say that its prevailing drive is toward a positive joy instead of a negative revelation of vice or folly that is seen as needing reform. When Shakespeare takes the rogue Falstaff and makes him into perhaps the greatest comic figure at the same time that he makes him strangely and marvelously appealing, he shows the gulf between himself and Jonson. He brings into being a figure of indubitable vice and folly whom even the Victorian moralist can yearn to rescue from the final kingly rejection by Hal. Almost all men seem to know that Falstaff is not put before them negatively but to the end that there should be positive joy taken in him. Shakespeare deals with him and with other disreputable or foolish or merely clownish figures related to him—such as Autolycus, Touchstone, or Launce—in a medieval comic spirit of acceptance which comes down from the moralities with certain modern extensions of feeling but with no radical change of quality. Falstaff and others of his Shakespearean kind spring from the Vice of the moralities by various lines of descent.

In the moral drama the Vice was a schemer against good, but, living up to his name, he tended to be an abstract of conscienceless iniquity in man rather than a Satanic figure. He was often enough a tempter of man but tended to be someone not of high rank in the army of evil when he was dramatized as a member of that army. More and more as the moral play developed, he was expected to provide low comedy by being thoroughly and irreformably the reprobate and his uninhibited jesting could become his chief reason for existence. Villains in Shakespeare who take unholy joy in their work and in their wit owe much to the Vice in his role as jesting schemer. Richard III acknowledges some of his own debt in an aside:

> Thus, like the formal Vice, Iniquity,
> I moralize two meanings in one word.
> (*Richard III*, III, i, 82–83)

Fools and clowns in Shakespeare are descended dramatically from the Vice as a low comic figure, however much they take quality also from attendant fools maintained after the medieval tradition in houses of the Tudor great. In a song Feste gives recognition to the Vice behind the fool:

> I'll be with you again,
> In a trice,
> Like to the old Vice,
> Your need to sustain.
> (*Twelfth Night*, IV, ii, 132–135)

Behind Falstaff in the same way is the Vice as jesting tempter and clever schemer who conquers the virtue of the hero and leads him into a roistering life, sometimes even a life of tavern haunting. But here we find Shakespeare giving an admirably comic twist to the inherited medieval formula. Hal is Mankind. And Falstaff, when Hal acts his father's part in the mock-interview scene, gets presented as the corrupter of this youthful Mankind. Falstaff is "that reverend vice, that grey iniquity" who tempts the Prince "in the likeness of an old fat man" and carries him "away from grace" (*1 Henry IV*, II, iv, 490 ff). The cream of the jest is that Falstaff is reprobate enough and more than witty enough to be a Vice but is quite incapable of misleading and dominating the Prince in the Vice's typical ways of deceit. The Prince is always dominant when we see him with Falstaff. Not only that, the Prince is thoroughly master of his fate and plans his period of roistering and also his triumphant final reform (to the vast disgust of those of us whose hearts have been won by Falstaff). When tricks are played between these two, the Prince plays them on Falstaff. It is never the other way around. In some lights poor Falstaff appears as a Vice outviced by his Mankind.

In the juxtaposition dramatically of low comedy and high seriousness, the medieval spirit is inclined to see nothing perilous but rather something for carefree acceptance. No matter how earnest this spirit is, it seems to have a strange capacity for being on good terms with the not-good that is found comic. It is, of course, capable of satire against the not-good, but often we find that instead of trying to crush the not-good with laughter, it welcomes it with laughter and leads it to a place reserved for it in opposition to the good. The not-good then responds in the basely comic way. In this process it is hard to discover any infection of the high seriousness of the drama. One thing, and perhaps the most important, that should be said in explanation is that the medieval spirit tends to take the mortal world as a realm of natural imperfection, where individual men are reformable but not the world as the world. Thus it may become possible at one time to engage religiously in contempt of the world and fix the mind and heart on a perfect otherworld but at another time, without being at all unreasonable, to enjoy the comic discords brought into being by the existence of both good and not-good in our world here below. One can enjoy the discords in a manner all the more carefree by being sure that they are not part of the ultimate scheme of things. Nor need the not-good get exaggerated ideas about itself, however much it is fondly accepted as witty in itself and a cause of wit. In comedy, a Mankind, or a Prince Hal, finally wins forgiveness and his reward, but a Vice, or a Falstaff, is shut out from the realm of happy ending. As a figure of the not-good in this world of imperfection he can never reform his ways and, no matter how engaging he is, he must suffer rejection when matters reach a certain point of seriousness. Even a Touchstone, who is not so fully a figure of the not-good and who is admitted to a group of lovers in a comedy, can have final happiness only dubiously by being assigned to a loving voyage victualed for but two months.

In the main, of course, Shakespearean comedy is a comedy of lovers. In one way its happy endings are joyous triumphs of fertility rites. Thus the love comedy is rooted in a far distant past, remnants of which were preserved in the Middle Ages; however, examination of a tradition that is peculiarly medieval in Shakespeare's love comedy must serve the present purpose.

The medieval culture, with a religion such as Christianity that could enthrone the concept of love and with a poet such as Dante that could abundantly justify the closing of his greatest work with the line

L'amor che move il sole e l'altre stelle,

could be expected to produce love comedy of a kind that had never been known in the ancient world. The English moral play begins as a drama exactly suiting Dante's idea of a divine comedy. Throughout the 15th century it mercifully rescues Mankind from the unhappy results of his yielding to temptation and, though it must not save him from the summons of Death, it is able to bring him to assurance of joy in Paradise. Only in the 16th century does the moral play treat its hero so unmercifully, both in what happens to him in this world and in his prospects in the next, that he takes on some importance for the beginning of Elizabethan tragedy. It is a divine manifestation of the love celebrated by Dante which rescues Mankind when the morality holds to the course of comedy. A resultant theme of mercy and forgiveness standing in opposition to but also in conjunction with justice is not entirely secularized when it becomes as important as it is for Shakespearean comedy, chiefly in *The Merchant of Venice*, *Measure for Measure*, *The Winter's Tale*, and *The Tempest*. The balancing of harsh justice and tender mercy and the final tipping of the balance toward mercy are here no simple matters, largely because of their background of Christian theology. The suggestions that the Duke in *Measure for Measure* and Prospero in *The Tempest* are figures of man playing God are strong. The suggestion is explicit at the beginning of *The Tempest* when Miranda expresses pity for those who have supposedly perished in the storm raised by her father's magic and says that had she "been any god of power" she would have sunk the sea within the earth before it should have drowned these unfortunates.

Another manifestation of the love celebrated by Dante is courtly love, by which woman is given a worshipful status that would have greatly amazed the ancient world. Courtly love too has no small place in Shakespearean comedy. At its highest reach in the Middle Ages it is the exaltation of a Beatrice to guideship in Paradise. Shakespeare's courtly love is of the flesh far more than Dante's and the rose in love's earthly garden is its goal rather than the rose of the beatific vision. But Shakespeare has technical interest in the fine points of courtly love and he is very conscious that its essence, even when woman yields herself in the flesh, is the elevation of woman into an embodiment of something that is infinitely desired beyond woman and yet is to be won only through love of woman. It has been well said of courtly love in one aspect that it is a feudalization of love: the faith which supports it puts the lady into a position like that of a *seigneur* and the lover into that of a vassal serving his liege lord. In his Renaissance version of courtly love Shakespeare has the worldly service demanded of the lady's vassal, but as he dramatizes this he introduces some notable overtones of religion.

For example, *Love's Labour's Lost* has to do with an attempt by a king and three courtiers to refine worldly knowledge (a proper Renaissance ambition) but to do it by a temporary, pseudo-monastic giving up of the world. Especially is love of ladies to be given up. The beginning of the play is even reminiscent of medieval contempt of the world and contempt of the flesh. It has the line:

The mind shall banquet, though the body pine.
(I, i, 25)

This is to be put beside lines on the soul and the body in Shakespeare's Sonnet 146 ("Poor soul, the centre of my sinful earth") which deserve to be called more essentially medieval because in them soul has not been transformed into mind:

Then, soul, live thou upon thy servant's loss,
And let that pine to aggravate thy store;
Buy terms divine in selling hours of dross;
Within be fed, without be rich no more.

The attempt of the King and his courtiers fails because ladies' eyes (a right courtly love theme) prove to be deeper reading than books. At the inconclusive end the lovers are to demonstrate their love by serving their ladies for the coming year, two of them in ways that recall the religious notes sounded at the beginning of the play. One lover is to forsake "all the pleasures of the world" and live in "some forlorn and naked hermitage" and the other is to "visit the speechless sick" and with wit to cheer "the pained impotent." We gather that the happy ending is only delayed. *Love's Labour's Lost* is in many respects a strangely profound early comedy of Shakespeare's, and not least so in what it does by joining worldliness and otherworldliness for its purposes.

In *The Two Gentlemen of Verona*, Shakespeare's

early concern with courtly love takes him into a more ordinary area of dramatic oppositions. But the struggle presented between two friends reared to follow the aristocratic code of honor in faith-keeping, one of whom proves faithless both in the service of love and in that of friendship, has an extraordinary ending that is religious if not other-worldly religious. Here Christian mercy and forgiveness play a part like that in the merciful moralities. The unvirtuous friend, in love with the virtuous friend's lady and even trying to take her by force in the most dishonorable fashion, is at once forgiven by the virtuous friend as soon as he expresses "hearty sorrow" and says, "Forgive me." The virtuous friend then even offers his lady to the other, excusing this lapse of faithfulness in love on the high ground that

> By penitence the Eternal's wrath's appeased.
> (V, iv, 81)

It is because the reformed friend is rehabilitated in love to the point of desiring his own lady again that all goes well.

Troilus and Cressida, a work issuing from Shakespeare's maturity, makes the Trojan war story, as it was romanticized in medieval tellings, into a play of courtly love so different in spirit from either of the two plays just considered that here all may be said to go the opposite of well. The drama is not without compassion but it lacks notably the gentle approach of Chaucer's telling of the love story. There is little true gaiety in it, though plenty of wit and scurrilous jesting. The religious note is no longer sounded and the reason for its absence is not merely the pagan setting. The young hero Troilus has infinite desire for faith-keeping but he is hemmed in by a world that produces wantonness in Cressida to accord with that in Helen and also produces modern ingloriousness in the Trojan war despite the dashes of romanticized medieval color given to it. Even as Troilus wins Cressida, he senses that in love "the will is infinite and the execution confined." When Cressida proves all too easily faithless and the disillusioned Troilus is left only with the desire to fight "cogging Greeks" until fated death shall overtake Troy and himself, there seems to be final justification for all the questioning that has gone on about granting the name of comedy to the play. Reasons have been given for calling it a comedy with the qualification "bitter." Reasons have also been given for calling it a "comicall satyre" of the Jonsonian order. It has even been thought of as having tragedy within it, if not having in full the quality of tragedy.

tragedy. That *Troilus and Cressida* challenges understanding in a way comparable to that of Shakespeare's major tragedies the present time is coming more and more to realize. There is a close poetic bond between it and *Hamlet*. But it is set apart from these major tragedies, or any of Shakespeare's tragedies, and perhaps is most plainly different in having a hero to whom Shakespeare refuses a tragic death within the action presented. Largely for the same reason, it is set apart from those medieval narrative tragedies which helped to bring about the acceptance of the hero's death as the rightful ending for a tragedy on the Elizabethan stage. These narrative tragedies include Chaucer's *Troilus and Criseyde*, their best single achievement, and also the short tragedies of his *Monk's Tale*. From Chaucer they go back for inspiration to Boccaccio's *De Casibus Virorum Illustrium* and reach forward through Lydgate's *Fall of Princes* to the Elizabethan *Mirror for Magistrates* and the many narratives of its particular kind which followed it. Medieval narrative tragedy had effect upon some of the moralities and through them increased its effect upon Elizabethan stage tragedy.

Death may be said to be the theme of themes for Gothic tragedy, narrative or dramatic. The later Middle Ages that conceived Gothic tragedy had come to make death a much favored subject of contemplation. They kept it before them by the spoken and written word, by pictorial treatment of conventional subjects like the Dance of Death or the Three Living and the Three Dead and by various representations in support of the reminder *memento mori.* All this was part of that religious exercise of contempt of the world practiced increasingly by late medieval man as a balance for his espousal of the world which produced the Renaissance. Also part of that exercise was the writing about and the depiction of Fortune and her wheel. The mortal world was seen as dangerously seductive. The more one found it attractive the more it needed to be regularly denied in the interests of that other world which was man's true home. In the words of Chaucer's poem "Truth":

A WHEEL OF FORTUNE FROM BARCLAY'S *The Shyp of Folys of the Worlde* (1509).

The wrastling for this world axeth a fal.
Her is non hoom, her nis but wildernesse.

In these two lines we find the informing spirit of medieval tragedy at its simplest. The sublunar world is a wilderness because it is irrational. Its ambitious activity is ruled over by Fortune and the man who wrestles for its prizes is on Fortune's wheel. The wheel is turned at intervals unexpectedly, always according to Fortune's whim, never according to the deserts of those on the wheel or any guiding principle at all. For anyone on the wheel disaster eventually comes.

The turning wheel is never reversed. A man who is able to cling to it may go to the top and at his height of good fortune may perhaps gain a crown. But the wheel must have its succeeding turns and with these he must go down. The completion of the descent is not merely loss of high position on the wheel but a fall from the wheel itself into death. This fall into death is the ultimate tragic truth, the ultimate tragic argument *de contemptu mundi.* The first tragic fall of man was into death for Adam and his was a fall from "hye prosperitee," as Chaucer tells briefly in his *Monk's Tale.* All men since have fallen into death and many have fallen thus from high prosperity in notable tragic fashion. In the conventional *ubi sunt* with its list of outstanding unfortunates and in the conventional *De Casibus* collection of stories one finds examples of transitory greatness. No man, however great, can secure himself by power or by merit in any worldly possession and therefore such a possession is to be contemned, even while one has it, to the end that pride of life shall be mortified.

Before Shakespearean tragedy could come to exist, a progressive change in man's view of the world had to take place. But even as the forming of a new world picture went on the old picture kept a strong appeal. Often the two pictures were presented side by side with an approval for both that seemed wholly oblivious of the contradictions between them. For tragedy the most important part of the new world picture was a measure of order resulting from a concept of cause and effect. This made it possible for the hero to have some part in shaping his tragedy through his choices of action.

In *Troilus and Criseyde* Chaucer does what is often done in *De Casibus* narratives as he writes a tragedy of courtly love. He builds his story upon the round of Fortune's wheel and magnifies Fortune's power. Troilus ascends on the wheel and at the high point of its turning, near the middle of the poem, wins joy with Criseyde. Then, after stanzas on the fickleness of Fortune, Troilus descends and Diomede rises on the wheel to gain Criseyde. Chaucer takes pains to show that Troilus is not notably at fault and that Criseyde is not to be harshly judged. He gives Troilus a long meditation blaming external necessity for his fall. The end of his fall is death. But he immediately rises to a realm where he can hear the music of the spheres, can laugh at those who weep for his death, and can know what it is to be free from "this wrecched world" with its blind delights that may not last. Chaucer has the medieval capacity to bring contempt of worldly love into the conclusion of this poem that makes much of that love.

More often than not, Shakespeare builds his tragedies upon a round of action like that on Fortune's wheel or upon what may be called a pyramid of balanced rise and fall related to action on the wheel. It is a form for tragedy profoundly different in effect from that which the Greeks created by their instinct for a late point of attack upon the fable to be dramatized. Shakespeare never comes very close to the typical *De Casibus* magnification of Fortune, but he reminds one of it most in *Romeo and Juliet* and *Richard II*, two early plays that may have been written within a year of each other. Romeo rises through about half of his tragedy to the joy of attaining Juliet and then almost at once is brought unwillingly to the killing of Tybalt and the sharp turn downward of his course. He marks the turn, as such a turn is conventionally marked in *De Casibus* narrative, by comment upon Fortune. But his comment is not of conventional length. It is merely, "O, I am fortune's fool!" (III, i, 141). Shakespeare is judicious in working from his source, a narrative poem by Arthur Brooke filled with references to Fortune, but in *Romeo and Juliet,* as has been sufficiently recognized, chance and the stars have large parts to play. In *Richard II* the hero falls from kingship on the wheel and Bolingbroke, who has been rising behind him, comes to be King in his place. Or, to use another conventional figure which Richard himself is made to use, the two men are buckets of Fortune counterpoised against each other in a well and Richard must be "down and full of tears" when Bolingbroke is "dancing in the air" (IV, i, 181–189). Richard can see almost nothing of his own contribution to his tragedy and talks of "sad stories of the death of kings" in *De Casibus* fashion and of "the antic" Death in Dance of Death fashion, implying that he simply goes the way of many others (III, ii, 155–170). But Shakespeare has made sure that we see beyond Fortune to what he cannot see.

We likewise see beyond Fortune when actions of rising and falling are balanced for Richard III and we see far beyond Fortune when such actions are balanced for Brutus in *Julius Caesar*, for Hamlet, for Macbeth, for Antony in *Antony and Cleopatra,* and for Coriolanus. In *Othello*, *King Lear*, and *Timon of Athens*, which may have been written in quick succession, there is for each hero a long fall after a brief period of prosperity and here in a special way we see far beyond Fortune. It does not need saying that when Shakespeare shows an order of tragic event encroaching upon Fortune's disorder, he never makes tragic justice a fully open book. But the order he shows does give weight to choice of action by human figures he creates, and to none more than Macbeth, despite the weight given to the acts of the witches when they tempt him.

The witches in *Macbeth* are supernatural tempters but they have ties with villain tempters of Shakespeare's who are mortal. Such figures, both supernatural and mortal, belong to an order not found in Greek tragedy, for their dramatic quality depends upon the Christian concept of Satanic temptation. They descend from the tempters of medieval plays and something has already been said about this descent with regard to the villain as a grim jester. *Macbeth's* witches are fiends in witch form descended from the devils of the moralities and other religious plays. His villain tempters, of whom Iago is chief, are descended just as legitimately from the Vice of the moralities.

The fool or clown, in whom the strain of the Vice merely as jester is obviously strong, has a place in Shakespearean tragedy as significant as that of the grotesque figure in Gothic religious art. That he was doubtless an outstanding success with Shakespeare's groundlings need not be counted against him—if indeed anyone in these days inclines to be snobbish about him. What he can mean for Shakespearean tragedy when he is at his best appears in Lear's fool. In much of *King Lear* this fool is another self of the hero, a self who sees while the ostensible kingly self is blind. In such a fool one finds what could bring Erasmus to take his praise of folly to the point of saying that "our Lord gave thanks that God had concealed the mystery of salvation from the wise, but he revealed it to babes, that is to fools." In Shakespeare, as in Erasmus, medieval folly is still medieval folly but it is given new dimensions by the Renaissance.

By being conducted to death as in the *De Casibus* story and in the Dance of Death, a Shakespearean protagonist has tragedy sealed for him as Gothic. The "fell sergeant, Death,/Is strict in his arrest" for Shakespeare's other tragic heroes no less than for Hamlet. But though death for the Shakespearean tragic hero can be release from "the rack of this tough world," as it is for Lear, it never makes his drama in full truth a medieval comment *de contemptu mundi*. Shakespearean tragedy never takes the direction of making the world into a wilderness of disorder worthy only to be abjured in favor of the other world. In this respect it is in large part beyond the medieval way of seeing man's condition, even when it has as much of medieval temper as it has in *Hamlet*.

In *Hamlet* death and the way man takes it are a theme always before us. King Hamlet has fallen to his death and Claudius, his murderer, has risen to the royal position on the wheel. Hamlet the son accepts the duty to avenge his father put upon him by an ancient code of honor, but he lives too much in a new world of doubt and multiple perception to let the code sweep him into deeds like those of a Laertes or a Fortinbras. For deep reasons that to him and to us seem incapable of final statement he cannot perform the act, counted rightful by him, of taking the place of Claudius on the wheel by pushing him down from it. Through almost exactly half the play there is a rise for Hamlet that takes him to a sought-for surety that Claudius killed his father. Then, at the height of his achievement and of Fortune's favor, he gets a chance to kill the praying, conscience-stricken King. He refuses it. With the killing of Polonius, he immediately begins a descent toward catastrophe. When he does eventually become Fortune's instrument for the King's death, he can only pull Claudius down to fall with him. The world through which Hamlet makes his way is "a sterile promontory" that can put suicide into one's thoughts and yet the other world is doubtful territory not to be counted on as a place to flee to from present ills. The *memento mori* is to be found in every graveyard and is cause for *ubi sunt* meditation. Even Caesars are food for worms. Nevertheless, man is "noble in reason" and "infinite in faculties" and is "the beauty of the world." And from the Middle Ages, capable of grim comedy in Dances of Death, stage devils, stage Vices, gargoyles, and fools, man inherits the ability to take a strange joy in the incongruities of all this. If one is a Hamlet, one can become a wry jester of the princely sort and even make common cause with a clown of nimble wit who digs graves. One can raise the question whether comedy and tragedy do not come together in ultimate reality. [Barbara Swain, *Fools and Folly during the Middle Ages and the Renaissance*, 1932; Willard Farnham, *The Medieval Heritage of Elizabethan Tragedy*, 1936; C. S. Lewis, *The Allegory of Love: A Study in Medieval Tradition*, 1936; Nevill Coghill, "The Basis of Shakespearian Comedy: A Study in Medieval Affinities," *Essays and Studies*, G. Rostrevor Hamilton, ed., English Association, New Series, III, 1950; Bernard Spivack, *Shakespeare and the Allegory of Evil*, 1958.]—W.F.

Meighen, Richard (fl. 1615–1641). London bookseller. Primarily a publisher of law books, Meighen, whose shop was located on the Strand, was one of a group of publishers under whose auspices Shakespeare's Second Folio (1632) was published. Allied with Meighen in the publication of F2 were Robert Allot, John Smethwicke, William Aspley, and Richard Hawkins.

Melun, vicomte de. A follower of Louis the dauphin who warned the traitorous English barons of his lord's sinister intentions toward them. It is not known if Melun did in fact have the English ancestry ascribed to him by Shakespeare.

In *King John*, Melun appears as a French count whose "grandsire was an Englishman." Dying from battle wounds, he warns the English noblemen who are fighting on the French side that it is Lewis' intention to have them executed after they have served their purpose (V, iv). [W. H. Thomson, *Shakespeare's Characters: A Historical Dictionary*, 1951.]

Melville, Herman (1819–1891). American novelist and poet. In his review of Hawthorne's *Mosses from an Old Manse* in *The Literary World*, August 17 and 24, 1850, Melville reveals his attitudes toward Shakespeare, noting that "much of the blind unbridled admiration that has been heaped upon Shakspeare, has been lavished upon the least part of him." Those who consider Shakespeare "as a mere man of Richard-the-Third humps and Macbeth daggers" have missed, Melville suggests, "those deep far-away things in him; those occasionally flashings-forth of the intuitive Truth in him; those short, quick probings at the very axis of reality; . . . the things that make Shakspeare, Shakspeare." In Hawthorne, as in Shakespeare, Melville discerned a power of blackness: "through the mouths of the dark characters of Hamlet, Timon, Lear, and Iago, he craftily says, or sometimes insinuates the things which we feel so terrifically true, that it were all but madness for any good man, in his own proper character, to utter, or even hint of them." In this review Melville argues that Shakespeare is by no means unapproachable, that the difference between Hawthorne and Shakespeare is not infinite but measurable, and that men "not very much inferior to Shakspeare, are this day being born on the banks of the Ohio."

Melville's verse shows his interest in Shakespeare's Falstaff. "Falstaff's Lament" dramatizes the character's feelings after Hal's reformation:

Here on this settle
He wore the true crown,
King of good fellows,
And Fat Jack was one—
Now, Beadle of England
In formal array—
Best fellow alive
On a throne flung away!

"In the Old Farm-House" pictures Melville, in the dead of the night, conversing with shadows from the past:

He laughs in white sheet,
  And I, I laugh too,
'Tis Shakespeare—good fellow—
  And Falstaff in view.

More important than Melville's insight into the dark side of Shakespeare or his versified treatment of Shakespeare and Falstaff is the profound influence which the poet had on Melville's language, on incidents in his fiction, on his characters, and on his essentially tragic world view. F. O. Matthiessen has pointed out in his *American Renaissance* (1941) the influence which Shakespeare had on Melville's language. According to Matthiessen, Melville, when writing *Moby-Dick* (1851), was liberated "through the agency of Shakespeare." Melville did not learn to express "the hidden life of men . . . until he encountered the unexampled vitality of Shakespeare's language." An example of Shakespearean influence, taken from Ahab's first long communication with the crew (chapter 36), can be printed as blank verse:

But look ye, Starbuck, what is said in heat,
That thing unsays itself. There are men
From whom warm words are small indignity.
I meant not to incense thee. Let it go.
Look! see yonder Turkish cheeks of spotted
  tawn—
Living, breathing pictures painted by the sun.

Matthiessen argues that Melville's reading of Shakespeare was a "catalytic agent, indispensable in releasing his work from limited reporting to the expression of profound natural forces. Lear's fool had taught him what Starbuck was to remark about poor Pip, that even the exalted words of a lunatic could penetrate to the heavenly mysteries."

Melville borrowed a number of dramatic devices from Shakespeare. Though Melville's scenes of comic relief, like those dealing with the black cook, Fleece, are often heavy-handed, he successfully adapted Shakespeare's more serious devices. Fedallah's prophecy of the things that must happen before Ahab will die is taken from the witches' prophecy in *Macbeth*. Ahab is told that Parsee will die before him, will return from the grave, and that only hemp can kill the captain of the *Pequod*. As it turns out Parsee does return from his watery grave, entangled in the lines pinioned to the white whale, and Ahab is caught in the hemp of the harpoon he hurls at Moby-Dick.

A number of Melville's characters are based on Shakespearean prototypes. Jackson in *Redburn* (1849), Babo in *Benito Cereno* (1855), and Claggart in *Billy Budd* (post. pub., 1924) are all lineal descendants of Iago. Ahab is related to Lear, and Pip is clearly based on Lear's fool. *Pierre* (1852) is apparently Melville's unsuccessful attempt to place Hamlet in 19th-century New York. [F. O. Matthiessen, *American Renaissance*, 1941; Charles Olson, *Call Me Ishmael*, 1947; A. L. Vogelback, "Shakespeare and Melville's *Benito Cereno*," *Modern Language Notes*, LXVII, 1952; G. R. Stewart, "The Two Moby-Dicks," *American Literature*, XXV, 1954; Edward Stone, "*Moby-Dick* and Shakespeare: A Remonstrance," *Shakespeare Quarterly*, VII, 1956.]—J.F.L.

memorial reconstruction. A means by which the texts of the BAD QUARTOS of Shakespeare's plays may have been recorded. According to the theory of memorial reconstruction, an actor (or actors) reconstructed the entire play from memory; evidence suggests that attempts at memorial reconstruction were usually made by actors who had had minor roles in the play. The circumstances that might have brought about memorial reconstructions are difficult to determine. They may have been initiated by Elizabethan printers who lured actors, or former actors, of Shakespeare's company into reconstructing the text for a fee; or, the initiators may have been the actors themselves. It is most probable that the circumstances varied in each case.

The theory was first advanced by W. W. Greg in 1910 when he suggested that the "bad quarto" of *The Merry Wives of Windsor* (1602) was based on a memorial reconstruction by the actor who played the Host of the Garter.

Peter Alexander made a similar observation as to the origin of the bad quartos of *2* and *3 Henry VI*; he suggested that the first was reported by the touring actors (in an abridged version of the play) who played Suffolk and Clifford, and that the second was reported by actors taking the roles of Warwick and Clifford.

G. I. Duthie has argued that the text of the bad quarto of *Hamlet* was the reported text or memorial reconstruction of the actor who played Marcellus, an officer of the guard. Duthie has also suggested that the "pied bull" quarto of *King Lear*, which is now generally classified among the bad quartos, was reconstructed from memory by the cast of the King's Men while on tour. Many scholars, however, adhere to the view that the source of the *King Lear* text is a STENOGRAPHIC REPORT, while Alice Walker and J. Dover Wilson argue that the play is partly a memorial reconstruction by the actors who played the appropriately perfidious roles of Goneril and Regan.

The reporters of the bad quarto of *Henry V* appear to have been the actors who played Gower and Exeter. In *Romeo and Juliet* the reporters were probably the actors who played Romeo and Paris in an abridged version of the play. Harry Hoppe (*The Bad Quarto of Romeo and Juliet*, 1948) suggests that these two actors were Gabriel Spencer and William Bird, who left Chamberlain's Men in 1597 to join the newly organized Pembroke's Men. Memorial reconstruction has also been seen as the source of one good quarto, the 1597 edition of *Richard III*, which may have been reconstructed by the entire company while on a provincial tour. [W. W. Greg, *The Shakespeare First Folio*, 1955.]

Menas. In *Antony and Cleopatra*, a pirate and a friend of Sextus Pompeius. While Pompey entertains the Roman triumvirs, with whom he has signed a peace treaty, Menas suggests that they cast adrift and murder Mark Antony, Octavius Caesar, and Aemilius Lepidus. Pompey's answer indicates that while the suggestion was good, it should have been carried out but not mentioned (II, vii).

Mendelssohn, Felix (1809–1847). German composer. Mendelssohn's great contribution to Shakespeare is his music for *A Midsummer Night's Dream.* He composed the overture when he was only 17, but the rest of the music—songs and choruses, **scherzo,** melodramas, nocturne, wedding march, and recitations with orchestral accompaniment—came much later, at the request of the king of Prussia. It was first played at the New Palace, Potsdam, in 1843. [Christopher Wilson, *Shakespeare and Music,* 1922.]

Menecrates. In *Antony and Cleopatra,* a friend to Pompey. Menecrates appears only in II, i to advise Pompey. Plutarch describes Menecrates as a famous pirate.

Menelaus. In Greek mythology, the king of Sparta, the brother of Agamemnon and the husband of Helen, whose abduction by Paris was the ostensible cause of the Trojan War. Menelaus appears prominently in Homer's *Iliad* as a general in the Greek army, and in three plays by Euripides. In *Troilus and Cressida,* Menelaus is one of the Greek generals and Helen's husband. He encounters and defeats his rival, Paris, on the battlefield, to the cackling commentary of Thersites:

> The cuckold and the cuckold-maker are at it. Now, bull! Now, dog! 'Loo, Paris, 'loo! Now, my double-henned sparrow! 'Loo, Paris, 'loo! The bull has the game: 'ware horns, ho!
>
> (V, vii, 9–12)

Menenius Agrippa. In *Coriolanus,* a patrician friend of the protagonist. Menenius tells the rebellious plebeians the fable of the belly and the members of the body, thus persuading them not to mutiny against the senators of Rome (I, i). When Coriolanus is forced to ask the plebeians' consent to his appointment as consul, Menenius begs the proud candidate not to reveal his contempt for the people. He later tries to dissuade the banished Coriolanus from leading a Volscian attack on Rome.

Menteith. In *Macbeth,* a Scottish nobleman. He fights with Malcolm's rebel army against Macbeth (V, iv).

Mercade. In *Love's Labour's Lost,* an attendant to the Princess of France. Mercade announces the death of the Princess' father (V, ii).

Merchant. In *Timon of Athens,* a minor character who enjoys Timon's generous patronage (I, i).

The Merchant of Venice.

Merchant of Venice, The. A comedy by Shakespeare.

Text. The best text is that of the First Quarto (1600), often known as the Heyes Quarto. The descriptive title reads: "The most excellent Historie of the Merchant of Venice. With the extreame crueltie of Shylocke the Iewe towards the sayd Merchant, in cutting a iust pound of his flesh: and the obtayning of Portia by the choyse of three chests. As it hath beene diuers times acted by the Lord Chamberlaine his Seruants. Written by William Shakespeare. At London, Printed by I. R. [James Roberts] for Thomas Heyes, and are to be sold in Paules Churchyard, at the signe of the Greene Dragon. 1600."

The Second Quarto (1619), a pirated reprint fraudulently dated 1600, is based on the Heyes Quarto. It was long thought to be the earlier of the two quartos, until the studies of A. W. Pollard proved that it was printed by William Jaggard for Thomas Pavier in 1619 along with nine other plays. The false date on the title page was designed to circumvent an order of the lord chamberlain on May 3, 1619, prohibiting the publication of any play belonging to the King's Men without their consent. The First Folio text (1623) was printed from the 1600 Quarto.

The printer's copy for Q1 was probably Shakespeare's own FOUL PAPERS. J. Dover Wilson's theory that the text was put together from the players' parts and the PLOT of the play (see ASSEMBLED TEXTS) has been generally discredited.

Date. The play was entered in the Stationers' Register on July 22, 1598: "xxij° Julij. James Robertes. Entred for his copie vnder the handes of bothe the wardens, a booke of the Marchaunt of Venyce, or otherwise called the Jewe of Venyce, Prouided, that yt bee not prynted by the said James Robertes or anye other whatsoeuer without lycence first had from the Right honorable the lord Chamberlen . . ." This entry is thought to represent an attempt of Shakespeare's company to prevent publication of a popular play (see BLOCKING ENTRY). The title is included in Meres' list in *Palladis Tamia* (1598). The earliest limits of the play may be set by the execution of Dr. López in June 1594 (see SOURCES below).

The most excellent

Historie of the Merchant of Venice.

VVith the extreame crueltie of *Shylocke* the Iewe towards the sayd Merchant, in cutting a iust pound of his flesh: and the obtayning of *Portia* by the choyse of three chests.

As it hath beene diuers times acted by the Lord Chamberlaine his Seruants.

Written by William Shakespeare.

AT LONDON,
Printed by *I. R.* for Thomas Heyes, and are to be sold in Paules Church-yard, at the signe of the Greene Dragon.
1600.

TITLE PAGE OF THE FIRST QUARTO OF *The Merchant of Venice* (1600).

Another topical allusion has been seen in the line "And see my wealthy Andrew dock'd in sand" (I, i, 27), apparently a reference to the Spanish ship *St. Andrew,* captured in the victorious English expedition to Cadiz. The news of the victory reached England in July 1596, which, unless that particular line were added in a revision of the play, would date the play between 1596 and 1598.

Sources. The play consists of the amalgam of two stories, from different sources: the casket story and the pound of flesh story. Most of the plot comes from the tale of Giannetto, the first tale of the fourth day of a collection of *novelle* called *Il Pecorone* (The Simpleton), collected or written by an otherwise unknown writer, Ser Giovanni Fiorentino. The relevant tale was written as early as 1378, but it first appeared in the collection published in 1558. Here we find "Belmonte" as the locale and most of the original plot—one of the many stories of the winning of an otherworld bride. The terms of wooing are curious: there are no caskets; the suitor must stay awake all night long or lose the desired lady. On the first two of three attempts the suitor is secretly given a sleeping potion and so falls asleep. On the third night he avoids the drug, stays awake, and wins the lady. Shakespeare, evidently realizing that this plot was unsuited for the stage, substituted a trial of the suitors by means of the caskets.

The casket story had been widely circulated. Shakespeare might have read it in one of three places: John GOWER's *Confessio Amantis* (1390; V, 2273–2434), an English poem of 35,000 lines in octosyllabic couplets; BOCCACCIO's *Decameron;* or, most likely, in the anonymous GESTA ROMANORUM, a huge collection of tales compiled on the continent in the 14th century, but first printed in 1472. Two English translations of the work appeared in the 16th century.

The pound of flesh story had also enjoyed wide circulation. It turns up in two versions that the poet easily could have read: "The Ballad of the Crueltie of Geruntus," probably written before 1590; and *The Orator,* a collection of orations, one of which (Number 95) is entitled "Of a Jew, who would for his debt have a pound of the flesh of a Christian." This work was translated into English probably by Anthony Munday from *Les Histoires Tragiques* by "Sylvain" (Alexander van der Busche), published in 1596. The dramatist may have found all the elements of the play in a lost English drama: Stephen Gosson, in his *School of Abuse* (1579), refers to a drama called THE JEW, which he describes as "representing the greediness of wordly choosers and the bloody minds of usurers." These phrases have been taken as a loose description of the casket and pound of flesh plots, but as *The Jew* is no longer extant, its relation to *The Merchant of Venice* must remain conjectural.

Shakespeare must also have been well acquainted with Marlowe's THE JEW OF MALTA, which was still being played at the Rose Playhouse by the Admiral's Men, with Edward Alleyn in the title role. Marlowe's Barabas, like Shylock, had one daughter and great wealth. He, too, hated the Christians, and was even more vindictive and remorseless than Shylock —in fact he was a monster of cruelty. Shakespeare owed something to *The Jew of Malta* in his portrayal of Shylock, but he transformed the type into a human being, still evil, but with recognizable human motives and actions.

A series of events in contemporary real life gave Shakespeare's play an absorbing topical interest. In 1586 Roderigo LÓPEZ, a Jewish-Portuguese doctor, became the queen's personal physician. His position at court involved him in political intrigue. He was assigned the position of interpreter and official guardian of Antonio Pérez, the half-Jewish pretender to the throne of Portugal. While serving in this double role, he was drawn by Spanish emissaries into a plot to assassinate Antonio. Later, the same agents sought, almost surely unsuccessfully, to induce López to poison the queen. Although the earl of Essex insisted on López' guilt, the queen remained unconvinced. Finally, however, in spite of López' protestations of innocence and her own reluctance, she signed his death warrant. On June 7, 1594 he was hanged, drawn, and quartered in the presence of a huge, derisive crowd. To capitalize on the London public's hostility toward López and all Jews, the Admiral's Men revived Marlowe's *The Jew of Malta;* during 1594 it played 15 times to crowded houses. While the López affair is not a formal source of *The Merchant of Venice,* it may have stimulated the poet to write a play about a villainous Jew. The allusion to a "wolf, . . . hang'd for human slaughter" (IV, i, 134) may be a reference to the fate of

López, the word "Wolf" possibly being a pun on his name.

Some critics believe that a play presented at the Rose Theatre on August 25, 1594, which Henslowe calls in his diary "the Venesyon Comodye," may have been the immediate source of Shakespeare's play, but it is not extant.—O. J. C.

Plot Synopsis. Act I. Although Antonio is a successful Venetian merchant whose argosies ply the seven seas, he is afflicted by a "want-wit sadness," unlike his loquacious young friend Gratiano, who hopes that all his wrinkles will come from mirth and laughter. Bassanio, another of Antonio's friends, is deeply in debt to him, but asks for an additional sum in order to woo a beautiful and wealthy lady of Belmont with whom he is in love. Unable to comply with Bassanio's request at the moment, Antonio authorizes him to raise the money in his name. He turns to Shylock, a Jewish usurer who hates Antonio, not only because he is a Christian, but because he has reviled Shylock's nation and lends money without taking interest. Shylock agrees to lend Antonio 3000 ducats for three months; if he is not repaid in time, however, he will demand a pound of the merchant's flesh. Bassanio objects to Antonio's signing such a bond, but the latter is confident that his ships will return laden with merchandise long before payment is due.

In Belmont, meanwhile, Portia, the lady loved by Bassanio, sighs over the terms of her father's will, according to which she must wed the suitor who, from three caskets of gold, silver, and lead, selects the one containing her portrait. With her maid Nerissa, she discusses the "parcel of wooers" from various nations who have thus far failed the test and declares herself relieved to see them depart. The only one of whom she speaks well is Bassanio.

Act II. Encountering his dim-sighted father, Old Gobbo, on the street, Launcelot Gobbo, Shylock's servant, convinces him of his identity only with considerable difficulty. Launcelot is unhappy in Shylock's service and prevails upon Bassanio to engage him. When he takes leave of Shylock's daughter, Jessica, she asks him to deliver a letter to Lorenzo, with whom she plans to elope. While Shylock is dining with Antonio, Jessica makes her escape dressed as a page, taking with her a large part of her father's treasure. It is later reported that upon discovering Jessica's flight, Shylock had bewailed the loss of his ducats as much as that of his daughter.

Among the suitors for Portia's hand is the Prince of Morocco, who boldly selects the golden casket and finds that it contains a death's-head and a scroll reading "All that glisters is not gold." Equally unlucky is the Prince of Arragon, who chooses the silver casket after analyzing the inscription that it bears: "Who chooseth me shall get as much as he deserves." Inside he finds the portrait of a blinking idiot.

Act III. Amid rumors that Antonio's ships have been wrecked, Shylock asserts that he will demand payment of his bond. When he is asked what Antonio's flesh would be good for, Shylock, recalling the gibes he has endured because of his faith, retorts: "To bait fish withal: if it will feed nothing else, it will feed my revenge."

Having arrived at Belmont, Bassanio insists on undergoing the test of the caskets at once, though Portia urges him to delay for a day or two. While musicians give him a hint in song, Bassanio studies the caskets and, wary of being deceived by external appearances, selects the one made of lead. Upon opening it, he is overjoyed to see a picture of Portia. When he asks whether she confirms the result of the test, she replies that she would wish to be fairer, richer, and wiser only to stand high in his estimation; as a sign of her submission, she gives him a ring which he vows to cherish forever. Gratiano, who with Nerissa had been a witness of the happy scene, reveals that Nerissa had promised to marry him if Bassanio won her mistress. Jessica and Lorenzo now arrive in the company of Salerio, who brings a letter from Antonio informing Bassanio that his ships are all lost and that Shylock is seeking payment of his bond; he asks Bassanio to come to Venice so that he can see him once more. Bassanio and Gratiano leave for Venice immediately after a double wedding. Portia, asking Lorenzo to remain as manager of her estate, announces her intention of retiring to a monastery with Nerissa until the return of their husbands, but after sending a mysterious message to her kinsman, Doctor Bellario, she informs Nerissa that they are to go to Venice in male disguise.

Act IV. In a court of justice, Shylock declares to the Duke of Venice that he is determined to have his bond, if only to satisfy the hate he bears

THE
EXCELLENT
Hiſtory of the Merchant of Venice.

With the extreme cruelty of *Shylocke* the Iew towards the ſaide Merchant, in cutting a iuſt pound of his fleſh. And the obtaining of *Portia*, by the choyſe of three Caskets.

Written by W. SHAKESPEARE.

Printed by *J. Roberts*, 1600

TITLE PAGE OF THE SECOND QUARTO OF *The Merchant of Venice* (1619). THIS EDITION WAS FALSELY DATED.

Antonio. Bassanio offers to pay twice the sum he owes, but the usurer insists on his pound of flesh; he warns that denial of his suit will prove the emptiness of Venetian law. The Duke states that he has asked a learned lawyer, Doctor Bellario, to render a decision, whereupon Nerissa, in the garb of a clerk, arrives with a letter from him saying that he cannot come because of illness, but that in his place he is sending a young colleague called Balthasar. The latter turns out to be Portia, dressed as a doctor of laws, who asks Shylock to temper the justice of his case by showing mercy to Antonio. The usurer refuses and hails the lawyer's wisdom when Portia declares that Antonio must prepare his bosom for the knife. Shylock's elation ends abruptly, however, when the lawyer reminds him that, according to Venetian law, he must not cut more than a pound of flesh nor shed a drop of Christian blood; otherwise he will lose both his property and his life. At this Shylock offers to settle for the 3000 ducats owed him, but Portia points out that as a penalty for seeking the life of a Venetian citizen, he must give half his wealth to the injured party and half to the state. The Duke, however, pardons Shylock and reduces the state's share of his property to a fine, while Antonio states that he will keep his half in trust for Jessica and Lorenzo if Shylock promises to embrace Christianity and bequeath all his wealth to his daughter and son-in-law upon his death. Shylock, his spirit crushed, can only consent to these terms.

Antonio and Bassanio thank the young doctor profusely for his services, but the only recompense that he will accept is the ring that Bassanio wears on his finger. Bassanio is at first unwilling to part with the ring, but relinquishes it at Antonio's urging. Nerissa whispers to Portia that the clerk will try to exact an identical reward from Gratiano.

Act V. In Portia's moonlit garden, the sweet stillness of the night inspires a lyrical colloquy between Jessica and Lorenzo. Portia and Nerissa arrive before daybreak, followed by Bassanio, Gratiano, and Antonio. Nerissa asks Gratiano for her ring and feigns disbelief when he states that he has given it to a lawyer's clerk. Portia chides Gratiano for parting so readily with his wife's gift, adding that she would be incensed if she were given a similar occasion for grief. Bassanio is now forced to confess what he has done with Portia's ring. Portia eventually agrees to forgive her husband and gives him a ring with the hope that he will keep this one better than the other. When Bassanio realizes that it is the same one he had given the lawyer, Portia and Nerissa reveal their masquerade to their dumbfounded spouses. Portia has good news for the others too: Jessica and Lorenzo learn that they will inherit Shylock's wealth, and Antonio is informed that three of his ships have returned safely to Venice.—H. D.

Comment. *The Merchant of Venice* is Shylock's play. Shakespeare has poured into a traditional figure so much more vitality than is necessary for the part that Shylock unfortunately has come to live a life independent of the story for which Shakespeare created him.

Shakespeare, designing Shylock to be the villain of the piece, began with the stereotyped Elizabethan conception of a Jewish usurer (moneylender). The

A
TRVE REPORT
OF SVNDRY HORRIBLE
Conſpiracies of late time detected to haue (by Barbarous murders) taken away the life of the *Queenes most excellent. Maieſtie*; whom Almighty God hath miraculouſly conſerued againſt the treacheries of her Rebelles, and the violences of her moſt puiſſant Enemies

AT LONDON
Printed by Charles Yetſweirt Esq.
1594.

TITLE PAGE OF A CONTEMPORARY ACCOUNT OF THE TRIAL OF DR. LÓPEZ.

name that the poet gave the character, "Shylock," was one to arouse the hostility of everyone who knew what it meant, for "Shylock" is an almost exact transliteration of the Hebrew "shalach," a word that in the King James version of the Bible is rendered as "cormorant," and any bird of prey was in Elizabethan times a conventional symbol of a usurer. Usury, the practice of taking interest for loans, was from the Middle Ages regarded as not only immoral, but also as actually a perversion of nature: since gold and silver were obviously sterile and barren, a moneylender was putting his money to an "unnatural act of generation." In accordance with this idea, Dante in his *Inferno* placed usurers in the same circle of hell as the sexual perverts. To present Shylock at the beginning of the play as a sly and calculating moneylender would suggest to any Elizabethan audience that a plot in which he was to play the villain would inevitably lead to tragedy.

Even though Shakespeare gives the murderous Jew of tradition traits of an almost sympathetic human being—witness his famous speech beginning "Hath not a Jew eyes"—the temper of the play is tragic as long as Shylock holds the stage. For it is the abduction of Jessica by one of the gentlemen-wastrels in Antonio's circle, and the group's ridicule of his deepest family and religious instincts that convert his smoldering hostility into a blazing fire of revenge. Only after Shylock's exit as a defeated villain does the spirit of comedy establish her reign. For this reason *The Merchant of Venice* can best e understood if regarded as Shakespeare's first agicomedy. To an Elizabethan audience Portia's lea for mercy would ring with religious overtones. Iany of the cycles of mystery plays contained a ast Judgment drama, in which Justice and Mercy ebate for the possession of mankind's soul. The dvocate for mercy is often the Virgin Mary. This ace of the mystery plays may explain the elevation nd earnestness through which Shakespeare transormed the mere clever quibbling of the Italian tale ito one of the most impressive scenes that he ever evised. Because of her remote descent from the 'irgin Mary, Portia's solemnity does not seem inppropriate to a trial of a criminal. Moreover, she no trivial *amorosa* of Italianate comedy, but the oet's first portrait of the ideal lady of the Renaisince—a woman of social grace, quick wit, and vely intelligence.

Antonio, like Portia, is a complex character whose ole would have sounded many overtones to an lizabethan audience. To begin with, he was the aost admired sort of gentleman, ideally devoted to is bosom friend, to whose "occasion" he is glad to evote his "purse, his person, and his extremest ieans." In this and other ways he is a romantic gure. To his contemporaries he may have had a roader significance. In a group of medieval tales alled *The Tale of Abraham and Theodore*, the escue of a borrower from the clutches of a usurer /as a symbol of man's redemption. In these tales, ie figure of Mankind signs a bond with the devil, ut when Satan attempts to claim his victim, the 'irgin appeals for mercy and God saves him. This escent from an allegorical figure may account for ntonio's mysterious melancholy—the inevitable ate of unredeemed man—and for his lack of any veryday relationship to any other character except assanio. Even the modern playgoer senses a hauntig quality in Antonio's nature.

It was one of the poet's master strokes to comine the pound of flesh and the casket plots, through ortia's disguise as a lawyer called in to pass judgient in the case of Shylock versus Antonio. J. Dover Wilson calls this ancient comic device the ivot of the action. The casket theme would have een more interesting to Elizabethans than it is to ur contemporaries. Modern producers find in the cenes telling the story little more than a chance to ring brilliant color to their staging by presenting ie Princes of Morocco and Arragon in gorgeous obes. To Shakespeare's audiences it had a larger ignificance. For to them the speeches of these reected suitors would have invited close attention, ecause of their delight in proverbial wisdom. The eflections of these two betray some flaw in their haracters or some false sense of values that renders hem unfit husbands for Portia. The motto on the ad casket, "Who chooseth me must give and azard all he hath," brings us to the scene in which assanio makes his crucial choice. His long soliloquy s he stands before the caskets, beginning "The vorld is still deceived with ornament" (III, ii, 74–07), is a variation on one of the poet's favorite hemes: the peril of mistaking appearance for reality. Vhile Bassanio stands pondering the significance of ie motto, Portia has a song sung, in which the hymes "bed," "head," "nourished," and the words "engender'd" and "fed," would suggest "lead" even to the slowest intelligence. J. Dover Wilson rejects the usual explanation that Portia is thus not too subtly guiding her suitor to the right choice. He believes that Shakespeare intended the song to give the audience a clue to the thoughts that pass through Bassanio's mind as he tries to solve the puzzle of the caskets.

With Shylock's exit, interest in the play is likely to flag. But it is a mistake to treat the trial scene as the end of the play. It is only the end of the tragic tension. Then Shakespeare is ready in the last act to crown the action with universal joy. The difficulty of establishing the atmosphere of romance is a challenge which forces him to invoke all the magic of his art. He transports us away from the turbulence of Venice and the strain of the trial to a moon-washed garden in Belmont and the inspired lyrical love dialogue of Lorenzo and Jessica. Here he bids us sit

> and let the sounds of music
> Creep in our ears: soft stillness and the night
> Become the touches of sweet harmony.
> (V, i, 55–57)

Nevertheless for many readers the over-all structure of the play is lacking in harmony and coherence. The gaiety of the lovers has a trivial, even callous quality when contrasted with the depth and intensity of the defeated villain.—O. J. C.

Stage History: England. The title page of the Heyes Quarto reads: "As it hath beene diuers times acted by the Lord Chamberlaine his Seruants." There is a tradition that Richard Burbage created the part of Shylock and made him a comic figure. We can deduce what actors before Edmund Kean made of the role by William Hazlitt's description of Kean's new interpretation of the part. Hazlitt begins, "We expected to see a decrepit old man bent with age and ugly with mental deformity, grinning with deadly malice . . . fixed on one unutterable purpose, revenge."

The first recorded performance was that given by the King's Men before the court at Whitehall on Shrove Sunday, February 10, 1605, and again on the following Tuesday. At the Restoration, it was one of the plays assigned to Thomas Killigrew, but there is no record of a performance of *The Merchant of Venice* as written by Shakespeare until 1741, for an adaptation entitled *The Jew of Venice*, by George Granville, later Lord LANSDOWNE, took *The Merchant*'s place on the stage. This version was first performed at Lincoln's Inn Fields in May 1701, with Thomas Betterton as Bassanio, assuming speeches intended for other characters. Anne Bracegirdle was Portia, and Thomas Doggett, in what John Downes said was one of his best comic roles, was Shylock. Much of the original was deleted, including both Gobbos, and large portions of the verse rewritten. Among the additions were a masque of Peleus and Thetis and a scene between Antonio and Shylock in prison. This tortuous "improvement," in which some of the prose speeches were converted into poetry by simply breaking the lines into equal lengths, held the stage at Lincoln's Inn Fields under John Rich's management, and afterwards at Covent Garden, from 1714 to 1735.

Then, in 1741, Charles Macklin dared to impersonate "the Jew that Shakespeare drew." His Shylock was no low-comedy figure, but a bloody, vengeful villain, filled with cunning and "terrifying ferocity." By the middle of this performance the audience was applauding the new Shylock and Macklin's reputation was made. He acted the part 22 times during that first season and his last appearance as Shylock was at Drury Lane on May 7, 1789. Macklin, almost 90 years old at the time, broke down in the early part of the performance and Thomas Ryder had to take on the part. One relic of Granville's approach was Kitty Clive's portrayal of Portia; she mimicked the oratorical manner of living judges and the courtroom technique of famous lawyers with whose mannerisms many of the audience were familiar.

In January 1742 Thomas Arne composed a song for Portia and soon afterward he wrote two songs for Lorenzo, one sung at Belmont, the other under Jessica's window before her elopement. Lorenzo thus became a singing role. Later more songs were introduced and even occasional dances. At Drury Lane in May 1754 David Garrick inserted a Pierrot's dance at the end of the third act and "a hornpipe" in the fifth. Although Garrick never acted in the comedy, he had chosen it for the opening of his management of Drury Lane on September 15, 1747.

In 1777 John Henderson established his reputation in London at the Haymarket with a brilliant performance of Shylock that John Philip Kemble called "the greatest effort that I ever witnessed on the stage." Kemble himself first appeared in the role in January 1784 at Drury Lane and played the part for the next 20 years with Sarah Siddons as Portia. When he assumed management of Covent Garden in 1803, he assigned Shylock's role to George Frederick Cooke, who had played this role in 1800. Cooke managed to retain the malignant aspect of the character, while tempering it somewhat with a solemn piety and a note of pathos. On January 26, 1814 Edmund Kean achieved a great personal triumph in the role with his romantic acting. All the critics of the time, led by Hazlitt, were loud in their praise. He divested Shylock of all his repulsive characteristics, presenting him as a man driven to catastrophe by a resentment that was amply justified. Perhaps his most striking innovation was his substitution of a little shabby black beard for the red one that had become sacrosanct.

William Charles Macready first appeared as Shylock at Covent Garden in 1823, endowing the character with traces of nobility that later actors developed and emphasized. Another successful Shylock, Charles Kean, staged an elaborate (and drastically cut) version in keeping with 19th-century taste at the Princess' on June 12, 1858; the setting attempted to re-create a picture of Venetian life. When Squire and Marie Bancroft staged their production at the Prince of Wales Theatre in Tottenham Court Road in 1875, the scenery was selected from views studied in Venice the previous year. Despite the exquisite Portia played for the first time by Ellen Terry, this production was a sad failure, largely because of the inadequate portrayal of Shylock by Charles Coughlin.

The most famous 19th-century production of *The Merchant of Venice* was that of Sir Henry Irving, which opened at the Lyceum Theatre on November 1, 1879. His Shylock was an aristocrat of an ancier race and religion, an outraged victim of prejudic proud and usually calm, only occasionally breakin out in scorn and rage. It became Irving's most fa mous role and his conception of the Jew has bee adopted, with some modifications, by most subse quent actors. The production, notable also for Elle Terry's enchanting Portia, was a gorgeous spectacl with revels in the Venetian streets and sympatheti Jews crowding the courtroom at the trial. I achieved the astonishing number of 250 consecutiv performances. Irving's production was exported t New York in 1883 where it played at the Sta Theatre.

Shylock continued to dominate the play in th 20th century, but occasionally the emphasis shifte as when Alan McKinnon directed Arthur Bourchie at the Garrick in 1905. While Bourchier's Shyloc was simply a vengeful, uncomplicated usurer, Mc Kinnon insisted that Antonio and Bassanio hold th stage to the last curtain. Then, in 1908 at H Majesty's Theatre, Beerbohm Tree presented h hysterically histrionic Jew, accompanied always b a repulsive Tubal. Tree outdid his predecessors i the role in the scene when Shylock returns to th empty house. Having repeatedly knocked, he thre open the door, calling, "Jessica!"; raged through th rooms; emerged crying and flung himself on th ground in a paroxysm of grief after sighting a di tant gondola; tore his clothes; and, finally, poure ashes over his head. For his trouble, Tree receive harsh criticism.

Matheson Lang's Shylock had all the outwar signs of servility, yet was more intelligent, discrim nating, and skillful than the Christians. This inte pretation, attributed to the counsel of Israel Zang will, was shown in December 1915 at the St. Jame In J. B. Fagan's *Merchant* at the Court in 191 Maurice Moscovitch played his first role in Englis —that of a harsh, realistic Shylock. During th last weeks of this production, Louis Bowumeeste a 74-year-old Dutch tragedian, took over for Mo covitch and is reported to have been so terrifyin in the role that a woman screamed and fainted fro fright. He spoke in Dutch and his son waved a hanc kerchief from the wings to cue the other actors.

The Merchant of Venice was included in the basi repertory of the touring companies. In Octob 1926 Frank Benson, then 69 years old, interrupte his provincial round with a matinee performanc as Shylock at the King's Theatre, Hammersmit displaying a briefly recaptured vigor. That sam year Terence Gray advertised his boredom with th play when he staged it at Cambridge. Under h direction, Portia delivered the mercy speech wit languid indifference, while the Duke played with yo-yo and the rest of the court yawned. The en of the decade saw the American actress Lucil Laverne play Shylock in a performance characte ized by the *Times* as having "occasionally left th Rialto; never the Contralto." This production wa presented at the Little; included in the cast was An drew Leigh as Launcelot, his first role after leavin his position as director at the Old Vic to pursue a acting career. Meanwhile, in that same year the ne Vic director, Harcourt Williams, staged *The Me chant*, starring Bremer Wills as Shylock. His pe ormance lacked distinction, but Granville-Barker vrote to the new director, "Antonio good if a little imid." That role had been played by John Gielgud.

There were three notable productions in 1932. The first, at the St. James, was an artistic success, vith Ernest Milton playing a proud Shylock. The econd was an emotional success: Frank Benson, reurning for the last time to Stratford-upon-Avon, ave a special matinee performance with a cast inluding many Old Bensonians. Lillian Braithwaite layed Portia; Cedric Hardwicke, Tubal; Robert)onat, Lorenzo; Nigel Playfair, Arragon—all acting 1 the traditional manner. The curtain fell when Benson's Shylock left the court. Then, in the sumier, Stratford presented Theodore Komisarjevsky's tartling fantastication of Shakespeare. While the oddering Duke drowsed, Portia, in horn-rimmed lasses, gave the "quality of mercy" speech; Antonio, n a ruff collar, was languidly indifferent to Randle Ayrton's incongruously traditional Shylock.

The Merchant was regularly performed during he early 1930's. In 1938, at Queen's Theatre, John Gielgud played a colorless, resentful Shylock oppoite the dominating role of Portia, acted by Peggy Ashcroft. The critics approved the gay Nerissa of Angela Baddeley and the contemplative Lorenzo of Alec Guinness in this production. The comedy was ncluded in Donald Wolfit's "black-out" tour of the rovinces during 1939, and scenes from the play vere shown at his lunchtime Shakespeare at the trand while the Battle of Britain raged in 1940. Volfit's production played in London in 1942, 945, 1946, and 1947 with the producer often sucessfully starring as Shylock. At Stratford, Baliol Iolloway impersonated Shylock for three consecuive years, beginning in 1940, in B. Iden Payne's roduction, and Michael Benthall staged the play or the Memorial Theatre first in 1947 and again in 948. Robert Helpmann was Shylock and Diana Vynyard, Portia in this last production.

Paul Rogers dominated at the Old Vic (1952/3) vith his strong Shylock, but at Stratford in 1953 the omantic aspect of the play gained prominence. Alhough Michael Redgrave played notably as Shyock, Peggy Ashcroft as Portia and Harry Andrews s Antonio gave especially fine portrayals. Among he latest Shylocks have been Emlyn Williams, who ssayed the part in Margaret Webster's Stratford roduction (1956), and Peter O'Toole, who played ie role in Michael Langham's 1960 production at ie same theatre.

Stage History: America. The earliest reference to performance of *The Merchant of Venice* is Sepmber 5, 1752 at Williamsburg, Virginia, with Miss eatrice Hallam as Jessica, Mrs. Lewis Hallam as 'ortia, and Lewis Hallam, Jr., as Launcelot. After David Douglass assumed control of the American Company, *The Merchant of Venice* was acted at nnapolis in 1760, at the Southwark Theatre in hiladelphia in 1766, and at the John Street Theatre 1 New York in 1768. The two later productions arred Lewis Hallam the younger as the Jew. The omedy was again acted in Philadelphia in 1773. John Ienry appeared as Shylock and continued in the art for many years with the Hallam company. The ollowing year, a company under Thomas Wignell resented the play at the New Theatre in Philadelphia; Chalmers portrayed Shylock, and Mrs. Whitlock (formerly Eliza Kemble, youngest sister of the famous family) was Portia.

Thomas Abthorpe Cooper appeared as Shylock in 1799 in association with Hallam. A year later John Hodgkinson played the lead role. James Fennell, between sojourns in jail, proved a poor Bassanio; Hallam was again Antonio, Mrs. Hodgkinson was Jessica; Joseph Jefferson and John Hogg were Launcelot and Old Gobbo. Cooper reappeared in the part in January 1803 and continued to make regular appearances as the Jew throughout the decade.

George Frederick Cooke's first New York appearance as Shylock was on November 30, 1810. He never sacrificed the essentials of the character to gain applause with grandstand theatrics. Cooke's sarcasm in his hatred for Antonio was devastating. As one critic commented, "The alternate passions of avarice and revenge were exquisitely portrayed" in his conception, which also infused a hint of domestic sentiment into his agonizing rage at the discovery of Jessica's elopement. Cooke played the part during his last season at the Olympic on September 27, 1811. Subsequent Shylocks included Henry Finn, who made his New York debut as the Jew on January 16, 1818, repeating the role in 1820 and 1830; and Robert Campbell Maywood, who appeared in 1819, in 1826 at the Chatham Garden, and on October 17, 1826 at the Lafayette Theatre. In December 1820 New Yorkers saw Edmund Kean's famous interpretation of the Jew at the Anthony Street Theatre in the most effective production of the drama seen in the United States up to that time. The following spring, after Boston and Philadelphia engagements, Kean played the part again in New York, but irate theatregoers, protesting the actor's failure to appear for a Boston performance, necessitated his departure for England. A few years later he returned to America and acted Shylock in 1825, and twice in 1826. Other Shylocks at this time were Lee, at the Park Theatre during the 1824/5 season, and Charles Kean, visiting New York in 1830.

In 1824 Henry Wallack led a Chatham Garden production and proved exceptionally fine in the courtroom scene. Wallack appeared again in 1824 and in 1832, when Mrs. Thomas Hamblin portrayed Portia. Edwin Forrest acted Shylock for the first time in New York on July 23, 1826 at the Bowery Theatre, and repeated the role the next year. Two instances of eccentric casting followed soon after at the Park: On December 19, 1827 the then 16-year-old Clare Fisher gave her interpretation of the Jew; on November 29, 1830 an even younger Shylock, Master Joseph Burke, 11, performed in the role. More conventional impersonators of that period included Thomas Hamblin who, with Mrs. Hamblin, appeared in 1830; and, during the 1832/3 season, Charles Kemble, starring opposite Fanny Kemble's Portia.

In December 1858 J. W. Wallack staged a scenically magnificent *Merchant of Venice* in which he restored Morocco and Arragon, but omitted the last act. In the leading role, Wallack was criticized for too much vehemence, but his injured Jew on the whole was commendable, presenting at the last a foiled but not defeated Shylock. Lester Wallack, his son, portrayed Bassanio in this production, which ran for 33 consecutive performances.

After a Boston appearance as Shylock in 1866, Edwin Booth, who had played the role in Australia (1854) and in London (1861), acted in a scenic revival at the Winter Garden in New York on January 28, 1867. The production ran for several weeks despite the *Times*' disappointment with Booth's Jew, criticized as too melodramatic and for indulging in meaningless noise and purposeless rage. Booth, nevertheless, continued to appear regularly in the role and among his Portias were Mary McVicker, Bella Bateman, and, in 1889, Helena Modjeska. Booth's contemporaries also seen as Shylock include Edward L. Davenport, whose inconsistent personation revealed, first, a crafty schemer turning ferocious halfway through, and finally, a majestically tragic figure; John McCullough, a conventional, uninteresting Shylock; and Lawrence Barrett, a cold, vengeful, and malicious moneylender.

Richard Mansfield assumed the role at Hermann's on October 23, 1893, infusing Shylock with every redeeming characteristic possible and intimating at the close of the trial scene that this highly sympathetic Jew has been driven to suicide. When Augustin Daly presented *The Merchant* in 1898—his last Shakespeare revival—he chose a comedian, Sydney Herbert, for the lead. Thus began a short-lived trend which saw Nathaniel Goodwin, noted for his comic impersonations, attempt the role soon after in 1901 and Edward Hugh Sothern, also gifted in comedy, adopt the part and act it often in repertory throughout the early part of the 20th century opposite Julia Marlowe's Portia. Sothern's Shylock pleased audiences, but critics disapproved of his benevolently avaricious Jew. During this period, however, Robert Mantell deviated from the pattern, presenting Shylock as a portrait in calculated treachery.

Besides Sothern and Mantell, New York audiences in the first two decades of the 20th century saw Shylock portrayed by Ben Greet, John Kellerd, Forbes-Robertson, Herbert Tree, and Albert Bruning. In 1922 Bruning assumed Tubal when David Belasco presented *The Merchant* at the Lyceum; David Warfield as Shylock presented a highly intelligent and striking representation, but never approached greatness. This production broke *Merchant* records with 92 performances. Shylock had been in Walter Hampden's repertory for several years when, in 1925, he produced the comedy at his own theatre opposite Ethel Barrymore, an ineffably lovely Portia hailed as magnificent in the trial scene. Hampden's Jew, however, dominated. His bitter and lonely man of intellect exacted no sympathy as an unsentimental and vindictive bigot getting the worst in a situation where, for once, Antonio, brought to life by William Sauter, became interesting and believable. George Arliss attempted the Jew for Winthrop Ames at the Broadhurst in 1928, and while the production was marked with care and taste, its Shylock, clearly an insidious plotter, failed to achieve emotional force. The supporting cast did better. Peggy Wood's Portia rang true, especially in a casual and winning reading of the mercy speech, and that usually unappealing clown Launcelot Gobbo, as played by Romney Brent, threatened to run away with the play. The Gobbos were again indulged to the limit when Maury Tuckerman and Noel Ainley assumed the parts in a liberally cut revival at the Time Square staged by Andrew Leigh in December 1930 In the same production Maurice Moscovitch depicted a fawning but essentially good-natured Shylock pitted against a masculinely gruff Portia (Selen Royle) in a trial scene noted for its lack of bitterness The sting was removed and little inspiration evident

In the early 1930's, performances of the play were given by repertory groups, including Fritz Leiber' and the Shakespeare Theatre Company's. Otis Skinner acted Shylock opposite Maude Adams' Portia in 1931; Ian Keith and Estelle Winwood played thos parts in Minneapolis and at the Alvin in 1935; and in 1942 John Carradine acted the Jew in San Francisco, later touring as Shylock, among other roles with his own repertory company.

A rather youngish Shylock portrayed by Luthe Adler bowed at the New York City Center in Marcl 1953. The distasteful elements of the Jew's characte were avoided in a colorless portrayal directed by Albert Marre using a highly intelligible text for a otherwise undistinguished production. Philip Bourneuf was an agreeable Antonio but Margaret Phillips' cool, somewhat heartless Portia was a frost pleader for mercy. Another attempt to humaniz Shylock was made in 1955 at The Club Theatre i Finch College. The dignified tragic martyr, "a villain without venom," of Clarence Derwent presente a usurer too self-pitying to be able to arouse sympathy. A month later, in February, the Shakespearewrights' Thomas Barbour portrayed a pitiless, fastidious, haughty Jew; and that June, Frederick Vall another dignified Shylock, played for the Shakespeare Festival at Stratford, Ontario, under Tyron Guthrie's direction. In 1957 the American Festival a Stratford, Connecticut, offered an especially affectin *Merchant* with Morris Carnovsky and Katharin Hepburn. Carnovsky as a thoroughly human villair self-loving and without compassion, avoided self pity and won sympathy for the Jew; as an intelligent, determined Portia, Miss Hepburn brought additional charm to an already attractive productio directed by Jack Landau.

Two of the latest *Merchants*, both staged in 196 benefited from exceptional Shylocks. A colorful, vigorous, rapid-fire production by the Gateway Company under the direction of Boris Tumarin, who als starred, appeared at the Gate Theatre. In a performance without hysteria, Tumarin ably exemplified self-possessed Jew whose trace of stoicism carrie him through the condemnation to penury with dignity. Carol Gustafson gave a generally competen interpretation of Portia, executing the legal maneuvers more comfortably than the romantic stratagem

Perhaps the most original interpretation of Shylock in America in modern times was rendered b George C. Scott, who acted in the New York Shakespeare Festival's presentation at Central Park in Jun 1962. Never before was the Jew more intelligen more sardonic, more terrifying, and, at the same tim more understandable. In a bitter, self-mocking portrayal, the usurer bargains for his pound of fles with ironic jest, indulges in vengeful wit, and the as his cynical hatred builds, screams for payment i fully obsessive fury. Here was a Shylock whose intellectual superiority over his shallow Venetian adversaries was unmistakable.—M.G.

Bibliography. TEXT: *The Merchant of Venice*, New Cambridge Edition, Arthur Quiller-Couch and J. Dover Wilson, eds., 1926; *The Merchant of Venice*, New Arden Edition, John Russell Brown, ed., 1955. DATE: New Cambridge Edition; New Arden Edition. SOURCES: Cecil Roth, "The Background of Shylock," *Review of English Studies*, IX, 1933; Geoffrey Bullough, *Narrative and Dramatic Sources of Shakespeare*, Vol. I, 1957; Kenneth Muir, *Shakespeare's Sources*, Vol. I, 1957. COMMENT: Harley Granville-Barker, *Prefaces to Shakespeare*, 1927–1947; T. M. Parrott, *Shakespearean Comedy*, 1949; J. Dover Wilson, *Shakespeare's Happy Comedies*, 1963. STAGE HISTORY: New Arden Edition; T. Allston Brown, *A History of the New York Stage . . . to 1901*, 1903; William Winter, *Shakespeare on the Stage*, 3 vols., 1911–1916; G. C. D. Odell, *Shakespeare from Betterton to Irving*, 1920; J. C. Trewin, *Shakespeare on the English Stage, 1900–1964*, 1964.

Selected Criticism

WILLIAM HAZLITT. In proportion as Shylock has ceased to be a popular bugbear, 'baited with the rabble's curse,' he becomes a half-favourite with the philosophical part of the audience, who are disposed to think that Jewish revenge is at least as good as Christian injuries. Shylock is *a good hater;* 'a man no less sinned against than sinning.' If he carries his revenge too far, yet he has strong grounds for 'the lodged hate he bears Antonio,' which he explains with equal force of eloquence and reason. He seems the depositary of the vengeance of his race; and though the long habit of brooding over daily insults and injuries has crusted over his temper with inveterate misanthropy, and hardened him against the contempt of mankind, this adds but little to the triumphant pretensions of his enemies. There is a strong, quick, and deep sense of justice mixed up with the gall and bitterness of his resentment. The constant apprehension of being burnt alive, plundered, banished, reviled, and trampled on, might be supposed to sour the most forbearing nature, and to take something from that 'milk of human kindness,' with which his persecutors contemplated his indignities. The desire of revenge is almost inseparable from the sense of wrong; and we can hardly help sympathizing with the proud spirit, hid beneath his 'Jewish gaberdine,' stung to madness by repeated undeserved provocations, and labouring to throw off the load of obloquy and oppression heaped upon him and all his tribe by one desperate act of 'lawful' revenge, till the ferociousness of the means by which he is to execute his purpose, and the pertinacity with which he adheres to it, turn us against him; but even at last, when disappointed of the sanguinary revenge with which he had glutted his hopes, and exposed to beggary and contempt by the letter of the law on which he had insisted with so little remorse, we pity him, and think him hardly dealt with by his judges. [*Characters of Shakespeare's Plays*, 1817.]

HEINRICH HEINE. When I saw this play at Drury Lane, there stood behind me in the box a pale, fair Briton, who at the end of the fourth act, fell weeping passionately, several times exclaiming, "The poor man is wronged." It was a face of the noblest Grecian style, with eyes large and black. I have never been able to forget those large, black eyes that wept for Shylock.

When I think of those tears, I have to rank *The Merchant of Venice* with the Tragedies, although the frame of the Piece is decorated with the merriest figures of Masks, of Satyrs, and of Cupids, and the Poet meant the Play for a Comedy. Shakespeare intended perhaps, for the amusement of "the general," to represent a tormented Werewolf, a hateful, fabulous creature that thirsts for blood, and of course loses his daughter and his ducats, and is ridiculed into the bargain. But the genius of the Poet, the Genius of Humanity that reigned in him, stood ever above his private will; and so it happened that in Shylock, in spite of all his uncouth grimacings, the Poet vindicates an unfortunate sect, which for mysterious purposes, has been burdened by Providence with the hate of the rabble both high and low, and has reciprocated this hate—not always by love. [*Shakespeares Mädchen und Frauen*, 1839; trans. in *Complete Works*, 1892–1895.]

BERNHARD TEN BRINK. If Shylock is prevented from carrying out his bloody intentions in regard to Antonio, even if he is remorselessly punished, mortally wounded in what he holds most dear, it is nothing more than poetic justice. It is only against his being forced to become a convert that our feelings justly rebel. The contemporaries of the poet doubtless attached no such importance to this point. But it is not merely poetic justice that our feelings demand. Shylock has come too close to us, we have learned to know too intimately the grounds of his hatred, of the intensity of his resentment, his figure has become too humanly significant, and the misfortune which overtakes him appeals too deeply to our sympathies, to permit us to be reconciled to the idea that his fate, which moves us so tragically, should be conceived otherwise than as a tragedy. ["Shakespeare as Comic Poet," *Five Lectures on Shakespeare*, 1895.]

GEORG M. BRANDES. The great value of *The Merchant of Venice* lies in the depth and seriousness which Shakespeare has imparted to the vague outlines of character presented by the old stories, and in the ravishing moonlight melodies which bring the drama to a close . . . .

The conclusion of *The Merchant of Venice* brings us to the threshold of a term in Shakespeare's life instinct with high-pitched gaiety and gladness. In this, his brightest period, he fervently celebrates strength and wisdom in man, intellect and wit in woman; and these most brilliant years of his life are also the most musical. His poetry, his whole existence, seem now to be given over to music, to harmony. [*William Shakespeare: A Critical Study*, 1896.]

E. E. STOLL. The time is past for speaking of Shakespeare as utterly impartial or inscrutable: the study of his work and that of his fellows as an expression of Elizabethan ideas and techniques is teaching us better. The puzzle whether *The Merchant of Venice* is not meant for tragedy, for instance, is cleared up when, as Professor Baker suggests, we forget Sir Henry Irving's acting, and remember that the title—and the hero—is not the "*Jew of Venice*" as he would lead us to suppose; that this comedy is only like others, as *Measure for Measure* and *Much Ado*, not clear of the shadow of the fear of death; and that in closing with an act where Shylock and his knife are forgotten in the unravelling of the mystery between the lovers and the crowning of Antonio's happiness in theirs, it does not, from the Elizabethan point of view, perpetrate an anti-climax, but, like many another Elizabethan play, carries to completion what is a story for story's sake. "Shylock is, and always has been the hero," says Professor Schelling. But why, then, did Shakespeare drop his hero out of the play for good before the fourth act was over? It is a trick which he never repeated—a trick, I am persuaded, of which he was not capable . . . .

By all the devices, then, of Shakespeare's dramaturgy Shylock is proclaimed, as by the triple repetition of a crier, to be the villain, though a comic villain or butt. Nor does the poet let pass any of the prejudices of that day which might heighten this impression. A miser, a money-lender, a Jew—all three had from time immemorial been objects of popular detestation and ridicule, whether in life or on the stage. The union of them in one person is in Shakespeare's time the rule, both in plays and in "character"-writing: to the popular imagination a money-lender was a sordid miser with a hooked nose. So it is in the acknowledged prototype of Shylock, Marlowe's "bottle-nosed" monster, Barabas, the Jew of Malta. ["Shylock, The Complete Villain," *Shakespeare Studies*, 1927.]

NEVILL COGHILL. We must not, therefore, think the ruse by which Portia entraps Shylock is some sly part of her character, for it is in the tradition; besides she gives Shylock every chance. Thrice his money is offered him. He is begged to supply a surgeon. But no, it is not in the bond. From the point of view of the medium of theatre, the scene is, of course, constructed on the principle of peripeteia, or sudden reversal of situation, one of the great devices of dramaturgy. At one moment we see Mercy a suppliant to Justice, and at the next, in a flash, Justice is a suppliant to Mercy. The reversal is as instantaneous as it is unexpected to an audience that does not know the story in advance . . . .

It will, of course, be argued that it is painful for Shylock to swallow his pride, abjure his racial faith, and receive baptism. But then Christianity is painful. If we allow our thoughts to pursue Shylock after he left the Court we may well wonder whether his compulsory submission to baptism in the end induced him to take up his cross and follow Christ. But from Antonio's point of view, Shylock has at least been given his chance of eternal joy, and it is he, Antonio, that has given it to him. Mercy has triumphed over justice, even if the way of mercy is a hard way. ["The Basis of Shakespearian Comedy: A Study in Medieval Affinities," *Essays and Studies*, n.s. III, 1950.]

BRENTS STIRLING. The verse is Shakespeare at his early lyrical best, but its exuberance is controlled by dramatic purpose and fitness. Salerio's opening virtuosity ending in his image of the "wealthy Andrew docked in sand," and Gratiano's lines on men whose faces "do cream and mantle like a standing pond," nicely fit the speakers and the situation. So do Shylock's passages of self-justification in I, iii and III, i. Not only are they expertly set going but they are enhanced by dramatic context. "Hath not a Je eyes" gains greatly from Salerio's taunting "What that good for?" which launches it, and from Shy lock's lines with Tubal which follow it and qualif its effect. Even the set pieces, the lyrical passages Act V, are dramatically paced. At this relativel early date Shakespeare had mastered the art of pc etry within the exacting medium of drama.

A unifying element of the verse is phrasal repet tion in varying forms for varying purposes. As rhythmic quality of Shylock's speech it runs steadil for four acts, but this important effect, already note has its counterparts. Begin, for example, with Shy lock's words: "Two thousand ducats in that, an other precious, precious jewels. I would my daughte were dead at my foot, and the jewels in her ea Would she were hearsed at my foot, and the duca in her coffin!" (III, i, 77–80) Compare this echoin of phrase with Portia's:

Though for myself alone
I would not be ambitious in my wish
To wish myself much better, yet for you
I would be trebled twenty times myself,
A thousand times more fair, ten thousand times
more rich,
That only to stand high in your account,
I might in virtues, beauties, livings, friends,
Exceed account.
(III, ii, 150–57)

Add another instance, Bassanio's speech at III, i 252–63, and observe finally how the unity in variet extends to the quite different but still analogous pas sages of V, i, 1–24 ("in such a night") and 192–20 ("the ring"). [Introduction to *The Merchant o Venice*, The Pelican Shakespeare, 1959.]

FRANK KERMODE. We are not likely, whether or n we share his high opinion of Shakespeare as a comi writer, to fall into Johnson's error when he di missed the reiteration of the word 'gentle' in th play as only another example of Shakespeare's weak ness for this 'fatal Cleopatra', the pun. 'Gentlenes in this play means civility in its old full sense, natur improved; but it also means 'Gentile', in the sense c Christian, which amounts, in a way, to the sam thing . . .

The Merchant of Venice, then, is 'about' judgmen redemption and mercy; the supersession in huma history of the grim four thousand years of un alleviated justice by the era of love and mercy. I begins with usury and corrupt love; it ends wit harmony and perfect love. And all the time it tell its audience that this is its subject; only by a deter mined effort to avoid the obvious can one mistak the theme of *The Merchant of Venice*. ["Th Mature Comedies," *Early Shakespeare*, Stratford Upon-Avon Studies 3, 1961.]

J. DOVER WILSON. . . . Portia's speech, one of th greatest sermons in all literature, an expression o religious thought worthy to set beside St. Paul' hymn in praise of Love, is of course addressed to th Jew. But I find it incredible that Shakespeare in tended it for Jews alone. The very fact that it i based throughout upon the Lord's Prayer, whic would mean nothing to a Hebrew, suggests that i was composed to knock at Christian hearts.

When Q accuses Shakespeare of not setting up th

leal of 'clemency, charity and specifically Christian harity', to oppose that of Cruelty and Revenge, he rangely forgets 'the quality of Mercy'. And Shy-ock, as I have said, is let off very lightly. He loses e money he had made by usury—that was only ght and proper. He is compelled to become a hristian—that was only an enforced benefit. But he as not hanged, drawn and quartered as Dr. Lopez as—much to Gratiano's disgust.

Shylock is a terrible old man. But he is the inevita-le product of centuries of racial persecution. Shake-peare does not draw this moral. He merely exposes e situation. He is neither for nor against Shylock. hakespeare never takes sides. Yet surely if he were ive today he would see in Mercy, mercy in the idest sense, which embraces understanding and for-iveness, the only possible solution of our racial atreds and enmities. [*Shakespeare's Happy Come-ies*, 1962.]

Merchants. In *The Comedy of Errors*, two minor peaking roles. In I, ii, the First Merchant advises ntipholus and Dromio of Syracuse to pretend that ey are from Epidamnum, lest their goods be con-scated and they be condemned to death under a cal edict forbidding foreign traders. In IV, i, the econd Merchant demands repayment of a debt from ngelo, who, in order to comply, must collect a ebt from Antipholus. In V, i, mistaking Antipholus f Syracuse for his brother, the Second Merchant in-ılts him and is challenged to a duel.

Merchant Taylors' School. English public school hose boys acted in the Elizabethan theatre. The Ierchant Taylors' School of London was founded 1 1561 with Richard Mulcaster (c. 1530–1611) as eadmaster. The boys' first recorded performances vere in 1572/3 when they played before the Mer-hant Taylors' Company at the Common Hall. The udience evidently misbehaved to the extent that the ignitaries of the Common Hall found that

> Everye lewd persone thinketh himself (for his penny) worthye of the chiefe and most comodious place withoute respecte of any other either for age or estimacion in the common weale.

'he boys were refused the use of the Common Hall, herefore, for 1574.

Under Mulcaster the boys gave several court per-ormances, including *Ariodante and Genevora*, prob-bly derived from Ariosto's *Orlando Furioso* and a ossible source of *Much Ado About Nothing*. In 586 Mulcaster resigned his position after a quarrel vith the Merchant Taylors. After that date regular erformances of plays ceased. [E. K. Chambers, *The Elizabethan Stage*, 1923.]

Mercutio. In *Romeo and Juliet*, the friend of Ro-neo whose ribald wit is matched by his hot temper. Iercutio is generally regarded as one of the greatest f Shakespeare's secondary heroes, and during his ppearances on the stage he virtually overshadows veryone else. It has been suggested that Mercutio is hakespeare's portrayal of Christopher Marlowe, vho, like Mercutio, was stabbed during an argument, nd who exhibited the same "mercurial" tempera-ent. [John W. Klein, "Was Mercutio Christopher Iarlowe?" *Drama*, Spring, 1961.]

Meres, Francis (1565–1647). Schoolmaster, critic, nd divine. Meres' PALLADIS TAMIA contains the most significant contemporary allusion to Shakespeare. Meres was educated at Cambridge, receiving his M.A. in 1591. In 1597 he was residing in London, where he doubtless became interested in the theatre and contemporary literature, interests reflected in the *Palladis Tamia* which he published in 1598. Meres translated from the Spanish *Grenada's Devotion* (1598) and *The sinners guyde* (1614), two homiletic religious guides by Luis de Granada. Meres, an An-glican divine, secured a living as rector of Wing in Rutland, retaining this office until his death.

Mérimée, Prosper. See FRANCE.

Mermaid Tavern. A 17th-century London tavern in Bread Street, Cheapside, the most famous gather-ing place for actors, playwrights, and others inter-ested in literature and the arts. At the Mermaid Tavern, according to Thomas Coryat (1577–1617) in his *Crudities* (1611), on the first Friday of every month young noblemen, aesthetes from the inns of court, actors, playwrights, including Shakespeare, Ben Jonson, and Beaumont and Fletcher, used to gather for drink and talk. Francis Beaumont has left us a vivid description of these meetings:

> What things have we seen
> Done at the Mermaid! heard what words that have been
> So nimble, and so full of subtile flame,
> As if that every one, from whence they came,
> Had meant to put his whole wit in a jest
> And had resolv'd to live a fool the rest
> Of his dull life.

Indirect evidence of Shakespeare's frequenting of the Mermaid has been provided by Leslie Hotson. Hotson has demonstrated that the William JOHNSON who acted as one of the poet's trustees in the pur-chase of the Blackfriars Gate-House was the land-lord of the Mermaid. [Leslie Hotson, *Shakespeare's Sonnets Dated*, 1949.]

Merry Conceited Humours of Bottom the Weaver. See Robert Cox.

Merry Devil of Edmonton, The (c. 1603). An anonymous play ascribed to Shakespeare during the latter half of the 17th century. The play was first en-tered in the Stationers' Register in 1607 and published in 1608. The title page describes it as "Acted, by his Maiesties Seruants, at the Globe . . ." The play was re-entered in the Register in 1653 by Humphrey Moseley as by "Wm. Shakespeare." The attribution to Shakespeare was also made by Francis Kirkman and Edward Archer in their respective catalogues of plays. One or two lines in the play seem to echo Fal-staff in *2 Henry IV* and the character of the Host may be derived from the Host of the Garter Inn in *The Merry Wives of Windsor*. However, there is no significant internal evidence that would indicate Shakespeare's authorship, and it is believed by some that Michael Drayton is the author. *The Merry Devil* was among the plays bound together in a vol-ume owned by Charles II under the title "Shake-speare, Vol. I."

Merry Jeste of a Shrewde and Curste Wyfe, Lapped in Morrelles Skin, A. See THE TAMING OF THE SHREW: *Sources*.

Merry Loungers, The. An anonymous 17th-cen-tury playlet, probably part of a college festivity. *The Merry Loungers* is notable for a passage in which some of Shakespeare's famous lines are garbled for comic effect:

> by hell it were an easy thing to pluck bright honor from the pale-faced moon—to morrow, to morrow & to morrow steals in a petty pace from day to day and all our yesterdays have lighted fools to their eternal homes, out-out brief candle-I am thy fathers spirit—(whistles and dances) well, but come lets go.

The lines are amusing testimony of Shakespeare early popularity.

THE

Merry VVives of WINDSOR.

Merry Wives of Windsor, The. A comedy by Shakespeare.

Text. The First Folio (1623) provides the authoritative text. It was apparently printed from a transcript of the King's Men's PROMPT-BOOK, or official acting version of the play, made by Ralph Crane, a professional scribe. It contains no stage directions; no "exits," except for those at the end of the scenes; and no "enters." Instead, at the head of each scene, there is a list of all the characters about to take part in it, in the order of their appearance. J. Dover Wilson's theory that the copy for the First Folio text had been concocted by stringing together the players' sides (parts), with the aid of the theatrical PLOT (see ASSEMBLED TEXTS), has not been widely accepted.

On January 18, 1602 an earlier version of the play was entered in the Stationers' Register:

> John Busby. Entred for his copie vnder the hand of master Seton, A booke called An excellent and pleasant conceited commedie of Sir John Faulstof and the merry wyves of Windesor vj[d]. Arthur Johnson. Entred for his Copye by assignement from John Busbye, A booke Called an excellent and pleasant conceyted Comedie of Sir John Faulstafe and the merye wyves of Windsor.

This earlier version was published in quarto in the same year with the following title page:

> A Most pleasaunt and excellent conceited Comedie, of Syr Iohn Falstaffe, and the merrie Wiues of Windsor Entermixed with sundrie variable and pleasing humors, of Syr Hugh the Welch Knight, Iustice Shallow, and his wise Cousin M. Slender. With the swaggering vaine of Auncient Pistoll, and Corporall Nym. By William Shakespeare. As it hath bene diuers times Acted by the right Honorable my Lord Chamberlaines seruants. Both before her Maiestie, and else-where. London Printed by T. C. [Thomas Creede] for Arthur Iohnson, and are to be sold at his shop in Powles Church-yard, at the signe of the Flower de Leus and the Crowne. 1602.

The 1602 edition is a "bad quarto," a mangle form of the play reported from memory by one ‹ the actors, probably the one who played the Ho (see MEMORIAL RECONSTRUCTION). It was reprinted i 1619 by William Jaggard.

Date. Recent scholarship has provided strong ev dence that *The Merry Wives of Windsor* was wri ten early in 1597 and first performed at initiatio ceremonies for the newly elected Knights of th Garter. The occasion was the Feast of St. Georg April 23, on which day the Knights staged a elaborate ceremony in the great hall at Windsc Castle. In 1597 two of the new knights were Georg Carey, Lord Hunsdon, the patron of Shakespeare company, and Frederick, duke of Württember satirized in the play as the "duke de Jamany mentioned below. These facts, together with th play's frequent allusions to Windsor Castle and th Garter, validate connecting the play with this occa sion. On this basis, the dates of the three Falsta plays can be established as follows: *1 Henry IV*, la 1596; *2 Henry IV*, early 1597; *The Merry Wives* c *Windsor*, April 1597.

Sources. No source for this comedy is extan However, we can perhaps determine its character b approaching the problem obliquely, beginning wit John DENNIS' report of the inception of the comedy appearing in his "Epistle Dedicatory" to *The Comi cal Gallant* (1702), his revision of Shakespeare comedy. He writes, "That this Comedy was nc despicable, I guess'd for several Reasons: First, know very well, that it hath pleas'd one of th greatest Queens that ever was in the world—Th Comedy was written at her command, and by he direction, and she was so eager to see it Acted, th she commanded it to be finished in fourteen day and was afterward, as Tradition tells us, very we pleas'd. At the Representation."

Nicholas Rowe, in his "Life of Shakespeare" pre

A

Most pleasaunt and excellent conceited Comedie, of Syr *Iohn Falstaffe*, and the merrie Wiues of *Windsor*.

Entermixed with sundrie variable and pleasing humors, of Syr *Hugh* the Welch Knight, Iustice *Shallow*, and his wise Cousin M. *Slender*.

With the swaggering vaine of Auncient *Pistoll*, and Corporall *Nym*.

By *William Shakespeare*.

As it hath bene diuers times Acted by the right Honorable my Lord Chamberlaines seruants. Both before her Maiestie, and else-where.

LONDON
Printed by T. C. for Arthur Iohnson, and are to be sold at his shop in Powles Church yard, at the signe of the Flower de Leuse and the Crowne.
1602.

TITLE PAGE OF THE FIRST QUARTO OF *The Merry Wives of Windsor* (1602). THIS IS A BAD QUARTO.

ixed to his six-volume edition of the *Works* (1709), mbellishes Dennis' account. He adds: "Queen Elizabeth was so well pleased with that admirable character of Falstaff in the two parts of *Henry IV* hat she commanded him [Shakespeare] to continue t for one more play and show him in love." Although the essential parts of this tradition have been ccepted by most critics, few believe that the dramatist could have composed a completely new play in so short a time. It seems likely, therefore, hat he remade, or at least revived, an old play, probably one already owned by his company. According to the speculations of William Green, Queen Elizabeth saw *1 Henry IV* during the 1596/7 Christmas revels, when Lord Hunsdon's Men played t at court. They acted before the queen six times between December 26 and 27, 1596 and February 597. One of the six plays then presented may well have been *2 Henry IV*. Captivated by Falstaff, she told her cousin George Carey, Lord Hunsdon, the patron of Shakespeare's company, that she would like to see a play in which the old rogue was in love. On April 17 Lord Hunsdon was appointed lord chamberlain and on April 23 was elected a Knight of the Garter. In gratitude to the queen for the high honors she had bestowed upon him, he commissioned Shakespeare, the company's playwright, to compose a play on Falstaff as a lover. Hunsdon was able to give Shakespeare only three weeks' notice, because he knew the date of his initiation only that long before it was to take place. Although 3 weeks is a little longer than Dennis' 14 days, it still was probably too short a time in which to turn out a completely new play, even for so skillful a craftsman as Shakespeare. Therefore he almost surely was forced to revive an old one.

Frequent efforts have been made to discover the characteristics of this suppositious source. As long ago as 1886 Fleay suggested that it may have been the *Jealous Comedy*, a drama Henslowe marks in his diary as "new" and records as being first performed on January 5, 1593 by the combined Admiral's and Strange's Men.

The Jealous Comedy was probably an example of Italian popular comedy, in which the characters are fixed types. Shakespeare had adopted many of them in *The Two Gentlemen of Verona*. Falstaff is no longer the merry roistering companion of Prince Hal. He has been thrust into the role of the *pedante* or schoolteacher. The characteristic business of this type of figure was to exhort his pupil to beware of illicit love, but later to be caught himself *in flagrante delicto* and publicly disgraced. This is Falstaff's situation. The features of his role that are identical with those of the pedants have been enumerated in the character of Holofernes in *Love's Labour's Lost*. One of the most revealing features of the pedant is the nature of his figures of speech. They are grammar-oriented. A good example occurs in Falstaff's description of Mrs. Ford's arts of seduction: "I can construe the action of her familiar style; and the hardest voice of her behaviour, to be Englished rightly, is, 'I am Sir John Falstaff's.'" Pistol's comment is, "He hath studied her will, and translated her will, out of honesty into English" (I, iii, 50–55). Thus, most of the time this debased Falstaff talks not like Prince Hal's boon companion, nor like the "high-falutin lover" that Arthur Quiller-Couch imagines his prototype to have been, but like the typical *pedante* of Italian comedy. Other characters in *The Merry Wives* are also developments of some of the fixed types of Italian popular comedy. The principal source of the play, then, is, in all probability, the suppositious *Jealous Comedy*.

Clear evidence of the topical origin of the horse-stealing scene appears in the Quarto text in Evans' warning to the Host:

> To have a care of your entertainments
> For there is three sorts of cosen garmombles,
> Is cosen all the Host of Maidenhead and
> Readings.
>
> (Q1, IV, v)

The reference is further clarified by Dr. Caius' pronouncement:

> I cannot tell vat is dat: but it is tell-a me dat you make grand preparation for a duke de Jamany.
>
> (IV, v, 87–89)

These are references to the career of a certain Count Mömpelgart, who became duke of Württemberg in 1593. A guest at Windsor Castle for two or three days in 1592, he became a laughingstock and a nuisance to the queen by sending a succession of envoys to importune her to nominate him to the Order of the Garter. The first of these envoys was incidentally engaged in buying horses for his master. After much delay the queen nominated Duke Frederick to the order in April 1596, and a knight elect of the order on April 23, 1597, *in absentia*. All these facts were well known to the courtiers and reference to the German lord would have aroused laughter among the attendants at the April 23 initiation.

The belief, held for many years, that in his portrait of Justice Shallow, Shakespeare was directing a satirical thrust at Sir Thomas Lucy has been undermined by Leslie Hotson, who has made a strong case for Shallow's being a portrait of a Surrey justice of the peace, William GARDINER. Slender is thought by Hotson to be a hit at William WAYTE, Gardiner's stepson, who sued for sureties of the peace against Shakespeare and others in 1596.

Hotson also argues that the name "Brooke," used by Master Ford in the quarto version of the play, is a satirical allusion to William Brooke, 7th Lord COBHAM and lord chamberlain from August 1596 until March 1597. William Green, however, suggests that the similarity was coincidental and that the name was changed to "Broome" in the First Folio, when the possible insult was discovered.—O. J. C.

Plot Synopsis. Act I. Robert Shallow, a country justice, and his cousin Slender claim that they have been wronged by Sir John Falstaff and those "cony-catching rascals" Bardolph, Nym, and Pistol. Referees in the dispute are the Host of the Garter Inn; Sir Hugh Evans, a Welsh parson; and Mr. Page, who invites them to dine at his home and "drink down all unkindness." Page has a daughter, Anne, whose other attractions are enhanced by the fact that she has £700 and "possibilities." She is sought in matrimony both by Slender, who is spurred to the chase by Shallow and Sir Hugh, and by Doctor Caius, a French physician. When Sir Hugh asks Mistress Quickly, Caius' housekeeper, to intercede on Slender's behalf, the peppery Frenchman challenges the parson to a duel. Mistress Quickly encourages both Slender and Caius, as well as Fenton, another gentleman in love with Anne.

Meanwhile, Falstaff, who is forced by poverty to discharge some of his followers, launches Bardolph in a career as a tapster at the Garter. He is convinced that Mrs. Page and her friend Mrs. Ford have favored him with "the leer of invitation," and since they control the purse strings in their households, he hopes to seduce them and use them as his "exchequers." He pens identical love letters to the ladies, and, when Nym and Pistol virtuously refuse to deliver them, he dismisses them both and entrusts the missives to his page, Robin. Nym and Pistol decide to avenge themselves by telling Page and Ford of Falstaff's intentions.

Act II. Mrs. Page and Mrs. Ford, far from succumbing to Falstaff's advances, agree to take revenge on the "greasy knight" by pretending to encourage his suit. Using Mistress Quickly as a go-between, Mrs. Ford informs Falstaff that her husband will be away from home that morning between 10 and 11. Meanwhile, Ford and Page have been told of Falstaff's designs by Pistol and Nym; Page h complete trust in his wife, but the suspicious For decides to test Mrs. Ford's fidelity. Posing as Master Brooke, he asks Falstaff's help in conqueri Mrs. Ford and offers to supply him with amp funds for the campaign. When Falstaff boasts of h forthcoming appointment with the lady, Ford, to mented by "the hell of having a false woman resolves to prevent the encounter.

Act III. Sir Hugh arrives at the field designate for his duel with Caius, but finds no sign of t Frenchman. The Host of the Garter Inn later r veals that he has deliberately sent the would-b duelists to different places and is able, without muc difficulty, to effect a reconciliation. Slender, mea while, continues to sigh for "sweet Anne Page" ar obtains the support of her father, though Mrs. Pag prefers the doctor. Fenton is rejected by Page b cause of his impoverished estate and his form association with the wild Prince Hal and Poins.

Falstaff has barely begun his wooing of Mrs. Fo when Mrs. Page bursts in to announce that Ford on his way with half the village at his heels. Falsta is obliged to hide in a basket under a pile of soil linen. Mrs. Ford's servants, following previous i structions, promptly leave with the basket ar deposit its contents in a muddy ditch near th Thames. When a thorough search of the house fai to uncover any trace of an intruder, Page reproach Ford for doubting his wife's virtue, but Ford r mains unconvinced. Their wives decide that Fa staff's "dissolute disease" calls for another dose the same medicine and agree to repeat their dece tion. Accordingly, the next day Mrs. Ford sen Mistress Quickly to offer him her apologies as we as an invitation to visit her again. Falstaff, despi his unhappiness over his ducking, readily assen When Ford, still in the guise of Master Brook learns of the assignation, he vows that the lechero Falstaff will not elude him a second time.

Act IV. Falstaff appears at Mrs. Ford's house the appointed hour only to be interrupted once mo by her jealous husband. She and Mrs. Page prev upon Falstaff to disguise himself in a gown belon ing to Mother Prat, the witch of Brentford; th neglect to inform him, however, that Mr. Fo loathes the old hag and has forbidden her to ent his house. Thus, when Falstaff makes his appearan in the witch's clothes, Ford drives him away with shower of blows.

Having decided that Falstaff has learned his lesso Mrs. Page and Mrs. Ford inform their husbands the hoax they had perpetrated on the old knigh Ford asks his wife's pardon and promises never aga to mistrust her. When Page suggests that they enj further sport with Falstaff, his wife reminds the of an old superstition dealing with the oak of Her the hunter in Windsor Forest; she proposes th they lure Falstaff to this supposedly haunted sp and descend upon him in the guise of fairies ar goblins. Page secretly resolves to use the occasion enable Slender to elope with Anne, while Mrs. Pa makes similar plans for Caius. Fenton, who has wo Anne's love, reveals to the Host of the Garter th she intends to deceive both her parents and mar him.

Act V. Falstaff, disguised as Herne the hunter and sporting a pair of horns, arrives in the forest at midnight and meets Mrs. Page and Mrs. Ford. Supposedly frightened by a noise, the ladies run off, whereupon Evans, in the garb of a satyr, enters with Pistol, Anne, Mistress Quickly, and others, all dressed as fairies and hobgoblins. As Falstaff lies on the ground, they pinch him and burn him with tapers, upbraiding him for his lasciviousness. Meanwhile, Caius steals away with a fairy clad in green and Slender with one dressed in white, while Fenton escapes with a third. The Pages and Fords now appear and unfold the entire scheme to the mortified Falstaff. After Slender and Caius have revealed that they have been duped into fleeing with boys, Anne and Fenton return to announce that they have just been married. Accepting the situation, Mr. Page wishes joy to his new son-in-law, and his wife invites the company, including Falstaff, to her home to "laugh this sport o'er by a country fire."—H. D.

Comment. The very first scene awakens false hopes that Shakespeare is about to write a new play about the authentic Falstaff and his old cronies. What better way to re-create his milieu than to introduce him in company with Bardolph, Pistol, and Nym, with fresh deviltry in prospect. They are ready to confront Justice Shallow, who has come to town in search of redress for injuries Falstaff had done him. Shallow has brought with him a country cousin named Slender, a typical English lout, whose principal enthusiasm is the racing of hounds on Cotsall. For his social graces he depends on his *Book of Songs and Sonnets* (see TOTTEL'S MISCELLANY) and his indispensable *Book of Riddles*. He has a grievance against Falstaff's crew: they have got him drunk in a tavern and picked his pockets. These two threads of a promising new plot are cut almost at once. They come to nothing. The author, apparently realizing that he did not have time to develop his source so thoroughly, left them dangling. The three rascals soon disappear. Bardolph becomes a drawer (barkeeper), while Nym and Pistol, discharged for refusing to carry Falstaff's love letters to Mistresses Ford and Page, turn against him and betray to the husbands of the merry wives Falstaff's plans for seducing them.

For Slender, however, Shakespeare has further use. Sir Hugh Evans, a Welsh parson and tutor to Page's boy, suggests that a marriage be arranged between Slender and Page's rich daughter, Anne. Shallow accepts the idea with enthusiasm and Slender becomes one of the three suitors of the *amorosa*, a conventional situation in Italianate comedy. The other two candidates for her hand are Dr. Caius and Master Fenton, the girl's favorite. This triplicate love story comes to hold as important a place in the organization of the play as the repeated duping of Falstaff. Shakespeare shows the importance that he gave to this theme by giving full play to the absurdities of both Slender and Dr. Caius. Seizing the chance to ridicule the Elizabethan gentry's preference for foreign doctors, he makes Dr. Caius French. Caius suffers from the paroxysms of excitement that Elizabethans thought were typical of Frenchmen. Slender's efforts to do his loutish best in his wooing of Anne Page form one of the funniest situations in the play. Clumsy, boorish lovers were often given comparable love scenes. A freshly conceived character put into a conventional situation serves, here as elsewhere in the poet's work, as a fortunate stimulus to his invention.

The Garter Inn, where Falstaff is lodged, and its Host at once call to mind the Boar's Head Tavern in *1* and *2 Henry IV* where Falstaff took his ease. This Host does more than serve his guests. He assumes some of the functions traditionally performed in Italian comedy by the tricky servant of the *amoroso*. This stock character's principal business is to help his master to win the *amorosa*, in spite of her parents' opposition to the match. The Host also initiates and precipitates the duel between Dr. Caius and Sir Hugh. In this plotting he is pure *zanni*, delighting in mischief for its own sake and in exposing the asininity of Master Fenton's rivals. Yet besides being a typical zany, the Host displays personal eccentricities from the moment of his first appearance. The editors of the Cambridge edition of this play were certain that the Host is a portrait of a real individual well known in Windsor. Their opinion was that "No one can doubt . . . that the part of mine Host of the Garter ridicules some actual personage . . . ."

Mistress Quickly brings to mind Falstaff's entourage even more surely than does the host. The hostess of the Boar's Head Tavern has become Dr. Caius' maid of all work, a natural declension. In her early scenes she exhibits her familiar warmhearted stupidity and her maundering abuse of the king's English. Later she becomes a busy go-between, a "good she-Mercury" offering help to each of Anne's three suitors. She says, "I will do what I can for them all three; for so I have promised, and I'll be as good as my word; but speciously for Master Fenton" (III, iv, 111–113). (He has just thrust money into her hand.) She also acts as go-between for the wives and their dupe. Burdened by so many duties, her original character disintegrates to such a degree that the dramatist does not hesitate to cast her as the fairy queen in the final masquelike scene. In that scene Falstaff, equipped with horns, in the guise of Herne the hunter, is pinched and pulled by fairies, who seek thus to purge him of his "unchaste desire." The little creatures were doubtless impersonated by the ten or more singing boys maintained as choristers by the Chapel Royal in Windsor Castle and trained to act. In this scene the denouement of the romantic plot is hastily acted out in pantomime. Dr. Caius and Slender are deceived into choosing the wrong images of Mistress Anne. Later each discovers that, instead of the girl, he has picked "a great lubberly boy," while Fenton, properly coached, steals away with the real *amorosa*. Anne's parents in a later scene are reconciled to the marriage they have tried to prevent. Throughout the comedy the threads of the definite plots are loosened in order to give scope to the eccentricities and imbecilities of a group of English villagers. Shakespeare put his imagination so generously into the service of these ridiculous folk that they excite bursts of laughter in every audience that watches them frolic on the stage. Despite the obvious structural defects of the play, its crowding of dramatic themes derived from various sources, it remains one of the most popular of Shakespeare's comedies. It communicates the sense of mirth and jollity that was a product of the comic verve of which he was master, particularly from the years 1596–1602.—O. J. C.

Stage History: England. A performance of the comedy was probably enacted on April 23, 1597, as explained above under *Date*. The First Quarto (1602) announces that the play "hath bene diuers times Acted by the right Honorable My Lord Chamberlaine's seruants Both before her Maiestie, and else-where." It was acted at Whitehall on November 4, 1604, and before Charles I and his queen, Henrietta Maria, by Lady Elizabeth's Servants at the Cockpit at Court on November 15, 1638. After the Restoration, it was one of the plays assigned to Thomas Killigrew, whose company, according to John Downes, acted it "but now and then." However, Samuel Pepys saw it three times between 1660 and 1667. In no one of these three performances did either the text or the actors please him at all. John DENNIS' adaptation, called *The Comical Gallant or The Amours of Sir John Falstaff*, was mounted at Drury Lane in 1702. It was acted by royal command on April 23, 1704, with Thomas Betterton as Falstaff, Anne Bracegirdle as Mistress Ford, and Elizabeth Barry as Mistress Page. The Falstaff of *The Merry Wives* was James Quin's most popular role. He first appeared in it on October 22, 1720 at Lincoln's Inn Fields, acting the part 18 times during the rest of the 1720/1 season, and, in December 1734, at Drury Lane for five successive evenings. The comedy's popularity continued throughout the 18th century. All the principal actors played Falstaff and the most popular actresses one of the two merry wives. The vogue persisted throughout the 19th century. In 1840 George Frederick Cooke played Falstaff at Covent Garden, with John Philip Kemble as Master Ford. Frederick Reynolds made an opera out of *The Merry Wives* in 1824, with music by Henry Bishop (see MUSIC BASED ON THE PLAYS). It was produced in February of that year with Elizabeth Vestris in the cast. Some of Bishop's music clung to many subsequent productions until 1851, when Charles Kean produced the comedy with the text purged of all its accretions for the opening of his first season as sole manager of the Princess' Theatre. He did retain one of the songs that had become popular to the words, "Fie on sinful fantasy." This production, with a cast which included Mr. and Mrs. Kean (Ellen Tree) playing Mr. and Mrs. Ford, George Bartley as Falstaff, and J. P. Harley as Slender, established the reputation of the house in a 25-night run. When Samuel Phelps staged the comedy at the Gaiety Theatre in December 1874, he substituted for the old favorite a song specially written for the production, "Love laid his sleepless head on a thorny rosy bed," with words by Swinburne and music by Sir Arthur Sullivan. The audience vocally protested the substitution.

In 1889 Beerbohm Tree in the role of Falstaff presented *The Merry Wives* as his first Shakespearean revival at the Haymarket, with Lady Tree playing Anne Page. At His Majesty's in 1902, he staged a three-act version, with Madge Kendal and Ellen Terry as Mistress Ford and Mistress Page. Oscar Asche upset the critics with his wintry version of the comedy, in opposition to the traditional "April and May" setting, at the Garrick in 1911. Although his interpretation of the season is supported in the text by Mistress Page's invitation to "laugh this sport o'er by a country fire," Page's description of "a raw, rheumatic day," and the tale of Herne the hunter who "doth all the winter time, at still midnight, walk round about an oak," Asche was condemned.

The critic James Agate called W. Bridges-Adams' 1923 production for Nigel Playfair's Lyric, Hammersmith, "a gorgeous success," but the play attracted only a small audience. Its cast—Edith Evans, an animated Mistress Page; Dorothy Green, a gay Mistress Ford; Roy Byford, an unpadded Falstaff; and Randle Ayrton, a frenzied Ford—were as yet not well known, and although the producer had an established reputation at Stratford-upon-Avon he was unfamiliar to London. Playfair recalled, "The magic blight of Shakespeare's name settled heavily on the box-office."

The magic of Ernest Milton's rendition of Master Ford amply compensated for scenic poverty at the Theatre Royal when, in 1924, Harold V. Neilson introduced him to Plymouth at one of his annual "festivals." As "Master Brooke," Milton tempted Falstaff with cleverly measured advances and withdrawals of the gold.

Oscar Asche badly mishandled his modern-dress version of the comedy when, in 1929, he altered the text to include a recitation of "The Charge of the Light Brigade," along with other unseemly innovations. The critics blasted him; the cast, which included Robert Atkins as Ford and Hay Petrie as Parson Hugh, opened at the Haymarket on July 26; the production was transferred to the Apollo the next day, where it lasted for less than a week.

During the 1929/30 season, the Cambridge Festival Theatre under Tyrone Guthrie staged *The Merry Wives*. In 1931 Baliol Holloway played Falstaff at the Duchess in his own production of the farce. The Winter Garden was the scene in 1932 of Frank Benson's unofficial farewell to London, in which he played Dr. Caius. Oscar Asche reverted to traditional staging for this production, which saw him in his last major role, that of Falstaff. Stanley Bell was enlisted into the effort to establish Shakespeare at the Manchester Hippodrome; but his nonscenic *Merry Wives* in May 1934, with Violet and Irene Vanbrugh as the Mistresses Ford and Page, was a financial failure. Theodore Komisarjevsky tried to breathe some new life into the dispirited Memorial Theatre at Stratford-upon-Avon with his imaginative production in 1935 employing a Viennese setting. Roy Byford's Falstaff wore whiskers and a scarlet hunting coat in this *Merry Wives*. Byford played Falstaff for Robert Atkins at the Ring in 1937. Those devoted wives, the Vanbrugh sisters, acted in this production as well as in Donald Wolfit's one-hour version for his lunchtime Shakespeare at the Strand in 1940. Wolfit took the role of Falstaff then and in 1942. That same year, Esmé Church produced *The Merry Wives* at the New Theatre. The comedy was largely neglected in London during the 1940's, but in 1951 Hugh Hunt revived it at the Old Vic, with Peggy Ashcroft as Mistress Page and Roger Livesey as Falstaff. Another Old Vic production for the 1955/6 season under Douglas Seale cast Wendy Hiller and Margaret Rawlings as the wives, with Paul Rogers introducing a note of unexpected nobility into the characterization of Falstaff.

Stratford witnessed a reversion to Oscar Asche's winter setting in Glen Byam Shaw's 1955 Christmasy version. Shaw was criticized as harshly as his innovating predecessor but cited the text in his defense. Since then, *The Merry Wives* has been ignored, except for the 1959/60 Old Vic season, when Alec McCowen gave a memorable interpretation of a stiff, rustic Ford.

Stage History: America. The Southwark Theatre in Philadelphia supplied the setting for the first production of *The Merry Wives* in America on March 2, 1770. The original cast can only be conjectured: it is assumed that Lewis Hallam played Ford, as he did for another *Merry Wives*, presented in Jamaica in 1779. The first *Merry Wives* in New York occurred on October 5, 1789 at the John Street for the benefit of Mrs. Harper. On this occasion, John Harper impersonated Falstaff. Before the 18th century closed, productions of the comedy were seen again in Philadelphia in 1790 and 1795 with Charles E. Whitlock the Falstaff in the latter production. In Boston in 1796 J. B. Williamson was Falstaff. Popular Falstaffs of the early 1800's included William Warren, Sr., in 1813 and Thomas Hilson in 1829. Of the two, Warren achieved the greater recognition for his fat knight, but his reputation was eclipsed when James Henry Hackett adopted the role on a visit to London in 1832. From then almost up to his death in 1871, Hackett virtually monopolized Falstaff, both in the comedy and in *1* and *2 Henry IV*. There were, however, others to attempt the part: John Dwyer at the National Theatre in 1839 and Charles Bass at Barton's Chambers Street Theatre in 1850. William E. Burton took the part of the Host in the latter production and three years later starred as a wildly comical Falstaff, with Thomas Placide giving support as Caius and Joseph Holman as Fenton in a presentation boasting completely new costumes and authentic scenery painted by Heilge. In 1858 Burton repeated the character for his benefit performance at Tripler Hall but, although undeniably a favorite with audiences, never came close to matching Hackett's steady efforts with the part.

A Park Theatre production in December 1838 starring Hackett included Charles Fisher as Sir Hugh and Charlotte Cushman as Mistress Page. Critical opinion divided over Hackett's interpretation of Falstaff, which gave no indication of the knight's noble origins but concentrated on the satirical humor, sensuality, and merry scorn of the character. Appearing with him in various productions were John Jack (who later exhibited Hackett's influence in his own Falstaff impersonation) as Shallow, Henry Placide as Caius, and James H. Stoddart as Slender.

Augustin Daly first presented *The Merry Wives* at his Fifth Avenue Theatre on November 19, 1872 with Charles Fisher as Falstaff, George Clarke and Fanny Davenport as the Fords, Louis James and Fanny Morant as the Pages, and William P. Davidge as Parson Hugh. During the 1885/6 season, he staged a more successful production, again with Fisher, whose Falstaff definitely reflected a noble birth; Ada Rehan and John Drew as the Fords; Virginia Dreher and Otis Skinner as the Pages; and Charles Leclercq as Evans. In both presentations James Lewis acted Slender. This later effort, for which Daly made his own arrangement of 4 acts and 11 scenes, was performed 35 times. A final Daly revival of the comedy opened in January 1898, introducing the inferior Falstaff of George Clarke and featuring again the merry Mistress Ford of Miss Rehan.

A somewhat deficient Falstaff appeared around the time of Daly's revivals. In 1885 William H. Crane adopted the role while his partner, Stuart Robson, portrayed Slender. Crane retained the fat knight in his repertory for a few years with only limited appeal and played the part for the last time at the Star Theatre opposite the Shallow and Slender of H. A. Weaver, Sr., and Joseph Wheelock, Jr.

In 1910 Louis Calvert acted Falstaff at the New with Edith Wynne Matthison and Rose Coghlan as the Mistresses Ford and Page. Herbert Tree and Constance Collier gave 12 performances at the New Amsterdam as Falstaff and Mistress Ford in 1916. That same year, when James K. Hackett's planned appearance in the role for which his father became famous was canceled because of illness, Thomas A. Wise substituted at the last moment as the fat knight, giving a superbly wicked impersonation rich with mellow humor. Viola Allen and Henrietta Crosman were not very successful as the merry wives, but Fuller Mellish presented a very capable Page and Charles W. Butler, a droll Host. The scenery and costumes in this production at the Criterion were more suggestive of the Arabian Nights than Windsor and added nothing to the proceedings. The next year Wise starred in Silvio Hein's revival at the Park Theatre opposite Constance Collier's Mistress Ford.

Otis Skinner, the Falstaff of a rowdy presentation at the Knickerbocker in March 1928, was one of the slimmest Falstaffs ever to appear. His reticent knight suffered the humiliations devised by the gay she-devil Mistress Page of Minnie Maddern Fiske and the handsomely flirtatious Mistress Ford of Henrietta Crosman under the direction of Harrison Grey Fiske. About this time Charles Coburn assumed the role of Falstaff, delighting audiences throughout the country with his impersonation. In 1934 he inaugurated the Mohawk Dramatic Festival at Union College, Schenectady, with a performance of *The Merry Wives* and, in 1946, took the comedy on tour for the Theatre Guild.

Critics blasted an Empire Theatre production directed by Robert Henderson in 1938 as a generally hysterical and infantile romp, alleviated only by Estelle Winwood's portrayal of Mistress Page. Even that, it was felt, grew shrill at times. Louis Lytton skimmed only the surface of the character, producing a silly Falstaff. Two later productions fared better. In 1956 an energetic presentation staged by Michael Langham for the Shakespearean Festival in Stratford, Ontario, featured the exceptional Falstaff of Douglas Campbell, and in 1959 the American Shakespeare Festival in Connecticut starred Larry Gates, a Falstaff who alternately posed as a conniving buffoon and a dignified profligate—a ponderous clown full of ludicrous self-esteem. The lively wives played by Nancy Wickwire (Mistress Ford) and Nancy Marchand (Mistress Page) contributed happily to the infectiously spirited presentation.

Richard Graham, taking the part of Falstaff in an Equity Library Theatre production at the Master Theatre in 1962, missed the sense of the ridiculous. The poorly conceived knight got little help from his supporting cast which, under the direction of Edward Payson Call, lacked vitality or humor.—M. G.

Bibliography. TEXT: *The Merry Wives of Windsor,* New Cambridge Edition, Arthur Quiller-Couch and J. Dover Wilson, eds., 1921. DATE: Leslie Hotson, *Shakespeare Versus Shallow,* 1931; William Green, *Shakespeare's "Merry Wives of Windsor,"* 1962. SOURCES: *Shakespeare's "Merry Wives of Windsor";* Sidney Thomas, "Source of *The Merry Wives of Windsor,*" *The Times Literary Supplement,* October 11, 1947; Geoffrey Bullough, *Narrative and Dramatic Sources of Shakespeare,* Vol. II, 1959. COMMENT: Oscar James Campbell, "The Italianate Background of *The Merry Wives of Windsor,*" *Essays and Studies in English and Comparative Literature,* Vol. VIII, 1932. STAGE HISTORY: New Cambridge Edition; T. Alston Brown, *A History of the New York Stage . . . to 1901,* 1903; William Winter, *Shakespeare on the Stage,* 3 vols., 1911–1916; G. C. D. Odell, *Shakespeare from Betterton to Irving,* 1920; C. B. Hogan, *Shakespeare in the Theatre, 1701–1800,* 2 vols., 1952, 1957; J. C. Trewin, *Shakespeare on the English Stage, 1900–1964,* 1964.

Selected Criticism

WILLIAM HAZLITT. *The Merry Wives of Windsor* is no doubt a very amusing play, with a great deal of humour, character, and nature in it: but we should have liked it much better, if any one else had been the hero of it, instead of Falstaff. We could have been contented if Shakespear had not been 'commanded to shew the knight in love.' Wits and philosophers, for the most part, do not shine in that character; and Sir John himself, by no means, comes off with flying colours. Many people complain of the degradation and insults to which Don Quixote is so frequently exposed in his various adventures. But what are the unconscious indignities which he suffers, compared with the sensible mortifications which Falstaff is made to bring upon himself? What are the blows and buffettings which the Don receives from the staves of the Yanguesian carriers or from Sancho Panza's more hard-hearted hands, compared with the contamination of the buckbasket, the disguise of the fat woman of Brentford, and the horns of Herne the hunter, which are discovered on Sir John's head? In reading the play, we indeed wish him well through all these discomfitures, but it would have been as well if he had not got into them. Falstaff in the *Merry Wives of Windsor* is not the man he was in the two parts of *Henry IV*. His wit and eloquence have left him. Instead of making a butt of others, he is made a butt of by them. [*The Characters of Shakespear's Plays,* 1817.]

G. G. GERVINUS. Great emphasis is laid throughout on honest knavery, in contrast to Falstaff's knavery . . . .

This simple but honest knavery celebrates its victory throughout over cunning and presumption. The crafty self-loving dig the pit and fall into i themselves; it is dug too strangely wide even for th simple, because self-conceited cunning estimates to lightly its opponent honesty. These words may b regarded as the soul of the play. It is a reflection t be drawn from no other of Shakespeare's dramas but only from this play of intrigue. All the under plot of the piece relates to this point and to thi lesson. The cunning host—a boaster full of mocker and tricks, who considers himself a great politicia and Machiavellian—teases the wavering, fencing D Caius and the pedantic Welshman Evans; the sam vexation befalls him as Falstaff, that the simple men who cannot even speak English, combine agains him, and cheat the crafty man about his horses . . . Alike in all these corresponding affairs does busines seek to ensnare honesty—cunning, simplicity– jealousy, innocence—and avarice, the inoffensiv nature; and their evil design reverts upon them selves. Unclouded honest sense is always superior t base passion. . . . The selfishness which we exhibite as the soul of Falstaff's nature appears at its highes climax when opposed to the virtue and simplicit which are its usual prey; in its vain security i considers the more subtle means of ensnaring as n longer necessary, and is thus ensnared in a gros trap. An egotist like Falstaff can suffer no severe defeat than from the honesty in which he does nc believe, and from the ignorance which he does no esteem. The more ridiculous side of self-love i therefore, in this play subjected to a ridiculou tragic-comic fall, which, as regards time and th development of the plot, precedes the serious comic tragic fall which meets Falstaff on the accession o the king, when the serious and mischievous side c his self-love was just on the point of a dangerou triumph. [*Shakespeare* 1849–1850; tr. 1863 as *Shakespeare Commentaries.*]

FRANK HARRIS. Had "The Merry Wives" been pro duced under ordinary conditions, one would hav had to rack one's brains to account for its feeblenes Not only is the genial Lord of Humour degraded i it into a buffoon, but the amusement of it is chiefl in situation; it is almost as much a farce as a comedy For these and other reasons I believe in the truth c the tradition that Elizabeth was so pleased with th character of Falstaff that she ordered Shakespeare t write another play showing the fat knight in love and that in obedience to this command Shakespear wrote "The Merry Wives" in a fortnight. For wha does a dramatist do when he is in a hurry to strik while the iron is hot and catch a Queen's fanc before it changes? Naturally he goes to his memor for his characters, to that vivid memory of yout which makes up by precision of portraiture for wha it lacks in depth of comprehension. And this is th distinguishing characteristic of "The Merry Wives. . . . Those who wish to measure the differenc between the conscious, deliberate work of the artis and the hurried slap-dash performance of the jou nalist, have only to compare the Falstaff of "Th Merry Wives" with the Falstaff of the two parts o "Henry IV." But if we take it for granted that "Th Merry Wives" was done in haste and to order, ca any inference be fairly drawn from the feeblenes of Falstaff and the unreality of his lovemaking? think so; it seems to me that, if Falstaff had been creation, Shakespeare must have reproduced him more effectively . . . .

The heart of the matter is that, whereas Shakespeare's men of action, when he is not helped by history or tradition, are thinly conceived and poorly painted, his comic characters—Falstaff, Sir Toby Belch, and Dogberry; Maria, Dame Quickly, and the Nurse, creatures of observation though they be, are only inferior as works of art to the portraits of himself which he has given us in Romeo, Hamlet, Macbeth, Orsino, and Posthumus. It is his humour which makes Shakespeare the greatest of dramatists, the most complete of men. [*The Man Shakespeare*, 1909.]

E. K. CHAMBERS. *The Merry Wives* . . . is admirably constructed, and moves, given competent interpreters, with astonishing vitality and go. On the modern stage it is apt to be overweighted by elaborate setting, which retards the rapidity of development essentially characteristic of a farce. But obviously Shakespeare cannot be held responsible for this, and the two central scenes, wherein the buck-basket plays its immortal part, fully attain that vivacity of action which so much of Elizabethan comedy, depending as it is apt to do upon fashions of verbal fence, unfortunately misses. Its complexities of domestic intrigue almost make the piece a farce in the modern sense; but it answers more precisely to the older conception of the form which prevailed in fifteenth-century France. Such farce you may define, if you will, as acted *fabliau*. And of acted *fabliau*, *The Merry Wives* is the best English specimen, just as Chaucer's *Miller's Tale* and *Reeve's Tale* are the best English specimens of *fabliau* in narrative. [*Shakespeare: A Survey*, 1925.]

J. DOVER WILSON. Bergson defined comedy as a criticism in the name of society of characters which show 'a special lack of adaptability' to social conventions and intercourse. Shakespearian comedy is rather a criticism of society itself and its conventions from the point of view of beings who through lack of intellect or education or adaptability or because they are outcasts like Shylock, are not recognized as full members of society. It has in fact a much closer affinity with the novels of Dostoevsky (e.g. *The Idiot*) than with the plays of Molière or Ibsen, possessing as it does tragic implications. Yet there is nothing whatever tragic about *The Merry Wives*. The jealousy of Master Ford supplies the only serious note in it, and that is not taken seriously by anyone but himself. It is even more consistently light-hearted than the gay *Love's Labour's Lost*, since it contains no messenger of Death to convert hilarity into sobriety at the close of the play. From first to last, all is merry, as the title promises. [*Shakespeare's Happy Comedies*, 1962.]

Mervailous Combat of Contrarieties. See CORIOLANUS: *Sources*.

Messala. In *Julius Caesar*, a friend of Brutus and Cassius. Messala brings Brutus news of Portia's death (IV, iii). After the battle of Philippi, however, he enters the service of Octavius (V, v). According to Plutarch, Octavius later remarked on the steadfast loyalty that Messala showed him at Actium, whereupon Messala replied, "You have always found me, Caesar, on the best and justest side."

Messallina. A Senecan melodrama by Nathanael Richards (fl. 1631–1641) first performed in 1634 or 1635 and published in 1640 as "*The Tragedy of Messallina The Roman Empresse.* As it hath beene Acted With generall applause divers times, by the Company of his Majesties Revells . . . 1640." This edition has an engraved title page containing a small picture of a stage. It is one of the four known contemporary reproductions of the Elizabethan stage, the others being the famous drawing of the Swan by Johannes DE WITT and engraved title pages of two other plays, *Roxana* and *The Wits*.

The play was performed by the King's Revels company at Salisbury Court. It has been assumed by some, therefore, that the picture represents the Salisbury Court stage. However, a close examination of the picture in comparison with that on the *Roxana* title page reveals that it is probably a direct copy of the *Roxana* engraving, and thus its value as an independent source of information about the structure of the early stage is considerably diminished.

Messenger. In *The Two Noble Kinsmen*, he describes to the royal company the impressive appearance of the knights who accompany Arcite and Palamon as they arrive to contest the hand of Emilia (IV, ii).

Metamorphoses. A long, elaborately structured Latin poem by OVID. The *Metamorphoses* consists of 15 books treating legends and tales of human and divine transfigurations from the time of the creation of the world to Julius Caesar. The poem is the most pervasive classical influence on Shakespeare's works. He consulted it frequently both in the original and in the English translation (1567) of Arthur GOLDING. Shakespeare is indebted to the *Metamorphoses* for the "tragical comedy" of Pyramus and Thisbe in *A Midsummer Night's Dream*, for the statue scene in *The Winter's Tale*, and for elements in *Titus Andronicus* and *The Tempest*, as well as for his narrative poem *Venus and Adonis*. The Bodleian Library owns a copy of a 1502 edition of *Metamorphoses* with the inscription "W^m^ Sh^r^" or "W^m^ Sh^re^" on the title page. A note on the inside of the front cover reads "This little Booke of Ovid was given to me by W. Hall who said it was once Will Shakespeares. T. N. 1682." The signature of Shakespeare on the title page is not generally accepted as genuine, but if the work is a forgery it is an extremely plausible one. Shakespeare is more likely to have owned a copy of this book than of any other. As Robert K. Root asserts, "With nearly all of the important episodes of the poem, with each of the fifteen books, save perhaps the twelfth and fifteenth, his [Shakespeare's] familiarity is clearly demonstrable." [Robert K. Root, *Classical Mythology in Shakespeare*, 1903.]

Meurice, Paul. See FRANCE.

Michael. In *2 Henry VI*, a follower of Jack Cade (IV, ii).

Michael, Sir. In *1 Henry IV*, a friend of Richard Scroop, Archbishop of York. The latter entrusts Sir Michael with dispatches to the lord marshal and to his cousin Scroop (IV, iv).

Middleton, Thomas (1570–1627). Dramatist. The son of a London bricklayer, Middleton was educated at Oxford. His first published works were a biblical paraphrase of *The Wisdom of Solomon* (1597) and a satire, *Microcynicon* (1599). In May 1602 he is mentioned in Philip Henslowe's diary as a collaborator with Dekker and Webster on a lost play, *Caesar's Fall*. In 1604 he added some minor elements to Dekker's *The Honest Whore* and began to write his realistic comedies of London life for the Children of Paul's. The best of these are *A Trick to Catch the Old One* (1608), *A Mad World, My Masters* (1604–1606), and *A Chaste Maid in Cheapside* (1611). In 1616 he began the collaboration with William ROWLEY which resulted in a number of plays, foremost of which is *The Changeling* (1622), one of the most remarkable dramas of the Jacobean age.

Middleton designed many of the lord mayor of London's annual pageants and in 1620 was rewarded with the title of city chronologer, a post he held until his death. His greatest success was his allegorical drama of the political intrigue that attended the negotiations for a marriage between Prince Charles (later Charles I) and the Spanish infanta in 1624. The play was called A GAME AT CHESSE, and it drew thousands of spectators each day before it was suppressed and Middleton imprisoned.

Middleton is most directly related to Shakespeare through his THE WITCH (c. 1610–1616), the play that contains the witches' songs indicated in the stage directions of *Macbeth*. For this reason Middleton is generally regarded as the author of the alleged interpolations in *Macbeth* (see MACBETH: *Text*). There is no general agreement as to what Middleton's share in *Macbeth* consists of, but it is thought to include, at the least, the witches' scene (III, v). His debt to Shakespeare is evidenced in *A Mad World, My Masters*, which echoes a number of Shakespearean lines, and in THE FAMILY OF LOVE, an imitation of *Romeo and Juliet*.

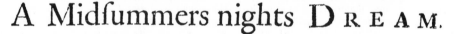

A Midſummers nights DREAM.

Midsummer Night's Dream, A. A romantic comedy by Shakespeare.

Text. The most reliable text is that of the First Quarto, printed late in 1600, shortly after having been entered in the Stationers' Register: "8 Octobris. Thomas Fyssher. Entred for his copie vnder the handes of master Rodes and the Wardens. A booke called A mydsommer nightes Dreame vj[d]." The title page of the Quarto reads: "A Midsommer nights dreame. As it hath beene sundry times publickely acted, by the Right honourable, the Lord Chamberlaine his seruants. Written by William Shakespeare Imprinted at London, for Thomas Fisher, and are to be soulde at his shoppe, at the Signe of the White Hart, in Fleetestreete. 1600."

The text is a reasonably accurate one, generally thought to be set up from the author's FOUL PAPERS, although J. Dover Wilson argues that a theatrical PROMPT-BOOK served as the printer's copy. The evidence is conflicting in some respects, but is best explained by W. W. Greg's conjecture that the entries which suggest a prompt-book are the bookkeeper's notes in the foul papers, made in preparation for the prompt-book.

The Second Quarto (1619, fraudulently dated 1600) reprints the First Quarto, with additional stage directions that suggest consultation with the prompt-book. The text of the First Folio (1623) reprints that of the Second Quarto. The Quartos contain no divisions into acts and scenes. Acts, but not scenes, are marked in the First Folio. The text is the fourth shortest play in the canon, running to only 2136 lines. This is one of the reasons for the almost universally held belief among critics that the play was written for a private performance, clearly a part of the festivities attendant upon an aristocratic wedding.

Date. Although the date of the play cannot be determined with certainty, some topical allusions make 1594–1595 the probable year of its composition. The most helpful of the allusions is Titania's description of the abnormally rainy year of 1594 (II, i, 81–117). So wet and windy was the weather that it completely changed the character of the seasons, until no one could tell which was which. The comedy, therefore, must have been written either in late 1594 or more probably in early 1595, before the audience had forgotten the flood, the failure of the harvests, the consequent rise in the price of food, and the widespread financial stringency.

Some critics find an allusion to the death of Robert Greene in 1592 in the lines

> 'The thrice three Muses mourning for the death
> Of Learning, late deceased in beggary.'
> That is some satire, keen and critical.
>
> (V, i, 52–54)

The death of Greene in wretched poverty made a strong impression on his fellow dramatists. The author's many pamphlets appearing from 1592 to 1595 contained moral warnings to the dissolute group of young university graduates, dubbed "wits," who during these years were establishing careers in the theatre. All these facts confirm the date 1594–1595 as most likely for the composition of the play.

A

Midſommer nights dreame.

As it hath beene ſundry times pub-*lickely acted, by the Right honoura-*ble, the Lord Chamberlaine his *ſeruants.*

Written by William Shakeſpeare.

¶Imprinted at London, for *Thomas Fiſher*, and are to be ſoulde at his ſhoppe, at the Signe of the White Hart, in *Fleeteſtreete.* 1600.

TITLE PAGE OF THE FIRST QUARTO OF *A Midsummer Night's Dream* (1600).

Sources. The plot is Shakespeare's invention. Each of its various elements had a separate source. The cross-wooing and the confused allegiance of two pairs of lovers was a convention of Italian comedy, which the poet had exploited in *The Two Gentlemen of Verona.* It is also a development of the errors motif of *The Comedy of Errors.* His knowledge of Theseus and the Amazon Queen Hippolyta he derived from CHAUCER's "The Knight's Tale," in which Chaucer refers to a great feast at their wedding. Shakespeare seems also to have read "The Life of Theseus" in North's translation (1579) of Plutarch's *Lives,* a work of which he later made extensive use when writing his Roman plays.

For the story of Pyramus and Thisbe, he had only to recall his reading in school of the tale in Ovid's METAMORPHOSES. The folklore about fairies, Puck, and Robin Goodfellow he could have learned from old wives' tales circulating in Stratford during his childhood. Midsummer Day was a joyously celebrated holiday in all parts of Merry England; and Midsummer Night was the time for a roundup of all sorts of fairies, witches, and spirits walking by night (see FOLK FESTIVALS). Oberon and Titania are names unknown to English folklore. In Ovid, Titania is a name for Circe. Oberon first was presented in English literature as king of the fairies in Robert Greene's *James IV* (c. 1591). Shakespeare, however, may have derived the names from the French romance *Huon of Bordeaux,* translated by Lord Berners in 1534. "Puck" as the name of a mischievous sprite goes back to Anglo-Saxon times. (He is also Kipling's "Puck of Pook's Hill.") Shakespeare may have read accounts of Robin Goodfellow, Puck's alternate name, in Reginald Scot's *Discoverie of Witchcraft* (1584). The names of all the laborers are related to their callings. Bottom was the bottom, or core, of the skein upon which a weaver's yarn was wound. Quince or quines were blocks of wood, an appropriate name for a carpenter. Snout meant the nozzle of a kettle, the mending of which was a tinker's principal business. Snug still means "close-fitting," a good name for a joiner. Flute was a bellows mender, whose principal job was to repair the fluted stops of church organs. Starveling is a natural descriptive word for tailors, who were supposed to be undersized and skinny. The last role may originally have been played by the actor John SINCKLO, who was noted for his "thin man" roles.

Many critics, the most recent of whom is J. Dover Wilson, believe that Titania's wooing of Bottom when he is sporting an ass' head is based on some details of the story of *Cupid and Psyche,* as told by a character in *The Golden Ass* of Lucius Apuleius (c. 125–192). The romance recounts the adventures of Lucius, a Greek youth, whom a witch transforms into an ass. Shakespeare could have read *The Golden Ass* in William Adlington's English translation (1566) of the Latin version of the Greek original. The lascivious matron who in Apuleius makes love to an ass Shakespeare transforms into Titania, who delicately woos Bottom. J. Dover Wilson finds similarities to Shakespeare's play in other parts of *The Golden Ass.*—O.J.C.

Plot Synopsis. Act I. In Athens, plans are under way for the wedding of Duke Theseus to Hippolyta, Queen of the Amazons, which is to take place on the night of the next new moon. To the ducal palace comes an angry father, Egeus, who accuses Lysander of bewitching his daughter Hermia, so as to make her fall in love with him, though she is already promised to Demetrius. When Hermia acknowledges her love for Lysander, Theseus tells her that, according to Athenian law, she must either die or enter a nunnery if she refuses to wed the man of her father's choice. He gives her until the new moon to reach a decision. The lovers, however, agree to flee from Athens together and arrange to meet the following night in a wood outside the city. They reveal their plan to Helena, Hermia's childhood friend, who had once been Demetrius' beloved and still cherishes a passion for him. Hoping to be restored to his favor, she decides to tell him of the lovers' projected flight.

Meanwhile, a group of artisans are preparing an interlude to be performed on the occasion of the Duke's wedding. The vehicle that their director, the carpenter Peter Quince, has chosen is "The most lamentable comedy, and most cruel death of Pyramus and Thisby." Nick Bottom, the weaver, is eager to play Pyramus—and most of the other parts as well. Francis Flute, the bellows-mender, is given the part of Thisbe. Robin Starveling, a tailor, is assigned the part of Thisbe's mother, and Tom Snout, a tinker, that of Pyramus' father. The role of Lion is given

A

Midſommer nights dreame.

As it hath beene ſundry times publikely *acted, by the Right Honourable*, the Lord Chamberlaine his *ſeruants.*

VVritten by VVilliam Shakeſpeare.

Printed by Iames Roberts, 1600.

TITLE PAGE OF THE SECOND QUARTO OF *A Midsummer Night's Dream* (1619). THIS EDITION WAS FALSELY DATED.

to Snug the joiner, despite the fact that he is "slow of study," since all he will have to do is roar.

Act II. In a wood near Athens, Oberon, king of the fairies, and his wife, Titania, have a falling-out over a lovely changeling boy whom she has adopted as her page, despite the objections of her husband, who wants to make him his attendant. When Titania refuses to surrender the lad, Oberon orders the knavish sprite Puck, or Robin Goodfellow, to bring him "a little western flower" upon which Cupid's bolt had once fallen, after missing the "fair vestal" against whom it had been aimed. If the eyelids of a sleeping person are anointed with the juice of this flower, he will lose his heart to the first living creature that he sees upon awaking. It is Oberon's design to force Titania to his will by having her fall in love with some wild animal. While Puck is executing this commission, Oberon witnesses a scene between Helena and Demetrius, who has followed Lysander and Hermia and now impatiently spurns the love of his discarded mistress. When Puck returns with the flower, Oberon tells him to seek Demetrius, whom he describes as "a disdainful youth" dressed in Athenian garb, and to daub his eyes with the magic juice.

Finding Titania asleep, Oberon squeezes the flower over her eyelids. Lysander and Hermia, having lost their way in the wood, also fall asleep nearby, each apart from the other, as becomes "a virtuous bachelor and a maid." Puck comes upon the young man and, mistaking him for Demetrius, drops the potion on his eyes. Demetrius and Helena now arrive, awaking Lysander, who promptly falls in love with Helena, though she is convinced that he is mocking her.

Act III. Near the spot where Titania lies asleep, the artisans rehearse their play. At Bottom's suggestion, they decide to add two prologues to assure the audience that Pyramus does not really kill himself and that the Lion is merely Snug. The mischievous Puck, who has watched the rehearsal with amusement, places an ass' head on Bottom's shoulders, causing his terrified companions to run away. Titania, awakening and catching sight of Bottom, is immediately smitten, and summons four fairies—Peaseblossom, Cobweb, Moth, and Mustardseed—to attend him.

Oberon is delighted to hear Puck's description of the "monster" who has captured Titania's fancy, but he is annoyed when he realizes that the sprite has sprinkled the love-juice on the eyelids of Lysander instead of Demetrius. As Demetrius lies asleep, Oberon corrects Puck's error, and upon awaking, the young man becomes enamored of the girl he had previously rejected. Helena is still certain that she is being made sport of, while Hermia, stunned by Lysander's abuse, accuses Helena of stealing her lover from her. Lysander and Demetrius, now rivals for Helena's affection, stalk off, resolved to settle the quarrel by combat. Following Oberon's instructions, Puck leads Demetrius and Lysander astray and, when they are overcome by drowsiness, anoints Lysander's eyelids with the antidote to love-juice. Hermia and Helena, meanwhile, have also fallen asleep beside their lovers.

Act IV. Seeing Titania asleep next to Bottom, Oberon, who has already obtained possession of the changeling child, takes pity on her and, after releasing her from her spell, is reconciled with her. Puck also removes the ass' head from Bottom's shoulders.

Having entered the forest during a hunt, Duke Theseus, Hippolyta, and Egeus startle the youthful lovers from their slumber. Now freed from the effects of the potion, but still somewhat dazed, Lysander explains that he and Hermia had fled to evade the Athenian law, while Demetrius avers his love for Helena and relinquishes his claim to Hermia. After Theseus declares that the two couples will be married along with him and Hippolyta, and they all return to Athens, Bottom awakes and makes his way to Quince's house, where his friends anxiously await him. Bottom gives the actors some last-minute instructions. Thisbe is to wear clean linen, the Lion must not pare his nails so that they can serve as claws, and none of them is to eat onions or garlic.

Act V. After the wedding, Duke Theseus asks Philostrate, master of the revels, whether he has arranged any masque or music for their entertainment. Finding a description of the artisans' interlude in a list Philostrate gives him, Theseus insists on seeing it, despite the former's remonstrances, asserting that "Never anything can be amiss, / When simpleness and duty tender it."

As Quince recites the prologue, riding it like "a rough colt," the other players enact a dumb show of the tragedy. During the play itself, Snout explains that he is the Wall between the homes of the ill-starred lovers and obligingly holds up his fingers when Pyramus wishes for a chink through which he might glimpse his beloved Thisbe. After the lovers have arranged to meet at "Ninny's tomb," the Lion and Moonshine enter, the latter announcing that the lanthorn he carries is the moon and that he is the man in the moon. When the tragedy has run its course, the actors perform a Bergomask dance, after which the Duke and his guests retire, for it is after midnight and fairy time is nigh. Heralded by Puck, the fairies, "following darkness like a dream," now appear; at the bidding of Oberon and Titania, they dance and sing, and then disperse throughout the house to bless the bridebeds of the sleeping lovers. Only Puck remains to promise amends for any offenses the "shadows" may have committed, asking the spectators to believe that they "have but slumber'd here / While these visions did appear."—H. D.

Comment. The only existing text is the version of the comedy designed to be presented in the great hall of an Elizabethan gentleman's country house, or possibly at the court, on an occasion at which Queen Elizabeth may have been present. Certain textual inconsistencies indicate that the play as we have it has been revised and that the lines which deal with the fantasy form only one of two textual layers. It has been suggested that the lower and older level largely consists of the dialogue of the lovers and other passages of wooden rhymed verse that Shakespeare must have written near the beginning of his career as a dramatist. The later and upper level would thus contain the lines written in celebration of the allegorically described wedding. It is filled with bursts of verbal music that Shakespeare hoped would charm the cultivated wedding guests. The upper level of the text may also have contained the half-buried topical allusions and personal satire.

The theme binding together the various strands of interest is "Love is a wholly irrational passion, the victim of whim and illusion. The behaviour of all the lovers is ridiculous."

Theseus and Hippolyta, having completed the ritual of courtship, are staid and serious and ready for marriage. They are the bride and groom for whose nuptials Philostrate has prepared the revels. Theseus is no Greek tyrant, but a thoroughly English gentleman, who has his ears attuned to the musical baying of his hounds in full cry (IV, i, 107–110).

Oberon's verses recited at the end of the play indicate that the play formed an important part of the celebration of the wedding. In these lines Oberon dispatches one of his minions to bless the marriage beds of all three couples, but in particular, the "best bride-bed."

> To the best bride-bed will we,
> Which by us shall blessed be;
> And the issue these create
> Ever shall be fortunate.
> (V, i, 410–413)

Many weddings of the nobility solemnized about the years 1594–1596 have been suggested as the occasion for which the play was written. One considered most likely by many historians is that of Elizabeth de Vere, the daughter of the earl of Oxford, to the earl of Derby, which took place on January 26, 1595. Another suggested wedding is that of Sir Thomas Heneage and the widowed countess of Southampton, the mother of Shakespeare's patron. This ceremony took place on May 2, 1594. Still another possible occasion was the wedding of Thomas Berkeley and Elizabeth Carey, the granddaughter of Lord Hunsdon, the patron of Shakespeare's company, on February 19, 1596.

The poet superficially differentiates the lovers involved in the imbroglio. Helena is the conventional rejected lovelorn maiden of romances, the incarnation of staunch fidelity to an inconstant man. Hermia is a more original creation; she is small, dark, and self-willed. She was accounted a vixen when she went to school. Bitterly resenting Helena's flings at her short stature, she returns her taunts with interest, applying to her epithets like "painted May-pole."

The two *amorosos* are not so sharply distinguished, though Demetrius is more like the traditional sighing, rejected lover, Lysander bolder and more resourceful. All four lovers religiously observe the rites of romantic worship—the moonlight serenade and the exchange of bracelets made of hair, of nosegays, of sweetmeats, and of rings. Love-making to them is an elaborate, fully prescribed ritual.

Shakespeare must have introduced Puck and the fairies into his first version of the confused lovers, for some of the couplets written for them are as mechanical and perfunctory as those in many of the exchanges of the lovers. Since other lines in their parts evoke magic as surely as any other verses that Shakespeare ever wrote, they are obviously a part of his final working over of his revised and expanded text.

Puck is the official jester at the court of Oberon, king of the fairies. He "jests to Oberon and makes him smile." He is also Oberon's confidential messenger. He is a tiny, insubstantial elf, like the other fairies. In all the legends he is bent on mischief, delighted to confuse and bewilder hapless mortals.

To this Ariel-like creature Shakespeare has given some of the traits of Robin Goodfellow, a loutish rustic and friendly sprite. One of his good deeds is to enter the kitchen and help with the housework in return for a bowl of cream and a mess of bread set out on the kitchen doorstep for him. The malicious tricks of which he boasts (II, i, 44–57) are cruder and more farcical than those that Puck displays in his own right. The other fairies, Peaseblossom, Cobweb, Moth, and Mustardseed, are almost wholly the figments of the poet's imagination.

About his fairies the poet has woven a delicate charm, delightfully translated by Mendelssohn into his famous incidental music to the play. Shakespeare evokes his magic by identifying the beauty of Oberon's realm with the flowers of the English countryside when drenched with moonlight. Titania sleeps in a bower on

> a bank where the wild thyme blows,
> Where oxlips and the nodding violet grows.
> (II, i, 249–250)

Theseus describes the art by which Shakespeare's

imagination gives to the airy nothing of the fairy world the local habitation of rural England as seen through the eye of its lover.

Into this world of gossamer-like texture, bully Bottom and his fellow artisans drop with a thud. Their performance of the "most lamentable comedy" is ridicule of the plays that the villagers in Shakespeare's day used to delight in acting. Among the entertainments offered to Queen Elizabeth when she went on a progress was a rustic show given by the folk of the countryside near the lord's estate where she was visiting. Bottom is the star of the troupe. Like most conceited amateurs, he feels competent to act all of the parts being assigned by the director. Having designed the part for Will Kempe, the company's low-comedy actor, Shakespeare expected Bottom to be a lout in the tradition of Launce in the *Two Gentlemen of Verona.* But he has progressed far beyond Launce's malapropisms and rural stupidity to become the comic embodiment of John Bull; like him he is firmly rooted to the earth and feels completely at home in every spot on its broad surface. Nothing abashes him or disturbs his colossal self-assurance. His experiences in fairyland do not give him an instant of wonder or perplexity. He is one of the funniest characters in all dramatic literature, the first of Shakespeare's comic characters to maintain through every change of taste and of literary fashion his irresistible appeal to laughter.

Some readers have seen broad hints of political and personal satire in the play. The first intimation of the presence of topical reference concealed in the action is in the instructions Oberon gives Puck as he dispatches him to fetch a flower that maidens ca "love in idleness." The verses begin

My gentle Puck, come hither. Thou rememberest
Since once I sat upon a promontory,
And heard a mermaid on a dolphin's back
Uttering such dulcet and harmonious breath
That the rude sea grew civil at her song
And certain stars shot madly from their spheres,
To hear the sea-maid's music.

(II, i, 148–154)

These lines have often been thought to describe th entertainments that the earl of Leicester offered th queen when she visited him for three weeks fror July 9th to 27th, 1575. J. Dover Wilson presents th arguments for this identification. A more likel identification may be that of E. K. Chambers, wh believes that the poetical description more defi nitely applies to a water fete presented to the quee by the earl of Hertford when she visited Elvethan his country estate, in 1591. A chart of the *mise-en scène,* first published in a contemporary pamphle now to be found in John Nichols' *Progresses an Public Processions of Queen Elizabeth* (3 vols. an Pt. 1 of Vol. IV, 1788–1821), shows a promontor extending into an artificial, crescent-shaped lake. O its surface floats a boat, on the deck of which mermaid can be discerned. The ship may have bee actually shaped like a dolphin, or the poet's imagi nation may have given it that form. One of th resemblances is the "shooting stars," which refers t the fireworks that Hertford provided for th occasion.

THE ELVETHAM ENTERTAINMENT, FROM NICHOLS' *Progresses.*

Edith Rickert has put forth an ingenious explana-on for this allusion to Hertford's fete, centering a complicated story of court intrigue and royal yranny. It begins with Hertford's secret marriage 1560 to Lady Catherine Grey, one of the queen's dies- in waiting, whom Titania describes as a votaress of my order" (i.e., of virginity). The ueen was greatly upset by the marriage, for Lady atherine was descended from Henry VIII's sister, he duchess of Suffolk. By Henry's will and by two cts of parliament, any legitimate child of Lady atherine had been proclaimed next heir to the hrone. So, when she gave birth to a son, the queen ensed the establishment of a new center of domestic ntrigue and threw her into prison. Then she con-rived to have an ecclesiastical court rule the mar-iage null and void, and the child illegitimate. While n prison, Catherine produced another son, and in 568, though she did not exactly "of that boy . . . lie," as Titania reports, she did succumb from the ueen's harsh treatment. In 1580 the earl, her hus-and, began secretly plotting to have the court's udgment reversed and the boy declared legitimate nd (at least) heir to his earldom of Hertford. His vater fete of 1591 was part of his campaign to ffect his result. In 1595 his machinations came to ight. The queen was furious. She at once sent him o the Tower, where he languished in peril of his ife. At this juncture in Hertford's career, *A Mid-ummer Night's Dream* was presented. If the rela-ion of the play to the crisis in Hertford's life be ccepted, the "little changeling boy" over the pos-ession of whom Titania and Oberon quarrel is one other than Hertford's son. In spite of his leading, the Queen remains obdurate. Titania's an-wer to Oberon is

> The fairy land buys not the child of me.
> (II, i, 122)

The fairy land is, of course, the water fete.

In addition to presenting the earl of Hertford's ituation, Shakespeare, according to Miss Rickert, makes one satiric thrust at the Scottish King James VI. At the mechanical's rehearsal (III, ii) of their play, they decide to adopt a simple way of keeping the ladies from being terrified at Snug's imperson-ation of a lion. In 1595 everyone in an audience of courtiers would have laughed, for it would recall one ludicrous example of King James' cowardice. As a part of a pageant, devised by the king himself to celebrate the christening of his son Henry at Sterling Castle on August 30, 1594, a lion was to draw in the baptismal car. But fearing danger to himself, at the last moment he decided to put a Moor into the harness for the lion, explaining that a lion would scare the ladies "out of their wits."

This bit of ridicule directed at King James has sent other critics searching for other satiric allusions to him in the play. And they have found many. The most amusing of their discoveries is that putting Bottom into the part of Pyramus is surely a home-thrust at the king, for in one of his letters to his cousin the queen, whom he hoped to marry, he re-minds her that she and he are not like Hero and Leander, but more like Pyramus and Thisbe,

> Devyded onlie by a wall
> Which in it had a bore
> Where through they spake

In the final speech written for Puck, the dramatist betrays a fear that he may have been too bold in his topical satire. The speech is a reiterated plea for pardon:

> If we shadows have offended, . . .
> Gentles, do not reprehend:
> If you pardon, we will mend.
> (V, i, 430–437, passim)

This is a simple explanation of this speech which the critics have had great difficulty in accounting for. This identification of Bottom with James seems to many preposterous. How could Shakespeare have dared to suggest to the queen that, if she refused to have Hertford's son made legitimate, Fate might cause her to respond to the wooing of her ridiculous cousin over the border? There are two answers to this objection. First, if Shakespeare really did give to Bottom some of the characteristics of King James, he would not have expected his audience completely to identify the two. The methods of Elizabethan allegory and analogy were never so crassly obvious. He could rely upon his gentle spectators to discern an occasional resemblance of Bottom to the king long enough for a burst of laughter. But the re-semblance, having been fleetingly suggested, dis-appeared and Bottom would return to devote him-self exclusively to the role of a fatuous weaver, concerned only with giving a star performance in the role of Pyramus.

The second reason for accepting the probability of the identification is that in the year 1594–1595, ridicule of James would have delighted the English court. While Shakespeare was writing the play, the relations between the royal neighbors became strained, for James was plotting with some of the queen's enemies to secure their approval of his suc-cession to the throne.

The reader may, if he chooses, ignore all the satire and topical reference that historians and scholars profess to find in *A Midsummer Night's Dream* and concentrate his attention upon its great dramatic and poetic values. Never has Shakespeare formed a more skillful union of multiple plots. Never has he written more exquisite poetry.—O. J. C.

Stage History: England. As explained above under *Comment*, topical references in the comedy make it likely that its first performance took place at court in 1595. On New Year's night 1604 the comedy was again given at court under the title *A Play of Robin Goodfellow*. In 1624 John Gee, in his *New Shreds of Old Snares*, refers to *The Comedy of Pyramus and Thisbe*. This title suggests that the clowns' in-terlude had already been cut off from the rest of the play to live a long dramatic life of its own. During the Puritan interregnum (1642–1660), the story of the mechanicals and their play became a droll called *The Merry Conceits of Bottom the Weaver* (1646). It was first published separately in 1661. Bottom was one of the roles in the repertory of the actor Robert Cox, who performed at fairs and taverns while the theatres were closed. The text is available in Francis Kirkman's collection of drolls entitled *The Wits; or, Sport upon Sport* (1672). The characters include all the mechanicals, Oberon, Titania, and "Pugg."

A Midsummer Night's Dream was one of the Shakespeare plays assigned to Thomas Killigrew and his King's Company. Samuel Pepys saw a performance on September 29, 1662, a play "which I had never seen before nor shall ever again, for it is the most insipid ridiculous play that I ever saw in my life." In 1692, Thomas Betterton, truckling to the Restoration taste for display, produced an operatic and spectacular show, based on Shakespeare's play, named *The Fairy Queen* at the Queen's Theatre (the new name given to Dorset Garden after the accession of James II).

Throughout the 18th century, various operatic versions of the comedy were staged. On October 19, 1716 John Rich produced as an afterpiece a work by Richard Leveridge called *A Comique Masque of Pyramus and Thisbe*, a mock opera intended as a burlesque of the then popular Italian operas. (For other operas, see MUSIC BASED ON THE PLAYS.) John Frederick Lampe's one-act amplification of Leveridge's opera, entitled *Pyramus and Thisbe*, followed at Covent Garden in 1745. THE FAIRIES was billed as "a new English opera" and introduced 28 songs. An alteration by David Garrick in three acts, this version was performed at Drury Lane in 1755. By November 23, 1763 there were 33 songs in Garrick's production, which gave way three nights later to George Colman's two-act treatment, *A Fairy Tale*, which reduced the number of songs to 13.

Not until November 1840, when Elizabeth Vestris and her husband, Charles Mathews, produced the play, was *A Midsummer Night's Dream* presented almost as Shakespeare wrote it, for the first time since 1642. In 1827, in Berlin, the German poet Ludwig Tieck supervised a revival of the play for which Mendelssohn wrote his celebrated overture. Mrs. Vestris introduced his music into her production. Her staging of the last scene was striking. At Oberon's command, the fairies trooped upon the stage, each bearing a twinkling, colored light. In the darkness, these little creatures formed into groups and danced.

Samuel Phelps surpassed Mrs. Vestris' accomplishment and truly realized Shakespeare's *Dream* with his enchanting, poetic production at Sadler's Wells in 1853. Bottom became one of Phelps' greatest roles after his revival of the piece. Three years later Charles Kean staged a severely cut version at the Princess' Theatre which achieved popular success, lasting for 150 performances. Puck in this production was played by Ellen Terry, then eight years old; at her first entrance she was seated on a mushroom that rose through a trap door.

The new century began with Beerbohm Tree's commercially successful revival of *A Midsummer Night's Dream* on January 10, 1900. For this lavish production, Tree's first comedy revival at Her Majesty's Theatre, every scenic marvel possible was displayed, even to the inclusion of live rabbits scampering in the wood. Tree acted Bottom, Lewis Waller was Lysander, Julia Neilson and Lady Tree (Helen Maud Holt) played Oberon and Titania. Frank Benson revived his pretentious 1889 Stratford production at the Lyceum on February 22, 1900, but he could hardly compete with Tree. In autumn of the next year Robert Courtneidge produced the play for Manchester, and another eight-year-old actress, Cicely Courtneidge, made her debut in the role of Peaseblossom. At the Adelphi, in November 1905, Oscar Asche's company achieved recognition with a production of the comedy, which was performed at that theatre again in December 1906. Asche took the role of Bottom and Lily Brayton played Helena.

A Midsummer Night's Dream was Harley Granville-Barker's last experimental production at the Savoy Theatre and, unveiled on February 6, 1914, it became his most controversial. Some critics complained that the innovations reduced the play to eccentricity, others defended it as Shakespeare's *Dream* revealed. Granville-Barker abandoned Mendelssohn for English folk tunes and used colored curtains to indicate changing scenes. But perhaps the most discussed aspect of Granville-Barker's presentation was his treatment of the fairies. Their hands and faces were gilded and their thigh-pieces made of bronze. Moving like marionettes, the "golden fairies" truly suggested their origins in another world. The play had 99 performances, with Lillah McCarthy playing Helena; Nigel Playfair, Bottom; Ion Swinley, Lysander; Baliol Holloway, Theseus; Donald Calthrop, Puck; and Dennis Neilson-Terry and Christine Silver, Oberon and Titania. The following year, Granville-Barker brought his production to Wallack's Theatre in New York, where the arguments were renewed.

Stratford-upon-Avon saw the play every two or three years from 1903, under Frank Benson, and from 1919, under W. Bridges-Adams. In 1915 Benson, with his company at the Court Theatre, played Theseus, to which role he unaccountably added a few lines from *Richard II*. There were productions at the Old Vic almost annually from 1914 to 1920 and Robert Atkins staged the comedy during three seasons from 1920 to 1925. In 1923 Donald Calthrop produced *A Midsummer Night's Dream* at the Kingsway Theatre, using simplified sets. His cast was an excellent one: Viola Tree as Helena, Nicholas Hannen and Athene Seyler as Oberon and Titania, Baliol Holloway as Bottom, and Frank Cellier as Quince. For those who had complained of the scenic paucity of Calthrop's production, the next year Basil Dean, a former stage manager for Beerbohm Tree, reverted to full spectacle. The stage at Drury Lane resembled a dense forest peopled by balletic fairies. An extraordinary cast included Leon Quartermaine (Lysander), Frank Vosper (Demetrius), Edith Evans (Helena), Gwen Ffrangcon-Davies (Titania), and D. Hay Petrie (Puck). This, the last Shakespearean production at Drury Lane for 13 years, ran for 96 performances.

The West End saw two productions of *A Midsummer Night's Dream* by Italia Conti's company, one in 1926 at the Winter Garden, and another, in 1927, at the Adelphi. Andrew Leigh directed the comedy at the Old Vic during the 1926/7 season with himself as Puck, Baliol Holloway as Bottom and Dorothy Massingham as Helena. It was with his production of *A Midsummer Night's Dream* on December 9, 1929 that Harcourt Williams finally and completely converted Old Vic audiences to Granville-Barker's notion of swiftly spoken verse. Williams, too, substituted Cecil Sharp's arrangement of folk tunes for Mendelssohn and dressed his green-faced fairies in seaweed rather than conventional filmy costumes. The fantasy succeeded, aided considerably by the performances of John Gielgud and Leslie French as Oberon and Puck. Williams staged the play for the Old Vic again in 1931, with Ralph Richardson as Bottom and Robert Harris as Oberon. Leslie French repeated his impersonation of Puck in this production and continued to play that role in presentations of the comedy at the Open Air throughout the 1930's. In the middle of this decade, the series of pleasant productions was interrupted by a controversial film version produced by Max Reinhardt. The cast for this movie included Dick Powell as Lysander, Victor Jory as Oberon, Mickey Rooney as Puck, and James Cagney as Bottom.

Two years later, during Christmas 1937, Tyrone Guthrie restored the fantasy in a triumphant, gauzy, balletic Victorian production at the Old Vic with Ralph Richardson as a dreamy, confused, amazed Bottom and Robert Helpmann as a dancing Oberon opposite Vivien Leigh's Titania. A natural for the Open Air Theatre, *A Midsummer Night's Dream* was produced as a pastoral annually from 1933 through 1940. During those years, Robert Atkins, Baliol Holloway, Leslie French, and Francis L. Sullivan played Bottom at Regent's Park; Phyllis Neilson-Terry regularly acted Oberon, giving the part over in 1938 to Jean Forbes-Robertson and, that autumn, to Gladys Cooper. The Birmingham Repertory Theatre staged the play in 1936; the Old Vic, in December 1938; Donald Wolfit at the Strand in 1941; Ben Iden Payne at Stratford in 1942, followed by Baliol Holloway's production at the Memorial Theatre the next year. In July 1942 at the Open Air, and the following December at the Westminster, Robert Atkins played Bottom in his own productions of the play. John Gielgud re-created his Oberon for the Haymarket in 1945, with Peggy Ashcroft as Titania in a Jacobean masque treatment of the comedy under the direction of Nevill Coghill.

In 1951 Tyrone Guthrie tried a second production of the play, but it lost much of its effectiveness, despite the Bottom of Paul Rogers. If a major fault was his too simple scenery, there was possibly less to commend in his Old Vic production of 1957, which buried Shakespeare beneath an expansive set and an elaborate ballet. This presentation was shown at Edinburgh for a preliminary season before being exported to America.

At Stratford, in 1959, Peter Hall staged a noisy production with Charles Laughton as Bottom, Mary Ure as Titania, and Cyril Luckham as Quince. This production was toned down in 1962, and finally achieved proper balance in its revival at the Aldwych in 1963. In between Hall's struggles with *A Midsummer Night's Dream,* Michael Langham produced it for the Old Vic (1960); Alec McCowen was Oberon and Douglas Campbell, who had directed a production of the comedy at Stratford, Ontario, in June of that year, played Bottom. Bad speech ruined Tony Richardson's 1962 Royal Court revival. David William presented the play at the Open Air in 1962 and 1963.

Stage History: America. The first performance of *A Midsummer Night's Dream* in America was given for the benefit of Ellen Hilson on November 9, 1826 at the Park Theatre, New York. She portrayed Puck on this occasion, while her husband, Thomas Hilson, an accomplished comedian, acted Bottom. A younger and as yet not fully appreciated comic actor, Henry Placide, was Snout; Catherine Hackett, wife of James H. Hackett, impersonated Hermia; and her sister, Mrs. Sharpe, appeared as Titania. In 1841 another production, emphasizing the fairy scenes, opened on August 30 at the Park Theatre but lasted only a short time; the 25-year-old Charlotte Cushman played Oberon opposite Mary Taylor's Titania and Eliza Knight's Puck.

William E. Burton, a superb interpreter of broad farce, portrayed Bottom in a revival at Burton's Theatre on Chambers Street which ran from February 3 to March 3, 1853. The following year he gave another production. Three days later, on February 6, 1854, a rival house, the Old Broadway, under E. A. Marshall's management, gave an opulent presentation of the comedy. There were two performances of the play at the Old Broadway in 1855. In 1859 Laura Keene presented a richly scenic revival at her theatre with an excellent cast that included Edward A. Sothern, father of E. H. Sothern, as Lysander. Miss Keene's Puck elicited favorable comment and the play was performed 40 times from April 18 to May 28. Charles Kean's acting version was used. A later production at Miss Keene's theatre (renamed the Olympic) on October 28, 1867 featured scenic marvels excelling in beauty those in any previous *Midsummer Night's Dream* on the American stage. The comedy achieved its longest American run of 100 nights.

Augustin Daly's first production of the play was seen at the Grand Opera House on August 19, 1873, with Fay Templeton as Puck. His second revival, opening at Daly's Theatre on January 31, 1888, boasted more lavish scenery and elaborate pageantry, and an excellent cast centered on James Lewis' pleasantly complacent, absurd Bottom. The young lovers, Otis Skinner and John Drew (Lysander and Demetrius) and Ada Rehan and Virginia Dreher (Helena and Hermia), ideally represented charming, romantic youth. This production lasted for more than 50 performances in the first season, and was revived in 1890 with a new cast which included Tyrone Power as Quince.

Other, less impressive, presentations of *A Midsummer Night's Dream* were offered by John W. Albaugh's Travelling Company, appearing at the Star Theatre in 1889; by Lewis James, Katherine Kidder and Company at the Grand Opera House in 1901; and in a Klaw-Erlanger revival at the New Amsterdam in 1903 with Nat C. Goodwin as Bottom. On September 21, 1906 the Astor Theatre opened with a presentation of the comedy that stressed spectacle over performance. Ben Greet, visiting America, played Bottom at the Garden Theatre in 1910. On February 16, 1915, a year after Harley Granville-Barker's controversial Savoy experiment, similar controversy greeted his unorthodox production at Wallack's with Ernest Cossart as Bottom.

A Midsummer Night's Dream, acted in German and transported by Max Reinhardt, who made his own version of the play, from the Deutsches Theater in Berlin and the Josefstadt in Vienna, opened at the Century Theatre on November 17, 1927. This was the New York debut of Reinhardt's troupe and critics were unanimous in their approval of the gorgeous spectacle, which used every conceivable mechanical device to dazzle the audience. Two performances excelled: the incomparable Oberon of Alexander Moissi and the devilish Puck of Vladimir Sokoloff. A makeshift and somewhat unglamorous *Midsummer Night's Dream* followed in 1932. This revival by the Shakespeare Theatre Company, as staged by Percival Vivian during a repertory season at the Jolson (later renamed The Shakespeare Theatre), was further weakened by a cast of many untrained actors.

Perhaps because of difficulties and expense in staging the fantasy, theatrical producers in New York have shown little interest in the play but, since the mid-1950's, several presentations have appeared in this country. In 1954 the Old Vic's production featuring the ballet stars Robert Helpmann and Moira Shearer as Oberon and Titania and Stanley Holloway as Bottom was performed at the Metropolitan Opera House. In 1956 the Shakespearewrights, directed by Norman Peck, overcame most of the production problems by presenting a scenically barren *Midsummer Night's Dream* at the Jan Hus Auditorium. Counting heavily on the antics of the mechanicals to compensate for the lack of magical wonders proved judicious, and a competent cast of tinkers provided sustained merriment during the Pyramus and Thisbe interlude. Most of the major portrayals failed, however, especially the too-belligerent Bottom of Robert Cass and a Puck devoid of urchin qualities, Philip Lawrence.

In 1958 the play as presented by the American Shakespeare Festival at Stratford, Connecticut, under Jack Landau's direction, relied heavily on the comic aspects to the almost complete annihilation of the poetic beauties of the text. Inga Swenson, Barbara Barrie, and June Havoc played Helena, Hermia, and Titania, while Hiram Sherman appeared as Bottom, Morris Carnovsky as Quince, Richard Easton as Puck, and Richard Waring as Oberon. The Festival in Stratford, Ontario, in 1960, too, concentrated on the comedy of the mechanicals, but with better effect, and the enjoyable buffoonery of the Pyramus and Thisbe interlude stole the show. Douglas Campbell directed this effort, with the accent in the fairy scenes on unabated movement at the expense of the poetry. John Dengel's Puck, who seemed to be everywhere at once, became an irritating distraction, but Helen Burns' Hermia was disconsolately droll and Kate Reid gave a comic portrayal of the bewildered Helena suddenly and unaccountably pursued by two lovesick males. The Connecticut Stratford Festival reached for the stars when they tried the comedy again in 1960, this time introducing Bert Lahr as Bottom in a production which later visited 18 cities. In 1961 Joseph Papp produced a lavish *Midsummer Night's Dream* for the New York Shakespeare Festival under Joel Friedman's direction and, once more, the horseplay overshadowed the poetic glories in the comedy. Fun and frolic abounded with the clumsy court-jester Puck of John Call, who reminded one commentator of "a cross between Mickey Rooney and Jackie Gleason," and the hilarious Bottom of Albert Quinton. Katharine Widdoes was a graceful Titania and James Earl Jones, a serious and fascinatingly satanic Oberon, "played lik Iago."

In March 1962 Frank McMullen directed the pla for the School of Drama at Yale. One of the most ir teresting productions was that staged in 1964 by Jac Sydow for the New York Shakespeare Festival Delacorte Mobile Theatre, which embarked on five-borough tour with the noble and commandin Oberon of Ted van Griethuysen, the impish Puck o Clyde M. Burton, and the broadly clowning Bottor of Clifton James bringing the Shakespearean theatr free to many who had never before seen a live prc duction of any play.—M. G.

Bibliography. TEXT: *A Midsummer Night's Drean* New Cambridge Edition, A. Quiller-Couch and Dover Wilson, eds., 1924; W. W. Greg, *The Edi torial Problem in Shakespeare*, 1939. DATE: Joh Draper, "The Date of *A Midsommer Night Dreame*," *Modern Language Notes*, LIII, 1938; Sid ney Thomas, "The Bad Weather in *A Midsumme Night's Dream*," *Modern Language Notes*, LXIV 1949. SOURCES: Geoffrey Bullough, *Narrative an Dramatic Sources of Shakespeare*, Vol. I, 195 COMMENT: New Cambridge Edition; Edith Ricker "Political Propaganda in *A Midsummer Night Dream*," *Modern Philology*, XXI, 1923; E. K. Cham bers, "The Occasion of *A Midsummer Night' Dream*," *Shakespearean Gleanings*, 1944. STAGE HIS TORY: New Cambridge Edition; T. Alston Brow *A History of the New York Stage . . . to 1901*, 190 William Winter, *Shakespeare on the Stage*, 3 vols 1911–1916; G. C. D. Odell, *Shakespeare from Be terton to Irving*, 1920; J. C. Trewin, *Shakespeare o the English Stage, 1900–1964*, 1964.

Selected Criticism

CHARLES KNIGHT. To offer an analysis of this subtl and ethereal drama would, we believe, be as unsatis factory as the attempts to associate it with the reali ties of the stage. With scarcely an exception, th proper understanding of the other plays of Shak spere may be assisted by connecting the apparentl separate parts of the action, and by developing an reconciling what seems obscure and anomalous i the features of the characters. But to follow out th caprices and illusions of the loves of Demetrius an Lysander, of Helena and Hermia;—to reduce to pro saic description the consequence of the jealousies o Oberon and Titania;—to trace the Fairy Quee under the most fantastic of deceptions, where grac and vulgarity blend together like the Cupids an Chimeras of Raffaelle's Arabesques;—and, finally, t go along with the scene till the illusions disappear— till the lovers are happy, and "sweet bully Bottom" is reduced to an ass of human dimensions;—such a attempt as this would be worse even than unreverential criticism. No,—the 'Midsummer-Night's Dream must be left to its own influences. [*Studies of Shakspere*, 1849.]

THOMAS KENNY. The "Midsummer Night's Dream" is Shakespeare's most characteristic invasion of th world of pure enchantment. In it he has found voice and a form for the idlest and most undefinabl movements of the human fancy. But there ar manifest, and perhaps to some extent inevitable limitations to the success with which he has accomplished this wonderful task. The versification more particularly in the rhyme, is often more o less languid and negligent . . . . The "Midsummer Night's Dream is not, perhaps, the perfection of frolicsome grace. It certainly is not the most rapt form of "harmonious madness" which it is possible to conceive. But in it we find the world of phantasy and the world of reality brought together with an ease and a truthfulness which had previously been unknown in any work of human hands. It was a new phenomenon in the manifestations of genius. It showed that a poet had at length arisen who, by the unaided force of imagination, and apparently without any intellectual effort, or the gratification of any personal predilection, could give an outward form to the most shadowy and fugitive images of the mind; and in this bright power he had neither predecessor nor follower among men. [*The Life and Genius of Shakespeare*, 1864.]

GEORG BRANDES. How is one to speak adequately of *A Midsummer Night's Dream*? It is idle to dwell upon the slightness of the character-drawing, for the poet's effort is not after characterisation; and, whatever its weak points, the poem as a whole is one of the tenderest, most original, and most perfect Shakespeare ever produced.

It is Spenser's fairy-poetry developed and condensed; it is Shelley's spirit-poetry anticipated by more than two centuries. And the airy dream is shot with whimsical parody. The frontiers of Elf-land and Clown-land meet and mingle.

We have here an element of aristocratic distinction in the princely couple, Theseus and Hippolyta, and their court. We have here an element of sprightly burlesque in the artisans' performance of Pyramus and Thisbe, treated with genial irony and divinely felicitous humour. And here, finally, we have the element of supernatural poetry, which soon after flashes forth again in *Romeo and Juliet*, where Mercutio describes the doings of Queen Mab. Puck and Pease-blossom, Cobweb and Mustardseed—pigmies who hunt the worms in a rosebud, tease bats, chase spiders, and lord it over nightingales—are the leading actors in an elfin play, a fairy carnival of inimitable mirth and melody, steeped in a midsummer atmosphere of mist-wreaths and flower-scents, under the afterglow that lingers through the sultry night. This miracle of happy inspiration contains the germs of innumerable romantic achievements in England, Germany, and Denmark, more than two centuries later . . . .

We have here no pathos. The hurricane of passion does not as yet sweep through Shakespeare's work. No; it is only the romantic and imaginative side of love that is here displayed, the magic whereby longing transmutes and idealises its object, the element of folly, infatuation, and illusion in desire, with its consequent variability and transitoriness. Man is by nature a being with no inward compass, led astray by his instincts and dreams, and for ever deceived either by himself or by others. This Shakespeare realises, but does not, as yet, take the matter very tragically. Thus the characters whom he here presents, even, or rather especially, in their love-affairs, appear as anything but reasonable beings. The lovers seek and avoid each other by turns, they love and are not loved again; the couples attract each other at cross-purposes; the youth runs after the maiden who shrinks from him, the maiden flees from the man who adores her; and the poet's delicate irony makes the confusion reach its height and find its symbolic expression when the Queen of the Fairies, in the intoxication of a love-dream, recognizes her ideal in a journeyman weaver with an ass's head. [*William Shakespeare: A Critical Study*, 1896.]

E. K. CHAMBERS. On *a priori* grounds, one might perhaps have expected that an unacademic writer, coming straight from the heart of Warwickshire, would have kept closer to the lines of the old folk beliefs about the 'good people,' and would even have shared in the habits of thought and imagination from which those beliefs took their rise. It is certainly not so with Shakespeare, who, for good or for evil, is a thorough child of the Renascence, and exhibits not only the Renascence love of quaint lore plundered from every quarter, but also the Renascence positive spirit, for which such lore has little meaning otherwise than as material for deliberate poetic craft. He takes his superstitions from learned and literary sources, just as he takes his natural history from the bestiaries, no less freely than from his own observation. Even when his material is of English origin, it is not always clear whether he has drawn it from reminiscences of his own Warwickshire boyhood or from some popular book, such as Reginald Scot's *Discovery of Witchcraft* or Harsnet's *Declaration of Popish Impostures*. It must not be assumed, therefore, that Shakespeare's use of the supernatural for dramatic purposes implies a belief in its actual and objective existence. Where it is not merely imposed upon him by his historical sources, it seems to serve one of two ends. Either it attunes the minds of the audience to a tragic or ironical issue, as for example in the terrible dreams of Richard Crookback before Bosworth Field; or it is a symbol, introduced by the poet as a recognition of a mystery, an unexplained element in the course of human affairs upon earth. This is its really important function in some of the greatest plays. [*Shakespeare: A Survey*, 1925.]

JOHN RUSSELL BROWN. If one wished to describe the judgment which informs *A Midsummer Night's Dream*, one might do so very simply: the play suggests that lovers, like lunatics, poets, and actors, have their own "truth" which is established as they see the beauty of their beloved, and that they are confident in this truth for, although it seems the "silliest stuff" to an outsider, to them it is quite reasonable; it also suggests that lovers, like actors, need, and sometimes ask for, our belief, and that this belief can only be given if we have the generosity and imagination to think "no worse of them than they of themselves."

The play's greatest triumph is the manner in which our wavering acceptance of the illusion of drama is used as a kind of flesh-and-blood image of the acceptance which is appropriate to the strange and private "truth" of those who enact the play of love. By using this living image, Shakespeare has gone beyond direct statement in words or action and has presented his judgment in terms of a mode of being, a relationship, in which we, the audience, are actually involved. And he has ensured that this image is experienced at first hand, for the audience of the play-within-the-play does not make the perfect reaction; one of them describes what this entails but it is left for us to make that description good. The success of the play will, finally, depend upon our reaction to its shadows. [*Shakespeare and His Comedies*, 1957.]

C. L. BARBER. If Shakespeare had called *A Midsummer Night's Dream* by a title that referred to pageantry and May games, the aspects of it with which I shall be chiefly concerned would be more often discussed. To honor a noble wedding, Shakespeare gathered up in a play the sort of pageantry which was usually presented piece-meal at aristocratic entertainments, in park and court as well as in hall. And the May game, everybody's pastime, gave the pattern for his whole action, which moves "from the town to the grove" and back again, bringing in summer to the bridal. These things were familiar and did not need to be stressed by a title . . . .

The humor of the play relates superstition, magic and passionate delusion as "fancy's images." The actual title emphasizes a sceptical attitude by calling the comedy a "dream." It seems unlikely that the title's characterization of the dream, "a midsummer night's dream," implies association with the specific customs of Midsummer Eve, the shortest night of the year, except as "midsummer night" would carry suggestions of a magic time. The observance of Midsummer Eve in England centered on building bonfires or "bonefires," of which there is nothing in Shakespeare's moonlight play. It was a time when maids might find out who their true love would be by dreams or divinations. There were customs of decking houses with greenery and hanging lights, which just possibly might connect with the fairies' torches at the comedy's end. And when people gathered fern seed at midnight, sometimes they spoke of spirits whizzing invisibly past. If one ranges through the eclectic pages of *The Golden Bough*, guided by the index for Midsummer Eve, one finds other customs suggestive of Shakespeare's play, involving moonlight, seeing the moon in water, gathering dew, and so on, but in Sweden, Bavaria, or still more remote places, rather than England. One can assume that parallel English customs have been lost, or one can assume that Shakespeare's imagination found its way to similarities with folk cult, starting from the custom of Maying and the general feeling that spirits may be abroad in the long dusks and short nights of midsummer. Olivia in *Twelfth Night* speaks of "midsummer madness" (III, iv, 61). In the absence of evidence, there is no way to settle just how much comes from tradition. But what *is* clear is that Shakespeare was not *simply* writing out folklore which he heard in his youth, as Romantic critics liked to assume. On the contrary, his fairies are produced by a complex fusion of pageantry and popular game, as well as popular fancy. Moreover, as we shall see, they are not serious in the menacing way in which the people's fairies were serious. Instead they are serious in a very different way, as embodiments of the May-game experience of eros in men and women and trees and flowers, while any superstitious tendency to believe in their literal reality is mocked. The whole night's action is presented as a release of shaping fantasy which brings clarification about the tricks of strong imagination. We watch a dream; but we are awake, thanks to pervasive humor about the tendency to take fantasy literally, whether in love, in superstition, or in Bottom's mechanical dramatics. As in *Love's Labour's Lost* the folly of wit becomes the generalized comic subject in the course of an astonishing release of witty invention, so here in the course of a more inclusive release of imagination, the folly of fantasy becomes the general subject, echoed back and forth between the strains of the play's imitative counterpoint. ["May Games and Metamorphoses on a Midsummer Night," *Shakespeare's Festive Comedy*, 1959.]

WOLFGANG CLEMEN. If the story of the craftsmen forms a satirical counterbalance to the plot of the lovers, then it is also true to say that the drama of Pyramus and Thisby initiates a twofold, even threefold kind of awareness. For what we get in this parody of the love tragedy is an exaggerated depiction of the four lovers' sentimentality, their high-flown protestations of love, and their pseudo-solemnity—a depiction in the form of a flashback that they themselves are now able to contemplate as spectators, serenely calm and reconciled with one another. The lovers' own relationships have likewise been a play that the fairies have found highly amusing, and these entanglements parallel the quarrel between Oberon and Titania, the quarrel from which the confusion among the lovers originated.

"The play within the play," superbly worked out by Shakespeare, makes us particularly aware that the entire drama has indeed been a "play," summoned into life by the dramatist's magic wand and just as easily made to vanish. When Puck refers in the first line of his epilogue ("If we shadows have offended") not merely to the fairies, previously termed "shadows," but also to all the actors who have taken part, we realize that Shakespeare is once more making it clear to us that we have been watching a "magic-lantern show," something where appearance, not reality, is the operative factor.

It is peculiarly ironic that Bottom, Quince, and company perform the tragedy of Pyramus and Thisby as an auspicious offering on behalf of the newly established love union, thereby, one might say, presenting the material of *Romeo and Juliet* in a comic and grotesque manner. Thus an exaggerated form of tragedy is employed so that the preceding scenes may be parodied as comedy. The play of Pyramus and Thisby parodies not only the torments of love, which the Athenian lovers can now look back on with serene calmness, but also the Senecan style of Elizabethan tragedy with its melodrama and ponderous conventions. Shakespeare parodies these conventions here by means of exaggeration or clumsy and grotesque usage—the too explicit prologue, for instance; the verbose self-explanation and commentaries; the stereotyped phrases for expressing grief; and the excessive use of such rhetorical devices as apostrophe, alliteration, hyperbole, and rhetorical question. [Introduction to *A Midsummer Night's Dream*, The Signet Classic Shakespeare, 1963.]

Mikulin, Grigóri Ivanovich (fl. 1601). Russian ambassador to the court of Queen Elizabeth. Mikulin was at Elizabeth's court on January 6, 1601 when a treaty of friendship between England and Russia was signed. Leslie Hotson has discovered a report by Mikulin describing the festivities that attended the signing of the treaty, among which was included, according to Hotson, the first performance of

Twelfth Night. In the scene in which Viola, disguised as a messenger, arrives at Lady Olivia's house, Hotson believes that Shakespeare satirized Mikulin, who had meticulously detailed instructions on how to behave and what to say during his visit. [Leslie Hotson, *The First Night of Twelfth Night,* 1954.]

Milan, Duke of. In *The Two Gentlemen of Verona,* Silvia's father. Having originally favored Thurio as his future son-in-law, the Duke eventually bestows his daughter on her true lover, Valentine, when Thurio refuses to fight for her.

Mildmay, Sir Humphrey (1592–?1666). Diarist. The oldest son of Sir Anthony Mildmay of Danbury, Essex, Mildmay apparently divided his time between managing his estates and attending the theatre. His diary and account book afford a valuable record of performances of plays in London from 1633 to 1642. Among the performances he records is one on May 6, 1635 "called ye More of Venice" (*Othello*).

Miles, Bernard (1907–). Actor and director. Miles made his first stage appearance in *Richard III.* Subsequent Shakespearean roles included that of Iago (1941), Christopher Sly in *The Taming of the Shrew* (1947), Caliban (1952), and Macbeth (1952). In 1951 he founded the Mermaid Theatre in St. John's Wood, a playhouse designed as a replica of an Elizabethan theatre. The theatre was reconstructed at Puddle Dock, London, in 1959.

miles gloriosus. See PLAUTUS.

Milhaud, Darius. See MUSIC BASED ON SHAKESPEARE: *20th century.*

military life. The army in Elizabethan England was characterized by corruption and inefficiency. There was no regular standing army, and the defense of the country was theoretically based on two 1557 statutes of Queen Mary and Philip II of Spain. The first, an Act for Arms and Armour, required "every nobleman, gentleman, or other temporal person" in the realm to keep, according to his means, a certain number of horses, weapons, and suits and other articles of defensive armor. The second, an Act for Taking of Musters, was intended to control such abuses as absences from musters and the prevalent practices of bribing the mustermasters or providing incompetents as substitutes for musters. In *1 Henry IV* Falstaff graphically describes his role as a dishonest mustermaster:

> If I be not ashamed of my soldiers, I am a soused gurnet. I have misused the king's press damnably. I have got, in exchange of a hundred and fifty soldiers, three hundred and odd pounds. I press me none but good householders, yeomen's sons; inquire me out contracted bachelors, such as had been asked twice on the banns; such a commodity of warm slaves, as had as lieve hear the devil as a drum; such as fear the report of a caliver worse than a struck fowl or a hurt wild-duck. I pressed me none but such toasts-and-butter, with hearts in their bellies no bigger than pins' heads, and they have bought out their services; and now my whole charge consists of ancients, corporals, lieutenants, gentlemen of companies, slaves as ragged as Lazarus in the painted cloth . . . A mad fellow met me on the way and told me I had unloaded all the gibbets and pressed the dead bodies. No eye hath seen such scarecrows . . . . and the villains march wide betwixt the legs, as if they had gyves on; for indeed I had the most of them out of prison. There's but a shirt and a half in all my company; and the half shirt is two napkins tacked together and thrown over the shoulders like a herald's coat without sleeves; and the shirt, to say the truth, stolen from my host at Saint Alban's, or the red-nose innkeeper of Daventry. But that's all one; they'll find linen enough on every hedge.
>
> (IV, ii, 12–53)

The Act for Taking of Musters provided that any man evading the muster would be subject to 10 days' imprisonment or a fine of 40 shillings. Mustermasters found discharging recruits for payment were subject to a fine of 10 times the amount they received. The acts, however, remained empty documents; the records of military service in Elizabeth's reign show that at times of crisis only limited numbers of men and arms could be mustered.

As Falstaff's speech suggests, the ranks of the troops of the shires were mostly filled with incompetents from the lower end of the social order; all others were able to buy their way out of service. This demoralizing situation was reflected in the methods employed to recruit troops: either the jails were opened and their inmates incorporated into the ranks, or recruits were impressed by press gangs. It became almost a tradition that on Easter Sunday, when the law compelled everyone to take the sacrament, press gangs would close the doors of the church and impress all the men inside.

Despite the abuses, corruption, and malpractices, some serious training did take place. In 1573, the year after the deployment of English troops in aid of Dutch insurgents at Alva, 3000 men of the London citizen army (the trainbands), in an effort to correct the sorry state of England's military, formed and drilled daily at Mile End, an old drill ground. It is interesting to note that almost all the instructors were foreigners; few Englishmen with the experience necessary for the task were available. Justice Shallow mentions the Mile End drills when he criticizes Wart (*2 Henry IV*, III, ii, 298–307).

Shakespeare was apparently unacquainted with the theoretical military literature of the day; many of the foreign terms common in English military jargon are not to be found in the plays. If any book may be said to have provided him with occasional theoretical knowledge of military affairs, then that book would have to be Plutarch. However, the playwright was aware of the drama, glory, and humor of military life, and such descriptive passages as appear in his plays are both vivid and eloquent. [J. W. Fortescue, "The Soldier," *Shakespeare's England,* 1916; Paul A. Jorgensen, *Shakespeare's Military World,* 1956.]

Miller, James (1706–1744). Clergyman and playwright. The son of a Dorsetshire clergyman, Miller went to Wadham, Oxford, and was to go into business but took holy orders instead. His first appointment was to a lectureship at Trinity Chapel. His creative efforts, plays and satirical writings, were undertaken to eke out a meager salary.

Other than his poetry, satire, and a political pamphlet attacking Robert Walpole (published posthumously) Miller's works were all adaptations of others, including Voltaire, Molière, and Shakespeare.

The Universal Passion, first acted at the Drury Lane in 1737, was Miller's version of *Much Ado About Nothing*. It includes interpolated non-Shakespearean passages from Molière's *Princess d'Elide* as well as lines from *Two Gentlemen of Verona* and *Twelfth Night*. *The Universal Passion* is a considerably "altered" version, to say the least; the characters in Miller's comedy are almost unrecognizable parallels to Shakespeare's, while the plot and act-scene sequences seem varied almost at random. In Act I, Bellario (Claudio) tells of his love for Lucilia (Hero), Joculo (a jester) describes life as a court jester, and Lucilia mockingly denigrates marriage. In the second act, Joculo discourses sarcastically about women, Lucilia tests Bellario's love, and Joculo jests with Delia (Margaret). In Act III, Bellario saves Gratiano's (Don Pedro's) life, the persiflage of Protheus (Benedick) and Liberia (Beatrice) is developed, and Joculo and Liberia discuss Protheus. The fourth act includes the transference of the Friar's speeches advising Lucilia's concealment to the character of Protheus, and in Act V Joculo makes love to Delia. Miller's version was performed 10 times in 1737 and revived for 2 performances in 1741. See MUCH ADO ABOUT NOTHING: *Stage History*. [*Dictionary of National Biography*, 1892; C. B. Hogan, *Shakespeare in the Theatre, 1701–1800*, 2 vols., 1952, 1957.]

Millington, Thomas (fl. 1583–1603). London bookseller active in the publication of unauthorized Shakespearean quartos. Millington was admitted to the Stationers' Company in 1591. His first book entry was *The First part of the Contention betwixt the two famous Houses of Yorke and Lancaster* (1594), the "bad quarto" of *2 Henry VI*. In the same year he was designated on the title page of *Titus Andronicus*, along with Edward White, as the distributor of that Quarto. In 1595 he published the bad quarto of *3 Henry VI* (*The true Tragedy of Richard, Duke of Yorke*). In conjunction with John Busby, he published the bad quarto of *Henry V* (1600). In 1602 he transferred the copyright of the bad quartos of *2 Henry VI* and *3 Henry VI* (the Second Quartos of which he had published in 1600) to Thomas Pavier. Pavier also received Millington's rights to *Titus Andronicus*, which had actually been published by John Danter but which apparently passed into Millington and White's possession after Danter's death about 1598. [R. B. McKerrow, ed., *A Dictionary of Printers and Booksellers . . . 1557–1640*, 1910.]

Mills, John (d. 1736). Actor. Mills joined the company at Drury Lane after Thomas Betterton and his faction had moved to Lincoln's Inn Fields in 1695. He remained at Drury Lane for 40 years, with the exception of some appearances at the Haymarket with the Drury Lane company from 1706 to 1708. His early parts were in comedies, such as Winlove (or Lucentio) in Lacy's *Sawny the Scot*, an adaptation of *The Taming of the Shrew*. Although he was criticized by Steele for excessive gesticulation, there is no doubt that Mills was one of the most competent actors of his time and he had an enormous repertory. His best parts were Prospero, Antonio (in Granville's *Jew Of Venice*), Macbeth, Julius Caesar, Buckingham (in Cibber's *King Richard the Third*), Falstaff (*2 Henry IV*), Titus Andronicus, Cassius, Lear, Othello, Hamlet, and Wolsey. [*Dictionary of National Biography*, 1885– ; C. B. Hogan, *Shak speare in the Theatre, 1701–1800*, 2 vols., 1952, 1957.

Milton, Ernest (1890–). Actor. Born in Sa Francisco, Milton moved to England at an early ag After appearing with a number of provincial com panies, he joined the Old Vic in 1918. He soon ros to become one of the mainstays of that troupe an in the next decade turned in creditable performance of many of the major Shakespearean roles. Amon his portrayals of this period were Shylock, Benedic Macbeth, Lear, Hamlet, and Palamon in the rarel played *The Two Noble Kinsmen*. In 1935 he had th leading role in *Timon of Athens* and in 1941 ap peared as Sir Andrew Aguecheek in *Twelfth Nigh* and as King John. In 1944 he appeared at the Ope Air Theatre as Leontes in *The Winter's Tale*.

Milton, John (1608–1674). Poet and author. Mil ton's career falls into three periods. Up to 1640 wa the time of education and travel, during which h wrote such works as "On the Morning of Christ' Nativity," "L'Allegro," "Il Penseroso," "Lycidas, and "Comus." From 1640, the year of his return fron the grand tour, until 1660 he was occupied with stat affairs. Except for a few sonnets he wrote prose dur ing this period, concerning himself with reforms i the church, the state, marriage, and education. Whe the Restoration forced him into political retiremen Milton returned to poetry and produced his majo works: *Paradise Lost* (1667), *Paradise Regaine* (1671), and *Samson Agonistes* (1671).

Milton's first printed work was the poem o Shakespeare—a 16-line epigram in heroic couplets– which appeared in the Second Folio (1632) o Shakespeare's works:

An Epitaph on the admirable Dramaticke Poet,
W. Shakespeare. 1630
What needs my *Shakespear* for his honour'd Bones,
The labour of an Age, in piled Stones
Or that his hallow'd reliques should be hid
Under a Star-ypointing *Pyramid*?
Dear Son of memory, great heir of Fame,
What needst thou such weak witnes of thy name?
Thou in our wonder and astonishment
Hast built thy self a live-long Monument.
For whil'st to th' shame of slow-endeavouring art
Thy easie numbers flow, and that each heart
Hath from the leaves of thy unvalu'd Booke,
Those Delphick lines with deep impression took,
Then thou our fancy of it self bereaving,
Dost make us marble with too much conceaving;
And so Sepulcher'd in such pomp dost lie
That Kings for such a Tombe would wish to die.

The poem develops two ideas, both derived from Ben Jonson's dedicatory poem in the First Folio: Shakespeare as "a monument without a tomb" and Shakespeare as a child of nature rather than of art. The latter idea is repeated in "L'Allegro" where "sweetest Shakespeare Fancy's child" is said to "warble his native wood-notes wild" in contrast to the "learned sock" of Jonson. The stress on Shakespeare as a child of nature is also found in the *Theatrum Poetarum* (1675) of Edward Phillips. Milton's nephew and biographer. Phillips seems to be echoing his uncle's opinions when he states of Shakespeare that no one "represented nature more purely to the life, and where the polishments of Art are most wanting, as probably his Learning was not extraordinary, he pleaseth with a certain wild and native elegeance."

In his prose work Milton occasionally made direct reference to Shakespeare; in his poetry, there are numerous verbal parallels as well as several episodes which suggest the influence of Shakespeare. For example, Satan's plotting against Adam and Eve recalls that of Iago against Othello and Desdemona; Satan's rebellion against the Father is occasioned by the exaltation of the Son, just as Iago's resentment is aroused by the promotion of Cassio. Adam's revulsion toward Eve after the fall echoes that of Antony toward Cleopatra. Satan's remorse at the opening of Book IV recalls the soliloquy of King Claudius. Numerous other parallels exist; for an exhaustive list, see Alwin Thaler, *Shakspere's Silences,* 1929; and the same author's supplementary essay in the *SAMLA Studies in Milton,* 1953.]

Minola, Baptista. See Baptista Minola.

miracle plays. See medievalism in Shakespeare.

Miranda. In *The Tempest,* Prospero's daughter and the heroine. A delicate portrait of a pure child of Nature, Miranda combines beauty, innocence, and compassion. Reared from infancy on the island and ignorant of her origins and her fellow man, she falls in love at first sight with the shipwrecked Ferdinand, having "no ambition to see a goodlier man." When Prospero tests the prince by having him pile up thousands of heavy logs, she generously offers to share his labors but he refuses.

Mirror for Magistrates, A. Tudor collection of verse biographies of tragic figures in English history. The *Mirror* had its inception in the reissue of John Lydgate's *Falle of Princes* (1431–1438) which in turn had been based on Boccaccio's *De Casibus Virorum Illustrium.* This edition of the *Falle* (1554) included an appendix containing biographies of English tragic heroes compiled by the editor, William Baldwin (d. 1564). There is evidence that soon afterwards a volume containing the English material was issued independently, but no copies survive. The earliest extant edition is that of 1559. Baldwin wrote many of the lives as well as the prose links and commentaries, but, as he explained in the Preface, he obtained the assistance of seven collaborators for additional material. The 19 lives in this edition follow the same formula: the ghosts of the dead heroes tell their stories in the form of a complaint, usually emphasizing how a sin or fault brought about its inevitable retribution. In 1563 Baldwin issued an expanded edition with eight new lives, two of which were destined to become famous: the tragedy of Henry, duke of Buckingham, by Thomas Sackville, and the complaint of Jane Shore by Thomas Churchyard (c. 1520–1604). The most notable feature of this edition was the celebrated "Induction" by Sackville, the most outstanding poetical work in the *Mirror.* Baldwin's work was carried on by John Higgins, who in 1574 issued *The First Part of the Mirror for Magistrates* consisting of 16 lives, all taken from the legendary history of early Britain. About this time numerous imitations—both collections and individual tragedies—began to appear. One such work having no connection with the original *Mirror* was Thomas Blenerhasset's (1550?–?1625) *The Second Part of the Mirror for Magistrates* (1578), a collection of 12 tragedies covering the period from Caesar's invasion of Britain to the Norman conquest. Interest had just about reached its peak in 1587 when an expansion of the original *Mirror* was published. After this, no new edition appeared until 1610 when Richard Niccols (1584–1616) recast much of the earlier material, adding a new Induction and 10 tragedies of his own. Niccols' edition was the last to appear until modern times.

The dedication to the 1559 edition explains the nature of the work: it is "a mirror for all men as well noble as others, to show the slippery deceits of the wavering lady [Fortune] and the due reward for all kinds of vices." By this mirror one can learn vicariously from history rather than from bitter experience. The principal moral inculcated is the divine nature of authority, the accountability of the ruler to God and of subjects to their ruler as God's vice-regent, and consequently the evils of rebellion. The *Mirror* is indicative both of the popular taste for historical narrative and of prevailing concepts of authority, and illustrative of the medieval tradition in tragedy (see medievalism in Shakespeare). It is natural to suspect that Shakespeare was influenced by the *Mirror* in his history plays—for example, in making Richard of Gloucester the actual murderer of King Henry VI—since there are frequent parallels in characters, situations, and themes. Although his indebtedness to the prose chronicles of the time is more direct and immediate, there is evidence that the *Mirror* provided hints and suggestions for his plays on the two Richards and on Henry IV and Henry VI. See Thomas Phaer. [Campbell, Lily B., *Shakespeare's Histories,* 1947.]

Misery of Civil-War, The. See John Crowne.

Mistress Overdone. See Overdone, Mistress.

Modena, Gustave. See Italy.

Modjeska, Helena (1840–1909). Polish-born American actress. Originally from Cracow, Modjeska was interested in a career as an actress from a very early age. In her teens she acted in the Polish provinces and Germany and subsequently returned to her native Cracow, where she became famous. She was soon to be the reigning actress at Warsaw's Imperial Theatre. In 1876, however, Modjeska emigrated to California to help found a Polish colony. When the venture failed, Modjeska learned English and in 1877 began acting at John McCullough's theatre in San Francisco. During the next 30 years she won great success in New York, London, and Poland. She played nine Shakespearean heroines, including Juliet, Rosalind, and Cleopatra. Although she was known for the poetry of her performances, her fine technique depended on careful, studied movements and an intellectual comprehension of the characters she portrayed. [*Dictionary of American Biography,* 1927– .]

Mohun, Michael (c. 1620–1684). Actor. Mohun was one of the chief actors in the King's Company, following the Restoration in 1660. Mohun, Charles Hart, and Henry Harris were the only serious rivals to Thomas Betterton. Mohun began his career as a boy actor under the tutelage of William Beeston, playing several adult roles at the Phoenix before his career was interrupted with the closing of the theatres in 1648. Naturally siding with the Royalists, he served with distinction and rose to the rank of major. He returned to the theatre with the Restoration, performing first at the Clare Market Theatre in Vere Street, then moving with the King's Company to the new theatre in Brydges Street, Drury Lane. Mohun and Hart were the leading members of the company and, although Mohun's most famous performances were second to Hart's—he played Cassius and Iago to Hart's Brutus and Othello—his dramatic personality was not overshadowed by his fellow player.

Molière. Born **Jean-Baptiste Poquelin** (1622–1673). French dramatist. Molière's comedies, composed in the tradition of the medieval farce and the *commedia dell'arte,* are penetrating studies of man's ruses, pretenses, and idiosyncracies. Such plays as *Tartuffe, The Would-be Gentleman,* and *The Misanthrope* are discerning glimpses of universal types which have remained unequaled in literary history.

Although Molière had no knowledge of the English language or of Shakespeare, the two playwrights have much in common. Both men were actors and dramatists, not philosophers, critics, or theorists, and they were well aware of the public's tastes and interests. They unhesitatingly borrowed from the works of their predecessors, but these borrowings served only as the basic materials from which they were to create works of art. The two dramatists tended to use similar plot devices, such as mistaken identity or disguise, and analogous dialogue techniques of soliloquies and asides. Although they used farce in their theatre, many of their plays, such as *Measure for Measure* or *The Miser,* can be more appropriately termed tragicomedy. Both were boldly original in the creation of characters, yet their inventive imaginations often paralleled one another: Harpagon is not far removed from Shylock, nor Tartuffe from Iago. Finally, the two playwrights absorbed their respective accumulated traditions—Shakespeare's lively Elizabethan age and Molière's golden period of Louis XIV—and brought them to perfection on the stage.

However, these traditions brought about marked differences in the creativeness of the two men. Shakespeare's tragedies and romantic comedies reflect the subjects of an adventurous time: the heroic history of England and Rome and the fanciful representation of Italy and Greece. Molière, on the other hand, described the people of his own era—a period of polished, prescribed, orderly existence. Shakespeare was perhaps the greater mastermind and Molière was never his equal in dramatized history, soul-searching tragedy, or graceful romantic comedy. Nevertheless, in the acute, perceptive observation of man's foibles, Molière surpassed his English counterpart. [E. E. Stoll, "Molière and Shakespeare," *Romanic Review,* XXXV, 1944.]—J.R.

Molloy, Charles. See ADAPTATIONS.

Mömpelgard, Count. See Frederick, duke of WÜRTTEMBERG.

Monck, Nugent (1877–1958). Actor and producer. As a young actor, Monck was influenced by William Poel of the Elizabethan Stage Society. His career was interrupted by World War I, after which he returned to Norwich, where he formed an amateur theatre group known as the Norwich Players. In 1921 he opened the MADDERMARKET THEATRE, which had been reconstructed with an Elizabethan stage, and for the next 30 years he guided the successful fortunes of that theatre. There he produced, with an amateur, always anonymous cast, all of Shakespeare's plays as well as numerous other Elizabethan plays. Monck, who frequently acted in his productions, delivered an account of the theatre to the Shakespeare Conference at Stratford-upon-Avon in 1957, the year before his death. [Nugent Monck, "The Maddermarket Theatre," *Shakespeare Survey 12,* 1959.]

Montagu, Elizabeth. Born **Elizabeth Robinson** (1720–1800). Writer and wit. Mrs. Montagu's literary salon, frequented by David Garrick, Sir Joshua Reynolds, Edmund Burke, and others, was the first to have the epithet "bluestocking" applied to it. Mrs. Montagu's *Essay on the Writings and Genius of Shakespear* (1769) is primarily an answer to Voltaire's harsh Shakespearean criticism. She argues that adherence to ancient rules and models is not the concern of a creative genius and that the plays of Corneille, and other French writers whom Voltaire praised, are cold and barren although they follow the rules. Voltaire did not appreciate Shakespeare's greatness, according to Mrs. Montagu, primarily because he did not understand his language.

Mrs. Montagu defends the mixture of comedy and tragedy in the history plays on the grounds that Shakespeare was inventing a new form which could not be judged by the old standards. In a close study of *Henry IV* she emphasizes that, considering the meagerness of Shakespeare's sources, his characterizations were accurate and complete. Elsewhere, she praises Shakespeare's use of ghosts and other supernatural beings because, unlike the ghosts of classical dramas, they play a necessary role in the action.

Mrs. Montagu especially praised *Macbeth* for showing "the pangs of guilt separate from the fear of punishment." She also studied *Julius Caesar* closely, lauding it above Corneille's similar play, *Cinna.* [Herbert Spencer Robinson, *English Shakespearian Criticism in the Eighteenth Century,* 1932.]

Montague. In *Romeo and Juliet,* the father of Romeo and enemy of the house of Capulet. After the death of the young lovers, Montague suffers a change of heart and says that he will erect a golden statue to the daughter of his former rival.

Montague, John Neville, marquis of (d. 1471). Younger brother of Warwick the Kingmaker. Awarded the earldom of Northumberland for his victory at Hexham (1464), Montague later defected to the Lancastrians when the lands and titles were restored to the original holder. In *3 Henry VI* Montague is a Yorkist but joins his brother on the Lancastrian side after Edward IV's marriage to Lady Grey; he is killed at Barnet.

Montague, Lady. In *Romeo and Juliet,* the mother of Romeo and wife of Montague. Lady Montague appears and speaks in only I, i. In V, iii, her husband announces that she has died of grief over Romeo's exile.

Montaigne, Michel Eyquem de (1533–1592). French essayist. Born at the family estate of Montaigne near Bordeaux, Montaigne was educated by a private tutor and at the Collège de Guyenne in Bordeaux, then at the height of its reputation; he later studied law, probably at Toulouse. With his formal education completed, Montaigne traveled extensively and on several occasions resided at court. In 1565 he married and a few years later retired to Montaigne to devote himself to a life of study and contemplation. However, he occasionally broke his retirement to

THE DISPUTED SHAKESPEARE SIGNATURE IN A COPY OF FLORIO'S TRANSLATION OF MONTAIGNE'S *Essays* (1603). (BRITISH MUSEUM)

travel and to serve as mayor of Bordeaux. During this period Montaigne began to record reflections on his reading and experiences, calling these writings *Essais*—thus coining a word for the new literary genre which he virtually originated. In 1580 he published two books of essays and in 1588 a third, together with revisions of the first two. A posthumous edition (*Essais*) appeared in 1595, edited by two friends, which has been accepted as the standard, even in preference to those issued during his lifetime.

For students of English literature, the name of Montaigne remains inseparable from that of John FLORIO, his Elizabethan translator. Florio's *Essayes* were published in 1603, but the title had been entered in the Stationers' Register three years previously and thus may have been known in manuscript prior to actual publication. It is probable that Shakespeare knew Florio, inasmuch as they both had a common patron in the earl of Southampton, a fact which increases the likelihood that Shakespeare may have read the manuscript before 1603.

The relationship of Shakespeare to Montaigne has been the subject of much speculation; down to about 1940 over 80 items on the subject had been recorded by Samuel A. Tannenbaum. The only instance of Shakespeare's direct indebtedness to Montaigne which has been generally accepted is Prospero's so-called commonwealth speech in *The Tempest:*

> I' th' commonwealth I would by contraries
> Execute all things; for no kind of traffic
> Would I admit; no name of magistrate . . .
> (II, i, 147 ff.)

It was first pointed out by Edward Capell that the source of this speech was to be found in Montaigne's essay "Of Cannibals" (I, 31), and it was subsequently agreed that Florio's translation was used. However, in a much later study of the question, Margaret T. Hodgen pointed out other parallels to this passage in works easily accessible to Shakespeare; not only was the thought a commonplace but the manner of expressing it was stereotyped. Thus Shakespeare followed the common practice of describing the primitive society in negatives and, if possible, in parallel constructions: ". . . no kind of traffic . . . no name of magistrate . . . letters should not be known . . . no use of metal . . . no occupation . . ." But Miss Hodgen believes that the weight of evidence still favors the view that Florio's Montaigne was the direct and immediate source.

In addition to this passage in *The Tempest,* numerous other discussions of the Montaigne-Shakespeare relationship were common in the 19th century. In some instances there was the claim that the two authors shared such common qualities as skepticism, tolerance, compassion, worldly wisdom, or a philosophical temper; others went further and insisted that such affinities were the result of a direct influence. *The Tempest* and *Hamlet* were the two plays most often cited as exemplifying the Montaigne-like Shakespeare. J. M. Robertson, the soundest and best known of such exponents, saw the skeptical and questioning Hamlet as a reflection of Montaigne. Jacob Feis maintained that Shakespeare consciously created Hamlet as an embodiment of Montaigne in order to sound a warning: Hamlet, like Montaigne, is a Renaissance humanist who cannot entirely free himself from the dogma of the past, and thus he brings disaster upon himself and upon those around him. In general, the professional Shakespeare scholars either ignored such theories or, like Walter Raleigh and J. C. Collins, dismissed them; Sidney Lee appears to be the only scholar on record who showed some agreement with Robertson. Exponents of the theory normally made uncritical use of parallel passages, read their own views into both Montaigne and Shakespeare, equated the views of Shakespeare with those of his characters, and leaned towards a strongly autobiographical interpretation of the plays; isolated speeches were often read as though they were as self-revelatory as Montaigne's essays.

A scholarly and objective approach to the question was made by George Coffin Taylor in *Shakespeare's Debt to Montaigne* (1925). Taylor listed about 100 passages in Shakespeare which he felt were too close to the Florio Montaigne to be coincidental and another 100 with a strong degree of probability; he also listed 750 words from Florio which Shakespeare used during and after 1603 but not before. While there is room to dispute the degree of certitude and probability in many of these parallels, the cumulative effect, after all allowances are made, remains impressive. Taylor concludes that the Florio Montaigne influence was strongest during and immediately after 1603 and that it receded until the composition of *The Tempest,* which again shows a strong influence. *Hamlet* leads with the number of parallel passages (51) with *Lear* in second place (23); in *The Tempest* there are 7 other parallels in addition to the commonwealth speech. The parallels are most frequent in the discursive and digressive portions of the speeches. Shakespeare's borrowings were largely verbal, without much indebtedness to the thought or philosophy of Montaigne; the alleged influence in regard to the latter can usually be explained by the common indebtedness to a particular author—to Plutarch, for example, who was a favorite of both. Often Shakespeare had the habit of picking up a thought of Montaigne's but then developing it in a direction of his own. [Jacob Feis, *Shakespeare and Montaigne,* 1884; J. M. Robertson, *Montaigne and Shakespeare,* 1897; Samuel A. Tannenbaum, *Elizabethan Bibliographies, No. 24: Michel Eyquem de Montaigne,* 1942; Margaret T. Hodgen, "Montaigne and Shakespeare Again," *Huntington Library Quarterly,* XVI, 1952.]—R.C.F.

Montano. In *Othello,* the Moor's predecessor as governor of Cyprus. After the murder of Desdemona, Montano takes Othello's weapon and places him under guard (V, ii).

Montemayor, Jorge de (c. 1521–61). Portuguese-born poet and novelist who spent most of his life in Spain and wrote in Spanish. His chief work is *Diana Enamorada,* a prose pastoral interspersed with verses. It concerns the misfortunes of two shepherd lovers, and employs disguises and the use of enchanted potions to restore happiness. Enormously popular, the work was translated into French by Nicolas Colin (1578), and into English by Bartholomew Yonge (1582, but not published until 1598). Shakespeare probably based his *Two Gentlemen of Verona* on a section of the *Diana,* a court performance of which was given by the Queen's Men in 1585, according to the Revels Accounts for that year. See TWO GENTLEMEN OF VERONA: *Sources.*

Montgomery, Sir John. An English knight, confused by Shakespeare with his brother, Sir Thomas Montgomery (d. 1495), who was an important adviser to Edward IV. In *3 Henry VI,* Sir John is a "trusty friend" of the Yorkists and upon Edward's return from Burgundy prevails upon him to claim the crown instead of merely the title of duke of York (IV, vii). [W. H. Thomson, *Shakespeare's Characters: A Historical Dictionary,* 1951.]

Montgomery, Philip Herbert, earl of. See Philip Herbert, 4th earl of PEMBROKE.

Montjoy. In *Henry V,* the chief French herald. Montjoy appears in III, vi and IV, iii bearing the French king's demand that, in view of his imminent defeat, Henry prepare to pay ransom commensurate with the damage he has caused. However, in IV, vii, after the battle of Agincourt, Montjoy admits that Henry has defeated the French.

monument. The memorial bust of Shakespeare located on the wall of Holy Trinity Church, Stratford. The poet's bust is flanked by two columns, on which a cornice rests. On the cornice are two figures representing Rest and Labour, between which are carved Shakespeare's arms, helm, and crest. Below the bust is a tablet with the following inscription:

IVDICIO PYLIVM, GENIO SOCRATEM, ARTE MARONEM:
TERRA TEGIT, POPVLVS MAERET, OLYMPVS HABET.

STAY PASSENGER, WHY GOEST THOV BY SO FAST?
READ IF THOV CANST, WHOM ENVIOVS DEATH HATH PLAST,
WITH IN THIS MONVMENT SHAKSPEARE: WITH WHOME,
QVICK NATVRE DIDE: WHOSE NAME DOTH DECK Y^{S} TOMBE,
FAR MORE THEN COST: SIEH ALL, Y^{T} HE HATH WRITT,
LEAVES LIVING ART, BVT PAGE, TO SERVE HIS WITT.
OBIIT AÑO DO^{I} 1616
AETATIS . 53 DIE 23 AP^{R}

The monument has been the subject of a great deal of conjecture and fancy. It was erected sometime between Shakespeare's death and the publication of the First Folio, for it is referred to in the prefatory poem which Leonard Digges prefixed to that volume:

thy Workes, by which, out-liue
Thy Tombe, thy name must: when that stone is rent, . . .

SHAKESPEARE'S MONUMENT IN HOLY TRINITY CHURCH. (SHAKESPEARE BIRTHPLACE TRUST)

The sculptor was Gheerart JANSSEN, whose shop wa located in London near the Globe Theatre, a fac which has led some to speculate that the monumen was commissioned by Shakespeare's fellow-actors rather than by his family. At the time of its carvin the bust was painted in life-like colors which subse quently wore off. It was whitewashed in 1793, and a attempt at restoring the colors was made in 186 From what traces of the original colors remain th eyes were apparently hazel and the hair auburn. Th bust displays a blandness and lack of detail whic suggests to some that it was carved from a deat mask model. See PORTRAITS OF SHAKESPEARE.

In 1656 Sir William Dugdale published an illustra tion of the monument which differs radically fron the monument as we know it. Either Dugdale's illus tration is inaccurate or the monument has been over hauled since the 17th century. There was a certai amount of alteration and repair which took place i 1748, but the extent and nature of these alteration have never been determined. The style of the wor and some of the figures on it bear a resemblance t the work on the tomb of Roger Manners, 5th earl o Rutland, a fact which has not gone unnoticed amon the advocates of the earl as the author of Shake speare's plays. See RUTLAND THEORY. [C. C. Stope *Shakespeare's Environment,* 1914; E. K. Chamber *William Shakespeare,* 1930.]

Moonshine. See Robin STARVELING.

Mopsa and Dorcas. In *The Winter's Tale,* tw shepherdesses who quarrel over the Clown in th sheep-shearing scene (IV, iv). Mopsa and Dorca

AN ENGRAVING OF SHAKESPEARE'S MONUMENT FROM DUGDALE'S *Antiquities of Warwickshire* (1656).

also dance and, with Autolycus, sing "Get you hence, for I must go."

More, Sir Thomas (1478–1535). Lord chancellor of England from 1529 to 1534. More, whose piety, learning, and wit had won him an international reputation, was one of the most respected men of his day. After the fall of Cardinal Wolsey, More reluctantly succeeded him as lord chancellor, knowing that he would soon be brought into conflict with his willful and headstrong king, Henry VIII. The conflict finally came to a climax when More refused to accept Henry as supreme head of the Church in England. In the following year he was beheaded for high treason. In addition to his famous *Utopia* (1516), More is probably the author of *The History of King Richard III* (written by 1513, first pub. 1543), although he may have merely translated this biography from the Latin of his patron, Cardinal Morton (c. 1420–1500). In any event the extant Latin version is markedly inferior to More's English rendering, which for its vigor and drama if not for its historical accuracy is often regarded as the first great biography in English literature. Not surprisingly, More's portrait of Richard, written during the reign of Richard's great enemy, Henry VII, is that of a hunchback villain steeped in murder and treachery. This view of Richard was later incorporated into the chronicles of Tudor historians and ultimately into Shakespeare's drama.

More himself was the subject of two distinguished biographies in the 16th century as well as of the play SIR THOMAS MORE, part of which is generally thought to be by Shakespeare. [R. W. Chambers, *Thomas More*, 1935.]

Morelli, Cesare. See MUSIC BASED ON SHAKESPEARE: *17th century*.

Morgan. In *Cymbeline*, the name taken by Belarius as a disguise, following his banishment by the King (III, iii).

Morgan or **Parker, Luce** (c. 1560–1610). A London prostitute and Leslie Hotson's candidate for the DARK LADY of the *Sonnets*. The brothel she operated was located in St. John Street, Clerkenwell. In 1600 she was arrested and confined to Bridewell Prison:

> Item yt is ordered that Luce Morgan alias Parker for that she is a notorious and lewde woman of her bodye and otherwise of evil conversacion shalbe presentlie committed to Brydewell there to be sett to worke till she shall become bounde with good & sufficient sureities for her good behaviour during her naturall lief.

An epitaph printed in 1656 indicates that she died of venereal disease.

According to Leslie Hotson, Luce Morgan is the Dark Lady of the *Sonnets*. He identifies her with a Luce Morgan who from 1579 to 1582 was serving the queen as gentlewoman of the bed chamber or privy chamber and with the "Lucy Negro" who is referred to as a prostitute in the 1594 *Gesta Grayorum:*

> *Lucy Negro*, Abess de Clerkenwell, holdeth the nunnery of Clerkenwell . . . by night-service in *Cauda*, and to find a choir of nuns . . . .

The epithet "Negro" was commonly used to refer to a dark-complexioned person.

Hotson's case for identifying her with the Dark Lady rests upon a number of concealed puns on her name which he claims to find in some of the sonnets. He has not, however, been able to turn up any information connecting her with Shakespeare or with his own candidate for Mr. W. H., William Hatcliffe. [Leslie Hotson, *Mr. W. H.*, 1964.]

Morgan, McNamara. See ADAPTATIONS; IRELAND.

Morgann, Maurice (1726–1802). Essayist and civil servant. Undersecretary of state in Shelburne's ministry, Morgan wrote primarily about politics. His *Essay on the Dramatic Character of Falstaff* (1777) is a striking anticipation of Romantic Shakespeare criticism, advocating the principle that "in Dramatic composition the *Impression* is the Fact" (see CHARACTER CRITICISM). In the essay, Morgann defends Falstaff against the charge of cowardice on the ground that nothing in the play supports it. It is a superimposed moral judgment rather than the impression from the play that causes censure of Falstaff despite a natural inclination to love and forgive him. A close study of *Henry IV* suggested to Morgann that good-natured humor and wit are the basic elements, not merely the adornments, of Falstaff's character. Morgann argued that our subjective approval of these traits should be the guide for our appreciation and judgment of the character. [Herbert Spencer Robinson, *English Shakespearian Criticism in the Eighteenth Century*, 1932.]

Morley, Thomas (1557–c. 1606). Musician and

composer. A pupil of William Byrd, Morley became one of the greatest Elizabethan composers of lute songs and madrigals. In 1588 he received a bachelor of music degree at Oxford and became organist at St. Paul's Cathedral in 1591. In 1592 he was made a Gentleman of the Chapel Royal and in 1598 was granted the monopoly of music printing, assigning it two years later to Thomas East.

Morley edited the madrigal collection *The Triumphes of Oriana* (1601), wrote the first comprehensive and most important English language treatise on composition of the Renaissance, *A Plaine and Easie Introduction to Practicall Musicke* (1597), and published consort lessons for six instruments, canzonets, madrigals, and balletts; it was in fact he who introduced the ballett, modeled on Gastoldi's *balletti,* to England.

From the fact that both Shakespeare and Morley lived from 1596 to 1601 in the parish of St. Helen's, Bishopsgate, scholars have speculated that the two men might have known each other, though the evidence supporting or disproving such a hypothesis is tenuous at best. Morley's *First Book of Ayres* (1600) contains a setting of "It was a lover and his lass" from *As You Like It* (V, iii), composed 1596, and in his *The First Booke of Consort Lessons* . . . (1599) is an air without words bearing the title "O mistress mine" and metrically suited to the lyric in *Twelfth Night* (II, iii). Despite scholarly research and speculation, it remains a moot point whether Morley wrote the music as settings of Shakespeare's lyrics, or whether Shakespeare wrote his words to fit Morley's music.

Morocco, Prince of. In *The Merchant of Venice,* the dark-complexioned foreign suitor of Portia who selects the golden casket in which lies "a carrion Death." The Prince of Morocco thereby loses his suit (II, vii).

Morris, Corbyn (d. 1779). Essayist. Morris is known primarily for his *Essay Towards Fixing the True Standards of Wit, Humour, Raillery, Satire and Ridicule* (1744). A considerable part of this study is devoted to Shakespeare's Falstaff, whom Morris considers the perfect combination of wit and humor. Contrasting Falstaff with the satirical characters of Ben Jonson's Subtle and Volpone, Morris observes that although the Jonson characters are clever and witty, they have no other redeeming graces and must ultimately be defeated and condemned. On the other hand, Falstaff—and, by extension, Shallow and Pistol—is not vicious, but naturally humorous and endearing, as well as clever. This and Shakespeare's rejection of artificial rules of propriety and poetic justice are, for Morris, what make Falstaff and the other comic characters so totally delightful. [Herbert Spencer Robinson, *English Shakespearian Criticism in the Eighteenth Century*, 1932.]

morris dance. See DANCING; FOLK FESTIVALS.

Mortimer, Sir **Edmund de** (1376–? 1409). Second son of Edmund de Mortimer, 3rd earl of March, and younger brother of Roger, 4th earl; in *1 Henry IV* erroneously called "Earl of March." With his brother-in-law Hotspur, Mortimer fought against Owen Glendower, who was leading the northern Welsh against Henry IV. Mortimer was defeated and imprisoned by Glendower, but soon married his daughter. This marriage confirmed the suspicions of the Lancastrian king Henry that Mortimer had sought an alliance with the Welsh in order to press the royal claims of his young nephew, Edmund, the 5th earl of March, who was descended from the line of the deposed Richard II. In a short time Mortimer, Glendower, and Hotspur had joined forces against the king, but were defeated. Mortimer died in Harlech castle, besieged by the king's forces. It was, however, through descent from Mortimer's family that the kings of the house of York, Edward IV and Richard III, were to justify their claims to the throne. In *1 Henry IV*, Shakespeare mistakenly assigns to Sir Edmund the rank and title to the crown of his nephew, the 5th earl of March. The scene (III, ii) in which the overconfident rebels divide England and Wales into three parts and place Mortimer on the throne actually occurred two years later, in 1405, with the earl of Northumberland as one of the three participants, rather than his son Hotspur, who had been killed in 1403.

Mortimer, Sir **John** and Sir **Hugh** (d. 1460). Uncles of Richard, duke of York. In *3 Henry VI,* they are killed at Wakefield (I, ii and iv).

Mortimer, Lady. In *1 Henry IV*, daughter of the Welsh rebel Owen Glendower, and wife of his captive, Edmund Mortimer. She appears in III, i, weeping at the prospect of parting with her husband. Unable to speak in English, she has no written lines; stage directions, however, indicate that "the lady speaks in Welsh."

Morton. In *2 Henry IV*, a retainer of the Earl of Northumberland. Morton brings word of Hotspur's death at Shrewsbury (I, i).

Morton, John, bishop of Ely. See John Morton, bishop of ELY.

Moseley, Humphrey (fl. 1627–1661). London bookseller. Moseley was the publisher of the first edition of Milton's *Poems* (1645) and of a number of other poets, including Donne, Davenant, and Henry Vaughan. He also published and sold a large number of plays. On September 9, 1653, he entered in the Stationers' Register "The merry Deuill of Edmonton by Wm Shakespeare and Henry ye first, Hen: ye 2d by Shakespeare, and Davenport." Under that same date Moseley entered the lost play *Cardenio* as having been written by Shakespeare and Fletcher. The first play is not generally regarded as Shakespeare's and the latter two are lost. On June 29, 1660, Moseley entered *The History of King Stephen, Duke Humphrey,* and *Iphis and Iantha* in the Register and attributed them to Shakespeare. None of these plays is extant. [H. R. Plomer, *A Dictionary of Booksellers and Printers . . . 1641–1667*, 1907.]

Moseley, Joseph. See John SHAKESPEARE.

Mossop, Henry (1729?–?1774). Actor. Educated at Trinity College, Dublin, Mossop made his first stage appearance in 1749 in Dublin, where he played Cassius. The following year he acted Richard III dressed in white satin. Vain and unmanageable, Mossop took offense at the theatre manager's alleged reference to him as a "coxcomb," and in 1751 he began to act for Garrick at Drury Lane. Under Garrick he scored an immediate success as Richard III, and in the following years played Macbeth, Othello, Wolsey, King John, Coriolanus, and the Duke in *Measure for Measure*. His Coriolanus was generally regarded as his greatest part. After adding Prospero and Hamlet to his repertory in 1757/8, Mossop quit London for Dublin and won considerable success as Iago to Spranger Barry's Othello. Later he acted such parts as Brutus, Timon, Hotspur, and Sempronius. From 1760 to 1770 he fought debts as manager of Dublin theatres, but failed. Having offended both Garrick and Mrs. Barry, he could not act in London, so his career was ended. [*Dictionary of National Biography*, 1885– .]

Moth. In *Love's Labour's Lost,* Don Armado's impertinent, witty page. Moth plays the infant Hercules in the dramatic presentation of the Nine Worthies (V, ii). Moth is thought to be a portrait of Thomas Nashe.

Moth. In *A Midsummer Night's Dream,* one of Titania's fairies who serves as a personal attendant on Bottom.

Mouffet or **Moffet, Thomas** (d. 1604). Physician, entomologist, and poet. Mouffet was the personal physician to a number of Elizabethan aristocrats and spent the last decade of his life on the estate of the countess of Pembroke at Wilton. He published a group of medical works and a Latin treatise on insects, *The Theatre of Insects* (1589). The latter work includes a lengthy treatment of spiders, which has given rise to the belief that Mouffet is the "Little Miss Muffet" of the old nursery rhyme.

Mouffet's poem *Of the Silkewormes, and their Flies* was published in 1599, far too late to be a source of *A Midsummer Night's Dream.* However, Shakespeare may have seen Mouffet's ludicrous verse in manuscript and parodied it. The poem includes a digression on the story of Pyramus and Thisbe which contains a number of parallels to Shakespeare's burlesque as well as the possible sources for the names Cobweb, Moth, and Bottom. [Kenneth Muir, *Shakespeare's Sources*, 1957.]

Mouldy, Ralph. In *2 Henry IV*, a "good-limbed" recruit interviewed by Falstaff. Mouldy purchases his release for 40 shillings (III, ii).

Moulton, Richard Green (1849–1924). Scholar. After receiving degrees from the University of London (1869) and Cambridge (1874), Moulton became associated with the university extension movement in both England and the United States. He joined the University of Chicago when it opened its doors in 1892 and served as professor of literary theory and interpretation until his retirement in 1919. Moulton wrote and edited several widely used texts on the subject of the Bible as literature, namely, *The Literary Study of the Bible* (1896), *A Short Introduction to the Literature of the Bible* (1901), and *The Modern Reader's Bible* (21 vols., 1896–1898; one-volume ed., 1907). In his *Shakespeare as a Dramatic Artist* (1885) he attempted to arrive at "an inductive science of literary criticism"; by intensive analyses of five plays, he drew certain conclusions concerning adaptation, plot, character, etc. He added more plays for analysis in subsequent editions, until the total reached nine in the third edition of 1892. Moulton supplemented this work with *The Moral System of Shakespeare* (1903), later enlarged and reissued under the title *Shakespeare as a Dramatic Thinker* (1907); Moulton described it as "a popular illustration of fiction as the experimental side of philosophy." A summary of his theories of literary criticism is contained in *The Modern Study of Literature* (1915).

Mountjoy, Christopher. See BELOTT-MOUNTJOY SUIT.

A mournefull Dittie, entituled *Elizabeths* losse, together with a welcome for King *Iames*.

To a pleasant new tune.

Farewell, farewell, farewell,
 braue Englands ioy:
Gone is thy friend
 that kept thee from annoy.
Lament, lament, lament
 you English Peeres,
Lament your losse
 possest so many yeeres.

Gone is thy Queene, the
 paragon of time,
On whom grim death
 hath spred his fatall line.
Lament, lament, &c.

Gone is that gem which
 God and man did loue,
She hath vs left
 to dwell in heauen aboue.
Lament, lament, &c.

You gallant Ladies
 of her Princely traine,
Lament your losse
 your loue, your hope, and gaine.
Lament, lament, &c.

Weepe wring your hands,
 all clad in mourning weeds,
Shew forth your loue,
 in tongue in hart and deeds.
Lament, lament, &c.

Full foure and fortie yeeres
 foure moneths seauen dayes,
She did maintaine this realme
 in peace alwayes.
Lament, lament, &c.

In spite of Spaines proud Pope,
 and all the rout,
Who Lyon like ran
 ranging round about.
Lament, lament, &c.

With traiterous plots to slay
 her Royall grace,
Her realme, her lawes
 and Gospell to deface,
Lament, lament, &c.

Yet time and tide God still
 was her defence,
Till for himselfe from vs
 hee tooke her hence
Lament, lament, &c.

We neede not to rehearse
 what care what griefe,
She still endured,
 and all for our reliefe.
Lament, lament, &c.

We neede not to rehearse
 what benefits,
You all inioyd, what pleasures
 and what gifts.
Lament, lament, &c.

You Virgins all bewayle
 your Virgin Queene,
That Phenix rare,
 on earth but sildome seene.
Lament, lament, &c.

With Angels wings she pearst
 the starrie skie,
When death, grim death,
 hath shut her mortall eye.
Lament, lament, &c.

You Nimphs that sing and bathe,
 in Fountaines cleere:
Come lend your helpe to sing
 in mournefull cheere.
Lament, lament, &c.

All you that doe professe
 sweet musicks Art,
Lay all aside, your Vyoll
 Lute and Harpe,
Lament, lament, &c.

Mourne Organs, Flutes,
 mourne Sagbuts with sad sound:
Mourne Trumpets shrill,
 mourne Cornets mute & round.
Lament, lament, &c.

You Poets all braue Shakspeare,
 Iohnson, Greene,
Bestow your time to write
 for Englands Queene.
Lament, lament, &c.

Returne your songs and Sonnets
 and your sayes:
To set forth sweete
 Elizabeths praise.
Lament, lament, &c.

In fine all you
 that loyall harts possesse,
With Roses sweete,
 bedeck hir Princely hearse.
Lament, lament, &c.

Bedeck that hearse
 sprong from that famous King
King Henrie the eight,
 whose fame on earth doth ring
Lament, lament, &c.

Now is the time that we
 must all forget,
Thy sacred name
 oh sweet Elizabeth.
Lament, lament, &c.

Praying for King Iames,
 as earst we prayed for thee,
In all submissiue loue
 and loyaltie.
Lament, lament, &c.

Beseeching God to blesse
 his Maiestie
With earthly peace
 and heauens felicitie.
Lament, lament, &c.

And make his raigne
 more prosperous here on earth
Then was the raigne
 of late Elizabeth.
Lament, lament, &c.

Wherefore all you
 that subiects true beare names:
Still pray with me, and say
 God saue King Iames.
Lament, lament, lament,
 you English Peeres,
Lament your losse enioyd
 so many yeeres.

FINIS.

Imprinted at London for T. P.

THE BALLAD, *A Mourneful Dittie* (1603).

Mourneful Dittie, A (1603). An anonymous ballad on the death of Queen Elizabeth, in 1603, exhorting Shakespeare, Jonson, and Greene to eulogize the dead queen. The full title of the ballad is "A Mourneful Dittie entituled Elizabeths Losse, together with a Welcome for King James." Of relevance is the following section:

> You poets all braue *Shakspeare, Johnson, Greene,*
> Bestow your time to write for Englands Queene.
> Lament, lament, lament you English Peeres;
> Lament your losse possest so many yeeres.

Either from ignorance or a reluctance to abandon a convenient rhyme for "Queene," the author included the name of Robert Greene, who had died a decade earlier in 1592. The blunder did not escape unnoticed, for in 1604 John Cooke (fl. 1604–1614) published a volume titled *Epigrames. served out in 52 severall Dishes for every man to tast without surfeting.* One of the epigrams in Cooke's volume contains an attack on the "hated fathers of vilde balladrie":

> Who er'e will go unto the presse may see
> The hated fathers of vilde balladrie;
> One sings in his base note the river Thames
> Shal sound the famous memory of noble King
> James;
> Another says that he will, to his death,
> Sing the renowned worthinesse of sweet Eliza-
> beth;
> So runnes their verse in such disordered straine,

And with them dare great majesty prophane;
Some dare do this; some other humbly craues
For helpe of Spirits in their sleeping graues,
As he that calde to *Shakespeare, Johnson, Greene,*
To write of their dead noble Queene.

[J. O. Halliwell-Phillipps, *Outlines of the Life of Shakespeare,* 1881.]

Mowbray, Thomas, Lord (1386–1405). Elder son of the first duke of Norfolk. In 1405, considering himself slighted by the crown, Mowbray lent his assistance to Archbishop Scrope in compiling a list of grievances against the government; the two were joined by the earl of Northumberland, and together they raised an army of revolt. At Shipton Moor, however, Westmorland's false promises induced the archbishop to dismiss his men. Instead of pardoning the rebel leaders and redressing their wrongs as he had pledged, Westmorland had them arrested. They were subsequently executed.

In *2 Henry IV,* Lord Mowbray plays much the same role as he did in history. He joins Archbishop Scroop and Lord Hastings in rebellion, but the false promises of Prince John persuade them to disband their forces; they are then arrested and sent to their deaths.

Mowbray, Thomas. See Thomas Mowbray, 1st duke of NORFOLK.

Mr. W. H. The dedicatee of the First Quarto of Shakespeare's *Sonnets.* The identity of Mr. W. H. is among the more fascinating problems of Shakespearean studies. The controversy stems from the cryptic dedication by Thomas Thorpe, the editor of the first edition:

TO.THE.ONLIE.BEGETTER.OF.
THESE.INSVING.SONNETS.
Mr.W.H. ALL.HAPPINESSE.
AND.THAT.ETERNITIE.
PROMISED.

BY.

OVR.EVER-LIVING.POET.

WISHETH.

THE.WELL-WISHING.
ADVENTVRER.IN.
SETTING.
FORTH.

T. T.

(REPRODUCED FROM THE 1609 QUARTO.)

The dedication is written in Thorpe's usual bombastic style and is probably intentionally obscure. Even put into the normal word order of an English sentence—"To Mr. W. H., the only begetter of these ensuing sonnets, the well-wishing adventurer in setting forth wisheth all happiness and that eternity promised by our ever-living poet"—the dedication remains puzzling.

Generally speaking, scholars have followed two lines of thought in connection with the identity of Mr. W. H.: some see him as the Fair Youth to whom most of the sonnets are addressed and others suggest that he is separate and distinct from the Fair Youth. The latter point of view was held by most of the early 19th-century critics, who took the term "begetter" in Thorpe's dedication to mean "getter" or "procurer" of the manuscript for the printer. The younger James Boswell, for example, in the 1821 edition writes, "W. H. was probably one of the friends to whom Shakespeare's *Sonnets* had been communicated and who furnished the printer with the copy." This anonymous "getter" became identified as William HALL, a stationer's assistant, who, according to Sir Sidney Lee (*A Life of William Shakespeare,* 1898) was professionally engaged in procuring copy for printers. Gerald Massey (1828–1907), in the *Athenaeum* of April 27, 1867, was the first to suggest that Mr. W. H. was Sir William HARVEY (or Hervey). Harvey was the third husband of the dowager countess of Southampton, the earl of Southampton's mother. Massey's theory has been reasserted by A. L. Rowse in his *William Shakespeare* (1963). If Harvey was Mr. W. H., Thorpe's dedication is properly inscribed. People in the Elizabethan age often spoke of a knight as Mister or Master. Proponents of this identification assume that the countess would naturally have in her possession a copy of the manuscript of the *Sonnets.* After her death, Harvey came upon this document, so the story goes, and gave or sold it to Thorpe. This theory is tenable only if the earl of Southampton be taken as the Fair Youth; it made little progress until it was enthusiastically adopted by Charlotte Stopes and supported in her *Life of Henry, Third Earl of Southampton* (1922).

To those for whom "begetter" means "inspirer," that is, for whom Mr. W. H. and the Fair Youth are one and the same person, one of the most popular choices for the role of Mr. W. H. has been Henry Wriothesley, the 3rd earl of SOUTHAMPTON. Southampton was the patron of various Elizabethan writers, and he was the only acknowledged patron of Shakespeare. To him Shakespeare dedicated his early erotic poems (see VENUS AND ADONIS and THE RAPE OF LUCRECE), in terms that reveal a growing intimacy. The partisans of Southampton adduce many facts besides these early dedications to support the view that he is W. H. They find circumstances of his life that are closely related to the sonnet story.

In 1590 William Cecil (Lord Burghley), then lord treasurer, sought to arrange a marriage between Southampton, who was his ward and then 17 years old, and his 15-year-old granddaughter, Lady Elizabeth Vere. But marriage was furthest from the youth's thoughts, for he was eager to enter upon a military career under the earl of Essex. Many persons, including his mother, put pressure upon him to contract so favorable a marriage, but he was obdurate. It was at this time that Shakespeare supposedly wrote his first 18 sonnets in which he urges the Fair Youth to marry and beget children, to insure the perpetuation of his beauty. Southampton's portrait drawn at the age of 19 shows him to be of a striking, almost feminine beauty. His long golden tresses fall over his left shoulder, and the features of his oval face are sensitive and delicate, just the sort of young man to inspire the affection that the poet in the *Sonnets* shows for his friend. The supporters of this attribution explain that Thorpe deliberately reversed the initials for Henry Wriothesley in order to conceal the name of the youth to whom the sonnets were addressed.

This ingenious explanation does not account for the absence of any record of Southampton's continued interest in Shakespeare or friendship for him after 1594. Equally curious is the lack of any reference to the young earl in Heminges' and Condell's dedication of the First Folio. This is a strong indication that Southampton had shown little or no interest in Shakespeare's plays. Other objections have been raised against Southampton's candidacy: it has been pointed out that the punnings on the name Will in Sonnets 135 and 136 are pointless unless the Fair Youth's name was, like the poet's, Will. Then too, if Shakespeare did not begin to write the sonnets until after the publication of *Lucrece* in 1594, Southampton was then 21 years of age—too mature a man to be addressed as a "lovely boy" (Sonnet 126).

William Herbert, 3rd earl of PEMBROKE, is the preferred candidate of many modern scholars. Pembroke clearly had a lifelong interest in Shakespeare's plays. To him and his brother Philip, the earl of Montgomery, the editors of the First Folio dedicated their volume, writing, "Since your Lordships have been pleased to think these trifles something heretofore and have prosecuted them and their author living with so much favour . . ."

It is true that any use of these great lords' names without an inclusion of all their titles was a Star Chamber offense. But Thorpe may have been bold and unscrupulous enough to risk prosecution if he thought he could in these devious ways conceal Mr. W. H.'s identity. Considering the Fair Youth's profligacy in the sonnet story, Thorpe would have felt concealment of his identity tactful, indeed necessary.

On the death of his father in January 1601, William Herbert became 3rd earl of Pembroke. The poet's relationship to the Pembroke family must have been established early in his career. His first plays, those written between 1589 and 1592, were produced by the company called Pembroke's Men. Their patron was William Herbert's father. His mother was the famous countess of PEMBROKE for whom her elder brother, Sir Philip Sidney, wrote *The Countess of Pembroke's Arcadia*. The relationship between an actor-servant with the family of his patron was sometimes close; between an actor-dramatist, already renowned as a poet, and the cultivated Pembroke household, it was likely to have been intimate. There apparently once existed a letter, unfortunately now lost, reported by William Cory to be extant in the year 1865, written by Lady Pembroke to her son in December 1603, in which she asks him to bring King James I to Wilton, the Pembroke estate, to see a performance of *As You Like It*. She adds as an afterthought, "We have the man Shakespeare with us."

In 1592, when Pembroke's Men began to produce Shakespeare's plays, William Herbert was 12 years old—an age at which the poet could have thought him a "lovely boy." If Pembroke's youth was the father to the man he became, he probably displayed at that early age some of the tastes which, ripening, united to make him an ideal Renaissance gentleman —dedicated to learning, a patron of the arts, and of an "affable, generous and magnificent disposition." He was, alas, "given to women," to whom his "licentious grace" made him irresistible. See Mary FITTON.

Having assumed that William Herbert was the recipient of all the sonnet letters, many scholars believe that Shakespeare thus addressed him first in 1595. In that year the youth's parents began to negotiate with Sir George Carey a marriage of their son with his daughter Elizabeth Carey. The youth may have refused to accede to his parents' wishes and at this critical juncture in their affairs, they may have sought the aid of a newly famous poet who had once worn their livery—William Shakespeare. They clearly hoped that an ornate poetic appeal might exert the influence that they desired on the cultured but recalcitrant lad.

In 1964 Leslie Hotson, in a volume entitled *Mr. W. H.*, introduced a new candidate for the role in the person of William Hatcliffe, of Hatcliffe, Lincolnshire. Certain phrases in the sonnets have convinced Hotson that Shakespeare is suggesting that Mr. W. H. was a prince of sorts. Since the queen would never tolerate any real prince near her throne, he suggests that the references are to the Prince of Purpoole, who presided over the annual Christmas revels at Gray's Inn. Hotson's belief that the date of the *Sonnets* was 1588–1589 forced him to seek the name of the prince of the revels for that year, and he found that he was a certain "Dominus de Purpoole Hatcliffe" (see William HATCLIFFE). Aside from the hidden references to a prince that Hotson finds in the *Sonnets* there is no evidence connecting Hatcliffe with Shakespeare.

Another celebrated candidate for Mr. W. H. is William HUGHES, a possibility suggested by a number of speculators, most notably by Oscar Wilde. Wilde's theory was put forth in his fictional biography, *The Portrait of Mr. W. H.* (1889).

To this group might be added a small array of lesser "W. H.'s" who have been put forth as candidates, including William Hathaway (b. 1578), Shakespeare's brother-in-law; William Hammond, a contemporary patron of letters; William Holgate (1590?–?1634), an aspiring poet and son of an innkeeper; another William Herbert or Harbert (1573–1656), the cousin of the 3rd earl of Pembroke; William Harrison, the Elizabethan historian; and finally "William Himself," a suggestion that has found favor with some of the advocates of the Baconian theory.

A host of candidates for the Fair Youth has also been put forth by some of those who believe him to be a person distinct from the Mr. W. H. Among these the best known are Robert Devereux, 2nd earl of Essex; Edmund Shakespeare, the younger brother of the poet; Robert Southwell, the Jesuit martyr; Will Kempe, an actor in Shakespeare's company; Walter Aston (b. 1583), the patron of Michael Drayton; and Charles Best, a minor poet whose inclusion is based upon the fact that the word "best" occurs 23 times in the *Sonnets*. [William Archer, "Shakespeare's Sonnets: The Case Against Southampton," *Fortnightly Review*, LXVIII, 1897; Sidney Lee, "Shakespeare and the Earl of Pembroke," *Fortnightly*

Review, LXIX, 1898; Sidney Lee, "Shakespeare and the Earl of Southampton," *Cornhill Magazine*, LXXVII, 1898; Arthur Acheson, *Shakespeare's Sonnet Story*, 1933; Lord Alfred Douglas, *The True History of Shakespeare's Sonnets*, 1933; *The Sonnets*, New Variorum Edition, Hyder E. Rollins, ed., 1944; J. Dover Wilson, *An Introduction to the Sonnets of Shakespeare*, 1964.]—O.J.C.

Mucedorus. An anonymous play first ascribed to Shakespeare in 1656. *Mucedorus*, one of the most popular plays on the Elizabethan stage, was first published in 1598 as

A most pleasant Comedie of Mucedorus, the Kings sonne of Valentia and Amadine the Kings daughter of Arragon, with the merie conceites of Mouse. Newly set foorth, as it hath bin sundrie times plaide in the honorable Cittie of London. Very delectable and full of mirth. *For William Jones.*

In 1610 an expanded version of the play was published in which it was described as having been acted by Shakespeare's company. Attempts have been made to ascribe the added parts of the play to Shakespeare but such conjectures have been generally rejected. The entire play was ascribed to Shakespeare in 1656 by Edward Archer in his catalogue of plays, and it was included in a volume in the library of Charles II marked "Shakespeare, Vol. I." [E. K. Chambers, *The Elizabethan Stage*, 1923.]

Much adoe about Nothing.

Much Ado About Nothing. A comedy by Shakespeare.

Text. The most authoritative text is that of the Quarto of 1600, bearing the title page: "Much adoe about Nothing. As it hath been sundrie times publikely acted by the right honourable, the Lord Chamberlaine his seruants. Written by William Shakespeare. London Printed by V. S. [Valentine Simmes] for Andrew Wise, and William Aspley. 1600." There is no division into acts and scenes. In the speech headings in IV, ii, the names "Kempe" and "Cowley," two low-comedy actors of Shakespeare's company, are substituted for Dogberry and Verges. This confusion has led to the suggestion that the printer's copy was the company's PROMPT-BOOK. However, all the other evidence in the text points to the author's FOUL PAPERS as the copy. The inconsistencies in the stage directions would have been intolerable in the company's prompt-book, whereas they are just the sort of errors that an author would be expected to make in preparing his first draft. The text of the First Folio was printed from the Quarto.

Date. The probable date of the first performance is late 1598. Under the date of August 4, 1600, *Much Ado*, along with *As You Like It*, *Henry V*, and Ben Jonson's *Every Man In his Humour*, was entered in the Stationers' Register with the notation "to be staied"—that is, not printed. This BLOCKING ENTRY was designed to prevent dishonest stationers from publishing unauthorized editions of the work. The play was re-entered in the Register later in the same month (August 23) in a typical entry announcing intention to publish. The title of the comedy does not appear in Meres' list in PALLADIS TAMIA, published in the autumn of 1598. The fact that Kempe, who created the role of Dogberry, left the Chamberlain's Men some time near the close of 1599, confirms the almost universally held opinion that *Much Ado* was written and first staged in the latter part of 1598.

Sources. C. T. Prouty has made an exhaustive study of the sources of the play, in which he discusses 16 possible dramatic and nondramatic works which Shakespeare might have used. The nondramatic versions derive either from ARIOSTO's epic *Orlando Furioso* (1516) or from the 22nd tale of Matteo BANDELLO's *Novelle* (1554). Shakespeare may have read Bandello in the original Italian or, more likely, in a French translation appearing in the third volume of Belleforest's *Histoires Tragiques* (1559). The story in Bandello tells how Sir Timbreo, in love with Fenicia, is made to believe that he has seen her talking with a lover at the window of her bedroom and consequently repudiates her. This is an old and widespread theme, which Ariosto had worked into cantos four to six of his *Orlando Furioso*. He calls the lady Ginevora and her suitor Ariodante. Sir John Harington's English translation of the epic appeared in 1591. Here, too, Shakespeare could have become acquainted with the tale. Spenser adapted and condensed the story in *The Faerie Queene* (II, iv), a version that Shakespeare doubtless read. Two lost plays have been suggested as the English sources of *Much Ado*. The first is *A historie of Ariodante and Genevora*, a drama played at court in 1583 by the boys of the Merchant Taylors' School and probably based on a poem by Peter Beverley, *Ariodante and Genevra* (1566). The second is *Fedele and Fortunio* (1585), an adaptation, probably by the versatile hack Anthony Munday, of an Italian play, *Il Fedele* (1579). *Panecia* (1574), a lost play acted at

Much adoe about Nothing.

As it hath been sundrie times publikely acted by the right honourable, the Lord Chamberlaine his seruants.

Written by William Shakespeare.

LONDON
Printed by V.S. for Andrew Wise, and William Aspley.
1600.

TITLE PAGE OF THE FIRST QUARTO OF *Much Ado About Nothing* (1600).

court on January 1, 1575, may have been an error for "Fenicia," the name of the lady in Bandello's version of the tale, but this is mere conjecture. One other Italian play, *Gli Duoi Fratelli Rivali,* bears a close resemblance to Shakespeare's plot, but the work was not published until 1601. It is highly unlikely that Shakespeare was familiar with it. The witty exchanges of Beatrice and Benedick may have been suggested by similar passages in Baldassare Castiglione's famous work *Il Libro del Cortegiano* (1528), which Shakespeare could have read in an English translation by Sir Thomas Hoby, entitled *The Courtier* (1561).—O. J. C.

Plot Synopsis. Act I. Leonato, Governor of Messina, welcomes Don Pedro, Prince of Arragon, who is returning to the city after a successful campaign against his bastard brother, Don John, with whom he is now reconciled. Also in the Prince's party are Claudio, a young Florentine who distinguished himself in the fighting, and Benedick, a lord from Padua. The latter renews his acquaintance with Beatrice, Leonato's niece, whom he greets as "my dear Lady Disdain." Like Benedick, she professes an aversion to matrimony. His "war-thoughts" being replaced by "soft and delicate desires," Claudio falls in love with Hero, Leonato's daughter, and confides his passion to Don Pedro, who promises to aid his suit by wooing her in his name. Overhearing their conversation, Borachio reports it to Don John, his master, who is "a plain-dealing villian," resentful of Claudio's recent triumphs and eager to cross him in every possible way.

Act II. At a ball in the home of Leonato, Beatrice informs her masked partner that Benedick is "a very dull fool" whose only talent is "devising impossible slanders"; she does not realize that she is addressing Benedick himself, who later inveighs against her caustic tongue, and flees when she enters the room. Meanwhile, Don Pedro has successfully conducted Claudio's suit for Hero, though for a moment the Florentine had thoughts that the Prince had betrayed him by seeking her for himself. Claudio would like to be married the very next day, but Leonato bids him to wait a week. Don Pedro suggests that they occupy themselves during the interval with the Herculean task of arranging a match between Beatrice and Benedick.

Hoping to thwart Claudio's marriage plans, Don John listens as Borachio expounds a scheme to cast suspicion on Hero's virtue. Borachio explains that he is in the favor of Margaret, Hero's waiting-woman. He will ask her to appear at Hero's window in her mistress's clothes while Don Pedro and Claudio are nearby, and speak to him in such a way as to convince them of her infidelity. Don John agrees to the plan, promising to reward Borachio with 1000 ducats.

As Benedick hides in a bower, Don Pedro, Leonato, and Claudio contrive to let him overhear a discussion of Beatrice's unrequited passion for him; she is likely to die if he does not return her affection, but she would rather die than admit her love. Hearing himself censured for his pride, Benedick is considerably chastened.

Act III. Hero and her maid Ursula, who are also in on the scheme, let Beatrice overhear their conversation about Benedick. They comment on the fact that he is wasting away with love for her; she is so disdainful, however, that she can find nothing pleasing in any man. Stung by these words, Beatrice resolves to banish her pride and tame her "wild heart" to Benedick's "loving hand."

On the day before the wedding, Don John informs the Prince and Claudio that Hero is disloyal and promises to show them proof if they will meet him near her chamber window that night. Claudio vows to shame his betrothed before the entire congregation if she is indeed unfaithful.

That night, having selected two citizens for the watch, Constables Dogberry and Verges give them instructions on the proper performance of their duty; Dogberry observes that since "they that touch pitch will be defiled," they should avoid contact with thieves and other disturbers of the peace. While the watch are at their post, they hear a drunken Borachio relate to Conrade, another of Don John's henchmen, how Claudio and Don Pedro had stationed themselves in Leonato's orchard and, seeing Margaret bid him good night, had mistaken her for Hero. The watch promptly arrest the two men and take them to Dogberry and Verges, who ask Leonato to question them. Leonato, however, is so busy with preparations for the wedding that he tells the constables to conduct the examination themselves.

Act IV. As Hero and Claudio stand before the altar, Friar Francis asks whether there is any impediment to the marriage. Leonato asserts that there is none and that he freely gives his daughter to Claudio. At this Claudio rejects Hero, stating that he will not knit his soul to "an approved wanton." The blush on her cheek, he says, betrays not modesty, but guilt. Leonato and Hero now appeal to Don Pedro, but the Prince supports his friend's allegations. Upon hearing Claudio's description of her supposed assignation, Hero faints, while the groom stalks off with the Prince and Don John. Hero revives and hears the bitter reproaches of her father, but Friar Francis is convinced of her innocence. He suggests that it be given out that she has died; since men prize what they have only after it is lost, Claudio may repent of his conduct, and her reputation may be redeemed. After the others have left the church, Benedick tells a weeping Beatrice that he thinks that Hero has been wronged. When he admits that he loves Beatrice and asks her to bid him do anything for her sake, she at once replies, "Kill Claudio." He is at first reluctant to undertake such a task, but, moved by her pleas, vows to bring Claudio to account.

Dogberry and Verges proceed to examine Borachio and Conrade before a sexton. Upon hearing the watchmen's account of the prisoners' conversation, the sexton orders them brought before Leonato. Angered at hearing himself called an ass by Conrade, Dogberry haughtily retorts that he is "a wise fellow, and, which is more, an officer, and, which is more, a householder, and . . . as pretty a piece of flesh as any is in Messina."

Act V. An apparently grief-stricken Leonato denounces Claudio for causing the death of his innocent daughter and challenges him to a duel. When Claudio and Don Pedro attempt to twit Benedick about Beatrice, he, too, challenges Claudio and states that henceforth he will forgo their company. He also informs them that Don John has fled from Messina. Just then Dogberry and Verges appear with Conrade and Borachio; Borachio reveals Don John's machinations against Claudio but maintains that Margaret was an innocent participant in the plot. The remorseful Claudio asks Leonato to impose a penance on him and readily agrees when Leonato asks him to marry the daughter of his brother, Antonio.

After a mournful visit to Hero's tomb, Claudio presents himself at Leonato's court the following day to wed the latter's niece, whose features are hidden by a mask. When she removes the mask, Claudio is amazed to see that the bride is Hero herself. Beatrice and Benedick again try to conceal their mutual affection, but when it is revealed that each has been secretly composing verses to the other, Benedick declares that he is ready to marry Beatrice "for pity." She replies that she will yield, but only "upon great persuasion." As pipers strike up a tune for dancing, a messenger brings word that Don John has been captured and is being returned to Messina.—H. D.

Comment. *Much Ado* is the first of Shakespeare's three so-called joyous comedies, the other two being *As You Like It* and *Twelfth Night*. The play is composed of two main plots: the Hero-Claudio story, which has some of the characteristics of a tragicomedy; and the Beatrice-Benedick story, a development of the ladies who mock the courtiers in *Love's Labour's Lost*. Perhaps from fear of allowing the Claudio-Hero plot to obscure the Benedick-Beatrice story Shakespeare treats it in a perfunctory fashion. It is not told in the language of the human heart. Claudio, though a brave soldier, is so inexperienced in the ways of love that he is glad to have Don Pedro do his courtship for him; yet, when Don Pedro obliges, Claudio suspects that he is wooing the girl for himself. The sole source of his knowledge of women is apparently medieval romance where a woman needed only to be chaste to be called virtuous; without chastity, she became "a rotten orange." Thus, when Claudio has what he believes to be ocular proof of Hero's lewdness, he can keep his escutcheon unstained only by impetuously exposing and denouncing her at the altar. His mood in the second marriage scene is almost as impulsive. He vows he will marry the cousin of the supposedly dead Hero, "were she an Ethiope." Believing himself responsible for Leonato's loss of his daughter, he feels honor bound to offer whatever restitution he can.

Don John is no motiveless villain. In Bandello's novel, Fenicia's slanderer is a rejected suitor. For this stale situation Shakespeare substitutes the forces in Don John's nature. His black depression is the result of his envy of Claudio. "That young start-up," he cries, who "hath all the glory of my overthrow." In "Of Envy" Bacon wrote that those most subject to envy were "deformed persons, old men and bastards." Don John is a bastard.

Beatrice and Benedick's merry war of words belongs to the dramatic tradition of love-game comedy, popularized by John Lyly. The thin substance of these comedies is the sprightly, witty conversation of ladies and gentlemen of high society. Shakespeare first adopted and refined this formula in *Love's Labour's Lost;* the masked dance in Act II of *Much Ado* is also a repetition of a similar interlude in *Love's Labour's Lost*.

Dover Wilson describes Beatrice as "the first woman in our literature, perhaps in the literature of Europe, who not only has a brain, but delights in the constant employment of it." One might add, in devoting all its resources to wit. She is interested in men only for their intelligence. Their constant appeals to love bore her: "I had rather hear my dog bark at a crow than a man swear he loves me." She is attracted to Benedick not by his sex-appeal but by his intelligence and his ability to sustain his part in their combats of wit. However, he is likely to come off second best in their verbal skirmishes, and seems a bit wistful in realizing that she plays the game more adroitly than he. It is Beatrice, he avers, who "speaks poniarde," and "every word a stab." Yet she is always free from malice. Neither believes for an instant that Hero is guilty. "Surely," Benedick exclaims to Beatrice, "I do believe your fair cousin wronged." Her response to Benedick's "Come bid me do anything for thee" is "Kill Claudio." This immediate demand that he defend Hero's honor in the most extreme fashion often shocks a modern reader, but Shakespeare designed it to be overwhelming proof of Beatrice's intense loyalty and sense of outrage. Beatrice is converted to love by one of the many scenes of eavesdropping scattered through the comedy. Hero contrives to have her overhear a conversation she carries on with Ursula about Beatrice's aversion to love:

> But Nature never framed a woman's heart
> Of prouder stuff than that of Beatrice;
>
> . . . she cannot love,
> Nor take no shape nor project of affection,
> She is so self-endeared.
> (III, i, 49–50, 54–56)

Although Beatrice may profess to scorn love, she does not relish having two of her intimate friends think that she is incapable of any form of affection. When Benedick, in a similarly contrived eavesdropping situation, hears that Beatrice is really consumed with love for him, he, too, realizes that the high spirit of their wit-combats is an expression of the exhilaration that love often produces in intellectual creatures like themselves. After Hero and Ursula have left the garden, Beatrice emerges from the arbor where she has been hiding, and in a perfunctory set speech announces her conversion not only to love but also to the kind of subjection to her husband that Elizabethans expected of their wives.

Shakespeare may have invented Dogberry and Verges to give the groundlings their expected chance for glee. The immortal Dogberry is a development of a type for which Dull, the doltish constable in *Love's Labour's Lost*, was a mere sketch. Moreover, Dogberry is a caricature of the night watchman of an Elizabethan village. His slowness of wit, his bustling incompetence, his prudent avoidance of an encounter with any evildoer, his all-night sleep on a churchyard bench were, and still are, good for sure-fire laughter. But Dogberry and Goodman Verges are more than isolated figures of fun. They occupy an important place in the structure of the comedy. Shakespeare realized that if he were to prevent his audiences from expecting Hero's fate to become tragic he would have to let them know that the plot of Don John and Borachio (the name means drunkenness) was going to be exposed in the nick of time. The two clowns of the watch prove to be just the characters to perform this service to the plot. Leonato, eager to be off to the wedding, barely listens to their attempt to tell him their important news. Hence the tediousness of the pair and their tantalizing tendency to skirt the important part of their story so exhausts Leonato's patience that he turns over the examination of the villains to Dogberry himself. While permitting the clumsy rustics to play a decisive role in averting a threatening tragedy, the scene produces the only important moment of suspense and tension in the entire play.—O. J. C.

Stage History. *Much Ado About Nothing* was one of 14 plays acted by the Lord Chamberlain's Men at court as part of the festivities celebrating the betrothal and marriage of Princess Elizabeth to the elector palatine in May 1613. The play, so filled with good acting parts, undoubtedly remained popular up to the time of the closing of the theatres in 1642. In a poem by Leonard DIGGES prefixed to John Benson's 1640 edition of Shakespeare's poems, the following lines appear:

> Let but *Beatrice*
> And *Benedick* be seene, lo, in a trice
> The Cockpit Galleries, Boxes all are full.

There is, however, no actual record of any other performance of the play throughout the 17th century. The lord chamberlain's record of December 12, 1660 set aside nine Shakespeare plays, including *Much Ado*, as the exclusive property of William Davenant's Duke's Company. These plays Davenant proposed "to reform and make fitt" the actors in his company. *Much Ado* was one of the first to suffer from his "improvements." Overzealousness in adapting *Measure for Measure* to contemporary taste prompted Davenant to furnish that play with Benedick-Beatrice material from *Much Ado* as a subplot. Samuel Pepys saw this hodgepodge, called *The Law Against Lovers*, performed on February 18, 1662 and found it "a good play." Dissenters from this opinion may have represented a majority, since there is no record of a revival.

John Rich revived Shakespeare's comedy at Lincoln's Inn Fields on February 9, 1721, announcing that the play had not been acted at that theatre for 30 years. Thus, although the genuine *Much Ado About Nothing* may have been performed one or more times around 1690, this is the earliest specific record of the play on a public stage. For Rich's production, Lacy Ryan was Benedick; Mrs. Croos, Beatrice; and James Quin probably played Leonato. The comedy disappeared for another 18 years, but some of Benedick's best lines appeared in Charles Johnson's *Love in a Forest*, a comedy based on *As You Like It*, published in 1723 and acted on January 9 of that year at Drury Lane. On February 28, 1737 *The Universal Passion*, an unnatural fusion by James Miller of *Much Ado About Nothing* and Molière's *La Princesse d'Elide*, was produced at Drury Lane. The similarity of the two themes resulted in a wearisome drama relieved only by music and dance elements. It was performed nine more times that season, probably owing its brief popularity to the appearance of Kitty Clive as Liberia (Beatrice); she later resurrected the piece for her benefit performance in 1741. Quin played Protheus (Benedick); Theophilus Cibber acted Joculo, a Touchstone-type jester; Elizabeth Butler was Lucilia (Hero); and Hannah Pritchard, Delia (Margaret). John Rich again restored the unalloyed *Much Ado* on November 2, 1727, this time at Covent Garden with Thomas and Elizabeth Vincent as Benedick and Beatrice. In March 1746 Covent Garden presented the comedy three times, now with Mrs. Pritchard acting Beatrice and Lacy Ryan as Benedick.

From David Garrick's first appearance as Benedick on November 14, 1748 until his retirement in 1776, *Much Ado* remained continuously in the Drury Lane repertory. The play was given 15 times during the first season, including an initial 8 successive performances, and it was revived once or more every year while Garrick was at Drury Lane. Mrs. Pritchard was his first Beatrice, playing opposite Garrick until 1756, when her daughter assumed the role. In 1762 and 1763 Mrs. John Palmer was Garrick's Beatrice, but it was in Elizabeth Pope, who appeared regularly in the part from 1764 to 1775, that a notable successor to Mrs. Pritchard was found. Drury Lane Dogberrys during this period were James Taswell (until 1758), Richard Yates (until 1766), and William Parsons (until 1776).

Covent Garden hardly dared to compete with Drury Lane's popular Benedick and revived the play in only two seasons while Garrick was appearing in the role. They gave it three performances in 1774 and one in 1775, with John Lee as Benedick in both productions and Edward Shuter, who had earlier been Garrick's Verges, as Dogberry. After Garrick's retirement, the Beatrices commanded the attention. Even John Henderson, beginning his Benedick portrayal at Bath in 1773 and giving his first London performance in the part on February 10, 1778 at Drury Lane, was unable to eclipse his predecessor. When Frances Abington, Garrick's Beatrice during the 1775/6 season, took the lead opposite Henderson at Covent Garden in 1783 and 1785, the heroine truly began her ascendancy. In 1786 and 1787 she again acted the part, to Joseph Holman's Benedick, and from 1789 through 1798 played opposite William Lewis. The next notable Beatrice was Elizabeth Farren, who first took the part at the Haymarket on August 17, 1787, and, when John Philip Kemble produced *Much Ado* at Drury Lane in April 1788, appeared as his Beatrice. Miss Farren was seen in seven separate revivals of the play up to 1797. The following year, Mrs. Jordan (the stage name of Dorothy Bland) took over the role opposite John Philip Kemble's Benedick to become the last prominent Beatrice of that century and for some time to come.

Benedick was one of Charles Kemble's more successful impersonations. He advanced to the role from that of Claudio in 1803 and continued playing it for many years. His Beatrices included Anne Brunton, Fanny Kemble, Helen Faucit, and Louisa Nisbett. In 1843, Macready, a failure as Benedick at Bath in 1815, staged *Much Ado* at Drury Lane, playing the hero to Mrs. Nisbett's Beatrice. Samuel Phelps never acted in the comedy but staged productions at Sadler's Wells with Henry Marston as Benedick to three different Beatrices: Miss Cooper (1848), Isabella Glyn (1850), and Mrs. Charles Young (1858). On November 20, 1858 Charles Kean presented a lavish *Much Ado,* his next-to-last revival as manager of the Princess' Theatre; he and his wife acted Benedick and Beatrice. The leading roles during this mid-century period were also played by J. W. Wallack and Charlotte Cushman, in her London debut year, 1845. William Creswick acted Benedick at the Surrey Theatre in 1850 and, in 1873, doubled as Benedick and Dogberry at the Holborn. The next year Creswick appeared at the Haymarket opposite the Beatrice of Helen Faucit. *Much Ado* had been performed at Manchester's Prince's Theatre in 1865, starring Mr. and Mrs. Charles Clavert. In 1875 Hermann Vezin and Ada Cavendish took the leading roles in John Hollingshead's Gaiety Theatre production. During 1879, Stratford's Barry Sullivan acted Benedick both at the Haymarket and at the Memorial Theatre, Stratford-upon-Avon.

On October 11, 1882 Henry Irving revived *Much Ado About Nothing* at the Lyceum. This production was the greatest achievement of his career. Irving cut Beatrice's visit to Hero on her wedding morning but restored Claudio's penance at the monument. Of the presentation George C. Odell comments, "The entire rendering of the play was as near to perfection as human art can go." Any deficiency in Irving's Benedick, still one of the best of his lighter impersonations, was amply compensated for by Johnston Forbes-Robertson's Claudio, and comparable performances in supporting roles. Ellen Terry as Beatrice gave one of the theatre's most famous impersonations, more delightful even than her Portia. Of Jessie Millward, Odell says, "the best Hero I have ever seen." The sets by Hawes Craven, W. Cuthbert, and William Telbin and the costumes by Alfred Thompson were magnificent. The play ran for 212 successive nights, after which it was interrupted by Irving's first American tour. When he returned to the Lyceum on May 31, 1884, he reopened with *Much Ado,* giving 31 more performances before ending on July 5. Ellen Terry re-created her legendary Beatrice in 1903 at the Imperial Theatre in Westminster, first opposite Oscar Asche and, later, Matheson Lang. For this production her son, Gordon Craig, impatient with attempts at precise scenic reproductions, designed simplified sets that shocked many but earned for Craig his place in theatrical history. The London run was brief, but Miss Terry took the production on three provincial tours.

Before Craig's innovations, George Alexander had presented a beautifully mounted *Much Ado* at the St. James in 1898. Alexander played Benedick opposite the Beatrice of Julia Neilson, but little is remembered but the scenery. In 1905 Beerbohm Tree miscast himself as Benedick for his own elaborate production, described by George Bernard Shaw as containing "endless larks in the way of stage business, carried out with much innocent enjoyment." Louis Calvert acted Dogberry in this splendidly staged presentation, and Lionel Brough was Verges; Basil Gill played Claudio; Laurence Irving, Don John; and Miriam Clements, Hero.

Frank Benson first staged the play at Stratford in 1891 and presented it during 12 later seasons up to 1914. His company had the advantage of George Weir's excellent Dogberry. In 1907 and 1908 Henry Ainley was Stratford's Benedick, first opposite Wynne Matthison and, in the second year, Constance Collier. Robert Lorraine acted Benedick in 1909 and again in 1910, when Violet Vanbrugh appeared as Beatrice. Miss Vanbrugh was Stratford's guest Beatrice again in 1913. Two years earlier Fred Terry and Julia Neilson had visited the Memorial Theatre to perform Benedick and Beatrice. Patrick Kirwan staged *Much Ado* there in 1914, with Arthur Bourchier as Benedick. In the summer of 1916 Ben Greet directed a *Much Ado* featuring Sybil Thorndike as Beatrice. The play was seen at Stratford under W. Bridges-Adams' direction throughout the 1920's; again in 1933, with George Hayes and Fabia Drake in the leading parts; and, in 1934, with Baliol Holloway (the Old Vic's Benedick of 1926) and Dorothy Black. In February 1926 Bridges-Adams had produced a *Much Ado* at the New with Henry Ainley and Madge Titheradge. There had been only two other productions of the comedy in the West End since Beerbohm Tree's revival in 1905: one at the King's Theatre, Hammersmith (1920), and the other at the Strand (1924). During the Old Vic 1918/9 season, Ernest Milton impersonated Benedick, and in 1926 Andrew Leigh produced a *Much Ado* with Edith Evans, newly arrived that season at the Vic, playing Beatrice. At the end of the next year, while the Old Vic was being rebuilt, Leigh presented the comedy at the Lyric, Hammersmith, with Lewis Casson and Sybil Thorndike as the principals. Henry Cass' *Much Ado* during the 1934/5 season, with Maurice Evans as Benedick and Mary Newcombe as Beatrice, was the last Vic production of the comedy for more than 20 years.

In January 1937 Robert Atkins, having presented the comedy twice at the Vic during the 1920's, staged it at the Ring, Blackfriars, with Jack Hawkins and Margaretta Scott, and began his summer Open Air Theatre productions of 1939 on June 3 with D. A. Clarke-Smith and Cathleen Nesbitt as Benedick and Beatrice. A month and a half earlier Stratford had attempted a *Much Ado* as the Shakespeare's Birthday play and to celebrate its own diamond jubilee. A power failure, which submerged the stage in gloom for 90 minutes, was corrected as Borachio spoke "What your wisdom could not discover, these shallow fools have brought to light." This unfortunate presentation, directed by B. Iden Payne, featured Alec Clunes and Vivienne Bennett in the leading roles.

While on a provincial tour in the fall of 1938, Donald Wolfit added Benedick to his repertoire and gave this portrayal for the first time in London during a repertory season at the Kingsway in early 1940. He repeated the role in 1945 opposite Rosalind Iden's Beatrice. That same year Robert Atkins produced another *Much Ado*, this time at Stratford, with Antony Eustrel and Clare Luce, and, in 1949, gave the play at the Open Air Theatre in Regent's Park with Antony Eustrel and Olive Gregg. Between Atkins' two productions there had been two London presentations. In 1946 Robert Donat appeared as Benedick opposite Renee Asherson's Beatrice in a production at the Aldwych which ran only a few weeks. The Bristol Old Vic came to the Embassy in 1947 with Hugh Hunt's modern-dress version of the comedy. Dogberry (William Devlin), costumed as an air-raid warden, rode a bicycle, and Benedick (Clement McCallin) was dressed as an Italian officer. Rosalie Crutchley was a convincing Beatrice.

John Gielgud's *Much Ado About Nothing* dominated the first half of the 1950's. In 1949 he directed Anthony Quayle and Diana Wynyard in Stratford's stylish production, which eventually grew into a theatre showpiece. The following season Gielgud, who had been Benedick at Stratford in 1931, acted the hero himself, while Peggy Ashcroft played Beatrice. Gielgud's rapid-fire delivery, the splendor of the dress, and the deft comic exaggeration all contributed to a memorable performance. George Rose was a wheezing Dogberry. In 1952 the Stratford production was brought to the stage of the Phoenix; this time Gielgud's leading lady was Diana Wynyard. The actor's low-toned, disbelieving first refusal to "Kill Claudio" eliminated the usual laugh and for once permitted the sincerity of the scene between Benedick and Beatrice to be realized. Paul Scofield played Don Pedro for this presentation. After a tour of the continent and the provinces with the comedy, Gielgud and a Stratford company returned to the London Palace in 1955 with a wholly perfected *Much Ado*. Peggy Ashcroft was once more Gielgud's Beatrice. In August 1959 this *Much Ado* with a new heroine, Margaret Leighton, performed for the Cambridge Drama Festival in Boston and opened the next month for a run at the Lunt-Fontanne in New York.

Since Gielgud's successes, *Much Ado* has been staged in England once at the Old Vic, in 1956 with Keith Michell and Barbara Jefford in Denis Carey's somewhat slow-moving production; twice at the Open Air (in 1956, produced again by Robert Atkins, who played Dogberry, and five years later under David Williams); and twice at Stratford, first, in 1958, produced by Douglas Seale in a lavish setting, which nevertheless left plenty of room for the comedy, with Michael Redgrave and Googie Withers at home as Benedick and Beatrice and again in 1961 with Christopher Plummer as Benedick. —M. G.

Bibliography. TEXT: *Much Ado About Nothing*, New Cambridge Edition, Arthur Quiller-Couch and J. Dover Wilson, eds., 1923; W. W. Greg, *The Editorial Problem in Shakespeare*, 1942. DATE: James G. McManaway, "Recent Studies in Shakespeare's Chronology," *Shakespeare Survey 3*, 1950. SOURCES: C. T. Prouty, *The Sources of Much Ado About Nothing*, 1950; Geoffrey Bullough, *Narrative and Dramatic Sources of Shakespeare*, Vol. II, 1958. COMMENT: David L. Stevenson, *The Love-Game Comedy*, 1946; J. Dover Wilson, *Shakespeare's Happy Comedies*, 1962. STAGE HISTORY: New Cambridge Edition; T. Alston Brown, *A History of the New York Stage . . . to 1901*, 1903; William Winter, *Shakespeare on the Stage*, 3 vols., 1911–1916; G. C. D. Odell, *Shakespeare from Betterton to Irving*, 1920; J. C. Trewin, *Shakespeare on the English Stage, 1900–1964*, 1964.

Selected Criticism

ANNA BROWNELL JAMESON. Shakespeare has exhibited in Beatrice a spirited and faithful portrait of the fine lady of his own time. The deportment, language, manners, and allusions are those of a particular class in a particular age; but the individual and dramatic character which forms the groundwork is strongly discriminated, and being taken from general nature, belongs to every age. In Beatrice, high intellect and high animal spirits meet, and excite each other like fire and air. In her wit, (which is brilliant without being imaginative,) there is a touch of insolence, not unfrequent in women when the wit predominates over reflection and imagination. In her temper, too, there is a slight infusion of the termagant; and her satirical humour plays with such an unrespective levity over all subjects alike, that it required a profound knowledge of women to bring such a character within the pale of our sympathy. But Beatrice, though wilful, is not wayward; she is volatile, not unfeeling. She has not only an exuberance of wit and gayety, but of heart, and soul, and energy of spirit; and is no more like the fine ladies of modern comedy,—whose wit consists in a temporary allusion, or a play upon words, and whose petulance is displayed in a toss of the head, a flirt of the fan, or a flourish of the pocket-handkerchief,—than one of our modern dandies is like Sir Philip Sidney.

In Beatrice, Shakespeare has contrived that the poetry of the character shall not only soften, but heighten its comic effect. We are not only inclined to forgive Beatrice all her scornful airs, all her biting jests, all her assumption of superiority; but they amuse and delight us the more, when we find her, with all the headlong simplicity of a child, falling at once into the snare laid for her affections; when we see *her*, who thought a man of God's making not good enough for her, who disdained to be o'ermastered by 'a piece of valiant dust,' stooping like the rest of her sex, vailing her proud spirit, and taming her wild heart to the loving hand of him whom she had scorned, flouted, and misused 'past the endurance of a block.' [*Shakespeare's Heroines;* originally published in *Characteristics of Women*, 1832.]

THOMAS CAMPBELL. Yet who, but Shakespeare, could dry our tears of interest for Hero, by so laughable an agent as the immortal Dogberry? I beg pardon for having allowed that Falstaff makes us forget all the other comic creations of our Poet. How could I have overlooked you, my Launce, and my Launce's dog, and my Dogberry? To say that Falstaff makes us forget Dogberry is, as Dogberry himself would say, 'most tolerable and not to be endured.' And yet Shakespeare, after pouncing this ridiculous prey, springs up, forthwith, to high dramatic effect in making Claudio, who had mistakenly accused Hero, so repentant as to consentingly marry another woman, her supposed cousin, under a veil, which, when it is lifted, displays his own vindicated bride.

At the same time, if Shakespeare were looking over my shoulder, I could not disguise some objections to this comedy, which involuntarily strikes me as debarring it from ranking among our Poet's most enchanting dramas. I am on the whole, I trust, a liberal on the score of dramatic probability. Our fancy and its faith are no niggards in believing whatsoever they may be delighted withal; but, if I may use a vulgar saying, 'a willing horse should not be ridden too hard.' Our fanciful faith is misused, when it is spurred and impelled to believe that Don John, without one particle of love for Hero, but out of mere personal spite to Claudio, should contrive the infernal treachery which made the latter *assuredly* jealous. Moreover, during one-half of the play, we have a disagreeable female character in that of Beatrice. Her portrait, I may be told, is deeply drawn, and minutely finished. It is; and so is that of Benedick, who is entirely her counterpart, except that he is less disagreeable. But the best-drawn portraits by the finest masters may be admirable in execution, though unpleasant to contemplate, and Beatrice's portrait is in this category. She is a tartar, by Shakespeare's own showing, and, if a natural woman, is not a pleasing representative of the sex. In befriending Hero, she almost reconciles us to her, but not entirely; for a good heart, that shows itself only on extraordinary occasions, is no sufficient atonement for a bad temper, which Beatrice evidently shows. [*The Dramatic Works of Shakespeare*, 1838.]

THOMAS MARC PARROTT. *Much Ado* is a play of action springing from character, but it is also a play of vivacious and amusing dialogue. In fact a great part of the fun of this play comes from the spoken word; often, indeed, the action halts while we listen to a rippling stream of speech. The text falls easily into verse and prose; easily but not equally, for about three-fourths of the whole is in prose, a new phenomenon in Shakespearean comedy. Shakespeare's rustics and clownish servants, indeed, had talked in prose; a merry gentleman like Mercutio might step from verse into prose and back again. Here for the first time, however, the dialogue of gentlefolk, male and female, is for the most part couched in prose. It seems as if Shakespeare is now convinced that for comedy of the lighter, less romantic type, prose is the proper vehicle. The conviction may have grown on him while he was creating Falstaff, his greatest comic figure, who seldom speaks a line of verse. The conjecture seems to be confirmed by the fact that King Henry's wooing of his French bride, perhaps the least romantic courtship in English drama, is all in prose. This scene is plainly meant to round off a drum-and-trumpet play with a concluding strain of comedy, and *King Henry V* was written in the same year as *Much Ado*.

Little need be said of the verse of this play. There are good lines here and there, but there is an absence alike of the lyric music of the *Dream* and the grave eloquence of *The Merchant*. The workmanlike verse is confined, almost without exception, to what is structurally the main, which is also the derived, plot, another proof, no doubt, of Shakespeare's slight regard for this action compared with his delight in the new theme and the two characters that he was adding to it. It is the prose and not the poetry of this play that lingers in the memory: the comic blunders of Dogberry, the wit-combats of the still defiant lovers, the scoffing comments of Benedick on love and marriage, the light-hearted jesting of Beatrice, and, best of all, the confession of their mutual love in simple unadorned prose. [*Shakespearean Comedy*, 1949.]

WYLIE SYPHER. By assuming the satyric mask Benedick and Beatrice are playing the role of boaster or *alazon* as well as the role of mocker. Their independence is, as Nietzsche would say, a privilege of the strong—and, in circumspect Messina, a transgression of the sentimental code. They have unwittingly been forced into a comic *hubris*, a heterodoxy, a pretension that they can occupy only with increasing difficulty. . . . Of course the assumption of the role of *alazon* is at least in part an affectation; we know that before the play opens there has already been a passage or two of hearts between them. The dilemma, however, remains: the comic fauns have been betrayed into posing as boasters—the Philistines in Messina would say as destroyers, nihilists. They have permitted themselves a single but unmistakable Nietzschean gesture.

Hence the full transformation, the completed metamorphosis, from *eiron* to clown, an entirely Socratic reversal occurring with the recognition or "discovery" that humbles the comic spirit itself and causes the dissembler to drop his mask. He no longer *plays* the fool. He *is* the fool. . . .

The satiric mask falls quickly from Beatrice and Benedick. When the situation in Messina hangs between farce and tragedy—between the devices of

Don Pedro as Lord of Misrule, and the devices of Don John as immoralist—we discover in Benedick the same wasted pity of which Mercutio, that other blasphemer, is capable. "Alas, poor hurt fowl!" remarks Benedick when he supposes that Claudio has been robbed of Hero by Don Pedro's wooing. "Now will he creep into sedges." The eavesdropping in Leonato's orchard, when by prearrangement Benedick and Beatrice overhear themselves accused of inhumanity, begins the discipline of suffering, the chastising of these comic fauns, whose virtue, according to the Socratic paradox, is a reflex of their innocence and whose humiliation is a warrant of their integrity. The triumph of comedy over farce, and over the Nietzschean dialectic, is the sudden realization of Benedick, then of Beatrice, "I must not seem proud. Happy are they that hear their detractions and can put them to mending." So they are reduced, and will be horribly in love; the world must be peopled. Benedick is not as he has been: "When I said I would die a bachelor, I did not think I should live till I were married." And Beatrice will tame her wild heart to Benedick's loving hand. The fauns are as pitiful and as helpless as Malvolio—"Alas, poor fool, how have they baffled thee!" ["Nietzsche and Socrates in Messina," *Partisan Review*, 1949.]

M. C. BRADBROOK. If *Romeo and Juliet* was a tragedy with its full complement of comedy, and *The Merchant of Venice* a comedy with an infusion of tragic pity and fear, *Much Ado About Nothing* is a comedy of Masks where the deeper issues are overlaid with mirth, and appear only at the climax of the play, the church scene. It is for this reason that so very mechanical a villain as Don John becomes a necessity of the plot. A true villain, like Shylock or Edmund or Richard III, would destroy the comedy: those who protest at the insufficiency of Don John should consider what would happen to the total composition if he were other than he is. The old worn device of a maid dressing up in her mistress's clothes—one of the commonplaces of European fiction for centuries—is also used for a special purpose. It is not perhaps so incredible as modern readers tend to think it: the story of Gratiano and Nerissa should have served as reminder that gentlewomen really might ape their mistresses, and talking with a man out at a window had happened in Shakespeare before without incurring moral disapprobation, even of the strictest; it was only as it happened on her wedding eve to the betrothed Hero that it took on the colouring of perfidy as well as lightness. Nevertheless the convention is used in a frankly conventional way; Margaret does not intervene when Claudio lodges his accusation, and Claudio does not fall upon the interloper and run him through like the hero of *A Blot in the Scutcheon*, both of which are obvious, natural, and probable, but inappropriate things for them to do. [*Shakespeare and Elizabethan Poetry*, 1951.]

FRANCIS FERGUSSON. One might say that *Much Ado* presents a comic vision of mankind which is also poetic, while the purpose of *The Comedy of Errors* is closer to that of the professional vaudevillian, who gauges his success by clocking the laughs: the provoking of thoughtless mirth, an almost reflex response. The difference between the two plays is clearest, perhaps, when one reflects that both are concerned with mistaken identity, but in *The Comedy of Errors* the mistake is simply a mistake in fact, while in *Much Ado* it is a failure of insight, or rather many failures of different kinds by the different characters.

Shakespeare accomplishes the *dénouement* of *The Comedy of Errors* in one swift scene. It is not difficult to correct an error in fact: it may be done instantly by providing the right fact: and as soon as both pairs of twins are on stage together, the error is gone. But correcting a failure of insight is a most delicate and mysterious process, which Shakespeare suggests, in *Much Ado*, in countless ways: through the symbolism of masks, night, and verbal ambiguities, and in peripeteias of his three variously comic subplots. [*The Human Image in Dramatic Literature*, 1957.]

GEORGE STEINER. The function of contrast is beautifully shown in *Much Ado About Nothing*. Nearly the entire play is written in prose. The few passages of verse are only a kind of shorthand to quicken matters. Indeed, with this play English prose established a firm claim to the comedy of intellect. Congreve, Oscar Wilde, and Shaw are direct heirs to Shakespeare's presentation of Beatrice and Benedick. Verse would mar the astringent, bracing quality of their love. They are lovers in the middle range of passion, enamoured neither of the flesh nor altogether of the heart, but caught in the enchantment of each other's wit. Their bright encounters show how intelligence gives to prose its real music. But in the last Act, poetry makes a memorable entrance. The setting is Hero's false tomb. Claudio, Don Pedro, and their musicians come to do it sorrowful honor. They sing a mournful lyric: "Pardon, goddess of the night." Then the prince turns to the players:

> Good morrow, masters, put your torches out.
> The wolves have prey'd, and look, the gentle day,
> Before the wheels of Phoebus, round about
> Dapples the drowsy east with spots of grey.

The lines cast a healing spell. They brush away the squalid machinations of the plot. At the touch of poetry, the entire play moves into a more luminous key. We know that disclosure is imminent and that the affair will end happily. This salutation to the morning, moreover, delivers a gentle rebuke to Beatrice and Benedick. Don Pedro invokes the pastoral and mythological order of the world. It has none of the sophistication of the lovers' prose. But it is more enduring. [*The Death of Tragedy*, 1961.]

Muir, Kenneth (1907–). Scholar; since 1951 King Alfred professor of English literature at the University of Liverpool. Muir has written on a variety of topics, with Shakespeare and Sir Thomas Wyatt as objects of special interest. He has edited Wyatt's *Collected Poems* (1949) and the *Unpublished Poems* (1961) and has written the *Life and Letters of Sir Thomas Wyatt* (1963). His works on Shakespeare are as follows: *The Voyage to Illyria: A New Study of Shakespeare* (with Sean O'Loughlin, 1937); *Shakespeare's Sources* (Vol. 1, *Comedies and Tragedies*, 1957); *Shakespeare and the Tragic Pattern* (1959); *Shakespeare as Collaborator* (1960); *Last Periods of Shakespeare, Racine, Ibsen* (1961); *Shakespeare: The Tragedies* (1961); *Shakespeare: Hamlet* (1963). For The New Arden Shakespeare he has edited *Macbeth* and *King Lear*. Muir has also edited some of Una Ellis-Fermor's papers, left unpublished at the time of her death, under the title *Shakespeare the Dramatist and Other Papers* (1961).

Munday or **Mundy, Anthony** (1560–1633). Dramatist and pamphleteer. Born in London, Munday was apparently a child actor before being apprenticed at the age of 16 to the printer John Allde. A year later he was publishing verse imitative in style and subject of *A Mirror for Magistrates*. In 1578 he was sent abroad to spy on the activities of English Catholic refugees in France and Italy. He gained admittance to the English College at Rome, where he collected material for an exposé of the machinations of the Catholics which he published as *The English Romayne Life* (1582). On returning to England, he continued his anti-Catholic activities, taking part in the capture of Edmund Campion (1540–1581), the Jesuit priest and poet. In 1584 he published *A Watchword to England*, an admonition against "traitors and treacherous practices."

By 1586 he was appointed a messenger of the Queen's Chamber, a part-time position which left him free to pursue his writing. He was actively writing plays, alone and in collaboration, until the end of Elizabeth's reign (1603). In 1598 he was cited in *Palladis Tamia* as "our best plotter," an epithet which may refer to Munday's particular adeptness in creating scenarios, or plot outlines, which were completed by others.

Munday's first extant play is *Fedele and Fortunio* (1584), an adaptation of an Italian play. The play was popular and may have been used by Shakespeare as one of his sources for *Much Ado About Nothing*, where he might have found not only the general outline of his plot, but the idea for the characters of Dogberry and Verges as well. Another of Munday's plays, *John a Kent* (1590), may have provided Shakespeare with incidents and ideas for *A Midsummer Night's Dream* (see A MIDSUMMER NIGHT'S DREAM: *Sources*). Munday is also the author of *The Downfall of Robert Earl of Huntingdon* (1598) and, in collaboration with Henry Chettle, its sequel, *The Death of Robert Earl of Huntingdon* (1598), two plays which may be the source of the greenwood adventures in *As You Like It* (see AS YOU LIKE IT: *Sources*). Philip Henslowe's diary reveals that Munday was one of the four authors who were paid £10 for *Sir John Oldcastle* (1599), one of the plays that Isaac Jaggard published in 1619 as Shakespeare's.

Munday's nondramatic work includes *Zelauto* or *The Fountaine of Fame* (1580), a long prose romance. Book III of the story includes an episode of Truculento, "an extorting Usurer," which is one of the secondary sources of *The Merchant of Venice*. Another possible source of the court scene in *Merchant of Venice* is the anecdote "Of a Jew, who would for his debt have a pound of the flesh of a Christian," included in *The Orator*, which was probably translated by Munday in 1596. See THE MERCHANT OF VENICE: *Sources*.

The original draft of SIR THOMAS MORE, the manuscript of which may contain three pages written by Shakespeare, is in Munday's handwriting. Munday is clearly part author of this play and, according to I. A. Shapiro, the sole author of the original version of the play. In addition to his own writing, Munday was also an editor. He is probably the "A. M." who edited *Bel-vedere* (1600), a dictionary of verse quotations, with copious citations from Shakespeare. See John BODENHAM. [I. A. Shapiro, "Shakespeare and Mundy," *Shakespeare Survey*, XIV, 1961.]

Munro, John [James] (c. 1883–1956). Scholar. In collaboration with F. J. Furnivall, Munro wrote *Shakespeare, Life and Work* (1908), a handbook for the general reader. *The Shakspere Allusion-Book* (1909) was the result of Munro's efforts to bring together, revise, and edit several previous works. For The Shakespeare Library series he edited two sources: *Romeus and Juliet* (1908) and *The Troublesome Reign of King John* (1913). Munro's final work was editing the six-volume *London Shakespeare* (1957), an annotated and critical edition.

Murderers, Two. In *2 Henry VI*, they are hired by the Duke of Suffolk to murder the Duke of Gloucester (III, ii).

Murray, [George] Gilbert (1866–1957). Scholar and critic. A classical scholar of great distinction, Murray wrote a pioneering work of Shakespearean criticism. His *Hamlet and Orestes* (1914) claims a common source for the Hamlet story and the Orestes myths, inaugurating a new school of Shakespearean criticism. See MYTHIC CRITICISM; HAMLET: *Selected Criticism*.

Murry, John Middleton (1889–1957). Editor and scholar. Educated at Christ's Hospital and Brasenose, Oxford, Murry became the editor of *Athenaeum* and of *Adelphi*. His contributions to Shakespearean scholarship include *Keats and Shakespeare* (1925), *Countries of the Mind* (2 vols., 1922, 1931), and *Shakespeare* (1936).

music based on Shakespeare. It has been said that Shakespeare's works have inspired more music than have the combined works of all other notable poets. While statistical demonstration of this assertion has never been attempted, it may nevertheless be regarded as substantially true. Grove's *Dictionary of Music* lists some 800 works based on Shakespeare, alphabetically arranged by plays and composers, and this compilation takes no notice of the countless unpublished pieces composed for performances and then forgotten. Again, it is more difficult to recall the names of composers who have *not* been inspired by Shakespeare (for example, J. S. Bach, Mozart, and Handel) than to run through the list of those who have. The following record is arranged chronologically to demonstrate how Shakespeare has permeated the world of music from his own time to the present.

17th century. The composers who may have contributed their efforts to the production of Shakespeare's works during his own lifetime (Thomas MORLEY, Robert JOHNSON, Thomas FORD, John HILTON, and John [Jack] WILSON) are mentioned in the entry MUSIC IN THE PLAYS. But before the appearance of the First Folio in 1623, perhaps even before Shakespeare's death, the practice of inserting additional music into his plays had begun. Hecate's lines in *Macbeth* (III, v, 3–35 and IV, i, 39–43) are generally regarded as the work of a later hand, probabl

Thomas Middleton's, and these passages contain the directions, "Music, and a song within: 'Come away, come away,' etc."; "Music, and a song: 'Black spirits,' etc."; and "Music. The Witches dance." Both of the songs appear in full in Middleton's play *The Witch,* together with the character of Hecate, who plays no essential part in Shakespeare. The song settings and dances were probably composed by Robert Johnson.

After 1660 there was a tendency to transform some of the plays into what were called "dramatic operas," "semi-operas," or even simply "operas," although opera, in the sense of a music-drama sung throughout, was not cultivated in England at this time. William DAVENANT, in his popular *Siege of Rhodes* (1656), a heroic drama, did produce a composition, consisting of airs, choruses, and long passages of recitative, which was sung from beginning to end. The music, none of which survives, was composed by Henry Lawes (1596–1662), Matthew Locke (c. 1630–1677), Charles Coleman (d. c. 1694), and George Hudson (fl. c. 1665). It did not resemble any of the Italian operas of the time, and its form had no successors or development in England. The same may be said of John Blow's (1649–1708) *Venus and Adonis* (c. 1682), which the unknown librettist did not base on Shakespeare's poem, and Henry PURCELL's *Dido and Aeneas* (c. 1689), to a libretto by Nahum Tate (1652–1715). These were experiments in the area of the dramatic cantata. Real opera at this time took root and flourished only in Italy and France.

In England "dramatic opera" was a direct descendant of the courtly Jacobean and Caroline MASQUE, characterized, in order of importance, by (1) spectacular scenery and elaborate costumes, (2) dances, (3) music—for the dances, for descriptive or "incidental" effects, for songs and choruses—and (4) dramatic action with spoken dialogue. When the first three of these elements were inserted into, or superimposed upon, a play for the popular theatre, the result was the sort of thing that happened to several of Shakespeare's plays, in which the music now played an increasingly important role. The dramatic texts which were used consisted of the notoriously distorted adaptations, not unlike the conversions of successful modern plays, such as Shaw's *Pygmalion* and O'Neill's *Anna Christie,* into "musicals." The most interesting of the Shakespearean "musicals" of the Restoration period are the following:

Macbeth was revived and mangled by Davenant in 1663, with additional music, some of which may have been selected from earlier compositions by Robert Johnson. In 1672 it was transformed into an "opera," with new scenery and stage-machines and a fresh musical score by Matthew Locke, of which a few fragments have survived. A still later score was provided for this Davenant version by John Eccles (1650–1735), probably sometime after 1698.

The Tempest, or The Enchanted Island was an elaborate distortion of Shakespeare's play, with the addition of several new characters, a chorus of devils, and a great deal of music. It was produced in 1667 by Davenant and John Dryden. In 1674 Thomas SHADWELL elaborated it into an "opera," with songs by John Banister (1630–1679) and Pelham Humfrey (1647–1674), a new air, "Arise, ye subterranean winds," set by Pietro Reggio (d. 1685), and incidental music by Giovanni Baptista Draghi (1640–1710) and Matthew Locke. The texts of Shakespeare's original songs were retained, including "Where the bee sucks" (V, i, 88–94). In 1695 Henry Purcell was commissioned to compose an entirely fresh score to Shadwell's libretto, set for an orchestra of 24 strings and 30 singing men and boys from the Chapel Royal. The two Shakespeare songs at the beginning of Act III, "Come unto these yellow sands," sung by Ariel and chorus, and "Full fathom five," sung, with chorus, by the non-Shakespearean Milcha, Ariel's companion-spirit, comprise the only settings of any of Shakespeare's actual words by the most celebrated English composer of the period.

Shadwell's elaboration of *Timon of Athens* appeared in 1678, with an added masque, set to music first by Louis Grabu (fl. 1665–1690) and later by Purcell.

The Fairy Queen, a mutilated version of *A Midsummer Night's Dream,* possibly by Elkanah Settle (1648–1724), was produced in 1692. It was embellished with many airs, including one sung by "a drunken poet," and four elaborate masques performed between the acts and at the end. All the music was composed by Purcell.

A curiosity of this period is an effective recitative setting, composed sometime after 1675 in the Italian operatic manner, of Hamlet's "To be or not to be" soliloquy (III, i, 56–88), with guitar accompaniment, supplied by one Cesare Morelli, and possibly inspired by Betterton's rendition of the lines. Its manuscript was discovered in the library of Samuel Pepys, preserved at Magdalen College, Cambridge. Morelli was employed as music master by Pepys between 1675 and 1679.

18th century. After the death of Purcell Shakespeare's reputation spread over all of continental Europe. The first opera based on *Hamlet* was composed by Domenico Scarlatti (1685–1757) in 1715. Carl Philip Emanuel Bach (1714–1788) composed an overture to the same tragedy. Franz Josef Haydn (1732–1809) wrote incidental music for both *Hamlet* and *King Lear.* For the latter he probably consulted a version based on the distortions of Nahum Tate, Garrick, and George Colman. The music consists of a festive overture, four intermezzi, and a triumphal march. Haydn may have received suggestions for this opus during his visits to London in 1790–1792 or 1794–1795, when the stage presented the tragedy without the Fool and ended it with the marriage of Edgar and Cordelia. At about the same time Haydn set Viola's speech "She never told her love" from *Twelfth Night* (II, iv, 113), as a canzonet for voice and piano, "composed for an English lady of position." In 1796 Carl Ditters von Dittersdorf (1739–1799) based an opera on *The Merry Wives of Windsor,* and in the same year Niccolò Antonio Zingarelli (1752–1837) produced his *Giulietta e Romeo* to a libretto by one Giuseppe Foppa, which omitted the parts of the Nurse, the Friar, Tybalt, and Montague. In this version, probably following Colley Cibber's revision, Juliet awakens before the death of Romeo.

During this century music for the plays continued to be produced in England. Between 1740 and 1750 Dr. Thomas Augustine ARNE set some 20 songs from the comedies, as well as incidental music for the original masque in *The Tempest.* John Christopher SMITH provided incidental music for *The Fairies*

(1755), another distortion of *A Midsummer Night's Dream,* and in 1756 for a similar "adaptation" of *The Tempest.* Dr. Charles Burney (1726–1814) set two songs from *A Midsummer Night's Dream,* "The woosell cock" (III, i, 128–131, 133–136) and "Up and down" (III, ii, 396–399), in 1762. In 1792 John Stafford Smith (1750–1836), antiquarian and composer of the tune to which *The Star-Spangled Banner* is now sung, set two songs from *As You Like It,* "Under the greenwood tree" (II, v, 1–8, 40–47, 52–59) and "What shall he have that kill'd the deer?" (IV, ii, 11–19) as "glees," or part songs, for four male voices.

19th century to 1850. Beethoven (1770–1827) composed his dramatic *Coriolan* overture (opus 62, 1807) for a "tragedy after Shakespeare" by Heinrich von Collin, but his inspiration was undoubtedly Shakespeare himself. Earlier in his career, when asked what he had in mind when writing his piano sonata, opus 31, no. 2, he is said to have replied, "Read Shakespeare's *Tempest.*"

Louis Spohr (1784–1859) wrote music for *Macbeth* in 1825. None of it was published except the overture, opus 75. Carl Maria von Weber (1786–1826) composed a curious and charming trio with chorus and guitar accompaniment to "Tell me where is fancy bred" (III, ii, 63–72) for a performance of *The Merchant of Venice* in Dresden in 1821. His opera *Oberon,* opus 9, based on *A Midsummer Night's Dream,* was first performed in 1826.

In England Sir Henry Rowley Bishop was the most prolific and successful provider of music for Shakespeare. Between 1816 and 1837 he produced operas, incidental music, and song settings for at least 12 of the plays. All of his work is competent and undistinguished.

In Italy Gioacchino Rossini produced his opera *Otello, o Il Moro di Venezia,* after a libretto by F. Berio di Salsa, in 1816. Vincenzo Bellini (1801–1835) achieved success with his opera based on *Romeo and Juliet, I Capuletti ed i Montecchi,* in 1830.

In Germany Franz Schubert (1797–1828) composed three songs, "Come, thou monarch of the vine" (*Antony and Cleopatra,* II, vii, 120–125), "Hark, hark, the lark" (*Cymbeline,* II, iii, 21–30), and "Who is Sylvia?" (*Two Gentlemen of Verona,* IV, ii, 39–53) in 1826; the last two gained the immediate and lasting affection of all audiences. Felix Mendelssohn (1809–1847) produced his popular *Midsummer Night's Dream* music (overture, songs and choruses, scherzo, melodramas—recitations with orchestral accompaniment—nocturne, and wedding march) between 1826 and 1843. Carl Otto Ehrenfried Nicolai (1810–1849) wrote his opera *Die lustige Weiber von Windsor* (*The Merry Wives of Windsor*) in 1849, to a text by H. S. Mosenthal; its overture has been a perennial success. Nicolai also set "It was a lover and his lass" (*As You Like It,* V, iii, 17–34) as opus 16, no. 2. Robert Schumann (1810–1856) produced a song, "When that I was and a little tiny boy" (*Twelfth Night,* end of play), and an overture to *Julius Caesar* among his last efforts at composition. His "Novelette," opus 21, no. 3, for piano ("Leicht und mit Humor—rasch und wild") is said to have been his idea for a witches' dance in *Macbeth.*

In France, Jacques François Fromental Elias Halévy (1799–1862) produced his opera *The Tempest,* with text by Eugène Scribe, in 1850. Hector Berlioz composed his "dramatic fantasia with choruses" on *The Tempest* in 1830; an overture to *King Lear,* opus 4, in 1831; *Roméo et Juliette,* opus 17, a "grande symphonie dramatique" to a text by Emile Deschamps, in 1839; the "Ballade sur la mort d'Ophélie et marche funèbre pour la dernière scène d'Hamlet, avec choeur" as opus 18, no. 3, in 1848 and the opera, "imité de Shakespeare," *Béatrice et Bénédict,* in 1862. The last received its first performance in the United States in Washington, D.C., on June 4, 1964 and was critically praised.

Enough works have been cited to show how powerfully Shakespeare captured the imagination of the Romantic school of musical composition throughout Europe. He was to wield even greater influence during the latter half of the century.

19th century, 1850–1900. In the European theatre of the 19th century there was an increasingly healthy tendency to eschew the wildest distortions of Shakespeare's texts and to present reasonably faithful, although drastically cut, versions of his plays. This cannot be said of the fantastic quasi-Shakespearean librettos supplied to or by the composers of operas. Their problems, of course, differed from those of theatrical producers, and they were compelled to adhere to the conventions of the opera house, which demanded recitatives and arias, vocal ensembles, ballets, and the like, with the result that the hand of Shakespeare himself was often unrecognizable.

Thus we find the Parisian Ambroise Thomas (1811–1896), whose music was always full of Gallic suavity, presenting *Le Songe d'une nuit d'été* (1850) to a text by Rosier and de Leuven, which bears very faint resemblance to Shakespeare's *A Midsummer Night's Dream* and adds the characters of Falstaff, Olivia, "Lord Latimer," Queen Elizabeth, and Shakespeare himself. In 1868, following a libretto by Michel Carré and Jules Barbier, Thomas produced *Hamlet* in which Laertes sings a patriotic Danish song, Ophelia's mad scenes become part of a ballet, Hamlet roars out drinking songs with the visiting players, the Queen, Laertes, and Polonius survive, Hamlet marries Ophelia and is crowned king of Denmark at the end, with the blessing of the Ghost.

Less outrageous treatments of Shakespeare included Richard Wagner's early and unsuccessful *Das Liebesverbot* (1835–1836), after *Measure for Measure;* Charles Gounod's *Roméo et Juliette* (1867), which enjoyed 100 performances in its first year; and Hermann Götz' *Der Widerspenstigen Zähmung* (1874, to a libretto by Joseph Victor Widmann, based on *The Taming of the Shrew*), which attained considerable popularity in Germany.

Giuseppe Verdi composed three Shakespearean operas which are still in the world's repertoire and probably remain the very best examples of the way in which a gifted composer can make use of Shakespeare without making either himself or the dramatist ridiculous. They are *Macbetto* (to a libretto by Francesco Piave, 1847 and revised in 1865); *Otello* (1887, libretto by Arrigo Boïto), in which even the insertion of an "Ave Maria" in addition to Desdemona's "Willow Song" does not impair the tragic effect; and *Falstaff* (1893), for which Boïto contrived a skillful amalgam of *Henry IV* and *The Merry Wives of Windsor.*

Bedřich Smetana (1824–1884) began work on an opera, *Viola,* during the last year of his life, using a libretto based on *Twelfth Night* by Eliška Krásnohorská. He finished only the first act, which was first performed, successfully, at the National Theatre in Prague in 1924. A tuneful operatic version of *Much Ado About Nothing* was produced by Sir Charles Villiers Stanford (1852–1924) to an eclectic text by Julian Sturgis, at Covent Garden in 1900. It has not been recently revived.

If Shakespeare's plays as heard in opera houses have in general left much to be desired, it may be said that the inspiration he provided to composers who were not manacled by idiotic texts was extremely fruitful. Musicians who were moved by the plays, and contented themselves with the writing of overtures, symphonic poems, incidental music, and song settings, created some of the most effective scores of the later 19th century. Among these are:

Franz Liszt (1811–1886): *Hamlet,* symphonic poem for orchestra, 1861; Friedrich von Flotow (1812–1883): incidental music for *The Winter's Tale,* 1859; Peter Cornelius (1824–1874): duet, "Come away, death" (*Twelfth Night,* II, iv, 52–68), opus 16, no. 3; Smetana: "Macbeth and the Witches" for piano (1859), the symphonic poem *Richard III,* 1862, and "Shakespeare March" for orchestra, 1864; Anton Rubinstein (1829–1894): overture to *Antony and Cleopatra,* opus 116; Johannes Brahms (1833–1897): "Come away, death" for female voices, two horns, and harp, opus 17, no. 2, and five of Ophelia's songs; Joseph Joachim (1831–1907): overtures to *Hamlet,* opus 4, and *Henry IV,* opus 7; Mily Alexeivich Balakirev (1837–1910): incidental music for *King Lear* (1861–1865); Peter Ilich TCHAIKOVSKY: symphonic poems and incidental music for *The Tempest* (1868), opus 18, *Romeo and Juliet* (1871), and *Hamlet* (1885), opus 67; Anton Dvořák (1841–1904): overture to *Othello* (1891).

In England Sir Arthur S. Sullivan (1842–1900) began his career as a serious composer at the age of 20 with incidental music for *The Tempest,* opus 1, following it with scores for performances of *The Merchant of Venice, The Merry Wives of Windsor, Henry VIII, Timon of Athens,* and *Macbeth.* During this period he also composed about a dozen Shakespeare songs and duets. He was destined to find more congenial inspiration in the texts supplied by W. S. Gilbert. Sir Charles Hubert H. Parry (1848–1918) also produced some 20 Shakespeare songs, more sophisticated than Sullivan's, as well as settings of five of the sonnets to Shakespeare's words, with German translations. Edward German (1862–1936) composed a symphonic poem, *Hamlet,* in 1897. He also provided music for six Shakespeare plays, of which only his dances for *Henry VIII* are still to be heard.

Hugo Wolf (1860–1903) composed a "Fairies' Song" (*Elfenlied*) in 1881, for women's voices, to words from Shakespeare's *A Midsummer Night's Dream.* In France, Vincent d'Indy (1851–1931) offered an overture to *Antony and Cleopatra* in 1875; Paul Dukas (1865–1935), an overture to *King Lear* in 1882; and Claude Debussy (1862–1918) wrote music to *King Lear* (1904), but only a bold *Fanfare* and a subtle *Sommeil de Lear* have survived.

20th century. The custom of demanding the provision of new music for Shakespeare persisted through the middle of this century. It resulted in a handful of curious operas, none of them more than vaguely reflecting Shakespeare's texts. In 1900 Frederick Delius (1862–1934) composed *Romeo und Julia auf dem Dorfe* (*A Village Romeo and Juliet*), in the form of a prologue and three acts, produced in Berlin in 1907, and conducted by Sir Thomas Beecham in London, 1910. "A Walk to the Paradise Garden" is the only item in this opus which may still be heard. Delius also wrote a charming setting of "It was a lover and his lass." Dr. Ralph Vaughan Williams (1872–1958) proved more faithful to Shakespeare's text when he based *Sir John in Love* (1929) on *The Merry Wives of Windsor.* His interest in the modal style of the music of the Renaissance lent a kind of quasi authenticity to his jolly score, which contained the now most often heard setting of "Greensleeves." To his other Shakespearean songs and part songs, Vaughan Williams added his more ambitious *Serenade to Music* in 1938, a cantata based on Act V of *The Merchant of Venice* ("How sweetly sleeps"), for 16 voices with orchestra. Ernest Bloch (1880–1959) completed a lyric drama, *Macbeth* (1910), to Edmond Flag's libretto; it never achieved popularity. Neither did Gian Francesco Malipiero's (1882–) "music dramas," *Giulio Cesare, Romeo e Giulietta,* and *Antonio e Cleopatra.* Dmitri Shostakovich (1906–) wrote some songs and incidental music for *Hamlet.* His *Lady Macbeth of Mtsensk,* produced in New York in 1935, is based on a novel by Leskov, rather than on the play. Full of bawdy humor and choral laments, it was consequently anathematized by the Soviet government. Benjamin Britten (1913–) created a chamber opera, *The Rape of Lucretia* (1946), which is full of dissonance and symbolism, and bears little relationship to Shakespeare's poem. In 1960 he wrote *A Midsummer Night's Dream.* Frank Martin's (1890–) opera *Der Sturm* (*The Tempest*) was written in 1956.

Again we find that composers who were satisfied to translate their own responses to Shakespeare simply into personal impressions or practical *Gebrauchsmusik* did the best service to Shakespeare in our own time. Engelbert Humperdinck (1854–1921) provided appropriate incidental music for *The Merchant of Venice, Romeo and Juliet, The Tempest, Twelfth Night, The Winter's Tale,* and *As You Like It* between 1905 and 1907. Edward Elgar (1857–1934) in his "symphonic study" *Falstaff,* opus 68; Edward MacDowell (1861–1908) in his orchestral *Hamlet and Ophelia,* opus 22; Richard Strauss (1864–1949) in his tone poem *Macbeth* (1890), opus 23; Jean Sibelius (1865–1957) in his incidental music and song settings for *Twelfth Night* and *The Tempest* (1909 and 1926); Florent Schmitt (1870–1958) in his music for Gide's translation of *Antony and Cleopatra* (1920); John Alden Carpenter (1876–1951) in his orchestral suite on "The seven ages of man" from *As You Like It* (II, vii, 139–166); John Ireland (1879–1962) in his incidental music to *Julius Caesar* and his song "When daffodils" from *The Winter's Tale* (IV, iii, 1–22); Sergei Prokofieff (1891–1953) in his *Romeo and Juliet* ballet of 1934, opus 64; Darius Milhaud (1892–) in his music for *Julius Caesar;* Arthur Honegger (1892–1955) in his overture, prelude, and Ariel songs for *The Tempest* in 1923; Philip Heseltine ("Peter Warlock," 1894–1930) in his several Shakespeare songs; Mario Castelnuovo-Tedesco (1895–) in his many songs, as well as overtures to *King John, The Taming of the Shrew, Twelfth Night, The Merchant of Venice, Julius Caesar,* and *The Winter's Tale;* and Aram Khachaturian (1903–) in his music for *Macbeth*—all have kept up the tradition of supplying musical commentaries on Shakespeare for concert halls and on the stage. In this spirit Aaron Copland (1900–) provided music for Orson Welles' production of *Five Kings,* and William Walton (1902–) made the impressive score for Sir Laurence Olivier's cinema production of *Henry V* in 1944. Carl Orff (1895–) has composed no less than six different sets of incidental music to *A Midsummer Night's Dream,* beginning in 1917. Of these, the fourth was published in 1944 but not performed; the fifth was first produced at Darmstadt in 1952 and succeeded impressively in both Germany and the U.S.; the last, composed in 1962, was performed at Stuttgart in 1964.

Skillfully irreverent hands have also seized upon Shakespeare to make him one of the most successful dramatists of the popular Broadway theatre. In 1938 Richard Rodgers (1902–) and Lorenz Hart (1895–1943), following a "book" by George Abbott, created *The Boys from Syracuse,* a hilarious farce which still holds the stage, after Shakespeare's *The Comedy of Errors.* Ten years later Cole Porter (1893–1964) made a "musical" out of *The Taming of the Shrew—Kiss Me, Kate*—the dialogue and sophisticated music of which delighted countless audiences. This is a throwback to the understandably popular "dramatic operas" of the Restoration period.

All of these efforts to attune Shakespeare to contemporary musical idioms have been highly admired, and Shakespeare has always been tough enough to endure an infinity of musical as well as other interpretations. But at the present time there is a growing tendency to persuade producers to return to the music, or the kind of music, which Shakespeare's own audiences might have heard. This tendency belatedly follows that of the theatrical profession in giving us a relatively "pure" Shakespeare in text and staging. Sir Steuart Wilson has compiled several sets of scores of the older music for the use of companies who are attempting to restore and reproduce the experiences of the theatregoers of Shakespeare's time. A notable contribution to this movement was made by Dr. Denis Stevens in his arrangement of "The Five Songs in *As You Like It*" for Bernard Miles' Mermaid Theatre production at the Royal Exchange in 1951. The researches and publications of Professors John H. Long and Frederick W. Sternfeld are giving powerful support to this trend. [Max Friedländer, "Shakespeares Werke in der Musik," *Jahrbuch der deutschen Shakespeare-Gesellschaft,* 37, 1901; Christopher Wilson, *Shakespeare and Music,* 1922; Edward J. Dent, *Foundations of English Opera,* 1928; *Grove's Dictionary of Music and Musicians,* Vol. VII, 1954; Robert Etheridge Moore, *Henry Purcell and the Restoration Theatre,* 1961; *Music to Shakespeare,* Alan Bonstead, ed., 1964; *Shakespeare in Music,* Phyllis Hartnoll, ed., 1964.]—E.B.

music in the plays. Shakespeare's familiarity with the music of his time is indicated by more than 5 passages in his works. His enthusiasm for this art manifested in the observations of many of his symp thetic characters. Lorenzo's lines in *The Merchant Venice* on "the sweet power of music" are typica

> The man that hath no music in himself,
> Nor is not moved with concord of sweet sounds,
> Is fit for treasons, stratagems and spoils;
> The motions of his spirit are dull as night
> And his affections dark as Erebus:
> Let no such man be trusted.
> (V, i, 83–88)

Only his less appealing characters, such as Shyloc contemn music. Even the bestial Caliban is capab of a musically aesthetic experience:

> The isle is full of noises,
> Sounds and sweet airs, that give delight and hurt not.
> Sometimes a thousand twangling instruments
> Will hum about mine ears, and sometimes voices
> That, if I then had waked after long sleep,
> Will make me sleep again: and then, in dreaming,
> The clouds methought would open and show riches
> Ready to drop upon me, that, when I waked,
> I cried to dream again.
> (*The Tempest,* III, ii, 144–152)

This passage has often been quoted by Englis musicians who have, perhaps fancifully, taken it t represent Shakespeare's impressions of the music o the British Isles. Possibly more indicative of Shake speare's considered views is the Duke's comment i *Measure for Measure* (IV, i) that "music oft hat such a charm / To make bad good, and good pro voke to harm."

Older quasi-philosophical notions, such as that o the "music of the spheres," were familiar to him, a indicated by Lorenzo's words:

> There's not the smallest orb which thou behold'st
> But in his motion like an angel sings,
> Still quiring to the young-eyed cherubins.
> Such harmony is in immortal souls;
> But whilst this muddy vesture of decay
> Doth grossly close it in, we cannot hear it.
> (*The Merchant of Venice,* V, i, 60–65)

Technical knowledge of both the theory and prac tice of music is illustrated in the observation of th King, in *Richard II* (V, v): "Music do I hear?/ Ha ha! keep time! How sour sweet music is, / Whe time is broke and no proportion kept!/ So is it i the music of men's lives."

"Broken music," a term used to indicate the employment of instruments of different choirs, suc as strings and woodwinds, in the same composition points up an amusing passage in the King's wooing of Princess Katharine in *Henry V* (V, ii, 262–264): "Come, your answer in broken music; for thy voice is music and thy English broken." Hamlet also, having called for the recorders (instruments more like reedless clarinets than like transverse flutes), begs Guildenstern to play (*Hamlet,* III, ii, 365 ff.), and hen his companion protests that he knows "no)uch of it," urges him on by saying, "'Tis as easy as ying. Govern these ventages [the holes or stops] ith your finger and thumb, give it breath with our mouth . . . ." And to further protestations he ursts out, "You would play upon me, you would eem to know my stops . . . Call me what instrument ou will, though you can fret me [frets are the uides for the fingers of players on plucked instruents], yet you cannot play upon me."

Very striking are Shakespeare's references to the gamut," the whole range of notes from bass to reble, indicated in various ways by the syllables *ut*, *e*, *mi*, *fa*, *sol*, *la*. An elementary bit of pedagogy on his subject may be observed in the comic music esson in *The Taming of the Shrew* (III, i). Even nore significant is the bastard Edmund's saying or nging the syllables *fa*, *sol*, *la*, *mi* in *Lear* (I, ii, 149) pon the entrance of his brother. The final note *mi* spelled "me" in the First Folio text; in the present ay the tone is called *ti* or *si*) makes the whole sequence an illustration of an interval extremely disordant to the Elizabethan ear, the fourth and eventh tones of the major scale. As the musicians nown to Shakespeare had been taught, "*Mi* contra *a* est *diabolus* in musica." Shakespeare's Edmund is roclaiming his deviltry in musical terms. Many furher examples of such use of musical devices could e cited.

Shakespeare was acutely aware of the emotional nd dramatic appeal of the actual music that could e recalled to the minds of his audiences. There vere the popular ballads with which everybody was amiliar. Silence sings "And Robin Hood, Scarlet, nd John" (*2 Henry IV*, V, iii, 107); the mad Ophelia's singing of ballad snatches, some of them ather salacious, has been thought to reveal some hings hidden in her subconscious; both Hamlet and ear's Fool used ballads for ironical touches, and Edgar chants "Child Rowland to the dark tower ame" (*King Lear*, III, iv, 187), which inspired Browning to write one of his most remarkable oems. Other characters allude to popular songs, uch as "Greensleeves," and Desdemona sings a subly altered version of the old "Willow Song" (*Othello*, IV, iii, 41 ff.). Nor did Shakespeare ignore he sophisticated "ayres" (art songs for lute and oice) which were being composed by the so-called utenist school of musicians in his time. Sir Hugh Evans (*Merry Wives of Windsor*, III, i, 17 ff.) sings "To shallow rivers," a paraphrase of Marlowe's 'Come live with me and be my love," of which a etting by William Corkine (fl. 1610), in his *Second Book of Ayres* (1612), survives. Here Sir Hugh amusingly combines it with Psalm 137, of which nany musical settings had become well known.

Musical resources. Shakespeare's theatres were adnirably equipped with musical resources. Many of the boy actors, who played all the female as well as the child roles, had had some training as choir singers; some of them were accomplished lutenists as well. The clowns were required to sing as well as dance, and even some of the male principals obviously were able to manage a song or to bear a part in a chorus or "catch" (a kind of humorous round or canon, in which the singers enter successively with an identical tune). The only forms of vocal music not attempted in the theatre were those of the sacred motet and the secular madrigal, highly elaborate contrapuntal works.

A large variety of instruments and instrumentalists was available: the family of plucked stringed instruments, the lute, cittern, pandora, and theorbo; the bowed viols, ranging from the high treble to the low bass viol da gamba. Of the woodwinds there were the fifes, flutes, and recorders, differing in size and range, and the oboes ("hautboys"), used for special effects. There was plenty of brass: horns and trumpets; and percussion in the form of kettledrums, tabors (small drums used for rustic music), and military drums. The musicians may have occupied a room or gallery of their own, situated behind or above the actors' stages (see MUSIC ROOM), although they occasionally performed onstage, offstage, or even under the stage. The only instruments not used in the theatre were the organ and the virginals, a popular keyboard instrument whose strings were sounded by wooden "chips," or "jacks," topped with quills. That Shakespeare knew this instrument is indicated by the jealous Leontes' "Still virginalling upon his palm" (*The Winter's Tale*, I, ii, 125–126) as he observes Polixenes caressing his wife's hand. More interesting is Sonnet 128, "How oft, when thou, my music, music play'st," in which the poet describes his lady's playing and envies the instrument's intimacy with her fingers. When Shakespeare mentions "the saucy jacks that kiss the tender inward of thy hand," he confuses the "chips" with the keys—a forgivable error.

Songs. Shakespeare's uses of vocal music in his plays were manifold, and always purposeful, ranging from appropriate moments of pure entertainment to those of complete and indispensable integration with the drama in order to illuminate character or carry the action forward. The music in general tends to become increasingly functional as Shakespeare develops his dramatic powers.

The following review of the songs and their uses is by no means complete; it presents only the most important and typical examples. Only the music which might possibly have been heard by Shakespeare himself is here identified, since a large number of the Elizabethan and early Jacobean settings have not survived. One question with regard to the extant settings has intrigued commentators: Was it Shakespeare's practice to compose a lyric to a tune which he had already heard, or did he write his verses independently, expecting or even commissioning a composer to provide original music? There is some evidence that he used both methods.

He sometimes required a song for which he found it unnecessary to provide words, as when Lady Mortimer (*1 Henry IV*, III, i, 249) simply sings "a Welsh song." A very moving scene is that in Brutus' tent (*Julius Caesar*, IV, iii, 257 ff.) at night, before the appearance of Caesar's ghost, when Brutus requires his boy Lucius to "touch thy instrument a strain or two." The stage direction reads simply "Music, and a song." Brutus: "This is a sleepy tune . . . Gentle knave, good night."

A purely decorative song is sung by the clown Feste as a kind of lighthearted epilogue to *Twelfth*

Night: "When that I was and a little tiny boy," with its recurrent "hey, ho, the wind and the rain," and the refrain, "For the rain it raineth every day." What is remarkable is that Shakespeare echoes himself in an ironically tragic manner when, at the height of the terror and tempest in *King Lear* (III, ii, 74–77), the Fool sings:

> He that has and a little tiny wit,—
> With hey, ho, the wind and the rain,—
> Must make content with his fortunes fit,
> For the rain it raineth every day.

Among the notable songs that have no specifically dramatic significance are "When daisies pied" and "When icicles hang by the wall," which bring *Love's Labour's Lost* to its conclusion, and Ariel's song in *The Tempest,* "Where the bee sucks" (V, i, 88–94), of which there survives a musical setting by Shakespeare's contemporary, Robert Johnson. This composer was born in 1582; some of his settings of music for *Macbeth, Cymbeline,* and *The Winter's Tale* have also been preserved in 17th-century collections.

By far the most numerous group of songs consists of those which, although not essential to the action, are nevertheless skillfully embedded in it and serve to illuminate either situation or character, or both. Among these may be included the ribald Mercutio's "An old hare hoar" (*Romeo and Juliet,* II, iv, 141–146); Balthasar's "Sigh no more" (*Much Ado About Nothing,* II, iii, 64–76), for which Thomas Ford (1580–1648) supplied a musical setting; "Blow, blow, thou winter wind" and "Under the greenwood tree" in *As You Like It* (II, vii, 174–179 and II, v, 1–8); and Pandarus' "Love, love, nothing but love" (*Troilus and Cressida,* III, i, 124–136), which fits the situation, the character of the singer, and the satirical mood of the whole play. In *The Winter's Tale* (IV, iv, 303–314), there is a vocal trio, sung by Autolycus, Dorcas, and Mopsa, "Get you hence," of which a contemporary setting survives, probably by Johnson. In *The Tempest* (I, ii, 376–386), there is Ariel's "Come unto these yellow sands," and later (II, ii, 184–189) Caliban's tipsy "No more dams I'll make for fish."

Sometimes Shakespeare used vocal music to indicate breaks in the action or the passage of time. Two notable instances occur in *As You Like It.* There is one brief scene (IV, ii) given over entirely to the rendition of a "catch" for men's voices, "What shall he have that kill'd the deer?" full of ribald puns on the word "horn." The surviving music, by one John Hilton (d. 1608) may at least resemble that which was originally composed for the play. The other is "It was a lover and his lass" (V, iii, 16–34), sung by Touchstone and two pages, to music unquestionably supplied by Shakespeare's contemporary, Thomas Morley. Morley was born in 1557; he was a Gentleman (singing man) of the Royal Chapel, organist at St. Paul's, editor of anthologies, composer of madrigals, services, motets, anthems, ayres, pieces for viols and virginals, and author of *A Plaine and Easie Introduction to Practicall Musicke* (1597)—in other words, a leading practitioner in all branches of the art. Between 1596 and 1599 he was Shakespeare's neighbor in the parish of St. Helen's in Bishopsgate Ward. It is inconceivable that the two men were not at least professional acquaintances. "It was a lover and his lass" appeared in Morley's *First Booke of Ayres or Little Short Songs* in 1600, about the time when Shakespeare's comedy was first acted. Morley died in 1603.

Many musical moments occur in the plays when the script demands songs in special categories; for instance:

Pedlars' songs. In *The Winter's Tale* Autolycus, posing as a pedlar plying his trade, sings "Lawn as white as driven snow" (IV, iv, 220–232), of which the earliest known setting is by John WILSON, possibly the Jack Wilson who was a singing boy in Shakespeare's company; and, in the same scene "Will you buy any tape?" (lines 322–330).

Drinking songs. These are fairly numerous. Three are assigned to Country Justice Silence in *2 Henry IV* (V, iii): "A cup of wine that's brisk and fine" (lines 48–50); "Do me right, and dub me knight Samingo" (lines 77–79), and "Do nothing but eat and make good cheer" (lines 18–23). In *Othello* (II, iii) Iago's drinking songs, "And let me the canakin clink, clink" (lines 71–75) and "King Stephen" (lines 92–99) help him to bring about the ruin of Cassio. In *Antony and Cleopatra* (II, vii, 120–125) a boy sings "Come, thou monarch of the vine," during which the whole party, with the exception of the shrewd Octavius, becomes excessively merry. And in *The Tempest* (II, ii, 48–56) the drunken nautical butler Stephano roars out "The master, the swabber, the boatswain and I."

Serenades. The two most famous Shakespeare songs in this genre are dramatically curious, in that both are delivered, not by the suitors of the ladies concerned, but by their deputies. In *Two Gentlemen of Verona* (IV, ii, 39–53), Thurio, "foolish rival to Valentine," is induced by the faithless Proteus to bring in musicians to perform "Who is Sylvia?" under the girl's window. In *Cymbeline* (II, iii, 21–30), the detestable Cloten employs professional musicians (instructing them in the most indecorous terms) to perform "Hark, hark, the lark," for which there has been preserved an anonymous manuscript of the music that may have been used or heard by Shakespeare.

Lullabies. Of this species Shakespeare produced one outstanding specimen, "You spotted snakes" in *A Midsummer Night's Dream* (II, ii, 9–24), to which Titania is lulled to sleep by her fairies.

Music for masques. Following the fashion of his time, Shakespeare introduced spectacular interludes into his plays, requiring elaborate stage effects, dancing, and, of course, music. There is such a masque toward the end of *As You Like It* (V, iv), for which he wrote the songs for Hymen and chorus, "Then there is mirth in heaven" (lines 114–121) and "Wedding is great Juno's crown" (lines 147–152). Similarly in *Cymbeline* (V, iv, 30–92), music and voices accompany the "vision of Posthumus" by rendering "No more, thou thunder-master show." Finally, in the betrothal-masque in *The Tempest* (IV, i, 106–117), we have the chorus "Honour, riches, marriage-blessing."

Dramatically purposeful songs. Most significant of all are those musical episodes which Shakespeare firmly integrated into his plays. There is in *The ſerchant of Venice* (III, ii, 63–72) the song ("whilst assanio comments on the caskets to himself") "Tell ne where is fancy bred?" Commanded by Portia, it lls up the time during Bassanio's meditation; it pro-ides philosophical reflections on the deceptiveness f outward appearances; and while he is wavering etween "gold, silver, and lead," it hints at the roper choice with its emphatic rhymes on *bred*, *ead*, and nouri*shed*.

In *Twelfth Night* (II, iii, 40 ff.), there is a com-lete, if miniature, comic secular cantata (a kind of nusical playlet), necessary to indicate passage of me, development of plot, atmosphere, mood, and haracterization. During this roisterous scene the lown sings "O mistress mine," the tune of which ppeared in Morley's *First Booke of Consort Lessons* 1599) within months of the first production of the lay. Whether Shakespeare used Morley's music or ſorley wrote the setting for Shakespeare's lyric is a uestion still in dispute. There follows the catch ung by Sir Toby Belch, the Clown, and Sir Andrew guecheek, "Hold thy peace, thou knave"; then a hree-men's-song, "Three merry men," and snatches f "There dwelt a man in Babylon," to the tradi-ional tune of "Greensleeves," and a ballad snatch, O, the twelfth day of December." The climax oc-urs with the entrance of the puritanical steward ſalvolio, who threatens the whole company of oisterers, saying, "If you can separate yourself and our misdemeanours, you are welcome to the house; not, an it would please you to take leave of her, he is very willing to bid you farewell." Sir Toby nmediately seizes upon the word "farewell," and egins singing "Farewell, dear heart," to the tune of obert Jones' "Farewell, dear love" (from his *First ooke of Songes & Ayres*, 1600), with comic altera-ions of the words and various spoken interjections, ntil Malvolio is forced to retire, with Sir Toby's Dost thou think, because thou art virtuous, there hall be no more cakes and ale?"

In *Measure for Measure* (IV, i, 1–9), a boy, pre-umably with a lute, sings, "Take, O, take those lips way." This is entirely appropriate as a song of onsolation for Mariana "of the moated grange," vho has been betrayed by the faithless Angelo. The arliest known setting is by John Wilson (1594–673), referred to above, who acted the part of althasar in *Much Ado*. Various publications of the 7th century contain his settings of "Sigh no more," Lawn as white as driven snow," and "Where the ee sucks." In *The Tempest* (I, ii, 396–404) Ariel ngs "Full fathom five thy father lies." He addresses to Ferdinand, who is convinced that his father has een drowned. It describes the decomposition of human body—a ghastly topic. Shakespeare trans-igures the revolting image into one of his prettiest ongs, thus emphasizing the point that even the most bhorrent physical facts are not to be taken seriously n this blithe fairy-tale comedy. The cheerful orig-nal setting by Robert Johnson is extant. Nothing ould be more indicative of Shakespeare's inspired se of song than this extraordinary composition.

Instrumental Music. Shakespeare hardly ever de-nanded incidental music merely for the music's sake. or him music was a fine dramatic tool. Of course e used it for purely practical purposes, as any other playwright, ancient or modern, has done. For dances, solo or ensemble, he could select from an unlimited supply of pavans, galliards, almains, corantos, and the like, which the composers of his time were turning out in great numbers. For rustic music he required the tabor and pipe. For marches he called for a "Danish march" in *Hamlet* (III, ii, 97) and a "dead march" at the end of *King Lear*. Hunting horns were required in *The Merry Wives of Windsor* (V, v, 107), *King Lear* (I, iii, 11 and iv, 8), and *A Midsummer Night's Dream* (IV, i, 107), although in the last instance Theseus seems to be prouder of the "music" of his hounds. For battles there were "the shrill trump, the spirit-stirring drum," and "th' ear-piercing fife" (*Othello*, III, iii, 351–352). How Shakespeare's battle music actually sounded may be realized by examining William Byrd's surviving score for *The Battle in My Ladye Nevells Booke* (c. 1591), which contains "The Marche before the Battell," "The Marche of Footmen," "The marche of horsmen," "The trumpetts," "The bagpipe and the drone," "The flute and the droome," "The marche to the fighte," "The retreat," "The buriing of the dead," "Ye soldiers dance," and "The galliard for the victorie." These pieces are arranged for keyboard, but the instrumentation is clearly indicated.

The use of fife and drum for festival torchlight processions is also indicated in Shylock's disparaging allusion to "the drum / And the vile squeaking of the wry-neck'd fife" in *The Merchant of Venice* (II, v, 29–30). For moments of pomp and circumstance there had to be elaborate trumpet "flourishes," as in *King Lear* (II, i, 81 and V, iii, 111 ff.); sometimes with the addition of kettledrums, as in *Hamlet* (I, iv, 11), and even cannon (V, ii, 286–288); and in *Coriolanus* (V, iv, 51), "Trumpets, hautboys, drums beat, all together." The "tucket" seems to have been a particular trumpet call by which its commander could be identified, as in *King Lear*: [*Tucket within.* "Hark, the Duke's trumpets" and "What trumpet's that?" Regan: "I know't; my sister's." (II, i, 81 and iv, 185–186).

Much more significant than these obvious uses of music for practical purposes is Shakespeare's employment of instrumental compositions to create a particular mood or emotional atmosphere. Most striking is the entrance of musicians, who simply "play music," in *The Merchant of Venice* (V, i, 68) so as to transport the audience from the near-tragedy of the severe court of Venice to the moonlit romance of Portia's garden at Belmont. Again, in *Antony and Cleopatra* (IV, iii, 12) when Antony's soldiers feel premonitions of oncoming disaster, "music of the hautboys as under the stage." And in *King Lear* (IV, vii), as the King begins to regain his sanity, music is used not only as atmosphere but also as therapy. The Doctor calls out, "Louder the music there!" In at least one other place Shakespeare deliberately uses music to define and highlight character: that of the sentimental Duke Orsino. As *Twelfth Night* opens, he declaims, "If music be the food of love, play on." The characterization is completed with the Duke's demand for "that old and antique song we heard last night" (II, iv, 3). The song is then sung by Feste. It is "Come away, death." [Richmond Noble,

Shakespeare's Use of Song, 1923; *William Byrd: Collected Works*, E. H. Fellowes, ed., Vol. XVIII, 1950; John H. Long, *Shakespeare's Use of Music*, 2 vols., 1955, 1961; F. W. Sternfeld, *Music in Shakespearean Tragedy*, 1963.]—E.B.

music room. In the Elizabethan theatre, a room for the performance of music offstage during a play. Of all the rooms in the Elizabethan theatre, the music room has been one of the most difficult to locate precisely. That such a room actually existed for purposes of allowing offstage music to be performed during the play is attested to by numerous stage directions within the texts of various plays. Probably located on the second level of the theatre, the music room was sometimes used for a chamber scene (in Killigrew's *Parson's Wedding* (1640), a bedroom scene in Act I is placed "above in the music room"); at other times it was apparently used for elevated battle scenes. (See PLAYHOUSE STRUCTURE.) Some theatres may not have had a special music room, for another text reveals that "the Fiddlers play in the tiring room," which was located behind the main stage. There is evidence that both the Red Bull in 1608 and the Swan in 1611 contained a music room. Other theatres before those dates, though they might not have had such a specified area, may have used one of the curtained rooms of the gallery to conceal musicians.

A recent controversy has centered on the question of whether there was a music room in the Globe, especially significant since so many of Shakespeare's plays call for music offstage and demand accompaniment for songs. The best evidence presented so far suggests that there was no music room over the stage at the Globe before 1609. After 1609, however, and as a result of productions by the King's Men at Blackfriars "private theatre" (which did have such a room), it is believed possible that such an innovation may have been incorporated into the Globe. The hypothesis advanced by J. Cranford Adams in 1942 that a music room may have been located on a third level of the tiring house has more recently been challenged and negated. [E. K. Chambers, *The Elizabethan Stage*, 1923; J. Cranford Adams, *The Globe Playhouse*, 1942; Richard Hosley, "Was There a Music Room in Shakespeare's Globe?" *Shakespeare Survey 13* (1960), 113-123.]—D.P.D.

Mustardseed. In *A Midsummer Night's Dream*, one of Queen Titania's fairies enlisted to attend Bottom.

Mutius. In *Titus Andronicus*, youngest son of Titus. When Titus attempts to prevent Bassianus from carrying off Lavinia, Mutius interferes on Bassianus' behalf and is killed by his father (I, i).

mythic criticism. A critical movement that attempts to explore the relationship of literature to primitive myth and ritual. Mythic criticism, which has developed out of insights provided by modern anthropology and Jungian psychology, focuses particularly on what are referred to as "archetypal" patterns or figures in literature. An archetype is a basic apprehension of, or response to, reality which lies embedded, in Jung's terms, within the "collective unconscious" of every individual and which is expressed in certain universal, continually recurring myths and rituals. These myths are embodied in literature and are the source of our profound emotional response to it. In Shakespearean studies, th mythic approach has generally derived from th thesis that drama as we know it is a later develop ment of primitive religious rituals organized aroun the myths of the seasons and of the ritualistic deat of the hero (tragedy) and his subsequent resur rection (comedy). Aside from this basic assumptior however, there is little agreement among critic themselves as to the function and relevance of myt in Shakespearean drama. Thus, it is less than ac curate to speak of these critics as representing "school" of criticism. Some of them, for exampl see a variety of basic myths underlying the plays others argue that the entire canon is the developmen of only one supremely significant, universal myth such as that of the redemption. Still other critic employ myth merely as an ancillary, supportiv feature of their critical analysis.

In Shakespearean criticism the mythic approac was introduced by the classical scholar Gilbert Mur ray in *Hamlet and Orestes* (1914). Murray's ex ploration of the archetypal roots of the legends o Hamlet and Orestes revealed both stories to b rooted in "the prehistoric and world-wide ritual bat tle of Summer and Winter, of Life and Death, whic has played so vast a part in the mental developmen of the human race . . . ." Somewhat similar ap proaches, although ones with more of a symboli than mythic orientation, are to be found in Coli Still's *Shakespeare's Mystery Play* (1921) and in th works of G. Wilson Knight (see SYMBOLISM). It wa not until the 1940's, however, that mythic criticisn assumed a real importance in Shakespearean studies In that decade George Kernodle's *From Art t Theatre* (1944) and Francis Fergusson's *The Idea o a Theatre* (1949) explored the ritual origins of th theatre and the significance of those origins in deter mining dramatic form. Fergusson's analysis of *Ham let* attempts to show the ritualistic pattern o "rhythm" as the determining element of the forn of the play. Other Shakespearean tragedies have bee analyzed from the standpoint of myth by Herber Weisinger ("The Myth and Ritual Approach t Shakespearean Tragedy," *Centennial Review*, 1957) Clifford Leech (*Shakespeare's Tragedies*, 1950); J. I M. Stewart (*Character and Motive in Shakespeare* 1949); and John Holloway (*The Sory of the Night* 1961).

Many of the critics who employ mythic element attempt to relate Shakespeare to specifically Christian origins, seeing the tragic heroes as Christ figure and in some cases citing biblical analogues to illuminate the themes of the plays. This has given rise to a debate on the religious values in the plays (see RELIGION). An example of this approach is Joseph A Bryant's *Hippolyta's View* (1961).

The mythical elements of the comedies have bee fruitfully explored by Northrop Frye and C. L Barber. Frye's "The Argument of Comedy," later incorporated into his *Anatomy of Criticism* (1957) is a particularly convincing analysis of the structure of comedy. Barber's *Shakespeare's Festive Comedy* (1951) is an examination of the "Saturnalian" elements in the comedies. Barber attempts to demonstrate the interplay between social and artistic form, in this case between the festival occasions of Elizabethan holidays, obscurely rooted in pagan ritual nd Shakespeare's embodiment of that form in his lays.

It is, however, Shakespeare's last plays, the romances, that have been the focus of the most conerted (and most controversial) mythic criticism. A lay like *The Winter's Tale*, for example, with its mphasis on death and regeneration, bears a strong nalogy to the myth of the seasons. The mythic interpretation of the romances has been advanced in a umber of articles, and even employed by critics not rdinarily associated with mythic criticism, such as . M. W. Tillyard (*Shakespeare's Last Plays*, 1938) nd Derek Traversi (*Shakespeare: The Last Phase*, 954).

The controversy over mythic criticism arises from he attempt to determine what precisely is the relaionship of primitive myth to a finished artistic achievement. The critics of the mythic approach have charged that its practitioners too often fail to recognize the very characteristics which distinguish a work of art. They are accused of identifying the play with the myth and of mistaking anthropology for literary criticism. Although there is justification for these charges, the best of the myth critics have given evidence of their awareness of the complexities and problems which underlie their critical method—problems which will have to be dealt with if the method is to assume a more important place in the criticism of Shakespearean drama. [Robert Hapgood, "Shakespeare and the Ritualists," *Shakespeare Survey 15*, 1962; Herbert Weisinger, "The Myth and Ritual Approach," *The Shakespeare Newsletter*, April–May, 1964.]—E.Q.

N

name. The origin of the name "Shakespeare" is obscured by history, but it apparently developed from an epithet conferred upon a valiant warrior. This possibility was recognized even in Shakespeare's time; as a contemporary account (*A Restitution of Decayed Intelligence*, 1605) put it, "Breakspear, Shakspear and the like, have been names imposed vpon the first bearers of them for valour and feats of arms." That the connection of the name with military valor continued to be made in Shakespeare's time is attested to by a reference in Fuller's *Worthies* (1662) to "the War-like sound of his Surname" (see Thomas FULLER) and by the alleged allusion to Shakespeare in Spenser's "Colin Clout's Come Home Again" (1595):

> A gentler shepherd may nowhere be found,
> Whose Muse, full of high thought's invention,
> Doth like himself heroically sound.

Roland Lewis has collected over 100 variant spellings of the name, the most common being "Shakespeare," "Shakspeare," "Shakespear," "Shakespere," "Shakspere," "Shaksper," "Shaxpere," "Shackspere." The six signatures generally accepted as authentically Shakespeare's give the following spellings: Belott-Mountjoy suit—Shaksp; Blackfriars Gate-House (purchase)—Shakspe; Blackfriars Gate-House (mortgage)—Shakspe; will (first sheet)—Shakspere; will (second sheet)—Shakspere; will (third sheet)—Shakspeare. Despite the fact that the name is not spelled "Shakespeare" in any of the six signatures, that form has become the dominant one in the 20th century. In support of the spelling is the fact that it is the one that recurs most frequently in contemporary allusions to the poet and on many documents, including the playwright's own will. The First Folio and the title pages of many of the early quartos also employ this spelling. "Shakespeare" is also the spelling on the tombs of Shakespeare's wife, his daughter Susanna, and her husband, John Hall. [B. Roland Lewis, *The Shakespeare Documents*, 1940.]

Nashe, Thomas (1567–?1601). Dramatist and pamphleteer. Born at Lowestoft, Suffolk, the son of a minister, Nashe was educated at Cambridge. His first book, *The Anatomie of Absurditie*, was entered in the Stationers' Register in 1588, but it was preceded in publication by an epistle which Nashe wrote as a Preface to Robert Greene's pamphlet *Menaphon* (1589). Addressed "To the Gentlemen Students of Both Universities," the epistle contains some caustic remarks on actors and on those dramatists who were not university trained (see UNIVERSITY WITS). There seems to be a clear reference, in the attack, to Kyd and to his authorship of the UR-HAMLET.

Nashe numbered among his patrons Sir George Carey (the lord chamberlain and patron of Shakespeare's acting company) and Archbishop Whitgift. The latter employed Nashe and John Lyly to answer the attacks of the pseudonymous Puritan pamphleteer Martin MARPRELATE. The controversy produced from both sides some of the most spirited prose of the period. Nashe's friendship with Greene and Lyly led to a quarrel with Spenser's friend Gabriel Harvey and the result was the scurrilous controversy carried on in pamphlets published by the two men. Harvey was clearly no match for Nashe, who indulged in some brilliantly satiric caricatures of his enemy. The controversy was finally suppressed as a public scandal in 1599 and Nashe's pamphlets were among those ordered burned by the archbishop (see John WHITGIFT). Some commentators believe that the controversy is the model for the disputes between Armado and Moth in *Love's Labour's Lost*. The belief that Nashe is satirized as Moth is based on numerous references in the play including the descriptions of Moth as "juvenal" (I, ii, 8; III, i, 67). As a satirist Nashe was more than once equated with Juvenal, most notably in the same passage of Robert Greene's *Groats-worth of Wit* which contains a celebrated attack on Shakespeare.

In 1592 Nashe reversed his former censure of the popular stage by defending it in his pamphlet *Pierce Penniless his Supplication to the Divell*. The pamphlet is important in the dating of the Henry VI plays for its reference to "brave Talbot . . . newe embalmed with the teares of ten thousand spectators" (see 1 HENRY VI: *Sources*). Of Nashe's dramatic work the only extant play written solely by him is *Summer's Last Will and Testament* (1592). In 1597 he had to flee London because of his part in the authorship of the scandalous THE ISLE OF DOGS (1597).

Nashe is distinguished as the originator of the picaresque novel in English. His *The Unfortunate Traveller, or the Life of Jack Wilton* (1594) is a racy and revealing picture of an Elizabethan rogue. In one line there is an echo of *Titus Andronicus*.

Pierce Penniless has been cited as the source of a number of elements in *Hamlet*, including the description of drinking as a Danish vice (I, iv, 15), Hamlet's references to cosmetics (III, i, 150; V, i, 213–214), and his advice to the players (III, ii, 1–50). J. Dover Wilson has argued that Nashe is the author of many sections of the three Henry VI plays and that he collaborated with Shakespeare on an earlier lost version of *The Taming of the Shrew*.

Nash Family. Stratford neighbors of Shakespeare. ***Thomas Nash*** (d. 1587) was a collector of the STRATFORD TITHES which were subsequently bought

The Nash Family

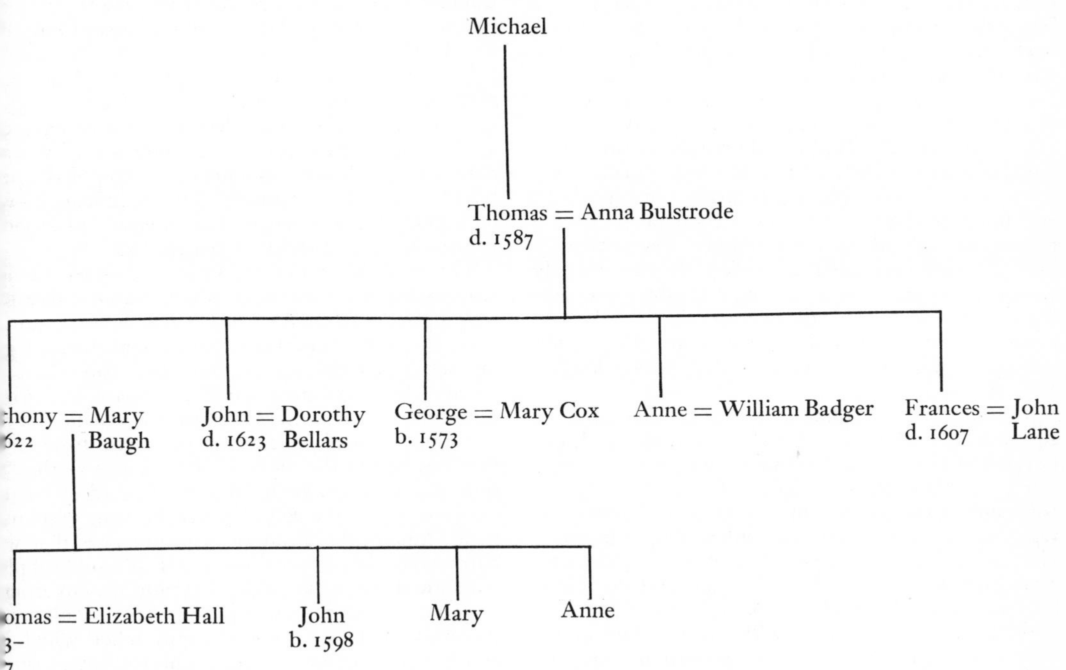

Shakespeare. He had two sons, Anthony and ın, both of whom were left 26s. 8d. by Shake-:are to purchase memorial rings. ***Anthony Nash*** (d. 2) was a witness to Shakespeare's purchase of land 1602 (see Old Stratford). He also witnessed an :eement between Shakespeare and William Rep-gham in 1614. In Shakespeare's will, he is de-ibed as "gentleman," and at his death in 1622 was e of the wealthiest men in Stratford.

His brother, ***John Nash*** (d. 1623), also witnessed akespeare's purchase of land in Old Stratford. He s one of the lessees, with Shakespeare, of the atford tithes. He was arrested in 1619 as the leader an anti-Puritan Stratford mob which opposed the tallation of the Puritan minister Thomas Wilson.

Anthony Nash's son ***Thomas*** (1593–1647) married akespeare's granddaughter Elizabeth Hall, the ly child of Susanna Shakespeare and John Hall. omas was educated at Lincoln's Inn and in 1622 erited some land, a house in Bridge Street, Strat-d, and an inn known as the Bear. When his her-in-law, John Hall, died in 1635, he left Nash "study of Books" at New Place. During the civil r Nash was an adherent of the royalist forces. In 43, as master of New Place, he entertained Queen :nrietta Maria during her sojourn in Stratford. ısh died in 1647 and was buried in the chancel of : Stratford church, immediately to the right of his ındfather-in-law, William Shakespeare. A shield owing the arms of the Nash, Hall, and Shakespeare nilies is carved on his tomb. [Joseph Q. Adams, *A fe of William Shakespeare*, 1923; Mark Eccles, *akespeare in Warwickshire*, 1961.]

Nathaniel, Sir. In *Love's Labour's Lost,* a hedge-priest and friend of Holofernes. As Alexander in the dramatic representation of the Nine Worthies (V, ii), Sir Nathaniel becomes dismayed by Berowne's jests and is unable to continue in his role. Costard defends Sir Nathaniel as a mild and honest man and considers him miscast as Alexander.

National Theatre Company. The performing wing of a British National Theatre, inaugurated in 1962, to be under the direction of Sir Laurence Olivier and subsidized by the British Government at £130,-000 per annum. The idea of a British National Theatre was discussed for nearly a century, but it was not until 1940/1 that a drive was instituted to raise funds and make the dream a reality.

The idea of the national theatre as a "museum of the drama" was elucidated by Olivier. However, to insure that such a museum would not become stuffy, conventional, or academic, Kenneth Tynan was chosen as literary manager.

The National Theatre took over the Old Vic, which gave its last performance June 16, 1963. The National Theatre Company's production of *Hamlet*, with Peter O'Toole, Michael Redgrave, and Diana Wynward, opened October 22, 1963 and ran for 27 performances, to mixed notices. This was followed by Olivier starring in and directing *Othello*, a production that has won unanimous acclaim.

Neilson, [Lilian] Adelaide. Real name **Elizabeth Ann Brown** (1848–1880). Actress. Born in Leeds, Adelaide Neilson had to overcome grim poverty. As a bar girl at a pub near the Haymarket Theatre, she early developed a reputation for declaiming Shakespeare, and in 1865 she made her acting debut at a Margate theatre as Juliet under the name of Lizzie Ann Bland. She adopted successively the names of Lilian Adelaide Lessont and Neilson. Her first London appearance was also in the role of Juliet in 1865. The critics were much impressed with her performance, describing her as beautiful, graceful, and possessing a musical voice. She was lauded for the graceful and tender early scenes which she was able to develop into scenes of tragic intensity at the end. In 1868 she played Rosalind in Edinburgh, and Rosalind and Juliet at the Drury Lane. She made many visits to the United States, playing Beatrice, Isabella, Viola, and Imogen. Her reputation as a tragedienne during the second half of the 19th century was unrivaled; her Juliet was regarded as perfect. In the comedy roles, however, it was noted that she was self-conscious and tended to overact; her Viola was merely "pretty," while her Rosalind was bright, yet lacking in poetry. [*Dictionary of National Biography*, 1885– .]

Neilson, William Allan (1869–1948). Scottish-born educator and scholar. Neilson was educated at Edinburgh and Harvard universities. After some years of teaching, he became president of Smith College in 1917 and served until 1939. "Neilson of Smith" was regarded as one of America's outstanding educators. His books include the scholarly *The Origins and Sources of the Courts of Love* (1899) and the popular handbooks: *Essentials of Poetry* (1912) and *The Facts about Shakespeare* (with A. H. Thorndike, 1913; rev., 1931). He also edited several anthologies: *English and Scottish Popular Ballads* (with R. A. Witham, 1909); *The Chief Elizabethan Dramatists Excluding Shakespeare* (1911); and *Chief British Poets of the Fourteenth and Fifteenth Centuries* (with K. G. T. Webster, 1916). His edition of *The Complete Plays and Poems of Shakespeare*, first published in 1906, was revised in 1942 with the collaboration of Charles Jarvis Hill. Neilson was also editor of The Tudor Shakespeare, *Webster's New International Dictionary of the English Language* (2nd ed., 1934), and *Webster's Biographical Dictionary* (1st ed., 1943, 2nd ed., 1948). [*Essays Contributed in Honor of President William Allan Neilson*, 1939; Margaret Farrand Thorp, *Neilson of Smith*, 1956.]

neoclassicism. Term used to describe the classicism that prevailed in England from the Restoration (1660) to the flowering of Romanticism at the end of the 18th century. English neoclassicism looked to classical literature (e.g., Vergil, Horace) and contemporary French neoclassical writings (e.g., the classical tragedy of Racine), not only as models for writing, but for attitudes toward life and art in general. The neoclassic period was marked by a high regard for order, reason, and rules. In art, this was expressed through form, logic, restrained emotion, symmetry, good taste, and decorum. The last was a crucial concept involving propriety; in drama it meant that style should be appropriate to situation, place, and character (e.g., a member of the lower orders should not speak majestic poetry).

A neoclassical stricture that applied only to drama and that gave rise to much debate in the 18th century was the concept of unity—specifically the unity of time, place, and action. These classical unities were derived somewhat erroneously from Aristotle. (Aristotle did insist on unity of action, warning at same time that this is not necessarily achieved focusing on one character; he simply mentions u of time as desirable, and unity of place is not m tioned by him at all.) Nevertheless the three uni developed into rules for effective drama in Italy d ing the Renaissance.

During the Restoration, the precepts of neocla cism naturally became the criteria for evaluating Looking back on their predecessors, the neoclassic applied their strictures to the literature of Eliza thans and Jacobeans—to none more than Shakespe —and found them wanting. The Renaissance—w its unbounded enthusiasm and intensity of respo to life—was considered a barbaric age.

The neoclassical evaluation of Shakespeare ran from outright rejection, of which Thomas RYME the supreme example, to the real appreciation John DRYDEN, who acknowledged Shakespeare's g ius and regretted his excesses and bad taste. France, VOLTAIRE attacked Shakespeare, compar him unfavorably with Racine and Corneille.) It the application of neoclassical principles to his w that resulted in the view of Shakespeare as the " tutor'd genius"—a great artist who could be excu his violation of the rules because he was ignorant them. Among the Shakespearean practices that w considered "incorrect" were his use of subpl which destroyed the unity of action; his covering large periods of time within one play, a violation the unity of time; his use of comic relief, which no place in neoclassical tragedy; his romantic settir and the anachronisms and inaccuracies wh cropped up in his historical plays. The view Shakespeare as ignorant of good practices in writ drama led to the "improvements" of his plays (ADAPTATIONS) in which his work was "corrected" make it conform to neoclassical standards. See CR CISM—17TH CENTURY; CRITICISM—18TH CENTURY.

Nerissa. In *The Merchant of Venice*, Portia's sp ited gentlewoman-in-waiting and confidante. Ner marries Gratiano and then, disguised as a law cle accompanies her mistress to Venice to save Antor

Nestor. In Greek legend and in Homer's *Iliad*, king of Pylos and the oldest and wisest of the Gre generals who fought at Troy, accustomed to off ing sage advice at considerable length. In *Troilus a Cressida*, Nestor appears as the garrulous but sa old counselor in the Greek camp. He aligns hi self with Ulysses in the attempt to rouse Achil from his retirement by declaring Ajax the "worth man."

Nestor's classical reputation for judicial wisdom reflected on the Shakespeare monument which li Nestor with Socrates and Vergil:

IVDICIO PYLIVM, GENIO SOCRATEM, ARTE MARONEM:
TERRA TEGIT, POPVLVS MAERET, OLYMPVS HABET.

The reference to "Pylivm" is to Nestor, the king Pylos.

Neville, Anne. See ANNE NEVILLE, LADY.

Neville, John (1925–). Actor and produc Neville studied for the stage at the Royal Acader of Dramatic Art and made his debut in a walk-role in *Richard II* in 1947. Subsequently, he appear with the Open Air Theatre, the Lowestoft reperto group, the Birmingham Repertory Company, a

Bristol and London Old Vic companies. His kespearean repertory covers a wide range of :s. He alternated with Richard Burton as Othello Iago in the Old Vic's 1955/6 production of *ello*, appeared in New York with the Old Vic 956, and toured the United States with them in 7/8. He directed *Henry V* for the Old Vic 60) and has directed at the Bristol Old Vic. *'ho's Who in the Theatre*, 1961.]

Jew Cambridge Shakespeare, The (1921–1962). A volume series of Shakespeare's works. The New nbridge has been edited on the basis of the scien- : bibliography set forth by A. W. Pollard and ers. The first play in the series, *The Tempest* 21), contains a general introduction by Sir Arthur iller-Couch and a textual introduction by J. ver Wilson. After the death of the former in 4, Wilson worked largely alone as general editor :he series.

Jewington Butts theatre. Elizabethan theatre lo- ed in the village of Newington in Surrey, a mile ay from London Bridge and separated from the akside by St. George's Fields. The history of the wington Butts is rather obscure. (Butts are tar- s in archery.) The theatre was probably built at ut the same time as the Curtain and the Theatre, 6. The first mention of the use of Newington tts as a theatre occurs in a letter from the privy incil to the Surrey justices of the peace in May :o:

> Notwithstanding their late order geven to the Lord Maiour to forbidd all playes within and bout the Cittie untill Michalmas next for avoyd- inge of infection, nevertheles certen players do playe sunderie daies every weeke at Newington Buttes on that parte of Surrey without the juris- diccion of the said Lord Maior contrary to their Lorships' order; their Lordships requier the Jus- ices not only to enquier who they be that disobey heir comaundement in that behalf, and not only o forbidd them expresly for playing in any of heis remote places nere unto the Cittie untill Michaelmas, but to have regard that within the recincte of Surrey none be permitted to play; if ny do to comitt them and to advertise, &c.

other letter to the justices of Surrey and the lord yor of London was sent by the privy council on y 11, 1586 and for a similar reason, that is, the cessity of avoiding large gatherings of people in ler to prevent the spread of plague. In 1591 or 2 the privy council authorized the reopening of Rose theatre and cited the inconvenient location the Newington Butts. See ROSE THEATRE.

The theatre at Newington was probably at least rtly under the control of Philip Henslowe. Hen- we's diary records 10 days of performances in 4 by Shakespeare's company, the Chamberlain's en, in combination with the Admiral's Men at the wington Butts theatre:

> In the name of god Amen beginige at Newington my Lord Admeralle men & my Lorde Chamberlen men As ffolowethe 1594.

June 3	[5?]	Heaster & Asheweros	viij^s.
4	[6?]	the Jewe of Malta	x^s.
5	[7?]	Andronicous	xij^s.
6	[8?]	Cutlacke	xj.^{s}
8	[10?]	ne Bellendon	xvij^s.
9	[11?]	Hamlet	viij^s.
10	[12?]	Heaster	v^s.
11	[13?]	the Tamyne of A Shrowe	ix^s.
12	[14?]	Andronicous	vij^s.
13	[15?]	the Jewe	iiij^s.

The performances at Newington Butts were limited in number, mostly because they were not profitable. Compared with the average receipts from the Rose that May of 41s., Newington yielded a daily average of 9s. The use of the Rose, however, had been curtailed because the authorities feared a recurrent outbreak of the plague. Their appearances at Newington Butts in 1594 were the first for the combined Admiral's-Chamberlain's company following the plague years of 1592–1594. A possibility exists that Sussex' Men also played at Newington Butts for eight days that spring, before the theatre was taken over by the Admiral's-Chamberlain's group. Thereafter the theatre fell into disuse; according to C. W. Wallace, by 1599 Newington was "only a memory." [E. K. Chambers, *The Elizabethan Stage*, 1923.]

New Place. The second largest mansion in Stratford, purchased by Shakespeare on the 4th of May, 1597. The property had two gardens, two orchards, and two barns. The house, built of brick and timbers, stood in nearly an acre of ground near the center of town. Shakespeare paid £60 for the place, a small price for so fine a property, but the house was apparently somewhat dilapidated. In the middle of the 16th century it was described as being "In great ruin and decay," but in Shakespeare's day the house was still a symbol of the owner's high social position. It had been built in the last part of the 15th century for Sir Hugh Clopton, lord mayor of London, who referred to it in his will (1496) as his "great house." It was properly so called. The lot had a frontage of 60 feet and was 70 feet long at its greatest depth. The house had 10 fireplaces and its gable was 28 feet high.

Shakespeare purchased the house from William UNDERHILL, a Catholic whose name had appeared on the 1592 recusancy returns along with John Shakespeare's. The fact that Shakespeare was able to buy one of the largest houses in his native town, which he had left about 10 years before in apparent poverty, has invited speculation. One of the explanations

NEW PLACE. THIS ENGRAVING IS FROM MALONE'S EDITION OF SHAKESPEARE (1790). IT WAS MADE FROM A DRAWING FOUND AT CLOPTON IN 1786.

is that his dedication of *Venus and Adonis* and *The Rape of Lucrece* to the earl of Southampton had been liberally rewarded by the earl. Nicholas Rowe, in his *Life of Shakespeare* (1709), writes: "There is one instance so singular in the magnificence of the patron of Shakespeare's that if I had not been assured that the story was handed down by Sir William Davenant, who was probably very well acquainted with his affairs, I should not have ventured to have inserted it that My Lord Southampton at one time gave him a thousand pounds to enable him to go through with a purchase which he heard he had a mind to." The tale is not improbable, except for the size of the gift. It was customary for a person accepting the dedication of a volume to reward the author with a gift of money, at least of £2, but wealthy patrons often gave much more. However, it was not necessary for the poet to seek help to finance a transaction involving only £60. By 1597 the acting profession had become very lucrative, and Shakespeare was a full sharer in the most successful company in London.

After repairing the house, Shakespeare settled his wife and daughters there. He stayed in it on his visits to Stratford and lived in it from about 1611, when he retired from active participation in the Globe, until his death in 1616.

The property remained in the hands of the poet's descendants (see Baldwin BROOKES) until the death of the last of them, his granddaughter Elizabeth Nash. On the death of her second husband, Sir John Bernard, it was sold to Sir Edward Walker. Walker lived there until his death in 1677, bequeathing it to the descendants of Sir Hugh Clopton, its original builder. In 1702 Sir John Clopton tore it down and erected a completely new structure in its place. That building was in turn demolished in 1759 by its owner, Francis Gastrell. However, there is extant a sketch of the frontage of the second structure made in 1737. It indicates that the house must have been an imposing building. [J. O. Halliwell-Phillipps, *A Historical Account of New Place*, 1864; Frank Simpson, "New Place," *Shakespeare Survey 5*, 1952.]

New Shakspere Society. A scholarly organization. The New Shakspere Society was founded in 1873 by F. J. Furnivall. Like the original Shakespeare Society (1840–1853), it endeavored to make available primary material. Under its sponsorship there appeared reprints of the First Folio and Quarto texts, parallel text editions, sources and analogues, plays by Shakespeare's contemporaries, documents illustrative of Elizabethan social history, etc. A total of eight series were projected, but one was abandoned and others left incomplete because of rival publications; thus the series of sources and analogues was discontinued because much of the same material was currently appearing in Gollancz's Shakespeare Library. Publication of scholarly research was the other major activity of the Society. The papers read at the annual meetings and later reprinted in the Society's *Transactions* (1874–1892) represent some of the most important scholarship of the period. Besides Furnivall, contributors included F. G. Fleay, James Spedding, Richard Simpson, J. K. Ingram, Nicolaus Delius, S. A. Brooke, R. G. Moulton, S. L. Lee, C. H. Herford, William Poel, and J. W. Hales. Many of the papers, especially those presented at the earlier meetings, were concerned with dating the plays means of VERSE TESTS—a favorite preoccupatior Furnivall and one of the stated objectives of Society. In 1894 the Society was disbanded.

New Way to Pay Old Debts, A. See Philip M SINGER.

New York Shakespeare Festival, The. A free matic festival held annually in New York City was the idea of Joseph Papp, its founder and p ducer-director, whose purpose was to encourage cultivate interest in poetic drama with emphasis Shakespeare's works, to establish an annual Sh speare summer festival, and to build a replica of Elizabethan playhouse. This idea was mode launched in 1954 in the Emanuel Presbyte Church on East 6th Street with $200 and ligh equipment from an old Bronx movie house. In 1 the city made the East River Amphitheatre avail to the company; then, a year later, with the help private grants and contributions, the troupe ope the summer season in Central Park on a tempor portable stage. Despite great financial difficulties other harassments, the festival was firmly establis in 1962 when the Delacorte Theatre was construc and opened on the Belvedere Lake site in Cen Park. With the purchase of a specially desig portable stage in 1964, a second company was ganized to give performances in parks and pl grounds in all parts of New York.

Aside from the annual summer festival in Cen Park, there have been many winter activities. Wi performances were held from 1957 to 1959 in Heckscher Theatre and since then the New Y Board of Education has sponsored productions the city high schools. These productions have come an important part of the curriculum of city schools. Under the auspices of the New Y State Council on the Arts, the festival has toured state of New York.

The most striking feature of Papp's conceptio that the performances are free. This, Papp felt, a vital element of the idea of a public theatre. T festival has been characterized not only by its de cratic spirit but by lively, robust productio among which have been *Romeo and Juliet*, *Jul Caesar*, *As You Like It*, *Titus Andronicus*, *Macbe The Two Gentlemen of Verona*, *Richard Twelfth Night*, *Antony and Cleopatra*, *Hamlet*, *T Tempest*, *Othello*, *The Merchant of Venice*, *Lo Labour's Lost* and *Coriolanus*. In 1964, as a depart from the strictly Shakespearean fare, Sophoc *Electra* was played.

Nicholson, Brinsley (1824–1892). Scholar. Af serving as a medical officer with the British army a number of years, Nicholson retired in 1870 a devoted the remainder of his life to scholarly acti ties. In 1875 he edited for the New Shakspere Soci the First Folio and the First Quarto of *Henry V*. then set about preparing a parallel text edition, b ill health intervened and the project was comple by P. A. Daniels in 1877. There followed edito work on Jonson, Chapman, and Donne. His editi of Jonson's plays for the Mermaid Series, not qu completed at the time of his death, was finished C. H. Herford (3 vols., 1893–1894). His work Donne formed the basis of the Muses' Library e tion (1896). Nicholson also edited Reginald Sco coverie of Witchcraft and read several papers to New Shakspere Society.

Nicholson, Samuel. See Acolastus, his After tte.

Nicolai, Carl Otto Ehrenfried. See music based on kespeare: *19th century to 1850.*

Nicoll, [John Ramsay] Allardyce (1894–). olar, professor emeritus of English language and rature at the University of Birmingham, editor of annual *Shakespeare Survey*. While a professor at mingham, Nicoll founded the Shakespeare Insti- at Stratford-upon-Avon in 1951 and remained director until his retirement in 1961. He is also a stee of the Shakespeare Birthplace Trust. His re than two dozen books deal with various aspects drama or the theatre: English and continental matic literature, history of the theatre, play pro-tion, etc. His several volumes of English stage ory are exhaustive studies of the periods from Restoration to the 20th century; in effect they continuations of the studies made by E. K. Cham-s and G. E. Bentley of the earlier periods. Two of books are concerned specifically with Shake-are: *Dryden as an Adapter of Shakespeare* (1922) *Studies in Shakespeare* (1927). He has also ed the works of Tourneur and Chapman's *mer* and has written the Introduction to *The zabethans* (1956), a profusely illustrated survey of period.

Nisbett, Louisa Cranstoun (c. 1812–1858). Actress. rn in London, Mrs. Nisbett began acting under name Miss Mordaunt as a child accompanying father, Frederick Hayes Macnamara. She made adult stage debut in 1826 as Lady Teazle in eenwich, followed by an appearance as Juliet at diff, and portrayals of Rosalind, Queen Katha-e, Portia, and Lady Macbeth at the Shakespeare morial Theatre, Stratford-upon-Avon. In 1829 appeared at Drury Lane, and in 1830 played trice at the Haymarket. In 1831, with her reputa-n already established, she quit the stage and mar-d, but, after her husband's death, returned to the ge in 1832.

At Drury Lane as Mrs. Nisbett, she began to play gamut of contemporary comedy roles. In 1835 appeared at Covent Garden in *Love's Labour's st* and as Mistress Ford in *The Merry Wives of ndsor*. In 1842 she played as Rosalind with Mac-dy. Her activities, however, were curtailed by ess, and she was forced to retire in 1851. During career she had established herself as one of the st beautiful women on the stage and one of the t comic actresses. [*Dictionary of National Biogra-y*, 1885– .]

oate of corne & malte. The title of a survey taken Stratford in 1598 which listed Shakespeare as the der of 10 quarters (80 bushels) of grain ("corne") barley ("malte"). The survey was made by the al justices of the peace upon the order of the vy council. In the 1590's English suffered a grain rtage which forced the price of grain up to an ationary level. To prevent the possibility of il-al hoarding of grain for brewing purposes, the vy council ordered local officials to record the nes of those in possession of large quantities of in. The situation in Stratford was apparently re distressing than elsewhere. Shakespeare's fellow townsman Abraham Sturley, in a letter to Richard Quiney which mentions Shakespeare in another connection, comments on the situation:

> . . . our neighbors are growne with the wantes they feele through the dearnes of corne, which heare is beionde all other countries that I can heare of deare and over deare, malcontent. Thei have assembled togeather in a great nomber, and travelled to Sir Tho. Luci on Fridai last to complaine of our malsters . . . 'I hope,' saith Tho. Grannams, 'if God send mi Lord of Essex downe shortli to see them [the "malsters"] hanged on gibbettes att their owne dores.

The "noate," or inventory, for Stratford was made on February 4, 1598. The list contained the name of virtually every householder in Stratford. Shakespeare's name was listed among those in the Chapel Street Ward: "Wm Shackspeare X. quarters."

It is not clear from the records whether Shakespeare's and his neighbors' activities were illegal, but the evidence would seem to indicate that they were.

In 1604, 20 bushels of malt belonging to Shakespeare were sold to Philip Rogers, for which Rogers failed to pay. [B. Roland Lewis, *The Shakespeare Documents*, 1940.]

Nokes or **Noke, James** (d. c. 1692). Actor. Little is known about Nokes' early life except that at one point he kept a toy shop in Cornhill. About 1659 he joined Rhodes' company at the Cockpit as one of six boy actors hired to play women's roles. An elder brother, Robert Nokes (d. c. 1673), was already a member of the company. In 1661 James Nokes was with the group of actors who became the Duke's Company under Davenant's direction at the Lincoln's Inn Fields Theatre. A performance by Nokes as Norfolk in *Henry VIII* was witnessed by Pepys in 1663/4, a year in which he also played the Constable of France in Lord Orrery's *Henry V*. His best role was Sir Martin Mar-all in the play of that name which Dryden adapted especially for Nokes from a translation of Molière's *L'Etourdi*. In 1672 Nokes played the Nurse in Nevil Payne's *Fatal Jealousy* and earned for himself the nickname of Nurse Nokes. Nokes played the Nurse again in the 1880 performance of Otway's *History and Fall of Caius Marius*, an adaptation of Shakespeare's *Romeo and Juliet*. The epilogue of Otway's play alludes to Nokes: "And now for you who here come wrapt in cloaks,/ Only for love of Underhill and Nurse Nokes."

In 1673 he played Polonius; Davies' *Dramatic Miscellanies* also conjectures that he played the Fool to Betterton's Lear. His specialty was broad comic roles and contemporary citations allude to him as excellent in this line. He retired wealthy. [*Dictionary of National Biography*, 1885– .]

Norden, John (1548–1625). Surveyor and topographer whose views of London provide the first and probably most accurate contemporary picture of the London theatres (see engravings of London). Norden's first view was printed in 1593 in his *Speculum Britanniae*, engraved by one Pieter van den Keere. The map, viewing London from the south, shows in the foreground the Bear Garden and the Rose theatre, the only playhouse on the Bankside at that time. A subsequent map, bearing the title *Civitas*

Londini and dated 1600, updates the 1593 map. The new map includes the two theatres built in the interim, the Swan (1595) and the Globe (1599). In Norden's picture the Globe is seen as the most southern and eastern of the Bankside theatres, just south of Maiden Lane. The most striking feature of the view, however, is that the three playhouses and the Bear Garden are all pictured as round buildings. The round exterior does not necessarily imply a round interior, however, it being possible to construct a polygonal inner frame. See PLAYHOUSE STRUCTURE. [I. A. Shapiro, "The Bankside Theatres; Early Engravings," *Shakespeare Survey 1*, 1948.]

Norfolk, duke of. ***Thomas Howard*** the elder (1443–1524), 1st earl of Surrey and 2nd duke of Norfolk (in the Howard family). Loyal to whoever occupied the throne, Howard, like his father, John Howard, had supported Richard III. He was imprisoned by Henry VII for some years, but gradually regained the king's confidence and his own earldom. Until the rise of Wolsey he was the chief advisor to Henry VIII, who made him duke of Norfolk in 1514. He reluctantly presided at the trial of his close friend Buckingham two years before his retirement from public life. His son ***Thomas Howard*** succeeded him as earl of SURREY (in which rank he appears in *Henry VIII*) and duke of Norfolk, and was the head of the anti-Wolsey group at the time of the cardinal's downfall. He was a son-in-law of the duke of Buckingham and an uncle of Anne Bullen, though he later presided over her trial.

In *Richard III*, the elder Howard, as the Earl of Surrey, appears as Richard's supporter at Bosworth Field (V, iii). In *Henry VIII*, the Duke of Norfolk combines events in the lives of both dukes, but is clearly intended to be the elder. He discusses with Buckingham (I, i) and later with other nobles (II, ii) the need to overthrow Wolsey, and eventually joins them in gloating over the Cardinal at his imminent downfall (II, ii). At other times he supports Queen Katharine's plea for tax relief to avert rebellion (II, ii), is present but takes no part when the privy council attempts to imprison Cranmer (V, iii), and is present at the coronation of Anne and the christening of the baby Elizabeth.

Norfolk, John Howard, 1st duke of (1430?–1485). An active Yorkist, Norfolk broke his oath to uphold the succession of Edward V by supporting Richard III and aiding in the imprisonment of the young princes. In *Richard III*, Norfolk and Surrey "have the leading of this foot and horse" in Richard's army. Norfolk shows the King a note which he found on his tent reading: "'Jockey of Norfolk, be not too bold,/For Dickon thy master is bought and sold'" (V, iii).

Norfolk, John Mowbray, 3rd duke of (1415–1461). Nephew by marriage of Richard, duke of York. In *3 Henry VI*, Norfolk is a supporter of the Yorkists (I, i and II, ii). Some authorities consider the Norfolk of this play to be the 4th duke of Norfolk whose daughter, Ann, was betrothed to Edward IV's younger son. [W. H. Thomson, *Shakespeare's Characters: A Historical Dictionary*, 1951.]

Norfolk, Thomas Mowbray, 1st duke of (c. 1366–1399). Second son of John, 10th Baron Mowbray, and Elizabeth, daughter of Margaret, countess of Norfolk. Mowbray joined the lords appellant their condemnation of Richard II's favorites in 1 but he and the king were later reconciled. When rebel duke of Gloucester died in Mowbray's custo the latter was said to have murdered him. Mowb denied responsibility for the deed, but was nevert less created duke of Norfolk in reward. Fearing his safety, however, Mowbray confided his app hensions to Henry Bolingbroke, who faithle accused Mowbray of treason. Richard banished h for life, and he died in Venice the following y

In *Richard II*, Mowbray is the custodian of Ri ard's uncle Gloucester, who has died in pris After a quarrel with Bolingbroke, who accuses h of embezzling royal funds and murdering Glouces Mowbray is banished by the King.

North, Sir **Thomas** (1535?–?1601). Translat Educated at Cambridge and Lincoln's Inn, No began his distinguished career with his translati through a French version, of Guevara's *El Relox Príncipes* as *The Diall of Princes* (1557). In 1570 translated *The Moral Philosophie of Doni*, a c lection of beast fables, from the Italian. His r achievement, however, is his rendering of PLUTARC *Lives* as *The Lives of the noble Grecians a Romanes* (1579). North's Plutarch, based not rectly on Plutarch but on a French version Jacques AMYOT, is one of the greatest translati in English literature. Shakespeare is indebted to as the chief source of *Julius Caesar*, *Antony a Cleopatra*, *Coriolanus*, and as one of the import sources of *Timon of Athens*. It has also been s gested as a minor source of *A Midsummer Nig Dream*.

The quality of North's translation is indicated Shakespeare's use, not only of the plots in gene but of whole passages from North's text, which w incorporated with relatively minor changes into texts of the plays. An example can be seen in following passage from North:

> I dare assure thee, that no enemy hath taken shall take Marcus Brutus alive, and I beseech G keep him from that fortune: for wheresoever be found, alive or dead, he will be found l himself.

In *Julius Caesar* Shakespeare translated Nort prose into the following blank-verse passage:

> I dare assure thee that no enemy
> Shall ever take alive the noble Brutus:
> The gods defend him from so great a shame!
> When you do find him, or alive or dead,
> He will be found like Brutus, like himself.
> (V, iv, 21–25)

[F. O. Matthiessen, *Translation: An Elizabethan A* 1931.]

Northbrooke, John. See ENEMIES OF THE STAGE.

Northcote, James (1746–1831). History and p trait painter, engraver, etcher, and writer on Northcote, originally a watchmaker, at the age 25 became a student and assistant to Sir Josh Reynolds. Northcote's training was thus classic rounded off in the traditional manner with a t of the continent. The nine paintings he contribu to BOYDELL'S SHAKESPEARE GALLERY show high co petence in drawing and composition, particularly ırial of the Princes in the Tower." His critical ıtings on Boydell's project are considered by some be of greater interest than the paintings he con-uted:

Now with regard to the Shakespeare Gallery, it was a subject of complaint that we painters didn't hoose the finest passages to paint from. It was a nistaken complaint, for pithy sayings . . . are ad-dressed to the ear, . . . and they are not suitable or painting . . .

istory painting," he adds, "ought to be called etical Painting, for its object is not to give in-mation, but to make an impression precisely the ne as poetry does, only by different means." 7. M. Merchant, *Shakespeare and the Artist*, 1959.]

Northern Lass, The. See Richard BROME.

Northumberland, Henry Percy, 1st earl of (1342–8). Though initially a supporter of Richard II, rthumberland grew disenchanted and cast his lot h Henry Bolingbroke, who, largely through the l's efforts and cooperation, was able to take the one as Henry IV. Northumberland and his son tspur defeated the Scots at Homildon Hill in 2 but rose in revolt against Henry when he re-ed to let them keep their prisoners' ransom ney or to help them recover Sir Edmund rtimer. After Hotspur's defeat and death at rewsbury, Northumberland gave himself up and s pardoned, only to lead another rebellion in 5. Forced to flee from England, he returned three ırs later. However, his band was met and defeated Rokeby's men on Bramham Moor, in which en-ınter Northumberland himself was killed.

In *Richard II*, Northumberland champions Boling-oke's cause, and in IV, i, when Richard is deprived his crown, presents the deposed King with a list his crimes. In *1 Henry IV*, Northumberland pre-nds to be ill in order to avoid appearing at the ttle of Shrewsbury. In *2 Henry IV* he leads Arch-hop Scroop to believe that he will support that elate's rebellion. Instead, Northumberland flees to otland, where he is soundly defeated.

Northumberland, Henry Percy, 3rd earl of (1421–61). A nobleman of the Lancastrian party who, in 60, defeated and killed the duke of York at Wake-ld. After helping Queen Margaret to overthrow earl of Warwick at the second battle of St. bans in 1461, Northumberland was killed at owton. In *3 Henry VI*, moved by York's passionate eech after capture, Northumberland says: "Had been slaughter-man to all my kin,/ I should not r my life but weep with him" (I, iv).

Northumberland, Henry Percy, 9th earl of (1564–32). Courtier and dilettante. Northumberland, a ect descendant of the Percys of Shakespeare's tories, succeeded to the earldom in 1585. He mar-d Dorothy Devereux, the sister of the earl of sex, in 1594, but the marriage was not a successful e and the two often lived apart. Not a Catholic nself, Northumberland was extremely sympa-etic to the Catholic cause; after the Gunpowder ot of 1605 his sympathies resulted in his imprison-ent in the Tower of London for 16 years. Al-ough he had not been implicated in the plot, he s found guilty of consorting with one of the otters and failing to assist in their apprehension.

Northumberland was a friend of Sir Walter Raleigh and, like him, a student of science, alchemy, and mathematics, and apparently a member of the "School of Night." Frances Yates has discovered an essay written by the earl to his wife, setting forth the thesis that scholarship and learning are infinitely preferable to female companionship. Miss Yates suggests that the young noblemen who express similarly pretentious opinions in *Love's Labour's Lost* are portraits of Northumberland, Raleigh, and their friends (see LOVE'S LABOUR'S LOST: *Comment*).

Northumberland's knowledge of Shakespeare's plays is evidenced by an allusion he made in 1628 to *1 Henry IV*. The context of the reference was a letter which he had written in connection with the somewhat involved arrangements for the marriage of his son to the daughter of the earl of Salisbury: "therefore my Lo: lett us runne in a straight line, without turnings and windings, as Henry Hotspurre, would have it, when Mortimer and he devided England in a mappe." [Frances Yates, *A Study of Love's Labour's Lost*, 1936; G. B. Harrison, "A New Shakespeare Allusion," *Shakespeare Quarterly*, VIII, 1957.]

Northumberland, Lady Maud. In *2 Henry IV*, the wife of the Earl of Northumberland, whom she persuades to flee to Scotland. Historically, she was Northumberland's second wife and the stepmother of Hotspur. [W. H. Thomson, *Shakespeare's Characters: A Historical Dictionary*, 1951.]

Northumberland MS. A manuscript apparently written between 1597 and 1603 which contains essays and tracts by Bacon and other miscellaneous matter. The title page of that portion of the manuscript which contains Bacon's essay "Of Tribute, or giving what is dew" is covered with scribbling, with the name "William Shakespeare" repeated frequently as well as the titles "Rychard the second" and "Rychard the third," two lines from *The Rape of Lucrece*, and a variation of the long word "honorificabilitudinitatibus" (*Love's Labour's Lost*, V, i, 44) appearing in the manuscript "honorificabilitudine." The scribbling gives all the appearance of idle doodling, but the advocates of the BACONIAN THEORY consider it a supremely important document in support of their view that Shakespeare's plays were written by Bacon. [E. K. Chambers, *William Shakespeare*, 1930.]

Norway. See SCANDINAVIA.

Nottingham, Charles Howard, 1st earl of (1536–1624). Lord high admiral under Elizabeth and patron of the Admiral's Men, the acting company which was the chief rival of Shakespeare's troupe. Howard held various positions at the Elizabethan court, including the office of lord chamberlain (1583–1585). In 1585 he was appointed lord high admiral and was in command of the forces in the victory over the Spanish Armada (1588). In 1596, he and Essex led a successful raid on the Spanish port of Cadiz, as a result of which he was made earl of Nottingham. See Henry Brooke, 8th Lord COBHAM.

Nottingham's Men. See ADMIRAL'S MEN.

Novelle. See Matteo BANDELLO.

Nurse. In *Romeo and Juliet*, Juliet's loquacious and bawdy confidante. Her name in the play is Angelica. The Nurse's earthy sensuality serves as a foil to Juliet's idealistic romanticism, and in this respect she serves as the female counterpart of Mercutio, Romeo's cynical and witty friend. Brilliant a creation as she is, the Nurse troubles some readers because of her seeming betrayal of the lovers' ideals. This, however, is quite consistent with her own ethical and intellectual limitations and what Samuel Johnson called the "great subtility of distinction" of her character, "at once loquacious and dishonest."

Nurse. In *Titus Andronicus*, one of three witnesses to the birth of Tamora's child by Aaron. When the Nurse brings the baby to its father, he murders her to preserve the secret of its birth (IV, ii).

Nym. In *The Merry Wives of Windsor*, a follower of Falstaff. Nym speaks a jargon of "humours," and when Falstaff orders him to deliver a love letter to Mistress Ford, this "Mars of malcontents" refuses to run such a "base humour." Dismissed for this subordinate behavior, Nym promises himself "humours of revenge" and informs Master Page Falstaff loves his wife. The character is often thou to be a caricature of Ben Jonson.

In *Henry V*, Nym appears as a corporal. Hav been betrothed to Mistress Quickly, he quarrels v Pistol, whom she marries; finally reconciled, h ever, Nym goes with Pistol and Bardolph on English campaign in France. Nym and Bardolph hanged for looting French churches.

Nymphs. In *The Two Noble Kinsmen*, they pear in the wedding procession of Theseus Hippolyta (I, i).

O

Oberon. In *A Midsummer Night's Dream*, jealous King of the fairies. When Titania refuses to surrender a "little changeling boy" to Oberon, who wants him for a page, he involves her in a humiliating passion for the foolish Bottom by anointing her eyes with Puck's magic potion. Oberon commissions Puck to use the same magic on Demetrius, causing him to fall in love with Helena. When all the lovers are properly paired, Oberon releases Titania from the spell and together they anticipate the fairy dance in honor of the marriage of Theseus and Hippolyta. (See SUPERNATURAL.)

Octavia. In *Antony and Cleopatra*, the sister of Octavius Caesar and wife of Antony. Octavia marries Antony as part of a scheme to reconcile the differences between him and her brother. Antony's disloyalty in abandoning her for Cleopatra precipitates the war culminating in the battle of Actium.

Octavius Caesar. See CAESAR, OCTAVIUS.

octavo. A printing term referring to a book made up of sheets folded 3 times to form 8 leaves (16 pages) about 5 inches wide and 7 inches long. Many of the earlier editions of *Venus and Adonis* and *The Rape of Lucrece* were printed in octavo. The abbreviation for octavo is O or 8vo. (For a list of octavo editions of Shakespeare's works, up to the publication of the First Folio, see QUARTO.)

Oenone and Paris. See Thomas HEYWOOD.

office-book. See Sir Henry HERBERT.

Okes, Nicholas (fl. 1596–1636). London printer who printed the First Quarto of *Othello* (1622). Okes was admitted as a freeman to the Stationers' Company in 1603. In 1608 he assumed control of the shop of George and Lionel Snowdon (fl. 1606–1608), and in that year Nathaniel Butter's "pied bull" edition of *King Lear* was printed there. In 1622 he printed Q1 of *Othello* for Thomas Walkley. [R. B. McKerrow, ed., *A Dictionary of Printers and Booksellers . . . 1557–1640*, 1910.]

Oldcastle, Sir John (c. 1377–1417). Soldier and friend of Henry V. Sir John, later Lord Cobham by virtue of his marriage to Jane, Lady Cobham, in 1409, served in the Welsh campaigns and was a commander of the forces against the French (1411). In 1413, he was arrested as an adherent of Lollardry, the 15th-century heretical reform movement instituted by John Wyclif (d. 1384) which anticipated many of the features of the Protestant Reformation. Oldcastle escaped from prison and led an attempt to overthrow the king. In 1417 he was captured and hanged; his body was burned while hanging. In the 16th century, Oldcastle was viewed as a martyr and was enshrined in John Foxe's hagiographical *Book of Martyrs* (1563). See Robert PARSONS.

Shakespeare's character Falstaff in the Henry IV plays was originally named Oldcastle. In *The Famous Victories of Henry the Fifth*, Shakespeare's probable source for some details of the Henry IV plays, one of the boon companions of Prince Hal was named Sir John Oldcastle. Shakespeare retained the name for his old rogue. The immediate success of the play, and particularly of the character, brought forth a strong protest from Oldcastle's descendants, members of the powerful Cobham family (see William Brooke, 7th Lord COBHAM; Henry Brooke, 8th Lord COBHAM). The name was changed to Falstaff, derived, with a shift in letters, from Sir John Fastolfe, a 15th-century soldier with a reputation for cowardice whose name Shakespeare had already used in his Henry VI plays (see Richard JAMES).

Falstaff's original name appears in both *1* and *2 Henry IV*. In the first, Hal addresses Falstaff as "my old lad of the castle" (I, ii, 47). In the second, one of Falstaff's speeches is marked "Old" in the 1600 quarto. The epilogue to *2 Henry IV* expressly states "for Oldcastle died a martyr, and this [Falstaff] is not the man." Oldcastle was vindicated in the Admiral's Men's play SIR JOHN OLDCASTLE.

Old Lady. In *Henry VIII*, a minor character. In II, iii, she teases Anne Bullen about the possibility of becoming Queen, and later (V, i) brings word to the King that Anne has given birth to a girl.

Old Man. In *King Lear*, a minor character. He appears in IV, i, guiding the blind Gloucester across the heath.

Old Stratford. A hamlet about a mile and a half north of Stratford. In 1602 Shakespeare purchased from William and John Combe 107 acres of farm land in Old Stratford for £320. The purchase established Shakespeare as an important landowner in the Stratford area, a position he further solidified in 1605 by his purchase of the Stratford tithes. The transaction involved land only, not any buildings which were on the property. Shakespeare's younger brother Gilbert acted as his agent in the transaction:

> This Indenture made the firste daie of Maye, in the fowre and fortieth yeare of the raigne of our Soveraigne Ladie Elizabeth, by the grace of God, of England, Fraunce and Ireland, Queene, Defendresse of the Faithe, &c., betweene William Combe of Warwicke, in the countie of Warrwick, esquier, and John Combe of Olde Stretford, in the countie aforesaide, gentleman, on the one partie, and William Shakespere of Stretford-uppon-Avon, in the countie aforesaide, gentleman, on thother partye; Witnesseth that the saide William Combe and John Combe, for and in consideracion of the

somme of three hundred and twentie poundes of currant Englishe money to them in hande, at and before the ensealinge and deliverie of theis presentes, well and trulie satisfied, contented and paide; wherof and wherwith they acknowledge themselves fullie satisfied, contented and paide, and therof, and of everie parte and parcell therof, doe clearlie, exonerate, acquite and discharge the saide William Shakespere, his heires, executors, administrators and assignes for ever by theis presentes, have aliened, bargayned, soldę, geven, graunted and confirmed, and by theis presentes, doe fullye, clearlie and absolutelie alien, bargayne, sell, give, graunte and confirme unto the saide William Shakespere, all and singuler those errable landes, with thappurtenaunces, conteyninge by estymacion fowre yarde lande of errable lande, scytuate, lyinge and beinge within the parrishe, feildes or towne of Olde Stretford aforesaide, in the saide countie of Warrwick, conteyninge by estimacion one hundred and seaven acres, be they more or lesse; and also all the common of pasture for sheepe, horse, kyne or other cattle, in the feildes of Olde Stretford aforesaide, to the saide fowre yarde lande belonginge or in any wise apperteyninge; and also all hades, leys, tyinges, proffittes, advantages and commodities whatsoever, with their and everie of their appurtenaunces to the saide bargayned premisses belonginge or apperteyninge, or hertofore reputed, taken, knowne or occupied as parte, parcell or member of the same, and the revercion and revercions of all and singuler the same bargayned premisses, and of everie parte and parcell therof, nowe or late in the severall tenures or occupacions of Thomas Hiccoxe and Lewes Hiccoxe, or of either of them, or of their assignes, or any of them; together also with all charters, deedes, writinges, escriptes, and mynumentes whatsoever, touchinge or concerninge the same premisses onlie, or only any parte or parcell therof; and also the true copies of all other deedes, evidences, charters, writinges, escriptes and mynumentes, which doe touche and concerne the saide premisses before bargayned and solde, or any parte or parcell therof, which the saide William Combe or John Combe nowe have in their custodie, or herafter may have, or which they may lawfullye gett, or come by, without suite in lawe; to have and to holde the saide fowre yarde of errable lande, conteyninge by estymacion one hundred and seaven acres, be they more or lesse, and all and singuler other premisses before by theis presentes aliened and solde, or mencioned or entended to be aliened and solde, and everie parte and parcell therof; and all deedes, charters, writinges, escriptes and mynumentes, before by theis presentes bargayned and solde unto the saide William Shakespere, his heires and assignes for ever, to the onlie proper use and behoofe of the saide William Shakespere, his heires and assignes for ever. And the saide William Combe and John Combe, for them, their heires, executors and administrators, doe covenant, promise, and graunte to and with the saide William Shakespere, his heires, executors and assignes, by theis presentes, that they, the said William and John Combe, are seazde, or one of them is seazed, of a good, sure, perfect and absolute estate, in fee simple, of th same premisses before by theis presentes bargayne and solde, or ment or mencioned to be bargayne and solde, without any further condicion or lym yttacion of use or estate, uses or estates; and th he, the said John Combe, his heires and assigne shall and will, from tyme to tyme, and at all tym herafter, well and sufficientlie save and keep harmles and indempnified as well the said fowr yardes of errable lande, conteyninge one hundre and seaven acres, and all other the premisses, wit their appurtenaunces, before bargayned and sold or mencioned or entended to be bargayned an solde, and everie parte and parcell therof, as als the saide William Shakespere, and his heires an assignes, and everie of them, of and from a former bargaynes, sales, leases, joyntures, dower wills, statutes, recognizances, writinges obligatori tynes, feoffamentes, entayles, judgmentes, execu cions, charges, titles, forfeytures and encombranc whatsoever, at any tyme before the ensealing herof, had, made, knowledged, done or suffred b the saide John Combe, or by the saide Willia Combe, or either of them, or by any other perso or persons whatsoever, any thinge lawfullye claym inge or havinge, from, by or under them, or eithe of them, the rentes and services herafter to be du in respect of the premisses before mencioned o entended to be bargayned and solde, to the cheif lorde or lordes of the fee or fees onlie excepte and foreprized. And the said William Combe an John Combe, for them, their heires, executors, ad ministrators and assignes, doe covenant, promis and graunte to and with the saide William Shak spere, his heires and assignes, by theis presente that they, the saide William and John Combe, o one of them, hathe right, full power and lawfu aucthoritie for any acte or actes done by them the saide William and John Combe, or by th sufferance or procurement of them, the saide Wi liam and John Combe, to geve, graunte, bargayn sell, convey and assure the saide fowre yardes o errable lande, conteyninge one hundred and seave acres, and all other the premisses before by the presentes bargayned and solde, or ment or mer cioned to be bargayned and solde, and everie par and parcell therof, to the saide William Shak spere, his heires and assignes, in suche manner an forme as in and by theis presentes is lymytte expressed, and declared; and that they, the said William and John Combe, and their heires an also all and everie other person and persons, an their heires, nowe or herafter havinge or clayn inge any lawfull estate righte, title or interest, o in or to the saide errable lande, and all other th premisses before by theis presentes bargayned an solde, with their and everie of their appurt naunces,—other then the chiefe lorde or lordes o the fee or fees of the premisses, for their rent and services only,—at all tymes herafter, during the space of fyve yeares next ensewinge the da herof, shall doe, cause, knowledge and suffer to b done and knowledged, all and every suche furth lawfull and reasonable acte and actes, thinge an thinges, devise and devises, conveyances and a surances whatsoever, for the further, more bett and perfect assurance, suretie, sure makinge an conveyinge of all the saide premisses before bargayned and solde, or mencioned to be bargayned and solde, with their appurtenaunces, and everie parte and parcell therof, to the saide William Shakespere, his heires and assignes, for ever, accordinge to the true entent and meaninge of theis presentes, as by the saide William Shakespere, his heires and assignes, or his or their learned counsell in the lawe, shal be reasonablye devized or advized, and required, be yt bye fyne or fynes with proclamacion, recoverye with voucher or vouchers over, deede or deedes enrolled, enrollment of theis presentes, feoffament, releaze, confirmacion or otherwise; with warrantie against the saide William Combe and John Combe, their heires and assignes, and all other persons clayminge by, from or under them, or any of them, or without warrantie, at the costes and charges in the lawe of the saide William Shakespere, his heires, executors, administrators or assignes, so as, for the makinge of any suche estate or assurance, the saide William and John Combe be not compeld to travell above sixe myles. And the saide William Combe and John Combe, for them, their heires, executors, administrators and assignes, doe covenant, promise and graunte to and with the saide William Shakespere, his heires, executors, administrators and assignes, by theis presentes, that the saide William Shakespere, his heires and assignes, shall or may, from tyme to tyme, from henceforth for ever, peaceably and quietlye have, holde, occupie, possesse and enjoye the saide fowre yardes of errable lande, and all other the bargayned premisses, with their appurtenances, and everie parte and parcell thereof, without any manner of lett, trouble, or eviccion of them, the said William Combe and John Combe, their heires or assignes; and without the lawfull lett, trouble or eviccion of any other person or persons whatsoever, lawfullie havinge or clayminge any thinge in, of or out of the saide premisses, or any parte therof, by, from or under them, the saide William Combe and John Combe, or either of them, or the heires or assignes of them, or either of them, or their or any of their estate, title or interest. In wytnes wherof the parties to theis presentes have enterchangeably sette their handes and seales, the daie and year first above written, 1602.—*W. Combe.—Jo. Combe.*—Sealed and delivered to Gilbert Shakespere, to the use of the within-named William Shakespere, in the presence of Anthony Nasshe, William Sheldon, Humfrey Maynwaringe, Rychard Mason, Jhon Nashe.

1 1610 Shakespeare confirmed his purchase and aid the Combes an additional £320 for 20 more cres of land in the same area.

Shakespeare's tenants on the Old Stratford land ere Thomas Hiccox and Lewis Hiccox (see HICCOX AMILY). This was probably the same Lewis Hiccox ho in 1603 converted into an inn a building in Ienley Street which John Shakespeare had willed his son William two years earlier. [J. O. Halliwell-hillipps, *Outlines of the Life of Shakespeare,* 1881.]

Old Vic Theatre. A playhouse built in 1818 and nown as the Royal Coburg Theatre, but renamed e Victoria after a visit from Princess Victoria in 1833. The early history of the Old Vic was relatively undistinguished, although from 1820 to 1831 it featured such outstanding performers as Kean and Macready. In 1879 Emma Cons (1838–1912), a former social worker, bought the freehold and the name of the theatre was changed to the Royal Victoria Hall and Coffee Tavern. Under her direction a committee was formed which purchased the theatre in 1886 on behalf of the people of London. The goal of Miss Cons and her associates was to provide wholesome entertainment for a large popular audience at reasonable prices. At the death of Miss Cons, the management of the theatre passed to her niece, Lilian BAYLIS, who introduced a series of innovations, including penny film shows. In October 1914, against the advice of all the knowledgeable theatre people in London, she began to experiment with productions of Shakespeare in repertory at popular prices, with the intention of developing a following among a large segment of the middle-class audience. During the first year eight of Shakespeare's plays were produced, and by 1923 the entire Shakespearean canon had been presented by a company which had already become world-famous.

This admirable record was achieved through the devotion of Miss Baylis, the highly talented actors in her company, and the generosity of Sir George Dance, who contributed more than £20,000 to the project. The Old Vic has numbered among its performers the greatest Shakespearean actors of this century, including Sir John Gielgud, Sir Laurence Olivier, Sir Ralph Richardson, Sir Donald Wolfit, Charles Laughton, Dame Sybil Thorndike, and Dame Edith Evans.

In May 1941 the theatre suffered severe damage in an air raid, and was not reopened until 1950. In November of that year the Old Vic, restored and renovated, opened with a production of *Twelfth Night.* In 1953, under the direction of Michael Benthall, it embarked on an ambitious "five-year plan" to repeat the earlier feat of staging all the plays of Shakespeare in the First Folio within a five-year period. During that time, the Old Vic drew more than 1,250,000 people, and concluded in 1958 with a production of *Henry VIII* with Sir John Gielgud as Wolsey and Dame Edith Evans as Queen Katharine.

In 1963 the long-sought National Theatre became a reality, and its birth necessitated the death of the Old Vic, which was absorbed by the NATIONAL THEATRE COMPANY. On June 14, 1963 the Old Vic company gave its last performance, a production of *Measure for Measure* which the London *Times* described as "the most emotionally charged event the British theatre has witnessed this century."

The following is a list of the Old Vic's directors since the introduction of repertory Shakespeare:

Mathison Lang, Hutin Britton, Estelle Stead, Andrew Leigh, and Ben Greet	1914–1915
Fisher White	1915
Ben Greet	1915–1918
George Foss	1918–1919
Russell Thorndike and Charles Warburton	1920
Robert Atkins	1921–1925
Andrew Leigh	1925–1929

Harcourt Williams	1929–1933
Tyrone Guthrie	1933–1934
Henry Cass	1934–1936
Tyrone Guthrie	1936–1943
John Burrell, Laurence Olivier, and Ralph Richardson	1944–1949
Hugh Hunt	1949–1950
Hugh Hunt, Glen Byam Shaw, George Devine, and Michel Saint-Denis	1950–1951
Tyrone Guthrie	1951–1952
Hugh Hunt	1952–1953
Michael Benthall	1953–1963

[*Who's Who in the Theatre*, 1961.]

Oldys, Sir William (1696–1761). Antiquarian and literary collector who is the source of several anecdotes about Shakespeare. Oldys was the author of brief biographies of Sir John Fastolfe, Sir Walter Raleigh, and Edward Alleyn. At his death he left a valuable collection of early manuscript fragments and notes, including notes to be used in a projected biography of Shakespeare. The notes on Shakespeare were subsequently printed in George Steevens' edition (1778) of Shakespeare's works. Oldys' notes contained a number of anecdotes, including the text of a ballad which Shakespeare was alleged to have written about Sir Thomas Lucy, and a variant version of the tradition that Shakespeare was the father of Sir William Davenant. Another of Oldys' anecdotes is the source of the tradition that Shakespeare played the role of old Adam in *As You Like It:*

> One of Shakespeare's younger brothers, who lived to a good old age, even some years, as I compute, after the restoration of *K. Charles II.* would in his younger days come to London to visit his brother *Will,* as he called him, and be a spectator of him as an actor in some of his own plays. This custom, as his brother's fame enlarged, and his dramatic entertainments grew the greatest support of our principal, if not of all our theatres, he continued it seems so long after his brother's death, as even to the latter end of his own life. The curiosity at this time of the most noted actors to learn something from him of his brother, &c. they justly held him in the highest veneration. And it may well be believed, as there was besides a kinsman and descendant of the family, who was then a celebrated actor among them, this opportunity made them greedily inquisitive into every little circumstance, more especially in his dramatick character, which his brother could relate of him. But he, it seems, was so stricken in years, and possibly his memory so weakened with infirmities (which might make him the easier pass for a man of weak intellects) that he could give them but little light into their enquiries; and all that could be recollected from him of his brother *Will,* in that station was, the faint, general, and almost lost ideas he had of having once seen him act a part in one of his own comedies, wherein being to personate a decrepit old man, he wore a long beard, and appeared so weak and drooping and unable to walk, that he was forced to be supported and carried by another person to a table, at which he was seated among some company, who were eating, and one of them sung a song.

Another anecdote deriving from Oldys describe a battle of wits alleged to have taken place betwee Shakespeare and Ben Jonson:

> Verses by Ben Jonson and Shakespeare,
> occasioned by the motto to the Globe
> Theatre—*Totus mundus agit histrionem.*
>
> *Jonson.*
>
> If, but *stage actors,* all the world displays,
> Where shall we find *spectators* of their plays?
>
> *Shakespeare.*
>
> Little, or much, of what we see, we do;
> We're all both *actors* and *spectators* too.

Oldys owned a copy of Gerard Langbaine's *Ac count of the English Dramatick Poets* (1691), on th margins of which he scribbled numerous annota tions, one of which asserted that

> Shakespear was not 29 years of age when he wrote his Henry the Fifth: For Tarlton who 5. acted in it died in 1592 or before. [*Against this*] 2.
> 2

Here Oldys had apparently confused Shakespeare' play with the earlier chronicle *The Famous Victorie of Henry V.* Oldys is also the source, according t Edmund Malone, of the tradition that Shakespear received only £5 for his *Hamlet.* See John Dow LAND. [E. K. Chambers, *William Shakespeare,* 1930.

Oliver. In *As You Like It,* the oldest son of Si Rowland de Boys and brother of Orlando an Jaques. Envious of Orlando and hoping to put a end to him, Oliver incites the wrestler Charle against his brother. When, after overcoming Charle in a match, Orlando leaves Duke Frederick's cour Oliver is sent to bring him back. Oliver follows hi brother into the Forest of Arden, where Orland generously saves him from attack by a lion. In change of heart, Oliver gives his land to Orland He subsequently marries Duke Frederick's daughte Celia.

Olivia. In *Twelfth Night,* a rich countess. Th beautiful and virtuous Olivia has been indulging i excessive mourning for her dead brother and in thi posture waters her room each day "with eye offending brine." She has abjured the sight and so ciety of men. Her romanticism, however, finds new outlet when she falls passionately in love wit Cesario, who is actually the disguised Viola. Aban doning her grief, Olivia goes in aggressive pursuit o the young Page.

When Sebastian, Viola's twin brother, appear Olivia mistakes him for her beloved and hurries hir off to a marriage ceremony. At the countess' nex encounter with Cesario, she addresses the Page a her husband, but he denies her.

The confusions are resolved when Sebastian re enters and Olivia is spared the embarrassment o having married a woman.

Olivier, Sir Laurence [Kerr] (1907–). Actor producer. Olivier's interpretations and production both on the stage and in films, have served to enlarg Shakespeare's audience to an extent that would b inconceivable to the 16th-century dramatist. Si

Laurence first appeared professionally in 1922 in an all-boy production of *The Taming of the Shrew.* From 1926 to 1928 he was with the Birmingham Repertory Company, playing in both *Henry IV* and *Henry VIII.* Primarily non-Shakespearean roles claimed him for the next seven years, and through them his reputation as an actor grew. In 1935 he abandoned work on a production of *Romeo and Juliet* to join John Gielgud's company, which was preparing a similar production. It proved a happy move. Olivier and Gielgud alternated in the roles of Romeo and Mercutio. In the period before World War II, Olivier did some non-Shakespearean film work both in England and in the United States, but London audiences also saw him as Hamlet in 1937, and as Sir Toby Belch, Henry V, Macbeth, Iago, and Coriolanus. In New York, he briefly portrayed Hamlet. In 1944 Sir Laurence performed Richard III. His portrayal touched off unqualified critical acclaim and Olivier's reputation as a Shakespearean actor of considerable merit was secure. In 1946, Olivier's film experience before the war was translated into permanent dramatic accomplishments. He produced and starred in a film version of *Henry V* and the following year presented *Hamlet* to cinema audiences. He was knighted the same year. His latest Shakespearean film, *Richard III*, was released in 1956 (see FILMS). In addition to his films, Sir Laurence has appeared with enormous success in the title roles of *King Lear*, *Titus Andronicus*, *Coriolanus*, Antony in *Antony and Cleopatra,* and *Othello*. The stage production of the latter was filmed in 1965. Since 1962 he has been the director of Britain's National Theatre, for which he produced *Hamlet* at the Old Vic Theatre. He was also the first director of the Chichester Festival (1962). See NATIONAL THEATRE COMPANY. [*Who's Who in the Theatre*, 1961; *Who's Who*, 1964.]

O'Neill, Eliza (1791–1872). Irish actress. Miss O'Neill was the daughter of the stage manager of the Drogheda Theatre, where she made her first stage appearance as a child. For two years she played in Dublin and Belfast; her Juliet was a high mark of the Dublin season. In 1814 she made her London debut as Juliet in a Covent Garden production, which established her immediately as a "younger and better Mrs. Siddons" in more than one contemporary estimation. For five years she was the favorite of the London stage, but in 1819 she married William Wrixon Becher, a well-to-do Irish member of parliament, and retired from the stage. [*Dictionary of National Biography*, 1885– .]

O'Neill, Eugene (1888–1953). American dramatist. O'Neill's formal education ended with his freshman year at Princeton, except for his attendance at George Pierce Baker's playwriting workshop at Harvard in 1914/15. His informal education derived from his reading, his 18 months as a seaman, a brief period as a reporter, and his sojourns in the artistic, intellectual, and political demimonde of Greenwich Village in the years following 1915. His early one-act plays were produced by the Provincetown Players in those years. In the course of writing some 75 plays, which ranged from realism and naturalism to the boldest expressionist experiments, he broke the historic sentimental and superficial mold of the American theatre and raised it to international artistic stature.

His earliest exposure to Shakespeare came through his father, actor James O'Neill. The elder O'Neill was fond of quoting and discussing Shakespeare and had played Othello to Edwin Booth's Iago and Macduff to Booth's Macbeth, as well as undertaking Hamlet, Mark Antony, Brutus, and other leading roles. Formal instruction at Harvard left Eugene cool to Shakespeare, but later, he said, he "explored Shakespeare with profit and pleasure untold."

The Shakespearean influence has been observed both in O'Neill's technique and in specific plots and characters. He revived the use of ghosts, soliloquies, and asides in order to probe hidden psychological depths and preterhuman areas beyond the scope of superficial "realism" and its conventional dialogues and character. In *The Emperor Jones* (1920), O'Neill uses monologues and apparitions to underline the collapse of Brutus Jones, the egomaniacal "king" of a Caribbean island who is destroyed by the feverish imaginings of his own brain. Soliloquies and asides are also used to round out character and theme in *The Hairy Ape* (1922), *The Great God Brown* (1926), *Strange Interlude* (1928), *Dynamo* (1929), and the unfinished *More Stately Mansions.*

Horst Frenz has suggested that *Mourning Becomes Electra* (1931) may have more in common with *Hamlet* than with the *Oresteia* of Aeschylus. The murder of Ezra Mannon and his dying words accusing his wife resemble the situation in *Hamlet.* In O'Neill's play Lavinia and Orin have an avenging role akin to Hamlet's, "mousetrapping" their guilty mother in a partial reconstruction of the crime. [Horst Frenz and Martin Mueller, "More Shakespeare and Less Aeschylus in Eugene O'Neill's *Mourning Becomes Electra,*" *American Literature*, 1965]—M. H.

Onions, C[harles] T[albut] (1873–1965). Lexicographer. A member of the staff of the *Oxford English Dictionary* from 1895, Onions became joint editor in 1914 and saw the work to its completion in 1933. He also edited the *Shorter Oxford English Dictionary* (1933). He used the Elizabethan material gathered for the preparation of these works as the basis for his *Shakespeare Glossary* (1911), an invaluable guide for the student. Replacing Sir Sidney Lee, he completed the editing of *Shakespeare's England* (2 vols., 1916), a collection of essays investigating every aspect of Elizabethan life.

Ophelia. In *Hamlet,* the daughter of Polonius and the beloved of Hamlet. A fragile and passive creature, Ophelia is overwhelmed by the tragic events around her. Hamlet's treatment of her in the nunnery scene (III, i) strikes some readers as unduly harsh. Others interpret it as the Prince's reaction to his mother's infidelity. Ophelia's mad scene (IV, v) is one of the great set pieces in the history of the theatre.

orchestra. A seating area on both sides of the stage and part of the first level of galleries in an Elizabethan theatre; the orchestra provided "gentlemen's rooms" in addition to those in the gallery over the stage (see PLAYHOUSE STRUCTURE; LORDS' ROOM). Thomas Heywood's *Gynaikeion: or, Nine Bookes of various History concerninge Women; inscribed* *by ye names of ye nine Muses* (1624) refers to it as "a place in the Theatre onely for the Nobilitie," and in Cotgrave's *Dictionary* (1611) it is "the senators' or noblemen's places in a theatre, between the stage and the common seats." The sketch of the Swan theatre by Johannes De Witt shows three tiers of galleries ringing the building with the word "orchestra" labeling the first or lowest gallery. It was not until the Restoration era that the orchestra area was used for musicians (last half of 17th century). The orchestra location may have been the most expensive seating area in the theatre, judging from Dekker's references in the *Guls Horn-booke* (1609) to nobles or lords who sat in "the twelve-penny room next to the stage." [Irwin Smith, *Shakespeare's Globe Playhouse*, 1956.]

Oregon Shakespearean Festival, The. A dramatic festival founded in 1935 by Professor Angus L. Bowmer and held annually in Ashland, Oregon. "America's First Elizabethan Theatre" is located in the mountainous, sunny valley of the Rogue River in southern Oregon.

Except for the omission of the galleries to allow for more adequate seating space, the Oregon theatre conforms to the measurements of the proposed Fortune theatre as stipulated in the 1599 contract between Philip Henslowe and Edward Alleyn with Peter Streete, the builder. These of course duplicate the plan of the Globe. The width of the Fortune stage, 43 feet, is here extended by omission of the galleries. The stage projects the stipulated 27½ feet, and is tapered. (The authenticity of this last detail cannot be determined from the Fortune plan.) Three balconies—lower, upper, and music balcony—conform to the 12, 11, and 9 feet specified for the galleries. The balanced side windows and doorways, and the railings and recesses, flanked by pillars and pilasters, lead up to the "heavens" and to the "hut." From the staff atop this hut, a flag bearing Shakespeare's arms floats some 50 feet overhead during performances. The 10 playing areas facilitate endless variation and improvisation in staging and affirm the fluidity, swiftness, and spectacular appeal of Elizabethan staging. Directors at Ashland make extensive use of banners, curtains, hangings, and other embellishments, yet stay well within what seems plausible restatement of devices and effects that would be familiar to Shakespeare's audience.

The only notable variation from known features of Elizabethan staging has been a movable extension of the upper balcony stage, called the "pavilion." It is a railed projection, with supporting side columns, which is used to compensate for restricted visibility in the side seats. This unit and the circular benches frequently placed around the bases of the two pillars are unobtrusive. They provide such effective support for action that they demonstrate the likelihood of the free use of such conveniences—platforms, ladders, benches—by Shakespeare's equivalent of the stage manager. In solving problems of movement, the use of an Elizabethan theatre confirms the contention of the best students of Shakespeare that full understanding of his plays demands that they be mounted on the kind of stage for which they were conceived. Among discoveries made here that suggest what the dramatist had in mind, the following are worth noting:

1. In massed movement, such as court scenes, processions, and combat, the open stage aids immensel in achieving the sense of freedom and naturalnes that the Chorus in *Henry V* urges. Overlapping o scenes accelerates action and changes, and diverts at tention from exits and the removal of bodies o properties.

2. Allegorical pageantry and masque, such as tha of Hymen in *As You Like It*, are greatly facilitatec Much action, certainly much comedy, is visual rathe than verbal. The burlesque masque that conclude *Love's Labour's Lost*, wherein Don Armado, Holo fernes, Costard, and others impersonate the Nin Worthies, and such play-within-the-play action a Bottom's "Pyramus and Thisbe" and "The Mouse trap" in *Hamlet*, with their stage audiences, are muc more effective with the multiple staging.

3. Of particular interest is the immense range o movement and position that enables the actor t sketch in broad strokes. Addresses to the audience in soliloquy or direct confidence, bring him down t the railing, back to a pillar bench, or in swift move ment across the entire stage. The pillars serve fo trees, for architectural units, or for abstract but tresses for emotion and body movement. In all thes effects the imagination of the audience is brough into play as it also is in filling out armies, mobs, an other suggested groups.

4. The symmetrical balancing of side doors an windows graphically depicts the opposed houses o the Roman stage and plot tradition, and also th medieval extension of allegorical "Houses" of Goo and Ill Fame. The locale is readily identifiable as th house of Antipholus, of Shylock, or of the Capule family. In subsequent scenes the same unit may serv for quite different settings. Small shelters over th doorways conform to the stage direction for a "pent house" roof, as in *Much Ado About Nothing*, whic along with the windows are among the few stipu lated architectural features in Shakespeare.

5. Physical positioning of playing areas, especiall of the balcony, makes special sets for castles, cit walls, and the like unnecessary and greatly speed performance by obviating set changes. The necessit for "covering speeches," such as those taking plac while Richard II descends from the balcony o Juliet's Nurse makes her way from the bedside t the family below, becomes apparent.

Finally, staging the plays in their original styl throws light on some of the difficulties and incon gruities that must have faced Elizabethan companies who were confronted with highly perceptive au diences from all social levels. These audiences migh readily accept a pillar as a tree, an enclosed space a an orchard or forest, but some of the action mad more trying demands on their tolerance. Attempts o actors to solve these problems are plainly referred t in Bottom's struggles toward authenticity, not t speak of Ben Jonson's jeers at crude naturalism. A notable instance is the problem of heaving aloft th dying Antony. Whatever solution Shakespeare' company may have adopted, the physical demand in raising an inert body the more than 12 feet to th balcony and over the railing are prodigious. Suc difficulties throw light on the many scenes whic Shakespeare presented through an expositor—for ex ample, Enobarbus' description of Cleopatra's barge— or otherwise avoided staging.

The performing company, drawn from all part

of the country, consists mainly of collegiate and semiprofessional players and teachers of acting. Four plays are given each season, but an extra play has often been added—either a less popular Shakespearean piece, such as *Titus Andronicus*, or a non-Shakespearean play, among which have been *The Duchess of Malfi, The Alchemist*, and *The Knight of the Burning Pestle*. The season of six weeks draws audiences totaling over 60,000. Plays are scheduled in rotation, enabling audiences to see four plays in as many nights. In 1957, performance of the entire cycle of the history plays was attained with *Henry VIII;* and in 1958 *Troilus and Cressida* completed the canon of Shakespeare's accepted plays. Each season includes at least one comedy, one tragedy, and one history play, the last being chosen from year to year according to the chronological order of reigns.

Closely associated with the festival is the Renaissance Institute, founded in 1955 by the late Dr. Margery Bailey of Stanford University. It offers a series of lectures and courses for college credit and publishes an annual volume of mimeographed studies on a wide variety of subjects related to the plays of the season.

Notable among directors at the festival have been B. Iden Payne, director of both the Dublin Abbey Players and the Stratford-upon-Avon company (1935–1942); James Sandoe; Allen Fletcher; Robert Loper; Richard Risso; Edward S. Brubaker; and Rod Alexander. All of these have served also as actors. [James Sandoe, "The Oregon Shakespeare Festival," *Shakespeare Quarterly*, I, 5–11, 1950; Herbert E. Childs, "On the Elizabethan Staging of *Hamlet*," *Shakespeare Quarterly*, XIII, 463–74, 1962.]—R. D. H.

Orff, Carl. See MUSIC BASED ON SHAKESPEARE: *20th century*.

Orlando. In *As You Like It*, youngest son of Rowland de Boys. Deprived by his brother Oliver of the education due his position, Orlando vows no longer to endure this unnatural treatment and demands his inheritance. A quarrel ensues, and Oliver afterward attempts to get rid of the brother he hates. Warned by the faithful servant Adam, Orlando flees to the Forest of Arden, where he comes upon the banished Duke, as well as his beloved Rosalind, who is disguised as the boy Ganymede. While walking in the forest, Orlando comes upon Oliver, who has been trailing him, asleep under a tree and threatened by a waiting lion. Nobly resisting the temptation of revenge, Orlando battles the beast and saves his brother. In one of the events of the happy denouement, Orlando marries Rosalind.

Orlando Furioso (c. 1591). A play by Robert GREENE which was based on Ariosto's epic poem *Orlando Furioso*, in the 1591 English translation of Sir John Harington. According to a contemporary rumor, Greene sold *Orlando Furioso* first to the Queen's Men and, after they went on tour in the provinces, to the Admiral's Men. The play was performed at court on December 6, 1591 and given at the Rose in February 1592. It was published by Cuthbert Burby in 1594. It is chiefly interesting in that it is the only Elizabethan play for which an actor's "PART" survives. The part was that apparently used by Edward Alleyn in playing the leading role. A comparison of the relevant lines of the part with that of the printed text reveals the printed version to be an extremely corrupt one, possibly a "bad quarto." [*Two Elizabethan Stage Abridgments: The Battle of Alcazar and Orlando Furioso*, W. W. Greg, ed., 1922.]

Orléans, Bastard of. Epithet for **Jean Dunois** (1402–1468). Illegitimate son of Louis, duke of Orléans. In the course of a brilliant military career, Dunois helped Joan of Arc to capture Orléans, and thereafter won many more battles against the English. With years of successful campaigning, he was able to expel the enemy from the country. In *1 Henry VI*, the Bastard presents Joan (La Pucelle) to the Dauphin, describing her as "a holy maid" destined to drive the English from France (I, ii).

Orléans, Charles, duke of (1391–1465). French poet and nephew of Charles VI. In *Henry V*, Orléans defends the Dauphin's reputation for valor against the insinuations of the Constable, and ridicules the "fat-brained" English for venturing into France (III, vii). Orléans is captured at Agincourt.

Orsino. In *Twelfth Night*, the Duke of Illyria. Orsino is in love with love and relishes his role of the languishing suitor. Projecting his passion for Olivia with all the appropriate sentiments, Orsino studiously maintains the melancholy disposition befitting his emotional state. But the Countess, who is in mourning for her brother, has abjured the company and sight of men, and refuses to receive Orsino's messengers. When Viola, disguised as the page Cesario, finally gains entry to plead the Duke's affections, she is informed by Olivia that, although the Countess presumes her wooer virtuous and knows he is noble and rich, she cannot love him. When Orsino at last realizes the futility of his suit, he accepts the love of Viola.

orthography. See SPELLING.

Orwell, George. Pen name of **Eric Arthur Blair** (1903–1950). Author. Educated at Eton, Orwell served with the imperial police in Burma from 1922 to 1927. After returning to Europe, he worked at various menial jobs and recorded his experiences in *Down and Out in Paris and London* (1933) and *The Road to Wigan Pier* (1937). *Homage to Catalonia* (1938) is an account of his activities during the early days of the Spanish Civil War. In *Animal Farm* (1945) he uses the beast epic as a means of satirizing Stalinism. *Nineteen Eighty-Four* (1949) depicts a future in which totalitarianism has been brought to its logical conclusion. Orwell's periodical articles were reprinted in several volumes and eventually gathered together in *Collected Essays* (1961). "Lear, Tolstoy and the Fool," originally published in 1947, is an answer to Tolstoy's attack on Shakespeare, particularly his *King Lear*. Orwell notes parallels between Tolstoy and Lear—both made a parade of renunciation yet both expected to retain the deference paid to authority—and concludes that what Tolstoy objected to in *Lear* was an intolerable image of himself. Orwell's study is a piece of brilliant psychological analysis, but like much of his literary criticism it contains elementary blunders in scholarship and reveals an insensitivity to many aspects of the play.

Osric. In *Hamlet*, a foppish courtier. In V, ii Osric announces that Claudius has wagered a bet on Hamlet in the forthcoming duel with Laertes, engages in a verbal duel with the Prince, and officiates at the fencing match. Osric is a minor gem of Shakespearean delineation who, in a few short lines, emerges unforgettably as a typical fawning, sycophantic Elizabethan courtier. He is characterized by Hamlet in the line "He did comply with his dug before he sucked it."

Ostler, Thomasina (b. 1594–d. post 1615). Daughter of John Heminges and widow of Shakespeare's fellow actor Will Ostler. Mrs. Ostler brought suit against her father in September 1615, claiming as executrix of her husband's estate—Ostler had died intestate the year before—Ostler's shares in the Globe and Blackfriars. These shares had been granted to Ostler by his fellow actors in 1612. Thomasina Ostler affirmed that shortly after her husband's death she had turned over Ostler's shares to her father and that her father had subsequently refused to return them. The week following the registry of her complaint in court, Heminges promised to satisfy her as to the value of the shares. When he had failed to do so by October 9, however, his daughter entered a common-law suit against him, estimating the value of the shares at £600.

Heminges' refusal to part with the shares was based upon a grant and assignment he claimed to have received from Ostler. The result of the suit is not recorded: presumably, since Heminges had them in his possession at the time of his own death, the court had decided in his favor. His reluctance to allow his daughter control over her property has been explained as stemming from a desire to avoid the complications which had been faced by the young widow of Augustine Phillips. (Mrs. Phillips had held her husband's shares, but had married an unreliable spendthrift, John Witter.) Heminges, too, apparently had good reason to doubt his daughter's stability: at this time she was also engaged in a suit charging Sir Walter Raleigh's mischievous son "Wat" (1593–1618) with insult and slander. [C. W. Wallace, *Advance Sheets from Shakespeare, The Globe and Blackfriars*, 1909; T. W. Baldwin, *The Organization and Personnel of the Shakespearean Company*, 1927.]

Ostler, Will[iam] (d. 1614). Actor. Ostler became a member of the King's Men, Shakespeare's company, in 1610, having begun his acting career as one of the Children of the Chapel. He appeared in the Children's production of Jonson's *Poetaster* in 1601. Upon reaching maturity he was "taken" into the King's Men to "strengthen the King's service" (see SHARER'S PAPERS). His first appearance in a cast list with the King's Men was in the *Alchemist* (1610). He played Antonio in *The Duchess of Malfi* (1614). An epigram in John Davies' *Scourge of Folly* (1611) bears witness to his reputation:

To the Roscius of these Times, Mr. W. Ostler.

Ostler, thou took'st a knock thou would'st have giv'n,
Neere sent thee to thy latest home: but O!
Where was thine action, when thy crown was riv'n,
Sole King of Actors! then wast idle? No:
Thou hadst it, for thou would'st bee doing? Thus
Good actors deeds are oft most dangerous;
But if thou plaist thy dying part as well
As thy stage parts, thou hast no part in hell.

The reference to "Sole King of Actors" has been taken by T. W. Baldwin to indicate that Ostler's specialty was the role of the king and other high nobles.

In 1611 he married Thomasina, the daughter of John Heminges. After Ostler's death in 1614, his wife sued her father for possession of Ostler's share in the Globe and Blackfriars theatres (see Thomasina OSTLER). [E. K. Chambers, *The Elizabethan Stage*, 1923; T. W. Baldwin, *The Organization and Personnel of the Shakespearean Company*, 1927.]

Oswald. In *King Lear*, the servant of Goneril. Oswald's devotion to his mistress and her evil designs is unwavering even at his death. This fact puzzled Dr. Johnson, who said, "I know not well why Shakespeare gives the Steward, who is a mere factor of wickedness, so much fidelity." It is perhaps explained by the strong hints in the play that the relationship between Oswald and Goneril is of a sexual nature which may be alluded to in Edgar's remarks about the servant who "served the lust of my mistress' heart and did the act of darkness with her" (III, iv, 89–90).

Othello. In the play which bears his name, a Moor and a professional soldier in the service of the Venetian state. Initially presented as a heroic and noble figure, Othello undergoes a radical deterioration in character during the course of the play. The grandeur and serene dignity with which he is invested in Act I is destroyed by Iago's diabolical intrigue, revealing a hitherto unobserved, fiercely barbaric strain in Othello's character. His towering rage prompts the play's most memorable lines, but it also effects a callousness which spills over into such crass outbursts as his "I will chop her into messes" (IV, i, 211). It is not until the final scene that he regains his heroic stature with his memorable farewell speech ("Soft you; a word or two before you go"—V, ii, 338–356). Some 20th-century critics, notably T. S. Eliot and F. R. Leavis, feel that Othello's regeneration is never realized, that the famous concluding speech is, in Eliot's words, "a terrible exposure of human weakness," and that Othello is here, as indeed throughout the play, guilty of self-dramatization. The result of this view has been a characterization of Othello as "the least heroic of Shakespeare's tragic heroes." This position, largely a reaction against the overestimation of Othello's nobility by A. C. Bradley and other 19th-century critics, has been cogently contested by John Holloway in *The Story of the Night* (1961). Holloway sees this final speech as the eloquent expression of Othello's sense of his own culpability and his suicide as the appropriate conclusion to it.

Another controversy generated by Othello is the question of his skin color. Some critics (among whom Coleridge must be numbered) have balked at the idea of interracial love and have suggested that to Shakespeare the term "Moor" represented not a Negro but merely someone of a dark complexion. The play's references, however (as well as those to Aaron, the Moorish villain of *Titus Andronicus*), make it clear that by "Moor" Shakespeare meant those physical characteristics associated with Negroes. [T. S. Eliot, *Selected Essays*, 1932; F. R. Leavis, *The Common Pursuit*, 1952; *Othello*, New Arden Edition, M. R. Ridley, ed., 1958.]

The Tragedy of OTHELLO, the Moore of *Venice.*

Othello. A tragedy by Shakespeare.

Text. *Othello* was entered in the Stationers' Register on October 6, 1621: "Thomas Walkley. Entred for his copie vnder the handes of Sir George Buck, and Master Swinhoe warden, The Tragedie of Othello, the moore of Venice, vj[d]." The First Quarto appeared the next year, 1622, under the following title: "The Tragoedy of Othello, The Moore of Venice. As it hath beene diuerse times acted at the Globe, and at the Black-Friers, by his Maiesties Seruants. Written by William Shakespeare . . . London, Printed by N. O. [Nicholas Okes] for Thomas Walkley, and are to be sold at his shop, at the Eagle and Child, in Brittans Bursse. 1622." The Quarto provides a good text, though shorter by about 160 lines than that of the First Folio. The omissions in the Quarto probably represent cuts in the acting version. The Quarto text, therefore, was probably set up from a transcript of the PROMPT-BOOK. The provenance of the First Folio text is a matter of controversy. It is based on either a copy of Q1 which had been collated with the prompt-book, or a copy of Q1 which had been corrected by reference to a FAIR COPY of the play.

Date. *Othello* was first performed at court on November 1, 1604 by Shakespeare's company and was almost surely written and first produced in the early part of that year. A supposed reference to the tragedy in Dekker and Middleton's *Honest Whore*, first produced in 1604, accords with the 1604 date.

Sources. Shakespeare found Othello's story in the seventh novella of the third decade of the *Hecatommithi*, a popular collection of tales made by Giovanni Battista Giraldi (surnamed CINTHIO). Each story is supposed to have been told by one of a group of 10 gentlemen and ladies on a sea voyage made after the sack of Rome in 1527. Of the characters in this tale only Desdemona has a familiar name, Disdemona. Othello's original is Christophoro Moro, the Moor. Iago is merely named Alfiero, the ensign; Cassio, *capo di squadra*, captain of a company. All the other chief characters in *Othello* have prototypes in the novella. Roderigo is only the soldier whom the captain struck. Though the Italian source is a tale of crass intrigue and brutal crime, the plot in all its essential features is like that of *Othello*. The wicked ensign lusts for Disdemona. When she spurns his advances, he decides to avenge the insult by accusing her of adultery with a captain, a friend of her husband. Thus the villain's motives are conventional and clear, as Iago's are the reverse. Yet the facts which Iago distorts to arouse Othello's wild suspicion and to feed his homicidal jealousy are practically the same as those in the source. For example, Cinthio's ensign steals the precious handkerchief from Disdemona while she is fondling her baby, and plants it in the captain's bedroom. He then gives the Moor visible proof of his wife's guilt by bringing him to a spot where he sees the captain's wife copying the embroidery on the handkerchief. Cinthio's version of the murder is sheer horror. The ensign and the Moor together beat her to death with a stocking filled with sand, and then pull down the ceiling of the murder-chamber on her dead body in order to make the killing seem an accident. The Italian tale adds a long-drawn-out aftermath in which Disdemona's relatives avenge the murder by killing the Moor. The ensign's

TITLE PAGE OF THE FIRST QUARTO OF *Othello* (1622).

THE

Tragœdy of Othello,

The Moore of Venice.

As it hath beene diuerſe times acted at the Globe, and at the Black-Friers, by *his Maieſties Seruants.*

Written by VVilliam Shakeſpeare.

LONDON,

ted by *N. O.* for *Thomas Walkley*, and are to be ſold at his ſhop, at the Eagle and Child, in Brittans Burſſe.

1622.

end was dreadful. While being tortured in an effort to force from him a confession of the crime, his body ruptured. "Thus did Heaven avenge the innocence of Disdemona." This is the farrago of horror that Shakespeare transformed into one of the greatest of his tragedies.

One of Shakespeare's most significant alterations of his source was his elevation of the character of Othello. For Othello's noble speech against the charge of having bewitched Desdemona (I, iii, 128–170) Shakespeare drew from Pliny's *Natural History*, translated by Philemon Holland in 1601. For background information he consulted *The Commonwealth and Government of Venice* (1543), originally in Latin and translated in 1599 by Lewis Lewkenor from an Italian version.—O.J.C.

Plot Synopsis. Act I. Othello, a noble Moor in the service of Venice, has aroused the hatred of his ensign Iago by disregarding Iago's claims to preferment and naming as his lieutenant one Michael Cassio, whom Iago despises as a textbook soldier. Iago, however, continues to serve Othello for his own ends. Having learned that the Moor has secretly wed Desdemona, the daughter of the senator Brabantio, Iago, accompanied by Roderigo, a rejected suitor of Desdemona, arouses Brabantio from his sleep to inform him that "an old black ram / Is tupping your white ewe." The outraged parent immediately seeks out Othello and accuses him of bewitching Desdemona, but the Moor interrupts to say that he has just received an urgent summons from the Duke of Venice.

Othello and Brabantio hurry to the Duke's council chamber, where the other senators are discussing a report that a Turkish fleet is on its way to Cyprus. Brabantio repeats his charge of witchcraft against Othello, who explains that he had often visited Brabantio's house at the senator's invitation and had captured Desdemona's interest with tales of his adventures. "She loved me for the dangers I had pass'd," he says, "And I loved her that she did pity them." When Desdemona herself arrives, she declares her devotion to Othello, who is appointed governor of Cyprus, and asks to be allowed to join him there. Iago, who is named to escort Desdemona to Cyprus, chides Roderigo for contemplating suicide because of her marriage; if Roderigo is generous with his purse, Iago will guarantee that he too will enjoy her favors. Iago, still brooding over Othello's slight to him and a rumor that his own wife, Emilia, had betrayed him with the Moor, resolves to kindle Othello's suspicions by suggesting that Desdemona and Cassio are overly familiar. The Moor will be easy to convince, for he has a good opinion of Iago and "thinks men honest that but seem to be so."

Act II. In Cyprus, Montano, Othello's predecessor as governor, is informed that a storm has destroyed the Turkish fleet. The tempest has also scattered the vessels of the Venetians, so that Cassio, Desdemona, Iago, Roderigo, and Emilia reach the island before Othello. Iago, who has observed with interest the cordial relations between Cassio and Desdemona, reaffirms his desire to arouse Othello's jealousy and enlists Roderigo's assistance in discrediting Cassio.

During a night of revelry, decreed by Othello to celebrate his marriage and Cyprus' escape from the Turkish attack, Cassio confides to Iago that he becomes intoxicated easily. Iago then contrives to make Cassio drunk and involves him in a public brawl with Roderigo and Montano. When Othello arrives and asks who started the fray, Iago, with seeming reluctance, names Cassio, who is relieved of his post as the Moor's lieutenant.

Act III. At Iago's suggestion, Cassio requests Desdemona to intercede for him, and she presses Othello to reinstate the disgraced officer. Expressing surprise to learn from Othello that Cassio has long been acquainted with Desdemona, Iago states several times that he believes Cassio to be an honest man, whereupon Othello asks him to reveal what is in his mind. After declaring his unwillingness to disclose his thoughts, Iago suddenly warns Othello to beware of jealousy, "the green-eyed monster which doth mock / The meat it feeds on." When Othello assures Iago that he would not be influenced by mere suspicion, Iago advises him to observe his wife's behavior with Cassio; he points out that she was once able to deceive her father and may regret marrying someone so different from her in background and complexion. Pondering Iago's words, Othello tells himself that if Desdemona proves faithless, he will not hesitate to discard her. His bitter reflections are cut short by the entrance of Desdemona and Emilia. As they converse, Desdemona drops a handkerchief which was Othello's first gift to her. Emilia picks it up and gives it to Iago, who had been asking her to steal it, planning to leave it in Cassio's lodgings. Lamenting his lost peace of mind, Othello upbraids Iago for calumniating Desdemona and asks for proof of her infidelity. Iago says that he has heard Cassio speak of her in his sleep and has seen him wipe his face with her handkerchief. When Othello asks Desdemona for the handkerchief, she replies that she does not have it and proceeds to renew her pleas on behalf of Cassio. Meanwhile, Cassio, who has found the handkerchief in his room, gives it to his sluttish mistress, Bianca.

Act IV. So tormented is Othello by his doubts of Desdemona that he falls into an epileptic trance at the feet of Iago, who exults over the efficacy of his "medicine." When Othello revives, Iago suggests that he stand nearby while Iago engages Cassio in a conversation about Desdemona. They actually discuss Bianca, who herself comes in to return the handkerchief, but Othello, who cannot hear what they are saying, believes that Cassio's ribald laughter is prompted by mention of Desdemona; he is equally shocked by the sight of the handkerchief. He vows to kill Desdemona and immediately acquiesces when Iago offers to dispose of Cassio.

Upon the arrival of letters from Venice recalling Othello and naming Cassio as his deputy in Cyprus, Desdemona expresses the hope that they may be reconciled, for the love she bears Cassio. Infuriated Othello strikes her. Later he accuses her of betraying him and calls her a whore, ignoring her protestations of innocence and Emilia's assurance that she is virtuous. In Emilia's opinion, "some busy and insinuating rogue" has planted false suspicions in Othello's mind. Desdemona is so distraught that she turns to Iago for advice, but he makes light of her concern Later she recalls her mother's maid, Barbara, who was forsaken in love and died singing a song of "willow," which Desdemona cannot drive from her mind.

Act V. At Iago's instigation, Roderigo tries to kill

Cassio, but merely wounds him; fearful of exposure, Iago then stabs Roderigo to death. In his bedchamber, Othello finds Desdemona asleep. As he puts out a burning light, he reflects that there is no "Promethean heat" that can rekindle Desdemona's light once it is extinguished. He awakens her with a kiss and tells her to prepare her soul for death. Ignoring her appeals for mercy and avowals of innocence, he smothers her. Suddenly he hears Emilia knocking at the door. When he admits her, Desdemona cries out, and Emilia asks who has done the deed. With her dying breath Desdemona replies: "Nobody; I myself. Farewell: / Commend me to my kind lord." After Othello confesses to Emilia that he is the murderer, Iago, Montano, and others appear in response to Emilia's shouts. She reaffirms her belief in Desdemona's virtue and when Othello mentions the handkerchief, declares that she had given it to Iago. Othello lunges at Iago, who fatally wounds Emilia and flees, but is soon captured and brought back into the room, where the Moor stabs him. Cassio, who is also present, explains how he had come by the handkerchief, and papers in Iago's pockets reveal to Othello the full story of Iago's villainy. Describing himself as "one that loved not wisely but too well," Othello stabs himself and dies upon the body of Desdemona.—H.D.

Comment. The subject of the play is a villain's wanton destruction of a marriage. The action, unlike that of *Hamlet* or *King Lear,* does not dilate the imagination, but holds it as in a vise to the central theme. No subplot and only the slightest flashes of comedy relieve the passionate intensity of the action. Nor is there any suggestion that, as in *Richard III,* superhuman forces control human action and guide it through the catastrophe to a morally invigorating conclusion. The poet offers no compensation for the triumph of evil, no counterpoise of spiritual insight. Once caught in an inextricable maze of wild passions, the characters hold us bastioned to the end of the plot against the intrusion of any morally regenerative influence, human or divine.

The lovers, Othello and Desdemona, are of completely different social traditions, even of race. The poet chooses a striking way of emphasizing the width of the gulf separating the pair. He makes it certain that his Othello is black, black as a Negro, much as we may be inclined to discount Iago's scornful phrases, like "old black ram" or "Barbary horse." A producer who wishes to preserve Shakespeare's intention must have his stage Othello black enough to pose a mystery to Desdemona. In present-day North America a Negro Othello is likely to pervert the meaning that Shakespeare gave the situation, to twist it into a problem of miscegenation, American style. This is disastrous to a correct interpretation of the action, for Othello is no struggler up from slavery for status, but an aristocrat, who fetches his "life and being" from "men of royal siege" (rank). Whether he fills Desdemona with wonder or with terror, he always leaves her spellbound. To her, and finally to her father, Othello becomes the incarnation of romance. He wears an aura of mystery. In these ways he bears no resemblance to Cinthio's savage barbarian. Shakespeare created a history for him from facts and fancies drawn partly from Venice's long years of warfare against the Turks, and partly from marvels he had read about in Pliny. This matter he worked into the descriptions Othello gave Desdemona and her father of the exploits of his youth:

> Wherein I spake of most disastrous chances,
> Of moving accidents by flood and field,
> Of hair-breadth scapes i' the imminent deadly breach,
> Of being taken by the insolent foe.
> (I, iii, 134–137)

The mystery begins with his birth. Of his mother we know only that she was a lady of high birth, adept in sorcery. The handkerchief that she gave her son was the gift of a sibyl, the descendant of a prophetess of ancient Babylon, Egypt, or Greece. Othello had wandered into regions stranger than the half-mythical place of his origin. He had stood at the foot of the mountains of the moon, whose heads touch heaven, where he had seen "The Anthropophagi and men whose heads / Do grow beneath their shoulders" (I, iii, 144–145). No visitant from faraway places in Shakespeare's plays is surrounded with atmosphere so heavy with romance. Yet, under the calm surface of this stately Moor lies the fury and the violence that Elizabethans expected Moors to betray when under stress. These intruders into Spain from Africa appeared in this guise in all the works of 16th-century fiction in which they appeared. In the popular Spanish Palmerin Romances (1511–1547) they are described as "barbarians" and "unbelieving hellhounds." This volatile mixture of tranquility and sleeping violence was supposed to characterize all dwellers in semitropical lands. Sir John Davies (1564–1628) enumerates these qualities in his *Microcosmos* (1603):

> For Southward men are cruel, moody, mad,
> Hot, black, lean leapers, lustful, used to vaunt,
> Yet wise in action, sober, fearful, sad.
> If good, most good, if bad, exceeding bad.

Shakespeare endows Othello with some of these traits, both admirable and offensive. Yet the common opinion of Othello, the dramatic character, is based on that of A. C. Bradley. His view is that Othello is ideally noble, strong and trustful, of a nature that makes him an easy victim of the malignity of a semidevil. This analysis, say the opponents of this interpretation, makes the play solely one of successful intrigue, in which there is no tragic flaw in the hero to make the catastrophe unmistakably his. The play then becomes a tragedy of undeserved suffering. Of those who take exception to this conception of the play and its hero, F. R. Leavis is the most persuasive. He believes that Othello is guilty of self-idealization. His success as a soldier of fortune has given him an inflated opinion of his own worth. In war self-dramatization becomes a virtue; in the unfamiliar Venetian high society into which his marriage has taken him, public virtues have become faults—at least infirmities. G. Wilson Knight makes the interesting suggestion that the storm which buffets the ships of Othello's company on its way to Cyprus is meant to impress an audience that the change in setting, as in Othello's emotional temper, is momentous. Iago is perceptive enough to appeal often to Othello's sense of self-importance. He flatters him when he protests, "I would not have your free and noble nature, / Out of self-bounty, be abused; look to 't" (III, iii, 199–200). As Othello approaches the climax, his self-idealization becomes at first blindness to Iago's machinations and, finally, brutal egotism: "I will chop her into messes: cuckold me!" (IV, i, 211).

In the scene of the murder his self-dramatization reaches its summit. He begins with his praise of his upraised sword and of the execution he has done with it:

Behold, I have a weapon;
A better never did itself sustain
Upon a soldier's thigh.
(V, ii, 259–261)

The speech at which he actually kills himself takes him back to the world of warriors where without anxiety and without perplexity he achieved glory and showed his loyalty to Venice:

And say besides, that in Aleppo once,
Where a malignant and a turban'd Turk
Beat a Venetian and traduced the state,
I took by the throat the circumcised dog,
And smote him, thus. [*Stabs himself.*]
(V, ii, 352–356)

This view of Othello, though it stains the familiar image, is a corrective of the highly idealized character that Bradley first created.

Iago's motives have proved a mystery to many critics. To be sure, he sets them forth clearly and vigorously. The first is his resentment against what he believes to be Othello's injustice in choosing Cassio, a mere military theorist, without firsthand acquaintance with warfare, for a position to which he, Iago, believes he has a better claim. That Cassio is a Florentine adds scorn to Iago's resentment. He knows that the city's prominent citizens are bankers who subsidize wars but never fight. It is not only his rival's promotion that provokes his indignation, but also his charm that induces in Iago a feeling of inferiority. Iago exclaims, "He hath a daily beauty in his life / That makes me ugly" (V, i, 19–20). Finally, he suspects that Othello has himself been Emilia's lover—"the thought whereof / Doth, like a poisonous mineral, gnaw my inwards" (II, i, 305–306). In a perverted nature like Iago's, these motives naturally launched a powerful drive toward vengeance. Many critics find that Iago's rehearsal of his motives does not adequately explain his automatic antagonism to beauty and goodness wherever they appear. They believe that the reasons Iago confesses to are only rationalizations of his powerful unacknowledged bent toward evil. These scholars have found justice in Coleridge's description of Iago's revelation of his motives as "the motive hunting of motiveless malignity." His phrase they interpret in terms of theatre tradition. They see him as a fresh incarnation of the Vice Dissimulation of many a morality play, who is by definition the personification of evil, the theological deadly opposite to Good. Like the Vice, Iago greatly enjoys himself while playing the part of arch-hypocrite and deceiver, laughing up his sleeve at the ease with which he leads the other characters by the nose. Like the Vice, too, he sneers at virtue. Again like the Vice, his allegiance is only to the devil. At intervals throughout the tragedy he admits that he is Satan's confederate. At the end of his first soliloquy, for example, in which he lays bare his program of villainy, he cries:

I have 't. It is engender'd. Hell and night
Must bring this monstrous birth to the world's light.
(I, iii, 409–410)

Satan is responsible for Iago's conviction that every human impulse is the result of close collaboration of self-seeking and sin. All his comments on men and their doings are permeated with a savage spirit of detraction. He stigmatizes Cassio's reputed military skill as "prattle without practice" and love of every sort as a "lust of the blood" and a "permission of the will" (sexual desire). He thus naturally interprets Cassio's courtesy to Desdemona as calculated stimulations to sexuality, Othello's kindness to Emilia as proof that he has seduced her, and Desdemona's attraction to Othello as an appetite for the abnormal in sex experience. His moral nihilism taints the idealism that any of the characters may express and also arouses the sneering laughter that satire often provokes.

Although all the dramatic action up to the catastrophe is the realization of Iago's plot, when he launched it, he did not foresee, much less plan, its tragic issue. As G. L. Kittredge points out, he is an opportunist, modifying his plot as each emergency and the need of preventing its exposure demand. As helplessly as his victims, he is swept along on a full tide to their common disaster. The first success of his scheme exhilarates him. His frustrated desire for action is at last released. Pleasure and action make the hours seem short, he exclaims, after he has assigned Cassio and Roderigo the parts they are to play in his tragedy of revenge. But the awful climax of the action completely silences him. He is either appalled by the horrors he has unwittingly created, or, like many an artist, after the completion of a masterpiece he expects it to speak for its creator. The other characters show little more individuality than the story demands. Desdemona is Shakespeare's portrait of the gentle lady of Cinthio's tale. He gives her the two positive traits that heroines in medieval and Renaissance narratives had to possess: chastity and fidelity to her lord and master. One of Desdemona's last speeches is a triumphant expression of her utter devotion to Othello, just after he has smothered her. To Emilia's cry, "O, who hath done this deed?" she has barely enough strength to gasp out her reply:

Nobody; I myself. Farewell:
Commend me to my kind lord: O, farewell!
(V, ii, 124–125)

Shakespeare adds youthful idealism and romantic yearning to these conventional features of a girl in love. She has not been attracted by any of the "curled darlings" of her natural social milieu; but the strange Othello with his stories of the dangers he has met at the eastern edge of the then known world stirs first her curiosity and then her imagination. He becomes her hero, the embodiment of the mystery that every sheltered girl believes surrounds the little area of the life with which she is familiar. Her father thinks that her infatuation is so unaccountable that it must be the result of black magic. He finds no other explanation for the girl who blushed at the mere recognition of her own erotic feelings "To fall in love with what she fear'd to look on!" (I, iii, 98). To this accusation, Othello answers,

> She loved me for the dangers I had pass'd,
> And I loved her that she did pity them.
> This only is the witchcraft I have used.
> (I, iii, 167–169)

Othello's explanation of their mutual love so much impresses the Duke of Venice, before whom he makes his defense, that he remarks, "I think this tale would win my daughter, too" (I, iii, 171). Desdemona's idealistic infatuation has given her no suspicion of the wild passions that rage beneath Othello's dark skin. Their first outbreak benumbs her mind, which explains the terrified confusion that prompts her reiterated pleas for Cassio at tragically inopportune moments and her childish prevarication about her lost handkerchief. Heaviest with tragic irony is her cry "Alas! he is betray'd and I undone" (V, ii, 76) when Othello tells her that Iago has killed Cassio. To Othello this exclamation is a clear betrayal of her guilt, and he stifles her in the manner of the violent barbarian he has again become.

The minor characters, Roderigo and Emilia, deserve only brief comment. Roderigo is a contemptible, loutish Venetian gentleman, whose stupidity is gross enough to be funny. Lust makes him Iago's easy dupe. Iago fleeces the credulous, lecherous fool, even as he forces him to serve the base purpose of his plot. Emilia is a representative of a conventional type in 16th-century Italian drama, the *balia*, a servant confidante. In Elizabethan drama she is often ineptly called "nurse." Like her Italian prototype, she is prone to speak the blunt and crass word and to be tolerant of sexual laxity. Yet her devotion to her mistress is inspired by her admiration of Desdemona's innocence and her purity. When Emilia learns, to her dismay, that she has been maneuvered into becoming Iago's accomplice, she pours upon him her burning abhorrence of him and his plot. She thus releases the pent-up emotions of the audience. Iago can shut her up only by thrusting his sword through her body. Her death yields her a moment of heroism. The intensity of the feelings aroused by Shakespeare's crowded Senecan denouement serves as a partial substitute for the protagonists' moral and spiritual triumph in *Hamlet* and *King Lear*.—O. J. C.

Stage History: England. The earliest recorded performance of *Othello* is that of November 1604, when the play was given before James I at Whitehall Palace (see REVELS ACCOUNTS). There is a record of a performance in September 1610 at Oxford, and another the previous April at the Globe. In 1629 and 1635 the play was shown at the Blackfriars (see Sir Humphrey MILDMAY), and at Hampton Court in 1636.

In his study of 17th-century allusions to Shakespeare, G. E. Bentley has shown that *Othello* was referred to in print more often than any other Shakespearean play except *The Tempest*. After the Restoration it became the property of the King's Company and so mercifully escaped William Davenant's "improvements." Pepys saw *The Moor of Venice* twice. The first time at the Phoenix in October 1660, Nathaniel Burt played Othello and Walter Clun was Iago. When he saw it for the second time, on February 6, 1669 at Drury Lane, Burt was again Othello; now Michael Mohun acted Iago, and Margaret Hughes, probably the first woman seen on the English public stage, Desdemona. A performance was given in Dublin in 1662. Drury Lane performances are recorded in 1674 and 1675, in 1683, when Thomas Betterton played Othello for the first time, and in 1684.

Othello was almost continuously on the stage throughout the 18th century. Betterton acted the Moor on May 21, 1703, with Anne Bracegirdle as Desdemona and John Verbruggen as Iago. He played the role regularly, first at Lincoln's Inn Fields and afterwards at the Haymarket and Drury Lane. Barton Booth succeeded Betterton as Othello and, according to Benjamin Victor, brought men to tears. He played the part in 1711 at Drury Lane opposite Mrs. Bradshaw's Desdemona and continued in it to 1727. Colley Cibber was Betterton's Iago at Drury Lane on March 24, 1709. His interpretation, a poor one of a transparent villain, reduced the character to implausibility. Nevertheless, Cibber carried on in the part until 1732. In 1722 James Quin's imposing, stolid, restrained Moor, dressed all in white, made his appearance at Lincoln's Inn Fields. The inner passion was missing from this too-respectable Othello, but Quin, who dominated the London stage of his time, acted the role until 1733 at that theatre, transferred to Drury Lane, and played it for the last time at Covent Garden on February 9, 1751. Iago during this period was played most often by Lacy Ryan, first opposite Quin at Lincoln's Inn Fields and afterwards at Covent Garden as late as 1759.

David Garrick acted Othello for the first time on March 7, 1745 at Drury Lane. His Desdemona was Susannah Cibber, who had taken that role first opposite Quin, and Charles Macklin was a plausible Iago. None of the passion was missing from Garrick's conception, but he was criticized for exaggerating the violence and completely neglecting the dignity of the role. Garrick tried the role again two days later and alternated with Thomas Sheridan as Othello and Iago in Dublin during that winter. He played it once more in June of the following year at Covent Garden before relinquishing the role to Spranger Barry, who was to become the great Othello of the period. Barry ideally synthesized the contrasted passions of love and jealousy in a powerful impersonation truly conveying all the nobility, tenderness, and consuming grief of the character. Barry first played the part with Macklin as Iago on October 4, 1746 and appeared in more than 20 revivals without serious competition up to February 9, 1775. Mrs. Cibber played opposite Barry from 1750 to 1753 and Ann Street (Mrs. Dancer), his future wife, played Desdemona from 1766 to 1780, after Barry's death. Both actresses gave fine, spirited performances of Desdemona. In 1749 Garrick played a believable Iago opposite Barry and, for a performance on March 11, 1751, Quin took the part of Iago to Barry's Othello.

At the end of the century John Philip Kemble was the ranking Othello. Although his portrayal lacked the emotional force inherent in the character and substituted mystery for agony, Kemble's productions were commercial successes. He played his first Othello on March 8, 1785 at Drury Lane. His sister, the majestic tragedienne Sarah Siddons, was a surprisingly tender and sympathetic Desdemona. They played these roles together again in 1787 and 1791 at Drury Lane and in 1792 and 1793 at the Haymarket; Robert Bensley was Iago. On March 12, 1794 the newly rebuilt Drury Lane opened, and on November 18 of that year the three re-created their respective roles. Kemble and Mrs. Siddons played the same roles at Drury Lane in 1797 and at Covent Garden in 1804, Mrs. Siddons for the last time. The following year, on May 22, 1805, Kemble played his last Othello. During this period, George Frederick Cooke appeared as an unmistakably villainous Iago, playing the role at Covent Garden in 1800, opposite Kemble again in 1804 and in 1808.

Barry's supremacy as Othello was unchallenged until Edmund Kean played the role at Drury Lane on May 5, 1814. Explosively violent and terrifying, grieved and pathetic, Kean overcame his short stature and managed to sustain the dignity of the Moor. Hazlitt praised this Othello as the "finest piece of acting in the world." When Kean invited Junius Brutus Booth, then only 21 and attracting much attention at Covent Garden, to play Iago opposite his Othello, the purpose was to disadvantage his young rival. Booth performed creditably, but Kean excelled himself. This match took place on February 20, 1817 at Drury Lane. Two days later, Booth absented himself to return to Covent Garden. In July of that year, he attempted Iago to the less formidable Othello of Charles Mayne Young. Meanwhile, Kean continued regularly in the title role and only occasionally acted Iago. On January 28, 1825 public opinion cried out against the apparent hypocrisy of his assuming the role of a husband lamenting his wife's infidelity when, less than two weeks before, he had been successfully sued for damages in an adultery case. But the magic of his portrayal triumphed over this obstacle and Kean continued to act Othello until the end of his career. He collapsed onstage and had to be carried off during a performance on March 25, 1833 at Covent Garden, in which his son, Charles Kean, played Iago and Charles' wife, Ellen Tree, Desdemona.

Lesser Othellos followed. William Charles Macready gave his intellectualized, but never great, conception of the Moor at Covent Garden on October 10, 1816. Five days later he was a smoldering, self-motivated Iago, commanding that role and improving and illuminating it through the years so that by 1832 Macready as Iago was able to stand against Kean's Othello. Macready continued in both parts throughout his career, giving the weaker impersonation much more often than Iago. Opposite his Othello were Helen Faucit in 1836, who gave the often overshadowed heroine intensity, and Fanny Kemble in 1849 at the Princess' Theatre. Macready played Iago opposite Samuel Phelps' Moor in October 1837. In August 1838 Phelps was Macready's Iago, but two months later the roles were again reversed. At Drury Lane in 1842 and 1843, Phelps acted first Iago and, in the later production, Othello. When, in 1844, he began his revivals at Sadler's Wells, he staged the play, and repeated it in all but 3 of his 17 years as manager, alternating in the two roles. He was better as Othello. He made his final Sadler's Wells appearance in the part on November 2, 1861, then continued acting both the Moor and Iago for more than 10 years at other theatres.

At the Princess' Theatre during the 1861/2 season the French actor Charles Fechter played first Othello and, afterward, Iago. He failed in the former portrayal but—as was often the case of inadequate Moors—succeeded with the latter impersonation. The novel Othello of this period was the American Negro Ira Aldridge. He played the role in 1826 at the Royalty, in 1833 at Covent Garden, and in 1865 at the Haymarket, giving a highly civilized, regulated portrayal where perhaps the opposite was expected. Aldridge's effective, but not inspired, impersonation was presented to admiring audiences throughout Europe.

Henry Irving first played the Moor on February 14, 1876 at the Lyceum Theatre, opposite the credible portrayal of Henry Forrester as Iago. Although the production ran for 49 performances, Irving's Othello was a failure. His interpretation differed greatly from the titanic Moor of the Italian Tommaso Salvini, who had acted the part at New York's Academy of Music in 1873 and at Drury Lane, opposite Edwin Booth's Iago, in 1875. While Salvini's Othello was openly sensual, intensely passionate, and finally totally despairing, Irving's feeble Moor was soft at first and only desperate at the last. As manager of the Lyceum, he revived the play in 1881 and alternated the leading roles with Edwin Booth, while Ellen Terry, who had previously played the role at the Princess' in 1863, acted Desdemona. William Terriss was Cassio. Iago became one of Irving's greatest characterizations, but Othello remained one of his poorest and, after this financially successful engagement, he never presented the play again. The deeply tender Desdemona of Miss Terry was thereby sacrificed.

IRA ALDRIDGE AS OTHELLO.

At Stratford-upon-Avon from 1880 to 1964 there were 24 revivals of *Othello*. Barry Sullivan played the Moor in the first and Frank Benson in the second (1886). In 1890 Benson appeared as Othello at the Globe Theatre while, at Stratford, Osmond Tearle produced the play and acted the title role. Stratford's final 19th-century *Othello* was staged in 1897, and Benson began his 20th-century productions of the play with one in 1900. Again in 1902 and 1905, the Memorial Theatre saw Benson play Othello opposite the Desdemona of his wife, Constance Featherstonehaugh.

The early 20th century saw two noble Othellos, each, however, presenting only half the man. The dignified Johnston Forbes-Roberston in 1902 at the Lyric Theatre was a very gentle Moor, in white turban and robes, who lacked the fierce power of the character. Oscar Asche was ferocious enough but missed the poetry. Forbes-Robertson played the Moor only once more, in 1913, at the Drury Lane. His wife, Gertrude Elliott, was Desdemona in both productions. During the summer of 1900, Asche and Lily Brayton acted Othello and Desdemona at Wigan and, in 1911, the two visited Stratford, where Asche produced the play for Benson. Earlier, in 1907, Lewis Waller and Evelyn Millard came from London to act the leads at the Memorial Theatre, having played the roles the previous year at the Lyceum with H. B. Irving as Iago. The Sicilian actor Giovanni Grasso created a terrifying, savage Moor at the Lyric in 1910, who, clutching his Iago by the throat, flung him to the floor. When Beerbohm Tree followed with a sumptuous production at His Majesty's in 1912, Othello became weaker and quieter. That summer Benson produced another Stratford *Othello*. In 1916 Philip Ben Greet, who staged *Othello* each season at the Old Vic from 1914/5 through 1916/7, brought his company to the Memorial Theatre, with Robert Atkins playing Iago. Matheson Lang, while acting in *Carnival* (written by Lang and H. C. M. Hardinge), the story of an actor and his wife who privately live their current stage impersonations of Othello and Desdemona, conceived of presenting matinee performances of Shakespeare's tragedy to precede the evening drama. His first afternoon *Othello* at the New Theatre on February 11, 1920 included Arthur Bourchier, Hilda Bayley, and Hutin Britton as Iago, Desdemona, and Emilia. Lang's Moor received critical praise, but the public preferred *Carnival* and his original plan of transferring *Othello* to the evening bill never materialized.

Godfrey Tearle played a restrained but authoritative Othello at the Court Theatre in 1921, opposite Basil Rathbone's lighthearted villain, and at the Prince's Theatre in 1925 for the Fellowship of Players, with Cedric Hardwicke as Iago. Another Othello in this tradition was Wilfrid Walter, who starred in Atkins' 1921/2 season at the Old Vic; he let loose the barbaric element before returning to final pitiable tenderness. Walter played the Moor again in 1930, this time for W. Bridges-Adams at Stratford, with George Hayes as Iago in a presentation which developed with repetition. Walter's penetrating conception of the character was fully approved. Hayes had previously been Iago to Ion Swinley's Othello at the Old Vic in Atkins' 1924 production. In 1927 the last Old Vic presentation of the decade was Andrew Leigh's, and had Baliol Holloway (who had acted Iago at Stratford in 1922) in the title role.

The second notable Negro Othello was Paul Robeson. He possessed all the physical qualities essential to an ideal portrayal of the Moor, but was unable to assert the full power inherent in the character. Although he was energetic and pathetic enough, the terror was missing, his tone monotonous. In 1930 Robeson appeared at the Savoy. Sybil Thorndike commanded full attention as Emilia in a cast which included Peggy Ashcroft as Desdemona and Ralph Richardson as Roderigo. Two years later Richardson was the Old Vic's "quite exceptionally honest Iago" (according to the *Times*), with Wilfrid Walter repeating his magnificent Othello. Edith Evans returned to the company, playing a coarse, indifferent Emilia in Harcourt Williams' production. Two months later at the St. James, Ernest Milton produced and starred in an *Othello* which closed just after opening. In January 1935 Abraham Sofaer was credited with a masterful performance of Othello, failing only during the murder scene. His Iago, Maurice Evans, was too easy to like and the villainy became pointless. That May, at the Westminster, Wilfrid Walter, in Hugh Hunt's production, played his last Othello. Tyrone Guthrie produced the play at the Old Vic in 1938 with Ralph Richardson as Othello and Laurence Olivier as Iago. Searching for a new interpretation of the play, thè director and Olivier supplied Iago with a subconscious homosexual attraction to Othello. The production was a notable failure. The next major Iago, Alec Clunes at Stratford in Robert Atkins' 1939 production, was recognizably malignant.

Donald Wolfit ushered in the next decade's *Othellos* with a production during a repertory season at the Kingsway in early 1940. On January 6, 1941 he staged a shortened version at the Strand, a full-text production following on the 25th of that month. Power without poetry characterized the Old Vic's Moor of 1942. He was Frederick Valk, the Czech actor, who appeared in Julius Gellner's production on the stage of the New Theatre opposite the sly, chilling Iago of Bernard Miles. In 1943 Baliol Holloway and Abraham Sofaer alternated the leading roles at Stratford. The next year Donald Wolfit produced another repertory season, this time at the Scala, including *Othello;* he again played the Moor himself, opposite Rosalind Iden's Desdemona. Two years later, another Wolfit season, with the producer as Iago, was presented at the Winter Garden. In his final West End repertory appearance in 1947 at the Savoy, Wolfit repeated Iago. At this time Peter Powell's fair production, with Jack Hawkins playing a temperate Othello and Anthony Quayle the villain, was playing at the Piccadilly. Quayle re-created Iago at Stratford in Godfrey Tearle's 1948 *Othello*. Others in the cast were Paul Rogers as Roderigo and Diana Wynyard as Desdemona. Tearle played Othello again during the next season, while Quayle assumed the title role in November 1952 (during a week of three productions previewed before an Australian tour) and in 1954, opposite Barbara Jefford's Desdemona. Quayle successfully developed the dignity and violence in his impressive impersonation of the Moor, a plain soldier agonized not with mean jealousy but with the unbearable sense that goodness has spoiled itself.

After Wolfit, the West End's interest in the drama lagged. It was produced at the Embassy Theatre in 1949 by André van Gyseghem, with Michael Aldridge and George Hagan, and by Orson Welles at the St. James Theatre in 1951. Welles brought the size, weight, and voice necessary to the image of the Moor. The production, altered to emphasize the eroticism, was suspenseful, but never highly passionate. Othello seethed quietly while the speeches flickered away, repressed to the last.

The Old Vic staged two *Othellos* during the 1950's. The first in 1951/2 was produced by Michael Langham, with Douglas Campbell as the Moor, Paul Rogers as Iago, and Irene Worth as Desdemona. Richard Burton and John Neville alternated the leads in 1956, each approaching the Moor from different directions. Burton presented the uncontrolled barbarian; Neville, the civilized, tender gentleman, pathetic in grief. Wendy Hiller acted Emilia and Rosemary Harris was Desdemona in this second Vic presentation, staged by Michael Benthall. The last productions of the decade were Stratford's. In 1956 Glen Byam Shaw directed Harry Andrews in the title role, opposite Emlyn Williams' conscienceless, demonic Iago, with Margaret Johnston as a courageous Desdemona and Diana Churchill as Emilia. Tony Richardson directed Paul Robeson, whose Othello rumbled monotonously, and Sam Wanamaker as Iago in 1959. The leading ladies were Mary Ure and Angela Baddeley, playing Desdemona and Emilia.

Stratford's 1961 production, a contrived affair produced by Franco Zeffirelli, was encumbered by complicated sets which delayed scene changes and could be saved neither by John Gielgud's Moor nor Ian Bannen's Iago. Dorothy Tutin was Desdemona and Peggy Ashcroft, Emilia.

The Old Vic's final season (1962/3) had an *Othello* directed by Casper Wrede. Leo McKern was praised for his coarse Iago, as was Catherine Lacy for her Emilia. Errol John acted the Moor. The National Theatre began its first season with *Hamlet* and *Othello* in 1963. John Dexter directed Laurence Olivier in a performance of the Moor which proved a resounding success. Olivier's characterization was indebted to the T. S. Eliot–F. R. Leavis interpretation of the hero as a self-dramatizing egoist. He played the role as an athletic man of action entranced by his own power in the earlier scenes, reverting under stress to savagery. Frank Finlay was Olivier's Iago.

Stage History: America. The first record of a New York performance of *Othello* was in December 1751 at the theatre in Nassau Street, with Robert Upton as the Moor. David Douglass staged the play and acted the title role on January 10, 1759 at the theatre on Cruger's Wharf, and again on January 25, 1762 for the benefit of the poor. When he played Othello on April 11, 1768, the younger Lewis Hallam acted Iago. Hallam was Iago opposite John Henry's Moor in 1791 and, in 1793, opposite John Hodgkinson. James Fennell retained the part for many years in his repertory, and Thomas Abthorpe Cooper was praised effusively for his interpretations of Othello and of Iago.

The first great American tragedian, Edwin Forrest, was an imposing, warmly passionate, noble Othello later, expressing fully the savage violence before reverting to a final solemnity. He played the Moor almost every year from 1826 to 1871, but abandoned his portrayal of Iago, criticized for lacking passion. Edwin Booth succeeded Forrest on the American stage, introducing a grave, "gentlemanly" Othello, tenderly passionate, always restrained. His Iago has been called the finest interpretation of the villain in his time. Booth managed to convey the inner evil while maintaining a congenial, sincere exterior. He acted both parts from 1860 to 1891, appearing in Great Britain, Germany, and Canada, as well as the United States. In 1862 he staged *Othello* at the Winter Garden and, in 1869, presented another elaborate revival of the drama at Booth's Theatre. Between these productions he acted Iago to the German tragedian Bogumil Dawison's Othello at the Winter Garden on December 29, 1866. In 1886 he briefly played Iago to Tommaso Salvini's Othello. What should have been a great theatrical experience, coming late in Booth's career, found him lacking the vitality necessary to his conception, and critics missed the fabled magnetism and charm. From 1888 to 1891 he alternated both roles with Lawrence Barrett—a partnership that ended sadly when, on March 18, Barrett collapsed during a performance as Othello and died two days later. Booth acted the Moor for the last time on the following April 1 and retired from the stage on April 4.

At the beginning of this century, *Othello* was included in Robert Mantell's repertory, his performance as the Moor adequately expressing the pathos, terror, and solemnity. In August 1942 Paul Robeson appeared as Othello for the first time in America at Cambridge, Massachusetts. Then, in October 1943, he acted the role in a Theatre Guild production at the Shubert which enjoyed a run of 295 performances. The motivation was lacking and Iago's dominance seemed to remove the tragedy from the play. There was a production at Stratford, Ontario, directed by Jean Gascon and George McCowan, with Douglas Campbell and Douglas Rain as Othello and Iago. The New York Shakespeare Festival Theatre, under Joseph Papp, staged the play during the summers of 1964 and 1965.—M.G.

Bibliography. TEXT: *Othello*, New Cambridge Edition, Alice Walker and J. Dover Wilson, eds., 1957; *Othello*, New Arden Edition, M. R. Ridley, ed., 1958. DATE: E. K. Chambers, *William Shakespeare*, 1930. SOURCES: J. M. French, "Othello Among the Anthropophagi," *PMLA*, XLIX, 1934; Kenneth Muir, *Shakespeare's Sources*, Vol. I, 1957. COMMENT: A. C. Bradley, *Shakespearean Tragedy*, 1904; E. E. Stoll, *Shakespeare Studies*, 1927; F. R. Leavis, "Diabolic Intellect and the Noble Hero," in *The Common Pursuit*, 1952; Helen Gardner, *The Noble Moor*, 1955; Bernard Spivack, *Shakespeare and the Allegory of Evil*, 1958. STAGE HISTORY: New Cambridge Edition; T. Alston Brown, *A History of the New York Stage . . . 1901*, 1903; William Winter, *Shakespeare on the Stage*, 3 vols., 1911–1916; G. C. D. Odell, *Shakespeare from Betterton to Irving*, 1920; Marvin Rosenberg, *The Masks of Othello*, 1961; J. C. Trewin, *Shakespeare on the English Stage, 1900–1964*, 1964.

Selected Criticism

THOMAS RYMER. Shakespeare in this Play calls 'em

e supersubtle venetians. Yet examine throughout e Tragedy there is nothing in the noble Desdemona, that is not below any Countrey Chamber-maid ith us. . . . we meet with nothing but blood and utchery, described much-what to the style of the st Speeches and Confessions of the persons executed Tyburn: with this difference, that there we have e fact, and the due course of Justice, whereas our oet against all Justice and Reason, against all Law, umanity and Nature, in a barbarous arbitrary way, xecutes and makes havock of his subjects, Hab-nab, they come to hand. Desdemona dropt her Handerchief; therefore she must be stifl'd. Othello, by w to be broken on the Wheel, by the Poets cunning escapes with cutting his own Throat. Cassio, for know not what, comes off with a broken shin. Jago urders his Benefactor Roderigo, as this were poetial gratitude. Jago is not yet kill'd, because there ever yet was such a villain alive. The Devil, if once e brings a man to be dipt in a deadly sin, lets him one, to take his course: and now when the Foul iend has done with him, our wise Authors take the nner into their poetical service; there to accomplish im, and do the Devils drudgery . . . .

What can remain with the Audience to carry ome with them from this sort of Poetry, for their se and edification? how can it work, unless (instead f settling the mind, and purging our passions) to elude our senses, disorder our thoughts, addle our rain, pervert our affections, hair our imaginations, orrupt our appetite, and fill our head with vanity, onfusion, Tintamarre, and Jingle-jangle, beyond hat all the Parish Clarks of London, with their old estament farces, and interludes, in Richard the secnds time cou'd ever pretend to? Our only hopes, or the good of their Souls, can be, that these people o to the Playhouse, as they do to Church, to sit still, ook on one another, make no reflection, nor mind e Play, more than they would a Sermon.

There is in this Play, some burlesk, some humour, nd ramble of Comical Wit, some shew, and some limickry to divert the spectators: but the tragical art is, plainly none other, than a Bloody Farce, ithout salt or savour. [*A Short View of Tragedy*, 693.]

SAMUEL JOHNSON. The beauties of this play impress emselves so strongly upon the attention of the eader, that they can draw no aid from critical illusation. The fiery openness of *Othello*, magnaniious, artless, and credulous, boundless in his confience, ardent in his affection, inflexible in his esolution, and obdurate in his revenge; the cool alignity of *Iago*, silent in his resentment, subtle in is designs, and studious at once of his interest and is vengeance; the soft simplicity of *Desdemona*, onfident of merit, and conscious of innocence, her rtless perseverance in her suit, and her slowness to ispect that she can be suspected, are such proofs of *hakespeare's* skill in human nature, as, I suppose, it vain to seek in any modern writer. The gradual rogress which *Iago* makes in the Moor's conviction, nd the circumstances which he employs to inflame im, are so artfully natural, that, though it will perps not be said of him as he says of himself, that he *a man not easily jealous*, yet we cannot but pity im when at last we find him *perplexed in the exeme*.

There is always danger, lest wickedness conjoined with abilities should steal upon esteem, though it misses of approbation; but the character of *Iago* is so conducted, that he is, from the first scene to the last, hated and despised.

Even the inferiour characters of this play would be very conspicuous in any other piece, not only for their justness but their strength. *Cassio* is brave, benevolent, and honest, ruined only by his want of stubbornness to resist an insidious invitation. *Rodorigo's* suspicious credulity, and impatient submission to the cheats which he sees practised upon him, and which by persuasion he suffers to be repeated, exhibit a strong picture of a weak mind betrayed by unlawful desires, to a false friend; and the virtue of *Æmilia* is such as we often find, worn loosely, but not cast off, easy to commit small crimes, but quickened and alarmed at atrocious villanies.

The Scenes, from the beginning to the end, are busy, varied by happy interchanges, and regularly promoting the progression of the story; and the narrative, in the end, though it tells but what is known already, yet is necessary to produce the death of *Othello*.

Had the scene opened in *Cyprus*, and the preceding incidents been occasionally related, there had been little wanting to a drama of the most exact and scrupulous regularity. [*The Plays of William Shakespeare*, 1765.]

WILLIAM HAZLITT. The picturesque contrasts of character in this play are almost as remarkable as the depth of the passion. The Moor Othello, the gentle Desdemona, the villain Iago, the good-natured Cassio, the fool Roderigo, present a range and variety of character as striking and palpable as that produced by the opposition of costume in a picture. Their distinguishing qualities stand out to the mind's eye, so that even when we are not thinking of their actions or sentiments, the idea of their persons is still as present to us as ever. These characters and the images they stamp upon the mind are the farthest asunder possible, the distance between them is immense: yet the compass of knowledge and invention which the poet has shown in embodying these extreme creations of his genius is only greater than the truth and felicity with which he has identified each character with itself, or blended their different qualities together in the same story. What a contrast the character of Othello forms to that of Iago! At the same time, the force of conception with which these two figures are opposed to each other is rendered still more intense by the complete consistency with which the traits of each character are brought out in a state of the highest finishing. The making one black and the other white, the one unprincipled, the other unfortunate in the extreme, would have answered the common purposes of effect, and satisfied the ambition of an ordinary painter of character. Shakespear has laboured the finer shades of difference in both with as much care and skill as if he had had to depend on the execution alone for the success of his design. [*The Characters of Shakespear's Plays*, 1817.]

JOHN QUINCY ADAMS. My objections to the character of *Desdemona* arise not from what *Iago*, or *Roderigo*, or *Brabantio*, or *Othello* says of her; but from what she herself *does*. She absconds from her father's house, in the dead of night, to marry a blackamoor. She breaks a father's heart, and covers his noble house with shame, to gratify—what? Pure love, like that of *Juliet* or *Miranda?* No! unnatural passion; it cannot be named with delicacy. Her admirers now say this is criticism of 1835; that the color of *Othello* has nothing to do with the passion of *Desdemona.* No? Why, if *Othello* had been white, what need would there have been for her running away with him? She could have made no better match. Her father could have made no reasonable objection to it; and there could have been no tragedy. If the color of *Othello* is not as vital to the whole tragedy as the age of *Juliet* is to her character and destiny, then have I read Shakespeare in vain. The father of *Desdemona* charges *Othello* with magic arts in obtaining the affections of his daughter. Why, but because her passion for him is *unnatural;* and why is it unnatural, but because of his color? [Letter to James Henry Hackett, reprinted in Hackett's *Notes, Criticisms, and Correspondence upon Shakespeare's Plays and Actors,* 1863.]

VICTOR HUGO. Iago near Othello is the precipice near the landslip. "This way!" he says in a low voice. The snare advises blindness. The lover of darkness guides the black. Deceit takes upon itself to give what light may be required by night. Falsehood serves as a blind man's dog to jealousy. Othello the negro and Iago the traitor pitted against whiteness and candor: what more formidable? These ferocities of darkness act in unison. These two incarnations of the eclipse conspire, the one roaring, the other sneering, for the tragic suffocation of light.

Sound this profound thing. Othello is the night, and being night, and wishing to kill, what does he take to slay with? Poison? the club? the axe? the knife? No; the pillow. To kill is to lull to sleep. Shakespeare himself perhaps did not take this into account. The creator sometimes, almost unknown to himself, yields to his type, so truly is that type a power. And it is thus that Desdemona, spouse of the man Night, dies, stifled by the pillow upon which the first kiss was given, and which receives the last sigh. [*William Shakespeare,* 1864; trans. M. B. Anderson, 1898.]

A. C. BRADLEY. Lastly, Othello's nature is all of one piece. His trust, where he trusts, is absolute. Hesitation is almost impossible to him. He is extremely self-reliant, and decides and acts instantaneously. If stirred to indignation, as 'in Aleppo once,' he answers with one lightning stroke. Love, if he loves, must be to him the heaven where either he must live or bear no life. If such a passion as jealousy seizes him, it will swell into a well-nigh incontrollable flood. He will press for immediate conviction or immediate relief. Convinced, he will act with the authority of a judge and the swiftness of a man in mortal pain. Undeceived, he will do like execution on himself.

This character is so noble, Othello's feelings and actions follow so inevitably from it and from the forces brought to bear on it, and his sufferings are so heart-rending, that he stirs, I believe, in most readers a passion of mingled love and pity which they feel for no other hero in Shakespeare, and to which not even Mr. Swinburne can do more than justice . . . . And pity itself vanishes, and love and admiration alone remain, in the majestic dignity and sovereign ascendancy of the close. Chaos has come and gon and the Othello of the Council-chamber and th quay of Cyprus has returned, or a greater and noble Othello still. As he speaks those final words i which all the glory and agony of his life—long ag in India and Arabia and Aleppo, and afterwards i Venice, and now in Cyprus—seem to pass before u like the pictures that flash before the eyes of drowning man, a triumphant scorn for the fetters c the flesh and the littleness of all the lives that mus survive him sweeps our grief away, and when he di upon a kiss the most painful of all tragedies leaves u for the moment free from pain, and exulting in th power of 'love and man's unconquerable mind [*Shakespearean Tragedy,* 1904.]

T. S. ELIOT. I have always felt that I have neve read a more terrible exposure of human weakness– of universal human weakness—than the last grea speech of Othello. I am ignorant whether anyon else has ever adopted this view, and it may appea subjective and fantastic in the extreme. It is usuall taken on its face value, as expressing the greatness i defeat of a noble but erring nature. . . . What Othell seems to me to be doing in making this speech i cheering himself up. He is endeavoring to escap reality, he has ceased to think about Desdemona, an is thinking about himself. Humility is the most diff cult of all virtues to achieve; nothing dies harde than the desire to think well of oneself. Othello suc ceeds in turning himself into a pathetic figure, b adopting an *aesthetic* rather than a moral attitud dramatising himself against his environment. H takes in the spectator, but the human motive is pr marily to take in himself. I do not believe that an writer has ever exposed this bovarysme, the huma will to see things as they are not, more clearly tha Shakespeare. ["Shakespeare and the Stoicism of Sen eca," in *Selected Essays of T. S. Eliot,* 1932.]

HARLEY GRANVILLE-BARKER. Out of Cinthio's Moo Shakespeare molds to his own liking the hero Othello, confident, dignified, candid, calm. He se up an Iago in total contrast to him; a common fel low, foul-minded and coarse-tongued, a braggart de crying in others the qualities he himself lacks, bitterl envious, pettily spiteful, morbidly vain. He ha abounding vitality, a glib tongue and a remarkabl faculty of adapting himself to his company, as w see when the cynical swagger which so impress Roderigo—that portentous "I am not what I am" an the like—turns to sober soldierly modesty wit Othello. Since Iago in the course of the play will at titudinize much and variously, and not only befo his victims but to himself, will exhibit such skill an a seemingly all but supernatural cunning, Shak speare, for a start, gives us this unvarnished view him, of the self, at any rate, that he shows to R derigo, whom he despises too much to care to che of anything but money . . . .

Othello has a quick and powerful imagination. It a gift which in a man of action may make either f greatness or disaster. It can be disciplined and r fined into a perceptiveness, which will pierce to th heart of a problem while duller men are scratchin its surface; it can divorce his mind from reality alt gether. How is it that, even under stress, Othell does not unarguably perceive Desdemona's inn ence and Iago's falsity? Instead his imagination only ›rves to inflame his passion. He is conscious of its nruliness.

> I swear 'tis better to be much abused
> Than but to know't a little.

-since imagination will multiply "little" beyond ıeasure; that, when passion has dislodged reason in im, is his first cry. Imagination begets monstrous otions:

> I had been happy, if the general camp,
> Pioneers and all, had tasted her sweet body,
> So I had nothing known . . . .

nd Iago keeps it fed with such kindred matter as ne tale of Cassio's dream, with picturings increas- ıgly physical, of her "naked with her friend a-bed," f Cassio's confessedly lying "with her, on her; what ou will!"—until the explicit obscenity leaves imagi- ation at a loss, and nature suspends the torment in he oblivion of a swoon. Later, self-torment takes the bscurer, perverser form of the "horrible fancy" vhich sees Desdemona as a whore in a brothel, him- elf among her purchasers; imagination run rabid . . . .

Othello's, we said, is a story of blindness and folly, f a man run mad. As the play is planned, evil works ll but unquestioned in him until it is too late. Of attle between good and evil, his soul the battle- round, even of a clarifying consciousness of the vil at work in him, there is nothing. Not until the nadman's deed is done, does "he that was Othello" vake to sanity again; his tragedy, then, to have roved from the seemingly securest heights of his soul's content" there is no depth of savagery to vhich man cannot fall. Yet, in face of the irrevocable leed savage and man are one. [*Prefaces to Shake- peare*, Vol. IV, 1946.]

ROBERT B. HEILMAN. Othello is the least heroic of hakespeare's tragic heroes. The need for justifica- ion, for a constant reconstruction of himself in ac- eptable terms, falls short of the achieved selfhood vhich can plunge with pride into great errors and ace up with humility to what has been done. All assion spent, Othello obscures his vision by trying o keep his virtues in focus. The Moor, the warrior, he survivor of exotic adventures, the romantic his- orian of self, is oddly affiliated with the middle-class ero, and in his kind of awareness we detect a pre- ision of later domestic drama.

It is these aspects of Othello's personality that are ost sight of when his ending is pictured as a rather lorious affair. His very defensiveness and sentiment nd sense of loss and of good intention not quite ex- licably gone awry win an affection which a stern acing of spiritual reality might not. . . .

In trying to win approval, from others and him- elf, Othello includes in his summation a one-line lefinition of himself which has been remembered etter than any other part of his apologia—as "one hat lov'd not wisely, but too well". Was his vice eally an excess of a virtue? Or should he have said 'not wisely, nor enough"? One can guess that the onstant quest of assurance might mean less a free iving of self than a taking for self. [*Magic in the Veb: Action and Language in Othello*, 1956.]

BERNARD SPIVACK. What indeed is Iago? In Shake- speare's most compact and painful tragedy he is the artisan of an intrigue that first alienates and then de- stroys a pair of wedded lovers, in an action fraught with the pathos that attends the loss of noble love and noble life. He is also the divisive agent of an- other kind of separation, probably a more tragic theme for the Elizabethans than for us—the divorce of friendship between two generous men. His vic- tims are a beautiful and pure-hearted Venetian woman, a noble and heroic Moorish prince, a loyal and ingenuous fellow soldier, his own honest wife, and a foolish gentleman whose wealth he has drained into his own pocket. He is a soldier, a liar, an adept at dissimulation and intrigue, a cynic, an egotist, a criminal. His crimes, he explains, are motivated by his resentment over the denial of an office to which he aspires and by his desire to recover it, by his sus- picion that he is a deceived husband and by his desire for revenge, and by his need ultimately to cover up his previous malefactions. He inflicts unendurable suffering, destroys love and friendship and four lives, and at the end moves off in defiant silence to torture and his own death . . . .

Labels . . . adhere only to surfaces and mock us with superficiality when we try to apply them to Shakespeare's depths. We detect the type with which he begins but lose it in the unique creation with which he ends. Applied to Iago, the Machiavellian label, while supplying some prefatory enlightenment, is too general to carry us very far into the moral meaning of his role. The high art that wrought him into the dense and exclusive design of his own play does not allow him to remain an undifferentiated specimen of villainous humanity according to the commonplace Elizabeth formula of the Machiavel. He is matched and specialized against a theme, and his evil refined into something rare through the ironic felicity of its polarization and the dramatic felicity of its operation within that theme. His cyni- cal naturalism in respect to human motives and rela- tionships is the first principle from which he moves, through a series of narrowing applications, until it creates his opinion of every other person in the play. It also creates something else: his opinion of his own situation. Unless we follow him closely through the descending gyres of his thought, we lose him and soon begin to wonder what he is talking about. Those of his words, however, which apply to the way we are now concerned with him are invariably consistent with the way he is morally organized, and perspicu- ous in the terms of that organization. He is wonder- fully opposed to the theme of the play as its anti- theme, and is, in fact, the most astonishing product of the Shakespearian technique of contrast. [*Shake- speare and the Allegory of Evil*, 1958.]

JOHN HOLLOWAY. . . . Othello's speech immediately before he stabs himself has been the object of some disparaging comment. Mr Eliot has said that Othello is 'cheering himself up'. Dr Leavis has used the words 'self-dramatization' and 'un-self-comprehending', has alleged that the tears Othello sheds are for the pathos of 'the spectacle of himself' (not, as one might suppose, for the major facts of the case), and sug- gests finally that in the closing lines Othello recalls, and re-enacts, 'his supreme moment of deliberate courage'. This—another attempt, be it noted, to don the tattered plumes of Bradley, and wing with them back before the play opens, or to and fro over a character's whole career—will not do. To have intervened in a street brawl, and (though in an unfriendly town) stabbed a man who may not even have been a soldier, is so far from looking like the supreme moment of deliberate courage in the life of a successful mercenary general, that on its own merits it is self-evidently a minor incident in that life.

That is detail, though. What is not a detail is that it seems as if both these critics, when they wrote what they did of the speech, were unaware of the convention within which it is written, and therefore of what must be looked for in it and how it must be judged. The last speech of a hero is no piece of private musing, but a conventional *genre.* It is the moment at which the character has a special privilege of comment: to sum up either his own life and what it stood for, or the causes of his death. These conventions are widespread in Elizabethan drama, but the cases of Gaunt, Hotspur, King Henry IV, Warwick in Henry VI, Hamlet and Antony make the point clear. All these either speak in the convention, or begin to but are prevented by death itself. It is also Othello's convention. His words should fall with an impersonality, and formality, upon the listener's ear. They are an authoritative and exact account of what has happened in the play. The character is stepping forward from his part to speak with the voice of that implicit chorus which so often speaks in Shakespeare.

What, then, of the seemingly irrelevant anecdote of the closing lines?

> Set you down this:
> And say besides that in Aleppo once,
> Where a malignant and a turban'd Turk
> Beat a Venetian and traduc'd the state,
> I took by th' throat the circumcised dog,
> And smote him—thus.
>
> (V, ii, 355–9)

It is not irrelevance. It is no mere self-indulgent re-enactment of a supreme or any other moment in Othello's past. Othello has been led to it by what he said two sentences before: that he is

> one whose hand
> *Like the base Indian,* threw away a pearl
> Richer than all his tribe
>
> (V, ii, 349–51)

He sees that he has not lived like a Venetian, but like a savage; and the idea leads him to the anecdote which, by its intense ironic charge, offers the final comment upon what he has done, offers a decisive comprehension of it. He has seen that the Turk, chief enemy of Venice, and the Moor, have become one. The 'circumcised dog' is himself. For what has Othello done in the case of Desdemona, daughter of a Senator, but 'beat a Venetian and traduce the state'? The earlier incident swims ironically up from the past because it reveals the ultimate contour of the present; and there is one sense in which Othello does indeed re-enact his past deed: he took vengeance on a little enemy of his society then, and this makes it clearer that he is doing the same thing upon a great one, now. The justice he wrought upon Desdemona was a false justice. This is not. The pattern of the tragedy is complete at last. ["Othello," *The Story o* *the Night,* 1961.]

W. H. AUDEN. Though the imagery in which h expresses his jealousy is sexual—what other kind o images could he use?—Othello's marriage is impor tant to him less as a sexual relationship than as a sym bol of being loved and accepted as a person, brother in the Venetian community. The monster i his own mind too hideous to be shown is the fear h has so far repressed that he is only valued for h social usefulness to the City. But for his occupatio he would be treated as a black barbarian.

The overcredulous, overgood-natured characte which, as Iago tells us, Othello had always displaye is a telltale symptom. He had *had* to be overcredu lous in order to compensate for his repressed sus picions. Both in his happiness at the beginning of th play and in his cosmic despair later, Othello remind one more of Timon of Athens than of Leontes.

Since what really matters to Othello is that Des demona should love him as the person he really i Iago has only to get him to suspect that she does no to release the repressed fears and resentments of a lif time, and the question of what she has done or no done is irrelevant. ["The Joker in the Pack," *Th* *Dyer's Hand and Other Essays,* 1962.]

ALVIN KERNAN. The movement of the play is fro Venice to Cyprus, from *The City* to the outpos from organized society to a condition much closer t raw nature, and from collective life to the life of th solitary individual. This movement is a characteristi pattern in Shakespeare's plays, both comedies an tragedies. . . .

This passage from Venice to Cyprus to fight th Turk and encounter the forces of barbarism is th geographical form of an action that occurs on th social and psychological levels as well. That is, ther are social and mental conditions that correspond t Venice and Cyprus, and there are forces at work i society and in man that correspond to the Turks, th raging seas, and "cannibals that each other eat." . .

What we have followed so far is a movement ex pressed in geographical and social symbols fror Venice to a Cyprus exposed to attack, from *The Cit* to barbarism, from Christendom to the domain o the Turks, from order to riot, from justice to wil revenge and murder, from truth to falsehood . . . .

Othello offers a variety of interrelated symbol that locate and define in historical, natural, socia moral, and human terms those qualities of being an universal forces that are forever at war in the uni verse and between which tragic man is always i movement. On one side there are Turks, cannibal barbarism, monstrous deformities of nature, the brut force of the sea, riot, mobs, darkness, Iago, hatre lust, concern for the self only, and cynicism. On th other side there are Venice, *The City,* law, senate amity, hierarchy, Desdemona, love, concern for oth ers, and innocent trust. As the characters of the pla act and speak, they bring together, by means of par allelism and metaphor, the various forms of the dif ferent ways of life . . . .

Othello's passage from Venice to Cyprus, from ab solute love for Desdemona to extinguishing the ligh in her bedchamber, and to the execution of himsel these are Shakespeare's words for tragic man. [Intro ıction to *Othello*, The Signet Classic Shakespeare, ›63.]

Otway, Thomas (1652–1685). Dramatist. Educated Oxford, Otway entered the theatre as an actor, ıt quickly turned to playwriting. In 1675 his first ay, *Alcibiades*, was produced. As the result of an ırequited love for the actress Elizabeth Barry (1658–13), he enlisted in the army and left England in 578. In 1679 he returned and produced his greatest agedies, *The Orphan* (1680) and *Venice Preserved* 682). Both plays starred Mrs. Barry and Thomas etterton. Otway's *History and Fall of Caius Marius* 679, pub. 1680) is a very free adaptation of the plot f *Romeo and Juliet* set against a background of oman history.

Unlike the original, Otway's play concentrates on ıe older generation and on civil discord between ıe patricians, led by Metellus (Capulet), and the ebellious plebeians, led by Marius (Montague). Vhen Metellus bypasses Marius and awards the posi- on of consul to Sylla, Marius, aided by his son oung Marius (Romeo), attempts a revolt, but it is nsuccessful.

Set against this action is what is left of Shake- peare's plot. Marius' son and Metellus' daughter Lavinia [Juliet]) are in love when the play opens. lthough Lavinia is to marry Sylla, she and Marius re secretly married, despite their parents' objec- ons. Young Marius proves himself a hero in battle nd his father gives his blessing to the match. The est of the love story follows Shakespeare fairly losely, except that the elder Marius kills his enemy nd is in turn killed by Sylla.

The romantic story and the political plot combine ery awkwardly in Otway's play. A saving grace is is realization of his indebtedness to Shakespeare. He oes not call his play an "improvement," but admits hat the best parts of his version are those he lifted odily from his source. *Caius Marius* was first pro- uced in 1679, and it held the stage for almost 100 ears. Some parts of this adaptation, notably the lov- rs' final scene together, continued to be played as ıte as the 19th century. [Hazelton Spencer, *Shake- peare Improved*, 1927.]

Outlaws. In *The Two Gentlemen of Verona*, the and of brigands who capture Valentine and subse- uently appoint him their captain. In IV, i, three of he Outlaws have speaking parts.

Overdone, Mistress. In *Measure for Measure*, a awd and keeper of a brothel. Mistress Overdone as had nine husbands and was "Overdone by the ıst." Worried about the proclamation that bawdy ouses must be closed, Mistress Overdone is assured y Pompey that she need not change her trade but vill receive special consideration, having "worn her] eyes almost out in the service" (I, ii). Never- heless she is sent to prison.

Overy, Edward (d. 1621). A witness to Shake- peare's purchase of the Blackfriars Gate-House. A rosperous businessman, Overy was a friend of John ackson, one of the trustees of the purchase. In his vill he left Jackson a bequest of £5. [Leslie Hotson, *hakespeare's Sonnets Dated*, 1949.]

Ovid [Publius Ovidius Naso] (43 B.C.–A.D. 18). Roman poet. One of the great poets of the Augustan ge—the period of the reign (27 B.C.–A.D. 14) of Caesar Augustus—Ovid was also a judge in the Roman courts. His personal life, however, was distinguished by a notable lack of judicial sobriety. He was married three times, and in A.D. 8 was banished from Rome for reasons that have remained obscure. In his banishment he devoted his life to poetry. He is the author of the METAMORPHOSES; the *Heroides*, a group of amorous epistles; the *Fasti*, a poetical calendar; the scandalous *Ars Amatoria;* and the *Tristia*, elegies occasioned by his exile.

In addition to extensive borrowings from the *Metamorphoses*, Shakespeare is indebted to Ovid for much of *The Rape of Lucrece*, which derives from the *Fasti*. Shakespeare used the *Heroides* in various places throughout his works: in the conversation of Lorenzo and Jessica in the garden at Belmont (*Merchant of Venice*, V, i, 1–24), for example. He was familiar with the *Ars Amatoria* and *Tristia* as well. [J. A. K. Thomson, *Shakespeare and the Classics*, 1952.]

Oxford, John de Vere, 13th earl of (1443–1513). A Lancastrian who aided Warwick in restoring Henry VI. Oxford escaped to France on the reinstatement of Edward IV, but returned to England in 1485 with Henry Tudor, earl of Richmond, who became Henry VII. In *3 Henry VI*, at King Lewis' palace in France, Oxford chides Warwick for abandoning King Henry and recalls that the Yorkists had caused the death of his own father and brother (III, iii). In *Richard III*, he appears briefly as a supporter of Richmond at Bosworth Field (V, ii).

Oxfordian theory. Term used to describe the theory that Edward de Vere, 17th earl of Oxford, is the author of the plays ascribed to Shakespeare. The Oxfordian theory, which has now outstripped the BACONIAN THEORY in popularity, was first put forth by J. Thomas Looney in his *"Shakespeare" Identified in Edward de Vere the Seventeenth Earl of Oxford* (1920). Looney's book resulted in the founding of the Shakespeare Fellowship, an ostensibly nonsectarian, anti-Stratfordian brotherhood, but one which rapidly became associated with the Oxfordian faction. The group received its greatest boost from the appearance of a biography of Oxford in 1928. The book, *The Seventeenth Earl of Oxford, 1550–1604*, by Bernard M. Ward, contained much new material on Oxford's life and tacit approval of the Oxfordian theory. The biography stimulated the prolific Percy Allen to pursue the case in a number of volumes published in the 1930's. Allen's most startling evidence, however, appeared in 1947 with the publication of his *Talks with Elizabethans Revealing the Mystery of "William Shakespeare."* In this volume Allen described his approach to the problem as follows, "Through the agency of a gifted medium, of wide experience and of unimpeachable integrity, I have, for many months past, been talking with the three above-named Elizabethans Oxford, Bacon and Shakespeare, from whom I have obtained . . . a final solution of the Shakespeare mystery . . ." The solution was that Shakespeare, Oxford, and others collaborated on the plays, with the major work being done by Oxford. Somewhat more pedestrian is the approach of Dorothy and Charlton Ogburn in their voluminous (1297 pages) *This Star of England:*

"*William Shakespeare*" *Man of the Renaissance* (1952, rev. ed. 1955). The work is essentially an elaborate restatement of the Oxfordian position, but it contains a number of surprising new "facts," not the least of which is that the earl of SOUTHAMPTON was the son of Oxford and Queen Elizabeth. The major objection to the Oxfordian theory by orthodox Shakespeareans has been the fact that Oxford died in 1604 and that in the orthodox chronology many of Shakespeare's greatest plays were written after that date. [Frank W. Wadsworth, *The Poacher from Stratford*, 1958.]

Oxford's Men. Acting company under the patronage of Edward de Vere, 17th earl of Oxford. The earl, himself interested in the drama to the extent of participating in court entertainments and writing some plays, sponsored a group of players from 1580 to about 1602. This company, evidently transferring to Oxford's patronage from that of the earl of Warwick, included two well-known figures: John (fl. 1575–1591) and Laurence (fl. 1571–1591) Dutton.

Oxford's Men may have occupied the Theatre in 1580, but for the most part their career was spent in the provinces. In 1583 John Dutton left Oxford's Men for the Queen's Men, a group formed that year which brought together the best individual actors then available. In 1584 Oxford's Men made their first appearance at court; their payee was John Lyly, who had been in the service of the earl of Oxford for a long time.

They are mentioned as having toured the provinces between 1585 and 1589/90, and they made no more appearances at court. In 1602 Oxford's Men merged with WORCESTER'S MEN. [E. K. Chambers, *The Elizabethan Stage*, 1923.]

Oxford University Dramatic Society. A theatrical society at Oxford commonly known as the O.U.D.S. Its formation was proposed in 1884 at the prompting of Arthur Bourchier, then an undergraduate at Chri Church, and some of his friends, including W. I Courtney and Cosmo Gordon Lang, later archbisho of Canterbury. The Society was launched in 188 with a production of *1 Henry IV*. Hotspur wa played by Bourchier and Lang spoke the Prologu From then until the outbreak of war in 1914, 32 productions were given. The O.U.D.S. was temporaril disbanded during the war, but was started again i 1919. In 1932, John Gielgud was invited to produc *Romeo and Juliet* and the production starred Christopher Hassall as Romeo, Peggy Ashcroft as Julie and Edith Evans as the Nurse. In the following yea Max Reinhardt directed what was to become one o the best known of O.U.D.S. productions—*A Midsummer Night's Dream*. In 1939, after a short perio of playing at the New Theatre, the O.U.D.S. move into the Oxford Playhouse with *The Duchess o Malfi* produced by Maurice Colbourne.

Shortly after World War II, the O.U.D.S. wa again suspended because of financial difficulties. A benevolent dictatorship was then formed by Nevil Coghill, a producer and senior member for over 3 years. The resulting organization, the Friends o O.U.D.S., made up of senior members of th O.U.D.S., maintained the high standards of previou productions and got the Society out of debt, pavin the way for its reestablishment in 1947.

The general policy of the O.U.D.S. is to presen plays that have been accepted as classics in order no to infringe upon the domain of the Experimenta Theatre Club. Each year four plays are produced o which one is usually by Shakespeare. O.U.D.S. productions have recently begun to tour. Three productions have been taken to France (*Richard II*, 1961 *Othello*, 1963; and *King Lear*, 1965) and the *Lear* wa also seen in Rome as well as in Caen, Paris, an Grenoble.

P

Page. In the Induction to *The Taming of the Shrew,* he disguises himself as a woman and pretends to be Sly's wife.

Page, Anne. In *The Merry Wives of Windsor,* the sweet young daughter of the Pages. Anne has £700 and three suitors. Although she considers Slender a fool and prefers marriage to Doctor Caius, Anne ends by deceiving both her father, who favors Slender, and her mother, who prizes the Doctor, and elopes with Fenton, whom she loves. Master and Mistress accept Anne's choice after the fact.

Page, Master George. In *The Merry Wives of Windsor,* a gentleman of Windsor. Master Page discredits Nym's information of Falstaff's intention to seduce his wife and suffers no jealous doubts of Mistress Page's virtue. Ford is subjected to Page's scorn when the attempt to expose an assignation between Falstaff and Mistress Ford fails. When Page's daughter Anne rejects Slender, the suitor he favors, and elopes with Fenton, the indulgent father readily accepts the marriage.

Page, Mistress Meg. In *The Merry Wives of Windsor,* one of the merry wives. The recipient of one of Falstaff's two identical love letters, Mistress Page joins forces with Mistress Ford in the humiliation of "this greasy knight." She initiates Falstaff's final abasement with her recollection of the old tale of Herne the Hunter. When her daughter Anne elopes with Fenton, thus disappointing Mistress Page's hope that she would marry Doctor Caius, the mother readily accepts her son-in-law, wishing him "many merry days."

Page, William. In *The Merry Wives of Windsor,* Anne Page's young brother. In IV, i, William replies to Sir Hugh Evans' foolish questions testing his knowledge of Latin; the scene evolves into a series of puns as Mistress Quickly takes words of the Latin doggerel for their English homonyms. Evans finally dismisses the boy, complimenting him for his power of memory.

Page to Falstaff. In *2 Henry IV,* a small boy put into Falstaff's service by Prince Hal. Falstaff describes him as "fitter to be worn in my cap than to wait at my heels" (I, ii). In *Henry V,* he accompanies Bardolph, Pistol, and Nym to France after Falstaff's death, but decides to leave their service because "their villany goes against my weak stomach, and therefore I must cast it up" (III, ii). Although not named here, he is probably the Robin of *The Merry Wives of Windsor.*

Painter. In *Timon of Athens,* a minor character who, in I, i, enjoys Timon's patronage. In V, i, having heard rumors of Timon's gold, the Painter goes to his benefactor's cave and attempts to renew their relationship. Timon drives him away.

Painter, William (c. 1540–1594). Translator. Painter was a schoolmaster and later a clerk of the ordnance in the Tower of London where he abused his position by the fraudulent appropriation of large sums of money. In 1566 he published the first volume of *The Palace of Pleasure* which contained 60 tales translated from a number of Italian, French, and Latin sources. *The Palace* was augmented in 1567 by publication of a second volume with 34 additional stories and by a combined edition of 101 tales published in 1575. *The Palace of Pleasure* was thus the largest collection of prose stories then available in English; it became the major source of plots for the Elizabethan playwrights. The stories came chiefly from the Italian *novelle* of Boccaccio, Matteo Bandello, Cinthio, Masuccio Salernitano, Giovanni Straparola, and Giovanni Fiorentino, as well as from classical sources such as Livy, Plutarch, and Herodotus. Painter's prose style, distinguished by its simplicity and directness, serves to underplay the somewhat lurid quality of the tales. Shakespeare probably drew upon several of Painter's translations of tales from Boccaccio's *Decameron* for the source of *All's Well That Ends Well,* and possibly also for some details of *The Rape of Lucrece* and *Romeo and Juliet.* See ALL'S WELL THAT ENDS WELL: *Sources.*

Palace of Pleasure, The. See William PAINTER.

Palamon. In *The Two Noble Kinsmen,* one of the kinsmen of the title and a nephew to Creon, King of Thebes. He and his cousin Arcite are captured by Theseus. On seeing Emilia from their prison window, both young men fall in love with her. After Arcite's banishment, Palamon is helped to escape by the Jailer's Daughter, who has fallen in love with him. Subsequently losing to Arcite the tournament for Emilia's hand, Palamon is about to be executed when news of his cousin's accidental death saves his life. He consequently wins Emilia.

Palatine's Men. See ADMIRAL'S MEN.

Palladis Tamia. A collection of miscellaneous essays by Francis MERES containing an important allusion to Shakespeare. *Palladis Tamia* was printed in 1598 as part of a series of literary commonplace books. The topics in the volume cover a broad range, including philosophy, morality, religion, and literary criticism. The reference to Shakespeare occurs in a section entitled "A Comparitiue discourse of our English Poets with the *Greeke, Latine, and Italian Poets*":

> As the soule of *Euphorbus* was thought to liue in *Pythagoras*: so the sweete wittie soule of *Ouid*

liues in mellifluous & hony-tongued *Shakespeare*, witnes his *Venus* and *Adonis*, his *Lucrece*, his sugred Sonnets among his priuate friends, &c.

As *Plautus* and *Seneca* are accounted the best for Comedy and Tragedy among the Latines: so *Shakespeare* among the English is the most excellent in both kinds for the stage; for Comedy, witnes his *Gentlemen of Verona*, his *Errors*, his *Loue labors lost*, his *Loue labours wonne*, his *Midsummers night dreame*, & his *Merchant of Venice*: for Tragedy his *Richard the 2. Richard* the *3. Henry the 4. King Iohn, Titus Andronicus* and his *Romeo* and *Iuliet*.

As *Epius Stolo* said, that the Muses would speake with *Plautus* tongue, if they would speak Latin: so I say that the Muses would speak with *Shakespeares* fine filed phrase, if they would speake English.

The reference to *Loue labours wonne* has prompted considerable speculation as to which play Meres had in mind (see LOVE'S LABOUR'S WON). Shakespeare's name also occurs in the list of the best lyric and love poets, and as best for both comedy and tragedy:

As *Pindarus*, *Anacreon* and *Callimachus* among the Greekes; and *Horace* and *Catullus* among the Latines are the best Lyrick Poets: so in this faculty the best among our Poets are *Spencer* (who excelleth in all kinds) *Daniel, Drayton, Shakespeare, Bretton* . . . .

These are our best for Tragedie, the Lorde *Buckhurst*, Doctor *Leg* of Cambridge, Doctor *Edes* of Oxforde, maister *Edward Ferris*, the Authour of the *Mirrour for Magistrates, Marlow, Peele, Watson, Kid, Shakespeare, Drayton, Chapman, Decker*, and *Beniamin Johnson* . . . .

The best for Comedy amongst us bee, *Edward* Earle of Oxforde, Doctor *Gager* of Oxforde, Maister *Rowley* once a rare Scholler of learned Pembrooke Hall in Cambridge, Maister *Edwardes* one of her Maiesties Chappell, eloquent and wittie *John Lilly, Lodge, Gascoyne, Greene, Shakespeare, Thomas Nash, Thomas Heywood, Anthony Mundye* our best plotter, *Chapman, Porter, Wilson, Hathway*, and *Henry Chettle* . . . .

These are the most passionate among us to bewaile and bemoane the perplexities of Loue, *Henrie Howard* Earle of Surrey, sir *Thomas Wyat* the elder, sir *Francis Brian*, sir *Philip Sidney*, sir *Walter Rawley*, sir *Edward Dyer, Spencer, Daniel, Drayton, Shakespeare* . . . .

The allusion is of great importance in determining the dates of the early plays and the *Sonnets*, as well as attesting to Shakespeare's stature among his contemporaries even at this comparatively early stage of his career.

In addition to mentioning *1 Henry IV* in his list of Shakespeare's plays, Meres quotes from the play in his account of Michael Drayton:

Michael Drayton . . . a man of vertuous disposition . . . which is almost miraculous . . . in these times . . . when there is nothing but rogery in villanous man . . . .

The phrase "there is nothing but roguery to be found in villanous man" occurs in the Shakespeare play (II, iv, 138–139).

Palladis Tamia, a second edition of which w published in 1634, is also notable for an erroneo account of the death of Christopher Marlowe, whi was accepted by scholars as fact until the publicati of Leslie Hotson's *The Death of Christopher Ma lowe* in 1925. [*Elizabethan Critical Essays*, G. Gre ory Smith, ed., 1904; *Francis Meres's Treatise "P etrie": A Critical Edition*, Don Cameron Allen, e 1933.]

Palmer, John (1744–1798). Actor. Born in Londo the son of a soldier, Palmer disregarded the advi of his father and Garrick to shun the theatre. Fro 1762 to 1766 he acted in a series of unsuccessful pr ductions, but in the ensuing two years he began establish himself and was engaged by Garrick. 1772 he went to Liverpool as a tragedian and the became a great favorite. He opened a new theat there with *As You Like It* in 1787, with himself Jaques. Ultimately his scandalous behavior and fina cial extravagance resulted in imprisonment for deb but by that time he had already played more tha 300 parts, including many major roles in Shak spearean plays. In tragedy he was most successful parts requiring dissimulation, which he evidentl possessed as a natural talent; thus Iago was one his best roles. He was excellent in comedy, especiall as Sir Toby Belch.

Charles Lamb characterized Palmer as a "gentl man with a slight infusion of the footman." He wa a colorful figure, and it was said that he induced th arresting officer to bail him out of debtors' priso that he was never ready on first nights, and that h ghost appeared after his death. [*Dictionary of Na tional Biography*, 1885– ; Charles Beecher Hogar *Shakespeare in the Theatre, 1701–1800*, 2 vols., 195 1957.]

Palsgrave's Men. See ADMIRAL'S MEN.

Pandar. In *Pericles*, proprietor of the Mytilen brothel. He is a conscientious tradesman willing t pay any price to revive a faltering business. A brie moment of misgiving over his offensive occupatio is interrupted by the arrival of a new recruit, th virtuous Marina, who subsequently threatens t ruin the Pandar's business by reforming his patron

Pandarus. In Greek legend, a Lycian leader, on of Priam's allies in the Trojan War; in *Troilus an Cressida*, Cressida's uncle and the matchmaker fo her and Troilus. Though in classical times Pandaru was depicted as an admirable archer and honored a a hero-god in his own country, and in Chaucer' *Troilus and Criseyde* he is a delightfully humorou old man, he came to be represented in medieval ro mance as despicable.

Part of the reason for the debasement of his char acter is historical: by Shakespeare's time the moder meaning of the word "pander," derived from Pan darus, had already been incorporated into the lan guage. Thus the Elizabethan audience expected t see Pandarus as a pander (procurer), just as it ex pected Cressida to be portrayed as a whore. Shake speare's Pandarus, however, is something more tha a lecherous, prurient old man wallowing in a kin of imaginative voyeurism. He is, as has been pointe out, more closely paralleled in Juliet's nurse, hi bawdiness being an aspect of his generally open an free, but not particularly scrupulous, nature. His be havior, however erroneous, is motivated by kindnes and friendship for the young lovers. [*Troilus an*

Cressida, New Variorum Edition, Harold Hillebrand and T. W. Baldwin, eds., 1953.]

Pandosto. See Robert GREENE.

Pandulph (d. 1226). Roman politician and papal legate, often confused with Cardinal Pandulfus Masca. In 1211 Pope Innocent III sent him to England to secure from King John the archbishopric of Canterbury for Stephen Langton. When King John refused the cardinal's request, Pandulph excommunicated him. Nevertheless, he opposed the intention of the French king to invade England. When, later, Pandulph excommunicated the great barons who forced John to sign the Magna Carta at Runnymede, the grateful king gave him the bishopric of Norwich.

In *King John*, Cardinal Pandulph appears as the papal legate who excommunicates John and prevails on Philip of France and Lewis the Dauphin to make war against the English. Pandulph subsequently persuades the Dauphin to claim the crown of England in the right of his wife, Lady Blanch.

Panthino. In *The Two Gentlemen of Verona*, a servant to Antonio, the father of Proteus. At the request of Antonio's brother, Panthino urges his master to send Proteus to seek his fortune in Milan (I, iii). Later he summons Proteus and Launce to the vessel that takes them to Milan (II, ii and iii).

Paris. In *Romeo and Juliet*, a nobleman whose betrothal to Juliet is arranged by her father. Paris is slain by Romeo at Juliet's tomb. The actor who originally played Paris (William Bird?) is thought to be one of the reporters of the "bad quarto" of *Romeo and Juliet*. See MEMORIAL RECONSTRUCTION.

Paris. In Greek legend and in Homer's *Iliad*, the son of Troy's King Priam and Hecuba; Paris' abduction of Helen caused the Trojan War. In *Troilus and Cressida*, he plays the same role; the poet emphasizes his idealistic and illusionary love for Helen.

Paris Garden. See BEARBAITING, BULLBAITING, AND COCKFIGHTING.

Parker Society, The. A scholarly society. The Parker Society was founded in 1841 for the purpose of reprinting the works of the major English Protestant writers of the 16th century. It was named in honor of Matthew Parker, Elizabeth's first Archbishop of Canterbury. When completed in 1855, its series of printed works consisted of 55 volumes including the index. With the exception of Richard Hooker, whose works are readily available elsewhere, the series contains the works of virtually all the important religious writers of the period—Bale, Becon, Coverdale, Cranmer, Grindal, Jewel, Latimer, Parker, Tyndale, Whitgift. The comprehensive index, more than 800 pages in length, is a guide to what the religious leaders had to say on the topics of the day.

Park Theatre. (1) In New York, the first important American theatre, originally called the New, was opened in 1798 with a performance of *As You Like It* in which the owner-actors John Hodgkinson (c. 1765–1805) and Lewis Hallam (c. 1740–1808) played Jaques and Touchstone, respectively. During 1798 Thomas Abthorpe Cooper (1776–1849) also played Hamlet. Although the Park was home to a good company, the querulous managers jeopardized its financial position. Under the succeeding manager, William Dunlap (1766–1839), the Park presented mostly contemporary drama, except for *Twelfth Night*, given in 1804. Cooper next managed the Park for owners Beekman and Astor, until in 1808 a controlling interest was bought by a businessman, Stephen Price (1783–1840), who managed it prosperously until his death. He engaged every important actor of the time, including Kean, Mathews, Kemble, Hackett, Forrest, and Macready, and although audiences apparently preferred the spectacles given elsewhere, Price maintained a repertory of classical and Shakespearean drama. In 1848 the Park burnt down, having suffered a decline after Price's death.

(2) A theatre opened in 1874 by Charles Albert Fechter at Broadway and 22nd Street, and managed from 1876 to 1882 (when it burned down) by Henry E. Abbey (1846–1896), one of the foremost American theatre managers.

(3) The first professional theatre in Brooklyn, managed by Sarah Crocker Conway (1834–1875) from 1864 until 1871, when she opened the larger Brooklyn Theatre. At the Park a good stock company supported important visiting stars. In 1873/4 Minne Maddern played in *Oliver Twist*, and appearances were also made by Adelaide Neilson and Edward Hugh Sothern. The competition from the Brooklyn Theatre led to a policy of variety and burlesque, but after the Brooklyn was destroyed, the Park again played host to an important stock company.

(4) The Majestic Theatre in Columbus Circle, opened in 1903, was called the Park from 1911 until 1925, when it was renamed the Cosmopolitan by Florenz Ziegfeld (1867–1932). [*The Oxford Companion to the Theatre*, Phyllis Hartnoll, ed., 1951.]

Parnassus Plays. Three anonymous plays, written between 1598 and 1602 and performed at St. John's College, Cambridge. The titles of the plays are *The Pilgrimage to Parnassus* (*1 Parnassus*), *The First Part of the Returne from Parnassus* (*2 Parnassus*), and *The Second Part of the Returne from Parnassus* (*3 Parnassus*). The plays are good examples of a certain type of UNIVERSITY DRAMA written by the students at Oxford and Cambridge. They are filled with satirical and topical allusions dealing with undergraduate life at Cambridge (*1 Parnassus*) and the difficulties impecunious young scholars faced after graduation (*2* and *3 Parnassus*). First performed during the 1601/2 Christmas revels, *3 Parnassus* was published in 1606 with the following title page:

> the Returne from Parnassus: Or The Scourge of Simony. Publiquely acted by the Students in Saint Johns Colledge in Cambridge.

In *3 Parnassus* two recent graduates, Studioso and Philomusus, attempt to obtain jobs as actors with Shakespeare's company, the Chamberlain's Men. They are to be auditioned by Richard Burbage and Will Kempe, who discuss the possibility of hiring the two graduates:

> *Burbage*. A little teaching will mend these faults, and it may bee besides they will be able to pen a part.
>
> *Kempe*. Few of the vniversity men pen plaies well, they smell too much of that writer *Ouid*, and that writer *Metamorphosis*, and talk too much of *Proserpina & Iuppiter*. Why heres our fellow *Shakespeare* puts them all downe, I and *Ben Ionson* too. O that *Ben Ionson* is a pestilent fellow, he brought vp Horace giuing the Poets a pill,

> but our fellow *Shakespeare* hath giuen him a purge that made him beray his credit.

Kempe's allusion to Jonson's "giuing the Poets a pill" has long been recognized as a reference to the WAR OF THE THEATRES, the literary feud which Jonson carried on against Dekker and Marston. Scholars, however, have been unable to agree on the exact nature of this apparent allusion to Shakespeare's participation in the "war" against Jonson. Some have suggested that Jonson is satirized as Jaques in *As You Like It* or as Nym, who frequently uses the word "humour," in *The Merry Wives of Windsor.* The most common view, however, sees Jonson in the characterization of AJAX in *Troilus and Cressida.* E. K. Chambers has suggested an alternative possibility, i.e., that the "purge" given to Jonson in Dekker and Marston's *Satiromastix* is alluded to here under the mistaken impression that the play, acted by Shakespeare's company, was written by Shakespeare.

Other important allusions to Shakespeare occur in *2 Parnassus,* in which the foolish courtier Gullio professes to be an ardent admirer of Shakespeare. His admiration expresses itself in such gushing and, to the author of the Parnassus plays, such ignorant sentiments as Gullio's comment:

> Let this duncified worlde esteeme of Spencer and Chaucer, I'le worshipp sweet Mr. Shakspeare, and to honoure him will lay his Venus and Adonis under my pillowe, as wee reade of one (I doe not well remember his name, but I am sure he was a kinge) slept with Homer under his bed's heade.

Gullio's disparagement of Spenser and Chaucer and his praise of Shakespeare are clearly presented here with irony. The author of the Parnassus plays apparently regarded Shakespeare as a good poet who was dissipating his talents on such trivial themes as romantic love. This opinion is made explicit in *3 Parnassus:*

> *Iudicio.* Who loues not *Adons* loue, or *Lucrece* rape?
> His sweeter verse contaynes hart throbbing line,
> Could but a graver subiect him content,
> Without loues foolish lazy languishment.

An attempt has been made to see in Gullio, the foolish courtier who dotes on Shakespeare, a satiric portrait of Shakespeare's patron Henry Wriothesley, earl of Southampton. Certain similarities between Southampton and Gullio have been admitted as evidence in support of this conjecture, including the fact that Gullio, like Southampton, is described as having served with Essex. Gullio is also shown as the patron of Ingenioso, another character in the play, and Ingenioso has been almost certainly identified as Thomas Nashe, who enjoyed Southampton's patronage on at least one occasion. This hypothesis is not acceptable to those who feel that Gullio represents a type rather than a specific individual.

The problem of the authorship of the plays has long puzzled critics. It is generally felt that they were not written by one man; scholars tend to suggest that the first play was written by one author and *2* and *3 Parnassus* by another. The identity of

THE
RETVRNE FROM
PERNASSVS:
Or
The Scourge of Simony.

Publiquely acted by the Students in Saint Iohns Colledge in *Cambridge,*

AT LONDON
Printed by *G. Eld,* for *Iohn Wright,* and are to bee sold at his shop at Christ church Gate.
1606.

TITLE PAGE OF *The Return from Parnassus* (1606).

the authors, however, remains a mystery. The view that John DAY was one of the authors is no longer accepted, and the suggestion that it was William Dodd, a student at Cambridge from 1598 to 1602 lacks any real authority. [*The Three Parnassus Plays* J. B. Leishman, ed., 1949.]—E.Q.

Parolles. In *All's Well That Ends Well,* a toadying follower of Bertram. Despised as if by acclamation, this worthless coward is nonetheless accepted by the Count of Rousillon as his boon companion. Variously called a "notorious liar," "vile rascal," "counterfeit lump of ore," and "owner of no one good quality," Parolles is succinctly appraised by Lafeu, who describes him as "a general offence." The extent of his villainy is exposed before Bertram when Parolles is blindfolded and tricked into betraying his unseen friend.

After Parolles' exposure, he rebounds from his disgrace and expresses delight simply in being alive. Parolles is sometimes considered to be a portrait of Barnabe BARNES.

Parrott, Thomas Marc (1866–1960). American scholar, professor at Princeton University. Parrott published many scholarly articles but, with the exception of his unfinished edition of Chapman (2 vols., 1910–1914) and *The Problem of Timon of Athens* (1923), his books have been guides for the student and general reader. His annotated edition of 23 plays and sonnets of Shakespeare has undergone many reprintings and two revisions (1929; rev., 1938, 1953). *William Shakespeare: A Handbook* (1934; rev., 1955) consists of essays on general topics. *A* *hort View of Elizabethan Drama* (with R. H. Ball, 943; rev., 1955) is one of the most useful of the horter surveys. Other works include *Shakespearean Comedy* (1949) and *A Companion to Victorian Literature* (with R. B. Martin, 1955). [*Essays in Dramatic Literature: The Parrott Presentation Volume*, Hardin Craig, ed., 1935.]

Parry, Charles Hubert H. See MUSIC BASED ON SHAKESPEARE: *19th century, 1850–1900.*

Parsons, Robert (1546–1610). Jesuit priest. Parsons was educated at Balliol College, Oxford. On graduation he became a tutor. Forced to resign for some unknown reason in 1574, he journeyed to Europe; at Louvain he was converted to Catholicism and in Rome joined the Society of Jesus in 1575. He then returned in disguise to England, where he set up a press and issued a number of polemical pamphlets. These tracts provoked parliament into enacting stricter measures against English Catholics. In 1580, Parsons returned to the continent where, for the next 30 years, he was a central figure in a number of intrigues directed against England.

Parsons wrote his numerous tracts under the pen name "N. D." (for Nicholas Dolman). One of these, *The Third Part of a Treatise, Intituled: Of three Conversions of England: conteyninge An Examen of the Calendar or Catalogue of Protestant Saints . . . by John Fox,* is an attack on Foxe's *Book of Martyrs.* Included in the *Book of Martyrs* had been an account of Sir John Oldcastle (the original name of Shakespeare's character Falstaff), whom Parsons describes as "a Ruffian-knight as all England knoweth, commonly brought in by comedians on their stages: he was put to death for robberyes and rebellion under the foresaid *K. Henry* the fifth." Parsons' identification of Falstaff with Oldcastle was probably a deliberate error on his part, since the Jesuit was one of the foremost exponents of the theory of EQUIVOCATION, or prudential lying. Parsons was condemned for casuistry by John Speed, English historian and author of a *History of Great Britaine* (1611), who asserted his conviction

> . . . that N. D. author of the three conuersions hath made *Ouldcastle* a Ruffian, a Robber, and a Rebell, and his authority taken from the *Stage-plaiers,* is more befitting the pen of his slanderous report, then the Credit of the iudicious, being only grounded from this Papist and his Poet, of like conscience for lies, the one euer faining, and the other euer falsifying the truth.

Speed's reference to "his Poet," if it is a direct allusion to Shakespeare, might be cited as evidence that Shakespeare was a Catholic. See RELIGION. [E. K. Chambers, *William Shakespeare,* 1930.]

part. In the Elizabethan theatre, the transcription of the lines of a particular character in a play made for the actor who was to play the role. There are a few extant examples of parts from medieval plays, but the only known Elizabethan part which has survived is that used by Edward Alleyn in the title role of Robert Greene's *Orlando Furioso.* The play was written in the autumn of 1591 and performed in February 1592 by the amalgamated company of the Admiral's and Strange's Men, of which Alleyn was the leading actor.

Alleyn's part contains about 530 lines written on sheets of paper which were pasted together in a long roll originally measuring 17½ feet in length and 6 inches in width. The part was evidently copied by a professional scribe with corrections and emendations added in Alleyn's own hand. Cues are given by indicating the last words of the preceding speaker. Stage directions, some of which are written in Latin, are indicated in the margin. See ASSEMBLED TEXTS.

Passionate Pilgrim, The (1599). A volume of po-

ONE SHEET OF ALLEYN'S PART TO GREENE'S *Orlando Furioso.* (DULWICH COLLEGE, BY PERMISSION OF THE GOVERNORS)

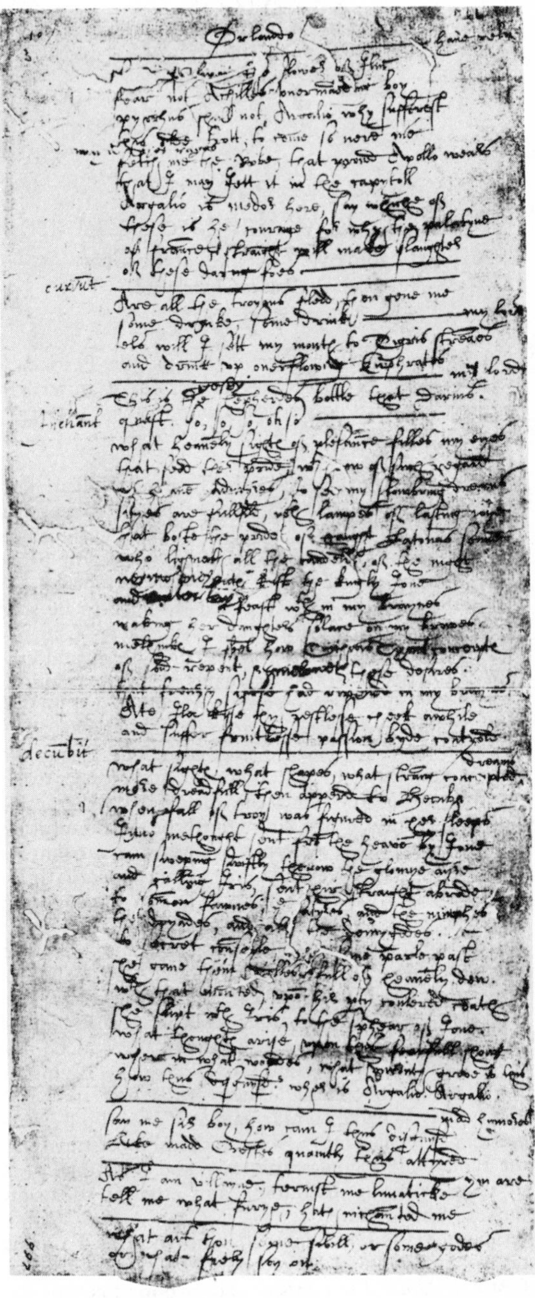

THE
PASSIONATE
PILGRIME.
By W. Shakespeare.

AT LONDON
Printed for W. Iaggard, and are
to be sold by W. Leake, at the Greyhound in Paules Churchyard.
1599.

TITLE PAGE OF THE SECOND OCTAVO OF *The Passionate Pilgrim* (1599). THERE IS ONLY ONE COPY OF THE FIRST EDITION EXTANT AND IT LACKS A TITLE PAGE.

etry attributed to Shakespeare. In 1599 William Jaggard, a somewhat disreputable publisher, collected a mélange of poems by a number of different authors and published them with the following title page: "The Passionate Pilgrime. By W. Shakespeare. At London Printed for W. Jaggard, and are to be sold by W. Leake, at the Greyhound in Paules Churchyard. 1599." This printing is actually the second edition of the book. Nothing remains of the first edition except two sheets preserved in the Folger Library. A third edition appeared in 1612.

There are a total of 20 poems in *The Passionate Pilgrim,* the last 6 of which appear in a section titled "Sonnets to sundry Notes of Musicke." Of the entire collection only 5 are known to be Shakespeare's. Poems I and II, for example, are corrupt versions of Shakespeare's Sonnets 138 and 144, and poems III, V, and XVI are extracts of three lyrical passages in *Love's Labour's Lost* (IV, iii, 56–69; IV, ii, 100–113; IV, iii, 101–120). Of the remaining poems, VIII and XX appeared in Richard Barnfield's *Poems In divers humors* (1598) and XIX consists of the first four stanzas of Marlowe's famous "The Passionate Shepherd to his Love" ("Come live with me and be my love") and the first stanza of Raleigh's "Nymph's Reply to the Shepherd." Poem XVII first appeared in Thomas Weelkes' *Madrigals to Three, Four, Five and Six Voices* (1597). The authorship of this and the remaining poems is unknown and their quality is so inferior as to discourage any attempt to assign them to Shakespeare.

The 1612 edition included nine additional poems taken from Thomas Heywood's *Troia Britannica: or Great Britaines Troy* (1609). Heywood violently objected to this action in the Epistle to his *Apologie for Actors* (1612), in which he refers to his and Shakespeare's displeasure with Jaggard's unethical practices: "Here likewise, I must necessarily insert a manifest injury done me in that worke, by taking the two Epistles of *Paris* to *Helen,* and *Helen* to *Paris* and printing them . . . vnder the name of another, . . whom I know much offended with M. Jaggard (that altogether vnknowne to him) presumed to make so bold with his name." As a result of this criticism Jaggard canceled the title page of the 1612 edition and replaced it with one that did not bear Shakespeare's name. [*The Poems,* New Arden Edition, F. T. Prince, ed., 1960.]

pastoralism. Literary genre dealing with shepherds and country life. Pastoralism celebrates the myth of innocence, of the world before the Fall. Pastoralism occurs in many literary forms but always presents a world in which man and nature are in harmony. Derived from the Greek poet Theocritus (fl. 270 B.C.), pastoral poetry received its finest expression in Elizabethan England in Edmund Spenser's *Shepheardes Calendar* (1579).

Pastoral prose found its earliest embodiment in the GREEK ROMANCES of the early Christian era; it was revitalized in the Renaissance by the appearance of Boccaccio's pastoral romance *Ameto* (1342). One of the most important of the Renaissance pastoral prose works was Jorge de Montemayor's *Diana Enamorada* (1542); this was translated from Spanish into English during the 1580's by Bartholomew Yonge and published in 1598. Original English works in the genre include Robert Greene's *Menaphon* (1589), Sir Philip Sidney's *Arcadia* (1590), and Thomas Lodge's *Rosalynde* (1590). See AS YOU LIKE IT: *Sources.*

In Italy, pastoral drama reached its apex in Giovanni Guarini's *Il Pastor Fido* (1585; pub. 1590). In England, pastoral drama grew out of mythological plays in pastoral settings, such as George Peele's *Arraignment of Paris* (1581) and John Lyly's *Woman in the Moon* (pub., 1597). This genre eventually developed into the pure pastoral drama of the early 17th century, the best examples of which are John Fletcher's *The Faithful Shepherdess* (1609–1610) Ben Jonson's *Sad Shepherd* (1629), and, according to some literary historians, Milton's *Comus* (1634).

The pastoral convention is a pervasive one in Shakespeare, revealing itself in early comedies, such as *Two Gentlemen of Verona,* and in his last plays, notably *The Winter's Tale.* The most striking use of pastoral elements, however, is found in his romantic comedies, particularly in *As You Like It,* which was based on the pastoral romance *Rosalynde.* Among the conventions of pastoralism that Shakespeare employs in this play are a country setting, an abiding interest in love on the part of its main characters, and ideal friendship (here between two women, Celia and Rosalind). It is, however, a mistake to regard it as a pastoral play. The oversimplified view of life which pastoralism embodies is never accepted *in toto* in the forest of Arden. There we are shown many more diverse approaches to life than the pastoral ideal admits of, ranging from the extreme pessimism of Jaques to the rustic simplicity of William and Audrey. The vision out of which *As You Like It* grew was much too broad and complex not to include criticism of the pastoral ideal as well as the leal itself. [W. W. Greg, *Pastoral Poetry and Pas-ral Drama*, 1906.]

Pastor Fido, Il. See PASTORALISM.

patent. See CHAMBERLAIN'S MEN.

Patience. In *Henry VIII,* an attendant of Queen atharine as she lies ill at Kimbolton (IV, ii). In er last hours, Katharine was actually attended by oña María de Salinas, a Spanish woman who had arried an English noble.

Patroclus. In Homer's *Iliad,* a loyal friend of chilles; in *Troilus and Cressida,* a commander of e Greek army. Patroclus tries, in both Homer and hakespeare, to persuade Achilles to take up arms nd rejoin the battle; but it is not until he is killed y the Trojans that the grief-stricken Achilles finally eenters the war against them.

patronage. The relationship between an artist and wealthy benefactor in which the artist is sub-idized. In Elizabethan times a poet tried to secure he patronage of a noble with elaborately flattering edications. However, a noble was not obliged to atronize a poet who had proffered him such a com-liment. Queen Elizabeth was, of course, the most opular potential patron of the period and she was he dedicatee of numerous books. Nearly rivaling lizabeth in popularity were Robert Dudley, earl f Leicester; William Cecil, Lord Burghley; Sir hilip Sidney; Henry Wriothesley, 3rd earl of outhampton; and Robert Devereux, 2nd earl of ssex. Leicester was widely known for his support f learning and his interest in the theatre. Burghley avored historians over poets and playwrights. Sid-ey was both patron and poet; Stephen Gosson's nauthorized and rather presumptuous dedication f the *Schoole of Abuse* to him moved Sidney to rite, in reply, his famous *Apologie for Poesie,* the irst great critical work in English. Essex, a some-ime poet himself, was the particular friend to poets, ut he had books of all sorts dedicated to him.

Though Southampton was evidently a man with great love of learning, he does not seem to have xtended patronage to many writers of his time. s the only man who can be positively identified s Shakespeare's patron, however, he has been re-varded with both glory and notoriety. *Venus and donis,* dedicated to Wriothesley in 1593, was ap-arently an offering to the nobleman for his rospective patronage; the supplicating, formal tone ndicates that Shakespeare either did not know Vriothesley at all or had only a very slight cquaintance with him:

> I know not how I shall offend in dedicating my unpolished lines to your lordship, nor how the world will censure me for choosing so strong a prop to support so weak a burden . . . .

But in *The Rape of Lucrece* a year later, the dedica-ion is one of intimacy and affection:

> The love I dedicate to your lordship is without end . . . . What I have done is yours; what I have to do is yours; being part in all I have, devoted yours.

The Rape of Lucrece was the last book Shakespeare himself gave out for publication. In 1609 Thomas Thorpe published Shakespeare's *Sonnets* setting forth a most puzzling dedication:

> To the onlie begetter of these insuing sonnets Mr. W. H. . . .

Speculation as to the identity of Mr. W. H. has remained speculation, and Southampton is only one among many candidates, those supporting him claiming that "W. H." is simply a reversal of his initials. Southampton reputedly made Shakespeare a gift of £1000, but this may be pure legend. If true, it is probably the most munificent gift in the history of patronage. See Henry Wriothesley, 3rd earl of SOUTHAMPTON. [D. Nichol Smith, "Authors and Patrons," *Shakespeare's England,* 1916.]

Paulina. In *The Winter's Tale,* wife of Antigonus, faithful lady-in-waiting of Hermione, and blunt, outspoken critic of Leontes. In partaking of these qualities of loyalty and frankness, Paulina functions as a sort of female equivalent to Kent in *King Lear.* Paulina's well-deserved triumph occurs in the final scene when she acts as author, producer, and director of the "statue scene" and is rewarded with the hand of Camillo.

Paul's Churchyard. See LONDON.

Pavier, Thomas (d. 1625). Publisher involved in the publication of several Shakespearean quartos. Originally a draper, Pavier transferred to the Stationers' Company in 1600. In that year a number of copyrights were assigned to him, including the "bad quarto" of *Henry V,* which had been published by

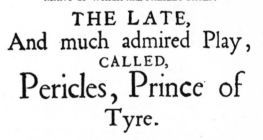

TITLE PAGE OF THE SECOND QUARTO OF *Pericles* (1619). THIS WAS ONE OF TEN SHAKESPEAREAN PLAYS PRINTED BY WILLIAM JAGGARD IN 1619, MANY OF WHICH ARE FALSELY DATED.

THE LATE,
And much admired Play,
CALLED,
Pericles, Prince of
Tyre.

With the true Relation of the whole History, aduentures, and fortunes of the saide Prince.

Written by W. SHAKESPEARE.

Printed for *T. P.* 1619.

Thomas Millington and John Busby, Kyd's *Spanish Tragedy*, and Lodge and Greene's *Looking Glasse for London*. Two years later Millington transferred the bad quartos of *2 Henry VI* (1594) and *3 Henry VI* (1595), as well as the good quarto of *Titus Andronicus* (1594) to him. Pavier apparently made no attempt to reprint these plays, however, until 1619 when he conjoined with the printer William JAGGARD to issue a collection of 10 Shakespearean and pseudo-Shakespearean plays. Pavier's contribution to the collection consisted of three of the Shakespearean plays mentioned above: *2* and *3 Henry VI* (here issued together as *The Whole Contention betweene the two Famous Houses, Lancaster and Yorke*) and *Henry V*. In addition Pavier was cited as the publisher of *Pericles* and of *1 Sir John Oldcastle*, which he had also published in 1600. The title page of 1619 Quartos of the latter two plays ascribed them to Shakespeare. [R. B. McKerrow, ed., *A Dictionary of Printers and Booksellers . . . 1557–1640*, 1910.]

Pavy, Salomon (c. 1590–1602). Actor. Pavy, whose first name is often erroneously listed as Salathiel, was a leading actor with the Children of the Chapel. His death at the age of 12 occasioned Ben Jonson's beautiful elegiac verse through which Pavy is best remembered. One verse is reproduced below:

> 'Twas a child, that so did thrive
>   In grace and feature,
> As Heaven and Nature seemed to strive
>   Which owned the creature.
> Years he numbered scarce thirteen
>   When Fates turned cruel,
> Yet three filled zodiacs had he been
>   The stage's jewel.

[G. E. Bentley, "A Good Name Lost: Ben Jonson's Lament for S.P.," *Times Literary Supplement*, May 30, 1942.]

Payne, B[en] Iden (1881–   ). Actor and director. Born in Newcastle-on-Tyne, Payne made his acting debut in 1899 with Benson's company in Worcester, and the following year appeared in *Henry V* in London. He directed and produced for various companies until 1920, and from 1919 to 1934 was visiting professor of drama at Carnegie Institute of Technology. He has also produced and directed plays for the Theatre Guild, New York, and the Goodman Repertory Theatre, Chicago. In July 1934 he was chosen to succeed W. Bridges-Adams as director of the Shakespeare Memorial Theatre. Under his direction *Antony and Cleopatra* was revived in 1935. In 1941 and 1942 he again directed the Memorial Theatre company before coming to the United States to teach at Carnegie, and Washington, Iowa, Missouri, Colorado, and Michigan universities. In 1945 he directed the Theatre Guild's production of *The Winter's Tale*, and since 1946 he has been guest professor of drama at the University of Texas.

Payne has directed many summer Shakespeare festivals in the United States: San Diego, 1949–1952, 1955, and 1957; Oregon, 1956 and 1961; and Alberta, 1958–1960, and 1962. He has received many honors for services to the theatre, and has written several plays. [*Who's Who in the Theatre*, 1961.]

Peacham, Henry (1576?–?1643). Schoolmaster, artist, and author. Educated at Oxford where he received an M.A. in 1598, Peacham became a promine member of London literary society in the earl years of the 17th century. Included among h friends at this time were Michael Drayton and Be Jonson. In 1622 he published his best-known worl *The Compleat Gentleman*, a guide to manners fo aspiring young English gentlemen. The work ir cludes an interesting survey of literature and th arts, but it omits the popular English drama an makes no mention of Shakespeare.

Peacham was once thought to be the artist wh drew an early illustration to *Titus Andronicus*, bu recent scholarship has come to doubt the ascriptio to him. See LONGLEAT MANUSCRIPT.

Peaseblossom. In *A Midsummer Night's Drean* one of Queen Titania's fairies assigned to wait upo Bottom.

Peck, Francis (1692–1743). Scholar and antiquary Peck claimed to have found an epitaph written b Shakespeare on Thomas Combe, matching the well known epitaph that Shakespeare was alleged to hav written about John Combe (see COMBE FAMILY) Peck's claim was printed in his "Explanatory an Critical Notes on divers Passages of Shakespeare' Plays," an appendix to his *New Memoirs of Milto* (1740):

> Every body knows *Shakespeare's* epitaph for *Joh a Combe*. And I am told he afterwards wrote an other for *Tom a Combe*, alias *Thin-Beard*, brothe of the said *John;* & that it was never yet printed It is as follows.
>
> *Thin* in *beard*, and thick in purse;
> Never man beloved worse:
> He went to th' grave with many a curse:
> The Devil & He had both one nurse.
>
> This is very sour.

[E. K. Chambers, *William Shakespeare*, 1930.]

Pedant. In *The Taming of the Shrew*, he is bullied by Tranio into impersonating Vincentio, the father of Lucentio (IV, ii). When the real parent arrives in Padua, the Pedant tries to have him arrested as a madman but runs off when the ruse is uncovered. He reappears at the banquet in the final scene.

Pedro, Don. In *Much Ado About Nothing*, the Prince of Arragon. The genial Don Pedro, victor in an almost bloodless action against his bastard brother, Don John, visits Leonato at Messina. Don Pedro is accompanied by Don John, with whom he is reconciled, and his distinguished officers Benedick and Claudio. He woos and wins Hero for Claudio and, to insure that the time between the engagement and the wedding passes quickly, undertakes one of "Hercules' labors"—to match Benedick and Beatrice in matrimony. The successful Cupid is, however, deceived by his treacherous brother and, believing himself dishonored for having arranged Claudio's betrothal to the "common stale," Hero, Don Pedro supports Hero's exposure before the wedding assembly. When the deception is uncovered, this honest nobleman offers to "bend under any heavy weight" to amend his mistake.

Peele, George (1556–1596). Playwright. Peele was born in London in the parish of St. James Garlickhithe. His father was the chief administrator of Christ's Hospital, a public asylum for orphans and

The Araygnement of Paris
A PASTORALL.
Presented before the Queenes Maiestie, by the Children of her Chappell

Imprinted at London by Henrie Marsh.
ANNO. 1584.

TITLE PAGE OF PEELE'S *Araygnement of Paris* (1584).

he aged. Peele was educated at Christ's Hospital and ater at Oxford, where he received two degrees. His irst known play is THE ARRAIGNMENT OF PARIS 1581), presented before the queen in 1584. It is one of the earliest examples in English drama of the pas-oral play. At this time Peele became associated with he UNIVERSITY WITS, among whom he was highly egarded, being cited by Nashe as "the atlas of po-try." He died in 1596, a victim of the pox, according o Meres in *Palladis Tamia* (1598).

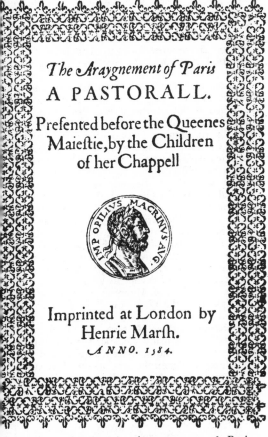

The posthumously published *Merrie Conceited 'ests of George Peele* (1607) is generally regarded as apocryphal, but the association of his name with a est book indicates that he had a reputation for loose iving (see THE PURITAN). Peele's plays include THE BATTLE OF ALCAZAR, *The Old Wives Tale* (1591), *Edward I* (c. 1593), and *David and Bethsabe* (1594). Peele has been suggested as Shakespeare's collabora-tor on *1 Henry VI* by a number of scholars, and J. Dover Wilson argues that *3 Henry VI* is Shake-speare's revision of a play principally by Peele (see 1 HENRY VI: *Text;* 3 HENRY VI: *Text*). Dugdale Sykes has argued that Peele is the author of *The Troublesome Raigne of King John*, the source of Shakespeare's *King John* (see KING JOHN: *Sources*). Several scholars have also detected a strong relation-ship between Peele's style and the style in Act I of *Titus Andronicus* (see TITUS ANDRONICUS: *Text*). Among those who reject attribution of EDWARD III to Shakespeare, there is a tendency to assign the play to Peele.

Pembroke, Henry Herbert, 2nd earl of (c. 1534–1601). Statesman and patron. The eldest son of the 1st earl of Pembroke was educated at Cambridge and succeeded to the earldom in 1570. He played an important role at the trials of the duke of Norfolk (1571/2), the earl of Arundel (1589), and Mary, Queen of Scots (1586); in the court intrigues during Elizabeth's reign, he sided with his intimate friend Leicester. In 1586 he was appointed president of Wales. Pembroke's third wife was Mary Sidney, the sister of Sir Philip Sidney who wrote his *Countess of Pembroke's Arcadia* for her, and to whom Edmund Spenser dedicated his *Ruines of Time*. A man of culture, Pembroke was a patron of antiquaries and chroniclers as well as the company of players known as PEMBROKE'S MEN.

Pembroke, Mary Herbert, countess of (1561–1621). The sister of Sir Philip SIDNEY and wife of Henry Herbert, 2nd earl of Pembroke, whom she married in 1577. A woman of excellent literary taste and of distinctive literary talent, the countess was the most famous patroness of literature of her time. She was praised by a host of poets, including Spenser, Daniel,

MARY HERBERT, COUNTESS OF PEMBROKE. ENGRAVING BY SIMON PASSE (1618). (NATIONAL PORTRAIT GALLERY)

and Jonson, and she inspired her brother's prose romance *Arcadia,* which she later revised and completed. She also completed a verse translation of the Psalms, begun by her brother, but to which she was the major contributor. Another of her literary efforts was *Antonius, A Tragoedie* (1590), an English translation of Robert Garnier's *Marc-Antoine* (1578) which may have provided Shakespeare with source material for *Antony and Cleopatra.*

The countess's estate at Wilton became an academy of learning where poets and artists were encouraged and supported. On December 2, 1603 Shakespeare's company performed at Wilton, while the court was residing there to escape the plague in London. According to a story printed in 1865 and regarded as credible by E. K. Chambers, there was in existence at one time a letter from the countess to her son, William Herbert, 3rd earl of Pembroke, telling him to invite James I to a performance of *As You Like It.* The letter concluded with the comment, "we have the man Shakespeare with us." For those who regard Herbert as the "Mr. W. H." of the *Sonnets,* this letter is cited as evidence of Shakespeare's intimacy with the Pembroke circle. Further evidence is thought to be present in Sonnet 3, where there is a reference to the beauty of the Fair Youth's mother:

> Thou art thy mother's glass, and she in thee
> Calls back the lovely April of her prime.

The beauty of the countess was proverbial, a fact most eloquently attested to in William Browne's famous epitaph on her:

> Underneath this sable hearse
> Lies the subject of all verse:
> Sidney's sister, Pembroke's mother;
> Death, ere thou hast slain another,
> Fair, and learn'd, and good as she,
> Time shall throw a dart at thee.

[F. B. Young, *Mary Sidney, Countess of Pembroke,* 1912; E. K. Chambers, *Shakespearean Gleanings,* 1944.]

Pembroke, Philip Herbert, 4th earl of (1584–1650). Younger brother of William Herbert, 3rd earl of Pembroke, whom he succeeded as lord chamberlain and with whom he acted as joint dedicatee of the First Folio. The nephew of Sir Philip Sidney, after whom he was apparently named, Philip Herbert was elevated to the peerage in 1605, when he was named earl of Montgomery, the title by which he was addressed in the dedicatory epistle to the First Folio. As earl of Montgomery he was the chief favorite of the Jacobean court during the early years of James I's reign. His good looks, skill in hunting and in the performances of masques at court earned him the highest preferment at court; however, his surliness and arrogance managed to make him many enemies. One of these was Shakespeare's patron, Henry Wriothesley, 3rd earl of Southampton, with whom Herbert quarreled in 1610.

Herbert was a generous patron of the arts, but he was habitually in debt, a fact which makes his selection as dedicatee of such an expensive volume as the Folio somewhat unusual. The explanation may lie in the fact that he was being rumored at the time as the logical candidate for the lord chamberlain's post held by his brother, who was expected to move up to th[e] more exalted position of lord treasurer. As lo[rd] chamberlain, Herbert would have considerable con[-]trol over the fortunes of the the King's Men; it wa[s] a politic move, therefore, to include him in th[e] dedication. If this was the thinking of Heminges an[d] Condell, it proved to be wise, for, in 1626, the ea[rl] succeeded his brother as lord chamberlain and, whe[n] William Herbert died in 1630, Philip Herbert als[o] succeeded to his brother's title, Pembroke. He re[-]mained lord chamberlain until 1641 when his espous[al] of the parliamentary faction caused him to be re[-]moved by the king. During the Civil War he openl[y] supported parliament and was attacked as a traitor i[n] royalist pamphlets of the time. His adherence to th[e] Puritan cause was all the more unusual in view of hi[s] personal life, which was marked by loose living an[d] a continuing fondness for (and patronage of) th[e] drama. He was the patron of Philip Massinger and i[n] 1647 was chosen by the King's Men as the dedicate[e] of the First Folio edition of the plays of Beaumon[t] and Fletcher. The dedication to that volume cites hi[s] earlier patronage of "the flowing compositions of th[e] . . . sweet Swan of Avon Shakespeare. . . ." [Dic[k] Taylor, "The Earl of Montgomery and the Dedica[-]tory Epistle to the First Folio," *Shakespeare Quar[-]terly,* XI, 1960.]

Pembroke, William Herbert, earl of (d. 1469). A soldier who won many victories for the Yorkists i[n] the Wars of the Roses. After his defeat and captur[e] at Hedgecote, Pembroke was beheaded by norther[n] Lancastrians. In *3 Henry VI,* Pembroke appears a[s] a supporter of Edward IV (IV, i).

Pembroke, William Herbert, 3rd earl of (1580–1630). Nobleman and courtier. Sometimes identifie[d]

WILLIAM HERBERT, 3RD EARL OF PEMBROKE. MINIATURE BY ISAAC OLIVER. (FOLGER SHAKESPEARE LIBRARY)

; the MR. W. H. of the *Sonnets*, Pembroke was the ›n of Henry Herbert, the 2nd earl of PEMBROKE, nd Mary Sidney, the sister of Philip Sidney. He ıcceeded to the earldom on the death of his father 1601. He was disgraced and imprisoned in 1601 'hen Mary FITTON bore him a stillborn illegitimate ›n. He held many important offices during the reign f James I: lord chamberlain of the royal household 1615–1625) and lord steward (1626–1630). He was hancellor of the University of Oxford in 1624 when ıe name of Broadgates Hall was changed to Pem-roke College in the chancellor's honor. In 1623 Jeminges and Condell dedicated the First Folio to Ierbert and his brother Philip, earl of Montgomery, ecause, as they explain in the dedication, both men haue been pleas'd to thinke these trifles some-thing, eeretofore; and haue prosequuted both them, and ıeir Authour liuing with so much fauour." The edication of the Folio to Herbert instead of South-mpton, Shakespeare's patron, is still the major point the argument identifying Pembroke as Mr. W. H. *The Sonnets*, New Variorum Edition, Hyder Rol-ns, ed., 1944.]

Pembroke, William Marshall or **Marshal** 1st earl f (d. 1219). A staunch follower of Henry II and is heirs. After serving Richard I, on whose behalf e fought Prince John's attempt to usurp the throne, embroke was nevertheless instrumental in aiding ›hn's accession to the throne on Richard's death in 199. He became one of King John's closest ad-isors. When Louis the dauphin invaded England in 216, the earl's son William fought on the French de. Pembroke himself, however, remained stead-stly loyal to John.

In *King John*, Pembroke, confused by Shakespeare 'ith his son, opposes the policies of the King and ins the lords who take up arms on the side of the ıvading Dauphin, Lewis. However, he returns to ›hn's side on learning that Lewis intends to kill ıe lords once his purpose is accomplished.

Pembroke's Men. Acting company under the pa-onage of Henry Herbert, 2nd earl of Pembroke. here is no contemporary account of Pembroke's len before 1592. In 1593 they are mentioned as ıving traveled in the provinces, with little or no nancial success, and in September that year Philip enslowe wrote Edward Alleyn and advised him ıat Pembroke's Men were all at home and had been or this five or six weeks." Henslowe added that the ur was such a failure that the men were forced to ıwn their costumes. On their provincial tour they ıd played at Rye, Bath, Ludlow, Bewdley, Shrews-ıry, Coventry, Ipswich, Leicester, and York (June 93); their rewards, listed in the provincial records, nged from 14s. to 40s.

To pay their debts they apparently also sold three their plays to booksellers, who published them in 94 and 1595. These dramas included Marlowe's *dward II; The Taming of A Shrew;* and *The True ragedy of Richard Duke of York* (a "bad quarto" *3 Henry VI*). It is probable that *The Contention York and Lancaster*, a bad quarto of *2 Henry VI*, as also a Pembroke's Men play, but their name es not appear on the title page of the 1594 edition. reliable edition of *Titus Andronicus* (1594) does, ›wever, contain their name on its title page. *The aming of A Shrew* remains of undetermined rela-tion to Shakespeare's *Taming of the Shrew*. All the above plays, except for *Edward II*, eventually be-came the property of Shakespeare's acting company, the Chamberlain's Men, and many scholars also be-lieve that Shakespeare belonged to Pembroke's Men before joining the Chamberlain's Men.

Nothing is known of the company's activities during 1595 and 1596. In 1597, however, Robert Shaw, Gabriel SPENCER, and William BIRD, who were probably former members of the Chamberlain's Men, as well as Richard Jones and Thomas Downton, formerly of the Admiral's Men, banded together to form a new company under the protection of Pem-broke. They contracted with Francis Langley, owner of the Swan theatre, to perform at that theatre. However, on July 28, 1597 they gave a performance of Thomas Nashe's scandalous *Isle of Dogs* which resulted in the closing of all the London theatres (see SWAN THEATRE). When the theatres were reopened, the actors refused to return to the Swan and began to perform under Henslowe's management at the Rose. Subsequently Pembroke's Men appear to have merged with Worcester's Men. [E. K. Chambers, *The Elizabethan Stage*, 1923.]

Pepys, Samuel (1633–1703). Diarist. Born in Lon-don and educated at Cambridge, Pepys secured a position as clerk of the acts in the naval office, later becoming secretary of the admiralty. His famous *Diary* is a record of his activities between 1660–1669. It is written in shorthand and was not translated until the 19th century. The *Diary* is a frank, unin-hibited portrait of the man and his time. Included among the many pleasures of his life was playgoing, and the *Diary* provides, among its other treasures, a unique history of the Restoration theatre and of Shakespearean productions of the period. Among the Shakespearean plays which Pepys saw (either in their original versions or in Restoration adaptations) were: *Hamlet, Henry IV, Henry V, Henry VIII, Macbeth, Merry Wives of Windsor, A Midsummer Night's Dream, Othello, Romeo and Juliet, The Tempest, Twelfth Night*, and *The Taming of the Shrew*. Extracts from the *Diary* are given below.

1660.

October 11.—Here, in the Park, we met with Mr. Salisbury, who took Mr. Creed and me to the Cockpitt to see "The Moore of Venice," which was well done. Burt acted the Moore; by the same token, a very pretty lady that sat by me, called out, to see Desdemona smothered.

December 5.—After dinner I went to the New Theatre and there I saw "The Merry Wives of Windsor" acted, the humours of the country gentleman and the French doctor very well done, but the rest but very poorly, and Sir J. Falstaffe as bad as any.

December 31.—In Paul's Church-yard I bought the play of "Henry the Fourth," and so went to the new Theatre and saw it acted; but my ex-pectation being too great, it did not please me, as otherwise I believe it would; and my having a book, I believe did spoil it a little.

1661.

June 4.—From thence [my Lord Crew's] to the Theatre and saw "Harry the 4th," a good play.

August 24.—To the Opera, and there saw "Hamlet, Prince of Denmarke," done with scenes very well, but above all, Betterton did the Prince's parts beyond imagination.

September 11.—Walking through Lincoln's Inn Fields observed at the Opera a new play "Twelfth Night," was acted there, and the King there; so I, against my own mind and resolution, could not forbear to go in, which did make the play seem a burthen to me, and I took no pleasure at all in it.

September 25.—To the Theatre, and saw "The Merry Wives of Windsor," ill done.

November 28.—After an hour or two's talk in divinity with my Lady, Captain Ferrers and Mr. Moore and I to the Theatre, and there saw "Hamlet" very well done.

1661–2.

March 1.—To the Opera, and there saw "Romeo and Juliet," the first time it was ever acted, but it is a play of itself the worst that ever I heard in my life, and the worst acted that ever I saw these people do, and I am resolved to go no more to see the first time of acting, for they were all of them out more or less.

1662.

September 29.—To the King's Theatre, where we saw "Midsummer's Night's Dream," which I had never seen before, nor shall ever again, for it is the most insipid ridiculous play that ever I saw in my life.

1662–3.

January 6.—After dinner to the Duke's House, and there saw "Twelfth-Night" acted well, though it be but a silly play, and not related at all to the name or day.

1663.

May 28.—By water to the Royall Theatre; but that was so full they told us we could have no room. And so to the Duke's house; and there saw "Hamlett" done, giving us fresh reason never to think enough of Betterton.

1663–4.

January 1.—Went to the Duke's house, the first play I have been at these six months, according to my last vowe, and here saw the so much cried-up play of "Henry the Eighth;" which, though I went with resolution to like it, is so simple a thing made up of a great many patches, that, besides the shows and processions in it, there is nothing in the world good or well done.

1664.

November 5.—To the Duke's house to a play, "Macbeth," a pretty good play, but admirably acted.

1666.

August 20.—To Deptford by water, reading "Othello, Moore of Venice," which I ever heretofore esteemed a mighty good play, but having to lately read "The Adventures of Five Houres," it seems a mean thing.

1666–7.

January 7.—To the Duke's house, and saw "Macbeth," which though I saw it lately, yet appears a most excellent play in all respects, but especially in divertisement, though it be a deep tragedy; which is a strange perfection in a tragedy, it bein most proper here, and suitable.

1667.

April 9.—To the King's house, and there sa "The Tameing of a Shrew," which hath some ver good pieces in it, but generally is but a mean play and the best part "Sawny", done by Lacy; an hath not half its life, by reason of the words, suppose, not being understood, at least by m [See John Lacy.]

April 19.—To the play-house, where we sa "Macbeth," which, though I have seen it often, y is it one of the best plays for a stage, and variet of dancing and musique, that ever I saw.

August 15.—Sir W. Pen and I to the Duke house, where a new play. The King and Cou there: the house full, and an act begun. And s went to the King's, and there saw "The Merr Wives of Windsor:" which did not please me all, in no part of it.

October 16.—To the Duke of York's house; * and I was vexed to see Young who is but a ba actor at best act Macbeth in the room of Betterto who, poor man! is sick: but Lord! what a preju dice it wrought in me against the whole play, an every body else agreed in disliking this fellow Thence home, and there find my wife gone home because of this fellow's acting of the part, sh went out of the house again.

November 1.—My wife and I to the King's play house, and there saw a silly play and an old on "The Taming of a Shrew."

November 2.—To the King's playhouse, an there saw "Henry the Fourth;" and, contrary t expectation, was pleased in nothing more than i Cartwright's speaking of Falstaffe's speech abou "What is Honour?"

November 6.—With my wife to a play, and th girl—"Macbeth," which we still like mightily though mighty short of the content we used t have when Betterton acted, who is still sick.

November 7.—At noon resolved with Sir W Pen to go to see "The Tempest," an old play o Shakespeare's, acted, I hear, the first day. * * Th house mighty full; the King and Court there: an the most innocent play that ever I saw; and curious piece of musick in an echo of half sen tences, the echo repeating the former half, whil the man goes on to the latter; which is might pretty. The play has no great wit, but yet good above ordinary plays.

November 13.—To the Duke of York's hous and there saw the Tempest again, which is ver pleasant, and full of so good variety that I canno be more pleased almost in a comedy, only the sea men's part a little too tedious.

December 12.—After dinner all alone to th Duke of York's house, and saw "The Tempest, which as often as I have seen it, I do like ver well, and the house very full.

1667–8.

August 31.—To the Duke of York's playhous and saw "Hamlet," which we have not seen thi year before, or more, and mightily pleased with i but above all with Betterton, the best part, I be lieve, that ever man acted.

1668–9.

December 30.—After dinner, my wife and I to the Duke's play-house, and there did see "King Harry the Eighth"; and was mightily pleased, better than I ever expected, with the history and shows of it.

January 15.—With my wife at my cozen Turner's where I staid, and sat a while, and carried The. and my wife to the Duke of York's house, to "Macbeth."

January 20.—To the Duke of York's house, and saw "Twelfth Night," as it is now revived; but, I think, one of the weakest plays that ever I saw on the stage.

February 6.—To the King's playhouse, and there in an upper box * * * did see "The Moor of Venice:" but ill acted in most parts; Mohun which did a little surprize me not acting Iago's part by much so well as Clun used to do: nor another Hart's, which was Cassio's; nor, indeed, Burt doing the Moor's so well as I once thought he did.

The Shakspere Allusion-Book, J. Munro, ed., 1909.]

Percy, Sir Charles (d. 1628). Brother of Sir Henry ercy, 9th earl of Northumberland. A descendant of hakespeare's Hotspur, Charles Percy was an aderent of the earl of ESSEX, serving under him in reland and acting as his lieutenant during the revolt. ercy was apparently the leader of the group who rranged for a performance of *Richard II* on the eve f the Essex rebellion. He was fined £5000 for his ole in the conspiracy. By marriage, Percy was lord f Dumbleton in Gloucestershire, not far from Stratord. As a friend of Southampton and Essex, he may vell have been acquainted with Shakespeare and may ave provided Shakespeare with some of the infornation about the Percys in *1 Henry IV*. In a letter, vritten about 1600, complaining of being stranded in he country, he alludes to two characters (Shallow nd Silence) from *2 Henry IV:*

> I am heere so pestred with contrie businesse that I shall not bee able as yet to come to London: If I stay heere long in this fashion, at my return I think you will find mee so dull that I shall bee taken for Justice Silence or Justice Shallow, wherefore I am to entreat you that you will take pittie of mee, and as occurrences shall searue, to send mee such news from time to time as shall happen, the knowledge of the which, thoutgh perhaps thee will not exempt mee from the opinion of a iustice Shallow at London, yet I will assure you, thee will make mee passe for a very sufficient gentleman in Glocestrshire.

The Shakspere Allusion-Book, J. Munro, ed., 1909.]

Percy, Henry (1342–1408). See Henry Percy, 1st arl of NORTHUMBERLAND.

Percy, Henry (1364–1403). See HOTSPUR.

Percy, Henry (1421–1461). See Henry Percy, 3rd arl of NORTHUMBERLAND.

Percy, Henry. See Henry Percy, 9th earl of ORTHUMBERLAND.

Percy, Lady. Born **Elizabeth Mortimer** (d. 1444). aughter of Edmund Mortimer, 3rd earl of March, nd wife of Henry Percy, known as Hotspur. She as arrested after her husband's defeat and death at hrewsbury, but was later released. In *1 Henry IV*, ady Percy follows Hotspur to Wales, where the rebels gather. Although Hotspur begs his high-spirited wife, Kate, for a song, she refuses him (III, i). In *2 Henry IV*, Lady Percy tells Hotspur's father, the earl of Northumberland, that he would wrong his son's ghost should he give to others in the rebellion the help which he denied to Hotspur. [W. H. Thomson, *Shakespeare's Characters: A Historical Dictionary*, 1951.]

Percy, Thomas. See Thomas Percy, earl of WORCESTER.

Perdita. In *The Winter's Tale*, the lost daughter of Leontes and Hermione, King and Queen of Sicilia, and the beloved of Florizel, Prince of Bohemia. Despite her humble surroundings, Perdita's true nobility irrepressibly manifests itself, leaving its impact on every character with whom she comes in contact.

She has been seen by a number of critics as a symbol of regeneration and rebirth, and as the agent of the transition which the play makes from its early concentration on sin and death to its concluding note of grace and renewal of life. The frequent references made in the play to Perdita's close resemblance to her mother are seen as an extension to her of Hermione's semi-divine spirit as a "goddess of Proserpine." Proserpine is the goddess of the seasons, and Perdita's appearance in her guise occurs in the fourth act when the dark winter of the first three acts is transformed into the lovely spring of Acts IV and V. See MYTHIC CRITICISM.

Perez, Antonio (c. 1540–1611). Secretary of state to Philip II of Spain. After becoming involved in a number of political and amorous intrigues, Perez was forced to leave Spain at the risk of his life. He traveled to the court of Henry of Navarre and eventually became a member of the household of the earl of Essex. Robert Gittings has argued that Don Armado, the boisterous Spaniard in *Love's Labour's Lost*, is a portrait of Perez. Among the evidence which he uses to support his thesis is the fact that Perez' epithet for himself was "el Peregrino"—the wanderer—and that the same word is used in Shakespeare's play to describe Armado: "He is too picked, too spruce, too affected, too odd, as it were, too peregrinate, as I may call it" (V, i, 14–16). See Gervase MARKHAM; Roderigo LOPEZ. [Robert Gittings, *Shakespeare's Rival*, 1960.]

performances of Shakespeare's plays. In the public playhouse performances took place in the afternoon, beginning at two or three o'clock, and lasted roughly two hours. Shakespeare's earlier plays were probably acted without any intermissions. The practice of having breaks developed with the music performed in the private playhouses by the boys between the acts. It gradually became the established custom to have one break at the end of Act I and another at the end of Act III.

Printed bills set up on posts and distributed by hand advertised the performances. The entrance fees were collected by "gatherers" at the main entrance and at another entrance to the stairs leading from the yard to the galleries. When the play was about to begin, a first trumpet was sounded to inform the prospective spectators and to alert the actors waiting in the tiring room. Upon a third sounding, the play began. Some of Shakespeare's dramas boasted prologues—three in *Henry V*—presented by an actor dressed in black. Backstage a PLOT of the play was hung up for the actors to consult. A prompter sat near the inner stage with the "book of the play." The play proper was sometimes followed by an epilogue spoken by some striking character in the piece—Puck in *A Midsummer Night's Dream*, Rosalind in *As You Like It*—to beg the audience to show its approval by applause. In the public playhouses the play was usually followed by an afterpiece called a JIG. It was a lyrical farce written in ballad measure and performed by the clown. It developed into a more elaborate affair in which as many as four actors took part.

An actor in the plays received his PART in manuscript, a full text of his own speeches with their cues, the last word or words of the speech preceding his own. We possess one playhouse manuscript of a part—that of the chief manuscript of Greene's *Orlando Furioso* preserved at Dulwich College. It was revised by Edward Alleyn, who played the principal role. See also PLAYHOUSE STRUCTURE. [Ronald Watkins, *On Producing Shakespeare*, 1950.]

Pericles. In *Pericles*, the titular hero, whose near-tragic misfortunes provide the basis of the play's action. Pericles is one of Shakespeare's most notable examples of the righteous man afflicted by fortun In the course of the play he is subjected to a seri of personal disasters, none of which can be traced any flaw in his character (see PERICLES: *Plot Sy opsis*). This apparently unmotivated suffering h suggested to some an analogy with the biblic story of Job. Others have probed Pericles' charact in an attempt to detect some hidden culpabilit Thus he has been seen as being mysteriously i volved with, or unconsciously attracted to, the ev with which he comes in contact.

This is not, however, the generally accepted vie The consensus is that Pericles is a model of Sto fortitude or Christian patience who suffers t slings and arrows of his fate, and in so doi achieves a mastery of it. His ultimate triumph thus a symbol of the perception and deeper unde standing which, as G. Wilson Knight suggest enables him to assimilate the tragic experien within that affirmative reconciliation with life th all of the romances can be seen to celebrate. [Wilson Knight, *The Crown of Life*, 1947; *Pericle* New Arden Edition, F. D. Hoeniger, ed., 1963.]

The much admired *Play*,

CALLED,

PERICLES, PRINCE of TYRE

Pericles. A romance by Shakespeare.

Text. *Pericles* was not included in either the First Folio (1623) or in the Second Folio (1632). It was taken into the second edition of the Third Folio (1664). The only authoritative text is that of the First Quarto of 1609. Part of the advertisement on the title page reads: "The Late, And much admired Play, Called Pericles, Prince of Tyre. With the true relation of the whole Historie, aduentures, and fortunes of the said Prince: As also, The no lesse strange, and worthy accidents, in the Birth and Life, of his Daughter Mariana. As it hath been diuers and sundry times acted by his Maiesties Seruants, at the Globe on the Banck-side. By William Shakespeare. Imprinted at London for Henry Gosson, and are to be sold at the signe of the Sunne in Pater-noster row, &c. 1609." The source of this Quarto text seems to have been a corrupt reported COPY. This theory would explain the large number of mislineations and verse printed as prose, and vice versa.

There were three compositors setting the type, at least half of the text being printed in a shop other than that of William White, who is listed as th printer on the title page. The compositors wer either careless or unable to decipher the handwritin of the copy.

Few scholars believe that the text is wholly o Shakespeare's composition. Many critics believe tha Shakespeare had nothing to do with Acts I and I but he is often considered to be the principal autho of Acts III, IV, and V. Various explanations hav been offered for these facts. The first is that *Pericle* is Shakespeare's incomplete revision or rewriting o an earlier play by another author. Because the las part appealed much more to his imagination than th first part, he began his revision with the last thre acts. Then, perhaps because his fellow actors were i a hurry to produce a play that might suit the taste o the Blackfriars audiences, he permitted his half-com pleted revision to be acted. A somewhat different ex planation is that he found that he did not have tim to meet the company's deadline and engaged a co laborator, perhaps George WILKINS, to work on th first two acts. A third explanation is that the tex

THE LATE,

And much admired Play,

Called

Pericles, Prince of Tyre

With the true Relation of the whole Historie, aduentures, and fortunes of the said Prince:

As also,

The no lesse strange, and worthy accidents, in the Birth and Life, of his Daughter MARIANA.

As it hath been diuers and sundry times acted by his Maiesties Seruants, at the Globe on the Banck-side.

By William Shakespeare.

Imprinted at London for *Henry Gosson*, and are to be sold at the signe of the Sunne in Pater-noster row, &c.

1609.

TITLE PAGE OF THE FIRST QUARTO OF *Pericles* (1609).

epresents Shakespeare's half-completed revision of ne first draft of a play of his own composition, ased on a lost earlier dramatization of the story of pollonius of Tyre.

Still another explanation, put forth by Philip Edards, derives from the printing history of Q1. dwards believes that the text was provided by two eporters attempting to reconstruct the original from emory (see MEMORIAL RECONSTRUCTION). The reorter of Acts I and II had only a sketchy recolleceon of the play, while the reporter of the last three cts was much more familiar with the original. Edards' hypothesis is designed to establish Shakespeare s the sole author of the play. Among those scholars ho have postulated a collaborator, the most popular hoices, in addition to Wilkins, have been William OWLEY, Thomas HEYWOOD, and John DAY.

Date. The play was entered in the Stationers' Regter on May 20, 1608: "20 Maij. Edward Blount. ntred for his copie vnder thandes of Sir George uck knight and Master Warden Seton A booke alled. the booke of Pericles prynce of Tyre." E. K. hambers argued that this entry referred to an older lay which Shakespeare revised in the winter of 608/9. Among scholars who believe that the entry refers to the play partly written by Shakespeare, there is a tendency to assign the play to 1607–1608. From the *Calendar of State Papers, Concerning Venice* we learn that Zorzi Giustinian, Venetian ambassador to the English court from January 5, 1606 to November 23, 1608, saw at court a "play called Pericles." Thus the limits of the play can be established as between 1606 and 1608, but within those limits there is considerable disagreement.

Sources. The ultimate source of *Pericles* is an old Latin tale of "Apollonius of Tyre," as retold by John Gower in his *Confessio Amantis* (1385–1393). The author or authors of *Pericles* also consulted the story as told in Laurence Twine's *The Patterne of Paynfull Adventures,* entered in the Stationers' Register in 1576. There are only two editions of the work extant, one undated, the other dated 1607. At points where the two sources differ, the authors of *Pericles* usually follow Gower. In 1608 George Wilkins published a novel, *The Painfull Adventures of Pericles, Prince of Tyre.* On the title page the author asserts that his work is "The True History of the Play of Pericles, as it was lately presented by the worthy and ancient poet John Gower." The novel is a prose version of *Pericles* based, most critics now believe, on a play, almost surely Shakespeare's, with a few additions from Twine's novel.

Wilkins' novel, if it is based on Shakespeare's play, provides a unique editorial possibility: that of being, in some instances, a more reliable index of the structure and action of the original play than the corrupt First Quarto.

G. L. Kittredge suggests that the name "Pericles" was a variation of "Pyrocles," the hero of Sir Philip Sidney's *Arcadia.* The change from "Apollonius" was doubtless made because that name could not be fitted into a line of iambic pentameters.—O.J.C.

Plot Synopsis. Act I. The poet Gower appears before the palace of King Antiochus of Antioch to tell of the King's incestuous relationship with his daughter, whom he has prevented from marrying by presenting all her suitors with a riddle they must solve or lose their lives. To Antioch comes young Pericles, Prince of Tyre, who, unmindful of the warnings of the King, is determined "to taste the fruit of yon celestial tree" or die in the attempt. Upon reading the riddle, however, he perceives the guilty secret of the King, who in turn realizes that his sin has been detected. Antiochus urges Pericles to remain in his court to undergo further tests, but the Prince is suspicious of the King's courtesy and hastily leaves, thereby barely escaping an assassin, Thaliard, engaged by the King. Pericles returns to Tyre, but, fearful that the King's hatred will pursue him there, secretly sets out once more, leaving wise old Helicanus as his deputy. Pericles makes for Tarsus, where he earns the gratitude of its governor, Cleon, and his wife, Dionyza, by bringing grain for the relief of the famine-plagued city.

Act II. Upon learning that he is still pursued by Thaliard, Pericles leaves Tarsus. During a severe storm at sea his ship is wrecked, and he is cast ashore at Pentapolis, where some kindly fishermen take pity on his hunger. When his rusty coat of armor is also saved, Pericles decides to take part in a tournament to be held by good King Simonides of Pentapolis to celebrate the birthday of his daughter Thaisa. Despite his bedraggled accoutrements, Pericles wins both the tourney and the love of Thaisa, who informs her father that she is determined to wed the knight of Tyre. Although Simonides approves of her choice, he feigns displeasure and accuses Pericles of bewitching her. After Pericles protests his honesty, Simonides gives his blessing to the match.

Act III. Continuing his tale, Gower states that Pericles receives letters informing him that Antiochus and his daughter are dead and that the citizens of Tyre are threatening to crown Helicanus unless Pericles returns within a year. Pericles sets sail for his native land, accompanied by Thaisa, who is expecting their first child. During a storm at sea, Thaisa dies giving birth to a daughter. Reluctantly acceding to the superstitions of the sailors, Pericles has his wife's body placed in a chest and thrown overboard. Washed ashore at Ephesus, the chest is taken to the house of Lord Cerimon, a skilled physician, who is able to revive Thaisa. Believing herself a widow, she then becomes a votaress in the nearby temple of Diana. Pericles, meanwhile, has proceeded to Tarsus and has left his infant daughter, Marina, in the care of Cleon and Dionyza.

Act IV. According to Gower, Pericles returns to Tyre while Marina grows to womanhood in Tarsus, winning widespread admiration for her accomplishments. Dionyza, however, is bitterly jealous because her own daughter has been completely overshadowed by Marina. She orders her servant Leonine to murder Marina, but, as he is about to perform the deed, she is abducted by pirates, who sell her to a brothel-keeper in Mytilene. So inviolable is her virtue that she not only refuses to yield to the demands of the brothel's clients, but even persuades them to renounce their dissolute habits. When she is interviewed by Lysimachus, the governor of Mytilene, he is deeply impressed by her modesty and bearing and, giving her gold, promises his protection. The brothel-keepers, meanwhile, have wearied of her "peevish chastity" and readily agree when she asks to be placed in an honest household where she can give instruction in music and needlework.

Act V. Having been told by Cleon and Dionyza that Marina is dead, the disconsolate Pericles sets sail for Tyre, but is driven by unfavorable winds to Mytilene, where he receives a shipboard visit from Lysimachus. When he learns from Helicanus the reason for the Prince's grief, Lysimachus orders that Marina be summoned, promising that she will raise his spirits "with her sweet harmony / And other chosen attractions." She sings for Pericles but gets no response; only when she mentions her own sorrows and exalted parentage does he reveal a spark of interest. As she tells her story, he gradually realizes that he has been reunited with the child he thought was dead. Suddenly, strange music lulls Pericles to sleep; in a vision he sees Diana, who bids him go to her temple in Ephesus. Upon arriving there with Marina and Lysimachus, Pericles describes his travails to the high priestess, who turns out to be Thaisa. A joyous reunion follows, during which Pericles announces the betrothal of Marina and Lysimachus. Hearing of the death of Simonides, Pericles declares that he and Thaisa will henceforth live at Pentapolis, while his son and daughter shall reign in Tyre.—H.D.

Comment. Since Shakespeare apparently had no dramatic source on which to model this drama th his company had commissioned him to write, he w impelled to invent and to fix the form and disti guishing features of a new type of play that came be known as a "romance." *Pericles* is his first exper ment in the creation of a new dramatic genre. F this reason the structure of the play is simple—a most bare. It is not complicated by subtleties characterization or by exploiting the emotions, eve those of the characters involved in the most heavil laden situations. The tale is the thing to catch and t hold the attention of the spectators. The events th crowd the story are strange and sensational, calc lated to excite surprise and wonder, sometimes eve sudden and transient awe. Witness the fire fro heaven that destroys the incestuous Antiochus an his daughter, Thaisa's almost literal resurrection fro the dead, and the landing of pirates just in time t prevent Leonine's murder of Marina. The scenes i the brothel have the attraction of the forbidden, not of the strange. Shakespeare cleanses these scen of some of their filthiness by turning Boult and th Bawd into comic figures. Marina's success in turnir away her would-be customers makes the futile effor of these employees of the brothel to perform the accustomed duties ridiculous:

> *Bawd.* How now! what's the matter?
> *Boult.* Worse and worse, mistress; she has her
> spoken holy words to the Lord Lysimachus.
> *Bawd.* O abominable!
>
> (IV, vi, 140–143)

The trials of Pericles form the central plot of th romance. His constant sea voyages become a symb of Everyman's progress through the perils and fru trations of life to a safe and peaceful harbor. Told i a Christian context, the journey would end in salv tion. Unlike the hero in most plays adopting th formula, Pericles is not active; he is passive. He do not conquer; he endures. F. D. Hoeniger sugges that the action of this play resembles that of certai miracle plays, where Patience, under the blows c misfortunes which God imposes to test His child submission to His will, is rewarded with beatitud Pericles, too, submits without protest to being th plaything of the gods, and is only freed from bond age by a vision of Diana which bids him hie to he temple at Ephesus and there make sacrifice to he She swears by her silver bow that he will be fort nate and happy thereafter.

Many of the themes first sounded in *Pericles* r appear in one or more of the later-written romance For example, the resurrection of Thaisa correspond to the coming to life of Hermione's supposed statu in *The Winter's Tale.* The sequence of a daughte lost, exposed to danger, found again, and instr mental in the reconciliation of her parents is als strikingly developed in *The Winter's Tale.* Th storms in *Pericles* that first cause separation and w and later reunion and blessed good fortune have counterpart in those of *The Tempest.* Dionyz Marina's wicked foster mother, corresponds to th second wife of Cymbeline, Imogen's evil stepmothe The apparently invincible power of evil in *Pericl* also dictates the action throughout most of *Cymb line* and *The Winter's Tale.* The passage of man years in Pericles' story becomes in *The Winter ale* the meaning of the action, for it illustrates the ower of time to heal and restore. The sudden turn f the action near the end of the play, away from ragedy to the creation of a celestial atmosphere in which all differences are composed and all sins forgiven, is common to *Pericles* and the other romances. *ericles* thus proves to be the basic structure on which the poet was to build his later, more elaborate omances.

In *Pericles* Shakespeare introduces some features of he MASQUE; there is some masquelike dancing when he six knights, heavy with armor, dance at Simonides' bidding, partly to arouse Pericles from his melncholy. There is much more song and instrumental nusic. Antiochus calls for music to introduce and ccompany the first entrance of his daughter, "aparell'd like the spring" (I, i, 12). While trying to evive the seemingly dead Thaisa, Cerimon twice sks for music:

> The rough and woeful music that we have,
> Cause it to sound, beseech you.
> The viol once more.
>
> (III, ii, 88–90)

Vhen Marina is brought before the speechless Periles, the others withdraw and she sings. Pericles is oo much absorbed in his grief to hear the song, but ot the members of the audience. Later, when Diana ppears to Pericles in a vision, he hears heavenly nusic that "nips" him into listening and lays "thick lumber" on his eyes. This "music of the spheres" is lesigned to arouse in Pericles, and also in the spectaor, a religious awe proper to recipients of a divine ommunication. The many introductions of music nto *Pericles* remind us of opera, which was one of he descendants of the masque.

Shakespeare's evocation of the medieval poet John Gower to serve as presenter and Chorus of the play ad no precedent. Gower's function is different from hat of the Chorus in *Henry V*, who speaks for the lramatist himself. Both Choruses keep the audience nformed about events not presented on the stage, nd thus hold scattered incidents together, but Gower also had pictorial value. His repeated appearnces in the quaint and severe garb of his day contantly remind the audience of the hallowed age of he story that is being dramatized. It also reinforces he religious aspect of the romance by associating he story with "the moral Gower."—O.J.C.

Stage History. *Pericles* was very popular in Shakepeare's day. Between 1609 and 1613 it was printed ix times with Shakespeare's name on the title page. ome lines in the anonymous pamphlet *Pimlyco or Runne Red-cap*, published in 1609, attest to its immeliate popularity with both high and low: "Amazde stood, to see a Crowde / Come to see *Shore* or *ericles*." A performance at court in late 1607 or arly 1608 was attended by the Venetian ambassador. *ericles* was also presented by CHOLMELEY'S MEN, a raveling troupe, at Gowthwaite Hall, Sir John York's mansion at Nidderdale in Yorkshire, on Febuary 2, 1610. The French ambassador was enterained at Whitehall on May 20, 1619 with various hows, including a performance of *Pericles*. The ecord of the occasion reads: "In the King's greate hamber they went to see the play of *Pirracles* Prince f Tyre, which lasted till two a clocke." The play was performed at least once at the Globe theatre between 1625 and June 10, 1631. Its continued popularity evidently irked Ben JONSON, who, after the failure of his *New Inn*, gibed at audiences in his *Ode to Himselfe* (1629) for preferring "some mouldy tale, Like *Pericles*" to his better dramas.

Pericles was the first of Shakespeare's plays to be produced (1660) after the Restoration. John Rhodes, former wardrobe-keeper at Blackfriars, established a group of actors and staged 13 plays at the Phoenix Theatre. *Pericles* was the only Shakespearean play in this repertoire. Thomas Betterton, then 25 years old, performed in the title role and was greatly praised. He played the part again at Salisbury Court early in 1661, but no other production is recorded until August 1, 1738, when Covent Garden staged an adaptation by George Lillo, entitled *Marina*. Lillo concocted a three-act drama out of the last two acts of *Pericles*, introducing some of his own fustian and a little 18th-century bawdry, the character of which can be inferred from the name given the bawd, "Mother Coupler."

Samuel Phelps' successful revival at Sadler's Wells ran for several weeks from October 14, 1854. This elaborate and costly spectacle in an oriental setting was the only important 19th-century production of *Pericles*. The verdict of the critics was laudatory, although they granted that the presentation was more for the eyes than the ears.

Pericles did not recover until May 1921 when Robert Atkins staged an excellent, unexpurgated production for the Old Vic Theatre with Rupert Harvey and Mary Sumner as Pericles and Marina. Since then the play's popularity has increased. In 1926 the Fellowship of Players acted the drama at the Scala, followed by a presentation at the Maddermarket Theatre, Norwich, in 1929. There were two productions in Germany in 1924 and an amateur adaptation performed in the United States at Smith College in 1920. During the 1930's *Pericles* was produced at the Cambridge Festival Theatre (1933) and, in America, at the Pasadena Playhouse (1936) under Gilmor Brown. The last production of the decade was Robert Atkins' uncut version at the Open Air Theatre in June 1939. Robert Eddison played Pericles and Margaret Vines was Marina.

Nugent Monck brought *Pericles* in 1947 to Stratford. The play was reduced to an hour and a half, with the first act completely eliminated. Paul Scofield was a romantic Prince and Daphne Slater a gentle Marina. Three years later Scofield and Miss Slater successfully re-created their roles in an uncut production by John Harrison at Rudolf Steiner Hall. In 1954 Douglas Seale staged a slightly cut *Pericles* for the Birmingham Repertory Theatre. This effective production, featuring Richard Pasco in a splendid performance of the hero and Doreen Aris as a tender, serious Marina, was especially noted for the intensely moving conversion and recognition scenes. That year, Arthur Lithgow staged the play at Antioch, Ohio, and, in 1957, another American production was seen in Ashland, Oregon. In Paris, René Dupuy produced *Pericles* at the Théâtre de l'Ambigu-Comique in 1957. Stratford saw an eloquent presentation the next year directed by Tony Richardson, who charged the atmosphere with sometimes too-noisy reminders of the sea theme. Edric

Connor was a calypso-singing Gower in this pictorial revival and Richard Johnson was properly romantic as a young Pericles. Geraldine McEwan lent poignance and beauty to the role of Marina.

Two productions of *Pericles* were staged in 1960, one at Barnard College in New York in April, and the other at Gniezno, Poland, in May.—M.G.

Bibliography. TEXT: *Pericles*, New Cambridge Edition, J. C. Maxwell, ed., 1956; *Pericles*, New Arden Edition, F. D. Hoeniger, ed., 1963; Philip Edwards, "An Approach to the Problem of *Pericles*," *Shakespeare Survey 5*, 1952; Kenneth Muir, *Shakespeare as Collaborator*, 1960. DATE: New Arden Edition; T. S. Graves, "On the Date and Significance of *Pericles*," *Modern Philology*, XIII, 1916. SOURCES: *The Painfull Adventures of Pericles*, Kenneth Muir, ed., 1953; Kenneth Muir, *Shakespeare's Sources*, Vol. I, 1957. COMMENT: New Arden Edition; Arthur Quiller-Couch, *Shakespeare's Workmanship*, 1918; John F. Danby, *Poets on Fortune's Hill*, 1952. STAGE HISTORY: New Cambridge Edition; New Arden Edition; G. C. D. Odell, *Shakespeare from Betterton to Irving*, 1920; J. C. Trewin, *Shakespeare on the English Stage, 1900–1964*, 1964.

Selected Criticism

G. G. GERVINUS. The tender nature of his (Pericles') character, which makes him anxious in moments of quiet action, renders him excited in misfortune, and robs him of the power of resistance in suffering. The same violent emotion, the same sinking into melancholy, the same change of his innermost feelings, which he remarks in himself in the first act, after his adventure in Antiochia, we see again rising in him after the supposed death of his wife and child; as at that time, he again casts himself upon the wide world and yields to immoderate grief, forgetful of men and of his duties, until the unknown daughter restores him to himself, and he at the same time recovers wife and child. The ecstatic transition from sorrow to joy is here intimated in the same masterly manner as the sudden decline from hope and happiness to melancholy and mourning was before depicted. As we said above, this is only sketched in outline; but there is a large scope left to a great actor to shape this outline into a complete form by the finishing touches of his representation. We therefore before suggested that Shakespeare may have chosen this play, in all other parts highly insignificant and trifling, only to prepare a difficult theme for his Burbage, who acted this character. [*Shakespeare*, 1849–1850; tr. 1863 as *Shakespeare Commentaries*.]

CAROLINE F. E. SPURGEON. *Pericles* alone of the romances has no sign of any running 'motive' or continuity of picture or thought in the imagery, a fact sufficient in itself to throw grave doubts on its authorship.

The proportion and subjects of the images in *Pericles* are, however, quite in keeping with Shakespeare's other plays: though as a whole they seem rather thin, and there is a very small proportion (eleven of the hundred and nine) of poetical images. A certain selection, though they fall under Shakespeare's usual headings, are flat, general, uninteresting and un-Shakespearian (e.g. the diamonds round a crown, spring and summer, the unplucked flower, 'groves, being topp'd', storm, snowball, 'pretty wrens', 'angel-eagle'). On the other hand, we find quite a fair number of images which are markedly 'Shakespearian' in quality. [*Shakespeare's Imagery*, 1935.]

G. WILSON KNIGHT. *Pericles* might be called Shakespearean morality play. The epilogue asserts as much, though it does no justice to the more important scenes, which so tower above the rest and which it would be a great error to relate too sharply to any known type of drama. These, whatever we think of them, are spontaneous, new creations. And yet, in spite of their superiority, they cannot be isolated. *Pericles* is too thoroughly organic a play for that, with all its running coherences of idea, image, and event . . . .

Whatever we think of certain parts, the whole, as we have it, is unquestionably dominated by a single mind; that mind is very clearly Shakespeare's; and Shakespeare's, too, in process of an advance unique in literature. [*The Crown of Life*, 1947.]

KENNETH MUIR. Journeys that end in lovers' meeting, scenes in which brother and sister, husband and wife, or parents and children meet again after long separation, when each believed the other dead, were frequent episodes in Elizabethan fiction—and in the Greek Romances on which they were sometimes based—and they have always been effective on the stage, whether in Greek tragedy or Latin comedy. Two of Euripides' most effective scenes are the meeting of Iphigenia and Orestes in Tauris and the restoration of Alcestis to her husband. Even the reunion of Egeon and his wife in *The Comedy of Errors* is a moving scene in a play which is largely farcical; the silent reunion of Isabella and Claudio is a little-recognized master-stroke in *Measure for Measure;* and the meeting of Viola and Sebastian in *Twelfth Night* is a touching climax to that play. The meeting of Pericles and Marina surpasses all these. Its effectiveness, and the effectiveness of the whole play, is due partly to Shakespeare's creation of a kind of myth which he could set up against the changes and chances of this mortal life. He is calling in a new world to redress the balance of the old, a new world in which the designs of evil men are frustrated and in which everything comes right in the end—the beautiful queen is not really dead, the beautiful princess is saved from murder and rape and the contamination of the brothel, and the hero, after more trials and tribulations than are normally the lot of man, is rewarded with unforeseen and unimagined happiness. Shakespeare is aware that his story is too good to be true, but such fables are a criticism of life as it is, and . . . a statement of faith. [*Shakespeare as Collaborator*, 1960.]

FRANK KERMODE. This version of the themes of sundering and reunion, the suffering king and the princess of magic virtue, is the prototype of the Romances. Marina, like Perdita and Miranda, has that 'better nature' which defies corruption, however harsh the world. And *Pericles* can help us with the later Romances in other ways. It is allegorical to the degree suggested by the foregoing, and not more. In the hands of Sidney and Spenser romance was a very flexible, but also an unstable, mode of ethical allegory. Spenser, whose poem Shakespeare knew perhaps as well as any other book, does not write allegory of unvarying intensity, but diversifies his master-allegory with subtle and even opportunistic figurations of a lesser kind. In Shakespeare there is good deal of this kind of thing, but his master-themes are invariably explicit and not figurative. He writes for the stage. He cannot put the Blatant Beast on the stage; he puts instead slanderers and louts. Florimell is pursued by a spotted monster 'that feeds on women's flesh', but Marina is sold into an actual brothel. The playwright cannot afford to neglect what Professor Danby calls 'the creaturely and existential'. In *Pericles* he comes nearer than anywhere else to a schematic presentation of themes inseparable from the very idea of romance-comedy, and there is in the nature of the case a strong element of parable. But it is wrong to impose detailed allegorical readings on the play. In the end, the theatre explains it; it is an act of concentration on the laws of comic form, a huge, perhaps inordinate, development of the comic recognition. The parabolic habit of romance touches it, more or less lightly, here and there. Truths, Truth itself perhaps, glint in the narrative, shiver and thresh in the net of language. But *Pericles* is, above all, the work of a great dramatist who had been much moved by a great poet, and who—not without a certain pride in easy mastery—wanted to do a new thing in the making of comedy. [*Shakespeare: The Final Plays,* 1963, No. 155 in "Writers and Their Work" series.]

WILLIAM EMPSON. I have no wish to deny that there is a good deal of religious or mystical feeling in the last plays; I think, indeed, that while he wrote them he was preparing his soul for death, but also that he would not regard the plays as a means of doing it. To continue turning them out had evidently become an unwelcome duty, though he carried on for three or four years. In the year that the Company got the use of the indoor Blackfriars Theatre Shakespeare somehow did not want to write another tragedy. Turning over a bad play by someone else, he felt that this kind of stuff would do; and during his subsequent years in harness he in effect just went on using that story again. *Pericles* did not pass without notice; terribly short of audience-gossip though we are, we find Shakespeare being jeered at for putting on such a salacious and catchpenny play. Some of it is, indeed, very peculiar, but not for being salacious.

The gallants leaving the brothel, for example (IV, v):

> *First Gentleman.* But to have divinity preached there! did you ever dream of such a thing?
> *Second Gentleman.* No, no. Come, I am for no more bawdy-houses; shall's go hear the vestals sing?

Here we meet a thrilling extremity of bad taste; plainly it was screwed up by the hand of the master. . . Or the delicious heroine herself, protesting her innocence (IV, i):

> I never spoke bad word, nor did ill turn
> To any living creature: believe me, la,
> I never killed a mouse, nor hurt a fly:
> I trod upon a worm once, 'gainst my will.
> But I wept for it.

The narrator Esther in *Bleak House* arouses the same electric nausea; it is done by implying "I'm such a good girl that I don't even *know* how good I am". In short, this is tear-jerks at their most reeking. ["Hunt the Symbol," *The Times Literary Supplement,* April 23, 1964.]

Peter. In *Romeo and Juliet,* a servant to Juliet's nurse. Peter sings "When griping grief" (IV, v), part of a song by Richard Edwards published in *The Paradise of Dainty Devises* (1576). Stage directions in Q2 indicate that this part was played by Will Kempe, the chief clown of Shakespeare's company, who undoubtedly made the most of the small part.

Peter, Friar. In *Measure for Measure,* a monk who assists Duke Vincentio in his plot to expose Angelo's misdeeds (V, i).

Peter of Pomfret. A prophet who predicted that King John would surrender his crown before Ascension Day, 1213. In *King John,* the King orders that Peter be imprisoned and hanged (IV, ii). The prophecy is fulfilled when, on Ascension Day, John settles his quarrel with Pope Innocent by making England a papal fief (V, i).

Peters, Matthew William (c. 1750–1814). Clergyman, painter, and engraver. Peters was born on the Isle of Wight and worked as a painter in Dublin. He subsequently took holy orders, but continued to paint. Peters contributed five paintings to BOYDELL's SHAKESPEARE GALLERY: two paintings illustrating scenes from *The Merry Wives of Windsor;* one from *Much Ado About Nothing;* and two from *Henry VIII.* His graceful work suggests a lighthearted nature, and the paintings from *Much Ado About Nothing* and *The Merry Wives of Windsor* are particularly charming. Of the pictures done from *Henry VIII,* the depiction of the Cardinal's visit to Queen Katharine is quite dramatic, while "The Baptism of Queen Elizabeth" is merely superficial. [W. M. Merchant, *Shakespeare and the Artist,* 1959.]

Peter Thump. See Thomas HORNER.

Petit, Jacques (fl. 1596). A French tutor and attendant of Anthony Bacon, brother of Francis, who recorded in a letter to Bacon a private performance of *Titus Andronicus.* The performance took place at the home of John Harington, later Lord Harington of Exton (d. 1613), cousin of the poet Sir John Harington. Harington's estate was at Burley-on-the-Hill in Rutland, where Petit was temporarily employed as a tutor. His letter, written in French, states that during the Christmas revels, probably on New Year's Day, 1596, a performance of *Titus Andronicus* was given by "Les commediens de Londres . . ." Petit does not describe the performance but merely interjects the terse critical comment "la monstre a plus valeu q̄ le suiect" ["the spectacle is worth more than the play"]. [Gustav Ungerer, "An Unrecorded Elizabethan Performance of *Titus Andronicus,*" *Shakespeare Survey 14,* 1961.]

Peto. In *1 Henry IV,* a collaborator with Falstaff, Bardolph, and Gadshill in the robbery of the travelers leaving the Rochester inn (II, ii). He subsequently tells Prince Henry that, as robbers, they were hard put to hide their fright. In *2 Henry IV,* he brings the Prince word of the rebellion (II, iv).

Petrarch. Anglicized surname of **Francesco Petrarca** (1304–1374). Italian humanist and poet. Educated for the law, Petrarch received the patronage of important civil and ecclesiastical rulers, including that of the popes then residing at Avignon. Frequent travels on diplomatic missions gave him the opportunity to meet the notable scholars of his day and to consult manuscripts scattered throughout Europe. Periods of retirement made it possible to carry on various literary activities. As a humanist Petrarch discovered, edited, annotated, and commented on forgotten Latin classics. As an author he was prolific and versatile, producing works in both prose and poetry and in both Latin and Italian. His Latin works include philosophical treatises, epistles to persons living and dead, biographical sketches of great Romans, and the unfinished epic *Africa,* which celebrates the deeds of Scipio Africanus in the conquest of Carthage. The principal Italian works are the *Canzoniere* (see SONNET SEQUENCE) and the *Trionfi*. The *Canzoniere* (literally, "the song book") consists primarily of sonnets addressed to Laura. Interspersed throughout are poems—usually sonnets but occasionally in other forms—dealing with different subjects.

The form, themes, images, and other elements used by Petrarch established a convention in sonneteering which lasted more than 200 years: the lover is caught in the meshes of love, he is like a ship in a storm, his tears are like floods and his sighs like tempests, he alternates between freezing and burning, his mistress is his "sweetest foe," her birthplace is a sacred shrine, she is an unattainable ideal, she inspires all that is noble in the lover. Such conventions were introduced into English by Sir Thomas Wyatt and the earl of SURREY, and were followed for a time by the Elizabethan sonneteers. Shakespeare made use of some Petrarchan elements, but in Sonnet 130 he ridiculed the conventional conceits. Petrarch's *Trionfi* is a series of symbolic imitations of a Roman triumph. The poet in a dream sees the triumph of Love, Chastity, Death, Fame, Time, and Eternity. Each triumphs over the preceding entity, until Eternity—that is, Christian immortality—ultimately triumphs over all. Certain themes of the *Trionfi*, particularly those of time and eternity, are used in Shakespeare's *Sonnets*.

Petruchio. In *The Taming of the Shrew,* an admitted fortune hunter. This swaggering and unmannerly gentleman of Verona arrives in Padua seeking a wealthy wife. Learning of Katharina's large dowry, Petruchio immediately presents himself as her suitor and confidently arranges a wedding date for the following Sunday. To curb his bride's headstrong humor, Petruchio plays the overly solicitous husband, finding fault with the accommodations and boisterously upbraiding his servants. By a series of practical jokes, he manages to discomfit Katharina into submissiveness. At Petruchio's insistence, his wife finally agrees that the sun is the moon; when her husband greets the aged Vincentio as a lovely young maiden, Katharina subscribes with her own portrait of the old man as a "young, budding virgin, fair and fresh and sweet."

Petruchio establishes his success in taming the shrew with a demonstration of Katharina's "new-built virtue and obedience" before the company of newlyweds.

Pettie, George (1548–1589). Translator and author. Pettie is the author of *A Petite Palace of Pettie His Pleasure* (1576), a collection of 12 tales based upon well-known classical stories. Pettie's book was designed to capitalize on the popularity of William Painter's *The Palace of Pleasure* (2 vols., 1566–1567) even to the extent of duplicating its title. It apparently succeeded, for Pettie's *Palace* was reprinted a number of times into the 17th century. One of the tales in the *Palace,* the account of the story of Pygmalion, has been suggested as the source of Hermione's resurrection in *The Winter's Tale.*

Pettie is also the author of *The Civile Conversation of M. Steeven Guazzo* (1581, 1586), a translation of an Italian work by Stefano Guazzo, by way of a French translation by Gabriel Chappuys. One passage in *The Civile Conversation* closely resembles Hamlet's attack on cosmetics in the nunnery scene (III, i). [Kenneth Muir, *Shakespeare's Sources,* Vol. I, 1957.]

Phaer, Thomas (c. 1510–1560). Translator, lawyer and physician. Educated at Oxford and Lincoln's Inn, Phaer was a government official in Wales and later a member of parliament. He wrote a number of popular legal and medical treatises, but his best-known work is his translation of the *Aeneid,* the first seven books of which were published in 1558. In 1562 a 2nd edition was published which contained 9 books and a portion of the 10th. The translation was later completed by Thomas Twine (1543–1613). Phaer's *Aeneid* was a popular and highly esteemed translation in the Elizabethan age. Shakespeare may be echoing it in certain passages of *The Tempest.* Phaer is also the author of the "Owen Glendower" section of *A Mirror for Magistrates,* which Shakespeare may have consulted for certain details in his portrait of Glendower in *1 Henry IV.*

Phaeton Sonnet, The. Name given to the anonymous poem attributed to Shakespeare because of its stylistic similarity to his known sonnets. The poem is part of the prefatory verse found in the *Second Fruites* of John Florio, published in 1591.

Phaethon to his Friend Florio.

Sweet friend, whose name agrees with thy increase,
How fit a rival art thou of the Spring!
For when each branch hath left his flourishing,
And green-locked Summer's shady pleasures cease,
She makes the Winter's storms repose in peace
And spends her franchise on each living thing:
The daisies sprout, the little birds do sing;
Herbs, gums, and plants do vaunt of their release.
So that when all our English wits lay dead
(Except the Laurel that is ever green),
Thou with thy fruits our barrenness o'erspread
And set thy flowery pleasance to be seen.
Such fruits, such flow'rets of morality,
Were ne'er before brought out of Italy.

[E. K. Chambers, *William Shakespeare,* 1930.]

Phebe. In *As You Like It,* a shepherdess. Disdaining the devoted Silvius, Phebe falls in love with Rosalind, who is disguised as the boy Ganymede. Phebe sends a love letter to Ganymede cruelly using Silvius as her messenger. Rosalind, having secured Phebe's promise that she will marry Silvius should circumstances compel her to withdraw her proposal to Ganymede, unmasks. The scornful Phebe is forced to marry her faithful Silvius.

Phelps, Samuel (1804–1878). Actor and theatre manager. Phelps abandoned a career in journalism to go on the stage. He made an initial reputation for himself as a tragedian on the York circuit, and was hired by Macready for Covent Garden, but he made his first London appearances as Shylock, Hamlet, Othello, and Richard III at the Haymarket. In 1843 he took over the management of Sadler's Wells Theatre, and made of it a center for the finest, most imaginative Shakespearean productions of his time. When he retired in 1862 he had produced all of Shakespeare except *Henry VI, Titus Andronicus, Troilus and Cressida*, and *Richard II*, including the first revival of *Antony and Cleopatra* (1849) in a century, and the first *Pericles* since the Restoration. He was best in Shakespeare's tragedies, especially as Lear and Othello, but he also played Bottom exceptionally well.

After his retirement from Sadler's Wells, Phelps made several appearances in London and the provinces, doing much Shakespeare, but also dramatizations of the novels of Sir Walter Scott; he made his last stage appearance as Cardinal Wolsey in 1878.

His work at Sadler's Wells had established a high standard in productions noted for their scenic beauty —without pageantry—and for the demands made on the many young actors who trained in them. [*Dictionary of National Biography*, 1885– ; *Oxford Companion to the Theatre*, Phyllis Hartnoll, ed., 1951.]

Philario. In *Cymbeline*, an Italian friend of Posthumus. Philario is Posthumus' host during his banishment in Italy and witnesses the wager on Imogen's virtue. When Iachimo returns from Britain claiming victory, Philario tries unsuccessfully to dissuade Posthumus from accepting the false "proofs" of Imogen's infidelity as "not strong enough to be believed of one persuaded well of" (II, iv).

Philaster. See John FLETCHER.

Philemon. In *Pericles*, servant of Cerimon. He is sent, in III, ii, to fetch fire and food for some shipwrecked people.

Philip II (1165–1223). King of France. He ascended the throne on the death of his father, Louis VII, in 1180. After Philip had established his position at home, he turned his attention abroad, and when the sons of England's Henry II rebelled against their father, Philip abetted them. Then, exchanging pledges of good faith with Henry's successor, Richard I, Philip failed to keep them. As a result, Richard joined with the Norman barons against the French king and defeated him in 1194. After Richard's death in 1199, King John signed a treaty with Philip, ceding to him Berri, Auvergne, and Brittany, as well as the guardianship of his nephew, Arthur. In 1202, however, war broke out again, and after some initial successes on the part of King John, Philip proceeded with the conquest of Normandy.

In *King John*, Philip supports Arthur's claim to the English throne and sends an ambassador to John demanding the surrender of his crown. Indignant, John forthwith invades France.

Philip II (1527–1598). King of Spain (1556–1598). Dedicated to the restoration of Catholic power in Europe, Philip was the most prominent and powerful ruler of his day. His marriage to Mary Tudor, queen of England (1553–1558), extended his power into England. His reign is marked by the long insurrection of his colonies in the Netherlands (1567–1579), his victory over the Turks at the Battle of Lepanto (1571), and his fierce rivalry with England in Europe, in the American colonies, and on the seas, culminating in the defeat of the Armada in 1588.

Feared and hated in England, Philip was nevertheless a respected enemy. One of the many explanations of the Shakespearean sonnet referring to the eclipse of the "mortal moone" (Sonnet 107) is that it alludes to Philip's death. [*The Sonnets*, Variorum Edition, Hyder Rollins, ed., 1944.]

Philips, Ambrose. See ADAPTATIONS.

Philip the Bastard. See Philip FAULCONBRIDGE.

Phillips, Augustine (d. 1605). Actor. Phillips appears in the acting list of Strange's Men in 1593, and had appeared with them in Tarlton's *Seven Deadly Sins* in 1590/1. His name, "Mr. Phillipps," is on the acting list for that play. He was one of the original Chamberlain's Men (Shakespeare's company) when they were formed in 1594. His name appears in the 1623 First Folio list of "principall Actors" in Shakespeare's plays.

He is on the actor lists of the company for 1598, 1599, and the official lists of 1603 and 1604. He was one of the King's Men who received four yards of red cloth from the Great Wardrobe for his participation in King James I's coronation procession through London in March 1604. In May 1595 a jig entitled "Phillips his gygg of the slyppers" was entered in the Stationers' Register. Phillips was called upon to testify regarding the performance his company gave of *Richard II* the evening prior to the Essex rebellion in 1601.

His will, executed on May 4, 1605, and probated by his widow May 13, 1605, is one source of information for the composition of Shakespeare's company. In it Phillips bequeathed £5 to be divided among the hired men of the company, 30s. in gold to his "Fellowe" actors William Shakespeare and Henry Condell, and to his "Servaunte" Christopher Beeston. He willed "twenty shillings in gould" each to his "fellowes" Lawrence Fletcher, Robert "Armyne," Richard "Coweley," Alexander Cook, and Nicholas Tooley. Almost immediately after Phillips' death, his widow married John Witter, thus forfeiting her inheritance. Phillips' share in the Globe later became the subject of a lawsuit brought by Witter and his wife. See John WITTER. [E. K. Chambers, *The Elizabethan Stage*, 1923.]

Phillips, Edward (1630–?1696). Biographer. The nephew of John Milton, of whom he wrote a biography, Phillips was also the author of one of the earliest biographical histories of the stage, *Theatrum Poetarum* (1675). His praise of Shakespeare in the *Theatrum* is profuse, although always qualified by the 17th-century characterization of Shakespeare as an untutored "natural" poet:

> *William Shakespear*, the Glory of the English Stage; whose nativity at *Stratford* upon *Avon*, is the highest honour that Town can boast of: from an Actor of Tragedies and Comedies, he became a *Maker;* and such a Maker, that though some others may perhaps pretend to a more exact *Decorum* and *oeconomie*, especially in Tragedy, never any express't a more lofty and Tragic heighth; never any represented nature more purely to the life,

and where the polishments of Art are most wanting, as probably his Learning was not extraordinary, he pleaseth with a certain wild and native Elegance; and in all his Writings hath an unvulgar style, as well in his *Venus and Adonis,* his *Rape of Lucrece* and other various Poems, as in his Dramatics.

Phillips also alludes to Shakespeare in his account of other Elizabethan dramatists:

> *Benjamin Johnson,* the most learned, judicious and correct, generally so accounted, of our *English* Comedians, and the more to be admired for being so, for that neither the height of natural parts, for he was no *Shakesphear,* nor the cost of Extraordinary Education . . . .
>
> *Christopher Marlow,* a kind of a second *Shakesphear* (whose contemporary he was) not only because like him he rose from an Actor to be a maker of Plays, though inferiour both in Fame and Merit; but also because in his begun Poem of *Hero* and *Leander,* he seems to have a resemblance of that clean and unsophisticated Wit, which is natural to that incomparable Poet . . . .
>
> *John Fletcher,* one of the happy *Triumvirat* (the other two being *Johnson* and *Shakespear*) of the Chief Dramatic Poets of our Nation, in the last foregoing Age, among whom there might be said to be a symmetry of perfection, while each excelled in his peculiar way: *Ben. Johnson* in his elaborate pains and knowledge of Authors, *Shakespear* in his pure vein of wit, and natural Poetic heighth; *Fletcher* in a courtly Elegance, and gentile familiarity of style . . . .

In his general comments he cites Shakespeare and Spenser as examples of "Poetic *Energie*" not "attainable by any Study or Industry":

> . . . let us observe *Spencer,* with all his Rustic, obsolete words, with all his rough-hewn clowterly Verses; yet take him throughout, and we shall find in him a gracefull and Poetic Majesty: in like manner *Shakespear,* in spight of all his unfiled expressions, his rambling and indigested Fancys, the laughter of the *Critical,* yet must be confess't a *Poet* above many that go beyond him in Literature some degrees.

Phillips is also the author of a Latin survey of dramatic verse, *Tractatulus de Carmine Dramatico Poetarum* (1669), which gives the following account:

> Gulielmus Shacsperius, qui praeter opera Dramatica, duo Poemata *Lucretiae stuprum à Tarquinio,* et *Amores Veneris in Adonidem,* Lyrica carmina nonnulla composuit: videtur fuisse, siquis alius, re verâ Poeta natus. [William Shakespeare, who besides his dramatic work, composed two poems *The Rape of Lucrece* and *Venus and Adonis* and some lyrical poetry: seems to have been, indeed, if ever there was such, a natural-born poet.]

[*The Shakspere Allusion-Book,* J. Munro, ed., 1909.]

Philo. In *Antony and Cleopatra,* a friend of Antony's. Philo appears only in the first scene, delivering the play's opening speech.

Philostrate. In *A Midsummer Night's Dream,* Theseus' Master of the Revels. Philostrate arranges the entertainments for the nuptial celebration and introduces the interlude, "Pyramus and Thisby," having advised Theseus that brief though the play is it is still too long (V, i).

Philoten. In *Pericles,* daughter of Cleon and Dionyza. Though Philoten does not appear in the play, she is mentioned by Gower in the Prologue to Act IV as being completely overshadowed by Marina, who thus arouses the enmity of Dionyza.

Philotus. In *Timon of Athens,* a servant of one of Timon's creditors. Philotus sues unsuccessfully for payment (III, iv).

Phoenix and the Turtle, The (1600). An untitled poem generally acknowledged to be by Shakespeare. It first appeared as one of a group of commendatory verses appended to a long poem by Robert Chester entitled LOVES MARTYR OR ROSALINS COMPLAINT (1601, 1611). Shakespeare's poem was also included in John BENSON's *Poems: Written by Wil. Shake-speare Gent.* (1640). It is a 67-line elegy written in strongly marked trochaic tetrameter. The poem begins with a summons to other birds to come to mourn the death of the phoenix and the turtledove:

> Love and constancy is dead;
> Phoenix and the turtle fled
> In a mutual flame from hence.
> (22–24)

The notion of the "mutual flame" sets up the subsequent theme of the mystical union of the two dead birds, a union made possible by love, which defies all the laws of reason and nature. The concluding 15 lines of the poem, the "threnos," celebrate the fusion of beauty (the phoenix) and fidelity (the turtledove). The poem, with its heavily allegorical and impersonal cast, is unlike any other work of Shakespeare, which has led some critics in the past to doubt its authenticity. It is now generally regarded as not only a legitimate but an important part of the Shakespearean canon, attracting a host of admirers and interpreters. Some have read the poem as a political allegory, suggesting that it refers to the tragic love affair of Elizabeth and Essex. Others have seen it as an allusion to Sir John SALISBURY, to whom *Love's Martyr* is dedicated; as a dirge for Anne Lyne (d. 1601), a Catholic recusant executed for harboring priests; or as a reference to Lucy Harington, countess of BEDFORD and her husband, Edward Russell, third earl of Bedford.

In recent years the philosophical and symbolic qualities of the poem have been explored. G. Wilson Knight has analyzed the poem in relation to the other poems in *Love's Martyr* and finds evidence to support his view that "The Phoenix and the Turtle," like the *Sonnets,* celebrates the fusion of the feminine and masculine principles, or "bisexual integration." J. V. Cunningham has found in the poem the embodiment of scholastic doctrine. The mystical relationship of the lovers is identical with that existing between the three persons of the Trinity as expounded by St. Thomas Aquinas. Other interpretations range from the theological to the biographical. Suggested sources for the poem include Ovid's *Amores* and an elegy on Sir Philip Sidney by Matthew Roydon. [*The Poems,* New Variorum Edition, Hyder Rollins, ed., 1938; *Poems,* New Arden Edition, F. T. Prince, ed., 1960; J. V. Cunningham, "Essence and the Phoenix," *ELH, A Journal of English Literary History*, XIX, No. 4, 1952; G. Wilson Knight, *The Mutual Flame*, 1955.]—E.Q.

Phoenix or **Cockpit theatre.** A playhouse located in the parish of St-Giles-in-the-Fields adjoining Drury Lane. The Phoenix was originally designed as a cockpit, an amphitheatre for the popular sport of cockfighting. In 1616 Christopher Beeston, the leader of Queen Anne's Men, leased the roofed building with the purpose of converting it into a private theatre. On March 4, 1617, shortly before Queen Anne's Men were scheduled to open, the playhouse was wrecked by a group of apprentices celebrating Shrove Tuesday. The rioters also destroyed the players' costumes and playbooks, thus contributing to the subsequent decline of Queen Anne's Men. The playhouse was repaired, however, and reopened three months later. Queen Anne's Men were replaced shortly thereafter by Prince Charles' Men, who occupied the theatre until 1622, and were themselves followed by Lady Elizabeth's Men. In the 1630's the theatre was occupied by the company of young actors known as "Beeston's Boys." Beeston died in 1638 and the company came under the control of his son, William. In 1649 the playhouse was badly damaged, but not destroyed, by government soldiers. It was reopened at the Restoration, but even before that, in 1658, the master diplomatist William Davenant had managed to secure government permission to stage his "operas" there. At the Restoration in 1660 the playhouse was occupied by a young company under the leadership of John Rhodes. The star of the company was Thomas Betterton. On October 11, 1660 Pepys saw a production of *Othello* there. From 1661 to 1665 a troupe under George Jolly occupied the theatre. Subsequently it fell into disuse. [Leslie Hotson, *The Commonwealth and Restoration Stage*, 1928.]

Phoenix Shakespeare Festival. A dramatic festival held annually at Phoenix, Arizona. In 1957 the first festival was held, under the auspices of the Alfred Knight Shakespearean Section of the Phoenix Little Theatre. Three different dramatic groups in the state each present a Shakespearean play in the spring at the host theatre in Phoenix. Other features of the festival are lectures and discussions and a country fair featuring Elizabethan songs and dances. Some critics have felt that the Little Theatre's proscenium stage puts Shakespearean plays at a disadvantage because it requires scenery. Director John Paul of Phoenix College solved this problem in his production of *Romeo and Juliet* by using a four-foot-high, curtained upper stage with side balconies, stairs, and a forestage, which enabled him to move the action continuously. For *The Tempest*, director Peter Maroney of the University of Arizona employed a scrim with moving light to suggest waves and rain for the opening scene and a backdrop of flexible plastic in tropical design for the following scenes. Other plays offered have included *Hamlet*, *Richard II*, *The Merchant of Venice*, and *Twelfth Night*. Arizona State College at Flagstaff and Arizona State University at Tempe have been participating institutions.—A.G.

Phrynia. In *Timon of Athens*, one of Alcibiades' two mistresses. In IV, iii, Timon gives Phrynia part of the treasure he has found, but curses her.

pied bull quarto. Name given to the first edition of *King Lear* (1608), published by Nathaniel Butter. The name comes from Butter's shop, located "at the signe of the Pide Bull," where the book was sold. Twelve copies of this quarto are extant, and they reveal many variants, an indication that correction and proofreading of the edition were done while the book was being printed. The second edition of *King Lear* bears the imprint "Printed for Nathaniel Butter. 1608," but it was actually printed in 1619 by William Jaggard, who altered the dates in order to circumvent an order of 1619 which forbade the printing of the King's Men's plays without their consent. Both the pied bull edition and the second edition are poor and apparently unauthorized texts. See King Lear: *Text*.

Pilon, Frederick. See adaptations; Ireland.

Pinch. In *The Comedy of Errors*, a schoolmaster and mountebank. Pinch is exhorted by Adriana to use his conjuring powers to bring Antipholus of Ephesus to his senses. He declares the twin, mistaken by Adriana for her husband, and Dromio, his servant, possessed by the devil and advises that they be consigned to "some dark room."

Pindarus. In *Julius Caesar*, a servant of Cassius. Pindarus erroneously reports that Titinius is taken by the enemy, leaving Cassius desolate and intent upon death. When Cassius commands Pindarus to kill him, the servant obeys. Although he is free now, Pindarus "yet would not so have been, durst I have done my will." He runs off far from Rome (V, iii).

piracy of plays. See printing and publishing.

Pirithous. In *The Two Noble Kinsmen*, an Athenian general. His friendship with Theseus, Duke of Athens, occasions a discussion between Hippolyta and Emilia on the relative merits of love between men and between women. Pirithous appoints the disguised Arcite to the service of Emilia, and later describes to Palamon his cousin's death.

Pisanio. In *Cymbeline*, the faithful servant of Posthumus. Pisanio is directed by the banished Posthumus to serve Imogen, and when commanded by his master to murder her, he suspects that Posthumus has been victimized by the "false Italian." Glumly, this steady servant accompanies Imogen to what she believes is a rendezvous with her husband. After disclosing Posthumus' orders to kill her, the honest Pisanio persuades Imogen to adopt the disguise of a boy and enter Lucius' service as a page. In the last act, he reveals Imogen's true identity.

Pistol. In *2 Henry IV*, Falstaff's ensign. In V, iii, Pistol brings his master news of the death of Henry IV. When Henry V subsequently turns against his old crony Falstaff, Pistol is arrested with him. In *The Merry Wives of Windsor*, Pistol is dismissed from Falstaff's service for refusing to deliver a love letter to Mistress Page. Pistol takes his revenge by informing Master Ford of Falstaff's designs on Mistress Ford. Resolving to court Mistress Quickly, he joins her in the baiting of Falstaff in Windsor Park.

In *Henry V*, Pistol has married Nell Quickly and is host of the Boar's Head Tavern. He leaves, however, for the English campaign in France, where, with his companions Bardolph and Nym, he takes to thievery. When in V, i, he hears of the death of his "Doll" (considered by some authorities to be a mistake for "Nell"), Pistol decides to return to England and turn procurer and cutpurse.

Pitoëff, Georges (1886–1939). Russian-born actor and director active in French theatre. Pitoëff began his work in the French-speaking theatre in 1908 at Geneva, Switzerland. From 1916 until his death, he and his wife, Ludmilla, presented a varied list of classic and modern plays in their repertory company, both in Geneva and in Paris. Pitoëff was not only the producer, director, and an actor in the company, but also created the sets and costumes for most of the plays.

As an actor he was especially adept at interpreting roles dealing with enigmatic characters, and it was natural that he should be particularly attracted to Shakespeare's *Hamlet*. He first appeared in the work during his 1920 production at Geneva, in an adaptation by Eugène Morand and Marcel Schwob. Constantly seeking new and different approaches to the difficult role, he produced and reappeared in six revivals of the play during his theatrical career. Besides *Hamlet*, he presented *Macbeth, Romeo and Juliet* (which he and Pierre-Jean Jouve adapted into French), and *Measure for Measure*.

Pitoëff felt that Shakespeare's work had a beauty of form and thought unequaled by other playwrights. The English dramatist, he noted, was an author who rejuvenated and invigorated those who came into contact with his works. He remained in awe of Shakespeare's verbal beauty and power and he always endeavored to emphasize those qualities in his productions. Known for his settings of *Hamlet* and *Macbeth*, Pitoëff followed one basic principle: the decor must aid in the expression of the essential part of the drama—the dialogue. Although the scenery should provide an effective synthetic and stylized background for the play, it nevertheless must remain as simple as possible, not detracting from the author's words.—J.R.

Planché, James Robinson (1796–1880). Dramatist, antiquary, and theatrical consultant. Planché was a remarkable man with many interests. He wrote burlesque melodramas, pantomimes, and serious opera libretti, including English texts for Weber's *Oberon* and Mozart's *Magic Flute*. He was an authority on heraldry and his *History of British Costume* (1834) is still in use as a reliable reference for modern designers. He was for a time the musical director of Vauxhall Gardens, as well as a designer and dramatist employed by Elizabeth Vestris. He inaugurated the 19th-century authentically costumed productions of Shakespeare's history plays with Charles Kemble's Covent Garden production of *King John* (1824). An account of the success of this production is given in his *Recollections and Reflections* (1872):

> Never shall I forget the dismay of some of the performers when they looked upon the flat-topped *chapeaux de fer* (*fer blanc,* I confess) of the twelfth century, which they irreverently stigmatized as *stewpans!* . . . When the curtain rose, and discovered King John dressed as his effigy appears in Worcester Cathedral, surrounded by his barons sheathed in mail, with cylindrical helmets and correct armorial shields, and his courtiers in the long tunics and mantles of the thirteenth century, there was a roar of approbation, accompanied by four distinct rounds of applause, . . . Receipts of from £400 to £600 nightly soon reimbursed the management for the expense of the production, and a complete reformation of dramatic costume became from that moment inevitable upon the English stage.

[W. M. Merchant, *Shakespeare and the Artist*, 1959; A. M. Nagler, *A Source Book in Theatrical History*, 1959.]

Plantagenet, Margaret (1473–1541). Second daughter of George, duke of Clarence. Henry VII married her to Sir Richard Pole. To make amends for the wrongs done her brother (Edward Plantagenet, earl of Warwick) by Richard III and Henry VII, King Henry VIII made Margaret countess of Salisbury in 1513. However, she was executed after her son Reginald Pole angered the king by his book *De Unitate Ecclesiastica*. In *Richard III*, Margaret is the maiden for whom Richard arranges a lowly match (IV, iii).

Plantagenet, Richard. See Richard Plantagenet, 3rd duke of York.

Platter, Thomas (fl. 1599–1600). Swiss physician who visited England in 1599 and wrote a description of London playgoing. Platter, who was in England from September 18 to October 20, 1599, recorded his attendance at a performance of *Julius Caesar* on September 21, 1599 and added an account of the practices of the London theatre. Platter's description is in German; the translation below is that of E. K. Chambers:

> After dinner on the 21st of September, at about two o'clock, I went with my companions over the water, and in the strewn roof-house saw the tragedy of the first Emperor Julius with at least fifteen characters very well acted. At the end of the comedy they danced according to their custom with extreme elegance. Two in men's clothes and two in women's gave this performance, in wonderful combination with each other. On another occasion, I also saw after dinner a comedy, not far from our inn, in the suburb; if I remember right, in Bishopsgate. Here they represented various nations, with whom on each occasion an Englishman fought for his daughter, and overcame them all except the German, who won the daughter in fight. He then sat down with him, and gave him and his servant strong drink, so that they both got drunk, and the servant threw his shoe at his master's head and they both fell asleep. Meanwhile the Englishman went into the tent, robbed the German of his gains, and thus he outwitted the German also. At the end they danced very elegantly both in English and in Irish fashion. And thus every day at two o'clock in the afternoon in the city of London two and sometimes three comedies are performed, at separate places, wherewith folk make merry together, and whichever does best gets the greatest audience. The places are so built, that they play on a raised platform, and every one can well see it all. There are, however, separate galleries and there one stands more comfortably and moreover can sit, but one pays more for it. Thus anyone who remains on the level standing pays only one English penny: but if he wants to sit, he is let in at a further door, and there he gives another penny.

If he desires to sit on a cushion in the most comfortable place of all, where he not only sees everything well, but can also be seen, then he gives yet another English penny at another door. And in the pauses of the comedy food and drink are carried round amongst the people, and one can thus refresh himself at his own cost.

The comedians are most expensively and elegantly apparelled, since it is customary in England, when distinguished gentlemen or knights die, for nearly the finest of their clothes to be made over and given to their servants, and as it is not proper for them to wear such clothes but only to imitate them, they give them to the comedians to purchase for a small sum.

What they can thus produce daily by way of mirth in the comedies, every one knows well, who has happened to see them acting or playing.

[G. Binz, "Londoner Theater und Schauspiele im Jahre 1599," *Anglia*, XXII, 456; E. K. Chambers, *The Elizabethan Stage*, 1923.]

Plautus, Titus Maccius (c. 254–184 B.C.). Roman comic dramatist. Plautus' early life was spent as a soldier, merchant, and itinerant corn miller. At the age of 45 he began writing plays based on the New Comedy that flourished in fourth-century Greece. He mingled elements of Menander's highly literate techniques with those of the coarse Roman farces based on early fertility rites and those of the Etruscan *saturae*, with their stock characters. The result was a vigorous, rough-and-tumble comedy. Nevertheless, Plautus' plays were not without charm, lent by his use of alliteration, assonance, puns, and coined words, as well as by his introduction of whole scenes of recitative meters (*cantica*) sung to a flute accompaniment. His plots were based largely on intrigue (*Mostellaria*) and mistaken identity (*Menaechmi*). He succeeded in producing 130 pieces, and the fact that 21 survive—more than the work of any other classical playwright—is a measure of his enduring popularity.

To the fastidious Augustan critics who followed, Plautus seemed crude, and his reputation declined. In the Middle Ages he was little regarded, but with the Renaissance he was reinstated as one of the great classical dramatists. One indirect route to Renaissance admiration led through German "education-drama" and Italian romance. Many adaptations for the Italian stage were produced in the 15th and 16th centuries: e.g., Ariosto's *I Suppositi* (1509), which was to form the basis for Gascoigne's *Supposes* (1566) and later became the subplot involving the wooing of Bianca in *The Taming of the Shrew*. Plautus made his way directly to Elizabethan court and academic circles through translations and adaptations, thus reinforcing broad English humor with his patterned plots: the mistaken identities, the clandestine love affairs, the separated families finally reunited with the restoration of long-lost children. The Elizabethans loved his farcical situations: the intrigues and confusions and ludicrous wrangles, the stage tricks like the perennially humorous beating on the gate, reflected in the porter scene of *Macbeth*. It was mainly from Plautus that the stock character types came, often bearing tag-names. To the *Pseudolus* (or *The Trickster*) the Elizabethans owed the crafty servant. The *Miles Gloriosus* furnished the prototype for a succession of braggart soldiers from Nicholas Udall's Roister Doister to Jonson's Captain Bobadil. Others who used the Plautine formulas were Thomas Heywood, Molière, and Dryden.

Shakespeare used translations of Plautus where they were available, but there is ample evidence that his grammar school education had enabled him to read the plays in Latin (at least well enough to extract the essentials), that he had a working knowledge of French and knew a little Italian. Hamlet's advice to the players, that "Seneca can not be too heavy, nor Plautus too light," as he prepares to welcome "the king," "the adventurous knight," "the lover," "the clown" (II, ii), attests to Shakespeare's familiarity with Latin drama and with these character types.

The plays of Shakespeare show Plautine elements down to the very end of his literary activity. Generally, however, the resemblances are more marked in the early plays, notably *The Comedy of Errors, The Taming of the Shrew, The Merry Wives of Windsor*, and portions of *The Two Gentlemen of Verona, Romeo and Juliet*, and *All's Well That Ends Well*. Certain devices of plot and characterization occur repeatedly. Plautus' use of a prologue recurs in each act of *Henry V*, in the Induction to *2 Henry IV*, as the chorus in Acts I and II of *Romeo and Juliet*, and as "Time, the Chorus" in Act IV of *The Winter's Tale*. The epilogues are also found at the end of *2 Henry IV* and *As You Like It*. The theme of the lost child restored and the family reunited climaxes *The Comedy of Errors, Winter's Tale*, and *Cymbeline*, and has echoes elsewhere. Plautus' *Aulularia* (*The Crock of Gold*), an account of how a young man elopes with a miser's daughter, recalls the Lorenzo-Jessica subplot of *The Merchant of Venice*. The Plautine woman disguised as a man (*Casina*) is reproduced in such heroines as Julia, Portia, Rosalind, Viola, and Imogen.

A ubiquitous figure, the braggart soldier is embodied in Don Armado, the fantastical Spaniard; in Parolles, the Italian bravo; in Bardolph, Nym, and Pistol; and, of course, in its richest flower, Falstaff. Numerous Renaissance analogues exist of the "trickster tricked," as Falstaff is in both *Henry IV* and *The Merry Wives of Windsor;* but it is in the latter play that he bears the closest resemblance to the explosive buffoonery of *Miles Gloriosus* and *Menaechmi*, both by his vaunts which, according to John Gassner, "reach the sublime by way of the ridiculous," and by the theme of the lecherous braggart who is duped into believing that his neighbor's wife is enamored of him.

The play most indebted to Plautus is *The Comedy of Errors*. Shakespeare drew on several plays of mistaken identity, certainly *Amphitruo, Menaechmi* (untranslated until 1595), and possibly *Miles Gloriosus*. The main plot derives from *Menaechmi*, in which one twin arranges to have lunch with a courtesan, but the other gets the lunch while the first is exposed to his wife. Shakespeare borrowed heavily from the second and third acts of the *Menaechmi*, but he adapted the stock Latin characters to Elizabethan types, so that Peniculus the parasite is replaced by the servant Dromio of

Ephesus, while Medicus the "quack" becomes Pinch, the lean-faced, conjuring schoolmaster. (Cf. Holofernes, the pedant of *Love's Labour's Lost.*) The twin servants were probably suggested by the *Amphitruo*. The framework of family misfortunes, only alluded to in the latter play, was complicated by Shakespeare, who developed a serious counterplot through the initial arrest of Aegeon and the calamitous events ensuing from the shipwreck. The change to a Christian setting enables Adriana, who displaces the courtesan as the central figure, to plead for the sanctity of marriage and allows for the moral disinfection of the play.

The influence of classical drama in general made Elizabethan playwrights more conscious of structure, the unities of time and place, and motivated behavior. [Cornelia C. Coulter, "The Plautine Tradition in Shakespeare," *Journal of English and Germanic Philology*, XIX, 1920.]—M.H.

Player. See First Player.

playhouse structure. The playhouses which stood for 40 years on the outskirts of the city of London, from the last years of Elizabeth I until the Puritan Revolution of 1642, were buildings altogether unique in time, place, and theatrical history. Nothing quite like them had ever been built before. Not until recent times has there been any attempt to repeat them; and in their own day, though there did exist here and there in Europe a few theatres, such as the famous Teatro Olimpico at Vincenza, built for rare aristocratic or academic patrons, there was no other city in the world but London which could show to visitors not only its cathedral, its monuments, its castle, and the halls and houses of its wealthy merchants, but also its popular theatre houses, not one but many. That group of them which stood on Bankside, the district on the south bank of the River Thames, can be seen in all contemporary drawings and engravings of the old city, a row of enigmatic, windowed tubs, each topped with a flag. In the engravings their claim on the attention is equaled only by that of London Bridge, the Tower, and Old St. Paul's; but unlike these landmarks the theatres have disappeared, leaving only a very inadequate descriptive record behind them. History likes to record the occasions, habits,

NORDEN'S FIRST VIEW OF BANKSIDE (1593) SHOWING THE BEAR GARDEN AND THE ROSE PLAYHOUSE.

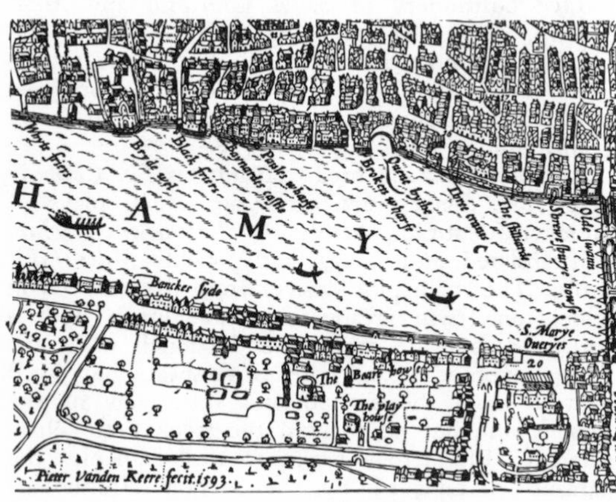

and houses of the great; commonplaces it takes for granted. And so the great playhouses of Elizabethan and Jacobean London, being the common places of amusement, were never fully pictured or described while they still existed. Perhaps they were thought too permanent to require it. What we now know of them has had to be pieced together from surviving scraps of evidence of many different kinds, all of which are incomplete but which, added together compose a picture, which, though not definitive may be completed reasonably well from an informed and resourceful imagination. In what follows here will be described, first, the principal surviving evidence and such conclusions as can be drawn from it, and, second, some recent theories designed to fill the final gap. It should be borne in mind that professional (and semi-professional) performances were continually being given in places such as the great halls of noble houses and palaces and of collegiate and legal groups such as the London inns of court (e.g. the Middle Temple Hall); and during the whole period under review, both before and after the setting up of specialized public playhouses professional companies acted regularly at certain inns in the city, such as the Cross Keys and the Bel Savage, which had long been renowned for this activity. It is necessary to remember that the style of theatrical presentation at the permanent theatres is likely to have been affected in some degree by the methods available at these other occasional places (plays being transferred from one to the other as needed) and that the architectural style of the permanent theatres has been thought by some authorities to have been affected by that of the public inns with which the actors had previously been familiar. The playhouses which will concern us here were of two kinds: public and private.

public playhouses. These were the large buildings already mentioned as familiar in the engraved views of London. Their chief characteristic was that they were built round an open yard, which enabled them to accommodate large audiences. On Bankside (southern outskirts of the city) were the Rose, the Swan, the Globe, and the Hope. There were two playhouses in Shoreditch (the northern outskirts)—the Theatre and the Curtain. In the Clerkenwell area (northwest outskirts) were the Fortune and the Red Bull. Of the last two, the Fortune was a square building, and the Red Bull may have been square also, though its shape is now not known. All the others were certainly round in plan, either circular or polygonal. There was also for a while a public theatre further out at Newington Butts, of which no details are known.

private playhouses. These were roofed theatres and therefore of necessity at the time smaller than the open "public" playhouses. The term "private" appears to have been used to designate those theatres that attracted the smaller and more select audiences who were prepared to pay higher prices for admission. They became increasingly fashionable with better-class patrons during the period under review. The three best known of these were the Blackfriars, a onetime monastic hall converted for theatrical purposes and originally used by a company of boy players (the Children of the

Chapel) but taken over in 1608 by the brothers Burbage for the King's Men, the company which also occupied the public Globe theatre; the Whitefriars, similar to the Blackfriars and first occupied by the Children of the King's Revels; and St. Paul's, occupied by a boys' company, the Children of Paul's. The building they used is not known, but is thought to have been either the choir school or convocation house of Old St. Paul's Cathedral. The chief interest of these playhouses for the present study is that although their structural features are not known, certain extant stage directions in plays written to be performed in them by companies also performing in public playhouses may help deductively to decide characteristics of staging and stage-building common to both.

It should be understood that although all these public and private playhouses shared common characteristics, and some were specifically copied from others, they all differed in some degree—in shape, size, or equipment—from each other, so that evidence of a particular practice at one playhouse will not necessarily apply to any other. With this caution in mind, however, it is reasonable to assume some general characteristic resemblance common to all. Modern students of the Elizabethan drama who have sought to isolate the characteristics of one particular theatre by studying selected plays known to have been specifically written for that theatre alone, do not seem so far to have uncovered any remarkable differences by this means. The present account will therefore concentrate chiefly on the physical features of the public playhouses, as being the most characteristic of their kind, and will assume a degree of common resemblance among them all.

ground plan and building material. These have to be considered together, since they are interdependent. On certain maps and engravings of Bankside (e.g., NORDEN, 1593; HONDIUS, 1610; HOLLAR, 1647) the playhouses are represented as circular buildings. Shakespeare in the Prologue to *Henry V* refers to the playhouse of its presentation (probably originally the Curtain) as a "wooden O." The Dutch eyewitness Johannes DE WITT, writing of his visit to the Swan in 1596, describes it as being built "of a concrete of flint stones . . . and supported by wooden columns . . . ," which seems in its context to indicate a circular outside wall of concrete, framed on the inside with wooden galleries. There are other sources, however, such as the panorama of London (c. 1616) by J. C. VISSCHER, which represent the playhouses not as circular buildings, but as polygonal, having flat sides suitable for timber-framed construction throughout—for a fully circular building all of timber is not a practical proposition. Both the timber and the concrete methods might have been used for different playhouses; but the evidence for all-timber construction *as a general rule* is the stronger. For instance, the surviving builder's contracts for the Fortune and Hope playhouses specify timber framing throughout; and when the first Globe was burnt down, it was stated by Ben Jonson to have had nothing left but the piles on which it was built; had it been of concrete, the shell would have remained. Since, then, the majority of public playhouses seem to have been built of timber throughout, these must have been polygonal, not circular. A polygonal structure with, say, 12 or 16 sides would from a little distance have a decidedly circular appearance, and might easily give rise to a representation such as that by Hollar in his 1647 Long View of London.

auditorium. Information concerning the interior appearance of the playhouses is chiefly gathered from the three sources already mentioned: the sketch which accompanied the letter of Johannes De Witt, and the contracts for building the Fortune and Hope playhouses. De Witt's sketch has had many critics, but its major statements are too widely corroborated from other evidence to be doubted. Not only do the hut and flag which he shows at the top of the building appear in every other picture of a public playhouse, drawn by independent witnesses, but the three galleries which he shows surrounding the central yard of the Swan are specified in the builders' contracts for both the Fortune and the Hope. Since the Fortune is known to have been built with one eye on the rival Globe it is reasonable to assume that the Globe, too, and its predecessor, the Theatre at Shoreditch, were equipped with the three tiers of galleries. The central yard around which these galleries were built, with the open sky above, was the logical outcome of structural and economic necessity. The requirements were for a house of the greatest possible audience capacity, all within a comfortable hearing distance of the stage, and for a good availability of daylight. The rounded playhouse with the open yard met these requirements well. To roof over so wide a yard, if possible at all with the ordinary constructional methods then available, would have been a prodigious task, and, being done, would have greatly reduced the light. The problem was solved on both counts by roofing only the galleries and the stage. It should also be remembered that there had been round-shaped bull- and bearbaiting arenas on Bankside for some time previous to the theatres, and these may have served as models; and the long practice of performances at inns, which meant probably in the inn-yards, had made customary the gathering of a standing yard-audience. The theatres for the first time provided the additional accommodation for a large seated audience in the galleries. The staircases which gave access to the galleries were housed on each side of the auditorium, projecting slightly from the outside wall of the main building, each under a gabled roof. To reach them, patrons had to go into the yard, where, on each side, there were steps leading up into the lowest gallery, and through this to the staircases beyond. Payments for admission were arranged progressively at each entrance, a coin to enter the yard, another at the lowest gallery, another at the staircase door, and so on.

Contemporary sources describe the several divisions of these galleries and their prices of admission in different ways which do not leave the locations clear. Mention is made of Gentlemen's Rooms, Twopenny Rooms, of "Twelve-penny roomes next the stage" of "Two Boxes in the lowermost storie fitt and decent for gentlemen to sitt in," of the lords' rooms, and others. There are references to gentlemen sitting "over the stage" and of a "Room over the tiring-house." The foregoing references apply severally to various theatres. In general it is reasonable to assume that the most favored gallery was the middle one, that the most expensive gentlemen's rooms (which may have been the same as lords' rooms) were next to the stage in the lowermost gallery, and that it was not unknown for high-class spectators to sit in rooms in that part of the middle gallery which came round to the back of the stage itself, that is "over the tiring-house." It is well known that fashionable visitors were also accustomed to sitting on stools upon the stage itself, a custom that Thomas Dekker, writing in 1609, clearly considered a nuisance; but it was a custom that may have prevailed only at the smaller and more crowded private playhouses.

It is generally assumed that one main gateway led into the yard from the outside. A report of the first Globe that, when it was on fire, the escaping audience had "but two narrow doors to get out," is taken by some authorities to refer to the main door into the yard and the actors' door in the backstage area. The present writer has found reason to think that at the Fortune, if not elsewhere, two auditorium doors may have been used; but, on the whole, reconstruction is best served by the idea of a single center entrance to the yard.

Roofs in the earlier theatres appear to have been mostly of thatch; but after the fire at the first Globe, which began in the thatching, its successor was roofed with tiles. The Fortune and the Hope were both tiled.

the stage. From the far side of the building facing the entrance and projecting into the center of the yard was the great rectangular wooden stage, built upon posts. Projecting over the stage at a height of approximately 24 feet was a roof and a hut-like superstructure, for all of which two great pillars rising from the stage provided forward support. At the rear the support was from the main frame of the building. This roof and superstructure is variously referred to as "the shadow" or "the heavens." (As an exception it should be noted that the stage of the Hope was specified in the contract to be built upon trestles so that it could be removed at need, and this made it necessary for "the Heavens all over the saide stage to be borne or carryed without any posts or supporters to be fixed or sett vpon the saide stage. . . ." To assist this, by reducing the weight, there was no hut superstructure over the stage at the Hope.)

The area beneath the stage was known as the hell. In some cases this was closed around with hangings, at others it may have been left open with the supporting posts in view. However, at the Fortune the underpart of the stage was permanently closed in with boards.

At the back of the projecting stage, where it was attached to the main building, was the so-called tiring-house, where the actors attired themselves and from which they came out into the play. In this stage-facing wall of the tiring-house were a number of openings. De Witt shows two double doors. Most authorities agree there must have been some sort of curtained opening between them. Above, at middle-gallery level, was a range of openings or windows overlooking the stage, which were often used as an upper part of the acting area itself (for example, in the balcony scene in *Romeo and Juliet*).

It is with the features of this permanent tiring-house façade and its use in play production that most conjectural interpretations tend chiefly to concern themselves, and to differ. Differences can be considerable, and some at present prevailing will be discussed in the last two sections of this article.

principal dimensions. The measurements given in the extant contract for building the Fortune may reasonably be used as a basis of assumption for the dimensions of other playhouses, such as the Globe, though it must be remembered that the Fortune was a square building. The principal measurements called for in the contract are: 80 feet for the over-all length of exterior wall; 55 feet for the interior width across the yard; 12 feet for the height of the bottom gallery; 11 feet for the height of the middle gallery; and 9 feet for the height of the top gallery. Allowing a thickness of, say, one foot for joists and flooring between galleries, and one foot for brick foundations, makes a total of 35 feet from the level of the yard to the eaves. The interior depth of the bottom gallery on plan was 12 feet 6 inches, with each of the two upper galleries overhanging by an additional 10 inches into the yard. The stage measured 43 feet wide and extended "to the middle of the yarde," that is, 27 feet 6 inches.

In the only other existing contract, that for the Hope, the only dimension given which is of use to us here is for the height of the principal posts of the bottom gallery, which were 12 feet, which tallies with measurements for the Fortune. For the most part it is stated in the contract that measurements at the Hope are to be the same as those at the Swan playhouse, which are now not known.

capacity. Estimates of the total audience capacity of the Fortune vary. Professor Harbage in *Shakespeare's Audience* (1941) calculated it at 2344. De Witt's account of 3000 at the Swan was probably an exaggeration, but it would seem that a capacity of 2000 for the average public playhouse may be considered a conservative figure.

uses of the stage. The salient stage of the Elizabethan playhouse stood out into the yard at a height of perhaps five feet or more above the ground, and onto it the actors sallied forth from the tiring-house which stood behind it, moving forward into the midst of the surrounding audience, of "groundlings" standing below, of seated crowds in the galleries around, and of gentlemen seated on the stage and in the nearby boxes. It is this movement of the actors back and forth, advancing and retiring, which distinguishes the Elizabethan stage practice from that of the modern proscenium stages, where the flow of movement tends to be from side to side, between the flanking wings. Thus the productions of the Elizabethan stage tended to have a processional character, to which even the bringing forward from the tiring-house of such necessary effects as thrones, beds, benches, or tables, along with the flags, drums, and costumes of the actors, contributed a part.

Scenery in the pictorial sense as an illusion of reality was not used, nor was there any means of showing it on the public stage; but a spectacular elaboration of stage properties was possible, and was frequently adopted. The stage directions in Thomas Heywood's plays of the *Four Ages* can be called in evidence to show the sort of effect that was popularly enjoyed: "Thunder and lightning . . . Jupiter appears in his glory under a Raine-bow, to whom they all kneele." "Hercules kills the Sea-Monster, the Trojans on the walles, the Greekes below." "Two fiery Buls are discovered, the Fleece hanging over them, and the Dragon sleeping beneath them: Medea with strange fiery-workes, hangs above in the aire in the strange habite of a Conjuresse," etc. The manager Henslowe's property-lists contain a rich record of tombs, chariots, altars, trees of golden apples, and the like, and his item "1 Hell mouth" shows how near the Elizabethan stage was to the practices of the medieval theatre whose hell mouth with its issue of devils had been a constant favorite. Other medieval methods also survived on the Elizabethan stage, notably, as scholars now tend to agree, some occasional and modified form of the "houses" which, standing around the acting area throughout the play, represented different parts of a city or of the world. This effect could be simplified by the use not of structures but of doors only, with nothing but the name of the supposed locality written above them. (Sir Philip Sidney speaks scornfully of "Thebes written in great letters upon an old door.")

The two great doors in the tiring-house wall at the Swan theatre have already been mentioned. Much speculation has been given to the space between them. Somewhere on the Elizabethan stage, space must be found for a curtained opening suitable for the effect known as a "discovery." With the drawing of a curtain "Prospero discovers [i.e., discloses, reveals] Ferdinand and Miranda playing at chess." Or, after Juliet drinks the potion, "She falls upon her bed within the curtains," and, later, after the family have mourned her supposed death, "they all but the Nurse go forth, casting rosemary on her and shutting the curtains." (See DISCOVERY SPACE.) There are many instances of the use of curtains in such a way that what is within them must be visible to all the audience around, and a reasonable location for such a curtained opening would be between the two doors of the tiring-house wall. Working from this hypothesis certain scholars in the past have assumed that this opening (sometimes referred to by them as the INNER STAGE), became increasingly used, and was in fact the origin of the modern proscenium arch; but this theory is now in decline. A curtained space of some sort, however, there had to be, and if it was not found in the wall of the tiring-house it must presumably have been built projecting forward from this onto the stage, as a sort of booth or tent.

Above the tiring-house doors, on a level with the middle gallery of the auditorium, was an open gallery (or a row of windows or a combination of both) which was very much used in Elizabethan drama. Indeed the frequency with which an "upper stage" or window was brought into action is one of its most characteristic features. The window of Juliet's bedchamber and the window from which Jessica throws down the casket of jewels to Lorenzo below are familiar examples among many. This upper stage was as much a feature of the indoor private playhouses as of the larger public ones on Bankside, and in the private theatres some part of it was used by the musicians. This may also have been the case in the public theatres. A reference to Ben Jonson as a dramatist who in his plays laid "no sieges to the music-room" would appear to indicate the changeable nature of the upper stage, one day a music room and the next a beleaguered city wall.

In the stage floor was a trap leading to the hell beneath, used for graves, apparitions, and the like. Above the stage was the roof called the heavens, with its similar opening for the descent of divine beings throned upon painted clouds, winch-operated from the hut aloft. There is evidence to show that not only this underside roof of the heavens but the whole playhouse, stage and auditorium alike, was colorfully decorated. At the Swan, for example, all the wooden posts and pillars of the house are known to have been painted to resemble marble.

Over the top of the house was a flagstaff, from which the playhouse flag was flown on days of performance.

theories of reconstruction. It has been attempted in all the foregoing to avoid controversial matter; but, unfortunately, what is definitely known about the Elizabethan playhouses falls short of what is necessary to make a complete reconstruction. The situation is aptly summarized by the case of the Fortune contract. Here we have detailed instructions for the building of everything but the stage. That, the contract says, was to be copied from the stage of the Globe, and a plan was attached to the contract to make all clear. But the plan is lost, and we are left with nothing but conjecture, based upon the interpretation of stage directions in printed plays surviving from the period, and some few letters and critical writings, all of value, but not unquestionable. From this point onward therefore, we are in the region of controversy.

It would be interesting to discuss the differences of interpretation and reconstruction made since the end of the last century, but space does not here permit. In the view of the present writer the carefulness of scholars has generally been successful in avoiding gross mistakes; but even so, interpretation has been clouded, formerly by the very undeveloped state of comparative theatrical research, and then by the inability of commentators at all times to imagine sympathetically a theatrical practice extremely different from their own. The former hindrance has been much removed in recent years; but the latter may still be with us, for critical interpretation in aesthetic matters is notoriously vulnerable to the aesthetic habits and visions of its own day. That having been said, it is proposed to conclude this account by giving very brief outlines of three different theories of reconstruction which have appeared in recent years. They will be given in the order of their first publication and without the critical argument upon which each is based, for which the interested reader must consult the works themselves.

1. John Cranford Adams (*The Globe Playhouse*, 1942) reconstructs the Globe as an octagonal building with dimensions based on the Fortune. Access to galleries is gained through passages on the outside of the building, not through the yard. The stage is not rectangular but narrows towards the front at the center of the yard. The tiring-house façade is three stories high (corresponding to the three galleries of the auditorium) built round three sides of a shallow curve facing inwards. The center wall has an opening on each of the three floors: at stage level an opening 12 feet high and 23 feet wide, called the Study; at middle story level, 11 feet high and 24 feet wide, called the Chamber, with, in front of it, on the stageward side of its frontal curtain, a long walkway or balcony called the Tarras; at top story level a smaller opening 9 feet high and 11 feet 6 inches wide, called the Music Gallery. There were openings in each of the two flanking walls of the tiring-house (each 12 feet wide): at stage level, a great double door; at middle level, a wide bay-window (standing forward on posts over the double doors below) called in each case a Window Stage; and on the top story, only the small windows lighting the storage loft. Above all is the heavens roof and the huts with winding gear, carried forward on two very tall posts standing on the stage.

The theory underlying this reconstruction is that in the majority of, if not all, Elizabethan plays, most scenes supposed to be taking place out of doors, or scenes not otherwise specifically localized, would be played on the main forward stage; all scenes indoors would be played either within the Study (at stage level) or in the Chamber on the upper floor, according to context. The Study and the Chamber, being closed by curtains, were available for limited changes of setting. Scenes at windows were played from the Window Stages flanking the Chamber, with the Tarras connecting them, the latter being used for scenes with balconies, city walls, etc. The topmost gallery was for the musicians, but could be used for play action when the context required it. So, in this reconstruction, action flows continuously between different locations and levels of the stage and tiring-house façade, those out of action being meanwhile prepared for ensuing scenes. The decoration of the house and stage building was based upon half-timbered Tudor styles.

2. C. Walter Hodges, in *The Globe Restored* (1953), bases his reconstruction upon the idea that the form of the stage itself derived from a traditional portable stage form, having a tent or booth at the back; this portable stage, being transferred to the arena of a permanent playhouse, was eventually built in and enlarged, resulting in a rectangular stage approximately 32 feet wide and 22 feet deep in a 16-sided polygonal building, the yard measuring approximately 55 feet across. Vertical measurements follow those of the Fortune. The tiring-house façade is a flat wall built across three bays of the polygon,

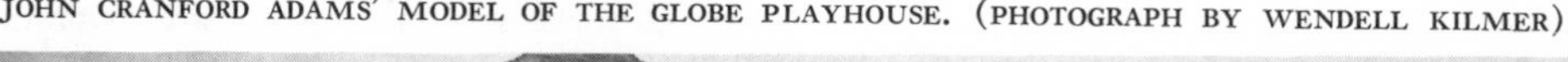

JOHN CRANFORD ADAMS' MODEL OF THE GLOBE PLAYHOUSE. (PHOTOGRAPH BY WENDELL KILMER)

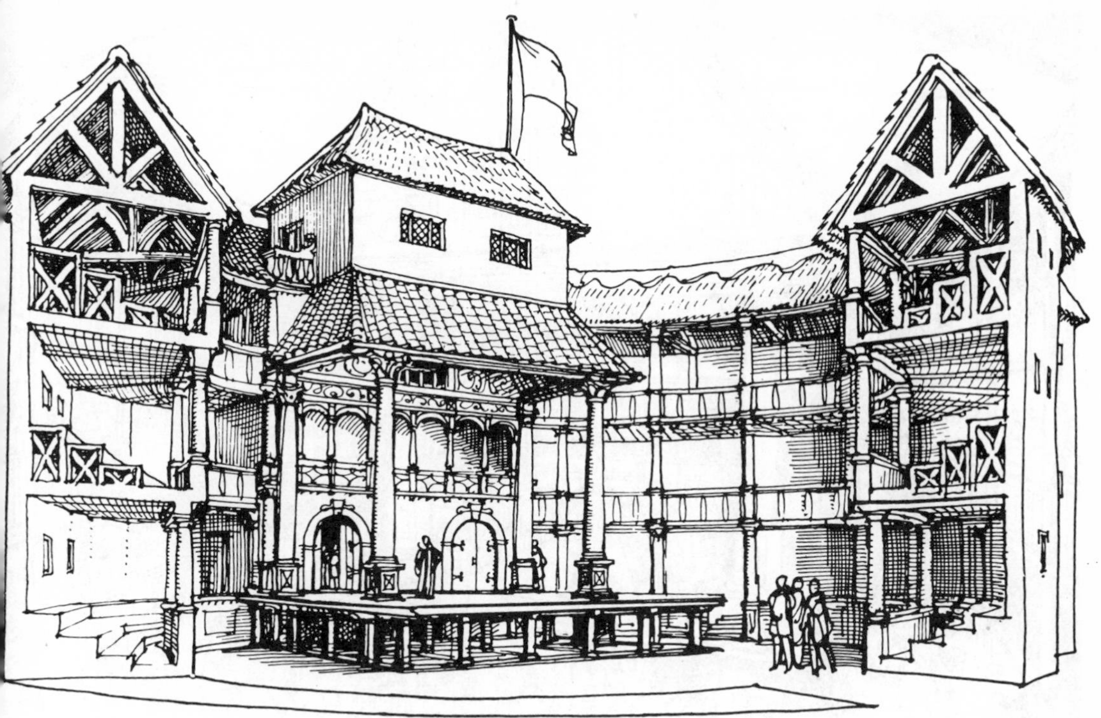

ELIZABETHAN PLAYHOUSE, 1595. C. WALTER HODGES' RECONSTRUCTION OF A TYPICAL PLAYHOUSE OF THIS PERIOD. THIS DRAWING IS BASED ON DE WITT'S SKETCH OF THE SWAN. (COURTESY OF COWARD-MC CANN, INC.)

two stories high, with two great doors at stage level and a range of arcaded openings above, similar to the screen and "minstrel's gallery" at the end of a typical Tudor Hall. The heavens roof is set at a height level with the middle of the top auditorium gallery, i.e., approximately 22 feet above the stage. The stage is very high (perhaps nearly 6 feet) to allow working headroom underneath, thus avoiding the need to dig a cellar in the ground, which is known on Bankside to have been swampy. The understructure of the stage is hidden by painted hangings from stage to ground at front and sides. Between the two doors on the stage is a curtain-hung opening with sometimes (or alternatively) a booth-like structure, also curtained, standing in front of it, forward of the tiring-house wall. All scenes are played on the main stage, often with conventionalized local settings ranged around as in medieval practice. The "discovery" opening and upper gallery of the tiring-house are used only where needed for immediate and specific action. Decoration of house, tiring-house, stage, and effects is very ornate in vernacular baroque style, based on contemporary processional devices, Flemish street theatres, etc.

3. Leslie Hotson's reconstruction, set forth in *Shakespeare's Wooden O* (1959), is based on the hypothesis that plays given privately at court and in collegiate halls, etc., were presented on a stage surrounded on all sides by the audience. This reconstruction assumes the same condition at public playhouses. In it the stage projects from the side of the building with two doors (as shown in De Witt) but these are only for access to scene storage, not for actors. The audience is on all sides, including seats on the stage between scene-storage doors and in the lords' room in the gallery above. Along both sides of the stage, starting from where it joins the building, stand two open structures, each of two stories, built of posts and closed all round with curtains, though these were usually drawn back to allow a view across the stage by the audience beyond. These upper and lower "houses" provide the various locations of the play. The tiring-house is beneath the stage (as in some medieval street theatres), and access to different parts of the stage is gained through trap doors in the floor within the curtained structures. In other respects this reconstruction follows usual lines.

further studies and selected bibliography. The three books referred to in the preceding section, though each arrives at a very different solution to the problems of reconstruction, have one thing in common: all have proposed new, even revolutionary, hypotheses. But they are so different that if any one of them is right, the others must be wrong. The reader may therefore be well advised, before making up his mind, to consult a more conservative scholarship from among the list given below:

The Elizabethan Stage (4 vols., 1923) by E. K. Chambers. This is still the best source book of collected information on the subject. Although Sir Edmund Chambers' reconstructive interpretations are now old-fashioned and may often be wrong, they are few, and do not cloud the value of the great body of information which he provides. In any case, he is always careful to dissociate his conjectures from his facts, so that the student is not misled.

The Elizabethan Playhouse and Other Studies

A DRAWING OF THE GLOBE PLAYHOUSE FOLLOWING HOTSON'S CONJECTURES. (THE MACMILLAN COMPANY)

(two series, 1912, 1913) and *The Physical Conditions of the Elizabethan Public Playhouse* (1927), by W. J. Lawrence. Three collections of essays which represent the best of imaginative scholarship during the first quarter of this century.

Henslowe's Diary (2 vols., 1904, 1908) and *The Henslowe Papers* (1907). An essential collection of source material, edited by Sir W. W. Greg.

The Staging of Elizabethan Plays at the Red Bull Theatre, by G. F. Reynolds. Published in 1940, this work inaugurated a new school of thinking which, on the assumption that conditions at the different playhouses may have differed sufficiently to have caused significant differences in techniques of production, attempts to isolate and study the productions of one theatre only, thus avoiding the pitfalls of over-indulgent synthesis. With cautious scholarship and richly fascinating detail, the author eventually commits himself to no final solution, but is inclined to favor the hypothesis of a curtained enclosure built forward like a booth against the façade of the tiring-house.

Modern studies of this subject may loosely be divided into a Left and a Right Wing. The Left Wing contains such conjectural works as those by Adams, Hotson and the present writer [C. Walter Hodges]. Of the more conservative Right Wing, the following should be mentioned:

Bernard Beckerman's *Shakespeare at the Globe* (1962) attempts to do for the Globe Playhouse what Reynolds did for the Red Bull, i.e., it studies in isolation only those plays known to have been performed at the Globe, as being the best means of investigating the methods of play presentation employed at that theatre. The author finds little evidence for such spectacular effects as Reynolds found at the Red Bull, and concludes among other things that there was probably not even a flying apparatus installed in the heavens area over the Globe stage. It is an excellent example of a carefully compounded, anti-romantic approach to the subject, which is typical of recent scholarship and very rewarding.

Other important studies in the same vein had been made, a few years earlier than Beckerman's, by Richard Hosley. In two papers, "The Gallery Over the Stage in the Public Playhouse of Shakespeare's Time" and "The Discovery-Space in Shakespeare's Globe," published respectively in *Shakespeare Quarterly*, Winter 1957, and *Shakespeare Survey 12*, 1959, Hosley scrutinizes the textual evidence for the nature and frequency of use of these areas of the stage. In "The Discovery-Space" he develops a theory that the whole of the tiring-house façade at stage level at the Swan and other theatres may have been fronted with a continuous arras, covering doors and all, but allowing room behind it for a discovery space.

Also in *Shakespeare Survey 12* is an investigation by Richard Southern, "On Reconstructing a Practicable Elizabethan Public Playhouse." Southern's collation of evidence that might have been thought too familiar and well worked to yield further fruit, e.g., the De Witt drawing of the Swan, provides an unexpectedly fresh and sensible view, especially of the arrangements of the auditorium.

Lastly should be mentioned A. M. Nagler's *Shakespeare's Stage* (1958), a concise book which selects conservatively among more recent theories and may be followed as a reliable introduction. The author finds reason to think that the two great stage posts, familiar in the Swan drawing and usually shown as one of the most characteristic features of a public playhouse, were not present at the Globe. —C. W. H.

plot or **plat.** In the Elizabethan theatre, a scene-by-scene outline of a play. The "plot" was prepared

THE "PLOT" OF *The Second Part of the Seven Deadly Sins.* (DULWICH COLLEGE, BY PERMISSION OF THE GOVERNORS) FOR A TRANSCRIPT SEE APPENDIX.

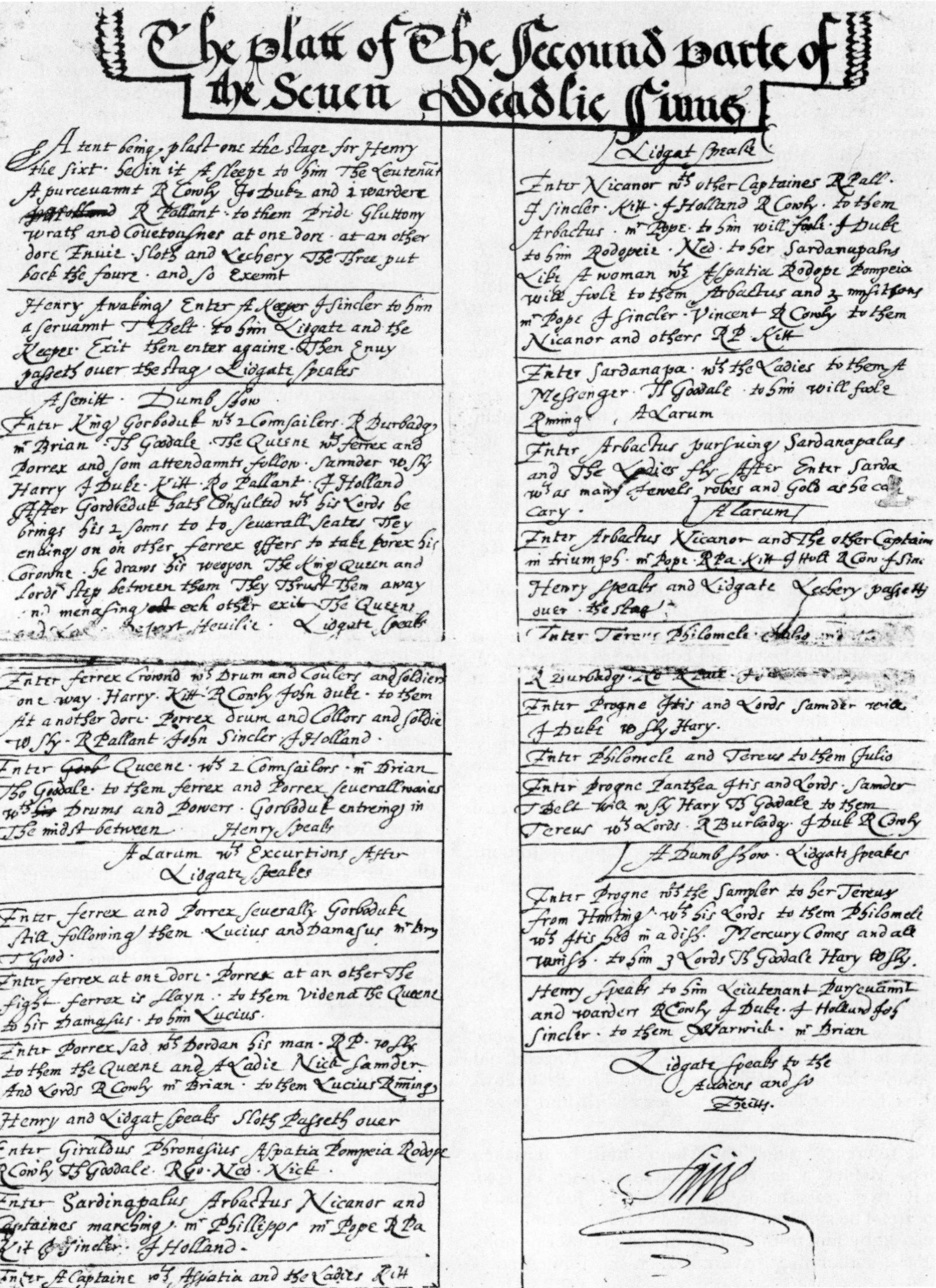

The platt of The Secound parte of the Seuen Deadlie Sinns

A tent being plast one the stage for Henry the sixt · he in it A sleepe to him The Leutenant A purceuannt R Cowly Jo Duke and 1 warder R Pallant · to them Pride · Gluttony wrath and Couetousnes at one dore · at an other dore Enuie · Sloth and Lechery The Three put back the foure · and so Exeunt

Henry Awaking Enter A Keeper J Sincler to him a seruannt T Belt · to him Lidgate and the Keeper · Exit then enter againe · Then Enuy passeth ouer the stag · Lidgate speakes

A senitt · Dumb show

Enter King Gorboduk wth 2 Counsailers · R Burbadg mr Brian · Th Goodale · The Queene wth ferrex and Porrex and som attendaunts follow · saunder wth Harry · J Duke · Kitt · Ro Pallant · J Holland · After Gordbeduk hath Consulted wth his Lords he brings his 2 sonns to to seuerall seates They enving on on other ferrex offers to take Porex his Corowne · he draws his weopon The King Queen and Lords step between them They Thrust Them away and menasing ech other exit The Queene and Lords Depart Heuilie · Lidgate speaks

Enter ferrex Crownd wth Drum and Coulers and soldiers one way Harry · Kitt · R Cowly John duke · to them At a nother dore · Porrex drum and Collors and soldie wth sly · R Pallant · John Sincler · J Holland ·

Enter Queene · wth 2 Counsailors · mr Brian Tho Goodale · to them ferrex and Porrex seuerall waies wth Drums and Powers · Gorboduk entreing in The midst between · Henry speaks

Alarum wth Excurtions After Lidgate speakes

Enter ferrex and Porrex seuerally Gorboduk still following them Lucius and Damasus mr Bry T Good ·

Enter ferrex at one dore · Porrex at an other The fight · ferrex is slayn · to them Videna the Queene to hir Damasus · to him Lucius.

Enter Porrex sad wth Dordan his man · R P · wth sly · to them the Queene and A Ladie Nick saunder And Lords R Cowly mr Brian · to them Lucius Running

Henry and Lidgat speaks · Sloth Passeth ouer

Enter Giraldus Phronesius Aspatia Pompeia Rodope R Cowly Th Goodale · R Go · Ned · Nick ·

Enter Sardinapalus Arbactus Nicanor and Captaines marching · mr Phillipps mr Pope R Pa Kit J Sincler · J Holland ·

Enter A Captaine wth Aspatia and the Ladies Kitt

Lidgat speake

Enter Nicanor wth other Captaines R Pall · J Sincler · Kitt · J Holland R Cowly · to them Arbactus · mr Pope · to him will foole · J Duke to him Rodopeie · Ned · to her Sardanupalus Like A woman wth Aspatia Rodope Pompeia will foole to them Arbactus and 3 musitions mr Pope J Sincler · Vincent · R Cowly to them Nicanor and others R P · Kitt

Enter Sardanapa wth the Ladies to them A Messenger · Th Goodale · to him will foole Running · A Larum

Enter Arbactus pursuing Sardanapalus and The Ladies fly · After Enter Sarda wth as many Jewels robes and Gold as he can cary · Alarum

Enter Arbactus Nicanor and The other Captains in triumph · mr Pope R Pa · Kitt · J Holt R Cow J Sinc

Henry speaks and Lidgate · Lechery passeth ouer · the stag

Enter Tereus Philomele Julio [illegible]

R Burbadg · [illegible]

Enter Progne Itis and Lords saunder will J Duke wth sly Hary ·

Enter Philomele and Tereus to them Julio

Enter Progne Panthea Itis and Lords · saunder T Belt · will wth sly Hary Th Goodale to them Tereus wth Lords · R Burbadg · J Duk R Cowly

A Dumb show · Lidgate speakes

Enter Progne wth the Sampler to her Tereus from Hunting wth his Lords to them Philomele wth Itis hed in a dish · Mercury Comes and all vanish · to him 3 Lords Th Goodale Hary wth Sly.

Henry speaks to him Leiutenant Pursuevant and warders R Cowly J Duke · J Holland Joh Sincler · to them Warwick · mr Brian

Lidgate speaks to the Audiens and so Endes.

for the actors and stagehands, listing the characters that were to appear in a given scene and the properties and sound effects required in it. The plot was written on two sheets of paper, which were pasted on both sides of a thin board. The board was hung from a peg by a small hole near the top. The sheets were divided into two columns by a double line running the full length of the paper. Scenes were marked by horizontal lines drawn across the columns; the names of the actors appeared next to the names of the characters they portrayed.

There are seven extant plots, two of which date from about 1590. These two plots, for Dead Man's Fortune and The Seven Deadly Sins, belonged either to the Admiral's Men or Strange's Men, or to an amalgamation of these two companies. The remaining five plots—for *Frederick and Basilia, 2* Fortune's Tennis, Troilus and Cressida, Battle of Alcazar, and *1 Tamar Cam*—date from the period 1597–1602. With the exception of the *Battle of Alcazar* none of the plays for which these plots were prepared has survived. The plot of *Troilus and Cressida* does not refer to the Shakespeare play but to a lost drama written by Henry Chettle and Thomas Dekker for the Admiral's Men around 1599. The term "author's plot" is used to designate the author's own outline of his play. The only extant author's plot, owned by the Folger Library, is for an anonymous play written sometime after 1627. An entry in Henslowe's diary records the date on which Ben Jonson "showed the Plotte unto the company," but the play is not named. See assembled texts. [W. W. Greg, *Dramatic Documents from the Elizabethan Playhouses*, 2 vols., 1931.]

Plume, Thomas (1630–1704). Archdeacon of Rochester (1679–1704), among whose manuscripts are several anecdotes relating to Shakespeare. Plume was born in Maldon, Essex, and educated at Christ's College, Cambridge. In his later years he was active in philanthropic work. In his native town of Maldon he financed the construction of a school and a library, to which he gave his books and manuscripts. The latter contain several references to Shakespeare and Ben Jonson, including a variant of the story (also told by Nicholas L'Estrange) of Shakespeare acting as a godfather to Ben Jonson's son and an account of Shakespeare's jesting epitaph for Jonson:

> Here lies Benjamin—w*i*th short hair up*on* his Chin—
> Who w*hi*le he lived was a slow thing—& now he's b*urie*d is no thing.

The manuscript also records an account of Shakespeare's father:

> He was a glovers son—*Si*r John Mennis saw once his old F*athe*r in h*is* shop—a merry Cheekd old man—*tha*t s*ai*d—Will was a g*oo*d Hon*est* Fellow, but he durst h*ave* crackt a jeast w*i*th him at any time.

The reference to Sir John Mennis must be mistaken since Mennis, a native of Kent, was born in 1599, only two years before the death of John Shakespeare. The story may have been told to Mennis and relayed by him to the author of the manuscript note, or the author may have mistaken Sir John Mennis for his older brother, Sir Matthew Mennis, born in 1593. [E. K. Chambers, *William Shakespeare*, 1930.]

Plumptre, James (1770–1832). Critic and dramatist. Plumptre was educated at Cambridge. He wrote a number of strongly didactic plays, highly moralistic in tone. His *Observations on Hamlet* (1796) is noteworthy as the first attempt to interpret the play as a political allegory. Plumptre argued that the play was written as an attack on the memory of Mary Queen of Scots, suggesting that Gertrude was modeled on Mary, and Hamlet on James I. [Herbert Spencer Robinson, *English Shakesperian Criticism in the Eighteenth Century*, 1932.]

Plutarch. Greek name **Ploutarchos** (c. 46–120). Greek biographer. Born at Chaeronea in Boeotia, Plutarch lived for some time in Rome, where he pursued a successful career as a rhetorician in the reign of the Emperor Trajan (98–117). Returning to his native Boeotia, Plutarch wrote his famous *Parallel Lives*. His 60-odd other works are generally grouped together as the *Moralia*, translated into English in 1603 by Philemon Holland.

In the Renaissance, *Parallel Lives* was one of the most popular and influential of classical works. It consists of 50 biographies of "noble" Greeks and Romans, 46 of which are arranged in pairs, with each pair linked by a short "comparison." Part of the reason for the work's popularity derives from the two excellent translations undertaken in the 16th century. The French translation (1559) by Jacques Amyot, a lively and vivid rendering, was in turn translated (1579) into English by Sir Thomas North. North's translation is the major source of *Julius Caesar*, *Antony and Cleopatra*, and *Coriolanus*. It is also a minor source for *A Midsummer Night's Dream* and *Timon of Athens*. In drawing from Plutarch, Shakespeare used not only his accounts of the lives, but also the interlinking "comparisons." See Antony and Cleopatra: *Sources;* Coriolanus: *Sources;* and Julius Caesar: *Sources*. [E. A. J. Honigman, "Shakespeare's Plutarch," *Shakespeare Quarterly*, X, 1959.]

Poe, Edgar Allan (1809–1849). American poet, critic, and short-story writer. In his famous "Letter to B—" Poe scorns people who believe Shakespeare a great writer but who have never read him. He would prefer to be among the "few gifted individuals who kneel around the summit, beholding, face to face, the master spirit who stands on the pinnacle."

It seems clear that Poe was fairly well versed in Shakespeare. His fiction, correspondence, and criticism are filled with Shakespearean quotations and allusions. There are 50 quotations from *Hamlet* alone.

W. B. Hunter, Jr., has argued that the image of "the mystic moon dripping an opiate vapor" in Poe's "The Sleeper" comes from a witch scene in *Macbeth*. Similarly, as Bryllion Fagin has pointed out, Poe's story "The Angel of the Odd" has a character reminiscent of Falstaff. More interesting than these negligible direct influences are Poe's critical comments on Shakespeare.

In a review of Hazlitt's *The Characters of Shakespeare's Plays* in the August 16, 1845 *Broadway Journal*, Poe speculated on the identification of Hamlet with Shakespeare, differentiated between Hamlet the man and Hamlet the character, and attributed the play's inconsistencies to Shakespeare's "impulsion to exaggerate." "In all commentary upon Shakespeare, there has been a radical error . . . . It is the error of attempting to expound his characters—to account for their actions—to reconcile his inconsistencies—not as if they were the coinage of a human brain, but as if they had been actual existences upon earth." Fagin has argued that in this review Poe displays an acquaintance with Shakespeare's characters "which he could have attained only by constant close reading of the plays themselves." Poe's knowledge of Shakespeare apparently had little effect on his tales or poetry, however. [William B. Hunter, Jr., "Poe's 'The Sleeper' and *Macbeth*," *American Literature*, XX, 1948; Bryllion Fagin, *The Histrionic Mr. Poe*, 1949; Edward Wagenknecht, *Edgar Allan Poe: The Man Behind the Legend*, 1963.]

Poel, William (1852–1934). Actor and producer. Poel is remembered for his pioneering attempts to restore Elizabethan stage conditions in the production of Shakespeare's plays. To this end, he founded in 1894 the Elizabethan Stage Society, which produced, beginning with *Twelfth Night* (1895), a host of Shakespearean and other Elizabethan plays. Poel's efforts in restoring the platform stage and in eliminating the elaborate décor of 19th-century Shakespearean production were not always successful, but they led to subsequent studies and performances of Shakespeare's plays and to the many reconstructions of the Elizabethan stage that exist today. [Robert Speaight, *William Poel and the Elizabethan Revival*, 1954.]

Poems. Generic title given to *Venus and Adonis* (1593), *The Rape of Lucrece* (1594), *The Phoenix and the Turtle* (1601), and, with suitable reservations, *The Passionate Pilgrim* (1599) and *A Lover's Complaint* (1609). The term is not used to include the *Sonnets*. None of these poems appeared in the First Folio. In fact, they were not published together until the 18th century. The title was first used in a collection published by John BENSON in 1640, with the title *Poems: Written by Wil. Shake-speare. Gent.* This collection, however, did not contain either *Venus and Adonis* or *The Rape of Lucrece*, but included instead many poems falsely attributed by Benson to Shakespeare. There are a number of other poems not in this collection which have been erroneously attributed to Shakespeare. Among these are an epitaph on Elias JAMES, a London brewmaster, and the so-called PHAETON SONNET.

Poet. In *Julius Caesar*, a nameless, obtrusive rhymester who breaks in on the quarreling generals to

TITLE PAGE AND FRONTISPIECE OF THE 1640 EDITION OF SHAKESPEARE'S POEMS. THE FRONTISPIECE WAS COPIED BY WILLIAM MARSHALL FROM THE DROESHOUT ENGRAVING.

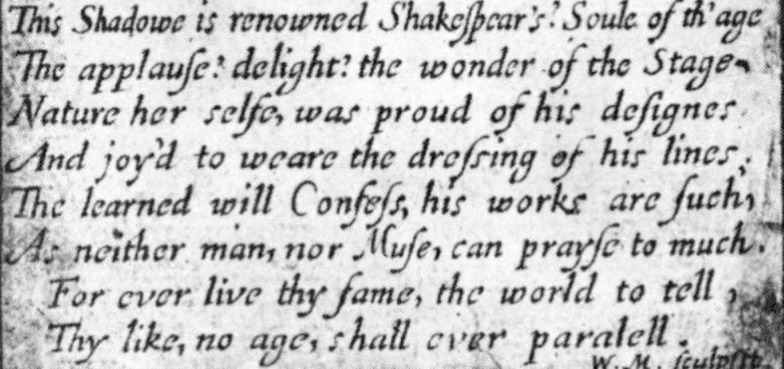

POEMS:

VVRITTEN

BY

WIL. SHAKE-SPEARE.

Gent.

Printed at *London* by *Tho. Cotes*, and are to be ſold by *Iohn Benſon*, dwelling in S^t. *Dunſtans* Church-yard.

spout his bad verse about love and friendship. Brutus is irritated by the "jigging fool" and orders the Poet out of the tent, but Cassius is amused and tolerant of the wretch (IV, iii). Plutarch recounts that Marcus Phaonius, a poet, forced entry to the generals' tent and quoted old Nestor's lines from Homer's *Iliad*.

Poet. In *Timon of Athens,* a minor character who, in I, i, enjoys Timon's patronage. In V, i, having heard rumors of Timon's gold, the Poet goes to his benefactor's cave and attempts to renew their relationship. Timon drives him away.

Poetaster. See WAR OF THE THEATRES.

Poetomachia. See WAR OF THE THEATRES.

Poins, Ned. In *1 Henry IV*, a joking friend of Prince Henry. It is Poins who proposes to the Prince that they disguise themselves and rob Falstaff and his accomplices of the loot they have stolen from the travelers (I, ii). He later joins Henry in mocking Francis the drawer, and, in *2 Henry IV,* suggests that they disguise themselves as drawers in order to spy on Falstaff.

Poland. The impact of Shakespeare's early influence in Poland is remarkable, especially since it flowed from Protestant England to Catholic Poland, two countries with no geographical, cultural, or linguistic connections, between which prior contacts were entirely mercantile, and in a period of such arduous transit as that of the religious wars. During the 16th century, Poland, more than double its present-day size, was one of the most advanced and prosperous kingdoms of Europe. Her cultural aspirations had long been congenial to those of western Europe and the hospitality of the Poles attracted an ever-growing number of foreign artists to their cities. Cracow, Danzig, and Elbing became destinations not only for the Scottish and English woolen merchants but also for many strolling players. With the influx of these actors interest in a secular drama mounted, and by 1554, when the first visit of a *commedia dell' arte* troupe is recorded, at least one or two of the most powerful nobles had already set aside chambers solely for "playing." By 1572 the visits of Italian troupes had become highly important.

By 1600 English traders were a common sight in the Baltic ports, and it is only natural that they brought news of their own culture and carried away reports of that of their hosts. Thus it is hardly surprising that Shakespeare should have known something of Poland, as readers of *Hamlet* and *The Comedy of Errors* may recall. Nor should it seem strange that something was known of the greatest English dramatist of his age in Poland while he was still alive.

There can be no doubt that the Italian troupes did much to provide enthusiastic audiences for those companies which followed them. When their eastward impetus finally carried them onto Polish soil, the earliest English comedians found hospitable conditions. Their first recorded performance took place in 1605 in Danzig on a hastily erected platform in the Dominican market place. They met with immense success. In September 1607 the company of John GREEN arrived in Elbing and, over a period of several weeks, performed their entire repertoire, which included at least five plays of Shakespeare and one of Marlowe. Their performances took place in a great hall built in 1599 at the behest of Andreas Mohrenberger von Barthowicz (1546–1609), the most cultured and influential member of the city council and very likely the man responsible for their having been invited. Nothing was heard of Green's company for several years until, in 1611, they reappeared along the Baltic coast, this time in Königsberg before the elector Johann Sigismund, who took them with him to Warsaw, the new capital, where they played to an audience of the leading nobles in the presence of King Sigismund III (1566–1632). This performance, the first of Shakespeare in Warsaw, took place on November 16, 1611 in the main hall of the royal castle. According to one source, the play given on this occasion was *The Taming of the Shrew*. Green's company returned to Warsaw during the winters of 1616 and 1618. By this time their repertoire had expanded to include *King Lear, Romeo and Juliet,* and *Julius Caesar.* Within four years they were followed by the company of Aaron Asken, which was granted royal patronage and remained in the palace until 1641. Asken's troupe performed *Hamlet, A Midsummer Night's Dream, Much Ado About Nothing, The Taming of the Shrew,* and *The Merry Wives of Windsor*.

Although the versions these early companies acted were entirely in English (at least until 1620, when the first German renditions appeared) and considerably garbled at that, their enormous vitality must have made itself felt. During this period, as rudimentary attempts at a Polish secular drama begin, we first detect the influence of Shakespeare. Among the surviving interludes of the early 17th century are several that include a Christopher Sly—Piotr Baryka's *The Peasant Who Became a King* (1637), the most notable among them—and that deal with the theme of a peasant clothed in majesty. Clumsy as they are, these early scenarios should be seen as the foundation upon which the later Polish national drama is erected, a foundation to which Shakespearean elements made an integral contribution.

Polish drama appears to have fallen before the invasion in 1655 by Charles X of Sweden, and a century of decay and strife followed. But the election of its last king, Stanislaus Augustus Poniatowski (1732–1798), in 1764 ushered into being a new period of brilliance, which can be compared only to the Enlightenment in France. In Poland, even more than elsewhere on the continent, French taste was the arbiter in all things. In the palaces French plays were performed almost exclusively. Neoclassical rules, especially those prescribed by Voltaire, dominated formal criticism. Nevertheless, this general resurgence of the arts created a favorable climate for the re-emergence of a national drama. A year after his accession the new king built Warsaw's first public theatre, aiding the formation of a group of writers, among whom were Franciszek Bohomolec (1720–1784), Franciszek Zabłocki (1750–1821), and Prince Adam Czartoryski (1734–1823). This group, in addition to their dramatic activities in the newly built theatre, founded a periodical, *The Monitor*, in whose pages appeared the first genuine criticism of Shakespeare. Czartoryski, the author of this piece in the 70th issue, had been partly educated in England, knew something of its literature (he had adapted a comedy by David Garrick), and appreciated the virtues of Shakespeare, in spite of his own neoclassical predilections. His article links Shakespeare with Addison, yet, with the exception of a few chronological errors—he has Shakespeare dead in 1556—the article is remarkably just and free from narrow prejudices. It was a fortunate coincidence that Shakespeare returned to prominence under the aegis of so influential an admirer at the very time that witnessed the second birth of Polish national drama. It was equally fortunate that there existed at the center of Polish culture, side by side with a widespread Gallophilism, strong romantic tendencies to which Shakespearean theatre appealed. The dramas written by the *Monitor* group, especially Bohomolec's *Twins* (1775) and Zabłocki's *Boaster* (1782), testify to the power of Shakespeare's influence.

The growth of that influence, however, had its opposition. The publication of Czartoryski's appreciation began a war of words between the followers of Voltaire, under a banner of "barbarous," and the partisans of a national drama, under one of "inspired"—a war that lasted well into the next century. Since Poland lacked a mature dramatic tradition, inevitably her playwrights found themselves pulled equally between Ducis, Molière, and Mercier on the one hand, and Shakespeare on the other. It did not help that Shakespeare was performed in French or German adaptations at this time. Neoclassicism seemed destined to become the abiding influence on Polish drama. *Hamlet,* the first translation of Shakespeare into Polish, by the "father of Polish theatre," Woljciech Bogusławski (1757–1829), was performed for the first time in Lẃow in 1797. It had been translated from a German version by Friedrich Ludwig Schröder (1744–1816) and bore only the remotest resemblance to the English original. Like most 18th-century adapters of Shakespeare, Bogusławski tailored *Hamlet* to suit the dimensions of a French aesthetic. He eliminated most of its violence and gave the play a happy ending. Bogusławski's Preface is a fine example of contradictions and Augustan rigidity, prejudiced, blind to its own shortcomings, but almost unwillingly laudatory.

> The tragic drama *Hamlet* which we offer here to the reader is entirely faithful to the plot of Shakespeare's original. However, structure, acts and scenes, as well as the ending, have been changed.
>
> A long play that takes five hours to perform, a play that in disregarding the conventions of drama, destroys the audience's interest: a play that, by presenting on stage low characters and ugly scenes, cheapens tragic grandeur: a play, lastly, whose ending disregards all moral purpose, punishing the guilty as well as the innocent with death; such a play could not be staged in an enlightened era without necessary improvements. Still, it could hardly be neglected because of other undeniable beauties which only Shakespeare's genius could create and make immortal.

Bogusławski's *Hamlet* initiated a new era of Polish interest in Shakespeare. Further translations in Polish followed. *Hamlet* was rendered in 1800 from an unidentified source, and again, in 1805, by Jan Kaminski (1777–1855), who used the Schröder version. In 1812 Schiller's version of *Macbeth* was translated by Stanislaw Regulski (1791–1831); an anonymous translation of *Much Ado About Nothing* appeared in 1825. It was at this time that first the tragedies and then the histories, especially *Henry IV*, which was staged in French in 1828, began to captivate Polish theatregoers. Shakespeare's popularity coincided with the appearance of the first of the superb tragedians who were to glorify the Polish stage until World War I. Actors like Kazimierz Owsinski (1752–1799), who had premiered the 1797 *Hamlet,* and Antoni Benza (1787–1859), whose Macbeth was the zenith of the 1810 season, demanded tragedies. Performances of Shakespeare flourished as never before.

After their initial impact, the Polish translations were little used. Performances in French and German were considered more polished and, as one critic pointed out, those translations had at least been made from English. One last, engaging attempt at a native version was Joseph Minasowicz' (1792–1849) *Othello* (1828), which he based on an Italian libretto by Francesco di Salsa for Rossini's opera *Otello.*

The first wave of Romanticism reached Poland at the end of the 1820's. With it, Shakespeare's position took on a new dimension. He was now actively regarded as the hope of a national drama. Poland's great poet Adam Mickiewicz (1798–1855) saw in Shakespeare the chief teacher of the young Polish playwrights. In a letter of 1828 he wrote:

> Again I say that our day needs first of all historical drama. Until now, it is true, no one has undertaken this in earnest. Schiller, despite his genius, merely copied Shakespeare's dramatic form. We, at least, imitate the spirit of Shakespeare, Schiller and Goethe, suiting it to our native needs. I would urge you to adapt a work by one of these great masters, preferably Shakespeare, whom I carry in the depths of my heart.

For Mickiewicz, as for many Romantic poets throughout Europe, Shakespeare represented the "kingdom of heaven," and his indebtedness to the English dramatist is visible throughout Mickiewicz' own works: the drama *Forefather's Eve,* the narrative poem *Pan Tadeusz,* and numerous critical ventures, such as the Sorbonne lectures of 1842. Polish dramatists and critics alike turned away from neoclassicism, aware that its tight rules stifled the climate Polish drama needed for its development. They called for more Shakespeare in Polish, and Maurycy Mochnacki (1804–1834), the brilliant critic of the *Gazeta Polska,* urged translators to go to the originals. In an epoch-making article, "Macbeth: Shakespeare's or Ducis' " (1829), he demonstrated the inadequacy of 18th-century French translations and counseled Polish actors, producers, writers, and audiences to approach the originals free from prejudices. Mochnacki's article paved the way for a new era of Shakespeare translation, inaugurated by Aleksander Tyszynski's (1811–1880) *King John,* which appeared in 1838. Tyszynski's play, translated from the original, is full of bombast and crudities. Yet he had shown his betters where to follow.

During the 19th century, Polish literature became one of the most important in Europe. Not only Mickiewicz, a major poet in any literature, but scores of other poets, playwrights, novelists, and critics produced works of considerable influence.

Although Shakespeare never generated a mania in Poland as he did in Germany, his name and work were, nevertheless, familiar in countless areas of Polish life. Writers like Franciszek Wezyk (1785–1862) sent the nation's youth to Shakespeare's histories to learn the nature of true patriotism. Exotic cults reconstructed the plays to dignify their own doctrines. It is for his influence on the literature of the time, however, that Shakespeare is deservedly famous. His aid in the establishment of a national drama cannot be underestimated. Such exceptional playwrights of the period as Alexander Fredro (1793–1876) and Julius Słowacki (1809–1849) found in Shakespeare their own inspiration. Fredro's first play, *Pan Geldhab* (1819), an interesting mixture of elements from Molière and Shakespeare, illustrates remarkably well how the two tendencies these playwrights represented confronted one another within the mainstream of Polish literature. Fredro never outgrew the Gallic influence. Słowacki, on the other hand, possessed no such bifurcated consciousness. His early work *Maria Stuart* (1830) is visibly "Schillerean." Yet once he came under the spell of Shakespeare, the result of his having seen Edmund Kean in *Richard III* during his visit to London in 1831, Słowacki heeded Mickiewicz and set himself the task of absorbing the spirit, not the manner, of his model. *Mindowe* (1832), Słowacki's next play, teems with the spirit of that "lump of foul deformity." His later plays, *Balladyna* (1834), *Mazeppa* (1839), and *Lilla Weneda* (1840), reveal how strongly the Shakespearean spirit had penetrated his own, though more subtly than before. Słowacki is of further interest because he is perhaps the only dramatist of the 19th century, certainly the only one of his immense stature, who is able to use Shakespeare without succumbing to the banality of formal imitation and who, moreover, educes from his native materials an existential profundity similar to that of the English dramatist.

Many other Polish dramatists of the same century, while less gifted, still deserve to be cited among Shakespeare's finest students. Such dramas as Josef Korzeniowski's (1797–1863) *Aniela* (1823), Josef Szujiski's (1835–1883) *Jerzy Lubomirski* (1862), Aleksander Swietochowski's (1849–1938) trilogy, *Immortal Souls* (1875), and Jan Kasprowicz' (1860–1926) *Napierski's Revolt* (1899) all demonstrate the benefits of Shakespeare's tutelage in technique, psychology, dramatical discrimination, and the use of Polish historical matter.

Although less noticeable in that genre, Shakespeare's effect on the 19th-century Polish novel was considerable. Novelists like Stefan Zeromskil (1864–1925) and Henryk Sienkiewicz (1846–1916) wrote under his influence; the latter, in particular, shows his enormous debt in *With Fire and Sword* (1884) and *The Deluge* (1886). The practice among the novelists, which was typified in the work of Sienkiewicz, was to create characters, particularly in historical fiction, who were amalgams of a great many favorite characters like Hotspur, Richmond, Henry V, or Pistol and Falstaff.

It is impossible to do more than suggest the indefatigable activity in Shakespeare's behalf in all phases of Polish literature during the 19th century. His plays were performed in every town and village by amateur and professional alike. The great acting tradition which had taken root in the preceding century bore fruit in such superb tragedians as Kazimierz Kaminsky (1865–1929), Boleslaw Ladnowski (1841–1911), Wincenty Rapacki (1841–1924), Boleslaw Leszcynski (1840–1918), whose creation of the role of Othello is legendary, and the immortal Modjeska (pseudonym of Helena Modrzejewska, 1844–1909), who triumphed in London, New York, and San Francisco. These actors not only demanded the opportunity of playing Shakespearean characters, but helped to perpetuate the practice, still in use, of judging an actor's merits on his creation of a Shakespearean role. It was fortunate for them that they lived in a time in which the finest translations of Shakespeare into Polish were being made. Tyszynski's lead in 1838 was followed by a joint effort by Ignacy Kefalinski (pseudonym of Archbishop Ignacego Holowinskiego, 1807–1855) and John of Dycalp (pseudonym of Joseph Jankowski, d. 1847). Their translations of eight plays, which appeared in three volumes between 1840 and 1847, while no more than adequate, were the most systematic and ambitious undertaking up to that time. Although individual plays were being translated, no effort was made to supersede this collection until 1862, when Stanislaw Kozmian (1837–1922), an excellent translator, actor, and director of the Cracow theatre, began staging his translations of *A Midsummer Night's Dream, King Lear, Two Gentlemen of Verona, King John, Richard II,* and *1* and *2 Henry IV*, which he published in three volumes at intervals from 1866 to 1877. Kozmian's translations demonstrated how well the Polish language, with its sibilance and verbal flourishes, could be suited to the English plays. His translations had the further virtue of being brilliantly stageworthy, with the result that after 1862 no French or German versions were acted again on the Polish stage. Neither of these collections, however, was complete and it was left to Joseph Ignacy Kraszewski (1812–1887), a leading novelist, to compile the first complete edition of Shakespeare's plays in Polish. This edition, in three volumes (1875–1877), relied on the existing translations of Kozmian, Leon Ulrich (1811–1885), and Josef Paszkowski (1817–1861), the three finest translators of Shakespeare during this era. In addition to the plays Kraszewski included his own life of the poet, interesting in its anticipation of the biographical method of the Danish critic Georg Brandes (1842–1927). One other complete edition in 10 volumes was issued in 1895 by the eminent philologist Dr. Henryk Biegeleisen (1855–1934). This edition consisted principally of the same translations used by Kraszewski, with but a few newer translations whose quality, though different, is not superior to the older ones. Of interest, however, are the series of essays on Shakespeare's dramatic method by Biegeleisen and an essay, "Shakespeare in Poland," by the literary historian and scholar Jan Zahorski (1858–1927).

Side by side with this enormous activity were the critical skirmishes which, although reduced, had hardly abated. The neoclassical bias of the preceding century persisted, though with little effect, in the criticism of Kazimierz Stadnicki (1790?–?1862), who failed to see anything of worth or beauty in all of

Shakespeare: Lear is a "senile mutterer," Hamlet "a self-pitying delinquent," and Lady Macbeth "a murderer's wife, and nothing more." Of greater consequence were the critics who censured Shakespeare for his lack of Catholic orthodoxy and for the materialistic ideals they read in his works. This school is one of the most interesting of the period and counted among its members Josef Szujiski, whom I have already mentioned as the author of a fine drama, *Jerzy Lubomirski* (deeply indebted to *Hamlet*), and the philosophical poet Zygmunt Kraszinski (1812–1859). Under the simultaneous influence of later Hegelians, such as the critic Hermann Ulrici, and the Catholic conservative Joseph De Maistre (1753–1821), these critics attempted to articulate, over a period of several decades, their reaction to Romantic individualism, to ethical and moral relativism, while proselytizing a view of art as "organic," not, however, in the Romantic sense of that term, but in a sense more nearly theistic. In a letter from Rome (1840, pub. 1852), Kraszinski expressed these doctrines as they affected his view of Shakespeare most clearly.

> The surface apparatus moves in him [Shakespeare], but the deeply eternal, the organic—where is that? Where in Shakespeare does one find the faith in existence? Where is there expressed that which harvests all that is dispersed, which unites all heterogeneous fragments, and reconciles all contradictions? Shakespeare is a mighty master of dissonance. But dissonances are only one half of life; where does he move toward harmony, universality; where does he march into the temple of endless truth and beauty?

He goes on in the same vein arguing that Shakespeare is primitive, devoid of spirituality, and short of true tragic stature because he fails to provide his age with the hope of resurrection. But in spite of such criticisms and worse invective Shakespeare continued to flourish and the number of his staunch admirers grew throughout the 19th century.

In the present century Polish Shakespeare scholarship has come of age, no longer merely following but forging ahead wherever the opportunity arose. In the first decade, under the influence of German philological critics, Polish scholars began the task of establishing Shakespeare's text, of analyzing it and contributing ably to the solution of many then unsolved problems. There have also been many interesting developments in criticism, with the contributions of the dramatist Stanislaw Wyspianski (1869–1907) and the critic and literary historian Jan Kott (1914–   ) the most exciting.

Wyspianski illustrates an imaginative rather than literalist approach. In a book of considerable size which served as the Introduction to Paszkowski's 1860 translation of *Hamlet* when it was reissued in 1901, Wyspianski argues a most interesting thesis. To understand what Shakespeare actually wrote, he claims, we must detach his mind from the theatre. Also partial to the historical approach, Wyspianski was interested principally in Shakespeare's philosophy. The heart of Wyspianski's view of *Hamlet* is based on the fact that Shakespeare himself played the part of the Ghost. The Ghost, he argues, must be the principal character of the play and any production must give the Ghost his proper importance. This, Wyspianski states, can be done by eliminating all the unjust characters and transferring them to the spirit world which is the kingdom of the Ghost. The spirit of Hamlet's father is not without its own sins and thus the play represents a triple problem of filial duty: young Fortinbras to his father, Hamlet to his, and Laertes to Polonius. The path of filial duty is clear but the sons cannot fully justify their deeds which are the fathers' responsibility, so they must perish in order to restore the balance of justice. Only young Fortinbras can live, because Hamlet's death removes his obligation and the play ends with the triumph of justice. This view resulted in one of the most interesting productions of *Hamlet* in 1901 and again in 1905. Admittedly classical in its bias it nevertheless shows that Polish Shakespeare criticism had come far enough by the turn of the century to venture to experiment.

Kott's views, while not so idiosyncratic, are still somewhat unusual. But like Wyspianski's they are solidly based on many years of careful textual study and have been refined in countless lectures which Kott, a professor at the University of Warsaw since the end of World War II, has given to his students. Kott's very interesting thesis, similar to that of his contemporary, the French actor-director Jean Louis Barrault (1910–   ), has been developed in a book, *Shakespeare, Our Contemporary*, translated into English (1964). In his book Kott points out that the age of Elizabeth, like our own, was a period of transition in which values lost their vitality long before new ones could replace them. He draws a number of astonishingly insightful and persuasive comparisons between *King Lear* and Samuel Beckett's (1906–   ) *Endgame* (1957). In a period in which there is no recourse to history, religion, or any fixed values, says Kott, the fool is at the center of the stage. What is absurd is natural to him. Thus, concentrating on Shakespeare's most "bitter fool," Kott demonstrates effectively that Shakespeare can be viewed most profitably through existentialist glasses.

While critical and scholarly activity concerning Shakespeare has increased, the tendency of young playwrights to go to his work for plunder has finally vanished, the last notable instances being Wyspianski's *Boleslaw the Bold* (1903) and Adolf Nowaczynski's (1876–1944) *Czar Dmitri* (1908) which, their obvious sources notwithstanding, are excellent historical dramas.

In the theatre the highest possible standards of production and design in the staging of Shakespeare have been attained in this century. Theatres like Julius Osterwa's (1885–1947) highly influential Reduta, the most important in Poland during its tenure (1919–1935), excelled in experimental productions of Shakespeare. The Reduta's productions of Wyspianski's *Hamlet* were instrumental in bringing about enormous changes in all facets of Polish theatre. Although Osterwa led his theatre eventually into National Repertory, others continued to stage Shakespeare far more frequently than any other playwright. Between 1913 and 1938, Warsaw's Teatre Polski gave 625 Shakespeare performances. After World War II, the ministry of culture in the new regime decreed a Shakespeare festival which opened on the poet's birthday on April 23, 1946 and did not close until August 31, 1947. During the 16 months 13 companies in 11 towns staged the entire Shakespeare canon among them, presenting 9 of the most beloved plays over and over.

Today Shakespeare is a national idol in Poland. Its people can look back on a cultural tradition that he, more than any single outside force and more than many internal forces, helped to sustain during its greatest crises. Hardly a writer exists after 1650 among the Poles who has not learned from Shakespeare in some way. Perhaps the most compelling explanation for his profound effect and lasting popularity is to be found in his having been brought to the Polish stage by living actors instead of in dry volumes, at a time when secular drama was being born. Performing actors transmit a popular rather than literary tradition and it is worth noting that the Poles never argued about whether Shakespeare should be performed, merely over the manner of his staging. If discord is a sign of vitality, then surely the confrontation of Shakespeare with Poland testifies to the vitality of both. [Josephine Calina, "Shakespeare in Poland," *Polish Review*, VI, 1946.]—O.LeW.

Polixenes. In *The Winter's Tale*, the King of Bohemia. Polixenes is the object of Leontes' jealousy in the early part of the play and the nemesis of Perdita and Florizel in the latter half. Polixenes' role is an ambiguous and ironic one, since he is first conceived of as the victim of injustice and later as its agent.

Pollard, A[lfred] W[illiam] (1859–1944). Scholar, bibliographer, and one of the pioneers in the development of modern textual criticism. Pollard was graduated from St. John's College, Oxford. He was employed in the department of printed books in the British Museum, where he acquired an expert knowledge of antiquarian books. In 1904 he became editor of *The Library*, a periodical devoted to bibliographical study.

Pollard's first Shakespearean study was his *Shakespeare Folios and Quartos . . . 1594–1685* (1909), a work which reestablished the authority of the early quartos by demonstrating that some of them had been printed from Shakespeare's manuscript. His other bibliographical studies included *Shakespeare's Fight with the Pirates* (1917; rev., 1920) and *The Foundation of Shakespeare's Text* (1923). He was also editor of the important collection *Shakespeare's Hand in The Play of Sir Thomas More* (1923). See SIR THOMAS MORE.

Pollard's greatest single scholarly work is his coeditorship with G. R. Redgrave of *A Short-Title Catalogue of Books Printed in England, Scotland and Ireland . . . 1475–1640* (2 vols., 1926). [W. W. Greg, "A. W. Pollard," *Dictionary of National Biography, 1941–1950*, 1959.]

Pollard, Thomas (1595?–?1654). Actor. Pollard was supplied to the King's Men in 1615 as a boy and by the 1630's he had developed a reputation for his performance of comic roles. In 1635 he was one of the three actors of the King's Men who petitioned the lord chamberlain for the right to share as housekeepers in the Globe and Blackfriars profits. The lord chamberlain later ordered Shank to surrender one share, to be divided among Pollard, Eyllaerdt Swanston, and Robert Benfield. See SHARERS' PAPERS.

When the theatres were suppressed after 1642 Pollard was one of those who continued to perform in defiance of the ban. In 1648 he was acting at the Phoenix when soldiers raided that playhouse. Shortly thereafter he retired to the country, where he died sometime before 1655. In his *Historia Histrionica* first published in 1699, James WRIGHT commented on the relative acting ability shown on the Jacobean and Caroline stages. Pollard is one of the actors he praises. [E. K. Chambers, *The Elizabethan Stage* 1923; G. E. Bentley, *The Jacobean and Caroline Stage*, 5 vols., 1941–1956.]

Polonius. In *Hamlet*, the father of Ophelia and Laertes and the Lord Chamberlain of Denmark Polonius delivers one of the play's most famous speeches (I, iii, 59–80), but the pragmatic wisdom of the lines is offset by the subsequent picture of him as a comic butt. He interprets Hamlet's feigned madness as a result of unrequited love for Ophelia, a theory which he tests by arranging a meeting between them during which he and Claudius act as spies. In another attempt to discover Hamlet's secret Polonius conceals himself behind an arras while Hamlet is talking to his mother. Here he is killed by Hamlet, who mistakes him for the King. Polonius' comic garrulity is underscored by his name in the First Quarto version of the play, where he is called Corambis, which means "tedious iteration." Hamlet's often harsh treatment of Polonius is explained by J Dover Wilson as a result of the fact that Hamlet is meant to overhear Polonius' plot to spy on him and Ophelia. See William Cecil, Lord BURGHLEY. [J Dover Wilson, *What Happens in Hamlet*, 1935.]

Polydore. In *Cymbeline*, the name which Belarius gives Guiderius upon kidnapping the infant whom he rears as his own son (III, iii).

Pompey. Anglicized name of **Sextus Pompeius** (75–35 B.C.). The younger son of Pompey the Great; in *Antony and Cleopatra*, a soldier against Roman imperialism. In the play, Pompey carries on his father's struggle against Roman imperialism. After Pompey has signed a treaty with the Roman triumvirs, Mark Antony, Octavius Caesar, and Aemilius Lepidus, battle breaks out again and he is defeated by Octavius.

Pompey Bum. In *Measure for Measure*, a clown, tapster, and bawd in the service of Mistress Overdone. When Angelo orders the closing of all the bawdy houses in Vienna, Pompey refuses to give up his trade and so is clapped into prison. The Provost offers him a pardon on the condition that he assist the executioner. Pompey gladly accepts, saying, "I have been an unlawful bawd time out of mind, but yet I will be content to be a lawful hangman."

Pope, Alexander (1688–1744). Poet, satirist. Despite the disadvantages of his dwarfish appearance his perpetual ill-health, and the restrictions imposed upon Roman Catholics in England, Pope became the outstanding poet of the Augustan period. He was acquainted with most of the leading literary figures of his time, including Addison and Swift, and his venomous pen won him many enemies and embroiled him in numerous controversies. His earliest poems were pastorals, chief among them *Windsor Forest* (1713). He brought the heroic couplet to unsurpassed perfection in his didactic poems *Essay on Criticism* (1711), *Moral Essays* (1731–1735), and *Essay on Man* (1733–1734) and in his satiric poems

The Rape of the Lock (1712, 1714), *The Dunciad* (1728; final edition, 1743), *Imitations of Horace* (1733–c. 1739), and *Epistle to Dr. Arbuthnot* (1735). His poems excel in their wit, lucidity, epigrammatic sharpness, and keen irony. He also composed lyrical poems and published a translation, in heroic couplets, of the *Iliad* and the *Odyssey*.

Pope's edition of Shakespeare was published in six quarto volumes in 1725. Additional volumes containing spurious plays and a list of 29 quartos, which Pope consulted but does not seem to have used, appeared in the second edition in 1728, along with a supplementary volume of the *Poems* by Dr. George Sewell. Pope used Rowe's text, which was the corrupt Fourth Folio, as a basis for his; the copy he sent to the press was Rowe's printed pages "corrected" as Pope thought necessary. He was one of the principal corrupters of the text, for his interest was that of a poet, and he omitted many words, sometimes whole lines, and inserted words that he believed improved the rhythm. He exercised his own judgment liberally, treating as interpolation whatever did not conform to his opinion of Shakespeare's style. He divided the scenes more distinctly, however, and made some improvements in the reading.

Lewis Theobald's *Shakespeare Restored: or, a Specimen of the Many Errors . . . by Mr. Pope in his Late Edition . . .*, published in 1726, took to task Pope's edition. Though the poet acknowledged certain of Theobald's emendations and incorporated them into his second edition, he retaliated by making Theobald the King of Dullness in the 1728 edition of his *Dunciad*. [D. Nichol Smith, *Eighteenth Century Essays on Shakespeare*, 1963.]

Pope, Thomas (d. before 1604). Actor. Pope was a member of the Chamberlain's Men from their formation in 1594. He had been one of a group of "instrumentister och springere" who toured the continent in 1586/7. He is evidently the Mr. Pope who took a male role in the revival of Tarlton's *Seven Deadly Sins* when it was given by Strange's or the Admiral's Men in 1590/1. He was with the group of Strange's Men who toured the provinces with Edward Alleyn in the summer of 1593; with several other members of that group Pope was then to join the newly formed Chamberlain's company. He became the joint payee (with John Heminges) for the Chamberlain's Men court performances for 1597 through 1599; his name is in the actor lists for *Every Man In his Humour* (1598) and *Every Man Out of his Humour* (1599); and there is an allusion to him in Samuel Rowlands' *The Letting of Humour's Blood in the Head-Vaine* (1600):

> What means Singer then,
> And Pope, the clowne, to speak so boorish, when
> They counterfaite the clownes upon the Stage?

T. W. Baldwin suggests that Pope played the high-comedy roles in Shakespeare's early comedies. He was, according to Baldwin, the quick-witted jester and word quibbler in contrast to Will Kempe, who played the dull country bumpkin. In *The Two Gentlemen of Verona*, for example, he might have played the part of Speed to Kempe's Launce. There has also been some conjecture that Pope might have created the role of Falstaff. The basis for this is that John Lowin was chosen to replace Pope in the company when Pope retired and it is known that Lowin played Falstaff.

Pope died sometime before February 13, 1604 (the date his will was probated). He was a man of some substance at the time of his death, but Robert Goughe is the only one of his fellow King's Men mentioned as a legatee. Pope left his interest in the Globe and Blackfriars to a Mary Clark, *alias* Wood, and to Thomas Bromley. Mary Clark soon thereafter married John Edmonds, an actor who was a member of Queen Anne's Men in 1618. In 1612 Pope's interest in these theatres was held by John and Mary Edmonds and Basil Nicoll (the latter presumably the trustee for Bromley). [E. K. Chambers, *The Elizabethan Stage*, 1923; T. W. Baldwin, *The Organization and Personnel of the Shakespearean Company*, 1927.]

Porter. In *Macbeth*, the drunken gatekeeper. In the scene immediately following the murder of Duncan, the Porter admits Macduff and Lennox into Glamis Castle at Inverness (II, iii). The Porter's intoxicated mutterings were for many years regarded as an artistic blemish on the play. Coleridge, for example, thought the scene an interpolation by another hand. This view was resoundingly discredited, however, by Thomas De Quincey's essay "On the Knocking at the Gate in *Macbeth*" (1823), a milestone in the history of Shakespearean criticism. De Quincey's essay demonstrates that, far from being irrelevant, the Porter scene reestablishes the claims of ordinary life temporarily suspended by the fiendish murder of Duncan. Subsequent critics have also noted that the Porter at the gate is a representation of the guardian of hell in the medieval morality plays and that Macduff's entrance is akin to Christ's descent into hell as pictured in the morality play *The Harrowing of Hell*. [*Selected Writings of Thomas De Quincey*, P. Van D. Stern, ed., 1937.]

Porter, Cole. See MUSIC BASED ON SHAKESPEARE: *20th century*.

Porter, Eric (1928–). Actor. Born in London, Porter was educated at Wimbledon Technical College. He made his debut at Cambridge in 1945 in a walk-on part in the Shakespeare Memorial Theatre company's production of *Twelfth Night*. This was followed by a season at Stratford-upon-Avon. In 1945 he joined the Traveling Repertory Theatre Company. After the war he toured Britain and Canada with Sir Donald Wolfit's company, and from 1948 to 1950 acted with the Birmingham Repertory Company. In 1952 he played Bolingbroke in Gielgud's *Richard II* in Hammersmith. In 1955 he acted for a season with the Old Vic as Banquo, Navarre, Christopher Sly, Bolingbroke, Jaques, and King Henry (*1* and *2 Henry IV*), and in 1955/6 played with the Bristol Old Vic as Lear. In 1960 he played with the Shakespeare Memorial Theatre as Malvolio, the Duke of Milan, Ulysses, and Leontes. From 1945 he appeared on television. [*Who's Who in the Theatre*, 1961.]

Porter, Henry (d. 1599). Playwright. Porter is first mentioned in Philip Henslowe's diary in 1596 as a playwright with the Admiral's Men. In 1598 he was listed in *Palladis Tamia*, along with Shakespeare and others, as among the best writers of comedy. His only extant play is *The Two Angry Women of Abingdon*, a comedy published in 1599. If the play was written earlier than *The Merry Wives of Windsor* it may have provided Shakespeare with some ideas for his comedy. Both plays contain the theme of marital jealousy and the device of a comic character being dunked into water. A number of verbal parallels and similarities in characterization have also been traced between Porter's comedy and *Romeo and Juliet.* According to Leslie Hotson, Porter is the same Henry Porter who was killed in a duel with a fellow playwright, John Day. [Leslie Hotson, *Shakespeare's Sonnets Dated,* 1949; J. M. Nosworthy, "The Two Angry Families of Verona," *Shakespeare Quarterly,* III, 1952.]

Porter's Hall. London theatre. Erection of Porter's Hall was authorized in a patent issued by James I in June 1615:

> Iames . . . did appoint and authorise Phillipp Rosseter and certaine others from tyme to tyme to provide, keepe, and bring vppe a convenient nomber of children, and them to practise and exercise in the quallitie of playing by the name of the children of the Revelles to the Queene, within the white ffryers in the Suburbs of our Cittie of London, or in any other convenient place where they the said Phillipp Rosseter and the rest of his partners should thinke fitting for that purpose, . . . whereas the said Phillipp Rosseter and the rest of his said partners have ever since trayned vppe and practised a convenient nomber of children of the Revelles for the purpose aforesaid in a Messuage or mansion house being parcell of the late dissolved Monastery called the white ffryers neere Fleetestreete in London, which the said Phillipp Rosseter did lately hold for terme of certaine yeres expired, And whereas the said Phillipp Roseter, together with Phillipp Kingman, Robert Iones, and Raphe Reeve, to continue the said service for the keeping and bringing vppe of the children for the solace and pleasure of our said most deere wife, and the better to practise . . . and exercise of the said children of the Revelles, All which premisses are scituate and being within the Precinct of the Blacke ffryers neere Puddlewharfe in the Suburbs of London, called by the name of the lady Saunders house, or otherwise Porters hall, and now in the occupation of the said Robert Iones . . . . [wee] . . . graunte lycense and authoritie . . . at their proper costes and charges to erect, build, and sett vppe . . . one convenient Playhouse for the said children of the Revelles, the same . . . to be vsed by the Children of the Revelles for the tyme being of the Queenes Maiestie, and for the Princes Players, and for the ladie Elizabeths Players, soe tollerated or lawfully lycensed to play exercise and practise them therein, Any lawe, Statute, Act of Parliament, restraint, or other matter or thing whatsoever to the contrary notwithstanding. Willing and commaunding you and every of you our said Maiors, Sheriffes, Iustices of peace, Bayliffes, Constables, headboroughes and all other our officers and ministers forthe tyme being, as yee tender our pleasure, to permitt and suffer them therein, without any your lettes, hinderance, molestacion, or disturbance whatsoever. . . .

Unfortunately, as a theater Porter's Hall turned out to be rather short-lived. Probably while it was still under construction, the residents of the Blackfriars petitioned the city to do away with the nuisance of the theatre situated "so neere vnto" the Church of St. Anne's as to interfere with worship. The city petitioned the privy council, which in turn gave the matter over to Sir Edward Coke, the lord chief justice. Coke decided in September 1615 that the Blackfriars precinct had been technically brought within the city's jurisdiction by the charter of 1608, and since Blackfriars was therefore no longer a suburb, construction of the building was to be discontinued.

Several plays, however, show evidence on their title pages of having been performed at Porter's Hall, and there are allusions to it in plays performed elsewhere.

By 1618, however, Porter's Hall was no longer in use as a playhouse. The Children of the Queen's Revels (see CHILDREN OF THE CHAPEL) ceased performing as a London company and possibly became a provincial touring troupe. [E. K. Chambers, *The Elizabethan Stage,* 1923.]

Portia. In *Julius Caesar,* Brutus' "true and honorable" wife. With gentle persistence Portia, who does not wish to dwell only "in the suburbs" of her husband's good pleasure, persuades Brutus to confide his secrets to her (II, i). When he is forced to flee from Rome after Caesar's assassination, Portia kills herself by swallowing hot coals.

Portia. In *The Merchant of Venice,* the heroine. An heiress whose material resources are matched by her charm and intellectual capacity, Portia is for many readers Shakespeare's ideal heroine. As such she has been the subject of some of the most extravagant encomia ever lavished upon a literary character. Effusiveness was particularly common among literary ladies of the 19th century, for whom Portia represented a paragon of the female sex. Typical was Mrs. F. A. Kemble, who described Portia in the *Atlantic Monthly* (June 1876) as "the laughter-loving, light-hearted, true-hearted, deep-hearted woman, full of keen perception, of active efficiency, of wisdom prompted by love, of tenderest unselfishness, of generous magnanimity; noble, simple, humble, pure, true, dutiful, religious and full of fun; delightful above all others, the woman of women."

Male critics, on the other hand, have been noticeably cooler in their estimation of this paragon. William Hazlitt, in one of his testier moments, decried her "affectation and pedantry." Later critics have noted the discrepancy between Portia's preaching about mercy and her application of that virtue to Shylock, whom she degrades in the trial scene with feminine relentlessness. Nevertheless most critics, even those who balk at her somewhat imperious nature, have been forced to acknowledge the admirable combination of feminine grace and intellectual strength in her nature. [*The Merchant of Venice,* New Variorum Edition, H. H. Furness, ed., 1888.]

portraits of Shakespeare. There are only two portraits of Shakespeare which merit consideration as authentic likenesses: the engraving by Martin Droeshout which appears as the frontispiece to the First Folio (1623), and the memorial bust (see MONUMENT) in Holy Trinity Church in Stratford-upon-

Avon. The Droeshout copper engraving was com-
iissioned by John Heminges and Henry Condell, he actors who prepared the First Folio of the plays or publication as a memorial tribute to Shakespeare; : was approved by them and by Ben Jonson (and ossibly by Anne Shakespeare, as well). Their ac-
eptance of this portrait of the man they knew well nd admired is our best guarantee of its adequacy s a likeness; however, their acceptance might indi-
ate only a conventional approval of the portrait. 'he engraving shows the head and shoulders of hakespeare as a fairly young man, dressed in the legant clothing of a courtier. The head is dispro-
ortionately large, and the chest and shoulders are ut of drawing. Since Droeshout was only 15 years ld when Shakespeare died, the engraving could nly have been done from an earlier portrait, prob-
bly just a line drawing of the head. This theory is ipported by two extant earlier proofs of the en-
raving (copies made before the final revision of the late) which indicate a similar disparity in the pro-
ortions of the head and shoulders.

The Stratford monument bust is also early; it is rst mentioned in the prefatory poem by Leonard)igges in the First Folio. Gerard JANSSEN, pre-
imably commissioned by Shakespeare's son-in-law)r. John Hall, carved the bust out of soft stone. It clearly an individualized portrait and not simply conventional funerary statue. The half-length fig-
re is simply dressed; one hand holds an upraised uill, while the other rests on a piece of paper.)riginally, the statue was painted, in order to indi-
ate in greater detail the poet's features, but it was hitewashed in 1793, and then repainted after that, 'hich accounts for its present dun color. Though ie monument in which it rests was repaired during ie 17th and 18th centuries, the bust, apart from the :painting, has not been touched. Most copies made f the bust have been misleading imitations; only the ists of George Bullock (1814) and Signor A. lichele (c. 1850) are considered valid.

The Flower portrait, donated to the Shakespeare lemorial Museum at Stratford by Mrs. Charles lower, is believed by some enthusiasts to be both a fe study and the original of the Droeshout engrav-
ig. The inscription, "*Willm Shakespeare,* 1609," is the only known example of cursive script of that ite, and is therefore suspect. Dated by experts as om the early 1600's, the portrait, though not the :iginal of the Droeshout, is probably the earliest of ie "disputed" portraits of Shakespeare which have me to light. There have been many copies made it; one, by William Blake, is now in the Man-
iester Corporation Art Gallery .

The portrait adorned with the most legends is the handos (known also as the "Davenant," "Stowe," "Ellesmere") portrait, now in the National Por-
ait Gallery. It is a highly romantic painting in the shionable Italian manner, and depicts Shakespeare a swarthy gentleman with an earring in his left r. Although it contrasts sharply with the two por-
aits considered authentic, it has had an immensely)pular appeal. A copy of this painting, executed by r Godfrey Kneller, hung above Dryden's desk. A rsion painted by Sir Joshua Reynolds is now lost, though the Roubiliac statue based on it and com-
issioned by David Garrick is now in the British Museum. One of the stories about the Chandos portrait, now no longer credited, attributed it to Richard Burbage. He is said to have given it to Joseph Taylor, a fellow actor of the King's Men; Taylor, in turn, is supposed to have bequeathed it to William Davenant, the self-styled illegitimate son or godson of Shakespeare. The verifiable history of the portrait, however, begins in 1848 with its sale among the other effects of the estate of the duke of Buckingham and Chandos; it was bought by the earl of Ellesmere, who subsequently presented it to the nation.

The "Kesselstadt death mask," now at Darmstadt, is purported to be the original death mask of the poet. Found by Dr. Ludwig Becker in 1849 in a Mainz rag shop, it has nothing intrinsic to connect it with Shakespeare; there is only the following inscription, "$A^{o}D\bar{m}$ 1616," repeated three times on its back. The skull is different in type from that shown in the Stratford bust and Droeshout portraits. The mask, despite its receding forehead, has a look of agreeable dignity and refinement, and this has probably helped to keep alive its claim to authenticity.

The Ely Palace portrait, purchased by Thomas Turton (d. 1864), bishop of Ely, in 1845, was discovered that year in a broker's shop. It bears the inscription "Æ 39 +1603." Several details similar to those in the proofs of the Droeshout engravings have caused its defenders to claim it as the Droeshout original. It shows a fleshy face with poorly articulated bone structure.

The Felton portrait, which first appeared in 1792, seems to be a portrait from life, though modern scholarship doubts its claim to be a likeness of Shakespeare. It was bought for £5 by Samuel Felton of Drayton, Shropshire, from a London dealer and, like the Ely portrait, has been defended as the original of the Droeshout print. It bore on its reverse the marking *Gul. Shakespear 1597 R.B.* (the last letters supposed by some to be the initials of Richard Burbage, though others have read them as *R.N.*) and is best known in engravings by Trotter and others, who added a body dressed in the clothes of the Droeshout print to the Felton head.

The Janssen portrait, so named after its supposed painter Cornelius Janssen, a fashionable 17th-century portrait painter, is artistically the least flawed of all the contested portraits of the poet. It is a fine example of period portraiture, but it is debatable whether its inscription, AE^{t} 46/1610 is proof of the identity of its subject. The most obvious doubt centers on the 6 in 46, which shows evidence of having been altered from an 0, possibly to conform to Shakespeare's age (46) in 1610. There are five excellent copies of the Janssen portrait still extant. It is sometimes called the Somerset portrait.

Both the Ely Palace portrait and the Felton portrait are similar in type and design to the Flower portrait, but neither of them can be dismissed with any authority as copies or adaptations, or ignored as impostures. Whatever the doubts concerning them and the Janssen, Flower, and Chandos portraits, these five paintings offer the best established claims of any portraits except the Droeshout engraving and the bust.

Among the more famous of the other portraits for

THE ASHBOURNE PORTRAIT. (FOLGER SHAKESPEARE LIBRARY)

THE CHANDOS PORTRAIT. (NATIONAL PORTRAIT GALLERY)

THE ELY PALACE PORTRAIT. (SHAKESPEARE BIRTH-PLACE TRUST)

THE JANSSEN PORTRAIT. (FOLGER SHAKESPEARE LIBRARY)

THE FIRST OR "PROOF" STATE OF THE DROESHOUT ENGRAVING. (FOLGER SHAKESPEARE LIBRARY)

THE DROESHOUT ENGRAVING IN ITS FINAL STATE.

THE FELTON PORTRAIT. (FOLGER SHAKESPEARE LIBRARY)

THE FLOWER PORTRAIT. (THE ROYAL SHAKESPEARE THEATRE)

which disputed, if not suspect, claims have been advanced are the Lumley portrait, said by one owner, George Rippon, to have been the original of the Chandos portrait; the Stratford or Hunt portrait, now in the "birthplace" at Stratford, restored and claimed by the picture cleaner Collins to be the original of the Stratford bust; and the Bath or Archer portrait, attributed to Frederigo Zuccaro and said to show Shakespeare about 1594, though it is improbable that Zuccaro was in England at that time and questionable that Shakespeare was as wealthy at 30, or ever as dandified, as the picture represents him.

In addition to two other portraits said to be by Zuccaro—the Boston Zuccaro or Joy portrait and the Cosway Zuccaro—mention should be made of the Burdett-Coutts portrait, which has certain mannerisms of 17th-century portraiture, but no recorded history, and the three-quarter-length Ashbourne portrait, sometimes known as the Kingston portrait. Inscribed AETATIS SVAE. 47. A° 1611, the portrait shows a fair-haired man in black resting his forearm on a skull and somewhat resembles the accepted likenesses of Shakespeare.

Unverifiable or unacceptable claims have been put forward for portraits having little apparent connection with Shakespeare, among them the Venice portrait at the Shakespeare Memorial, the Jacob Tonson, the Soest, the Hampton Court, the H. Danby Seymour, and the Lytton portraits. All that can relevantly be said of the Welcombe portrait is that it bears a resemblance to the Chandos and Boston Zuccaro; of the Duke of Leeds portrait that, like the Droeshout engraving, it shows a wired band about the neck; and of the Charlecote portrait that it shows the wired band and its subject bald.

Scholarship has dismissed the claims of certain well-known portraits, admitting that, though they are not of Shakespeare, they are fine paintings of somebody. Into this group fall the Aston Cantlow, the Crooks, the Gilliland, the Gwennet, the Grafton or Winston, the Rendelsham, the Sanders, the Thorne Court, and the Wilson portraits, to mention only the better known.

At the present time many portraits exist in a great variety of media. There are miniatures, including the beautiful but unauthenticated Welbeck Abbey and Somerville miniatures; engravings on wood, steel, and copper. There are stained-glass portraits, sculptured figures and monuments, including the statue in the Poet's Corner in Westminster Abbey, based on the Chandos portrait and executed in 1740. There are wood carvings, medals, coins, pottery heads, intaglio portraits on gems, and numerous others. Most of them are obviously derived from one or another of the better-known 17th-century portraits, and some are forgeries or pure invention. Among the recorded portraits which, because they are lost, cannot be authenticated, are the earl of Oxford, the Challis, and the countess of Zetland portraits, the last destroyed by fire. Despite the wealth of portraits, however, the consensus of modern scholars is that only the Stratford bust and the Droeshout engraving are authentically of Shakespeare. (M. H. Spielmann, *The Title-Page of the First Folio*, 1924.)

Portugal. Although the name of Shakespeare and his reputation were generally known in early 18th-century Portugal, a genuine acquaintance with his works was slow to mature. Quite early, literary people in Portugal knew the names of Shakespeare's most significant characters and the stories told in his most famous plays, but direct acquaintance with the text was rare.

Francisco Luis Ameno's *Ambleto em Dania* (about 1755) is an opera based on *Hamlet*. Only a fragment of it exists in manuscript, and Carolina Michaëlis de Vasconcellos argues that it was based upon an Italian or Spanish version rather than Shakespeare's play. Vicente Pedro Nolasco da Cunha, the translator of Sappho, Homer, Vergil, Racine, and Schiller wrote *Julius Cäsar*, a play which he designated a drama in imitation of Shakespeare. It exists only in manuscript and dates from the middle of the 18th century.

Three-quarters of the plays performed on the Portugese stage in the 18th and 19th centuries were adapted from foreign dramas. The "translators" of Sophocles, Metastasio, Racine, and Addison used a free hand and did not intend to render the original accurately. Often they produced "imitations" rather than translations. Rebello da Silva's *Othello* (1856) appears to be a free rendition of Alfred de Vigny rather than Shakespeare. In any event it is a simplification of Shakespeare's plot into sentimental, tearful prose.

Antonio Feliciano de Castilho, who apparently translated Anacreon without understanding a word of Greek and Goethe's *Faust* without seeing a page of it in the original, turned his attention to Shakespeare. He claimed that his *Sonho de uma Noite de S. João* (1875) was translated directly from Shakespeare's *Midsummer Night's Dream*. Carolina Michaëlis de Vasconcellos doubts this assertion but admits that Castilho is of more worth poetically and closer to Shakespeare than is Rebello da Silva.

The king of Portugal, Louis I, anonymously published a translation of *Hamlet* in 1877, the first attempt to render Shakespeare into Portugese as he is in the original. Michaëlis notes that this translation is most successful when it echoes the more rhetorical passages in Shakespeare but less so when dealing with the witty, the grotesque, and the gross. Bulhão Pato's *Hamlet* (1879) remedies this difficulty, although at times his translation leans on François Victor Hugo's French. These two translators, along with Antonio Petronillo Lamarao, established in Portugal the tradition of Shakespearean translations which are as faithful to the original as is possible. In recent years the scholarship of Luis Cardin and the translation of the complete works undertaken by the Faculty of Letters at the University Coimbra have been important developments. [Carolina Michaëlis de Vasconcellos, "Shakespeare in Portugal," *Shakespeare-Jahrbuch*, XV, 1880.]—A.B.

Posthumus Leonatus. In *Cymbeline*, husband of Imogen, and a "poor but worthy gentleman." Banished for having secretly married the King's daughter, Posthumus proves an easy victim for the cunning of Iachimo and is provoked into making a wager on his wife's constancy. Unable to reject Iachimo's false evidence of Imogen's infidelity, Posthumus indicts women for "all faults that may be named, nay, that hell knows," and orders her killed. Nevertheless h suffers remorse at word of her death and despair at Iachimo's revelation of her innocence. When the living Imogen forgives him his lack of faith in her, Posthumus matches her generosity by forgiving the penitent Iachimo.

Preston, Thomas. See CAMBYSES.

Priam. In Greek legend, in Homer's *Iliad,* and in *Troilus and Cressida,* the king of Troy when that city was sacked by the Greeks. In Shakespeare's play Priam presides over the debate between Hector and Troilus (II, ii), but has no voice in the final decision to continue the war against the Greeks. He is equally ineffectual in his attempt to dissuade Hector from meeting Achilles in battle (V, iii). Priam's lack of authority is the dramatic expression of one of the play's themes—the overthrowing of "degree." See TROILUS AND CRESSIDA: *Comment.*

Price, Hereward Thimbleby (1880–1964). American scholar, professor at the University of Michigan. Price's scholarly activities were largely in the area of philological and textual studies, to wit, *A History of Ablaut in the Strong Verbs from Caxton to the End of the Elizabethan Period* (1910), *The Text of Henry V* (1920), *Foreign Influences on Middle English* (1947), and *Construction in Shakespeare* (1951). At the time of his death he had completed editing the New Variorum Edition of *Titus Andronicus.*

Priest. In *Hamlet,* a minor character who appears as a member of Ophelia's funeral procession in V, i. When Laertes asks why the ceremony is so scanty, the Priest replies that her obsequies have been as far enlarged as they can without dishonoring the service of the dead and that, but for command from high authority, she would not even be buried in consecrated ground, for her death was "doubtful."

Prince Charles' Men [Duke of York's Men]. A company of actors under the patronage of Charles I when he was the duke of York and, later, prince of Wales. The earliest records of the company, which may have been a continuation of LENNOX' MEN, date from 1608. In 1610 they received, along with all the London companies, a patent "to use and exercise the arte and quality of playing Comedyes, Tragedies, Histories, Enterludes, Moralles, Pastoralles, Stage-playes, and such other like . . . ." The company appeared at court frequently for the entertainment of the children of the royal family. The chief playwright was William ROWLEY, who also acted as payee for the company. In 1614 they amalgamated with LADY ELIZABETH'S MEN under an arrangement with Philip Henslowe. When Henslowe died in 1616 the combination was dissolved and Prince Charles' Men appeared at the Hope theatre and later at the Red Bull. In 1619 the company came under the direction of Christopher BEESTON and moved to the Phoenix, probably returning to the Red Bull in 1622. They are also recorded as having been at the Curtain that year. The company disbanded in 1625 when Prince Charles succeeded to the throne. [G. E. Bentley, *The Jacobean and Caroline Stage,* 5 vols., 1941–1956.]

Prince Henry's Men. See ADMIRAL'S MEN.

Princess of France. See FRANCE, PRINCESS OF.

Princess's Theatre. Former exhibition hall converted into a theatre in 1840. At first, the Princess's was used primarily for opera, but in 1850 Edmund Kean's son Charles assumed control and began to mount Shakespearean productions in the grand manner. His productions of *Macbeth, King John, Richard III,* and *Henry VIII* have been described as "miracles of stage craft." The *Henry VIII,* for example, is notable for the first use of limelight. The Princess's was destroyed by fire in 1880 and rebuilt the following year by Wilson Barrett (1847–1904), who ran it successfully for a number of years, alternating popular melodramas with generally unsuccessful Shakespearean productions. After 1902 the theatre was bought by an American syndicate which experienced difficulties with alterations and the lease, and the Princess's fell into disuse.

printing and publishing. In Elizabethan times book publication was a virtual monopoly of the Stationers' Company, an organization of printers and publishers incorporated in 1557. Not only did the Company have the sole printing rights in the kingdom (with the exception of the university presses at Oxford and Cambridge), but it was empowered to search the premises of anyone concerned with the book trade and seize any book printed in violation of the existing licensing and censorship laws. Under an edict of 1586 all books were required to be licensed, that is, submitted for the perusal of the archbishop of Canterbury or one of his deputies before they could be published. The wardens of the Stationers' Company were expected to see that these rules were complied with and to demand proof of licensing before entering a book in the STATIONERS' REGISTER. The Register may also have functioned as a kind of copyright register (see COPYRIGHT). The Register did record the date of publication of every book issued by the Company, and it has become an invaluable source of bibliographical information.

Playwrights in Shakespeare's day were considerably less interested in having their plays published than they were in having them produced. Most authors wrote specifically for an acting company which paid them directly for their plays, and it was not to the advantage of the acting company to sell a play as long as it could be profitably produced. Acting companies would, however, frequently authorize publication of plays, or would give the playwright permission to publish. Shakespeare's First Folio (1623) was authorized and edited by the actor-sharers of the King's Men, and Ben Jonson himself oversaw the publication of his first folio collection (1616).

Once sold, the rights to a play belonged in perpetuity to the printer, even if the play had been sold without the author's knowledge or consent. Without an author's supervision of the printing, the correction of errors, or the initiation of necessary changes, texts suffered corruption in the publication process. Some printers, in fact, "improved" or changed the text as it suited them; some changed poetry to prose, or prose to poetry, for reasons of space; some were unable to read the copyist's handwriting; and few were meticulous about proofreading. Several different types of COPY could reach a printer: the FOUL PAPERS, or author's last complete draft from which a clean, or fair, copy was transcribed; a FAIR COPY, without prompter's notes; the theatre's PROMPT-BOOK; a stenographic version made during a performance (see STENOGRAPHIC REPORT); or a version made from an actor's memory (see MEMORIAL RECONSTRUCTION). Garbled or corrupt texts were the almost invariable result of the memorial versions (which were probably the sources of the BAD QUARTOS of Shakespeare's plays). [R. B. McKerrow, "Booksellers, Printers, and the Stationers' Trade," *Shakespeare's England*, 1916.]

Pritchard, Hannah. Born **Hannah Vaughan** (1711–1768). Actress. Mrs. Pritchard's first contact with the theatre was as a singer at the fairs in and around London. While in her teens, she attracted the attention of Theophilus Cibber and joined his company at the Haymarket. In 1730, having established something of a reputation in comic roles, she joined the Drury Lane company and remained there for the balance of her career.

Mrs. Pritchard may have formalized her acting style at this time under the influence of James Quin, the leading actor of the day. This style, accenting articulation, was to mark her as "old-fashioned" in the latter part of her career. Mrs. Pritchard's early roles were mainly comic, and she received great praise for her 1740 performance of Rosalind to Quin's Jaques in *As You Like It*. David Garrick arrived at the Drury Lane that year and, in subsequent seasons, Mrs. Pritchard moved to even greater acclaim in tragic portrayals. Her finest role was Lady Macbeth, which she first offered in 1748 and again 20 years later at her farewell performance. Other of her memorable tragic roles were Juliet, the Queen in *Hamlet*, and Queen Katharine in *Henry VIII*. [*Dictionary of National Biography*, 1885– ; *Oxford Companion to the Theatre*, Phyllis Hartnoll, ed., 1951.]

private theatres. See PLAYHOUSE STRUCTURE.

privy council. The group of high-ranking noblemen who served as the English monarch's personal staff (the use of the term dates from the late 14th century). The council was the supreme executive and judicial body of the state. It issued its orders through the lords lieutenant of the counties of the realm and the local magistrates. Members of the privy council were privileged with direct access to the monarch. During Elizabeth's reign the number of members was never large, thus enabling her to retain firm control over the body. In 1600 there were only 11 members of the council; this was further reduced the following year when the most famous of her councillors, the earl of Essex, was executed for treason. The council was an active body, meeting almost every day to decide cases ranging from the trivial to the most significant. In its judicial role the council sat in Star Chamber. Here were decided cases which did not lie within the jurisdiction of the ordinary courts. One of the members of the council was Lord Hunsdon, lord chamberlain, in charge of the operation and organization of the royal household and the patron of Shakespeare's company until 1603.

The lord chamberlain and his fellow privy councillors were directly concerned with plays and the theatre in two ways. Their principal interest lay in the control and censorship of plays in order to prevent any suggestion of treason or heresy. As this function grew in importance, eventually becoming a responsibility of the Master of the Revels, the council became more and more the agency of the court which acted as a counterforce to Puritan opposition to the stage (see ENEMIES OF THE STAGE). Without th council's numerous decisions in defense of the play ers, the Elizabethan theatre might have been sup pressed long before Shakespeare ever came to Lon don.

problem plays. In connection with Shakespeare, term used to describe those of his plays in whic point of view is ambiguous. Thus, in Shakespearea criticism the term calls attention, not to social prob lems, but to the problems of interpretation the play evoke in the mind of the reader.

The term was first used in connection with Shake speare by F. S. Boas in 1896 to describe the ambigu ities and complexities of *Hamlet*, *All's Well Tha Ends Well*, *Troilus and Cressida*, and *Measure fo Measure*. Subsequent criticism has not used the terr with reference to *Hamlet;* the other three plays men tioned, however, are frequently referred to as "prob lem plays" or "problem comedies." There has bee a consequent tendency to view the three plays a closely related in chronology and in their ironic even cynical view of life. The validity of this view has been questioned, however, and in a recent book *The Problem Plays of Shakespeare* (1963), on th subject, Ernest Schanzer has reapplied the term t refer to *Julius Caesar* and *Antony and Cleopatr* along with *Measure for Measure*. See COMICAL SATIRE

Proculeius. In *Antony and Cleopatra*, a friend o Octavius Caesar. After Antony's death, Octavius send Proculeius to reassure Cleopatra that she will not b humiliated by her new master (V, i and ii).

Prokofieff, Sergei. See MUSIC BASED ON SHAKESPEARE *20th century*.

prologue. In drama, the formal address to the audi ence which precedes a play. The prologue in th Elizabethan theatre was generally written in verse modeled on the prologues to the Latin comedies o Plautus and Terence. Six plays in the Shakespearea canon contain prologues. These are *Romeo an Juliet*, *2 Henry IV*, *Henry V*, *Troilus and Cressid Pericles*, and *Henry VIII*. It is interesting to not that Shakespeare's prologues, as well as his epilogue (see EPILOGUE), were written during two periods i his career: at the time immediately preceding an immediately following his so-called "tragic period (1600–1607). An explanation is suggested by the fac that prologues and epilogues were out of fashion i the early years of the 17th century, and regaine popularity only after the first decade.

The most interesting of Shakespeare's prologues i the famous "Prologue armed" prefaced to the 160 edition of *Troilus and Cressida*, with its apparen reference to the War of the Theatres:

Prologue

In Troy, there lies the scene. From isles of
    Greece
The princes orgulous, their high blood chafed,
Have to the port of Athens sent their ships,
Fraught with the ministers and instruments
Of cruel war: sixty and nine, that wore
Their crownets regal, from the Athenian bay
Put forth toward Phrygia; and their vow is made
To ransack Troy, within whose strong immures
The ravish'd Helen, Menelaus' queen,
With wanton Paris sleeps; and that's the quarrel.
To Tenedos they come;

And the deep-drawing barks do there disgorge
Their warlike fraughtage: now on Dardan plains
The fresh and yet unbruised Greeks do pitch
Their brave pavilions: Priam's six-gated city,
Dardan, and Tymbria, Helias, Chetas, Troien,
And Antenorides, with massy staples
And corresponsive and fulfilling bolts,
Sperr up the sons of Troy.
Now expectation, tickling skittish spirits,
On one and other side, Trojan and Greek,
Sets all on hazard: and hither am I come
A prologue arm'd, but not in confidence
Of author's pen or actor's voice, but suited
In like conditions as our argument,
To tell you, fair beholders, that our play
Leaps o'er the vaunt and firstlings of those broils,
Beginning in the middle, starting thence away
To what may be digested in a play.
Like or find fault; do as your pleasures are:
Now good or bad, 'tis but the chance of war.

n *Henry V* there is a prologue for each act. The irst of these is well known for its reference to the layhouse as "this wooden O" (see CURTAIN THEA-RE) and the prologue to Act V for its allusion to he earl of Essex's expedition to Ireland:

Were now the general of our gracious empress,
As in good time he may, from Ireland coming,
Bringing rebellion broached on his sword,
How many would the peaceful city quit,
To welcome him!

The prologue to *Romeo and Juliet* is noteworthy or its memorable description of the hero and heroe as "a pair of star-crossed lovers." Of the remaing prologues, that which prefaces *Henry VIII* is enerally assigned to his presumed collaborator on he play, John Fletcher (see HENRY VIII: *Text*); he prologue to *2 Henry IV* is spoken by Rumour nd serves to bridge the gap between the action of his play and *1 Henry IV;* and the prologues before ach act of *Pericles*, spoken by GOWER, are of unertain authorship. [Clifford Leech, "Shakespeare's rologues and Epilogues," *Studies in Honor of . W. Baldwin*, 1958.]

Promos and Cassandra. See George WHETSTONE.

prompt-book. The copy of a play adapted from he author's manuscript for use on the stage.

In the Elizabethan theatre the prompt-copy was nown simply as the "book," and the prompter was eferred to as the BOOK-KEEPER or "book-holder." he prompt-book was usually prepared by the comany's scribe, although some extant examples of rompt-books indicate that the author himself preared the prompt-copy. It provided the official cting version of the play and was generally shorter nd contained more specifically detailed stage direcons than the author's original manuscript. After its reparation the book was submitted to the Master f the Revels to be licensed for performance.

According to W. W. Greg, there are 15 Elizaethan prompt-books extant, listed here in Greg's onjectured chronological order:

1. *John a Kent*, c. 1590?
2. *Sir Thomas More*, c. 1594?
3. *Thomas of Woodstock*, c. 1592–95?

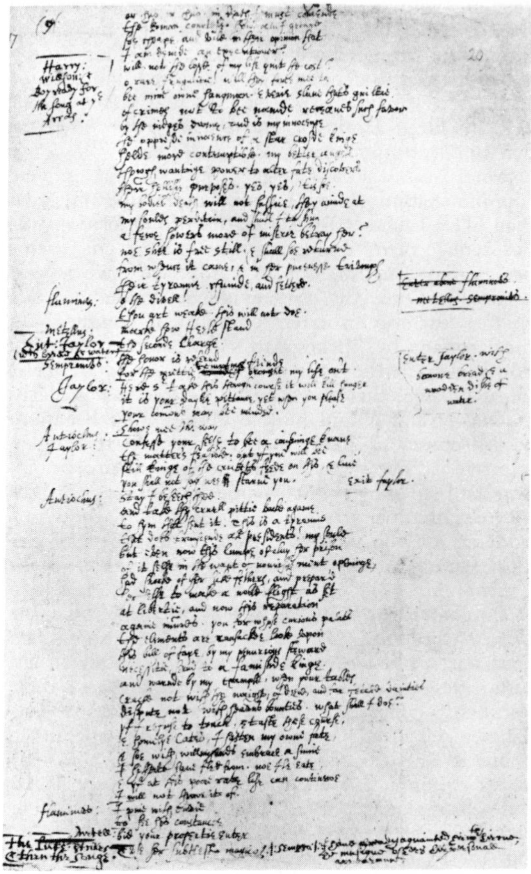

A PAGE OF MANUSCRIPT OF MASSINGER'S *Believe As You List* (1631) THAT WAS USED AS THE PROMPT COPY. THE BOOK-KEEPER HAS ANNOTATED THE MANUSCRIPT WITH CUES AND DIRECTIONS. AT THE TOP LEFT HE HAS WRITTEN, "HARRY: WILSON: & BOY READY FOR THE SONG AT YE ARRAS." (BRITISH MUSEUM)

4. *Edmond Ironside*, c. 1590–1600?
5. *Charlemagne*, c. 1605?
6. *The Second Maiden's Tragedy*, 1611.
7. *Sir John Van Olden Barnavelt*, 1619.
8. *The Two Noble Ladies*, 1622–?
9. *The Welsh Embassador*, c. 1623.
10. *The Parliament of Love*, 1624.
11. *The Captives*, 1624.
12. *The Honest Man's Fortune*, 1624.
13. *Believe As You List*, 1631.
14. *The Launching of the Mary*, 1633.
15. *The Lady Mother*, 1635.

Of these the most famous is that for SIR THOMAS MORE, three pages of which are generally thought to be in Shakespeare's handwriting.

Five of these 15 plays have careful act-scene divisions, 7 others feature act divisions only. Another distinctive feature of these books is the occasional use, in the speech headings, of the name of the actor instead of the character. See ACT-SCENE DIVISION.

Scholars are increasingly of the opinion that in cases where a play had been published, the printed version, with annotations and corrections added from the original prompt-copy, came to be used as the official prompt-book for that play. This theory has been used to account for the First Folio texts of *Titus Andronicus, Richard II,* and *King Lear.* [W. W. Greg, *Dramatic Documents from the Elizabethan Playhouses,* 1931.]

prompter. See BOOK-KEEPER.

pronunciation. Though much more like our own than like Chaucer's, Shakespeare's pronunciation was different in many important particulars from that of present-day English. For its study, we have at our disposal not only the usual evidence of spellings and rhymes but also an extensive body of comment on the language by Shakespeare's own contemporaries. For it was in the 16th century, a period of great social change, that the English people, particularly the newer upper and middle classes, first began to be self-conscious about their speech and to seek to improve it. The many books on English pronunciation and spelling which appeared during Shakespeare's lifetime provide us with a large body of evidence on the spoken English of the period; the most famous of these works were John Hart's *An Orthographie* (1569), William Bullokar's *A Booke at Large for the Amendment of Orthographie for English Speech* (1580), and Richard Mulcaster's *The First Part of the Elementarie* (1582). Though such authorities are often mutually contradictory, their testimony, when combined with other types of evidence, yields a body of reasonably dependable phonetic data. It must be borne in mind that in that period, as in our own, there were extensive social and chronological differences in English speech, more cultivated or more old-fashioned usages existing side by side with newer or less well established types of pronunciation.

In this article the sounds of Shakespeare's English are compared with those of present-day American English, labeled "PD."

The so-called long vowels in *beet, boat,* and *bought* were pronounced as in PD English. But the vowel of *beat,* and of other words spelled with *ea,* was not the same as that of *beet,* as it is now, but was identical with the vowels of *bait* and *bate,* being an open mid-vowel very much like that of PD *fair.* Thus, in Hamlet's injunction "Speak the speech" (III, ii, 1), the vowel of *speak* was different from that of *speech,* which already had its PD pronunciation. In Shakespeare's English there were a number of sets of homonyms of the type of *beat* : *bait* : *bate,* such as *mead* : *maid* : *made* and *peal* : *pail* : *pale.* Though their pronunciation has changed, *bait* and *bate* are still homonyms today, but *beat* is now a homonym of *beet* rather than of *bait* and *bate.* It is generally believed that the present pronunciation of *beat* has come down unchanged from a variant, perhaps nonstandard, pronunciation which existed in London alongside the more conservative type described above. In words with *oo,* such as *food, good, blood* (which now have three different vowel sounds), Shakespeare's English had two types of pronunciation. Words of the types of *food* and *good* had the vowel of PD *food;* those of the type of *blood* had the vowel of PD *good* and, as we shall see, were perfect rhymes with *bud* and other "short *u*" words. The vowels of *grow* and *cause* were pronounced as at present.

The diphthongs of *bite* and *bout,* which had been simple vowels in Chaucer ("long" *i* and *u* respectively), had apparently not yet attained their PD pronunciation, the first element of each diphthong then having the value of the second vowel of *sofa;* this type of pronunciation is still heard in some conservative speech areas, such as the Tidewater region of Virginia. The diphthong of *toil* and *joy* seems to have been given its PD pronunciation by many speakers of Shakespeare's time, but the evidence of rhymes and puns suggests that many other speakers pronounced these words with the vowel of *tile.* This latter type of pronunciation lasted a long time in English and is still found, in spellings like *jine* and *pizen,* in American dialect writings of the 19th century. The verb *rile,* for *roil,* is still current. The diphthong of *few* and *due* was pronounced in Shakespeare's time as in PD English.

The so-called short vowels in *bit, bet, bat* were pronounced as in PD English; the first vowel of *bodkin* was probably somewhat rounded, as in PD British English or in the speech of eastern New England. In *put* and *bud,* which today have different vowels, there may have been a good deal of variation, older and more conservative speakers using the vowel of PD *put* in words of both types—in which case *bud* and *blood* would have been perfect rhymes though with a different vowel than now. The PD pronunciations of *bud* and *blood* may also have been in use, but to what extent we cannot know. Rhymes such as *art* : *convert* and *deserts* : *parts* (Sonnets 14, 17) suggest that words with *er* followed by a consonant were pronounced with the vowel of PD *sergeant;* all these words except *sergeant* (and *clerk* in British English) have been changed to their present pronunciation with *ur* through the influence of the spelling.

In the consonants, also, Shakespeare's pronunciation differed in several respects from our own. In words beginning with *kn* and *gn,* such as *knight, know, gnat, gnaw,* the initial *k* and *g* may still have been pronounced, at least by conservative speakers. In words with medial *ssi, ti,* and *si,* such as *mission, nation, vision,* the older pronunciations *mis-yon, viz-yon,* and the like were in the process of being replaced by the newer pronunciations with *sh* and *zh* but how far the process had gone by the end of the 16th century is uncertain.

The stress patterns of native English words have changed very little since the Anglo-Saxon period and by Shakespeare's time most of the French words borrowed during the Middle English period had been adapted to English stress. But in many of the longer words of Latin origin, borrowed either directly or through French, the stress had not yet become fixed, and Shakespeare and his contemporaries were free, to a greater degree than modern poets, to shift the accent of a word for metrical convenience. Examples are: canónized (*Hamlet,* I, iv, 47), cómmendable (*Hamlet,* I, ii, 87), córrosive (*2 Henry VI,* III, ii, 403), demónstrate (*Othello,* I, i, 61), and démonstràble (*Othello,* III, iv, 142), persév́er (*Comedy of Errors,* II, ii, 217), and perséverance (*Troilus and Cressida,* III, iii, 150), sepúlchre (*Two Gentlemen,* IV, ii, 118 and *Richard II,* I, iii, 196).

The system of pronunciation described above seems to have prevailed during most of the 17th century, but by the beginning of the 18th century stand ırd English must have been pronounced much like PD American English. Many of the features of PD British English, such as the "broad *a*" in *half* and *pass*, are later innovations. [Helge Kökeritz, *Shakespeare's Pronunciation*, 1953; E. J. Dobson, *English Pronunciation 1500–1700*, 2 vols., 1957.]—E.V.K.D.

Prospero. In *The Tempest*, the exiled Duke of Milan, whose potent magic enables him to control the destiny of each character in the play. Prospero's power is so absolute, his knowledge so pervasive, and his justice and mercy so obscurely intermingled that many critics have seen in him a God-figure and viewed the play as an allegory of divine judgment. An older group of critics, more biographically than theologically oriented, tend to see in Prospero a portrait of Shakespeare himself and to regard the speech in which he promises to abjure his magic (V, , 34–37) as Shakespeare's farewell to his art.

Although their vocabularies differ, both groups of critics are responding to the same phenomenon—the unique status of Prospero among Shakespearean characters. For Prospero alone of the poet's creations seems to be in control of his own destiny. This semidivine status separates him from the action of the play and, to some extent, alienates him from the audience. The result is that despite his undoubted virtue and wisdom, Prospero is a rather unappealing character.

Many modern readers are put off by what they describe as the "moralizing schoolteacher" aspect of Prospero. They accuse him of lacking a sense of humor and deplore his harsh treatment of Ferdinand, Ariel, and even of Caliban. The source of this reaction probably lies in the fact that he too frequently has everything his own way—even with himself. In Prospero there are no signs of the inner conflict which a modern audience is accustomed to looking for in a dramatic character. His struggle and conflict have been undergone before the play begins. Nevertheless his final decision—to pursue "virtue" rather than "vengeance" in dealing with his enemies —is a dramatic choice and one which marks him as a truly noble figure. [*The Tempest*, New Variorum Edition, H. H. Furness, ed., 1892.]

Protestantism. See RELIGION.

Proteus. In *The Two Gentlemen of Verona*, one of the gentlemen of the play's title, an inconstant friend and lover. Proteus betrays Valentine by thwarting his friend's attempts to elope with Silvia and, unfaithful to his troth with Julia, sues for Silvia's affections himself. When his perfidious behavior is uncovered, Proteus is ashamed; but he is forgiven, first by Valentine, then by Julia.

provincial tours. While Shakespeare as a boy may have rejoiced at the appearance of players on tour visiting Stratford-upon-Avon, he undoubtedly did not relish the opportunity to tour the provinces himself with his own acting company from 1592–1594, when the plague occasioned the closing of the London theatres. The plague, attributed by the Puritans to the moral corruption of society and the wrath of God, visited London in cycles, and necessitated the closing of the theatres in 1563, 1592–1594, and 1603. From 1564 to 1587 and 1604 to 1609, the plague was endemic from July to November, reaching a climax in September and October. Some years—1579, 1580, and 1604—were relatively free of plague, while in others—1588–1591, 1595–1602, and 1610–1616—incidence was negligible. Between 1609 and 1625, the plague did not represent a serious threat. E. K. Chambers has suggested that a parallel exists between the years of relative freedom from the plague and the period of the greatest development of Elizabethan drama. (The theatres were also closed for political reasons; see THE ISLE OF DOGS.)

Actors were as aware of the serious economic consequences as of the health hazard imposed by the plague. They attempted to forestall the use of plague as an excuse for the Puritanical London authorities to close the theatres. In their patents of 1619 and 1625, the King's Men appealed to the showings of the plague bill—an official count of weekly deaths from plague—as the criteria for keeping the theatres open. The patents permit plays if weekly deaths do not exceed 40 in number. Players did not maintain a reserve fund for emergencies; profits were usually divided weekly or even daily. When the theatres were closed, they resorted to provincial tours as a last measure to ensure survival. A tour meant a reversion to the players' earlier status as "strowlers" or minstrels, at best, and vagabonds at worst. On tour, in fact, they were expected by their relatively unsophisticated audiences to tumble and perform acrobatics or "feats of activity." The most discouraging aspect of the provincial tour was, however, its paucity of audiences and consequent lack of profit. The pittances gathered in a small town in no way compared with the gate receipts at the London theatres, even though provincial audiences regarded players well and welcomed them hospitably for the most part. Frequently, however, players were enjoined from performing because of local opposition; and, if they misbehaved (or were charged with misbehavior) they were far from their patrons, and could not rely on privileged intervention from their lords or royal patrons.

A possible consequence of a provincial tour was the corruption of play texts. Scholars have pointed to the variant version of *Titus Andronicus* used by Pembroke's Men while traveling, and it has been suggested that the "bad quartos" of *2 Henry VI* (1594), *3 Henry VI* (1595), *Romeo and Juliet* (1597), and *Henry V* (1600) are the results of necessary abridgements while Shakespeare's company (either Pembroke's, Strange's, or Chamberlain's) was on tour. Companies normally limited the number of actors taken on tour to under 10; hired men were left in London; and, consequently, roles were eliminated altogether or the actors resorted to doubling. Frequently, they did not take along all their promptbooks; if a play was requested (by a nobleman offering them the hospitality of his manor) which was not immediately available, it could be presented by means of a memorial reconstruction, which, ultimately, found its way into print as a bad quarto of a play (see MEMORIAL RECONSTRUCTION; BAD QUARTO). Scenes were also deleted because elaborate scenery could not be carried about the countryside in the single wagon usually used to transport apparel and players.

An account of the visit of some players to the town of Gloucester about 1574 is recorded in the quasi-autobiographical treatise *Mount Tabor* (1639) by one R. Willis:

> In the City of *Gloucester*, the manner is (as I think it is in other like corporations) that when Players of Enterludes come to towne, they first attend the Mayor, to enforme him what noble-mans servants they are, and so to get licence for their publike playing; and if the Mayor like the Actors, or would shew respect to their Lord and Master, he appoints them to play their first play before himselfe, and the Aldermen and common Counsell of the City; and that is called the Mayors play, were every one that will comes in without money, the Mayor giving the players a reward as hee thinks fit, to shew respect unto them. At such a play my father tooke me with him, and made me stand betweene his leggs, as he sate upon one of the benches, where wee saw and heard very well.

Willis' experience might have paralleled Shakespeare's. At the age of 12, for example, Shakespeare might have been taken to see Warwick's Men, Worcester's Men, or, in the following year, Leicester's Men, headed by James Burbage.

Performances in rural towns were given in various places: the guildhall, on scaffolding in the town square or town inn yard, in churches, churchyards, and (at Great Yarmouth) in a "game house." After the performance, the players were sometimes treated to the hospitality of the town; this might consist of "wine and suger," a "drinkinge," a "banket," breakfast at their inn, or "Wine and chirries," as in the Gloucester house of a "Mr. Swordbearer." Remuneration was scanty, though the few shillings offered players at the beginning of Elizabeth's reign was increased to £2 or £3 by 1616. Patronage was important: a warrant from a patron was an absolute necessity, and after 1581 players were expected to present a license from the Master of the Revels as well. One patent frequently served for more than one traveling company, if the evidence of a company of Worcester's Men, for example, appearing in two widely separated towns on the same day, is sufficient.

The hazards of the journey consisted in more than bad roads, dependence on good weather, avoidance of the plague, hostility of the Puritans, and opposition by local authorities. The tract RATSEIS GHOST describes the meeting of the highwayman Gamaliel Ratsey and some traveling players:

> . . . [he] came by chance into an inne where that night there harbored a company of players; . . . In the morning, Ratsey made the players taste of his bountie, and so departed . . . About a weeke after, hee met with the same players, although hee had so disguised himselfe with a false head of hayre and beard that they could take no notice of him; and lying, as they did before, in one inne together, hee was desirous they should play a private play before him, . . . Ratsey heard their play, and seemed to like that, . . . and verie liberally out with his purse and gave them fortie shillings, with which they held themselves very richly satisfied, for they scarce had twentie shillings audience at any time for a play in the countrey. But Ratsey thought they should not enjoy it long, although he let them beare it about them till the next day in their purses; for the morning beeing come, and they having packt away their luggage and some part of their companie before in a waggon, discharged the house and followed them presently. Ratsey . . . overtook them; . . . and having made a desperate tender o their stocke into Ratseyes handes, he bad then play for more, for, sayes hee, it is an idle profession that brings in much profite, and every nigh were you come, your playing beares your charge and somewhat into purse. Besides, you have fidler fare,—meat, drink and mony. If the worst be, it i but pawning your apparell, for as good actors an stalkers as you are have done it, though now they scorne it; . . . and because you are now destitut of a maister, I will give you leave to play under my protection for a senights space, . . .

As time went on the players' reluctance to travel increased. D. Lupton's *London and the Countrey Carbonadoed* (c. 1632) says that

> Sometimes they fly into the country: but 'tis suspicion that they are either poor, or want clothes or else company, or a new play; or, do as som wandering sermonists, make one sermon travel an serve twenty churches.

For the individual playing companies' itineraries se ADMIRAL'S MEN; CHAMBERLAIN'S MEN; LEICESTER' MEN; PEMBROKE'S MEN; QUEEN'S MEN; STRANGE' MEN; SUSSEX' MEN; WARWICK'S MEN. [J. T. Murray *English Dramatic Companies, 1558–1642*, 1910; E. K Chambers, *The Elizabethan Stage*, 1923; E. K. Chambers, *William Shakespeare*, 1930; G. E. Bentley, *Th Jacobean and Caroline Stage*, 5 vols., 1941–1956.]–M.R.

Provost. In *Measure for Measure*, governor of th Viennese prison. Hoping that Angelo will relent i his harsh judgment of Claudio, the kindly Provos questions the Deputy's order to execute him and, a a witness to Isabella's plea for her brother's life, pray that she will avail where he has failed. In like fashio he enlists Pompey's services as an assistant to the executioner, promising him a pardon. The Duke recognizes this gentle officer's humanity, which earns h tribute, . . . "seldom when/ The steeled gaoler is th friend of men."

Prynne, William (1600–1669). Puritan pamphletee and fierce opponent of the stage. Educated at Oxfor and Lincoln's Inn, Prynne very early acquired a fanatical allegiance to Calvinism.

In 1633 his *Histrio-mastix, The Players Scourge*, violent attack on "Stage-playes, Play-poets and Stage players," was published. A volume of more than 100 pages, *Histrio-mastix* is a furious invective again the "godlessness" of stage plays. It was written in th year of the publication of the Second Folio, and includes, in a lament of the growing popularity of play-books, a specific mention of the Folio edition of Shakespeare's and Jonson's plays:

> * Ben Johnsons, Shackspeers, and others.
>
> † Shackspeers Plaies are printed in the best Crowne paper, far better than most Bibles.
>
> ‡ Above forty thousand Play-bookes have been printed and vented within these two yeares.

> * Some Play-books since I first undertooke subject, are growne from *Quarto* into *Folio;* wh yet beare so good a price and sale, that I car but with griefe relate it, they are now † n printed in farre better paper than most Octavo Quarto *Bibles*, which hardly finde such vent they: And can then one *Quarto* Tractate aga Stage-playes be thought too large, when as it n assault such ample Play-house *Volumes*? Besi our *Quarto*-Play-bookes since the first sheetes this my Treatise came unto the Presse, have c forth in such ‡ abundance, and found so m customers, that they almost exceede all num one studie being scarce able to holde them, and yeares time too little to peruse them all.

In the course of his attack Prynne also railed at the practice of feminine performers in dramatic entertainments, which he branded as "whorishly impudent." The remark was taken to be a direct aspersion on Queen Henrietta Maria, consort of Charles I, who had recently taken a role in a court masque, *The Shepherd's Paradise*. The result was that Prynne was imprisoned and suffered the loss of both of his ears. Despite the dire penalty inflicted on its author, *Histrio-mastix* was extremely popular among the Puritans and was influential in eventual suppression of the theatres. Prynne spent the rest of his contentious life engaged in a series of debates and quarrels for which he suffered further penalties. [E. W. Kirby, *William Prynne: a Study in Puritanism*, 1931.]

psychoanalytic criticism. See Sigmund FREUD; Ernest JONES.

psychology. Modern scholarship, in revealing the main tenets of Elizabethan psychology, has made an important contribution to the understanding of Shakespeare's plays. It is not, however, a master key which unlocks the hearts of the men and women in the dramatic universe of his creation. For Shakespeare did not manufacture characters that were mechanical dolls whose workings were governed by an intricate set of pushbuttons in a complex system of psychology. He created them from his own observation of humanity in accordance with the general view of the nature of man dominant in his time and in accordance with the dramatic conventions of his theatre. His characterization is not dependent on the jumbled and conflicting details of the pseudo-science of Elizabethan psychology, but he uses its terminology, its general concepts, and the empirical data which it sought to explain. The studies in Elizabethan psychology by modern scholars are therefore useful. Before we can illustrate this usefulness we must look at their findings.

Elizabethan psychology, which was based on classical and medieval authority and governed by the Renaissance penchant for finding analogies between all things in the universe, may be summarized in a simplified rough sketch which disregards the many differences in detail. The body of man is a microcosm ("a small world") that contains within itself parallels and correspondences to the world at large. Just as the universe is made up of four elements—air, fire, water, earth—so the body has four humors. These humors are fluids which are the product of digestion and which, according to the color and qualities of the humor dominant in a person, determine his complexion, not only in the sense of facial hue, but in the larger Elizabethan sense of physical and mental constitution. The four humors—blood, choler, phlegm, and melancholy—have their seats in different organs and nourish different parts of the body. A man in whom they existed in the proper proportions would have perfect health of body and peace of mind, his reason being in absolute command of his passions, as God intended it to be. Such an ideal, however, is seldom, if ever, attained in actual life, where men are subject in some degree to the dominance of one of the humors.

The best kind of temperament, a word which for Elizabethans meant "balance of humors," is that of the person of the sanguine humor, which results from an excess of blood. Blood, like air, is hot and moist, and heat and moisture are vital necessities which a man is born with, but progressively loses, until in old age he becomes cold and dry. Blood is a red and sweet fluid; the person of sanguine humor is, therefore, ruddy, fair, agreeable, cheerful, courageous. However, in his overabundance of vitality, he may tend to be lustful, riotous, and impractical in his optimism. Choler, a yellow and bitter fluid, is, like fire, hot and dry; the characteristic defects of the choleric man, who is lean and yellowish of complexion, are, therefore, anger, rashness, and pride. Phlegm, a whitish and tasteless fluid, is, like water, cold and moist; the characteristic defects of the phlegmatic man, who is pale and fat, are torpidity and dullness. Melancholy, a black and sour fluid, is, like earth, cold and dry; the melancholic man, who is lean and swarthy, is, therefore, morose and introspectively fearful.

One's native disposition is dependent on the planet under the influence of which one was born (the word "influence" originally meant the power over men flowing from the stars). Those of sanguine humor were born under the influence of Jupiter, hence are of a "jovial" disposition, and those of melancholic humor were born under the influence of Saturn, hence are of a "saturnine" disposition. Those born under the influence of Mercury are of a "mercurial" disposition, that is, are of an unstable nature, varying from one humor to another.

The four humors are affected not only by the planets and stars, but by periods of life, seasons, social positions, national origins, the kinds of food eaten, the days of the week, and the hours of the day. The sanguine humor, for instance, is associated with youth, spring, and the nobility; the melancholic humor is associated with old age, winter, and base occupations. One's native disposition may therefore be modified on occasion or even completely changed in the course of time.

The excitation of the passions has a physiological effect. It may increase the strength of one's dominant humor if one allows himself to give way repeatedly to the passions to which he is disposed, or it may gradually establish another humor as dominant if one is strongly provoked to passions to which one is not naturally disposed. A cold and dry passion, such as sorrow or fear, causes the spleen to discharge melancholy and at the same time causes the heart to contract, withholding blood and cooling and drying the body. A hot and dry passion, such as anger, causes the gall to discharge choler and at the same time causes the heart to expand, sending the heated blood boiling through the body. A hot and moist passion, such as joy or desire, opens the heart, the dispersed blood warming and moistening the body. Thus passions alter the temperament, and the alteration of the temperament in turn tends to make these passions habitual. Sudden extreme passion may cause the heart to break by violently contracting or expanding it, and thus bringing about death. Certain expressions that we have retained in the language, such as "he vented his spleen," "it made my blood boil," "it warmed the cockles of my heart," and "she died of a broken heart" were for the Elizabethans literal statements of fact, not figures of speech.

The passions should be ruled by the reason, through which man distinguishes good from evil;

but since the fall of Adam the passions have been unreliable subjects, always threatening to rebel. When they assume not merely temporary dominance but absolute mastery over the reason, using it to secure their own ends, man is confirmed in sin. He is punished by mental torment in this life and damnation in the next life.

The fact that many terms of this psychological doctrine became a part of the popular language indicates how widely it was known. Dramatists who used it need not have read deeply in esoteric treatises, just as today those who speak of repressions, Oedipus complexes, and inferiority complexes need not be students of Freud and Adler.

Of the more than 150 passages in which Shakespeare is thought to refer to humoral psychology, one may be cited here for illustration. When Othello remarks to Desdemona that her hand is moist, she replies (III, iv, 37), "It yet hath felt no age nor known no sorrow." Age and sorrow, as we have seen, dry the body through depriving it of blood ("Dry sorrow drinks our blood," says Romeo [III, v, 59]). Othello, pretending to jest, finds Desdemona's hot, moist hand to be a symptom of hot-blooded lust and prescribes the standard treatment: "fasting," which reduces the amount of blood in addition to mortifying the body, and "prayer," by which one may combat the "young and sweating devil" of lust "that commonly rebels."

Although Shakespeare makes use of humoral psychology, his characters are far from being mere illustrations of psychological types. Interpretive criticism can, however, make use of this psychology in its analysis. The students of Elizabethan psychology have, for instance, contributed to the analysis of the most discussed character in world literature. "His morose brooding," says Lawrence Babb of Hamlet, "his weary despondency, his suicidal impulses, his cynical satire, his sudden changes of mood and unpredictable fits and starts of rash activity are all in keeping with the Elizabethan idea of the melancholic. The melancholy man, moreover, is traditionally a person who reflects rather than acts . . . ." However, susceptibility to abrupt shifts of mood, it should be noted, is not the trait of the man of native melancholic temperament but of the man of "unnatural melancholy," which comes from the combustion of one of the normal humors as a result of immoderate passion or some other cause. As one afflicted by "unnatural melancholy," Hamlet resembles earlier malcontent revengers on the Elizabethan stage who, weakened by their grief and unnerved by the return of a loved one from the grave, were temporarily unable to carry out the mission they had accepted.

To say this is not, however, to reduce Hamlet to a pathological case (his vision of corruption is shown to have validity, and we have to come to terms with it) or to fail to differentiate him from the cruder, less individualized members of the dramatic type to which he belongs. Moreover, it does not require a scholar returned from the grave of dead ideas to explain Hamlet's essential nature. A. C. Bradley's description (*Shakespearean Tragedy*, 1904) of the Prince as an idealist disillusioned by the revelations that came to him after his mother's hasty marriage, and unable to act in his depression, is, as Babb has pointed out, in accordance with what scholars have revealed about Elizabethan ideas concerning melancholy. A knowledge of how Elizabethans regarded the bitter malcontent that Hamlet has become enriches Bradley's portrait of him as well as corroborates its accuracy.

More important than the aid Elizabethan psychology gives in the analysis of individual characters is the contribution it makes toward the understanding of certain broad features of Shakespeare's characterization. His tragic heroes, for instance, can be seen as exemplifying the men of whom Hamlet says (I, iv, 23–31) that, though they have many good qualities, they bear "the stamp of one defect" with which they were either born or which they acquired through the "o'ergrowth of some complexion, / Oft breaking down the pales and forts of reason" or through "some habit that too much o'er-leavens / The form of plausive manners"—that is, through the growing dominance of a humor which breaks down the defenses of reason or through habit spoiling a good quality by overdeveloping it. As Bradley said of the tragic heroes, they have "a marked one-sidedness, a predisposition in some particular direction" and "desire, passion, or will attains in them a terrible force."

Whereas the hero of Shakespearean tragedy is a man with stronger passions than those of most men—passions which bring about his downfall but spring from a force of character that has potentialities for good as well as evil and that raises him above ordinary persons—the villain is a man of superior intellectual ability whose reason is not in conflict with his passion but serves it. His reason, as Hamlet phrases it (III, iv, 88), acts as a pander to satisfy sensual desire, perverting itself by not fulfilling its proper function. Richard III may seem utterly passionless in his cool, diabolical cunning, but his mother tells us (*Richard III*, IV, iv, 167–172) that from birth he was given over to wildness, only in his "age confirm'd" becoming subtle in his bloody ways, "more mild but yet more harmful, kind in hatred." Iago does not rage or lose control over himself when he says that he believes that Emilia had an affair with Othello, as Othello does when he is convinced that Desdemona has been unfaithful, but his reason is governed by his malevolent hatred. Hardened by what Hamlet calls "damned custom" (III, iv, 37), habit that confirms in sin and damns, the heart of the Shakespearean villain is incapable of being wrung by ordinary human feeling. That he acts cold-bloodedly in the service of his master passion makes him the more frightening a figure.

Shakespeare's comedy has been properly counterposed to Ben Jonson's "comedy of humors," but it too has its "humors" characters—characters ridden by a single ruling passion, mechanical in their responses, hostile to gaiety and life, sometimes comical, sometimes sinister, sometimes both, the counterparts of the villains in his tragedy. Of this company are Shylock, Don John, Duke Frederick, and Malvolio. Shylock, asked by the Duke why he wishes Antonio's life, replies (*Merchant of Venice*, IV, i, 40–62) that he has no answer save that it is his "humor" and "a lodgèd hate" he bears Antonio: his deep-lying, irrational hatred dominates him to the point where he is even ready to give up his money to be able to kill Antonio. Don John asks his tool Conrade why Conrade, professing to have been "born under Saturn" (*Much Ado*

About Nothing, I, iii, 12), urges him to be reasonable in his malcontentism. Duke Frederick, of a "rough and envious disposition" (*As You Like It*, I, ii, 253), smolders with suppressed wrath at each of his appearances before he flares up. Malvolio, "sick of self-love" (*Twelfth Night*, I, v, 97), finds nothing to his taste and is a kill-joy, as Richard, who "loves Richard" (*Richard III*, V, iii, 183), hates "the idle pleasures of these days" (I, i, 31) and is a killer.

The hero of Shakespearean comedy, on the other hand, is a gentleman, with the balanced personality of the gentleman, although his love-melancholy, from which he emerges at the conclusion of the play, may evoke some amusement. In his triumph, as Northrop Frye says, "the normal individual is freed from the bonds of a humorous society, and a normal society is freed from the bonds imposed on it by humorous individuals." In the resolution of Shakespearean tragedy, the chaos that threatened the universe is quelled, and order is, although at a grievous cost, restored to the body politic. This body is now headed by a ruler who is in full command of the "little world of man" (*King Lear*, III, i, 10) that is his own internal nature, as well as in command of a social organism that has survived by purging itself of the source of its disturbance. Shakespeare's drama may be concerned with individuals, but Elizabethan psychology, in its emphasis on the analogies between man, society, and the cosmos, helped to give that drama wider implications. [Ruth L. Anderson, *Elizabethan Psychology and Shakespeare's Plays*, 1927; Lily B. Campbell, *Shakespeare's Tragic Heroes: Slaves of Passion*, 1930; John W. Draper, *The Humors and Shakespeare's Characters*, 1945; Louise C. Turner Forest, "A Caveat for Critics Against Invoking Elizabethan Psychology," *Publications of the Modern Language Association*, LXI, 6, 1946; Lawrence Babb, *The Elizabethan Malady: A Study of Melancholia in English Literature from 1580–1642*, 1951.]—P.N.S.

psychomachia. A type of Christian allegory in which Good and Evil wage a war for possession of a human soul. The term derives from the title of a poem by Prudentius (fl. 400), an early Christian poet whose *Psychomachia* is an allegorized and Christianized version of the great battles portrayed in pre-Christian epics. The tradition of the psychomachia was later incorporated as an important part of the medieval morality play.

Bernard Spivack has argued that the psychomachia constitutes the basic pattern upon which *Othello* rests, with Desdemona and Iago representing the contending forces of Good and Evil. [Bernard Spivack, *Shakespeare and the Allegory of Evil*, 1958.]

Publilius Syrus (fl. 1st cent. B.C.). Roman dramatist and epigrammatist, whose *Sententiae*, a collection of maxims, had a strong influence on Shakespeare. Born a slave in Antioch, Syria, Publilius Syrus came to Rome where his considerable abilities soon won him his freedom. He wrote plays (now lost) for which he was honored by Julius Caesar. His *Sententiae* were widely known throughout medieval Europe and were published by Erasmus in 1514 as a Latin textbook. According to Charles G. Smith, there are 180 lines in Shakespeare that parallel the Latin maxims of Publilius Syrus, including one that may have been the inspiration for Ulysses' speech on degree in *Troilus and Cressida* (I, iii, 75 ff.). [Charles G. Smith, *Shakespeare's Proverb Lore*, 1963.]

Publius. In *Julius Caesar*, a senator. Publius is one of those who escort Caesar to the Senate house on the ides of March (II, ii). After the assassination, L. Cornelius Cinna remarks that Publius is "quite confounded with this mutiny."

Publius. In *Titus Andronicus*, son of the tribune Marcus Andronicus, and nephew to Titus. Publius humors the supposedly mad Titus (IV, iii) and helps him take revenge on Demetrius and Chiron (V, ii).

Pucelle, Joan la. See JOAN OF ARC.

Puck. In *A Midsummer Night's Dream*, a mischievous fairy in the service of Oberon. Puck is also referred to in Shakespeare's plays by the names Robin Goodfellow and Hobgoblin. "Puck" or "pouke" originally was the term used to describe a type of devil or evil spirit. Shakespeare seems to have been the first writer to identify him with Robin Goodfellow, who practiced merry pranks and was chief of the spirits in medieval English folklore who haunted England. Although he was capable of assuming a variety of shapes, Robin was unfailingly distinguished by his tricks, his laughter, and his broom, with which—when properly propitiated—he accomplished the domestic chores of whatever English country house or cottage he was thought to be inhabiting. In *A Midsummer Night's Dream*, Shakespeare invokes this fanciful folk hero as the presiding genius of the mishaps and delusions which abound in his fragile fantasy-world. See SUPERNATURAL.

Pudsey, Edward (d. 1613). A resident of Sutton Coldfield, Yorkshire. Pudsey's notebook, written about 1610, contains numerous quotations from seven Shakespearean plays: *The Merchant of Venice*, *Titus Andronicus*, *Romeo and Juliet*, *Richard II*, *Richard III*, *Much Ado About Nothing*, and *Hamlet*. In most cases the quotations are literal extracts from the known quarto versions of the plays. In one or two cases, however, there are variations from the printed text, the most interesting of which is from *Much Ado About Nothing* (II, iii, 142–144): the notebook reads "writ a letter of a sheet of paper & found Frist

WOODCUT OF ROBIN GOODFELLOW FROM AN ELIZABETHAN BALLAD.

between the sheete" where the Quarto and Folio read, "O when she had writ it, & was reading it over, she found Benedicke and Beatrice betweene the sheete." Pudsey's notes also contain quotations from a play identified as "Irus." Richard Savage, who first published the notes, thought they might refer to a lost play of Shakespeare, but they have since been shown to be extracts from George Chapman's *The Blind Beggar of Alexandria.* [*Edward Pudsey's Booke*, Richard Savage, ed., 1888; E. K. Chambers, *The Elizabethan Stage,* 1923; Juliet Gowan, "Edward Pudsey's Booke . . .," *Research Opportunities in Renaissance Drama*, VIII, 1965.]

punctuation. The punctuation in the early quartos and folios of Shakespeare's plays was regarded by most 18th- and 19th-century editors as careless and illogical, and was therefore disregarded. In 1911 Percy Simpson published his *Shakespearian Punctuation,* which set forth the argument that the punctuation in the early editions was a reflection of Shakespeare's own. Simpson's thesis was that Shakespeare's punctuation was designed as a guide to actors delivering their lines, not as an aid to a reader. It was an instrument of oral effectiveness, not of grammar or logic. Thus, Simpson argued, in a given passage, a series of clauses which Shakespeare wished to have delivered rapidly would be separated only by commas culminating at the end of the passage in a full stop (period). Simpson's thesis was radically modified by A. W. Pollard, who argued that only certain passages in the early texts reflected Shakespeare's original punctuation, and that by and large the punctuation in these texts was inserted not by Shakespeare but by the compositors in the printing houses (see COMPOSITOR). Pollard's conjecture is supported by the punctuation of Hand D, generally thought to be Shakespeare's, in the manuscript of *Sir Thomas More*. Hand D's punctuation is extremely light: in 77 lines there are only 25 commas, 4 full stops and 2 semicolons. None of the quartos is so lightly punctuated. Thus the general tendency of modern scholars is to regard the punctuation in the early quartos and First Folio as the work of the printing house compositors, which on rare occasions reproduces the original Shakespearean pointing. One who takes notable exception to this view is J. Dover Wilson, who believes, for example, that Q2 *Hamlet* (1604) reproduces, virtually unaltered, the punctuation of Shakespeare's foul papers. The more accepted position is represented by Philip Edwards, whose analysis of Q1 *Pericles* (1609) postulates three compositors: X, whose punctuation was heavy and varied; Z, whose punctuation was relatively light; and Y, whose punctuation was very light. In the Folio text of *Hamlet*, that portion of the text set by Compositor A is marked by the frequent use of semicolons, while that set by Compositor B is totally lacking in semicolons. [A. W. Pollard, *Shakespeare's Fight with the Pirates,* 1917; J. Dover Wilson, *The Manuscript of Shakespeare's Hamlet,* 1934; Philip Edwards, "An Approach to the Problem of *Pericles,*" *Shakespeare Survey 5*, 1952.]—E.Q.

Purcell, Henry (1659–1695). Outstanding composer of the English Baroque. The son of a Gentleman of the Chapel Royal, Purcell himself served in that institution as a chorister from about 1668 to 1673. In 1679 he became organist of Westminster Abbey, succeeding John Blow, who had in all probability been his teacher. In 1682 he was appointed organist of the Chapel Royal, and the following year he was made keeper of the king's instruments.

Purcell's stage music includes one opera, *Dido and Aeneas* (c. 1689, libretto by Nahum Tate), and five so-called "English operas," full-length musicodramatic works with spoken dialogue and elaborate scenic effects, similar to masques: *Dioclesian* (1690); *King Arthur* (1691), libretto by Dryden; *The Fairy Queen* (1692), libretto adapted, perhaps by Elkanah Settle, from Shakespeare's *A Midsummer Night's Dream; The Indian Queen* (1695), libretto by Dryden and Sir Thomas Howard; and *The Tempest, or the Enchanted Island* (?1695), libretto by Thomas Shadwell, based on Shakespeare. From 1680 to 1695 Purcell composed incidental music for 43 plays, including works of Tate, Beaumont and Fletcher, Davenant, Dryden, Shadwell, Congreve, Ravenscroft, and Aphra Behn. Among these was a production in 1694 of Shadwell's *The History of Timon of Athens, the Man-Hater*, based on Shakespeare. In 1699 a masque of *Dido and Aeneas* utilizing Purcell's music was performed as part of Charles Gildon's version of *Measure for Measure.*

After his death at the age of 36, Purcell was buried beneath the Westminster Abbey organ. He was without question the most gifted and original British composer of his age and one of the greatest that Britain has produced in any age.

TITLE PAGE OF THE 1625 EDITION OF PURCHAS' *Pilgrimage*, WHICH INCLUDES A SOURCE OF *The Tempest.*

Purchas, Samuel (c. 1575?–1626). Clergyman and editor. As vicar of a parish on the Thames, Purchas encountered many seamen. He collected their stories in a series of popular travel books: *Purchas, his Pilgrimage. or Relations of the World and the Religions observed in All Ages—And places discovered* (1613) and *Purchas, His Pilgrim Microcosmos, Or the Historie of Man* (1619). He also completed Richard HAKLUYT's *Principal Navigations* (1625), which included a letter about a shipwreck by William STRACHEY: "A True Reportory of the Wracke." Strachey's letter, dated July 15, 1610, is a minor source of *The Tempest*. Since Purchas' volume was not, however, published until 1625, it is generally believed that Shakespeare must have seen Strachey's account in manuscript. See THE TEMPEST: *Sources*.

Puritan, The. Also **The Puritan Widow.** An anonymous play published as Shakespeare's in the Third Folio (1664). In 1607 the Stationers' Register recorded

> 6 Augusti. George Elde Entred for his copie vnder thandes of Sir George Bucke knight and the wardens a book called the comedie of the Puritan Widowe vj[d].

A quarto version was published that year as

> The Puritaine Or The Widdow of Watlingstreete. Acted by the Children of Paules. Written by W. S. Imprinted at London by G. Eld. 1607.

The play, probably written in 1606, was a satire on the Puritans and was based on a jest-book titled *The Merrie Conceited Jests of George Peele* (1605). The play contained a number of topical allusions generally directed at Puritan hypocrisy. Some commentators have also found in it an allusion to *Macbeth* and a parody of the last act of *Othello*, but such suggestions are based on only the most tenuous textual identifications.

Scholars have been all but unanimous in rejecting ascription of the authorship to Shakespeare. The play has been ascribed to Wentworth SMITH, but it is generally believed that it was written by Thomas Middleton. [Baldwin Maxwell, *Studies in the Shakespeare Apocrypha*, 1956.]

Puritanism. See ENEMIES OF THE STAGE; Martin MARPRELATE; RECUSANCY; RELIGION.

Pushkin, Alexander. See RUSSIA.

Puttenham, George (d. 1590). Elizabethan critic. Puttenham is generally regarded as the author of *The Arte of English Poesie* (1589), one of the best extant examples of Elizabethan literary criticism. Puttenham's treatise was the first publication of Shakespeare's fellow Stratfordian Richard Field, who was later to publish Shakespeare's *Venus and Adonis* and *Rape of Lucrece*. W. L. Rushton has argued that Shakespeare's extensive knowledge of rhetorical figures (see RHETORIC) derives from Puttenham. [W. L. Rushton, *Shakespeare and "The Arte of English Poesie,"* 1909.]

Pyramus. See Nick BOTTOM.

Q

quarto. A printing term, commonly abbreviated as Q or 4to, which designates a book size. The term derives from the fact that the pages of a quarto are about one-fourth the size of the sheet of paper they are printed on. Four pages are printed on each side of the sheet and the sheet is folded twice, to produce a gathering of 4 leaves, or 8 numbered pages. The size of the trimmed pages varies, since it is determined by the size of the initial sheet. In Shakespeare's time quartos were about 7 inches wide and 9 inches long, the ideal size for the publication of a play. See also FOLIO; OCTAVO.

Eighteen (19, if *Taming of A Shrew* be accepted as a "bad quarto") of Shakespeare's plays were published in quarto before their subsequent publication in the First Folio. *Pericles*, which was omitted from the First Folio, was printed in quarto in 1609. Quarto was also the format of the first editions of *Venus and Adonis* (1593), *The Rape of Lucrece* (1594), and the *Sonnets* (1609).

Frequently neglected by earlier editors who relied almost exclusively on the folio editions of the plays, the quartos have come to play an increasingly important role in the attempts of modern scholars to establish a definitive text. (See Edward CAPELL.) Even the so-called BAD QUARTOS can be of help in resolving textual difficulties. See TEXTUAL CRITICISM.

The following is a list of all the known quarto and octavo (designated as O) editions of Shakespeare's plays, sonnets, and poems up to the printing of the First Folio in 1623.

1593 *Venus & Adonis*, Q1, Field
1594 *2 Henry VI*, Q1 (bad; "The First Part of the Contention . . ."), Creede for Millington
Lucrece, Q, Field for Harrison
Shrew, Q1 (bad; "A Shrew"), Short for Burby
Titus, Q1, Danter for White & Millington
Venus & Adonis, Q2, Field
1595 *3 Henry VI*, Q1 (bad; really in octavo; "The True Tragedie . . ."), Short for Millington
1595? *Venus & Adonis*, O1 (fragment), Field for Harrison?
1596 *Shrew*, Q2 (bad), Short for Burby
Venus & Adonis, O2, Field for Harrison
1597 *Richard II*, Q1, Simmes for Wise
Richard III, Q1, Simmes for Wise
Romeo, Q1 (bad), by Danter
1598 *1 Henry IV*, Q1, Short for Wise
LLL, Q, White for Burby
Lucrece, O1, Short for Harrison
Richard II, Q2 & Q3, Simmes for Wise
Richard III, Q2, Creede for Wise
1599 *1 Henry IV*, Q2, Stafford for Wise
Passionate Pilgrim, probably O1 and O2 (with 5 poems by Shakespeare), Judson for Jaggard
Romeo, Q2, Creede for Burby
Venus & Adonis, O3, Short for Leake
Venus & Adonis, O4, Bradock for Leake
1600 *2 Henry IV*, Q, Simmes for Wise & Aspley
Henry V, Q1 (bad), Creede for Millington & Busby
2 Henry VI, Q2 (bad), Simmes for Millington
3 Henry VI, Q2 (bad), White for Millington
Lucrece, O2 & O3, Harrison for Harrison
Merchant, Q1, Roberts for Heyes
MND, Q1, Allde or Bradock for Fisher
Much Ado, Q, Simmes for Wise & Aspley
Titus, Q2, Roberts for White
1601 *Phoenix & Turtle*, Q1 (in *Love's Martyr*), Field for Blount
1602 *Henry V*, Q2 (bad), Creede for Pavier
Merry Wives, Q1 (bad), Creede for Johnson
Richard III, Q3, Creede for Wise
Venus & Adonis, O5 (date uncertain), Bradock for Leake
Venus & Adonis, O6, Raworth for Leake
Venus & Adonis, O7, Lownes for Leake
Venus & Adonis, O8, for Leake
1603 *Hamlet*, Q1 (bad), Simmes for Ling & Trundell
1604 *Hamlet*, Q2, Roberts for Ling
1 Henry IV, Q3, Simmes for Law
1605 *Richard III*, Q4, Creede for Law
1607 *Lucrece*, O4, Okes for Harrison
Shrew, Q3 (bad), Simmes for Ling
1608 *1 Henry IV*, Q4, for Law
Lear, Q1, Okes or Snowden for Butter
Richard II, Q4, White for Law
1609 *Pericles*, Q1 & Q2, White for Gosson
Romeo, Q3, for Smethwick
Sonnets and *A Lover's Complaint*, Q, Eld for Thorpe
Troilus, Q, Eld for Bonian & Walley
1611 *Hamlet*, Q3, for Smethwick; Q4, for Smethwick, is undated
Pericles, Q3, by Stafford
Phoenix & Turtle, Q2 (in *The Anuals of great Brittaine*, the new title on a reissue of *Love's Martyr*), Allde for Lownes
Titus, Q3, Allde for White
1612 *Passionate Pilgrim*, O3, by Jaggard
Richard III, Q5, Creede for Law
1613 *1 Henry IV*, Q5, White for Law

1613? *Romeo,* Q4, probably for Smethwick
1615 *Richard II,* Q5, for Law
1616 *Lucrece,* O5, Snodham for Jackson
1617 *Venus & Adonis,* O9, Stansby for Barrett
1619 *Henry V,* Q3 (bad, falsely dated 1608), Jaggard for Pavier
2 & 3 Henry VI, Q3 (bad: "The Whole Contention . . ."; reprints "The First Part of the Contention . . ." & "The True Tragedie . . ."), Jaggard for Pavier
Lear, Q2 (falsely dated 1608), Jaggard for Pavier
Merchant, Q2 (falsely dated 1600), Jaggard for Pavier
Merry Wives, Q2 (bad), Jaggard for Pavier
MND, Q2 (falsely dated 1600), Jaggard for Pavier
Pericles, Q4, Jaggard for Pavier
1622 *1 Henry IV,* Q6, Purfoot for Law
Othello, Q, Okes for Walkley
Richard III, Q6, Purfoot for Law

The octavo editions of these works are sometimes, for ease of reference in scholarly discussions, given Q numbers which place them in a continuous sequence with the quarto editions. Thus the editions of *Venus and Adonis* are referred to, not as Q1, Q2, O1, O2, etc., but as Q1, Q2, Q3, and so on.

The texts of successive editions of each work were for the most part simply reprinted from the immediately preceding edition. There is a growing opinion that many of the plays in the First Folio which had been published previously were set from quarto texts that had been marked with additions, deletions, and changes derived from some sort of manuscript copy—foul papers, prompt-book, etc. See COPY. [E. K. Chambers, *William Shakespeare,* 1930.]

Quayle, Anthony (1913–). Actor, producer, and director. Born in Lancashire, Quayle was educated at Rugby and studied acting at the Royal Academy of Dramatic Art. He made his acting debut in 1931 in *Robin Hood* and that same year played Hector in *Troilus and Cressida* in Cambridge. He was in many Old Vic productions of the 1930's, playing Guildenstern, Laertes, Horatio, Demetrius, Cassio, the King (*Henry V*), and Surrey (*Richard II*).

After the war he continued to be interested in Shakespearean roles and productions, and in 1948 became director of the Shakespeare Memorial Theatre at Stratford-upon-Avon. He played in many of his own productions, the 1954 *Othello,* for example, and brought the company to New York in 1956, the year he resigned his directorship. In 1957 he appeared at the Paris Festival as Aaron, and also in Venice, Belgrade, Vienna, and Warsaw. [*Who's Who in the Theatre,* 1961.]

Queen. In *Cymbeline,* the King's second wife. Loathing her husband, the Queen plots to win his throne for Cloten, her son by an earlier marriage. An attempt to marry Cloten to Cymbeline's daughter Imogen having failed, the Queen schemes to achieve her end by poisoning both the King and his daughter. Her plans come to nothing, and when Cloten fails to return home from a journey to Wales, the Queen falls sick in despair. In V, v, Cornelius reports her dying confession and repentance.

Queen Anne's Men. See WORCESTER'S MEN.

Queen Elizabeth's Men. See QUEEN'S MEN.

Queen Henrietta's Men. A company of actors formed after the long plague of 1625. Queen Henrietta's Men were managed by Christopher Beeston (see BEESTON FAMILY). It was composed largely of hitherto unknown actors with a small group from LADY ELIZABETH'S MEN and Queen Anne's company. The new company apparently prospered until 1630 when the theatres were again closed as a result of the plague. With the reopening of the theatres the company continued to be popular, becoming the chief rival of the King's Men in the 1630's. The principal playwright for the group in those years was James SHIRLEY and the company's home was the Phoenix theatre in Drury Lane. Their success continued until 1636 when yet another epidemic of plague closed the theatres. During this period the company was disbanded, and a new company was formed the following year. The chief playwright of the new company was Richard Brome, and its theatre was the Salisbury Court, where the company performed until the suppression of the theatres in 1642. [G. E. Bentley, *The Jacobean and Caroline Stage,* 5 vols., 1941–1956.]

Queen of Bohemia's Men. See LADY ELIZABETH'S MEN.

Queens, Three. In *The Two Noble Kinsmen,* they appear at the wedding celebration of Theseus and Hippolyta. With the aid of the bride and her sister, Emilia, the Queens persuade Theseus to avenge them on Creon, King of Thebes, who is responsible for the deaths of their husbands (I, i).

Queen's Men [Queen Elizabeth's Men] (1583–1603). Elizabethan acting company. The Revels Accounts for 1582/3 registered disbursement of 20s. for the traveling expenses of

> Edmond Tylney Esquire Master of the office being sent for to the Courte by Letter from Mr Secreatary dated the xth of Marche 1582. To choose out a companie of players for her maiestie.

A company of 12 men was selected, including Richard Tarlton and actors from various established London companies. They enjoyed the status of servants to the queen and received wages and liveries as grooms of the chamber.

Their first summer (1583 by the new calendar) was spent touring the provinces. Upon their return to London the privy council petitioned the city authorities for permission for the company to play in the city. They received a license to play at the Bull and the Bear, but only on holidays. Sir Francis Walsingham wrote an additional letter asking leave to play on weekdays as well. In the city records of the exchange, the names of the following players were entered: "Robert Wilson, John Dutton, Richard Tarleton, John Laneham, John Bentley, Thobye Mylles, John Towne, John Synger, Leonall Cooke, John Garland, John Adams, [and] William Johnson." They appeared at court that season on December 26 and 29, 1583 and March 3, 1584. Disturbances in the vicinity of the Middlesex theatres in 1584 resulted in suppression of all plays by the city. They continued to alternate provincial tours with London seasons until 1588.

During this period it is not certain at which London theatres they played each winter. By extending references to Tarlton, who performed exclusively with the Queen's Men, some idea of where the group might have been playing is derived, including the THEATRE, the CURTAIN THEATRE, the Bell, the Bull, the Bel Savage, and various inn yards. In 1589 they may have played in some anti-Martinist plays during the Marprelate controversy. The anti-Martinist plays were suppressed, and it has been noted that the Queen's Men began their provincial tour rather early that year. Various performance records reveal that the Queen's Men may have been split into two groups on their provincial tours; the group was so large that even in London they required the facilities of two inn yards during the winter seasons. In 1590/1 they appeared in combination with Sussex' Men at Southampton, Gloucester (also with the Admiral's Men), and Coventry, and at Faversham with Essex' Men.

By 1591/2 their popularity was on the wane; they gave only one performance at court, compared to six for Strange's Men (then combined with the Admiral's Men). In September 1592 they elicited a protest from the Cambridge University authorities for having played despite a plague-inspired ban on the gathering of large crowds. They gave no performance at court in 1592/3. The following year, upon their return from the provinces, they gave their last recorded court performance. In April 1594 they are known to have performed at one of Philip Henslowe's theatres, either in association or amalgamation with Sussex' Men. Of the five plays given, only one, *King Leire*, was from the Queen's Men's repertory. At that point they disappeared from the London stage.

In 1594 and 1595, nine of their plays were recorded in the Stationers' Register and then published: *A Looking Glass for London and England*, *King Leire*, *James IV*, *The Famous Victories of Henry V*, *The True Tragedy of Richard III*, *Selimus*, Peele's *Old Wives' Tale*, *Valentine and Orson*, and *Sir Clyomon and Clamydes*. [E. K. Chambers, *The Elizabethan Stage*, 1923.]

Queen to Richard II. See ISABELLA OF VALOIS.

Quickly, Mistress. In *1* and *2 Henry IV*, hostess of the Eastcheap tavern. Falstaff states, in *1 Henry IV*, III, ii, that Mistress Quickly's tavern is a bawdy house where the pockets of the clientele are picked. Though it is clear in this play that she is married, in *2 Henry IV* Mistress Quickly has become a widow. Claiming that Falstaff has broken a promise to marry her, she enters an action against him for the 30 shillings that she gave him at the time of his proposal (II, i). At the end of the play Mistress Quickly is arrested with Doll Tearsheet on the charge of having assisted in beating a man to death.

In *The Merry Wives of Windsor*, Mistress Quickly is housekeeper for Doctor Caius and a professional go-between. Impartial in the busy performance of her services on behalf of Anne Page's suitors, and professing to "know Anne's mind," she gives equal encouragement to each (I, iv). Privately, however, she holds the opinion that none is acceptable. Mistress Quickly is also employed by the merry wives to deliver their messages to Falstaff. Pistol, recognizing the financial rewards of her loving labors, resolves to marry her.

In *Henry V*, Mistress Quickly is referred to as Nell Quickly and has married Pistol. After de-

The Quiney Family

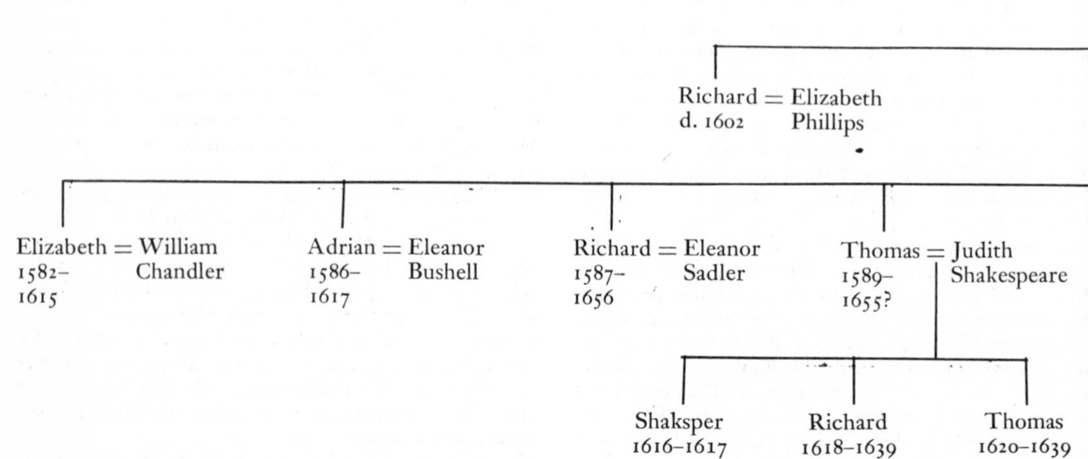

scribing the death of Falstaff in II, iii, she bids farewell to her husband, who is leaving for the English campaign in France. Pistol's reference in V, i, to "Doll," who died "i' the spital," is taken by some authorities to be a mistake for "Nell."

Quiller-Couch, Sir Arthur T. (1863–1944). Scholar. After graduation from Trinity College, Oxford, in 1882, Quiller-Couch worked for a decade as a journalist in London. In 1892 he retired to his native Cornwall and, under the pseudonym "Q," achieved a wide audience with his numerous, versatile works: novels, tales, essays, poems, parodies, and anthologies. For his activities he was knighted in 1910 and in 1912 was appointed fellow of Jesus College and King Edward VII professor of English literature at Cambridge. The fact that he came to university teaching relatively late in life and after a successful career as a popular author influenced his teaching and scholarship. He was popular with undergraduates owing to his stimulating and entertaining lectures. He was also influential in helping to free Cambridge from an overemphasis of the philological aspects of literature. Many of his lectures were collected and published in book form: *On the Art of Writing* (1916) and several volumes of *Studies in Literature* (1918, 1927, 1929). A number of his Cambridge lectures on Shakespeare were published as *Shakespeare's Workmanship* (1918). With J. Dover Wilson he became joint editor of the New Cambridge edition of *The Works of Shakespeare*, writing a general introduction for the initial volume, *The Tempest* (1921). In 1932 he delivered the Annual Shakespeare Lecture of the British Academy, a talk entitled "Paternity in Shakespeare." *Memories and Opinions*, an unfinished autobiography, with an introduction by S. C. Roberts, was published shortly after his death in 1944. [Fred Brittain, *Arthur Quiller-Couch: A Biographical Study*, 1947.]

Quin, James (1693–1766). Actor. Born in London, the illegitimate son of a Dublin barrister and the grandson of a former lord mayor, Quin was educated in Dublin, where he went on the stage. One of his earliest roles was Cleon in Shadwell's adaptation of *Timon of Athens*. He appeared at Drury Lane for the first time in 1714 and established his reputation with his 1716 portrayal of Richard III. His other roles were Gloucester in *King Lear*, Cinna in Thomas Otway's *Caius Marius*, an adaptation of *Romeo and Juliet*, and Aaron in *Titus Andronicus*. In 1718 he made his first appearance at Lincoln's Inn Fields as Hotspur and spent the following 14 years there. He played Antony in *Julius Caesar* and after 1719 many of the tragic leads, such as Macbeth, Brutus, and Coriolanus.

In 1732 he moved to Covent Garden, where he played Othello, Falstaff, Hector, Thersites, the Duke (*Measure for Measure*), the King (*1 Henry IV*), Buckingham (*Richard III*), the Ghost, Lear, and Apemantus. He played Othello for the first time in 1734 at Drury Lane, where he remained for the next seven years, adding to his repertory Richard III, Jaques, Antonio (*Merchant of Venice*), and Proteus (Benedick) in *The Universal Passion*, Miller's adaptation of Shakespeare's *Much Ado About Nothing*. From 1742 to the end of his career he played at Covent Garden where, in 1745, he was the original King John in Colley Cibber's *Papal Tyranny in the Reign of King John*. In 1746 Quin, Garrick, and

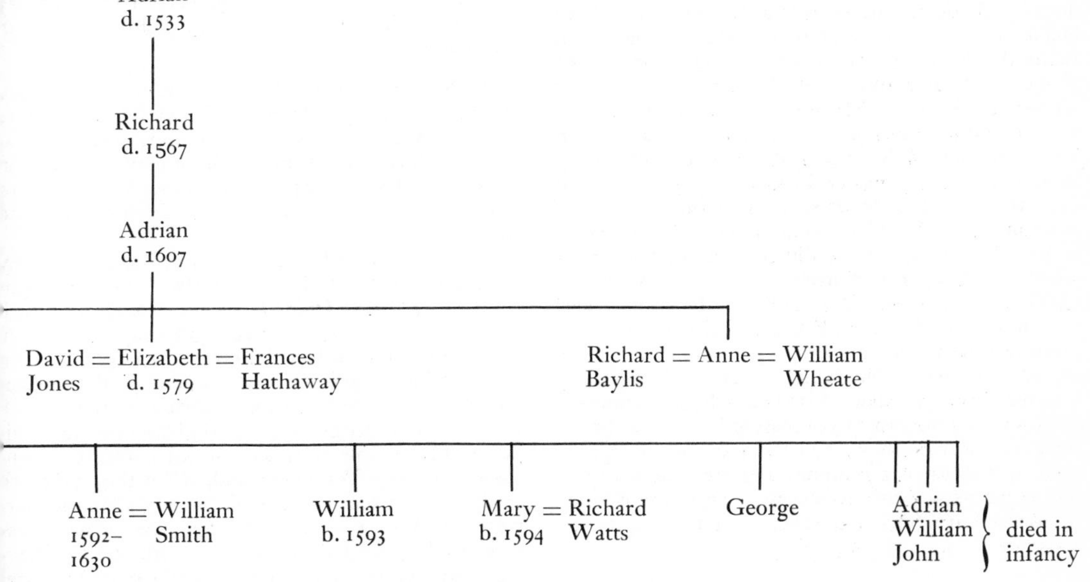

Mrs. Cibber were engaged by Rich for a Covent Garden performance of *The Fair Penitent*. So popular were all three that often they could not continue in their roles because of the cheering. In a rivalry over who could play Richard III better, Garrick won, but Quin was the better Falstaff.

In 1749 Quin created the role of Coriolanus in Thomson's adaptation of Shakespeare's play. The following year he received the huge salary of £1000 a year, the highest amount ever given a player at Covent Garden. In 1751 Quin played for the first time King John in Shakespeare's play, made his debut as Iago, and then retired to Bath. Thereafter he performed only in benefit performances. He was almost, but not quite, a great actor. His Othello, Macbeth, Lear, and Richard were bad, but he was good as the Duke in *Measure for Measure*, Henry VIII, Falstaff, Brutus, and the Ghost in *Hamlet*. Garrick epitomized him as "Pope Quin," who damns all churches but his own. Two portraits of him ascribed to Hogarth hang in the Garrick Club, and a Gainsborough is in Buckingham Palace. [*Dictionary of National Biography*, 1885– ; Charles Beecher Hogan, *Shakespeare in the Theatre, 1701–1800*, 2 vols., 1952, 1957.]

Quince, Peter. In *A Midsummer Night's Dream*, a carpenter. Author and director of "The most lamentable comedy, and most cruel death of Pyramus and Thisby," Quince recites its prologue "like a child on a recorder" (V, i).

Quiney, Judith. See Judith SHAKESPEARE.

Quiney Family. An important Stratford family whose members included friends and relatives of Shakespeare. ***Adrian Quiney*** (d. 1607) was a prosperous mercer and one of the original aldermen under the charter granted to Stratford in 1553. He served as town bailiff in 1559, 1571, and 1582. His house was located in High Street, very near John Shakespeare's house in Henley Street. Adrian's son ***Richard*** (d. 1602) was a friend and neighbor of Shakespeare, and author of the only extant letter written to the poet. He was born sometime before 1557. In 1588 he was selected as an alderman and in 1592 as bailiff of Stratford. As a representative of Stratford, Quiney visited London every year from 1597 to 1601. His business in London involved a petition from Stratford requesting a dispensation from taxes because of the difficult financial straits in which the town found itself at this time. While in London, he conducted a number of business and personal affairs for himself and his friends, of which there is some record in extant correspondence. During his stay there in the winter of 1597/8 he received a letter from Abraham STURLEY which mentioned Shakespeare's interest in purchasing land in the Stratford area near Shottery. On his next visit he apparently was short of the money required for his London expenses and on this occasion he wrote a letter to Shakespeare (dated October 25, 1598) requesting a loan of £30:

> Loveinge Contreyman, I am bolde of yow as of a ffrende, craveinge yowr helpe with xxx^{ll} uppon m^{r} Bushells & my securytee or m^{r} Myttons with me. m^{r} Rosswell is nott come to London as yeate & I have especiall cawse. Yow shall ffrende me muche in helpeing me out of all the debettes I owe in London I thancke god & muche quiet my mynde which wolde nott be indebted. I am now towardes the Cowrte in hope of answer for th dispatche of my Buysenes. Yow shall nether loas creddytt nor money by me the Lorde wyllinge nowe butt perswade yowr selfe soe as I hope yow shall nott need to feare butt with all harti thanckefullnes I wyll holde my tyme & conter yowr ffrende & yf we Bargaine farther yow shalb the paiem*aster* yowr selfe. My tyme biddes m hasten to an ende & soe I committ thys yowr ca & hope of yowr helpe. I feare I shall nott be back thys night ffrom the Cowrte. Haste. The Lord be with yow & with us all amen. ffrom the Bell i Carter Lane the 25 october 1598. Yowrs in a kyndenes Ryc. Quyney. [Addressed] H[aste] T my Loveinge good ffrend & contreymann Mr Wm Shackespere deliver thees. [Seal] On a bend thre trefoils slipped.

At the same time Quiney was apparently still negoti ating with Shakespeare for the possible purchase o the land alluded to by Sturley. On October 30, 159 Quiney's father Adrian wrote him, apparently i response to a letter from his son indicating som sort of transaction with Shakespeare:

> Yow shalle, God wylling, receve from your wyf by ye baylye, thys brynger, aswrance of x^{s} . . Yff yow bargen with Mr Sha.. or receve mone therfor, brynge your money home yf yow maye I see howe knite stockynges be sold, ther ys gre byinge of them at Evysshome. Edward Wheat an Harrye, your brother man, were both at Evyshom thys daye senet, and, as I harde, bestow 20^{ll}. the in knyt hosseyngs, wherefore I thynke yow may doo good, yff yow can have money . . . [Ad dressed] To my lovynge sonne Rycharde Qwyne at the Belle in Carter Leyne deliver thesse i London.

On November 4, another letter written by Sturle indicates that "Mr. Wm. Shak. would procure v money." Shakespeare's assistance apparently took a least two forms: the loan which Quiney requested i his letter of October 25 and the business arrangemen referred to in the correspondence from Sturley an Adrian Quiney.

In 1601, the year before his death, Richard Quiney was again elected bailiff of Stratford. He had eigh children. ***Thomas Quiney*** (1589–c. 1662), his thir son, married Shakespeare's younger daughter, Judith A vintner, Thomas leased a tavern in High Street i 1611. On February 10, 1616 he and Judith Shakespeare were married during a period of the church year when marriages were forbidden without a license. The couple were summoned before the consistory court in Worcester and, when they failed t appear, were excommunicated. Shortly after the marriage, on March 26, 1616, Quiney was brought before the Stratford court where he admitted to having had "carnal intercourse" with one Margare Wheeler, who had died in childbirth 11 days before These two incidents are probably related; that is Quiney's hasty, unlicensed marriage to Judith was probably a calculated attempt to avoid marriage with Margaret Wheeler, whose pregnancy was well advanced by February. The most striking aspect of this scandal was that on March 25 Shakespeare revised his will in a manner indicating his lack of confidence in Quiney. See Judith SHAKESPEARE.

Quiney and Judith had three children, all of whom died before reaching adulthood. In 1617 Quiney was chosen as a constable of Stratford and in 1621 as chamberlain. In 1633 he appeared to be in some financial difficulty, but as late as 1650 he was still in business as a vintner, selling wine to the Stratford corporation in that year. The idea that he left Stratford for London in 1652 is not supported by any extant evidence. He was still alive in 1655, when he bequeathed an annuity to his brother Richard. [E. I. Fripp, *Master Richard Quyny*, 1924; Mark Eccles, *Shakespeare in Warwickshire*, 1961; Hugh A. Hanley, "Shakespeare's Family in Stratford Records," *The Times Literary Supplement*, May 21, 1964.]

Quintus. In *Titus Andronicus*, one of Titus' sons. With his brother Martius, Quintus falls into the pit where Tamora's sons have thrown the body of Bassianus. He and Martius are accused of having murdered him and are executed.

R

Racine, Jean (1639–1699). French dramatist. The leading tragic playwright during the time of Louis XIV, Racine is the author of some of the best-known works of the French theatre. Beginning with *Andromaque* in 1667, he achieved fame with such plays as *Britannicus* (1669), *Bérénice* (1670) and *Phèdre* (1677).

Although he stands beside Shakespeare as one of the greatest writers of tragedy in theatrical history, Racine differs considerably from his English counterpart. The French writer sees drama as the recounting of a spiritual crisis at a particular moment, and his range of vision centers on the interaction of a small group of people at this moment of intensity. This knack of concentrating on a specific period contributes greatly to his success in delving into the mysteries of the mind of man and in evoking a psychological realism. Moreover, Racine is also able to compose his neoclassic tragedies on a rigid structure with no subplots or distractions, and applies Aristotle's rules of the dramatic unities of time, setting, and action effortlessly and effectively. Shakespeare, on the other hand, tends to treat not only the moment of crisis, but the entire development of circumstances relating to the crisis. His vision of adventure appears to take in the whole of life, a full rendering of human activity, in a form that is free and diverse, frequently mixing comic and tragic elements.

Both dramatists have the right to be called poets, yet each uses a distinctly different method. Shakespeare's style of writing brings forth all the emphatic, extraordinary, and bold qualities of the English language, coupled with a master imagination. Racine, however, creates a commanding flow of sound and music, using a vocabulary barely exceeding 1500 words. While Shakespeare's triumph is based upon the highly colored splendor of his language, Racine is able to achieve his own poetic effect through the beauties and subtleties of restraint, clarity, and refinement, and he shows that the simplest means are often capable of expressing the highest art. [Stendhal, *Racine et Shakespeare*, 2 vols., 1823, 1825.]—J.R.

Radcliffe, Samuel (1614–1648). Principal of Brasenose College, Oxford. Radcliffe is presumed to be the compiler of a commonplace book which contains several quotations from Shakespeare. Among these is a passage which, according to Radcliffe, had been inserted into a sermon given by one Nicholas Richardson at St. Mary's Church in 1620. The passage is interesting because the quotation appears to have been taken from a quarto version of *Romeo and Juliet* (II, ii, 177–182). The text as given below, however, varies from any of the known earlier versions, thus suggesting the possibility of a lost early edition of the play:

> Tis' almost morning I would haue thee gone
> And yet no farther then a wantons bird,
> That lets it hop a little from his hand,
> Like a poore prisoner, in his twisted gyues,
> Then with a silken thread plucks it back againe
> So iealous louing of his liberty. *Tragedy of Romeo and Juliet. 4⁰: pag. 84. . . .*

[E. K. Chambers, *William Shakespeare*, 1930.]

Ragozine. In *Measure for Measure*, a notorious pirate who dies in prison. The Provost, required to send Claudio's head to Angelo, sends that of Ragozine instead (IV, iii). Ragozine does not appear on stage.

Rainolds, John. See ENEMIES OF THE STAGE.

Raleigh, Sir **Walter** (1552?–1618). Poet, soldier, courtier, explorer, and historian. Raleigh's fame as an historical personage has tended to overshadow his considerable achievement as a lyric poet. Although a large portion of his work is not extant, his reputation has grown on the basis of his surviving poems.

WALTER RALEIGH. PORTRAIT BY AN UNKNOWN ARTIST. (NATIONAL PORTRAIT GALLERY)

Among these is the well-known "Nymph's Reply to the Shepherd," an ironic rebuttal of the pastoral ideal presented in Marlowe's "Passionate Shepherd" ("Come live with me and be my love"). Both Marlowe's poem and the first stanza of Raleigh's were published among the mélange of poems in THE PASSIONATE PILGRIM (1599), attributed by the printer to Shakespeare.

During the 1580's Raleigh was the queen's reigning favorite but his fortunes declined with the arrival at court of the earl of Essex and completely collapsed when Raleigh committed the grave error of marrying one of the queen's maids of honor.

The rivalry between Essex and Raleigh has led some commentators, operating on the assumption that Shakespeare was a partisan of Essex, to see satirical portraits of Raleigh variously as Diomedes or as Ajax in *Troilus and Cressida*. G. B. Harrison has suggested that a follower of Raleigh, possibly Matthew Roydon, may have written *Willobie his Avisa* (1594) as an attack on Shakespeare and the earl of Southampton in response to an alleged portrait of Raleigh as Tarquin in Shakespeare's *Rape of Lucrece*. Others have viewed Raleigh as the major figure of the so-called school of night and identified him with the figure of Don Armado in *Love's Labour's Lost*. See SCHOOL OF NIGHT. [*Willobie His Avisa*, G. B. Harrison, ed., 1926; M. C. Bradbrook, *The School of Night: A Study in the Literary Relationships of Ralegh*, 1936.]

Raleigh, Sir Walter Alexander (1861–1922). Scholar. Educated at the universities of London and Cambridge, Raleigh taught at Liverpool and Glasgow before assuming the position of professor of English literature at Oxford in 1904. There he achieved a popular following comparable to that of Sir Arthur Quiller-Couch at Cambridge. He was knighted in 1911. Disavowing elaborate theories and systems, his method was to exhibit what was great in literature by reading selected passages and commenting on them. This is basically the same method he used in his books, most of which are extended appreciative essays on the major English authors—Milton, Wordsworth, Shakespeare, and Johnson. His first book, *The English Novel* (1891), was a pioneer effort in the field, and his *Robert Louis Stevenson* (1895) appeared the year following the novelist's death. His *Shakespeare* (1907), written for the English Men of Letters series, is still a good general introduction. Raleigh also edited *Johnson on Shakespeare* (1908), a collection of relevant documents and an adequate selection of notes.

Ralph Roister Doister. A comedy by Nicholas Udall (1505–1556). First performed about 1553, the play is the earliest extant English comedy to employ the five-act construction of Roman comedy. The main character is derived from the *miles gloriosus* (braggart warrior) figure of Roman comedy, a type to which Falstaff bears some resemblance.

Rambures, Lord (d. 1415). Master of the French crossbows at Agincourt. In *Henry V*, Rambures joins the other French nobles in discrediting English courage before the battle (III, vii). Rambures is later listed among the casualties.

Rape of Lucrece, The. A narrative poem by Shakespeare.

Text. The poem was entered for copyright in the

LVCRECE.

LONDON.

Printed by Richard Field, for Iohn Harriſon, and are to be ſold at the ſigne of the white Greyhound in Paules Churh-yard. 1594.

TITLE PAGE OF THE QUARTO OF *The Rape of Lucrece* (1594).

Stationers' Register on May 9, 1594 and printed in the same year with the title: "Lucrece. London. Printed by Richard Field, for Iohn Harrison, and are to be sold at the signe of the white Greyhound in Paules Churhyard. 1594." FIELD, a native of Stratford, had also printed *Venus and Adonis*. *Lucrece* was dedicated as follows:

> To the Right Honourable, Henry Wriothesley, Earle of Southhampton, and Baron of Titchfield. The love I dedicate to your Lordship is without end: wherof this Pamphlet without beginning is but a superfluous Moity. The warrant I have of your Honourable disposition, not the worth of my untutored Lines makes it assured of acceptance. What I have done is yours, what I have to doe is yours, being part in all I have, devoted yours. Were my worth greater, my duety would shew greater, meane time, as it is, it is bound to your Lordship; To whom I wish long life still lengthned with all happinesse. Your Lordships in all duety. William Shakespeare.

The poem was reprinted seven times before 1640 and was surpassed in popularity only by its predecessor, *Venus and Adonis*. It is written in a seven-line stanza, rhyming *a b a b b c c*, called rhyme royal.

The text of the Quarto is a good one; like that of *Venus and Adonis*, it was carefully printed and probably set up from the author's FAIR COPY. Shakespeare may himself have seen it through the press and read and corrected proof.

Date. In his dedication to *Venus and Adonis*,

Shakespeare promised to honor his patron with "some graver labour." This is generally regarded as a reference to *Lucrece,* thus fixing the date of composition between the publication of *Venus and Adonis* in 1593 and the entry of *Lucrece* in the Stationers' Register, 1594.

Sources. The primary source is the story of Lucrece as told by Ovid in his *Fasti,* a work not translated into English by 1594. Secondary sources are Livy's *History of Rome* (*Ab urbe condita Libri,* Book I, chapters 57–59); a paraphrase of the tale in English in William Painter's *Palace of Pleasure* (1566 and 1575); Chaucer's version of the story in his *Legend of Good Women* (lines 1680–1883); and another version by John Gower in his *Confessio Amantis* (1390, 1393). Most of these earlier versions are considerably shorter than Shakespeare's poem, which runs to 1855 lines. Its episodes, sentiment, and tone are like those in Samuel Daniel's *Complaint of Rosamond* (1592), a narrative poem in which the spirit of Rosamond Clifford, the mistress of Henry II, laments her fate.

Argument. *The Rape of Lucrece* is prefaced by an "argument," or summary, of the action. This Argument may have been written by Shakespeare; if so, however, it contains some details which are strangely inconsistent with the poem. For example, the Argument speaks of Lucrece's sending two messengers after the flight of Tarquin, while the poem itself mentions only one. If the Argument was written by Shakespeare, it is one of the few extant examples of his non-dramatic prose. The text is given below.

> Lucius Tarquinius, for his excessive pride surnamed Superbus, after he had caused his own father-in-law Servius Tullius to be cruelly murdered, and, contrary to the Roman laws and customs, not requiring or staying for the people's suffrages, had possessed himself of the kingdom, went, accompanied with his sons and other noblemen of Rome to besiege Ardea. During which siege the principal men of the army meeting one evening at the tent of Sextus Tarquinius, the king's son, in their discourses after supper every one commended the virtues of his own wife; among whom Collatinus extolled the incomparable chastity of his wife Lucretia. In that pleasant humour they all posted to Rome; and intending, by their secret and sudden arrival, to make trial of that which everyone had before avouched, only Collatinus finds his wife, though it were late in the night, spinning amongst her maids: the other ladies were all found dancing and revelling, or in several disports. Whereupon the noblemen yielded Collatinus the victory, and his wife the fame. At that time Sextus Tarquinius being inflamed with Lucrece' beauty, yet smothering his passions for the present, departed with the rest back to the camp; from whence he shortly after privily withdrew himself, and was, according to his estate, royally entertained and lodged by Lucrece at Collatium. The same night he treacherously stealeth into her chamber, violently ravished her, and early in the morning speedeth away. Lucrece, in this lamentable plight, hastily dispatcheth messengers, one to Rome for her father, another to the camp for Collatine. They came, the one accompanied with Junius Brutus, the other with Publius Valerius; and finding Lucrece attired in mourning habit, demanded the cause of her sorrow. She, first taking an oath of them for her revenge, revealed the actor, and whole manner of his dealing, and withal suddenly stabbed herself. Which done, with one consent they all vowed to root out the whole hated family of the Tarquins; and bearing the dead body to Rome, Brutus acquainted the people with the doer and manner of the vile deed, with a bitter invective against the tyranny of the king: wherewith the people were so moved, that with one consent and a general acclamation the Tarquins were all exiled, and the state government changed from kings to consuls.

Comment. Some of Shakespeare's contemporaries found the eroticism of *Venus and Adonis* offensive. Doubtless to avoid a repetition of this sort of criticism, he wrote a second work that he hoped would establish the moral soundness of his Muse. To accomplish this purpose he chose another story from Ovid, which, as he retold it, became an exaltation of chastity and an execration of lust. The work betrays an even greater indulgence in rhetorical artifice than he had shown in his first poem. In fact, the poet directed more of his invention to the decoration of his theme than to the theme itself. As Douglas Bush writes, "Declamation roars while Passion sleeps." For example, while Tarquin is standing beside Lucrece's bed, mad to possess her, she devotes 80 lines to an attempt to dissuade him from the rape. After the deed is done, the poem becomes Lucrece's long lament:

> Thus ebbs and flows the current of her sorrow,
> And time doth weary time with her complaining.
>
> (1569–1570)

Line 1298 of the poem reads, "Conceit and grief an eager combat fight"—and conceit is the obvious winner. Whatever beauty a modern reader can find in *The Rape of Lucrece* is the music of sorrow that rings on many occasions and in many keys throughout the poem. Yet, the popularity of the poem was equaled only by that of *Venus and Adonis.* By 1616 it had run through 6 editions and a poetic anthology compiled at the end of the 1590's contained 19 quotations from *Lucrece.*

Joseph Quincy Adams points out that Henry Willoughby's *Willobie his Avisa,* which came out in the same year as *The Rape of Lucrece,* is both an imitation of Shakespeare's poem and a tribute to it. He advertises it as insinuating "how honest maids and women should be on their guard considering the glory and praise that commends a spotless life." He declares that his purpose is to celebrate a "Britain Lucrecia." In 1600 Thomas Middleton wrote a continuation of Shakespeare's poem, in the same stanza, entitled *The Ghost of Lucrece,* of which a unique copy is in the Folger Library. [*Poems,* New Variorum Edition, Hyder E. Rollins, ed., 1938; Douglas Bush, *Mythology and the Renaissance Tradition in English Literature,* 1932, rev. ed. 1963; Don Cameron Allen, "Some Observations on the Rape of Lucrece," *Shakespeare Survey 15,* 1962.]—O.J.C.

Ratcliff or **Radcliffe, Sir Richard** (d. 1485). One of Richard III's chief advisors and included, with Sir Francis LOVEL and Sir William Catesby, in Colingbourne's insulting couplet about Richard's reign. In *Richard III,* Ratcliff supervises the execution of Rivers, Grey, and Vaughan at Pomfret Castle (III, ii) and is present at the battle of Bosworth Field, where he is killed.

Ratseis Ghost. An anonymous pamphlet published in 1605 which provides information about traveling acting companies in Elizabethan England. The tract also contains an allusion to *Hamlet* and a reference to a successful actor thought by some to be Shakespeare. The references occur in a chapter describing a fictional encounter between Gamaliell Ratsey, a highwayman, and a troupe of strolling players. The incident is evidence of the impecunious condition of acting companies traveling in the provinces. See PROVINCIAL TOURS.

The alleged Shakespearean reference occurs in Ratsey's description of certain players:

> . . . whom Fortune hath so wel favored that, what by penny-sparing and long practise of playing, are growne so wealthy that they have expected to be knighted, or at least to be conjunct in authority and to sit with men of great worship on the bench of justice . . . . Get thee to London, for if one man were dead, they will have much neede of such a one as thou art. There would be none in my opinion fitter then thyselfe to play his parts. My conceipt is such of thee, that I durst venture all the money in my purse on thy head to play Hamlet with him for a wager. There thou shalt learne to be frugall,—for players were never so thriftie as they are now about London—and to feed upon all men, to let none feede upon thee; to make thy hand stranger to thy pocket, thy hart slow to performe thy tongues promise; and when thou feelest thy purse well lined, buy thee some place or lordship in the country, that, growing weary of playing, thy mony may there bring thee to dignitie and reputation; then thou needest care for no man, nor not for them that before made thee prowd with speaking their words upon the stage.

The allusion to the affluent player who buys himself "some place . . . in the country" is regarded by some as a reference to Shakespeare's purchase of New Place in 1597, although it is much more likely a reference to Edward Alleyn, the leading actor of his day, who in 1605 purchased a country home at Dulwich. [J. O. Halliwell-Phillipps, *Outlines of the Life of Shakespeare*, 1881.]

Ravenscroft, Edward (1650–1697). Dramatist. Ravenscroft's revisions of earlier plays include an adaptation of *Titus Andronicus* produced in 1686. He was educated at Middle Temple, where he wrote his first play while recuperating from an illness. His best-received play was *The London Cuckolds* (1681), an enormously popular slapstick farce which continued to be played for 70 years. Ravenscroft's version of Shakespeare's play is titled *Titus Andronicus, or the Rape of Lavinia*. It includes a prefaced Address which is often cited in connection with Shakespeare's authorship of *Titus* (see DISINTEGRATION):

> I think it a greater theft to Rob the dead of their Praise, than the Living of their Money. That I may not appear Guilty of such a Crime, 'tis necessary I should acquaint you, that there is a Play in Mr. *Shakespears* Volume under the name of *Titus Andronicus,* from whence I drew part of this. I have been told by some anciently conversant with the Stage, that it was not Originally his, but brought by a private Author to be Acted, and he only gave some Master-touches to one or two of the Principal Parts or Characters; . . .

Ravenscroft's version of *Titus Andronicus* does not differ markedly from Shakespeare's play. There are minor structural changes and some condensation, but the only really noteworthy alteration is a rather limited shift in emphasis away from scenes of physical horror. Quintus and Martius do not fall into Aaron's pit, but are discovered looking into it. Titus' hand is not cut off onstage, and the celebrated scene in which the various dismembered organs are carried offstage is altered so that Lavinia does not carry Titus' hand in her mouth. That grisly task is not eliminated, however, merely assigned to the child Junius (young Lucius). Ravenscroft's intention seems to have been to save the real horrors for the end. Aaron spends the entire last scene on the rack before he is finally burned to death—an original elaboration of the action in Shakespeare.

An occasional modernization and a few rewritten passages are Ravenscroft's only changes in Shakespeare's diction. See TITUS ANDRONICUS: *Stage History.*

Rawlidge, Richard (fl. 1628). Author of a pamphlet against immoderate drinking. Rawlidge's *A Monster Lately Found out and Discovered or the Scourging of Tiplers* (1628) includes a diatribe against the theatres as places "filled with . . . sinnes." Rawlidge also alludes to the prohibition of the inn theatres: the Bell, Cross Keys, Bull, and Bel Savage, which he identifies not by name but by location. About 1596 these inns, which were located within the city of London, were forced to cease operation as theatres, and the players, in Rawlidge's words, were "thrust . . . out of the Citty." Rawlidge expresses fairly accurately the Puritans' rationale:

> London hath within the memory of man lost much of hir pristine lustre, . . . by being . . . filled with . . . sinnes, which . . . are . . . maintained, in Play-houses, Ale-houses, Bawdy-houses, Dicing-houses, . . . All which houses, and traps for Gentlemen, and others, of such Receipt, were formerly taken notice of by many Citizens, and well disposed graue Gentlemen . . . whervpon some of the pious magistrates made humble suit to the late Queene Elizabeth of euer-living memorie, and her priuy Counsaile, and obteined leaue from her Majesty to thrust those Players out of the Citty and to pull downe the Dicing houses: which accordingly was affected, and the Play-houses in *Gracious street, Bishopsgate-street,* nigh *Paules,* that on *Ludgate* hill, the *White-Friars* were put down, and other lewd houses quite supprest within the Liberties, by the care of those religious senators, . . . and surely had all their successors followed their worthy stepps, sinne would not at this day haue beene so powerfull, and raigning as it is.

[E. K. Chambers, *The Elizabethan Stage*, 1923.]

Raworth, Robert (fl. 1602–1647). London printer. Raworth printed, in octavo, the eighth edition of *Venus and Adonis* (1602). His shop was located in Old Fish, near St. Mary Magdalene's Church. Raworth's edition of *Venus and Adonis* introduced a number of new readings into the poem. He also published Thomas Heywood's *English Traveller* (1633) and an edition of the Italian pastoral play *Il Pastor Fido*. [*The Poems*, New Variorum Edition, Hyder Rollins, ed., 1938.]

recusancy. In Elizabethan England the refusal, particularly on the part of Roman Catholics, to acknowledge the authority of the Church of England. The Act of Supremacy (1559), issued in the first year of Elizabeth's reign, affirmed the authority of the queen in religious matters. This was followed by an Act of Uniformity which enforced attendance of the laity at Church of England services on Sundays and holy days. Failure to attend services usually resulted in a fine and occasionally in imprisonment. At the beginning of Elizabeth's reign almost all recusants were Catholic, but as Puritan disaffection with Anglicanism grew, more and more Puritans became recusants. In 1591, in the wake of rumors of a second Spanish Armada, a royal proclamation was issued calling for a commission in each county to report on the names and activities of "Popish recusants." Among the list of returns for Stratford in 1592 is the name "Mr. John Shakespeare," the poet's father. Some scholars, notably Edgar I. Fripp, the Stratford historian, have argued that John Shakespeare's recusancy was a result of his Puritan, not Catholic, sympathies, but most authorities reject this idea (see John Shakespeare). Included in the same list of recusants were a George Bardolfe and a William Fluellen, two names used by Shakespeare for characters in *1* and *2 Henry IV* and *Henry V*.

In 1606 the discovery of the Gunpowder Plot led to new antirecusant regulations, including a fine for failure to receive Communion on Easter Sunday. The purpose of the regulation was to punish "persons popishly affected." Among 21 persons in Stratford who were charged with this offense in that year was Susanna Shakespeare, the poet's elder daughter. The record indicates that she did not immediately appear to answer the charge; when she did later appear, she was dismissed without penalty. Other persons on the list included Hamnet and Judith Sadler, godparents to Shakespeare's two other children, and two persons, John Wheeler and his son John, whose names were also on the 1592 recusant list with John Shakespeare's. The weight of the evidence seems to indicate Susanna's Catholic sympathies, but this must be counterbalanced by the fact that the following year she married Dr. John Hall, who was, from all accounts, a staunch Puritan. See religion. [John de Groot, *The Shakespeares and The Old Faith*, 1946; Hugh A. Hanley, "Shakespeare's Family in Stratford Records," *The Times Literary Supplement*, May 21, 1964.]

Recuyell of the Histories of Troy. See William Caxton.

Red Bull theatre. London theatre located in Clerkenwell, Middlesex, to the north of the city. The Red Bull was built shortly before 1606; the original lease was held by Aaron Holland. According to the *Historia Histrionica* (1699) of James Wright, the Red Bull as well as the Globe and Fortune "were large houses, and lay partly open to the weather: and there they always acted by daylight."

The patent granted to Queen Anne's Men in 1609 indicates that their usual houses were the Curtain and the Red Bull. This company was the first to use the Red Bull, beginning at some time between 160[illegible] and 1606, remaining there until at least 1617 (and probably playing there intermittently until 1619) when they are supposed to have moved to the Cockpit theatre in Drury Lane. See Worcester's Men.

The Red Bull was noted for the rowdiness and vulgarity of its clientele; according to Wright, it and the Fortune "were mostly frequented by citizens and the meaner sort of people." In May 1610 a group of men were summoned before the Middlesex justices of the peace and charged with having committed "a notable outrage at the playhouse called the Red Bull." In March 1614 one Alexander Fulsis was charged with picking a pocket of a purse and £3 at the theatre. The bad reputation of the place was alluded to by many writers of satire. George Wither, in his *Abuses Stript, and Whipt* (1613), a collection of satirical writings, remarks of a bad poet that

> His poetry is such as he can cull
> From plays he heard at Curtain or at Bull.

In *Albumazar* (1614), a play by Thomas Tomkis, a character says:

> Then will I confound her with compliments drawn from the plays I see at the Fortune and Red Bull, where I learn all the words I speak and understand not.

Edmund Gayton's pamphlet, *Pleasant Notes upon Don Quixot* (1654), bears evidence of his contempt for that theatre and its actors:

> I have heard that the poets of the Fortune and Red Bull had always a mouth-measure for their actors (who were terrible tear-throats) and made their lines proportionable to their compass, which were sesquipedales, a foot and a half.

The plays with which the Red Bull acting companies amused the citizenry included the Queen's Men's productions of Thomas Heywood's *The Rape of Lucrece* (between 1603 and 1608); John Webster's *The White Devil* (between 1609 and 1612); *The Birth of Merlin* (c. 1608), an anonymous work attributed to "William Shakespear and William Rowley"; and Heywood's *Ages* plays—*The Golden Age* (c. 1611), *The Silver Age* (c. 1612), *The Brazen Age* (c. 1613), and *The Iron Age* (c. 1613). In 1637 Thomas Heywood wrote a special Prologue and Epilogue for his play *Pleasant Diologues and Dramma's* with the following note:

> A young witty lad playing the part of Richard the third: at the Red Bull: the Author because hee was interested in the play to incourage him, wrot him this Prologue and Epilogue.

E. K. Chambers interprets this as alluding to an exceptional performance of Shakespeare's *Richard III*, probably at some time before 1619.

Some scholars conjecture that in 1619 at the death of their patron, Queen Anne, some of the members of the Red Bull company remained at the theatre, while others, such as Christopher Beeston, joined Prince Charles' Men at the Cockpit. When he left, according to legal records, Beeston took "all the furniture and apparell." At some time before 1625 the Red Bull was altered and enlarged; however, little is known of the companies which played there after that time. The "Red Bull Company" is cited in an entry in the office-book of Sir Henry Herbert, the Master of the Revels:

> Received from Mr. Hemming, in their company's name, to forbid the playing of Shakespeare's plays, to the Red Bull Company, this 11 of April, 1627,—5l. 0. 0.

The "Mr. Hemming" is John Heminges, business manager of the King's Men, Shakespeare's company, until his death. Whichever company occupied the Red Bull, in London it apparently was familiarly called the Red Bull company, while in the provinces it was called the King's company. The latter was probably the same group which in 1629 received a royal patent as "His Majesty's servants for the city of York." Scholars speculate that they may have comprised the remnants of the old Prince Charles' Men and other companies which had survived the long closing of the theatres because of the plague in 1625.

The Red Bull continued in use until the Commonwealth, and some performances were probably given during the time the theatres were supposed to be officially closed. It was reopened at the Restoration and remained in use until 1663. It has been suggested that during this latter period the theatre was roofed over, but Chambers tends to accept the word of Wright that it was "open to the weather." [E. K. Chambers, *The Elizabethan Stage*, 1923; George F. Reynolds, *The Staging of Elizabethan Plays at the Red Bull Theater 1605–1625*, 1940.]

Redgrave, Sir **Michael [Scudamore]** (1908–). Actor, producer, author, director, and theatre manager. Born in Bristol, Redgrave was educated at Cambridge, and was a schoolmaster for a short period. His professional acting debut was in Liverpool in 1934; he played with the Liverpool Repertory Company for the next two years. In 1936 he began to act with the Old Vic in such roles as Ferdinand (*Love's Labour's Lost*), Orlando (*As You Like It*), Laertes, and Chorus (*Henry V*). In 1937 he joined Sir John Gielgud's company at the Queen's and played Bolingbroke in *Richard II*. He did Aguecheek in the Phoenix's 1938 presentation of *Twelfth Night*, and Macbeth at the Aldwych in 1947 and again in New York in 1948. He played with the Old Vic in 1950 as Berowne and Hamlet. His Hamlet was also given at the Zurich and Holland festivals and at Elsinore's Kronborg Castle in 1950.

In 1951 he acted with the Shakespeare Memorial Theatre at Stratford-upon-Avon as Richard II and Hotspur and directed *2 Henry IV*. In 1953 he was again with the Memorial Theatre as Shylock, Lear, and Antony in *Antony and Cleopatra*. His performance in *Tiger at the Gates* in New York won him great acclaim. In 1958 he was again at Stratford as Hamlet and Benedick in *Much Ado About Nothing*. He also performed Hamlet in Moscow and Leningrad in 1958/9, and gave solo performances of Shakespeare in Holland and Hungary.

He has made many films since 1938, has written two plays, *The Seventh Man* and *Circus Boy*, and adapted Henry James' *Aspern Papers* for the stage. He was knighted in 1959. His books include *The Actor's Ways and Means* (1955), *Mask or Face* (1958), and *The Mountebank's Tale* (1959), a novel. [*Who's Who in the Theatre*, 1961.]

Red Lion Inn. Elizabethan playing-inn. The only extant reference to the Red Lion Inn occurs in the following memorandum which deals with the quality of workmanship in constructing scaffolding in the innyard:

> Courte holden the xv[th] daie of Julie 1567, Annoque Regni Reginae Eliz. nono by M[r] William Ruddoke, M[r] Richard More, Henrye Whreste & Richard Smarte wardeins, & M[r] Bradshawe. Memorandum that at courte holden the daie & yeare abovesayd that, whear certaine varyaunce, discord & debate was betwene Wyllyam Sylvester carpenter on thone partie & John Brayen grocer on thother partie, yt is agreed, concluded & fullie determyned by the saide parties . . . that Wyllyam Buttermore, . . . [et al] . . . shall with expedicon goe & peruse suche defaultes as are & by them shalbe found of in & aboute suche skaffoldes, as he the said Willyam hathe mad at the house called the Red Lyon in the parishe of Stebinyhuthe, & the said Willyam Sillvester shall repaire & amend the same with their advize substancyallie, as they shall thinke good. And that the said John Brayne, on Satterdaie next ensuenge the date above written, shall paye to the said Willyam Sylvester the some of eight poundes, tenne shillinges, lawfull money of England, & that after the playe, which is called the storye of Sampson, be once plaied at the place aforesaid the said John shall deliver to the said Willyam such bondes as are now in his custodie for the performaunce of the bargaine . . . .

Chambers suggests that John Brayne, grocer, was the brother-in-law of James Burbage, who financed the construction of Burbage's Theatre in 1576. Stebinyhuthe was probably the parish of Stepney in Middlesex, then located east of the city of London, past Whitechapel, and not within the city's jurisdiction. [E. K. Chambers, *The Elizabethan Stage*, 1923.]

Reed, Isaac (1742–1807). Scholar. An attorney and bibliophile, Reed collected a magnificent library which many scholars, including Dr. Johnson and Edmund Malone, used. Reed himself was the editor of *Biographia Dramatica* (2 vols., 1782), a valuable biographical history of English drama. In 1785 he revised his friend George Steevens' edition of Shakespeare (10 vols.). After Steevens' death, Reed completed and published that editor's expanded edition which ran to 21 volumes and is known as the First Variorum (1803). Reed was characterized by Joseph Ritson as "superior to all others in his knowledge of English literature." See VARIORUM EDITIONS.

Regan. In *King Lear*, the second daughter of the King. Although lacking the forceful and fierce qualities of her sister Goneril, Regan is capable of no less cruelty. To many the pettiness of her personality renders her more loathsome than her sister. A. C. Bradley (*Shakespearean Tragedy*, 1904) found her "the most hideous human being . . . that Shakespeare ever drew."

Reggio, Pietro. See MUSIC BASED ON SHAKESPEARE: *17th century*.

Rehan, Ada. Real name **Crehan** (1860–1916). American actress. Born in Limerick, Ireland, Ada

Rehan was educated in Brooklyn and made her first appearance on the stage in Newark in 1874 in *Across the Continent*. The following year she joined the Drews' stock company in Philadelphia, and then journeyed to Louisville, where she played Ophelia in Edwin Booth's *Hamlet*. She was, however, essentially a comedienne. From 1879 to 1899 she played with Augustin Daly's company in more than 200 roles, including Bianca, Celia, Rosalind, Cordelia, Desdemona, Lady Anne, Mistress Ford, Olivia, Viola, Katharine (*Henry V*), Ursula, Beatrice, Helena, Princess of France, Julia, Miranda, and Portia. Her most famous role was Katharina in *The Taming of the Shrew*, which she first played in an 1887 New York production which also included the Induction for the first time in that city.

She made her first London appearance at Toole's Theatre in 1884, revisiting that city in 1886, 1888, 1890, 1893, and 1895. Following Daly's death, she toured the United States in *The Taming of the Shrew, The Merchant of Venice, Twelfth Night, School for Scandal, Much Ado About Nothing*, and *Twelfth Night*. She made her last appearance on the stage in 1906. [*Who's Who in the Theatre*, 1914.]

Reignier or **Regnier, René**, duke of **Anjou** (1409–1480). Also king of Naples, Sicily, and Jerusalem. René attended the coronation of Charles VII of France in 1429. On coming into possession of the duchy of Lorraine, he was challenged by Antoine de Vaudémont, who gained the help of the Burgundians. After his capture by Burgundy in 1431, René was imprisoned for a year and then released on parole. Again made a prisoner in 1435, René was ransomed after two years. He participated in the peace parley of 1444 at Tours, and as a consequence his daughter Margaret was married to Henry VI of England. In *1 Henry VI*, Reignier loyally supports the Dauphin and Joan (La Pucelle). When the Earl of Suffolk captures his daughter Margaret, Reignier acquiesces to her marriage with Henry VI.

Reinhardt, Max. Real name **Goldmann** (1873–1943). Viennese-born theatre manager, producer, and director. Reinhardt began his theatrical career as an actor with the Salzburg Stadt Theater in 1893. In 1894 he made his Berlin debut at the Deutsches Theatre, with which he maintained a long association. In 1902 he began managing the Kleines Theatre in Berlin, but the following year ceased to act, and devoted all his creative energies to producing and directing. Among his most famous productions were *Oedipus Rex*, the *Oresteia*, and *Faust* in Berlin in 1911. In 1912 he brought *Oedipus Rex* to Covent Garden, where it was much acclaimed. In 1920 Reinhardt founded the Salzburg Festival and every year gave his production there of *Jedermann*, the morality play *Everyman* as adapted by Hugo von Hofmannsthal.

Reinhardt's many notable productions include *A Midsummer Night's Dream* (Covent Garden, 1912; Oxford University Dramatic Society, 1933; and Hollywood, 1934), *Macbeth, Julius Caesar, Hamlet, The Comedy of Errors*, and *Agamemnon*. In 1933, when Hitler came to power in Germany, Reinhardt took up residence in the United States, where he worked until his death. Reinhardt believed that the theatre was a medium to be considered separately from dramatic literature and his productions were noted for their many innovations in staging: the use of visual devices, the arena stage, and the effective use of crowds. [*Who's Who in the Theatre*, 1939; *Oxford Companion to the Theatre*, Phyllis Hartnoll, ed., 1951.]

religion. There are two major problems which arise in considering the relationship of religion and Shakespeare. The first is the fairly concrete biographical problem of his religious affiliation, Anglican, Catholic, or Puritan. The second is the not entirely unrelated, but more remote and conjectural problem of the religious values (or lack of them) which inhere in his plays. The latter problem has received considerable attention in recent years; the answer to the former continues to elude researchers.

As with most famous Shakespearean conundrums the facts concerning his denominational adherence have been obscured by the prejudices and *a priori* theorizing of the commentators. Catholic students such as H. S. Bowden (*The Religion of Shakespeare*, 1899) and Clara Longworth de Chambrun (*Shakespeare, A Portrait Restored*, 1957), see Shakespeare as a staunch adherent of the old faith, while Protestants, such as the Reverend Thomas Carter (*Shakespeare, Puritan and Recusant*, 1897), view him as a child of the Reformation. Notable among scholars who argue that Shakespeare was an orthodox member of the Church of England are Joseph Quincy Adams (*A Life of William Shakespeare*, 1923) and Sidney Lee (*A Life of William Shakespeare*, 1898).

As far as the biographical issues are concerned, it is generally conceded that Shakespeare's father was a Catholic (see John SHAKESPEARE) and it has recently been discovered that the poet's daughter Susanna was listed with a group of recusants in 1607 (see Susanna SHAKESPEARE; RECUSANCY). Stratford itself, in the 16th century, was fairly well divided in the matter of religious preferences. Although the governing body of the town, the Stratford corporation, had become pronouncedly Puritan by the end of Shakespeare's life, in his formative years it apparently did not display any religious preference. The schoolmaster at the Stratford grammar school from 1571 to 1575, years during which Shakespeare would have been in attendance, was Simon HUNT, who later became a Jesuit. Shakespeare's friends and relatives included members of both faiths. His son-in-law John Hall was apparently an ardent Protestant, while the will of his maternal grandfather, Robert Arden, with its reference to "the blessed Lady St. Mary," is that of a Catholic. Among his London acquaintances, his patron, the earl of Southampton, was the scion of one of the leading Catholic families in Elizabethan England, and the family with which he lodged for a time in London, the Mountjoys, were French Huguenots.

Religious allusions in Elizabethan plays were limited by government censorship. Nevertheless, it can be seen that Shakespeare toned down the anti-Catholicism of his source in writing *King John* (see KING JOHN: *Sources*) and that he betrayed a noticeable lack of anticlerical bias in his characterizations of the friars in *Romeo and Juliet* and *Measure for Measure*. On the other hand, in *Macbeth* he did not hesitate to condemn the Jesuit doctrine of EQUIVOCATION or to use Samuel Harsnett's anti-Catholic *Declaration of Egregious Popish Impostures* as an important source for *King Lear*.

In 1611 the historian John Speed, addressing a poemic to the Jesuit Robert Parsons, alluded to Parsons and Shakespeare as "this Papist and his Poet." The proprietary "his" may or may not be significant. However, it seems reasonable to expect that if Shakespeare's Catholicism was public knowledge, there would have been references to it in contemporary allusions to him.

According to Richard DAVIES, writing at the end of the 17th century, Shakespeare "dyed a Papist," a view to which E. K. Chambers and J. O. Halliwell-Phillipps were inclined to lend credence. But Davies' phrase seems to imply a late conversion rather than a lifelong adherence. G. B. Harrison, arguing from a Catholic position, suggests that Shakespeare was in his early life a Catholic, that he lapsed into skepticism during the period of the tragedies and problem plays, and that he was subsequently reconciled to Catholicism. Despite this and other more or less plausible conjectures, the tendency among scholars in the absence of convincing contrary evidence, is to view Shakespeare as a conforming member of the Church of England.

It is in the second problem, however, that of the religious values in the plays, that scholars and critics of the 20th century have been more interested. This interest derives, as does so much of modern Shakespearean criticism, from a formulation in A. C. Bradley's *Shakespearean Tragedy* (1904). Bradley asserts that "Elizabethan drama was almost wholly secular" and that Shakespeare's tragic cosmos is one on which no theological observation impinges. Bradley was not denying that Shakespeare himself was a man of faith, but merely emphasizing that he rigorously excluded the religious view from his tragedies. In the Bradleyan conception of tragedy, death was the ultimate, irremediable fact into which the Christian doctrine of eternal life and redemption represented an irreconcilable intrusion. The view contrary to Bradley's is said to develop from the criticism of G. Wilson Knight, although Knight himself denies any attempt to fix his interpretation within an orthodox Christian mold (see SYMBOLISM). Knight and some of the more orthodox Christian interpreters of the plays do, however, share some of the assumptions of MYTHIC CRITICISM, particularly those which relate tragedy to the ritual sacrifice of the hero who atones for the sins of the community. Other Christian analyses, such as Paul N. Siegel's *Shakespearean Tragedy and the Elizabethan Compromise* (1957), attempt to find the basis of Shakespearean tragedy in Renaissance Christian humanism and the medieval allegorical tradition which lay behind it. The tendency to view the plays as representative of Biblical analogies and allegories is also pronounced in the essays of Roy W. Battenhouse, in G. R. Elliott's *Dramatic Providence in Macbeth* (1958), in J. A. Bryant's *Hippolyta's View* (1961), and in M. D. H. Parker's *The Slave of Life* (1955). A sharp corrective to these views has been issued by Roland M. Frye (*Shakespeare and Christian Doctrine*, 1963), who criticizes the "theologizing analyses of the School of Knight." Frye argues that the plays are filled with theological allusions but that these allusions are peripheral, not essential, to the design of the plays. [John H. De Groot, *The Shakespeares and The Old Faith*, 1946; G. B. Harrison, "Shakespeare's Religion," *Commonweal*, XLVIII, July 2, 1948; M. D. H. Parker, *The Slave of Life*, 1955; Roy W. Battenhouse, "Shakespearean Tragedy: A Christian Approach," and Sylvan Barnet, "Some Limitations of a Christian Approach to Shakespeare," *ELH*, XXII, 1955; Aldous Huxley, "Shakespeare and Religion," *Show*, February, 1964.]—E.Q.

religious life in Elizabethan England. Despite the prominence of religious life in Elizabethan England, Elizabeth's reign was, at least in the early years, a time of relative freedom and peace; this is particularly true if her reign is compared with the tumult and religious suppression of the reigns of Edward VI and Mary before her and the Puritan era after her. One of Elizabeth's first concerns as queen was to effect a religious settlement that would establish religious and national unity under the crown. Noncommittal herself, she re-established the Protestant prayer book, but with alterations designed to make it more palatable to the Catholics. The Elizabethan prayer book became the only authorized form of worship in England and the people were required to attend services in their parish churches and were fined if they did not. For the first 10 years of the reign, the Elizabethan settlement was accepted without difficulty, most of the recalcitrant clergy being Catholic bishops appointed by Mary (see ACT OF SUPREMACY). However, the papal bull *Regnans in excelsis* (1570) of Pius V, excommunicating Elizabeth, agitated an otherwise relatively harmonious situation. Foreign seminaries began to send their missionaries into England; measures against Roman Catholics became more severe and Elizabeth's earlier tolerance was replaced with the suspicion that every Catholic, now that she was excommunicated, was a potential traitor. In the period 1570–1603, 180 Catholics were executed.

The intensification of anti-Catholic feeling led the party of reform to criticize Elizabeth's settlement as too moderate. Actually, a dissatisfied Protestant element had been foreseen by the writer of the *Devise for Alteratione of Religione* at the ascension of Elizabeth to the throne, and there was even a strong dissenting group before the death of Edward VI. Under Mary these reformers exiled themselves to Switzerland and Germany where they absorbed the teachings of Calvin. The disciplinarian controversy grew and developed and the Puritans eventually demanded that a Presbyterian discipline, like that of Geneva, be established. Of course this agitation culminated in the Puritan Revolution of the 17th century. But during Elizabeth's reign the political results of the controversy were negligible whereas the social and religious ramifications were considerable. It had the pernicious effect of seriously restricting private life and conduct with a stringent code of morals—the arts and sports, for example, were regarded as evil temptations—and the mistrust of popery amounted to an absurd prejudice which legislated against traditional forms of recreation, particularly stage plays, as the "dregs of Antichrist." See ENEMIES OF THE STAGE.

Certain books were required at religious services: the English Bible, a psalter, the Book of Common Prayer, the two tomes of the homilies, and a translation of Erasmus' *Paraphrases*. It was insisted that the readings be clear and the words distinguishable. Certain "popish" practices were eschewed, such as the overuse of the organ, the prolonged ringing of bells for a dying person ("one short peal" before burial and one after was permitted), the procession on Rogation days was conducted "without wearing any surplices, carrying of banners or hand-bells, or staying at crosses or other suchlike popish ceremonies." The most basic function of the clergy was catechism or indoctrination. The ministry, before evening prayer on every Sunday and holy day, was to hear the recitations of children, apprentices, and servants. The parents and masters of children and apprentices who failed to send their charges for instruction were inquired into; the minister had a list of these young people and called certain of them for questioning and instruction on Sundays and holy days. Failure to know the catechism was deemed a significant omission. Parishioners were required to receive Holy Communion three times a year at the least. Church attendance and the general behavior of the parishioners on Sundays and holy days were closely observed. See RELIGION. [Rev. Ronald Bayne, "Religion," *Shakespeare's England*, 1916.]—J.C.

Remaines of a Greater Worke Concerning Britain. See William CAMDEN.

René of Anjou. See René REIGNIER, or Regnier, duke of Anjou.

Replingham, William (fl. 1614). A Warwickshire attorney who was associated with his cousin Arthur Mainwaring in the attempt to enclose land in Welcombe where Shakespeare owned tithes (see ENCLOSURE). On October 28, 1614 Replingham signed an agreement with Shakespeare, assuring the latter that the proposed enclosure would not adversely affect Shakespeare's income from the land, but that if it did, Replingham would recompense Shakespeare for any loss suffered. The agreement gives similar assurance to Thomas Greene, Shakespeare's friend and kinsman, who also owned a portion of the tithes:

> Vicesimo octavo die Octobris, anno Domini 1614. Articles of agreement indented made betweene William Shackespeare, of Stretford in the county of Warwicke, gent., on the one partye, and William Replingham, of Greete Harborowe in the countie of Warwicke, gent., on the other partie, the daye and yeare abouesaid. Inter alia Item, the said William Replingham, for him, his heires, executours and assignes, doth covenaunte and agree to and with the said William Shackespeare, his heires and assignes, That he, the said William Replingham, his heires or assignes, shall, uppon reasonable request, satisfie, content and make recompence unto him, the said William Shackespeare or his assignes, for all such losse, detriment and hinderance as he, the said William Shackespeare, his heires and assignes, and one Thomas Greene, gent., shall or maye be thought, in the viewe and judgement of foure indifferent persons, to be indifferentlie elected by the said William and William, and their heires, and in default of the said William Replingham, by the said William Shackespeare or his heires onely, to survey and judge the same, to sustayne or incurre for or in respecte of the increasinge [decreasinge] of the yearelie value of the tythes they the said William Shackespeare and Thomas doe joyntlie or seuerallie hold and enioy in the said fieldes, or anie of them, by reason of anie inclosure or decaye of tyllage there ment and intended by the said William Replingham; and that the said William Replingham and his heires shall procure such sufficient securitie vnt the said William Shackespeare and his heires, fo the performance of theis covenauntes, as shalbe devised by learned counsell. In witnes whereof th parties abouesaid to theis presentes interchange ablie their handes and seales have put, the day and yeare first aboue wrytten.

[E. K. Chambers, *William Shakespeare*, 1930; F Roland Lewis, *The Shakespeare Documents*, 1940.]

Revels Accounts. Records of the expenditure involved in the performance of plays and masque at court. The Revels Accounts were drawn up b the Revels Office and presented for payment to th treasurer of the chamber, at whose office an abstrac of the Revels Accounts was recorded (see CHAMBE ACCOUNTS). The payments were made by th treasurer on warrant from the privy council unt 1614 and, after that, on warrant from the lor chamberlain. The Accounts provide a valuabl record of the history of entertainments at cour and particularly in those cases where the Account mention the name of the play for which the pay ment was to be made. The extant Accounts for th reign of Elizabeth unfortunately deal only with th period from 1571 to 1589, thus not covering an Shakespearean plays.

Two Accounts exist for the reign of James I, on for the years 1604/5 and another for 1611/2, con cerning which there has been a great deal of con troversy. These Jacobean Accounts were printed i 1842 by Peter CUNNINGHAM and their authenticit

THE 1604/1605 REVELS ACCOUNTS. (PUBLIC RECORD OFFICE)

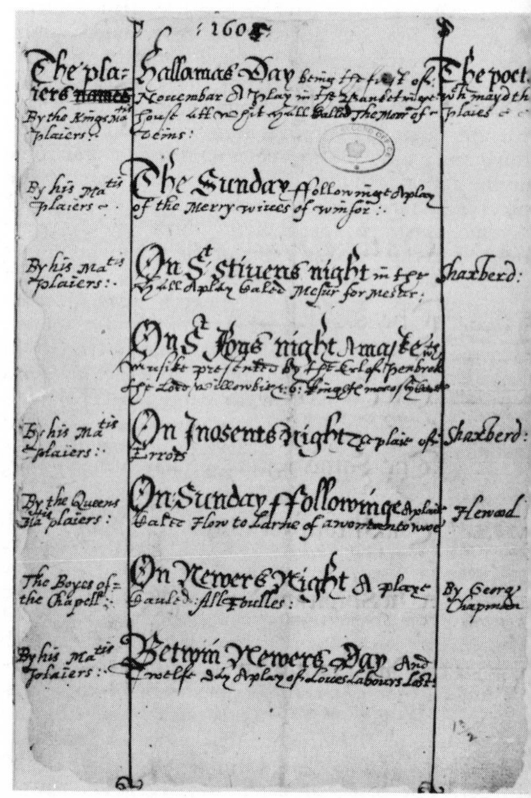

The plaiers names | Hallamas Day being the first of Nouembar A play in the Banketinge house att Whithall called The Moor of Venis: | The poets which mayd the plaies

By the Kings Matis plaiers:

By his Matis plaiers: | The Sunday ffollowinge A play of the Merry wiues of winsor:

By his Matis plaiers: | On St Stiuens night in the Hall A play Caled Mesur for Mesur: | Shaxberd:

On St Jons night A maske with musike presented by the Erll of Penbrok the Lord Willowbie & 6 knightes more of the court

By his Matis plaiers: | On Inosents Night the plaie of Errors: | Shaxberd:

By the Queens Matis plaiers: | On Sunday ffollowinge A plaie Called How to Larne of a woman to wooe: | Heiwood

The Boyes of the Chapell: | On Newers Night A playe Cauled All Foulles: | By George Chapman

By his Matis plaiers: | Betwin Newers Day And Twelfe day A play of Loues Labours Lost:

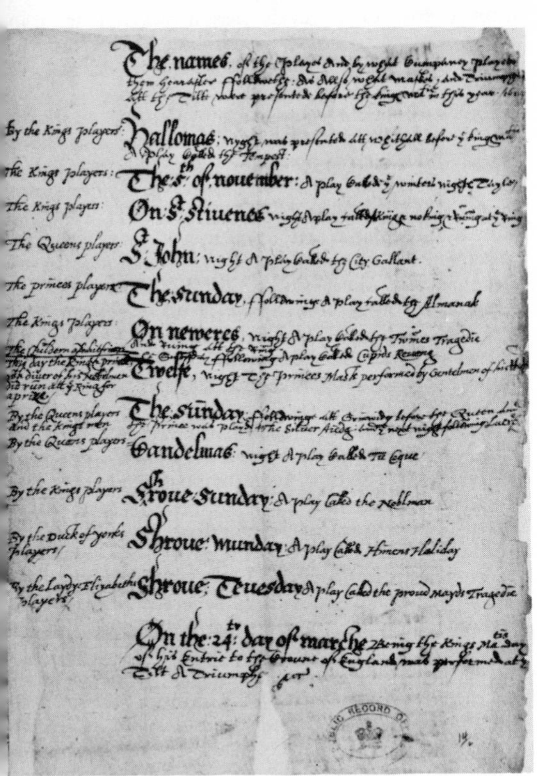

THE 1611/1612 REVELS ACCOUNTS. (PUBLIC RECORD OFFICE)

has frequently been questioned. The strongest support for their reliability comes from the so-called "Malone Scrap," an apparent extract of the Accounts included among the papers of the scholar Edmond Malone. Malone died in 1812, thus his knowledge of the Accounts would preclude the possibility of a forgery by Cunningham. Samuel A. Tannenbaum and other scholars, however, have argued that both the Accounts and the "Malone Scrap" are forgeries perpetrated by John Payne Collier, who was closely associated with Cunningham in the Shakespeare Society. Despite this suspicion, the Accounts, which have been subjected to microscopic examination, are generally regarded by scholars as genuine documents of the Jacobean period. The two entries for 1604/5 and 1611/2 are as follows:

[1604/5]

The Plaiers.		The Poets wch mayd the plaies.
By the Kings matis plaiers.	Hallamas Day being the first of Nouembar A play in the Banketinge house att Whithall called The Moor of Venis.	
By his Matis plaiers.	The Sunday ffollowinge A Play of the Merry Wiues of Winsor.	
By his Matis plaiers.	On St Stiuens Night in the Hall A Play caled Mesur for Mesur.	Shaxberd.
By his Matis plaiers.	On Inosents Night The Plaie of Errors.	Shaxberd.
By the Queens Matis plaiers.	On Sunday ffollowinge A plaie cald How to Larne of a woman to wooe.	Hewood.
The Boyes of the Chapell.	On Newers Night A playe cauled: All Foulles.	By Georg Chapman.
By his Matis Plaiers.	Betwin Newers Day and Twelfe day A Play of Loues Labours Lost.	
By his Matis plaiers.	On the 7 of January was played the play of Henry the fift.	
By his Matis plaiers.	The 8 of January A play cauled Euery on out of his Umor.	
By his Matis plaiers.	On Candelmas night A playe Euery one In his Umor.	
	The Sunday ffollowing A playe provided and discharged.	
By his Matis plaiers.	On Shrousunday A play of the Marthant of Venis.	Shaxberd.
By his Matis plaiers.	On Shroumonday A Tragidye of The Spanishe Maz.	
By his Matis players.	On Shroutusday A play cauled the Martchant of Venis againe comanded By the Kings Matie.	Shaxberd.

[1611/2]

By the Kings Players:	Hallomas nyght was presented att Whithall before ye Kinges Matie a play called the Tempest.
The Kings players:	The 5th of Nouember: A play called ye winters nightes Tayle.
The Kings players:	On St Stiuenes night A play called A King & no King.
The Queens players:	St John night x A Play called the City Gallant.

The Princes players.	The Sunday followinge A play called the Almanak.
The Kings players.	On Neweres night A play called the Twiñes Tragedie.
The Childern of Whitfriars.	The Sunday following A play called Cupids Reueng.
By the Queens players and the Kings Men.	The Sunday following [Twelfth Night] att Grinwidg before the Queen and the Prince was playd the Siluer Aiedg: and ye next night following Lucrecia.
By the Queens players.	Candelmas night A play called Tu Coque.
By the Kings players.	Shroue Sunday: A play called the Noblman.
By the Duck of Yorks players.	Shroue Sunday: A play called the Noblman.
By the Ladye Elizabeths players.	Shroue Teuesday A play called the proud Mayds Tragedie.

[E. K. Chambers, *The Elizabethan Stage*, 1923.]

Revels Office. The department of the royal household responsible for providing theatrical entertainment at court. The operation of the Revels Office was under the direction of the MASTER OF THE REVELS, who was assisted by three other officers and a large number of workmen. Their purpose was

> . . . the Apparelling, Disgyzing, ffurnishing, ffitting Garnishing & orderly setting foorthe of men, women, & Children: in sundry Tragedies, Playes, Maskes and sportes with their apte howses of paynted Canvas & properties incident suche as mighte most lyvely expresse the effect of the histories plaied & Devises in Maskes this yeare showen at the Coorte for her Maiesties Regall Disporte & Recreation.

As the above extract indicates, costuming was the major task of the Revels Office. Costumes were usually elaborate and expensive. Scenery and other stage properties were extensively used. As court entertainments became more elaborate, the task and size of the Revels Office increased.

The court revels took place during the Christmas season and at Shrovetide, the three days preceding Ash Wednesday. Preparations were begun as early as the previous October, when the Master held auditions for the plays and masques to be performed at court. After the plays were selected, a horde of carpenters, dressmakers, and property men would begin the work which would be conducted with feverish activity until the night of the performance. The average cost of a revels season was about £30 under Elizabeth and considerably more than that during the reigns of the Stuarts. See REVELS ACCOUNTS.

Under the mastership of Sir Thomas Cawarden (1545–1559), the Revels Office was located at Blackfriars. Cawarden's successor, Sir Thomas Benger (1560–1572), moved the Office to the former site of St. John of Jerusalem Hospital in 1560. There it remained until 1608 when it was moved to Whitefriars; subsequently, it was located in Cheapside, in the parish of St. Mary Bowe. [E. K. Chambers, *The Elizabethan Stage*, 1923; *Studies in the Elizabethan Theatre*, Charles T. Prouty, ed., 1961.]

revenge. One of the common motifs of Renaissance English tragedy was revenge, which was developed through three themes: God's revenge for sin or Divine Justice; public revenge for crimes against the state, which was meted out at the hands of kings; and private revenge or the individual vendetta, which was forbidden by both God and state. A brief examination of the social background of revenge tragedy is necessary before defining the genre.

Elizabethan law punished avengers who took the law into their own hands as severely as it did the original criminals, for personal vengeance was regarded not only as disrespect for the law, but also as a legacy from the not-too-distant lawless past; it was seen as a threat against the authority of the state and, by implication, against civilization itself. Religion explicitly forbade private revenge; properly, it was God's domain ("Vengeance is mine; I will repay, saith the Lord"), and theologians and preachers wrote and spoke against it from the pulpit. Some scholars believe that the Elizabethan audiences were prevented from sympathizing with the revenge hero because of their moral and religious education; at the least, the audiences were aware of official disapproval.

By the 1620's it was clear that, whatever the Elizabethan attitude had been, the Jacobeans condemned private revenge both officially and popularly. James I insisted on obedience to the law prohibiting dueling in a number of edicts (1610, 1613, and 1618). The Puritan attacks on the stage increased in number and in harshness. A proliferation of arguments was leveled against revenge by powerful moralists.

However, the very amount of sermonizing and literature against private revenge suggests that traditionally in the 16th century and the first two decades of the 17th there was strong popular sympathy for those who took revenge under certain circumstances. Personal honor was regarded by Elizabethans as a proper matter of life and death. According to popular sentiment, revenge was permissible for base injuries, acts especially bestial and dishonorable; for self-defense, when the injured party could not get redress from the state because of the lack of legal proof (the duel was the common means of retribution in these cases); and for murder, which demanded blood to restore the honor of both the victim and his kin. Especially, revenge for a murdered father was popularly regarded as a dreadful but sacred duty required for the public good. In Italy, civil law in the 16th century could, in fact, refuse the heir of a murdered man his estate until the victim was avenged. Count Romei in *The Courtiers Acad-*

nie (translated c. 1598), a document well known to nglishmen, defined the proprieties for honorable venge.

Against this contradiction between the official ode and the public sentiment, the revenge tragedies f the Renaissance, particularly *Hamlet,* should be iewed.

The two strongest influences on the development f revenge tragedy were Seneca and the Italian *ovelle.* Seneca, first translated into English about e mid-16th century, wrote tragedies characterized y blood revenge for murders or outrageous injuries, d by a multitude of horrors. Ghosts, dissembling vengers, innocent accomplices, hellish punishments, icide, and dramatic irony are all evident in Seneca's ree major blood tragedies: *Thyestes, Medea,* d *Agamemnon.* Elizabethan writers, particularly homas Kyd, adopted from Seneca the device of the host (making this supernatural sanction of revenge crease the tragic dignity of the hero), a psychogical or emotional treatment of character, and etorical trappings to display the general "philophical" approach to life on the part of the hero.

A far more important source was the Italian *ovelle* and such writings as Machiavelli's, whose ery name was to Englishmen a synonym for "vilin." Italians were notorious in England for their engeful jealousy, and for their vindictiveness in all atters of honor. Italianate revenge was always rerded with moral aversion because of the deceitful eapons and sinister intrigue attached to carrying it ut. Poison was the traditional means of vengeance, eing both safe and secret. From Italianate sources me the literary conventions of expiatory suicide; complices, often hired; occasional madness; roantic love in the person of a woman avenger; the eneral air of intrigue; the use of poison; and, most nportant, the Machiavellian villain, such as Lorenzo *The Spanish Tragedy* and Claudius in *Hamlet,* oth of whom have important roles opposing the ero. In Shakespeare, the Italianate revenge is typied by Laertes in *Hamlet,* who in his blind wrath is oth quick and bloody, but without regard for his uty as a subject, for his conscience, or even for the lvation of his soul. Beginning with Christopher arlowe's *The Jew of Malta* (c. 1589), totally alianate, villain-centered dramas began to appear. evenge is an important part of the plot structure of ese plays, but the real focus of interest is the genal villainy and evil of the central figure. The plays this sub-tradition ultimately dominate the genre n the stage of the second and third decades of the 7th century, and further testify to an implicit shift popular attitude toward total disapproval of reenge.

Thomas Kyd's *The Spanish Tragedy* (c. 1589) ecame the model for Elizabethan writers, being the rst English drama to make revenge the dominant otive of both character and plot, and leading to e final catastrophe in which murderers and avengrs alike are killed (the latter by suicide). Other evices in Kyd's play that became conventional were e use of a ghost, intrigue, violent and bloody tion, parallelisms in the development of the plot, e use of deceit to accomplish the revenge, draatic irony, justifiable hesitation on the part of the ero for reasons of moral scruple, madness due to overwhelming grief, and a Machiavellian villain. There are also a variety of minor conventions: the exhibition of the victim's body, the wearing of black by the avenger, the reading of a book before a philosophical soliloquy, letters written in blood, and melancholia in the hero, among others. A final significant characteristic of *The Spanish Tragedy* was the fact that the hero, whose motive for revenge is just and sympathetic, enters increasingly into a world of moral darkness as he attempts to carry out his vengeance; Hieronimo finally turns into the Italianate villain and forfeits by his excesses the sympathy of the audience.

The school of Kyd produced a number of plays modeled on *The Spanish Tragedy. Titus Andronicus* is one, though Shakespeare differs from Kyd in many respects. Other plays properly in this school are John Marston's *Antonio's Revenge* (c. 1599), his *The Malcontent* (1604), Cyril Tourneur's *The Revenger's Tragedy* (c. 1606–1607), his *The Atheist's Tragedy* (1607–1611), George Chapman's *The Revenge of Bussy D'Ambois* (1610), and John Fletcher's *Valentinian* (1610–1614).

In Shakespeare, the foremost example of the treatment of revenge is *Hamlet.* Here the contradiction between code and tradition is resolved in the Christian denial of criminal revenge, which provides the moral obstacles to the hero in his attempt to fulfill vengeance. Other examples of the explicit Christian denial of revenge are in *Richard II* (I, i, 152–156) and *The Tempest* (V, i, 25–28). Revenge as a minor motif in Shakespeare also appears in *Richard III, Romeo and Juliet, Julius Caesar, Macbeth, Othello,* and *Coriolanus.*

For a full discussion of revenge in *Hamlet,* see Paul N. Siegel's *Shakespearean Tragedy and the Elizabethan Compromise* (1957) and Ashley H. Thorndike's "Hamlet and Contemporary Revenge Plays," *PMLA,* XXVI (1902). [Lily B. Campbell, "Theories of Revenge in Renaissance England," *Modern Philology,* XXVIII, 1931; Fredson Bowers, *Elizabethan Revenge Tragedy: 1587–1642,* 1940.]—S.K.

Revenger's Tragedy, The. See CYRIL TOURNEUR.

revision. In the Elizabethan theatre, the practice of altering and updating old plays for periodical revivals on the stage. From 1597 to 1603, for example, the Admiral's Men revived 23 old plays, of which 4 underwent substantial revision. Thus, the practice does not seem to have been as common as has been assumed by the proponents of the DISINTEGRATION theory, who argue that Shakespeare regularly revised his own and others' old plays.

The strongest evidence of a revision by Shakespeare of one of his own plays is contained on the title page of the First Quarto of *Love's Labour's Lost* (1598), which is described as "newly corrected and augmented by W. Shakespeare." This may refer to a revision by the author, or it may refer, as does a similar title page for the good quarto of *Romeo and Juliet* (1599), to the prior appearance of a "bad quarto." The former theory, however, is usually regarded as more tenable.

There has been a general tendency to reject any view of the young Shakespeare as a mere reviser of other men's plays. This new position stems directly from Peter Alexander's demonstration that *2* and *3*

Henry VI (thought since the time of Edmund Malone to be revisions of the CONTENTION PLAYS) are in reality original dramas of which the Contention plays are bad quartos. Nevertheless, many scholars still view *Titus Andronicus* and *The Merry Wives of Windsor* as revisions by Shakespeare of older plays either by himself or others. Finally, there is one other important example of Shakespeare's participation in a revision: the manuscript of SIR THOMAS MORE, three pages of which are thought to be in Shakespeare's hand. However, the many unanswered questions about this play preclude the possibility of drawing any definite conclusions concerning revision. [E. K. Chambers, *William Shakespeare,* 1930; E. A. J. Honigmann, *The Stability of Shakespeare's Text,* 1965.]

Reynaldo. In *Hamlet,* the servant of Polonius sent by his old master to spy on Laertes in Paris (II, i).

Reynolds, Frederick (1764–1841). Dramatist and adapter of Shakespeare's plays. Educated at Middle Temple, which he left in 1782 in order to write plays, Reynolds is responsible for nearly 100 tragedies and comedies of which 20 or so were popular in his day. Between 1816 and 1828 he produced a number of operatic versions of Shakespearean plays, namely, *A Midsummer Night's Dream* (1816), *The Comedy of Errors* (1819), *Twelfth Night* (1820), *The Two Gentlemen of Verona* (1821), *The Tempest* (1821), *The Merry Wives of Windsor* (1824), and *The Taming of the Shrew* (1828). Reynolds' adaptations of Shakespeare ultimately earned him a reputation for degradation of the drama.

Reynolds, Sir **Joshua** (1723–1792). Portrait and history painter. Founding member and president of the Royal Academy, Reynolds proudly upheld the artistic principles formalized by the French Academy (see ART). It is said that a £500 note insured his endorsement of BOYDELL'S SHAKESPEARE GALLERY, but he would have undoubtedly sympathized with Boydell's aim in any case.

Reynolds defended the tradition of classical (rather than historical) dress in the dispute over "The Death of Wolfe," by Benjamin WEST. In an address (1771) given at the time, he laid down the rules of history painting as he saw it, describing the restraint necessary in the handling of universal passions and the capacity of history painting to arouse general response and excite moral sentiments. He advised that local and petty details of character and circumstance be avoided or suppressed:

> . . . it is not enough in Invention that the Artist should restrain and keep under all the inferior parts of his subject; he must sometimes deviate from vulgar and strict historical truth, in pursuing the grandeur of his design. . . .

Reynolds contributed three paintings to Boydell's project: a delightful "Puck" with Titania and Bottom in the background; "Macbeth and the Witches"; and the "Death of Cardinal Beaufort" from *Henry VI,* generally considered the best painting in the collection. Reynolds approved of borrowing from classical art, and it is not surprising that he was able in the latter painting to incorporate a group of figures from Nicolas Poussin's "Death of Germanicus." What is surprising, however, is his borrowing the twisted posture of the dying Beaufort from a painting by Henry Fuseli. [W. M. Merchant, *Shak speare and the Artist,* 1959.]

Reynolds, William (1575–1633). Stratford lan owner to whom Shakespeare left 26s. 8d. in his w to buy a ring. He was the son of William (d. 161 and Margaret (d. 1615) Reynolds, who were su pected of harboring priests in 1604. At his paren death, he inherited all of their property, which increased, thus becoming one of the largest lan holders in Stratford. In 1619 he was named as o of a group of anti-Puritans who had attacked ar libeled the Puritan vicar Thomas Wilson. [Ma Eccles, *Shakespeare in Warwickshire,* 1961.]

rhetoric. Shakespeare is supreme in his langua and in the range and vitality of the people he h created through his language. Hotspur, for exampl speaks at one time with colloquial informality, tell you what . . . such a deal of skimble-skamb stuff," while at another time he soars to a peak expressing the chivalric ideal, "methinks it were easy leap to pluck bright honour from the pal faced moon." Biblical and classical allusions intensif and enrich multiple meanings. Such is the phra "whoreson Achitophel." As Hilda Hulme has note it can be no mere coincidence that Falstaff alone all Shakespeare's characters should utter this nam for with amazingly apt and complex implications once comic and tragic, wide and deep, it glanc both backward and forward and ironically intimat his own ultimate rejection as misleader of the King son.

The extraordinary flexibility, richness, and pow of Shakespeare's language are due in part to h genius, in part to the changing linguistic forms of h time which promoted a lively spirit of free creativ ness, and in part to what is the main concern this article, the general theory of composition the prevailing. T. W. Baldwin has demonstrated co vincingly, not only that Shakespeare gained from th Latin textbooks regularly studied in Renaissan grammar schools a thorough and systematic know edge of rhetoric and logic and employed techniqu and materials derived from them, but also that could and did count on the spontaneous response his audience. See EDUCATION.

To enable the modern reader better to understan and enjoy the approximately 200 Renaissance figur of speech, amazing in their analysis of thought an expression, they were reclassified in 1947 accordin to their four basic functions: in creating grammatic effects, such as antithesis through repetition, and promoting the three modes of persuading othe which Aristotle treats in his *Rhetoric,* namely, b appealing to their reason (*logos*); to their feelin (*pathos*); to their confidence in the speaker's cha acter, his competence, and his good will toward the (*ethos*). Philip Melanchthon's classification of a proximately 40 figures of thought under topics logic and Henry Peacham's subdivisions introduce in the 1593 revision of his 1577 *Garden of Eloquen* testify to their awareness of the intrinsic relationshi between logic and rhetoric.

Even the vices of language and the fallacies logic studied in the schools provided the dramati with means to create comic effects. Thus, recalling most rare vision, Bottom says that eye hath n heard, ear hath not seen what his dream was; by th misplacing he communicates his own grotesque wonder without any mockery of St. Paul. At the rehearsal, he expresses his naïve ebullience when he eagerly offers to play Thisby and speak "in a monstrous little voice" or the lion and "roar as gentle as any sucking dove." The unique humor of Dogberry is compounded of an inept sense of importance, prescribing inane penalties in instructing the watchmen, dividing one offense into six through synonyms, and especially substituting for the word he means its contrary, as when he exclaims, "O villain! Thou wilt be condemned into everlasting redemption for this." The guilty conspirator arrested by the watchmen ironically points up to the supposedly wise the incongruity basic to the comic, "What your wisdoms could not discover, these shallow fools have brought to light." Fallacious reasoning likewise is often comic because of the incongruity between the appearance of sound logic and the underlying sophistry. Thus, Feste proves, with her permission, that Olivia is a fool because she mourns a brother whose soul is in heaven. Accused of declaring falsely that Prince Hal owes him £1000, Falstaff wriggles out of the difficulty and emerges triumphant by translating the charge into a metaphor and magnifying it into a compliment, "A thousand pounds, Hal? A million, thy love is worth a million; thou owest me thy love."

On the other hand, Shakespeare uses fallacious argument as a powerful device to characterize his villains. When the hired assassins tell Clarence in prison that his brother Richard has sent them to murder him, he exclaims, "It cannot be, for he . . . swore with sobs that he would labour my delivery." The murderer replies, "Why so he doth, when he delivers you from this earth's thraldom to the joys of heaven." Sheer effrontery and resourcefulness in argument are exemplified when Richard admits he killed the sons of Edward IV's Queen but seeks her aid in wooing her daughter Elizabeth. "If I did take the kingdom from your sons, to make amends, I'll give it to your daughter . . . . Plead what I will be, not what I have been." The Queen finally consents and goes her way while Richard reflects, "Relenting fool, and shallow, changing woman!" Iago, a master of innuendo, plays each of his victims against the other to his own evil advantage. He counsels Cassio to regain Othello's esteem by Desdemona's intercession so that "by how much she strives to do him good" Iago's insinuations will "turn her virtue into pitch, and out of her own goodness make the net that shall enmesh them all."

Returning to the fourfold classification of the figures of speech, we note that Renaissance poets were zestful makers of language and freely used one part of speech as another. Most striking are the nouns Shakespeare used as verbs: "the thunder would not peace at my bidding"; Lord Angelo "dukes it well"; "knee the way into his mercy"; "a hand that kings have lipped." Often negatives enhance the effect: "I am unkinged by Bolingbroke"; "Let me unkiss the oath 'twixt thee and me"; "A little to disquantity your train"; "lest her . . . beauty unprovide my mind again." Shakespeare asserts likeness through vivid metaphor: "'Tis deepest winter in Lord Timon's purse"; Angelo's "blood is very snow-broth"; Rosencrantz is a sponge "that soaks up the King's countenance"; Antony "o'er green Neptune's back with ships made cities."

We perceive a notable growth of skill in using the figures of repetition that emphasize grammatical structure as Shakespeare advances from his obvious apprenticeship in the early plays to varied and deeply moving use of the same figure when he achieved mastery of his art. The figures differ, depending, for example, on the placing of the repeated words: with a few words between; with no words between; at the beginning or the end of parallel phrases; in one order and then in the reverse order. The following exemplify the first kind only. Othello heaps up irony as he bitterly inveighs against Desdemona in the presence of her astounded kinsman Lodovico, "Ay, you did wish that I would make her turn. Sir, she can turn, and turn; and yet go on, and turn again." Macbeth utters his cynical survey of life beginning "Tomorrow and tomorrow and tomorrow." Antony uses this figure with a colloquial ease genuinely dramatic when he bids farewell successively to his servitors after his defeat, "Give me thy hand, thou hast been rightly honest. So hast thou; And thou, and thou, and thou. You have served me well." On the other hand, each of the following exemplifies a different figure of repetition: "Out, out, brief candle"; "Farewell the tranquil mind; farewell content"; "What dost thou think? Think, my lord? . . . By heaven, he echoes me; as if there were some monster in his thought!"; "heaven hath pleased . . . to punish me with this, and this with me."

Shakespeare's contemporaries perceived the multiple meanings of a word and responded to its deliberate ambiguity by discerning the parts and the whole, as one recognizes each of the tones in a musical chord. Three figures of speech, later called puns, repeat the ambiguous word. "To England will I steal, and there I'll steal"; "I cannot say whore—It does abhor me now I speak the word"; *Doctor* (observing Lady Macbeth's sleepwalking): "Well, well, well." *Gentlewoman:* "Pray God it be, Sir." The fourth and most subtle figure uses a word with two meanings but does not repeat it. Perhaps the most powerful and deeply moving pun in Shakespeare is Kent's assertion of what longer life would mean to Lear: "He hates him that would upon the rack of this tough world stretch him out longer." Another, even more subtle pun might be present when Gloucester, now aware of Edmund's treachery but not of Edgar's true love, protests he cannot read the paper Lear thrusts before his eyeless sockets, "Were all thy letters suns, I could not see one." Does not our mind leap to "sons"?

To persuade his listeners a speaker may employ the topics and forms of logic in one or more of the three modes of persuasion: to convince their minds (*logos*); to rouse their emotions to pity, anger, exultation (*pathos*); to impress them with such confidence in his character, both as to his competence and his good will toward them, that they think and act as he urges (*ethos*). Antony's oration over Caesar combines *ethos*, *logos*, and *pathos* in an expert manipulation of the minds and feelings of the crowd. First, he seemingly accepts what Brutus has just told them, that Caesar was ambitious; this must be true because Brutus is an honorable man (*ethos*). Next, he undermines this assertion by contrasting what

Brutus says with what Caesar was and did (*logos*). Then he turns toward Caesar's coffin and weeps (*pathos*), while citizens comment on his threefold persuasion, "much reason in his sayings," "his eyes are red as fire with weeping," "There's not a nobler man in Rome than Antony . . . We'll hear him, we'll follow him, we'll die with him." Finally, roused to the highest pitch, the crowd rushes away to burn and destroy.

Shakespeare easily excels his contemporaries in adapting devices to every conceivable dramatic purpose. In impregnating scenes of human urgency with the tension of genuine debate, he so fuses thought and feeling, character and plot that they become almost indistinguishable and thereby more intense, moving both mind and heart. This is particularly evident in the great tragedies. Iago represents the most remarkable instance of ironical dramatic *ethos*, for by the very same words and acts he causes the other persons in the play to think well of him and the audience to think ill. Desdemona and Hermione argue with dignity and cogency before judges at a public trial. Isabel contends with superb skill and honesty against the craft and deceit of Angelo. Beatrice, Benedick, Rosalind, and Touchstone are skillful fencers with words, adept at the quick retort, the pert reply. The gravediggers match the court clowns in light sophistry even though the subject of their banter is suitably grim. Each person speaks in his own idiom, be it that of villain, queen, or clown. With equally authentic accent, Shakespeare adapts language to the garrulous, the shallow, the ignorant, the grave. Mainly by a skillful use of the vices of language he travesties the affectation of Osric, the pedantry of Holofernes, the bombast of Glendower, the garrulity of Juliet's nurse and Justice Shallow, the scurrility of Thersites. By means of fallacious argument he creates the light sophistic of Touchstone, the cynical mockery of Apemantus, the barbed shafts of the fool in *Lear*. Through mastery of argumentation (*logos, pathos, ethos*), characters whom he has endowed with natural eloquence full of personal and vivid touches engage both the intellect and the feelings of the audience, whether they voice with experienced tongue cogent analytic thought on grave affairs or in soliloquy unburden the heart of poignant doubt or fear or grief. Thought and imagery commensurate with the genuine stress of a compelling problem or passion forge language which by appealing simultaneously to the reason and the imagination confers beauty as well as vision. The style echoes the mood with sureness whether it shifts from unruffled deliberation to hysterical excitement or from stern self-control to unbridled emotion in the movement of living drama. Shakespeare's creative art illustrates most fully the variety and compass of the Renaissance theory of composition.

The formal training which Shakespeare received contributed not only to the breadth and stature of his thought but also to the richness of the gorgeous panoply with which he invested it. With figures of repetition he weaves a haunting harmony of sound. Language, fresh, vibrant, exuberant, and free, effects sudden and vivid concentrations of meaning by a poetically superb and daring use of nouns as verbs, of the transferred epithet, the compound epithet, metaphor, subtle puns, negative terms. Through inverted word order, parenthesis, the omission or addition of conjunctions, Shakespeare secures such control over movement and rhythm that, like a figure skater, he may dart, poise, turn, plunge, go where he will, his words fraught with wisdom and deep feeling—and all this but an art subservient to the larger art of plot construction, character creation, and profound insight into human nature and its problems. [Bibliography: the traditionalists: Aristotle, Cicero, Quintilian, Horace, Aphthonius, Erasmus, Lily, Melanchthon, Cox, Wilson, Rainolde, Lever, Blundeville; the figurists, whose whole treatment was in some 10 figures: Susenbrotus, Sherry, Peacham, Puttenham, Day; the Ramists: Ramus, Talaeus, Fenner, Fraunce, Butler, Hoskyns. Selected modern studies: G. Willcock, "Shakespeare and Rhetoric," *Essays and Studies by Members of the English Association*, No. 18, 1934; A. H. Gilbert, "Logic in the Elizabethan Drama," *Studies in Philology*, October, 1935; Hardin Craig, *The Enchanted Glass*, 1936; W. G. Crane, *Wit and Rhetoric in the Renaissance*, 1937; L. Osborn, *The Life, Letters, and Writings of John Hoskyns*, 1937; F. P. Wilson, "Shakespeare and the Diction of Common Life," *Proceedings of the British Academy*, 1941; F. R. Johnson, "Two Renaissance Textbooks of Rhetoric: Aphthonius' *Progymnasmata* and Rainolde's *A Booke Called the Foundacion of Rhetorike*," *Huntington Library Quarterly*, August, 1943; T. W. Baldwin, *William Shakspere's Small Latine and Lesse Greeke*, 2 vols., 1944; R. Tuve, *Elizabethan and Metaphysical Imagery*, 1947; Hilda Hulme, *Explorations in Shakespeare's Language*, 1962; for fuller bibliography see Sister Miriam Joseph, C.S.C., *Shakespeare's Use of the Arts of Language*, 1947, or *Rhetoric in Shakespeare's Time*, 1962.]—S.M.J.

Rice, John (fl. 1607–1630). Actor. Rice was a boy apprenticed to John Heminges of the King's Men in 1607; that year he delivered Ben Jonson's verse speech to the king at a dinner in the Merchant Taylors' hall. In 1610 he participated in further pageantry, this time representing the nymph Corinea at the city of London's salute to Prince Henry when the latter became prince of Wales. The following year Rice became one of the original members of Lady Elizabeth's Men.

By 1619, however, he had rejoined the King's Men, for he is in the cast list of the King's Men's production of *Sir John Van Olden Barnavelt* in which the prompter's notes name him a captain and a servant. T. W. Baldwin and E. K. Chambers suggest that he was taken into the King's company as a replacement for Nathan Field, who left that year. Rice's name appears in the acting lists of the First Folio of Shakespeare's plays (1623), and the quarto of *The Duchess of Malfi* (pub. 1623). His presence in the *Duchess of Malfi* quarto without an alternate actor being designated for the same role is a circumstance which has led scholars to conclude that Rice was with the company in 1614, when the play was originally given, and from 1619 to 1623, when the company revived it. Rice was also named in the new patent granted the company at the accession of Charles I in 1625.

It is generally thought that Rice left the company by 1629. Scholars suggest that Rice may have taken holy orders, citing as evidence John Heminges' will, probated in 1630, in which a legacy is bequeathed to

"John Rice Clerke of St Saviours in Southwarke." E. K. Chambers, *The Elizabethan Stage*, 1923; T. W. Baldwin, *The Organization and Personnel of the Shakespearean Company*, 1927; G. E. Bentley, *The Jacobean and Caroline Stage*, 5 vols., 1941–1956.]

Rich or **Riche, Barnabe** (1540?–1617). Author and soldier. Entering the military service in 1562, Rich fought in the low countries and in Ireland, eventually rising to the rank of captain. He is the author of numerous books and pamphlets. In 1581 he published *Riche his Farewell to Militarie profession*, a collection of eight stories "gathered together for the only delight of the courteous gentlewomen both of England and Ireland." One of these tales is "Of Apollonius and Silla" based on a story in Matteo Bandello's *Novelle* by way of François de Belleforest's French translations. Rich's tale is the direct source of *Twelfth Night* (see TWELFTH NIGHT: *Sources*). He is also the author of *The Straunge and Wonderfull Adventures of Don Simonides* (1581, 1584), a two-part romance written in the then fashionable style of euphuism. He may be the R. B. who wrote GREENE'S FUNERALLS.

Rich, John (c. 1682–1761). Theatre manager and pantomimist. Son of Christopher Rich, John Rich and his brother took over Lincoln's Inn Fields Theatre at the death of their father in 1714. Rich's company was composed of those who had left the Drury Lane: Kean, the Bullocks, Pack, Spiller, and Griffin. It was a capable company, although not of the same rank as the Drury Lane's under Cibber, Wilks, and Booth. In 1716, Rich instituted the first of a long series of successful pantomimes, in which he played Harlequin. In 1728 Rich produced *The Beggar's Opera* by John Gay. Refused by Drury Lane, this production was described by a contemporary wit as having made "Gay rich, and Rich gay." In 1732 Rich's company opened the season with *Hamlet* at their new house, Covent Garden, inaugurating a star-studded, artistically successful management of that house. In 1746, when Rich hired Garrick, Quin, and Mrs. Cibber, the house showed a £8,500 profit for the season. He had a reputation for encouraging the best actors, but they did not like him and accused him of prompting hostile public demonstrations in order to render them more amenable to his discipline.

In 1750/1, the Covent Garden witnessed the competition of Garrick and Barry as rival Romeos, and in 1755 rivalry as King Lear. Rich's talent for pantomime undoubtedly aided the actors under his jurisdiction in developing proficiency at their craft, but he was uneducated and illiterate. Rich's portrait, attributed to Hogarth, and a picture of him as Harlequin are in the Garrick Club. [*Dictionary of National Biography*, 1885– .]

Richard II (1367–1400). King of England; in *Richard II*, the fatally flawed hero. The son of Edward "the Black Prince," who died before becoming king, Richard succeeded his grandfather, Edward III (1312–1377). His coronation ceremony was the most splendid England had ever seen, and the pomp and majesty of that event was to become the hallmark of Richard's reign (1377–1399). Under the tutelage of his chief counselor and guardian, John of

RICHARD II. PORTRAIT BY AN UNKNOWN ARTIST. (NATIONAL PORTRAIT GALLERY)

Gaunt, Richard developed into an early version of the divine-right monarch—an absolute ruler standing above law and tradition. His arrogance and pretentiousness reached their apex when, after the death of John of Gaunt, he seized his old adviser's lands, thus depriving Gaunt's son, Henry Bolingbroke, of his inheritance. Bolingbroke's successful usurpation of Richard's crown is the nominal center of interest in Shakespeare's play. Actually, however, the play focuses much more acutely on Richard's own personality.

Shakespeare's Richard is presented as intelligent, sensitive, and eloquent. These attributes are, however, undermined by the frivolous, self-indulgent, and self-dramatizing strains in his character. The complex combination of these qualities produces Shakespeare's first great tragic hero. See RICHARD II: *Comment*.

The Life and Death of King Richard the Second.

Richard II. A history play by Shakespeare.

Text. The First Quarto (1597) furnishes a good text, except for the omission of the abdication scene (IV, i, 154–318). It is advertised as follows: "The Tragedie of King Richard the second. As it hath beene publikely acted by the right Honourable the Lorde Chamberlaine his Seruants. London Printed by Valentine Simmes for Androw Wise, and are to be sold at his shop in Paules church yard at the signe of the Angel. 1597." The text is derived from a manuscript version, quite possibly Shakespeare's FOUL PAPERS. Later quartos appeared in the following years: two in 1598, one in 1608, and one in 1615. The text of each one of these quartos is based on its immediate predecessor. The abdication scene was published for the first time in the Fourth Quarto (1608) "With new additions of the Parliament Sceane, and the deposing of King Richard, As it hath been lately acted by the Kinges Majesties seruantes, at the Globe." The text of the First Folio was apparently based on that of the Third and Fifth Quartos, occasionally collated with the prompt-book, or official acting version of the play, which would have belonged to Shakespeare's company. The prompt-book must have been the source of the Folio's version of the abdication scene, which differs from the less satisfactory account in the Fourth and Fifth Quartos. The deposition scene was probably a part of the original play but was cut from the first three quartos. Queen Elizabeth saw parallels between herself and Richard and so was strongly opposed to any presentation on the stage of his deposition (see William LAMBARDE). Only after James was safely settled on the throne were the actors allowed to stage this controversial scene.

Date. The play was entered in the Stationers' Register on August 29, 1597: "Andrew Wise. Entred for his Copie by appoyntment from master Warden Man, The Tragedye of Richard the Second vj^d^." Parallels between *Richard II* and the first four books of Samuel Daniel's epic *The Civil Wars* (1595) have been cited as evidence for a date of 1595. A letter written by Sir Edward HOBY on December 7, 1595, inviting Sir Robert Cecil to his house to see "K. Richard present him-selfe," has also been adduced as evidence of the 1595 date. But we cannot be sure whether Sir Edward's reference is to a performance of Shakespeare's *Richard II*. There were other plays about Richard II current at the time. The piece in question may even have been Shakespeare's *Richard III*.

Sources. For the historical material, Shakespeare went to the second edition of HOLINSHED's *Chronicles* (1587) and, if the play was written in 1595 probably to the first four books of Daniel's CIVIL WARS. For picturesque incidents he drew on other books, such as the report of the poor groom to the imprisoned Richard. The groom tells of how proudly Richard's horse Barbary carried Bolingbroke, his new master, at Bolingbroke's coronation: "That horse that thou so often hast bestrid" (V, v, 79). This incident was probably suggested by a similar story in Jean FROISSART's *Chronicles* in which a greyhound deserts his master for a new one when the master is struck by misfortune. Shakespeare could have read this tale in Lord Berners' English translation of Froissart (2 vols., 1523–1525). *Thomas of Woodstock*, an anonymous play of the early

TITLE PAGE OF THE FIRST QUARTO OF *Richard II* (1597).

THE

Tragedie of King Richard the se-cond.

As it hath beene publikely acted by the right Honourable the Lorde Chamberlaine his Seruants.

LONDON

Printed by Valentine Simmes for Androw Wise, and are to be sold at his shop in Paules church yard at the signe of the Angel.

1597.

590's, has often been related to *Richard II*. Al-
hough it treats an earlier part of Richard's reign, ome historians argue that it formed the first part f a hypothetical chronicle source of *Richard II*.

The structure of *Richard II* is like that of Mar-
owe's *Edward II* (c. 1593). Marlowe's original chievement in his play is his subjection of hisorical events to the revelation of a weak but ttractive personality. Shakespeare copied and im-
roved Marlowe's formula in *Richard II*. His King, ke Edward, is also the slave of irrational impulses. -O. J. C.

Plot Synopsis. Act I. At Windsor Castle, King ichard listens to the allegations of his cousin Ienry Bolingbroke, son of John of Gaunt, Duke of ancaster, who accuses Thomas Mowbray, Duke f Norfolk, of embezzling royal funds and of lotting the recent death of the Duke of Gloucester. Vhen Bolingbroke and Mowbray refuse to be econciled, Richard orders that a trial by combat e held at Coventry to settle the dispute. Just before he combat begins, however, Richard decides to anish both contenders—Mowbray for life, Boling-
roke for 10 years, which he reduces to 6. Richard ater remarks on the signs of popular affection hown Bolingbroke as he made his way into exile. The King himself is preparing to leave for Ireland, vhere a rebellion has broken out, when he is sum-
noned to the bedside of the dying John of Gaunt.

Act II. Gaunt anxiously awaits Richard's arrival, opeful that the young monarch will heed the ounsels of a dying man. When the King arrives, Gaunt warns him against the flatterers by whom he s surrounded, and rebukes him for his irresponsi-
ility in administering the royal revenue. Richard's nly response is to berate his uncle as "a lunatic ean-witted fool." As soon as Gaunt dies, Richard onfiscates his property, overruling the protests of he Duke of York, who reminds him of Boling-
roke's rights. Angered by Richard's high-handed-
ess, Henry Percy, Duke of Northumberland, eviews with Lord Ross and Lord Willoughby the King's misdeeds, revealing that the banished Bol-
ngbroke has set sail for England with an army of 000 men.

As Sir John Bushy tries to comfort Queen Isabel, vho is grieving over Richard's departure for Ireland, ir Henry Green bursts in with the news that Bolingbroke has landed and that he has won he allegiance of such powerful magnates as North-
mberland and his son Harry. In Gloucestershire, Bolingbroke explains to York, who is acting as egent in Richard's absence, that he has violated is sentence of banishment only to claim his in-
eritance as Duke of Lancaster.

Act III. Arriving in Wales, Richard expresses his oy at touching his kingdom once again and his con-
idence that Bolingbroke's rebellion will soon col-
apse. Despite the encouragement of York's son, the oyal Duke of Aumerle, and the Bishop of Carlisle, he King's confidence fades as he learns from the Earl of Salisbury and Sir Stephen Scroop that he as been deserted by all, even by the Duke of York. n despair, Richard seeks refuge at Flint Castle. When Bolingbroke arrives before the castle and earns that Richard is within, he asks to see him, promising to lay down his arms if his sentence of banishment is revoked and his property is restored. Richard, who appears on the walls of the castle, grants Bolingbroke's demands. Despite his cousin's fair words, however, he realizes that he retains only a shadow of his former power.

Meanwhile, in the garden of the Duke of York, Queen Isabel seeks some amusement to drive away her cares. A gardener appears, accompanied by two servants, one of whom wonders why they should take pains with their garden while disorder prevails in England. The gardener retorts that if Richard had tended his garden as zealously as they do theirs, he would not be faced with the loss of his crown. At this, the Queen makes her presence known and learns that Bolingbroke has brought Richard to London.

Act IV. At a session of parliament in London, Sir John Bagot, an erstwhile adherent of King Richard, accuses Aumerle of complicity in Gloucester's death and is supported by Lord Fitzwater, who alleges that Mowbray had made a similar charge. When Bolingbroke states that settlement of the quarrel will have to wait until Mowbray can be recalled to England, the Bishop of Carlisle discloses that Mowbray has died in Venice. Bolingbroke announces that he intends to depose the King, and, ignoring the Bishop's objection that no subject can judge his sovereign, he summons Richard, who is deprived of his crown. When Northumberland presents him with a list of his alleged crimes, Richard refuses to read the document. The deposed King calls for a looking-glass and, after bitterly examining the image that it reveals, dashes it to the ground. After Bolingbroke leaves, the Abbot of Westminster confides to Aumerle and the Bishop of Carlisle that he has de-
vised a plan to do away with Bolingbroke.

Act V. As Richard is being led to the Tower of London, he is espied from a window by Queen Isabel, who chides him for showing such meekness in adversity. Northumberland interrupts their colloquy to state that Richard is to be taken to Pom-
fret instead, while Isabel must return to her native France. Addressing Northumberland as the "ladder wherewithal / The mounting Bolingbroke ascends my throne," Richard foresees an era of discord, caused by the animosity that is bound to erupt between Northumberland and Bolingbroke.

After Bolingbroke's coronation as Henry IV, the Duke of York discovers that his son, Aumerle, is implicated in the Abbot of Westminster's plot to murder the new King. Denouncing Aumerle as a villain and traitor, and brushing aside his wife's frantic pleas, he determines to expose the conspiracy to the King. Aumerle and his mother also speed to Windsor Castle and succeed in obtaining a pardon from the King, though Henry's clemency does not extend to the other conspirators.

As Richard, a prisoner in Pomfret Castle, ruefully reflects upon his fallen condition, he is murdered by Sir Pierce of Exton, who claims to be acting on a hint from the King. When Exton returns to Windsor Castle with the coffin, Henry repudiates the murderer, though he admits that he had wished Richard dead. He announces that he will make a voyage to the Holy Land to expiate the deed.—H. D.

Comment. When the London theatres reopened in the spring of 1594, after the great London plague of 1592 had kept them closed for over a year, Shakespeare resumed the writing of chronicle history plays. He embarked upon an ambitious project: the construction of a sequence of four connected history plays: *Richard II* (1595), *1 Henry IV* (1596), *2 Henry IV* (1597), and *Henry V* (1599).

Richard II is a self-conscious poet, whose speeches and attitudes are those of an actor playing the parts that Fate has assigned him. Shakespeare wrote this play shortly after finishing his *Venus and Adonis* (1593) and *The Rape of Lucrece* (1594) and while he was working on his sonnets. By making Richard a frustrated actor and poet he was able to fill many of the King's speeches with the lyrical beauty that he had cultivated in his poems. This verse is different in structure and in tone from that of his earlier plays. The new poetical manner is like that of a liturgy. In his weakness and his propensity for disaster, Richard is like Marlowe's Edward II. Yet he is a more sympathetic character. Edward's effeminacy is often repulsive, involved as it is with homosexuality. Richard's posturing, at once pathetic and absurd, takes the form of eloquent and beautiful verse which becomes a kind of musical accompaniment to the attitudes he strikes.

Richard II, unlike Richard III, is no obvious criminal. He is a self-absorbed lyric poet reciting lines that he invents extempore. For example, returning from Ireland he learns that Bolingbroke has grown "strong and great in substance and in power" (III, ii, 35); but instead of taking the military action that the situation demands, he lapses into sheer elegy. Woe is the emotion that the actor playing the part should at this moment express, and Richard does so in extravagantly figurative speech. He cries:

of comfort no man speak
. . . . .
For God's sake, let us sit upon the ground
And tell sad stories of the death of kings.
(III, ii, 144, 155–156)

The deposition scene marks the high point of the plot and of the characterization of Richard. For the moment at which he must divest himself of all his royal regalia, he designs a tableau that he hopes will make the scene memorable. He assigns to each actor his "business." He begins by turning to Bolingbroke and saying,

Here, cousin;
On this side my hand, and on that side yours.
Now is this golden crown like a deep well
That owes two buckets, filling one another.
(IV, i, 182–185)

Richard's delight in a happy phrase is as great as his imagined skill as a stage director. After he has unkinged himself, he calls for a mirror, hoping that he can see there traces of grief in his face. When he can discern no signs of sorrow, he hurls the mirror to the ground, shattering the glass and his own image with it. Bolingbroke's comment on this theatrical gesture is:

The shadow of your sorrow hath destroy'd
The shadow of your face.
(IV, i, 292–293)

This quip so delights Richard that he completel forgets his plight and gives his full attention t savoring the felicity of the conceit. He turns t Bolingbroke with childish eagerness, crying:

Say that again.
The shadow of my sorrow! ha! let's see:
'Tis very true . . .
(IV, i, 293–295)

and he proceeds to analyze the figure and to comment on its propriety. Even when awaiting hi execution in Pomfret Castle's dungeon, he forget the grim reality of his situation in busily tryin to develop a poetic similitude between his prison an the great world beyond its walls. Though unable t work it out at once, he insists "I'll hammer it out. In this situation he becomes absurd—a strangel comic figure. But later he gains, for the nonc tragic stature by killing with an axe two confederates of Exton, his executioner.

Richard's royal incompetence has involved hir in the crimes that old Gaunt enumerates in dying speech that has become Shakespeare's mos famous patriotic utterance (II, i, 5–68). The Kin has been seduced by base flatterers whom he ha made boon companions. He has squandered hi wealth on them and sought to replenish it wit grievous taxation. These policies, though they hav alienated his subjects, do not justify Bolingbroke actions. A king, according to the accepted politica doctrine of the age, was God's deputy on earth, s that it was sacrilegious to raise a hand against hin Bolingbroke's part in Richard's deposition an death was therefore a sin for which he suffere punishment in both parts of *Henry IV*.

In *Richard II* Shakespeare solves the problem o getting rid of a bad king. Richard undoes himsel. Though full of genuine pathos, the passage verge on absurdity when Richard insists that his situatio is more desperate than was Christ's when betraye by Judas. Richard's appeals for sympathy are thu neutralized by his exaggerated sensibility towar himself and his exaggerated apathy toward the concerns of everyone else. He is, therefore, not a conventional tragic protagonist, nor is the play a customary tragedy. Nevertheless, the decline in Richard's fortunes is in inverse proportion to his growt as a dignified human being, and the last act amount to a regeneration of Richard the man, even as i chronicles the defeat of Richard the King.—O. J. C

Stage History. The first recorded performance o *Richard II* took place at the Globe theatre on February 7, 1601, the day before Essex' abortive risin (see earl of Essex). The circumstances of the production are described in a deposition made b Augustine Phillips. The next known performanc was given on September 30, 1607 by members o the ship's company of His Majesty's Ship *Dragon* when off Sierra Leone on its way to the East Indie (see William Keeling). According to Sir Henr Herbert's office-book, the play was produced at th Globe on January 12, 1631.

The first performance of the history after th Restoration was in a version made by Nahum Tat in 1680. It was suppressed (in spite of his changin the names of the characters and calling the pla *The Sicilian Usurper*) after playing for two day t the Theatre Royal in 1681. An adaptation made ·y Lewis THEOBALD, the famous editor of Shakespeare, appeared in 1719 at Lincoln's Inn Fields. It vas more successful and was included in the epertoire for at least another season. In 1738 the hakespeare play at last enjoyed a long run, at Covent Garden.

Another adaptation, by Richard Wroughton, vas presented at Drury Lane in March 1815, with Edmund Kean playing Richard. This version was cted 13 times that season and revived regularly luring the next 5 years. Both John Vandenhoff and Charles Macready appeared occasionally in the itle role, but not until Charles Kean's production n 1857 did the play achieve real popularity, running for 85 performances. The main feature of this how was an elaborate spectacle of the deposed Richard's humiliating entry into London in Bolingbroke's train.

On November 11, 1899 Harley Granville-Barker, ged 22, played a single performance of *Richard II* or William Poel in the lecture room of London University in Burlington Gardens, but the West End had no performance of *Richard II* until Frank Benson brought it to the Lyceum in March 1900, 2 years after Kean's production. Benson's success nfluenced Beerbohm Tree, who presented a decorative production and played a haunted and touchng Richard in 1903 at His Majesty's. Thereafter, Tree staged the drama in his Shakespeare festivals of 1905 and 1910, and for its own run in November 906, while Benson showed it at Stratford-upon-Avon every year except 1912 from 1901 through 913. Russell Thorndike appeared as Richard for producer Ben Greet during the Old Vic's 1916/7 eason and coproduced the play with Charles Warburton for the 1919/20 season.

In 1929, both George Hayes at Stratford and John Gielgud at the Old Vic excelled in their portrayals of the agonized King. Hayes had played he role for Robert Atkins at the Old Vic in 1924 nd would take the part again under Atkins at Stratford 20 years later. In between, he acted Richard for Tyrone Guthrie in 1933 and B. Iden Payne in 1941. Gielgud was playing his first season t the Old Vic in 1929 and, in this performance produced by Harcourt Williams, he came close to completely captivating the critics. The next year Ralph Richardson joined the Old Vic and played Bolingbroke to Gielgud's Richard. In 1937 Gielgud e-created his Richard II in his own production at he Queen's Theatre with a cast which included Michael Redgrave, Leon Quartermaine, and Peggy Ashcroft. He has since played the role as far afield s Rhodesia (1953).

Maurice Evans played Richard II at the Old Vic n 1934 and at New York's St. James in 1937. He ad remarkable success subsequently touring in the part in the United States. Many notable Richards ollowed. Alec Guinness in Ralph Richardson's 947 production at the New Theatre presented a proud, unsympathetic weakling; Paul Scofield, directed by Gielgud in 1952 at the Lyric, spoke with precision and sharp intonation. Michael Redgrave at Stratford was an effeminate, foppish king in the first half, pathetic in the second half, and always highly yrical, in Anthony Quayle's 1951 production, staged on Tanya Moiseiwitsch's permanent wooden set incorporating Elizabethan features.

In Joan Littlewood's production for the Theatre Workshop, Stratford East, in 1955, the poetry was butchered and Harry Corbett's Richard bordered on lunacy. But at the Old Vic, the chilling verse spoken by John Neville's king held the stage during the 1954/5 and 1955/6 seasons. One of the most recent stagings was that by Peter Hall at Stratford in 1964, with the capricious, cruel Richard of David Warner, detached both from the government of the country and from his own downfall. In this production Eric Porter, with quiet assurance, played a Bolingbroke always in command.—M.G.

Bibliography. TEXT: *Richard II*, New Cambridge Edition, J. Dover Wilson, ed., 1939; *King Richard II*, New Variorum Edition, Matthew Black, ed., 1955; *King Richard II*, New Arden Edition, Peter Ure, ed., 1956. DATE: New Variorum Edition; New Arden Edition. SOURCES: New Variorum Edition; *Woodstock, a Moral History*, A. P. Rossiter, ed., 1946; *Samuel Daniel's Civil Wars*, Laurence Michel, ed., 1958. COMMENT: E. M. W. Tillyard, *Shakespeare's History Plays*, 1944; John Palmer, *Political Characters of Shakespeare*, 1945; Leonard Dean, "Richard II: the State and the Image of the Theater," *PMLA*, LXVII, 1952. STAGE HISTORY: New Cambridge Edition; G. C. D. Odell, *Shakespeare from Betterton to Irving*, 1920; J. C. Trewin, *Shakespeare on the English Stage, 1900–1964*, 1964.

Selected Criticism

SAMUEL TAYLOR COLERIDGE. . . . I will now advert to the character of the King. He is represented as a man not deficient in immediate courage, which displays itself at his assassination; or in powers of mind, as appears by the foresight he exhibits throughout the play: still, he is weak, variable, and womanish, and possesses feelings, which, amiable in a female, are misplaced in a man, and altogether unfit for a king. In prosperity he is insolent and presumptuous, and in adversity, if we are to believe Dr. Johnson, he is humane and pious. I cannot admit the latter epithet, because I perceive the utmost consistency of character in Richard: what he was at first, he is at last, excepting as far as he yields to circumstances: what he shewed himself at the commencement of the play, he shews himself at the end of it . . . .

From the beginning to the end of the play he pours out all the peculiarities and powers of his mind: he catches at new hope, and seeks new friends, is disappointed, despairs, and at length makes a merit of his resignation. He scatters himself into a multitude of images, and in conclusion endeavours to shelter himself from that which is around him by a cloud of his own thoughts. Throughout his whole career may be noticed the most rapid transitions—from the highest insolence to the lowest humility—from hope to despair, from the extravagance of love to the agonies of resentment, and from pretended resignation to the bitterest reproaches. The whole is joined with the utmost richness and copiousness of thought, and were there an actor capable of representing Richard, the part would delight us more than any other of Shakespeare's master-pieces,—with, perhaps, the single exception of King Lear. [*Shakespearean Criticism* by S. T. Coleridge, T. M. Raysor, ed., Everyman Library Edition, 1960.]

WALTER PATER. In no other play perhaps is there such a flush of those gay, fresh, variegated flowers of speech—color and figure, not lightly attached to, but fused into, the very phrase itself—which Shakespeare cannot help dispensing to his characters, as in this "play of the Deposing of King Richard the Second," an exquisite poet if he is nothing else, from first to last, in light and gloom alike, able to see all things poetically, to give a poetic turn to his conduct of them, and refreshing with his golden language the tritest aspects of that ironic contrast between the pretensions of a king and the actual necessities of his destiny. What a garden of words! With him, blank verse, infinitely graceful, deliberate, musical in inflection, becomes indeed a true "verse royal," that rhyming lapse, which to the Shakespearean ear, at least in youth, came as the last touch of refinement on it, being here doubly appropriate. His eloquence blends with that fatal beauty, of which he was so frankly aware, so amiable to his friends, to his wife, of the effects of which on the people his enemies were so much afraid, on which Shakespeare himself dwells so attentively as the "royal blood" comes and goes in the face with his rapid changes of temper.

. . . the play of *Richard the Second* does, like a musical composition, possess a certain concentration of all its parts, a simple continuity, an evenness in execution, which are rare in the great dramatist. With *Romeo and Juliet*, that perfect symphony (symphony of three independent poetic forms set in a grander one which it is the merit of German criticism to have detected), it belongs to a small group of plays, where, by happy birth and consistent evolution, dramatic form approaches to something like the unity of a lyrical ballad, a lyric, a song, a single strain of music.

. . . his coronation, by the pageantry, the amplitude, the learned care, of its order, so lengthy that the king, then only eleven years of age, and fasting, as a communicant at the ceremony, was carried away in a faint, fixed the type under which it has ever since continued. And nowhere is there so emphatic a reiteration as in *Richard the Second* of the sentiment which those singular rites were calculated to produce. . . . But this, too, in the hands of Shakespeare, becomes for him, like any other of those fantastic, ineffectual, easily discredited, personal graces, as capricious in its operation on men's wills as merely physical beauty, kindling himself to eloquence indeed, but only giving double pathos to insults which "barbarism itself" might have pitied—the dust in his face, as he returns, through the streets of London, a prisoner in the train of his victorious enemy. "How soon my sorrow hath destroyed my face!" he cries, in that most poetic invention of the mirror scene, which does but reinforce again that physical charm which all confessed. The sense of "divine right" in kings is found to act not so much as a secret of power over others, as of infatuation to themselves. And of all those personal gifts the one which alone never altogether fails him is just that royal utterance, his appreciation of the poetry of his own hapless lot, an eloquent self-pity, infecting others in spite of themselves, till they too become irresistibly eloquent about him. [*Appreciations*, 1889.]

WILLIAM BUTLER YEATS. I cannot believe that Shakespeare looked on his Richard II. with any but sympathetic eyes, understanding indeed how ill-fitted he was to be King, at a certain moment of history, but understanding that he was lovable and full of capricious fancy, "a wild creature" as Pater has called him. The man on whom Shakespeare modelled him had been full of French elegancies, as he knew from Holinshed, and had given life a new luxury, a new splendour, and been "too friendly" to his friends, "too favourable" to his enemies. And certainly Shakespeare had these things in his head when he made his King fail, a little because he lacked some qualities that were doubtless common among his scullions, but more because he had certain qualities that are uncommon in all ages. To suppose that Shakespeare preferred the men who deposed his King is to suppose that Shakespeare judged men with the eyes of a Municipal Councillor weighing the merits of a Town Clerk; and that had he been by when Verlaine cried out from his bed, "Sir you have been made by the stroke of a pen, but I have been made by the breath of God," he would have thought the Hospital Superintendent the better man. He saw indeed, as I think, in Richard II. the defeat that awaits all, whether they be Artist or Saint, who find themselves where men ask of them a rough energy and have nothing to give but some contemplative virtue, whether lyrical phantasy, or sweetness of temper, or dreamy dignity, or love of God, or love of His creatures. He saw that such a man through sheer bewilderment and impatience can become as unjust or as violent as any common man, any Bolingbroke or Prince John, and yet remain "that sweet lovely rose." The courtly and saintly ideals of the Middle Ages were fading, and the practical ideals of the modern age had begun to threaten the unuseful dome of the sky; Merry England was fading, and yet it was not so faded that the Poets could not watch the procession of the world with that untroubled sympathy for men as they are, as apart from all they do and seem, which is the substance of tragic irony. ["At Stratford on Avon," *Ideas of Good and Evil,* 1903; reprinted in *Essays and Introductions*, 1961.]

PETER URE. But just as Richard's miscalculation and capricious fancy give us an insight into his weakness, so the kind of attention we pay to his sufferings will be to some extent determined by what commentators have diagnosed as the theatricality with which he expresses them. "He throws himself into the part of the deposed monarch", says Pater, "[and] falls gracefully as on the world's stage." Here again we are in danger of confusing Shakespeare's medium, which is a play designed to cast light above all others on to Richard, with the dramatic character. The gracefulness, the enthusiasm, the loquacity, the taking of the centre of the stage and the consciousness of onlookers are Shakespeare's own powers and the means which he uses to give us Richard as fully and centrally as he can; they are not attributes of the character, for Richard is no more an actor than he is a poet. We are not to suppose that because a character in a play speaks a great deal, he is necessarily fond of the sound of his own voice, or because he continually takes the centre of the stage, that he necessarily enjoys playing a part. The Richard who luxuriates in his own destruction is a product of some such suppositions; it also springs from an unwillingness to recognize the appeal of the tradition of the "complaint" and *The Mirror for Magistrates*, from which Richard's lamentations and reproaches in part descend. It is not Richard who stages the impressive and symbolical scenes in which he appears, . . . but Shakespeare, who desired to set before us the honoured spectacle of the fallen king . . . .

The play, then, is not simply about a weak but legitimate monarch out-generalled by an able usurper. By showing us this subject in terms of Richard's suffering, Shakespeare adds a further dimension; and extends this beyond the mere pathos of a spectacular fall from glory to dishonour. Shakespeare seems to have used all the skill then at his command to give voice to the inwardness of his protagonist and to show him alive and exciting within the area of his peculiarly exact and individual tragic dilemma: the king who must. As Hazlitt said, "the part of Richard himself gives the chief interest to the play", and with it all the more important problems of its interpretation connect. [Introduction to *Richard II*, New Arden Edition, 1956.]

Richard III (1452–1485). King of England; in *2* and *3 Henry VI*, the Duke of Gloucester, a leader of the Yorkist faction and the assassin of Henry VI; in *Richard III*, the murderous, Machiavellian usurper of the crown of England. The picture which Shakespeare gives of Richard—a malevolent hunchback guilty of wholesale murder in his ruthless ascent to the throne—is essentially in accord with the account of Tudor historians who, writing during the reign of Richard's enemies, did not hesitate to attribute every evil act to him.

Although certainly a usurper and probably a murderer, the historical Richard was only a child of his time whose ferocity and cold-bloodedness could be matched by many of his contemporaries. It is true, however, that Richard's personal character was not such as to inspire loyalty, a fact which eventually led to his downfall, for his defeat at Bosworth by Richmond was largely the result of desertion by his allies. Richard was, nevertheless, a competent administrator and a skillful and brave soldier, the latter fact making it unlikely that his physical deformity was as great as Shakespeare seems to indicate.

The greatness of Shakespeare's characterization, however, does not lie in its historical accuracy

RICHARD III. PORTRAIT BY AN UNKNOWN ARTIST. (NATIONAL PORTRAIT GALLERY)

but in its imaginative embodiment of the abstract idea of evil. Here the playwright was working with a precedent. He based his portrait of Richard on the VICE of medieval drama, the zestful, disarmingly candid demi-devil whose unmotivated malevolence is a feature of many morality plays. Shakespeare's hunchback, like the medieval figure, dominates the action by the sheer force of his personality. His strength derives from the totality of his commitment to evil, and thus he achieves a kind of diabolic dignity which can be matched only by Milton's Lucifer. Richard is Shakespeare's first great villain, the ancestor of Edmund and Iago. See RICHARD III: *Comment*.

The Tragedy of Richard the Third: With the Landing of the Earl of Richmond, and the Battel at Bosworth Field.

Richard III. A history play by Shakespeare.

Text. "The tragedie of kinge Richard the Third with the death of the Duke of Clarence" was entered in the Stationers' Register on October 20, 1597 and published in the same year. Before the appearance of the First Folio, five other quartos were published (Q2, 1598; Q3, 1602; Q4, 1605; Q5, 1612; Q6, 1622), evidence of the play's continued popularity. Each one of the quartos advertised the play as "by William Shake-speare" or "William Shakespeare." The Folio text was based largely on Q6 or Q3, haphazardly collated with a theatrical manuscript. Each of the quartos was printed from its predecessor. This chronology would ordinarily establish the 1597 Quarto as the basis for the text; however, Q1's claim to authority is somewhat weakened by the generally held opinion that the source of this text is a MEMORIAL RECONSTRUCTION made by a group of Shakespeare's company who went on tour during the period from July to October in 1597, when the London theatres were shut down. This theory helps to account for the absence of 200 lines in this Quarto which are present in the Folio. Thus a modern text of the play is necessarily "eclectic"—i.e., based upon both the Folio and Q1.

Date. *The Tragedy of King Richard III* was probably written in 1592–1593. The drama is so closely connected a sequel to the Henry VI histories, which Shakespeare completed in 1592, that he must have begun *Richard III* immediately after finishing the trilogy. The high percentage of end-stopped lines points to an early phase of his career.

Sources. The chief source of the historical material in *Richard III* is the second edition of Raphael HOLINSHED'S *Chronicles of England, Scotland and Ireland* (1587 ed.). For most of the events in the career of Richard, Duke of Gloucester, later Richard III, Holinshed took verbatim the account of Edward HALLE'S chronicle entitled *The union of the two noble and illustre famelies of Lancastre and York* (1548). The sources of much of Halle's material were Sir Thomas More's *The Life of Richard III* (1513) and Polydore Vergil's *Historia Anglica* (1534).

In *The Tragedy of King Richard III* Shakespeare assembles and pieces together many earlier traditions of tragedy by way of dramatizing the career of a hunchbacked royal criminal. Richard has many forebears. His most direct ancestor is a stock figure in the morality plays, the Vice Dissimulation (see MEDIEVIALISM IN SHAKESPEARE). This Vice practiced his arts of deception in a gay, self-congratulatory manner, imitated by Richard in his easy conquest of Lady Anne (I, iii).

The play betrays Shakespeare's heritage from the tragedies of Seneca in the prominence of motives of revenge, in the presentation of characters afflicted with hybris, and in the portrayal of Queen Margaret as a veritable Fury, whose laments and cries for revenge resound like the voice of Destiny. Shake-

TITLE PAGE OF THE FIRST QUARTO OF *Richard III* (1597).

THE TRAGEDY OF
King Richard the third.

Containing,
His treacherous Plots against his brother Clarence:
the pittiefull murther of his iunocent nephewes:
his tyrannicall vsurpation: with the whole course
of his detested life, and most deserued death.

As it hath beene lately Acted by the
Right honourable the Lord Chamberlaine his seruants.

AT LONDON
Printed by Valentine Sims, for Andrew Wise,
dwelling in Paules Chuch-yard, at the
Signe of the Angell.
1597.

speare also borrows some of the lyrical features of Seneca's imitation of Greek tragedy. Margaret, meeting Elizabeth, the widow of Edward IV, and Richard's mother, the Duchess of York, before the palace (IV, iv), becomes the leader of a chorus of lamentation that forms a musical interlude in the farrago of crime. Still another lyrical feature of pseudo-Greek tragedy is *stichomythia*, the classical name for the excited dialogues in which two characters answer each other in one-line aphorisms.

Richard adopts as guides for his tyranny some of the immoral moral precepts announced by Niccolò MACHIAVELLI in his political treatise, *Il Principe*, 1509. *The Prince* is a collection of maxims which Machiavelli believed, if applied to the Italian situation, would ensure the rise of an autocrat to sovereign power. His advice is nakedly pragmatic, free from any moral restraints. The prince is urged to adopt the ferocity of the lion or the cunning of the fox, depending on the nature of the situation confronting him.

In *Tamburlaine the Great* (1587), and in the character Barabas in *The Famous Tragedy of the Rich Jew of Malta* (c. 1589), Marlowe had created Machiavellian villains who could have served as partial models for the figure of Richard. Already in *3 Henry VI* (III, ii, 193), Richard has verified the relationship by boasting that he will "set the murderous Machiavel to school."—O. J. C.

Plot Synopsis. Act I. Although England's civil discord has apparently ended with the triumph of the House of York and the accession of Edward IV, the turbulent soul of the King's brother Richard, Duke of Gloucester, is not at rest. Since his deformities prevent him from savoring the wanton pleasures in which the King delights, he is "determined to prove a villain" and has contrived to turn the King against his brother George, Duke of Clarence, with a prophecy that someone with the initial "G" would be the murderer of Edward's heirs. On a London street, he meets Clarence, who is being taken to the Tower. Apparently sympathizing with his plight, Richard asserts that the King's lowborn Queen, Elizabeth Grey, and her brother, Earl Rivers, are responsible for his arrest. From Lord Hastings, himself recently freed from the Tower, Richard learns that the King is seriously ill. This news causes him to reflect that Clarence must die before Edward if he, Richard, the youngest of the three brothers, is to realize his ambitions.

Richard then encounters the Lady Anne as she mourns over the body of her father-in-law, Henry VI, whom Richard has recently slain, as he had earlier slain her husband Edward. At first she replies to Richard's honeyed words with abuse, even when he protests that he had killed only in order to win her as his wife. Pretending to be wounded by her scorn, he gives her his sword and bares his breast to her, but she refuses to be his executioner. He eventually succeeds in half convincing her of his sincerity and persuading her to wear his ring.

In the palace, Richard bickers with the Queen, Rivers, and her son Lord Grey, scornfully alluding to their sudden advancement and accusing them of sowing dissension in the court. Unobserved, Queen Margaret, widow of Henry VI, witnesses the scene with grim satisfaction. She emerges to hurl a stream of curses at the Queen and her kindred, but saves her bitterest epithets for "that poisonous bunch-back'd toad," the Duke of Gloucester.

Meanwhile, the Duke of Clarence tells his jailer, Sir Robert Brackenbury, of a dream in which he had drowned and been assailed by the spirits of those he had wronged. Two murderers engaged by Richard enter with a commission ordering Brackenbury to deliver Clarence to their hands. After vainly pleading for his life, Clarence is stabbed, and his body immersed in a butt of malmsey wine. One of the murderers is so stricken by conscience that he decides to forgo his share of the fee.

Act II. The ailing Edward, anxious to restore amity to the court, prevails upon Queen Margaret and her kinsmen to swear friendship to Lord Hastings and the Duke of Buckingham. Richard also takes part in the outwardly cordial scene, only to plunge the company into gloom by reporting the death of Clarence. Edward, believing himself responsible, is disconsolate.

The fragile peace between the rival factions is shattered when Edward dies and is succeeded by the youthful Prince of Wales. Both Queen Elizabeth and the dowager Duchess of York, Richard's mother, are alarmed to learn that Rivers, Grey, and Sir Thomas Vaughan, sent to Wales to escort the Prince to London, have been arrested by Richard and Buckingham. The Queen decides to seek sanctuary with her younger son, the Duke of York.

Act III. Arriving in London with Richard and Buckingham, Prince Edward remarks on the absence of his other uncles. After Buckingham prevails upon Cardinal Bourchier to remove the Duke of York from sanctuary, Edward is reunited with his brother, who proves at Richard's expense that he has a sharp and lively wit. The two boys depart for the Tower where, at Richard's suggestion, they are to lodge until the coronation.

Richard and Buckingham then dispatch Sir William Catesby to ascertain how Lord Hastings would react if Richard were to be declared king. Hastings informs Catesby that he would rather lose his head than consent to Richard's usurpation of the crown. However, when Lord Stanley urges him to be wary of the boar—an allusion to Richard's device—Hastings scoffs at his fears. Stanley reminds him that the Queen's kinsmen, who are to be executed that very day, had once felt as confident as he. At a council meeting in the Tower later that day, Hastings again affirms his belief in the Duke's good will toward him, but his words are belied when Richard suddenly accuses Hastings of bewitching him. As he is led to the place of execution, Hastings sadly recalls Stanley's warning and the curses of Queen Margaret.

After convincing the Mayor of London that "the dangerous and unsuspected" Hastings deserved to die, Richard instructs Buckingham to address the citizenry at Guildhall and to suggest that, since the late King had been contracted to another woman at the time of his marriage to Lady Grey, his children are illegitimate; he is also to hint that Edward himself was not the son of the late Duke of York. Buckingham returns to report that, although the crowd had remained unmoved by his harangue, some of his own followers had shouted "God save King Richard." When the Mayor arrives with some citizens, they find Richard deep in pious meditation. Buckingham and the Mayor offer him the crown, but Richard refuses peremptorily, yielding only after repeated entreaties.

Act IV. Before the Tower, Queen Elizabeth, the Duchess of York, and Anne, now Richard's wife, try to visit the young Princes, but their way is barred by Brackenbury, who states that the "King" has ordered that they be refused access. They are stunned when Lord Stanley arrives to summon Anne to Westminster to be crowned as Richard's queen.

Richard, uneasy despite his coronation, informs Buckingham that the Princes in the Tower are a threat to his security, and when the Duke fails to respond to the hint, he engages an impoverished gentleman, Tyrell, to dispose of the lads. Convinced that he must marry Elizabeth, daughter of the late King, in order to strengthen his position, he instructs Catesby to spread the news that Anne is gravely ill. When Buckingham reminds the King that he had promised to reward his services with the earldom of Hereford, Richard tartly replies that he is not "in the giving vein." Alarmed, Buckingham determines to flee.

Queen Elizabeth and the Duchess of York are mourning the death of the Princes when they are accosted by Margaret, who boasts that she is cloyed with the revenge she had craved. Despite the injuries that Richard has inflicted on her kindred, Queen Elizabeth agrees to convey his proposal of marriage to her daughter, persuaded by his description of the blessings the union would bring to her family and the kingdom.

Messengers now bring word that the Earl of Richmond, heir to the Lancastrian claim to the throne, is on his way to England from Brittany, having won the support of the Duke of Buckingham. Confused and alarmed by the ill tidings, the King becomes suspicious when Stanley, Richmond's stepfather, offers to fight the rebels, and orders him to leave his son as an assurance of his loyalty. Richard soon learns that Buckingham has been taken prisoner, but that Richmond has landed at Milford Haven in Wales.

Act V. At Bosworth Field the opposing parties prepare to give battle on the morrow. Richard's sleep is troubled by the appearance of the ghosts of his victims, who foretell his defeat and the triumph of Richmond. Awakening, the King acknowledges the pangs of conscience that afflict him, realizes that "there is no creature loves me," but succeeds in banishing his fears. Just before the battle starts, he learns that Stanley has thrown his support to Richmond. Although Richard fights valiantly, refusing to withdraw after his horse is slain, he is killed by Richmond. The victorious Earl is hailed as King Henry VII. He declares that he will marry Edward's daughter Elizabeth in order to unite the white rose and the red.—H. D.

Comment. The second and third parts of *Henry VI,* together with *Richard III,* form a dramatized history of the Wars of the Roses, a conflict between the Houses of York and Lancaster; *3 Henry VI* presents what seems at the moment a final phase of the war, with the Yorkists triumphant and Edward IV firmly established on the throne. More important for the future is the emergence of the cacodemon, Richard of York. It is he who is to initiate and direct the plots that form the substance of *Richard III.* It is he who unifies the action of both *3 Henry VI* and *Richard III.* With a few bold strokes Shakespeare etches the image of the insidious devil indelibly on our minds. His wickedness in the Henry plays culminates in his stabbing to death Prince Edward in the battle of Tewkesbury (1471) and in his murder of King Henry in the Tower of London. In *Richard III* Shakespeare often recalls for his audience murders that the King has committed in the two previous dramas. In stylized speeches Queen Margaret, Queen Elizabeth, and the Duchess of York lament his homicides. Queen Margaret begins the wailing:

> I had an Edward, till a Richard kill'd him;
> I had a Harry, till a Richard kill'd him:
> Thou hadst an Edward, till a Richard kill'd him;
> Thou hadst a Richard, till a Richard killed him.
> (IV, iv, 40–43)

Shakespeare keeps alive the idea that Richard is a subhuman monster by the animal imagery that his detractors employ in their references to him. Margaret calls him an "elvish-mark'd, abortive, rooting hog" (I, iii, 228). In another passage she warns Queen Elizabeth's kindred to

> take heed of yonder dog!
> Look, when he fawns, he bites.
> (I, iii, 289–290)

And Richmond after he has slain him, cries, "The day is ours, the bloody dog is dead" (V, v, 2).

Richard's villainy is a complex of many stage traditions. The most obvious is that of the cruel tyrant of Seneca's tragedy, whom Marlowe had transformed into a Tamburlaine, threatening heaven in high, astounding terms. His despotic deeds fill a play with violence and blood. In addition to the tyrant and the theme of revenge, the play employs the Greek and Senecan artifice of the onset of hybris, the name the ancients gave to the strutting self-assurance of a guilty creature, blind to the imminent retribution. The cause of this half-insane illusion they described in the aphorism "Whom the gods would destroy, they first make mad." Richard deludes Hastings and later Buckingham into believing that they are deep in his confidence just before he turns upon them and, with trumped-up accusations of "treachery," dooms them to instant death. Their surprise provokes scornful laughter. Such incidents serve as good examples of Richard's diabolic humor.

Margaret's anomalous position in the tragedy stamps her as a character out of Seneca. She has no historical right to a part in the events dramatized in *Richard III.* She left England for France in 1475 and died there without ever returning. The part that the dramatist wrote for her is not that of a human being. She seems much more like a direct descendant of the Senecan Furies, those hellish creatures who appeared on the earth in order to stimulate the vengeance to be enacted for ancient crimes. Margaret's curses are more than expressions of a thwarted woman's anger; they are the pronouncements of Destiny.

The stylized choral lamentations and *stichomythia* described above in the discussion of sources form two of the lyrical features of the play. This latter rhetorical device is illustrated at length in a passage (IV, iv, 344–367) in which Queen Elizabeth repels Richard's efforts to persuade her to woo her daughter for him. The two characters successfully play what A. P. Rossiter calls a game of rhetorical tennis as follows:

King Richard. Be eloquent in my behalf to her.
Queen Elizabeth. An honest tale speeds best being plainly told.
King Richard. Then in plain terms tell her my loving tale.
Queen Elizabeth. Plain and not honest is too harsh a style.
(IV, iv, 357–360)

In addition to his sinister characteristics Richard displays those of a comedian. M. M. Reese describes him as Shakespeare's "first great comic character." Elizabethan audiences would recognize him as a member of the family of the Vice, a stock character in the morality plays, where he was named "Dissimulation," "False Semblant," or "Iniquity." Richard admits in an aside his relationship to this character:

Thus, like the formal vice, Iniquity,
I moralize two meanings in one word.
(III, i, 82–83)

Richard finds amusement in the ease with which he leads his victims by the nose. His effortless success in having Clarence imprisoned provokes a characteristically ironical outburst:

Simple, plain Clarence! I do love thee so,
That I will shortly send thy soul to heaven,
If heaven will take the present at our hands.
(I, i, 118–120)

These are not features of a Senecan tyrant or of a Machiavellian villain; they are family traits of the Vice.

Richard embellishes his art of deception with histrionic ability, and even lures Buckingham into imitating it ineptly in a scene that gives Shakespeare the chance for one of his best passages requiring "ham" acting. Buckingham boasts of his acting skill, assuring Richard:

Tut, I can counterfeit the deep tragedian;
Speak and look back, and pry on every side,
Tremble and start at wagging of a straw,
Intending deep suspicion: ghastly looks
Are at my service, like enforced smiles.
(III, v, 5–9)

Serving as a background of this account of Richard's comic villainy is a historico-philosophical interpretation of the play. E. M. W. Tillyard believes that Shakespeare's main object in writing *Richard III* was to present an example of the working out of God's will in English history. The play certainly develops with increasing clarity the theme of divine retribution and the providential reunion of a tragically divided England. This conception, which he derived from Halle, Shakespeare gave in *Richard III* impressive dramatic expression. In *3 Henry VI*, Queen Margaret, standing helplessly by whilst Richard and his brothers, Clarence and Edward, stab her son Prince Edward to death, curses each of the murderers, prophesying that he will feel the wrath of God's vengeance. The application of this divine judgment forms the play's moral architecture. Richard's deserved punishment, foreshadowed by evidences of a supernal presence, may be regarded as forming the great central arch of the dramatic structure. The requitals suffered by Clarence, by the Queen's kindred, by Hastings, and by Buckingham, form the supporting arches. Each of these minor catastrophes is a demonstration of the ways of God's retributive justice.

The Richard of the last play of the tetralogy, having made away with all his domestic rivals for the crown, is free to act as he pleases. In his famous opening soliloquy he lays bare his intentions and his reasons for initiating a program of crime. The "weak piping time of peace" offers him no chance for the only kind of activity for which an ugly hunchbacked creature is fitted. Unable to caper nimbly in a lady's chamber to the lascivious tinkling of a lute, he is bored. To relieve the boredom, he decides to prove a villain, "subtle, false and treacherous," and describes the first step he will take in his pursuit of the crown. His success suffers no interruption until he hears spoken for the first time the name "Richmond," the enemy who is fated to kill him. Then the shadow of Nemesis falls upon him and the intimation of the presence of that awful goddess darkens his intelligence and enfeebles his will. He abruptly cancels orders he has just given and strikes the bearer of bad news. The appearances of the spectres of all whom he has murdered cheer Richmond and dismay him. They form an authentic prophecy of the issue of the morrow's battle. The supernatural visitants throw Richard into a state of shock, which seems briefly to split his personality, for he carries on an excited dialogue with himself, as in the following lines:

What do I fear? myself? there's none else by:
Richard loves Richard; that is, I am I.
Is there a murderer here? No. Yes, I am:
Then fly. What, from myself? Great reason why:
Lest I revenge. What, myself upon myself?
(V, iii, 182–186)

There is another possible explanation for these tortuous lines. In a contemporary Dutch play of Lambert van den Bosch on the subject of Richard's career definitely related to Shakespeare's drama, *De Roode en Witte Roos of Lankaster en Jork* (1651; The White Rose and the Red), at this point in the story there appears among the other ghosts a *Doppelgänger*, a ghostly wraith of Richard himself. In folklore the appearance of this figure is a sure sign of impending death. It is interesting to speculate that Shakespeare originally had a *Doppelgänger* crowd in among the other ghosts; and that when his fellows acted the scene, they had the incoherent lines read as a dialogue between Richard and his wraith. When the weird illusion disappears, he voices the despair of which it was a manifestation:

I shall despair. There is no creature loves me;
And if I die, no soul shall pity me.
(V, iii, 200–201)

This is a despondent parallel to his cocky boast made in *3 Henry VI:*

I have no brother, I am like no brother;
And this word 'love,' which greybeards call divine,
Be resident in men like one another
And not in me: I am myself alone.
(V, vi, 80–83)

When, with daybreak, comes need for military action, Richard is himself again. "Come bustle, bustle," he cries to his men and banishes the terrors of the night with his zest for planning strategy for the impending battle. His exhortations are meant as much for himself as for his soldiers:

Let not our babbling dreams affright our souls:
Conscience is but a word that cowards use.
(V, iii, 308–309)

With this sacrilegious boast on his lips, he rushes boldly into battle to be slain by Richmond in single combat.

This Richmond, Shakespeare endows with no distinct human personality. He is less a man than God's instrument, chosen to accomplish the union of the Houses of York and Lancaster and to bring peace to the land long stricken with the woes of civil war. Richmond never lets his men, or Shakespeare his audience, forget that God is his ally. He assures his soldiers that "God and our good cause fight upon our side" and that their enemy is

One that hath ever been God's enemy:
Then, if you fight against God's enemy,
God will in justice ward you as his soldiers.
(V, iii, 252–254)

The orders that he issues after his victory promise that he will be a perfect governor. First of all he recognizes that degree is to be of pre-eminent importance in the society at whose summit he is to sit. His command for the burial of the slain is "Inter their bodies as becomes their birth." He then proclaims a pardon for all the deserters from Richard's army, and ends by lauding the "smooth-faced peace" that Richmond and Elizabeth, by God's fair ordinance conjoined together, are fated to establish and maintain. Then, applying the play's political lesson to a current Tudor situation, he begs God to prevent the rival factions, who support different pretenders to the succession of the aging Queen, from bringing back the carnage and chaos of civil war. He ends his solemn exhortation with a prayer:

Now civil wounds are stopp'd, peace lives again:
That she may long live here, God say amen!
(V, v, 40–41)

This was a petition that every Elizabethan audience in the 1590's must have joined in with a sevenfold amen.–O. J. C.

Stage History: England. Richard BURBAGE, who soon became the most famous actor in Shakespeare's company, made his first hit in the part of Richard Crookback. How far into the 17th century the great popularity of the role and the play lasted we do not know. There is a record of a performance at court on November 16, 1633 but none of any revival of the tragedy during the Restoration.

In 1700 Colley Cibber constructed a version called KING RICHARD III, which held the stage until very recently. Cibber concocted his adaptation by stringing together bits taken from *3 Henry VI*, *Richard II*, and *Richard III*. He even interpolated part of the first scene of *2 Henry IV* and 14 lines from the 4th chorus of *Henry V* and a little verse of his own invention into Richard's soliloquy before the final battle. Some of the most famous lines, such as "Off with his head; so much for Buckingham," and "Richard's himself again," are pure Cibber. To make room for all this extraneous material, the adapter omitted completely the part of Margaret and those of the other wailing women. He also eliminated Clarence and Stanley. Cibber himself, although his reputation was made in impersonations of fops played Richard until 1739.

Two years later, in 1741, David Garrick chose the part in Cibber's adaptation for his London debut at Goodman's Fields and from 1742 to 1776 this version was produced every year, except four, at the Drury Lane. John Philip Kemble first played Richard in 1783; his impersonation of the King was subdued almost refined in manner, vastly different from Garrick's sardonic menace. As manager of Covent Garden, Kemble staged a slight revision of Cibber's version in 1811, restoring some of Shakespeare's language and acting in the title role with great success. Queen Elizabeth in this production was played by Kemble's sister, the great Sarah Siddons. Notable performances of Richard during the first half of the 19th century include those of George Frederick Cooke, Edmund Kean, and Junius Brutus Booth. On March 13, 1821 Charles Macready made the bold experiment of presenting a text in which he had restored most of Shakespeare's *Richard III*, while prudently retaining the most popular of Cibber's gags. Much to his disappointment, the critics and the public so definitely preferred Cibber's version that Macready was obliged to revert to it. During the season of 1837 Charles Kean first won acclaim on the London stage in Cibber's *Richard III*. Later in 1850, he gave the work a lavishly spectacular production with a cast of over 100 actors.

To Samuel Phelps goes the honor of really restoring Shakespeare's play to the English stage, even to the antiphonal wailings of the three bereft mothers. This production was brought out at Sadler's Wells on February 20, 1845. Critics rejoiced in the restoration of all of Margaret's part, but thought Richard better developed in Cibber's version. The public response to this noble revival is suggested by the fact that when Phelps staged *Richard III* again in November 1861, it was in Cibber's version.

Henry Irving's restored Shakespearean version played first at the Lyceum in January 1877, was cut so drastically that the plot at times became unintelligible. His revival of the piece in 1896 was as unsuccessful as the original. In March 1889 Richard Mansfield revived *Richard III* at London's Globe in a spectacular production which he later brought to America. Wishing to have the drama show Richard's progress in crime, he had each one of the five acts carefully dated on the playbill. Although Mansfield preserved most of the text of the original it was much condensed. Omitting Margaret, he also followed Cibber in beginning his performance with the scenes in *3 Henry VI* dealing with the murder of Henry VI.

Richard III was in the basic repertory of Frank Benson's company, with Benson in the title role. He offered productions regularly from 1886 through 1915 at Stratford-upon-Avon and, in 1911, the Co-operative Cinematograph Company released a two-reel film of Benson's *Richard* as acted at Stratford's Memorial Theatre. He produced the drama for Beerbohm Tree's fifth and seventh annual Shakespeare Festivals at His Majesty's. Genevieve Ward acted Queen Margaret in both London productions and at Stratford in 1908 and 1909. She also appeared in that role opposite Sir John Martin Harvey's Richard, a debonair monster, in 1916 at His Majesty's. One of Robert Atkins' first portrayals at the Old Vic was of Richard III in Ben Greet's production during the 1915/6 season, a quietly menacing characterization he re-created in his own Vic productions during the 1920/1 and 1922/3 seasons. Perhaps the most outstanding performances of the King in this decade were given by Baliol Holloway, who played the role for W. Bridges-Adams at Stratford in 1921 and 1923. His sinister Gloucester was first seen by West End audiences in December 1923 when Holloway acted with The Fellowship of Players at the Regent. Two years later the classical actor, with his instinctive feeling for Shakespeare, played Richard with cynical gusto opposite Edith Evans, equally successful as Margaret. He played the cunning villain again in 1927 and in his own production at the New in 1930, when he received a standing ovation for this dashing, theatrical presentation.

There was an Open Air production in 1934 which had Peter Glenville in the lead; two Vic productions, Henry Cass' in 1937 and Tyrone Guthrie's the next year, with Emlyn Williams as Richard. In 1939, Stratford offered its only *Richard III* of the 30's in Iden Payne's production, with John Laurie as Gloucester, Dorothy Green as Margaret, and Alec Clunes as Richmond. Donald Wolfit's incredible wartime lunch-hour Shakespeare at the Strand included a shortened version of *Richard III* on January 8, 1941 and a full production the following January. His sometimes remote, yet zestful Richard was admired by those critics who preferred their Shakespeare straight. Wolfit played the title role again in 1944 during a season at the Scala in which he presented *Richard III*, as well as other Shakespeare plays. Rosalind Iden, his wife, was Lady Anne.

The definitive performance of Richard can be credited to Laurence Olivier, who ideally combined intelligence with boldly dramatic strength in an extraordinary characterization of the King's full personality. Thoughtful, active, wickedly buoyant, with pallid complexion, long beaked nose, and limp black hair, Olivier, crouched on the throne, truly presented the diabolical Richard in all his cynical humors. Sybil Thorndike, who had played Margaret more than 25 years before for the Old Vic, was once again chillingly rancorous in the role. This Vic production, produced by John Burrell, opened on September 13, 1944 at the New Theatre and included Ralph Richardson as Richmond, Nicholas Hannen as Buckingham, and Joyce Redmond as Lady Anne. During 1948 Olivier toured Australia and New Zealand with an Old Vic company in a three-play repertory which included *Richard III*. In 1949 he returned to the New Theatre to re-enact Richard, this time opposite Vivien Leigh's Lady

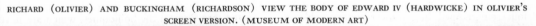

RICHARD (OLIVIER) AND BUCKINGHAM (RICHARDSON) VIEW THE BODY OF EDWARD IV (HARDWICKE) IN OLIVIER'S SCREEN VERSION. (MUSEUM OF MODERN ART)

Anne. Olivier's terrifying, malignant King was preserved in a film version which he himself directed in 1955. Critical opinion was divided on this carefully cut (Margaret was omitted), well-performed movie, whose cast included John Gielgud playing Clarence; Cedric Hardwicke, Edward IV; Ralph Richardson, Buckingham; and Alec Clunes, Hastings.

In 1953 Glen Byam Shaw directed a Stratford *Richard III* with Marius Goring in the title role, Harry Andrews as Buckingham, and Yvonne Mitchell as Lady Anne. That same year, Tyrone Guthrie opened the first season of the Shakespeare Festival Theatre at Stratford, Ontario, Canada, with *Richard III,* starring Alec Guinness. An Old Vic production in 1957, played by Robert Helpmann, Barbara Jefford, and Fay Compton as Gloucester, Lady Anne, and Margaret, and produced by Douglas Seale, had little success. Stratford failed with *Richard III* in 1961, mediocre despite an impressive cast (Christopher Plummer as Richard, Edith Evans as Margaret), and the Old Vic's 1961/2 production under Colin Graham was equally inadequate, however talented its cast of Paul Daneman, Robert Eddison, and Eileen Atkins acting Richard, Clarence, and Lady Anne, respectively. Meanwhile, *An Age of Kings* was being presented to television audiences. Produced in 1961, these programs spanned Shakespearean histories from *Richard II* through *Richard III.*

The latest major production of *Richard III* was in Peter Hall's *The Wars of the Roses* trilogy, first staged at Stratford in 1963, then presented at the Aldwych in 1964, returning later that year for another Stratford season. The text was arranged by John Barton into a coherent, logical narrative and included the three parts of *Henry VI* (the last half of *2 Henry VI* and *3 Henry VI* was titled *Edward IV*) and *Richard III.* Ian Holm was a Gloucester trapped in a power struggle, his maliciousness and mischievousness hardened into cruelty and manipulation, the torment of his deformity revealed in the soliloquies. He was joined by Peggy Ashcroft as a half-insane, vindictive Margaret.

Stage History: America. The American productions of *Richard III* followed closely the English fashions. Edmund Kean, on his American tours of 1820 and 1825, found *Richard III* his most popular vehicle. It was the first part Junius Brutus Booth played on his American tour during 1821. The wild ruffian of his portrayal was much admired. His son Edwin Booth established his reputation in 1852 with his impersonation of Richard, at first emphasizing his wiles and deceit but later adopting more and more of his father's interpretation of the role. He restored Shakespeare's version of the play to the American stage with a production in 1876 in Brooklyn, New York. *Richard III* was the vehicle selected by Robert Mantell when he began a successful comeback into theatrical prominence with a production of Cibber's version at the Princess Theatre in New York on December 5, 1904. And when John Barrymore gave his memorable performance of the villain King in 1920, he adopted Richard Mansfield's acting version. A 1965 production of the play by Sir Tyrone Guthrie at his theatre in Minneapolis starred Hume Cronyn. An unusual and provocative production, it emphasized the play's cynicism and wit. Cronyn portrayed Richard as a diabolical jester, the embodiment of black humor. In addition to stage performances, there were two American films of the play, the first released in 1908, the second in 1913.—M.G.

Bibliography. Text: David L. Patrick, *The Textual History of Richard III,* 1936; *Richard III,* New Cambridge Edition, J. Dover Wilson, ed., 1954; Fredson Bowers, "The Copy for the Folio *Richard III,*" *Shakespeare Quarterly,* X, 1959. Date: New Cambridge Edition. Sources: Sidney Thomas, *The Antic Hamlet and Richard III,* 1943; Geoffrey Bullough, *Narrative and Dramatic Sources of Shakespeare,* III, 1960. Comment: August Goll, *Criminal Types in Shakespeare,* translated from the Danish by Mrs. Charles Weekes, 1909; C. V. Boyer, *The Villain as Hero in Elizabethan Tragedy,* 1914; E. M. W. Tillyard, *Shakespeare's History Plays,* 1944; Wolfgang Clemen, *The Development of Shakespeare's Imagery,* 1951; Irving Ribner, *The English History Play in the Age of Shakespeare,* 1957; M. M. Reese, *The Cease of Majesty,* 1961; A. P. Rossiter, *Angel with Horns,* 1961. Stage History: New Cambridge Edition; T. Alston Brown, *A History of the New York Stage . . . to 1901,* 1903; William Winter, *Shakespeare on the Stage,* 3 vols., 1911–1916; G. C. D. Odell, *Shakespeare from Betterton to Irving,* 1920; J. C. Trewin, *Shakespeare on the English Stage, 1900–1964,* 1964.

Selected Criticism

ANONYMOUS. The Qualities which constitute Richard's Character are such as require a nice Discernment of Spirits, otherwise the Actor will be likely to fail in the distinguishing Singularities of this very complicated Hero. This, we imagine, is the Case in many Scenes, as this Actor performs them. The deep designing Villainy of Richard is generally converted into Rant in the Soliloquies, which are never agitated with the Passions, except where Joy transports him. They are mostly Situations of dark, cool, and deliberate Wickedness, and should be uttered with deep and grave Tones of Voice, and a gloomy Countenance. These two Requisites Nature has denied this Performer, tho' she has been very liberal to him in Qualifications for Love, Grief and enraged Tenderness. Accordingly, he does not seem to carry with him that covered Spirit of Enterprize, which is so peculiar a Mark of the Character. He is too turbulent in all the Scenes where he is alone; and the Humour of Richard, which never should take off the Mark, is with him too free and open. Richard's Pleasantry never rises to Mirth; it always proceeds from what the Poet calls the *mala mentis gaudia,* the wicked Pleasures of the Mind; and it should therefore never become totally jocund, but should ever be a mixed Emotion of Joy and Malice. [Review of Spranger Barry's Richard III, *The London Chronicle,* Jan. 29–Feb. 1, 1757; reprinted in *The English Dramatic Critics,* James Agate, ed., 1932.]

SAMUEL JOHNSON. This is one of the most celebrated of our authour's performances; yet I know not whether it has not happened to him as to others, to be praised most when praise is not most deserved. That this play has scenes noble in themselves, and very well contrived to strike in the exhibition, cannot be denied. But some parts are trifling, others shocking, and some improbable. [*The Plays of William Shakespeare*, 1765.]

CHARLES LAMB. But of Mr Cooke's *Richard: . . . His habitual jocularity*, the effect of buoyant spirits, and an elastic mind, rejoicing in its own powers, and in the success of its machinations. This quality of unstrained mirth accompanies *Richard*, and is a prime feature in his character. It never leaves him; in plots, in stratagems, and in the midst of his bloody devices, it is perpetually driving him upon wit, and jests, and personal satire, fanciful allusions, and quaint felicities of phrase. It is one of the chief artifices by which the consummate master of dramatic effect has contrived to soften the horrors of the scene, and to make us contemplate a bloody and vicious character with delight. No where, in any of his plays, is to be found so much of sprightly colloquial dialogue, and soliloquies of genuine humour, as in *Richard*. This character of unlaboured mirth Mr Cooke seems entirely to pass over, and substitutes in its stead the coarse, taunting humour, and clumsy merriment, of a low-minded assassin.

His personal deformity.—When the *Richard* of Mr Cooke makes allusions to his own *form*, they seem accompanied with *unmixed distaste* and *pain*, like some obtrusive and *haunting* idea— But surely the *Richard* of Shakspeare mingles in these allusions a perpetual reference to his own powers and capacities, by which he is enabled to surmount these petty objections; and the joy of a defect *conquered*, or *turned* into an advantage, is one cause of these very allusions, and of the satisfaction, with which his mind recurs to them. These allusions themselves are made in an ironical and good humoured spirit of exaggeration—the most bitter of them are to be found in his self-congratulating soliloquy spoken in the very moment and crisis of joyful exultation on the success of his unheard of courtship. [Review of George Frederick Cooke as Richard III, 1802; reprinted in *Lamb's Criticism*, E. M. W. Tillyard, ed., 1923.]

JAMES RUSSELL LOWELL. I think these are the three qualities—subtlety of poetic expression, humor, and eloquence—which we should expect to find in a play of Shakespeare's and especially in an historical play. Of each and all of these we find less in "Richard III.," as it appears to me, than in any other of his plays of equal pretensions; for although it is true that in "Richard II." there is no humorous character, the humor of irony is many times present in the speeches of the king after his dethronement. There is a gleam of humor here and there in "Richard III.," as where Richard rebukes Buckingham for saying "'zounds,"—

"O do not swear, my Lord of Buckingham;"

and there are many other Shakespearian touches; but the play as a whole appears to me always less than it should be, except in scenic effectiveness, to be reckoned a work from Shakespeare's brain and hand alone, or even mainly,—less in all the qualities and dimensions that are most exclusively and characteristically his. This I think to be conclusive, for, as Goethe says very truly, if there be any defect in the most admirable of Shakespeare's plays, it is that they are more than they should be. The same great critic, speaking of his "Henry IV.," says with equal truth "that, were everything else that has come down to us of the same kind lost, [the arts of] poesy and rhetoric could be re-created out of it."

The first impression made upon us by "Richard III." is that it is thoroughly melodramatic in conception and execution. Whoever has seen it upon the stage knows that the actor of Richard is sure to offend against every canon of taste laid down by Hamlet in his advice to the players. He is sure to tear his passion to rags and tatters; he is sure to split the ears of the groundlings; and he is sure to overstep the modesty of nature with every one of his stage strides. Now, it is not impossible that Shakespeare, as a caterer for the public taste, may have been willing that the groundlings as well as other people should help to fill the coffers of his company, and that the right kind of attraction should accordingly be offered them. It is therefore conceivable that he may have retouched or even added to a poor play which had already proved popular; but it is not conceivable that he should have written an entire play in violation of those principles of taste which we may deduce more or less clearly from everything he wrote. [*The Complete Writings of James Russell Lowell*, 1904.]

WOLFGANG CLEMEN. The omnipresence of the hero, Richard III, is a striking feature of this drama. We have already said that the whole action depends upon him. But not only that—we feel his presence even when he is not upon the stage. Images are partly responsible for this. Again and again, the impression which Richard's nature makes upon the other characters and which lingers with them is reflected in their speeches, generally in the form of animal-imagery. The fundamental image for him is that of the repulsive dog, an image, of which we find traces as early as the last part of *Henry VI*. In the great scene of lament in the fourth act Queen Margaret finds the most impressive formulation of this image:

> From forth the kennel of thy womb hath crept
> A hell-hound that doth hunt us all to death:
> That dog, that had his teeth before his eyes,
> To worry lambs and lap their gentle blood . . .
> (IV. iv. 47)

Richard III appears further as *poisonous toad*, as *foul hunchback'd toad, bottled spider, as hedge-hog, elvish-mark'd, abortive, rooting hog. . . .*

We cannot exaggerate the imaginative value of these revolting animal-images. Without our becoming conscious of it, the repulsive figure of the hunchbacked Richard as we see it upon the stage is repeatedly transformed into animal bodies conforming to his nature, and thus his brutal, animal character is illuminated from this angle too. *Richard III* is Shakespeare's first play in which the chief character is delineated by symbolical images recurring as a *leitmotif*. In *Henry VI* the animal images, which are occasionally employed for individual combatants, are not yet differentiated. Talbot as well as Clifford and Salisbury are all compared to lions. None of these characters is made to differ from the others by means of the images appertaining to him. When Shakespeare compares the warriors to bears, wolves, steers, eagles, etc., he is not thinking of the individuals; he is seeking to create the general atmosphere of battle and war. In *Richard III*, however, the imagery begins to serve individual characterization. [*The Development of Shakespeare's Imagery*, 1951.]

A. P. ROSSITER. On the face of it, he [Richard] is the demon-Prince, the cacodemon born of hell, the misshapen toad, etc. (all things ugly and ill). But through his prowess as actor and his embodiment of the comic Vice and impish-to-fiendish humour, he offers the false as more attractive than the true (the actor's function), and the ugly and evil as admirable and amusing (the clown's game of value-reversals). You can say, "We don't take him seriously." I reply, "That is exactly what gets most of his acquaintances into Hell: just what the devil-clown relies on." But he is not only this demon incarnate, he is in effect God's agent in a predetermined plan of divine retribution: the "scourge of God." Now by Tudor-Christian historical principles, this plan is *right*. Thus, in a real sense, Richard is a King who "can do no wrong"; for in the pattern of the justice of divine retribution on the wicked, he functions as an avenging angel. Hence my paradoxical title, "Angel with Horns."

The paradox is sharpened by what I have mainly passed by: the repulsiveness, humanely speaking, of the "justice." God's will it may be, but it sickens us: it is as pitiless as the Devil's (who is called in to execute it). The contrast with Marlowe's painless, dehumanized slaughterings in *Tamburlaine* is patent.

This overall system of *paradox* is the play's unity. It is revealed as a constant displaying of inversions, or reversals of meaning: whether we consider the verbal patterns (the *peripeteias* or reversals of act and intention or expectation); the antithesis of false and true in the histrionic character; or the constant inversions of irony. Those verbal capsizings I began by talking about, with their deliberate reversals to the opposite meaning in equivocal terms, are the exact correlatives of both the nature of man (or man in power: Richard) and of the nature of events (history); and of language too, in which all is conveyed. [*Angel with Horns*, 1961.]

Richardson, John (fl. 1582). A friend and neighbor of Richard Hathaway who, in 1582, stood surety along with Fulke Sandells at the granting of a marriage license for Hathaway's daughter Anne and Shakespeare (see MARRIAGE). Standing surety involved a promise to pay a sum of £40 to the representatives of the bishop of Worcester if the marriage were later found to be invalid. A year prior to the marriage, Richardson had acted as a witness to Richard Hathaway's will. [Mark Eccles, *Shakespeare in Warwickshire*, 1961.]

Richardson, Sir Ralph (1902–). Actor. Born in Gloucestershire, Richardson made his acting debut in Brighton in 1920. In 1921 he acted Lorenzo in a production of *The Merchant of Venice* at Lowestoft, and for the next four years toured the provinces. In 1926 he appeared with the Birmingham Repertory Theatre, and in 1928 in London as Tranio in a modern-dress *Taming of the Shrew*. He has acted with the Old Vic on innumerable occasions in many roles, beginning with the Prince of Wales in a 1930 production of *1 Henry IV*. Since then his Shakespearean repertory has encompassed Caliban, Bolingbroke, Enobarbus, Sir Toby Belch, Don Pedro, Kent, Faulconbridge, Petruchio, Bottom, Henry V, Brutus, Iago, the Ghost and First Gravedigger in *Hamlet*, Othello, Falstaff, John of Gaunt, Timon, and Mercutio. In 1944 he became a joint director at the Old Vic's New Theatre, and has appeared as well at the Shakespeare Memorial Theatre, Stratford-upon-Avon. Since 193 he has turned in memorable performances in many films, including *Richard III*. [*Who's Who in the Theatre*, 1961.]

Richardson, William (1743–1814). Scottish author and educator. In his *Philosophical Analysis and Illustration of Some of Shakespeare's Remarkable Characters*, Richardson attempts to define four of Shakespeare's characters—Macbeth, Hamlet, Jaques, and Imogen—psychologically and morally, drawing from each a philosophical lesson. Thus, Macbeth is an example of a naturally honest man driven to villainy by an overriding passion; Jaques is a naturally sociable figure turned antisocial through disappointment.

In the *Essays on Shakespeare's Dramatic Characters . . .* (1784) Richardson treats Richard III, Lear and Timon in similar fashion; in an article published in 1789 in *Essays on Shakespeare's . . . Sir John Falstaff and on his Female Characters*, he emphasizes Falstaff's unhappy end.

The 1784 *Essays* also note dramatic faults in Shakespeare, namely, Shakespeare's disregard for the classical unities, his occasional historical and geographical errors, and, most of all, his juxtaposition of tragedy and comedy and the presentation of dignified figures in trivial situations. [Herbert Spencer Robinson, *English Shakespearian Criticism in the Eighteenth Century*, 1932.]

Richardus Tertius. See Thomas LEGGE.

Riche, Barnabe. See Barnabe RICH.

Richmond, Henry Tudor, earl of. See HENRY VII.

Ridley, Maurice Roy (1890–). Scholar, lecturer in English at Bedford College, London. Ridley is the editor of the *New Temple Shakespeare* (1934–1936) and the New Arden editions of *Antony and Cleopatra* (1954) and *Othello* (1958). He is also the author of *Shakespeare's Plays, a Commentary* (1937).

Ristori, Adelaide. See ITALY.

Ritson, Joseph (1752–1803). Scholar. A splenetic and often pedantic scholar, Ritson is chiefly noted for his heated attacks on contemporary Shakespearean scholars. His *Remarks, critical and illustrative, on the Text and Notes of the last Edition of Shakespeare* (1783) is a vitriolic onslaught on the Johnson-Steevens edition (1778). In *The Quip Modest* (1788) he scornfully attacked Isaac Reed and Edmund Malone. Ritson is also credited with being one of the first scholars to detect the forgeries of William Henry Ireland. He never completed his projected edition of Shakespeare, but he did produce a valuable history of early English literature in his *Bibliographia Poetica* (1802).

Rival Poet, The. Designation for the poet referred to in Sonnets 78–83, 85, and 86.

Throughout these sonnets Shakespeare modestly refers to one or more rivals for the favor of his patron. He calls him "a worthier pen" (79, 6) and "a better spirit" to whom he is "inferior far" (80, 2, 7). He asserts that this competitor has been taught by spirits to write "above a mortal pitch" (86, 6). Assuming that Shakespeare would apply these phrases only to poets of considerable merit, some critics have limited their choice of the Rival Poet to the greater of Shakespeare's contemporaries. Their availability is usually judged by the similarity of their achievements to those of the poet described in Sonnet 86:

> Was it the proud full sail of his great verse,
> Bound for the prize of all too precious you,
> That did my ripe thoughts in my brain inhearse,
> Making their tomb the womb wherein they grew?
> Was it his spirit, by spirits taught to write
> Above a mortal pitch, that struck me dead?
> No, neither he, nor his compeers by night
> Giving him aid, my verse astonished.
> He, nor that affable familiar ghost
> Which nightly gulls him with intelligence,
> As victors of my silence cannot boast;
> I was not sick of any fear from thence:
> But when your countenance fill'd up his line,
> Then lack'd I matter; that enfeebled mine.

Spenser has been chosen for the honor on the ground that he was the only poet of the age of whom Shakespeare would have been likely to be jealous. The "affable familiar ghost," explain the partisans of Spenser, is Chaucer, the "most sacred happie spirit" of the Faerie Queene (Frank Mathew, *An Image of Shakespeare*, 1922). Marlowe was early nominated for the rivalship, because "the proud full sail of his great verse" could easily be taken as an imaginative description of Marlowe's "mighty line." He was at the peak of his power and popularity when Shakespeare came to London, but he died in 1593, too soon to be a rival sonneteer. And there is no evidence whatever that he was acquainted with either Southampton or Pembroke. A. L. Rowse in his *William Shakespeare* (1963) accepts Marlowe as the Rival Poet. He asks "Was not *Hero and Leander* (1593) written in competition with *Venus and Adonis* (1592)? And *Hero and Leander* begins with a salute to his rival's theme, for upon Hero's sleeve is embroidered a grove "Where Venus in her naked glory strove / To please the careless and disdainful eyes / Of proud Adonis that before her lies." Samuel Daniel was groomed for the position largely because Shakespeare is thought to have found inspiration in Daniel's poems—for Lucrece in *The Complaint of Rosamond* (1592) and for important features of his sonnets in Daniel's sequence, *Delia* (1592).

Throughout the sequence Shakespeare alludes indirectly and cryptically to the poems of rivals who he fears are superseding him in the favor of his patron. One of the most significant expressions of his anxiety occurs in Sonnet 76. There he asks, in effect, "If my verses are so monotonous, so devoid of novelty, why do I not adopt some of the 'new-found methods' and 'compounds strange' of my avant-garde contemporaries?" These phrases aptly describe John Donne's early metaphysical poems, and make him another candidate for the Rival Poet. George Chapman has become the candidate favored by most Shakespeareans, because he, best of all claimants, fits the description of the poet and his work presented in Sonnet 86. Although the phrase "The proud full sail of his great verse" is a good description of Marlowe's poetry, it is an even better characterization of the 14-syllabled, rhymed lines (so-called fourteeners) in which Chapman cast his translation of the first seven books of the *Iliad* that appeared in 1598. The phrase "his compeers by night" may well be a reference to Chapman's poem "The Shadow of Night." The allusion to "night" also suggests, according to Arthur Acheson, M. C. Bradbrook, and Frances Yates, Chapman's association in a SCHOOL OF NIGHT, a group organized by Sir Walter Raleigh for the study of mathematics and astronomy. Miss Bradbrook's thesis is that this group is being satirized in *Love's Labour's Lost* where there is a reference (frequently emended by modern editors) to a "schoole of night." Thomas Harriott or Hariot, a famous mathematician and astronomer, was apparently the intellectual leader of the school. George Chapman and Marlowe were the first two poets who joined the group. Chapman's studies took a different direction from those of his colleagues. Being a mystic, he became interested in psychic phenomena and spiritualism. A good guess is that the affable familiar ghost to which Shakespeare jestingly refers was the spirit or *anima* of Homer, which Chapman asserted came to him in a vision and prompted him while he was at work translating the *Iliad*. Shakespeare's insinuation that this spirit was a bad angel who duped him is playfully satiric, as is his pretense that the rival's ideas were so transcendental that they forced Shakespeare in shame to bury his much simpler thoughts. Other candidates suggested for the role of Shakespeare's rival have included Ben Jonson, Michael Drayton, and the less well known figure put forth by Sidney Lee, Barnabe BARNES. Robert Gittings' *Shakespeare's Rival* (1960) identifies the Rival Poet as Gervase (Jarvis) MARKHAM, a minor poet and a member of the so-called Southampton Circle. [*The Sonnets*, New Variorum Edition, Hyder Rollins, ed., 1944.]—O. J. C.

Rivers, Anthony Woodville, 2nd Earl (1442?–1483). Eldest son of Richard Woodville, 1st Earl Rivers, and Jacquetta, widow of John of Lancaster, duke of Bedford. After his marriage to Elizabeth, daughter of Lord Scales, Woodville succeeded to the title held by his father-in-law. With the Lancastrians at the battle of Towton, Woodville afterward abandoned that party for the Yorkist king, Edward IV. Accompanying the king to exile in Holland, Woodville, now Earl Rivers, returned with him to England in 1471 and fought at the victorious battle of Barnet. When Edward died, Rivers, his half-brother Richard Grey, and Sir Thomas Vaughan were arrested by order of the duke of Gloucester, and executed.

In *3 Henry VI*, Rivers appears in IV, iv, where Queen Elizabeth informs him of Edward's capture by Warwick's army. In *Richard III* Rivers says, just before his execution: "To-day shalt thou behold a subject die/ For truth, for duty, and for loyalty."

Roberts, James (fl. 1564–1608). London printer and publisher. Roberts issued a number of Shakespeare quartos. Admitted to the Stationers' Company in 1564, he married the widow of the printer John Charlewood (d. 1593) and secured Charlewood's numerous copyrights, including the exclusive right to print the acting companies' playbills. His relationship with Shakespeare's company appears to have been close, for he seems to have acted as its agent among the stationers in the players' often futile efforts to prevent publication of popular plays. In 1598 he entered *The Merchant of Venice* in the Stationers' Register, with the surprising proviso that "yt

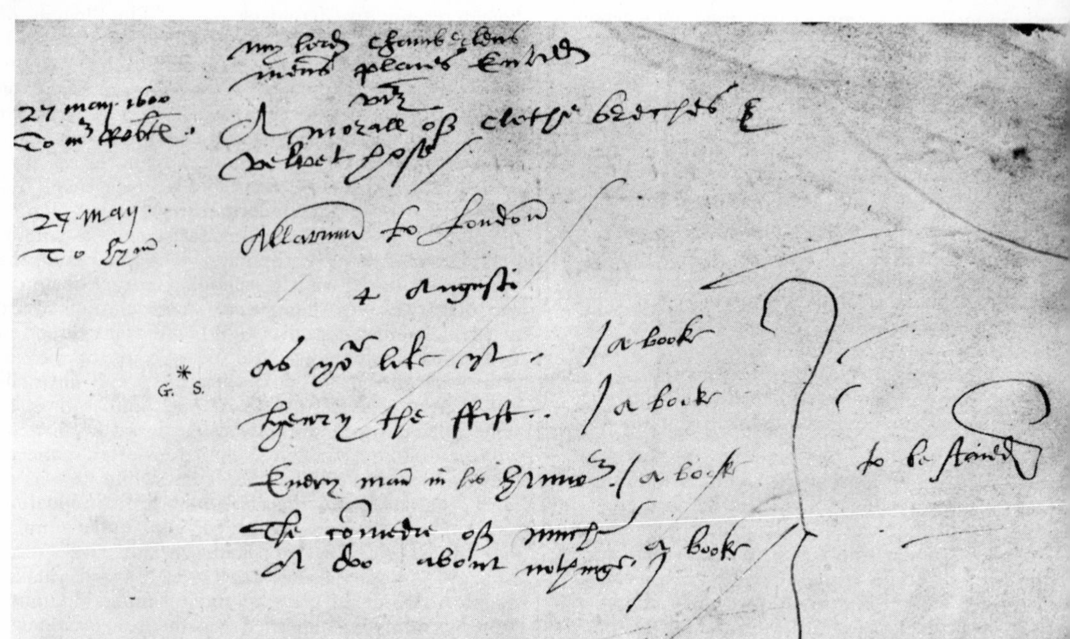
27 may 1600
To mr Robte.
27 may.
To him

my lord chamberlens
menns plaies Entred
viz
A morall of clothe breches &
velvet hose
Allarum to London
4 Augusti
As you like yt. / a booke
Henry the ffift. / a booke
Every man in his humor. / a booke
The commedie of muche
A doo about nothinge. / a booke
to be staied

G. * S.

ROBERTS' BLOCKING ENTRY OF 1600 IN THE STATIONERS' REGISTER. NOT A FORMAL ENTRY IN THE REGISTER, THIS IS REALLY A MEMORANDUM ON A SPARE PAGE. (STATIONERS' HALL, BY PERMISSION OF THE WORSHIPFUL COMPANY OF STATIONERS) FOR A TRANSCRIPT SEE APPENDIX.

bee not prynted." Two years later (1600) he did print the First Quarto of that play. In 1600 he also printed the Second Quarto of *Titus Andronicus* and made what has been described as a BLOCKING ENTRY in the Stationers' Register for *As You Like It, Henry V, Much Ado About Nothing*, and Jonson's *Every Man In his Humour*. Another apparent attempt to forestall publication was his registration of *Hamlet* in 1602. If this was his aim it was unsuccessful, for in 1603 Nicholas Ling published an unauthorized "bad quarto" of the play. In the following year, however, Ling and Roberts combined as publisher and printer of the good Second Quarto of *Hamlet* (1604). Again in 1603 Roberts registered, but did not print, *Troilus and Cressida*. In 1608 Roberts sold his business to William Jaggard, who in 1619 printed a number of Shakespearean plays with false dates on the title pages in order to avoid a government order prohibiting the publication of the King's Men's plays without their consent. Two of these 1619 Quartos, *A Midsummer Night's Dream* and *The Merchant of Venice*, bear the imprint of Roberts and the date 1600. Roberts had printed the 1600 Quarto of *The Merchant*, but the printer of *A Midsummer Night's Dream* in 1600 is generally thought to be either Edward Allde or Richard Bradock. Roberts printed comparatively few plays during his career, but it is interesting that all of the plays he entered in the Stationers' Register belonged to Shakespeare's company. [R. B. McKerrow, ed., *A Dictionary of Printers and Booksellers . . . 1557–1640*, 1910.]

Roberts, John. See Sir William BISHOP.

Robertson, J[ohn] M[ackinnon] (1856–1933). Scholar and politician. One of the foremost exponents of the DISINTEGRATION theory of Shakespeare's texts, Robertson was also a wide-ranging social critic and an active man of affairs. He serve as a member of parliament from 1906 to 1918 an wrote a number of respected books on a wide variet of topics, including religion, economics, and socia science.

In the field of Shakespearean studies, he was disciple of F. G. Fleay, whose VERSE TESTS and othe statistical data first publicized the theory that a larg part of the Shakespeare canon contained much ma terial not written by him. Robertson was particularl prone to "discovering" the work of Marlowe an Chapman embedded in the Shakespeare texts. H tentatively expounded his theories first in *Did Shake speare Write Titus Andronicus?* (1905), developin his thesis at greater length in *Shakespeare and Chap man* (1917). His position was most elaborately pre sented, however, in *The Shakespeare Canon* (5 vols 1922–1930), in which he analyzed in detail each o the plays. Although generally rejected today, hi theories had considerable influence in their time They were the basis, for example, of the famou essay "Hamlet and His Problems" by T. S. ELIOT.

Robertson is also the author of *The Baconia Heresy: A Confutation* (1913) and *Montaigne an Shakespeare* (1897; enlarged, 1909). [*Dictionary o National Biography, 1931–1940*, 1949.]

Robin. In *The Merry Wives of Windsor*, a littl page to Falstaff. Robin delivers Falstaff's love letter to the merry wives, and when sent by his master t attend Mistress Page, he tells her that he woul rather walk in front of her like a man than follow Falstaff like a dwarf. Accordingly, Robin joins in the plots at Falstaff's expense. (See also PAGE T FALSTAFF.)

Robin Goodfellow. See PUCK.

Robin Hood plays. See FOLK FESTIVALS.

Robinson, John (fl. 1616). One of the witnesses to Shakespeare's will. Conceivably, he is the same John Robinson who is mentioned in the will as a tenant of Shakespeare's London property, the Blackfriars Gate-House:

> . . . And alsoe All that Messuage or tenemente with theppurtenaunces wherein one John Robinson dwelleth, scituat lyeing & being in the blackfriers in London nere the Wardrobe, & all other my landes tenementes and hereditamentes whatsoever.

If the John Robinson who signed the will is not the same man as the occupant of the gatehouse, he was probably one of Shakespeare's Stratford servants.

Robinson, the tenant, was still occupying the gatehouse in 1618, when, in accordance with the directions in Shakespeare's will, the house was transferred in trust (see BLACKFRIARS GATE-HOUSE):

> Memorand, that the xj.th daye of Februarye in the yeres within written, John Robynson, tenant of the premysses withinmencioned, did geve and delyver unto John Greene withinnamed to the use of Susanna Hall within-named, sixe pence of lawefull money of England, in name of attornement, in the presence of Matt: Benson: John Prise. Per me Rychardum Tyler.

[J. O. Halliwell-Phillipps, *Outlines of the Life of Shakespeare*, 1881.]

Robinson, Richard (d. 1648). Actor. According to E. K. Chambers, Robinson was conceivably the son of James Robinson, a member of the syndicate managing the Children of the Chapel in 1600, and a boy actor with the Children at Blackfriars. Robinson was with the King's Men from 1611, playing that year in *Catiline*. According to a passage in *The Devil Is an Ass*, given by the King's Men in 1616, Robinson was still a boy actor playing women's roles. He is listed in the 1623 quarto of *The Duchess of Malfi* as the second actor to play the Cardinal, succeeding Henry Condell in that role; and he is in the actor list of the First Folio of Shakespeare's plays which was also published that year.

At some time after Richard Burbage's death (1619), Robinson probably married his widow, Winifred, for she is mentioned in the SHARERS' PAPERS dispute as Mrs. Robinson. Robinson continues to appear in extant acting lists of the King's Men. The *Historia Histrionica* of James Wright refers to the actors "*Hart* and *Clun*," who "were bred up Boys at the *Blackfriers* . . . *Hart* was *Robinson's* Boy or Apprentice." Wright also refers to "*Pollard*, and *Robinson*" who "were Comedians" at Blackfriars, but the latter allusion is probably to another actor; there seem to have been several Robinsons on the stage at the time, and a "Robbins" who actually was a comedian (see James WRIGHT). Wright also says that Robinson was killed in 1645, when he took up arms for the king, but scholars credit the burial listed in the registry of St. Anne's, Blackfriars, of "Richard Robinson a Player" on March 23, 1648. [E. K. Chambers, *The Elizabethan Stage*, 1923; T. W. Baldwin, *The Organization and Personnel of the Shakespearean Company*, 1927; G. E. Bentley, *The Jacobean and Caroline Stage*, 5 vols., 1941–1956.]

Roche, Robert (1576–1629). Poet and divine who made an early allusion to Shakespeare. Roche's only extant work, *Eustathia or the Constancie of Susanna*, was published in 1599. In his apologetic Preface "To the Reader" Roche acknowledges his inability to match Shakespeare's *Rape of Lucrece:* "Expect not heere, th' invention, or the vaine Of *Lucrece rape-write*."

Roche's *Eustathia* is a long, dull poem which fully justifies his modesty. [William Sloane, "Four Early Shakspere Allusions," *Shakespeare Association Bulletin*, 1938.]

Roche, Walter (fl. 1559–1575). Master of the Stratford grammar school from Christmas 1569 to Michaelmas 1571. A native of Lancashire, Roche was educated at Oxford, receiving his B.A. in 1559. In 1573 and 1575, he and John Shakespeare served as witnesses to two deeds enacted in those years. If Shakespeare attended the Stratford school, Roche would have been the schoolmaster during his early years. Roche lived in Chapel Street, three doors from New Place, the house Shakespeare bought in 1597. Roche was succeeded as master by Simon Hunt.

Rocke of Regard. See George WHETSTONE.

Roderigo. In *Othello*, a Venetian gentleman smitten with love for Desdemona. Pretending to aid Roderigo in his suit, Iago persuades him that he must murder his supposed rival, Cassio. When Cassio escapes with a wound, Iago kills Roderigo to prevent revelation of the plot.

Rodgers, Richard. See MUSIC BASED ON SHAKESPEARE: *20th century*.

Rogers, Paul (1917–). Actor. Born at Plympton, Devon, and educated at Newton Abbot, Rogers studied acting at Michael Chekhov's Theatre Studio and made his debut at the Scala in 1938. In 1939 he appeared at Stratford-upon-Avon and then went into repertory at Colchester. After World War II he played a wide variety of parts with the Bristol Old Vic, including Tybalt and Bottom, and then joined the London Old Vic. His roles have included Don Armado, Dull, Osric, the First Player, Malvolio, Doctor Caius, Iago, the Third Witch, Shylock, Henry VIII, Macbeth, Petruchio, Touchstone, Falstaff, Leontes, Mercutio, John of Gaunt, Pandarus, Hamlet, and Lear. In 1957 he toured Australia for the Elizabethan Theatre Trust Drama Company as Hamlet, and has been in films and television since 1952. He is also the author of a preface to the Folio Society edition of *Love's Labour's Lost* (1959). [*Who's Who in the Theatre*, 1961.]

Rogers, Philip. Stratford apothecary whom Shakespeare sued for debt in 1604. Rogers had purchased from Shakespeare malt amounting to 35s. 10d., for which he refused to pay. Shakespeare appealed to the Stratford court of record, which functioned as a small-claims court. The case was brought before the court in July 1604, but the records relating to the suit are not extant and the determination of the case is not known. Rogers, whose apothecary shop was located in High Street, appears to have been in financial difficulty at this time.

Some doubt has been entertained as to whether the William Shakespeare in this case is the dramatist, but the only other William Shakespeare who might qualify does not begin to appear in local records until after 1620. [B. Roland Lewis, *The Shakespeare Documents*, 1940.]

Rogers, Richard (fl. 1656). Bookseller. In association with William Ley (fl. 1640–1656) Rogers published in 1656 a catalogue of plays which falsely ascribed a number of plays to Shakespeare. Among these were the history plays *Edward II*, *Edward III*, *Edward IV*, and the comedy *The London Prodigal*. [W. W. Greg, *A List of English Plays Written Before 1643 . . .*, 1900.]

rogues and vagabonds. Economic and social changes in the 16th century greatly increased the number of unemployed men in England and added to the growing confraternity of thieves, swindlers, vagabonds, and beggars that infested both the highways and the towns. Many slid into a life of crime from simple inclination or dislike of honest work; others, such as minstrels, players, and peddlers, whose occupations kept them traveling, found themselves grouped by association (and ultimately by law) with vagabonds (see ACTORS). Husbandmen, through no fault of their own, found themselves dispossessed of their farms either after the dissolution of the monasteries and the confiscation of church lands or as a result of the general change in which land that had once been farmed was being turned into pasture for sheep (see ENCLOSURE).

Wandering on the roads or flocking to an increasingly crowded London, such men were outside the law simply by virtue of being unemployed; in order to live they often took to begging or thieving. Poor laws of varying stringency were enacted during Elizabeth's reign. These attempted to provide relief for those who were unable to work because of physical disability, to punish those who preferred begging and thievery to honest work,

TITLE PAGE OF A 17TH-CENTURY TREATISE ON BEGGING.

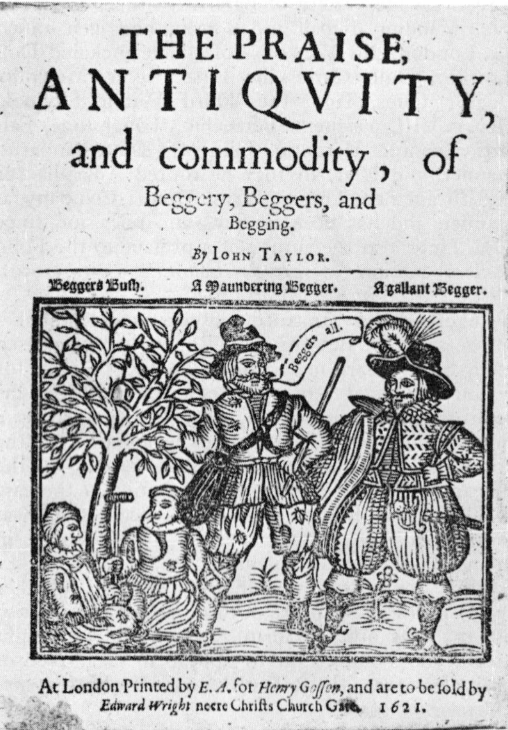

THE PRAISE, ANTIQVITY, and commodity, of Beggery, Beggers, and Begging.

By IOHN TAYLOR.

At London Printed by E. A. for Henry Goffon, and are to be sold by Edward Wright neere Christs Church Gate. 1621.

and to extract a certain amount of enforced charit from the rich. The punishments for vagrancy an begging were severe; whipping or branding wa common for a first offense, and a second was con strued as a felony, which meant the gallows.

However, even the threat of the hangman ha little effect in discouraging thievery and vaga bondage; indeed, so numerous were rogues an vagabonds that there was established among then a kind of thieves' guild with a multitude of fin rules and regulations, a hierarchy of sorts, and peculiar argot known as the pelting speech, peddlers French, or thieves' cant. In the nomenclature of th pelting tongue, types of rogues included palliard or clapperdogens, men who went ragged an blistered their legs with arsenic to gain sympath and contributions; Abraham men, who pretende madness and begged for anything they might con vert to money; counterfeit cranks, who feigne sickness and used soap to produce a realistic foar at the mouth; dummerers, who doubled up thei tongues and carried a forged notice asserting tha they were dumb; priggers or prancers, who robbe on the highways; and others. The terms of thei trade were couched in the canting tongue so tha they would be unintelligible if overheard by a would-be victim. Each of their various swindle was known as a certain art or law as, for instance Barnard's law for enticing a dupe into a crooked game of cards. There was a certain amount of appreciation for art and finesse in thievery, indicated by the esteem in which the foist, or pickpocket, was held, in comparison to the less skillful nip, or cutpurse. Autolycus, one of Shakespeare's rogues, is a "snapper-up of unconsidered trifles" (*Winter's Tale*, IV, iii, 26); ready to snatch whatever he can, he is not too proud to use his knife as well as his fingers:

> I picked and cut most of their festival purses.
> (IV, iv, 626)

Falstaff, another famous rogue, is a somewhat more honorable fellow, but even he feels the pinch of want at times and is not above a bit of swindling or cony-catching (see CONY-CATCHING PAMPHLETS):

> I, I, I myself sometimes, leaving the fear of God on the left hand and hiding mine honour in my necessity, am fain to shuffle, to hedge and to lurch.
> (*Merry Wives of Windsor*, II, ii, 23–26)

Bardolph and Nym, "sharpers attending on Falstaff," are of a more thoroughly rascally breed:

> They will steal any thing, and call it purchase. Bardolph stole a lute-case, bore it twelve leagues, and sold it for three half-pence. Nym and Bardolph are sworn brothers in filching.
> (*Henry V*, III, ii, 44–48)

[Charles Whibley, "Rogues and Vagabonds," *Shakespeare's England*, 1916.]

Rolfe, William James (1827–1910). American educator. Leaving Amherst after three years without taking a degree, Rolfe spent the next 20 years as a schoolmaster in his native Massachusetts. His introduction of English literature into the curriculum was recognized as a sweeping reform, and gained him honorary degrees from Harvard (1859) and Amherst (1865, 1887). In 1868 he retired from regular teaching in order to devote himself to traveling, lecturing, and the preparation of school texts. He issued two separate editions of Shakespeare, each in 40 volumes (1871–1884 and 1903–1906), which became the most widely used texts in American schools. Despite the expurgations which Rolfe felt obligated to make, his work received high praise from outstanding scholars on both sides of the Atlantic. Rolfe also published numerous periodical notes on Shakespeare and two biographies: *Shakespeare the Boy* (1896) and *A Life of William Shakespeare* (1904), the latter with a bibliography that is a useful guide to 19th-century authorities. His other works include editions of Scott and Tennyson, guide and travel books, a series of science texts, and books of an educational nature. In 1907 he estimated that he had written or edited 144 volumes exclusive of periodical articles.

Rolli, Paolo. See ITALY.

Rollins, Hyder [Edward] (1889–1958). American scholar. Rollins succeeded G. L. Kittredge, with whom he had studied, as Gurney professor of English at Harvard in 1939. He edited all of the major Elizabethan "poetical miscellanies," including the famous *Tottel's Miscellany* (2 vols., 1928–1929), as well as the variorum editions of *Shakespeare's Poems* (1938) and *Sonnets* (1944). In 1947 Rollins was named general editor of the Fourth Variorum (see VARIORUM EDITIONS). In the final years of his life he devoted himself to the Romantic period, editing the standard edition of *The Letters of John Keats* (2 vols., 1958).

Romeo. The hero of *Romeo and Juliet.* Romeo, who first appears as a moon-struck adolescent, is transformed in the course of the play into a figure of tragic stature. Although never without boyish charm and vitality, he is in the early parts of the play a somewhat posturing, self-indulgent adolescent. His infatuation with Rosaline is more pose than passion and is quite rightly the subject of Mercutio's witty cynicisms. But beneath this elegant and trivial façade lie the real, untested capacities of his character, capacities which are eventually proved when caught up in the inexorable tragic action. He moves from innocence to experience through the inevitable path of suffering, but in so doing creates transcending love which enables him to affirm life even while losing it. Romeo has been called an early model of Hamlet, with whom he shares a tendency toward melancholy and a fondness for verbal quibbles.

It has been suggested that the actor who originally played Romeo (possibly Gabriel Spencer) was one of the reporters for the "bad quarto" of the play published in 1597. See MEMORIAL RECONSTRUCTION.

Romeo and Juliet. A tragedy by Shakespeare.

Text. The First Quarto of *Romeo and Juliet* was printed in 1597, entitled "An Excellent conceited Tragedie of Romeo and Iuliet, As it hath been often (with great applause) plaid publiquely by the right Honourable the L. of Hunsdon his Seruants." This is a "bad quarto," clearly a pirated edition. The text was put together from a MEMORIAL RECONSTRUCTION made by one or two actors who had appeared in an abridged version of the play. The text of Q1 is corrupt, full of inaccuracies, and with many speeches abridged.

A Second Quarto appeared in 1599, entitled "The Most Excellent and lamentable Tragedy of Romeo and Iuliet. Newly corrected, augmented and amended: As it hath bene sundry times publiquely acted, by the right Honourable the Lord Chamberlaine his Servants." It had 700 more lines than Q1. Q2 was apparently launched under the auspices of the company in order to correct the false impression of the work inevitably given by Q1. Q2 was either set up from Q1, after it had been corrected from and collated with Shakespeare's FOUL PAPERS, or it was set directly from the foul papers, with occasional consultation of Q1. The former thesis is that of the editors of The New Cambridge Edition, the latter that of Richard Hosley. Sometimes the prompter's notes intrude into the stage directions: for example, at IV, v, 102, instead of Q1's "Enter Peter," Q2 has "Enter Will Kempe," the actor who played Peter. Quartos subsequent to Q2 are Q3, 1609; Q4, undated; and Q5, 1637. Q3 served as copy for the First Folio.

Date. Conjectures about the date of *Romeo and Juliet* have ranged from 1591 to 1596. The earlier date is preferred by those who see in the Nurse's remark "'Tis since the earthquake now eleven years" (I, iii, 23) an allusion to the London earthquake of 1580. The later date is preferred by those who detect in the text allusions to the expedition to Cadiz under Essex in 1596 and by those who connect the reference on the title page

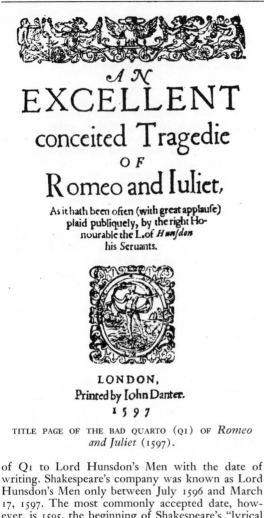

A N
EXCELLENT
conceited Tragedie
OF
Romeo and Iuliet,
As it hath been often (with great applause)
plaid publiquely, by the right Honourable the L. of *Hunsdon*
his Seruants.

LONDON,
Printed by Iohn Danter.
1597

TITLE PAGE OF THE BAD QUARTO (Q1) OF *Romeo and Juliet* (1597).

of Q1 to Lord Hunsdon's Men with the date of writing. Shakespeare's company was known as Lord Hunsdon's Men only between July 1596 and March 17, 1597. The most commonly accepted date, however, is 1595, the beginning of Shakespeare's "lyrical period" and the year in which William Covell's *Polimanteia*, a work with which Shakespeare was probably familiar, alluded to an earthquake of 1584.

Sources. Shakespeare derived the plot of his play from a poem by Arthur Brooke, in poulter's measure, entitled *The Tragicall Historye of Romeus and Juliet* (1562). The theme of the tragedy of two noble young lovers was very popular during the Italian Renaissance. The first version of the tale that contained details like those in *Romeo and Juliet* was in Masuccio Salernitano's *Il Novellino* (1474). Luigi da Porto composed a *novella* (short story) the plot of which was in its essential features like that of Shakespeare's tragedy. Its title was *Istoria novellamente ritrovata di due Nobili Amanti* (1535). The line from Da Porto to the playwright passes through Matteo Bandello's *Le Novelle di Bandello* (1560), which were translated into English by Sir Geoffrey Fenton in 1567. The romance was also included, with others from Bandello, in William Painter's *The Palace of Pleasure* (1566, 1567, 1575). Bandello's *novella* was the source of a French version by Pierre Boaistuau which appeared in Belleforest's *Histoires Tragiques* (1559). Brooke's poem seems to have been based on this French translation rather than upon Painter's English translation of Bandello.

Brooke writes in his Preface, "Though I saw the same argument set forth on the stage with more commendation than I can look for . . . yet the same matter penned as it is, may serve to lyke good effect." This remark suggests the possibility that Shakespeare may have seen the lost play and gained from it some inspiration. However, Brooke's poem seems to have been Shakespeare's only direct source. Brooke gave him the entire plot and occasional turns of phrase. His *Romeus and Juliet* has important differences from the original Italian tale. In the *novella* Juliet awakens in the tomb in time to carry on a brief conversation with Romeo. In Brooke, as in Shakespeare, Juliet recovers from her trance after her lover has taken the fatal poison and in despair stabs herself to death with his dagger. Brooke developed the character of the Nurse, but Mercutio, barely foreshadowed in Brooke, is largely Shakespeare's inspired creation.

The poet transforms the spirit of his immediate source. Brooke wrote in the manner of a severe Puritan moralist. He says that his purpose in telling the story is to warn youth against servitude to "dishonest desire" and against disobedience to parents and neglect of the good advice of friends. Brooke's Juliet is a "wily wench," who waxes merry over her successful deception of her mother. She puts her parents off the scent of Romeo by pretending to be much attracted to Paris, and cunningly sets her cap for him. Romeo's expressions of love never rise above the conventional complaints of a lovelorn sonneteer, and Friar Laurence's cell is little better than a house of assignation. The deaths of such a pair, contaminated by the wicked world in which they live, is deserved punishment for sin. Shakespeare greatly increased the dramatic excitement of Brooke's tale by changing his months into days. In this way he introduces a sense of headlong hurry of the eager lovers.—O. J. C.

Plot Synopsis. Act I. In Verona, the "ancient grudge" between the families of Montague and Capulet bursts forth once more in a public brawl involving members of both households. Escalus, the Prince of Verona, is so vexed by the disturbance that he decrees the death penalty for anyone taking part in a similar fray. Romeo, young scion of the Montagues, has not participated in the brawl, for he is totally absorbed by his bootless passion for the fair Rosaline, who has forsworn love. Benvolio, Romeo's kinsman, urges him to forget Rosaline by finding a new mistress and, when he learns that she is to be a guest in the house of Capulet that night, he suggests that Romeo go himself so that he may compare her with the other beauties present.

Among those invited to Capulet's festivity is Paris a young nobleman who hopes to win the hand and heart of Juliet, Capulet's daughter. After impatiently listening to the reminiscences of Juliet's garrulous Nurse, Lady Capulet informs her daughter, who is not yet 14, of the proposed match and bids her "read o'er the volume of young Paris' face" at the ball that night.

Romeo, wearing a mask, sets out for the Capulet ball in the company of Benvolio and another kinsman, Mercutio. The dejection of the lovelorn youth arouses the mirth of the irrepressible Mercutio, who conjectures that Romeo has been visited by Queen Mab, the "fairies' midwife," who delivers men of their dreams. At the ball, Romeo and Juliet meet and fall in love at once, though each is dismayed to learn the identity of the other. Meanwhile, Juliet's cousin Tybalt has recognized Romeo by his voice, but is prevented from challenging him by Capulet, who will not let him harm a guest.

Act II. Having eluded Benvolio and Mercutio, Romeo hides in Capulet's orchard and hears Juliet express her love for him despite the fact that he bears the hated name of Montague. After he makes his presence known, Juliet again avows her passion, apologizing for the swiftness with which she has let herself be won, but promising to "prove more true / Than those that have more cunning to be strange." At daybreak Romeo leaves, declaring that he will send for her so that they can be married. Later in the day, the two lovers are secretly wed in the cell of a Franciscan monk, Friar Laurence, who hopes that the alliance will turn their "households' rancour to pure love."

Act III. Seeking to renew his quarrel with the Montagues, Tybalt accosts Benvolio and Mercutio on the street. Romeo also arrives on the scene but, as he is purged of hatred toward the Capulets because of his marriage to Juliet, answers Tybalt's insults with gentle words. Exasperated by Romeo's meekness, Mercutio draws his sword and is mortally wounded by Tybalt. His anger rekindled by the death of Mercutio, Romeo kills Tybalt and flees as the outraged citizenry approaches. After he hears Benvolio's account of the melee, Prince Escalus exiles Romeo.

Juliet's grief at hearing of Tybalt's death becomes even keener when she learns that Romeo has been banished for the deed. She sends the Nurse to bring him to her for a final leave-taking. The Nurse finds him in Friar Laurence's cell, loudly bemoaning his fate. When he draws his sword to kill himself, he is sternly rebuked by the monk, who declares that his "wild acts denote / The unreasonable fury of a beast."

Romeo hurries to Juliet's side and remains with her until the song of the lark, harbinger of the morn, forces him to bid his bride a reluctant farewell. After Romeo's departure for exile in Mantua, Juliet's father, who attributes her tears to sorrow over Tybalt's death, announces that she is to marry Count Paris on the following Thursday. When she protests, he becomes incensed and, seconded by his wife, threatens to turn her out of the house if she refuses to obey him. The anguished Juliet turns to the Nurse for comfort, but the latter observes that since Romeo is banished, she may as well marry Paris, compared to whom Romeo is a "dishclout."

Act IV. Learning of Juliet's predicament, the well-meaning Friar Laurence offers her a way out. She is to tell her parents that she will marry Paris as they command. Then, on the eve of the wedding she is to drink a liquid which will give her the semblance of death; after 42 hours, during which she will lie in the family vault, she will awake from her slumber. Meanwhile, Friar Laurence will have informed Romeo of the scheme, and he can return to take her with him to Mantua. Juliet fol-

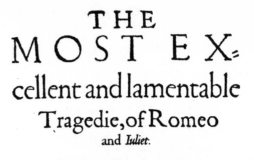

THE
MOST EX-
cellent and lamentable
Tragedie, of Romeo
and *Iuliet.*

Newly corrected, augmented, and amended:

As it hath bene sundry times publiquely acted, by the right Honourable the Lord Chamberlaine his Seruants.

LONDON
Printed by Thomas Creede, for Cuthbert Burby, and are to be sold at his shop neare the Exchange.
1599.

TITLE PAGE OF THE GOOD QUARTO (Q2) OF *Romeo and Juliet* (1599).

lows the friar's advice and, while her father makes preparations for the wedding feast, swallows the potion, dreading all the while the prospect of waking in the vault where Tybalt recently was laid.

Act V. In Mantua, Romeo is told of Juliet's death by his servant Balthasar, who has hastened from Verona with the news. The grief-stricken youth decides to return to Verona, and purchases poison from an apothecary whose poverty leads him to wink at the law forbidding such sales. Meanwhile, Friar John, who was to deliver Friar Laurence's letter explaining the plan to Romeo, reports that he had been detained in Verona by a quarantine.

Paris, coming to strew flowers on Juliet's bier, discovers Romeo in the vault of the Capulets and assumes that he intends to desecrate the bodies interred there. Romeo begs Paris to leave, but the Count refuses and is slain by Romeo. Finding Juliet's body inside the tomb, Romeo gives her a last embrace, drinks the poison, and dies. Friar Laurence arrives and finds the corpses of Romeo and Paris just as Juliet awakens. He tries to take her away from the tragic scene but, frightened by a noise, himself flees. Juliet, seeing Romeo with the cup of poison in his hand, surmises what has happened and stabs herself with his dagger. After being summoned by Paris' page, the watchmen of the churchyard, baffled by the pitiful sight, send for Prince Escalus and the Montagues and Capulets. They hear the story of the star-crossed lovers from the lips of Friar Laurence, who both blames and excuses himself for his part in the affair. Realizing that their hatred was the cause of the tragedy, Montague and Capulet make a tardy peace and promise to erect gold statues of "true and faithful" Juliet and her Romeo.—H.D.

Comment. Though *Romeo and Juliet* is a lyric tragedy, it has been strongly influenced by Seneca. Fortune and an unfavorable configuration of the stars are blamed for the final catastrophe. Chance weaves some of the strands of the tragic pattern. It is chance that takes Romeo to the dance where he first sees Juliet. It is chance that brings him to the duel between Tybalt and Mercutio at a crucial moment. It is chance that keeps Friar John quarantined and so unable to let Romeo know of Friar Laurence's plan to unite him with Juliet. Finally, it is bad luck for Juliet to awaken from her trance just too late to prevent Romeo's drinking of his dram of poison. This brooding of astrological Fate over the operations of chance is Shakespeare's way of adapting Senecan Fortune to the events of his story.

Romeo and Juliet also displays much of the bloodshed and horror of a typical Senecan tragedy, already given full play in *Titus Andronicus.* The scene in the graveyard in and around Juliet's tomb, with Tybalt lying exposed in his bloody sheet, Romeo's obsession with the worms (Juliet's chambermaids, he calls them), and the final strewing of the stage with the dead, forms a scene of horror quite in the approved Senecan fashion. A preparation for this scene is Juliet's terrified anticipation of the horrible sights she will see when she awakens from her drugged sleep in the vault. It is also calculated to produce Senecan thrills for their own sake.

However, much of the action is not reminiscent of Roman melodrama. Romeo is like Marlowe's characters in demanding the fulfillment of his heart's desire at once. Shakespeare makes it clear that the headlong course of Romeo's passion invites inevitable disaster. "These violent delights," exclaims Friar Laurence, "have violent ends." And Juliet interrupts the ecstasy of her first exchange of vows with Romeo to confess,

> I have no joy in this contract to-night:
> It is too rash, too unadvised, too sudden;
> Too like the lightning, which doth cease to be
> Ere one can say "It lightens."
>
> (II, ii, 117–120)

The rashness of Romeo's actions at all the critical moments of the plot and the impetuosity of all the Montagues and Capulets seem to have been aroused by the intense heat of an Italian summer. Mercutio hints that the weather is partly responsible for the headlong, reckless action of most of the characters:

> The day is hot, the Capulets abroad,
> And, if we meet, we shall not scape a brawl;
> For now, these hot days, is the mad blood stirring.
>
> (III, i, 2–4)

Italian, too, are the soft-scented nights in which the nightingale sings till dawn, a perfect setting for fervent love.

Romeo's affectation of love for Rosaline has led him to adopt the moods proper to the post-Petrarch sonneteers. He knows that sighs, tears, and despair are evidence of the true love of a rejected suitor, so he casts himself in the role of a youth thus afflicted. He repairs to his private chamber, shuts up his windows, and cultivates a black mood. His father reports that under a sycamore tree

> Many a morning hath he there been seen,
> With tears augmenting the fresh morning's dew.
>
> (I, i, 137–138)

And after Romeo's release from this pose by true love, Friar Laurence remembers:

> Jesu Maria, what a deal of brine
> Hath wash'd thy sallow cheeks for Rosaline!
>
> (II, iii, 69–70)

Romeo's language is as self-conscious and contrived as his behavior. He plays with figures of speech that often become a parody of the verbal extravagances of the later Petrarchists:

> Why, then, O brawling love! O loving hate!
> O any thing, of nothing first create!
>
> (I, i, 182–183)

But his sight of Juliet sweeps away every trace of insincerity. His first brief exchange with her at the dance preserves almost nothing of his self-admired artificiality. To be sure, he does adopt the romantic fiction that he is a pilgrim visiting her as though for worship at a shrine. And the appropriate ceremony, as Harley Granville-Barker suggests, has about it "something sacramental, something shy, grave and sweet."

That Romeo reverts to this mannered strain of speech for a moment after he has leapt over the wall into Juliet's garden is no wonder. It is his way of silencing Mercutio's indecencies that ring in his ears. But Juliet's simple intensity at once burns away the last vestige of his insincerity. His deepest nature responds to such lines as

> My bounty is as boundless as the sea,
> My love as deep; the more I give to thee,
> The more I have, for both are infinite.
>
> (II, ii, 133–135)

Whatever Juliet's supposed age, love has matured her, revealing emotional deeps hitherto hidden from her. This discovery has lent her dignity and courage far beyond the capacity of any child. Why Shakespeare fixes her age as 14 years is a question never satisfactorily answered. Cynics maintain that the poet took this way of assuring his audiences that Romeo is her very first lover.

The fatal duel comes immediately after his moment of ecstasy with Juliet. His accidental responsibility for Mercutio's death is the source of all the disastrous events that follow one another with fateful speed. Mercutio, who thus plays an important part in Shakespeare's version of the story, is almost wholly the poet's invention. His prototype in Brooke's poem is a rival for Juliet's hand, appearing only briefly at the dance as a bold fellow among shy ladies. The poet makes of this shadowy creature so original and vigorous a figure that jesting commentators say that Shakespeare had to kill him off to prevent his stealing the show. He is the sensual

Romeus and Juliet Fo. 1

There is beyonde the Alps,
a towne of auncient fame,
Whose bright renoune yet shineth clere,
Verona men it name.
Bylt in an happy time,
bylt on a fertile soyle:
Maynteined by the heauenly fates,
and by the townish toyle.
The fruitfull hilles aboue,
the pleasant vales belowe,
The siluer streame with chanell depe,
that through the towne doth flow:
The store of springes that serue
for vse, and eke for ease:
And other moe commodities,
which profite may and please.
Eke many certaine signes
of thinges betyde of olde,
To fyll the houngry eyes of those
that curiously beholde:
Doe make this towne to bee
preferde aboue the rest
of Lumbard townes, or at the least
compared with the best.
In which while Escalus,
as prince alone did raigne,
To reache rewarde vnto the good,
To pay the lewde with payne,
Alas (I rewe to thinke)
an heauy happe befell:
Which Boccace skant (not my rude tong)
were able forth to tell,
Within my trembling hand,
my penne doth shake for feare:
And on my colde amased head,
vpright doth stand my heare.

A. i. But

THE FIRST PAGE OF BROOKE'S *Romeus and Juliet*. THE TITLE PAGE OF THIS UNIQUE COPY OF THE SECOND EDITION IS MISSING. (HUNTINGTON LIBRARY)

nan as opposed to the idealistic Romeo, a devil-may-are, scoffing realist who finds ridiculous everything hat seems to him affected or highfalutin.

Juliet, like many of the poet's tragic protagonists n the brink of catastrophe, finds herself utterly lone. The complications of her situation isolate her rom everyone to whom she might naturally turn or comfort and support. Capulet sees in her refusal o marry the man of *his* choice a rebellion against arental authority. Lady Capulet echoes her husband. The Nurse's solution of the girl's tragic plight is bhorrent. To the sensual old woman, love is only form of physical pleasure in which romance and oyalty are stupid intrusions. Let Juliet forget Romeo; his banishment is as final as death. Let her narry the Count Paris: "O, he's a lovely gentle-nan! / Romeo's a dishclout to him" (III, v, 220–221). n another situation Juliet cries, "Is there not pity itting in the clouds, / That sees into the bottom of ny grief?" (III, v, 198–199). The increasing pathos f her plight threatens to make of the play a "she ragedy," but Shakespeare rescues it at this point rom a lachrymose conclusion by turning our in-erest to a more vital issue, to the self-destruction f a slave of passion. After Romeo has received the alse news of Juliet's death he acts like a man drunk vith desperation. Shakespeare would have his audience realize that so passion-driven a man courts disaster.

Although Shakespeare the playwright took his plot from Brooke's poem, Shakespeare the poet found none of love's radiance there, and no language that could express idealistic erotic feeling. He could, however, have found the language of love fully and beautifully developed in the many collections of songs and sonnets that appeared in England for many years before 1596. When Romeo and Juliet speak from their hearts, they borrow the idiom of the simple songs and lyrics that made England during the 16th century a symphony of spontaneous music. From one point of view these early English lyrics may be considered as one of the sources of the play. Four conventional lyric patterns are embedded in the text. The first exchange between the lovers (I, v, 95–100) forms a sonnet. Juliet's soliloquy as she impatiently awaits Romeo in the evening (III, ii, 1–31) is a serena. The lovers' farewell at parting in the morning after their night together (III, v, 1–59) takes the form of a medieval lyric called in Provençal an "alba" (the word means "dawn"), usually a lament of lovers that dawn has come so soon. And Paris' valediction as he strews flowers at Juliet's tomb (V, iii, 12–17) is an elegy.

Stoll in his *Shakespeare's Young Lovers* (1937) insists that the characters in this play are meant to interest audiences not psychologically, but merely poetically, and he seeks to show that the two lovers are distinguished emotionally by the difference in the character of their figures of speech. Romeo's imagination has a wider range. It may soar above the earth and its concerns as it does in the lines beginning

O, speak again, bright angel! for thou art
As glorious to this night, being o'er my head,
As is a winged messenger of heaven.
(II, ii, 26–28)

or it may explore the far reaches of the earth:

I am no pilot; yet, wert thou as far
As that vast shore wash'd with the farthest sea,
I would adventure for such merchandise.
(II, ii, 82–84)

Juliet's imagination is more earthbound, filled with experiences of her childhood. A good example of her limited but equally intense flights of fancy is the figure of "a child's captive bird," which exposes her unwillingness to have Romeo leave, mingled with fear that if he goes he will be caught.

'Tis almost morning; I would have thee gone:
And yet no further than a wanton bird.
(II, ii, 177–178)

It is Shakespeare's achievement that so early in his career he could endow each of the disparate elements in *Romeo and Juliet* with an urgency new in Elizabethan tragedy and present the emotions of the chief characters with a fire-new beauty that has converted the old tale of a youth and a girl into the most popular romantic tragedy in the English-speaking world.—O.J.C.

Stage History: England. From the time of its first staging, *Romeo and Juliet* has been one of the most often and most successfully produced of all of Shakespeare's plays. The enthusiasm of some of the earliest readers of the tragedy can be inferred from the condition of the First Folio owned by the Bodleian Library of Oxford, which acquired it in 1623 and chained it to shelves where the undergraduates might have easy access to it. Though all the pages are worn, most crumpled is the one containing the lyric parting of the pair after their night of love (III, v). That the drama must have been equally approved on the stage is evident from the title pages of three quartos (1597, 1599, and 1609) which attest to many performances by Shakespeare's company. However, no actual record of a production before the closing of the theatres in 1642 exists.

In 1662 Davenant revived the work with Mary Saunderson, afterwards Mrs. Betterton, as Juliet and Betterton as Mercutio. Pepys was very scornful of everything about this production, pronouncing it ". . . the worst that ever I heard in my life and the worst acted. . . ." Doubtless to render the work more pleasing to Restoration taste, James Howard turned it into a tragicomedy, "preserving Romeo and Juliet alive." And for a number of years whenever the drama was revived it was played one night as a tragedy and the next as a tragicomedy. During the season of 1679/80 Otway lifted a number of scenes from *Romeo and Juliet* and gave them to young Marius and Lavinia, the lovers in his *The History and Fall of Caius Marius*. In this strange mixture of ancient Rome and Renaissance Italy, Betterton played Caius Marius, Elizabeth Barry was Lavinia. This patchwork flourished, missing only an occasional season up to 1727. Shakespeare's play did not appear again until 1744, when Theophilus Cibber had the courage to revive something approaching the original at the Haymarket. Cibber did not dare dispense with Otway's intensification of the pathos in the catastrophe and retained Juliet's awakening before her lover's death for the tear-evoking dialogue of farewell.

When on November 29, 1748 David Garrick staged his own adaptation of *Romeo and Juliet,* which survived on the stage until 1845, this scene was again included, though in a revised and superior form. Garrick's alteration as a whole adhered more closely to the genuine than did Cibber's. Spranger Barry and Mrs. Cibber appeared in the title roles. For the remainder of the century, *Romeo and Juliet* appeared uninterruptedly, and from 1751–1800, according to C. B. Hogan, it was acted more times than any other Shakespeare play, totaling 399 performances. In September 1750 rival presentations were staged at Covent Garden, where Barry and Mrs. Cibber played the lovers, and at Drury Lane, where Garrick assumed the role of Romeo to George Anne Bellamy's Juliet. Although Garrick was initially victorious with 13 performances to 12 at Covent Garden, the undeclared *Romeo and Juliet* war continued. The tragedy was staged every season at Drury Lane from 1750 until late 1772 and in eight seasons between 1776 and 1796; Covent Garden productions appeared in all but one year (1780) during that half-century. Henry Woodward successfully and regularly acted Mercutio, first at Drury Lane, then at Covent Garden from 1763 to 1776. John Palmer assumed that role at Drury Lane in 1758 and played the part there each season until 1767, the year before his death. Garrick continued as Romeo up to 1761, while Barry played the youn lover at Covent Garden every year until 1758, the at the Haymarket in 1766 and 1767, and finally a Drury Lane on December 22, 1767, and April 11 1768. Besides the admired, forceful Juliet of Mrs Cibber, who appeared as the heroine until 1763, an the natural, ardent portrayal of Miss (later Mrs.) Bellamy, who played the role to 1770, other Juliet included Miss Nossiter and Miss Pritchard (afterward Mrs. Palmer). Both made their acting debut in the role, the former at Covent Garden on October 10, 1753, the latter at Drury Lane on Octobe 9, 1756.

After Garrick, the most famous actors gave th play only the barest recognition. John Philip Kembl first staged it in 1788 for two performances and i 1789, when Sarah Siddons made her only Londo appearance as Juliet on May 11. Kemble acte Romeo in both productions, but for his final *Rome and Juliet* at Drury Lane in 1796, that part wa assigned to Barrymore, while Mrs. Jordan playe her first Juliet. Charles Kemble portrayed Paris Later, the hero of the tragedy became one o Charles' most successful acting roles. When the elde Kemble brother opened his management of Coven Garden in 1803 with *Romeo and Juliet,* he prudently cast Charles as the young lover, a characterization which was re-created in revivals up t 1828. Kemble's finest portrayal, however, was o Mercutio, which he acted for the first time o October 5, 1829. This presentation was especiall memorable for the triumphant debut of Fann Kemble, then only 19 years old, as Juliet. Kembl as Mercutio appeared with another great Julie Helen Faucit, on March 10, 1836, when the Rome was George Bennett. Another famous debut ha

FANNY KEMBLE AS JULIET.

occurred in 1810 when, at 17, William Charles Macready successfully interpreted the young hero at Birmingham. This triumph was followed by success in the part later at Bath but, although his initial London appearance as Romeo in 1817 at Covent Garden was warmly received, Macready performed the part only twice more, in January 1822. As manager of Covent Garden, he did, however, produce the play, offering two performances in 1838 with himself in the role of Friar Laurence, while J. R. Anderson and Helen Faucit played the principals. Anderson and Miss Faucit repeated their portrayals at Drury Lane in 1852, and in 1855, when Barry Sullivan was the Haymarket's Romeo, Miss Faucit again acted Juliet.

Edmund Kean essayed the role of Romeo unsuccessfully in January 1815. His son Charles was only 17 when he assumed the lover's role on December 22, 1828 at Drury Lane. The following year young Kean played the part at the Haymarket, where he also re-created his Romeo in 1841 opposite Ellen Tree's Juliet. Before this Miss Tree had essayed the male lead, acting Romeo in revivals spanning the years 1829 and 1836. Her Juliet in 1832 was the superlative Fanny Kemble. Another female who played the hero during this time, Priscilla Horton, acted the part in 1834 at the Victoria. It was, therefore, less than revolutionary when Charlotte Cushman appeared as Romeo opposite her sister Susan's Juliet on December 29, 1845. The novelty of this Haymarket revival consisted in the elimination of Otway's contribution of Juliet's death scene awakening. The production was an emphatic success and ran for 3 nights each week until July 11, 1846, for a total of 84 performances. In January 1855 Miss Cushman again acted Romeo for London audiences to Ada Swanborough's Juliet, and later that year switched to the heroine's role at the Theatre Royal opposite W. R. Bedford's Romeo.

Samuel Phelps' first revival of *Romeo and Juliet* was performed 15 times, opening on September 5, 1846. Almost 13 years elapsed before his second *Romeo and Juliet*. Then, in February 1859, Phelps presented Mrs. Charles Young as the heroine. There followed a third production during September and October of that year, with Caroline Heath as Juliet. Mr. and Mrs. Hermann Vezin starred in an 1861 revival. During the last year of his management at Sadler's Wells, 1862, Phelps offered his final *Romeo and Juliet*.

For 15 years from 1865, Adelaide Neilson was indisputedly the most popular Juliet. Her first appearance at the Royalty on July 17 attracted little attention, but inaugurated a series of later successes both in London and America, where she visited on four occasions. Her most spectacular acclaim came after a Drury Lane performance on December 19, 1870 opposite J. B. Howard's Romeo. In 1882, when Henry Irving presented the tragedy as his first elaborate Shakespeare production at the Lyceum, he and Ellen Terry were the star-crossed lovers. In this performance minor characters succeeded where the stars failed; performances by Mrs. Stirling as the Nurse and George Alexander as Paris were praised, but Irving lacked the romantic nature of Romeo and Miss Terry missed the tragic elements of Juliet. Nevertheless, the scenic artistry of the production carried this revival for 161 performances. The acting fared better when William Terriss reverted to Romeo and Mary Anderson interpreted Juliet at the Lyceum two years later during Irving's absence in America. This revival opened on November 1, 1884 and continued throughout the winter. When Miss Anderson's accomplished Juliet appeared the next year in New York, her Romeo was Johnston Forbes-Robertson. Previously, in March 1881, this actor had made his debut as Romeo at the Court Theatre opposite Helena Modjeska, whose effectiveness as Juliet suffered from her Polish accent. Still, critics received her more sympathetically than Forbes-Robertson's later Juliet, Mrs. Patrick Campbell, who appeared in his Lyceum production in 1895.

Frank Benson, after an initial failure with the play at the Imperial in 1881, went on to present 12 successful revivals of the tragedy at the Memorial Theatre. Even before this theatre existed, Stratford-upon-Avon had seen *Romeo and Juliet* in 1864, and, after its building in 1879, witnessed productions by Edward Compton's company (1882) and the Bernard-Alleyn management (1885). During Benson's tenancy at the theatre, he and his wife almost always portrayed the title roles, but on two occasions guest performers assumed these parts. In 1908, Henry Ainley and Constance Collier played Romeo and Juliet and, in 1911, Lewis Waller and Madge Titheradge took the roles. Earlier, in 1905, Waller's sternly dispassionate Romeo appeared opposite the disappointing Juliet of Evelyn Millard at the Imperial. This production of the tragedy had followed a tame presentation at the Court in 1904 starring Charles Lander and Thyrza Norman. It had preceded the last offering by William Poel's Elizabethan Stage Society, which, in May 1905, gave four performances of the drama on the stage of the Royalty. For this production Poel cast Esme Percy, then 17, and Dorothy Minto, 14, as the young lovers; George Bernard Shaw, who counted an audience of little more than a handful, remarked that the tragedy "for the first time became endurable" when acted with the youthful ardor of the leading players. In 1907 E. H. Sothern and his wife, Julia Marlowe, were unable to equal their successes in America with a repertory which included *Romeo and Juliet*, shown at the Waldorf on May 2. Yet, despite London's dismal record with the tragedy during the first decade of the 1900's, the next season two more *Romeo and Juliets* appeared, one in February 1908 at the Royalty Theatre, with Paul Lovett and Ine Cameron, the second in the following month at the Lyceum with Matheson Lang and Nora Kerin. Gerald Lawrence and Fay Davis took the title roles at the Court in 1909, after which a lavishly staged *Romeo and Juliet* bowed at the New Theatre on September 2, 1911, introducing the widely acclaimed Juliet of the 18-year-old Phyllis Neilson-Terry. When Beerbohm Tree offered his typically spectacular *Romeo and Juliet*, Miss Neilson-Terry again managed to draw attention from the scenery, appearing opposite Philip Merivale, while Tree played Mercutio. Earlier that season, in March, Harcourt Williams and Lilian Hallows acted the lovers at the Prince's, but the first significant dramatic contribution to the tragedy in this century awaited a Lyric

Theatre presentation in April 1919 which saw the title roles mere appendages to those of Mercutio and the Nurse. Leon Quartermaine won enthusiastic ovations for his portrayal of the Veronese gallant, and the 71-year-old Ellen Terry was alternately gay, endearing, and strong in her last great Shakespearean role as the Nurse. Nugent Monck's Maddermarket Theatre players acted their first *Romeo and Juliet* in 1920 and that same year the Everyman Theatre Company at Hampstead presented Nicholas Hannen and Muriel Pratt in the title roles. H. K. Ayliff directed the play at Birmingham in 1922, with Ion Swinley and Gwen Ffrangcon-Davies; when he later produced the tragedy at the Regent in 1924, Romeo was given to John Gielgud, just 20 years old, his dramatic abilities as yet undeveloped. Miss Ffrangcon-Davies' Juliet saved the day and, when Gielgud fell ill, she was rejoined by Ion Swinley, who gave way to Ernest Milton until the production's original Romeo recuperated and completed the six-weeks' run. Milton had previously portrayed the young hero opposite Mary Sumner's Juliet for Robert Atkins' Old Vic production during the 1920/1 season. The Old Vic had staged two earlier *Romeo and Juliets* and, afterward, on April 12, 1926, Andrew Leigh directed its fourth production with Frank Vosper as Romeo and Nell Carter as Juliet. Edith Evans began the outline of her later complete portrait of the Nurse, and Baliol Holloway acted Mercutio with his usual excellence. In December of that year the Fellowship of Players appeared in the tragedy at the Strand, featuring Laurence Anderson and Jean Forbes-Robertson's highly commended interpretation of the young heroine. Sir Johnston's daughter repeated her successful portrayal for Andrew Leigh at the Old Vic in 1928; her Romeo was poignantly played by Eric Portman, with Ernest Milton as Mercutio.

Meanwhile at Stratford, W. Bridges-Adams produced the tragedy three times in a decade, first in 1919, again in 1926; in the summer of 1929 he added the tragedy to the spring program, with George Hayes and Joyce Bland in the title roles. Three more productions of the drama complete his *Romeo and Juliet* record at Stratford during the 1930's. In two of these, in 1933 and 1934, John Wyse and Rachel Kempson were among the finest lovers in Memorial Theatre presentations; George Hayes portrayed Mercutio in the earlier production.

Gielgud played Romeo for the second time at the Old Vic in September 1929, this time under Harcourt Williams' rapid direction and with impressive support from Adele Dixon as Juliet and Martita Hunt as the Nurse. Then, in the spring of 1932, Gielgud staged *Romeo and Juliet* with an Oxford University Dramatic Society company, enhanced by the professional talents of Peggy Ashcroft and Edith Evans. The amateurs in the Oxford cast included Christopher Hassall as Romeo, William Devlin as Tybalt, George Devine as Mercutio, and Hugh Hunt as Friar Laurence—all on the threshold of careers in the Shakespearean theatre. This production foreshadowed Gielgud's supreme success with the tragedy three years later. This same year presentations were offered at the Embassy by A. R. Whatmore, costarring Sebastian Shaw and Joyce Bland, and at the Kingsway with Peter Dearing, the producer, as Romeo, opposite Mary Casson. In March 1933, Harcourt Williams directed his second Old Vic *Romeo and Juliet* and Peggy Ashcroft played her second Juliet. Marius Goring was Romeo and Malcolm Keen, Mercutio. Meanwhile, Edith Evans was strengthening her portrayal of the Nurse in New York performances during December 1934 with Katharine Cornell's Juliet at the Martin Beck Theatre. Then, on October 17, 1935, Laurence Olivier, having abandoned his own production of the tragedy to join forces with Gielgud, opened under his direction as Romeo in the longest recorded run of the play, 186 performances, to Peggy Ashcroft's Juliet at the New Theatre. Gielgud at first played Mercutio and Edith Evans eloquently rendered her perfected portrait of the Nurse. Six weeks later, the male stars exchanged roles and, although Gielgud's Mercutio had given new meaning to the Queen Mab speech, the switch proved more comfortable for both actors. Olivier did not turn his back on Romeo, for in 1940 he again played that part in his own production, which he directed at the 51st Street Theatre in New York.

Robert Donat, unable to appear in Gielgud's production, had also canceled his planned revival of the tragedy in 1935. His opportunity to play Romeo was deferred until October 1939, when he acted with an Old Vic company under producer Murray Macdonald at Streatham Hill. Constance Cummings portrayed Juliet in this promising but unfulfilled production. After Bridges-Adams' withdrawal, Stratford staged a *Romeo and Juliet* directed by Randle Ayrton in 1936, with Peter Glenville and Pamela Brown; two under Ben Iden Payne with Francis James and Valerie Tudor in the title roles in 1938 and Godfrey Kenton and Margaretta Scott in 1941; and another staged by Robert Atkins in 1945, starring David Peel and Moira Lister. At the King's, Hammersmith, producer Clare Harris cast Basil C. Langton and Renee Asherson as the young lovers in a *Romeo and Juliet* opening on March 1, 1946. The following year, Peter Brook discarded much of the scenery and also overlooked some of the plot. Academic dismay persuaded him, however, to restore the Friar's vital vial scene after initial performances. This Stratford cast included the gifted Daphne Slater as Juliet, Laurence Payne as Romeo, and Beatrix Lehmann as the Nurse, but Paul Scofield's delivery of the Queen Mab speech stole all the honors for Mercutio. Later that October the production was repeated at His Majesty's. Before, in August, John Wyse, an earlier successful Romeo, directed Allan Cuthbertson and Isabel Dean in the title parts at the Boltons.

Five years elapsed before a major *Romeo and Juliet* appeared in London. Then, in 1952, two presentations of the tragedy opened one month apart. The Cambridge Marlowe Society acted the play under George Rylands and John Barton at the Scala in August, and Hugh Hunt directed the Old Vic's first attempt with the drama in nearly 20 years that September, with a convincingly enraptured heroine in Claire Bloom and an unabashedly romantic hero in Alan Badel. Between this and the next Old Vic production of the play, Stratford offered a routine *Romeo and Juliet* in 1954, produced by Glen Byam Shaw and featuring Laurence Harvey and Zena

Walker. Robert Helpmann directed the 1956 Vic presentation (hampered by the dangerously cramped sets of Loudon Sainthill), which opened in June and, in the fall, was included in a repertory tour of the United States and Canada. The company, starring the Romeo of John Neville opposite Claire Bloom, with Paul Rogers as Mercutio, appeared at New York's Winter Garden that October.

In 1958, Glen Byam Shaw (Benvolio at the New in 1935) directed his second production of the tragedy at Stratford, with Richard Johnson and Dorothy Tutin. The final Old Vic production of the play, under the direction of Franco Zeffirelli, who doubled as designer, opened on October 4, 1960. Zeffirelli's uncompromisingly realistic view of the tragedy often sacrificed first the rapturous and then the tragic elements, with many unfortunate cuts. The rival houses resembled New York street gangs and the controversial production had many outspoken advocates who effected a respectable run. John Stride and Judi Dench were properly young and rash as the lovers. Alec McCowen, his Queen Mab speech badly hacked, was Mercutio. The costumes were Peter Hall's.

In closing the record of the play in England, mention should be made of Edith Evans' last appearance as the Nurse—a portrayal that spanned 35 years—at Stratford in 1961. Peter Wood directed this production with Brian Murray as Romeo, Dorothy Tutin (who had improved her former characterization) as Juliet, and Ian Bannen as Mercutio.

Stage History: America. The tragedy was first seen in the United States in an amateur production in Philadelphia in 1730; in 1754, it was produced with Rigby and Mrs. Hallam as Romeo and Juliet. New York's interest in the play lagged during the 18th century, when only 12 productions were shown in that city, but in all but 7 years from 1800 to 1839 and thereafter through 1894, *Romeo and Juliet* enjoyed annual runs on the New York stage. Lydia Kelly started the vogue of female Romeos in the United States, taking the male lead in 1829. This practice was continued by Charlotte Cushman, then Mrs. H. B. Conway (the most frequent female interpreter of Romeo), and finally by Fay Templeton in 1875. In 1869 Edwin Booth and Mary McVickers acted the title roles in a production bowing at Booth's Theatre on February 3 for a 10-week run. Fourteen years later Maurice Barrymore and Madame Modjeska played the young lovers in a final presentation before Booth's Theatre closed. The last quarter of the 19th century produced two popular American Juliets, Adelaide Neilson and Mary Anderson, followed by Julia Marlowe at the beginning of the 20th century. Comparable Romeos were rare, but Edwin Booth and Lawrence Barrett won acclaim with their portrayals of the hero. A bizarre presentation which advertised George Rignold playing Romeo to seven different Juliets in one night fell short of its boast when Adelaide Neilson absented herself from the balcony scene. This affair took place on May 31, 1877, and is memorable only as a theatrical oddity.

In many appearances, beginning in 1904, Miss Marlowe's Romeo was played by her husband, Edward H. Sothern, whose skillful but unimpassioned performance was overshadowed by his wife's ardent, piteous, heroic Juliet. In many of their repertory appearances in the tragedy, Eugenia Woodward played the Nurse and Frederick Lewis, Mercutio. During the early decades of the present century, Robert Mantell often portrayed Romeo opposite Genevieve Hamper. In 1922 Arthur Hopkins produced the tragedy starring McKay Morris and Ethel Barrymore in the title roles. Morris was an ineffective lover, but Miss Barrymore, while at times perhaps too worldly-wise, gave an exquisite and moving impersonation of Juliet. However, the greatest acclaim was accorded Basil Sydney's brilliant Mercutio. The following year brought a new *Romeo and Juliet* record: Beginning on January 24, the drama, as staged by Frank Reicher, ran for more than 150 performances at the Henry Miller Theatre. Jane Cowl presented a youthful, poetic, and imaginative heroine opposite the spirited and romantic Romeo of Rollo Peters. Peters also designed the sets for this well-paced production, notable for an especially excellent, subdued tomb scene. Able support was given by Dennis King, a gallant, musical Mercutio, and Jessie Ralph as a coarse, humorous Nurse. In 1930 Eva Le Gallienne played Juliet for the Civic Repertory Theatre, with Donald Cameron as Romeo. Katharine Cornell portrayed Juliet at the Erlanger Theatre in Buffalo during November 1933, a year before appearing in that role at the Martin Beck Theatre in New York, with Edith Evans playing the Nurse and Maurice Evans, Romeo. In December 1937 the Pasadena Playhouse completed its staging of all Shakespeare's plays with a production of *Romeo and Juliet*, starring a 16-year-old actor and 14-year-old actress in the title roles.

A much-heralded New York stage debut of the popular motion picture actress Olivia de Haviland as Juliet in March 1951 ended after 49 performances. Oliver Messel designed visually exciting sets for this production staged by Peter Glenville, who used a carefully pruned text. Although Jack Hawkins as Mercutio gave a poor reading of the Queen Mab speech, his performance for the most part won praise, and critical opinion delighted in Evelyn Varden's whimsical and unscrupulous Nurse; Douglas Watson as a virile, believable Romeo received favorable notices. But Miss de Haviland's heroine was disappointing—her conscientious, knowledgeable interpretation lacked sensitivity. In 1958 the American Shakespeare Festival in Stratford, Connecticut, offered an uninspired *Romeo and Juliet* with Richard Easton and Inga Swenson as the young lovers. In June 1960 Michael Langham directed the tragedy for the Shakespeare Memorial Theatre at Stratford, Ontario, with Bruno Gerussi and Julie Harris as Romeo and Juliet, Christopher Plummer as Mercutio, and Kate Reid as the Nurse. The theatre in Stratford, Connecticut, received mixed reviews for its second revival in the summer of 1965 when Terence Scammell and Maria Tucci played the lovers, Lillian Gish, the Nurse, and John Cunningham, Mercutio. One critic called the results catastrophic, another, "credible and touching."

Romeo and Juliet has been produced more often on film than any other Shakespeare play. Theda Bara was the heroine in a 1916 silent movie, and the last American film version of the tragedy, directed by George Cukor in 1936, starred Leslie Howard and Norma Shearer as the lovers, with John Barrymore as Mercutio. This last, a lavish affair employing mechanically brilliant technical effects, was badly cut and a dramatic failure. An Anglo-Italian film, directed by Renato Castellani in 1953, received a similarly hostile critical reception for its emphasis on scenery and pictorial effects (filmed in Verona and Mantua) to the subordination of the poetic value of the play.—M. G.

Bibliography. TEXT: *Romeo and Juliet*, New Cambridge Edition, G. I. Duthie and J. Dover Wilson, eds., 1955; Harry R. Hoppe, *The Bad Quarto of Romeo and Juliet*, 1948; Richard Hosley, "Quarto Copy for Q2 *Romeo and Juliet*," *Studies in Bibliography*, IX, 1957. DATE: New Cambridge Edition; Sidney Thomas, "The Earthquake in *Romeo and Juliet*," *Modern Language Notes*, LXIV, 1949. SOURCES: Geoffrey Bullough, *Narrative and Dramatic Sources of Shakespeare's Plays*, Vol. I, 1957; Kenneth Muir, *Shakespeare's Sources*, Vol. I, 1957. COMMENT: Harley Granville-Barker, *Prefaces to Shakespeare*, Vol. II, 1930; Elmer Edgar Stoll, *Shakespeare's Young Lovers*, 1937; H. B. Charlton, *Shakespearian Tragedy*, 1948; D. A. Stauffer, *Shakespeare's World of Images*, 1949; Clifford Leech, *Shakespeare's Tragedies*, 1950. STAGE HISTORY: New Cambridge Edition; G. C. D. Odell, *Shakespeare from Betterton to Irving*, 1920; J. C. Trewin, *Shakespeare on the English Stage, 1900–1964*, 1964.

Selected Criticism

SAMUEL JOHNSON. This play is one of the most pleasing of our Author's performances. The scenes are busy and various, the incidents numerous and important, the catastrophe irresistibly affecting, and the process of the action carried on with such probability, at least with such congruity to popular opinions, as tragedy requires.

Here is one of the few attempts of *Shakespeare* to exhibit the conversation of gentlemen, to represent the airy sprightliness of juvenile elegance. *Mr. Dryden* mentions a tradition, which might easily reach his time, of a declaration made by *Shakespeare*, that *he was obliged to kill* Mercutio *in the third act, lest he would have been killed by him.* Yet he thinks him *no such formidable person, but that he might have lived through the play, and died in his bed,* without danger to a poet. *Dryden* well knew, had he been in quest of truth, that, in a pointed sentence, more regard is commonly had to the words than the thought, and that it is very seldom to be rigorously understood. *Mercutio's* wit, gaiety and courage, will always procure him friends that wish him a longer life; but his death is not precipitated, he has lived out the time allotted him in the construction of the play; nor do I doubt the ability of *Shakespeare* to have continued his existence, though some of his sallies are perhaps out of the reach of *Dryden;* whose genius was not very fertile of merriment, nor ductile to humour, but acute, argumentative, comprehensive, and sublime.

The Nurse is one of the characters in which the Authour delighted: he has, with great subtilty of distinction, drawn her at once loquacious and secret, obsequious and insolent, trusty and dishonest.

His comick scenes are happily wrought, but his pathetick strains are always polluted with some unexpected depravations. His persons, however distressed, *have a conceit left them in their misery, a miserable conceit.* [*The Plays of William Shakespeare*, 1765.]

WALTER WHITER.

"And lips, O you
"The doors of breath, *seal* with a righteous kiss
"A *dateless* bargain to ENGROSSING death."
(*Romeo and Juliet*, Act V. S. iii)

Mr. Malone thinks that ENGROSSING is here used i its *clerical* or legal sense. The reader however wi surely be of opinion, that no adequate meanin can be annexed to *engrossing Death* under such a interpretation. The sense, which the word common bears, was certainly intended by the Poet, thoug he was led to make use of this peculiar term by th legal ideas with which it is connected. It is how ever somewhat extraordinary, that the writer himse should not have been impressed with the effect c so glaring an ambiguity. There is no subject, fro which our Poet is so delighted to draw his allusion as the *Seal* and *Bond*. Our Commentators have not, believe, observed the strange coincidence betwee this last speech of Romeo, and a former one at th beginning of the play, in which he anticipates h approaching misfortunes.

"O, here,
"Will I set up my everlasting rest;
"And shake the yoke of inauspicious *stars*
"From this world-wearied flesh.—Eyes, look
"your last!
"Arms, take your last embrace! and lips, O you
"The doors of breath, *seal* with a righteous kiss
"A *dateless bargain* to engrossing death!
"Come, bitter conduct, come unsavoury guide!
"Thou desperate pilot, now at once run on
"The dashing rocks, thy *sea-sick* weary *bark!*"
(*Romeo and Juliet*, Act V. S. iii)

"My mind misgives,
"Some consequence, yet hanging in the *stars,*
"Shall *bitterly* begin his fearful *date*
"With this night's revels; and *expire the term*
"Of a despised life, *clos'd* in my breast,
"By some vile *forfeit* of untimely death:
"But he, that hath the *steerage* of my *course,*
"Direct my *sail!*"
(*Romeo and Juliet*, Act I. S. iv.)

The curious reader will not fail to observe th the ideas drawn from the *Stars,* the *Law,* and th *Sea,* succeed each other in the same order, thoug with a different application, in both speeches. W may add likewise, that the *bitter* cause of Romeo death is to be found in the latter speech; thoug I am well aware that the word *bitterly* was su gested to the Poet by the impression on his min of the peculiar species of death, which he ha himself destined for the character; and that was not intentionally selected for the purpose attributing to Romeo a presentiment of the *mod* by which the *date* of his existence was to *expire.* This singular coincidence in the accumulation images apparently so remote cannot surely be co sidered as the effect of chance, or as the produ of imitation. It is certainly derived from son latent association; which I have in vain attempte to discover. There is scarcely a play of our Autho vhere we do not find some favourite vein of meta-hor or allusion by which it is distinguished. [*A pecimen of a Commentary on Shakespeare,* 1794.]

SAMUEL TAYLOR COLERIDGE. In "Romeo and Juliet" he principal characters may be divided into two lasses: in one class passion—the passion of love—is rawn and drawn truly, as well as beautifully; but he persons are not individualised farther than as the ctor appears on the stage. It is a very just descrip-ion and development of love, without giving, if I nay so express myself, the philosophical history of it -without shewing how the man became acted upon y that particular passion, but leading it through all he incidents of the drama, and rendering it pre-lominant . . . .

Another remark I may make upon "Romeo and uliet" is, that in this tragedy the poet is not, as I ave hinted, entirely blended with the dramatist,—at east, not in the degree to be afterwards noticed in Lear," "Hamlet," "Othello," or "Macbeth." Capulet nd Montague not unfrequently talk a language only elonging to the poet, and not so characteristic of, nd peculiar to, the passions of persons in the situ-tions in which they are placed—a mistake, or rather n indistinctness, which many of our later dramatists ave carried through the whole of their productions. . . . Romeo became enamoured of the idea he had ormed in his own mind, and then, as it were, chris-ened the first real being of the contrary sex as en-lowed with the perfections he desired. He appears o be in love with Rosaline; but in truth he is in love nly with his own idea. He felt that necessity of eing beloved which no noble mind can be without. Then our poet, our poet who so well knew human ature, introduces Romeo to Juliet, and makes it not nly a violent but a permanent love—a point for vhich Shakespeare has been ridiculed by the ig-orant and unthinking. Romeo is first represented in state most susceptible of love, and then, seeing uliet, he took and retained the infection.

This brings me to observe upon a characteristic of hakespeare, which belongs to a man of profound hought and high genius. It has been too much the ustom, when anything that happened in his dramas ould not easily be explained by the few words the oet has employed, to pass it idly over, and to say hat it is beyond our reach, and beyond the power of hilosophy—a sort of terra incognita for discoverers -a great ocean to be hereafter explored. Others have reated such passages as hints and glimpses of some-hing now nonexistent, as the sacred fragments of an ncient and ruined temple, all the portions of which re beautiful, although their particular relation to ach other is unknown. Shakespeare knew the human nind, and its most minute and intimate workings, nd he never introduces a word, or a thought, in vain r out of place: if we do not understand him, it is ur own fault or the fault of copyists and typogra-hers; but study, and the possession of some small ock of the knowledge by which he worked, will nable us often to detect and explain his meaning. He ever wrote at random, or hit upon points of char-cter and conduct by chance; and the smallest frag-nent of his mind not unfrequently gives a clue to a nost perfect, regular, and consistent whole. [*Shake-pearean Criticism* by S. T. Coleridge, T. M. Raysor, d., Everyman Library Edition, 1960.]

JOHN QUINCY ADAMS. Tragedy, according to the admirable definition of Aristotle, is a poem imitative of human life, and the object of which is to purify the soul of the spectator by the agency of terror and pity. The terror is excited by the incidents of the story and the sufferings of the person represented; the pity, by the interest of sympathy with their characters. Terror and pity are moved by the mere aspect of human sufferings; but the sympathy is strong or weak, in proportion to the interest that we take in the *character* of the sufferer. With this definition of tragedy, "Romeo and Juliet" is a drama of the highest order. The incidents of terror and the sufferings of the principal persons of the drama arouse every sympathy of the soul, and the interest of sympathy with Juliet. She unites all the interest of ecstatic love, of unexampled calamity, and of the peculiar tenderness which the heart feels for innocence in childhood. Most truly, then, says the Prince of Verona, at the conclusion of the play—

> "For never was a story of more wo
> Than this of Juliet and her Romeo."

The age of Juliet seems to be the key to her character throughout the play, an essential ingredient in the intense sympathy which she inspires; and Shakespeare has marked it, not only in her discourse, but even in her name, the diminutive of tender affections applied only to childhood. If Shakespeare had exhibited upon the stage a woman of nineteen, he would have dismissed her nurse and called her Julia. She might still have been a very interesting character, but the whole color and complexion of the play must have been changed. An intelligent, virtuous woman, in love with a youth of assorted age and congenial character, is always a person of deep interest in the drama. But that interest is heightened and redoubled when, to the sympathy with the lover, you add all the kind affectations with which you share in the joys and sorrows of the child. There is childishness in the discourse of Juliet, and the poet has shown us why; because she had scarcely ceased to be a child. [Letter to James Henry Hackett, reprinted in Hackett's *Notes, Criticisms and Correspondence upon Shakespeare's Plays and Actors,* 1863.]

JOHANN LUDWIG TIECK. Shakespeare was eminently right in not closing the tragedy with the death of Juliet, however much our modern impatience may demand it. Not only do the affecting reconciliation of the two old foes and the vindication of Friar Lawrence make the continuation necessary, but so it must be chiefly in order that, after misfortune has done its worst, the true idea of the tragedy, its glorified essence, may rise before our souls that up to this point have been too sorely tried and too violently affected to perceive the inmost meaning of the poem, or to take a painful yet clear survey of it. . . . It is a pity that on the stage much of the Nurse's vulgar babble, as well as Mercutio's flying witticisms, must be omitted. We are no longer innocent enough and unconstrained enough to listen to these jests simply as jests; our propriety is instantly aroused; on such occasions, and on much milder ones, it never allows itself to be caught napping. How, in more modern pieces, it applauds much worse things, and feels thereby much edified and strengthened, is no riddle to those who see that in this respect we live in a world turned upside down. In a tragedy like this, where love is the theme that is treated under its manifold aspects, the contrast of joking and laughter should not be forgotten. Through the whole piece, as in a many-voiced musical symphony, the voices of the young people at one time mingle in unison, then separate and flow onward in contrast; Benvolio the sedate, Tybalt the furious, Mercutio the witty, Romeo the enthusiast, Paris the tender, refined youth; indeed, we may even add the tone of command of the young Prince, whom I have always thought to be quite young, and have imagined as a counterpart to the others. [*Dramaturgische Blätter*, Vol. I, 1826; reprinted in *Romeo and Juliet*, New Variorium Edition, H. H. Furness, ed., 1871.]

DONALD A. STAUFFER. . . . from the religious imagery of the wooing to the feasting imagery of the Capulet vault, when Romeo's wit plays its "lightning before death," the power of love is idealized; and true love, as though it were a hyphenated compound, echoes through the play.

Shakespeare has found skill adequate to his ambition. Nothing but the finest part of pure love inhabits his scenes of romantic enchantment—the courtship at the ball, the moonlit wooing, the bridal night. He has intensified its purity by contrasting it with Romeo's first posings, with Capulet's bargainings and tantrums, with Mercutio's bawdry, with the Friar's benign philosophizing, and with the nurse's loose opportunism. He has shown that love makes lovers fearless. He sings its hymn in Juliet's epithalamium; and consecrates it as rising above life, in the successive draughts, of sleep and of death, which each lover drinks to the other. His favorite theme of Death the Bridegroom he has introduced when the lean abhorred monster, in Romeo's imaginings, keeps Juliet "in dark to be his paramour."

Above all, he has brought out the pathos of love by violent contrasts. Time hurries all things away, and in the lightning imagery the kiss and the consummation are as fire and powder. Frail love, surrounded by disasters, becomes a thing of light in blackness, itself "like a rich jewel in an Ethiop's ear." All is loneliness: Juliet is deserted by her father, then by her mother, then by her nurse, until she is left only with the power to die, or to consign herself to the horrible vault. Romeo is exiled–and indeed through the middle scenes "banished! banished!" beats like a pulse. Desperate and exiled, love knows only enemies, ranging from the vulgar nurse to "love-devouring death" itself.

The secret of the play is that the deaths of the lovers are *not* the result of the hatred between the houses, nor of any other cause except love itself, which seeks in death its own restoring cordial. Love conquers death even more surely than it conque hate. It sweeps aside all accidents, so that fate itself seems powerless. Time is conquered, in that first stirring of a belief that Shakespeare came later to trust completely: that the intensity of an emotion towers above its temporal duration or success. [*Shakespeare's World of Images*, 1949.]

WOLFGANG CLEMEN. In Shakespeare's work, conventional style and a freer, more spontaneous mode of expression are not opposite poles which may be definitely assigned to different periods. It is impos sible to say that with a certain play, the conventiona style comes to an end, and that from then on, a new style exclusively prevails. There are many transition and interrelationships, and in some plays which stan at the turning-point between the young and the ma ture Shakespeare, the most traditional and conven tional wording is to be found together with a direc and surprising new language which allows us t divine the Shakespeare of the great tragedies. *Rome and Juliet* is the best example of this co-existence o two styles. H. Granville-Barker has shown how bot in separate scenes and in the dramatic structure new spontaneity often breaks through the conven tional vestment, but is still not yet strong enough t pervade the whole of the play. The same thing ma now be shown to hold for the imagery as well.

. . . *Romeo and Juliet* shows at several points ho Shakespeare produces a closer harmony between th imagery and the characters, between the inner an outer situation and the theme of the play. But eve here, we have not yet what we should call "dra matic" imagery. With its rich poetic decoration, it abundance of epithets, its personifications, the im agery is still predominantly of a descriptive char acter. Thus the long description of Queen Mab ap pears as an extra-dramatic moment in the structur of the play. . . . In *Romeo and Juliet* Shakespeare i still writing in a style which leaves nothing unsaid This tendency towards complete representatio clarification, amplification and description is never theless favourable to the development of a poeti diction of great wealth and colour in which th metaphorical element can freely unfold. For, com pared to earlier plays, we find in *Romeo and Julie* an increase of metaphors used where formerly a co ceit or an elaborate comparison would have bee inserted. These, it is true, have not yet disappeare but the growing predilection for metaphors seem significant and suggests the way Shakespeare will g Viewed from this angle, too, *Romeo and Juliet*, ap pears as a play of transition. [*The Development o Shakespeare's Imagery*, 1951.]

Romeus and Juliet, The Tragicall Historye of. Se Arthur BROOKE.

Romney, George (1734–1802). Artist. An importa portrait painter, Romney's reputation was based o his fashionable portraits of pretty women. Howeve he had always aspired to producing history painting and he eagerly accepted an invitation to contribut to BOYDELL'S SHAKESPEARE GALLERY. Five notebook in the Folger Library contain studies for *King Lea Macbeth*, and *The Tempest*, and there are man preliminary sketches for "The Infant Shakespeare. Most of these drawings are in line and wash an show an inventiveness and freedom of treatment th are almost wholly absent from the finished painting that he finally submitted. Three of Romney's paint ings for the gallery are "Cassandra Raving," a elaborate painting of Lady Hamilton in classic costume; an illustration of the opening scene of *Th Tempest;* and "The Infant Shakespeare Nursed b Nature and the Passions," an allegorical painting i the classical style. [W. M. Merchant, *Shakespear and the Artist*, 1959.]

Rosalind. In *As You Like It*, the beautiful, witt daughter of the banished Duke. Rosalind is retaine at the usurping Frederick's court as a companion fc daughter Celia. After Orlando's victory over arles the wrestler, Rosalind, smitten with love, wards his bravery with a chain from her neck. owever, Frederick's malice toward Rosalind's father is rekindled and she is soon banished from urt. Accompanied by Celia and the jester Touchne, Rosalind journeys to the Forest of Arden, guised as the boy Ganymede. There she renews r acquaintance with Orlando, who has fled from s brother Oliver. After reading his verses to Rosad, Ganymede teases Orlando into indulging in a ake-believe courtship which she promises will cure s love for his lady. Finally casting aside her playful le, Rosalind, having gained the consent of her ther (who is also in Arden Forest), marries Orndo.

Rosaline. In *Love's Labour's Lost,* the clever oung lady-in-waiting to the Princess of France. An rly portrait of Beatrice in *Much Ado About Noth-g,* Rosaline shares with that heroine sparkling wit d verbal dexterity. Rosaline's chief combatant in er verbal duels is the ironic Berowne, for whom she more than a match. Her final triumph occurs when erowne declares his love. She accepts under the roviso that Berowne will spend the next year visitg hospitals so that his sharp wit may be softened charity.

Rosaline. In *Romeo and Juliet,* the girl with whom omeo is in love at the beginning of the play. Rosane never appears on stage and she is soon forgotten fter Romeo meets Juliet.

Rose, George (1920–). Actor. Rose was a nember of the Old Vic from 1944 to 1948. He has ppeared in a large number of Shakespearean roles, ncluding Autolycus in *The Winter's Tale* (1951) nd Dogberry in *Much Ado About Nothing* (1959). n 1964 he scored a success as the First Gravedigger n the John Gielgud production of *Hamlet* in New ork.

Rosenbach, A[braham] S[imon] W[olf] (1876–952). American book collector and dealer. Born in hiladelphia, Rosenbach became a book collector at n early age, following the example of his uncle, Moses Polock, whose combined bookshop and publishing house on Commerce Street had become a endezvous for publishers, writers, and collectors. Rosenbach studied at the University of Pennsylvania, ecame a teaching fellow after receiving his bacheor's degree, and obtained the doctorate in 1901. Abandoning teaching for the book trade, in 1904 he ssued his first catalogue from 1320 Walnut Street, n address which was to be famous for over 50 years; e later established an office and residence in New York.

With his growing reputation as a collector and dealer, Rosenbach received important commissions; e played a major role in assembling the collections of Henry E. Huntington and Pierpont Morgan. He ecounted his experiences in numerous periodical articles which were later collected in book form: *The Unpublishable Memoirs* (1917), *Books and Bidders* (1927), and *A Book Hunter's Holiday* (1936). He also published a number of monographs on American, Jewish, and theatrical bibliography and history. Among the several learned societies to which he belonged was the Shakespeare Association of America, of which he served as president from 1934 to 1949.

Rosenbach's dealings in Shakespeareana were both numerous and important. In 1922 he set a record by paying £8,600 for a copy of the First Folio, only to exceed that record in 1933 by paying £14,500 for another copy. He built up an extensive collection through the purchase of such notable Shakespeare libraries as those of Mardsen J. Perry (containing the bulk of J. O. Halliwell-Phillipps' collection) and Sir George Holford. Shortly before his death, Rosenbach sold the remainder of his Shakespeare holdings to the Swiss collector Martin Bodmer. This transaction was the most important since 1914 when the Duke of Devonshire sold his collection to Henry E. Huntington. [Edwin Wolf 2nd with John F. Fleming, *Rosenbach: A Biography,* 1960; John F. Fleming, "The Rosenbach-Bodmer Shakespeare Folios and Quartos," *Shakespeare Quarterly,* III, 1952.]

Rosencrantz and Guildenstern. In *Hamlet,* schoolmates of Hamlet's invited by Claudius to spy on the Prince (II, ii). Although Rosencrantz and Guildenstern are usually regarded as treacherous fellows, there is nothing in the text, other than Hamlet's unnatural suspicions, to support the idea that they are acting from anything but the best motives.

Rose theatre. Elizabethan playhouse, owned by Philip Henslowe. The Rose was located on the Bankside in Southwark in the area known as the Liberty of the Clink. The site, a rose garden at an earlier date, was located midway between the areas later occupied by the Hope and the Globe theatres. In January 1587 Henslowe concluded an agreement with a grocer, John Cholmley, for partnership in a "playe howse now in framinge and shortly to be ereckted and sett vppe vpone" the site. Henslowe was to set up the "saide play house with all furniture thervnto belonginge with as muche expedicion as maye be," pay the rent for the land, and repair the bridges and wharves on the property by the following Michaelmas. Cholmley was to pay any additional maintenance expenses and pay Henslowe the sum of £816 in quarterly installments. In return Cholmley was to have half the profits which accrued from "any playe or playes, that shalbe showen or played there or otherwysse howsoever." Both partners were to select the players to play in the Rose, and either by themselves or by assignment collect admission fees, except for friends whom they permitted to enter "for nothinge."

The construction of the Rose in 1587 established the Bankside area as a rival to the northerly "fields" in the presentation of plays. The closing of the Rose because of the plague in 1591/2 caused a serious hardship for the watermen engaged in ferrying playgoers across the Thames. The watermen petitioned the privy council to reopen the Rose; Henslowe's players had in the meantime been performing at Newington Butts theatre, located in an area that proved to be unprofitable to all. In recognition of the watermen's plight, the privy council ordered the reopening of the Rose with the following warrant (probably late 1592):

> Whereas not longe since vpon some Consideracions we did restraine the Lorde Straunge his servauntes from playinge at the Rose on the banckside, and enioyned them to plaie three daies at Newington Butts, Now forasmuch as wee are

satisfied that by reason of the tediousnes of the waie and that of longe tyme plaies haue not there bene vsed on working daies, And for that a nomber of poore watermen are therby releeved, Youe shall permitt and suffer them or any other there to exercise them selues in such sorte as they haue don heretofore, And that the Rose maie be at libertie without any restrainte, solonge as yt shalbe free from infection of sicknes, . . .

Henslowe's diary, which detailed his financial transactions from 1592 to 1597, indicates that the Rose was a highly profitable venture. Its average daily profit in May 1594 was 41s., compared with the 9s. per diem which had been taken at Newington Butts. The diary lists in detail the plays performed by Strange's Men at the Rose during the period February 19 to June 22, 1592, with gate receipts. In 1592, too, the diary records £108 spent for extensive repairs to the Rose. The plague permitted only short playing seasons at all theatres during this period (1592–1594). In 1593/4 there is a note of Sussex' Men having played from December 26 to February 6, and of Sussex' and the Queen's Men playing together (see AMALGAMATION) April 1–8, 1594.

After 1594 the Admiral's Men, headed by Edward ALLEYN, was the company which used the Rose almost exclusively. Henslowe's relations with the company were amicable (especially since Alleyn had married his stepdaughter in 1592); Henslowe took a share of the Rose's profits as his due as lessee. He did not collect rent from the players. This was the same arrangement as the housekeepers at the Globe had essayed. There were differences, however, in Henslowe's relations with players who used the theatre after the Admiral's Men moved to his Fortune theatre in 1600. Henslowe collected half the proceeds of the gallery admissions (those that were calculated from the gallery entrances, not from the exterior doors). He remained responsible for the repairs. Otherwise, all expenses were charged to the players. In 1600 Pembroke's Men are noted as playing at the Rose, in defiance of the privy council order limiting acting companies to the Admiral's at the Fortune and the Chamberlain's Men at the Globe. Henslowe's diary records only two unprofitable performances for them, however. WORCESTER'S MEN were in occupancy at the Rose by 1603; they stayed there possibly until 1604, when they established themselves at the Red Bull. Henslowe's lease on the land was due to expire in 1605, and certainly no plays after that date are recorded there. The Rose was pulled down by 1606. During that year a man named Edward Box of Bread Street was taxed for the site of "the late playhouse in Maid lane," which was the location of the Rose. When presented with the tax bill, Henslowe had replied that it was "out of his hands." Chambers conjectures that the site remained in use for purposes of amusement even after the building was pulled down, and that some other building on the property might have retained the name "the Rose." Alleyn's papers record payment of "tithe dwe for the Rose" in 1622, and in his edition of the variorum, Edmund Malone found an entry in the office-book of the Master of the Revels Sir Henry Herbert that after 1620 the Rose and the Swan were used for prizefights. [E. K. Chambers, *The Elizabethan Stage*, 1923.]

Ross, Thane of. In *Macbeth,* a Scottish noblem[an]. In IV, iii, Ross brings Macduff word that Macb[eth] has murdered Lady Macduff and her "babes." [He] then joins the rebels against Macbeth.

Ross, William de, 7th Lord (d. 1414). L[ord] treasurer of England under Henry IV. In *Rich[ard] II,* Ross goes over to Bolingbroke's cause af[ter] Richard confiscates the property of John of Ga[unt] and thereby deprives Gaunt's son Henry of [his] rightful legacy (II, i). [W. H. Thomson, *Sha[ke]speare's Characters: A Historical Dictionary,* 195[1].]

Rosseter, Philip (d. 1624). Lutenist and theatri[cal] manager. Rosseter was a lutenist at court from 16[04] to 1624 (or 1623, old style calendar) with the title [of] lute of the privy chamber. The lutenist enjoy[ed] higher status than the other court musicians; he sa[ng,] played, and composed his own songs. In 1601, R[os]seter and Thomas Campion (1567–1620) compos[ed] their *Booke of Ayres,* which was published in 16[01]. Rosseter fell heir to Campion's property at the l[at]ter's death in 1620.

In theatrical enterprises, Rosseter's concerns ce[n]tered about the CHILDREN OF THE CHAPEL (also [some]times known as the Children of the Queen's Revel[s]). He is named as a patentee in the license granted t[o the] Queen's Revels in 1610, was their payee in t[he] Chamber Accounts list of rewards to the acti[ng] companies in 1612 and 1613, and was their manag[er] from their reorganization in 1617. Rosseter also he[ld] the lease on the Whitefriars theatre from 1609 [to] 1615; in 1615 he was issued a patent for the constru[c]tion of a theatre in the Blackfriars to be known [as] PORTER'S HALL THEATRE. In 1613 he appeared [in] Chapman's *Middle Temple and Lincoln's I[nn] Masque,* with John and Robert Dowland a[nd] Thomas Ford. In several of his enterprises as theat[re] manager, Rosseter was associated with Philip Hen[s]lowe. [E. K. Chambers, *The Elizabethan Stage,* 192[3]; G. E. Bentley, *The Jacobean and Caroline Stag[e],* 5 vols., 1941–1956.]

Rossini, Gioacchino (1792–1868). Italian compose[r]. Rossini's three-act opera *Otello* is the earliest ope[ra] based on the play. The librettist was Marquis Beri[o]. It was first produced at the Teatro del Fond[o], Naples, in 1816, and was popular for many yea[rs] until Verdi's masterpiece of 1887 overshadowed i[t]. The music was in many ways ahead of its time an[d] still has considerable dramatic impact. [Christoph[er] Wilson, *Shakespeare and Music,* 1922.]

Rotheram, Thomas, archbishop of York. Se[e] Thomas Rotheram, archbishop of YORK.

Rousillon, Countess of. In *All's Well That End[s] Well,* Bertram's mother and Helena's guardian. [A] truly aristocratic lady who regards her ward as [a] daughter, the Countess favors Helena's love for he[r] son and encourages her to follow him to Paris.

Rowe, Nicholas (1674–1718). Dramatist, poet, firs[t] editor, and first authoritative biographer of Shake[speare]. Abandoning law for literature, Rowe becam[e] a successful writer of tragic drama. Modeled on ear[lier] historical tragedies, his plays have a tone of mora[l] dignity and lofty, patriotic idealism, qualities whic[h] clash strongly with the licentiousness of Restoratio[n] drama and make him a forerunner of the Augusta[n] stage. His best-known plays are *The Tragedy o[f] Jane Shore* "Written in Imitation of Shakespeare'[s] Style" (1714), and *The Fair Penitent* (1703), whic[h] was praised by Samuel Johnson. Rowe had severa[l] minor political appointments and in 1715 became poet laureate, succeeding Nahum Tate. He was buried in Westminster Abbey.

Rowe's edition of Shakespeare, the first critical and illustrated one to appear, was published in six octavo volumes in 1709; a second edition, extended to nine volumes to include the *Poems*, appeared in 1714. The plays followed the order of the Folios, with the doubtful plays placed at the end. Rowe used the corrupt Fourth Folio for his text, and although he did not consult the quartos or First Folio, he made certain emendations which are the correct readings. His experience as a dramatist led him to make many technical improvements: the division of the plays into acts and scenes, the mention of entrances and exits of the players, and a list of *dramatis personae* at the head of each play. Further, he modernized the spelling, punctuation, and grammar, thus making Shakespeare more intelligible to 18th-century audiences and readers and paving the way for future editions.

His *Some Account of the Life, &c. of Mr. William Shakespear*, the first formal biography, appeared as an introduction to the 1709 edition and became the standard work for the 18th century, subsequent editors of Shakespeare having reprinted it in altered form. Much of the material in the way of theatrical traditions, legends, and anecdotes was collected for Rowe by Thomas Betterton at Stratford, and we owe its preservation to Shakespeare's first editor. See John HALES; Sir Thomas LUCY; ELIZABETH I. [D. Nichol Smith, *Eighteenth Century Essays on Shakespeare*, 1963.]

Rowington. A village about 12 miles northwest of Stratford. Rowington was a Catholic stronghold and the home of a number of individuals surnamed Shakespeare, but there is no indication of any direct relationship between them and the Shakespeare family of Stratford. Among the Rowington branch was a William Shakespeare listed in 1605 as a trained soldier.

Rowlands, Samuel (1570?–?1628). Satirist. A prolific writer, Rowlands was the author of a number of lively pamphlets satirizing the London of his day. His work contains two allusions to Shakespearean plays. The first of these occurs in his *Whole Crew of Kind Gossips* (1609), in which a husband whose wife has complained of his drunkenness makes the following rejoinder:

> In sober sadnesse I do speake it now,
> And to you all I make a solemne vow,
> The chiefest Art I have I will bestow
> About a worke cald taming of the Shrow.

Rowlands' *The Night Raven* (1620) alludes to *Hamlet* or to the earlier version of the play, the so-called *Ur-Hamlet:*

> I will not cry *Hamlet Revenge* my greeves,
> But I will call *Hang-man Revenge* on theeves.

Rowley, Samuel (1575?–?1624). Actor and dramatist, sometimes said to be the brother of William ROWLEY, but there is no evidence to support this conjecture. Samuel Rowley was a member of the Admiral's Men, for whom he revised Christopher Marlowe's *Dr. Faustus* in 1601 and 1602, possibly adding the inferior comic scenes in that play. He remained with the Admiral's when they became first the Prince's Men and later when their patron was the Elector Palatine. Rowley is best known for his history play *When You See Me, You Know Me* (1605), which is one of the sources of *Henry VIII*. The anonymous play *The Famous Victories of Henry V*, which is one of the sources of Shakespeare's plays relating to that monarch, has been attributed to Rowley by H. Dugdale Sykes. [H. Dugdale Sykes, *Sidelights on Elizabethan Drama*, 1924.]

Rowley, William (1585?–1642). Actor and dramatist. The earliest known reference to Rowley is as an actor with the Duke of York's Men (Prince Charles' Men) in 1608. He is listed as an actor with the King's Men in 1625. As a playwright his chief virtue seemed to be a knowledge of what was theatrically effective, a sense which he used to great advantage in his collaborations with more gifted writers. He worked with Dekker and Ford on *The Witch of Edmonton* (1621), with Webster on *A Cure for a Cuckold* (1625), and with Fletcher on *The Maid in the Mill* (1623). His most fruitful association, however, was with Thomas Middleton, with whom he wrote *A Fair Quarrel* (1617); *The Changeling* (1622), their most distinguished effort; and *The Spanish Gypsy* (1623). In Middleton's scandalous success, *A Game at Chess* (1624), Rowley probably played the role of the Fat Bishop. He was apparently at this time a member of the King's Men. A quarto published in 1662 by Francis Kirkman and Henry Marsh has the following title page: "*The Birth of Merlin* . . . written by William Shakespear, and William Rowley." The play is usually regarded as Rowley's but not Shakespeare's. Sidney Lee and others have also suggested that Rowley was one of the collaborators with Shakespeare on *Pericles*, but the suggestion has been rejected by recent editors. [G. E. Bentley, *The Jacobean and Caroline Stage*, 5 vols., 1941–1956.]

Rowse, A[lfred] L[eslie] (1903–). Historian, fellow of All Souls College, Oxford. Beginning with *Sir Richard Grenville of the Revenge* (1937), Rowse has gained a wide audience for his books on Elizabethan England, most notably *The England of Elizabeth* (1950), *An Elizabethan Garland* (1953), *The Expansion of Elizabethan England* (1955), *The Elizabethans and America* (1959), and *Sir Walter Ralegh* (1962). In recent years he has moved into the field of literary scholarship with *William Shakespeare, A Biography* (1963), an edition of Shakespeare's *Sonnets* (1964), and *Christopher Marlowe, A Biography* (1964). A lively controversy arose from the claim, made in his life of Shakespeare, that he had been able, by means of historical investigation and the use of historical method, to solve "for the first time, and definitely, the problem of the sonnets." He explained that all previous attempts had failed because the task had been undertaken by literary scholars lacking the proper historical training. Now, thanks to the historian, all problems are solved except for the identity of Shakespeare's mistress, "something we are never likely to know." Rowse's claims drew a quick response. It was suggested that he had drawn upon the works of literary scholars without adding anything substantially new; that, for example, his identification of Mr. W. H. as the earl of Southampton had been offered as long ago as 1817 by Nathan Drake. Rowse repeated his claims in the Introduction to his edition of the *Sonnets*, published the following year, but with more modesty and with a gesture of reconciliation toward the literary scholars.

Roxana. A tragedy in Latin written about 1592 by William Alabaster (1567–1640) for an academic performance at Trinity College, Cambridge. The play was not published until 1632. A small postage-stamp-size engraving on the title page of this edition contains one of the four pictures of the Elizabethan stage known to be extant. The other three pictures are the famous drawing of the Swan by Johannes DE WITT and the engraved title pages of two other plays, *Messallina* and *The Wits*. The *Roxana* engraving shows a stage tapering toward the front and surrounded by a short railing. At the rear of the stage are curtains and above these spectators' rooms similar to those in de Witt's Swan drawing.

It has been suggested that the *Roxana* engraving represents a picture of the academic stage upon which the play was originally produced. This seems unlikely, however, in view of the fact that the edition appeared 40 years after the production. It is more plausible to assume that the artist drew a picture of a stage with which he was familiar.

Royal Shakespeare Theatre (originally **Shakespeare Memorial Theatre**). A theatre at Stratford-upon-Avon. It was 263 years after Shakespeare's death before Stratford-upon-Avon had a theatre dedicated to his work. Earlier there had been little drama seen

THE SMALL DRAWING OF A STAGE (HERE ENLARGED MANY TIMES) ON THE TITLE PAGE OF ALABASTER'S *Roxana* (1630).

there—occasional strolling actors, the "Garrick" Ju bilee of 1769, which celebrated the dramatist whil using no more than half a line from the plays, an intermittent commemorations that ended with th Tercentenary Festival of 1864. A ring of poplars i a paddock behind Old Town now marks the site o the 12-sided wooden pavilion used as a theatre fo the festival fortnight. These matters aside, there ha been nothing. Though a small theatre building wa opened in December 1827 on a part of the site o Shakespeare's Great Garden, it was never more tha a minor provincial house. During its last 30 year from 1842, it had dwindled into a nondescript publi building.

It took the faith and fire of a townsman, whos name is still potent, to establish what had bee needed. Charles Edward Flower, a wealthy brewe son of Edward Fordham Flower (mayor in 1864) proposed during the 1870's that Shakespeare's tow should have Shakespeare's theatre. He gave for th purpose two acres upon the Bancroft, or rive meadow, where cattle had grazed in Shakespeare' day and where Garrick's "Rotunda" had stood i 1769. Flower led the subscribers, giving much of th £20,000 himself; and the Shakespeare Memorial As sociation set about erecting "a small theatre in whic to have occasional performances of Shakespeare' plays," and also a library and picture gallery beside i

Outside Stratford there was disbelief in the idea o a permanent theatre in this remote market town. Sev eral writers on the opening day, April 23, 1879, cam to gibe. The building, designed by Messrs. Dodgshu and Unsworth, of Westminster, proved externally t be a strange "modern Gothic" structure with plum cake turrets, odd gables, walls of staring red bric and a band of half-timbering: a motley block, fron a distance as flimsy in aspect as a cardboard cutou A critic called it "a piece of pinchbeck 19th-centur medievalism." Nine years later, however, Osca Wilde found it "one of the loveliest building erected in England for many years." The theatr proper held 800 persons on the ground floor and i dress circle and gallery. An intimate place, excelle for speaking and listening, it had a cramped, shallo stage: the proscenium was 27 feet 6 inches in heigh with an opening of 26 feet.

For the opening night Charles Flower had assem bled a company to perform *Much Ado About Noth ing*, including Helen Faucit—who, though retire agreed to act on this occasion—as Beatrice and Barr Sullivan as Benedick. Miss Kate Field, an America living in Stratford, recited the dedication ode b Westland Marston.

The festival continued for a fortnight, Sulliva playing Hamlet and also Jaques in *As You Like I* After the premiere, Ellen Wallis succeeded Hele Faucit as Beatrice. London critics, their horizo bounded by Leicester Square and by Clare Marke were persistently resentful. Shakespeare had sough his intellectual life in London. Would he need a memorial an addition to the list of petty provinci theatres? Stratford took no notice. During the ne few years various managers conducted festivals o the dramatist's birthday. There was also such an ou of-season pleasure as the debut of the young Cal fornian actress Mary Anderson as Rosalind in Augu 1885.

At Easter in the following year, Stratford first met the actor who, with Charles Flower, was one of the true pillars of the Memorial Theatre. He was Frank Robert BENSON, a man of 27. Son of a Hampshire squire and educated at Winchester and New College, Oxford, he had had very brief acting experience with Irving and had toured with two provincial companies. When his second provincial manager, heavily in debt, abandoned his company during a Scottish weekend, young Frank Benson took it over: the Bensonian company was born. Its fellowship would endure for over four decades, the best-loved band of brothers in British stage record.

Benson, handsome and impetuous, was an idealist with a passionate loyalty to Shakespeare. He faced problems of production with a fresh, probing mind. Always he had a genius for enlisting young players; his company again and again renewed its strength. With him it was perpetually four o'clock on a May morning, and his work kept the freshness of daybreak. As a man of business he was unpractical, an idealist who could not read a balance sheet; but to the end he remained the visionary, the dedicated Shakespearean whose "life was homage."

From the spring of 1886 until the spring of 1919 Benson and his company missed only five Stratford years. Other managers controlled three early festivals (1889, 1890, 1895), and there was a break in 1917 and 1918 during the first world war. Otherwise, the theatre, for its townsfolk and for the increasing number of festival visitors, meant Benson. His visit every spring was a personal refreshment after the company's winter months of "begging friar" toil around the industrial towns. With him there came in time many young players of repute: Mrs. Benson, who had been Constance Fetherstonhaugh—not a specially good actress, but a personality comparable with her husband; the comedian George R. Weir; and such players as Frank Rodney, Oscar Asche, O. B. Clarence, Alfred Brydone, Arthur Whitby, Henry Ainley, and Matheson Lang.

Financially, the arrangement (a division of festival proceeds—60 per cent to Benson, 40 per cent to the theatre) would be much the same as at any other touring "date"; but the Governors subsidized a special production annually of one of the lesser-known plays. By 1904 the Stratford festival had completed 25 years. Within a decade spring season attendances had grown from 4000 to 14,000. Charles Flower died in 1892. His brother Edgar, who succeeded him as chairman, died in 1903, and was followed in turn by his son, Archibald Dennis Flower (later knighted).

In 1904 the spring festival covered three weeks. Benson packed into this period as many as 13 Shakespeare plays and the Oresteian trilogy of Aeschylus. Over the years his work had included such plays as *Timon of Athens, Coriolanus, Antony and Cleopatra,* and an uncut *Hamlet,* and in 1901 he had given a special historical cycle, six of the plays in what was known as "the week of kings." On his night he could be a fine and sensitive actor—his Richard II remained unexampled—and he has been undervalued by writers who noted mannerisms of speech and gait and who began a legend, later exaggerated beyond reason, that as a touring manager he was obsessed with sports. This was not so, though he did regard an actor's physical fitness and stamina important and encouraged his company to play games.

Besides developing young talent, Benson drew leading players to Stratford for special performances: Ellen Terry, Tree, Forbes-Robertson, Lewis Waller—these and others came as the festivals grew in quality and acclaim. By 1910 there was a summer season as well as one in the spring; before long each lasted for a month.

War brought inevitable change. The festivals went on bravely for three years, and in the spring of 1916 King George V knighted Frank Benson during the Shakespeare Tercentenary matinee at Drury Lane Theatre. Then, during 1917 and 1918, a time of dangerous pressure, the Stratford Memorial did not open. After the war it was hard to regain the careless rapture of 1913. Following a makeshift spring program in 1919, the theatre passed under the joint control of its Governors and London's Shakespeare Memorial National Theatre Committee. This group believed that an advance towards a National Theatre would be the creation of a permanent company or companies, which in due time would be adequately endowed. Meanwhile it was possible at the moment to give practical aid to Stratford.

Benson was invited to direct the festival and to conduct its school of acting, on condition (it was stringent) that he no longer appeared himself. When he refused the terms, W. Bridges-Adams succeeded him in August 1919. Bridges-Adams was an experienced young Shakespearean director whom the veteran Ben Greet publicly nicknamed "Unabridges." He wished to see the plays "as plays, irrespective of mutilations made to suit the whim of a star or the exigencies of stage carpentry—in short, straight Shakespeare played by a balanced cast." For seven years he directed with high skill. During 1925 the theatre was incorporated under royal charter, with the king as patron, and a council—Alderman Flower as its chairman—as administrators. Under this charter the Memorial could not be run as a commercial undertaking: its profits must go solely to the future promotion of its objects.

In the very next year, on March 6, 1926, the building was burned to a shell one gusty afternoon. No-

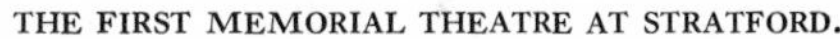

THE FIRST MEMORIAL THEATRE AT STRATFORD.

body ever discovered the cause: maybe a match dropped carelessly. Thanks to a slant in the wind at a critical moment, library and picture gallery were saved intact. Bernard Shaw sent Shavian congratulations: "It will be a tremendous advantage to have a proper modern theatre; there are a few other theatres I should like to see burned."

For six years the festivals were confined to the Stratford-upon-Avon Picture House, which Bridges-Adams converted with immense craft and resource. Much of his work there is remembered warmly, with the performances by such players as Dorothy Green (an Old Bensonian), Dorothy Massingham, Wilfrid Walter, George Hayes, and Roy Byford. During three consecutive winters a festival company toured the United States and Canada. Americans contributed with special generosity (£137,000 out of a final £316,000) to the fund for a new Memorial theatre erected to the design of Elisabeth Scott, who won an open competition. And on April 23, 1932 the prince of Wales flew to Stratford to open a great building of red and silver-gray brick that stood astride the Bancroft, roughly midway between Shakespeare's birthplace in Henley Street and Holy Trinity Church, where he was buried.

This theatre was entirely different from the endeared eccentricity that had gone. Externally, it was austere, ungarnished. There were critics to call it both a factory and a tomb. But, in general, its internal luxury pleased everyone—its foyers, its bronze, steel, marble, its variety of woods, its exceedingly intricate stage mechanism. Costing £177,000, it held nearly 1000 people. Its stage was very deep, with a proscenium opening 30 feet wide. An expert wrote hopefully: "The shape of the theatre resembles a giant horn and is so designed that the players can be heard in all parts of the stage, and the sound distributed evenly through the auditorium."

Everything appeared set for success; but it would be 14 years before the Memorial theatre found itself. Audiences between 1932 and 1939 were surprising: they rose from 115,000 to 200,000. From 1933 the festival, split no longer into two parts, lasted through spring and summer from Easter to Michaelmas. But critics were harsh. Stratford offered salaries too low to tempt the most eminent actors from London for so long a period. Because of the tourist industry, as many plays as possible had to be contained within one week; in April first nights jostled each other. Moreover, the impressive theatre was no friend to its players. A chasm separated the stage from the front of the stalls; Baliol Holloway, one of the distinguished Shakespeareans of his period, said that it could be like playing to Boulogne from the beach at Folkestone. Projection was difficult. Actors began to long for the temporary theatre at the Picture House, or for the old theatre, the hollow circle of blackened brick (behind the new Memorial) that one day would be converted into a conference hall. Though there were fine companies, the gulf between actors and audience began to nag at the mind like a misprint in a fine edition.

Even so, audiences grew. At the end of 1934 the brilliant Bridges-Adams decided to resign as a warning to the Governors against complacency based on a belief that tourist support was sure, whatever the Stratford standard. Bridges-Adams had begun to invite guest directors (they included Tyrone Guthrie and Theodore Komisarjevsky) and guest designers. This policy was preserved by his successor, B. Iden Payne, an Old Bensonian who for twenty years had worked in America. A gently academic director, his staging influenced by the austerity of William Poel, he came at Stratford's most difficult hour: his reign is remembered principally for the rise of Donald Wolfit, whose Hamlet and Ulysses were warmly applauded, and for such a production as Komisarjevsky's *King Lear,* staged on a long flight of steps, with the veteran Randle Ayrton in the noblest portrait of his career. The Second World War brought heavy restrictions. Still, even if Stratford had reverted to a Midland market town, the festival managed to keep going. Iden Payne left at the end of 1942 to lecture in America; Milton Rosmer had one season (1943) and Robert Atkins two (1944–1945). Atkins knew the dangers of the theatre's stage and immediately brought all action forward. But at the end of 1945 he too, resigned. It was then, for the first complete postwar festival, that of 1946, that Sir Barry Jackson crossed from the BIRMINGHAM REPERTORY THEATRE to begin three famous seasons of renaissance. The chairman of the Governors was Lieutenant-Colonel (later Sir) Fordham Flower, who had succeeded his father, Sir Archibald, in 1944. Barry Jackson, a confirmed Shakespearean, had expansive plans. He chipped off the barnacles of complacency and false tradition. He recruited eight directors for the first eight plays. He improved unsatisfactory conditions backstage; he made the theatre attractive to London actors—though he preferred to discover stars than to import them—and he saw to other things: the housing of costumes, the storage of scenery, and the enlargement and refitting of workshops, until the Memorial theatre was self-supporting.

During his term he brought to Stratford the contentious productions of the young Peter Brook (whose *Love's Labour's Lost* in 1946 was a work of genius) and an actor of growing mastery, Paul Scofield; both had been at the Birmingham Repertory Theatre. Most people regretted, as he himself did, Jackson's departure at the end of 1948, an unpublicized surrender to an insistence on youth: ironical when one realized that Barry Jackson, of all people, was himself a prime discoverer and encourager of youth in the British classical theatre. He was succeeded by Anthony Quayle, aged 34. Within the next decade most of the major names of the British stage came to Stratford. Thus, John Gielgud headed the 1950 cast and appeared as Benedick in his own revival of *Much Ado About Nothing,* tested in the previous year with another company. Peggy Ashcroft was his Beatrice. He also appeared as Angelo in Peter Brook's *Measure for Measure* and as Lear. In 1951 the interior of the Memorial Theatre was remodeled, and its circle was curved to break the blank side walls; the chasm between actors and audience vanished. It was the year of a festival sequence of four historical plays (*Richard II* to *Henry V*) with a cast headed by Michael Redgrave, Anthony Quayle and Richard Burton.

During 1953 Glen Byam Shaw, much loved and fastidious, became codirector of the Memorial Theatre with Quayle, and from the end of 1956 he conducted it alone until December 1959. Festivals in the

1950's were now up, now down, but—whatever the sierra of achievement—they were consistently and overwhelmingly supported by Shakespeareans from all over the world. These audiences saw certain historic revivals. Michael Redgrave and Peggy Ashcroft (1953) were the best Antony and Cleopatra of their time, in a production by Shaw. Peter Brook, in 1955, completed the full range of Shakespeare at Stratford by staging *Titus Andronicus,* with Laurence Olivier majestic as Titus: a collector's rare primitive in which the night and the season were lanced with fire. Olivier, who had found the heart of Macbeth in the same summer, returned to play Coriolanus in 1959. Redgrave brought his Hamlet in 1958, and Charles Laughton (1959) was a provocative Lear. This, in Glen Byam Shaw's production, was Laughton's return to Shakespeare in Britain after 25 years. That season also, one of the major British actresses, Edith Evans, appeared as the Countess of Rousillon in an idiosyncratic and mannered version of *All's Well That Ends Well* by Tyrone Guthrie and as Volumnia in *Coriolanus.*

The producer of *Coriolanus,* Peter Hall, a Cambridge graduate aged 29, became director of the Memorial Theatre in 1960 and planned its full-scale reorganization. Hall wanted to create an ensemble, a Stratford company that, remaining undispersed, would find in time a proper cohesion and style. Within the next two years Peter Brook and the French director Michel Saint-Denis, long respected in Britain, joined him as a triumvirate at the head of what was now the Royal Shakespeare Company: the theatre had been renamed the Royal Shakespeare Theatre in the spring of 1961. By then it had a London home at the Aldwych, taken over for a repertory of non-Shakespearean classics, new plays, and a few revivals transferred from Stratford. The Aldwych stage was altered to one of the same size as that at Stratford, which had again been redesigned, with a projecting wedge.

At first the new Royal Shakespeare organization, suffering from severe growing pains, had more success in London than in Stratford. Generally its Shakespeare revivals were unsure, marred by their indifferent speech. Then standards improved, and various productions—especially *Troilus and Cressida* (1960), staged by Peter Hall and John Barton in a sandy cockpit; *As You Like It,* directed by Michael Elliott on a swelling green knoll, with Vanessa Redgrave as Rosalind; and a historical sequence of *The Wars of the Roses* (1963)—proved that Stratford development was on the right lines. *The Wars of the Roses,* a two-part conflation (by John Barton) of the three chronicles of *Henry VI,* followed by *Richard III,* was repeated in Quatercentenary year as the end of a full historical progress that began with *Richard II:* seven plays in all, the most challenging and successful of Shakespearean feats under the new regime. Another major success, *King Lear* (1962–1963), was directed by Peter Brook in a production—set in what seemed to be a world of leather and rusted metal—that managed to be at once modern and timeless. It had Paul Scofield as a Lear who became, movingly, the victim of his own arrogance. In 1964 the Royal Shakespeare Company took this production, and one of *The Comedy of Errors,* on tour through Eastern Europe and later to New York.

At the time of the Quatercentenary the Royal Shakespeare Theatre (Lord Avon as its president, Sir Fordham Flower as its chairman) stood with the newly founded National Theatre at the crest of the British stage. It was estimated then that annually about 750,000 people paid more than £500,000 to see Royal Shakespeare productions. In spite of its feats—or probably because of them, for the repertoire system is costly—the company needs as much financial aid as it can get. In 1964 the Arts Council of Great Britain contributed £80,000.

Stratford, with many of its players under long-term contract, looks forward to years of intense creative work. The company exists "to build a strong bridge between the classical theatre and the truly popular theatre of our time." At Stratford its Shakespeare exists in a world of experiment. Peter Brook holds that production and settings must be moved "away from romance, away from fantasy, away from decoration . . . . We must all look beyond an outer liveliness to an inner one."

It is in this mood that Stratford-upon-Avon—which has seen stage fashion veer from careful realism to imaginative if sometimes freakish austerity—goes into the fifth century since Shakespeare's birth. The Royal Shakespeare Theatre, weathered externally, has settled into the landscape and riverscape. Its seasons last now for nine months in a year. All is very far removed from the pioneering night in 1879 when carriages, driving along Waterside in a drench of rain, reached a gas-lit "modern Gothic" theatre that first celebrated the town's own dramatist.—J.C.T.

Roydon, Matthew (fl. 1560–1622). Poet. Roydon was educated at Cambridge where he received an M.A. in 1580. He was a friend of the leading poets of his day, including Sidney, Marlowe, Spenser, and Chapman, and has been identified as a member of the so-called SCHOOL OF NIGHT. G. B. Harrison has argued that Roydon is the author of WILLOBIE HIS AVISA, which, according to Harrison, he wrote as a reply to Shakespeare's alleged attack on Raleigh in *The Rape of Lucrece.* [*Willobie His Avisa,* G. B. Harrison, ed., 1926.]

Rubinstein, Anton. See MUSIC BASED ON SHAKESPEARE: *19th century, 1850–1900.*

Rugby. In *The Merry Wives of Windsor,* the servant of Doctor Caius. A simple man, Rugby is a foil for his volatile master and the strong-minded housekeeper, Mistress Quickly.

Rumour. In *2 Henry IV,* the Presenter. In the Induction, he brings word to the Earl of Northumberland that his son Hotspur has won the battle of Shrewsbury. The news proves to be false.

Runciman, John (1744–1768). Watercolorist and history painter. Runciman died in Naples, where he had gone for the sake of his health, at the age of 24. "King Lear in the Storm" (1767), painted shortly before his death, is a remarkable work, historically as well as artistically. Its dramatic organization anticipates the school of history painting of the next generation; its violent interplay of human emotions and natural elements belongs to the height of Romantic painting. Runciman approached his subject with a radical freshness of vision. There is nothing in the painting that suggests the stage; the setting of the picture neglects and even contradicts the textual description of the heath scene, for it shows Lear and his companions at the edge of a stormy sea. Nevertheless, the painting strikes the viewer as being somehow wholly true to Shakespeare. This intuition is confirmed by noting the many textual references to sea storms in the heightened language of the heath scene. The painting is not an illustration of the play, but an interpretation of it, presented with sensitivity and power. See ART. [W. M. Merchant, *Shakespeare and the Artist*, 1959.]

Russell, Thomas (1570–1634). Shakespeare's friend and one of the overseers of his will (the other was Francis COLLINS). Russell was born in the village of Strensham, located on the Avon, not far from Stratford. In 1590 he married Katherine Bampfield and thus became allied with the family of Henry Willoughby, the apparent author of WILLOBIE HIS AVISA. In a transaction dated 1591, Willoughby's and Russell's names are mentioned together in a manner which strongly suggests friendship between the two. This is important, for if Shakespeare knew Russell at this time, Russell represents a direct link between Shakespeare and Henry Willoughby, thus strengthening the argument that the "W. S." referred to in Willoughby's poem is Shakespeare. Russell's wife died during the 1590's, and he subsequently married again. His second wife was Anne Digges, the widow of Thomas Digges, a prominent London astronomer and mathematician. By this marriage Anne was the mother of Sir Dudley Digges (1583–1639), a leading member of the Virginia Company, and of Leonard DIGGES, the young admirer of Shakespeare who wrote two poems in honor of the dramatist. Although prevented from remarrying by certain provisions in her husband's will, Anne entered into a common-law relationship with Russell and with her family went to live at his estate in Alderminster, four miles from Stratford. The impediments in the will were finally removed and the couple were officially married on August 26, 1603. The nature and length of Shakespeare's friendship with Russell is not known, but it was evidently a close one, to judge by the appointment of Russell as overseer of the will and of Shakespeare's bequest to him of £5. [Leslie Hotson, *I, William Shakespeare*, 1937.]

Russia. According to frequent Soviet Russian claims, Shakespeare has found a second home in Russia. He is published in larger-selling editions in Russia than in Great Britain and other English-speaking countries, and productions on Soviet stages (not only in Russian, but in many other languages of the U.S.S.R.) are said to take place more often and to be attended by bigger audiences than anywhere else in the world. Be this as it may, the tremendous popularity and respect which Shakespeare has enjoyed in Russia in the last 130 years—since the days of Pushkin—cannot be disputed. At the same time, it is paradoxical that along with the admiration for Shakespeare and his domestication, almost naturalization, in Russia, two of the most severe attacks ever launched against him have also been made in Russia: Tolstoy's, moral and aesthetic, around the turn of the century, and the Soviet-Marxist, social and political, during the first two decades of the Soviet regime. Shakespeare, however, easily survived these two onslaughts, and the love for him in Russia today is extremely strong.

The first Russian contacts with Shakespeare, in greatly changed form, were indirect and faint—through German actors and playwrights who learned their craft from English players in the 17th century, and then went on tours to Russia, where they in turn acquired native disciples. However, information about exactly what plays were produced in Russia by such wandering troupes is indefinite and vague. The first publication of Shakespeare, in greatly adapted form, came not from such grass roots of popular drama and staging, but from the opposite side—literary adaptation. Alexander Sumarokov (1718–1777), the first Russian nobleman to devote himself to literature as a profession, wrote almost a score of neoclassical tragedies and comedies. His second play was an adaptation of *Hamlet* (1748, prod. 1750), and it is this version which marks the entrance of Shakespeare into Russian literary and dramatic history. Sumarokov probably used Pierre-Antoine de La Place's French translation (*Théâtre Anglois*, 1745–1748) of Shakespeare; there is no evidence that he knew any English. The tragedy is greatly transmuted, in accordance with neoclassical taste. The ghost is turned into a dream; the main characters are provided with confidants and confidantes. Polonius and Claudius plan to murder Gertrude (who is persuaded by Hamlet's oratory to repent and to join his side), as well as Hamlet, and then to marry Claudius to Ophelia. Hamlet, however, eludes 50 assassins and presents himself to the jubilant people at the end, triumphant in all respects.

Sumarokov's *Hamlet* went through six editions in the 1780's. Various other adaptations were made in the second half of the 18th century. Catherine the Great herself, who in addition to all her other activities found time to write 14 comedies, 5 comic operas, and 3 historical plays, adapted *The Merry Wives of Windsor* under the title *What it Means to Have a Basket and Linen*. She also made a free translation of *Timon of Athens*. The former play, particularly, is interesting in its prosaic, matter-of-fact language and the Russification of many of the English features of its original.

Shakespeare was further popularized by the sentimentalist Nikolay Karamzin (1766–1826), who translated *Julius Caesar* in 1787, and praised Shakespeare in his *Letters of a Russian Traveler*, although he preferred reading him to seeing him. At least the Haymarket Theatre production of *Hamlet*, during his visit to London, pleased him less than Shakespeare on the printed page.

After 1800, the number of translations of Shakespeare's plays increased, as did critical discussions and allusions to Shakespeare. He was becoming domiciled in Russia, although the transplantation was still for the most part a double one: Russian critics and translators relied on French and German mediators. Their response was often based more on acquaintance with, and impressions from, French and German critics, than the original text. Neoclassical and German romantic comments on Shakespeare—praise and dispraise—dominated Russian thinking. Alexander Pushkin, the great poet, was the man who completed the process of borrowing from Europe and then went on to his own original interpretations and adaptations of Shakespeare. His relationship to Shakespeare was close. It was Shakespeare who helped him free himself from the Byronic influences of the years 1820 to 1824. The historical drama *Boris Godunov*

(1825) was consciously influenced by Shakespeare. Without dependence on 18th-century ideas of decorum and characterization, Pushkin created free, broadly conceived human beings, drawn from various social classes, ignoring the classical "unities," and reconstructing a past rich in feudal disorder and dynastic contests. Shakespeare was to Pushkin the model of how to create "loose and simple types" with "deep frankness of popular passions."

Pushkin based several works on Shakespeare. His *Count Nulin* (1825) is a racy Russification of *The Rape of Lucrece*—in which, however, the rural Lucrece gets the better of the would-be seducer, whom she sends packing with a slap. His *Angelo* (1833) is a partly dramatic, partly narrative poem in 535 lines, summarizing the chief plot of *Measure for Measure*. Pushkin considered this his best work.

Every great Russian writer since Pushkin has had his say about Shakespeare. Many wrote essays on him, some alluded to him indirectly, or adapted him, or gave their opinion in personal letters and through characters they created. Stage productions of Shakespeare were among the most important in Russian theatrical history; famous actors made their name in their Shakespearean roles.

The heroine of novelist Nikolay Leskov's (1831–1895) *Lady Macbeth of Mtsensk* (1865) was a passionate, violent Russian woman who murdered her husband as well as other people and fell victim to her lover (and to the law), but destroyed the lover as well as herself in a final outburst.

Ivan Turgenev, the first of the great Russian novelists to win fame in the West, served throughout his life as a two-way bridge for West European-Russian cultural contacts. In two of his stories, "Hamlet of Shchigrovo" and "King Lear of the Steppes," Turgenev borrowed Shakespearean titles to indicate the similarities between his very Russian, local characters and Shakespearean heroes. In his essay, *Hamlet and Don Quixote* (1860), he took the two characters to be "the antitypes of human nature, the two poles of the axletree on which that nature turns," and presented Cervantes' character as a model to be emulated by Russians, and Hamlet as closest to what in Turgenev's opinion they were—and ought to avoid being.

Turgenev, then, was preaching to the Russians of his day—using Shakespeare's *Hamlet* as a text. He saw Hamlet in Goethe's tradition, as an inactive thinker paralyzed by scruples due to excessive analysis, whereas Don Quixote was a doer of deeds, resolute, perhaps foolish and ridiculous, but at least someone who had the courage of his convictions. "Hamlet is beyond all else analysis, egoism, skepticism personified."

Ivan Goncharov, on the other hand, wrote an article about Hamlet in which he interpreted him as being far from a skeptic or egoist. He emphasized the idea of the role which Hamlet was called upon to perform. Much like mid-20th-century commentators, Goncharov envisaged Hamlet in the play as determined by the extraordinary situation into which he was plunged, and, in a very romantic fashion, he conceived of Hamlet as a personality separable from the role, the man he would have been, in Goncharov's view, if he had lived under normal, everyday circumstances.

Fyodor Dostoevsky admired Shakespeare as a great Western genius, but never used his character types as titles, nor did he ever give an extended critical discussion of his works, although he did make passing references to them, for example, the several comments he made on *Othello* in *The Brothers Karamazov* in speaking of jealousy. His notebooks show him to have been preoccupied with Shakespeare at the time when he was writing *The Possessed*. The last wanderings of Stepan Trofimovich in that novel, it is perhaps not too much to suggest, remind the reader of the heath and storm scenes in *King Lear*.

Lev Tolstoy occupies a very special place in the history of Shakespeare in Russia. Throughout his life, he showed himself to be highly irritated by Shakespeare's reputation, and he wrote several extended attacks against him. The following note which he wrote after reading *Julius Caesar* is typical of Tolstoy: "Amazingly foul. If I were young and healthy, I'd write an article about it. To rid people of the necessity of pretending that they like it." When he wrote "Shakespeare and the Drama" (pub. 1906), he was not very young (75), but still full of vigor in his hostility to the English dramatist. In that lengthy study, he recapitulated his onslaughts against Shakespeare which he had made in *What Is Art* (1897–1898) and elsewhere, affirmed that he re-read Shakespeare—tragedies, comedies, and history plays—in Russian, English, and German—and still "invariably underwent the same feelings: repulsion, weariness, and bewilderment." He then undertook to explain the reason for his negative reaction. In a detailed analysis of *King Lear*, and in other chapters, he attacked Shakespeare mainly for his characters' insufficient motivation, lack of realism, and absence of probability and verisimilitude. Tolstoy's essay reads like the cavils of a literal-minded legalist, unable to understand the conventions of poetic drama. Tolstoy ridiculed Shakespeare's language, showing no grasp whatever of metaphor. He spoke of poetic drama as if it were to be judged by the rules of evidence in a courtroom. Shakespeare's "amoralism" comes under specially strong fire. According to Tolstoy, the plays corresponded to "the irreligious and immoral frame of mind of the upper classes of Shakespeare's time."

Tolstoy's essay brought about a correspondence between George Bernard Shaw and Tolstoy, but his rejection of Shakespeare was too sweeping even for Shaw, who found it necessary to disagree with the Russian novelist in the end.

Translations. N. Ketcher was the first to publish a translation of Shakespeare's collected works (1841). The first collected edition of translations by different hands, edited by Nikolai Nekrasov (1821–1878) and Gerbel, appeared between 1865 and 1867, containing 34 dramas in verse and prose. Outstanding were the translations of Alexander Druzhinin (1824–1864), Kroneberg, and Alexander Ostrovsky (1823–1886). Other one-man translations of the collected works by Sokolovsky and Kanshin appeared, and a huge edition, that of Brokhhaus-Efron or Vengerov, was published between 1902 and 1904.

Stage Productions. Moscow and Petersburg, particularly the Imperial Theatres—the Maly in Moscow, and the Alexandrinsky in Petersburg—were the scenes of the most important Russian productions of classical Shakespearean repertory. Vasily Karatygin (1802–1853), who acted with great pathos and bombast, was the star tragedian in Petersburg, whereas his rival in Moscow was Pavel Mochalov (1800–

1848). The controversy about the merits of the two great actors, often centered on their Hamlets, is reflected in periodical literature, and plays an important role in the essay about *Hamlet* by the critic Visarion Belinsky. Later in the century. Mikhail Shchepkin (1788–1863), a serf actor, led a movement toward greater simplicity and realism in acting. Between 1856 and 1867, the triumphant tour of the American Negro Ira Aldridge included the roles of Othello and Shylock.

For a time, after 1860, Shakespeare, along with other foreign classics, was eclipsed on the stage by native Russian plays—Ostrovsky's, Pisemsky's, and Turgenev's. Another trend was away from concentration on Shakespeare's tragedies; in the later 1860's, more of his comedies began to be produced.

There were other foreign visitors who introduced new styles of acting and producing, ranging from the Meiningen company (1885) to the Italians Ernesto Rossi (from 1877 to 1895) and Tommaso Salvini (1895). Russian actors and actresses outstanding in Shakespearean roles included Yuzhin-Sumbatov and Fedotova. The Moscow Art Theatre presented *The Merchant of Venice* (1898) (a failure, however), *As You Like It* (1899), *Julius Caesar* (1903), and *Hamlet* (1911) with the famous actor Vasili Kachalov.

Shakespeare in the U.S.S.R. In the social and ideological turmoil of the Revolution and Civil War, Shakespeare's position was no more assured than that of any established reputation or institution. His fortunes in Russia since 1917 have followed the vagaries of Soviet attitudes to literature in general.

At first, some extremists questioned Shakespeare's right to survival in a "classless society," which would require only classless literature. Professor Nusinov, for example, wrote that the characters depicted in traditional classics "express in one form or another the passions and experiences of all classes which recognized private property. Inasmuch as these characters sprang out of the inevitability of private property and the oppression of man by man, the experiences embodied in such characters will gradually become alien to the people of a classless society." Eventually, however, less iconoclastic views prevailed. The Marxist Maxim Gorky and the Symbolist Alexander Blok, for instance, agreed on the necessity of preserving Shakespeare as part of the heritage of world culture.

Marxist critics (see MARXIST CRITICISM), sociological in their approach, were divided on how to place Shakespeare. To some of them (for example, Vladimir Friche), Shakespeare's work was aristocratic in leaning, even reactionary, feudal. To others (for example, A. A. Smirnov), Shakespeare appeared to have loved the people "with a vital and healthy love." He was a bourgeois writer who, however, hated bourgeois greed and Philistinism and transcended bourgeois ideology to such an extent that members of his own class were still unable to understand the revolutionary elements in his work. The latter, favorable approach gradually won official endorsement.

Many new translations of Shakespeare's works were made since 1917. S. Marshak made a superb version of Shakespeare's sonnets; Boris Pasternak translated several of the tragedies and wrote an interesting essay on his work as translator.

Stage productions flourished during the first four years after the Revolution; in the 1920's, various experimental, original, sometimes extremely radical adaptations were performed; in the 1930's, with the liquidation of Meyerhold and other representatives of "formalism" and "modernism" on the stage, conventional productions began to predominate. Since the death of Stalin, Shakespeare is safely enthroned as an officially accepted classic. There are numerous Shakespeare conferences, anthologies, productions; Soviet Shakespearean scholarship in recent years has been voluminous and increasingly valuable. It has even included some studies of imagery of more than local interest.

The history of Shakespeare in Russia, since Sumarokov and Catherine the Great in the 18th century to our days, shows the amazing versatility and adaptability of Shakespeare, as well as the proneness of the Russians to seek (and find) in their imported classics ideas and models (moral, social, literary, psychological) that will be immediately, practically usable in their own day and in their own country. [André Lirondelle, *Shakespeare en Russie*, 1912; Ernst Friedrichs, "Shakespeare in Russland," *Englische Studien*, Vol. 50, 1916; Ernest Simmons, "Catherine the Great and Shakespeare," *PMLA*, XLVII, 1932; E. Blum, "Shakespeare in the U.S.S.R.," *Shakespeare Association Bulletin*, 1945.]—G.G.

Rutland, Edmund, earl of (1443–1460). In *3 Henry VI,* as in history, the young son of Richard Plantagenet, duke of York. At the battle of Wakefield Edmund is ruthlessly murdered by Clifford, "that cruel child-killer," in revenge for the previous death of Clifford's father.

Rutland, Francis Manners, 6th earl of (1578–1632). Courtier. The brother of Roger Manners, 5th earl of Rutland, to whose title he succeeded upon the latter's death in 1612, Rutland was a prominent member of the Jacobean court, and entertained James I at his estate Belvoir on a number of occasions.

In the account book of Rutland's steward, there is the following item dated March 31, 1613:

> Item, 31 Martii, to Mr Shakspeare in gold about my Lorde's impreso, xliiij^s^; to Richard Burbage for paynting and making yt, in gold xliiij^s^.—iiij^li^. viij^s^.

Since Richard Burbage, the actor, is also known to have been a painter, it is generally assumed that this item refers to the actor and the dramatist. An *impresa* was a painted paper shield on which were written verse epithets or mottoes. [E. K. Chambers, *William Shakespeare*, 1930.]

Rutland theory. Term used to describe the idea that Roger Manners, 5th earl of Rutland (d. 1612), is the author of the plays ascribed to Shakespeare. The Rutland theory was first advanced in 1906 by the German Peter Alvor in *Das Neue Shakespeare-Evangelium*. Demonstrating a conservatism rare in anti-Stratfordian circles, he claimed only the authorship of the comedies for Rutland. Alvor's claims were both repudiated and enlarged by Karl Bliebtreu in his *Die Lösung der Shakespeare-Frage* (1907), who claimed Rutland as the author of all the plays. Bliebtreu's views were developed in America by Lewis Bostelmann and in Belgium by Célestin Demblon. Demblon's *Lord Rutland est Shakespeare* (1912) argues that in the plays are concealed accounts of Rutland's life, which he traces in considerable detail. The next considerable presentation of Rutland's case was Pierre Porohovshikov's *Shakespeare Unmasked* (1940, 1955), which admitted Francis Bacon as a minor collaborator with Rutland, thus enabling Porohovshikov to find the alleged Baconian ciphers embedded in the text of the First Folio (1623). (See BACONIAN THEORY.) The most recent advocate of the case for Rutland is Claud W. Sykes (*Alias William Shakespeare?*, 1947), who, employing "the methods of Sherlock Holmes," comes to the inevitable conclusion. Despite their claims, the advocates of Rutland have as yet been unable to produce any evidence that he wrote literature of any type. See CLAIMANTS.

Ryan, Lacy (c. 1694–1760). Actor. Born in England, of Irish descent, Ryan was intended for the law, but left his studies in 1710 to play Rosencrantz in a Greenwich production of *Hamlet*. In 1711 he appeared at Drury Lane as Lorenzo in Granville's *Jew of Venice* and Granius (Benvolio) in Otway's *Caius Marius*, adaptations of Shakespeare's *Merchant of Venice* and *Romeo and Juliet*. From 1718 to 1732 he was at the Lincoln's Inn Fields Theatre. In 1732 he moved with the Lincoln's Inn Fields company to their new theatre at Covent Garden where he remained until February 1760. He established an undisputed claim to the roles of lovers in tragedy and fine gentlemen in comedy. His most important original role was the Bastard in Colley Cibber's *Papal Tyranny in the Reign of King John*, an alteration of Shakespeare's play. He gave his best performances as Edgar, Ford, Iago, Mosca (*Volpone*), Cassius, and Macduff. He was almost in the first rank of actors, and was undoubtedly one of the most versatile actors of his time. Garrick mocked him for his drawling, croaking voice and the damaged features resulting from a jaw injury, but when Garrick went to see him as Richard III intending to laugh, he admired Ryan's performance so much that he improved his own interpretation as a result.

Ryan's many parts in Shakespearean plays included Claudio (*Measure for Measure*), Cymbeline, Ferdinand, Ford, Geraldo (Hortensio in John Lacy's *Sauny the Scot*), the Ghost, Gloucester (*1 Henry VI*), Gratiano, Hamlet, Henry VI (in Cibber's version of *Richard III*), Hotspur, Iago, Jaques, Laertes, Lorenzo, Lucius (*Titus Andronicus*), Macduff, Orlando, King Philip (*King John*), Polixenes, Posthumus, Richard II, Richmond, Shylock, Sylla (Paris in Otway's *Romeo and Juliet*), Troilus, Ursaces (Posthumus in D'Urfey's version of *Cymbeline*), Vernon, Wolsey, and the Prince of Wales (*1* and *2 Henry IV*). [*Dictionary of National Biography*, 1885– ; Charles Beecher Hogan, *Shakespeare in the Theatre, 1701–1800*, 2 vols., 1952, 1957.]

Ryan, Richard (1796–1849). Biographer and bookseller. Ryan is the reputed editor of *Dramatic Table Talk or Scenes, Situations, and Adventures, serious and comic, in Theatrical History and Biography* (1825) in which appeared the following anecdote about Shakespeare and Queen Elizabeth:

> It is well known that Queen Elizabeth was a great admirer of the immortal Shakspeare, and used frequently (as was the custom of persons of great rank in those days) to appear upon the stage before the audience, or to sit delighted behind the scenes, when the plays of our bard were performed. One evening, when Shakspeare himself was personating the part of a King, the audience knew of her Majesty being in the house. She crossed the stage when he was performing, and, on receiving the accustomed greeting from the audience, moved politely to the poet, but he did not notice it! When behind the scenes, she caught his eye, and moved again, but still he would not throw off his character, to notice her: this made her Majesty think of some means by which she might know, whether he would depart, or not, from the dignity of his character while on the stage.—Accordingly, as he was about to make his exit, she stepped before him, dropped her glove, and recrossed the stage, which Shakspeare noticing, took up, with these words, immediately after finishing his speech, and so aptly were they delivered, that they seemed to belong to it:
>
> 'And though now bent on this high embassy,
> Yet *stoop* we to take up our *Cousin's* glove!'
>
> He then walked off the stage, and presented the glove to the Queen, who was greatly pleased with his behaviour, and complimented him upon the propriety of it.

The incident is as unlikely as it is charming. [E. K. Chambers, *William Shakespeare*, 1930.]

Rylands, George (1902–). Scholar. Former university lecturer in English at Cambridge, Rylands has served as a governor of the Old Vic and supervised the recording of Shakespeare's plays for the British Council. His Shakespearean anthology, *The Ages of Man* (1939), provided the text for Sir John Gielgud's successful one-man reading from Shakespeare. He is also the author of "Shakespeare's Poetic Energy," a British Academy Lecture delivered in 1951.

Rymer, Thomas (1641–1713). Antiquary, critic. As historiographer royal, Rymer wrote a great work on English foreign policy in 15 volumes. His learning, however, did not fit him for literary criticism. He was a dogmatic adherent to the critical principles of neoclassicism and found Elizabethan literature, with its frequent disregard of classical aesthetic doctrines, barbaric. His critical judgments were first put forth in the preface he appended to his translation of René Rapin's *Reflections on Aristotle's Treatise of Poesie* (1674). In 1678 he published *The Tragedies of The Last Age consider'd and Examin'd by the Practice of the Ancients, and by the Common sense of all Ages*. In the preface Rymer mentions Shakespeare, but makes no critical judgments of his works. These he reserved for his *Short View of Tragedy* (1693) in which he delivers his famous denunciation of *Othello*.

His principal demands, as set forth in *Short View*, are that the construction of a play be probable, and that characterization adhere to the principles of decorum, that is, that fixed characteristics belonging to a nationality, a class, an age group, or a profession should be observed. Through a rigorous application of these standards, he arrives at comments like "[Othello's] love and jealousy are no part of a soldier's character." To give an important place in the fable to a handkerchief, he asserts, is improbable and beneath the dignity of tragedy. He accepts the critical doctrine of the age that every play should present a moral, and with heavy humor he suggests that the moral of *Othello* is "a warning to all good Wives, that they look well to their Linnen." Giving up his fooling, his final view is that "the tragical part [of *Othello*] is plainly none other than a Bloody Farce without salt or savor." Rymer was equally severe in his treatment of *Julius Caesar*. He castigates Shakespeare for the freedom with which he interpreted the historical figures of that play:

> He might be familiar with *Othello* and *Iago,* as his own natural acquaintance; but *Caesar* and *Brutus* were above his conversation. To put them in Fools Coats, and make them Jack-puddens in the *Shakespear* dress, is a *Sacriledge* . . . . The Truth is, this authors head was full of villanous, unnatural images, and history has only furnish'd him with great names, thereby to recommend them to the World.

Long regarded as the *locus classicus* of bad criticism, Rymer's remarks have come to be seen as representative, if rather undistinguished, specimens of orthodox neoclassicism. His stoutest defender has been T. S. Eliot, who, while admitting that Rymer's views were "wrong-headed," argued that he had never seen an adequate refutation of Rymer's criticism of *Othello.* [*Dramatic Essays of the Neo-Classical Age,* Henry Hatch Adams and Baxter Hathaway, eds., 1950; Curt A. Zimansky, *The Critical Works of Thomas Rymer,* edited with an Introduction and Notes, 1956.]

S

Sadler, Hamnet (d. 1624) and **Judith** (d. 1614). Friends of Shakespeare and evidently the godparents of Shakespeare's twins, Hamnet and Judith, born in 1585. Hamnet, whose name also appears as "Hamlet," was a baker with a shop at the corner of High Street and Sheep Street. His shop was destroyed by fire in 1595, and the extant records indicate that he was continually in financial difficulty from that time on. In 1606 Hamnet and Judith were listed as recusants along with Susanna Shakespeare (see RECUSANCY). In 1616 he witnessed Shakespeare's will and received a legacy of 26s. 8d. to buy a memorial ring. [Mark Eccles, *Shakespeare in Warwickshire*, 1961.]

Sadler's Wells Theatre. Playhouse built on the grounds of a former medicinal spring. The original Sadler's Wells Theatre was used primarily for musical interludes with an occasional dramatic offering, such as *The Tempest* in 1764. In 1765 the old building was torn down and a new one was erected; it was not until 1844, however, under the direction of Samuel Phelps that the theatre attained any distinction. Phelps began his career at Sadler's Wells with a production of *Macbeth* (1844), and for the next 19 years his were the most consistently distinguished Shakespearean productions of the time. A decline followed Phelps' reign, and it was not until 1931, when Lilian BAYLIS took over its management, that its former high reputation was revived. Construction was begun on a new theatre, which opened in 1931 with a production of *Twelfth Night*. Since that time, the theatre has become world-famous for its own opera and ballet companies; in October 1956 the Sadler's Wells Ballet Company was granted a royal charter and became the Royal Ballet.

St. Helen's Parish. District in the northeast section of London within the ward of Bishopsgate where Shakespeare resided in 1596. His name is included in a list of those living in St. Helen's Parish who had defaulted in the payment of a tax, the assessment for which had been made in October 1596. He is also listed in a second assessment made in October 1598 as residing in "St. Hellen's parishe." A subsequent list for the year 1599, however, indicates that he had moved to Southwark in the Liberty of the Clink. His failure to pay his taxes is generally explained by the assumption that he moved from St. Helen's Parish sometime in 1596, for in November of that year he was named in a court order as a resident of Southwark. Shakespeare's assessment indicates that his taxable goods were valued at £5, £2 more than the same assessment lists for Richard Burbage, the leading actor of Shakespeare's company. From this fact Joseph Quincy Adams concluded that at this time Shakespeare might have been living in London with his family. [J. Q. Adams, *A Life of William Shakespeare*, 1923.]

Salarino and Salanio. In *The Merchant of Venice*, friends of Antonio and Bassanio. Salarino helps Lorenzo to elope with Jessica (II, vi) and commiserates with Antonio after his arrest (III, iii). In II, viii, Salarino and Salanio discuss Shylock's reaction to Jessica's flight, and in III, i, the news that one of Antonio's ships has been lost.

Salerio. In *The Merchant of Venice*, the friend of Gratiano and Bassanio who, in III, ii, reports that Antonio's ships are lost. Salerio is present at Antonio's trial.

Salisbury or **Salusbury, Sir John** (1566?–1612). Poet and patron. A native of Lleweni, Denbyshire, in 1586 Salisbury married Ursula Stanley, illegitimate daughter of Henry Stanley, 4th earl of Derby. Their first child, Jane, was born in 1587. In 1601 Robert Chester's LOVE'S MARTYR appeared. This collection of poems, including Shakespeare's THE PHOENIX AND THE TURTLE, was dedicated to Salisbury. These facts have been cited by some scholars as evidence that Sir John, his wife, and his daughter are the subjects of that mysterious collection of verse. Sir John is said to represent the Turtle, his wife the Phoenix, and their daughter the new Phoenix rising from their union. Another theory set forth is that the poem refers to an unhappy love affair which allegedly took place between Sir John and his wife's sister. Neither theory, however, has met with general acceptance.

Salisbury, John Montacute, 3rd earl of (1350?–1400). Son of Sir John de Montacute, who was the brother of William, 2nd earl. On his recommendation of Richard II's marriage to Isabella of Valois, Salisbury rose high in the king's favor. He went with Richard to Ireland in 1399, and after Henry Bolingbroke invaded England, returned with the king to Flint, where the latter surrendered to Henry. A participant in the unsuccessful plot of the abbot of Westminster against Henry IV (1400), Salisbury was executed by the mob at Cirencester.

In *Richard II*, as in history, Salisbury is Richard's loyal supporter. Taking part in the conspiracy to murder Henry IV, he is captured and beheaded.

Salisbury, Richard Neville, 1st earl of (1400–1460). Eldest son of Ralph, 1st earl of Westmorland, and husband of Alice Montacute, daughter of the 4th earl of Salisbury, whose title Richard inherited in 1429. For some time Salisbury's position in the struggle between the royal party and the duke of York was ambiguous, due, no doubt, to his family connections with both factions. In 1447 he participated in the arrest of Humphrey, duke of Gloucester, but when Henry became insane in 1453, Salisbury supported York's claim to the title of protector, and he himself became chancellor. On the king's recovery, he was discharged from his post and thereafter aided York. Wounded and captured at Wakefield, Salisbury was subsequently beheaded at Pontefract.

In *2 Henry VI,* Salisbury opposes the schemes of Gloucester's enemies and after Gloucester's death demands that Suffolk be exiled for his murder. As a Yorkist he fights against the royal army at St. Alban's.

Salisbury, Robert Cecil, 1st earl of (c. 1563–1612). Statesman. The son of Elizabeth's chief minister, William Cecil, Lord BURGHLEY, Robert Cecil emulated his father by becoming the most powerful English statesman of his day. During Elizabeth's reign, he succeeded Sir Francis Walsingham as secretary of state, a post to which he was appointed in 1596 despite the opposition of his greatest enemy, the earl of Essex. Essex had favored, among others, William Davison for the post. Immediately after the appointment was made Davison's son Francis wrote the following comment to his father:

> If he [Essex] be vanquished . . . all the world shall never make me confess, but that bumbasted legs are a better fortification than bulwarks, and St. GOBBO a far greater and more omnipotent saint than either St. PHILIP or St. DIEGO.

The allusion "St. Gobbo" here refers to Cecil, who was extremely small and suffered from a curvature of the spine. The name "Gobbo" may have been suggested by that of the clown in *The Merchant of Venice.*

Despite the opposition of Essex, Cecil continued to play an important role in Elizabeth's government. After his father's death in 1598 he had no allies among the various factions jostling for power around the aged queen. Nevertheless, by virtue of his undoubted ability and cleverness, he managed to main tain his power. He solidified his position in 160 after the Essex rebellion had been quelled, despit the attempt of the earl, during his trial, to impug Cecil's loyalty. It was largely through Cecil's inter vention that Essex' chief lieutenant and Shakespeare patron, the earl of Southampton, was spared th death penalty. After the execution of Essex, Ceci began secret negotiations to insure the succession o James VI of Scotland to the English throne. Jame rewarded him by creating him Viscount Cranborn in 1604 and earl of Salisbury the following year. I 1608 he was appointed lord treasurer, a post in whic he unsuccessfully tried to order the chaotic financia affairs of the king.

In 1595 Cecil was invited to a performance o either *Richard II* or *Richard III* (see Sir Edwar HOBY), and his home at Hatfield may have been th scene of a 1605 production of *Love's Labour's Los* (see Sir Walter COPE).

Salisbury, Thomas de Montacute or **Montague** 4th earl of (1388–1428). Grandfather of Warwic the Kingmaker and one of the ablest and most pop ular English officers in the war against France. I *Henry V* Salisbury fights at Agincourt (IV, iii) and in *1 Henry VI* he is killed by a cannon sho while observing the city of Orléans from a "secre grate" (I, iv).

Salisbury, William de Longsword, 3rd earl o (d. 1226). Illegitimate son of Henry II. He was a advisor and friend to King John until 1216 when, fo a short time, he joined the dauphin Louis in his at tempted invasion of England. After John's deat Salisbury rejoined the English side and fought for hi nephew, Henry III. He subsequently aided the regen Hubert de Burgh, as administrator and soldier. In *Kin John,* Salisbury, dubious about John's policies an suspecting the King of having murdered his nephe Arthur, joins the English lords who have defecte to the side of Lewis the Dauphin. On learning o the Dauphin's intention to murder the defector

ROBERT CECIL (FAR RIGHT), LATER FIRST EARL OF SALISBURY, LED THE ENGLISH DELEGATION TO THE SOMERSET HOUSE CONFERENCE IN 1604 THAT ENDED THE WAR WITH SPAIN. (NATIONAL PORTRAIT GALLERY)

nce his aim is achieved, Salisbury returns to King ohn's camp.

Salisbury Court theatre. A playhouse located in alisbury Court to the east of Whitefriars precinct. 'he Salisbury Court theatre was built in 1629 by ichard Gunnell and William Blagrove. It was oofed, being designed as a private theatre. The first ompany to occupy it was the CHILDREN OF THE ING'S REVELS, who were replaced by PRINCE HARLES' MEN in 1631. From 1637 to the closing of ne theatres in 1642 it was occupied by Queen Henritta's Men. According to a contemporary report, he theatre was "pulled down by a company of oldiers set on by the sectaries of these sad times on aturday, the 24 day of March, 1649." However, the rm "pulled down" means "destroyed on the inside" nd in 1660 the playhouse was repaired and opened. Jntil 1661 it was occupied by Davenant's DUKE'S OMPANY. The building was finally destroyed in the reat fire of 1666. [J. Q. Adams, *Shakespearean Playouses*, 1917.]

Salisbury manuscript. A manuscript which conains a poem written about the time of the publicaon of the First Folio. The poem is a paean to Ieminges and Condell, the editors of the Folio, for heir efforts in preserving Shakespeare's works:

To my good freandes m^r^ John Hemings
& Henry Condall.

To yowe that Joyntly with vndaunted paynes
vowtsafed to Chawnte to vs thease noble
straynes,
how mutch yowe merrytt by it is not sedd,
butt yowe haue pleased the lyving, loved the
deadd,
Raysede from the woambe of Earth a Ritcher
myne
then Curteys Cowlde with all his Castelyne
Associattes, they dydd butt digg for Gowlde,
Butt yowe for Treasure mutch moare mani-
follde.

The MS is part of a collection that belonged to ne Salisbury family of Lleweni, Wales. One memer of the family, Sir John SALISBURY, was the edicatee of Robert Chester's *Love's Martyr*, to vhich Shakespeare contributed *The Phoenix and he Turtle*. It has been suggested that the author of nis poem was Sir John's son Sir Henry Salisbury d. 1632).

Salvini, Tommaso (1829–1916). Italian actor. Salini was born in Milan, of actor parents, and made is first stage appearances at the age of 14 in Goldoni's comedies. In 1847 he joined Adelaide istori's company, playing Paolo in Silvio Pellico's *rancesca da Rimini* and Romeo in *Romeo and uliet*. In 1849 he was involved with Garibaldi in the attle to make Rome an Italian city.

In the 1850's and 1870's he made frequent tours, with ppearances in Spain, Portugal, the United States, razil, South America, Austria, Germany, London, nd Paris. In London in 1875 he met and married a oung Englishwoman, Carlotta Sharpe (1854–1878). His appearance in *La Morte Civile* by Giacometti in aris in 1877 won him the praise of Zola and Hugo. In 1885, he performed Coriolanus in North Amera and the Ukraine, with great success, and toured New York, San Francisco, Philadelphia, and Boston with Edwin Booth as Iago in *Othello*. In 1889 he married an American, Genoveffa (Genevieve) Bearman. Although he retired from the stage in 1890, he took part in Rome's celebration of Adelaide Ristori's 80th birthday in 1902. His own 80th birthday was celebrated throughout Italy in 1909.

Salvini was a memorable Othello and in the 1876 London production he appeared in the play for 30 consecutive nights, instead of his usual four times a week. His son, Alessandro (1861–1896), was also an actor who enjoyed some success. Salvini's *Ricordi, anedotti ed impressioni* (1895) appeared in part in English as *Leaves from the Autobiography of Tommaso Salvini* in 1893. [*Enciclopedia Biografica e Bibliografica "Italiana,"* 1944; *Oxford Companion to the Theatre*, Phyllis Hartnoll, ed., 1951.]

Sampson. In *Romeo and Juliet*, a servant to Capulet. Sampson is a truculent fellow who bites his thumb at Abraham and Balthasar, beginning the brawl that leads to Prince Escalus' ban on street fighting (I, i).

Sandells, Fulke (b. 1551). A yeoman of Shottery who in 1582 acted as surety, with John Richardson, at the granting of a marriage license to Anne Hathaway and Shakespeare. Sandells was a friend of Anne's father Richard Hathaway and in 1581 acted as one of the supervisors of Hathaway's will. It was customary when the bridegroom was a minor (Shakespeare was 18) to have friends of the bride acting as surety. See MARRIAGE. [Mark Eccles, *Shakespeare in Warwickshire*, 1961.]

San Diego National Shakespeare Festival. An annual summer presentation of some of Shakespeare's plays at San Diego, California. Its first productions, 50-minute versions of some of Shakespeare's dramas, were staged in the 1935/6 Pacific International Exposition. They were mounted on the Old Globe Theatre, an open-air theatre built along the lines of London's Bankside Globe playhouse by theatre architect Thomas Wood Stevens. Shakespeare scholar B. Iden Payne adapted several plays for Exposition productions. It was not, however, until after the Second World War that the organization established its annual Shakespeare Festival. The festival was launched in 1949 with a production of *Twelfth Night* directed by Payne.

The producing director-in-residence of the yearround schedule of productions at the Old Globe is Craig Noel, who has held that post since 1947 and who was instrumental in establishing the summer Shakespeare Festival. During the winter season the Old Globe Theatre presents 10 contemporary plays with nonprofessional local talent under Noel's supervision. With the summer festival, however, it became apparent that really fine productions of Shakespeare could be achieved only with highly trained professionals in the leading roles. Noel organized a professional repertory company, consisting of a core of members of Equity. This group of 12 is supported by a group—the scholarship acting company—of nonprofessionals. A large group of apprentices chosen from applications further their interest in, and knowledge of, the theatre through the work they do during the summer festival in the various phases of theatrical production.

The Old Globe Theatre is located in Balboa Park,

which provides for the building a handsomely landscaped setting and an enclosed "village green," the scene of the 16th-century singing and dancing that precede all performances. Adjacent to the theatre are several smaller buildings, notably the Falstaff Tavern, where arena productions of current plays are staged.

The stage of the Old Globe is a raised platform with a curtained "inner stage," with a second stage above it, side doors and windows, and two massive posts supporting the "heaven," a cover over the apron stage. These are the distinguishing features of Shakespeare's stage, and although the dimensions are considerably reduced, the proportions are consistently in scale. Conventional seating is provided for about 400 spectators. The directors of the theatre have sought to recover the Elizabethan style in costuming and staging.

The San Diego National Shakespeare Festival has restricted its productions to the dramas of strong box-office appeal, except for *All's Well That Ends Well* and *Measure for Measure*. The 23 plays presented in San Diego since 1949 are all those to be found in standard collections. Since 1954 three plays have been presented each summer.

Reviews of many of the productions have appeared in *The Shakespeare Quarterly*. The critical consensus seems to be that, though the theatre has not established its claim to be a faithful replica of the Old Globe in all of its distinguishing features, through its 15 seasons it has given its audience a good idea of the intimate relationship existing between audience and actor in the Elizabethan theatre and of the importance the dramatist and actor attached to recitation of the verse and to the audience's response to all its rhetorical subtleties.—R.D.H.

Sands, Lord. In *Henry VIII*, Sands joins the LORD CHAMBERLAIN in scoffing at continental fashions, before attending Wolsey's banquet (I, iii and iv). Sands also marches with the nobles who conduct Buckingham to his execution. This character was probably Sir William Sands, who was made a baron by Henry VIII in 1526, and the same year succeeded the earl of Worcester as lord chamberlain, although Worcester probably has that function throughout Shakespeare's play.

Satiro-mastix. See WAR OF THE THEATRES.

Saturninus. In *Titus Andronicus*, son of the deceased emperor of Rome. When Titus declines election as emperor, Saturninus, elected in his place, promises to marry Titus' daughter Lavinia. Bassianus, however, thwarts his brother Saturninus by claiming Lavinia as his betrothed and carrying her off. The Emperor consequently marries Tamora, Queen of the Goths and an enemy of Titus. In one of a series of schemes carried out by Tamora and her lover Aaron, Titus' two sons Quintus and Martius are executed on mistaken suspicion of having murdered Bassianus. In revenge, Titus invites Saturninus and Tamora to a banquet, where he feeds Tamora the flesh of her dead sons and kills her. Saturninus thereupon kills Titus and is in turn killed by Titus' son Lucius.

Saunderson, Mary (d. 1712). Actress. Mary Saunderson was one of the first women to act in Shakespearean drama. In 1661, she was a member of the Duke's Company at Lisle's Tennis Court under Davenant, and the following year married the illustrious Thomas BETTERTON, also a member of th company. She played opposite her husband in man roles, excelling in Shakespearean characterization She achieved such success with her portrayal Lady Macbeth that Cibber praised her above Mr Barry. She assisted in the careers of several youn Thespians, including Anne Bracegirdle. Survivin her husband by two years, she benefited from pension bestowed by Queen Anne.

Sauny the Scot. See THE TAMING OF THE SHREW *Stage History;* John LACY.

Savage, Richard (1847–1924). Secretary and Li brarian of the Shakespeare Birthplace Trust fro 1884 to 1910. He edited the published accounts of th parish registers of Stratford (3 vols., 1897–1905) an the minutes and accounts of the Stratford corpora tion (3 vols., 1921–1924). He is also the editor *Edward Pudsey's Book* (1888). See Edward PUDSE

Savage, Thomas (c. 1552–1611). London acquain ance of Shakespeare to whom, along with Willia LEVESON, Shakespeare and four other sharers in th Chamberlain's Men granted a half-interest in th ground lease of the Globe. The purpose of the gra was to enable Leveson and Savage to regrant th half-interest to the five actor-sharers, with each act receiving a fifth part of the interest. (See GLO THEATRE.)

Savage was a native of Rufford in Lancashire. H cousin, whom he mentions in his will, was the wido of Sir Thomas Hesketh, in whose acting compan Shakespeare might have spent the early years of h career (see William SHAKESHAFTE). [Leslie Hotso *Shakespeare's Sonnets Dated*, 1949.]

Saxo Grammaticus (1150?–?1200). Danish historia and poet. He is the author of *Gesta Danorum* o *Historiae Danicae* (c. 1185–1200), a chronicle histor of Denmark which includes the story of Hamle His narrative contains the basic features of Shake speare's plot as well as the major characters: Am lethus (Hamlet), Feng (Claudius), and Geruth (Gertrude). Saxo's story circulated widely in MS In 1514 it was printed in Paris and later reprinted. I was the direct source of the Hamlet story told b François de Belleforest in his *Histoires Tragique* which in turn was probably the source of the Ur HAMLET. [Israel Gollancz, *The Sources of Hamle* 1926.]

Say, James Fiennes, Baron (d. 1450). A captai for Henry V during the French campaigns. Sa became lord chamberlain to Henry VI. A followe of William de la Pole, duke of Suffolk, Say wa charged with partial responsibility for the surrende of Anjou and Maine. When Cade defeated Staffor and the lords threatened to join the rebels if Sa were not imprisoned, Henry sent him to the Towe In 1450, Lord Scales surrendered Say to the rebel who executed him. In *2 Henry VI*, Say appears a the Lord Treasurer. Captured by Cade and accuse of extortion, of selling the English possessions i France, of corrupting the youth of the realm b erecting a grammar school, and of other crimes, Sa is led off to be executed.

Scales, Thomas de, 7th Baron (1399?–1460). loyal adherent to the house of Lancaster. Afte serving for many years in the French campaign Scales returned to England. Strongly supportin Henry VI, he raised an army in 1450 in defens

;ainst Jack Cade's rebel mob. Ten years later he :fended the Tower against Salisbury's Yorkists. inally surrendering for lack of food, Scales was urdered by some London boatmen.

In *1 Henry VI*, Scales is reported captured by the rench at Patay (I, i), and in *2 Henry VI*, he is in ommand of the Tower when Cade's rebellious oops reach London (IV, v).

Scandinavia. Before 1700 P. J. Coyet, Swedish mbassador in London, and his countryman Urban iärne, the well-known physician, are known to ıve owned a copy of the Folio of 1632. The unique py of the Quarto edition of *Titus Andronicus* 594) was found in Sweden, although it is not ıown when it reached there. It was presented to ıd identified at the University Library in Lund in)05 as a hitherto unknown edition and, like so any other Shakespeare volumes, has found its way the Folger Library in Washington, D.C. Shakeeare's name was first mentioned by the Dane öger Reenberg in a poem (1703) and at the same me short accounts of Shakespeare appear in Denıark. An early Swedish traveler in England, Bengt errner, the astronomer, saw *Hamlet*, *Macbeth*, and *'enry VIII* in 1759, but did not mention Shakeeare's name in his diary. Indirectly some knowldge of Shakespeare could be obtained from the wedish and Danish translations of extracts from Adison's *Spectator* published about 1730–1740, where uotations from Shakespeare's plays are found.

translations. Denmark achieved the first Scandinaian translation, Johannes Boye's *Hamlet*, anonyously published in 1777. The actor and poet Peter oersom began his work of turning Shakespeare into anish in 1807. He had published 10 plays before his eath in 1817. The standard edition of Shakespeare Danish (1861–1870) is the work of Edvard embcke, but Valdemar Österberg's translations of dozen plays (latest edition 1927–1930) come closer rendering Elizabethan language. There are also a ood many other attempts in the rich field of Danish anslations.

The first Swedish translation of a whole play was ıade by Erik Gustaf Geijer, historian and poet, with *lacbeth* (1813). He was followed by Bishop Johan Ienrik Thomander with five plays (1825), including omedies, histories, and tragedies. These two were ıe forerunners of Sweden's "classical" translator, arl August Hagberg (1810–1864), who presented a omplete Swedish version of Shakespeare's dramatic orks in 1847–1851 (latest edition revised by Nils Iolin 1927–1930). Hagberg's work is still considered nsurpassed by many critics, although he may not ways have done full justice to the lyrical elements the plays, such as the songs. Modern poets have lled this gap, for example Erik Blomberg with his anslations of many of Shakespeare's songs. Per Iallström's versions followed in 1922–1931. Interestg attempts have recently been made by two versale scholars: Björn Collinder (1894–) and Åke hlmarks (1911–). In the series *Levande litratur* (which includes much from Shakespeare, eginning with *Cymbeline*, translated by Molin in 960), Collinder published his translations of *King ear*, *Macbeth*, *Othello*, *Romeo and Juliet*, and *As ou Like It* in 1960–1963. His translations were also dited with parallel English and Swedish texts in 1964. Ohlmarks began his comprehensive work of a new complete Shakespeare by publishing *Comedies* (1963) and *Histories* (1964). There are also many separate renderings, such as Allan Bergstrand's *A Midsummer Night's Dream* (1946). The *Sonnets*, previously presented in Swedish by C. R. Nyblom in 1871, have recently been translated by K. A. Svensson (1964).

The Norwegians got their first rendering of *Macbeth* from Niels Hauge in 1855. A standard translation of most of the plays was edited in 1923–1942 in Riksmål, for a long time the official written language, by a team of scholars and poets under the editorship of Adam Trampe Bödtker. Special attention has been paid to the last volume's *Troll kan temmes* (*The Taming of the Shrew*), translated by Gunnar Larsen. Of very great interest are Shakespearean translations into Landsmål, the new form of language based on the "best dialects." Its short, vigorous word forms and rich vocabulary seem to make it an excellent medium for rendering Shakespeare's language. Its founder, Ivar Aasen (1813–1896), translated fragments from Shakespeare. In his *Pröver af Landsmålet i Norge* (1853) is included a scene from *Romeo and Juliet* (II, ix) in Nynorsk. Landsmål is particularly suitable for popular language, like that in the Launcelot Gobbo scenes in *The Merchant of Venice*, translated by Olav Madshus and Arne Garborg (1905). Aasen's follower in our own time, Henrik Rytter (1877–1950), published his fine rendering of 23 of Shakespeare's plays in 1932–1933. Herman Wildenvey's *As You Like It or: Life in the Woods* (1912) is more an adaptation than a translation of Shakespeare's play. In the last few years translations have been numerous. The *Sonnets* were rendered into Norwegian by H. O. Christophersen in 1945. Of great interest were the translations by André Bjerke: *A Midsummer Night's Dream* (1958) and *Hamlet* (1959) which were very effective on the stage. Other impressive interpretations are Inger Hagerup's *Macbeth* (1958) and *Richard III* (1961), *Romeo and Juliet* by Gunnar Reiss-Andersen in the same year, and Lorentz Eckhoff's *Antony and Cleopatra* and Hartvig Kiran's *Macbeth*, both in 1962. The classical Finnish translation was rendered by Paavo Cajander (1846–1913), who translated 36 dramas and many of the sonnets. A modern translation into Finnish has been done by Yrjö Jylhä (1903–1956).

performances. German-born Gottfried Seuerling came from the continent to produce *Romeo and Juliet* in Norrköping, Sweden, in 1776, and later in several places both in Sweden and Finland. His production was based partly on a French version by Jean François Ducis, partly on a German one by Christian Weisse. The first performance of *Hamlet* in Scandinavia took place in Gothenburg in 1787, probably in a Swedish translation from English. Hamlet was played by Andreas Widerberg. The famous drama was not performed in the Danish and Swedish capitals until 1813 (in Copenhagen) and 1819 (in Stockholm). Scenes from *Hamlet* were given in Christiania (now Oslo) in 1830. *Macbeth* was performed there in Foersom's Danish version in 1844. At that time the tragedy had aroused deep interest in Scandinavia. The first Finnish tragedy, J. F. Lagervall's *Ruunulinna* (1832), is an "imitation" of *Macbeth*. Already in 1835, the Finnish poet J. L.

Runeberg (1804–1877), the author of *Ballads of Ensign Stål,* had referred to *Macbeth* as a model drama. After a first night in Stockholm in 1838, an acting company toured Finland with this tragedy in the same year. The play was subject to lively discussion. Runeberg wrote a paper called "Is Macbeth a Christian Tragedy?" (1842). His answer was in the affirmative.

The 1850's, when Hagberg's translation had gained ground and the actor Edvard Swartz had fascinated audiences with his Hamlet (1853), begin a new epoch. A third peak period came in the 1920's, when the producer Per Lindberg, often in cooperation with Knut Ström, staged a whole series of Shakespeare plays, first in Gothenburg, then in Stockholm. In Norway Sille Beyer's Danish adaptation of *As You Like It* was performed by student actors in 1852. The performance of *Henry IV* in 1867, when Björnstjerne Björnson (1832–1910) was still director of Christiania Teater, the Norwegian national stage, was a notable one. It resulted from Björnson's desire to give the actor Johannes Brun an opportunity to display his genius in the greatest of comic roles, and Brun's Falstaff has remained a classic in Norwegian theatrical history. It might also be mentioned that a Swedish traveling company under August Lindberg played *Hamlet* in Bergen in 1895. Many interesting productions can be registered in the decade 1945–1955. *Julius Caesar* was acted in 1947 at the Nationalteatret, Oslo, and in the next year the Swedish producer Sandro Malmqvist visited Det Norske Teater with his production of *A Midsummer Night's Dream* and won high praise from the critics. *As You Like It* was played in Trondheim in 1949, *Cymbeline* in an operatic version in 1951. *Macbeth* at the Nationalteatret in Oslo in 1955 was a thrilling performance, largely the result of Mrs. Tore Segelcke's interpretation of Lady Macbeth. In Denmark, where open-air performances are popular, *A Midsummer Night's Dream, Twelfth Night,* and other comedies have been thus presented. The yearly representations of *Hamlet* at Kronborg Castle in Elsinore have been noteworthy.

Olaf Poulsen, the master of comic art on the Danish national stage, played Bottom and Sir Toby Belch. His nephew, Johannes Poulsen, started a Shakespeare renaissance with a series of performances beginning in 1927. Interest in Shakespeare is running high today in Swedish theatres in Stockholm, Gothenburg, Malmö, and other towns. Dramatiska Teatern, the national stage, under the director Karl Ragnar Gierow, has presented plays that are practically new to the Swedish public: *Measure for Measure* (1958) and *King John* (1961), the latter a first performance for Sweden. Both were produced by Alf Sjöberg, who admirably displayed his inventive power. Malmö Stadsteater, which has a spacious stage, seems to fit Shakespeare's romances excellently. Performances there have included *The Winter's Tale* (1959), produced by Sandro Malmqvist, and *The Tempest* (1963), produced by the Dane Helge Refn. Another producer at this theatre was Ingmar Bergman with his *Macbeth.* Riksteatern, the national traveling company in Sweden, has produced Shakespeare yearly. Of great importance to Swedish schools has been the *Shakespeare Society* at Umeå College, founded by the teacher Margreta Söderwall, who has toured with her pupil-actors both in he native country and abroad.

actors. Outstanding Scandinavian Hamlets have in cluded the Swedish August Lindberg (both manage and actor), Anders de Wahl, Gösta Ekman, and th Norwegian Ingolf Schanche—leading actors wh traveled all over Scandinavia—and the present-da actors Per Oscarsson and Ulf Palme. A renowne Rosalind was the Norwegian actress Johanne Dyb wad; the Swedish actress Inga Tidblad has been brilliant interpreter of Shakespeare's women's part such as Viola, Rosalind, and Beatrice.

criticism. When in 1865 Norway's great autho Björnstjerne Björnson, then manager of Christiani Teater, produced *A Midsummer Night's Dream* i Öhlenschläger's translation, he received adverse re views. But he refuted his critics in convincing term and eloquently acknowledged his debt to Shakespear Otherwise, criticism in Norway has been on th whole meager. There existed no book about Shake speare before Lorentz Eckhoff published his volume *William Shakespeare* (1939; 2nd edition, 1948) an *Shakespeare, Spokesman of the Third Estate* (1954 An important contribution is Edvard Beyer's stud *Problemer omkring oversettelser av Shakespeare dramatikk* (*Problems Concerning Translations o Shakespeare's Dramas,* 1956). Denmark was responsi ble for the most important contribution, the grea work by Georg Brandes, *William Shakespeare* (vols., 1895–1896). Filled with profound intuitiv understanding, it aroused interest everywhere, in cluding lively debate. Already, in his *Kritiker o Portraiter* (1870), he had given an analysis of Shake speare's art which proved of great interest to Augus Strindberg (1849–1912). In Otto Jespersen (1860 1943) Denmark had a scholar whose works on Shake speare's language have been of the greatest impo tance, for example, his *Growth and Structure of th English Language* (9th edition, 1956). Poul Rubov has given a fine account of the Danish translation *Shakespeare paa Dansk* ("Shakespeare in Danish" 1932), and Valdemar Österberg has produced ver valuable textual criticism. A good specimen of Swed ish literary criticism is Henrik Schück's comprehen sive work *Shakspere och hans tid* ("Shakespeare an His Time"; 1916), in particular his illuminating out line of the Elizabethan background. In the same yea came August Brunius' *Shakespeare och scene* ("Shakespeare and the Stage"). More recentl Gustaf Fredén's *William Shakespeare* (1958) an Gunnar Sjögren's many studies have attracted muc attention.

influence. The far-reaching influence of Shake speare can only be hinted at. Blank verse in more o less Shakespearean style appears sporadically in Den mark, for example, in Johannes Ewald's opera *Balder's Död* ("Balder's Death," 1775) and *Fiskern* ("Fishermen"; 1779). Jens Baggesen in *Labyrinthe* (1792) found sublime expressions for his worship o Shakespeare. The Swedish poet Bishop Frans Mi chael Franzén was another Shakespeare enthusiast; h saw Shakespeare's plays acted in England in 1795 an wrote some fine blank verse in Swedish. Commo tendencies can often be traced between England an Scandinavia. Many traits that originate in Shake speare can be found in the dramatic products of th Romantic movement, including the fairy tales, and i he historical dramas. Adam Öhlenschläger's *Sankt Hans Aftenspil* ("St. John's Evening Play"; in *Digte*, 803) is pretty nearly a Danish *Midsummer Night's Dream*. The influence of Shakespeare is best studied n August Strindberg's dramas. *Master Olof* and other lays grew out of impulses from Shakespeare coupled vith the pursuit of the native tradition of the hisorical drama. Much could be said about Shakepeare's influence on modern playwrights. It is obious in the great Danish dramatist Kaj Munk (1898–944), both in his lyric and dramatic poetry. In nodern poetry a Shakespearean influence is often erceptible, as for instance in the imagery of Birger jöberg's *Kriser och Kransar* ("Crises and Wreaths"; 926) and in Gierow's blank-verse drama *Rovdjuret* "Rapacious Beast"; 1941).

The events of the Jubilee Year in the theatres and n television and radio were too many to be enumerted here, but a few examples might be mentioned. On television all the Scandinavian countries have aken part in the production of Shakespeare's plays. There has been a Danish-English performance of *Hamlet* from Kronborg Castle in Elsinore, a Norvegian *The Tempest*, a Finnish *As You Like It*, and a Swedish *Henry IV*. John Gielgud's tour in Sweden and Finland with his *Ages of Man* aroused much atention. A retrospective exhibition, "Shakespeare in Gothenburg 1781–1964," was arranged by the Teaterhistoriska Samfundet and a traveling exhibition of Shakespeare literature was brought together by the British Council. Festival performances, commemoraion speeches, and lectures abounded. [Nils Molin, *Shakespeare och Sverige intill 1800-talets mitt* ("Shakespeare and Sweden Until the Middle of the 19th Century), 1931; Alf Henriques, *Shakespeare og Danmark indtil 1840* ("Shakespeare and Denmark Until 1840"), 1941; Lorentz Eckhoff, "Shakespeare in Norwegian Translations," *Shakespeare Jahrbuch*, 92, 1956.]—N.M.

Scarlatti, Domenico. See MUSIC BASED ON SHAKESPEARE: *18th century*.

Scarus. In *Antony and Cleopatra*, a loyal friend to Antony. For his valor, Cleopatra promises Scarus a uit of golden armor (IV, viii).

Schlegel, A[ugust] W[ilhelm] von (1767–1845). German critic and translator. Born in Hanover and educated at the university of Göttingen, Schlegel became professor of literature and fine arts at Jena and ater professor of literature at Bonn. He translated works by Camões, Cervantes, Calderón, and Dante. His most famous translations are those of 13 Shakepearean plays, still regarded as the best German ranslation of Shakespeare. As a Romantic critic Schlegel attacked the works of Friedrich von Schiler, Christoph Wieland, and August von Kotzebue.

In *Lectures on Dramatic Art and Literature* (1809–1811, tr., 1815) Schlegel refutes the neoclassical view that Shakespeare was a wild, untutored genius and defends the propriety of Shakespeare's anachronisms, his figurative language, his portrayal of violence on the stage, and his admixture of comic scenes in tragedy. To Schlegel, Shakespeare appears to be "a profound artist, and not a blind and wildly luxuriant genius." He considers the conventional view an "extravagant error." In other art forms, Schlegel argues, such a view refutes itself, "for in them acquired knowledge is an indispensable condition before anything can be performed." He has found in the works of poets "given out for careless pupils of nature, without any art or school discipline . . . a distinguished cultivation of the mental powers, practice in art, and views worthy in themselves and maturely considered."

In reply to the contention that Shakespeare often violated good taste and decorum Schlegel argues that

> . . . if the effeminacy of the present day is to serve as a general standard of what tragical composition may exhibit to human nature, we shall be forced to set very narrow limits to art, and everything like a powerful effect must at once be renounced. If we wish to have a grand purpose, we must also wish to have the means, and our nerves should in some measure accommodate themselves to painful impressions when, by way of requital, our mind is thereby elevated and strengthened.

Schmidt, Alexander (1816–1887). German scholar. Schmidt's most important work is the *Shakespeare-Lexicon* (2 vols., 1874–1875), described in the subtitle as "a complete dictionary of all the English words, phrases and constructions in the works of the poet." The definitions and explanations are entirely in English. Schmidt also edited several plays of Shakespeare and contributed articles on textual criticism.

Schmitt, Florent. See MUSIC BASED ON SHAKESPEARE: *20th century*.

scholarship—18th century. Shakespearean scholarship can be said to have begun only in the 18th century. The FIRST FOLIO (1623), coming as it did only a few years after the death of Shakespeare, was simply a reprint of the works of a contemporary author, issued to supply a demand. The subsequent folios which appeared in the course of the 17th century attempted no more than to correct obvious errors, modernize the spelling, and, in the case of the Third Folio, to add some plays attributed to the author (see APOCRYPHA). There was little in the way of a scholarly or critical edition as it is conceived today. That concept developed in the course of the 18th century; furthermore, the 18th century is a convenient unit in that each editor—from Rowe in 1709 to Malone in 1790—used the edition of his predecessor, thereby establishing an unbroken continuity of text.

Nicholas ROWE occupies the distinguished position of being Shakespeare's first editor. His edition (6 vols., 1709), despite its limitations, made the text accessible and prepared the way for works of sounder scholarship. On the basis of his experience as a working dramatist, Rowe recognized the value of such aids as the dramatis personae, the division into acts and scenes (see ACT-SCENE DIVISION), and the indication of exits and entrances—all of which he supplied. For the text he simply took what was most readily available—the Fourth Folio of 1685—and made such minor alterations as modernizing the spelling and emending (see EMENDATION) a few obscure passages. Rowe also has the distinction of being the first formal biographer of Shakespeare, although the brief life which he wrote for his edition is untrustworthy on a number of points.

Alexander POPE used Rowe's text for his edition (6 vols., 1725) to which George SEWELL added a seventh volume consisting of the poems and a history of the stage. Pope had access to a number of quartos—he listed 29 in his edition of 1728—but he made little use of them in textual collation. He was highly subjective and personal in his emendations, freely making changes in accordance with current ideas of correctness and relegating to the bottom of the page passages which he felt were inferior. Lewis THEOBALD pointed out Pope's shortcomings in *Shakespeare Restored* (1726), and Pope retaliated by ridiculing his critic in *The Dunciad* (1728). Theobald then brought out his own edition (7 vols., 1733), the first in which standards of classical scholarship were applied to an English work. Basing his text on the First Folio, Theobald made use of a larger number of quartos than earlier editors and drew upon his extensive knowledge of Elizabethan literature and history. A half century was to elapse before an edition of comparable scholarship was to appear.

Sir Thomas HANMER's edition (6 vols., 1744) was the work of a country gentleman and scholarly amateur. It was sought after by reason of the excellent Gravelot engravings and other qualities of good bookmanship, but in scholarship it was poor; essentially it was Rowe's text emended according to the editor's intuitive judgments without reference to documentary sources. Among questions wrapped in obscurity and still a matter of dispute is the degree to which William WARBURTON collaborated with Hanmer. Some notes of Warburton were included in this edition, but Warburton soon brought out one of his own (8 vols., 1747) with a preface in which he denounced Hanmer and insisted that the latter's use of his notes had been unauthorized. Warburton also denounced Theobald but did not hesitate to incorporate into his own edition some of the best fruits of Theobald's scholarship. Warburton, as friend and literary executor of Pope, would have a natural antipathy toward Pope's enemies; also, as expected, he used Pope's text. The next major edition was that of Dr. Samuel JOHNSON who had proposed a new edition in 1745 and again in 1756; it was not until 1765 that it finally appeared in eight volumes. It proved to be a disappointment in regard to text. Although Johnson recognized the value of the First Folio and of collation with the quartos, he was content to reprint the Warburton text with few changes. The chief merits of his edition are the critical preface and the commonsense judgments displayed in the critical notes.

A new era—sometimes called "the quarto era"—began in the 1760's (see QUARTO). With the exception of Theobald, editors had heretofore been content to print what was essentially the Fourth Folio with some modifications based on a limited degree of collation; the line of descent from Rowe consisted of questionable scholarship applied to a defective original. A fresh start was made by Edward CAPELL who was conscious of the deficiencies of both Rowe and Hanmer; upon the appearance of the latter's edition in 1744, Capell began to collect quartos with the intention of using them as the basis for an edition. He spent about 20 years at the task. He began to send copy to the printer in 1760, but it was not until 1768 that the 10-volume work was completed. The critical apparatus was published separately at a later date: notes to nine of the plays appeared i 1774, but those for the entire edition in 1783, tw years after his death. Capell has failed to receiv some of the credit due him because the evidence sup porting his emendations did not appear until a late date, by which time another competent scholar ha issued an edition.

George STEEVENS was meanwhile proceeding alon lines similar to those of Capell. In 1766 he publishe the quartos of 20 plays from the collection of Davi Garrick. His edition of the complete works followe a few years later (10 vols., 1773). Although he base his text on Johnson, Steevens was more than a mer reviser; he drew upon his extensive knowledge o Elizabethan literature and upon his study of th quartos to supply those elements which Johnso lacked. Revised editions appeared in 1778 and i 1785, the latter undertaken by his friend Isaac REE

Among Steevens' collaborators was Edmund MALONE, who provided an essay on the CHRONOLOGY c the plays for the 1778 edition; in 1780 Malone adde two more volumes to the Steevens edition—th poems, the apocryphal plays in the Third Folio, an a lengthy history of the stage. Eventually Steeven and Malone had a falling out, and Malone set ou on his own, issuing a 10-volume edition in 1790. Ap parently Steevens was stimulated by this edition, fo in 1793 he published his fourth edition, revised an augmented, in 15 volumes. Malone then turned t other scholarly activities, but he still continued t gather material with the intent of publishing a re vised edition. After his death in 1812, his collectio and notes passed into the hands of James Boswel the younger, who incorporated them into the Thir Variorum edition of 1821. See VARIORUM EDITIONS.—R. C. F.

scholarship—19th century. The 19th century sav significant changes in Shakespearean scholarship de spite a degree of continuity with the previous age In general, there was a shift from individual to col laborative effort, with a marked increase in th scope and depth of scholarship. Both continuity an change are exemplified by the first edition to appea in the century, the 21-volume First Variorum (se VARIORUM EDITIONS) in 1803 under the editorship o Isaac REED. The title page refers to this as the "fifth" edition, that is, the fifth in the series begun in 177 by George Steevens. Steevens had made a step in th direction of a variorum edition by including John son's notes, but Reed, his successor, carried th process a step further and brought out an editio which was literally *cum notis variorum*—"with note of various others"—in this case both Johnson an Steevens. The Second Variorum (1813) was a re print of the First with a few minor alterations, ap pearing a few years after the death of Reed. Mean while, James BOSWELL the younger was following similar procedure with Edmund Malone's edition The Third Variorum (21 vols., 1821) is Boswell' revision of Malone's 1790 edition, augmented b much additional material which Malone had bee working on at the time of his death. The Thir Variorum was the last with such a title for half century, until the appearance of the first volume o the New Variorum in 1871 under the editorship o H. H. FURNESS. Furness received his inspiration fron Boswell, but he so greatly expanded the scope of hi own series that it cannot be regarded as a revision of the Third Variorum.

Editions with other objectives made their appearance. The German scholar Nikolaus Delius prepared an edition (2 vols., 1854) valued for its text which Furnivall used in his LEOPOLD SHAKESPEARE (1877). High praise has been accorded the edition (6 vols., 1857) of Alexander DYCE for its readable text together with its useful notes and glossary. Several editions aimed at a mass audience were supplied by Charles KNIGHT from the 1830's to the 1860's. When Shakespeare began to be a subject for school study, suitable editions were provided in the form of one play to a volume with introduction, notes, and glossary. At least once during each decade from the middle of the century a new series appeared, the most important of which were those of H. H. Hudson, W. J. Rolfe, A. W. Verity, and Sir Israel Gollancz. It was often through such series as these that the fruits of current scholarship were made accessible to the student and general reader. The greatest achievement of 19th-century scholarship in the establishment of a text was The Cambridge Shakespeare (9 vols., 1863–1866), under the editorship of W. G. Clark, J. Glover, and W. A. Wright, which drew upon the collection of quartos bequeathed to Cambridge by Edward Capell. As much as any other edition the Cambridge became the standard text, being accepted for such purposes as line numbering; the reprinting of the Cambridge text in the one-volume Globe (1864) has made it readily accessible to all. The end of the 19th century saw the inauguration of another major undertaking, The Arden Shakespeare, with W. J. Craig and R. H. Case as general editors, the first volume of which appeared in 1899. Although not advertised as a variorum edition, it has served a similar purpose for advanced scholars by reason of its scholarly text with variants, critical notes from various sources, lengthy introductions, and excerpts from important sources.

The increased consciousness of textual integrity together with modern methods of textual reproduction resulted in the publication of facsimile editions. In 1864 Lionel Booth published a three-volume edition of the First Folio in so-called "type facsimile," i.e., a careful reprinting of the original but not a true facsimile in the sense of being an exact reproduction. Exact reproduction was made possible by such systems as photolithography, which Howard Staunton used in his facsimile of the First Folio (1866). J. O. Halliwell-Phillipps used direct photographic reproduction reduced in size to make a more convenient volume (1876). For the quartos, the most important 19th-century facsimiles are those of Halliwell-Phillipps (lithography, 48 vols., 1862–1876) and of F. J. Furnivall (photolithography, 43 vols., 1880–1889). The New York Shakespeare Society sponsored a useful work in the Bankside Shakespeare (22 vols., 1888–1906), edited by James Appleton Morgan, in which the folio and quarto texts are reproduced side by side.

The collaborative nature of 19th-century scholarship is exemplified by the formation of Shakespeare societies which held regular meetings, published papers, and sponsored the reprinting of primary source material. First in time is the SHAKESPEARE SOCIETY, founded in 1840 by John Payne COLLIER in cooperation with G. L. Craik, Alexander Dyce, Charles Knight, and J. O. Halliwell-Phillipps. In addition to publishing its *Papers* at intervals, it reprinted a number of old plays and documents relating to the Elizabethan theatre. The Society was disbanded in 1853 following the disclosure of Collier's forgeries. In 1873 F. J. FURNIVALL founded a successor in the New Shakspere Society. Much of the most important scholarship of two decades was first made known in the papers read at the Society's meetings and later published in its *Transactions* (1874–1892); the Society was also responsible for the reprinting of a number of Shakespeare's sources. In Philadelphia a Shakespeare Society was founded in 1842, and one in New York in 1885 which issued 13 publications from 1885 to 1903. Germany was responsible for what has proved to be the most enduring of such societies, the Deutsche Shakespeare-Gesellschaft, founded in Weimar in 1865. With the exception of the years 1944–1947, its *Jahrbuch* has appeared without interruption from 1865 to the present, serving as a medium of publication for outstanding scholars of Germany and elsewhere. As an impetus behind much of the most significant scholarly activity of the 19th century, the societies played a dominant role comparable to that of the universities in the 20th. R. C. F.

scholarship—20th century. With the exception of the *Shakespeare Jahrbuch*, no Shakespeare periodical survived from the 19th into the 20th century; at the turn of the century there was no standard bibliography, no active school of textual bibliography, no reputable facsimiles of the four folios; DISINTEGRATION of the canon was rampant and the Baconians (see CLAIMANTS) were very active. The New Shakspere Society had ceased functioning in 1884. J. O. Halliwell-Phillipps, astute collector and prolific publisher, had died in 1889. He knew there was much to be discovered and in 1884 had written *Memoranda Intended for the Use of Amateurs . . . Sufficiently Interested . . . to Make Searches in the Public Record Office on the Chance of Discovering New Facts Respecting Shakespeare* which listed 30 documentary areas for investigation. In his footsteps followed Charlotte Carmichael Stopes who by painstaking investigation of public records in Warwickshire and London added numerous details to the extant knowledge of Shakespeare's family and friends. In 1903 F. J. Furnivall, passing some time at the local registry office in Compton, found a dozen references between 1575 and 1654 to the Shakespeares of that area, some of them to another William Shakespeare.

documentary research. The early years of the 20th century were remarkably fruitful in new discoveries about Shakespeare. In 1900, a Mr. Pearson showed Sidney Lee a document he discovered in the Tixall Library that listed 23 persons who reportedly got their coats-of-arms under false pretenses. Under a drawing of a coat-of-arms were the words "Shakespeare Ye Player." In 1904, Dr. Andrew Clark sent to F. J. Furnivall extracts from the Plume manuscript, thus announcing to the world a new anecdote about Shakespeare being a glover's son (see Thomas PLUME).

On November 18, 1905, C. W. Wallace of the University of Nebraska announced the first of his valuable finds. In two of the three documents he discovered at this time Shakespeare's name figured with six others in a petition to Sir Thomas Egerton, lord chancellor, requiring Matthew Bacon to relinquish the deeds to the Blackfriars Gate-house in which Shakespeare had an interest. These papers, covering the dates April 26, May 15, and May 22, 1615, show Shakespeare's continued interest in London affairs within a year of his death in 1616.

Within six weeks Wallace published another discovery in *The Times* of London. This was a record of payment in the Belvoir Castle account books of Francis Manners, 6th earl of Rutland, on March 31, 1613, to Mr. Shakespeare and Richard Burbage of 44s. in gold for the making of a heraldic shield (impresa) which was used on King James' Accession Day on March 24. The close relationship of Richard Burbage with William Shakespeare makes it virtually certain that the Mr. Shakespeare referred to was William and not the John Shakespeare who was a bitmaker to the king.

Wallace and his wife went on to examine five million documents in their quest for Shakespearean and dramatic history and succeeded in turning up, in 1910, records which gave new particulars about Shakespeare's holdings in the Globe and Blackfriars theatres. Their findings, first announced in *The Times* and later expanded in the *Century* magazine (LXXX, 1910), detailed the papers in Thomasina Ostler's suit against her father, who had seized her husband's shares in the Blackfriars theatre after the latter had died intestate. These documents revealed Shakespeare's interests in the Blackfriars (1/7) and the Globe (1/14) at that time (1615). Wallace also discovered the court of requests documents in the suit of John Witter against Heminges and Condell and in the suit of Robert Keysar against Richard Burbage and others.

The Wallaces' most important discovery was the depositions made by Shakespeare and others in the Belott-Mountjoy suit, which revealed that Shakespeare had been the principal agent in arranging the marriage of apprentice Stephen Belott to Mary Mountjoy.

A worthy successor to the scholarly researching of Wallace was Leslie Hotson, who, taking a hint from Halliwell-Phillipps, began his labors among the documents of the Queen's Bench. In 1931 Hotson's *Shakespeare versus Shallow* brought forth the details of the quarrel of William Wayte with Shakespeare, Francis Langley, and others. From these details, Hotson arrived at his theory that in *The Merry Wives of Windsor*, William Gardiner and Wayte are being satirized as Shallow and Slender (see William Gardiner). On the basis of his discoveries, Hotson also moved the date of composition of the play to some time before the inhibition of plays on July 28, 1597. See The Merry Wives of Windsor: *Date*.

Hotson also discovered the relationship of Leonard Digges, one of Shakespeare's eulogists in the First Folio, to Thomas Russell whom Shakespeare had appointed as one of the overseers of his will (*I, William Shakespeare*, 1937).

Hotson's later theories have been less persuasive. His argument that Love's Labour's Won is *Troilus and Cressida* is unacceptable; his dating of Sonnet 107 (*Shakespeare's Sonnets Dated*, 1949) is scarcely more acceptable; his theory of an arena theatre (*Shakespeare's Wooden O*, 1959) with spectator sitting on four sides and actors' entrances mad through trapdoors in the stage is impossible to con ceive of (see playhouse structure); his brilliant re construction of the first performance of *Twelft Night* (*The First Night of Twelfth Night*, 1954) i interesting, but not fully proved; and his remarkabl theory that the Mr. W. H. of the *Sonnets* is Willian Hatcliffe is virtually impossible to accept. The ex ternal evidence that Hotson brings to bear on hi theory, however, proves him to be a master of liter ary investigation.

biography. The attempt to reconstruct Shake speare's personality and biography from his play was an undertaking characteristic of the turn of th century. When Edward Dowden in 1878 divide Shakespeare's life into four periods according to th style and biographical influences in the plays, h summed up the opinion of many others—notabl Coleridge and the German romantics—and animate a whole school of writers, including Swinburne Frank Harris, Bernhard Ten Brink, and Geor Brandes, who sought the life of Shakespeare in th plays. Dramatic tragedy, they thought, could onl come from personal tragedy: the death of his so Hamnet, the fall of Southampton and Essex, the per fidy of the Dark Lady, the death of his father, an the approaching death of Elizabeth. The serene an optimistic romances represent Shakespeare's maturit in a period of convalescence.

Frank Harris, for example, in his *The Man Shake speare and His Tragic Life Story* (1909), in seekin the man in his works, elaborated an earlier theor that Mary Fitton was the Dark Lady of the *Sonnet* and asserted that Shakespeare revealed himself in th characters of Romeo, Jaques, and Hamlet.

In 1909 Sidney Lee's essay on the "Impersona Aspect of Shakespeare's Art" began the formal op position to the biographical theories—an oppositio already expressed by Carlyle's "On Shakespeare" (i *On Heroes and Hero Worship*) and by Browning i his poem "At the Mermaid." Shakespeare's play have such variety that for every view he expressed i them, it is possible to cite a contrary view. Lee an his successors think that public tastes rather tha personal affairs dictated the themes of the plays. Per haps the best statement of this opinion was made b C. J. Sisson in his lecture (1934) on "The Mythica Sorrows of Shakespeare," in which he refutes an rejects the "mythical sorrows" that were supposed t have affected Shakespeare's output of plays and de clares rather that Shakespeare rose to the heights o tragedy through the growth of his own power an artistic genius.

Though G. L. Kittredge in 1936 ("The Ma Shakespeare," *Shakespeare Association Bulletin*, XI also denied that it was possible to find Shakespear in his plays—and E. K. Chambers among many other agreed—the new psychological school still sough for Shakespeare's personality. E. A. Armstrong' *Shakespeare's Imagination: A Study of the Psychol ogy of Association and Inspiration* (1946) attempte to analyze Shakespeare's artistic personality, con sidering image clusters based on reading, past ex periences, memories, and emotions. Since some o this comes from the deep roots of the subconscious psychoanalytic studies are not entirely invalid. I *The Personality of Shakespeare* (1953), Harol

Grier McCurdy based his conclusions on the presumption that each play represents Shakespeare's mind at the time: Shakespeare uses himself and his imagination; his own insecurity and striving for recognition are apparent; his characters get older as he gets older; he was sensitive to his surroundings; he may have been a latent homosexual; he had some distrust in affairs involving women; *Hamlet* and *Coriolanus* were composed under the influence of the death of his parents; and the wrongs done to John Shakespeare were reflected in the wrongs done to Hamlet's father.

In 1964 Leonard F. Manheim in his article "The Mythical Joys of Shakespeare: Or, What You Will" (in *Shakespeare Encomium*, Anne Paolucci, ed., The City College Papers, I) noted that Sisson's use of the term "mythical" was equivocal and fraught with meanings like "nonexistent" and "grossly exaggerated." Using the word rather in the sense of "that which is the product of a non-conscious, 'mythopoeic' drive to explain phenomena which are not rationally understood, or which are so understood but are not, on the psychodynamic level, acceptable to the mind," he interpreted *Twelfth Night* as a fantasy through which Shakespeare gave himself "grounds for [irrational] joy" by re-creating for a while his son Hamnet in the body of Judith—through the characters of the "drowned" Sebastian in the person of the male-disguised Viola-Cesario.

In the field of regular biography, the 20th century has been prolific. Except for Hotson's work in the 1930's, most of the major biographical discoveries were made in the first 15 years. With or without discoveries, biographies rolled from the presses. If they had little new to offer, their authors presented the facts from new perspectives with different emphases to a public that seemed ready to absorb all that was offered. By 1900 Sidney Lee's *Life* (1898) was in the fourth of eleven printings and revisions that were made up to 1925. Lee's work remained standard until the appearance of Joseph Quincy Adams' *Life* in 1923. Hamilton Wright Mabie's biography of 1900 was a less scholarly though popular work which went through four editions by 1912.

In 1904 Daniel Henry Lambert published his *Cartae Shakespeareanae: Shakespeare Documents*, a small but useful book which reprinted in whole or in part, in chronological order, 161 documents illustrating the life of Shakespeare. More useful was William Allan Neilson and Ashley Horace Thorndike's *The Facts about Shakespeare* (1913) which, because of its conciseness, tables, charts, bibliographies, and appendices, found favor as a school text and reached 21 editions by 1931. In the first 20 years of the century, aside from Wallace's work, the major portion of new research was done by Charlotte Carmichael Stopes, who in her lifetime wrote about 100 separate articles, some of them collected into books: *Shakespeare's Warwickshire Contemporaries* (1897; revised edition 1907), *Shakespeare's Family and Friends* (1901), *Shakespeare's Environment* (1914), and *Shakespeare's Industry* (1916).

The next 40 years were remarkably productive in Shakespearean biography. Joseph Quincy Adams collected virtually all that was useful in his *Life of William Shakespeare* (1923); John Semple Smart's *Shakespeare: Truth and Tradition* (1928) was called one of the best biographies of the century because of its rational approach; Edgar I. Fripp, successor to Halliwell-Phillipps and Mrs. Stopes in intensive ransacking of Warwickshire records, brought out within nine years *Master Richard Quyny, Bailiff of Stratford-upon-Avon* (1924), *Shakespeare's Stratford* (1928), *Shakespeare's Haunts near Stratford* (1929), *Shakespeare Studies: Biographical and Literary* (1930), and in 1938 his posthumously published two-volume *Shakespeare Man and Artist*, not the easiest book to read nor the best arranged, but certainly one of the most interesting and fact-laden biographies that has yet appeared; a reprint came out in 1965. C. F. Tucker Brooke's *Shakespeare of Stratford* (1926) and Pierce Butler's *Materials for the Life of Shakespeare* (1932) provide excellent resource materials.

If any life is now considered standard it is E. K. Chambers' *William Shakespeare: A Study of Facts and Problems* (2 vols., 1930). Actually, the biography proper in these volumes is contained in the first three chapters of Volume I. The rest of the volume is concerned with the text, printing, authenticity, chronology, and sources of the plays. The second volume with its eight appendices divided into 169 sections presents the essential documents on which the biography is based. Because of its comprehensiveness and the usually dispassionate objectivity of Chambers' vast scholarship, the biography is indispensable.

Numerous biographies have appeared since the work of E. K. Chambers. The most useful of these are J. Dover Wilson's *The Essential Shakespeare* (1932); Peter Alexander's *Shakespeare's Life and Art* (1939); John Middleton Murry's *Shakespeare* (1936); Hazleton Spencer's *Art and Life of William Shakespeare* (1940), two-thirds of which is concerned with criticism and theatrical history of the plays; Marchette Chute's *Shakespeare of London* (1949); Ivor Brown's *Shakespeare* (1949) and *Shakespeare in His Time* (1960); M. M. Reese's *Shakespeare: His World and His Work* (1953), a thorough survey; Henri Fluchère's *Shakespeare* (1953); F. E. Halliday's *Shakespeare: A Pictorial Biography* (1956) and his *Shakespeare* (1961); Giles Dawson's brief but circumspect *Life of William Shakespeare* in the Folger Shakespeare Library Series (1958); G. E. Bentley's *Shakespeare: A Biographical Handbook* (1961), a very useful survey; Peter Quennell's *William Shakespeare* (1963); and A. L. Rowse's *William Shakespeare* (1963).

Reserved for special mention are two biographies of resource materials in the tradition of Halliwell-Phillipps, Stopes, and Chambers. Mark Eccles in his *Shakespeare in Warwickshire* (1961) presents a minute survey of the affairs of those in some way related to Shakespeare in his Stratford environment which is useful in itself and suggestive of further areas of investigation. Perhaps the most ambitious work of this century is B. Roland Lewis' *The Shakespeare Documents* (1940). In two large volumes Lewis collected 276 primary records, documents, Stationers' Register entries, etc., printed them verbatim, translated those in Latin into English, printed facsimiles and illustrations of 59 of them, drew up many genealogical tables, and presented the explanatory scholarship in 115 chapters.

In 1946 E. K. Chambers published a series of lectures, *Sources for a Biography of Shakespeare*, which noted that there were still tenurial, ecclesiastical, municipal, occupational, court, national, and personal records which might profitably be searched for new biographical details. In 1964 the Public Record Office printed a booklet of the 28 Shakespeare documents and records in that office (*Shakespeare in the Public Records*, N. E. Evans).

A task for which scholarship is sorely needed is to fill in the lacuna between 1585 and 1592, the so-called lost years. For this period much has been proposed by scholars though little has been accepted. Arthur Acheson in *Shakespeare's Lost Years in London, 1586–92* (1920) makes Shakespeare an intimate of the earl of Southampton, and member of the earl of Pembroke's men in 1591. Arthur Gray suggests that Shakespeare was made a page in the home of Henry Goodere of Polesworth in Arden (northern Warwickshire), and was probably a teacher or tutor there before going to London (*A Chapter in the Early Life of Shakespeare: Polesworth in Arden*, 1926). In 1932 J. Dover Wilson in his *The Essential Shakespeare*, which he subtitled "A Biographical Adventure," leaned toward Shakespeare's Catholicism and says that "if . . . he received his education as a singing-boy in the service of some great Catholic nobleman, it would help to explain how he became an actor, since the transition from singing-boy to stage-player was almost as inevitable at that period as the breaking of the male voice in adolescence." The tradition that Shakespeare was a schoolmaster in the country may refer, says Wilson, to Shakespeare's stay at Southampton's seat at Titchfield during the 1593/4 plague. Oliver Baker's hypothesis (*In Shakespeare's Warwickshire and the Unknown Years*, 1938) is that Shakespeare was in Lancashire with Alexander Houghton (see William SHAKESHAFTE). William Bliss (*The Real Shakespeare*, 1947) conjectured that Shakespeare sailed around the world with Drake though B. C. L'Estrange Ewen (*Shakespeare No Seaman*, 1938) declared that Shakespeare knew some of the terms but none of the art of seamanship. Leslie Hotson (*Shakespeare's Sonnets Dated and other Essays*, 1949) would have us believe that during these years Shakespeare wrote more than a hundred of his best sonnets. Cecil G. Gray (*Notes & Queries*, Dec. 23, 1950) suggests that Shakespeare might have been tutor to Lord Herbert of Cherbury, a relative of the earl of Pembroke, and E. B. Everitt (*The Young Shakespeare*, 1954) would have us believe that Shakespeare in the early years was writing the old *King Leir*, *Edmund Ironside*, *Edward III* and other plays during his association with the Queen's Men, whom he left in 1589 to join Pembroke's. Alfred Harbage also pondered Shakespeare's being a tutor in a private household and thinks that *Love's Labour's Lost* was composed as early as 1588/9 (*Philological Quarterly*, XLI, 1962).

Other theories include that he was articled to a lawyer for three years (E. I. Fripp); that he was a soldier (Duff Cooper, *Sergeant Shakespeare*, 1949); that he was a printer (William Blades, *Shakespeare and Typography*, 1872, and William Jaggard, *Shakespeare Once a Printer and Bookman*, 1934). Refutations have come from Sir Dunbar Plunket Barton (*Links Between Shakespeare and the Law*, 1929); Paul S. Clarkson and C. T. Warren (*The Law of Property in Shakespeare and the Elizabethan Drama*, 1942); and Paul Jorgensen (*Shakespeare's Military World*, 1956). Of the many professions in which the young Shakespeare is supposed to have been engaged during the lost years, only the tradition that he was a schoolmaster in the country is generally accepted (see BEESTON FAMILY). In *William Shakespeare*, E. K. Chambers concludes that "after all the careful scrutiny of clues and all the patient balancing of possibilities, the last word for a self-respecting scholarship can only be nescience."

Scholars have pointed out Shakespeare's knowledge of music, gardening, animal lore, horses, the supernatural, national character, economics, sports and pastimes, heraldry, home life, birds, the Bible, medicine, and so on, finding in Shakespeare an omniscience which is a tribute to the dramatist as well as to the investigating scholars.

textual and related studies. Interest in the authenticity of the copy or text—the actual manuscript that went to the printer—has become a dominant feature of 20th-century scholarship. The bibliographical method that has arisen from this interest led Peter Alexander (*Shakespeare's Henry VI and Richard III*, 1929) to conclude that the Contention plays are "bad quartos" of *2* and *3 Henry VI* and *Richard III* and not, as formerly thought, earlier plays by other men. This hypothesis, generally accepted, led to a re-examination of Robert Greene's attack on Shakespeare in A GROATS-WORTH OF WIT. Other prominent names in the field of textual criticism are W. W. Greg, A. W. Pollard, and Fredson Bowers. See TEXTUAL CRITICISM.

Renewed interest in reproductions of folios and quartos has been another consequence of textual criticism. Halliwell-Phillipps and F. J. Furnivall had superintended lithographic and photolithographic reproductions of the quartos in the late 19th century and W. W. Greg began an edition in collotype, now being continued by Charlton Hinman. The reprinting of the First Folio in a fine collotype facsimile in 1902 was a noted event and the issue went out of print almost immediately. Methuen reprinted (1904, 1910) the four folios by photographic process; J. Dover Wilson published collotype editions of single plays from the folio; and the long-awaited halftone folio facsimile promised by the Oxford University Press under the editorship of W. W. Greg was unfortunately dropped when it was learned that the Yale University Press had in preparation an edition in photo offset. The latter appeared in 1955 under the editorship of Helge Kökeritz and Charles Tyler Prouty. The ill-starred production of this volume was detailed by Fredson Bowers in *Modern Philology* (August 1955), wherein he shows that careless platemakers, desirous of eliminating show-through, painted between the lines and obliterated ascenders of h's and descenders of y's, making them look like n's and v's, and eliminated tails of commas, making them print as periods, etc.

Further advances in bibliographical scholarship will be made when the "old spelling" Shakespeare finally sees print. The principles for this edition were laid down in 1939 when Ronald B. McKerrow published his *Prolegomena for the Oxford Shakespeare*. Alice Walker assumed the editorship of this edition after the death of McKerrow in January 1940. Charlton Hinman's demonstration in *The Printing and Proof Reading of the First Folio* (1963) of the stints of th arious compositors has added to our appreciation of 1e complications in that volume and the commercial ale of his collating machine may foster similar stud-:s elsewhere. A more definitive if not fully authori-ative text is to some extent closer to reality.

Whether any Shakespearean manuscripts will ever e discovered cannot be predicted. The play of *Sir 'homas More* printed from a manuscript in 1844 and ttributed to Shakespeare by Richard Simpson in 871 (*Notes & Queries*, VIII, July 1) was subjected a great deal of paleographical and literary scrutiny y Sir Edward Maunde Thompson (*Shakespeare's Iandwriting*, 1916) who came to the definite con-lusion that the three-page "addition" of 147 lines of Hand D" are in the handwriting of William Shake-peare. Seven years later Sir Edward, A. W. Pollard, V. W. Greg, J. Dover Wilson, and R. W. Chambers -an impressive band of scholars—wrote a collection f essays (*Shakespeare's Hand in the Play of 'Sir 'homas More,'* 1923) which supported the same con-lusion. A whole bibliography of articles soon ap-eared with Dr. Samuel A. Tannenbaum (*Shake-peare and Sir Thomas More*, 1929) in the forefront f those who denied Shakespeare's hand in the play. 'he attribution is based on only six known signatures f Shakespeare. See HANDWRITING; SIR THOMAS MORE.

Another area in which 20th-century scholars have vorked, not always achieving fully acceptable con-lusions, is the matter of Shakespeare's punctuation. n 1911 Percy Simpson (*Shakespearean Punctuation*) naintained that Shakespeare punctuated his plays not rammatically but dramatically, as a guide to the ctor reading the lines. Sir Sidney Lee objected (in 922), implying that there were more examples pro han con, to which Simpson replied that it was not a natter of the number of examples but their value in nterpreting a work of art. Ashley Thorndike in an rticle on "Parentheses in Shakespeare" (*The Shake-peare Association Bulletin*, IX, 1934) would not gree with Simpson, thinking that there was too nuch contamination between Shakespeare's auto-raph copy and the final appearance in print. Peter Alexander in 1932 (*TLS*, p. 195) and later in *Shake-peare's Punctuation* (1945) found too much variance etween quartos and folios to make a definitive case, ut Richard Flatter (*Shakespeare's Producing Hand*, 948) did find that Shakespeare's punctuation al-owed for dramatic pauses, stage business, etc. Cer-ainly the problem is complicated by the number of imes that grammatical punctuation and dramatic 1ecessity for a pause overlap. In A. C. Partridge's tudy of *Orthography in Shakespeare and Eliza-bethan Drama* (1964) the dramatic value of the unctuation in the good quartos is affirmed as being ased on an elocutionary principle but not exclu-ively. If Shakespeare was "a trainer of actors" then 'it is right to suppose that playhouse punctuation of is manuscripts, at any rate in the set speeches, was is own." The folio punctuation, however, could ave been subject to the practice of a professional cribe, a member of the company, the printer's com-ositors, or to a shortage of punctuation marks. The olio punctuation therefore is probably a synthesis or tratification of different practices.

Shakespearean scholarship in the 20th century has een facilitated by the existence of various periodi-cals in which scholars are able to vent their opinions and discoveries: *New Shakespeareana* lasted eight years, from 1902 to 1909; *The Shakespeare Review* ran for six issues in 1928; *The Shakespeare Association Bulletin*, valuable for its classified bibliographies, lasted from 1924 to 1949, after which, in 1950, it became the distinguished *Shakespeare Quarterly*, now under the editorship of James G. McManaway of the Folger Shakespeare Library. Annual volumes of *Shakespeare Survey* began to appear in 1948, under the editorship of Allardyce Nicoll. *The Shakespeare Newsletter*, published six times during the school year, was established in 1951 under the editorship of Louis Marder; *Shakespeare Studies* (Japan), edited by Jiro Ozu, was established in 1962; and *Shakespeare Studies* (U.S.A.), under the editorship of J. Leeds Barroll, began annual publication in 1965. The *Shakespeare Jahrbuch*, founded in 1865, continues publication, with 1965 having two volumes published individually by the rival East and West branches of the unfortunately divided Shakespeare Society of Germany.

The 20th century has also seen the publication of a number of encyclopedic volumes of useful reference value. H. R. D. Anders' *Shakespeare's Books* (1904) lists all that Shakespeare is supposed to have read. C. T. Onions' *Shakespeare Glossary* (1911) is a useful supplement to Alexander Schmidt's still-unsurpassed *Shakespeare Lexicon* (1874, 3rd edition, 1902). F. G. Stokes' *Dictionary of the Characters and Proper Names in the Works of Shakespeare* (1924) gives histories of the English historical characters and very handily summarizes each appearance of every character in the plays. In 1925 Edward Sugden published his monumental *Topographical Dictionary to the Works of Shakespeare and His Fellow Dramatists* which lists not only every place name in Shakespeare, but covers 639 English plays to 1660. W. H. Thomson's *Shakespeare's Characters: A Historical Dictionary* (1951) gives succinct historical accounts of the characters in Shakespeare's chronicle plays. F. E. Halliday's *A Shakespeare Companion 1564–1964* (1964) is a valuable handbook to Shakespearean lore.

Many encyclopedic works dealing with dramatic scholarship have been published, among them William Winter's *Shakespeare on the Stage* (5 vols., 1911 and following); G. C. D. Odell's *Shakespeare from Betterton to Irving* (1920); and C. B. Hogan's *Shakespeare in the Theatre 1701–1800* (2 vols., 1952, 1957), which lists all the London productions of Shakespeare and his adapters.

Several bibliographies have been published in the 20th century, notably William Jaggard's *Shakespeare Bibliography* (1911), 36,000 alphabetical entries of much of what was produced up to that time, but which is weak in American editions and references to periodical literature; Walther Ebisch and L. L. Schücking's *Shakespeare Bibliography* (1931) and *Supplement* (1937) are valuable for their coverage of German as well as English materials and for their system of classification; and Gordon Ross Smith's *Classified Shakespeare Bibliography, 1936–1958* (1963), which continues the work of Ebisch and Schücking. A very useful annotated bibliography of the plays is Ronald Berman's *A Reader's Guide to Shakespeare's Plays* (1965). A monumental annotated bibliography of Shakespeare and Music is under preparation by

Charles Haywood of Queens College. The commemorative issue of *The Shakespeare Newsletter* (April-May 1964) has a convenient list of books in print on Shakespeare and a chronological list of doctoral dissertations from 1867 to 1963.

The 300th anniversary (1916) of Shakespeare's death brought forth an excellent volume, *Shakespeare's England,* which is still a very useful and scholarly survey of all aspects of Elizabethan life in its especial relationship to Shakespeare. (*Shakespeare Survey 17* of 1964 is a similar venture.) Another excellent volume of 1916, the *Book of Homage to Shakespeare,* edited by Sir Israel Gollancz, is a large compilation of eulogy and scholarly articles. The 300th anniversary (1923) of the publication of the First Folio brought forth a volume of *Studies in The First Folio,* distinguished by contributions from M. H. Spielmann on Shakespeare's portraits with 46 plates, and other essays by J. Dover Wilson, Sir Sidney Lee, W. W. Greg, R. Crompton Rhodes, Allardyce Nicoll, and an introduction by Sir Israel Gollancz. The 400th anniversary (1964) of Shakespeare's birth spawned dozens of commemorative issues of periodicals and *festschrift* volumes, which along with articles in the usual periodicals more than tripled the usual output of Shakespeareana for a total of more than 3500 items. The assessment of 1964 scholarship will probably reveal no major biographical, critical, or bibliographical discoveries, but the sum total reveals that interest in Shakespeare during the fifth century will probably remain undiminished.

Histories of Shakespeare's reputation tell the story of the past. Ivor Brown and George Fearon humorously trace the reputation of Shakespeare in Stratford (*This Shakespeare Industry,* called *The Amazing Monument* in the English edition, 1939). F. E. Halliday's *The Cult of Shakespeare* (1957) traces the highlights of the affairs of the devotees over the centuries, and Louis Marder in *His Exits and His Entrances: The Story of Shakespeare's Reputation* (1953) wrote a detailed anecdotal volume which surveys the 370 years from 1592 to 1962 in all its varied aspects.

To know what Shakespeareans have done, foolishly and wisely, is a good foundation for continued progress. A listing of tasks and problems for future scholarship—about 50 of them—will be found in *The Shakespeare Newsletter* (XIV, 1964; and XV, 1965). See also CRITICISM—20TH CENTURY.—L. M.

School of Night. A phrase in *Love's Labour's Lost* possibly referring to an intellectual coterie led by Sir Walter Raleigh. The phrase occurs in the lines "Black is the badge of hell, / The hue of dungeons and the schoole of night" (IV, iii, 254–255). For many years it was regarded as a misprint and emended to "suit of night." In 1903, however, Arthur Acheson argued that the phrase, and indeed all of *Love's Labour's Lost,* was a hit at Raleigh and a group of his friends who apparently had intellectual pretensions similar to the young noblemen in Shakespeare's play. That such a group, centered around Raleigh, actually existed is not positively known, but there is a reference to "Sir Walter Rauley's Schoole of Atheisme" in a pamphlet published in 1592. The inference is that Raleigh and some of his friends were pursuing astronomical and occult studies, that they were the natural rivals of another court clique led by the earls of Essex and Southampton, and that Shakespeare was an adherent of the Essex faction. Among the group thought to be associated with Raleigh was Thomas Harriot, a well-known mathematician, Henry Percy, 9th earl of NORTHUMBERLAND, and the poets Matthew ROYDON and George CHAPMAN. Chapman's poem *The Shadow of Night* (pub. 1594) is a glorification of the life of study and contemplation as opposed to the frivolities of woman's companionship. It is also a paean to blackness and night. This connotation together with the imputation of "black" atheism, associated with the Raleigh group, lends, for many scholars, considerable substance to Acheson's argument. [Arthur Acheson, *Shakespeare and the Rival Poet,* 1903; Muriel C. Bradbrook, *The School of Night: A Study in the Literary Relationships of Ralegh,* 1936.]

Schubert, Franz. See MUSIC BASED ON SHAKESPEARE: *19th century to 1850.*

Schücking, Levin Ludwig (1878–1964). Scholar. Schücking was the editor of *Character Problems in Shakespeare's Plays* (1919, trans., 1922) and *Shakespeare and the Tragic Style of His Time* (1947). With Walther Ebisch he edited *A Shakespeare Bibliography* (1931; *Supplement,* 1937), a valuable list of early 20th-century Shakespearean commentary.

Schumann, Robert. See MUSIC BASED ON SHAKESPEARE: *19th century to 1850.*

Scofield, Paul (1922–). Actor. Born in Sussex, Scofield studied for the stage at London's Mask Theatre School. He made his professional debut in 1940 in *Desire Under the Elms.* From 1944 to 1946 he was a member of the Birmingham Repertory Theatre, where he played the Clown in *The Winter's Tale* and Philip the Bastard in *King John.* In 1946, 1947, and 1948 he appeared at the Shakespeare Memorial Theatre in Stratford-upon-Avon in such roles as Henry V, Armado, Malcolm, Lucio, Mercutio, Sir Andrew Aguecheek, Cloten, Pericles, the Bastard, Bassanio, Hamlet, Troilus, and Roderigo, repeating many of these roles in London productions as well. In 1952/3 he appeared as Richard II with Sir John Gielgud in the latter's season in Hammersmith. In 1955 he toured as Hamlet, playing in Moscow and London. In 1962 he appeared in the title role of Peter Brook's "existentialist" production of *King Lear.* [*Who's Who in the Theatre,* 1961.]

Scoloker, Anthony (fl. 1604). Author of the poem *Daiphantus, or the Passions of Love* (1604). In the *Epistle* to the poem there is a reference to

> *Friendly Shakespeare's Tragedies,* where the *Commedian* rides, when the *Tragedian* stands on Tiptoe: Faith it should please all, like Prince *Hamlet.* But in sadnesse, then it were to be feared he would runne mad: Insooth I will not be moonesicke, to please: nor out of my wits though I displeased all.

Later in the poem he alludes to *Hamlet,* indicating Hamlet's appearance on the stage in Shakespeare's time:

> Put off his cloathes; his shirt he onely weares,
> Much like mad-*Hamlet;* thus as Passion teares.

[*The Shakspere Allusion-Book,* J. Munro, ed., 1909.]

Scot or **Scott, Reginald** (1538?–1599). Author. Scot

belonged to the landed gentry, was a member of parliament (1588–1589), and probably served as a justice of the peace. His *Discovery of Witchcraft* (1584) is an exhaustive encyclopedia of contemporary beliefs on witchcraft, spirits, alchemy, magic, and related subjects. Scot consulted hundreds of authors and drew upon his personal experience in the courts of law. He attacked belief in witches, astrology, and alchemy on the basis of both reason and revelation; he attributed such beliefs to the work of willful impostors and to mental disturbance. Scot's work was in turn attacked, notably by James VI of Scotland, who called his book "damnable" and attempted a refutation in his *Daemonology* (1597). It seems possible that Shakespeare used material from Scot in writing *Macbeth*.

Scott, Sir Walter (1771–1832). Scottish novelist, poet, and lawyer. Interested in old ballads, Scott collected and published three volumes of them: *Minstrelsy of the Scottish Border* (1802–1803). *The Lay of the Last Minstrel* (1805) was the first in his series of metrical romances, after which he turned to historical fiction: the Waverley novels (1814–1819), *Kenilworth* (1821), *Quentin Durward* (1823), among many others. He died in Abbotsford in 1832, his health broken by pressure of a financial reversal.

Scott's acquaintance with Shakespeare began at an early age. As a boy he read the plays avidly and witnessed a number of productions in Edinburgh. There were private performances in the Scott home as well, with Walter himself playing Richard III, for he thought his limp could substitute for the hump. (See LAMENESS.) His interest never flagged. In an essay on "Drama" in the Supplement to the *Encyclopædia Britannica* (1819) he stressed the order that Shakespeare had brought to the English stage. The Waverley novels contain over 200 quotations from Shakespeare, especially in the chapter headings, and the interpolated lyrics in many of his novels seem to derive from the songs in Elizabethan drama. An edition of Shakespeare for which Scott was to write a long prefatory biography and notes was planned by Archibald Constable, but only three volumes (II, III, and IV) seem to have been printed (1826), of which but one copy of one volume (III) is extant. Whether Scott ever wrote the biography, therefore, is unknown. [W. M. Parker, "Scott's Knowledge of Shakespeare," *Quarterly Review*, CCXC, 1952.]

Scroop or **Scrope, Henry le,** 3rd Baron (1376?–1415). Eldest son of Stephen, 2nd Baron Scrope of Masham. He was a close friend and trusted counselor of the young prince who became King Henry V. Unaccountably, however, he joined the conspiracy of the earl of Cambridge. When the plot against Henry's life was discovered, Scrope, along with his associates Cambridge and Sir Thomas Grey, was condemned to death and beheaded. In *Henry V*, he appears as Lord Scroop who, with his fellow traitors Cambridge and Grey, has been bribed by the French to murder the King. The plot is uncovered (II, ii) and the three are executed.

Scroop, Richard. See Richard Scroop or Scrope, archbishop of YORK.

Scroop or **Scrope,** Sir **Stephen** (d. 1408). Third son of Richard, 1st Baron Scrope of Bolton, and brother of the earl of Wiltshire. Like Wiltshire, Sir Stephen was one of those who remained loyal to Richard II after the landing of Henry Bolingbroke. He was, however, taken into the confidence of the new king, who appointed Scrope deputy lieutenant of Ireland. In *Richard II*, Scroop brings news to Richard in Wales that his adherents Bushy, Green, and Wiltshire have all lost their heads at the hands of Bolingbroke (III, ii). [W. H. Thomson, *Shakespeare's Characters: A Historical Dictionary*, 1951.]

Sea Captain. In *2 Henry VI*, the pirate by whose ship the Duke of Suffolk is captured. Describing the ills that Suffolk's "devilish policy" has inflicted on England, the captain orders that his head be struck off "on our longboat's side" (IV, i).

Sea Captain. In *Twelfth Night*, the captain of Viola and Sebastian's ship, wrecked off the Illyrian coast. The Sea Captain wins Viola's trust and agrees to present her as a eunuch to Duke Orsino (I, i).

seating and prices. See AUDIENCES.

Sebastian. In *The Tempest*, brother of Alonso. Callously mocking Gonzalo's attempts to console Alonso, Sebastian nevertheless accurately describes the King's desperation with the words "He receives comfort like cold porridge." More weak than evil, Sebastian is incited by Antonio to murder his brother, but fails when Ariel awakens the intended victim. Sebastian demonstrates neither gratitude nor remorse when included in Prospero's generous pardon.

Sebastian. In *Twelfth Night*, twin brother of Viola. While sight-seeing in Illyria in front of Olivia's house, Sebastian is mistaken for Cesario, who is in reality Viola disguised, and is challenged to a duel by Sir Andrew Aguecheek. Immediately after wounding his assailant, the astonished Sebastian is claimed by Olivia. In wonder at the madness of this dream world, he nevertheless accepts Olivia's marriage proposal, and the knot is promptly tied. Thereupon follows the confrontation of Sebastian with Cesario, and Viola's true identity is revealed.

Second Folio. The second edition of Shakespeare's collected plays, published in 1632. The Second Folio was printed by Thomas COTES, who took over the business of the printers of the First Folio, William and Isaac Jaggard, on the latter's death in 1627. The publishers of the Folio were Robert Allot, John Smethwicke, Richard Hawkins, William Aspley, and Richard Meighen. The title page reads:

> Mr. William Shakespeares Comedies, Histories, and Tragedies. Published according to the true Originall Coppies. The second Impression. [Droeshout portrait.] London, Printed by Tho. Cotes, for Robert Allot, and are to be sold at his shop at the signe of the blacke Beare in Pauls Church-yard. 1632. [Some copies have one "p" in "Copies." Others have John Smethwicke, Richard Hawkins, William Aspley, or Richard Meighen for Allot.]

According to M. W. Black and M. A. Shaaber, there were 1,679 changes made in this reprinting of the First Folio, an average of two per page. Thus it is clear that the Second Folio was rather carefully edited by someone who corrected the text according to his own sense of clarity and reasonableness. In a surprisingly large number of cases, his judgment proved to be correct, for more than 800 of his emendations have been accepted by modern editors.

The preliminary matter of the volume reprints from the First Folio Ben Jonson's verses, Heminges and Condell's preface, the poems by Leonard Digges, "I. M.," and Hugh Holland, and adds Milton's poem on Shakespeare and the admirable poem signed I. M. S. See The FRIENDLY ADMIRER. [M. W. Black and M. A. Shaaber, *Shakespeare's Seventeenth-Century Editors*, 1937.]

Second Maiden's Tragedy, The (c. 1611). An anonymous play licensed for the stage in 1611 but not published in its own time. The play is preserved in manuscript in the British Museum. Stage directions in the manuscript give the names of two actors, Richard Robinson and Robert Gough, thus making it clear that the play was acted by the King's Men. On the last leaf of the manuscript is an ascription of the authorship, written in a later hand, to "Thomas Goffe" (1591–1629), an obscure 17th-century playwright. Another hand has crossed this out and substituted the name "George Chapman." This in turn has been crossed out and replaced with the words "By Will Shakspear." The play is probably the same one entered September 9, 1653 in the Stationers' Register by Humphrey Moseley as "The Maid's Tragedie, 2d. part." Evidence indicates that the attribution to Shakespeare was made at some time during the latter half of the 17th century. There is no internal evidence to support attribution of the play to Shakespeare, however. [W. W. Greg, *Dramatic Documents from the Elizabethan Playhouses*, 1931.]

Sedley, Sir Charles (1639?–1701). Lyric poet and playwright. Sedley wrote three plays during his lifetime, but he is best known for his love lyrics. Among his contemporaries he had a reputation for being a rake and a wit. One of his plays is *Antony and Cleopatra* (1677), written in heroic couplets, which, though it bears the same title, is not related to Shakespeare's play.

Sedley also wrote a verse prologue which served as the preface to a play, *The Wary Widdow* (1693), written by his friend Henry Higden (fl. 1686). Sedley's prologue defends Shakespeare against the strictures of neoclassical critics such as Thomas Rymer, who had attacked *Othello:*

> But against old as well as new to rage,
> Is the peculiar Phrensy of this Age.
> Shackspear must down, and you must praise no
>   more
> Soft Desdemona, nor the Jealous Moor:
> Shackspear whose fruitfull Genius, happy Wit
> Was fram'd and finisht at a lucky hit
> The Pride of Nature, and the shame of Schools,
> Born to Create, and not to Learn from Rules;
> Must please no more, his Bastards now deride
> Their Fathers Nakedness they ought to hide,
> But when on Spurs their Pegasus they force,
> Their Jaded Muse is distanc'd in the Course.

[*The Shakspere Allusion-Book*, J. Munro, ed., 1909.]

See If You Like It. See COMEDY OF ERRORS: *Stage History*.

Sejanus (1603). A tragedy by Ben JONSON performed by the King's Men in 1603. Shakespeare is listed as one of the actors in a note published in the Jonson First Folio (1616) edition of *Sejanus*. It has been suggested that Shakespeare played the role of Tiberius on the assumption that he specialized in "kingly parts" (see John DAVIES). In the preface t the First Quarto edition of the play (1605) Jonso indicated that "a second Pen had good share" c the play as originally written and that he had re written that portion, choosing "to put weaker (an no doubt less pleasing [lines] of mine own, then t defraud so happy a *Genius* of his right." The refe ence to an original collaborator has led some schola to assume that Shakespeare was the "Genius" t whom Jonson alludes, but the "second pen" probabl belongs to George Chapman. Whoever the co laborator, the play in its original form provoke considerable displeasure in the privy council wher Jonson was called to answer charges "of Popery an of Treason." Jonson was apparently saved from pur ishment by the intervention of the lord chamberlai [*Ben Jonson*, C. H. Herford and Percy Simpso eds., 11 vols., 1925–1952.]

Seleucus. In *Antony and Cleopatra*, an attendar on Cleopatra, and her treasurer. When called t verify Cleopatra's inventory of her wealth, Seleucu does not bear out her claim, but says she has fa more wealth than she admits to (V, ii).

Sempronius. In *Timon of Athens*, one of the flat tering lords who take advantage of Timon's generos ity but show him little in return. In III, iii, Sem pronius, feigning offense at being the last to be aske for money, denies Timon's request.

Sempronius. In *Titus Andronicus*, a relative o Titus. He does not speak, but joins in humorin the supposedly mad Titus by shooting arrows wit messages to the gods (IV, iii).

Seneca, Lucius Annaeus (c. 4 B.C.–A.D. 65). Roma philosopher and dramatist. Known as Seneca th Younger, he came from a distinguished family an became tutor to Nero. In addition to a large bod of writing on Stoic philosophy and civic affairs, h composed nine tragedies: *Hercules Furens* (*Hercule Mad*), *Thyestes*, *Phoenissae*, *Phaedra* (*Hippolytus*) *Oedipus*, *Troades* (*Hecuba*), *Medea*, *Agamemnon* and *Hercules Oetaeus*. Fashioned after late Gree tragedy, they were, like the dramas of Euripides divided into five parts. A certain lack of sensibility the flat characterizations, and the formal characte of the Latin language turned Seneca's plays int pieces for declamation rather than production. Sen ecan drama is characterized by sensational theme involving crime and retribution, adultery, incest revenge, and unnatural murder. Other staples are th informative chorus, the revenge motif (see REVENGE) a protagonist in conflict with one or more adver saries, main characters who confide in a friend, an supernatural visitants like Furies, deities, and ghosts

Medieval writers, notably Dante and John Lydgate regarded Seneca as one of the great tragedians, an his elegant rhetoric had tremendous appeal in Renais sance Italy, France, and England. The strong infusio of classical learning in the Elizabethan gramma school (which educated Shakespeare) and in the uni versity spread to the playwrights, and Seneca wa the sole surviving Latin author for tragedies. Sedu lous imitations of Seneca were written first for th cultivated audience at the academies and the inns o court, then for the popular stage, where they wer mixed with morality and farcical elements. The best known example of the type is GORBODUC, a Senecan "tragedy of blood" recounting the dissension, mur er, and civil war that evolve from the division of 1 English kingdom between a king's sons. In two spects this blank-verse drama deviated from the enecan formula: in the dramatization of an entire ory instead of the moment of crisis, and in the dict presentation of acts of brutality which were voided in accordance with the principle of classical ecorum.

An English translation of Seneca's plays by various ands, called *Seneca His Tenne Tragedies*, was pubshed in 1581; and about 1589 Thomas Kyd mixed omantic intrigue with the standard Senecan elements achieve possibly the most popular Elizabethan lood-and-thunder drama, *The Spanish Tragedy*. yd was probably the author of an early (now lost) ersion of *Hamlet* (see UR-HAMLET).

Polonius' comment on the players, for whom Seneca cannot be too heavy, nor Plautus too light" *Hamlet*, II, ii), attests Shakespeare's familiarity ith these Latin sources. Shakespeare's debt to Senca in the early 1590's is clearly seen. The strong, rude, high-flown tragic style of his histories from *Ienry VI* to *Richard II* caused them to be termed rhetorical tragedies." Geoffrey Bullough has pointed ut the influence of Seneca's *Troades*, which introuces three generations, each with its memories and riefs, on *Richard III*. Richard's wooing of Anne (I,), whose husband he murdered, suggests *Hercules urens*, which contains a similar wooing wherein the surper Lycus, who has murdered her father and wo brothers, courts Megaera, wife of the absent Iercules. In *King John*, the dying speech of the ing recalls Hercules' outcries in *Hercules Oetaeus*, nd is even closer to the English translation. Another cho of these outcries occurs later in *Antony and leopatra*.

In Shakespeare's early tragedy *Titus Andronicus* as vell, the revenge theme, involving the cannibalistic horrid banquet," may be taken from the story of Atreus in Seneca's *Thyestes*, retold in several Elizaethan story collections. The sacrifice of the captive o requite the vengeful spirit of the dead (I, i), vhich is the mainspring of the entire action, is also ound in Seneca's *Troades*. *Julius Caesar* is pervaded y the Senecan spirit. Influenced by the Roman's hesis in his widely known moral essay *De Beneiciis*, one critic maintains, Shakespeare delineated Brutus' equivocal role in the conspiracy as involving, ot a conflict between republican and monarchical heories, but rather a conflict of naïve illusions with olitical realities.

The later tragedies as well reflect the influence of he classical dramatist. *Hamlet* contains such Senecan taples as the vengeful ghost superintending the acion, the articulation of plot and subplots, the Machiavellian villain, the hesitant avenger, madness eal and feigned, murders and other violence, dumb how and play-within-play, and the dramatic death of the hero—much of it framed in sententious declanation. This legacy, transmitted by Kyd, was of ourse irradiated and transformed by Shakespeare's enius.

Kenneth Muir finds many parallels in *Macbeth* vith both the *Hercules* and the *Agamemnon* in situaion and emotional texture. The list of parallels inludes "the healing powers of sleep, the murderer's orrified reawakening after the deed, the sense of guilt, the feeling that all the oceans of the world would not cleanse the blood from his hands, the contrast between the tyrant and the good king." Cassandra's prediction of the future in Act V of *Agamemnon* recalls two passages in *Macbeth:* the aside in which he indicates the beginning of temptation and the soliloquy of the imagined dagger. The adage of Seneca's nurse which in the English version of *Agamemnon* reads, "The thing he fears he doth augment who heapeth sin to sin" might be taken as the theme of Shakespeare's drama.

Many of Shakespeare's allusions to classical mythology are in the Senecan mode; but the Senecan fustian of Pistol and even some of Falstaff's clownish bombast evince Shakespeare's awareness of an outmoded style. [Karl J. Holzknecht, *The Backgrounds of Shakespeare's Plays*, 1950; Kenneth Muir, *Shakespeare's Sources: Comedies and Tragedies*, 1957; Geoffrey Bullough, *Narrative and Dramatic Sources*, Vol. III, 1960.]—M. H.

Serlio, Sebastiano (1475–1554). Italian architect and stage designer whose precepts on theatre construction and scenery had a strong influence on the Renaissance stage. Serlio's observations were published in his *Architettura* (7 vols., 1537–1551) of which the second volume is given over to a description of a stage which he had constructed at Vicenza. The most important part of his description is that which dwells on scenery. Serlio, reproducing the classic stage of Roman drama, divided his scenery into three types: tragic, comic, and satiric. His importance, however, derives from his position as the foremost expositor of perspective scenery. Perspective scenery was then an entirely new concept, and it was not until the 17th century that it was introduced into England. Serlio's concepts were adapted to English court performances, such as Inigo JONES' staging of Ben Jonson's *Masque of Blackness* (1605). Perspective scenery was not introduced into the public theatres, however, until after the Restoration.

Servant of the Chief Justice. In *2 Henry IV*, a minor character. His master tells him to fetch Falstaff, whom the servant has recognized on a London street. Falstaff, anxious to avoid the Chief Justice, feigns deafness and misunderstanding and heaps a torrent of humorous abuse on the servant (I, ii).

Servilius. In *Timon of Athens*, a servant to Timon. Servilius tries unsuccessfully to borrow money from Lucius on behalf of his master (III, ii).

Settle, Elkanah. See MUSIC BASED ON SHAKESPEARE: *17th century*.

Seven Deadly Sins, The. A lost play attributed to the comic actor Richard TARLTON. The only extant part of *The Seven Deadly Sins* is the PLOT, found in the papers of Philip Henslowe and Edward Alleyn preserved at Dulwich College. The play was apparently written in two parts for Tarlton's company, the Queen's Men, at some time before his death (1588), and passed into the possession of Strange's Men about 1590/1. The plot, or outline of the play used as a record of entrances and exits, is important; on it are listed the names of the actors who, a few years later, formed the nucleus of the Chamberlain's Men, Shakespeare's company. In the male roles were "Mr. Brian" (George Bryan), "Mr. Phillipps" (Augustine Phillips), "R. Burbadg" (Richard Burbage),

"R. Cowley" (Richard Cowley), "John Duke," "Ro. Pallant" (Robert Pallant, not in Chamberlain's), "John Sincler" (John Sincklo), "Tho. Goodale," "W. Sly" (Will Sly), "Harry" (possibly Henry Condell), "Kitt" (possibly Christopher Beeston); and "J. Holland" and "Vincent" (not otherwise identifiable). Taking parts as women were "Saunder" (Alexander Cooke?), "Nick" (Nicholas Tooley), "R. Go." (Robert Goughe), and "Will," "Ned," and "T. Belt," who are not otherwise identifiable.

The plot outlines the second part of the play; it consists of three parts, titled Envy, Sloth, and Lechery, and an Induction. This division has led to suggestions by scholars that the various parts of the play compose the unidentified *Three, Four,* and *Five Plays in One* listed in Henslowe's diary. Scholars further conjecture that the play was a serious one, using classical themes. Envy is illustrated by episodes of Ferrex and Porrex; Sloth by Sardanapalus; and Lechery by Tereus. The episodes are punctuated by a dialogue-commentary on the action spoken by characters representing Henry VI and the poet John Lydgate.

The handwriting of the plot has been identified as the same as that of "Hand C" of the manuscript of SIR THOMAS MORE and as that of the book-keeper of FORTUNE'S TENNIS. [W. W. Greg, *Dramatic Documents from the Elizabethan Playhouses*, 1931.]

Sewell, George (1690?–1726). Author. By training a physician, Sewell was unsuccessful at his profession and became a literary hack, turning out poems, plays, translations, and political pamphlets. Nothing came of his literary ambitions, and he died a pauper. In 1725 he published a volume containing some of the nondramatic works of Shakespeare along with an essay on the stage, a glossary, and remarks on the plays. This book was issued as the seventh volume of Pope's edition of the works.

Sexton. In *Much Ado About Nothing,* a minor character. In IV, ii, the Sexton prompts Dogberry in the questioning of Borachio and Conrade.

Seyton. In *Macbeth,* an officer in attendance on Macbeth. In V, iii, Seyton confirms the reports of the advance of English soldiers; two scenes later, he reports the death of Lady Macbeth.

Shadow, Simon. In *2 Henry IV,* one of the men conscripted by Justice Shallow and selected by Falstaff to serve in the army (III, ii).

Shadwell, Thomas (1642?–1692). Dramatist. Shadwell is best known to posterity as the subject of John Dryden's merciless satire *MacFlecknoe* (1682). He was born in Norfolk and educated at Cambridge and Middle Temple. After traveling abroad, he became a playwright, producing 18 plays between 1668 and 1692. Shadwell was opposed to the prevailing Restoration comedy of manners, and declared himself to be a disciple of Ben Jonson and the comedy of humors. In 1682 he quarreled with Dryden, a feud which resulted in Dryden's portrait of Shadwell in *MacFlecknoe.* With the revolution of 1688 Shadwell succeeded Dryden as poet laureate and historiographer royal, positions he held until his death.

Two of Shadwell's plays are Shakespearean adaptations. *The Tempest, or the Enchanted Island* (1674) is an operatic version, with a later score by Henry Purcell (1595?), of the Dryden-Davenant adaptation, THE TEMPEST, OR THE ENCHANTED ISLAND. The opera was enormously popular with Restoration audienc Except for the addition of several songs, the text almost wholly that of Dryden and Davenant. Th order of the scenes is slightly changed, and Milcha introduced very early in the opera, but the radic transformation of the play is basically independe of language. It consists of an almost overwhelmin emphasis on the visual and spectacular, achieved b a variety of machines and props. Spirits and devi rise out of trap doors, Ariel and Milcha fly aroun on wires and pulleys, and a table disappears twic Elaborate sets, costumes, and dances complete th visual feast. The spirit of the opera is discernible i this brief account of the finale, where Prospero is en tertaining the company with his magic: "Neptun Amphitrite, Oceanus and Tethys appear in a Chari drawn with Sea-horses; on each side of the Chario Sea-gods and Goddesses, Tritons and Nereides They are joined by a chorus of winds in a series songs and dances. Finally the sun rises in the sky an Ariel flies down from it to hang suspended in th air while the entire company joins in singing "Whe the Bee Sucks." The opera was published in 1674, th year of its first production at Dorset Garden.

Shadwell duplicated this success with a secon adaptation, *The History of Timon of Athens, th Man-Hater* (1678). Although *Timon of Athens* do not lend itself to romantic elaboration as graceful as *The Tempest* does, Shadwell adds a love story the original plot. Timon in his glory is introduced having two women, his mistress Evandra and his b trothed Melissa. Despite his love for Evandr Timon's sense of honor keeps him from breakin with Melissa, who is really attracted only by h wealth. When he becomes bankrupt, he loses n only his friends but his fiancée, too, while his r jected mistress remains faithful and offers him h savings. When Timon discovers gold, Melissa retur to him, but he refuses to take her back; and when h dies Evandra, who has never wavered in her lov kills herself.

Other parts of the play are also changed: Dem trius (Shakespeare's Flavius) is not consistently loy to Timon but leaves him when the others reject hi His role is, in part, taken over by Evandra. Alcibiad is brought closer to the main action by having M lissa turn to him each time his fortunes rise high than Timon's.

Shadwell's adaptation of *Timon* is coherent an dramatic, on the whole, and except where his pl required new speeches and scenes, he did not tamp with Shakespeare's dialogue. Shadwell's *Timon Athens* was published in 1678 and first produced the same year at Dorset Garden; later productions the play incorporated songs by Henry Purce [Hazelton Spencer, *Shakespeare Improved,* 1927.]

Shakeshafte, William (fl. 1581). Actor or servan Shakeshafte was mentioned in the will, dated Augu 3, 1581, of Alexander Houghton of Lea, Lancashir which included a bequest of his stock of play cloth and musical instruments to his brother Thomas. Th will adds, however, that if Thomas did not wish keep players "then yt ys my wyll that Sir Thom Heskethe knyghte shall have the same instrumen and play clothes. And I most hertelye requyre th said Sir Thomas to be ffrendlye unto ffoke Gyllon and William Shakeshafte nowe dwellynge with m and eyther to take theym unto his Servyce or els to helpe theym to some good master as my tryste ys he wyll." William Shakeshafte and "ffoke Gyllome," then, were in the service of Alexander Houghton in 1581, either as servants or actors. It has been suggested by some that this Shakeshafte was Shakespeare and that during the so-called lost years (1585–1592, a period in Shakespeare's life about which nothing is known) he was a provincial actor. Shakespeare's grandfather, Richard, was sometimes known as "Shakeschaft," and it is possible that Shakespeare might have used that variant in 1581, since Elizabethans often varied the spelling of their own names. E. K. Chambers argues that it is entirely possible for William Shakeshafte to have passed from the service of Houghton to that of Sir Thomas Hesketh and from there to that of Lord Strange, whose acting company later became the Lord Chamberlain's Men, Shakespeare's company. But this connection between Shakeshafte and Shakespeare, however plausible, remains conjectural. Allan Keen and Roger Lubbock have elaborated on this conjecture to support their thesis that the annotations in a copy of the 1550 edition of Halle's *Chronicles*, the ownership of which has been traced to someone in Lea, Lancashire, are in Shakespeare's hand. [E. K. Chambers, *Shakespearean Gleanings*, 1944; Allan Keen and Roger Lubbock, *The Annotator*, 1954.]

Shakespeare, Anne (1571–1579). Shakespeare's younger sister who died in childhood. Anne's baptism and burial were recorded in the Stratford Parish Register for 1571 and 1579: "1571, Sept. 28 C. Anna filia magistri Shakspere" and "1579, Apr. 4. Anne daughter to Mr. John Shakspere." [B. Roland Lewis, *The Shakespeare Documents*, 1940.]

Shakespeare, Edmund (c. 1580–1607). Brother of the poet, who may be the "Edmond Shakspeare a player" who was buried from St. Mary Overies Church in Southwark on December 31, 1607. Edmund, the youngest child of John and Mary Shakespeare, was baptized on May 3, 1580; his godfather probably was his uncle, Edmund Lambert. He apparently followed his older brother's career in London, although there is no evidence connecting the Stratfordian with the actor. There are only two references to the actor: a notice of his burial, and an earlier one, in the burial register in St. Giles Cripplegate on August 12, 1607, that reads: "Edward sonne of Edward Shackspeere, Player: baseborne." [Mark Eccles, *Shakespeare in Warwickshire*, 1961.]

Shakespeare, Gilbert (1566–1612). A younger brother of Shakespeare. Gilbert was baptized on October 13, 1566. He apparently followed his older brother to London, for in 1597 he acted as surety for William Sampson, a clockmaker of Stratford. He is listed at this time as a resident of St. Bride's Parish, London, and his occupation is given as a haberdasher. In 1602 he acted as his brother William's agent in the latter's purchase of land in Old Stratford. On March 5, 1610 he served as a witness to a lease, signing his name "Gilbart Shakesper." On February 3, 1612 his burial is recorded in the Stratford Register: "Gilbert Shakspeare, adolescens." The term "adolescens" was probably used here to mean "bachelor." [Mark Eccles, *Shakespeare in Warwickshire*, 1961.]

Shakespeare, Hamnet (1585–1596). Shakespeare's son, who died in his childhood. Hamnet and his twin sister Judith were baptized on February 2, 1585: "Hamnet and Judeth sonne and daughter to William Shakspere." The godparents of the twins were probably Shakespeare's neighbors, Hamnet and Judith Sadler. The name "Hamnet," which is of Norman origin, was spelled in a number of ways during the 16th century, including the form "Hamlet." Shakespeare's son died at the age of 11 and was buried on August 11, 1596.

Shakespeare, Henry (d. 1596). Shakespeare's uncle. The brother of John Shakespeare, Henry was a farmer whose principal holding was located at Snitterfield. He also was the tenant of a farm at Ingon in the parish of Hampton Lucy. He had two children, Lettice (b. 1582) and James (1585–1589).

Henry's name is mentioned in a number of records. He was fined in 1574, 1583, and 1596. In 1580 he was excommunicated for failure to pay his tithe. In 1586 he borrowed £22 from Nicholas Lane, his brother John acting as surety. As a result of Henry's failure to pay the entire debt, Lane later sued John for the debt. In September 1596 Henry was imprisoned for debt and died shortly thereafter. He was buried on December 29. [Mark Eccles, *Shakespeare in Warwickshire*, 1961.]

Shakespeare, Joan (b. 1558). Elder sister of William Shakespeare, baptized on September 15, 1558. She apparently died in childhood, since another sister of Shakespeare's, also named Joan, was born in 1569. See Joan Hart.

Shakespeare, John (d. 1601). Father of William. John Shakespeare migrated to Stratford in 1551 from Snitterfield, a smaller village to the north. His father, Richard Shakespeare, was a tenant on one of Robert Arden's farms. In Stratford John set himself up as a whittawer or glover (see Thomas Plume), and a dealer in agricultural products, particularly hides and wool. John, therefore, was not a butcher, as has often been falsely alleged. A glover's business was the preparation and sale of the softer kinds of leather, from which girdles, caps, laces, purses, and other pieces of wearing apparel were made. His was a dignified and lucrative business. By 1556 he had so greatly prospered that he was able to buy or lease two houses in Stratford, one a double house in Henley Street, one half of which, now referred to as the "woolshop," was used for his business. The other half, held on a lease, he converted into a residence in which he later installed his bride, Mary Arden. The other real estate was a house in Greenhill Street with a garden and a barn. This he bought as an investment. His social position was enhanced by his marriage to Mary Arden, the youngest and the favorite daughter of Robert Arden of Wilmcote, a wealthy "gentleman of worship," that is, of fine reputation (see Arden Family). In his will he left Mary, besides some money, an estate of 50 acres of land, called Asbies. John had married an heiress. In anecdotes compiled by Archdeacon Thomas Plume of Rochester about 1656 a Sir John Mennes reports an encounter with the father, whom he describes as "a merry-cheek't old man that said, 'Will was a good honest fellow, but he darest have crackt a jeast with him at any time.' "

John Shakespeare's marriage to Mary Arden just a year after she had come into her inheritance gave his

The Families of Shakespeare, Arden, and Webbe

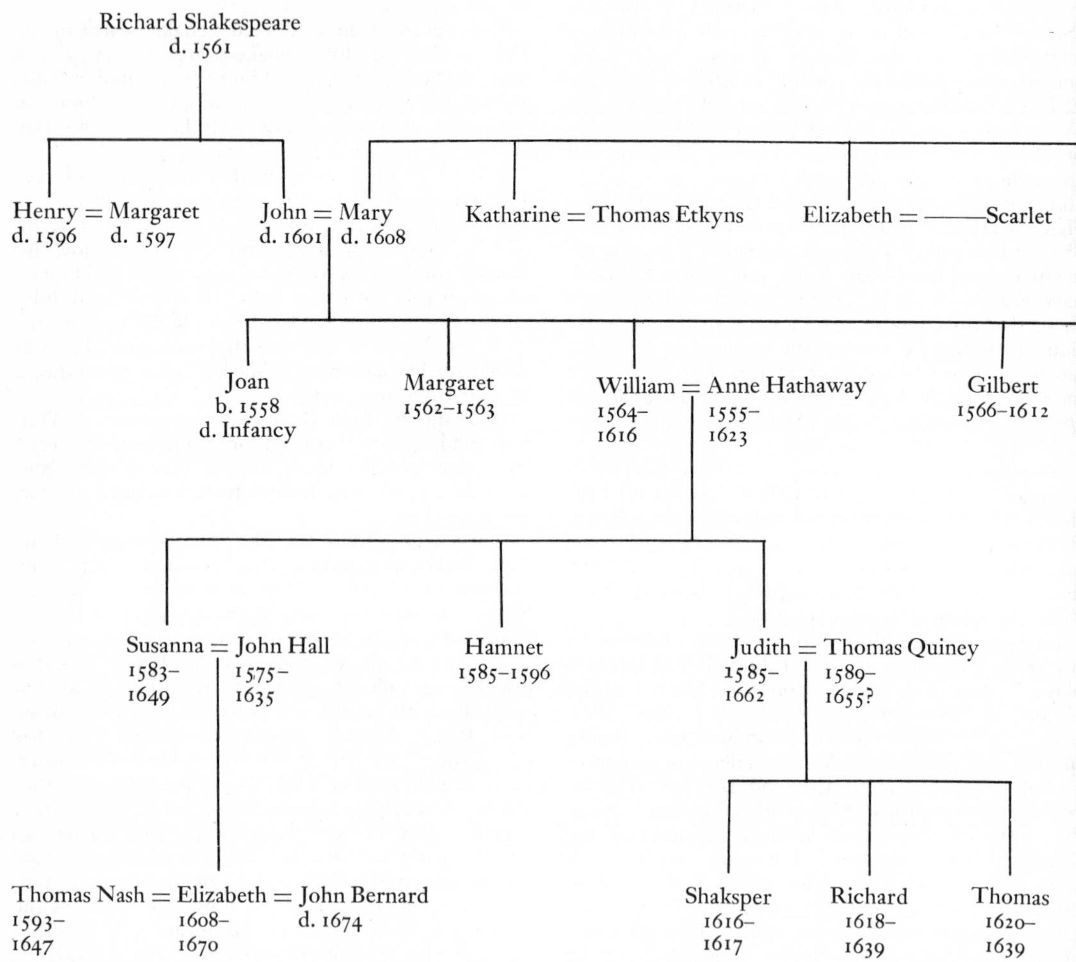

career a fresh impetus. As a man of substance, he was elected first to petty municipal offices, such as ale taster and inspector of all the bread sold in Stratford. He then became in succession an alderman, one of the two chamberlains or treasurers of the Stratford corporation (1561–1563), and finally in 1568 high bailiff. The high bailiff performed the duties of mayor, of justice of the peace, of the queen's chief officer, and of the judge of the court of record. While holding the office of bailiff, John Shakespeare licensed the Queen's company and the earl of Worcester's company to appear in Stratford's Guild Hall.

His first two children, Joan and Margaret, died in infancy. William, born in 1564, was his third child. Five other children were born to the couple: Gilbert, in 1566; Joan, in 1569; Anne, in 1571; Richard, in 1574; and Edmund in 1580, who, like his brother, became an actor.

It has often been assumed that John Shakespeare was almost entirely uneducated; that, though he could probably read and certainly knew how to keep accounts, he could write with difficulty, if at all. This belief is founded on the fact that Shakespeare's father signed both public and private documents, not with his name, but with a cross. Moreover, no example of his autograph has ever turned up.

Today a man who substitutes a cross for his signature certainly does not know how to write. But in the 16th century this method of attesting was not necessarily proof of illiteracy. When the cross was first placed upon legal documents, it was a symbol of the Holy Cross and proof that the man who made

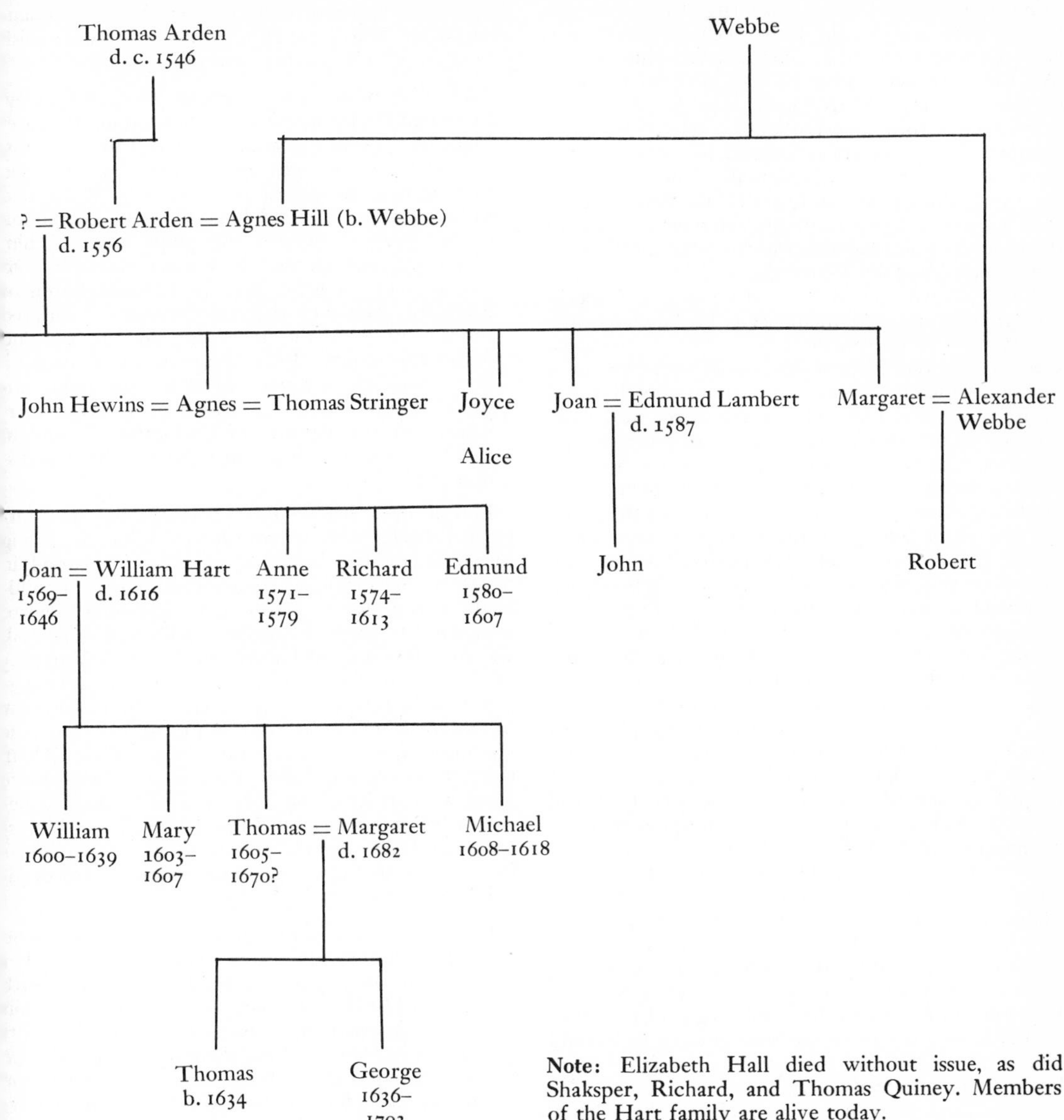

Note: Elizabeth Hall died without issue, as did Shaksper, Richard, and Thomas Quiney. Members of the Hart family are alive today.

it gave his assent religious sanctity. That is, it was the equivalent of an oath. In early English charters men of the highest education—noblemen, abbots, bishops, and even kings—signed with a cross. And this medieval habit prevailed down into Elizabethan times, particularly in villages like Stratford-upon-Avon.

Furthermore, while John Shakespeare was one of the two chamberlains of Stratford, he and his colleagues actually kept the accounts themselves. The town clerk made an explicit declaration of this fact. And their bookkeeping involved a good deal of writing. They had, for example, to set down the items for which the town's money was spent. John Shakespeare and his companion in office kept the books so well that the pair continued to do so the following year, although their nominal successors were supposed to perform all the duties of the office. It would have been strange if the burghers of Stratford had chosen an illiterate man for the important offices that Shakespeare's father held.

In 1577 John Shakespeare began to find himself in financial difficulties. He mortgaged a house and land, part of his wife's inheritance (see LAMBERT FAMILY), and had to part with her property in Snitterfield. But he never became poor. He was never forced to part with the three houses he owned in Stratford. In 1580 he was summoned to appear before the court at Westminster. This order he ignored, and was penalized £20 for his nonappearance. He also gave surety to the amount of £20 for the appearance in court of a friend, John Audeley. When he too failed to appear, the court added £20 to Shakespeare's original fine. Forty pounds was a large sum of money at the time and would have been imposed only against a man whom the court believed able to pay. We can only guess what he had done to incur so severe a penalty. It may have been his continued attendance at forbidden Catholic services. This guess is supported by the appearance of his name in 1592 on a list of citizens who habitually failed to attend the parish church (see RECUSANCY). On September 6, 1586 John was deprived of his alderman's gown on the ground of his long absences from the meetings of the council (see John WHEELER).

The so-called will of John Shakespeare, properly interpreted, reinforces the belief in his fidelity to the old faith. This document is not a will in the legal sense of the term, but a devotional testament of a man who solemnly declares his intention to live and to die a Catholic. The will was discovered in the latter part of the 18th century by a workman, Joseph Moseley, who was repairing the roof of the house in Henley Street known as Shakespeare's "birthplace." He found it carefully hidden between the rafters and the tiles on the roof. John JORDAN copied the original, which then unaccountably disappeared, but not until the sound and careful scholar Edmund Malone had examined it. From a study of the handwriting he pronounced it a genuine document of the latter half of the 16th century. The style of the testament, however, is florid and not Elizabethan, not the sort that a Yorkshire yeoman could possibly have mastered. Hence most 19th-century biographers of Shakespeare branded it a clumsy forgery.

But we now know that this testament was the English version of a widely circulated ecclesiastical formula. Written originally in Italian, apparently the composition of Saint Charles Borromeo, it was carried by the missionary Jesuits all over the world. They had it translated into many languages and signed by their converts in the various countries which they visited. Either the Catholic mission of 1580 or that headed by Robert Southwell four years later evidently took copies of this testament into England and circulated them to be signed by English Catholics in order to stiffen their loyalty to the old church. It would seem that one of those faithful adherents was John Shakespeare.

These facts make it highly probable that Shakespeare's father remained a Catholic to the day of his death and that the poet was brought up in a household devoted to the old religion. John Shakespeare died in 1601 and was buried in Stratford-upon-Avon on September 8. [Joseph Quincy Adams, *A Life of William Shakespeare*, 1923; John Henry de Groot, *The Shakespeares and The Old Faith*, 1946.]—O.J.C.

Shakespeare, Judith (1585–1662). Shakespeare's younger daughter, twin sister of Hamnet. On February 10, 1616 Judith, then 31 years of age, married Thomas Quiney (see QUINEY FAMILY), her junior by 4 or 5 years. Their marriage was solemnized at a time when ecclesiastical law prescribed a special license for all marriages taking place between Septuagesima Sunday and the Sunday after Easter, which in 1616 covered the period from January 28 to April 7. Since the couple never obtained this license, they were excommunicated.

A document has recently been discovered in the Kent County archives office which helps to explain the couple's apparent haste in marrying. The document, dated March 26, 1616, is in Latin, the English translation of which is here given:

> The office of the judge against Thomas Quiney Presented for incontinence with a certain Margaret Wheelar, . . . he appeared, and when the said presentment was brought against him, he confessed that he had had carnal intercourse with the said Wheelar and submitted himself to the correction of the Judge, wherefor the judge enjoined him public penance clothed in a sheet (according to custom) for three Sundays in the said church of Stratford. And then the said Quyney . . . offered the sum of 5s. to the use of the poor of the said parish and requested that the penance imposed on him should be remitted, wherefor the judge enjoined him to acknowledge his fault in his own attire before the Minister of Bishopton . . . and to certify this at the next court. And so he was dismissed.

Eleven days before this presentment, the Margaret Wheeler with whom Quiney admitted having carnal intercourse "and her child" were buried in Stratford, her death apparently resulting from childbirth. This discovery throws new light on a hitherto unexplained change in Shakespeare's will. The will was first drawn up in January 1616, but on March 25 of that year it was altered in such a fashion as to suggest that Shakespeare was uncertain about his new son-in-law. Judith received £100 as her marriage "porcion" and the interest on another £150. Then the will specifies, if Judith were to die within three years without issue, the £150 was to be divided between his granddaughter Elizabeth Hall and his sister Joan Hart. (In the following extract, brackets indicate words that were scratched out in the original document.)

> But if my saied daughter Judith be lyving att thend of the saied three Yeares or anie yssue of her bodye, then my will ys & soe I devise & bequeath the saied Hundred & ffyftie poundes to be sett out by my executours & overseers for the best benefit of her & her issue & the stock not to be paied vnto her soe long as she shalbe marryed & covert Baron [by my executours & overseers,] but my will ys that she shall have the consideracion yearelie paied vnto her during her lief & after her deceas the saied stock and consideracion to bee paied to her children if she have Anie & if not to her executours or assignes she lyving the saied terme after my deceas. Provided that yf such husbond as she shall att thend of the saied three Yeares be marryed vnto or attaine after doe sufficientlie Assure vnto her & thissue of her bodie landes Awnswereable to the porcion by this my will gyven vnto her & to be adiudged soe by my executours & overseers then my will ys that the said cl[li] shalbe paid to such husbond as shall make such assurance to his owne vse . . . .

In other words, Shakespeare was insuring for his daughter and her heirs a stable income, married as she was to a man whose instability and infidelity had just been discovered.

Judith had three children. One, Shakespeare, died

at the age of six months. The other two, Richard and Thomas, died in 1639 a few weeks apart, probably as the result of an epidemic. Judith herself lived on until 1662, dying at the age of 77. She was buried at Stratford on February 9, 1662. [E. K. Chambers, *William Shakespeare*, 1930; Hugh A. Hanley, "Shakespeare's Family in Stratford Records," *The Times Literary Supplement*, May 21, 1964.]

Shakespeare, Margaret (1562–1563). Shakespeare's elder sister who died in infancy a year before he was born. Margaret's baptism and burial are recorded in the Stratford Parish Register: "1562, December 2 Margareta filia Johannis Shakspere . . . ; 1563, April 30 Margareta filia Johannis Shakspere." [B. Roland Lewis, *The Shakespeare Documents*, 1940.]

Shakespeare, Richard (d. c. 1560). Shakespeare's grandfather. Although there is no direct proof that Richard Shakespeare was the father of the poet's father, the available evidence makes it highly probable. Richard Shakespeare was a farmer at Snitterfield, a village near Stratford. He is first mentioned in the Snitterfield records in 1529. He farmed land on two manors in Snitterfield and rented a house belonging to Robert Arden, Shakespeare's maternal grandfather. He died sometime before February 10, 1561 when the administration of his estate was granted to his son John, who is almost certainly Shakespeare's father. Richard had at least one other son, Henry Shakespeare, and possibly a third, Thomas Shakespeare. [Mark Eccles, *Shakespeare in Warwickshire*, 1961.]

Shakespeare, Richard (1574–1613). A younger brother of Shakespeare, baptized on March 11, 1574. Nothing is known of him other than the dates of his baptism and burial. The latter took place on February 4, 1613.

Shakespeare, Susanna (1583–1649). Shakespeare's elder daughter. Susanna was baptized on May 26, 1583, six months after the marriage of William and Anne Shakespeare. Nothing is known of her early life until the appearance of her name in 1606 in a recusant list for failing to receive Communion on Easter Sunday (see recusancy). In 1607 she was married to John Hall, a physician. In 1612 Hall purchased a house in Old Town, near Stratford, but so far as is known never lived there. The only dwelling at which the Halls are known to have resided is New Place, both before and after Shakespeare's death.

They were living at New Place in 1613 when Susanna brought a suit, in the consistory court of Worcester Cathedral, for defamation against John Lane. Susanna charged that Lane had slandered her in asserting that she ". . . had the runninge of the raynes & had been naught with Rafe Smith at John Palmer." The precise implication of Lane's assertion is not clear; in any event Susanna's character was vindicated by the court, which promptly had Lane excommunicated for slander.

Susanna and her husband were the executors of Shakespeare's will, and she was named heir to his houses and lands, with the provision that the property in turn be bequeathed to any male children she might have. In 1635 Hall died, naming Susanna executrix of his nuncupative will, as a result of which she was sued for recovery of a debt (see Baldwin Brookes). She continued to live at New Place with her daughter and son-in-law, Thomas Nash, acting as hostess to Queen Henrietta Maria during the latter's visit in 1643. In 1647 her son-in-law died, bequeathing New Place and the Blackfriars property to his cousin Edward Nash (see Nash Family). The bequest was successfully challenged in court by Susanna and her daughter Elizabeth, who established their sole right to the property. On July 11, 1649 Susanna died; she was buried in the chancel of Holy Trinity Church in Stratford. Her gravestone, with a cut of the Shakespeare arms impaled by the Hall arms, was inscribed with the following epitaph:

Witty above her sexe, but that's not all,
Wise to salvation was good Mistris Hall,
Something of Shakespeare was in that, but this
Wholy of him with whom she's now in blisse.
Then, Passenger, hast nere a teare,
  To weepe with her that wept with all;
That wept, yet set her self to chere
  Them up with comforts cordiall.
Her love shall live, her mercy spread,
  When thou has't ner'e a teare to shed.

In 1707 her bones were disinterred and the inscription on the stone erased. Before the erasure, however, it was copied by William Dugdale in his *Antiquities of Warwickshire* (1656), and Dugdale's text was used as a basis for the inscription on the restored stone in 1844. [B. Roland Lewis, *The Shakespeare Documents*, 1940; Mark Eccles, *Shakespeare in Warwickshire*, 1961; Hugh A. Hanley, "Shakespeare's Family in Stratford Records," *The Times Literary Supplement*, May 21, 1964.]

Shakespeare, Thomas (fl. 1563–1583). A tenant farmer on the Snitterfield manor and possibly an uncle of the poet's. Thomas Shakespeare is cited in the Snitterfield records as a copyholder in 1563, 1578, 1581, and 1583. On the latter two dates he was also fined for minor offenses. He had at least one son, ***John*** (b. 1581). He may be the "Thomas Greene alias Shakspere" who was buried at Stratford in 1590. [Mark Eccles, *Shakespeare in Warwickshire*, 1961.]

Shakespeare, William (1564–1616). Poet, actor, and playwright. The documented facts of Shakespeare's life are as sparse as the legends are prolific. Yet more is known about him than most other playwrights of his day and certainly enough is known to make possible a reconstruction of the major events and activities of his life and to weed out the more fantastic myths that have naturally gathered about his name.

Stratford. Shakespeare was born in Stratford-upon-Avon; the exact date of his birth is unknown (see birthday) but traditionally is considered to be April 23, 1564. His father was John Shakespeare, a glover. Extant records show his father to have been a prominent and respected citizen and property owner in Stratford. Two of the buildings he owned, adjacent to one another, are generally designated as the woolshop and the birthplace and the latter is traditionally believed to be the place of Shakespeare's birth although there is no real evidence for this belief. Shakespeare's father held several public offices in the town, including the equivalent of the modern office of mayor. Shakespeare's mother, Mary Arden, was probably connected with an old and respected family of the county of Warwickshire (see Arden Family).

Although the Tudor records of the Stratford grammar school have long since disappeared, it is all but certain that, at the age of six or seven, Shakespeare entered school there to learn what all other Elizabethan schoolboys learned—Latin (see EDUCATION). Just when Shakespeare's schooling ended and why are not certain, but it is possible, as Nicholas Rowe reports from hearsay in his biography (1709), that Shakespeare left school to help his father in business. If this story is true, he would have been about 13, a time when records show a sudden fall in the fortunes of John Shakespeare—an inexplicable financial decline and withdrawal from public eminence from which he never recovered.

In 1582, when he was 18, Shakespeare married Anne Hathaway (see HATHAWAY FAMILY); the marriage is documented by extant records (see MARRIAGE). The baptism of their first child, Susanna, is recorded in the Stratford parish register under the date of May 26, 1583 (see Susanna SHAKESPEARE). Two years later, under the date of February 2, the baptism of the twins Hamnet and Judith is recorded. Hamnet, Shakespeare's only son, died at the age of 11 on August 11, 1596, as recorded in the parish register. (See Judith SHAKESPEARE.) Susanna Shakespeare eventually married John HALL, a physician, and their daughter, Elizabeth HALL, was Shakespeare's last living descendant at the time of her death in 1670.

The years between the birth of Judith and Hamnet, 1585, and an allusion to Shakespeare by Robert Greene in 1592, are the so-called lost years; documentary evidence as to Shakespeare's whereabouts and activities during this period is totally lacking. It has been conjectured that he is the William SHAKESHAFTE, probably a provincial actor, who is mentioned in the will of Alexander Houghton. Another story derives from William BEESTON, who asserted that Shakespeare was a schoolmaster in the country. Nothing, however, can be confirmed about this period in Shakespeare's life except that he left his family during it and that by the time Robert Greene alluded to him, he was firmly established in London, acting, and prominent enough as a playwright to provoke Greene's jealousy and ire.

In his move to London, however, Shakespeare by no means severed his ties with Stratford. During the 20 years he was in London, he carried on many business transactions, among them the purchase of land, in Stratford and it is clear that he continued to think of it as his home. In 1597, for example, he bought NEW PLACE, a large, handsome house, and there installed his family. A town inventory (see NOATE OF CORNE & MALTE) in the next year shows that Shakespeare was storing grain in the barns of his new property. The correspondence between the Stratfordians Abraham STURLEY and Richard Quiney (see QUINEY FAMILY) seems to indicate that they considered Shakespeare their fellow townsman. Other business activities of Shakespeare's in Stratford when he was living in London include his purchases in 1602 of land in OLD STRATFORD (see COMBE FAMILY) and of a cottage across CHAPEL LANE from the garden of New Place. In 1605 he made his largest known investment, purchasing an interest in the lease of the STRATFORD TITHES; this investment later involved him in a controversy over ENCLOSURE (see William REPLINGHAM). In 1604, 1608, and 1609, records show that Shakespeare brought suit for recovery of deb against John ADDENBROOK and Philip ROGERS. In 161 he contributed to the HIGHWAYS SUBSCRIPTION. All evi dence seems to indicate an uninterrupted interest i the town on his part, and his position there seems t have been one of some distinction, helped, no doub by his growing reputation in London. As early a 1596 his reputation must have been such as to mak him able to help his father secure the COAT OF ARM that the latter had applied for 20 years before.

Sometime around 1612, after 20 years of writin and acting for London's foremost acting company Shakespeare moved back to Stratford. He died o April 23, 1616; the cause and circumstances of hi death are unknown. In apparent lack of trust of hi son-in-law, Thomas Quiney, Shakespeare altered hi WILL just a month before he died. He was buried i the chancel of the HOLY TRINITY CHURCH and severa years later a monument was erected, presumably b his family (see MONUMENT; EPITAPH). The monumen was carved by Gheerart Janssen and is one of tw extant likenesses of Shakespeare considered to b authentic (see PORTRAITS OF SHAKESPEARE). See als RELIGION.

London. The allusion of Robert GREENE to Shake speare in his pamphlet A GROATS-WORTH OF WI places Shakespeare definitely in London in 1592. Th allusion refers to him as both an actor and a play wright and indicates that he had achieved som reputation by that time. Shakespeare's residence i London has been surmised from the reports of ta collectors which place him in ST. HELEN'S PARISH be fore 1596 and on the Bankside in SOUTHWARK, nea the Globe theatre, in 1597. Evidence confirming hi residence in Southwark is found in a writ serve against Shakespeare and Francis LANGLEY by th sheriff in that district. The complainant was a Wil liam WAYTE and the quarrel involved Willian GARDINER, but the details of the dispute are n longer known.

How Shakespeare came to join the lord chamber lain's acting company and where he got his training —the training of actors in his day was extremel rigorous and the profession highly competitive—i not known. It is reasonable to assume that he starte out as a HIRED MAN, possibly in Pembroke's Men, o was a member of Strange's Men when they re-forme to become the Lord Chamberlain's Men. In any case he emerges as a member of Chamberlain's Men i 1594. His position as a leading actor and SHARER i the company is attested to by a record of paymen in that year from the Master of the Revels to th Chamberlain's Men for a performance at court. Such payments were usually made to the two or thre most prominent actors in the company, and in thi case the payment was made to Will Kempe, Richar Burbage, and Shakespeare. See CHAMBERLAIN'S MEN ACTING COMPANIES.

In 1598 the leading actors of the Chamberlain' Men took the first steps toward the construction o their own playhouse, the GLOBE theatre. The troup probably moved there sometime during 1599 and it reputation steadily rose until it was of unrivale prominence. The high achievement of this company was due in part to its unique organization. The usua arrangement for acting companies was one in which the actors leased their theatres from theatre owner

William Shakespeare

of

Stratford-upon-Avon

---

hakespeare never lost touch with the country town where he was born. At the eight of his career as a London playwright Shakespeare still involved himself with ocal affairs in Stratford. It was in Stratford that he invested the money that he arned in London. In his middle age, when his writing days were nearly over, he eturned to Stratford, where he spent the rest of his life. On the following pages re pictured some of the places that Shakespeare knew as a resident of Stratford, s well as some of the documents that testify to his continued interest in his home own.

THE COUNTI OF WARWICK THE SHIRE TOWNE AND CITIE OF COVENTRE described
WARWICKE
Septentrio
Occidens
Meridies
Parte of Stafford Shire
PART OF WORCESTER
SHIRE
Gloucester Shire
Parte of
HEMLINFORD HUNDRED
BARLICHWAYE HUNDRED
PART OF KINETON HUND
Bermicham
Sutton Cosfeld
Cosfeld Wast
Colshill
Solihull
Henley in Arde
Feckenham
Aulcester
Stretford upon Auen
Shipston
Warwick
Evesholme
Campden
Tamworth
Kineton
Oxford
Rob: Rich E.
Anno Domini 1610.
THE SCALE OF MILES
1 2 3 4 5 6 7
A SCALE OF PASES
40 80 120 160 200
Performed by Iohn Speede. And are to be sold by Thomas Basset in Fleetstreet, and Richard Chiswell in St Pauls Churchyard.

THE COUNTY OF WARWICKSHIRE IN 1610. THIS MAP IS FROM JOHN SPEED'S *Theatre of the Empire of Great Britaine.*

THE "BIRTHPLACE" IN HENLEY STREET. IT IS ACTUALLY TWO ADJOINING BUILDINGS. THE ONE ON THE LEFT IS TRADITIONALLY THOUGHT TO BE THE ONE IN WHICH SHAKESPEARE WAS BORN. (SHAKESPEARE BIRTHPLACE TRUST)

"GULIELMUS FILIUS JOHANNES SHAKSPERE"—SHAKESPEARE'S CHRISTENING AS RECORDED IN THE STRATFORD PARISH REGISTER. (SHAKESPEARE BIRTHPLACE TRUST)

HOLY TRINITY CHURCH, STRATFORD, WHERE SHAKESPEARE WAS CHRISTENED. THE MAIN BUILDING DATES FROM THE 13TH CENTURY; THE AISLES WERE ADDED IN THE 14TH CENTURY AND THE CHANCEL IN THE 15TH. THE POINTED SPIRE, WHICH IS TOTALLY ALIEN TO THE REST OF THE BUILDING, WAS CONSTRUCTED IN THE 18TH CENTURY. SHAKESPEARE IS BURIED IN THE NAVE. (SHAKESPEARE BIRTHPLACE TRUST)

THE STRATFORD GRAMMAR SCHOOL. NO RECORDS HAVE SURVIVED TO PROVE THAT SHAKESPEARE ATTENDED SCHOOL IN THIS ROOM, BUT IT IS PERFECTLY REASONABLE TO ASSUME THAT HE DID. (SHAKESPEARE BIRTHPLACE TRUST)

ROBERT ARDEN'S HOUSE AT WILMCOTE. SHAKESPEARE'S MOTHER WAS BORN IN THIS LARGE AND PLEASANT FARMHOUSE. (SHAKESPEARE BIRTHPLACE TRUST)

THE HATHAWAY FARMHOUSE AT SHOTTERY, NOW KNOWN AS ANNE HATHAWAY'S COTTAGE. IT IS LIKELY THAT SHAKESPEARE'S WIFE WAS BORN HERE. (SHAKESPEARE BIRTHPLACE TRUST)

PAGES FROM THE PARISH REGISTER OF HOLY TRINITY, ON WHICH THE CHRISTENINGS OF SHAKESPEARE'S THREE CHILDREN ARE RECORDED: SUSANNA ON MAY 26, 1583, AND THE TWINS HAMNET AND JUDITH ON FEBRUARY 2, 1585. (SHAKESPEARE BIRTHPLACE TRUST)

EXEMPLIFICATION OF THE FINE OF NEW PLACE, MAY 4, 1597. THE FINE WAS A COLLUSIVE LAWSUIT BY WHICH THE TRANSFER OF PROPERTY BETWEEN WILLIAM UNDERHILL AND SHAKESPEARE WAS EFFECTED; IT ESTABLISHED SHAKESPEARE AS THE NEW OWNER OF NEW PLACE, THE SECOND LARGEST HOUSE IN STRATFORD. THE FINE IS WRITTEN IN LATIN. (SHAKESPEARE BIRTHPLACE TRUST)

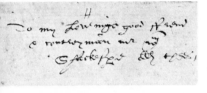

THE "NOATE OF CORNE & MALTE." ON FEBRUARY 4, 1598, THE TOWN OF STRATFORD TOOK A CENSUS OF THE AMOUNT OF GRAIN AND BARLEY (CORNE & MALTE) THAT WAS BEING STORED BY THE RESIDENTS. IN THE CHAPEL STREET WARD SHAKESPEARE WAS LISTED AS THE OWNER OF 10 QUARTERS OF GRAIN (80 BUSHELS). BELOW SHAKESPEARE ON THE LIST IS JULIUS SHAW, SHAKESPEARE'S NEIGHBOR, WHO 18 YEARS LATER WITNESSED SHAKESPEARE'S WILL. (SHAKEPEARE BIRTHPLACE TRUST)

A LETTER TO SHAKESPEARE FROM HIS STRATFORD FRIEND RICHARD QUINEY ASKING FOR A LOAN, OCTOBER 25, 1598. THIS IS THE ONLY LETTER TO SHAKESPEARE THAT HAS SURVIVED. FOR A TRANSCRIPT SEE *Quiney Family*. (SHAKESPEARE BIRTHPLACE TRUST)

A MEMO IN THE HAND OF THOMAS GREENE, SHAKESPEARE'S "COSEN," CONCERNING THE WELCOMBE ENCLOSURE, SEPTEMBER 5, 1614. THIS NOTE, HEADED "AUNCIENT FFREEHOLDERS IN THE FFIELDS OF OLDSTRATFORD AND WELCOMBE," BEGINS "M[r] SHAKSPEARE. 4. YARD LAND. NOE COMMON NOR GROUND BEYOND GOSPELL BUSHE, NOE GROWND IN SANDFIELD, NOR NONE IN SLOWE HILL FIELD BEYOND BISHOPTON NOR NONE IN THE ENCLOSURE BEYOND BISHOPTON." THE PROPERTY DESCRIBED IS THE OLD STRATFORD ESTATE WHICH SHAKESPEARE BOUGHT IN 1602 FROM WILLIAM AND JOHN COMBE. (SHAKESPEARE BIRTHPLACE TRUST)

HALL'S CROFT. SHAKESPEARE'S DAUGHTER SUSANNA MARRIED JOHN HALL, A DOCTOR. IT WAS IN THIS HOUSE, NEAR HOLY TRINITY, THAT THEY LIVED UNTIL THEY MOVED TO NEW PLACE, WHICH SHAKESPEARE LEFT TO THEM. NO DOUBT HALL ATTENDED SHAKESPEARE IN HIS FINAL ILLNESS. (SHAKESPEARE BIRTHPLACE TRUST)

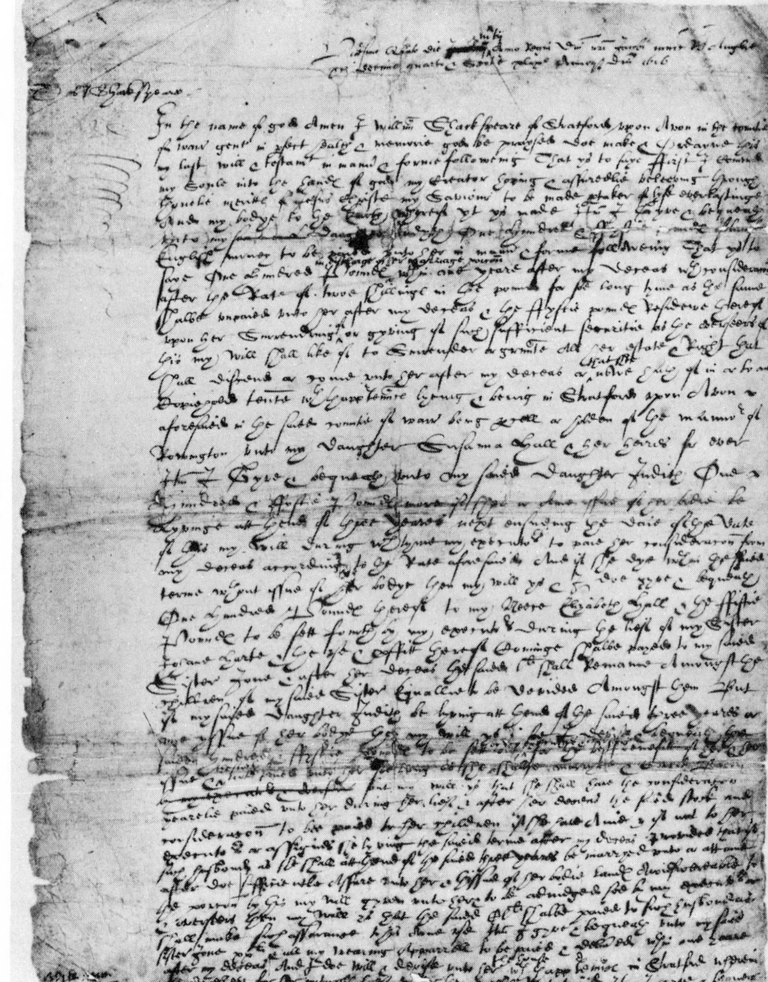

THE FIRST SHEET OF SHAKESPEARE'S WILL. HIS SIGNATURE, NOW ILLEGIBLE, IS IN THE LOWER LEFT CORNER.

THE SECOND SHEET OF THE WILL. THIS SHEET IS SIGNED IN THE LOWER RIGHT CORNER.

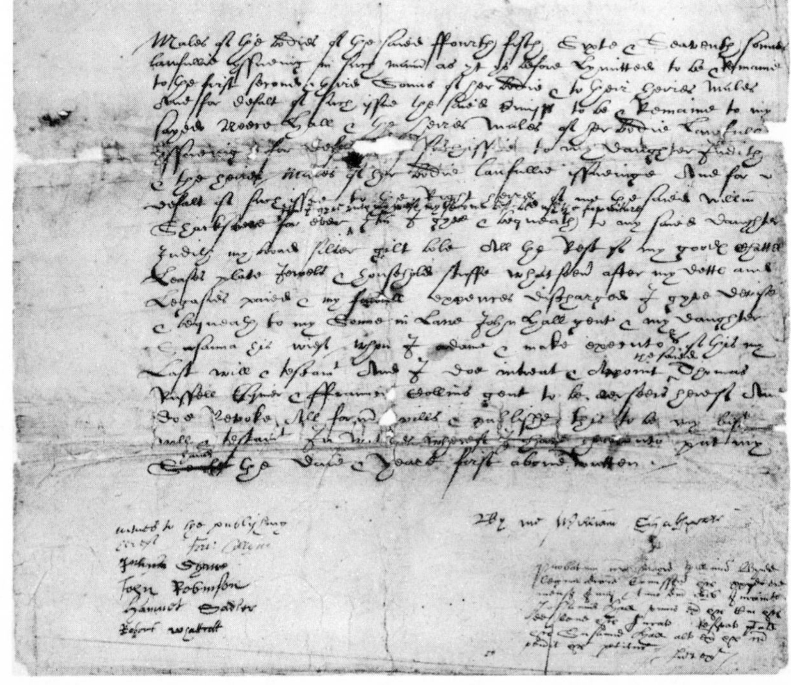

THE THIRD SHEET OF THE WILL. IT IS THIS SHEET WHICH CONTAINS THE FAMOUS INTERLINEATION OF THE SECOND BEST BED. FOR A TRANSCRIPT OF THE ENTIRE DOCUMENT SEE *will*. (PUBLIC RECORD OFFICE)

ONE MONTH AFTER SHAKESPEARE COMPLETED AND SIGNED HIS WILL HIS BURIAL WAS RECORDED IN THE STRATFORD PARISH REGISTER: "APRILL 25 [1616] WILL SHAKSPERE GENT." EIGHT DAYS EARLIER WILLIAM HART, SHAKESPEARE'S BROTHER-IN-LAW, WAS BURIED. (SHAKESPEARE BIRTHPLACE TRUST)

THE GRAVE OF SHAKESPEARE IN HOLY TRINITY. HIS WIFE ANNE IS BURIED ON HIS LEFT. (SHAKESPEARE BIRTHPLACE TRUST)

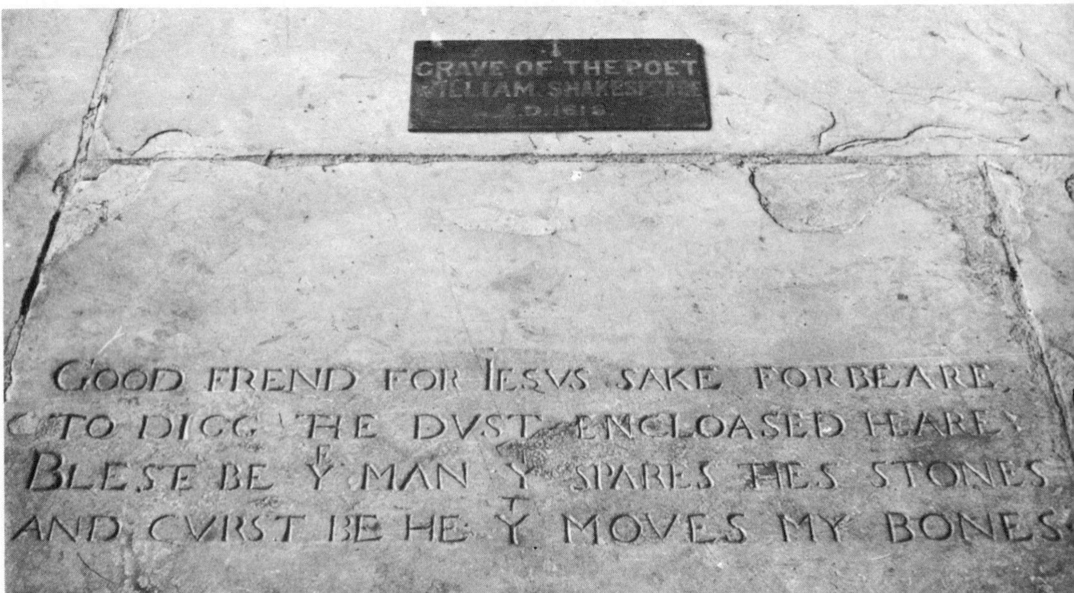

who were usually in no other way connected with the theatre; they were often businessmen with conflicting interests. In the case of the Globe, half the ownership was given to Cuthbert and Richard Burbage, the latter the leading actor of the company, and the other half was divided equally among five actor-sharers, including Shakespeare. Thus actors were owners or HOUSEKEEPERS as well, and almost all profits from the work of the actors remained with the actors. In 1603, on the death of Queen Elizabeth, all the acting companies came under the patronage of members of the royal family, and the Chamberlain's Men, as the finest acting company in London, became King James' troupe, the King's Men. As such, Shakespeare and his fellows attained even greater distinction, received a new patent, and were entitled to wear royal livery. In 1608 the King's Men rented a second theatre, the BLACKFRIARS, a private theatre. Seven men, including Shakespeare, each had a share in the theatre.

Very little reliable evidence exists as to the parts Shakespeare played in his own or other men's plays. However, a mixture of gossip and tradition attributes to him the role of Adam in *As You Like It* and the Ghost in *Hamlet.* John DAVIES in an epigram in *The Scourge of Folly, consisting of Satyrical Epigrams and others* (c. 1610) is responsible for the idea that Shakespeare often played the part of King in his own plays. It is on this basis that T. W. Baldwin infers that Shakespeare's line as an actor was that of an old man of high rank about whom the center of action revolves, like the fatherly Duncan in *Macbeth.* Other roles that Baldwin assigns to Shakespeare are the following:

THE CAST OF THE FIRST PERFORMANCE OF JONSON'S *Sejanus.* FROM JONSON'S *Complete Workes* (1616).

This Tragœdie vvas first
acted, in the yeere
1603.

By the Kings Maiesties
SERVANTS.

The principall Tragœdians were,

RIC. BVRBADGE. WILL. SHAKE-SPEARE.
AVG. PHILIPS. IOH. HEMINGS.
WILL. SLY. HEN. CONDEL.
IOH. LOWIN. ALEX. COOKE.

With the allowance of the Master of REVELLS.

Duke of Florence (*All's Well That Ends Well*)
Lepidus (*Antony and Cleopatra*)
Duke of Ephesus (*Comedy of Errrors*)
Charles VI (*Henry V*)
Cicero or Cinna (*Julius Caesar*)
Friar Peter (*Measure for Measure*)
Duke (*Merchant of Venice*)
Friar Francis (*Much Ado About Nothing*)
Duke (*Othello*)
Escalus (*Romeo and Juliet*)
Vincentio (*Taming of the Shrew*)
Sea Captain (*Twelfth Night*)
Antonio (*Two Gentlemen of Verona*)

Shakespeare is mentioned in the casts of characters of two of Ben Jonson's plays—EVERY MAN IN HIS HUMOUR and SEJANUS—and there is a tradition that in the first he played the elder Knowell. The dates of these two plays, 1598 and 1603 respectively, indicate that Shakespeare continued to act fairly late in his career, even after he was a successful playwright and poet.

Shakespeare apparently retired to Stratford sometime before May 11, 1612, for, in a deposition of that date in regard to the BELLOT-MOUNTJOY suit, he describes himself as a resident of Stratford. It is likely, however, that he went to London occasionally—in this instance to serve as witness in a suit. In 1613 Shakespeare is recorded as having designed, with Richard Burbage, an impresa for Francis Manners, 6th earl of RUTLAND. It was about this time that he purchased the BLACKFRIARS GATE-HOUSE, another indication that he had not retired from London completely.

Running simultaneously with Shakespeare's career as an actor was, of course, his career as playwright and poet. Shakespeare's development (see SHAKESPEARE, WILLIAM: HIS PLAYS AND POEMS) into a writer whom many consider the supreme literary artist of all time, during a period of unparalleled intellectual and artistic vigor whose greatest achievement was its drama, is the happiest coincidence in English literary history. Shakespeare's involvement with several aspects of the theatre—as actor, theatre owner, and playwright—though unique even in his own time, was possible because playwrights in general had a more intimate relationship with the theatre and actors than is the case today. Most modern productions of Shakespeare give very little idea of the theatrical conditions in which he worked. The structure of the theatre in Shakespeare's time, for example, afforded far greater intimacy between actor and audience than is possible in modern-day theatres (see PLAYHOUSE STRUCTURE). The audience itself was far more heterogeneous than is the modern theatre audience, and Shakespeare appealed to everyone (see AUDIENCES). The division of a play into acts and scenes was not provided by Shakespeare, but was the work of later editors to make the plays conform to the theatrical conventions of a later day (see ACT-SCENE DIVISION). Thus an Elizabethan production, without such breaks, had much greater continuity and fluidity of action and the audience's attention did not lapse because of changes of scene, curtain raisings and droppings, and the like. See PERFORMANCES OF SHAKESPEARE'S PLAYS.

Like all playwrights of the time, Shakespeare was

very much influenced in his writing by the nature and size of his company. A common device, DOUBLING, made it possible for a company of, say, 15 actors to play twice that many roles or more. Shakespeare usually knew who was going to act the parts in his plays and wrote them to suit the talents of the actors in his company (see CAST). Shakespeare was most certainly influenced by the fact that in his day women did not act and female roles were impersonated by boy actors whose voices had not yet changed. The tenure of the boys as female impersonators was necessarily limited and their range of expression must also have been limited. This situation undoubtedly accounts for the small number of women in proportion to men in the plays. G. E. Bentley points out that in all of Shakespeare's plays he assigns the largest part to women in only four of them; that the types of women in the plays are extremely limited compared with the types of men; and that Shakespeare never wrote a role which would require a boy actor to sustain a normal, maternal attitude. Thus, many phases of Shakespeare's art can be fully appreciated only when seen against the background of his theatre. See ACTORS.

Of the 36 plays published in the FIRST FOLIO (1623), the first collected edition of Shakespeare's plays, only 18 had been previously published. These were published in QUARTO, the usual format for play publication in Elizabethan times. Again, modern practices differ so radically from Elizabethan that confusion has arisen about the publication of Shakespeare's plays. The central difference between publication today and in Shakespeare's day is that the writer had nothing to do with the publication of his own works (see PRINTING AND PUBLISHING); he did not own them, had no COPYRIGHT, and therefore no legal rights concerning their printing. His play was the property of the acting company for whom he wrote it and, in general, acting companies jealously guarded their plays so that they would be exclusively part of their repertories (see BLOCKING ENTRY). This state of affairs is partially responsible for the publication of corrupt versions of Shakespeare's plays (see BAD QUARTOS) and for false attributions to Shakespeare of other men's work (see APOCRYPHA). As a result, the authenticity of the Shakespearean canon has been subject to painstaking investigation on the part of modern scholars (see CANON). For a full discussion of the plays, see under the individual titles.

Authors usually had more of a hand in the publication of their nondramatic works. In the case of two of Shakespeare's poems—*Venus and Adonis* and *The Rape of Lucrece*—Shakespeare obviously had some control of their printing and even wrote dedications for them. Both were dedicated to Henry Wriothesley, 3rd earl of SOUTHAMPTON, and, taken together with the dedication in the SONNETS, have aroused speculation, often wild, about the relationship of Shakespeare to his patron. The dedication in the *Sonnets* was the publisher's and its enigmatic phrasing has caused endless conjecture about Shakespeare's life. Such conjecture is the result of reading the *Sonnets* as biography and is based on the attempts to determine the identity—Southampton is a favorite candidate—of MR. W. H., the dedicatee.

There are many contemporary references to Shakespeare's plays and his works, some direct and som[e] oblique: Robert Greene's angry allusion to Shake[-]speare was apologized for by Greene's publishe[r] Henry CHETTLE; Francis Meres, in the list of play[s] included in his PALLADIS TAMIA, includes several o[f] Shakespeare's plays and praises him highly; a numbe[r] of the plays were entered in the STATIONERS' REGIS[-]TER; the Chamberlain's Men, and especially Shake[-]speare, are referred to in the PARNASSUS PLAYS[;] Gabriel HARVEY asserts that *Venus and Adonis* i[s] more popular with youth, but that the "wiser sort[s]" prefer *Lucrece* and *Hamlet.* Tributes by his contem[-]poraries are included in the First Folio by Ben JON[-]SON, Leonard DIGGES, Hugh HOLLAND, James Mabb[e] (see M., I.), and, of course, by Shakespeare's fellow actors John HEMINGES and Henry CONDELL, who pre[-]pared the volume for publication. For other contem[-]porary references of note see WILLOBIE HIS AVISA[;] Michael DRAYTON; Richard BARNFIELD; John MARS[-]TON; John WEEVER; John BODENHAM; John MANNING[-]HAM; Robert PARSONS; Anthony SCOLOKER; William CAMDEN; William BARKSTEAD; John WEBSTER; Rich[-]ard CAREW; William DRUMMOND. Among some o[f] the notices after his death are those by William BASSE; John TAYLOR; John MILTON; John BENSON.

This long list might give the impression that Shake[-]speare's fame as the greatest of England's writer[s] began in his own day. However, Shakespeare's repu[-]tation was neither as high nor of the same kind as i[t] is today and its history is not a dull collection o[f] high praise from every generation alike. The history of his reputation, in fact, is interesting in that it re[-]flects the artistic standards and values of each perio[d] in subsequent literary history (see CRITICISM—17TH CENTURY; CRITICISM—18TH CENTURY; CRITICISM—19TH CENTURY; CRITICISM—20TH CENTURY).

legends. There are many stories about Shakespeare in contemporary, Caroline, and Restoration writing that purport to add to his biography and that form what E. K. Chambers calls the Shakespeare-mythos[.] The value of these stories is twofold: they contribute to the reconstruction of his life and the history of hi[s] reputation. Caution, however, must be taken in as[-]sessing the value of statements about Shakespeare be[-]cause of the universal tendency on the part of people to create myths about the past, especially about he[-]roes. It is best to accept the general drift of these tra[-]ditions and see them in light of other evidence rathe[r] than adhere to details.

London, Oxford, and Stratford are the three mai[n] sources of tradition about Shakespeare. The Stratford tradition is miscellaneous and testifies to the fact tha[t] Stratfordians were early aware of Shakespeare's rep[-]utation and that the town had become a place o[f] pilgrimage as early as 1630. Thomas PLUME set down several anecdotes about Shakespeare, among them that he was a glover's son. The story that Shake[-]speare wrote an epitaph on John Combe was re[-]corded by Lieutenant HAMMOND and Nichola[s] BURGH in the 17th century. Another story concern[s] Shakespeare's death following a drinking bout with Ben Jonson (see John WARD; BIDFORD). The tradition that Shakespeare left Stratford because he was caught stealing deer on the property of Sir Thomas LUCY was recorded by Richard DAVIES and Joshua BARNES[.] The curse on Shakespeare's tomb is attributed to him by Mr. DOWDALL and William HALL. If the various anecdotes about Shakespeare are not to be trusted, they do show that a local mythology was early created under the pressure of interest and curiosity from the outside.

The Oxford tradition is concerned exclusively with the legend that Sir William DAVENANT was the natural son of Shakespeare which, though the result of local tradition, had tacit confirmation from Davenant himself.

The London tradition is largely theatrical and yields information about Shakespeare as an actor, about his relationship with Ben Jonson, and about the composition of some of his plays. Stories about Shakespeare and Jonson were recorded by Nicholas L'ESTRANGE and Thomas FULLER. Notices about the composition of his plays were written by Richard JAMES, Edward RAVENSCROFT, and John DOWNES, and the anonymous ESSAY AGAINST TOO MUCH READING discusses Shakespeare's method as a writer. The line of transmission of the London tradition is mainly from Davenant to his associate Thomas Betterton, from whom it finds its way to Alexander Pope and others in the 18th century, including Sir William OLDYS.

These stories all appeared, some of them much embellished, in early attempts at biography. Shakespeare is treated in several early collective biographies, notably those by Edward PHILLIPS, William WINSTANLEY, Gerard LANGBAINE, and Charles GILDON. These are interesting more for an early view of his reputation than for any specific biographical data they yield. More anecdotal are the notices of Shakespeare by Sir William BISHOP, Sir Hugh CLOPTON, and John AUBREY. The dearth of strictly contemporary references to Shakespeare is due in part to the fact that until 1709—when Nicholas ROWE made the first attempt to reconstruct the life of Shakespeare for his *Life*—there was no systematic research into the playwright's life and many who might have provided information or recollections about him died without being consulted. Later notices—those that appeared in the 18th and 19th centuries—are to be regarded with great skepticism. Finally, it might be noted that, unlike the various traditions that derive from recorded notices comparatively close to Shakespeare's time, the notion that his plays were written by someone else materialized, unsupported by fact or tradition, in the 19th century. See CLAIMANTS. [E. K. Chambers, *William Shakespeare*, 1930; Marchette Chute, *Shakespeare of London*, 1949; Mark Eccles, *Shakespeare in Warwickshire*, 1961; G. E. Bentley, *Shakespeare: A Biographical Handbook*, 1961.] —J.C.

Shakespeare, William: His Plays and Poems. Any attempt to give an account of Shakespeare's development as a poet and a playwright is fraught with difficulties. To begin with, we cannot be certain of the exact order in which he wrote his works. However, we can be reasonably sure of determining the successive stages of his intellectual and artistic growth.

Another difficulty is that, unlike the work of most other dramatists, Shakespeare's plays do not follow one another in logical progression. *Twelfth Night*, for example, does not grow out of *As You Like It*, nor is *Othello* a foretaste of *King Lear*. Moreover, we must not assume that the story of the poet's growth will explain his achievements or that it will reveal any of the secrets of his mind and heart, for his inspiration was not his private experience but that of all mankind. That was partly what Ben Jonson meant when he said Shakespeare was "for all time." Nevertheless, Shakespeare was also of an age, the Elizabethan age. It is said that great drama is likely to be produced at a time of a transition from one epoch to another; it reflects the clash of two views of life. Such a situation existed in 16th-century England. At that time the carefully ordered and articulated medieval society was rudely shaken by the revolt of many intellectual leaders against some of the political, religious, and moral conceptions of the Middle Ages and the institutions that embodied them. This conflict in society produced a similar struggle in sensitive minds, and Shakespeare's mind was uniquely responsive. As his career blossomed, it was subjective drama that more and more occupied his mind and deepened his art. His specific views of the problems of the spirit can be found in the plots of his plays and the flights of his poetry. In this study, therefore, we are simply trying to determine in a general way the order taken by the procession of vehicles, each one of which conveyed one of his significant views of life and recorded one of his impulses to artistic creation.

No one knows just when and under what conditions Shakespeare first wrote his dramas. Until recently most scholars believed that he began his career by revising plays belonging to his company or by collaborating with some of the University Wits: Robert Greene, George Peele, and perhaps Thomas Nashe. But now the early plays—*The Comedy of Errors*, *Titus Andronicus*, and the three parts of *Henry VI*—are thought to be wholly Shakespeare's work.

The Early Plays. At present there is general agreement that *The Comedy of Errors* is the poet's first acted drama, produced as early as 1589, and that *Titus Andronicus* was written at about the same time. It is natural that his first drama should be an imitation of the Latin comedies he had studied in the grammar school. He had perhaps even taken part in a production of one of them directed by the master of the school.

In *The Comedy of Errors* the young playwright shows remarkable technical skill for a novice. He takes full advantage of his doubling of identical twins. It enables him to multiply the mistakes in identity (errors), each one of which is given a prepared spot in the plot and follows its predecessors with breathless speed until every character's confusion mounts with the hilarity of the audience to a climax. Then the Dromios face each other, and the laughter suddenly subsides—although even at the very last the Antipholuses cannot tell which Dromio is which.

The poet's varying of meters to fit the situations which the lines record shows a similar artistic sophistication. Only about half of the comedy is written in blank verse, and that is end-stopped and monotonously regular in its beat. This is varied by verse in alternated rhymes, usually in lyrical passages, like Antipholus of Syracuse's wooing of Luciana (III, ii). Finally, some of the low-comedy scenes, particularly the speeches of the Dromios, are written in rhymed

A Ryght
Pithy, Pleasaunt and me
rie Comedie: In-
tytuled Gammer gur-
tons Nedle: Played on
Stage, not longe
ago in Chri-
stes
Colledge in Cambridge.

Made by Mr. S. Mr. of Art.

Imprented at London in
Fleetestreat beneth the Con-
duit at the signe of S. John
Evangelist by Tho-
mas Colwell.

TITLE PAGE OF THE EARLY COMEDY *Gammer Gurton's Needle* (1575). MR. S, THE AUTHOR, IS THOUGHT TO BE WILLIAM STEVENSON.

doggerel, rough anapaestic tetrameter, which goes as follows:

> Say what you will, sir, but I know what I know;
> That you beat me at the mart, I have your hand
> to show.
>
> (III, i, 11–12)

This is the verse form of many pre-Shakespearean comedies, like *Gammer Gurton's Needle* (1552) and *Ralph Roister Doister* (1553).

The artificial balance and symmetry of the characters in *The Comedy of Errors,* as in *Titus Andronicus,* is modeled on the ingenious construction that John Lyly gave to all his works, nondramatic as well as dramatic. Shakespeare may have seen some of his predecessor's plays on the stage before the companies for which Lyly wrote were "restrained" from acting, between the years 1591 and 1599. At any rate Shakespeare named his identical twins Dromio after a boy-servant to Old Memphio in *Mother Bombie* (1589–1590). Shakespeare could have learned all the tricks of Lyly's florid style from reading one or both of his Euphuistic novels (1579 and 1580). In the early stages of his career Shakespeare prized ingenuit particularly in the application of the lessons in rhe oric and logic he had learned at school to th speeches of some of his characters; for example, t those of the Dromios, illustrated in the followin passage:

> The capon burns, the pig falls from the spit,
> The clock hath strucken twelve upon the bell;
> My mistress made it one upon my cheek:
> She is so hot because the meat is cold;
> The meat is cold because you come not home;
> You come not home because you have no
> stomach;
> You have no stomach having broke your fast;
> But we that know what 'tis to fast and pray
> Are penitent for your default to-day.
>
> (I, ii, 44–52)

The lines form a mass of parallelisms, contrasts, an employments of the "topics" of logic.

No doubt believing that every comedy shou have some love interest, the poet introduced into th farce Luciana to be wooed and won by Antipholu of Syracuse, whose stanzaic courting (III, ii, 29–3 is based on Erasmus' rules for writing letters (se EDUCATION). This being the author's first attempt t compose a love-address, it is a complicated and aw ward amplification of a figure of speech. *The Com edy of Errors* thus proves to be a school play. A most every feature of the work is the application a textbook lesson. Shakespeare the playwright di not dare in 1589 to depend wholly on his unaide slowly developing professional skill.

Titus Andronicus is also a school play, exploitin the features of the tragedies of Seneca. They we the approved models for Tudor tragedy, as those Plautus were for Tudor comedy. *Titus* is no thought to be the dramatist's first tragedy, writte as early as 1589.

Although Shakespeare may have borrowed all th horrors packed into *Titus Andronicus* from Ovid tale of Philomela and Procne, in its piling of vendet upon vendetta the tragedy is correctly described Senecan. If the playwright did not study Seneca Latin at school, he could have read his works some of the English translations made between th years 1560 and 1580. They were all collected and i sued in a single volume by Thomas Newton in 158 entitled *Seneca, his tenne Tragedies, translated in English.* This volume was the probable source of th poet's knowledge of Seneca. However, Thom Kyd's *Spanish Tragedy* (1588–1589), the most pop lar play of its age, acted by both the Admiral's an the Lord Chamberlain's Men, exhibited all of Se eca's distinctive characteristics. In this play alo Shakespeare could have become familiar with a Seneca's stock in trade that he borrowed througho his professional career.

Some of the dramatist's additions to Titus' role ha been first introduced into Ovid's story by Joh GOWER in his *Confessio Amantis* (1390, 1393). Suc was Titus' serving up of the severed heads in she of pastry, and such was the important part played his version by abstractions. Tamora, taking note Titus, calling upon Revenge for aid, disguises herse and her two sons as Revenge, Murder, and Ra (V, ii). Gower also added madness to Titus' affli tions. Besides being actually mad, Titus feigns madness. Therefore, here, as in *Hamlet,* a spectator finds it hard to decide where feigned madness ends and real madness begins.

It is of no importance to determine whether Shakespeare derived these features of Titus' role from Gower or from his later derivatives, *The Spanish Tragedy,* for example. What is important is the realization that in *Titus Andronicus* Shakespeare adopts the manner of classical medieval narratives. In this tragedy, as in the three parts of *Henry VI,* Shakespeare often employs figures of speech the effective use of which he had been taught at school. Chiron, recognizing the lines of Horace that had been attached to a bundle of weapons brought in by Lucius, exclaims,

> O, 'tis a verse in Horace; I know it well:
> I read it in the grammar long ago.
> (IV, ii, 22–23)

It does appear twice, once with Horace's name attached, in William Lily's Latin grammar, a textbook used in all Tudor grammar schools. Every member of an Elizabethan audience who had gone to such a school would also have recognized the set speeches and remembered what emotion each one the grammarians taught was intended to express. When, for example, the grammar-trained playgoer heard Tamora's vain entreaty to spare the life of her sons (I, i, 104–120), he might have taken delight in remembering that his school textbook had labeled this kind of appeal "vehement supplication." It was doubtless the fact that the declamatory passages had the authority of learned works of rhetoric that led the poet to extend them to a greater length than their dramatic value warranted.

It is a relief to find in this wilderness of regularly accented blank verse, overweighted with figures of rhetoric and reference to classical mythology, two characters who speak the language of everyday life: the clown, the first of the poet's typical low-comedy bumpkins (IV, iii, 77–120), and the motiveless Aaron, a reincarnation of the morality Vice, who explains his own villainy in terms of primitive psychological theory: "Aaron will have his soul black like his face" (III, i, 206).

The First Chronicles. The analysis of these two plays written as early as 1589–1590 shows that at that point in his career Shakespeare had not yet learned to speak with his own voice or to have views of his own on the human condition.

Having tried his hand at an imitation of Roman comedy and of Seneca's form of a Roman tragedy, the playwright turned to the composition of a type of drama that had no classical prototype: the history play. Nevertheless, he diligently applied to it the lessons he had learned in the grammar school and through strict attention to contemporary plays that in their use of language hewed closely to classical models. Although restrained from excessive use of the arts of rhetoric by his practical need as a dramatist to interrupt long speeches with action, he began in the Henry VI plays to exploit as freely as he dared the rhetorical devices for intensifying, amplifying, and varying simple expressions. The device that he found most useful was Amplification. He constructed many speeches delivered on the battlefield with lavish use of this device, having frequent recourse to complicated metaphors, series of comparisons, and allusions to classical mythology. Queen Margaret's speech to her forces on the eve of the battle of Tewkesbury forms an overingenious 36-line development of a metaphor of the sea and shipwreck (*3 Henry VI,* V, iv, 1–36). In it Warwick is "our anchor"; Montague, "our top-mast"; Oxford, "another anchor"; Somerset, "another goodly mast"; the friends of France, "our shrouds and tacklings," etc. The values in this long speech are only rhetorical, not at all dramatic. King Henry's praise of a shepherd's life, often a symbol of peace, is largely composed of passages illustrating the rhetorical figure of Repetition. There are 3 in 16 lines (*3 Henry VI,* II, v, 22–37). One of the most extended of the three begins:

> So many hours must I tend my flock,
> So many hours must I take my rest,
> So many hours must I contemplate, etc.

The figure of Repetition illustrated in this passage, written in a minor key, gives it an elegiac quality that wins sympathy for the humiliated king, chid from the battle by his wife, the Amazon Margaret of Anjou.

As Gladys Willcock points out, Shakespeare in the Henry dramas gives metaphor a "new status." He employs it to give passages of physical violence and horror aesthetic distance by associating them with classical story or myth. Young Clifford's threats before he joins the battle of Saint Alban's form a good example of the poet's adaptation of this rhetorical device:

> Henceforth I will not have to do with pity:
> Meet I an infant of the House of York,
> Into as many gobbets will I cut it
> As wild Medea young Absyrtus did.
> (*II Henry VI,* V, ii, 56–59)

Shakespeare's generous use of the figures of rhetoric in the three Henry VI plays fills the lines with as much book language as stage language. This even balance between literary and dramatic idiom persisting in many of his early plays gives them a distinctive character more admired in his age than at any time since.

In spite of his continuing concern with literary conventions, the young playwright began in the histories to demonstrate a growing mastery of drama as a medium intended for the theatre. Indeed, his choice of English history as the subject of four consecutive plays suggests a practical theatre man's awareness of the demands of his audience. The patriotism aroused by the defeat of the Armada in 1588 had awakened among Elizabethans an intense curiosity about England's past. It was about two years later that Shakespeare, no doubt hoping to exploit this lively interest, began at the age of 26 to plan and compose his tetralogy dealing with the Wars of the Roses: the three parts of *Henry VI* and *Richard III.* In 1548 a second issue of Edward HALLE's chronicle, *The union of the two noble and illustre famelies of Lancastre and York,* had appeared and in 1550 a third; a second and enlarged edition of Holinshed's *Chronicles* was published in 1587. These volumes offered

Shakespeare material that he could effectively dramatize.

Although *1 Henry VI* sets the stage for the main subject of the tetralogy, the Wars of the Roses, the growing conflict is significant less for its own sake than as the background and cause of Lord Talbot's needless death while defending England's interests in France. The playwright's chief concern is that

> The fraud of England, not the force of France,
> Hath now entrapp'd the noble-minded Talbot.
> (IV, iv, 36–37)

Talbot is the true hero of the play. Shakespeare presents him and the other English captains as paragons of courage, loyalty, and righteousness, whereas the French are repulsive examples of deceit, cowardice, and satanic evil. The exaggeration of this contrast seems to a modern audience sheer jingoism. Yet, if its principal purpose was to excite a patriotic Elizabethan audience to transports of delight, it also served to emphasize the dramatic irony that is central to the play: the heroic Talbot dies less a victim of the pusillanimous French than of his own countrymen, the English nobles, who pursue their selfish interests at home and leave their captains to die unsupported in the field. In this way Shakespeare effectively introduced the political lesson that he propounded in all the plays based on the chronicles: English armies fighting abroad are always victorious except when they are frustrated by division and perfidy on the home front. Had he been willing merely to cater to the nationalistic fervor of his audience, the young dramatist would hardly have chosen as his subject a period of national disarray caused by long years of civil war and a succession of weak or tyrannical kings. Instead, he shrewdly turned this fervor to his own homiletic intent.

Two other reasons have been suggested for his choice of the Wars of the Roses as a subject. The first, as developed by Professor Virgil Whitaker, is that the battles and other important incidents of these wars had taken place near Warwick or Coventry, towns not far from Stratford-upon-Avon. The first battle of Barnet had been fought not more than 30 miles away. The oldest citizens of the place still alive during Shakespeare's youth would have been children during the reign of Richard III, and their memories of these exciting events taking place not far from their hearthstones must have become part of local lore.

A second reason for his choice of the Wars of the Roses was that the method devised by Halle for unifying in his chronicle the confused history of the struggle to the death of the Houses of York and Lancaster suited Shakespeare's need to achieve a dramatic unity. Halle's declared purpose was to show how the turmoil following the forced abdication of Richard II and his subsequent murder had issued in the God-approved and God-directed union of the Houses of York and Lancaster under the Tudor King Henry VII. Shakespeare adopted Halle's moral pattern for his tetralogy.

Whether he did so for more than dramaturgical reasons, it is interesting that in his histories Shakespeare more often discerned the direction of God than of the more pagan alternative of Fortune. Nonetheless, he did not ignore the influence of the stars, which occupies a ground between pagan and Christian concepts. Bedford's first speech in *1 Henry VI* blames the heavens for Henry V's death:

> Comets, importing change of times and states,
> Brandish your crystal tresses in the sky,
> And with them scourge the bad revolting stars
> That have consented unto Henry's death!
> (I, i, 2–5)

Talbot once accuses "malignant and ill-boding stars" of responsibility for the desperate situation of his forces and of himself, their general. Even thus early in his career, in dealing with serious issues of life Shakespeare always asserts or assumes the existence of a force which is more powerful than those of any man or group of men and which holds poor mortals completely under its control, whether it be called Providence, the heavens, or Fortune. This is his major metaphysical conception and it introduces a touch of pessimism into all his thoughtful treatments of the graver issues of life.

In *2 Henry VI* Shakespeare reveals social attitudes that prevail throughout nearly all his later plays. His treatment of Cade's rebellion reveals his view of the lower classes and first betrays his characteristic lack of interest in social evils of any sort. To him Cade and his followers are a disorganized mob of yokels with no idea of the nature of the abuses for which they were seeking redress or of the reforms they are demanding. This muddle-headedness he presents as comic. Yet he has enough amused understanding of the people to make his ridicule of their stupidity free from malice. This attitude toward them persisted throughout his work, except for his treatment of the crowd in *Julius Caesar* and *Coriolanus*.

It is significant for Shakespeare's development as a dramatist that many of the most theatrically effective scenes in *1 Henry VI* are unhistorical: for example the Robin Hood-like episode of Talbot and the Duchess of Auvergne (II, ii, 34–60) and the scene in the Temple Garden (II, iv) in which a representative of each of the two warring factions plucks a rose, one red, the other white—symbols of their antagonism. Shakespeare here begins to display his genius in converting history or legend into striking scenes, a facility we shall see illustrated in detail in *Richard III*. The lessons he was learning as an actor in a producing organization began to be invaluable to an apprentice dramatist.

In adapting chronicle material to the demands of "theatre" in the plays of the tetralogy, Shakespeare invented scenes of striking detail for the plot or the characters. Whitaker enumerates some characteristic examples of this transformation. In *Richard III*, for example, the scene in which Richard appears in religious exercise between two bishops (III, vii) is based on a phrase in Halle's chronicle. The ghosts who appear to Richard and Richmond before the battle of Bosworth Field are derived from Holinshed's remark that Richard's excuse for his low spirits had been a dream of being "pulled and haled by devils." And Richard's famous cry for a horse was suggested by a mere prosaic statement in Holinshed that some of his soldiers had brought him a horse on which to flee after his possible defeat. Shakespeare clearly had developed an actor's eye for theatrical scenes.

3 Henry VI is largely devoted to the development of Richard of Gloucester until at the end of the play he emerges as the melodramatic villain who is to dominate the action of *Richard III*. The influence of Marlowe upon Shakespeare is first unmistakable in the creation of this villain-hero. The author of the two parts of *Tamburlaine* concentrates our interest on a single dominating character, a warrior who aspires to more power and greater eminence than fate has in store for him. So, when he reaches the top of his achievement, he falls precipitously. Mortimer in Marlowe's *Edward II* describes the fate of such an overreaching aspirant for power and fame as one bound to Fortune's wheel:

> There is a point to which, when they aspire,
> They tumble headlong down.
> (V, vi, 60–61)

Shakespeare, following Marlowe's lead, converts the many scattered events dramatized in the last phases of the Wars of the Roses into Richard's deeds. Shakespeare usually saw history in terms of human character, rather than in those of political forces or political intrigues.

He also learned from Marlowe how to make blank verse an effective expression of dramatic value. *Gorboduc* (1561), the first English tragedy written in that verse form, established it as the obligatory medium for translations of Seneca and for plays written in his manner. The blank verse of these early dramas seldom escaped sounding a mechanical iambic beat. Marlowe's strong flood of emotion relieved the monotony by substituting for its stiff regularity the natural rhythms of excited speech.

The declamatory, formalized verse of *2* and *3 Henry VI* and *Richard III*, different in kind from that Shakespeare had before written, is obviously his successful imitation of Marlowe's mighty line. However, he varied its music with many of the rhetorical figures with which he had already decorated his style and also with tirades, aphorisms, and antiphonal laments like those in Seneca and his Tudor imitators.

The poet also endowed Richard with many characteristics of the so-called Machiavellian villain. At the end of a long soliloquy in *3 Henry VI*, he exclaims:

> I'll play the orator as well as Nestor,
> Deceive more slily than Ulysses could,
> And, like a Sinon, take another Troy.
> I can add colours to the chameleon,
> Change shapes with Proteus for advantages,
> And set the murderous Machiavel to school.
> (III, ii, 188–193)

This passage, characteristically overcharged with classical references and others of similar import, proves that the playwright possessed some knowledge of the subversive moral principles that the Elizabethans believed that Machiavelli had enunciated in *Il Principe* (*The Prince*, written 1513–1517). When we realize that Richard also has in his nature many characteristics of the Vice Dissimulation of the morality plays, we begin to understand why Richard of Gloucester has come to be regarded as the prototype of all subsequent villains in English melodrama, and the play as the dramatist's first masterpiece—one that through the years has continued to be a favorite of actors and audiences. No play of mere violence and bloodletting could have attained to this eminence among the great dramatic tragedies of the Western world. Its excellencies are numerous. It is the first of Shakespeare's dramas to display a moral architecture. It teaches the first of the political lessons that Shakespeare saw latent in the historical events he had ordered into a play: Civil discord shakes a nation into chaos and inevitably raises a tyrant to supreme power. This pronouncement leads to another of more general significance: Long addiction to evil disorders the criminal's judgment and paralyzes his will. Richard's final soliloquy brings home the stern lesson of his career: God promises that sins will be punished and that tyrants, like Gloucester, will be doomed and damned.

Two Italianate Comedies. After writing his four plays on a stormy period in English history, Shakespeare turned once more to farce (if we may assume that *The Taming of the Shrew* was his next play). He may have adapted a contemporary play called *The Taming of A Shrew* (see THE TAMING OF THE SHREW: *Sources*); but the theme was widespread in folk tales. This time the playwright found his model, not in the Roman comedies that he knew from school, but in Italian comedies of his own time. From these he borrowed the Italianate servants: Tranio, a quick-witted companion for his master and a bold, ingenious plotter in his behalf, and Grumio, his slow-witted fellow. This contrast of a clever and a dull servant would be a source of much mirth also in Shakespeare's later comedies. Gremio, Bianca's rich but senile lover, has been a figure of fun from the days of Roman comedy to the present.

Bianca, the second of the three amorosas, has the usual three suitors of Italian comedy: Lucentio and Hortensio, genuine amorosos, and Gremio. Here, however, Shakespeare elaborated on the form, seizing the opportunity to introduce in the three methods of wooing adopted by the two young gentlemen and Petruchio (III, i) one of those artificial balances found in Lyly's novels and comedies. Lucentio woos under cover of parsing a passage from Vergil in the approved grammar school fashion, Hortensio woos by way of music, Petruchio by a strong display of masculine force.

Shakespeare makes every effort to immerse the action of this comedy in an authentic Italian atmosphere. Gregor Sarrazini believes that the dramatist shows so much more accurate, detached knowledge of northern Italy, of Padua and Mantua, in this play and, in later works, of Verona and Venice, than he could have learned from books of travelers or from their own mouths, that during his so-called lost years he must have traveled in northern Italy. See ITALY IN THE PLAYS.

Petruchio and Hortensio exchange greetings in Italian. The former addresses the latter as follows: "*Con tutto il cuore, ben trovato,*" and Hortensio replies, "*Alla nostra casa ben venuto, molto honorato signor mio Petruchio.*" These are phrases that would appear near the beginning of any handbook for learning Italian. A. L. Rowse states categorically that the poet found these phrases in Claude Desainliens' handbook for learning Italian and French entitled *Campo di Fior* (1583), printed by Richard Field, Shakespeare's Stratford friend who had become an important London printer, issuing, among other significant works, *Venus and Adonis*. During his first years in London, Shakespeare was evidently seeking through reading to supplement the small knowledge of contemporary thought and letters that he gained in school.

Once again, however, he added something of his own to a familiar model. In the many fabliaux dealing with ways of taming shrewish wives, the farcical violence of the two principals is left unexplained. Shakespeare took pains to account for it, and thus turned puppets into human beings. The girl's fury he showed to be a natural result of her envy of Bianca's power to attract men and of her resentment at her father's obvious preference for her sister. Petruchio's wild coercion of his bride is only his stormy method of attracting her by making a show of his virility. The playwright was beginning to find it interesting to convert even his low-comedy figures into recognizable men and women.

The Two Gentlemen of Verona, probably written before the theatres were closed by the plague during most of the years 1592 and 1593, marks a new direction in Shakespeare's comic art. It is a romantic comedy of gentle manners and cultivated emotions. We can only guess how he became acquainted with the codes of conduct of the world of fashion. He may have met and attracted some of the young lordlings who, like the earl of Southampton, frequented the theatres. Or he may have had a chance to observe the polished manners of the gentry when his company visited the great houses of aristocrats like that of the earl of Pembroke and his cultivated countess. Or he may have learned all that he needed to know about courtiers and their manners from his reading of Lyly's novels and plays.

The comedy breaks sharply with the techniques of his school pieces. He employs but few topics of invention. When he does, they are appropriate to the situation and the character speaking. Queen Margaret's amplification of the metaphor of the sea and shipwreck in *3 Henry VI* was a sheer independent tour de force. Julia's extended comparison of her love to the current of a stream is as obvious a figure of amplification, but it possesses many dramatic and poetic values absent from the earlier example:

The current that with gentle murmur glides,
Thou know'st, being stopp'd, impatiently doth
rage;
But when his fair course is not hindered,
He makes sweet music with the enamell'd stones,
Giving a gentle kiss to every sedge
He overtaketh in his pilgrimage,
And so by many winding nooks he strays
With willing sport to the wild ocean.
Then let me go and hinder not my course:
I'll be as patient as a gentle stream
And make a pastime of each weary step,
Till the last step have brought me to my love;
And there I'll rest, as after much turmoil
A blessed soul doth in Elysium.
(II, vii, 25–38)

These lines have the grace and the sweet intensity of a girl's confession of love. It is also a characterization of the pathetically devoted creature that Julia has become. The wooden parallel structure of much of the verse in *The Comedy of Errors* becomes in one of Valentine's speeches a burst of lyrical beauty:

Except I be by Silvia in the night,
There is no music in the nightingale;
Unless I look on Silvia in the day,
There is no day for me to look upon.
(III, i, 178–181)

The song "Who is Silvia? What is she?"—familiar in Schubert's setting to the entire Western world—in its context seems to make Julia, who hears it sung to a rival, utterly forlorn.

The contrasted servants of Italianate comedy are here more sharply differentiated than in *The Taming of the Shrew*, and their "business" more fully developed. Speed's comic business is the torrent of words that he pours from his mouth in breathless hurry. Launce continues partly to rely on the time-honored stupidities of the slow-witted servant, for example, mistaking a word for another of simila sound. His long, often coarse monologues are comic routines, like the *lazzi* of the clown in the *commedia dell' arte*. The most famous of these, his monologue as he fondles his dog Crab, is the authentic coarse talk of an English bumpkin devoted to his ill-trained cur. The passage, precious for its discovery of a new fund of the dramatist's humor, derived from the vocabulary and the exactly imitated speech rhythms of a low-class dolt.

The theme of the play is the superiority of friendship to love and the struggle between the authority of each. Just why Shakespeare chose to treat thi subject at this stage of his career we can only guess It is possible that his ardent friendship with th youthful lord that he celebrates in his sonnets may have led him to glorify the emotion dramatically The ideal friendship demanding the sacrifice of lov at its altar is an old medieval theme. Many gentleme of Elizabethan England paid allegiance to this cult o friendship, which had been given new life in th Renaissance. It had scriptural sanction in the love o David and Jonathan. Richard Edwards, in his affect ing play *Damon and Pythias* (1565, pub. 1571), gav the subject wide currency. And John Lyly, in hi *Euphues: The Anatomy of Wit* (1578), paid it ex travagant tribute, ranking it far above love. H writes, "The love of man to woman is a thing com mon and of course; the friendship of men is infinit and immortal," and much more to the same effec Lyly may have influenced Shakespeare's choice o theme in this comedy as much as he did its style. Se TWO GENTLEMEN OF VERONA: *Comment*.

Male friendship seems the more profound if lov between the sexes is seen as trivial. Love in comed before *Two Gentlemen of Verona* had almost un formly been treated as foolish and courtship as ab surd. Lyly, in all his plays except *Midas*, mocked a love and ridiculed doting lovers. Shakespeare fo lowed his lead to the extent of making Valentine worship of Silvia silly. He put flowers of rhetoric a the service of such a lover. Valentine, in describin Silvia's beauty to Proteus, indulges in what Proteu stigmatizes as "braggardism." The lady has to hol up the train of her dress

lest the base earth
Should from her vesture chance to steal a kiss

And, of so great a favour growing proud,
Disdain to root the summer-swelling flower
And make rough winter everlastingly.
(II, iv, 159–163)

Many of the situations and devices first employed ı *The Two Gentlemen* Shakespeare develops into ome of the most successful incidents of his later lays. Julia's discussion of her suitors with her lady ı waiting, Lucetta, serves as a model for the diaogue between Portia and Nerissa on the same subect in *The Merchant of Venice* (I, ii, 1–133). Valenine's rope ladder and Silvia's pretext of going for onfession at a friar's cell is repeated in *Romeo and uliet*. Valentine's lament at his banishment is a foreaste of Romeo's frantic complaint to the Friar at his anishment from Verona (III, iii, 29–51). And peed's listing of the special marks of a lover (II, i, 8–34) is like Rosalind's similarly satiric list of the ıfallible marks of a lover that her uncle has taught er to recognize (*As You Like It*, III, ii, 392–404). 'alentine's flight to the forest and his encounter with he friendly outlaws is like the escape of the charcters in *As You Like It* to the hospitality of Arden; : reflects the spirit of the Robin Hood ballads.

Prized more for its promise than for any substanial achievement, Shakespeare's first romantic comedy olds within the bounds of its simple structure poentialities that the poet was to develop into some of he brightest displays of his genius.

The Poems. The closing of the theatres because of he prevalence of the plague during the years 1592 nd 1593 interrupted Shakespeare's career as an actorramatist and presented him with both the leisure nd the necessity to apply his gifts to other forms. lthough a poet's career entailed practical risks, then s now, the young poet must have welcomed the hange in one respect, for he shared the common iew that writing poetry was a higher form of acivity than turning out plays for the public theatres. n Sonnet 111 he would later bid his friend

with Fortune chide,
. . . . .
That did not better for my life provide
Than public means which public manners breeds.
Thence comes it that my name receives a brand,
And almost thence my nature is subdued
To what it works in, like the dyer's hand.

'here is little doubt for which achievement he ished to be remembered: the preservation of the lays is owed to the efforts of others, the poems hakespeare seems to have seen through the press imself.

Poets like Spenser and Marlowe were achieving iccess with long poems on themes of classical myhology, modeled in part on the idyls of the Alexanrian poets. Shakespeare emulated them in the style nd form of his first poem, as well as in his choice of story from Ovid—a choice well adapted to the rotic but refined tastes of the nobility, on whose atronage every poet had to depend. He told the ale of the amorous goddess Venus spurned by the andsome Adonis, who is repelled by her importuate advances. The young poet made the most of the pportunities the story afforded for sensuous decription; but, like a true dramatist, he expressed the youth's repudiation of lust with as much persuasive sympathy as he did the goddess's urging of it. Like a dramatist, too, he could describe at length such a scene as a stallion's pursuit of a mare so that it became not merely a digression extended and elaborated for its own sake, in the fashion of the idyl, but an incident that adds to the emotional impact of the whole poem.

Douglas Bush describes *Venus and Adonis* as the creation of a "Renaissance Ovid." He means, one must suppose, that the poem is merely an ornate retelling of a classical myth. Other critics, however, believe that Shakespeare had something important to say in the work. Lu Emily Pearson, in her *Elizabethan Love Conventions* (1933), explains that *Venus and Adonis* emphasizes the contrast between sacred and profane love. Venus represents naked passion that destroys all that it touches, while Adonis represents chaste love—reason in love. A more acceptable view is that Adonis represents, rather, the inseparable union of love with beauty. As in the Sonnets, here Shakespeare assumes that beauty must be forever recreated. Venus is the stimulus for that re-creation through the propagation of offspring. That is the only way of preserving beauty in all the forms of nature. The sexual impulse is therefore of so great importance in the universal scheme of life that Venus is justified in being crassly, almost brutally, insistent on having her way with Adonis. Though to a modern reader this interpretation may seem overingenious, it would not have seemed so to an adept in the Platonic doctrine of love. When Adonis dies with Venus' desire unsatisfied, with him will go beauty and love, and chaos will come again.

To judge from the dedication of his next poem, Shakespeare's suit for noble patronage was successful. He addressed the new work, as he had *Venus and Adonis*, to the young earl of Southampton in fulfillment of his promise in the earlier dedication to produce "some graver labour." *The Rape of Lucrece* is indeed graver, and a great deal longer, but its more ambitious purpose is not fully achieved. The poet had learned the light touch appropriate to the comedy of love, but, at the age of 29, he did not yet have the maturity to sustain an elevated passion throughout so extended a work. His tragic sense was still attuned to the horrors and the uncomplicated opposition of evil and virtue characteristic of the Senecan melodrama of his *Titus Andronicus*. Indeed, there are so many parallels between this play and the poems that some scholars have argued that *Titus* must have been written at about the same time as the poems.

The charge of wantonness that had been leveled against *Venus and Adonis* was not repeated against *Lucrece*, a glorification of chastity. Gabriel Harvey explained the universal commendation of this second poem by writing, "The younger sort take much delight in Shakespeares Venus, and Adonis: but his Lucrece, & his tragedie of Hamlet . . . have it in them to please the wiser sort."

Vestiges of a dramatic structure are vaguely discernible beneath the rhetorical decoration of the poem. It depicts the disastrous fall of a slave of passion. Tarquin is of the family of tyrants who served as villain-protagonists in typical Senecan melodramas and their English imitations. To satisfy his lust, he risks and loses everything—position, honor, and fame—and gains only disgust and despair. Lucrece is the tyrant's helpless victim, who awakens the same sort of pity as does Desdemona.

In this second poem Shakespeare has lost none of that delight in rhetoric which he had displayed in *Venus and Adonis*. The course of the story is continually interrupted by long rhetorical or decorative passages. After the rape has been committed, Lucrece compares herself to Hecuba, which gives her a chance to paint, in 200 lines (1368–1569), an elaborate picture of the siege of Troy. She expresses her grief and despair not directly but by ingenious conceits and labored imaginative expressions.

Nonetheless, the poem is not without fine passages. The most powerful section is the protracted scene in which the heroine inveighs against Opportunity and apostrophizes Time. Here the poet, freed of the requirement that action in the theatre must not remain long suspended, is able to exploit to its fullest potential a rhetorical device that he had used less effectively in *Titus Andronicus* and would use again in his next two history plays, *King John* and *Richard II*. The poem's real beauty lies in the music of sorrow sung in many modes:

For sorrow, like a heavy-hanging bell,
Once set on ringing, with its own weight goes.
(1493–1494)

It is the incessant tolling of this bell behind all the tortuous ingenuity of thought and language that gives the poem its occasional power and beauty.

The Sonnets. The period during which Shakespeare wrote his Sonnets is too uncertain to make any close connection between their composition and the poet's other activities beyond pointing to affinities with some of the earlier plays, *Love's Labour's Lost* in particular, in which are imbedded seven actual sonnets. It reveals more of Shakespeare's development as an artist to compare his Sonnets with those of his contemporaries. Beginning with Sir Philip Sidney, whose *Astrophel and Stella* started the sonnet-making vogue in 1591, most Elizabethan poets adopted the form of the Italian sonnet, immortalized by Petrarch, which lent itself to the display of verbal virtuosity. Shakespeare, however, preferred a variation popularized by Henry Howard, earl of Surrey. In permitting seven rhymes instead of only five it gave the poet greater freedom.

Like his contemporaries, Shakespeare delighted in elaborate conceits and in word plays such as the manifold pun on his name in Sonnets 135 and 136. Although this preoccupation with verbal effects was more acceptable to his contemporaries than it is to modern readers, it sometimes worked to the detriment of the poems, for Shakespeare tended to be impatient of the technical discipline required to make these effects come off. If the modesty of his sonnets on the Rival Poet can be taken as genuine, he was aware of his technical deficiencies. His "tongue-tied Muse" would hold still, he declared in Sonnet 85,

And like unletter'd clerk still cry "Amen"
To every hymn that able spirit affords
In polish'd form of well-refined pen.

He asserted, however, "I think good thoughts whilst other write good words," and promised in Sonnet 82 "when they have devised / What strained touches rhetoric can lend," to portray his friend "in true plain words." To whatever degree the poet may here have been trying to convert a recognized failing into a virtue, it is certainly true that "plain words" were among Shakespeare's most striking contributions to the sonnet. He revitalized the form in other significant ways as well, broadening its range of subject matter and deepening its range of feeling. He addressed his first 126 sonnets to a young man, and 2[illegible] of the last 28 to a woman. And this woman is far from the unapproachable lady of the Italian convention. Her face is foul, her body "the wide world's common place." She betrays the poet with his dearest friend. His only consolation is "that she who makes me sin awards me pain."

One of the most striking features of the Sonnets is the poet's use of the language of love and of passion when addressing his Friend. This fact has led many critics to suspect that his feelings for the youth were homosexual (see HOMOSEXUALITY). However, these critics have neglected to weigh the fervent allegiance Renaissance gentlemen paid to the cult of male friendship. It became a symbol of the mystical union of the soul with God. All this explains the poet's eagerness to describe his feelings for the young lord, which he calls "dear religious love," and his willingness to express it in the vocabulary usually employed only for man's love of woman.

M. M. Reese, among other critics, has pointed out that "love" in the poetry of Renaissance authors was "often the symbol for their passionate apprehension of beauty . . . Beauty fades, but must be born again." Shakespeare expresses this conception succinctly in the first two lines of his first sonnet:

From fairest creatures we desire increase,
That thereby beauty's rose might never die.

So throughout the sequence he makes war upon "this bloody tyrant time," the "ceaseless lackey to Eternity." Mark Van Doren has written that "in so far as the sequence has unity, it is organized about the theme of 'Time's decay' . . . of Beauty moving to the ultimate decay. Its leitmotif is the 'ravages of Time, swift-footed, terrible Time.'" The poet delights in any form of generation—that of a flower no less than that of a "lovely boy." For he saw that the end of each of these forms was the creation of new beauty. These threads of mutability, of beauty in the making, of plenitude, and of immortality, interwoven with the themes of individual sonnets, create and sustain the rich texture of the sequence.

Having become fully attuned to the play and counterplay of the themes announced and developed in the sequence, the sensitive reader begins to realize that enveloping the Sonnets is an atmosphere created by the beauty and variety of the world in which every idea expressed in the series is born and every incident in the *drame à trois* is sustained. The poet ranges from the trivial to the ineffable, from the "careful housewife" who, while pursuing a runaway chicken, leaves behind her crying babe, to the roar of the waves of the sea as they surge upon a pebbled beach, or to the cosmic sense of "the wide world dreaming on things to come." These individual nemes united to create a sonnet sequence that in its each and intensity transcends all other lyrics, great nd small, of the Elizabethan age.

Love's Labour's Lost. Shakespeare continued to iden the scope of his reading and to extend the ange of his interests, particularly during the plague ears 1592–1594, while he was writing his poems. The esults of this process of self-education were almost once apparent in his plays when he was again able turn to the theatre. Their traces are evident in *ove's Labour's Lost*, completed before the end of 594. The academy established in the play by erdinand, King of Navarre, seems to have been inpired by a description of a similar group founded y Henry III of France in the 16th century.

Accounts of the goings-on at a French court learly fascinated the poet and he recaptured their pirit in a play that he probably wrote for a private udience that included members of the nobility. Once again using the repartee of the characters in ohn Lyly's novels and his comedies as a model, he lled the verbal exchanges of the guests with their osts at Nérac with the speed and charm of his own it. However, he never became so deeply involved the delight that his characters take in their exuerant cleverness as not to see the affectation and stentation in their self-conscious conversation.

The low-comedy figures and their ridiculous play f the Nine Worthies form an antimasque to the nasquelike occupations of the gentry with their singg, dancing, and disguising. In these farcical figures hakespeare seems to make fun of his own tendency the earlier plays to overcharge his dialogue with e rhetorical figures he had been taught to use at chool. Holofernes, the pedant, is a pretentious and norant instructor of the arts of rhetoric. The topic at he and others of his kind thought the most imortant was invention, which enabled a school boy introduce into his prose as many flowers of rhetric as he could pluck from his mind. Of equal nportance with this injunction was a veneration for Ovid, who in his *Metamorphoses* illustrated many of e felicities of composition. All these points are avestied in Holofernes' speeches. He boasts to Nathaniel that his pedantry "is a gift that I have, mple, simple; a foolish extravagant spirit, full of orms, figures, shapes, objects, ideas, apprehensions, otions, revolutions..." (IV, ii, 67–70). His emptyeaded praise of Ovid is another of the author's hits the absurdity of much of the instruction of rhetric he received at school. Holofernes pontificates: .. for the elegancy, facility, and golden cadence of oesy, caret. Ovidius Naso was the man: and why, ndeed, Naso, but for smelling out the odoriferous owers of fancy, the jerks of invention? Imitari is othing" (IV, ii, 125–130).

In some important respects the comedy marks hakespeare's emancipation from some of the exavagancies and pedantries of his earlier style.

Since Shakespeare wrote *Love's Labour's Lost* at bout the same time that he was at work on his sonets and his other poems, he found it possible to ansfer some of his new-found poetic versatility to is play, which is the most uniformly lyrical of all is comedies.

The drama contains another significant relationship to the sonnets. G. L. Kittredge long ago suggested that there is some connection between Rosaline of the play and the Dark Lady of the sonnets. Indeed, the resemblances are so close that each might serve as a portrait of the same maid of honor. The girls are alike in being brunettes and morally loose. Berowne describes Rosaline as

> A wightly wanton with a velvet brow,
> With two pitch-balls stuck in her face for eyes;
> Ay, and, by heaven, one that will do the deed
> Though Argus were her eunuch and her guard.
> (III, i, 198–201)

The play contains many other allusions to Rosaline's easy virtue, as in the following exchange between Rosaline and Katharine:

> *Ros.* Look, what you do, you do it still i' the dark.
> *Kath.* So do not you, for you are a light [unchaste] wench.
> (V, ii, 24–25)

Berowne describes Cupid as:

> Dread prince of plackets, king of codpieces,
> Sole imperator and great general
> Of trotting 'paritors...
> (III, i, 186–188)

A paritor, in this context a pimp, was the summoning officer of an ecclesiastical court. So Cupid, in becoming the summoning officer of a court of love, becomes a pimp. This function of the god of love is an appropriate assignment for one of the disillusioned suitors of the giddy Rosaline to make. Rosaline is the first, and perhaps the only, character in all the plays who with any warrant can be thought to be a likeness of a living person in Shakespeare's milieu.

The comedy contains more bawdry and more sustained sly obscenity than almost any other of the poet's plays. The conversation of Boyet with the three ladies, in the course of which he and Rosaline sing a suggestive song (IV, i, 120–142), is so lewd that Maria interrupts the fine flow of their dirty wit, protesting, "Come, come, you talk greasily; your lips grow foul." We may guess that in giving bawdry free play he was truckling to what he had heard was the preoccupation and the taste of Queen Elizabeth's entourage.

In this play the young dramatist reveals his sensitivity to the charm of a cultivated society such as he half-imagined it to be and half-knew it from his acquaintance with young aristocrats such as the earl of Southampton.

King John. The precise order in which Shakespeare composed his next four plays is far from certain. Even if that order were known, it would hardly make the course of the poet's artistic growth the easier to trace, for these plays are extraordinarily various. *Romeo and Juliet* is a lyrical tragedy; *A Midsummer Night's Dream* is a romantic comedy; *King John* and *Richard II*, though both history plays, are so different in kind and quality that it is hard to believe that they were written at the same stage of the author's career. As extraordinary as the variety of these plays, however, is the manner in which the lyrical impulse that had filled *Love's Labour's Lost* with music continues unabated (except in *King John*) through such basically different dramatic forms.

Shakespeare had been so successful with his tetralogy of history plays, finished not long before the temporary closing of the London theatres during the plague, that it was natural for him to return to this profitable medium. He apparently thought it unwise to take up the story of English monarchs where he had left it, with Henry VII's seizure of the throne. Such a continuation would have carried him dangerously close to the queen's immediate ancestors and their controversial policies. He therefore turned to the reigns of John and Richard II, so far into England's medieval past that, in spite of certain parallels with contemporary events, they might seem politically unexceptionable as dramatic material. In point of historical chronology, though not necessarily of date of composition, *King John* was the earlier of the two histories. Besides being safe subject matter, John's reign offered positive advantages to the author. By toning down the extremely anti-Catholic temper of the anonymous play *The Troublesome Raigne of John, King of England,* his principal source, he could prove both to his predominantly Protestant audience and to the Catholic earl of Southampton, whose favor he was courting, that he could write a play on a religious subject and maintain a judicious attitude toward the conflict. This was like the nonsectarian judicial attitude of the queen toward religion. But a more compelling reason for his choice of John's reign was the opportunity to dramatize its events in a way that would make them serve as a favorable commentary on the politico-religious struggle in which Queen Elizabeth was constantly involved. The king's denial of the papal legate's authority to question his reasons for preventing Stephen Langton from occupying the archbishop's see had led to his excommunication. This would call to mind the papal bull of 1569 excommunicating Elizabeth and so aiding the joint papal and French support of Mary Stuart's efforts to supplant Elizabeth on the throne. Yet John's eagerness to accomplish Prince Arthur's death would recall in flattering contrast the queen's reluctance to send Mary to the block.

The Bastard's great speech on commodity (expediency; II, i, 561–598) would remind his audience of King Henry IV of France's justification of his conversion to Catholicism as necessary political expediency. These examples show that the dramatist for the nonce had adopted the official conception of history as a mirror of contemporary policy.

Shakespeare uses the historical material to develop two strains of interest. His first concern is with the King's defense of his throne against the united forces of the Catholic powers of Philip, King of France, and the Duke of Austria. Avoiding the historic, but essentially undramatic, issue of John's weak title to the kingship, he makes his second strain of interest the King's bad character. In this phase of his plot Shakespeare betrayed his lack of interest in history as an accurate record of the past; only those events attracted him that he could transform into effective theatre.

In pursuit of this end the dramatist in several scenes substituted striking theatre for the logic of history. John's reasons for blinding the young Prince Arthur, plausibly explained in *The Troublesom Raigne,* are entirely omitted in *King John,* as ar those of the monk for poisoning the King and th circumstances in which the deed was accomplishe In the first instance, the shock to the audience whe Hubert appears with hot irons to burn out the boy eyes may add to the dramatic impact, but it mak the lad's entreaties seem an almost mawkish appe for tears. In the second case, the playwright devot all his attention to John's pain-racked death. T emphasize its horror, he draws upon his store Senecan imagery, of which he never again mak such ample use. We are told how the bowels of th "resolved" monk, who served as the King's taste "suddenly burst out" (V, vi, 29–30). The King i his death agony employs the same sort of repulsi language figuratively, crying:

> There is so hot a summer in my bosom,
> That all my bowels crumble up to dust.
> (V, vii, 30–31)

And he continues,

> And none of you will bid the winter come
> To thrust his icy fingers in my maw.
> (*Ibid.,* 36–37)

Shakespeare had demonstrated in his first historic play, *1 Henry VI,* his capacity to depict the issues history in theatrically effective scenes. In *King Jol* he carried this practice to an extreme, with the resu that dramatic importance attaches, not to John th usurper, but to John the unstable man. The pl makes no clear comment on the King's inability face, much less to solve, problems of statecraft, fo eign and domestic.

King John is a transitional play, marking a pau in Shakespeare's development. In it he refurbish some of his now familiar rhetorical artifices, his dr matic devices, and his character types. In the proce he extended their scope at the same time that adapted them more effectively to the larger plan the drama. In some instances, notably that of th scoffing commenter, the Bastard, he carried them the highest possible pitch of their development.

The extent to which the play looks both forwa and back in the course of its author's development strikingly shown in two nearly consecutive speech of Constance, Arthur's mother, in the fourth scene Act III. After Arthur leaps from the wall of h castle prison only to dash himself to pieces on t stones below, Constance adds to the pathos of th boy's fate by uttering a mad diatribe against Deat a rhetorical figure that the poet had developed length in Lucrece's invective against Opportunity *The Rape of Lucrece.* Constance's invective is fill with macabre properties of the graveyard, linki her grief to horror, to death and dissolution:

> Death, death; O amiable lovely death!
> Thou odoriferous stench! sound rottenness!
> Arise forth from the couch of lasting night,
> Thou hate and terror to prosperity,
> And I will kiss thy detestable bones
> And put my eyeballs in thy vaulty brows.
> (III, iv, 25–30)

This passage is undiluted rhetoric, in the mazes which sincere emotion is lost. Later in this sce however, Constance utters another lament. Dominated by a simple figure, it expresses moving grief:

> Grief fills the room up of my absent child,
> Lies in his bed, walks up and down with me,
> Puts on his pretty looks, repeats his words,
> Remembers me of all his gracious parts,
> Stuffs out his vacant garments with his form;
> Then, have I reason to be fond of grief?
> (III, iv, 93–98)

A Lyrical History Play. The differences between *King John* and *Richard II*, written at about the same time, are striking. *Richard II* marks a new development in Shakespeare's art and, indeed, in English tragedy. The catastrophe is caused, not by a villain, not by Fate, not by the pressure of events over which the protagonist has no control, but by a serious flaw in that protagonist's nature. Richard's character is his fate. Absorbed in his own charm and the histrionic felicity of his actions, he lets self-love crowd love for England off the stage on which he is playing his part.

Shakespeare developed with so much originality this tragic protagonist that Richard became only partly tragic. Our attitude toward him is so objective, so near to being satiric, that he arouses none of the Aristotelian terror and only a little pity.

In creating his first tragic protagonist whose character precipitates his catastrophe, Shakespeare uncovered a rich vein of original material. It is not surprising that he was unable to exploit it to fullest effect. *Richard II* is only a partly successful representation of this type of tragedy. The lessons he learned from it, however, helped him to shape triumphantly his later tragic heroes, beginning with the Brutus and Cassius of *Julius Caesar*.

Richard II marks another new development in the poet's composition of his "histories." E. M. W. Tillyard finds detailed evidence in the play of the poet's new knowledge of the customs of chivalry and of his intuitive sensing of its atmosphere. This suggests that, after completing *King John*, he had read extensively in writers on the Middle Ages (see RICHARD II: *Sources*). This saturation of the new play with the spirit of the Middle Ages sets it off from all the rest of Shakespeare's "histories."

The playwright wrote *Richard II* shortly after he had finished his *Venus and Adonis* and *The Rape of Lucrece* and while he was working on his sonnets. By making Richard a frustrated actor and dramatic poet, he was able to fill many of the King's speeches with the lyrical beauty that he had cultivated in his poems. This verse is different in structure and in tone from that of his earlier plays, which derived from Marlowe. It marks, therefore, the end of his imitation of Marlowe's mighty line, of the long sweep of his pentameters.

The poet's preoccupation with poetry and a poetical monarch sometimes works to the disadvantage of the drama. Its charm is individual and particular. Although much happens in the play, the events seem to take place in an atmosphere more congenial to the creation of a mood than to the holding of excited attention of an audience to a page of English history. For the first time in his theatrical career, Shakespeare the poet dominates Shakespeare the playwright.

Romeo and Juliet. It was during this same period that, having achieved considerable success with his chronicle plays and his romantic comedies, Shakespeare tried his hand once more at tragedy, which he had not attempted since his early exercise, *Titus Andronicus*. He did not break all at once with classical tradition. Though *Romeo and Juliet*, like most English dramas of the type written in the late 16th century, is an essentially lyric tragedy, it still retains many characteristics of Senecan tragedy. Fortune plays an important role in precipitating the catastrophe; the fate of the lovers is written in the stars. The Prologue promises that we are to see the tragic end of a "pair of star-crossed lovers," and throughout the action both protagonists express premonitions of the blows of ill-chance. Romeo's mind misgives that

> Some consequence yet hanging in the stars
> Shall bitterly begin his fearful date
> With this night's revels.
> (I, iv, 107–109)

Even the feud between the two families is merely one of the powerful instruments of Fate. Pure chance is responsible for several of the crucial events: Friar John's quarantine and Juliet's too-late wakening, for example.

There is much Senecan horror in *Romeo and Juliet*. Not only does the long final scene take place in a tomb, with the bloody corpse of Tybalt lying nearby—to which three more dead are added before the play ends—but the terrors of the scene are extended through anticipation in Juliet's fears before she drinks the potion, and intensified through Romeo's morbid dwelling upon the worms that are to be "Juliet's chambermaids."

In these respects Shakespeare still depended on his classical models, but the young playwright's developing dramatic powers and his growing knowledge of human nature would not permit him to let his characters be mere pawns of Fate. He knew, like Friar Laurence, that "violent delights have violent ends." It is not only quarrelsome blades like Mercutio and Tybalt who invite their own deaths; the lovers themselves precipitate the final tragedy by their youthful insistence on the immediate gratification of their desires.

If *Romeo and Juliet* still owes much to Seneca, in other respects it seems at first glance merely a continuation of the work the dramatist had been doing shortly before its writing. The first two acts are constructed on the model of *The Two Gentlemen of Verona* and *Love's Labour's Lost*, in which flowers of rhetoric stream from the lips of doting lovers. Romeo's posturing love for Rosaline is portrayed with the same appeal to rhetorical extravagance. His behavior in the first two acts is, moreover, as preposterously extravagant as his speech. Romeo, his father reports, often sits at daybreak in a sycamore grove, "With tears augmenting the fresh morning's dew" (I, i, 138). Later, he

> private in his chamber pens himself,
> Shuts up his windows, locks fair daylight out
> And makes himself an artificial night.
> (I, i, 144–146)

Thus far in the play Shakespeare seems to have adopted the satirical attitude toward love that was characteristic of all English love comedies, including his own, since Lyly. He even includes, in Mercutio, the typical common-sense observer to comment upon the lover's folly. But here again Shakespeare transcends his model and makes the familiar conventions serve higher dramatic ends. Their very familiarity works to his advantage. An Elizabethan audience would have scoffed with Mercutio at Romeo's infatuation with Rosaline and laughed with Friar Laurence at the speed with which he forgets her once he meets Juliet. But Romeo's new love turns out to be, not merely genuine, but stronger than the fear of death itself. Mercutio, the wittiest of the scoffers, is no longer needed to ridicule a doting lover, and becomes a crucially serious figure who, by his own death, precipitates the final tragedy. The audience, forced to revise its expectations and transfer its emotional loyalty, would be the more deeply moved. Similarly, Shakespeare worked into his larger dramatic scheme the stock characters that he adapted from *commedia dell' arte*. The Nurse is a garrulous *balia*, Capulet and Montague conventional examples of the Irate Old Man. As such, they are amusing in their own right. But, as the lovers' plight grows steadily more desperate, their insensitivity and crudeness greatly heighten the pathos of Juliet's complete isolation in the face of impending tragedy.

In a unique way Shakespeare combined characteristics of romantic comedy with three of the traditional elements of tragedy: fate, disorder in society, and a protagonist in whom passion triumphs over reason. If he did not succeed in joining these elements quite seamlessly, he nevertheless gave them a dramatic urgency and a poetic beauty that were an enduring achievement.

A Midsummer Night's Dream. Although *A Midsummer Night's Dream* is a romantic comedy, a form of drama that Shakespeare had earlier tried with considerable success, it would have added little to his stature if the troubles of its two pairs of lovers were all it had to offer. The confusions caused by Puck's mistaking one *amoroso* for another are more ingenious than those of *The Comedy of Errors,* but the sentiments of the lovers and most of the rhymed couplets in which they express them are far from being "the stuff that dreams are made on." Yet *A Midsummer Night's Dream* is one of Shakespeare's most original plays, for in it he invented fairies—or, at least, fairies as the English-speaking world has imagined them ever since. Before the poet made Oberon, Titania, and their fairy band seem as real as they are insubstantial, English fairies were man-sized creatures of folklore who were usually malevolent. These malign and awkward beasts he converted into tiny, gay creatures, companions of butterflies and moonbeams.

Inspired as it was, the creation of a wholly new and dreamlike world peopled with fairies was not Shakespeare's only achievement in *A Midsummer Night's Dream.* His "base mechanicals" were by far the most successful low-comedy characters that he had yet conceived, perhaps because, instead of basing them on stock characters of Roman or Italian comedy, he drew them directly from his own appreciative observation of clumsy village theatricals. The pompous Bottom and his fellow players are as hilariously recognizable today as they were in 1595.

Having created two worlds at opposite extremes—the moonlight and gossamer realm of the fairies an the real and earthbound one of village artisans— Shakespeare ingeniously blended these worlds wit a more conventional one of nobles and aristocrati lovers. The elaborate but unified structure of thi masquelike comedy reveals the easy mastery of com plicated dramatic organization that the playwrigh had acquired. And his lyrical impulse assumed nev and exquisite forms. He created a variety of music all in the same key. The royal pair, Theseus an Hippolyta, speak in dignified formal blank verse The lovers usually address each other in rhyme couplets, showing that their love is never to be fille with deep emotion. The fairies, except when Obero speaks, employ trochaic tetrameter (four-syllable lines that dance. Bottom and his company speak i prose; but when they impersonate Pyramus an Thisbe they use a ballad meter made ridiculous b alliteration and emphatic repetition.

Never before had Shakespeare shown so fully th range of his imagination and his skill in adapting hi art to completely new and strange situations.

The Merchant of Venice. *The Merchant of Venic* probably written in 1596, marks the author's creatio of a more elaborate comedy than he had designe before. Although he wove disparate themes into reasonably coherent plot, as he had in *A Midsumme Night's Dream,* it was his enrichment of the individ ual themes that constituted his new achievement i the play. His treatment of Shylock, though no wholly successful, is nonetheless a striking example o the poet's intellectual growth. Designing him to b the villain of the piece, he modeled him on a typicall melodramatic figure in earlier Tudor drama, o which Barabas in Marlowe's *The Jew of Malta* i the most famous example. But Shakespeare becam interested in his villain as a human being. He at tributed to him a father's affection for his daughte a widower's love of a dead wife, and a yearning fo the austere dignity of his Old Testament forebear and for the respect due an ancient religion. Shake speare gave such power to Shylock's defense in th trial scene that at its end many spectators feel lik the "pale Briton" at a 19th-century performanc whom the poet Heine reported as "weeping pas sionately" and several times exclaiming, "The poo man is wronged!" In thus humanizing Shylock's rol Shakespeare threw the character out of focus, so tha he seems at the end a pathetically defeated old ma instead of a proper villain who deserves the hosti laughter of the spectators. Some critics go so far a to insist that *The Merchant of Venice* is the poet first tragicomedy. Hardin Craig's comment th Shakespeare wrote us one play and we insist o reading another is unfair; the author himself largely to blame for the ambivalent attitudes take by most audiences and readers toward Shyloc Dover Wilson believes that this ambivalence resul from the collision between Shakespeare's "pitile observation" on the one hand, and his understandin and divine compassion on the other.

Shakespeare deepened in a similar fashion the fab of the three caskets, originally an oriental tale illu trating perverse judgment. Without ignoring th chance that it offered for colorful stage display, h attempted to attach symbolic significance to th choice of each suitor. In the expansion of Portia ole he avoided the dangers that beset him in his nlargement of Shylock's. In her he created a new kind of *amorosa*. She is no lovelorn maiden in pursuit of a lover or a husband, no quick-witted participant in a love-game of wit, but a woman of lignity and self-command. Only such a cool, intellectual aristocrat is well cast as a legal expert and as devotee of Christian mercy. Yet she is willing, in act eager, to decline into an ideal Elizabethan wife who commits her wealth and herself to "her lord, er governor, her king."

If Shakespeare did not quite succeed in blending he diverse elements of this play into a unified whole, he changes that he wrought individually on these lements manifest a new depth in his art.

Henry IV and Henry V. The 1590's mark a substantial growth in Shakespeare's knowledge of contemporary political thought and in his interest, particularly, in the cares and duties of a king and the vil of rebellion against his authority. He seems to ave remembered some of the Homilies that he had eard read in church, particularly "An Exhortation Concerning Good Order and Obedience to Rulers nd Magistrates" and the six-part "Homily Against Disobedience and Wilfull Rebellion." This reading ears fruit in both of the Henry IV plays.

Shakespeare's finest achievement in this double rama is the creation of his greatest comic figure, Sir John Falstaff. However, no discovery of the nethods he employed in bringing Falstaff to life and o enumeration of the comic traditions that meet to ive him deathless substance throw any light on the way Shakespeare transformed one of the tavern-aunters in the Prodigal Son morality plays into a omic masterpiece. This remains one of the mysteries f genius. Falstaff may be said to exhibit best Shakespeare's power, at its peak in 1597–1598, of converting facts in the chronicles and figures of traditional tory into living dramatic figures.

Another of the evidences in *1* and *2 Henry IV* of he poet's progress toward artistic maturity is that ere for the first time he attempts to dramatize rowth of character, a triumph that Elizabethan ramatists seldom attempted and almost never chieved. Shakespeare, however, is partially successful in his presentation of the development of a madap prince into a mature military captain. In this ndertaking he makes valuable use of a contrast he raws between Hotspur and Prince Hal. Each represents a different epoch's attitude toward war. Hotspur, a spiritual child of the age of chivalry, regards war, not as an instrument of national policy, but as highway to honor. The extravagance of the metaphors that Shakespeare puts into his mouth shows hat he often goes astray in the mazes of his imagination, and so loses touch with reality. Hal is never bsessed with his delight in his loose companions, for e realizes at every step of his involvement with hem just what he is doing and why. The difference etween these two warriors symbolizes that between he madcap Prince and the master officer into which e develops.

In *2 Henry IV*, Shakespeare reveals for the first me an interest in contemporary social grievances. The scenes in which he describes Falstaff's career as recruiting officer have a double purpose. They reeal new forms of Sir John's comic "business" and serve as an attack on a deplorable evil. In a soliloquy in *1 Henry IV*, Falstaff describes in his devil-may-care fashion how he takes bribes from able-bodied men on the draft list who are loath to go to war; this leaves him with only those recruits who are penniless and poor-spirited. He jocosely admits the fact in a soliloquy:

> . . . I am a soused gurnet. I have misused the king's press damnably. I have got, in exchange of a hundred and fifty soldiers, three hundred and odd pounds . . . . A mad fellow met me on the way and told me I had unloaded all the gibbets and pressed the dead bodies. No eye hath seen such scarecrows.
>
> (*1 Henry IV*, IV, ii, 12–16; 39–42)

In *2 Henry IV* Shakespeare designs a scene in which we see the actual operation of this scandalous misuse of the draft (*2 Henry IV*, III, ii, 259 ff.). It is a new way of making the audience laugh at Falstaff—at his droll way of choosing and drilling his wretched recruits and at his mischievous encouragement of his confederate Justice Shallow's imbecilities. Yet, behind this clowning, Shakespeare makes a direct attack on a cruel injustice in Elizabethan life, the disgraceful treatment of the common soldier. Many pamphlets written in the late 16th century lament the degradation of the professional soldier. Barnabe Rich, for example, in his *Allarme to England* (1578) insists that recruits are chosen at the pleasure and convenience of the local constable (of which Justice Shallow is a type). In London this officer forcibly enlisted soldiers by scouring the prisons of thieves and the streets of rogues and vagabonds. The plight of conscripts returning from campaigns in France or the Low Countries was often desperate. Receiving no pension, they were forced to beg or turn petty thieves. Barnabe Googe (1540–1594) quotes Sir William Drury as saying that these "veterans could look forward to one of three ends of their careers: to be slain, to beg, or to be hanged." Shakespeare attacks this cynical attitude of the pamphleteer toward the common soldier. Falstaff, unconcerned about the fate of his men, announces: "I have led my ragamuffins where they are peppered: there's not three of my hundred and fifty left alive; and they are for the town's end, to beg during life" (*1 Henry IV*, V, iii, 36–40). His response to the Prince's comment on his troops, "I did never see such pitiful rascals," is "Tut, tut; good enough to toss; food for powder, food for powder; they'll fill a pit as well as better: tush, man, mortal men, mortal men" (*1 Henry IV*, IV, ii, 70–73).

These scenes produce a complicated aesthetic reaction. By making Falstaff both the agent and object of his satire, the playwright accomplishes his main purpose, that is, he reduces but does not completely destroy the delight of an audience in his fooling. At the same time he mitigates the severity of the satire in which he is at bottom sincere. In this masterful fashion the author keeps the spirit of the play comic even while insinuating into the laughter strong disapproval of a social scandal.

It is now believed that Shakespeare interrupted his series of history plays after *1* or *2 Henry IV* in order to write *The Merry Wives of Windsor* for a performance during the 1597 Feast of the Garter (see

Date in entry for the play). Writing in a hurry in order to meet a deadline, the playwright had no time in which to invent new characters, so most of them are developments of those in his earlier plays. Some figured in the comic underplots of *Henry IV*, others were stock characters from Italianate comedy that he had used before in other guises.

The central plot is another example of the love story of an *amorosa*, here Anne Page, who has three suitors. Typically, her parents and two foolish suitors are outwitted, and she marries her young lover, Master Fenton, in an elaborate series of deceits planned by Mistress Quickly. Upon this simple plot Shakespeare grafted that of the duping of a philanderer, who gives pious advice about the way to control erotic impulses, but is caught in a stupid attempt to seduce two women at the same time. Doubtless because the Falstaff of *Henry IV* had proved so popular, Shakespeare gave his name to this character and even introduced almost unchanged some of his cronies from the earlier plays: Bardolph, Pistol, and Nym. But the character who has appropriated Falstaff's name is a completely different man. His mind, which in *Henry IV* moved gaily ahead of those who tried to dupe him, is the slowest and dullest in the farce. Detached from the dramatic tradition of the *miles gloriosus* and the tavern-haunter, he here belongs to that of the *pedante* of Italian comedy; he has become a blood brother to Tartuffe—a new portrait in Shakespeare's gallery of frauds—but drawn too hastily to achieve stature in his new role.

Shakespeare was more successful with some of the minor characters in the play. Slender is an original representative of a stock figure in Elizabethan drama, the witless bumpkin. Shallow has brought him to town in the hope that he can be maneuvered into marrying an heiress. The playwright, as often discerning the human being behind the comic type, manages to arouse sympathy for the shy, white-faced rustic's efforts to carry on a conversation with Anne Page—an absurd mixture of childish boasting and bashful self-distrust. Sir Hugh Evans and Dr. Caius represent a development of the dramatist's interest in quaint national traits. Sir Hugh is a relative of the Welshman of *Henry IV;* Dr. Caius is another excitable, wildly gesticulating Frenchman, who happens to be a doctor. Had Shakespeare had ample time to develop this rich variety of characters, *The Merry Wives of Windsor* might have proved to be one of his most delightful comedies. As it stands the play shows the unfortunate results of necessarily hurried composition.

Completing the twice-interrupted tetralogy of history plays begun with *Richard II*, Shakespeare wrote *Henry V* in 1599. Ignoring the technical advances he had made in *Richard II* over the Henry VI plays, he returned to the strictly chronological method that he had adopted in his first histories. Yet the form is appropriate enough in an epic drama like *Henry V*, and in it the poet was able to subordinate the panoply of drum-and-trumpet plays to a serious consideration of the development of an ideal English warrior-king, begun in *1* and *2 Henry IV*. In so doing, he produced a new kind of history play, one that becomes, in large part, a dissertation on the obligations of kingship and the proper conduct of war.

Shakespeare created his ideal epic hero by making Henry the embodiment of all the qualities demande of a king by the familiar Homilies, and by authoriti on government, such as Sir Thomas Elyot. True t the principle that, before involving his nation in wa a monarch should obtain the sanction of its highe religious, as well as civil, authorities, Henry turns f counsel to the Archbishop of Canterbury. As furth evidence of his devout Christian faith, the Kir prays alone before the battle of Agincourt and, ha ing won the victory, cries, "Take it, God, / For it none but thine!" (IV, viii, 116–117). No other ep hero, except Aeneas, is so subservient to divine wi In this, his last history play to be written without collaborator, Shakespeare remained true to that v sion of history governed by the will of God whic he had discerned in his first chronicle play, *1 Hen VI*.

If, as many scholars believe, *Henry V* reflects tl political activity of the earl of Essex in 1599, then it unique among the histories in this concern with tl personal fortunes of a contemporary lord. The pre arations for the King's expedition to France may l imagined as a picture of the excited activity readying the equipment for Essex' ill-fated exped tion to Ireland. Essex, moreover, was then urgir that all the parties and nations that composed Gre Britain form a closely knit union through their c operation in the conduct of a foreign war. In *Hen V* a Welshman, an Irishman, and a Scotsman, thoug each is drawn with his supposed comical idiosyncr sies, all prove as bold as lions in helping to reali Henry's very similar political dream.

Henry V is usually regarded as Shakespeare's fine expression of patriotism, of its inspiration and i obligations. It is implicit in all that the King and h cohorts do and flamingly voiced in his exhortation his troops before Harfleur and on the morning Agincourt. These orations exemplify the rhetoric feature first illustrated in Queen Margaret's addre to her troops before the battle of Tewkesbury *Henry VI*, V, iv, 1–38). But, whereas Margare endless elaboration of a single metaphor was o viously designed to win the admiration of an auc ence trained in rhetoric, Henry's simple eloquen and his appeals to courage ring true. They might w serve to "stiffen the sinews, summon up the bloo (III, i, 1–34).

The prologues in *Henry V* show that the dram tist had become increasingly aware that he could n adequately represent the struggles of masses of m even on his flexible Elizabethan stage. Admitting th his "cockpit" could not "hold the vasty fields France," Shakespeare turned to the composition tragedies in which the struggles took place, not much on battlefields as in the minds and souls of t protagonists.

Julius Caesar. The first such tragedy was *Juli Caesar*, written in the same year (1599) as *Henry* In this play Shakespeare introduced two trag protagonists who meet disaster, each for a differe reason. He had already created in Richard II protagonist who brought down catastrophe on l head through a flaw in his own nature. In *Juli Caesar* the playwright elaborated this theme in t characters of both Brutus and Caesar. He did moreover, with such mature perception of the co plexity of human nature and of the problems political ethics that these two characters have been for centuries subject to a range of interpretation that has varied with the temper of the age. Brutus has been seen, according to the predisposition of his audiences, as a heroic idealist, a hypocritical regicide, or an earnest man who reluctantly makes a wrong moral choice. In *Dr. Faustus* Marlowe had followed the practice of certain late morality plays by externalizing such a conflict as a debate between a good and a bad angel, with a man's soul for the prize. Shakespeare transferred this confrontation to the mind of Brutus, showing glimpses of the battle in some of Brutus' soliloquies. Perhaps the most revealing is the one that he speaks just after deciding that he must kill Caesar. In it he runs over the reasons that have brought him to this conclusion (II, i, 10–34). They are full of fallacies and forced conclusions. Although he acknowledges that he possesses no evidence to suggest that Caesar is sure to become a tyrant, he feels that, if he should ever gain absolute power, he might become a despot. On this shaky moral foundation he builds his determination to commit regicide, thus becoming the architect of the social chaos that the murder precipitates and indirectly inviting the catastrophe that overtakes him. Brutus is thus Shakespeare's first tragic hero who, in spite of a noble nature and a sense of high purpose, is brought low because he makes a wrong moral choice. The self-communings by which he arrives at this choice are a foretaste of the deeper debates soon to trouble the soul of Hamlet—an equally noble hero whose acts, also undertaken through a sense of duty, bring disaster upon himself and the state.

Shakespeare's dramatization of the fall of Caesar, the subsidiary protagonist, was at once conventional and original. The poet was traditional in adopting the pessimistic view, first advanced by the Greeks, that all human life had the same pattern, rising to prosperity and power and then inevitably falling to ruin and death. This was the view of human destiny that proved most popular with medieval and Renaissance writers and was the subject of many tragedies of the 16th and early 17th centuries. But, although Caesar's fall fits this accepted pattern, it resulted, not from the inevitable operation of Fate, but from a fatal weakness in his own nature. Shakespeare's Caesar, like his Brutus, is so full of the contradictions of human nature that he appears to some audiences a portrait of nobility and magnanimity, to others a vainglorious tyrant. Most of the playwright's allusions to Caesar in his other works acknowledge him to be an indomitable conqueror and a great man. In *Julius Caesar*, however, Shakespeare followed a French Renaissance tradition in placing great emphasis on Caesar's arrogant self-assurance. As a result, Caesar appears as one of his deeply flawed tragic heroes.

The two orations delivered at Caesar's funeral show that the poet is no longer an apprentice in the practice of the art of rhetoric. He has become a master in its use. Both speeches are composed of transfigured figures taught in the grammar schools. Brutus' speech is an example of pure *logos*, an appeal to reason. It is appropriately written in simple Attic prose. Antony appeals first to the crowd's belief in his competence for the occasion and his judgment (ethos), but finally only to the crowd's emotions (pathos), revealing at the same time his own overwhelming emotion. He thus expertly manipulates the feeling of his audience until he converts it into a howling mob, determined to wreck, burn, and kill. Thus, by the masterful use of rhetoric Shakespeare creates one of the greatest scenes of mob violence in all literature.

Julius Caesar marks one of the author's greatest steps toward the perfection of his professional skill. It also gives evidence of a new deep realization of the complexity of human nature and of the ambiguity of moral and political justice.

Three Romantic Comedies. During the years at the turn of the century when Shakespeare was designing his last great history play and his first great tragedy, he also wrote three romantic comedies: *Much Ado About Nothing*, *As You Like It*, and *Twelfth Night*, the last two of which are undoubtedly his finest work in that genre. *Much Ado About Nothing* (1598–1599) is the first of what David Stevenson appropriately calls "love-game" comedies. In his copy of the Second Folio, King Charles I inscribed as title for the comedy, *Benedict and Beatrice.* He clearly thought, as do most modern readers, that their story is the most memorable part of the comedy. Their running battle of wit is not an invention new to this play. It is rather a development of the banter of Berowne and Rosaline in *Love's Labour's Lost.* This play in turn had imitated John Lyly's method of making situations of comic drama out of a widespread Renaissance literary controversy between two basic attitudes toward love. These were, on the one hand, the exaggerated concept of love invented by the troubadours that had become the essence of courtly romance and, on the other hand, a skeptical, realistic rejection of the tenets of this religion of love. In this debate the man was usually a devotee, the woman a skeptic. Shakespeare's contribution to this debate was the use of these mocking lovers to satirize outmoded rituals of courtship.

The invention of Dogberry added new luster to Shakespeare's comic art. The humors of the country constable and the headborough are nothing like those of the clowns and yokels previously displayed by the low-comedy actors in Shakespeare's company. These had generally been developments of traditional stereotypes, often Italianate, even when they were transported to the Boar's Head Tavern. Dogberry and his companion Verges have been chosen from the life of rural England. (John Aubrey, in fact, names a constable of Long Crendon, Buckinghamshire, as the lout of whom Dogberry is a portrait.) In creating this pair of noddies, the poet opened wide the door upon the endless variety of Elizabethan life.

Compared with the Beatrice-Benedick subplot, the main plot seems perfunctory and sensational. J. Dover Wilson has suggested that the quarreling lovers became so popular with audiences that the author fattened their parts with new repartee at the expense of the verse of the main plot, which had to be cut proportionately.

As You Like It, probably written in 1600, soon after the completion of *Much Ado About Nothing*, is also basically a love-game comedy. Yet here Shakespeare treats the game both more subtly and more satirically. Orlando and Rosalind are the bantering pair. Orlando exhibits in exaggerated form the extravagant conduct of a romantic lover, hanging love rhymes on trees and carving the name of his Rosalind on their bark. In his verses he endows her with all the charms of the heroines of old: Helen's beauty, Cleopatra's majesty, and Lucretia's modesty. Rosalind's ridicule of these exaggerations is always gay and imaginative: "O most gentle pulpiter! what tedious homily of love have you wearied your parishioners withal!" and "I was never so berhymed since Pythagoras' time, that I was an Irish rat, which I can hardly remember" (III, ii, 163–165, 186–188). Disguised as Ganymede, Rosalind taunts Orlando with his absurdities. He can only answer, a little sheepishly, that neither rhyme nor reason can tell how much he loves her. Her response is that love is only a madness and deserves a whip, as madmen do. But in effect Shakespeare adds a new dimension to the love-game encounter by permitting it to develop (rather more convincingly than in *Much Ado*) into a genuine love affair both humanly sound and romantically satisfying.

Touchstone, one of the agents of satire in this comedy, ridicules the excesses of Orlando, that devoted descendant of enamored knights, with his account of his own strange capers long since, when he was wooing Jane Smile. In the end, however, Touchstone himself is persuaded into marriage with the foul but honest Audrey.

If, in the character of Touchstone, Shakespeare was merely refining some of the witty clowns of his earlier comedies, in Jaques he created a new kind of figure, who was both the agent and the victim of satire. Shakespeare's target was the founders of a contemporary satiric vogue (see AS YOU LIKE IT: *Comment*). Like them, Jaques imagines that he will "Cleanse the foul body of the infected world, / If they will patiently receive my medicine" (II, vii, 60–61), but the playwright shows Jaques' affected satirical attitude to be only ridiculous presumption.

As You Like It, more unified in tone and spirit than *Much Ado About Nothing*, was the poet's first triumph in his newly adopted form of romantic comedy. In *Twelfth Night*, probably his next attempt at the form (1600–1601), he created a comic masterpiece. Evidently thinking that he had exhausted the comic potentialities of the love-game, Shakespeare wrote a straightforward comedy. In this, the last of his pure comedies, he concerned himself less with inventing new devices than with putting old ones to new and richer uses. He returned to his earliest attempt at comedy, *The Comedy of Errors*, to borrow a pair of twins, separated by shipwreck, each unaware of the other's presence in the city. From *The Two Gentlemen of Verona*, his first romantic comedy, he borrowed even more. There, as in *Twelfth Night*, a forlorn girl, disguised as a page, takes service with the man she loves (or comes to love), and is sent to court on his behalf a lady, who straightway falls in love with the girl, imagining her to be a youth. Though in the later comedy poignancy is mixed with humor in the situations that arise from this love imbroglio, Shakespeare revealed a new and rare sympathy with a girl's emotions. This is particularly true of the scene in which the Duke sends Viola to woo Olivia for him and she affirms that she knows "Too well what love women to men may owe." Almost as tender are the scenes in which Olivia betra her love to the Duke's messenger. They are writte in verse that, for sheer loveliness, is nowhere su passed in Shakespeare or any other English poe They stand at the summit of his achievement i lyrical splendor.

Some of Shakespeare's satirical attitude toward th extravagances of chivalric love survives from th love-game comedies. Orsino is trying to feel the lov that the sonneteers celebrated. That emotion is he shown to be aesthetic sensuality: Orsino is not long ing for love, but for prolongation of his desire f excess of it. Olivia, too, is a sentimentalist, in lov with grief. Viola brings, along with the messages sh carries between them, fresh air that stimulates bot Olivia and Orsino to give up their self-absorbe brooding and to return to the world where love not a fever, but a tonic for natural emotions.

In the richly comic underplot of the conflict be tween Sir Toby Belch and his cronies and Malvoli Shakespeare adopted Ben Jonson's method of expo ing fools and knaves. Sir Andrew Aguecheek is fellow to Jonson's gulls, but outdoes them all in she fatuity. Malvolio is much like an Elizabethan humo less bluenose in his intolerance of gaiety, his worsh of propriety, and his itch to bring everyone to h own bigoted way of appraising his fellow men. S Toby resembles Falstaff both in his figure and in h role as a kind of highly localized Lord of Misrul However, instead of being the ruins of a chape going Puritan, he is the remains of a decayed gentl man; he speaks Spanish on one occasion, French c another, and when half-drunk he throws a morsel theological learning at his familiars. Although the were traditional Elizabethan figures of fun, Shak speare stamped each one with an originality th makes their scenes rank with the finest in all lo comedy.

Three "Dark" Comedies. Shakespeare never aga wrote a happy comedy. His next three plays th contain elements of comedy—*All's Well That En Well, Troilus and Cressida, Measure for Measure* are often called, in F. S. Boas' term, "problem plays They do indeed present a problem for the reader playgoer, for he is never sure where the playwrig intended the sympathies of his audience to lie. No of the plays has a hero, only one a female charact whose behavior is unambiguously that of a heroin In all the plays the actions of the supposed hero heroine are motivated by love for a person wh proves to be patently unworthy of such devotio The reader is left with a sense that the author viewing his characters from a distance and with pessimistically ironic, if not cynical, eye. It is hard surprising that none of these "dark" comedies h ever achieved popularity.

Many theories have been advanced to account f the disturbingly pessimistic tone of these play which followed hard upon the happy comedies, *You Like It* and *Twelfth Night*. One frequent heard explanation is that about 1600 Shakespeare b came the victim of depression caused by some pe sonal disappointment or grief: perhaps the infideli of his dark mistress, the failure of Essex' *Putsch*, or severe illness. If one must assume at all that an a thor's work is an accurate reflection of his state mind during its composition, it is safe enough to b lieve that Shakespeare shared the *Weltschmerz* that assailed many thoughtful Elizabethans at the turn of the century. There were many reasons for this widespread depression. The new astronomy called into doubt many cherished traditional beliefs. Men were dismayed to learn that matter above the moon was not, as they had been taught, exempt from corruption. Decay, therefore, permeated every form of life and mutability became the universal lord. Closely related to these concepts was the ominous belief that the earth was nearing its end; for it had all but completed its allotted time of 6000 years and was suffering from the ills of old age. For this reason, all earth's creatures and even the vegetation, lacking their pristine vigor, had become smaller and weaker. These ideas produced in many serious-minded men profound dejection, which Shakespeare may have shared.

A more objective reason for the unhappy spirit of the dark comedies is the strong infusion of satire with which Shakespeare treated the three plays. This critical temper had taken refuge in the drama after the restraining order of June 1, 1599, issued jointly by the archbishop of Canterbury and the bishop of London, which required that "Noe Satyres or Epigrams be printed hereafter" (see Archbishop WHITGIFT). Ben Jonson found a way of avoiding this prohibition by inventing a new type of comedy, which he called "comicall satyre." His first attempt in this new form was *Every Man Out of his Humour*, which was produced by the Chamberlain's Men in 1599. In this play Jonson employed a twofold satirical method. First, he invented characters who exemplified the forms of folly or knavery that he wished to satirize, then made them, through an exaggerated display of their own absurdity, bring down upon their heads the ridicule of the other characters and of the audience. Second, he introduced two kinds of commentator to point up the satire by ridiculing the victims. One of these, a spokesman for the author, castigated the knave or gull with the professed intent of reforming. The other indulged in the most scurrilous abuse for its own sake, usually with extravagant and absurd verbal display.

Shakespeare was clearly influenced by these Jonsonian devices in all three of the problem plays. Their harshness (compared to the kindlier satire to which he subjected such foolish creatures as Malvolio and Sir Andrew Aguecheek) accounts in part for the bitter tone of these comedies. Parolles, in *All's Well That Ends Well*, is tricked into exposing his own knavery, then derisively ejected from the scene in a characteristically Jonsonian fashion. Angelo, in *Measure for Measure*, is treated in a similar manner. In the first act, the disguised Duke, explaining his own plans to Friar Thomas, reveals the satirical plan of the author:

> Lord Angelo is precise;
> Stands at a guard with envy; scarce confesses
> That his blood flows, or that his appetite
> Is more to bread than stone: hence we shall see,
> If power change purpose, what our seemers be.
> (I, iii, 50–54)

Angelo, in short, is elevated solely so that he may betray the depths of his own knavery for the edification of the audience. Having been brought low, Angelo is permitted to confess his faults and promise to reform, an alternative open to the Jonsonian figure of scorn.

Shakespeare also adopted one of the Jonsonian commentators, the scurrilous buffoon. He appears in *All's Well That Ends Well* as the clown, Lavache, a foul-tongued rogue who delights in gross and tortured figures of speech. He also appears in the guise of Thersites, in *Troilus and Cressida*. Although he is well matched to his Homeric original, Thersites' preposterous figures of speech identify him as a buffoon of comical satire. The absurdly salacious Pandarus, too, has many of the buffoon's characteristics.

The presence of these grotesque and often distasteful characters does much to set the satirical tone of the dark comedies, to prepare the audience to expect an ironic view of life. True love cannot grow under the ministrations of a Pandarus; his lascivious introduction of the lovers at their assignation (III, ii) is a cue that their affair will end in frustration and absurdity. Nobility and heroism (at least, in literature) cannot long withstand the presence of a Thersites; and Shakespeare's Greeks and Trojans are far from noble. (Homer, writing a heroic saga, took care to eject Thersites early from the action.)

The problem plays have still another characteristic in common that contributes to their dark coloration. In each the action is precipitated by strong sexual attraction that seems to some degree irrational. Angelo is not a straightforwardly lustful villain; he is a fanatical puritan who must punish in others the impulses that he tries to deny in himself. Helena is not openly the "clever wench" of Boccaccio and the medieval tales, eager to lure a husband or lover into her bed; she is a modest and refined young woman. Nevertheless, she not only relentlessly pursues a man who despises her, but resorts to trickery to get herself with child by him. In *Measure for Measure* in particular this element of sexual self-deceit tends to curdle the comic aspects of the situation. In Helena's case, the obvious unworthiness of the man she is pursuing calls into question the nature of her love, or of love itself. (As Enobarbus says in another connection, "The loyalty well held to fools does make / Our faith mere folly.") In *Troilus and Cressida* (where a pessimistic view of love is in keeping with the tone of the play as a whole) something similar happens to the hero. Like Romeo, an ardent, youthful, sometimes sensual lover, Troilus ignores the guide of reason in the Trojan council of war to become a slave of passion. However, because the object of this passion is not an innocent, loving Juliet, but a transparently faithless Cressida, the passion itself appears ridiculous. At the end of the play Troilus is equally futile as a lover and as a warrior.

At this stage of his career Shakespeare may have taken a deeply pessimistic view of life that is reflected in the problem plays. What is certain is that he was no longer content to take a simple view of human motivation. In *Julius Caesar*, his first mature tragedy, he had shown an awareness of the complexity with which the elements are mixed in human nature. In the dark comedies he seems equally determined to present this complexity, but unsure both of how to adapt it to the demands of comedy and how to reveal his own attitude toward the characters sufficiently to guide the responses of his audience.

Hamlet. During the period at the turn of the century when Shakespeare was writing the problem plays, which many audiences find his most baffling and disturbing works, he also wrote what is almost universally regarded as the greatest of his tragedies. *Hamlet* stands at the top of the poet's achievement. It marks, in the first place, a great advance in his technical skill as a playwright. No sooner are the opening scenes on the battlements established and the characters introduced than Marcellus, in the 21st line of the play, asks, "What, hath this thing appear'd again to-night?" and creates a tension that will not be released until the final scene. The Ghost who immediately crosses the stage sharpens expectation and deepens the ominous mood. Horatio interprets the apparition as a portent of disaster to Denmark in the war with Norway for which the nation is preparing —an assumption which will seem, for much of the play, to have been false, but in the end will turn out to be disastrously accurate. Horatio's droning recital of the causes of the disturbed relations between the two nations is intentionally made tedious so that the second appearance of the Ghost will come with an added shock of surprise. At the end of the scene the protagonist of the play is mentioned for the first time, and in connection with a supernatural being of uncertain intent. But the playwright shrewdly postpones revealing the purpose of the Ghost's visitation until he can, in the second scene, introduce Hamlet in relation to the other principal characters in the drama that is to follow. Hamlet, clothed in black, sits apart from the resplendent courtiers, alone with his brooding melancholy. This is an effective visual means of presenting, even before he speaks, Hamlet's isolation from everyone. At last, in the final scene of the first act, Shakespeare lets his audience learn why the Ghost is doomed to walk the night. With his admonition to Hamlet a new suspense is created that will last out the play, through Hamlet's repeated efforts to corroborate the Ghost's horrible tale and his endeavors to kill the King, until his pent-up emotions explode in a general catastrophe. In none of Shakespeare's plays written before *Hamlet* is his professional expertise as a dramatist so clearly demonstrated.

The isolation of Hamlet during the early part of the tragedy results in another important development of the poet's art. Provided with no constant companion, as he had been in earlier dramatic versions of the story, he is forced to express his emotional responses to the pressures put upon him in soliloquies that give us the first clearly philosophical lyrics that Shakespeare had ever written. To most audiences they are the glory of his genius. They serve as convincing evidence of his new intellectual maturity. They reveal, moreover, the surprising breadth and depth of his reading. Of crucial importance to the play, for example, are his evident familiarity with treatises on the neurotic character of melancholy and his knowledge of Christian teaching on the subject of ghosts. These go far to explain the protagonist's irrational behavior and his hesitation in carrying out the Ghost's commands. At his first confrontation with "this thing," he betrays the doubts that would have assailed every thoughtful Englishman of the age who considered the problem of the nature of spirits, evil as well as good. These doubts, which account for much of the continuing suspense in the play, Hamlet expresses in his first words addressed to the Ghost:

> Be thou a spirit of health or goblin damn'd,
> Bring with thee airs from heaven or blasts from
> hell,
> Be thy intents wicked or charitable,
> Thou comest in such a questionable shape
> That I will speak to thee.
>
> (I, iv, 40–44)

In some of Hamlet's lines can be seen the first clea reflection of certain philosophical doctrines curren in Tudor England. The "dread of something afte death" that is the subject of the "To be or not to be' soliloquy (III, i, 56–88) was an active fear in every Christian mind that he will spend eternal life in hel rather than in heaven. J. V. Cunningham has pointe out that Hamlet's courageous willingness to "suffe the slings and arrows of outrageous fortune" and hi looking forward to death as a release from th "whips and scorns of time" are pure Stoicism. Tha Hamlet, and doubtless his creator, associated God' providence with the Stoic destiny is clear fron Hamlet's conversation with Horatio just before th fatal duel:

> there's a special providence in the fall of a spar row. If it be now, 'tis not to come; if it be not t come, it will be now; if it be not now, yet it wil come: the readiness is all.
>
> (V, ii, 230–234)

Hamlet clearly shows that for him the ideal man i the Stoical man, with the Stoic's attitude towar death. In stressing the importance of Horatio's friend ship, he says,

> for thou hast been
> As one, in suffering all, that suffers nothing,
> A man that fortune's buffets and rewards
> Hast ta'en with equal thanks.
> . . . . .
> Give me that man
> That is not passion's slave, and I will wear him
> In my heart's core, ay, in my heart of heart,
> As I do thee.
>
> (III, ii, 70–73, 76–79)

Shakespeare seems also to have been acquainte with Renaissance neo-Platonism. In describing t Rosencrantz and Guildenstern the depth of his mel ancholy, Hamlet places man's position in the univer sal creation as halfway between that of animals an that of angels:

> What a piece of work is a man! how noble i reason! how infinite in faculty! in form and mov ing how express and admirable! in action how lik an angel! in apprehension how like a god! th beauty of the world! the paragon of animals! An yet, to me, what is this quintessence of dust?
>
> (II, ii, 316–322)

This idea of a hierarchy in created beings is neo Platonic, but also fundamental to much medieva thought.

This complex of ideas incorporated in *Hamle* marks a great step forward in giving Shakespeare' plays a wide relevance to human destiny. For Ham let, more than any other of Shakespeare's character indeed of any other character in fiction, seems to b a representative modern man at large in literature.

Othello. Although the basic plot line of *Hamlet* i

imple enough, Shakespeare gave the play a texture f great complexity through richness of characteriza- ion, subtlety of interplay between the characters, nd the profound philosophical implications per- eived by the intellectual protagonist. *Othello,* on he other hand, though it was his next tragedy, is one f the most simply organized of all his tragedies. It as a single theme, and the poet avoided obscuring r weakening its impact through dividing the in- erest or introducing nonessential complexities. The rotagonist, a straightforward military man, is not iven to philosophy. There is no one to relate the lay to universal natural order or to any other loctrines of the age. In this microcosm without a nacrocosm, everything that happens results from he machinations of an unambiguously evil villain nd the gullibility of nearly everyone else in the lay.

Perhaps Shakespeare believed that jealousy, even in n essentially noble character, is too petty a motiva- ion to sustain the action of a philosophical tragedy. or whatever reason, he concentrated on the details f what was, in its source (see OTHELLO: *Sources*), a rutally melodramatic plot, riveting the audience's ttention on every step of the villain's diabolical cheming. But, characteristically transforming every- hing he touched, Shakespeare turned a crude and nsympathetic figure into the noble and generous Moor, whose fall, even though due to a foolish and nworthy motive, reaches tragic proportions. Be- ause the poet succeeded in making it believable that uch a large-hearted character should easily succumb o the insinuations of the villain, many explanations ave been advanced to explain this behavior. For ex- mple, in spite of his consciousness of his own merit,)thello is too ready to believe that a white girl night come to regret her marriage to a black man, which has so horrified her father that he can attrib- te it only to drugs or bewitchment. Or the Moor's ong years of service in the fabulous countries of the ast have made him unfamiliar with the social life of Venice and unable accurately to judge the behavior f its high-born ladies. Or, although Desdemona has egged not to be bereft of "the rites for which I ove him" (I, iii, 258), Othello ignores this aspect of heir love. Requesting the Duke of Venice to let her o with him to Cyprus, he says,

> I therefore beg it not,
> To please the palate of my appetite,
> Nor to comply with heat—the young affects
> In me defunct—and proper satisfaction,
> But to be free and bounteous to her mind.
> (I, iii, 262–266)

f this passage is to be taken literally, it is not sur- rising that Othello is thrown into a panic when Iago egins to talk in crass sexual terms of the woman e has so unrealistically idealized.

It is probably a mistake to separate the question of)thello's gullibility from that of the other characters vhom Iago entraps in his schemes with consummate ase—Cassio, Roderigo, and Emilia. E. E. Stoll has xplained Iago's facile success by pointing out that e is a representative of a popular dramatic type, the alumniator, whose dramatic function is precisely to e believed. Iago is also descended, like Shakespeare's rst great villain, Richard III, from another stock haracter, the Vice of the morality plays. This ancestry accounts for the cynical pleasure he shows in his own villainy, taking the audience into his confidence as he plans each step in trapping two enemies at once. Shakespeare, who had used the Vice as model for a villain before, and would use it again in *King Lear,* may well have known that this traditional character's delight in his own ingenuity was infectious and would help to make his too-easy success with his elaborate schemes seem more plausible than it actually was.

King Lear. In Hamlet's soliloquies Shakespeare had written his first essays in philosophical speculation. In *King Lear* he built an entire play upon a structure similar to one which had been invented for purposes of philosophical or ethical instruction: that of the morality play. Lear, like Everyman, is Man at the end of his days when he is called to account for the conduct of his life and must take stock of his true assets. Like Everyman, Lear is deserted by his fair-weather friends and sustained by those whom he has despised and rejected. He repents of his besetting sin of pride, is redeemed, and dies, ready for heaven. As in many morality plays, the good characters—Cordelia, Kent, and Edgar—are balanced by a like number of evil ones—Goneril, Regan, and Edmund. Although they are individualized human beings as well, all these characters can be seen as personifications of moral qualities: Kent as Truth, Cordelia as Love, Edgar as Knowledge, the evil sisters as Lust and the Cruelty that is likely to accompany it. The action, particularly of the evil characters, is pushed to such extremes that the play often seems to be an *exemplum* on pride and the wrath that follows its frustration. It is no accident that, during a period when the theatre was in disrepute in Puritan America, *King Lear* could be played as a dramatized tract entitled *The Crime of Filial Ingratitude.*

Lear is representative ruler, as well as representative man. As head of the state he has sacred duties of leadership. In laying them down, along with those of head of a family, he incurs tragic guilt and introduces chaos into both family and state. This social disarrangement is reflected in the derangement in Lear's mind and spirit and also in the elements. The tempest on the heath is not only a symbol of the storm in Lear's mind; it is outraged Nature's protest against the anarchy which Lear has introduced into her realm. Lear begs "the great gods / That keep this dreadful pother o'er our heads" to expose man's hidden vices in the hope that he himself and the world will be forever purged of them (III, ii, 49–59). Shakespeare had given shape and significance to his history plays with his philosophical conviction that a legitimate temporal monarch rules as a representative of divine will and that failure to respect that rule leads to disruption in the state. Though Richard II was seriously flawed as man and ruler, his deposition brought divine retribution upon his successor and led to the disastrous anarchy of the Wars of the Roses. In *King Lear* Shakespeare added new significance to this concept. It is the ruler himself who, through pride and the abdication of his sacred responsibilities, brings catastrophe upon himself and the state.

In *King Lear* the poet extended this idea, moreover, into still another aspect of rule: social responsibility. In the prayer that Lear offers while he stands before the hovel lashed by the wind (III, iv, 28–36) is Shakespeare's first hint of the importance of sympathy for "poor naked wretches." The prayer ends,

> Take physic, pomp;
> Expose thyself to feel what wretches feel,
> That thou mayst shake the superflux to them,
> And show the heavens more just.
>
> (III, iv, 33–36)

Gloucester at a similar stage of his redemption strikes the same note. Giving a purse to "poor Tom," he says,

> Here, take this purse, thou whom the heavens' plagues
> Have humbled to all strokes: that I am wretched
> Makes thee the happier: heavens, deal so still!
> Let the superfluous and lust-dieted man,
> That slaves your ordinance, that will not see
> Because he doth not feel, feel your power quickly;
> So distribution should undo excess,
> And each man have enough.
>
> (IV, i, 67–74)

Both redeemed men expect the state as well as the individual to be their purveyor of exact and equal justice.

The salvation of Lear through love does not prove as lasting as he expects when, in a state of exaltation, he goes to prison with Cordelia. In the last scene he is mad again. Did Shakespeare mean to convey by this that only beyond death can man finally conquer evil? Does its hopelessness indicate that the poet's view of life was deeply pessimistic? Or does it mean that, as Middleton Murry believed, Shakespeare was out of his philosophical depth in *King Lear*? Whatever the answer, he never again attempted to dramatize a metaphysical interpretation of human experience. His later tragic protagonists—Antony, Timon, and Coriolanus—are merely men destroyed by their slavery to one or another of the passions. None of them has any allegorical significance. Only in his last play did he, in Prospero and Miranda, establish the kind of spiritual union between father and daughter that is destroyed in *King Lear* at the very moment of its expected consummation.

Macbeth. After finishing *King Lear* (1605), with its fully developed "echo plot" and its complexity of meaning, Shakespeare returned in *Macbeth* to the simple dramatic structure he had used in *Othello*. He devoted his full imaginative powers to concentrating the greatest possible intensity on a straightforward plot line. Everything irrelevant to this single plot was shorn away. Like *Othello*, *Macbeth* has no "comic relief," except for the Porter's scene—and that turns out to be a shrewd device for increasing suspense at a crucial moment in the action. The scenes in which Hecate leads the Witches in songs and dances were not written by Shakespeare. The long scene between Macduff and Malcolm at the English court (IV, iii) has often been regarded as an inept interruption to the action, but it actually serves three purposes central to the theme. Malcolm's shrewdness in testing Macduff's moral character demonstrates his own fitness to rule, without which the eventual defeat of Macbeth would prove a hollow victory. His suspicion of Macduff and the news brought by Ross combine to reveal the depth and extent of Macbeth's villainy and, by proving him tyrant, to justify the war against him to the Eliza bethan audience—for the slaying of a tyrant was be lieved by all political theorists of the age to be a jus act in the eyes of both man and God. Finally, th English scene, like the Fortinbras scenes in *Hamle* gives the action wider scope and significance than i would have if seen merely as an internal politica struggle.

There are two protagonists in *Macbeth,* but Lad Macbeth's part in the murder and its aftermath serve as a parallel and contrast to that of her husband, an this, too, contributes to the strength of the main plo Lady Macbeth is not, like Gloucester in the ech plot of *King Lear,* involved in a separate actio although the guilt that she shares with Macbet instead of binding them together with bonds of ap prehension and wicked triumph, drives them apar each to live in solitude with his private agony, eac to take a solitary road to despair and death. Thi concentration of interest on a single, continuous ac tion made *Macbeth* the shortest of Shakespeare tragedies, hardly more than half the length of th First Folio text of *Hamlet*.

The rise and fall of a tyrant was a familiar subje in Elizabethan tragedy. In *Macbeth,* as in so man other of his plays, Shakespeare matched an extern conflict with an internal one in the heart of his pro tagonist, thereby adding a new depth to what woul otherwise have been merely a sequence of violer events. Throughout the drama Macbeth is tor between ruthless ambition and paralyzing fear. I his first scene in the play (I, iii) after learning th the first of the Witches' prophecies has come tru he is thrown into a dark reverie in which he revea that he has long dreamed of "the swelling act of th imperial theme" and of the desperate deed that migl win him the crown. Yet, he mutters, "the horri image" of the deed "doth unfix my hair / And mal my seated heart knock at my ribs." His momentar disorientation in this scene presages the hallucinator terrors that will totally unman him after his murde both of Duncan (II, ii) and of Banquo (III, iv Thenceforward his courage is sustained by t prophecies of the Witches and, when they ha proved false, by sheer desperation.

In *Macbeth* Shakespeare further developed, wi immense theatrical effect, a device that he had intr duced in *Hamlet,* where it also served multip purposes. The ominous appearance of the Ghost the very beginning of the earlier play arouses su pense that involves the protagonist, its second appea ance sets Hamlet on the course of revenge that is t action of the play, its third serves to "whet h blunted purpose," and thus hurry the drama on t ward its bloody end. Moreover, the Ghost, thoug clearly intended to be real, is also a reflection Hamlet's own fears and suspicions. "I doubt son foul play," he says, on merely hearing of the Ghos appearance. The Witches perform almost identic functions in *Macbeth*. The announced intention these creatures (in the seventh line of the play) meet with Macbeth immediately associates him wi evil. In the third scene they set the action of the pl in motion by rousing his latent ambition with th prophecy. In their third and last appearance (IV, they hasten it toward its conclusion by persuadi

Macbeth with further prophecies to "be bloody, bold, and resolute." In *Macbeth,* even more clearly than in *Hamlet,* the supernatural beings, although real, are also embodiments of the protagonist's dark and hidden thoughts. "Thou hast harp'd my fear aright," Macbeth tells the First Apparition. His first line in the play, "So foul and fair a day I have not seen" (I, iii, 38), is an echo of the chant (I, i, 11) of the Witches—whom he has not yet seen. Thus the playwright found a brilliantly effective means of representing visually the dominant thoughts of two of his greatest protagonists even before they appear onstage.

Antony and Cleopatra. Immediately after completing his shortest tragedy, which, with *Othello,* was also his most concentrated in dramatic effect, Shakespeare wrote the most episodic of his tragic dramas. He revived the technique of his early chronicle plays in order to paint a colorful backdrop for what is also his most exotic, and erotic, tragedy. For the first time in either a tragedy or a history play political events, treated with unsurpassed vividness and economy of characterization, account for almost the entire action of the play, yet are ultimately subordinated in importance to the private drama of the two protagonists. This drama, as in Shakespeare's first successful tragedy, *Romeo and Juliet,* is a love that triumphs over death. Yet two loves, or two plays, could hardly be more different. *Antony and Cleopatra* portrays a mature, proudly sensual love between two great, yet deeply flawed protagonists. The key to understanding is certainly to be found in Shakespeare's own attitude toward those characters. Yet, as in so many of his later plays, the playwright does not reveal his attitude in unambiguous terms. His dramatic purposes, clearly different from those of any earlier play, are therefore subject to a wide variety of interpretations. The two most generally held views are (1) that the play is an unillusioned portrayal of the crippling effect of passion on mankind's aspirations toward nobility and greatness, and (2) that it celebrates the transcendent experience of human love, through which man may overcome even the fact of death. Since these two views are diametrically opposed, they can best be considered separately.

According to many "neo-realist" critics, *Antony and Cleopatra* was for Shakespeare an attempt to write a tragedy about protagonists who are so subject to human frailties that they have little of the grandeur of conventional tragic heroes. Seen in this way, the momentous events of the play serve mainly to lend significance to the decline of Antony and Cleopatra and their love, which would otherwise be hardly the stuff of tragedy. When the play begins Antony, "the triple pillar of the world," has already been "transformed / Into a strumpet's fool" (I, i, 12–13). The once-brilliant general ignores the duties of his position as ruler of the eastern segment of the Roman empire while he indulges himself in middle-aged dalliance with a queen who has earlier bestowed her favors on Julius Caesar and Pompey the Great, not to mention "hotter hours, / Unregister'd in vulgar fame"—as Antony reminds her in one of their unedifying quarrels (III, xiii, 118–119). Although he still has moments of magnanimity and an occasional fitful flash of his old nobility, his moral stamina, undermined by his soft life in the East, cannot assert itself for long even in Rome. He is a decayed aristocrat who, having failed to remain true to his somewhat outmoded ideals, is no longer a match for the coldly practical realism of Caesar. He flees back to Cleopatra, whose subtle flatteries sustain him in the illusion that he is still "the demi-Atlas of this earth." Even in his final battle his courage is only that of desperation. Even his attempted suicide is a ludicrous failure.

Seen from this relentlessly realistic perspective, Cleopatra, too, conforms to none of the traditional demands for a tragic figure. In life self-willed, capricious, and self-indulgent, she is in death theatrically effective rather than tragically moving. She is not regenerated by love, for the love of Antony and Cleopatra is not of a kind that matures and ennobles; it is pure sexual attraction elevated to the level of ritual. To this love Cleopatra imagines that she remains true in death. But her motives for taking her life are far from being purely those of loyalty to Antony. After his death she is still sufficiently interested in life to try through trickery to salvage half her fortune and to threaten to scratch out the eyes of the man who foils her scheme. She determines to die as much to escape the indignity of adorning Caesar's triumphal procession as to give consummate expression to a wife's grief. In spite of her plan to die "after the high Roman fashion," she actually does so in a sensuously ostentatious oriental manner, having long "pursued conclusions infinite / Of easy ways to die" (V, ii, 358–359).

To those for whom Shakespeare's two protagonists fail to achieve the heights of his earlier tragic heroes, *Antony and Cleopatra* may represent a falling off from the four great tragedies, or it may indicate that the poet was exhausting his interest in the conventional forms of tragedy and searching, if not for new forms, at least for ways of modifying the old.

Critics and audiences who regard the play as one of Shakespeare's greatest tragedies agree that it is a new development in his art. They believe, however, that the key to the playwright's attitudes toward the protagonists of his tragedies must not, as in the history plays, be sought in their effect upon the state: Antony's rebellion was less disastrous for Rome than either Hamlet's private vendetta or Lear's domestic ill-judgment, though both are unmistakable tragic heroes. The true significance of a protagonist is to be found in the regard he inspires in other characters and, above all, in the language of the playwright. This view, popular with Romantic critics, has received strong support from studies of the imagery in *Antony and Cleopatra.*

No other drama of Shakespeare's approaches *Antony and Cleopatra* in the worldwide scope of its action or in the cosmic significance assigned to the deeds of its principal characters. The extent of the action is shown in scenes which range over much of the Roman World. Constant emphasis is put upon the world-shaking importance of the events and the principal figures. Octavia, speaking of Antony, tells Caesar, "Wars 'twixt you twain would be / As if the world should cleave" (III, iv, 30–31). In the scene aboard Pompey's ship, Menas points out how easily Pompey might be "lord of all the world" by disposing at one blow of the "three world-sharers"—Antony, Caesar, and Lepidus:

> Thou art, if thou darest be, the earthly Jove:
> Whate'er the ocean pales, or sky inclips,
> Is thine, if thou wilt ha't.
>
> (II, vii, 73–75)

And Pompey, Antony, and Caesar end by dancing in a circle to the refrain, "Cup us, till the world go round!"

The language in which Antony is described by others regularly belies his often ignoble behavior. The Soothsayer tells him,

> Thy demon, that's thy spirit which keeps thee, is
> Noble, courageous, high, unmatchable,
> Where Caesar's is not.
>
> (II, iii, 19–21)

Before killing himself to avoid killing Antony, Eros begs his general, "Turn from me, then, that noble countenance, / Wherein the worship of the whole world lies" (IV, xiv, 85–86). Antony achieves grandeur even in his failings. When Caesar complains that he is "the abstract of all faults / That all men follow," Lepidus replies that "His faults in him seem as the spots of heaven, / More fiery by night's blackness" (I, iv, 9–10, 12–13). Even his chief adversary, Caesar, is deeply moved at Antony's death:

> The breaking of so great a thing should make
> A greater crack: the round world
> Should have shook lions into civil streets,
> And citizens to their dens: the death of Antony
> Is not a single doom; in the name lay
> A moiety of the world.
>
> (V, i, 14–19)

But it is Cleopatra who tolls Antony's knell with the overtones that have rung throughout the play:

> I dream'd there was an Emperor Antony:
> O, such another sleep, that I might see
> But such another man! . . .
> His face was as the heavens; and therein stuck
> A sun and moon, which kept their course, and
> lighted
> The little O, the earth. . . .
> His legs bestrid the ocean: his rear'd arm
> Crested the world: his voice was propertied
> As all the tuned spheres, and that to friends;
> But when he meant to quail and shake the orb,
> He was as rattling thunder. For his bounty,
> There was no winter in 't; an autumn 'twas
> That grew the more by reaping: his delights
> Were dolphin-like; they show'd his back above
> The element they lived in: in his livery
> Walk'd crowns and crownets; realms and islands
> were
> As plates dropp'd from his pocket.
>
> (V, ii, 76–92)

She is describing not an ordinary mortal but a creature who, from the first lines of the play, has been seen as an earthly war god. Philo speaks of "his goodly eyes, / That o'er the files and musters of the war / Have glow'd like plated Mars" (I, i, 2–4). Enobarbus will not, as Lepidus requests, entreat his captain "to soft and gentle speech," but "to answer like himself: if Caesar move him, / Let Antony look over Caesar's head / And speak as loud as Mars" (II, ii, 3–6). Before his final defeat (IV, iii) his soldiers hear strange music in the earth and know that " 'Tis the god Hercules, whom Antony loved, / Now leaves him."

If Antony is a Mars incarnate, Cleopatra is his Venus; it is Venus who sails down the Cydnus on her barge to meet Antony, as the practical soldier Enobarbus rapturously describes the event (II, ii, 195–223). And the pair have no doubt that their love, like the love of gods, transcends earthly custom. Antony makes this clear in the first scene of the play:

> Let Rome in Tiber melt, and the wide arch
> Of the ranged empire fall! Here is my space.
> Kingdoms are clay: our dungy earth alike
> Feeds beast as man: the nobleness of life
> Is to do thus; when such a mutual pair
> And such a twain can do 't.
>
> (I, i, 33–38)

To this concept of their love Cleopatra, for all her frailty and womanish caprice, is true to the last. She wishes

> To throw my sceptre at the injurious gods;
> To tell them that this world did equal theirs
> Till they had stol'n our jewel.
>
> (IV, xv, 75–77)

She dies, certainly not "after the high Roman fashion," but like an oriental goddess-queen, eager "to rush into the secret house of death, / Ere death dare come to us" (IV, xv, 81–82). "I am again for Cydnus, / To meet Mark Antony," she tells Charmian (V, ii, 228–229), and calmly issues her last instructions:

> Give me my robe, put on my crown; I have
> Immortal longings in me.
>
> . . . . .
>
> Methinks I hear
> Antony call; I see him rouse himself
> To praise my noble act.
>
> . . . . .
>
> Husband, I come:
> Now to that name my courage prove my title!
> I am fire and air; my other elements
> I give to baser life.
>
> (V, ii, 282–292 *passim*)

To those who find the key to this tragedy in the characters' evaluation of themselves and who place emphasis upon the qualities of the poetry in which they express themselves, *Antony and Cleopatra* is one of Shakespeare's supreme achievements. To those who prefer to judge the characters through a dispassionate view of their behavior and its consequences, the obvious imperfections of the pair make them unable to support a truly great tragedy, and even the bright flashes of the poetry seem sparks from a slowly dying fire.

Timon of Athens and Coriolanus. A striking characteristic of Shakespeare's last tragedies was his attempt to deal in the form of tragedy with what Willard Farnham has called "deeply flawed" protagonists. Antony, Cleopatra, and Coriolanus are so much at the mercy of their human frailties that, fo many audiences and critics, these faults have almost obscured their virtues. Between the two tragedies in which these characters appear, Shakespeare wrote a play in which even the protagonist's virtues are shown to be flaws. If *Timon of Athens* was designed to be the tragedy of a magnificent Renaissance man who practiced on a grand scale charity, hospitality, and generosity, but was destroyed by his anger at the ingratitude and meanness of his beneficiaries, it is a most unsuccessful one. But the temper and tone of the play are established, not by Timon's "virtuous" deeds of the first two acts, but by his violent misanthropy and the bursts of invective he indulges in during the remainder of the play. This is the mood of formal satire, and the play is more easily understood in the context of satire than of tragedy. The two phases of Timon's conduct are presented as folly. His histrionic generosity is a virtue in excess; his violent expressions of hatred of mankind are so extreme as to make audiences laugh. Timon's actions more logically awake scornful laughter than pity and terror, yet the course of the play is cast in the mold of tragedy. Shakespeare may have intended in *Timon of Athens* to write a tragical satire, as he may have tried in the problem plays to write a comical satire. The result, unfortunately, was satisfactory neither as tragedy nor as satire. Shakespeare may have recognized that he could not form an effective union of the two elements and stopped working on the play.

Coriolanus has for its protagonist a man with as many faults as Antony or Cleopatra, but little of their grace. In this, the last of his tragedies, the playwright once again dealt with a principal character in whom the elements are so mixed that his creator's own attitude toward him can hardly be discerned. Therefore, since the subject of the play is the perennial social conflict between rich and poor and the position of the protagonist is associated with a familiar political posture found in all periods, the reactions of both audiences and critics to the play tend to correspond with their political views. Coriolanus, a patrician, is violently scornful of the plebeians, whom he greets in his first lines in the play with the words,

> What's the matter, you dissentious rogues,
> That, rubbing the poor itch of your opinion,
> Make yourselves scabs?
>
> (I, i, 168–170)

If this attitude does not endear Coriolanus to the plebeians, neither does it incline in his favor critics of a firmly democratic persuasion. They point out that he brings down disaster on his own head and on the state through his inordinate contempt for the people and his rigidity of character. And, indeed, the accusation of the First Citizen often seems justified by the protagonist's subsequent acts: "What he hath done famously, he did it . . . to please his mother, and to be partly proud; which he is, even to the altitude of his virtue" (I, i, 36–37, 39–41). Coriolanus is a slave to his own rage when his vast pride is hurt. His actions can be governed by persons shrewd enough to play upon his always predictable emotional reactions—the tribunes, his mother, and, finally, Aufidius. He functions well only in war, where his nearly perpetual rage can be channeled toward useful ends; but even there he is ready enough to turn his much vaunted courage against his own country when he is offended. He dies, not gloriously in battle, but ignominiously cut down and trampled by envious conspirators in a foreign land, who have first justified the deed by provoking him to one last rage. Since this is not the noble end of Shakespeare's earlier tragic heroes, it has been often regarded as indicative of the poet's own attitude toward his protagonist.

Coriolanus' shortcomings as a tragic hero are so many and so obvious that some critics have argued that he is intentionally cast in the mold of Timon—that *Coriolanus* is, in fact, the playwright's second and successful attempt to write a tragic satire. According to this view the protagonist is intentionally held up to scorn. Like all victims of satire, he is the subject of endless and usually hostile comment from other characters, beginning with the angry citizens in the first scene. It has been suggested that Shakespeare patterned his play on Jonson's *Sejanus*, to which it bears structural resemblances. Menenius, moreover, occasionally shows the delight in extravagant and sometimes vulgar ridicule characteristic of a Jonsonian buffoon. A psychological interpretation of Coriolanus' character—which accords well enough with either a tragic or a satiric view of the play—emphasizes the influence of his mother, Volumnia, who clearly loves her only son more for the warlike fame that redounds to her glory than for himself, "If my son were my husband," she tells his wife, "I should freelier rejoice in that absence wherein he won honour than in the embracements of his bed where he would show most love" (I, iii, 2–6). The general's fearful scorn and anger stand against the world but quail before those of his mother at the two crucial points in the play when she opposes him. When he refuses to beg the plebeians for the honor of the consulship, Volumnia—who herself "was wont / To call them woollen vassals, things created / To buy and sell with groats" (III, ii, 8–10)—upbraids him for being "too absolute" until he pleads, "Pray, be content: / Mother, I am going to the market-place; / Chide me no more" (III, ii, 130–132). When Coriolanus is about to attack his native city and "all the swords / In Italy, and her confederate arms, / Could not have made this peace" (V, iii, 207–209), Volumnia's taunt "This fellow had a Volscian to his mother" wins a final capitulation that he knows to be his death warrant:

> O mother, mother!
> What have you done? Behold, the heavens do ope,
> The gods look down, and this unnatural scene
> They laugh at. O my mother, mother! O!
> You have won a happy victory to Rome;
> But, for your son,—believe it, O, believe it,
> Most dangerously you have with him prevail'd,
> If not most mortal to him. But, let it come.
>
> (V, iii, 182–189)

Volumnia, having a second time persuaded her son to abandon the martial "absoluteness" that she had herself inculcated in him, returns home to be greeted as "our patroness, the life of Rome!" Coriolanus goes to a sordid death in exile.

Those critics who regard the protagonist's absoluteness as a virtue find a key to his tragedy in his reproach to Volumnia:

Why did you wish me milder? would you have
me
False to my nature? Rather say I play
The man I am.

(III, ii, 14–16)

His arrogance and rigidity are virtues on the battlefield, for which he has been so single-mindedly reared. Disaster results when he is persuaded momentarily to repudiate his own nature in humbly seeking civil honors which, at best, he little cares for. Coriolanus is unquestionably one of Shakespeare's most deeply flawed protagonists—but the playwright portrays the tribunes, his chief opponents, as demagogues without redeeming traits; the plebeians are, for the most part, fickle and cowardly; Menenius is bland and devious; Volumnia is coldly self-centered; Aufidius, who should be the protagonist's Volscian counterpart, has none of the martial virtues but bravery. In such a world Coriolanus' absoluteness may seem a quality as rare and noble as it is doomed. In this view of the play his moment of compassion, in full knowledge of its fatal consequences for himself, redeems his faults and lends him a tragic stature that is only heightened by the ignominy of the death that he has knowingly embraced.

In *Coriolanus,* his last tragedy, Shakespeare once again refused to reveal his own attitudes toward the characters he created. Instead, he presented them with the multiplicity of faults and virtues common to human nature and thus forced his audiences ever since to interpret their acts as best they might, reliving in the theatre the ambiguous complexity of human experience.

The Romances. The four romances that followed *Coriolanus* have always been the subject of much speculation and debate. These, the last plays that Shakespeare wrote alone—*Pericles, Cymbeline, The Winter's Tale,* and *The Tempest*—represent so radical a departure from all that he had written before that they make us wonder what was his purpose in creating them. The most widely accepted explanation of his reason is that advanced by G. E. Bentley. He argues that in his romances Shakespeare was seeking appropriate ways of entertaining an audience that was new for his company—the aristocrats who gathered at the Blackfriars theatre. Shakespeare's company had leased this theatre to serve as a house for its winter season in 1608. Up to that year Blackfriars had been used successively by the Children of the Chapel Royal and the Children of the Queen's Revels. The shows of these boys had largely formed the taste of their patrons. The theatrical features of these dramas were designed to display the talents of choirboy actors, many of whom, besides being singers, were accomplished instrumentalists and dancers. It was therefore natural for the dramatists who wrote for the children to introduce into their plays music and dancing, and sometimes even miniature masques. Thus it is argued that in his efforts to hold the interest of the erstwhile patrons of the boys' companies, Shakespeare featured in his romances many of the spectacular characteristics that had previously charmed the ladies and gentlemen of quality who formed the Blackfriars audiences. Though their theatrical taste was more sophisticated than that of the throngs who frequented the Globe, it was less catholic. It expected suspense, surprise, scenes of forgiveness, reconciliation, and even of rebirth that united to produce a happy ending that somehow suggested profundity.

Of these romances *The Tempest* alone broke new ground in Shakespeare's techniques and in the world of his ideas. In this play as in no other of his works he strictly observed the unities of time, place, and action as they were understood by Renaissance critics. In conceiving of Prospero's magic and its power, Shakespeare was tapping a new source of knowledge that carried his imagination into regions into which it had never before ventured. From a partial and often confused idea of one aspect of neo-Platonism, he derived his ideas of white magic that form the source of *The Tempest.* The demons that are under the wizard's control are also fugitives from neo-Platonism. They form an amalgam of the demons of folklore and those defined in neo-Platonic writings. They thus become partially identified with forces of nature, particularly with its elements. Ariel, for example, is a spirit of air. Caliban, according to W. C. Curry (to whose *Shakespeare's Philosophical Patterns* [1937] I am at this point deeply indebted), bears traces of an aquatic spirit, as when Trinculo makes fun of Caliban's fishlike appearance and his fishy smell. But Shakespeare makes little of Caliban as a water sprite, choosing instead to explain that the monster had been begotten by the devil on Sycorax, a witch.

The plays also sound overtones of pagan religion and myth. The sequence of events is reminiscent of the Greek myth of the seasons. Perdita's adventures in *The Winter's Tale* are a counterpart of those of Persephone and her mother, Demeter. Perdita's apparent death and prolonged disappearance parallel Persephone's departure into the lower world at the onset of winter, and her joyous reunion with her earthly mother is like the blooming of all nature at Persephone's return to her earth-mother (see MYTHIC CRITICISM). In another religious context the romances can be seen as allegorical expositions of Christian doctrine, with reconciliation serving as a symbol of redemption.

Opinions of the poetic and dramatic excellence of the romances are sharply divided. The unfavorable positions range from the mild disapproval of Sir Arthur Quiller-Couch and H. B. Charlton—that all the romances, except *The Tempest,* betray a loss of dramatic skill, and only a flaccid control of language—to the sharp rejection of commentators, led by Lytton Strachey, who dismiss the romances as the work of a tired and bored author, capable of turning out only potboilers. Contemporary critics, however have tended to rehabilitate these last heirs of Shakespeare's invention. They insist that the poetry of the romances has never been surpassed in any other of Shakespeare's plays, that they reveal a master technician in their unity of construction, their beauty of design, and their richness of connotation. It is this last quality that has led an entire school of critics to search for a meaning beyond meaning in the romances and to find it in allegory and myth. A study of this last stage of the growth of Shakespeare's mind and art assures us that, to the end of his work for the stage, he continued to seek new sources for inspiration and to explore new ways of converting the materials that he found into the substance of dramas of more and more exotic beauty and of more and more depth.—O. J. C.

Bibliography. E. E. Stoll, *Othello, An Historical and Comparative Study*, 1915; Lytton Strachey, "Shakespeare's Final Period," *Books and Characters*, 1922; Douglas Bush, *Mythology and the Renaissance Tradition in English Literature*, 1932, rev. ed., 1963; John Middleton Murry, *Shakespeare*, 1936; H. B. Charlton, *Shakespearian Comedy*, 1938; E. M. W. Tillyard, *Shakespeare's History Plays*, 1944; D. L. Stevenson, *The Love-Game Comedy*, 1946; G. E. Bentley, "Shakespeare and the Blackfriars Theatre," *Shakespeare Survey 1*, 1948; Willard Farnham, *Shakespeare's Tragic Frontier*, 1950; J. V. Cunningham, *Woe and Wonder: The Emotional Effect of Shakespearean Tragedy*, 1951; M. M. Reese, *Shakespeare: His World and His Work*, 1953; Virgil Whitaker, *Shakespeare's Learning*, 1953; Gladys D. Willcock, *Language and Poetry in Shakespeare's Plays*, 1954; J. Dover Wilson, *Shakespeare's Happy Comedies*, 1962; A. L. Rowse, *William Shakespeare*, 1963.

Shakespeare Association. See SCHOLARSHIP—20TH CENTURY.

Shakespeare Association Bulletin. The official periodical of the SHAKESPEARE ASSOCIATION OF AMERICA from 1924 to 1948. The *Shakespeare Association Bulletin* featured an annual bibliography by Samuel Tannenbaum, who also served as its editor from 1934 to 1947. In 1949 the *Bulletin* ceased publication and was succeeded in the following year by the SHAKESPEARE QUARTERLY.

Shakespeare Association of America, The. A scholarly society. It was founded in 1923; its first president was the Shakespeare scholar Ashley H. Thorndike. In 1924 the organization began issuing the SHAKESPEARE ASSOCIATION BULLETIN, the official publication of the association until 1948 when its format was altered and its name changed to SHAKESPEARE QUARTERLY. The second president of the association was the distinguished bibliophile Abraham S. W. Rosenbach, who served from 1934 until his death in 1952. He was succeeded by Arthur C. Houghton, Jr., who relinquished the post in 1956. Mrs. Donald F. Hyde succeeded him as president.

Shakespeare Institute of the University of Birmingham, The. A postgraduate and research institute in Birmingham, England. Established in 1951 by Professor Allardyce Nicoll, then head of the university's English department, it owes its existence to his vision and energy and to generous financial support, at its inception and subsequently, provided by the firm of Scribbans-Kemp through the personal interest of H. Oliver-King. Professor Nicoll retired in 1961 and was succeeded by the present director, Professor T. J. B. Spencer.

The Institute's central concern is the work of the poet and actor-dramatist whose name it bears, and the environment—material, spiritual, and intellectual —in which he lived and worked; but it aims to study Shakespeare in the light of a full knowledge of dramatists, poets, and prose-writers who were his predecessors or contemporaries, or immediately under his influence. It therefore encourages study of any aspect of 16th- or 17th-century Europe relevant to its main interest and works in close connection not only with the English department of the university but also with many other departments in the Faculty of Arts.

Some of the activities of the Institute are carried on at Stratford-upon-Avon (20 miles southeast of the main university site in Birmingham) in a large old house known as "Mason Croft." Its 18th-century façade is in Church Street, on the side opposite the 15th-century almshouses and grammar school; at the back are large and beautiful gardens stretching all the way to Rother Street. During the first quarter of this century Mason Croft was the home of the novelist Marie Corelli, who repaired it and added the great music room that now serves as a lecture and conference hall. Miss Corelli also extended and embellished the gardens, which make an admirable setting for the outdoor functions of the biennial International Shakespeare Conference and of the annual Shakespeare Summer School. These, and similar meetings, are held at Mason Croft. The library and the research activities of the Institute are housed in a large Victorian mansion, "Westmere," standing in extensive and exceptionally beautiful grounds in Edgbaston Park Road, Birmingham, on the periphery of the main university site. This gives members of the Institute ample library facilities for everyday work, and enables them to attend the numerous theatrical productions in Birmingham in addition to those at Stratford. It also allows members of all departments in the university to join easily and fully in the research activities of the Institute.

The primary resources of the Institute's library are its collection of microfilms of books and manuscripts, mostly of the period 1500–1660. These now number well over 20,000, and are steadily increasing. They include microfilms of all known manuscripts of English plays (and many in Latin) up to 1700, of many manuscript songbooks of the same period, and, for the Elizabethan and Jacobean period, such diverse material as virtually all the Italian *commedia dell' arte* plays, the Register of the Stationers' Company, and the City of London's repertories and journals. All these microfilms, together with the Institute's own collection of printed books and periodicals (now running into many thousands, and growing steadily) are available for study by members of the Institute or by accredited visiting scholars. The Institute library is open on practically every day of the year. Additional library resources are available nearby in the university library (some 800 yards from the Institute) and in the Birmingham Municipal Reference Library, whose Shakespeare Memorial Collection is perhaps the most complete of its kind and, for students of Shakespeare and Elizabethan literature, a working collection of inestimable value. The Municipal Reference Library also possesses a vast collection of early deeds and other manuscripts relating to Warwickshire and adjoining counties, many still unexamined and uncatalogued. A little further afield similar collections of deeds and manuscripts, many still awaiting study, can be found in the county record office at Warwick (21 miles away) and in the Shakespeare Centre at Stratford-upon-Avon, which possesses also a small but important collection of early printed books.

Initially the Institute staff consisted of a director, a senior fellow and assistant director (1951–1959: Professor C. J. Sisson), and three junior fellows. From 1952 to 1959 the Charles Henry Foyle Trust provided a fellowship to enable a visiting scholar of senior status to work at the Institute for a year and join in its collaborative activities. Holders of this Foyle Fellowship included Professors R. C. Bald (Chicago), Arthur Brown (London), Clifford Leech (Toronto), L. C. Martin (Liverpool), and Baldwin Maxwell (Iowa). Among recipients of other awards who have elected to hold them at the Shakespeare Institute are Professor Mark Eccles (Wisconsin), Marvin Felheim (Michigan), Toyoichi Hirai (Hosei), Richard Hosley (Missouri), Jiro Ozu (Tokyo), Johnstone Parr (Alabama), A. C. Sprague (Bryn Mawr), and Drs. Zdenek Stribrny (Prague) and Henryk Zbierski (Poznan).

Among former junior fellows are Dr. John Brown, Professor R. A. Foakes, B. A. Harris, and E. A. Honigmann. In addition to the three junior fellowships, other fellowships are being established as a result of generous aid recently received from the Ford Foundation and the Gulbenkian Foundation for development of the Institute's work.

The Institute has always worked in close association with the university's English department, many of whose members took an active part in the work of the Institute from its inception. This close relationship continues, notwithstanding the inevitable changes of staff in both establishments, and the Institute's work has profited greatly thereby.

In founding the Institute, Professor Nicoll was prompted by belief that the tasks now confronting Shakespearean scholars are too large for individuals to tackle singlehanded and require collaboration by researchers working together along agreed lines. Such cooperation has already created new tools for scholarly research; for example, the Institute's elaborate chronological index of English books printed before 1641, from which one can find out easily which new publications or new editions were issued, certainly or probably, in any month, or even week, of the period. This in turn has made possible the "Books and Readers" series of dissertations, which is surveying the content and characteristics of the output of the press as this varied during Shakespeare's lifetime. Other "tools" in preparation are an index of "literary relations" to help trace centers of patronage and literary cliques, a register of plays giving dates of composition and performances, concordances (already available for much of the work of Robert Greene, Anthony Munday, Cyril Tourneur, and John Webster), and an index of first lines of all poems written between 1500 and 1641.

Members of the Institute devote much time to preparing authoritative editions of writings of 16th- and 17th-century authors. A scholarly paperback edition of Shakespeare (one play to each volume) is in active preparation, under the general editorship of Professor Spencer; editions of the works of John Ford and Greene are being prepared also.

As well as contributing numerous articles to periodicals, members of the Institute have published a considerable number of books. *Shakespeare Survey*, published annually by the Cambridge University Press, and edited by Professor Nicoll, now extends to 17 volumes. *Stratford-upon-Avon Studies*, edited by Dr. J. R. Brown and B. A. Harris, is another series still in progress. Professor Nicoll's publications include *Shakespeare* (1952), *Chapman's Homer* (2 vols., 1956), *The Elizabethans* (1957), and a revision of his *History of English Drama from the Restoration* (6 vols., 1952–1959). Professor Sisson edited *The Complete Works of Shakespeare* (1954) and published his *New Readings in Shakespeare* (1956). Dr. J. R. Brown published *Shakespeare and his Comedies* (1957) and edited *The Merchant of Venice* (1955) for The New Arden Shakespeare and *The White Devil* (1960) for The Revels Plays. Professor Foakes has edited *The Comedy of Errors* (1952) and *Henry VIII* (1957) for The New Arden Shakespeare and, in collaboration with R. T. Rickert (another member of the Institute), a new edition of *Henslowe's Diary* (1961). E. A. Honigmann edited *King John* (1954) for The New Arden Shakespeare. Professor Baldwin Maxwell published *Studies in the Shakespeare Apocrypha* (1956). Professor Martin edited Robert Herrick's *Poetical Works* (1956) and Henry Vaughan's *Poetical Works* (1957). T. J. B. Spencer edited an illustrated volume, *Shakespeare: a Celebration* (1964), and a new edition of those of Plutarch's *Lives* known to have been studied by Shakespeare (Penguin Books, 1964).

The Institute accepts for training a limited number of postgraduates working on 16th- and 17th-century subjects for higher degrees (M.A. or Ph.D.) of the university. Tuition is entirely by seminars and individual supervision, but members of the Institute may also, if they wish, attend any lectures given in the university.

Scholars engaged in independent research and wishing to use the Institute are welcomed and given facilities for carrying on their work there.—I. A. S.

Shakespeare Jahrbuch. See JAHRBUCH DER DEUTSCHEN SHAKESPEARE-GESELLSCHAFT.

Shakespeare Memorial Theatre. See ROYAL SHAKESPEARE THEATRE.

Shakespeare Newsletter, The. A miscellany of Shakespearean news, published six times a year by its founder and editor, Louis Marder. The newsletter, which contains articles of both scholarly and popular interest, was founded in New York in 1950. It was published at Kent State University, Ohio, until August 1965. It is now published at the University of Illinois-Chicago.

Shakespeare Quarterly. The official publication of the SHAKESPEARE ASSOCIATION OF AMERICA. The successor to the SHAKESPEARE ASSOCIATION BULLETIN, it was first published in 1950. The *Shakespeare Quarterly* includes the most extensive annual Shakespeare bibliography, articles and book reviews of scholarly interest, and reviews of current Shakespeare productions. The summer issue of the 1956 volume of the *Quarterly* presented an extensive supplement, edited by G. Blakemore Evans, to the New Variorum Edition of *1 Henry IV*. In 1964 the *Quarterly* celebrated Shakespeare's 400th anniversary by issuing a large collection of critical studies, published simultaneously in book form as *Shakespeare 400*. The editor of the *Quarterly* is James G. McManaway of the Folger Shakespeare Library.

Shakespeare's company. See CHAMBERLAIN'S MEN.

Shakespeare Society. A scholarly organization. The Shakespeare Society was founded in London in 1840 by J. P. Collier in collaboration with G. L.

Craik, A. Dyce, J. O. Halliwell-Phillipps, and Charles Knight. During a period of 12 years the society published 48 volumes of primary material; the volumes were issued without numbers, but they are sometimes referred to by the numbers assigned by W. T. Lowndes, *Bibliographer's Manual of English Literature* (4 vols., 1834; Vol. IV, Pt. 2, p. 2341). Included are some of the most important documents in early English dramatic history: Dyce's edition of *Sir Thomas More,* Gosson's *School of Abuse,* Henslowe's diary, extracts from the registers of the Stationers' Company, the plays of Heywood, texts of the Coventry and Chester cycles, etc. The society was discredited when it was revealed that Collier had inserted forged material in some of his documents, and in 1853 it was disbanded. See NEW SHAKSPERE SOCIETY.

Shakespeare Studies. An annual volume containing articles and reviews relating to Shakespearean scholarship. First published in 1965, the volume is edited by its founder, J. Leeds Barroll of the University of Cincinnati.

Shakespeare Survey. A series of annual volumes dealing with Shakespearean studies and production throughout the world. The *Survey,* the first volume of which was published in 1948, is edited by Allardyce Nicoll. Each volume is devoted to a specific area of Shakespearean studies, generally introduced by retrospective surveys of that field of study. The areas which have been covered, annually from 1948 to 1965, are the following:

1. Shakespeare and his Stage
2. Shakespearean Production
3. The Man and the Writer
4. Interpretation
5. Textual Criticism
6. The Histories
7. Style and Language
8. The Comedies
9. *Hamlet*
10. The Roman Plays
11. The Last Plays
12. The Elizabethan Theatre
13. *King Lear*
14. Shakespeare and his Contemporaries
15. The Poems and Music
16. Shakespeare in the Modern World
17. Shakespeare in His Own Age
18. Shakespeare Then Till Now

Shallow, Robert. In *2 Henry IV,* a country justice. Shallow recruits from the inhabitants of Cotswold a group of "sufficient men" for the King's service under Falstaff. When Falstaff returns from his campaign, Shallow houses him and lends him a thousand pounds. In *The Merry Wives of Windsor* he is Slender's cousin. Now a doddering 80 years old, Shallow boasts that he has seen the time when he could make "fellows skip like rats" and that his finger still itches when he sees a sword drawn. Sir John Falstaff is threatened with a "Star Chamber" suit by the Justice for having beaten his men, killed his deer, and broken open his lodge. Later, Shallow, who has secured Master Page's consent to his cousin's suit, pushes Slender into an interview with Anne, but it is Shallow who has to declare Slender's love for her. The character of Shallow is generally thought to be an attack on Sir Thomas LUCY, although Leslie Hotson argues that Shallow is based on William GARDINER, justice of the peace at Southwark.

Shank or **Shanks, John** (d. 1636). Actor. Shank apparently had a long career in the theatre, beginning with Pembroke's Men in the 1580's and later serving with Queen Elizabeth's Men. In 1610 he was listed with Prince Henry's company, joining the King's Men sometime between 1613 and 1619. Shank's name can be found in both the 1619 patent and the First Folio list of actors (1623). Evidently he had succeeded Robert Armin as the company's clown after Armin's death in 1615. In 1633 his purchase of three shares in the Globe and two in Blackfriars from John Heminges' son William involved him in a dispute with his fellow actors (see SHARERS' PAPERS). His death was registered in the parish of St. Giles', Cripplegate, January 27, 1636. His son John Shank, Jr., was also an actor, playing at the Fortune about 1640.

His career as a comedian is recalled in the *Historia Histrionica* of James WRIGHT, and an allusion attributed to "W. Turner's *Dish of Stuff, or a Gallimaufry*" appears in Collier's *Memoirs of the Principal Actors in the Plays of Shakespeare* (1846):

That's the fat fool of the Curtain,
  And the lean fool of the Bull:
Since Shancke did leave to sing his rhimes,
  He is counted but a gull:
The players on the Bankside,
  The round Globe and the Swan,
Will teach you idle tricks of love,
  But the Bull will play the man.

Collier dated the verses at 1662, but according to E. K. Chambers the theatres mentioned indicate a much earlier date. [E. K. Chambers, *The Elizabethan Stage,* 1923; G. E. Bentley, *The Jacobean and Caroline Stage,* 5 vols., 1941–1956.]

sharer. In the Elizabethan theatre, a member of an acting company who was a part-owner of the company, received a portion of the company's profit, and was responsible, along with his fellow sharers, for its expenses. An actor sharer is to be distinguished from actors who were HIRED MEN, that is, salaried employees of the company. In Shakespeare's company the sharers were also generally HOUSEKEEPERS, that is, owners of the theatre building as well (see CHAMBERLAIN'S MEN). A sharer's interest in a company apparently ceased upon his retirement, transfer, or death. [T. W. Baldwin, *The Organization and Personnel of the Shakespearean Company,* 1927.]

sharers' papers. Term used to describe the documents resulting from a dispute among the members of the King's Men in 1635. The term "sharers' papers" is a misnomer in that the dispute actually refers not to the sharers, the owners of the acting company, but to the housekeepers, the owners of the theatre. In Shakespeare's company, of course, the housekeepers and the sharers were usually the same persons except that while one's share in the acting company generally ceased upon retirement, the part-ownership of the theatre remained the property of the individual, to be sold or bequeathed to his heirs.

In 1635 three actor-sharers with the King's Men, Thomas Pollard, Robert Benfield, and Eyllaerdt

Swanston, petitioned the lord chamberlain for the right to purchase shares in the Globe and Blackfriars theatres, specifically a portion of those shares owned by John Shank who had purchased his shares from William Heminges, the son of John Heminges. Shank owned three shares in the Globe and two in the Blackfriars; the players were demanding the right to purchase from Shank one share in the Globe and one in Blackfriars, as well as two other Globe shares, one belonging to Cuthbert Burbage and the other to Mrs. Winifred Robinson, the remarried widow of Richard Burbage. The petition was answered by Shank, who warned the lord chamberlain against establishing such a dangerous precedent:

> . . . to all young men that shall follow heerafter, that they shall allwayes refuse to doe his Ma[ty] service, vnless they may haue whatsoeuer they will though it bee other mens estates.

Cuthbert Burbage, Richard Burbage's son William, and Mrs. Robinson also replied to the charges in the petition. Their answer was much the same as Shank's except that it was prefaced by a history of the Globe and Blackfriars, which affords us invaluable information about those theatres:

> The father of us, Cutbert and Richard Burbage, was the first builder of playhowses, and was himselfe in his younger yeeres a player. The Theater hee built with many hundred poundes taken up at interest.—The players that lived in those first times had onely the profitts arising from the dores, but now the players receave all the commings in at the dores to themselves and halfe the galleries from the houskepers. Hee built this house upon leased ground, by which meanes the landlord and hee had a great suite in law, and, by his death, the like troubles fell on us, his sonnes; wee then bethought us of altering from thence, and at like expence built the Globe, with more summes of money taken up at interest, which lay heavy on us many yeeres, and to ourselves we joyned those deserveing men, Shakspere, Hemings, Condall, Philips and others, partners in the profittes of that they call the House, but makeing the leases for twenty-one yeeres hath beene the destruction of ourselves and others, for they dyeing at the expiration of three or four yeeres of their lease, the subsequent yeeres became dissolved to strangers, as by marrying with their widdowes, and the like by their children.—Thus, Right Honorable, as concerning the Globe, where wee ourselves are but lessees. Now for the Blackfriers, that is our inheritance; our father purchased it at extreame rates, and made it into a playhouse with great charge and troble; which after was leased out to one Evans that first sett up the boyes commonly called the Queenes Majesties Children of the Chappell. In processe of time, the boyes growing vp to bee men, which were Underwood, Field, Ostler, and were taken to strengthen the Kings service; and the more to strengthen the service, the boyes dayly wearing out, it was considered that house would bee as fitt for ourselves, and soe purchased the lease remaining from Evans with our money, and placed men players, which were Hemings, Condall, Shakspeare, &c.

The lord chamberlain decided in favor of the petitioners, requiring Shank to sell his shares in the theatres. Shank then entered a further petition stating that in compliance with the lord chamberlain's order he had made the players an offer which they had rejected. The lord chamberlain then ordered the establishment of a board of inquiry to determine a fair price for the shares. The outcome of the inquiry is not known, but the shares were still in Shank's possession in December 1635 when he made his will. [J. O. Halliwell-Phillipps, *Outlines of the Life of Shakespeare*, 1881; G. E. Bentley, *The Jacobean and Caroline Stage*, 5 vols., 1941–1956.]

Sharpham, Edward (1576–1608). Dramatist. Educated at Middle Temple, Sharpham was a negligent student and was never called to the bar. His playwriting career is obscure, but he is known to be the author of two plays, *The Fleir*, acted at Blackfriars by the Children of the King's Revels in 1605/6, and *Cupid's Whirligig* (1607). *The Fleir* is chiefly notable for its borrowings from *1 Henry IV* and from the scene from *King Lear* (I, iv, 9–42) in which Kent lists his qualifications as a serving man. The play is also the source of our knowledge of a stage tradition concerning the performance of *A Midsummer Night's Dream*, namely, Flute as "Thisbe" stabs himself with his scabbard: "Faith like *Thisbe* in the play, a has almost kil'd himselfe with the scabberd." [*The Shakspere Allusion-Book*, J. Munro, ed., 1909.]

Shaw, George Bernard (1856–1950). Irish playwright and critic. Born in Dublin and educated at Wesleyan Connexional School, Shaw was the most important dramatist writing in English during the late 19th and early 20th centuries. After unsuccessfully trying his hand at the novel, Shaw began in 1885 to write the dramas which were collected in his *Plays Pleasant and Unpleasant* (1898). Among these are *Mrs. Warren's Profession*, a study of prostitution; *Arms and the Man*, a satire on the military; and *Candida*, a sympathetic treatment of the emancipated woman.

The plays which followed continued to reveal Shaw's antiromantic, unsentimental view of life, and a concept of society in keeping with socialistic sentiments. They include *Man and Superman* (1903), *Major Barbara* (1905), *Pygmalion* (1913), and *Saint Joan* (1923). As a critic Shaw produced *The Perfect Wagnerite* (1898) and *The Quintessence of Ibsenism* (1891), an early defense of the Norwegian playwright. Shaw's most important criticism is contained in the lengthy and brilliant essays with which he prefaced his plays.

It is rather difficult to take seriously much of Shaw's criticism of Shakespeare. As Edwin Wilson points out in the Introduction to *Shaw on Shakespeare* (1961), Shaw attacked Shakespeare "with an impudence that had not been seen before, nor is likely to be seen again." As dramatic critic for the *Saturday Review*, Shaw wrote that *Cymbeline* is "for the most part stagey trash of the lowest melodramatic order"; its author wrote "for an afternoon, but not for all time." Shaw's witty assaults upon Shakespeare are not entirely sophomoric, however, for he considered Shakespeare "one of the towers of the Bastille, and down he must come." Shaw's hostility was due in large measure to his conviction that productions of hakespeare were interfering with the acceptance of bsen and the new theatre. Furthermore, Shakespeare nd Shaw did not share the same social conscience nd moral scruples. Other factors which limited his ppreciation of Shakespeare were Shaw's inability to ccept the tragic view of life and his insistence that rt must be didactic.

Although he often despised Shakespeare's ideas, haw praised his art, even suggesting that "in manner nd art nobody can write better than Shakespeare, ecause, carelessness apart, he did the thing as well s it can be done within the limits of human faculty." haw waxed eloquent when he praised the harmonies f Shakespeare's "word-music." He also praised and rew attention to the satirical comedies, which had een neglected.

Shaw, Glen Byam (1904–). Actor and director. Born in London, Shaw was educated at the Vestminster School and made his London debut at Iammersmith in 1925. In 1926 he played in repertory t J. B. Fagan's Oxford Playhouse. He has appeared n America and England. Among his Shakespearean ortrayals are Laertes (1934), Benvolio (1935), Sir tephen Scroop, Gratiano (1937/8), and Horatio in ondon and at Kronborg Castle, Helsingor (Elsinore, 939). Among the Shakespearean productions Shaw as directed are *Richard II* with Gielgud at the Oxord University Drama Society (1935), *The Merchant f Venice* with Gielgud (1938), and *Antony and Cleopatra* (1946). In 1947 he was appointed director f the Old Vic School and the Theatre Centre. In 949 he directed *As You Like It* for the Young Vic Company, and in 1951, *Henry V* at the Old Vic.

In 1952 Shaw became co-director with Anthony Quayle of the Shakespeare Memorial Theatre at tratford-upon-Avon. That year he directed *Coriolanus,* and the following year, *Richard III,* with Quayle. Shaw directed *Romeo and Juliet* and *Troilus nd Cressida* in 1954, *Macbeth* and *The Merry Wives f Windsor* in 1955. In 1956 Quayle resigned as coirector, but Shaw continued, directing *Othello* 1956), *As You Like It* (1957), *Julius Caesar* (1957), *Hamlet* (1958), *Romeo and Juliet* (1958), and *King Lear* (1959). Then Shaw, too, resigned, but returned o produce *King Lear* at Stratford in 1960. [*Who's Who in the Theatre,* 1961.]

Shaw, July (1571–1629). Stratford friend and eighbor of Shakespeare. A prosperous wool merhant, Shaw lived on Chapel Street, two doors away rom Shakespeare's New Place. He was successful nough to be styled "gentleman" by 1613, the year n which he was elected an alderman of Stratford. His friendship with Shakespeare is evidenced by the act that he served as a witness to the latter's will in 616. [Mark Eccles, *Shakespeare in Warwickshire,* 961.]

Shelley, Percy Bysshe (1792–1822). Romantic poet. A native of Sussex, Shelley's political and religious adicalism brought about his expulsion from Oxford n 1811. When his wife's suicide aroused public cenure of his libertine conduct, he took Mary Godwin, ow his second wife, to Italy where, befriended by Byron, Shelley wrote his finest poems: "Ode to the West Wind" (1819), "To a Skylark" (1820), "Adonis" (1821). He was drowned in the Bay of Lerici in 822. Contemporary biographers and his own letters attest to Shelley's deep knowledge and appreciation of Shakespeare. Numerous entries made in his journal while he was writing his greatest work mention his reading Shakespeare, stressing that he read certain plays aloud. In 1817, when he was considering turning his talents primarily to drama, he acted in Shakespearean plays at Marlow. His verse plays reflect this knowledge, especially *The Cenci* (1819), the plot of which suggests both *Macbeth* and *Othello* and in which may be found verbal references to many of the other tragedies as well. Standard Shakespearean imagery (animal images, especially of the hunt, the world as a stage, etc.) dominate the play. Critics have noted over 60 references to Shakespeare in Shelley's work, and cite the elegy for Keats, "Adonais," as especially filled with verbal echoes of Shakespeare. [David L. Clark, "Shelley and Shakespeare," *PMLA,* LIV, 1939; Frederick L. Jones, "Shelley and Shakespeare: A Supplement," *PMLA,* LIX, 1944.]

Shepherd. In *The Winter's Tale,* reputed father of Perdita. This good-hearted old shepherd, discovering the abandoned infant Perdita, takes "it up for pity" and raises the child as his daughter. While he exerts paternal discipline, the old Shepherd also shows fatherly appreciation for Perdita's accomplishments and proudly reports that she does everything well. Condemned by Polixenes to hang for his involvement in the proposed betrothal of his foster child and Florizel, the Shepherd is advised by his son to prove that Perdita is a foundling. He is rewarded when Perdita's identity is discovered, and is made "a gentleman born."

Shepherd, Old. In *1 Henry VI,* father of La Pucelle (Joan of Arc). When he laments his daughter's approaching death, La Pucelle scornfully denies having come of such humble parentage. The Shepherd then curses her and calls on the girl's captors to burn her, since "hanging is too good" (V, iv).

Sheridan, Richard Brinsley (1751–1816). Playwright. Best known as the author of two great comedies, *The Rivals* (1775) and *The School for Scandal* (1777), Sheridan was also directly involved in Shakespearean production as a theatre owner. In 1776 he became part owner and manager of the Drury Lane Theatre, having purchased it from David Garrick. During Sheridan's ownership the great Shakespearean tradition established by Garrick was continued by John Philip Kemble. Sheridan had a less happy experience as a Shakespearean entrepreneur when he oversaw the production of *Vortigern,* a pseudo-Shakespearean effort of William Henry IRELAND.

Sheridan, Thomas (1719–1788). Irish actor and author. The father of the playwright Richard Brinsley Sheridan, Thomas Sheridan began his career playing Richard III in Dublin. He went to London in 1744 and played Hamlet both at Drury Lane and at Covent Garden. In that year he also played Brutus and Macbeth and Othello. Other leading Shakespearean roles played by Sheridan were King John (1760), Richard III (1754, in Colley Cibber's adaptation), Romeo (1754), and Shylock (1754).

Sheridan also wrote a version of *Coriolanus* derived from James Thomson's adaptation. Sheridan's adaptation is a considerably shortened form in which, with the exception of a few lines, the entire first act is omitted. Sheridan played the leading role at Drury Lane in 1754. [Charles Beecher Hogan, *Shakespeare in the Theatre, 1701–1800*, 2 vols., 1952, 1957.]

Sheriff. In *1 Henry IV*, he enters the Boar's Head Tavern where Prince Henry and his friends are carrying on uproariously, and asks for "A gross fat man" (II, iv).

Sheriff of Wiltshire. In *Richard III*, he leads the Duke of Buckingham to execution. Historically this sheriff was Henry Long (d. 1490). [W. H. Thomson, *Shakespeare's Characters: A Historical Dictionary*, 1951.]

Shirley, James (1596–1666). Dramatist. Born in London and educated at Oxford and Cambridge, Shirley lost his position as headmaster of the grammar school at St. Albans when he was converted to Catholicism in 1625. He took up playwriting in order to support himself. Between 1625 and the closing of the theatres in 1642, he produced a large number of plays, of which 31 are extant. He quickly established himself as a court favorite, even "collaborating" with King Charles on one play, *The Gamester* (1634), "made by Sherley . . . out of a plot of the King's." At the death of Philip Massinger in 1640, Shirley became chief playwright for the King's Men. In the civil war, he served with the king's forces and after the war he resumed his old profession of schoolmaster. He died, according to a contemporary account, "overcome with affrightments, disconsolations and other miseries" endured in the Great Fire of 1666.

In general Shirley was a worthy inheritor of the great tradition of English Renaissance drama. Although his plays are more closely related to those of Jonson and Beaumont and Fletcher, his debt to Shakespeare can be seen in a number of his plays. In 1691 Gerard Langbaine asserted that in Shirley's masque *The Triumph of Beautie* (1646), "our Author has imitated *Shakespear*, in the Comical part of his *Midsummer Nights Dream;* and *Shirley's* Shepheard *Bottle*, is but a Copy of *Shakespear's Bottom, the Weaver*."

Shoemaker's Holiday, The. See Thomas DEKKER.

Shore, Jane (c. 1445–1527). Mistress of Edward IV. The wife of a goldsmith, Jane Shore became Edward's mistress in 1470. Although she exercised considerable political power for a time, she was imprisoned for witchcraft after the death of Edward and died in poverty. Her story, as recounted in narrative verse by Thomas Churchyard for the 1563 edition of *A Mirror for Magistrates*, won considerable popularity during the Elizabethan age. She is alluded to in *Richard III* (I, i, 73; III, i, 185).

Shoreditch. In Elizabethan times a northern suburb of London and the location of the first two public theatres, the Theatre and the Curtain. Shoreditch had an unsavory reputation as the home of prostitutes and pickpockets. Many actors lived there, including Richard Burbage. According to the unreliable John Aubrey, Shakespeare "lived in Shoreditch, wouldnt be debouched, and if invited to writ; he was in paine." [Edward H. Sugden, *A Topographical Dictionary to . . . Shakespeare . . .*, 1925.]

Short, Peter (d. 1603). London printer at whose shop in Bread Street a number of Shakespearean quartos were printed. Short was admitted to the Stationers' Company in 1589 and soon established an active business. In 1598 he printed the First Quarto of *1 Henry IV* as well as the second edition of *The Rape of Lucrece*, printed in octavo. In that year he also printed Francis Meres' *Palladis Tamia.* In 1599 he printed the fifth edition of *Venus and Adonis* which contains many readings not found in any other edition, but which was a carelessly printed text. He was also the printer and publisher of the anonymous *Taming of A Shrew* (1594). Short died in 1603 and his widow married the stationer Humphrey Lownes. [R. B. McKerrow, ed., *A Dictionary of Printers and Booksellers . . . 1557–1640*, 1910.]

Shostakovich, Dmitri. See MUSIC BASED ON SHAKESPEARE: *20th century*.

Shottery. A small hamlet about a mile from Stratford and the home of Shakespeare's wife, Anne Hathaway. The Hathaways lived at Hewlands Farm which Anne's grandfather John Hathaway had leased in 1543. This may be the land which Shakespeare was reportedly interested in buying, according to a letter from Abraham STURLEY to Richard Quiney. The purchase apparently never went through, however and in 1610 Hewlands Farm was sold to Bartholomew Hathaway, Shakespeare's brother-in-law. [Mark Eccles, *Shakespeare in Warwickshire*, 1961].

Shrewsbury, John Talbot, 1st earl of (1388?-1453). Second son of Richard, 4th Baron Talbot of Goodrich Castle. Talbot had a long and brilliant career as a soldier: with the duke of Bedford in France, Talbot won many battles until his capture by the French at Patay in 1429. He was held prisoner for two years. On his release, Talbot participated in the highly successful campaign of Philip, duke of Burgundy, in northwest France After capturing Bordeaux and the surrounding country, he was finally defeated and killed at Castillon.

In *1 Henry VI,* Talbot appears as leader of the English armies. Trapped by the French at Patay, he foils the Countess of Auvergne in her attempt to capture him unawares. When Talbot retakes Rouen from Joan (La Pucelle), Henry rewards him with the title of Earl of Shrewsbury. He is killed trying to take Bordeaux.

Shylock. In *The Merchant of Venice,* a wealthy Jewish moneylender. Shylock, although he appears in only five scenes, has emerged as one of Shakespeare's greatest and most controversial characters Easily dominating the light, not to say frivolous, romantic action of the play, he is an alternately anguished, alternately ludicrous human being. Theatre history, however, suggests that it has been simpler to treat him as exclusively tragic or comic without probing the complexity of his nature. Thus, stage renditions of Shylock have ranged from early 18th century characterizations of a broadly farcical figure to Sir Henry Irving's portrait of a martyred Old Testament patriarch. See THE MERCHANT OF VENICE *Stage History*.

The critical history of Shylock's character has covered a similarly wide range. He has been pictured by E. E. Stoll and others as a comic villain whom the Elizabethan audience would have hissed and hooted off the stage. The tragic Shylock, according to Stoll is not Shakespeare's creation, but the product of 19th century sentimentality. Many modern readers, how

·er, consider that Stoll's picture of Shylock, while ·ccessful in giving a unified tone to the play, ·minishes his character to a point which the play ·self contradicts. They tend to agree more, although ·t completely, with the tragic view of Shylock en-·rsed in the 19th century by Heinrich Heine and ·illiam Hazlitt. Heine and Hazlitt located the roots Shylock's passionate hatred and consuming desire ·r revenge in the centuries of persecution and ·loquy to which his people had been subjected. ·heirs is a view of a Shylock who is "more sinned ·ainst than sinning," which, although in some re-·ects is a more satisfactory account of the charac-·r's impact on readers and viewers, nevertheless in-·oduces a further problem. The tragic Shylock, set ·wn in the middle of *The Merchant of Venice,* ·ursts the mold of that fragile, fanciful play. This ·ylock belongs, as Granville-Barker has suggested, · "a greater play that Shakespeare was yet to write." ·hus for some, the character and the play which he ·ominates are irreconcilable. This is the reaction of ·any modern readers for whom the treatment of ·hylock in the court scene is a remote but disturbing ·minder of the Nazi atrocities.

The foregoing response calls attention to the most ·exed problem of the play, the question of anti-·emitism in the characterization of Shylock. Despite ·e fact that the subject of racial prejudice has been ·ersistently pronounced irrelevant to the concerns of ·e play, the debate over the attitude toward Jews ·mbodied in the portrait of Shylock has raged for ·enturies. Shakespeare has been pictured as the first ·reat defender of the Jews in Western literature and ·s a "Jew-hater." A great deal of scholarship and ·ritical judiciousness has gone into supporting both ·f these views, but nothing like a conclusive answer ·as yet appeared. What does seem clear is that ·hakespeare could have known few, if any, Jews ·ersonally, and that for him and for his audiences, a ·Jew" was less a man than a symbol. Anti-Semitism ·n Elizabethan England was a theoretical position ·ather than a living reality, since Jews had been ban-·shed from England in 1290 and were not readmitted ·ntil 1655. Although there may have been a small ·umber of them in England during Shakespeare's ·ifetime, they would have been very few. As Martin ·Holmes (*Shakespeare's Public,* 1962) has suggested, ·the race had become unfamiliar and exotic." It is ·lso clear that Shylock, whatever his faults, is no ·nere racial stereotype but a powerful and fiercely ·uman character. [E. E. Stoll, *Shakespeare Studies,* ·927; T. Lelyveld, *Shylock on the Stage,* 1960; Edgar ·Rosenberg, *From Shylock to Svengali,* 1960; Bernard ·Grebanier, *The Truth About Shylock,* 1962.]—E.Q.

Sibelius, Jean. See MUSIC BASED ON SHAKESPEARE: ·oth century.

Sicilian Usurper, The. See Nahum TATE.

Sicinius Velutus and **Junius Brutus.** Leaders of the ·lebeians' revolt of 464 B.C., in which, refusing to ·oil for the patricians, the workers seceded from ·Rome to the Mons Sacer. In *Coriolanus,* Sicinius ·Velutus and Junius Brutus appear as people's trib-·unes. Stirring up popular ill-will against Coriolanus, ·hey effect his banishment, but when he leads the ·Volscians against Rome, they deny having wronged ·him and induce Menenius to attempt to dissuade ·him from attacking.

Siddons, Sarah. Born **Sarah Kemble** (1755–1831). Actress. Universally recognized as the greatest actress of the 18th century, Mrs. Siddons was described by William Hazlitt as "not less than a goddess, or than a prophetess inspired by the gods," and Lord Byron considered her worth a Cooke, Kemble, and Kean all put together.

Mrs. Siddons was the daughter of Roger Kemble, a Midland actor-manager, and sister of John Philip and Charles Kemble (see KEMBLE FAMILY). She proved to be an infant prodigy and was received affectionately by her audiences for her poetry recitals. Her first role was that of Ariel in *The Tempest* and in the cast was William Siddons, whom she married six years later in 1773 at 18. The young couple toured the provinces until David Garrick, hearing of her talents, brought her to Drury Lane in 1775 to make her debut as Portia in *The Merchant of Venice.* It was a most untimely and unfortunate engagement; the critics were harsh and uncompromising and Mrs. Siddons left London. The provinces welcomed her and she played at Manchester and Bath under the tutelage of Tate Wilkinson and John Palmer. At Bath, from 1778 to 1781, she scored notable successes as Lady Macbeth, Constance in *King John,* and a score of other roles. Drury Lane sent for her again in 1781, and this time London audiences and critics alike were unanimous in their praise.

Mrs. Siddons' early provincial triumphs were primarily made in Shakespearean characterizations, but her London performances were, at first, primarily non-Shakespearean. It was not until 1783, as Isabella in *Measure for Measure* and as Constance, that she played Shakespeare at the Drury Lane. Later, in 1785, she portrayed Lady Macbeth, as well as Desdemona. In 1786, she played Ophelia and Portia. These roles, especially Lady Macbeth and Constance, which were her finest, were repeated throughout her career. Other notable portrayals were of the queens in *Hamlet, Richard II,* and *Henry VIII,* Volumnia in *Coriolanus,* and Hermione in *The Winter's Tale.* The Drury Lane was the scene of most of Mrs. Siddons' memorable performances; in 1790, however, ill health and entanglements with a parsimonious management represented by Richard Sheridan caused a permanent dissociation. From 1790 to 1806, Mrs. Siddons did not appear regularly on the stage. In 1806, she joined her brother John Philip Kemble at Covent Garden, where, although she played several seasons, she restricted herself to the roles her public loved best. Her most popular characterization was always Lady Macbeth and in 1812 she re-created it for the last time. [*Dictionary of National Biography,* 1885– ; *Oxford Companion to the Theatre,* Phyllis Hartnoll, ed., 1951.] E. V. G.

Sidney, Sir Philip (1554–1586). Poet and courtier. Sidney was regarded by his contemporaries as the ideal embodiment of the age, the gentleman who served with distinction as a poet, patron, scholar, courtier, diplomat, and soldier. His promising career was cut short at the age of 32 when he was fatally wounded at the battle of Zutphen. None of Sidney's writings was printed during his lifetime. *An Apologie for Poetrie,* which exists in a slightly different version entitled *In Defence of Poesie,* was written about 1580–1582, apparently in response to Stephen Gosson's *School of Abuse* (1579) which had been dedi-

SIR PHILIP SIDNEY. PORTRAIT BY AN UNKNOWN ARTIST. (NATIONAL PORTRAIT GALLERY)

cated to Sidney; both versions were published in 1595. Sidney, however, did not mention Gosson by name, nor did he attempt a direct refutation. His object was a comprehensive defense of letters cast in the form of a classical oration. The result is an epitome of Renaissance literary criticism, embodying various principles of Plato, Aristotle, and Horace and showing the influence of such contemporary Italian critics as Julius Caesar Scaliger and Antonio Minturno. The comments on drama, though brief, mark the beginning of dramatic criticism in England; Sidney's chief concern is to uphold the unities and to attack the mixed form of tragicomedy. But Sidney was more at home with poetry and romance. His ARCADIA, an unfinished pastoral romance, was first published in 1590. With *Astrophel and Stella*, Sidney wrote one of the earliest SONNET SEQUENCES in English; the work was inspired by his unsuccessful courtship of Penelope Devereux, later Lady Rich. Its unauthorized publication in 1591 is credited with launching the vogue of sonnet sequences in the 1590's. Not until 1598 did an authorized version appear, when all of Sidney's principal works were published under the supervision of his sister, Mary Herbert, countess of PEMBROKE. [John Buxton, *Sir Philip Sidney and the English Renaissance*, 1954.]

Silence. In *2 Henry IV*, a country justice and Shallow's cousin. During a late-evening party in Shallow's orchard, Silence drinks and sings lustily until Falstaff orders that he be carried to bed (V, iii).

Silius. In *Antony and Cleopatra*, one of the officers in the army of Ventidius. Silius tries to persuac Ventidius to pursue the defeated and retreating Pa thians, but his commander rejects his suggestio (III, i).

Silvia. In *The Two Gentlemen of Verona*, th beautiful and kind daughter of the Duke of Mila Wooed by Thurio, Valentine, and Proteus, Silvia won by the faithful Valentine.

Silvius. In *As You Like It*, a young shephe whose love for the disdainful Phebe is unrequite Silvius slavishly delivers Phebe's love letter t Rosalind, who is disguised as a boy. His devotio is rewarded when Rosalind, who considers th love has made Silvius a coward, reveals her sex.

Simmes or **Sims, Valentine** (d. ?1622). Londo printer of several Shakespeare quartos. Simmes w admitted to the Stationers' Company in 1585 an four years later was arrested as one of the compos tors in the printing of the MARPRELATE pamphlet This was the first of a long series of brushes with th authorities that Simmes underwent for his illeg printing activities. In 1622 he was prohibited fro working as a master printer and was retired from th Stationers' Company with a small pension. H Shakespearean publications include the printing c the First Quartos of *Richard III* (1597) and *Richar II* (1597), as well as the Second and Third Quart of the latter. In 1600 he printed *2 Henry IV* an *Much Ado About Nothing*, and in 1603 the "ba quarto" of *Hamlet*. [R. B. McKerrow, ed., *A Dic tionary of Printers and Booksellers . . . 1557–164* 1910.]

Simonides. In *Pericles*, King of Pentapolis an father of Thaisa. Pericles says of Simonides, "He a happy king, since he gains from his subjects th name of good by his government." When the shabb stranger knight, Pericles, is victor in a tournamer celebrating Thaisa's birthday, Simonides, uncor cerned with outward appearances, shows him marke favor. Although Simonides privately commends h daughter's decision to marry Pericles or no on he feigns displeasure and accuses the Prince o having bewitched Thaisa. Soon abandoning th pretense, however, Simonides bestows his patern blessing on the match.

Simpcox, Saunder, and his wife. In *2 Henry V* they persuade the credulous King that Simpco eyesight has been restored by St. Alban after lifetime of blindness. Simpcox is exposed by th Duke of Gloucester (II, i). An incident of thi kind occurred during the reign of Henry VI whe a blind man came to St. Albans with his wif begged for several days, and claimed to be healec Gloucester put him in the stocks. [W. H. Thomsor *Shakespeare's Characters: A Historical Dictionar* 1951.]

Simple. In *The Merry Wives of Windsor*, servant to Slender. Simple carries to Mistre Quickly a letter from Sir Hugh Evans asking he to assist in Slender's suit for Anne Page. He hide in a closet when Doctor Caius arrives and, upo being discovered, is sent by Caius to deliver challenge to Evans (I, iv). In IV, v, Falstaff an the Host of the Garter Inn poke fun at him.

Simpson, Percy (1865–1962). Scholar. A lecturer a Oxford and a fellow of Oriel, Simpson first attracte attention by the theory set forth in his *Shakespeari* *unctuation* (1911). Simpson maintained that the ınctuation was rhythmical rather than logical, that ıe marks were intended as a guide to the speaker in ıaking pauses, without regard to abstract principles. mong others, A. W. Pollard and Dover Wilson ac- ːpted the theory, but the present tendency is to re- ırd the compositor, rather than Shakespeare, as the ıe responsible for the punctuation. Other works ıclude *Proof-Reading in the Sixteenth, Seventeenth, ıd Eighteenth Centuries* (1935) and *The Theme of evenge in Elizabethan Tragedy* (1935). *Studies in lizabethan Drama* (1955) includes an essay on the evelopment of Shakespeare's versification and one n his use of Latin authors. Simpson's most monu- ıental achievement was his collaboration with C. H. Ierford and E. M. Simpson in editing the works of en Jonson (11 vols., 1925–1952).

Sims, Valentine. See Valentine SIMMES.

Sincklo or **Sincler, John** (fl. 1590–1604). Actor. ıncklo has been tentatively identified as a member f the combined Admiral-Strange's company in 590/1, possibly Pembroke's Men in 1592/3, and from 594 to 1604 as one of Chamberlain's Men. Sincklo is ıentioned in the "plot" of *2 Seven Deadly Sins* 1590/1), and in the stage directions of *3 Henry VI:* Enter Sinklo and Humfrey." He is also mentioned ı the Folio Induction to *The Taming of the Shrew,* ı the role of a Player, and in the Quarto *2 Henry V*, in which he appears as the First Beadle.

It has been suggested that Sincklo was noted for laying roles requiring a thin man, including Robert 'aulconbridge in *King John* (Faulconbridge's thin- ess is mocked by his brother the Bastard), the ıpothecary in *Romeo and Juliet,* and Robin Starve- ng in *A Midsummer Night's Dream.*

Sir John Oldcastle (c. 1600). A play by Michael)rayton, Anthony Munday, Richard Hathaway, and ːobert Wilson. *Sir John Oldcastle* was commissioned y Philip Henslowe for the Admiral's Men, presum- bly to offset the picture of Oldcastle given in the haracter of Falstaff whom Shakespeare had origi- ally named Oldcastle (see Sir John OLDCASTLE). In *ir John Oldcastle,* the presentation of the knight as he morally upright Protestant martyr is consistent vith the historical facts. The play was published in 600 as:

> The first part Of the true and honorable historie, of the life of Sir John Old-castle, the good Lord Cobham. As it hath been lately acted by the right honorable the Earle of Notingham Lord high Ad- mirall of England his seruants.... V.S. for Thomas Pavier....

ɜy this time a second part (now lost) to the Old- astle play had evidently been written, probably by)rayton alone. In 1602 the play was transferred to Vorcester's Men, and Thomas Dekker was paid £2 os. for additions to this and other plays.

The first part was reprinted in 1619 by William aggard as one of a collection of falsely dated Shake- pearean and pseudo-Shakespearean plays which he nd Thomas Pavier brought out in that year. The itle page of the 1619 Quarto adds "Written by Wil- iam Shakespeare." The play was included among he seven plays that were added to the Third Folio 1664) and Fourth Folio (1685).

Sir Thomas More. An extant manuscript play, three pages of which are generally believed to be in Shakespeare's handwriting. The manuscript is preserved in the Harleian collection at the British Museum, the earliest known owner being John Murray, an 18th-century collector of rare books and manuscripts. The manuscript is in such disrepair that it is not available for examination. In 1911, however, it was reproduced in typographical facsimile, masterfully edited by W. W. Greg in a work which is one of the finest examples of English literary scholarship.

The aspect of the manuscript which has attracted the most attention is the problem of identifying the seven different handwritings to be found therein. Greg's initial distinctions are still generally accepted as accurate. The play was apparently written by one author, identified as "Hand S," and submitted for licensing to Edmund Tilney, the Master of the Revels. Tilney apparently rejected the manuscript because of certain controversial passages. Some time later the manuscript was taken up again; the controversial passages were removed and replaced by five additions to the play written in five different hands, identified as hands "A" to "E." On the basis of existing paleographical evidence, the assignment of the six hands is as follows: S, Anthony Munday; A, Henry Chettle; B, Thomas Heywood; C, an anonymous book-keeper; D, William Shakespeare; and E, Thomas Dekker. The seventh hand in the manuscript is that of Tilney, to whom apparently the revised manuscript was resubmitted, and who rejected the second attempt as well.

There is all but unanimous agreement that Munday wrote the original manuscript, that Chettle wrote the first addition, and Dekker the last addition. S. A. Tannenbaum's assertion that Hand C was Thomas Kyd's was refuted by Greg, who showed that it was the hand of the same scribe or book-keeper who copied the "plot" of *The Seven Deadly Sins.* Hand B is generally accepted as belonging to Thomas Heywood, although some doubt of this is still expressed by certain scholars.

The most important problem is the identity of Hand D. The definitive establishment of this as Shakespeare's is made extremely difficult by the fact that six signatures constitute the only recognized extant examples of his hand (see HANDWRITING). This identification was first made by Sir Edward Maunde Thompson who analyzed and compared the signatures with the writing of Hand D and declared them to be the same. To Sir Edward's paleographical evidence were added a number of literary arguments in favor of Shakespeare's authorship, which were collected in a symposium edited by A. W. Pollard as *Shakespeare's Hand in the Play of Sir Thomas More* (1923). These included Dover Wilson's argument that the writing style of Hand D explained some errors and abnormal spellings occurring in printed texts of Shakespeare, and R. W. Chambers' exposition—later amplified in his *Man's Unconquerable Mind* (1939)—that the development of ideas in the section by Hand D was similar to Shakespeare's. Chambers' argument is a particularly brilliant and convincing one, demonstrating a remarkable correspondence between the mind of Shakespeare and that of Hand D.

Despite the seeming conclusiveness of the arguments, however, some scholars rejected the theory.

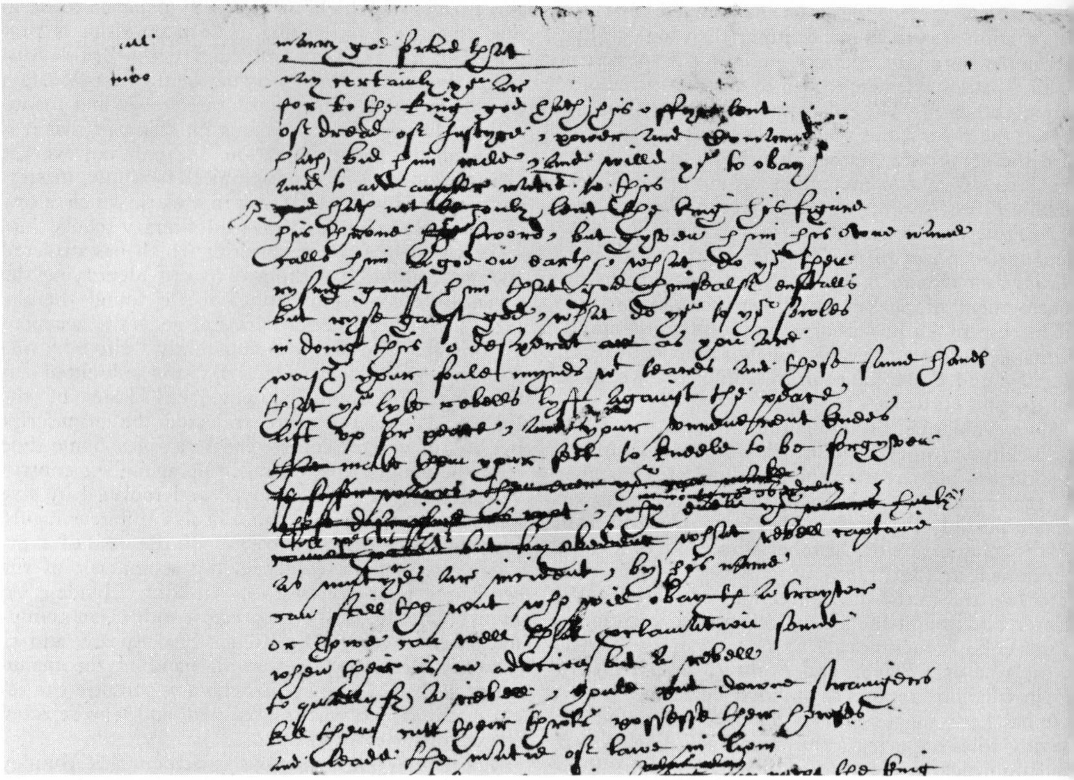

A PAGE FROM THE "HAND D" ADDITION TO THE MANUSCRIPT OF *Sir Thomas More.* (BRITISH MUSEUM) FOR A TRANSCRIPT SEE APPENDIX.

Chief of these was Tannenbaum whose *The Booke of Sir Thomas Moore* (1927) and *Shakspere and Sir Thomas Moore* (1929) disputed the paleographical evidence. However, further evidence was forthcoming in Caroline Spurgeon's study of Shakespeare's imagery (*Review of English Studies*, VI, 1930), which revealed that Hand D's recurrent simile of the mob as water overflowing its banks and 11 other images in Hand D's addition were strikingly similar to those used by Shakespeare elsewhere. The suggestion has also been advanced that Shakespeare is the author of the addition to the play written by Hand C, the professional scribe.

Another major problem in connection with the play is the date. The scribe, Hand C, was apparently with the Admiral's Men after 1597. Thus, if the play is dated after that date we are faced with a seemingly inexplicable paradox of Shakespeare's collaborating on a play for the company which was the chief rival of his own. Internal stylistic evidence, however, seems to date Hand D's addition close to Shakespeare's tragic period (1599–1607), but there is no generally accepted date. The best conservative estimate is 1594–1595. [S. A. Tannenbaum, *Shakspere and Sir Thomas Moore*, 1929; Harold Jenkins, "A Supplement to Sir Walter Greg's Edition of *Sir Thomas More*," Malone Society Collections, VI, 1962.]

Sisson, C[harles] J[asper] (1885–). Scholar; editor of the *Modern Language Review* (1926–1957); professor at London University (1928–1951); and fellow of the Shakespeare Institute. An early work of Sisson's is *Shakespeare in India* (1926). In *Lo Plays of Shakespeare's Age* (1936) he drew upon va ious sources, including allusions to nonextant play to re-create the social life and theatrical milieu of th Elizabethan age. *New Readings in Shakespeare* (vols., 1956) consists of textual and critical notes t the plays. His *Shakespeare's Tragic Justice* was pub lished in 1961. Sisson delivered the 1934 Annu Shakespeare Lecture of the British Academy, "Th Mythical Sorrows of Shakespeare" (reprinted i *Studies in Shakespeare*, Peter Alexander, ed., 1964 Sisson has also edited a one-volume edition of th *Complete Works* (1954).

Sitwell, Dame Edith (1887–1964). Poet, member c a distinguished literary family; created a dame of th British Empire in 1954. Dame Edith first capture attention with *Wheels*, a series of annual anthologi of poetry, the first of which was published in 191 Volumes of her own poems began to appear at fr quent intervals, with important collections in *Th Canticle of the Rose* (1949) and *Collected Poem* (1954). Her critical works include *A Poet's Note book* (1943), which contains a section on Shak speare, and *A Notebook on William Shakespear* (1948). Both are correctly titled "notebooks," th is, they are not formally organized discussions bu collections of eclectic, impressionistic, and subjectiv notes. Considerable attention is devoted to technic matters in which Dame Edith drew upon her ow experience as a poet. In such matters as vowel ha mony, however, her conclusions are sometimes i valid because she did not consider the factor c ound changes which have taken place since the 16th entury. Dame Edith's interest in Queen Elizabeth reulted in two impressionistic biographical sketches, *anfare for Elizabeth* (1946; film script, 1953) and *he Queens and the Hive* (1962).

Siward (d. 1055). Danish warrior; son of Beorn, arl of Northumberland; and son-in-law of Ealdred, arl of Bernicia. Siward killed his wife's uncle and ook his earldom; he was subsequently made earl f Huntingdon. The uncle of Malcolm III of Scotand, he undertook to restore his sister's son to the cottish throne and in 1054 invaded Scotland with 0,000 men. He succeeded only in placing Malcolm n the throne of Cumbria. In *Macbeth*, Siward eads the English troops sent into Scotland by Edvard the Confessor to aid Malcolm against Macbeth. W. H. Thomson, *Shakespeare's Characters: A Hisorical Dictionary*, 1951.]

Siward, Young. Real name, **Osborn** (d. 1054). Eldest son of Siward, earl of Northumberland. He vent with his father's invading force into Scotland, hallenged Macbeth, and was killed by him in ingle combat. In *Macbeth*, Young Siward, on earning his opponent's name, says: "The devil himself could not pronounce a title/ More hateul to mine ear" (V, vii). [W. H. Thomson, *Shakespeare's Characters: A Historical Dictionary*, 951.]

Skinner, Otis (1858–1942). American actor. Born in Cambridge, Massachusetts, Skinner made his first stage appearance in Philadelphia in 1877 and played in stock there for two years. In 1880 he appeared with Edwin Booth as the wounded Officer in *Macbeth;* he also appeared in *Much Ado About Nothing*, *Richard III*, *Othello*, *Hamlet*, and *The Taming of the Shrew*. He next appeared with Lawrence Barrett in *Julius Caesar* in 1882. From 1884 until 1888 he acted in Augustin Daly's company as Master Page, Lucentio, and Lysander.

In 1889 he joined the Booth-Modjeska company at the Broadway Theatre and played Claudio, Bassanio, Laertes, and Macduff in their Shakespearean productions. In 1890 he acted Romeo with another company, then rejoined Modjeska for the next two years, performing Orlando, Henry VIII, Leonatus, Benedick, and Hamlet. In 1903 he acted with Ada Rehan as Shylock and Petruchio. He was also a creditable Falstaff in *1 Henry IV* in 1926 and in a 1928 *Merry Wives of Windsor*. He accompanied Maude Adams playing Shylock on her 1931/2 tour; and in 1932 he acted Thersites in New York. He wrote four books: *Footlights and Spotlights*, *Mad Folk of the Theatre*, *One Man in His Time*, and *The Last Tragedian*. [*Who's Who in the Theatre*, 1939.]

Slender, Abraham. In *The Merry Wives of Windsor*, a moronic cousin of Shallow and suitor to Anne Page. Fully "dissolved and dissolutely" agreeable to marriage with "sweet Anne Page," Slender relies completely on the good offices of Shallow and Sir Hugh Evans to handle his courtship. For his own part, this simpleton tells Anne that he would have little or nothing to do with her and advises her to consult her father, who supports this match, for information on its development (III, iv). Master Page arranges for Slender to elope with Anne during the mayhem at Windsor Park, but Anne deceives her father and elopes with Fenton, while Slender mistakenly runs off with a fairy in white, who turns out to be a postmaster's boy. The character of Slender may have been based on William WAYTE.

Sly, Christopher. In the Induction to *The Taming of the Shrew*, a drunken tinker. Sly is transported, while in an alcoholic stupor, to a nobleman's chamber and is dressed in finery. He awakes surrounded by attendants and a "wife" who assure him he has just recovered from 15 years of lunacy. The comedy, "The Taming of the Shrew," is performed to distract Sly and prevent a recurrence of his illness. See TAMING OF THE SHREW: *Sources*.

Sly, Will[iam] (d. 1608). Actor. Sly was a member of the Chamberlain's Men, Shakespeare's company, from 1594 to 1605, and appears in all the extant acting lists for 1598 to 1605. He is listed in the "plot" of Tarlton's *Seven Deadly Sins*, which the amalgamated Admiral's Men-Strange's Men gave in 1590/1. In an inventory of the Admiral's Men properties, taken in 1598 and recorded in Henslowe's papers, there is an item: "Perowes sewt, which Wm Sley were." Pero is a female character in Chapman's play *Bussy D'Ambois* (1604). (Although *Bussy* dates from 1604, scholars, such as E. K. Chambers, have suggested that Chapman had adapted a "relic of an obsolete play," which had been given by the Admiral's Men at some date before 1594, when Sly ceased to be a member of that company.)

Sly's name appears in the acting lists for the following plays: Jonson's *Every Man In his Humour* (1598), *Every Man Out of his Humour* (1599), *Sejanus* (1603), *Volpone* (1605); in the Induction written by Webster for Marston's *The Malcontent*,

WILLIAM SLY. PORTRAIT BY AN UNKNOWN ARTIST. (DULWICH COLLEGE, BY PERMISSION OF THE GOVERNORS.)

given by the King's Men in 1604, he appears in his own character.

The portrait of Sly in the gallery at Dulwich College shows him to be a decided personality. According to T. W. Baldwin, Sly took youthful, romantic, or soldierly parts (Lewis in *King John*, the Dauphin in *Henry V*); and mercurial roles (Tybalt in *Romeo and Juliet*, Hotspur in *Henry IV*, Laertes in *Hamlet*, Claudio in *Measure for Measure*, Macduff in *Macbeth*, and Edmund in *King Lear*). Baldwin surmises that Hotspur's excitable temperament is a replica of Sly's own.

Sly was an overseer and legatee of Augustine Phillips' will (made in 1605). In his own nuncupative (oral) will he left legacies to Cuthbert Burbage and James Sandes of the King's Men, and the rest of his property to the family of Robert Browne. Sly's death disrupted the King's Men's sharers' arrangements concluded with Burbage over the lease of the Blackfriars theatre. [E. K. Chambers, *The Elizabethan Stage*, 1923; T. W. Baldwin, *The Organization and Personnel of the Shakespearean Company*, 1927.]

Smart, John Semple (1868–1925). Scholar. Born in Glasgow, Smart studied at St. Andrews and at several continental universities. In 1907 he was appointed Queen Margaret College Lecturer at the University of Glasgow. His scholarly works include a study of James Macpherson and an annotated edition of Milton's sonnets, the latter a major achievement in Milton scholarship. At the time of his death Smart left unfinished a work on Shakespeare which was issued posthumously as *Shakespeare—Truth and Tradition* (1928) with a memoir by W. Macneile Dixon. The completed portion consists of several chapters on the life and background of Shakespeare in which myths and assumptions are subjected to a meticulous examination. Smart's views on textual and critical questions survive only in fragments pieced together by his pupil, Peter Alexander, who subsequently developed some of his mentor's embryonic ideas. For example, Smart's contention that *The True Tragedy of Richard Duke of York* was a "bad quarto" of *3 Henry VI* was demonstrated at length by Alexander in his *Shakespeare's Henry VI and Richard III* (1929).

Smetana, Bedřich. See MUSIC BASED ON SHAKESPEARE: *19th century, 1850–1900*.

Smethwicke, John (d. 1641). London bookseller who was among the publishers who issued the First Folio (1623) and the Second Folio (1632). Smethwicke was admitted as a freeman to the Stationers' Company in 1597, eventually rising to the position of Master of the company in 1639. In 1607 Nicholas Ling's copyrights, which included *Love's Labour's Lost*, *Hamlet*, and *Romeo and Juliet*, were transferred to him. He published three quartos of *Hamlet:* Q3 (1611), Q4 (no date), and Q5 (1637). He also published three quartos of *Romeo and Juliet:* Q3 (1609), Q4 (no date), and Q5 (1637). [R. B. McKerrow, ed., *A Dictionary of Printers and Booksellers . . . 1557–1640*, 1910.]

Smirke, Robert (1752–1845). Painter and illustrator. A popular painter, Smirke contributed the largest number (26) of paintings to BOYDELL'S SHAKESPEARE GALLERY. Only occasionally successful with romantic scenes, such as the unusually sympathetic treatment he gives the normally comic "Anne Page, Slende and Simple," Smirke's real talent lay in comedy. H humor has an ironic tinge, and his "Sly in Bed," fro the Induction to *The Taming of the Shrew*, is ha dled with a particularly effective communication the mock heroic. His flair for caricature makes hi most successful in wholly humorous scenes, such "Escalus, Froth, and Elbow" from *Measure f Measure*. [W. M. Merchant, *Shakespeare and th Artist*, 1959.]

Smith. In *2 Henry VI*, a weaver and follower Jack Cade. Smith is the principal accuser of th unfortunate Clerk of Chatham (IV, ii).

Smith, John Christopher (1712–1795). Musicia Born in Germany, Smith went to England as a chil A friend and protégé of the composer Handel, h also numbered among his acquaintances David Ga rick. He composed the music for Garrick's operati version of *The Tempest* (see THE TEMPEST: *Stag History*). Smith also wrote 28 songs for *The Fairie* Garrick's musical adaptation of *A Midsumme Night's Dream*, first performed in 1755. [C. Hogan, *Shakespeare in the Theatre, 1701–1800*, vols., 1952, 1957.]

Smith, John Stafford. See MUSIC BASED ON SHAKE SPEARE: *18th century*.

Smith, [Lloyd] Logan Pearsall (1865–1946). Amer ican-born author. Smith studied at Haverford an Harvard. He moved to England and continue his studies at Balliol College, Oxford, receivin the degrees of B.A. (1903) and M.A. (1906). 1913 he became a naturalized British citizen. Smit received some recognition for his *Trivia* (1902; rev 1918), a collection of aphorisms and thoughts. Othe works include a biography of Sir Henry Wotto and popular introductions to the study of languag *On Reading Shakespeare* (1933) is a brief volume o appreciation, largely impressionistic in nature; Smit deprecates the excessive attention to historical back ground as represented in the works of E. E. Stol he defends the reading of Shakespeare, opposing th view that the only valid way to experience the play is to see them on the stage. Smith also wrote *Milto and His Modern Critics* (1940), a similar defens against what he considered the pedantry of moder scholarship. *Unforgotten Years*, his autobiography was published in 1938.

Smith, Wentworth (fl. 1601–1603). Playwrigh thought by some to be the "W. S." whose initial appear on the title page of the apocryphal Shake spearean plays THOMAS LORD CROMWELL and TH PURITAN. All that is definitely known of Smith' career is that from 1601 to 1603 he collaborated o 15 plays for Philip Henslowe's Admiral's an Worcester's companies. None of these plays i extant.

Smith is probably the author of *The Hector o Germany*, a play published in 1615 by "W. Smith." In his prefatory Epistle to the play Smith indicate that some years before he had written a play for th Chamberlain's Men, a fact which strengthens th case for ascription to him of co-authorship o *Thomas Lord Cromwell*, which was a Chamberlain' play. [Baldwin Maxwell, *Studies in the Shakespear Apocrypha*, 1956.]

Smith, William (fl. 1596). Poet who may be th

W. S." listed on the title page of LOCRINE, a play nce attributed to Shakespeare. Smith, a poetic disci-le of Edmund Spenser, is the author of a sonnet equence titled *Chloris, or the Complaint of the 'assionate Despised Shepheard* (1596). When a selec-ion from *Chloris* was published in the anthology *ngland's Helicon* (1600), the author was listed as W. S.," while in the same volume a selection of erse from *Love's Labour's Lost* is ascribed to "W. hakespeare." Thus there is some basis for associat-ng the initials with Smith. There is no extant evi-ence that Smith ever wrote plays, although the 8th-century scholar William Warburton claimed to ave owned a manuscript play called *St. George for ngland* by "Will Smithe."

Smith may also be the "W. S." whose "sonnetes" vere entered in the Stationers' Register in 1596, but he volume, if ever printed, is not extant. [Baldwin Maxwell, *Studies in the Shakespeare Apocrypha*, 956.]

Smock Alley theatre. See IRELAND.

Snare. In *2 Henry IV*, a sheriff's officer who ssists Fang in the arrest of Falstaff (II, i).

Snitterfield. A village located about three and one-alf miles north of Stratford. It was the home of hakespeare's paternal grandfather, Richard Shake-peare, who was a tenant farmer on land owned by Robert Arden of Wilmcote, Shakespeare's maternal randfather. Arden apparently left Shakespeare's arents a small portion of this land, which they sold n 1579 to Robert Webbe for £4.

Snout, Tom. In *A Midsummer Night's Dream*, a vorrisome Athenian tinker. Originally cast in the ole of Pyramus' father in the dramatic interlude, Snout represents Wall, "the wittiest partition," at the ctual performance (V, i).

Snowden, George and Lionel. See Nicholas OKES.

Snug. In *A Midsummer Night's Dream*, an Athen-an joiner who is assigned the role of Lion in the dramatic interlude. Although Snug is "slow of study" (I, ii), he "roars well."

Soer, Dorothy. See William WAYTE.

Soliman and Perseda (c. 1589–1592). An anony-nous Elizabethan play entered in the Stationers' Register on November 10, 1592 as "The tragedye of Salamon and Perceda." The play contains a bragging knight, Basilisco, who delivers a speech (V, iii, 63 ff.) imilar to Falstaff's "catechism on honour" (*1 Henry V*, V, i, 127 ff.). There is also an allusion to Basilisco n *King John* (I, i, 244). [*1 Henry IV*, New Arden Edition, A. R. Humphreys, ed., 1960.]

Solinus. In *The Comedy of Errors*, the Duke of Ephesus. Because of the hostility between his city nd Syracuse, Solinus condemns Aegeon, a merchant of Syracuse, to death for landing in Ephesus, but grants him one day in which to secure his ransom nd avoid execution. He pardons Aegeon when the question of mistaken identities is resolved.

Somerset, Edmund Beaufort, 2nd duke of (d. 1455). Younger brother of John Beaufort, 1st duke of Somerset. He succeeded the duke of York as regent in France, but during his rule many of the English possessions there were lost. Somerset con-sequently became most unpopular at home. When Henry VI suffered his first fit of insanity in 1453, York, who had become protector, imprisoned Somerset in the Tower. On the king's return to sanity and the duke's restoration to authority, York went to battle against Somerset, who was killed in the battle at St. Albans.

In *2 Henry VI*, Somerset continues the quarrel between his brother, John Beaufort, and the Duke of York. When Somerset is made Regent of France, York demands his removal. Assured that his enemy is in the Tower, York is infuriated to find him with Queen Margaret. He goes to battle against the Lancastrians, and Somerset is killed at St. Albans.

Somerset, Edmund Beaufort, 4th duke of (1438?–1471). Younger brother of Henry Beaufort, 3rd duke of Somerset, whose title Edmund inherited after Henry's execution by the Yorkists in 1464. In *3 Henry VI*, Edmund joins Warwick's forces after King Edward's marriage to Lady Grey (IV, i). He is beheaded after the battle of Tewkesbury (V, v).

Somerset, John Beaufort, 3rd earl, later 1st duke of (1403–1444). Second son of John Beaufort, 1st earl. He succeeded to the earldom in 1419 on the death of his brother Henry. The following year Beaufort went to France to serve under King Henry V, but was captured by the French. After his ran-som he continued to fight under Henry VI. Beau-fort was made duke of Somerset in 1443 and named captain-general in Aquitaine and Normandy. Angered, however, at the appointment of the duke of York as France's regent instead of himself, Somerset returned to England. He died the follow-ing year, possibly by suicide.

In *1 Henry VI*, Somerset appears first as earl, and later as duke. When in London's Temple Garden he quarrels with Richard Plantagenet, the latter invites those who support him to join him in pluck-ing a white rose. Somerset responds by plucking a red one. The quarrel continues throughout the play.

Somerville, Sir John. In *3 Henry VI*, a Lan-castrian who reports to Warwick that Clarence is near Coventry (V, i). The character has been identified with Sir Thomas Somerville (d. 1500) of Gloucestershire. [W. H. Thomson, *Shakespeare's Characters: A Historical Dictionary*, 1951.]

Somerville, Sir **William** (d. 1616). A native of Edstone, near Stratford, Sir William was knighted in 1603. According to a letter written in 1616, Somer-ville was a close friend of Shakespeare and the first owner of the miniature portrait of the dramatist attributed to Nicholas Hilliard and known as the Hilliard Miniature.

Sir William's brother, ***John Somerville*** (1560–1583), was married to a daughter of Edward Arden, a distant relative of Shakespeare's mother. Somer-ville and Edward Arden, both ardent Catholic recu-sants, were executed for an attempt in 1583 to assassinate Queen Elizabeth. [Edgar I. Fripp, *Shake-speare, Man and Artist*, 1938.]

Sonnets, The. A collection of 154 sonnets by Shakespeare.

Text. The only authoritative text of the Sonnets is that of the 1609 Quarto, entered in the Stationers' Register for Thomas Thorpe as follows: "20 Maij Thomas Thorpe Entred for his copie vnder thandes of master Wilson and master Lownes Warden A

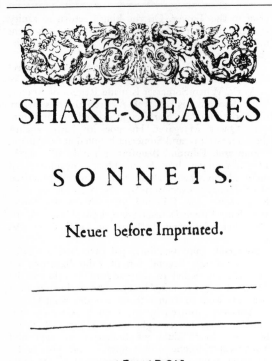

SHAKE-SPEARES

SONNETS.

Neuer before Imprinted.

AT LONDON
By *G*. *Eld* for *T. T.* and are
to be solde by *Iohn Wright*, dwelling
at Christ Church gate.
1609.

TITLE PAGE OF THE 1609 QUARTO OF THE *Sonnets*.

Booke called Shakespeares sonnettes." The title page of the Quarto reads: "Shake-speares sonnets Neuer before Imprinted. At London By G. Eld for T. T. and are to be solde by Iohn Wright dwelling at Christ Church gate [or, on some copies, "by William Aspley"]. 1609." The text is as reliable as that of one of the good quartos of the plays. It must have been based on Shakespeare's autograph copy or on a careful transcription of it.

The copy had obviously been surreptitiously obtained and shows clear evidence that it had not been proofread by the author. Texts of 138 and 144 had been previously published in 1599 by William Jaggard, with his son, who published the First Folio. The volume in which they appeared, *The Passionate Pilgrim*, was a collection of 20 lyrics by various poets. The text of neither of these sonnets is exactly like that of Thorpe's Quarto. That of Sonnet 144 contains so many variants that some critics believe it to be a memorial text. In any case, these texts are generally considered inferior to those of the 1609 Quarto.

The complete authenticity of the 1609 text has been repeatedly questioned. A number of the sonnets in the collection are of such an allegedly inferior artistic quality or (an important point with 19th-century scholars) of such a dubious moral quality that they have frequently been assigned to other poets. The "disintegrators" of Shakespeare (see DISINTEGRATION) have been particularly prone to find evidence of other hands in the collection. However objective evidence in support of these theses has not been advanced.

In 1640 there appeared a second edition of the *Sonnets*, bearing the following title: "Poems: Written by Wil. Shake-speare. Gent. Printed at London by Tho. Cotes, and are to be sold by Iohn Benson dwelling in St. Dunstans Church-yard, 1640." In addition to poems by other authors, the volume contained all but eight of the sonnets, but completely rearranged, under such titles as "The Glory of Beauty" and "Injurious Time." The texts of the sonnets in BENSON's Quarto are less authoritative than those of the 1609 Quarto. Few responsible critics now believe that the sonnets, or groups of sonnets in the 1609 Quarto are in exactly the right chronological order, although Thorpe's division into two parts—the first 126 sonnets to, or about, a young aristocrat; the remaining group to the same man, but about a dark lady—is generally accepted as official. However, a recent study of the sonnet order by Hilton Landry has yielded the suggestion that there is no narrative underlying the collection and no two-group division into which the poems naturally fall.

Date. The first intimation of the existence of a collection of sonnets written by Shakespeare appears in MERES' list in PALLADIS TAMIA (1598). In it the author includes the poet's "sugared sonnets among his private friends." We cannot now determine which sonnets of those published in Thorpe's 1609 Quarto Shakespeare had circulated among his close personal friends. Certain of those in the 1609 publication display conduct of the recipient of the poems so scandalous that Shakespeare certainly would have been loath to give it publicity. J. Dover Wilson calls the sonnets which divulge the young man's shameful conduct the poet's "secret or private sonnets." Those free from such revelations and more faithful to the conventions of the sonnet tradition, he designates as his "sugared or portfolio sonnets." The years 1592 to 1595 were those of the greatest vogue of the sequences. Sir Philip Sidney's *Astrophel and Stella* (1591) was at once imitated by English poets of every degree of ability and of every social station. The first to appear in 1592 were Samuel Daniel's *Delia* and Henry Constable's (1562–1613) *Diana*. They were followed by scores of collections appearing from 1592 to 1595. The flood then began to recede, so that by 1597 the popularity of the form had subsided.

Until recently most scholars believed that Shakespeare at once joined the throng in friendly rivalry with his contemporaries and so fixed the date of his activity in this field as 1592–1595. Moreover, some of his plays written during those years, particularly *Love's Labour's Lost*, show a lively interest in the sonnet, indeed almost a compulsion to experiment with its use. Into the text of this comedy he introduced seven sonnets, weaving some of them into the texture of the play, leaving others as independent amatory lyrics. Many parallels in thought, phrase and imagery can be discerned between the Sonnets and other of Shakespeare's early work, including his erotic poems. These similarities strengthen the case for the dating of 1592–1595. The critics who base their study on the development of the poet's style believe that by 1597 Shakespeare was so fully oc ıpied with the composition of his dramas that he ould have had no inclination toward further prac- :e of an outmoded poetic fashion.

A study of the relation of parts of the sonnet story › events in the lives of the two principal claimants ›r the position of Mr. W. H., Henry Wriothesley, ıird earl of Southampton (1573–1624) and William :erbert, third earl of Pembroke (1580–1630), results the establishment of nearly the same date for the ›et's first work on the Sonnets. In the early 1590's ord Burghley, Southampton's guardian, was making ıliant efforts to arrange a marriage for his ward ith his granddaughter, Lady Elizabeth Vere. But ıe young earl was so vigorously opposed to the idea ıat in 1594 he secured a release from the engage- ent by paying a forfeit of £5000, and the next year ıtered upon his intrigue with Elizabeth Vernon. herefore the years 1592–1594 were those in which ıakespeare's poems urging marriage would lend ıpport to Burghley's project. Similar unsuccessful :gotiations beginning in 1595 were made for Pem- :oke's marriage to Elizabeth Carey, granddaughter the lord chamberlain, Lord Hunsdon. This would : the natural time for Pembroke's parents to appeal their retainers to urge in verse that their son ıould marry.

Leslie Hotson suggested a much earlier date than ıy time in the 1590's, by a fresh interpretation of ıe line in Sonnet 107, "The mortal moon hath her :lipse endured." Taking mortal to mean "deadly," ıd the moon as the crescent, moon-shaped order in hich the commanders of the Spanish Armada drew ɔ their ships, he fixed the date as early as 1588–1589. 'his date has been accepted by few, if any, scholars ı the field.

It is not known just when Shakespeare ceased send- ıg poetic missives to his young friend. The so-called ıted sonnet, 107, may refer to the poet's escape om a seriously threatening danger to himself and › the queen in the year 1601. Other critics believe ıat it refers to her death in 1603, which would carry ıe date of some of the poems to the year 1603. If ıe couplet concluding Sonnet 124,

THE SPANISH ARMADA IN A HALF-MOON-SHAPED BATTLE FORMATION. THIS MAP BY ROBERT ADAMS IS FROM A CONTEMPORARY ACCOUNT OF THE RUNNING SEA BATTLE.

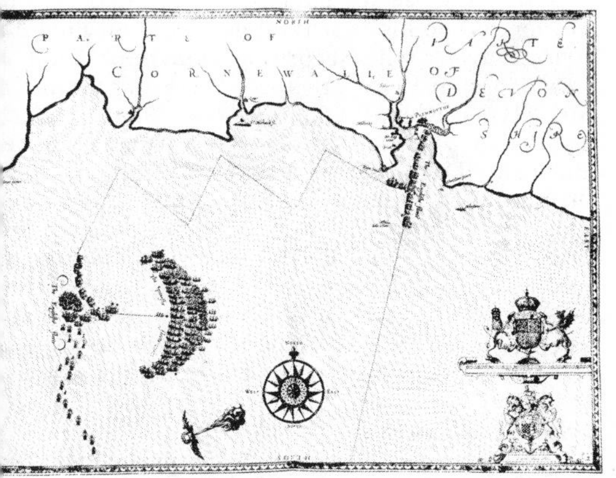

> To this I witness call the fools of time,
> Which die for goodness, who have lived for crime.

refers to the misguided Jesuits who planned the Gunpowder Plot for November 5, 1605, as J. Dover Wilson believes probable, Shakespeare must have continued to address sonnets to Pembroke at least until some time in early 1606.

Sources. If the sonnets are taken to be half-concealed autobiography, their sources must be found in the lives of Shakespeare, a young friend (probably either the earl of Southampton or the earl of Pembroke), and a dark temptress, of whom Mary Fitton is a type. If they are merely literary exercises, as Sir Sidney Lee impressively argues in his "Vogue of the Elizabethan Sonnets," affixed to his enlarged edition of his *Life of William Shakespeare* (1915), then they must assume their proper place in the vogue of the sonnet that invaded all the literature of western Europe for 300 years. Petrarch, its originator, established some of the conventions of the type. Almost all of his 317 sonnets, called canzoniere, he addressed to a lady, half-real and half-ideal, whom he named Laura. Although Shakespeare probably did not read Petrarch in Italian, he could have become acquainted with his sonnets through those of Thomas Wyatt and the earl of Surrey, many of which are translations of Petrarch. Sir Philip Sidney's sonnets were first published surreptitiously in 1591 under the title *Sir Philip Sidney, His Astrophel and Stella.* As Astrophel, Sidney became the lover of Stella, the star. He, like Petrarch, contrived to make the individual poems of his sequence seem to be episodes in an unhappy love affair, in Sidney's case with Penelope Devereux, afterward Lady Rich. Shakespeare had clearly read Sidney's sonnets, but some critics find a much stronger influence upon him from Samuel Daniel's *Delia.* Twenty-eight of Daniel's sonnets were first published as an appendix to *Astrophel and Stella* and 35 were brought out in a single volume in 1592, with a dedicatory sonnet to the countess of Pembroke.

The partisans of Daniel detect in Shakespeare's sequence close imitations of his contemporary's "sugared style," that is, his penchant for "conceits," overingenious figures of speech. They also discover in *Delia* imagery identical to that in the Sonnets and methods of linking together individual poems like those used by Shakespeare. Yet, compared to Daniel's shadowy figures, Shakespeare's characters are creatures of flesh and blood.

Fully as great as the influence of Daniel was that of Ovid's *Metamorphoses* in Arthur Golding's translation (1565–1567). Among the conventions originating in Ovid and in Horace, and also present in Petrarch, Shakespeare most often exploits the "eternizing" theme, the notion that a poet's praise of his patron confers upon the great man earthly immortality. It is his only sure protection from the ravages of time. Thirteen of Shakespeare's Sonnets are on this theme, which he announces in Sonnet 55:

> Not marble, nor the gilded monuments
> Of princes, shall outlive this powerful rhyme.

In Sonnet 64 Shakespeare follows Ovid in choosing the ceaseless encroachment of the sea upon the land as a striking example of the ruin following in the wake of eternal change:

> When I have seen the hungry ocean gain
> Advantage on the kingdom of the shore,
>
> . . . . .
>
> Ruin hath taught me thus to ruminate,
> That Time will come and take my love away.

Mutability regarded from a different point of view becomes "The Triumph of Time." The word triumph calls to mind the ancient Roman custom of celebrating the conquests of a war hero with colorful processions moving through the streets of the capital. Petrarch created visionary imitations of these pageants, that of Chastity, of Death, of Fame, of Time, and finally, of Eternity. Shakespeare glorifies only one of these triumphs, that of Time—evidence of his obsession with the tragic effects of mutability.

Subject Matter. Shakespeare's collected sonnets consist of 154 poems. The last two, 153 and 154, are different versions of the same epigram in the GREEK ANTHOLOGY, a collection of 4500 fugitive pieces of Greek poetry by more than 300 writers. Assuming that the sequence is autobiographical, many modern critics find in the remaining 152 poems a story of a tense little drama involving three persons: a Poet; his Friend, probably a lord of high degree; and a woman, a brunette, now universally known as the Dark Lady. The first 126 sonnets are poetical letters sent singly or in groups to the Friend; those from 127 to 152 inclusive are about the woman, but probably also sent to the Friend. The one-sided correspondence begins with the Poet's dispatch, perhaps at the suggestion of the noble youth's parents, of 17 poetical letters urging him to marry and beget children. This "embassage" establishes an acquaintance with the boyish aristocrat that soon ripens into an ardent friendship. The sequence records the frustrations and the triumphs of this relationship, one of its most critical trials being the rivalry of another poet (see RIVAL POET) for the affection and the favor of the Friend. The "plot" mounts to a dangerous crisis. The handsome and licentious lord steals the Poet's mistress. Shakespeare describes certain episodes in his wooing and winning of the lady. The two men share her favors for a while, each secretly from the other. When the Poet learns the truth, he explains and forgives his Friend's treachery. But that does not prevent him from bitterly attacking the lady's looseness and her deceit nor from execrating the lust that she excites in him. In the end the Poet breaks all ties with her and begins to build on a firm foundation a friendship that apparently lasted as long as he lived.

Form. PETRARCH, who initiated the Renaissance vogue of the sonnet, divided each of his quatorzains, as the form was then usually called, into two parts: an octave consisting of two quatrains, rhyming *a b b a,* and a sestet of two three-line stanzas. The form that Shakespeare adopted, 3 quatrains of 10-syllabled lines and a concluding couplet, had been introduced into the English sonnet tradition by Sir Thomas Wyatt and perfected by Henry Howard, earl of Surrey. The sonnets of these two poets first appeared in *Tottel's Miscellany* (1557). This form was adopted by almost all of the Tudor sonneteers. Shakespeare commonly places a strong pause in sense at the end of each quatrain, the strongest at the end of the second. He manages the form with ease and grace, evoking from it a variety of music. Th couplet frequently sums up the essence of the poen More often it introduces what Tucker Brooke calle "a surprising negative." But in most of the sonnet the last two lines bring the poem swiftly to the eartl

Comment. Shakespeare mercifully spares his read ers the iteration of some of the most tiresome c Petrarchan conventions. He does not luxuriate in th woe of a rejected suitor. He seldom laments th agony of a sleepless night. He avoids most of th comparisons of the lady with objects of natur beauty. Instead, in Sonnet 21 he ridicules such com parison and in Sonnet 130 cries,

> My mistress' eyes are nothing like the sun;
> Coral is far more red than her lips' red.

The happy truth is that Shakespeare has liberate more than half of his sonnets from the tyranny o Petrarchan convention, and so is free to sound nev notes in the lyric chorus of his age. In Sonnet 30 hi tears flow "For precious friends hid in death's date less night." It is his lack of "this man's art and tha man's scope" that discourages him (Sonnet 29). In blacker mood in Sonnet 66 he sees everywhere th victory of folly and evil over wisdom and virtue "And captive good attending captain ill." The mos striking of the poet's innovations is his confessio that his attraction to the Dark Lady is mere sensual ity, and that yielding to it is followed by repulsio and remorse. But it is her deceit and infidelity th most painfully torture him. Although her lover aware of her duplicity, he refuses (Sonnet 138) t recognize it for what it is:

> When my love swears that she is made of truth
> I do believe her, though I know she lies.

When he escapes completely from the spell she cas upon him, he curses the lust that she arouses in hin He knows it is "The expense of spirit in a waste c shame" (Sonnet 129). And in the deepest searchin of his soul he discovers that he must "Buy tern divine in selling hours of dross" (Sonnet 146).

In these sacred sonnets Shakespeare transcends th world of thought and feeling in which the other son neteers of his day live and move and have thei being. Supporting the expression of these themes ar a number of general conceptions. Of them, that c Plenitude is perhaps the most important.

Shakespeare's fidelity to this idea brings him fir of all joy in nature's abundance. It explains h distress at his friend's failure to have children. Pro creation was to him a natural good and he alludes t its instruments with surprising frankness.—O. J. C

Bibliography. TEXT: *Sonnets,* New Variorum Ed tion, Hyder Rollins, ed., 1944; *The Sonnets, Son and Poems of Shakespeare,* Oscar James Campbel ed., 1965. DATE: New Variorum Edition; Lesli Hotson, *Shakespeare's Sonnets Dated,* 1949. COM MENT: Edward Hubler, *The Sense of Shakespeare Sonnets,* 1952; John Blair Leishman, *Themes an Variations in Shakespeare's Sonnets,* 1961; Hilto Landry, *Interpretations in Shakespeare's Sonnet* 1963; J. Dover Wilson, *An Introduction to the Son nets of Shakespeare,* 1964; *Shakespeare's Sonnet* A. L. Rowse, ed., 1964.

Selected Criticism

GEORGE STEEVENS. We have not reprinted the Son nets, & c. of Shakespeare, because the strongest a of Parliament that could be framed, would fail to compel readers into their service; notwithstanding these miscellaneous Poems have derived every possible advantage from the literature and judgement of their only intelligent editor, Mr. Malone, whose implements of criticism, like the ivory rake and golden spade in Prudentius, are on this occasion disgraced by the objects of their culture.—Had Shakespeare produced no other works than these, his name would have reached us with as little celebrity as time has conferred on that of Thomas Watson, an older and much more elegant sonnetteer. ["A Note on Shakespeare's Sonnets, & c.," *The Plays of William Shakespeare*, 1793.]

GEORGE CHALMERS. Of those Amatory Verses [the sonnets], it may be truly said, that as a whole poem, which is often tied together by a very slight ligature, they have two of the worst faults, that can degrade any writing; they are obscure; and they are tedious. Spenser, who furnished the model of them, has his obscurities, and tediousness; but he has withal, more distinctness, in his topicks, and more facility, in his style: Shakspeare plainly endeavoured to go beyond the mark of his rivalry; but, in affecting the sublime, he sunk, by a natural cadence, into the unintelligible. Spenser having no rival, and only a single object, caught at such topicks of praise, as he thought would please the most, and adopted such a style, as he could most easily manage. Of such a poet, as Shakspeare, it may easily be conceived, that he has many happy phrases, and elegant lines, though they are generally darkened by conceit, and marred by affectation; with as many happy phrases, and elegant lines, Spenser has fewer conceits and less affectation; having from inheritance, as fruitful a garden of images, which he watered from a deeper fountain of learning. Shakspeare, "fancy's sweetest child," shows sometimes a manifest superiority in *imagination* over Spenser, when this wonderful poet is forming the same images. By an effort of his creative powers, Shakspeare appears to have carried away the palm, in this great quality of a true poet, from his illustrious rival, even when Spenser put forth his whole strength, in cultivating the same field. [*A Supplemental Apology for the Believers in the Shakspeare-papers*, 1799.]

SAMUEL TAYLOR COLERIDGE. I believe it possible that a man may, under certain states of the moral feeling, entertain something deserving the name of love towards a male object—an affection beyond friendship, and wholly aloof from appetite. In Elizabeth's and James's time it seems to have been almost fashionable to cherish such a feeling; and perhaps we may account in some measure for it by considering how very inferior women of that age, taken generally, were in education and accomplishment of mind to the men. . . . I mention this with reference to Shakespeare's sonnets, which have been supposed, by some, to be addressed to William Herbert, Earl of Pembroke, whom Clarendon calls the most beloved man of his age, though his licentiousness was equal to his virtues. I doubt this. I do not think that Shakespeare, merely because he was an actor, would have thought it necessary to veil his emotions towards Pembroke under a disguise, though he might probably have done so, if the real object had perchance been a Laura or Leonora. It seems to me that the sonnets could only have come from a man deeply in love, and in love with a woman; and there is one sonnet which, from its incongruity, I take to be a purposed blind. These extraordinary sonnets form, in fact, a poem of so many stanzas of fourteen lines each; and, like the passion which inspired them, the sonnets are always the same, with a variety of expression,—continuous, if you regard the lover's soul—distinct, if you listen to him, as he heaves them sigh after sigh. [*Shakespearean Criticism* by S. T. Coleridge, T. M. Raysor, ed., Everyman Library Edition, 1960.]

BARRETT WENDELL. The *Sonnets*, then, alter any conception of Shakspere's individuality which might spring from the plays we have read. Even though they tell nothing of the facts of his life, the *Sonnets* imply very much concerning the inner truth of it. No one, surely, could have written these poems without a temperament in every sense artistic, and a consciously mastered art. Nor could any one have expressed such emotion and such passion as underlie the *Sonnets* without a knowledge of suffering which no sane poise could lighten, like that of the chronicle-histories; nor any such cheerful sanity, or such robust irony as the comedies express; nor any such sentimental sense of tragedy as makes *Romeo and Juliet* perennially lovely. Whoever wrote the *Sonnets* must have known the depths of spiritual suffering; nor yet have known how to emerge from them. Such a Shakspere, unlike what we have known hitherto, is not unlike the Shakspere who will reveal himself in the plays to come. [*Elizabethan Literature*, 1894.]

BENEDETTO CROCE. The *Sonnets* are also based upon Italian models, where we find exhortations addressed to admired youth set upon a pinnacle, similar to those that passed between Venus and Adonis. The beautiful youth, posing as Adonis, and treated like him, became very common in our lyric poetry of the time of Marino, in the seventeenth century, as were also love sonnets addressed to ladies, possessing some peculiar characteristic, such as red hair or a dark complexion, or even something different or unfamiliar in their beauty, such as too lofty or too diminutive a stature.

Notwithstanding this literary tendency in his inspiration, Shakespeare does not cease to be a poet, because he is never altogether able to separate himself from himself, everywhere he infuses his own thoughts and modes of feeling, those harmonies, peculiar to himself, those movements of the soul, so delicate and so profound. This has endowed the *Sonnets* with the aspect of a biographical mystery, of a poem containing some hidden moral and philosophical sense. When we read verses such as

> The canker-blooms have full as deep a dye
> As the perfumed tincture of the roses,
> Hang on such thorns and play as wantonly
> When summer's breath their masked buds discloses:
> But, for their virtue only is their show,
> They live unwoo'd and unrespected fade,
> Die to themselves. Sweet roses do not so;
> Of their sweet deaths are sweetest odours made.
> (54, 5–12)

we feel the commonplace of literature, revived with lyric emotion. Note too in the *Sonnets* their pensiveness, their exquisite moral tone, their wealth of psychological allusions, in which we often recognise the poet of the great plays. Sometimes there echoes in them that malediction of the chains of pleasure, which will afterwards become [as in 129] *Antony and Cleopatra;* at others we hear Hamlet, tormented and perplexed; yet more often we catch glimpses of reality as appearance and appearance as reality, as in the *Dream* or the *Tempest*. The truth is that the soul of Shakespeare, poured into a fixed and therefore inadequate mould, his lyrical impulse confined to the epigrammatic, cause the poetry to flow together there, but deny to it complete expansion and unfolding. [*Ariosto, Shakespeare and Corneille*, 1920.]

ARTHUR MIZENER. The pattern which one of Shakespeare's sonnets aims to establish in the reader's mind is not the pattern of logic aimed at by the metaphysical poem; his typical sonnet is rather a formal effort to create in the reader's mind a pattern, externally controlled, very like the pattern of the mind when it contemplates, with full attention but for no immediately practical purpose, an object in nature. Such a pattern is not built simply of logical relations nor does it consist simply of what is in perfect focus; it is built for all the kinds of relations known to the mind, as a result of its verbal conditioning or for other reasons, which can be invoked verbally. The building of a verbal construct calculated to invoke such a pattern requires the use of every resource language as a social instrument possesses, and it involves a structure of figurative language which at least approaches, in its own verbal terms, the richness, the density, the logical incompleteness of the mind. ["The Structure of Figurative Language in Shakespeare's Sonnets," *The Southern Review*, V, 1940.]

EDWARD HUBLER. Perhaps we can learn more of Shakespeare's poetic practice if we turn to a structural pattern with which he always succeeded. No sonnet beginning with "When" is an undistinguished poem. Naturally there is nothing magical in the word. It is simply that "when" introduces a subordinate clause which must, perhaps after more subordinate matter, lead to a main clause, thus creating an arrangement of logically ordered elements in an emphatic sequence. When the arrangement can be readily made to coincide with the sonnet length, the structure avoids Shakespeare's most characteristic faults as a sonnetteer—the tacked-on couplet and the broken back. He is almost certain to succeed when the parts of the sonnet stand in a "When I, Then I, Then I, So" relationship, or in some variant of it. It was an excellent pattern for a poet impatient with technical problems. But if the pattern did not reach to the end of the sonnet, or if there was no "so" or "for" notion to follow the logical sequence, the couplet, as in the fifteenth sonnet, stood in danger of seeming to be tacked on. Too often the development of the idea ends with the quatrains, and the couplet fails to share the power in which the quatrains were conceived. In such instances the couplet is poetically, but not intellectually, false. It seems, to use Shakespeare's words, to have been begotten in "the ventricle of memory . . . and delivered upon the mellowing of occasion." ["Form and Matter," *The Sense of Shakespeare's Sonnets*, 1952.]

PATRICK CRUTTWELL. The 1590's are the crucial years. In the Elizabethan *fin-de-siècle* there occurred a change, a shift of thought and feeling, which led directly to the greatest moment in English poetry: the "Shakespearean moment," the opening years o the seventeenth century, in which were written a the supreme Shakespearean dramas. The 1590 brought about that deep change of sensibility whic marks off the later from the earlier Elizabethan which alters the climate from that of *Arcadia* an *The Faerie Queene* to that which welcomed *Hamle* which probably demanded the Shakespearean rewri ing of that drama from its crude original blood-an thunder Kyd, and which found its other great po in the person of Donne. To think of the Elizabetha age as a solid, unchanging unity is utterly misleadin Within it there were two generations and (roughl corresponding to those generations) two mentaliti In the 1590's the one "handed over" to the othe Such a statement is, of course, the grossest simplific tion; in the realms of the mind and the imaginatic things do not happen as neatly as that. And in fac the 1590's are intensely confused, precisely becau the "handing over" was then taking place; new an old were deeply entangled, and all generalizatio must be loaded with exceptions. But there *was* a old, and there *was* a new, and the task of criticism to analyse and distinguish.

Of all the poetry then written, none shows bett what was really happening than the Sonnets o Shakespeare. They deal with far more than th personal events which make up their outward m terial; they show an intensely sensitive awareness o the currents and cross-currents of the age. The have hardly received the properly critical attentio that they deserve; real criticism, it may be, h fought shy of them because of the fatal and futi attraction they have exercised on the noble army o cranks, who are far too busy identifying the youn man, the dark lady, the rival poet, and Willia Shakespeare, to bother about the quality of th poetry. But the Sonnets are, in their own right, an quite apart from external "problems," poems of gre and intriguing interest, as well as of beauty; they a much more subtle and varied than a casual readin reveals. The sweet and unchanging smoothness o their form is extremely deceptive; and it is partl this—the contrast between spirit and form—whic makes them, of all the works of the 1590's, the be adapted to help us to a comprehension of the age development in poetry. For what they show is blending of new and old, the new *in* the old, and th new growing through the old; they use a form (th sonnet-sequence) which was above all the chose form of the old, and in that form they say somethin completely at odds with the old, and destined to co quer it. [*The Shakespearean Moment*, 1955.]

sonnet sequence. A series of sonnets united b some common theme. Almost from its inception th sonnet had been regarded both as an independe poem and as a unit in a larger whole. PETRARCH s the standard for the form, theme, and imagery of th sonnet and inaugurated the practice of linking th separate sonnets to form a unit. His *Canzoniere* co sists of more than 300 poems, the majority of whic are sonnets addressed to Laura. The sequence is fu ther divided into two parts, those addressed t Laura in life and those to her after her death. Th first group records conflicting emotions and desire an uncertain mind, and a vacillating will. The secon reveals a greater unity of thought and feeling; th oet is at first desolate, but gradually he is consoled y the realization that Laura has won for herself ernal life and that she infuses her lover with the ope of salvation and ultimate reunion with her. hese two groups illustrate the two general forms at the sonnet sequence was to take: a loose associaon around a common theme or object of devotion, nd a unified work in which the sonnets form links a patterned development or progression.

Petrarch was widely imitated in Italy, France, and ltimately in England. The first English sonnets—hose by Sir Thomas Wyatt and the earl of SURREY -were published in *Tottel's Miscellany* (1557). Neither attempted a sequence but merely wrote inividual sonnets which, for the most part, were ardly more than translations or paraphrases of oreign models. Nor did the publication of these onnets exert any great immediate influence. Only a prinkling of sonnets appeared for about a generation. Thomas Watson's *Hecatompathia* (1582) night be considered the first English sonnet sequence. It consists of a sequence of 100 poems which he author termed "sonnets," although they are 18 nes in length and the structural division is different rom that of the traditional sonnet. No one seems o have followed Watson in using this form.

The 1590's saw an outburst of sonnet sequences. The earliest was Sir Philip Sidney's *Astrophel and tella* (1591), which relates the unsuccessful courthip of Stella ("the star," Penelope Devereux) by strophel ("the star seeker," Sidney). This edition ontained a number of poems by other authors, inluding some sonnets by Samuel Daniel. Daniel was hereby stimulated to issue an edition under his own irection. In the following year he published *Delia,* sequence of 50 sonnets dedicated to Sidney's sister, he countess of Pembroke. As with subsequent soneteers, Daniel drew heavily upon Petrarchan conentions, a fact which makes it hazardous to interpret he work as an expression of personal feeling. *Diana* y Henry Constable (1562–1613) was also published n 1592. The fashion for sonnet sequences was now n full swing. In 1593 three of them appeared: *Phyllis* y Thomas Lodge, *Parthenophil and Parthenophe* y Barnabe Barnes, and *Licia* by Giles Fletcher the Elder. The following year, three more cycles were ublished: Michael Drayton's *Idea's Mirror,* William Percy's *Coelia,* and the anonymous *Zepheria.* That ame year Daniel and Constable issued revised and ugmented editions of their earlier works. *Amoretti,* major work by Edmund Spenser, was published in 595. It is a sonnet sequence in which conventional lements are used to convey the poet's love for Elizaeth Boyle, his future wife. Also appearing in 1595 vere *Cynthia* by Richard Barnfield, *Emaricdulfe* by "E. C.," and *Alcilia* by "I. C." Three more cycles vere published in the following year: *Chloris* by William Smith, *Diella* by Richard Linche (fl. 1596–1601), and *Fidessa* by Bartholomew Griffin (d. 1602). The vogue had spent its force. In 1597 only one sequence appeared, Robert Tofte's *Laura;* as he title indicates, the author drew upon Petrarch, out he departed sufficiently from convention to give happy ending to the story. Of uncertain date is he *Caelica* by Fulke Greville, first published in 1633, ive years after the poet's death. The title page tates that the work was written in the author's "youth and familiar exercise with Sir Philip Sidney." A comparison of the sonnets of the two men suggests that they set about to write competitive versions on a number of set themes.

Thus in a period of a few years the sonnet sequence flourished and died. It was about a decade after its apparent end that the greatest cycle of the era—Shakespeare's—made its appearance. See SONNETS: *Sources.*

Son that has killed his father. In *3 Henry VI,* he is grief-stricken to discover that the man whom he has killed in battle is his own father, who was fighting on the opposite side (II, v).

Soothsayers. The soothsayers in Shakespeare attest to Elizabethan belief in the SUPERNATURAL; dramatically, their augury heightens the tension of expectation. Soothsayers appear in three of Shakespeare's plays: in *Julius Caesar* (I, ii; II, iv; III, i) his "beware the ides of March" strikes an ominous note of impending catastrophe; in *Antony and Cleopatra* (I, ii; II, iii) he tells two of Cleopatra's attendants that they will outlive her and informs Antony that Caesar's fortunes will rise higher than Antony's. In *Cymbeline* alone is the soothsayer's divination welcome: in IV, ii, he tells Lucius of impending victory for Rome, and the play ends (V, v) on the note struck by his favorable interpretation of the label Posthumus finds on his bosom after waking from his vision.

Sothern, Edward Hugh (1859–1933). Actor. Son of E. A. Sothern (1826–1881), Sothern was educated in London and made his first stage appearance with his father in New York. In 1881 he made his London debut and there met Julia Marlowe, who became his second wife in 1911. He toured the United States with John McCullough, and from 1884 to 1898 he was the leading man in Frohman's Lyceum company. He made his first appearance with Julia Marlowe in *Romeo and Juliet* in Chicago in 1904 and then came to New York with *Much Ado About Nothing* and *Hamlet.*

In 1905 Sothern and Marlowe toured with *The Taming of the Shrew, The Merchant of Venice,* and *Twelfth Night,* with Sothern as Petruchio, Shylock, and Malvolio. In 1907 they presented a Shakespearean season at the Lyric, New York, with *Romeo and Juliet, Hamlet, Merchant of Venice,* and *Twelfth Night,* and took to London their productions of *Twelfth Night, Romeo and Juliet,* and *Hamlet.* They were an immediate artistic success, but upon their return to New York, they dissolved the combination. Sothern then joined a company in Chicago, where he gave a successful Hamlet. In 1909 Miss Marlowe and Sothern took the leads in *Antony and Cleopatra* and toured in Shakespearean repertory the following year. They gave *Macbeth* (1910) in New York, and made further tours in 1912/3 and 1916. In 1923, Sothern played Leonatus in *Cymbeline* at the Jolson Theatre, and in 1928 gave a lecture tour with dramatized readings.

In 1924 he and his wife presented scenery, costumes, and properties for 10 Shakespearean productions to the Shakespeare Memorial Theatre at Stratford-upon-Avon. For most of his life Sothern was one of the leading exponents of romantic, light Shakespearean production in the United States. He also wrote two plays, *Whose Are They?* and *I Love,*

Thy Lovest, He Loves, as well as *My Remembrances* (1917). His films included *The Chattel* and *An Enemy to the King.* [*Who's Who in the Theatre,* 1933; *Oxford Companion to the Theatre,* Phyllis Hartnoll, ed., 1951.]

sources. There are four preliminary difficulties which must be mentioned before discussing Shakespeare's use of his sources. First, so many Elizabethan books have been lost, and so many plays, which Shakespeare may have known as actor or spectator, were never published, that we cannot always be certain that he did not derive information from them rather than from works which he appears to have used. Second, there was a great deal of common knowledge, repeated in book after book, and a particular source for such commonplaces is often impossible to determine. Third, the extent of Shakespeare's knowledge of foreign languages is still a matter of debate. He knew Latin and French, he probably knew some Italian, and he may have known a smattering of Spanish. The only evidence that he knew any Greek is Jonson's remark that he had "small Latin and less Greek." We cannot be certain that his French was sufficient for him to read medieval chronicles, though his Italian apparently enabled him to read Ariosto, Cinthio, and a number of plays. Fourth, there is still controversy about the relation of some of Shakespeare's plays to other plays of the period. Most critics now believe that *The Taming of A Shrew* was derived from Shakespeare's play and was not its source—though they may have had a common source; most critics, but not all, believe that *The Troublesome Raigne of John King of England* was the source of *King John;* and although the two CONTENTION PLAYS are now known to be "bad quartos" of *2* and *3 Henry VI,* there are still some critics who believe that Shakespeare was revising the work of others. It is thought by many that certain plays were based on lost dramatic sources, including *Richard II, The Two Gentlemen of Verona, The Merry Wives of Windsor, Pericles,* and *Hamlet.*

The extent of Shakespeare's library is unknown. Only one book bears a signature that can seriously be considered Shakespeare's—William Lambarde's *Archaionomia* (1568), a collection of Anglo-Saxon laws; but there is no evidence that the poet ever read it. He shows such familiarity with Ovid's *Metamorphoses,* both in the original and in Arthur Golding's translation, that it is reasonable to assume that he possessed copies of both. The same may be said of the Geneva version of the Bible (the Bishops' version he would hear in church), Holinshed's *Chronicles,* North's translation of Plutarch's *Lives,* and Florio's translation of Montaigne's *Essais.*

We can deduce from our knowledge of the curriculum (as examined in T. W. Baldwin's various volumes) and from some echoes in his plays and poems what books Shakespeare is likely to have read at school. We know what sources he used for most of his plays, but we do not know what scores of books he may have read in his search for plots. However economical he was, he must have read many books which have left no visible mark on his plays.

Yet a large number of echoes have been traced in his plays, sometimes when he was deliberately imitating something he had read, but often unconsciously. He probably read Samuel Harsnett *Declaration of Egregious Popishe Impostures* order to obtain local color in depicting the feign demoniac, Edgar. But he echoed many of Harsnett words and phrases in parts of *King Lear* in whic Edgar does not appear, and there is a belated ech of the same pamphlet six years later in *Th Tempest.* In the same way, Shakespeare consulte Lewis Lewkenor's (fl. 1599) translation of Co tarini's *The Commonwealth and Government Venice* when he was writing *Othello;* and, thoug he picked up one or two details for providing loc color, he also echoed phrases from Lewkeno address to the reader and his epistle dedicator Lewkenor, for example, says, "I would willing endure to haue mine eares inclined" to the mouth a traveler, as Desdemona would "seriously inclin to the traveler's tales of Othello.

Shakepeare's mind seems to have played the san trick when he was writing *Twelfth Night.* For th main plot he used a tale in Barnabe Riche's *Farewe to Militarie Profession,* but there are echoes in th third scene of the play of Riche's apology gentlewomen that he was not a good dancer in h epistle dedicatory.

There is some evidence that Shakespeare use dictionaries of quotations as an aid to compositio When he was writing of Bolingbroke's banishmen for example, he seems to have looked up *patria* an *exilium* in Erasmus' *Adagia* and there found quot tions from Ovid and Cicero. In the same way h probably looked up *avaritia,* when writing a stan in *The Rape of Lucrece* (855–861), and there foun quotations from an ode and satire of Horace' These linked up in his mind (as T. W. Baldwi has demonstrated) with Luke 12:15–21 and the no on the passage in the Geneva version. There some evidence that for another stanza in *Lucre* he used Mirandola's *Flores,* which was a popul school textbook.

The book which provided Shakespeare with mo material than any other was Holinshed's *Chronicle* All the English histories, *King Lear, Macbeth,* an *Cymbeline* were based on this book, though a these plays had other sources as well. The mai source of the first four English histories was, i fact, Edward Halle's *The union of the two nob and illustre famelies of Lancastre and York;* an here and there Shakespeare used Robert Fabyan *The New Chronicles of England and France* (fo *1 Henry VI*), John Foxe's *Book of Martyrs* (fo *2 Henry VI*), and the anonymous play *The Tru Tragedy of Richard III.* For the remaining hi tories, Holinshed replaced Halle as the main sourc but Shakespeare consulted all the relevant boo he could find—for *Richard II,* the anonymous pla *Thomas of Woodstock;* Samuel Daniel's poem *Th Civile Wars;* Berners' translation of Froissart; *Th Mirror for Magistrates;* and, some believe, th *Chronicque de la Traïson et mort de Richart De* and Créton's poem on the same subject. For *Hen IV* and *Henry V,* he read the old play *The Famo Victories of Henry V,* Samuel Daniel, *The Mirr for Magistrates,* and several minor sources; an for *Henry VIII,* written at the very end of h career, he consulted John Foxe and *When You S Me, You Know Me,* a play by Samuel Rowley.

T. W. Baldwin has shown that *The Comedy*

Errors, based on Plautus' *Menaechmi,* with one scene derived from the same author's *Amphitruo,* was reconstructed "into the *Andria* formula of Terentian structure." Shakespeare added hints from Gascoigne's *Supposes,* from *Apollonius of Tyre,* and from Acts 19. R. Warwick Bond suggested that the framework was influenced by Cecchi's *L'Ammalata,* but this is more likely to be an analogue than a source.

The Two Gentlemen of Verona may be based on a lost play, *Felix and Philiomena,* performed in 1585, or from Jorge Montemayor's *Diana,* which Shakespeare could have read in a French translation. *The Taming of the Shrew* may be based on a play which also formed the basis of *The Taming of A Shrew.* The Bianca scenes owe a good deal to Gascoigne's *Supposes.*

No direct source has been discovered for *A Midsummer Night's Dream,* though details were derived from Chaucer's "Knightes Tale," North's translation of Plutarch's life of Theseus, Greene's *James IV,* and Lyly's *Endimion.* The Pyramus and Thisbe interlude is derived from Golding's Ovid, from Chaucer's version in *The Legend of Good Women,* from Thomas Mouffet's *Of the Silkewormes, and their Flies* (which was not printed until 1599), and one or two other versions of the tale, from all of which Shakespeare picked up absurd phrases.

It seems probable that the rather tenuous plot of *Love's Labour's Lost* was Shakespeare's invention, though some details he may have derived from contemporary history and some of the comic characters from Italian comedy. With *The Merchant of Venice* we are on surer ground. Although before 1579 there was a play called *The Jew,* which represented "the greediness of wordly choosers and bloody minds of usurers," and a play by Dekker called *The Jew of Venice,* Shakespeare probably dramatized the Pound of Flesh story from *Il Pecorone.* The trial scene is influenced by a speech of a Jew in Piot's translation of Alexander Silvayn's *The Orator* (1596). Jessica's elopement was suggested by another version of the Pound of Flesh story, Munday's *Zelauto* (1580), with which there are several verbal parallels, and also by Marlowe's *Jew of Malta,* in which Abigail turns Christian. Jessica's disguise was Shakespeare's addition. The Caskets plot was derived from R. Robinson's translation of the *Gesta Romanorum* (1595).

Geoffrey Bullough prints a number of analogues of *The Merry Wives of Windsor,* including a tale from *Il Pecorone* of a lover who escapes in a basket of clean linen, a story of a duped husband in *Tarltons Newes out of Purgatorie,* and a tale of a deceitful wife in Riche's *Farewell to Militarie Profession.* All these Shakespeare probably knew; and he knew also the *Casina* of Plautus, which may have given hints for the Anne Page underplot. The horse-stealing episodes (which are clumsily handled in the play) probably relate in some way to the visit of Frederick Count Mömpelgard to England in 1592 and his subsequent attempts to obtain the Order of the Garter. It is possible, if Shakespeare wrote the play in the traditional fortnight, that he used an immediate source which has not survived.

There is the same difficulty with *Much Ado About Nothing.* The Hero plot derives ultimately from two distinct sources, Ariosto's *Orlando Furioso* and a tale by Bandello, for some details come from one version and some from another. But there were two lost plays by which Shakespeare may have been influenced: *Ariodante and Jenevra* (1583), based on Ariosto, and *The Matter of Panecia* (1575), which is thought to be about Bandello's heroine, Fenicia. The Beatrice-Benedick plot may be Shakespeare's invention—he may have taken a hint from Castiglione's *The Courtier* in Hoby's translation—and he was probably responsible for the union of the two plots, for the substitution of a villain for a rival in love as an accuser of the heroine, and, of course, for the invention of Dogberry and his associates.

As You Like It is indisputably based on *Rosalynde* (1590). Thomas Lodge's novel is charming and slow-moving, interspersed with long euphuistic speeches, eclogues, and other poems. Shakespeare retained the main outlines of the story, but he makes the usurping Duke the brother of the outlawed Duke in order to provide a parallel to the other plot in which Orlando is cheated of his rights by a villainous brother. Both villains repent in Shakespeare's play; in Lodge's novel Torismond is killed. Shakespeare omits an episode in which Rosader and the repentant Saladyne save Ganymede and Aliena from a gang of ruffians; and Rosader has previously saved Saladyne from a lion, whereas Orlando has to cope with a snake as well as a lioness. Both here, in the first scene where Orlando tells Adam what he already knows, and in the sudden repentances of his villains, Shakespeare is laughing at the conventions of romance. Lodge rewards Adam by making him Captain of the King's guard; Shakespeare's Adam is nearly 80, but his character contrasts neatly with the second childishness of the seventh age of man as described by Jaques. Shakespeare introduces a number of new characters—Le Beau, Touchstone, Jaques, Audrey, and William, all of whom provide an astringent element to what might otherwise be oversweet, and Amiens, to sing several of the songs. But the most significant alterations are in the transformation of Rosalind into Shakespeare's wittiest heroine and (as I have argued elsewhere) in the different levels of pastoral—the noble outlaws, the country bumpkins, the tradition of the eclogues (closest to Lodge), and the amateur shepherd and shepherdess, Ganymede and Aliena. Each of these sets off the others.

The main source of *Twelfth Night* is Riche's tale of Apolonius and Silla in his *Farewell to Militarie Profession,* but there are several Italian plays and novels which may have given Shakespeare a few hints. In Gonzaga's *Gl'Inganni,* a disguised woman takes the name of Cesare; in Secchi's play of the same title another woman disguises herself as a page for love of a man; in another of Secchi's plays, *L'Interesse,* we have the situation of a girl disguised as a man in love with a man who loves another woman, and there is a comic duel in which a man fights with a woman in disguise; and, closest of all, in the anonymous *Gl'Ingannati,* in which there is a reference to the feast of the Epiphany, Lelia, disguised as Fabio, becomes Flamineo's page, and Isabella, to whom she is sent on a love-embassy, falls in love with her. The situation is resolved, as in *Twelfth Night*, by the arrival of the heroine's lost brother. Lelia's story was also told by Bandello and Cinthio, two authors from whom Shakespeare derived the plots of other plays.

Shakespeare omitted from Riche's tale an attempted rape of Silla and her brother's getting Julina with child. *Twelfth Night* is nearer in spirit to the Italian comedies, although Lelia has apparently been raped during the sack of Rome, and although Shakespeare's poetry transforms a comedy of intrigue. The gulling of Malvolio was apparently his invention, but he may have picked up hints from an incident concerning Sir William Knollys' objection to revelers at Court and from pamphlets by Harsnett and others on the exorcisms of William Darrell.

The sources of *Troilus and Cressida* are even more complex. They include Chaucer's narrative poem, some books of Chapman's translation of the *Iliad*, Caxton's *Recuyell of the Historyes of Troy*, Lydgate's *Troy Book*, and Greene's *Euphues his Censure to Philautus*. For dramatic and satiric purposes Shakespeare, influenced by Henryson's sequel to Chaucer's poem, blackened the character of Pandarus and made Cressida capitulate to Diomed without a struggle. In the same way, in the war scenes, he used Thersites as a kind of chorus to denigrate the Greek leaders, who are no longer the heroic figures depicted by Homer.

The main source of *Measure for Measure* is Whetstone's two-part play *Promos and Cassandra*, but Shakespeare made some drastic alterations. From the prose version of the tale in Whetstone's *Heptameron of Civil Discourses* Shakespeare took the name of his heroine. It is also probable that he had read Cinthio's two versions of the story, for the *Hecatommithi* was the source of *Othello*, written about the same time, and the dramatic version *Epitia* (not published until 1583, five years after Whetstone's play), which is closer in spirit to Shakespeare's play than any other versions of the story, including one or two suggestive verbal parallels.

Shakespeare diverged from all previous versions in not allowing his heroine to consent to the proposal to ransom her brother at the price of her chastity, and in making her a novice; he alone does not marry her to her seducer; he alone provides a substitute in the Deputy's bed; and he alone makes the crime for which the brother is condemned premarital intercourse instead of rape. The purpose of these changes was threefold: to make the conflict in the heroine's mind more agonizing, to remove the monstrous marriage, and to subordinate the plot itself to the theme of justice, mercy, and forgiveness.

All's Well That Ends Well derives either from Boccaccio's *Decameron* (III.9) or William Painter's *The Palace of Pleasure*. The two versions of the tale differ very little; but in Painter's, Beltramo sleeps with Giletta many times before she conceives; in Boccaccio's and Shakespeare's, only once. Shakespeare follows his source fairly closely, but he makes Helena poor and says nothing about her many suitors; he does away with the King's reluctance to approve of Helena's choice, arguing that virtue is the true nobility; he omits Giletta's months of rule in Roussillon before she leaves for Florence; he conflates the characters of Giletta's hostess and Diana's mother; he complicates the last act by having Bertram arrested on suspicion of murdering his wife and by introducing Diana to accuse him; and, in place of the twins with which Giletta presents Beltramo, Helena's child is not yet born by the end of the play. The biggest changes however, are in the characterization, especially of the Countess, and in the introduction of the Parolles underplot, and both these have the effect of lowering our opinion of Bertram.

The main plot of *Cymbeline* is taken from a tale in Boccaccio's *Decameron* (II.9), but Shakespeare also used an English variant of the same story entitled *Frederyke of Jennen*, from which he took a number of details not to be found in Boccaccio. In linking this wager story concerning merchants with an old play, *The Rare Triumphs of Love and Fortune* Shakespeare altered the social milieu, and made his heroine a princess. The historical framework of the play was taken from Holinshed and *The Mirror for Magistrates*, and for the battle Shakespeare went to the Scottish section of the *Chronicles*, which he may have come across when he was writing *Macbeth*.

Shakespeare took the plot of *The Winter's Tale* from Greene's *Pandosto*, but he also consulted Francis Sabie's poem "The Fisshermans Tale" (1595) based on Greene's novel. He follows Greene most closely in the speech he gives Hermione at her trial but there are a few verbal echoes from Greene and Sabie scattered through the play. He made a large number of minor alterations (for example Perdita is taken to Bohemia by Antigonus, not set adrift in a boat) and two major ones. Bellaria actually dies on hearing of the death of her son but Hermione recovers; and at the end of Greene's novel Pandosto falls in love with Fawnia, his daughter, and commits suicide on learning who she is. Shakespeare, obsessed with reconciliation and forgiveness, restores the wronged Hermione to the penitent Leontes and by the marriage of Florizel and Perdita reconciles Leontes and Polixenes.

No direct source of *The Tempest* has been discovered and it is possible that Shakespeare invented it. But he picked up hints from accounts of the Bermudas shipwreck, from *The Rare Triumphs of Love and Fortune*, from one of Erasmus' *Colloquies* from Ovid's *Metamorphoses*, from Florio's translation of Montaigne's *Essais*, and from Robert Eden's *History of Travaile*.

The main source of *Romeo and Juliet* was Arthur Brooke's poem "Romeus and Juliet," but Shakespeare also consulted Painter's version of Bandello's tale and, as Brooke says he saw a performance of a play on the subject, Shakespeare may have seen that, too. He adopts a more sympathetic attitude to the lovers than Brooke had done and he does not condemn the behavior of Friar Laurence. He creates the characters of Mercutio and Tybalt from casual references by Brooke and makes the nurse more real and vital. The main change, however, is the speeding up of the action. Weeks elapse in Brooke's poem between the first meeting of Romeus and Juliet and their marriage, and more weeks elapse between the marriage and the killin of Tybalt, which Romeus does in self-defense. The action of the play is condensed into a few days and this emphasizes the passionate impulsiveness of the lovers, their marriage being consummated in the knowledge that Romeo must leave at dawn. Romeo's last speech in the tomb contains echoes of *Astrophel and Stella* and Daniel's *Complaint of Rosamond*.

North's translation of Plutarch's *Lives* provided Shakespeare with the plots of his three Roman plays and *Timon of Athens*. *Julius Caesar* is based on the lives of Caesar (for the first half of the play), Antony and Brutus (for the remainder). *Antony and Cleopatra* is a condensed dramatization of the last 10 years of the life of Antony, though Shakespeare omits the account of the Parthian campaign. For both these plays, however, Shakespeare also used a translation of Appian, as Ernest Schanzer has demonstrated; and for *Antony and Cleopatra* he also used the Countess of Pembroke's version of Garnier's *Antonie* and Daniel's *Cleopatra*. For *Coriolanus* he used, besides Plutarch's life, the versions of Menenius' fable given by Livy, Sidney, Averell, and Camden.

Shakespeare's verbal indebtedness to North's translation is comparatively little in *Julius Caesar*, considerable in *Antony and Cleopatra*, and extensive in *Coriolanus*. The substance, and many of the actual words, of the speeches of Coriolanus are to be found in North's prose. Here, for example, is part of the speech in which the hero reveals himself to his old enemy, Aufidius:

> I am Caius Marcius, who hath done to thy self particularly, and to all the Volscians generally, great hurt and mischief, which I cannot deny for my surname of Coriolanus which I bear. For I never had other benefit nor recompense, of all the true and painful service I have done, and the extreme dangers I have been in, but this only surname: a good memory and witness of the malice and displeasure thou shouldest bear me. Indeed the name only remaineth with me: for the rest, the envy and the cruelty of the people of Rome have taken from me, by the sufferance of the dastardly nobility and magistrates, who have forsaken me, and let me be banished by the people.

My name is Caius Martius, who hath done
To thee particularly and to all the Volsces
Great hurt and mischief; thereto witness may
My surname, Coriolanus: the painful service,
The extreme dangers and the drops of blood
Shed for my thankless country are requited
But with that surname; a good memory,
And witness of the malice and displeasure
Which thou should'st bear me: only that name
    remains;
The cruelty and envy of the people,
Permitted by our dastard nobles, who
Have all forsook me, hath devour'd the rest;
And suffer'd me by the voice of slaves to be
Whoop'd out of Rome.

(IV, v, 71–84)

In spite of the closeness with which Shakespeare follows North, he makes several changes in the play for dramatic reasons. He fuses three separate insurrections into one; he makes the characters of the Tribunes less sympathetic in order to provide the hero with more excuse for his conduct; and he creates Menenius from a man in Plutarch whose one function is to tell the fable of the body and its members.

Although Shakespeare was greatly indebted to North's translation, it would be wrong to pretend that the task of dramatization was simple. It has been said that he hardly ventures "to rearrange, much less to alter, the actions recorded by the historian"; but he does rearrange and he does expand mere hints in Plutarch. His genius as a playwright is displayed as effectively in the minor changes he made in dramatizing Plutarch as in the major changes he had to make in dramatizing the story of Lear. In the same way his greatness as a poet can be seen from the slight changes he had to introduce in order to convert North's prose into verse, as well as in speeches for which there is no known source. He imposes order on the rambling prose of North, omitting and adding, rearranging and condensing. Sometimes he adds a vivid metaphor or a more precise epithet. But perhaps the major factor in the transmutation is the magnificence of the great Shakespearean rhythm. The rhythm could be demonstrated only by an extended comparison, but the other changes can be illustrated by the concluding sentences of the two descriptions of Antony's first meeting with Cleopatra:

> So that in the end, there ran such multitudes of people one after another to see her, that Antonius was left post alone in the market-place, in his imperial seat to give audience.

                The city cast
Her people out upon her; and Antony,
Enthroned i' the market-place, did sit alone,
Whistling to the air; which, but for vacancy,
Had gone to gaze on Cleopatra too
And made a gap in nature.

(II, ii, 218–223)

Othello, written about the same time as *Measure for Measure*, was derived from Cinthio's *Hecatommithi*, probably the original rather than Gabriel Chappuys' French translation. Shakespeare deviated from his source in a number of ways. The most important of these concerns Iago's motives: the corresponding character in the source is motivated by his thwarted love for Desdemona and his hatred of the two men who have succeeded, as he thinks, in winning her affections, the Moor and Cassio—none of the three men is given a name by Cinthio. Iago steals the handkerchief while Desdemona is fondling his child: Shakespeare's heroine (more dramatically) forgets the precious handkerchief only when it proves too small to bind Othello's head. Cassio gives the handkerchief to his wife, not to a harlot, and the alteration is used by Iago to arouse Othello's fury. The murder of Desdemona is carried out by Iago, who beats her to death with a sandbag, and the two men conceal the crime by making part of the ceiling fall. Cassio accuses the Moor before the Signiory, having been informed by Iago of the attack on him and of Desdemona's murder, for which the villain blames the Moor. The Moor is banished and eventually killed by Desdemona's kinsmen, while Iago is tortured to death for another crime altogether. Shakespeare's deviations from the events have a fivefold effect: they convert the Moor into a much nobler figure and, by giving him a glamorous past, enable us to believe in the marriage; they make Iago both more complex and more evil; they make Othello aware of the truth, so that he executes himself and Iago is exposed before the end of the play; and the leisurely narrative of the novel is speeded up in such a way as to make Othello's jealousy credible on the stage.

Shakespeare was doubtless attracted to the story of Macbeth by the fact that King James was reputed to be Banquo's descendant and was known to have approved of Matthew Gwinn's Latin playlet on the witches' prophecies; but in Holinshed's *Chronicles*, Banquo was one of Macbeth's accomplices. Shakespeare therefore made use of Donwald's murder of King Duff at the instigation of his wife, while the King was a guest in his castle. This had the effect of whitewashing Banquo; and Shakespeare made the story more dramatic by giving Lady Macbeth a more active role and by making Macbeth commit the actual deed—Donwald employs four servants for the purpose.

The rest of the play is based on Holinshed's account of Macbeth, although Shakespeare keeps verbally close to his source only in the scene where Macbeth first encounters the weird sisters and in the testing of Macduff by Malcolm (IV, iii). But the poet made many alterations for the sake of dramatic effect: for example, the three campaigns described by Holinshed are combined into one; Duncan is made venerable and saintly instead of young and feeble; the 10 years during which Macbeth ruled well are suppressed; and the banquet scene (suggested, perhaps, by De Loier's *Treatise of Specters*), the porter scene (with its topical references to the Gunpowder Plot), and Lady Macbeth's sleepwalking and death were added. One other example will show the brilliance of Shakespeare's plotting. In Holinshed's account Macduff comes to England knowing that his family has been killed. In the play he has not yet heard the news, and this not merely makes Malcolm's suspicions more plausible but enables the breaking of the news to provide a splendid climax to the scene.

Recent critics have argued that Shakespeare consulted other accounts of Macbeth—William Stewart's manuscript poem entitled "Buik of the Croniclis of Scotland," Skene's *Scots Acts*, Leslie's *De origine, Moribus, et Rebus Gestis Scotorum*, and Buchanan's Latin *History of Scotland*. It is unlikely that Shakespeare read Stewart and Skene; but there is some evidence that he knew the other two books, as they seem to have left their mark both on the imagery and on the characterization.

Shakespeare took the precaution of studying James I's writings; and even if we discount some of H. N. Paul's arguments in *The Royal Play of "Macbeth,"* there are undoubted parallels with *Daemonologie* and possible echoes of *A Counterblast to Tobacco*, the *Basilikon Doron*, and *The True Law of Free Monarchies*. Shakespeare had also been studying Seneca's *Hercules Furens*, of which there are a number of echoes; and there are echoes, too, of several of Shakespeare's own works, the most significant being from *Lucrece* and *Richard III*.

The other great tragedy which exemplifies Shakespeare's use of multiple sources is *King Lear*. There were dozens of versions of the Lear story and Shakespeare knew several of them—the old play of *King Leir*, the brief accounts by Holinshed and in Spenser's *Faerie Queene*, the anecdote of the lovetest in Camden's *Remaines*, and Cordilla's complaint in *The Mirror for Magistrates*. There are echoes from all these in Shakespeare's play. He combined the Lear story with the episode of the Paphlagonian King from Sidney's *Arcadia*, and he picked up hints from neighboring chapters in that book, as he likewise echoed passages in Holinshed adjacent to the story of Lear. He went to Harsnett's *Declaration*, as we have seen, for details of the storm scenes; and it has been argued that he had been reading Florio's translation of Montaigne's *Essais*.

Sidney's story, in which the favored son betrays his father and the ill-treated son returns good for evil, provided a neat parallel with the story of Lear's treatment at the hands of his daughters, and Shakespeare used various devices to weld the plots together. The evil son, Edmund, is made the object of the affections of the two evil daughters; and, because of his ambitions, he orders the execution of Lear and Cordelia. The good son, Edgar, is responsible for the downfall of Goneril and the death of Edmund. More significant than the plot linkage, however, is the thematic parallelism: for example, the madness of Lear parallels both the blindness of Gloucester and the feigned madness of Poor Tom.

The source play had ended with the restoration of Leir to the throne; but in all the other versions of the story, Cordelia, after her father's death, is overthrown by a rebellion of her nephews and she commits suicide in prison. To avoid this, and to bring Cordelia's death within the compass of the play, which had to end with the death of the hero, Shakespeare reverses the result of the battle and substitutes a murder for the suicide.

The main source of *Hamlet* was probably a lost play, possibly by Thomas Kyd. It is not known whether Shakespeare consulted prose versions of the Hamlet story by Saxo Grammaticus or Belleforest.

The study of Shakespeare's sources is no substitute for criticism; but, now and again, the knowledge of the source may enable us to choose between rival interpretations. We know from Plutarch, for example, that Cleopatra lies about her treasure in order to delude Octavius, not because she intends to live. Sometimes, too, the knowledge that Shakespeare deviated from his sources (for example, in *Measure for Measure*, *Othello*, and *The Winter's Tale*) may cause us to ask the questions that will lead us to a true interpretation. [H. R. D. Anders, *Shakespeare's Books*, 1904; S. Guttman, *The Foreign Sources of Shakespeare's Works*, 1947; V. K. Whitaker, *Shakespeare's Use of Learning*, 1953; Geoffrey Bullough *Narrative and Dramatic Sources of Shakespeare*, 8 vols., 1957–1966; Kenneth Muir, *Shakespeare's Sources*, I, 1957.]—K.M.

Southampton, Elizabeth Wriothesley, countess of. Born **Elizabeth Vernon** (d. c. 1648). The wife of Henry Wriothesley, 3rd earl of SOUTHAMPTON, and one of the candidates for the Dark Lady of the *Sonnets*. She was the daughter of Sir John Vernon of Hodnet who died in 1591, and she became a ward of her cousin, the earl of Essex, who secured her a position at court as one of the queen's ladies-in-waiting. By 1595 court gossip had linked her name with Southampton's, and in 1598 she became pregnant, at which time she was secretly married to the earl. It is on the basis of these events that she is designated the Dark Lady by some of those who identify Southampton as the Fair Youth of the *Sonnets* (see Mr. W. H.). Her subsequent life, however, is distinguished by a singular devotion to her husband hardly consistent with the immoral wanton pictured in Shakespeare's poems. When the queen became apprised of the secret marriage, she ordered the imprisonment of the earl and his "new coined Countess." They were released shortly after, and Southampton joined Essex in the disastrous expedition to Ireland. During the expedition the countess wrote many letters to her husband, including one which contains an unsolved contemporary allusion:

> Al the nues I can send you that I thinke wil make you mery is that I reade in a letter from London that Sir John Falstaf is by his Mrs Dame Pintpot made father of a godly milers thum, a boye thats all heade and veri litel body; but this is a secrit.

It has been suggested that this is a reference to Shakespeare, but the more likely explanation seems to be that she is referring to an acquaintance whose behavior or girth was Falstaffian. Leslie Hotson convincingly argues that the allusion is to the enemy of Essex and Southampton, Henry Brooke, 8th Lord Cobham. [C. C. Stopes, *The Life of Henry, Third Earl of Southampton*, 1922; Leslie Hotson, *Shakespeare's Sonnets Dated*, 1949.]

HENRY WRIOTHESLEY, 3RD EARL OF SOUTHAMPTON. ENGRAVING BY SIMON PASSE (1617). (HUNTINGTON LIBRARY)

Southampton, Henry Wriothesley, 3d earl of (1573–1624). Shakespeare's patron. Born at Cowdray House on October 6, 1573, Southampton was between 9 and 10 years younger than Shakespeare. He succeeded to his title in 1581 when he was eight years old. He had been baptized and brought up a Catholic, but as a ward of the state, he came under the guardianship of William Cecil, Lord Burghley, whose attempt to arrange a marriage for him with Lady Elizabeth Vere failed (see Mr. W. H.). Southampton went to St. John's College, Cambridge, where he showed a precocious talent for the arts and developed a keen interest in literature. He graduated M.A. in 1589. At the age of 17 he was presented at court where the queen showed him extraordinary marks of her favor. Almost at once he became a generous patron of poets and other men of letters. Shakespeare's dedication to him of *Venus and Adonis* and *The Rape of Lucrece* is proof that his reputation as a generous patron was well known. In 1594 Thomas Nashe dedicated to him his *The unfortunate traveller or The Life of Jack Wilton*, and Gervase Markham dedicated to him his poem *The Most Honorable Tragedy of Sir Richard Grenville* (1595). He took into his service as a teacher of Italian John Florio, whose Italian-English dictionary, *A World of Words* (1598), was associated with Southampton's name. Nicholas Rowe on the authority of Sir William Davenant states in his *Life of Shakespeare* (1709) that Southampton once gave the poet a gift of £1000, possibly as the recognition of the dedication of his poems. If the sonnets urging marriage were really addressed to Southampton, they must have been written and dispatched before the beginning of his affair with Elizabeth Vernon in 1595, which ended with a forced marriage in 1598 (see Elizabeth Wriothesley, countess of Southampton). This disgraceful episode brought down upon him the wrath of the queen who sent him for a brief stay in Fleet Prison.

The earl apparently developed a notable interest in the drama. Rowland White in a letter to Sir Robert Sidney wrote, "My Lord Southampton and Lord Rutland [Francis Manners, 6th earl of Rutland] come not to Court—They pass away their time merely in going to plays every day."

Early in his life Southampton became a great admirer of Robert Devereux, 2nd earl of Essex, and after his arrival in London he attached himself to him, taking part in Essex' expedition to Cadiz in 1596 and to the Azores in 1597. In 1601, when Essex attempted to seize control of the government, Southampton joined the ill-fated rebellion, with the result that he was captured and sentenced to death (see topical references). Through the intercession of Sir Robert Cecil, however, the penalty was commuted to a prison sentence. Southampton was released with the accession of James I in 1603. His prison experience apparently did not dampen his enthusiasm for the theatre, since in January of 1605 Shakespeare's company presented a revival of *Love's Labour's Lost* at Southampton's London house. He continued to be active in military and court affairs until his death in 1624. [A. L. Rowse, *Shakespeare's Southampton*, 1965.]

Southwark. A borough in the county of Surrey on the south side of the Thames. In Elizabethan times Southwark was a suburb of London, to which it was connected by London Bridge, and was outside the jurisdiction of the city fathers. Within Southwark was the district known as the Bankside where most of the Elizabethan theatres were built, including the Hope, the Rose, the Globe, and the Swan. Southwark also contained a number of inns, prisons, and a fairgrounds.

Southwell, John. A priest who was arrested for his aid in the alleged treason of Eleanor Cobham, the duchess of Gloucester. Southwell died in the Tower before execution could be carried out. In *2 Henry VI*, Southwell acts as a conjuror for the Duchess, and is condemned to hang. [W. H. Thomson, *Shakespeare's Characters: A Historical Dictionary*, 1951.]

Southwell, Robert (c. 1561–1595). Poet. Educated at Douai and Paris, Southwell was ordained a Jesuit priest and in 1586 returned to England with Father Henry GARNET. During this time Catholic priests were outlawed in England under penalty of death. After six years of secret missionary activities, Southwell was apprehended. He spent several years in prison before he was finally executed.

Southwell's earliest poetic work was his *Marie Magdalens funerall tears* (1594). Another collection of verse, *Saint Peters complaynt*, was published shortly after his death in 1595 but had been circulated in manuscript form as early as 1591. Christopher Devlin has argued, rather unconvincingly, that a dedication written by Southwell urging poets to devote their lyric skills to religious rather than profane subjects was directed to Shakespeare and was responsible for the poet's shift in theme from the explicitly amorous *Venus and Adonis* to the more consciously moral *The Rape of Lucrece*. The basis of Devlin's argument is the address of the dedication, not published until 1616, "To my worthy good cousin, Master W.S." [Christopher Devlin, *The Life of Robert Southwell, Poet and Martyr*, 1956.]

Soviet Union. See RUSSIA.

Spain. The history of Shakespeare's works, reputation, and influence in Spain has followed an irregular but upward-moving course over the past 200 years. It begins with the rarely relieved gloom of the early translations, drawn for the most part from the incomplete and bowdlerized French versions of Jean François Ducis. Ducis was a neoclassicist who knew no English; he set six of his plays in regular Alexandrine couplets, basing his "translation" on *Le Théâtre Anglois* of P. A. de La Place. De La Place, in turn, had translated only the major scenes, preserving the continuity by summarizing the minor scenes. Ducis dropped characters, changed names, tampered with motives and simplified the plots of the plays. His translations dominated Spanish Shakespearean productions from 1772, when Ramón de la Cruz translated his *Hamlet* into Spanish, until the last third of the 19th century. The only translations of complete plays directly from the English throughout this period were Leandro Fernández de Moratín's faithfu prose *Hamlet* (1798), with notes reflecting a nec classical bias, and José García de Villalta's not-so faithful verse *Macbeth* (1838).

Although the return, in 1832, of many educate Spaniards who had taken refuge in England durin the War of Independence and the reign of Ferdinand VII, "The Desired," presaged a renewed interest in Shakespeare, his reputation was not yet quit secure. The rise of his prestige resulting from the appearance of *Don Alvaro, O la Fuerza del Sino* (1835 by the Duque de Rivas, *El Trovador* (1836) of Antonio García Gutiérrez, and *Los Amantes de Teru* of Juan Eugenio Hartzenbusch—three plays by returned exiles manifesting a strong Shakespearean influence—was countered by the continuing popularit of two farces translated from the French, *Shakespeare Enamorado* (1810) and *El Sueño de un Noche de Verano* (1852; not Shakespeare's *A Midsummer Night's Dream*). The first, by Alexandr Duval, depicted Shakespeare as the ludicrously jealous lover of an actress; the second, by Joseph Rosie and Adolphe de Leuven, presented him as th drunken lover of Queen Elizabeth I. *Un Dram Nuevo* (1867) by Manuel Tamayo y Baus, castin Shakespeare in a noble role, did little to redress th balance.

Not until 1857, when touring Italian opera companies began performing operas by Rossini, Bellin and Verdi based on fairly accurate Shakespearea texts, did Shakespeare's reputation move upward toward the attainment of its present position. The success of the Italian productions led to new translation among them those of two resident Englishmen, Jame (Jaime) Clark (1844–1875) and William (Guillermo MacPherson (1824–1898). In 1881, on the occasion o the Calderón Bicentenary, Marcelino Menéndez Pelayo, the father of modern Spanish scholarshi with some of these new translations available to hin could declare that Shakespeare was the world's greatest dramatist, not excluding Calderón himself.

Shakespeare's influence kept pace with his reputation. Two plays demonstrating this influence are *Lo Favoritos* (1892), based on an episode in *A Midsummer Night's Dream*, and *Cuento de Amor* (1899), recast of *Twelfth Night*, both by Jacinto Benavent (1866–1954), the Nobel prize-winning dramatist.

Translation. Serious translation of Shakespear into Spanish begins with MacPherson and Clark, notwithstanding the work of Moratín and Villalta; si plays in Francisco José Orellana's series, *Teatro Selecto Antiguo y Moderno, Nacional y Extranjer* (1868); and a few fragments, including the "To b or not to be" soliloquy from *Hamlet*, by José Marí Blanco-Crespo (Joseph Blanco-White). In the 1870 Clark brought out 5 volumes of translations, 10 play in all, following the English original as to verse o prose. At about the same time, MacPherson published his first translation, *Hamlet* (1873), and followed it with 22 others, including 9 of the 10 translated by Clark, the sole exception being *Much Ad About Nothing*. Between 1885 and 1897 his translations were collected in eight volumes and frequentl reprinted. The only plays still not translated at th turn of the century were: *Richard II, Henry V,* a of *Henry VI, Henry VIII, Pericles, Timon of Athens, All's Well That Ends Well, Comedy of Error*

Love's Labour's Lost, Two Gentlemen of Verona, and *Twelfth Night.* The Spanish critics admired the translations in general, but accused Clark of amplifying and MacPherson of curtailing the original text. Alfonso Par, a noted Spanish Shakespearean scholar, criticized both for attempting to translate in verse and contrasted them with the Marqués de Dos Hermanas (1829–1901), who translated three plays, the poems, and the sonnets in prose.

In the four decades following the MacPherson and Clark translations, several attempts were made, but did not get beyond three or four plays. Menéndez y Pelayo translated four plays, Benavente translated one, and Gregorio Martínez Sierra, another noted Spanish playwright, did three. Not until the 1920's, with the systematic appearance of translations by Luis Astrana Marín (1889–1959), were a large number of plays rendered again by a single translator. Since World War II, Marín has dominated the scene with his *Obras Completas de William Shakespeare,* a prose translation of all the plays and poems, the first such translation entirely from the English text and the only complete Spanish translation. At the time of his death, Marín was engaged in bringing out a revised, bilingual edition. Other important figures in post-World War II translation are Salvador de Madariaga, whose verse-for-verse and prose-for-prose *Hamlet* is set in a 17th-century Spanish verse style, and Doña Angelina Damian de Bulart, who did a verse translation of the sonnets in 1944.

Information concerning translations in the minor dialects is sketchy. There are no translations at the present time in Galician. There is a Basque *Macbeth.* In Catalán, a language more amenable to translation from the English than Castilian Spanish, there is a good translation by José María de Sagarra, a highly regarded poet. Before his death in 1964, seven volumes had appeared containing translations of more than half the plays.

Stage Production. Except for Moratín's early *Hamlet,* Orellana's six plays were the only translations not expressly intended for stage production. On the stage, the pattern of garbled adaptations which the Spanish theatre audiences have always associated with the name of Shakespeare was set at the very beginning of their acquaintance with his works. The only production before 1802 consisted of the five performances of Ramón de la Cruz's translation of Ducis' *Hamlet* in 1772. It was played in Madrid, not surviving long enough to be taken to Barcelona.

Between 1802 and 1900 there were 1081 performances of Shakespeare plays or adaptations in these two major cities and countless others in provincial towns. From 1802 to 1833 there were 170 performances, the first success being *Othello,* followed by *Romeo and Juliet.* Although *Hamlet* and *Macbeth* were performed during this period, they were usually unsuccessful. The romantic period, 1833 to 1857, saw the addition of *King John, A Midsummer Night's Dream,* and *Richard III* to the repertory, of which the last mentioned was accorded an especially warm reception. There were 168 performances of these seven plays during this period. During the realistic period, 1857 to 1900, six more plays were added: *The Merchant of Venice, King Lear, Antony and Cleopatra, The Taming of the Shrew, Twelfth Night,* and *Coriolanus. Hamlet, Othello,* and *The Taming of the Shrew* enjoyed particular popularity. The increase in Shakespeare's popularity is attested to by the 743 performances staged during this period.

The only significant event since 1900 has been the nationalization of the Teatro Nacional in 1940. No longer a commercial enterprise, the Teatro has now turned its attention to raising the taste of the theatre-going public. A different Shakespeare play was performed each season from 1940 to 1947. As of 1948, Shakespeare productions were thriving, but the stage texts were still generally mangled versions of the originals. [Alfonso Par, *Contribución a la Bibliografía Española de Shakespeare,* 1930; Alfonso Par, *Shakespeare en la Literatura Española,* 1935; Alfonso Par, *Representaciones Shakespearianas en España,* 2 vols., 1936, 1940; Sir Henry Thomas, "Shakespeare in Spain," *Proceedings of the British Academy,* XXXVI, 1950; Thomas A. Fitzgerald, "Shakespeare in Spain and Spanish America, *Modern Language Journal,* XXXV, 1951.]—A.B.

Spalding, William (1809–1859). Critic. Spalding contributed a number of articles on Shakespeare to the *Edinburgh Review.* In 1833 he published *Letter on Shakespere's Authorship of the Two Noble Kinsmen,* in which he set forth in an authoritative manner the case for Shakespeare's part-authorship of the play. See THE TWO NOBLE KINSMEN: *Selected Criticism.*

Spanish Tragedy, The. See Thomas KYD.

Spedding, James (1808–1881). Scholar. After graduation from Cambridge, Spedding served for a decade in the colonial office. He left in 1841 to devote his life to the study of Francis Bacon. In 1847 he began work on an edition of Bacon in collaboration with R. E. Ellis and D. D. Heath. For reasons of health, Ellis was forced to resign, leaving the bulk of the work to Spedding who had the occasional assistance of Heath, who edited most of the legal writings. The *Works* appeared in seven volumes from 1857 to 1859, followed by the *Letters and Life* (7 vols., 1861–1874); a condensation of the latter was published as the *Life and Times* (2 vols., 1878). Spedding occasionally turned his attention to problems of Shakespeare scholarship. In the *Gentleman's Magazine* (August 1850) he published an article maintaining that the greater part of *Henry VIII* was by Fletcher, with Shakespeare responsible only for I, i and ii; II, iii and iv; III, ii, 1–203; and V, i. Immediately afterward, Samuel Hickson published a letter giving additional evidence and stating that he had anticipated Spedding's contention by several years (*Notes and Queries,* August 24, 1850); Spedding called attention to this letter and made some additional observations in the October 1850 issue of the *Gentleman's Magazine.* These comments of Spedding and Hickson, together with an article in support by F. G. Fleay, were reprinted in 1874 as an appendix to the *Transactions of the New Shakspere Society.* This material constitutes one of the first manifestations of the "disintegration theory," i.e., the attribution to other playwrights of passages from works accepted in the Shakespeare canon. Spedding also became concerned with Shakespeare's part in the play *The Booke of Sir Thomas Moore* (British Museum MS Harley 7368). Richard Simpson (1820–1876) had maintained, on the basis of internal evidence, that several portions of this play were composed by Shakespeare and that these portions were possibly in Shakespeare's own hand (*Notes and Queries,* July 1, 1871). Spedding agreed with Simpson on this attribution and was even more firmly convinced that the handwriting was Shakespeare's (*Notes and Queries,* September 21, 1872). As Spedding's reputation as a Bacon scholar grew, advocates of Bacon as the author of the plays attributed to Shakespeare attempted to enlist his support for their cause, but he remained unconvinced. His views were set forth in a letter addressed to Nathaniel Holmes, who wrote *The Authorship of Shakespeare* (1866), one of the most widely read books on the subject. The letter was reprinted by Spedding in *Reviews and Discussions* (1879), along with the article on Shakespeare's part in SIR THOMAS MORE and reviews of two London productions of Shakespeare. Spedding's other activities in Shakespeare scholarship consisted in reading several papers before meetings of the New Shakspere Society.

Speed. In *The Two Gentlemen of Verona,* quick-witted servant who attends Valentine. Speed and his master are captured by outlaws (IV, i).

spelling. In Shakespeare's time no standard system of spelling existed in English. Extant manuscripts and letters indicate a total lack of uniformity: a given word was frequently spelled more than one way on the same page. Printed material was somewhat more consistent, but even here the most important determinant in spelling a word was frequently the space or lack of space which a compositor had available in setting up a line of type. Added to this is the fact that the compositors' personal spelling habits were frequently reflected in the text (see COMPOSITOR). Thus it is extremely difficult to determine Shakespeare's own spelling from an examination of the early quartos. The best evidence, if it could be confirmed, is that provided by the manuscript of *Sir Thomas More,* three pages of which are thought to be in Shakespeare's hand. In arguing the case for Shakespeare's authorship of these three pages, Dover Wilson has shown that certain unusual spellings in the passage are duplicated in other Shakespearean texts. Of these the most notable is the word "silence" which is spelled "scilens" in the passage in *Sir Thomas More.* This same spelling is frequently used in the speech prefixes to Q1 of *2 Henry IV* to indicate Justice Silence. Aside from an unusual spelling like "scilens" the *Sir Thomas More* fragment, if it is by Shakespeare, reveals that he was a fairly normal, conservative speller who usually chose full spellings such as "sonne," "hee," and "goe," and who used an "ie" ending in preference to a "y." [J. Dover Wilson, et al., *Shakespeare's Hand in "The Play of Sir Thomas More,"* 1923; A. C. Partridge, *Orthography in Shakespeare and Elizabethan Drama,* 1964.]

Spencer, Gabriel (d. 1598). Actor. Spencer was with Pembroke's, the Admiral's Men, and probably also with the Chamberlain's Men. The earliest mention of him occurs in 1597, when he was one of the members of the newly reorganized Pembroke's Men, under contract to Francis Langley, at the Swan theatre. This new company had a short-lived existence, for in July 1597 their production of the scandalous ISLE OF DOGS infuriated the authorities to the extent that all the London theatres were ordered closed, and Spencer, another actor, Robert Shaw, and Ben Jonson, part author of the play, were imprisoned. After his release from prison Spencer joined the Admiral's Men. He remained with them until September 1598, when he was killed by Ben Jonson in a duel resulting from a quarrel.

There is some evidence to suggest that before joining Pembroke's Men in 1597, Spencer belonged to Shakespeare's company. In the stage directions to the Folio text of *3 Henry VI* (I, ii, 48), the name "Gabriel" is thought to refer to Spencer. On the basis of this conjecture, it has been suggested that Spencer may have been the reporter of the "bad quarto" of *Romeo and Juliet.* See MEMORIAL RECONSTRUCTION. [Harry R. Hoppe, *The Bad Quarto of Romeo and Juliet,* 1948.]

Spencer, Theodore (1902–1949). American critic. Spencer's most significant contribution to Shakespearean studies is his elucidation of the traditional, and often implicit, doctrines that lie behind Elizabethan literature. He is the author of *Death and Elizabethan Tragedy* (1936), a study of the attitude toward death in the plays of Shakespeare and his contemporaries, and *Shakespeare and the Nature of Man* (1942), a closely detailed survey of the Elizabethan view of the universe as a harmoniously ordered, hierarchical structure. Central to this view is the vision of man as a microcosm—a small world mirroring the larger one. See HISTORICAL CRITICISM.

Spenser, Edmund (c. 1552–1599). Poet. Spenser received early recognition as one of the major poets of his day with the publication of *The Shepheardes Calendar* (1579), a series of 12 pastoral eclogues. After serving Lord Grey of Wilton as secretary in Ireland, he returned to London to supervise the publication of the first three books (1590) of *The Faerie Queene;* the remaining books appeared in 1596. Other works include *Complaints* (1591), an expression of his disappointment at failing to receive court preferment; *Colin Clouts Come home againe* (1595), an allegorical description of his journey to London; *Astrophel* (1595), an elegy on Sir Philip Sidney; *Amoretti* (1595), a sonnet sequence commemorating Spenser's courtship of Elizabeth Boyle; *Epithalamion* (1595), a hymn in honor of Spenser's own marriage; *Prothalamion* (1596), a celebration of the double marriage of the daughters of the earl of Worcester; and *Fowre Hymnes* (1596), a Christian-Platonic praise of human and divine love. *A View of the Present State of Ireland,* a prose treatise defending the policy of Lord Grey, circulated in manuscript form about 1596 but was not printed until 1633.

Spenser has been credited with making one of the earliest allusions to Shakespeare. In *Colin Clout Come home againe,* the poet Aëtion is praised as a gentle shepherd whose muse, "full of high thought invention," does "like himselfe Heroically sound." The argument is that Shakespeare was the only poet of this time who both dealt with heroic subject matter and who had a surname of heroic sound. (See NAME.) The belief that "our pleasant Willy" in "The Teares of the Muses," published in *Complaints* refers to Shakespeare has not been generally accepted. Numerous verbal parallels suggest that Shakespeare was familiar with Spenser's works. A recent trend in scholarship has been the study of themes and techniques common to these two poets but modified by the demands of their respectiv genres. [W. B. C. Watkins, *Shakespeare and Spenser*, 1950; A. F. Potts, *Shakespeare and the Faerie Queene*, 1958.]

Spohr, Louis. See MUSIC BASED ON SHAKESPEARE: *19th century to 1850*.

Sprague, Arthur Colby (1895–). American scholar, professor emeritus at Bryn Mawr. Sprague's first book was *Shakespeare and the Audience* (1935), a study of the physical aspects of the Elizabethan theatre and its influence on the structure of the drama. His *Shakespeare and the Actors: The Stage Business* (1944) covers the period 1660–1905. *Shakespearian Players and Performances* (1953) is a discussion of famous actors and their performances. His *Shakespeare's Histories* appeared in 1964.

Spurgeon, Caroline (1869–1942). Scholar. Professor of English at the University of London, Miss Spurgeon edited *Keats's Shakespeare* (1928), an edition which provides Keats' annotations. Her most important book is *Shakespeare's Imagery* (1935), an original study which attempts "to point out several directions in which the detailed examination of Shakespeare's images seems . . . to throw new light on the poet and his work." By comparing Shakespeare's images with those of his contemporaries and by pointing to characteristic attitudes expressed in Shakespeare's images—his sympathy for snails and horses, for instance—Miss Spurgeon attempts to characterize Shakespeare's personality. Shakespeare's imagery, she argues, "unwittingly lays bare his own innermost likes and dislikes, observations and interests, associations of thought, attitudes of mind and beliefs." Her study of Shakespeare's imagery also provides evidence about "Hand D" in SIR THOMAS MORE. See IMAGERY.

Stafford, Sir Humphrey (1439–1469). A Yorkist who was nevertheless executed by Edward IV for withdrawing troops needed to put down a Yorkshire rebellion. Sir Humphrey was a cousin of the Staffords killed by Cade's rebels. In *3 Henry VI*, King Edward orders Stafford to levy men (IV, i). The Lord Stafford reported dead in I, i, 7, was another Stafford and a Lancastrian.

Stafford, Sir Humphrey. He was knighted by King Henry VI and made governor of Calais. On his return to England, Stafford was killed by Jack Cade's rebel mob. In *2 Henry VI*, Stafford and his brother, William, lead the King's forces against Cade at Blackheath. In the ensuing skirmish, both brothers are killed. [W. H. Thomson, *Shakespeare's Characters: A Historical Dictionary*, 1951.]

Stafford, Simon (d. c. 1630). Printer. Stafford is the printer of the Second Quarto (1599) of *1 Henry IV* and of the *True Chronicle History of King Leir* (1605), the source of Shakespeare's *King Lear*.

Stafford, Sir William. See Sir Humphrey STAFFORD.

stage directions. The great majority of stage directions printed in the early Shakespearean quartos and folio are now thought to have originated with the playwright himself and not, as was formerly thought, with the book-keeper. It has come to be recognized that most of the extant directions are of the type that would have naturally occurred to the playwright rather than the individual (book-keeper or prompter) concerned with performances of the plays. Shakespeare's stage directions are usually characterized by vagueness or by the suggestion of alternative actions. Some of the purposes for which Shakespeare used stage directions include the following:

1. To name a character on his first appearance, such as "Enter . . . a Schoolemaster call'd Pinch" (*Comedy of Errors*, IV, iv).
2. To indicate disguises, such as "Enter Rosalind for Ganymede, Celia for Aliena, and Clown, alias Touchstone" (*As You Like It*, II, iv).
3. To call for sound effects, such as "A flourish of trumpets . . ." (*Hamlet*, I, iv).
4. To indicate groupings of characters, such as "All gather to see them" (*Comedy of Errors*, V, i).
5. To "discover" or display a scene, such as "Here Prospero discovers Ferdinand and Miranda playing at chess." (*Tempest*, V, i). See DISCOVERY SPACE.
6. To indicate a specific acting area, such as "Enter Romeo and Juliet aloft" (*Romeo and Juliet*, III, v).

Shakespeare also, of course, used stage directions to indicate some necessary action on stage. Probably the best-known example of the latter type is, "Exit pursued by a bear" (*Winter's Tale*, III, iii). [W. W. Greg, *The Shakespeare First Folio*, 1955.]

stage imagery. Stage imagery is created by the persons, properties, and actions visible or audible on stage when a play is in production. Its function is analogous to that of the allegorical picture in the emblem books of the Renaissance: to present the essential truth for instantaneous comprehension by the eye; while the dialogue, like the emblem book's verses, explicates and elaborates the image for the benefit of methodical, discursive reason. In Shakespeare's plays, the stage imagery works with the verbal imagery of the dialogue to create a visible expression of the themes of a given play.

All of the basic stage action of each of Shakespeare's plays is not only significant but emblematic, as a whole and in parts. That is to say, each *scene* is emblematic—not just the garden scene in *Richard II*, but every scene in *Richard II;* each *stage property* is emblematic—the murderer's torch, Falstaff's cushion, Richard III's prayer book, as well as the crown Richard II so reluctantly hands over to Bolingbroke, or the one Prince Hal takes from his father's pillow. Each particular *gesture* is emblematic—the Judas kiss, the throwing of dice, the drinking of wine; any *tableau* or *movement* may be emblematic, as when Henry VI creates the picture of his virtual abdication by climbing down from his throne and wandering off stage after the good Duke Humphrey Gloucester, now in disgrace, leaving Margaret on the throne and in control of the realm.

While each of Shakespeare's stage images is unique and can be understood mainly in terms of the context he gives it, it is also true that the significance of a given stage image is not determined merely by the particular context in which it appears, but rather each stage image is a coherent part of the recognized body of visual symbolism which had been built up in Western Europe over several centuries. In some cases, as in the blinding of Gloucester, the image could be traced at least as far back as *Oedipus Rex.* Yet it was the Renaissance, probably, which was the golden age of stage emblems, for the "emblematic habit of mind" shows itself everywhere. Clothing, embroidery, colors, jewels, impresas and badges, painted cloths, street pageants, emblem books, stained-glass windows, illustrations in prayer books, all were speaking pictures to the Elizabethans. Playwrights and playgoers had an additional mode of communication in the conventional scenes derived from medieval mysteries and moralities, as well as those born on the popular stage. When Ben Jonson, for instance, went to work on a new masque, he would turn to the *Iconologia* of Cesare da Ripa and find his allegorical characters already rigged out in full conventional costume and attributes, down to the last detail. The writer of mimetic plays used his visual vocabulary less obviously, but the mode of representation is essentially the same—choice from a large but finite number of conventional stage emblems. To put it another way, Elizabethan and Jacobean plays, including those of Shakespeare, are composed of a number of visual *topoi* or commonplaces arranged in a meaningful series.

Perhaps the best way to convey the richness of Shakespeare's use of conventional stage imagery is to sketch some of the emblematic connotations of two of his most famous scenes. An obvious example is Cleopatra's death scene. The adders are a realization of the snakes and serpents of old Nile conjured up verbally throughout the play: all the tenors—Furies, passions, tortures, pleasures, poisons, metamorphoses, loves, "joy of the worm," Cleopatra herself—are made visible at last in the vehicle, the snake itself. We have been prepared by Enobarbus' description to perceive the Queen in state as an entrancing quean, or Voluptas; a woman with vipers at her breasts is the sign of Luxuria; and the serpents' teeth seem to bring only drowsy pleasure. At the same time Cleopatra becomes maternal at last, speaking to the creatures as babes nursing at her breasts, transforming herself into a Madonna or Charity. In this one obstinately ambivalent scene, as throughout the play, Cleopatra remains faithful to all the contradictory extremes of her own nature and of human love itself.

Perhaps an even clearer example of Shakespeare's manipulation of a conventional scene to clarify his own dramatic purposes is Lady Macbeth's sleepwalking scene. In earlier plays there appear a number of examples of one conventional scene, the image of female penitence based on the type of Mary Magdalene and familiar to Elizabethans as the punishment meted to unfaithful wives. Shakespeare uses the scene to show the disgrace of Dame Eleanor in *2 Henry VI*, II, iv, after she has attempted treason by witchcraft. The stage direction in *The First Part of the Contention* gives a fair idea of the scene: "Enter Dame Elnor Cobham barefoote, and a white sheet about her, with a waxe candle in her hand, and verses written on her backe and pind on . . . ." A later penitent—punished for treason as well as adultery—is Jane Shore, both in *The True Tragedy of Richard III* and in Heywood's *2 Edward IV*. The stage direction in the latter play reads, "Enter the two Parators, with Mistris Shoare in a white sheet, barefooted, with her haire about her eares, and in her hand a waxe taper." It is explained that she also has a letter (unspecified) branded on her forehead. Then the dialogue gives a long explanation of the conventional moral significance of each of the visible signs of her repentance (a simple strategy strongly reminiscent of the contemporary emblem books).

The next time Shakespeare uses the scene it is Lady Macbeth who advances haltingly across the stage clad in a white gown and carrying her lighted candle even though her eyes are darkened by sleep; one should perceive at once the ironic reference to that conventional scene of *Penitentia*. Though innocent of adultery, Lady Macbeth is fatally estranged from her husband by misguided devotion. She has in fact led him to be unfaithful to human kind, to his own nobility. In addition, Lady Macbeth is consciously guilty of that greater infidelity, treason. She still will not admit to unexpected remorse for that crime; but when her conscious mind is no longer in control when she is asleep, her burden of guilt forces her to do endless and fruitless penance.

Minor details in the scene cast their own allusions: the disheveled hair is a sign of Grief, as in *King John* and the candle, like the torch in any Jacobean tragedy, denotes a scene of moral as well as physical darkness. When Lady Macbeth sets down the candle and attempts purification by washing her hands she alludes to the traditional emblem of Pilate as well as to the earlier scene in the play—"A little water clear us of this deed." In fact the entire play makes use of the conventional visual symbolism—the banquet scene alludes to the Last Supper; Macbeth's bloody daggers identify him with Cain, the first murderer and also with despairing Suicide; at the end of the play his traitor's head is brought on triumphantly by Macduff, who plays David to the beheaded tyrant or a John the Baptist who is able to behead the slayer of innocents, the Herod of this play. The innocents slaughtered in this play, the bloody babes, are also literally represented upon the stage, as is the cloak of manliness. In short, *Macbeth's* stage imagery makes us see that Shakespeare's poetry is not restricted to the written word. Mimetic and symbolic both at once, the stage imagery makes the whole play poetry.

For a full-length study of the major stage images of the period see Martha Hester Golden, "The Iconography of the English History Play," unpublished Ph.D. thesis, Columbia University, 1964. Available on microfilm, this work includes pertinent bibliography and an index of stage emblems. [Alice Sylvia Griffin *Pageantry on the Shakespearean Stage*, 1951; Guy de Tervarent, *Attributs et symboles dans l'art profane 1450–1600: dictionnaire d'un langage perdu*, 2 vols. 1958, 1959; Maurice Charney, *Shakespeare's Roman Plays: The Function of Imagery in the Drama* 1961.]—M.H.G.

Stanford, Charles Villiers. See MUSIC BASED ON SHAKESPEARE: *19th century, 1850–1900*.

Stanhope, John, [1st Lord **Stanhope of Harrington**] (c. 1545–1617). Courtier and nobleman whose duties at court included acting as vice chamberlain (chief assistant to the lord chamberlain) and treasurer of the chamber. In the latter post, which he held from 1596 to 1617, Stanhope was responsible for the disbursement of payments made to actors and musicians for performances at court (see CHAMBER ACCOUNTS). His records include payments for performances at Whitehall during the Christmas season of 1612/3 when among the plays given were *1* and *2 Henry IV*, *Much Ado About Nothing*, *The Tempest*, *The Winter's Tale*, *Othello*, and *Julius Caesar*.

Stanley, Sir John. In *2 Henry VI*, Stanley is the escort of the Duchess of Gloucester on her banishment to the Isle of Man. Historically, Eleanor Cob am was probably committed to the care of Sir ohn's father, Sir Thomas Stanley, who was governor of the Isle of Man. He died in 1458 or 1459. W. H. Thomson, *Shakespeare's Characters: A Historical Dictionary*, 1951.]

Stanley, Sir Thomas; later 1st earl of Derby 1435?–1504). Husband, first of Eleanor Neville, Varwick's sister, then of Margaret Beaufort, countss of Richmond. An agile supporter of the crown, e gave his allegiance in turn to Henry VI, Edward V, Edward V, and Richard III, defecting from the ast to support his stepson Henry, earl of Richmond.)n his accession as Henry VII in 1485, Richmond ewarded Stanley by making him earl of Derby. In *Richard III*, Stanley professes friendship for the surper, declaring: "I never was nor never will be alse." Mistrusting Stanley, nevertheless, Richard olds his son, George, hostage after bidding him nuster his forces against Richmond (IV, iv).

Stanley, Sir William (d. 1495). Son of Thomas, st Baron Stanley. Having supported Edward IV, ir William resisted Richard III's attempts to retain is loyalty. He fought for the earl of Richmond at Bosworth, where his arrival with 3000 men turned he battle in Richmond's favor. Later, however, Sir William joined Perkin Warbeck's rebellion against King Henry VII. He was accused of treason and eheaded. In *3 Henry VI*, Sir William helps Edward V to escape from Middleham Castle but does not peak (IV, v). In *Richard III*, he is mentioned as ne of the men of "noble fame and worth" who ave turned against the King (IV, v).

Stanley Family. An aristocratic Shropshire family or whom Shakespeare is alleged to have written two pitaphs. Sir ***Thomas Stanley*** (d. 1576) of Winwick, Shropshire, and Sir ***Edward Stanley*** (d. 1609) were he brothers of ***Henry Stanley***, 4th earl of Derby (c. 1531–1593). On the tomb in which Sir Thomas and is wife are buried were engraved two epitaphs which William Dugdale in 1664 claimed to have been nade by Shakespeare. An anonymous manuscript lating from the reign of Charles I also ascribes the verses to Shakespeare. The subjects of the verses are Sir Thomas and Sir Edward, but another Sir Edward Stanley, the son of Sir Thomas, is more likely o be the person interred in the monument. If he is, here can be no question that Shakespeare did not write the epitaphs, since Sir Edward died in 1632, 16 years after Shakespeare. The two verses are copied as follows in the manuscript:

Shakspeare   An Epitaph on Sr Edward Standly.
Ingraven on his Toombe in Tong Church.

Not monumentall stones preserves our Fame;
Nor sky-aspiring Piramides our name;
The memory of him for whom this standes
Shall out live marble and defacers hands
When all to times consumption shall bee given,
Standly for whom this stands shall stand in Heaven.

On Sr Thomas Standly

Idem, ibidem
Ask who lies heere but doe not wheepe;
Hee is not deade; Hee doth but sleepe;
This stony Register is for his bones,
His Fame is more perpetuall, then these stones,
And his owne goodnesse wth him selfe being gone,
Shall live when Earthly monument is nonne.

Star Chamber. See PRIVY COUNCIL.

Starveling, Robin. In *A Midsummer Night's Dream*, an Athenian tailor who believes that the killing should be left out of the dramatic interlude. Originally assigned the role of Thisby's mother, Starveling plays Moonshine in the actual performance. The audience, however, interrupts his attempts to recite his one line, and he "wanes" early (V, i).

Stationers' Register. A record kept by the Stationers' Company in which members of the company recorded works they intended to publish. The Stationers' Company was the organization of printers and publishers that held a monopoly of the printing trade in Tudor England. It was incorporated in 1557 with the provision "that no person shall practise or exercise the art or mystery of printing . . . unless the same person is . . . one of the society . . . ." This provision enabled the government to maintain a stricter control over the publication of all printed material, since it still required each publication to be licensed by the governmental authorities. See John WHITGIFT.

The governing body of the Stationers' Company was the court of assistants under the direction of the master and two wardens of the company. The court dealt largely with disputes between members over infringements and violations of copyright privilege. It was the court which granted the stationer the

THE FIRST MENTION OF SHAKESPEARE BY NAME IN THE STATIONERS' REGISTER. (STATIONERS' HALL, BY PERMISSION OF THE WORSHIPFUL COMPANY OF STATIONERS) FOR A TRANSCRIPT SEE APPENDIX.

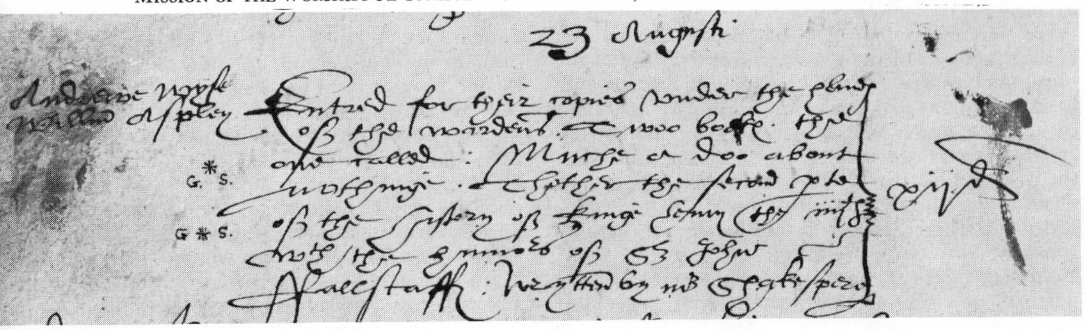

right to enter his copy in the Register. The Register was kept by the clerk of the company to record the licenses and entrances of copies, and it is this document that forms the basis of much of our information concerning the literature of the period. The procedure indicated by the Register is itself somewhat obscure. It has not been possible, for example, to determine precisely how copyright was secured. It used to be assumed that simply recording a work in the Register achieved copyright, but this view has recently been challenged (see COPYRIGHT). Another problem concerns the so-called staying or BLOCKING ENTRIES, the nature of which has not as yet been clearly determined. The Register is also obscure as to the procedure involved in the transfer of copyrights from one stationer to another. Despite these problems, the Register provides one of the best sources of information in establishing the terminal date (see CHRONOLOGY) of a play and sometimes provides further information, such as the nature of the copy. For example, the entry in 1608 for *Pericles:* "A booke called The Booke" enables us to infer that the prompt-book (the official acting version of a play) or a transcript of the prompt-book was submitted as copy, at least for registration purposes. The Register also occasionally cites actual performances, as in the entry for *King Lear:*

> 26 Novembris. Nathanael Butter John Busby. Entred for their Copie under thandes of Sir George Buck knight and Thwardens A booke called. Master William Shakespeare his historye of Kinge Lear, as yt was played before the Kinges maiestie at Whitehall vppon Sainct Stephens night at Christmas Last, by his maiesties servantes playinge vsually at the Globe on the Banksyde . . . .

[Leo Kirschbaum, *Shakespeare and the Stationers,* 1955.]

Steele, Sir **Richard** (1672–1729). Critic, essayist, and dramatist. Steele founded *The Tatler* (1709–1711), a journal of politics and society, contributing articles under the name of Isaac Bickerstaff. He and Joseph Addison also published *The Spectator* (March 1711–December 1712), another London journal, justly famous for its humor, wisdom, and polished style.

Like Addison, Steele does not try to measure Shakespeare by arbitrary rules, but judges the plays by his emotional reaction to them. Steele is a particularly moral and didactic writer, and his opinions of the plays are based on the lessons or inspirations that can be drawn from them; Hamlet's experience, for example, will "dwell strongly upon the minds of the audience and would certainly affect their behavior."

For pure entertainment, Steele prefers scenes such as the visitations of the ghosts in *Richard III* and the opening chorus of *Henry V*, which appeal strongly to the emotions and excite the imagination. In this context, he makes one criticism: many potentially exciting scenes are spoiled by a distance between the poet and his characters, so that the tragic events seem to be merely described rather than experienced. [Herbert Spencer Robinson, *English Shakespearian Criticism in the Eighteenth Century*, 1932.]

Steevens, George (1736–1800). Scholar and editor. The son of a sea captain, Steevens was educated at Cambridge but did not take a degree. In 1766 he published an edition of 20 of Shakespeare's plays reprinted from 20 quartos. He collaborated with Dr Johnson in producing a 10-volume edition of the plays (1773), which was revised and reprinted in 1778, and further revised by Isaac Reed in 1785. In an attempt to displace the authority of Edmund MALONE's edition of 1790, Steevens published a final edition in 1793 (15 vols.). Given to controversy and practical jokes, Steevens inserted into his notes salacious glosses attributed to two clergymen whom he disliked, and he was not above an occasional forgery.

Steevens' most important single scholarly achievement was his inclusion of *Pericles* in the Shakespeare canon. His exclusion of Shakespeare's poems, on the other hand, was based on his opinion that "the strongest act of Parliament that could be framed would fail to compel readers into their service." He was, nevertheless, a fine scholar and his editions were invaluable sources for later scholars and served as the basis for the first two VARIORUM EDITIONS.

Stendhal. Pen name of **Marie Henri Beyle** (1783–1842). French novelist, biographer, and critic. Born in Grenoble, Stendhal settled in Paris after serving as a dragoon in Napoleon's army. He is remembered primarily for his realistic novels, *Le Rouge et le Noir* (1830) and *La Chartreuse de Parme* (1839).

Stendhal's *Racine et Shakespeare* (1823) established him as one of the leaders in the literary battle raging between Classicists and Romantics. All good art, he argues in this book, was Romantic in its day. Stendhal believed that the addition of strangeness to beauty constituted the character of Romantic art. Therefore, he argues, the writer must be entirely free in his choice of subject and treatment. Great writers are not concerned merely with academic proprieties and conventional types, but respond, like Dante, Shakespeare, and Molière, to the unique spirit of their times. See FRANCE.

stenographic report. A means by which the texts of the BAD QUARTOS of Shakespeare's plays may have been recorded. According to the theory of stenographic report, the texts for these quartos were taken from shorthand reports made surreptitiously by publishers' agents during performances of plays.

The practice of shorthand was not unknown in Elizabethan England. In 1588 Timothy Bright published his *Characterie*, a very primitive and awkward stenographic style that relied heavily on the use of synonyms. It was apparently used in the reporting of sermons, which were popular reading matter at the time. In 1632 Thomas Heywood, in the prologue to his play *If You Know Not Me You Know Nobody*, complained that 25 years earlier the play had been pirated by means of stenographic report: ". . . some by Stenography drew The plot: put it in print: (scarce one word trew)." Despite this evidence, the theory has not been generally respected as the basis for the Shakespearean bad quartos, largely because the only shorthand system efficient enough to report plays (and probably the system used in reporting Heywood's play) was John Willis' *Stenography*, not published until 1602, by which time almost all of the Shakespearean bad quartos had been published. Furthermore, a stenographer would find it difficult to avoid discovery while taking notes. The more generally accepted view of the source of the bad quartos

CHARACTERIE.
AN ARTE
of shorte, swifte,
and secrete wri-
ting by Charac-
ter.

Inuented by Timothe
Bright, Doctor of
Phisike.

Imprinted at London by
I. Windet, the Assigne
of Tim. Bright.
1588.
Cum priuilegio Regiæ Maiestatis.
Forbidding all other to print
the same.

TITLE PAGE OF BRIGHT'S TREATISE ON SHORTHAND (1588).

s the theory of MEMORIAL RECONSTRUCTION. [W. W. Greg, *The Editorial Problem in Shakespeare*, 1942.]

Stephano. In *The Merchant of Venice*, a servant to Portia. Stephano brings word to Jessica and Lorenzo of Portia's return to Belmont (V, i).

Stephano. In *The Tempest*, the King of Naples' drunken butler. The rare four-legged monster afflicted with ague whom this coarse drunkard, Stephano, resolves to cure and sell for a handsome price is, in reality, Trinculo and Caliban shivering with fear under the gaberdine. Stephano applies his medication, Caliban tastes the "celestial liquor" and, under its influence, promises the Butler sovereignty of the island if he will kill Prospero. The murderous plot is thwarted by Ariel, who leads the three varlets "red-hot with drinking" into a stagnant pool and later sets on them spirits in the shape of dogs. Stephano and his companions receive merciful treatment when brought before Prospero.

Stevens, Denis. See MUSIC BASED ON SHAKESPEARE: *20th century*.

Steward. In *All's Well That Ends Well*, a minor character. In I, iii the Steward tells the Countess of Helena's love for Bertram.

Still, Colin (1888–). Scholar. Still's *Shakespeare's Mystery Play* (1921), revised and reissued in 1936 as *The Timeless Theme*, is a highly symbolic interpretation of *The Tempest*. It exerted a strong influence on a number of later critics, notably G. Wilson Knight. See MYTHIC CRITICISM.

Stoll, E[lmer] E[dgar] (1874–1959). American scholar and critic. Stoll, who was for many years a professor of English at the University of Minnesota, is notable chiefly as an opponent of impressionism in Shakespearean criticism (see CRITICISM—20TH CENTURY) and for his insistence that Shakespeare should be studied in terms of the conventions of Elizabethan drama. From the publication of his first book, *Othello* (1915), Stoll declared himself an opponent of the then dominant school of character analysis represented by the criticism of A. C. Bradley and argued for an examination of the plays in the context of the period. (See HISTORICAL CRITICISM.) He developed this thesis with increasing belligerence in all of his work. His books on Shakespeare include *Hamlet* (1919), *Shakespeare Studies* (1927), *Poets and Playwrights* (1930), *Art and Artifice in Shakespeare* (1933), *Shakespeare's Young Lovers* (1937), *Shakespeare and Other Masters* (1940), and *From Shakespeare to Joyce* (1944).

Stopes, Charlotte Carmichael (1841–1929). Scholar. An ardent suffragette, Miss Stopes' interest in Shakespeare was intensified because of her belief that he had a profound understanding of women. In 1888 she defended Shakespeare's claim to authorship in her *Bacon-Shakespeare Question*. She then began her extensive studies of Shakespeare's background and environment in *Shakespeare's Warwickshire Contemporaries* (1897), *Shakespeare's Family* (1901), *Shakespeare's Environment* (1914), *Shakespeare's Industry* (1916). At the age of 81, she published *The Life of Henry, third Earl of Southampton* (1922), in which she identified Southampton as the friend of the *Sonnets*, William Harvey as MR. W. H., and Jacqueline Field as the Dark Lady. She is also the author of *The True Story of the Stratford Bust* (1904), *Burbage and Shakespeare's Stage* (1913), and *Early Records Illustrating the Personal Life of Shakespeare* (1927).

Stow, John (c. 1525–1605). Chronicler and antiquarian. Stow's antiquarian studies were literary as well as historical. Thus in 1561 he edited *The workes of Geffrey Chaucer*, an edition which included many apocryphal poems attributed to the poet. He also edited the works of the medieval historian Matthew Paris (d. 1259).

His own historical work is incorporated in his *A Summarie of Englyshe Chronicles* (1565) and his *Annales* [*The Chronicle of England*] in 1580. He is best known, however, for *A Survay of London* (1598), a systematic account of the history, geography, architecture, and institutions of the city of London in Shakespeare's time. Both the *Summarie* and the *Annales* were later expanded by Edmund HOWES. In one of Howes' enlarged editions there is a list of the London theatres and a description of the burning of the Globe.

Strachey, William. See THE TEMPEST: *Sources*.

Strangers. In *Timon of Athens,* three men who tell Lucius of his friend's economic ruin. When Lucius rejects the request for money borne by Timon's servant, the Strangers condemn his behavior and those flatterers for whom "policy sits above conscience" (III, ii).

Strange's Men [Derby's Men]. Two Elizabethan acting companies under the patronage of Henry Stanley, 4th earl of Derby, popularly known as Lord Strange, and his son Ferdinando Stanley, also called Lord Strange. In the 1580's Strange's Men and Derby's Men gave joint performances, with the result that it is extremely difficult to distinguish them in the records. In any event their early history is obscure, and it is not until the end of the decade that the troupe of actors who were later to form the nucleus of the Chamberlain's Men clearly emerged as a distinct company under the patronage of Ferdinando Stanley.

In 1589 they were performing at the Cross Keys Inn within the city of London in defiance of the lord mayor's order suppressing all plays within the city limits. Their violation of the prohibition resulted in imprisonment for some of the members of the troupe.

In 1590 they amalgamated with the Admiral's Men at the Theatre and possibly also the Curtain (see AMALGAMATION). The following year the Admiral's Men quarreled with the owner of the Theatre, James Burbage, and left to play under Philip Henslowe at the Rose; the evidence seems to indicate that Strange's Men left with them. In the winter of 1591/2 the combined Admiral's-Strange's Men, under the leadership of Edward Alleyn, gave six performances at court. In the spring of 1592 the company was at the Rose where in 18 weeks it performed 23 plays, including *Harey Vj* and *Titus and Vespasian,* two plays which are either identical to, or the sources of, Shakespeare's *1 Henry VI* and *Titus Andronicus.* The following year an outbreak of the plague forced the company to leave London for a provincial tour. The following license to travel was granted May 6, 1593:

> Edward Allen, servaunt to the right honorable the Lord Highe Admiral, William Kemp, Thomas Pope, John Heminges, Augustine Phillipes and Georg Brian, being al one companie, servauntes to our verie good the Lord the Lord Straiinge, ar restrained their exercize of playing within the said citie and liberties thereof, yet it is not therby ment but that they shal and maie in regard of the service by them don and to be don at the Court exercize their quallitie of playing comodies, tragedies and such like in anie other cities, townes and corporacions where the infection is not, so it be not within seaven miles of London or of the Coort, that they maie be in the better readines here-after for her Majesty's service whensoever they shalbe therunto called.

At this point in the history of the combined Admiral's-Strange's company it is clear that Strange's Men was the dominant group but that the Admiral's Alleyn was the star performer. After September 25, 1593, while the company was still on tour, Ferdinando Stanley became 5th earl of Derby and his troupe became known as Derby's Men. Within six months, however, Stanley died, leaving the compan without a patron. By June of 1594 the company ha returned to London and the amalgamation had bee dissolved. Two new companies were formed: on was the Admiral's Men under the leadership of Ed ward Alleyn and the other under the patronage o the lord chamberlain, Henry Lord Hunsdon (se CHAMBERLAIN'S MEN). The latter group was compose of the actors mentioned in the travel license of Ma 6, 1593: Pope, Heminges, Kempe, Phillips, an Bryan. After a short period (10 days) at the Newing ton Butts theatre, the troupe moved to the Theatr when they were probably joined by the two me who were to make of it the outstanding acting com pany in London: Richard Burbage and Williar Shakespeare. It has been suggested that Shakespear may indeed have been a minor member of the ol Strange's (Derby's) Men and then joined the Cham berlain's company, but there is no evidence to sup port such a conjecture.

At the same time that Derby's Men were becom ing the Chamberlain's company, a provincial com pany was formed under the patronage of Williar Stanley, 6th earl of Derby. This circumstance has le some scholars to credit Stanley with authorship c the plays and poems usually attributed to Shak speare. See DERBYITE THEORY. [E. K. Chambers, *Th Elizabethan Stage,* 1923.]

Straparola, Giovanni (d. c. 1557). Italian poet an novelist. He is the author of *Tredici piacevoli not* (1550–1554), an enormously successful collection c tales which are by turns obscene and fantastic. Th collection ran through 20 editions in a short time an was translated into French (1560–1563). Williar Painter borrowed a few of Straparola's stories for h *Palace of Pleasure* (1566), among which is the tale c Filenio, the duped lover, which may be an importar source of *The Merry Wives of Windsor.* [Geoffre Bullough, *Narrative and Dramatic Sources of Shak speare,* Vol. II, 1958.]

Stratford gild. See GILD OF THE HOLY CROSS.

Stratford Shakespearean Festival, Canada, Th

THE STAGE AT STRATFORD, ONTARIO. (PHOTOGRAPH BY PETER SMITH)

A dramatic festival held at Stratford, Ontario. In 1952, a young newspaperman named Tom Patterson proposed to the civic leaders of Stratford that an annual festival of Shakespeare's plays be held there. They sent him to England to investigate the possibility. There he consulted wtih Tyrone Guthrie, who agreed to direct two plays the following summer in Stratford. Alec Guinness agreed to star in them. The stage was to be a revolutionary one—an "open" stage, incorporating the Elizabethan acting areas, and designed by Tanya Moiseiwitsch, based on Dr. Guthrie's conviction that "a play can be best presented by getting as near as possible to the manner in which the author envisaged its performance." As daring as the venture itself, this stage was later to serve as the model for Shakespearean stages throughout the United States and England. Basically, it was a modern, artistic entity combining the main features of the Elizabethan stage. A large platform was surrounded on three sides by the audience; at the back stood a graceful columned structure that could be curtained to resemble the alcove of the Elizabethan inner stage. An acting area on its roof served as an upper stage, reached from the main platform by visible stairs at each side.

Doubt whether a festival of Shakespearean plays could succeed in a region where most of the population had never seen any play staged prompted caution and economy. A permanent building over the stage was held in abeyance, and a large, blue canvas circus tent was erected to serve as the auditorium, giving the event a festive, carnival air.

If the stage made history when the festival opened in the summer of 1953, so did the productions and the audiences. The productions, applauded by critics for their artistic achievement and by audiences for their excitement, were a tense and colorful *Richard III*, with Guinness as an introspective Richard, and a graceful *All's Well That Ends Well*, with Irene Worth as an appealing Helena and Guinness illuminating the small role of the ailing king. The actors came upon the curtainless stage from the front, through entrances tunneled beneath the first rows of seats, and down the aisles as well as from side entrances. They came rushing in with banners and spears in *Richard III* and dancing in for the court scene in *All's Well That Ends Well*. In crowd scenes the action seemed to envelop the entire auditorium; in quiet scenes the intimacy between actor and audience proved a revelation. Under bright lights, the actors formed kaleidoscopic patterns in costumes brilliantly created by Miss Moiseiwitsch to lend color to the production and character to their wearers. Exposed, with no shadows or scenery to cover defects, the actor had to depend on his own skill and on Shakespeare's magnificent lines—and neither failed him.

To the town of Stratford with its one main street and rural hotel streamed visitors from all the provinces of Canada, from throughout the United States, from England, from Europe. Townspeople rented out rooms in their own homes, and parishioners of local churches cooked large-scale lunches and dinners. The festival was a success.

Not only a new Shakespeare festival and a new stage, but also a new style of Shakespearean acting was launched that summer. Using Canadian actors whose professional experience previously had been almost entirely confined to radio and television, Dr. Guthrie created a striking ensemble, actors who combined with their North American virility a respect for the poetry that bespoke their English ties. One of the greatest achievements of the festival has been the continuing development of such a company.

Guthrie, who created the character and style of the company, was to continue with them for two more years, directing *The Taming of the Shrew* in 1954, *The Merchant of Venice* in 1955 (*Measure for Measure* and *Julius Caesar* being the other plays in those respective years), and returning in 1957 with a production of *Twelfth Night* to celebrate the opening of the new, permanent building. These three presentations demonstrated the notable characteristics of a Guthrie Shakespearean production: illumination of the text and an over-all unity of style that brought out the theme of the play; brilliant use of the cast in ensemble; fluid staging as the characters moved in choreographic fashion around the open stage; effective stillness with tableaux in which each character was both an individual and an integral part of the over-all picture; inventive yet convincing use of the nonperiod setting; and the choice of an able cast, in this instance, young Canadians who were to become the festival's future stars. *The Taming of the Shrew* was as romantic as it was farcical, presented in a style reminiscent of the American Southwest; *The Merchant of Venice* offered Frederick Valk as a dignified Shylock, driven to hatred when the things he most loved were threatened.

So strong a native company had been built up by 1956 that Guthrie's successor, Michael Langham, could use them to advantage that year in an energetic *Merry Wives of Windsor* and a stirring *Henry V*. The Canadian Christopher Plummer was excellent as a stalwart, yet sensitive Henry, and French Canadian actors effectively portrayed elegant, graceful French soldiers.

In 1957 the adventuresome new theatre building opened. Designed by Robert Fairfield, it proved ideal for the stage and auditorium, retaining the carnival spirit, with gay colors and a geometric roof that was compared to a piecrust and to a partly opened umbrella. The productions were Guthrie's haunting *Twelfth Night* and a *Hamlet* directed by Langham. Set in the Cavalier period, *Twelfth Night* contrasted the wild farce of the drinking, letter, and dueling scenes, as interludes in a melancholy world in which Feste was an old man and Viola, played by Siobhan McKenna, seemed always aware that disappointment might be her fate. Plummer's Hamlet was notable for its many facets—mad, Oedipal, stalwart, and indecisive—but the result was confusion. In five years the festival had come of age, achieved a permanent home, and become a landmark both on the Canadian scene and in the theatrical world. The company appeared on Broadway and at the Edinburgh festival. Retaining the spirit with which it was founded, it became established, but it never became an Establishment.

In 1958 Plummer returned to demonstrate his ample talents in Shakespearean comedy as Benedick in *Much Ado About Nothing*, opposite the spirited Beatrice of Eileen Herlie. But in *The Winter's Tale* he failed to make the character of Leontes convincing. Jason Robards, Jr., imported from Broadway, was unconvincing as Hotspur in *1 Henry IV*.

The festival has drawn almost entirely upon English directors. Peter Hall, who was later to become managing director of the Royal Shakespeare Company, directed *As You Like It* with Miss Worth in 1959. Also offered that year was *Othello*, with Douglas Campbell, a permanent member of the company, in the title role and Douglas Rain and Frances Hyland, both outstanding Canadian actors, as Iago and Desdemona. In 1960 Douglas Seale came from England to direct *King John* with Rain in the title role as a human, even sympathetic John, while Langham directed *Romeo and Juliet*, with Bruno Gerussi and Julie Harris as the lovers and Plummer as Mercutio. The following year, 1961, proved noteworthy: Paul Scofield was the star and renovations were made to the stage. Mr. Scofield was brilliant in two strongly contrasted roles, a rugged Coriolanus in a production set in 19th-century France, and a dusty Armado in *Love's Labour's Lost*. The festival's first Canadian director, George McCowan, staged *Henry VIII*, with Campbell in the title role. Miss Moiseiwitsch and Brian Jackson redesigned the stage. They provided an entrance from the rear of the platform, with a movable back wall, heightened the stage balcony, reduced the number of its pillars to five from nine, and added two side entrances.

In 1962 Plummer starred again, this time in a *Macbeth* directed by Peter Coe of England, whose novel but confusing interpretation was that Macbeth grows in nobility and self-knowledge as the play progresses. In *The Tempest*, John Colicos was as outstanding as Caliban as he had been as Petruchio in *The Taming of the Shrew*, an indication of his important future contributions to the festival. The following year Colicos appeared in the title role of *Timon of Athens* in a production staged by Langham in modern dress, with a musical score by Duke Ellington. Many of the play's commentaries seemed particularly pertinent in the modern setting. Jean Gascon, a French Canadian, directed *The Comedy of Errors* in *commedia dell' arte* style, and the third offering was *Troilus and Cressida*, with Peter Donat and Martha Henry in the title roles. The following spring the company with great success visited Chichester, England, where the festival stage was inspired by the one in Canada.

By 1964 the native company had grown so strong that they could portray the leads as well as supporting roles in two major plays for the celebration of Shakespeare's 400th anniversary. Colicos, who had developed his talents in a variety of Shakespearean roles, attempted the most difficult assignment of his career, King Lear. Another Shakespearean king, Richard II, was portrayed by William Hutt, who had enacted numerous roles with the festival during its first decade. Langham and Stuart Burge directed.

In 12 summers, the Stratford Shakespearean Festival, set in a remote Ontario town, had become a major contributor to the modern Shakespearean stage. It had developed native actors into a virile young company, impressive both for its ensemble and its stars, whose united aim was to serve the stage excitement and the poetry of Shakespeare. And its stage, born of Dr. Guthrie's conviction that a Shakespearean stage best serves Shakespeare, has revolutionized Shakespearean production in the 20th century.—A. G.

Stratford Shakespeare Festival, Connecticut. See American Shakespeare Festival.

Stratford tithes. Name given to the rentals received from former monastery lands which, after the Reformation, had been granted to the town of Stratford. The Stratford corporation, the governing body of the town, leased the tithes to individuals who were responsible for the collection of the rents. These individuals, in turn, often subleased the tithes. In 1605 Shakespeare purchased one of these subleases from one Ralph Hubaud. His purchase covered the rentals in the neighboring hamlets of Old Stratford, Welcombe, and Bishopton. The purchase price was £440, in addition to which Shakespeare had to pay £5 a year to the holder of the main lease, John Barker, and £17 a year to the Stratford corporation. The first half of the sale document deals with the prior history of the tithes and the second half, extracts of which are printed below, with the assignment of the lease to Shakespeare:

> This indenture made the foure and twentythe daye of Julye . . . Betweene Ralphe Hubaude of Ippesley in the countye of Warr., esquier, on thone parte and William Shakespear of Stratforde-upon-Avon in the sayed countye of Warr., gent., on thothe parte . . . . This indenture nowe witnesseth that the sayed Raphe Hubaude, for and in consideration of the somme of foure hundred and fourtye poundes of lawfull Englishe money to him by the sayed William Shakespear, before thensealinge and delivery of thees presents, well and truelye contented and payed, whereof and of everye parte and parcell whereof hee, the sayed Raphe Hubaude dothe by thees presentes acknowledge the receipt and thereof and of everye parte and parcell thereof dothe clerelye acquite, exonerate and discharge the sayed William Shakespear, his executors and administrators, for ever by thees presentes,—hathe demised, graunted, assigned and sett over, and by thees presentes dothe demise, graunte, assigne and sett over unto the sayed William Shakespear, his executors and assignes, the moytie or one half of all and singuler the sayed tythes of corne, grayne, blade and heye, yearelye, and from tyme to tyme cominge, encreasinge, reneweinge, arrysinge, groweinge, issueinge or happenynge, or to bee had, receyved, perceyved or taken out, of, upon or in the townes, villages, hamlettes, groundes and fyeldes of Stratforde, Olde Stratforde, Welcombe and Bushopton aforesayed in the sayed countye of Warr., and alsoe the moytie or one half of all and singuler the sayed tythes of wooll, lambe, and other smalle and pryvie tythes, herbage, oblacions, obvencions, alterages, mynumentes and offeringes whatsoever, yearelye, and from tyme to tyme cominge, encreasinge, reneweinge or happeninge, or to bee had, receyved, perceyved or taken, within the parishe of Stratforde-upon-Avon aforesayed . . . the sayed William Shakespeare, his executors, administrators or assignes, shall and will, duringe the residewe of the sayed terme of fourescore and twelve yeares which bee yet to comme and unexpired, yearelie content and paye the severall rentes above mencioned, vidlt., seaventene poundes to the

baylief and burgesses of Stratford aforesayed, and fyve poundes to the sayed John Barker, his executors or assignes, att the dayes and places aforesayed in which it ought to bee payed accordinge to the purporte and true meaninge of thees presentes, and thereof shall and will discharge the saied Raphe Hubaude, his executors, administrators and assignes. In witnes whereof the partyes abovesayed to thees presentes interchangeablie have sett their seales the daie and yeare fyrst above written.—*Raffe Hubaud.*—Sealde and delivered in the presence of William Hubaud, Anthony Nasshe, Fra: Collyns.

In 1611 Shakespeare and two other holders of subleases, Richard Lane and Thomas Greene, brought a complaint before the court of chancery. In it they charged that certain other subleaseholders, chiefly William Combe, were failing to pay their share of the rent due the main leaseholder, Barker. Since subleaseholders were responsible to Barker as a group, Shakespeare and the other complainants were forced to make up the difference or risk losing their leases:

To the Right Honorable Thomas Lord Ellesmere, Lord Chauncellour of England. In humble wise complayninge, shewen unto your honorable good Lordshipp, your dayly oratours Richard Lane, of Awston in the county of Warwicke, esquire, Thomas Greene, of Stratford-uppon-Avon in the said county of Warwicke, esquire, and William Shackspeare, of Stratford-uppon-Avon . . . Richard Lane and William Shackspeare, and some fewe others of the said parties, are wholly, and against all equity and good conscience, usually dryven to pay the same for preservacion of their estates of and in the partes of the premisses belonginge unto them; and albeyt your said oratours have taken greate paynes and travayle in entreatinge and endevoringe to bringe the said parties of their owne accordes, and without suite of lawe, to agree every one to a reasonable contribucion toward the same residue of the said rente of xxvij.*li.* xiij.*s.* iiij.*d.*, accordinge to the value of such of the premisses as they enjoy, and onely for their respectyve tymes and termes therein, yet have they refused, and denied, and styll doe refuse and deny, to be perswaded or drawen thereunto, and some of them beinge encoraged, as yt should seme, by some frendly and kind promise of the said Henry Barker, assignee of the said John Barker, that they should find favour, thoughe their said estates should be all forfeyted, have given yt forth that they should be glade and cared not a whitt yf the estates of some or all the said premisses should be forfeyted, for they should doe well enoughe with the sayd Henry Barker. In tender consideracion whereof, and for soe much as yt is against all equitye and reason that the estates of some that are willinge to paie a reasonable parte toward the said residue of the said rente of xxvij.*li.* xiij.*s.* iiij.*d.*, haveinge respecte to the smalnes of the values of the thinges they doe possesse, should depend uppon the carlesnes and frowardnes or other practices of others, which will not paie a reasonable parte or anie thinge at all toward the same; and for that yt is most agreeable to all reason, equity and good conscience, that every person, his executors and assignes, should be ratably charged with a yearely porcion toward the said residue of the sayd rente, accordinge to the yearely benefitt he enjoyeth or receaveth; and for that your oratours have noe meanes, by the order or course of the common lawes of this realme, to enforce or compell anie of the said partyes to yeald anie certayne contrybucion toward the same, and soe are and styll shal bee remediles therein unles they may be in that behalf relieved by your Lordshippes gracious clemency and relyef to others in such lyke cases extended . . . .

In reply to the complaint, William Combe agreed to pay more rent. Shakespeare's interest in the tithes was sold by his heirs to the Stratford corporation in 1625. See also ENCLOSURE. [J. O. Halliwell-Phillipps, *Outlines of the Life of Shakespeare*, 1881; Gerald Eades Bentley, *Shakespeare: A Biographical Handbook*, 1961.]

Stratford-upon-Avon. Although in 1564 Stratford was a quiet country village of not more than 2000 inhabitants, most of them tradesmen and their families, it was an important market town, the center of a rich agricultural region. Since the town had never been walled, the streets were broad and straight. The houses were built of stucco with timber, the beams showing, and with thatched roofs. Each prosperous villager had his own barn and garden. Under a new charter granted in 1553 by Edward VI, it became an independent, self-governing community ruled by a corporation composed of the officers of the old religious guilds that it had superseded. This body regulated the affairs of every citizen, even to the smallest details of his conduct. It fined those who let their pigs loose in the streets or allowed refuse to collect before their houses, a misdemeanor for which the poet's father was once fined. It was also severe on those given to profanity and condemned shrewish wives to a ducking in the Avon. The authorities administered religious affairs with a firm hand. They

THE SEAL OF THE BOROUGH OF STRATFORD-UPON-AVON. (SHAKESPEARE BIRTHPLACE TRUST)

fined a citizen who did not bring his family and servants to church every Sunday, for such neglect was strong evidence that the culprit was a recusant, a devotee of the old faith (see RECUSANCY). The regions adjacent to the town were among the most beautiful in all England. There were primeval forests near—the Forest of Arden and the woodland in Warwickshire, and also a wealth of flowering meadows. The vicinity of Stratford was also rich in historical associations. Within seven miles was the town of Warwick, with its magnificent castle, a relic of the days of chivalry and, more recently, the center of the Wars of the Roses, which Shakespeare was to dramatize in *2* and *3 Henry VI* and *Richard III*. Kenilworth Castle, the seat of the earl of Leicester, Queen Elizabeth's favorite, was not much farther away. In 1575 the earl lavishly entertained the queen there on one of her progresses. In places like these Shakespeare learned to feel the charm and romance of England's storied past. [Sir William Dugdale, *Antiquities of Warwickshire*, 1656; E. I. Fripp, *Shakespeare's Stratford*, 1928; Marchette Chute, *Shakespeare of London*, 1949.]

Strato. In *Julius Caesar*, a servant of Brutus. At Philippi, after the other servants have fled, Brutus asks Strato to hold his master's sword while he runs on it, Strato's life having had "some smatch of honor in it." Strato agrees to do this service but first must shake his master's hand (V, v).

Strauss, Richard. See MUSIC BASED ON SHAKESPEARE: *20th century*.

Strindberg, August (1849–1912). Swedish dramatist, novelist, and essayist, described by George Bernard Shaw as "the only genuinely Shakespearean modern dramatist." Because his plays have not become dated, like those of his pioneering contemporaries Zola and Ibsen, and because of his seminal dramaturgic experiments, Strindberg's reputation continues to grow. His plays cover the spectrum of dramatic types: satirical fantasy (*Lucky Pehr's Journey*, 1880), chronicle history (*Gustavus Vasa*, 1899), realism (*Miss Julie*, 1888), naturalism (*The Father*, 1887), tragicomedy (*Crimes and Crimes*, 1899), and expressionism (*A Dream Play*, 1902).

Although the first translations of Shakespeare had not come to Sweden until the late 18th century, by Strindberg's time a cult of Shakespeare had grown up, along with deliberate imitations which quickly fell into sentimental stereotypes. According to the autobiographical *Son of a Servant* (1886), Strindberg went through a mechanical study of the Elizabethan in school and university, but in 1864 he "devoured all Shakespeare in Hagberg's translation." A performance of *Hamlet* in the same year marked "a milestone in my dark life."

One of Strindberg's earliest plays, the historical tragedy *Hermione* (1869), shows a serious emulation of the Shakespearean manner with the classical five acts, monologues, stock effects, a third-act forewarning and a fifth-act general catastrophe. The blank verse ends on the inevitable rhymed couplet. There are borrowings from *Hamlet* (deaths by stabbing and poisoned wine), and especially from *Julius Caesar*. Brutus is represented by the idealistic but misguided patriot Kriton, Cassius by the demagogue Kreon, and Caesar by Philippos, with parallel scenes and dialogue.

After encountering the critic Georg Brandes, wh attacked the prevalent sentimental interpretations Shakespeare and demonstrated his detailed realis Strindberg scaled down his heroes and langua from superhuman to real (a change which parallel one in Shakespeare's own development). He r studied Shakespeare and criticized *Hamlet* on th basis, he said, of his "thorough knowledge of all th poet's works, the chief of which he had read in th original and whose principal commentators he ha studied." *Master Olaf* (1881) shows Strindberg transition from romantic to realistic impulses. F the structural innovations in this play he looked *Henry IV*, with the comment, "Tragic and comi great and small, alternate as in life." The "Me lanspel" adapts the scene between Trinculo an Caliban (*Tempest*, II, ii). The opening of Act V in debt to Ophelia's funeral scene in *Hamlet*. Marte the most human and attractive character, reflec the whimsical humor of Falstaff.

Gustavus Vasa also showed many parallels wit *Henry IV*. There is the contrast between a rebellio ridden, troubled King and an irresponsible son wit his questionable companions. Jakob Israel, son the King's political enemy, serves as foil to Er much as Hotspur, son of Henry's opponent, do to Prince Hal, while both meet an untimely deat Goran's cynical humor, notably in the inn scen suggests the inspiration of Falstaff. The next pla *Erik XIV*, continues the historical chain in the sam way that *Henry V* follows *2 Henry IV:* with th death of the old King, and the coronation and reig of the reformed young monarch.

While Strindberg's history plays show the cleare Shakespearean influences, other dramas also demo strate their indebtedness. Martin Lamm has pointe out the striking similarities between Othello and th hero of *The Father*—each is a military man draw larger than life and self-destroyed by a consumin jealous torment over his wife's fidelity. Strindberg reference to Othello's "Satanic misunderstandings and his doubt about his own progeny point as muc to *The Father* as to Shakespeare's tragedy. And th Captain's outcry in the closing death scene is clearl Shakespearean. The theme of a leader destroyed b woman's lust for power also echoes *Macbeth* an *King Lear*. See SCANDINAVIA. [Joan Bulman, *Strind berg and Shakespeare: Shakespeare's Influence o Strindberg's Historical Drama*, 1933.]—M.H.

Stringer, Thomas (fl. 1560–1583). Shakespeare uncle. Stringer was the second husband of Agne sister of Mary Arden, whom he married in 1550 (se ARDEN FAMILY). From 1560 to 1583 he leased land i Bearley and Snitterfield, the home of Richard Shake speare, the poet's grandfather. Stringer had two son John (b. 1554) and Arden (b. 1556). He purchase the share in the Arden estate belonging to his sister in-law Katharine Edkins and in 1576 sold it to an other sister-in-law, Margaret Arden, and her husban Edward Cornwell. [Mark Eccles, *Shakespeare i Warwickshire*, 1961.]

Stubbes, Philip (fl. 1581–1591). Puritan pamphle teer. Stubbes, born in Norfolk, moved to Londo where he became active in civic affairs. His chie claim to fame, however, rests upon the ferocious at tacks upon the stage which he launched in his *Th Anatomie of Abuses* (1583) and *The Second part o*

The Anatomie of Abuses (1583) (see ENEMIES OF THE STAGE). Stubbes' pamphlets are models of the art of invective, as well as being testimony to the popularity of plays in London:

> All Stage-playes, Enterluds, and Commedies are either of diuyne or prophane matter: If they be of diuine matter, then are they most intollerable, or rather Sacrilegious; for that the blessed word of God is to be handled reuerently, grauely, and sagely, with veneration to the glorious Maiestie of God, which shineth therin, and not scoffingly, flowtingly, and iybingly, as it is vpon stages in Playes and Enterluds, without any reuerence, worship, or veneration to the same. The word of our Saluation, the price of Christ his bloud, & the merits of his passion, were not giuen to be derided and iested at, as they be in these filthie playes and enterluds on stages & scaffolds, or to be mixt and interlaced with bawdry, wanton shewes, & vncomely gestures, as is vsed (euery Man knoweth) in these playes and enterludes . . . . Doo these Mockers and Flowters of his Maiesty, these dissembling Hipocrites, and flattering Gnatoes, think to escape vnpunished? beware, therfore, you masking Players, you painted sepulchres, you doble dealing ambodexters, be warned betymes, and, lik good computistes, cast your accompts before, what wil be the reward thereof in the end, least God destroy you in his wrath: abuse God no more, corrupt his people no longer with your dregges, and intermingle not his blessed word with such prophane vanities. For at no hand it is not lawfull to mixt scurrilitie with diuinitie, nor diuinitie with scurrilitie . . . . Vpon the other side, if their playes be of prophane matters, than tend they to the dishonor of God, and norishing of vice, both which are damnable. So that whither they be the one or the other, they are quite contrarie to the Word of grace, and sucked out of the Deuills teates to nourish vs in ydolatrie, hethenrie, and sinne. And therfore they, cariyng the note, or brand, of GOD his curse vppon their backs, which way soeuer they goe, are to be hissed out of all Christian kingdomes, if they wil haue Christ to dwell amongst them. . . . Do they not maintaine bawdrie, infinit folery, & renue the remembrance of hethen ydolatrie? Do they not induce whordom & vnclennes? nay, are they not rather plaine deuourers of maydenly virginitie and chastitie? For proofe wherof, but marke the flocking and running to Theaters & curtens, daylie and hourely, night and daye, tyme and tyde, to see Playes and Enterludes; where such wanton gestures, such bawdie speaches, such laughing and fleering, such kissing and bussing, such clipping and culling, Suche winckinge and glancinge of wanton eyes, and the like, is vsed, as is wonderfull to behold. Then, these goodly pageants being done, euery mate sorts to his mate, euery one bringes another homeward of their way verye freendly, and in their secret conclaues (couertly) they play the Sodomits, or worse . . . .

Stubbes' argument and rhetoric were attacked and ridiculed by Thomas Nashe in his *Anatomie of Absurdity* (1589). [E. K. Chambers, *The Elizabethan Stage*, 1923.]

Students, The. An anonymous 18th-century adaptation of *Love's Labour's Lost*, published in 1762. The prologue to the play clearly acknowledges the indebtedness to Shakespeare:

> All Congreve's wit, the polish'd scenes require,
> All Farquhar's humour, and all Hoadly's fire.
> Our bard, advent'ring to the comic land,
> Directs his choice by Shakespeare's happier hand;
> Shakespeare! who warms with more than magic art,
> Enchants the ear, whilst he instructs the heart;
> Yet should he fail, he hopes, the wits will own,
> There's enough of Shakespeare's still, to please the town.

The alteration, which omits the characters of Holofernes and Sir Nathaniel, is a dull and spiritless affair. It was apparently never performed on the stage. [*Love's Labour's Lost*, New Variorum Edition, H. H. Furness, ed., 1904.]

Sturley, Abraham (d. 1614). Shakespeare's fellow townsman. Educated at Queen's College, Cambridge, Sturley settled in Stratford around 1580 and was chosen alderman in 1591 and chamberlain in 1594. From 1599 to 1601 he corresponded with his friend Richard QUINEY during the latter's visits to London. Two of these letters allude to Shakespeare:

> This is one speciall remembrance from y[r] fathers motion. It semeth bj him that our countriman, M[r] Shaksper, is willinge to disburse some monei vpon some od yardeland or other att Shottri or neare about vs; he thinketh it a verj fitt patterne to move him to deale in the matter of our tithes. Bj the instruccions v can geve him theareof, and bj the frendes he can make therefore, we thinke it a faire marke for him to shoote att, and not unpossible to hitt. It obtained would advance him in deede, and would do vs muche good . . . [January 24, 1598].

> Y[r] letter of the 25 of October came to mj handes the laste of the same att night per Grenwaj, which imported . . . that our countriman M[r] Wm. Shak. would procure vs monej, which I will like of as I shall heare when, and wheare, and howe; and I praj let not go that occasion if it may sort to any indifferent condicions . . . [November 4, 1598].

The first reference to Shakespeare indicates that in 1598, shortly after having purchased New Place, Shakespeare was interested in acquiring land (see SHOTTERY). The "matter of our tithes," of which Sturley speaks, was not, however, a reference to the Stratford tithes which Shakespeare purchased in 1605.

The letters indicate that Sturley and Quiney were in financial straits, probably as a result of two large fires which raged in Stratford in 1594 and 1595. In the first of these, Sturley's house was burned down. Subsequently his fortunes improved, however, and he served the town on a number of missions. By the time of his death he had received a grant of arms. See also NOATE OF CORNE & MALTE. [Mark Eccles, *Shakespeare in Warwickshire*, 1961.]

style. In the work of an artist, all things are subsumed under the heading of "style," including the selection of subjects, the ordering of materials, and the moral, emotional, and aesthetic aims which seem to govern the selection and ordering. "Style" in its widest sense is the stamp of the creator upon the thing he creates, and has been defined as "the man himself." If we say that the works of Shakespeare bear the stamp of a wise, original, and vital man in his quest for the true and the beautiful, we have (unlikely though it may seem) said something about his "style," especially if we add that this lofty activity never impaired his relish for the merely strange, exciting, and comical.

Even as applied narrowly to the kind and quality of the language he used, the topic covers a range of phenomena which defies summary treatment. Like all true artists, Shakespeare developed; hence there is a vast distinction in styles between, let us say, *Henry VI* (c. 1591), *Richard II* (c. 1596), *Hamlet* (c. 1601), and *The Tempest* (c. 1611). Moreover, Shakespeare was a dramatist, and like all true members of that special literary guild, he varied his style according to dramatic need, whether that of broad farce, stage epic, high tragedy, or poetic romance, and according to the personality and function of the various characters. Although written within a few years of each other, *The Merry Wives of Windsor*, *Julius Caesar*, and *Hamlet* are quite distinct in style, with the first written mostly in a racy, homespun prose, the second in incisive, "public" verse, and the third in richly imaginative, "involuted" prose and verse. Within a single play there may be a multiplicity of styles. If Hamlet, Polonius, and the First Gravedigger had all been made to speak in the same style, the style of *Hamlet* as a whole would not be the marvelous thing it is. How is one to describe something whose very essence is variability?

We must speak only of the common denominators, those features of Shakespeare's discourse which remain constant whatever the type of play, whoever the speaker, and whether the latter is speaking rhymed verse, blank verse, or prose. The similarity which underlies the variety, what Coleridge would have called "unity in multeity," is the *fitness* of style to the speaker and the occasion. The various media, rhymed verse, blank verse, and prose, do not appear at random, but according to which of the three will function best on the given occasion; and the same principle holds true of the over-all mode of various passages, oratorical, lyrical, or intimate and realistic. This quality of *fitness* was gradually achieved and is pervasive only after Shakespeare emerged from what has been called his "lyrical period" of the mid-nineties. From the very beginning, there is the proper "decorum" (fitness) in the speech of the comic characters and in the farces as a whole, but at the beginning the oratorical grandeur or lyrical sweetness of particular passages in serious contexts is apt to be sometimes gratuitous. Thus the chilly and practical Lady Capulet during her first scene in *Romeo and Juliet* grows fanciful about the unwed lover as an unbound book, less because such a speech seems natural to her than because the poet felt impelled to write it. Yet in this same play, the accents of her husband, her daughter, and the latter's Nurse are precisely right throughout. The undeveloped style of even the Henry VI plays, in this matter of fitness, as in the stiffness of the verse and the mechanical nature of the imagery, need not distract us in our search for the common denominator in style if we are sensitive to promise, the intimations of futu power.

The texts of the plays consist of the utterances the characters as they speak to each other, them selves, or the audience. One grand feature of Shak speare's style, even when the medium is rhyme verse, is that in spite of the highly condensed, figur tive, and "literary" quality of the utterances, we st seem to be hearing genuine living speech. An in pression of naturalness is conveyed through the co stant infiltration of plain words and colloquial tur of speech so as to dissipate any impression of boo ishness. Although a particular speech may in fact b organized with cunning logic, it will contain th appearance of false starts, digressions, and the lik so as to sound like something orally improvise rather than something preorganized and revised. Th impression of spontaneity is reinforced by the a ticulation of speech to speech. Each dialogue seem an organic growth, with each speech in it apparentl suggested by the preceding speech. No speech is separate entity, but a rejoinder, a commentary, passionate agreement, or the like. We seem not to b hearing speeches but witnessing communication.

The unique union which Shakespeare achieved be tween the colloquial and the literary, between th "natural" and the inimitable, would have been im possible except for his feeling for language. He love it for its own sake, and respected it as his sole ex ploitable possession—the one with which he mus create and conquer. He seems never to have forgot ten a word which he had read or heard, or to hav failed to examine its adaptability, its power to expres something new as well as old, or several things a once. He himself was the creator of a number o words (including "critic" and "critical"!) now i common use, and a host of now-common idiomati expressions, such as "cudgelling" one's brain "breathing" one's last, "falling" to blows, and "bury ing" one's head in one's hands. Certainly a commo feature of Shakespeare's style is the verbal resource fulness. In an age intoxicated with words and multi plying their number in a way which alarmed an incensed the conservative, he used a greater numbe of different words and word-forms than any othe writer, or than any other before or since. The mer number need not be considered a virtue, since writ ers (for instance, Racine) have achieved fine literar effects with a vocabulary one-tenth the size of hi The point is that in Shakespeare's case, by no mean typical, quantity improved rather than impaire quality—lent variety, expressiveness, and grace to basically strong and simple verbal texture. *Usua* words are *usually* employed, unusual ones when the are inevitable; for instance, the plain word "love" occurs on an average of once in every 10 to 15 line while the fine word "incarnadine" appears only onc in the more than 100,000 lines. Shakespeare neve grew enamored of the imposing citizens of his worl of words, but let them appear only on state oc casions. Although it is not quite true that he neve repeated, he was not given to exploiting his successe In the line "The rank of osiers by the murmurin stream," the adjective "murmuring" is so *right* tha we might expect its frequent use; "murmuring surge" occurs in one later play and then is permanentl abandoned—that is, by Shakespeare, for a host o ter writers have set streams and surges "murmur-g." With what seems like sheer profligacy, Shake-eare was sparing even in the use of his own inven-ons, never once using the word again after being e first to create the "gnarled" oak, the "pedantical" rm, and the "lack-lustre" eye.

Some of the verbal stylists of the English Renais-nce were consciously selective: the translators of e Bible favored the native "English" diction, others ent in militantly for new Latinisms. Spenser fa-red the archaic or pseudo-archaic, Lyly the more ltivated "flowers of rhetoric," and Nashe the jaun-ness of slangy conceits. In contrast, citizenship was mpletely open in Shakespeare's world of words. e loved to pair and intermingle Romance and atinate words with those of Teutonic origin ("I now not where is that Promethean heat / That can y light relume"), and to graft the prefixes and ffixes from one linguistic heritage upon the roots the other (preferring "dishearten" to "discour-ge"). The combination of the elegance, exactitude, d euphony of the Latin derivatives with the rength and pungency of the Teutonic permitted a ecial kind of orchestration. Subtlety of meaning uld be accompanied with appropriate and illustra-ve sound. One can hear the very cry of pain and rotest in the Ghost's voice as the Latinisms re-rberate after the Teutonic prelude,

> Cut off even in the blossoms of my sin,
> Unhousel'd, disappointed, unaneled . . .
> (*Hamlet*, I, v, 76–77)

d the tones of terrified revulsion in Claudio's vision death, where "obstruction," "sensible," and "mo-on" tune in with "cold," "rot," and "clod":

> Ay, but to die, and go we know not where;
> To lie in cold obstruction and to rot;
> This sensible warm motion to become
> A kneaded clod . . .
> (*Measure for Measure*, III, i, 118–121)

egardless of whether the effects are achieved by riety or by simple repetition, meaning is consonant ith sound in Shakespeare as in no other writer in ual measure. The effect of repetition is illustrated Hamlet's "O villain, villain, smiling damned vil-in," Shylock's "What, what, what? Ill luck, ill ck?" or Macbeth's "Tomorrow and tomorrow and morrow. . . ." Without knowing the meaning of e words, a listener could detect by the sounds amlet's rage, Shylock's glee, and Macbeth's despair -just as he could hear the "touches of sweet har-ony" as Lorenzo describes the music of the spheres Still quiring to the young-eyed cherubins."

Shakespeare could work and play with words multaneously, delighting in them for their own sake the same time that he was disciplining them to his urpose. When he writes that

> Golden lads and girls all must,
> As chimney-sweepers, come to dust.
> (*Cymbeline*, IV, ii, 262–263)

e have an example of what Johnson considered his most fatal defect, his inability to resist a pun. But tually it is the very pun—"come to dust"—in this lemn dirge which creates the image of the sooty ttle urchins with whom the golden lads are mere equals in mortality. It may be argued that it is the glint of mirth that gives the lines their poignance, and yet this is one of the more doubtful instances. In general, Shakespeare's puns shade into his serious word-play by such imperceptible degrees that we cannot pinpoint the place where joking ends and poetry begins.

The same thing might be said about the distinction between his rhetoric and his poetry. In spite of the apparent freedom and diversity of his expression, no writer has shown a greater fondness for patterned speech than Shakespeare. His lines are full of artifice, with every rhetorical device of the Renaissance manuals employed time and time again. Whenever we have verbal balance, repetition, parallelism, and contrast in the lines, we have the conscious patterning sometimes stigmatized as "artificial," and we have it all the time. Juliet's "Parting is such sweet sorrow," despite its apparent "artlessness," could be used as illustration in at least three sections of a rhetorical manual: "sweet sorrow" (verbally self-contradictory) is the figure of speech known as the oxymoron; the initial sibilant of the last three words is alliteration; and the way in which a disyllable both opens and closes the phrase constitutes one form of rhetorical parallelism or balance.

The rhetorical patterns were used with increasingly subtle modifications, so that they continue to satisfy our desire for symmetry and order even when scarcely visible. We would never think of calling the style of *The Tempest* rhetorical, and yet there is as much use of balance, repetition, and contrast in the arrangement of the words as there is in the admittedly rhetorical *Richard III.* The difference is that the devices in his later plays lie beneath the surface of the language rather than upon it. In like manner the conspicuous features of the iambic pentameter verse line (the alternating beat, the distinct pause at the line-end, etc.) become less and less conspicuous as Shakespeare mastered the form and adapted it to his purpose. The verse seems more and more "conversational" without ceasing to be verse. See RHETORIC.

The imagery becomes more and more functional, meaning less visible as decoration, without becoming less abundant. It becomes actually more abundant, as well as more original and apt. The poet seems to have retained in his mind's eye all he had ever seen. The figures of babes used by cartographers to represent the winds convert in his lines to a symbol of pity in a pitiless time—the "naked new-born babe / Striding the blast." It is a strange image, such as would generate only in the fevered mind of a Macbeth. At the opposite extreme is Celia's image of the lovelorn Orlando, whom she finds under a tree "like a dropped acorn." Its playfulness is neither more nor less characteristic of Shakespeare's style than Macbeth's "naked babe" or than the frightful images that sear the eyes and distort the lips of King Lear. The images can summon up in a single line a whole world of wonder (". . . of anters vast and deserts idle"), or the long-past days of youth ("We have heard the chimes at midnight, Master Shallow"), or the specter of complete futility ("It [life] is a tale told by an idiot"). The imagery enriches the prose as it does the verse, so that the prose is never prosaic. A series of kindred images can reach through a play, helping to create its atmosphere and carry its theme, like those of enchanted moonlight in *A Midsummer Night's Dream*, of contrasted light and darkness in *Romeo and Juliet*, and of blood in *Macbeth*. As a poet it was Shakespeare's function to make ideas, values, and emotions visible to us, to make the ideal real, the abstract concrete—to give to "airy nothings a local habitation and a name." He does it largely through his imagery. See IMAGERY.

Shakespeare's language would not have its immense power to touch our minds and emotions were it not for its tactile quality. In the best sense, it is ingratiating. Truths familiar to us through Biblical texts, classical maxims, and popular proverbs are recorded in a fashion that freshens the familiar. The familiarity lets our spirits greet the lovely words halfway. And there is always the invocation of the most constant world of human experience, that of nature and domestic life—the raw cold of winter (when "coughing drowns the parson's saw"), the warmth of spring (when "maidens bleach their summer smocks"), the recurrent miracle of dawn (with the sun "in rosy mantle clad"). At some time in our past, we seem all to have lain on the "bank where the wild thyme grows," as we have all seen the "daffodils that come before the swallow dares." Such things do not change, whatever else does, and their natural preservative will save Shakespeare's style from ever becoming stale. [F. P. Wilson, *Shakespeare and the Diction of Common Life*, 1941; W. H. Clemen, *The Development of Shakespeare's Imagery*, 1951; B. I. Evans, *The Language of Shakespeare's Plays*, 1952; A. Harbage, *Shakespeare: A Reader's Guide*, 1963; *Shakespeare Survey* 7, 1954, A. Nicoll, ed., contains a survey of works on style by M. C. Bradbrook and others.]—A. H.

Suffolk, Charles Brandon, 1st duke of (d. 1545). Son of Sir William BRANDON, he was long a favorite of Henry VIII, but temporarily lost royal favor when he secretly married the king's sister, widow of Louis XII of France. Though his restoration to favor may have been Wolsey's work, Suffolk later opposed the cardinal. In *Henry VIII*, Suffolk is one of the nobles who taunt Wolsey at his downfall (III, ii). He is high-steward at the coronation of Anne Bullen (IV, i) and is present at the christening of Elizabeth (V, v). He is the most cautious of the lords who attempt to imprison Cranmer (IV, iii). In V, i, he has been playing an unspecified game with the King.

Suffolk, William de la Pole, 4th earl and 1st duke of (1396–1450). Second son of Michael, 2nd earl of Suffolk, and brother of Michael, 3rd earl, whose title he inherited. Suffolk fought in the French wars under Henry V and the duke of Bedford, succeeding, on Salisbury's death, to the chief command of the English forces. He returned to England after the crowning of Henry VI and subsequently married the widowed countess of Salisbury. After arranging King Henry's marriage with Margaret of Anjou, Suffolk was able, with the queen's help, to overthrow his bitter enemy the duke of Gloucester. In 1448 he was made a duke.

Because Anjou and Maine were ceded to France when Margaret became queen of England, Suffolk had become exceedingly unpopular. After England had suffered further losses in France, he was accused of having sold the kingdom and was committed to the Tower. In an attempt to save Suffolk, the king banished him for five years; however, his ship was intercepted and he was summarily beheaded.

In *1 Henry VI*, Suffolk, joining the Lancastrians, plucks a red rose in the Temple Garden. At Angiers he captures Margaret of Anjou and falls in love with her, but since he is already married, Suffolk arranges her marriage to Henry VI. In *2 Henry VI* he is made Duke by King Henry, who is grateful to Suffolk for having secured him his Queen. Suffolk succeeds in having the Duchess of Gloucester tried for sorcery and later banished, and in having the Duke murdered. When Salisbury and Warwick subsequently demand that Suffolk be banished, the King acquiesces. As he parts from Margaret, she confesses her love for him. Captured off the coast of Kent, Suffolk is murdered by a seaman named Walter Whitmore. The love affair between Suffolk and Margaret portrayed by Shakespeare is probably not historically true.

Sullivan, Arthur S. See MUSIC BASED ON SHAKESPEARE: *19th century, 1850–1900*.

Sullivan, [Thomas] Barry (1821–1891). Irish actor. Sullivan began his career with touring companies in Ireland (especially in Cork), the English provinces and Scotland, where he managed a theatre in Aberdeen for three years. In 1852 he made his first London appearance, as Hamlet, at the Haymarket. The reception accorded this performance resulted in

TITLE PAGE OF ROBERT HARRISON'S STUDY OF THE SUPERNATURAL, *Of Ghostes and spirites* (1572).

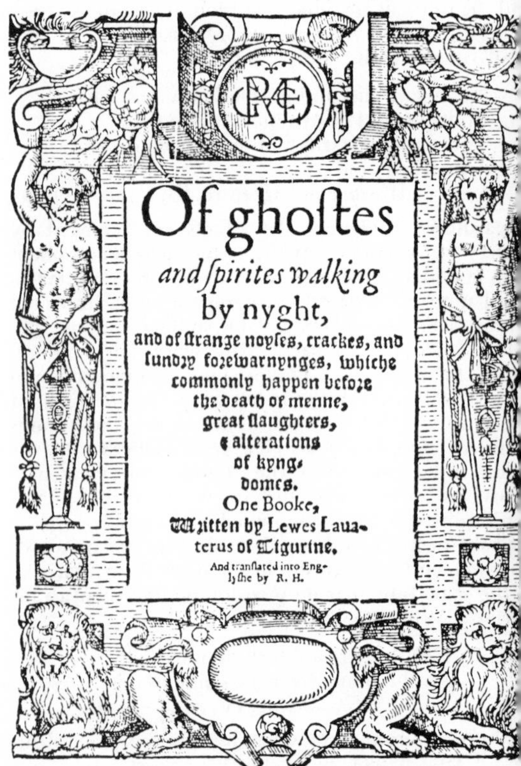
Of ghoſtes
and ſpirites walking
by nyght,
and of ſtrange noyſes, crackes, and
ſundry forewarnynges, whiche
commonly happen before
the death of menne,
great ſlaughters,
& alterations
of kyng-
domes.
One Booke,
Written by Lewes Laua-
terus of Tigurine.
And tranſlated into Eng-
lyſhe by R. H.

Printed at London by Henry Benneyman
for Richard VVatkyns. 1572.

ꞔason at Sadler's Wells under Samuel Phelps. In 858 Sullivan toured the United States and Australia. ı 1876 his 60-night run as Richard III at Drury Lane ʼas interrupted when a supporting player ran a word through Sullivan's eye, but he continued to ct, appearing as Benedick in *Much Ado About Nothing* at the opening of the Shakespeare Memorial ʼheatre, Stratford-upon-Avon, in 1879.

After 1879 he no longer appeared in London, but is career continued in the provinces and Ireland. y the time of his death, he claimed to have played ichard III and Hamlet 3500 times and he had porrayed 300 different characters, including 50 to 60 of hakespeare's. In *Macbeth* alone, for example, he ad been Seyton, Malcolm, Lennox, Ross, Banquo, lacduff, and Macbeth; and in *Hamlet*, Rosencrantz, laudius, the Ghost, and Hamlet. His popularity was rimarily among less sophisticated audiences, alıough at one time George Bernard Shaw considered im a great actor. His acting was marked by vigor nd forcibly delivered lines, and his Hamlet was redited with being the most faithful "mental porraiture" of the time. [G. B. Shaw, *Sullivan, Shakepear, and Shaw*, 1948; E. J. West, "Barry Sullivan: havian and Actual," *Educational Theatre Journal*, I, December 1949; *Oxford Companion to the Theatre*, hyllis Hartnoll, ed., 1951.]

supernatural, the. Elizabethans of all classes beeved in the power of supernatural agencies. These opular beliefs are reflected in at least half of Shakepeare's plays. Witches, ghosts, demons, divination, nd an interest in astrology are among the superatural phenomena of which Shakespeare makes ramatic use (see GHOSTS AND APPARITIONS). Four ramas in particular—*A Midsummer Night's Dream, Hamlet, Macbeth,* and *The Tempest*—deal signifiantly with the supernatural. Cumberland Clark in is *Shakespeare and the Supernatural* (1932) points ut that Shakespeare's attitude toward the superatural, as expressed in these plays, varies considerbly. It begins with "lighthearted, amused tolerance," hanges to "serious meditation . . . and apprehenon," and emerges with a "renewed faith and condence in good."

Belief in witchcraft is the most extravagant and ensational asp ct of Elizabethan superstition. A witch" ordinarily was a decrepit old hag whom eople thought to be in league with Satan. The evil, it was believed, had given strange powers to itches. They could fly through the air, vanish, raise torms, and inflict people and animals with disease. hakespeare mentions such a hag in *The Merry Wives of Windsor*, and in *1 Henry VI* he includes oan of Arc in this category. A rarer kind of witch is epresented by the Weird Sisters in *Macbeth*, creaures who are not of this world.

Few Englishmen of the late 16th and early 17th enturies doubted the reality of witchcraft. When Reginald Scot published *The discoverie of Witchraft* (1584), an exposé of superstitious beliefs, King ames ordered the book burnt, and replied to Scot ersonally in his *Daemonologie* (1597). King James, believer in witchcraft, was energetic in his efforts o stamp it out.

The magician, like the witch, was believed to have he power of summoning devils to aid him in evil nterprises. In return for supernatural assistance, he sells his soul to the devil. Marlowe's Doctor Faustus is the most significant Elizabethan example of such a magician. Prospero in *The Tempest* is Shakespeare's original adaptation of the good magician who employs "white magic" as opposed to Faustus' demoniacally inspired black magic.

The form of the supernatural which Shakespeare utilizes most frequently is the ghostly apparition. Shakespeare makes use of two kinds of ghosts, the objective and the subjective. The objective ghost, such as Hamlet's father, is supposed to be actually present and apparent to a number of people at the same time. The subjective ghost, such as Banquo in *Macbeth* and Caesar in *Julius Caesar*, is a figment of the viewer's imagination. At times Shakespearean ghosts appear in dreams, as do the apparitions to Richard III before the battle of Bosworth and to Posthumus in *Cymbeline*.

Another preternatural type that Shakespeare employed was the fairy. Fairies or "little people" meddled in human affairs and played mischievous pranks, but they were relatively harmless. The little people of popular superstition were often cruel and evil, but on Shakespeare's stage the type is helpful, happy, and friendly, as are the diminutive creatures of *A Midsummer Night's Dream* (see FAIRIES).

In a number of plays Shakespeare gives instances of various superstitious beliefs. He uses the supposed ability of dying men to see into the future at the death of John of Gaunt in *Richard II* and of Hotspur in *1 Henry IV*. Also in *1 Henry IV* Gadshill refers to the belief that fern seeds were invisible and that whoever could gather them had the power to make himself invisible. The plays contain examples of

WOODCUT SHOWING VARIOUS WITCHES FROM MATTHEW HOPKINS' *The Discovery of Witches* (1647).

popular bird lore, plant lore, and superstitious notions about spiders and toads.

Shakespeare's plays contain something like a running debate on the subject of astrology. Cassius in *Julius Caesar* is a skeptic when he tells Brutus that the fault "is not in our stars, / But in ourselves." Similarly, Helena in *All's Well That Ends Well* argues that "Our remedies oft in ourselves do lie, / Which we ascribe to heaven." Lafeu in the same play attacks the new philosophy. We make "trifles of terrors," he complains. Instead of "ensconcing ourselves into seeming knowledge" we should "submit ourselves to an unknown fear." In *King Lear* Gloucester expresses a firm belief in the baneful effects of eclipses. Edmund, however, considers belief in the influence of the stars on human affairs to be humbug and hypocrisy:

> This is the excellent foppery of the world, that, when we are sick in fortune,—often the surfeit of our own behaviour,—we make guilty of our disasters the sun, the moon, and the stars: as if we were villains by necessity; fools by heavenly compulsion; knaves, thieves, and treachers, by spherical predominance; drunkards, liars, and adulterers, by an enforced obedience of planetary influence; and all that we are evil in, by a divine thrusting on: an admirable evasion of whoremaster man, to lay his goatish disposition to the charge of a star! My father compounded with my mother under the dragon's tail; and my nativity was under Ursa major; so that it follows, I am rough and lecherous. Tut, I should have been that I am, had the maidenliest star in the firmament twinkled on my bastardizing.
>
> (I, ii, 129 ff.)

Iago, another villain, similarly argues that a man is responsible for his actions, that " 'tis in ourselves that we are thus, or thus." As Clark has suggested, characters like Edmund and Iago, "the men who pursue their own advantage and shrink from no steps to attain their end," are the ones who "pronounce the more reasonable, sane, and scientific opinions." Shakespeare seems also to justify popular superstitious beliefs by prefacing disaster and tragedy with dreams and meteorological omens.

In his plays Shakespeare frequently made use of popular superstitions. At times, as in the case of *A Midsummer Night's Dream*, Shakespeare adapted folk beliefs with considerable originality. Shakespeare's ghosts are often strongly characterized and are always functionally related to the plot; he never indulges in Gothic excess or in the supernatural for its own sake. This world, its comedy and its tragedy, is always at the center of Shakespeare's stage.

Shakespeare portrays fairyland in *A Midsummer Night's Dream*, a play in which he gave "to airy nothing / A local habitation and a name." Ignoring the unpleasant aspects of the folk tradition, Shakespeare creates delightful creatures and, as Clark suggests, "writes in a happy, carefree vein, drawing prodigally on his imagination." Though prone to mischief, the little people of this play are not endowed with any real influence upon the lives of men and they seem incapable of genuine malice. Though relatively harmless, the little people of Titania and Oberon's world have many of the powers ascribed to elves and fairies in the folk tradition. Puck ca[n] make himself invisible and assume any shape h[e] pleases. The quarrel between Titania and Obero[n] affects the weather. Only once in this play are th[e] darker aspects of superstition portrayed. With th[e] coming of dawn we are told "ghosts, wandering her[e] and there, / Troop home to churchyards: damne[d] spirits all, . . ." Clark argues that Shakespeare's con[-]ception of fairies "as tiny, benevolent, aery being[s] influenced all subsequent literature on the subjec[t] and finally dispelled the old ideas of malicious, evi[l] awful creatures who had to be obeyed and propiti[-]ated."

The second of the great plays with a significan[t] use of the supernatural is *Hamlet*. Shakespeare, i[n] portraying the ghost of Hamlet's father, is quit[e] faithful to popular notions about ghosts. He appear[s] at the dead of night, terrifies the sentries at Elsinor[e] and does not speak until spoken to. A common opin[-]ion regarding ghosts was that they were evil spirit[s] impersonating the deceased. Hamlet's doubts abou[t] the identity of the ghost are therefore warranted b[y] Elizabethan ghost lore. Shakespeare, a master a[t] stagecraft, so effectively prepared for the appearanc[e] of the ghost that this scene is one of the most success[-]ful even in the 20th century. In addition to his dra[-]matic impact, the ghost provides the audience with [a] great deal of information necessary for understand[-]ing the play, a brilliant way of handling expositior[n]. The ghost in Hamlet has no direct power to reveng[e] himself. He must persuade Hamlet, a human agen[t].

The Shakespearean play into which the super[-]natural enters most significantly is *Macbeth*. I[n] *Hamlet* the ghost appears to reveal what happene[d] in the past. The three witches in *Macbeth* appear t[o] reveal what will happen in the future. Though Mac[-]beth seems to retain his free will, the Weird Sister[s] exercise greater power over human destiny than d[o] preternatural beings in any other play. The Weir[d] Sisters can vanish at will, assume all sorts of shape[s] and control the weather, but they do not have th[e] power to take human life. In Shakespearean traged[y] the hero is always responsible for his action or in[-]action. The two sets of prophecies are fulfille[d] through Macbeth's actions rather than preternatura[l] machinations. So completely is Macbeth's destiny i[n] his own hands that critics have argued, somewha[t] unconvincingly, that Shakespeare meant the witche[s] to be a symbolic representation of Macbeth's inwar[d] temptations.

The dagger floating in the air just before the mur[-]der of the King and the subjective ghost, Banqu[o] are meant to be understood as hallucinations, in al[l] probability. Macbeth calls the dagger "a false crea[-]tion, proceeding from the heat oppressed brain" an[d] Lady Macbeth speaks of the ghost as the "painting" of Macbeth's fear.

In *The Tempest* Shakespeare allows man to hav[e] complete control over the forces of evil. Prosper[o] frees Ariel from the sorceries of Caliban's mothe[r] the witch Sycorax. Prospero is the master of bot[h] Ariel and Caliban and throughout the play his wor[d] is law. Shakespeare suggests that though man nee[d] not fear the preternatural, magical forces are bes[t] left alone. Prospero's command over spirits and th[e] laws of nature results from deliberate study. H[e] never uses these powers with malice. Unlike *A Mid* mmer Night's Dream*, Shakespeare's other play ealing with a fairyland, *The Tempest* has elicited number of allegorical interpretations. The preter- atural creatures of the earlier play are presented xclusively for our entertainment. In *The Tempest* rospero's control of nature and the supernatural ould appear to be a comment upon life and art.

In addition to these four plays in which the super- atural elements are highly significant, Shakespeare as included influences of the unseen world in at ast a dozen other plays. Most significant are the hosts and prophecies in *Julius Caesar* and *Richard I*. In *1 Henry VI*, Joan of Arc is represented as a itch. In *2 Henry VI*, a spirit foretells the fate of ing Henry, the Duke of Suffolk, and the Duke of omerset. In this play Shakespeare contrasts true and igned manifestations of the supernatural. In *The Ierry Wives of Windsor*, Anne Page and her troupe f elves and fairies plague Falstaff. *Troilus and Cres- da, King Lear, Antony and Cleopatra, Pericles, ymbeline*, and *The Winter's Tale* contain instances f prophecy, portents, divination of omens, visions, d one unconventional ghost, Hermione, who is not tually dead. [Margaret Lucy, *Shakespeare and the upernatural*, 1908; Cumberland Clark, *Shakespeare d the Supernatural*, 1932.]— J. F. L.

Supposes. See George GASCOIGNE.

sureties of the peace. See CAWDREY FAMILY; Wil- am GARDINER.

Surrey, earl of. An English title held by various milies from the 12th to the 16th centuries. In the 5th century the title was held by the Howard mily, who were also dukes of NORFOLK. When homas Howard the elder, earl of Surrey, regained 1514 his hereditary rank of duke of Norfolk, hich his father had lost at the fall of Richard III, is son Thomas Howard succeeded to the rank of rl. He in turn became duke of Norfolk on the eath of his father in 1524 and the title of earl of urrey fell to his young son, Henry Howard. In *Ienry VIII*, although much of the action takes place ter this date, the Earl of Surrey is clearly intended be the younger Thomas Howard. He returns from eland (where Wolsey had sent him to prevent his pporting his father-in-law, Buckingham) in time join his father and the other nobles in gloating ver the Cardinal's downfall (III, ii). He is present ter for the coronation of Anne Bullen, his niece.

Surrey, Earl of. In *2 Henry IV*, the King asks urrey and the Earl of Warwick if they have read ertain letters pertaining to the northern rebellion. nly Warwick speaks (III, i). This character was robably Thomas Fitzalan (1381–1415), earl of rundel and Surrey.

Surrey, Henry Howard, earl of (c. 1517–1547). ourtier and poet. The eldest son of the 3rd duke of orfolk, Surrey was favored by Henry VIII while s cousin, Catherine Howard, was queen (1540– 42). After Catherine's execution, he was increas- gly the victim of plots emanating from his power- l rivals, the Seymour family. His impetuous nature ade him vulnerable, and in 1547 he was executed trumped-up charges of treason. During his life- me Surrey's poems circulated in manuscript; 40 of em appeared in *Tottel's Miscellany* (1559). Along ith Thomas Wyatt, Surrey introduced the sonnet to English. He established the so-called English or Shakespearean form, consisting of three quatrains and a couplet (see SONNET SEQUENCE). His translation (1557) of Books II and IV of Vergil's *Aeneid* is historically important in that it introduced blank verse into English, but otherwise it is undistinguished. Surrey is also important for metrical reforms which helped set the standards for the subsequent age.

Surrey, Thomas Holand or **Holland,** duke of; later 3rd earl of **Kent** (1374–1400). Eldest son of Thomas, 2nd earl of Kent. Surrey was made a duke of Surrey by Richard II in 1397 in reward for supporting the king against the lords appellant, and the next year he was appointed earl marshal of England in anticipation of the duel between Henry Bolingbroke and the duke of Norfolk. On Henry's accession as king, Surrey lost his title (1399). Subsequently becoming involved in a conspiracy against Henry, he was captured and beheaded.

In *Richard II*, Surrey defends the Duke of Aumerle against the accusation of Sir John Bagot that he murdered Gloucester (IV, i). Surrey is later implicated in the plot of the Abbot of Westminster to kill Henry, and is himself killed.

Surveyor to the Duke of Buckingham. In *Henry VIII*, the Surveyor, having been dismissed from his position, testifies falsely against his former master (I, ii). This character was Charles Knevet, or Knyvet, who functioned as steward of the estates of the duke of Buckingham, to whom he was related.

Sussex' Men (1569–1594). Elizabethan acting company under the patronage of the 2nd, 3rd, and 4th earls of Sussex. Sussex' Men's first recorded performance was at Nottingham on March 16, 1569. Thereafter they played largely in the provinces, but made occasional appearances at court during the Christmas seasons. Sussex became the lord chamberlain in July 1572, so that at any time between 1572 and 1583 when a company is cited as the Lord Chamberlain's Men, it is Sussex' that is meant. (A later company of Chamberlain's Men was under the patronage of Henry Carey, 1st Lord Hunsdon.) The only actor known to be part of Sussex' was John Adams, a clown. In 1590 they evidently traveled in combination with the Queen's Men to such places as Southampton, Gloucester, and Coventry, and are mentioned as playing alone in 1592/3 at Sudbury, Ipswich, York, Newcastle, and Winchester.

The troupe played at Philip Henslowe's Rose from December 26, 1593 to February 6, 1594. During this short season the only "new" play they presented was *Titus Andronicus* (see TITUS ANDRONICUS: *Date*). Thereafter the company is no longer recorded as having appeared at court or on the London stage; up to 1618, however, there is evidence that a group of actors called Sussex' Men were touring the provinces. [John Tucker Murray, *English Dramatic Companies, 1558–1642*, 1910; E. K. Chambers, *The Elizabethan Stage*, 1923.]

Swanston, Eyllaerdt or **Elliard** (d. 1651). Actor. With the King's Men from 1624 to 1642, Swanston is first recorded with Lady Elizabeth's Men in 1622. He joined the King's Men in 1624, possibly as a replacement for John Underwood. In 1635 he was one of the three actors who attempted to become housekeepers (see SHARERS' PAPERS). He became one of the leading members of the company, acting in the title roles of *Othello* and *Richard III*. Swanston was a rarity among his fellow actors, a partisan of parliament against the king during the civil war. [G. E. Bentley, *The Jacobean and Caroline Stage*, 5 vols., 1941–1956.]

Swan theatre. Elizabethan theatre. The Swan was located in the manor of Paris Garden on the Bankside in Southwark. The land was sold to Francis LANGLEY for £850 by Thomas Cure the younger, into whose possession it had fallen. The location of the Swan, from a survey of the site made in November 1624, was at the northeast corner of the manor grounds, east of the manor house, and 26 poles (a pole is equal to 5½ yards) south of Paris Garden stairs. On the survey map the Swan is a double-outlined circle, divided into 12 parts, with a small porch or tiring-house jutting out to the road. Chambers thinks the theatre was ready for use by 1595. In 1596 Johannes de Witt visited London and made his well-known drawing of the Swan (see PLAYHOUSE STRUCTURE). By 1597 Langley had concluded an agreement with Pembroke's Men for their use of the Swan. Under the terms of lease, Langley was to prepare it and furnish apparel (which he estimated at £300). In return, Langley would receive his owner's half of the gallery receipts as rent and half of t actors' moiety in repayment for the sums he h advanced them. The problems which arose over t Pembroke's Men's presentation of *The Isle of Do* on July 28, 1597 led to their practical dissolution a company. Several actors were jailed, and the leadi actors joined the Admiral's Men at the Rose. Langl engaged the latter in a suit for breach of contra and was evidently able to put together some sort acting company, for the Swan remained open a wh longer. It was, however, no longer in use by a regul company thereafter.

THE SWAN THEATRE. THIS DRAWING, A COPY OF ONE MADE BY JOHANNES DE WITT, IS THE ONLY KNOWN VIEW OF AN ELIZABETHAN PLAYHOUSE. DE WITT VISITED LONDON IN 1596, AT WHICH TIME THE ORIGINAL OF THIS DRAWING MUST HAVE BEEN MADE. BECAUSE OF THE BIRD'S-EYE PERSPECTIVE, IT HAS BEEN SUPPOSED THAT DE WITT MADE HIS SKETCH FROM MEMORY. (UNIVERSITY LIBRARY, UTRECHT, MS 842, FOL. 132)

Allusions to it appear in various works betwe 1598 and 1611. *Palladis Tamia* (1598) alludes to it the scene of a challenge in "extemporall" verse Robert Wilson:

> And so is now our wittie Wilson, who for learni and extemporall witte in this facultie is witho compare or compeere, as, to his great and etern commendations, he manifested in his challenge the *Swanne* on the Banke Side.

On May 15, 1600 the privy council permitted t place to exhibit "feats of activity" by Peter Bromvi When Langley died in 1601, the property fell in the hands of Hugh Browker, a prothonotary of t court of common pleas, and remained with his fami until 1655. On February 7, 1602 the Swan played hc to fencers, and on November 6, 1602 Richard Ve nar's *England's Joy* was advertised for the Swa *England's Joy* was, according to its posted bill, to a satirical spectacle of recent English history; i stead, Vennar was arrested before the performan and the disappointed audience in the Swan "r venged themselves upon the hangings, curtair chairs, stooles, walles, and whatsoever came in thei way, very outragiously, and made great spoile."

By 1611 plays were again being given at the Swa The *Roaring Girl*, given at the Fortune, mentions knight who "lost his purse at the last new play i' t Swan." The *Chast Mayd in Cheape-side* (pub. 163 on its title page indicates that it was "Often acted the Swan on the Banke-side." This was one of t plays belonging to Philip Henslowe's Lady Eliz beth's Men, who had taken over the Swan in 161 The accounts of the Paris Garden overseers list th receipts from the Swan for every year from Apr 1611 to 1615. When the Hope was opened in 161 the Swan fell into disuse. The Hope was, in fac modeled on the Swan. (See HOPE THEATRE.) In 162 the overseers' accounts recorded one payment fro actors using the Swan, and the office-book of S Henry Herbert, the Master of the Revels, indicat that both the Swan and the Rose were used as late 1620 for prizefights. In 1632 *Holland's Leaguer* pr vides the last contemporary allusion to the Swan:

> The last which stood, and as it were shak'd hand with this Fortresse, [i.e., the Hope] beeing in tim past as famous as any of the other, was now falle to decay, and like a dying *Swanne*, hanging dow her head, seemed to sing her owne dierge.

The building appears on maps of the Bankside b Visscher (1616) and the Merian group (1638), bu not in Hollar's (1647). [E. K. Chambers, *The Eliza bethan Stage*, 1923.]

Sweden. See SCANDINAVIA.

Swinburne, Algernon Charles (1837–1909). Poet, playwright, and man of letters. A great admirer of the Elizabethan drama, Swinburne once said, "when I write plays it is with a view to their being performed at the Globe, the Red Bull, or the Black Friars." The Elizabethan influence comes through most strongly in Swinburne's Mary Stuart trilogy (*Chastelard*, 1860; *Bothwell*, 1874; *Mary Stuart*, 1881) in which many characters have distinct Shakespearean prototypes.

Swinburne wrote three books on Shakespeare: *A Study of Shakespeare* (1880), *Shakespeare* (1909), and *Three Plays of Shakespeare* (1909). In the first he pays special attention to the progress of Shakespeare's prosody, a progress apparent not to the metrical statistician, but rather to the critic who is himself a poet. Perhaps Swinburne's finest criticism is of *King Lear*, which he compares to the work of Aeschylus, the one tragic poet greater, in his opinion, than Shakespeare. He calls *Lear* "the most terrible work of human genius" for it reveals nature as unnatural. Swinburne extends his comparison between Shakespeare and Aeschylus in his last book, asserting that although the author of the *Oresteia* was the finer poet, the author of *Othello* was unexcelled in dramatic creation. [Gaynell Spivey, "Swinburne's Use of Elizabethan Drama," *Studies in Philology*, XLI, 1944.]

Swinley, Ion (1891–1937). Actor. Swinley made his dramatic debut in a 1911 production of *A Midsummer Night's Dream*. At Stratford-upon-Avon in 1913 he appeared as Troilus in a Memorial Theatre production of *Troilus and Cressida*. Subsequent Shakespearean roles included those of Henry V, Hamlet, Prospero, and Romeo. At his premature death in 1937 he was described as the finest Shakespearean actor of his time. [J. C. Trewin, *Shakespeare on the English Stage, 1900–1964*, 1964.]

symbolism. The word "symbolism" as used in current literary and dramatic disquisition is not covered by the dictionary definition of it as a *conventional* sign. Rather it means some effect, person, object, or descriptive passage which automatically radiates significances flowering from that effect's intrinsic nature. The meanings are not imposed by a convention, as they may be in allegory, but spring *inevitably* from the symbol used. Though in one sense infinite, they are in another strictly limited. For example, the much discussed Falcon in Ibsen's *Brand*, despite the evidence for the reading of it at one point as "the spirit of compromise," inevitably suggests, as does the falcon throughout Shakespeare, a strong aspiration. Any external evidence that counters the intrinsic meaning must accordingly be either inaccurate or misunderstood. The laws of symbolism are rigid, and its analysis a severely disciplined study.

Symbolism exists to give sensory form to values and powers not otherwise easy to express; at the limit, to extrasensory dimensions of being, and spirit realities. Under poetic handling normal events may themselves assume an aura of symbolical suggestion; through imagery and atmosphere they may shade into the numinous. All imaginative writing is to this extent symbolical. But usually, and certainly for our present, Shakespearean, purpose, we do well to limit the term to elements where normal realism is, or appears to be, negated, or broken through; to effects which stick out, strangely but meaningfully. In Shakespeare such effects tend to involve the supernatural, though we must not forget that they grow from a soil of semisymbolic naturalism; they do not impinge from a completely alien world. They have strong dramatic quality.

Shakespeare's major symbolisms were not properly focused until recently. Imaginative tonings and the occasional dominant image (e.g., fire in *Coriolanus*) were handled by A. C. Bradley; and imagery became a primary study with Caroline Spurgeon and Wolfgang Clemen (see IMAGERY). But the major symbolisms have proved less inviting. Colin Still's *Shakespeare's Mystery Play* (1921; revised and enlarged as *The Timeless Theme*, 1936) faced them in *The Tempest*, seeing its events in depth and relating them to ancient myth and ritual; but his enquiry was, though brilliant, limited to one obviously symbolic, drama. Probably the first real advance into the more general study of Shakespeare's symbolism was made at Oxford by John Masefield in his Romanes Lecture *Shakespeare and Spiritual Life* (1924), wherein he took seriously and probed metaphysically the supernatural portents of *Julius Caesar*, *Hamlet*, and *Macbeth*. These had too often been treated by commentators as little more than a writer's obedience to his "sources," or to traditional superstition. The older critics would have called them "machinery," the term applied in the 18th century to Pope's sylphs in *The Rape of the Lock*. But the word "machinery" is not so derogatory as it sounds. It suggests power and action; and that is exactly how such symbolisms function; they are dynamic, and geared to the human action. It is symbolism in this sense to which my own works have been primarily, though not exclusively, devoted.

There were two related discoveries, both of which may be supposed to involve "symbolism." One was the recognition of the death-reversals in *Pericles* and *The Winter's Tale* as dramatic equivalents to a truth beyond tragedy; the other—it came, so far as I can recall, second—the recognition within separate plays of imagistic and intellectual coherences as spatial areas of the mind, at high moments crystallizing into direct dramatic symbolisms of supernatural or semisupernatural quality. Both discoveries derived equally from the willingness to see within the Shakespearean world, as Keats puts it in *Hyperion*, "the depth of things" (*The Fall of Hyperion;* I, 304); that is, to accept every effect in its own right as exerting lines of force according to its intrinsic nature over and above the surface story. These were my main contributions. Imagistic coherences were simultaneously being studied by Caroline Spurgeon (*Leading Motives in the Imagery of Shakespeare's Tragedies*, 1930; *Shakespeare's Iterative Imagery*, 1931). F. C. Kolbe in *Shakespeare's Way* (1930) played on various keymotifs not limited to imagery and touching events, but his results remained, in the main, sketchy. Apart from Masefield's Romanes Lecture the major symbolic agencies were not being accorded their due of centrality.

A peculiarly rich discovery of the new method was made in my reading of the three Apparitions in Act IV, scene i of *Macbeth:* the Armed Head, the Bloody Child, the Crowned and Tree-bearing Child. These appear as spiritualistic materializations, recalling the spirit-raising scene of *2 Henry VI* (I, iv); but they are also carefully made to constitute an exact symbolism. They are, it is true, related prophetically to the events of the fifth act, but they simultaneously exist more metaphysically as a compressed miniature of the total drama, showing: (1) death, destructive and self-destructive; (2) life-born-out-of-death; and (3) human life backed by nature and raised by the crown to a yet higher status, so that the second child-figure compactly denotes nature, man, and the surpassing of man in royalty. The two child-figures relate to this particular play's pervading use of child-thoughts throughout, and those in turn to the many thoughts of life-forces in nature and human feasting. Nowhere else can we so plainly see how the major symbols may flower from a semi-symbolic soil; and also how they may function ambivalently, since Macbeth is encouraged by their *words* while remaining blind to the *drama* of their visually symbolic statement.

Since these three Apparitions together dramatize conflict, they come to thunder. The following procession of kings, suggesting a creative harmony undisturbed by the brief conflict, comes naturally to music. We have here a peculiarly compact example of Shakespeare's recurring symbolic contrast of thunder-tempests and music. In *The Shakespearian Tempest* it was shown how this recurring balance applies to a large part of Shakespeare's universe, not alone as imagery but as event: in the romantic comedies, the tragedies, and the final plays. The tempest-music symbolism, often taking the form of the sea as variously fierce and calm, acts as a principle of unity in Shakespeare's world. Atmosphere, imagery, and thought all vary: the unity lies in the symbolism.

In the historical dramas tempests are tragic impressions in the imagery, and there are cosmic portents; and music as a backwater of peace countering violence functions in *Richard II* and both parts of *Henry IV* as in the tragedies. But the dominant *symbolism* of the history sequence is the Crown, existing, despite the inadequacies of its various possessors, as a sacred symbol aiming to raise man and his community beyond man and to link the temporal to the eternal. This symbol too applies widely throughout Shakespeare, since nearly all his plays are royalistically centered. There are accordingly two principles of unity in Shakespeare: (1) tempests-and-music and (2) the crown. Their mutual relation, which I first expressed in *The Olive and the Sword* (1944), though the relevant passage did not appear in the abbreviated version included in *The Sovereign Flower* (1958), is found in the Shakespearean will to transmute human conflicts through the agency of the royalistic intuition to a harmony. This harmony is finally stated in Cranmer's prophecy of the Elizabethan and Jacobean ages in *Henry VIII*, where crown and ruler coalesce. The involvement is localized, contemporary, and specific, in the manner of Aeschylus, Vergil, and Dante. But what was for Shakespeare an actuality becomes symbolic for us, taking its place beside Aeschylus' Athens and Vergil's Rome.

The relation of symbolism to realism, in the popular sense of the word, is well seen in Shakespeare's use of gold and riches in *The Merchant of Venice* and *Timon of Athens*. In the former, Max Plowman was the first to analyze in depth the contrast money-values and life-values ("pound of fles "heart") in the trial scene; and in my book on Shak spearean production I grouped this reading, not or with the three caskets as symbols of true and fa wealth, but also with Portia's "infinite bank-balanc read as a symbol of the true; for by symbolism t material may at any moment assume sacramen properties. In *Timon of Athens* gold has similar tw way pointings: it both stimulates avarice and acts the expression of a bounteous and warm heart. the later scenes Timon's new-found gold adds to prophetic stature; as outcast, he is still sought aft in performance the gold *inevitably* helps to build the dramatic power of his Promethean personali When Caroline Spurgeon criticizes my emphasis gold in *Timon of Athens*, observing that there we in fact no gold metaphors, we see the divergence her approach from mine. The gold in *Timon* is pa of the symbolic action, more important than imager It is with a stage eye that Shakespeare's symbolis must be read.

Symbolism continually leads us from the ordina into the imponderables. The handkerchief in *Othel* a domestic object in a domestic world, assumes s pernal power, to become, as Othello's reiteratio drive home, a primary agent. Middleton Murry, wh though a pervading influence behind the new Shak spearean movement, was not generally at ease wi symbolism as such, was nevertheless the first to o serve that Desdemona's "Sure, there's some wond in this handkerchief" is not merely an acceptance Othello's account of it, but a sudden realization, view of Othello's extraordinary behavior, of magic in action. In making the handkerchief a supe natural force in relation to conjugal infidelity Shak speare was, as Byron, according to Thomas Medwi observed, in close accord with Oriental lore: "T handkerchief is the strongest proof of love, not on among the Moors, but all Eastern nations."

In *King Lear* the supernatural is not directly dr matized, but Edgar as pretended madman, nake fantastic in behavior, and talking of the fiends th torment him, blends with the appalling tempest ar wild heath to give us as strong a sense of the supe normal as any apparition. It is Shakespeare's mo elaborate and complex raising of realism to syr bolism.

Symbols may, however, be less obviously based realism. Ghosts have undoubtedly been seen, b even so they come as strangers, if not aliens, as fro another dimension. We meet them in *Richard I*, *Julius Caesar*, *Hamlet*, and *Macbeth*. They are dark toned and directly related to the drama's deeper i sues; they function as authoritative entities, and t one in *Hamlet* as a dramatic agent. In *Hamlet* t Ghost is described in terms of folklore and religio eschatology, but it has dramatically a more genera ized import. Bradley was in part right to relate i "majestic" qualities to its function as an instrume of supernal judgment; but it is also a spirit sufferi in purgatory. It remains ambiguous. My own readir has been comprehensive, seeing it as a symbol death invading life; just as the Weird Sisters in *Ma beth* are symbols of evil. Then there are the appea ances of divine beings. Such are Hymen in *As Yo Like It*, Hecate in *Macbeth*, Diana in *Pericles*, Apol

The Winter's Tale, Jupiter in Cymbeline, the ngels in Henry VIII. The academic and stage rection of Jupiter has at last been reversed. That it ould have taken so long, and been an unaided bat-, shows how blind commentary may be to staging d therefore to symbolism. Jupiter was always pontially a superb stage power, and as such he is now ing recognized.

Academic understanding has regularly been held by (1) a lack of stage sense and (2) fear of the pernatural. When a work may be written off as holly "fanciful," acceptance comes more easily. he fairies and spirits of *A Midsummer Night's ream* and *The Tempest* grow from what may be lled a highly imaginative soil; within their world ey are expected. Nevertheless they, and their soil, e all symbolically loaded and active and demand alysis in depth.

In *Pericles* and *The Winter's Tale* a human story self takes on supernatural quality and so becomes, this extent, symbolic. The death-reversals come n us, dramatically, as resurrections. During these unions and revivals with their sacred tonings and usic, we experience a reversal of death, just as at e conclusions of *Hamlet* and *King Lear* we experice death. That Leontes and Hermione must within e fiction be supposed to die later is dramatically relevant: they do not exist after the action. Within e structure of a happy-ending romance a deathversal is felt pressing for statement and recognition. hat it may strain the form is arguable; but its presce is dramatically, if not logically, indisputable. /e may say that the form is so manipulated and olded as to "symbolize" a difficult truth regarding mmortality."

Though there is so much else in Shakespeare, we all only receive his total work as a harmony if we low his symbolism to be our guide. The study of haracters" alone leaves us with a wealth of human nderstanding, rich but chaotic; the study of thought d imagery in isolation will plunge us into a misading medievalism. Both, the humanistic and the ctrinal, are legitimate constituents; but neither, r both together, gives us the essence. Academically ere is always the temptation to concentrate on ese more easily definable elements, separately or gether; but the dramatic essence will not be found so simple a scheme as (1) the philosophic and agistic overlay of (2) a human story. It lies rather the knotting together of these two elements rough symbolism; and this knotting together can ly come from intuition of a third reality, or diension, whereby the disparity is dissolved; and so e have various indications of a supernature, not denable in orthodox terms and yet out-spacing realm, as the resolving agent.

Except for the crown's religious associations in e histories, the authoritative Duke in *Measure for easure* disguised as a friar and finally pronouncing dgment "like power divine" (V, i, 370), and the ngels in *Henry VIII*, Shakespeare never employs a hristian symbolism. All the symbolic agencies which e have noted are either naturalistic or pagan. When lendower's spirit-controlling powers so unequivolly cut across Shakespeare's most strongly realistic ama, *1 Henry IV*, they do so with an occult, but t a Christian, authority. Cerimon's and Prospero's arts, or magic, are naturalistic, or spiritualistic, not in any orthodox sense doctrinal. It is, in part, because the study of Shakespeare's symbolism eventually forces us into categories involving occult and spiritualistic possibilities that the academic mind has proved so reluctant in investigation.

There are many complications. Shakespeare labors to harmonize opposing cultures: Renaissance humanism and medieval doctrine. He uses symbols of disorder, natural and cosmic, to point, it would appear, his moral; so that he might well seem to be composing "morality" plays with "order" as his deity and fifth-act ritual conclusions in the contemporary manner as symbolic judgments corresponding to the Judgment conclusions to the Mystery cycles. And yet matters are not so simple; nor will a great poetic dramatist base his lifework on an abstract concept. Symbols outspace the concepts which they suggest. The crown, in plays variously Christian or pagan, is irreducible to abstract concepts on the one side or—at least until Cranmer's prophecy in *Henry VIII*—its human tenants on the other. Richard III before Bosworth knows that the natural portents may apply equally to Richmond and himself; and the Gardeners in *Richard II* appear to adduce their gardening analogy to blame the King both for nurturing weeds and for not cutting off in good time the revolutionary who arises to root them out. In *Julius Caesar* the portents are highly intricate and variously viewed: to Cassius, Caesar's assassination is an act of order; to Antony, the reverse; and to Brutus, ambivalent; and every curve is faced and traced by Shakespeare's symbolic artistry. "Order" may apply to the individual, to lovers, to the family, the state, the cosmos; and any one "order" may, as in *Romeo and Juliet*, conflict with another, or others. In *Troilus and Cressida* Ulysses' "order" speech is balanced against the tragic mysticism of Agamemnon and Nestor; the communal necessity is balanced against the personal and the spiritual. The contrast here dramatized is peculiarly important, for it helps us to see why in *Macbeth*, though the disorder-symbols (II, iv) appear clearly to condemn the hero's crime, his tragic soul-strength asserts itself with considerable dramatic authority against them; almost, it would seem, against destiny itself.

This soul-strength is dramatized in *Timon of Athens*, wherein the hero assumes the powers elsewhere housed in external symbolism. There is, necessarily, no tempest; what symbols there are, such as the gold and, as in *King Lear*, animal references, Timon dominates; he speaks as an equal of the cosmic lights which he finally rejects for the sea, which functions, mainly through sound, for its surf should be heard, as what we may call a symbol of "nirvana." There is more here than satire, or hatred; nor is Timon a misguided hero. The stage impact counters such negative and partial readings. Following Edgar in *King Lear*, Timon's nakedness marks his approach as man or superman to some beyond-human yet human-rooted dimension, his physical stature and new-found gold together exerting on the stage positive and Promethean radiations. Humanity and symbolism are identified.

The process continues, differently, in *Antony and Cleopatra*, which is throughout so imaginatively fabricated, almost inflated, that only once does a direct symbolism need to assert itself in the mysterious music (IV, iii) that is said to denote the leaving of Antony by "the god Hercules, whom Antony loved." Here, as with the Apparitions of *Macbeth* and the later scenes of *Timon of Athens,* a stage recognition is essential. While suggesting Antony's fall as a soldier, the music, *as music,* in Shakespeare regularly love's language, inevitably also supports the countering love theme. The music's ambivalence is underlined by the Soldiers' words directly preceding the more explicit interpretation regarding "the god Hercules" (which itself significantly includes the word "loved"): "It signs well, does it not?"—"No." "Peace, I say! What should this mean?" The effect in the theatre registers before any of the spoken words, and continues after, dissolving tragedy in harmony. Nowhere can we so plainly see how dangerous it may be for the study of Shakespeare's symbolism to read the text as literature without living the experience as drama.

This knitting of the human essence to the symbolic leads on to the beyond-tragedy reversals of the last period. It is as though, having used various symbolisms, especially symbolisms of order, as his semichoric—though generally as ambivalent as a Greek oracle—pointers, Shakespeare finds the human essence asserting itself in *Macbeth* against the symbolism and then in *King Lear, Timon of Athens,* and *Antony and Cleopatra* drawing level with it and assuming its properties. No precise doctrinal solution is stated. Prospero's island in *The Tempest* itself endures disorder and the revolutionary Caliban may attract actors as the drama's star part, developing as it does the rough nature-contacts of *King Lear* and *Timon of Athens,* as Ariel symbolizes the aspiring poetry that counters them; while Prospero, Shakespeare's achieved, but troubled—and testy—superman, has, as best he may, to control both.

Our final trusts must be placed in: (1) the cogent yet noncommittal unifiers, the tempest-music opposition and the crown; (2) the tragic aspirations and later death-reversals, for the *individual;* and (3) Shakespeare's last play, the semiritualistic *Henry VIII,* balancing church and state, theology and humanism—though not in the cause of any abstraction such as "order" or "nationalism" but exactly located and thence, and *only* thence, widely symbolic—for the community.

The researches here recorded have not as yet been widely understood and developed. With a few notable exceptions, among them Roy Walker's study of *Macbeth* (*The Time is Free,* 1949), the ingrained academic reluctance to face the supernatural has led to a playing down, and often an ignoring, of the major symbolisms, accompanied by an overemphasis on intellectual and imagistic detail; and also on moral doctrine. Symbolic interpretation is concerned less with morals than with metaphysics; but there has been, as so often in the past, a tendency to take the easier course of moralizing. Scholarship has too often behaved as does Macbeth in listening to the Apparitions' words while failing to focus their visual quality; it has read and interpreted the text as word-sequences without sense of the stage totality.

In consequence scholars have responded to what I have designated the plays' "spatial" qualities as isolated patterns of static thought imposed on the action instead of as an indissoluble part of that dynami… dimension from within which the great symboli… agencies themselves function. Shakespeare's thought world is often medievally toned; but his dramati… action is of Renaissance quality. Commentators hav… been led to take Othello's and Macbeth's words regarding their own damnation at their face value instead of recognizing them as froth on the fierce current which, whatever else it does, cannot withou… distortion of the dramatic impact be supposed to lea… to hell. While making Shakespearean drama a serie… of Christian moralities, with "order," which ca… mean anything or nothing, as a deceptive guide, the… have remained blind to the major symbolic powers none of which—except for the examples that w… have noted in *Measure for Measure* and *Henry VII…* —are Christian.

A better response has come from poets. The movement we are discussing was heralded by John Masefield's Romanes Lecture and the first, and it is sti… the finest, published reaction to my reading of th… final plays, in *Myth and Miracle* and elsewhere, wa… T. S. Eliot's *Marina* (1930). In his essay "Music i… Shakespeare" W. H. Auden has discussed and developed the exposition of Shakespeare's music symbolism set out in *The Shakespearian Tempest.* Franci… Berry's *The Shakespeare Inset* (1965) surveys a majo… yet hitherto neglected element of Shakespeare's symbolic artistry.

From the first the new approach demanded wha… may be called a new "focal length"; and symbolisr… could not be high-lighted without a correspondin… shadowing of what had come to be known as "character" study. Nevertheless, A. C. Bradley's analys… of Shakespeare's personages remain for the mos… part unshaken, though on occasion he attempts t… render logical Shakespeare's dramatic and poeti… compressions by character enquiries which appea… within the new focus, irrelevant. Bradley may on occasion ask awkward questions regarding offstag… events where a final interpretation recognizes th… necessity of silence; but they are usually questior… which throw into relief problems which a sensitiv… actor of the role concerned does well, provisionall… to face.

The keynote of symbolic interpretation is the replacing of the moral by the metaphysical; and Bradley's approach, as in, especially, his first essay o… *King Lear,* has at least as much of the one as of th… other. I do not deny that my own first attacks o… "character" study inevitably involved certain elements in Bradley's work; but I was not thinking primarily of him, but of a whole century's commentary. That I regarded Bradley as a part-precursor c… my own labors is clear from my earliest, 1928, "manifesto," reprinted in *The Sovereign Flower.* Failur… to recognize his part in the story of Shakespearea… interpretation is a symptom of failure in understanding of the imaginative extensions that have complemented, without invalidating, his achievement.

In conclusion, the case for the study of Shakespeare's symbolism may be stated as follows: the isolation of plot, character, imagery, or philosoph… leads, in each instance, to distortion, if not error; bu… the study of symbolism, even its study in apparer… isolation, does not; for it is impossible to discus… these major symbols at all adequately without simu…

neously discussing the total drama. [The items alded to above include Max Plowman's "Money and e Merchant," *The Adelphi*, September, 1931; hn Middleton Murry's *Shakespeare*, 1936; and /. H. Auden's "Music in Shakespeare," *Shakeeare Criticism, 1935–1960*, Anne Ridler, ed., 1963. y own works are as follows: *The Wheel of Fire*, 30, enlarged 1949; *The Imperial Theme*, 1931, with new Preface 1951; *The Shakespearian Tempest*, 1932, with a new Preface 1953; *The Crown of Life*, 1946, incorporating *Myth and Miracle; The Sovereign Flower*, 1958, incorporating *The Olive and the Sword*, 1944; *The Christian Renaissance*, 1933, revised 1962, contains a chapter defining symbolism; *The Golden Labyrinth*, 1962; *Shakespearian Production*, 1964, an enlarged version of *Principles of Shakespearian Production*, 1936.]—G.W.K.

T

Tabourer. In *The Two Noble Kinsmen,* a drummer for the morris dance in the forest (III, v).

Tailor. In *The Taming of the Shrew,* a minor speaking role in IV, iii. To torment Katharina, Petruchio has the Tailor show her a fine gown but, calling it ugly, Petruchio refuses to let her have it.

Taine, Hippolyte Adolphe (1828–1893). French critic, philosopher, and historian. Born at Vouziers in Ardennes, Taine studied at Paris and became known with the publication in 1853 of his critical analysis of La Fontaine's *Fables.* In *Etudes sur les philosophes français du dix-neuvième siècle* (1857) Taine reveals his positivistic principles. His *Origines de la France contemporaine* (1875–1894), though it condemns the royalists, attacks the leaders of the Revolution and Napoleon. Taine is best known to the English-speaking world for his *Histoire de la littérature anglaise* (1863).

As a literary critic, Taine emphasizes the influence of "race, environment, and epoch" and views literary development as a dialectic in which one period gives way to its antithesis, an idea which he derived from Hegel. A fortunate concurrence of racial tendencies, environmental factors, and the spirit of an age produces great artistic achievement, as in the music of 18th-century Germany, the painting of 17th-century Holland and Flanders, and the poetry of 16th-century England. When Taine discusses Shakespeare in his history of English literature, he focuses attention on naturalistic characteristics. The Elizabethans, he argues, portrayed "genuine and primitive man beside himself, aflame, the slave of animal impulses, and the plaything of his dreams, entirely given up to the present moment, compacted of lusts, contradictions and follies."

Talbot, John (1388?–1453). See John Talbot, 1st earl of SHREWSBURY.

Talbot, John (1413?–1460). Son of John Talbot, 1st earl of Shrewsbury. Young Talbot was killed while fighting at Northampton for the Lancastrians. In *1 Henry VI,* this valiant youth is killed with his father while trying to take Bordeaux (IV, vii).

Tales from Shakespeare (1807). Prose narrative versions of Shakespeare's plays written for children by Mary and Charles LAMB. The *Tales* have long been a children's classic and have constituted for many generations of children their introduction to Shakespeare. There are 20 tales, the histories and romance plays being omitted. Mary Lamb wrote the comedies and her brother Charles wrote the tragedies. The method which the two authors used to construct the tales was to weave into the story as many as possible of Shakespeare's own words. The *Tales* have been translated into many languages. Their influence in Japan was such that they were first taken for Shakespeare's originals (see JAPAN).

Tamburlaine the Great (c. 1587). A tragedy two parts by Christopher MARLOWE. It was enter in the Stationers' Register in 1590 and publish the same year as "Tamburlaine the Great. Wh from a Scythian Shephearde by his rare and wo derfull Conquests became a most puissant a mightye Monarque. And (for his tyranny, a terrour in Warre) was tearmed, The Scourge God. Deuided into two Tragicall Discourses, as th were sundrie times shewed vpon Stages in the Citie London, By the right honorable the Lord Admyra his seruantes. Now first, and newlie published."

Tamburlaine is the story of the Scythian shephe the scourge of God (which God is never clea the "Rogue of Volga," come down from the hi of Samarcanda, armed with incredible physic strength, fierce looks, irresistible powers of spee to overwhelm the regions now known as the Midd East. *Tamburlaine,* with Edward Alleyn in the tit role, was immediately successful. Rivaled at the b office only by Thomas Kyd's *The Spanish Traged* *Tamburlaine* established Marlowe as the golden b of the London theatre.

Invulnerable to the power of mortal man, Tar burlaine holds the "Fates fast bound in ir chains . . . ." After he discards his shepherd's s for a coat of armor and a curtle ax, he tours t Levant, accompanied by barbarian hordes, wi signal success. He captures Zenocrate, daughter the Soldan of Egypt, defeats the armies of Pers overwhelms the Turks, whose emperor and empre Bajazeth and Zabina, he encages. Having no achieved earth's "perfect bliss and sole felicity / T sweet fruition of an earthly crown," Tamburlai begins to manifest signs of unfriendliness towa humankind. He feeds Bajazeth and Zabina wi scraps he tosses from his table; when it pleases hi he forces Bajazeth to serve as a footstool. Mea while, Tamburlaine has acquired an impressive c lection of tents—white, red, and black. When he la siege to a city, as he does to Damascus late in t first part, he pitches the white tents. While they a up the city can surrender without reprisal. Aft 24 hours, the color changes to red; the citizens this point may expect mercy, their governors nor On the third day, when the black tents go up, t point of no return has passed, and all are subject fire, sword, and rape.

Tamburlaine's triumph at Damascus breaks t wills of Bajazeth and Zabina. They split their sku against the bars of the cages in which they ha been brutally confined. Zenocrate, distressed at t ight of them, cheers up when she learns that her ather, who has fought for Damascus, has survived nd been pardoned. As the first part of the play nds, Tamburlaine crowns her queen of Persia and nnounces that their marriage will be solemnized t once.

The second part of *Tamburlaine* is anticlimactic, factitious sequel provoked by the popularity of he original. Having become conqueror of the vorld, little is left for Tamburlaine but to experience uffering. Much time has passed. Tamburlaine now as three sons; their mother, prematurely aged, is lead in the second act.

For the first time Tamburlaine, the dealer of a nillion deaths, feels death personally. His reaction s what one might expect:

> What, is she dead? Techelles, draw thy sword,
> And wound the earth, that it may cleave in
> twain . . . .

Anticipating Shakespeare's Northumberland when e learns of his son Hotspur's death ("Let heaven iss earth! now let not Nature's hand / Keep the vild flood confined! let order die!") and King Lear n the storm-tormented heath ("And thou, all-haking thunder, / Smite flat the thick rotundity o' he world! / Crack nature's moulds, all germens pill at once, / That make ingrateful man!"), Tam-urlaine, in a frenzy of egocentric protest and a elf-pitying sense of outrage, refuses to accept the act of death. He decrees that Zenocrate be "Em-alm'd with cassia, ambergris, and myrrh, / Not apt in lead, but in a sheet of gold . . . ." Her body vill be carried with him until he dies, when they hall share one epitaph. The city that saw her death e orders burnt to the ground, never to be rebuilt; statue of Zenocrate is set upon its ashes. Not until he last scene of *Romeo and Juliet*—with the golden tatues of the star-cross'd lovers—do we come across comparable example of materialistic fatuity.

Meanwhile, Callapine, son of Bajazeth, has escaped rom Tamburlaine's thraldom and mustered a host hat threatens the great man's security. Tamburlaine ttempts to instill in his sons his own zest for war y cutting his arm and requiring them to wash heir hands in his blood. Tamburlaine easily defeats Callapine, but has no satisfaction from the victory vhen he learns that his son Calyphas has lolled in is tent during the battle. Tamburlaine stabs the 'effeminate brat" and has him buried by Turkish oncubines who then for their pains are loosed to he soldiery.

The last act of Tamburlaine's blazing career is a aranoid orgy of atrocity that ends in death, prob-ably because Marlowe could see no future in the ubject. Tamburlaine harnesses the captive kings and viceroys to his chariot. "With bits in their nouths, reins in his left hand, and in his right hand whip with which he scourgeth them," Tambur-aine complains: "Holla, ye pamper'd jades of Asia! / What, can ye draw but twenty miles a-day . . . ?" He orders the governor of Babylon anged and shot for not surrendering his city on lemand. All Babylonian survivors are drowned. The Alcoran and all books of Mohammedan super-tition are burned, and in his penultimate expression of outrageous *hybris* Tamburlaine defies Mahomet to wreak vengeance on his head. Mahomet seems happy to oblige. Tamburlaine, as he plans a triumphal junket into Persia, finds himself "distemper'd suddenly . . . ." He calls for a map to see what there is left of the world for his sons to conquer (he envisions what is now known as the Suez Canal); he turns the management of his king-drawn chariot over to his son Amyras and, gazing upon the hearse of Zenocrate, speaks his final line: "For Tamburlaine, the scourge of God, must die." If Marlowe meant to suggest retributive justice by this ending, and he probably did, he kept the fact secret from his protagonist. Tamburlaine departs this life regretting only that his sons and friends will be deprived of his egotistical presence; he is convinced that he and Zenocrate, reunited, will be translated to a "higher throne"; then let the gods beware!

Many critics assume that Marlowe exerted a formative influence on Shakespeare, most clearly to be seen in the influence of *Tamburlaine* on *Richard III*. A. L. Rowse in *William Shakespeare* (1963), for example, writes, "Shakespeare's grand tribute to Marlowe was *Richard III*, a play so Marlovian in inspiration that one is inclined to think of it as written the year of his death—with him in mind." The likeness of the two plays can easily be overstated, as Rowse has done. The two tragedies are alike in their concentration upon character, attaining a unity that Shakespeare had not been able to compass in his *Henry VI* chronicle histories. Shakespeare may have achieved the monolithic nature of *Richard III* by imitating the structure of *Tamburlaine*. Richard, like Tamburlaine, seeks exceptional power, is deterred by no moral or religious scruples from attaining his ends. There the similarities end. Richard plots to reach a definite goal; Tamburlaine's aspiration is the essential element in human living. "Our souls," he explains, "still climbing after knowledge infinite, are always moving as the restless spheres." Richard III is never free from the dictates of Christian morality united with the Greek idea of *hybris*. Marlowe's spirit is a probing skepticism. Tamburlaine is no atheist, but the worshiper of a God of power and beauty. This conception he explains in a speech to Arcanes:

> he that sits on high and never sleeps,
> Nor in one place is circumscriptible,
> But everywhere fills every continent
> With strange infusion of his sacred vigor.

Beauty is also an attribute of this God, and Zenocrate, as the symbol of beauty, converts the bloody conqueror into a lover and produces a conflict in him between love and honor. There is absolutely nothing of this romantic identification of beauty and love in Richard's cynical relationship with women; with Anne for example. Nor is there any tribute to beauty or consciousness of its power faintly suggestive of Marlowe's lyrical incantation of beauty in the famous passage beginning, "What is beauty, saith my sufferings then?" Marlowe here overreaches the finest passages of eloquence in *Richard III* as his mighty line surpasses in its dynamic power and grandeur any verse imitative of Marlowe's in *Richard III*.—G. W. M.

Taming of A Shrew, The. See TAMING OF THE SHREW: *Sources*.

The Taming of the Shrew.

Taming of the Shrew, The. An early comedy by Shakespeare.

Text. The only authoritative text is that of the First Folio (1623), derived from a manuscript which probably served as the players' PROMPT-BOOK. The textual problem is complicated by the difficulty in determining the relationship between this play and an anonymous play, *The Taming of A Shrew* ("A Pleasant Conceited Historie, called the Taming of a Shrew. As it was sundry times acted by the Right honorable the Earle of Pembrook his seruants. Printed at London by Peter Short and are to be sold by Cutbert Burbie, at his shop at the Royall Exchange. 1594"), published in 1594 and reprinted in 1596 and 1607.

For many years *The Taming of A Shrew* was regarded as the direct source of Shakespeare's play. Recently, however, a majority of scholars have come to believe that the anonymous play is merely a BAD QUARTO either of *The Taming of the Shrew*, or of an earlier play from which both *The Taming of A Shrew* and Shakespeare's play derive. There is, however, no evidence of an earlier play. Its existence has been assumed because the divergences between the two extant plays are much wider than those between a bad quarto of any other play and its Folio version (see below in the discussion of *Sources*). On the other hand, those scholars, like Peter Alexander, who deny the existence of an older play and argue that *A Shrew* is a bad quarto of *The Shrew* invoke the principle that the existence of an entity should not be assumed where it is not needed. The publishers of the First Folio apparently regarded *A Shrew* as a previously published version of *The Shrew*, for they failed to include the latter in their entries of previously unpublished plays in the Stationers' Register.

A related problem centers on the authorship of *The Taming of the Shrew*. Many scholars, among them T. M. Parrott and E. K. Chambers, have argued that the play is not entirely Shakespeare's and have generally assigned the rather insipid subplot of Bianca and her suitors to an anonymous collaborator. Among the candidates suggested as collaborators have been Thomas Lodge, Robert Greene, and George Chapman. More recent scholarship, however, has come to regard the play as entirely Shakespeare's.

Date. The play is not mentioned by Francis Meres in his *Palladis Tamia* in 1598 (unless it be the play that he calls *Love's Labour's Won*), but it is generally regarded as being much earlier. Henslowe's diary records a performance of "the tamynge of A shrowe" in June of 1594, during which time Shakespeare's company (the Lord Chamberlain's Men) was playing at Henslowe's theatre in Newington Butts. It seems likely therefore that the play referred to here (despite the designation "A shrowe") is Shakespeare's farce and not the anonymous play, which belonged to the earl of Pembroke's company. If this supposition is correct, the play can be dated sometime around 1593, although many feel that this is a revision of a still earlier version written before 1590.

Sources. Whether *The Taming of A Shrew* is the source or merely a corrupt version of Shakespeare's play, it presents some interesting parallels to *The Taming of the Shrew*. Both plays feature an Induction in which the story of Christopher Sly is recounted, although Shakespeare's account is almost twice the length of that in *A Shrew*. This Induction is a truncated dramatization of another widely spread story. It is most easily available to an English reader in a tale from *The Arabian Nights* called "The Sleeper Awakes," but the story is essentially the same in all its versions: some gentlemen out hunting come upon a peasant or an artisan lying dead drunk before an alehouse. They carry him to the castle of one of them and dress him in fine clothes. When he awakes they convince him that he is really the gentleman he seems to be. In Shakespeare's play the victim, Christopher Sly, disappears long before the first act is finished. But in *A Shrew* he remains to the end, interrupting the actors with ridiculous comments. This comedy is provided with an epilogue in which Sly, again in a drunken stupor, is carried back to the refuse heap from which he was picked up. When he awakens there, he realizes that his dream has been instructive, for it has inspired him with the courage to adopt Petruchio's method of taming a shrewish wife. The absence of this ironically appropriate ending in *The Taming of the Shrew* can best be explained by assuming that the manuscript on which the Folio text was based lacked a few of its final pages.

Whatever the relationship of *A Shrew* to *The Shrew*, it is clear that Shakespeare's play provides a verve and gusto, as well as a richness of characterization, which is only hinted at in the anonymous play. Scholars who view the latter as merely a bad quarto of *The Shrew* have looked elsewhere to find Shakespeare's source. The taming of a shrewish wife was a theme widely current in the folklore of both East and West, and in literary form as well. Richard Hosley argues that the major source of the play is a popular ballad called *Her egynneth a Merry Jest of a Shrewde and Curste Vyfe, Lapped in Morrelles Skin, for her Good ehaviour* (c. 1550). The ballad recounts a "tam-ıg" in which the shrew is severely beaten, then 'rapped in the skin of a dead horse, Morel. Though ıe details of the action are considerably more :ude and barbaric than in Shakespeare's play, the asic plot is the same. Hosley further argues that ıe more humane elements in the play derive from "colloquy" by Erasmus, translated into English in 557, "A Mery Dialogue, Declaringe the Prop-:tyes of Shrowde Shrewes and Honest Wyves." 'his colloquy contains an *exemplum* (an anecdote 'ith a moral)—said to be based on the early married fe of Sir Thomas More—in which the "taming" of ıe wife is achieved without the use of physical ɔrce.

The subplot of *The Taming of the Shrew* derives om George Gascoigne's *Supposes* (1566), a classi-ıl comedy of intrigue. Gascoigne's play was in ırn a translation of Ariosto's *I Suppositi* (1509). *upposes* may have suggested to Shakespeare the alian setting of his comedy.—O. J. C.

Plot Synopsis. Induction. Christopher Sly, a ınker, is found in a drunken stupor on a heath by lord returning from a hunt with several re-ıiners. As a joke the lord has Sly taken to his house, laced in a sumptuous chamber, and dressed in ɔstly garments. When Sly awakens, he is told that : is a noble gentleman who has been touched by ınacy and has been asleep for 15 years. Sly at first ısists that he is "by birth a pedlar, by education a ırd-maker, by transmutation a bear-herd, and now y present profession a tinker," but he eventually lows himself to be convinced that he is indeed a reat personage and married to a lovely lady (who actually the lord's page in disguise). Meanwhile, ıe lord has engaged a troupe of players, who resent a "pleasant comedy" to help banish the ınker's malady.

Act. I. Lucentio, the son of Vincentio, a wealthy isan merchant, has arrived in Padua, where he plans ɔ dedicate himself to study, though his servant ranio hopes that his devotion to Aristotle will not ıuse him to neglect Ovid. The young men listen Baptista, a rich Paduan gentleman, announces ıat his daughter Bianca will remain unmarried and ɔnfined to her home until her older sister, Katha-ına, is wed. Dismayed by Baptista's decision, ianca's suitors, Gremio and Hortensio, agree to ɔrget their rivalry long enough to find a husband ɔr Katharina—a task of no mean proportions, for ıe is a "fiend of hell" whose shrewish ways have riven off prospective mates. Lucentio, meanwhile, as fallen in love with Bianca and decides to gain dmittance to her house by posing as a tutor, since aptista has expressed the desire to have his daugh-rs receive instruction in music and poetry. Tranio, n the other hand, is to take the place of Lucentio. nother newcomer to Padua is Petruchio, a pros-:rous Veronese, who informs Hortensio that he seeking a rich wife. Hortensio tells him about atharina's wealth and beauty, warning him, how-'er, that she is "renown'd in Padua for her scold-ıg tongue." Petruchio at once determines to have :r, regardless of her fiery temper. "Think you a ttle din can daunt mine ears?" he asks. "Have I not in my time heard lions roar?" Gremio and Hortensio agree to share the expenses of Petruchio's courtship, but each presses his campaign for Bianca. Hortensio asks Petruchio to introduce him into Baptista's house as a music teacher, while Gremio promises to recommend the services of the disguised Lucentio, who, in return, is to encourage the old man's suit. Tranio, dressed as Lucentio, also declares himself a candidate for Bianca's hand.

Act II. Arriving at Baptista's house in the company of Hortensio and the others, Petruchio states that he is anxious to meet Katharina, of whose beauty, wit, and amiability he has heard so much. He also presents Hortensio as the music teacher Licio, and Lucentio is introduced by Gremio as a young scholar called Cambio. Petruchio assures Baptista that he will win Katharina's love and that he is "as peremptory as she is proud-minded." He is not even cowed by the fact that Katharina responds to the music teacher's instruction by breaking his lute over his head. Ignoring her blows and her protests, he announces that they will be wed on Sunday. Gremio and Tranio, who still pretends to be Lucentio, then vie for Bianca's hand by boasting of the riches that they can give her. Baptista prefers Tranio's offer, but insists that his father, Vincentio, guarantee the settlement.

Act III. Under the jealous eye of Hortensio, Lucentio, in the guise of the tutor Cambio, reveals his true identity to Bianca, as well as his love for her, during a Latin lesson. On Sunday, Petruchio keeps the wedding party waiting. He finally arrives dressed in shabby clothes and riding a sway-backed nag and refuses to change into more suitable attire. During the ceremony he behaves like a madman, knocking the priest down and tossing wine in the sexton's face. Afterwards he will not stay for the wedding feast but whisks Katharina away as if he were rescuing her from thieves.

Act IV. Grumio, Petruchio's attendant, arrives at his master's country house to warn Curtis and the other servants that the newlyweds are on their way. According to Grumio, the trip from Padua was full of misadventures: Katharina's horse stumbled, Petruchio beat Grumio with such fury that Katharina had to wade through the mud to restrain him, and then both horses ran away. On their arrival, Petruchio finds fault with all his servants, declares that the supper is burnt, and dashes the food to the floor while Katharina urges him to be patient. There is, however, a reason behind Petruchio's apparent lunacy: like the falconer, he must tame his wild bird and "make her come and know her keeper's call."

In Padua, Hortensio and Tranio witness a tender scene between Bianca and Lucentio. Hortensio, realizing that Bianca loves her tutor, decides to settle for a wealthy widow who dotes on him. Biondello, another of Lucentio's servants, reports that he has found a Mantuan pedant who resembles Vincentio. He and Tranio tell the gullible pedant that the Duke of Padua has decreed the death penalty for Mantuans who enter his territories and offer to protect him if he will pose as Lucentio's father.

Katharina, meanwhile, has not been permitted to eat or sleep for days. When a tailor and a haberdasher arrive with new clothes for her, Petruchio declares that nothing is satisfactory and soothes her by declaring that "'tis the mind that makes the body rich." During the return trip to Padua he comments on the moonlight and when Katharina points out that it is the sun that is shining, he retorts that if he is crossed, he shall go back. She decides to submit: "What you will have it named, even that it is; / And so it shall be so for Katharine." Meeting an old man on the road, Petruchio addresses him as a young girl and Katharina immediately concurs, only to be contradicted by her husband. The man turns out to be Vincentio, who is on his way to Padua to pay a surprise visit to Lucentio.

Act V. Petruchio, Katharina, and Vincentio arrive at Baptista's house to find the pedant there claiming to be Lucentio's father. Vincentio, learning that Tranio is passing himself off as his son, assumes that the former has murdered his master; but, before he can give away the deception, he is himself arrested on the orders of Tranio and Baptista. The confusion is cleared up by the appearance of Bianca and Lucentio, who have just been secretly married.

At the banquet that follows, Petruchio wagers 100 crowns with Lucentio and Hortensio, who has married the widow, that his wife is more obedient than theirs. Bianca and the widow refuse to heed their husbands' summons, but the docile Katharina comes at once. At Petruchio's bidding, she instructs the other wives on their conjugal obligations, asserting that "Such duty as the subject owes the prince / Even such a woman oweth to her husband."—H. D.

Comment. This play often has been thought to be the mysterious *Love's Labour's Won,* mentioned in Meres' list in his PALLADIS TAMIA. Petruchio's wooing, unlike that of other lovers in Shakespeare's comedies, involves a lot of physical labor. Like *The Comedy of Errors,* this play is crowded with action, much of it sheer physical farce. It is full of slapstick and rant. Yet the poet contrives to give the farcical goings-on some human significance. Petruchio is made to play his part with so much amused gusto that he easily becomes the hero of his own created farce. Much of his raving and storming is showing off for Katharina's benefit. Although his methods of taming are harsh and violent, he talks to her in an ironically restrained fashion that never insults the proud, ardent girl that she is. The author makes it clear that her violence is a natural explosion of jealousy of her sister's power to attract suitors, while she only repels them. Her trouncing of the mealy-mouthed Bianca to force her to tell which of her suitors she likes best betrays her lively interest in men. Katharina resents also her father's obvious preference for Bianca. She crows, "*She* is your treasure, *she* must have a husband" (II, i, 32). Beneath the cloak of her violence Katharina is as eager for a mate as most of Shakespeare's marriageable girls. After Petruchio has won her love, she becomes submissive not only to him, but also to the love she has always secretly craved. When, near the end of the play, she is ashamed to kiss in public, Petruchio says, "Why, then let's home again," and she answers, "Nay, I will give thee a kiss: now pray thee, love, stay" (V, i, 153).

As poetry *The Taming of the Shrew* is one of Shakespeare's least distinguished plays. Nevertheless, it has been one of his most successful on the stage.—O. J. C.

Stage History: England. The first recorded performance of the comedy is that noted in Philip Henslowe's diary as given in June 1594 by the Lord Chamberlain's Servants at Newington Butts. According to the records of Sir Henry Herbert, Master of the Revels, *The Taming of the Shrew* was acted on November 26, 1633 at St. James' palace before the king and queen, and there is further reference to a revival in Herbert's accounts for 1663/4.

In 1667 John LACY, the low comedian of the King's Company, made an adaptation of the play called *Sauny the Scot.* Sauny, a substitute for Grumio, was acted by Lacy and was made the chief character in the comedy. He spoke the dialect of a North Countryman which Samuel Pepys complained he could not understand at all. The farce is largely written in prose with, as G. C. D. Odell points out, "phrases from Shakespeare glancing shyly out of the enveloping Scotch mist." The scene is London and most of the characters have been given English names. Lacy cut out the Induction and mangled and vulgarized the work. For example, he introduced a bedroom scene in which Sauny starts to undress Margaret (Katharina). On January 24, 1716 Christopher Bullock's farce *The Cobler of Preston,* an amplification of Shakespeare's Christopher Sly episode, was produced at Lincoln's Inn Fields. Ten days later, Charles Johnson's identically titled elaboration of the Induction was presented at Drury Lane. In his Preface, Bullock boasts that, getting wind of Johnson's "entertainment," he wrote his play in two days and got it staged in three. In spite of this hurry, Bullock's is the funnier of the two works. One reason for the comparative dullness of Johnson's farce is that he dragged in current politics. A century later, the politics were removed and a love story added to a revision of Johnson's *Cobler* which was set to music and acted at Drury Lane on September 29, 1817. Its minor success was attributable to Joseph Munden's exceedingly droll Sly. Meanwhile, *Sauny the Scot* was very popular, and by the time it was printed in 1698, Bullock was appearing as Sauny; George Powell playing Petruchio; Susanna Verbruggen, the Shrew; and Susannah Cibber, Bianca. A ballad farce by "J. Worsdale, Portrait Painter," based on Lacy's adaptation and titled *A Cure for a Scold,* was acted on February 25, 1735 at Drury Lane. Sauny, renamed Archer, is refined and anglicized, his part greatly reduced. Salway took this role; Charles Macklin played Manley (Petruchio); Kitty Clive was Peg (Katharina); and Hannah Pritchard, Flora (Bianca). The work was seen again in 1750, but both it and the often revived *Sauny the Scot* were banished when *Catherine and Petruchio,* David Garrick's abbreviated alteration of *The Taming of the Shrew,* appeared at Drury Lane. On March 18, 1754, at her benefit, Mrs Pritchard acted Catherine in this version; in 1756 Mrs. Clive was the heroine. Harry Woodward acted Petruchio in both presentations and Richard Yates played Grumio. Garrick eliminated the Induction material, the wooing of Bianca, and the character of Gremio. His condensation in three acts enjoyed great popularity as an afterpiece and held the stage until late in the 19th century. John Philip Kemble presented this version, Frederick Reynolds used the abridgment for his opera *The Taming of the Shrew*, presented at Drury Lane in 1828, and William Charles Macready also retained Garrick's play while managing at Covent Garden and Drury Lane.

On March 16, 1844 Shakespeare's comedy was restored and acted in its entirety for what was probably the first time since before the closing of the theatres. The revival, undertaken by Benjamin Webster, who was then managing the Haymarket, was staged amazingly by J. R. Planché in an approximation of the Elizabethan manner without scenery and spectacle; two screens and a pair of curtains constituted the entire dramatic apparatus, while placards denoted scene changes. A drop scene represented a view of London, including a reproduction of the Globe theatre. Webster acted Petrucio (his spelling), and Ada Nisbett, Katharina. This admirable production was repeated in 1847, with the first Sly and Grumio, Strickland and John Buckstone, being replaced by Edward Lambert and Robert Keeley. When Samuel Phelps also selected the original for his revival on November 15, 1856, at Sadler's Wells, he played Christopher Sly with great success. Occasionally he reverted to the still popular *Catherine and Petruchio* (Kemble preferred this spelling), and *The Taming of the Shrew* awaited public favor in London until Augustin Daly presented his superb American production at the Gaiety Theatre on May 29, 1888. Despite disconcerting and unnecessary scene transpositions which sometimes had the effect of cramping the action, Daly's tastefully staged revival was an immediate success, owing much to the magnificent portrayal of Katharina by Ada Rehan. This production had previously replaced *Catherine and Petruchio*, which had been continuously on the American stage since Lewis Hallam the younger acted the hero at the John Street Theatre in 1768 opposite Margaret Cheer. Daly had presented it for the first time on January 18, 1887, at Daly's Theatre in New York. John Drew appeared then and in the London performance opposite Miss Rehan. In 1893 the play was chosen to open the new Daly's Theatre in London on March 12 and Miss Rehan again gave her impersonation of Katharina, still remembered as one of the greatest Shakespearean representations, this time with George Clarke as Petruchio.

Since then, the play has been produced regularly. Frank Benson offered Stratford-upon-Avon's first *Taming of the Shrew* in 1893 and, from 1896 to the spring of 1917 when he presented cut versions of *Richard III* and the comedy on one bill, he staged 14 productions of the play at the Memorial Theatre at Stratford. Benson and his wife Constance acted the leads at Stratford, yielding to a guest performance by Arthur Bourchier and Violet Vanbrugh during the festival's 1912 spring season. The Bensons appeared as the principals at the Comedy Theatre in 1901 and for Beerbohm Tree's sixth and seventh annual Shakespeare festivals at His Majesty's in 1910 and 1911. Two other Petruchios appeared in the West End during this time. Oscar Asche, larger than life at the Adelphi, doubled as the hero and Sly, giving performances there in 1904, 1906, and 1908, and at the Apollo in 1916. His furious Katharina was played by his wife, Lily Brayton, in every production. Sly was a permanent fixture in Martin Harvey's presentations at the Prince of Wales' Theatre in 1913 and His Majesty's in 1916. Seated in the orchestra with his back to the audience throughout the play, he was played first by Charles Glenney, who proved a better drunken tinker than his successor, Rutland Barrington. The Katharina to Harvey's Petruchio was Nina de Silva in both presentations, for which a single set, a stylized picture of a 15th-century summerhouse with a garden background, was devised.

The Oxford University Dramatic Society acted the play in February 1907, and the Birmingham Repertory company presented it in June 1918. There were productions at the Old Vic every season from 1914 through 1921, the first by Matheson Lang and Hutin Britton, three under Ben Greet, one directed by George Foss, another by Russell Thorndike and Charles Warburton, and finally one under Robert Atkins, who staged the comedy a second time for the 1922/3 season and again with the Old Vic company at the New Oxford, when George Hayes and Florence Saunders acted Petruchio and Katharina.

The Taming of the Shrew was included in the basic repertory of the touring companies headed by Edward Dunston, Charles Doran, and Henry Baynton. Early in 1922 Baynton arrived at the Savoy for matinee performances of his repertory, which included his powerful Petruchio. That spring Laurence Olivier made his first stage appearance in a presentation of the comedy at Stratford given by the boys of All Saints Choir School. His part was Katharina. In 1925 and 1927, Andrew Leigh had gifted shrews for his Old Vic productions. The first Katharina, Edith Evans, so realistically simulated the pangs of hunger that one observer claimed the candy vendors took shelter "as at the approach of a rapacious army." Her Petruchio, the seasoned Baliol Holloway, always held his audience. The second of Leigh's female interpreters of the fiery heroine was Sybil Thorndike, who acted opposite Lewis Casson at the Lyric Theatre at Hammersmith while the Old Vic Theatre was in the process of rebuilding. Another notable actress, Dorothy Green, renowned for her Lady Macbeth and Cleopatra, portrayed Katharina at the Apollo in 1926 opposite Robert Loraine.

The farce was happily adapted to modern dress for Barry Jackson when he staged it at the Court Theatre in 1928 for producer H. K. Ayliff. A dilapidated Ford replaced the donkey for the journey to Padua; Scott Sunderland was Petruchio and Eileen Beldon, Katharina. Frank Pettingell as Sly sat in a box throughout the night with his attendant Lord, Laurence Olivier, and Ralph Richardson appeared in the role of Tranio. When Harcourt Williams directed the play at the Old Vic in 1931, Richardson was promoted to Petruchio, playing opposite Phyllis Thomas. Stratford under W. Bridges-Adams gave the comedy almost every year or two from 1920 through 1933, when Anew McMaster and Madge Compton appeared as the principals. In 1936 B. Iden Payne produced the play for the Memorial Theatre with Donald Wolfit, who like Olivier made his first stage appearance in *The Taming of the Shrew.* Edith Evans was less successful than originally with Katharina when she re-created the role at the New Theatre in 1937 for Claude Gurney's production, costarring Leslie Banks. Although in the early stormings Miss Evans surpassed herself, her voice could not sustain the strain. Arthur Sinclair, when not doubling as Pedant, watched the proceedings from bed as Sly. Alec Clunes and Elspeth Duxbury were Lucentio and Bianca. The Vic presented Maurice Evans and Cathleen Nesbitt in 1935 and, in 1939, Tyrone Guthrie dressed his Petruchio, Roger Livesey, in red, white, and blue corsets at his marriage to Katharina, Ursula Jeans. That year saw another innovator, Theodore Komisarjevsky, undertake the comedy for Stratford, with Alec Clunes, Vivienne Bennett, and Jay Laurier, the Petruchio, Katharina, and Sly.

Wolfit re-created Petruchio in his own productions for repertory seasons in 1940 at the Kingsway Theatre, with Rosalinde Fuller, and in 1953 at the King's Theatre at Hammersmith, with Rosalind Iden. The farce was acted in four separate Open Air Theatre revivals. In 1941 Patrick Kinsella and Claire Luce starred, while Russell Thorndike essayed Sly. The next year, George Street and Mary Martlew were the Park's Petruchio and Katharina and, in 1950, Antony Eustrel and Ruth Lodge took the leads. Leslie French directed and acted Grumio, a role he had taken at the Old Vic in 1931, for the theatre's last *Taming of the Shrew* in June 1958, which had Bernard Brown and Cecilia Sonnenberg as the hero and heroine, while Robert Atkins played Baptista. B. Iden Payne staged the farce in three consecutive seasons at Stratford, beginning in 1940. For the second of these productions Baliol Holloway tamed Freda Jackson, 16 years after he had performed the same service for Edith Evans. Atkins produced still another *Shrew,* this one at Stratford with Antony Eustrel and Patricia Jessel in 1944. In 1947 the Old Vic company brought the comedy to the New Theatre under the auspices of John Burrell, whose Petruchio, the handsome Trevor Howard, quietly endangered Patricia Burke, while Bernard Miles, a cherubic drunk, looked on. Denis Carey produced the next Old Vic presentation in 1954 with Paul Rogers and Ann Todd and, the following year, an Old Vic company toured Australia with the *Shrew* in its repertory.

Stratford-upon-Avon saw Michael Benthall's production in 1948, with Anthony Quayle and Diana Wynyard. George Devine directed the play in 1953 and 1954, first with Marius Goring and Yvonne Mitchell, then with Keith Michell and Barbara Jefford. John Barton directed a production in 1960 with Peter O'Toole and Peggy Ashcroft as Petruchio and Katharina, Jack MacGowran as Sly, and Patrick Wymark as Grumio. This production was redirected by Maurice Daniels before its improved presentation at the Aldwych in September 1961. The cast changes included a new hero, Derek Godfrey, and a Katharina, to some reminiscent of Ada Rehan, Vanessa Redgrave. This last treatment was transferred intact to Stratford for the following season.

Stage History: America. Shakespeare's *Shrew* was never acted on the American stage until Augustin Daly produced it late in the 19th century. Befo that, Garrick's adaptation, *Catherine and Petruchi* invariably replaced the original from its first Amer can enactment on November 21, 1766 at the Sout wark in Philadelphia. In it Margaret Cheer made h theatrical debut as the heroine with Lewis Hallar the younger, as Petruchio. The following April th condensed variant made its initial New York appea ance with the Philadelphia cast and thereafter almo every prominent actor and actress played the leadin characters in the comedy.

Daly's brilliantly staged production of the origin text gained immediate success and ran for 137 co secutive performances from the opening on Januar 18, 1887. The acting version used naturally delete all coarse language and much of the first act cor versation between Lucentio and Tranio, but the I duction, never before acted in America in any forn was included. Ada Rehan portrayed a Katharir whose shrewishness was only skin deep, but her v rago could be menacing, sullen, and savage, meltin at the end into ideally sweet feminine tendernes Her first Petruchio, John Drew, personified charn ing virility and boisterousness without brutality. I later revivals, during the last decade of the centur one of the best Petruchios, George Clarke, playe the hero opposite Miss Rehan, investing the cha acter with shrewdness, staunch resolve, and often gentle humor. Charles Richman and Otis Skinne succeeded to the role after Daly's death.

The Induction was eliminated once again in 190 when E. H. Sothern and Julia Marlowe produce the comedy, first in Cleveland and later at th Knickerbocker in New York on October 16. Usin an unskillfully condensed text, they acted *The Shre* in the broadest farcical spirit possible and althoug their production was handsome, their performanc left much to be desired. Miss Marlowe presented wicked and witty Katharina, "a lovely fish-wife. Her interpretation, one of unabated fire and forc never hinted at the gentler nature beneath an Sothern's Petruchio evaporated in noisy fuming an bluster.

Margaret Anglin's revival, seen in San Francisco i 1913, was noted chiefly for its strict adherence to th original text, and while there were some cuts, onl Shakespeare's language was used. However, by th time this production reached New York's Hudson i March 1914, the Induction, initially included, wa abandoned and the scenically bland production wa slow and colorless. Miss Anglin, costarring with Er Blind, gave a completely lackluster performance a Katharina. The once fiery she-devil became a sulle ladylike grouch—a mere frump—and her Petruchi was equally commonplace. The supporting cast in cluded Sidney Greenstreet, whose performance a Biondello was, according to one critic, "a gross car cature of humanity" that "would have disgraced th callowest amateur."

In 1925 H. K. Ayliff's modern-dress version ap peared at the Garrick with Mary Ellis and Bas Sydney in the title roles and an enormously funn Curtis played by Maria Ouspenskaya. *The Shre* was also acted by Fritz Leiber's Chicago repertor during the 1929/30 season, and in 1933 the Shake speare Theatre Company gave 15 performances in a undistinguished production of the comedy.

Probably the most notable presentation of the play in this century was given at the Guild in September 1935 starring Alfred Lunt and Lynn Fontanne under the direction of Harry Wagstaff Gribble. The comedy was low; the horseplay, superb; and both the explosive Kate and her domineering Petruchio captured to perfection the spirit of comic irreverence. P. Thomas Gomez was featured as Grumio, and Sidney Greenstreet's amusing portrayal of a corpulent Baptista humorously communicated the distracted parent's hopefulness and fearfulness. The production ran for 129 performances and was revived at the Alvin five years later when Herbert Hoover attended with the first-night audience on February 5.

In 1951 a shrill, slapstick production under Margaret Webster bowed at the New York City Center with a fierce and fiery Claire Luce and a roaring, strutting Ralph Clanton. Critics called it "*Kiss Me Kate* without music" with everyone reaching strenuously for laughs.

The *Shrews* that followed represented improvements. The Stratford Shakespearean Festival in Canada gave two productions: one in 1954 directed by Tyrone Guthrie and presented in a style reminiscent of the American Southwest and another in 1962 by Michael Langham. The later presentation, decorative and antic, employed much inventive stage business and its excellent cast (Kate Reid as the heroine, William Needles as Gremio, and Peter Donat as Hortensio) included an outstanding Petruchio, the handsomely persuasive John Colicos. In 1956 the American Shakespeare Festival in Connecticut presented the comedy under Norman Lloyd's direction and one of the latest productions in New York was given by the Phoenix Company at the Phyllis Anderson Theatre in 1963. Nan Martin, a brawling, willful Katharina, managed to elicit sympathy from the outset in this visually beautiful presentment which saw her at the last radiantly loving toward the madcap ruffian of Robert Gerringer.—M.G.

Bibliography. TEXT: *The Taming of the Shrew*, New Cambridge Edition, Arthur Quiller-Couch and J. Dover Wilson, eds., 1928; R. Houk, "The Evolution of *The Taming of the Shrew*," *PMLA*, LVII, 1942; Hardin Craig, "*The Shrew* and *A Shrew*," *Elizabethan Studies in Honor of George F. Reynolds*, 1945; Karl Wentersdorf, "The Authenticity of *The Taming of the Shrew*," *Shakespeare Quarterly*, V, 1954; Peter Alexander, "A Case of Three Sisters," *The Times Literary Supplement*, July 8, 1965. DATE: James G. McManaway, "Recent Studies in Shakespeare's Chronology," *Shakespeare Survey* 3, 1950. SOURCES: Geoffrey Bullough, *Narrative and Dramatic Sources of Shakespeare*, I, 1957; Richard Hosley, "Sources and Analogues of *The Taming of the Shrew*," *Huntington Library Quarterly*, 27, 1964. COMMENT: H. B. Charlton, *Shakespearian Comedy*, 1938. STAGE HISTORY: New Cambridge Edition; T. Allston Brown, *A History of the New York Stage . . . to 1901*, 1903; William Winter, *Shakespeare on the Stage*, 3 vols., 1911–1916; G. C. D. Odell, *Shakespeare from Betterton to Irving*, 1920; J. C. Trewin, *Shakespeare on the English Stage, 1900–1964*, 1964.

Selected Criticism

BARRETT WENDELL. Altogether, the more one considers this perennially amusing play, the less substantial one finds it; after all, it proves to be only a hack-made farce. It is a good farce, however; though fun is the most evanescent trait of any literary period, it is lastingly funny; and, considering that in all likelihood it proceeds from at least three distinct hands, it has surprising unity of diverting effect. Such unity of effect can hardly be accidental. There is no reason for not attributing it to the practised and skilful hand of Shakspere, revising and completing the cruder work of others. [*William Shakspere, A Study in Elizabethan Literature*, 1894.]

GEORGE BERNARD SHAW. The Taming of the Shrew is a remarkable example of Shakespear's repeated attempts to make the public accept realistic comedy. Petruchio is worth fifty Orlandos as a human study. The preliminary scenes in which he shews his character by pricking up his ears at the news that there is a fortune to be got by any man who will take an ugly and ill-tempered woman off her father's hands, and hurrying off to strike the bargain before somebody else picks it up, are not romantic; but they give an honest and masterly picture of a real man, whose like we have all met. The actual taming of the woman by the methods used in taming wild beasts belongs to his determination to make himself rich and comfortable, and his perfect freedom from all delicacy in using his strength and opportunities for that purpose. The process is quite bearable, because the selfishness of the man is healthily goodhumored and untainted by wanton cruelty, and it is good for the shrew to encounter a force like that and be brought to her senses. Unfortunately, Shakespear's own immaturity, as well as the immaturity of the art he was experimenting in, made it impossible for him to keep the play on the realistic plane to the end; and the last scene is altogether disgusting to modern sensibility. No man with any decency of feeling can sit it out in the company of a woman without being extremely ashamed of the lord-of-creation moral implied in the wager and the speech put into the woman's own mouth. Therefore the play, though still worthy of a complete and efficient representation, would need, even at that, some apology. But the Garrick version of it, as a farcical afterpiece!—thank you: no. [Article in the *Saturday Review*, November 6, 1897.]

FRANK HARRIS. The women characters in *The Taming of the Shrew* hardly deserve consideration. Neither Katharina nor Bianca is worthy to be called a woman's portrait; we only know a trait or two of them, and the widow is not even outlined. But the play itself has another and deeper interest for us as throwing light on Shakespeare's life and character. In spite of the enormous success it has had on the stage and the fact that it has held its place in popular liking even to our time, it is a wretchedly poor farce, and the theme is utterly unworthy of the master. Some of the play does not read like him; but his hand is quite plainly revealed in the scenes between Katharina and Petruchio; in fact the taming of the shrew is his. One cannot but wonder why Shakespeare ever put hand to such a paltry subject. The answer comes pat to those who believe that he himself had been married unhappily to a jealous, ill-tempered scold. Marriage had been a defeat to him: he could not but see that; in this play he will comfort his pride by showing how even a shrew can be mastered; how violence can be subdued by violence. The moment one looks at the play from this point of view, its sub-conscious purpose becomes clear to one and its faults are all explained. [*The Women of Shakespeare*, 1911.]

THOMAS MARC PARROTT. It is in this combat, this clash of wills, that the true dramatic value of *The Shrew* consists. In the hands of a modern dramatist it might easily have reached a tragic conclusion. But Shakespeare was no Ibsen; it was probably a psychical impossibility for him to conceive a Kate turning her back on her husband and slamming the door after her as she goes out into the world. For him to have entertained such a conception would have been to break with a medieval convention of long standing. We have already seen how Noah and his sons use physical force to get his recalcitrant wife into the Ark; and Tom Tyler calls in a friend to beat his shrewish wife into temporary submission. In a rude ballad, A Merry Jest of a Shrewd and Curst Wife, extant in Shakespeare's youth, the shrew is not only well beaten, but finally wrapped in the salted hide of an old horse. It is to the credit of the author of *A Shrew* that he disdains this sort of merry jest; Ferando never lays a hand on Kate; no more does Petruchio, though once he threatens jestingly to return the blow she gives him with a counterbuff. Shakespeare, who knew all about hawks, knew better than to make Petruchio try to tame his haggard by the use of force; his explosions of violence are wordy rather than physical, directed at others rather than at Kate, and they are, in effect, comic exaggerations of her own fierce insistence upon her will. Kate is keen-sighted enough to see the absurdity of her husband's behavior and, when at last she comes to recognize it as a fantastic distortion of her own, she is ready to renounce the role of a virago and assume that of an obedient and loving wife. [*Shakespearean Comedy*, 1949.]

JOHN RUSSELL BROWN. Great payment only results in great payment—Nature's bounteous largess is cherished only 'in *bounty*'—and Petruchio does not merely receive; he and Kate exchange kisses, and find contentment in mutual generosity. Adriana saw only one side of the contract of love and it seemed monstrous and unfair; Katharina's speech on the duty of wives and the paying of 'tribute' is joyful and elated because, in some mysterious way, she has confidence in Petruchio's love and in his willingness to give away his loan of Nature's bounty. There is no doubt at the end of *The Shrew* that he or she who gives most, not in the terms of commercial wealth but in terms of the contract of love, must inevitably get most. To present the happiness of this contract in lively dramatic terms is the great achievement of *The Shrew*. It is sometimes called a brutal and degrading play, but this could only be true if Katharina's submission had been abject, or if Petruchio, in triumph, had put his foot upon her hand; what happens, in fact, is that Petruchio and Katharina exchange kisses and her speech is confident and joyful, the most sustained and spirited speech in the whole play. Viewed against Shakespeare's ideal of love's wealth, this comedy presents, in its own gay, hilarious way, a profound mystery —how in love 'Property was thus appalled', how 'Either was the other's mine'. [*Shakespeare and His Comedies*, 1957.]

MAYNARD MACK. . . . toward the beginning of Shakespeare's career, we have Sly in *The Taming of the Shrew*. Even in the anonymous play *A Shrew*, but much more in Shakespeare's version, we confront in Sly's experience after being thrown out of the alehouse what appears to be an abstract and brief chronicle of how stage illusion takes effect. Sly, having fallen briefly into one of those mysterious sleeps that Shakespeare elsewhere attributes to those who are undergoing the power of a dramatist, wakes to find the identity of a rich lord thrust upon him, rejects it at first, knowing perfectly well who he is ("Christopher Sly, old Sly's son, of Burtonheath . . . . Ask Marian Hacket, the fat alewife of Wincot, if she know me not"), then is engulfed by it, accepts the dream as reality, accepts also a dressed-up players' boy to share the new reality with him as his supposed lady, and at last sits down with her beside him to watch the strolling players put on *The Taming of the Shrew*. Since Sly's newly assumed identity has no result whatever except to bring him face to face with a play, it is tempting to imagine him a witty paradigm of all of us as theatergoers, when we awake out of our ordinary reality of the alehouse, or whatever other reality ordinarily encompasses us, to the superimposed reality of the playhouse, and find that there (at any rate, so long as a comedy is playing) wishes are horses and beggars do ride. Sly, to be sure, soon disengages himself from the strollers' play and falls asleep; but in Shakespeare's version—the situation differs somewhat in *A Shrew*—his engagement to his identity as a lord, though presumably broken when the play ends, stretches into infinity for anything we are ever told.

This way of considering Sly is the more tempting in that the play as a whole manipulates the theme of displaced identity in a way that can hardly be ignored. For what the Lord and his Servants do in thrusting a temporary identity on Sly is echoed in what Petruchio does for Kate at a deeper level of psychic change . . . .

Petruchio's stratagem is thus more than an entertaining stage device. It parodies the idolatrousness of romantic love which, as Theseus says, is always seeing Helen in a brow of Egypt; but it also reflects love's genuine creative power, which can on occasion make the loved one grow to match the dream. ["Engagement and Detachment in Shakespeare's Plays," *Essays on Shakespeare and Elizabethan Drama*, Richard Hosley, ed., 1962].

DEREK TRAVERSI. Petruchio's entire attitude . . . reflects a commonsense which is the necessary counterpoise of idealism, saving it from the dangers of empty posturing and self-gratifying excess. Repeating a device already used in *The Comedy of Errors*, the lesson is driven home by the attitude of his servant, Grumio, in whom, at his better moments, a similar sense of reality prevails. Typical, in the capacity it shows of seeing his own situation dispassionately, of casting upon it a wry, unprejudiced glance, is Grumio's account of his cold journey home in the company of his master and of the strange new bride he has so inexplicably chosen to bring with him [IV, i]. Grumio and his like know that there is, after all, a limit to any man's capacity to impose himself, to play at being under all circumstances the master of the situations in which he finds himself; and it is this knowledge that enables him to share with his fellow-servant Curtis the admission, uttered in plain, uncompromising prose, that 'winter tames man, woman, and beast; for it hath tamed my old master, and my new mistress, and myself, fellow Curtis.' There are worse points of view from which we may choose to consider the apparent crudity of Petruchio's own attitudes and behavior. [*Shakespeare: The Early Comedies*, rev. ed., 1964, No. 129 in "Writers and Their Work" series.]

Tamora. In *Titus Andronicus*, queen of the Goths. Captured by Titus with her three sons, Tamora marries the emperor Saturninus. Titus having sacrificed Tamora's eldest son Alarbus, the Empress and her Moorish lover Aaron plot revenge. As a result of their scheming, Titus' daughter Lavinia is raped and mutilated, two of his sons are falsely executed for murder, and Titus himself is deprived of a hand. In revenge, Titus murders Tamora's two surviving sons, serves them to her in a pie, and kills her.

Tannenbaum, Samuel A[aron] (1874–1948). Hungarian-born physician and scholar. Tannenbaum emigrated to the U.S. as a child. In 1898 he received his M.D. from Columbia, but by this time had developed an interest in the two areas to which he would devote his life—psychology and Shakespeare. He studied in Europe under Freud, returning to America in order to practice psychotherapy. His scholarly study of Shakespeare centered on Elizabethan handwriting, which he treated in his *Problems in Shakspere's Penmanship* (1927) and *The Handwriting of the Renaissance* (1930). Dr. Tannenbaum rejected the generally accepted theory that Shakespeare's handwriting is extant in a manuscript version of SIR THOMAS MORE. He engaged in another heated controversy when he contended in his *Shakspere Forgeries in the Revels Accounts* (1928) that the manuscript was a forgery. Dr. Tannenbaum was the editor of the *Shakespeare Association Bulletin* from 1934 to 1947 and the compiler, with his second wife, Dorothy, of a large number of valuable bibliographies of the individual Shakespearean works and of the major Elizabethan dramatists and poets. His large personal library now forms the basis of the University of North Carolina's Tannenbaum Shakespeare Collection. [John S. McAleer, "The Gladiatorial Dr. Tannenbaum," *Bulletin of the New York Public Library*, LXVI, 1962.]

Tarlton, Richard (d. 1588). Actor. Tarlton was the famous clown of the Queen's Men, a group he joined at their formation in 1583. His origins are obscure, and little reliable information is available. A good deal of biographical "data" appeared in the various pamphlets which were printed following his death. These include a ballad, "Tarltons Farewell" (1588); "Tarltons repentance of his farewell to his frends in his sicknes a little before his deathe" (1589); "a pleasant dyttye dialogue wise betwene Tarltons ghost and Robyn Good Fellow" (1590); and, most famous of all, the collection known as *Tarltons Jests*, published posthumously and attributed to Tarlton. (The earliest extant edition dates from 1611, but the second of the three parts of the *Jests* was entered in the Stationers' Register August 4, 1600 and the first part must therefore be dated even earlier.)

Tarlton allegedly owned the Saba tavern in Gracechurch Street, where he was also said to be the scavenger of the ward, "and often the Ward complained of his slacknesse, in keeping the streets cleane." He was also supposed to be the owner of an ordinary (a tavern) in Paternoster Row. This story conflicts with another account of his origins, which, given in Fuller's *Worthies*, has it that he was keeping his father's swine at Condover when a servant of the earl of Leicester overheard his witty remarks and brought him to court.

Various accounts describe Tarlton as having a squint and a flat nose. His clothes included a suit of russet (homespun reddish-brown cloth of coarse texture), a buttoned cap, wide puffed breeches, short ankle-strapped boots, and a belt with a leather purse attached to it. He carried a tabor (a small drum with a head like a tambourine) and a pipe and had a trick of standing on one toe.

His clowning technique was ad lib rather than planned. Hamlet's advice to the players (*Hamlet*, III, ii, 42–50) may have been prompted by Tarlton's practice:

> And let those that play your clowns speak no more than is set down for them; for there be of them that will themselves laugh, to set on some quantity of barren spectators to laugh too; though, in the mean time, some necessary question of the play be then to be considered: that's villanous, and shows a most pitiful ambition in the fool that uses it.

Tarlton was Queen Elizabeth's favorite clown, and he allegedly took the greatest liberties in his frequent appearances before her. According to *A Full Account of the Character of Queen Elizabeth* (1693) by Edmund Bohun (1645–1699), on one occasion "he pointed at Sir Walter Raleigh and said 'See, the Knave commands the Queen,' for which he was corrected by a frown from the Queen . . . ." The same source also relates Tarlton's gibes at the power of the earl of Leicester. Of his roles, few are definitely known. One that is known is his doubling the roles of clown and judge in *The Famous Victories of Henry the Fifth*, a play given by the Queen's Men "at the Bull in Bishopsgate," which Tarlton himself may have written. He is credited with having written THE SEVEN DEADLY SINS, of which only the "plot" is extant. He is also the author of several jigs (farces in rhyme, sung and danced to popular tunes), which he performed. There has also been some speculation that he might have taken the roles of Pedringano in Kyd's *Spanish Tragedy;* Bullethrumble in *Selimus;* and the Mouse in *Mucedorus*.

His reputation survived well past his death. Taverns and fighting cocks were named after him. A "Tarlton Inn" is the scene of the action of William Percy's *Cuck-Queanes and Cuckolds Errants* (1601), where Tarlton is said to be the inn's "quondam controller and induperator." Scholars have conjectured that Tarlton was the model for Yorick whose skull Hamlet recovers from the graveyard and who is described as "a fellow of infinite jest, of most excellent fancy" (*Hamlet*, V, i, 203–204). [E. K. Chambers, *The Elizabethan Stage*, 1923.]

Tasso, Torquato (1544–1595). Italian poet. Educated for the law, Tasso turned to literature at an early age, publishing his first work, *Rinaldo* (1562), at 18. Later he served as court poet to the powerful Este family. At the Este court he did his best work although suffering from intermittent bouts of the insanity to which he finally succumbed completely. He died in a monastery in Sant'Onofrio in 1595.

Tasso's greatest achievement is his *Gerusalemme Liberata* (1581), an epic poem on the Christian conquest of Jerusalem in the first crusade. The poem, translated into English in 1594 by Richard Carew and in 1600 by Edward Fairfax, was used by Edmund Spenser in *The Faerie Queene* and possibly by Shakespeare in *Cymbeline*. Tasso's pastoral play *Aminta* (1573; pub. 1581) was the source of Berowne's speech in *Love's Labour's Lost* (IV, iii, 302), beginning "From women's eyes this doctrine I derive." [Sidney Lee, *Elizabethan and Other Essays*, 1929.]

Tate, Nahum (1652–1715). Irish-born dramatist. Tate specialized in adaptations of the Elizabethan dramatists, particularly Shakespeare. A graduate of Trinity College, Dublin, Tate came to London in 1673, where he secured the patronage of the Tory leader, Lord Dorset. He collaborated with John Dryden on the second part of *Absalom and Achitophel* (1682), and in 1692 succeeded Thomas Shadwell as poet laureate. He was given to heavy drinking, as a result of which he was often in debt and, at his death, in hiding from his creditors. His Elizabethan adaptations include *Injur'd Love: or, the Cruel Husband* (1707) from Webster's *The White Devil; Cuckold's Haven* (1685), based on *Eastward Ho!;* and an adaptation of Jonson's *The Devill is an Asse*. His contemporary reputation, however, rested largely on his adaptations of Shakespeare's *King Lear, Richard II*, and *Coriolanus*.

Tate's *The History of King Lear* is the most infamous of Restoration adaptations. In Tate's hands *Lear* becomes a simpler and more cheerful play, with the Fool and the King of France eliminated, a romance between Cordelia and Edgar added, and most of Lear's kingdom restored to him.

Tate objected to the rapid and arbitrary action of the first scene and corrected it by inventing motivations for both Lear and Cordelia. Cordelia refuses to answer her father because she loves Edgar and hopes to scare off her other suitors. Since Lear disapproves of her choice and perceives her purpose, his wrath has some justification. Edgar woos Cordelia in spite of Lear's hostility, but she rejects him, ostensibly because he cannot support her, but really to test his sincerity. He contemplates suicide, but decides rather to adopt a disguise, so that he can continue to watch over her.

The rationalization of the play has a deadening effect on its most passionate scenes. Without the Fool or the mad trial, the storm and heath scenes become flat. The elimination of the King of France leaves Cordelia with nothing to do but wander about the heath looking for her father until she is captured by Edmund, saved by Edgar (to whom she repledges her love), and once again captured by Edmund.

It is the ending of the play, however, that is Tate's greatest crime. After Goneril and Regan poison each other and Edgar kills Edmund, the scene shifts to the prison, where the soldiers have come to kill Lear and Cordelia. The King, with remarkable strength and agility, snatches a weapon and manages to kill two of the soldiers before Edgar and Albany arrive to help. Albany gives all but a third of the kingdom to Lear, who in turn gives it to Cordelia and Edgar. Lear then retires with Kent and Gloucester to spend the rest of his life in peaceful contemplation.

Anyone who could so pervert Shakespeare's plot could not be expected to respect his poetry. Although Tate incorporates whole passages from the original in his adaptation, he completely rewrites the rest, making no attempt to match the spirit or style of his model. *The History of King Lear*, first produced in 1681, held the stage for 150 years. It was not until William Charles Macready's production in 1838 that the original version was performed. See George COLMAN.

In *The History of King Richard the Second* Tate chooses to treat the story as pure fiction rather than as history, and suffers no qualms about altering personalities, particularly the King's, to suit his purposes. In a foreword to his *King Richard II*, he presents his excuse:

> My Design was to engage the pitty of the Audience for him in his Distresses, which I cou'd never have compass'd had I not before shewn him a Wise, Active and Just Prince.

Tate obviously could not allow the audience to sympathize with a hero whose morals were dubious and accordingly eliminates all subtlety of characterization and any elements that might complicate the audience's response to the story. All the references to Richard's tyranny in the first half of the play are removed. Among the deletions are the scene at the end of Act I in which Richard wishes for Gaunt's death, and most of Gaunt's eulogy of England. Richard doesn't seize his uncle's property, but only borrows it, promising to return it "with interest" once the emergency is over. On the other hand, Bolingbroke is made less of a patriot and more of a usurper. His farewell to England in the first act is rewritten to eliminate sentiment and present his fully matured plans for revolution. In an altogether original scene at the end of Act II Bolingbroke flatters a rioting mob into begging him to seize the crown much in the manner of Richard III. Other major alterations include an emphasis on the love of Richard and his queen, meant to make him more sympathetic and the reduction of York to the level of a buffoon. Verbal alterations are extensive, but follow no discernible pattern.

Although *King Lear* was written earlier, *Richard II* was Tate's first produced adaptation. It was staged at Dorset Garden in 1680, only to be suppressed after two performances by the king, who, with some justification, suspected personal allusions. Tate quickly rewrote the play as *The Sicilian Usurper*, mainly by changing all the names, but the adaptation of the adaptation was unsuccessful.

The Ingratitude of a Common-wealth: Or, the Fall of Caius Martius Coriolanus (1681) is not so violently butchered an adaptation as Tate's *King Lear* nor are its characters changed to introduce new themes, as in his version of *Richard II*. Tate does emphasize the chaotic state of the commonwealth described in the play and pointedly notes its application to his contemporaries, but the major alteration is a complete change in the tone of the final act. Here he suddenly drops *Coriolanus* and apparently adopts *Titus Andronicus* as his model. Following in rapid succession are the assassination of Coriolanu (who manages, however, to stay alive through most of the act), the attempted rape of Virgilia and her suicide, a description of the torture of the boy Martius, the sight of the mad Volumnia raving over her grandson's mangled but still-living body, a sentimental parting of Coriolanus and his son, and—finally—their deaths. There is no dramatic reason for all this Senecan horror, and the only explanation for the combination of four acts of political comment with a bloodbath conclusion is that it represents an attempt to gain popularity on every level. Tate's efforts were unsuccessful, however, and the play failed very soon after its first production in the winter of 1681/2. [Hazelton Spencer, *Shakespeare Improved*, 1927.]—G.M.B.

Taurus, Statilius. In *Antony and Cleopatra*, the commander of Octavius Caesar's army at Actium (III, viii).

Taverner, William. See ADAPTATIONS.

Taylor, Edward (d. 1797). Author. The *Cursory Remarks on Tragedy* published anonymously in 1772 has been attributed to William Richardson, but is probably the work of Edward Taylor. It presents a dogmatic and unrelenting condemnation of Shakespeare for his violation of poetic justice, the unities, and other classical criteria. Taylor acknowledges Shakespeare's talent as a writer of comedy and the superiority of his poetry at its best, but he considers him an inferior tragedian, greatly overrated by virtue of national prejudice.

Taylor, John (c. 1578–1653). Poet, known as the "water poet." Employed as a waterman on the Thames, Taylor ferried passengers across the river. He was also a celebrated "character" about London known for his many trips around England and to the continent. His accounts of these voyages, liberally sprinkled with gossip and personal editorials, were printed in penny pamphlets. His verse was largely satiric and topical.

A good deal of Taylor's business as a waterman was dependent upon the theatrical trade in Southwark. Customers came from London wishing to attend the Globe, the Swan, or the Hope theatres. About 1614 a number of theatres opened to the north and west of London, thus depriving the watermen of potential customers. Taylor was selected as spokesman for the Thames watermen and a petition to the king was drawn up, attempting to prevent the operation of any theatre within four miles of London excepting those in Southwark. The King's Men, who wished to protect their winter home at Blackfriars, instituted a counter suit. Nothing came of either suit and Taylor was accused by his fellow watermen of having been bribed by the players. Taylor had a number of writers among his acquaintance, including Ben Jonson and Thomas Coryat (c. 1577–1617). He also was a friend of John Jackson, one of Shakespeare's trustees in his purchase of the Blackfriars Gate-house. Taylor probably knew Shakespeare as well and alludes to him in one of his verses, *The Praise of Hemp-seed* (1620):

> In paper, many a Poet now suruiues
> Or else their lines had perish'd with their liues.
> Old Chaucer, Gower, and Sir Thomas More,
> Sir Philip Sidney, who the Lawrell wore,
> Spencer, and Shakespeare did in Art excell,
> Sir Edward Dyer, Greene, Nash, Daniell.
> Siluester, Beumont, Sir John Harrington,
> Forgetfulnesse their workes would ouer run,
> But that in paper they immortally
> Doe liue in spight of death, and cannot die.

[Robert Southey, *Lives of the Uneducated Poets*, 1831; E. K. Chambers, *The Elizabethan Stage*, 1923.]

Taylor, Joseph (1586–1652). Actor. Taylor acted with Lady Elizabeth's Men from 1611 to 1616, when he joined Prince Charles' company. He established a reputation as an actor with the latter group before moving to the King's Men late in 1619. He was evidently taken on as a replacement for Richard Burbage, who had died in March 1619. James WRIGHT, in the *Historia Histrionica*, says that he played Hamlet "incomparably well"; according to John Downes, he had been trained by "the Author Mr. Shakespear." This is unlikely, however, since Taylor joined the group after Shakespeare's death (see John DOWNES).

Taylor was a leading actor with the King's Men for the rest of his life, assuming with John LOWIN the joint management of the company, and being listed with Lowin and Swanston as payees for the company's court performances. In 1639 he was appointed to the post of Yeoman of the Revels, evidently through the influence of the Master of the Revels, Sir Henry Herbert.

Taylor's name appears in the list of the principal actors in the 1623 First Folio of Shakespeare's plays. His name seconds Burbage's as Ferdinand in the 1623 quarto of *The Duchess of Malfi*. T. W. Baldwin has suggested that Taylor's roles were those requiring a handsome, dashing figure, either a young lover or a near-villain.

After the closing of the theatres, nostalgia for the old actors provoked many reminiscences. Two years after Taylor's death, in 1654, Edmund Gayton published his *Pleasant Notes upon Don Quixot*, where he mentions that "*Taylor acting Arbaces* in *A King and No King* or *Swanston D'Amboys*, were shadows to him . . . ." In Gayton's *Wit Revived* (1655), there is the following allusion:

> Q. *Which of our Tailors were the most famous?*
> A. The Plaier and the Sculler.

The "Sculler" he mentions is evidently the "water poet" John Taylor. The 1658 edition of Richard Flecknoe's *Enigmaticall Characters* alludes to Taylor as Mosca in *Volpone:*

> *Of one that imitates the good companion another way* . . . He is on, who now the stage is down Acts the *Parasites* part at Table; and since *Tailors* death, none can play *Mosco's* part so well as he.

[E. K. Chambers, *The Elizabethan Stage*, 1923; T. W. Baldwin, *The Organization and Personnel of the Shakespearean Company*, 1927; G. E. Bentley, *The Jacobean and Caroline Stage*, 5 vols., 1941–1956.]

Tchaikovsky, Peter Ilich (1840–1893). Russian composer. One of Tchaikovsky's earliest and most enduring successes was his "Fantasy Overture, Romeo and Juliet" (1869). Four years later he published another "Fantasy Overture," this time based on *The Tempest*, which is infrequently played today. A third "Fantasy Overture," on *Hamlet* (1885), is not one of the composer's more inspired works. He used some themes from this work in the complete incidental music he composed for a production of *Hamlet* in Petrograd in 1891. Of all Tchaikovsky's works, the *Romeo and Juliet* overture is still one of the most popular. [Christopher Wilson, *Shakespeare and Music*, 1922.]

Tearle, Sir Godfrey (1884–1953). Actor. Son of the actor Osmond Tearle (1852–1901) and his second wife, Marianne Conway (Minnie) Levy, Godfrey Tearle made his debut as the Duke of York in *Richard III* at Burnley in 1893. From 1899 to 1901 he acted with his father's company, commencing what proved to be a long and distinguished career in Shakespearean and other roles. He appeared as Hamlet, Othello, Shylock, Brutus, Romeo, Silvius, Lodovico, Master Page, Octavius, Marcellus, Lorenzo, Cassius, Sir Henry Guildford (in the "all-star" 1915 revival of *Henry VIII*), Horatio (in the 1930 Haymarket "all-star" *Hamlet*), and Antony (*Julius Caesar* and *Antony and Cleopatra*). From 1916 to 1919 his career was interrupted by service with His Majesty's Forces, but after the war he returned to the theatre and in 1924 managed and produced at the Apollo. He appeared as Brutus in a modern-dress *Julius Caesar* at His Majesty's Theatre in 1939, and as Othello and Macbeth at the Shakespeare Memorial Theatre, Stratford-upon-Avon, in 1948 and 1949. He was in films from early in his career, including a *Romeo and Juliet* with Tearle as Romeo. In 1932 he became the first president of the British Actors' Equity Association, and in 1935 he was vice chairman of the London Theatre Council. He was knighted in 1951. [*Who's Who in the Theatre*, 1952.]

Tearsheet, Doll. In *2 Henry IV*, Falstaff's mistress. At the play's end she is sent to prison as a harlot who has caused several men's deaths. In *Henry V*, Pistol reports that she is "dead i' the spital" (V, i).

THE TEMPEST.

Tempest, The. A romance by Shakespeare.

Text. The only authoritative text of *The Tempest* is that of the First Folio (1623). A part of the play may have been cut in this text to make room for a masque (IV, i, 60–138). This masque is suitable for the celebration of a betrothal and probably served as a feature of the entertainment offered to the visiting elector palatine during the winter of 1612/3. The entertainment culminated in his betrothal to the Princess Elizabeth, the daughter of Charles I, on December 27, 1612. The subsequent marriage of the royal pair took place on February 14, 1613. The play, however, had been presented earlier at court on "Hallomass Nyght" November 1, 1611.

The stage directions of the Folio are both more elaborate and more specific than those for any other of the plays except *Henry VIII*. It is possible that the editors, John Heminges and Henry Condell, having decided to place *The Tempest* first in the Folio, gave it unusual editorial care, so that it could serve as a formal model for the plays to follow.

The text is accurately divided into acts and scenes. *The Tempest* is one of four plays in the volume provided with a list of the dramatis personae. It is disfigured by some inconsistencies for which the editors may not be responsible. Some passages of distinctly rhythmical speeches have been set as prose. This is evident in a few of Caliban's speeches in which there are hidden rhymes. The Folio text was set up from a transcript carefully prepared by Ralph Crane, the scribe for the King's Men.

Date. As noted above, the play was presented at court on November 1, 1611. If this was not the first performance of the romance, it suggests that it was successful on the stage shortly before. The date for the composition of the play is almost certainly 1611.

Sources. The only undisputed source for any part of *The Tempest* is a minor one, Montaigne's essay "On Cannibals," which Shakespeare could have read in John Florio's English translation (1603). In this essay Montaigne opines that the New World furnishes an example of a completely natural life uncorrupted by civilization. In his speeches in the second act (II, i, 145–169, *passim*), Gonzalo describes how he would organize society on Prospero's island, had he a plantation there. His comments form a satire of the romantic concept of primitivism. He himself characterizes his program as "merry fooling."

Die Schöne Sidea, composed by Jacob AYRER of Nürnberg, was first proposed as a source of *The Tempest* by the German Romantic novelist Ludwig Tieck. This was one of the dramas published in Ayrer's *Opus Theatricum* (1618). The similarities between the two dramas are features of the basic story of which the German and the English play are parallel developments: the benevolent magician; a captive, log-bearing prince; the magician's daughter, who falls in love with the prisoner; the bewitching of the prince's sword when he tries to attack the magician; and the eventual happy union of the lovers.

Some critics have speculated that Ayrer's play might be a German redaction of an earlier play on the same subject, an *Ur-Tempest*, played by English comedians in Germany before 1605. But no evidence exists to establish any direct relationship between the two plays.

A more likely source of important features of *The Tempest* is a type of *commedia dell' arte* pastoral tragicomedy well known in 16th-century Italy. Ferdinando Neri was the first to collect and to publish a group of these plays, under the title of *Scenari delle Maschere in Arcadia* (1913). The scene of these marine pastorals is always the same as that of Shakespeare's romance, a remote island demiparadise appropriately called "Enchanted Arcadia" or "Lost Island." The center of some of these plays is a benevolent magician (there were many "Magi" scenarios in the popular Italian drama of the 16th century) equipped with the conventional insignia of his art, a staff and a book. His white magic enables him to control beneficent familiar spirits, as well as satyrs, devils, and the other malevolent creatures. All of these subjects he imprisons in a cave that is always the center of the stage in Renaissance "pastoral" or "satyrical" sets (see Sebastiano SERLIO). From this cavern the magician calls forth his subjects when he wishes them to do his bidding. The purpose of all his magic is to settle old quarrels and to bring about the marriage of the young lovers. In *La Nave* ("the ship"), one of these scenarios, the first scene is set on a doomed vessel in a violent storm, with the terrified passengers "lamenting, wailing and crying for help." At the end of this scene the vessel sinks, taking all hands down with it. Next we see the shipwrecked company crawling from the sea. The low-comedy figures arrive in grotesque fashion: for example, one of the buffoons is belched from the mouth of a whale. In *La Pazzia* ("madness"), another of the scenarios, Gratiano develops a farcical routine, a series of *lazzi* much like those of Stephano when he comes upon Caliban and Trinculo hidden under a gaberdine (II, ii, 58–117). In *Il Capriccio* ("the grotesquerie"), as Miss Kathleen Lea has pointed out, there is a banquet that rises from the ground and is later snatched away by spirits. In another of these scenarios, *Li Tre Satiri* ("the three satyrs"), a native of the island conspires with some of the shipwrecked intruders to steal the magician's book and so to learn how to use his magic powers. But the mage becomes aware of their plot, thwarts it, and leads the action to a happy ending.

The similarities between these scenarios and details of *The Tempest* are too many and too close to be explained as coincidence. That the printed texts of these *scenari* are only chance survivals of a type of no obstacle to establishing their relationship to Shakespeare's romance. Commedia dell'arte companies seldom published their scenarios until after the plays had become stale dramatic fare. Moreover, these *scenari* are only chance survivals of a type of popular comedy represented by scores of scenarios like those under discussion. How Shakespeare became acquainted with these or similar commedie dell' arte is too complicated a problem to be explored here. The dramatic construction of these comedies makes it probable that the poet planned to have *The Tempest* culminate in the frustration of Caliban's plot. The defeat of the conspiracy is of major importance to the dramatic action. Prospero treats it in a mere aside:

> I had forgot that foul conspiracy
> Of the beast Caliban and his confederates
> Against my life: the minute of their plot
> Is almost come.
>
> (IV, i, 139–142)

One possible explanation for Shakespeare's perfunctory dealing with this turning point in the action may be that the lines describing Prospero's foiling of the conspiracy were in the original text and that these were replaced by the masque which may have been inserted for the performance at the royal betrothal of the Princess Elizabeth. This theory of course rests on the hypothesis that the masque is an addition to the text and not an original element of it.

Certain pamphlets dealing with the wreck of the ship *The Sea-Venture* furnished Shakespeare with some details of the storm with which *The Tempest* opens. This ship was one of the nine of a fleet under the command of Sir Thomas Gates and Sir George Somers that in June 1609 sailed for Virginia in order to bolster John Smith's colony. It was separated by a hurricane from the rest of the vessels and wrecked on the coast of Bermuda. Of the three works describing this Virginia voyage, the one that Shakespeare knew best was a letter, written by William Strachey, dated July 15, 1610. Although not published until it appeared in *Purchas His Pilgrimes* in 1625, Strachey's letter may have been known earlier to Shakespeare through his personal connections with the Virginia Company, the sponsors of the voyage. Other accounts of the wreck were given in Sylvester Jourdain's *A Discovery of the Bermudas* (1610) and in the Virginia Company's official report *The True Declaration of the Estate of the Colonie in Virginia* (1610). It was on these descriptions, particularly Strachey's, of the hurricane that Shakespeare modeled his first scene in *The Tempest*. From them he also learned something about the animals and the vegetation of the New World. However, the Bermuda pamphlets were not the poet's only source of knowledge of America. The name "Setebos" he found in Robert Eden's *History of Travaile* (1577). There the Patagonians are reported to have called upon "theyr Devill Setebos" for help in times of fear and of danger.—O.J.C.

Plot Synopsis. Act I. After a severe storm at sea wrecks their vessel, King Alonso of Naples; his brother Sebastian; Alonso's son, Ferdinand; and Antonio, the usurping Duke of Milan, are cast ashore on an enchanted island inhabited by Prospero, the rightful Duke, and his daughter, Miranda. During the storm, Prospero reveals to Miranda that 12 years earlier his brother Antonio, with Alonso's connivance, had taken advantage of Prospero's absorption in his studies of magic to usurp his title. Prospero and Miranda, then only three years old, had been cast adrift in a boat and were able to survive only because Gonzalo, a kindly Neapolitan lord, had provided them with food and clothes and had also brought Prospero his precious books. Eventually they landed on this island, once the home of the foul witch Sycorax, now dead. Having been abandoned here by some sailors, she gave birth to a brutish creature called Caliban, whom Prospero now employs as his servant, after vainly trying to civilize him. Sycorax had brought with her a slave, the spirit Ariel, whom she imprisoned in a cloven pine until Prospero released him. Ariel is obliged to serve Prospero, but he longs for the freedom that his master has promised him. The storm which brings the King and his followers to the island is raised by Prospero, who has perfected his knowledge of the occult since his exile from Milan. He assures Miranda, however, that no harm will come to any of the castaways.

At his master's bidding, Ariel makes himself invisible and leads a bewildered Ferdinand to Prospero's cell by his singing. As Prospero has expected, Ferdinand falls in love with Miranda, who, remembering no other man but her father, eagerly returns the young Prince's affection. Prospero, however, fears that Ferdinand may have made too easy a conquest and pretends to disapprove of their romance.

Act II. Meanwhile, Alonso, Sebastian, and Antonio have landed in another part of the island, together with Gonzalo and other lords. Alonso, who had been returning from Tunis, where his daughter had married the King, is disconsolate to think that he has now lost Ferdinand, his only son. Lulled by Ariel's music, they all fall asleep, except Sebastian and Antonio, who uses this opportunity to persuade Sebastian to kill the King, his brother, so as to fall heir to the crown of Naples. He reminds Sebastian that he, Antonio, won the duchy of Milan by similar means and has never been troubled by pangs of conscience. As they plan the murder, Ariel, who has heard their conversation, sings in Gonzalo's ear to wake him, thus foiling the conspirators.

As Caliban grumblingly gathers wood, he is espied by Trinculo, a drunken jester from the wrecked ship, who hides under Caliban's cloak when the storm begins again. To the same spot comes Stephano, another bibulous survivor, who takes repeated swigs from a bottle he has managed to rescue. He shares the bottle with Caliban, who is pleased with the "celestial liquor" and who offers to worship Stephano as his god.

Act III. To test Ferdinand's sincerity, Prospero has given him the arduous task of carrying and heaping thousands of logs. As Prospero looks on, Miranda pleads with Ferdinand to let her share his labor, and they exchange vows of eternal devotion. Stephano and Trinculo, meanwhile, continue their drinking, while Ariel observes them undetected. At Caliban's suggestion, they decide to kill Prospero; then Stephano can be king of the island, Miranda will be his queen, and Trinculo and Caliban his viceroys. Upon hearing the notes of Ariel's tabor and pipe, they defer their plot and follow the mysterious tune.

Alonso and the other members of his party are completely exhausted, though Antonio and Sebastian are still planning to assassinate the King. While Prospero stands above, invisible to them, several strange beings lay a banquet before them and invite them to eat. As Alonso is about to take the first mouthful, the banquet vanishes, and Ariel appears in the shape of a harpy, amid thunder and lightning. Reminding Alonso, Antonio, and Sebastian of their crimes against Prospero and his daughter, Ariel declares that the powers have taken revenge by depriving Alonso of his son and warns the King that "lingering perdition" shall henceforth dog his steps. Gonzalo observes that Alonso, Antonio, and Sebastian now seem like desperate men, for they are beginning to feel the pricks of conscience.

Act IV. Declaring himself satisfied with Ferdinand's conduct, Prospero gives Miranda to him but warns him not to violate her maidenhood before their union can be sanctified by holy rite. To celebrate the betrothal a masque is held in which Iris, Ceres, and Juno bestow their blessings on the couple. Suddenly Prospero remembers Caliban's conspiracy, of which Ariel had informed him, and abruptly ends the masque. Ferdinand is disturbed by Prospero's anger, but the latter declares that the actors, spirits all, have melted into the air, just as the world and everything in it will someday dissolve "And, like this insubstantial pageant faded, / Leave not a rack behind." Summoned by Prospero, Ariel reveals that he has led Caliban and his cohorts into a stagnant pool where they have sunk in slime up to their chins. At Prospero's bidding, Ariel brings in some gaudy apparel, which he hangs on a line. After Prospero and Ariel make themselves invisible, Caliban, Stephano, and Trinculo enter, the latter two bemoaning the loss of their bottle. Dazzled by the garments, they hurriedly put them on and forget all about their plans, while Caliban fumes in vain. Then spirits, in the shape of dogs, run in and drive them out.

Act V. Ariel informs Prospero that, as he ordered, the King and his followers are imprisoned in a nearby grove of lime trees. When Ariel remarks that Prospero would be moved if he could see their mournful appearance, Prospero is impressed by the fact that Ariel, who is but air, has more compassion for them than he, a fellow mortal. Losing his desire for vengeance in view of the prisoners' penitence, he asks Ariel to bring them to him and abjures his magical powers, destroying his staff and book. When the King and the others arrive, enchanted by Ariel's music, they enter a charmed circle before Prospero's cell. Dressed in the attire he wore as duke of Milan, Prospero reveals himself to Alonso and explains how he came to the island. Then he bids them look into his cell, where Ferdinand and Miranda are seen playing chess. Following Prospero's instruction, Ariel comes in with the wrecked ship's master and boatswain, who report that the vessel has been mysteriously made seaworthy again and that all the mariners are back on board. After ordering Ariel to release Caliban and his friends, who arrive drunk and wearing their stolen finery, Prospero invites the King and his train into his cell. He announces that in the morning they can set out for Naples for the wedding of Ferdinand and Miranda, after which he will return to Milan. Lastly, he gives Ariel his long-sought freedom.—H.D.

Comment. The elaborate masque of Ceres, the Roman goddess of fertility, is a betrothal masque honoring Ferdinand and Miranda. It emphasizes in its picturesque manner some of the themes of the play itself: the insistence on chastity, for example, and on the plenitude of the Golden Age. Frank Kermode suggests that the verses written for this masque are the author's subtle caricature of the poetry that had become fashionable for the masque. Other critics find a more intimate relationship between the mode of the masque and *The Tempest*. Prospero has been thought to be like a masque "presenter," in that the characters come and go at his behest. His famous speech in which he dismisses the revelers, beginning "Our revels now are ended" (IV, i, 148–160), contains allusions to the scenes and properties of a masque. These are obvious in the following lines:

> The solemn temples, the great globe itself,
> Yea, all which it inherit, shall dissolve
> And, like this insubstantial pageant faded,
> Leave not a rack behind.
> (IV, i, 153–156)

"Rack," although it was used to define a bank of natural clouds, was applied particularly to stage clouds. And these stage clouds in masques were sometimes used to "dissolve" a scene. Some scholars adopt the extreme view that the entire play is a kind of adapted masque which provided opportunities for music, dancing, and much scenic display, features in which Blackfriars audiences delighted. But this idea has not been widely accepted.

The characters in *The Tempest* have grown under the hands of a genius to proportions that little resemble the puppet-like figures of the scenarios. Prospero is a typical magician and conjurer of esoteric tradition, but he is much more. He is a neo-Platonic mage, possessing the powers of a holy adept in the sacred learning of white magic. Until he has donned his magic robe he is powerless, but clad in the garment, he brings us to the realm of occult charm that lies beyond normal human experience, of visions of mysterious beauty that always suffuse wish-fulfillment. In these ways he becomes the most substantial king of fairyland ever to have appeared in folk tales or myth. His powers are the result of deep and prolonged study, while the witch Sycorax has learned her black magic from communion with the devil.

Prospero's aerial spirits are benevolent sprites obedient to the interposition of divine powers. Through them he can fill the air with magical music. "Where should this music be?" asks Ferdinand, "i' the air or the earth? / It sounds no more: and, sure, it waits upon / Some god o' the island" (I, ii, 387–389).

Shakespeare has carefully developed Prospero's dramatic role. We realize that, at first, the mage took selfish delight in using his occult energy a bit ruthlessly and arrogantly. But when he realizes that Miranda has grown to maturity, cut off from all human beings but himself, he decides to employ his art to establishing her in a brave new world of men and women. His elaborate plan for inducing his enemies to make peace with him is partly an act of parental devotion. For his daughter is not Ferdinand's Miranda, but Prospero's Miranda. We see her through his eyes and his emotions. She is the last and the most captivating of the poet's romantic heroines. She comes from noble stock and is therefore beautiful, as the wicked are inevitably ugly. Although the embodiment of chastity, she is frank in her offers of love to Ferdinand. She is so avid of new experience and so enthusiastic in her greeting of the many goodly creatures of the world into which her father introduces her that she seems more than a lively, ardent girl; she becomes almost a symbol of innocent, eager hope.

Caliban represents, in Kermode's phrase, "nature without nurture." He is a brute; his name is an anagram of cannibal. Most Elizabethan spectators, particularly those who had attended any kind of a royal entertainment, would identify him at once as a "wodewose," or wild man of the woods. The vogue of employing this strange creature in court shows and disguisings grew as the 16th century advanced. In shows of its late decades he became brutal and lecherous, like the classical satyrs. Caliban is also a goblin who must endure the punishment of rendering menial services to the king of fairyland. Although some of the characters in the play refer to Caliban as a mooncalf, a word that meant "monster" and sometimes "congenital idiot," he is never mindless or impervious to the wonder of some of Prospero's magic. He is an amalgam of a savage, of a dimwitted boy, and, E. E. Stoll adds, of a badly trained dog. Over this strange mixture Shakespeare's imagination, humor, and poetry play to bring to life one of the most original and robust of his creations. The poet's idea of a proper savage may have been influenced by American Indians who had been brought back to England by travelers returning from the New World and exhibited in London side shows. That he may have gazed on some of these transplanted Indians does not mean that he designed Caliban to be an American aborigine. He is rather an Old World mythical creature that aroused a new interest in spectators who had seen American Indians.

It is possible that Shakespeare expected the more thoughtful in his audiences to see social significance in Caliban, for the brute becomes an inept revolutionary. He mistakes a drunken butler and his companion steward for gods, and their intoxicants for celestial liquor. His jaw drops in awe at the sight of the reeling clowns and he at once promises them groveling allegiance, if they will but free him from Prospero's tyranny. Once satisfied on their meeting this condition, he marches off with the drunken clowns to his expected triumph in tipsy revolutionary ardor.

Ariel is representative of the conventional sprite through which a magician often had to act. Because Prospero has released him from the cloven pine in which Sycorax had trapped him, he is bound to serve the mage for a fixed term. Only after he has completed it will he be able to rejoice in the untrammeled freedom that is his natural state. This is what similar creatures have been forced to do since the 13th-century *chanson de geste, Huon de Bordeaux*. Ariel is also a fairy like Puck; he is a diminutive thing, associated with butterflies and moonbeams. He dances and flits his way through the play, often breaking into song. In these songs music and magic unite to make them the most exquisite of all the songs that scatter through the play. Like a lark's caroling, they seem to drop from the upper air. Literal-minded critics take Ariel to be a symbol of the poet's imagination, or more crassly, of his poetry, as Caliban is of his prose. More esoteric interpreters, seeing Ariel as half-angel and half-bird, regard him as a symbol of grace at the service of man's longing for the sort of absolute liberty to be found only in Paradise.

A disturbing suspicion that *The Tempest* holds

depths of meaning hidden under its surface has inspired the same searchers for absolutes to find allegory, symbol, and myth in this, as in his other romances. Their approach has been greatly influenced by the contemporary interest in anthropology and comparative religion. G. Wilson Knight has become the acknowledged leader of the searchers for recondite significances in *The Tempest*. For him this play is a "myth of immortality." D. G. James, in his *Scepticism and Poetry* (1937), describes what he believes was Shakespeare's reason for turning to myth and symbol: having come to feel that life was too various and contradictory to have its significance embodied in a logically constructed play concerned with the conflicts of human beings, he became convinced that myth was a better vehicle for conveying to his audiences his ever-deepening apprehension of life's mystery.

There remains to be considered the idea held by many earlier critics that Shakespeare designed Prospero's invocations of magic to be an allegory of his own dramatic career. They saw in Prospero's glorious speech following the fading out of the spirits who had presented the masque of Ceres, the poet's melancholy farewell to the stage and all the creatures with which he had peopled it. But this theory becomes absurd in such passages as that in which Prospero boasts that his potent art has "bedimm'd / The noontide sun, called forth the mutinous winds" (V, i, 41–42). A playwright making so extravagant a boast of his own powers would have seemed to any audience, and particularly to one at court, to have taken complete leave of his senses. The speech is more wisely regarded as the most impressive of the poet's many monodies on mutability—another reluctant tribute to the might of Time, the destroyer which brings home to us that

> We are such stuff
> As dreams are made on, and our little life
> Is rounded with a sleep.
> (IV, i, 156–158)

It is appropriate to the dramatic situation and to the emotion it awakens in Prospero. Like the great monologues of many of Shakespeare's characters, it rises far above comment on a specific situation, to ring with universal meaning.

It is a relief to leave this mass of subjective comment and conjecture to the consideration of the probable reactions of the Blackfriars audiences to *The Tempest* for which the original version was probably written. It conforms to their aesthetic predilections, satisfying their appetite for surprise, wonder, and the strange. The drunken *lazzi* of the low-comedy characters were the kind of physical farce that the audiences preferred to comedy of character or even of situation. And the masque and suggestions of anti-masque were exactly the kind of display for which the stage of their fashionable Blackfriars theatre was created.

The diverse materials of Shakespeare's sources passing through the prism of his imagination became forms of iridescent beauty, creating in the process one of the world's most intellectually luminous and theatrically entertaining dramas.—O.J.C.

Stage History. On November 1, 1611 "a play Called the Tempest" was acted before the court at Whitehall. During the winter of 1612/3 *The Tempest* was among the plays performed as part of the festivities celebrating the betrothal and marriage of Princess Elizabeth to the elector palatine (see above under *Text*). On November 7, 1667 Samuel Pepys attended a performance of *The Tempest, or The Enchanted Island* at the Duke's Theatre in Lincoln's Inn Fields. This was William DAVENANT's adaptation, composed with some assistance from Dryden. It has been characterized by George C. D. Odell as "the worst perversion of Shakespeare in the two-century history of such atrocities." Miranda is supplied with a male counterpart in the character of Hippolito, a youth who has never seen a woman, as well as a younger sister, Dorinda. Additional companions to the island's original inhabitants include a sister, Sycorax, for Caliban and for Ariel a female sprite, Milcha. Sebastian and the plot against the King of Naples are omitted, along with much of Shakespeare's language. Pepys enjoyed the play, however, and, after seeing it seven times more, recorded that he "could not be more pleased almost in a comedy." The public concurred, and the Davenant-Dryden *Tempest* drove Shakespeare's play from the stage until the late 18th century. Thomas SHADWELL altered the alteration, expanding Milcha's role and transforming it into an opera, with music by Henry Purcell. His version, printed in 1674, was elaborately staged with many mechanical devices at Dorset Garden in 1673. It is not known which *Tempest*, the original or the adapted version, was performed at Lincoln's Inn Fields on October 13, 1702, but the Drury Lane productions on June 4, 1714 and January 2, 1729 were decidedly of the Davenant-Dryden alteration. Shakespeare briefly deposed Davenant and Dryden at Drury Lane on January 31 and May 19, 1746 with Denis Delane as Ferdinand, Charles Macklin as Stephano, and Kitty Clive as Ariel. Unfortunately, the following year, on December 26, the perversion was restored. In 1756 David Garrick compiled another alteration, based on Davenant-Dryden's *Tempest*, with music by John Christopher Smith. It was billed as "a new English Opera." Perhaps regretting the opera, Garrick restored Shakespeare's text a year later, in a performance featuring Henry Mossop and Edward Berry as Prospero and Caliban; Richard Yates took the part of Trinculo and Miss Pritchard (daughter of Hannah Pritchard) was Miranda.

What appears to have been Shakespeare's *Tempest* was revived at Drury Lane every year but two from this production until 1787, although Richard Brinsley Sheridan's adaptation, with music by Thomas Linley, Jr., was probably performed in 1777. Yates continued to act Trinculo through 1767 and Miss Pritchard (who became Mrs. Palmer) played Miranda through 1768.

The first recorded production of *The Tempest* at Covent Garden was an anonymous operatic version ("mutilation," according to the *Morning Post*), with musical selections from Purcell, J. C. Smith, Thomas Arne, and John A. Fisher. It was acted in 1776, 1777, and 1779. These were the only Covent Garden attempts with *The Tempest* in the 18th century. There was another alteration—this one designed to be performed by puppets—produced at the Patagonian Theatre, Exeter Exchange in 1779/80. In 1788 a pantomime based on *The Tempest* entitled *The Duke of Milan* was given at the Royalty Theatre.

In 1789 John Philip Kemble restored Hippolito

d Dorinda in a version largely from Davenant and ryden, mingled with some Shakespeare. This alter- ion was first staged at Drury Lane on October 13 d performed at least nine times that year and seven e next. Every season, from November 9, 1791 rough 1794, the Drury Lane company acted this *empest* at the Haymarket. Its production was re- med at the Drury Lane on February 22, 1797 and esented nine more times before the close of the ntury. During this time, Dorinda's role exceeded importance that of Miranda, and the leading ac- esses of the day preferred her part. Elizabeth Far- n, Mary Logan Gibbs, and Dorothy Jordan all im- rsonated the more popular sister. Kemble restored ore of the original poetry and eliminated much of e earlier music for his second version, in which he mself played Prospero, staged at Covent Garden in 06. Charles Kemble was Ferdinand and his wife, orinda. This version was presented at Covent Gar- n up to 1815 and was the basis of an "operatized" eatment arranged by Frederick REYNOLDS and enry Rowley BISHOP which appeared at Covent arden on May 15, 1821. Charles Macready played rospero, but most of the characters were assigned singers, with Maria Foote as Ariel. Macready was rospero again in Alfred Bunn's Drury Lane revival *The Tempest,* as "altered by Dryden and Dave- nt," in 1833, but in 1838, his second season as man- ger of Covent Garden, he staged Shakespeare's play ith only slight alterations. Dorinda and Hippolito ere successfully banished from this carefully anned production, which was given 55 times. elen Faucit played Miranda and Priscilla Horton oubled in the roles of Ceres and a high-flying Ariel. muel Phelps, the Antonio of Macready's produc- on, was Prospero in his own Sadler's Wells revivals Shakespeare's *Tempest* in 1847, 1855, and 1860. n July 1, 1857 Charles Kean gave a scenically su- rb representation of the original, sacrificing, how- er, many of the poetic beauties of the text. The orm spectacle was a special triumph, and mechani- l devices convincingly contrived the magical ele- ents of the play. Kean was Prospero; John Ryder, aliban; Carlotta Leclercq, Miranda; and Kate Terry, riel. Perhaps the most novel casting of Caliban in is century was for a Queen's Theatre production November 1871: the handsome George Rignold, ter universally acclaimed for his portrayal of King enry V, acted the savage "with tusks and paste- ard jaws." The revival was with full spectacle and cluded songs, ballets, and the masque. Ryder acted rospero in this and two later productions in 1875; e at the Gaiety on April 10, with Osmond Tearle Ferdinand, the other in June at the Crystal Palace. Frank Benson staged Stratford-upon-Avon's first *empest* in 1891 and followed with four other pro- uctions spanning the first decade of the 20th cen- ry. In 1900 his company appeared in the play at the yceum, with Benson as Caliban. A revival followed the Court Theatre in 1903, modestly produced by hn Leigh, who attempted Caliban. When Beer- hm Tree accepted the scenic challenges offered by *he Tempest,* he ravaged the text and centered the oduction on Caliban, the role reserved for himself. he ship foundered on a noisy sea in the opening ene and faded on the horizon at the close, while aliban, a cringing brute, stretched "his arms towards in mute despair." The production appeared at His Majesty's Theatre in 1904. Alternately titled by A. B. Walkeley *The Girl From Prospero's Island,* it was repeated during Tree's second and third annual Shakespeare Festivals in the two following years. There was a Birmingham production by John Drink- water in 1915, noticed largely for Barry Jackson's ex- periment in color. The Old Vic presented *The Tem- pest* every season from 1914 through 1921. During the war years, when actors were scarce, Sybil Thorn- dike assumed many male roles, among them Ferdi- nand. When Robert Atkins joined the Old Vic company under Ben Greet in 1915, he appeared as Prospero. He returned as director in 1920 to play Caliban, an impersonation he repeated for over 40 years. W. Bridges-Adams produced the play during his first season at Stratford (1919), with Basil Rath- bone and Joyce Carey as Ferdinand and Miranda. He subsequently staged three revivals; the last, in 1934 with Baliol Holloway (Caliban), Neil Porter (Prospero), and Rachel Kempson (Ariel), is one of the best productions in the history of the Memorial Theatre.

After a 14-year gap since Tree's last appearance as Caliban, his daughter Viola Tree managed an Ald- wych revival (1921) which introduced a new and too-human savage in her coproducer, Louis Calvert. Henry Ainley was Prospero and Miss Tree ap- peared as Juno. In 1926 Henry Baynton's company acted *The Tempest* at the Savoy; in his cast was the young John Gielgud, who took the part of Fer- dinand. During the Old Vic's 1923/4 season, Robert Atkins directed his second *Tempest,* with Ion Swin- ley as Prospero. Three seasons later, Andrew Leigh guided a production at Stratford, with Prospero and Caliban played by Neil Porter and Baliol Holloway. In 1930 John Gielgud and Ralph Richardson acted these roles for Harcourt Williams, who, in 1933, elected to end his Old Vic career by portraying Pros- pero opposite the Caliban of Malcolm Keen and Peggy Ashcroft's Miranda. In September of that year, Atkins re-created his Caliban for the first *Tempest* at the Open Air Theatre in Regent's Park, while Leslie French, the Old Vic's 1930 Ariel, again played the spirit. French appeared regularly at the Open Air throughout the decade with his imperson- ation of Ariel and, in 1939, directed *The Tempest* for the Oxford University Dramatic Society. The 1933 Prospero was the impressively authoritative John Drinkwater. In 1936 and 1937 the island adequately and naturally represented in the Park was inhabited by Ion Swinley's Prospero. Baliol Holloway's Caliban was followed in the later production by Russell Thorndike's. From then on, Robert Atkins' outstand- ing impersonation of the savage was given in every Open Air *Tempest.* In 1938 his master was played by Philip Merivale, in 1943 by Wilfrid Walter, in 1955 by Robert Eddison in a production by David Wil- liam, and, finally, in 1960, by Alan Judd.

When Tyrone Guthrie staged *The Tempest* for the Vic-Wells in 1934, he represented the island with little more than a single log and some seaweed. Charles Laughton governed this seemingly unpros- perous domain, his Prospero a little too benevolent; Caliban was almost lovable as portrayed by the mild, amiable Roger Livesey. Ariel was the production's salvation. Elsa Lanchester's enchanting performance of the sprite is as yet unequaled. Stratford continued with more or less regular productions of the play;

one in 1935 by Randle Ayrton and in 1938, 1941, and 1942 under B. Iden Payne.

The Tempest was the last Old Vic production before the bombing in 1940 forced the company to the provinces and later damaged part of the theatre. The production struck the emotional tone appropriate for the time, with the ascetic Prospero of John Gielgud especially effective in the reconciliation and farewell scenes. Jack Hawkins acted Caliban and Jessica Tandy, Miranda, under the direction of George Devine and Marius Goring. In 1957 Gielgud's Prospero, contemplative and with a knowledge of himself and the nature of man learned over the years of exile, appeared in Peter Brook's subtly staged *Tempest* at Stratford and again in December when it was transferred to Drury Lane. Alec Clunes was Caliban; Cyril Luckham, Gonzalo; and Doreen Aris, Miranda. Robert Harris, who had been Stratford's Prospero in Eric Crozier's over-mechanized production in 1946, and again in 1947 under Norman Wright's direction, played Alonso. Stratford had also had two productions of *The Tempest* by Michael Benthall. The first, in 1951, presented a masque treatment which began with an inauspicious, stylized shipwreck scene, but eventually found dry land. Michael Redgrave was a powerful, still human, Prospero; Alan Badel a radiant Ariel. Hugh Griffith played Caliban and Hazel Penwarden, Miranda. In 1952 *The Tempest* was less successful when Ralph Richardson portrayed a preoccupied Prospero at Stratford, with Michael Hordern as Caliban, Margaret Leighton as Ariel.

Robert Helpmann produced an Old Vic *Tempest* in 1954, with Richard Burton as Caliban and Michael Hordern as Prospero, while Claire Bloom portrayed Miranda. In 1959 Douglas Seale, using a text edited by George Rylands and music by Purcell and Locke, staged the Davenant-Dryden mutilation. In 1962 Oliver Neville restored the original to the Old Vic. Alastair Sim, 30 years absent from the Shakespearean stage, played Prospero as a mild-mannered, fanciful ruler.

There were two silent film versions of *The Tempest*, one American production released in 1910 and one French in 1912. Both were aesthetic failures, 20 minutes of a 50-minute version being devoted to the storm. A television production in 1960 also concentrated too heavily on scenic effects and mechanical contrivances, with a miniature Ariel soaring in the air and a large Caliban creeping on the ground.—M. G.

Bibliography. TEXT: *The Tempest*, New Cambridge Edition, Arthur Quiller-Couch and J. Dover Wilson, eds., 1921; *The Tempest*, New Arden Edition, Frank Kermode, ed., 1954. DATE: New Arden Edition. SOURCES: W. W. Newell, "The Sources of Shakespeare's *The Tempest*," *Journal of American Folklore*, XVI, 1903; Kathleen M. Lea, *Italian Popular Comedy*, 1934; J. M. Nosworthy, "The Narrative Sources of *The Tempest*," *Review of English Studies*, XXIV, 1948. COMMENT: New Arden Edition; Enid Welsford, *The Court Masque*, 1927; G. Wilson Knight, *The Shakespearian Tempest*, 1932. STAGE HISTORY: New Cambridge Edition; G. C. D. Odell, *Shakespeare from Betterton to Irving*, 1920; J. C. Trewin, *Shakespeare on the English Stage, 1900–1964*, 1964.

Selected Criticism

JOHN DRYDEN.

As when a Tree's cut down, the secret Root
Lives under ground, and then new branches shoot
So, from old *Shakespear's* honour'd dust, this day
Springs up and buds a new reviving Play.
Shakespear, who (taught by none) did first impart
To *Fletcher* Wit, to labouring *Johnson* Art.
He, Monarch-like, gave those his Subjects Law,
And is that Nature which they paint and draw.
Fletcher reach'd that which on his heights did grow,
Whilst *Johnson* crept and gather'd all below.
This did his Love, and this his Mirth digest:
One imitates him most, the other best.
If they have since out-writ all other Men,
'Tis with the drops which fell from *Shakespear's* pen.
The Storm which vanish'd on the neighb'ring shore,
Was taught by *Shakespear's* Tempest first to roar.
That Innocence and Beauty which did smile
In *Fletcher*, grew on this *Enchanted Isle*.
But *Shakespear's* Magick could not copy'd be,
Within that Circle none durst walk but he.
I must confess 'twas bold, nor would you now
That liberty to vulgar Wits allow,
Which work by Magick supernatural things:
But *Shakespear's* Pow'r is Sacred as a King's
Those Legends from old Priesthood were receiv'd
And he then writ, as People then believ'd.
But, if for *Shakespear* we your grace implore,
We for our Theatre shall want it more:
Who by our dearth of Youths are forc'd t'employ
One of our Women to present a Boy.
And that's a transformation, you will say,
Exceeding all the Magick in the Play.

[Prologue to *The Tempest*, the Davenant–Dryd[e]n adaptation, published 1670.]

SAMUEL TAYLOR COLERIDGE. In this play Shakespea[re] has especially appealed to the imagination, and [he] has constructed a plot well adapted to the purpos[e]. According to his scheme, he did not appeal to a[ny] sensuous impression (the word "sensuous" is autho[r]ised by Milton) of time and place, but to t[he] imagination, and it is to be borne in mind, that [of] old, and as regards mere scenery, his works may [be] said to have been recited rather than acted—that [is] to say, description and narration supplied the pla[ce] of visual exhibition: the audience was told to fan[cy] that they saw what they only heard described; t[he] painting was not in colours but in words.

This is particularly to be noted in the first scene—a storm and its confusion on board the king's shi[p]. The highest and the lowest characters are broug[ht] together, and with what excellence! Much of t[he] genius of Shakespeare is displayed in these happ[y] combinations—the highest and the lowest, the gaye[st] and the saddest; he is not droll in one scene a[nd] melancholy in another, but often both the one a[nd] the other in the same scene. Laughter is made [to] swell the tear of sorrow, and to throw, as it wer[e] poetic light upon it, while the tear mingles tenderness with the laughter. Shakespeare has evinced the power, which above all other men he possessed, that of introducing the profoundest sentiments of wisdom, where they would be least expected, yet where they are most truly natural. One admirable secret of his art is, that separate speeches frequently do not appear to have been occasioned by those which preceded, and which are consequent upon each other, but to have arisen out of the peculiar character of the speaker. [*Shakespearean Criticism* by S. T. Coleridge, T. M. Raysor, ed., Everyman Library Edition, 1960.]

WILLIAM HAZLITT. *The Tempest* is one of the most original and perfect of Shakespear's productions, and he has shown in it all the variety of his powers. It is full of grace and grandeur. The human and imaginary characters, the dramatic and the grotesque, are blended together with the greatest art, and without any appearance to it. Though he has here given 'to airy nothing a local habitation and a name,' yet that part which is only the fantastic creation of his mind has the same palpable texture and coheres 'semblably' with the rest. As the preternatural part has the air of reality, and almost haunts the imagination with a sense of truth, the real characters and events partake of the wildness of a dream. The stately magician Prospero, driven from his dukedom, but around whom (so potent is his art) airy spirits throng numberless to do his bidding; his daughter Miranda ('worthy of that name') to whom all the power of his art points, and who seems the goddess of the isle; the princely Ferdinand, cast by fate upon the haven of his happiness in this idol of his love; the delicate Ariel; the savage Caliban, half brute, half demon; the drunken ship's crew—are all connected parts of the story, and can hardly be spared from the place they fill. Even the local scenery is of a piece and character with the subject. Prospero's enchanted island seems to have risen from out of the sea; the airy music, the tempest-tossed vessel, the turbulent waves, all have the effect of the landscape background of some fine picture. Shakespear's pencil is (to use an allusion of his own) 'like the dyer's hand, subdued to what it works in.' Everything in him, though it partakes of 'the liberty of wit,' is also subjected to 'the law' of the understanding. For instance, even the drunken sailors, who are made reeling ripe, share, in the disorder of their minds and bodies, in the tumult of the elements, and seem on shore to be as much at the mercy of chance as they were before at the mercy of the wind and waves. These fellows with their sea-wit are the least to our taste of any part of the play; but they are as like drunken sailors as they can be, and are an indirect foil to Caliban, whose figure acquires a classical dignity in the comparison. [*Characters of Shakespear's Plays*, 1817.]

VICTOR HUGO. Many commentators agree in the belief that *The Tempest* is the last creation of Shakespeare. I will readily believe it. There is in *The Tempest* the solemn tone of a testament. It might be said that, before his death, the poet, in this epopee of the ideal, had designed a codicil for the Future. In this enchanted isle, full of 'sounds and sweet airs that give delight,' we may expect to behold Utopia, the promised land of future generations, Paradise regained. Who in reality is Prospero, the king of this isle? Prospero is the shipwrecked sailor who reaches port, the exile who regains his native land, he who from the depths of despair becomes all-powerful, the worker who by his science has tamed matter, Caliban, and by his genius the spirit, Ariel. Prospero is man, the master of Nature and the despot of destiny; he is the man-Providence!

The Tempest is the supreme denouement, dreamed by Shakespeare, for the bloody drama of Genesis. It is the expiation of the primordial crime. The region whither it transports us is the enchanted land where the sentence of damnation is absolved by clemency, and where reconciliation is ensured by amnesty to the fratricide. And, at the close of the piece, when the poet, touched by emotion, throws Antonio into the arms of Prospero, he has made Cain pardoned by Abel. [*Œuvres complètes de Shakespeare*, 1859–1866; translation from *The Tempest*, New Variorum ed., 1892.]

JAMES RUSSELL LOWELL. If I read *The Tempest* rightly, it is an example of how a great poet should write allegory,—not embodying metaphysical abstractions, but giving us ideals abstracted from life itself, suggesting an under-meaning everywhere, forcing it upon us nowhere, tantalizing the mind with hints that imply so much and tell so little, and yet keep the attention all eye and ear with eager, if fruitless, expectation. Here the leading characters are not merely typical, but symbolical,—that is, they do not illustrate a class of persons, they belong to universal Nature. . . . The whole play indeed is a succession of illusions, winding up with those solemn words of the great enchanter who had summoned to his service every shape of merriment or passion, every figure in the great tragi-comedy of life, and who was now bidding farewell to the scene of his triumphs. [*Among my Books*, 1870.]

EDWARD DOWDEN. I should describe Prospero as the man of genius, the great artist, lacking at first in practical gifts which lead to material success, and set adrift on the perilous sea of life, in which he finds his enchanted island, where he may achieve his works of wonder. He bears with him Art in its infancy—the marvellous child, Miranda. The grosser passions and appetites—Caliban—he subdues to his service, '*Mir.* 'Tis a villain, sir, I do not love to look on. *Pros.* But as 'tis We cannot miss him'; and he partially informs this servant-monster with intellect and imagination; for Caliban has dim affinities with the higher world of spirits. But these grosser passions and appetites attempt to violate the purity of art. Caliban would seize on Miranda, and people the island with Calibans; therefore his servitude must be strict. And who is Ferdinand? Is he not, with his gallantry and his beauty, the young Fletcher in conjunction with whom Shakspere worked upon *The Two Noble Kinsmen* and *Henry VIII*? Fletcher is conceived as a follower of the Shaksperian style and method in dramatic art; he had 'eyed full many a lady with best regard,' for several virtues had liked several women, but never any with whole-hearted devotion, except Miranda. And to Ferdinand the old enchanter will entrust his daughter, 'a third of his own life.' But Shakspere had perceived the weak point in Fletcher's genius—its want of hardness of fibre, of patient endurance, and of a sense of the solemnity and sanctity of the service of art. And therefore he finely hints to his friend, that his winning of Miranda must not be too light and easy. It shall be Ferdinand's task to remove some thousands of logs and pile them, according to the strict injunction of Prospero. 'Don't despise drudgery and dryasdust work, young poets,' Shakspere would seem to say, who had himself so carefully laboured over his English and Roman histories; 'for Miranda's sake such drudgery may well seem light.' Therefore, also, Prospero surrounds the marriage of Ferdinand to his daughter with a religious awe. Ferdinand must honour her as sacred, and win her by hard toil. But the work of the higher imagination is not drudgery —it is swift and serviceable among all the elements, fire upon the topmast, the sea-nymph upon the sands, Ceres the goddess of earth, with harvest blessings, in the Masque. It is essentially Ariel, an airy spirit,—the imaginative genius of poetry, but recently delivered in England from long slavery to Sycorax. Prospero's departure from the island is the abandoning by Shakspere of the theatre, the scene of his marvellous works: 'Graves at my command Have waked their sleepers, oped, and let them forth By my so potent art.' Henceforth Prospero is but a man; no longer a great enchanter. He returns to the dukedom he had lost in Stratford-upon Avon, and will pay no tribute henceforth to any Alonzo or Lucy of them all. [*Shakspere—His Mind and Art*, 1875.]

FRANK KERMODE. Learning is a major theme in the play; we learn that Miranda is capable of it and Caliban not, and why this should be so; but we are also given a plan of the place of learning in the dispositions of providence. Prospero, like Adam, fell from his kingdom by an inordinate thirst for knowledge; but learning is a great aid to virtue, the road by which we may love and imitate God, and "repair the ruins of our first parents", and by its means he is enabled to return. The solicitude which accompanied Adam and Eve when "the world was all before them" went also with Prospero and Miranda when they set out in their "rotten carcass of a butt".

> By foul play, as thou say'st, were we heav'd thence,
> But blessedly holp hither.
>
> (I. ii. 62–3)

They came ashore "by Providence divine"; and Gonzalo leaves us in no doubt that Prospero's fault, like Adam's, was a happy one:

> Was Milan thrust from Milan, that his issue
> Should become kings of Naples? O rejoice
> Beyond a common joy! . . .
>
> (V. i. 205–7)

He had achieved the great object of Learning, and regained a richer heritage. But he is not learned in only this rather abstract sense; he is the learned prince. Like Boethius, he had been a natural philosopher, and had learnt from Philosophy that "to hate the wicked were against reason." He clearly shared the view that "no wise man had rather live in banishment, poverty, and ignominy, than prosper in his own country . . . For in this manner is the office of wisdom performed with more credit and renown, where the governors' happiness is participated by the people about them." And Philosophy, though ambiguously, taught both Boethius and Prospero "the way by which thou mayest return to thy country."

There is nothing remarkable about Prospero's a[m]bition to regain his own kingdom and strengthen [his] house by a royal marriage. To be studious and co[n]templative, but also to be able to translate knowled[ge] into power in the active life, was the object of [his] discipline; the Renaissance venerated Scipio for [his] demonstration of this truth, and Marvell's Horati[an] Ode speaks of Cromwell in the same terms.

> The chiefe Use then in man of that he knowes,
> Is his paines taking for the good of all . . .
> Yet *Some seeke knowledge, merely but to know,*
> And idle Curiositie that is . . .

Prospero is not at all paradoxical in presenting hi[m]self at the climax as he was "sometime Milan". Y[et] he does not intend merely to look after his world[ly] affairs; every third thought is to be his grave. "T[he] end of the active or doing life ought to be the b[e]holding; as of war, peace, and as of paines, rest." T[he] active and contemplative lives are complementary.

In all respects, then, Prospero expresses the qua[li]ties of the world of Art, of the *non vile*. These qua[li]ties become evident in the organized contrasts b[e]tween his world and the world of the vile; betwe[en] the worlds of Art and Nature. [Introduction to *T[he] Tempest*, Arden Shakespeare, sixth edition, 1958.]

Tempest, The, or the Enchanted Island. An ada[p]tation of Shakespeare's *The Tempest* by Jo[hn] DRYDEN and William DAVENANT, first acted at Lisl[e's] Tennis Court in 1667 and published in 1670. T[he] Dryden-Davenant *Tempest* was one of the most su[c]cessful of the Restoration adaptations; its populari[ty] was exceeded only by that of the opera based on [it] by Thomas SHADWELL. *The Tempest, or the E[n]chanted Island* was undoubtedly the least faithful [of] all the Restoration adaptations in terms of adheren[ce] to the spirit and language of the original play. Mo[st] of the changes in the story (and the idea of t[he] adaptation itself) are Davenant's, while most of t[he] text is probably Dryden's. The many suggestive a[nd] bawdy speeches—the scenes between Dorinda a[nd] Miranda and between them and their young me[n], for example, are filled with double entendre—a[re] both a marked contrast to Davenant's customa[ry] prudishness and alien to the spirit of Shakespear[e's] romance.

Davenant's structural changes are meant to esta[b]lish a formal balance in the play. Several new cha[r]acters appear. Hippolito, heir to the dukedom [of] Mantua and one who "never saw Woman," is a ma[le] counterpart of Miranda. He is eventually betroth[ed] to her newly invented sister, Dorinda; she, in tur[n], serves as Miranda's companion and sounding boar[d]. Caliban is given a hideous sister, Sycorax, and Ari[el] a sweetheart named Milcha. Among the deletions a[re] the Antonio-Sebastian conspiracy, Ferdinand's pili[ng] of the logs, the appearance and disappearance of t[he] magical feast (it does take place offstage), a[nd] Prospero's farewell to his magic.

The prime attraction which *The Tempest* offer[ed] Davenant was undoubtedly its opportunity for t[he] presentation of a gaudy spectacle. While Shak[e]speare's storm is merely suggested in a brief a[nd] chaotic scene, the adaptation presents a careful a[nd] extravagant staging. In the adaptation, too, a masq[ue] of Vices greets the gentlemen landing on the islar[d] and attempts to persuade them to repent their si[ns], while the finale presents Ariel and Milcha perfor[m] g a sarabande. [Hazelton Spencer, *Shakespeare* ·*proved*, 1927.]

Temple Grafton. A small village five miles west of ·ratford. Shakespeare's marriage license, issued on ·ovember 27, 1582, authorized a marriage "inter ·illelmum Shaxpere et Annam Whateley de Temple ·rafton." Annam Whateley is generally regarded as ·e clerk's error for Anne Hathaway, but the "Tem- ·e Grafton" is more puzzling; one explanation for · appearance on the license is that the couple, if ·atholic, may have been married in Temple Grafton · "Old John Frith," a Catholic priest who, be- ·use of his advanced age, was tolerated at a time ·hen Catholic services were suppressed. See Anne ·HATELY. [M. D. H. Parker, *The Slave of Life*, ·55.]

Tennyson, Alfred, Lord (1809–1892). Poet. Born at ·mersby, in Lincolnshire, Tennyson was writing at ·e age of five. He attended Trinity College, Cam- ·idge, although he was never graduated. There he ·rote *Poems, Chiefly Lyrical* (1830) which, along ·ith his next volume, *Poems* (1832), was savagely ·viewed. But *Poems* (2 vols., 1842), which included ·ocksley Hall" and "Ulysses," was well received. · 1850 he published his great elegy for Arthur ·enry Hallam, *In Memoriam,* and was appointed ·et laureate. Later works include *Maud* (1855), ·*ylls of the King* (1859), *Enoch Arden* (1864), and ·umber of plays.

Echoes of Shakespeare (especially of *The Tem-* ·*st*) in Tennyson's early play *The Devil and the* ·*idy* (pub. 1830) bear out Hallam Tennyson's con- ·ntion that his father read much Shakespeare as a ·y. The play was in blank verse, which Tennyson ·nsidered "the finest vehicle of thought in the lan- ·age of Shakespeare and Milton." To complete the ·cle of Shakespeare's English chronicles, Tennyson ·rote an "historical trilogy"—*Harold* (pub. 1876), ·*cket* (pub. 1879), *Queen Mary* (pub. 1875)—using ·*ing John* as his model, especially in *Queen Mary*. But the influence of Shakespeare was not confined · form. Tennyson seems to have had *Troilus and* ·*essida* (III, iii, 150–153) in mind while writing ·Jlysses" (ll. 22–24) and perhaps *Hamlet* as well ·V, iv, 33–35 for ll. 3–5). He called *Maud* (1855), ·hich he preferred above all his other poems, "a ·tle *Hamlet*," high praise indeed, for he considered ·*amlet* "the greatest creation in literature that I know ·," greater even than *Lear*, which is "too titanic" to · acted. Tennyson's reading of Shakespeare was so ·ute that F. J. Furnivall, the founder of the New ·akspere Society, often sought his advice on texts, ·e poet's ear being particularly helpful in deciding ·hich parts of *Pericles, Henry VI,* and *Henry VIII* ·ere properly accreditable to Shakespeare.

On his deathbed, according to Tennyson's son, the ·-year-old poet called for a copy of Shakespeare ·hich opened to a favorite passage from *Cymbeline* ·Hang there like fruit, my soul,/Till the tree die!" ·, v, 263–264). The volume is buried with him in ·estminster Abbey. [Hallam Tennyson, *Alfred* ·*ord Tennyson: A Memoir by His Son,* 1897; E. A. ·ooney, Jr., "Tennyson's Earliest Shakespeare Paral- ·s," *Shakespeare Association Bulletin,* XV, 1940; ·ouglas Bush, "Tennyson's 'Ulysses' and 'Hamlet,'" ·*odern Language Review,* XXXVIII, 1943.]

tents. In Elizabethan staging, properties made of ·in or cloth, mostly square in shape, which were pitched on the boards of a stage and used to suggest an armed camp in a battle scene. Shakespeare's plays abound in references to tents. In *Richard III,* for example, Richard appears on Bosworth Field, where he instructs his servants to pitch his tent: "Up with my tent there! here will I lie to-night;/But where to-morrow?" (V, iii, 7–8).

In *Julius Caesar,* the action in Act IV switches from the field in front of Brutus' tent (scene ii) to the tent's interior (scene iii). In a battlefield scene two tents were erected on the stage, with the action alternating between them to suggest the camp of the enemy and that of the protagonist. Tents could be quite elaborate; they were furnished with tables, chairs, doors (made of curtains), and even had locks on the doors. In the "plot" of *2 Seven Deadly Sins,* Henry VI is directed to lie asleep in "A tent being plast one the stage" while dumb-shows enter through the two "dores." [E. K. Chambers, *The Elizabethan Stage,* 1923.]

Terence [Publius Terentius Afer] (190?–?159 B.C.). Roman comic dramatist. Born in Carthage, Terence was brought to Rome as a slave but was educated and emancipated by a master who recognized his talent. In addition, his personal grace made him welcome in the higher circles of society. As part of the Greek Revival, he followed Plautus in adapting the comedies of Menander. His six plays, of which the best known are probably *Andria* and *Phormio,* were produced 166–160 B.C.

Like his Greek and Roman exemplars, Terence wrote a comedy of manners, using the same stock situations (involving intrigue and coincidence) and characters (e.g., the crafty parasite); but he differs from Plautus in several ways. Terence uses irony rather than ridicule; instead of relying on animation and a somewhat gross virility, he shows refinement of sentiment; he avoids crude vernacular speech, and his style is economical, yet supple; there are many delicate touches in his characterization. What he loses in vigor he makes up in elegance.

Terence was the only classical playwright whom the medieval churchmen could tolerate. With the revival of Latin drama in the 16th century, he was especially favored in the schools. Terentian style became the basis of the English grammar school, taking precedence over that of Plautus and even of Horace. His influence spread from the schools through the university men to the public stage, and he was widely imitated. Nicholas Udall, a schoolmaster who had published a work on Terence, showed his familiarity with Terentian play structure in his *Ralph Roister Doister,* the first regular English comedy (c. 1553). He embodied in his comic hero the braggart soldier Thraso of Terence's *Eunuchus,* as well as Plautus' *miles gloriosus.* John Lyly's euphuistic style was in debt to Terence; Molière copied his *Phormio* in *Les Fourberies de Scapin;* and Sir Richard Steele adapted his *Andria* in *The Conscious Lovers.*

Shakespeare owes some debt to Terence in matters of characterization, plot, style, and especially structure. In the use of such stock characters as the braggart soldier (Parolles; Bardolph, Nym, and Pistol; and, of course, Falstaff), it is difficult to separate Terence's influence from that of Plautus. The cheerful insolence and ingenuity of Terence's crafty parasite Phormio find numerous echoes in

Shakespeare. Professor T. W. Baldwin has shown how adroitly Shakespeare adapted to *Twelfth Night* the formula of *Andria*, built around the elements of a clever servant and a shipwrecked family finally reunited. Here and in *A Midsummer Night's Dream*, with its pairs of confused lovers floundering at cross-purposes, the comedy is modulated by a certain Terentian sympathetic ruefulness over human nature. And something of the balance and elegance of Shakespeare's early style can be traced back through Lyly to Terence.

Not the least of Terence's contributions to Shakespearean comedy was the element of form. As revived in the academy, classical drama generally called attention to structure, coherence of plot, the unities of time and place, and motivated entrances and exits. Terence had constructed his plays in five stages which he called acts; these divisions were explicated to Elizabethans by the Roman grammarian Donatus as a further development of the Aristotelian demand for a beginning, a middle, and an end. The influence of the grammar school, where Terence was drilled into Renaissance students, disposed educated Englishmen and the public generally to the five-act division. Thus, argues Baldwin, Shakespeare probably learned of this structure firsthand in school as well as through exposure to his predecessors in five-act comedy, Udall and Lyly. These influences blend in such early plays as *Love's Labour's Lost, The Comedy of Errors, The Two Gentlemen of Verona, Romeo and Juliet,* and *All's Well That Ends Well,* all of which Shakespeare divided into five acts and into scenes. [T. W. Baldwin, *William Shakspere's Five-Act Structure,* 1947.]—M. H.

Terry, Dame **[Alice] Ellen** (1847–1928). Actress. Born in Coventry, Ellen Terry came of a large family of actors, which included her father, Benjamin Terry, her mother, Sarah Ballard, three of her sisters, and a brother. As a child she made her debut as Mamillius in Charles Kean's production of *The Winter's Tale* in 1856, followed by performances of Puck (1856), Arthur (1858), and Fleance (1859). In 1862 she began acting in Bristol, doing Titania the following year before returning to the Haymarket in London. Her roles there included Hero, Desdemona, and Nerissa. In 1864 she married a 47-year-old painter, George Frederic Watts, from whom she was separated the following year. In 1867 she played for the first time opposite Henry Irving, in Garrick's *Catherine and Petruchio.*

From 1868 to 1874 she lived in retirement with E. W. Godwin and bore two children, Edith and Edward Gordon Craig. She returned to the stage in 1874 and acted for Charles Reade. In 1875 she scored a great success as Portia in *The Merchant of Venice.* In the same year she married her second husband, Charles Clavering Wardell, who acted as Charles Kelly. They separated in 1881. In 1878 she went to act for Henry Irving as Ophelia. Thereafter, until about 1902, Miss Terry and Irving were inseparable. She played the leads in all his productions and accompanied him on eight visits to America. Her great Shakespearean roles during this time included Ophelia, Juliet, Desdemona, Beatrice, Viola, Lady Macbeth, Queen Katharine, Cordelia, Imogen, and Volumnia. To Irving must go the credit for choosing plays which set off her great talent, but her succe[ss] was equally due to her beauty, her voice, her char[m] and vitality, and most of all to her intelligence, sym[]pathy, and hard work.

In 1902 she played Queen Katharine at the Shak[e]speare Memorial Theatre under the direction [of] Frank Benson, and later that year she played Mistre[ss] Page for Herbert Beerbohm Tree. In 1903 she beg[an] to manage the Imperial Theatre, Westminster, whe[re] she produced critical, though not financial, success[es] staged, as in the case of *Much Ado About Nothin[g]* by her son Gordon Craig.

In 1906 she celebrated the 50th anniversary of h[er] debut with a jubilee matinee at Drury Lane. A[l]though her memory was beginning to fail, she unde[r]took lecture tours and some new roles, such as He[r]mione in 1906. In 1907, while in Pittsburgh, she ma[r]ried James Usselmann, a young American actor i[n] her American touring company who acted und[er] the name of James Carew. In 1925 she made her la[st] appearance in the theatre, on the stage of the Lyri[c] Hammersmith.

In 1903, aided by Christopher St. John, she ha[d] delivered lectures on Shakespeare which owed man[y] of their ideas to George Bernard Shaw. These we[re] published in 1932 as *Four Lectures on Shakespear[e],* Christopher St. John, editor. Also published posthu[]mously were *Ellen Terry's Memoirs,* with notes an[d] additional chapters by Edith Craig and St. Joh[n] (1933), and *Ellen Terry and Bernard Shaw, A Co[r]respondence,* St. John, editor (1931). Miss Terry wa[s] created Dame of the British Empire in 1925. He[r] house at Small Hythe, Tenterden, Kent, was bough[t] by public subscription and made into an Elle[n] Terry Museum. [*Dictionary of National Biography* 1885– .]

Testament of Cresseid. See Robert Henryson.

textual criticism. Textual criticism of Shakespear[e] has only one object: to recover as nearly as may b[e] in the most minute detail, precisely what Shakespea[re] wrote, both in content and in form. By content [is] meant the exact words, what are often called th[e] "substantives" of a text; by form is meant the tex[]ture in which these words are clothed, such as the[ir] spelling, punctuation, capitalization, and division[—]what are often called the "accidentals" of a text. I[n] some part, because most current editions of Shake[]speare are modernized, the "accidentals" have bee[n] of less concern than the recovery of the word[s] themselves; nevertheless, these forms have their par[t] in the total picture of Shakespeare's intentions, an[d] the comparative neglect of the evidence they yiel[d] has tended to solidify a conventional text that i[n] many small questions of meaning is far remove[d] from the evidence of the original documents.

The process of recovery of Shakespeare's word[s] and their accidentals differs with the evidence fo[r] each play and hence can never be entirely uniform[.] Thus it is the additional responsibility of textua[l] critics to assay the weight that can be placed upo[n] the evidence and the confidence that may be fe[lt] in the conclusions drawn in respect to the recover[y] of the texts, in whole or in part. Indeed, althoug[h] it is true that the recovery of Shakespeare's exac[t] words is the ultimate aim of textual criticism, th[e] meaning of "recovery" is by no means restricte[d] to the process of discovering and correcting specifi[c] ror. Instead, a critic "recovers" Shakespeare's text ost notably by identifying those documents in hich the texts are preserved in their most authoritive form and rejecting all other versions that have d no access to fresh authority. This process alone ovides us with the overwhelming majority of the ords that, on the available evidence, we must beve are authentically Shakespeare's. Thereafter, the rrection by emendation is a separate procedure. ometimes the process of selection is complicated the conflicting claims of two or more texts that em from independent authoritative traditions. In ch cases, the textual critic's task is more complex nce he must attempt to discover the line of transission of these texts back to Shakespeare's lost orking papers and to estimate the effects of this ansmission on the variant forms that the texts ve taken. Only after a clear view has been gained the nature and extent of the authority in these ocuments can the matter of a choice of readings etween their variants be attempted on any logical sis.

Textual criticism, then, is often more concerned ith establishing the nature and authority of texts their original documentary form (see COPY) than is in the secondary process of recovering true adings from occasional corruptions. As a result, uch of the scholarship devoted to Shakespearean xtual criticism is not in the least aimed at the oblem of emending any single specific reading. his last is only the final operation in the construcon of a definitive text after all other matters have een settled.

In the past, textual criticism was often a subjective t not susceptible of rule since the taste and learng of the individual critic were almost alone in estion. Taste and learning are still the most imrtant endowments a critic can possess when he mes to the final operation on a text, but in some nsiderable part, stemming from Sir Walter Greg's 28 British Academy lecture "Principles of Emendaon in Shakespeare," a methodological approach has olved that provides a factual basis for literary iticism applied to text. This new approach, of itical bibliography, attempts to study the transission of the Shakespeare texts in their earliest thoritative documents by endeavoring to deterine the specific conditions that produced these ocuments. An estimate of their trustworthiness, en, can start with the physical evidence. Indeed, e heart of the method consists in supplying a echanical explanation for all phenomena mechanilly produced by the printing process whenever ch an explanation can be arrived at on the reverable evidence. On occasion such bibliographical idence limits the number of possibilities open to e finishing touches of critical explanation, which ust necessarily refer back to values, or opinion, as e basis for judgment. The most informed textual iticism joins the bibliographical and the critical assigning to each its proper complementary role.

We begin, then, with the conditions that proiced the original Shakespeare texts on which all iticism must rest. No evidence exists to suggest at Shakespeare ever concerned himself with the inting of any of his plays or the accuracy of the xts given to the printer. With a few exceptions, the manuscripts came to the press from the theatrical company and, before the posthumous collection made in the First Folio of 1623, they seemed to represent the copy the company could best spare. Actually, these conditions may have given us some texts that are superior to what we should have obtained had the company been less careless, since to the company the PROMPT-BOOK was the single authoritative document. A textual critic, however, knows that prompt-books were usually scribal transcripts and that corruption of the text increases with every agent intervening between the author and the end result. When a text has been set up directly from a Shakespeare manuscript, even one in not wholly legible shape perhaps, only the compositor comes between us and the original. But for every scribe who copies out fair the author's worked-over papers, inadvertent as well as sophisticating errors are introduced; and if only one form of text derived from such a chain of transmission is preserved, most of the errors will be so ingrained as not to be recognized for what they are. For example, well over a hundred readings in *Hamlet* that are certainly not Shakespeare's would be accepted without quibble if the Folio alone had been preserved and we had not had the Second Quarto, printed from a source nearer the holograph (if not the holograph itself), to provide us with what Shakespeare wrote in these cases of transmissional corruption.

The earliest task of the textual critic, therefore, is to try to identify the kind of manuscript that served as printer's copy for a Shakespeare first edition and for any later authoritative form of the text. If the manuscript is taken to be autograph, the critic will be inclined to give the benefit of the doubt to difficult words or phrases, less likely to be the invention of the compositor than of the author, and he will feel that they can represent Shakespeare's own, or else in some recoverable form a recognizably corrupt version of what Shakespeare wrote. But though the printed text might be superficially cleaner and more correct if the printer's copy were a scribal transcript, the critic will know that it is sure to harbor corruptions of a different sort from the first, and he may be emboldened to question doubtful or not entirely characteristic readings that in the first text would pass scrutiny without comment.

Although various inquiries into the nature of the lost manuscripts have been speculative in the extreme, some bibliographical progress has been made in identifying the sources of a few. For instance, a theatrical scribe, Ralph Crane, has been identified as the inscriber of the manuscripts that were given to the Folio printer for *The Two Gentlemen of Verona*, *The Merry Wives of Windsor*, and *The Winter's Tale*. Certain preserved Crane manuscripts furnish valuable evidence to isolate his characteristics in the Shakespeare texts so that they need not be confused with the author's or compositor's. Or, in another example, the same two compositors who set the Second Quarto *Hamlet* in James Roberts' shop also set *The Merchant of Venice*. Thus the very marked differences in the accidentals of both prints cannot be ascribed to the printer but must reflect a fundamental variation in the manuscript copy. If the Second Quarto of *Hamlet* were set from Shakespeare's working papers, as is usually assumed, then the manuscript behind *The Merchant* cannot be the autograph that critics on slight evidence have customarily assigned as copy. Similarly, it is now known from the spelling evidence of the Folio print, independent of its two compositors, that halfway through the preparation of the copy behind *1 Henry VI* the inscriber changed, and so do the characteristics of the manuscript. In the past, investigations of a general sort have attempted to isolate the physical characteristics of theatrical manuscripts and to search for these stigmata in the printed texts, drawing suitable conclusions from the positive or the negative evidence discovered. More searching investigations now try to isolate the characteristics of the various compositors who set the Shakespeare texts and then to ascribe to the manuscript those details that run counter to the known and predictable habits of the several workmen.

Four major textual situations exist in the original documents that provide the sources for critical study.

The first, and simplest, are those cases in which only one edition was set from any manuscript, and all later editions were simple reprints without authority. The purest examples come in plays printed for the first time in the Folio. *The Two Gentlemen of Verona* is such a play, and so is *Macbeth*, and *Antony and Cleopatra*, each of which represents a different state of textual transmission. *Two Gentlemen* was printed from Ralph Crane's transcript of a manuscript whose nature is not known. *Macbeth* seems to represent a scribal copy made from a prompt-book in a severely cut version for the stage worked up at a date later than the original writing and containing some lines by another hand. Serious as are its deficiencies, it is the only text we have. *Antony and Cleopatra* may have been set from the most authoritative possible source, Shakespeare's own manuscript, probably without cutting for the stage; the evidence for this is slight, however.

These single texts offer the fewest problems in recovery capable of solution by textual criticism, largely because they provide the smallest evidence with which to work. The obvious errors can be identified and corrected by an informed editor. Readings that make some but not a wholly satisfactory sense can also yield, on occasion, to the methods of literary criticism. An editor, for example, can sometimes decide what Shakespeare must have written in one place by utilizing the evidence of what he wrote somewhere else. When Cleopatra bids the Messenger from Antony, "Ram thou thy fruitful tidings in mine ears," no editor need be misled by "fruitful" and the easy handwriting confusion between *in* and *m* to emend, as some have done, to "Rain thou thy fruitful tidings." That the witness of the print is correct is almost certainly indicated by such parallels as "thrusting this report into his ears" from *Julius Caesar*, or "You cram these words into my ears" in *The Tempest*. Rightly or wrongly, the frequent critical approval of "the dead vast and middle of the night" taken from the bad First Quarto of *Hamlet* as against the good Second Quarto and Folio readings "dead wast" (i.e., waste) rests chiefly on the parallel with "that vast of night" in *The Tempest*.

Yet analogies of this sort must be used wi caution. The Ghost, approving of Hamlet's resol tion, remarks in the Second Quarto that if Ham had behaved otherwise he would have been dul than "the fat weed that roots on Lethe whar Guided by a quotation from *Antony and Cleopat* about the vagabond flag that moves back and for with the current of the stream and so "rots itself motion," most editors have decided that the Fol was correct when it printed "the fat weed that r on Lethe wharf." But a critic might well consid that a "wharf" is a bank, and the *Antony and Cle patra* water image need have no direct applicati to the *Hamlet* word, for the waters of the river forgetfulness merely flow past the "fat weed" abo them on the bank and therefore can have nothi to do with its rotting. That Shakespeare did n write "roots" is still to demonstrate.

Sometimes an inspired guess gives us with absolu conviction of rightness what Shakespeare must ha written, even though we rely on faith and not concrete evidence. Partly of this nature is Willia Warburton's emendation of the Second Quarto a Folio *Hamlet* "good kissing carrion" to "god kissi carrion," with its long series of reverberations purity and corruption, and its layers of word-pla Very likely the faint parallel Warburton invok from *Cymbeline* of "common-kissing Titan" w an afterthought and not the progenitor of t inevitable reading. A more famous example, perha because made without analogy, was Theobald's teration of "a table of green fields" in *Henry V* "a babbl'd of green fields," even though mode critics take some of the fun out of life by suggesti that "talk'd" (which indeed was the original su gestion) is more probable than "babbl'd." S EMENDATION.

Bibliographical examination of the text may pr vide suggestions for emendation or, at the least, m reveal mechanical conditions that cannot be ignor by a critic. In *Love's Labour's Lost*, IV, iii, 181–18 Berowne asks, in the authoritative Quarto, "Wh shall you see mee write a thing in rime? / Or gro for Ione? or spende a minutes time. . . ." The Fol reprint makes the second line more explicit: "C grone for *Ioane?*" Of six copies checked by S Walter Greg for his facsimile edition of the Quart five read "Ione"; but one, "Loue." The Globe a Kittredge texts prefer "love," but Richard Dav (New Arden Edition) and Peter Alexander choo "Joan." Either makes sense, although critics w prefer *Joan* have not faced up to the fact that th is a country-wench name inappropriate in the pre ent context. The fact is that the variant *Ione-Lo* is a press-alteration made during the course printing the outer forme of sheet E. Only one oth variant appears in this forme, the correction another page in the same five copies that pri "Ione" of the turned second letter "p" in loose spaced "paper."

Criticism alone could not settle on this eviden which was the earlier and which the later varian but the analytical bibliographer can demonstra from the copies containing a press-variant in t opposite forme that "Loue" was the original rea ing. For David the demonstration of this order w sufficient to settle the authority of *Joan*, but t case is not so simple. The real question is wheth e agent who made the change while the sheet as in press referred back to manuscript copy for s authority, or whether he ordered the alteration n his own. In general it is a rare press-corrector of ays at this time who consults the manuscript, and this particular book no other known press-variant substantive or requires anything like consultation f copy; all merely correct obvious misprints or ightly improve the accidentals. The normal interretation of the bibliographical evidence is that the ress-corrector was in fact sophisticating his copy hen he took "Loue" to be a misprint and changed to "Ione." A literary critic who accepts as Shakeeare's true reading the press-corrector's alteration stead of the word set by the compositor from his opy should have stronger evidence to back him up an has yet been presented.

On other occasions, the information that is acımulating about the general habits and relative curacy of some of the compositors who set Shakeeare texts may suggest the need for emendation f doubtful readings that yet make some sense. If, or instance, a suspected reading comes in the work f Compositor A of the First Folio (see COMPOSITOR), e know that most of his departures from copy will e rather literal misreadings from which the true ord might be recovered, whereas his fellow, Comositor B, is more likely to crowd his memory with o much copy material before he turns to his cases set type, and therefore serious errors can result om his memorial confusion that creates paraphrases d substitutions. Also, Compositor B is inclined to nker with the meter of verse, and sometimes he eliberately changes words that he thinks are not uite right. Thus not only the incidence of error ill be higher in B's work than in A's, but also the ature of the error might differ, and a textual critic tempting to recover true readings from suspected orruption can govern himself accordingly.

The second textual situation is only slightly more omplex. This occurs when only one edition exists f a play printed from manuscript, always one bere the Folio, but the editors of the Folio made a uick comparison of the early Quarto with their ayhouse copy and wrote in minor changes before nding the marked printed edition to Jaggard's op. Usually these alterations do not affect the text ut reflect the Folio editors' concern for such theatcal matters as the stage directions or speech prexes. Such minor Folio alteration happened to a w plays, like *The Merchant of Venice*, and a critic ust come to some conclusions about the source d accuracy of the changes. In *Titus Andronicus* e Folio editors failed to alter any details of the rinted Quarto text, but from their playhouse manuript they did add a new scene not present in the rly editions.

The third situation is much more troublesome. ere the earliest edition in print is what is known chnically as a BAD QUARTO. In the details of their rigin it is likely that these "bad quartos" vary idely, but they all have one point in common: that there is no transcriptional link with any Shakeeare autograph. The theory that fits these curious xts best is that they are all reports of the acted xt, that is, MEMORIAL RECONSTRUCTIONS—on a few casions by an actor who had participated, like the arcellus-Voltimand actor of *Hamlet*. Some of Shakespeare's most popular plays were pirated in this manner, among them *Hamlet, King Lear, Henry V, Richard III, Romeo and Juliet*, and *The Merry Wives of Windsor*. For some of these, *Romeo and Juliet* and *Hamlet* for example, Shakespeare's company issued a better text within a few years of the unauthorized publication; but most of these plays, such as *King Lear, Richard III*, and *Merry Wives of Windsor*, had to wait until the Folio for an improved version.

For some of these plays, such as *Hamlet, Romeo and Juliet*, and *Merry Wives of Windsor*, the good new text was set directly from a manuscript furnished by the acting company. Yet it is cause for uneasiness that, in every improved bad-quarto play, editors have felt it necessary occasionally to go back to the bad version in preference to the good in order to recover what they felt Shakespeare really wrote. This process began in the 18th century when the nature of the bad texts was not understood and they were thought on the whole to be Shakespearean first drafts. It is from the 18th century, for example, that the quite indefensible reading "a rose by any other name would smell as sweet" in *Romeo and Juliet* from the bad quarto has got itself firmly fixed in tradition instead of the manifestly correct Second Quarto's "rose by any other word." Yet, as with certain of the omissions in the Folio *Merry Wives of Windsor*—notably the phrase "Give me thy hand, terrestrial; so" addressed by the Host to Caius—no question exists that sometimes a bad text can preserve the right reading.

The situation grows even more complex when the manuscript that stands behind the good text was not itself used as printer's copy; but, instead, this copy was made up by bringing the earlier printed bad quarto into general conformity with the manuscript by interlineation, substitution, and often additions on attached slips of paper. It is quite demonstrable that the good Folio text of such plays as *King Lear* and *Richard III* was typeset from such extraordinarily marked-up printed copy.

Four particular problems arise when the transmission of the text passes through such an annotated printed quarto.

First, the compositor may have had more than usual difficulty in reading some of the cramped insertions, and errors may creep in.

Second, the scribe is in some sense copying out the manuscript again and is therefore liable to error. It is quite possible for him to change a correct reading in the printed copy to an incorrect one under the illusion that he is making a required alteration. Or, an incorrect reading may be altered, not to a correct one but to another error.

Third, depending upon the nature of the manuscript used by the Folio (especially if it is at some remove from Shakespeare's autograph), the possibility exists that it will contain errors, corrections of which are found in the actor's memory as reflected in the bad quarto.

Fourth, the scribe may miss some differences between print and manuscript and fail to correct errors in the printed copy, in which case a critic seldom can be entirely certain that he is reading what Shakespeare did not write instead of a common reading approved in both manuscript and reported text. Under these difficult conditions it is not strange that the recovery of the true text from two or more faulty witnesses is subject to more than ordinary debate. It has been estimated that more than 140 readings common to the Quarto and Folio texts of *Richard III* represent scribal failure to correct error in the Quarto and hence are subject to editorial emendation. The evidence for *King Lear* is so remarkably at variance sometimes as to make unanimity of critical opinion an almost hopeless prospect. Nevertheless, the modern tendency is to take it that—despite all the various sources of possible error in the good text—a strong presumption in its favor should exist and that especially powerful reasons should operate if its readings are to be rejected in favor of plausible but automatically suspect variants from the bad quarto. For instance, few critics will now object on literary grounds to *ponderous* in Cordelia's aside, "I am sure my love's / More ponderous than my tongue," and choose as Shakespearean the glib and conventional bad quarto "More richer than my tongue" preferred by earlier editors.

The fourth category represents a puzzling situation. Here such plays as *Othello, Troilus and Cressida, Hamlet,* and perhaps *2 Henry IV* were originally printed in quarto in good texts that were either Shakespearean autographs or else were derived from the original papers at only a short remove. Yet when these plays came to be printed in the Folio, we find there another good text although one of a different tradition. The reason for the rejection of the earlier printed good texts can be most obscure. Copyright problems just possibly may have dictated the shift in *Troilus and Cressida* which had initially started in the Folio as a simple reprint, but certainly not in *Hamlet* or in *2 Henry IV*.

If both texts are authoritative, the choice of readings is often not a clear-cut one between corruption and correction such as is ordinarily found in the bad-quarto revisions in the Folio, where the weight on correction is manifestly in favor of the altered text.

Instead, the variant may represent, just about as often, correctness in the original good edition, and corruption in the altered Folio version, if the manuscript used for the Folio, though authoritatively derived, were farther removed in its line of transmission from Shakespeare's original than the manuscript used as printer's copy for the earlier quarto.

This state of affairs seems to be present in *Hamlet,* which runs the gamut of modes of textual transmission. *Hamlet* was first printed in 1603 in a reported bad-quarto text. In late 1604 a revised good quarto was published, generally thought to have been set up from an ill-written manuscript in Shakespeare's own hand, although the evidence is speculative. In 1623 the printers of the Folio produced a version that seems to have a theatrical origin and thus to have passed through the hands of several scribes, with ensuing corruptions. Ordinarily, the more literary version of the Second Quarto, the one (whatever its nature) printed from a manuscript closest to Shakespeare, would have pre-eminent authority, and any Folio variant would need to show cause why it should be accepted as a substitute. For many readings this textual logi is quite accurate in its application.

On the other hand, a textual critic must balanc at least two additional factors. First, the tw compositors of the Second Quarto had seriou trouble reading a difficult manuscript. For all o Act I it is clear that the first compositor referre for assistance to a copy of the bad quarto, and thu some readings in the Second Quarto may no represent what were in the manuscript copy bu instead may derive from an actor's faulty memor as reproduced in the 1603 text. Second, many erro were made when the bad quarto was no longer o assistance, and we must presume that the Foli manuscript in a number of cases had these word right. To these may be added a rather speculativ third factor, the possibility that between the in scription of the form of the manuscript represente by the Second Quarto and the prompt-book forn seemingly represented at some remove by th Folio, Shakespeare may have introduced a fe revisions.

In the various places where the bad quarto ca act as a witness, it can tell us what the actor re membered from his part. That is, when the tw Quartos agree against the Folio, we seem to be i possession of what Shakespeare wrote in his ow papers and was transferred verbatim to the origin prompt-book. For instance, when the two earl texts read "jump at this dead hour," and the Foli "just at this dead hour," we not only may suspec the Folio substitution of a colorless normal wor for a vigorous, unusual one, but we have th evidence that the actor remembered "jump," an that Shakespeare's manuscript seems to have rea "jump." However, this logic is less compelling i the first act, since the possibility must always b contemplated that an agreement like "jump" wa taken over by the Second from the bad quart That this contingency is to be respected may b shown by the agreement of both Quartos in Marcel lus' query, "Why such daily cost of brazen cannon? whereas the Folio provides the incontestably co rect reading "cast."

Correspondingly, agreement between Folio an bad quarto as against Second Quarto might b significant, as in the manifestly correct assignmen to Marcellus instead of to Horatio of the lin "What, has this thing appeared again tonight? Yet in viewing such concurrences a critic will nee to recall that both bad quarto and Folio tex ultimately stem from the same prompt-book, an this may have contained an error not present i Shakespeare's own papers. Agreement of the ba quarto and Folio texts of *The Merry Wives o Windsor* in the error in Nym's remark abou stealing "at a minute's rest" instead of the corre "minim's rest" demonstrates such a transmission c error.

Yet a textual critic's troubles do not confin themselves to the question of the variants alon Common readings in *Hamlet* in Second Quarto an Folio like "good kissing carrion" and "pious bond (for *pious bawds*) are clearly in need of emend tion, yet their origin is almost inexplicable if bot texts were set from independent manuscripts. Th crucial matter of the physical transmission of th ext then comes in question; and in spite of some lifficulties that remain to be worked out, it would eem most probable on the evidence that the Folio vas not set directly from manuscript but from a opy of the Second Quarto that had been altered n various respects by comparison with the new nanuscript. This physical fact, if fact it be, completely changes the whole textual logic bearing on he shared reading. The critic can no longer take t as axiomatic that agreement between the two ood authorities is proof of a reading's authenticity. On the contrary, the identical Folio form may represent not what was in the Folio manuscript but instead an oversight by the scribe annotating the econd Quarto for the printer.

At the present time Shakespearean textual criticism has reached something of a point of rest in espect to the single-text plays in the first two ategories. Very few previously unsuggested editorial emendations of any marked importance are ikely to be proposed, and the literary critic can lo little more than pick and choose among known lternatives. The complex texts of the third and ourth categories still suffer from eclectic literary diting in which, mostly on grounds of taste, a ritic will agree or disagree with traditional choices out without the application of any rigorous textual heory derived from the origin, transmission, and elationship of the two authorities to limit or to uide his selection.

In the meantime, however, background studies hat will eventually lead to a re-evaluation of tradiion are proceeding with some vigor. Unsolved roblems of transmission, such as still obtain in *Hamlet*, *King Lear*, and *Richard III*, will ultimately e settled on a factual basis. The modern weapon as turned out to be the science of compositor tudy, by which an attempt is made to strip the eil of print from a text and thus to recover a umber of the precise details of the underlying nanuscript. Now that the resources of electronic omputers can be applied to large-scale textual reearch, the means are at last available to determine n scientific and not on impressionistic evidence nough of the basic manuscript characteristics in a umber of plays so that the scribes can be sorted ut, classified, and the nucleus of play texts set rom Shakespeare's own holographs can be isolated or intensive and detailed study.

The end in view is a bold one: to discover from he maximum penetration of the physical facts the ew evidence that can be applied to the textual riticism of Shakespeare. It is such evidence alone hat can lead to an authoritative, modern revaluation of the results of the great critical effort f a hundred years ago that produced the standard Globe text. On the basis of this new technical nowledge that has been accumulating since World Var II, the definitive text designed to replace the Globe will be constructed from the combined pplication of bibliographical, linguistic, and critcal scholarship of a kind that could not have been nvisaged by an earlier generation. [W. W. Greg, *Principles of Emendation in Shakespeare*, 1928; W. W. Greg, *The Editorial Problem in Shakespeare*, 1942; Alice Walker, *Textual Problems of the First Folio*, 1953; Fredson Bowers, *On Editing Shakespeare and the Elizabethan Dramatists*, 1955; W. W. Greg, *The Shakespeare First Folio*, 1955; Charlton Hinman, *The Printing and Proof-reading of the First Folio of Shakespeare*, 1963; Fredson Bowers, *Bibliography and Textual Criticism*, 1964; Fredson Bowers, "Today's Shakespeare Texts and Tomorrow's," *Studies in Bibliography*, XIX, 1966.] —F. B.

Thackeray, William Makepeace (1811–1863). Novelist. Born in Calcutta, Thackeray went to Cambridge and then to the continent to study first law, then art. Successful at neither, he began writing the satiric "Yellowplush" articles for *Fraser's Magazine*. His greatest novel, *Vanity Fair* (1848), was followed by *Pendennis* (1850), *Henry Esmond* (1852), *The Newcomes* (1855), and *The Virginians* (1859). A common theme in Thackeray's novels is love for an unworthy person, and wherever he uses it (as in *Vanity Fair*, *Pendennis*, and *The Virginians*), he alludes to Titania and Bottom, and when a lady eagerly listens to a courter, it is as if she is playing Desdemona to his Othello. There are many Hal-Falstaff relationships, and George Warrington (*The Virginians*) quotes from Hamlet's soliloquies to describe his own plight. In speaking of *Hamlet* in that novel and again in "Picture Gossip," Thackeray makes a point of defending Gertrude. *Hamlet*, *Othello*, *A Midsummer Night's Dream*, and *Macbeth* are the plays most alluded to. Criticisms of contemporary productions of Shakespeare are common in his letters, Charles Macready's performances being particularly disparaged. In an essay, "Round the Christmas Tree," Thackeray witnesses a burlesque pantomime of *Hamlet* and remonstrates, "But, gentlemen, if you don't respect Shakespeare, to whom will you be civil?" [Edward Vandiver, "Thackeray and Shakespeare," *Furman Studies*, XXXIV, 1951.]

Thaisa. In *Pericles*, daughter of King Simonides of Pentapolis, wife of Pericles, and mother of Marina. Independent of parental consent and ignorant of Pericles' pedigree, Thaisa determines to marry him or no one. She accompanies her husband on his return voyage to Tyre and, believed dead after giving birth to a daughter, is buried at sea. Thaisa's coffin is washed ashore at Ephesus, where she is resurrected by the wonder-working physician, Cerimon. Presuming Pericles dead, a mourning Thaisa becomes a votaress at the temple of the goddess Diana in Ephesus. Fourteen years later she is reunited with her husband and child.

Thaliard. In *Pericles*, a lord of Antioch. Employed by Antiochus to murder Pericles, Thaliard considers discretion the better part of valor and pursues his assignment without questioning its motivation.

Theatre, the. The first building in England to serve primarily as a public theatre. The Theatre was built in 1576 by James Burbage on land leased from Giles Alleyn. The site was in the liberty of Halliwell (or Holywell), St. Leonard's, Shoreditch, which lay outside the Bishopsgate entrance to the north of the city of London and was beyond the jurisdiction of the hostile civic authorities. Burbage's lease on the property was to run for a period of 21 years. The cost of the new building (estimated by contemporaries, after its completion, at 1000 marks or £666) was borne by John Brayne, the brother-in-law of Burbage and a reluctant partner in what he considered a perilous venture. The friction between Burbage and Brayne intensified over the years, resulting in a considerable body of litigation, which has incidentally provided scholars with a record of the Theatre's early years. When Brayne died in 1586 his widow, together with Brayne's friend, Robert Miles, continued the long-standing feud, which erupted into a full-scale Donnybrook on November 16, 1590. On that day the widow and Miles stationed themselves at the gallery entrance in order to collect her share of the receipts, in accordance with a procedure ordered by the courts. Burbage, however, attempted to intimidate the pair and with the aid of his two sons, Cuthbert and Richard, expelled them from the premises. Richard Burbage (who later became the leading actor in Shakespeare's company), wielding a broomstick, described himself as paying Miles his moiety with a beating. The litigation continued for five more years and, with Miles evidently losing heart in the battle, was dismissed ultimately from the courts. E. A. J. Honigmann suggests that the entire imbroglio is reproduced in certain fictional incidents added by Shakespeare to *King John.* Honigmann compares Richard Burbage's role to that of the Bastard and the widow's with that of Constance. This conjecture is advanced by Honigmann to support his theory that *King John* was written in 1590 for the combined Admiral-Strange company; the theory has not as yet been generally accepted, however. See KING JOHN: *Date.*

In the meantime the Theatre had provoked a controversy of another kind. It had become the focus of the furious Puritan attack upon the stage; it was cited as being a principal source of moral corruption and disorder and the habitat of cutpurses and prostitutes. In the face of such outspoken opposition Burbage experienced some difficulty in renewing his lease, which expired in 1597. In February of that year Burbage died and his son Cuthbert (Burbage had already legally transferred the lease to him in 1589) continued negotiations with the landlord. Unable to arrive at an agreement, Cuthbert, acting on a proviso in his lease, instructed the carpenter Peter Street to dismantle the Theatre and transport the timber through the city and across the Thames to the Bankside. It was with this timber that the Globe was constructed. See GLOBE THEATRE.

The physical details of the Theatre are a matter of conjecture, but apparently it was constructed of timber with a certain amount of ironwork. According to Johannes De Witt, a traveller who wrote (1596) about his visit to London, it was the shape of an "amphitheatrum." It had a tiring-house and three galleries, one of which was divided into upper rooms for spectators to stand or sit in. There is no extant information regarding the nature or shape of the stage. The money was taken by appointed collectors, placed in locked boxes, and later doled out to those entitled to it. The admission to the building itself was 1d, with an additional 1d or 2d for a place in the gallery. The players evidently shared the entrance fees, while the owners of the house divided the gallery receipts. In 1585 Burbage, Brayne, and Henry Lanman, the owner of the neighboring Curtain theatre, had agreed to use the Curtain for seven years as an "Esore" (an easer) to the Theatre: the prof from both theatres were to be equally divided.

The first company to occupy the Theatre w probably Leicester's Men (from 1576 to 1578), w whom James Burbage had been associated as a play in 1574. They were possibly followed by Warwic Men (later known as Oxford's Men), who play there until at least 1583. That year witnessed t formation of the Queen's Men, which caused a ge eral rearrangement of all the major companies. It certain that the Queen's Men played at the Thea regularly, but not exclusively, during the 1580's. 1590/1 the Admiral's Men, probably already am gamated with Strange's Men, were playing there. quarrel of the Admiral's Men with Burbage caus them to move over to Henslowe's Rose theatre. 1594 Richard Burbage became one of the new formed Chamberlain's Men (Shakespeare's co pany) and that company occupied the Theatre un 1596; that year *Hamlet* was acted there for the fi time. Later in 1596 the Burbages' difficulty with th landlord caused the Chamberlain's Men to remove the Curtain theatre. In 1597 all London theatres we ordered shut down as a result of a scandalous pe formance of THE ISLE OF DOGS. It is likely that t Theatre was never reopened, for by 1598 it was r ferred to in a satire in E. Guilpin's *Skialetheia* being unoccupied:

> but see yonder,
> One, like the unfrequented Theater,
> Walkes in darke silence and vast solitude.

[E. K. Chambers, *The Elizabethan Stage,* 1923; *Ki John,* New Arden Edition, E. A. J. Honigmann, e 1954.]

Theobald, Lewis (1688–1744). Classical schol dramatist, Shakespearean editor and critic. Theoba (pronounced Tib'bald) translated three plays Sophocles and two of Aristophanes. He wrote trag comedies, operas, masques, and collaborated with t actor and manager of the Drury Lane Theatre, Jo Rich (1692–1761), in the production of pantomim In 1726 he produced *Shakespeare Restored: or Specimen of the many Errors as well committed, unamended, by Mr. Pope in his late edition of th Poet. Designed not only to correct the said editio but to restore the True Reading of Shakespeare all the Editions ever yet publish'd.* Pope struck ba by making him the King of Dullness of the first ed tion of the *Dunciad* (1728). In 1733 Theobald's ed tion of the plays in seven volumes appeared. In it a some of his happiest textual emendations. The mo famous appears in Mrs. Quickly's account of Fa staff's death (*Henry V,* II, iii, 9–44). Both t Quarto and the Folio readings were "His nose was sharp as a pen and a Table of greene fields." The la ter phrase he emended to read "'a babbled of gree fields." This emendation has been adopted by t majority of modern editors (see EMENDATION). The bald also studied Shakespeare's sources, particular Holinshed's *Chronicles* and North's translation Plutarch's *Lives,* and consulted 41 quartos, of whic 28 were earlier than the First Folio. His reputatic suffered a severe decline in the latter half of the 18 century, largely at the hands of the very scholars ar editors who capitalized on his pioneer efforts. Mode opinions of his work are divided: some consider hi ıe of the greatest and fairest of Shakespeare critics, hers see him as a narrow pedant with great textual mpetence.

A less commendable aspect of Theobald's career is s activity as an "adapter" of Shakespeare's plays. In 19 he presented a version of *Richard II*, revised to nform to neoclassical ideas of unity of action and gnity of character. The play was presented at incoln's Inn Fields in 1719/20 and was moderately ccessful (see RICHARD II: *Stage History*). In 1728 heobald printed a play titled *Double Falsehood*, hich he claimed was a modernized version of a lost ıakespearean play, *Cardenio*. Theobald claimed at the lost play was written by Shakespeare in the st years of his life as a present for his "natural," i.e. egitimate, daughter. Either Theobald was fabricatg the existence of this play or the copies which he aimed to have seen have been unaccountably lost. Iodern scholarship is still undecided on this point. e CARDENIO. [R. F. Jones, *Lewis Theobald: His ontribution to English Scholarship*, 1919; D. Nichol nith, *Shakespeare in the Eighteenth Century*, 1928.]

Thersites. In Homer's *Iliad*, a deformed, vituperave officer in the Greek army at the siege of Troy, hose constant railing at his chiefs was ended when chilles felled him with his fist and killed him. In *roilus and Cressida*, Thersites appears as a foulouthed, cynical commentator whose blistering use of the major characters establishes the general ne of the play. Thersites reduces all human motition to one impulse, lechery: "Lechery, lechery; ill, wars and lechery; nothing else holds fashion" V, ii, 195–196). He fulfills the role ordinarily played the Fool in Shakespearean drama, that of the deched commentator who punctures the pretensions d illusions of the protagonists. However, Thersites an infinitely more negative character than any of ıakespeare's Fools. His criticism is not that of the onic, balanced commentator on human foibles, but e scurrilous ranting of one who is made, in Coledge's words, "to despise and be despicable."

In the attempt to see, in *Troilus and Cressida*, alluons to the War of the Theatres, Thersites has been riously presented as Shakespeare's portrait of the ten abusive satirist John Marston, or Ben Jonson. Iost critics who see this topical allegory in the ay, however, argue that Jonson is portrayed in the gure of Ajax. Others, notably J. Dover Wilson and . B. Harrison, have suggested that the play is an legorical description of the fortunes of the earl of ssex in 1600, the year before his abortive rebellion. this view, Thersites is thought to be a representaon of Henry CUFFE, Essex' personal secretary. See PICAL REFERENCES. [G. B. Harrison, "Shakespeare's opical Significances," *Times Literary Supplement*, ovember 20, 1930; J. Dover Wilson, *The Essential hakespeare*, 1932; O. J. Campbell, *Comicall Satyre d Shakespeare's Troilus and Cressida*, 1938.]

Theseus. In ancient Greek legend, the chief hero Attica, performer of innumerable exploits, and ver of Hippolyta. In *A Midsummer Night's Dream*, heseus appears as the Duke of Athens. Making arngements for his approaching marriage to Hiplyta, he orders his Master of the Revels to prepare nerriments" for the occasion. The dramatic interde, "Pyramus and Thisby," is accordingly rehearsed r performance. Meanwhile, Theseus cautions Hermia to yield to her father's will by marrying Demetrius. When, later, the four sleeping lovers awaken from their woodland dreams to discover that Demetrius loves Helena and Lysander loves Hermia, the Duke approves the new matches and invites the couples to join him and Hippolyta in a triple wedding ceremony.

In *The Two Noble Kinsmen* Theseus, again the Duke of Athens, interrupts the celebration of his marriage to Hippolyta to wage a successful war against Creon, King of Thebes. Later, he mediates the contest between the noble kinsmen, Arcite and Palamon, for the hand of Emilia, sister to Hippolyta.

Thierry and Theodoret. See John FLETCHER.

Third Folio. The third collected edition of Shakespeare's plays, published in 1663 and then reprinted in 1664 with seven new plays added to the original 36. These seven additional plays include six generally regarded as apocryphal, namely, *The London Prodigal*, *Thomas Lord Cromwell*, *Sir John Oldcastle*, *The Puritan*, *A Yorkshire Tragedy*, and *Locrine*. One of the seven plays, however, *Pericles*, is now accepted into the canon. The title page of the Third Folio reads as follows:

> Mr. William Shakespear's Comedies, Histories, and Tragedies. Published according to the true Original Copies. The third Impression. And unto this Impression is added seven Plays, never before Printed in Folio. viz. Pericles Prince of Tyre. The London Prodigall. The History of Thomas Ld. Cromwell. Sir John Oldcastle Lord Cobham. The Puritan Widow. A Yorkshire Tragedy. The Tragedy of Locrine. London, Printed for P. C. 1664.

The bibliographical evidence indicates that the seven plays were not originally planned for inclusion in the volume but added as an afterthought. The Third Folio appears to have been carefully proofread but not against the previous edition, which was the printer's copy. [M. W. Black and M. A. Shaaber, *Shakespeare's Seventeenth-Century Editors*, 1937.]

Thirlby, Styan (c. 1686–1753). Successively a clergyman, physician, and lawyer. Most of Thirlby's scholarly work was accomplished early in his career when, as a fellow of Trinity College, Cambridge, he edited several works of the Church Fathers. Eventually he obtained a sinecure through the influence of Sir Edward Walpole. Thirlby contributed some notes to Theobald's edition (1733) of Shakespeare and made some vague remarks about plans to bring out an edition of his own. Nothing came of the project except for some notes and a few attempts at emendation made in the margin of his personal copy which, after his death, became the property of Walpole. Walpole then loaned it to Samuel Johnson when the latter was working on his edition of Shakespeare. In this manner some of Thirlby's material passed into Johnson's edition, suitably acknowledged by the word "Thirlby" in the appropriate place.

Thisby. See Francis FLUTE.

Thomas, Ambroise. See MUSIC BASED ON SHAKESPEARE: *19th century, 1850–1900*.

Thomas, Friar. In *Measure for Measure*, a minor character whom the Duke of Vienna asks for help in assuming the disguise of a friar. The Duke reveals to Friar Thomas that he wants to spy on Angelo (I, iii).

Thomas Lord Cromwell. An anonymous play attributed to Shakespeare. It was first published in quarto in 1602 with the following title page:

> The True Chronicle Historie of the whole life and death of Thomas Lord Cromwell. As it hath beene sundrie times publikely Acted by the Right Honorable the Lord Chamberlaine his Seruants. Written by W. S. Imprinted at London for William Iones, and are to be sold at his house neere Holburne conduict, at the signe of the Gunne. 1602.

The play was reprinted in 1613, again as written by "W. S.," and included in the Third and Fourth Folios of 1664 and 1685, respectively. Few, if any, critics assign the play to Shakespeare, although A. W. von Schlegel regarded it as among Shakespeare's masterpieces. Swinburne, on the other hand, characterized it as "shapeless, spiritless, bodiless, soulless, senseless, helpless, worthless rubbish . . . ." The play is based on the account of Cromwell's life given in Foxe's *Book of Martyrs* and has been ascribed to Wentworth SMITH. [Baldwin Maxwell, *Studies in the Shakespeare Apocrypha*, 1956.]

Thomas of Woodstock. See WOODSTOCK.

Thomson, James (1700–1748). Scottish poet and playwright. Educated at Edinburgh University, Thomson came to London planning to become a clergyman. With the appearance of "Winter" (1726), however, he turned his full attention to poetry. The four poems constituting *The Seasons* were published in 1730. His only other major poem, *The Castle of Indolence*, was finished the year he died. Thomson also wrote a number of neoclassical tragedies, including *Sophonisba* (1730) and *Coriolanus*, shortly before his death. The latter, although an adaptation of Shakespeare's play, bears little resemblance to it. Thomson's play is set entirely in the Volscian camp after Coriolanus' exile from Rome. His popularity there provokes the jealousy of Tullius (Aufidius, in Shakespeare), who is not, however, among the conspirators who murder Coriolanus in the final act. The roles of his mother and wife, so crucial in Shakespeare's version, are almost eliminated. They are reduced to one scene in the final act in which they implore Coriolanus to spare Rome. Thomson's blank verse is decorous and rhetorical, but his tragedy lacked the dramatic activity which filled Shakespeare's. The play has never been revived since its first season, 1749, when Thomson's friend, the actor James Quin, produced it at Covent Garden with himself in the title role. There was, however, a successful adaptation of both Thomson and Shakespeare done by Sheridan in 1754. [G. C. D. Odell, *Shakespeare from Betterton to Irving*, 1920.]

Thorndike, A[shley] H[orace] (1871–1933). American scholar; from 1900, professor of English at Columbia University. Thorndike's first book was *The Influence of Beaumont and Fletcher on Shakespeare* (1901). His *Shakespeare's Theater* (1916) is a study of the audience, theatres, companies, and acting. In collaboration with William Allan Neilson, Thorndike wrote *The Facts About Shakespeare* (1913) and edited The Tudor Shakespeare (39 vols., 1911–1913). He delivered the Annual Shakespeare Lecture of the British Academy, "Shakespeare in America," in 1927. Thorndike was also first president of the Shakespeare Society of America.

Thorndike, Dame **Sybil** (1882–). Actress and theatre manager. Born in Gainsborough, Syb Thorndike studied music at the Guildhall School an for the stage at Ben Greet's Academy. Her first stag appearance was with Greet's Pastoral Players in 190 in Cambridge. She toured the United States wit Greet, performing mostly Shakespearean repertory In 1914 she joined Greet at the Old Vic, where dur ing the next four years she played nearly all th principal female Shakespearean leads—Adriana, Lad Macbeth, Rosalind, Portia, Viola, Constance, Bea trice, Imogen, Queen Margaret (*Richard III*), an Mistress Ford—as well as the male roles of Launcelo Gobbo, Ferdinand (*The Tempest*), and Puck She enjoyed great success in the role of Hecub in a 1919/20 production of *The Trojan Women* In 1921 she played at the Odeon with J. K Hackett and in 1922 assumed the management of th New Theatre. In 1927/8 she rejoined the Old Vic accompanying them on their South African tour th following year and on later tours. She has been i films since 1921, and in 1931 she was created Dam Commander of the Order of the British Empire. He biography, written by her brother, Russell Thorn dike (1885–), was published in 1929, and in 193 Dame Sybil and her brother collaborated on a biog raphy of Lilian Baylis. She is married to Sir Lewi T. Casson. [*Who's Who in the Theatre*, 1961.]

Thorpe, Thomas (1570–1635). Publisher of Shake speare's *Sonnets* (1609). Thorpe became a freema of the Stationers' Company in 1594. In 1600 he pro cured the manuscript of Christopher Marlowe' translation of *Lucans First Book*, which he published From that time on he devoted himself to acquirin unpublished manuscripts. In 1604 he published *Th Malcontent* by John Marston and in 1605 Ben Jon son's *Sejanus*. In 1609 he acquired by some unknow means (see MR. W. H., Sir William HARVEY, Wil liam HALL) the manuscript of Shakespeare's *Son nets*, which he published in that year with a dedica tion to "Mr. W. H.," whom he described as th "onlie begetter of these insuing sonnets," thus settin off one of the most famous (and often fatuous) pur suits in literary history.

In this connection it is interesting to note that i the next year Thorpe published a volume which h dedicated, in extremely obsequious terms, to Wil liam Herbert, earl of Pembroke and one of th candidates for the title of Mr. W. H. Thorpe ha been identified with the Thomas Thorpe who serve as mayor of Norwich in 1615. [*Dictionary of Na tional Biography*, 1885.]

Thurio. In *The Two Gentlemen of Verona*, Valen tine's rival for Silvia, favored by her father for hi wealth. Thurio follows Silvia when she sets out t join Valentine but cravenly renounces his clain when challenged by Valentine to fight for her.

Thyreus, called **Thidias** in the First Folio. In *An tony and Cleopatra*, a friend of Octavius Caesar's Thyreus is sent by Caesar to lure Cleopatra fron Antony with promises of anything she may desire While kissing her hand, Thyreus is surprised by An tony, who has him whipped (III, xiii).

Tieck, [Johann] Ludwig (1773–1853). German au thor, major figure in the Romantic movement. Alon with his creative work in fiction and drama, Tiec maintained a lifelong devotion to Shakespeare an the Elizabethan dramatists, a devotion which bega ring his student days at Göttingen. *Kaiser Ok-ianus* (1804), one of his earlier plays, shows ong influences of *Cymbeline* and *The Winter's le. Alt-Englische Theater* (2 vols., 1811) consists of nslations of pre-Shakespearean dramas together th historical-critical introductions. A similar work his *Shakespeares Vorschule* (2 vols., 1823, 1829). *chterleben* (1826) is a novel set in Elizabethan gland with a cast of characters including Shake-eare, the earl of Southampton, the Dark Lady, ristopher Marlowe, and others. Tieck's most im-rtant undertaking in the field was his preparation the standard German translation of Shakespeare. 'hen A. W. von Schlegel left unfinished his trans-ion of the complete works, Tieck continued the k. Aided by his daughter Dorothea and her hus-nd, Graf Wolf Baudissin, he translated the re-ining plays and edited the entire work. The hlegel-Tieck translation made Shakespeare a Ger-n classic and laid the foundation for subsequent erman scholarship and criticism (see GERMANY). From his earliest days Tieck had contemplated a mprehensive book on Shakespeare, and for the rpose of gathering additional material he made a p to England in 1817. Nothing came of the project such, partly for the reason that much of his ma-ial appeared as prefaces in the works mentioned ove and in other critical writings. The latter are cluded in his *Kritische Schriften* (Leipzig, 4 vols., 48–1852). An essay on *Hamlet*, "Observations ncerning Characters in *Hamlet*," is available in *akespeare in Europe* (1963), edited by Oswald Winter. The fragments of Tieck's unfinished ok on Shakespeare were edited by Henry Lüdeke d published as *Das Buch über Shakespeare* (1920). dwin H. Zeydel, *Ludwig Tieck and England*, 31, and *Ludwig Tieck, the German Romanticist*, 35.]

Tillyard, E[ustace] M[andeville] W[etenhall] 889–1962). Scholar. Educated at Jesus College, mbridge, Tillyard was elected fellow in 1912 and bsequently served as Master of Jesus (1945–1959) d University Lecturer in English (1926–1954). His holarly publications have been primarily in the glish Renaissance with special attention devoted Milton and Shakespeare.

In the area of Shakespearean scholarship Tillyard's jor work is *Shakespeare's History Plays* (1944), study of the background of Elizabethan historical ought with an examination of the two cycles of story plays, *King John*, and *Macbeth*. Briefer orks, given originally as lectures, are *Shakespeare's st Plays* (1938), devoted to *Cymbeline*, *The Win-'s Tale*, and *The Tempest;* and *Shakespeare's oblem Plays* (1949), an examination of *Hamlet*, *oilus and Cressida*, *All's Well That Ends Well*, d *Measure for Measure*. *The Elizabethan World cture* (1943) is an exposition of several Renaissance mmonplaces such as the concepts of DEGREE and rrespondence; these commonplaces are illustrated the *Orchestra* (1596) of Sir John Davies, a work hich Tillyard edited in 1945 and discussed again his *Five Poems* (1948; reissued in 1955 as *Poetry d Its Background*). Among other works on the enaissance, *The Epic Strain in the English Novel* (1955) contains a brief comparison between Scott's *Heart of Midlothian* and *Measure for Measure*. *Essays, Literary and Educational* (1962), one of several volumes of collected essays and lectures, contains four items on Shakespeare and two others on Tudor literature. *Some Mythical Elements in English Literature* (1961), the Clark Lectures for 1959–1960, includes a lecture on two Tudor myths, that of pedigree and that of divine appointment. See HISTORICAL CRITICISM.

Tilney, Edmund (d. 1610). Master of the Revels (1579–1609). Tilney began his career as the author of a prose treatise, *A Briefe and Pleasant Discourse of Duties in Mariage* (1568), dedicated to Queen Elizabeth. He was appointed to the Revels post on July 24, 1579 and remained in office for 30 years. Unfortunately, comparatively few Revels Accounts of the period of his mastership are extant. It was during Tilney's administration that the jurisdiction of the MASTER OF THE REVELS was widened to include the privilege of reading and licensing all plays before their performance. Evidence of the type of censorship Tilney employed in licensing plays can be seen in the manuscript of *Sir Thomas More* (which may also contain additions by Shakespeare). Tilney's censorship is focused on the "Ill May-Day" scenes of that play and the references to aliens as fomenters of the riots recorded therein. Tilney was succeeded in his post by his nephew Sir George Buc.

Timandra. In *Timon of Athens*, one of Alcibiades' two mistresses. In IV, iii, Timon gives Timandra part of the treasure he has found, but curses her.

Time. In *The Winter's Tale*, the Chorus. At the beginning of Act IV, Time relates that 16 years have elapsed, Leontes is still repenting his jealousy, and Perdita is "now grown in grace equal with wondering."

Timon. The central figure of *Timon of Athens* and one of Shakespeare's most enigmatic creations. Timon, who in the course of the play moves from the extreme of magnanimity to the limits of misanthropy, is the source of a question still unresolved by students of the play: what is the authorial attitude toward him? Is he meant to be regarded as an object of satire, tragic rather than comic satire, but satire nonetheless? Or did Shakespeare intend him as an orthodox tragic hero, radically flawed but not without the dignity and stature of the heroes of the great tragedies? The kind of response made to the character depends to a large degree on the nature of the impression which the character makes in the first act. His indiscriminate prodigality has been seen by some as ludicrous, by others as an example of a loving and generous heart. Lying somewhere between these two views is the idea that Timon is a preliminary portrait of King Lear. But whether or not he is, in Coleridge's phrase, "a Lear of the satirical drama" or, in G. Wilson Knight's view, a more universally significant Lear, he remains one of Shakespeare's most inscrutable creations. See TIMON OF ATHENS: *Selected Criticism*. [G. Wilson Knight, *The Wheel of Fire*, 1930; O. J. Campbell, *Shakespeare's Satire*, 1943.]

Timon, or the Misanthrope. See LUCIAN.

THE LIFE OF TYMON OF ATHENS.

Timon of Athens. A tragedy by Shakespeare.

Text. This play was first published in the First Folio (1623), where it is included among the tragedies, between *Romeo and Juliet* and *Julius Caesar*. This position was originally planned for *Troilus and Cressida*. However, the printing of that play was held up because of the publishers' inability to secure the copyright. Thus, it is probable that the editors of the Folio had not intended to include *Timon of Athens* in their volume, but were forced to do so in order to fill the space left empty by the temporary removal of *Troilus and Cressida*. Searching among the manuscripts and other papers of their company, they may have found a manuscript of *Timon of Athens* which they thought might serve their purpose. However, it did not fit the vacant space exactly. The editor had to leave out a whole quire of paper, leaving a gap between pages 98 and 109. He also had to leave one page completely blank, and to use another that had been left empty for names of the actors who had played the roles in the play. In spite of this necessary tinkering, in went *Timon*. The text is, in George Lyman Kittredge's words, "a strange jumble of good verse, limping metre and out and out prose."

The copy for the text was probably a combination of Shakespeare's FOUL PAPERS, in an extremely primitive state, and (where these were too illegible for the printer) a transcript of them made by a professional scribe, Ralph Crane.

The early critics thought that this text betrayed the presence of a collaborator, but that opinion is no longer widely held. Instead, the generally accepted belief is that the text represents either an incomplete original play or an unfinished redaction of an older play. The inevitable question is "Why did Shakespeare leave *Timon of Athens* unfinished?" E. K. Chambers' answer is that he stopped because he was in an emotional state bordering on a nervous breakdown when the sustained effort of dramatic creation became overwhelming. G. B. Harrison finds another reason for this abandonment of a project in full career: sheer boredom with Timon and his story. A more probable explanation is that the playwright found that he could not convert Timon into an acceptable tragic protagonist.

Date. The date of the play remains uncertain. Verse tests have little value when applied to so rough a text as that of *Timon*. However, the results of such tests of meter as have been made, combined with similarity of mood and style, make it possible to place the composition of *Timon* anywhere between 1605 and 1609, that is, between *King Lear* (1605) and *Pericles* (1608–1609). A recent attempt has been made to push the date of this play back to the time of *Troilus and Cressida* (1601–1602 The basis for this radically early dating is its leged affinity with *Troilus* in regard to the satiric cynical, even misanthropic view of humanity whi appears in both plays.

The obvious affinities of *Timon* are with *Le* Sir Walter Raleigh boldly suggested that *Timon* theme and temper was a first sketch for *King Le* Other critics prefer to place *Timon* between *Cori lanus* (1608) and the romances (1608-1609), belie ing that, if rightly read, it contains the germ of t romances. Shakespeare may have come upon Timo story while reading North's translation of Plutarc "Life of Marcus Antonius" in preparation for composition of *Antony and Cleopatra*, for an a count of Timon's career appears as a digression that "Life." Based on all this indirect evidence, good guess is that the year 1606–1607 is the mo likely date for the composition of *Timon of Athe*

Sources. Shakespeare had long been familiar wi Timon and his story. In *Love's Labour's Lost* 1593), Berowne includes Timon in a series of e amples of extreme absurdity:

> To see great Hercules whipping a gig [top],
> And profound Solomon to tune a jig,
> And Nestor play at push-pin with the boys,
> And critic Timon laugh at idle toys!
> (IV, iii, 167–170)

One possible source of *Timon* is an anonymo academic play, *Timon*, written sometime betwe 1581 and 1590 and printed for the first time Alexander Dyce for the Shakespeare Society 1842. This drama, like Shakespeare's, shows Tim both in his prosperity and in his destitution. The are other resemblances between the two plays th cannot be coincidental. The chief objection to t attribution of source is that this play had not be printed when Shakespeare was at work on *Timon*. He clearly knew the digression on Tim in Plutarch: from it the poet took the account Timon's death, his burial on the seashore, and t epitaph. He may also have read Lucian's amusi dialogue, *Timon Misanthropus*, if not in Greek, th in either a Latin or a French translation. Fro Lucian came Timon's discovery of the gold, t arrival of the parasites whom he drives away wi blows, and also the visit of the senators to off him "special dignities." From Lucian, too, came tw examples of Timon's generosity: the freeing of o of his petitioner's friends from prison, and t gift that makes possible the marriage of anoth petitioner's daughter.—O. J. C.

Plot Synopsis. Act I. Timon is a noble Atheni so renowned for his liberality and good nature th oets, painters, and tradesmen flock to his home to ek his patronage. When he learns that his friend entidius has been imprisoned for a debt of five lents, he immediately sends him the money; nor oes he hesitate to provide his servant Lucilius with e sum he needs to wed the daughter of a rich d Athenian. He is a splendid host, scorning cereony where true friendship exists. Only the churlh Apemantus fails to respond to Timon's kindliess and derides him for believing the honeyed ords of the flatterers who surround him. But imon, who loves his friends and holds that men e born to do good to one another, continues to estow costly gifts with a prodigal hand, to the ismay of his steward, Flavius, who knows that his aster's fortune is nearly exhausted.

Act II. When his creditors begin to press for ayment, Timon is at last forced to listen to Flavius, ho informs him that he has lost all his property. or a moment Timon suspects the steward of disonesty, but Flavius affirms his integrity and reinds Timon that he has often tried to curb his rodigality. Timon is not seriously alarmed by lavius' revelations, however, for he expects much om the bounty of his friends and dispatches rvants to the lords Lucius and Lucullus, and to entidius, who has recently inherited his father's reat estate.

Act III. When Flaminius, Timon's servant, asks ucullus for 50 talents on behalf of his master, ucullus refuses, piously maintaining that he had ften advised Timon to spend less. He then atmpts to bribe Flaminius to say that he has not ound Lucullus, but the youth throws the money ack. Lucius regrets that he lacks the means to elp Timon; Sempronius, another friend, also reses, declaring himself offended because Timon had ot turned to him first.

After he finds his home beseiged by the servants f his creditors, the very men who accepted his ifts and later refused to help him, Timon decides feast his false friends once again. Scenting an nprovement in Timon's fortune, they appear at is house with apologies for having denied his reuests for money. He offers them an imposing rray of covered dishes, but when the lids are reoved, they are found to contain warm water. enouncing his guests as "smiling, smooth, dested parasites," Timon dashes the water in their ces, throws the dishes at them, and drives them ut of his house.

In the senate house of Athens, meanwhile, the nators have been listening to the captain Alcibiades, ho asks them to show mercy to a soldier conemned for killing a man while drunk. He reminds em of the soldier's military record and of his own ictories, but the senators are unyielding. Indeed, angered are they by the importunity of Alcibiaes that they order him to leave Athens within 48 ours.

Act IV. With a curse on all Athenians, Timon aves the city and betakes himself to a cave in e woods, where he expects to find "the unkindest east more kinder than mankind." Digging for roots, e comes upon a treasure of gold, but reburies most f it upon hearing a drum. The drum signals the pproach of Alcibiades, who has taken arms against the Athenians. Timon rejects Alcibiades' offer of friendship, but when he learns that the captain needs money to press his campaign against Athens, he supplies him with gold, urging him to devastate the city and to spare none of its inhabitants. He also gives gold to Alcibiades' rapacious mistresses, Phrynia and Timandra.

After the departure of the captain, Timon receives a visit from Apemantus, who scoffs at his new mode of existence because it stems from necessity, not conviction; he would be a courtier again were he not a beggar. Timon retorts that the lowborn Apemantus, who has never known man's flattery and ingratitude, has no reason for hating humanity. After an exchange of insults, Timon drives Apemantus away. Soon some thieves appear, their greed whetted by reports of Timon's treasure. Declaring that at least they are thieves professed and work not "in holier shapes," he gives them a share of his gold. Timon is now joined by his faithful steward, who, after dividing his own wealth among Timon's former servants, had gone in search of his master. Convinced that he has found one honest man, Timon gives him the rest of his fortune, exhorting him to show charity to no human being.

Act V. Having heard rumors of Timon's gold, a poet and a painter seek him out to offer him their services; instead of gold, however, they receive beatings. Some Athenian senators who request his aid against Alcibiades are also unsuccessful, for he informs them that their countrymen may end their woes simply by hanging themselves. When Alcibiades appears before the city's walls, the senators argue that all the citizens do not deserve punishment at his hands and ask him to take revenge only on those who offended him. Alcibiades bows to their entreaties, promising to sacrifice only his enemies and Timon's. Just before Alcibiades enters the city, a soldier arrives to report the death of Timon. He bears a waxen impression of the inscription on his tomb: "Here lie I, Timon; who, alive, all living men did hate."—H. D.

Comment. The subject of the play is misanthropy. Most of the earlier versions of Timon's story treat his fanatical hatred of man and all his works, and his withdrawal from repellent association with human beings in order to live like a beast in the wilderness near the sea. Shakespeare's account differs from all the earlier versions in his devotion of the first two acts of his tragedy to the events that produced Timon's misanthropy. In this he differs from the traditional misanthrope figure, who has no life story behind him to account for his attitude.

The critics are in substantial agreement about the theme of the play. It serves as a vivid illustration of the Pauline warning, "The love of money is the root of all evil." The newly established money economy of Shakespeare's day, with its necessary financial instrument of usury, gave the Biblical proverb a new meaning and a new urgency. Most critics also agree that the topic of the play is the self-destruction of an intrinsically noble man through his complete slavery to the passion of anger fortified by contempt.

There are, however, sharp differences among critics on other aspects of this strange play. One group finds Timon an unsatisfactory tragic protagonist. He arouses none of the sympathy that most of Shakespeare's other tragic heroes do, even Othello and Lear. In fact, his conduct is repellent to most readers. Critics of this persuasion see something histrionic in his generosity, a certain smugness in the display of his munificence. His generosity is his response, not to the appeals of true friends, but to the flattery of sycophants who

> Rain sacrificial whisperings in his ear,
> Make sacred even his stirrup, and through him
> Drink the free air.
>
> (I, i, 81–83)

His automatic benevolence is really foolish prodigality, for he has already learned from his steward that he is bankrupt. After his self-banishment from Athens his conduct is either repulsive or ridiculous. He does nothing but rail in more and more strident tones, until he seems to be on the verge of madness. Presently Apemantus joins him in antiphonal curses until, in a burst of fury, he pelts the intruder with stones.

Shakespeare illustrates, both in the scenes of Timon's generosity and in those of his vituperation, a form of construction different from that of his other tragedies. There, each character is introduced prepared to play his part in a well-constructed plot. Here, where there is no real plot, the dramatist forms the dramatis personae into a procession of individuals, each playing the same role. Three flatterers file by in order, each figuratively with his hand out; three bandits come to steal nuggets of Timon's new-found gold; two, then two more senators visit him to entreat him to return to Athens. This is the method of formal satire loosely adapted to the purposes of tragedy. Timon's choice of the site for his grave is a final expression of his mania. He will establish his everlasting mansion

> Upon the beached verge of the salt flood;
> Who once a day with his embossed froth
> The turbulent surge shall cover.
>
> (V, i, 219–221)

In these lines he seeks to be associated for eternity with turbulence and senseless destruction—to create a posthumous life for his misanthropy. Although there is nothing in the text to substantiate his suicide, many critics feel that the inference is unavoidable. At any rate, he is dead before the end of the play. The conclusion brings no reconciliation of the destructive elements of Timon's nature and only an uncertain view of a new synthesis of social forces, similar to that which Fortinbras promises at the end of *Hamlet*.

Many critics reject all the assumptions of this negative view of Timon and of the satirical implications of the drama. To be sure, as Willard Farnham explains, Timon's is a deeply flawed goodness, yet his nature remains intrinsically fine. His essential nobility has been smirched and led astray by the venality of Athens. Flavius explains that Timon has been

> Undone by goodness! Strange, unusual blood,
> When man's worst sin is, he does too much good!
> Who, then, dares to be half so kind again?
> For bounty, that makes gods, does still mar men.
>
> (IV, ii, 38–41)

This passage makes it clear that Shakespeare he presents excessive goodness as a tragic flaw. B this defect did not prevent most of the other cha acters from stamping him as noble; Flavius an Timon's other servants show concern and affectio for him.

Although critics of this school find little wit which to sympathize in his behavior after he settl in his cave in the wilderness, they do find h situation pathetic. Alcibiades sounds this note c pathos in his final speech, which serves as a bene diction on the dead Timon:

> rich conceit
> Taught thee to make vast Neptune weep for aye
> On thy low grave, on faults forgiven. Dead
> Is noble Timon: of whose memory
> Hereafter more.
>
> (V, iv, 77–81)

Shakespeare evidently counted upon the con trast he drew between Timon and both Alcibiade and Apemantus to keep his conception of Timon' character clear. Alcibiades makes common caus with Timon against the greed for gold that hurrying Athens to ruin. He, like Timon, is ban ished. But the senate's injustice does not provok him to hate the entire human race. His reaction t this injury is controlled and pragmatic. Once out side the walls, an outlaw, he can more effectivel rally his troops for an incursion. Athens onc captured, he will "use the olive with my sword Make war breed peace, make peace stint war. His half-objective attitude toward the moral de terioration of Athens and toward his own banish ment throws into strong relief Timon's frenzy an his unbridled invective. Yet it is because he lack Timon's sensibility, even though it be tragicall intense, that he can become a stolidly efficien cleanser of Athens.

Whatever our view of Timon the misanthrope we can see that every character in this strange pla and every utterance points at Timon. The ex hibition of his abnormal conduct in two sharpl contrasted situations is the sole substance of th tragedy. It serves as a substitute for plot. The resul is extreme intensity, without relief and withou diversion, that renders the play at once tedious an gripping.—O. J. C.

Stage History. There is no record of a productio of *Timon of Athens* on the Jacobean stage. Fron Shakespeare's day to the late 19th century, excep for a performance at the Smock Alley Theatre i Dublin on June 3, 1761, only adaptations of th play were staged. The first of these was Thoma SHADWELL's *The History of Timon of Athens, th Man Hater*, presented at Dorset Garden in 1678. Th chief variation which helped popularize this altera tion was the addition of two female characters loving Evandra, the faithful mistress, and flirtatiou Melissa, the unfaithful one. This resulted in th triteness inevitable with the introduction of mis conceived "love interest" to the plot. Another featur that greatly enhanced the popularity of Shadwell' *Timon* was the inclusion of a masque with musi by Purcell which John DOWNES claims "wonderfull pleas'd the Court and City." Thomas Bettertor presumably took the title role for the original pres entation, while Henry Harris played Apemantus

Irs. Betterton (Mary Sanderson) was Evandra; Irs. Shadwell (Anne Gibbs), Melissa. Shadwell's laptation was frequently revived and, from 1701 1737, was produced at the Haymarket, Drury ane, and Covent Garden. Timon was played everal times by Barton Booth and lesser actors. ames Quin preferred Apemantus and appeared in nat part at Covent Garden in 1733, 1734, and in Drury Lane revival on March 20, 1740.

In 1768 James Love (stage name of James Dance) ltered *Timon* "from Shakespeare and Shadwell," ut his version, performed at the Theatre Royal n Richmond Green, was never seen in London. 'his was followed by Richard Cumberland's adaptation, which was produced at Drury Lane on December 4, 1771 and performed 11 times between hen and February 6, 1772. It starred Spranger arry; his wife, Ann Street Barry, played Evanthe, new character who was Timon's daughter. vanthe's amorous involvements with Alcibiades and ucius overshadow her father's affairs. David Garick staged the play with excellent scenery, but it iled. A further, never published, alteration of hadwell's play by Thomas Hull was presented or its only performance at Covent Garden on lay 13, 1786, with Joseph G. Holman in the tle role.

The first attempt to restore Shakespeare's text o the stage was made by George Lamb and prouced at Drury Lane on October 28, 1816. For his ersion, Lamb interpolated some of Cumberland's naterial in the last scene, but, on the whole, the lay is Shakespeare's with omissions only. Because lcibiades' mistresses were eliminated along with he feminine inventions of Shadwell and Cumberand, the drama was without a single female charcter. However, Edmund Kean's remarkable perormance as Timon more than compensated for the ack of romantic diversions.

The next producer to approach the play was amuel Phelps. He did it with great care, and, ossibly for the first time, the entire cast of Shakepeare's *Timon* (with only one exception, the Fool) vas presented. Although full scenic display was ccorded the productions at Sadler's Wells in 1851 nd 1856, the text, almost pure Shakespeare except or a few theatrically necessary cuts, was never ubmerged, and Phelps' impersonation of Timon eceived excellent notices. The first revival was resented at least 40 times from its initial appearance o Christmas 1851. In it Henry Marston portrayed lcibiades, transferring to the role of Apemantus n the later production; while George Bennett first layed Apemantus.

Frank Benson admired *Timon* and undertook its roduction at Stratford-upon-Avon in 1892, perorming in a specially arranged three-act version. The drama was acted once on April 22 and twice n Shakespeare's birthday, the 23rd. However, the ublic's interest in the tragedy could be sustained nly briefly and the attitude of regarding *Timon* s little more than a novelty piece has persisted to he present day. John Leigh's revival of the tragedy t the Court Theatre in May 1904 was based on Benson's acting version. Leigh played the title ole, Hermann Vezin was Apemantus, and Frank Cooper, Alcibiades. Although this was the first ondon *Timon* since 1856, no one was impressed and the play had to await Robert Atkins' inclusion in his Folio productions at the Old Vic to become worthy of notice. Atkins himself played Timon when his revival appeared on May 1, 1922. In 1928 W. Bridges-Adams produced the drama at the Stratford-upon-Avon Picture House, starring Wilfrid Walter, with George Hayes as Apemantus. Nugent Monck from the Maddermarket Theatre in Norwich staged *Timon* at the Westminster in 1935. Cutting "certain comic scenes that are obviously not by Shakespeare" and condensing "other repetitive scenes," Monck insisted on swiftness of performance. Ernest Milton, attempting the part of Timon, was too eccentric, and Harcourt Williams was unconvincing as Apemantus. Music was composed for this production by Benjamin Britten, then 21 years old.

The play's timeless theme made it easily adaptable to the modern-dress version arranged by Barry Jackson for the Birmingham Repertory in 1947. The characters were transformed into contemporary Athenians, Apemantus occupying himself with crossword puzzles. The setting for the second half of the play was a bomb crater guarded by a large howitzer. A special performance of this production was given before a conference of Shakespearean scholars in the Assembly Hall at Stratford without scenery and using music supplied by Ravel recordings.

Tyrone Guthrie, considering the tragedy a satire against materialism, enlivened his 1952 production for the Old Vic with some inappropriate low comedy. He represented the senators as harassed grotesques and introduced a great deal of horseplay at the close of the first banquet scene. André Morell was Timon, and appeared again in that role at the Zurich Festival later in the year. The next production, again at the Old Vic, came only four years later—on September 5, 1956. Michael Benthall offered a cut version of the tragedy; his Timon, Ralph Richardson, was unsuccessful with the verse.

American productions have been few and far between. Gilmor Brown staged *Timon* in 1936 at the Pasadena Playhouse in the second of his summer festivals devoted to Shakespeare's Greco-Roman dramas. In the Antioch (Ohio) Festival of 1953, it was given nine performances; and in 1963 a very successful modern-dress production of the tragedy was mounted at the Stratford, Ontario, Festival.—M. G.

Bibliography. Text: *Complete Works*, G. L. Kittredge, ed., 1936; *Timon of Athens*, New Cambridge Edition, J. Dover Wilson and J. C. Maxwell, eds., 1957; *Timon of Athens*, New Arden Edition, H. J. Oliver, ed., 1959; *Timon of Athens*, Pelican Edition, Charlton Hinman, ed., 1964. Date: New Cambridge Edition; New Arden Edition. Sources: Willard Farnham, *Shakespeare's Tragic Frontier*, 1950; E. A. J. Honigmann, "Timon of Athens," *Shakespeare Quarterly*, XII, 1961. Comment: Oscar James Campbell, *Shakespeare's Satire*, 1943; Willard Farnham, *Shakespeare's Tragic Frontier*, 1950; Clifford Leech, *Shakespeare's Tragedies*, 1950. Stage History: New Cambridge Edition; G. C. D. Odell, *Shakespeare from Betterton to Irving*, 1920; J. C. Trewin, *Shakespeare on the English Stage, 1900–1964*, 1964.

Selected Criticism

samuel johnson. The play of *Timon* is a domestick Tragedy, and therefore strongly fastens on the attention of the reader. In the plan there is not much art, but the incidents are natural, and the characters various and exact. The catastrophe affords a very powerful warning against that ostentatious liberality, which scatters bounty, but confers no benefits, and buys flattery, but not friendship. [*The Plays of William Shakespeare*, 1765.]

BARRETT WENDELL. In *Timon* there is such weakness of creative imagination that we can hardly realize how what goes on might really occur anywhere. The merit of *Timon,* in short, so far as it has any, lies wholly in isolated passages, notable for firmness of phrase. It is just such merit as we should expect to survive, no matter how fully imaginative impulse should desert a poet like Shakespeare. After about twenty years of faithful work, his masterly style was bound to have become a fixed habit of expression. Had he failed now and again to phrase single thoughts with ultimate felicity, he would almost have been writing in a new language. Apart from this mere survival of style, *Timon* throughout indicates exhaustion of creative energy. Its impotently "humourous" treatment of character reminds one, rather painfully, of the first symptoms of creative weakness in *Coriolanus*. Its general mood, too, is colder, more cynical, darker even than that. The misanthropy which underlies *Timon,* indeed, is savage enough to suggest the more masterly misanthropy of Swift. [*William Shakspere, A Study in Elizabethan Literature*, 1894.]

FRANK HARRIS. "Timon" marks the extremity of Shakespeare's suffering. It is not to be called a work of art, it is hardly even a tragedy; it is the causeless ruin of a soul, a ruin insufficiently motived by complete trust in men and spendthrift generosity. If there was ever a man who gave so lavishly as Timon, if there was ever one so senseless blind in trusting, then he deserved his fate. There is no gradation in his giving, and none in his fall; no artistic crescendo. The whole drama is, as I have said, a scream of suffering, or rather, a long curse upon all the ordinary conditions of life. The highest qualities of Shakespeare are not to be found in the play. There are none of the magnificent phrases which bejewel "Lear"; little of high wisdom, even in the pages which are indubitably Shakespeare's, and no characterization worth mentioning. The honest steward, Flavius, is the honest Kent again of "Lear," honest and loyal beyond nature; Apemantus is another Thersites. Words which throw a high light on Shakespeare's character are given to this or that personage of the play without discrimination. One phrase of Apemantus is as true of Shakespeare as of Timon and is worth noting:

> "The middle of humanity thou never knewest, but the extremity of both ends."

The tragic sonnet-note is given to Flavius:

> What viler thing upon the earth than friends
> Who can bring noblest minds to basest ends!

In so far as Timon is a character at all he is manifestly Shakespeare, Shakespeare who raves against the world, because he finds no honesty in men, no virtue in women, evil everywhere—"boundless thefts in limited professions." [*The Man Shakespeare*, 1909.]

MARK VAN DOREN. If Aristotle was right when he called plot the soul of tragedy, "Timon of Athens" has no soul. There are those who claim to know that Shakespeare's soul is in it, exposed at a crisis which experts on the inner lives of authors can read at a glance; but that is an additional way of saying that the play does without complications. Its action is the simplest that can be imagined. Upon the refusal of four friends to lend him money when he needs it Timon passes from the extreme of prodigality to the extreme of misanthropy. "The middle of humanity," whence tragedy no less than comedy derives its strength, he never knows; he knows "but the extremity of both ends." The words are those of Apemantus, who as the churl of the piece is privileged also to say that Timon's transformation is from a madman to a fool, from a flashing phoenix to a naked gull. Apemantus is a harsh critic, but he is a critic. The author's interest is entirely confined to the absolutes of Timon's illusion and disillusion. Not only has he taken no pains to motivate his hero's change of mind, for the episode of the friends' ingratitude is perfunctory; he has taken no pains whatever to put more than lyric force into Timon's utterances before and after. The play is two plays casually joined at the middle; or rather two poems, two pictures, in swan white and raven black. The contrast is all. [*Shakespeare*, 1939.]

tireman. A hired man in an Elizabethan acting company who dressed the actors, maintained the wardrobe and properties, and set up properties on stage. In the roofed private theatres, the tireman took charge of the lights; the Induction of Marston's *What You Will* (pub. 1607) directs "Enter Tireman with lights." The tireman also dressed the hair and beards of the actors. In Marston's *2 Antonio and Mellida* (pub. 1602), a character complains that the "tiring man hath not glued on my beard half fast enough." A tirewoman was in charge of dressing the hair of women who participated in the Elizabethan and Jacobean court masques. As a property man, a tireman with a stool in the Induction to Marston's *The Malcontent* (pub. 1604) follows the entering "W. Sly."

During the performances of plays the tireman stationed himself in an alcove near the stage, close to the screens and properties stored in the tiring-house. He could also be called upon to act occasionally. See HIRED MEN. [E. K. Chambers, *The Elizabethan Stage*, 1923.]

tiring-house. The area at the back of the projecting stage, in the main building of 16th- and 17th-century theatres, where the actors remained when not in action on stage, and to and from which they made their exits and entrances. (See PLAYHOUSE STRUCTURE.) The name tiring-house derives from "attiring" or the donning of costumes, as the actor John Alleyn referred to it in his deposition in the Theatre dispute of 1591: "the Attyring housse or place where the players make them readye." The famous actor Richard Tarlton was described in the heyday of his career (in the 1580's) by Henry Peacham in *Thalia's Banquet* (1620): "Tarlton when his head was onely seene,/ The Tire-house door and Tapistrie betweene."

The tiring-house was the actors' "green room."

ere were stationed the book-keeper, or prompter, e tireman, the stage-keeper (who apparently kept e theatre clean), grooms, and other necessary at- ndants and musicians (see HIRED MEN). The tire- ouse's external doors gave access to the street, and nce the tiring-house was usually roofed over, it as provided with "convenient windowes and lightes azed," as in the Fortune theatre. Tiring-houses ere also part of the structure of the private thea- es.

The front of the tiring-house was the "scene" or *aena*, in the sense understood in Renaissance staging f

> a skaffold, a pavillion, or forepart of a theatre where players make them readie, being trimmed with hangings, out of which they enter upon the stage.

he tiring-house front was also the *domus* of plays iven at court. The modern use of the word "scene," om *scena*, refers to this tiring-house façade, which ven in the medieval stage was not merely a wall but shelter for performers. As early as 1520, the English ntertainers were familiar with the staging require- ents set forth by continental authorities such as ominic Mancini. *The Englysshe Mancyne upon the oure Cardynale Vertues* (1520), a translation of Iancini, describes "a disgyser y^t^ goeth into a secret orner callyd a scene of the pleyinge place to haunge his rayment." The prologue to *Acolastus* 1540) mentions "our scenes, that is to saye, our laces appoynted for our players to come forth of." E. K. Chambers, *The Elizabethan Stage*, 1923.]

Titania. In *A Midsummer Night's Dream*, Queen f the fairies. Having refused Oberon possession of changeling boy, Titania is put by him under a agic spell and suffers a humiliating infatuation for ottom. Eventually released from this enchantment, he is reunited with the fairy King. See SUPERNATURAL.

tithes. See STRATFORD TITHES.

Titinius. In *Julius Caesar*, a friend to Brutus and assius. A brave soldier, Titinius is sent by Cassius o discover "whether yond troops are friend or nemy" and is mistakenly believed to be captured. itinius returns with a victory wreath from Brutus, to find Cassius dead. Grieving that "the sun of Rome is set," this heroic friend places the garland crown on his general's brow and, so that all may "see how [he] regarded Caius Cassius," kills himself with Cassius' sword (V, iii).

titles. Distinguishing names for literary, dramatic, and other works. In the Elizabethan stage it was customary to provide double or alternate titles for plays, for example, *Twelfth Night; or What You Will.* The practice seems to have been occasioned by the desire to provide eye-catching and provocative phrases for advertising handbills. In other cases plays would come to be known popularly by the names of the hero or other significant character portrayed therein. Allusions originating in the 16th and 17th centuries therefore refer to the *Henry IV* plays as *Oldcastle* or *Falstaff* (see 1 HENRY IV: *Stage History*), and to *Twelfth Night* as *Malvolio. Othello* was referred to as *The Moor of Venice* (see OTHELLO: *Stage History*); and *Henry VIII* (according to the account of the burning of the Globe written by Sir Henry WOTTON) apparently had the alternate title *All is True.* [W. J. Lawrence, *Those Nut-Cracking Elizabethans*, 1935.]

Titus. In *Timon of Athens*, a servant of one of Timon's creditors. Titus sues unsuccessfully for payment (III, iv).

Titus Andronicus. In the tragedy of the same name, a noble Roman general. Upon returning to Rome in triumph after a ten-year campaign against the Goths, he rejects the crown offered to him by the people and selects Saturninus as emperor.

A stern Roman *paterfamilias*, he does not mourn his 22 sons who lost their lives honorably, but tearfully begs the authorities to spare Martius and Quintus, unjustly condemned for the murder of Bassianus. His grief reaches new depths when he beholds his ravished and mutilated daughter Lavinia; instead of seeking relief in lamentation, however, he asks his son Lucius and brother Marcus to join him in plotting "some device of further misery,/ To make us wonder'd at in time to come." After he has avenged himself on Tamora, he imitates the example of the Roman hero Virginius by slaying Lavinia to end her shame and is in turn killed by Saturninus.

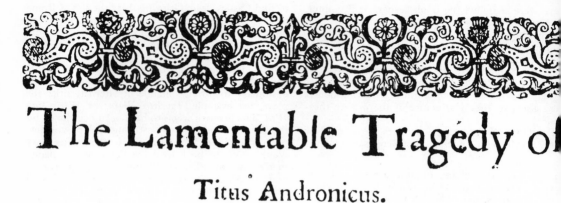

The Lamentable Tragedy of Titus Andronicus.

Titus Andronicus. An early tragedy by Shakespeare.

Text. On February 6, 1594, the printer John Danter entered in the Stationers' Register "a booke intituled a Noble Roman Historye of Tytus Andronicus. . . . Entred also . . . the ballad thereof." This entry is generally regarded as referring to Shakespeare's play, which was published by Danter later that year, although it has also been suggested that the entry refers to a prose history which was the source of the play. The existence of the First Quarto (1594), now considered the most authoritative text of the play, was unknown until 1904 when a single copy (presently in the Folger Shakespeare Library) was discovered in Sweden. This Quarto, entitled "The Most Lamentable Romaine Tragedie of Titus Andronicus: As it was Plaide by the Right Honourable the Earle of Darbie, Earle of Pembrooke, and Earle of Sussex their Seruants. London, Printed by Iohn Danter, and are to be sold by Edward White & Thomas Millington, at the little North doore of Paules at the signe of the Gunne," was reprinted with some minor changes in 1600 and 1611. The 1611 Quarto provided the basis for the First Folio text, with the exception of a few scattered lines and one entire scene—III, ii—that do not appear in the Quarto. This scene must have been copied from a manuscript or printed version of the play no longer extant.

Shakespeare's authorship of *Titus Andronicus* has long been questioned because many critics are loath to believe that the "gentle" Shakespeare could have devised this jumble of horrors. However, his authorship is made probable by its inclusion in the First Folio and its appearance in Meres' list of plays in Palladis Tamia (1598) among the poet's "excellent tragedies."

The first author to attribute the play to a different playwright was Edward Ravenscroft. In an Address prefixed to his "improvement" of *Titus Andronicus*, Ravenscroft states: "I have been told by some anciently conversant with the Stage that it was not Originally his, but brought by a private Authour to be Acted, and he only gave some Master-touches to one or two of the Principal Parts or Characters." Ravenscroft cites no authority for this story; yet most 18th-century scholars, including Lewis Theobald and Dr. Johnson, held this view.

Some modern scholars, including Dover Wilson, believe that Shakespeare had a collaborator, whose hand is most apparent in Act I, and that the ma was George Peele. J. M. Robertson thought th the suspected collaborator was Thomas Kyd an that he devised the plot. Of late, however, criti are prone to accept the whole play as Shakespeare

TITLE PAGE OF THE UNIQUE COPY OF THE FIRST QUARTO OF *Titus Andronicus* (1594). THIS WAS THE FIRST SHAKESPEAREAN PLAY TO BE PUBLISHED IN A FORM NOW CONSIDERED AUTHORITATIVE. (FOLGER SHAKESPEARE LIBRARY)

THE MOST LA-
mentable Romaine
Tragedie of Titus Andronicus:

As it was Plaide by the Right Ho-
nourable the Earle of *Darbie*, Earle of *Pembrooke*,
and Earle of *Sussex* their Seruants.

LONDON,
Printed by Iohn Danter, and are
to be sold by *Edward White* & *Thomas Millington*,
at the little North doore of Paules at the
signe of the Gunne,
1594.

lone and to detect in it foreshadowing of some f the poet's mature tragedies, particularly *Othello* nd *King Lear.*

Date. In his diary under the date of January 24, 594, Philip Henslowe records the performance of Titus & Ondronicus" with the designation "ne" new]. However, Henslowe's "ne" does not necesarily indicate an entirely new play; it may refer o an older play that had recently been revised. 'hus T. W. Baldwin argues that the original *Titus* vas written in 1589 by a playwright other than hakespeare and revised in 1594 by Shakespeare nd Peele. Several other clues must be considered in ttempting to determine the date. One of these is till another entry in Henslowe's diary, dated April 1, 1592, for a play, also designated "ne," titled Tittus and Vespacia." This may or may not be he same play as *Titus Andronicus.* Another is a eference in the anonymous *A Knack to Knowe a Cnave*, a performance of which is recorded on une 10, 1592. The play contains an allusion to 'itus' conquest of the Goths, which is an allusion ither to Shakespeare's source or to his play. Finally, here is the celebrated comment of Ben Jonson, writng in 1614, in the Induction to *Bartholomew Fair.* onson ridicules the old-fashioned taste of

> Hee that will sweare, *Ieronimo* [Kyd's *Spanish Tragedy*], or *Andronicus* are the best playes, yet, shall passe unexpected at, heere, as a man whose Iudgement shewes it is constant, and hath stood still, these five and twentie, or thirtie yeeres . . .

Although Jonson is probably using round numbers, is assertion, which pushes the date of the play back o 1589, cannot lightly be disregarded. The question f the play's date remains unresolved.

Sources. A discussion of the source of *Titus* nust of necessity revert to the Stationers' Register ntry mentioned above. An 18th-century chapbook, liscovered in 1936 at the Folger Library under he title of *The History of Titus Andronicus . . .*, ears a strong resemblance to Shakespeare's play. According to one conjecture, this chapbook is the lescendant of the book entered in the Stationers' Register in 1594. The theory receives strong support from the fact that the entry notes "also the ballad hereof" and that a ballad (also published in Percy's *Reliques* as "Titus Andronicus's Complaint") s printed with and derived from the chapbook. Whether or not the chapbook is a reprint of the ook entered in 1594, it is now generally regarded s a version of what must have been Shakespeare's najor source.

The situation is further complicated by the existence of two other dramatic versions of the tory, one in Dutch and another in German. The Dutch version, by Jan Vos (1610–1667), is entitled *Aran en Titus* (1641); the German version is the nonymous *Tragoedia von Tito Andronico* (1620). Both of these plays seem to be indebted either to Shakespeare or to his source. They are thought by ome to be related to the "Tittus and Vespacia" nentioned above.

For certain incidents in the play Shakespeare nay have drawn upon classical stories. From Ovid's ale of Philomela and Procne in Book VI of his *Metamorphoses* he may have adopted the "quaint device" by which a raped and mutilated girl reveals the name of her ravisher. He could have modeled on Seneca's *Thyestes* Titus' murder of Tamora's sons and his serving of a pie made of their flesh for their mother to eat. Titus' sacrificial murder of Lavinia retells a similar story in Seneca's *Troades*, where Virginius executes his daughter to save her from the lustful advances of Appius.—O. J. C.

Plot Synopsis. Act I. After spending 10 years in battle against the "barbarous" Goths, Titus Andronicus and his four sons return in triumph to Rome with their prisoners: the Gothic Queen Tamora; her sons, Alarbus, Demetrius, and Chiron; and Aaron, her Moorish lover. Ignoring Tamora's pleas for mercy, Titus orders that Alarbus be sacrificed to the shades of his dead sons. Marcus Andronicus, Titus' brother and a tribune of the people, urges the victorious general to declare himself a candidate for the vacant imperial throne, in competition with the late Emperor's two sons, Saturninus and Bassianus. Refusing the honor, Titus advises the people to crown Saturninus, who thereupon expresses his desire to wed Lavinia, Titus' daughter. She, however, is already affianced to Bassianus, who abducts her with the aid of her brothers. During the scuffle, Titus kills one of his own sons, Mutius, for hindering his pursuit of Bassianus. Fearful of Titus' influence, Saturninus angrily accuses him of complicity in Bassianus' action and declares that he will marry Tamora, who advises him to feign amity toward the Andronici until she can exact her revenge.

Act II. Both of Tamora's surviving sons, Demetrius and Chiron, are determined to possess Lavinia, although she is married to Bassianus. At the suggestion of Aaron, they decide to assault her during a forthcoming hunt. On the day in question, Lavinia and Bassianus surprise Tamora and her paramour in the forest. When her sons arrive on the scene, she claims that Bassianus and Lavinia have threatened her with torture, whereupon Demetrius and Chiron stab Bassianus and ravish Lavinia, cutting off her tongue and hands so that she cannot disclose the identity of her attackers. Bassianus' body is thrown into a pit, to which Aaron lures Martius and Quintus, sons of Titus. With Tamora's help, he then succeeds in convincing Saturninus that they are guilty of the murder of his brother.

Act III. Despite Titus' piteous entreaties, his two sons are condemned to death, and a third, Lucius, is banished for attempting to rescue his brothers. Aaron reports that the Emperor will spare Titus' sons if he, Marcus, or Lucius will cut off his hand and send it to him as a sign of good faith. Marcus and Lucius are eager to make the sacrifice, but Titus deceives them and sends his own hand, which Aaron severs at Titus' bidding. The hand is returned to Titus with the heads of his sons. Vowing to right the wrongs that have been committed against his family, Titus dispatches Lucius to the land of the Goths to raise an army there.

Act IV. Titus has left Rome, together with Lavinia, Marcus, and a young son of Lucius. Using her stumps to turn the pages of Ovid's *Metamorphoses* to the story of Philomela, who had suffered a fate similar to hers, Lavinia is able to acquaint her father with the details of her misfortune. Then, holding a staff in her mouth, she writes the names of the culprits on the sand. Titus decides to return to Rome to press for satisfaction at the court. He sends Demetrius and Chiron a gift of weapons with a cryptic message, which they are too dull to comprehend but which Aaron recognizes as an allusion to their guilt. Tamora now gives birth to a boy, fathered by the Moor Aaron. Demetrius and Chiron declare that the infant must die, but Aaron proposes that another child be substituted.

Titus, apparently bereft of his reason, seeks redress from heaven, affixing scrolls addressed to the gods on arrows and scattering them throughout Rome, to the annoyance of the Emperor. Saturninus becomes even more alarmed when he learns that a large Gothic army led by Lucius is marching on Rome.

Act V. Aaron, who has fled from Rome with his child, is captured by a soldier in Lucius' army. After Lucius has sworn that he will not harm the infant, Aaron states that he has been the author of the crimes against the Andronici; he exults in his villainy, asserting that he has "done a thousand dreadful things / As willingly as one would kill a fly."

Hoping that Titus can be persuaded to separate Lucius from his alliance with the Goths, Tamora disguises herself as Revenge and calls upon the seemingly demented old man, accompanied by her sons, who are dressed as Rape and Murder. At her request, he agrees to summon Lucius to a feast to be attended by the Emperor and prevails upon her to leave Rape and Murder behind. Revealing that his madness was but feigned, he cuts their throats while Lavinia holds a basin between her stumps to receive their blood.

Lucius arrives at the home of Titus for his meeting with the Emperor. Dressed as a cook and assisted by Lavinia, Titus serves the meal, urging his guests to taste the dishes placed before them. Suddenly, he kills Lavinia, thus ending her dishonor. He then identifies Demetrius and Chiron as her assailants, adding that the dead youths have been baked in a pie, of which their mother has eaten. At this he stabs the Empress, whereupon Saturninus kills Titus and is himself slain by Lucius.

Addressing the people of Rome, Marcus and Lucius describe the heinous misdeeds of Tamora and her sons and the wrongs endured by the Andronici. The response of the citizens is to hail Lucius as Rome's new emperor. After condemning Aaron to death by starvation, he orders funeral rites for Saturninus and for Titus and Lavinia, but commands that the body of Tamora be thrown to the beasts and birds of prey.—H. D.

Comment. *Titus Andronicus*, as E. M. W. Tillyard has made clear, is a play rich in political doctrine. The action begins with a dispute over the succession to the crown, a subject that agitated Elizabethans during the last decades of the 16th century. Saturninus, the late Emperor's son, claims the throne by right of primogeniture. Bassianus, the younger son, bases his claim upon superior merit and demands that the issue be decided by popular election. At this juncture, Marcus Andronicus announces that the people already have held such an election and have chosen Titus for the position. However, on his return from his conquest of the Goths, Titus refuses the honor and names Saturninus as any sound political thinker of Elizabethan England would, holding the doctrine of primogeniture sacred. This does not end the civil strife, however, for Saturninus is later murdered. Only at the end of the play is the turmoil stilled by the accession to the throne of the sole remaining legal claimant, Titus' son Lucius. Marcus Andronicus, speaking for the author, warns the "sons of Rome" against civil strife and urges them, "uproar sever'd" as they are, to knit themselves together again under their new emperor. Shakespeare teaches this same lesson in many of his later chronicle history plays.

Titus Andronicus contains many other seeds that were to burgeon into flower in the later tragedies. Titus' real madness or his revenge under the cover of pretended madness Shakespeare was to develop with great subtlety and theatrical power in *Hamlet*. Also, like Othello, Titus is a simple warrior, strong in battle but in other aspects of civilized life an easy victim of an evil schemer. Titus is most like Lear, a pathetic old man verging on senility, who is driven to destruction by spurts of wild anger and folly. Aaron is a full but distorted model for Iago. It is in potentialities for artistic development rather than in actual achievement that *Titus*, as the first of Shakespeare's tragedies, invites respect and serious study.—O. J. C.

Stage History. We can infer the early popularity of *Titus Andronicus* from statements on the title page of the Second (1600) and Third Quarto (1611) that the play had been performed sundry times by the Lord Chamberlain's Men. There is record of a performance given at the manor of Sir John Harington on New Year's Day 1596. (See Jacques PETIT.) Another performance may be reflected in the illustration of a scene from the play in the LONGLEAT MANUSCRIPT. At the Restoration, it was one of the nine plays assigned to the King's Men at Drury Lane. It is doubtful, however, whether this company ever presented it, for RAVENSCROFT's adaptation, first staged in 1686, was the version preferred by Restoration audiences. There were only three productions in the 19th century, memorable because Aaron was played by Ira ALDRIDGE, a great American Negro actor, who had secured his reputation with his portrayal of Othello at London's Royalty in 1826.

In October 1923 Robert Atkins mounted Shakespeare's *Titus* at the Old Vic with Wilfrid Walter as Titus and George Hayes as Aaron. The audience listened respectfully until the succession of murders in the last act occurred and then burst into laughter. It was 32 years before the tragedy recovered. In 1955 Peter Brook produced the first *Titus* ever displayed at Stratford-upon-Avon. With Laurence Olivier's appearance as a grizzled warrior, rather than conquering hero, Titus was immediately made real. Later, as a truly tragic figure of grief and suffering, Olivier overcame the poverty of the words with the beauty of his vocalization. Vivien Leigh played Lavinia; Anthony Quayle, Aaron; Maxine Audley, Tamora; Alan Webb, Marcus Andronicus, in this production, which was again staged in 1957, this time at the Stoll Theatre, London. Two years earlier the play had been acted by Wilfrid Walter and George Hayes (Titus and Aaron) on the B.B.C. Third Programme under producer Wilfrid Grantham and, at this same time, performed by the Marlowe Society at Cambridge. The Old Vic attempted *Titus* again in April 1957, including it on a double bill with *The Comedy of Errors.* Derek Godfrey played Titus under Walter Hudd's direction; Keith Michell was Aaron, and Barbara Jefford, Tamora. Birmingham Repertory offered a *Titus* in 1963 when it celebrated its golden jubilee with a season of three plays. Derek Jacobi played Aaron for this production directed by Ronald Eyre.—M. G.

Bibliography. TEXT. *Titus Andronicus,* New Cambridge Edition, J. Dover Wilson, ed., 1948; *Titus Andronicus,* New Arden Edition, J. C. Maxwell, ed., 1953. DATE: New Cambridge Edition; New Arden Edition; T. W. Baldwin, *On the Literary Genetics of Shakspere's Plays, 1592–1594,* 1959. SOURCES: Howard Baker, *Induction to Tragedy,* 1939; Horst Oppel, *Titus Andronicus: Studien zur dramengeschichtlichen Stellung von Shakespeares früher Tragödie,* 1961. COMMENT: H. B. Charlton, *Shakespearian Tragedy,* 1948; M. C. Bradbrook, *Shakespeare and Elizabethan Poetry,* 1951; H. T. Price, *Construction in Shakespeare,* 1951. STAGE HISTORY: G. C. D. Odell, *Shakespeare from Betterton to Irving,* 1920; J. C. Trewin, *Shakespeare on the English Stage, 1900–1964,* 1964.

Selected Criticism

SAMUEL JOHNSON. All the editors and criticks agree with Mr. *Theobald* in supposing this play spurious. I see no reason for differing from them; for the colour of the stile is wholly different from that of the other plays, and there is an attempt at regular versification, and artificial closes, not always inelegant, yet seldom pleasing. The barbarity of the spectacles, and the general massacre which are here exhibited, can scarcely be conceived tolerable to any audience; yet we are told by *Johnson,* that they were not only born but praised. That *Shakespeare* wrote any part, though *Theobald* declares it *incontestable,* I see no reason for believing.

The chronology of this play does not prove it not to be *Shakespeare's.* If it had been written twenty-five years, in 1614, it might have been written when *Shakespeare* was twenty-five years old. When he left *Warwickshire* I know not, but at the age of twenty-five it was rather too late to fly for deer-stealing.

Ravenscroft, who, in the reign of *Charles* II. revised this play, and restored it to the stage, tells us in his preface, from a theatrical tradition I suppose, which in his time might be of sufficient authority, that this play was touched in different parts by *Shakespeare,* but written by some other poet. I do not find *Shakespeare's* touches very discernible. [*The Plays of William Shakespeare,* 1765.]

CHARLES KNIGHT. [Tamora] is the presiding genius of the piece; and in her we see, as we believe, the outbreak of that wonderful conception of the union of powerful intellect and moral depravity which Shakspere was afterwards to make manifest with such consummate wisdom. Strong passions, ready wit, perfect self-possession, and a sort of oriental imagination, take Tamora out of the class of ordinary women . . . .

Aaron, the Moor, in his general conception is an unmitigated villain—something alien from humanity —a fiend, and therefore only to be detested. But Shakspere, by that insight which, however imperfectly developed, must have distinguished his earliest efforts, brings Aaron into the circle of humanity; and then he is a thing which moves us, and his punishment is poetical justice. One touch does this —his affection for his child:

> Come on, you thick-lipp'd slave, I'll bear you hence;
> For it is you that puts us to our shifts:
> I'll make you feed on berries, and on roots,
> And feed on curds and whey, and suck the goat,
> And cabin in a cave; and bring you up
> To be a warrior, and command a camp.

Did Shakspere put in these lines, and the previous ones which evolve the same feeling, under the system of a cool editorial mending of a second man's work? The system may do for an article; but a play is another thing. [*Studies of Shakspere,* 1849.]

H. T. PRICE. *Titus* . . . resembles Shakespeare's other work, both comedy and tragedy, in that it is built upon the principle of contrast. We have the contrasting pairs or groups: Titus-Aaron, Lavinia-Tamora, Saturninus-Bassianus, the sons of Titus-the sons of Tamora. Not only are members of the opposite party contrasted, there are also contrasts within the same party. Marcus, as we shall see, by his mildness throws into higher relief the sterner traits of Titus. Contrast dominates the play and informs every scene of it. As we have already noted, whatever is fine in the Romans appears finer still in comparison with the vices of their opposites. On the one hand we have courage, stern probity, honor, but also stubbornness, hardness, and stupidity, on the other hand, slipperiness, trickiness, intrigue, the lie, foulness of every sort. None of the dramatists who are supposed to have had a hand in the play, could conceive a plan so intricate or adhere to it so closely, once it was conceived. But Shakespeare goes farther. He uses contrast to heighten incident and situation as well as character. Act II.ii. and iii. are admirable examples of Shakespeare's technique. The delightful freshness of dawn and the beauty of the woods are not described for their own sake, still less are they, as some critics assert, a homesick reminiscence of Stratford. They are written in cold blood with the deliberate purpose of accentuating by contrast the horrors that follow . . . .

We come to an important aspect of the plot which scholars tend to overlook. *Titus* is a political play, and Shakespeare is the most political of all dramatists. His work excited the admiration of statesmen like Gladstone and Bismarck, who both wondered how he managed to penetrate so many secrets of their profession. Shakespeare's political interest shows itself in various ways. He likes to connect his heroes with an action involving the fortunes of the state, he is skilful in tracing the course of political intrigue, and he delights in exposing those kinks of character or intellect which unfit even men of action for public life. The real hero of his political plays is the state. In some plays it is England, in others it is Rome. Now *Titus* centres round an affair of state, and its hero is no particular person but it is Rome herself. All the characters are viewed in their relation to Rome and they are set against Rome as a background. This theme is sustained throughout the play; it dominates the fifth act as the first. No member of that writers' syndicate—large as it is—which the revisionists credit with *Titus* has Shakespeare's deep love of the state or his understanding of the criss-cross currents of politics. The intense political interest of Titus points to the man who wrote Shakespeare's historical and Roman plays, and it points to no one else. ["The Authorship of *Titus Andronicus*," *Journal of English and Germanic Philology*, XLVII, 1943.]

J. C. MAXWELL. It is, I think, the one play of Shakespeare which could have left an intelligent contemporary in some doubt whether the author's truest bent was for the stage, and this in spite of its superiority in sheer competence over most contemporary drama. It is true that the drama of the time had, as a whole, close connections with non-dramatic poetry, but even when allowances have been made for that, we may still feel with Miss Bradbrook that *Titus* is "more like a pageant than a play." What is not yet present is any sustained power of building up to a climax: as W. H. Clemen puts it, "instead of preparing us for *one* great event, for *one* climax, and leading us through all the stages of development up to this peak, Shakespeare overwhelms us from the first act on with 'climaxes,' with a multiplicity of fearful events and high-sounding words." Professor Clemen, in the discussion from which this extract is taken, is specially concerned with Shakespeare's failure to make the imagery of the play subserve a genuinely dramatic purpose, and I have nothing to add to his account. But in concentrating on Shakespeare's failure to do what he does with increasing mastery in his mature plays, there is a danger of overlooking how far he has already got. He has a sense of the play as a whole, and a sense of the individual episode. It is principally in bringing the two into relation that he is still deficient. So too on the side of language: the individual phrase or line, and the rhetorical outline of a speech, are often successful; what is lacking is commonly the sense of appropriateness of speech to situation and character, and above all the power to convey a real impression of dramatic interchange: "the characters are not yet talking with *each other*, but are delivering pompous orations to the audience."

Yet the very fact that we can point to so many things that are wrong with *Titus* is itself evidence of dramatic life: no one dwells on defects, and suggests improvements, in the irremediably dull and worthless. And even if the things in *Titus* which look forward to the later tragedies derive most of their interest from what becomes of them in those tragedies, they have some impressiveness in their inchoate state. *Romeo and Juliet* is on almost every count a vastly superior play to *Titus*, but it could be maintained that *Titus* is strictly speaking more *promising*. The author of *Romeo and Juliet* could conceivably have gone in that play as far as he was destined to go in tragedy—and indeed Shakespeare's tragic development does not exactly proceed through *Romeo and Juliet*—but the author of *Titus* was obviously going *somewhere:* though it was not yet certain whether he would steer clear of violent episodic melodrama on the one hand and exaggeratedly Ovidian narrative in dialogue on the other. [Introduction to *Titus Andronicus*, New Arden Edition, 1953.]

EUGENE WAITH. The theme of *Titus Andronicus* is too commonplace to attribute to any one source. It is, I take it, the opposition of moral and political disorder to the unifying force of friendship and wise government, a theme in which Shakespeare was interested all his life. Tillyard noted several years ago the relation of this tragedy to the history plays, and it extends to the Roman plays, to *King Lear*, *Macbeth* and much else that Shakespeare wrote. Marcus states the theme at the end of the play:

> You sad-faced men, people and sons of Rome,
> By uproar severed, as a flight of fowl
> Scattered by winds and high tempestuous gusts,
> O, let me teach you how to knit again
> This scattered corn into one mutual sheaf,
> These broken limbs again into one body.
> (V, iii, 67–72)

The rape and mutilation of Lavinia is the central symbol of disorder, both moral and political, resembling in this respect the rape of Lucrece as Shakespeare portrays it. The connexion between the two sorts of disorder is made explicit in the play's two references to Tarquin, once as ravisher (IV, i, 64–5) and once as the evil, exiled king (III, i, 299). The association is still present in Shakespeare's mind many years later, when he has Macbeth speak of "wither'd murder" moving "with Tarquin's ravishing strides" (II, i, 55).

The integrating force, which through most of the play is too weak to impose itself upon chaos, appears in the guise of friendship, brotherly love, justice, and gratitude. Marcus addresses Titus at the beginning of the play as the "friend in justice" to the people of Rome (I, i, 180), and at the end calls Lucius "Rome's dear friend" (V, iii, 80). Brotherly love is demonstrated in the bizarre episodes of Quintus losing himself in the effort to help his brother Martius out of the pit, and of Marcus offering his hand for that of Titus. The absence of brotherly love appears in the first scene in the quarrel of Saturninus and Bassianus, and injustice and ingratitude are the subjects of complaint throughout the play.

The theme of *Titus Andronicus* is at least consonant with what many interpreters supposed Ovid to be saying. Friendship is one of the ordering forces; Golding uses this word in translating Ovid's account of how the strife between the elements was ended. He says that God, separating "each from other did them bind / In endless friendship to agree" (I, 24–5). Titus laments the departure of justice by quoting "Terras Astraea Reliquit" from Ovid's description of the iron age, just before the time of the giants and the flood. Disorder is represented by the acts of wanton violence and one of the most powerful metaphors in the play, "Rome is but a wilderness of tigers" (III, i, 54), seems to echo Golding's lines about disorder in the state. ["The Metamorphosis of Violence in *Titus Andronicus*," *Shakespeare Survey 10*, 1957.]

Tofte, Robert (d. 1620). Poet and translator. Tofte's poem *Alba, the months minde of a melan-*

choly lover (1598) contains a reference to *Love's Labour's Lost* which is useful in dating that play (see LOVE'S LABOUR'S LOST: *Date*).

Tolstoy, Count Lev (1828–1910). Russian novelist and moral philosopher. With Dostoevsky, Tolstoy made the Russian realistic novel a literary genre that ranks in importance and influence with classical Greek drama and Elizabethan drama. His major works are *Anna Karenina* (1875–1877) and the monumental *War and Peace* (1865–1869).

Along with George Bernard Shaw, Tolstoy is one of Shakespeare's most severe critics of repute. In "Shakespeare and the Drama" (1906), an essay attacking Shakespeare, Tolstoy presented a detailed analysis of *King Lear* in which he dismissed Shakespeare's play as improbable and unnatural and announced his preference for Shakespeare's source (see KING LEIR). It is precisely Tolstoy's eminence in world literature which has brought such notoriety to his essay. If the essay had been written by anyone of lesser stature it would have long ago been dismissed as a supreme example of harebrained criticism. As the considered judgment of one great artist on another, however, the essay has provoked considerable comment, notably George ORWELL's famous essay "Lear, Tolstoy and the Fool" (1947). Orwell suggested that Tolstoy unconsciously identified with Lear and saw in the play a vision of life which threatened his own religious and philosophical beliefs. See RUSSIA. [*Tolstoy on Shakespeare*, trans. V. Tchertkoff, 1907.]

Tom o' Bedlam. See EDGAR.

Tooley [Wilkinson], Nicholas (c. 1575–1623). Actor. Tooley was with the King's Men, Shakespeare's acting company, from about 1605 to 1623. He was probably an apprentice of Richard Burbage (whom he epitomizes in his will as his "late Master"), and was an intimate of the entire Burbage clan. Tooley became a full member of the King's Men after 1603/4, and his name is in the acting lists of many plays. The only known role directly attributable to him, however, is Forobosco in *The Duchess of Malfi*, and he is one of "seuerall mad men, N. Towley, I. Vnderwood, &c." in that same play (1619–1623). T. W. Baldwin has conjectured that he was one of the company's best comic actors, but there is very little evidence available to confirm that notion. Tooley's will, dated June 3, 1623, contains references to Cuthbert Burbage, "in whose house I do now lodge," Richard Burbage, Henry Condell, and four fellow members of the King's Men. His burial is recorded in the register of St. Giles's, Cripplegate. [E. K. Chambers, *The Elizabethan Stage*, 1923; G. E. Bentley, *The Jacobean and Caroline Stage*, 5 vols., 1941–1956.]

Topas, Sir. In *Twelfth Night*, the name adopted by the clown, Feste, when he disguises himself as a curate (IV, ii).

topical references. Players, said Hamlet, are "the abstract and brief chronicles of the times: after your death you were better have a bad epitaph than their ill report while you live." That also was the opinion of Queen Elizabeth I and her privy council, who kept a close watch over the theatres. Surviving records show that every few months there was trouble. Between 1597 and 1605, Ben Jonson was twice censured and twice imprisoned for comments which were considered too saucy; but the dramatists, eager to please their patrons, continued to comment as boldly as they dared on public and private events and personalities. Topicalities are common in Elizabethan plays, varying all the way from plays directly dramatizing recent events and scandals to obvious or oblique comment and gags intended to raise an immediate laugh. Playgoers in the time of Shakespeare were alert to hidden meanings.

Shakespeare also took risks. Contemporaries saw certain parallels between the troubles of their own times and events in the reign of Richard II, and the followers of Essex bribed Shakespeare's company to play *Richard II* as propaganda for their rebellion. Much was made of the incident at Essex' trial. Some also regarded the passage describing Bolingbroke's courtship of the common people (I, iv, 23–36) as a direct reference to Essex. Moreover certain passages in *2 Henry IV* were considered so topical that when the play was first printed in 1600, it was thought safer to omit them. See 2nd earl of ESSEX; William LAMBARDE.

Compared with other playwrights, Shakespeare was sparing with *direct topicalities*. The most famous is the reference to Essex in *Henry V*, where the Chorus in the Prologue to Act V describes the King's return to London in these words (italics mine):

> The mayor and all his brethren in best sort,
> Like to the Senators of the antique Rome,
> With the plebeians swarming at their heels,
> Go forth and fetch their conquering Caesar in.
> As *by a lower but loving likelihood,*
> *Were now the general of our gracious Empress,*
> *As in good time he may, from Ireland coming,*
> *Bringing rebellion broached on his sword,*
> *How many would the peaceful city quit,*
> *To welcome him!*

On March 27, 1599, Essex set out from London to make up his command and everywhere as he passed (in the words of Stowe's *Annals*) "the people pressed exceedingly to behold him, especially in the highways, for more than four miles space, crying and singing, 'God bless your Lordship,' 'God preserve your Honour' etc."

Again in *Hamlet*, Rosencrantz tells Hamlet of the "aery of children, little eyases" who "so berattle the common stages—so they call them—that many wearing rapiers are afraid of goose quills and dare scarce come thither" (II, ii, 353 ff.). The reference is obviously to the War of the Theatres which was waged in the boys' theatres in 1600 and 1601 between Ben Jonson and John Marston.

Direct topicalities also abound in *Love's Labour's Lost*, a play written for a society audience; but most of them refer to matters of private interest to the audience who identified the originals of Holofernes and Don Armado, and understood the significance of such lines as

> The fox, the ape, the humble-bee,
> Were still at odds, being but three.
> Until the goose came out of door,
> And stay'd the odds by adding four.
> (III, i, 90–93)

Unfortunately modern scholars have lost the key to the meanings of most of the allusions in this play. See LOVE'S LABOUR'S LOST: *Sources*.

Far more subtle are Shakespeare's *topical significances*, of which there are many. Usually they take the form of remarks or situations which are entirely suitable to their context in the play but which had a special significance to the original hearers. For example, from the late summer of 1598 and till his death in February 1601, Essex and his affairs caused much gossip and speculation, not all favorable. Shakespeare made his contribution in *Much Ado* when Hero sends a message to Beatrice to

> steal into the pleached bower,
> Where honeysuckles, ripen'd by the sun,
> Forbid the sun to enter, *like favourites*
> *Made proud by princes, that advance their pride*
> *Against that power that bred it.*
>
> (III, i, 7–11)

Another oblique reference to Essex occurs in *Hamlet*. On February 8, 1601, Essex made his futile rebellion when he tried to raise support in the city of London for an attack on Whitehall Palace. When false news was brought to the old queen that Essex was winning in the city, she went on with her dinner as usual and observed calmly that He that placed her in that seat would preserve her in it; and when the lord admiral was setting out with his little army of loyal supporters, she could hardly be prevented from going with them "to see if ever a rebel of them durst show their faces against her."

No one watching *Hamlet* in the months following the rebellion could have missed the significance of the passage where Claudius confronts Laertes when he breaks into the palace at the head of a mob of rebellious Danes:

> What is the cause, Laertes,
> That thy rebellion looks so giant-like?
> Let him go, Gertrude; do not fear our person:
> *There's such divinity doth hedge a king,*
> *That treason can but peep to what it would,*
> *Acts little of his will.*
>
> (IV, v, 120–125)

The topical significances in *Troilus and Cressida* are more elaborate. The play, as so often, is made up of several interwoven stories. One of these, which Shakespeare took from Chapman's recent translation of *Seven Books of the Iliades of Homer* (1598), concerns Achilles, supported by Patroclus and Thersites, who sulks in his tent and criticizes Agamemnon and the other Greek generals. The situation is very similar to what was happening in the later months of 1600 when Essex and his particular followers, the earl of Southampton and his malcontent secretary Henry Cuffe, railed at the queen's privy councillors. The situation was indeed far nearer to actual events than to Homer's *Iliad*. Moreover, the identification of Achilles with Essex had already been made by Chapman who dedicated his translation to Essex as "Most true Achilles (whom by sacred prophecy Homer did but prefigure in his admired object) . . ."

The great speech of Ulysses on "Degree" (I, iii, 75–137) was an eloquent survey of the apprehensions of all prudent men of affairs. Yet the speech remains entirely relevant to its place in the play. Such is Shakespeare's skill in perceiving the universal in the particular that this speech is always relevant whenever order is threatened by insubordination.

In writing *Othello*, Shakespeare used two pieces of gossip as material for a situation and a speech. In 1578, King Sebastian of Portugal, fighting against the Moors in Africa, was killed at the battle of Alcazar but the body was never found, and from time to time pretenders appeared who claimed to be the missing king. On January 17, 1599, John Chamberlain wrote to his friend Dudley Carleton:

> The news comes now very hot that Sebastian the King of Portugal that was said to be slain in the battle in Barbary is at Venice, and hath made so good trial of himself that the Venetians allow him and maintain almost four score persons about him at their charge. They say he tells very strange stories, how he with fourteen more escaped from the battle and got up into the mountains, and so by many adventures he went and he went till he came into Ethiopia or Prester John's land, meaning from thence to have gone into the East Indies, but understanding that they were yielded and sworn to the King of Spain durst not proceed, but turned back again, and *per tot discrimina* in this long pilgrimage (wherein he hath been taken, bought and sold twelve or thirteen times) got at last to Venice . . .

The story caused much excitement in England in 1601 and 1602; three accounts were printed and the Admiral's Men dramatized the tale. Othello's account of the tales he told to Desdemona was seemingly based on this story, though the "men whose heads do grow beneath their shoulders" were taken from Raleigh's account of his voyage to Guiana:

> Her father loved me; oft invited me;
> Still questioned me the story of my life,
> From year to year, the battles, sieges, fortunes,
> That I have passed.
> I ran it through, even from my boyish days,
> To the very moment that he bade me tell it;
> Wherein I spake of most disastrous chances,
> Of moving accidents by flood and field,
> Of hairbreadth 'scapes i' the imminent deadly breach,
> Of being taken by the insolent foe
> And sold to slavery, of my redemption thence
> And portance in my travels' history:
> Wherein of antres vast and deserts idle,
> Rough quarries, rocks and hills whose heads touch heaven,
> It was my hint to speak,—such was the process;
> And of the Cannibals that each other eat,
> The Anthropophagi and men whose heads
> Do grow beneath their shoulders . . .
>
> . . . which I observing,
> Took once a pliant hour, and found good means
> To draw from her a prayer of earnest heart
> That I would all my pilgrimage dilate . . .
>
> (I, iii, 128–153)

The second instance occurs at the beginning of the play. Iago enters seething with rage because—in spite of his vast experience of the wars—Othello has promoted Cassio over his head; and Cassio is a mere stu-lent of wars, a "bookish theoric." In the Cádiz expedition of 1596, Sir Francis Vere, one of the most experienced and distinguished of all professional officers, served as second in command of the land army under Essex. In 1597, to Vere's loudly expressed chagrin, Essex chose Lord Mountjoy as his second in command over Vere—a choice which was severely criticized because Mountjoy was a mere "book soldier." Actually, when he was given the difficult task of succeeding Essex after his failure in Ireland, Mountjoy showed himself a most skillful general.

But *Othello* is not in any sense a topical play about Vere, Mountjoy, or Sebastian. Rather, Shakespeare used incidents in real life just as he used effective passages from books of all kinds. The same process can be seen in *Lear*.

The old folk tale of the king and his three daughters had been included in Holinshed's *Chronicles*, but in writing the play Shakespeare used several scraps gleaned from recent events and books. *Lear*, as the title page of the First Quarto shows, was acted before James I and the court at Whitehall on December 26, 1606. The play was seemingly written between February and December. In February appeared a quite remarkable story of strange incidents in Croatia, including the birth of three sons to one woman, of which one had four heads that uttered strange things. The editor and translator, one Edward Gresham, an almanac maker, observed in his preface that such things were divine signs of portending disaster:

> The Earth's and Moon's late and horrible obscurations, the frequent eclipsations of the fixed bodies; by the wandering, the fixed stars, I mean the planets, within these few years more than ordinary, shall without doubt (salved divine inhibition) have their effects no less admirable, than the positions unusual. Which Peucer with many more too long to rehearse out of continual observation and the consent of all authors noted to be, new leagues, traitorous designments, catching at kingdoms, translation of empire, downfall of men in authority, emulations, ambition, innovations, factious sects, schisms, and much disturbance and troubles in religion and matters of the Church, with many other things infallible in sequent such orbical positions and phenomenes.

Shakespeare seems to have been amused, as well he might be, by this effusion. He adapted some of Gresham's verbiage for Gloucester's apprehension:

> These late eclipses in the sun and moon portend no good to us: though the wisdom of nature can reason it thus and thus, yet nature finds itself scourged by the sequent effects: love cools, friendship falls off, brothers divide: in cities, mutinies; in countries, discord; in palaces, treason; and the bond cracked 'twixt son and father. . . .
>
> (I, ii, 112–119)

A little later, Edmund, who despises his father's notions, ironically continues the tale to Edgar:

> I am thinking, brother, of a prediction I read this other day, what should follow these eclipses. . . . I promise you, the effects he writes of succeed unhappily; as of unnaturalness between the child and the parent; death, dearth, dissolutions of ancient amities; divisions in state, menaces and maledictions against king and nobles; needless diffidences, banishment of friends, dissipation of cohorts, nuptial breaches, and I know not what.
>
> (I, ii, 152–163)

The similarity of phrase and rhythm is so close that it can hardly be accidental.

Again, on March 29 and 30 occurred the worst storm in living memory, which caused great damage all over Europe. There is no suggestion of a storm in any of the other versions of the Lear story; it may be more than coincidence that this was the inspiration for sending Lear out into his storm; and that the same storm was the basis for the wild night which followed the murder of Duncan in *Macbeth* (I, iv).

Again, Edgar, about to disguise himself to escape the wrath of his father, pauses to explain

> I heard myself proclaim'd;
> And by the happy hollow of a tree
> Escaped the hunt. No port is free; no place,
> That guard, and most unusual vigilance,
> Does not attend my taking.
>
> (II, iii, 1–5)

Similar precautions, including the closing of the ports, had quite recently been taken to apprehend the plotters in the Gunpowder treason of November 1605; and such broadcast proclamations were then a novelty.

Again, as Lear goes mad and attaches himself to the Bedlam beggar, he sagely observes (III, iv, 159–160):

> First let me talk with this philosopher.
> What is the cause of thunder?

—a remark which would have raised a laugh in the court audience at Whitehall, for in December 1606 many were also asking the same question after a disaster at Bletchingley in Surrey where the spire of the church was struck and destroyed by lightning and the bells melted, an event which was variously interpreted, and evoked a *Discourse* from one Simon Harward on the several causes and kinds of lightning, all fantastic.

Any one of these parallels may be accidental; but there are too many of them scattered throughout Shakespeare's plays. They are seldom obvious to the casual reader, for they can only be perceived by one who is so familiar with what was happening when the play was being written that he comes to his reading with the same kind of knowledge as the original spectator. But it would be surprising if it were otherwise. Shakespeare is a writer of universal interest because he was so acutely aware of everything that happened around him. [The background for the events of Shakespeare's times is to be found in the vast mass of contemporary records. The following are typical and useful collections: *Annales, or a General Chronicle of England*, begun by John Stowe and continued by Edmund Howes, 1631; *Letters and Memorials of State . . . from the originals at Penhurst Place*, etc., Arthur Collins, 2 vols., 1746; *Memoirs of the Reign of Queen Elizabeth . . . from the original papers . . . of Anthony Bacon and other manuscripts*, Thomas Birch, 2 vols., 1754; *The Elizabethan Journals, being a record of those things most talked about during the years 1591–1603,* G. B. Harrison, 3 vols., 1928–1933; *A Jacobean Journal . . . 1603–1606,* G. B. Harrison, 1941; *A Second Jacobean Journal . . . 1607–1610,* G. B. Harrison, 1958.]—G. B. H.

Tottel's Miscellany. Popular title for the anthology published by Richard Tottel (d. 1594) as *Songes and Sonettes, written by the ryght honorable Lorde Henry Haward late Earle of Surrey, and other* (1557). Although not the first collection of poems, *Tottel's Miscellany* became the most famous and successful of the Elizabethan collections. The total of 271 pieces in the first edition were attributed as follows: 40 to the earl of Surrey, 97 to Thomas Wyatt, 40 to Nicholas Grimald (1519–1562), and 94 to "Uncertain Authors." Within the next 30 years, 9 editions appeared and the number of poems increased to 310.

In addition to the poets already mentioned, there are works by Geoffrey Chaucer, John Heywood, Lord Vaux, Sir John Cheke, John Harrington, and others. Most of the poems are amorous lyrics, but the collection includes other genres, such as satire, elegy, and pastoral. There is likewise a variety of metrical forms, including sonnet, terza rima, ottava rima, rime royal, heroic couplet, blank verse, poulter's measure. Both for its intrinsic merit and for its historical value, *Tottel's Miscellany* is one of the major works of the Elizabethan era. Shakespeare quoted from Tottel in *Hamlet.* The song of the first gravedigger (V, i, 69 ff.) is a slight variation of three stanzas taken from No. 212 in Tottel, "The Aged Lover Renounceth Love." And in *The Merry Wives of Windsor* Slender refers to the work: "I had rather than forty shillings I had my Book of Songs and Sonnets here" (I, i, 205–206). According to a letter from David Garrick to George Steevens, Shakespeare owned a copy of *Tottel's Miscellany*, and that copy may be the one now in the collection of Arthur A. Houghton, Jr. [John F. Fleming, "A Book from Shakespeare's Library," *Shakespeare Quarterly*, XV, 1964.]

Touchstone. In *As You Like It*, the keen-witted jester at Duke Frederick's court. Taking a satirical view of human extravagances, Touchstone ridicules romantic vagaries and burlesques the pompous posturings of court manners. In Arden Forest he parodies Orlando's poem to Rosalind, commenting that the tree on which it was found "truly . . . yields bad fruit" (III, ii). Touchstone, however, does not completely disassociate himself from man's foibles. In his own outlandish fashion, he courts Audrey, "an ill-favored thing," and dismisses her former lover, mild-mannered William, with exaggerated threats. Not merely a buffoon, Touchstone is a philosophic commentator who "uses his folly like a stalking horse and under the presentation of that he shoots his wit" (V, iv). See Robert ARMIN.

Tourneur, Cyril (c. 1575–1626). Dramatist. Tourneur was probably the son of Capt. Richard Turnor who served in the Netherlands. He was apparently employed in the diplomatic service as a courier to that country after 1613. In 1625 he sailed with Sir Edward Cecil (1572–1638) on his unsuccessful expedition against the Spanish at Cadiz. On the return voyage, Tourneur was put ashore at Kinsale, Ireland, where he died on February 28.

Tourneur's first publication was a contribution to the then fashionable genre of verse satire titled *The Transformed Metamorphosis* (1600). Of the two extant plays with which he is credited, only *The Atheist's Tragedy* (1611) is indisputably his. *The Revenger's Tragedy* (1606) is generally assigned to Tourneur, although a number of scholars claim it for Thomas Middleton. *The Atheist's Tragedy* has a number of Shakespearean echoes. Like *Hamlet* it calls into question the somewhat primitive and oversimplified ethic of the revenge play, and in a speech on justice and mercy there is a distinct recollection of Portia's famous lines from *The Merchant of Venice* (IV, i, 184–202).

Tranio. In *The Taming of the Shrew*, a servant of Lucentio. Impersonating his master, Tranio pretends to be a suitor for Bianca to frustrate Lucentio's competitors. Outbidding Gremio in the matter of a dowry settlement, Tranio is given Baptista's consent to marry his daughter on condition that his father will vouch for the agreement. He bullies a Pedant into impersonating Lucentio's father and runs off when the arrival of the real parent reveals the ruse.

travel. Foreign travel was regarded, in Elizabethan England, as an integral part of the educational experience of every gentleman. So much was this true that there was definite official encouragement of travel and in certain instances Elizabeth is known to have paid at least part of some travelers' expenses. This attitude reflected a Renaissance abhorrence of insularity and parochialism. Oxford and Cambridge sometimes allotted their fellows funds to cover the cost of travel for two or more years after they had taken their degrees. Younger students, sons of noblemen, were often sent abroad on continental tours, accompanied by governors and tutors, in order to travel from one important university to another, attending lectures given by the distinguished professors of the day. Paris, Montpellier, Padua, and Bologna each had its share of English students, including, for example, William Harvey, who received his M.D. from Padua in 1602. Indeed, Italy was undoubtedly the most popular of the countries visited by English tourists. The interest during the Renaissance in the study of ancient cultural history (as recorded in Italy's works of art and monuments) was responsible for this attraction (see LEARNING IN ELIZABETHAN ENGLAND). Venice was the most popular Italian city with both English and other foreign travelers.

The individual's particular mode of travel was usually determined by his rank and means. The gentleman preferred his own retinue of horses and servants. Younger persons en route to continental schools most often used the public coach system which prevailed through France, Holland, Germany, and Poland. A more economical means of travel was afforded by simply buying a horse at the outset of a journey and selling it at the journey's end.

The quality of inns varied greatly from country to country. French inns were considered rather sumptuous, often providing silk sheets and silver plate. The inns in the north of Germany were notoriously poor, and the hosts' bad manners were proverbial. Beds were uncomfortable and meals were available only at fixed times. The inns in the south of Germany were considerably better, while Poland was noted for the worst accommodations.

There, hard benches were provided for sleeping, and travelers were required to provide their own bedding.

The most famous and incomparable inns by contemporary standards were to be found in England itself. They were large and pleasant, able to provide more-than-acceptable food at practically a moment's notice. There were usually many inns in a given town and their keen competition resulted in great benefit to the traveler.

Within England itself there was a considerable amount of travel; people were lured from place to place by considerations of health, education, commerce, and in the case of London, desire to better their fortunes. There were many roads running throughout the country, some no more than footpaths, and most in a general state of disrepair. The four main highways were those from London to Dover, to Bristol, to Chester, and to Berwick-on-Tweed. By the end of the 16th century, maps and itineraries, noting the distances between towns, were available.

The most rapid mode of travel was by the post-horse relay system which occasionally set some rather impressive records at times of national crisis. This system evolved primarily as a means of facilitating communication from London to outlying districts. The government made no provision for transporting private communications; this was handled mainly by the carrier system which was introduced in the 16th century. Private persons did, however, benefit from the existence of the post-horses; individuals were able to hire them for travel in instances of emergency, when speed was required. Otherwise, the usual mode of travel for an English gentleman was his own horses, and he usually stopped for refreshment and rest at the pleasant English inns en route.

Walking remained the time-honored means of travel among the poorer classes. Students did a great deal of walking, and most of the acting companies moved about on foot.

English people traveling in England were usually involved in matters of business; for pleasure, i.e., travel for its own sake, they went abroad. Foreign travelers in England, however, were interested in the pleasures and enticements of the country; hence, some of the most interesting accounts of travel in England have come from continental Europeans.

Travers. In *2 Henry IV*, a retainer of the Earl of Northumberland. Travers informs his master of the defeat at Shrewsbury (I, i).

Traversi, Derek A. (1912–). Critic. Educated at Merton College, Oxford, Traversi has given lectures for the British Institute and the British Council in various foreign countries. His *An Approach to Shakespeare* (1938) is a survey of the plays which stresses close analysis of the text. In *Shakespeare: The Last Phase* (1954) Traversi discusses the symbolic unity of the late comedies. Later works are *Shakespeare: From Richard II to Henry V* (1957) and *Shakespeare: The Roman Plays* (1963). See CRITICISM—20TH CENTURY.

Trebonius. In *Julius Caesar*, one of the conspirators. Trebonius agrees with Brutus that Antony's death should not be added to Caesar's. With the other conspirators he accompanies Caesar to the Senate house, ironically promising to stay so near him "that your best friends shall wish I had been further." His role in the assassination is to draw Mark Antony aside while the petition is presented; after the killing he reports that Antony has run home "amazed." In Plutarch's account, Decius Brutus Albinus holds Antony outside with contrived conversation.

Tree, Ellen (1805–1880). Actress. Born of a London theatrical family, Ellen Tree made her debut at a private theatre. Her first appearance at Covent Garden was in an operatic version of *Twelfth Night* in 1822/3 when she and her sister played Olivia and Viola. Toward the end of the 1820's she began to gain a reputation as a fine actress. Among her Shakespearean roles was Romeo, which she played to Fanny Kemble's Juliet in 1832, as well as Rosalind, Beatrice, and Portia, which she played on an American tour in 1836 to 1839. In 1842 she married Charles Kean and thereafter she and her husband acted together, she playing Viola, Desdemona, Lady Macbeth, Hermione, Constance, the Queen (*Richard II*), Queen Katharine, and the Chorus in *Henry V*. She retired from the stage when Kean died in 1868. [*Dictionary of National Biography*, 1885– .]

Tree, Sir Herbert Beerbohm. Stage name of **Herbert Draper Beerbohm** (1853–1917). Actor and theatre manager. Although Tree's major contribution to the theatre is to be found in the areas of lavish production and new devices in stagecraft, he was also a major actor of his day. He began his professional career with the stage name Herbert Beerbohm Tree in 1878 after several years of amateur work in London. He spent several months in the provinces before venturing to appear professionally in London. It was years, however, before he gained a reputation with his portrayal of the Reverend Robert Spalding in *The Private Secretary*, and became the manager of the Haymarket. It proved a very successful business venture for the next 10 years. In 1889, at the Haymarket, he produced *The Merry Wives of Windsor*, in which he was critically acclaimed as Falstaff. With his production of *Hamlet* in 1892, his efforts as producer began to obscure his talents as an actor. His productions of *Hamlet*, and later, *Henry IV* (1895), *Julius Caesar* (1898), *King John* (1899), *Twelfth Night* (1901), and *The Tempest* (1904) aroused great animosity in the critics. His acting had been favorably compared by some with that of Phelps and Irving, but his productions were decried with bitter invective. His elaborations were sometimes at the cost of the text, both in cutting and scene shifting. He did not, however, allow these critical salvos to deter him, for in 1910, 1911, and 1912, he produced, respectively, *Henry VIII*, *Macbeth*, and *Othello*, outdoing in special effects and elaborations his earlier productions. While never the favorite of the drama critics, he was beloved by his audiences of average London theatregoers. He was knighted in 1909.

Tressel and Berkeley. In *Richard III*, two gentlemen attending Lady Anne (I, ii). They do not speak.

Tres Sibyllae. See Matthew GWINNE.

Trewin, John Courtenay (1908–). Drama critic and author. Born in Cornwall and educated at Plymouth College, Trewin is one of the most able and prolific of contemporary drama critics and chroniclers. Since 1937 he has been a frequent contributor to *The Observer,* becoming a member of its editorial staff, its literary editor, and its second drama critic. He has been drama critic of *Punch* (1944–1945), *John o' London's* (1945–1954), *The Illustrated London News* (1946–), *The Sketch* (1947–1959), *The Lady* (1949–), *The Birmingham Post* (1955–), and radio-drama critic for *The Listener* (1951–1957). His books dealing with performance and production of Shakespearean plays are numerous: *The Shakespeare Memorial Theatre* (1932); *Stratford-upon-Avon* (1950); *The Stratford Festival* (1953), with T. C. Kemp; and *Shakespeare on the English Stage, 1900–1964* (1964). Among his works are biographies of notable performers: *Edith Evans* (1954); *Mr. Macready* (1955); *Sybil Thorndike* (1955); *Paul Scofield* (1956); *Alec Clunes* (1958); and *John Neville* (1961). *Benson and the Bensonians* (1960) and *The Birmingham Repertory Theatre* (1963) are studies of two groups which have contributed greatly to the performance of Shakespeare's plays in the 20th century.

Trinculo. In *The Tempest,* Alonso's jester. Coming upon the grotesque Caliban, drunken Trinculo considers that in England "not a holiday fool there but would give a piece of silver" to see this freak. He takes shelter under the monster's cloak, philosophizing that "Misery acquaints a man with strange bedfellows," and is there discovered by Stephano. When Caliban hatches his plot to kill Prospero so that Stephano may rule the island, Trinculo joins the conspiracy.

Troilus. In classical myth, one of the sons of Priam, killed by Achilles in the Trojan War; his love for Cressida, first celebrated in medieval romance, forms no part of the classic tale. In *Troilus and Cressida,* Troilus appears as the young hero. In II, ii, he tries to persuade Hector not to end the war by surrendering Helen to the Greeks; scoffing at the objection of his brother Helenus and at the dire prophecies o[f] his sister Cassandra, he argues that, regardless of th[e] dictates of reason, it would be dishonorable for th[e] Trojans to desist from an enterprise already under[-]taken and that the war will enable them to wi[n] fame and glory.

Although Troilus assures Cressida that "the mora[l] of my wit/Is—plain and true; there's all the reac[h] of it," some critics have detected in his characte[r] an ambiguity that they have found disturbing but i[n] keeping with the complexity of the play itself[.] Ulysses, one of the few reliable sources of informa[-]tion in the play, describes him thus:

> The youngest son of Priam, a true knight,
> Not yet mature, yet matchless, firm of word,
> Speaking in deeds and deedless in his tongue;
> Not soon provoked, nor being provoked soon
> calm'd;
> His heart and hand both open and both free;
> For what he has he gives, what thinks he shows;
> (IV, v, 96–101)

[*Troilus and Cressida,* New Variorum Edition, Har[-]old Hillebrand and T. W. Baldwin, eds., 1953[;] Robert Kimbrough, *Shakespeare's Troilus and Cres[-]sida and Its Setting,* 1964.]

Troilus and Cressida (c. 1599). A lost play o[n] which, according to Philip Henslowe's diary, Henr[y] Chettle and Thomas Dekker were working in Apri[l] 1599. The play was intended for the Admiral's Me[n] and is probably the same play to which a fragmen[-]tary extant "plot" belongs. All that remains of th[e] plot is the lower half of the front sheet, so it is no[t] possible to identify it with any certainty. From th[e] portion that does remain there does not appear t[o] be any relationship between this play and Shake[-]speare's. [W. W. Greg, *Dramatic Documents fro[m] the Elizabethan Playhouses,* 1931.]

THE TRAGEDY OF

Troilus and Creſsida,

Troilus and Cressida. A play by Shakespeare.

Text. The play was printed only once before its publication in the First Folio. However, midway through the printing of the First Quarto, its title page was changed, so that it exists in two states. The original title page (designated QA) had the following title: "The Historie of Troylus and Cresseida. As it was acted by the Kings Maiesties seruants at the Globe. Written by William Shakespeare." Before the text was completely printed, this title page was canceled and replaced with a new title page (QB) that omits any reference t[o] the play's having been performed: "The Famou[s] Historie of Troylus and Cresseid. Excellently ex[-]pressing the beginning of their loues, with th[e] conceited wooing of Pandarus Prince of Licia." I[n] addition to a new title page, QB also contained [a] remarkable epistle to the reader:

A neuer writer, to an euer
reader. Newes.

Eternall reader, you haue heere a new play, neue[r]

THE
Historie of Troylus
and Cresseida.

As it was acted by the Kings Maiesties
seruants at the Globe.

Written by William Shakespeare.

LONDON
Imprinted by *G.Eld* for *R Bonian* and *H. Walley*, and
are to be sold at the spred Eagle in Paules
Church-yeard, ouer against the
great North doore.
1609.

THE FIRST-ISSUE TITLE PAGE OF *Troilus and Cressida* (1609). SOMETIME DURING THE PRINTING OF THE FIRST QUARTO THIS TITLE PAGE WAS SUPPLANTED BY THE CANCEL TITLE PAGE.

stal'd with the Stage, neuer clapper-clawd with the palmes of the vulger, and yet passing full of the palme comicall; for it is a birth of your braine, that neuer under-tooke any thing commicall, vainely: And were but the vaine names of commedies changde for the titles of Commodities, or of Playes for Pleas; you should see all those grand censors, that now stile them such vanities, flock to them for the maine grace of their grauities: especially this authors Commedies, that are so fram'd to the life, that they serue for the most common Commentaries, of all the actions of our liues shewing such a dexteritie, and power of witte, that the most displeased with Playes, are pleasd with his Commedies. And all such dull and heauy-witted worldlings, as were neuer capable of the witte of a Commedie, comming by report of them to his representations, haue found that witte there, that they neuer found in them selues, and have parted better wittied then they came: feeling an edge of witte set vpon them, more than euer they dreamd they had braine to grinde it on. So much and such sauored salt of witte is in his Commedies, that they seeme (for their height of pleasure) to be borne in that sea that brought forth *Venus*. Amongst all there is none more witty then this: And had I time I would comment upon it, though I know it needs not, (for so much as will make you thinke your testerne well bestowd) but for so much worth, as euen poore I know to be stuft in it. It deserues such a labour, as well as the best Commedy in *Terence* or *Plautus*. And beleeue this, that when hee is gone, and his Commedies out of sale, you will scramble for them, and set vp a new English Inquisition. Take this for a warning, and at the perrill of your pleasures losse, and Iudgements, refuse not, nor like this the lesse, for not being sullied, with the smoaky breath of the multitude; but thanke fortune for the scape it hath made amongst you. Since by the grand possessors wills I beleeue you should have prayd for them rather then beene prayd. And so I leaue all such to be prayd for (for the states of their wits healths) that will not praise it. Vale.

There are two explanations of these contradictions between the statements on the two title pages of the quarto. The first is that elaborated by W. W. Lawrence, who supposes that the play was a failure at the Globe. The editors, therefore, anticipated a problem in selling a piece that had been unsuccessful in the theatre. Therefore, they cut out all references to stage performances, and in their blurb made its failure to please the crowd seem to recommend the volume to intelligent readers. Another possibility is that someone informed the editors that the play had never been acted at the Globe, or indeed given any public performance, and they inserted in Quarto B a new title page and a Preface. A third explanation, first offered by Peter Alexan-

THE CANCEL TITLE PAGE OF *Troilus and Cressida* (1609).

THE
Famous Historie of
Troylus *and* Cresseid.

Excellently expressing the beginning
of their loues, with the conceited wooing
of *Pandarus* Prince of *Licia*.

Written by William Shakespeare.

LONDON
Imprinted by *G.Eld* for *R.Bonian* and *H. Walley*, and
are to be sold at the spred Eagle in Paules
Church-yeard, ouer against the
great North doore.
1609.

der, is that the play was written for a special audience, probably of barristers, and produced at one of the inns of court, and, in spite of the advertisement in Quarto A, never acted before a popular audience. See below under *Comment.*

The relation of the Folio to the Quarto is obscure and its explanation complicated. The editors of the Cambridge Edition believed that the copy for the Folio was a transcript of Shakespeare's original manuscript, revised and slightly altered by the author himself, and that before the printing of the Folio the manuscript had been tampered with by another hand. Earlier critics agreed that the battle scenes, scenes 4 to 10 of the last act, were not Shakespeare's work, nor was the strange, inconclusive ending. The modern critical tendency is to consider Shakespeare the sole author of the Folio text and the ending a mark of his originality, in complete harmony with his design for the work.

The copy for the Folio text appears to have been the 1609 Quarto used in conjunction with Shakespeare's original manuscript. The copy for the Quarto, it is generally believed, was a transcript of Shakespeare's FOUL PAPERS, designed for reading, not acting. On the basis of this evidence it would appear that the Folio was the more authoritative text. In fact, however, the Folio text was so hastily and ineptly composed and printed that the Quarto is generally superior. The Folio, on the other hand, includes some 45 lines not in the Quarto, as well as the prologue. Thus a modern text of the play should be "eclectic," that is, based upon a judicious editorial selection from both the Quarto and Folio texts. See PROLOGUE.

Date. The earliest record of the play is an entry, generally regarded as a BLOCKING ENTRY, inserted by James Roberts in the Stationers' Register, dated February 7, 1603: "The booke of Troilus and Cresseda as yt is acted by my lord Chamberlen's Men." Shakespeare composed this play when the vogue of satiric comedy was at the height of its popularity, from 1599, when Jonson's *Every Man Out of his Humour* (which he called "comicall satyre") was first staged, until 1604. The play is thought to contain allusions to two other Jonson plays, *Cynthia's Revels* (1600) and *The Poetaster* (1601). Robert Kimbrough argues that Ulysses' speech on "degree" is parodied by Thomas Middleton in his *Family of Love,* which Kimbrough dates 1602. A reasonable date for *Troilus and Cressida* is 1601–1602.

Sources. Shakespeare showed an interest in the medieval tale of *Troilus and Cressida* from the beginning of his literary career. He devotes lines 1366–1561 of *The Rape of Lucrece* to a description of the skillful painting of the Troy story and a characterization of the principal actors in the old tale, "sly Ulysses, grave Nestor and Helen, the strumpet, who began the stir." There are also references to the story scattered throughout the plays; one of the most famous is Pistol's stigmatizing the whore Doll as a "lazar kite of Cressid's kind." Shakespeare made some use of Chaucer's treatment of the love story in *Troilus and Criseyde.* Shakespeare's play follows exactly the order of events in Chaucer's poem and adopts Chaucer's conception of some of the characters, notably Pandarus. The poet's idea of the Greeks came from books I, II, VI–XI, a XVIII of Chapman's translation of the *Iliad* (1598 with help from Arthur Hall's translation of the fi 10 books of the *Iliad* (1581). However, it is a mi take to approach a reading of Shakespeare's pl by way of Chaucer or Chapman, for the events the drama belong to a different tradition. The hero of the Homeric war story had suffered a degener tion on their way from ancient Greece through t Middle Ages to the Renaissance. For the treatme of both the Greek and Trojan warriors, Shak speare's principal source was William Caxton *Recuyell of the Historyes of Troy* (1475). Oth details of the camp scenes derive from John Ly gate's *The Troy Book* (c. 1412–1420). Both of the 15th-century treatments, as well as Chaucer's poe are in turn based upon the medieval tales of Tr collected by Guido delle Colonne as *Histor Troiana* (1287). To medieval writers faithful to t ideals of chivalry, Achilles became the embodime of savage cruelty and the rest of the Greeks undisciplined crowd of cowards and bullies. A though the Trojan Hector had become a model chivalric courtesy, as a group the Trojan soldie had declined into an undisciplined mob, unable obey the dictates either of conscience or reason.

The love story had suffered a similar degener tion. This was the natural result of the scorn medieval Christians, devoted to the ideals of chival and courtly love, for the manners and morals primitive Greece. Conduct admirable in a fema Greek slave violated all the canons of a system ideal amorous behavior. Thus Cressida, who Homer was one of Cupid's saints, had become creature to deplore and deride. Shakespeare's sourc for his debased conception of Cressida were, fir Robert Henryson's *Testament of Cressid,* written the late 15th century. It was printed in Thynne edition of Chaucer (1532), and thought to be t work of the older writer. Henryson presents Cre sida as a beggar afflicted with leprosy, at the tin often confused with syphilis. Perhaps Shakespea also had read George Whetstone's *Rock of Rega* (1576), in which she is made a moral warnin Whetstone even puts into her mouth some of h preaching:

> You ramping gyrles, which rage with wanton lust,
> Behold in me the bitter blowness of change.

By Shakespeare's time the elements of the story ha become fixed: Cressida was a wanton, sometimes harlot; Troilus, an eager young warrior brought grief through his love for a disreputable woma and Pandarus, a leering pimp. It is not true th Shakespeare was incapable of appreciating Chaucer Criseyde or that she repelled his realistic sense a that, therefore, he deliberately debased her. She w only one of the many Cressidas appearing in wor of literature with which Shakespeare was familia And she was the Cressida who could best be fitt into the poet's plan for his drama.—O. J. C.

Plot Synopsis. Act I. Seven years have elaps since the princes of Greece first laid siege to Tr to avenge the abduction of Helen, Menelaus' wi by Paris, son of King Priam of Troy. Troil Priam's youngest son, has fallen deeply in lo with Cressida, the daughter of Calchas, a Trojan priest who has joined the enemy. Although Cressida returns Troilus' affection, she believes that "men prize the thing ungain'd more than it is" and has decided to conceal her feelings. Fanning the flames of their passion is Cressida's uncle, Pandarus, who willingly serves as their go-between.

During a conference in the Greek camp, Agamemnon, commander of the besieging forces, reveals that he is dissatisfied with the sluggish progress of the war. In the opinion of Ulysses, Prince of Ithaca, the morale of the Greeks has been sapped by the conduct of Achilles, their chief warrior, who, swollen with self-esteem, lies in his tent all day, laughing at the rude jests of his friend Patroclus. The discussion is interrupted by the arrival of Aeneas, another Trojan warrior, who bears a challenge from Priam's son Hector to any Greek "that holds his honour higher than his ease." Ulysses realizes that the challenge is aimed at Achilles, but he advises his comrades to rebuff Achilles by choosing the "dull brainless" Ajax to face Hector instead.

Act II. The venerable Nestor has conveyed the Greek peace terms to the Trojans, stating that the war will end immediately if Helen is restored to them. Hector urges his kinsmen to accede to the Greek demands, and his judgment is confirmed by the prophecies of his sister Cassandra, who foresees the ruin of Troy if Helen is not returned. The more sentimental Troilus, however, argues that they cannot honorably repudiate the actions of Paris. As for Paris, he would not retract a single one of his steps. Despite his misgivings, Hector allows himself to be convinced by his brothers.

Agamemnon, seeking an interview with Achilles, is turned away at his tent by Patroclus, who says that Achilles will not take the field on the morrow, nor will he deign to give an excuse for his behavior. Agamemnon asks Ajax to talk to Achilles, but Ulysses and Nestor, stuffing the gullible Ajax with praise, convince him that he would demean himself by requesting any favors from Achilles.

Act III. Through the good offices of Pandarus, Troilus and Cressida are brought together at last. She confesses that she has long loved Troilus and swears eternal fealty, expressing the hope that her name become a byword for falseness if she should be unfaithful to him.

As a reward for his services to the Greek cause, Calchas asks that Cressida be brought to the Grecian camp in exchange for Antenor, a captured Trojan general. Agamemnon agrees to this proposal and sends Diomedes to effect the exchange. Acting on the suggestion of Ulysses, Agamemnon and Ajax snub Achilles, who inquires whether they have forgotten his achievements. Ulysses replies that men bestow their praise and affection only on the hero of the moment and that Achilles is being eclipsed by Ajax. Fearful for his reputation and eager for a glimpse of Hector, Achilles asks the scurrilous Thersites to prevail upon Ajax to invite Hector to Achilles' tent after the forthcoming combat.

Act IV. Taking a sorrowful farewell of his beloved Cressida, Troilus gives her a sleeve as a token of his devotion and draws her repeated promises of fidelity. He warns her to beware of the blandishments of the Greek youths and is quick to resent Diomedes' frank appreciation of her beauty. When Diomedes arrives with Cressida in the Greek camp, her coquettish manner and the alacrity with which she bestows kisses on the Greek leaders move Ulysses to observe that "her wanton spirits look out / At every joint and motive of her body."

The combat between Hector and Ajax ends after a single passage at arms, when Hector, pointing out that his opponent is related to Troy's royal family, declares his reluctance to shed the blood of a kinsman. Hector then enjoys an amicable visit with the Greeks. Only Achilles proves churlish, boasting that he will kill the Trojan Prince. Troilus, who is a member of Hector's party, learns from Ulysses that Diomedes is openly enamored of Cressida.

Act V. Accompanied by Ulysses and Thersites, Troilus watches as Diomedes pays court to Cressida. Diomedes asks for a pledge from her, and, after a show of reluctance, she gives him Troilus' sleeve and consents to his returning the next night. Troilus, who can scarcely credit what he has seen, bitterly inveighs against "false Cressida" and vows to kill Diomedes.

The following day, Hector insists on going into battle, despite the forebodings of Cassandra and his wife, Andromache. During the fighting, Troilus challenges Diomedes, but their duel is inconclusive. Patroclus' death at the hands of Hector spurs Achilles to revenge. He finds Hector unarmed but does not hesitate to order his Myrmidon followers to fall upon the defenseless Trojan. Troilus brings the ill-tidings to the Trojan forces, adding that Hector's corpse is being dragged by the tail of Achilles' horse. For Pandarus, the disillusioned youth has only insults. The old man remarks that all go-betweens must endure such abuse, and wonders "why should our endeavour be so loved and the performance so loathed."—H. D.

Comment. Critics agree that *Troilus and Cressida* is the most puzzling of Shakespeare's plays. On the title page of Quarto B it is described as a "Famous History," but in the Preface to Quarto B it is more than once referred to as a "comedy."

The play occupies an ambiguous position in the Folio, between the histories and the tragedies, and it is the only play in the Folio which is not included in the "Catalogue" (table of contents) at the beginning of the book. It used to be thought that this ambivalent position was a reflection of the editors' uncertainty about the nature of the play with which they were dealing. Recent studies of the printing of the Folio have offered another explanation, however. This thesis is that the editors originally planned to include the play among the tragedies, right after *Romeo and Juliet*. However, they discovered, after setting three pages of the play in type, that they had not secured the copyright from the publisher of the 1609 Quarto. Apparently there was some difficulty in securing copyright, so that the printing of the play was postponed and renewed at a later date after the tragedies had been printed.

Whatever the explanation for the phenomenon, the ambiguous position of the play is entirely appropriate, for it is probably best understood, not as comedy, tragedy, or history, but as a satiric play, for which Ben Jonson furnished a model in his *Every Man Out of his Humour* (1599). To this drama Jonson gave the appropriate name "comicall satyre." Some critics have detected in the harsh, bitter spirit of the play the satiric temper. W. W. Lawrence writes, "We may call Shakespeare's picture of the Troy story an experiment in the middle ground between comedy and tragedy." This "middle ground" was that which Jonson claimed as the proper field for his "Comicall Satyre." Other critics are confident that the spirit of the play is precisely that of satire; that it is, indeed, a reflection of the bitter satiric spirit of Marston, who developed the figure of Malcontent. F. S. Boas asserts that the play is "a merciless satire of the high-flown ideal of love fostered by the medieval cycle of romance" and by "savage scorn" for "the feudal code of love and honor." But, curiously, no one of these critics pays any attention to the form in which Shakespeare clothed this satiric spirit. It is patently that which Jonson invented for his COMICAL SATIRES.

Troilus and Cressida appears to have been written for a more sophisticated audience than that normally gathered at the Globe. The long, closely reasoned philosophical disquisitions and the meditative soliloquies are not the sort to hold the attention of a popular audience. Yet Shakespeare could hardly have designed the work for a court performance; its scurrility would have offended the queen. As Peter Alexander points out, "The spectators at times are addressed directly and familiarly by the most scurril characters in most scurril terms." And in its impudent epilogue the poet implies that there will be hissing, except from as many in the audience that "be here of Pandar's Hall" and "Brethren and sisters of the hold-door trade." Alexander was the first to suggest that Shakespeare wrote the play for an audience of barristers gathered at one of the INNS OF COURT for some festal occasion. This conjecture explains so many of the problems of interpretation that have tortured critics of the play that we adopt it as a working hypothesis.

The principal characters in both the war story and the love encounters end their dramatic careers in frustration and their actions in futility. Shakespeare, by exposing their follies and misconduct without presenting their reform, substitutes cynical amusement for the satisfaction expected by an audience at the close of a comedy. The Greek host is in a chaotic state, because the warriors' pursuit of selfish personal ends has destroyed the basis of any successful social effort. The observance of "degree" or rank—the series of subordinations of each individual to his rightfully constituted superior in the social scale—has been ignored. In this part of the play the poet is attacking not the institution of war, but war as waged by an anarchistic mob. Ulysses announces the author's thesis:

> O, when degree is shaked,
> Which is the ladder to all high designs,
> The enterprise is sick!
> . . . . .
> Take but degree away, untune that string,
> And, hark, what discord follows!
> (I, iii, 101–103, 109–110)

The action of the drama, so far as it concerns both groups of military leaders, illustrates Ulysses' text. Among the Greeks Achilles is the chief architect c the chaos. He lies in his tent mocking the plans o the general staff, while his homosexual friend Pa roclus amuses him by imitating the manner an pose of the other Greek generals. Ajax, a lou grown absurdly conceited, also keeps to his ten Ulysses starts the ball rolling by devising a schem that he believes will purge Achilles of his pride an bring him back to his companions-in-arms. Th essence of his plot is to induce Ajax instead o Achilles to meet Hector in single combat. Afte causing Ajax to burn with pugilistic zeal, he ha the former fellow warriors of Achilles file by hin making contemptuous gestures. This maneuver pro duces the effect that Ulysses desires. Achilles ask himself, "Whither hath fled my reputation?" an ponders the question in a soliloquy of seductive elo quence (III, iii, 75–92).

The imaginative fluency of this passage must no be interpreted as the poet's attempt to gain sym pathy for Achilles and his situation. It is the poeti mode in which Shakespeare casts the language o almost all the dramatis personae; rhetorical splendo that he designed to delight the discriminating tast of the members of an inns of court audience. H does not attempt to make this vivid language a forn of character depiction. In this play the ideas of ever character, even of those patently ridiculed, ar expressed with unvarying philosophical and imagina tive fervor. One of the most famous of these pas sages of high seriousness clothes one of Ulysses arguments designed to persuade Achilles to rejoi the Greek army. He points out that heroic action if it is to be admired, must be continuous. Ma quickly forgets the past achievements of others They become one of the victims of Time th destroyer:

> For beauty, wit,
> High birth, vigour of bone, desert in service,
> Love, friendship, charity, are subjects all
> To envious and calumniating time.
> (III, iii, 171–174)

Ulysses, by the mere threat of putting Ajax i Achilles' place, accomplishes his purpose. Achille recognizes his conduct to be folly. In satiric play of the same type as *Troilus and Cressida,* he woul at this point be purged of his folly and renounce it But at the crucial moment he remembers his lov for Polyxena and realizes that the dictates of chival ric love forbid his seeking the death of her kinsman This is one of the points in the play that have per suaded many critics, including Boas, to believe tha it contains much ridicule of the *fin amor*, of medieva chivalry. The fact that exaggerated acts of devotio of medieval lovers and their amorous protestation were imitated by the queen's pretended adorer would have increased the audience's relish of satir of *fin amor*.

The degradation of Ajax was not entirely Shake speare's doing. It had been hinted at in classica sources and developed in William Caxton. Som scholars believe that Shakespeare designed Ajax t play a part in the so-called War of the Theatres i which Jonson, Marston, and Dekker were involved The only justification for this assumption is a speec of the actor Will Kempe in the second part of *The Return from Parnassus*, an academic play written 1601–1602. Kempe cries, "O that Ben Jonson is a pestilent fellow; he brought up Horace giving the poets a pill [i.e., in *The Poetaster*] but our poet Shakespeare hath given him a purge that made him bewray his credit." Scholars are agreed that, if anywhere the playwright did administer this purge, he embodied it in the character of Ajax.

Attached to the exposure and ridicule of Achilles is Thersites, who had appeared with all his grossness in the *Iliad*. To discover his derivation is not to explain his dramatic function in the play; consequently scholars have busily sought to define his role. They usually put him down as a chorus or a court fool, Ajax' licensed jester, a variation of the wise fool who appears full grown in *King Lear*. But the wise fool always exerts his efforts to clear the eyes of his master from dangerous illusions; he never, like Thersites, makes criticism an end in itself. Thersites is, rather, a railer, a detractor, and a buffoon in exactly the same sense as is Carlo Buffone in Jonson's *Every Man Out of his Humour*. Like Carlo's, his diatribes are designed to evoke simultaneously amusement and aversion. His penchant for bold adulterate similes is as incorrigible as that of his forebear, as his following description of Ajax illustrates:

> Why, he stalks up and down like a peacock,—a stride and a stand: ruminates like an hostess that hath no arithmetic but her brain to set down her reckoning: bites his lip with a politic regard, as who should say "There were wit in this head, an 'twould out;" and so there is, but it lies as coldly in him as fire in a flint, which will not show without knocking. The man's undone for ever; for if Hector break not his neck i' the combat, he'll break 't himself in vain-glory. He knows not me: I said "Good morrow, Ajax;" and he replies "Thanks, Agamemnon." What think you of this man that takes me for the general? He's grown a very land-fish, languageless, a monster. A plague of opinion! a man may wear it on both sides, like a leather jerkin.
>
> (III, iii, 251 ff.)

This store of similes, though mannered, is not unduly virulent. Nor is his metaphorical excoriation of Patroclus as Achilles' "masculine whore" unduly severe for an established satiric convention of scourging sexual sins with Juvenal's savagery. Thersites' comments on individual and group follies run the gamut from wisdom to Billingsgate. Thersites has been universally described as "the most unShakespearean figure" in all the poet's work. The real explanation is that the poet was unsuccessful in his attempt to transform the Homeric Thersites into one of the indispensable characters in the momentarily popular satiric comedy. His failure was due to the emotional intensity with which Shakespeare treated his buffoon, which to many readers makes Thersites more disgusting than amusing.

The Trojans in the play are, as definitely as the Greeks, a crowd of recalcitrant individuals who deliberately forsake reason. Hector, like Ulysses among the Greeks, represents wisdom. He argues that common sense should convince them that Helen is not worth the sacrifice they will have to make in protecting Paris' possession of his captive girl. Hector's advice provokes a wild protest from Troilus:

> Nay, if we talk of reason,
> Let's shut our gates and sleep: manhood and honour
> Should have hare-hearts, would they but fat their thoughts
> With this crammed reason: reason and respect
> Make livers pale and lustihood deject.
>
> (II, ii, 46–50)

Hector condemns this knightly concept of honor, branding such talk as that of immature men, "Whom Aristotle thought / Unfit to hear moral philosophy," and warns Troilus and Paris, the adulterous lovers, that

> The reasons you allege do more conduce
> To the hot passion of distemper'd blood
> Than to make up a free determination
> 'Twixt right and wrong, . . .
>
> (II, ii, 166–171)

These wise words prove to be prophetic. Troilus obeys the dictates of irrational pleasure and becomes the slave of the temptress Cressida. He follows undirected courses of revenge and is left at the end of the play rushing wildly and futilely after Achilles. Troilus the warrior and Troilus the lover are different aspects of a life over which Troilus the man has deliberately abandoned all rational control.

Since all the world loves a lover, many critics find it difficult to believe that Shakespeare treats the love of Troilus and Cressida derisively. Yet he must have designed certain episodes in the story to awaken laughter with a touch of moral reprehension. Literary tradition had already rendered Cressida, in the language of W. W. Lawrence, a "byword for a loose and faithless woman." Many critics take Troilus for an idealistic, ardent youth, seduced and ruined by a sensual and calculating wench. But as Hyder Rollins points out, the sensuality of his desire when for the first time he is to meet Cressida alone is unmistakable. His soliloquy on that occasion (III, ii, 19–28) betrays him to be an expert in sexual gratification. His is a gourmet's anxiety that his lying with Cressida will be so exquisite a delight that he will, thereafter, lose nice distinctions in sexual experience. On the chance that anyone in the sophisticated audience, after hearing Troilus' expressions of the agony of unsatisfied desire should be in doubt about the nature of the encounter he is anticipating, Pandarus bustles in to comment on the meeting in a manner unmistakable even to a "thrice repured" mind. G. B. Harrison does not exaggerate when he writes that Pandarus leads in Cressida with "greasy chuckles of satisfaction" and all but puts the lovers to bed together on the stage. Cressida has used all her arts of coquetry to tease and intensify her lover's passion, so that the consummation will come at the most ardent moment for each of them. No one would expect happy results from this carnal encounter. We next see the pair on the morning after their night together. Like Romeo and Juliet, they sing an *aubade*, but their matutinal exchange is accompanied, not by the sweet notes of the lark, but by the cawing of ribald crows. Theirs is the fretful dialogue of two sated sensualists. To prolong the enjoyment of the experienced gentlemen of the audience, Pandarus comes in with a wealth of suggestive comments. In the actual scene of parting Troilus' expression of the agony he feels is never insincere, but it sometimes borders on hysteria and sometimes is unintentionally funny. When he exclaims "Cressid, I love thee in so 'strained' a purity" (the Folio has "strange"), the audience, having just witnessed the erotic encounter of the passionate pair, would surely have laughed. Because everyone familiar with Cressida's reputation would have known that she would prove false, Troilus' reiterated "be true" becomes an ironic leitmotif of the scene of parting. From this strained antiphonal, Cressida goes straight to the Greek camp, and soon is explaining the transfer of her favors from Troilus to Diomedes in flippant couplets. The commentator Ulysses is conveniently at hand to keep the attitude of the audience derisive: "Fie, fie upon her! / There's language in her eye, her cheek, her lip" (IV, v, 54–55).

Cressida is not a wicked creature, merely a willing victim of irresistible desire, and a cunning flirt, to boot. She does not deserve the punishment at the end of the play that many commentators think Shakespeare should have made her suffer. As for Troilus, his apologists believe that his exclamations at the sight of Cressida in Diomedes' arms are a moving expression of "impassioned agony," that it is "one of the most poignant scenes of eavesdropping in all Shakespeare." But it would have been inept dramatic construction to win sympathy for Troilus by underscoring the pathos of his devotion just before he was to be shown acting with mad futility. Perhaps Shakespeare expected his audience to accept Troilus' own description of his confused soliloquy as "madness of discourse." In tortured language he seeks to preserve his image of a faithful Cressida in the face of contradictory fact. He is here a disordered lover and becomes almost at once a disordered warrior. At the end of the jumbled battle scenes to which the fifth act is almost wholly devoted we last see him shaking his fist at the "vile, abominable Grecion tents," and threatening to haunt the murderer Achilles "like a wicked conscience." The issue of the war story and that of the love story come together in a common failure. Achilles has shamefully triumphed over Hector. This done, he returns to shameful inaction with the same excuse he had earlier made. The rules of chivalry did not permit a lover to seek the life of a brother of his ladylove, Polyxena. Futility is the logical end of a youth's love for a faithless woman. Futility is the logical result of a war waged by a mob of selfish individuals incapable of submitting themselves to the discipline of leadership. Futility is the logical denouement of a play organized and developed in the manner of a satirical comedy fashioned after Ben Jonson's "comicall satyres."—O. J. C.

Stage History. During the Restoration, *Troilus and Cressida* was given its earliest recorded performance anywhere at the Smock Alley Theatre in Dublin (see IRELAND). In England, Dryden's alteration, *Troilus and Cressida, or Truth Found To Late*, first performed at Dorset Garden in 167 displaced the original, holding the stage until 173 after which *Troilus and Cressida* appears to ha been completely ignored until the 20th centur Dryden's version, noted for plot unity and t addition of some effective scenes, reformed t character of Cressida, representing her as faithf to Troilus throughout. Some unfortunate abrid ments, especially in Ulysses' Time speech, invol the loss of much of the poetry of the genuin but additions, one (reminiscent of the quarrel sce between Brutus and Cassius) in which Troilus a Hector argue and reconcile, and another betwe Troilus and Diomedes have been much admire Thomas Betterton and Mary Lee played the tit roles in the first production, while Mary Bette ton acted the expanded role of Andromache. T play was acted 10 times in the 18th century. revival at Drury Lane in 1709 had Robert Wil as Troilus and Mrs. Bradshaw as Cressida, wi Betterton playing Thersites and Barton Booth, Ach les. Subsequent stagings at Lincoln's Inn Fields 1720, 1721, and twice in 1723 and two revivals Covent Garden, on December 20, 1733 and Janua 7, 1734, complete the performance record of Dr den's play. Lacy Ryan acted Troilus in all fi productions and James Quin, having portray Hector earlier, transferred to the role of Thersit after 1723. Anna Boheme was Cressida until Nover ber 1723. Covent Garden's Cressida was Mrs. Chri topher Bullock.

What little notice Charles Fry attracted wh he revived Shakespeare's play on June 1, 1907 at t Great Queen Street Theatre (with himself Thersites, Lewis Casson as Troilus, and Olive Ke nett as Cressida) was unfavorable. It only served convince critics that *Troilus and Cressida* as Shak speare wrote it was unmanageable. However, 1912, William Poel demonstrated that a cohere pattern could be established and, employing ne staging methods, presented his Elizabethan Sta Society in the problem play at the King's Ha Covent Garden, on the 10th, 15th, and 18th December. Some drastic cuts eliminated much the best poetry from Ulysses' Time speech ar Troilus' farewell to Cressida in IV, iv, and com pletely omitted the hero's despair over Hecto death. Black and purple curtains draped the othe wise bare stage, on which Edith Evans, a 24-yea old amateur, as Cressida eloquently suggested t wanton in a perfect portrayal of the mocki beauty. Poel, who played Pandarus, indulged a ty ical casting eccentricity in assigning Thersite Aeneas, and Paris to actresses. Esme Percy w Troilus, but, when the production was repeate at Stratford-upon-Avon the following May 12t Ion Swinley assumed that role.

In March 1922 the Marlowe Society acted t play at Cambridge with an all-male cast that w praised for its vigor but criticized for overemphasi ing the comic elements of the play. When the grou directed by Frank Birch, brought the production f a week's run in June to the Everyman Theatr Hampstead, actresses were assigned to the fema roles; Enid Baddeley portrayed Cressida. A brillia performance by Dennis Robertson as Pandarus w

.rticularly commended; in 1932, when Birch pre-nted the play at the Cambridge Festival Theatre, obertson repeated his characterization. The Mar-we Society under George Rylands accounted for ree more productions; its second in 1940, another 1948, and a final one in association with John rton and Robin Midgley in 1956. Rylands was so responsible for a televised *Troilus and Cressida* esented by the British Broadcasting Company in ptember 1954. Another university group, the xford University Dramatic Society, offered two oductions, one in 1938 produced by Nevill Cog-ll and shown at Exeter College, the second in 56 at St. John's.

The Old Vic first staged the play on November 1923 under Robert Atkins. Despite a talented st–Ion Swinley again as Troilus, Florence unders as Cressida, Hay Petrie as Thersites, and eorge Hayes as Ajax–the *Times* characterized e revival as necessarily dull. In 1928 Nugent onck produced the drama with the Norwich ayers at the Maddermarket Theatre. In 1936 Iden Payne, having previously directed a *Troilus d Cressida* at the Carnegie Institute of Technology Pittsburgh, Pennsylvania, in 1934, produced Strat-rd's second effort with the play. His cast in-ıded Donald Eccles and Pamela Brown in the le roles, Donald Wolfit as Ulysses, Randle Ayr-n as Pandarus, James Dale as Thersites, and osalind Iden as Cassandra. Two years later a odern-dress version was staged at the Westminster Michael MacOwan. The Trojans wore khaki, e Greeks, blue uniforms. Robert Harris and Ruth odge were Troilus and Cressida, Stephen Murray, seedy, leftist reporter-in-raincoat Thersites. Pan-rus became a dandified rogue at the hands of ax Adrian and Ulysses took on a new significance hen Robert Speaight infused meanness into his aracterization of a clever and eloquent diplomat. he antiwar theme was timely that September after e temporary reprieve of the Munich pact. Regent's rk was the scene of a production in 1946 by obert Atkins, with John Byron, intense and mpathetic as Troilus, and Patricia Hicks, too cuous as Cressida; Russell Thorndike appeared as ndarus. Twelve years after its second *Troilus d Cressida*, Stratford staged another production, is by Anthony Quayle, who, as he had in 1932 Cambridge, played Hector. Paul Scofield and eather Stannard were the lovers; Diana Wynyard, elen; and Noel Willman and Esmond Knight, ndarus and Thersites. William Devlin played gamemnon in the next Stratford Memorial Theatre oduction in 1954, but, aside from his reliable rformance and Malcolm Pride's attractive set, ntributed, as had its predecessor, little that was w to the experience. Glen Byam Shaw directed is *Troilus and Cressida*, with Laurence Harvey d Muriel Pavlow in the title roles and Anthony uayle now as Pandarus, while Keith Michell ayed Achilles.

Tyrone Guthrie cut only the prologue for the ld Vic's second revival in 1956, which saw the reeks wearing pre-World War I German uni-rms and the Trojans in costumes designed for e occasion. Cressida first appeared in a hobble-irted riding habit and Wendy Hiller's Helen of Troy played a flirtatious piano. All was biting satire, the complicated and poetic passion buried beneath the comic. John Neville and Rosemary Harris had a bad time as Troilus and Cressida, but Paul Rogers played the old roué Pandarus excellently, and Clifford Williams was effective as Thersites, a squalid wartime correspondent. The production was transported to New York later that year, and Neville transferred to the role of Thersites when it opened at the Winter Garden. Michael Croft presented his Youth Theatre in the play in September 1958 at the Lyric Theatre, Hammersmith. Two years later, Peter Hall and John Barton produced a *Troilus and Cressida* at Stratford; it was revived during an Edinburgh Festival in 1962 (perhaps the play's first production in Scotland) and seen again the following October at the Aldwych. Love and honor wasted away on a sand-covered platform against Leslie Hurry's scorching, dark red backcloth. Dorothy Tutin, first opposite Denholm Elliott and later Ian Holm, steadily improved her Cressida, her characterization finally fully developed at the Aldwych. Max Adrian was once more effective as Pandarus; Peter O'Toole played Thersites; Eric Porter, Ulysses; and Derek Godfrey, Hector. Elizabeth Sellars appeared as Helen.

To mark the Birmingham Repertory Theatre's golden jubilee and to complete its record of Shakespeare revivals, John Harrison produced a *Troilus and Cressida* in a season of three plays in 1963 (*Henry VIII* and *Titus Andronicus* were the others), with Derek Jacobi as Troilus.

A majority of the productions of *Troilus and Cressida* seen in the United States have been staged by amateur university societies. The first of these was acted by the all-male Dramatic Association at Yale under Edgar Woolley in 1916. In 1927 Rockford College in Illinois presented an all-female cast in its production. B. Iden Payne's production in 1934 came between that and a Western Reserve University presentation in 1947 in Cleveland, Ohio, produced by Eric Capon. The next year Harvard students performed the play 10 times.

Of the professional revivals, one at Moss' Broadway Theatre on June 6, 1932 received the widest recognition, but that was almost unanimously negative. James Lawler and Edith Barrett played the title roles; Eugene Powers and Otis Skinner won some good notices as Pandarus and Thersites; Charles Coburn's Ajax was ignored; but Blanche Yurka's Helen earned modest praise. Here again the verdict that the play could not, and therefore should not, be staged re-echoed. Nevertheless, Gilmor Brown included it in his Pasadena Playhouse revivals during 1936, and, in 1941, the Theatre Intime at Princeton in July and the Civic Theatre in Washington in December offered *Troilus and Cressida*. It was also given, with little critical success, in New York's Shakespeare Festival in Central Park August 10–28, 1965.–M. G.

Bibliography. TEXT: *Troilus and Cressida*, New Variorum Edition, H. N. Hillebrand, ed., 1953; *Troilus and Cressida*, New Cambridge Edition, Alice Walker and J. Dover Wilson, eds., 1957; W. W. Greg, *The Shakespeare First Folio*, 1955. DATE: Abbie Findlay Potts, "*Cynthia's Revels, Poetaster,* and *Troilus and Cressida*," *Shakespeare Quarterly*, V, 1954; Robert Kimbrough, *Shakespeare's Troilus and Cressida and its Setting*, 1964. SOURCES: Hyder E. Rollins, "The Troilus-Cressida Story from Chaucer to Shakespeare," *PMLA*, XXXII, 1917; Robert Presson, *Shakespeare's Troilus and Cressida and the Legends of Troy*, 1953. COMMENT: Peter Alexander, "*Troilus and Cressida*, 1609," *Library*, IX, 1928; W. W. Lawrence, *Shakespeare's Problem Comedies*, 1931; Oscar James Campbell, *Comicall Satyre and Shakespeare's Troilus and Cressida*, 1938; Kenneth Muir, "Troilus and Cressida," *Shakespeare Survey 8*, 1955; Robert Ornstein, *The Moral Vision of Jacobean Tragedy*, 1960; *Shakespeare's Troilus and Cressida and its Setting*. STAGE HISTORY: New Variorum Edition; New Cambridge Edition; G. C. D. Odell, *Shakespeare from Betterton to Irving*, 1920; J. C. Trewin, *Shakespeare on the English Stage, 1900–1964*, 1964.

Selected Criticism

G. WILSON KNIGHT. The theme is this. Human values are strongly contrasted with human failings. Now in Shakespeare there are two primary "values," Love and War. These two are vividly present in *Troilus and Cressida*. But they exist in a world which questions their ultimate purpose and beauty. The love of Troilus, the heroism of Hector, the symbolic romance which burns in the figure of Helen—these are placed beside the "scurril jests" and lazy pride of Achilles, the block-headed stupidity of Ajax, the mockery of Thersites. The Trojan party stands for human beauty and worth, the Greek party for the bestial and stupid elements of man, the barren stagnancy of intellect divorced from action, and the criticism which exposes these things with jeers. The atmospheres of the two opposing camps are thus strongly contrasted, and the handing over of Cressida to the Greeks, which is the pivot incident of the play, has thus a symbolic suggestion. Now these two primary aspects of humanity can be provisionally equated with the concepts "intuition" and "intellect," or "emotion" and "reason." In the play this distinction sometimes assumes the form of an antinomy between "individualism" and "social order." Now human values rest on an intuitive faith or an intuitive recognition: the denial of them—which may itself be largely emotional—if not directly caused by intellectual reasoning, is very easily related to such reasoning, and often looks to it for its own defence. Cynicism is eminently logical to the modern, post-Renaissance mind. Therefore, though aware that my terms cannot be ultimately justified as exact labels for the two faculties under discussion, I use them for my immediate purpose to point the peculiar dualism that persists in the thought of this play. Thus "intellect" is considered here as tending towards "cynicism," and "intuition" in association with "romantic faith"—a phrase chosen to suggest the dual values, Love and War. We can then say that the root idea of *Troilus and Cressida* is the dynamic opposition in the mind of these two faculties: intuition and intellect. [*The Wheel of Fire*, 1930.]

S. L. BETHELL. *Troilus and Cressida* is a consciously philosophical play. Normally Shakespeare's philosophical notions are incarnated in character and action; and his poetic thought, always concrete and image-filled, relates to character and action directl and only indirectly to whatever general truths ma be implied. The 'To-morrow, and to-morrow' spee((*Macb.* v.v.19) expresses directly Macbeth's reactic to his wife's death, and merely implies the atheis ('dusty death', 'Signifying nothing') which has r sulted from his gradual hardening in crime. *Troilus and Cressida*, on the other hand, the thougł only partially embodied in character and actio flows over into the dialogue, which, though usual concrete enough and full of imagery, is frequent developed almost independently of the situation which it refers. Ulysses' great speech on 'degre (*T.a.C.* I. iii. 75) begins and ends with Troy, but much more concerned with generalities of politic philosophy than with the Trojan war: in *Troil and Cressida* the story is an excuse for thought rath than the embodiment of thought. The metaphysic problems of the tragedies must, from the first, ha presented themselves to Shakespeare in terms of co crete experience; but in *Troilus and Cressida* he pu sues philosophical abstractions with the impassion eagerness of Donne. Problems of time and value ar their mutual relations are thrust forward for th audience's attention:

> Time hath, my lord, a wallet at his back,
> Wherein he puts alms for oblivion.
> (*T.a.C.* III. iii. 145–146)

As in Donne, philosophy is usually apprehended terms of sense-experience, but occasionally even th bare bones of abstract thinking appear, e.g. Troilus' crucial but awkward query: 'What is augh but as 'tis valued?' (II. ii. 52).

In such a play it is no wonder to find characte with something of a 'morality' flavour. As Thersit recalls the old Vice, so Ulysses conveys some su gestion of an abstract Worldly Wisdom. Most of th characters in *Troilus and Cressida* express themselv philosophically, but Ulysses has an especially lar share of such speeches, including the famous 'degre speech and the speech on Time. With him ev more than the others, what he says is infinitely mo important than why he says it, and at times even h behaviour is hard to interpret on naturalistic grounc [*Shakespeare and the Popular Dramatic Traditio* 1944.]

UNA ELLIS-FERMOR. It would seem, then, th this play is an attempt, upon a scale whose vas ness is measured by the intensity with which eve faculty of the poet's mind is engaged, to find th image (of absolute value) in the evidence of mar achievement, in the sum or parts of his experien or, if nowhere else, in the processes of creati imagination. Troilus's love, Agamemnon's chivalr Ulysses's vision of the hierarchy of state are a thus, experimental images, in which are tested th absolute value of man's passion, intellect, and in agination. In face of this test, this "quid hoc a aeternitatem?", all fail. There is no absolute quali the evidence for which does not resolve itself in a mere subjective illusion of blood or fancy, a 'ma Idolatrie, To make the seruice greater then the Go (II. ii. 58–59). The creations of man's spirit, hither exalted, are now seen to have survived only b chance, at the mercy all the time of a stronge natural law of destruction; what in another moc might have appeared tragic accidents, the counterpoint in a fuller harmony, are now seen, instead, to reveal an underlying law to which all is recurrently and inescapably subject. This is the ultimate, indeed the only surviving absolute in *Troilus and Cressida*. The faculty that could perceive degree and the ordered form of a universe, the imagination itself, has been touched and the images of form no longer rise at its command. "There is no more to say." The dark night of the soul comes down upon the unilluminated wreckage of the universe of vision. The play of *Troilus and Cressida* remains as one of the few living and unified expressions of this experience. The grand scale of this catastrophe blinds us. We do not willingly imagine this overthrow; some at least of us never to the end comprehend it, for it is like a note too deep for our hearing, or a landscape too vast for our experiencing. We probably come nearer to understanding the tragedies than this play which is no tragedy and is yet perhaps the record of the profoundest catastrophe in man's experience. "Moving of th'earth brings harms and fears, Men reckon what it did and meant, But trepidation of the spheres, Though greater far, is innocent." If we turn from this attempt to understand the nature of the underlying ideas in *Troilus and Cressida* and consider the form through which these ideas are revealed, we see that what has been achieved is in fact what we suggested at the outset. The idea of chaos, of disjunction, of ultimate formlessness and negation, has by a supreme act of artistic mastery been given form. It has not been described in more or less abstract terms; it has been imagined. What seemed to be an absolute limitation of drama has been transcended and shown, in this rare achievement, to be but relative. And in this case, even more than in either of those which we have just considered, the subduing of content to form is no mere act of virtuosity; it has a further significance as an instance of one of the ultimate functions of art. That the experience on which this play rests is of profound significance at any time, and of peculiar significance to our own, needs no discussion. [*The Frontiers of Drama*, 1945.]

Troublesome Raigne of John King of England, The. See King John: *Sources*.

True Tragedy of Richard Duke of York. See Contention plays.

Trundle or **Trundell, John** (fl. 1603–1626). London publisher of plays and ballads. In 1603 Trundle and Nicholas Ling were the joint publishers of the "bad quarto" of Hamlet. Trundle was apparently an intimate of the London theatrical world; Jonson makes a jesting reference to him as a publisher of ballads in the revised version of *Every Man In his Humour* (1616): "Will if this be read with patience, Ile be gelt, and troll ballads for Mr. Iohn Trvndle, yonder, the rest of my mortalitie." [Leo Kirschbaum, *Shakespeare and the Stationers*, 1955.]

Trussell, John (fl. 1595). Poet. Trussell's *The First Rape of Faire Helen* (1595) bears some resemblances to Shakespeare's *Rape of Lucrece*. The only other works definitely attributed to Trussell are three prefatory poems published with *The Triumphs over Death* (1595), a devotional tract written by the Jesuit poet and martyr Robert Southwell. There has been no positive identification of Trussell. He may be related to the Trussell family of Billesley, a hamlet near Stratford. If this is the case he may also have been a distant relative of Shakespeare, since Shakespeare's maternal grandmother, the wife of Robert Arden, was probably a Trussell. Stratford records show that in 1592 John Shakespeare and Thomas Trussell, an attorney, jointly appraised the goods of Henry Field.

The First Rape of Faire Helen, a narrative poem of 1918 lines, recounts the story of the rape of Helen by Theseus and of her subsequent marriage to Menelaus. The poem bears some resemblances to Shakespeare's account of Lucrece, but they are not nearly extensive enough to justify the claim of some that Trussell's work is a plagiarism of *Lucrece*. Those who hold the view that Trussell is closely imitating Shakespeare have also suggested that a prefatory sonnet, published with the poem, is addressed to Shakespeare:

> To praise thy worth or to applaud thy wit,
> Or to commend thy pleasing Poetrie:
> Were but to shew my insufficiencie,
> Which cannot equall what thy selfe hast writ.
> for thou maist challenge not vnworthily,
> true Vertues merits, Fames eternitie,
> Vpon thy browes perpetually to sit.
> Then what need I to laud thy Poesie,
> (which cannot pen thy praise effectuallie)
> Sith Phoebus Laurell will eternize it.
> yet since our friendship and our amitie.
> commaunded me as much: (and hee,
> Qui tua non laudat deteriora dabit)
> I haue aduentur'd, as each eye may see,
> to shame my selfe in seeking praise for thee.
>
> I. T.

[M. A. Shaaber, "'The First Rape of Faire Helen' by John Trussell," *Shakespeare Quarterly*, VIII, 1957.]

Tubal. In *The Merchant of Venice*, a Jew who informs Shylock that Jessica has been squandering his money and jewels in Genoa. Tubal also conveys the more welcome news that Antonio is ruined (III, i).

Tuckfield, Thomas (fl. 1624–1626). Actor. Tuckfield was probably a hired man with the King's Men. In 1624 his name, "Thomas Tuckfeild," appeared on a list of 21 "Musitions and other necessary attendantes" of the company exempted from arrest by Sir Henry Herbert, the Master of the Revels. His name appears also in one of the stage directions affixed to the First Quarto of Shakespeare and Fletcher's *Two Noble Kinsmen*, which was printed in 1634. The stage direction, which reads "some Attendants, T. Tucke: Curtis," probably dates from a revival of the play given by the King's Men about 1626. See Curtis Greville. [G. E. Bentley, *The Jacobean and Caroline Stage*, 5 vols. 1941–1956.]

Turgenev, Ivan. See Russia.

Turkey. In Turkey, where European-style legitimate theatre started in the 1840's, Shakespeare's tragedies and comedies have steadily gained renown since 1860, when *Othello* was offered in Istanbul as the first Shakespeare play to be produced in Turkish. Later years saw performances of *Hamlet*, *Romeo and Juliet*, *The Comedy of Errors*, and *The Merchant of Venice*. The earliest published translations were an abridged adaptation of *Othello* (1877) and the full Turkish versions of *The Merchant of Venice* (1885) and *The Comedy of Errors* (1888). Occasional Shakespearean influences crept into the plays of Namik Kemal (1840–1888), a pioneering dramatist, and Abdülhak Hamit Tarhan (1852–1937), whose tragedies captivated the Turkish audiences between 1875 and 1920. Shakespeare exerted virtually no influence on Turkish playwriting after Tarhan's heyday but dominated Turkey's dramatic repertory. In the early part of the 20th century Shakespeare productions received fresh impetus from Dr. Abdullah Cevdet's translations of the major tragedies, published between 1908 and 1912, and from the *Othello* performances of Kâmil Riza, who achieved fame as "Othello Kâmil."

Shakespeare's pre-eminence on the Turkish stage was firmly established by the Istanbul City Theatre, founded in 1914. Under the aegis of Muhsin Ertuğrul (1892–), the City Theatre presented nearly 50 productions of 21 Shakespeare plays in its first 50 years. Muhsin Ertuğrul personally staged 10 of Turkey's 13 *Hamlets* since 1914. His *Hamlet* production in the 1959/60 season, featuring Engin Cezzar in the title role, ran for 170 performances—one of the world's longest runs for *Hamlet*. The City Theatre also presents opulent Shakespeare productions in summer at the open rotunda on the Bosphorus fortress built in the mid-15th century.

The State Theatre in Ankara has presented 10 Shakespeare productions since its establishment in 1940. Private theatres in major cities, troupes touring the countryside, the People's Houses (community culture centers active between 1930 and 1950), college theatres, and Turkish radio have also contributed to Shakespeare's popularity in Turkey. In rural areas a loose adaptation of *Othello*, entitled *Black Man's Revenge*, is a perennial favorite.

The 400th anniversary of the playwright's birth was lavishly celebrated in Turkey. Istanbul saw six Shakespeare plays produced by the City Theatre and one by the private Küçük Sahne. The City Theatre celebrated its 50th anniversary in 1964 with an open-air production of *Coriolanus*. In Ankara, the State Theatre produced two Shakespeare plays and gave a Shakespeare recital. Later it performed *Julius Caesar* at the International Theatre Festival in Paris and at the ancient Greek theatre at Aspendos before an audience of 15,000.

Twenty-one Shakespeare plays have been produced in Turkey with 14 remaining untranslated ar two unproduced although translations are availabl Prior to the 1940's, most Shakespeare translatio were made from French and German versions; th thus showed little regard for accuracy and, being bookish prose, conveyed none of Shakespeare's dr matic intensity and poetic effects. In the 1940's ar 1950's, when over 30 Shakespeare translations ca out, well-qualified translators, including Orhan B rian, Nurettin Sevin, Yusuf Mardin, Halide Ed Adivar, and İrfan Şahinbaş, working from the En lish originals, secured precision of meaning ar strengthened the poetic elements, although they, to failed to convey Shakespeare's dramatic power. N Turkish versions of any of the poems are availabl and only about 50 of the sonnets have been tran lated.

Shakespeare scholarship in Turkey has yet to d velop. Very few of the books, pamphlets, and art cles on Shakespeare may be considered original co tributions. There are perhaps only two studies whic would merit mention: Mina Urgan's book on clow in the Elizabethan age and her treatise on *Macbet*

Shakespeare expresses nothing but contempt f Turks, referring to them as "malignant," "base," "ci cumcised dog," etc. He imputes to them treacher cruelty, lack of honor, wanton behavior, and lu Turks, in Shakespeare's eyes, are barbarous infide Most Turkish translations and productions of Shak speare's plays have dropped or softened the poe disparaging references to Turks.

In modern Turkey, no playwright—native or fo eign—has enjoyed as wide a fame as Shakespeare or many productions. Perhaps in no other non-Englis speaking country which has remained outside of t mainstream of Western culture until recent tim has Shakespeare been as dominant a theatrical for as in 20th-century Turkey. [John W. Drap "Shakespeare and the Turk," *Journal of English a Germanic Philology*, LV, 1956; Türk Tiyatro Dergisi, *Türkiye de Shakespeare* (articles by Muhs Ertuğrul, Arslan Kaynardag, Kemal Tözem, a Z. K.), Combined Issue, July-September 1962; Met And, "Shakespeare in Turkey," *Theatre Researc Recherches Théâtrales*, VI, 2, 1964.]—T. S. H.

Tutor to Rutland. In *3 Henry VI*, he vainly be Clifford not to kill the young earl. The tut is spared because of his priestly calling (I, ii Historically, Rutland's tutor was Sir Robert Asp (fl. 1460), a priest.

Twelfe-Night, Or what you will.

Twelfth Night; or, What You Will. A comedy by hakespeare.

Text. The only authoritative text is that of the irst Folio (1623). There are no earlier editions. 'he text is a good one, probably based on a ıeatrical PROMPT-BOOK. It is divided into acts and :enes; the rather detailed stage directions indicate ıe work of a BOOK-KEEPER. One striking error in ıe text is the name Violenta substituted for Viola ı a stage direction (I, v, 57). The same name is rroneously inserted into a stage direction of *All's Vell That Ends Well* (III, v).

Date. A date some time between 1600 and 1602 ıay be accepted as the probable time for the comosition of *Twelfth Night*. There are contemporary :ports of early performances which help to date ıe play. John MANNINGHAM notes in his diary that n Candlemas, February 2, 1602 he saw *Twelfth Night* acted at the Middle Temple, where he lived. He describes the occasion as follows: "At our feast wee had a play called 'Twelue Night, or What You Will,' much like the Commedy of Errores or Menechmi in Plautus, but most like an neere to that in Italian called *Inganni*." Manningham makes it clear that it was Shakespeare's play that he saw, by going on to commend as "a good practice" (clever device) the trick played on Malvolio, which he describes in detail. Other pieces of circumstantial evidence support a date between 1600 and 1602. Maria's reference (III, ii, 85) to "the new map with the augmentation of the Indies" refers to a map drawn (c. 1599) by Emerie Molyneux; it shows the East Indies in greater detail than any map previously drawn of this region. Fabian's boast (II, v, 197), "I will not give my part in this sport for a pension of thousands to be paid from the Sophy"

THE WRIGHT-MOLYNEUX MAP OF THE WORLD TO WHICH MARIA REFERS. THE DATE OF THIS MAP (C. 1599) HAS GIVEN A CLUE TO THE DATING OF *Twelfth Night*. (HUNTINGTON LIBRARY)

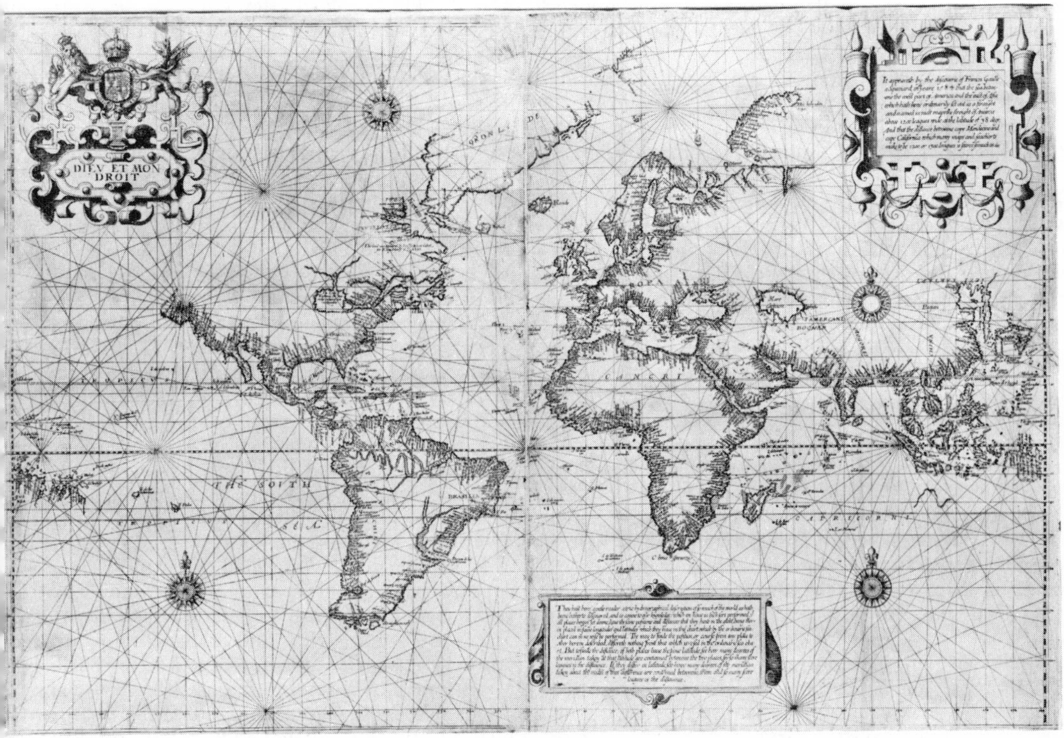

is probably an allusion to Sir Robert Shirley's return on the ship *Sophy* from Persia in 1599 with rich gifts from the shah.

In advancing a specific date for the first performance of *Twelfth Night*, Leslie Hotson has presented convincing evidence to support his belief that this comedy was first acted at court on the Feast of the Epiphany—that is, Twelfth Night—January 6, 1601. This production was the high point of the entertainment offered Don Virginio Orsino, a Tuscan duke, during his official visit to Queen Elizabeth. Hotson's theory falls just short of being incontestable, with the result that many scholars feel that a somewhat later date, perhaps January 6, 1602, would be more appropriate. They argue that the references to Orsino would be more appropriate after his visit than during it.

Sources. The *Inganni* (Deceits), to which Manningham (see above) compares *Twelfth Night*, is doubtless the author's mistake for the anonymous *Gli' Ingannati:* Although there existed two Italian plays entitled *Inganni*—one by Nicolò Secchi, published in 1562, and one by Curzio Gonzaga, published in 1592—neither of these plays resembles Shakespeare's except in incidental details. The plot of *Gli' Ingannati*, on the other hand, closely resembles that of Shakespeare's comedy. It was first acted at Siena in 1531 under the auspices of one of the bourgeois academies (literary clubs) popular throughout 16th-century Italy. First published in 1537, the play was so popular that by 1585 it had gone through eight Italian editions. *Gli' Ingannati* was translated into French by Charles Estienne, first as *Le Sacrifice* (1543) and later as *Les Abusez* (1549, 1556). The French version was in turn translated into Latin by an English scholar at Cambridge, where it was performed in 1595 in connection with a visit of the earl of Essex. The title of the Latin version is *Laelia*.

Shakespeare's main source, however, is Barnabe RICHE's "Of Apolonius and Silla," the second story in his *Farewell to Militarie Profession* (1581). Riche's story is derived ultimately from *Gli' Ingannati*, by way of prose versions in Bandello's *Novelle* (1554) and François de Belleforest's *Histoires Tragiques* (1571). According to Leslie Hotson's theory, the character of Malvolio is based on Sir William KNOLLYS, Elizabeth's puritanical comptroller of the household and a familiar object of ridicule in court circles.—O. J. C.

Plot Synopsis. Act I. Orsino, Duke of Illyria, is in love with Olivia, a wealthy noblewoman, but she is in mourning because of the death of a brother and will not even receive the Duke's emissary. Olivia's aloofness merely fans the ardor of the Duke, who takes into his service a youth called Cesario and asks him to pay court to her on his behalf. In reality, Cesario is a maiden named Viola who was shipwrecked on the Illyrian coast after being separated from her brother. Having decided to wear male attire and seek temporary employment with the Duke, she now finds herself in love with him.

Olivia's prolonged mourning is not to the liking of her riotous uncle, Sir Toby Belch, who is warned by her maid Maria that Olivia is displeased with his late hours and excessive drinking. Maria is also critical of Sir Andrew Aguecheek, a foolish but affluent knight whom Sir Toby has advanced as candidate for his niece's hand. Sir Andrew is wil ing to concede defeat, but Toby persuades him stay a month longer. Other members of Olivia household include her clown, Feste, and her co ceited and ill-tempered steward, Malvolio. Wh Viola arrives to woo Olivia in the Duke's name, s gains entrance only with difficulty. Olivia aga rejects the Duke's suit, but is so charmed by t youthful envoy that she invents an excuse for givi him her ring.

Act II. Sir Toby and Sir Andrew are enjoying bibulous evening, enlivened by Feste's singing, wh Maria enters to complain about their "caterwau ing." She is soon followed by Malvolio, who d clares that Olivia has threatened to evict Toby if does not mend his ways. Annoyed at the steward impertinence, Sir Toby demands, "Dost thou thin because thou art virtuous, there shall be no mo cakes and ale?" When Malvolio departs, Mar derides him as "an affectioned ass" who conside himself irresistible. She proposes that they take a vantage of his failing by leading him to believe th Olivia has fallen in love with him.

Duke Orsino luxuriates in his passion for Oliv and, undaunted by previous failures, bids Viola renew his suit. He scoffs at her suggestion that son woman may be as deeply in love with him as he with Olivia; no feminine heart, he claims, could ho a passion as large as his.

Sir Toby and his fellow conspirators can bare restrain their anger when they overhear Malvol consider the possibility of marrying Olivia ar lording it over her uncle. His ruminations are c short when he comes across a love letter written a hand that resembles Olivia's, but is actuall Maria's. He convinces himself that he is the u identified man to whom it is addressed and resolv to follow its instructions for winning Olivia's favo to be surly with the servants, to smile in h presence, and to wear yellow stockings cros gartered. The eavesdroppers chortle as Maria poin out that Olivia loathes yellow and will undoubted find Malvolio's smiles at variance with her mela choly air.

Act III. Viola, still in the guise of Cesario, pa another visit to Olivia, who makes no secret of h infatuation. The favors that she bestows on Cesar offend Sir Andrew, who is persuaded by Sir Tob and Fabian, another of Olivia's servants, to challen the youth. Sir Toby is confident, however, th neither Sir Andrew nor Cesario has enough coura to fight the other.

Meanwhile, Viola's twin brother, Sebastian, wh was saved from drowning by a sea captain calle Antonio, has arrived in Illyria. Though Antonio sought by the Illyrian authorities for an old offens he not only insists on accompanying Sebastian, b gives him his purse as well.

A smiling Malvolio, clad in yellow stocking appears before Olivia and archly quotes passag from her letter. She concludes that he is ma Sir Toby's fun with Sir Andrew also procee apace. The aggrieved suitor pens a letter challengin Viola, but Toby, finding it unsatisfactory, express the knight's displeasure himself. Viola is naturall puzzled by the challenge and protests that she is r fighter. Sir Toby, however, reports that Cesar s a skilled swordsman, causing the timorous Sir Andrew to regret his challenge. Just as the re-uctant duelists have drawn their swords, Antonio ppears and tries to end the dispute, but is himself rrested by some officers. Mistaking Viola for ebastian, he asks for his money and is dismayed vhen she replies that she does not know him.

Act IV. On the street before Olivia's house ebastian is accosted by Sir Andrew, who strikes im. Sebastian is about to retaliate when Olivia in-ites him into her home. She later appears with a riest and asks Sebastian to accompany her to the hapel so that they can be secretly married. Despite is bewilderment, he meekly complies.

Meanwhile, Feste, pretending to be good Sir Topas the curate, interrogates Malvolio, who has een locked in a dark room. When Toby proposes hat they end their prank because of Olivia's dis-leasure with him, Feste agrees to bring Malvolio light and writing materials.

Act V. While the Duke and Viola are waiting for n interview with Olivia, the officers return with ntonio, who accuses Viola of the basest ingrati-ude. Olivia compounds Viola's confusion by re-roaching her for faithlessness. When the priest ipports Olivia's assertion that Cesario is her hus-and, even the Duke spurns Viola. Sir Andrew and n inebriated Sir Toby burst in, loudly calling for surgeon. They claim that Cesario, who they be-eved was a coward, has given them a thorough rashing. The mystery is dispelled when Sebastian nters to apologize for his attack on Olivia's kins-ian. He and Viola soon realize that they are brother nd sister.

Olivia is reminded of Malvolio, who is released nd shows her the letter that has been the cause of is woes. Upon seeing the handwriting, she guesses iat the author was Maria. Fabian explains that Maria as incited by him and Sir Toby, who has married er in recompense. Malvolio vows revenge on the t of them, but the Duke hopes that he can be acified. To Viola he predicts that when he sees er in feminine clothes, she will become "Orsino's iistress and his fancy's queen."—H. D.

Comment. The main romantic plot—Viola's love r the Duke—is the poet's development of a typical alianate comic situation, both of COMMEDIA LL' ARTE (popular comedy) and of the *commedia udita* (learned comedy) based on Terence and lautus. The common elements include a pair of distinguishable twins and a girl disguised as a ge, who follows her errant lover abroad and in-iuates herself into his service. She usually adopts is stratagem in order to recover his love; in *welfth Night* it is merely in order to protect her-lf, a timid and modest girl, from the advances rude men. When, like her Italianate model, she lks under the protection of her disguise about her thetic situation, Shakespeare composes for her me of the loveliest lyrics that he ever wrote. The mplications arising out of a sentimental girl's lling in love with a girl disguised as a page are so conventional in Italianate comedy. All these ements in the main plot are like those in a fairy ory. They form a strong contrast to the realistic, oad comedy of the subplot that unfolds in livia's manor house. Since Olivia's establishment is in a transitional stage between a medieval castle and a Tudor country house, it contains some of the elements of the older, fast-disappearing organization (see ELIZABETHAN LIFE IN THE PLAYS). Sir Toby is a relic of the armed retainers who were the neces-sary defenders of the castle. Their drunken goings-on were tolerated in those days because their services were of first importance. In Elizabethan England, having lost their military importance, they had become, like Toby, only a nuisance. Sir Andrew is a survival of the uninvited guests to whom the manor offered hospitality as a matter of course. Malvolio is the major-domo who was responsible for the successful operation of Olivia's domestic estab-lishment.

In organizing these characters into a subplot, Shakespeare imitates Ben Jonson's method of con-structing a satiric comedy. Maria and her fellow conspirators, in forming a trap in which to hold Malvolio while they expose his absurdity, are adopt-ing and improving on Jonson's method of driving a fool out of his "humour." Malvolio's humour is self-love. His colossal conceit so completely upsets his sense of social values that he, a household servant, aspires to marriage with the lady of the manor. The plot forces him into an exaggerated display of his absurd way of ingratiating himself with her. Follow-ing the instructions of Maria's forged letter, he dons yellow stockings, which were part of the conventional costume of a servingman. As he wreathes his face in grimaced smiles, kisses his hands, and adopts all the absurdities of conduct recommended in Maria's letter of malicious advice, Olivia is sure that he has lost his mind. This gives Sir Toby a chance to improve upon the original plot. At his suggestion Malvolio is given the usual Elizabethan treatment for an insane man: he is bound and cast into a dark prison. This has seemed so brutal to many actors that they have often pre-sented him as the pathetic victim of cruel horseplay. That certainly was not Shakespeare's intention. When at the end of the play Malvolio frantically rushes offstage, shouting, "I'll be revenged on the whole pack of you," Shakespeare expected his audiences to follow him with the scornful laughter that he, taught by Jonson, thought it was the business of comical satire to arouse.

Sir Andrew Aguecheek bears a strong family like-ness to Jonson's country gulls. He is a complete ninny who mistakes Sir Toby's rowdy conduct for the manners of a complete gentleman. Sir Toby delights in forcing the devotion of his "dear manni-kin" into more and more exhibitions of fatuity.

Feste is an example of the all-licensed fool whom great lords, and even kings, kept at their courts to furnish amusement, well into the 16th century. Feste is apparently the first part that Shakespeare wrote for Robert Armin, who during the year 1599 succeeded Will Kempe as the low-comedy actor in the Chamberlain's Men. He is a typical court fool, amusing his mistress with impudence and chop logic that is boring to most modern audiences. Armin had a good voice and so Shakespeare gave him a number of songs to sing during the course of the play. Some critics assign Feste a position of great importance, seeing in him the directing spirit of the drama. H. N. Hudson declared he is "the highest wisdom in the play and the lowest buffoonery, hence Shake-speare's ideal fool."

Malvolio's harassed exit introduces one of the poet's most successful final ensemble scenes. Each character enters singly to write an effective "finis" to his comic business. Nowhere else has the poet brought all the strands of a complicated plot to a more skillful denouement. Nor has he more deftly mingled in one scene romantic feeling, merriment, and derision.—O. J. C.

Stage History: England. If Leslie Hotson's theory, explained above under *Date*, is correct, the first performance of *Twelfth Night* was on January 6, 1601. The earliest recorded performance is that noted by John Manningham as occurring on February 2, 1602. Under the title *Malvolio*, by which it was apparently better known, the play was presented at the palace at Whitehall on February 2, 1622. In his commendatory poem prefixed to John Benson's edition of Shakespeare's poems, Leonard DIGGES alludes to the box-office appeal of "Malvoglio that crosse garter'd Gull."

With the reopening of the theatres in 1660, the play became the property of Sir William Davenant's Duke's Company. In his diary Samuel PEPYS noted his attendance at three different performances of the play—the earliest on September 11, 1661—none of which he enjoyed. The cast which Pepys saw included Thomas Betterton as Sir Toby and Henry Harris as Sir Andrew Aguecheek.

In 1703 William BURNABY produced a monstrosity entitled *Love Betrayed or The Agreeable Disappointment*. The stated purpose of this adaptation of *Twelfth Night* was to produce a text that could serve as a libretto for an opera or a masque. Burnaby's changes were radical in both character and plot. For example, he merged Malvolio and Sir Andrew into one character called Taquilet, and split Maria into two—a witty confidante of the heroine and an amorous old serving-woman.

Not until 1741, at the beginning of Garrick's reign at the Drury Lane, did the play again find favor. In January of that year Charles Macklin first impersonated Malvolio, which remained for years undisputedly his role. With Hannah Pritchard as Viola and Kitty Clive as Olivia, the play became a popular favorite. After 1741 the comedy was staged at both Drury Lane and Covent Garden year after year until about 1819, the role of Malvolio invariably being given to the principal actor.

In the early 19th century, music began to be introduced into the play. One of the productions most embellished with music was that staged at Covent Garden on November 8, 1820. The songs sung by Viola were written by Henry Rowley Bishop; a note in the playbill announced that "in the course of the comedy will be introduced Songs, Glees and Choruses, the Poetry selected entirely from the Plays, Poems and Sonnets of Shakespeare."

Throughout the 19th century, there was a strong mutual influence of the English and American productions. The Hallam Company produced the play in New York in 1804. The American sisters Charlotte and Susan Cushman, who had startled London and New York as Romeo and Juliet, produced *Twelfth Night*, with Charlotte as Viola and Susan as Olivia. Charles Kean chose the comedy for the opening of his triumphant repertory season at the New Princess Theatre in September 1850. There were 40 performances during the 1850/1 season, staged with the scenic splendor that was featur in all of Kean's productions. His wife, Ellen Tr scored a hit as Viola. Sir Henry Irving cast hi self as Malvolio in a production at the Lyceu Theatre in July 1884. His production sacrific characterization to the splendor of the ensemb scenes. He made Malvolio an almost tragic figu a sentimental interpretation which exerted an u fortunate influence on subsequent impersonatio of the character. Ellen Terry, who confessed th the production was one of Irving's least successf and styled it "dull, lumpy, and heavy," was a fa cinating Viola. The critics found alluring A Rehan's portrayal of this role, known backstage the "breeches part." Beginning on January 8, 18 at Daly's Theatre in London, she played Viola 119 consecutive performances, a phenomenally lo run for the time.

The early 20th century saw contrasting interpr tations of *Twelfth Night*. In 1901 Beerbohm Tr staged what *Punch* labeled a "swardy" producti of the comedy at His Majesty's. Tree's Malvol was an insufferably haughty martinet shadowed b four "minor" images who straightened to attenti at their master's voice. Then, in 1903, William Poe Elizabethan Stage Society staged, in the words Max Beerbohm, an "instructive" rather than "d lightful" *Twelfth Night;* but the artist Byam Sha congratulated Poel, wishing "that others wou follow [his] noble example and allow us to list to Shakespeare."

Harley Granville-Barker followed an experiment production of *The Winter's Tale* with an equal nontraditional *Twelfth Night*, which opened November 15, 1912 at the Savoy and played 1 performances. His wife, Lillah McCarthy, play Viola, with Evelyn Millard as Olivia. Henry Ainl presented a three-dimensional portrayal of Malvol —a priggish, conceited steward, the absurdly hoo winked lover, and the pathetic, overwrought pr oner. Sir Toby and Sir Andrew were restored their gentlemen's status; and Hayden Coffin, r cruited from the musical comedy stage, sustain as Feste the latent melancholy of the text. Jol Masefield wrote to Granville-Barker, "You got t full flavour and power from it and made one fe that one was listening to one of the world's maste at his happiest."

James Bernard Fagan gave a traditional stagi of the play at the Court in 1918, in which Herbe Waring made Malvolio perpetually pompous.

In the summer of 1932 Sydney Carroll cho *Twelfth Night* for his trial matinee at the Op Air Theatre in Regent's Park. Rain drenched t audience and performers, who included Jean Forbe Robertson as a gravely wistful Viola and Phyl Neilson-Terry as a colorful and slightly reg Olivia who sang the last verse of Feste's farew song. This same version, produced by Robert Atki began the first season of the Open Air Theatre June 5, 1933, playing to an audience of more th 3000.

During the 1930's, *Twelfth Night* was played most continuously in London and was a standa play in the repertoire of the touring compani The memorable "ring" soliloquy of Edith Evans Viola highlighted Harcourt Williams' production f the Old Vic in 1932. Five years later, under Tyro uthrie's direction, Laurence Olivier happily over-ayed Sir Toby; Jessica Tandy doubled in the role Viola and Sebastian, with resultant damage to e recognition scene; and Alec Guinness portrayed wraithlike Sir Andrew. At the Phoenix in the tumn of 1938 a production, unmemorable except r Peggy Ashcroft's Viola and Michael Redgrave's guecheek, achieved the distinction of being the st Shakespearean play to be televised in its entirety om a theatre.

In 1939 *Twelfth Night* was in the repertoire of oductions presented by Donald Wolfit during his st "black-out" tour. When his autumn tour had to canceled in 1940, scenes from the comedy were cluded in his lunchtime Shakespeare season at the rand Theatre. Wolfit also traveled to the R.A.F. mps in East Anglia during the fall of 1943 with *welfth Night.*

Robert Atkins' successful production of the play r Stratford-upon-Avon in 1945 introduced the merican actress Claire Luce in an intelligent por-ayal of Viola. Alec Guinness presented a mild *welfth Night* for the Old Vic, playing at the New heatre during the 1948/9 season. This production atured a revolving set by Michael Warre; admit-dly ingenious, it nonetheless irritated at least one itic, who felt that "a permanent set should never t us know it is there." Sir Cedric Hardwicke as r Toby dominated this Illyrian scene. Two seasons ter the Old Vic returned from the New Theatre ith Hugh Hunt's *Twelfth Night*, which was iticized for its drab piazza set but congratulated r Peggy Ashcroft's shining Viola.

In 1955 John Gielgud's production for Stratford-on-Avon presented Vivien Leigh playing Viola pposite her husband, Sir Laurence Olivier, as a in-lipped, lisping Malvolio. The comic balance of e play was somewhat distorted at Stratford in 1958 hen Dorothy Tutin acted Viola against the flighty, attering Olivia of Geraldine McEwan. The Strat-rd company under producer Peter Hall performed the Aldwych in 1960, with Eric Porter imperson-ing Malvolio.

In 1959, and again in 1962, *Twelfth Night* was esented at the Open Air Theatre, first by Robert tkins, and later by Denis Carey. Performances by e Old Vic were seen during both the 1960/1 d 1961/2 seasons; and in 1964 John Franklyn-obbins staged his matinee production at the omedy Theatre with Barry Boys as Malvolio.

Stage History: America. The first recorded per-rmance of the comedy in America occurred on ay 5, 1794 at the Theatre in Federal Street, Boston, d its first New York enactment came on June 11, 04 at the Park. *Twelfth Night* was rarely repre-nted during the early part of the 19th century, but August 10, 1824 a talented cast, which included enry Wallack as Malvolio, performed the play at e Chatham Garden; and with William E. Burton's itial production at his Chambers Street Theatre on arch 29, 1852, the play's popularity rose steadily. A arse but genial comedian, Burton no doubt amply led the role of Sir Toby, supported by Lester Wal-ck as Aguecheek, William R. Blake as Malvolio, d Henry Placide as Feste. In subsequent revivals, rton's cast varied and, in 1853, Charles Fisher as-med Malvolio—a performance described as "a finely finished bit of eccentric comedy" which would have been improved with a suggestion of false pride and self-importance. James William Wallack produced *Twelfth Night* in 1856 with John Dyott's severe Malvolio and Charles M. Walcott's Sir Andrew, a study in servile credulity. In 1869 Augustin Daly presented his first revival of the comedy at his Fifth Avenue Theatre with an exceptional cast including Mrs. Scott-Siddons exhibiting anxiety and coy pleasure as Viola; Fanny Davenport, an exuberant Maria; William P. Davidge in a perfect display of jocund humor as Toby Belch—more than just a sot, distinctly a person of importance; and George Clarke as a grimly conceited and absurd Malvolio. When Daly presented his second *Twelfth Night* in 1877, Adelaide Neilson appeared as Viola and Charles Fisher again portrayed Malvolio, but his finest presentation of the play was effected in 1893 at Daly's. Then two musical numbers were lifted for the comedy: "Come unto these yellow sands" from *The Tempest* and "Who is Sylvia?" naturally substituting the name "Olivia," from *The Two Gentlemen of Verona.* George Clarke acted Malvolio in this production with James Lewis as a carousing Sir Toby never forgetful of the consequence of his knighthood. The most outstanding performance of the revival was Ada Rehan's debut as Viola. Her comedy impersonations were unmatched, and as a bold, ironic, and wistful dissembler whose sympathetic consideration for the misguided Olivia revealed a generous, gentle nature, Miss Rehan performed brilliantly.

The importance of Sir Toby and Sir Andrew was heightened in a perversion of the comedy written by Charles Webb and acted by William H. Crane and Stuart Robson at the Fifth Avenue in 1881. The less talented Robson proved better as Aguecheek than Crane as Belch, the latter investing his characterization with nothing more than drunken boisterousness. That same year, Helena Modjeska acted Viola for the first time in Washington and, in 1882, appeared in the part at Booth's, achieving only minimum effectiveness as the shipwrecked maiden.

An attempt to underplay the fanciful and romantic aspects of *Twelfth Night* and to equate life in Illyria with everyday existence elsewhere was produced by Viola Allen, who acted Viola, and presented on February 8, 1904 and again in 1905 at the Knickerbocker. Ben Greet, operating from the same theatre, staged the play a few weeks after Miss Allen's first appearance in the comedy. He used a single simplified set and achieved greater effect through the efforts of a more competent cast including his own commendable Malvolio. In 1905 Edward Hugh Sothern and Julia Marlowe undertook a production of *Twelfth Night*, giving what came to be recognized as their best Shakespearean portrayals. Miss Marlowe's richly gay Viola (first acted by her in 1887) "created the illusion of truth without sacrificing the enchantment of poetry" and Sothern's perfectly conceived and admirably executed interpretation of a pompous yet worthy Malvolio ideally embodied all the character's eccentricity without sacrificing his substance. They acted the comedy in repertory seasons to 1913 and, for Miss Marlowe's return to the stage in 1919, after an absence of five years, revived it at the Shubert in an impressionistic set using draperies and flat backgrounds against a green-gray cyclorama. Rowland Buckstone was Sir Toby; J. Sayre Crawley, Aguecheek; and Vernon Kelso, Feste. Miss Marlowe's unimpaired vocal powers impressed, but Sothern's high comedy, "just on the border of tears," enthralled.

With a few exceptions, most other performances of the play during that period were disappointing. Annie Russell's Viola and Louis Calvert's Toby in 1910 at the New count as failures, but Ferdinand Gottschalk's Aguecheek evinced all the vacuous conceit of the silly knight clearly shown to harbor sincere resentment over Olivia's preference for Cesario. In 1914 a *Twelfth Night* at the Hudson lacked distinction with a cast including Margaret Anglin (Viola), Fuller Mellish (Malvolio), and Sidney Greenstreet (Sir Toby), and that same year another production at the Liberty was notable chiefly as the American debut of Phyllis Neilson-Terry giving her enormously successful impersonation of Viola.

The worthy efforts of Fritz Leiber as Malvolio and Vera Allen as Viola for two performances during a repertory season in 1930 were eclipsed by a production on October 15 of that year at Maxine Elliott's presented by Kenneth MacGowan and Joseph Verner Reed which ran for 65 nights. Feste turned the pages of a huge book to reveal each new scene of a charmingly staged *Twelfth Night* starring Jane Cowl as Viola and Leon Quartermaine as Malvolio. In November 1932 the Shakespeare Theatre Company presented the play starring Ian Maclaren, an arrogant, effeminate blockhead, and Curtis Cooksey, a barely audible Belch, and in 1940 Helen Hayes assumed Viola at the St. James opposite Maurice Evans' Malvolio. The Chekhov Players presented a highly improvised, stylized production at the Little in 1941, featuring Beatrice Straight as Viola, Ford Rainey as Sir Toby, Hurd Hatfield as Sir Andrew, and Alan Harkness as Feste (see *Selected Criticism*, below). Less than three years later a well-acted production was presented at the Drama Workshop of the New School for Social Research. Eugene van Grona portrayed an effeminate and pathetically foolish Malvolio while the Falstaffian Sir Toby of Gerald de Lancey amused consistently. Darrin Dublin was downright funny as Aguecheek and Elaine Stritch, while not a fully realized Feste, sang delightfully. In the rather small role of Sebastian, Marlon Brando proved satisfactory.

In 1949 an engaging but only modestly diverting *Twelfth Night*, having been given at the Ann Arbor Dramatic Festival, opened at the Empire on October 3. Valentine Windt directed the handsome production, presenting a humorous and zesty Viola (Frances Reid); Philip Tonge and Carl Benton Reid as the drunken mischiefmakers Andrew and Toby; and the swaggering, comical, occasionally touching Malvolio of Arnold Moss. Nina Foch was Olivia. To celebrate the opening of a new permanent building at the Stratford Shakespeare Festival in Ontario, in June 1957, Tyrone Guthrie staged a production of *Twelfth Night* set in the Cavalier period. The wild roistering of Douglas Campbell's Sir Toby and Christopher Plummer's Aguecheek contrasted with the haunting melancholy of Bruno Gerussi's old man Feste. The highly talented cast also included Siobhan McKenna, an alert Viola, Douglas Rain as Malvolio, Frances Hyland as Olivia, and Lloyd Bochner as Orsino. The New York Shakespeare Festival offer a mediocre production in 1958 with only two sol performances—those of Arthur Quinton, a heart vulgar, cowardly Toby, and Meredith Dallas, va and vulnerable as a fastidious Malvolio. Sedge Mi ler's fluttering Sir Andrew was only intermittent effective, while Carol Gustafson seemed too brash Viola and Peggy Bennion somewhat brittle as Olivi But that same year an Old Vic company indulged inspired clowning at the Broadway with a delightf production featuring Barbara Jefford as Viola; Jo Neville, a cowardly Aguecheek; Joss Ackland, blustering Sir Toby; and Richard Wordsworth, pompous but rather likable Malvolio. A Regenc period *Twelfth Night* presented by the Americ Shakespeare Festival in 1960 was dismissed by Walt Kerr as "calculated nonsense."—M. G.

Bibliography. TEXT: *Twelfth Night*, New Car bridge Edition, A. Quiller-Couch and J. Dov Wilson, eds., 1926; W. W. Greg, *The Editori Problem in Shakespeare*, 1939. DATE: Leslie Hotso *The First Night of "Twelfth Night,"* 1954. SOURCE *The First Night of "Twelfth Night"*; Geoffr Bullough, *Narrative and Dramatic Sources Shakespeare*, Vol. II, 1958. COMMENT: H. N Hudson, *Shakespeare, His Life, Art, and Charact* 2 vols., 1872; C. L. Barber, *Shakespeare's Festi Comedy*, 1959. STAGE HISTORY: New Cambrid Edition; T. Alston Brown, *A History of the Ne York Stage . . . to 1901*, 1903; William Wint *Shakespeare on the Stage*, 3 vols., 1911–1916; G. C. Odell, *Shakespeare from Betterton to Irving*, 192 J. C. Trewin, *Shakespeare on the English Stag 1900–1964*, 1964.

Selected Criticism

A. W. SCHLEGEL. This comedy unites the ente tainment of an intrigue, contrived with gre ingenuity, to the richest fund of comic characte and situations, and the beauteous colours of ethereal poetry. In most of his plays Shakespea treats love more as an affair of the imagination th the heart; but here we are particularly remind by him that, in his language, the same wor *fancy*, signified both fancy and love. The love the music-enraptured Duke to Olivia is not mere a fancy, but an imagination; Viola appears at fi to fall arbitrarily in love with the Duke, whom s serves as a page, although she afterwards touch the tenderest chords of feeling: The proud Oliv is entangled by the modest and insinuating messeng of the Duke, in whom she is far from suspecting disguised rival, and at last, by a second deceptio takes the brother for the sister. To these, whi I might call ideal follies, a contrast is formed the undisguised absurdities to which the enterta ing tricks of the ludicrous persons of the pie give rise, in like manner under pretence of lo . . . . These [comic] scenes are as admirably co ceived and significant as they are laughab [*A Course of Lectures on Dramatic Literatu* 1809–1811; trans. John Black, 1846.]

WILLIAM HAZLITT. This is justly considered as o of the most delightful of Shakespear's comedi It is full of sweetness and pleasantry. It is perha too good-natured for comedy. It has little sati and no spleen. It aims at the ludicrous rather th the ridiculous. It makes us laugh at the follies nankind, not despise them, and still less bear any ll-will towards them. Shakespear's comic genius esembles the bee rather in its power of extracting weets from weeds or poisons than in leaving a ting behind it. He gives the most amusing exaggeraion of the prevailing foibles of his characters, but n a way that they themselves, instead of being ffended at, would almost join in to humour; he ather contrives opportunities for them to show hemselves off in the happiest lights, than renders hem contemptible in the perverse construction of he wit or malice of others . . . .

Shakespear's comedy is of a pastoral and poetical ast. Folly is indigenous to the soil, and shoots ut with native, happy, unchecked luxuriance. bsurdity has every encouragement afforded it; nd nonsense has room to flourish in. Nothing is unted by the churlish, icy hand of indifference r severity. The poet runs riot in a conceit, and dolizes a quibble. His whole object is to turn he meanest or rudest objects to a pleasurable acount. The relish which he has of a pun, or of he quaint humour of a low character, does not nterfere with the delight with which he describes beautiful image or the most refined love. *Characters of Shakespear's Plays,* 1817.]

CHARLES LAMB. Malvolio is not essentially ludicrous. Ie becomes comic but by accident. He is cold, ausre, repelling; but dignified, consistent, and, for hat appears, rather of an over-stretched morality. Iaria describes him as a sort of Puritan; and he night have worn his gold chain with honour in one f our old round-head families, in the service of a ambert, or a Lady Fairfax. But his morality and his nanners are misplaced in Illyria. He is opposed to ne proper *levities* of the piece, and falls in the unqual contest. Still his pride, or his gravity (call it hich you will) is inherent, and native to the man, ot mock or affected, which latter only are the fit bjects to excite laughter. His quality is at the best nlovely, but neither buffoon nor contemptible. His earing is lofty, a little above his station, but probaly not much above his deserts. We see no reason hy he should not have been brave, honourable, ccomplished. His careless committal of the ring to ne ground (which he was commissioned to restore Cesario), bespeaks a generosity of birth and feelg. His dialect on all occasions is that of a gentlean, and a man of education. We must not confound im with the eternal old, low steward of comedy. Iis is master of the household to a great Princess; a ignity probably conferred upon him for other reects than age or length of service. Olivia, at the rst indication of his supposed madness, declares that e 'would not have him miscarry for half of her owry.' Does this look as if the character was meant appear little or insignificant? Once, indeed, she ccuses him to his face—of what?—of being 'sick of lf-love,'—but with a gentleness and considerateness hich could not have been, if she had not thought at this particular infirmity shaded some virtues. His buke to the knight, and his sottish revellers, is sensie and spirited; and when we take into consideraon the unprotected condition of his mistress, and e strict regard with which her state of real or dismbled mourning would draw the eyes of the world oon her house-affairs, Malvolio might feel the honour of the family in some sort in his keeping; as it appears not that Olivia had any more brothers, or kinsmen, to look to it—for Sir Toby had dropped all such nice respects at the buttery hatch. That Malvolio was meant to be represented as possessing estimable qualities, the expression of the Duke in his anxiety to have him reconciled, almost infers. 'Pursue, and entreat him to a peace.' Even in his abused state of chains and darkness, a sort of greatness seems never to desert him. He argues highly and well with the supposed Sir Topas, and philosophises gallantly upon his straw. There must have been some shadow of worth about the man; he must have been something more than a mere vapour—a thing of straw, or Jack in office—before Fabian and Maria could have ventured sending him upon a courting-errand to Olivia. There was some consonancy (as he would say) in the undertaking, or the jest would have been too bold even for that house of misrule. ["On Some of the Old Actors," *The Essays of Elia,* 1822; reprinted in *Lamb's Criticism,* G. M. W. Tillyard, ed., 1923.]

WILLIAM ARCHER. I confess that Malvolio has always been to me one of the most puzzling of Shakespeare's creations. The theory, so popular with German, and with some English, commentators, which makes of him a satirical type of the Puritan as Shakespeare conceived him, will not hold ground for a moment. It is founded on one or two detached speeches wrested from their context. Maria says of him that 'he is sometimes a kind of a Puritan,' only to say in the next breath that 'the devil a Puritan' is he; and when Sir Andrew expresses a desire to beat him, Sir Toby derisively asks, 'What, for being a Puritan? Thy exquisite reason, dear knight.' Is it likely that Shakespeare was himself guilty of the stupidity which even Sir Toby ridicules in his gull? . . . There is nothing of the typical Puritan in Malvolio . . . If I may hazard a theory, I should say that he is not a Puritan, but a Philistine. The radical defect of his nature is a lack of that sense of humour which is the safety-valve of all our little insanities, preventing even the most expansive egoism from altogether over-inflating us. He takes himself and the world too seriously. He has no intuition for the incongruous and grotesque, to put the drag upon his egoistic fantasy, 'sick of self-love.' His face, not only smileless itself, but contemptuous of mirth in others, has acted as a damper upon the humour of the sprightly Maria and the jovial Sir Toby; he has taken a set pleasure in putting the poor Clown out of countenance by receiving his quips with a stolid gravity. Hence the rancour of the humorists against a fundamentally antagonistic nature; hence, perhaps, their whim of making him crown his absurdities by a forced smile, a grimace more incongruous with his pompous personality than even cross-garters or yellow stockings. He is a being, in short, to whom the world, with all its shows and forms, is intensely real and profoundly respectable. He has no sense of its littleness, its evanescence, without which he can have no true sense of its greatness and its mystery. [*Macmillan's Magazine,* August, 1884.]

STARK YOUNG. I have never, in a long list of *Twelfth Night* productions, seen certain motifs and themes of the play turn out so clear; I have never heard reading that made them so reckless and irresponsible, as they should be, but yet so exact to the play's intention. The melancholy of Olivia and of Orsino, for example, is usually taken in the declamatory vein, heavy, amatory and unconvincing. But as Mr. Chekhov directs it, the theme is a competition in romantic egotism, in which Viola and her love are delicately included, though Orsino will not have it that she nor any woman can ever love as he does, not any age or inclination equal his despair. Their several loves thus achieve a due placement, sociable, sensible and romantic, so that our hearts shall be wrung by them, musical, elegiac, delirious, as by the lute's playing of some sad, sweet song or by some momentary fading sweetness on the air. In this production we have the delightful experience of finding that what in most productions of the play have been mere dull flats of emotion can take on variety, vigor and something of the rose of spring and all its fatal lovely music.

The reading of the jester's lines turns out mere gibberish in most Shakespeare productions, so much so as to make you wonder why intelligent princes ever had these perky, punning bores around them, as historically we know they did. Here in Feste we hear distinctly the burlesque of philosophic system and thought that Shakespeare intended; grave echoes appear, laments, quips and poignant topsy-turvy. In this case it is entirely right that the clown should be the one who sings, that a story which begins with music should sing itself out with a song. [From a review in *New Republic* of a production by the Chekhov Theatre Players at the Little Theatre, New York, Dec. 1, 1941; reprinted in Young's *Immortal Shadows*, 1948.]

JOSEPH H. SUMMERS. . . . the play does not resolve into a magic blessing of the world's fertility as does *A Midsummer Night's Dream.* We have been promised a happy ending, and we receive it. We are grateful that the proper Jacks and Jills have found each other, but the miracle is a limited miracle, available only to the young and the lucky. Not every Jack has his Jill even in Illyria, and after the general unmasking, those without love may seem even lonelier. Malvolio, of course, is justly punished. He has earned his mad scene, and with the aid of Feste he has made it comic. As a result of his humiliation he has also earned some sort of redress. Yet he is ridiculous in his arrogance to the end, and his threatened revenge, now that he is powerless to effect it, sustains the comedy and the characterization and prevents the obtrusion of destructive pathos.

It is Feste rather than Malvolio who finally reminds us of the limitations and the costs of the romantic vision of happiness with which we have been seduced. However burdensome, masking is his career, and romantic love provides no end for it. Alone on the stage at the end of the play, he sings a song of unfulfilled love which shows the other side of the coin. For Feste, as for his audience, the mask can never be finally discarded: the rain it raineth every day . . . .

Twelfth Night is the climax of Shakespeare's early achievement in comedy. The effects and values of the earlier comedies are here subtly embodied in the most complex structure which Shakespeare had yet created. But the play also look forward: the pressure to dissolve the comedy, t realize and finally abandon the burden of laughter is an intrinsic part of its "perfection." Viola clear-eyed and affirmative vision of her own an the world's irrationality is a triumph and we desir it; yet we realize its vulnerability, and we come t realize that virtue in disguise is only totally trium phant when evil is not in disguise—is not trul present at all. Having solved magnificently th problems of this particular form of comedy Shakespeare was evidently not tempted to repea his triumph. After *Twelfth Night* the so-calle comedies require for their happy resolutions mor radical characters and devices—omniscient and omn present Dukes, magic, and resurrection. Mor obvious miracles are needed for comedy to exi in a world in which evil also exists, not merel incipiently but with power. ["The Masks of Twelft Night," *The University of Kansas City Review* Vol. 22, Autumn, 1955.]

C. L. BARBER. Malvolio has been called a satiric portrait of the Puritan spirit, and there is som truth in the notion. But he is not hostile to holida because he is a Puritan; he is like a Puritan be cause he is hostile to holiday. Shakespeare eve mocks, in passing, the thoughtless, fashionable anti athy to Puritans current among gallants. S Andrew responds to Maria's "sometimes he is kind of Puritan," with "if I thought that, I'd be him like a dog" (II. iii. 151-153). "The devil Puritan he is, or anything constantly," Mar observes candidly, "but a time-pleaser" (II. iii. 15 160). Shakespeare's two greatest comic butts, Ma volio and Shylock, express basic human attitud which were at work in the commercial revolutio the new values whose development R. H. Tawne described in *Religion and the Rise of Capitalism* But both figures are conceived at a level esthetic abstraction which makes it inappropria to identify them with specific groups in the mingle actualities of history: Shylock, embodying ruthle money power, is no more to be equated with actu bankers than Malvolio, who has something of t Puritan ethic, is to be thought of as a portrait actual Puritans. Yet, seen in the perspective literary and social history, there is a curious a propriateness in Malvolio's presence, as a kind foreign body to be expelled by laughter, in Shak speare's last free-and-easy festive comedy. He a man of business, and, it is passingly suggested, hard one; he is or would like to be a rising ma and to rise he *uses* sobriety and morality. O could moralize the spectacle by observing that, the long run, in the 1640's, Malvolio *was* reveng on the whole pack of them.

But Shakespeare's comedy remains, long af 1640, to move audiences through release to clarifi tion, making distinctions between false care a true freedom and realizing anew, for successi generations, powers in human nature and socie which make good the risks of courtesy and liber And this without blinking the fact that "the r it raineth every day." ["Testing Courtesy a Humanity in *Twelfth Night*," *Shakespeare's Festi Comedy*, 1959.]

JOHN HOLLANDER. The Action of *Twelfth Nigh*

ndeed that of a Revels, a suspension of mundane ffairs during a brief epoch in a temporary world f indulgence, a land full of food, drink, love, lay, disguise and music. But parties end, and the eveller eventually becomes satiated and drops eavily into his worldly self again. The fact that lays were categorized as "revells" for institutional urposes may have appealed to Shakespeare; he eems at any rate to have analyzed the dramatic nd moral nature of feasting, and to have made it ne subject of his play. His analysis is schematized n Orsino's opening speech.

The essential action of a revels is: To so surfeit ne Appetite upon excess that it "may sicken and o die". It is the Appetite, not the whole Self, owever, which is surfeited: the Self will emerge t the conclusion of the action from where it has been hidden. The movement of the play is toward this emergence of humanity from behind a mask of comic type. ["Twelfth Night and the Morality of Indulgence," *Sewanee Review,* Vol. 67, 1959.]

Twine, Laurence (c. 1540–?). Translator whose *The Patterne of Painefull Adventures* provided one of the sources of *Pericles.* Twine graduated from Oxford in 1564, after which he entered the ministry. *The Patterne of Painefull Adventures* was entered in the Stationers' Register in 1576 and probably printed then although no copy of that date has survived. The only extant copies are those of an undated edition published about 1594 and another edition printed in 1607. The 1607 edition may have been the immediate occasion for the play. See PERICLES: *Sources.*

THE Two Gentlemen of Verona.

Two Gentlemen of Verona, The. A comedy by hakespeare.

Text. The sole authority for the text is that f the First Folio (1623). This has been greatly bridged, probably in order to meet the requirements of a performance on some special occasion see ABRIDGED TEXTS). The only directions are the exits" at the end of each scene; there are no roper "entrances." Instead, at the head of each ene is a list of the characters who are to appear it. J. Dover Wilson advances the theory that the PY for the play was made by stringing together e players' parts, including their cues, which had een transcribed from the PROMPT-BOOK and had en been handed to each actor to memorize (see SEMBLED TEXTS). This conjecture also would count for the relative brevity of the text, which ns to 2380 lines, considerably less than the normal 00-line text of an Elizabethan play. A more ausible explanation, however, is that the copy ven to the printers was a transcript of the comny's prompt-book made by Ralph Crane, a prosional scribe.

There are indications that this text, to use the rases of Dover Wilson, "has been hacked about d drastically abridged, in order to meet the reirements of a particular performance or comny." There are also signs that it has been mpered with, such as the intrusion of an unmetrical e that is so devoid of meaning that it defies endation.

Date. The date of the play has not been determined with any certainty; highly conjectural estimates range from 1590 to 1595. The earlier date is currently favored, largely as a result of the marked immaturities and crudities in the play's structure.

Sources. The main features of the plot of *The Two Gentlemen of Verona* are based on the episode of Felix and Felismena in a chivalric and pastoral romance entitled *Diana Enamorada* (1542). It was written in Spanish by the Portuguese author Jorge de MONTEMAYOR. Shakespeare probably could not read the work in Spanish, but there was a French translation by Nicolas Collin (1578, 1587). The English translation by Bartholomew Yonge, though not published until 1598, had been completed in 1582. Shakespeare may possibly have read Yonge's version in a circulated manuscript. It is more probable that he became acquainted with the story in an anonymous lost play entitled *The History of Felix and Philiomena,* acted at court "by her majesty's servants on the Sunday next after New Years day" (1585). This was probably a pastoral play based on Montemayor. Some resemblances to the plot of *The Two Gentlemen* appear in Henry Wotton's English translation of Jacques d'Yver's "Le Printemps d'Yver" (1572), to which Wotton gave the title "A Courtlie controversie of Cupid's Cautels [tricks] . . . translated out of French, as neare as our English phrase will permit, by H. W., Gentleman" (1578). Parallels to the story also occur in one of the scenarios of Flaminio Scala's collection of 50 scenarios published as *Il Teatro delle Favole rappresentative . . . composa da Flaminio Scala Comico del Sereniis Sig. Duca di Mantova, Venetii, 1611.* These are texts of *commedia dell'arte,* acted for many years before their publication.

A parallel for the last scene of the play, in which Valentine with apparent nonchalance hands Silvia over to his friend Proteus, is found in "The wonderful history of Titus and Gisippus, and whereby is fully declared the figure of perfet amitie," which appears in Book II, Chapter XII, of Sir Thomas Elyot's *The Governour* (1531). The two youths are bound together, not only by the sacred bonds of "dear religious love," but also by their exact resemblance to each other. They are almost literally one soul in bodies twain. When Titus confesses to Gisippus "all blusshinge and ashamed" that he is desperately in love with the young gentlewoman to whom Gisippus is affianced, and had in due time become "amorouse," Gisippus, kissing and embracing Titus, renounces all his "titles and interest" that he now has or might have in this "faire mayden," and arranges to have Titus consummate the marriage made to Gisippus by putting his own ring on the maiden's finger and undoing "her gyrdell of virginitie." The maiden's feelings concern the friends as little as those of Silvia affect Valentine and Proteus. The universal obloquy and derision that his action is certain to receive, and even the hatred of his kindred, will be as nothing compared to the felicities he is thus able to give his friend. The incident in the tale is like that of the play in being an *exemplum* of sacrifices a true friend will make for what Shakespeare calls his "lover."—O. J. C.

Plot Synopsis. Act I. As he prepares to set out from Verona to seek advancement in Milan, Valentine takes leave of his friend Proteus and chides him for letting his love for Julia keep him "living dully sluggardized at home." Although Proteus has a champion in Julia's maid Lucetta, Julia declares herself indifferent to him and, without reading it, tears up a letter he has sent her. But her interest in the contents of the bits of torn paper indicates that she is smitten with him after all. Their romance is interrupted, however, by the decision of Proteus' father, Antonio, to send him to Milan.

Act II. To the disgust of his quick-witted page, Speed, Valentine has fallen in love with Silvia, daughter of the Duke of Milan. When Silvia, who had asked Valentine to compose some verses for one she loves, tells him that the lines are for him, Speed is surprised at the obtuseness of his master, who does not realize that he is the favored one.

After Proteus bids Julia a tender farewell in Verona, the lovers exchange rings as a token of their fidelity. Launce, Proteus' servant, is also unhappy about leaving Verona, though his "cruel-hearted" dog, Crab, has not shed a single tear over their impending departure.

When Proteus arrives at the court of the Duke of Milan, Valentine and Silvia receive him warmly. Valentine informs Proteus that he and Silvia are in love but that her father prefers a wealthier suitor, Thurio. It is Valentine's intention to run away with Silvia, gaining access to her chamber at night by means of a corded ladder. The fickl Proteus, however, has become infatuated with Silvi himself. Though he is sensible of his obligations t Julia and to Valentine, he decides to tell the Duk of the lovers' projected flight. Meanwhile, Julia ignorant of the faithlessness of Proteus and longin to see him, decides to disguise herself as a bo and go to Milan.

Act III. Explaining that he is motivated by lov for the Duke, not hatred for Valentine, Proteu betrays the planned elopement to Silvia's fathe The Duke thereupon catches Valentine with ladder and a compromising letter to Silvia an banishes him without exposing the treachery o Proteus. When Thurio complains that Valentine' exile has not increased Silvia's affection for him the wily Proteus, still determined to win her fo himself, offers to extol Thurio's virtues to her whil blackening Valentine's character.

Act IV. Valentine and Speed, wandering in forest near Mantua, are accosted by a band o outlaws who had turned to banditry after bein banished from their homes for various minor crime Impressed by Valentine's appearance and accom plishments, they propose to make him their leade Valentine accepts the offer on condition that the refrain from molesting women or the poor.

Proteus, who has been unable to sway Silvi from her devotion to Valentine, continues to le Thurio believe that he is genuinely interested i furthering his suit. At a suggestion of Proteu Thurio engages musicians to praise Silvia's charm in song before her chamber window. After Thurio' departure, Proteus hastens to express his own lov for Silvia, who responds to his blandishments wit scorn. Neither of them realizes that Julia, sti dressed as a boy, is a horrified witness of th scene. Learning that her father is going to forc her to marry Thurio, Silvia resolves to flee Valentine's side and asks Sir Eglamour, a knigh who had vowed chastity upon his lady's grav to accompany her.

Launce, meanwhile, has been having difficulti with Crab, who, despite his master's training, do not know how to behave himself in society. Launc himself becomes the subject of Proteus' ire whe he reports that Silvia had refused the dog th he had taken her at his master's bidding an adds that he had been compelled to offer Cra since the little dog that Proteus had given him ha been stolen. Dismissing Launce, Proteus orders h new page, Sebastian, who is actually Julia in di guise, to take Silvia a letter and a ring in exchang for a picture of herself. Julia sorrowfully observ that it is the very ring that she had given Prote upon his departure from Verona. Silvia refuses accept the gift and expresses her sympathy for th girl whom Proteus has forsaken.

Act V. Silvia carries out her plan of fleeing Mantua and is pursued by Proteus and Thuri She is captured by the outlaws but is quick rescued by Proteus, who is about to exact h reward by force when he is stopped by Valentin Shamed by his friend's reproaches, Proteus as Valentine's forgiveness and the latter, declarin himself satisfied, offers to surrender Silvia to hi At this Julia, who has accompanied Proteus in h male attire, swoons and accidently reveals the rin hat Proteus had given her in Verona. She now iscloses her identity, rebuking Proteus for his ickleness. He acknowledges his inconstancy, which .e describes as the one error that mars man's erfection, and admits that Julia is as attractive as ilvia. The outlaws now bring in two other risoners, the Duke and Thurio, who lays claim o Silvia. But when Valentine threatens him with odily harm, the craven Thurio hastily renounces er, whereupon the Duke, decrying Thurio's faint-eartedness, offers her to Valentine. After Valentine as also prevailed upon the Duke to pardon his fel-ow outlaws, they all return to Milan for the mar-iage of the two couples, who shall share "one feast, ne house, one mutual happiness."—H. D.

Comment. In structure the play closely resembles hat of many 16th-century Italian comedies, both opular (COMMEDIA DELL' ARTE) and literary (*com-edia erudita*). Like them, it is the story of the vooing of the first *amorosa*, Silvia, by three suitors: 'alentine, the preferred lover; Proteus, his rival; and 'hurio, a poltroon. Julia, the second *amorosa*, like nany of her sisters in Italian comedy, takes on the isguise of a page; she enters into the service of 'roteus, her faithless lover, and carries his love mes-ages to her rival. Two other figures conventional n Italianate drama are the contrasted servants: peed, the quick-witted jester and word quibbler, nd Launce, the dull-witted bumpkin.

When the poet wrote this comedy, he was under he influence of John LYLY, not only in the choice f his theme but also in his manner of treating . Shakespeare's imitation, however, betrays a 'prentice hand" in the nonchalant way in which e has Proteus give Silvia over to his rival

> And, that my love may appear plain and free
> [gentle and generous],
> All that was mine in Silvia I give thee.
> (V, iv, 82–83)

'he balanced structure of the comedy is another ndication of Lyly's influence: two lovers, two adies, two servants. The poet also imitates Lyly's onstant use of antitheses, puns, quips, and other orms of wordplay, although in Shakespeare the onceit sometimes generates a music to which yly's ear was deaf, as in Valentine's lament:

> Except I be by Silvia in the night,
> There is no music in the nightingale;
> Unless I look on Silvia in the day,
> There is no day for me to look upon.
> (III, i, 178–181)

n even purer lyric is the serenade the hired usicians sing under Silvia's window, "Who is ilvia? What is she?" (see MUSIC IN THE PLAYS). 'he large amount of prose in the play is still urther evidence of Shakespeare's faithful disciple-hip to Lyly. But in the matter of language the oet excelled his master. For example, he casts aunce's triumphantly comic monologue with Crab, is dog, in the authentic speech of the lower lasses.

In other respects the comedy reflects Elizabethan igh life and the spirit of courtly romance. Valen-ine and Proteus, as the title makes clear, are lizabethan aristocrats. Valentine, like other Eliza-ethan gentlemen, scornful of unadventurous young men, embarks on a voyage to see the wonders of the world and to seek honor, which he holds vastly superior to love. Yet on his travels he falls in love and becomes a chivalric "servant" to a lady and mistress. Proteus is a traitor to the Renaissance ideal of a gentleman, false both to love and to friendship. The high-born girls also are sharply differentiated. Silvia is a mere sketch, a conventional *amorosa*, who remains true to the ideals of courtly etiquette. Julia is a more original creation, a passion-ate, reckless girl with none of Silvia's poise. Eglamour is a copy of a figure familiar to medieval romance. On the grave of his dead mistress he vows to devote his life to the service of ladies in need. His offer to act as Silvia's guide and protector on her perilous journey to join the banished Valentine is quite in character.—O. J. C.

Stage History. This comedy through the years has seldom attracted either producers or actors. The first recorded performance was one directed by David Garrick at Drury Lane on December 22, 1762. But this was an "improvement" made by Benjamin VICTOR, who changed the arrangement of the scenes and wrote some new material for the last act, so that he could devise one more confrontation of Launce and Speed and thus en-hance the final scene of the play. Shakespeare's own play, with only a few alterations, was first staged at Covent Garden on April 17, 1784. John Philip Kemble mounted the real Shakespeare at Drury Lane in 1790, but he used Victor's version when he produced *The Two Gentlemen of Verona* at Covent Garden on April 21, 1808, and this production failed. Frederick REYNOLDS' musical treatment of the comedy was presented at Covent Garden on November 29, 1821, and played 29 performances during the first season. The music was composed by Henry Rowley Bishop, and Maria Tree sang the role of Julia. William Charles Mac-ready staged Shakespeare's play at Drury Lane on December 29, 1841, and *The Two Gentlemen* failed again. Both Charles Kean and Samuel Phelps tried with productions in the 1850's and met with similarly apathetic audiences, who perhaps con-sidered the comedy a poor predecessor of *Twelfth Night*. In 1895 Augustin Daly at Daly's Theatre in London did not fare any better, even though his cast included Ada Rehan playing Julia.

The first staging of the unpopular comedy in the 20th century was remarkable in that Harley Granville-Barker produced it and even took the part of the servant Speed. This was in 1904 at the Court Theatre, and Barker had agreed to stage *The Two Gentlemen* on the condition that he could present Shaw's *Candida* at six matinees. Lewis Casson played the First Outlaw and Sir Eglamour in this almost forgotten production. In 1910 Beer-bohm Tree invited William Poel's Elizabethan Stage Society to His Majesty's Theatre, where, on April 20th, they acted the comedy on a specially built apron stage. Stratford had allowed 20 years to elapse after Osmond Tearle's well-forgotten 1890 production before staging the play again, this time with Frank Benson's company. *The Two Gentlemen* was in the Old Vic's repertory, and the company under Ben Greet performed the play at Stratford-upon-Avon in the summer of 1916.

There were two productions in 1925: W. Bridges-

Adams' at Stratford and Robert Atkins' at the Apollo with The Fellowship of Players (John Gielgud as Valentine, Ion Swinley as Proteus).

Then 13 years passed before B. Iden Payne produced it at Stratford in 1938 with Gyles Isham playing Valentine, and another 11 years until Robert Atkins fitted *The Two Gentlemen* into a single performance with *The Comedy of Errors* at the Open Air in 1949.

Somewhat surprisingly, it was a production of *The Two Gentlemen* by the Bristol Old Vic which enhanced the London Vic's rather dismal 1951/2 season. Under Denis Carey's direction, with John Neville's Valentine, the presentation managed to bring the springlike, youthful qualities of the play to life within a Renaissance masque framework. Another memorable production was staged at the Old Vic during its 1956/7 season—this time produced by Michael Langham in a lush, romantic Regency setting, with Keith Michell as Proteus and Barbara Jefford as Julia.

The play's notorious record of regrettable productions was supplemented when, in 1960, Peter Hall staged it at Stratford. Brittle speech by the leading players did not help. Two performances were notable, however: Eric Porter as the Duke of Milan and Derek Godfrey as Proteus.—M. G.

Bibliography. TEXT: *The Two Gentlemen of Verona*, New Cambridge Edition, A. Quiller-Couch and J. Dover Wilson, eds., 1921. DATE: New Cambridge Edition. SOURCES: Oscar James Campbell, "Two Gentlemen of Verona and Italian Comedy," *Studies in Shakespeare, Milton and Donne*, 1925; T. W. Baldwin, *Shakespere's Five-Act Structure*, 1947; Ralph M. Sargent, "Sir Thomas Elyot and the Integrity of *The Two Gentlemen of Verona*," *PMLA*, LXV 1950; Geoffrey Bullough, *Narrative and Dramatic Sources of Shakespeare*, Vol. I, 1957. COMMENT: H. B. Charlton, *Shakespearian Comedy*, 1938; John F. Danby, "Shakespearean Criticism and *Two Gentlemen of Verona*," *Critical Quarterly*, II, 1960. STAGE HISTORY: New Cambridge Edition; G. C. D. Odell, *Shakespeare from Betterton to Irving*, 1920; J. C. Trewin, *Shakespeare on the English Stage, 1900-1964*, 1964.

Selected Criticism

SAMUEL JOHNSON.

> It is observable (I know now for what cause) that the stile of this comedy is less figurative, and more natural and unaffected than the greater part of this author's, tho' supposed to be one of the first he wrote.—POPE.

To this observation of Mr. *Pope*, which is very just, Mr. *Theobald* has added, that this is one of *Shakespear's worst plays, and is less corrupted than any other*. Mr. *Upton* peremptorily determines, *that if any proof can be drawn from manner and style, this play must be sent packing and seek for its parent elsewhere. How otherwise*, says he, *do painters distinguish copies from originals, and have not authours their peculiar style and manner from which a true critick can form as unerring a judgment as a Painter?* I am afraid this illustration of a critick's science will not prove what is desired. A Painter knows a copy from an original by rules somewhat resembling these by which criticks know a translation, which if it be literal, and literal it must be to resemble the copy of picture, will be easily distinguished. Copies a known from originals even when the painter copi his own picture; so if an authour should literal translate his work he would lose the manner an original . . . .

But by the internal marks of a composition v may discover the authour with probability, thou seldom with certainty. When I read this play cannot but think that I discover both in the serio and ludicrous scenes, the language and sentimen of *Shakespear*. It is not indeed one of his mo powerful effusions, it has neither many diversiti of character, nor striking delineations of life, b it abounds in γνωμαι beyond most of his plays, a few have more lines or passages which, singly co sidered, are eminently beautiful. I am yet inclin to believe that it was not very successful, and su pect that it has escaped corruption, only becau being seldom played it was less exposed to t hazards of transcription. [*The Plays of Willia Shakespeare*, 1765.]

WILLIAM HAZLITT. This is little more than the fi outlines of a comedy loosely sketched in. It is t story of a novel dramatised with very little labo or pretension; yet there are passages of hi poetical spirit, and of inimitable quaintness humour, which are undoubtedly Shakespear's, a there is throughout the conduct of the fable careless grace and felicity which marks it for his . . The style of the familiar parts of this come is indeed made up of conceits—low they may be f what we know, but then they are not poor, b rich ones. The scene of Launce with his dog (n that in the second, but that in the fourth act) a perfect treat in the way of farcical drollery a invention; nor do we think Speed's manner proving his master to be in love deficient in v or sense, though the style may be criticised as n simple enough for the modern taste. [*Characters Shakespear's Plays*, 1817.]

G. G. GERVINUS. The piece treats of the essen and the power of love, and especially of its influen upon judgment and habit generally, and it is n well to impute to it a more defined idea. T twofold nature of love is here at the outset e hibited with that equal emphasis and that perfe impartiality which struck Goethe so powerfully Shakespeare's writings. The poet facilitated t solving of this double problem by an aesthe artifice peculiar to himself, which we find especia evident in this youthful work, and which we repeated in almost all his dramas. The structu and design of the play are carried out in a str parallelism; the characters and events are so exac placed in relation and contrast to each other t not only those of a similar nature, but even th of a contrary one, serve mutually to explain ea other . . . .

Not alone are the servants Speed and Launce plac in characteristic opposition to their masters, witty Speed to the simple Valentine, the awkw Launce to the clever Proteus; not alone are th stationed by the side of their masters as disinterest observers, to whose extreme simplicity that apparent which in the infatuation of passion esca the understanding of the wise; so that Speed p ceives the love of Silvia before his master, a ven the simple Launce sees through the knavish ricks of his lord; but they are also by actions of heir own placed as a parody by the side of the ıain action, in a manner which invests even the ommonest incidents with a high moral value. .aunce's account of his farewell may be regarded s a parody of Julia's silent parting from Proteus; ıe scene in which Speed "thrusts himself" into .aunce's love affairs and "will be swinged for it," aricatures the false intrusion of Proteus into 'alentine's love; but a deeper sense still lies in ıe stories of the rough Launce and his dog Crab, ıe very senses which undoubtedly occur to the entle reader as the most offensive. To the silly emi-brute fellow, who sympathizes with his beast lmost more than with men, his dog is his best riend. He has suffered stripes for him, he has taken is faults upon himself, and has been willing to acrifice everything to him. At last, self-sacrificing ke Valentine and Julia, he is willing to resign even ıis friend; he is ready to abandon his best possession) do a service to his master. With this capacity or sacrifice, this simple child of nature is placed y the side of Proteus—that splendid model of ıanly endowments, who, self-seeking, betrayed riend and lover. [*Shakespeare*, 1849–1850; tr. 1863 ; *Shakespeare Commentaries*.]

GEORGE P. BAKER. Could there be a more complete onfession of dramatic ineptitude than that last cene? It fails to do everything for which we have een looking. Valentine, after communing with imself in a way that foreshadows the banished uke in *As You Like It*, withdraws as he sees rangers coming through the forest. Proteus, who accompanied by the faithful Julia, still disguised a page, has found Silvia and is trying to force is love upon her. Valentine, overhearing, bursts orth and denounces his friend. If Shakespeare did ot wish to "hold" the scene of the avowal of his ve by Proteus through letting Julia take some art in it, or by prolonging the play of emotion etween Proteus and Silvia, he had, on the re- pearance of Valentine, an opportunity for a rong scene in which the play and interplay of the elings of the four characters might lead at last a happy solution. Yet this is his weak handling f the situation:—

Valentine. Now I dare not say
I have one friend alive; thou would'st disprove me.
Who should be trusted now, when one's right hand
Is perjured to the bosom? Proteus,
I am sorry I must never trust thee more,
But count the world a stranger for thy sake.
The private wound is deepest; O time most accursed,
'Mongst all foes that friends should be the worst!
Proteus. My shame and guilt confounds me.
Forgive me, Valentine: if hearty sorrow
Be a sufficient ransom for an offence.
I tender 't here: I do as truly suffer
As e'er I did commit.
Valentine. Then I am paid;
And once again I do receive thee honest.
Who by repentance is not satisfied,
Is nor of heaven nor earth, for these are pleased.
By penitence the Eternal wrath's appeased:
And, that my love may appear plain and free,
All that was mine in Silvia, I give thee.

It is hard enough to believe that Valentine would forgive so promptly, but that he would go as far as to offer to yield up Silvia is preposterous. That touch came simply to motivate the sudden swooning of Julia at the news. Only a little less absurd is the sudden swerve into rightmindedness of Proteus when Julia has revealed herself. After all these startling surprises, however, perhaps one is ready to agree to Julia's glad acceptance of the changeable affections of so worthless a person as Proteus. Is it not clear that in this scene the momentary effect, the start of surprise, mean far more to the dramatist than truth to life and probability? Having lured his audience on by writing scenes which constantly promised complicated action ahead, when the closing in of the afternoon at last drives him to bay, he gets out of his difficulties in the swiftest possible fashion, but with complete sacrifice of good dramatic art, the rich possibilities of his material, and truth to life. [*The Development of Shakespeare as a Dramatist*, 1907.]

H. B. CHARLTON. Romance, and not comedy, has called the tune of *The Two Gentlemen of Verona*, and governed the direction of the action of the play. That is why its creatures bear so little resemblance to men of flesh and blood. Lacking this, they are scarcely dramatic figures at all; for every form of drama would appear to seek at least so much of human nature in its characters. But perhaps the characters of the Two Gentlemen are comic in a sense which at first had never entered the mind of their maker. Valentine bids for the sympathy, but not for the laughter of the audience: the ideals by which he lives are assumed to have the world's approbation. But in execution they involve him in most ridiculous plight. He turns the world from its compassionate approval to a mood of sceptical questioning. The hero of romantic comedy appears no better than its clowns. And so topsy-turvy is the world of romance that apparently the one obvious way to be reputed in it for a fool, is to show at least a faint sign of discretion and of common sense. Thurio, for instance, was cast for the dotard of the play, and of course he is not without egregious folly. But what was meant in the end to annihilate him with contempt, turns out quite otherwise. Threatened by Valentine's sword, he resigns all claim to Silvia, on the ground that he holds him but a fool that will endanger his body for a girl that loves him not. The audience is invited to call Thurio a fool for thus showing himself to be the one person in the play with a modicum of worldly wisdom, a respect for the limitations of human nature, and a recognition of the conditions under which it may survive. Clearly, Shakespeare's first attempt to make romantic comedy had only succeeded so far that it had unexpectedly and inadvertently made romance comic. The real problem was still to be faced. [*Shakesperian Comedy*, 1938.]

DEREK TRAVERSI. *The Two Gentlemen of Verona* ... needs to be seen, if it is to come to life at all, as an early experiment in the use of convention for positive ends. As such it points to later and more successful developments. Many devices used in later comedies—the disguising of her sex as woman's resourceful response to betrayal, the relation between the intriguing villain and the friend who unwisely trusts him, even (for the brief moment of the bandit episode at the end of the play) the contrast between court artifice and the simple life of the forest—appear here for the first time. We must see in them, beyond such obvious absurdities as Valentine's offhand renunciation, in the last scene, of his love for the benefit of none other than his betrayer, a first essay in the more meaningful patternings of the later comedies. In these, conventions not altogether dissimilar, though immensely deepened and developed, become instruments for the exploration of human relationships, more especially in love, and fo the expression of a true attitude to love itself: a attitude in which poetry and realism, romance an comedy are variously combined. Although it woul be dangerous to read too much into this early piece it is worth noting that it ends, like its greater suc cessors, with a reconciliation of conflicting opposites the uniting of its lovers and the return of its outlaw to civilized and social living: a reconciliation th unreality of which stresses indeed the inadequat use to which its conventions are put, but which ha possibilities of development once the dramati poetic, and human contents of the action have bee simultaneously expanded. [*Shakespeare: The Earl Comedies*, rev. ed., 1964, No. 129 in "Writers an Their Work" series.]

The Two Noble Kinſmen.

Two Noble Kinsmen, The. A romance by Shakespeare and John Fletcher.

Text. The earliest and best text of the play is that of a Quarto published in 1634 with the title: "The Two Noble Kinsmen: Presented at the Blackfriers by the Kings Maiesties Servants, with great applause: Written by the memorable Worthies of their time; Mr John Fletcher, and Mr William Shakespeare, Gent." The copy for this Quarto may have been the authors' FOUL PAPERS, which had been subsequently marked by the company's BOOK-KEEPER in order to prepare a PROMPT-BOOK of the play. If foul papers served as copy, it would explain the numerous errors and unpolished quality of the play, particularly of those scenes assigned to Shakespeare. This text was reprinted in the second folio edition of Fletcher's works (1679), but not in the Shakespeare First Folio, or in any subsequent edition of the plays during the 17th century—not even in that of 1664 that added seven plays to the canon. Fletcher's contribution can be recognized by the effeminate character of its verse with its many weak, unstressed line endings and its two plots side by side throughout the play, with no intrinsic connection between them.

The parts of the play that are obviously not from Fletcher's pen many scholars have ascribed to Shakespeare, believing that the resemblances in both metric and theatric features between *The Two Noble Kinsmen* and the poet's last plays are close, and that the parts of *The Two Noble Kinsmen* that scholars usually assigned to the two authors agree with those assigned to Fletcher and Shakespeare in *Henry VIII*.

Among the English Romantic devotees of Shakespeare, Lamb and Coleridge were emphatically of the opinion that the poet collaborated with Fletcher i composing the drama. A minority, to which Shelle was a notable adherent, were sure that Shakespea had not written a single line of *The Two Nob Kinsmen*. Many of those who reject Shakespear authorship of the play have argued that Philip Ma singer was Fletcher's collaborator. Various theori as to the nature of the collaboration have been a vanced: (1) that Shakespeare helped his "apprenti Fletcher" to plan the play and wrote certain scen notably the first scene of the first act and the in portant first scene of the fifth act, to give him t right sort of start; (2) that Fletcher planned the pl and wrote some of the text, but left it unfinished a that Shakespeare later completed it. All scholars a agreed that Fletcher invented the subplot of t jailer's enamored, mad daughter and wrote all of h part. There is substantial agreement that Shak speare's share of the play consists of the followin Act I, scenes 1–3; Act III, scene 1; and all of Act except scene 2.

Date. Although no evidence exists to fix the da of composition and first performance of the pl scholars are agreed that 1613 is the most likely da On February 20, 1613 Francis Beaumont's *Masq of the Inner Temple and Grayes Inn* was first p sented at court. The morris dance in *Two No Kinsmen* (III, v) reproduces that in Beaumo *Masque* and was probably inserted shortly after t court performance.

Sources. The events of the main plot follow clos those of Chaucer's *Knight's Tale*. Lost plays on t subject were staged in 1566 and 1594 respective and Shakespeare had used the wedding of These and Hippolyta as the setting for the May Day rites of *A Midsummer Night's Dream.* The borrowings from various plays of Shakespeare and the imitations of his scenes and situations are unmistakable. They will be examined below under *Comment.*—O. J. C.

Plot Synopsis. Act I. The marriage celebration of Theseus, Duke of Athens, and Hippolyta is interrupted by the appearance of three queens who have come to entreat the Duke to avenge them for their husbands slain by Creon, King of Thebes. Hippolyta and her sister, Emilia, are moved to learn that the dead men have not been allowed burial; they plead the queens' cause to Theseus, who finally agrees to act and dispatches his captain, Artesius, to prepare for war.

In the palace of Thebes, Arcite and Palamon, two noble kinsmen and nephews of Creon, discuss the corruption in Thebes under their uncle's tyrannical rule. They would like to leave the country, but Valerius, a nobleman, tells them of the impending war with Athens and they realize they have no choice but to stay and fight for Creon.

At the gates of Athens, Hippolyta and Emilia bid farewell to Theseus' general, Pirithous. He extols the great bond between himself and the Duke. Emilia claims that the bond of love between women is stronger; she reminisces to Hippolyta of a childhood friend who died. Her attachment to the girl was so great that Emilia claims she will never love a man.

Amid the carnage in the field outside Thebes, Theseus enters, the victor. The three queens give him their thanks. The Duke inquires after Arcite and Palamon, who have been wounded and captured. He praises their courage and warlike skills, and asks that they be cared for. In another part of the field the queens claim their husbands' hearses.

Act II. The Athenian jailer and his daughter's wooer are discussing marriage arrangements when the daughter enters, praising the virtues of the noble cousins.

Meanwhile, Palamon regrets the loss of the fame he would have achieved as a warrior, while Arcite grieves over the fact that he will have no wife and children to remember him. But the two rejoice that they are together; they love one another, and will consider prison a sanctuary from the corrupt world outside. From their prison window they see Emilia walking in the garden, and both immediately fall in love with her. Their common praise turns to arguments and threats. Arcite is then taken to see the Duke. When Palamon learns that his cousin has been banished from Athens while he must remain there a prisoner, he vows to escape.

In the country outside Athens the banished Arcite fears that his cousin will somehow win Emilia. When he overhears some country boys talking about the games and amusements they will perform for the Duke, he decides to disguise himself as one of them to gain Emilia's attention.

Meanwhile, the jailer's daughter has fallen in love with Palamon. Though acknowledging herself to be "mean and base," she is determined to gain his love.

Arcite, who has distinguished himself in the sports and by his wit, wins the praises of the court and is made servant to Emilia. Meanwhile, the jailer's daughter has freed Palamon and led him to the woods, where she expects to join him.

Act III. In the forest on May Day Arcite soliloquizes on his good fortune. Palamon, still in shackles and weakened from his experiences in prison, comes upon his cousin and calls him a traitor. He wants to fight him immediately for Emilia's love, but Arcite insists on first helping him regain his strength. In another part of the forest the jailer's daughter is searching for Palamon, for she has learned that her father is to be hanged for the prisoner's escape. Unable to find Palamon, she goes mad.

Arcite brings food and drink to his cousin and reminds him of past pleasures in Thebes, but Palamon remains determined to fight for Emilia. Arcite agrees to bring swords and armor once he realizes he cannot dissuade his cousin from a duel.

The jailer's daughter, wandering about distractedly, falls in with a group of country folk who perform a dance before the royal entourage, the performance enlivened by the pun-filled monologue of a schoolmaster. A short distance away the noble kinsmen are preparing to fight, but stop when they hear Theseus approaching. Palamon's insistence on continuing the fight is interrupted by the Duke. Palamon impulsively reveals their identities and begs the Duke let them finish their combat. Theseus agrees, but Hippolyta, fearing for Emilia's reputation, begs her to intercede. Emilia asks that the two be banished, but the cousins insist on fighting. Since Emilia cannot choose between them, Theseus decides that they shall return and fight within a month; whoever wins shall marry Emilia, whoever loses shall be executed.

Act IV. The jailer has been pardoned, but he and the wooer are concerned about his daughter's madness. In the palace Emilia is comparing pictures of the cousins, trying to decide upon one of them but unable to do so. When she learns that the fight is about to begin, she is saddened that one or both of them will die because of her, "the sacrifice" to her "unhappy beauty." Meanwhile, the court is extolling the virtues of the two and their attendant knights.

The jailer and the wooer engage a doctor, who advises the wooer to impersonate Palamon in order to help the jailer's daughter regain her sanity.

Act V. Kneeling at altars near the field of combat, the cousins pray—Arcite to Mars, and Palamon to Venus—for success. Emilia prays at the altar of Diana.

At the prison the wooer, impersonating Palamon, gains the confidence of the jailer's daughter. The doctor now advises, over the jailer's protests, that the wooer sleep with her.

Emilia refuses to witness the combat of the cousins, although Theseus insists that "of this war" she is "the treasure." The winner must force his opponent to touch the pillar of a pyramid the Duke has had erected. Arcite is victorious, and the unhappy Emilia receives him, asking only that she be charged "to live to comfort this unfriended, / This miserable prince, that cuts away / A life more worthy from him than all women."

A block is prepared for the beheading of Palamon and his attendant knights, who reconcile themselves to their death by contemplating the honor which they have gained as warriors. Palamon inquires about the condition of the jailer's daughter. When he learns she is well and will marry, he offers her his purse, the knights following suit. As Palamon places his head on the block, a messenger rushes in, followed immediately by Pirithous. The latter tells how Arcite's black horse, frightened by a spark, has thrown his rider and trampled him.

The royal family enters with the dying Arcite. Palamon entreats him for a few last words to "one that yet loves thee dying." Before he dies, Arcite gives his cousin Emilia, "and with her all the world's joy." Theseus comments on the subtle game fortune has played and they all adjourn to prepare the funeral of Arcite and the wedding of Palamon and Emilia.—M. H. H.

Comment. Assuming that the relationship of Fletcher to Shakespeare in 1613 remained that of apprentice to master, we are prepared to find in *The Two Noble Kinsmen* features of other plays designed for the King's Men and their audiences of the Blackfriars theatre. The most striking of these likenesses are the elaborate pageants. The *Two Noble Kinsmen* opens with an expertly contrived religious ceremony before the Temple of Hymen—a brilliant nuptial procession accompanied by music and song. This is interrupted by the sharply contrasted ceremonious entrance of three widowed queens clad in black, who fall at the bridegroom's feet to beg his aid in forcing Creon to permit the burial of their husbands, slain in battle. Another equally effective religious procession, this time to the altars of Mars, Venus, and Diana, forms the first scene of the fifth act. These and other routines of pageantry in this play are unsurpassed by any similar spectacle in Shakespeare's romances. The substitution of sensational situations for those revealing character is a foretaste of Fletcher's settled manner of truckling to the decadent taste of the Jacobean gentry. Such is the struggle between the consecrated demands of Palamon and Arcite's friendship and those of their love-aroused enmity. Extreme contrasts, calculated to startle and waylay, form the warp and woof of the play's fabric. Witness Palamon's sudden emergence from a bush, still shackled, while the forest resounds with the shouting of youths and maidens joyously out a-Maying.

All that happens in the third act takes place, some of it inappropriately, in a forest near Athens, counterpart of the "wood near Athens" of *A Midsummer Night's Dream*. There Gerrold, a schoolmaster like Holofernes of *Love's Labour's Lost*, directs for Theseus a "country pastime"—a morris dance. Fletcher's "sly obscenity," often not very sly, forces its way even into this dance of the yokels and their wenches; for the Bairan (Batavian) who is admonished to "carry his tail without offense and scandal to the ladies" (III, v, 34–35) is surely the second appearance of "the strange Indian with the great Tool" who is mentioned in the fifth act of *Henry VIII*. The obscenity is painfully obvious in the ravings of the jailer's mad daughter. They are often reminiscent of Lady Macbeth's sleepwalking scene and of Ophelia's confused images and her pathetic betrayals of obsession with sex, the result of the frustration of her love for Hamlet on the very eve of its expected fruition. There is no pathos or delicacy in the jailer's daughter's expression of her passion for Palamon. She is a picture of a lowborn wench insanely beset with sex. Fletcher exploits th ludicrous conduct of a baseborn girl in love with gentleman. Vulgarity is implicit in such a relation ship, a situation that Shakespeare consistently avoid:

The character of no one of the persons in the pla is well drawn. Each tends to adapt himself to th demands of the scenes in which he appears. Th image of Emilia is blurred with each of her appear ances. Her one speech in the first scene introduce her as a dignified and natural patrician girl, an im pression confirmed by her prayer to Diana in th first scene of the fifth act. But in the third scene o the first act she is a different creature, whose lov for a girl, the dead Flavinia, proves to her

> That true love 'tween maid and maid may be
> More than in sex divided.
>
> (I, iii, 81–82)

Therefore she is sure that she will not "love an that's called man." This little glimpse of homosexual ity having afforded a momentary thrill, the autho: constrained by his story, presents Emilia, not only i love, but equally in love with two men at the sam time. To her, they are "equal precious"; she is will ing to marry either as fate determines the result o their duel. As a symbol of her innocent indecisior she wears Arcite's picture "on her right side" an Palamon's "on her left." For a creature so easil blown hither and thither by circumstance, the autho can with difficulty supply motives for her actions. I is the greatest weakness of Fletcher's art that most c his characters are weakly motivated. Almost all tha they charmingly and nobly do is the result of un reflecting impulse.

Fletcher does make some effort to distinguish be tween the two cousins. Each is a gentle perfec knight, a paragon of chivalric behavior, but Palamo is more energetic and practical in performance tha the gentler tempered Arcite. Emilia, in a monologu while the knights are fighting offstage, expatiates o this difference. Arcite is "gently visaged," "Merc and manly courage are bedfellows in his visage' Palamon

> Has a most menacing aspect; his brow
> Is graved, and seems to bury what it frowns on.
>
> . . . . .
>
> Melancholy
> Becomes him nobly. So does Arcite's mirth
> But Palamon's sadness is a kind of mirth . . .
>
> (V, iii, 44–46; 49–52)

and so on in the vocabulary of a not very bright an entirely unemotional girl. Her only anxiety, it ap pears, is that if Arcite wins her, Palamon migh wound him to "the spoiling of his figure." Howeve inept this balancing of charms, it does prepare us fc Palamon's triumph and makes Arcite's death a sent mental tragedy for everyone except Emilia.

Clearly the most profitable way of approaching th study of *The Two Noble Kinsmen* is by way Fletcher's other romances, rather than by way c Shakespeare's incomparable last plays. Seen from th point of view, the play can be enjoyed for its fluen well-mannered verse, which tells a colorful tale c gentle deeds, full of surprises and swift changes fortune. Its characters are objectively observed an judged, not probed surgeon-like; the discovery of motives in a complex of emotions is not the purpose of the authors. *The Two Noble Kinsmen*, except for Shakespeare's romances, can be enjoyed as one of the best of Jacobean romantic tragedies.—O. J. C.

Stage History. The earliest recorded reference to a performance of *The Two Noble Kinsmen* is in an undated note by Sir George Buc, Master of the Revels, which lists the play among a group of dramas apparently being considered for performance at court. At the Restoration the play was adapted by Sir William Davenant, under the title of *The Rivals*. Pepys attended a performance on September 10, 1664, describing it as "no excellent play, but good acting in it." He saw it again on December 2 and applauded the performances of Thomas Betterton and Henry Harris. In his adaptation Davenant eliminated the subplot of the Jailer's Daughter and changed the ending. The play was apparently a great success and was given before Charles II on November 19, 1667, its last recorded performance until the 20th century.

Over 260 years were to elapse before *The Two Noble Kinsmen*, in any form, was to appear on the English stage. The play was not revived until March 12, 1928, when it was presented at the Old Vic with Ion Swinley in the role of Palamon.—M. G.

Bibliography. TEXT: *The Two Noble Kinsmen*, C. H. Herford, ed., 1897; *The Complete Works of Shakespeare*, G. L. Kittredge, ed., 1936; William Spalding, *Letter on Shakspeare's Authorship of The Two Noble Kinsmen*, 1833; Frederick O. Waller, "Printer's Copy for *The Two Noble Kinsmen*," *Studies in Bibliography* XI, 1958. SOURCES: *The Complete Works of Shakespeare*. COMMENT: Theodore Spencer, "The Two Noble Kinsmen," *Modern Philology*, Vol. 36, 1938; Kenneth Muir, *Shakespeare as Collaborator*, 1960. STAGE HISTORY: Arthur Colby Sprague, *Beaumont and Fletcher on the Restoration Stage*, 1926.

Selected Criticism

WILLIAM SPALDING. The application of the distinctive qualities of Shakspeare's tone of thought to the spirit of *The Two Noble Kinsmen*, is a task for your own judgment and discrimination, and would not be aided by suggestions of mine. I have stated the result to which I have been led by such an application; and I am confident that you will be able to reach the same conclusion by a path which may be shorter than any which I could clear for you. In connexion however with this inquiry, I would direct your attention to one other truth possessing a clear application here. Shakspeare's thoughtfulness goes the length of becoming a Moral distinction and excellence. That such a difference does exist between Shakspeare and Fletcher, is denied by no one; and the moral tone of this play, in those parts which I have ventured to call Shakspeare's, is distinctly a higher one than Fletcher's. It is uniform and pure, though the moral inquisition is less severe than Shakspeare's often is. If Massinger or Jonson had been the poet alleged to have written part or the whole of the work, it would have been difficult to draw any inference from this circumstance by itself; but when the question is only between Shakspeare and Fletcher, even an abstinence from gross violation or utter concealment of moral truth is an important element in the decision; and the positively high strain here maintained is a very strong argument in favor of the purer writer . . . .

Our last words are claimed by the proper subject of our inquiry. Have I convinced you that in the composition of *The Two Noble Kinsmen*, Shakspeare had the extensive participation which I have ascribed to him? It is very probable that my reasoning is in many parts defective; but I place so much confidence in the goodness of the cause itself, that I would unhesitatingly leave the question, without a word of argument, to be determined by any one, possessing a familiar acquaintance with both the poets whose claims are to be balanced, and an ordinarily acute discernment of their distinguishing qualities. I am firmly persuaded that the subject needs only to have attention directed to it; and my investigation of it cannot have been a failure in every particular. The circumstances attending the first publication of the drama do not, in the most unfavorable view which can with any fairness be taken of them, exclude us from deciding the question of Shakspeare's authorship by an examination of the work itself; and it is unnecessary that the effect of the external evidence should be estimated one step higher. Do the internal proofs allot all to Fletcher, or assign any share to Shakspeare? The Story is ill-suited for the dramatic purposes of the one poet, and belongs to a class of subjects at variance with his style of thought, and not elsewhere chosen by him or any author of the school to which he belonged: both the individual and the class accord with the whole temper and all the purposes of the other poet, and the class is one from which he has repeatedly selected themes. It is next to impossible that Fletcher can have selected the subject; it is not unlikely that Shakspeare may have suggested it; and if the execution of the plan shall be thought to evince that he was in any degree connected with the work, we can hardly avoid the conclusion that it was by him that the subject was chosen. The proof here, (which I think has not been noticed by any one before me,) seems to me to be stronger than in any other branch of the argument. The Scenical Arrangement of the drama offers points of resemblance to Shakspeare, which, at the very least, have considerable strength when they are taken together, and are corroborative of other circumstances. The execution of that large proportion of the drama which has been marked off as his, presents circumstances of likeness to him, so numerous that they cannot possibly have been accidental, and so strikingly characteristic that we cannot conceive them to be the product of imitation. Even if it should be doubted whether Shakspeare chose the subject, or arranged any part of the plot, it seems to me that his claim to the authorship of these individual parts needs only examination to be universally admitted; not that I consider the proof here as stronger than that which establishes his choice of the plot, but because it is of a nature to be more easily and intuitively comprehended. [*A Letter on Shakspeare's Authorship of The Two Noble Kinsmen*, 1833.]

THEODORE SPENCER. The Shakespearean parts of the play, however . . . *are* worth careful analysis, for they illustrate what was happening to Shakespeare at the end of his career more clearly than anything in *The Tempest* or *Henry VIII*. The most striking fact that stands out is that Shakespeare seems no longer to be interested in process or in change and hence is no longer interested in the development of character. Whether he wrote the lines or not, what is apparently his state of mind is summed up in Theseus' address to the gods in the last speech of the play:

Let us be thankful
For that which is, and with you leave dispute
That are above our question.

And in this acceptance of "that which is," there is a mingling—it is of course inevitable—of an awareness of good and an awareness of evil, the one felt almost ecstatically, though never, as in *The Winter's Tale*, entirely so; the other felt as being continually in the background, though never pressing into the immediate situation. The speeches of Theseus, of the queens, of Palamon and Arcite are contemplative, not active, and what change occurs in the main characters is very superficial.

The story itself, to be sure, demands remoteness, a pageant-like treatment, and a slighting of differences in character, but though Shakespeare must obviously have seen this, his seeing it does not satisfactorily account for the almost unnecessary *stasis* of his presentation. . . . The style of the Shakespearean parts of *The Two Noble Kinsmen*, as Palamon's address to Venus so clearly shows, is the style of an old man, a style that reveals, to be sure, an expert technique in handling words, and a mastery of incantation, but which has little concern for the tricks that would please an audience, and which is, in a sense, dramatically stagnant. After studying Shakespeare's part of the play, we feel that his return to Stratford and his abandonment of writing were almost inevitable. In fact, it is possible to wonder whether his retirement was entirely voluntary. The shareholders in the Globe knew what the public wanted; the differences between Shakespeare's slow pageantry—its faded, difficult magnificence, its elaborate remoteness—and Fletcher's easy, accomplished manipulation, were clear enough to anyone with an eye on the box office: Fletcher's style was obviously much better adapted to the increasing superficiality of the popular taste. One can even imagine a deputation calling on Shakespeare—it is not an agreeable thought—to suggest that, all things considered, it would be wise to go home and write no more. ["The Two Noble Kinsmen," *Modern Philology*, Vol. 36, 1938.]

KENNETH MUIR. I think it is significant that nearly all Shakespeare's last plays contain theophanies. Diana appears in *Pericles;* Jupiter appears in *Cymbeline;* in *The Winter's Tale* there is an oracle and a vision; in *Henry VIII* a vision. All these plays contain references to God or the gods in their final speeches, and the epilogue of *The Tempest* ends with a prayer for forgiveness:

my ending is despair
Unless I be reliev'd by prayer,
Which pierces so that it assaults
Mercy itself, and frees all faults.
As you from crimes would pardon'd be,
Let your indulgence set me free.

In this respect *The Two Noble Kinsmen* conforms to the pattern of the plays of the last period. In other respects it differs considerably. Shakespeare is no longer obsessed with the necessity of forgiveness; he no longer deals with the reconciling of the fathers through the love of the children, with the restoration of the lost wife or child, with the recovery of a lost kingdom. Instead of the evil jealousy of Leontes and Posthumus, the murderous ambition of Antonio and Sebastian, there is only the comparatively sympathetic rivalry of Palamon and Arcite—the evil Creon never appears.

The plot of the play does not really allow much depth or subtlety of characterization. If, for example, Emilia's dilemma were allowed to be more than pathetic, if she were given a will of her own or the reality of an Imogen, the ending of the play would be more difficult to accept. In any case Fletcher lacked the poetic sensitiveness to develop Emilia along the lines of her portrait in the third scene of the play. But it is quite possible that the playgoers at the Blackfriars preferred the slickness, the smartness, and the sentimentality of the Fletcher scenes to the gnarled toughness of Shakespeare's final style.

It is reasonable to suppose that the play was written in something of a hurry. Perhaps Shakespeare, on one of his last visits to London, was prevailed upon to help his old fellows by writing something for the Blackfriars theatre, as they were short of new plays for the forthcoming season. Shakespeare, who wished to return to Stratford within a fortnight, agreed to sketch out a play and to write as much as he could in the time. Fletcher, who may have collaborated with him already in *Henry VIII*, would write the remaining scenes, and make any necessary alterations in the parts written by Shakespeare. It is not a play that adds anything to his reputation; but no other English dramatist, then or since then, has equalled the dramatic verse in the first scenes of Act I and Act V. [*Shakespeare as Collaborator*, 1960.]

Tybalt. In *Romeo and Juliet*, the cousin of Juliet whose death at the hands of Romeo marks the turning point of the play. Tybalt is both arrogant and pompous and as such is the perfect foil for the man whom he kills, Mercutio (III, i).

Tyler, Richard (1566–1636). A friend of Shakespeare to whom the poet bequeathed money to buy a ring in the first draft of his will (in January 1616), but whose name was replaced by Hamnet Sadler's in the final draft. The reason for Shakespeare's apparent change of heart toward Tyler may be found in the charge, made public in March 1616, that Tyler had appropriated public funds for his own use.

Tyler, born about the same time as Shakespeare, may have been one of his schoolmates. Two of his daughters, Judith (b. 1593) and Susanna (b. 1597), bear the same names as the poet's daughters and his son William (b. 1598) may have been Shakespeare's godchild. In 1618 his signature appears on a document relating to the transfer of Shakespeare's London property, the Blackfriars Gate-House. [Mark Eccles, *Shakespeare in Warwickshire*, 1961.]

Tyler, Thomas (1826–1902). Scholar. Though primarily concerned with Biblical studies, Tyler was one of the original members of the New Shakspere Society and made occasional contributions to Shakespeare scholarship, e.g., *The Philosophy of Hamlet*

(1874). In his edition of Shakespeare's *Sonnets* (1890) he made a conjecture on the identity of the Dark Lady. Assuming that Mr. W. H. was William Herbert, earl of Pembroke, Tyler was the first to suggest that the Dark Lady might be Mary Fitton, Pembroke's mistress. His conjecture was taken as a certainty by Frank Harris in *The Man Shakespeare and His Tragic Life Story* (1909). G. B. Shaw made use of the idea in his *Dark Lady of the Sonnets* (1910).

Tynan, Kenneth (1927–). Dramatic critic. Born in Birmingham, Tynan was educated at Oxford. In 1949 he began his career as a director of the Lichfield Repertory Company, and the following year directed *Othello* for an Arts Council tour. His only acting role was the First Gravedigger in Sir Alec Guinness' *Hamlet* in 1951. Tynan is best known for dramatic criticism, which he has written for *The Spectator* (1951/2), *Evening Standard* (1952/3), *Daily Sketch* (1953/4), *The Observer* (1954–1958, 1960–), and *The New Yorker* (1958–1960). He was also script editor at Ealing Films from 1956 to 1958, and has written *He That Plays the King* (1950), *Persona Grata* (1953), *Alec Guinness* (1953), *Bull Fever* (1955), and *Curtains* (1961). He is a frequent contributor to many periodicals. Tynan became literary adviser to the National Theatre Company in 1963. [*Who's Who in the Theatre,* 1961; *The New York Times,* March 18, April 3, 1963.]

Tyrrel, Sir **James** (d. 1502). An ardent Yorkist, knighted after the battle of Tewkesbury. Tyrrel also supported Richard III, for whom he is said to have carried out the murder of the princes in 1483. For this crime he was beheaded during the reign of Henry VII. In *Richard III,* Tyrrel, having suborned Dighton and Forrest to do "this ruthless piece of butchery," reports to Richard that he has seen the Princes dead (IV, iii).

Tyrwhitt, Thomas (1730–1786). Scholar. Educated at Oxford and the Middle Temple, Tyrwhitt was a civil servant until 1768, at which time he retired to devote himself entirely to scholarship. He early became a master of languages and gained a deserved reputation for his knowledge of both classical and modern philology. In 1766 there appeared his *Observations and Conjectures upon some Passages of Shakespeare.* This and other fruits of his scholarship he made available to Steevens for his edition of 1778, to Malone (1778), and to Reed (1785). Of his several classical editions, Aristotle's *Poetics* (1794) is the most notable. Tyrwhitt's chief claim to fame rests on his edition of Chaucer's *Canterbury Tales* (5 vols., 1775–1778); the text was the best-edited English classic to that time, and the accompanying essay on Chaucer's language was the first to set forth the correct principles of versification. Tyrwhitt was also apparently the first in modern times to call attention to *Palladis Tamia,* Meres' collection of essays, important for their allusions to Shakespeare.

U

Ulrici, Hermann (1806–1884). German scholar, professor of philosophy at the University of Halle from 1834 until his death. In addition to several philosophical treatises, Ulrici published studies in Greek poetry and on Shakespeare. His *Uber Shakespeares Dramatische Kunst* (1839; English translation, 1846) was an early attempt to trace the growth and development of Shakespeare's dramatic art. In the third edition of 1876 (translated into English that same year), Ulrici presented in a final form the fruits of a lifetime of reflection; he somewhat modified his earlier romantic enthusiasms and put greater emphasis on the unity of plot and the development of character. Excerpts from his work have been reprinted in the New Variorum Shakespeare. Ulrici also edited *Gallerie zu Shakespeares Dramatische Werken* (1847), a collection of essays by German scholars on the principal plays.

Ulysses. The Roman name of Odysseus, an important figure of many Greek myths, the hero of Homer's *Odyssey* and a prominent character in that poet's *Iliad.* In *Troilus and Cressida,* Ulysses appears as a Greek general. His long speech on "degree" is the most famous passage in the play. Ulysses has, like most of the characters and, indeed, the entire play, been subject to a wide range of interpretation. Some commentators have considered him the play's hero and the author's spokesman, while others have seen him as a corrupt Machiavellian whose eloquently voiced ideals are belied by his crafty intrigues.

Both views would appear to be extreme. Ulysses is neither the play's hero nor one of the objects of mockery. His role is not significant enough for the former and he is presented in too admirable a light to be considered among the latter. He is rather the touchstone of the traditional values of order and degree which are capriciously destroyed by individual self-indulgence and willfulness.

Underhill, William (1555–1597). The owner of New Place, who sold it to Shakespeare in 1597. Underhill held an important position in Warwickshire, despite the fact that he had earlier been imprisoned as a Catholic recusant. His father purchased New Place in 1567 and he inherited it on the latter's death in 1570. Shakespeare bought the house for £60. Shortly after the purchase, on July 7, 1597, Underhill was poisoned by his son Fulke. Fulke was executed in 1599, and his younger brother Hercules inherited his father's estate when he came of age in 1602. In that year Hercules confirmed the sale of the house to Shakespeare. The confirmation, which probably served to clear the title, involved a restatement of the original document with Hercules' name substituted for his father's. One other change is th addition of two orchards (*duobus pomariis*) whicl are not cited in the earlier document.

> Inter Willielmum Shakespeare generosum queren tem et Herculem Underhill generosum deforcian tem, de uno mesuagio duobus horreis duobu gardinis et duobus pomariis cum pertinenciis i Stretford-super-Avon . . .
>
> [Between William Shakespeare, gentleman, com plainant and Hercules Underhill, gentleman, de forciant, concerning one house, two barns, tw gardens, and two orchards with their appurte nances in Stratford upon Avon . . .]

[Tucker Brooke, *Shakespeare of Stratford,* 1926.]

Underwood, John (d. 1624). Actor. Underwood' career as an actor began with the Children of th Chapel at some time about 1601. According to th deposition of the Burbage family in the SHARER PAPERS dispute, Underwood, Will Ostler, and Natha Field were taken into the "King's service" at th time the family acquired the Blackfriars theatr (1608). Underwood appears in the casts of th Chapel's productions of *Cynthia's Revels* and *Th Poetaster* and in over 20 extant cast lists of the King Men's plays. The only part he is definitely known t have played is that of Delio in Webster's *Duchess o Malfi* (pub. 1623), as given bv the King's Men 1614 and, in revival, 1619–1623.

His will, dated October 4, 1624, indicates that h owned shares in the Globe, Blackfriars, and Curtai theatres which he assigned to Henry Condell an two other executors to be held in trust for his fiv minor children. Underwood's name is among thos of the "principall Actors" in the First Folio c Shakespeare's plays (1623). [E. K. Chambers, *Th Elizabethan Stage,* 1923; G. E. Bentley, *The Jacobea and Caroline Stage,* 5 vols., 1941–1956.]

Union of the Two Noble and Illustre Famelies c Lancastre and York, The. See Edward Halle.

United States. Evidence of interest in Shakespea in 17th-century America is slender. There is n record suggesting that a copy of his works w included in any New England book collectio John Harvard's library contained comedies c Plautus and Terence and even a copy of a Can bridge University play, but no Shakespeare. Cor sidering the attitude of the Puritans toward the stag the situation is not at all surprising. It is clea nevertheless, that some Shakespearean verse was rea and admired in the Bay Colony. John Cotton's so Seaborn, who graduated from Harvard in 165 copied into his college notebook a lyric fro

Measure for Measure, "Take, Oh, Take Those Lips Away," which he got from an anthology published in London in 1641.

In the South, traces of Shakespeare are similarly sketchy. A 1777 catalogue of the library of the Virginian William Byrd (1674–1744) refers to folios of Jonson and Shakespeare, but there is no proof that these go back to the 17th century. The library of the Carter family, with its emphasis on books of practical value, contained little literature and no Shakespeare. Another Virginian, Captain Arthur Spicer, listed the title *Macbeth* in an inventory made in 1699, perhaps the only reference to a copy of a Shakespearean play recorded in 17th-century America.

on the stage. During the following century Shakespeare's works were on the shelves of American book collections, and his plays were presented on the fledgling American stage. In 1730 there was an amateur performance of *Romeo and Juliet* in New York. Professional productions, dating from about midcentury, brought *Richard III*, *Othello*, and *Hamlet* to audiences in Charleston, Williamsburg, Philadelphia, and New York. Managers of the first theatrical companies, such as Lewis Hallam (1740–1808) and David Douglass (?–1786), frequently found themselves beleaguered by the clergy and the police, however.

In New England, moral objections prevented the establishment of a theatre. After a production in 1750 of *The Orphan*, by Thomas Otway (1652–1685), Boston immediately passed a law prohibiting the repetition of any such "means of disseminating licentious maxims." This law kept theatrical performances from Boston until the British army occupied the city in 1775. In 1792 the sheriff appeared on the stage to close Boston's first theatrical season, which had offered *Hamlet* and *Richard III*.

Attempts to evade restrictive laws were ingenious; in the autumn of 1761 Douglass produced *Othello* at the King's Arms Tavern in Newport, Rhode Island. The playbill described the performance as "A series of moral dialogues in five parts, depicting the evil effects of jealousy and other bad passions and proving that happiness can only spring from the pursuit of virtue." At Providence, the following year, Douglass erected a "schoolhouse" for the production of a variety of moral dialogues, but the Rhode Island Assembly banned their performance.

Objections to the theatre were somewhat less strenuous in other sections of the country, though the Pennsylvania Assembly prohibited stage plays in 1700, classifying them among "rude and riotous sports." Throughout the early 18th century a number of laws against theatrical performances were enacted in Philadelphia but immediately revoked by authorities in England. The building permit for Douglass' Society Hall Theatre (1759) ordered that it be built outside city limits, a condition suggesting Elizabethan London.

In New York and Virginia opposition was less widespread. Indeed, in the *Virginia Gazette*, published in Williamsburg, one critic praised the literary heritage of the drama, mentioning Sophocles, Corneille, Shakespeare, and Molière. Since men like Milton and Addison wrote plays, he argued, the genre "must needs be very blameless."

In July of 1753 Hallam printed an article in the New York *Mercury* in defense of theatrical productions. In addition to the "instruction" hidden in the plays of "the immortal Shakespeare," Hallam emphasized the decorum of performances which were meant to provide polite society with rational diversion. He appeals to a class-conscious refinement based upon imitation of London's social life. Playgoing, apparently, had become a symbol of status. During the crisis over England's imposition of the Stamp Act (1765), a mob broke into the Chapel Street Theatre in New York, scattered the audience, and set fire to the building, an indication that theatrical performances were associated with the elite and with the mother country.

Until the eve of the Revolution the American theatre was a makeshift affair. Performances were given in hastily erected buildings and often in the public rooms of inns. The plays of Shakespeare held their own in the colonial theatre, and were offered in about the same proportion as on the London stage. Acting companies ordinarily opened a series of performances with a play by Shakespeare. Success in London determined which plays were acted. *Richard III* in Cibber's version appears to have been the most popular Shakespearean play.

The New Theatre in Southwark outside Philadelphia and the John Street Theatre in New York, permanent buildings constructed (in 1766 and 1767 respectively) solely for theatrical productions, were landmarks in the history of the American theatre. The New Theatre gave performances for 100 nights during its first season and was used as a playhouse for some 50 years. At the John Street Theatre Douglass produced at least 10 Shakespearean plays the first season, including *Antony and Cleopatra* and *Cymbeline*.

On October 20, 1774, a decree from the continental congress discouraged "every species of extravagance and dissipation," signaling the close of professional theatres for the duration of the war. The professional theatre gave way to amateur performances, the most significant of which took place in New York, Boston, and Philadelphia during the British occupation. In New York at the John Street Theatre, renamed the Theatre Royal, some officers of General Howe's command performed *Richard III*, *Macbeth*, *King Lear*, and *Katherine and Petruchio*, Garrick's version of *The Taming of the Shrew*. Despite the objections of congress, the American army occasionally produced theatricals, even at Valley Forge. A curious example was the production of the then little-known *Coriolanus* at Portsmouth, New Hampshire, in 1778. An epilogue, written for the occasion, interprets Coriolanus as a man suffering from "his country's base ingratitude," a fate which the soldiers at Portsmouth apparently felt they shared.

The attitudes of prominent 18th-century Americans toward Shakespeare are enlightening. Often he is thought of not as a playwright, but as a source of political or moral wisdom. To support his own views on class structure in society, John Adams, in a commentary on the Italian historian Davila, quotes Ulysses' speech on degree from *Troilus and Cressida* (I, iii, 75 ff.). Jefferson's reasons in a letter of 1771 advising a friend to buy the works of Shakespeare are moral and pragmatic. When he drew up a reading schedule for law students, Jefferson suggested Shakespeare as light bedtime reading which would develop "the full powers of the English language." Washington, however, got his Shakespeare by going to the theatre, a pleasurable ingredient in a gentleman's social life. He does not seem to have distinguished between Shakespeare and other dramatists. "Dined with Mr. James Delancey and went to the play at Hull's Tavern in the evening," reads an entry in his journal for May 28, 1773. The play that night was *Hamlet.*

After the war professional theatre revived, and Shakespeare was played on the American stage more than any other dramatist. The new theatres erected in Philadelphia, Boston, and New York were comparable to those in London. Their most commanding attraction was a touring British star, such as Fanny Kemble or Edmund Kean, for in 19th-century America, as in England, the actor was the central concern of the playgoer. Shakespeare had become venerable, a representative of culture, a link with England, and leading roles in his plays were considered a test of an actor's artistry. Shakespeare so presided over the American theatrical world that the niche above the central door of New York's New Park Theatre (1821) held his bust, and the tympanum over the stage of the new Chestnut Street Theatre (1822) in Philadelphia depicted Shakespeare with the muses of tragedy and comedy.

Romantic criticism affected the portrayal of Shakespeare on the English and the American stage. Kean, who appeared in America as early as 1820, advocated a subjective and impulsive style, contrary to established acting traditions. His Othello, Hamlet, Shylock, and Lear were enthusiastically appreciated. Junius Brutus Booth, another British actor who played Shakespeare in the romantic style, was likewise successful in America. James Hackett, the American, went in the direction of "method" acting, studying the part critically and developing a psychological interpretation of the role. He rebuked his contemporary, Edwin Forrest, for uncritical violence and frenzy. J. B. Booth's son Edwin Booth culminated the achievement of 19th-century Shakespearean acting in America by combining an intellectual approach with artistic integrity in his great portrayal of Hamlet.

The plays of Shakespeare went west with touring acting companies. Performances in frontier towns ranged from soliloquies declaimed above the din of a saloon to professional productions of plays such as *Hamlet, Macbeth, Othello,* and *Richard III* by the Booths and William Chapman, Jr., and Caroline Chapman at the Jenny Lind Theatre in San Francisco during the summer of 1852.

literary influence. Shakespeare, pre-eminent on the American stage, did less handsomely in American schools. Throughout the century set pieces from the plays furnished material for books on oratory and elocution. Shakespeare was introduced to common schools in readers like Thomas Sheridan's *Lectures on the Art of Reading.* Passages from Shakespeare provided moral instruction in the famous McGuffey readers, which began to flourish in the 1830's. The poet was first introduced to American undergraduates in 1784 through quotations in Hugh Blair's *Lectures on Rhetoric and Belles Lettres.* But Shakespeare did not become part of the literary curriculum of colleges until nearly a century had passed.

In America, as in England, the traditional curriculum for undergraduates concentrated on the classics. They were expected to read "modern literature" on their own. The list of subscribers to an 1807 edition of Shakespeare's works includes more than half the students at Harvard. In an address delivered before the Modern Language Association of America in 1889, James Russell Lowell advocated the teaching of modern literature in colleges. Meanwhile, single plays, issued at Boston and New York in stage versions, argue the development of a reading public for Shakespeare among playgoers. For the most part, early American editions were aimed at the general reader. The first, Bioren and Madan's *Shakespeare,* published in Philadelphia in 1795–1796, commends itself for avoiding scholarly apparatus: "An American reader," the editors assert, "is seldom disposed to wander through the wilderness of verbal criticism."

The impact of Shakespeare on the minds of prominent 19th-century Americans was often profound. Ralph Waldo EMERSON refers to Shakespeare more than to any other writer, but his comments take the form of superlative generalizations; Shakespeare, as the representative poet, is invoked as a god and his works quoted like scripture. Emerson commends him in glowing adjectives, rationalizes his bawdry, and tries to ignore the fact that he wrote for the stage. In his lecture "Shakespeare or the Poet," which he worked into *Representative Men* (1850), Emerson belittles anything that might come between Shakespeare's sublimity and the reader, such as theatres, actors, scholarly research, and Shakespeare societies.

Walt WHITMAN saw Shakespeare's plays on the New York stage; he read "stormy passages from *Julius Caesar* or *Richard*" on the Broadway bus and declaimed Shakespeare "to the surf and sea-gulls" at Coney Island. "It seems a shame," he remarks, "to pick and choose from the riches Shakespeare left us, to criticize his infinitely royal, multiform quality." Whitman did not, however accept the "almost luny worship of Shakespeare" prevalent at the time, and he did not think Shakespeare the "all-in-all of literature." Whitman's adulation was qualified because he found in Shakespeare principles "non-acceptable to America and democracy."

Lincoln, though he picked up his education "under the pressure of necessity," found time to acquaint himself with the works of Shakespeare. When he was president, he sometimes read Shakespeare aloud and often went to performances of the plays. John Hay, then his secretary, records in his diary that Lincoln read to him from *Henry VI* and *Richard III* until his "eyelids caught his [Lincoln's] considerate notice" and the President sent him to bed. Lincoln was sufficiently acquainted with the text of Shakespeare to dispute Hackett's rendition of certain lines. When Hackett visited the White House on December 13, 1863, Hay noted that Lincoln shared "a very intimate knowledge of those plays of Shakespeare where Falstaff figured." Lincoln's familiarity with the text of Shakespeare, however did not influence his own diction or style.

Herman MELVILLE was profoundly influenced by hakespeare. During the winter of 1849, as he was)out to write *Moby Dick*, Melville apparently ent through all of Shakespeare and found there a)lackness" which made him the "profoundest of inkers." Melville's review (1850) of *Mosses from ι Old Manse* praises Hawthorne for probing, like hakespeare, the darker aspects of human life. Melille found several levels of meaning in Shakespeare's lays, an insight which may account for his major :vision of *Moby Dick*. He included devices from *'ing Lear* and *Macbeth* and echoed Shakespeare's ,nguage throughout the book, particularly in Ahab's)liloquies. Like Emerson, Melville saw in the works f Shakespeare the reflected image of his own soul.

The worship of Shakespeare in the 19th century as made his works classroom classics. A high-:hool student can expect to study in detail plays ke *Romeo and Juliet, Macbeth*, and *Julius Caesar* ; part of his English curriculum. In college he 'ill read additional plays and be introduced to hakespearean scholarship and to problems of inter-retation. Separate plays have been made available to :udents and the general reader in inexpensive paper-ack editions.

the 20th century. Despite the decline of repertory ompanies and the rivalry of contemporary drama-sts, Shakespeare continues to be successful on roadway. The staging of Shakespeare in the 20th entury evinces a tendency to experiment. Elaborate erformances, such as Herbert Beerbohm Tree's *Ienry VIII*, for which a portion of Westminster ιbbey was realistically reconstructed on the stage, ave given way to anachronous costuming and :tting, as in performances in modern dress. In 1937, t the Mercury Theatre in New York, Orson Welles layed Julius Caesar against the bare pipes and rick of backstage walls, an attempt to re-create ıe simplicity of Elizabethan productions. Modern ıterpretations of the plays are usually unsentimental, :flecting the tendency to construe Shakespeare 'ithout tears. From John Gielgud's Hamlet in the 930's to Richard Burton's in the 1960's celebrated ritish actors have drawn audiences to Shakespeare n Broadway.

Shakespeare has had limited success in motion ictures even when played by eminent actors. The ıedium, which is relentlessly visual, may clash with ıe elaborate verbal texture of the plays. Recently hakespeare has been presented to American audi-nces on television. In February of 1959 the Old 'ic Company played *Hamlet* on the DuPont Show f the Month. The following year the Hallmark Iall of Fame presented *The Tempest. The Age of Kings*, a series of five plays filmed by BBC, had :s premiere in January of 1961.

A most significant contemporary development has een the popularity of Shakespeare festivals. In 1954 he American Shakespeare Festival Theatre and ιcademy received a grant of $200,000 from the Rockefeller Foundation to found a permanent Shake-pearean theatre at Stratford, Connecticut. The fol-owing year the Stratford company played *Julius Caesar* and *The Tempest*. In 1957 the New York hakespeare Festival opened, offering free perform-nces of four plays in the open air in Central Park. hakespeare was played under the stars in Toledo, Ohio, and festivals were inaugurated at colleges such as Antioch and Hofstra. (See below, *regional productions in the U.S.*) The 1962 season included eight Shakespeare festivals across the nation. The fourth centennial of Shakespeare's birth was the occasion of amateur and professional performances of Shakespeare's plays in cities and on campuses throughout the country.

scholarship. Washington IRVING's essay "On the Boar's Head Tavern" in his *Sketch Book* (1819) satirizes Shakespearean scholarship and editors who "send up mists of obscurity from their notes at the bottom of each page." Literary Americans of the 19th century preferred rhapsodic criticism, like that of Emerson, to scholarly commentary. Edgar Allan POE, in a passage often quoted, pictures Dr. Johnson as a clumsy elephant unable to cope with the airy creatures of Shakespeare's imagination. An interest in Shakespearean scholarship developed in the United States after the Civil War, when the plays were studied in colleges as a linguistic discipline.

Henry N. Hudson, editor of the *Harvard Shakespeare* (1880/1), was one of the first Americans to devote himself to Shakespearean scholarship. His early lectures, published in two volumes in 1848 and aimed at the general reader, romanticize Shakespeare in the Schlegel-Coleridge tradition and emphasize the poet's moral value. These tendencies continue in Hudson's more scholarly work, *Shakespeare, His Life, Art and Character*, 1872. Richard Grant White, his contemporary, became an authority on the First Folio and one of the earliest to detect Collier's forgeries. James Russell Lowell, reviewing White for the *Atlantic Monthly* in 1859, insisted upon the importance of establishing a text free of sacrilegious 18th-century emendations. Thus romantic Shakespeare worship contributed to the demand for accurate texts of the plays. This demand would lead to H. H. Furness' New Variorum editions begun in 1871.

Another fortunate result of 19th-century Shakespeare worship is the famous collection of Henry Clay Folger which his family gave to the nation in 1932. Inspired by Emerson, Folger began what has become the most valuable collection of Shakespeareana in the world, housed in the FOLGER SHAKESPEARE LIBRARY in Washington, D. C.

Despite the prevalence of "new criticism" and the application of insights derived from modern psychology and anthropology to literary studies, the contribution of American Shakespearean scholars in the 20th century has been largely historical in its approach and often aimed at an understanding of the Elizabethan theatre and Shakespeare as a dramatist. George F. Reynolds' *Some Principles of Elizabethan Staging* (1905) was a pioneer work in this direction. Both George P. Baker of Harvard and James Brander Matthews of Columbia emphasized Shakespeare the playwright, not Shakespeare the poet.

A. H. Thorndike's *Shakespeare's Theater* (1916), Joseph Q. Adams' *Shakespearean Playhouses* (1917), and John C. Adams' *The Globe Playhouse: Its Design and Equipment* (1942) are examples of books which deal with Shakespeare's theatre. Lily B. Campbell has written about the machinery employed on the Elizabethan stage, and T. W. Baldwin has described the organization and personnel of the Shakespearean acting company. From George Lyman Kittredge to Hardin Craig, the approach to Shakespeare has been essentially historical. Significant biographical information has been unearthed by C. W. Wallace and Leslie Hotson. The trend of 20th-century American scholarship is typified in the work of E. E. Stoll, who has attempted a realistic understanding of Shakespeare's accomplishment in relation to the theatre in which he and his contemporaries did their work. [The best single source on this subject is Esther C. Dunn, *Shakespeare in America*, 1939.]—J. F. L.

regional productions in the U.S. Shakespearean productions in towns and cities throughout the United States have flourished, almost disappeared, and flourished again. By the 1890's touring companies were trouping Shakespeare's plays to almost every town that boasted an auditorium; in 1906 more than 200 stock companies in major American cities were presenting Shakespeare. Soon after this time, rising costs made extensive touring impractical, and the stock companies were replaced by a cheaper form of entertainment, the movies.

It was just before and after World War I that live theatre, of which Shakespeare was a staple, began its revival around the country in little theatres (groups of nonprofessional civic actors) and drama departments of colleges, where students produced and acted in the classics and received credit for their theatre courses. By 1964 there were 1800 college and university theatres presenting a series of plays each season, most of them offering a Shakespeare play regularly. As the director is generally a professional and the students are preparing for careers in the theatre or to teach theatre, these productions of Shakespeare are at the least competent and at the best entertaining and exhilarating. They provide the majority of the Shakespearean productions seen by American audiences. In the main the directors pay careful attention to the text and incorporate the best of modern scholarship into the productions. One significant achievement of the university productions is that they were the pioneers in this country in presenting the plays on stages that either were replicas of an Elizabethan stage or incorporated some of its features. Before the "open" stage was used professionally, there were such stages in regular use for Shakespeare at Hofstra and Antioch colleges, at the University of Illinois, and at the OREGON SHAKESPEARE FESTIVAL.

A major handicap to adequate presentation has been the youth of the student actors, who may be convincing as Hamlet or Romeo, but not as Lear or Macbeth. Some college theatres assign the principal roles to graduate students or invite professional actors to head a student cast. For example, Colleen Dewhurst and George C. Scott have appeared as Portia and Shylock in a production of *The Merchant of Venice* at the University of Utah, and Jeffrey Lynn as Macbeth at Bowling Green State University, Ohio. Both these theatres offer Shakespeare plays regularly. Other such theatres include those at Stanford University, the University of Vermont, the University of Kansas at Lawrence, the University of Texas (where B. Iden Payne directs the annual Shakespeare production), Ohio Wesleyan (where R. C. Hunter directed 41 Shakespeare plays from 1921 to his retirement in 1959), the Universit of Nebraska, and the College of William and Mary.

Productions sometimes are experimental. The Rin Theatre at the University of Miami offers Shakespeare in the round; at Baylor University in Texas Paul Baker has directed a "multiple Hamlet," i which Burgess Meredith, supplemented by studen actors, portrayed "the various facets of Hamlet' character."

Often a state university sends its production of Shakespeare on tours of nearby high schools an colleges; a pioneer in such ventures is the Universit of Minnesota, which has toured many outstandin productions, among them *King Lear* and *Romeo and Juliet*. A Shakespeare festival is an annual even at many colleges and universities, including Colorado University, Northwestern University, Hofstr College, and Rice Institute in Houston. See HOFSTR COLLEGE SHAKESPEARE FESTIVAL; COLORADO UNIVERSITY SHAKESPEARE FESTIVAL.

Fewer community theatres attempt Shakespeare but among those that have done so successfully ar the Tulsa Little Theatre, the Topeka Civic Theatre the Phoenix Little Theatre (host to the annua PHOENIX SHAKESPEARE FESTIVAL), and the theatr of Western Springs, Illinois. Since 1940 the Cleveland Play House has annually staged a Shakespear play especially for student audiences. Production are offered at its Euclid-77th Theatre on an ope stage designed with Shakespeare plays in mind Recently a production of *The Comedy of Error* there was followed by the Rodgers-Hart *Boys from Syracuse*. See GREAT LAKES SHAKESPEARE FESTIVAL SAN DIEGO SHAKESPEARE THEATRE.

Among the professional drama schools which als serve as community theatres, both the Goodma Memorial Theatre in Chicago and the Pasaden Playhouse in California offer Shakespeare productions annually; the latter has produced the entir canon.

Resident professional companies at universities offering Shakespeare and other classics, have appeared at the University of Michigan and at Princeton University, where the Association of Producin Artists offered a season of six Shakespeare plays i 1960/1. Professional companies which have bee touring in Shakespearean plays for 15 years are th state-supported Barter Theatre at Abingdon, Virginia, and Players, Inc., a company made up o graduates of the drama department of Catholi University in Washington, D.C. The latter grou has performed Shakespeare for American service men and community audiences in France, Germany and Italy, including a lively *Taming of the Shrew* in 1958, with Joanne Ellspermann and Laurence Luckinbill in the leading roles.

In 1962 and 1963 new theatres were establishe in Minneapolis and Seattle with resident professiona companies, generally trained in the university theatres. Both of these theatres offer annual performances of Shakespeare plays, as does the Aren Stage in Washington, D.C.—A. G.

Universal Passion, The. See James MILLER.

university drama. Term used to describe th Tudor and Stuart plays performed at Oxford an Cambridge. The medieval tradition of miracle an morality plays was liturgical and popular in origi and had no impact on the academic stage. The latte wed its development to the dominance of HUMAN-M and the renewed interest in classical languages. the beginning of the 16th century these plays, ritten in Latin, amounted to little more than adap-tions of the Latin drama, particularly of Plautus nd Terence. By the middle of the century, how-ver, the academic playwrights began to explore ew themes while retaining the classical five-act ormula. The earliest extant examples of this type re Nicholas Grimald's *Christus Redivivus* (1543), nd his *Archipropheta* (1548), both of which were erformed at Oxford. In 1566 Elizabeth visited Ox-ord, where she attended a performance of *Palamon nd Arcyte,* a play based on Chaucer's "Knight's ale," the same story that Shakespeare and Fletcher sed for *The Two Noble Kinsmen.*

The best known of the plays performed at Oxford nd Cambridge is *Gammer Gurton's Needle* (pub. 575), the first "regular" English comedy. Other sser-known plays, however, are more directly re-ted to Shakespeare. These include a play about ichard III, *Richardus Tertius,* by Thomas Legge, cted at Cambridge in 1580, and *Laelia,* acted at ueen's College in 1595, an adaptation of the Italian rose comedy *Gli' Ingannati* which used the same tory as *Twelfth Night.* Later examples of university rama are the PARNASSUS PLAYS, a trilogy performed t St. John's College, Cambridge, about 1598, 1600, nd 1601, which contain a number of contemporary llusions, including a reference to Shakespeare's articipation in the War of the Theatres.

On August 27, 1605 King James visited Oxford, vhere he was greeted with a salute or "conceit," vhich might have given Shakespeare the idea for the vitches' scenes in *Macbeth* (see MACBETH: *Sources*). F. S. Boas, *University Drama in the Tudor Age,* 914.]

University Wits. Name used to designate a group f Elizabethan pamphleteers and playwrights, edu-ated at Cambridge or Oxford, who wrote plays for he professional theatre in the latter part of the 580's. The chief figures in the group were Christo-her MARLOWE, Robert GREENE, George PEELE, Thomas NASHE, and Thomas LODGE. Aside from the normous contributions to the development of Eng-ish drama made by the individuals, such as Marlowe, n the group, its chief distinctions seem to have been taste for dissolute living, a strong strain of profes-ional jealousy, and, very probably, an intense dislike or "unlettered" competitors like Shakespeare.

upper stage. Gallery above the stage in an Eliza-ethan playhouse. In the drawing of the Swan thea-re, this area is shown to project slightly over the cenic wall (or tiring-house façade) and is divided nto six small compartments by short vertical pillars. The area was used for seating spectators, as a MUSIC ROOM, and as an additional level available for the actors to perform on. Ascent and descent of actors to and from various stage levels is a characteristic of the Elizabethan theatre: classical and neoclassical stage traditions usually confined the action to a single level.

The upper stage had various functions. In plays such as *The Battle of Alcazar,* the "plot" of which is extant, a stage direction reads, "Enter aboue Neme-sis." Nemesis is the "divine presenter" and from above controls the actions of the lower stage players who, as her puppets, merely execute her commands. In *James IV* the presenters are Bohan, a Scot, and Oberon, king of fairies; they appear in an Induction, remove to the "Gallery," and later reappear in order to comment on the action. In the anonymous play *The Taming of A Shrew,* the character Will Sly is similarly brought forth for the Induction, but re-moved during the Induction's first scene. He reap-pears in the second scene, evidently above, and criti-cizes the play. At the end, by means of an epilogue, the lord in the play orders a servant to "lay" Sly

> in the place where we did find him,
> Just underneath the alehouse side below.

In Shakespeare's *Taming of the Shrew,* the second scene of the Induction takes place "aloft"; the pre-senters "sit" while viewing the play and comment once according to the stage direction, "The Pre-senters aboue speakes." The presenters were sent above where, without obstruction to the action, they were visible to the audience. As a rule, they fur-nished a prologue or epilogue and departed. In some plays they are required to remain on the lower level, generally because the upper area is required for use as a tower or wall, as in *Soliman and Perseda.* The presenters functioned as "idealized spectators," ac-cording to E. K. Chambers, in lieu of the ordinary mortals who had once occupied the area. See PLAY-HOUSE STRUCTURE; LORDS' ROOM.

The frequent use of this area for a chamber (Hero's room in *Much Ado About Nothing,* Fal-staff's room in *Merry Wives of Windsor,* Brabantio's room in *Othello,* and Celia's room in *Volpone*) has led to a considerable scholarly controversy. The ar-gument concerns the possibility of using this room space to play interior scenes which probably could not otherwise have been seen by spectators located in the pit and lower galleries. [E. K. Chambers, *The Elizabethan Stage,* 1923.]

Upton, John (1707–1760). Critic. Educated at Merton College, Oxford, Upton held a number of church livings during his lifetime. He contributed to the 18th-century debate over Shakespeare's learning in his *Critical Observations on Shakespeare* (1746). Upton argued that Shakespeare was well versed in classical literature. [Herbert Spencer Robinson, *English Shakesperian Criticism in the Eighteenth Century,* 1932.]

Ur-Hamlet. Name given to the lost play believed to have been the direct source of *Hamlet.* The earli-est reference to the *Ur-Hamlet* is in Thomas Nashe's Preface to Robert Greene's *Menaphon* (1589), which contains an allusion to "whole Hamlets . . . handfulls of tragical speaches." A further reference in the same passage to the "kidde in Aesop" has led many critics to assume that the play was written by Thomas KYD. The play was later mentioned in Hens-lowe's diary as having been performed on June 1, 1594 at Newington Butts by the amalgamated com-panies of the Admiral's Men and Chamberlain's Men. The fact that the receipts for this performance were a mere 8s. suggests that the play had been on the boards for some time and was no longer popular. In 1596 Thomas Lodge's *Wit's Miserie* alluded to "the Visard of ye ghost which cried so miserably at ye Theator, like an oister wife, Hamlet, revenge." Lodge's reference to the Theatre, which up to 1596 was the home of the Chamberlain's Men, is an indication that the play was the property of Shakespeare's company. A reference in Dekker's *Satiromastix* (1601)—"my name's Hamlet revenge: thou hast been at Parris garden hast not?" (IV, i, 150)—is generally regarded as an allusion to the *Ur-Hamlet* rather than Shakespeare's play since the phrase "Hamlet revenge" does not occur in Shakespeare. The phrase is also used in a pamphlet by Samuel Rowlands, published in 1602.

Numerous attempts have been made to reconstruct the old play and to establish its relationship not only to the Shakespearean play as it is now known but to the "bad quarto" (Q1) of *Hamlet* and to the German version, DER BESTRAFTE BRUDER-MORD. [Isra Gollancz, *The Sources of Hamlet*, 1926.]

Ursula. In *Much Ado About Nothing*, a gentl woman who attends Hero. As a participant in he mistress' scheme to make Beatrice fall in love wit Benedick, Ursula praises Benedick "more than eve man did merit." She is happily rewarded to observ her fish devouring the bait (III, i).

Urswick, Sir **Christopher** (1448–1522). Priest an diplomat. Urswick became confessor to Margare Beaufort and subsequently helped to bring about th marriage of her son Henry VII and Elizabeth c York (1484). In *Richard III*, Urswick is sent by th Earl of Derby with a message to Richmond (IV, v

V

Valentine. In *Titus Andronicus,* a relative of itus. He does not speak, but joins in humoring e supposedly mad Titus by shooting arrows with essages to the gods (IV, iii).

Valentine. In *Twelfth Night,* a gentleman who rves as Duke Orsino's emissary to Olivia. Valentine ports that he was not admitted to her presence and at she plans to mourn her dead brother for seven ars (I, i).

Valentine. In *The Two Gentlemen of Verona,* ie of the gentlemen of the play's title. Valentine es to the court of the Duke of Milan to acquire orldly experience and falls in love with the Duke's ughter, Silvia. Banished as a result of the conniving his friend and rival, Proteus, Valentine becomes ptain of a band of outlaws, and Silvia, fleeing her me in search of Valentine, is captured by them. hen Proteus rescues her and then threatens to rape r, Valentine comes to Silvia's assistance and ultiately wins her hand. He forgives his friend's eachery.

Valentini, Domenico. See ITALY.

Valeria. In *Coriolanus,* a friend of Virgilia. Durg a visit to Virgilia, Valeria praises Marcius' son, ings news of the siege of Corioli, and tries unccessfully to persuade her friend to leave the ouse (I, iii). In V, iii, she accompanies Volumnia d Virgilia when they plead with Coriolanus to are Rome.

Valerius. In *The Two Noble Kinsmen,* a Theban obleman. He announces to Arcite and Palamon the nminence of war with Athens (I, ii).

Valpy, Richard (1754–1836). Schoolmaster and lapter. A graduate of Pembroke, Oxford, possessor f M.A., B.D., and D.D. degrees, and a noted antiuarian as well, Valpy was headmaster of the Readg School from 1781 to 1831, and in that period ised its standards immeasurably. He was an inired and dedicated teacher and adapted English, atin, and Greek plays for presentation by his boys n important school occasions. Usually they were mited to performance at the town hall, for the benfit of local charities, but his *King John* was prented at Covent Garden in 1803. He also adapted hakespeare's *3 Henry VI* as *The Roses; or King lenry the Sixth; an Historical Tragedy* (1795); another adaptation was *The Merchant of Venice, a omedy* (1802). [*Dictionary of National Biography,* 892; George C. Branam, *Eighteenth-Century Adaptations of Shakespearean Tragedy,* 1956.]

Vanbrugh, Violet (1867–1942). Actress. Born Viot Augusta Mary Barnes, Miss Vanbrugh made her rst appearance on the stage in *Faust and Loose* in 1886 at Toole's Theatre. In 1892 a chance meeting with Henry Irving resulted in her understudying Ellen Terry in his production of *Henry VIII.* In 1893 she understudied Ada Rehan at Augustin Daly's Theatre, and in 1893/94 played Olivia in *Twelfth Night.* She married Arthur Bourchier, a member of Daly's company, in 1894 and moved with him to the Royalty Theatre when Bourchier became its manager. In 1906 she acted Lady Macbeth to her husband's Macbeth at the Stratford Memorial Theatre and again at the Garrick Theatre, London. In subsequent years she portrayed Beatrice, Queen Katherine (for Sir Herbert Beerbohm Tree), and Mistress Ford (to Ellen Terry's Mistress Page in 1911). Of her many parts, Queen Katherine and Mistress Ford won her her greatest successes.

In 1937 she and her sister Dame Irene Vanbrugh (d. 1949) opened an open-air theatre in Regent Park. Of her films, *Pygmalion* (1938) is most notable. Miss Vanbrugh was a pioneer in advocating a theatrical career for serious, well-brought-up young women, and her reminiscences, *Dare To Be Wise* (1925), offered advice to young actresses. The Vanbrugh Theatre, the private theatre of the Royal Academy of Dramatic Art, was opened in 1954 and was named in honor of both Vanbrugh sisters. (*Dictionary of National Biography, 1941–1950,* 1959.)

Van Buchell, Arend. See Johannes DEWITT.

Vandenhoff, John M. (1790–1861). Actor. Born in Salisbury of parents of Dutch extraction, Vandenhoff was educated by the Jesuits with a view to the priesthood. After teaching classics for a year, he took to the stage and in 1808 made his first appearance at Salisbury, followed by appearances with Edmund Kean at Exeter and Weymouth. In 1813/4 he appeared as King Henry in *1 Henry IV* in a production at Bath, and later joined a troupe with headquarters at Liverpool. Billed as Vandenhoff from Liverpool, he made his London debut at Covent Garden as Lear in 1820, performing also Sir Giles Overreach and Coriolanus. He left Covent Garden after a short period, in disgust over his treatment by Macready, and made several tours. Among his successful Shakespearean roles were Macbeth, Cassius, and Othello. His Coriolanus was especially popular. He played Hamlet in 1834, and Faulconbridge, Hotspur, and Cassius in 1838. In 1837 he visited America. In the following years he appeared mostly in the provinces; on one occasion at Edinburgh as Wolsey with Henry Irving in an 1857 production of *Henry VIII.* He made his farewell appearances at Liverpool in 1858 as Brutus and Wolsey. His children, George (1813–1885) and Charlotte Elizabeth (1818–1860), also pursued careers in the theatre and played in many Shakespearean productions; Charlotte Elizabeth was especially successful as Juliet and Cordelia.

Although Vandenhoff enjoyed some popular acclaim, his critical reception was far from satisfactory. His Coriolanus was considered imitative of Kemble's, and his Othello and Macbeth deficient in pathos and passion. As Iago, Vandenhoff was said to have assumed a "mask of impulsive lightheartedness and *bonhomie*" and a "detestable gaiety in his soliloquies and asides." [*Dictionary of National Biography*, 1885– ; *Oxford Companion to the Theatre*, Phyllis Hartnoll, ed., 1951.]

variorum editions. Editions of a literary work which contain, in addition to the text, a collection of annotation and comment by earlier editors and critics as well as a list of all variant readings in the text. There have been four variorum editions of Shakespeare's text, the first of which was published in 1803 under the editorship of Isaac Reed, although the major share of the work was done by George STEEVENS, who died in 1800. The First Variorum consisted of 21 volumes, based primarily on Steevens' early editions of the plays alone. (He was so contemptuous of the poems and sonnets that he refused to include them in any of his editions.) Steevens' edition also contained a glossary, notes by Dr. Johnson and himself, and extensive contributions from Edmund Malone, George Chalmers, and Richard Farmer. The Second Variorum, a reprint of the First, was published in 1813.

The Third Variorum, known as the Boswell-Malone Variorum, was printed in 1821. Based on the text of Edmund MALONE, who died in 1812, it was edited by James Boswell the younger. This edition, one of the monuments of Shakespeare scholarship, includes three volumes of prefatory matter, including prefaces from most of the 18th-century editions of the plays; Richard Farmer's *Essay on the Learning of Shakespeare;* Rowe's *Life of Shakespeare;* Malone's *Life of Shakespeare* and his *History of the Stage;* extracts from the *Stationers' Register;* and Henslowe's diary, as well as numerous, invaluable notes to the plays.

The scope and size of the Fourth (or New) Variorum may be gauged by the fact that although it was begun in 1871 and work on it has continued steadily, it is still incomplete. The New Variorum was initiated by the American scholar Horace H. Furness and continued by his son H. H. Furness, Jr. In 1936 the project came under the supervision and sponsorship of the Modern Language Association of America. The general editor from 1936 was Joseph Quincy Adams. Adams was succeeded in 1947 by Hyder Rollins, who acted as general editor until his death in 1958. The present (1966) general editor is James G. McManaway.

The volumes of the New Variorum are as follows:

Vol.		
I	Romeo and Juliet	1871
II	Macbeth	1873
III & IV	Hamlet	1877
V	King Lear	1880
VI	Othello	1886
VII	The Merchant of Venice	1888
VIII	As You Like It	1890
IX	The Tempest	1892
X	A Midsummer Night's Dream	189
XI	The Winter's Tale	189
XII	Much Ado About Nothing	189
XIII	Twelfth Night	190
XIV	Love's Labour's Lost	190
XV	Antony and Cleopatra	190
XVI	Richard III	190
XVII	Julius Caesar	191
XVIII	Cymbeline	191
XIX	King John	191
XX	Coriolanus	192
XXI	1 Henry IV (Supplement in 1956)	193
XXII	The Poems	193
XXIII	2 Henry IV	194
XXIV & XXV	Sonnets	194
XXVI	Troilus and Cressida	195
XXVII	Richard II	195

Forthcoming titles are *Titus Andronicus*, T. F Price, ed., and *Comedy of Errors*, T. W. Baldwin, e

Varrius. In *Antony and Cleopatra*, a friend t Pompey. In II, i, Varrius informs Pompey of An tony's imminent arrival in Rome.

Varrius. In *Measure for Measure*, a friend of Duk Vincentio. Although Varrius appears twice (IV, and V, i), he does not speak. His name is omitte from the list of actors in the Folio text.

Varro and Claudius. In *Julius Caesar*, two servan of Brutus. Varro and Claudius sleep in their master tent on the night before Philippi (IV, iii).

Varro's Servants. In *Timon of Athens*, two serv ants of a lord to whom Timon owes money. The try vainly to collect the debt.

Vaughan, Sir **Thomas** (d. 1483). An ardent York ist. Vaughan waged many battles for Edward IV who made him counselor to his heir, Prince Edwar After the king died, Vaughan, Sir Richard Grey and Earl Rivers were escorting the young Edwar V to London for his coronation when they wer arrested by Richard, duke of Gloucester. The thre men were subsequently executed for treason. I *Richard III*, Vaughan joins his associates in cursin the usurper and his fellows: "You live that sha cry woe for this hereafter" (III, iii).

Vaughan Williams, Ralph. See MUSIC BASED O SHAKESPEARE: *20th century*.

Vaux, Sir **Nicholas** (d. 1523). Courtier and soldie Son of Sir William Vaux, he was restored by Henr VII to the estates stripped from his father. I *Henry VIII*, II, i, Buckingham is delivered into hi charge by Sir Thomas Lovell for execution.

Vaux, Sir **William** (d. 1471). A loyal Lancastria who was killed at Tewkesbury. In *2 Henry V* Vaux informs Queen Margaret that Cardinal Beau fort is dying (III, ii).

Venice, Duke of. In *The Merchant of Venice*, merciful and kind judge who presides at Antonio trial. The Duke of Venice warns Antonio that Shy lock is an inhuman wretch (IV, i).

Ventidius. In *Antony and Cleopatra*, a general i Antony's army. Having defeated the Parthians i battle, Ventidius, aware that Antony might be jeal ous of his general's success, does not pursue them

Ventidius. In *Timon of Athens*, a man who Timon rescues from debtors' prison (I, i). Late when Timon is pressed by creditors, Ventidius, al ough he has recently inherited his father's great tate, refuses to help his former benefactor.

Venus and Adonis. A narrative poem by Shakeeare.

Text. The best text is that of the First Quarto, refully printed from what was probably the poet's IR COPY. Its title page reads:

Venus and Adonis Vilia miretur vulgus: mihi flauus Apollo Pocula Castalia plena ministret aqua. ["Let the base crowd admire what is low but let golden-haired Apollo serve me cups filled with water from the Muse's spring."] London Imprinted by Richard Field, and are to be sold at the signe of the white Greyhound in Paules Church-yard. 1593.

Richard Field was not only the printer of *Venus d Adonis* but its publisher also. He was the son of Stratford tanner. Undoubtedly he and the poet ere friends, and the excellence of the printed text tests to their close cooperation on this Quarto and e first edition of *Lucrece* the following year. The dedication reads:

To the Right Honourable Henrie Wriothesley, Earle of Southampton, and Baron of Titchfield.

Right Honourable, I know not how I shall offend in dedicating my vnpolisht lines to your Lordship, nor how the worlde will censure mee for choosing so strong a proppe to support so weake a burthen, onelye if your Honour seeme but pleased, I account my selfe highly praised, and vowe to take aduantage of all idle houres, till I haue honoured you with some grauer labour. But if the first heire of my inuention proue deformed, I shall be sorie it had so noble a god-father: and neuer after eare so barren a land, for feare it yeeld me still so bad a haruest, I leaue it to your Honourable suruey, and your Honor to your hearts content which I wish may alwaies answere your owne wish, and the worlds hopefull expectation. Your Honors in all dutie, William Shakespeare.

TITLE PAGE OF *Venus and Adonis* (1593).

VENVS

AND ADONIS

Vilia miretur vulgus: mihi flauus Apollo Pocula Castalia plena ministret aqua.

LONDON

Imprinted by Richard Field, and are to be sold at the signe of the white Greyhound in Paules Church-yard.

1593.

The phrase "first heire of my inuention" may refer either to Shakespeare's first major poetic effort, or to his first published poem.

A second edition was published in 1594 by John Harrison, who had secured the copyright from Field. Field remained the printer, however. The poem was reprinted—this time in octavo rather than quarto—in 1595. The poem's popularity is attested to by the numerous subsequent reprints, in 1596, 1599, 1602, 1610, 1617, and 1620.

Date. *Venus and Adonis* was entered in the Stationers' Register in April 1593. The generally accepted conjecture is that the poem was written shortly before this date, during the period August 1592 through April 1593, when the theatres were shut down as a result of the plague.

Sources. The major sources of the poem are the stories of Venus and Adonis and of Hermaphroditus and Salmacia in Ovid's *Metamorphoses*. Shakespeare undoubtedly knew the original, but he was certainly also familiar with Arthur Golding's translation of the *Metamorphoses,* published in 1567. The verse form of *Venus and Adonis* is a six-line stanza rhyming *a b a b c c*, one that had become popular for many different sorts of poems. Spenser had employed it in his elegy on the death of Sir Philip Sidney entitled *Astrophel*, a poem not published until 1595, but probably written as early as 1590. It is also the meter of Thomas Lodge's erotic poem *Scilla's Metamorphoses* (1589), which treats the love of the sea-god Glaucus for the coy Scilla. This poem set the style that became the favorite of the cultivated gentlemen of the court, the inns of court, and of the universities. They reserved their highest enthusiasm for the sensuous love stories about mythological figures drawn from the works of Ovid. Lodge's descriptive title of his poem contains the phrase "very fit for young courtiers to peruse and coy dames to remember." Marlowe's *Hero and Leander* (1593) is the best of the Ovidian romances. It contains the most successful combination of the genre's distinctive characteristics: descriptions of natural beauty, voluptuous development of erotic situations, and an ornate style. These are also the elements of which Shakespeare has composed his poem.

"The Sheepheards Song of Venus and Adonis" by H. C. (probably Henry Chettle), first published in *England's Helicon* (1600), is undoubtedly not a source but a copy of Shakespeare's poem.

Comment. The influence of Ovid appears in almost every line of *Venus and Adonis.* Throughout the Renaissance he was the "amorous school master," and the "amorous" element was distinctly physical. Venus offers all the delights of sexual love with unabashed frankness. As a background to her attempts at seduction, Shakespeare paints many pictures of life in the open as he had known it at Stratford and its environs: the coursing of "poor Wat" the hare, for example, is for many readers the finest passage in the poem (679–708). There are also many little vignettes of animals he had lovingly observed:

> Like a dive-dapper peering through a wave,
> Who, being look'd on, ducks as quickly in.
> (86–87)

or

> Like a milch doe, whose swelling dugs do ache,
> Hasting to feed her fawn hid in some brake.
> (875–876)

Most striking of all its features is its rhetorical ornamentation. It is filled with encomia, complaints, diatribes, and declamation. The story is little more than a string upon which Shakespeare hung his rhetorical jewels. One critic has called the poem "a pageant of gesture." The style also is ingeniously wrought with a plethora of antitheses, epigrams, and alternatives. Venus' diatribe against Death (931–954) and her curse of love (1135–1164) are good examples of the florid verse.

Although these outmoded ornaments are not to modern taste, they were greatly admired by the audience for which the poem was written. The enthusiasm with which the work was greeted was intense and prolonged. It went through 10 editions in the space of 10 years. The undergraduates' delight is amusingly satirized by the author of *The Return from Parnassus*, a play presented at Cambridge University in 1601. He puts in the mouth of a foolish undergraduate named Gullio a rhapsody: "Let the duncified world esteem of Spenser and Chaucer. I'll worship sweet master Shakespeare, and, to honor him, will lay his *Venus and Adonis* under my pillow." The praise of more sober critics was sincere and discriminating. For here, for the first time, the poet had given his verses a glow and an animation seldom absent from either his later lyrical or dramatic poetry.—O.J.C.

Bibliography. TEXT: *The Poems*, New Variorum Edition, Hyder Rollins, ed., 1938; *The Poems*, New Arden Edition, F. T. Prince, ed., 1960. COMMENT: Douglas Bush, *Mythology and the Renaissance Tradition in English Poetry*, 1932.

Verdi, Giuseppe (1813–1901). Italian composer. The musical genius of Verdi came to full fruition in his old age with his two great Shakespearean operas, *Falstaff* and *Otello*. *Macbetto*, produced in 1847 at the Pergola in Florence, is a less mature work and suffers from a routine libretto by Piave, but it has many passages of considerable power and is still often performed.

After producing *Aïda* in 1871, Verdi, wealthy and famous, withdrew from musical activity. For 15 years he wrote no more operas, though he made several attempts to write a *King Lear;* a complete libretto of the play has been found in Verdi's handwriting. He was drawn out of his retirement by a splendid libretto that Arrigo Boïto (1842–1918) had written from Shakespeare's *Othello*, closely following the play. The opera is a lyric drama in four acts, without an overture. Shakespeare's first act, set in Venice, is omitted; the entire action takes place in Cyprus. Presented at La Scala in 1887, *Otello* was an immediate success.

Falstaff, which appeared six years later, is a product of the same collaboration. Boïto's libretto, based on *The Merry Wives of Windsor* and passages fr[o] *Henry IV*, is written in three acts of two scenes ea[ch] and is a masterful adaptation. The music of Verd[i's] first comic opera combines complexity of structu[re] with transparency of texture in a brilliant but m[el]low and sunny score. [Christopher Wilson, *Shak[e]speare and Music*, 1922.]

Verges. In *Much Ado About Nothing*, a headb[or]ough and Dogberry's partner. In III, iii, Verges [as]sures Dogberry that the watchmen are good a[nd] true, and proffers advice while the Constable charg[es] them with their night duties. Later, Verges, "a go[od] old man" who "will be talking," announces to Le[o]nato the arrest of Borachio and Conrade, and wh[en] the rogues are examined, he is present to affirm Do[g]berry's conclusions.

Vergil. Full Latin name **Publius Vergilius Ma[ro]** (70–19 B.C.). Roman poet. In Elizabethan Englan[d] Vergil was regarded as the supreme classical po[et]. The basis of the esteem in which he was held was [his] great epic poem the *Aeneid*, the sixth book of whi[ch] was popularly supposed to have contained a prop[h]ecy of the birth of Christ. The *Aeneid* was tran[s]lated into the Scottish dialect in 1513 by Bish[op] Gavin Douglas (c. 1474–1522). Books II and IV we[re] translated (1557) into English by Henry Howa[rd], earl of SURREY, and became the first English poet

TITLE PAGE OF PHAER'S TRANSLATION OF VERGIL'S *Aeneid* (1584).

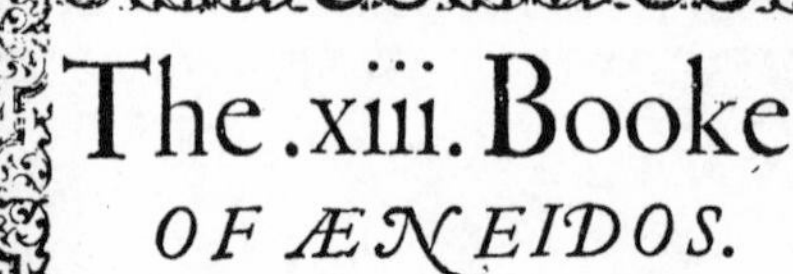

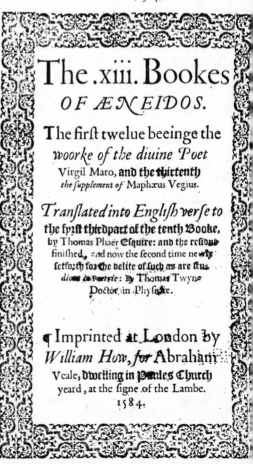

The .xiii. Bookes
OF ÆNEIDOS.
The first twelue beeinge the woorke of the diuine Poet Virgil Maro, and the thirtenth the supplement of Maphæus Vegius.
Translated into English verse to the first thirdpart of the tenth Booke, by Thomas Phaer Esquire: and the residue finished, and now the second time newly setforth for the delite of such as are studious in Poetrie: By Thomas Twyne Doctor in Physicke.
¶ Imprinted at London by William How, for Abraham Veale, dwelling in Paules Church yeard, at the signe of the Lambe.
1584.

. blank verse; the entire work was Englished by homas Phaer and Thomas Twine (1543–1613) as *he Whole XII Bookes of the Aeneidos* (1573). ıakespeare's allusions to the *Aeneid* usually refer to ıe episodes of the destruction of Troy in Book II or the story of Dido in Book IV. The most famous of ıese is the Player's speech in *Hamlet* (II, ii, 472–36), recounting the sack of Troy and the death of riam. See First Player.

Verity, Arthur Wilson (1863–1937). Scholar. Eduıted at Trinity College, Cambridge, Verity won the arness Prize in 1885 for his essay *The Influence of hristopher Marlowe on Shakspere's Earlier Style* 1886). There followed the editing of the works of :veral playwrights: Thomas Heywood, Nathan ield, Sir George Etheredge. But Verity's most imortant editorial work was done on Shakespeare and Iilton. For the Pitt Press series he edited 13 plays, ıch in a single volume (1890–1905), and he proided various works of Milton with extensive annoıtion; his edition of *Paradise Lost* (1910) is the most :arned in modern times.

Vernon. In *1 Henry VI*, Vernon plucks a white ose in the Temple Garden, thus allying himself vith the Yorkist faction (II, iv). After a quarrel vith Basset, a Lancastrian, Vernon asks King Henry ermission to meet Basset in personal combat but refused (IV, i). This character may have been ıodeled on Sir Richard Vernon (d. 1452), speaker f the house of commons in the Leicester parliaıent. [W. H. Thomson, *Shakespeare's Characters: 1 Historical Dictionary*, 1951.]

Vernon, Elizabeth. See Elizabeth, countess of outhampton.

Vernon, Sir Richard. In *1 Henry IV*, a member of Iotspur's rebellion. Vernon cooperates with the arl of Worcester when the latter decides not to elay Henry's offer of peace to Hotspur, and is ubsequently captured at the battle of Shrewsbury nd executed. Historically, it was Baron Shipbrook, ir Richard's second son, who joined the rebellion gainst Henry, helped to lead the forces at Shrewsury, and was captured and beheaded. [W. H. Thomson, *Shakespeare's Characters: A Historical Dictionary*, 1951.]

verse tests. A means by which an attempt is made o establish the authenticity or chronology of poetiıal works. As applied to Shakespeare, a statistical nalysis is made of each play, tabulating the variaions in the length of lines, the number of syllables, he distribution of stresses and pauses, and the proortion of blank verse to prose and rhyme. The reults are then compared to facts as established by xternal evidence, and conclusions are drawn conerning the period of Shakespeare's life during which he play was probably written. The evidence gathered from verse tests is also used to establish authenicity. The technique of the verse test did not come nto general use until the middle of the 19th century, ut groundwork had been laid about a century beore. In "Remarks on Shakespeare," an appendix to he sixth edition of Thomas Edwards' *Canons of Criticism* (1758), Richard Roderick called attention o three peculiarities of *Henry VIII* as compared with Shakespeare's other plays: (1) the frequency of edundant syllables—twice the number in any other play; (2) the placing of the caesura, or main pause, later in the line than in the other plays; and (3) the disproportionately large number of inverted feet. These facts were simply noted without any attempt to draw conclusions as to the authorship or the chronology.

Edmund Malone, however, concerned himself with the latter in his "An Attempt to ascertain the Order in which the Plays attributed to Shakspeare were written," published in the second edition (1778) of Steevens' Shakespeare. For the most part Malone relied on external evidence, but he did note the high proportion of rhymes as a sign of earlier work. A century was to elapse before the subject was pursued further. In 1857 Charles Bathurst published his *Remarks on the Differences in Shakespeare's Versification in . . . His Life*, the first work in which the whole subject of Shakespeare's versification was examined in relation to the chronology of the plays; Bathurst noted in particular the gradual change in redundant final syllables and in the coincidence of the rhythmical pauses with line endings.

The subject now attracted the attention of F. J. Furnivall who, in his prospectus for the New Shakspere Society, stated that ascertaining the order of the plays by metrical tests would be one of the principal objects of the Society. Papers on the subject were read to the Society by Furnivall himself and by F. G. Fleay, J. K. Ingram, and F. S. Pulling (see the Society's *Transactions*, 1873, 1874, 1879, and 1885). Fleay made an important contribution with the statistical table in which he enumerated for each play the total number of lines together with a breakdown into blank verse, prose, and rhyme; abnormally short and long lines; and lines with redundant syllables. After presenting the table to the Society in 1874, he reprinted it with corrections in his *Shakespeare Manual* (1876) and made further corrections for inclusion in C. M. Ingleby's *Shakespeare, the Man and the Book* (2 vols., 1877–1881). Despite inaccuracies which still remained, his table continued to be the standard guide for many years. Fleay was concerned less with chronology than with using the verse test to reject as spurious plays and passages formerly attributed to Shakespeare. Hence he became one of the first of the "disintegrators," to be followed by such scholars as J. M. Robertson who used the verse test for the same purpose. (See disintegration.) Meanwhile, this technique was adopted by several German scholars—Hertzberg, König, Conrad—who concentrated on a portion of the canon or on an individual play in order to present a more accurate analysis. G. G. Gervinus in his *Shakespeare* (4 vols., 1849–1850; Eng. trans., 2 vols., 1862) used the verse test along with other techniques to divide Shakespeare's work into three distinct periods and to trace the development of his art. Furnivall was influenced by this work and, in a long introduction to the English translations, summarized and developed further the theories of Gervinus. The substance of this introduction was reprinted in the Leopold Shakespeare (1877). Among scholars the verse test no longer commands the respect that it once did; increased awareness of the complicated factors involved in the transmission and publication of the text makes it hazardous to place too much reliance on this one test. For a balanced discussion and the most reliable tables to date, see E. K. Chambers, *William Shakespeare: A Study of Facts and Problems* (2 vols., 1930), Vol. I, 243–274.

VERSE TABLE

	1. TOTAL LINES	2. LINES OF PROSE	3. LINES OF BLANK VERSE	4. LINES OF RHYMED VERSE	5. % RHYME TO VERSE	6. % RUN-ON LINES	7. % BROKEN-END SPEECHES	8. FEMININE ENDINGS	9. LIGHT ENDINGS	10. WEAK ENDINGS
1 H. VI	2677	2	2357	318	10	10	1	191	3	1
2 H. VI	3162	551	2515	96	3	11	1	332	2	1
3 H. VI	2904	3	2773	128	3	10	1	366	3	0
R III	3619	83	3384	152	4	13	3	638	4	0
Titus	2523	41	2352	130	4	12	3	200	5	0
C of E	1777	244	1155	378	19	13	1	198	0	0
Shrew	2647	625	1871	151	4	8	4	371	1	1
Two G	2292	654	1510	128	7	12	6	269	0	0
L L L	2785	1051	584	1150	62	18	10	26	3	0
R & J	3050	455	2101	466	17	14	15	168	6	1
R II	2757	0	2228	529	19	20	7	258	4	0
M N D	2174	470	746	798	43	13	17	59	0	1
K John	2570	0	2438	132	5	18	13	151	7	0
M of V	2658	633	1883	142	5	22	22	325	6	1
1 H. IV	3176	1493	1607	76	3	23	14	92	5	2
2 H. IV	3446	1813	1420	72	3	21	17	221	1	0
Much Ado	2825	2105	644	76	5	19	21	145	1	1
H. V	3381	1440	1504	58	3	22	18	336	2	0
M W W	3018	2664	214	26	6	20	21	54	1	0
J C	2477	176	2269	32	1	19	20	413	10	0
A Y L I	2856	1659	926	217	6	17	22	230	2	0
T N	2690	1752	762	176	14	15	36	167	3	1
Hamlet	3929	1211	2444	135	3	23	52	528	8	0
T & C	3496	1188	2065	186	9	27	31	463	6	0
All's Well	2966	1478	1203	279	19	28	74	349	11	2
Oth	3316	685	2528	103	3	20	41	679	2	0
M M	2820	1154	1577	89	4	23	51	377	7	0
Timon	2374	701	1513	160	9	33	63	334	16	5
Lear	3328	925	2234	169	3	29	61	580	5	1
Mac	2106	158	1692	108	6	37	77	420	21	2
A & C	3059	287	2732	40	1	43	78	666	71	28
Cor	3406	829	2549	28	1	46	79	710	60	44
Per	1140[a]	337	781	22	3	25	71[b]	171	15	5
Cym	3339	526	2607	122	3	46	85	799	78	52
W T	3074	876	2107	59	0	38	88	675	57	43
Tem	2062	464	1445	64	0.1	42	85	472	42	25
H. VIII	1167[a]	7	1154	6	0.5	39	72	374	45	37
T N K	1131[a]	57	1050	24	2	30		312	50	34

[a] Shakespeare's part [b] Bradley's figure

Cols. 1–4. These figures are Fleay's as corrected by Chambers. For some plays the figures from columns 2, 3, and 4 if added together will not equal the figure in column 1. The difference represents lines of a metric quality that is distinct from the rest of the play. Chambers calls these lines "external." Examples of external lines are Pistol's bombast in *2 Henry IV*, *Henry V*, and *The Merry Wives*, the player's speech from *Hamlet*, choruses, interludes, prologues, epilogues, etc.

Col. 5. These figures are from G. König's *Der Vers in Shakespeares Dramen* (1888). They represent the proportion of rhymed five-foot lines to all five-foot lines.

Col. 6. From König. A run-on line in poetry is the opposite of an end-stopped line. The following example from *The Tempest* illustrates both:

Pros. Now does my project gather to a head: (*end-stopped*)
My charms crack not; my spirits obey; and time (*run-on*)
Goes upright with his carriage. How's the day?
(V, i, 1–3)

Col. 7. From König. A broken-end speech is one that ends in mid-line, such as:

Pros. A devil, a born devil, on whose nature
Nurture can never stick; on whom my pains,
Humanely taken, all, all lost, quite lost;
And as with age his body uglier grows,
So his mind cankers. I will plague them all,
Even to roaring.
(*The Tempest*, IV, i, 188–193)

Col. 8. Fleay's figures. A line with a feminine ending has an extra, unstressed syllable at the end, such as "How weary, stale, flat and unprofitable."

Cols. 9, 10. J. K. Ingram's figures from the *Transactions* of the New Shakspere Society

874). Lines with light or weak endings are exgerated forms of run-on lines. Light endings are onosyllables other than conjunctions and prepositions that are lightly stressed due to the sense of the etry. Weak endings are monosyllabic conjunctions and prepositions which Ingram termed roclitic."

Had I been any god of power, I would (*light*)
Have sunk the sea within the earth or ere
It should the good ship so have swallow'd and (*weak*)
The fraughting souls within her.
(*The Tempest*, I, ii, 10–13)

Vestris, Elizabeth (1797–1856). Actress and mangeress. Known to her company as Madame Vestris, ucia Elizabeth Bartolozzi was born in London, the ughter of a famous Italian engraver. After a rudientary education in music she married at the age of 5 Auguste Armand Vestris (1788–1825), a dancer d ballet-master at the King's Theatre, who left her 1820. She made her singing debut in 1815 at the ing's in *Il Ratto di Proserpina* and was an imediate success. In 1824, she played Ariel to lacready's Prospero, Luciana in *Comedy of Errors,* d Mistresses Ford and Page.

In 1831 she opened, in partnership with Maria oote who left shortly thereafter, the Olympic heatre where a series of extravaganzas, including e *Olympic Revels*, was staged by Planché. Among e comedians and burlesque actors she engaged for er company was Charles Mathews, whom she maried in 1838. In the following year, the couple underok the management of Covent Garden. See Charles IATHEWS.

Vice. A character in morality plays. Vice was origally the abstraction of all the vices, and, as such, a ompanion to the Devil whom he plagued and often rove off the stage with his dagger of lath. In the ourse of time he became a sardonic intriguer who, nder such names as Sensual Suggestion, Ill Repute, mbidexter, and Iniquity, deceived and seduced frail umanity. He scoffed with cynical amusement at the agic events on stage. Traces of his character can be een in two of the foremost Shakespearean villains, go and Richard III. See MEDIEVALISM IN SHAKEPEARE. [Bernard Spivack, *Shakespeare and the Allegory of Evil*, 1958.]

Victor, Benjamin (d. 1778). Dramatist. Victor dapted Shakespeare's *The Two Gentlemen of erona* for the stage in 1762. His alterations are, on the hole, slight ones designed to clarify certain obscure otives of the characters. This version was first produced on December 22, 1762 at the Drury Lane in he first production given any version during the 8th century; it was also the first recorded performnce ever given Shakespeare's play. The original play vas not produced until 1784 (see THE TWO GENTLEMEN OF VERONA: *Stage History*). Victor was treasrer of Drury Lane from 1760 until his death, and is he author of *The History of the Theatres of London and Dublin, from the Year 1730.* [*With*] *An Annual Register of Plays from 1712*, 2 vols. (1761), *The History of the Theatres of London, from the Year 1760* (1771), as well as a fictionalized account of contemporary scandal, *The Widow of the Wood* (1755). [C. B. Hogan, *Shakespeare in the Theatre 1701–1800*, 2 vols., 1952, 1957.]

Vigny, Alfred de. See FRANCE.

Vincentio. In *Measure for Measure*, the Duke of Vienna. Having failed to enforce Vienna's laws against immorality, Vincentio relinquishes his powers to Angelo, "a man of stricture and firm abstinence," and gives out the word that he has gone to Poland. In reality, he disguises himself as a friar called Lodowick and remains in Vienna to observe Angelo's conduct in office. When Angelo promises to spare Claudio's life if his sister Isabella will give herself to him, it is Friar Lodowick who devises the plan that saves both the condemned man and Isabella's honor. At the end of the play he orders Angelo to marry Mariana, who has begged for his life, and declares his own love for Isabella.

Vincentio. In *The Taming of the Shrew*, an old gentleman from Pisa, Lucentio's father. While traveling to Padua to visit his son, Vincentio learns from Petruchio that Lucentio has married Bianca. In a confrontation with his impersonator, the Pedant, Vincentio is almost jailed, but Lucentio arrives in time to acknowledge his real father.

Viola. In *Twelfth Night*, Sebastian's twin sister. Cast ashore in a strange land, Viola recognizes the need for self-protection and adopts the disguise of a boy. Viola acts the part of the page Cesario with obvious delight, and although she has fallen in love with the Duke, she faithfully carries his messages to Olivia. Keenly aware of the absurdity of the passions loosed in Illyria, and in contrast to the sentimental Orsino and Olivia, Viola recognizes the illogic of her love. She accepts it with simplicity, leaving its resolution to time: "O Time, thou must untangle this, not I! It is too hard a knot for me to untie!" Viola's patience is rewarded when, in the end, Orsino marries her. [Joseph H. Summers, "The Masks of Twelfth Night," *University of Kansas City Review*, XXII, 1955.]

Violenta. In *All's Well That Ends Well*, a friend and neighbor of Diana's mother. Violenta appears only in III, v, and does not speak.

Virgilia. In *Coriolanus*, the protagonist's gentle and loyal wife, who quietly keeps her house, awaiting her husband's return from war. In V, iii, Virgilia goes with her son and mother-in-law to Coriolanus' tent and helps to dissuade him from leading a Volscian attack on Rome.

Visscher, Claes Janszoon de (1586–1652). Dutch engraver, whose *View of London* was long regarded as the most reliable guide to the shapes and locations of the Elizabethan theatres. There are two extant copies of the Visscher engraving, one in the Folger Library bearing the signature "Visscher excudit." The other copy, in the British Museum, is signed "J. C. Visscher delineavit" and "Ludovicus Hondius lusit" and dated 1616. In both copies the Globe is pictured as an octagonal building, although it is slightly larger in the British Museum print than in that of the Folger. The Folger print is probably a later copy of that in the British Museum.

The traditional view of the Globe as an octagon rests upon Visscher's prints, but Visscher's authority as a dependable source has been undermined by recent evidence indicating that in his engravings he

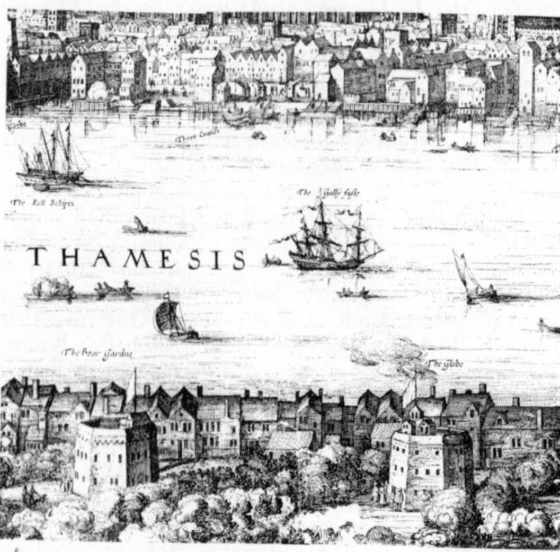

PART OF VISSCHER'S VIEW OF LONDON SHOWING THE GLOBE AND THE BEAR GARDEN. (FOLGER SHAKESPEARE LIBRARY)

borrowed extensively from the earlier maps of John Norden and Ralph Agas. This fact, together with the many inaccuracies in Visscher's representation of Southwark, calls into question the reliability of his picture of the Globe. [I. A. Shapiro, "The Bankside Theatres: Early Engravings," *Shakespeare Survey 1*, 1948; Irwin Smith, *Shakespeare's Globe Playhouse*, 1956.]

Voltaire. Pen name of **François-Marie Arouet** (1694–1778). French satirist, philosopher, historian, dramatist, and poet. Voltaire was an exile in England when he first mentioned Shakespeare (*Essai sur la poésie épique*, 1727). Credit must go to three subsequent works—the preface to *Oedipe* (1730), the *Discours sur la tragédie* (1731), and *Lettres philosophiques* (1734; *v.* no. XVIII)—for introducing the "essential" Shakespeare, the Shakespeare of the tragedies, to continental Europe. *That* they did. Before Voltaire, the Elizabethan dramatist was virtually unknown except to his countrymen; after Voltaire, he was forever free from the bonds of insularity. See FRANCE.

Nor did the introduction itself, as far as it went, display "the petty cavils of a petty mind" (the words were Samuel Johnson's at a much later date). Voltaire's oft-repeated appraisal of Shakespeare as a forceful genius, natural and sublime, but with not one grain of taste, actually reflected Dryden's and Pope's, Lord Chesterfield's and Lord Bolingbroke's, in short, a consensus of British opinion under the Restoration. He even conceded, graciously enough for a French classicist, that Shakespeare's "flaws" were only a ransom paid to the "barbarity" of the times. Further references to the barbarian's "coarse but appealing irregularities" clearly suggest that might teach the civilized a thing or two; so that, a very real sense, Voltaire was out to prescribe so of Shakespeare's strong honey, while measuring hi self, through a series of tests, how much of a d French tragedy could stand (*Eryphile* vs. *Haml* 1732; *Zaïre* vs. *Othello*, 1732; *Brutus*, 1731; *La M de César*, 1735).

Overzealous responses played havoc with this c culated boldness. The prefaces to *Mérope* (1744) a *Sémiramis* (1749) betray Voltaire's incipient fe lest the French classical tradition be subverted disfigured at the hands of the "Anglomaniacs." Fe gave way to panic in his *Appel à toutes les natio de l'Europe* (1761), prompted by an anonymo (British?) encomium of Shakespeare at the exper of Corneille; and panic turned to hysterical fu when Pierre Le Tourneur, Shakespeare's new tra lator, leveled a thinly veiled attack against the se appointed "censors" whose crusades for freedom d not extend to the realm of art. Voltaire, more us to stinging than to being stung, arraigned "the scou drel" before the French Academy (*Lettre à l'Acad mie Française*, 1776). Not even the "apotheosis" te dered him at the performance of his last trage (*Irène*, 1778) could placate his feelings. Beneath th emotional turmoil, however, his thought remain too constant for his own good. "I do *not* despi Shakespeare," he had written Horace Walpole (Ju 17, 1768) in despairing self-defense against the show of broadsides that poured from abroad, especial Britain, after 1761. Indeed he did not—and all to some pathos attaches to the fact that the rise Shakespeare's star, having escaped his control, ca to portend the decline and fall of his critical empi [Thomas R. Lounsbury, *Shakespeare and Voltair* 1902; Gustave Lanson's critical edition of Voltair *Lettres philosophiques*, 1909.]—J-A.B.

Voltimand. In *Hamlet*, one of the two courtie whom Claudius dispatches to Norway in a diploma attempt to prevent Fortinbras' invasion of Denma (I, ii). The mission is successful.

Volumnia. In *Coriolanus*, the protagonist's do ineering mother. Sharing his loathing for th plebeians, Volumnia advises Coriolanus neverthele to hide his true feelings until the people have co firmed his appointment as consul. In V, iii, sh goes with Coriolanus' wife and son to his ten where she persuades him not to lead the Volscia against Rome.

Volumnius. In *Julius Caesar*, a friend and follow of Brutus and Cassius. When Brutus appeals to h old schoolmate to hold Brutus' sword while he ru on it, Volumnius refuses, saying, "That's not an offi for a friend." With the approach of the victo Volumnius flees (V, v). Plutarch made selectio from Volumnius' own written account of the dea of Brutus.

Vortigern and Rowena. See William Henry IR LAND.

W

Wadeson, Anthony. See Look About You.

Wagner, Richard (1813–1883). German composer. is only known contribution to Shakespearean music the two-act opera *Das Liebesverbot*, which was ised on *Measure for Measure*. It was performed ıly twice, in 1836, at the theatre of Magdeburg, here the composer was musical director. The score as not published until 1922–1923; in 1923 the opera as revived in Germany. The music is bright and gh-spirited; the libretto is based rather loosely on ie play and Wagner shifted the locale from Vienna Sicily. [Christopher Wilson, *Shakespeare and Iusic*, 1922.]

Walker, Alice. Scholar. In 1936 Miss Walker lited, in collaboration with G. D. Willcock, George uttenham's *The Arte of English Poesie*. Her most nportant work is *Textual Problems of the First olio* (1953), in which attention is focused on six lays: *Richard III*, *King Lear*, *Troilus and Cressida*, *Henry IV*, *Hamlet*, and *Othello*. Her thesis is that ie text of the First Folio was based on quartos hich had been collated with manuscripts having ome degree of authenticity. This thesis had previusly been set forth regarding the first three plays ientioned and a fair degree of acceptance obtained. liss Walker extended the argument to include the ther three. One of the provocative conclusions eached is that modern editors are justified in emendıg the text with much more freedom than they have itherto been accustomed. In 1960 Miss Walker gave ie British Academy's Annual Shakespeare Lecture n "Edward Capell and his Edition of *Shakespeare*," which has been reprinted in *Studies in Shakespeare*, 'eter Alexander, ed. (1964).

Walker, Henry (d. 1616). The London minstrel rom whom Shakespeare purchased the Blackfriars Gate-House in 1613. A native of Herefordshire near Vales, Walker was a member of the Minstrels', or Iusicians', company of London, the only organizaon licensed to present public performances of music ı London. He had purchased the gatehouse from Iatthew Bacon for £100 in 1604, although he does ot appear to have occupied it until some time later. Leslie Hotson, *Shakespeare's Sonnets Dated*, 1949.]

Walkley, Thomas (fl. 1619–1658). Bookseller who ublished the First Quarto (1622) of *Othello*. Walkey was admitted as a freeman of the Stationers' Company in 1618. He entered *Othello* in the Stationrs' Register on October 6, 1621 and published it in he following year, providing a text superior, acording to one recent editor, to that of the First 'olio. Walkley prefaced the text with an epistle from the Stationer to the Reader," in which he refers to Shakespeare's reputation as the greatest advertisement for the work. See Othello: *Text*. [*Othello*, New Arden Edition, M. R. Ridley, ed., 1958.]

Wall. See Tom Snout.

Wallace, C[harles] W[illiam] (1865–1932). American scholar who discovered a number of important documents relating to Shakespeare. Educated at various American and German universities, Wallace was for many years a member of the faculty at the University of Nebraska. In his later years he enjoyed considerable financial success drilling for oil in Texas.

The most important of his Shakespearean discoveries was the Belott-Mountjoy suit; the deposition for the suit includes the best extant example of Shakespeare's handwriting. Wallace also uncovered many documents relating to the ownership and distribution of shares of the Globe and Blackfriars theatres. His publications include *Globe Theatre Apparel* (1909), *Keysar v. Burbadge and Others* (1910), *The Evolution of the English Drama up to Shakespeare* (1912), and *Shakespeare and his London Associates*, University of Nebraska Studies, X, 1910.

Walley, Henry (fl. 1608–1655). Bookseller and Master of the Stationers' Company in 1655. In association with Richard Bonian, Walley was the publisher of the First Quarto of *Troilus and Cressida*, published in 1609 and reissued in the same year. The second issue contains an interesting Epistle to the reader, presumably written by the publishers. See Troilus and Cressida: *Text*.

Walpole, Horace (1717–1797). Novelist and critic. Born in London, the son of England's first prime minister, Walpole attended Eton and Cambridge. In 1757 he established the Strawberry Hill Press near Twickenham where he printed poems of his friend Thomas Gray and his own gothic novel, *The Castle of Otranto* (1765). Walpole's literary criticism has long been attacked, including his criticism of Shakespeare. With his summary of *A Midsummer Night's Dream* as "forty times more nonsensical than the worst translation of any Italian opera-books" in mind, Macaulay said of Walpole that "no writer surely was ever guilty of so much false and absurd criticism." But neither can it be denied that Walpole was at times an astute critic. He attacked Voltaire's criticism of Shakespeare, Addison's *Cato* in comparison to *Julius Caesar*, and the popular contemporary adaptations of Shakespeare's plays. He especially took Garrick to task for omitting the gravedigger's scene from his *Hamlet*. And before Johnson's Preface appeared, Walpole had already defended Shakespeare's transcendence of the classical rules. Most of Walpole's valid criticism, unfortunately, appears in two notebooks as yet unpublished, his *Miscellany* and *Book of Materials*.

Although Walpole wrote that his concept of the "comic relief" scene, especially the joking menial, was inspired by Shakespeare, and although many of the trappings of the gothic novel may be traced back to Elizabethan drama, neither a direct nor important Shakespearean influence is apparent in his own writings. [Jesse M. Stein, "Horace Walpole and Shakespeare," *Studies in Philology*, XXXI, 1934; Clyde Kilby, "Horace Walpole on Shakespeare," *Studies in Philology*, XXXVIII, 1941.]

Walton, William. See MUSIC BASED ON SHAKESPEARE: *20th century*.

Warburton, William (1698–1779). Churchman and scholar. Born in Nottinghamshire, Warburton took orders in 1723 and six years later received the living at Brant Broughton which he held for 18 years; in 1759 he became bishop of Gloucester. He gained the attention of Alexander Pope when, reversing an earlier position, he wrote a series of articles defending the orthodoxy of Pope's *Essay on Man*. He became Pope's literary executor and in 1751 edited his works. He also published several theological works. Warburton's edition of Shakespeare (8 vols., 1747) was based on Pope's text. Its publication was stimulated by the appearance of the edition of Thomas HANMER (1744), which contained some notes made by Warburton. Warburton asserted that the use of this material had been without his authorization, but it is possible that he was rationalizing a position taken after a quarrel with the former collaborator. The origin of the Hanmer-Warburton dispute is obscure as is the degree of Warburton's association with Hanmer. In his preface Warburton attacked both Lewis Theobald and Hanmer, although he incorporated material from the Theobald edition into his own. He in turn was attacked by Thomas Edwards (1699–1757) in his *Supplement to Mr. Warburton's edition of Shakespeare* (1747), reissued in the following year as *The Canons of Criticism*. The popularity of this controversy is attested to by the fact that Edwards' book went through six editions during Warburton's lifetime. As an editor of Shakespeare, Warburton has not been held in high regard, but he nevertheless made a few significant textual emendations. Hamlet's "a god kissing carrion" (II, ii, 182), Warburton's emendation of the "good kissing carrion" of the quarto and folio versions, was greatly admired by Dr. Johnson and has been accepted by many subsequent editors. [Arthur W. Evans, *Warburton and the Warburtonians*, 1932.]

Ward, John (fl. 1649–1681). Churchman and diarist. John Ward was the vicar of Stratford Parish from 1662 to 1681. From the years 1648 to 1679 he kept a diary published as the *Diary of John Ward* (C. Severn, ed., 1839). Extracts from the period 1661–1663 contain the following information about Shakespeare:

> Shakespear had but 2 daughters, one whereof M. Hall, ye physitian, married, and by her had one daughter, to wit, ye Lady Bernard of Abbingdon.
>
> I have heard y^t M^r. Shakespeare was a natural wit, without any art at all; hee frequented ye plays al^l his younger time, but in his elder days lived at Stratford: and supplied ye stage with 2 plays every year, and for y^t had an allowance so large, y^t he spent att ye rate of a 1,000*l*. a year, as I have heard
>
> Remember to peruse Shakespears plays and be versd in *them*, y^t I may not be ignorant in y matter.
>
> Shakespear, Drayton, and Ben Jonson, had merry meeting, and itt seems drank too hard, fo Shakespear died of a feavour there contracted.

Ward's estimate of Shakespeare's income must b greatly exaggerated. His entire cash estate was no more than £350.

One further note in Ward's diary is interesting i revealing the possible source of his information abou Shakespeare: "A letter to my brother, to see Mr Queeny, to send for Tom Smith for the acknow edgment." "Mrs. Queeny" would be Judith Quiney Shakespeare's daughter, who died in 1662. [*Th Shakspere Allusion-Book*, J. Munro, ed., 1909.]

Warlock, Peter (Philip Heseltine). See MUSI BASED ON SHAKESPEARE: *20th century*.

Warner, William (c. 1558–1609). Poet and trans lator whose English version of Plautus' *Menaechm* may have provided the direct source of *The Comed of Errors*. Although Shakespeare's play is generall dated earlier than Warner's translation (entered i the Stationers' Register on June 10, 1594 and pub lished in the following year), it is possible tha Shakespeare may have seen Warner's work in manu script. This possibility is strengthened by the adver tisement, prefacing Warner's work, which indicate that the translation was originally made, not for pub lication, but "for the use and delight of his privat friends, who in Plautus owne words are not able t understand them." Added to this is the fact tha Warner's patron was Henry Carey, Lord Hunsdon the lord chamberlain and patron of Shakespeare' company. A few verbal correspondences have als been cited as evidence of Shakespeare's indebtednes to Warner. However, it can be argued, as it has bee by T. W. Baldwin, that the indebtedness runs in th other direction, that it was Warner who borrowe from Shakespeare.

Warner was also the author of *Albion's Englan* (1586–1606), a long historical epic which recount the legendary origins of the English nation. *Albion' England* was extremely successful in its time and wa continually reprinted and expanded by Warner until in its final form it totaled 16 books. In 159 Warner was cited by Francis Meres as ranking wit Spenser as "our chief heroical makers." [*Comedy o Errors*, Heath's American Arden Shakespeare, T. W Baldwin, ed., 1928; Geoffrey Bullough, *Narrativ and Dramatic Sources of Shakespeare*, Vol. I, 1957 *The Comedy of Errors*, New Arden Edition, R. A Foakes, ed., 1962.]

War of the Theatres or **Poetomachia.** Name give to a stage quarrel occurring between the years 159 and 1602. The exact nature of the quarrel has lon been disputed by scholars with the result that a vari ety of interpretations of the "war" has been offered It has been viewed as a personal feud between Be Jonson, John Marston, and Thomas Dekker; as conflict between the popular public theatres and th private coterie theatres; as a commercial rivalry be tween the two leading theatrical companies, th Chamberlain's Men and the Admiral's Men; as mock feud trumped up for its box-office appeal; and finally, as an abortive encounter between the contrasting artistic principles of Shakespeare and Jonson. The majority of these views depend to a large degree on the implications which scholars have derived from some isolated and fragmentary evidence. What the evidence does suggest is that sometime about 1599 there was an outbreak of a personal quarrel among certain playwrights, that the quarrel became complicated by extra-personal issues, and that Shakespeare became involved not in the personal feud but in the larger aspects of the problem.

The earliest dramatic expression of the quarrel probably occurred in 1599 in Marston's *Histriomastix*. The play contains the character of Chrisoganus, modeled on Jonson. Jonson thereupon parodied Marston's somewhat pompous style in two plays, *Every Man Out of his Humour* (1599) and *Cynthia's Revels* (1600). In the latter play he coupled Marston with Dekker as braggarts and inflated ignoramuses. Jonson later denied rather unconvincingly that he had intended any satire on the two dramatists in this play. Marston and Dekker were so little convinced that they began at once to prepare an answer to *Cynthia's Revels*. Jonson evidently got wind of their plan and working for 15 weeks at a speed unusual for him, anticipated his enemies' satire by completing *The Poetaster* and having it performed by the Children of Blackfriars in 1601. That the play was an attack upon Marston is known from Jonson's later comment, recorded by William Drummond, that "he had many quarrels with Marston, beat him, and took his pistol from him, wrote his Poetaster upon him." The play's most famous scene is the one in which Horace (Jonson) forces Crispinus (Marston) to swallow a purge of his brain and his bowels which causes him to vomit some of the pretentious words of his vocabulary.

In the meantime Dekker and Marston had finished their play, *Satiro-mastix* or *The Untrussing of the Humorous Poet* (1601), which was staged both at a private theatre by the Children of Paul's and at the Globe by the Chamberlain's Men. This play was probably the last dramatic note sounded in the quarrel and the dispute between Jonson and Marston, who in 1605 collaborated on *Eastward Ho!*

Alfred Harbage has argued that behind this quarrel between Jonson and Marston lies a more profound disagreement in which Marston and Jonson are aligned in opposition to Shakespeare, Dekker, and Heywood. Harbage's thesis is that Marston and Jonson, writing their plays primarily for the small, select private theatres, are directing their principal satire at the unlearned popular theatre playwrights, of whom Shakespeare was the most successful example. This opposition is, according to Harbage, an aspect of the radical cultural division between the private and the public theatres. He cites as part of his supporting evidence the commentary on the quarrel revealed in the PARNASSUS PLAYS, a series of satires of contemporary life written at that time by undergraduates at Cambridge University. In one of these plays a character remarks, "that Ben Jonson is a pestilent fellow; he brought up Horace giving the poets a pill, but our fellow Shakespeare hath given him a purge that made him beray his credit." Harbage argues that the "purge" referred to was the satire of Jonson in *Satiro-mastix*, a play which the author of the Parnassus play mistakenly attributed to Shakespeare because the play had been first performed by his company, the Chamberlain's Men. Other critics have argued that the "purge" was administered in *Troilus and Cressida* in the character of AJAX.

Central to the Harbage hypothesis is the famous allusion to the children's companies in *Hamlet* (II, ii). He argues that the comments refer directly to the satiric thrusts ("goosequills") which the private theatres had been directing at the popular plays ("the common stages"). The relevant passages from the play occur when Rosencrantz explains to Hamlet why the "tragedians of the city" have been forced to undertake the provincial tour which brought them to Elsinore:

> *Hamlet*. How comes it? do they grow rusty?
> *Rosencrantz*. Nay, their endeavour keeps in the wonted pace: but there is, sir, an aery of children, little eyases, that cry out on the top of question, and are most tyrannically clapped for't: these are now the fashion, and so berattle the common stages—so they call them—that many wearing rapiers are afraid of goosequills and dare scarce come thither.
> *Hamlet*. What, are they children? who maintains 'em? how are they escoted? Will they pursue the quality no longer than they can sing? will they not say afterwards, if they should grow themselves to common players—as it is most like, if their means are no better—their writers do them wrong, to make them exclaim against their own succession?
> *Rosencrantz*. 'Faith, there has been much to do on both sides; and the nation holds it no sin to tarre them to controversy; there was, for a while, no money bid for argument, unless the poet and the player went to cuffs in the question.
> (II, ii, 352 ff)

Most scholars agree that in the passage Shakespeare is revealing the anxiety over the economic threat which the boy companies must have constituted at this time. Whether or not the passage is indicative of a more profound disagreement involving differing cultural, moral, and social attitudes is still open to question. [J. H. Penniman, *The War of the Theatres*, 1897; R. A. Small, *The Stage-quarrel between Ben Jonson and the so-called Poetasters*, 1899; R. B. Sharpe, *The Real War of the Theatres: Shakespeare's Fellows in . . . Rivalry with the Admiral's Men, 1594–1603 . . .*, 1935; Alfred Harbage, *Shakespeare and the Rival Traditions*, 1952; John J. Enck, "The Peace of the Poetomachia," *PMLA*, 77, September 1962; Robert Kimbrough, *Shakespeare's Troilus and Cressida and its Setting*, 1964.]—E. Q.

Warren, John (fl. 1640). Poet. Warren contributed a commendatory verse to the 1640 edition of Shakespeare's *Poems:*

Of Mr. William Shakespeare.

What, lofty *Shakespeare*, art againe reviv'd?
And *Virbius* like now show'st thy selfe twise liv'd,
Tis [Benson's] love that thus to thee is showne,
The labours his, the glory still thine owne.
These learned Poems amongst thine after-birth,
That makes thy name immortall on the earth,

Will make the learned still admire to see,
The Muses gifts so fully infus'd on thee.
Let Carping *Momus* barke and bite his fill,
And ignorant *Davus* slight thy learned skill:
Yet those who know the worth of thy desert,
And with true judgement can discerne thy Art,
Will be admirers of thy high tun'd straine,
Amongst whose number let me still remaine.

[*The Shakspere Allusion-Book*, J. Munro, ed., 1909.]

Wars of the Roses, The. See 3 Henry VI: *Stage History*.

Wart, Thomas. In *2 Henry IV*, one of the men conscripted by Justice Shallow and selected by Falstaff to serve in the army (III, ii).

Warton, Joseph (1722–1800). Critic and educator. In a series of five essays published in 1753 in *The Adventurer*, Warton discussed Shakespeare's plays, particularly *The Tempest* and *King Lear*. While criticizing what he considered Shakespeare's lapses from unity and his at times excessively poetic language, Warton admired Shakespeare's creative imagination, consistent characterization, and superb poetry. In general, he felt that Shakespeare's faults were far outweighed by his virtues.

For Warton, *The Tempest* represents the best example of Shakespeare's creative power. He notes many occasions on which Shakespeare suggests tremendous passion through understatement. A subjective critic, Warton praised those passages that most moved him. [Herbert Spencer Robinson, *English Shakesperian Criticism in the Eighteenth Century*, 1932.]

Warwick, Edward Plantagenet, earl of (1475–1499). Eldest son of George, duke of Clarence, and Isabella Neville, daughter of Warwick the Kingmaker. He was orphaned at three and brought up by his aunt Ann, duchess of Gloucester. Imprisoned in Sheriff Hutton Castle by his uncle Richard III, Warwick was later transferred to the Tower by Henry VII. He remained there until his execution for allegedly conspiring against that king. In *Richard III*, Ned Plantagenet and his sister Margaret mourn the death of their father with the Duchess of York (II, ii). King Richard later reveals that he has imprisoned the boy (IV, iii).

Warwick, Richard Beauchamp, earl of (1382–1439). Warrior and diplomat. Under Henry IV he fought against Owen Glendower and the Percys, subsequently accompanying Henry V on his invasion of France. Warwick became one of the king's most trusted ministers, and on Henry's deathbed was commissioned with the care of the infant Henry VI. In 1437 he was appointed lieutenant of Normandy and remained in France until his death two years later.

In *2 Henry IV*, Warwick is the King's counselor. In III, i, he reassures Henry that "Rumour doth double, like the voice and echo, /The numbers of the fear'd." Shakespeare's reference to Warwick as "cousin Nevil" in the foregoing scene is a confusion based on the fact that his youngest daughter, Anne, married Richard Neville, who later became earl of Warwick. In *Henry V*, Warwick is one of the leaders of the English forces in France. He speaks only one line: "How now, how now! what's the matter?" (IV, viii). In *1 Henry VI*, he plucks a white rose in the Temple Garden, thus allying himself with the Yorkist faction. In V, iv, he joins in the condemnation of Joan (La Pucelle).

Warwick, Richard Nevil or **Neville,** earl of. Calle the Kingmaker (1428–1471). Eldest son of Richar Neville, earl of Salisbury, and husband of Ann Beauchamp, daughter of Richard Beauchamp, earl o Warwick, to whose title Neville succeeded. Sup porting the duke of York's claim to the thron Warwick brought the captive King Henry VI t London after a victory at Northampton (1460 After York was killed at Wakefield that year an Queen Margaret defeated at Towton in 1461, Wa wick joined the new duke of York and was instru mental in making him King Edward IV.

Warwick's friendship with Edward ended whe the king married Elizabeth Woodville (Lady Grey while the earl was negotiating a marriage betwee Edward and Bona of Savoy. Joining Louis XI c France and Queen Margaret in an invasion of Eng land (1470), Warwick helped to depose Edwar and to restore Henry VI to the throne. In 147 however, Edward's army defeated the earl at Barne where he was killed.

In *2 Henry VI*, Warwick joins his father, the Ea of Salisbury, in accusing Suffolk of Gloucester murder. As a Yorkist he fights against the roya army at St. Alban's. In *3 Henry VI*, Warwick is re sponsible for the crowning of York's son as Edwar IV. On going to Europe to obtain the hand c Princess Bona for the King, Warwick is angered t learn that Edward has meanwhile married Lad Grey. He consequently makes peace with Quee Margaret and joins the Lancastrian party. Afte Edward is captured by Warwick's invading army, h escapes and, meeting Salisbury's forces at Barne defeats and kills him. Warwick dies in battle.

Warwick's Men. A company of actors under th patronage of Ambrose Dudley, earl of Warwic (1528–1590). Warwick's Men appeared in London a early as 1562 and gave two court performances du ing the Christmas season of 1564/5. During the perio of 1574/5 the troupe performed regularly at Stra ford. In the next five years they appeared at cou frequently, but in 1580 the company left Warwick service and became known as OXFORD'S MEN.

Wayte, William (d. 1603). Stepson of Williar GARDINER who in 1596 claimed sureties of the peac against Francis LANGLEY, the owner of the Swan the atre, William Shakespeare, Dorothy Soer, and Ann Lee. Wayte's petition was filed in response to a earlier petition for sureties of the peace which Lang ley had entered against Gardiner and Wayte. Sure ties of the peace were court orders requiring th posting of bonds by the defendants as assurances tha they would keep the peace for a specified perio Leslie Hotson, who discovered the court document has traced the careers of Gardiner and Wayte in de tail. He has found that Wayte was the dupe of th unscrupulous Gardiner, by whom he was defraude of his inheritance. Wayte also evidently acted a Gardiner's agent in his dealings with Langley an Shakespeare. On the basis of these documents an other evidence, Hotson argues that Gardiner an Wayte are the prototypes of Justice Shallow and h cousin Abraham SLENDER in *The Merry Wives o Windsor*. Wayte died in the plague of 1603. [Lesli Hotson, *Shakespeare Versus Shallow*, 1931.]

Webbe Family. Shakespeare's cousins. ***Alexande Webbe*** (d. 1573) married Margaret Arden, the siste of Shakespeare's mother (see ARDEN FAMILY). H was a resident of Bearley, a hamlet near Snitterfiel

Vebbe leased the house in Snitterfield which be-nged to Shakespeare's grandfather, Richard Shake-eare, on the latter's death in 1561. In his will, dated 573, he named John Shakespeare of Stratford as one f his overseers:

I, Alexander Webbe of the parishe of Snitterfield and in the countie of Warwick, husbandman, doe make this, my last will and testament, inmanner and forme folloinge,—fyrst, I geve and bequeth my sowle to Allmightie God, my Maker, Savior, and Redemer, and my bodie to be buried in the parishe churchyard of Snitterfild, and there to lye in a full, suer, and perfect hope of resurrection both as well of the quicke as of the deade. Item, I geve and bequeth to Robart Webbe, my eldest sonne, x.li. of good and lawfull money of England, to be payed unto him within four years after the date hereof. Item, I geve and bequeth to Edward Webbe, my sonne, x.li. of good and lawfull money, to be payde unto him at the full age of xviij.th years . . . . The residue of my goodes, movable and unmovable whatsoe ever, I doe geve unto Margarett, my wiffe, whome I doe make my full and sole executrix, as well to gather upp my debettes as to paye thesse my legacies; and also I will that she doe see my children vertusly brought up, and my funerall to be well executed and donne, and my bodie honestly brought whome, and that she doe fulfill my last will and testament as my hope is in her. Moreover I doe institute, appoynte, and ordaine to be my overseers to see this my last will and testament performed, satisfied and fulfilled, according to my will, John Shackespere of Stretford-upon-Aven, John Hill of Bearley, and for theyre paynes taken I geve them xij.d apece. Wittnes, John Wager, Henry Shaxspere, William Maydes, with others.—Probatum Wigornie, etc., xv.º Julij, 1573 . . . .

Webbe's widow married Edward CORNWELL in 574. Webbe left six children, the oldest of whom as ***Robert Webbe*** (d. 1597), who in 1578 bought is mother's shares of the Arden estate. In the fol-wing year he purchased the share in the estate held y Shakespeare's parents and in 1581 the share held y Edmund and Joan Lambert, thus securing the ajor portions of the entire estate of Robert Arden. 1581 he married Mary Perkes, by whom he had ven children. At his death his goods were assessed : a value of £51. [J. O. Halliwell-Phillipps, *Out-nes of the Life of Shakespeare*, 1881; Mark Eccles, *hakespeare in Warwickshire*, 1961.]

Weber, Carl Maria von. See MUSIC BASED ON SHAKE-EARE: *19th century to 1850.*

Webster, John (1580?–?1634). Dramatist. There is ss known about Webster than about any other ajor figure of Elizabethan literature. E. K. Cham-ers has suggested that he may be identified with an ctor of the same name who toured in Germany in 596. His name first appears in Philip Henslowe's iary in 1602 where he is listed as a collaborator with nthony Munday, Thomas Middleton, Thomas Dek-er, and Michael Drayton on "sesers ffalle" (*Caesar's all*). In 1604 he wrote an Induction to John Mar-on's *The Malcontent* and in the following year col-borated with Dekker on *Westward Ho!* (1605) and *orthward Ho!* (1605). His masterpieces are *The hite Devil* (1609–1612) and THE DUCHESS OF MALFI (1613/14), two of the greatest plays in the English language. Tragedies of horror derived from Italian novelle, both plays combine an intensity and power of language which convey an unforgettable vision of evil. In both plays there are occasional verbal parallels to Shakespeare, but according to R. W. Dent comparatively few signs of borrowing. Webster apparently thought rather less of Shakespeare than of other of his contemporaries, if we are to judge by his comment in the Epistle to *The White Devil:*

> . . . For mine owne part I haue euer truly cherisht my good opinion of other mens worthy Labours, especially of that full and haightned stile of Maister *Chapman:* The labor'd and vnderstanding workes of Maister *Johnson;* The no lesse worthy composures of the both worthily excellent Maister *Beamont* & Maister *Fletcher:* And lastly (without wrong last to be named), the right happy and copious industry of M. *Shake-speare*, M. *Decker*, & M. *Heywood* . . .

Webster is also thought to be the author of the group of 32 new characters added to the fifth edition of Sir Thomas Overbury's *Characters* (1615), a collection of sketches of types of people. [R. W. Dent, *John Webster's Borrowing*, 1960.]

Webster Family. Actors and theatrical producers. ***Benjamin Nottingham Webster*** (1797–1882), a prominent character actor who claimed descent from Sir George Buc, an Elizabethan Master of the Revels, began acting in 1818. His Shakespearean repertory included Pompey, Old Gobbo, Roderigo, Oswald, Bardolph, Verges, Feste, and Gratiano. In 1847 he performed at Covent Garden as Petruchio in a benefit to raise money to purchase Shakespeare's house. At various periods between 1837 and 1879 he managed the Haymarket, Adelphi, and Princess' theatres.

The grandson of the elder Webster, ***Benjamin Webster*** (1864–1947) was meant for the bar, but turned to the stage instead. Among his earliest appearances was one with Henry Irving and a tour in the United States with Ellen Terry; he also acted in the companies of Alexander, Terry, and Boucicault. In 1939 he went to the United States, where he enjoyed a high reputation. One of his best later parts was Montague in Laurence Olivier and Vivian Leigh's *Romeo and Juliet*. His wife, Dame ***May Whitty*** (1865–1948), was a distinguished actress who enjoyed a long, outstanding career on the English and American stage and in films.

Margaret Webster (1905–), the daughter of Benjamin Webster and Dame May Whitty, made her debut in 1917 and has included many Shakespearean roles in her repertory. Since 1935 she has been an active producer and director in both the United States and England. Among the plays she has directed have been *Richard II* (1951), *Richard III* (1953), *The Merchant of Venice* (Stratford-upon-Avon, 1956), *Measure for Measure* (Old Vic, 1957), and *Antony and Cleopatra* (1963). She has also staged the operas *Macbeth* (1957) and *The Taming of the Shrew* (1958) for the New York City Opera Company. In 1946/7 she was a director and producer for the American Repertory Theatre, and she staged the Shakespearean productions at the 1939 New York World's Fair. She is the author of *Shakespeare Without Tears* (1942), a book based on her experiences as an actress and director. [*Dictionary of National Biography*, 1885- ; *The Oxford Companion to the Theatre*, Phyllis Hartnoll, ed., 1951.]

Weever, John (1576–1632). Poet. Born in Lancashire and educated at Cambridge, Weever published his first book of poems in 1599 under the title *Epigrammes in the oldest Cut, and newest Fashion*. Included in the collection are an epigram on the actor Edward Alleyn and others on the leading poets of the time, including one on Shakespeare:

Ad Gulielmum Shakespeare.

Honie-tong'd *Shakespeare* when I saw thine issue
I swore *Apollo* got them and none other,
Their rosie-tainted features cloth'd in tissue,
Some heauen born goddesse said to be their mother:
Rose-checkt *Adonis* with his amber tresses,
Faire fire-hot *Venus* charming him to loue her,
Chaste *Lucretia* virgine-like her dresses,
Prowd lust-stung *Tarquine* seeking still to proue her:
Romea Richard; more whose names I know not,
Their sugred tongues, and power attractiue beuty
Say they are Saints althogh that Sts they shew not
For thousands vowes to them subiectiue dutie:
They burn in loue thy children *Shakespear* het them,
Go, wo thy Muse more Nymphish brood beget them.

Weever is also the author of *The Mirror of Martyrs or the life and death of Sir John Oldcastle* ... (1601), written in response to the controversy aroused by Shakespeare's portrait of Sir John Oldcastle as Falstaff. In the same poem Weever makes reference to another Shakespeare play in the lines:

The many-headed multitude were drawne
By *Brutus* speach, that *Caesar* was ambitious,
When eloquent *Mark Antonie* had showne
His vertues, who but *Brutus* then was vicious?

Later in his life Weever devoted himself to antiquarian studies, publishing in 1632 his *Ancient Funerall Monuments*, an invaluable record of tombstone inscriptions in Great Britain.

Weird Sisters. See WITCHES, THREE.

Welcombe. A small hamlet about a mile and a half northeast of Stratford and one of the sites of the STRATFORD TITHES purchased by Shakespeare in 1605.

Welles, [George] Orson (1915-). American actor, producer, and director. Born in Kenosha, Wisconsin, Welles was a painter and news correspondent before embarking on a career in the theatre. He made his acting debut in Dublin in *Hamlet* in 1931 and then returned to the United States to tour as Mercutio with Katharine Cornell in her *Romeo and Juliet* (1933). In 1934 Welles organized and became manager of the Woodstock (Illinois) Theatre Festival, and later that year played the Chorus and Tybalt in a New York production of *Romeo and Juliet*. In 1936 he became director of the Negro People's Theatre, for which he directed an all-Negro *Macbeth*. In 1937 he became a director of the Federal Theatre Project in New York, and produced series of Columbia recordings of Shakespearean play for children. In 1937 he founded his own Mercur Theatre, which opened that November with a modern-dress production, without scenery, of *Juliu Caesar*, in which Welles played Brutus.

Welles' best-known Shakespearean impersonatio is Othello, which he played in London for the firs time in 1951, directing his own production. He als played and directed *King Lear* for the New Yor City Center in 1956. He has played in innumerabl films, including his own production of *Macbet* (1947). [*Who's Who in the Theatre*, 1961.]

Wendell, Barrett. See CRITICISM—19TH CENTURY.

West, Benjamin (1738–1820). American portrai and history painter. West first studied art in his na tive Philadelphia, and his talent so impressed his fel low citizens that they subscribed to a fund and pai his way to Italy so that he could study there. In 175 West arrived in Rome, where Winckelmann's neo classical theories and the new archaeological dis coveries were inspiring the young generation o painters. West's neoclassic style differed from that o the French and German schools, for his conceptio of history painting included not only Greek an Roman history, but English history and even con temporary events. After three years in Italy he wen to London, where his new style was acclaimed an his career firmly established.

West's "Death of Wolfe," exhibited at the Roya Academy in 1771, became the center of a storm o controversy focused on the propriety in histor painting of using costume contemporary with th event depicted. The Royal Academy, under th presidency of Sir Joshua REYNOLDS, censured Wes saying that "obedience to the rules of art is mor important than obedience to the reality of facts," bu West stoutly defended the propriety of fact. Th dispute marked the emergence of nationalist feelin and historical accuracy in history painting. It is in teresting to note that during the period of disput over West's painting there was a simultaneous aban donment of anachronistic costuming in the theatr throughout Europe and England.

West contributed two paintings, to BOYDELL SHAKESPEARE GALLERY: "King Lear in the Storm" an "Ophelia appearing before the King and Queen." Se ART. [Edgar Wind, "Revolution of History Paint ing," *Warburg* II, 1938.]

Westall, Richard (1765–1836). Painter and illustra tor. Westall studied art at the school of the Roya Academy. His oil paintings were neither distin guished nor popular, however, and he turned to boo illustration and watercolor painting. He produced 2 pictures for BOYDELL'S SHAKESPEARE GALLERY, an the designs for Boydell's edition of Milton. His illus trations for the Bible and the Book of Commo Prayer were well suited to the public taste an gained him much approval. His last employment wa as drawing instructor to the then Princess Victori

Westminster, William de Colchester, abbot c (d. 1420). One of the commissioners sent to th Tower to obtain the resignation of Richard II c England. Abbot Colchester seems to have bee reconciled to the idea of a change in power pric to the accession of Henry, and there is no evidenc that he plotted against the new king. Abbot Co hester spent 60 years at Westminster, ruling it for 4. Although there has been some argument that the bbot of the play was not William de Colchester ut his successor, Richard Harweden, the identification of Colchester is generally accepted.

In *Richard II*, Abbot Colchester appears as a supporter of the King and, together with Aumerle, lots against Bolingbroke. The conspiracy is uncovered by Aumerle's father, the Duke of York, nd Abbot Colchester's consequent death is reported n the last scene. (W. H. Thomson, *Shakespeare's Characters: A Historical Dictionary*, 1951.)

Westminster School. Choir school and grammar chool in the abbey of Westminster, whose students participated in various dramatic presentations in the Elizabethan and Jacobean theatre. Their theatrical ctivity would seem to date from the 14th century; beginning in 1369 there is a record of the boys' participation in celebrations of the BOY-BISHOP.

The most illustrious Westminster headmaster, Nicholas Udall, was appointed in 1555 but held the post only a year (see RALPH ROISTER DOISTER). In 561 the boys appeared at a lord mayor's pageant; in 562 they gave a play at the annual dinner of the Society of Parish Clerks; and in 1566 Mr. Taylor, "Mr of the quirysters," received payment for their ervices at the Ironmongers' pageant.

In 1564 the boys gave their first court performnces in Terence's *Heautontimorumenus* and Plautus' *Miles Gloriosus*. In 1565/6 they gave *Sapientia Solomonis* before Elizabeth. Taylor's mastership terminated in the following year. The next known choirmaster was John Billingsley of whom there is mention in the records of a 1572 performance of *Paris and Vienna*. There were performances recorded for Shrovetide 1566/7 and Christmas, 1567/8. On New Year's Day 1574 the boys presented *Truth, Faithfulness and Mercy* under the direction of William Elderton.

Although court performances were not recorded after 1574, the college accounts cite dramatic expenditures until 1640. [E. K. Chambers, *The Elizabethan Stage*, 1923.]

Westmorland, Ralph Neville, 1st earl of (1364–1425). Eldest son of John, 5th Baron Neville. He was made earl in 1397 by Richard II. When Richard expelled Henry Bolingbroke from the kingdom, Westmorland sided against the king and joined Bolingbroke when he invaded England in 1399. During the Percy revolt of 1403, Westmorland, at Henry IV's behest, turned back the rebel forces and two years later intercepted those led by Archbishop Scrope. Weak in numbers himself, Westmorland feigned satisfaction with the demands of Scrope and Thomas Mowbray. He induced the archbishop to dismiss his men, whereupon he arrested the two leaders and turned them over to the king.

In *1 Henry IV*, Westmoreland supports the King against the rebels, who are led by Hotspur and Thomas Percy, earl of Worcester. He appears at the battle of Shrewsbury, where the mutinous forces are defeated. In *2 Henry IV*, Westmoreland assists John of Lancaster in duping the rebels into dismissing their army. In *Henry V*, he expresses to Henry, on the eve of Agincourt, a despondent wish for 10,000 more men, thus prompting the King's famous St. Crispin speech (IV, iii).

Westmorland, Ralph Neville, 2nd earl of (d. 1484). Grandson of the 1st earl of Westmorland. He was less active as a Lancastrian than his brothers, one of whom was killed at Towton. In *3 Henry VI*. Westmoreland berates Henry as a "faint-hearted and degenerate king" when the latter names York as his heir (I, i).

W. H., Mr. See MR. W. H.

Whatcott, Robert (fl. 1613–1616). One of the witnesses to Shakespeare's will. He may have been a servant of Shakespeare or of his son-in-law John Hall. In 1613 he appeared as a witness for Shakespeare's daughter Susanna in a defamation of character suit which she brought against John Lane. Nothing else is known of him. [Mark Eccles, *Shakespeare in Warwickshire*, 1961.]

Whately or **Whateley, Anne.** The name that appears on Shakespeare's marriage license. A true account of Shakespeare's matrimonial affairs has been made difficult because of a license issued by the bishop of Worcester on November 27, 1582—the day before the signing of the Hathaway bond—authorizing a marriage "inter Willelmum Shaxpere et Annam Whateley de Temple Grafton," a small village about five miles from Stratford. The usual explanation for this is that the clerk mistook the Latin Annam Hathaway for Anna Whately and that the license was for Anne Hathaway's marriage. Detractors of the poet find in the license an explanation for his hurried marriage: the girl's mother and brother, getting wind of the poet's plan to marry another woman, forced him into a kind of shotgun wedding (see MARRIAGE). Another explanation is that the prospective groom was not the dramatist, but another of the many William Shakespeares who resided in Worcestershire. See TEMPLE GRAFTON. [Sir Sidney Lee, *A Life of William Shakespeare*, new ed., 1915.]

Whately, Thomas (d. 1772). Author. Whately's *Remarks on Some of the Characters of Shakespeare* was written about 1770 and published posthumously in 1785. Whately's primary critical standard in the work is the successful creation of distinct personalities; thus he concerns himself specifically with Shakespeare's characters, rather than the plots or construction of the plays.

In comparing Shakespeare's Macbeth and Richard III as essentially different characters acting under similar circumstances, Whately praises Shakespeare for creating two figures of such individuality despite their superficially identical situations. Whately intended to discuss several other characters, but *Remarks* was left unfinished at his death. [Herbert Spencer Robinson, *English Shakespearian Criticism in the Eighteenth Century*, 1932.]

Wheatley, Francis (1747–1801). Engraver and landscape, portrait, and genre painter. Wheatley was a pupil of Richard Wilson (1714–1782) and one of the painters who worked on the decorations for Vauxhall Gardens. He is best known for his series of genre engravings, *The Cries of London*, but his landscapes and treatments of rural subjects were greatly admired. He was a popular artist, and contributed 13 paintings to BOYDELL'S SHAKESPEARE GALLERY. "Perdita distributing Flowers," illustrating a scene from *The Winter's Tale*, is generally considered the most successful. Although a few of his paintings are strangely pompous, Wheatley's style is usually delicate and sprightly, recalling the earlier work of

Francis Hayman and Hubert Gravelot. [W. M. Merchant, *Shakespeare and the Artist*, 1959.]

Wheeler, John (d. 1592). Friend and associate of John Shakespeare. Wheeler and John Shakespeare were both prominent members of the Stratford council, the governing body of the town. About 1577, however, they began to absent themselves from the regular meetings of the council. In 1586 they were replaced by two new members "for that m^r^ wheler dothe desyre to be put out of the Companye & m^r^ Shaxspere dothe not come to the halles when they be warned nor hathe not done of Longe tyme."

The 1592 recusancy list, which includes the name of John Shakespeare, also lists John Wheeler and his son, John. John Wheeler, Jr., was also cited in the 1607 recusant list which included Susanna Shakespeare, the poet's daughter. See RECUSANCY. [Mark Eccles, *Shakespeare in Warwickshire*, 1961.]

Wheeler, Margaret. See Judith SHAKESPEARE.

Whetstone, George (1544?–?1587). Author and adventurer. In 1573 Whetstone enlisted to serve in the Low Countries where he met George Gascoigne and Thomas Churchyard. He also took part in Sir Humphrey Gilbert's voyage to Newfoundland in 1578/9, visited Italy in 1580, and fought at Zutphen in 1586. Besides his travels and adventures, he wrote a number of miscellaneous works. His *The Rocke of Regard* (1576) is a collection of 68 pieces in prose and verse modeled on the *Poesies* of his friend Gascoigne, many of them adapted from the Italian *novelle* then in vogue. *Promos and Cassandra* (1578) is a play in two parts adapted from Cinthio; its chief interest today lies in the fact that Shakespeare used it as one of the main sources for *Measure for Measure* (see MEASURE FOR MEASURE: *Sources*). Whetstone retold the same story in prose for his *Heptameron of Civill Discourses* (1582; reissued in 1593 as *Aurelia*), a work modeled on the Italian convention of interlocking tales and debates. [Thomas C. Izard, *Whetstone: Mid-Elizabethan Gentleman of Letters*, 1942; Charles T. Prouty, "George Whetstone and the Sources of *Measure for Measure*," in *Shakespeare 400*, James G. McManaway, ed., 1964.]

White, Edward (fl. 1565–1612). London publisher of the Second and Third Quartos of *Titus Andronicus* (1600, 1611). White made his first entry in the Stationers' Register in 1577. In 1594 his shop by the Little North Door of St. Paul's Churchyard at the sign of the Gun was designated as the selling place of the First Quarto of *Titus Andronicus*, printed and published by John Danter. After Danter's death (c. 1598) White and Thomas Millington apparently received the copyright of the play, which they in turn transferred in 1602 to Thomas Pavier. The terms of the transfer apparently allowed White to continue publishing the play, for he brought out a second edition of *Titus* in 1600 and a third edition in 1611.

White, Richard Grant (1821–1885). American scholar. A native of Brooklyn, White began his career as a musical and literary critic for a number of New York newspapers. Although actively engaged in professional writing all his life, he found time to pursue a deep interest in Shakespeare. His 12-volume edition, *The Works of William Shakespeare* (1857–1866; reprinted in 1883 as the *Riverside Shakespeare*), was the finest American edition of its day. He was also the author of two other volumes on Shakespeare: *Shakespeare's Scholar* (1854) and *Studies i Shakespeare* (1886).

White, William (fl. 1583–1615). London printe who printed several Shakespearean quartos. Whit was admitted as a freeman to the Stationers' Con pany in 1583. In 1598 he printed for Cuthbert Burb the First Quarto of *Love's Labour's Lost*, the firs play with Shakespeare's name on the title page, and carelessly printed text. In 1600 he printed the Secon Quarto of *The True Tragedie of Richard Duke o York*, a "bad quarto" of *3 Henry VI*. In 1609 h printed Q1 and Q2 of *Pericles* in a text which is ex tremely corrupt. White also printed Q4 of *Richar II*, which was the first quarto to include the deposi tion scene, omitted in all previous editions. Se RICHARD II: *Text*. [R. B. McKerrow, ed., *A Diction ary of Printers and Booksellers . . . 1557–1640*, 1910.

White Devil, The. See John WEBSTER.

Whitefriars. A playhouse located within the pre cinct of the former priory of the White Friars (Car melites) on the north side of the Thames. Th Whitefriars was the second private theatre to b built in London. It was roofed and apparently rec tangular in shape. The earliest record in existence o a theatre at that location is a lease dating from 160 The CHILDREN OF THE KING'S REVELS were the firs occupants, and they were succeeded by the Childre of the Queen's Revels (1609–1613). In 1613 th Queen's Revels amalgamated with an adult company Lady Elizabeth's Men. The amalgamation was dis solved in 1616. By 1629 Whitefriars was no longer i use, having been replaced by the Salisbury Cour theatre.

Whitehall. A royal palace located between West minster and Charing Cross. Whitehall was originall the property of the Dominican Order, later the resi dence of the archbishop of York. It became a roya palace under Henry VIII. In Elizabeth's time it wa occasionally used for the performance of plays, bu in the reign of James I it came to be employed mor frequently for the elaborate masques in which th Stuart queens, Anne and Henrietta Maria, loved t indulge, such as Ben Jonson's *Masque of Blacknes* (1605) and *Masque of Queens* (1609). These per formances took place in the large Banqueting Hal built in Elizabeth's time and rebuilt by Inigo Jone after a fire in 1619. The Whitehall ground also con tained a small cockpit which came to be used for les elaborate theatrical presentations. See COCKPIT A COURT. [Edward H. Sugden, *A Topographical Dic tionary to . . . Shakespeare . . .*, 1925.]

Whitgift, John (c. 1530–1604). Archbishop of Car terbury (1583–1604) and close friend and confidan of Queen Elizabeth. Whitgift, the son of a wealth merchant, was educated at Cambridge where he be came a confirmed adherent of the Anglican religior He was ordained in 1560 and rose rapidly in th church, becoming bishop of Worcester in 1577 an archbishop of Canterbury in 1583. He gained the re spect and trust of the queen, who called him he "little black husband." In 1586 he was given the au thority to peruse and license all manuscripts bein prepared for publication, as well as the power to de stroy the press of any printer who failed to compl with his wishes. Whitgift was, in effect, chief censo of all publications. The major objects of his censor ship were the Puritans who, in 1588, defied the licens ng requirement and published, under the pseudonym f Martin MARPRELATE, a series of attacks on Angli-ans in general and Whitgift in particular. Whitgift's esponse was a ruthless campaign against the Mar-relate authors. He himself contributed a pamphlet arly in the controversy directed against the Puritan uthors' "licentious libertie."

Whitgift did not personally censor all the manu-cripts submitted; he had a staff assigned for that urpose. However, he occasionally issued the license n his own hand; an instance of this occurred in 1593 vhen he licensed Shakespeare's *Venus and Adonis.* n 1599 the archbishop engaged in another rigorous ensorship campaign when, in conjunction with the ishop of London, he issued a decree ordering the urning of a long list of books on the grounds of heir being either scurrilously satiric or heavily rotic. Among these were several Ovidian narrative oems which had attempted, in a more coarse man-er, to capitalize on the popularity of *Venus and ldonis*. There was a great deal of satiric literature ncluded: the pamphlets produced in the controversy etween Gabriel Harvey and Thomas NASHE, the *Elegies* of Christopher Marlowe, the *Epigrams* of Sir ohn Davies, John Marston's satiric poem *Metamor-phosis of Pygmalion's Image,* and WILLOBIE HIS AVISA, a puzzling poem which many scholars believe ontains allusions to Shakespeare's life. Whitgift's lecree also added "that no satires or epigrams be rinted hereafter." On June 4, 1599 the condemned ooks were publicly burned in a ceremony which as come to be known as the "bishops' bonfire."

Whitman, Walt[er] (1819–1892). American poet. ournalist and author of *Democratic Vistas* (1871), Whitman is best known for his book of poems *Leaves of Grass* (1855). In subsequent editions Whit-nan expanded the *Leaves of Grass,* adding new oems and revising others. The poet saw the ninth dition through the press in 1892, the year of his leath.

In *Democratic Vistas* Whitman describes the poet s a seer and emphasizes his function as a prophet ooking into the future. The poet, according to Whitman, should be in the vanguard, leading the rest of society into a bright, democratic future. Through-out his career Whitman referred to Shakespeare as n exponent of "feudal" literature, "the poet of lords nd ladies and their side of life." Shakespeare, he felt, ad written "for the court and for the young nobil-ty and gentry." Whitman argued that many great iterary works, including Shakespeare's, are "poison-us to the idea of the pride and dignity of the com-non people, the life-blood of democracy." He elieved that America had to "surmount the gor-geous history of feudalism, or else prove the most remendous failure of time." Accordingly, Whitman uggested that America's Civil War, the nation's final truggle for democracy, was a literary subject more mpressive than Homer's siege of Troy or the French Wars described by Shakespeare. R. C. Harrison has rgued that in reaction to "feudal" literature Whit-nan determined to become the poet of democracy.

Whitman criticized Shakespeare's style as well as is politics. In the face of contemporary Shakespeare-vorship, Whitman maintained that Shakespeare was full of conceits" and "over-ornate," and that his tyle was "tangled and florid" with "countless prolixities." He was willing to grant, however, that "to the deepest soul, it seems a shame to pick and choose from the riches Shakespeare has left us—to criticize his infinitely royal, multiform quality—to gauge, with optic glasses, the dazzle of his sun-like beams."

Whitman admired the "movement, intensity of life," and "action" depicted in Shakespeare's plays. He considered Shakespeare the "dramatist of passions at their stormiest out-stretch." He found the humor of the comedies "very broad, obvious, often brutal, coarse," while he found that of the tragedies "more remote, subtle, illusive." Whitman's criticism of Shakespeare, though it appears to be based upon a genuine reaction to the plays, cannot be considered original or significant. Of more interest, perhaps, is the extent of his knowledge of Shakespeare, and the influence of Shakespeare on his writing.

R. C. Harrison maintains "it is clear that the poet read extensively and intensively the sonnets, but more particularly the plays of Shakespeare." As an avid theatre-goer Whitman saw a considerable number of Shakespeare's plays on the New York stage, often reading the text before seeing one performed. Whitman was particularly impressed by Junius Brutus Booth's Richard III, Lear, Shylock, and Iago; he also admired Tom Hamblin as Macbeth and Faulconbridge, John H. Clarke as the Ghost in *Hamlet* and as Prospero in *The Tempest,* Charles Kean as King John, Ellen Tree as Queen Constance, and James H. Hackett as Falstaff.

C. J. Furness has argued that Whitman "seems to have studied somewhat assiduously the critical and scholarly works on Shakespeare current in his day." Although Whitman wrote a number of newspaper and magazine articles on Shakespeare and took notes on Shakespeare's biography, sources, financial holdings, relation to contemporaries, and the criticism of Malone, Pope, Voltaire, and Emerson, his knowledge of Shakespearean scholarship has been overestimated, as Floyd Stovall maintains. The larger part of Whitman's notes on Shakespeare are on eight sheets of paper and appear to have been taken principally from John Payne Collier's biography of Shakespeare (1844). Although the poet read Dowden's *Shakspere: A Critical Study of His Mind and Art* (1874) in 1888, his knowledge of Shakespeare was more limited than has been generally supposed. Stovall concludes that he was thoroughly familiar with the 8 or 10 plays popular in the 1830's and 1840's.

R. C. Harrison has collected evidence which argues that Whitman's writing, particularly his prose, is "saturated with the poetry of Shakespeare." His tentative study finds Whitman quoting 45 characters from 23 plays. As Stovall points out, however, the "echoes" are often proverbial and of "slight value" as evidence of acquaintance with the text. Furthermore, most of the references are from Whitman's "trite and sententious" writings in the 1840's or his "garrulous talk" of the late 1880's.

Whitman had doubts about Shakespeare's "feudalism" and his ornate style, but he genuinely relished the stormy passages and dramatic scenes in plays like *Richard III.* Though curious about Shakespeare's sources, his stage, and his biography, Whitman was not a Shakespearean scholar. Finally, Whitman's verse hardly reveals a trace of Shakespearean influence. [Richard C. Harrison, "Walt Whitman and

Shakespeare," *PMLA*, XLIV, 1929; Clifton J. Furness, "Walt Whitman's Estimate of Shakespeare," *Harvard Studies and Notes in Philology and Literature,* XIV, 1932; Alwin Thaler, *Shakespeare and Democracy,* 1941; Floyd Stovall, "Whitman, Shakespeare, and Democracy," *Journal of English and Germanic Philology,* LI, 1952; Floyd Stovall, "Whitman's Knowledge of Shakespeare," *Studies in Philology,* XLIX, 1952.]—J. F. L.

Whitmore, Walter. In *2 Henry VI,* one of a crew of pirates. Whitmore loses an eye "in laying the prize aboard." In retaliation he beheads his captive, the Duke of Suffolk (IV, i).

Whittington, Thomas (d. 1601). The shepherd employed by Richard Hathaway, Shakespeare's father-in-law. On March 25, 1601 Whittington made his will, in which he mentioned Shakespeare and his wife:

> Item I geve and bequeth unto the poore people of Stratford 40s. that is in the hand of Anne Shaxspere, wyf unto Mr Wyllyam Shaxspere, and is due debt unto me, beyng payd to myne Executor by the said Wyllyam Shaxspere or his assigns, according to the true meanyng of this my wyll . . . .

[B. Roland Lewis, *The Shakespeare Documents,* 1940.]

Whitty, Dame May. See WEBSTER FAMILY.

Widow. In *All's Well That Ends Well,* a Florentine and Diana's mother. The Widow solicits and secures Helena as her lodger. Helena, in turn, purchases the Widow's "friendly help" with ready gold and the promise of a generous dowry for her daughter. The cooperative old lady thereupon settles the arrangements for the counterfeit seduction of Bertram.

Widow. In *The Taming of the Shrew,* she is wed by Hortensio after he loses his suit for Bianca (IV, ii).

Wife for a Month, A. See John FLETCHER.

Wilde, Oscar (1854–1900). Irish-born dramatist, essayist, novelist, poet. Educated at Trinity College, Dublin, and Oxford, Wilde became a disciple of Walter Pater. A novel, *The Picture of Dorian Gray* (1891), was followed by a series of drawing-room comedies, most notably *Lady Windermere's Fan* (1892) and *The Importance of Being Earnest* (1895). Convicted on morals charges, he wrote an apologia, *De Profundis,* in prison (1897, pub. 1905).

In *The Portrait of Mr. W. H.* (1889), Wilde sets forth in fictional form a theory of the sonnets based on the identification of MR. W. H. Following a suggestion by the 18th-century critic Thomas Tyrwhitt, Wilde creates a character who, mainly on the basis of various puns (as in Sonnet 20: "A man in hue, all 'hues' in his controlling"), identifies W. H. as Willie Hughes, a boy actor. Wilde's young scholar commits suicide to manifest his faith in the theory, and his story is told by a nameless narrator who investigates further and builds a detailed interpretation of the sonnets based on the presumed existence of Willie Hughes.

The sonnets, he holds, are not independent from, but intimately connected with, Shakespeare's plays. Obscure lines become clear when read as a study of "the true relations between the art of the actor and the art of the dramatist." The marriage which is urged for Willie Hughes is marriage to Shakespeare' Muse (as in Sonnet 82), his agreement to go on th stage. The boy's beauty suits him perfectly for fe male roles, and it is for him that Shakespeare create his immortal women. The poet's devotion become so intense that Shakespeare finally sees in the boy no only "a most delicate instrument for the presentatio of his art, but the visible incarnation of his idea o beauty."

The rival poet is Marlowe, who lures Willi Hughes from the Globe to play Gaveston in hi *Edward II.* Although Wilde's narrator cannot iden tify the Dark Lady by name, he decides that she wa "the profligate wife of some old and wealthy citizen' who had an especial liking for actors. She has becom enamored of Willie Hughes, and Shakespeare, to di vert her attention from his beloved actor, addresse some sonnets to her. But the stratagem is not wholl successful, for Shakespeare himself is temporarily en thralled, more by the beauty of his own verse tha by the woman. It is she who was the citizen's wif in the anecdote about Shakespeare and Burbage (se John MANNINGHAM), but the other actor was no Burbage, Wilde's narrator insists, but the pretty Wil lie Hughes.

The story ends with the narrator, whose enthusi asm is spent by his burst of energy, skeptical of hi own theory, realizing that it rests entirely on on whose very existence can in no way be verified [Oscar Wilde, "The Portrait of Mr. W. H.," *Th Riddle of Shakespeare's Sonnets,* Edward Hubler ed., 1962.]—R.E.L.

Wilkins, George (fl. 1603–1608). Author. Virtuall nothing is known about Wilkins. His earliest know work is *Three Miseries of Barbary: plague, famin civill warre* (c. 1606), a pamphlet calling upon Lon doners to repent. His *The Miseries of Inforst Mar iage* (1607) is a play which was performed b Shakespeare's company and is closely related t *A Yorkshire Tragedy* (1608), generally ascribed t Heywood. It seems likely that the two men collabo rated on a play based on the prose pamphlet *Tw Unnatural Murthers* (1604), with Heywood's versio containing the original ending, and that Wilkins sub sequently rewrote the play with a new ending. Othe works, also written in collaboration, are *Jests t make you Merie* (1607, with Thomas Dekker) an *The Travels of Three English Brothers* (1607, wit John Day and Samuel Rowley).

Wilkins is also the author of *The Painfull Adven tures of Pericles Prince of Tyre* (1608), a nove based on the play performed by Shakespeare's com pany. Since it is commonly held that *Pericles* wa not entirely the work of Shakespeare, suggestion have been made that Wilkins had a hand in the dra matic version as well. Both Percy Allen (*Shake speare, Wilkins and Jonson as Borrowers,* 1928) an Henry Dugdale Sykes (*Sidelights on Shakespear* 1919) maintain that the play was substantially Wil kins' with revisions made by Shakespeare and tha Wilkins wrote *The Painfull Adventures* followin the success of the stage version. Kenneth Muir sug gests that Wilkins and Heywood collaborated on play, that Shakespeare's version superseded it on th stage, and that the prose version then followed.

Wilkins is probably also the author of *The Histor of Iustine* (1606), a translation of the *Historiaru*

Philippicarum of Justinus (fl. 3rd century A.D.). The ascription of this work to Wilkins strengthens the case for his authorship of an earlier stage version, for *The History of Iustine* contains a number of parallels with *Pericles,* including the names Pericles and Lysimachus. [*The Painfull Adventures of Pericles Prince of Tyre,* Kenneth Muir, ed., 1953; E. A. J. Honigmann, *The Stability of Shakespeare's Text,* 1965.]

Wilkinson, Tate (1739–1803). Actor and theatrical manager. The son of a clergyman, Wilkinson was educated at Harrow before becoming an actor. He was most noted for his imitations of contemporary members of the theatrical profession, including Peg Woffington, John Rich, David Garrick, Thomas Sheridan, and Spranger Barry. Unfortunately his own acting style was almost completely imitative of whatever actor's interpretation he happened to fancy. Thus, he played Othello at Bath and at Drury Lane in 1759 so nearly in Spranger Barry's manner that many thought Barry himself was playing the role. In Portsmouth in 1758 he played a variety of Shakespearean roles, including Romeo, Hotspur, Richard III, Horatio, Lear, Hamlet, and Petruchio.

From 1766 Wilkinson took over the management of several theatres. In 1773 he produced his own adaptation of *Hamlet.* Wilkinson collected a number of minor dramatic works of the 18th century. He also wrote *Memoirs of his own Life* (4 vols., 1790). [*Dictionary of National Biography,* 1885– ; Charles Beecher Hogan, *Shakespeare in the Theatre, 1701–1800,* 2 vols., 1952, 1957.]

Wilks, Robert (1665–1732). Actor. Popular with the audiences of his time, Wilks was excellent in comedy and was a truly fine tragedian. His first Shakespearean role, that of Othello, which he played at the Smock Alley Theatre in Dublin, earned him an opportunity in London and sometime later he filled the vacancy at the Drury Lane created by the death of Mountfort. Wilks' most popular role was that of Sir Harry Wildair, and at a time when Shakespeare was definitely not the rage, he scored successes as Macduff and Hamlet. In addition, his name appeared on the repertory bill, along with Barton Booth's and Colley Cibber's, of *Othello, Julius Caesar,* and *1 Henry IV.*

Wilks, with Colley Cibber and Thomas Doggett (who later gave way to Barton Booth), sublet the Drury Lane in 1711 and set in motion that theatre's revival. He continued both his joint-managership and his acting career until his death.

will. Shakespeare's will has long been the happy hunting ground of those seeking confirmation of their predetermined convictions about the poet's private life. As a result, it is popularly regarded as an explosive, revelatory document laying bare his innermost thoughts. The pedestrian truth, however, is that the will is a rather conventional straightforward account of Shakespeare's bequests to family and friends, differing neither in form nor tone from most early 17th-century wills.

It was first drawn up in January 1616 and revised, shortly before the poet's death, on March 25 of the same year. The revision mainly concerned the bequest to the poet's daughter Judith, who had married Thomas Quiney on February 2, 1616. Shortly after the marriage it became known that Quiney had been involved in an illicit relationship with another woman (see Judith SHAKESPEARE), and the changes in the will reflect the poet's lack of confidence in his son-in-law.

Both the original and revised drafts of the will were drawn up by Francis COLLINS, who, along with Thomas RUSSELL, was also one of the overseers of the will. The major provisions of the testament are designed to insure that his property pass to his male descendants. If this was Shakespeare's purpose, it was foiled by fate—an irony he doubtless would have appreciated—for his last direct descendant was his granddaughter, Elizabeth Hall. The legatees and their bequests are as follows:

Judith Shakespeare: £150, the interest on another £150, and a silver-gilt bowl.

Susanna Hall (Shakespeare's elder daughter): New Place, the Henley Street property, the property in Old Stratford, Blackfriars Gate-house and all of his other property.

Joan Hart (Shakespeare's sister): the occupancy of the Henley Street house at an annual rent of 12d for the rest of her life, and all of his clothing.

William, Michael, and Thomas Hart (sons of Joan Hart): £5 each.

Elizabeth Hall (Shakespeare's granddaughter): all of his plate, except for the bowl given to Judith.

Thomas Combe (Stratford neighbor): his sword.

Thomas Russell (friend and overseer): £5.

Francis Collins (overseer): £13, 6s 8d.

Hamnet Sadler, Anthony Nash, John Nash (Stratford neighbors): 26s 8d each to buy memorial rings.

John Heminges, Richard Burbage, and Henry Condell (fellow actors): 26s 8d each to buy memorial rings.

"the Poore of Stratford": £10.

Anne Shakespeare (the poet's wife): "my second best bed."

The famous "second best bed" has caused countless conjectures about Shakespeare's relationship with his wife. However, according to the law of the time it was not necessary for Shakespeare to have mentioned his wife at all in order to have her properly provided for. She automatically received the income from one-third of his estates for the rest of her life. The second-best bed was apparently a special remembrance, possibly included at his wife's request.

The text of his will, as transcribed by E. K. Chambers, is given below. Chambers' additions and comments are enclosed in square brackets; matter crossed out in the will is enclosed in broken brackets; and additions and corrections made in the will appear in italics.

Sheet 1

> Vicesimo Quinto die ⟨Januarij⟩ *Martij* Anno Regni Domini nostri Jacobi nunc Regis Anglie &c decimo quarto & Scotie xlix° Annoque domini 1616.

T[*estamentum*] W[*illel*]mj Shackspeare.

R[*ecognoscatu*]r. In the name of god Amen I William Shackspeare of Stratford vpon Avon in the countie of Warr gent in perfect health & memorie god be praysed doe make & Ordayne this my last will & testament in manner & forme followeing. That is to saye ffirst I Comend my Soule into the handes of god my Creator, hoping & assuredlie beleeving through thonelie merittes of Jesus Christe my Saviour to be made partaker of lyfe everlastinge, And my bodye to the Earth whereof yt ys made. Item I Gyve & bequeath vnto my ⟨sonne in L⟩ daughter Judyth One Hundred & ffyftie poundes of lawfull English money to be paied vnto her in manner & forme followeing; That ys to saye, One Hundred Poundes *in discharge of her marriage porcion* within one yeare after my deceas, with consideracion after the Rate of twoe shillinges in the pound for soe long tyme as the same shalbe vnpaied vnto her after my deceas, & the ffyftie poundes Residewe thereof vpon her Surrendring *of*, or gyving of such sufficient securitie as the overseers of this my will shall like of to Surrender or graunte, All her estate & Right that shall discend or come vnto her after my deceas or *that shee* nowe hath of in or to one Copiehold tenemente with thappurtenaunces lyeing & being in Stratford vpon Avon aforesaied in the saied countie of Warr, being parcell or holden of the mannour of Rowington, vnto my daughter Susanna Hall & her heires for ever. Item I Gyve & bequeath vnto my saied daughter Judith One Hundred & ffyftie Poundes more if shee or Anie issue of her bodie be Lyvinge att thend of three Yeares next ensueing the daie of the date of this my will, during which tyme my executours to paie her consideracion from my deceas according to the Rate aforesaied. And if she dye within the saied terme without issue of her bodye then my will ys & I doe gyve & bequeath One Hundred Poundes thereof to my Neece Elizabeth Hall & the ffiftie Poundes to be sett fourth by my executours during the lief of my Sister Johane Harte & the vse & profitt thereof Cominge shalbe payed to my saied Sister Jone, & after her deceas the said l^{li} shall Remaine Amongst the children of my saied Sister Equallie to be devided Amongst them. But if my saied daughter Judith be lyving att thend of the saied three Years or anie yssue of her bodye, then my will ys & soe I devise & bequeath the saied Hundred & ffyftie poundes to be sett out *by my executours & overseers* for the best benefitt of her & her issue & *the stock* not *to be* paied vnto her soe long as she shalbe marryed & covert Baron ⟨by my executours & overseers,⟩ but my will ys that she shall have the consideracion yearelie paied vnto her during her lief & after her deceas the saied stock and consideracion to bee paied to her children if she have Anie & if not to her executours or assignes she lyving the saied terme after my deceas. Provided that yf such husbond as she shall att thend of the saied three Yeares be marryed vnto or attaine after doe sufficientlie Assure vnto her & thissue of her bodie landes Awnswereable to the porcion by this my will gyven vnto her & to be adiudged soe by my executours & overseers then my will ys that the said cl^{li} shalbe paied to such husbond as shall make such assurance to his owne vse. Item I gyve & bequeath vnto my saied sister Jone xx^{li} & all my wearing Apparrell to be paied & deliuered within one yeare after my deceas, And I doe will & devise vnto her *the house* with thappurtenaunces in Stratford wherein she dwelleth for her naturall lief vnder the yearli Rent of xij^{d}. Item I gyve and bequeath

[(*In left margin now illegible*) William Shakspere

Sheet 2

Vnto her three sonns Welliam Harte [*blank*] Har & Michaell Harte ffyve poundes A peece to be paye within one Yeare after my deceas. ⟨to be sett ou for her within one Yeare after my deceas by my executours with thadvise & direccions of my over seers for her best proffitt vntill her Marriage an then the same with the increase thereof to be paie vnto her.⟩ Item I gyve & bequeath vnto ⟨her⟩ *th saied Elizabeth Hall* All my Plate *(except my bro silver & gilt bole)* that I now have att the date o this my will. Item I gyve & bequeath vnto th Poore of Stratford aforesaied tenn poundes, t m^{r} Thomas Combe my Sword, to Thomas Russel Esquier ffyve poundes, & to ffrauncis Collins of th Borough of Warr in the countie of Warr gen thirteene poundes Sixe shillings & Eight pence t be paied within one Yeare after my deceas. Iten I gyve & bequeath to ⟨m^{r} Richard Tyler thelder *Hamlett Sadler* xxvj^{s} viij^{d} to buy him A Ringe *to William Raynoldes gent xxvj^{s} viij^{d} to buy hin A Ringe*, to my godson William Walker xx^{s} i gold, to Anthonye Nashe gent xxvj^{s} viij^{d}, & t Mr John Nashe xxvj^{s} *viij^{d}* ⟨in gold,⟩ *& to my ffellowes John Hemynge Richard Burbage & Henry Cundell xxvj^{s} viij^{d} A peece to buy then Ringes*. Item I Gyve Will bequeath & Devise vnt my daughter Susanna Hall *for better enabling o her to performe this my will & towardes the per formans thereof* All that Capitall Messuage o tenemente with thappurtenaunces *in Stratfor aforesaied* Called the newe place wherein I now dwell & twoe messuages or tenementes with thappurtenaunces scituat lyeing & being in Henley streete within the borough of Stratford aforesaied And all my barnes stables Orchardes garden landes tenementes & hereditamentes whatsoeve scituat lyeing & being or to be had Receyved per ceyved or taken within the townes Hamlettes vil lages ffieldes & groundes of Stratford vpon Avon Oldstratford Bushopton & Welcombe or in anie o them in the saied countie of Warr, And alsoe Al that Messuage or tenemente with thappurtenaunce wherein one John Robinson dwelleth, scituat lye ing & being in the blackfriers in London nere th Wardrobe, & all other my landes tenementes an hereditamentes whatsoever; To Have & to hol All & singuler the saied premisses with their Ap purtennaunces vnto the saied Susanna Hall for & during the terme of her naturall lief, & after he Deceas to the first sonne of her bodie lawfulli yssueing & to the heires Males of the bodie of th saied first Sonne lawfullie yssueing, & for defalt o such issue to the second Sonne of her bodie law fullie issueing and ⟨so⟩ to the heires Males of th bodie of the saied Second Sonne lawfullie yssue inge, & for defalt of such heires to the third Sonn of the bodie of the saied Susanna Lawfullie yssue ing and of the heires Males of the bodie of th saied third sonne lawfullie yssueing, And for defal of such issue the same soe to be & Remaine to th ffourth ⟨sonne⟩ ffyfth sixte & Seaventh sonnes of her bodie lawfullie issueing one after Another & to the heires

2 Willim̃ Shakspere

Sheet 3

Males of the bodies of the said fourth fifth Sixte & Seaventh sonnes lawfullie yssueing, in such manner as yt ys before Lymitted to be & Remaine to the first second and third Sonns of her bodie & to their heires Males; And for defalt of such issue the said premisses to be & Remaine to my sayed Neece Hall & the heires males of her bodie Lawfullie yssueing, and for defalt of issue to my daughter Judith & the heires Males of her bodie lawfullie yssueing, And for defalt of such issue to the Right heires of me the saied William Shackspere for ever. *Item I gyve vnto my wief my second best bed with the furniture* Item I gyve & bequeath to my saied daughter Judith my broad silver gilt bole. All the Rest of my goodes chattels Leases plate Jewels & householde stuffe whatsoever, after my dettes and Legasies paied & my funerall expences discharged, I gyve devise & bequeath to my Sonne in Lawe John Hall gent & my daughter Susanna his wief whom I ordaine & make executours of this my Last will and testament. And I doe intreat & Appoint *the saied* Thomas Russell Esquier & ffrauncis Collins gent to be overseers hereof. And doe Revoke All former wills & publishe this to be my last will and testament. In witnesse whereof I have hereunto put my ⟨Seale⟩ *hand* the daie & Yeare first aboue Written.

By me William Shakspeare.

witnes to the publishing
hereof. Fra: Collyns
Julyus Shawe
John Robinson
Hamnet Sadler
Robert Whattcott

[*Endorsed*] Probatum coram magistro Willielmo Byrde legum doctore Comissario &c xxij[do] die mensis Junij Anno domini 1616. Juramento Johannis Hall vnius executoris &c Cui &c de bene &c Jurato. Reservata potestate &c Susanne Hall alteri executori &c cum venerit &c petitura

Inventorium exhibitum

The will consists of three pages; all three were signed by the dramatist. The absence of any reference to the plays or to the shares in the Globe and Blackfriars theatres is frequently cited by the "anti-Stratfordians" to deny Shakespeare's authorship. Shakespeare, however, did not consider the plays his personal property, since they belonged to the King's Men and to the publishers of those plays which had appeared in quartos. His shares in the Blackfriars and Globe were presumably sold before this document was drawn up.

The will is preserved at the office of the Principal Probate Registry at Somerset House, London. It was discovered in 1847 by Joseph Greene. An inventory of Shakespeare's personal effects which had been attached to the will is lost. [E. K. Chambers, *William Shakespeare*, 1930; G. E. Bentley, *Shakespeare: A Biographical Handbook*, 1961.]—E.Q.

William. In *As You Like It*, a rustic who is in love with Audrey. Touchstone, who has claimed Audrey for himself, warns William to shun her company, otherwise Touchstone will kill him "a hundred and fifty ways" (V, i).

Williams, [George] Emlyn (1905–). Actor, dramatist, producer, and director. Born in Wales, Williams received an M.A. from Oxford, where he was a member of the Oxford University Dramatic Society. He made his London debut in 1927 at the Savoy and later joined the Buxton Old Vic company, taking such roles as Oswald and playing in Ibsen's *Ghosts*. In 1937 he played with the Old Vic as Angelo (*Measure for Measure*) and Richard III. In 1956 he appeared as Shylock, Iago, and Angelo at the Shakespeare Memorial Theatre, Stratford-upon-Avon. He has directed many plays and has appeared in films since 1932. His plays include *A Murder Has Been Arranged* (1930), *Night Must Fall* (1935), and *The Corn Is Green* (1938). [*Who's Who in the Theatre*, 1961.]

Williams, [Ernest George] Harcourt (1880–1957). Actor and producer. Williams made his first stage appearance in Belfast as the Duke of Bedford in F. R. Benson's production of *Henry V* in 1898. He remained with Benson's company for five years, and made his first London appearance as Sir Thomas Grey in *Henry V* in 1900. In 1903 he toured with Ellen Terry, after having appeared as Romeo and Orsino in Benson's productions. His other Shakespearean roles included Gratiano, Claudio, Orlando, Clarence, and Charles VI of France (*Henry V*). The last role he repeated in Sir Laurence Olivier's film of the play. In 1923 he played Shakespeare in G. B. Shaw's *The Dark Lady of the Sonnets* at the Kingsway Theatre and in 1925 was the Player King in John Barrymore's *Hamlet* at the Haymarket.

In May 1929 he was appointed producer at the Old Vic, and was subsequently involved in 50 productions, appearing as Brutus, John of Gaunt (*Richard II*), and the Ghost in *Hamlet*. In 1940/1 he worked with the Drama Repertory Company of the British Broadcasting Company and rejoined the Old Vic at the New Theatre in 1944. His later roles included Glendower, the Lord Chief Justice (*2 Henry IV*), and Leonato. Williams published two books: *Tales from Ebony* (1934) and *Four Years at the Old Vic* (1935). [*Oxford Companion to the Theatre*, Phyllis Hartnoll, ed., 1951; *Who's Who in the Theatre*, 1957.]

Williams, Michael. In *Henry V*, a soldier in the English army at Agincourt. Quarreling with the disguised King on the eve of the battle, Williams exchanges gloves with him, for in this way they will be able to recognize each other later (IV, i). After the battle, Henry gives Williams' glove to Fluellen, whom Williams then accosts and strikes. Fluellen orders the soldier arrested, but Henry soon frees him and rewards him with a gloveful of money.

Williams, Sir Roger (c. 1540–1595). Soldier. A native of Wales, Williams was a professional soldier, a seasoned veteran of many wars. His last years were spent in the service of the earl of Essex, of whom he was an extravagant admirer. Dover Wilson and others believe that the doughty Welshman, Fluellen, in *Henry V* is Shakespeare's sympathetic portrait of Sir Roger. Wilson has also advanced the theory that Williams is one of the pseudonymous authors of the Marprelate tracts. See Martin MARPRELATE. [*Henry V*, New Cambridge Edition, J. Dover Wilson, ed., 1947; Geoffrey Bullough, *Narrative and Dramatic Sources of Shakespeare*, Vol. IV, 1962.]

Willobie his Avisa (1594). A narrative poem thought to contain allusions to Shakespeare's personal life. The poem was entered in the Stationers' Register September 3, 1594 and published the same year with the title *Willobie his Avisa. Or, the true Picture of a modest Maid, and of a Chast and constant wife. In Hexameter verse.* It was attributed to "Henry Willoby."

The work is introduced by a student of Oxford, Hadrian DORRELL, in an "Epistle Dedicatory" and an "Epistle to the gentle and courteous Reader." In the latter, authorship of the poem is attributed to "my very good friend and chamber fellow [at Oxford] M. Henry Willobie, a young man and a scholar of very good hope." A Henry Willobie of West Knoyle, Wiltshire, attended St. John's College, Oxford, in 1591; he subsequently transferred to Exeter College, from which he was graduated in 1595. He died sometime between 1597 and 1605, the date of the fourth edition of the poem—in which there is included a new poem, "The Victory of English Chastity," by Thomas Willobye, described as "Frater Henrici Willoby nuper defuncti" ("Brother of Henry Willoby lately deceased"). There was no "Hadrian Dorrell" enrolled at Oxford at that time, although a "Thomas Darrell" was in attendance at Brasenose College.

Dorrell's epistle is followed by two commendatory poems, one signed "Abell Emet," the other signed "Contraria Contrarijs: Vigilantius: Dormitanus." The latter has been conjecturally identified by Leslie Hotson as Robert Wakeman ("Vigilantius") and Edmund or Edward Napper ("Dormitanus"), both students at Oxford in the 1590's.

The poem itself relates the tale of the beautiful Avisa, wife of an innkeeper, upon whose virtue many assaults, all unsuccessful, are made. Avisa remains true to her husband, and the poem is ostensibly a paean to her fidelity and chastity. Among her rejected suitors is "Henrico Willobego," H. W., who, in despair at his rejection, turns for advice to his "friend W. S. who not long before had tryed the curtesy of the like passion, and was now newly recouered . . . he [W. S.] determined to see whether it would sort to a happier end for this actor then it did for the old player." The odd conjunction of the initials "W. S." and the reference to him as "the old player" is to many scholars irrefutable evidence of Shakespeare's identity; the poem is also seen as providing a clue to the relationship of the Fair Youth, Dark Lady, and poet of the *Sonnets*.

The case for Shakespeare's identity is further strengthened by an allusion to *The Rape of Lucrece* by "Contraria Contrarijs: Vigilantius: Dormitanus" in the commendatory verse:

> *Yet* Tarquyne *pluckt his glistering grape,*
> *And* Shake-speare, *paints poore Lucrece rape.*

In addition, W. S. attempts to console H. W. in the words

> She is no Saynt, she is no Nonne,
> I thinke in tyme she may be wonne.

which paraphrase lines in *Titus Andronicus* (II, i, 82–83):

> She is a woman, therefore may be woo'd;
> She is a woman, therefore may be won.

The lines, in fact, suggest several parallels with lines occurring in various places in Shakespeare's writings; in Sonnet 41:

> Gentle thou art and therefore to be won,
> Beauteous thou art, therefore to be assailed.

in *1 Henry VI* (V, iii, 78–79):

> She's beautiful and therefore to be woo'd;
> She is a woman, therefore to be won.

and in *Richard III* (I, ii, 228–229):

> Was ever woman in this humour woo'd?
> Was ever woman in this humour won?

G. B. Harrison, in his edition (1926) of the poem, argues that "Henry Willobie" is merely the assumed name of Matthew Roydon, a follower of Raleigh, who wrote the poem as a veiled attack on Raleigh's enemies in the Essex circle, particularly against Shakespeare's patron, Henry Wriothesley, earl of Southampton, to whom the initials "H. W." could easily apply. The case for Willobie as the author, however, is strengthened by Hotson's discovery that Willobie was related to Shakespeare's friend Thomas Russell.

The idea that the poem contains hidden allusions to contemporary persons is supported by two other facts. The first of these is that in 1596 a poem, *Penelopes Complaint: or a Mirror for wanton Minions* by Peter Colse, was published which appears to be a direct refutation of *Willobie his Avisa*. Colse in his dedication refers to the fact that "an unknown author hath of late published a pamphlet called *Avisa*" which Colse characterizes as "vain glorious." *Penelopes Complaint*, a rough English paraphrase of certain passages from the *Odyssey*, makes no mention of *Willobie his Avisa*, but in one of the commendatory Latin verses prefixed to *Penelopes Complaint* there is a strong contrast drawn between "Penelope" and "Avisa," to the detriment of "Avisa." Since Colse's poem is dedicated to the wife of Sir Ralph Horsey, lord lieutenant of Dorsetshire and a friend of Southampton, it has been conjectured that *Willobie his Avisa* contains an attack on Horsey. The conjecture is supported by depiction of one of Avisa's rejected suitors, "Cavaleiro," as having "wanny cheeks" and "shaggy locks."

The second circumstance pointing to *Willobie his Avisa* as a contemporary allusion is that the poem was one of the books directed to be burned in 1599 in the "bishops' bonfire" of Archbishop Whitgift. The books burned on that occasion were primarily pornographic or contained personal satire of an offensive nature. *Willobie his Avisa* apparently was classed in the second category. [Leslie Hotson, *I, William Shakespeare*, 1937; Tucker Brooke, *Essays on Shakespeare and Other Elizabethans*, 1948.]

Willoughby, William de, 5th Baron (d. 1409). A member of parliament during the reigns of Richard

II and Henry IV. In *Richard II*, Lord Willoughby joins Bolingbroke's cause after Richard confiscates the property of John of Gaunt and thereby deprives Gaunt's son, Bolingbroke, of his rightful legacy (II, i). [W. H. Thomson, *Shakespeare's Characters: A Historical Dictionary*, 1951.]

Wilmcote. A hamlet in the parish of Aston Cantlow two and one half miles northwest of Stratford, and the home of Shakespeare's mother, Mary Arden. Robert Arden, the poet's grandfather, held two estates there, ASBYES, which he bequeathed to his daughter, and a copyhold farm which may also have been willed to Mary Arden.

Wilson, Frank Percy (1889–1963). Scholar. Wilson was a professor at Leeds (1929–1936), London (1936–1947), and Oxford (1947–1957). An early work was *The Plague in Shakespeare's London* (1927). *Elizabethan and Jacobean* (1945), expanded from a series of lectures, considers the differences between the literatures of the two periods; the final chapter is devoted to Shakespeare. Other works include *Marlowe and the Early Shakespeare* (1953) and *Seventeenth Century Prose* (1960). [*Elizabethan and Jacobean Studies Presented to Frank Percy Wilson*, H. J. Davis and H. L. Gardner, eds., 1959.]

Wilson, Henry (fl. 1624–1631). Musician with the King's Men, included in the list of "Musitions and other necessary attendantes" of the company exempted from arrest in 1624. Wilson was sued for debt by John Heminges, Shakespeare's fellow actor, in 1628. He is described in the warrant as a "fiddler." In the prompt-book of Philip Massinger's *Believe As You List* (1631), he is mentioned in a stage direction: "Harry: Willson: & Boy ready for the song at ye Arras." [G. E. Bentley, *The Jacobean and Caroline Stage*, 5 vols., 1941–1956.]

Wilson J[ohn] Dover (1881–1969). Scholar. One of the most productive and stimulating scholars of the 20th century, Wilson first became infatuated with Shakespeare as an undergraduate at Cambridge. His earliest Shakespearean effort was his edition of *Life in Shakespeare's England* (1911), a collection of contemporary accounts of Elizabethan life. Shortly thereafter, under the influence of A. W. Pollard, he began the intensive paleographical and bibliographical studies that have been the central focus of his career. As one of the contributors to *Shakespeare's Hand in The Play of Sir Thomas More* (1923), Wilson concentrated on the orthographic characteristics of the manuscript of SIR THOMAS MORE in order to demonstrate that many of the misprints in early editions of Shakespeare's plays could be directly traced to the scribal peculiarities of the handwriting of "D." Having thus established the likelihood of the identity of "Hand D" with Shakespeare, Wilson used the manuscript as the source of his study of the copy for *Hamlet*, in *The Manuscript of Shakespeare's Hamlet* (2 vols., 1934).

Wilson has also published a number of valuable critical studies of Shakespeare. His *The Essential Shakespeare* (1932) is an imaginative treatment of the poet's development. *What Happens in Hamlet* (1935) is a highly regarded and influential study of the play, which includes among its arguments the theory that Hamlet's knowledge of Polonius' presence in the nunnery scene (III, i) is a result of his having overheard Polonius' announced intention to spy on him. This theory has been adopted in many recent stagings of *Hamlet*. Other critical studies by Wilson include *The Fortunes of Falstaff* (1943) (see FALSTAFF) and *Shakespeare's Happy Comedies* (1962). In 1964 Wilson produced his *An Introduction to the Sonnets of Shakespeare . . .*, in which he argues for William Herbert, 3rd earl of Pembroke, as the Fair Youth of the *Sonnets* (see MR. W. H.).

Despite these considerable achievements, Wilson's greatest contribution to Shakespearean studies is his editorship of The New Cambridge Shakespeare. Begun in 1921, under the joint editorship of Wilson and Sir Arthur Quiller-Couch, the edition, devoting a separate volume to each play, was the first to make use of the discoveries and methodology of scientific bibliographical criticism (see TEXTUAL CRITICISM). As the first volumes appeared, the edition became something of a storm center as a result of the ingenious but often fanciful accounts of the various stages of composition and revision which, according to Wilson, the manuscript of the play had undergone. Many of these reconstructions derived from Wilson's essentially disintegrationist theories (see DISINTEGRATION). Others resulted in highly original explanations for textual idiosyncrasies, such as that of ASSEMBLED TEXTS. Despite the lack of universal acceptance of his theories, the edition, completed in 1962, is among the most valuable of the 20th century. Not the least valuable aspect of the edition is Wilson's often controversial emendations, such as his substitution of "sullied flesh" for "solid flesh" in the first soliloquy of *Hamlet* (see EMENDATION).

Wilson, John (1595–1674). Instrumentalist, singer, and composer. It is probable that in Wilson's earlier years he sang in plays and wrote music to lyrics for stage productions. An accomplished lutenist, he became one of King Charles' musicians in 1635. Despite his royalist ties, he was appointed professor of music at Oxford in 1656, and with the Restoration became one of King Charles II's musicians. He was made a Gentleman of the Chapel Royal in 1662.

Wilson published a memorial tribute to Charles I, the *Psalterium Carolinium* (1657), and the collection *Cheerfull Ayres or Ballads* (1660), which includes his setting of Autolycus' song "Lawn as white as driven snow" from *The Winter's Tale*. He also contributed songs to numerous collections published in the third quarter of the 17th century.

Wilson is in all probability the same "Iacke Wilson" mentioned in a stage direction in *Much Ado About Nothing* (II, i) in the First Folio. In this case he would have played Balthasar and sung "Sigh no more, ladies." There is some possibility, generally discounted by scholars, that the Wilson referred to could have been another John Wilson (1585?–?1641), one of a band of public musicians who played for entertainments in the city of London.

Wilson, Robert (d. 1600). Actor and playwright. Wilson belonged to Leicester's Men in 1572, and he is alluded to by a number of contemporary writers as a distinguished actor. In 1583 he joined the Queen's Men. His acting is cited by Francis Meres in *Palladis Tamia* (1598) for its "extemporall witte" and his work as a dramatist for being among "the best for comedy." As a playwright he was one of the group of industrious hacks engaged by Philip Henslowe to supply plays to the Admiral's Men. One of his collaborations was SIR JOHN OLDCASTLE (1599), the play later published by William Jaggard as Shakespeare's.

Wilson, Steuart. See MUSIC BASED ON SHAKESPEARE: *20th century*.

Wily Beguiled (pub. 1606). An anonymous play probably originally produced at Cambridge sometime between 1596 and 1606. *Wily Beguiled* was published in 1606 with the following title page:

> A Pleasant Comedie, Called Wily Beguilde. The Chiefe Actors be these: A poore Scholler, a rich Foole, and a Knaue at a shifte. *H. L. for Clement Knight.*

The play is interesting primarily because of numerous imitations of lines in *Romeo and Juliet* and *The Merchant of Venice*. The imitations include parallels with the exchange between Lorenzo and Jessica in Act V of *The Merchant of Venice* and with Capulet's excoriation of Juliet for her refusal of Paris in Act III of *Romeo and Juliet*.

Winchester, bishop of. See Stephen GARDINER, bishop of Winchester.

Winchester, Henry Beaufort, bishop of (d. 1447). Second illegitimate son of John of Gaunt and Catherine Swynford, born at Beaufort Castle in Anjou. Richard II declared him legitimate in 1397. Rising rapidly, Beaufort was made bishop of Winchester in 1404, became tutor to the prince of Wales under King Henry IV, and on the accession of Henry V, was created chancellor. When the king died, Winchester was named a guardian of the infant Henry VI and sat on the council of regency. Later, as a result of a long and bitter quarrel with his nephew Humphrey, duke of Gloucester, Winchester resigned his post of chancellor.

In 1426 the pope named him cardinal of St. Eusebius and appointed him legate in Germany, Hungary, and Bohemia; but on Winchester's return to London, Gloucester refused to recognize him as legate and tried to deprive him of his bishopric. When Winchester subsequently became head of the Lancastrian faction in the kingdom, Gloucester promptly allied himself with the house of York. Turning to the war with France, Winchester tried several times to arrange a peace, but he met with no success. He died a few weeks after the mysterious death of his old enemy, Gloucester.

In *1 Henry VI*, Beaufort is the great-uncle of the King and rival of Gloucester, who accuses him of the murder of Henry V. After crowning Henry VI in Paris, Beaufort later appears as a cardinal. In *2 Henry VI*, agreeing with Queen Margaret and Suffolk that Gloucester must be put out of the way, Beaufort offers to provide the executioner. Later, while lying delirious on his deathbed, the Cardinal betrays his part in the Duke's murder.

Windsor. A town on the south bank of the Thames, 21 miles from London and the seat of one of the royal palaces, Windsor Castle. At the castle, the Chapel of St. George, built by Edward III, is used for the installation of the Knights of the Garter, at whose election day on April 23, 1597 *The Merry Wives of Windsor* was first performed. See THE MERRY WIVES OF WINDSOR: *Date*. [Edward H. Sugden, *A Topographical Dictionary to the Works of Shakespeare . . .*, 1925.]

Winstanley, William (c. 1628–1698). Biographer and literary historian. Winstanley is best known for his *Lives of the most Famous English Poets* (1687), a largely unoriginal compilation of early literary histories such as Edward Phillips' *Theatrum Poetarum* (1675) and Thomas Fuller's *History of the Worthies of England* (1662). Winstanley's account of Shakespeare was derived entirely from Phillips and Fuller and contains no new biographical information. The same work, however, contains an interesting defense of Richard III and deprecates the picture of him given in Shakespeare's play:

> The Life of King *Richard* the Third.
>
> But as Honour is always attended on by Envy, so hath this worthy Princes fame been blasted by malicious traducers, who like *Shakespear* in his Play of him, render him dreadfully black in his actions, a monster of nature, rather than a man of admirable parts.

[*The Shakspere Allusion-Book*, J. Munro, ed., 1909.]

The VVinters Tale.

Winter's Tale, The. A romance by Shakespeare.

Text. For the text of *The Winter's Tale* the sole authority is that of the FIRST FOLIO (1623). It is fully divided into acts and scenes, the verse regularly arranged, and the punctuation elaborate. This text was probably set either from Shakespeare's FOUL PAPERS or from a carefully transcribed manuscript of a PROMPT-BOOK that Sir Henry Herbert, Master of the Revels, reports on August 19, 1623 as lost. This report, together with the appearance of massed entrances in the text, has led J. Dover Wilson to suggest that the text was assembled from the individual actors' parts (see ASSEMBLED TEXTS). Wilson's theory, however, has not been generally accepted.

From the investigations of a number of scholars, beginning with Sir Sidney Lee, it has become clear that *The Winter's Tale* was nearly omitted from the First Folio. Isaac Jaggard, its printer, had set up only 13 of the comedies and was well on his way with the histories before a manuscript of *The Winter's Tale* turned up.

Date. Simon Forman saw *The Winter's Tale* at the

Globe theatre on May 15, 1611. In 1842 Peter Cunningham discovered in the cellar of Somerset House two lost account books of the Revels Office, one for 1604/5, the other for 1611/2; these records have been established as genuine. In the latter book the following entry appears: "The Kings Players on the 5th of November, 1611. A play called ye winters nightes Tayle." It is thought that the antimasque dance of the satyrs in the play (IV, iv, 352) was suggested by the satyr who sang and danced in Jonson's *Masque of Oberon,* acted at court on January 1, 1611. The text of this masque contains the following stage directions: "After the satyrs had sung a song to the moon, the song ended they fell suddenly into an antic dance, full of gesture and swift motion and continued it till the crowing of the cock." That Shakespeare borrowed his antimasque from Jonson is made probable by the words in which the Servant introduces the "saltiers" (his mistake for satyrs): "One three of them, by their own report, sir, hath danced before the king" (IV, iv, 345–346). Shakespeare seems to have further imitated Jonson in placing the satyrs' antimasque after his dance of the shepherds. If these two pieces of evidence are accepted as convincing, Shakespeare must have written *The Winter's Tale* sometime between the performance of Jonson's masque, January 1, 1611, and the day, May 15, 1611, that Simon Forman reports having seen it.

Sources. The source of the main plot of *The Winter's Tale* is Robert Greene's novel *Pandosto, or the Triumph of Time,* printed in 1588, and reprinted in 1607 with the title *Dorastus and Fawnia,* the running title in the original edition. Shakespeare follows his source closely, carrying over to his play all the characters in *Pandosto* except Mopsa. In *Pandosto* Mopsa is the typical shrewish wife of folklore, ready to cudgel her man whenever she thinks necessary. Shakespeare appropriates only her name, which he gives to one of the shepherdesses. He adds new characters, of which Autolycus is the most important. Although related to a figure in *Pandosto,* Autolycus is a fresh and brilliant creation. His pranks are like those that Greene describes in his CONY-CATCHING PAMPHLETS. In one of them Greene describes the way that one of these tricksters picks the pockets of members of a crowd while he holds their attention by singing ballads. The miracle of a statue's coming to life Shakespeare doubtless first found in the story of Pygmalion and Galatea told in Ovid's *Metamorphoses,* one of his school texts.

Shakespeare has Bohemia and Sicilia change places. Greene's king and queen of Bohemia become the rulers of Sicilia and Greene's king of Sicilia becomes the monarch of Bohemia. Thus, the famous Arcadian scene of Act IV is not set in the traditional Arcadia, Sicily. This change forces the poet to give Bohemia a seacoast, a mistake that has distressed many critics from Ben Jonson down to the present. Shakespeare also radically changed the ending of the story, and with it the meaning of the action. In *Pandosto* the queen dies immediately after her trial, and her husband later commits suicide, partly because of his feelings of guilt over his violent passion for his daughter, awakened in him when she and her princely love were cast by a storm onto the shore of his kingdom—a sexual complication that Shakespeare omits. Some of the changes that he made in the Greene story may have been suggested by Francis Sabie's *The Fissherman's Tale* and its second part, *Flora's Fortune,* both published in 1595.—O.J.C.

Plot Synopsis. Act I. Leontes, King of Sicilia, is enjoying a visit from his childhood friend Polixenes, King of Bohemia. When Polixenes proposes to return to his homeland, Leontes vainly exhorts him to prolong his stay and asks his wife, Hermione, to add her entreaties to his own. Her success, however, together with the attentions she pays Polixenes, is enough to arouse the jealousy of her husband; soon he becomes convinced that she has been unfaithful to him and that Polixenes is the father of the unborn child she bears. He even believes that the Crown Prince, Mamillius, is not really his son. Leontes reveals his suspicions to the Lord Camillo; the latter asserts his faith in the Queen's virtue, but reluctantly agrees to poison Polixenes provided Leontes will restore Hermione to favor. Polixenes, noticing the changed manner of his host, persuades Camillo to disclose the King's design to him and decides to leave at once, taking Camillo with him.

Act II. The flight of Polixenes serves only to confirm Leontes' belief in his guilt. Ignoring Hermione's avowals of innocence and the protests of his courtiers, Leontes orders that Mamillius be taken from her and that she be arrested. While she is in prison, she gives birth to a daughter. The Lady Paulina brings the infant to the King in the belief that the sight of the innocent babe will assuage his wrath, but he declares that the child is a bastard and drives Paulina from his presence with a torrent of abuse. He orders Antigonus, Paulina's husband, to take the child "to some remote and desert place" and to leave it there at the mercy of the elements. It is then announced that the Lords Cleomenes and Dion, whom Leontes had sent to the oracle at Delphi, have arrived with the sealed verdict of Apollo's priest.

Act III. Leontes brings Hermione before a court of justice and formally accuses her, not only of adultery, but also of conspiring with Polixenes and Camillo to murder him. Although he threatens her with death, she replies that her life is of little value now that she has lost his favor, "the crown and comfort" of her existence. She asks that Apollo be her judge, whereupon Cleomenes and Dion are summoned to deliver the oracle, which states that Hermione is chaste, that Leontes is a tyrant, and that he "shall live without an heir, if that which is lost be not found." The others hail the verdict as a vindication of Hermione, but Leontes merely declares that "there is no truth at all i' the oracle" and orders the trial to continue. Suddenly, a servant reports that Mamillius has died of fear over the Queen's plight. At this Hermione swoons and is carried away on the verge of death. Upon seeing the results of his defiance of the gods, the King regrets his rashness and resolves to seek a reconciliation with Hermione, Polixenes, and Camillo. But his repentance comes too late; bitterly upbraiding him for his jealousy, Paulina announces that the Queen is dead.

Antigonus, following the instructions of a sorrowful white-robed creature he has seen in a vision, names his tiny charge Perdita and leaves her on the stormy coast of Bohemia. After Antigonus has been chased away from the scene by a bear, the child is found by an old Shepherd. His clownish son then reports that the bear has killed Antigonus and that the ship that brought him to Bohemia has been wrecked with the loss of all on board.

Act IV. Sixteen years have passed. Raised by the old Shepherd as his daughter, Perdita has grown into a young woman of such beauty and grace that she has won the love of Prince Florizel, son of Polixenes. Though Perdita was not aware of Florizel's identity at first, and believed him to be a humble swain called Doricles, she now fears that the King will force him to desert her because of the difference in their rank. Meanwhile, Polixenes and Camillo, who have heard that Florizel is infatuated with a shepherdess, don disguises and pay a visit to the Shepherd's cottage while sheepshearing is in progress. Perdita welcomes them with garlands of midsummer blooms, causing the King to observe that she "is the prettiest low-born lass that ever / Ran on the green-sward." The gambols of the shepherds are interrupted by the arrival of Autolycus, a roguish peddler who has already relieved the Clown of the money with which he planned to buy dainties for his sweetheart. Autolycus dazzles the shepherds with his ribbons, trinkets, and ballads and warns the Clown to be wary, since "there are cozeners abroad." Polixenes, alarmed by Florizel's obvious devotion to Perdita, resolves to part them and discloses his identity just as the lovers are about to plight their troth. He threatens Florizel with disinheritance and Perdita with death if they do not end their relationship at once. After Polixenes storms out in a rage, Perdita asks Florizel to leave, but the Prince refuses to abandon her. Upon hearing that Florizel has decided to flee, Camillo suggests that he and Perdita go to Sicilia, where Leontes will surely welcome them. When Autolycus reappears after disposing of all his "trumpery," Camillo orders him to change clothes with Florizel. Camillo, who has long yearned to see Sicilia again, plans to inform Polixenes of the lovers' flight in the hope of inducing him to follow them and of accompanying the King himself. Meanwhile, the Shepherd, fearful of Polixenes' anger, has decided to tell him that Perdita is not his daughter, and to show him the bundle of costly garments and jewels that he had found with the infant. Autolycus, taking advantage of his new finery to dupe the Shepherd and his son into believing that he is a great courtier, persuades them to go aboard the lovers' ship instead.

Act V. Leontes' penitence for his follies has been so severe that Cleomenes beseeches him to forgive himself. Paulina, however, is unrelenting in her praise of Hermione's virtues and draws from the King a promise not to remarry until he finds a twin to the dead Queen. When Florizel arrives with Perdita, Leontes receives them warmly, but a moment later it is reported that Polixenes has landed in pursuit of the runaways and has seized the Shepherd and the Clown.

The Sicilian court is soon astir with the news of the revelations that followed the examination of the Shepherd's bundle and of Leontes' joyous reunion with his daughter. At the request of Perdita, Paulina, whose happiness is marred only by the knowledge of her widowhood, lets them see a statue of Hermione which she has in her house. Leontes is astonished by its resemblance to the Queen, though he remarks that the sculptor had given Hermione wrinkles that she did not possess while alive. When Leontes declares that he wishes to kiss the statue, Paulina states that she can make it move. At this the figure of Hermione descends from its pedestal and embraces Leontes. She now reveals that she has been alive all these years, hoping to see the fulfillment of the oracle. After urging Paulina to marry Camillo, Leontes begs the forgiveness of Hermione and Polixenes and introduces to his wife her future son-in-law.—H.D.

Comment. The title has about the same significance as that of an old wives' tale: the kind of story that an old crone, sitting in a chimney corner, might tell when winter has driven all the household into the kitchen. Little Mamillius says, "A sad tale's best for winter: I have one / Of sprites and goblins" (II, i, 25–26). And he begins, "There was a man . . . . Dwelt by a churchyard."

The Winter's Tale is composed of two distinct halves. The first three acts display many of the features of a Blackfriars romance, one oriented to the aristocratic audience which that theatre attracted. Like them, the drama sacrifices the development of character to the concoction of sensational situations, to swift changes in the relations of character to character, and, above all, to surprises. Shakespeare, however, is at pains to lend credibility to some of the operations of sheer chance. In *Pandosto* the abandoned baby is put into an open boat which is guided by the sea and the wind to Sicilia; there is no Antigonus to place the little girl in a desert country near the sea. On the other hand, Shakespeare disposes of Antigonus a bit too irresponsibly. The stage direction reads: "Exit Antigonus pursued by a bear"—and that is the last we see of him. The terrified Clown later reports the destruction of the ship by the stormy sea, the piteous cries of its drowning company, and a bear's tearing Antigonus to pieces.

Shakespeare endeavors to make credible many other events that in *Pandosto* are due to the intervention of fortune. For example, he gives the return journey of Perdita and Florizel to Sicily a plausibility it lacks in Greene's romance. There the fleeing lovers are carried to Leontes' court by fortunate mischance. But in *The Winter's Tale* Camillo plans every step of their journey in the hope that their meeting with Leontes will lead to his own return to Sicilia. Again, the unlikelihood of a child's dying of grief a day after learning of his mother's disgrace is mitigated by earlier reports to the King that the child, though ill, is recuperating ("He took good rest to-night"; II, iii, 10). His subsequent death, therefore, is caused by physical illness, only complicated by grief and shame. The introduction of the sheepshearing festival into Act IV brings into a tale of the strange and remote the realism of the familiar English countryside. The poet selects neither Pan nor a mournful shepherdess to introduce his audience into a sylvan Arcadia, but a country lout on his way to buy dainties at an English sheepshearing feast. This rustic is soon joined by Autolycus, one of the merry petty thieves who haunted English fairs and other country gatherings. The happy bumpkins whom he gulls are redolent of the soil. They have an appetite for songs and an open-mouthed eagerness to hear the latest broadside ballads and to sing them in parts. These country folk step into *The Winter's Tale* from Shakespeare's own merry England.

Shakespeare also gives the figures of a traditional

pastoral transforming touches of reality. (See PASTORALISM.) He changes the pastoral heroine into a girl with instincts as natural and sound as those of her mother. She realizes better than Florizel the dangers into which their love is likely to lead them; if she should lose him, she is prepared to milk her ewes and weep.

Leontes' mad suspicions and madder jealousy seem to have been created more for the febrile emotional crises that they produce than for the display of the ravages that an errant emotion can wreak upon a normal human being. E. M. W. Tillyard suggests that Leontes' seizure is like one of the god-sent lunacies of its victims in Greek drama, a temporary insanity like that visited upon Ajax or Hercules. Shakespeare presents Leontes' affliction as a full-grown obsession. Only those unfamiliar with the devastating effects of jealousy upon reason will deny that Leontes' deeds are those of a normal man, though a deeply afflicted man and a weak one whom his courtiers and especially Paulina regard with faint contempt. The change that the report of the death of Mamillius and Paulina's announcement of Hermione's deathlike swoon produce in Leontes is too sudden to arouse any emotions other than surprise and bewilderment. However, it is a striking example of the sort of theatrical effect that became the distinguishing mark of a Blackfriars romance. Time helps to cure Leontes' distemper and to bring about his reconciliation with his daughter. His contrition brings a realization that Hermione was peerless among women. In this mood Florizel's appearance awakens in the King deep regret for the loss of his friend and a poignant longing for his own children. But his delight is short-lived, for he at once learns that Florizel has deceived Polixenes. We anticipate one of the poet's long-drawn-out denouements, settling everything happily. Fortunately he disappoints us. For this conventional finale he substitutes a single *coup-de-théâtre* that surprises us and most of the characters in the play. He brings Hermione's supposed statue to life. There is a tradition that, at an early 19th-century production, as Hermione began to descend from her pedestal, the audience rose as one man and in a trance started to walk toward her. In spite of the hypnotic attraction of this sensational turn in the plot, the poet holds our attention to the human significance of the scene. Hermione's first embrace is for her husband, but her first words form a prayer to the gods to rain blessings on her daughter. The scene, touched with religious solemnity, is charged with joy and hope. We become assured that the mistakes and sins of the earlier generation will be redeemed in the happy future promised by the union of Florizel and Perdita. The feelings of peace and security induced by the reunion and reconciliation of those who have been alienated by suspicion and misunderstanding run deep. For our minds, swept clean by assaults of sorrow, grief, and despair, are conditioned to accept as certain the triumph of time, its power to heal and restore. See MYTHIC CRITICISM.—O.J.C.

Stage History. Except for the performance which Simon Forman saw at the Globe in 1611 (see above under *Date*), all of the seven productions of *The Winter's Tale* recorded before 1642 took place at court. The play was one of the dramas presented as part of the festivities devised to celebrate Princess Elizabeth's marriage in 1612; it was played before King James on other occasions and at least once at the court of Charles I. In 1741 Henry Giffard revived the play, which, so far as we know, had not been staged for over 100 years, at the newly built Goodman's Fields Theatre. That same year it was presented at Covent Garden featuring Hannah Pritchard in the role of Paulina.

In the 18th century the play was frequently shorn of all its plot except the story of Florizel and Perdita. The most famous and the best of the abbreviations was the one made by David Garrick. It was called FLORIZEL AND PERDITA and was first produced at Drury Lane on January 21, 1756. Except for the scene in which the Shepherd and Clown discover Perdita, Garrick's "improvement" consisted of material taken from the last two acts of *The Winter's Tale* and preceded by long prose expositions from Garrick's own pen. These take the form of a dialogue between Camillo and a "Gentleman," who obligingly relate to each other the plot of the first three acts. In spite of his amputation of all the first part of Shakespeare's play, Garrick had the effrontery in his preface to write of his "plan / To spill no drop of that immortal man." However, his adaptation so completely satisfied the audiences at Drury Lane that it held the stage for the rest of the century. Less successful were ADAPTATIONS made by MacNamara Morgan for the Smock Alley Theatre in Dublin (1756) and by Thomas Hull for Covent Garden (1773). In 1771 George COLMAN, in a version of the romance "as originally written by Shakespeare," did restore most of the original, but his effort fell far short of the popularity of Garrick's *Florizel and Perdita,* and after one season gave way to the abbreviation.

In the early 19th century *The Winter's Tale* returned to the London stage in something like its original form. On March 25, 1802 John Philip Kemble produced a version that was nearly complete Shakespeare. He did, however, omit the speech of Time as Chorus and used Garrick's ending. Kemble was a greatly admired Leontes. Sarah Siddons was Hermione, the last new part she added to her repertoire. In November 1823 William Charles Macready appeared as Leontes at Drury Lane and continued to play the part there for more than two years. In 1845 Samuel Phelps produced the play at Sadlers' Wells.

In 1856 Charles Kean gave the work a spectacular performance at the Princess' Theatre, embellished with music and dancing and adorned with numerous pseudohistorical representations of the architecture of ancient Syracuse. Having changed the scene of Act IV from Bohemia to Bithynia, he was able to clothe the shepherds in classical Greek dress; in this garb he put them through a wild Bacchic revel. This was the farrago of pageantry and stage machinery in which Ellen Terry had her first speaking part, in the role of the child Mamillius. This production played 102 consecutive performances. In September 1887 Mary Anderson staged a charming revival of *The Winter's Tale* in which she strove especially for scenic beauty. The mounting required 13 different sets, not unusual in an age when the action of a Shakespearean play was consistently smothered by sumptuous settings. Yet Miss Anderson in the double role of Perdita and Hermione captivated the critics as no other actress in these roles had ever done. In

1895 a company in which Sir Henry Irving played Leontes presented the play at Stratford-upon-Avon.

At His Majesty's Theatre in September 1906, Beerbohm Tree presented a three-act revival of *The Winter's Tale*, with Ellen Terry as Hermione, one of her last great roles. The scenery included a cascading brook at which Autolycus washed his face while singing, "When daffodils begin to peer."

Then, in 1912, Harley Granville-Barker chose *The Winter's Tale* in his attempt to discover "some means of acting Shakespeare naturally and appealingly from the full text." For this production at the Savoy, he designed a platform stage consisting of three acting areas and abolished footlights. Only six lines were cut from the text and, under Granville-Barker's direction, the company was urged to speak swiftly, but always with an ear to the "musical structure of the verse." This bold venture roused a critical storm. Although his cast, including Lillah McCarthy and Henry Ainley, gave inspired performances and he attracted many warm disciples, the public did not support Granville-Barker. After six weeks the play was withdrawn.

At Stratford during the 1920's there were two productions, one in 1921 and another in 1925. The West End saw the Fellowship of Players present the play in 1923 at the Lyric Theatre and again at Prince's Theatre with Harcourt Williams as Leontes and Lilian Braithwaite as Hermione.

In 1931 and 1932 the drama was staged at Stratford, Randle Ayrton playing Leontes and Dorothy Massingham in the role of Hermione. An Old Vic production in 1933 featured Peggy Ashcroft as Perdita, with Malcolm Keen as Leontes. Michael MacOwan directed *The Winter's Tale* for the Old Vic during the 1935/6 season.

Jack Hawkins played Leontes at the Open Air Theatre in 1937; Baliol Holloway took the part in B. Iden Payne's production in Stratford during that year and again in 1942. There was another Stratford *Winter's Tale* under Dorothy Green in 1943 and the Open Air presented Ernest Milton and Cecily Byrne as Leontes and Hermione in 1944.

Anthony Quayle's 1948 version at Stratford, with Esmond Knight, Diana Wynyard, and Paul Scofield as a slow-paced Clown, reverted to the traditional appearance of a live bear in pursuit of Antigonus. In 1951 Peter Brook staged a stark and successful *Winter's Tale* at the Phoenix Theatre. His cast included John Gielgud, Diana Wynyard, and Flora Robson (Leontes, Hermione, and Paulina). Gielgud interpreted Leontes as jealous from his first appearance onstage, an interesting attempt to make plausible the character's unmotivated jealousy. See Leontes.

Wendy Hiller was the Old Vic's Hermione in 1955, opposite Paul Rogers' Leontes and Margaret Rawlings' Paulina. *The Winter's Tale* by Peter Wood, emphasizing the acting over the production, presented Eric Porter as Leontes in 1960.

In America *The Winter's Tale* was revived at the Theatre Guild in New York during the 1945/6 season. The skillful acting of Henry Daniell as Leontes made even the King's half-insane jealousy credible. Seen through this actor's eyes, the Queen's success in persuading Polixenes to prolong his visit is but the least of what the excited husband suspects to be betrayals of intimacy between the two. Eva Le Gallienne played Hermione. Florence Reed was a splendid Paulina, doing more than her share in persuading the audience to accept the fantasy as truth. To the surprise of the critics, the production was a great popular success.

The Stratford Shakespearean Festival, Ontario, directed by Douglas Campbell, presented the drama in 1958. Eileen Herlie was Paulina, with Christopher Plummer as Leontes, Charmian King as Hermione, and Douglas Rain as the Clown.—M.G.

Bibliography. Text: *The Winter's Tale*, New Cambridge Edition, Arthur Quiller-Couch and J. Dover Wilson, eds., 1931; *The Winter's Tale*, New Arden Edition, J. H. P. Pafford, ed., 1963. Date: New Arden Edition. Sources: New Arden Edition; E. A. J. Honigmann, "Secondary Sources of *The Winter's Tale*," *Philological Quarterly*, XXXIV, 1955; Kenneth Muir, *Shakespeare's Sources*, Vol. I, 1957. Comment: S. L. Bethell, *The Winter's Tale*, 1947; Gerald E. Bentley, "Shakespeare and the Blackfriars Theatre," *Shakespeare Survey 1*, 1948; E. C. Pettet, *Shakespeare and the Romance Tradition*, 1949; E. M. W. Tillyard, *Shakespeare's Last Plays*, 1938, 1951. Stage History: New Cambridge Edition; New Arden Edition; G. C. D. Odell, *Shakespeare from Betterton to Irving*, 1920; J. C. Trewin, *Shakespeare on the English Stage, 1900–1964*, 1964.

Selected Criticism

CHARLOTTE LENNOX. It has been mentioned as a great praise to Shakespear that the old paltry story of *Dorastus and Fawnia* served him for a Winter's Tale, but if we compare the conduct of the incidents in the Play with the paltry Story on which it is founded, we shall find the original much less absurd and ridiculous. . . . Shakespear seems to have preserved the queen alive for the sake of her representing her own statue in the last scene—a mean and absurd contrivance: for how can it be imagined that Hermione, a virtuous and affectionate wife, would conceal herself during sixteen years in a solitary house, though she was sensible that her repentant husband was all that time consuming away with grief and remorse for her death: and what reason could she have for chusing to live in such a miserable confinement when she might have been happy in the possession of her husband's affection and have shared his throne? How ridiculous also in a great Queen, on so interesting an occasion to submit to such buffoonery as standing on a pedestal, motionless, her eyes fixed, and at last to be conjured down by a magical command of Paulina. . . . The novel has nothing in it half so low and improbable as this contrivance of the statue; and indeed wherever Shakespear has altered or invented, his *Winter's Tale* is greatly inferior to the old paltry story that furnished him with the subject of it. [*Shakespear Illustrated*, 1753.]

A. W. SCHLEGEL. *The Winter's Tale* is as appropriately named as *A Midsummer Night's Dream*. It is one of those tales which are peculiarly calculated to beguile the dreary leisure of a long winter evening, which are attractive and intelligible even to childhood, and which, animated by fervent truth in the delineation of character and passion, invested with the decoration of a poetry lowering itself, as it were, to the simplicity of the subject, transport even manhood back to the golden age of imagination. The calculation of probabilities has nothing to do with such nderful and fleeting adventures, ending at last in neral joy; and accordingly, Shakespeare has here :en the greatest liberties with anachronisms and ographical errors; he opens a free navigation be- een Sicily and Bohemia, makes Giulio Romano the ntemporary of the Delphic Oracle, not to mention ner incongruities. [*A Course of Lectures on Dra- ıtic Literature*, 1809–1811; trans. John Black, 1846.]

THOMAS CAMPBELL. After a hundred perusals of this y I sat down to it, for the last time, fresh from ıding Mrs Lennox's objections to it; and a dread- l list of them she seems at first sight to make out; t when you come to the piece itself, some of those jections disappear, as if conscious of their false- od, and the rest insensibly melt away. . . . Mrs nnox says, that the Statue scene is low and ridicu- ıs. I am sure Mrs Siddons used to make it appear us in a different light. Let Mrs Lennox and her llowers, if she has any, get a patent for this belief. 'hen a projector asked a reward from James I. for ving invented the art of flying, the King offered m a patent for it; the humbler privilege of an ex- ısive right to crawl upon all-fours ought to be ven to the believers of Shakespeare's Statue scene ing low and ridiculous. [*Dramatic Works of akespeare*, 1838.]

VICTOR HUGO. From its earliest publication this ay has been the subject of a mistake; placed by the litors of the First Folio in the list of Comedies, it s been accepted according to its label, and held to : an old wife's tale or as a light and fanciful impro- sation, and not, as it should have been, one of the ost serious and profound dramas of the poet. *The 'inter's Tale* is no comedy; it is a tragedy, more agic even than *Cymbeline*. Assuredly the death of ntigonus, and far more that of Mamillius, move us ore deeply than the death of Cloten. But it is not one by this double catastrophe that *The Winter's 'ale* is a drama; it is so by its general composition, y its impassioned tone, and by the ascending scale f its chief scenes. Therein Shakespeare's style is no nger that of *Much Ado About Nothing*. In this tter comedy Shakespeare carefully spares the spec- tor all painful emotions; he admits him beforehand to the secret of all situations, whereby the spec- tor, already set at ease by the very title of the play, eed never distress himself over imaginary misfor- nes whereof he foresees the issue. When Claudio aves us to pray at the tomb of his betrothed, we ever let ourselves be moved at this grief; we know ıe tomb is empty; we have been expressly told that lero is not dead, and that at the decisive moment e will reappear. But on the contrary in *The Win- r's Tale*, the poet keeps the secret to himself; not r a single instant does he admit us to the councils f Fate. He wishes us to be involved in the despair f his characters; he would have us, like Leontes, be- eve in the death of Hermione, and to the very last e leaves us the dupes of Paulina's device. Hence it that the dénoument is profoundly solemn. Then, ıen our anxiety is at its height; and when the statue irs, when marble becomes flesh, when the queen escends from the pedestal, it cannot be but that we re present at some magic invocation by a super- atural power, and at this unexpected resurrection, ve feel an indescribable emotion of wonder and sur- rise. [*Œuvres complètes de Shakespeare*, 1859–1866; translation from *The Winter's Tale*, New Variorum ed., 1898.]

F. J. FURNIVALL. The last complete play of Shakspere, as it is, the golden glow of the sunset of his genius is over it, the sweet country air all through it; and of few, if any of his plays, is there a pleasanter picture in the memory than of *Winter's Tale*. As long as men can think, shall Perdita brighten and sweeten, Hermione ennoble, men's minds and lives. How happily, too, it brings Shakspere before us, mixing with his Stratford neighbours at their sheep-shearing and country sports, enjoying the vagabond pedlar's gammon and talk, delighting in the sweet Warwickshire maidens, and buying them 'fairings,' telling goblin stories to the boys, 'There was a man dwelt by a church-yard,'—opening his heart afresh to all the innocent mirth, and the beauty of nature around him. [*Leopold Shakespeare*, 1877.]

G. WILSON KNIGHT. The truth shadowed, or revealed, is only to be known, if at all, within the subjective personality, the 'I' not easily linked into an objective argument. It is precisely this mysterious 'I' in the audience that the more important persons of drama, and in especial tragedy, regularly objectify. Now within the 'I' rest all those indefinables and irrationalities of free-will and guilt, of unconditioned and therefore appallingly responsible action with which *The Winter's Tale* is throughout deeply concerned; as in Leontes' unmotivated sin for which he is nevertheless in some sense responsible, with his following loss of free-will, selling himself in bondage to dark powers, and a consequent enduring and infliction of tyranny. The outward effects are suspicion, knowledge of evil and violent blame; with a final spreading and miserable knowledge of death ('There was a man dwelt by a churchyard'—II.i.28), leading on, with Paulina's assistance, to repentance. Time is throughout present as a backward-flowing thing, swallowing and engulfing; we are sunk deep in the consciousness of dead facts, causes, death. Now over against all this stands the creative consciousness, existing not in present-past but present-future, and with a sense of causation not behind but ahead, the ever-flowing in of the new and unconditioned, from future to present: this is the consciousness of freedom, in which 'every wink of an eye some new grace will be born' (V.ii.124). Hence our poetry plays queer tricks with time, as in the 'boy eternal' passage where consciousness is confined to 'to-day' and 'to-morrow': in Florizel's dreams of immediate perfection eternalized; in thought of 'eternity' (which includes the future, being over-dimensional to the time-stream) as the creative origin; and in Paulina's annoyance at the poet-gentleman's ready submission to time the destroyer. Freedom is creation, and therefore art; and hence our emphases on art, in the flower-dialogue, in notice of Julio Romano's skill, in the statue-scene; and here we approach a vital problem. It is precisely the creative spirit in man, the unmotivated and forward 'I', that binds him to 'great creating Nature', the 'great nature' by whose laws the child is 'freed and enfranchised' from the womb (II.ii.60–1): he is one with that nature, in so far as he is free. Our drama works therefore to show Leontes, under the tutelage of the Oracle, as painfully working himself from the bondage of sin and remorse into the freedom of nature, with the aptly-named Paulina as conscience, guide, and priestess. The resurrection is not performed until (i) Leontes' repentance is complete and (ii) creation is satisfied by the return of Perdita, who is needed for Hermione's full release. Religion, art, procreation, and nature (in 'warmth', 'breath' and 'eating') are all contributory to the conclusion, which is shown as no easy release, but rather a gradual revelation, corresponding to Pericles' reunion with Marina, under terrific dramatic pressure and fraught with an excitement with which the watcher's 'I' is, by most careful technique, forced into a close subjective identity, so that the immortality revealed is less concept than experience. Nor is it just a reversal of tragedy; rather tragedy is contained, assimilated, transmuted; every phrase of the resurrection scene is soaked in tragic feeling, and the accompanying joy less an antithesis to sorrow than its final flowering. The depths of the 'I', which are tragic, are being integrated with the objective delight which is nature's joy. ["Great Creating Nature," *The Crown of Life*, 1947.]

FRANK KERMODE. In its identification of the thematic and the theatrical, this is a true work of Shakespeare's. It is, of course, more complex than my account suggests. The survival of Hermione authenticates Perdita's beauty; time, which has seemed the destroyer, is a redeemer. At one masterly moment Perdita herself stands like a statue beside the supposed statue of her mother, to remind us that created things work their own perfection and continuance in time, as well as suffer under it. And in the end the play seems to say (I borrow the language of Yeats) that "whatever is begotten, born and dies" is nobler than "monuments of unageing intellect"—and also, when truly considered, more truly lasting.

Such a formula may justly attract the complaint that it is partial and moralizing. The play is a great one, with a natural energy that supports all it says about natural power; its scheme is deep-laid and its language fertile in suggestion. It will not be trapped by the historian, though he can speak of the vogue of tragicomic romance and compare Perdita with Pastorella. It will not, either, be caught in the net of allegory. To say that Hermione suffers, dies, and is restored to life, is not to suggest a parallel that the author missed, but equally not to hit his true intention. All truths, he might argue, are related to the Truth; all good stories will have—to use the term of Erich Auerbach—a "figural" quality. *The Winter's Tale*, like many other stories, deals with sin and forgiveness, and with the triumph of time—also a Christian theme. But we value it not for some hidden truth, but for its power to realize experience, to show something of life that could only be shown by the intense activity of intellect and imagination in the medium of a theatrical form. It is not a great allegory or a great argument, but a great play. [Introduction to *The Winter's Tale*, The Signet Classic Shakespeare, 1963.]

Wise or **Wythes, Andrew** (fl. 1589–1603). London publisher of several Shakespeare quartos. Wise entered the Stationers' Company as a freeman in 1589, his shop being located at the sign of The Angel in St. Paul's Churchyard. In 1597 he published the First Quartos of *Richard II* and *Richard III*. He probably purchased the manuscripts of these plays from Shakespeare's company, which may have been in financ trouble as a result of the closing of the theatres 1597. (See ISLE OF DOGS.) In 1600, in conjuncti with William Aspley, he published the First Quar of *2 Henry IV* and *Much Ado About Nothing*. I had published the First Quarto of *1 Henry IV* b fore, in 1598. Wise's publications, all good quart and generally good texts, suggest that he was friendly terms with Shakespeare's company. In 16 he transferred his rights to *Richard II*, *Richard I* and *1 Henry IV* to Matthew Law. There is record of his further activity.

Witch, The (c. 1610–1616). A play by Thom MIDDLETON, two songs from which were interpolat into the stage directions of *Macbeth*. *The Witch* extant in manuscript in the handwriting of Ral Crane, the scrivener of the King's Men. The sta directions occur in *Macbeth* at III, v, 33 [So within: "Come away, come away," etc.] and at I i, 43 [Music and a song: "Black Spirits," etc.]. T full texts of both of these songs are found in *T Witch*, a fact which has led a number of comment tors to suggest that the two scenes in *Macbeth* which the songs occur were written by Middleto [*The Witch by Thomas Middleton*, W. W. Gr and F. P. Wilson, eds., Malone Society Reprin 1950.]

Witches, Three. In *Macbeth*, three "secret, blac and midnight hags" who practice supernatural ar The Witches appear briefly in I, i, then again in iii, where they greet Macbeth as "thane of Glamis "thane of Cawdor," and "king hereafter." They th hail Banquo as "lesser than Macbeth, and greater a man who shall beget kings, though he himself none. In IV, i, they conjure for Macbeth thr apparitions: the first, an armed head, warns hi against Macduff; the second, a bloody child, te him that "none of woman born shall harm Macbeth and the third, a child crowned, with a tree in h hand, tells Macbeth that he shall not be vanquish till Birnam wood comes to Dunsinane hill again him. See SUPERNATURAL.

Wits, or Sport Upon Sport, The. See Robert Co

Witter, John (fl. 1606–1620). A London reside who married the widow of Shakespeare's fello actor Augustine Phillips. When Phillips died 1605, his share as a housekeeper of the Globe pass to his widow. Under the terms of the will, howeve she forfeited her share upon her remarriage in 16 In 1611 the actor John Heminges, who succeede Phillips' widow as executor of the will, leased Phi lips' share to the Witters. When the Globe burn down in 1613, the Witters were unable to meet the portion of the cost of rebuilding the new theat and the share lapsed into Heminges' hands; he ga one-half of it to Henry Condell. However, in Ap 1619, Witter brought a suit against Heminges ar Condell. In their reply to the suit, the defendants e plained how the original shares had been conceive (see GLOBE THEATRE), thus providing important d tails about the organization of Shakespeare's com pany. Witter was characterized in the reply as profligate who had long since deserted his wife, d ceased at the time of the trial. The court decided favor of Heminges and Condell. [C. W. Wallac *Shakespeare and his London Associates*, 1910.]

Witts Recreations. An anonymous collection

ppets of verse published in 1640 which includes an igram on Shakespeare:

To Mr. William Shake-spear.

Shake-speare, we must be silent in thy praise,
'Cause our encomion's will but blast thy Bayes,
Which envy could not, that thou didst so well;
Let thine own histories prove thy Chronicle.

'he Shakspere Allusion-Book, J. Munro, ed., 1909.]

Woffington, [Margaret] Peg (c. 1714–1760). Irish-rn actress. After a poverty-stricken childhood and brief career as a fruit-monger in Dublin, Peg 'offington played Ophelia there in 1737 in her first ·ious performance on the stage. In 1740 she played r the first time Sir Harry Wildair in *The Constant uple*. This role was to prove her most captivating d her appearance in trousers won more approval om audiences than did performances of her suc-ssors in the part, Woodward and Garrick. In 1740 e made her debut at Covent Garden under Rich and anged her name from Miss to Mrs. Woffington. 1741 she began to play with Garrick at Drury ne; her roles included Nerissa, Rosalind, Helena, d Cordelia to Garrick's Lear. By the following ar she and Garrick, known lovers, had begun to e in a Bow Street *ménage à trois* with Charles acklin. She continued to play in London and ıblin until her last performance as Rosalind in 57. In the course of her career she had portrayed e major female leads and supporting roles in Shake-eare's plays and contemporary adaptations: Ad-ına, Lady Anne, Desdemona, Mistress Ford, elena, Hippolito (in Dryden and Davenant's ver-on of *The Tempest*), Isabella, Queen Katharine, ıdy Macbeth, Ophelia, Lady Percy, Portia (in *lius Caesar* and *The Merchant of Venice*), Queen ertrude, and Viola Veturia (Volumnia in Sheri-ın's alteration of *Coriolanus*). She had accumulated great degree of notoriety and an unprecedented ıount of money. She was considered the hand-mest actress of her time, and although her morals ere not above reproach, her greatest successes were roles of ladies of rank and elegance. Augustin aly wrote the *Life of Peg Woffington* (1888). *)ictionary of National Biography*, 1892; Charles ·echer Hogan, *Shakespeare in the Theatre, 1701–oo*, 2 vols., 1952, 1957.]

Wolf, Hugo. See MUSIC BASED ON SHAKESPEARE: *th century, 1850–1900.*

Wolfit, Sir Donald (1902–). Actor and man-ɾer. Born in Newark-on-Trent, Notts, Sir Donald ade his first stage appearance at York in 1920 as ondello in *The Taming of the Shrew*, which he so played in 1924 in London. For the next two ːars he acted and directed for the Arts League of ːrvice and in 1927 acted with the Sheffield Reper-ry Company. In 1929/30 he played Tybalt, Cassius, ouchstone, Macduff, and Claudius with the Old ic, and the following year toured Canada with Sir arry Jackson's company. In 1933 he played Hamlet the Arts Theatre Club's production of the First uarto of *Hamlet*. In 1936 and 1937 he took part in ıe Shakespearean productions at the Shakespeare Iemorial Theatre, Stratford-upon-Avon, as Hamlet, rsino, Cassius, Kent, Ulysses, Tranio, Gratiano, on Pedro, Iachimo, Ford, Touchstone, and Autoly-ıs. In September 1937 he formed his own Shake-spearean company, touring as Hamlet, Macbeth, Shylock, and Malvolio. In February 1940 he opened his first London season of Shakespeare, playing Hamlet, Shylock, Petruchio, Malvolio, Othello, and Benedick. In 1940, during the Battle of Britain, he inaugurated a three-month season of "lunch hour" Shakespeare, and acted Touchstone, Falstaff (*Merry Wives of Windsor*), Richard III, and Bottom. During World War II he made many Shakespearean tours. When the war was over, he went to New York, where his company offered *King Lear*, *The Merchant of Venice*, *Volpone*, and *Hamlet*. In 1949 he presented four months of Shakespearean repertory at Camden, and in 1950 his company gave nine classical plays at the Malverne Festival and on tour; in 1951 they performed *Twelfth Night* before Queen Elizabeth II. In 1953, a new company under Wolfit's direction presented *Oedipus Tyrannus*, *Oedipus Colonus*, and *1 Henry IV* at Hammersmith, and in 1959 and 1960 Wolfit took a company on a Shakespearean recital tour to Africa, Italy, the United States, Canada, Australia, Asia, and the Near East. He has completed one volume of a proposed multivolume autobiography, *First Interval* (1955). He was knighted in 1957. [*Who's Who in the Theatre*, 1961.]

Wolsey, Thomas (1475?–1530). Bishop of Lincoln and Tournai, archbishop of York, cardinal, and lord chancellor; in *Henry VIII*, he implements the King's divorce of Queen Katharine and opposes his marriage to Anne Bullen.

Of obscure parentage, Thomas Wolsey was a brilliant student at Oxford, where he later founded Cardinal (now Christ Church) College. In 1503 he became chaplain to Henry VII and successfully completed several diplomatic missions. He rose even more rapidly under Henry VIII, and by 1511 dominated the privy council. He supported Henry in the divorce of Katharine, arranging to have himself made papal legate (with Cardinal Campeius) to try the case. He intended, however, that the king should marry a French princess, not Anne Bullen. His failure to win the pope's approval for the divorce was a strong factor in his sudden fall from favor. Having long since alienated the anti-clerical nobles by his power, his fantastic arrogance, and his ambition (he secretly maneuvered to be declared pope), he was banished to his see of York. He died a year later, faced with charges of treason.

In Shakespeare's time Wolsey's career was regarded as an ideal example of the operation of the Wheel of Fortune, wherein one is raised to the height of good fortune only to be precipitously cast down to the depths of despair. This conception was essential to the medieval notion of tragedy (see MEDIEVALISM IN SHAKESPEARE) and to the tragic movement of *Henry VIII*. Wolsey's tragedy, however, is only one of the play's themes. He thus never succeeds in emerging as the main character, although he is usually conceded to be the most memorable.

Woman Killed With Kindness, A. See Thomas HEYWOOD.

Wonderful Year, The. See Thomas DEKKER.

Woods, William. See ADAPTATIONS.

Woodstock. An anonymous play of uncertain date dealing with the early years of the reign of Richard II and the murder of Richard's uncle, Thomas of Woodstock, duke of Gloucester. A. P. Rossiter has argued that the picture of John of Gaunt in Shakespeare's *Richard II* is derived from the character of Woodstock in this play, presuming that *Woodstock* was an earlier play than *Richard II*. The problem of the date of Woodstock is complicated by the fact that it was not printed in Shakespeare's time and is extant in manuscript (Egerton MS 1994). E. K. Chambers and W. W. Greg have dated the play between 1592 and 1595, before Shakespeare's, and Chambers is inclined to the belief that *Richard II* was designed as a sequel to *Woodstock;* but the view has been rejected by an editor of *Richard II*, Peter Ure. What is clear, however, is Shakespeare's knowledge of the anonymous play, a fact attested by the frequent verbal echoes of it in *Richard II*. [*Woodstock, a Moral History*, A. P. Rossiter, ed., 1946; *King Richard II*, New Arden Edition, Peter Ure, ed., 1956.]

Woodvile or **Woodville, Richard** (d. c. 1441). A loyal retainer of Henry V, later chamberlain to the duke of Bedford, and finally constable of the Tower of London. In *1 Henry VI*, Woodvile is only lieutenant of the Tower. Following the orders of the Bishop of Winchester, he refuses to admit the Duke of Gloucester (I, iii). [W. H. Thomson, *Shakespeare's Characters: A Historical Dictionary*, 1951.]

Woodward, Henry (1714–1777). Actor. Woodward was the son of a tallow chandler in Southwark. After a few years at the Merchant Taylors' School, he joined John Rich's pantomime troupe at Lincoln's Inn Fields in 1729. From 1730 to 1736 he acted with the Goodman's Fields Theatre company in many varied roles, including Simple (*The Merry Wives of Windsor*) and Prince John (*1* and *2 Henry IV*). In 1737 he moved to Drury Lane, where he remained until 1747 (with a brief engagement at Covent Garden in 1741) and played a repertory of more than 50 roles, including 40 Shakespearean characters, among them Sir Andrew Aguecheek, Ariel, Falstaff (*2 Henry IV*), Launcelot Gobbo, Mercutio, Petruchio (in Garrick's *Catherine and Petruchio*), Touchstone, and a Mustacho and Ventoso, two characters added by Dryden and Davenant in their version of *The Tempest*. He played in Dublin in 1747 and returned to Drury Lane the following year. Woodward's Mercutio in the Garrick-Barry *Romeo and Juliet* rivalry of 1757/8 was a personal triumph. His last appearance was as Stephano in *The Tempest* in 1777. During his life he was hailed as an unmatched comedian; although his figure was said to be good enough for tragedy, he was most adept at delineating the fop and the coxcomb. Some accused him of overacting, but he was universally lauded as Parolles, Osric, Lucio, Touchstone, Aguecheek, and Mercutio. [*Dictionary of National Biography*, 1885– .]

Wooer. In *The Two Noble Kinsmen*, suitor to the Jailer's Daughter. On the Doctor's advice, he impersonates Palamon, thus helping to cure the girl's madness (V, ii).

woolshop. Name given by James O. Halliwell-Phillipps to a house in Henley Street, Stratford, purchased by John Shakespeare in 1556. The "woolshop" is adjacent to the house known as the BIRTHPLACE, although on the basis of existing evidence Shakespeare is more likely to have been born in the woolshop than in the birthplace. Halliwell-Phillipps' designation was based on his conjecture that John Shakespeare used this building, situated east of t birthplace, for the storage of wool. In the 17 century the building became an inn known first "The Maidenhead" and later as "The Maidenhe and Swan." In 1847 it was sold, with the birthpla to the Shakespeare Birthplace Committee. [J. Halliwell-Phillipps, *Outlines of the Life of Shak speare*, 1881.]

Worcester. The county town of Worcestershi The town apparently had a regular playhouse ear in the 16th century. In Shakespeare's time the dioc of Worcester included the town of Stratford. T consistory court of Worcester contains the registr tion of Shakespeare's marriage. The town is allud to in two of Shakespeare's plays: *King John* (V, v 99) and *1 Henry IV* (IV, i, 125). [Edward Sugden, *A Topographical Dictionary to the Wor of Shakespeare . . .*, 1925.]

Worcester, Thomas Percy, earl of (1344?–140 Younger brother of Henry Percy, 1st earl of Nort umberland. He served Edward III in internal affa and in war. Subsequently appointed steward Richard II's household, Worcester accompanied th king on his last expedition to Ireland. After Bolin broke's successful landing, however, he joined t invader. For four years Worcester was a loyal su porter of Henry IV; then, inexplicably turni traitor, he joined his nephew Hotspur in op rebellion against the king. When Henry attempt to make a compromise with the rebels before t fateful battle of Shrewsbury, Worcester deliberate misrepresented the king's proposals and incited h associates to immediate battle. He was taken prison and beheaded.

In *1 Henry IV*, Worcester joins his brothe Northumberland, and his nephew, Hotspur, in t rebellion against Henry IV. Before the battle Shrewsbury, Henry offers Worcester a full pard for himself and his associates, but the Earl, inste of passing on the King's message, delivers to Ho spur a challenge to immediate battle. In the su sequent fighting, Worcester is captured and e ecuted.

Worcester's Men (1555–1603) **[Queen Anne's M** (1603–1619)]. Acting company under the patrona successively, of William Somerset (1526–1589), 3 earl of Worcester; Edward Somerset (1553–1628 4th earl of Worcester; Henry Somerset (b. 1577 5th earl of Worcester; and Anne (1574–1619), que consort of England. The first Worcester's Men, provincial company, is known to have visited Str ford-upon-Avon in 1568/9, 1574/5, 1581/2, a 1583/4. In 1583 the 3rd earl licensed, or perhaps r newed the license of, a group which included E ward Alleyn, then only 16, Robert and Edwa Browne, Richard Jones, and James Tunstall. All these, excepting Robert Browne, later became A miral's Men.

After provincial visits in 1585, this early compa is heard of no more, and in 1589/90 a company und the patronage of the 4th earl enters the records. T second company, too, was mainly provincial unt 1601, by which time its patron held several hig court posts and felt, perhaps, that a London acti company was more in keeping with his prestige.

In March 1602 the privy council, seeking to lim the number of companies permitted to play in Lo ɔn, ordered Worcester's to join Oxford's Men and ıe two to play at the Boar's Head Inn exclusively. y August the company had entered into some sort agreement with the theatrical entrepreneur Philip enslowe, for they were receiving advances from m for the purchase of play-books and costumes. o theatre is mentioned, but presumably the com- ıny was playing at the Rose, which the Admiral's en had vacated when they moved to the newly ıilt Fortune in 1600. The names of the players cited the diary include John Duke, Thomas Blackwood, Villiam Kempe, John Thare, John Lowin, Thomas eywood, Christopher Beeston, and Robert Pallant. he diary also recorded 12 new plays and the price enslowe paid for them—the usual price was £6, ith an occasional £1 or £2 premium. Among the ays were *A Medicine for a Curst Wife* by Dekker ıd *Sir John Oldcastle*. The latter was an older Ad- iral's play which Dekker was hired (at £2 10s.) to ɔctor for Worcester's.

The company was not called to court in 1602/3, ıt the diary records a rather large expenditure evertheless, a total of £234 11s. 6d. for the 7 months diary entries. On May 9, 1603 the diary notes a sumption of playing after the death of Queen lizabeth, but the plague sent the company out of ondon along with the other companies, and the ary records no more entries pertaining to Worces- r's Men.

In 1603 they were taken under the patronage of ueen Anne. A letter of the privy council, dated pril 9, 1604, permitted the resumption of playing ıd noted that their theatre was the Curtain. The ɔmpany received cloth for the March 15, 1604 ronation procession of James and Anne. The actors mentioned were "Christopher Beeston, Robert Lee, John Duke, Robert Palante, Richard Purkins, Thomas Haward, James Houlte, Thomas Swetherton, Thomas Grene, and Robert Beeston." Another letter, a draft patent for a royal license, located the company at the Boar's Head as well as at the Curtain. The title page of George Wilkins, William Rowley, and John Day's *Travels of Three English Brothers* (entered in the Stationers' Register in 1607) indicates that this play was given by Queen Anne's Men at the Curtain, but a passage in Beaumont and Fletcher's *The Knight of the Burning Pestle* (1607) mentions that it was also given at the RED BULL THEATRE. In 1607/8 the company appeared at court five times. In 1611/2 they joined with Shakespeare's company, the King's Men, in performing Heywood's *Silver Age* and *Rape of Lucrece* and in 1614/5 gave three plays at court on their own.

Some of the members of the company are thought to have formed several concurrent provincial touring companies, under the single patent granted to Queen Anne's Men, between 1605 and 1617. In 1619 the queen died and the list of actors who received mourning for her funeral on May 13 indicates the changing makeup of the company; they include Robert Lee, Richard Perkins, Christopher Beeston, Robert Pallant, Thomas Heywood, James Holt, Thomas Swinnerton, Martin Slater, Ellis Wroth, John Comber, Thomas Basse, John Blaney, William Robinson, John Edmonds, Thomas Drewe, Gregory Sanderson, and John Garret.

In spite of the queen's patronage, the company appears to have been in severe financial straits from 1612 to 1617. Early in 1617 the company attempted to transfer its activities from the Red Bull to the newly completed Cockpit theatre. On the 4th of March that year the Cockpit was sacked by apprentices in a traditional Shrove Tuesday riot. The company returned to the Red Bull while repairs were completed and then moved to the Cockpit in June that year. The riot, however, had wreaked havoc on a company that could ill afford even the most minor setback.

In Christmas 1618/9, a performance of Middleton's *Inner Temple Masque or Masque of Heroes* was given at the Inner Temple. The character of Dr. Almanack was taken by Joseph Taylor, while other parts were taken by members of the group of Prince Charles' Men, which succeeded the Queen Anne's Men at the Cockpit-Phoenix a few months thereafter. The play alludes to the Shrove Tuesday misfortune, the low state of the Queen Anne's Men, and their occupancy of a so-called unlucky theatre.

The London company came to an end with the death of the queen in 1619, although a provincial company could be found touring and calling themselves "Servants to the Late Queen Anne." Christopher Beeston forced out whatever remnants of the company had attempted to stay at his Phoenix theatre and introduced Prince Charles' Men. [E. K. Chambers, *The Elizabethan Stage*, 1923; G. E. Bentley, *The Jacobean and Caroline Stage*, 5 vols., 1941–1956.]

QUEEN ANNE OF DENMARK, THE WIFE OF JAMES I. SHE WAS AN ENTHUSIASTIC PATRON OF THE THEATRE. (NATIONAL PORTRAIT GALLERY)

Wordsworth, William (1770–1850). Romantic poet. One of the early leaders of English romanticism, Wordsworth published, with his friend Coleridge, the epoch-making *Lyrical Ballads* in 1798. Wordsworth's preface to the second edition (1800) became the manifesto of the romantic movement.

Wordsworth's appreciation of Shakespeare, whom he considered, with Homer, the world's greatest poet, is well established. Shakespearean influences in Wordsworth's poetry are more difficult to trace. Russell Noyes has found influences from *Hamlet* in "Ode: Intimations of Immortality" as well as a direct reference (l. 147, "like a guilty thing") to the play. A letter written by his sister Dorothy when Wordsworth was working on the poem indicates that he was reading *Hamlet* at the time. In his long autobiographical poem *The Prelude* (pub. post. 1850), Wordsworth drew on Prospero's speech in *The Tempest* (V, i, 33–57). [J. C. Maxwell, "Wordsworth and Prospero," *Notes & Queries*, Old Series, 194, 1949; Russell Noyes, "Wordsworth's 'Ode: Intimations of Immortality' and *Hamlet*," *Notes & Queries*, New Series, 3, 1956.]

Worsdale, James. See ADAPTATIONS.

Wotton, Sir **Henry** (1568–1639). Poet, diplomat, and translator. Educated at Oxford and Middle Temple, in 1595 Wotton became an agent of the earl of Essex for the purpose of securing intelligence information. He later served as ambassador to Venice and as provost at Eton. Wotton was a friend of John Donne, and intended to write a biography of the poet. He died before beginning the work, however, but another friend, Izaak Walton (1593–1683), did accomplish this task.

In a letter written on July 2, 1613 to his nephew Sir Edmund Bacon, Wotton described the burning of the Globe theatre during a performance of *Henry VIII* (which Wotton here calls *All is true*):

> The King's Players had a new Play, called *All is true*, representing some principal pieces of the Reign of *Henry* the *8th*, which was set forth with many extraordinary Circumstances of Pomp and Majesty, even to the matting of the Stage; the Knights of the Order, with their Georges and Garter, the Guards with their embroidered Coats, and the like: sufficient in truth within a while to make Greatness very familiar, if not ridiculous. Now, King *Henry* making a Masque at the Cardinal *Wolsey's* House, and certain Cannons being shot off at his entry, some of the Paper, or other stuff, wherewith one of them was stopped, did light on the Thatch, where being thought at first but an idle smoak, and their Eyes more attentive to the show, it kindled inwardly, and ran round like a train, consuming within less than an hour the whole House to the very ground.

[*The Shakspere Allusion-Book*, J. Munro, ed., 1909.]

Wright, James (1643–1713). Theatrical historian. Wright's *Historia Histrionica: an Historical Account of the English Stage* (1699) is an important source of information about the theatre during the period of the Commonwealth and Restoration. It also sheds light upon the activities of Shakespeare's company. *The Historia* is written in the form of a dialogue between Lovewit, partisan of Restoration drama, and Truman, an old playgoer whose memory stretches back to the period before the closing of the theatres:

> *Lovew.* . . . But pray, Sir, what Master Parts can you remember the old *Black-friers* Men to Act, in *Johnson, Shakespear,* and *Fletcher's* Plays?
>
> *Trum.* What I can at present recollect I'll tell y *Shakespear,* (who as I have heard was a mu better Poet than Player) *Burbadge, Hemmin* and others of the Older sort, were Dead bef I knew the Town; but in my time, before t Wars, *Lowin* used to Act, with mighty A plause, *Falstaffe, Morose, Vulpone,* and *Ma mon* in the *Alchymist; Melancius* in the *Mai Tragedy,* and at the same time *Amyntor* w play'd by *Stephen Hammerton,* (who was first a most noted and beautiful Woman Act but afterwards he acted with equal Grace a Applause, a Young Lover's Part); *Tayler* act *Hamlet* incomparably well, *Jago, Truewit* in t *Silent Woman,* and *Face* in the *Alchymi Swanston* used to Play *Othello: Pollard,* a *Robinson* were Comedians, so was *Shank,* w used to Act Sir *Roger,* in the *Scornful La* These were of the *Blackfriers.* Those of prin pal Note at the *Cockpit,* were, *Perkins, Mich Bowyer, Sumner, William Allen,* and *Bird,* en nent Actors. and *Robins,* a Comedian. Of t other Companies I took little notice.
>
> *Lovew.* Were there so many companies?
>
> *Trum.* Before the Wars, there were in being these Play-houses at the same time. The *Blac friers,* and *Globe* on the *Bank-side,* a Wint and Summer House, belonging to the same Co pany, called the King's Servants; the *Cock pit Phaenix,* in *Drury-lane,* called the Queen's Ser ants; the private House in *Salisbury-court,* call the Prince's Servants; the *Fortune* near *Whit cross-street,* and the *Red Bull* at the upper e of St. *John's-street:* The two last were most frequented by Citizens, and the meaner sort People. All these Companies got Money, a Liv'd in Reputation, especially those of t *Blackfriers,* who were Men of grave and sob Behaviour.
>
> *Lovew.* Which I admire at; That the Town mu less than at present, could then maintain Fi Companies and yet now Two can hardly Subsi
>
> *Trum.* Do not wonder, but consider, That th the Town was then, perhaps, not much mo than half so Populous as now, yet then the Pric were small (there being no Scenes) and bett order kept among the Company that cam which made very good People think a Play Innocent Diversion for an idle Hour or two, t Plays themselves being then, for the most pa more Instructive and Moral . . . .
>
> *Lovew.* What kind of Playhouses had they befo the Wars?
>
> *Trum.* The *Black-friers, Cockpit,* and *Salisbur court,* were called Private Houses, and we very small to what we see now. The *Cockpit* w standing since the Restauration, and *Rhod* company acted there for some time.
>
> *Lovew.* I have seen that.
>
> *Trum.* Then you have seen the other two, in e fect; for they were all three Built almost exact alike, for Form and Bigness. Here they had Pi for the Gentry, and Acted by Candle-light. T *Globe, Fortune,* and *Bull,* were large House and lay partly open to the Weather, and the they alwaies Acted by Daylight.
>
> *Lovew.* But prithee, *Truman,* what became of the

Players when the Stage was put down, and the Rebellion raised?

Trum. Most of 'em, except *Lowin, Tayler* and *Pollard,* (who were superannuated) went into the King's Army, and like good Men and true, Serv'd their Old Master, tho' in a different, yet more honourable, Capacity.

n author of considerable versatility, Wright wrote number of books on a variety of subjects. He also llected old plays which unfortunately were not eserved after his death. [G. E. Bentley, *The cobean and Caroline Stage,* 5 vols., 1941–1956.]

Wright, Louis B[ooker] (1899–). American orary director and historian. Before assuming the osition of director of the Folger Shakespeare Liary in 1948, Wright had been for 16 years a mem-r of the permanent research group at the Henry Huntington Library. During that time he also ctured at a number of universities, edited the *untington Library Quarterly* (1946–1948), and rved on the editorial board of several other scholly journals. His first and best-known book is *iddle-Class Culture in Elizabethan England* (1935). e continued his investigations of popular culture ith *The Atlantic Frontier: Colonial American vilization* (1947) and *The Cultural Life of the merican Colonies* (1957). Wright has also been tive in editing a number of different works. With irginia A. LaMar he is editor of The Folger Liary General Reader's Shakespeare, a paperback ries containing illustrations drawn from the Folger ibrary collection. With the same collaborator he ited *Life and Letters in Tudor and Stuart England* 962), a collection of booklets originally issued inpendently by the Folger Library. This work, the st of a projected series, has among its distinctive atures numerous outstanding illustrations and usel annotated bibliographies. The Pelican *Henry V* as edited by Wright and Virginia Freund. His *akespeare for Everyman* appeared in 1964.

Wright, William Aldis (1836?–1914). Scholar. Vright served Trinity College, Cambridge, as liarian, senior bursar, and vice-master, but never ld a teaching position. His first scholarly work as in the field of biblical studies and took the form contributions to Sir William Smith's *Dictionary the Bible* (3 vols., 1860–1863). Then, with William eorge Clark, he edited the nine-volume Cambridge lition of Shakespeare (1863–1866), one of the most portant in modern scholarship. The editors were e first to enumerate the previous editions and to ake an attempt at establishing the relationship beveen them. For the most part, the emendations and itical apparatus have stood the test of time. The ne-volume Globe, based on the Cambridge edition, opeared in 1864 and remains a standard guide. Vright edited the *Journal of Philology* from 1868 1913. Among other texts which he edited are acon's *Advancement of Learning* (1869), the Engsh works of Roger Ascham (1904), and the Authored Version of the Bible (5 vols., 1909). A personal iend of Edward FitzGerald, he published the latr's *Letters and Literary Remains* in 1889.

Wriothesley, Elizabeth. See Elizabeth, countess of OUTHAMPTON.

Wroughton, Richard. See ADAPTATIONS.

Wroxall. A small village about 12 miles north of Stratford which may have been the home of Shakespeare's ancestors. In 1417 an Elizabeth Shakspere was living in Wroxall and in 1464 a Richard Schackspeire and his wife Margery were residents. Between 1504 and 1546 a William Shakespeare is recorded there, and two John Shakespeares are mentioned in local records between 1507 and 1534. In 1501 the prioress of the Wroxall Abbey was an Isabel Shakspere. [Mark Eccles, *Shakespeare in Warwickshire,* 1961.]

Württemberg, Frederick, duke of. German duke whose activities in England are alluded to in the horse-stealing incident in *The Merry Wives of Windsor* (IV, iii; IV, v). Frederick succeeded to the title of duke of Württemberg on August 8, 1593. The year before that, as Count Mömpelgard, he had visited England, been given two audiences with the queen and been entertained by the country's leading nobles, including the earl of Essex. During his visit, however, he developed an obsessional desire to become a Knight of the Garter and began besieging the English court with letters and ambassadorial missions in his behalf. After several delays the duke was elected to the Order of the Garter on April 23, 1597, the celebration for which *The Merry Wives of Windsor* was probably written. See MERRY WIVES OF WINDSOR: *Date; Sources.*

In the quarto version of the play there is a reference, in the context of the horse-stealing episode, to "cosen garmombles," a phrase which is usually regarded as a punning reference to Mömpelgard. During his 1592 visit, the count had been unable to secure fresh horses at one point in his itinerary and this may be the incident to which Shakespeare is here alluding. The actual horse-stealing episode itself, however, may have been suggested by another scandal (see le sieur Aymar de CHASTES), which Shakespeare associated with the duke of Württemberg in order to capitalize on the fact that the duke was being nominated as a Knight of the Garter on the very day on which the first performance of the play was to be held. [William Green, *Shakespeare's Merry Wives of Windsor,* 1962.]

Wyndham, George (1863–1913). Statesman and author. Educated at Eton and Sandhurst, Wyndham served for a time with the army. After his marriage in 1887 he resigned his commission and entered politics. He represented Dover in parliament from 1889 until his death, and served as chief secretary for Ireland, 1900–1905. In 1892, while his party was in opposition, Wyndham found time for literary activities. He became associated with William Ernest Henley and contributed to the latter's periodicals. He also wrote the introduction to Sir Thomas North's translation of Plutarch's *Lives* (1895/6) for Henley's Tudor Translations. His long prefatory essay and notes, written for *Shakespeare's Poems* (1898), remains one of the best introductions to the subject. *Ronsard and La Pléiade* (1906), a selection with verse translations, also has an excellent introductory essay. A group of his essays, including those on Shakespeare and North, have been selected by Charles Whibley and published as *Essays in Romantic Literature* (1919). [J. W. Mackail and Guy Wyndham, *Life and Letters of George Wyndham,* 2 vols., 1925.]

Wythes, Andrew. See Andrew WISE.

Y

Yates, Richard (c. 1706–1796). Actor. Yates began his career as one of the "the great Mogul's company of Comedians" at the Haymarket. In 1737 he began a two-year engagement at Covent Garden, in comic roles such as Wart in *2 Henry IV*. From 1739 to 1767 he played chiefly with the Drury Lane company, originating many non-Shakespearean roles such as Sir Oliver Surface in *School for Scandal* (1777) as well as playing most of Shakespeare's clowns. He was Autolycus in *Winter's Tale* and Lavache in the first revival of *All's Well* after the Restoration. He played the clowns in *Twelfth Night* and *Measure for Measure,* Pistol, Fluellen, Trinculo, Malvolio, Touchstone, Shallow, Dogberry, Falstaff, Launce, Bottom, and Shylock. He was the original Grumio in Garrick's *Catherine and Petruchio,* an adaptation of *The Taming of the Shrew,* in 1754. In 1756 he married an actress, Mary Ann Graham, the second Mrs. Yates, whose career later eclipsed her husband's. After 1767 Yates was apparently employed only intermittently. In Edinburgh in 1773 he played Othello, Touchstone, and Shylock; he reappeared at Covent Garden in 1782. In retrospect, critics held him unequaled as an impersonator of Shakespearean clowns. His best roles were the First Gravedigger in *Hamlet* and Autolycus. His portrayals were independent of any tricks or special costumes. [*Dictionary of National Biography,* 1885– .]

Yeats, William Butler (1865–1939). Irish poet and playwright. Born in Dublin, Yeats first intended to follow his father's career as a painter, but he soon turned to poetry. He achieved recognition with *The Wanderings of Oisin* (1889) and became involved in the literary life of London in the 1890's. On his return to Dublin he served with the Abbey Theatre and took part in the Irish nationalist movement; both activities had a decisive influence on his later work. *The Countess Cathleen,* his first drama, was written in 1892 and produced in 1899. In addition to poetry and drama, Yeats' work includes literary and dramatic criticism, autobiography, and letters. There is no complete edition of his works, but important volumes are the *Collected Poems* (1956), *The Variorum Edition of Yeats' Poetry* (1957), *Collected Plays* (1952), and *Autobiographies* (1955). Several collections of his letters have been published, the most comprehensive of which is that edited by Allan Wade (1954).

Although Yeats made constant reference to Shakespeare in his letters, no specific influence is discernible in either the poems or the plays. There are, however, suggestions of Shakespeare's *Sonnets* in the later poems. Yeats was rereading the early plays and the sonnets in 1934/5, and the poems written durin that period, like the *Sonnets,* at times express mood of disillusionment and disgust. Yeats contributed a essay on Shakespeare, "At Stratford-on-Avon printed in *Ideas of Good and Evil* (1903), and r printed in *Essays and Introductions* (1961). The e say was occasioned by his visit to Stratford in 19 where he read in the library of the Shakespeare In stitute and attended six performances of the histo plays. Yeats noted that the critics of the 19th centur tended to exalt those heroes who had some utility the state and to neglect those—Coriolanus, Hamle Timon, and Richard II—who did not. He believe that Shakespeare looked with favor on Richard admiring him as a man while recognizing his unfi ness to be a king, and judging him superior to th men who deposed him. By contrast, Henry IV coarse, violent, remorseful, and, ultimately, a failur Yeats also observed that the characters tend to b complements of each other: "Richard II is an u ripened Hamlet; Henry IV is a ripened Fortinbras See CRITICISM—20TH CENTURY.

Yorick. In *Hamlet,* the former court jester Elsinore. The discovery of his skull prompts Ham let's famous apostrophe: "Alas, poor Yorick! I kne him, Horatio, a fellow of infinite jest, of most e cellent fancy" (V, i, 202–204). The reference Yorick is traditionally regarded as an allusion to th famous Elizabethan clown Richard Tarlton.

York, Cicely Neville, duchess of (d. 1495). Daugh ter of Ralph Neville, 1st earl of Westmorland, ar Joan Beaufort. Cicely married Richard Plantagene 3rd duke of York, in 1438. In *Richard III,* as history, she is the mother of Edward IV, Richar the Duke of Gloucester, and George, Duke Clarence. In II, ii, while mourning with her gran children the death of their father, Clarence, sh receives the news of Edward's death. In IV, iv, sh curses Richard, calling him a toad.

York, Edmund of Langley, 1st duke of (134 1402). Fifth son of Edward III. York was thr times appointed regent on Richard II's absences fro the country. When the king went to Ireland in 139 York was initially loyal to him in opposition Henry Bolingbroke. Finding few supporters f Richard, however, York defected to the usurpe party and joined Bolingbroke on his victorio march to Bristol.

In *Richard II,* York appears as a weak old m who tries unsuccessfully to keep peace between h two nephews, Richard and Bolingbroke. After th latter has been crowned Henry IV, York discove that his own son, the Duke of Aumerle, is involv a plot to murder Henry. He exposes the plot to e King.

York, Edward of Langley, 2nd duke of. See Edard of Norwich, duke of AUMERLE.

York, Joan Holland, duchess of (d. 1434). Third ughter of Thomas, earl of Kent, and probably e second wife of Edmund of Langley, 1st duke York. Aumerle, portrayed by Shakespeare as an Holland's son, was actually the son of York's rst wife. In *Richard II*, the Duchess secures umerle's pardon for plotting against Henry IV, espite his father's demand that he be executed for s crime (V, iii). [W. H. Thomson, *Shakespeare's haracters: A Historical Dictionary*, 1951.]

York, Richard, duke of (1472–1483). Second son of dward IV and Elizabeth Woodville. In 1478 he as married to Anne, daughter of John Mowbray, uke of Norfolk. After the king's death he was onsigned to the Tower with his brother, Edward , and there the two boys were murdered, it is ought, by smothering with pillows. In *Richard I*, the Duke discomfits the usurping King with his arp wit (III, i).

York, Richard le Scroop or **Scrope,** archbishop of 350?–1405). Fourth son of Henry, 1st Baron crope of Masham. Though he submitted to the ccession of Bolingbroke as Henry IV, Scrope rned with the Percys against the king. After ublishing a manifesto declaring that he sought a ore just government, the archbishop took up arms ith Thomas Mowbray in 1405 and led 8000 men Shipton Moor. There they met the king's army nder the earl of Westmorland. After a meeting in hich Westmorland agreed to the requirements of e manifesto, York dismissed his men. Immediately Vestmorland withdrew from his promise and rested the archbishop and Mowbray, who were uickly tried and executed.

In *1 Henry IV*, Archbishop Scroop supports lotspur and his uncle the earl of Worcester in eir rebellion. He does not, however, fight in the attle of Shrewsbury. In *2 Henry IV*, Prince John f Lancaster treacherously deceives Scroop into ismissing his forces, whereupon the Archbishop is rested and executed.

York, Richard Plantagenet, 3rd duke of (1411–460). Son of Richard, earl of Cambridge, and Anne lortimer. Plantagenet became duke of York when is uncle, Edward of Langley, was killed at Aginourt (1415). Becoming involved in a long struggle ith Edmund Beaufort, 2nd duke of Somerset, York onsigned his enemy to the Tower when King lenry VI suffered his first fit of insanity. On the ng's recovery, however, York was relieved of his ost as protector and Somerset was restored to ower. With the aid of Salisbury and Warwick, ork then gathered a force behind him and battled e royal army at St. Albans, where he won a ictory (1455). On Henry's second attack of innity, York again became protector but was again moved from his post on the king's recovery.

After a period of refuge in Wales, York returned England, where, in 1460, he claimed the crown. arliament then moved that Henry would continue reign with York as protector, and that the latter ould succeed to the throne on the king's death. ueen Margaret, angered that this decision bypassed er son, Edward, renewed hostilities against York, who was defeated and killed at the battle of Wakefield. His head, crowned with paper, was placed on the walls of the city of York.

In *1 Henry VI*, the Duke of York appears first as Richard Plantagenet. When in London's Temple Garden he quarrels with John Beaufort, 3rd earl of Somerset, Plantagenet invites those who support him to join him in plucking a white rose. Somerset responds by plucking a red one. In *2 Henry VI*, York is the head of the White Rose faction. His rivals, Cardinal Beaufort and Suffolk, in order to rid themselves of York, send him to Ireland to suppress a rebellion. When, at St. Albans, York's army emerges victorious over the Lancastrians, he heads for London. In *3 Henry VI*, York is the pretender to the throne. Yielding to his sons' pressure to usurp it, York sets out to do so, but is defeated by Queen Margaret.

York, Thomas Rotheram, archbishop of (1423–1500). His ancestry is disputed. A trusted friend of Edward IV, Rotheram was imprisoned by Richard III for his continued loyalty to Queen Elizabeth after Edward's death. On his release after Richard's coronation, Rotheram took little part in public affairs. In *Richard III*, Rotheram resigns his seal to Queen Elizabeth on receiving the news that her brother Earl Rivers and her son Lord Grey have been imprisoned by the usurper. Rotheram offers to conduct the Queen to sanctuary (II, iv).

Yorkshire Tragedy, A. A domestic tragedy entered in the Stationers' Register in 1608 and published the

TITLE PAGE OF THE SECOND QUARTO OF *A Yorkshire Tragedy* (1619). LIKE THE FIRST QUARTO IT IS INCORRECTLY ASCRIBED TO SHAKESPEARE.

A

YORKSHIRE

TRAGEDIE.

Not so New, as Lamentable

and True.

Written by W. SHAKESPEARE.

Printed for *T. P.* 1619:

same year. Both the entry and the quarto listed the author as "W. Shakespeare.":

> A Yorkshire Tragedy. Not so New as Lamentable and true. Acted by his Maiesties Players at the Globe. Written by W. Shakespeare. At London Printed by R. B. for Thomas Pauier and are to bee sold at his shop on Cornhill, neere to the exchange. 1608.

It was reprinted in 1619 by William Jaggard, again ascribed to Shakespeare, and included in the Third (1664) and Fourth (1685) Folios.

The play is based on a sensational multiple murder committed in 1605 by a man named Walter Calverley who, in a fit of insanity, killed two of his children and wounded his wife (see DOMESTIC TRAGEDY). Few if any scholars accept Shakespeare as the sole author of the work, although some regard certain scenes as not unworthy of him. The two leading candidates for the authorship are Thomas Heywood and George Wilkins. If the play was acted by the King's Men, it is not unlikely that Shakespeare touched up or added one or two scenes. [Baldwin Maxwell, *Studies in the Shakespeare Apocrypha*, 1956.]

Young, Charles Mayne (1777–1856). Actor. Born in London and educated at Eton and the Merchant Taylors' School, Young made his professional debut in 1807 at the Haymarket as Hamlet. He also acted Hotspur and Petruchio before moving to Covent Garden, and later supported Kemble in *Othello* and *Macbeth,* occasionally replacing him in starring roles. After 1811, Young replaced Kemble altogether Covent Garden and was the leading actor of t London stage until challenged by Kean and Ma ready. Young continued to act until 1832. During h career he played many Shakespearean parts—I chimo, Prospero, Jaques, Coriolanus, Antony (*A tony and Cleopatra*), Richard III, Cassius, the Du (*Measure for Measure*), Falstaff, King John, Brutu and Lear. His best parts were Hamlet, Macbet Prospero, and Cassius, although some critics charg him with imitating Kemble. [*Dictionary of Nation Biography*, 1885– .]

Young, Edward (1683–1765). Poet. Young's *Th Complaint; or, Night-Thoughts on Life, Death an Immortality* (1742–1745) gave rise to the school "graveyard poets." His *Conjectures on Origin Composition,* published in 1759, is in favor of ori inality and independence in literature, taking excep tion to the theory that writers were to study an imitate the classics. For him, Shakespeare was t perfect example of a great literary talent who cou ignore and rise above the rules and conventions b cause he was the equal of the ancient writers o whose works the rules are based.

Young also cites Shakespeare in his argument th scholarship is not the same as genius. He subscrib to the image of Shakespeare as an untutored an natural writer, and suggests that greater learnir might have hampered him. [Herbert Spencer Robi son, *English Shakesperian Criticism in the Eigh eenth Century*, 1932.]

Z

Zeffirelli, G. Franco. Real name **Corsi** (1923–). pera and stage producer and designer. Educated in lorence, since 1949 Zeffirelli has designed and pro- iced operas and plays in all the major Italian cities, well as at many of the festivals on the continent, Great Britain, and in the United States. He di- cted and designed a production of *Romeo and lliet* at the Old Vic in 1960, the opera *Falstaff* at ovent Garden in 1961, and later in New York, and elaborate *Othello* at Stratford-upon-Avon in 1961. *Who's Who*, 1964.]

Zoffany, John. Born **Johann Zoffanyi** (1733–1810). ainter. German-born, Zoffany emigrated to Eng- nd in 1758 and won royal patronage and popular cclaim for his portraiture. He specialized in painting ramatic conversation pieces, which were group por- raits of actors set against a theatrical backdrop. He as a friend of David Garrick, and many of his con- ersation pieces are valuable to dramatic historians or the information they provide about contemporary stage design. His only theatrical conversation piece based on a Shakespearean play is the murder scene from *Macbeth*, played by Garrick and Mrs. Pritchard (see ART). His studies of Garrick in various roles, including the title role of *The Alchemist*, reveal Garrick's development of the more realistic technique of acting then replacing the erstwhile stilted theatricality of the stage. [W. M. Merchant, *Shakespeare and the Artist*, 1959.]

Zuccarelli, Francesco (1702–1788). Italian-born painter, employed in Venice and London. Zuccarelli was a founding member of the Royal Academy. He is especially known for his landscapes, and his "Macbeth and the Witches" (now in the Stratford Gallery) is a landscape suggested by the play, but is by no means a literal depiction of the scene. Zuccarelli is generally held to have been primarily a decorative painter, and his reputation, with his contemporaries as well as later critics, was not very high. [W. M. Merchant, *Shakespeare and the Artist*, 1959.]

Appendixes

Chronology of Events

Related to the Life and Works of William Shakespeare

Extracted from a compilation by Louis Marder

NOTE: The symbol . . indicates that only the year of the event is known.

1552

pril 29 John Shakespeare, the poet's father, first appears in the town records of Stratford as having a house in Henley Street, either as owner or tenant.

1556

ct. 2 John Shakespeare buys a tenement in Greenhill Street from George Turnor and a house (the "woolshop") and garden in Henley Street from Edward West.

ov. 24 In his will Robert Arden leaves to his youngest daughter, Mary, all his land in Wilmcote (about sixty acres), called Asbies, and the crop upon it, with ten marks (£6. 13s. 4d.).

1557

. Probably in this year John Shakespeare and Mary Arden are married in Aston Cantlow.

1558

ept. 15 Joan, first child of John and Mary Shakespeare, christened.

ov. 17 Elizabeth Tudor accedes to the throne.

1562

ec. 2 Margaret, second child of John and Mary Shakespeare, christened.

1563

pril 30 Margaret Shakespeare buried.

1564

pril 26 Notice of baptism of William, third child of John and Mary Shakespeare, entered in parish register, Holy Trinity Church, Stratford.

1566

July 4 John Shakespeare elected Alderman.

Oct. 13 Gilbert, fourth child of John and Mary Shakespeare, baptized.

1568

Sept. 4 John Shakespeare elected high bailiff, highest public office in Stratford.

. . *Archaionomia*, by William Lambarde, keeper of the records in the Tower, published; an extant copy contains a Shakespeare signature which some accept as genuine.

1569

April 15 Joan, fifth child of John and Mary Shakespeare, christened. Their first child, also named Joan, had presumably died.

. . Professional players first act in Stratford.

1571

Sept. 5 John Shakespeare elected Chief Alderman.

Sept. 28 Anne, sixth child of John and Mary Shakespeare, christened.

. . William probably enters grammar school, seven years being the usual age for admission.

1574

March 11 Richard, seventh child of John and Mary Shakespeare, christened.

1575

. . Queen Elizabeth visits Kenilworth Castle, near Stratford. William may have witnessed the pageantry, which is

. . possibly reflected in *A Midsummer Night's Dream.*

. . John Shakespeare buys property in Henley Street.

1576

April 13 James Burbage leases from Giles Alleyn land for building a playhouse to be called the Theatre on a site north of Bishopsgate in the parish of St. Leonard's, Shoreditch, in the liberty of Holywell, outside the jurisdiction of the city of London.

. . Later record indicates John Shakespeare applied for a coat of arms (see 1596).

1577

. . John Shakespeare begins to have financial difficulties, as shown in municipal records at Stratford.

. . Curtain theatre built just south of the Theatre.

1578

Nov. 14 John Shakespeare borrows £40 by mortgaging a house and fifty-six acres in Wilmcote, a part of his wife's inheritance.

1579

April 4 Anne Shakespeare buried.

1580

May 3 Edmund, eighth child of John and Mary Shakespeare, baptized.

1581

Aug. 3 A "William Shakeshafte," an actor, mentioned in the will of Alexander Houghton of Lea in Lancashire.

Sept. 1 Richard Hathaway of Shottery, husbandman, wills ten marks to his daughter Agnes (Anne) to be paid on the day of her marriage.

1582

Nov. 27 Marriage license issued by the office of John Whitgift, bishop of Worcester, to William Shakespeare and Anne Whateley [Hathaway] of Temple Grafton.

Nov. 28 Bond of £40 entered in the bishop of Worcester's register by Fulke Sandells and John Richardson to permit the marriage of William Shakespeare and Anne Hathaway after only one asking of the banns.

1583

May 26 Susanna, first child of William and Anne Shakespeare, baptized.

. . Earl of Oxford's players act in Stratford in the season 1583/4.

. . Earl of Worcester's players act in Stratford in the same season.

. . Earl of Essex' players act in Stratford in the same season.

1585

Feb. 2 Hamnet and Judith, twins of Willia and Anne Shakespeare, christened.

. . Unnamed company of players at Stra ford.

1587

. . Earl of Essex' Men at Stratford.

. . Earl of Leicester's Men at Stratfor

. . Rose Theatre built by Philip Hen lowe on the Bankside, Southwark, the liberty of the Clink.

1588

Sept. 3 Richard Tarlton buried, his death prob ably ending the fortunes of t Queen's Men.

Sept. 4 Earl of Leicester dies.

1589

. . Allusion to a Hamlet play (the *U Hamlet*) in Thomas Nashe's prefa to Robert Greene's *Menaphon.*

1591

. . *The Troublesome Raigne of John Kin of England* anonymously publishe in two parts for Sampson Clarke.

1592

March 3 *Harey the vj* acted by Strange's Me at the Rose.

April 11 *Tittus and Vespacia* performed b Strange's men. Again on April 2 May 3, 8, 15, 24, and June 6. See TITU ANDRONICUS: *Text.*

Sept. 3 Robert Green dies.

Sept. 20 Greene's pamphlet *Groats-worth of W* entered in Stationers' Register; it ca tigates Shakespeare as an "upsta crow."

Sept. 25 John Shakespeare named in a list recusants in Warwickshire.

Oct. 22 Edward Alleyn marries Joan Woo ward, stepdaughter of Henslowe, an forms partnership with Henslowe.

Dec. 8 Henry Chettle's *Kind-Harts Dream* entered in Stationers' Register; pre ace contains his apology for Greene attack on Shakespeare.

. . Severe plague in London; plays re strained much of year after June.

1593

April 18 Shakespeare's *Venus and Adonis* (Q entered in Stationers' Register b Richard Field.

May 6 Privy council grants license to trav to Edward Alleyn, of the Lor Admiral's Men, and William Kemp Thomas Pope, John Heminges, Au gustine Phillips, and George Brian Strange's Men.

May 30 Christopher Marlowe killed.

. . Theatrical performances restraine throughout year because of plagu acting companies, including the Earl of Pembroke's Men (possibly Shakespeare's company) face hard times.

1594

n. 23 *Titus Andronicus* performed by Sussex' Men, probably at the Rose.

n. 28 *Titus Andronicus* performed again.

b. 6 *Titus Andronicus* performed again.

On this day also *Titus Andronicus* entered in Stationers' Register by John Danter. A ballad of the same name was entered at the same time.

arch 12 *The First Part of the Contention betwixt the two famous Houses of Yorke and Lancaster* entered in Stationers' Register. See HENRY VI: *Text*.

ay 2 *The Taming of A Shrew* entered in Stationers' Register by Peter Short, who printed Q1 for Cuthbert Burby.

ay 9 *The Ravyshement of Lucrece* entered in Stationers' Register by John Harrison, for whom it was printed, as *The Rape of Lucrece* (Q1), by Richard Field.

une 5 & 12 *Titus* performed at Newington Butts in Surrey beyond the Bankside.

une 11 *Ur-Hamlet* performed at Newington Butts by the Lord Admiral's Men and the Lord Chamberlain's Men.

une 13 *The Taming of A Shrew* or *The Taming of the Shrew* performed at Newington Butts, presumably by the Lord Chamberlain's Men.

une 25 Richard Field assigns copyright of *Venus and Adonis* to "Master Harrison Senior."

une Regular performances of plays begin again for first time since 1592.

une Newly formed Chamberlain's Men first mentioned.

uly 20 *Locrine* entered in Stationers' Register by Thomas Creede; published in 1595 and again in Q3, 1664.

ug. 27 "Venesyon Comedy" first performed. See THE MERCHANT OF VENICE.

ept. 3 *Willobie his Avisa* entered in Stationers' Register; Shakespeare mentioned in commendatory verses.

ept. 22 Stratford devastated by fire. Part of Shakespeare property in Henley Street may have been burned or torn down.

ec. 26–27 Richard Burbage, William Kempe, and Shakespeare act with Chamberlain's Men at Greenwich Palace; paid March 15, 1595.

ec. 28 *The Comedy of Errors* performed at Gray's Inn, presumably by the Chamberlain's Men.

. *Titus Andronicus* (Q1) anonymously published.

. *Venus and Adonis* (Q2) printed by Richard Field for John Harrison.

. Earl of Pembroke's Men dissolved; Chamberlain's Men may have taken over some of their plays, including *Titus Andronicus*, *The Taming of the Shrew*, and *Hamlet*.

. . Robert Southwell, in his *Saint Peters Complaint with other Poems*, makes possible allusion to *Venus and Adonis*.

. . Chamberlain's Men perform in Cambridge and Ipswich, 1594/5.

1595

March 15 Payment of £20 for plays presented before queen during Christmas of 1594 by lord chamberlain mentions Shakespeare by name.

Sept. Fire in Stratford.

Dec. 9 *Richard II* or *Richard III* may have been performed for Sir Edward Hoby.

. . *The true Tragedie of Richard Duke of Yorke* anonymously printed by Peter Short for T. Millington; generally regarded as a bad quarto of *3 Henry VI*.

. . *Venus and Adonis* published in octavo.

1596

June 25 Harrison assigns copyright of *Venus and Adonis* to William Leake.

July 22 Henry Carey, Lord Hunsdon, lord chamberlain and patron of the Chamberlain's Men, dies. Shakespeare's company comes under patronage of George Carey, 2nd Lord Hunsdon.

Aug. 11 Hamnet Shakespeare is buried at Stratford, aged 11.

Sept. 11–17 Lord Hunsdon's Men perform in Guildhall at Bristol.

Oct. 20 Grant of arms, applied for twenty years earlier, made to John Shakespeare.

Oct. William Shakespeare is living in parish of St. Helen's, Bishopsgate; assessed 5s. on goods valued at £5.

Nov. 3 Francis Langley asks for an injunction against William Gardiner and his stepson William Wayte, who have threatened to close Langley's newly built Swan theatre.

Nov. 29 Wayte, fearing attack, secures writ of attachment to enforce keeping of the peace by Langley, Shakespeare, Dorothy Soer, and Anne Lee. Writ was issued to sheriff of Surrey, so Shakespeare must have moved to the south bank of the Thames in the liberty of the Clink.

. . *Venus and Adonis* (Q4) printed.

. . Swan theatre built by Langley in 1595 or 1596 in Paris Garden on the Bankside; a Dutch visitor, Johannes De Witt, estimates the audience at 3,000.

1597

Jan. 1–6 Chamberlain's Men at palace at Whitehall.

March 17 George Carey, 2nd Lord Hunsdon, appointed lord chamberlain.

April 22–23 Feast of the Garter, possible date of first performance of *The Merry Wives of Windsor*.

May 4 Shakespeare purchases New Place, two barns, and two cottages in Stratford from William Underhill for £60.

July 28 Production of *The Isle of Dogs* at the Swan causes the city council to close the theatres for a time.

Aug. 29 *Richard II* entered in Stationers' Register by Andrew Wise.

Oct. 20 *Richard III* entered in Stationers' Register by Wise.

Nov. 15 Shakespeare owes 5s. to the collectors of the subsidy in Bishopsgate ward, St. Helen's Parish, London; he defaults, having probably moved away.

. . *Romeo and Juliet* (Q1) printed in part by John Danter; unregistered.

. . *Richard II* (Q1) printed by Valentine Simmes for Wise.

. . *Richard III* (Q1) printed by Simmes for Wise.

1598

Jan. 1 Chamberlain's Men at Whitehall.

Jan. 6 Chamberlain's Men at Whitehall.

Jan. 24 Abraham Sturley writes from Stratford to Richard Quiney in London saying that Quiney's father has suggested that Richard approach Shakespeare about buying land near Shottery.

Feb. 9 Act of 1572 modified so that the patron of an acting company must have the rank of at least a baron. Admiral's Men and Chamberlain's Men have monopoly in London.

Feb. 25 *1 Henry IV* entered in Stationers' Register by Andrew Wise; printed for him by Peter Short later in the year.

July 22 *The Merchant of Venice* entered in Stationers' Register by James Roberts.

Sept. 7 Francis Meres' *Palladis Tamia* entered in Stationers' Register.

Sept. Ben Jonson's *Every Man In his Humour* performed on some day before Sept. 20; Shakespeare one of the principal players.

Oct. 1 An indenture lists Shakespeare as in default in payment of taxes in St. Helen's Parish, Bishopsgate, London.

Oct. 25 Richard Quiney in London addresses a letter to Shakespeare asking for a loan of £30 or £40 but apparently does not have it delivered.

Oct. 30 On about this date Adrian Quiney writes to his son Richard about a proposed bargain with Shakespeare.

Oct. Late in this month or early in November another letter from Adrian Quiney to his son indicates that the loan is still under consideration.

Nov. 4 Sturley again writes Richard Quiney from Stratford mentioning the loan.

Dec. 26 Chamberlain's Men at Whitehall.

Dec. The Theatre demolished.

. . *Love's Labour's Lost* (Q1) printed by William White for Cuthbert Burby.

. . *Richard III* (Q2) printed by Thomas Creede for Andrew Wise.

. . *Richard II* (Q2 and Q3) printed by Va entine Simmes for Wise.

. . *The Rape of Lucrece* (Q2) printed b Peter Short for John Harrison.

. . Shakespeare, now alluded to as "gentl man" in town records, sells the Stra ford Corporation a load of stone.

. . Shakespeare among principal actors c Chamberlain's Men, as recorded i 1616 Folio of Jonson's works und *Every Man In his Humour.*

1599

Jan. 1 Chamberlain's Men at Whitehall.

Feb. 20 Chamberlain's Men at palace at Rich mond.

Feb. 21 Land for Globe theatre leased b Nicholas Brend to leading sharehold ers in Chamberlain's Men, includin Shakespeare.

Sept. 21 Thomas Platter of Basle attends a per formance of *Julius Caesar* at th Globe.

Oct. 6 Shakespeare's name appears in tax rec ords as owing taxes in St. Helen's Par ish, Bishopsgate.

. . *Romeo and Juliet* (Q2) printed b Thomas Creede for Cuthbert Burby

. . *1 Henry IV* (Q2) printed by Simo Stafford for Andrew Wise.

. . *Venus and Adonis* (O3) printed b Peter Short for William Leake.

. . *Venus and Adonis* (O4) printed b Richard Bradock for William Leake.

. . John Weever's poem "Ad Guglielmur Shakespeare" published, praising th poet for his *Venus and Adonis.*

. . Thomas Savage and William Leveso appointed trustees of the Globe the atre by Shakespeare and his fellov shareholders.

. . *The Passionate Pilgrim* attributed t Shakespeare by its publisher, Williar Jaggard. Unregistered.

1600

Jan. 8 Philip Henslowe signs contract fo building the Fortune theatre.

Aug. 4 *Henry V*, *As You Like It*, and *Muc Ado About Nothing* entered in Sta tioners' Register by James Roberts thought to be a "blocking entry."

Aug. 14 Rights to *Henry V* transferred in Sta tioners' Register to Thomas Pavier who had secured the copyrights fron Thomas Millington and John Busby

Aug. 23 *Much Ado About Nothing* and *2 Henry IV* entered in Stationers' Register a by Shakespeare. First mention o Shakespeare by name in Register.

Oct. 6 Shakespeare is listed on the tax record as owing 13s. 4d. on the pipe roll fo the county of Sussex, which include Surrey for tax purposes.

Oct. 8 *A Midsummer Night's Dream* entere in Stationers' Register by Thoma Fisher.

Oct. 28 Copyright of *The Merchant of Venice* transferred by James Roberts to Thomas Hayes, for whom he printed Q1.

. *Much Ado About Nothing* (Q1) printed by Valentine Simmes for Andrew Wise and William Aspley.

. *A Midsummer Night's Dream* (Q1) printed by Allde or Bradock for Thomas Fisher.

. *Henry V* (Q1) printed by Thomas Creede for Thomas Millington and John Busby.

. *2 Henry IV* (Q1) printed by Simmes for Wise and Aspley.

. *The Merchant of Venice* (Q1) printed by James Roberts for Thomas Hayes.

. *Titus Andronicus* (Q2) printed by Roberts for Edward White.

. *The First Part of the Contention betwixt the two famous Houses of Yorke and Lancaster* (Q2) printed by Simmes for Thomas Millington. See 2 HENRY VI.

. *The true Tragedie of Richard Duke of Yorke* (Q2) printed by William White for Millington.

. *The Rape of Lucrece* (O2 and O3) printed and published by John Harrison.

. Thomas Morley's *First Book of Airs or Little Short Songs* published; contains a setting of "It Was a Lover and His Lass," a song in *As You Like It*.

1601

Feb. 6 A performance of *Richard II* arranged for the following day by friends of the earl of Essex as inspiration for his revolt.

Feb. 8 Robert, earl of Essex, leads a revolt.

Feb. 19 Essex and earl of Southampton tried and condemned.

Feb. 25 Essex executed, Southampton spared.

March 25 Thomas Whittington, Joan Hathaway's shepherd, bequeaths to the poor of Stratford 40s. owed him by Anne Shakespeare.

Sept. 8 John Shakespeare buried in Stratford.

. For razing the Theatre, the Burbages are sued by Giles Alleyn, who had leased the site to their father. Alleyn records that the timber was used by them in building the Globe theatre.

. *Love's Martyr* published; includes "The Phoenix and the Turtle," ascribed to Shakespeare.

. *The Returne from Parnassus*, Part 1, published; a university play containing many references to Shakespeare.

1602

Jan. 18 *The Merry Wives of Windsor* entered in Stationers' Register by John Busby, transferred on same day to Arthur Johnson.

May 1 Shakespeare purchases from William and John Combe 107 acres of farmland in Old Stratford, agreeing to pay £320.

July 26 *Hamlet* entered in Stationers' Register by James Roberts.

Aug. 11 *Thomas Lord Cromwell* entered in Stationers' Register as by "W. S." Appears in F3 (1664).

Sept. 28 Walter Getley surrenders to William Shakespeare a cottage and one-quarter acre of land in Chapel Lane across from the garden of New Place.

. . *The Merry Wives of Windsor* (Q1) printed by Thomas Creede for Arthur Johnson.

. . *Henry V* (Q2) printed by Creede for Thomas Pavier.

. . *Richard III* (Q3) printed by Creede for Andrew Wise.

. . *The Returne from Parnassus*, Part 2, an undergraduate play at Cambridge, mentions Shakespeare in connection with Richard Burbage.

1603

Jan. 1 *A Midsummer Night's Dream* performed at Hampton Court.

Jan. 25 Copyright of *Richard II* transferred to Matthew Law by Andrew Wise.

Feb. 7 *Troilus and Cressida* entered in Stationers' Register by James Roberts.

March 24 Queen Elizabeth dies.

April London theatres closed because of the plague.

May 7 The new king, James I, arrives in London.

May 19 Patent granted to Chamberlain's Men by James I renames them King's Men; Shakespeare's name mentioned in patent.

May *Hamlet* (Q1) printed by Valentine Simmes for Nicholas Ling and John Trundell.

June 25 Copyrights to *1 Henry IV*, *Richard II*, and *Richard III* transferred to Matthew Law by Andrew Wise.

Dec. 2 King's Men paid £30 for acting a play, possibly *As You Like It*, before the king at Wilton.

Oct. 24–Dec. 12 During the winter Shakespeare appeared in a performance of Ben Jonson's *Sejanus*, the last record of his acting.

. . Henry Chettle's poem *Englandes Mourning Garment* entered in Stationers' Register; it contains lines exhorting Shakespeare to write something in honor of the late queen.

1604

March 15 Shakespeare mentioned in accounts of Sir George Home, master of the great wardrobe, as receiving 4½ yards of red cloth for appearing in procession with the King's Men at the coronation of James I.

April Shakespeare listed as one of King's Men

in margin of a privy council warrant for a play.

July Shakespeare sues Philip Rogers for debt of 3s. 10d.

Aug. 9–27 Twelve members of King's Men paid £21. 12s. for eighteen days' attendance at Somerset House during visit of Spanish envoy.

Nov. 1 *Othello* first performed at palace at Whitehall.

Nov. 4 *The Merry Wives of Windsor* performed at court.

Dec. 26 *Measure for Measure* performed at court.

. . *Hamlet* (Q2) printed by James Roberts for Nicholas Ling.

. . *1 Henry IV* (Q3) printed by Valentine Simmes for Matthew Law.

1605

Jan. 1–6 *Love's Labour's Lost* performed at court sometime before Jan. 6.

Jan. 7 *Henry V* performed at court.

Feb. 10 *The Merchant of Venice* performed at court.

Feb. 12 *The Merchant of Venice* again performed at court, commended by the king.

May 4 Augustine Phillips wills Shakespeare, his fellow actor, 30s. in gold.

July 24 Shakespeare buys a quarter interest in the lease of Stratford tithes for £440.

. . *Richard III* (Q4) printed by Thomas Creede for Matthew Law.

. . *The London Prodigal* printed by Creede for Nathaniel Butter as by Shakespeare.

1606

May 5 Susanna Shakespeare listed with a group of recusants who had failed to receive Communion on Easter Sunday.

May 27 Act passed imposing a fine of £10 for "abuse of the holy name of God in stageplays."

Dec. 26 *King Lear* performed by King's Men before the King at Whitehall.

1607

Jan. 22 Copyrights of *Romeo and Juliet*, *Love's Labour's Lost*, and *The Taming of A Shrew* transferred to Nicholas Ling by Cuthbert Burby.

June 5 Susanna Shakespeare married in Holy Trinity Church to John Hall, a physician of Stratford.

July–Nov. Theatres closed because of plague.

Aug. 6 *The Puritan* entered in Stationers' Register by George Eld as by "W.S."; though probably by Wentworth Smith, it was included in F3 in 1664.

Aug. 7 *Macbeth* possibly performed at Hampton Court for visiting King Christian IV of Denmark.

Aug. 12 Register of St. Giles' church, Cripplegate, records burial of Edward, son of Edward Shakespeare, player.

Sept. 5 *Hamlet* performed aboard the Brit ship *Dragon* at Sierra Leone.

Nov. 26 Nathaniel Butter and John Busby en *King Lear* in Stationers' Regist Printed 1608.

Dec. 31 An actor named Edmund Shakespea possibly William Shakespeare's young brother, buried at St. Saviour's chur in Southwark, the parish in which t Globe is located.

1608

Feb. 21 Elizabeth, daughter of John and S anna Shakespeare Hall, christened.

March 31 *Hamlet* possibly again performed abo the *Dragon*.

May 2 *A Yorkshire Tragedy* entered in S tioners' Register by Thomas Pavi as by W. Shakespeare; it was includ in F3, 1664.

May 20 *Antony and Cleopatra* and *Pericles* e tered in Stationers' Register by E ward Blount.

Aug. 9 Shakespeare, Richard and Cuthb Burbage, Thomas Evans, John He inges, Henry Condell, and Willi Sly lease the Blackfriars theatre f a period of twenty-one years.

Aug. 17 Sly's death increases shares of oth lessors from one seventh to one sixt

Sept. 7 Shakespeare's mother, Mary, buried Stratford.

Oct. 16 Shakespeare stands as godfather, eith in person or by proxy, to Willi Walker of Stratford.

Dec. 17 Arrest of John Addenbrooke for a de to Shakespeare entered by Thom Greene in court record at Stratfor

. . *Pericles* seen by Venetian ambassad Zorzi Giustinian sometime betwe Jan. 5 and Nov. 23.

. . *King Lear* (Q1) printed by Nicho Okes or George and Lionel Snowd for Nathaniel Butter.

. . *Richard II* (Q4) printed by Willia White for Matthew Law.

. . *1 Henry IV* (Q4) printed for Matthe Law.

. . *A Yorkshire Tragedy* printed by Ric ard Bradock for Thomas Pavier.

1609

Jan. 28 Richard Bonian and Henry Walley ent *Troilus and Cressida* in Stationer Register (see 1603).

May 20 Shakespeare's Sonnets entered in St tioners' Register by Thomas Thorp

Sept. 9 Thomas Greene, calling himself Shak speare's "cousin," indicates in a men orandum that he has been occupyin New Place and may do so for anoth year.

Christmas season King's Men perform thirteen plays b fore the royal family at Whitehall.

. . *Pericles* (Q1 and Q2) printed for Henr Gosson.

. *Troilus and Cressida* (Q1) printed by George Eld for Bonian and Walley.

1610

b. 8 Robert Keysar brings suit against the actor-sharers of the King's Men.

. Shakespeare assures conveyance of his Old Stratford land bought in 1602.

1611

pril 21 *Cymbeline* seen by Simon Forman between this date and April 29, as noted in his *Booke of Plaies*.

ay 15 *The Winter's Tale* performed at the Globe theatre, as noted by Forman.

. *Pericles* (Q3) printed by Simon Stafford.

. *Hamlet* (Q3) printed for John Smethwick.

. *Titus Andronicus* (Q3) printed by Edward Allde for Edward White.

. *Love's Martyr*, containing Shakespeare's poem "The Phoenix and the Turtle," is reissued as *The Anuals of Great Brittaine*.

1612

n. 28 Bill of complaint endorsed by Stephen Belott against his father-in-law, Christopher Mountjoy.

b. 3 Gilbert Shakespeare buried at Stratford. On the same day Mountjoy answers Belott's bill of complaint.

ay 5 Belott replies to Mountjoy's answer.

ay 11 Shakespeare among witnesses in Belott-Mountjoy suit; his residence is given as Stratford, suggesting that he is by this time in semi-retirement at New Place.

ct. 16 Frederick V, elector palatine and future king of Bohemia, arrives in England to marry Elizabeth, daughter of James I.

ov. 1 *The Tempest* performed by King's Men.

ov. 5 *The Winter's Tale* performed by King's Men.

ov. 6 Henry, Prince of Wales, dies.

. *Richard III* (Q5) printed by Thomas Creede for Matthew Law.

1613

n. 28 John Combe, a Stratford neighbor, bequeathes Shakespeare £5.

eb. 14 Richard Shakespeare buried.

arch 10 Shakespeare purchases the Blackfriars Gate-House in London.

arch 31 Shakespeare and Richard Burbage receive 44s. each for impresa of earl of Rutland.

ay 20 King's Men paid for performances of *Much Ado About Nothing*, *The Tempest*, *The Winter's Tale*, *1* and *2 Henry IV*, *Othello*, and *Julius Caesar* during marriage festivities of Frederick V and Elizabeth.

une 8 *Cardenio* acted by King's Men for ambassador of Savoy; in 1653 Humphrey Moseley registered this play as by Shakespeare and John Fletcher.

June 29 Globe theatre burns during first performance of *Henry VIII* as noted on July 2 in letter of Sir Henry Wotton to Sir Edmund Bacon.

July 15 Susanna Shakespeare Hall sues John Lane for defamation in the consistory court at Worcester Cathedral.

1614

June Globe theatre reopens.

July 9 Fire in Stratford burns fifty-four houses.

Sept. 5 Document made by Thomas Greene shows that Shakespeare owns about 127 acres of land.

Nov. 17 Shakespeare and his son-in-law Dr. John Hall are in London on business connected with the Stratford tithes, as noted in Thomas Greene's diary.

1615

April 26 Shakespeare is party to a suit to have Matthew Bacon turn over deeds and papers to the Blackfriars property, inherited from his mother, Anne, but subsequently sold to the King's Men.

May 22 Court orders Bacon to deliver papers to court for transfer to proper owners.

Sept. Thomas Greene again alludes to Shakespeare in reference to possible enclosure of his land.

. . *Richard II* (Q5) printed for Matthew Law.

1616

Jan. 25? Francis Collins draws up Shakespeare's will.

Feb. 10 Judith Shakespeare married to Thomas Quiney, a vintner.

March 12 Thomas and Judith Shakespeare Quiney excommunicated, probably for having married without a license during the Lenten season.

March 25 Shakespeare revises his will.

March 26 Thomas Quiney in court to answer charges that he had illicit relations with one Margaret Wheeler.

April 23 Shakespeare dies.

April 25 Shakespeare's burial recorded in register of Holy Trinity church.

June 22 Shakespeare's will probated by Dr. John Hall in London.

Nov. 23 Shakespeare, son of Thomas and Judith Shakespeare Quiney, baptized.

. . *The Rape of Lucrece* (O5) printed by Thomas Snodham for Roger Jackson.

. . Folio of Ben Jonson's works published.

1617

Feb. 16 William Leake assigns copyright of *Venus and Adonis* to William Barrett.

. . Dr. John Hall and Susanna Shakespeare pay "fine of admittance" for occupying New Place after Shakespeare's death.

. . *Venus and Adonis* (O9) printed by William Stansby for William Barrett.

1618

Feb. 10 John Jackson, John Heminges, and William Johnson convey their trusteeship of the Blackfriars property to John Greene and Matthew Morris, acting in the interest of Susanna Shakespeare Hall.

Dec. In conversations with William Drummond during this and the following month, Ben Jonson alludes to Shakespeare's art and knowledge, as noted in Drummond's diary.

1619

May 3 Lord chamberlain directs Stationers' Company in a letter that no plays of the King's Men be printed without their consent.

May 20 *Pericles* performed in the king's chambers for the royal party and French guests.

July 8 Laurence Hayes asserts his right to the copyright of *The Merchant of Venice*, which William Jaggard had surreptitiously printed earlier in the year for Thomas Pavier.

Christmas season *The Winter's Tale*, *Two Noble Kinsmen*, *Hamlet*, and *2 Henry IV* performed at court.

. . Star Chamber bill charges John Nash, William Reynolds, John Lane (earlier sued by Susanna Shakespeare Hall for defamation), and others with riot and libel against a Puritan vicar, Wilson.

1621

Oct. 6 *Othello* entered in Stationers' Register for Thomas Walkley.

1622

April 22 Elizabeth (1608–1670), daughter of Dr John and Susanna Shakespeare Hall, marries Thomas Nash.

. . *Othello* (Q1) printed by Nicholas Okes for Thomas Walkley.

. . *1 Henry IV* (Q6) printed by Thomas Purfoot for Matthew Law.

. . *Richard III* (Q6) printed by Purfoot for Law.

1623

Feb. 2 *Malvolio* (*Twelfth Night*) performed at court by King's Men.

Aug. 6 Anne Hathaway Shakespeare dies at 67

Nov. 8 Edward Blount and Isaac Jaggard enter *The Tempest*, *Two Gentlemen of Verona*, *Measure for Measure*, *The Comedy of Errors*, *As You Like It*, *All's Well That Ends Well*, *Twelfth Night*, *The Winter's Tale*, *3 Henry VI*, *Henry VIII*, *Coriolanus*, *Timon of Athens*, *Julius Caesar*, *Macbeth*, *Antony and Cleopatra*, and *Cymbeline* in the Stationers' Register preparatory to printing the First Folio.

. . The First Folio is printed by Jaggard and Blount for William Jaggard, Blount, John Smethwick, and William Aspley.

Transcripts of Documents

Henslowe's diary, 1599:

1\.

this 14th of October 1599

Receaued by me Robt Shaa of phillip Henslowe to pay H. Chettle [f] in full paiment of a booke Called the stepmothers tragedy for the vse of the Company iiijli J say Receaued——— } 4li

2\.

this 16th of october 99

Receued by me Thomas downton of phillipp [H] Henchlow to pay Mr mvnday Mr drayton & Mr Wilsson & harthway for the first pte of the lyfe of Sr Jhon Ouldcasstell & in earnest of the Secvnd pte for the vse of the compayny ten pownd J say receued——— } 10li

3\.

Receved by me Samuell Rowlye of phyllyp henchloe for harrye chettell in Earneste of the playe of patient Gryssell for the Vse of the Comepanye——— } xxs

4\.

Lent vnto Robarte shaw the 1 of novmber 1599 to lent vnto Mr willsones the some of——— } xs

5\.

Lente vnto Robart shaw the i of novmber 1599 to Lend vnto wm harton in earneste of A Boocke called the tragedie of John cox some of——— } xxs

6\.

as A gefte

Receved of Mr hincheloe for Mr Mundaye & the Reste of the poets at the playnge of Sr John oldcastell the ferste tyme——— } xs

7\.

Receaued of mr Ph: Hinchlow by a note vnder the hand of mr Rob: Shaw in full payment for the second pt of Henrye Richmond sold to him & his Companye the some of eight pownds Current moneye the viijt daye of November *1599*——— } viijli

By me *R Wilson*

l s d
some 25 – 00 – 00

The company mentioned is the Admiral's then playing at the Rose theatre. The various entries on the page of the diary were made by different people: Robert Shaw, 1; Thomas Downton, 2; Samuel Rowley, 3 and 6; Robert Wilson, 7; Henslowe entered items 4 and 5 and added up the total at the bottom of the page.

The "plot" of *The Seven Deadly Sins*:

THE PLATT OF THE SECOUND PARTE OF
THE SEUEN DEADLIE SINNS

A tent being plast one the stage for Henry the sixt · he in it A sleepe to him The Leutenat A purceuaunt R Cowly Jo Duke and i wardere [J Holland] R Pallant : to them Pride · Gluttony Wrath and couetousnes at one dore · at an other dore Enuie · Sloth and Lechery · The Three put back the foure · and so Exeunt

---

Henry Awaking Enter A Keeper J sincler · to him a seruaunt T Belt · to him Lidgate and the Keeper · Exit then enter againe · Then Enuy passeth ouer the stag · Lidgate speakes

---

A senitt · Dumb show ·
Enter King Gorboduk wth 2 Counsailers · R Burbadg mr Brian · Th Goodale · The Queene wth ferrex and Porrex and som attendaunts follow · saunder w sly Harry J Duke · Kitt · Ro Pallant · J Holland After Gordbeduk hath Consulted wth his Lords he brings his 2 sonns to to seuerall seates · They enuing on on other ferrex offers to take Porex his Corowne · he draws his weopon The King Queen and Lords step between them They Thrust Them away and menasing [ect] ech other exit · The Queene and L Depart Heuilie · Lidgate speaks

---

Enter ferrex Crownd wth Drum and Coulers and soldiers one way · Harry · Kitt · R Cowly John duke · to them At a nother dore · Porrex drum and Collors and soldie W sly · R Pallant · John Sincler · J Holland ·

Enter [Gorb] Queene · wth 2 Counsailors · mr Brian Tho Goodale · to them ferrex and Porrex seuerall waies wth [his] Drums and Powers · Gorboduk entreing in The midst between · Henry speaks

---

A Larum wth Excurtions After
Lidgate speakes

Enter ferrex and Porrex seuerally Gorboduke still following them · Lucius and Damasus mr Bry T Good ·

Enter ferrex at one dore · Porrex at an other The fight ferrex is slayn: to them Videna The Queene to hir Damasus · to him Lucius ·

Enter Porrex sad wth Dordan his man · R P · w sly : to them the Queene and A Ladie Nick saunder And Lords R Cowly mr Brian · to them Lucius Runing

---

Henry and Lidgat speaks Sloth Passeth ouer

Enter Giraldus Phronesius Aspatia Pompeia Rodope R Cowly Th Goodale · R Go · Ned · Nick · Enter Sardinapalus Arbactus Nicanor and Captaines marching · mr Phillipps mr Pope R Pa Kit J sincler · J Holland ·

Enter A Captaine wth Aspatia and the Ladies Kitt

Lidgate speake

Enter Nicanor wth other Captaines R Pall · sincler · Kitt · J Holland R Cowly · to the[m] Arbactus · mr Pope · to him will foole · J Duk[e] to him Rodopeie · Ned · to her Sardanapalu[s] Like A woman wth Aspatia Rodope Pompeia wi[ll] foole to them Arbactus and 3 musitions mr Pop[e] J sincler · Vincent R Cowly to them Nicanor an[d] others R P · Kitt

---

Enter sardanapa · wth the Ladies to them A Mes senger · Th Goodale · to him will foole Runin[g] A Larum

---

Enter Arbactus pursuing Sardanapalus and Th[e] Ladies fly · After Enter Sarda wth as many Jewel[s] robes and Gold as he ca cary ·

A larum

Enter Arbactus Nicanor and The other Captains i[n] triumph · mr Pope · R Pa · Kitt J Hall R Co[wly] · J Sinc

---

Henry speaks and Lidgate Lechery passeth ouer the stag

Enter Tereus Philomele · Julio and R Burbad[g] · Ro R Pall · J si

---

Enter Progne Jtis and Lords saunder will J Duke w sly Hary ·

Enter Philomele and Tereus to them Julio

Enter Progne Panthea Jtis and Lords · saunder T Belt will w sly Hary Th Goodale to them Tereu[s] wth Lords · R Burbadg · J Duk R Cowly

A Dumb show · Lidgate speake[s]

Enter Progne wth the Sampler to her Tereus fro[m] Hunting · wth his Lords to them Philomele wth Jtis hed in a dish · Mercury Comes and all Vanis[h] · to him 3 Lords Th Goodale Hary w sly ·

Henry speaks to him Leiutenant Purseuaunt an[d] warders R Cowly J Duke · J Holland Joh sincle[r] · to them Warwick · mr Brian

---

Lidgate speaks to the
Audiens and so
Exitts ·

---

finis

Hand D" in *Sir Thomas More.* This is part of Moore's speech as he tries to quell the rioters:

ll

marry god forbid that

noo

nay certainly yo^u ar
for to the king god hath his offyce lent
of dread of Iustyce, power and Comaund
hath bid him rule, and willd yo^u to obay
and to add ampler matie. to this
he [god] hath not [le] only lent the king his figure
his throne [his] sword, but gyven him his owne name
calls him a god on earth, what do yo^u then
rysing gainst him that god himseaif enstalls
but ryse gainst god, what do yo^u to yor sowles
in doing this o desperat [ar] as you are.
wash your foule mynds w^t teares and those same hands
that yo^u lyke rebells lyft against the peace
lift vp for peace, and your vnreuerent knees
[that] make them your feet to kneele to be forgyven
[is safer warrs, then euer yo^u can make]
[whose discipline is ryot; why euen yor [warrs] hurly] [in in to yor obedienc.]
[cannot pceed but by obedienc] tell me but this what rebell captaine
as mutynes ar incident, by his name
can still the rout why will obay [th] a traytor
or howe can well that pclamation sounde
when ther is no adicion but a rebell
to quallyfy a rebell, youle put downe straingers
kill them cutt their throts possesse their howses
and leade the matie of lawe in liom

Roberts' blocking entry in the Stationers' Register:

27 may 1600 — my lord chamberlens
To Mr Robts — men plaies Entred
viz
A morall of clothe breches &
Veluet hose /

27 may
To hym — Allarum to London

4 Augusti
As yo^u like yt /a booke
Henry the ffift /a booke
Every man in his Humo^r /a booke
The Commedie of muche
A doo about nothinge /a booke
} to be staied

Shakespeare in the Stationers' Register:

23 Augusti [1600]

Andrew Wyse
Willm Aspley Entered for their copies vnder the handes
of the wardens Twoo bookes, the
one called Muche a Doo about
nothinge. Thother the second pte
of the History of Kinge Henry the iiij^th xij^d
wth the hummours of Sr John
Ffallstaff: Wrytten by Mr Shakespere

Declared Accounts of 1594:

To **Willm Kempe** Willm Shakespeare & Richarde Burbage seruantes to the Lord Chambleyne vpon the councelles warr^t dated at Whitehall xv^to Martii 1594 for twoe seuerall comedies or Enterludes shewed by them before her Matie in xpmas [Christmas] tyme laste paste viz^d vpon St Stephens daye & Innocentes daye xiij^l vj^s viij^d and by waye of her ma^tes Rewarde vj^l xiij^s iij^d.

George Buc's allowance of *The Second Maiden's Tragedy*:

This second Maydens tragedy (for it hath
no name inscribed) may wth the reformatio-
ns bee acted publikely. 31. octob^r
1611. / G. Buc

Genealogical Table of the Houses of York and Lancaster

The table below traces the history of the English crown for 277 years: from 1327 when Edward III was crowned to 1603 when Elizabeth I died. The period began with the Hundred Years War (1337-1453), which saw the English gain then lose a vast French empire. Even before the French wars were concluded civil strife erupted at home. From 1455 to 1485 the bitter Wars of the Roses raged, and the crown became the plaything of the great noble families. One hundred and fifty years of fighting abroad and on their own soil had decimated the ranks of the important feudal houses of Plantagenet, York, Lancaster, and others. A new English dynasty was founded at Bosworth where Henry Tudor, Elizabeth's grandfather, was given the crown. Nine of Shakespeare's plays (*Richard II; 1 & 2 Henry IV; Henry V; 1, 2, & 3 Henry VI; Richard III;* and *Henry VIII*) chronicle the events of these years. The table includes many of the characters who people the plays. The names of reigning monarchs are written in small capitals.

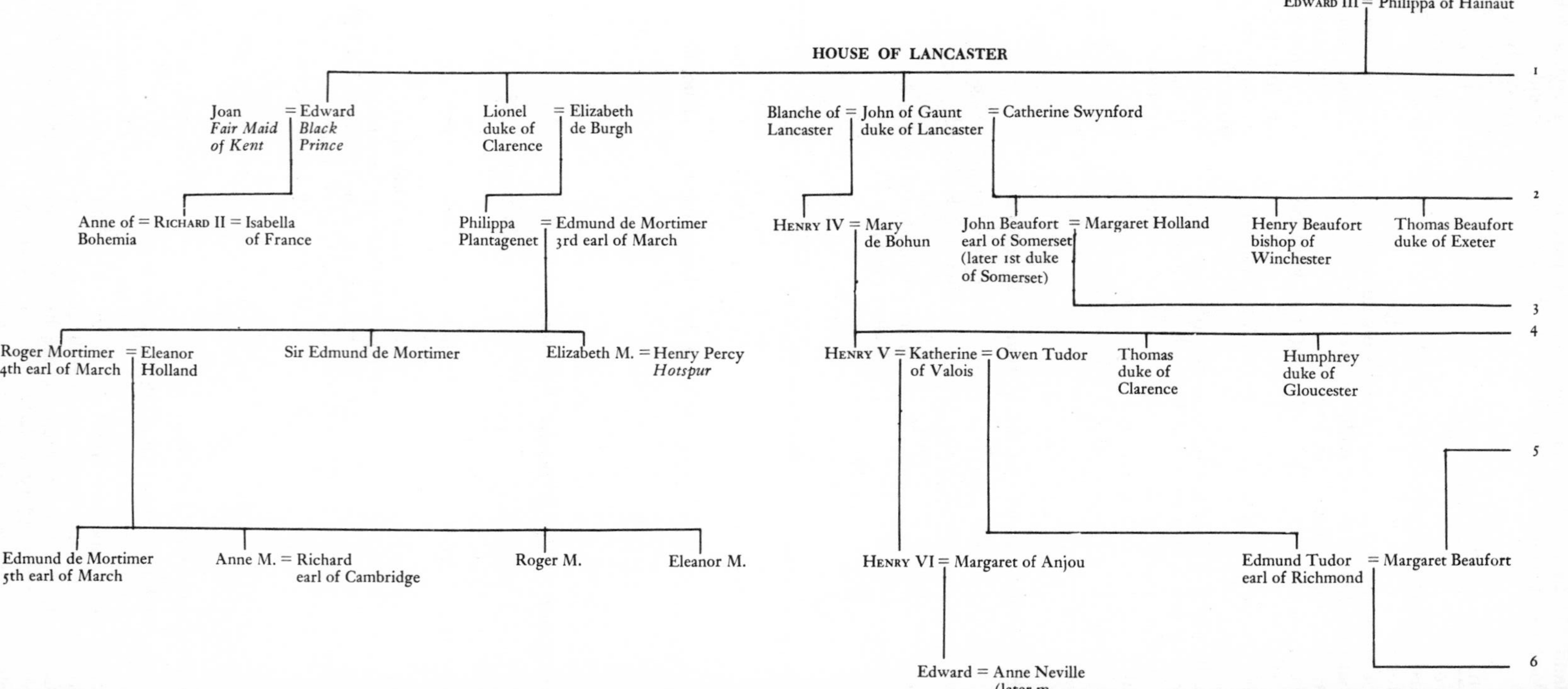

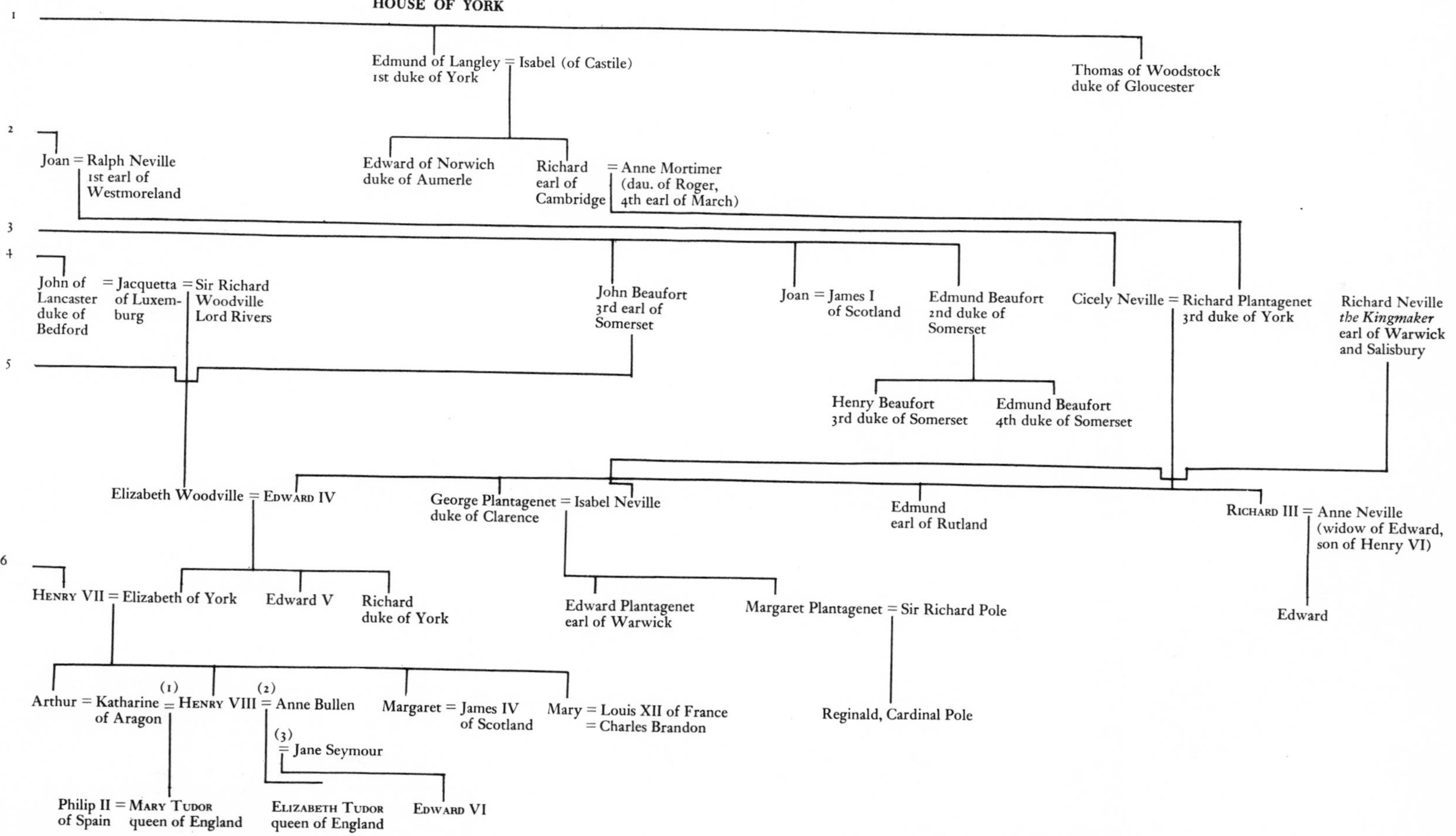

HOUSE OF YORK
1
Edmund of Langley = Isabel (of Castile)
1st duke of York
Thomas of Woodstock
duke of Gloucester
2
Joan = Ralph Neville
1st earl of
Westmoreland
Edward of Norwich
duke of Aumerle
Richard
earl of
Cambridge
= Anne Mortimer
(dau. of Roger,
4th earl of March)
3
4
John of
Lancaster
duke of
Bedford
= Jacquetta
of Luxem-
burg
= Sir Richard
Woodville
Lord Rivers
John Beaufort
3rd earl of
Somerset
Joan = James I
of Scotland
Edmund Beaufort
2nd duke of
Somerset
Cicely Neville = Richard Plantagenet
3rd duke of York
Richard Neville
the Kingmaker
earl of Warwick
and Salisbury
5
Henry Beaufort
3rd duke of Somerset
Edmund Beaufort
4th duke of Somerset
Elizabeth Woodville = Edward IV
George Plantagenet = Isabel Neville
duke of Clarence
Edmund
earl of Rutland
Richard III = Anne Neville
(widow of Edward,
son of Henry VI)
6
Henry VII = Elizabeth of York
Edward V
Richard
duke of York
Edward Plantagenet
earl of Warwick
Margaret Plantagenet = Sir Richard Pole
Edward
Arthur = Katharine
of Aragon
(1)
= Henry VIII
(2)
= Anne Bullen
(3)
= Jane Seymour
Margaret = James IV
of Scotland
Mary = Louis XII of France
= Charles Brandon
Reginald, Cardinal Pole
Philip II = Mary Tudor
of Spain
queen of England
Elizabeth Tudor
queen of England
Edward VI

A Selected Bibliography

This bibliography is arranged according to the following outline

I. CRITICISM

A. Bibliographies

B. Shakespeare's Life

- *1. General*
- *2. Special*
- *3. Family, Friends, and Environment*

C. Textual Criticism

- *1. Elizabethan Printing Practices*
- *2. The Shakespearean Texts*

D. Sources and Influences

E. The Theatre

- *1. Playhouses*
- *2. Dramatic Background*

F. Stage History

G. General Criticism

H. Special Studies

- *1. Imagery and Language*
- *2. Themes*
- *3. Translations*
- *4. Classroom Use of Shakespeare*
- *5. Critical Anthologies and Histories*
- *6. Art*
- *7. Music*
- *8. Shakespeare's Influence*

I. Histories

J. Comedies

- *1. General*
- *2. Problem Plays*
- *3. Romances*

K. Tragedies

L. Claimants

II. THE WORKS OF SHAKESPEARE

A. Collected Editions

B. Chronology

C. The Plays and Poems

1–37. The plays in alphabetical order. 38. Poems. 39. Sonnets. 40. Apocryphal plays.

Abbreviations

AR *Antioch Review*
BJRL *Bulletin of the John Rylands Library*
BUSE *Boston University Studies in English*
CE *College English*
CHEL *Cambridge History of English Literature*
CQ *Critical Quarterly*
CRAS *Centennial Review of Arts and Sciences* (Michigan State)
DUJ *Durham University Journal*
E&S *Essays & Studies* (English Association)
EC *Essays in Criticism*
EIE *English Institute Essays*
EJ *English Journal*
ELH *Journal of English Literary History*
ES *English Studies*
HLQ *Huntington Library Quarterly*
JEGP *Journal of English and Germanic Philology*
JGE *Journal of General Education*
JRUL *Journal of the Rutgers University Library*
KN *Kwartalnik Neofilologiczny*, Warsaw
KR *Kenyon Review*
MLN *Modern Language Notes*
MLQ *Modern Language Quarterly*
MLR *Modern Language Review*
MP *Modern Philology*
N&Q *Notes & Queries*
PAPS *Proceedings of the American Philosophical Society*
PMLA *PMLA Publications of the Modern Language Association of America*
PQ *Philological Quarterly*
PR *Partisan Review*
QJS *Quarterly Journal of Speech*
REL *Review of English Literature*
RES *Review of English Studies*
RS *Research Studies*
SAB *Shakespeare Association Bulletin*
SB *Studies in Bibliography*
SEL *Studies in English Literature*
SJ *Shakespeare-Jahrbuch*
SN *Shakespeare Newsletter*
SP *Studies in Philology*
SQ *Shakespeare Quarterly*
SR *Sewanee Review*
SS *Shakespeare Survey*
TDR *Tulane Drama Review*
TLS *Times Literary Supplement*
TN *Theatre Notebook*
TxSE *Texas Studies in English*
UTQ *University of Toronto Quarterly*
VQR *Virginia Quarterly Review*
YR *Yale Review*
ZAA *Zeitschrift für Anglistik und Amerikanist* East Berlin

Short Titles

Adams *Joseph Quincy Adams Memorial Studies.* James G. McManaway, Giles E. Dawson, Edwin E. Willoughby, eds. Washington, D.C., 1948.

Barker-Harrison Granville-Barker, Harley, and G. B. Harrison. *A Companion to Shakespeare Studies.* Garden City, 1960.

Bullough Bullough, Geoffrey B. *Narrative and Dramatic Sources of Shakespeare.* 6 vols. London, 1957–1966.

Chambers Chambers, E. K. *William Shakespeare: A Study of Facts and Problems.* 2 vols. Oxford, 1930.

Clemen Clemen, Wolfgang H. *The Development of Shakespeare's Imagery.* Cambridge, Mass., 1951.

Coleridge *Coleridge's Shakespearean Criticism.* T. M. Raysor, ed. 2 vols. Cambridge, Mass., 1930.

Greg Greg, W. W. *The Shakespeare First Folio: Its Bibliographical and Textual History.* Oxford, 1955.

Hazlitt Hazlitt, William. *Characters of Shakespear's Plays.* Everyman's Library. New York, 1936.

Hinman Hinman, Charlton. *The Printing a Proof-Reading of the First Folio Shakespeare.* 2 vols. Oxford, 1963.

Honigmann Honigmann, E. A. J. *The Stability Shakespeare's Texts.* London, 1965.

Johnson *Johnson on Shakespeare.* Sir Walter Raleigh, ed. London, 1908.

Muir Muir, Kenneth. *Shakespeare's Sourc* Vol. I. Comedies and Tragedies. Lo don, 1957.

New Cambridge *The Works of William Shakespea* New Cambridge Edition. Arth Quiller-Couch and John Dover W son, eds. Cambridge, 1921–1965.

Odell Odell, George C. D. *Shakespeare fro Betterton to Irving.* 2 vols. Lond 1920.

Trewin Trewin, J. C. *Shakespeare on the En lish Stage, 1900–1964: A Survey Productions.* London, 1964.

Van Doren Van Doren, M. *Shakespeare,* 1939.

Winter Winter, W. *Shakespeare on the Sta* 3 vols. London, 1911–1916.

I. CRITICISM

A. Bibliographies

Annual bibliographies of Shakespeare studies appear in the following periodicals:

Shakespeare Quarterly (formerly *The Shakespeare Association Bulletin*).
Shakespeare-Jahrbuch (Jahrbuch der Deutsch Shakespeare-Gesellschaft).
Studies in Philology.
PMLA

An annual review of Shakespeare studies appears i

Shakespeare Survey (Cambridge).
The Year's Work in English Studies.

;GARD, W. *Shakespeare Bibliography . . .* Stratford-upon-Avon, 1911.

SCH, W. and L. L. SCHÜCKING. *A Shakespeare Bibliography*. Oxford, 1931. Supplement, 1930–1935. Oxford, 1937.

ITH, G. R. *A Classified Shakespeare Bibliography, 1936–1958*. University Park, Pa., 1963.

RMAN, R. *A Reader's Guide to Shakespeare's Plays: A Discursive Bibliography*. Chicago, 1965.

B. Shakespeare's Life

1. General

ambers I, 1–26; *Barker-Harrison*, 1–8.

WE, N. *Some Account of the Life, &c of Mr. William Shakespear*, London, 1709.

AKE, N. *Shakespeare and His Times*. 2 Vols. London, 1817.

OTTOWE, A. *The Life of Shakespeare; Enquiries into the Originality of His Dramatic Plots and Characters; and Essays on the Ancient Theatres and Theatrical Usages*. 2 Vols. London, 1824.

IGHT, C. *William Shakspere: a Biography*. London, 1843.

DSON, H. N. *Shakespeare, His Life, Art and Characters*. 2 Vols. Boston, 1872.

LEBY, C. M. *Shakespeare, the man and the book, being a collection of occasional papers on the bard and his writings*. 2 Vols. London, 1877–81.

ALLIWELL-PHILLIPPS, J. O. *Outlines of the Life of Shakespeare*. London, 1882.

E, S. *A Life of William Shakespeare*. London, 1898.

ADLEY, A. C. *Shakespeare the Man*. London, 1909.

ARRIS, F. *The Man Shakespeare and His Tragic Life-story*. New York, 1909.

AMS, J. Q. *A Life of William Shakespeare*. London, 1923.

OOKE, C. F. T. *Shakespeare of Stratford*. New Haven, 1926.

HELLING, F. E. *Shakespeare Biography and Other Papers Chiefly Elizabethan*. Philadelphia, 1937.

IPP, E. I. *Shakespeare, Man and Artist*. Oxford, 1938.

AMBERS, SIR E. K. *Shakespearean Gleanings*. Oxford, 1944.

UTE, M. *Shakespeare of London*. New York, 1949.

ESE, M. M. *Shakespeare: His World and His Work*. New York, 1953.

ALLIDAY, F. E. *Shakespeare in his Age*. London, 1956.

——. *Shakespeare*. New York, 1961.

——. *Shakespeare: A Pictorial Biography*, new ed. New York, 1964.

OWN, I. *Shakespeare in His Time*. Edinburgh, 1960.

JENNELL, P. *Shakespeare: A Biography*. Cleveland and New York, 1963.

WSE, A. L. *William Shakespeare: A Biography*. New York, 1963.

LEXANDER, P. *Shakespeare*. Home Univ. Lib. of Mod. Knowledge, 252. London and New York, 1964.

2. Special

RTER, T. *Shakespeare, Puritan and Recusant*. Edinburgh and London, 1897.

ADDEN, D. H. *The Diary of Master William Silence*. London, 1897.

SARRAZIN, G. *William Shakespeares Lehrjahre*. Eine literarhistorische Studie. Weimar, 1897.

STOPES, C. C. *Shakespeare's Warwickshire Contemporaries*. Stratford-upon-Avon, 1897.

BOWDEN, H. S. *The Religion of Shakespeare*. London, 1899.

MOULTON, R. G. *The Moral System of Shakespeare*. New York, 1903.

———. *Shakespeare as a Dramatic Thinker, A Popular Illustration of Fiction as the Experimental Side of Philosophy*. New York and London, 1907.

BEECHING, H. C. "On the Religion of Shakespeare." *Shakespeare's Works*. Stratford, 1907, Vol. 10.

WILSON, J. D. *The Essential Shakespeare*. Cambridge, 1932.

———. "Malone and the Upstart Crow." *SS 4* (1951), 56–58.

BAKER, O. *In Shakespeare's Warwickshire and the Unknown Years*. London, 1937.

MUIR, K., and S. O'LOUGHLIN. *The Voyage to Illyria*. London, 1937.

HARBAGE, A. "A Contemporary Attack Upon Shakspere?" *SAB*, XVI (1941), 42–48.

HEALY, T. F. "Shakespeare Was an Irishman." *American Mercury*, LI (1941), 24–32.

BROOKE, C. F. T. "The License for Shakespeare's Marriage." *MLN*, LVII (1942), 687–688.

MCMANAWAY, J. G. "The License for Shakespeare's Marriage." *MLN*, LVII (1942), 450–451.

DE GROOT, J. H. *The Shakespeares and "The Old Faith."* New York, 1946.

DUFF COOPER, SIR A. *Sergeant Shakespeare*. London and Toronto, 1949.

SCOTT-GILES, C. W. *Shakespeare's Heraldry*. London, 1950.

MCCURDY, H. G. *The Personality of Shakespeare: A Venture in Psychological Method*. New Haven, 1953.

EVERITT, E. B. *The Young Shakespeare: Studies in Documentary Evidence*. Copenhagen, 1954.

HARDING, D. P. "Shakespeare the Elizabethan." *Shakespeare: of an Age and for all Time*. The Yale Shakespeare Festival Lectures, 1954, pp. 13–32.

KEEN, A., and R. LUBBOCK. *The Annotator: the Pursuit of an Elizabethan Reader of Halle's "Chronicle" Involving Some Surmises About the Early Life of William Shakespeare*. London, 1954.

AUSTIN, W. B. "A Supposed Contemporary Allusion to Shakespeare as a Plagiarist." *SQ*, VI (1955), 373–380.

ISAACS, J. *Shakespeare's Earliest Years in the Theatre. Proceedings of the British Academy*, XXXIX, London, 1955.

LAW, R. A. "Guessing About the Youthful Shakespeare." *TxSE*, XXXIV (1955), 43–50.

BROWN, I. *How Shakespeare Spent the Day*. London, 1963.

ALEXANDER, P. "The Schoolmaster from the Country." *TLS*, April 23, 1964.

FALCONER, A. F. *Shakespeare and the Sea*. New York, 1964.

HALLIDAY, F. E. *A Shakespeare Companion, 1564–1964*, rev. ed. New York, 1964.

3. Family, Friends, and Environment

FRENCH, G. R. *Shakespeareana Genealogica*. London, 1869.

STOPES, C. C. *Shakespeare's Family, being a record*

of the ancesters and descendants of William Shakespeare, with some account of the Ardens. New York, 1901.

———. *Shakespeare's Environment.* London, 1918.

ELTON, C. I. *William Shakespeare, His Family and Friends.* ed. A. Hamilton Thompson. London, 1904.

The Victoria History of the County of Warwick. London. Vol. II. ed. William Page. 1908. Vol. III. gen. ed. L. F. Salzman, local ed. Philip Styles. 1945. Vol. IV. ed. L. F. Salzman. 1947.

SAVAGE, R., and E. I. FRIPP. *Minutes and Accounts of the Corporation of Stratford-upon-Avon and Other Records 1553–1620.* 3 Vols. London, 1921, 1924, 1926.

FRIPP, E. I. *Shakespeare's Stratford.* Oxford, 1928.

———. *Shakespeare's Haunts Near Stratford.* Oxford, 1929.

HOTSON, L. *I, William Shakespeare, do Appoint Thomas Russell, Esquire . . .* London, 1937.

———. "Maypoles and Puritans." *SQ*, I (1950), 205–207.

GRAY, A. *Shakespeare's Son-in-Law, John Hall.* Cambridge, Mass., 1939.

SHIELD, H. A. "Links with Shakespeare." *N & Q*, 191 (1946), pp. 112–114; 194 (1949), pp. 30–32, 320, 536–537; 195 (1950), pp. 114–115, 205–206, 385–386; 196 (1951), pp. 250–252; 197 (1952), pp. 156–157, 387–389; 198 (1953); pp. 280–282, 405–406; n.s. II (1955), pp. 94–97, 513–514; n.s. III (1956), pp. 423–424; n.s. IV (1957), pp. 522–523; n.s. V (1958), pp. 526–527.

ECCLES, M. *Shakespeare in Warwickshire.* Madison, Wis., 1961.

SUTHERLAND, R. C. "The Grants of Arms to Shakespeare's Father." *SQ*, XIV (1963), 379–385.

HANLEY, H. A. "Shakespeare's Family in Stratford Records." *TLS* (May 21, 1964), p. 441.

C. Textual Criticism

1. Elizabethan Printing Practices

LOUNSBURY, T. R. *The Text of Shakespeare, its history from the publication of the quartos and folios down to and including the publication of the editions of Pope and Theobald.* New York, 1906.

MCKERROW, R. B. *A Dictionary of the Printers and Booksellers in England, Scotland, and Ireland, and of Foreign Printers of English Books, 1557–1640.* London, 1910.

ARBER, E., ed. *A Transcript of the Registers of the Company of Stationers of London, 1554–1640.* 5 Vols. London, 1875–1894. Continued in *A Transcript of the Registers of the Worshipful Company of Stationers, 1640–1708.* ed. G. E. B. Eyre. 3 Vols. 1913–1914.

PLOMER, H. R. *A Dictionary of the Booksellers and Printers . . . in England, Scotland, and Ireland, 1641–1667.* Bibliogr. Soc., 1907. Continued for 1668–1725, Bibliogr. Soc., 1922.

GREG, W. W. "An Elizabethan Printer and His Copy." *Library*, 1925, pp. 102–118.

———. "The Rationale of Copy-text." *SB*, III (1950), 19–36.

ALBRIGHT, E. M. *Dramatic Publication in Englan 1580–1640.* New York, 1927.

2. The Shakespearean Texts

Chambers I, 126–242; *Barker-Harrison*, 263–2 *Greg; Hinman.*

KNIGHT, C. *Old Lamps or New? a Plea for the Ori nal Editions of the Text of Shakspere: formi an Introductory Notice to the Stratford Shakspe* 1853.

BARTLETT, H. C., and A. W. POLLARD. *A Census Shakespeare's Plays in Quarto, 1594–1709.* N Haven, 1916.

GREG, W. W. "On Certain False Dates in Shak spearian Quartos." *Library*, n.s., IX (1908), 208–2

———. *Principles of Emendation in Shakespea* Oxford, 1928.

———. *The Editorial Problem in Shakespeare: Survey of the Foundations of the Text*, 3rd e Oxford, 1954.

POLLARD, A. W. *Shakespeare Folios and Quartos.* study in the bibliography of Shakespeare's pla 1594–1685. London, 1909.

———. *Shakespeare's Fight With the Pirates and t Problems of the Transmission of His Text.* Ca bridge, 1920.

NEIDIG, W. J. "The Shakespeare Quartos of 161 *MP*, VIII (1910), 145–64.

RHODES, R. C. *Shakespeare's First Folio.* Oxford, 19

SPIELMANN, M. H., J. D. WILSON, SIR S. LEE, R. RHODES, W. W. GREG, and A. NICOLL. *Studies in t First Folio.* Intro. Sir Israel Gollancz. Oxford, 19

BLACK, M. W., and M. A. SHAABER. *Shakespeare's Se enteenth Century Editors, 1632–1685.* New Yo 1937.

MCKERROW, R. B. *Prolegomena for the Oxford Shak speare.* Oxford, 1939.

HART, A. *Stolne and Surreptitious Copies: A Compa ative Study of Shakespeare's Bad Quartos.* Oxfo 1942.

KIRSCHBAUM, L. "An Hypothesis Concerning t Origin of the Bad Quartos." *PMLA*, LX (194 697–715.

———. *Shakespeare and the Stationers.* Columb Ohio, 1955.

MCMANAWAY, J. G. "Where Are Shakespeare's Ma uscripts?" *The New Colophon*, II (1950), 357–3

———. "The Year's Contributions to Shakespeare Study. III: Textual Studies." *SS.* Annually in ea issue. 1948 ——.

WALKER, A. *Textual Problems of the First Foli "Richard III," "King Lear," "Troilus & Cressid "2 Henry IV," "Othello."* Shakespeare Proble Series VII, gen. ed. J. Dover Wilson. Cambrid 1953.

———. "Compositor Determination and Other Pro lems in Shakespearian Texts." *SB*, VII (1955), 3–

———. "The Shifting Text." *TLS*, April 23, 1964.

BOWERS, F. *On Editing Shakespeare and the Eliz bethan Dramatists.* Philadelphia, 1955.

———. "What Shakespeare Wrote." *SJ*, XCVIII (196 24–50.

HINMAN, C. "Cast-off Copy for the First Folio Shakespeare." *SQ*, VI (1955), 259–273.

SHROEDER, J. W. *The Great Folio of 1623: Shak*

speare's Plays in the Printing House. Hamden, Conn., 1956.

WILLIAMS, P., JR. "New Approaches to Textual Problems in Shakespeare." *SB*, VIII (1956), 3–14.

CRAIG, H. *A New Look at Shakespeare's Quartos.* Stanford, Calif., 1961.

TURNER, R. K., JR. "Analytical Bibliography and Shakespeare's Text." *MP*, LXII (1964), 51–58.

D. Sources and Influences

Bullough; Muir.

FARMER, R. *Essay on the Learning of Shakespeare.* Cambridge, 1767.

COLLIER, J. P., and W. C. HAZLITT, eds. *Shakespeare's Library. A collection of the plays, romances, novels, poems, and histories employed by Shakespeare in the composition of his works.* 6 Vols. 2nd ed. London, 1875.

BOAS, F. S. *Shakspere and His Predecessors,* London, 1896.

BOSWELL-STONE, W. G. *Shakspere's Holinshed.* London, 1896.

ANDERS, H. R. D. *Shakespeare's Books.* Berlin, 1904.

MOORMAN, F. W. "Shakespeare's History-Plays and Daniel's 'Civile Wars'." *SJ.*, XL (1904), 69–83.

ROUSE, W. H. D., ed. *Shakespeare's Ovid, being Arthur Golding's translation of the "Metamorphoses."* London, 1904.

LUCAS, F. L. *Seneca and Elizabethan Tragedy.* Cambridge, 1922.

NEWTON, T., ed. *Seneca His Tenne Tragedies.* Tr. Thomas Newton. Introd. by T. S. Eliot. 2 Vols. London, 1927.

BAKER, H. *Induction to Tragedy. A Study in the Development of Form in "Gorboduc," "The Spanish Tragedy" and "Titus Andronicus."* Baton Rouge, La., 1939.

BALDWIN, T. W. *William Shakspere's Small Latine and Lesse Greeke.* 2 Vols. Urbana, Ill., 1944.

———. *Shakspere's Five-Act Structure: Shakspere's Early Plays on the Background of Renaissance Theories of Five-Act Structure from 1470.* Urbana, Ill., 1947.

———. *On the Literary Genetics of Shakspere's Poems and Sonnets.* Urbana, Ill., 1950.

———. "Shakspere's Aphthonian Man." *MLN*, LXV (1950), 111–112.

GUTTMAN, S. *The Foreign Sources of Shakespeare's Works: An Annotated Bibliography of the Commentary Written on this Subject between 1904 and 1940.* New York, 1947.

THALER, A. *Shakespeare and Sir Philip Sidney; The Influence of "The Defense of Poetry."* Oxford, 1947.

PETTET, E. C. *Shakespeare and the Romance Tradition.* London, 1949.

WATKINS, W. B. C. *Shakespeare and Spenser.* Princeton, N.J., 1950.

RÖHRMAN, H. *Marlowe and Shakespeare: A Thematic Exposition of Some of Their Plays.* Arnhem, Netherlands, 1952.

THOMSON, J. A. K. *Shakespeare and the Classics.* London, 1952.

WILSON, F. P. *Marlowe and the Early Shakespeare.* Oxford, 1953.

HONIGMANN, E. A. J. "Shakespeare's *Lost Source-Plays.*" *MLR*, XLIX (1954), 293–307.

SCHRICKX, W. *Shakespeare's Early Contemporaries. The Background of the Harvey-Nashe Polemic and "Love's Labour's Lost."* Antwerp, 1956.

SPENCER, T. J. B. "Shakespeare and the Elizabethan Romans." *SS 10* (1957), 27–38.

WILSON, J. D. "Shakespeare's 'Small Latin'—How Much?" *SS 10* (1957), 12–26.

PRICE, H. T. "Shakespeare's Classical Scholarship." *RES*, ns, IX (1958), 54–55.

ZITNER, S. P. "Gosson, Ovid, and the Elizabethan Audience." *SQ*, IX (1958), 206–208.

MINCOFF, M. "Shakespeare and Lyly." *SS 14* (1961), 15–24.

SMITH, C. G. *Shakespeare's Proverb Lore: His Use of the Sententiae of Leonard Culman and Publilius Syrus.* Cambridge, Mass., 1963.

E. The Theatre

1. Playhouses

CHAMBERS, E. K. *The Elizabethan Stage.* 4 Vols. Oxford, 1923.

BENTLEY, G. E. *The Jacobean and Caroline Stage.* 5 Vols. Oxford, 1941–56.

VENEZKY, A. *Pageantry on the Shakespearean Stage.* New York, 1951.

HODGES, C. W. *The Globe Restored.* London, 1953.

NAGLER, A. M. *Shakespeare's Stage,* tr. from the German by Ralph Mannheim. New Haven, Conn., 1958.

ADAMS, J. C. *The Globe Playhouse.* Rev. ed. New York, 1961.

HOSLEY, R. "The Shakespearean Theater." *SN*, XIV (1964), 32–33.

———. "Shakespearian Stage Curtains: Then and Now." *CE*, XXV (1964), 488–492.

SMITH, I. *Shakespeare's Blackfriars Playhouse.* New York, 1965.

2. Dramatic Background

Chambers I, 27–125; *Barker-Harrison*, 9–43.

GILDERSLEEVE, V. C. *Government Regulation of the Elizabethan Drama.* New York, 1908.

CHAMBERS, E. K. *The Elizabethan Stage.* 4 Vols. Oxford, 1923.

LAWRENCE, W. J. *Those Nut-Cracking Elizabethans.* London, 1935.

LINTHICUM, M. C. *Costume in the Drama of Shakespeare and his Contemporaries.* Oxford, 1936.

HARBAGE, A. "Elizabethan Acting." *PMLA*, LIV (1939), 685–708.

———. *Shakespeare's Audience.* New York, 1941.

———. *Shakespeare and the Rival Traditions.* New York, 1952.

HARRISON, G. B. *Elizabethan Plays and Players.* London, 1940.

PURDOM, C. B. *Producing Shakespeare.* London, 1950.

JOSEPH, B. L. *Elizabethan Acting.* Oxford, 1951.

PRIOR, M. E. "The Elizabethan Audience and the Plays of Shakespeare." *MP*, XLIX (1952), 101–123.

DE BANKE, C. *Shakespearean Stage Production: Then & Now.* New York, 1953.

WILSON, F. P. "The Elizabethan Theatre." *Neophil*, XXXIX (1955), 40–58.

BECKERMAN, B. *Shakespeare at the Globe, 1599–1609*. New York, 1962.

BENTLEY, G. E. *Shakespeare and His Theatre*. Lincoln, Nebr., 1964.

F. Stage History

Odell; Trewin; New Cambridge; Winter; Barker-Harrison, 332–353.

LAMB, C. *Essays on the Tragedies of Shakespeare considered with Reference to Their Fitness for Stage Representation. Charles Lamb's Works*. London, 1818.

HACKETT, J. H. *Notes, Criticisms, and Correspondence Upon Shakespeare's Plays and Actors*. New York, 1863.

LEE, S. *Shakespeare and the Modern Stage, With Other Essays*. London, 1907.

POEL, W. *Shakespeare in the Theatre*. London, 1913.

SPENCER, H. *Shakespeare Improved*. The Restoration versions in quarto and on the stage. Cambridge, Mass. and Oxford, 1927.

LAWRENCE, W. J. *Speeding Up Shakespeare*. London, 1937.

SPRAGUE, A. C. *Shakespeare and the Actors. The Stage Business in His Plays (1660–1905)*. Cambridge, Mass., 1944.

———. *Shakespearian Players and Performances*. Cambridge, Mass., 1953.

———. *The Stage Business in Shakespeare's Plays: A Postscript*. Society for Theatre Research Pamphlet Series, No. 3. London, 1953.

BROWN, J. R. "On the Acting of Shakespeare's Plays." *QJS*, XXXIX (1953), 474–484.

MCMULLEN, F. "Producing Shakespeare." *Shakespeare: of an Age and for all Time*. The Yale Shakespeare Festival Lectures, 1954, pp. 55–57.

HARBAGE, A. *Theatre for Shakespeare*. Toronto, 1955.

WEBSTER, M. *Shakespeare Today*. London, 1956.

GASKILL, W. "Staging Shakespeare Now." *TLS*, April 23, 1964.

KNIGHT, G. W. *Shakespearian Production, with Especial Reference to the Tragedies*. London, 1964.

SHATTUCK, C. H. *The Shakespeare Promptbooks: A Descriptive Catalogue*. Urbana, Illinois, 1965.

G. General Criticism

SCHLEGEL, A. W. *Vorlesungen Über Dramatische Kunst und Literatur*. 1809–1811.

CAMPBELL, T. *Remarks on the Life and Writings of William Shakespeare*. 1838.

HUNTER, J. *New Illustrations of the Life, Studies, and Writings of Shakespeare*. 2 Vols. London, 1844–45.

HUDSON, H. N. *Lectures on Shakespeare*. 2 Vols. New York, 1848.

KNIGHT, C. *Studies of Shakespeare . . .* London, 1851.

WHITE, R. G. *Shakespeare's Scholar: Being Historical and Critical Studies of His Text, Characters, and Commentators; With an Examination of Mr. Collier's Folio of 1623*. New York, 1854.

HUGO, V. *William Shakespeare*. Paris, 1864.

WISEMAN, NICHOLAS CARDINAL. *Shakespeare; a Lec ture*. 1865.

DOWDEN, E. *Shakspere: A critical study of his min and art*. London, 1875.

ELZE, K. *Abhandlungen zu Shakespeare*. Halle, 187 Eng. trans., 1888.

SWINBURNE, A. C. *A Study of Shakespeare*. Londo 1880.

TEN BRINK, B. *Five Lectures on Shakespeare*. Tran by J. Franklin. London, 1895.

COLLINS, J. C. *Studies in Shakespeare*. London, 190.

RALEIGH, W. *Shakespeare*. London, 1907.

SAINTSBURY, G. "Shakespeare, Life and Plays." *CHEI* V (1910), 165–222.

MASEFIELD, J. *William Shakespeare*, rev. ed. Londo 1911.

SMEATON, O. *Shakespeare, His Life and Work*. Lon don, 1912.

GOLLANCZ, I., ed. *A Book of Homage to Shakespear* Oxford, 1916.

KITTREDGE, G. L. *Shakspere*. Cambridge, Mass., 191

MATTHEWS, B., and A. H. THORNDIKE, eds. *Shak spearean Studies*. New York, 1916.

QUILLER-COUCH, A. *Shakespeare's Workmanshi* London, 1918.

CROCE, B. *Ariosto, Shakespeare e Corneille*. Ba Italy, 1920. English tran. by Douglas Ainslie. Lon don, 1921.

LAWRENCE, W. J. *Shakespeare's Workshop*. Oxfor 1928.

SISSON, C. J. *The Mythical Sorrows of Shakespear* Oxford, 1934.

———. *Shakespeare*. Writers and Their Work, N 58. London, 1955.

MURRY, J. M. *Shakespeare*. London, 1936.

WILSON, R. *The Approach to Shakespeare*. Londo 1938.

HARRISON, G. B. *Introducing Shakespeare*. Londo 1939.

RIDLEY, M. R. *On Reading Shakespeare*. Londo 1940.

SPENCER, H. *The Art and Life of William Shak speare*. New York, 1940.

GRANVILLE-BARKER, H. *Prefaces to Shakespeare*. Vols. Princeton, N.J., 1946; 1947.

HARBAGE, A. *As They Liked It: An Essay on Shak speare and Morality*. New York, 1947.

———. *Shakespeare and the Rival Traditions*. Ne York, 1952.

———. *William Shakespeare: A Reader's Guide*. Ne York, 1963.

ELLIS-FERMOR, U. *Shakespeare the Dramatist*. Lon don, 1948.

———. *Shakespeare the Dramatist, and other Paper* ed. Kenneth Muir. London and New York, 196

STAUFFER, D. A. *Shakespeare's World of Images: T Development of His Moral Ideas*. New York, 194

HOLZKNECHT, K. J. *The Backgrounds of Shakespeare Plays*. New York, 1950.

SANDERS, G. *Shakespeare Primer*. New York, 1950.

ALEXANDER, P. *A Shakespeare Primer*. London, 195

BRADBROOK, M. C. *Shakespeare and Elizabethan P etry: A Study of his Earlier Work in Relation the Poetry of the Time*. London, 1951.

DUTHIE, G. I. *Shakespeare*. London, 1951.

GODDARD, H. C. *The Meaning of Shakespeare*. Ch cago, 1951.

SEWELL, A. *Character and Society in Shakespeare.* Oxford, 1951.
NICOLL, A. *Shakespeare.* London, 1952.
FLUCHÈRE, H. *Shakespeare.* London, 1953.
HOLLOWAY, J. "Dramatic Irony in Shakespeare." *Northern Miscellany of Literary Criticism,* I (1953), 3–16.
PARROTT, T. M. *William Shakespeare: A Handbook.* Rev. ed. New York, 1953.
REESE, M. M. *Shakespeare: His World and His Work.* New York, 1953.
SPALDING, K. J. *The Philosophy of Shakespeare.* New York, Oxford, and Toronto, 1953.
FORD, B., ed. *The Age of Shakespeare.* Aylesbury and London, 1955.
TRAVERSI, D. A. *An Approach to Shakespeare,* 2nd ed., rev. New York, 1956.
KNIGHTS, L. C. *Some Shakespearean Themes.* London, 1959.
LUDOWYK, E. F. C. *Understanding Shakespeare.* Cambridge, 1962.
MATTHEWS, H. *Character and Symbol in Shakespeare's Plays: A Study of Certain Christian and pre-Christian Elements in Their Structure and Imagery.* Cambridge, 1962.
ARTHOS, J. *The Art of Shakespeare.* London and New York, 1964.
GRACE, W. J. *Approaching Shakespeare.* New York and London, 1964.
HOLLAND, N. *The Shakespearean Imagination.* New York, 1964.
HOROWITZ, D. *Shakespeare: An Existentialist View.* London, 1965.

H. Special Studies

1. Imagery and Language

Parker-Harrison, 116–135; *Clemen.*
AYSCOUGH, S. *An Index to the Remarkable Passages and Words Made Use of by Shakespeare.* London, 1790.
WHITER, W. *A Specimen of a Commentary on Shakespeare.* London, 1794.
CLARKE, M. C. *The Complete Concordance to Shakspere,* being a verbal index to all the passages in the dramatic works of the poet. New and rev. ed. London, 1870.
SCHMIDT, A. *Shakespeare-Lexicon.* Berlin, 1874–1875, 1886.
BARTLETT, J. *A New and Complete Concordance or Verbal Index to Words, Phrases, and Passages in the Dramatic Works of Shakespeare, With a Supplement Concordance to the Poems.* London, 1906.
ONIONS, C. T. *A Shakespeare Glossary.* Oxford, 1911.
SIMPSON, P. *Shakespearian Punctuation.* Oxford, 1911.
KELLNER, L. *Shakespeare-Wörterbuch.* Leipzig, 1922.
SPURGEON, C. F. E. *Shakespeare's Imagery and What It Tells Us.* Cambridge, 1935.
ELLIS-FERMOR, U. *Some Recent Research in Shakespeare's Imagery.* Oxford, 1937.
WILSON, F. P. *Shakespeare and the Diction of Common Life.* Oxford, 1941.
BORNSTEIN, L. H. "Analysis of Imagery: A Critique of Literary Method." *PMLA,* LVII (1942), 638–653.
ALEXANDER, P. *Shakespeare's Punctuation.* London, 1945.
ARMSTRONG, E. A. *Shakespeare's Imagination.* London, 1946.
MIRIAM JOSEPH, SISTER, C. S. C. *Shakespeare's Use of the Arts of Language.* New York, 1947.
RANSOM, J. C. "On Shakespeare's Language." *SR,* LV (1947), 181–198.
DOWNER, A. S. "The Life of Our Design." *Hudson Review,* II (1949), 242–263.
MOROZOV, M. M. "The Individualization of Shakespeare's Characters through Imagery." *SS 2* (1949), 83–106.
STAUFFER, D. A. *Shakespeare's World of Images: The Development of His Moral Ideas.* New York, 1949.
PASTERNAK, B. "Shakespeare's Imagery and Rhythm," tr. by Peter Meadows. *Arena,* I (1950), 33–37.
CRANE, M. *Shakespeare's Prose.* Chicago, 1951.
KÖKERITZ, H. *Shakespeare's Pronunciation.* New Haven, 1953.
PARTRIDGE, A. C. *The Accidence of Ben Jonson's Plays, Masques and Entertainments.* Cambridge, 1953.
———. "Shakespeare's Orthography in *Venus and Adonis* and Some Early Quartos." *SS* 7 (1954), 35–47.
———. *Orthography in Shakespeare and Elizabethan Drama: A Study of Colloquial Contractions, Elision, Prosody and Punctuation.* London and Lincoln, Nebr., 1964.
HALLIDAY, F. E. *The Poetry of Shakespeare's Plays.* London, 1954.
BORINSKI, L. "Shakespeare's Comic Prose." *SS 8* (1955), 57–68.
PARTRIDGE, E. *Shakespeare's Bawdy: A Literary and Psychological Essay and a Comprehensive Glossary.* London, 1947; New York, 1948; new ed., rev. 1955.
WILLCOCK, G. D. *Language and Poetry in Shakespeare's Early Plays.* London, 1955. *Proceedings of the British Academy,* XL, 103–117.
HULME, H. M. *Explorations in Shakespeare's Language: Some Problems of Lexical Meaning in the Dramatic Text.* London, 1962.
JORGENSEN, P. A. *Redeeming Shakespeare's Words.* Berkeley, Calif., and Los Angeles, 1962.

2. Themes

CURRY, W. C. *Shakespeare's Philosophical Patterns.* Baton Rouge, La., 1937.
MARY BONAVENTURE MROZ, SISTER, O. S. F. *Divine Vengeance: A Study in the Philosophical Backgrounds of the Revenge Motif as it Appears in Shakespeare's Chronicle History Plays.* Washington, D. C., 1941.
HARBAGE, A. *As They Liked It.* New York, 1947.
DORAN, M. *Endeavors of Art: A Study of Form in Elizabethan Drama.* Madison, Wis., 1953.
BARNET, S. "Some Limitations of a Christian Approach to Shakespeare." *ELH,* XXII (1955), 81–92.
BUSH, G. *Shakespeare and the Natural Condition.* Cambridge, Mass., 1956.
BRYANT, J. A., JR. *Hippolyta's View: Some Christian Aspects of Shakespeare's Plays.* Lexington, Ky., 1961.

JENKINS, H. "The Tragedy of Revenge in Shakespeare and Webster." *SS 14* (1961), 45–55.
SEN GUPTA, S. C. *The Whirligig of Time*. Bombay, 1961.
VYVYAN, J. *Shakespeare and Platonic Beauty*. London and New York, 1961.
WATSON, C. B. *Shakespeare and the Renaissance Concept of Honor*. Princeton, N.J., 1961.
FRYE, R. M. *Shakespeare and Christian Doctrine*. Princeton, N.J., 1963.
RIGHTER, A. *Shakespeare and the Idea of the Play*. New York, 1963.
BERRY, F. *The Shakespeare Inset*. London, 1965.

3. *Translations*

SCHLEGEL, A. W., ed. *Shakspeares Dramatische Werke*. 8 Vols. Berlin, 1797–1801. 9.Bd., 1 Abt. Berlin, 1810.
SCHLEGEL, A. W. and L. TIECK, eds. *Shakespeares Dramatische Werke*. 12 Vols. Berlin, 1839–1840.
Oeuvres Complètes de W. Shakespeare. Translated by François-Victor Hugo. 18 Vols. Paris, 1856–1867.
Oeuvres Complètes de Shakespeare. Translated by E. Montégut. 10 Vols. Paris, 1867–1873.
William Shakespeare. Dziela Dramatyczne. Shakespeare's plays in Polish translation by J. Kasprowicz, J. Korzeniowski, St. Kozmian, K. Ostrowski, A. Pajgert, J. Paszkowski, E. Porebowicz and L. Ulrich. With an introd. by Roman Dyboski, and with a study on Shakespeare in Poland by L. Bernacki. 6 Vols. Warsaw, 1911–1913.

4. *Classroom Use of Shakespeare*

HAYDEN, H. *The Immortal Memory: A New Approach to the Teaching of Shakespeare*. London, 1936.
TAYLOR, R. V. *Shakespeare for Senior Schools*. London, 1937.
PEAT, R. C. *Presenting Shakespeare*. London, 1947.
WOOD, S. *The New Teaching of Shakespeare in Schools*. London, 1948.
MARTIN, M. W. "Shakespeare in Today's Classroom." *English Journal*, XLIV (1955), pp. 228–229. *SN*, V (1955), p. 18.
FIDONE, W. "An Above-average Class Studies *Hamlet*." *English Journal*, XLV (1956), 470–476.
ILLSLEY, W. A. *A Shakespeare Manual for Schools*. Cambridge, 1957.

5. *Critical Anthologies and Histories*

Barker-Harrison, 293–311.
SMITH, D. N. *Shakespeare in the 18th Century*. Oxford, 1928.
BRADBY, A., ed. *Shakespeare Criticism, 1919–1935*. Oxford, 1936.
SMIRNOV, A. A. *Shakespeare: A Marxist Interpretation*, tr. by Sonia Volochova and others. New York, 1936.
HALLIDAY, F. E. *Shakespeare and His Critics*. London, 1949.
BRADBROOK, M. C. "Fifty Years of the Criticism of Shakespeare's Style." *SS* 7 (1954), 1–11.
WEISINGER, H. "An Examination of the Myth and Ritual Approach to Shakespeare." *Myth and Mythmaking*, ed. Henry A. Murray. New York, 1960. pp. 132–140.
———. "Myth, Method, and Shakespeare." *JGE*, XV (1964), 29–49.
HAPGOOD, R. "Shakespeare and the Ritualists." *SS 15* (1962), 111–124.
EASTMAN, A. M. and G. B. HARRISON, eds. *Shakespeare's Critics from Jonson to Auden: A Medley of Judgments*. Ann Arbor, Mich., 1964.

6. *Art*

HARTMANN, S. *Shakespeare in Art*. Boston, 1901.
FAIRCHILD, ARTHUR H. R. *Shakespeare and the Arts of Design (Architecture, Sculpture, and Painting)* Univ. of Missouri Studies, XII, No. 1. Columbia Mo., 1937.
MERCHANT, W. M. *Shakespeare and the Artist*. Oxford, 1959.

7. *Music*

Barker-Harrison, 136–160.
WILSON, C. *Shakespeare and Music*. London, 1922.
LONG, J. H. *Shakespeare's Use of Music: A Study of the Music and Its Performance in the Original Production of Seven Comedies*. Gainesville, Fla. 1955.
MANIFOLD, J. S. *The Music in English Drama*. From Shakespeare to Purcell. London, 1956.
AUDEN, W. H. "Music in Shakespeare." *Encounter* IX (1957), 31–44.
SENG, P. J. "Music in Shakespeare." *Encounter*, (1958), 67–68.
STERNFELD, F. W. *Music in Shakespearean Tragedy* London and New York, 1963.

8. *Shakespeare's Influence*

COHN, A. *Shakespeare in Germany in the Sixteenth and Seventeenth Centuries: an Account of the English Actors in Germany and the Netherlands, and of the Plays Performed by them During the Same Period*. Berlin and London, 1864.
DUNN, E. *Shakespeare in America*. New York, 193[illegible]
MUIR, K. "The Future of Shakespeare." *Penguin New Writing*, XXVIII (1946/47), 101–121.
FLUCHÈRE, H. "Shakespeare in France: 1868–1948." *SS 2* (1949), 115–124.
LEVIN, H. "Shakespeare Today." *PAPS*, CVI (1962), 422–426.
CLEMEN, W. "Shakespeare and the Modern World." *SS 16* (1963), 57–62.
LEWINTER, O., ed. *Shakespeare in Europe*. Cleveland 1963.
BRENNECKE, E. and H. *Shakespeare in Germany 1590–1700*. Chicago, 1964.
PEYRE, H. "Shakespeare and Modern French Criticism." *The Persistence of Shakespeare Idolatry: Essays in Honor of Robert W. Babcock*, ed. Herbert M. Schueller. Detroit, 1964, pp. 1–46.
SUTHERLAND, J. and J. HURSTFIELD, eds. *Shakespeare's World*. London, 1964.
WEIGAND, H. J. "Shakespeare in German Criticism." *The Persistence of Shakespeare Idolatry: Essays in Honor of Robert W. Babcock*, ed. Herbert M. Schueller. Detroit, 1964, pp. 105–133.

I. Histories

Courtenay, T. P. *Commentaries On the Historical Plays of Shakespeare.* 2 Vols. London, 1840, 1861.

Marriott, J. A. R. *English History in Shakespeare.* London, 1918.

Tillyard, E. M. W. *Shakespeare's History Plays.* London, 1944.

Palmer, J. *Political Characters of Shakespeare.* London, 1945.

Chapman, R. "The Wheel of Fortune in Shakespeare's Historical Plays." *RES*, n.s., I (1950), 1–7.

Bethell, S. L. "The Comic Element in Shakespeare's Histories: A Paper Read at the Shakespeare Conference at Stratford-upon-Avon, 1951." *Anglia*, LXXI (1952).

Richardson, A. D., III. "The Early Historical Plays." *Shakespeare: of an Age and for all Time.* New Haven, 1954.

Ribner, I. *The English History Play in the Age of Shakespeare.* Princeton, N.J., 1957.

Traversi, D. *Shakespeare: From Richard II to Henry V.* Stanford, Calif., 1957.

Reese, M. M. *The Cease of Majesty: A Study of Shakespeare's History Plays.* London, 1961; New York, 1962.

Knights, L. C. *William Shakespeare, The Histories:* Richard III, King John, Richard II, Henry V. Writers and Their Work, 151. London, 1962.

Leech, C. *William Shakespeare, The Chronicles:* Henry VI, Henry IV, The Merry Wives of Windsor, Henry VIII. Writers and Their Work, No. 146. London, 1962.

J. Comedies

1. General

Adams, pp. 429–437.

Charlton, H. B. *Shakespearian Comedy.* London, 1938.

Hollowell, A. *Shakespeare's Use of Comic Materials in Tragedy: A Survey of Criticism.* Chapel Hill, N.C., 1940.

Campbell, O. J. *Shakespeare's Satire.* New York and London, 1943.

Gordon, G. *Shakespearian Comedy and Other Studies*, ed. Sir Edmund Chambers. Oxford, 1944.

Palmer, J. *Comic Characters of Shakespeare.* New York, 1946.

Knight, G. W. *The Crown of Life: Essays in Interpretation of Shakespeare's Final Plays.* Oxford, 1947.

Frye, N. "The Argument of Comedy." *EIE*, 1948. New York, 1949.

———. "Characterization in Shakespearian Comedy." *SQ*, IV (1953), 271–277.

Parrott, T. M. *Shakespearean Comedy.* New York, 1949.

Coghill, N. "The Basis of Shakespearian Comedy." *Essays and Studies*, n.s., III (1950), 1–28.

Sen Gupta, S. C. *Shakespearian Comedy.* Calcutta, 1951.

Barber, C. L. "The Saturnalian Pattern In Shakespeare's Comedy." *SR*, LIX (1951), 593–611.

Thompson, K. F. "Shakespeare's Romantic Comedies." *PMLA*, LXVII (1952), 1079–93.

Desai, C. N. *Shakespearean Comedy.* Indore City, M. B., India, 1953.

Bradbrook, M. C. *The Growth and Structure of Elizabethan Comedy.* London, 1955.

Brown, J. R. "The Interpretation of Shakespeare's Comedies." *SS 8* (1955), 1–13.

Cecil, D. "Shakespearean Comedy." *The Fine Art of Reading and Other Literary Studies.* New York, 1957.

Tillyard, E. M. W. *The Nature of Comedy and Shakespeare.* London, 1958.

Evans, B. *Shakespeare's Comedies.* Berkeley, Calif., 1960.

Traversi, D. *William Shakespeare, The Early Comedies:* The Comedy of Errors, The Taming of the Shrew, The Two Gentlemen of Verona, Love's Labour's Lost, The Merchant of Venice. Writers and Their Work, No. 129. London and New York, 1960.

Draper, J. *Stratford to Dogberry.* 1961.

Kermode, F. "The Mature Comedies." *Early Shakespeare.* Stratford-upon-Avon Studies, 3. London and New York, 1961, pp. 211–227.

Doran, M. " 'Discrepant Awareness' in Shakespeare's Comedies." *MP*, LX (1962), 51–55.

Hunter, G. K. *William Shakespeare, The Late Comedies:* A Midsummer-Night's Dream, Much Ado About Nothing, As You Like It, Twelfth Night. Writers and Their Work, No. 143. London and New York, 1962.

Wilson, J. D. *Shakespeare's Happy Comedies.* London, 1962.

2. Problem Plays

Lawrence, W. W. *Shakespeare's Problem Comedies.* New York, 1931.

Charlton, H. B. "Shakespeare's 'Dark Comedies.' " *BJRL*, XXI (1937), 78–128.

Tillyard, E. M. W. *Shakespeare's Problem Plays.* Toronto, 1949; London, 1950.

Ure, P. *William Shakespeare, The Problem Plays:* Troilus and Cressida, All's Well That Ends Well, Measure for Measure, Timon of Athens. Writers and Their Work, No. 140. London and New York, 1961.

———. "The Enigmatic Problem Plays." *SN*, XIV (1964), 22–23.

Schanzer, E. *The Problem Plays of Shakespeare: A Study of* Julius Caesar, Measure for Measure, Antony and Cleopatra. London, 1963.

Lever, J. W. "Shakespeare and the Problem Play." *DUJ*, XXV (1964), 86–88.

3. Romances

Tillyard, E. M. W. *Shakespeare's Last Plays.* London, 1938.

Knight, G. W. *The Crown of Life: Essays in Interpretation of Shakespeare's Final Plays*, 2nd ed. London, 1948.

Pettet, E. C. *Shakespeare and the RomanceTradition.* London, 1949.

Traversi, D. *Shakespeare: The Last Phase.* London, 1954.

LEECH, C. "The Structure of the Last Plays." *SS 11* (1958), 19–30.

KERMODE, F. *William Shakespeare, The Final Plays:* Pericles, The Winter's Tale, The Tempest, The Two Noble Kinsmen. Writers and Their Work, 155. London, 1963.

FRYE, N. *A Natural Perspective: The Development of Shakespearean Comedy and Romance.* New York, 1964.

SMITH, H. "Shakespeare's Romances." *HLQ,* XXVII (1964), 279–287.

HUNTER, R. G. *Shakespeare and the Comedy of Forgiveness.* New York, 1965.

K. Tragedies

LAMB, C. *On the Tragedies of Shakespeare Considered With Reference to Their Fitness for Stage Representation.* London, 1818.

BRADLEY, A. C. *Shakespearean Tragedy.* London, 1904.

CAMPBELL, L. B. *Shakespeare's Tragic Heroes: Slaves of Passion.* New York, 1930.

SPENCER, T. *Death and Elizabethan Tragedy.* Cambridge, Mass., 1936.

———. *Shakespeare and the Nature of Man.* New York, 1942.

FAIRCHILD, A. H. R. *Shakespeare and the Tragic Theme.* Univ. of Missouri Studies, XIX, No. 2. Columbia, Mo., 1944.

PRIOR, M. E. *The Language of Tragedy.* New York and Oxford, 1947.

CHARLTON, H. B. *Shakespearian Tragedy.* Cambridge, 1948.

CUNNINGHAM, J. V. "'Tragedy' in Shakespeare." *ELH,* XVII (1950), 30–35.

———. *Woe or Wonder: The Emotional Effect of Shakespearean Tragedy.* Denver, Colo., 1951.

FARNHAM, W. *Shakespeare's Tragic Frontier: The World of His Final Tragedies.* Berkeley, Calif., 1950.

LEECH, C. *Shakespeare's Tragedies: And Other Studies in Seventeenth-Century Drama.* London, 1950.

MINCOFF, M. "The Structural Pattern of Shakespeare's Tragedies." *SS 3* (1950), 58–65.

HARRISON, G. B. *Shakespeare's Tragedies.* London, 1951.

WEISINGER, H. *Tragedy and the Paradox of the Fortunate Fall.* East Lansing, Mich., 1953.

———. "The Myth and Ritual Approach to Shakespearean Tragedy." *The Centennial Review of Arts and Science,* I (1957), 142–166.

SPEAIGHT, R. *Nature in Shakespearian Tragedy.* London, 1955.

HENN, T. R. *The Harvest of Tragedy.* London, 1956.

MULLER, H. J. *The Spirit of Tragedy.* New York, 1956.

STIRLING, B. *Unity in Shakespearean Tragedy. The Interplay of Theme and Character.* New York, 1956.

BATTENHOUSE, R. "Shakespearean Tragedy." *The Tragic Vision and the Christian Faith,* ed. Nathan A. Scott. New York, 1957.

———. "Shakespearean Tragedy as Christian: Some Confusions in the Debate." *CRAS,* VIII (1964), 77–98.

KNIGHT, G. W. *The Wheel of Fire: Essays in Interpretation of Shakespeare's Sombre Tragedies,* Intro. by T. S. Eliot, 5th rev. ed. New York, 1957.

MAXWELL, J. C. "Shakespeare's Roman Plays: 1900–1956." *SS 10* (1957), 1–11.

SIEGEL, P. N. *Shakespearean Tragedy and the Elizabethan Compromise.* New York, 1957.

WILSON, H. S. *On the Design of Shakespearian Tragedy.* Toronto, 1957.

MACK, M. "The Jacobean Shakespeare: Some Observations on the Construction of the Tragedies." *Jacobean Theater.* Stratford-upon-Avon Studies, 1, gen. eds. John Russell Brown and Bernard Harris. London and New York, 1960, pp. 11–41.

RIBNER, I. *Patterns in Shakespearian Tragedy.* London, 1960.

ROSEN, W. *Shakespeare and the Craft of Tragedy.* New York, 1960.

CHARNEY, M. *Shakespeare's Roman Plays: The Function of Imagery in the Drama.* Cambridge, Mass., 1961.

HOLLOWAY, J. *The Story of the Night: Studies in Shakespeare's Major Tragedies.* London, 1961.

MUIR, K. *William Shakespeare: The Great Tragedies*—Hamlet, Othello, King Lear, Macbeth. Writers and Their Work, No. 133. London, 1961.

SISSON, C. J. *Shakespeare's Tragic Justice.* London, 1962.

HARBAGE, A., ed. *Shakespeare: The Tragedies: A Collection of Critical Essays.* Englewood Cliffs, N.J., 1964.

HEILMAN, R. B. "To Know Himself: An Aspect of Tragic Structure." *REL,* v, ii (1964), 36–57.

L. Claimants

BACON, D. S. *The Philosophy of the Plays of Shakespeare Unfolded.* London, 1857. ("Raleigh" school")

HOLMES, N. *The Authorship of Shakespeare.* New York, 1866. (Bacon)

DONNELLY, I. *The Great Cryptogram: Francis Bacon's Cipher in the So-called Shakespeare Plays.* 2 Vols. New York, 1888. (Bacon)

GREENWOOD, G. G. *The Shakespeare Problem Restated.* London, 1908. (Bacon)

LANG, A. *Shakespeare, Bacon, and the Great Unknown.* London, 1912. (Bacon)

ROBERTSON, J. M. *The Baconian Heresy. A Confutation.* London, 1913. (Refutes Bacon)

BAXTER, J. T. *The Greatest of Literary Problems. The Authorship of the Shakespeare Works.* Boston, 1915. (Bacon)

LEFRANC, A. *Sous le Masque de 'William Shakespeare.* 2 vols. Paris, 1918–1919. (Derby)

LOONEY, J. T. *"Shakespeare" identified in Edward de Vere, the 17th Earl of Oxford.* London, 1920. (Oxford)

ALLEN, P. *The Case for Edward de Vere, 17th Earl of Oxford, as "W. Shakespeare."* London, 1930. (Oxford)

SPURGEON, C. "The Use of Imagery by Shakespeare and Bacon." *RES,* IX (1933). (Refutes Bacon)

CORNWALL, A. B. *Francis the First: Unacknowledged King of Great Britain and Ireland known to the World as Sir Francis Bacon, Man of Mystery and Cipher.* Birmingham, 1936. (Bacon) ampbell, O. J. "Shakespeare Himself." *Harper's* (July, 1940), pp. 172–185. (Supports Shakespeare)

rooks, A. *Will Shakespeare and the Dyer's Hand.* New York, 1943. (Dyer)

rundry, W. G. C. *Francis Bacon: a Map of Days, a Guide to his Homes and Haunts.* London, 1946. (Bacon)

Voodward, F. L. *Bacon and the Cipher Story.* Chicago, 1947. (Bacon)

)gburn, D. and C. *This Star of England: Shakespeare, Man of the Renaissance.* New York, 1952. (Oxford)

Ioffman, C. *The Murder of the Man Who Was Shakespeare.* New York, 1955. (Marlowe)

Gibson, H. N. *The Shakespeare Claimants: A Critical Survey of the Four Principal Theories Concerning the Authorship of the Shakespearean Plays.* London and New York, 1962. (Bacon, Oxford, Derby, Marlowe.)

McManaway, J. G. *The Authorship of Shakespeare.* Washington, D.C., 1962. (Supports Shakespeare)

McMichael, G. and E. M. Glenn, eds. *Shakespeare and His Rivals: A Casebook on the Authorship Controversy.* New York, 1962. (Survey)

Crow, J. "Heretics Observed." *TLS*, April 23, 1964. (Survey)

Harris, W. "An Early Baconian." *Manchester Review*, x (1964), 126–127. (Bacon)

II. THE WORKS OF SHAKESPEARE

A. Collected Editions

Hanmer, Sir Thomas.] *The Works of Shakespear.* Carefully revised and corrected by Sir Thomas Hanmer. 6 Vols. Oxford, 1743–1744, 1770–1771.

Warburton, William.] *The Works of Shakespear in Eight Volumes.* The genuine text, collated . . . , corrected and emended . . . by Mr. Pope and Mr. Warburton. 8 Vols. London, 1747.

Johnson, Samuel.] *The Plays of William Shakespeare, in Eight Volumes.* With the corrections and illustrations of various commentators, to which are added notes by Samuel Johnson. 8 Vols. London, 1765, 1768.

Steevens, George.] *Twenty of the Plays of Shakespeare,* . . . Publ. from the originals by George Steevens. 4 Vols. London, 1766.

Capell, Edward.] *Mr. William Shakespeare His Comedies, Histories, and Tragedies,* . . . Republished in Ten Volumes by Edward Capell. 10 Vols. London, 1767–1768.

Steevens, George, and Samuel Johnson.] *The Plays of William Shakespeare.* With the corrections and illustrations of various commentators, to which are added notes by Samuel Johnson and George Steevens. 10 Vols. London, 1773. Second edn., rev. and augmented by I. Reed. 10 Vols. London, 1778. Supplement to second edn. by Edmond Malone, 2 Vols. London, 1780. Third edn., 14 Vols., London 1785. Fourth edn., 15 Vols., London 1793.

Malone, Edmond.] *The Plays and Poems of William Shakespeare, in Ten Volumes.* Collated verbatim with the most authentic copies . . . with notes by E. Malone. 10 Vols. London, 1790.

Reed, Isaac.] *The Plays of William Shakspeare* . . . With the corrections and illustrations of various commentators, to which are added notes by Samuel Johnson and George Steevens. 5th ed., rev. and augmented by I. Reed, with a glossarial index. 21 Vols. [The First Variorum Edition.] London, 1803.

Reed, Isaac.] *The Plays of William Shakspeare* . . . With corrections and illustrations of various commentators, to which are added notes by Samuel Johnson and George Steevens. 6th edn. rev. and augmented by I. Reed. 21 Vols. [The 2nd Variorum Edition.] London, 1813.

Boswell, James.] *The Plays and Poems of William Shakspeare,* with the corrections and illustrations of various commentators, comprehending a life of the poet, and an enlarged history of the stage by the late Edmond Malone, with a new glossarial index, ed. J. Boswell. 21 Vols. [The 3rd Variorum Edition.] London, 1821.

[Singer, S. W.] *The Dramatic Works of William Shakespeare.* With notes, original and selected by Samuel Weller Singer, and a life of the poet by C. Symmons. 10 Vols. London, 1826.

[Knight, Charles.] *The Pictorial Edition of the Works of Shakspere.* 8 vols. London, 1839–42.

[Halliwell-Phillipps, J. O.] *The Works of William Shakespeare.* The text formed from a new collation of the early editions . . . By J. O. Halliwell. 16 Vols. London, 1853–1865.

[Clark, W. G., J. Glover, and W. A. Wright.] *The Works of Shakespeare.* 9 vols. [The Cambridge Shakespeare.] Cambridge, 1863–1866.

[Clark, William G., and William A. Wright.] *The Works of William Shakespeare.* London, 1864. [The Globe Edition, which is the standard for line numbering.]

[White, Richard Grant.] *The Works of William Shakespeare.* 12 Vols. Boston, 1857–1866.

[Furness, Horace Howard, and Horace Howard Furness, Jr.] *A New Variorum Edition of the Works of Shakespeare.* Philadelphia, 1871– .

[Furnivall, F. J.] *The Leopold Shakespeare.* The poet's works, in chronological order, from the text of Delius. Intro. by F. J. Furnivall. London, 1877.

[Hudson, Henry N.] *The Complete Works of William Shakespeare.* With a life of the poet, explanatory footnotes, critical notes, and a glossarial index by Henry N. Hudson. 20 Vols. Boston, 1881.

[Dyce, Alexander.] *The Works of Shakespeare.* The text rev. by Alexander Dyce. 3rd ed., 1895–1901.

[Morgan, Appleton.] *The Bankside Shakespeare.* 22 Vols. New York, 1888–1906.

[Herford, C. H.] *The Works of Shakespeare.* With introductions and notes. 10 Vols. London, 1899–1900.

[Craig, W. J.] *The Oxford Shakespeare.* The complete works of Shakespeare, ed. with a glossary by W. J. Craig. Oxford, 1891.

[Porter, Charlotte, and Helen A. Clarke.] *The American First Folio Edition.* 40 Vols. New York, 1903–1912.

[Furnivall, F. J., and W. G. Boswell-Stone.] *The Old Spelling Shakespeare*. London, 1904.

[Craig, W. J., 1899–1906, and R. H. Case, 1909–1924.] *The Arden Shakespeare*. 37 Vols. London, 1899–1924.

[Neilson, William Allan and Ashley Horace Thorndike.] *The Tudor Shakespeare*. 40 Vols. New York and London, 1911–1913.

[Cross, Wilbur L., and C. F. T. Brooke.] *The Yale Shakespeare*. 40 Vols. New Haven and Oxford, 1918–1928.

[Quiller-Couch, Sir Arthur, and John Dover Wilson.] *The Works of Shakespeare. The New Cambridge Shakespeare*. Cambridge, 1921–1962.

[Farjeon, H.] *The Works of Shakespeare*. 7 Vols. (The Nonesuch Press Shakespeare.) London, 1929–1934.

[Ridley, M. R.] *The New Temple Shakespeare*. 39 Vols. London, 1934–1936.

[Kittredge, G. L.] *The Works of Shakespeare*. Boston, 1936.

[Houghton, R. E. C. *et al.*] *The New Clarendon Shakespeare*. Oxford, 1938–

[Alexander, P.] *The Works of Shakespeare*. London, 1951.

[Craig, H.] *Shakespeare*. Chicago, 1951.

[Ellis-Fermor, U., H. F. Brooks, H. Jenkins *et al.*] *The New Arden Shakespeare*. London and Cambridge, Mass., 1951–

[Sisson, C. J.] *The Complete Works of Shakespeare*. London, 1954.

[Kökeritz, H., C. T. Prouty *et al.*] *The Yale Shakespeare*, Revised edition. New Haven, 1954–

[Munro, J. J.] *The London Shakespeare*. 6 Vols. London, 1957.

[Alexander, P.] *The Heritage Shakespeare*. 3 Vols. New York, 1958.

Noteworthy paperback editions include:

Bantam. O. J. Campbell, A. Rothschild, S. Vaughan, eds.

Folger. L. B. Wright, V. A. LaMar, eds.

Laurel. F. Fergusson, C. J. Sisson, eds.

Pelican. A. Harbage, ed.

Penguin. G. B. Harrison, ed.

Signet. S. Barnet, ed.

B. Chronology

Chambers, I, 243–274.

McManaway, J. G. "Recent Studies in Shakespeare's Chronology." *SS 3* (1950), 23–33.

Feuillerat, A. *The Composition of Shakespeare's Plays: Authorship, Chronology*. New Haven, 1953.

Mincoff, M. "The Chronology of Shakespeare's Early Works." *ZAA*, xii (1964), 173–182.

C. The Plays and Poems

1. All's Well That Ends Well

Modern Editions: New Cambridge, A. Quiller-Couch and J. Dover Wilson, eds. Cambridge, 1929; Penguin, G. B. Harrison, ed. London, 1955; New Arden, G. K. Hunter, ed. London, 1959; Laurel, Francis Fergusson and C. J. Sisson, eds. New York, 1961; Signet, Sylvan Barnet, ed. New York, 196[illegible]; Pelican, Jonas Barish, ed. Baltimore, 1964.

Textual Studies: *Chambers*, I, 449–452; *Greg*, pp. 351–353; *Hinman, passim.*

Thiselton, A. E. *Some Textual Notes On "All Well That Ends Well."* London, 1900.

Tolman, A. H. *What Has Become of Shakespeare's Play "Love's Labour's Won"?* Chicago, 1902.

Sources: *Bullough*, II, 375–396; *Muir.*

Stage History: *Odell, passim; Trewin, passim; New Cambridge*, pp. 187–189.

Criticism: *Johnson*, pp. 99–102; *Coleridge*, I, 112–11[illegible]; *Hazlitt*, pp. 329–332; *Van Doren*, pp. 178–185.

Lawrence, W. W. *Shakespeare's Problem Comedie[s]*. New York, 1931.

Tillyard, E. M. W. *Shakespeare's Problem Play[s]*. Toronto, 1949.

Bradbrook, M. C. "Virtue Is the True Nobility: Study of the Structure of *All's Well That Ends Well.*" *RES*, n.s., i (1950), 289–301.

Wilson, H. S. "Dramatic Emphasis in *All's Well That Ends Well.*" *HLQ*, xiii (1950), 217–240.

Leech, C. "The Theme of Ambition in *All's Well That Ends Well.*" *ELH*, xxi (1954), 17–29.

Carter, A. H. "In Defense of Bertram." *SQ*, v[illegible] (1956), 21–31.

Knight, G. W. *The Sovereign Flower*. London, 1958.

King, W. N. "Shakespeare's Mingled Yarn." *MLQ*, xxi (1960), 33–44.

Nagarajan, S. "The Structure of *All's Well That Ends Well.*" *EC*, x (1960), 24–31.

Turner, R. "Dramatic Conventions in *All's Well That Ends Well.*" *PMLA*, lxxv (1960), 497–502.

Adams, J. F. "*All's Well That Ends Well:* The Paradox of Procreation." *SQ*, xii (1961), 261–270.

Calderwood, J. L. "The Mingled Yarn of *All's Well.*" *JEGP*, lxii (1963), 61–76.

———. "Styles of Knowing in *All's Well.*" *MLQ*, xxv (1964), 272–294.

LaGuardia, E. "Chastity, Regeneration, and World Order in *All's Well That Ends Well.*" *Myth and Symbol: Critical Approaches and Applications*, ed. Bernice Slote. Lincoln, Neb., 1963, pp. 119–13[illegible].

Ranald, M. L. "The Betrothals of *All's Well That Ends Well.*" *HLQ*, xxvi (1963), 179–192.

Halio, J. L. "*All's Well That Ends Well.*" *SQ*, xv, (1964), 33–43.

Hapgood, R., and R. Y. Turner. "Dramatic Conventions in *All's Well That Ends Well.*" *PMLA*, lxx[illegible] (1964), 177–182.

2. Antony and Cleopatra

Modern Editions: Arden, R. H. Case, ed. London, 1906; New Variorum, Howard H. Furness, ed. Philadelphia, 1907; G. L. Kittredge, ed. Boston, 1941; New Cambridge, J. Dover Wilson, ed. Cambridge, 1950; New Arden, M. R. Ridley, ed. London, 1954; Yale, P. Phialas, ed. New Haven, Conn., 1955; Pelican, M. Mack, ed. Baltimore, 196[illegible]; Laurel, Francis Fergusson and C. J. Sisson, ed. New York, 1961; Signet, Barbara Everitt, ed. New York, 1964.

Textual Studies: *Chambers*, I, 476–478; *Greg*, pp. 398–403; *Hinman, passim.*

BAYFIELD, M. A. *A Study of Shakespeare's Versification, With an Inquiry into the Trustworthiness of the Early Texts . . . Including a Revised Text of Antony and Cleopatra.* Cambridge, 1920.

Sources: *Bullough,* V, 215–452; *Muir.*

BROOKE, C. F. T., ed. *Shakespeare's Plutarch.* (Vol. II containing the main sources of *Antony and Cleopatra* and of *Coriolanus.*) Oxford, 1909.

WESTBROOK, P. D. "Horace's Influence on Shakespeare's *Antony and Cleopatra.*" *PMLA,* LXII (1947), 392–398.

NORMAN, A. M. Z. "Daniel's *The Tragedie of Cleopatra* and *Antony and Cleopatra.*" *SQ,* IX (1958), 11–18.

Stage History: *Odell, passim; Trewin, passim; New Cambridge,* pp. xxxvii–xlvi; *Winter* III, 431–467.

Criticism: *Johnson,* pp. 179–180; *Coleridge,* I, 85–89; *Hazlitt,* pp. 228–232; *Van Doren,* pp. 230–243; *Clemen,* pp. 159–167.

STOLL, E. E. "Cleopatra." *MLR,* XXIII (1928), 145–63.

LEAVIS, F. R. "*Antony and Cleopatra* and *All For Love:* A Critical Exercise." *Scrutiny,* V (1937), 158–169.

KNIGHT, G. W. *The Imperial Theme.* Oxford, 1931.

SPENCER, T. *Shakespeare and the Nature of Man.* New York, 1942.

PALMER, J. *Political Characters of Shakespeare.* London, 1945.

GRANVILLE-BARKER, H. *Prefaces to Shakespeare.* 2 Vols. Princeton, N. J. 1946, 1947.

WIMSATT, W. K., JR. "Poetry and Morals." *Thought,* XXIII (1948), 281–299.

CECIL, D. *Poets and Storytellers.* London, 1949.

KNIGHTS, L. C. "On the Tragedy of *Antony and Cleopatra.*" *Scrutiny,* XVI (1949), 318–323.

DANBY, J. F. *Poets on Fortune's Hill: Studies in Sidney, Shakespeare, Beaumont and Fletcher.* London, 1952.

PEARSON, N. H. "*Antony and Cleopatra.*" *Shakespeare: Of an Age and for all Time.* New Haven, 1954, pp. 125–147.

BARNET, S. "Recognition and Reversal in *Antony and Cleopatra.*" *SQ,* VIII (1957), 331–334.

WARNER, A. "A Note on *Antony and Cleopatra.*" *English,* XI (1957), 139–144.

BARROLL, J. L. "Antony and Pleasure." *JEGP,* LVII (1958), 708–720.

STEIN, A. "The Image of Antony." *KR,* XXI (1959), 586–606.

MUIR, K. "The Imagery of *Antony and Cleopatra.*" *KN,* VIII (1961), 249–264.

DAICHES, D. "Imagery and Meaning in *Antony and Cleopatra.*" *ES,* XLIII (1962), 343–358.

HARRIER, R. C. "Cleopatra's End." *SQ,* XIII (1962), 63–65.

BURKE, K. "Shakespearean Persuasion." *AR,* XXIV (1964), 19–36.

PROSER, M. N. *The Heroic Image in Five Shakespearean Tragedies.* Princeton, N.J., 1965.

3. *As You Like It*

Modern Editions: New Variorum, Howard H. Furness, ed. Philadelphia, 1890; Arden, J. W. Holme, ed. London, 1914; New Cambridge, A. Quiller-Couch and J. Dover Wilson, eds. Cambridge, 1926; G. L. Kittredge, ed. Boston, 1939; Yale, S. Burchell, ed. New Haven, Conn., 1954; Pelican, R. Sargent, ed. Baltimore, 1959; Laurel, Francis Fergusson and C. J. Sisson, eds. New York, 1961; Signet, Albert Gilman, ed. New York, 1963; Bantam, O. J. Campbell, Alfred Rothschild and Stuart Vaughan, eds. New York, 1965.

Textual Studies: *Chambers,* I, 401–404; *Greg,* pp. 293–295; *Hinman, passim.*

Sources: *Bullough,* II, 143–266; *Muir.*

THORNDIKE, A. H. "The Relation of *As You Like It* to Robin Hood Plays." *JEGP,* IV (1901), 59–69.

STOLL, E. E. "Shakspere, Marston, and the Malcontent Type." *MP,* III (1905–1906), 281–3.

GREG, W. W., ed. Lodge's *Rosalynde,* being the original of Shakespeare's *As You Like It.* Oxford, 1907.

TOLMAN, A. H. "Shakespeare's Manipulation of His Sources in *As You Like It.*" *MLN,* XXXVII (1922), 65–76.

BAIRD, R. C. "*As You Like It* and Its Source." *Essays in Honor of Walter Clyde Curry.* Nashville, Tenn., 1954.

FELVER, C. S. "Robert Armin, Shakespeare's Source for Touchstone." *SQ,* VII (1956), 135–137.

Stage History: *Odell, passim; Trewin, passim; New Cambridge,* pp. 167–171; *Winter II,* 215–341.

SHATTUCK, C. H. *Mr. Macready Produces* As You Like It: *A Prompt Book Study.* Chapbook No. 5–6. Urbana, Ill., 1962.

Criticism: *Coleridge,* I, 103–105; *Hazlitt,* pp. 338–341; *Van Doren,* pp. 127–135; *Adams,* pp. 157–182.

SMITH, J. "*As You Like It.*" *Scrutiny,* IX (1940), 9–32.

WILCOX, J. "Putting Jaques into *As You Like It.*" *MLR,* XXXVI (1941), 388–394.

BARBER, C. L. "The Use of Comedy in *As You Like It.*" *PQ,* XXI (1942), 353–367.

BENNETT, J. W. "Jaques' Seven Ages." *SAB,* XVIII (1943), 168–174.

CAMPBELL, O. J. *Shakespeare's Satire.* Oxford, 1943.

PALMER, J. *Comic Characters of Shakespeare.* New York, 1946.

HARBAGE, A. *As They Liked It.* New York, 1947.

PARROTT, T. M. *Shakespearean Comedy.* New York, 1949.

GOLDSMITH, R. H. "Touchstone: Critic in Motley." *PMLA,* LXVIII (1953), 884–895.

JENKINS, H. "As You Like It." *SS 8* (1955), 40–51.

JONES, W. "William Shakespeare as William in *As You Like It.*" *SQ,* XI (1960), 228–231.

HALIO, Jay. L. " 'No Clock in the Forest': Time in *As You Like It.*" *SEL,* II (1962), 197–207.

DORAN, M. " 'Yet Am I Inland Bred.' " *SQ,* XV (1964), 99–114.

4. *The Comedy of Errors*

Modern Editions: Arden, H. Cunningham, ed. London, 1906; New Cambridge, A. Quiller-Couch and J. Dover Wilson, eds. Cambridge, 1922; Yale, R. D. French, ed. New Haven, Conn., 1926; T. W. Baldwin, ed., 1928; Penguin, G. B. Harrison, ed., 1948; Penguin, G. B. Harrison, ed. London, 1955; New Arden, R. A. Foakes, ed. London, 1962; Pelican, Paul Jorgensen, ed. Baltimore, 1964. Folger, Louis B. Wright and Virginia La Mar, eds. New York, 1963.

Textual Studies: *Chambers,* I, 305–312; *Greg,* pp. 200–202; *Hinman, passim.*

Thomas, S. "The Date of *The Comedy of Errors.*" *SQ,* vii (1956), 377–384.

Sources: *Bullough,* I, 3–54; *Muir.*

Rouse, W. H. D., ed. *The Menaechmi,* the original of Shakespeare's *Comedy of Errors.* The Latin text together with the Elizabethan translation. London, 1912.

Stage History: *Odell, passim; Trewin, passim; New Cambridge,* pp. xxvi–xxx.

Criticism: *Johnson,* p. 97; *Coleridge,* I, 99; *Hazlitt,* pp. 351–361; *Van Doren,* pp. 33–36.

Gaw, A. "The Evolution of *The Comedy of Errors.*" *PMLA,* xli (1926), 620–66.

Elliott, G. R. "Weirdness in *The Comedy of Errors.*" *UTQ,* ix (1939), 95–106.

Parks, G. B. "Shakespeare's Map for *The Comedy of Errors.*" *JEGP,* xxxix (1940), 93–97.

Baldwin, T. W. *Shakspere's Five-Act Structure: Shakspere's Early Plays on the Background of the Renaissance Theories of Five-Act Structure from 1470.* Urbana, Ill., 1947.

Highet, G. A. *The Classical Tradition.* New York, 1949.

Fergusson, F. "*The Comedy of Errors* and *Much Ado About Nothing.*" *SR,* lxii (1954), 24–37. (Reprinted in *The Human Image in Dramatic Literature.* New York, 1957.)

Feldman, A. B. "Portals of discovery." *American Imago,* xvi (1959), 77–107.

Brooks, H. "Themes and Structure in *The Comedy of Errors.*" *Early Shakespeare.* Stratford-upon-Avon Studies, 3. London, 1961, pp. 55–71.

Barber, C. L. "Shakespearian Comedy in *The Comedy of Errors.*" *CE,* xxv (1964), 493–497.

5. *Coriolanus*

Modern Editions: E. K. Chambers, London, 1898; Arden, W. Craig and R. Case, eds. London, 1922; New Variorum, Howard H. Furness, Jr., ed. Philadelphia, 1928; Pelican, Harry Levin, ed. Baltimore, 1956; New Cambridge, J. Dover Wilson, ed. Cambridge, 1960; Laurel, Francis Fergusson and C. J. Sisson, eds. New York, 1962; Alice Walker, ed. London, 1964.

Textual Studies: *Chambers,* I, 478–480; *Adams,* pp. 239–252; *Greg,* pp. 404–407; *Hinman, passim.*

Sources: *Bullough,* V, 453–563; *Muir.*

Pettet, E. C. "*Coriolanus* and the Midlands Insurrection of 1607." *SS 3* (1950), 34–42.

Heuer, H. "From Plutarch to Shakespeare: a Study of Coriolanus." *SS 10* (1957), 50–59.

Stage History: *Odell, passim; Trewin, passim; New Cambridge,* pp. xli–liii; *Winter* III, 196–231.

Criticism: *Johnson,* pp. 177–178; *Coleridge,* I, 89–91; *Hazlitt,* pp. 214–221; *Van Doren,* pp. 243–248; *Clemen,* pp. 154–158.

MacCallum, M. W. *Shakespeare's Roman Plays and Their Background.* London, 1910.

Tolman, A. H. "The Structure of Shakespeare's Tragedies, With Special Reference to *Coriolanus.*" *MLN,* xxxvii (1922), 449–58.

Traversi, D. A. "*Coriolanus.*" *Scrutiny,* vi (1937–38).

Draper, J. W. "Shakespeare's *Coriolanus:* a study in Renaissance Psychology." *West Virginia Bulletin (Philological Studies),* iii (1939), 22–36.

Thaler, A. *Shakespeare and Democracy.* Knoxvill[e], Tenn., 1941.

Campbell, O. J. *Shakespeare's Satire.* New Yor[k], 1943.

Maxwell, J. C. "Animal imagery in *Coriolanus*[."] *MLR,* xlii (1947), 417–421.

Jorgensen, P. A. "Shakespeare's Coriolanus: Eliza[-]bethan Soldier." *PMLA,* lxiv (1949), 221–235.

Farnham, W. *Shakespeare's Tragic Frontier: Th[e] World of His Final Tragedies.* Berkeley, Calif[.], 1950.

Honig, E. "*Sejanus* and *Coriolanus:* A Study i[n] Alienation." *MLQ,* xii (1951), 407–421.

Ribner, I. "The Tragedy of Coriolanus." *ES,* xxx[iv] (1953), 1–9.

Enright, D. J. "*Coriolanus:* Tragedy or Debate?" *EC,* iv (1954), 1–9.

Knight, G. W. *The Imperial Theme.* 3rd ed., re[-]printed with minor corrections. London, 1955.

MacLure, M. "Shakespeare and the Lonely Dragon[."] *UTQ,* xxiv (1955), 109–120.

Jorgensen, P. A. *Shakespeare's Military World.* Be[r]keley, Calif., 1956.

Sen, S. K. "What Happens in *Coriolanus.*" *SQ,* [ix] (1958), 331–345.

Oliver, H. J. "Coriolanus as a Tragic Hero." *SQ,* (1959), 53–60.

Zeeveld, W. G. "*Coriolanus* and Jacobean Politics[."] *MLR,* lvii (1962), 321–334.

Proser, M. N. *The Heroic Image in Five Shakespear[-]ean Tragedies.* Princeton, 1965.

6. *Cymbeline*

Modern Editions: Arden, E. Dowden, ed. Londo[n], 1903; New Variorum, Howard H. Furness, Jr., e[d]. Philadelphia, 1913; Yale, S. B. Hemingway, ed. Ne[w] Haven, Conn., 1924; New Arden, J. M. Nosworth[y], ed. London, 1955; Penguin, G. B. Harrison, e[d]. London, 1957; New Cambridge, J. C. Maxwel[l], ed. Cambridge, 1960; Pelican, Robert Heilman, e[d]. Baltimore, 1964; Laurel, Francis Fergusson an[d] C. J. Sisson, eds. New York, 1964.

Textual Studies: *Chambers,* I, 484–487; *Greg,* p[p]. 412–414; *Hinman, passim.*

Sources: *Muir.*

Wilson, H. S. "*Philaster* and *Cymbeline.*" *EIE,* 195[-] pp. 146–167.

Stage History: *Odell, passim; Trewin, passim; Ne[w] Cambridge,* pp. xliii–lv; *Winter* III, 41–166.

Shaw, G. B. *Cymbeline Refinished.* A Variation o[n] Shakespeare's Ending. In *Geneva, Cymbeline Re[-]finished and Good King Charles.* London, 1946.

Criticism: *Johnson,* pp. 181–184; *Coleridge,* I, 11[5–]119; *Hazlitt,* pp. 179–186; *Van Doren,* pp. 262–27[-] *Clemen,* pp. 205–213.

Tillyard, E. M. W. "*Shakespeare's Last Plays.*" Lon[-]don, 1938.

Stephenson, A. A. "The Significance of *Cymbeline.*" *Scrutiny,* x (1942), 329–338.

Knight, G. W. *The Crown of Life.* London, 1947.

Camden, C. "The Elizabethan Imogen." *The Ric[e] Institute Pamphlet,* xxxviii (1951), 1–17.

Wright, C. T. "The Queen's Husband: Some Ren[-]aissance Views." *Studies in English,* iii (1957), 133[-]138.

Brockbank, J. P. "History and Histrionics in *Cymbeline*." *SS 11* (1958), 42–49.

ones, Emrys. "Stuart Cymbeline." *EC*, XI (1961), 84–99.

Hoeniger, F. D. "Irony and Romance in *Cymbeline*." *SEL*, II (1962), 219–228.

Marsh, D. R. C. *The Recurring Miracle: A Study of* Cymbeline *and the Last Plays*. Durban, Rep. of So. Africa, 1964.

wander, H. "*Cymbeline* and the 'Blameless Hero.'" *ELH*, XXXI (1964), 259–270.

rye, N. *A Natural Perspective: The Development of Shakespearean Comedy and Romance*. New York, 1965.

7. *Hamlet*

Raven, A. A. *A Hamlet Bibliography and Reference Guide, 1877–1935*. Chicago, 1936.

Conklin, P. S. *A History of "Hamlet" Criticism, 1601–1821*. New York, 1947.

Leech, C. "Studies in *Hamlet*, 1901–1955," *SS 9* (1956), 1–15.

Modern Editions: New Variorum, Howard H. Furness, ed. Philadelphia, 1877; Arden, Edward Dowden, ed. London, 1899; J. Q. Adams, ed. 1929; New Cambridge, J. Dover Wilson, ed. Cambridge, 1934; G. L. Kittredge, ed. Boston, 1939; Yale, T. Brooke and J. R. Crawford, eds. New Haven, Conn., 1957; Pelican, W. Farnham, ed. Baltimore, 1957; Folger, Louis B. Wright and Virginia LaMar, eds. New York, 1957; Bantam, O. J. Campbell, Alfred Rothschild and Stuart Vaughan, eds. New York, 1961; Signet, Edward Hubler, ed. New York, 1963. Weiner, Albert, ed. *Hamlet: The First Quarto, 1603*. Great Neck, New York, 1962; Cyrus Hoy, ed. New York, 1963.

Textual Studies: *Chambers*, I, 408–425; *Greg*, pp. 299–333; *Hinman, passim; Honigmann, passim.*

Gray, H. D. "The First Quarto of *Hamlet*." *MLR*, X (1915), 171–80.

De Groot, H. *Hamlet, Its Textual History*. An inquiry into the relations between the first and second quartos and the first folio of *Hamlet*. Amsterdam, 1923.

Van Dam, B. A. P. *The Text of Shakespeare's Hamlet*. London, 1924.

Lawrence, W. J. "The Date of Hamlet." *TLS*, April 8, 1926, p. 263.

Wilson, J. D. *The Manuscripts of Shakespeare's Hamlet*. Cambridge, 1934.

Alexander, P. "The Text of Hamlet." *RES*, XII (1936), 385–400.

Cairncross, A. S. *The Problem of Hamlet: A Solution*. London, 1936.

Duthie, G. I. *The Bad Quarto of Hamlet: A Critical Study*. Cambridge, 1941.

avage, D. S. *Hamlet and The Pirates*. London, 1950.

Walker, A. *Textual Problems of the First Folio*. Cambridge, 1953.

——. "Collateral Substantive Texts (with special reference to *Hamlet*)." *SB*, VII (1955), 51–67.

owers, F. "The Printing of Hamlet, Quarto 2." With "Addendum." *SB*, VII (1955), 41–50; VIII (1956), 267–269.

——. "Hamlet's 'Sullied' or 'Solid' Flesh: A Bibliographical Case-history." *SS 9* (1956), 44–48.

——. "The Textual Relation of Q2 to Q1 *Hamlet* (1)." *SB*, VIII (1956), 39–66.

Brown, J. R. "The Compositors of *Hamlet* Q2 and *The Merchant of Venice*." *SB*, VII (1955), 17–40.

Jenkins, H. "The Relation Between the Second Quarto and the Folio Text of *Hamlet*," *SB*, VII (1955), 69–83.

Honigmann, E. A. J. "The Date of *Hamlet*." *SS 9* (1956), 24–34.

Nosworthy, J. M. *Shakespeare's Occasional Plays. Their Origin and Transmission*. London, 1965.

Sources: *Muir*.

Corbin, J. *The Elizabethan Hamlet*. A study of the sources, and of Shakespeare's environment to show that the mad scenes had a comic aspect now ignored. London, 1895.

Creizenach, W. "*Der Bestrafte Brudermord* and Shakespeare's *Hamlet*." *MP*, II (1904–1905), 249–60.

Lewis, C. M. *The Genesis of Hamlet*. New York, 1907.

Corpus Hamleticum. Hamlet in Sage und Dichtung, Kunst und Musik. Hrsg. von Josef Schick. Berlin, 1912.

Malone, K. *The Literary History of Hamlet. I. The Early Tradition*. Heidelberg, 1923.

Gollancz, I. *The Sources of Hamlet, With An Essay on the Legend*. Oxford, 1926.

Babb, L. "Hamlet, Melancholy and the Devil." *MLN*, LIX (1944), 120–122.

——. *The Elizabethan Malady: A Study of Melancholia in English Literature from 1580–1642*. East Lansing, Mich., 1951, pp. 106–110.

Caldiero, F. "The Source of Hamlet's 'What a piece of work is a man.'" *N & Q* (September 29, 1951), 421–424.

Bennett, J. W. "Characterization in Polonius' Advice to Laertes." *SQ*, IV (1953), 3–9.

——. "These Few Precepts." *SQ*, VII (1956), 275–276.

Quinlan, M. J. "Shakespeare and the Catholic Burial Services." *SQ*, V (1954), 302–306.

Muir, K. "Henry Swinburne and Shakespeare." *N&Q*, n.s. IV (1957), 285–286.

Stage History: *Odell, passim; Trewin, passim; New Cambridge*, pp. lxix–xcvii; *Winter* I, 320–442.

Spriggs, C. O. "Hamlet on the Eighteenth Century Stage." *Quarterly Journal of Speech*, XXII (1936).

Gilder, R. *John Gielgud's Hamlet: A Record of Performance*. New York, 1937.

McManaway, J. G. "The Two Earliest Prompt Books of *Hamlet*." *Papers of the Bibliographical Society of America*, XLII (1949), 288–320.

Fry, C. "Letters to an Actor Playing *Hamlet*." *SS 5* (1952), 58–61.

Mander, R., and J. Mitchenson—compilers. *Hamlet through the Ages. A Pictorial Record From 1709*. London, 1952.

Griffin, A. B. "Jean-Louis Barrault Acts Hamlet." *SQ*, IV (1953), 163–164.

Downer, A. S. "The *Hamlet* Year." *SQ*, V (1954), 155–165.

Browne, E. M. "English Hamlets of the Twentieth Century." *SS 9* (1956), 16–23.

Isaacs, J., ed. *William Poel's Prompt-Book of Fratricide Punished*. London, 1957.

Overmyer, G. *America's First Hamlet*. New York, 1957.

Byrne, M. St. C. "The Earliest *Hamlet* Prompt Book in an English Library." *TN*, xv (1960), 21–31.
Hunt, H. *Old Vic Prefaces*. London, 1954.
Criticism: *Johnson*, pp. 189–196; *Coleridge*, I, 18–44; II, 192–198, 272–275; *Hazlitt*, pp. 232–237; *Van Doren*, pp. 161–172; *Adams*, pp. 295–313; *Clemen*, pp. 106–118.
Bradley, A. C. *Shakespearean Tragedy*. London, 1904.
Murray, G. *Hamlet and Orestes*. Oxford, 1914.
Stoll, E. E. *Hamlet*. Minneapolis, 1919.
Robertson, J. M. *The Problem of Hamlet*. London, 1919.
Jones, E. *A Psycho-Analytic Study of Hamlet*. London, 1922.
———. *Hamlet and Oedipus*. London, 1949.
Conrad, B. R. "Hamlet's Delay." *PMLA*, xli (1926), 680–7.
Wilson, J. D. *What Happens in Hamlet*. Cambridge, 1935.
Beatty, J. M. "The King in *Hamlet*." *SAB*, xi (1936), 238–249.
Farnham, W. "*Hamlet*." *The Medieval Heritage of Elizabethan Tragedy*. Berkeley, Calif., 1936.
Frassati, A. *La Volontà in Amleto*. Bologna, 1936.
Cazamian, L. "Humor in Hamlet." *Rice Institute Pamphlet*, xxiv (1937), 214–228.
Schücking, L. L. *The Meaning of "Hamlet."* Oxford, 1937.
Spencer, T. "*Hamlet* and the Nature of Reality." *ELH*, v (1938), 253–277.
Draper, J. W. *The Hamlet of Shakespeare's Audience*. Durham, N.C., 1939.
Greg, W. W. "The Mouse-Trap." *MLR*, xxxv (1940), 8–10.
Knights, L. C. "Prince Hamlet." *Scrutiny*, ix (1940), 148–160.
———. *An Approach to Hamlet*. Stanford, Calif., 1961.
Doran, M. "That Undiscovered Country." *PQ*, xx (1941), 413–427.
Hankins, J. E. *The Character of Hamlet and Other Essays*. Chapel Hill, N.C., 1941.
Campbell, O. J. "What is the Matter With Hamlet?" *Yale Review*, xxxii (1942), 309–322.
Fowlie, W. "Swann and Hamlet: A Note on the Contemporary Hero." *PR*, ix (1942), 195–202.
Lewis, C. S. *Hamlet: The Prince or the Poem?* London, 1942.
Barfield, O. "The Form of Hamlet." *Romanticism Comes of Age*. London, 1944, pp. 85–103.
Sypher, W. "Hamlet: the Existential Madness." *Nation*, 162 (June 21, 1946), 750–751.
Charlton, H. B. *Shakespearian Tragedy*. Cambridge, 1948, pp. 83–112.
Madariaga, S. de. *On Hamlet*. London, 1948.
Prior, M. E. "The Thought of Hamlet and the Modern Temper." *ELH*, xv (1948), 261–285.
Walker, R. *The Time is Out of Joint:* a study of "Hamlet." London, 1948.
Barbarow, G. "Hamlet Through a Telescope." *Hudson Review*, ii (1949), 98–117.
Fergusson, F. *The Idea of a Theatre*. Princeton, 1949.
Fiedler, L. "The Defense of Illusion and the Creation of Myth: Device and Symbol in the Plays of Shakespeare." *English Institute Essays: 1948*. New York, 1949, pp. 74–94.
Flatter, R. *Hamlet's Father*. New Haven, 1949.
Connolly, T. F. "Shakespeare and the Double Man." *SQ*, i (1950), 30–35.
Duncan, E. "Unsubstantial Father: A Study of the *Hamlet* symbolism in Joyce's *Ulysses*." *University of Toronto Quarterly*, xix (1950), 126–140.
Huhner, M. *Shakespeare's Hamlet*. New York, 1950.
Mincoff, M. "The Structural Pattern of Shakespeare's Tragedies." *SS 3* (1950), 58–65.
Nosworthy, J. M. "*Hamlet* and the Player Who Could Not Keep Counsel." *SS 3* (1950), 74–82.
Williamson, C. C. H., ed. *Readings on the Character of Hamlet, 1661–1947*. London, 1950.
Battenhouse, R. W. "The Ghost in Hamlet: A Catholic 'Linchpin'?" *SP*, xlviii (1951), 161–192.
———. "Hamlet's Apostrophe on Man: Clue to the Tragedy." *PMLA*, lxvi (1951), 1073–1113.
Cunningham, J. V. *Woe or Wonder: The Emotional Effect of Shakespearean Tragedy*. Denver, 1951, pp. 11–37.
Elliott, G. R. *Scourge and Minister: A Study of Hamlet as a Tragedy of Revengefulness and Justice*. Durham, N.C., 1951.
Empson, W. "The Staging of *Hamlet*." *TLS* (November 23, 1951), p. 749.
———. "Hamlet When New." *SR*, lxi (1953), 15–42, 185–205.
James, D. G. *The Dream of Learning: An Essay on "The Advancement of Learning," "Hamlet," and "King Lear."* Oxford, 1951.
Craig, H. "A Cutpurse of the Empire." *A Tribute to George C. Taylor*, Arnold Williams, ed. Chapel Hill, N.C., 1952.
Johnson, S. F. "The Regeneration of Hamlet." *SQ*, iii (1952), 187–207.
Kenner, H. "Joyce's *Ulysses:* Homer and Hamlet." *Essays in Criticism*, ii (1952), 85–104.
Mack, M. "The World of Hamlet." *Yale Review*, xl (1952).
Reik, T. *The Secret Self*. New York, 1952.
Joseph, B. L. *Conscience and the King: A Study of Hamlet*. London, 1953.
Altick, R. D. "Hamlet and the Odor of Mortality." *SQ*, v (1954), 167–176.
Bonjour, A. "Hamlet and the Phantom Clue." *ES*, xxxv (1954), 253–259.
Goodman, P. *The Structure of Literature*. Chicago, 1954.
Highet, G. "The Madness of Hamlet." *A Clerk of Oxenford*. London, 1954.
Polanyi, K. "Hamlet." *Yale Review*, xliii (1954), 336–350.
Alexander, P. *Hamlet: Father and Son*. Oxford, 1955.
Bowers, F. "Hamlet as Minister and Scourge." *PMLA*, lxx (1955), 740–749.
———. "Dramatic Structure and Criticism: Plot in *Hamlet*." *SQ* xv, ii (1964), 207–218.
De Rougemont, D. "Kierkegaard and Hamlet: Two Danish Princes." *The Anchor Review*, i (1955), 99–127.
Goddard, H. C. "Hamlet to Ophelia." *CE*, xvi (1955), 403–415.
Foakes, R. A. "Hamlet and the Court of Elsinore." *SS 9* (1956), 35–43.
Kitto, H. D. F. *Form and Meaning in Drama: A*

Study of Six Greek Plays and of "Hamlet." London, 1956.

Kirschbaum, L. "Hamlet and Ophelia." *PQ*, xxxv (1956), 376–393.

——. *Two Lectures on Shakespeare: In Defense of Guildenstern and Rosencrantz;* The Tempest—*Apologetics or Spectacle*. Oxford, 1961.

Santayana, G. *Essays in Literary Criticism*. New York, 1956, pp. 120–136.

Coles, B. *Shakespeare's Four Giants: Hamlet, Macbeth, Othello, Lear*. Rindge, N. H., 1957.

Heilbrun, C. "The Character of Hamlet's Mother." *SQ*, viii (1957), 201–206.

West, R. *The Court and the Castle*. New Haven, 1957.

Aronson, A. "More Matter, with Less Art: A Study in the Rhetoric of Hamlet." *The Visvabharati Quarterly*. West Bengal, India, 1958.

Wilson, E. C. "Polonius in the Round." *SQ*, ix (1958), 83–85.

Levin, H. *The Question of Hamlet*. New York, 1959.

Babcock, W. *Hamlet: A Tragedy of Errors*. Lafayette, Ind., 1961.

Miriam Joseph, Sister. "Discerning the Ghost in Hamlet." *PMLA*, lxxvi (1961), 493–502.

——. "*Hamlet*, A Christian Tragedy." *SP*, lix (1962), 119–140.

Devlin, C. *Hamlet's Divinity and Other Essays*. Introd. by C. V. Wedgwood. Carbondale, Ill., 1963.

Siegel, P. N. "Discerning the Ghost in *Hamlet*." *PMLA*, lxxviii (1963), 148–149.

Brown, J. R., and B. Harris, eds. *Hamlet*. Stratford-upon-Avon Studies, 5. London, 1964.

Kott, J. "Hamlet of the Mid-Century." *Encounter*, xxiii, ii (1964), 33–39.

8. 1 Henry IV

Modern Editions: Arden, R. P. Cowl and A. E. Morgan, eds. London, 1914; Yale, S. B. Hemingway, ed. New Haven, Conn., 1917; New Variorum, S. B. Hemingway, ed. Philadelphia, 1936; G. L. Kittredge, ed. Boston, 1940; New Cambridge, J. Dover Wilson, ed. Cambridge, 1946; Pelican, M. A. Shaaber, ed. Baltimore, 1957; New Arden, A. R. Humphreys, ed. London, 1960; J. L. Sanderson, ed. New York, 1962; Signet, Maynard Mack, ed. New York, 1964; Bantam, O. J. Campbell, Alfred Rothschild and Stuart Vaughan, eds. New York, 1964.

Textual Studies: *Chambers,* I, 375–384; *Greg*, pp. 262–276; *Hinman, passim.*

Crundell, H. W. "The Text of *1 Henry IV*." *N&Q*, 177 (1939), 347–349.

Sources: *Bullough*, IV, 155–343.

Wilson, J. D. "The Origins and Development of Shakespeare's *Henry IV*." *Library*, 4th Series, xxvi (1945), 2–16.

Stage History: *Odell, passim; Trewin, passim; New Cambridge*, pp. xxix–xlvi; *Winter*, III, 297–382.

Craig, H. "The Dering Version of Shakespeare's *Henry IV*." *PQ*, xxxv (1956), 218–219.

Criticism: *Johnson*, pp. 113–118; *Hazlitt*, pp. 277–285; *Van Doren*, pp. 97–114; *Adams*, pp. 429–437.

Charlton, H. B. *Shakespearian Comedy*. London, 1938.

McLuhan, H. M. "*Henry IV*, A Mirror for Magistrates." *UTQ*, xvii (1948), 152–160.

Traversi, D. A. "*Henry IV—Part I*." *Scrutiny*, xv (1948), 24–35.

Barber, C. L. "From Ritual to Comedy: An Examination of *Henry IV*." *English Stage Comedy. English Institute Essays*, 1954, pp. 22–51.

Unger, L. "Deception and Self-deception in Shakespeare's *Henry IV*." *The Man in the Name: Essays on the Experience of Poetry*. Minneapolis and Oxford, 1956.

Langbaum, R. *The Poetry of Experience: The Dramatic Monologue in Modern Literary Tradition*. New York, 1957.

Mack, M. "Engagement and Detachment in Shakespeare's Plays." *Essays on Shakespeare and the Elizabethan Drama in Honor of Hardin Craig*, Richard Hosley, ed. Columbia, Mo., 1962, pp. 275–296.

9. Falstaff

Morgann, M. *An Essay on the Dramatic Character of Sir John Falstaff*. London, 1777.

Richardson, W. *Essays on Shakespeare's Dramatic Character of Sir John Falstaff, and on His Imitation of Female Characters*. London, 1789.

Hackett, J. H. *Falstaff; a Shakesperian Tract*. Privately printed. 1840.

Bradley, A. C. "The Rejection of Falstaff." *Oxford Lectures On Poetry*. London, 1909.

Stoll, E. E. "Falstaff." *Shakespeare Studies*. New York, 1927.

Empson, W. *Some Versions of Pastoral*. London, 1935.

——. "Falstaff and Mr. Dover Wilson," *KR*, xv (1953), 213–262.

Phillips, G. W. *Lord Burghley in Shakespeare: Falstaff, Sly and Others*. London, 1936.

Draper, J. W. "Falstaff and the Plautine Parasite." *Classical Jour.*, xxxiii (1938), 390–401.

Shirley, J. W. "Falstaff, An Elizabethan Glutton." *PQ*, xvii (1938), 271–287.

Pushkin, A. "Notes on Shylock, Angelo and Falstaff," tr. by Albert Siegel. *SAB*, xvi (1941), 120–121.

Wilson, J. D. *The Fortunes of Falstaff*. Cambridge, 1943.

Boughner, D. C. "Traditional Elements in Falstaff." *JEGP*, xliii (1944), 417–428.

——. "Vice, Braggart, and Falstaff." *Anglia*, lxxii (1954), 35–61.

Levin, H. "Falstaff Uncolted." *MLN*, lxi (1946), 305–310.

Hotson, J. L. "Earl of Essex and Falstaff." *Shakespeare's Sonnets Dated, and Other Essays*. London and Toronto, 1949.

McCutchan, J. W. "Similarities Between Falstaff and Gluttony in Medwall's *Nature*." *SAB*, xxiv (1949), 214–219.

Wilson, E. "J. Dover Wilson on Falstaff." *Classics and Commercials*, 1951, pp. 161–167.

Bryant, J. A., Jr. "Shakespeare's Falstaff and the Mantle of Dick Tarlton." *SP*, li (1954), 149–162.

Fiehler, R. "How Oldcastle Became Falstaff." *MLQ*, xvi (1955), 16–28.

SPIVACK, B. "Falstaff and the Psychomachia." *SQ*, VIII (1957), 449–459.

WILLIAMS, P. "The Birth and Death of Falstaff Reconsidered." *SQ*, VIII (1957), 359–365.

HUNTER, G. K. "Shakespeare's Politics and the Rejection of Falstaff." *CQ*, I (1959), 229–236.

FLEISSNER, ROBERT F. "Falstaff's Green Sickness Unto Death." *SQ*, XII (1961), 47–55.

SENG, PETER J. "Songs, Time, and the Rejection of Falstaff." *SS 15* (1962), 31–40.

10. 2 Henry IV

Modern Editions: American Arden, L. Winstanley, ed., 1918; Arden, R. P. Cowl and A. E. Morgan, eds. London, 1923; Yale, S. B. Hemingway, ed. New Haven, Conn., 1921; New Variorum, M. A. Shaaber, ed. Philadelphia, 1940; New Cambridge, J. Dover Wilson, ed. Cambridge, 1946; Pelican, Allan Chester, ed. Baltimore, 1957; Laurel, Francis Fergusson and C. J. Sisson, eds. New York, 1962; Folger, Louis B. Wright and Virginia LaMar, eds. New York, 1961; Bantam, O. J. Campbell, Alfred Rothschild and Stuart Vaughan, eds. New York, 1964; New Arden, A. R. Humphreys, ed. London, 1965.

Textual Studies: *Chambers*, I, 375–384; *Greg*, pp. 262–276; *Hinman, passim.*

McMANAWAY, J. G. "The Cancel in the Quarto of *2 Henry IV*." *Studies in Honor of A. H. R. Fairchild. Univ. Missouri Studies*, Vol. 21, No. 1. Columbia, Mo., 1946.

SMITH, J. H. "The Cancel in the Quarto of *2 Henry IV* Revisited." *SQ*, XV, iii (1964), 173–178.

Sources: *Bullough*, IV, 249–346.

Stage History: *Odell, passim; Trewin, passim; Winter* III, pp. 297–382.

Criticism: *Johnson*, pp. 119–125; *Hazlitt*, pp. 277–285; *Van Doren*, pp. 97–114.

LAW, R. A. "Structural Unity in the Two Parts of *Henry IV*." *SP*, XXIV (1927), 223–42.

DEAN, L. F. "Shakespeare's Treatment of Conventional Ideas." *SR*, LII (1944), 414–423.

HOTSON, J. L. "Ancient Pistol." *YR* XXXVIII (1948), 51–66.

SHAABER, M. A. "The Unity of *Henry IV*." *Adams.*

TRAVERSI, D. A. "*Henry IV—Part II.*" *Scrutiny*, XV (1948), 117–127.

STEWART, J. I. M. *Character and Motive in Shakespeare.* London, 1949.

CAIN, H. E. "Further Light on the Relations of *1* and *2 Henry IV*." *SQ*, III (1952), 21–38.

LEECH, C. "The Unity of *2 Henry IV*." *SS 6* (1953), 16–24.

HUNTER, G. K. "*Henry IV* and the Elizabethan Two-Part Play." *RES*, n.s. V (1954), 236–248.

JENKINS, H. *The Structural Problem in Shakespeare's "Henry the Fourth."* London, 1956.

DICKINSON, H. "The Reformation of Prince Hal." *SQ*, XII (1961), 33–46.

11. Henry V

Modern Editions: Arden, H. Evans, ed. London, 1903; G. L. Kittredge, ed. Boston, 1945; New Cambridge, J. Dover Wilson, ed. Cambridge, 1947; New Arden, J. H. Walter, ed. London, 1954; Yal R. J. Dorius, ed. New Haven, Conn., 1955; Pel can, Louis B. Wright and Virginia LaMar, e Baltimore, 1957; Laurel, Francis Fergusson ar C. J. Sisson, eds. New York, 1962.

Textual Studies: *Chambers*, I, 388–396; *Greg*, p 282–288, *Hinman, passim.*

NICHOLSON, B. "The Relation of the Quarto to th Folio Version of *Henry V*." *Trans. New Shaks Soc.*, 1879–1882.

PRICE, H. T. *The Text of Henry V.* Newcastl under-Lyme, 1920.

SMITH, W. D. "The *Henry V* Choruses in the Fir Folio." *JEGP*, LIII (1954), 38–57.

CAIRNCROSS, A. S. "Quarto Copy for Folio *Henry V*" *SB*, VIII (1956), 67–93.

HOTSON, J. L. "Falstaff's Death and the Greenfield's" *TLS*, April 6, 1956.

HULME, H. M., P. URE, and F. W. BATESON. "Th Critical Forum: A Table of Green Fields." *EIC*, v (1957), 222–226.

Sources: *Bullough*, IV, 347–432.

Stage History: *Odell, passim; Trewin, passim; Ne Cambridge*, pp. xlviii–lvi.

Criticism: *Johnson*, pp. 126–133; *Coleridge*, I, 15 160; *Hazlitt*, pp. 285–291; *Van Doren*, pp. 143–15

YEATS, W. B. *Ideas of Good and Evil.* New Yorl 1903.

ALBRIGHT, E. M. "The Folio Version of *Henry V* i Relation to Shakespeare's Times." *PMLA*, XLI (1928), 722–56.

SPENCER, H. *The Mind and Art of William Shake speare.* New York, 1940.

TRAVERSI, D. A. "Henry the Fifth." *Scrutiny*, (1941), 352–374.

———. *Shakespeare from Richard II to Henry V* London, 1957.

WILSON, J. D. *The Fortunes of Falstaff.* Cambridg 1943.

CAMPBELL, L. B. *Shakespeare's Histories.* San Marin Calif., 1947.

JORGENSEN, P. A. "The courtship scene in Henry V. *MLQ*, XI (1950), 180–188.

GILBERT, A. "Patriotism and Satire in Henry V. *Studies in Shakespeare*, Mathews and Emery, ed Miami, 1953.

STRIBRNY, Z. *Shakespeare's History Plays.* Pragu 1959.

BRADDY, H. "Shakespeare's Henry V and the Frenc nobility." *Texas Studies in Literature and Lan guage*, III (1961), 189–196.

REESE, M. M. *The Cease of Majesty: a study o Shakespeare's history plays.* London, 1961.

12. Henry VI

Modern Editions: Arden, H. C. Hart, ed. 3 Vols London, 1909–10; Yale, C. F. Tucker Brooke, ed 3 Vols. New Haven, Conn., 1918–23; New Cambridge, J. Dover Wilson, ed. Cambridge, 1952 New Arden, A. S. Cairncross, ed. 3 Vols. London 1957–1964; Laurel, Francis Fergusson and C. J Sisson, eds. New York, 1963.

Textual Studies: *Chambers*, I, 277–293; *Greg*, pp 176–189; *Hinman, passim.*

WHITE, R. G. *Essay on the Authorship of the Thre*

Parts of King Henry the Sixth. Cambridge, Mass., 1859.

Kenny, T. *The Life and Genius of Shakspeare*. London, 1864.

Alexander, P. *Shakespeare's Henry VI and Richard III*. Introd. by A. W. Pollard. Cambridge, 1929.

Doran, M. *Henry VI, Parts II and III, Their Relation to the Contention and the True Tragedy*. Iowa City, Ia., 1928.

McKerrow, R. B. "A Note on the Bad Quartos of *2* and *3 Henry VI* and the Folio Text." *RES*, xiii (1937), 64–72.

Jordan, J. E. "The Reporter of *Henry VI, Part 2*." *PMLA*, lxiv (1949), 1089–113.

Kirschbaum, L. "The Authorship of *I Henry VI*." *PMLA*, lxvii (1952), 809–822.

Feuillerat, A. *The Composition of Shakespeare's Plays: Authorship, Chronology*. New Haven, 1953.

Kernan, A. B. "A Comparison of the Imagery in *3 Henry VI* and *The True Tragedie of Richard, Duke of York*." *SP*, li (1954), 431–442.

Prouty, C. T. *The Contention and Shakespeare's 2 Henry VI: A Comparative Study*. New Haven and Oxford, 1954.

McManaway, J. G. "*The Contention* and *2 Henry VI*." *Brunner Festschrift. Wiener Beiträge zur Englischen Philologie*, lxv (1957), 143–155.

Sources: *Bullough*, III, 23–217.

Law, R. A. "The Chronicles and the Three Parts of *Henry VI*." *TxSE*, xxxiii (1955), 13–32.

Stage History: *Odell, passim; Trewin, passim; New Cambridge, 1*, pp. li–lv; *3*, xxxix–xlv.

Wilson, J. D. and T. C. Worsley. *Shakespeare's Histories at Stratford, 1951*. London, 1952.

Jackson, Sir B. "On Producing *Henry VI*." *SS 6* (1953), 49–52.

Criticism: *Johnson*, pp. 134–145; *Hazlitt*, pp. 292–298; *Van Doren*, pp. 10–19; *Clemen*, pp. 40–46.

Stirling, B. *The Populace in Shakespeare*. New York, 1949.

Boas, F. S. "Joan of Arc in Shakespeare, Schiller, and Shaw." *SQ*, ii (1951), 35–45.

Wilson, F. P. *Marlowe and the Early Shakespeare*. Oxford, 1953.

Leech, C. "The Two-Part Play. Marlowe and the Early Shakespeare." *SJ*, 94 (1958), 90–106.

Quinn, C. M. "Providence in Shakespeare's Yorkist Plays." *SQ*, x (1959), pp. 45–52.

Brockbank, J. P. "The Frame of Disorder—*Henry VI*." *Early Shakespeare*. Stratford-upon-Avon Studies, 3. London and New York, 1961, pp. 73–79.

Mincoff, M. "*Henry VI, Part III* and *The True Tragedy*." *ES*, xlii (1961), 273–288.

Berman, R. S. "Fathers and Sons in the Henry VI Plays." *SQ*, xiii (1962), 487–497.

13. Henry VIII

Modern Editions: Arden, C. K. Pooler, ed. London, 1915; Yale, J. M. Berdan and C. F. Tucker Brooke, eds. New Haven, Conn., 1925; New Arden, R. A. Foakes, ed. London, 1957; Penguin, G. B. Harrison, ed. London, 1958; New Cambridge, J. C. Maxwell, ed. Cambridge, 1962.

Textual Studies: *Chambers*, I, 495–498; *Greg*, pp. 422–425; *Hinman, passim.*

Spedding, J. "On the Several Shares of Shakspere and Fletcher in the Play of *Henry VIII*." *Trans. New Shaksp. Soc.*, 1874.

Nicholson, M. H. "The Authorship of *Henry VIII*." *PMLA*, xxxvii (1922), 484–502.

Partridge, A. C. *The Problem of "Henry VIII" Reopened*. Cambridge, 1949.

Foakes, R. A. "On the First Folio Text of *Henry VIII*." *SB*, x (1958), 55–60.

Mincoff, M. "Henry VIII and Fletcher." *SQ*, xii (1961), 239–260.

Sources: *Bullough*, IV, 435–510.

Law, R. A. "Holinshed and *Henry the Eighth*." *TxSE*, xxxvi (1957), 1–11.

Stage History: *Odell, passim; Trewin, passim; New Cambridge*, pp. xxxviii–l; *Winter* I, 516–564.

Criticism: *Johnson*, pp. 148–153; *Hazlitt*, pp. 303–306; *Van Doren*, pp. 289–293.

Wiley, P. L. "Renaissance Exploitation of Cavendish's *Life of Wolsey*." *SP*, xliii (1946), 121–146.

Knight, G. W. *The Crown of Life*. London, 1947.

Kermode, F. "What is Shakespeare's *Henry VIII* About?" *Durham University Journal*, n.s. ix (1948), 48–55.

Stribrny, Z. *Shakespeare's History Plays*. Prague, 1959.

Reese, M. M. *The Cease of Majesty: a study of Shakespeare's history plays*. London, 1961.

Muir, K. *Last Periods of Shakespeare, Racine, Ibsen*. Detroit, 1961.

Tillyard, E. M. W. "Why Did Shakespeare Write Henry VIII?" *CQ*, iii (1961), 22–27.

14. Julius Caesar

Modern Editions: New Variorum, Howard H. Furness, Jr., ed. Philadelphia, 1913; G. L. Kittredge, ed. Boston, 1939; New Cambridge, J. Dover Wilson, ed. Cambridge, 1949; New Arden, T. S. Dorsch, ed. London, 1955; Yale, A. Kernan, ed. New Haven, Conn., 1959; Pelican, S. Johnson, ed. Baltimore, 1960; Signet, William and Barbara Rosen, eds. New York, 1963; Bantam, O. J. Campbell, Alfred Rothschild and Stuart Vaughan, eds. New York, 1961.

Textual Studies: *Chambers*, I, 396–401; *Greg*, pp. 289–292; *Hinman, passim.*

Smith, W. D. "The Duplicate Revelation of Portia's Death." *SQ*, iv (1953), 153–161.

Stirling, B. "*Julius Caesar* in Revision." *SQ*, xiii (1962), 187–205.

Sources: *Bullough*, V, 3–214; *Muir.*

Ayres, H. M. "Shakespeare's *Julius Caesar* in the Light of Some Other Versions." *PMLA*, xxv, n.s., xviii (1910), pp. 183–227.

Bush, D. "*Julius Caesar* and Elyot's *Governour*." *MLN*, lii (1937), 407–408.

Schanzer, E., ed. *Shakespeare's Appian*. A Selection from the Tudor Translation of Appian's *Civil Wars*. Liverpool, 1956.

Ornstein, R. "Seneca and the Political Drama of *Julius Caesar*." *JEGP*, lvii (1958), 51–56.

Stage History: *Odell, passim; Trewin, passim; New Cambridge*, pp. xxxiv–xliii; *Winter*, II, 541–630.

Hunt, H. *Old Vic Prefaces*. London, 1954.

WALKER, R. "Unto Caesar: A Review of Recent Productions," *SS 11* (1958), 128–135.

Criticism: *Johnson*, pp. 197–201; *Coleridge*, I, 13–18; *Hazlitt*, pp. 195–199; *Van Doren*, pp. 152–161.

KNIGHT, G. W. *The Imperial Theme*. Oxford, 1931.

GRANVILLE-BARKER, H. *Prefaces to Shakespeare*. 2 Vols. Princeton, N. J., 1946, 1947.

PALMER, J. *Political Characters of Shakespeare*. New York, 1946.

CHARLTON, H. B. *Shakespearian Tragedy*. Cambridge, 1948.

STIRLING, B. *The Populace in Shakespeare*. New York, 1949.

FELHEIM, M. "The Problem of Time in *Julius Caesar*." *HLQ*, XIII (1950), 399–405.

SCHANZER, E. "A neglected source of *Julius Caesar*." *N&Q*, 199 (1954), 196–197.

———. "The Problem of *Julius Caesar*." *SQ*, VI (1955), 297–308.

STIRLING, B. *Unity in Shakespearian Tragedy*. New York, 1956.

———. "Brutus and the Death of Portia," *SQ*, X (1959), 211–217.

RIBNER, I. "Political issues in *Julius Caesar*." *JEGP*, LVI (1957), 10–22.

BONJOUR, A. *The Structure of "Julius Caesar."* Liverpool, 1958.

HALL, V. "*Julius Caesar:* a play without political bias." *Studies in the English Renaissance Drama. In Memory of K. L. Holzknecht*. New York, 1959.

SMITH, G. R. "Brutus, Virtue and Will," *SQ*, X (1959), 367–379.

PAOLUCCI, A. "The Tragic Hero in *Julius Caesar*." *SQ*, XI (1960), 329–333.

DEAN, L. F. "Julius Caesar and Modern Criticism." *EJ*, L (1961), 451–456.

BROWN, J. R. "Shakespeare's Subtext: I." *TDR*, VIII, i (1963), 72–94.

RABKIN, N. "Structure, Convention, and Meaning in *Julius Caesar*." *JEGP*, LXIII (1964), 240–254.

PROSER, M. N. *The Heroic Image in Five Shakespearean Tragedies*. Princeton, 1965.

15. King John

Modern Editions: G. C. Moore Smith, ed. 1900; New Variorum, Howard H. Furness, Jr., ed. Philadelphia, 1919; New Cambridge, J. Dover Wilson, ed. Cambridge, 1936; New Arden, E. A. J. Honigmann, ed. London, 1954; Penguin, G. B. Harrison, ed. London, 1957; Pelican, Irving Ribner, ed. Baltimore, 1962; Laurel, Francis Fergusson, ed. New York, 1963.

Textual Studies: *Chambers*, I, 364–367; *Greg*, pp. 248–255; *Hinman, passim.*

LAW, R. A. "On the Date of *King John*." *SP*, LIV (1957), 119–127.

Sources: *Bullough*, IV, 1–152.

Stage History: *Odell, passim; Trewin, passim; New Cambridge*, pp. lxiii–lxxix; *Winter* III, 468–509.

SHATTUCK, C. H., ed. *William Charles Macready's* King John: *A Facsimile Prompt-Book*. Urbana, Ill., 1962.

Criticism: *Johnson*, pp. 103–109; *Coleridge*, I, 141–142; *Hazlitt*, pp. 306–312; *Van Doren*, pp. 88–97; *Adams*, pp. 183–197.

CAMPBELL, L. B. *Shakespeare's Histories*. San Marino, Calif., 1947.

BONJOUR, A. "The Road to Swinstead Abbey: A Study of the Sense and Structure of *King John*." *ELH*, XVIII (1951), 253–274.

CALDERWOOD, J. L. "Commodity and Honour in *King John*." *UTQ*, XXIX (1960), 341–356.

16. King Lear

TANNENBAUM, S. A. *Shakespeare's "King Lear": A Concise Bibliography*. Elizabethan Bibliographies No. 16. New York, 1940.

Modern Editions: New Variorum, Howard H. Furness, ed. Philadelphia, 1880; G. L. Kittredge, ed. Boston, 1939; G. I. Duthie, ed. 1949; New Arden, K. Muir, ed. London, 1952; Folger, Louis B. Wright and Virginia LaMar, eds. New York, 1957; Pelican, A. Harbage, ed. Baltimore, 1958; New Cambridge, J. Dover Wilson and G. I. Duthie, eds. Cambridge, 1960; Laurel, Francis Fergusson and C. J. Sisson, eds. New York, 1960; Signet, Russel Fraser, ed. New York, 1963; Bantam, O. J. Campbell, Alfred Rothschild and Stuart Vaughan, eds. New York, 1964.

Textual Studies: *Chambers*, I, 463–470; *Greg*, pp. 375–388; *Hinman, passim; Honigmann*, pp. 121–129.

The History of King Leir, 1605. The Malone Society Reprints, 1907.

VAN DAM, B. A. P. *The Text of Shakespeare's "Lear,"* ed. H. DeVocht. Materials for the Study of the Old English Drama, No. 10. Louvain, 1935.

GREG, W. W. *The Variants in the First Quarto of "King Lear."* London, 1940.

KIRSCHBAUM, L. *The True Text of "King Lear."* Baltimore, 1945.

WILLIAMS, P., JR. "The Compositor of the 'Pied Bull' *Lear*." *Papers Bibl. Soc. Univ. Virginia*, I (1948–49), 59–68.

DUTHIE, G. I. *Elizabethan Shorthand and the First Quarto of "King Lear."* Oxford, 1950.

WALKER, A. "*King Lear*—the 1608 Quarto." *MLR*, XLVII (1952), 376–378.

WILLIAMS, P. "Two Problems in the Folio Text of *King Lear*." *SQ*, IV (1953), 451–460.

CAIRNCROSS, A. S. "The Quartos and the Folio Text of *King Lear*." *RES*, n.s. VI (1955), 252–258.

Sources: *Muir.*

LEE, S., ed. *The Chronicle History of King Leir, the Original of Shakespeare's "King Lear."* London, 1909.

HENDERSON, W. B. D. "Montaigne's *Apologie of Raymond Sebond*, and *King Lear*." *SAB*, XIV (1939), 209–225; *SAB*, XV (1940), 40–56.

MUIR, K. "Samuel Harsnett and *King Lear*." *RES*, II (1951), 11–21.

Stage History: *Odell, passim; Trewin, passim; New Cambridge*, pp. lvi–lxix; *Winter* II, 342–480.

BROOKE, C. F. T. "*King Lear* on the Stage." *Essays on Shakespeare and Other Elizabethans*. New Haven, 1948.

SUTHERLAND, W. O. S., Jr. "Polonius, Hamlet, and Lear in Aaron Hill's *Prompter*." *SP*, XLIX (1952), 605–618.

SPENCER, C. "A Word for Tate's *King Lear*." *SEL*, III (1963), 241–251.

iticism: *Johnson*, pp. 154–162; *Coleridge*, I, 54–67; *Hazlitt*, pp. 257–272; *Van Doren*, pp. 204–216; *Adams*, pp. 337–349. *Clemen*, pp. 133–153.
ADLEY, A. C. *Shakespearean Tragedy*. London, 1904.
IGHT, G. W. *The Wheel of Fire: Essays in Interpretation of Shakespeare's Sombre Tragedies*, 4th ed. London and New York, 1949.
ANVILLE-BARKER, H. *Prefaces to Shakespeare*. 2 Vols. Princeton, N. J., 1946, 1947.
UIR, E. *The Politics of King Lear*. Glasgow Univ. Pub. No. 72. Glasgow, 1947.
MPBELL, O. J. "The Salvation of Lear." *ELH*, XV (1948), 93–109.
ILMAN, R. B. *This Great Stage: Image and Structure in "King Lear."* Baton Rouge, 1948.
NBY, J. F. *Shakespeare's Doctrine of Nature: A Study of "King Lear."* London, 1949.
THIAN, J. M. *"King Lear": A Tragic Reading of Life*. Toronto, 1949.
WELL, E. *"King Lear." Atlantic Monthly*, May, 1950, pp. 57–62.
IPSON, W. *The Structure of Complex Words*. London, 1951.
ILLIAMS, G. W. "The Poetry of the Storm in *King Lear*." *SQ*, II (1951), 57–71.
GEL, P. N. "Adversity and the Miracle of Love in *King Lear*." *SQ*, VI (1955), 325–336.
ORRIS, I. "Cordelia and Lear." *SQ*, VIII (1957), 141–158.
WOTTNY, W. M. T. "Lear's Questions." *SS 10* (1957), 90–97.
OST, W. "Shakespeare's Rituals and the Opening of *King Lear*." *Hudson Review*, X (1958), 577–585.
ACLEAN, H. "Disguise in *King Lear*." *SQ*, XI (1960), 49–54.
EST, R. "Sex and Pessimism in *King Lear*." *SQ*, XI (1960), 55–60.
IPSON, W., K. MUIR, J. F. DANBY, and E. JONES. "The New *King Lear*." *CQ*, III (1961), 67–75.
NNETT, J. W. "The Storm Within: The Madness of Lear." *SQ*, XIII (1962), 137–155.
ASER, R. A. *Shakespeare's Poetics, in Relation to King Lear*. London, 1962.
VIDSON, C. "'My poor fool is hang'd!'" *Universitas*, I (1963), 57–61.
IGHTS, L. C. "*King Lear as Metaphor*." *Myth and Symbol: Critical Approaches and Applications*, ed. Bernice Slote. Lincoln, Neb. 1963, pp. 21–38.
SHUTZ, H. L. "Cordelia and the Fool." *RS*, XXXII (1964), 240–260.
IIDT, K. "The Quarto and the Folio *Lear*." *ES*, XLV (1964), 149–162.
TON, W. R. *King Lear and the Gods*. San Marino, Calif., 1965.
ACK, M. *King Lear in Our Time*. Berkeley, 1965.

17. Love's Labour's Lost

odern Editions: New Variorum, Howard H. Furness, ed. Philadelphia, 1904; New Cambridge, A. Quiller-Couch and J. Dover Wilson, eds. Cambridge, 1923; Yale, W. Cross and C. T. Brooke, eds. New Haven, Conn., 1925; New Arden, Richard David, ed. London, 1951; Penguin, G. B. Harrison, ed. London, 1953; Folger, Louis B. Wright and Virginia LaMar, eds. New York, 1962; Pelican, Alfred Harbage, ed. Baltimore, 1963.
Textual Studies: *Chambers*, I, 331–338; *Greg*, pp. 219–224; *Hinman, passim; Honigmann, passim.*
KIRSCHBAUM, L. "Is *The Spanish Tragedy* a leading case? Did a bad quarto of *Love's Labour's Lost* ever exist?" *JEGP*, XXXVII (1938), 501–512.
PARSONS, H. *Emendations to Three of Shakespeare's Plays: "Merry Wives of Windsor," "Love's Labour's Lost," "Comedy of Errors."* London, 1953.
Sources: *Bullough*, I, 425–442; *Muir*.
CAMPBELL, O. J. "*Love's Labour's Lost* Restudied." *Studies in Shakespeare, Milton and Donne*. New York, 1925.
SORENSEN, F. "The Masque of the Muscovites in *Love's Labour's Lost*." *MLN*, L (1935), 499–501.
BRADBROOK, M. C. *The School of Night. A Study in the Literary Relationships of Sir Walter Ralegh*. Cambridge, 1936.
YATES, F. A. *A Study of "Love's Labour's Lost."* Shakespeare Problems, V. Cambridge, 1936.
BOUGHNER, D. C. "Don Armado and the *Commedia dell' Arte*." *SP*, XXXVII (1940), 201–224.
PHELPS, J. "The Source of *Love's Labour's Lost*." *SAB*, XVII (1942), 97–102.
OPPEL, H. "Gabriel Harvey." *SJ*, 82/83 (1949), 34–51.
MARAÑÓN, G. *Antonio Pérez, Spanish Traitor*, tr. by Charles D. Ley. London, 1954.
SCHRICKX, W. *Shakespeare's Early Contemporaries. The Background of the Harvey-Nashe Polemic and "Love's Labour's Lost."* Antwerp, 1956.
UNGERER, G. *Anglo-Spanish Relations in Tudor Literature*. Bern and Madrid, Artes Gráficas Clavileño, 1956.
Stage History: *Odell, passim; Trewin, passim; New Cambridge*, pp. lix–lxii; *Winter* III, 167–195.
HUNT, H. *Old Vic Prefaces*. London, 1954.
Criticism: *Johnson*, pp. 86–88; *Coleridge*, I, 92–99; *Hazlitt*, pp. 332–334; *Van Doren*, pp. 45–51.
CHARLTON, H. B. *Shakespearian Comedy*. London, 1938.
GRANVILLE-BARKER, H. *Prefaces to Shakespeare*. 2 Vols. Princeton, N. J., 1946, 1947.
PALMER, J. *Comic Characters of Shakespeare*. New York, 1946.
PARROTT, T. M. *Shakespearean Comedy*. New York, 1949.
DESAI, C. N. *Shakespearean Comedy*, Indore City, M. B., India, 1953.
BARBER, C. L. *Shakespeare's festive comedy*. Princeton, 1959.
HARBAGE, A. "*Love's Labor's Lost* and the Early Shakespeare." *PQ*, XLI (1962), 18–36.
HOY, C. "*Love's Labour's Lost* and the Nature of Comedy." *SQ*, XIII (1962), 31–40.

18. Macbeth

TANNENBAUM, S. A. *Shakespeare's "Macbeth": A Concise Bibliography*. New York, 1939.
Modern Editions: E. K. Chambers, ed. London, 1893; New Variorum, Howard H. Furness, Jr., ed. Philadelphia, 1903; J. Q. Adams, ed., 1931; G. L. Kittredge, ed. Boston, 1939; New Cambridge, J. Dover Wilson, ed. Cambridge, 1947; New Arden, K. Muir, ed. London, 1951; Yale, E. Waith, ed. New Haven,

Conn., 1954; Pelican, A. Harbage, ed. Baltimore, 1956; Folger, Louis B. Wright and Virginia LaMar, eds. New York, 1959; Bantam, O. J. Campbell, Alfred Rothschild and Stuart Vaughan, eds. New York, 1961; Signet, Sylvan Barnet, ed. New York, 1963.

Textual Studies: *Chambers*, I, 471–476; *Greg*, pp. 389–397; *Hinman, passim.*

NOSWORTHY, J. M. *Shakespeare's Occasional Plays. Their Origin and Transmission.* London, 1965.

Sources. *Muir.*

PAUL, H. N. *The Royal Play of Macbeth.* Philadelphia, 1950.

Stage History: *Odell, passim; Trewin, passim; New Cambridge*, pp. lxix–lxxxii; *Winter*, I, 443–515.

PURDOM, C. B. *The Crosby Hall Macbeth.* London, 1951.

Criticism: *Johnson*, pp. 167–176, 202–206; *Coleridge*, I, 67–82; II, 269–272; *Hazlitt*, pp. 186–194; *Van Doren*, pp. 216–230; *Adams*, pp. 269–277.

BRADLEY, A. C. *Shakespearean Tragedy.* London, 1904.

KNIGHT, G. W. *The Imperial Theme.* Oxford, 1939.

SPENDER, S. "Time, Violence and *Macbeth.*" *Penguin New Writing*, III (1940–1941), 115–120.

DORAN, M. "That Undiscovered Country. A Problem Concerning the Use of the Supernatural in *Hamlet* and *Macbeth.*" *Renaissance Studies in Honor of Hardin Craig.* Stanford, Calif., 1941. *PQ*, XX (1941), 413–427.

SMITH, F. M. "The Relation of *Macbeth* to *Richard the Third.*" *PMLA*, LX (1945), 1003–20.

BROOKS, C. "The Naked Babe and the Cloak of Manliness." In *The Well Wrought Urn.* New York, 1949.

WALKER, R. *The Time Is Free: A Study of "Macbeth."* London, 1949.

EMPSON, W. "Dover Wilson on *Macbeth.*" *KR*, XIV (1952), 84–102.

FERGUSSON, F. "*Macbeth* as the Imitation of an Action." *EIE, 1951.* New York, 1952, pp. 31–43.

STIRLING, B. "The Unity of *Macbeth.*" *SQ*, IV (1953), 385–394.

MAHOOD, M. M. *Shakespeare's Word Play.* London, 1956.

PACK, R. "*Macbeth:* The Anatomy of Loss, *YR*, XLV (1956), 533–548.

WINTERS, Y. "Problems for the Modern Critic of Literature." *Hudson Review*, IX (1956), 325–386.

LAWLOR, J. "Mind and Hand: Some Reflections on the Study of Shakespeare's Imagery." *SQ*, VIII (1957), 179–193.

HYDE, I. "*Macbeth:* A Problem." *English*, XIII (1960), 91–94.

HARCOURT, J. B. "'I Pray You, Remember the Porter.'" *SQ*, XII (1961), 393–402.

McCARTHY, M. "General Macbeth." *Harpers*, CCXXIV (June 1962), 35–39.

HUNTLEY, F. L. "*Macbeth* and the Background of Jesuitical Equivocation." *PMLA*, LXXIX (1964), 390–400.

PAOLUCCI, A. "*Macbeth* and *Oedipus Rex:* A Study in Paradox." *1564–1964: Shakespeare Encomium*, ed. Anne Paolucci. The City College Papers, I. New York, 1964, pp. 44–70.

PROSER, M. N. *The Heroic Image in Five Shakespearean Tragedies.* Princeton, 1965.

19. Measure for Measure

Modern Editions: Arden, H. Hart, ed. London, 190 New Cambridge, A. Quiller-Couch and J. Dov Wilson, eds. Cambridge, 1922; Yale, D. Hardin ed. New Haven, Conn., 1954; Penguin, G. B. Ha rison, ed. London, 1954; Pelican, R. C. Bald, e Baltimore, 1956; Signet, S. Nagarajan, ed. Ne York, 1964; New Arden, J. W. Lever, ed. Londo 1965.

Textual Studies: *Chambers*, I, 452–457; *Greg*, p 354–356; *Hinman, passim; Honigmann, passim.*

THISELTON, A. E. *Some Textual Notes On "Measu for Measure."* London, 1901.

LEVER, J. W. "The Date of *Measure for Measure* *SQ*, X (1959), 381–388.

Sources: *Bullough*, II, 399–530; *Muir.*

Stage History: *Odell, passim; Trewin, passim; Ne Cambridge*, pp. 160–165.

MERCHANT, W. M. *Shakespeare and the Artist.* O ford, 1959.

Criticism: *Johnson*, pp. 75–80; *Coleridge*, I, 113–11 *Hazlitt*, pp. 345–349; *Van Doren*, pp. 185–19 *Adams*, pp. 129–139.

KNIGHT, G. W. *The Wheel of Fire.* London, 1930.

CHAMBERS, R. W. *The Jacobean Shakespeare a "Measure for Measure."* Oxford, 1937.

BRADBROOK, M. C. "Authority, Truth, and Justice *Measure for Measure.*" *RES*, XVII (1941), 385–39

KNIGHTS, L. C. "The Ambiguity of *Measure f Measure.*" *Scrutiny*, X (1942), 222–233.

LEAVIS, F. R. "The Greatness of *Measure for Mea ure.*" *Scrutiny*, X (1942), 234–247.

TRAVERSI, D. A. "*Measure for Measure.*" *Scrutiny*, (1942), 40–58.

WILSON, F. P. *Elizabethan and Jacobean.* Oxfor 1945.

BATTENHOUSE, R. W. "*Measure for Measure* a Christian Doctrine of the Atonement." *PMLA*, L (1946), 1029–59.

DODDS, W. M. T. "The Character of Angelo in *Mea ure for Measure.*" *MLR*, XLI (1946), 246–255.

PARROTT, T. M. *Shakespearean Comedy.* New Yor 1949.

POPE, E. M. "The Renaissance Background of *Mea ure for Measure.*" *SS 2* (1949), 66–82.

SMITH, R. M. "Interpretations of *Measure for Mea ure.*" *SQ*, I (1950).

SYPHER, W. "Shakespeare as Casuist: *Measure f Measure.*" *SR*, LVIII (1950), 262–280.

KRIEGER, M. "*Measure for Measure* and Elizabeth Comedy." *PMLA*, LXVI (1951), 775–784.

LASCELLES, M. *Shakespeare's "Measure for Measure* London, 1953.

SIEGEL, P. N. "*Measure for Measure:* The Signi cance of the Title." *SQ*, IV (1953), 317–320.

COGHILL, N. "Comic Form in *Measure for Measure* *SS 8* (1955), 14–26.

STEVENSON, D. L. "Design and Structure in *Measu for Measure:* A New Appraisal." *ELH*, XX (1956), 256–278.

ORNSTEIN, R. "The Human Comedy: *Measure f Measure.*" *Univ. of Kansas City Review*, XX (1957), 15–22.

SCHANZER, E. "The Marriage-Contracts in *Measu for Measure.*" *SS 13* (1960), 81–89.

uthall, R. "*Measure for Measure* and the Protestant Ethic." *EC*, xi (1961), 11–33.

unkel, W. "Law and Equity in *Measure for Measure*." *SQ*, xiii (1962), 275–285.

20. The Merchant of Venice

annenbaum, S. A. *Shakespeare's "The Merchant of Venice": A Concise Bibliography.* New York, 1941.

odern Editions: New Variorum, Howard H. Furness, ed. Philadelphia, 1888; New Cambridge, A. Quiller-Couch and J. Dover Wilson, eds. Cambridge, 1926; G. L. Kittredge, ed. Boston, 1945; New Arden, J. R. Brown, ed. London, 1955; Pelican, Brents Stirling, ed. Baltimore, 1959; Yale, A. D. Richardson, ed. New Haven, Conn., 1960; Bantam, O. J. Campbell, Alfred Rothschild and Stuart Vaughan, eds. New York, 1962.

extual Studies: *Chambers,* I, 368–375; *Greg,* pp. 240–247; *Hinman, passim.*

cKenzie, D. F. "Compositor B's role in *The Merchant of Venice* Q2 (1619)." *SB*, ii (1949), 75–90.

rown, J. R. "The compositors of *Hamlet* Q2 and *The Merchant of Venice.*" *SB*, vii (1955), 17–40.

urces: *Bullough,* I, 445–514; *Muir.*

egel, P. N. "Shylock and the Puritan usurers." *Studies in Shakespeare,* A. D. Matthews and C. M. Emery, eds. Miami, 1953.

age History: *Odell, passim; Trewin, passim; New Cambridge,* pp. 178–186; *Winter* I, 129–231.

mallwood, O. "The Stage-History of *Merchant of Venice.*" Abstr. *University of Oklahoma Bulletin,* Jan., 1939.

elyveld, T. B. *Shylock on the Stage: Significant Changes in the Interpretation of Shakespeare's Jew. Microf. Ab.*, xi (1951), 772. New York, 1951.

unt, H. *Old Vic Prefaces.* London, 1954.

arnovsky, M. "Mirror of Shylock." *Tulane Drama Review,* iii (1958), 35–45.

nsheimer, H. *Shylock: The History of a Character or the Myth of the Jew.* Foreword by John Middleton Murry. London, 1960.

rown, J. R. "The Realization of Shylock: A Theatrical Criticism." *Early Shakespeare. Stratford-upon-Avon Studies,* 3. London and New York, 1961, pp. 187–209.

riticism: *Johnson,* pp. 81–82; *Hazlitt,* pp. 320–324; *Van Doren,* 79–87.

toll, E. E. "Shylock." *JEGP*, x (1911), 236–79. Enlarged in *Shakespeare Studies.* New York, 1927.

——. "Shakespeare's Jew." *UTQ*, viii (1939), 139–154.

annigan, J. E. "Shylock and Portia." *SAB*, xiv (1939), 169–175.

urry, J. M. "The Significance of Shylock." *Adelphi*, xxii (1945), 1–5.

almer, J. *Comic Characters of Shakespeare.* New York, 1946.

athan, N. "Shylock, Jacob and God's Judgment." *SQ*, i (1950), 255–259.

ranville-Barker, H. *Prefaces to Shakespeare.* 2 Vols., Princeton, N.J., 1946, 1947.

ever, J. W. and N. Nathan. "Shylock, Portia and the values of Shakespearean comedy." *SQ*, iii (1952), 383–388.

Graham, C. B. "Standards of Value in *The Merchant of Venice.*" *SQ*, iv (1953), 145–151.

Brown, J. R. *Shakespeare and his comedies.* London, 1957.

Freud, S. "The Theme of the Three Caskets." *Collected Papers.* iv (1925), 244–256.

Evans, B. *Shakespeare's Comedies.* Oxford, 1960.

Tillyard, E. M. W. "The Trial Scene in *The Merchant of Venice.*" *REL*, ii, iv (1961), 51–59.

Grebanier, B. *The Truth About Shylock.* New York, 1962.

21. The Merry Wives of Windsor

Modern Editions: Arden, Henry Hart, ed. London, 1904; New Cambridge, A. Quiller-Couch and J. Dover Wilson, eds. Cambridge, 1921; Penguin, G. B. Harrison, ed. London, 1957; Pelican, Fredson Bowers, ed. Baltimore, 1963.

Textual Studies: *Chambers,* I, 425–438; *Greg,* pp. 334–337; *Hinman, passim.*

Bracy, W. *"The Merry Wives of Windsor": The History and Transmission of Shakespeare's Text.* Univ. of Missouri Studies, xxv, No. 1. Columbia, Mo., 1952.

Nosworthy, J. M. *Shakespeare's Occasional Plays. Their Origin and Transmission.* London, 1965.

Sources: *Bullough,* II, 3–58; *Muir.*

Crofts, J. E. V. *Shakespeare and the Post Horses. A New Study of "The Merry Wives of Windsor."* London, 1937.

Boughner, D. C. "Traditional Elements in Falstaff." *JEGP*, xliii (1944), 417–428.

Draper, J. W. "The Humor of Corporal Nym." *SAB*, xiii (1938), 131–138.

Stage History: *Odell, passim; Trewin, passim; New Cambridge,* pp. 135–138; *Winter* III, 383–430.

Hunt, H. *Old Vic Prefaces.* London, 1954.

Criticism: *Johnson,* pp. 93–94; *Coleridge,* I, 102–103; *Hazlitt,* pp. 349–351; *Van Doren,* pp. 115–118.

Charlton, H. B. *Falstaff.* Manchester, England, 1935.

——. *Shakespearian Comedy.* London, 1938.

Parrott, T. M. *Shakespearean Comedy.* New York, 1949.

Sen Gupta, S. C. *Shakespearian Comedy.* Calcutta, 1950; New York, 1951.

Hemingway, S. B. "On Behalf of that Falstaff." *SQ*, iii (1952), 307–311.

Reik, T. "Comedy of Intrigue." *The Secret Self.* New York, 1952, pp. 63–75.

Green, W. Shakespeare's *Merry Wives of Windsor.* Princeton, N.J., 1962.

22. A Midsummer Night's Dream

Modern Editions: New Variorum, Howard H. Furness, ed. Philadelphia, 1895; E. K. Chambers, ed. London, 1897; Arden, H. Cunningham, ed. London, 1905; New Cambridge, A. Quiller-Couch and J. Dover Wilson, eds. Cambridge, 1924; G. L. Kittredge, ed. Boston, 1939; Penguin, G. B. Harrison, ed. London, 1953; Signet, Wolfgang Clemen, ed. New York, 1963; Bantam, O. J. Campbell, Alfred Rothschild and Stuart Vaughan, eds. New York, 1965.

Textual Studies: *Chambers,* I, 356–363; *Greg,* pp. 240–247; *Hinman, passim.*

Thomas, S. "The Bad Weather in *A Midsummer Night's Dream*." *MLN*, LXIV (1949), 319–322.

Turner, R. K., Jr. "Printing Methods and Textual Problems in *A Midsummer Night's Dream* Q1." *SB*, XV (1962), 33–55.

Sources: *Bullough*, I, 367–422; *Muir*.

Rickert, E. "Political Propaganda and Satire in *A Midsummer Night's Dream*." *MP*., XXI (1923), pp. 53–89, 133–55.

Chambers, E. K. "The Occasion of *A Midsummer Night's Dream*." *Shakespearean Gleanings*. Oxford, 1944.

Generosa, Sister M. "Apuleius and *A Midsummer Night's Dream:* Analogue or Source, Which?" *SP*, XLII (1945), 198–204.

Poirier, M. "Sidney's Influence upon *A Midsummer Night's Dream*." *SP*, XLIV (1947), 483–489.

Muir, K. "Pyramus and Thisbe: A Study in Shakespeare's Method." *SQ*, V (1954), 141–153.

Doran, M. "Pyramus and Thisbe Once More." *Essays on Shakespeare and the Elizabethan Drama in Honor of Hardin Craig*, Richard Hosley, ed. Columbia, Mo., 1962, pp. 149–161.

Staton, W. F., Jr. "Ovidian Elements in *A Midsummer Night's Dream*." *HLQ*, XXVI (1963), 165–178.

Stage History: *Odell, passim; Trewin, passim; New Cambridge*, pp. 160–168; *Winter* III, 232–296.

Criticism: *Johnson*, pp. 67–71; *Coleridge*, I, 100–102; *Hazlitt*, pp. 244–248; *Van Doren*, pp. 61–67.

Charlton, H. B. *Shakespearian Comedy*. London, 1938.

Law, R. A. "The 'Pre-Conceived Pattern' of *A Midsummer Night's Dream*." *TxSE*, XXIII (1943), 5–14.

Bethurum, D. "Shakespeare's comment on medieval romance in *A Midsummer-Night's Dream*." *MLN*, LX (1945), 85–94.

Schanzer, E. "The Central Theme of *A Midsummer Night's Dream*." *UTQ*, XX (1951), 233–238.

———. "The Moon and the Fairies in *A Midsummer Night's Dream*." *UTQ*, XXIV (1955), 234–246.

Siegel, P. N. "*A Midsummer Night's Dream* and the Wedding Guests." *SQ*, IV (1953), 139–144.

Bonnard, G. "Shakespeare's purpose in *Midsummer-Night's Dream*." *SJ*, XCII (1956), 268–279.

Nemerov, H. "The Marriage of Theseus and Hippolyta." *KR* XVIII (1956), 633–641.

Olsen, P. A. "*A Midsummer Night's Dream* and the Meaning of Court Marriage." *ELH*, XXIV (1957), 95–119.

Briggs, K. M. *The Anatomy of Puck*. London, 1959.

Merchant, W. M. "*A Midsummer-Night's Dream:* a visual re-creation." *Early Shakespeare*, Stratford-upon-Avon Studies 3 (1961), 165–185.

23. *Much Ado About Nothing*

Modern Editions: New Variorum, Howard H. Furness, ed. Philadelphia, 1899; New Cambridge, A. Quiller-Couch and J. Dover Wilson, eds. Cambridge, 1923; Arden, G. Trenery, ed. London, 1924; G. L. Kittredge, ed. Boston, 1941; C. T. Prouty, ed. New York, 1948; Pelican, J. W. Bennett, ed. Baltimore, 1958; Signet, D. L. Stevenson, ed. New York, 1963.

Textual Studies: *Chambers*, I, 384–388; *Greg*, pp. 277–281; *Hinman, passim.*

Sources: *Bullough*, II, 61–139; *Adams*, pp. 537–5 *Muir*.

Scott, M. A. "The Book of the Courtyer: A Possi Source of Benedick and Beatrice." *PMLA*, n.s., IX (1901), 475–502.

Prouty, C. T. *The Sources of "Much Ado Ab Nothing": A Critical Study, Together with Text of Peter Beverley's "Ariodanto and Ieneu* New Haven, 1950.

Potts, A. F. *Shakespeare and The Faerie Quee* Ithaca, 1958.

Stage History: *Odell, passim; Trewin, passim; N Cambridge*, pp. 159–164.

Criticism: *Johnson*, pp. 97–98; *Hazlitt*, pp. 335–3 *Van Doren*, pp. 119–127.

Draper, J. W. "Benedick and Beatrice." *JEGP*, (1942), 140–149.

Palmer, J. *Comic Characters of Shakespeare*. N York, 1946.

Smith, J. "*Much Ado About Nothing*." *Scruti* XIII (1946), 342–357.

Stevenson, D. L. *The Love-Game Comedy*. N York, 1946.

Sypher, W. "Nietzsche and Socrates in Messin *PR*, XVI (1949), 702–713.

Neill, K. "More ado about Claudio." *SQ*, III (195 91–107.

Fergusson, F. "*Comedy of Errors* and *Much A About Nothing*." *SR*, LXII (1954), 24–37.

Jorgensen, P. A. "*Much Ado About Nothing*." *S* V (1954), 287–295.

McPeek, J. "The Thief 'Deformed.'" *BUSE*, (1960), 65–84.

Wey, J. "To Grace Harmony: Musical Design *Much Ado About Nothing*." *BUSE*, IV (196 181–188.

Everett, B. "*Much Ado About Nothing*." *CQ*, (1961), 319–335.

Owen, C. "Comic Awareness." *BUSE*, V (1961), 1 207.

Gilbert, A. "Two Margarets: The Composition *Much Ado About Nothing*." *PQ*, XLI (1962), 61–

Kirschbaum, L. *Character and Characterization Shakespeare*. Detroit, 1962.

24. *Othello*

Tannenbaum, S. A. *Shakespeare's "Othello": A Co cise Bibliography*. New York, 1943.

Modern Editions: New Variorum, Howard H. F ness, ed. Philadelphia, 1886; G. L. Kittredge, Boston, 1941; New Cambridge, J. Dover Wils and A. Walker, eds. Cambridge, 1957; Yale, Brooke and L. Mason, eds. New Haven, Con 1957; New Arden, M. R. Ridley, ed. London, 19 Pelican, G. E. Bentley, ed. Baltimore, 1958; Le ard Dean, ed. New York, 1961; Bantam, O. Campbell, Alfred Rothschild and Stuart Vaugh eds. New York, 1962; Signet, Alvin Kernan, New York, 1963.

Textual Studies: *Chambers*, I, 457–463; *Greg*, 357–374; *Hinman, passim; Honigmann*, pp. 1 120; *Adams*, pp. 373–389.

Walker, A. "The 1622 Quarto and the First Fo Texts of *Othello*." *SS* 5 (1952), 16–24.

Rosenberg, M. "On the Dating of *Othello*." XXXIX (1958), 72–74.

urces: *Muir.*

LLOCK, W. A. "The Sources of *Othello*." *MLN*, XL (1925), 226–8.

UIR, K. "Holland's Pliny and *Othello*." *N & Q*, 198 (1953), 513–514.

——. "Shakespeare and Lewkenor." *RES*, VII (1956), 182–183.

VACK, B. *Shakespeare and the Allegory of Evil.* New York, 1958.

AMS, M. S. "'Ocular Proof' in *Othello* and Its Source." *PMLA*, LXXIX (1964), 234–241.

NES, E. *Othello's Countrymen: The African in English Renaissance Drama.* Oxford, 1965.

age History: *Odell, passim; Trewin, passim; New Cambridge*, pp. lvii–lxix; *Winter* I, 232–319.

LLOTSON, G. "*Othello* and *The Alchemist* at Oxford in 1610." *Essays in Criticism and Research.* Cambridge, 1942.

SENBERG, M. *The Masks of Othello: The Search for the Identity of Othello, Iago, and Desdemona by Three Centuries of Actors and Critics.* Berkeley, Calif., and Los Angeles, 1961.

iticism: *Johnson*, 197; *Coleridge*, I, 44–54, 124–125; *Van Doren*, pp. 192–203; *Adams*, pp. 523–535; *Clemen*, pp. 119–132.

OLL, E. E. *Othello, An Historical and Comparative Study.* Minneapolis, 1915.

——. "Another *Othello* Too Modern." *Adams*, pp. 351–371.

——. "Iago Not A Malcontent." *JEGP*, LI (1952), 163–167.

EAVIS, F. R. "Diabolic Intellect and the Noble Hero: A Note on *Othello*." *Scrutiny*, VI (1937). Reprinted in *The Common Pursuit.* New York, 1952.

RAPER, John W. "The Jealousy of Iago." *Neophil*, XXV (1939), 50–60.

IRSCHBAUM, L. "The Modern Othello." *ELH*, XI (1944), 283–296.

RIOR, M. E. "Character in Relation to Action in *Othello*." *MP*, XLIV (1947), 225–237.

AYMOND, W. O. "Motivation and Character Portrayal in *Othello*." *UTQ*, XVII (1947), 80–96.

LLEN, D. C. "Three Notes on Donne's Poetry with a Side Glance at *Othello*." *MLN*, LXV (1950), 102–106.

RDAN, H. H. "Dramatic Illusion in *Othello*." *SQ*, I (1950), 146–152.

MPSON, W. *The Structure of Complex Words.* London, 1951.

VEBB, H. J. "The Military Background in *Othello*." *PQ*, XXX (1951), 40–52.

ETHELL, S. L. "Shakespeare's Imagery: The Diabolic Images in *Othello*." *SS 5* (1952), 62–80.

OWOTTNY, W. M. T. "Justice and Love in *Othello*." *UTQ*, XXI (1952), 330–344.

LLIOTT, G. R. *Flaming Minister: A Study of "Othello" as Tragedy of Love and Hate.* Durham, N.C., 1953.

IEGEL, P. N. "The Damnation of *Othello*." *PMLA*, LXVIII (1953), 1068–78.

——. "The Damnation of *Othello*: An Addendum." *PMLA*, LXXI (1956), 279–280.

IUBLER, E. "The Damnation of *Othello*: Some Limitations on the Christian View of the Play." *SQ*, IX (1958), 295–300.

ARDNER, H. *The Noble Moor. Proceedings of the British Academy, 1955*, XLI, 189–205. Oxford, 1956.

GÉRARD, A. "'Egregiously an Ass': The Dark Side of the Moor. A View of Othello's Mind." *SS 10* (1957), 98–106.

HEILMAN, R. B. *Magic in the Web: Action and Language in "Othello."* Lexington, Ky., 1956.

——. "'Twere Best not Know Myself: Othello, Lear, Macbeth." *SQ*, XV, ii (1964), 89–98.

LANGBAUM, R. *The Poetry of Experience: The Dramatic Monologue in Modern Literary Tradition.* New York, 1957.

ARTHOS, J. "The Fall of *Othello*." *SQ*, IX (1958), 93–104.

MACK, M. "The Jacobean Shakespeare." *Jacobean Theatre.* London, 1960.

AUDEN, W. H. "The Alienated City: Reflections on *Othello*." *Encounter*, XVII (Aug. 1961), 3–14.

HOLLOWAY, J. *The Story of the Night.* London, 1961.

LEVIN, H. "*Othello* and the Motive Hunters." *CRAS*, VIII (1964), 1–16.

PROSER, M. N. *The Heroic Image in Five Shakespearean Tragedies.* Princeton, 1965.

25. Pericles, Prince of Tyre

Modern Editions: Arden, K. Deighton, ed. London, 1907; New Cambridge, J. C. Maxwell, ed. Cambridge, 1956; Penguin, G. B. Harrison, ed. London, 1958; New Arden, F. D. Hoeniger, ed. London, 1963; Signet, Ernest Schanzer, ed. New York, 1965.

Textual Studies: *Chambers*, I, 518–528; *Greg*, pp. 74–76.

FLEAY, F. G. "On the Play of *Pericles*." *Trans. New Shaksp. Soc.*, 1874.

HASTINGS, W. T. "Exit George Wilkins?" *SAB*, XI (1936), 67–83.

EDWARDS, P. "An Approach to the Problem of *Pericles*." *SS 5* (1952), 25–49.

HOENIGER, F. D. "How significant are textual parallels? A new author for *Pericles*?" *SQ*, XI (1960), 27–37.

Sources. *Bullough*, VI; *Muir.*

PARROTT, T. M. "*Pericles:* The Play and the Novel." *SAB*, XXIII (1948), 105–113.

WILKINS, G. *The Painfull Adventures of Pericles, Prince of Tyre*, ed. Kenneth Muir. Liverpool, 1953.

Stage History: *Odell, passim; Trewin, passim; New Cambridge*, pp. xxx–xl.

Criticism: *Van Doren*, pp. 253–262.

DELIUS, N. "Über Shakespeares *Pericles, Prince of Tyre*." *SJ*, III (1868), 175–204.

CRAIG, H. "Shakespeare's Development as a Dramatist in the Light of His Experience." *SP*, XXXIX (1942), 226–238.

KNIGHT, G. W. *The Crown of Life: Interpretation of Shakespeare's Final Plays.* Oxford, 1947.

ARTHOS, J. "*Pericles, Prince of Tyre:* A Study in the Dramatic Use of Romantic Narrative." *SQ*, IV (1953), 257–270.

BARKER, G. A. "Themes and Variations in Shakespeare's *Pericles*." *ES*, XLIV (1963), 401–414.

26. Richard II

Modern Editions: Cambridge, J. Dover Wilson, ed. Cambridge, 1939; G. L. Kittredge, ed. Boston, 1941; New Variorum, Matthew Black, ed. Philadelphia,

1955; New Arden, P. Ure, ed. London, 1956; Yale, R. T. Petersson, ed. New Haven, Conn., 1957; Pelican, Matthew Black, ed. London, 1957; Signet, Kenneth Muir, ed. New York, 1963.

Textual Studies: *Chambers*, I, 348–356; *Greg*, pp. 236–239; *Hinman, passim.*

Sources: *Bullough*, III, 353–491*; Adams*, pp. 199–216.

ALBRIGHT, E. M. "Shakespeare's *Richard II* and the Essex Conspiracy." *PMLA*, XLII (1927), 686–720.

TILLOTSON, K. "Drayton and *Richard II:* 1597–1600." *RES*, XV (1939), 172–179.

WILKINSON, B. "The Deposition of Richard II and Accession of Henry IV." *English Historical Review*, LIV (1939), 215–239.

WILSON, J. D. "The Political Background of Shakespeare's *Richard II* and *Henry IV.*" *SJ*, LXXV (1939), 36–51.

ROSSITER, A. P., ed. *Woodstock: A Moral History.* London, 1946.

Stage History: *Odell, passim; Trewin, passim; New Cambridge*, pp. lxxvii–xcii.

O'CONNELL, R. L. "A Stage History of *Richard II.*" *Listener*, LI (1954), 225.

MCMANAWAY, J. G. "*Richard II* at Covent Garden." *SQ*, XV, ii (1964), 161–175.

Criticism: *Johnson*, pp. 110–112; *Coleridge*, I, 142–156; *Hazlitt*, pp. 272–277; *Van Doren*, pp. 68–79; *Clemen*, pp. 53–62.

DORAN, M. "Imagery in *Richard II* and in *Henry IV.*" *MLR*, XXXVII (1942), 113–122.

RIBNER, I. "Bolingbroke, a True Machiavellian." *MLQ*, IX (1948), 117–184.

BONNARD, G. A. "The Actor in *Richard II.*" *SJ*, 87/88 (1952), 87–101.

DEAN, L. F. "*Richard II:* The State and the Image of the Theater." *PMLA*, LXVII (1952), 211–18.

STIRLING, B. "Bolingbroke's 'Decision'." *SQ*, II (1951), 27–34.

BOGARD, T. "Shakespeare's Second Richard." *PMLA*, LXX (1955), 192–204.

PROVOST, F. "The Sorrows of Shakespeare's Richard II." *Studies in English Renaissance Literature*, ed. Waldo F. McNeir. Baton Rouge, La., 1962, pp. 40–55.

27. *Richard III*

Modern Editions: Bankside, E. Calkins, ed. London, 1891; Arden, A. H. Thompson, ed. London, 1907; New Variorum, Howard H. Furness, Jr., ed. Philadelphia, 1908; Yale, Jack R. Crawford, ed. New Haven, Conn., 1927; American Arden, Hazelton Spencer, ed. Boston, 1933; New Cambridge, J. Dover Wilson, ed. Cambridge, 1954; Laurel, Francis Fergusson and C. J. Sisson, eds. New York, 1958; Signet, Mark Eccles, ed. New York, 1964.

Textual Studies: *Chambers*, I, 294–305; *Greg*, pp. 190–199; *Hinman, passim.*

GREG, W. W. "*Richard III—Q5* (1612)." *Library*, n.s. XVII (1936), 88–97.

PATRICK, D. L. *The Textual History of "Richard III."* Stanford, Calif., 1936.

WILSON, J. D. "On Editing Shakespeare with Special Reference to the Problems of *Richard III.*" *Talking of Shakespeare*, ed. John Garrett. London, 1954.

———. "The Composition of the Clarence Scenes *Richard III.*" *MLR*, LIII (1958), 211–214.

WALTON, J. K. *The Copy for the Folio Text "Richard III."* Auckland, N.Z., 1955.

CAIRNCROSS, A. S. "The Quartos and the Folio Te of *Richard III.*" *RES*, VIII (1957), 225–233.

SHAPIRO, I. A. "*Richard II* or *Richard III* or . . . *SQ*, IX (1958), 204–206.

Sources: *Bullough* III, 221–349.

CAMPBELL, O. J. *The Position of "The Roode Witte Roos" in the Saga of King Richard I* Madison, Wis., 1919.

SPARGO, J. W. "Clarence in the Malmsey-Butt *MLN*, LI (1936), 166–173.

DEAN, L. F. "Literary Problems in More's *Richa III.*" *PMLA*, LVIII (1943), 22–41.

CAMPBELL, L. B. *Shakespeare's Histories.* San Marin Calif., 1947.

WILSON, J. D. "Shakespeare's *Richard III* and *T True Tragedy of Richard the Third, 1594.*" *S* III (1952), 299–306.

KENDALL, P. M. *Richard the Third.* London, 1955.

BROOKE, N. "Marlowe as Provocative Agent." *SS* (1961), 34–44.

Stage History: *Odell, passim; Trewin, passim; Ne Cambridge*, pp. xlvi–lxi; *Winter* I, 68–128.

Criticism: *Johnson*, pp. 146–147; *Hazlitt*, pp. 29 303; *Van Doren*, pp. 19–27; *Clemen*, pp. 47–52.

RANK, O. "Shakespeares Vaterkomplex." *Das Inze Motiv in Dichtung und Sage*, Leipzig, 1912.

LEWIS, W. *The Lion and the Fox: The Role of t Hero in the Plays of Shakespeare.* London, 1927.

THOMAS, S. *The Antic Hamlet and Richard III.* Ne York, 1943.

LAW, R. A. "*Richard the Third:* A Study in Shak speare's Composition." *PMLA*, LX (1945), 689–69

CLEMEN, W. H. "Tradition and Originality in Shak speare's *Richard III.*" *SQ*, V (1954), 247–257.

———. *Kommentar zu Shakespeares "Richard II* Göttingen, W. Germany, 1957.

ROSSITER, A. P. *Angel with Horns, and Other Shak speare Lectures*, ed. Graham Storey. London ar New York, 1961.

28. *Romeo and Juliet*

TANNENBAUM, S. A. and D. R. *Shakespeare's "Rom and Juliet" (a Concise Bibliography).* New Yor 1950.

Modern Editions: New Variorum, Howard H. Fu ness, ed. Philadelphia, 1871; Arden, E. Dowden, e London, 1900; G. L. Kittredge, ed. Boston, 194 Yale, R. Hosley, ed. New Haven, Conn., 195 New Cambridge, G. I. Duthie and J. Dover Wi son, eds. Cambridge, 1955; Laurel, Francis Fe gusson and C. J. Sisson, eds. New York, 1958; Fo ger, Louis B. Wright and Virginia LaMar, ed New York, 1960; Pelican, John Hankins, ed. Balt more, 1960; Bantam, O. J. Campbell, Alfred Roth child and Stuart Vaughan, eds. New York, 196 Signet, Joseph Bryant, ed. New York, 1964.

Textual Studies: *Chambers*, I, 338–347; *Greg*, p 225–235; *Hinman, passim; Honigmann, passim.*

HOPPE, H. R. *The Bad Quarto of "Romeo an Juliet": A Bibliographical and Textual Study.* Co nell Studies in English, XXXVI. Ithaca, N.Y., 194

APER, J. W. "The Date of *Romeo and Juliet.*" *RES*, XXV (1949), 55–57.

IOMAS, S. "The Bibliographical Links Between the First Two Quartos of *Romeo and Juliet.*" *RES*, XXV (1949), 110–114.

——. "The Earthquake in *Romeo and Juliet.*" *MLN*, LXIV (1949), 417–419.

——. "Henry Chettle and the First Quarto of *Romeo and Juliet.*" *RES*, n.s. I (1950), 8–16.

OSLEY, R. "The Corrupting Influence of the Bad Quarto on the Received Text of *Romeo and Juliet.*" *SQ*, IV (1953), 11–33.

INMAN, C. "The Proof-Reading of the First Folio Text of *Romeo and Juliet.*" *SB*, VI (1954), 61–70.

urces: *Bullough*, I, 269–363; *Muir*.

UNRO, J. J., ed. *Brooke's 'Romeus and Juliet' being the original of Shakespeare's 'Romeo and Juliet.'* London, 1908.

SCHER, R. *Quellen zu Romeo und Julia*. Bonn, 1922.

ALLEY, H. R. "Shakespeare's Debt to Marlowe in *Romeo and Juliet.*" *PQ*, XXI (1942), 257–267.

LLEN, N. B. "Shakespeare and Arthur Brooke." *Delaware Notes*, 17th Series (1944), 91–110.

OORE, O. H. *The Legend of Romeo and Juliet.* Columbus, Ohio, 1950.

OSWORTHY, J. M. "The Two Angry Families of Verona." *SQ*, III (1952), 219–226.

age History: *Odell, passim; Trewin, passim; New Cambridge*, pp. xxviii–lii; *Winter* II, 107–214.

OSLEY, R. "The Use of the Upper Stage in *Romeo and Juliet.*" *SQ*, V (1954), 371–379.

ROWN, J. R. "S. Franco Zeffirelli's *Romeo and Juliet.*" *SS 15* (1962), 147–155.

ONE, G. W., Jr. "*Romeo and Juliet:* The Source of Its Modern Stage Career." *SQ*, XV, ii (1964), 191–206.

riticism: *Johnson*, pp. 185–188; *Coleridge*, I, 2–12; *Hazlitt*, pp. 248–257; *Van Doren*, pp. 51–61; *Clemen*, pp. 63–73.

OLL, E. E. *Shakespeare's Young Lovers.* Oxford, 1937.

HARLTON, H. B. "*Romeo and Juliet*" *as an Experimental Tragedy*. London, 1939.

RAPER, J. W. "Shakespeare's Star-Crossed Lovers." *RES*, XV (1939), 16–34.

RANVILLE-BARKER, H. *Prefaces to Shakespeare.* 2 Vols. Princeton, N.J., 1946, 1947.

AIN, H. E. "*Romeo and Juliet:* A Reinterpretation." *SAB*, XXII (1947), 163–192.

OWLING, L. E. "The Thematic Framework of *Romeo and Juliet.*" *PMLA*, LXIV (1949), 208–220.

URRANT, G. H. "What's in a Name? A Discussion of *Romeo and Juliet.*" *Theoria*, VIII (1956), 23–36.

ICKEY, F. M. *Not Wisely But Too Well: Shakespeare's Love Tragedies.* San Marino, Calif., 1957.

AWLOR, J. "*Romeo and Juliet.*" *Early Shakespeare.* Stratford-upon-Avon Studies, 3. London and New York, 1961, pp. 123–143.

EGEL, P. N. "Christianity and the Religion of Love in *Romeo and Juliet.*" *SQ*, XII (1961), 371–392.

29. The Taming of the Shrew

odern Editions: Bankside, A. Frey, ed. London, 1888; Arden, R. Bond, ed. London, 1904; New Cambridge, A. Quiller-Couch and J. Dover Wilson, eds. Cambridge, 1928; Penguin, G. B. Harrison, ed. London, 1951; Yale, T. Bergin, ed. New Haven, Conn., 1954; Laurel, Francis Fergusson and C. J. Sisson, eds. New York, 1958; Pelican, Richard Hosley, ed. Baltimore, 1964.

Textual Studies: *Chambers*, I, 322–328; *Greg*, pp. 210–216; *Hinman, passim*.

ASHTON, F. H. "The Revision of the Folio Text of the *Taming of the Shrew.*" *PQ*, VI (1927), pp. 151–60.

VAN DAM, B. A. P. "*The Taming of A Shrew.*" *ES*, X (1928), 97–106.

WENTERSDORF, K. "The Authenticity of *The Taming of the Shrew.*" *SQ*, V (1954), 11–32.

PRIOR, M. E. "Imagery as a Test of Authorship." *SQ*, VI (1955), 381–386.

WALDO, T. R., and T. W. HERBERT. "Musical terms in *The Taming of the Shrew;* evidence of single authorship." *SQ*, X (1959), 185–199.

HOSLEY, R. "Was There a 'Dramatic Epilogue' to *The Taming of the Shrew?*" *SEL*, I, ii (1961), 17–34.

Sources: *Bullough*, I, 57–158; *Muir*.

GRAY, H. D. "*The Taming of a Shrew.*" *PQ*, XX (1941), 325–333.

DUTHIE, G. I. "*The Taming of a Shrew* and *The Taming of the Shrew.*" *RES*, XIX (1943), 337–356.

PARROTT, T. M. "*The Taming of a Shrew*—A New Study of an Old Play." *Elizabethan Studies and Other Essays: In Honor of George F. Reynolds.* Denver, Colo., 1945, 155–165.

CRAIG, H. "The Shrew and A Shrew: Possible Settlement of an Old Debate." *Elizabethan Studies and Other Essays: In Honor of George F. Reynolds.* Denver, Colo., 1945, 150–154.

SHROEDER, J. W. "*The Taming of a Shrew* and *The Taming of the Shrew:* A Case Reopened." *JEGP*, LVII (1958), 424–443.

HOSLEY, R. "Sources and Analogues of *The Taming of the Shrew.*" *HLQ*, XXVII (1964), 289–308.

Stage History: *Odell, passim; Trewin, passim; New Cambridge*, pp. 181–186; *Winter* II, 481–540.

CRUNDELL, H. W. "*The Taming of the Shrew* on the XVII Century Stage." *N&Q*, 173 (1937).

Criticism: *Johnson*, pp. 95–96; *Hazlitt*, pp. 341–345; *Van Doren*, pp. 36–40.

DRAPER, J. W. "Kate the Curst." *Journal of Nervous and Mental Diseases*, 89 (1939), 757–764.

HOUK, R. A. "The Evolution of *The Taming of the Shrew.*" *PMLA*, LVII (1942), 1009–38.

———. "Shakespeare's Heroic Shrew." *SAB*, XVIII (1943), 121–132, 175–186.

SISSON, C. J. "*Taming of the Shrew.*" *Drama*, XXXVII (Autumn, 1955), 25–27.

BRADBROOK, M. C. "Dramatic Role as Social Image; A Study of *The Taming of the Shrew.*" *SJ*, 94 (1958), 132–150.

BROOKS, C. "Shakespeare's Romantic Shrews." *SQ*, XI (1960), 351–356.

SERONSY, C. " 'Supposes' as the Unifying Theme in the *Taming of the Shrew.*" *SQ*, XIV (1963), 15–30.

30. The Tempest

Modern Editions: New Variorum, H. H. Furness, ed. Philadelphia, 1892; Arden, M. Luce, ed. London, 1902; New Cambridge, A. Quiller-Couch and J. Dover Wilson, eds. Cambridge, 1921; G. L. Kittredge, ed. Boston, 1939; New Arden, F. Kermode, ed. London, 1954; Yale, D. Horn, ed. New Haven, Conn., 1955; Pelican, N. Frye, ed. Baltimore, 1958; Signet, Robert Langbaum, ed. New York, 1964; Bantam, O. J. Campbell, Alfred Rothschild and Stuart Vaughan, eds. New York, 1964.

Textual Studies: *Chambers,* I, 490–494; *Greg,* pp. 418–421; *Hinman, passim.*

Sources: *Muir.*

NEWELL, W. W. "Sources of Shakespeare's *Tempest.*" *Journ. of Amer. Folklore,* XVI (1903).

HOTSON, J. L. *I, William Shakespeare.* London, 1937.

JOURDAIN, S. *A Discovery of the Barmudas Otherwise Called the Isle of Divels (1610).* Introd. by Joseph Q. Adams. Scholars' Facsimiles and Reprints, Third Ser. New York, 1940.

NOSWORTHY, J. M. "The Narrative Sources of *The Tempest.*" *RES,* XXIV (1948), 281–294.

GOLDSMITH, R. H. "The Wild Man on the English Stage." *MLR,* LII (1958), 481–491.

Stage History: *Odell, passim; Trewin, passim; New Cambridge,* pp. 109–111.

CAMPBELL, O. J. "Miss Webster and *The Tempest.*" *Amer. Scholar,* XIV (1946), 271–281.

MOSS, A. "We are Such Stuff . . ." *Theatre Arts,* XXIX (1945), 407–408.

Criticism: *Johnson,* pp. 64–66; *Coleridge,* I, 126–137; II, 169–181; *Hazlitt,* pp. 238–244; *Van Doren,* pp. 280–288; *Clemen,* pp. 182–194.

STILL, C. *The Timeless Theme: A Critical Theory Formulated and Applied.* London, 1936.

WILSON, J. D. *The Meaning of The Tempest.* Newcastle, 1936.

CURRY, W. C. *Shakespeare's Philosophical Patterns.* Baton Rouge, La., 1937.

KOSZUL, A. "Ariel." *ES,* XIX (1937), 200–204.

HANKINS, J. E. "Caliban, the Bestial Man." *PMLA,* LXII (1947).

AUDEN, W. H. "The Sea and the Mirror." *For the Time Being.* New York, 1945.

HOWARTH, R. G. *Shakespeare's "Tempest,"* rev. ed. Sydney, Australia, 1947.

DOBRÉE, B. "The Tempest." *Essays and Studies of the English Association* (1952), 13–25.

WILSON, H. S. "Action and Symbol in *Measure for Measure* and *The Tempest.*" *SQ,* IV (1953), 375–384.

KNOX, B. "*The Tempest* and the Ancient Comic Tradition." *English Stage Comedy, EIE,* 1954, pp. 52–73.

LOWENTHAL, L. *Literature and the Image of Man: Sociological Studies of the European Drama and Novel, 1600–1900.* Boston, 1957.

GESNER, C. "*The Tempest* as Pastoral Romance." *SQ,* X (1959), 531–544.

ORGEL, S. K. "New Uses of Adversity: Tragic Experience in *The Tempest.*" *In Defense of Reading,* eds. Reuben A. Brower and Richard Poirier. New York, 1962, pp. 110–132.

31. Timon of Athens

Modern Editions: Arden, K. Deighton, ed. London, 1905; Penguin, G. B. Harrison, ed. London, 1956; New Cambridge, J. C. Maxwell, ed. Cambridge, 1957; New Arden, H. J. Oliver, ed. London, 1959; Laurel, Francis Fergusson and C. J. Sisson, eds. New York, 1963; Signet, Maurice Charney, New York, 1965; Pelican, Charlton Hinman, Baltimore, 1965.

Textual Studies: *Chambers,* I, 480–484; *Greg,* 408–411; *Hinman, passim.*

Sources: *Bullough,* VI; *Muir.*

ADAMS, J. Q. "*Timon of Athens* and the Irregul[arities] of the First Folio." *JEGP,* VII (1907–1908), 63.

Stage History: *Odell, passim; Trewin, passim; N[ew] Cambridge,* pp. xliii–liv.

WILLIAMS, S. T. "Some Versions of *Timon* [of] *Athens* On the Stage." *MP,* XVIII (1920), 269–85.

KNIGHT, G. W. "*Timon of Athens* and Its Drama[tic] Descendants." *REL,* II (1961), 9–18.

Criticism: *Johnson,* pp. 163–165; *Coleridge,* I, 83–[...] 108–109; *Hazlitt,* pp. 210–213; *Van Doren,* pp. 2[...] 253; *Clemen,* pp. 168–176.

PARROTT, T. M. *The Problem of Timon of Athe[ns]* London, 1923.

WECTER, DIXON, "Shakespeare's Purpose in *Timon* [of] *Athens.*" *PMLA,* XLIII, (1928), 701–21.

WOODS, A. H. "Syphilis in Shakespeare's Tragedy [of] *Timon of Athens.*" *The American Journal of P[sy]chiatry,* 91 (1934), 95–107.

DRAPER, J. W. "The Psychology of Shakespea[re's] Timon." *MLR,* XXXV (1940), 521–525.

CAMPBELL, O. J. *Shakespeare's Satire.* New Yo[rk,] 1943.

FARNHAM, W. "The Beast Theme in Shakespea[re's] *Timon.*" *Essays and Studies by Members of* [the] *Department of English.* Univ. California Pu[bl.] Eng., Vol XIV. Berkeley, Calif., 1943, pp. 49–56.

COLLINS, A. S. "*Timon of Athens:* a Reconside[ra]tion." *RES,* XXII (1946), 96–108.

MAXWELL, J. C. "Timon of Athens." *Scrutiny,* [...] (1948), 195–208.

KNIGHT, G. W. *Christ and Nietzsche.* London, 19[...]

LEECH, C. *Shakespeare's Tragedies.* London, 1950.

EMPSON, W. *The Structure of Complex Wor[ds.]* London, 1951.

THOMSON, P. "The Literature of Patronage, 15[...] 1630." *EC,* II (1952), 267–284.

SPENCER, T. J. B. "Shakespeare Learns the Value [of] Money: Shakespeare at Work on *Timon* [of] *Athens.*" *SS 6* (1953), 75–78.

ELLIS-FERMOR, U. *Shakespeare the Dramatist.* Lo[n]don, 1961.

HONIGMANN, E. A. J. "*Timon of Athens.*" *SQ,* [...] (1961), 3–20.

COOK, D. "*Timon of Athens.*" *SS 16* (1963), 83–[...]

32. Titus Andronicus

Modern Editions: *Titus Andronicus.* The Fi[rst] Quarto, 1594. Reproduced in facsimile from t[he] unique copy in the Folger Shakespeare Libra[ry.] Intro. by Joseph Quincy Adams. New York, 19[...] New Cambridge, J. Dover Wilson, ed. Cambrid[ge,] 1948; New Arden, J. C. Maxwell, ed. Lond[on,] 1953; Penguin, G. B. Harrison, ed. London, 19[...] Signet, Sylvan Barnet, ed. New York, 1964.

Textual Studies: *Chambers,* I, 312–322; *Greg,* [...] 203–209; *Hinman, passim.*

CRAWFORD, C. "The Date and Authenticity of Ti[tus] Andronicus." *SJ,* XXXVI (1900), 1–65.

E, H. T. "The Authorship of *Titus Andronicus*." GP, XLII (1943), 55–81.

LLERAT, A. *The Composition of Shakespeare's ays: Authorship, Chronology*. New Haven, 1953.

TRELL, P. L., and G. W. WILLIAMS. "Roberts' mpositors in *Titus Andronicus* Q2." *SB*, VIII 956), 27–38.

, R. F. "The Composition of *Titus Andronicus*." *10* (1957), 60–70.

ces: *Bullough*, VI; *Muir*.

, R. A. "The Roman Background of *Titus Anonicus*." *SP*, XL (1943), 145–153.

ENT, R. M. "The Source of *Titus Andronicus*." , XLVI (1949), 167–183.

SON, J. D. "*Titus and Vespasian* and Professor lexander." *MLR*, XLVI (1951), 250.

EL, H. *Titus Andronicus. Studien zur dramengehichtlichen Stellung von Shakespeares früher ragödie*. Heidelberg, 1961.

e History: *Odell, passim; Trewin, passim; New mbridge*, pp. lxvi–lxxi.

SON, J. D. "*Titus Andronicus* on the Stage in 95." *SS 1* (1948), 17–22.

ERER, G. "An Unrecorded Elizabethan Performce of *Titus Andronicus*." *SS 14* (1961), 102–109.

icism: *Coleridge*, I, 1–2; *Van Doren*, pp. 28–33; *lemen*, pp. 21–29.

E, H. T. "The Language of *Titus Andronicus*." *pers of the Michigan Academy of Science, Arts, d Letters*, XXI (1935), 501–507.

—. *Construction in Shakespeare*. Ann Arbor, ich., 1951.

YARD, E. M. W. *Shakespeare's History Plays*. ondon, 1944.

MONDE, W. H. "The Ritual Origin of Shakeeare's *Titus Andronicus*." *International Journal Psycho-Analysis*, XXXVI (1955), 61–65.

TH, E. M. "The Metamorphosis of Violence in *itus Andronicus*." *SS 10* (1957), 38–49.

MERS, E. "Wilderness of Tigers: Structure and ymbolism in *Titus Andronicus*." *EC*, x (1960), 5–289.

NCER, T. J. B. *William Shakespeare, The Roman ays:* Titus Andronicus, Julius Caesar, Antony d Cleopatra, Coriolanus. Writers and Their /ork, 157. London, 1963.

33. Troilus and Cressida

NNENBAUM, S. A. and D. R. *Shakespeare's "Trois and Cressida": A Concise Bibliography*. New ork, 1943.

lern Editions: Arden, K. Deighton, ed. London, 06; Warwick, B. Dobrée, ed. London, 1938; New ariorum, H. Hillebrand and T. W. Baldwin, eds. hiladelphia, 1953; Yale, J. Campbell, ed. New aven, Conn., 1956; New Cambridge, J. Dover Vilson and A. Walker, eds. Cambridge, 1957; elican, V. K. Whitaker, ed. Baltimore, 1958; gnet, Daniel Seltzer, ed. New York, 1963.

tual Studies: *Chambers*, I, 438–449; *Greg*, pp. 8–350; *Hinman, passim; Honigmann*, pp. 78–95.

XANDER, P. "*Troilus and Cressida, 1609*." *Library*, S., IX (1928), 267–86.

LKER, A. "The Textual Problems of *Troilus and ressida*." *MLR*, XLV (1950), 459–464.

LLIAMS, P., "Shakespeare's *Troilus and Cressida:* The Relationship of Quarto and Folio." *SB*, III (1950), 131–143.

GREG, W. W. "The Printing of Shakespeare's *Troilus and Cressida* in the First Folio." *Papers of the Bibl. Soc. of Amer.*, XLV (1951), 273–282.

NOSWORTHY, J. M. *Shakespeare's Occasional Plays. Their Origin and Transmission*. London, 1965.

Sources: *Bullough*, VI; *Muir*.

TATLOCK, J. S. P. "The Siege of Troy in Elizabethan Literature, Especially in Shakespeare and Heywood." *PMLA*, XXX, n.s., XXIII (1915), 673–770.

ROLLINS, H. E. "The Troilus-Cressida Story from Chaucer to Shakespeare." *PMLA*, XXXII, n.s., XXV (1917), 383–429.

PRESSON, R. K. *Shakespeare's "Troilus and Cressida" and the Legends of Troy*. Madison, Wis., 1953.

BRADBROOK, M. C. "What Shakespeare Did to Chaucer's *Troilus and Criseyde*." *SQ*, IX (1958), 311–319.

BULLOUGH, G. "The Lost *Troilus and Cressida*." *E&S*, XVII (1964), 24–40.

Stage History: *Odell, passim; Trewin, passim; New Cambridge*, pp. xlvii–lvi.

Criticism: *Coleridge*, I, 108–111; *Hazlitt*, pp. 221–227; *Van Doren*, pp. 172–178.

EMPSON, W. *Some Versions of Pastoral*. London, 1935.

CAMPBELL, O. J. *Comicall Satyre and Shakespeare's "Troilus and Cressida."* San Marino, Calif., 1938.

BETHELL, S. L. *Shakespeare and the Popular Dramatic Tradition*. Intro. by T. S. Eliot. London, 1944.

ELLIS-FERMOR, U. *The Frontiers of Drama*. London, 1945.

RICHARDS, I. A. "*Troilus and Cressida* and Plato." *Hudson Review*, I (1948), 362–376.

WYNEKEN, H. "*Troilus and Cressida*." Dramaturg. Blätter, II (1948), 140–142.

TILLYARD, E. M. W. *Shakespeare's Problem Plays*. Toronto, 1949.

DUNKEL, W. D. "Shakespeare's *Troilus*." *SQ*, II (1951), 331–334.

KNIGHTS, L. C. "*Troilus and Cressida* Again." *Scrutiny*, XVIII (1951), 144–157.

KENDALL, P. M. "Inaction and Ambivalence in *Troilus and Cressida*." *James Southall Wilson Festschrift*, 1952, pp. 131–145.

NOWOTTNY, W. M. T. " 'Opinion' and 'Value' in *Troilus and Cressida*." *EC*, IV (1954), 282–296.

POTTS, A. F. "*Cynthia's Revels, Poetaster*, and *Troilus and Cressida*." *SQ*, V (1954), 297–302.

KERMODE, F. "Opinion, Truth and Value." *EC*, V (1955), 181–187.

HARRIER, R. "Troilus Divided." *Studies in the English Renaissance Drama. In Memory of K. L. Holzknecht*. New York, 1959.

MORRIS, B. "The Tragic Structure of *Troilus and Cressida*." *SQ*, X (1959), 481–491.

KAULA, D. "Will and Reason in *Troilus and Cressida*." *SQ*, XII (1961), 271–283.

MAIN, W. W. "Character Amalgams in Shakespeare's *Troilus and Cressida*." *SP*, LVIII (1961), 170–178.

FOAKES, R. A. "*Troilus and Cressida* Reconsidered." *UTQ*, XXXII (1963), 142–154.

FARNHAM, W. "Troilus in Shapes of Infinite Desire." *SQ*, XV, ii (1964), 257–264.

KIMBROUGH, R. *Shakespeare's* Troilus & Cressida *and Its Setting*. Cambridge, Mass., 1964.

34. Twelfth Night

Modern Editions: New Variorum, Howard H. Furness, ed. Philadelphia, 1901; Arden, M. Luce, ed. London, 1906; New Cambridge, A. Quiller-Couch and J. Dover Wilson, eds. Cambridge, 1930; G. L. Kittredge, ed. Boston, 1941; Mark Eccles, ed. New York, 1948; Yale, W. Holden, ed. New Haven, Conn., 1954; Pelican, C. T. Prouty, ed. Baltimore, 1958; Laurel, Francis Fergusson and C. J. Sisson, eds. New York, 1960; Folger, Louis B. Wright and Virginia LaMar, eds. New York, 1960; Bantam, O. J. Campbell, Alfred Rothschild and Stuart Vaughan, eds. New York, 1964; Signet, Herschel Baker, ed. New York, 1965.

Textual Studies: *Chambers*, I, 404–407; *Greg*, pp. 296–298; *Hinman, passim.*

Sources: *Bullough*, II, 269–372; *Muir.*

LUCE, M., ed. *Rich's* Apolonius and Silla, *an original of Shakespeare's* Twelfth Night. London, 1912.

HOTSON, J. L. *The First Night of "Twelfth Night."* London, 1954.

KAUFMAN, H. A. "Nicolò Secchi as a Source of *Twelfth Night.*" *SQ*, v (1954), 271–280.

Stage History: *Odell, passim; Trewin, passim; New Cambridge*, pp. 173–179; *Winter* II, 1–106.

HUNT, H. *Old Vic Prefaces.* London, 1954.

Criticism: *Johnson*, pp. 91–92; *Coleridge*, I, 105–107; *Hazlitt*, pp. 313–318; *Van Doren*, pp. 135–143.

DRAPER, J. W. *The "Twelfth Night" of Shakespeare's Audience.* Palo Alto, Calif., 1950.

SUMMERS, J. "The Masks of *Twelfth Night.*" *University of Kansas City Review*, XXII (1955), 25–32.

BROWN, J. R. *Shakespeare and His Comedies*, London, 1957.

SALINGAR, L. G. "The Design of *Twelfth Night.*" *SQ*, IX (1958), 117–39.

BARBER, C. L. *Shakespeare's Festive Comedy*, Princeton, 1959.

NAGARAJAN, S. "What You Will." *SQ*, x (1959), 61–66.

HOLLANDER, J. "*Twelfth Night* and the morality of indulgence." *SR*, LXVII (1959), 220–238.

HARDY, B. *Twelfth Night.* London, 1962.

MANHEIM, L. F. "The Mythical Joys of Shakespeare; or, What You *Will.*" *Shakespeare Encomium.* Anne Paolucci, ed. The City College Papers, I. New York, 1964, pp. 100–112.

35. The Two Gentlemen of Verona

Modern Editions: Arden, R. Bond, ed. London, 1906; New Cambridge, A. Quiller-Couch and J. Dover Wilson, eds. Cambridge, 1921; Yale, Karl Young, ed. New Haven, Conn., 1924; Penguin, G. B. Harrison, ed. London, 1956; Pelican, Berners Jackson, ed. Baltimore, 1964. Folger, Louis B. Wright and Virginia LaMar, eds., New York, 1964.

Textual Studies: *Chambers*, I, 329–331; *Greg*, pp. 217–218; *Hinman, passim.*

Sources: *Bullough*, I, 203–268; *Muir.*

CAMPBELL, O. J. "*The Two Gentlemen of Verona* and Italian Comedy." *Studies in Shakespeare, Milton and Donne.* New York, 1925.

ALLEN, M. S. "Brooke's *Romeus and Juliet* as a source for the Valentine-Sylvia plot in *Two Gentlemen of Verona.*" *Studies in English (University of Texas)*, XVIII (1938), 25–46.

ATKINSON, D. F. "The source of *Two Gentleme Verona.*" *SP*, XLI (1944), 223–234.

SARGENT, R. M. "Sir Thomas Elyot and the Inte of *The Two Gentlemen of Verona.*" *PMLA*, (1950), 1166–1180.

Stage History: *Odell, passim; Trewin, passim; Cambridge*, pp. 105–106.

Criticism: *Johnson*, pp. 72–74; *Hazlitt*, pp. 318- *Van Doren*, pp. 40–44.

QUILLER-COUCH, SIR A. *Shakespeare's Workman.* Cambridge, 1918.

PARKS, G. B. "The Development of *Two Gentle of Verona.*" *Huntington Lib. Bull.*, No. II (1937), 1–11.

BALDWIN, T. W. *Shakspere's Five-Act Struc Shakspere's Early Plays on the Backgroun Renaissance Theories of Five-Act Structure f 1470.* Urbana, Ill., 1947.

GODDARD, H. C. *The Meaning of Shakespeare.* cago, 1951.

PERRY, T. A. "Proteus, wry-transformed travel *SQ*, v (1954), 33–40.

DANBY, J. "Shakespeare Criticism and *Two Ge men of Verona.*" *CQ*, II (1960), pp. 309–321.

BROOKS, H. "Two Clowns in a Comedy. . . ." *E* XVI (1964), 91–100.

36. The Two Noble Kinsmen

Modern Editions: Temple, C. H. Herford, ed. York, 1897; C. F. T. Brooke, ed. (in *The Sh speare Apocrypha*). New York, 1908; G. L. tredge, ed. (in *The Complete Works*) Bos 1940.

Textual Studies: *Chambers*, I, 528–532.

WALLER, F. O. "Printer's Copy for *The Two N Kinsmen.*" *SB*, XI (1958), 61–84.

Sources:

THORNDIKE, A. H. *The Influence of Beaumont Fletcher upon Shakespeare.* Worcester, Mass.,

Stage History:

SPRAGUE, A. C. *Beaumont and Fletcher on the Re ration Stage.* Cambridge, Mass., 1926.

Criticism:

SPENCER, T. "*The Two Noble Kinsmen.*" *MP*, x (1939), 255–276.

MINCOFF, M. "The Authorship of *The Two N Kinsmen.*" *ES*, XXXIII (1952), 97–115.

MUIR, K. *Shakespeare as Collaborator.* London, 1

37. The Winter's Tale

Modern Editions: New Variorum, Howard H. ness, ed. Philadelphia, 1898; New Cambridge, Quiller-Couch and J. Dover Wilson, eds. C bridge, 1931; Pelican, B. Maxwell, ed. Baltim 1956; S. L. Bethell, ed. London, 1956; New Ar J. H. Pafford, ed. London, 1963; Signet, Fr Kermode, ed. New York, 1963.

Textual Studies: *Chambers*, I, 487–490; *Greg*, 415–417; *Hinman, passim.*

TANNENBAUM, S. A. "Textual and Other Notes *The Winter's Tale.*" *PQ*, VII (1928), 358–367.

Sources: *Muir.*

THOMAS, P. G., ed. *Greene's 'Pandosto', or 'Dora and Fawnia', Being the Original of Shakespe 'Winter's Tale'.* Oxford, 1907.

IGMANN, E. A. J. "Secondary Sources of *The Winter's Tale*." *PQ*, XXXIV (1955), 27–38.
ge History: *Odell, passim; Trewin, passim; New ambridge*, pp. 185–193.
icism: *Johnson*, pp. 89–90; *Coleridge*, I, 119–125; *azlitt*, pp. 324–329; *Van Doren*, pp. 271–280; *lemen*, pp. 195–204.
HELL, S. L. "*The Winter's Tale*": *A Study*. London, 1947.
GHT, G. W. *The Crown of Life*. London, 1947.
TET, E. C. *Shakespeare and the Romance Tradition*. London, 1949.
NIGER, F. D. "The Meaning of *The Winter's Tale*." *UTQ*, XX (1950), 11–26.
EL, P. N. "Leontes, a jealous Tyrant." *RES*, n.s. I 1950), 302–307.
JOUR, A. "The Final Scene of *The Winter's Tale*." *ES*, XXXIII (1952), 193–208.
ENEUS, R. J. "The Inception of Leontes' Jealousy *The Winter's Tale*." *SQ*, IV (1953), 321–326.
ANT, J. R. JR. "Shakespeare's Allegory: *The Winter's Tale*." *SR*, LXIII (1955), 202–222.
E, N. "Recognition in *The Winter's Tale*." *Essays on Shakespeare and the Elizabethan Drama in Honor of Hardin Craig*, Richard Hosley, ed. Columbia, Mo., 1962, pp. 235–246.
ANZER, E. "The Structural Pattern of *The Winter's Tale*." *REL*, V, ii (1964), 72–82.

38. Poems

dern Editions: G. Wyndham, ed., 1898; Arden, . K. Pooler, ed. London, 1911, 1927; Yale, A. euillerat, ed. New Haven, Conn., 1927; New emple, M. R. Ridley, ed. London, 1935; New ariorum, H. E. Rollins, ed. Philadelphia, 1938; enguin, G. B. Harrison, ed. London, 1959; New rden, F. T. Prince, ed. London, 1960; O. J. ampbell, ed. New York, 1964.
RNESS, H. K. *A Concordance to Shakespeare's Poems*, An Index to Every Word Therein Contained. Philadelphia, 1874.
rces: *Bullough*, I, 161–202; *Muir*.
ticism: *Hazlitt*, pp. 357–361; *Van Doren*, pp. 1–9.
CA, L. R. *Elizabethan Narrative Poetry*. New Brunswick, N. J., 1950.
ITH, H. *Elizabethan Poetry: A Study in Conventions, Meaning, and Expression*. Cambridge, Mass., 953.
NCE, F. T. *William Shakespeare: The Poems*. Writers and Their Work, 165. London and New York, 1963.

VENUS AND ADONIS

RTRIDGE, A. C. "Shakespeare's Orthography in *Venus and Adonis* and Some Early Quartos." *SS* (1954), 35–45.
AABER, M. A. "*The First Rape of Faire Hellen* by ohn Trussel." *SQ*, VIII (1957), 407–448.
ADBROOK, M. C. "Beasts and Gods: Greene's *Groats-worth of Witte* and the Social Purpose of *Venus and Adonis*." *SS 15* (1962), 62–72.
LMATIER, M. A. "A Suggested New Source in Ovid's *Metamorphoses* for Shakespeare's *Venus and Adonis*." HLQ, XXIV (1961), 163–169.
BKIN, N. "Venus and Adonis and the Myth of Love." *Pacific Coast Studies in Shakespeare*, Waldo McNeir, ed. Eugene, Ore., 1965.

THE RAPE OF LUCRECE

KUHL, E. P. "Shakespeare's *Rape of Lucrece*." *Renaissance Studies in Honor of Hardin Craig*, 1941, pp. 160–168.
ALLEN, D. C. "Some observations on *The Rape of Lucrece*." *SS 15* (1962), 89–98.

THE PHOENIX AND THE TURTLE

FAIRCHILD, A. H. R. "The Phoenix and Turtle." *Englische Studien*, XXXIII (1904), 337–84.
NEWDIGATE, B. H. "'The Phoenix and the Turtle': Was Lady Bedford the Phoenix?" *TLS* (Oct. 24, 1936), p. 862.
CUNNINGHAM, J. V. "'Essence' and *The Phoenix and Turtle*." *ELH*, XIX (1952), 265–276.
ONG, W. J. "Metaphor and the Twinned Vision." *SR*, LXIII (1955), 193–201.
RICHARDS, I. A. "The Sense of Poetry: Shakespeare's *The Phoenix and the Turtle*." *Daedalus*, 87, iii (1958), 86–94.
ELLRODT, R. "An Anatomy of 'The Phoenix and the Turtle'." *SS 15* (1962), 99–110.
MATCHETT, W. H. *The Phoenix and the Turtle*. The Hague, 1965.

39. The Sonnets

TANNENBAUM, S. A. *Shakespeare's Sonnets*. Elizabethan Bibliographies, 10. New York, 1940.
Modern Editions: E. Dowden, ed. London, 1881; G. Wyndham, ed., 1898; Samuel Butler, ed., 1899; W. H. Hadow, ed., 1907; Variorum, R. M. Alden, ed. Philadelphia, 1916; Arden, C. K. Pooler, ed. London, 1918; Yale, E. B. Reed, ed. New Haven, Conn., 1923; T. G. Tucker, ed., 1924; Tucker Brooke, ed., 1936; Penguin, G. B. Harrison, ed. London, 1938; New Variorum, H. E. Rollins, ed. 2 Vols. Philadelphia, 1944; Pelican, D. Bush, ed. Baltimore, 1961; Oscar James Campbell, ed. New York, 1964; Signet, William Burto, ed., Intro. by W. H. Auden, New York, 1964.
Arrangement and Date:
GRAY, H. D. "The Arrangement and the Date of Shakespeare's Sonnets." *PMLA*, XXX, n.s., XXIII (1915), 629–44.
BRAY, D. *The Original Order of Shakespeare's Sonnets*. London, 1925.
FORT, J. A. *A Time-Scheme for Shakespeare's Sonnets*. London, 1929.
SCHAAR, C. *Elizabethan Sonnet Themes and the Dating of Shakespeare's Sonnets*. Lund, Sweden, 1962.
LANDRY, H. *Interpretations in Shakespeare's Sonnets*. Perspectives in Criticism, 14. Berkeley, Calif., and Los Angeles, 1963.
Biographical Interpretations:
BOADEN, J. *On The Sonnets of Shakespeare*, identifying the person to whom they were addressed and elucidating several points in the poet's history. London, 1837.
TYLER, T. *The Herbert-Fitton Theory of Shakespeare's Sonnets*. A Reply. London, 1898.
ACHESON, A. *Shakespeare and the Rival Poet*. Displaying Shakespeare as a satirist and proving the

identity of the patron and the rival of the sonnets. London and New York, 1903.
———. *Mistress Davenant, the Dark Lady of Shakespeare's Sonnets.* London, 1913.
———. *Shakespeare's Sonnet Story, 1592–8.* With an appendix, including a monograph on 'The Crosse Inn and the Tavern of Oxford', by E. Thurlow Leeds. London, 1922.
NISBET, U. *The Onlie Begetter.* London, 1936.
ANGELL, P. K. "Light on the Dark Lady: A Study of Some Elizabethan Libels." *PMLA,* LII (1937), 652–674.
DOUGLAS, LORD ALFRED. "Shakespeare and Will Hughes." *TLS* (May 21, 1938), p. 353.
MURRY, J. M. "Chapman the Rival Poet." *TLS,* June 4, 1938, pp. 253–309.
ANGELL, P. K., and T. W. BALDWIN. " 'Light on the Dark Lady.' " *PMLA,* LV (1940), 598–602.
GRAY, H. D. "Shakespeare's Rival Poet." *JEGP,* XLVII (1948), 365–373.
BROWN, I. "Shak.'s Dark Lady." *Dark Ladies.* London, 1957, pp. 253–309.
WILDE, O. *The Portrait of Mr. W. H.,* ed. with Introd. by Vyvyan Holland. London, 1958.
GITTINGS, R. *Shakespeare's Rival: A Study in Three Parts.* London, 1960.
WILSON, J. D. *Shakespeare's Sonnets: An Introduction for Historians and Others.* Cambridge, 1963.

Criticism:

ROBERTSON, J. M. *The Problems of the Shakespear Sonnets.* London, 1926.
EMPSON, W. *Some Versions of Pastoral.* London, 1935.
YOUNG, H. McC. *The Sonnets of Shakespeare: A Psycho-Sexual Analysis.* Menasha, Wis., 1936.
MUIR, K., and S. O'LOUGHLIN. *The Voyage to Illyria.* London, 1937.
BRAY, D. *Shakespeare's Sonnet Sequence.* London, 1938.
RANSOM, J. C. *The World's Body.* New York, 1938.
MIZENER, A. "The Structure of Figurative Language in Shakespeare's Sonnets." *Southern Rev.,* V (1940), 730–747.
HOTSON, J. L. *Shakespeare's Sonnets Dated, and Other Essays.* London, 1949.
———. "More Light on Shakespeare's Sonnets." *SQ,* II (1951), 111–118.
HUBLER, E. "Three Shakespearean Myths: Mutability, Plenitude, and Reputation." *EIE, 1948.* New York, 1949, pp. 95–119.
———. *The Sense of Shakespeare's Sonnets.* Pri ton, N. J., 1952.
BALDWIN, T. W. *On the Literary Genetics of S spere's Poems and Sonnets.* Urbana, Ill., 1950.
BATESON, F. W. "Elementary My Dear Hotsoı Caveat for Literary Detectives." *EC,* I (1951), 88.
BERRYMAN, J. "Shakespeare at Thirty." *Hudson view,* VI (1953), 175–203.
CRUTTWELL, P. *The Shakespearean Moment.* Lon 1954.
KNIGHT, G. W. *The Mutual Flame: An Interp tion of Shakespeare's Sonnets.* London, 1955.
LEVER, J. W. *The Elizabethan Love Sonnet.* Lon 1956.
BLACKMUR, R. P. "A Poetics for Infatuation." XXIII (1961), 647–670.
LEISHMAN, J. B. *Themes and Variations in Sh speare's Sonnets.* London and New York, 1961.
HUBLER, E., and others. *The Riddle of Shakespe Sonnets.* New York, 1962.
KRIEGER, M. *A Window to Criticism: Shakespe Sonnets and Modern Poetics.* Princeton, N.J.,
WILLEN, G. and V. B. REED, eds. *A Casebook Shakespeare's Sonnets.* New York, 1964.

40. *Apocryphal Plays*

Shakespeare's Doubtful Plays. Ed. with introd each play by A. F. Hopkinson. 3 Vols. Lon 1891–1895.
BROOKE, C. F. T., ed. *The Shakespeare Apocry* Being a collection of 14 plays which have ascribed to Shakespeare. Oxford, 1908.
MAXWELL, B. *Studies in the Shakespeare Apocry* New York, 1956.

SIR THOMAS MORE

BALD, R. C. "*The Booke of Sir Thomas More* an Problems." *SS 2* (1949), 44–61.
STIRLING, B. *The Populace in Shakespeare.* York, 1949.
NOSWORTHY, J. M. "Shakespeare and *Sir Tho More.*" *RES,* n.s., VI (1955), 12–25.
SHAPIRO, I. A. "The Significance of a Date." (1955), 100–105.
WILSON, J. D. "The New Way with Shakespe Texts: An Introduction for Lay Readers. III Sight of Shakespeare's Manuscripts." *SS 9* (19 69–80.